Collins German Dictionary & Grammar

HarperCollins Publishers
Westerhill Road
Bishopbriggs
Glasgow
G64 2QT

Seventh Edition 2014

Reprint 10 9 8 7 6 5 4 3 2 1 0

ISBN 978-0-00-745302-3

www.collinsdictionary.com
www.collins.co.uk

A catalogue record for this book is available from the British Library

Typeset by Davidson Publishing Solutions

Printed in India by Gopsons Papers Ltd

Acknowledgements
We would like to thank those authors and publishers who kindly gave permission for copyright material to be used in the Collins Corpus. We would also like to thank Times Newspapers Ltd for providing valuable data.

EDITOR
Susie Beattie

CONTRIBUTORS
Horst Kopleck
Joyce Littlejohn
Val McNulty
Helen Newstead
Maggie Seaton

TECHNICAL SUPPORT
Thomas Callan
Agnieszka Urbanowicz
Dave Wark

FOR THE PUBLISHER
Gerry Breslin
Catherine Love
Evelyn Sword

Contributors to the previous edition
Gaëlle Amiot-Cadey, Elspeth Anderson, Dagmar Förtsch, Ilse MacLean, Gisela Moohan, Hildegard Pesch, Robin Sawers, Ulrike Seeberger, Veronika Schnorr, Eva Vennebusch, Beate Wengel

Inhalt

Contents

Einleitung

Sie möchten Englisch lernen oder vielleicht bereits vorhandene Kenntnisse vertiefen. Sie möchten sich auf Englisch ausdrücken, englische Texte lesen oder übersetzen, oder Sie möchten sich ganz einfach mit Englisch sprechenden Menschen unterhalten können. Ganz gleich ob Sie Englisch an der Schule oder an der Universität lernen, in einem Büro oder in einem Unternehmen tätig sind: Sie haben sich den richtigen Begleiter für Ihre Arbeit ausgesucht! Dieses Buch ist der ideale Helfer, wenn Sie sich in englischer Sprache ausdrücken und verständlich machen wollen, ob Sie nun sprechen oder schreiben. Unser Wörterbuch ist ganz bewusst praktisch und modern, es räumt vor allem der Alltagssprache und der Sprache, wie sie Ihnen in Zeitungen und Nachrichten, im Geschäftsleben, im Büro und im Urlaub begegnet, großen Raum ein. Wie in allen unseren Wörterbüchern haben wir das Hauptgewicht auf zeitgenössische Sprache und idiomatische Redewendungen gelegt.

Wie man dieses Buch benutzt

Im Folgenden geben wir einige Erklärungen darüber, wie die Einträge Ihres Wörterbuchs aufgebaut sind. Unser Ziel: Wir wollen Ihnen so viel Information wie möglich bieten, ohne dabei an Klarheit und Verständlichkeit einzubüßen.

Die Wörterbucheinträge

Ein typischer Eintrag in Ihres Wörterbuchs besteht aus folgenden Elementen:

Lautschrift

Wie die meisten modernen Wörterbücher geben wir die Aussprache mit Zeichen an, die zum „internationalen phonetischen Alphabet" gehören. Weiter unten (auf den Seiten xii und xiii) finden Sie eine vollständige Liste der Zeichen, die in diesem System benutzt werden. Die Aussprache englischer Wörter geben wir auf der englisch-deutschen Seite unmittelbar hinter dem jeweiligen Wort in eckigen Klammern an. Die deutsche Aussprache erscheint im deutsch-englischen Teil ebenfalls auf diese Weise unmittelbar hinter den Worteinträgen. Allerdings wird sie nicht immer angegeben, zum Beispiel bei zusammengesetzten Wörtern wie Liebesbrief, deren Bestandteile schon an anderer Stelle im Wörterbuch zu finden sind.

Grammatik-Information

Alle Wörter gehören zu einer der folgenden grammatischen Klassen: Substantiv, Verb, Adjektiv, Pronomen, Artikel, Konjunktion, Präposition, Interjektion, Abkürzung. Substantive können im Deutschen männlich, weiblich oder sächlich sein. Verben können transitiv, intransitiv, reflexiv oder auch unpersönlich sein. Die Wortart folgt auf die Lautschrift und ist in KAPITÄLCHEN angegeben. Wo bei Übersetzungen eine Geschlechtsangabe erforderlich ist, wird diese in *Kursivschrift* gegeben.

Oft gehören Wörter zu zwei oder mehr grammatischen Klassen. So kann das deutsche Wort **gut** ein Adjektiv („good") oder auch ein Adverb („well") sein, und das englische Wort **spell** ist sowohl ein Substantiv („Zauber") als auch ein Verb („schreiben, buchstabieren"). Das Verb **reden** ist manchmal transitiv, d. h. es hat ein Objekt („sie redet Unsinn"), manchmal intransitiv, d.h. es wird ohne Objekt gebraucht („er redet ständig vom Wetter"). Zur besseren Übersichtlichkeit sind verschiedene Wortarten durch das Symbol ▸ abgegrenzt; alle Beispielsätze werden dann unter den entsprechenden grammatischen Kategorien gegeben.

Bedeutungsunterschiede

Die meisten Wörter haben mehr als eine Bedeutung. So kann z.B. **Rad** einen Teil eines Autos oder Fahrrads bezeichnen, aber auch ein Wort für das Fahrrad selbst sein. Andere Wörter haben je nach Kontext verschiedene Übersetzungen; so bedeutet das Verb **to recede** abhängig vom Subjekt des Satzes entweder „zurückgehen" oder „verschwinden". Damit Sie in jedem Zusammenhang immer die richtige Übersetzung finden, haben wir die Einträge nach Bedeutungen eingeteilt: jede Kategorie wird durch einen „Verwendungshinweis" bestimmt, der *kursiv* gedruckt ist und in

Klammern steht. Die beiden Beispiele von oben sehen dann so aus:

Rad NT wheel; (*Fahrrad*) bike
recede VI (*tide*) zurückgehen; (*lights etc*) verschwinden

Andere Wörter haben in verschiedenen Sachzusammenhängen unterschiedliche Bedeutungen. Das Wort **Rezept** z. B. bezeichnet eine Koch- oder Backanleitung, bezieht sich in medizinischen Zusammenhängen jedoch auf ärztlich verordnete Medikamente. Wir zeigen Ihnen, welche Übersetzung Sie auswählen sollten, indem wir wieder in Klammern solche Fachgebiete in *kursiven* Buchstaben angeben, mit dem Anfangsbuchstaben großgeschrieben, im vorigen Fall *Koch* als Abkürzung für *Kochen* und *Med* als Abkürzung für *Medizin*:

Rezept NT (*Koch*) recipe; (*Med*) prescription

Sie finden eine Liste aller in diesem Wörterbuch benutzten Abkürzungen für solche Sachgebiete auf den Seiten viii–x.

Übersetzungen
Die meisten deutschen Wörter können mit einem einzigen englischen Wort übersetzt werden und umgekehrt. Aber manchmal gibt es eine solche genaue Entsprechung nicht. In diesen Fällen haben wir eine ungefähre Entsprechung angegeben, gekennzeichnet durch ≈. Dies ist z. B. der Fall bei **Gymnasium** mit den englischen bzw. amerikanischen Äquivalenten „grammar school" und „high school", die aufgrund der unterschiedlichen Ausbildungssysteme lediglich ungefähre Entsprechungen sein können.

Gymnasium NT ≈ grammar school (BRIT), high school (*US*)

Manchmal kann man nicht einmal ein ungefähres Äquivalent finden. Besonders oft ist das der Fall beim Essen, insbesondere bei lokalen Spezialitäten wie dieser schottischen Speise:

haggis (SCOT) N *Gericht aus gehackten Schafsinnereien und Haferschrot, im Schafsmagen gekocht*

Hier wird statt einer Übersetzung (die es einfach gar nicht gibt) eine Erklärung gegeben, die durch *Kursivschrift* als solche kenntlich gemacht ist.

Im Deutschen wissen Sie , in welcher Situation Sie den Ausdruck **ich bin pleite** verwenden würden, wann Sie **ich bin knapp bei Kasse** sagen und wann **ich bin in Geldschwierigkeiten**. Wenn Sie jedoch Englisch verstehen oder selbst sprechen wollen, ist es wichtig zu wissen, welcher Ausdruck etwa höflich ist und welcher nicht. Um Ihnen hierbei zu helfen, haben wir für umgangssprachliche Ausdrücke die Kennzeichnung (*umg*) bzw. (*inf*) verwendet. Besonders anstößige Ausdrücke sind zusätzlich mit einem Ausrufezeichen versehen, also (*umg!*) bzw. (*inf!*), um den Benutzer zu warnen, diese nur mit großer Vorsicht zu verwenden. Angaben wie (*umg*) oder (*inf*) werden bei Übersetzungen in der Regel nicht wiederholt, wenn das Sprachniveau der Zielsprache dem der Ausgangssprache entspricht.

Schlüsselwörter
Im Text als **SCHLÜSSELWÖRTER** hervorgehobene Einträge, wie etwa **to be** und **to do** und ihre deutschen Entsprechungen **sein** und **machen**, werden als Grundelemente der Sprache besonders ausführlich behandelt.

Landeskundliche Informationen
In durch einen senkrecht verblassenden Balken abgesetzten Artikeln werden landeskundliche Aspekte in deutsch- und englischsprachigen Ländern behandelt. Die Themen umfassen Politik, Ausbildung, Medien und Feiertage, z. B. **Bundestag**, **Abitur**, **BBC** und **Hallowe'en**.

Introduction

You may be starting to learn German, or you may wish to extend your knowledge of the language. Perhaps you want to read and study German books, newspapers and magazines, or perhaps simply have a conversation with German speakers. Whatever the reason, whether you're a student, a tourist or want to use German for business, this is the ideal book to help you understand and communicate. This modern, user-friendly dictionary gives priority to everyday vocabulary and the language of current affairs, business and tourism. As in all Collins dictionaries, the emphasis is firmly placed on contemporary language and expressions.

How to use this dictionary

You will find below an outline of the way in which information is presented in your dictionary. Our aim is to give you the maximum amount of information whilst still providing a text which is clear and user-friendly.

Entries

A typical entry in your dictionary will be made up of the following elements:

Phonetic transcription

Phonetics appear in square brackets immediately after the headword. They are shown using the International Phonetic Alphabet (IPA), and a complete list of the symbols used in this system can be found on pages xii and xiii.

Grammatical information

All words belong to one of the following parts of speech: noun, verb, adjective, adverb, pronoun, article, conjunction, preposition, exclamation, abbreviation. Nouns can be singular or plural and, in German, masculine, feminine or neuter. Verbs can be transitive, intransitive, reflexive or impersonal. Parts of speech appear in SMALL CAPS immediately after the phonetic spelling of the headword. The gender of the translation appears in *italics* immediately following the key element of the translation.

Often a word can have more than one part of speech. Just as the English word **next** can be an adjective or an adverb, the German word **gut** can be an adjective ("good") or an adverb ("well"). In the same way the verb **to walk** is sometimes transitive, i.e. it takes an object ("to walk the dog") and sometimes intransitive, i.e. it doesn't take an object ("to walk to school"). To help you find the meaning you are looking for quickly and for clarity of presentation, the different part of speech categories are separated by a solid black triangle ▶.

Meaning divisions

Most words have more than one meaning. Take, for example, **punch** which can be, amongst other things, a blow with the fist or an object used for making holes. Other words are translated differently depending on the context in which they are used. The intransitive verb **to recede**, for example, can be translated by "zurückgehen" or "verschwinden" depending on *what* is receding. To help you select the most appropriate translation in every context, entries are divided according to meaning. Each different meaning is introduced by an "indicator" in *italics* and in brackets. Thus, the examples given above will be shown as follows:

> **punch** N (*blow*) Schlag *m*; (*tool*) Locher *m*
> **recede** VI (*tide*) zurückgehen; (*lights etc*) verschwinden

Likewise, some words can have a different meaning when used to talk about a specific subject area or field. For example, **bishop**, which in a religious context means a high-ranking clergyman, is also the name of a chess piece. To show English speakers which translation to use, we have added "subject field labels" in italics with initial capitals and in brackets, in this case (*Rel*) and (*Chess*):

bishop N (*Rel*) Bischof *m*; (*Chess*) Läufer *m*

Field labels are often shortened to save space. You will find a complete list of abbreviations used in the dictionary on pages viii to x

Translations

Most English words have a direct translation in German and vice versa, as shown in the examples given above. Sometimes, however, no exact equivalent exists in the target language. In such cases we have given an approximate equivalent, indicated by the sign ≈. Such is the case of **high school**, the German equivalent of which is "Oberschule *f*". This is not an exact translation since the systems of the two countries in question are quite different:

high school N ≈ Oberschule *f*

On occasion it is impossible to find even an approximate equivalent. This may be the case, for example, with the names of culinary specialities like this German cake:

Streuselkuchen M *cake with crumble topping*

Here the translation (which doesn't exist) is replaced by an explanation. For increased clarity the explanation, or "gloss", is shown in *italics*.

Register

In English you instinctively know when to say **I'm broke** *or* **I'm a bit short of cash** and when to say **I don't have any money**. When you are trying to understand someone who is speaking German, however, or when you yourself try to speak German, it is especially important to know what is polite and what is less so. To help you with this, we have added the register labels (*umg*) and (*inf*) to colloquial or offensive expressions. Those expressions which are particularly vulgar are also given an exclamation mark (*umg!*) or (*inf!*), warning you to use them with extreme care. Please note that the register labels (*umg*) and (*inf*) are not always repeated in the target language when the register of the translation matches that of the word or phrase being translated.

Keywords

Words labelled in the text as **KEYWORDS**, such as **be** and **do** or their German equivalents **sein** and **machen**, have been given special treatment because they form the basic elements of the language. This extra help will ensure that you know how to use these complex words with confidence.

Cultural information

Entries which appear next to a fading vertical bar explain aspects of culture in German- and English-speaking countries. Subject areas covered include politics, education, media and national festivals, for example **Bundestag**, **Abitur**, **BBC** and **Hallowe'en**.

Abkürzungen / Abbreviations

Abkürzungen		Abbreviations
Abkürzung	*abk, abbr*	abbreviation
Adjektiv	*adj*	adjective
Verwaltung	*Admin*	administration
Adverb	*adv*	adverb
Landwirtschaft	*Agr*	agriculture
Akkusativ	*akk, acc*	accusative
Anatomie	*Anat*	anatomy
Architektur	*Archit*	architecture
Artikel	*art*	article
Kunst	*Art*	
Astrologie	*Astrol*	astrology
Astronomie	*Astron*	astronomy
attributiv	*attrib*	attributive
Kraftfahrzeuge	*Aut*	automobiles
Hilfsverb	*aux*	auxiliary
Luftfahrt	*Aviat*	aviation
Bergbau	*Bergb*	mining
besonders	*bes*	especially
Biologie	*Biol*	biology
Botanik	*Bot*	botany
britisch	*Brit*	British
Kartenspiel	*Cards*	
Chemie	*Chem*	chemistry
Film	*Cine*	cinema
Handel	*Comm*	commerce
Komparativ	*comp*	comparative
Computer	*Comput*	computers
Konjunktion	*conj*	conjunction
Bauwesen	*Constr*	building
zusammengesetztes Wort	*cpd*	compound
Kochen und Backen	*Culin*	cooking
Dativ	*dat*	dative
bestimmt	*def*	definite
diminutiv	*dimin*	diminutive
dekliniert	*dekl*	declined
kirchlich	*Eccl*	ecclesiastical
Volkswirtschaft	*Econ*	economics
Eisenbahn	*Eisenb*	railways
Elektrizität	*Elek, Elec*	electricity
besonders	*esp*	especially
und so weiter	*etc*	et cetera
etwas	*etw*	something
Euphemismus	*euph*	euphemism
Ausruf	*excl*	exclamation
Femininum	*f*	feminine
übertragen	*fig*	figurative
Film	*Film*	cinema
Finanzen	*Fin*	finance
formell	*form*	formal
'phrasal verb', bei dem Partikel und Verb nicht getrennt werden können	*fus*	fused: phrasal verb where the particle cannot be separated from the verb
gehoben	*geh*	elevated

Genitiv	*gen*	genitive
Geografie	*Geog*	geography
Geologie	*Geol*	geology
Geometrie	*Geom*	geometry
Grammatik	*Gram*	grammar
Geschichte	*Hist*	history
scherzhaft	*hum*	humorous
Imperfekt	*imperf*	imperfect
unpersönlich	*impers*	impersonal
unbestimmt	*indef*	indefinite
umgangssprachlich (! vulgär)	*inf* (!)	informal (! particularly offensive)
untrennbares Verb	*insep*	inseparable
Interjektion	*interj*	interjection
Interrogativ	*interrog*	interrogative
unveränderlich	*inv*	invariable
unregelmäßig	*irreg*	irregular
jemand	*jd*	somebody
jemandem	*jdm*	(to) somebody
jemanden	*jdn*	somebody
jemandes	*jds*	somebody's
Rechtswesen	*Jur*	law
Kartenspiel	*Karten*	cards
Kochen und Backen	*Koch*	cooking
Komparativ	*komp*	comparative
Konjunktion	*konj*	conjunction
Rechtswesen	*Law*	law
Sprachwissenschaft	*Ling*	linguistics
wörtlich	*lit*	literal
literarisch	*liter*	literary
Literatur	*Liter*	literature
Maskulinum	*m*	masculine
Mathematik	*Math*	mathematics
Medizin	*Med*	medicine
Meteorologie	*Met*	meteorology
Militärwesen	*Mil*	military
Bergbau	*Min*	mining
Musik	*Mus*	music
Substantiv	*n*	noun
nautisch	*Naut*	nautical
Nominativ	*nom*	nominative
norddeutsch	*Nordd*	North Germany
Neutrum	*nt*	neuter
Zahlwort	*num*	numeral
Objekt	*obj*	object
oder	*od*	or
veraltet	*old*	
sich	*o.s.*	oneself
österreichisch	*Österr*	Austria
Parlament	*Parl*	parliament
pejorativ	*pej*	pejorative
Person/persönlich	*pers*	person/personal
Pharmazie	*Pharm*	pharmacy
Fotografie	*Phot*	photography
Physik	*Phys*	physics
Physiologie	*Physiol*	physiology

Plural	*pl*	plural
Politik	*Pol*	politics
possessiv	*poss*	possessive
Partizip Perfekt	*pp*	past participle
Präfix	*präf, pref*	prefix
Präposition	*präp, prep*	preposition
Präsens	*präs, pres*	present
Pronomen	*pron*	pronoun
Psychologie	*Psych*	psychology
Imperfekt	*pt*	past tense
Radio	*Radio*	radio
Eisenbahn	*Rail*	railways
Religion	*Rel*	religion
Relativ-	*rel*	relative
Rundfunk	*Rundf*	broadcasting
jemand (-en, -em)	*sb*	somebody
Schulwesen	*Sch*	school
Naturwissenschaft	*Sci*	science
Schulwesen	*Scol*	school
schottisch	*Scot*	Scottish
Singular	*sing*	singular
Skisport	*Ski*	skiing
etwas	*sth*	something
Süddeutschland	*Südd*	South German
Suffix	*suff*	suffix
Superlativ	*superl*	superlative
Technik	*Tech*	technology
Telekommunikation	*Tel*	telecommunications
Theater	*Theat*	theatre
Fernsehen	*TV*	television
Typografie	*Typ*	typography
umgangssprachlich (! vulgär)	*umg(!)*	colloquial (! particularly offensive)
Universität	*Univ*	university
unpersönlich	*unpers*	impersonal
unregelmäßig	*unreg*	irregular
untrennbar	*untr*	inseparable
unveränderlich	*unver*	invariable
(nord)amerikanisch	*US*	(North)American
gewöhnlich	*usu*	usually
und so weiter	*usw*	et cetera
Verb	*vb*	verb
intransitives Verb	*vi*	intransitive verb
reflexives Verb	*vr*	reflexive verb
transitives Verb	*vt*	transitive verb
Wirtschaft	*Wirts*	economy
Zoologie	*Zool*	zoology
zusammengesetztes Wort	*zW*	compound
ungefähre Entsprechung	≈	cultural equivalent
eingetragene Marke	®	registered trademark

German noun endings

After many noun entries on the German-English side of the dictionary, you will find two pieces of grammatical information, separated by commas, to help you with the declension of the noun, e.g. **-, -n** or **-(e)s, -e**. The first item shows you the genitive singular form, and the second gives the plural form. The hyphen stands for the word itself and the other letters are endings. Sometimes an umlaut is shown over the hyphen, which means an umlaut must be placed on the vowel of the word, e.g.:

DICTIONARY ENTRY	GENITIVE SINGULAR	PLURAL
Mann *m* **-(e)s, ¨-er**	**Mannes** *or* **Manns**	**Männer**
Jacht *f* **-, -en**	**Jacht**	**Jachten**

This information is not given when the noun has one of the regular German noun endings below, and you should refer to this table in such cases. Similarly, genitive and plural endings are not shown when the German entry is a compound consisting of two or more words which are to be found elsewhere in the dictionary, since the compound form takes the endings of the LAST word of which it is formed, e.g.:

for **Nebenstraße** *see* **Straße**
for **Schneeball** *see* **Ball**

Regular German noun endings

NOM	GEN	PL
-ant *m*	-anten	-anten
-anz *f*	-anz	-anzen
-ar *m*	-ar(e)s	-are
-chen *nt*	-chens	-chen
-ei *f*	-ei	-eien
-elle *f*	-elle	-ellen
-ent *m*	-enten	-enten
-enz *f*	-enz	-enzen
-ette *f*	-ette	-etten
-eur *m*	-eurs	-eure
-euse *f*	-euse	-eusen
-heit *f*	-heit	-heiten
-ie *f*	-ie	-ien
-ik *f*	-ik	-iken
-in *f*	-in	-innen
-ine *f*	-ine	-inen
-ion *f*	-ion	-ionen
-ist *m*	-isten	-isten
-ium *nt*	-iums	-ien
-ius *m*	-ius	-iusse
-ive *f*	-ive	-iven
-keit *f*	-keit	-keiten
-lein *nt*	-leins	-lein
-ling *m*	-lings	-linge
-ment *nt*	-ments	-mente
-mus *m*	-mus	-men
-schaft *f*	-schaft	-schaften
-tät *f*	-tät	-täten
-tor *m*	-tors	-toren
-ung *f*	-ung	-ungen
-ur *f*	-ur	-uren

Lautschrift

NB: Alle Vokallaute sind nur ungefähre Entsprechungen.

Phonetic symbols

NB: All vowels sounds are approximate only.

Vokale		Vowels
m*a*tt	[a]	
F*ah*ne	[aː]	
Vat*er*	[əɾ]	
	[ɑː]	c*al*m, p*ar*t
	[æ]	s*a*t
R*en*dezvous	[ã]	
Ch*an*ce	[aː]	
	[ɑ̃ː]	cli*en*tele
*E*tage	[e]	
S*ee*le, M*eh*l	[eː]	
W*ä*sche, B*e*tt	[ɛ]	*e*gg
z*äh*len	[ɛː]	
T*ein*t	[ɛ̃ː]	
mach*e*	[ə]	*a*bove
	[əː]	b*ur*n, *ear*n
K*i*ste	[ɪ]	p*i*t, awfull*y*
V*i*tamin	[i]	
Z*ie*l	[iː]	p*ea*t
*O*ase	[o]	
*o*ben	[oː]	
Champign*on*	[õ]	
Sal*on*	[õː]	
M*o*st	[ɔ]	c*o*t
	[ɔː]	b*or*n, j*aw*
*ö*konomisch	[ø]	
bl*ö*d	[øː]	
G*ö*ttin	[œ]	
	[ʌ]	h*u*t
z*u*letzt	[u]	p*u*t
M*u*t	[uː]	p*oo*l
M*u*tter	[ʊ]	
Ph*y*sik	[y]	
K*ü*bel	[yː]	
S*ü*nde	[ʏ]	

Diphthonge		Diphthongs
Styling	[ai]	
weit	[aɪ]	buy, die, my
umbauen	[au]	house, now
Haus	[aʊ]	
	[eɪ]	pay, mate
	[ɛə]	pair, mare
	[əu]	no, boat
	[ɪə]	mere, shear
Heu, Häuser	[ɔʏ]	
	[ɔɪ]	boy, coin
	[uə]	tour, poor

Konsonanten		Consonants
Ball	[b]	ball
mich	[ç]	
	[tʃ]	child
fern	[f]	field
gern	[g]	good
Hand	[h]	hand
ja	[j]	yet, million
	[dʒ]	just
Kind	[k]	kind, catch
links, Pult	[l]	left, little
matt	[m]	mat
Nest	[n]	nest
lang	[ŋ]	long
Paar	[p]	put
rennen	[r]	run
fast, fassen	[s]	sit
Chef, Stein, Schlag	[ʃ]	shall
Tafel	[t]	tab
	[θ]	thing
	[ð]	this
wer	[v]	very
	[w]	wet
Loch	[x]	loch
fix	[ks]	box
singen	[z]	pods, zip
Zahn	[ts]	
genieren	[ʒ]	measure

Andere Zeichen		Other signs
glottal stop	|	Knacklaut
main stress	[ˈ]	Hauptton
long vowel	[ː]	Längezeichen

Irregular German verbs

* with "sein"

INFINITIV	PRÄSENS 2., 3. SINGULAR	PRÄTERITUM	PARTIZIP PERFEKT
abwägen	wägst ab, wägt ab	wog ab	abgewogen
ausbedingen	bedingst aus, bedingt aus	bedang *od* bedingte aus	ausbedungen
backen	bäckst, bäckt	backte *od* buk	gebacken
befehlen	befiehlst, befiehlt	befahl	befohlen
beginnen	beginnst, beginnt	begann	begonnen
beißen	beißt, beißt	biss	gebissen
bergen	birgst, birgt	barg	geborgen
bersten*	birst, birst	barst	geborsten
betrügen	betrügst, betrügt	betrog	betrogen
bewegen	bewegst, bewegt	bewog	bewogen
biegen	biegst, biegt	bog	gebogen
bieten	bietest, bietet	bot	geboten
binden	bindest, bindet	band	gebunden
bitten	bittest, bittet	bat	gebeten
blasen	bläst, bläst	blies	geblasen
bleiben*	bleibst, bleibt	blieb	geblieben
braten	brätst, brät	briet	gebraten
brechen*	brichst, bricht	brach	gebrochen
brennen	brennst, brennt	brannte	gebrannt
bringen	bringst, bringt	brachte	gebracht
denken	denkst, denkt	dachte	gedacht
dreschen	drischst, drischt	drosch	gedroschen
dringen*	dringst, dringt	drang	gedrungen
dürfen	darfst, darf	durfte	gedurft
empfangen	empfängst, empfängt	empfing	empfangen
empfehlen	empfiehlst, empfiehlt	empfahl	empfohlen
empfinden	empfindest, empfindet	empfand	empfunden
erbleichen*	erbleichst, erbleicht	erbleichte	erblichen
erlöschen*	erlischst, erlischt	erlosch	erloschen
erschrecken*	erschrickst, erschrickt	erschrak	erschrocken
erwägen	erwägst, erwägt	erwog	erwogen
essen	isst, isst	aß	gegessen
fahren*	fährst, fährt	fuhr	gefahren
fallen*	fällst, fällt	fiel	gefallen
fangen	fängst, fängt	fing	gefangen
fechten	fichtst, ficht	focht	gefochten
finden	findest, findet	fand	gefunden
flechten	flichtst, flicht	flocht	geflochten
fliegen*	fliegst, fliegt	flog	geflogen
fliehen*	fliehst, flieht	floh	geflohen
fließen*	fließt, fließt	floss	geflossen
fressen	frisst, frisst	fraß	gefressen
frieren	frierst, friert	fror	gefroren
gären*	gärst, gärt	gor	gegoren
gebären	gebierst, gebiert	gebar	geboren
geben	gibst, gibt	gab	gegeben
gedeihen*	gedeihst, gedeiht	gedieh	gediehen
gehen*	gehst, geht	ging	gegangen

*with "sein"

INFINITIV	PRÄSENS 2., 3. SINGULAR	PRÄTERITUM	PARTIZIP PERFEKT
gelingen*	–, gelingt	gelang	gelungen
gelten	giltst, gilt	galt	gegolten
genesen*	genest, genest	genas	genesen
genießen	genießt, genießt	genoss	genossen
geraten*	gerätst, gerät	geriet	geraten
geschehen*	–, geschieht	geschah	geschehen
gewinnen	gewinnst, gewinnt	gewann	gewonnen
gießen	gießt, gießt	goss	gegossen
gleichen	gleichst, gleicht	glich	geglichen
gleiten*	gleitest, gleitet	glitt	geglitten
glimmen	glimmst, glimmt	glomm	geglommen
graben	gräbst, gräbt	grub	gegraben
greifen	greifst, greift	griff	gegriffen
haben	hast, hat	hatte	gehabt
halten	hältst, hält	hielt	gehalten
hängen	hängst, hängt	hing	gehangen
hauen	haust, haut	haute	gehauen
heben	hebst, hebt	hob	gehoben
heißen	heißt, heißt	hieß	geheißen
helfen	hilfst, hilft	half	geholfen
kennen	kennst, kennt	kannte	gekannt
klimmen*	klimmst, klimmt	klomm	geklommen
klingen	klingst, klingt	klang	geklungen
kneifen	kneifst, kneift	kniff	gekniffen
kommen*	kommst, kommt	kam	gekommen
können	kannst, kann	konnte	gekonnt
kriechen*	kriechst, kriecht	kroch	gekrochen
laden	lädst, lädt	lud	geladen
lassen	lässt, lässt	ließ	gelassen
laufen*	läufst, läuft	lief	gelaufen
leiden	leidest, leidet	litt	gelitten
leihen	leihst, leiht	lieh	geliehen
lesen	liest, liest	las	gelesen
liegen	liegst, liegt	lag	gelegen
lügen	lügst, lügt	log	gelogen
mahlen	mahlst, mahlt	mahlte	gemahlen
meiden	meidest, meidet	mied	gemieden
melken	melkst, melkt	melkte *od* molk	gemolken
messen	misst, misst	maß	gemessen
misslingen*	–, misslingt	misslang	misslungen
mögen	magst, mag	mochte	gemocht
müssen	musst, muss	musste	gemusst
nehmen	nimmst, nimmt	nahm	genommen
nennen	nennst, nennt	nannte	genannt
pfeifen	pfeifst, pfeift	pfiff	gepfiffen
preisen	preist, preist	pries	gepriesen
quellen*	quillst, quillt	quoll	gequollen
raten	rätst, rät	riet	geraten
reiben	reibst, reibt	rieb	gerieben

* with "sein"

INFINITIV	PRÄSENS 2., 3. SINGULAR	PRÄTERITUM	PARTIZIP PERFEKT
reißen*	reißt, reißt	riss	gerissen
reiten*	reitest, reitet	ritt	geritten
rennen*	rennst, rennt	rannte	gerannt
riechen	riechst, riecht	roch	gerochen
ringen	ringst, ringt	rang	gerungen
rinnen*	rinnst, rinnt	rann	geronnen
rufen	rufst, ruft	rief	gerufen
salzen	salzt, salzt	salzte	gesalzen
saufen	säufst, säuft	soff	gesoffen
saugen	saugst, saugt	sog *od* saugte	gesogen *od* gesaugt
schaffen	schaffst, schafft	schuf	geschaffen
schallen	schallst, schallt	scholl	geschollen
scheiden*	scheidest, scheidet	schied	geschieden
scheinen	scheinst, scheint	schien	geschienen
scheißen	scheißt, scheißt	schiss	geschissen
schelten	schiltst, schilt	schalt	gescholten
scheren	scherst, schert	schor	geschoren
schieben	schiebst, schiebt	schob	geschoben
schießen	schießt, schießt	schoss	geschossen
schinden	schindest, schindet	schindete	geschunden
schlafen	schläfst, schläft	schlief	geschlafen
schlagen	schlägst, schlägt	schlug	geschlagen
schleichen*	schleichst, schleicht	schlich	geschlichen
schleifen	schleifst, schleift	schliff	geschliffen
schließen	schließt, schließt	schloss	geschlossen
schlingen	schlingst, schlingt	schlang	geschlungen
schmeißen	schmeißt, schmeißt	schmiss	geschmissen
schmelzen*	schmilzt, schmilzt	schmolz	geschmolzen
schneiden	schneidest, schneidet	schnitt	geschnitten
schreiben	schreibst, schreibt	schrieb	geschrieben
schreien	schreist, schreit	schrie	geschrien
schreiten	schreitest, schreitet	schritt	geschritten
schweigen	schweigst, schweigt	schwieg	geschwiegen
schwellen*	schwillst, schwillt	schwoll	geschwollen
schwimmen*	schwimmst, schwimmt	schwamm	geschwommen
schwinden*	schwindest, schwindet	schwand	geschwunden
schwingen	schwingst, schwingt	schwang	geschwungen
schwören	schwörst, schwört	schwor	geschworen
sehen	siehst, sieht	sah	gesehen
sein*	bist, ist	war	gewesen
senden	sendest, sendet	sandte	gesandt
singen	singst, singt	sang	gesungen
sinken*	sinkst, sinkt	sank	gesunken
sinnen	sinnst, sinnt	sann	gesonnen
sitzen	sitzt, sitzt	saß	gesessen
sollen	sollst, soll	sollte	gesollt
speien	speist, speit	spie	gespien
spinnen	spinnst, spinnt	spann	gesponnen
sprechen	sprichst, spricht	sprach	gesprochen
sprießen*	sprießt, sprießt	spross	gesprossen
springen*	springst, springt	sprang	gesprungen

* with "sein"

INFINITIV	PRÄSENS 2., 3. SINGULAR	PRÄTERITUM	PARTIZIP PERFEKT
stechen	stichst, sticht	stach	gestochen
stecken	steckst, steckt	steckte *od* stak	gesteckt
stehen	stehst, steht	stand	gestanden
stehlen	stiehlst, stiehlt	stahl	gestohlen
steigen*	steigst, steigt	stieg	gestiegen
sterben*	stirbst, stirbt	starb	gestorben
stinken	stinkst, stinkt	stank	gestunken
stoßen	stößt, stößt	stieß	gestoßen
streichen	streichst, streicht	strich	gestrichen
streiten	streitest, streitet	stritt	gestritten
tragen	trägst, trägt	trug	getragen
treffen	triffst, trifft	traf	getroffen
treiben*	treibst, treibt	trieb	getrieben
treten*	trittst, tritt	trat	getreten
trinken	trinkst, trinkt	trank	getrunken
trügen	trügst, trügt	trog	getrogen
tun	tust, tut	tat	getan
verderben	verdirbst, verdirbt	verdarb	verdorben
verdrießen	verdrießt, verdrießt	verdross	verdrossen
vergessen	vergisst, vergisst	vergaß	vergessen
verlieren	verlierst, verliert	verlor	verloren
verschleißen	verschleißt, verschleißt	verschliss	verschlissen
verschwinden	verschwindest, verschwindet	verschwand	verschwunden
verzeihen	verzeihst, verzeiht	verzieh	verziehen
wachsen*	wächst, wächst	wuchs	gewachsen
wägen	wägst, wägt	wog	gewogen
waschen	wäschst, wäscht	wusch	gewaschen
weben	webst, webt	webte *od* wob	gewoben
weichen*	weichst, weicht	wich	gewichen
weisen	weist, weist	wies	gewiesen
wenden	wendest, wendet	wandte	gewandt
werben	wirbst, wirbt	warb	geworben
werden*	wirst, wird	wurde	geworden
werfen	wirfst, wirft	warf	geworfen
wiegen	wiegst, wiegt	wog	gewogen
winden	windest, windet	wand	gewunden
wissen	weißt, weiß	wusste	gewusst
wollen	willst, will	wollte	gewollt
wringen	wringst, wringt	wrang	gewrungen
zeihen	zeihst, zeiht	zieh	geziehen
ziehen*	ziehst, zieht	zog	gezogen
zwingen	zwingst, zwingt	zwang	gezwungen

DEUTSCH–ENGLISCH

GERMAN–ENGLISH

Aa

a

A[1], a [a:] NT A, a; **A wie Anton** ≈ A for Andrew, ≈ A for Able (*US*); **das A und O** the be-all and end-all; (*eines Wissensgebietes*) the basics *pl*; **wer A sagt, muss auch B sagen** (*Sprichwort*) in for a penny, in for a pound (*Sprichwort*)
A[2] ABK (= *Autobahn*) ≈ M (BRIT)
à [a:] PRÄP (*bes Comm*) at
a. ABK = **am**
AA NT ABK (= *Auswärtiges Amt*) F.O. (BRIT)
Aachen ['a:xən] (**-s**) NT Aachen
Aal [a:l] (**-(e)s, -e**) M eel
aalen ['a:lən] (*umg*) VR: **sich in der Sonne ~** to bask in the sun
a. a. O. ABK (= *am angegebenen od angeführten Ort*) loc. cit.
Aas [a:s] (**-es, -e** *od* **Äser**) NT carrion; **Aasgeier** M vulture

SCHLÜSSELWORT

ab [ap] PRÄP *+dat* from; **ab Werk** (*Comm*) ex works; **Kinder ab 12 Jahren** children from the age of 12; **ab morgen** from tomorrow; **ab sofort** as of now
▸ ADV **1** off; **links ab** to the left; **der Knopf ist ab** the button has come off; **ab nach Hause!** off home with you!; **ab durch die Mitte!** (*umg*) beat it!
2 (*zeitlich*): **von da ab** from then on; **von heute ab** from today, as of today
3 (*auf Fahrplänen*): **München ab 12.20** leaving Munich 12.20
4: **ab und zu** *od* **an** now and then *od* again

abändern ['aplɛndərn] VT: **~ (in** *+akk*) to alter (to); (*Gesetzentwurf*) to amend (to); (*Strafe, Urteil*) to revise (to)
Abänderung F alteration; (*von Gesetzentwurf*) amendment; (*von Strafe, Urteil*) revision
Abänderungsantrag M (*Parl*) proposed amendment
abarbeiten ['aplarbaıtən] VR to slave away
Abart ['apla:rt] F (*Biol*) variety
abartig ADJ abnormal
Abb. ABK (= *Abbildung*) illus.
Abbau ['apbaʊ] (**-(e)s**) M *+gen* dismantling; (*Verminderung*) reduction (in); (*Verfall*) decline (in); (*Min*) mining; (*über Tage*) quarrying; (*Chem*) decomposition
abbaubar ADJ: **biologisch ~** biodegradable
abbauen VT to dismantle; (*verringern*) to reduce; (*Min*) to mine; (*über Tage*) to quarry; (*Chem*) to break down; **Arbeitsplätze ~** to make job cuts
Abbaurechte PL mineral rights *pl*
abbeißen ['apbaısən] *unreg* VT to bite off
abbekommen ['apbəkɔmən] *unreg* VT: **etwas ~** to get some (of it); (*beschädigt werden*) to get damaged; (*verletzt werden*) to get hurt
abberufen ['apbəru:fən] *unreg* VT to recall
Abberufung F recall
abbestellen ['apbəʃtɛlən] VT to cancel
abbezahlen ['apbətsa:lən] VT to pay off
abbiegen ['apbi:gən] *unreg* VI to turn off; (*Straße*) to bend ▸ VT to bend; (*verhindern*) to ward off
Abbiegespur F turning lane
Abbild ['apbılt] NT portrayal; (*einer Person*) image, likeness; **abbilden** ['apbıldən] VT to portray; **Abbildung** F illustration; (*Schaubild*) diagram
abbinden ['apbındən] *unreg* VT (*Med: Arm, Bein etc*) to ligature
Abbitte ['apbıtə] F: **~ leisten** *od* **tun (bei)** to make one's apologies (to)
abblasen ['apbla:zən] *unreg* VT to blow off; (*fig: umg*) to call off
abblättern ['apblɛtərn] VI (*Putz, Farbe*) to flake (off)
abblenden ['apblɛndən] VT (*Aut*) to dip (BRIT), to dim (*US*) ▸ VI to dip (BRIT) *od* dim (*US*) one's headlights
Abblendlicht ['apblɛntlıçt] NT dipped (BRIT) *od* dimmed (*US*) headlights *pl*
abblitzen ['apblıtsən] (*umg*) VI: **jdn ~ lassen** to send sb packing
abbrechen ['apbrɛçən] *unreg* VT to break off; (*Gebäude*) to pull down; (*Zelt*) to take down; (*aufhören*) to stop; (*Comput*) to abort ▸ VI to break off; (*aufhören*) to stop; **sich** *dat* **einen ~** (*umg: sich sehr anstrengen*) to bust a gut
abbremsen ['apbrɛmzən] VI to brake, to slow down
abbrennen ['apbrɛnən] *unreg* VT to burn off; (*Feuerwerk*) to let off ▸ VI (*Hilfsverb sein*) to burn down; **abgebrannt sein** (*umg*) to be broke
abbringen ['apbrıŋən] *unreg* VT: **jdn von etw ~** to dissuade sb from sth; **jdn vom Weg ~** to

divert sb; **ich bringe den Verschluss nicht ab** (*umg*) I can't get the top off

abbröckeln ['apbrœkəln] VI to crumble off *od* away; (*Börse: Preise*) to ease

Abbruch ['apbrʊx] M (*von Verhandlungen etc*) breaking off; (*von Haus*) demolition; (*Comput*) abort; **jdm/etw ~ tun** to harm sb/sth; **Abbrucharbeiten** PL demolition work *sing*; **abbruchreif** ADJ only fit for demolition

abbrühen ['apbry:ən] VT to scald

abbuchen ['apbu:xən] VT to debit; (*durch Dauerauftrag*): **~ (von)** to pay by standing order (from)

abbürsten ['apbʏrstən] VT to brush off

abbüßen ['apby:sən] VT (*Strafe*) to serve

ABC-Waffen PL ABK (= *atomare, biologische und chemische Waffen*) ABC weapons

abdampfen ['apdampfən] VI (*fig: umg: losgehen/-fahren*) to hit the road

abdanken ['apdaŋkən] VI to resign; (*König*) to abdicate

Abdankung F resignation; (*von König*) abdication

abdecken ['apdɛkən] VT to uncover; (*Tisch*) to clear; (*Loch*) to cover

abdichten ['apdɪçtən] VT to seal; (*Naut*) to caulk

abdrängen ['apdrɛŋən] VT to push off

abdrehen ['apdre:ən] VT (*Gas*) to turn off; (*Licht*) to switch off; (*Film*) to shoot ▸ VI (*Schiff*) to change course; **jdm den Hals ~** to wring sb's neck

abdriften ['apdrɪftən] VI to drift (away)

abdrosseln ['apdrɔsəln] VT to throttle; (*Aut*) to stall; (*Produktion*) to cut back

Abdruck ['apdrʊk] M (*Nachdrucken*) reprinting; (*Gedrucktes*) reprint; (*Gipsabdruck, Wachsabdruck*) impression; (*Fingerabdruck*) print; **abdrucken** VT to print

abdrücken ['apdrʏkən] VT to make an impression of; (*Waffe*) to fire; (*umg: Person*) to hug, to squeeze ▸ VR to leave imprints; (*abstoßen*) to push o.s. away; **jdm die Luft ~** to squeeze all the breath out of sb

abdüsen ['apdy:sən] (*umg*) VI to dash *od* whizz off

abebben ['ap|ɛbən] VI to ebb away

Abend ['a:bənt] (**-s, -e**) M evening; **gegen ~** towards (the) evening; **den ganzen ~ (über)** the whole evening; **zu ~ essen** to have dinner *od* supper; **heute ~** this evening; **Abendanzug** M dinner jacket (BRIT), tuxedo (US); **Abendbrot** NT supper; **Abendessen** NT supper; **abendfüllend** ADJ taking up the whole evening; **Abendgymnasium** NT night school; **Abendkasse** F (*Theat*) box office; **Abendkleid** NT evening gown; **Abendkurs** M evening classes *pl*; **Abendland** NT West; **abendlich** ADJ evening; **Abendmahl** NT Holy Communion; **Abendrot** NT sunset

abends ADV in the evening

Abend- zW: **Abendvorstellung** F evening performance; **Abendzeitung** F evening paper

Abenteuer ['a:bəntɔʏər] (**-s, -**) NT adventure; (*Liebesabenteuer*) affair; **abenteuerlich** ADJ adventurous; **Abenteuerspielplatz** M adventure playground; **Abenteuerurlaub** M adventure holiday

Abenteurer (**-s, -**) M adventurer; **Abenteurerin** F adventuress

aber ['a:bər] KONJ but; (*jedoch*) however ▸ ADV: **oder ~** or else; **bist du ~ braun!** aren't you brown!; **das ist ~ schön** that's really nice; **nun ist ~ Schluss!** now that's enough!

Aber NT but

Aberglaube ['a:bərglaʊbə] M superstition

abergläubisch ['a:bərglɔʏbɪʃ] ADJ superstitious

aberkennen ['ap|ɛrkɛnən] *unreg* VT: **jdm etw ~** to deprive sb of sth, to take sth (away) from sb

Aberkennung F deprivation

abermalig ADJ repeated

abermals ADV once again

Abertausend, abertausend ['a:bərtaʊznt] NUM: **Tausend und ~** thousands upon thousands

Abf. ABK (= *Abfahrt*) dep.

abfahren ['apfa:rən] *unreg* VI to leave, to depart ▸ VT to take *od* cart away; (*Film*) to start; (*Film, TV: Kamera*) to roll; (*Strecke*) to drive; (*Reifen*) to wear; (*Fahrkarte*) to use; **der Zug ist abgefahren** (*lit*) the train has left; (*fig*) we've/you've *etc* missed the boat; **der Zug fährt um 8.00 von Bremen ab** the train leaves Bremen at 8 o'clock; **jdn ~ lassen** (*umg: abweisen*) to tell sb to get lost; **auf jdn ~** (*umg*) to really go for sb

Abfahrt ['apfa:rt] F departure; (*Autobahnabfahrt*) exit; (*Ski*) descent; (*Piste*) run; **Vorsicht bei der ~ des Zuges!** stand clear, the train is about to leave!

Abfahrts- zW: **Abfahrtslauf** M (*Ski*) downhill; **Abfahrtstag** M day of departure; **Abfahrtszeit** F departure time

Abfall ['apfal] M waste; (*von Speisen etc*) rubbish (BRIT), garbage (US); (*Neigung*) slope; (*Verschlechterung*) decline; **Abfalleimer** M rubbish bin (BRIT), garbage can (US)

abfallen *unreg* VI (*lit, fig*) to fall *od* drop off; (*Pol, vom Glauben*) to break away; (*sich neigen*) to fall *od* drop away; **wie viel fällt bei dem Geschäft für mich ab?** (*umg*) how much do I get out of the deal?

abfällig ['apfɛlɪç] ADJ disparaging, deprecatory

Abfallprodukt NT (*lit, fig*) waste product

abfangen ['apfaŋən] *unreg* VT to intercept; (*Person*) to catch; (*unter Kontrolle bringen*) to check; (*Aufprall*) to absorb; (*Kunden*) to lure away

Abfangjäger M (*Mil*) interceptor

abfärben ['apfɛrbən] VI (*lit*) to lose its colour; (*Wäsche*) to run; (*fig*) to rub off

abfassen ['apfasən] VT to write, to draft

abfeiern ['apfaɪərn] (*umg*) VT: **Überstunden ~** to take time off in lieu of overtime pay

abfertigen ['apfɛrtɪgən] VT to prepare for dispatch, to process; (*an Grenze*) to clear; (*Kundschaft*) to attend to; **jdn kurz ~** to give sb short shrift

Abfertigung F preparing for dispatch, processing; (*an Grenze*) clearance; (*Bedienung: von Kunden*) service; (: *von Antragstellern*): **~ von** dealing with
abfeuern ['apfɔʏərn] VT to fire
abfinden ['apfɪndən] *unreg* VT to pay off ▶ VR to come to terms; **sich mit jdm ~/nicht ~** to put up with/not to get on with sb; **er konnte sich nie damit ~, dass …** he could never accept the fact that …
Abfindung F (*von Gläubigern*) payment; (*Geld*) sum in settlement
abflachen ['apflaxən] VT to level (off), to flatten (out) ▶ VI (*fig: sinken*) to decline
abflauen ['apflaʊən] VI (*Wind, Erregung*) to die away, to subside; (*Nachfrage, Geschäft*) to fall *od* drop off
abfliegen ['apfli:gən] *unreg* VI to take off ▶ VT (*Gebiet*) to fly over
abfließen ['apfli:sən] *unreg* VI to drain away; **ins Ausland ~** (*Geld*) to flow out of the country
Abflug ['apflu:k] M departure; (*Start*) take-off; **Abflughalle** F departure lounge; **Abflugterminal** ['apflu:ktœrmɪnəl] (**-s, -s**) M departure terminal; **Abflugzeit** F departure time
Abfluss ['apflʊs] M draining away; (*Öffnung*) outlet; **Abflussrohr** NT drainpipe; (*von sanitären Anlagen*) wastepipe
abfragen ['apfra:gən] VT to test; (*Comput*) to call up; **jdn etw ~** to question sb on sth
abfrieren ['apfri:rən] *unreg* VI: **ihm sind die Füße abgefroren** his feet got frostbitten, he got frostbite in his feet
abfrühstücken ['apfry:ʃtykən] (*umg*) VT (*jdn*) to fob off, to snub; (*Sache*) to get through with
Abfuhr ['apfu:r] (**-, -en**) F removal; (*fig*) snub, rebuff; **sich *dat* eine ~ holen** to meet with a rebuff
abführen ['apfy:rən] VT to lead away; (*Gelder, Steuern*) to pay ▶ VI (*Med*) to have a laxative effect
Abführmittel NT laxative, purgative
Abfüllanlage F bottling plant
abfüllen ['apfʏlən] VT to draw off; (*in Flaschen*) to bottle
Abgabe ['apga:bə] F handing in; (*von Ball*) pass; (*Steuer*) tax; (*einer Erklärung*) giving
abgabenfrei ADJ tax-free
abgabenpflichtig ADJ liable to tax
Abgabetermin M closing date; (*für Dissertation etc*) submission date
Abgang ['apgaŋ] M (*von Schule*) leaving; (*Theat*) exit; (*Med: Ausscheiden*) passing; (: *Fehlgeburt*) miscarriage; (*Abfahrt*) departure; (*der Post, von Waren*) dispatch
Abgangszeugnis NT leaving certificate
Abgas ['apga:s] NT waste gas; (*Aut*) exhaust; **Abgase** exhaust fumes *pl*; **Abgasgrenzwert** M exhaust emission standard; **Abgassonderuntersuchung** F exhaust emission test
ABGB NT ABK (ÖSTERR: = *Allgemeines Bürgerliches Gesetzbuch*) Civil Code in Austria
abgeben ['apge:bən] *unreg* VT (*Gegenstand*) to hand *od* give in; (*Ball*) to pass; (*Wärme*) to give off; (*Amt*) to hand over; (*Schuss*) to fire; (*Erklärung, Urteil*) to give; (*darstellen*) to make ▶ VR: **sich mit jdm/etw ~** to associate with sb/bother with sth; **„Kinderwagen abzugeben"** "pram for sale"; **jdm etw ~** (*überlassen*) to let sb have sth
abgebrannt ['apgəbrant] (*umg*) ADJ broke
abgebrüht ['apgəbry:t] (*umg*) ADJ (*skrupellos*) hard-boiled, hardened
abgedroschen ['apgədrɔʃən] ADJ trite; (*Witz*) corny
abgefahren ['apgəfa:rən] PP *von* **abfahren**
abgefeimt ['apgəfaɪmt] ADJ cunning
abgegeben ['apgəge:bən] PP *von* **abgeben**
abgegriffen ['apgəgrɪfən] ADJ (*Buch*) well-thumbed; (*Redensart*) trite
abgehackt ['apgəhakt] ADJ clipped
abgehalftert ['apgəhalftərt] ADJ (*fig: umg*) run-down, dead beat
abgehangen ['apgəhaŋən] PP *von* **abhängen** ▶ ADJ: **(gut) ~** (*Fleisch*) well-hung
abgehärtet ['apgəhɛrtət] ADJ tough, hardy; (*fig*) hardened
abgehen ['apge:ən] *unreg* VI to go away, to leave; (*Theat*) to exit; (*Post*) to go; (*Med*) to be passed; (*sterben*) to die; (*Knopf etc*) to come off; (*abgezogen werden*) to be taken off; (*Straße*) to branch off; (*abweichen*): **von einer Forderung ~** to give up a demand ▶ VT (*Strecke*) to go *od* walk along; (*Mil: Gelände*) to patrol; **von seiner Meinung ~** to change one's opinion; **davon gehen 5% ab** 5% is taken off that; **etw geht jdm ab** (*fehlt*) sb lacks sth
abgekämpft ['apgəkɛmpft] ADJ exhausted
abgekartet ['apgəkartət] ADJ: **ein abgekartetes Spiel** a rigged job
abgeklärt ['apgəklɛ:rt] ADJ serene, tranquil
abgelegen ['apgəle:gən] ADJ remote
abgelten ['apgɛltən] *unreg* VT (*Ansprüche*) to satisfy
abgemacht ['apgəmaxt] ADJ fixed; **~!** done!
abgemagert ['apgəma:gərt] ADJ (*sehr dünn*) thin; (*ausgemergelt*) emaciated
abgeneigt ['apgənaɪkt] ADJ averse; **ich wäre nicht ~, das zu tun** I wouldn't mind doing that
abgenutzt ['apgənʊtst] ADJ worn, shabby; (*Reifen*) worn; (*fig: Klischees*) well-worn
Abgeordnete(r) ['apgəlɔrdnətə(r)] F(M) elected representative; (*von Parlament*) member of parliament
Abgesandte(r) ['apgəzantə(r)] F(M) delegate; (*Pol*) envoy
abgeschieden ['apgəʃi:dən] ADV (*einsam*): **~ leben/wohnen** to live in seclusion
abgeschlagen ['apgəʃla:gən] ADJ (*besiegt*) defeated; (*erschöpft*) exhausted, worn-out
abgeschlossen ['apgəʃlɔsən] PP *von* **abschließen** ▶ ADJ *attrib* (*Wohnung*) self-contained
abgeschmackt ['apgəʃmakt] ADJ tasteless; **Abgeschmacktheit** F lack of taste; (*Bemerkung*) tasteless remark

abgesehen ['apgəze:ən] ADJ: **es auf jdn/etw ~ haben** to be after sb/sth; **~ von ...** apart from ...
abgespannt ['apgəʃpant] ADJ tired out
abgestanden ['apgəʃtandən] ADJ stale; (*Bier*) flat
abgestorben ['apgəʃtɔrbən] ADJ numb; (*Biol, Med*) dead
abgestumpft ['apgəʃtʊmpft] ADJ (*gefühllos: Person*) insensitive; (*Gefühle, Gewissen*) dulled
abgetakelt ['apgəta:kəlt] ADJ (*fig*) decrepit, past it
abgetan ['apgəta:n] ADJ: **damit ist die Sache ~** that settles the matter
abgetragen ['apgətra:gən] ADJ worn
abgewinnen ['apgəvɪnən] *unreg* VT: **jdm Geld ~** to win money from sb; **einer Sache etw/Geschmack ~** to get sth/pleasure from sth
abgewogen ['apgəvo:gən] ADJ (*Urteil, Worte*) balanced
abgewöhnen ['apgəvø:nən] VT: **jdm/sich etw ~** to cure sb of sth/give sth up
abgießen ['apgi:sən] *unreg* VT (*Flüssigkeit*) to pour off
Abglanz ['apglants] M (*auch fig*) reflection
abgleiten ['apglaɪtən] *unreg* VI to slip, to slide
Abgott ['apgɔt] M idol
abgöttisch ['apgœtɪʃ] ADJ: **~ lieben** to idolize
abgrasen ['apgra:zən] VT (*Feld*) to graze; (*umg: Thema*) to do to death
abgrenzen ['apgrɛntsən] VT (*lit, fig*) to mark off; (*Gelände*) to fence off ▶ VR: **sich ~ (gegen)** to dis(as)sociate o.s. (from)
Abgrund ['apgrʊnt] M (*lit, fig*) abyss
abgründig ['apgrʏndɪç] ADJ unfathomable; (*Lächeln*) cryptic
abgrundtief ADJ (*Hass, Verachtung*) profound
abgucken ['apgʊkən] VT, VI to copy
Abguss ['apgʊs] M (*Kunst, Metallurgie: Vorgang*) casting; (*: Form*) cast
abhaben ['apha:bən] (*umg*) *unreg* VT (*abbekommen*): **willst du ein Stück ~?** do you want a bit?
abhacken ['aphakən] VT to chop off
abhaken ['apha:kən] VT to tick off (BRIT), to check off (*US*)
abhalten ['aphaltən] *unreg* VT (*Versammlung*) to hold; **jdn von etw ~** (*fernhalten*) to keep sb away from sth; (*hindern*) to keep sb from sth
abhandeln ['aphandəln] VT (*Thema*) to deal with; **jdm die Waren/10 Euro ~** to do a deal with sb for the goods/beat sb down 10 euros
abhandenkommen [ap'handən-] VI to get lost
Abhandlung ['aphandlʊŋ] F treatise, discourse
Abhang ['aphaŋ] M slope
abhängen ['aphɛŋən] *unreg* VT (*Bild*) to take down; (*Anhänger*) to uncouple; (*Verfolger*) to shake off ▶ VI (*Fleisch*) to hang; **von jdm/etw ~** to depend on sb/sth; **das hängt ganz davon ab** it all depends; **er hat abgehängt** (*Tel: umg*) he hung up (on me *etc*)
abhängig ['aphɛŋɪç] ADJ: **~ (von)** dependent (on); **Abhängigkeit** F: **Abhängigkeit (von)** dependence (on)
abhärten ['aphɛrtən] VT to toughen up ▶ VR to toughen (o.s.) up; **sich gegen etw ~** to harden o.s. to sth
abhauen ['aphaʊən] *unreg* VT to cut off; (*Baum*) to cut down ▶ VI (*umg*) to clear off *od* out; **hau ab!** beat it!
abheben ['aphe:bən] *unreg* VT to lift (up); (*Karten*) to cut; (*Masche*) to slip; (*Geld*) to withdraw, to take out ▶ VI (*Flugzeug*) to take off; (*Rakete*) to lift off; (*Karten*) to cut ▶ VR: **sich ~ von** to stand out from, to contrast with
abheften ['aphɛftən] VT (*Rechnungen etc*) to file away; (*Nähen*) to tack, to baste
abhelfen ['aphɛlfən] *unreg* VI *+dat* to remedy
abhetzen ['aphɛtsən] VR to wear *od* tire o.s. out
Abhilfe ['aphɪlfə] F remedy; **~ schaffen** to put things right
abholen ['apho:lən] VT (*Gegenstand*) to fetch, to collect; (*Person*) to call for; (*am Bahnhof etc*) to pick up, to meet
Abholmarkt M cash and carry
abholzen ['aphɔltsən] VT (*Wald*) to clear, to deforest
abhorchen ['aphɔrçən] VT (*Med*) to listen to, to sound
abhören ['aphø:rən] VT (*Vokabeln*) to test; (*Telefongespräch*) to tap; (*Tonband etc*) to listen to; **abgehört werden** (*umg*) to be bugged
Abhörgerät NT bug
abhungern ['aphʊŋərn] VR: **sich** *dat* **10 Kilo ~** to lose 10 kilos by going on a starvation diet
Abi ['abi] **(-s, -s)** NT (*Sch umg*) = **Abitur**
Abitur [abi'tu:r] **(-s, -e)** NT *German school-leaving examination*, ≈ A-levels *pl* (BRIT); **(das) ~ machen** to take one's school-leaving exam *od* A-levels

> The **Abitur** is the German school-leaving examination which is taken at the age of 18 or 19 by pupils at a **Gymnasium**. It is taken in four subjects and is necessary for entry to a university education.

Abiturient(in) [abituri'ɛnt(ɪn)] M(F) candidate for school-leaving certificate
abkämmen ['apkɛmən] VT (*Gegend*) to comb, to scour
abkanzeln ['apkantsəln] (*umg*) VT: **jdn ~** to give sb a dressing-down
abkapseln ['apkapsəln] VR to shut *od* cut o.s. off
abkarten ['apkartən] (*umg*) VT: **die Sache war von vornherein abgekartet** the whole thing was a put-up job
abkaufen ['apkaʊfən] VT: **jdm etw ~** to buy sth from sb; **das kauf ich dir nicht ab!** (*umg*) I don't believe you
abkehren ['apke:rən] VT (*Blick*) to avert, to turn away ▶ VR to turn away
abklappern ['apklapərn] (*umg*) VT (*Kunden*) to call on; (*: Läden, Straße*): **~ (nach)** to scour (for), to comb (for)
abklären ['apklɛ:rən] VT (*klarstellen*) to clear up, to clarify ▶ VR (*sich setzen*) to clarify
Abklatsch ['apklatʃ] **(-es, -e)** M (*fig*) (poor) copy
abklemmen ['apklɛmən] VT (*Leitung*) to clamp

abklingen ['apklɪŋən] *unreg* VI to die away; (*Rundf*) to fade out
abknallen ['apknalən] (*umg*) VT to shoot down
abknöpfen ['apknœpfən] VT to unbutton; **jdm etw ~** (*umg*) to get sth off sb
abkochen ['apkɔxən] VT to boil; (*keimfrei machen*) to sterilize (by boiling)
abkommandieren ['apkɔmandi:rən] VT (*Mil: zu Einheit*) to post; (*zu bestimmtem Dienst*): **~ zu** to detail for
abkommen ['apkɔmən] *unreg* VI to get away; **(vom Thema) ~** to get off the subject, to digress; **von der Straße/einem Plan ~** to leave the road/give up a plan
Abkommen (**-s, -**) NT agreement
abkömmlich ['apkœmlɪç] ADJ available, free
Abkömmling M (*Nachkomme*) descendant; (*fig*) adherent
abkönnen ['apkœnən] (*umg*) *unreg* VT (*mögen*): **das kann ich nicht ab** I can't stand it
abkoppeln ['apkɔpəln] VT (*Anhänger*) to unhitch
abkratzen ['apkratsən] VT to scrape off ▸ VI (*umg*) to kick the bucket
abkriegen ['apkri:gən] (*umg*) VT = **abbekommen**
abkühlen ['apky:lən] VT to cool down ▸ VR (*Mensch*) to cool down *od* off; (*Wetter*) to get cool; (*Zuneigung*) to cool
Abkunft ['apkʊnft] (-) F origin, birth
abkürzen ['apkʏrtsən] VT to shorten; (*Wort*) to abbreviate; **den Weg ~** to take a short cut
Abkürzung F abbreviation; (*Weg*) short cut
abladen ['apla:dən] *unreg* VI to unload ▸ VT to unload; (*fig: umg*): **seinen Ärger (bei jdm) ~** to vent one's anger (on sb)
Ablage ['apla:gə] F place to keep/put sth; (*Aktenordnung*) filing; (*für Akten*) tray
ablagern ['apla:gərn] VT to deposit ▸ VR to be deposited ▸ VI to mature
Ablagerung F (*abgelagerter Stoff*) deposit
ablassen ['aplasən] *unreg* VT (*Wasser, Dampf*) to let out *od* off; (*vom Preis*) to knock off ▸ VI: **von etw ~** to give sth up, to abandon sth
Ablauf M (*Abfluss*) drain; (*von Ereignissen*) course; (*einer Frist, Zeit*) expiry (BRIT), expiration (US); **nach ~ des Jahres/dieser Zeit** at the end of the year/this time
Ablaufdatum NT (ÖSTERR) expiry date; (*von Lebensmitteln*) use-by *od* best-before date
ablaufen ['aplaʊfən] *unreg* VI (*abfließen*) to drain away; (*Ereignisse*) to happen; (*Frist, Zeit, Pass*) to expire ▸ VT (*Sohlen*) to wear (down *od* out); **~ lassen** (*abspulen, abspielen: Platte, Tonband*) to play; (*Film*) to run; **sich** *dat* **die Beine** *od* **Hacken nach etw ~** (*umg*) to walk one's legs off looking for sth; **jdm den Rang ~** to steal a march on sb
Ableben ['aple:bən] NT (*form*) demise (*form*)
ablegen ['aple:gən] VT to put *od* lay down; (*Kleider*) to take off; (*Gewohnheit*) to get rid of; (*Prüfung*) to take, to sit (BRIT); (*Zeugnis*) to give; (*Schriftwechsel*) to file (away); (*nicht mehr tragen: Kleidung*) to discard, to cast off; (*Schwur, Eid*) to swear ▸ VI (*Schiff*) to cast off
Ableger (**-s, -**) M layer; (*fig*) branch, offshoot
ablehnen ['aple:nən] VT to reject; (*missbilligen*) to disapprove of; (*Einladung*) to decline, to refuse ▸ VI to decline, to refuse
Ablehnung F rejection; (*von Einladung*) refusal; **auf ~ stoßen** to meet with disapproval
ableisten ['aplaɪstən] VT (*form: Zeit*) to serve
ableiten ['aplaɪtən] VT (*Wasser*) to divert; (*deduzieren*) to deduce; (*Wort*) to derive
Ableitung F diversion; (*Deduzierung*) deduction; (*von Wort*) derivation; (*Wort*) derivative
ablenken ['aplɛŋkən] VT to turn away, to deflect; (*zerstreuen*) to distract ▸ VI to change the subject; **das lenkt ab** (*zerstreut*) it takes your mind off things; (*stört*) it's distracting
Ablenkung F deflection; (*Zerstreuung*) distraction
Ablenkungsmanöver NT diversionary tactic; (*um vom Thema abzulenken*) red herring
ablesen ['aple:zən] *unreg* VT to read; **jdm jeden Wunsch von den Augen ~** to anticipate sb's every wish
ableugnen ['aplɔʏgnən] VT to deny
ablichten ['aplɪçtən] VT to photocopy; (*fotografieren*) to photograph
abliefern ['apli:fərn] VT to deliver; **etw bei jdm/einer Dienststelle ~** to hand sth over to sb/in at an office
Ablieferung F delivery
abliegen ['apli:gən] *unreg* VI to be some distance away; (*fig*) to be far removed
ablisten ['aplɪstən] VT: **jdm etw ~** to trick *od* con sb out of sth
ablösen ['aplø:zən] VT (*abtrennen*) to take off, to remove; (*in Amt*) to take over from; (*Fin: Schuld, Hypothek*) to pay off, to redeem; (*Methode, System*) to supersede ▸ VR (*auch*: **einander ablösen**) to take turns; (*Fahrer, Kollegen, Wachen*) to relieve each other
Ablösung F removal; (*von Fahrer, Wache*) relieving
abluchsen ['aplʊksən] (*umg*) VT: **jdm etw ~** to get *od* wangle sth out of sb
Abluft F (*Tech*) used air
ABM PL ABK (= *Arbeitsbeschaffungsmaßnahmen*) *job-creation scheme*
abmachen ['apmaxən] VT to take off; (*vereinbaren*) to agree; **etw mit sich allein ~** to sort sth out for o.s.
Abmachung F agreement
abmagern ['apma:gərn] VI to get thinner, to become emaciated
Abmagerungskur F diet; **eine ~ machen** to go on a diet
Abmarsch ['apmarʃ] M departure;
abmarschbereit ADJ ready to start
abmarschieren ['apmarʃi:rən] VI to march off
abmelden ['apmɛldən] VT (*Auto*) to take off the road; (*Telefon*) to have disconnected; (*Comput*) to log off ▸ VR to give notice of one's departure; (*im Hotel*) to check out; **ein Kind von einer Schule ~** to take a child away from a school; **er/sie ist bei mir abgemeldet** (*umg*) I don't

want anything to do with him/her; **jdn bei der Polizei ~** to register sb's departure with the police

abmessen ['apmɛsən] *unreg* VT to measure

Abmessung F measurement; (*Ausmaß*) dimension

abmontieren ['apmɔnti:rən] VT to take off; (*Maschine*) to dismantle

ABM-Stelle F *temporary post created as part of a job creation scheme*

abmühen ['apmy:ən] VR to wear o.s. out

abnabeln ['apna:bəln] VT: **jdn ~** (*auch fig*) to cut sb's umbilical cord

abnagen ['apna:gən] VT to gnaw off; (*Knochen*) to gnaw

Abnäher ['apnɛ:ər] (**-s, -**) M dart

Abnahme ['apna:mə] F *+gen* removal; (*Comm*) buying; (*Verringerung*) decrease (in)

abnehmen ['apne:mən] *unreg* VT to take off, to remove; (*Führerschein*) to take away; (*Prüfung*) to hold; (*Maschen*) to decrease; (*Hörer*) to lift, to pick up; (*begutachten: Gebäude, Auto*) to inspect ▸ VI to decrease; (*schlanker werden*) to lose weight; (*Tel*) to pick up the phone; **jdm etw ~** (*Geld*) to get sth out of sb; (*kaufen, auch umg: glauben*) to buy sth from sb; **kann ich dir etwas ~?** (*tragen*) can I take something for you?; **jdm Arbeit ~** to take work off sb's shoulders; **jdm ein Versprechen ~** to make sb promise sth

Abnehmer (**-s, -**) M purchaser, customer; **viele/wenige ~ finden** (*Comm*) to sell well/badly

Abneigung ['apnaɪgʊŋ] F aversion, dislike

abnicken ['apnɪkən] (*umg*) VT: **etw ~** to nod sth through

abnorm [ap'nɔrm] ADJ abnormal

abnötigen ['apnø:tɪgən] VT: **jdm etw/Respekt ~** to force sth from sb/gain sb's respect

abnutzen ['apnʊtsən] VT to wear out

Abnutzung F wear (and tear)

Abo ['abo] (**-s, -s**) (*umg*) NT = **Abonnement**

Abonnement [abɔn(ə)'mã:] (**-s, -s** *od* **-e**) NT subscription; (*Theaterabonnement*) season ticket

Abonnent(in) [abɔ'nɛnt(ɪn)] M(F) subscriber

abonnieren [abɔ'ni:rən] VT to subscribe to

abordnen ['ap|ɔrdnən] VT to delegate

Abordnung F delegation

Abort [a'bɔrt] (**-(e)s, -e**) M (*veraltet*) lavatory

abpacken ['appakən] VT to pack

abpassen ['appasən] VT (*Person, Gelegenheit*) to wait for; (*warten auf*) to catch; (*jdm auflauern*) to waylay; **etw gut ~** to time sth well

abpausen ['appaʊzən] VT to make a tracing of

abpfeifen ['appfaɪfən] *unreg* VT, VI (*Sport*): **(das Spiel) ~** to blow the whistle (for the end of the game)

Abpfiff ['appfɪf] M final whistle

abplagen ['appla:gən] VR to struggle (away)

Abprall ['appral] M rebound; (*von Kugel*) ricochet

abprallen ['appralən] VI to bounce off; (*Kugel*) to ricochet; **an jdm ~** (*fig*) to make no impression on sb

abputzen ['appʊtsən] VT to clean; (*Nase etc*) to wipe

abquälen ['apkvɛ:lən] VR to struggle (away)

abrackern ['aprakərn] (*umg*) VR to slave away

abraten ['apra:tən] *unreg* VI: **jdm von etw ~** to advise sb against sth, to warn sb against sth

abräumen ['aprɔʏmən] VT to clear up *od* away; (*Tisch*) to clear ▸ VI to clear up *od* away

abreagieren ['apreagi:rən] VT: **seinen Zorn (an jdm/etw) ~** to work one's anger off (on sb/sth) ▸ VR to calm down; **seinen Ärger an anderen ~** to take it out on others

abrechnen ['aprɛçnən] VT to deduct, to take off ▸ VI (*lit*) to settle up; (*fig*) to get even; **darf ich ~?** would you like your bill (Brit) *od* check (US) now?

Abrechnung F settlement; (*Rechnung*) bill; (*Aufstellung*) statement; (*Bilanz*) balancing; (*fig: Rache*) revenge; **in ~ stellen** (*form: Abzug*) to deduct; **~ über** *+akk* bill/statement for

Abrechnungszeitraum M accounting period

Abrede ['apre:də] F: **etw in ~ stellen** to deny *od* dispute sth

abregen ['apre:gən] (*umg*) VR to calm *od* cool down

abreiben ['apraɪbən] *unreg* VT to rub off; (*säubern*) to wipe; **jdn mit einem Handtuch ~** to towel sb down

Abreibung (*umg*) F (*Prügel*) hiding, thrashing

Abreise ['apraɪzə] F departure

abreisen VI to leave, to set off

abreißen ['apraɪsən] *unreg* VT (*Haus*) to tear down; (*Blatt*) to tear off ▸ VI: **den Kontakt nicht ~ lassen** to stay in touch

abrichten ['aprɪçtən] VT to train

abriegeln ['apri:gəln] VT (*Tür*) to bolt; (*Straße, Gebiet*) to seal off

abringen ['aprɪŋən] *unreg* VT: **sich** *dat* **ein Lächeln ~** to force a smile

Abriss ['aprɪs] (**-es, -e**) M (*Übersicht*) outline; (*Abbruch*) demolition

abrollen ['aprɔlən] VT (*abwickeln*) to unwind ▸ VI (*vonstattengehen: Programm*) to run; (*: Veranstaltung*) to go off; (*: Ereignisse*) to unfold

Abruf ['apru:f] M: **auf ~** on call

abrufen *unreg* VT (*Mensch*) to call away; (*Comm: Ware*) to request delivery of; (*Comput*) to recall, to retrieve

abrunden ['aprʊndən] VT to round off

abrupt [ab'rʊpt] ADJ abrupt

abrüsten ['aprʏstən] VI to disarm

Abrüstung F disarmament

abrutschen ['aprʊtʃən] VI to slip; (*Aviat*) to sideslip

Abs. ABK = **Absender**; (= *Absatz*) par., para

absacken ['apzakən] VI (*sinken*) to sink; (*Boden, Gebäude*) to subside

Absage ['apza:gə] (**-, -n**) F refusal; (*auf Einladung*) negative reply

absagen VT to cancel, to call off; (*Einladung*) to turn down ▸ VI to cry off; (*ablehnen*) to decline; **jdm ~** to tell sb that one can't come

absägen ['apzɛ:gən] VT to saw off

absahnen ['apza:nən] VT (*lit*) to skim; **das Beste für sich ~** (*fig*) to take the cream

Absatz ['apzats] M (*Comm*) sales *pl*; (*Jur*) section; (*Bodensatz*) deposit; (*neuer Abschnitt*) paragraph; (*Treppenabsatz*) landing; (*Schuhabsatz*) heel; **Absatzflaute** F slump in the market; **Absatzförderung** F sales promotion; **Absatzgebiet** NT (*Comm*) market; **Absatzplus** NT increase in sales; **Absatzprognose** F sales forecast; **Absatzschwierigkeiten** PL sales problems *pl*; **Absatzziffern** PL sales figures *pl*

absaufen ['apzaʊfən] *unreg* (*umg*) VI (*ertrinken*) to drown; (: *Motor*) to flood; (: *Schiff etc*) to go down

absaugen ['apzaʊgən] VT (*Flüssigkeit*) to suck out *od* off; (*Teppich, Sofa*) to hoover®, to vacuum

abschaben ['apʃa:bən] VT to scrape off; (*Möhren*) to scrape

abschaffen ['apʃafən] VT to abolish, to do away with

Abschaffung F abolition

abschalten ['apʃaltən] VT, VI (*lit, umg*) to switch off

abschattieren ['apʃati:rən] VT to shade

abschätzen ['apʃɛtsən] VT to estimate; (*Lage*) to assess; (*Person*) to size up

abschätzig ['apʃɛtsɪç] ADJ disparaging, derogatory

Abschaum ['apʃaʊm] **(-(e)s)** M scum

Abscheu ['apʃɔʏ] **(-(e)s)** M loathing, repugnance; **abscheuerregend** ADJ repulsive, loathsome; **abscheulich** ADJ abominable

abschicken ['apʃɪkən] VT to send off

abschieben ['apʃi:bən] *unreg* VT to push away; (*Person*) to pack off; (*ausweisen: Ausländer*) to deport; (*fig: Verantwortung, Schuld*): **~ (auf** +*akk*) to shift (onto)

Abschied ['apʃi:t] **(-(e)s, -e)** M parting; (*von Armee*) discharge; **(von jdm) ~ nehmen** to say goodbye (to sb), to take one's leave (of sb); **seinen ~ nehmen** (*Mil*) to apply for discharge; **zum ~** on parting

Abschiedsbrief M farewell letter

Abschiedsfeier F farewell party

abschießen ['apʃi:sən] *unreg* VT (*Flugzeug*) to shoot down; (*Geschoss*) to fire; (*umg: Minister*) to get rid of

abschirmen ['apʃɪrmən] VT to screen; (*schützen*) to protect ▶ VR (*sich isolieren*): **sich ~ (gegen)** to cut o.s. off (from)

abschlaffen ['apʃlafən] (*umg*) VI to flag

abschlagen ['apʃla:gən] *unreg* VT (*abhacken, Comm*) to knock off; (*ablehnen*) to refuse; (*Mil*) to repel

abschlägig ['apʃlɛ:gɪç] ADJ negative; **jdn/etw ~ bescheiden** (*form*) to turn sb/sth down

Abschlagszahlung F interim payment

abschleifen ['apʃlaɪfən] *unreg* VT to grind down; (*Holzboden*) to sand (down) ▶ VR to wear off

Abschleppdienst M (*Aut*) breakdown service (BRIT), towing company (US)

abschleppen ['apʃlɛpən] VT to (take in) tow

Abschleppseil NT towrope

abschließen ['apʃli:sən] *unreg* VT (*Tür*) to lock; (*beenden*) to conclude, to finish; (*Vertrag, Handel*) to conclude; (*Versicherung*) to take out; (*Wette*) to place ▶ VR (*sich isolieren*) to cut o.s. off; **mit abgeschlossenem Studium** with a degree; **mit der Vergangenheit ~** to break with the past

abschließend ADJ concluding ▶ ADV in conclusion, finally

Abschluss ['apʃlʊs] M (*Beendigung*) close, conclusion; (*Comm: Bilanz*) balancing; (*von Vertrag, Handel*) conclusion; **zum ~** in conclusion; **Abschlussfeier** F (*Sch*) school-leavers' ceremony; **Abschlussprüfer** M accountant; **Abschlussprüfung** F (*Sch*) final examination; (*Univ*) finals *pl*; **Abschlussrechnung** F final account; **Abschlusszeugnis** NT (*Sch*) leaving certificate, diploma (*US*)

abschmecken ['apʃmɛkən] VT (*kosten*) to taste; (*würzen*) to season

abschmieren ['apʃmi:rən] VT (*Aut*) to grease, to lubricate

abschminken ['apʃmɪŋkən] VR to remove one's make-up ▶ VT (*umg*): **sich** *dat* **etw ~** to get sth out of one's mind

abschmirgeln ['apʃmɪrgəln] VT to sand down

abschnallen ['apʃnalən] VR to unfasten one's seat belt ▶ VI (*umg: nicht mehr folgen können*) to give up; (: *fassungslos sein*) to be staggered

abschneiden ['apʃnaɪdən] *unreg* VT to cut off ▶ VI to do, to come off; **bei etw gut/schlecht ~** (*umg*) to come off well/badly in sth

Abschnitt ['apʃnɪt] M section; (*Mil*) sector; (*Kontrollabschnitt*) counterfoil (BRIT), stub (US); (*Math*) segment; (*Zeitabschnitt*) period

abschnüren ['apʃny:rən] VT to constrict

abschöpfen ['apʃœpfən] VT to skim off

abschrauben ['apʃraʊbən] VT to unscrew

abschrecken ['apʃrɛkən] VT to deter, to put off; (*mit kaltem Wasser*) to plunge into cold water

abschreckend ADJ deterrent; **abschreckendes Beispiel** warning; **eine abschreckende Wirkung haben, ~ wirken** to act as a deterrent

abschreiben ['apʃraɪbən] *unreg* VT to copy; (*verloren geben*) to write off; (*Comm*) to deduct; **er ist bei mir abgeschrieben** I'm finished with him

Abschreibung F (*Comm*) deduction; (*Wertverminderung*) depreciation

Abschrift ['apʃrɪft] F copy

abschuften ['apʃʊftən] (*umg*) VR to slog one's guts out (*umg*)

abschürfen ['apʃʏrfən] VT to graze

Abschuss ['apʃʊs] M (*eines Geschützes*) firing; (*Herunterschießen*) shooting down; (*Tötung*) shooting

abschüssig ['apʃʏsɪç] ADJ steep

Abschussliste F: **er steht auf der ~** (*umg*) his days are numbered

Abschussrampe F launch(ing) pad

abschütteln ['apʃʏtəln] VT to shake off

abschütten ['apʃʏtən] VT (*Flüssigkeit etc*) to pour off

abschwächen ['apʃvɛçən] VT to lessen; (*Behauptung, Kritik*) to tone down ▶ VR to lessen

abschweifen ['apʃvaɪfən] VI to wander; (*Redner*) to digress
Abschweifung F digression
abschwellen ['apʃvɛlən] *unreg* VI (*Geschwulst*) to go down; (*Lärm*) to die down
abschwenken ['apʃvɛŋkən] VI to turn away
abschwören ['apʃvøːrən] *unreg* VI *+dat* to renounce
absehbar ['apzeːbaːr] ADJ foreseeable; **in absehbarer Zeit** in the foreseeable future; **das Ende ist ~** the end is in sight
absehen *unreg* VT (*Ende, Folgen*) to foresee ▸ VI: **von etw ~** to refrain from sth; (*nicht berücksichtigen*) to leave sth out of consideration; **jdm etw ~** (*erlernen*) to copy sth from sb
abseilen ['apzaɪlən] VT to lower down on a rope ▸ VR (*Bergsteiger*) to abseil (down)
abseits ADV out of the way ▸ PRÄP *+gen* away from
Abseits ['apzaɪts] NT (*Sport*) offside; **im ~ stehen** to be offside; **im ~ leben** (*fig*) to live in the shadows; **Abseitsfalle** F (*Sport*) offside trap
absenden ['apzɛndən] *unreg* VT to send off, to dispatch
Absender M sender
Absendung F dispatch
absetzbar ['apzɛtsbaːr] ADJ (*Beamter*) dismissible; (*Waren*) saleable; (*von Steuer*) deductible
absetzen ['apzɛtsən] VT (*niederstellen*) to put down; (*aussteigen lassen*) to drop (off); (*abnehmen; auch Theaterstück*) to take off; (*Comm: verkaufen*) to sell; (*Fin: abziehen*) to deduct; (*entlassen*) to dismiss; (*König*) to depose; (*streichen*) to drop; (*Fußballspiel, Termin*) to cancel; (*hervorheben*) to pick out ▸ VI: **er trank das Glas aus, ohne abzusetzen** he emptied his glass in one ▸ VR (*sich entfernen*) to clear off; (*sich ablagern*) to be deposited; **das kann man ~** that is tax-deductible
Absetzung F (*Fin: Abzug*) deduction; (*Entlassung*) dismissal; (*von König*) deposing; (*Streichung*) dropping
absichern ['apzɪçərn] VT to make safe; (*schützen*) to safeguard ▸ VR to protect o.s.
Absicht ['apzɪçt] F intention; **mit ~** on purpose; **absichtlich** ADJ intentional, deliberate
absichtslos ADJ unintentional
absinken ['apzɪŋkən] *unreg* VI to sink; (*Temperatur, Geschwindigkeit*) to decrease
absitzen ['apzɪtsən] *unreg* VI to dismount ▸ VT (*Strafe*) to serve
absolut [apzo'luːt] ADJ absolute
Absolutheitsanspruch M claim to absolute right
Absolutismus [apzoluː'tɪsmʊs] M absolutism
Absolvent(in) M(F): **die Absolventen eines Lehrgangs** the students who have completed a course
absolvieren [apzɔl'viːrən] VT (*Sch*) to complete
absonderlich [ap'zɔndərlɪç] ADJ odd, strange
absondern VT to separate; (*ausscheiden*) to give off, to secrete ▸ VR to cut o.s. off
Absonderung F separation; (*Med*) secretion
absorbieren [apzɔr'biːrən] VT (*lit, fig*) to absorb
abspalten ['apʃpaltən] VT to split off
Abspannung ['apʃpanʊŋ] F (*Ermüdung*) exhaustion
absparen ['apʃpaːrən] VT: **sich** *dat* **etw ~** to scrimp and save for sth
abspecken ['apʃpɛkən] (*umg*) VT to shed ▸ VI to lose weight
abspeichern ['apʃpaɪçərn] VT (*Comput*) to save
abspeisen ['apʃpaɪzən] VT (*fig*) to fob off
abspenstig ['apʃpɛnstɪç] ADJ: **(jdm) ~ machen** to lure away (from sb)
absperren ['apʃpɛrən] VT to block *od* close off; (*Tür*) to lock
Absperrung F (*Vorgang*) blocking *od* closing off; (*Sperre*) barricade
abspielen ['apʃpiːlən] VT (*CD etc*) to play; (*Sport: Ball*) to pass ▸ VR to happen; **vom Blatt ~** (*Mus*) to sight-read
absplittern ['apʃplɪtərn] VT, VI to chip off
Absprache ['apʃpraːxə] F arrangement; **ohne vorherige ~** without prior consultation
absprechen ['apʃprɛçən] *unreg* VT (*vereinbaren*) to arrange ▸ VR: **die beiden hatten sich vorher abgesprochen** they had agreed on what to do/say *etc* in advance; **jdm etw ~** to deny sb sth; (*in Abrede stellen: Begabung*) to dispute sb's sth
abspringen ['apʃprɪŋən] *unreg* VI to jump down/off; (*Farbe, Lack*) to flake off; (*Aviat*) to bale out; (*sich distanzieren*) to back out
Absprung ['apʃprʊŋ] M jump; **den ~ schaffen** (*fig*) to make the break (*umg*)
abspulen ['apʃpuːlən] VT (*Kabel, Garn*) to unwind
abspülen ['apʃpyːlən] VT to rinse; **Geschirr ~** to wash up (BRIT), to do the dishes
abstammen ['apʃtamən] VI to be descended; (*Wort*) to be derived
Abstammung F descent; (*von Wort*) derivation; **französischer ~** of French extraction *od* descent
Abstand ['apʃtant] M distance; (*zeitlich*) interval; **davon ~ nehmen, etw zu tun** to refrain from doing sth; **~ halten** (*Aut*) to keep one's distance; **~ von etw gewinnen** (*fig*) to distance o.s. from sth; **mit großem ~ führen** to lead by a wide margin; **mit ~ der Beste** by far the best
Abstandssumme F compensation
abstatten ['apʃtatən] VT (*form: Dank*) to give; (*: Besuch*) to pay
abstauben ['apʃtaʊbən] VT, VI to dust; (*umg: mitgehen lassen*) to help oneself to, to pinch; **(den Ball) ~** (*Sport*) to tuck the ball away
Abstauber(in) ['apʃtaʊbər(ɪn)] **(-s, -)** (*umg*) M(F) (*Person*) somebody on the make
abstechen ['apʃtɛçən] *unreg* VT to cut; (*Tier*) to cut the throat of ▸ VI: **~ gegen** *od* **von** to contrast with
Abstecher **(-s, -)** M detour
abstecken ['apʃtɛkən] VT (*Fläche*) to mark out; (*Saum*) to pin

abstehen ['apʃte:ən] *unreg* VI (*Ohren, Haare*) to stick out; (*entfernt sein*) to stand away
Absteige F cheap hotel
absteigen ['apʃtaɪgən] *unreg* VI (*vom Rad etc*) to get off, to dismount; **in einem Gasthof ~** to put up at an inn; **(in die Zweite Liga) ~** to be relegated (to the second division); **auf dem absteigenden Ast sein** (*umg*) to be going downhill, to be on the decline
abstellen ['apʃtɛlən] VT (*niederstellen*) to put down; (*entfernt stellen*) to pull out; (*hinstellen: Auto*) to park; (*ausschalten*) to turn *od* switch off; (*Missstand, Unsitte*) to stop; (*abkommandieren*) to order off; (*ausrichten*): **~ auf** *+akk* to gear to; **das lässt sich nicht/lässt sich ~** nothing/something can be done about that
Abstellgleis NT siding; **jdn aufs ~ schieben** (*fig*) to cast sb aside
Abstellraum M storeroom
abstempeln ['apʃtɛmpəln] VT to stamp; (*fig*): **~ zu** *od* **als** to brand as
absterben ['apʃtɛrbən] *unreg* VI to die; (*Körperteil*) to go numb
Abstieg ['apʃti:k] **(-(e)s, -e)** M descent; (*Sport*) relegation; (*fig*) decline
Abstiegskampf M (*Sport*) relegation battle
abstimmen ['apʃtɪmən] VI to vote ▶ VT: **~ (auf** *+akk*) (*Instrument*) to tune (to); (*Interessen*) to match (with); (*Termine, Ziele*) to fit in (with) ▶ VR to agree
Abstimmung F vote; (*geheime Abstimmung*) ballot
abstinent [apsti'nɛnt] ADJ (*von Alkohol*) teetotal
Abstinenz [apsti'nɛnts] F teetotalism
Abstinenzler(in) **(-s, -)** M(F) teetotaller
abstoßen ['apʃto:sən] *unreg* VT to push off *od* away; (*anekeln*) to repel; (*Comm: Ware, Aktien*) to sell off
abstoßend ADJ repulsive
abstottern ['apʃtɔtərn] (*umg*) VT to pay off in instalments
abstrahieren [apstra'hi:rən] VT, VI to abstract
abstrakt [ap'strakt] ADJ abstract ▶ ADV abstractly, in the abstract
Abstraktion [apstraktsi'o:n] F abstraction
Abstraktum [ap'straktʊm] **(-s, Abstrakta)** NT abstract concept; (*Gram*) abstract noun
abstrampeln ['apʃtrampəln] VR (*fig: umg*) to sweat (away)
abstreifen ['apʃtraɪfən] VT (*abtreten: Schuhe, Füße*) to wipe; (*abziehen: Schmuck*) to take off, to slip off
abstreiten ['apʃtraɪtən] *unreg* VT to deny
Abstrich ['apʃtrɪç] M (*Abzug*) cut; (*Med*) smear; **Abstriche machen** to lower one's sights
abstufen ['apʃtu:fən] VT (*Hang*) to terrace; (*Farben*) to shade; (*Gehälter*) to grade
abstumpfen ['apʃtʊmpfən] VT (*lit, fig*) to dull, to blunt ▶ VI to become dulled
Absturz ['apʃtʊrts] M fall; (*Aviat*) crash
abstürzen ['apʃtʏrtsən] VI to fall; (*Aviat*) to crash
absuchen ['apzu:xən] VT to scour, to search
absurd [ap'zʊrt] ADJ absurd
Abszess [aps'tsɛs] **(-es, -sse)** M abscess

Abt [apt] **(-(e)s, Äbte)** M abbot
Abt. ABK (= *Abteilung*) dept.
abtasten ['aptastən] VT to feel, to probe; (*Elek*) to scan; (*bei Durchsuchung*): **~ (auf** *+akk*) to frisk (for)
abtauen ['aptaʊən] VT, VI to thaw; (*Kühlschrank*) to defrost
Abtei [ap'taɪ] **(-, -en)** F abbey
Abteil [ap'taɪl] **(-(e)s, -e)** NT compartment
abteilen ['aptaɪlən] VT to divide up; (*abtrennen*) to divide off
Abteilung F (*in Firma, Kaufhaus*) department; (*Mil*) unit; (*in Krankenhaus, Jur*) section
Abteilungsleiter(in) M(F) head of department; (*in Kaufhaus*) department manager(ess)
abtelefonieren ['aptelefoni:rən] (*umg*) VI to telephone to say one can't make it
Äbtissin [ɛp'tɪsɪn] F abbess
abtönen ['aptø:nən] VT (*Phot*) to tone down
abtöten ['aptøtən] VT (*lit, fig*) to destroy, to kill (off); (*Nerv*) to deaden
abtragen ['aptra:gən] *unreg* VT (*Hügel, Erde*) to level down; (*Essen*) to clear away; (*Kleider*) to wear out; (*Schulden*) to pay off
abträglich ['aptrɛ:klɪç] ADJ *+dat* harmful (to)
Abtragung F (*Geol*) erosion
Abtransport **(-(e)s, -e)** M transportation; (*aus Katastrophengebiet*) evacuation
abtransportieren ['aptranspɔrti:rən] VT to transport; (*aus Katastrophengebiet*) to evacuate
abtreiben ['aptraɪbən] *unreg* VT (*Boot, Flugzeug*) to drive off course; (*Kind*) to abort ▶ VI to be driven off course; (*Frau*) to have an abortion
Abtreibung F abortion
Abtreibungsparagraf M abortion law
Abtreibungsversuch M attempted abortion
abtrennen ['aptrɛnən] VT (*lostrennen*) to detach; (*entfernen*) to take off; (*abteilen*) to separate off
abtreten ['aptre:tən] *unreg* VT to wear out; (*überlassen*) to hand over, to cede; (*Rechte, Ansprüche*) to transfer ▶ VI to go off; (*zurücktreten*) to step down; **sich** *dat* **die Füße ~** to wipe one's feet; **~!** (*Mil*) dismiss!
Abtritt ['aptrɪt] M (*Rücktritt*) resignation
abtrocknen ['aptrɔknən] VT to dry ▶ VI to do the drying-up
abtropfen ['aptrɔpfən] VI: **etw ~ lassen** to let sth drain
abtrünnig ['aptrʏnɪç] ADJ renegade
abtun ['aptu:n] *unreg* VT to take off; (*fig*) to dismiss; **etw kurz ~** to brush sth aside
aburteilen ['ap|ʊrtaɪlən] VT to condemn
abverlangen ['apfɛrlaŋən] VT: **jdm etw ~** to demand sth from sb
abwägen ['apvɛ:gən] *unreg* VT to weigh up
abwählen ['apvɛ:lən] VT to vote out (of office); (*Sch: Fach*) to give up
abwälzen ['apvɛltsən] VT: **~ (auf** *+akk*) (*Schuld, Verantwortung*) to shift (onto); (*Arbeit*) to unload (onto); (*Kosten*) to pass on (to)
abwandeln ['apvandəln] VT to adapt
abwandern ['apvandərn] VI to move away
Abwärme ['apvɛrmə] F waste heat

abwarten ['apvartən] VT to wait for ▶ VI to wait; **das Gewitter ~** to wait till the storm is over; **~ und Tee trinken** (*umg*) to wait and see; **eine abwartende Haltung einnehmen** to play a waiting game

abwärts ['apvɛrts] ADV down; **mit ihm/dem Land geht es ~** he/the country is going downhill

Abwasch ['apvaʃ] (**-(e)s**) M washing-up; **du kannst das auch machen, das ist (dann) ein ~** (*umg*) you could do that as well and kill two birds with one stone

abwaschen *unreg* VT (*Schmutz*) to wash off; (*Geschirr*) to wash (up)

Abwasser ['apvasər] (**-s, -wässer**) NT sewage; **Abwasseraufbereitung** F sewage treatment; **Abwasserkanal** M sewer

abwechseln ['apvɛksəln] VI, VR to alternate; (*Personen*) to take turns

abwechselnd ADJ alternate

Abwechslung F change; (*Zerstreuung*) diversion; **für ~ sorgen** to provide entertainment

abwechslungsreich ADJ varied

Abweg ['apve:k] M: **auf Abwege geraten/führen** to go/lead astray

abwegig ['apve:gıç] ADJ wrong; (*Verdacht*) groundless

Abwehr ['apve:r] (-) F defence; (*Schutz*) protection; (*Abwehrdienst*) counter-intelligence (service); **auf ~ stoßen** to be repulsed; **abwehren** VT to ward off; (*Ball*) to stop; **abwehrende Geste** dismissive gesture; **Abwehrreaktion** F (*Psych*) defence (BRIT) *od* defense (US) reaction; **Abwehrstoff** M antibody

abweichen ['apvaıçən] *unreg* VI to deviate; (*Meinung*) to differ; **vom rechten Weg ~** (*fig*) to wander off the straight and narrow

abweichend ADJ deviant; (*Meinungen*) differing

Abweichler (**-s, -**) M (*Pol*) maverick

Abweichung F (*zeitlich, zahlenmäßig*) allowance; **zulässige ~** (*Tech*) tolerance

abweisen ['apvaızən] *unreg* VT to turn away; (*Antrag*) to turn down; **er lässt sich nicht ~** he won't take no for an answer

abweisend ADJ (*Haltung*) cold

abwenden ['apvɛndən] *unreg* VT to avert ▶ VR to turn away

abwerben ['apvɛrbən] *unreg* VT: **(jdm) ~** to woo away (from sb)

abwerfen ['apvɛrfən] *unreg* VT to throw off; (*Profit*) to yield; (*aus Flugzeug*) to drop; (*Spielkarte*) to discard

abwerten ['apvɛrtən] VT (*Fin*) to devalue

abwertend ADJ pejorative

Abwertung F devaluation

abwesend ['apve:zənt] ADJ absent; (*zerstreut*) far away

Abwesenheit ['apve:zənhaıt] F absence; **durch ~ glänzen** (*ironisch*) to be conspicuous by one's absence

abwickeln ['apvıkəln] VT to unwind; (*Geschäft*) to transact, to conclude; (*fig: erledigen*) to deal with

Abwicklungskosten ['apvıkluŋskɔstən] PL transaction costs *pl*

abwiegen ['apvi:gən] *unreg* VT to weigh out

abwimmeln ['apvıməln] (*umg*) VT (*Person*) to get rid of; (*: Auftrag*) to get out of

abwinken ['apvıŋkən] VI to wave it/him *etc* aside; (*fig: ablehnen*) to say no

abwirtschaften ['apvırtʃaftən] VI to go downhill

abwischen ['apvıʃən] VT to wipe off *od* away; (*putzen*) to wipe

abwracken ['apvrakən] VT (*Schiff*) to break (up); **ein abgewrackter Mensch** a wreck (of a person)

Abwurf ['apvʊrf] M throwing off; (*von Bomben etc*) dropping; (*von Reiter, Sport*) throw

abwürgen ['apvʏrgən] (*umg*) VT to scotch; (*Motor*) to stall; **etw von vornherein ~** to nip sth in the bud

abzahlen ['aptsa:lən] VT to pay off

abzählen ['aptsɛ:lən] VT to count (up); **abgezähltes Fahrgeld** exact fare

Abzählreim ['aptsɛ:lraım] M counting rhyme (*e.g. eeny meeny miney mo*)

Abzahlung F repayment; **auf ~ kaufen** to buy on hire purchase (BRIT) *od* the installment plan (US)

abzapfen ['aptsapfən] VT to draw off; **jdm Blut ~** to take blood from sb

abzäunen ['aptsɔynən] VT to fence off

Abzeichen ['aptsaıçən] NT badge; (*Orden*) decoration

abzeichnen ['aptsaıçnən] VT to draw, to copy; (*unterschreiben*) to initial ▶ VR to stand out; (*fig: bevorstehen*) to loom

Abziehbild NT transfer

abziehen ['aptsi:ən] *unreg* VT to take off; (*Tier*) to skin; (*Bett*) to strip; (*Truppen*) to withdraw; (*subtrahieren*) to take away, to subtract; (*kopieren*) to run off; (*Schlüssel*) to take out, to remove ▶ VI to go away; (*Truppen*) to withdraw; (*abdrücken*) to pull the trigger, to fire

abzielen ['aptsi:lən] VI: **~ auf** *+akk* to be aimed at

Abzocke ['aptsɔkə] (*umg*) F rip-off

Abzug ['aptsu:k] M departure; (*von Truppen*) withdrawal; (*Kopie*) copy; (*Subtraktion*) subtraction; (*Betrag*) deduction; (*Rabatt*) discount; (*Rauchabzug*) flue; (*von Waffen*) trigger; (*Korrekturfahne*) proof; (*Phot*) print; **jdm freien ~ gewähren** to grant sb safe passage

abzüglich ['aptsy:klıç] PRÄP *+gen* less

abzweigen ['aptsvaıgən] VI to branch off ▶ VT to set aside

Abzweigung F junction

Accessoires [aksɛso'a:rs] PL accessories *pl*

ach [ax] INTERJ oh; **~ so!** I see!; **mit A~ und Krach** by the skin of one's teeth; **~ was** *od* **wo, das ist doch nicht so schlimm!** come on now, it's not that bad!

Achillesferse [a'xılɛsfɛrzə] F Achilles heel

Achse ['aksə] (**-, -n**) F axis; (*Aut*) axle; **auf ~ sein** (*umg*) to be on the move

Achsel ['aksəl] (**-, -n**) F shoulder; **Achselhöhle** F armpit; **Achselzucken** NT shrug (of one's shoulders)

Achsenbruch M (*Aut*) broken axle
Achsenkreuz NT coordinate system
acht NUM eight; **~ Tage** a week
Acht[1] [axt] (**-, -en**) F eight; (*beim Eislaufen etc*) figure (of) eight
Acht[2] (**-**) F attention; **hab ~** (*Mil*) attention!; **~ geben** = **achtgeben**; **sich in ~ nehmen (vor** *+dat*) to be careful (of), to watch out (for); **etw außer ~ lassen** to disregard sth
achtbar ADJ worthy
achte(r, s) ADJ eighth
Achteck NT octagon
Achtel NT eighth; **Achtelnote** F quaver, eighth note (*US*)
achten VT to respect ▶ VI: **~ (auf** *+akk*) to pay attention (to); **darauf ~, dass ...** to be careful that ...
ächten ['ɛçtən] VT to outlaw, to ban
Achterbahn F roller coaster
Achterdeck NT (*Naut*) afterdeck
achtfach ADJ eightfold
achtgeben *unreg* VI: **~ (auf** *+akk*) to take care (of); (*aufmerksam sein*) to pay attention (to)
achthundert NUM eight hundred
achtlos ADJ careless; **viele gehen ~ daran vorbei** many people just pass by without noticing
achtmal ADV eight times
achtsam ADJ attentive
Achtstundentag M eight-hour day
Achtung ['axtʊŋ] F attention; (*Ehrfurcht*) respect ▶ INTERJ look out!; (*Mil*) attention!; **alle ~!** good for you/him *etc*!; **~, fertig, los!** ready, steady, go!; **„~ Hochspannung!"** "danger, high voltage"; **„~ Lebensgefahr/Stufe!"** "danger/ mind the step!"
Achtungserfolg M reasonable success
achtzehn NUM eighteen
achtzig NUM eighty; **Achtziger(in)** (**-s, -**) M(F) octogenarian
ächzen ['ɛçtsən] VI: **~ (vor** *+dat*) to groan (with)
Acker ['akər] (**-s, Äcker**) M field; **Ackerbau** M agriculture; **Ackerbau und Viehzucht** farming
ackern VI to plough; (*umg*) to slog away
a conto [a 'kɔnto] ADV (*Comm*) on account
a. d. ABK = **an der**: *bei Ortsnamen*
a. D. ABK = **außer Dienst**
A. D. ABK (= *Anno Domini*) A.D.
ad absurdum [at ap'zʊrdʊm] ADV: **~ führen** (*Argument etc*) to reduce to absurdity
ADAC (**-**) M ABK (= *Allgemeiner Deutscher Automobil-Club*) *German motoring organization*, ≈ AA (BRIT), ≈ AAA (*US*)
ad acta [at 'akta] ADV: **etw ~ legen** (*fig*) to consider sth finished; (*Frage, Problem*) to consider sth closed
Adam ['a:dam] M: **bei ~ und Eva anfangen** (*umg*) to start right from scratch *od* from square one
Adapter [a'daptər] (**-s, -**) M adapter
adaptieren [adap'ti:rən] VT to adapt
adäquat [adɛ'kva:t] ADJ (*Belohnung, Übersetzung*) adequate; (*Stellung, Verhalten*) suitable
addieren [a'di:rən] VT to add (up)
Addis Abeba ['adɪs'a:beba] (**- -s**) NT Addis Ababa
Addition [aditsi'o:n] F addition
ade INTERJ bye!
Adel ['a:dəl] (**-s**) M nobility; **~ verpflichtet** noblesse oblige
adelig ADJ noble
Adelsstand M nobility
Ader ['a:dər] (**-, -n**) F vein; (*fig: Veranlagung*) bent
Adhäsionsverschluss [athɛzi'o:nsfɛrʃlʊs] M adhesive seal
Adjektiv ['atjɛkti:f] (**-s, -e**) NT adjective
Adler ['a:dlər] (**-s, -**) M eagle
adlig ADJ = **adelig**
Admiral [atmi'ra:l] (**-s, -e**) M admiral
Admiralität F admiralty
adoptieren [adɔp'ti:rən] VT to adopt
Adoption [adɔptsi'o:n] F adoption
Adoptiveltern PL adoptive parents *pl*
Adoptivkind NT adopted child
Adr. ABK (= *Adresse*) add.
Adrenalin [adrena'li:n] (**-s**) NT adrenalin
Adressant [adrɛ'sant] M sender
Adressat [adrɛ'sa:t] (**-en, -en**) M addressee
Adressbuch NT directory; (*privat*) address book
Adresse [a'drɛsə] (**-, -n**) F (*auch Comput*) address; **an der falschen ~ sein** (*umg*) to have gone/ come to the wrong person; **absolute ~** absolute address; **relative ~** relative address
adressieren [adrɛ'si:rən] VT: **~ (an** *+akk*) to address (to)
Adria ['a:dria] (**-**) F Adriatic Sea
Adriatisches Meer [adri'a:tɪʃəs me:r] NT (*form*) Adriatic Sea
ADSL NT ABK (= *Asymmetric Digital Subscriber Line*) ADSL
Advent [at'vɛnt] (**-(e)s, -e**) M Advent; **der erste/ zweite ~** the first/second Sunday in Advent
Advents- ZW: **Adventskalender** M Advent calendar; **Adventskranz** M Advent wreath
Adverb [at'vɛrp] NT adverb
adverbial [atvɛrbi'a:l] ADJ adverbial
aero- [aero] PRÄF aero-
Aerobic [ae'ro:bik] (**-s**) NT aerobics *sing*
Affäre [a'fɛ:rə] (**-, -n**) F affair; **sich aus der ~ ziehen** (*umg*) to get (o.s.) out of it
Affe ['afə] (**-n, -n**) M monkey; (*umg: Kerl*) berk (BRIT)
Affekt (**-(e)s, -e**) M: **im ~ handeln** to act in the heat of the moment
affektiert [afɛk'ti:rt] ADJ affected
Affen- ZW: **affenartig** ADJ like a monkey; **mit affenartiger Geschwindigkeit** (*umg*) like a flash; **affengeil** (*umg*) ADJ magic, fantastic; **Affenhitze** (*umg*) F incredible heat; **Affenliebe** F: **Affenliebe (zu)** blind adoration (of); **Affenschande** (*umg*) F crying shame; **Affentempo** (*umg*) NT: **in** *od* **mit einem Affentempo** at breakneck speed; **Affentheater** (*umg*) NT: **ein Affentheater aufführen** to make a fuss
affig ['afɪç] ADJ affected

Afghane [afˈgaːnə] (**-n, -n**) M Afghan
Afghanin [afˈgaːnɪn] F Afghan
afghanisch ADJ Afghan
Afghanistan [afˈgaːnɪstaːn] (**-s**) NT Afghanistan
Afrika [ˈaːfrika] (**-s**) NT Africa
Afrikaans [afriˈkaːns] (-) NT Afrikaans
Afrikaner(in) [afriˈkaːnər(ɪn)] (**-s, -**) M(F) African
afrikanisch ADJ African
afroamerikanisch [ˈaːfro|ameriˈkaːnɪʃ] ADJ Afro-American
After [ˈaftər] (**-s, -**) M anus
AG (-) F ABK (= *Aktiengesellschaft*) ≈ plc (BRIT), ≈ corp., inc. (US)
Ägäis [ɛˈgɛːɪs] (-) F Aegean (Sea)
Ägäisches Meer NT Aegean Sea
Agent(in) [aˈgɛnt(ɪn)] M(F) agent
Agententätigkeit F espionage
Agentur [agɛnˈtuːr] F agency; **Agenturbericht** M, **Agenturmeldung** F (news) agency report
Aggregat [agreˈgaːt] (**-(e)s, -e**) NT aggregate; (*Tech*) unit; **Aggregatzustand** M (*Phys*) state
Aggression [agrɛsiˈoːn] F aggression
aggressiv [agrɛˈsiːf] ADJ aggressive
Aggressivität [agrɛsiviˈtɛːt] F aggressiveness
Aggressor [aˈgrɛsoːr] (**-s, -en**) M aggressor
Agitation [agitatsiˈoːn] F agitation
Agrarpolitik F agricultural policy
Agrarstaat M agrarian state
AGV F ABK (= *Arbeitsgemeinschaft der Verbraucherverbände*) *consumer groups' association*
Ägypten [ɛˈgʏptən] (**-s**) NT Egypt
Ägypter(in) (**-s, -**) M(F) Egyptian
ägyptisch ADJ Egyptian
aha [aˈhaː] INTERJ aha!
Aha-Erlebnis NT sudden insight
ahd. ABK (= *althochdeutsch*) OHG
Ahn [aːn] (**-en, -en**) M forebear
ahnden [ˈaːndən] VT (*geh: Freveltat, Verbrechen*) to avenge; (*Übertretung, Verstoß*) to punish
ähneln [ˈɛːnəln] VI *+dat* to be like, to resemble ▸ VR to be alike *od* similar
ahnen [ˈaːnən] VT to suspect; (*Tod, Gefahr*) to have a presentiment of; **nichts Böses ~** to be unsuspecting; **du ahnst es nicht!** you have no idea!; **davon habe ich nichts geahnt** I didn't have the slightest inkling of it
Ahnenforschung F genealogy
ähnlich [ˈɛːnlɪç] ADJ *+dat* similar (to); **das sieht ihm (ganz) ~!** (*umg*) that's just like him!, that's him all over!; **Ähnlichkeit** F similarity
Ahnung [ˈaːnʊŋ] F idea, suspicion; (*Vorgefühl*) presentiment; **keine ~!** no idea
ahnungslos ADJ unsuspecting
Ahorn [ˈaːhɔrn] (**-s, -e**) M maple
Ähre [ˈɛːrə] (**-, -n**) F ear
AHS F ABK (ÖSTERR: = *allgemeinbildende höhere Schule*) ≈ secondary school
Aids [eːdz] (-) NT Aids; **aidskrank** ADJ suffering from Aids; **Aidstest** M Aids test
Airbag [ˈɛːbɛːg] (**-s, -s**) M (*Aut*) airbag
Akademie [akadeˈmiː] F academy
Akademiker(in) [akaˈdeːmikər(ɪn)] (**-s, -**) M(F) university graduate
akademisch ADJ academic
Akazie [aˈkaːtsiə] (**-, -n**) F acacia
Akk. ABK = **Akkusativ**
akklimatisieren [aklimatiˈziːrən] VR to become acclimatized
Akkord [aˈkɔrt] (**-(e)s, -e**) M (*Mus*) chord; **im ~ arbeiten** to do piecework; **Akkordarbeit** F piecework
Akkordeon [aˈkɔrdeɔn] (**-s, -s**) NT accordion
Akkordlohn M piece wages *pl*, piece rate
Akkreditiv [akrediˈtiːf] (**-s, -e**) NT (*Comm*) letter of credit
Akku [ˈaku] (**-s, -s**) (*umg*) M (*Akkumulator*) battery
akkurat [akuˈraːt] ADJ precise; (*sorgfältig*) meticulous
Akkusativ [ˈakuzatiːf] (**-s, -e**) M accusative (case); **Akkusativobjekt** NT accusative *od* direct object
Akne [ˈaknə] (**-, -n**) F acne
Akribie [akriˈbiː] F (*geh*) meticulousness
Akrobat(in) [akroˈbaːt(ɪn)] (**-en, -en**) M(F) acrobat
Akt [akt] (**-(e)s, -e**) M act; (*Kunst*) nude
Akte [ˈaktə] (**-, -n**) F file; **etw zu den Akten legen** (*lit, fig*) to file sth away
Akten- ZW: **Aktendeckel** M folder; **Aktenkoffer** M attaché case; **aktenkundig** ADJ on record; **Aktennotiz** F memo(randum); **Aktenordner** M file; **Aktenschrank** M filing cabinet; **Aktentasche** F briefcase; **Aktenzeichen** NT reference
Aktie [ˈaktsiə] (**-, -n**) F share; **wie stehen die Aktien?** (*hum: umg*) how are things?
Aktien- ZW: **Aktienbank** F joint-stock bank; **Aktienemission** F share issue; **Aktiengesellschaft** F public limited company (BRIT), corporation (US); **Aktienindex** M share index; **Aktienkapital** NT share capital; **Aktienkurs** M share price
Aktion [aktsiˈoːn] F campaign; (*Polizeiaktion, Suchaktion*) action
Aktionär(in) [aktsioˈnɛːr(ɪn)] (**-s, -e**) M(F) shareholder
Aktionismus [aktsioˈnɪsmʊs] M (*Pol*) actionism
Aktionsradius [aktsiˈoːnzraːdiʊs] (**-, -ien**) M (*Aviat, Naut*) range; (*fig: Wirkungsbereich*) scope
aktiv [akˈtiːf] ADJ active; (*Mil*) regular
Aktiv (**-s**) NT (*Gram*) active (voice)
Aktiva [akˈtiːva] PL assets *pl*
aktivieren [aktiˈviːrən] VT to activate; (*fig: Arbeit, Kampagne*) to step up; (*Mitarbeiter*) to get moving
Aktivität [aktiviˈtɛːt] F activity
Aktivposten M (*lit, fig*) asset
Aktivsaldo M (*Comm*) credit balance
Aktivurlaub M activity holiday
aktualisieren [aktualiˈziːrən] VT (*Comput*) to update
Aktualität [aktualiˈtɛːt] F topicality; (*einer Mode*) up-to-dateness

aktuell [aktu'ɛl] ADJ topical; (*Mode*) up-to-date; **eine aktuelle Sendung** (*Rundf, TV*) a current affairs programme
Akupunktur [akupuŋk'tu:ər] F acupuncture
Akustik [a'kʊstɪk] F acoustics *pl*
akustisch [a'kʊstɪʃ] ADJ acoustic; **ich habe dich rein ~ nicht verstanden** I simply didn't catch what you said (properly)
akut [a'ku:t] ADJ acute; (*Frage*) pressing, urgent
AKW NT ABK = **Atomkraftwerk**
Akzent [ak'tsɛnt] **(-(e)s, -e)** M accent; (*Betonung*) stress; **Akzente setzen** (*fig*) to bring out *od* emphasize the main points; **Akzentverschiebung** F (*fig*) shift of emphasis
Akzept **(-(e)s, -e)** NT (*Comm: Wechsel*) acceptance
akzeptabel [aktsɛp'ta:bl] ADJ acceptable
akzeptieren [aktsɛp'ti:rən] VT to accept
AL F ABK (= *Alternative Liste*) *siehe* **alternativ**
Alarm [a'larm] **(-(e)s, -e)** M alarm; (*Zustand*) alert; **~ schlagen** to give *od* raise the alarm; **Alarmanlage** F alarm system; **alarmbereit** ADJ standing by; **Alarmbereitschaft** F stand-by
alarmieren [alar'mi:rən] VT to alarm; **die Polizei ~** to call the police
Alaska [a'laska] **(-s)** NT Alaska
Albaner(in) [al'ba:nər(ɪn)] **(-s, -)** M(F) Albanian
Albanien [al'ba:niən] **(-s)** NT Albania
albanisch ADJ Albanian
albern ['albərn] ADJ silly
Albtraum ['alptraʊm] M nightmare
Album ['albʊm] **(-s, Alben)** NT album
Alcopops ['alkopɔps] PL alcopops *pl*
Aleuten [ale'u:tən] PL Aleutian Islands *pl*
Alge ['algə] **(-, -n)** F alga
Algebra ['algebra] **(-)** F algebra
Algerien [al'ge:riən] **(-s)** NT Algeria
Algerier(in) **(-s, -)** M(F) Algerian
algerisch [al'ge:rɪʃ] ADJ Algerian
Algier ['alʒi:ər] **(-s)** NT Algiers
ALGOL ['algɔl] **(-(s))** NT (*Comput*) ALGOL
Algorithmus [algo'rɪtmʊs] M (*Comput*) algorithm
alias ['a:lias] ADV alias
Alibi ['a:libi] **(-s, -s)** NT alibi
Alimente [ali'mɛntə] PL alimony *sing*
Alkohol ['alkohɔl] **(-s, -e)** M alcohol; **unter ~ stehen** to be under the influence (of alcohol); **alkoholarm** ADJ low alcohol; **Alkoholexzess** M binge drinking; **alkoholfrei** ADJ non-alcoholic; **alkoholfreies Getränk** soft drink; **Alkoholgehalt** M proof
Alkoholika [alko'ho:lika] PL alcoholic drinks *pl*, liquor (*US*)
Alkoholiker(in) [alko'ho:likər(ɪn)] **(-s, -)** M(F) alcoholic
alkoholisch ADJ alcoholic
Alkoholverbot NT ban on alcohol
All [al] **(-s)** NT universe; (*Raumfahrt*) space; (*außerhalb unseres Sternsystems*) outer space
allabendlich ADJ every evening
allbekannt ADJ universally known
alle ADJ *siehe* **alle(r,s)**

SCHLÜSSELWORT

alle(r, s) ADJ **1** (*sämtliche*) all; **wir alle** all of us; **alle Kinder waren da** all the children were there; **alle Kinder mögen ...** all children like ...; **alle beide** both of us/them; **sie kamen alle** they all came; **alles Gute** all the best; **alles in allem** all in all; **vor allem** above all; **das ist alles andere als ...** that's anything but ...; **es hat alles keinen Sinn mehr** nothing makes sense any more; **was habt ihr alles gemacht?** what did you get up to?
2 (*mit Zeit- oder Maßangaben*) every; **alle vier Jahre** every four years; **alle fünf Meter** every five metres
▸ PRON everything; **alles was er sagt** everything he says, all that he says; **trotz allem** in spite of everything
▸ ADV (*zu Ende, aufgebraucht*) finished; **die Milch ist alle** the milk's all gone, there's no milk left; **etw alle machen** to finish sth up

alledem ['alәde:m] PRON: **bei/trotz** *etc* **~** with/in spite of *etc* all that; **zu ~** moreover
Allee [a'le:] **(-, -n)** F avenue
allein [a'laɪn] ADJ, ADV alone; (*ohne Hilfe*) on one's own, by oneself ▸ KONJ (*geh*) but, only; **von ~** by oneself/itself; **nicht ~** (*nicht nur*) not only; **~ schon der Gedanke** the very *od* mere thought ..., the thought alone ...; **alleinerziehend** ADJ single-parent; **Alleinerziehende(r)** F(M), **Alleinerzieher(in)** M(F) single parent; **Alleingang** M: **im Alleingang** on one's own; **Alleinherrscher(in)** M(F) autocrat; **Alleinhersteller(in)** M(F) sole manufacturer
alleinig [a'laɪnɪç] ADJ sole
allein- ZW: **Alleinsein** NT being on one's own; (*Einsamkeit*) loneliness; **alleinstehend** ADJ single; **Alleinunterhalter(in)** M(F) solo entertainer; **Alleinvertretung** F (*Comm*) sole agency; **Alleinvertretungsvertrag** M (*Comm*) exclusive agency agreement
allemal ['alә'ma:l] ADV (*jedes Mal*) always; (*ohne Weiteres*) with no bother; *siehe auch* **Mal**
allenfalls ['alәn'fals] ADV at all events; (*höchstens*) at most
allerbeste(r, s) ['alәr'bɛstә(r, s)] ADJ very best
allerdings ['alәr'dɪŋs] ADV (*zwar*) admittedly; (*gewiss*) certainly
Allergie [aler'gi:] F allergy
allergisch [a'lɛrgɪʃ] ADJ allergic; **auf etw** *akk* **~ reagieren** to be allergic to sth
allerhand (*umg*) ADJ *unver* all sorts of; **das ist doch ~!** that's a bit much!; **~!** (*lobend*) good show!
Allerheiligen NT All Saints' Day

> **Allerheiligen** (All Saints' Day) is a public holiday in Germany and in Austria. It is a day in honour of all the saints. **Allerseelen** (All Souls' Day) is celebrated on November 2nd in the Roman Catholic Church. It is customary to visit cemeteries and place lighted candles on the graves of deceased relatives and friends.

aller- zW: **allerhöchste(r, s)** ADJ very highest; **es wird allerhöchste Zeit, dass …** it's really high time that …; **allerhöchstens** ADV at the very most; **allerlei** ADJ *unver* all sorts of; **allerletzte(r, s)** ADJ very last; **der/das ist das Allerletzte** (*umg*) he's/it's the absolute end!; **allerneuste(r, s)** ADJ very latest

Allerseelen (**-s**) NT All Souls' Day; *siehe auch* **Allerheiligen**

allerseits ADV on all sides; **prost ~!** cheers everyone!

Allerwelts- IN zW (*Durchschnitts-*) common; (*nichtssagend*) commonplace

allerwenigste(r, s) ADJ very least; **die allerwenigsten Menschen wissen das** very few people know that

Allerwerteste(r) M (*hum*) posterior (*hum*)

alles PRON everything; *siehe auch* **alle(r,s)**

allesamt ADV all (of them/us *etc*)

Alleskleber (**-s, -**) M all-purpose adhesive

Allgäu ['algɔʏ] NT *part of the alpine region of Bavaria*

allgegenwärtig ADJ omnipresent, ubiquitous

allgemein ['algəmaɪn] ADJ general ▶ ADV: **es ist ~ üblich** it's the general rule; **~ verständlich** generally intelligible; **im A~** in general; **im allgemeinen Interesse** in the common interest; **auf allgemeinen Wunsch** by popular request; **Allgemeinbildung** F general *od* all-round education; **allgemeingültig** ADJ generally accepted; **Allgemeinheit** F (*Menschen*) general public; **Allgemeinheiten** PL (*Redensarten*) general remarks *pl*; **Allgemeinwissen** NT general knowledge

Allheilmittel [al'haɪlmɪtəl] NT cure-all, panacea (*bes fig*)

Alliierte(r) [ali'i:rtə(r)] F(M) ally

all- zW: **alljährlich** ADJ annual; **allmächtig** ADJ all-powerful, omnipotent; **allmählich** ADJ gradual ▶ ADV gradually; **es wird allmählich Zeit** (*umg*) it's about time; **Allradantrieb** M all-wheel drive; **allseitig** ADJ (*allgemein*) general; (*ausnahmslos*) universal; **Alltag** M everyday life; **alltäglich** ADJ daily; (*gewöhnlich*) commonplace; **alltags** ADV on weekdays; **Alltagskultur** F everyday culture

Allüren [a'ly:rən] PL odd behaviour (BRIT) *od* behavior (US) *sing*; (*eines Stars etc*) airs and graces *pl*

all- zW: **allwissend** ADJ omniscient; **Allzeithoch** NT all-time high; **Allzeittief** NT all-time low; **allzu** ADV all too; **allzu gern** (*mögen*) only too much; (*bereitwillig*) only too willingly; **allzu oft** all too often; **allzu viel** too much

Allzweck- ['altsvɛk-] IN zW all-purpose; **Allzweckreiniger** (**-s, -**) M multi-purpose cleaner

Alm [alm] (**-, -en**) F alpine pasture

Almosen ['almo:zən] (**-s, -**) NT alms *pl*

Alpen ['alpən] PL Alps *pl*; **Alpenblume** F alpine flower; **Alpenveilchen** NT cyclamen; **Alpenvorland** NT foothills *pl* of the Alps

Alphabet [alfa'be:t] (**-(e)s, -e**) NT alphabet

alphabetisch ADJ alphabetical

alphanumerisch [alfanu'me:rɪʃ] ADJ (*Comput*) alphanumeric

Alptraum ['alptraʊm] M = **Albtraum**

SCHLÜSSELWORT

als [als] KONJ **1** (*zeitlich*) when; **damals als …** (in the days) when …; **gerade als …** just as …; (*gleichzeitig*) as

2 (*in der Eigenschaft*) than; **als Antwort** as an answer; **als Kind** as a child

3 (*bei Vergleichen*) than; **ich kam später als er** I came later than he (did) *od* later than him; **lieber … als …** rather … than …; **alles andere als** anything but; **nichts als Ärger** nothing but trouble; **so viel/so weit als möglich** (*bei Vergleichen*) as much/far as possible

4: **als ob/wenn** as if

alsbaldig [als'baldɪç] KONJ: **„zum alsbaldigen Verbrauch bestimmt"** "for immediate use only"

also ['alzo:] KONJ so; (*folglich*) therefore; **~ wie ich schon sagte** well (then), as I said before; **ich komme ~ morgen** so I'll come tomorrow; **~ gut** *od* **schön!** okay then; **~, so was!** well really!; **na ~!** there you are then!

alt ADJ old; **ich bin nicht mehr der Alte** I am not the man I was; **alles beim Alten lassen** to leave everything as it was; **ich werde heute nicht ~ (werden)** (*umg*) I won't last long today/tonight *etc*; **~ aussehen** (*fig: umg*) to be in a pickle

Alt [alt] (**-s, -e**) M (*Mus*) alto

Altar [al'ta:r] (**-(e)s, -äre**) M altar

alt- zW: **Altbau** M old building; **Altbauwohnung** F flat (BRIT) *od* apartment (US) in an old building; **altbekannt** ADJ well-known; **altbewährt** ADJ (*Methode etc*) well-tried; (*Tradition etc*) long-standing; **Altbier** NT *top-fermented German dark beer*; **alteingesessen** ADJ old-established; **Alteisen** NT scrap iron

Altenheim NT old people's home

Altenteil ['altəntaɪl] NT: **sich aufs ~ setzen** *od* **zurückziehen** (*fig*) to retire from public life

Alter ['altər] (**-s, -**) NT age; (*hohes*) old age; **er ist in deinem ~** he's your age; **im ~ von** at the age of

älter ['ɛltər] ADJ (*comp*) older; (*Bruder, Schwester*) elder; (*nicht mehr jung*) elderly

altern ['altərn] VI to grow old, to age

alternativ ADJ alternative; **~ leben** to live an alternative way of life

Alternativ- [altɛrna'ti:f] IN zW alternative

Alternative [altɛrna'ti:və] F alternative

Alternativ- zW: **Alternativmedizin** F alternative medicine; **Alternativszene** F alternative scene; **Alternativtechnologie** F alternative technology

alters ['altərs] ADV (*geh*): **von** *od* **seit ~ (her)** from time immemorial

Alters- zW: **Altersarmut** F old-age poverty; **altersbedingt** ADJ related to a particular age; (*durch hohes Alter*) caused by old age;

Altersgrenze F age limit; **flexible Altersgrenze** flexible retirement age; **Altersheim** NT old people's home; **Altersrente** F old age pension; **Altersruhegeld** NT retirement benefit; **altersschwach** ADJ (*Mensch*) old and infirm; (*Auto, Möbel*) decrepit; **Altersversorgung** F provision for old age

Altertum ['altərtu:m] NT antiquity

altertümlich ADJ (*aus dem Altertum*) ancient; (*veraltet*) antiquated

alt- ZW: **altgedient** ADJ long-serving; **Altglas** NT used glass (*for recycling*), scrap glass; **Altglascontainer** M bottle bank; **althergebracht** ADJ traditional; **Altherrenmannschaft** F (*Sport*) *team of players over thirty*; **altklug** ADJ precocious; **Altlasten** PL legacy *sing* of dangerous waste; **Altmaterial** NT scrap; **Altmetall** NT scrap metal; **altmodisch** ADJ old-fashioned; **Altpapier** NT waste paper; **Altstadt** F old town

Altstimme F alto

Altwarenhändler M second-hand dealer

Altweibersommer M Indian summer

Alu ['a:lu] (*umg*) ABK = **Arbeitslosenunterstützung**; **Aluminium**

Alufolie ['a:lufo:liə] F tinfoil

Aluminium [alu'mi:niʊm] (**-s**) NT aluminium (BRIT), aluminum (*US*); **Aluminiumfolie** F tinfoil

Alzheimerkrankheit ['altshaɪmər'kraŋkhaɪt] F Alzheimer's disease

am [am] = **an dem**; **am Sterben** on the point of dying; **am 15. März** on March 15th; **am letzten Sonntag** last Sunday; **am Morgen/Abend** in the morning/evening; **am besten/schönsten** best/most beautiful

Amalgam [amal'ga:m] (**-s, -e**) NT amalgam

Amateur [ama'tø:r] M amateur

Amazonas [ama'tso:nas] (**-**) M Amazon (river)

Ambiente [ambi'ɛntə] (**-**) NT ambience

Ambition [ambitsi'o:n] F: **Ambitionen auf etw** *akk* **haben** to have ambitions of getting sth

Amboss ['ambɔs] (**-es, -e**) M anvil

ambulant [ambu'lant] ADJ outpatient

Ambulanz F (*Krankenwagen*) ambulance; (*in der Klinik*) outpatients' department

Ameise ['a:maɪzə] (**-, -n**) F ant

Ameisenhaufen M anthill

amen ['a:mən] INTERJ amen

Amerika [a'me:rika] (**-s**) NT America

Amerikaner [ameri'ka:nər] (**-s, -**) M American; (*Gebäck*) *flat iced cake*

Amerikanerin F American

amerikanisch ADJ American

Ami ['ami] (**-s, -s**) (*umg*) M Yank; (*Soldat*) GI

Amme ['amə] (**-, -n**) F (*veraltet*) foster mother; (*Nährmutter*) wet nurse

Ammenmärchen ['amənmɛ:rçən] NT fairy tale *od* story

Amok ['a:mɔk] M: **~ laufen** to run amok *od* amuck

Amortisation [amɔrtizatsi'o:n] F amortization

amortisieren [amɔrti'zi:rən] VR to pay for itself

Ampel ['ampəl] (**-, -n**) F traffic lights *pl*

amphibisch [am'fi:bɪʃ] ADJ amphibious

Ampulle [am'pʊlə] (**-, -n**) F (*Behälter*) ampoule

amputieren [ampu'ti:rən] VT to amputate

Amsel ['amzəl] (**-, -n**) F blackbird

Amsterdam [amstər'dam] (**-s**) NT Amsterdam

Amt [amt] (**-(e)s, Ämter**) NT office; (*Posten*) post; (*Pflicht*) duty; (*Tel*) exchange; **zum zuständigen ~ gehen** to go to the relevant authority; **von Amts wegen** (*auf behördliche Anordnung hin*) officially

amtieren [am'ti:rən] VI to hold office; (*fungieren*): **als ... ~** to act as ...

amtierend ADJ incumbent

amtlich ADJ official; **amtliches Kennzeichen** registration (number), license number (*US*)

Amtmann (**-(e)s,** *pl* **-männer** *od* **-leute**) M (*Verwaltung*) senior civil servant

Amtmännin F (*Verwaltung*) senior civil servant

Amts- ZW: **Amtsarzt** M medical officer; **amtsärztlich** ADJ: **amtsärztlich untersucht werden** to have an official medical examination; **Amtsdeutsch, Amtsdeutsche** NT officialese; **Amtseid** M: **den Amtseid ablegen** to be sworn in, to take the oath of office; **Amtsgeheimnis** NT (*geheime Sache*) official secret; (*Schweigepflicht*) official secrecy; **Amtsgericht** NT county (BRIT) *od* district (*US*) court; **Amtsmissbrauch** M abuse of one's position; **Amtsperiode** F term of office; **Amtsperson** F official; **Amtsrichter** M district judge; **Amtsschimmel** M (*hum*) officialdom; **Amtssprache** F official language; **Amtsstunden** PL office hours *pl*; **Amtsträger** M office bearer; **Amtswechsel** M change of office; (*in Behörde*) rotation (in office); **Amtsweg** M: **auf dem Amtsweg** through official channels; **Amtszeit** F period of office

amüsant [amy'zant] ADJ amusing

Amüsement [amyzə'mã:] NT amusement

amüsieren [amy'zi:rən] VT to amuse ▶ VR to enjoy o.s.; **sich über etw** *akk* **~** to find sth funny; (*unfreundlich*) to make fun of sth

SCHLÜSSELWORT

an [an] PRÄP *+dat* **1** (*räumlich: wo?*) at; (*auf, bei*) on; (*nahe bei*) near; **an diesem Ort** at this place; **an der Wand** on the wall; **zu nahe an etw** too near to sth; **unten am Fluss** down by the river; **Köln liegt am Rhein** Cologne is on the Rhine; **an der gleichen Stelle** at *od* on the same spot; **jdn an der Hand nehmen** to take sb by the hand; **sie wohnen Tür an Tür** they live next door to one another; **es an der Leber** *etc* **haben** (*umg*) to have liver *etc* trouble

2 (*zeitlich: wann?*) on; **an diesem Tag** on this day; **an Ostern** at Easter

3: **arm an Fett** low in fat; **jung an Jahren sein** to be young in years; **an der ganzen Sache ist nichts** there is nothing in it; **an etw sterben** to die of sth; **an (und für) sich** actually

▶ PRÄP *+akk* **1** (*räumlich: wohin?*) to; **er ging ans**

Fenster he went (over) to the window; **etw an die Wand hängen/schreiben** to hang/write sth on the wall; **an die Arbeit gehen** to get down to work
2 (*zeitlich: woran?*): **an etw denken** to think of sth
3 (*gerichtet an*) to; **ein Gruß/eine Frage an dich** greetings/a question to you
▶ ADV **1** (*ungefähr*) about; **an die Hundert** about a hundred; **an die 10 Euro** around 10 euros
2 (*auf Fahrplänen*): **Frankfurt an 18.30** arriving Frankfurt 18.30
3 (*ab*): **von dort/heute an** from there/today onwards
4 (*angeschaltet, angezogen*) on; **an sein** (*umg*) to be on; **das Licht ist an** the light is on; **ohne etwas an** with nothing on; *siehe auch* **am**

anal [a'na:l] ADJ anal
analog [ana'lo:k] ADJ analogous; (*Comput*) analog
Analogie [analo'gi:] F analogy
Analogrechner [ana'lo:krɛçnər] M analog computer
Analphabet(in) [an|alfa'be:t(ɪn)] (**-en, -en**) M(F) illiterate (person)
Analyse [ana'ly:zə] (**-, -n**) F analysis
analysieren [analy'zi:rən] VT to analyse (BRIT), to analyze (US)
Anämie [anɛ'mi:] (**-, -n**) F anaemia (BRIT), anemia (US)
Ananas ['ananas] (**-,** - *od* **-se**) F pineapple
Anarchie [anar'çi:] F anarchy
anarchisch [a'narçɪʃ] ADJ anarchic
Anarchist(in) [anar'çɪst(ɪn)] (**-en, -en**) M(F) anarchist
Anästhesist(in) [an|ɛste'zɪst(ɪn)] (**-en, -en**) M(F) anaesthetist (BRIT), anesthesiologist (US)
Anatomie [anato'mi:] F anatomy
anbaggern ['anbagərn] VT (*umg*) to chat up (BRIT), to come on to (US)
anbahnen ['anba:nən] VR to open up; (*sich andeuten*) to be in the offing; (*Unangenehmes*) to be looming ▶ VT to initiate
Anbahnung F initiation
anbändeln ['anbɛndəln] (*umg*) VI to flirt
Anbau ['anbaʊ] M (*Agr*) cultivation; (*Gebäude*) extension
anbauen VT (*Agr*) to cultivate; (*Gebäudeteil*) to build on
Anbaugebiet NT: **ein gutes ~ für etw** a good area for growing sth
Anbaumöbel PL unit furniture *sing*
anbehalten ['anbəhaltən] *unreg* VT to keep on
anbei [an'baɪ] ADV enclosed (*form*); **~ schicken wir Ihnen** … please find enclosed …
anbeißen ['anbaɪsən] *unreg* VT to bite into ▶ VI (*lit*) to bite; (*fig*) to swallow the bait; **zum A~ aussehen** (*umg*) to look good enough to eat
anbelangen ['anbəlaŋən] VT to concern; **was mich anbelangt** as far as I am concerned
anberaumen ['anbəraʊmən] VT (*form*) to fix, to arrange
anbeten ['anbe:tən] VT to worship
Anbetracht ['anbətraxt] M: **in ~** *+gen* in view of
Anbetung F worship
anbiedern ['anbi:dərn] (*pej*) VR: **sich ~ (bei)** to curry favour (with)
anbieten ['anbi:tən] *unreg* VT to offer ▶ VR to volunteer; **das bietet sich als Lösung an** that would provide a solution
anbinden ['anbɪndən] *unreg* VT to tie up; (*verbinden*) to connect
Anblick ['anblɪk] M sight
anblicken VT to look at
anbraten ['anbra:tən] *unreg* VT (*Fleisch*) to brown
anbrechen ['anbrɛçən] *unreg* VT to start; (*Vorräte*) to break into ▶ VI to start; (*Tag*) to break; (*Nacht*) to fall
anbrennen ['anbrɛnən] *unreg* VI to catch fire; (*Koch*) to burn
anbringen ['anbrɪŋən] *unreg* VT to bring; (*Ware*) to sell; (*festmachen*) to fasten; (*Telefon etc*) to install
Anbruch ['anbrʊx] M beginning; **~ des Tages** dawn; **~ der Nacht** nightfall
anbrüllen ['anbrʏlən] VT to roar at
Andacht ['andaxt] (**-, -en**) F devotion; (*Versenkung*) rapt interest; (*Gottesdienst*) prayers *pl*; (*Ehrfurcht*) reverence
andächtig ['andɛçtɪç] ADJ devout
andauern ['andaʊərn] VI to last, to go on
andauernd ADJ continual
Anden ['andən] PL: **die ~** the Andes *pl*
Andenken ['andɛŋkən] (**-s, -**) NT memory; (*Reiseandenken*) souvenir; (*Erinnerungsstück*): **ein ~ (an** *+akk*) a memento (of), a keepsake (from)
andere(r, s) ADJ other; (*verschieden*) different; **am anderen Tage** the next day; **ein anderes Mal** another time; **kein anderer** nobody else; **alles ~ als zufrieden** anything but pleased, far from pleased; **von etwas anderem sprechen** to talk about something else; **es blieb mir nichts anderes übrig als selbst hinzugehen** I had no alternative but to go myself; **unter anderem** among other things; **von einem Tag zum anderen** overnight; **sie hat einen anderen** she has someone else
andererseits ADV on the other hand
andermal ADV: **ein ~** some other time
ändern ['ɛndərn] VT to alter, to change ▶ VR to change
andernfalls ADV otherwise
andernorts ['andərn'ɔrts] ADV elsewhere
anders ADV: **~ (als)** differently (from); **wer ~?** who else?; **niemand ~** no-one else; **wie nicht ~ zu erwarten** as was to be expected; **wie könnte es ~ sein?** how could it be otherwise?; **ich kann nicht ~** (*kann es nicht lassen*) I can't help it; (*muss leider*) I have no choice; **~ ausgedrückt** to put it another way; **jemand/irgendwo ~** somebody/somewhere else; **~ aussehen/klingen** to look/sound different; **~ lautend** = **anderslautend**
andersartig ADJ different
Andersdenkende(r) F(M) dissident, dissenter

anderseits ['andər'zaɪts] ADV = **andererseits**
anders- ZW: **andersfarbig** ADJ of a different colour; **andersgläubig** ADJ of a different faith; **andersherum** ADV the other way round; **anderslautend** ADJ: **anderslautende Berichte** reports to the contrary; **anderswo** ADV elsewhere; **anderswoher** ADV from elsewhere; **anderswohin** ADV elsewhere
anderthalb ['andərt'halp] ADJ one and a half
Änderung ['ɛndərʊŋ] F alteration, change
Änderungsantrag ['ɛndərʊŋsǀantra:k] M (*Parl*) amendment
anderweitig ['andər'vaɪtɪç] ADJ other ▶ ADV otherwise; (*anderswo*) elsewhere
andeuten ['andɔʏtən] VT to indicate; (*Wink geben*) to hint at
Andeutung F indication; (*Wink*) hint
andeutungsweise ADV (*als Anspielung, Anzeichen*) by way of a hint; (*als flüchtiger Hinweis*) in passing
andichten ['andɪçtən] VT: **jdm etw ~** (*umg: Fähigkeiten*) to credit sb with sth
Andorra [an'dɔra] (**-s**) NT Andorra
Andorraner(in) [andɔ'ra:nər(ɪn)] M(F) Andorran
Andrang ['andraŋ] M crush; **es herrschte großer ~** there was a huge crowd
andrehen ['andre:ən] VT to turn *od* switch on; **jdm etw ~** (*umg*) to unload sth onto sb
androhen ['andro:ən] VT: **jdm etw ~** to threaten sb with sth
Androhung F: **unter ~ von Gewalt** with the threat of violence
anecken ['anǀɛkən] (*umg*) VI: **(bei jdm/allen) ~** to rub (sb/everyone) up the wrong way
aneignen ['anǀaɪgnən] VT: **sich** *dat* **etw ~** to acquire sth; (*widerrechtlich*) to appropriate sth; (*sich mit etw vertraut machen*) to learn sth
aneinander [anǀaɪ'nandər] ADV at/on/to *etc* one another *od* each other; **sich ~ gewöhnen** to get used to each other; **aneinanderfügen** VT to put together; **aneinandergeraten** VI to clash; **aneinanderlegen** VT to put together
anekeln ['anǀe:kəln] VT to disgust
Anemone [ane'mo:nə] (**-, -n**) F anemone
anerkannt ['anǀɛrkant] ADJ recognized, acknowledged
anerkennen ['anǀɛrkɛnən] *unreg* VT to recognize, to acknowledge; (*würdigen*) to appreciate; **das muss man ~** (*zugeben*) you can't argue with that; (*würdigen*) one has to appreciate that
anerkennend ADJ appreciative
anerkennenswert ADJ praiseworthy
Anerkennung F recognition, acknowledgement; (*Würdigung*) appreciation
anerzogen ['anǀɛrtso:gən] ADJ acquired
anfachen ['anfaxən] VT (*lit*) to fan into flame; (*fig*) to kindle
anfahren ['anfa:rən] *unreg* VT to deliver; (*fahren gegen*) to hit; (*Hafen*) to put into; (*umg*) to bawl at ▶ VI to drive up; (*losfahren*) to drive off
Anfahrt ['anfa:rt] F (*Anfahrtsweg, Anfahrtszeit*) journey; (*Zufahrt*) approach
Anfall ['anfal] M (*Med*) attack; **in einem ~ von** (*fig*) in a fit of
anfallen *unreg* VT to attack ▶ VI (*Arbeit*) to come up; (*Produkt, Nebenprodukte*) to be obtained; (*Zinsen*) to accrue; (*sich anhäufen*) to accumulate; **die anfallenden Kosten/Reparaturen** the costs/repairs incurred
anfällig ['anfɛlɪç] ADJ delicate; **~ für etw** prone to sth
Anfang ['anfaŋ] (**-(e)s, -fänge**) M beginning, start; **von ~ an** right from the beginning; **zu ~** at the beginning; **~ fünfzig** in one's early fifties; **~ Mai/1994** at the beginning of May/1994
anfangen ['anfaŋən] *unreg* VT to begin, to start; (*machen*) to do ▶ VI to begin, to start; **damit kann ich nichts ~** (*nützt mir nichts*) that's no good to me; (*verstehe ich nicht*) it doesn't mean a thing to me; **mit dir ist heute (aber) gar nichts anzufangen!** you're no fun at all today!; **bei einer Firma ~** to start working for a firm
Anfänger(in) ['anfɛŋər(ɪn)] (**-s, -**) M(F) beginner
anfänglich ['anfɛŋlɪç] ADJ initial
anfangs ADV at first; **wie ich schon ~ erwähnte** as I mentioned at the beginning; **Anfangsbuchstabe** M initial *od* first letter; **Anfangsgehalt** NT starting salary; **Anfangsstadium** NT initial stages *pl*
anfassen ['anfasən] VT to handle; (*berühren*) to touch ▶ VI to lend a hand ▶ VR to feel
anfechtbar ['anfɛçtba:r] ADJ contestable
anfechten ['anfɛçtən] *unreg* VT to dispute; (*Meinung, Aussage*) to challenge; (*Urteil*) to appeal against; (*beunruhigen*) to trouble
anfeinden ['anfaɪndən] VT to treat with hostility
anfertigen ['anfɛrtɪgən] VT to make
anfeuchten ['anfɔʏçtən] VT to moisten
anfeuern ['anfɔʏərn] VT (*fig*) to spur on
anflehen ['anfle:ən] VT to implore
anfliegen ['anfli:gən] *unreg* VT to fly to ▶ VI to fly up
Anflug ['anflu:k] M (*Aviat*) approach; (*Spur*) trace
anfordern ['anfɔrdərn] VT to demand; (*Comm*) to requisition
Anforderung F +*gen* demand (for); (*Comm*) requisition
Anfrage ['anfra:gə] F inquiry; (*Parl*) question
anfragen ['anfra:gən] VI to inquire
anfreunden ['anfrɔʏndən] VR to make friends; **sich mit etw ~** (*fig*) to get to like sth
anfügen ['anfy:gən] VT to add; (*beifügen*) to enclose
anfühlen ['anfy:lən] VT, VR to feel; **es fühlt sich gut an** it feels good
anführen ['anfy:rən] VT to lead; (*zitieren*) to quote; (*umg: betrügen*) to lead up the garden path
Anführer(in) (**-s, -**) M(F) leader
Anführung F leadership; (*Zitat*) quotation
Anführungszeichen PL quotation marks *pl*, inverted commas *pl* (BRIT)
Angabe ['anga:bə] F statement; (*Tech*) specification; (*umg: Prahlerei*) boasting; (*Sport*)

service; **Angaben** PL (*Auskunft*) particulars *pl*; **ohne ~ von Gründen** without giving any reasons; **Angaben zur Person** (*form*) personal details *od* particulars
angeben ['ange:bən] *unreg* VT to give; (*anzeigen*) to inform on; (*bestimmen*) to set ▶ VI (*umg*) to boast; (*Sport*) to serve
Angeber(in) (**-s, -**) (*umg*) M(F) show-off
Angeberei [ange:bə'raɪ] (*umg*) F showing off
angeblich ['ange:plɪç] ADJ alleged
angeboren ['angəbo:rən] ADJ *+dat* inborn, innate (in); (*Med, fig*): **~ (bei)** congenital (to)
Angebot ['angəbo:t] NT offer; (*Comm*): **~ (an** *+dat*) supply (of); **im ~** (*umg*) on special offer; **~ und Nachfrage** supply and demand
angeboten ['angəbo:tən] PP *von* **anbieten**
Angebotspreis M offer price
angebracht ['angəbraxt] ADJ appropriate
angebrannt ['angəbrant] ADV: **das Fleisch schmeckt ~** the meat tastes burnt; **es riecht hier so ~** there's a smell of burning here
angebrochen ['angəbrɔxən] ADJ (*Packung, Flasche*) open(ed); **was machen wir mit dem angebrochenen Abend?** (*umg*) what shall we do with the rest of the evening?
angebunden ['angəbʊndən] ADJ: **kurz ~ sein** (*umg*) to be abrupt *od* curt
angefangen PP *von* **anfangen**
angegeben PP *von* **angeben**
angegossen ['angəgɔsən] ADJ: **wie ~ sitzen** to fit like a glove
angegriffen ['angəgrɪfən] ADJ: **er wirkt ~** he looks as if he's under a lot of strain
angehalten ['angəhaltən] PP *von* **anhalten** ▶ ADJ: **~ sein, etw zu tun** to be required *od* obliged to do sth
angehaucht ['angəhaʊxt] ADJ: **links/rechts ~ sein** to have left-/right-wing tendencies *od* leanings
angeheiratet ['angəhaɪratət] ADJ related by marriage
angeheitert ['angəhaɪtərt] ADJ tipsy
angehen ['ange:ən] *unreg* VT to concern; (*angreifen*) to attack; (*bitten*): **jdn ~ (um)** to approach sb (for) ▶ VI (*Feuer*) to light; (*umg: beginnen*) to begin; **das geht ihn gar nichts an** that's none of his business; **gegen jdn ~** (*entgegentreten*) to fight sb; **gegen etw ~** (*entgegentreten*) to fight sth; (*Missstände, Zustände*) to take measures against sth
angehend ADJ prospective; (*Musiker, Künstler*) budding
angehören ['angəhø:rən] VI *+dat* to belong to
Angehörige(r) F(M) relative
Angeklagte(r) ['angəkla:ktə(r)] F(M) accused, defendant
angeknackst ['angəknakst] (*umg*) ADJ (*Mensch*) uptight; (*: Selbstbewusstsein*) weakened
angekommen ['angəkɔmən] PP *von* **ankommen**
Angel ['aŋəl] (**-, -n**) F fishing rod; (*Türangel*) hinge; **die Welt aus den Angeln heben** (*fig*) to turn the world upside down
Angelegenheit ['angəle:gənhaɪt] F affair, matter
angelernt ['angəlɛrnt] ADJ (*Arbeiter*) semi-skilled
Angelhaken M fish hook
angeln ['aŋəln] VT to catch ▶ VI to fish; **Angeln** (**-s**) NT angling, fishing
Angelpunkt M crucial *od* central point; (*Frage*) key *od* central issue
Angelrute F fishing rod
Angelsachse ['aŋəlzaksə] (**-n, -n**) M Anglo-Saxon
Angelsächsin ['aŋəlzɛksɪn] F Anglo-Saxon
angelsächsisch ['aŋəlzɛksɪʃ] ADJ Anglo-Saxon
Angelschein M fishing permit
angemessen ['angəmɛsən] ADJ appropriate, suitable; **eine der Leistung angemessene Bezahlung** payment commensurate with the input
angenehm ['angəne:m] ADJ pleasant; **~!** (*bei Vorstellung*) pleased to meet you; **das Angenehme mit dem Nützlichen verbinden** to combine business with pleasure
angenommen ['angənɔmən] PP *von* **annehmen** ▶ ADJ assumed; (*Kind*) adopted; **~, wir ...** assuming we ...
angepasst ['angəpast] ADJ conformist
angerufen ['angəru:fən] PP *von* **anrufen**
angesäuselt ['angəzɔʏzəlt] ADJ tipsy, merry
angeschlagen ['angəʃla:gən] (*umg*) ADJ (*Mensch, Aussehen, Nerven*) shattered; (*: Gesundheit*) poor
angeschlossen ['angəʃlɔsən] ADJ *+dat* affiliated (to *od* with), associated (with)
angeschmiert ['angəʃmi:rt] (*umg*) ADJ in trouble; **der/die Angeschmierte sein** to have been had
angeschrieben ['angəʃri:bən] (*umg*) ADJ: **bei jdm gut/schlecht ~ sein** to be in sb's good/bad books
angesehen ['angəze:ən] PP *von* **ansehen** ▶ ADJ respected
Angesicht ['angəzɪçt] NT (*geh*) face
angesichts ['angəzɪçts] PRÄP *+gen* in view of, considering
angespannt ['angəʃpant] ADJ (*Aufmerksamkeit*) close; (*Nerven, Lage*) tense, strained; (*Comm: Markt*) tight, overstretched; (*Arbeit*) hard
Angest. ABK = **Angestellte(r)**
angestammt ['angəʃtamt] ADJ (*überkommen*) traditional; (*ererbt: Rechte*) hereditary; (*: Besitz*) inherited
Angestellte(r) ['angəʃtɛltə(r)] F(M) employee; (*Büroangestellte*) white-collar worker
angestrengt ['angəʃtrɛŋt] ADV as hard as one can
angetan ['angəta:n] ADJ: **von jdm/etw ~ sein** to be taken with sb/sth; **es jdm ~ haben** to appeal to sb
angetrunken ['angətrʊŋkən] ADJ inebriated
angewiesen ['angəvi:zən] ADJ: **auf jdn/etw ~ sein** to be dependent on sb/sth; **auf sich selbst ~ sein** to be left to one's own devices

angewöhnen ['angəvø:nən] VT: **jdm/sich etw ~** to accustom sb/become accustomed to sth
Angewohnheit ['angəvo:nhaɪt] F habit
angewurzelt ['angəvʊrtsəlt] ADJ: **wie ~ dastehen** to be rooted to the spot
angiften ['angɪftən] (*pej, umg*) VT to snap at
Angina [aŋ'gi:na] (**-, Anginen**) F tonsillitis; **Angina Pectoris** (**-**) F angina
angleichen ['anglaɪçən] *unreg* VT, VR to adjust
Angler ['aŋlər] (**-s, -**) M angler
angliedern ['angli:dərn] VT: **~ (an** *+akk*) (*Verein, Partei*) to affiliate (to *od* with); (*Land*) to annex (to)
Anglist(in) [aŋ'glɪst(ɪn)] (**-en, -en**) M(F) English specialist; (*Student*) English student; (*Professor etc*) English lecturer/professor
Angola [aŋ'go:la] (**-s**) NT Angola
angolanisch [aŋgo'la:nɪʃ] ADJ Angolan
angreifen ['angraɪfən] *unreg* VT to attack; (*anfassen*) to touch; (*Arbeit*) to tackle; (*beschädigen*) to damage
Angreifer(in) (**-s, -**) M(F) attacker
angrenzen ['angrɛntsən] VI: **an etw** *akk* **~** to border on sth, to adjoin sth
Angriff ['angrɪf] M attack; **etw in ~ nehmen** to make a start on sth
Angriffsfläche F: **jdm/etw eine ~ bieten** (*lit, fig*) to provide sb/sth with a target
angriffslustig ADJ aggressive
angst ADJ: **jdm ist ~** sb is afraid *od* scared; **Angst** [aŋst] (**-, Ängste**) F fear; **Angst haben (vor** *+dat*) to be afraid *od* scared (of); **Angst um jdn/etw haben** to be worried about sb/sth; **jdm Angst einflößen** *od* **einjagen** to frighten sb; **jdm Angst machen** to scare sb; **nur keine Angst!** don't be scared; **angstfrei** ADJ free of fear; **Angsthase** (*umg*) M chicken, scaredy-cat
ängstigen ['ɛŋstɪgən] VT to frighten ▸ VR: **sich ~ (vor** *+dat od* **um)** to worry (o.s.) (about)
ängstlich ADJ nervous; (*besorgt*) worried; (*schüchtern*) timid; **Ängstlichkeit** F nervousness
Angstschweiß M: **mir brach der ~ aus** I broke out in a cold sweat
angurten ['angʊrtən] VT, VR = **anschnallen**
Anh. ABK (= *Anhang*) app.
anhaben ['anha:bən] *unreg* VT to have on; **er kann mir nichts ~** he can't hurt me
anhaften ['anhaftən] VI (*lit*): **~ (an** *+dat*) to stick (to); (*fig*): **~** *+dat* to stick to, to stay with
anhalten ['anhaltən] *unreg* VT to stop ▸ VI to stop; (*andauern*) to persist; (*werben*): **um die Hand eines Mädchens ~** to ask for a girl's hand in marriage; **(jdm) etw ~** to hold sth up (against sb); **jdn zur Arbeit/Höflichkeit ~** to get sb to work/teach sb to be polite
anhaltend ADJ persistent
Anhalter(in) (**-s, -**) M(F) hitch-hiker; **per ~ fahren** to hitch-hike
Anhaltspunkt M clue
anhand [an'hant] PRÄP *+gen* with; **~ eines Beispiels** by means of an example
Anhang ['anhaŋ] M appendix; (*Leute*) family; (*Anhängerschaft*) supporters *pl*; (*Comput*) attachment
anhängen ['anhɛŋən] *unreg* VT to hang up; (*Wagen*) to couple up; (*Zusatz*) to add (on); (*Comput*) to append; **sich an jdn ~** to attach o.s. to sb; **eine Datei an eine E-Mail ~** (*Comput*) to attach a file to an email; **jdm etw ~** (*umg: nachsagen, anlasten*) to blame sb for sth, to blame sth on sb; (*: Verdacht, Schuld*) to pin sth on sb
Anhänger (**-s, -**) M supporter; (*Aut*) trailer; (*am Koffer*) tag; (*Schmuck*) pendant; **Anhängerschaft** F supporters *pl*
Anhängeschloss NT padlock
anhängig ADJ (*Jur*) sub judice; **etw ~ machen** to start legal proceedings over sth
anhänglich ADJ devoted; **Anhänglichkeit** F devotion
Anhängsel (**-s, -**) NT appendage
anhauen ['anhaʊən] (*umg*) VT (*ansprechen*): **jdn ~ (um)** to accost sb (for)
anhäufen ['anhɔʏfən] VT to accumulate, to amass ▸ VR to accrue
Anhäufung ['anhɔʏfʊŋ] F accumulation
anheben ['anhe:bən] *unreg* VT to lift up; (*Preise*) to raise
anheimelnd ['anhaɪməlnt] ADJ comfortable, cosy
anheimstellen [an'haɪmʃtɛlən] VT: **jdm etw ~** to leave sth up to sb
anheizen ['anhaɪtsən] VT (*Ofen*) to light; (*fig: umg: Wirtschaft*) to stimulate; (*verschlimmern: Krise*) to aggravate
anheuern ['anhɔʏərn] VT, VI (*Naut, fig*) to sign on *od* up
Anhieb ['anhi:b] M: **auf ~** straight off, first go; **es klappte auf ~** it was an immediate success
anhimmeln ['anhɪməln] (*umg*) VT to idolize, to worship
Anhöhe ['anhø:ə] F hill
anhören ['anhø:rən] VT to listen to; (*anmerken*) to hear ▸ VR to sound; **das hört sich gut an** that sounds good
Anhörung F hearing
Animierdame [ani'mi:rda:mə] F nightclub/bar hostess
animieren [ani'mi:rən] VT to encourage, to urge on
Anis [a'ni:s] (**-es, -e**) M aniseed
Ank. ABK (= *Ankunft*) arr.
ankämpfen ['ankɛmpfən] VI: **gegen etw ~** to fight (against) sth; (*gegen Wind, Strömung*) to battle against sth
Ankara ['aŋkara] (**-s**) NT Ankara
Ankauf ['ankaʊf] M: **~ und Verkauf von ...** we buy and sell ...; **ankaufen** VT to purchase, to buy
Anker ['aŋkər] (**-s, -**) M anchor; **vor ~ gehen** to drop anchor
ankern VT, VI to anchor
Ankerplatz M anchorage
Anklage ['ankla:gə] F accusation; (*Jur*) charge; **gegen jdn ~ erheben** (*Jur*) to bring *od* prefer charges against sb; **Anklagebank** F dock
anklagen ['ankla:gən] VT to accuse; **jdn (eines Verbrechens) ~** (*Jur*) to charge sb (with a crime)

Anklagepunkt M charge
Ankläger(in) ['anklɛːgər(ɪn)] **(-s, -)** M(F) accuser
Anklageschrift F indictment
anklammern ['anklamərn] VT to clip, to staple ▶ VR: **sich an etw** *akk, dat* **~** to cling to sth
Anklang ['anklaŋ] M: **bei jdm ~ finden** to meet with sb's approval
ankleben ['ankleːbən] VT: **„Plakate ~ verboten!"** "stick no bills"
Ankleidekabine F changing cubicle
ankleiden ['anklaɪdən] VT, VR to dress
anklicken ['anklɪkən] VT (*Comput*) to click on
anklingen ['anklɪŋən] VI (*angeschnitten werden*) to be touched (up)on; (*erinnern*): **~ an** *+akk* to be reminiscent of
anklopfen ['anklɔpfən] VI to knock
anknipsen ['anknɪpsən] VT to switch on; (*Schalter*) to flick
anknüpfen ['anknʏpfən] VT to fasten *od* tie on; (*Beziehungen*) to establish; (*Gespräch*) to start up ▶ VI (*anschließen*): **~ an** *+akk* to refer to
Anknüpfungspunkt M link
ankommen ['ankɔmən] *unreg* VI to arrive; (*näher kommen*) to approach; (*Anklang finden*): **bei jdm (gut) ~** to go down well with sb ▶ VI UNPERS: **er ließ es auf einen Streit/einen Versuch ~** he was prepared to argue about it/to give it a try; **es kommt darauf an** it depends; (*wichtig sein*) that is what matters; **es kommt auf ihn an** it depends on him; **es darauf ~ lassen** to let things take their course; **gegen jdn/etw ~** to cope with sb/sth; **damit kommst du bei ihm nicht an!** you won't get anywhere with him like that
ankreiden ['ankraɪdən] VT (*fig*): **jdm etw (dick *od* übel) ~** to hold sth against sb
ankreuzen ['ankrɔʏtsən] VT to mark with a cross
ankündigen ['ankʏndɪgən] VT to announce
Ankündigung F announcement
Ankunft ['ankʊnft] **(-, -künfte)** F arrival
Ankunftszeit F time of arrival
ankurbeln ['ankʊrbəln] VT (*Aut*) to crank; (*fig*) to boost
Anl. ABK (= *Anlage*) enc(l).
anlachen ['anlaxən] VT to smile at; **sich** *dat* **jdn ~** (*umg*) to pick sb up
Anlage ['anlaːgə] F disposition; (*Begabung*) talent; (*Park*) gardens *pl*; (*Beilage*) enclosure; (*Tech*) plant; (*Einrichtung: Mil, Elek*) installation(s *pl*); (*Sportanlage etc*) facilities *pl*; (*umg: Stereoanlage*) (stereo) system; (*Fin*) investment; (*Entwurf*) layout; **als ~ *od* in der ~ erhalten Sie ...** please find enclosed ...; **Anlageberater(in)** M(F) investment consultant; **Anlagekapital** NT fixed capital
Anlagenabschreibung F capital allowance
Anlagengeschäft NT investment deal; (*Branche*) investment banking
Anlagevermögen NT capital assets *pl*, fixed assets *pl*
anlangen ['anlaŋən] VI (*ankommen*) to arrive

Anlass ['anlas] **(-es, -lässe)** M: **~ (zu)** cause (for); (*Ereignis*) occasion; **aus ~** *+gen* on the occasion of; **~ zu etw geben** to give rise to sth; **beim geringsten/bei jedem ~** for the slightest reason/at every opportunity; **etw zum ~ nehmen** to take the opportunity of sth
anlassen *unreg* VT to leave on; (*Motor*) to start ▶ VR (*umg*) to start off
Anlasser **(-s, -)** M (*Aut*) starter
anlässlich ['anlɛslɪç] PRÄP *+gen* on the occasion of
anlasten ['anlastən] VT: **jdm etw ~** to blame sb for sth
Anlauf ['anlaʊf] M run-up; (*fig: Versuch*) attempt, try
anlaufen *unreg* VI to begin; (*Film*) to be showing; (*Sport*) to run up; (*Fenster*) to mist up; (*Metall*) to tarnish ▶ VT to call at; **rot ~** to turn *od* go red; **gegen etw ~** to run into *od* up against sth; **angelaufen kommen** to come running up
Anlauf- ZW: **Anlaufstelle** F place to go (with one's problems); **Anlaufzeit** F (*fig*) time to get going *od* started
anläuten ['anlɔʏtən] VI to ring
anlegen ['anleːgən] VT to put; (*anziehen*) to put on; (*gestalten*) to lay out; (*Kartei, Akte*) to start; (*Comput: Datei*) to create; (*Geld*) to invest ▶ VI to dock; (*Naut*) to berth; **etw an etw** *akk* **~** to put sth against *od* on sth; **ein Gewehr ~ (auf** *+akk***)** to aim a weapon (at); **es auf etw** *akk* **~** to be out for sth/to do sth; **strengere Maßstäbe ~ (bei)** to lay down *od* impose stricter standards (in); **sich mit jdm ~** (*umg*) to quarrel with sb
Anlegeplatz M landing place
Anleger(in) **(-s, -)** M(F) (*Fin*) investor
Anlegestelle F landing place
anlehnen ['anleːnən] VT to lean; (*Tür*) to leave ajar; **(sich) an etw** *akk* **~** to lean on *od* against sth
Anlehnung F (*Imitation*): **in ~ an jdn/etw** following sb/sth
Anlehnungsbedürfnis NT need of loving care
anleiern ['anlaɪərn] (*umg*) VT to get going
Anleihe ['anlaɪə] **(-, -n)** F (*Fin*) loan; (*Wertpapier*) bond
anleiten ['anlaɪtən] VT to instruct
Anleitung F instructions *pl*
anlernen ['anlɛrnən] VT to teach, to instruct
anlesen ['anleːzən] *unreg* VT (*aneignen*): **sich** *dat* **etw ~** to learn sth by reading
anliegen *unreg* VI (*Kleidung*) to cling
Anliegen ['anliːgən] **(-s, -)** NT matter; (*Wunsch*) wish
anliegend ADJ adjacent; (*beigefügt*) enclosed
Anlieger **(-s, -)** M resident; **~ frei** no thoroughfare – residents only
anlocken ['anlɔkən] VT to attract; (*Tiere*) to lure
anlügen ['anlyːgən] *unreg* VT to lie to
Anm. ABK (= *Anmerkung*) n.
anmachen ['anmaxən] VT to attach; (*einschalten*) to switch on; (*Salat*) to dress; **jdn ~** (*umg*) to turn sb on; (*umg: ansprechen*) to chat sb up (BRIT), to come on to sb (US); (*umg: beschimpfen*) to have a go at sb

anmalen ['anma:lən] VT to paint ▶ VR (*pej: schminken*) to paint one's face *od* o.s.
Anmarsch ['anmarʃ] M: **im ~ sein** to be advancing; (*hum*) to be on the way; **im ~ sein auf** *+akk* to be advancing on
anmaßen ['anma:sən] VT: **sich** *dat* **etw ~** to lay claim to sth
anmaßend ADJ arrogant
Anmaßung F presumption
Anmeldeformular ['anmɛldəfɔrmʊla:r] NT registration form
anmelden VT to announce; (*geltend machen: Recht, Ansprüche, zu Steuerzwecken*) to declare; (*Comput*) to log on ▶ VR (*sich ankündigen*) to make an appointment; (*polizeilich, für Kurs etc*) to register; **ein Gespräch nach Deutschland ~** (*Tel*) to book a call to Germany
Anmeldeschluss M deadline for applications, registration deadline
Anmeldung F registration; (*Antrag*) application; **nur nach vorheriger ~** by appointment only
anmerken ['anmɛrkən] VT to observe; (*anstreichen*) to mark; **jdm seine Verlegenheit** *etc* **~** to notice sb's embarrassment *etc*; **sich** *dat* **nichts ~ lassen** not to give anything away
Anmerkung F note
Anmut ['anmu:t] (-) F grace
anmuten VT (*geh*): **jdn ~** to appear *od* seem to sb
anmutig ADJ charming
annähen ['annɛ:ən] VT to sew on
annähern ['annɛ:ərn] VR to get closer
annähernd ADJ approximate; **nicht ~ so viel** not nearly as much
Annäherung F approach
Annäherungsversuch M advances *pl*
Annahme ['anna:mə] (-, -n) F acceptance; (*Vermutung*) assumption; **Annahmestelle** F counter; (*für Reparaturen*) reception; **Annahmeverweigerung** F refusal
annehmbar ['anne:mba:r] ADJ acceptable
annehmen *unreg* VT to accept; (*Namen*) to take; (*Kind*) to adopt; (*vermuten*) to suppose, to assume ▶ VR *+gen* to take care (of); **jdn an Kindes statt ~** to adopt sb; **angenommen, das ist so** assuming that is so
Annehmlichkeit F comfort
annektieren [anɛk'ti:rən] VT to annex
anno ['ano] ADJ: **von ~ dazumal** (*umg*) from the year dot
Annonce [a'nõ:sə] (-, -n) F advertisement
annoncieren [anõ'si:rən] VT, VI to advertise
annullieren [anʊ'li:rən] VT to annul
Anode [a'no:də] (-, -n) F anode
anöden ['anlø:dən] (*umg*) VT to bore stiff
anomal [ano'ma:l] ADJ (*regelwidrig*) unusual, abnormal; (*nicht normal*) strange, odd
anonym [ano'ny:m] ADJ anonymous
Anorak ['anorak] (-s, -s) M anorak
anordnen ['anlɔrdnən] VT to arrange; (*befehlen*) to order
Anordnung F arrangement; (*Befehl*) order; **Anordnungen treffen** to give orders
anorganisch ['anlɔrga:nɪʃ] ADJ (*Chem*) inorganic
anpacken ['anpakən] VT to grasp; (*fig*) to tackle; **mit ~** to lend a hand
anpassen ['anpasən] VT (*Kleidung*) to fit; (*fig*) to adapt ▶ VR to adapt
Anpassung F fitting; (*fig*) adaptation
Anpassungsdruck M pressure to conform (*to society*)
anpassungsfähig ADJ adaptable
anpeilen ['anpaɪlən] VT (*mit Radar, Funk etc*) to take a bearing on; **etw ~** (*fig: umg*) to have one's sights on sth
Anpfiff ['anpfɪf] M (*Sport*) (starting) whistle; (*Spielbeginn: Fußball etc*) kick-off; (*umg: Tadel*) roasting
anpöbeln ['anpø:bəln] VT to abuse; (*umg*) to pester
Anprall ['anpral] M: **~ gegen** *od* **an** *+akk* impact on *od* against
anprangern ['anpraŋərn] VT to denounce
anpreisen ['anpraɪzən] *unreg* VT to extol; **sich ~ (als)** to sell o.s. (as); **etw ~** to extol (the virtues of) sth; **seine Waren ~** to cry one's wares
Anprobe ['anpro:bə] F trying on
anprobieren ['anprobi:rən] VT to try on
anpumpen ['anpʊmpən] (*umg*) VT to borrow from
anquatschen ['ankvatʃən] (*umg*) VT to speak to; (*Mädchen*) to try to pick up
Anrainer ['anraɪnər] (-s, -) M neighbour (BRIT), neighbor (US)
anranzen ['anrantsən] (*umg*) VT: **jdn ~** to tick sb off
anraten ['anra:tən] *unreg* VT to recommend; **auf A~ des Arztes** *etc* on the doctor's *etc* advice *od* recommendation
anrechnen ['anrɛçnən] VT to charge; (*fig*) to count; **jdm etw hoch ~** to think highly of sb for sth
Anrecht ['anrɛçt] NT: **~ auf** *+akk* right (to); **ein ~ auf etw haben** to be entitled to sth, to have a right to sth
Anrede ['anre:də] F form of address
anreden VT to address
anregen ['anre:gən] VT to stimulate; **angeregte Unterhaltung** lively discussion
anregend ADJ stimulating
Anregung F stimulation; (*Vorschlag*) suggestion
anreichern ['anraɪçərn] VT to enrich
Anreise ['anraɪzə] F journey there/here
anreisen VI to arrive
anreißen ['anraɪsən] *unreg* VT (*kurz zur Sprache bringen*) to touch on
Anreiz ['anraɪts] M incentive
anrempeln ['anrɛmpəln] VT (*anstoßen*) to bump into; (*absichtlich*) to jostle
anrennen ['anrɛnən] *unreg* VI: **gegen etw ~** (*gegen Wind etc*) to run against sth; (*Mil*) to storm sth
Anrichte ['anrɪçtə] (-, -n) F sideboard
anrichten VT to serve up; **Unheil ~** to make mischief; **da hast du aber etwas angerichtet!** (*umg: verursacht*) you've started something there all right!; (*: angestellt*) you've really made a mess there!

anrüchig ['anrʏçɪç] ADJ dubious
anrücken ['anrʏkən] VI to approach; (*Mil*) to advance
Anruf ['anru:f] M call; **Anrufbeantworter** M (telephone) answering machine, answerphone
anrufen *unreg* VT to call out to; (*bitten*) to call on; (*Tel*) to ring up, to phone, to call
anrühren ['anry:rən] VT to touch; (*mischen*) to mix
ans [ans] = **an das**
Ansage ['anza:gə] F announcement
ansagen VT to announce ▶ VR to say one will come; **angesagt sein** to be recommended; (*modisch sein*) to be the in thing
Ansager(in) (-**s**, -) M(F) announcer
ansammeln ['anzaməln] VT to collect ▶ VR to accumulate; (*fig: Wut, Druck*) to build up
Ansammlung F collection; (*Leute*) crowd
ansässig ['anzɛsɪç] ADJ resident
Ansatz ['anzats] M start; (*Haaransatz*) hairline; (*Halsansatz*) base; (*Verlängerungsstück*) extension; (*Veranschlagung*) estimate; **die ersten Ansätze zu etw** the beginnings of sth; **Ansatzpunkt** M starting point; **Ansatzstück** NT (*Tech*) attachment
anschaffen ['anʃafən] VT to buy, to purchase ▶ VI: **~ gehen** (*umg: durch Prostitution*) to be on the game; **sich** *dat* **Kinder ~** (*umg*) to have children
Anschaffung F purchase
anschalten ['anʃaltən] VT to switch on
anschauen ['anʃaʊən] VT to look at
anschaulich ADJ illustrative
Anschauung F (*Meinung*) view; **aus eigener ~** from one's own experience
Anschauungsmaterial NT illustrative material
Anschein ['anʃaɪn] M appearance; **allem ~ nach** to all appearances; **den ~ haben** to seem, to appear
anscheinend ADJ apparent
anschieben ['anʃi:bən] *unreg* VT (*Fahrzeug*) to push
Anschiss ['anʃɪs] (*umg*) M: **einen ~ bekommen** to get a telling-off *od* ticking-off (*bes* BRIT)
Anschlag ['anʃla:k] M notice; (*Attentat*) attack; (*Comm*) estimate; (*auf Klavier*) touch; (*auf Schreibmaschine*) keystroke; **einem ~ zum Opfer fallen** to be assassinated; **ein Gewehr im ~ haben** (*Mil*) to have a rifle at the ready; **Anschlagbrett** NT notice board (BRIT), bulletin board (US)
anschlagen ['anʃla:gən] *unreg* VT to put up; (*beschädigen*) to chip; (*Akkord*) to strike; (*Kosten*) to estimate ▶ VI to hit; (*wirken*) to have an effect; (*Glocke*) to ring; (*Hund*) to bark; **einen anderen Ton ~** (*fig*) to change one's tune; **an etw** *akk* **~** to hit against sth
anschlagfrei ADJ: **anschlagfreier Drucker** non-impact printer
Anschlagzettel M notice
anschleppen ['anʃlɛpən] (*umg*) VT (*unerwünscht mitbringen*) to bring along
anschließen ['anʃli:sən] *unreg* VT to connect up; (*Sender*) to link up; (*in Steckdose*) to plug in; (*fig: hinzufügen*) to add ▶ VI: **an etw** *akk* **~** (*zeitlich*) to follow sth ▶ VR: **sich jdm/etw ~** to join sb/sth; (*beipflichten*) to agree with sb/sth; **sich an etw** *akk* **~** (*angrenzen*) to adjoin sth
anschließend ADJ adjacent; (*zeitlich*) subsequent ▶ ADV afterwards; **~ an** +*akk* following
Anschluss ['anʃlʊs] M (*Elek, Eisenb, Tel*) connection; (*weiterer Apparat*) extension; (*von Wasser etc*) supply; (*Comput*) port; **im ~ an** +*akk* following; **~ finden** to make friends; **~ bekommen** to get through; **kein ~ unter dieser Nummer** number unobtainable; **den ~ verpassen** (*Eisenb etc*) to miss one's connection; (*fig*) to miss the boat; **Anschlussflug** M connecting flight
anschmiegen ['anʃmi:gən] VR: **sich an jdn/etw ~** (*Kind, Hund*) to snuggle *od* nestle up to *od* against sb/sth
anschmiegsam ['anʃmi:kza:m] ADJ affectionate
anschmieren ['anʃmi:rən] VT to smear; (*umg*) to take in
anschnallen ['anʃnalən] VT to buckle on ▶ VR to fasten one's seat belt
Anschnallpflicht F: **für Kinder besteht ~** children must wear seat belts
anschnauzen ['anʃnaʊtsən] (*umg*) VT to yell at
anschneiden ['anʃnaɪdən] *unreg* VT to cut into; (*Thema*) to introduce
Anschnitt ['anʃnɪt] M first slice
anschreiben ['anʃraɪbən] *unreg* VT to write (up); (*Comm*) to charge up; (*benachrichtigen*) to write to; **bei jdm gut/schlecht angeschrieben sein** to be well/badly thought of by sb, to be in sb's good/bad books
anschreien ['anʃraɪən] *unreg* VT to shout at
Anschrift ['anʃrɪft] F address
Anschriftenliste F mailing list
Anschub M (*bei Firmengründung*) start-up (funds *pl*)
Anschuldigung ['anʃʊldɪgʊŋ] F accusation
anschwärzen ['anʃvɛrtsən] VT (*fig: umg*): **jdn ~ (bei)** to blacken sb's name (with)
anschwellen ['anʃvɛlən] *unreg* VI to swell (up)
anschwemmen ['anʃvɛmən] VT to wash ashore
anschwindeln ['anʃvɪndəln] (*umg*) VT to lie to
ansehen ['anze:ən] *unreg* VT to look at; **jdm etw ~** to see sth (from sb's face); **jdn/etw als etw ~** to look on sb/sth as sth; **~ für** to consider; **(sich** *dat***) etw ~** to (have a) look at sth; (*Fernsehsendung*) to watch sth; (*Film, Stück, Sportveranstaltung*) to see sth; **etw (mit) ~** to watch sth, to see sth happening
Ansehen (-**s**) NT respect; (*Ruf*) reputation; **ohne ~ der Person** (*Jur*) without respect of person
ansehnlich ['anze:nlɪç] ADJ fine-looking; (*beträchtlich*) considerable
anseilen ['anzaɪlən] VT: **jdn/sich ~** to rope sb/o.s. up
an sein ['anzaɪn] *siehe* **an**

ansetzen ['anzɛtsən] VT (*festlegen*) to fix; (*entwickeln*) to develop; (*Fett*) to put on; (*Blätter*) to grow; (*zubereiten*) to prepare ▸ VI (*anfangen*) to start, to begin; (*Entwicklung*) to set in; (*dick werden*) to put on weight ▸ VR (*Rost etc*) to start to develop; **~ an** *+akk* (*anfügen*) to fit on to; (*anlegen, an Mund etc*) to put to; **zu etw ~** to prepare to do sth; **jdn/etw auf jdn/etw ~** to set sb/sth on sb/sth
Ansicht ['anzɪçt] F (*Anblick*) sight; (*Meinung*) view, opinion; **zur ~** on approval; **meiner ~ nach** in my opinion
Ansichtskarte F picture postcard
Ansichtssache F matter of opinion
ansiedeln ['anzi:dəln] VT to settle; (*Tierart*) to introduce ▸ VR to settle; (*Industrie etc*) to get established
ansonsten [an'zɔnstən] ADV otherwise
anspannen ['anʃpanən] VT to harness; (*Muskel*) to strain
Anspannung F strain
Anspiel ['anʃpi:l] NT (*Sport*) start of play
anspielen VT (*Sport*) to play the ball *etc* to ▸ VI: **auf etw** *akk* **~** to refer *od* allude to sth
Anspielung F: **~ (auf** *+akk***)** reference (to), allusion (to)
Ansporn ['anʃpɔrn] **(-(e)s)** M incentive
Ansprache ['anʃpra:xə] F (*Rede*) address
ansprechen ['anʃprɛçən] *unreg* VT to speak to; (*bitten, gefallen*) to appeal to; (*Eindruck machen auf*) to make an impression on ▸ VI: **~ auf** *+akk* (*Patient*) to respond (to); (*Messgerät*) to react (to); **jdn auf etw** *akk* **(hin) ~** to ask sb about sth
ansprechend ADJ attractive
Ansprechpartner M contact
anspringen ['anʃprɪŋən] *unreg* VI (*Aut*) to start ▸ VT (*anfallen*) to jump; (*Raubtier*) to pounce (up)on; (*Hund: hochspringen*) to jump up at
Anspruch ['anʃprʊx] **(-s, -sprüche)** M (*Recht*): **~ (auf** *+akk***)** claim (to); **den Ansprüchen gerecht werden** to meet the requirements; **hohe Ansprüche stellen/haben** to demand/ expect a lot; **jdn/etw in ~ nehmen** to occupy sb/take up sth
anspruchslos ADJ undemanding
anspruchsvoll ADJ demanding; (*Comm*) upmarket
anspucken ['anʃpʊkən] VT to spit at
anstacheln ['anʃtaxəln] VT to spur on
Anstalt ['anʃtalt] **(-, -en)** F institution; **Anstalten machen, etw zu tun** to prepare to do sth
Anstand ['anʃtant] M decency; (*Manieren*) (good) manners *pl*
anständig ['anʃtɛndɪç] ADJ decent; (*umg*) proper; (*groß*) considerable; **Anständigkeit** F propriety, decency
anstandshalber ['anʃtantshalbər] ADV out of politeness
anstandslos ADV without any ado
anstarren ['anʃtarən] VT to stare at
anstatt [an'ʃtat] PRÄP *+gen* instead of ▸ KONJ: **~ etw zu tun** instead of doing sth
anstauen ['anʃtaʊən] VR to accumulate; (*Blut in Adern etc*) to congest; (*fig: Gefühle*) to build up
anstechen ['anʃtɛçən] *unreg* VT to prick; (*Fass*) to tap
anstecken ['anʃtɛkən] VT to pin on; (*Ring*) to put *od* slip on; (*Med*) to infect; (*Pfeife*) to light; (*Haus*) to set fire to ▸ VR: **ich habe mich bei ihm angesteckt** I caught it from him ▸ VI (*fig*) to be infectious
ansteckend ADJ infectious
Ansteckung F infection
Ansteckungsgefahr F danger of infection
anstehen ['anʃte:ən] *unreg* VI to queue (up) (BRIT), to line up (US); (*Verhandlungspunkt*) to be on the agenda
ansteigen ['anʃtaɪgən] *unreg* VI to rise; (*Straße*) to climb
anstelle, an Stelle [an'ʃtɛlə] PRÄP *+gen* in place of
anstellen ['anʃtɛlən] VT (*einschalten*) to turn on; (*Arbeit geben*) to employ; (*umg: Unfug treiben*) to get up to; (: *machen*) to do ▸ VR to queue (up) (BRIT), to line up (US); (*umg*) to act; (: *sich zieren*) to make a fuss, to act up; **was hast du wieder angestellt?** what have you been up to now?
Anstellung F employment; (*Posten*) post, position; **~ auf Lebenszeit** tenure
ansteuern ['anʃtɔʏərn] VT to make *od* steer *od* head for
Anstich ['anʃtɪç] M (*von Fass*) tapping, broaching
Anstieg ['anʃti:k] **(-(e)s, -e)** M climb; (*fig: von Preisen etc*) increase
anstiften ['anʃtɪftən] VT (*Unglück*) to cause; **jdn zu etw ~** to put sb up to sth
Anstifter **(-s, -)** M instigator
Anstiftung F (*von Tat*) instigation; (*von Mensch*): **~ (zu)** incitement (to)
anstimmen ['anʃtɪmən] VT (*Lied*) to strike up (with); (*Geschrei*) to set up ▸ VI to strike up
Anstoß ['anʃto:s] M impetus; (*Ärgernis*) offence (BRIT), offense (US); (*Sport*) kick-off; **der erste ~** the initiative; **ein Stein des Anstoßes** (*umstrittene Sache*) a bone of contention; **~ nehmen an** *+dat* to take offence at
anstoßen *unreg* VT to push; (*mit Fuß*) to kick ▸ VI to knock, to bump; (*mit der Zunge*) to lisp; (*mit Gläsern*) to drink a toast; **an etw** *akk* **~** (*angrenzen*) to adjoin sth; **~ auf** *+akk* to drink (a toast) to
anstößig ['anʃtø:sɪç] ADJ offensive, indecent; **Anstößigkeit** F indecency, offensiveness
anstrahlen ['anʃtra:lən] VT to floodlight; (*strahlend ansehen*) to beam at
anstreben ['anʃtre:bən] VT to strive for
anstreichen ['anʃtraɪçən] *unreg* VT to paint; **(jdm) etw als Fehler ~** to mark sth wrong
Anstreicher(in) **(-s, -)** M(F) painter
anstrengen ['anʃtrɛŋən] VT to strain; (*strapazieren: jdn*) to tire out; (: *Patienten*) to fatigue; (*Jur*) to bring ▸ VR to make an effort; **eine Klage ~ (gegen)** (*Jur*) to initiate *od* institute proceedings (against)
anstrengend ADJ tiring
Anstrengung F effort

Anstrich ['anʃtrɪç] M coat of paint
Ansturm ['anʃtʊrm] M rush; (*Mil*) attack
ansuchen ['anzu:xən] VI: **um etw** ~ to apply for sth
Ansuchen ['anzu:xən] (**-s, -**) NT request
Antagonismus [antago'nɪsmʊs] M antagonism
antanzen ['antantsən] (*umg*) VI to turn *od* show up
Antarktis [ant'larktɪs] (-) F Antarctic
antarktisch ADJ Antarctic
antasten ['antastən] VT to touch; (*Recht*) to infringe upon; (*Ehre*) to question
Anteil ['antaɪl] (**-s, -e**) M share; (*Mitgefühl*) sympathy; ~ **nehmen an** +*dat* to share in; (*sich interessieren*) to take an interest in; ~ **an etw** *dat* **haben** (*beitragen*) to contribute to sth; (*teilnehmen*) to take part in sth
anteilig ADJ proportionate, proportional
anteilmäßig ADJ pro rata
Anteilnahme (-) F sympathy
Antenne [an'tɛnə] (**-, -n**) F aerial; (*Zool*) antenna; **eine/keine ~ für etw haben** (*fig: umg*) to have a/no feeling for sth
Anthrazit [antra'tsi:t] (**-s, -e**) M anthracite
Anthropologie [antropolo'gi:] (-) F anthropology
Anti- ['anti] IN ZW anti; **Antialkoholiker** M teetotaller; **antiautoritär** ADJ anti-authoritarian; **Antibabypille** F (contraceptive) pill; **Antibiotikum** (**-s, -ka**) NT antibiotic; **Antiheld** M antihero
antik [an'ti:k] ADJ antique
Antike (**-, -n**) F (*Zeitalter*) ancient world; (*Kunstgegenstand*) antique
Antikörper M antibody
Antillen [an'tɪlən] PL Antilles *pl*
Antilope [anti'lo:pə] (**-, -n**) F antelope
Antipathie [antipa'ti:] F antipathy
antippen ['antɪpən] VT to tap; (*Pedal, Bremse*) to touch; (*fig: Thema*) to touch on
Antiquariat [antikvari'a:t] (**-(e)s, -e**) NT secondhand bookshop; **modernes ~** remainder bookshop/department
antiquiert [anti'kvi:rt] (*pej*) ADJ antiquated
Antiquitäten [antikvi'tɛ:tən] PL antiques *pl*; **Antiquitätenhandel** M antique business; **Antiquitätenhändler(in)** M(F) antique dealer
Antisemitismus [antizemi'tɪsmʊs] M anti-semitism
antiseptisch [anti'zɛptɪʃ] ADJ antiseptic
Antiviren- ADJ (*Comput*) antivirus; **Antivirensoftware** F antivirus software
Antlitz ['antlɪts] (**-es, -e**) NT (*liter*) countenance (*liter*), face
antörnen ['antœrnən] (*umg*) VT (*Drogen, Musik*) to turn on ▶ VI: **... törnt an** ... turns you on
Antrag ['antra:k] (**-(e)s, -träge**) M proposal; (*Parl*) motion; (*Gesuch*) application; **einen ~ auf etw** *akk* **stellen** to make an application for sth; (*Jur etc*) to file a petition/claim for sth
Antragsformular NT application form
Antragsgegner(in) M(F) (*Jur*) respondent
Antragsteller(in) (**-s, -**) M(F) claimant; (*für Kredit etc*) applicant
antreffen ['antrɛfən] *unreg* VT to meet
antreiben ['antraɪbən] *unreg* VT to drive on; (*Motor*) to drive; (*anschwemmen*) to wash up ▶ VI to be washed up; **jdn zur Eile/Arbeit ~** to urge sb to hurry up/to work
Antreiber (**-s, -**) (*pej*) M slave-driver (*pej*)
antreten ['antre:tən] *unreg* VT (*Amt*) to take up; (*Erbschaft*) to come into; (*Beweis*) to offer; (*Reise*) to start, to begin ▶ VI (*Mil*) to fall in; (*Sport*) to line up; (*zum Dienst*) to report; **gegen jdn ~** to play/fight against sb
Antrieb ['antri:p] M (*lit, fig*) drive; **aus eigenem ~** of one's own accord
Antriebskraft F (*Tech*) power
antrinken ['antrɪŋkən] *unreg* VT (*Flasche, Glas*) to start to drink from; **sich** *dat* **Mut/einen Rausch ~** to give o.s. Dutch courage/get drunk; **angetrunken sein** to be tipsy
Antritt ['antrɪt] M beginning, commencement; (*eines Amts*) taking up
antun ['antu:n] *unreg* VT: **jdm etw ~** to do sth to sb; **sich** *dat* **etwas ~** (*Selbstmord begehen*) to kill oneself; **sich** *dat* **Zwang ~** to force o.s.
anturnen ['antœrnən] (*umg*) VT = **antörnen**
Antwerpen [ant'vɛrpən] (**-s**) NT Antwerp
Antwort ['antvɔrt] (**-, -en**) F answer, reply; **um ~ wird gebeten** RSVP
antworten VI to answer, to reply
anvertrauen ['anfɛrtraʊən] VT: **jdm etw ~** to entrust sb with sth; **sich jdm ~** to confide in sb
anvisieren ['anvizi:rən] VT (*fig*) to set one's sights on
anwachsen ['anvaksən] *unreg* VI to grow; (*Pflanze*) to take root
Anwalt ['anvalt] (**-(e)s, -wälte**) M lawyer; (*fig: Fürsprecher*) advocate; (*: der Armen etc*) champion
Anwältin ['anvɛltɪn] F *siehe* **Anwalt**
Anwalts- ZW: **Anwaltshonorar** NT retainer, retaining fee; **Anwaltskammer** F *professional association of lawyers*, ≈ Law Society (BRIT); **Anwaltskosten** PL legal expenses *pl*
Anwandlung ['anvandlʊŋ] F caprice; **eine ~ von etw** a fit of sth
anwärmen ['anvɛrmən] VT to warm up
Anwärter(in) ['anvɛrtər(ɪn)] M(F) candidate
anweisen ['anvaɪzən] *unreg* VT to instruct; (*zuteilen*) to assign
Anweisung F instruction; (*Comm*) remittance; (*Postanweisung, Zahlungsanweisung*) money order
anwendbar ['anvɛntba:r] ADJ practicable, applicable
anwenden ['anvɛndən] *unreg* VT to use, to employ; (*Gesetz, Regel*) to apply
Anwender(in) (**-s, -**) M(F) user; **Anwenderprogramm** NT (*Comput*) application program; **Anwendersoftware** F application package
Anwendung F use; (*auch Comput*) application, app
anwerfen ['anvɛrfən] *unreg* VT (*Tech*) to start up

anwesend ['anve:zənt] ADJ present; **die Anwesenden** those present
Anwesenheit F presence
Anwesenheitsliste F attendance register
anwidern ['anvi:dərn] VT to disgust
Anwohner(in) ['anvo:nər(ɪn)] **(-s, -)** M(F) resident
Anwuchs ['anvu:ks] M growth
Anzahl ['antsa:l] F: **~ (an** *+dat*) number (of)
anzahlen VT: **100 Euro ~** to pay 100 euros as a deposit
Anzahlung F deposit, payment on account
anzapfen ['antsapfən] VT to tap
Anzeichen ['antsaɪçən] NT sign, indication; **alle ~ deuten darauf hin, dass ...** all the signs are that ...
Anzeige ['antsaɪgə] **(-, -n)** F (*Zeitungsanzeige*) announcement; (*Werbung*) advertisement; (*Comput*) display; (*bei Polizei*) report; **gegen jdn ~ erstatten** to report sb (to the police)
anzeigen VT (*zu erkennen geben*) to show; (*bekannt geben*) to announce; (*bei Polizei*) to report
Anzeigenteil M advertisements *pl*
anzeigepflichtig ADJ notifiable
Anzeiger M indicator
anzetteln ['antsɛtəln] (*umg*) VT to instigate
anziehen ['antsi:ən] *unreg* VT to attract; (*Kleidung*) to put on; (*Mensch*) to dress; (*Schraube, Seil*) to pull tight; (*Knie*) to draw up; (*Feuchtigkeit*) to absorb ▶ VR to get dressed
anziehend ADJ attractive
Anziehung F (*Reiz*) attraction
Anziehungskraft F power of attraction; (*Phys*) force of gravitation
Anzug ['antsu:k] M suit; **im ~ sein** to be approaching
anzüglich ['antsy:klɪç] ADJ personal; (*anstößig*) offensive; **Anzüglichkeit** F offensiveness; (*Bemerkung*) personal remark
anzünden ['antsʏndən] VT to light
Anzünder M lighter
anzweifeln ['antsvaɪfəln] VT to doubt
AOK (-) F ABK (= *Allgemeine Ortskrankenkasse*) *siehe* **Ortskrankenkasse**

> The **AOK** (Allgemeine Ortskrankenkasse) forms part of a compulsory medical insurance scheme for people who are not members of a private scheme. In every large town there is an independently run AOK office. Foreign nationals may also receive help from these offices if they fall ill while in Germany.

APA F ABK (= *Austria Presse-Agentur*) *Austrian news agency*
apart [a'part] ADJ distinctive
Apartheid [a'pa:rthaɪt] F apartheid
Apartment [a'partmənt] **(-s, -s)** NT flat (BRIT), apartment (*bes US*)
Apathie [apa'ti:] F apathy
apathisch [a'pa:tɪʃ] ADJ apathetic
Apenninen [apɛ'ni:nən] PL Apennines *pl*
Aperitif [aperi'ti:f] **(-s, -s** *od* **-e)** M aperitif
Apfel ['apfəl] **(-s, Äpfel)** M apple; **in den sauren ~ beißen** (*fig: umg*) to swallow the bitter pill; **etw für einen ~ und ein Ei kaufen** (*umg*) to buy sth dirt cheap *od* for a song; **Apfelmus** NT apple purée; (*als Beilage*) apple sauce; **Apfelsaft** M apple juice
Apfelsine [apfəl'zi:nə] **(-, -n)** F orange
Apfeltasche F apple turnover
Apfelwein M cider
apl. ABK = **außerplanmäßig**
APO, Apo ['a:po] (-) F ABK (= *außerparlamentarische Opposition*) *extraparliamentary opposition*

> The **APO** was an extraparliamentary opposition group formed in West Germany in the late 1960s by those who felt that their interests were not being sufficiently represented in parliament. It was disbanded in the 1970s. Some of its members then formed the RAF, a terrorist organisation. Some formed the Green Party (**die Grünen**).

apolitisch ['apoli:tɪʃ] ADJ non-political, apolitical
Apostel [a'pɔstəl] **(-s, -)** M apostle
Apostroph [apo'stro:f] **(-s, -e)** M apostrophe
Apotheke [apo'te:kə] **(-, -n)** F pharmacy, chemist's (shop) (BRIT)

> The **Apotheke** is a pharmacy where prescribed drugs and other medicines only available on prescription are sold. It also sells toiletries. The pharmacist is qualified to give advice on medicines and treatment.

Apotheker(in) **(-s, -)** M(F) pharmacist, (dispensing) chemist (BRIT)
App [ap] **(-s)** F app
Appalachen [apa'laxən] PL Appalachian Mountains *pl*
Apparat [apa'ra:t] **(-(e)s, -e)** M piece of apparatus; (*Fotoapparat*) camera; (*Telefon*) telephone; (*Rundf, TV*) set; (*Verwaltungsapparat, Parteiapparat*) machinery, apparatus; **am ~** on the phone; (*als Antwort*) speaking; **am ~ bleiben** to hold the line
Apparatur [apara'tu:r] F apparatus
Appartement [apart(ə)'mã:] **(-s, -s)** NT flat (BRIT), apartment (*bes US*)
Appell [a'pɛl] **(-s, -e)** M (*Mil*) muster, parade; (*fig*) appeal; **zum ~ antreten** to line up for roll call
appellieren [apɛ'li:rən] VI: **~ (an** *+akk*) to appeal (to)
Appetit [ape'ti:t] **(-(e)s, -e)** M appetite; **guten ~!** enjoy your meal; **appetitlich** ADJ appetizing; **Appetitlosigkeit** F lack of appetite
Applaus [ap'laʊs] **(-es, -e)** M applause
Appretur [apre'tu:r] F finish; (*Wasserundurchlässigkeit*) waterproofing
approbiert [apro'bi:rt] ADJ (*Arzt*) registered, certified
Apr. ABK (= *April*) Apr.
Aprikose [apri'ko:zə] **(-, -n)** F apricot
April [a'prɪl] **(-(s), -e)** (*pl selten*) M April; **jdn in den ~ schicken** to make an April fool of sb; *siehe auch* **September**; **Aprilwetter** NT April showers *pl*

apropos [apro'po:] ADV by the way, that reminds me
Aquaplaning [akva'pla:nɪŋ] (**-(s)**) NT aquaplaning
Aquarell [akva'rɛl] (**-s**, **-e**) NT watercolour (BRIT), watercolor (US)
Aquarium [a'kva:riʊm] NT aquarium
Äquator [ɛ'kva:tɔr] (**-s**) M equator
Äquivalent [ɛkviva'lɛnt] (**-(e)s**, **-e**) NT equivalent
Ar [a:r] (**-s**, **-e**) NT OD M (*Maß*) are (*100 m²*)
Ära ['ɛ:ra] (-, **Ären**) F era
Araber(in) ['a:rabər(ɪn)] (**-s**, **-**) M(F) Arab
Arabien [a'ra:biən] (**-s**) NT Arabia
arabisch ADJ Arab; (*Arabien betreffend*) Arabian; (*Sprache*) Arabic; **Arabischer Golf** Arabian Gulf; **Arabisches Meer** Arabian Sea; **Arabische Wüste** Arabian Desert
Arbeit ['arbaɪt] (-, **-en**) F work; (*Stelle*) job; (*Erzeugnis*) piece of work; (*wissenschaftliche*) dissertation; (*Klassenarbeit*) test; **Tag der ~** Labour (BRIT) *od* Labor (US) Day; **sich an die ~ machen, an die ~ gehen** to get down to work, to start working; **jdm ~ machen** (*Mühe*) to put sb to trouble; **das war eine ~!** that was a hard job!
arbeiten VI to work ▶ VT to make ▶ VR: **sich nach oben/an die Spitze ~** (*fig*) to work one's way up/to the top
Arbeiter(in) (**-s**, **-**) M(F) worker; (*ungelernt*) labourer (BRIT), laborer (US)
Arbeiter- zW: **Arbeiterfamilie** F working-class family; **Arbeiterkammer** F (ÖSTERR) Chambers of Labour; **Arbeiterkind** NT child from a working-class family; **Arbeitermitbestimmung** F employee participation; **Arbeiterschaft** F workers *pl*, labour (BRIT) *od* labor (US) force; **Arbeiterselbstkontrolle** F workers' control; **Arbeiter-und-Bauern-Staat** M (DDR) workers' and peasants' state; **Arbeiterwohlfahrt** F workers' welfare association
Arbeit- zW: **Arbeitgeber** (**-s**, **-**) M employer; **Arbeitnehmer** (**-s**, **-**) M employee
Arbeits- IN ZW labour (BRIT), labor (US)
Arbeitsagentur F job agency
arbeitsam ADJ industrious
Arbeits- zW: **Arbeitsamt** NT employment exchange, Job Centre (BRIT); **Arbeitsaufwand** M expenditure of energy; (*Industrie*) use of labour (BRIT) *od* labor (US); **Arbeitsbedingungen** PL working conditions *pl*; **Arbeitsbeschaffung** F (*Arbeitsplatzbeschaffung*) job creation; **Arbeitserlaubnis** F work permit; **arbeitsfähig** ADJ fit for work, able-bodied; **Arbeitsgang** M operation; **Arbeitsgemeinschaft** F study group; **Arbeitsgericht** NT industrial tribunal; **arbeitsintensiv** ADJ labour-intensive (BRIT), labor-intensive (US); **Arbeitskonflikt** M industrial dispute; **Arbeitskraft** F worker; **Arbeitskräfte** PL workers *pl*, labour (BRIT), labor (US); **arbeitslos** ADJ unemployed, out-of-work; **Arbeitslose(r)** F(M) unemployed person; **die Arbeitslosen** *pl* the unemployed *pl*; **Arbeitslosengeld** NT unemployment benefit; **Arbeitslosenhilfe** F unemployment benefit; **Arbeitslosenunterstützung** F unemployment benefit; **Arbeitslosenversicherung** F *compulsory insurance against unemployment*; **Arbeitslosigkeit** F unemployment; **Arbeitsmarkt** M job market; **Arbeitsmoral** F attitude to work; (*in Betrieb*) work climate; **Arbeitsniederlegung** F walkout; **Arbeitsplatte** F (*Küche*) work-top, work surface; **Arbeitsplatz** M place of work; (*Stelle*) job; **Arbeitsplatzrechner** M (*Comput*) work station; **Arbeitsplatzverlust** M job loss; **Arbeitsrecht** NT industrial law; **arbeitsscheu** ADJ workshy; **Arbeitsschutz** M *maintenance of health and safety standards at work*; **Arbeitsspeicher** M (*Comput*) main memory; **Arbeitstag** M work(ing) day; **Arbeitsteilung** F division of labour (BRIT) *od* labor (US); **Arbeitstier** NT (*fig: umg*) glutton for work, workaholic; **arbeitsunfähig** ADJ unfit for work; **Arbeitsunfall** M industrial accident; **Arbeitsverhältnis** NT employee-employer relationship; **Arbeitsvermittler(in)** M(F): **(privater) Arbeitsvermittler** employment officer, job placement officer; **Arbeitsvermittlung** F (*Amt*) employment exchange; (*privat*) employment agency; **Arbeitsvertrag** M contract of employment; **Arbeitszeit** F working hours *pl*; **Arbeitszeitkonto** NT record of hours worked; **Arbeitszeitmodell** NT model of working hours; **Arbeitszeitregelung** F regulation of working hours; **Arbeitszeitverkürzung** F reduction in working hours; **Arbeitszimmer** NT study
Archäologe [arçɛo'lo:gə] (**-n**, **-n**) M arch(a)eologist
Archäologin [arçɛo'lo:gɪn] F arch(a)eologist
Arche ['arçə] (-, **-n**) F: **die ~ Noah** Noah's Ark
Architekt(in) [arçi'tɛkt(ɪn)] (**-en**, **-en**) M(F) architect
architektonisch [arçitɛk'to:nɪʃ] ADJ architectural
Architektur [arçitɛk'tu:r] F architecture
Archiv [ar'çi:f] (**-s**, **-e**) NT archive
ARD F *German broadcasting corporation*

> The **ARD** (Arbeitsgemeinschaft der öffentlich-rechtlichen Rundfunkanstalten der Bundesrepublik Deutschland) is the name of the German broadcasting corporation founded as a result of several mergers after 1945. It is financed by licence fees and advertising and transmits the First Programme nationwide as well as the Third and other regional programmes. News and educational programmes make up about a third of its transmissions.

Arena [a're:na] (-, **Arenen**) F (*lit, fig*) arena; (*Zirkusarena, Stierkampfarena*) ring
arg [ark] ADJ bad, awful ▶ ADV awfully, very; **es zu ~ treiben** to go too far
Argentinien [argɛn'ti:niən] (**-s**) NT Argentina, the Argentine

Argentinier(in) (**-s**, **-**) M(F) Argentine, Argentinian (BRIT), Argentinean (US)
argentinisch [argɛn'ti:nɪʃ] ADJ Argentine, Argentinian (BRIT), Argentinean (US)
Ärger ['ɛrgər] (**-s**) M (*Wut*) anger; (*Unannehmlichkeit*) trouble; **jdm ~ machen** *od* **bereiten** to cause sb a lot of trouble *od* bother; **ärgerlich** ADJ (*zornig*) angry; (*lästig*) annoying, aggravating
ärgern VT to annoy ▶ VR to get annoyed
Ärgernis (**-ses**, **-se**) NT annoyance; (*Anstoß*) offence (BRIT), offense (US), outrage; **öffentliches ~ erregen** to be a public nuisance
arg- ZW: **arglistig** ADJ cunning, insidious; **arglistige Täuschung** fraud; **arglos** ADJ guileless, innocent; **Arglosigkeit** F guilelessness, innocence
Argument [argu'mɛnt] NT argument
argumentieren [argumɛn'ti:rən] VI to argue
Argusauge ['argʊslaʊgə] NT (*geh*): **mit Argusaugen** eagle-eyed
Argwohn M suspicion
argwöhnisch ADJ suspicious
Arie ['a:riə] F aria
Aristokrat(in) [arɪsto'kra:t(ɪn)] (**-en**, **-en**) M(F) aristocrat
Aristokratie [arɪstokra:'ti:] F aristocracy
aristokratisch ADJ aristocratic
arithmetisch [arɪt'me:tɪʃ] ADJ arithmetical; **arithmetisches Mittel** arithmetic mean
Arkaden [ar'ka:dən] PL (*Bogengang*) arcade *sing*
Arktis ['arktɪs] (**-**) F Arctic
arktisch ADJ Arctic
arm [arm] ADJ poor; **~ dran sein** (*umg*) to have a hard time of it
Arm (**-(e)s**, **-e**) M arm; (*Flussarm*) branch; **jdn auf den ~ nehmen** (*fig: umg*) to pull sb's leg; **jdm unter die Arme greifen** (*fig*) to help sb out; **einen langen/den längeren ~ haben** (*fig*) to have a lot of/more pull (*umg*) *od* influence
Armatur [arma'tu:r] F (*Elek*) armature
Armaturenbrett NT instrument panel; (*Aut*) dashboard
Armband NT bracelet; **Armbanduhr** F (wrist) watch
Arme(r) F(M) poor man/woman; **die Armen** the poor
Armee [ar'me:] (**-**, **-n**) F army; **Armeekorps** NT army corps
Ärmel ['ɛrməl] (**-s**, **-**) M sleeve; **etw aus dem ~ schütteln** (*fig*) to produce sth just like that
Ärmelkanal M (English) Channel
Armenien [ar'me:niən] (**-s**) NT Armenia
Armenier(in) [ar'me:niər(ɪn)] (**-s**, **-**) M(F) Armenian
armenisch [ar'me:nɪʃ] ADJ Armenian
Armenrecht NT (*Jur*) legal aid
Armer M *siehe* **Arme(r)**
Armlehne F armrest
Armleuchter (*pej, umg*) M (*Dummkopf*) twit (BRIT), fool
ärmlich ['ɛrmlɪç] ADJ poor; **aus ärmlichen Verhältnissen** from a poor family
armselig ADJ wretched, miserable; (*mitleiderregend*) pathetic, pitiful
Armut ['armu:t] (**-**) F poverty
Armutsgrenze F poverty line
Armutsrisiko NT poverty risk
Armutszeugnis NT (*fig*): **jdm/sich ein ~ ausstellen** to show sb's/one's shortcomings
Aroma [a'ro:ma] (**-s**, **Aromen**) NT aroma; **Aromatherapie** F aromatherapy
aromatisch [aro'ma:tɪʃ] ADJ aromatic
arrangieren [arã:'ʒi:rən] VT to arrange ▶ VR to come to an arrangement
Arrest [a'rɛst] (**-(e)s**, **-e**) M detention
arretieren [are'ti:rən] VT (*Tech*) to lock (in place)
arrogant [aro'gant] ADJ arrogant
Arroganz F arrogance
Arsch [arʃ] (**-es**, **Ärsche**) (*umg!*) M arse (BRIT), ass (US); **leck mich am ~!** (*lass mich in Ruhe*) get stuffed! (*umg!*), fuck off! (*umg!*); **am ~ der Welt** (*umg*) in the back of beyond; **Arschkriecher** (*umg!*) M arse licker (*umg!*), crawler; **Arschloch** (*umg!*) NT (*Mensch*) bastard (*umg!*)
Arsen [ar'ze:n] (**-s**) NT arsenic
Art [a:rt] (**-**, **-en**) F (*Weise*) way; (*Sorte*) kind, sort; (*Biol*) species; **eine ~ (von) Frucht** a kind of fruit; **Häuser aller ~** houses of all kinds; **einzig in seiner ~ sein** to be the only one of its kind, to be unique; **auf diese ~ und Weise** in this way; **das ist doch keine ~!** that's no way to behave!; **es ist nicht seine ~, das zu tun** it's not like him to do that; **ich mache das auf meine ~** I do that my (own) way; **Schnitzel nach ~ des Hauses** chef's special escalope
arten VI: **nach jdm ~** to take after sb; **der Mensch ist so geartet, dass ...** human nature is such that ...
Artenschutz M protection of endangered species
Arterie [ar'te:riə] F artery
Arterienverkalkung F arteriosclerosis
Artgenosse ['a:rtgənɔsə] M animal/plant of the same species; (*Mensch*) person of the same type
Arthritis [ar'tri:tɪs] (**-**, **-ritiden**) F arthritis
artig ['a:rtɪç] ADJ good, well-behaved
Artikel [ar'ti:kəl] (**-s**, **-**) M article
Artillerie [artɪlə'ri:] F artillery
Artischocke [arti'ʃɔkə] (**-**, **-n**) F artichoke
Artist(in) [ar'tɪst(ɪn)] (**-en**, **-en**) M(F) (circus) performer
Artistik [ar'tɪstɪk] (**-**) F artistry; (*Zirkus-/Varietékunst*) circus/variety performing
Arznei [a:rts'naɪ] F medicine; **Arzneimittel** NT medicine, medicament
Arzt [a:rtst] (**-es**, **Ärzte**) M doctor; **praktischer ~** general practitioner, GP
Ärztekammer F ≈ General Medical Council (BRIT), State Medical Board of Registration (US)
Arzthelfer(in) M(F) doctor's assistant
Ärztin ['ɛ:rtstɪn] F woman doctor; *siehe auch* **Arzt**
ärztlich ['ɛ:rtstlɪç] ADJ medical
Arztpraxis F doctor's practice; (*Räume*) doctor's surgery (BRIT) *od* office (US)
As [as] (**-ses**, **-se**) NT (*Mus*) A flat; *siehe auch* **Ass**

Asbest [as'bɛst] (**-(e)s, -e**) M asbestos
Asche ['aʃə] (-, **-n**) F ash
Aschen- ZW: **Aschenbahn** F cinder track; **Aschenbecher** M ashtray; **Aschenbrödel** NT (*Liter, fig*) Cinderella; **Aschenputtel** NT (*Liter, fig*) Cinderella
Aschermittwoch M Ash Wednesday
Aserbaidschan [azɛrbaɪ'dʒa:n] (**-s**) NT Azerbaijan
aserbaidschanisch ADJ Azerbaijani
Asiat(in) [azi'a:t(ɪn)] (**-en, -en**) M(F) Asian
asiatisch ADJ Asian, Asiatic
Asien ['a:ziən] (**-s**) NT Asia
asozial ['azotsia:l] ADJ antisocial; (*Familie*) asocial
Asoziale(r) (*pej*) F(M) *dekl wie adj* antisocial person; **Asoziale** PL antisocial elements
Aspekt [as'pɛkt] (**-(e)s, -e**) M aspect
Asphalt [as'falt] (**-(e)s, -e**) M asphalt
asphaltieren [asfal'ti:rən] VT to asphalt
Asphaltstraße F asphalt road
Ass [as] (**-es, -e**) NT ace
aß *etc* [a:s] VB *siehe* **essen**
Ass. ABK = **Assessor(in)**
Assekurant(in) [aseku'rant(ɪn)] (**-en, -en**) M(F) underwriter
Assemblersprache [ə'sɛmblərʃpra:xə] F (*Comput*) assembly language
Assessor(in) [a'sɛsɔr, -'so:rɪn] (**-s, -en**) M(F) *graduate civil servant who has completed his/her traineeship*
Assistent(in) [asɪs'tɛnt(ɪn)] M(F) assistant
Assistenzarzt [asɪs'tɛntsa:rtst] M houseman (BRIT), intern (US)
Assoziation [asotsiatsi'o:n] F association
assoziieren [asotsi'i:rən] VT (*geh*) to associate
Ast [ast] (**-(e)s, Äste**) M branch; **sich** *dat* **einen ~ lachen** (*umg*) to double up (with laughter)
AStA ['asta] (**-(s), -(s)**) M ABK (= *Allgemeiner Studentenausschuss) students' association*
Aster ['astər] (-, **-n**) F aster
ästhetisch [ɛs'te:tɪʃ] ADJ aesthetic (BRIT), esthetic (US)
Asthma ['astma] (**-s**) NT asthma
Asthmatiker(in) [ast'ma:tikər(ɪn)] (**-s, -**) M(F) asthmatic
astrein ['astraɪn] ADJ (*fig: umg: moralisch einwandfrei*) straight, on the level; (*: echt*) genuine; (*prima*) fantastic
Astrologe [astro'lo:gə] (**-n, -n**) M astrologer
Astrologie [astrolo'gi:] F astrology
Astrologin F astrologer
Astronaut(in) [astro'naʊt(ɪn)] (**-en, -en**) M(F) astronaut
Astronautik F astronautics
Astronom(in) [astro'no:m(ɪn)] (**-en, -en**) M(F) astronomer
Astronomie [astrono'mi:] F astronomy
ASU F ABK (= *Arbeitsgemeinschaft selbstständiger Unternehmer) association of private traders*; (= *Abgassonderuntersuchung*) exhaust emission test
ASW F ABK (= *außersinnliche Wahrnehmung*) ESP
Asyl [a'zy:l] (**-s, -e**) NT asylum; (*Heim*) home; (*Obdachlosenasyl*) shelter
Asylant(in) [azy'lant(ɪn)] (**-en, -en**) M(F) asylum seeker
Asylrecht NT (*Pol*) right of (political) asylum
A.T. ABK (= *Altes Testament*) O.T.
Atelier [atəli'e:] (**-s, -s**) NT studio
Atem ['a:təm] (**-s**) M breath; **den ~ anhalten** to hold one's breath; **außer ~** out of breath; **jdn in ~ halten** to keep sb in suspense *od* on tenterhooks; **das verschlug mir den ~** it took my breath away; **einen langen/den längeren ~ haben** to have a lot of staying power; **atemberaubend** ADJ breathtaking; **Atembeschwerden** PL breathing difficulties *pl*; **atemlos** ADJ breathless; **Atempause** F breather; **Atemwege** PL (*Anat*) respiratory tract; **Atemzug** M breath
Atheismus [ate'ɪsmʊs] M atheism
Atheist(in) M(F) atheist; **atheistisch** ADJ atheistic
Athen [a'te:n] (**-s**) NT Athens
Athener(in) (**-s, -**) M(F) Athenian
Äther ['ɛ:tər] (**-s, -**) M ether
Äthiopien [ɛti'o:piən] (**-s**) NT Ethiopia
Äthiopier(in) (**-s, -**) M(F) Ethiopian
äthiopisch ADJ Ethiopian
Athlet(in) [at'le:t(ɪn)] (**-en, -en**) M(F) athlete
Athletik F athletics *sing*
Atlanten PL *von* **Atlas**
Atlantik [at'lantɪk] (**-s**) M Atlantic
atlantisch ADJ Atlantic; **der Atlantische Ozean** the Atlantic Ocean
Atlas ['atlas] (**-** *od* **-ses, -se** *od* **Atlanten**) M atlas; **Atlasgebirge** NT Atlas Mountains *pl*
atmen ['a:tmən] VT, VI to breathe
Atmosphäre [atmo'sfɛ:rə] (-, **-n**) F atmosphere
atmosphärisch ADJ atmospheric
Atmung ['a:tmʊŋ] F respiration
Ätna ['ɛ:tna] (**-(s)**) M Etna
Atom [a'to:m] (**-s, -e**) NT atom
atomar [ato'ma:r] ADJ atomic, nuclear; (*Drohung*) nuclear
Atom- ZW: **Atombombe** F atom bomb; **Atomenergie** F nuclear *od* atomic energy; **Atomgegner** M: **Atomgegner sein** to be antinuclear; **Atomkern** M atomic nucleus; **Atomkraft** F nuclear power; **Atomkraftwerk** NT nuclear power station; **Atomkrieg** M nuclear *od* atomic war; **Atomlobby** F nuclear lobby; **Atommacht** F nuclear *od* atomic power; **Atommeiler** M nuclear reactor; **Atommüll** M nuclear waste; **Atomphysik** F nuclear physics *sing*; **Atompilz** M mushroom cloud; **Atomsperrvertrag** M (*Pol*) nuclear non-proliferation treaty; **Atomsprengkopf** M nuclear *od* atomic warhead; **Atomstrom** M *electricity generated by nuclear power*; **Atomtest** M nuclear test; **Atomtestgelände** NT nuclear testing range; **Atomwaffen** PL nuclear *od* atomic weapons *pl*; **atomwaffenfrei** ADJ (*Zone*) nuclear-free; **Atomwirtschaft** F nuclear industry; **Atomzeitalter** NT atomic age

Attachment [a'tɛtʃmɛnt] NT (*Comput*) attachment
Attacke [a'takə] (**-, -n**) F (*Angriff*) attack
Attentat [atɛn'ta:t] (**-(e)s, -e**) NT: **~ (auf** *+akk*) (attempted) assassination (of)
Attentäter(in) [atɛn'tɛ:tər(ɪn)] (**-s, -**) M(F) (would-be) assassin
Attest [a'tɛst] (**-(e)s, -e**) NT certificate
Attraktion [atraktsi'o:n] F attraction
attraktiv [atrak'ti:f] ADJ attractive
Attrappe [a'trapə] (**-, -n**) F dummy; **bei ihr ist alles ~** everything about her is false
Attribut [atri'bu:t] (**-(e)s, -e**) NT (*Gram*) attribute
At-Zeichen ['attsaɪçən] NT (*Comput*) at symbol
ätzen ['ɛtsən] VI to be caustic
ätzend ADJ (*lit: Säure*) corrosive; (*Geruch*) pungent; (*fig: umg: furchtbar*) dreadful, horrible; (*: toll*) magic
Aubergine [obɛr'ʒi:nə] (**-, -n**) F aubergine, eggplant (*US*)

SCHLÜSSELWORT

auch [aʊx] ADV **1** (*ebenfalls*) also, too, as well; **das ist auch schön** that's nice too *od* as well; **er kommt — ich auch** he's coming — so am I, me too; **auch nicht** not ... either; **ich auch nicht** nor I, me neither; **oder auch** or; **auch das noch!** not that as well!; **nicht nur ..., sondern auch ...** not only ... but also ...
2 (*selbst, sogar*) even; **auch wenn das Wetter schlecht ist** even if the weather is bad; **ohne auch nur zu fragen** without even asking
3 (*wirklich*) really; **du siehst müde aus — bin ich auch** you look tired — (so) I am; **so sieht es auch aus** (and) that's what it looks like
4 (*auch immer*): **wer auch** whoever; **was auch** whatever; **wozu auch?** (*emphatisch*) whatever for?; **wie dem auch sei** be that as it may; **wie sehr er sich auch bemühte** however much he tried

Audienz [aʊdi'ɛnts] (**-, -en**) F (*bei Papst, König etc*) audience
Audimax [aʊdi'maks] NT (*Univ etc: umg*) main lecture hall
audiovisuell [aʊdiovizu'ɛl] ADJ audiovisual
Auditorium [aʊdi'to:riʊm] NT (*Hörsaal*) lecture hall; (*geh: Zuhörerschaft*) audience

SCHLÜSSELWORT

auf [aʊf] PRÄP *+dat* (*wo?*) on; **auf dem Tisch** on the table; **auf der Reise** on the way; **auf der Post/dem Fest** at the post office/party; **auf der Straße** on the road; **auf dem Land/der ganzen Welt** in the country/the whole world; **was hat es damit auf sich?** what does it mean?
▶ PRÄP *+akk* **1** (*wohin?*) on(to); **auf den Tisch** on(to) the table; **auf die Post gehen** to go to the post office; **auf das Land** into the country; **etw auf einen Zettel schreiben** to write sth on a piece of paper; **auf eine Tasse Kaffee/eine Zigarette(nlänge)** for a cup of coffee/a smoke; **die Nacht (von Montag) auf Dienstag** Monday night; **auf einen Polizisten kommen 1.000 Bürger** there is one policeman to every 1,000 citizens
2: **auf Deutsch** in German; **auf Lebenszeit** for my/his lifetime; **bis auf ihn** except for him; **auf einmal** at once; **auf seinen Vorschlag (hin)** at his suggestion
▶ ADV **1** (*offen*) open; **auf sein** to be open; **das Fenster ist auf** the window is open
2 (*hinauf*) up; **auf und ab** up and down; **auf und davon** up and away; **auf!** (*los!*) come on!; **von klein auf** from childhood onwards
3 (*aufgestanden*) up; **auf sein** (*Person*) to be up; **ist er schon auf?** is he up yet?
▶ KONJ: **auf dass** (so) that

aufarbeiten ['aʊflarbaɪtən] VT (*erledigen: Korrespondenz etc*) to catch up with
aufatmen ['aʊfla:tmən] VI to heave a sigh of relief
aufbahren ['aʊfba:rən] VT to lay out
Aufbau ['aʊfbaʊ] M (*Bauen*) building, construction; (*Struktur*) structure; (*aufgebautes Teil*) superstructure
aufbauen ['aʊfbaʊən] VT to erect, to build (up); (*gestalten*) to construct; (*gründen*): **~ (auf** *+dat*) to found (on), to base (on) ▶ VR: **sich vor jdm ~** to draw o.s. up to one's full height in front of sb; **sich eine Existenz ~** to make a life for oneself
aufbäumen ['aʊfbɔymən] VR to rear; (*fig*) to revolt, to rebel
aufbauschen ['aʊfbaʊʃən] VT to puff out; (*fig*) to exaggerate
aufbegehren ['aʊfbəge:rən] VI (*geh*) to rebel
aufbehalten ['aʊfbəhaltən] *unreg* VT to keep on
aufbekommen ['aʊfbəkɔmən] *unreg* (*umg*) VT (*öffnen*) to get open; (*Hausaufgaben*) to be given
aufbereiten ['aʊfbəraɪtən] VT to process; (*Trinkwasser*) to purify; (*Text etc*) to work up
Aufbereitungsanlage F processing plant
aufbessern ['aʊfbɛsərn] VT (*Gehalt*) to increase
aufbewahren ['aʊfbəva:rən] VT to keep; (*Gepäck*) to put in the left-luggage office
Aufbewahrung F (safe)keeping; (*Gepäckaufbewahrung*) left-luggage office (BRIT), baggage check (*US*); **jdm etw zur ~ geben** to give sb sth for safekeeping
Aufbewahrungsort M storage place
aufbieten ['aʊfbi:tən] *unreg* VT (*Kraft*) to summon (up); (*Armee, Polizei*) to mobilize
Aufbietung F: **unter ~ aller Kräfte ...** summoning (up) all his/her *etc* strength ...
aufbinden ['aʊfbɪndən] *unreg* VT: **lass dir doch so etwas nicht ~** (*fig*) don't fall for that
aufblähen ['aʊfblɛ:ən] VR to blow out; (*Segel*) to billow out; (*Med*) to become swollen; (*fig: pej*) to puff o.s. up
aufblasen ['aʊfbla:zən] *unreg* VT to blow up, to inflate ▶ VR (*umg*) to become big-headed
aufbleiben ['aʊfblaɪbən] *unreg* VI (*Laden*) to remain open; (*Person*) to stay up

a

aufblenden ['aʊfblɛndən] VT (*Scheinwerfer*) to turn on full beam
aufblicken ['aʊfblɪkən] VI to look up; **~ zu** (*lit*) to look up at; (*fig*) to look up to
aufblühen ['aʊfbly:ən] VI to blossom; (*fig*) to blossom, to flourish
aufblühend ADJ (*Comm*) booming
aufbocken ['aʊfbɔkən] VT (*Auto*) to jack up
aufbrauchen ['aʊfbraʊxən] VT to use up
aufbrausen ['aʊfbraʊzən] VI (*fig*) to flare up
aufbrausend ADJ hot-tempered
aufbrechen ['aʊfbrɛçən] *unreg* VT to break open, to prise (BRIT) *od* pry (US) open ▶ VI to burst open; (*gehen*) to start, to set off
aufbringen ['aʊfbrɪŋən] *unreg* VT (*öffnen*) to open; (*in Mode*) to bring into fashion; (*beschaffen*) to procure; (*Fin*) to raise; (*ärgern*) to irritate; **Verständnis für etw ~** to be able to understand sth
Aufbruch ['aʊfbrʊx] M departure
aufbrühen ['aʊfbry:ən] VT (*Tee*) to make
aufbrummen ['aʊfbrʊmən] (*umg*) VT: **jdm die Kosten ~** to land sb with the costs
aufbürden ['aʊfbʏrdən] VT: **jdm etw ~** to burden sb with sth
aufdecken ['aʊfdɛkən] VT to uncover; (*Spielkarten*) to show
aufdrängen ['aʊfdrɛŋən] VT: **jdm etw ~** to force sth on sb ▶ VR: **sich jdm ~** to intrude on sb
aufdrehen ['aʊfdre:ən] VT (*Wasserhahn etc*) to turn on; (*Ventil*) to open; (*Schraubverschluss*) to unscrew; (*Radio etc*) to turn up; (*Haar*) to put in rollers
aufdringlich ['aʊfdrɪŋlɪç] ADJ pushy; (*Benehmen*) obtrusive; (*Parfüm*) powerful
aufeinander [aʊflaɪ'nandər] ADV on top of one another; (*schießen*) at each other; (*warten*) for one another; (*vertrauen*) each other; **Aufeinanderfolge** F succession, series; **aufeinanderfolgen** VI to follow one another; **aufeinanderfolgend** ADJ consecutive; **aufeinanderlegen** VT to lay on top of one another; **aufeinanderprallen** VI (*Autos etc*) to collide; (*Truppen, Meinungen*) to clash
Aufenthalt ['aʊflɛnthalt] M stay; (*Verzögerung*) delay; (*Eisenb*: *Halten*) stop; (*Ort*) haunt
Aufenthalts- ZW: **Aufenthaltserlaubnis** F, **Aufenthaltsgenehmigung** F residence permit; **Aufenthaltsraum** M day room; (*in Betrieb*) recreation room
auferlegen ['aʊflɛrle:gən] VT: **(jdm) ~** to impose (upon sb)
auferstehen ['aʊflɛrʃte:ən] *unreg* VI UNTR to rise from the dead
Auferstehung F resurrection
aufessen ['aʊflɛsən] *unreg* VT to eat up
auffahren ['aʊffa:rən] *unreg* VI (*herankommen*) to draw up; (*hochfahren*) to jump up; (*wütend werden*) to flare up; (*in den Himmel*) to ascend ▶ VT (*Kanonen, Geschütz*) to bring up; **~ auf** +*akk* (*Auto*) to run *od* crash into
auffahrend ADJ hot-tempered
Auffahrt F (*Hausauffahrt*) drive; (*Autobahnauffahrt*) slip road (BRIT), entrance ramp (US)
Auffahrunfall M pile-up
auffallen ['aʊffalən] *unreg* VI to be noticeable; **angenehm/unangenehm ~** to make a good/bad impression; **jdm ~** (*bemerkt werden*) to strike sb; **das fällt gar nicht auf** nobody will notice
auffallend ADJ striking
auffällig ['aʊffɛlɪç] ADJ conspicuous, striking
auffangen ['aʊffaŋən] *unreg* VT to catch; (*Funkspruch*) to intercept; (*Preise*) to peg; (*abfangen*: *Aufprall etc*) to cushion, to absorb
Auffanglager NT reception camp
auffassen ['aʊffasən] VT to understand, to comprehend; (*auslegen*) to see, to view
Auffassung F (*Meinung*) opinion; (*Auslegung*) view, conception; (*auch*: **Auffassungsgabe**) grasp
auffindbar ['aʊffɪntba:r] ADJ to be found
aufflammen ['aʊfflamən] VI (*lit, fig*: *Feuer, Unruhen etc*) to flare up
auffliegen ['aʊffli:gən] *unreg* VI to fly up; (*umg*: *Rauschgiftring etc*) to be busted
auffordern ['aʊffɔrdərn] VT to challenge; (*befehlen*) to call upon, to order; (*bitten*) to ask
Aufforderung F (*Befehl*) order; (*Einladung*) invitation
aufforsten ['aʊffɔrstən] VT (*Gebiet*) to reafforest; (*Wald*) to restock
auffrischen ['aʊffrɪʃən] VT to freshen up; (*Kenntnisse*) to brush up; (*Erinnerungen*) to reawaken ▶ VI (*Wind*) to freshen
aufführen ['aʊffy:rən] VT (*Theat*) to perform; (*in einem Verzeichnis*) to list, to specify ▶ VR (*sich benehmen*) to behave; **einzeln ~** to itemize
Aufführung F (*Theat*) performance; (*Liste*) specification
auffüllen ['aʊffʏlən] VT to fill up; (*Vorräte*) to replenish; (*Öl*) to top up
Aufgabe ['aʊfga:bə] (-, -**n**) F task; (*Sch*) exercise; (*Hausaufgabe*) homework; (*Verzicht*) giving up; (*von Gepäck*) registration; (*von Post*) posting; (*von Inserat*) insertion; **sich** *dat* **etw zur ~ machen** to make sth one's job *od* business
aufgabeln ['aʊfga:bəln] VT (*fig*: *umg*: *jdn*) to pick up; (: *Sache*) to get hold of
Aufgabenbereich M area of responsibility
Aufgang ['aʊfgaŋ] M ascent; (*Sonnenaufgang*) rise; (*Treppe*) staircase
aufgeben ['aʊfge:bən] *unreg* VT (*verzichten auf*) to give up; (*Paket*) to send, to post; (*Gepäck*) to register; (*Bestellung*) to give; (*Inserat*) to insert; (*Rätsel, Problem*) to set ▶ VI to give up
aufgeblasen ['aʊfgəbla:zən] ADJ (*fig*) puffed up, self-important
Aufgebot ['aʊfgəbo:t] NT supply; (*von Kräften*) utilization; (*Eheaufgebot*) banns *pl*
aufgedonnert ['aʊfgədɔnərt] (*pej, umg*) ADJ tarted up
aufgedreht ['aʊfgədre:t] (*umg*) ADJ excited
aufgedunsen ['aʊfgedʊnzən] ADJ swollen, puffed up

aufgegeben ['aʊfgəge:bən] PP *von* **aufgeben**
aufgehen ['aʊfge:ən] *unreg* VI (*Sonne, Teig*) to rise; (*sich öffnen*) to open; (*Theat: Vorhang*) to go up; (*Knopf, Knoten etc*) to come undone; (*klar werden*) to become clear; (*Math*) to come out exactly; **~ (in** *+dat***)** (*sich widmen*) to be absorbed (in); **in Rauch/Flammen ~** to go up in smoke/flames
aufgeilen ['aʊfgaɪlən] (*umg*) VT to turn on ▶ VR to be turned on
aufgeklärt ['aʊfgəklɛ:rt] ADJ enlightened; (*sexuell*) knowing the facts of life
aufgekratzt ['aʊfgəkratst] (*umg*) ADJ in high spirits, full of beans
aufgelaufen ['aʊfgəlaʊfən] ADJ: **aufgelaufene Zinsen** *pl* accrued interest *sing*
Aufgeld NT premium
aufgelegt ['aʊfgəle:kt] ADJ: **gut/schlecht ~ sein** to be in a good/bad mood; **zu etw ~ sein** to be in the mood for sth
aufgenommen ['aʊfgənɔmən] PP *von* **aufnehmen**
aufgeregt ['aʊfgəre:kt] ADJ excited
aufgeschlossen ['aʊfgəʃlɔsən] ADJ open, open-minded
aufgeschmissen ['aʊfgəʃmɪsən] (*umg*) ADJ in a fix, stuck
aufgeschrieben ['aʊfgəʃri:bən] PP *von* **aufschreiben**
aufgestanden ['aʊfgəʃtandən] PP *von* **aufstehen**
aufgetakelt ['aʊfgəta:kəlt] ADJ (*fig: umg*) dressed up to the nines
aufgeweckt ['aʊfgəvɛkt] ADJ bright, intelligent
aufgießen ['aʊfgi:sən] *unreg* VT (*Wasser*) to pour over; (*Tee*) to infuse
aufgliedern ['aʊfgli:dərn] VR: **sich ~ (in** *+akk***)** to (sub)divide (into), to break down (into)
aufgreifen ['aʊfgraɪfən] *unreg* VT (*Thema*) to take up; (*Verdächtige*) to pick up, to seize
aufgrund, auf Grund [aʊf'grʊnt] PRÄP *+gen*: **~ von** on the basis of; (*wegen*) because of
Aufgussbeutel ['aʊfgʊsbɔʏtəl] M sachet (containing coffee/herbs *etc*) for brewing; (*Teebeutel*) tea bag
aufhaben ['aʊfha:bən] *unreg* VT (*Hut etc*) to have on; (*Arbeit*) to have to do
aufhalsen ['aʊfhalzən] (*umg*) VT: **jdm etw ~** to saddle *od* lumber sb with sth
aufhalten ['aʊfhaltən] *unreg* VT (*Person*) to detain; (*Entwicklung*) to check; (*Tür, Hand*) to hold open; (*Augen*) to keep open ▶ VR (*wohnen*) to live; (*bleiben*) to stay; **jdn (bei etw) ~** (*abhalten, stören*) to hold *od* keep sb back (from sth); **sich über etw/jdn ~** to go on about sth/sb; **sich mit etw ~** to waste time over sth; **sich bei etw ~** (*sich befassen*) to dwell on sth
aufhängen ['aʊfhɛŋən] *unreg* VT (*Wäsche*) to hang up; (*Menschen*) to hang ▶ VR to hang o.s.
Aufhänger (-s, -) M (*am Mantel*) hook; (*fig*) peg
Aufhängung F (*Tech*) suspension
aufheben ['aʊfhe:bən] *unreg* VT (*hochheben*) to raise, to lift; (*Sitzung*) to wind up; (*Urteil*) to annul; (*Gesetz*) to repeal, to abolish; (*aufbewahren*) to keep; (*ausgleichen*) to offset, to make up for ▶ VR to cancel itself out; **viel A~(s) machen (von)** to make a fuss (about); **bei jdm gut aufgehoben sein** to be well looked after at sb's
aufheitern ['aʊfhaɪtərn] VT, VR (*Himmel, Miene*) to brighten; (*Mensch*) to cheer up
Aufheiterungen PL (*Met*) bright periods *pl*
aufheizen ['aʊfhaɪtsən] VT: **die Stimmung ~** to stir up feelings
aufhelfen ['aʊfhɛlfən] *unreg* VI (*lit: beim Aufstehen*): **jdm ~** to help sb up
aufhellen ['aʊfhɛlən] VT, VR to clear up; (*Farbe, Haare*) to lighten
aufhetzen ['aʊfhɛtsən] VT to stir up
aufheulen ['aʊfhɔʏlən] VI to howl; (*Sirene*) to (start to) wail; (*Motor*) to (give a) roar
aufholen ['aʊfho:lən] VT (*Zeit*) to make up ▶ VI to catch up
aufhorchen ['aʊfhɔrçən] VI to prick up one's ears
aufhören ['aʊfhø:rən] VI to stop; **~, etw zu tun** to stop doing sth
aufkaufen ['aʊfkaʊfən] VT to buy up
aufklappen ['aʊfklapən] VT to open; (*Verdeck*) to fold back
aufklären ['aʊfklɛ:rən] VT (*Geheimnis etc*) to clear up; (*Person*) to enlighten; (*sexuell*) to tell the facts of life to; (*Mil*) to reconnoitre ▶ VR to clear up
Aufklärung F (*von Geheimnis*) clearing up; (*Unterrichtung, Zeitalter*) enlightenment; (*sexuell*) sex education; (*Mil, Aviat*) reconnaissance
Aufklärungsarbeit F educational work
aufkleben ['aʊfkle:bən] VT to stick on
Aufkleber (-s, -) M sticker
aufknöpfen ['aʊfknœpfən] VT to unbutton
aufkochen ['aʊfkɔxən] VT to bring to the boil
aufkommen ['aʊfkɔmən] *unreg* VI (*Wind*) to come up; (*Zweifel, Gefühl*) to arise; (*Mode*) to start; **für jdn/etw ~** to be liable *od* responsible for sb/sth; **für den Schaden ~** to pay for the damage; **endlich kam Stimmung auf** at last things livened up
aufkreuzen ['aʊfkrɔʏtsən] (*umg*) VI (*erscheinen*) to turn *od* show up
aufkündigen ['aʊfkʏndɪgən] VT (*Vertrag etc*) to terminate
aufladen ['aʊfla:dən] *unreg* VT to load; (*Handy etc*) to charge; (*Handykarte etc*) to top up ▶ VR (*Batterie etc*) to be charged; (*neu aufladen*) to be recharged; **jdm/sich etw ~** (*fig*) to saddle sb/o.s. with sth
Auflage ['aʊfla:gə] F edition; (*Zeitung*) circulation; (*Bedingung*) condition; **jdm etw zur ~ machen** to make sth a condition for sb
Auflagehöhe, Auflagenhöhe F (*von Buch*) number of copies published; (*von Zeitung*) circulation
auflassen ['aʊflasən] *unreg* (*umg*) VT (*Hut, Brille*) to keep on; (*Tür*) to leave open; **die Kinder länger ~** to let the children stay up (longer)

auflauern ['aʊflaʊərn] VI: **jdm ~** to lie in wait for sb
Auflauf ['aʊflaʊf] M (*Koch*) pudding; (*Menschenauflauf*) crowd
auflaufen *unreg* VI (*auf Grund laufen: Schiff*) to run aground; **jdn ~ lassen** (*umg*) to drop sb in it
Auflaufform F (*Koch*) ovenproof dish
aufleben ['aʊfle:bən] VI to revive
auflegen ['aʊfle:gən] VT to put on; (*Hörer*) to put down; (*Typ*) to print ▸ VI (*Tel*) to hang up
auflehnen ['aʊfle:nən] VT to lean on ▸ VR to rebel
Auflehnung F rebellion
auflesen ['aʊfle:zən] *unreg* VT to pick up
aufleuchten ['aʊflɔʏçtən] VI to light up
aufliegen ['aʊfli:gən] *unreg* VI to lie on; (*Comm*) to be available
auflisten ['aʊflɪstən] VT (*auch Comput*) to list
auflockern ['aʊflɔkərn] VT to loosen; (*fig: Eintönigkeit etc*) to liven up; (*entspannen, zwangloser machen*) to make relaxed; (*Atmosphäre*) to make more relaxed, to ease
auflösen ['aʊflø:zən] VT to dissolve; (*Missverständnis*) to sort out; (*Konto*) to close; (*Firma*) to wind up; (*Haushalt*) to break up; **in Tränen aufgelöst sein** to be in tears
Auflösung F dissolving; (*von Rätsel*) solution; (*von Bildschirm*) resolution
aufmachen ['aʊfmaxən] VT to open; (*Kleidung*) to undo; (*zurechtmachen*) to do up ▸ VR to set out
Aufmacher M (*Presse*) lead
Aufmachung F (*Kleidung*) outfit, get-up; (*Gestaltung*) format
aufmerksam ['aʊfmɛrkza:m] ADJ attentive; **auf etw** *akk* **~ werden** to become aware of sth; **jdn auf etw** *akk* **~ machen** to point sth out to sb; **(das ist) sehr ~ von Ihnen** (*zuvorkommend*) (that's) most kind of you; **Aufmerksamkeit** F attention, attentiveness; (*Geschenk*) token (gift)
aufmöbeln ['aʊfmø:bəln] (*umg*) VT (*Gegenstand*) to do up; (*beleben*) to buck up, to pep up
aufmucken ['aʊfmʊkən] (*umg*) VI: **~ gegen** to protest at *od* against
aufmuntern ['aʊfmʊntərn] VT (*ermutigen*) to encourage; (*erheitern*) to cheer up
aufmüpfig ['aʊfmʏpfɪç] (*umg*) ADJ rebellious
Aufnahme ['aʊfna:mə] (-, -n) F reception; (*Beginn*) beginning; (*in Verein etc*) admission; (*in Liste etc*) inclusion; (*Notieren*) taking down; (*Phot*) shot; (*auf Tonband etc*) recording; **Aufnahmeantrag** M application for membership *od* admission; **aufnahmefähig** ADJ receptive; **Aufnahmeleiter** M (*Film*) production manager; (*Rundf, TV*) producer; **Aufnahmeprüfung** F entrance test; **Aufnahmestopp** M (*für Flüchtlinge etc*) freeze on immigration
aufnehmen ['aʊfne:mən] *unreg* VT to receive; (*hochheben*) to pick up; (*beginnen*) to take up; (*in Verein etc*) to admit; (*in Liste etc*) to include; (*fassen*) to hold; (*begreifen*) to take in, to grasp; (*beim Stricken: Maschen*) to increase, to make; (*notieren*) to take down; (*fotografieren*) to photograph; (*auf Tonband, Platte*) to record; (*Fin: leihen*) to take out; **es mit jdm ~ können** to be able to compete with sb
aufnötigen ['aʊfnø:tɪgən] VT: **jdm etw ~** to force sth on sb
aufoktroyieren ['aʊflɔktroaji:rən] VT: **jdm etw ~** (*geh*) to impose *od* force sth on sb
aufopfern ['aʊflɔpfərn] VT to sacrifice ▸ VR to sacrifice o.s.
aufopfernd ADJ selfless
aufpassen ['aʊfpasən] VI (*aufmerksam sein*) to pay attention; (*vorsichtig sein*) to take care; **auf jdn/etw ~** to look after *od* watch sb/sth; **aufgepasst!** look out!
Aufpasser(in) (-s, -) (*pej*) M(F) (*Aufseher, Spitzel*) spy, watchdog; (*Beobachter*) supervisor; (*Wächter*) guard
aufpflanzen ['aʊfpflantsən] VR: **sich vor jdm ~** to plant o.s. in front of sb
aufplatzen ['aʊfplatsən] VI to burst open
aufplustern ['aʊfplu:stərn] VR (*Vogel*) to ruffle (up) its feathers; (*Mensch*) to puff o.s. up
aufprägen ['aʊfprɛ:gən] VT: **jdm/etw seinen Stempel ~** (*fig*) to leave one's mark on sb/sth
Aufprall ['aʊfpral] (-(e)s, -e) M impact
aufprallen VI: **auf etw** *akk* **~** to hit sth, to crash into sth
Aufpreis ['aʊfpraɪs] M extra charge
aufpumpen ['aʊfpʊmpən] VT to pump up
aufputschen ['aʊfpʊtʃən] VT (*aufhetzen*) to inflame; (*erregen*) to stimulate
Aufputschmittel NT stimulant
aufraffen ['aʊfrafən] VR to rouse o.s.
aufräumen ['aʊfrɔʏmən] VT, VI (*Dinge*) to clear away; (*Zimmer*) to tidy up
Aufräumungsarbeiten PL clearing-up operations *pl*
aufrecht ['aʊfrɛçt] ADJ (*lit, fig*) upright
aufrechterhalten *unreg* VT to maintain
aufregen ['aʊfre:gən] VT to excite; (*ärgerlich machen*) to irritate, to annoy; (*nervös machen*) to make nervous; (*beunruhigen*) to disturb ▸ VR to get excited
aufregend ADJ exciting
Aufregung F excitement
aufreiben ['aʊfraɪbən] *unreg* VT (*Haut*) to rub raw; (*erschöpfen*) to exhaust; (*Mil: völlig vernichten*) to wipe out, to annihilate
aufreibend ADJ strenuous
aufreihen ['aʊfraɪən] VT (*in Linie*) to line up; (*Perlen*) to string
aufreißen ['aʊfraɪsən] *unreg* VT (*Umschlag*) to tear open; (*Augen*) to open wide; (*Tür*) to throw open; (*Straße*) to take up; (*umg: Mädchen*) to pick up
Aufreißer (-s, -) M (*Person*) smooth operator
aufreizen ['aʊfraɪtsən] VT to incite, to stir up
aufreizend ADJ exciting, stimulating
aufrichten ['aʊfrɪçtən] VT to put up, to erect; (*moralisch*) to console ▸ VR to rise; (*moralisch*): **sich ~ (an** *+dat***)** to take heart (from); **sich im Bett ~** to sit up in bed
aufrichtig ['aʊfrɪçtɪç] ADJ sincere; (*ehrlich*) honest; **Aufrichtigkeit** F sincerity

aufrollen ['aʊfrɔlən] VT (*zusammenrollen*) to roll up; (*Kabel*) to coil *od* wind up; *siehe auch* **wiederaufrollen**
aufrücken ['aʊfrʏkən] VI to move up; (*beruflich*) to be promoted
Aufruf ['aʊfru:f] M summons; (*zur Hilfe*) call; (*des Namens*) calling out
aufrufen *unreg* VT (*Namen*) to call out; (*auffordern*): **jdn ~ (zu)** to call upon sb (for); **einen Schüler ~** to ask a pupil (to answer) a question
Aufruhr ['aʊfru:r] **(-(e)s, -e)** M uprising, revolt; **in ~ sein** to be in uproar
Aufrührer(in) **(-s, -)** M(F) rabble-rouser
aufrührerisch ['aʊfry:rərɪʃ] ADJ rebellious
aufrunden ['aʊfrʊndən] VT (*Summe*) to round up
aufrüsten ['aʊfrʏstən] VT, VI to arm
Aufrüstung F rearmament
aufrütteln ['aʊfrʏtəln] VT (*lit, fig*) to shake up
aufs [aʊfs] = **auf das**
aufsagen ['aʊfza:gən] VT (*Gedicht*) to recite; (*geh: Freundschaft*) to put an end to
aufsammeln ['aʊfzaməln] VT to gather up
aufsässig ['aʊfzɛsɪç] ADJ rebellious
Aufsatz ['aʊfzats] M (*Geschriebenes*) essay, composition; (*auf Schrank etc*) top
aufsaugen ['aʊfzaʊgən] *unreg* VT to soak up
aufschauen ['aʊfʃaʊən] VI to look up
aufscheuchen ['aʊfʃɔʏçən] VT to scare, to startle
aufschichten ['aʊfʃɪçtən] VT to stack, to pile up
aufschieben ['aʊfʃi:bən] *unreg* VT to push open; (*verzögern*) to put off, to postpone
Aufschlag ['aʊfʃla:k] M (*Ärmelaufschlag*) cuff; (*Jackenaufschlag*) lapel; (*Hosenaufschlag*) turn-up (BRIT), cuff (US); (*Aufprall*) impact; (*Preisaufschlag*) surcharge; (*Tennis*) service
aufschlagen ['aʊfʃla:gən] *unreg* VT (*öffnen*) to open; (*verwunden*) to cut; (*hochschlagen*) to turn up; (*aufbauen: Zelt, Lager*) to pitch, to erect; (*Wohnsitz*) to take up ▶ VI (*aufprallen*) to hit; (*teurer werden*) to go up; (*Tennis*) to serve; **schlagt Seite 111 auf** open your books at page 111
aufschließen ['aʊfʃli:sən] *unreg* VT to open up, to unlock ▶ VI (*aufrücken*) to close up
Aufschluss ['aʊfʃlʊs] M information
aufschlüsseln ['aʊfʃlʏsəln] VT: **~ (nach)** to break down (into); (*klassifizieren*) to classify (according to)
aufschlussreich ADJ informative, illuminating
aufschnappen ['aʊfʃnapən] VT (*umg*) to pick up ▶ VI to fly open
aufschneiden ['aʊfʃnaɪdən] *unreg* VT to cut open; (*Brot*) to cut up; (*Med: Geschwür*) to lance ▶ VI (*umg*) to brag
Aufschneider **(-s, -)** M boaster, braggart
Aufschnitt ['aʊfʃnɪt] M (slices of) cold meat
aufschnüren ['aʊfʃny:rən] VT to unlace; (*Paket*) to untie
aufschrauben ['aʊfʃraʊbən] VT (*festschrauben*) to screw on; (*lösen*) to unscrew
aufschrecken ['aʊfʃrɛkən] VT to startle ▶ VI (*unreg*) to start up
Aufschrei ['aʊfʃraɪ] M cry
aufschreiben ['aʊfʃraɪbən] *unreg* VT to write down
aufschreien *unreg* VI to cry out
Aufschrift ['aʊfʃrɪft] F (*Inschrift*) inscription; (*Etikett*) label
Aufschub ['aʊfʃu:p] **(-(e)s, -schübe)** M delay, postponement; **jdm ~ gewähren** to grant sb an extension
aufschürfen ['aʊfʃʏrfən] VT: **sich** *dat* **die Haut/das Knie ~** to graze *od* scrape o.s./one's knee
aufschütten ['aʊfʃʏtən] VT (*Flüssigkeit*) to pour on; (*Kohle*) to put on (the fire); (*Damm, Deich*) to throw up; **Kaffee ~** to make coffee
aufschwatzen ['aʊfʃvatsən] (*umg*) VT: **jdm etw ~** to talk sb into (getting/having *etc*) sth
Aufschwung ['aʊfʃvʊŋ] M (*Elan*) boost; (*wirtschaftlich*) upturn, boom; (*Sport: an Gerät*) mount
aufsehen ['aʊfze:ən] *unreg* VI to look up; **~ zu** (*lit*) to look up at; (*fig*) to look up to; **Aufsehen** **(-s)** NT sensation, stir; **großes Aufsehen erregen** to cause a sensation; **aufsehenerregend** ADJ sensational
Aufseher(in) **(-s, -)** M(F) guard; (*im Betrieb*) supervisor; (*Museumsaufseher*) attendant; (*Parkaufseher*) keeper
auf sein ['aʊfzaɪn] *siehe* **auf**
aufseiten, auf Seiten [aʊf'zaɪtn] PRÄP +*gen*: **~ von** on the part of
aufsetzen ['aʊfzɛtsən] VT to put on; (*Flugzeug*) to put down; (*Dokument*) to draw up ▶ VR to sit upright ▶ VI (*Flugzeug*) to touch down
Aufsicht ['aʊfzɪçt] F supervision; **die ~ haben** to be in charge; **bei einer Prüfung ~ führen** to invigilate (BRIT) *od* supervise an exam
Aufsichtsrat M board (of directors)
aufsitzen ['aʊfzɪtsən] *unreg* VI (*aufgerichtet sitzen*) to sit up; (*aufs Pferd, Motorrad*) to mount, to get on; (*Schiff*) to run aground; **jdn ~ lassen** (*umg*) to stand sb up; **jdm ~** (*umg*) to be taken in by sb
aufspalten ['aʊfʃpaltən] VT to split
aufspannen ['aʊfʃpanən] VT (*Netz, Sprungtuch*) to stretch *od* spread out; (*Schirm*) to put up, to open
aufsparen ['aʊfʃpa:rən] VT to save (up)
aufsperren ['aʊfʃpɛrən] VT to unlock; (*Mund*) to open wide; **die Ohren ~** (*umg*) to prick up one's ears
aufspielen ['aʊfʃpi:lən] VR to show off; **sich als etw ~** to try to come on as sth
aufspießen ['aʊfʃpi:sən] VT to spear
aufspringen ['aʊfʃprɪŋən] *unreg* VI (*hochspringen*) to jump up; (*sich öffnen*) to spring open; (*Hände, Lippen*) to become chapped; **~ auf** +*akk* to jump onto
aufspüren ['aʊfʃpy:rən] VT to track down, to trace
aufstacheln ['aʊfʃtaxəln] VT to incite
aufstampfen ['aʊfʃtampfən] VI: **mit dem Fuß ~** to stamp one's foot
Aufstand ['aʊfʃtant] M insurrection, rebellion
aufständisch ['aʊfʃtɛndɪʃ] ADJ rebellious, mutinous

aufstauen ['aʊfʃtaʊən] VR to collect; (*fig: Ärger*) to be bottled up
aufstechen ['aʊfʃtɛçən] *unreg* VT to prick open, to puncture
aufstecken ['aʊfʃtɛkən] VT to stick on; (*mit Nadeln*) to pin up; (*umg*) to give up
aufstehen ['aʊfʃte:ən] *unreg* VI to get up; (*Tür*) to be open; **da musst du früher** *od* **eher ~!** (*fig: umg*) you'll have to do better than that!
aufsteigen ['aʊfʃtaɪgən] *unreg* VI (*hochsteigen*) to climb; (*Rauch*) to rise; **~ auf** *+akk* to get onto; **in jdm ~** (*Hass, Verdacht, Erinnerung etc*) to well up in sb
Aufsteiger (-s, -) M (*Sport*) promoted team; **(sozialer) ~** social climber
aufstellen ['aʊfʃtɛlən] VT (*aufrecht stellen*) to put up; (*Maschine*) to install; (*aufreihen*) to line up; (*Kandidaten*) to nominate; (*Forderung, Behauptung*) to put forward; (*formulieren: Programm etc*) to draw up; (*leisten: Rekord*) to set up
Aufstellung F (*Sport*) line-up; (*Liste*) list
Aufstieg ['aʊfʃti:k] **(-(e)s, -e)** M (*auf Berg*) ascent; (*Fortschritt*) rise; (*beruflich, Sport*) promotion
Aufstiegschance F prospect of promotion
aufstöbern ['aʊfʃtø:bərn] VT (*Wild*) to start, to flush; (*umg: entdecken*) to run to earth
aufstocken ['aʊfʃtɔkən] VT (*Vorräte*) to build up
aufstoßen ['aʊfʃto:sən] *unreg* VT to push open ▸ VI to belch
aufstrebend ['aʊfʃtre:bənd] ADJ ambitious; (*Land*) striving for progress
Aufstrich ['aʊfʃtrɪç] M spread
aufstülpen ['aʊfʃtʏlpən] VT (*Ärmel*) to turn up; (*Hut*) to put on
aufstützen ['aʊfʃtʏtsən] VT (*Körperteil*) to prop, to lean; (*Person*) to prop up ▸ VR: **sich ~ auf** *+akk* to lean on
aufsuchen ['aʊfzu:xən] VT (*besuchen*) to visit; (*konsultieren*) to consult
auftakeln ['aʊfta:kəln] VT (*Naut*) to rig (out) ▸ VR (*pej, umg*) to deck o.s. out
Auftakt ['aʊftakt] M (*Mus*) upbeat; (*fig*) prelude
auftanken ['aʊftaŋkən] VI to get petrol (BRIT) *od* gas (US) ▸ VT to refuel
auftauchen ['aʊftaʊxən] VI to appear; (*gefunden werden, kommen*) to turn up; (*aus Wasser etc*) to emerge; (*U-Boot*) to surface; (*Zweifel*) to arise
auftauen ['aʊftaʊən] VT to thaw ▸ VI to thaw; (*fig*) to relax
aufteilen ['aʊftaɪlən] VT to divide up; (*Raum*) to partition
Aufteilung F division; (*von Raum*) partition
auftischen ['aʊftɪʃən] VT to serve (up); (*fig*) to tell
Auftr. ABK = **Auftrag**
Auftrag ['aʊftra:k] **(-(e)s, -träge)** M order; (*Anweisung*) commission; (*Aufgabe*) mission; **etw in ~ geben (bei)** to order/commission sth (from); **im ~ von** on behalf of; **im ~** *od* **i. A. J. Burnett** pp J. Burnett
auftragen ['aʊftra:gən] *unreg* VT (*Essen*) to serve; (*Farbe*) to put on; (*Kleidung*) to wear out ▸ VI (*dick machen*): **die Jacke trägt auf** the jacket makes one look fat; **jdm etw ~** to tell sb sth; **dick ~** (*umg*) to exaggerate
Auftraggeber(in) (-s, -) M(F) client; (*Comm*) customer
Auftragsbestätigung F confirmation of order
auftreiben ['aʊftraɪbən] *unreg* (*umg*) VT (*beschaffen*) to raise
auftrennen ['aʊftrɛnən] VT to undo
auftreten ['aʊftre:tən] *unreg* VT to kick open ▸ VI to appear; (*mit Füßen*) to tread; (*sich verhalten*) to behave; (*fig: eintreten*) to occur; (*Schwierigkeiten etc*) to arise; **als Vermittler** *etc* **~** to act as intermediary *etc*; **geschlossen ~** to put up a united front
Auftreten (-s) NT (*Vorkommen*) appearance; (*Benehmen*) behaviour (BRIT), behavior (US)
Auftrieb ['aʊftri:p] M (*Phys*) buoyancy, lift; (*fig*) impetus
Auftritt ['aʊftrɪt] M (*von Schauspieler*) entrance; (*lit, fig: Szene*) scene
auftrumpfen ['aʊftrʊmpfən] VI to show how good one is; (*mit Bemerkung*) to crow
auftun ['aʊftu:n] *unreg* VT to open ▸ VR to open up
auftürmen ['aʊftʏrmən] VR (*Gebirge etc*) to tower up; (*Schwierigkeiten*) to pile *od* mount up
aufwachen ['aʊfvaxən] VI to wake up
aufwachsen ['aʊfvaksən] *unreg* VI to grow up
Aufwand ['aʊfvant] **(-(e)s)** M expenditure; (*Kosten*) expense; (*Luxus*) show; **bitte, keinen ~!** please don't go out of your way
aufwändig ['aʊfvɛndɪç] ADJ, ADV costly
Aufwandsentschädigung F expense allowance
aufwärmen ['aʊfvɛrmən] VT to warm up; (*alte Geschichten*) to rake up
aufwarten ['aʊfvartən] VI (*zu bieten haben*): **mit etw ~** to offer sth
aufwärts ['aʊfvɛrts] ADV upwards; **es geht ~** things are looking up; **Aufwärtsentwicklung** F upward trend
aufwecken ['aʊfvɛkən] VT to wake(n) up
aufweichen ['aʊfvaɪçən] VT to soften; (*Brot*) to soak
aufweisen ['aʊfvaɪzən] *unreg* VT to show
aufwenden ['aʊfvɛndən] *unreg* VT to expend; (*Geld*) to spend; (*Sorgfalt*) to devote
aufwendig ['aʊfvɛndɪç] ADJ, ADV costly
aufwerfen ['aʊfvɛrfən] *unreg* VT (*Fenster etc*) to throw open; (*Probleme*) to throw up, to raise ▸ VR: **sich zu etw ~** to make o.s. out to be sth
aufwerten ['aʊfvɛrtən] VT (*Fin*) to revalue; (*fig*) to raise in value
Aufwertung F revaluation
aufwickeln ['aʊfvɪkəln] VT (*aufrollen*) to roll up; (*umg: Haar*) to put in curlers; (*lösen*) to untie
aufwiegeln ['aʊfvi:gəln] VT to stir up, to incite
aufwiegen ['aʊfvi:gən] *unreg* VT to make up for
Aufwind ['aʊfvɪnt] M up-current; **neuen ~ bekommen** (*fig*) to get new impetus

aufwirbeln ['aʊfvɪrbəln] VT to whirl up; **Staub ~** (*fig*) to create a stir
aufwischen ['aʊfvɪʃən] VT to wipe up
aufwühlen ['aʊfvy:lən] VT (*lit: Erde, Meer*) to churn (up); (*Gefühle*) to stir
aufzählen ['aʊftsɛ:lən] VT to count out
aufzeichnen ['aʊftsaɪçnən] VT to sketch; (*schriftlich*) to jot down; (*auf Band*) to record
Aufzeichnung F (*schriftlich*) note; (*Tonbandaufzeichnung, Filmaufzeichnung*) recording
aufzeigen ['aʊftsaɪgən] VT to show, to demonstrate
aufziehen ['aʊftsi:ən] *unreg* VT (*hochziehen*) to raise, to draw up; (*öffnen*) to pull open; (*: Reißverschluss*) to undo; (*Gardinen*) to draw (back); (*Uhr*) to wind; (*großziehen: Kinder*) to raise, to bring up; (*Tiere*) to rear; (*umg: necken*) to tease; (*: veranstalten*) to set up; (*: Fest*) to arrange ▶ VI (*Gewitter, Wolken*) to gather
Aufzucht ['aʊftsʊxt] F (*das Großziehen*) rearing, raising
Aufzug ['aʊftsu:k] M (*Fahrstuhl*) lift (BRIT), elevator (US); (*Aufmarsch*) procession, parade; (*Kleidung*) get-up; (*Theat*) act
aufzwingen ['aʊftsvɪŋgən] *unreg* VT: **jdm etw ~** to force sth upon sb
Aug. ABK (= *August*) Aug.
Augapfel ['aʊklapfəl] M eyeball; (*fig*) apple of one's eye
Auge ['aʊgə] (**-s, -n**) NT eye; (*Fettauge*) globule of fat; **unter vier Augen** in private; **vor aller Augen** in front of everybody, for all to see; **jdn/etw mit anderen Augen (an)sehen** to see sb/sth in a different light; **ich habe kein ~ zugetan** I didn't sleep a wink; **ein ~/beide Augen zudrücken** (*umg*) to turn a blind eye; **jdn/etw aus den Augen verlieren** to lose sight of sb/sth; (*fig*) to lose touch with sb/sth; **etw ins ~ fassen** to contemplate sth; **das kann leicht ins ~ gehen** (*fig: umg*) it might easily go wrong
Augenarzt M eye specialist, ophthalmologist
Augenblick M moment; **im ~** at the moment; **im ersten ~** for a moment; **augenblicklich** ADJ (*sofort*) instantaneous; (*gegenwärtig*) present
Augen- ZW: **Augenbraue** F eyebrow; **Augenbrauenstift** M eyebrow pencil; **Augenhöhe** F: **in Augenhöhe** at eye level; **Augenmerk** NT (*Aufmerksamkeit*) attention; **Augenoptiker(in)** (**-s, -**) M(F) optician; **Augenschein** M: **jdn/etw in Augenschein nehmen** to have a close look at sb/sth; **augenscheinlich** ADJ obvious; **Augentropfen** PL eyedrops *pl*; **Augenweide** F sight for sore eyes; **Augenwischerei** F (*fig*) eye-wash; **Augenzeuge** M eye witness
Augenzeugin F eye witness
August [aʊ'gʊst] (**-(e)s** *od* **-, -e**) (*pl selten*) M August; *siehe auch* **September**
Auktion [aʊktsi'o:n] F auction
Auktionator [aʊktsio'na:tɔr] M auctioneer
Aula ['aʊla] (**-, Aulen** *od* **-s**) F assembly hall

SCHLÜSSELWORT

aus [aʊs] PRÄP +*dat* **1** (*räumlich*) out of; (*von ... her*) from; **er ist aus Berlin** he's from Berlin; **aus dem Fenster** out of the window
2 (*gemacht/hergestellt aus*) made of; **ein Herz aus Stein** a heart of stone
3 (*auf Ursache deutend*) out of; **aus Mitleid** out of sympathy; **aus Erfahrung** from experience; **aus Spaß** for fun
4: **aus ihr wird nie etwas** she'll never get anywhere
▶ ADV **1** (*zu Ende*) finished, over; **aus sein** to be over; **es ist aus mit ihm** he is finished, he has had it; **aus und vorbei** over and done with
2 (*ausgeschaltet, ausgezogen*) off; **aus sein** to be out; **Licht aus!** lights out!
3 (*in Verbindung mit von*): **von Rom aus** from Rome; **vom Fenster aus** out of the window; **von sich aus** (*selbstständig*) of one's own accord; **von mir aus** as far as I'm concerned
4: **aus und ein gehen** to come and go; (*bei jdm*) to visit frequently; **weder aus noch ein wissen** to be at one's wits' end; **auf etw** *akk* **aus sein** to be after sth

Aus [aʊs] (-) NT (*Sport*) outfield; **ins ~ gehen** to go out
ausarbeiten ['aʊslarbaɪtən] VT to work out
ausarten ['aʊslartən] VI to degenerate; (*Kind*) to become overexcited
ausatmen ['aʊsla:tmən] VI to breathe out
ausbaden ['aʊsba:dən] (*umg*) VT: **etw ~ müssen** to carry the can for sth
Ausbau ['aʊsbaʊ] M extension, expansion; (*Entfernung*) removal
ausbauen VT to extend, to expand; (*herausnehmen*) to take out, to remove
ausbaufähig ADJ (*fig*) worth developing
ausbedingen ['aʊsbədɪŋən] *unreg* VT: **sich** *dat* **etw ~** to insist on sth
ausbeißen ['aʊsbaɪsən] *unreg* VR: **sich** *dat* **an etw** *dat* **die Zähne ~** (*fig*) to have a tough time of it with sth
ausbessern ['aʊsbɛsərn] VT to mend, to repair
Ausbesserungsarbeiten PL repair work *sing*
ausbeulen ['aʊsbɔʏlən] VT to beat out
Ausbeute ['aʊsbɔʏtə] F yield; (*Gewinn*) profit, gain; (*Fische*) catch
ausbeuten VT to exploit; (*Min*) to work
ausbezahlen ['aʊsbətsa:lən] VT (*Geld*) to pay out
ausbilden ['aʊsbɪldən] VT to educate; (*Lehrling, Soldat*) to instruct, to train; (*Fähigkeiten*) to develop; (*Geschmack*) to cultivate
Ausbilder(in) (**-s, -**) M(F) instructor, instructress
Ausbildung F education; (*von Lehrling, Soldat*) training, instruction; (*von Fähigkeiten*) development; **er ist noch in der ~** he hasn't finished his education; (*Lehrling*) he's still a trainee
Ausbildungs- ZW: **Ausbildungsförderung** F (provision of) grants for students and trainees;

(*Stipendium*) grant; **Ausbildungsplatz** M (*Stelle*) training vacancy
ausbitten ['aʊsbɪtən] *unreg* VT: **sich** *dat* **etw ~** (*geh*: *erbitten*) to ask for sth; (*verlangen*) to insist on sth
ausblasen ['aʊsbla:zən] *unreg* VT to blow out; (*Ei*) to blow
ausbleiben ['aʊsblaɪbən] *unreg* VI (*Personen*) to stay away, to not come; (*Ereignisse*) to fail to happen, to not happen; **es konnte nicht ~, dass ...** it was inevitable that ...
ausblenden ['aʊsblɛndən] VT, VI (*TV etc*) to fade out
Ausblick ['aʊsblɪk] M (*lit, fig*) prospect, outlook, view
ausbomben ['aʊsbɔmbən] VT to bomb out
ausbooten ['aʊsbo:tən] (*umg*) VT (*jdn*) to kick *od* boot out
ausbrechen ['aʊsbrɛçən] *unreg* VI to break out ▶ VT to break off; **in Tränen/Gelächter ~** to burst into tears/out laughing
Ausbrecher(in) (**-s, -**) (*umg*) M(F) (*Gefangener*) escaped prisoner, escapee
ausbreiten ['aʊsbraɪtən] VT to spread (out); (*Arme*) to stretch out ▶ VR to spread; **sich über ein Thema ~** to expand *od* enlarge on a topic
ausbrennen ['aʊsbrɛnən] *unreg* VT to scorch; (*Wunde*) to cauterize ▶ VI to burn out
ausbringen ['aʊsbrɪŋən] *unreg* VT (*ein Hoch*) to propose
Ausbruch ['aʊsbrʊx] M outbreak; (*von Vulkan*) eruption; (*Gefühlsausbruch*) outburst; (*von Gefangenen*) escape
ausbrüten ['aʊsbry:tən] VT (*lit, fig*) to hatch
Ausbuchtung ['aʊsbʊxtʊŋ] F bulge; (*Küste*) cove
ausbügeln ['aʊsby:gəln] VT to iron out; (*umg*: *Fehler, Verlust*) to make good
ausbuhen ['aʊsbu:ən] VT to boo
Ausbund ['aʊsbʊnt] M: **ein ~ an** *od* **von Tugend/Sparsamkeit** a paragon of virtue/a model of thrift
ausbürgern ['aʊsbʏrgərn] VT to expatriate
ausbürsten ['aʊsbʏrstən] VT to brush out
Ausdauer ['aʊsdaʊər] F stamina; (*Beharrlichkeit*) perseverance
ausdauernd ADJ persevering
ausdehnen ['aʊsde:nən] VT, VR (*räumlich*) to expand; (*zeitlich, auch Gummi*) to stretch; (*Nebel, fig*: *Macht*) to extend
ausdenken ['aʊsdɛŋkən] *unreg* VT (*zu Ende denken*) to think through; **sich** *dat* **etw ~** to think sth up; **das ist nicht auszudenken** (*unvorstellbar*) it's inconceivable
ausdiskutieren ['aʊsdɪskuti:rən] VT to talk out
ausdrehen ['aʊsdre:ən] VT to turn *od* switch off
Ausdruck ['aʊsdrʊk] (**-s, -drücke**) M expression, phrase; (*Kundgabe, Gesichtsausdruck*) expression; (*Fachausdruck*) term; (*Comput*) hard copy; **mit dem ~ des Bedauerns** (*form*) expressing regret
ausdrucken VT (*Text*) to print out
ausdrücken ['aʊsdrʏkən] VT (*auch vr*: *formulieren, zeigen*) to express; (*Zigarette*) to put out; (*Zitrone*) to squeeze
ausdrücklich ADJ express, explicit ▶ ADV expressly
Ausdrucks- ZW: **Ausdrucksfähigkeit** F expressiveness; (*Gewandtheit*) articulateness; **ausdruckslos** ADJ expressionless, blank; **ausdrucksvoll** ADJ expressive; **Ausdrucksweise** F mode of expression
Ausdünstung ['aʊsdʏnstʊŋ] F (*Dampf*) vapour (BRIT), vapor (US); (*Geruch*) smell
auseinander [aʊsl aɪ'nandər] ADV (*getrennt*) apart; **weit ~** far apart
auseinander- ZW: **auseinanderbringen** *unreg* VT to separate; **auseinanderfallen** *unreg* VI to fall apart; **auseinandergehen** *unreg* VI (*Menschen*) to separate; (*Meinungen*) to differ; (*Gegenstand*) to fall apart; (*umg*: *dick werden*) to put on weight; **auseinanderhalten** *unreg* VT to tell apart; **auseinanderklaffen** VI to gape open; (*fig*: *Meinungen*) to be far apart, to diverge (wildly); **auseinanderlaufen** *unreg* VI (*Menge*) to disperse; (*umg*: *sich trennen*) to break up; **auseinanderleben** VR to drift apart; **auseinandernehmen** *unreg* VT to take to pieces, to dismantle; **auseinanderschreiben** *unreg* VT to write as separate words; **auseinandersetzen** *unreg* VT to set forth, to explain ▶ VR (*sich verständigen*) to come to terms, to settle; (*sich befassen*) to concern o.s.; **sich mit jdm auseinandersetzen** to talk with sb; (*sich streiten*) to argue with sb; **Auseinandersetzung** F argument
auserkoren ['aʊslɛrko:rən] ADJ (*liter*) chosen, selected
auserlesen ['aʊslɛrle:zən] ADJ select, choice
ausersehen ['aʊslɛrze:ən] *unreg* VT (*geh*): **dazu ~ sein, etw zu tun** to be chosen to do sth
ausfahrbar ADJ extendable; (*Antenne, Fahrgestell*) retractable
ausfahren ['aʊsfa:rən] *unreg* VI to drive out; (*Naut*) to put out (to sea) ▶ VT to take out; (*Aut*) to drive flat out; (*ausliefern*: *Waren*) to deliver; **ausgefahrene Wege** rutted roads
Ausfahrt F (*des Zuges etc*) leaving, departure; (*Autobahnausfahrt, Garagenausfahrt*) exit, way out; (*Spazierfahrt*) drive, excursion
Ausfall ['aʊsfal] M loss; (*Nichtstattfinden*) cancellation; (*das Versagen*: *Tech, Med*) failure; (*von Motor*) breakdown; (*Produktionsstörung*) stoppage; (*Mil*) sortie; (*Fechten*) lunge; (*radioaktiv*) fallout
ausfallen ['aʊsfalən] *unreg* VI (*Zähne, Haare*) to fall *od* come out; (*nicht stattfinden*) to be cancelled; (*wegbleiben*) to be omitted; (*Person*) to drop out; (*Lohn*) to be stopped; (*nicht funktionieren*) to break down; (*Resultat haben*) to turn out; **wie ist das Spiel ausgefallen?** what was the result of the game?; **die Schule fällt morgen aus** there's no school tomorrow
ausfallend ADJ impertinent
Ausfallstraße F arterial road
Ausfallzeit F (*Maschine*) downtime
ausfegen ['aʊsfe:gən] VT to sweep out

ausfeilen ['aʊsfaɪlən] VT to file out; (*Stil*) to polish up
ausfertigen ['aʊsfɛrtɪgən] VT (*form*) to draw up; (*Rechnung*) to make out; **doppelt ~** to duplicate
Ausfertigung F (*form*) drawing up; (*von Rechnung*) making out; (*Exemplar*) copy; **in doppelter/dreifacher ~** in duplicate/triplicate
ausfindig ['aʊsfɪndɪç] ADJ: **~ machen** to discover
ausfliegen ['aʊsfli:gən] *unreg* VI to fly away ▸ VT to fly out; **sie sind ausgeflogen** (*umg*) they're out
ausfließen ['aʊsfli:sən] *unreg* VI: **~ (aus)** (*herausfließen*) to flow out (of); (*auslaufen: Öl etc*) to leak (out of); (*Eiter etc*) to be discharged (from)
ausflippen ['aʊsflɪpən] (*umg*) VI to freak out
Ausflucht ['aʊsflʊxt] **(-, -flüchte)** F excuse
Ausflug ['aʊsflu:k] M excursion, outing
Ausflügler(in) ['aʊsfly:klər(ɪn)] **(-s, -)** M(F) tripper (BRIT), excursionist (US)
Ausfluss ['aʊsflʊs] M outlet; (*Med*) discharge
ausfragen ['aʊsfra:gən] VT to interrogate, to question
ausfransen ['aʊsfranzən] VI to fray
ausfressen ['aʊsfrɛsən] *unreg* (*umg*) VT (*anstellen*) to be up to
Ausfuhr ['aʊsfu:r] **(-, -en)** F export, exportation; (*Ware*) export ▸ IN ZW export
ausführbar ['aʊsfy:rba:r] ADJ feasible; (*Comm*) exportable
ausführen ['aʊsfy:rən] VT (*verwirklichen*) to carry out; (*Person*) to take out; (*Hund*) to take for a walk; (*Comm*) to export; (*erklären*) to give details of; **die ausführende Gewalt** (*Pol*) the executive
Ausfuhrgenehmigung F export licence
ausführlich ADJ detailed ▸ ADV in detail;
Ausführlichkeit F detail
Ausführung F execution, performance; (*von Waren*) design; (*von Thema*) exposition; (*Durchführung*) completion; (*Herstellungsart*) version; (*Erklärung*) explanation
Ausfuhrzoll M export duty
ausfüllen ['aʊsfʏlən] VT to fill up; (*Fragebogen etc*) to fill in; (*Beruf*) to be fulfilling for; **jdn (ganz) ~** (*Zeit in Anspruch nehmen*) to take (all) sb's time
Ausg. ABK (= *Ausgabe*) ed.
Ausgabe ['aʊsga:bə] F (*Geld*) expenditure, outlay; (*Aushändigung*) giving out; (*Schalter*) counter; (*Ausführung*) version; (*Buch*) edition; (*Nummer*) issue
Ausgang ['aʊsgaŋ] M way out, exit; (*Ende*) end; (*Ausgangpunkt*) starting point; (*Ergebnis*) result; (*Ausgehtag*) free time, time off; **ein Unfall mit tödlichem ~** a fatal accident; **kein ~** no exit
Ausgangs- ZW: **Ausgangsbasis** F starting point; **Ausgangspunkt** M starting point; **Ausgangssperre** F curfew
ausgeben ['aʊsge:bən] *unreg* VT (*Geld*) to spend; (*austeilen*) to issue, to distribute; (*Comput*) to output ▸ VR: **sich für etw/jdn ~** to pass o.s. off as sth/sb; **ich gebe heute Abend einen aus** (*umg*) it's my treat this evening
ausgebeult ['aʊsgəbɔʏlt] ADJ (*Kleidung*) baggy; (*Hut*) battered
ausgebucht ['aʊsgəbu:xt] ADJ fully booked
Ausgeburt ['aʊsgəbu:rt] (*pej*) F (*der Fantasie etc*) monstrous product *od* invention
ausgedehnt ['aʊsgəde:nt] ADJ (*breit, groß, fig: weitreichend*) extensive; (*Spaziergang*) long; (*zeitlich*) lengthy
ausgedient ['aʊsgədi:nt] ADJ (*Soldat*) discharged; (*verbraucht*) no longer in use; **~ haben** to have come to the end of its useful life
ausgefallen ['aʊsgəfalən] ADJ (*ungewöhnlich*) exceptional
ausgefuchst ['aʊsgəfʊkst] (*umg*) ADJ clever; (*listig*) crafty
ausgegangen ['aʊsgəgaŋən] PP *von* **ausgehen**
ausgeglichen ['aʊsgəglɪçən] ADJ (well-)balanced; **Ausgeglichenheit** F balance; (*von Mensch*) even-temperedness
Ausgehanzug M good suit
ausgehen ['aʊsge:ən] *unreg* VI (*auch Feuer, Ofen, Licht*) to go out; (*zu Ende gehen*) to come to an end; (*Benzin*) to run out; (*Haare, Zähne*) to fall *od* come out; (*Strom*) to go off; (*Resultat haben*) to turn out; (*spazieren gehen*) to go (out) for a walk; (*abgeschickt werden: Post*) to be sent off; **mir ging das Benzin aus** I ran out of petrol (BRIT) *od* gas (US); **auf etw akk ~** to aim at sth; **von etw ~** (*wegführen*) to lead away from sth; (*herrühren*) to come from sth; (*zugrunde legen*) to proceed from sth; **wir können davon ~, dass ...** we can proceed from the assumption that ..., we can take as our starting point that ...; **leer ~** to get nothing; **schlecht ~** to turn out badly
ausgehungert ['aʊsgəhʊŋərt] ADJ starved; (*abgezehrt: Mensch etc*) emaciated
Ausgehverbot NT curfew
ausgeklügelt ['aʊsgəkly:gəlt] ADJ ingenious
ausgekocht ['aʊsgəkɔxt] (*pej, umg*) ADJ (*durchtrieben*) cunning; (*fig*) out-and-out
ausgelassen ['aʊsgəlasən] ADJ boisterous, high-spirited, exuberant; **Ausgelassenheit** F boisterousness, high spirits *pl*, exuberance
ausgelastet ['aʊsgəlastət] ADJ fully occupied
ausgeleiert ['aʊsgəlaɪərt] ADJ worn; (*Gummiband*) stretched
ausgelernt ['aʊsgəlɛrnt] ADJ trained, qualified
ausgemacht ['aʊsgəmaxt] ADJ settled; (*umg: Dummkopf etc*) out-and-out, downright; **es gilt als ~, dass ...** it is settled that ...; **es war eine ausgemachte Sache, dass ...** it was a foregone conclusion that ...
ausgemergelt ['aʊsgəmɛrgəlt] ADJ (*Gesicht*) emaciated, gaunt
ausgenommen ['aʊsgənɔmən] KONJ except; **Anwesende sind ~** present company excepted
ausgepowert ['aʊsgəpaʊərt] ADJ: **~ sein** (*umg*) to be tired, to be exhausted
ausgeprägt ['aʊsgəprɛ:kt] ADJ prominent; (*Eigenschaft*) distinct
ausgerechnet ['aʊsgərɛçnət] ADV just, precisely; **~ du** you of all people; **~ heute** today of all days

ausgeschlossen ['aʊsgəʃlɔsən] PP *von* **ausschließen** ▸ ADJ (*unmöglich*) impossible, out of the question; **es ist nicht ~, dass …** it cannot be ruled out that …
ausgeschnitten ['aʊsgəʃnɪtən] ADJ (*Kleid*) low-necked
ausgesehen ['aʊsgəze:ən] PP *von* **aussehen**
ausgesprochen ['aʊsgəʃprɔxən] ADJ (*Faulheit, Lüge etc*) out-and-out; (*unverkennbar*) marked ▸ ADV decidedly; **~ gut** really good
ausgestorben ['aʊsgəʃtɔrbən] ADJ (*Tierart*) extinct; (*fig*) deserted
ausgewogen ['aʊsgəvo:gən] ADJ balanced; (*Maß*) equal
ausgezeichnet ['aʊsgətsaɪçnət] ADJ excellent
ausgiebig ['aʊsgi:bɪç] ADJ (*Gebrauch*) full, good; (*Essen*) generous, lavish; **~ schlafen** to have a good sleep
ausgießen ['aʊsgi:sən] *unreg* VT (*aus einem Behälter*) to pour out; (*Behälter*) to empty; (*weggießen*) to pour away
Ausgleich ['aʊsglaɪç] **(-(e)s, -e)** M balance; (*von Fehler, Mangel*) compensation; (*Sport*): **den ~ erzielen** to equalize; **zum ~** *+gen* in order to offset sth; **das ist ein guter ~** (*entspannend*) that's very relaxing
ausgleichen ['aʊsglaɪçən] *unreg* VT to balance (out); (*Konflikte*) to reconcile; (*Höhe*) to even up ▸ VI (*Sport*) to equalize; **ausgleichende Gerechtigkeit** poetic justice
Ausgleichssport M keep-fit activity
Ausgleichstor NT equalizer
ausgraben ['aʊsgra:bən] *unreg* VT to dig up; (*Leichen*) to exhume; (*fig*) to unearth
Ausgrabung F excavation
ausgrenzen ['aʊsgrɛntsən] VT to shut out, to separate
Ausgrenzung F shut-out, separation
Ausguck ['aʊsgʊk] M look-out
Ausguss ['aʊsgʊs] M (*Spüle*) sink; (*Abfluss*) outlet; (*Tülle*) spout
aushaben ['aʊsha:bən] *unreg* (*umg*) VT (*Kleidung*) to have taken off; (*Buch*) to have finished
aushalten ['aʊshaltən] *unreg* VT to bear, to stand; (*umg: Geliebte*) to keep ▸ VI to hold out; **das ist nicht zum A~** that is unbearable; **sich von jdm ~ lassen** to be kept by sb
aushandeln ['aʊshandəln] VT to negotiate
aushändigen ['aʊshɛndɪgən] VT: **jdm etw ~** to hand sth over to sb
Aushang ['aʊshaŋ] M notice
aushängen ['aʊshɛŋən] *unreg* VT (*Meldung*) to put up; (*Fenster*) to take off its hinges ▸ VI to be displayed ▸ VR to hang out
Aushängeschild NT (shop) sign; (*fig*): **als ~ für etw dienen** to promote sth
ausharren ['aʊsharən] VI to hold out
aushäusig ['aʊshɔʏzɪç] ADJ gallivanting around, on the tiles
ausheben ['aʊshe:bən] *unreg* VT (*Erde*) to lift out; (*Grube*) to hollow out; (*Tür*) to take off its hinges; (*Diebesnest*) to clear out; (*Mil*) to enlist
aushecken ['aʊshɛkən] (*umg*) VT to concoct, to think up
aushelfen ['aʊshɛlfən] *unreg* VI: **jdm ~** to help sb out
Aushilfe ['aʊshɪlfə] F help, assistance; (*Person*) (temporary) worker
Aushilfs- ZW: **Aushilfskraft** F temporary worker; **Aushilfslehrer(in)** M(F) supply teacher; **aushilfsweise** ADV temporarily, as a stopgap
aushöhlen ['aʊshø:lən] VT to hollow out; (*fig: untergraben*) to undermine
ausholen ['aʊsho:lən] VI to swing one's arm back; (*zur Ohrfeige*) to raise one's hand; (*beim Gehen*) to take long strides; **zum Gegenschlag ~** (*lit, fig*) to prepare for a counter-attack
aushorchen ['aʊshɔrçən] VT to sound out, to pump
aushungern ['aʊshʊŋərn] VT to starve out
auskennen ['aʊskɛnən] *unreg* VR to know a lot; (*an einem Ort*) to know one's way about; (*in Fragen etc*) to be knowledgeable; **man kennt sich bei ihm nie aus** you never know where you are with him
auskippen ['aʊskɪpən] VT to empty
ausklammern ['aʊsklamərn] VT (*Thema*) to exclude, to leave out
Ausklang ['aʊsklaŋ] M (*geh*) end
ausklappbar ['aʊsklapba:r] ADJ: **dieser Tisch ist ~** this table can be opened out
auskleiden ['aʊsklaɪdən] VR (*geh*) to undress ▸ VT (*Wand*) to line
ausklingen ['aʊsklɪŋən] *unreg* VI to end; (*Ton, Lied*) to die away; (*Fest*) to come to an end
ausklinken ['aʊsklɪŋkən] VT (*Bomben*) to release ▸ VI (*umg*) to flip one's lid
ausklopfen ['aʊsklɔpfən] VT (*Teppich*) to beat; (*Pfeife*) to knock out
auskochen ['aʊskɔxən] VT to boil; (*Med*) to sterilize
auskommen ['aʊskɔmən] *unreg* VI: **mit jdm ~** to get on with sb; **mit etw ~** to get by with sth; **Auskommen (-s)** NT: **sein Auskommen haben** to get by; **mit ihr ist kein Auskommen** she's impossible to get on with
auskosten ['aʊskɔstən] VT to enjoy to the full
auskramen ['aʊskra:mən] (*umg*) VT to dig out, to unearth; (*fig: alte Geschichten etc*) to bring up
auskratzen ['aʊskratsən] VT (*auch Med*) to scrape out
auskugeln ['aʊsku:gəln] VR: **sich** *dat* **den Arm ~** to dislocate one's arm
auskundschaften ['aʊskʊntʃaftən] VT to spy out; (*Gebiet*) to reconnoitre (BRIT), to reconnoiter (US)
Auskunft ['aʊskʊnft] **(-, -künfte)** F information; (*nähere*) details *pl*, particulars *pl*; (*Stelle*) information office; (*Tel*) inquiries; **jdm ~ erteilen** to give sb information
auskuppeln ['aʊskʊpəln] VI to disengage the clutch
auskurieren ['aʊskuri:rən] (*umg*) VT to cure
auslachen ['aʊslaxən] VT to laugh at, to mock

ausladen ['aʊsla:dən] *unreg* VT to unload; (*umg: Gäste*) to cancel an invitation to ▸ VI (*Äste*) to spread
ausladend ADJ (*Gebärden, Bewegung*) sweeping
Auslage ['aʊsla:gə] F shop window (display)
Auslagen PL outlay *sing*, expenditure *sing*
Ausland ['aʊslant] NT foreign countries *pl*; **im ~** abroad; **ins ~** abroad
Ausländer(in) ['aʊslɛndər(ɪn)] **(-s, -)** M(F) foreigner; **ausländerfeindlich** ADJ hostile to foreigners, xenophobic; **Ausländerfeindlichkeit** F hostility to foreigners, xenophobia
ausländisch ADJ foreign
Auslands- ZW: **Auslandsaufenthalt** M stay abroad; **Auslandsgespräch** NT international call; **Auslandskorrespondent(in)** M(F) foreign correspondent; **Auslandsreise** F trip abroad; **Auslandsschutzbrief** M international travel cover; **Auslandsvertretung** F agency abroad; (*von Firma*) foreign branch
auslassen ['aʊslasən] *unreg* VT to leave out; (*Wort etc*) to omit; (*Fett*) to melt; (*Kleidungsstück*) to let out ▸ VR: **sich über etw** *akk* **~** to speak one's mind about sth; **seine Wut** *etc* **an jdm ~** to vent one's rage *etc* on sb
Auslassung F omission
Auslassungszeichen NT apostrophe
auslasten ['aʊslastən] VT (*Fahrzeug*) to make full use of; (*Maschine*) to use to capacity; (*jdn*) to occupy fully
Auslauf ['aʊslaʊf] M (*für Tiere*) run; (*Ausfluss*) outflow, outlet
auslaufen *unreg* VI to run out; (*Behälter*) to leak; (*Naut*) to put out (to sea); (*langsam aufhören*) to run down
Ausläufer ['aʊslɔʏfər] M (*von Gebirge*) spur; (*Pflanze*) runner; (*Met: von Hoch*) ridge; (*: von Tief*) trough
ausleeren ['aʊsle:rən] VT to empty
auslegen ['aʊsle:gən] VT (*Waren*) to lay out; (*Köder*) to put down; (*Geld*) to lend; (*bedecken*) to cover; (*Text etc*) to interpret
Ausleger (-s, -) M (*von Kran etc*) jib, boom
Auslegung F interpretation
Ausleihe ['aʊslaɪə] **(-, -n)** F issuing; (*Stelle*) issue desk
ausleihen ['aʊslaɪən] *unreg* VT (*verleihen*) to lend; **sich** *dat* **etw ~** to borrow sth
auslernen ['aʊslɛrnən] VI (*Lehrling*) to finish one's apprenticeship; **man lernt nie aus** (*Sprichwort*) you live and learn
Auslese ['aʊsle:zə] **(-, -n)** F selection; (*Elite*) elite; (*Wein*) choice wine
auslesen ['aʊsle:zən] *unreg* VT to select; (*umg: zu Ende lesen*) to finish
ausliefern ['aʊsli:fərn] VT to hand over; (*Comm*) to deliver ▸ VR: **sich jdm ~** to give o.s. up to sb; **~ (an** *+akk*) to deliver (up) (to), to hand over (to); (*an anderen Staat*) to extradite (to); **jdm/etw ausgeliefert sein** to be at the mercy of sb/sth
Auslieferungsabkommen NT extradition treaty
ausliegen ['aʊsli:gən] *unreg* VI (*zur Ansicht*) to be displayed; (*Zeitschriften etc*) to be available (to the public); (*Liste*) to be up
ausloggen ['aʊslɔgən] VI (*Comput*) to log out *od* off
auslöschen ['aʊslœʃən] VT to extinguish; (*fig*) to wipe out, to obliterate
auslosen ['aʊslo:zən] VT to draw lots for
auslösen ['aʊsløːzən] VT (*Explosion, Schuss*) to set off; (*hervorrufen*) to cause, to produce; (*Gefangene*) to ransom; (*Pfand*) to redeem
Auslöser (-s, -) M trigger; (*Phot*) release; (*Anlass*) cause
ausloten ['aʊslo:tən] VT (*Naut: Tiefe*) to sound; (*fig geh*) to plumb
ausmachen ['aʊsmaxən] VT (*Licht, Radio*) to turn off; (*Feuer*) to put out; (*entdecken*) to make out; (*vereinbaren*) to agree; (*beilegen*) to settle; (*Anteil darstellen, betragen*) to represent; (*bedeuten*) to matter; **das macht ihm nichts aus** it doesn't matter to him; **macht es Ihnen etwas aus, wenn …?** would you mind if …?
ausmalen ['aʊsma:lən] VT to paint; (*fig*) to describe; **sich** *dat* **etw ~** to imagine sth
Ausmaß ['aʊsma:s] NT dimension; (*fig*) scale
ausmerzen ['aʊsmɛrtsən] VT to eliminate
ausmessen ['aʊsmɛsən] *unreg* VT to measure
ausmisten ['aʊsmɪstən] VT (*Stall*) to muck out; (*fig: umg: Schrank etc*) to tidy out; (*: Zimmer*) to clean out
ausmustern ['aʊsmʊstərn] VT (*Maschine, Fahrzeug etc*) to take out of service; (*Mil: entlassen*) to invalid out
Ausnahme ['aʊsna:mə] **(-, -n)** F exception; **eine ~ machen** to make an exception; **Ausnahmeerscheinung** F exception, one-off example; **Ausnahmefall** M exceptional case; **Ausnahmezustand** M state of emergency
ausnahmslos ADV without exception
ausnahmsweise ADV by way of exception, for once
ausnehmen ['aʊsne:mən] *unreg* VT to take out, to remove; (*Tier*) to gut; (*Nest*) to rob; (*umg: Geld abnehmen*) to clean out; (*ausschließen*) to make an exception of ▸ VR to look, to appear
ausnehmend ADJ exceptional
ausnüchtern ['aʊsnʏçtərn] VT, VI to sober up
Ausnüchterungszelle F drying-out cell
ausnutzen ['aʊsnʊtsən] VT (*Zeit, Gelegenheit*) to use, to turn to good account; (*Einfluss*) to use; (*Mensch, Gutmütigkeit*) to exploit
auspacken ['aʊspakən] VT to unpack ▸ VI (*umg: alles sagen*) to talk
auspfeifen ['aʊspfaɪfən] *unreg* VT to hiss/boo at
ausplaudern ['aʊsplaʊdərn] VT (*Geheimnis*) to blab
ausposaunen ['aʊspozaʊnən] (*umg*) VT to tell the world about
ausprägen ['aʊsprɛ:gən] VR (*Begabung, Charaktereigenschaft*) to reveal *od* show itself
auspressen ['aʊsprɛsən] VT (*Saft, Schwamm etc*) to squeeze out; (*Zitrone etc*) to squeeze
ausprobieren ['aʊsprobi:rən] VT to try (out)

Auspuff ['aʊspʊf] **(-(e)s, -e)** M (*Tech*) exhaust; **Auspuffrohr** NT exhaust (pipe); **Auspufftopf** M (*Aut*) silencer (BRIT), muffler (US)
ausquartieren ['aʊskvarti:rən] VT to move out
ausquetschen ['aʊskvɛtʃən] VT (*Zitrone etc*) to squeeze; (*umg: ausfragen*) to grill; (*: aus Neugier*) to pump
ausradieren ['aʊsradi:rən] VT to erase, to rub out
ausrangieren ['aʊsrɑ̃ʒi:rən] (*umg*) VT to chuck out; (*Maschine, Auto*) to scrap
ausrauben ['aʊsraʊbən] VT to rob
ausräumen ['aʊsrɔʏmən] VT (*Dinge*) to clear away; (*Schrank, Zimmer*) to empty; (*Bedenken*) to put aside
ausrechnen ['aʊsrɛçnən] VT to calculate, to reckon
Ausrechnung F calculation, reckoning
Ausrede ['aʊsre:də] F excuse
ausreden ['aʊsre:dən] VI to have one's say ▸ VT: **jdm etw ~** to talk sb out of sth; **er hat mich nicht mal ~ lassen** he didn't even let me finish (speaking)
ausreichen ['aʊsraɪçən] VI to suffice, to be enough
ausreichend ADJ sufficient, adequate; (*Sch*) adequate
Ausreise ['aʊsraɪzə] F departure; **bei der ~** when leaving the country; **Ausreiseerlaubnis** F exit visa
ausreisen ['aʊsraɪzən] VI to leave the country
ausreißen ['aʊsraɪsən] *unreg* VT to tear *od* pull out ▸ VI (*Riss bekommen*) to tear; (*umg*) to make off, to scram; **er hat sich** *dat* **kein Bein ausgerissen** (*umg*) he didn't exactly overstrain himself
ausrenken ['aʊsrɛŋkən] VT to dislocate
ausrichten ['aʊsrɪçtən] VT (*Botschaft*) to deliver; (*Gruß*) to pass on; (*Hochzeit etc*) to arrange; (*in gerade Linie bringen*) to get in a straight line; (*angleichen*) to bring into line; (*Typ etc*) to justify; **etwas/nichts bei jdm ~** to get somewhere/nowhere with sb; **jdm etw ~** to take a message for sb; **ich werde es ihm ~** I'll tell him
ausrotten ['aʊsrɔtən] VT to stamp out, to exterminate
ausrücken ['aʊsrʏkən] VI (*Mil*) to move off; (*Feuerwehr, Polizei*) to be called out; (*umg: weglaufen*) to run away
Ausruf ['aʊsru:f] M (*Schrei*) cry, exclamation; (*Verkünden*) proclamation
ausrufen *unreg* VT to cry out, to exclaim; **jdn ~ (lassen)** (*über Lautsprecher etc*) to page sb
Ausrufezeichen NT exclamation mark
ausruhen ['aʊsru:ən] VT, VI, VR to rest
ausrüsten ['aʊsrʏstən] VT to equip, to fit out
Ausrüstung F equipment
ausrutschen ['aʊsrʊtʃən] VI to slip
Ausrutscher (-s, -) (*umg*) M (*lit, fig*) slip
Aussage ['aʊsza:gə] **(-, -n)** F (*Jur*) statement; **der Angeklagte/Zeuge verweigerte die ~** the accused/witness refused to give evidence
aussagekräftig ADJ expressive, full of expression
aussagen ['aʊsza:gən] VT to say, to state ▸ VI (*Jur*) to give evidence
Aussatz ['aʊszats] **(-es)** M (*Med*) leprosy
aussaugen ['aʊszaʊgən] VT (*Saft etc*) to suck out; (*Wunde*) to suck the poison out of; (*fig: ausbeuten*) to drain dry
ausschalten ['aʊsʃaltən] VT to switch off; (*fig*) to eliminate
Ausschank ['aʊsʃaŋk] **(-(e)s, -schänke)** M dispensing, giving out; (*Comm*) selling; (*Theke*) bar
Ausschankerlaubnis F licence (BRIT), license (US)
Ausschau ['aʊsʃaʊ] F: **~ halten (nach)** to look out (for), to watch (for)
ausschauen VI: **~ (nach)** to look out (for), to be on the look-out (for)
ausscheiden ['aʊsʃaɪdən] *unreg* VT (*aussondern*) to take out; (*Med*) to excrete ▸ VI: **~ (aus)** to leave; (*aus einem Amt*) to retire (from); (*Sport*) to be eliminated (from), to be knocked out (of); **er scheidet für den Posten aus** he can't be considered for the job
Ausscheidung F (*Aussondern*) removal; (*Med*) excretion; (*Sport*) elimination
ausschenken ['aʊsʃɛŋkən] VT to pour out; (*am Ausschank*) to serve
ausscheren ['aʊsʃe:rən] VI (*Fahrzeug*) to leave the line *od* convoy; (*zum Überholen*) to pull out
ausschildern ['aʊsʃɪldərn] VT to signpost
ausschimpfen ['aʊsʃɪmpfən] VT to scold, to tell off
ausschlachten ['aʊsʃlaxtən] VT (*Auto*) to cannibalize; (*fig*) to make a meal of
ausschlafen ['aʊsʃla:fən] *unreg* VI, VR to have a lie-in ▸ VT to sleep off; **ich bin nicht ausgeschlafen** I didn't have *od* get enough sleep
Ausschlag ['aʊsʃla:k] M (*Med*) rash; (*Pendelausschlag*) swing; (*von Nadel*) deflection; **den ~ geben** (*fig*) to tip the balance
ausschlagen ['aʊsʃla:gən] *unreg* VT to knock out; (*auskleiden*) to deck out; (*verweigern*) to decline ▸ VI (*Pferd*) to kick out; (*Bot*) to sprout; (*Zeiger*) to be deflected
ausschlaggebend ADJ decisive
ausschließen ['aʊsʃli:sən] *unreg* VT to shut *od* lock out; (*Sport*) to disqualify; (*Fehler, Möglichkeit etc*) to rule out; (*fig*) to exclude; **ich will mich nicht ~** myself not excepted
ausschließlich ADJ exclusive ▸ ADV exclusively ▸ PRÄP *+gen* excluding, exclusive of
ausschlüpfen ['aʊsʃlʏpfən] VI to slip out; (*aus Ei, Puppe*) to hatch out
Ausschluss ['aʊsʃlʊs] M exclusion; **unter ~ der Öffentlichkeit stattfinden** to be closed to the public; (*Jur*) to be held in camera
ausschmücken ['aʊsʃmʏkən] VT to decorate; (*fig*) to embellish
ausschneiden ['aʊsʃnaɪdən] *unreg* VT to cut out; (*Büsche*) to trim

Ausschnitt ['aʊsʃnɪt] M *(Teil)* section; *(von Kleid)* neckline; *(Zeitungsausschnitt)* cutting (BRIT), clipping (US); *(aus Film etc)* excerpt
ausschöpfen ['aʊsʃœpfən] VT to ladle out; *(fig)* to exhaust; **Wasser** *etc* **aus etw** ~ to ladle water *etc* out of sth
ausschreiben ['aʊsʃraɪbən] *unreg* VT *(ganz schreiben)* to write out (in full); *(Scheck, Rechnung etc)* to write (out); *(Stelle, Wettbewerb etc)* to announce, to advertise
Ausschreibung F *(Bekanntmachung: von Wahlen)* calling; (: *von Stelle)* advertising
Ausschreitung ['aʊsʃraɪtʊŋ] F excess; **Ausschreitungen** riots *pl*
Ausschuss ['aʊsʃʊs] M committee, board; *(Abfall)* waste, scraps *pl*; *(Comm: auch:* **Ausschussware***)* reject
ausschütten ['aʊsʃʏtən] VT to pour out; *(Eimer)* to empty; *(Geld)* to pay ▶ VR to shake (with laughter)
Ausschüttung F *(Fin)* distribution
ausschwärmen ['aʊsʃvɛrmən] VI *(Bienen, Menschen)* to swarm out; *(Mil)* to fan out
ausschweifend ['aʊsʃvaɪfənt] ADJ *(Leben)* dissipated, debauched; *(Fantasie)* extravagant
Ausschweifung F excess
ausschweigen ['aʊsʃvaɪgən] *unreg* VR to keep silent
ausschwitzen ['aʊsʃvɪtsən] VT to sweat out
aussehen ['aʊsze:ən] *unreg* VI to look; **gut** ~ to look good/well; **wie siehts aus?** *(umg: wie stehts?)* how's things?; **das sieht nach nichts aus** that doesn't look anything special; **es sieht nach Regen aus** it looks like rain; **es sieht schlecht aus** things look bad; **Aussehen** (-s) NT appearance
aus sein ['aʊssaɪn] *siehe* **aus**
außen ['aʊsən] ADV outside; *(nach außen)* outwards; ~ **ist es rot** it's red (on the) outside
Außen- ZW: **Außenantenne** F outside aerial; **Außenarbeiten** PL work *sing* on the exterior; **Außenaufnahme** F outdoor shot; **Außenbezirk** M outlying district; **Außenbordmotor** M outboard motor
aussenden ['aʊszɛndən] *unreg* VT to send out, to emit
Außen- ZW: **Außendienst** M outside *od* field service; *(von Diplomat)* foreign service; **Außenhandel** M foreign trade; **Außenminister** M foreign minister; **Außenministerium** NT foreign office; **Außenpolitik** F foreign policy; **Außenseite** F outside; **Außenseiter(in) (-s, -)** M(F) outsider; **Außenspiegel** M *(Aut)* outside mirror; **Außenstände** PL *(bes Comm)* outstanding debts *pl*, arrears *pl*; **Außenstehende(r)** F(M) outsider; **Außenstelle** F branch; **Außenwelt** F outside world
außer ['aʊsər] PRÄP *+dat (räumlich)* out of; *(abgesehen von)* except ▶ KONJ *(ausgenommen)* except; ~ **Gefahr sein** to be out of danger; ~ **Zweifel** beyond any doubt; ~ **Betrieb** out of order; ~ **sich** *dat* **sein/geraten** to be beside o.s.; ~ **Dienst** retired; ~ **Landes** abroad; ~ **wenn** unless; ~ **dass** except; **außeramtlich** ADJ unofficial, private
außerdem KONJ besides, in addition ▶ ADV anyway
außerdienstlich ADJ private
äußere(r, s) ['ɔʏsərə(r, s)] ADJ outer, external; **Äußere(s)** NT exterior; *(fig: Aussehen)* outward appearance
außer- ZW: **außerehelich** ADJ extramarital; **außergewöhnlich** ADJ unusual; **außerhalb** PRÄP *+gen* outside ▶ ADV outside; **außerirdisch** ADJ extraterrestrial; **Außerkraftsetzung** F repeal
äußerlich ADJ external; **rein ~ betrachtet** on the face of it; **Äußerlichkeit** F *(fig)* triviality; *(Oberflächlichkeit)* superficiality; *(Formalität)* formality
äußern VT to utter, to express; *(zeigen)* to show ▶ VR to give one's opinion; *(sich zeigen)* to show itself
außer- ZW: **außerordentlich** ADJ extraordinary; **außerplanmäßig** ADJ unscheduled; **außersinnlich** ADJ: **außersinnliche Wahrnehmung** extrasensory perception
äußerst ['ɔʏsərst] ADV extremely, most
außerstande, außer Stande [aʊsər'ʃtandə] ADV *(nicht in der Lage)* not in a position; *(nicht fähig)* unable
äußerste(r, s) ADJ utmost; *(räumlich)* farthest; *(Termin)* last possible; *(Preis)* highest; **mein äußerstes Angebot** my final offer
Äußerste(s) NT: **bis zum Äußersten gehen** to go to extremes
äußerstenfalls ADV if the worst comes to the worst
Äußerung F *(Bemerkung)* remark, comment; *(Behauptung)* statement; *(Zeichen)* expression
aussetzen ['aʊszɛtsən] VT *(Kind, Tier)* to abandon; *(Boote)* to lower; *(Belohnung)* to offer; *(Urteil, Verfahren)* to postpone ▶ VI *(aufhören)* to stop; *(Pause machen)* to have a break; **jdn/sich einer Sache** *dat* ~ to lay sb/o.s. open to sth; **jdm/etw ausgesetzt sein** to be exposed to sb/sth; **was haben Sie daran auszusetzen?** what's your objection to it?; **an jdm/etw etwas** ~ to find fault with sb/sth
Aussicht ['aʊszɪçt] F view; *(in Zukunft)* prospect; **in ~ sein** to be in view; **etw in ~ haben** to have sth in view; **jdm etw in ~ stellen** to promise sb sth
Aussichts- ZW: **aussichtslos** ADJ hopeless; **Aussichtspunkt** M viewpoint; **aussichtsreich** ADJ promising; **Aussichtsturm** M observation tower
Aussiedler(in) ['aʊszi:dlər(ɪn)] (-s, -) M(F) *(Auswanderer)* emigrant

> **Aussiedler** are people of German origin from East and South-East Europe who have resettled in Germany. Many come from the former Soviet Union. They are given free German language tuition and receive financial help. The number of Aussiedler increased dramatically in the early 1990s.

aussöhnen ['aʊszø:nən] VT to reconcile ▸ VR (*einander*) to become reconciled; **sich mit jdm/etw ~** to reconcile o.s. with sb/to sth
Aussöhnung F reconciliation
aussondern ['aʊszɔndərn] VT to separate off, to select
aussorgen ['aʊszɔrgən] VI: **ausgesorgt haben** to have no more money worries
aussortieren ['aʊszɔrti:rən] VT to sort out
ausspannen ['aʊsʃpanən] VI (*erholen*) to relax ▸ VT to spread *od* stretch out; (*Pferd*) to unharness; **er hat ihm die Freundin ausgespannt** (*umg*) he's nicked his girlfriend
aussparen ['aʊsʃpa:rən] VT to leave open
aussperren ['aʊsʃpɛrən] VT to lock out
Aussperrung F (*Industrie*) lock-out
ausspielen ['aʊsʃpi:lən] VT (*Karte*) to lead; (*Geldprämie*) to offer as a prize ▸ VI (*Karten*) to lead; **ausgespielt haben** to be finished; **jdn gegen jdn ~** to play sb off against sb
Ausspielung F (*im Lotto*) draw
ausspionieren ['aʊsʃpioni:rən] VT (*Pläne etc*) to spy out; (*Person*) to spy on
Aussprache ['aʊsʃpra:xə] F pronunciation; (*Unterredung*) (frank) discussion
aussprechen ['aʊsʃprɛçən] *unreg* VT to pronounce; (*zu Ende sprechen*) to speak; (*äußern*) to say, to express ▸ VR (*sich äußern*): **sich ~ (über** +*akk*) to speak (about); (*sich anvertrauen*) to unburden o.s. (about *od* on); (*diskutieren*) to discuss ▸ VI (*zu Ende sprechen*) to finish speaking; **der Regierung das Vertrauen ~** to pass a vote of confidence in the government
Ausspruch ['aʊsʃprʊx] M remark; (*geflügeltes Wort*) saying
ausspucken ['aʊsʃpʊkən] VT to spit out ▸ VI to spit
ausspülen ['aʊsʃpy:lən] VT to wash out; (*Mund*) to rinse
ausstaffieren ['aʊsʃtafi:rən] VT to equip, to kit out; (*Zimmer*) to furnish
Ausstand ['aʊsʃtant] M strike; **in den ~ treten** to go on strike; **seinen ~ geben** to hold a leaving party
ausstatten ['aʊsʃtatən] VT (*Zimmer etc*) to furnish; **jdn mit etw ~** to equip sb *od* kit sb out with sth
Ausstattung F (*Ausstatten*) provision; (*Kleidung*) outfit; (*Aussteuer*) dowry; (*Aufmachung*) make-up; (*Einrichtung*) furnishing
ausstechen ['aʊsʃtɛçən] *unreg* VT (*Torf, Kekse*) to cut out; (*Augen*) to gouge out; (*übertreffen*) to outshine
ausstehen ['aʊsʃte:ən] *unreg* VT to stand, to endure ▸ VI (*noch nicht da sein*) to be outstanding; **ich kann ihn nicht ~** I can't stand him
aussteigen ['aʊsʃtaɪgən] *unreg* VI to get out, to alight; **alles ~!** (*von Schaffner*) all change!; **aus der Gesellschaft ~** to drop out (of society)
Aussteiger(in) (*umg*) M(F) dropout
ausstellen ['aʊsʃtɛlən] VT to exhibit, to display; (*umg: ausschalten*) to switch off; (*Rechnung etc*) to make out; (*Pass, Zeugnis*) to issue
Aussteller(in) M(F) (*auf Messe*) exhibitor; (*von Scheck*) drawer
Ausstellung F exhibition; (*Fin*) drawing up; (*einer Rechnung*) making out; (*eines Passes etc*) issuing
Ausstellungsdatum NT date of issue
Ausstellungsstück NT (*in Ausstellung*) exhibit; (*in Schaufenster etc*) display item
aussterben ['aʊsʃtɛrbən] *unreg* VI to die out; **Aussterben** NT extinction
Aussteuer ['aʊsʃtɔʏər] F dowry
aussteuern ['aʊsʃtɔʏərn] VT (*Verstärker*) to adjust
Ausstieg ['aʊsʃti:k] **(-(e)s, -e)** M (*Ausgang*) exit; **~ aus der Atomenergie** abandonment of nuclear energy
ausstopfen ['aʊsʃtɔpfən] VT to stuff
ausstoßen ['aʊsʃto:sən] *unreg* VT (*Luft, Rauch*) to give off, to emit; (*aus Verein etc*) to expel, to exclude; (*herstellen: Teile, Stückzahl*) to turn out, to produce
ausstrahlen ['aʊsʃtra:lən] VT, VI to radiate; (*Rundf*) to broadcast
Ausstrahlung F radiation; (*Rundf, TV*) broadcast; (*fig*) charisma
ausstrecken ['aʊsʃtrɛkən] VT, VR to stretch out
ausstreichen ['aʊsʃtraɪçən] *unreg* VT to cross out; (*glätten*) to smooth out
ausstreuen ['aʊsʃtrɔʏən] VT to scatter; (*fig: Gerücht*) to spread
ausströmen ['aʊsʃtrø:mən] VI (*Gas*) to pour out, to escape ▸ VT to give off; (*fig*) to radiate
aussuchen ['aʊszu:xən] VT to select, to pick out
Austausch ['aʊstaʊʃ] M exchange; **austauschbar** ADJ exchangeable
austauschen VT to exchange, to swop
Austauschmotor M replacement engine; (*gebraucht*) factory-reconditioned engine
Austauschstudent(in) M(F) exchange student
austeilen ['aʊstaɪlən] VT to distribute, to give out
Auster ['aʊstər] **(-, -n)** F oyster
austoben ['aʊsto:bən] VR (*Kind*) to run wild; (*Erwachsene*) to let off steam; (*sich müde machen*) to tire o.s. out
austragen ['aʊstra:gən] *unreg* VT (*Post*) to deliver; (*Streit etc*) to decide; (*Wettkämpfe*) to hold; **ein Kind ~** (*nicht abtreiben*) to have a child
Austräger ['aʊstrɛ:gər] M delivery boy; (*Zeitungsausträger*) newspaper boy
Austragungsort M (*Sport*) venue
Australien [aʊs'tra:liən] **(-s)** NT Australia
Australier(in) **(-s, -)** M(F) Australian
australisch ADJ Australian
austreiben ['aʊstraɪbən] *unreg* VT to drive out, to expel; (*Teufel etc*) to exorcize; **jdm etw ~** to cure sb of sth; (*bes durch Schläge*) to knock sth out of sb
austreten ['aʊstre:tən] *unreg* VI (*zur Toilette*) to be excused ▸ VT (*Feuer*) to tread out, to trample; (*Schuhe*) to wear out; (*Treppe*) to wear down; **aus etw ~** to leave sth
austricksen ['aʊstrɪksən] (*umg*) VT (*Sport, fig*) to trick

austrinken ['aʊstrɪŋkən] *unreg* VT (*Glas*) to drain; (*Getränk*) to drink up ▸ VI to finish one's drink, to drink up
Austritt ['aʊstrɪt] M emission; (*aus Verein, Partei etc*) retirement, withdrawal
austrocknen ['aʊstrɔknən] VT, VI to dry up
austüfteln ['aʊstʏftəln] (*umg*) VT to work out; (*ersinnen*) to think up
ausüben ['aʊsly:bən] VT (*Beruf*) to practise (BRIT), to practice (US), carry out; (*innehaben: Amt*) to hold; (*Funktion*) to perform; (*Einfluss*) to exert; **einen Reiz auf jdn ~** to hold an attraction for sb; **eine Wirkung auf jdn ~** to have an effect on sb
Ausübung F practice, exercise; **in ~ seines Dienstes/seiner Pflicht** (*form*) in the execution of his duty
ausufern ['aʊslu:fərn] VI (*fig*) to get out of hand; (*Konflikt etc*): **~ (zu)** to escalate (into)
Ausverkauf ['aʊsfɛrkaʊf] M sale; (*fig: Verrat*) sell-out
ausverkaufen VT to sell out; (*Geschäft*) to sell up
ausverkauft ADJ (*Karten, Artikel*) sold out; (*Theat: Haus*) full
auswachsen ['aʊsvaksən] *unreg* VI: **das ist (ja) zum A~** (*umg*) it's enough to drive you mad
Auswahl ['aʊsva:l] F: **eine ~ (an** *+dat***)** a selection (of), a choice (of)
auswählen ['aʊsvɛ:lən] VT to select, to choose
Auswahlmöglichkeit F choice
Auswanderer ['aʊsvandərər] **(-s, -)** M emigrant
Auswanderin ['aʊsvandərɪn] F emigrant
auswandern VI to emigrate
Auswanderung F emigration
auswärtig ['aʊsvɛrtɪç] ADJ (*nicht am/vom Ort*) out-of-town; (*ausländisch*) foreign; **das Auswärtige Amt** the Foreign Office (BRIT), the State Department (US)
auswärts ['aʊsvɛrts] ADV outside; (*nach außen*) outwards; **~ essen** to eat out; **~ spielen** to play away; **Auswärtsspiel** NT away game
auswaschen ['aʊsvaʃən] *unreg* VT to wash out; (*spülen*) to rinse (out)
auswechseln ['aʊsvɛksəln] VT to replace; (*Sport*) to substitute
Ausweg ['aʊsve:k] M way out; **der letzte ~** the last resort; **ausweglos** ADJ hopeless
ausweichen ['aʊsvaɪçən] *unreg* VI: **jdm/etw ~** (*lit*) to move aside *od* make way for sb/sth; (*fig*) to sidestep sb/sth; **jdm/einer Begegnung ~** to avoid sb/a meeting
ausweichend ADJ evasive
Ausweichmanöver NT evasive action
ausweinen ['aʊsvaɪnən] VR to have a (good) cry
Ausweis ['aʊsvaɪs] **(-es, -e)** M identity card; (*Pass*) passport; (*Mitgliedsausweis, Bibliotheksausweis etc*) card; **~, bitte** your papers, please
ausweisen ['ausvaɪzən] *unreg* VT to expel, to banish ▸ VR to prove one's identity
Ausweis- ZW: **Ausweiskarte** F identity papers *pl*; **Ausweiskontrolle** F identity check; **Ausweispapiere** PL identity papers *pl*
Ausweisung F expulsion
ausweiten ['aʊsvaɪtən] VT to stretch
auswendig ['aʊsvɛndɪç] ADV by heart; **~ lernen** to learn by heart
auswerfen ['aʊsvɛrfən] *unreg* VT (*Anker, Netz*) to cast
auswerten ['aʊsvɛrtən] VT to evaluate
Auswertung F evaluation, analysis; (*Nutzung*) utilization
auswickeln ['aʊsvɪkəln] VT (*Paket, Bonbon etc*) to unwrap
auswirken ['aʊsvɪrkən] VR to have an effect
Auswirkung F effect
auswischen ['aʊsvɪʃən] VT to wipe out; **jdm eins ~** (*umg*) to put one over on sb
Auswuchs ['aʊsvu:ks] M (out)growth; (*fig*) product; (*Missstand, Übersteigerung*) excess
auswuchten ['aʊsvʊxtən] VT (*Aut*) to balance
auszacken ['aʊstsakən] VT (*Stoff etc*) to pink
auszahlen ['aʊstsa:lən] VT (*Lohn, Summe*) to pay out; (*Arbeiter*) to pay off; (*Miterben*) to buy out ▸ VR (*sich lohnen*) to pay
auszählen ['aʊstsɛ:lən] VT (*Stimmen*) to count; (*Boxen*) to count out
auszeichnen ['aʊstsaɪçnən] VT to honour (BRIT), to honor (US); (*Mil*) to decorate; (*Comm*) to price ▸ VR to distinguish o.s.; **der Wagen zeichnet sich durch ... aus** one of the car's main features is ...
Auszeichnung F distinction; (*Comm*) pricing; (*Ehrung*) awarding of decoration; (*Ehre*) honour (BRIT), honor (US); (*Orden*) decoration; **mit ~** with distinction
ausziehen ['aʊstsi:ən] *unreg* VT (*Kleidung*) to take off; (*Haare, Zähne, Tisch etc*) to pull out ▸ VR to undress ▸ VI (*aufbrechen*) to leave; (*aus Wohnung*) to move out
Auszubildende(r) ['aʊstsʊbɪldəndə(r)] F(M) trainee; (*als Handwerker*) apprentice
Auszug ['aʊstsu:k] M (*aus Wohnung*) removal; (*aus Buch etc*) extract; (*Kontoauszug*) statement; (*Ausmarsch*) departure
autark [aʊ'tark] ADJ self-sufficient (*auch fig*); (*Comm*) autarkical
Auto ['aʊto] **(-s, -s)** NT (motor-)car, automobile (US); **mit dem ~ fahren** to go by car; **~ fahren** to drive
Autoatlas M road atlas
Autobahn F motorway (BRIT), expressway (US)

> **Autobahn** is the German for a motorway. In the former West Germany there is an widespread network but in the former **DDR** the motorways are somewhat less extensive. There is no overall speed limit but a limit of 130 km per hour is recommended and there are lower mandatory limits on certain stretches of road. As yet there are no tolls payable on German Autobahns.

Autobahn- ZW: **Autobahnauffahrt** F motorway access road (BRIT), on-ramp (US); **Autobahnausfahrt** F motorway exit (BRIT), off-ramp (US); **Autobahndreieck** NT motorway

(BRIT) *od* expressway (*US*) junction; **Autobahnkreuz** NT motorway (BRIT) *od* expressway (*US*) intersection; **Autobahnzubringer** M motorway feeder *od* access road

Autobiografie [autobiogra'fi:] F autobiography

Auto- ZW: **Autobombe** F car bomb; **Autobus** M bus; (*Reisebus*) coach (BRIT), bus (*US*); **Autofähre** F car ferry; **Autofahrer(in)** M(F) motorist, driver; **Autofahrt** F drive; **Autofriedhof** (*umg*) M car dump

autogen [auto'ge:n] ADJ autogenous; **autogenes Training** (*Psych*) relaxation through self-hypnosis

Autogramm [auto'gram] NT autograph

Automat (**-en, -en**) M machine

Automatik [auto'ma:tɪk] F automatic mechanism (*auch fig*); (*Gesamtanlage*) automatic system; (*Aut*) automatic transmission

automatisch ADJ automatic

Automatisierung [automati'zi:rʊŋ] F automation

Automechaniker(in) M(F) car mechanic

Automobilausstellung [automo'bi:lausʃtɛlʊŋ] F motor show

autonom [auto'no:m] ADJ autonomous

Autopsie [autɔ'psi:] F post-mortem, autopsy

Autor ['autɔr] (**-s, -en**) M author

Auto- ZW: **Autoradio** NT car radio; **Autoreifen** M car tyre (BRIT) *od* tire (*US*); **Autoreisezug** M motorail train; **Autorennen** NT motor race; (*Sportart*) motor racing

Autorin [au'to:rɪn] F authoress

autoritär [autori'tɛ:r] ADJ authoritarian

Autorität F authority

Auto- ZW: **Autoschalter** M drive-in bank (counter); **Autoschlüssel** M car key; **Autotelefon** NT car phone; **Autounfall** M car *od* motor accident; **Autoverleih** M, **Autovermietung** F car hire (BRIT) *od* rental (*US*)

AvD (**-**) M ABK (= *Automobilclub von Deutschland*) *German motoring organization*, ≈ AA (BRIT), ≈ AAA (*US*)

Axt [akst] (**-, Äxte**) F axe (BRIT), ax (*US*)

AZ, Az. ABK (= *Aktenzeichen*) ref.

Azoren [a'tso:rən] PL (*Geog*) Azores *pl*

Azteke [ats'te:kə] (**-n, -n**) M Aztec

Azubi [a'tsu:bi] (**-s, -s**) (*umg*) F(M) ABK = **Auszubildende(r)**

Bb

b

B¹, b [beː] NT (*letter*) B, b; **B wie Bertha** ≈ B for Benjamin, ≈ B for Baker (*US*); **B-Dur/b-Moll** (the key of) B flat major/minor
B² [beː] F ABK = **Bundesstraße**
Baby ['beːbi] (**-s, -s**) NT baby; **Babyausstattung** F layette; **Babyklappe** F *anonymous drop-off point for unwanted babies*; **Babynahrung** F baby food; **Babyraum** M (*Flughafen etc*) nursing room; **babysitten** VI to babysit; **Babysitter** ['beːbisɪtər] (**-s, -**) M baby-sitter; **Babyspeck** (*umg*) M puppy fat
Bach [bax] (**-(e)s, Bäche**) M stream, brook
Backblech NT baking tray
Backbord (**-(e)s, -e**) NT (*Naut*) port
Backe (**-, -n**) F cheek
backen ['bakən] *unreg* VT, VI to bake; **frisch/knusprig gebackenes Brot** fresh/crusty bread
Backenbart M sideboards *pl*
Backenzahn M molar
Bäcker(in) ['bɛkər(ɪn)] (**-s, -**) M(F) baker
Bäckerei [bɛkə'raɪ] F bakery; (*Bäckerladen*) baker's (shop)
Bäckerjunge M (*Lehrling*) baker's apprentice
Back- zW: **Backfisch** M fried fish; (*veraltet*) teenager; **Backform** F baking tin (BRIT) *od* pan (*US*); **Backhähnchen** NT fried chicken in breadcrumbs; **Backobst** NT dried fruit; **Backofen** M oven; **Backpflaume** F prune; **Backpulver** NT baking powder; **Backstein** M brick
bäckt [bɛkt] VB *siehe* **backen**
Backwaren PL bread, cakes and pastries *pl*
Bad [baːt] (**-(e)s, Bäder**) NT bath; (*Schwimmen*) swim; (*Ort*) spa; **ein ~ nehmen** to have *od* take a bath
Bade- zW: **Badeanstalt** F swimming pool; **Badeanzug** M bathing suit; **Badehose** F bathing *od* swimming trunks *pl*; **Badekappe** F bathing cap; **Bademantel** M bath(ing) robe; **Bademeister** M swimming pool attendant
baden ['baːdən] VI to bathe, to have a bath ▶ VT to bath; **~ gehen** (*fig: umg*) to come a cropper
Baden-Württemberg ['baːdən'vʏrtəmbɛrk] NT Baden-Württemberg
Bade- zW: **Badeort** M spa; **Badesachen** PL swimming things *pl*; **Badetuch** NT bath towel; **Badewanne** F bath(tub); **Badezimmer** NT bathroom
baff [baf] ADJ: **~ sein** (*umg*) to be flabbergasted
BAföG, Bafög [baːføk] NT ABK = **Bundesausbildungsförderungsgesetz**; *see note*

> **Bafög** is the system which awards grants for living expenses to students at universities and certain training colleges. The amount is based on parental income. Part of the grant must be paid back a few years after graduating.

BAG (-) NT ABK (= *Bundesarbeitsgericht*) *German industrial tribunal*
Bagatelle [baga'tɛlə] (**-, -n**) F trifle
Bagdad ['bakdat] (**-s**) NT Baghdad
Bagger ['bagər] (**-s, -**) M excavator; (*Naut*) dredger
baggern VT, VI to excavate; (*Naut*) to dredge
Baggersee M (flooded) gravel pit
Bahamas [ba'haːmas] PL: **die ~** the Bahamas *pl*
Bahn [baːn] (**-, -en**) F railway (BRIT), railroad (*US*); (*Weg*) road, way; (*Spur*) lane; (*Rennbahn*) track; (*Astron*) orbit; (*Stoffbahn*) length; **mit der ~** by train *od* rail/tram; **frei ~** (*Comm*) carriage free to station of destination; **jdm/etw die ~ ebnen** (*fig*) to clear the way for sb/sth; **von der rechten ~ abkommen** to stray from the straight and narrow; **jdn aus der ~ werfen** (*fig*) to shatter sb; **Bahnbeamte(r)** M railway (BRIT) *od* railroad (*US*) official; **bahnbrechend** ADJ pioneering; **Bahnbrecher(in)** (**-s, -**) M(F) pioneer
BahnCard® (**-, -s**) F rail card (*allowing 50% or 25% reduction on tickets*); **Bahndamm** M railway embankment
bahnen VT: **sich einen Weg ~** to clear a way
Bahnfahrt F railway (BRIT) *od* railroad (*US*) journey
Bahnhof M station; **auf dem ~** at the station; **ich verstehe nur ~** (*hum: umg*) it's all Greek to me
Bahnhofshalle F station concourse
Bahnhofsmission F *charitable organization for helping rail travellers*

> The **Bahnhofsmission** is a charitable organization set up by and run jointly by various churches. They have an office at railway stations in most big cities to which people in need of advice and help can go.

Bahnhofswirtschaft F station restaurant
Bahn- ZW: **bahnlagernd** ADJ (*Comm*) to be collected from the station; **Bahnlinie** F (railway (BRIT) *od* railroad (US)) line; **Bahnschranke** F level (BRIT) *od* grade (US) crossing barrier; **Bahnsteig** M platform; **Bahnsteigkarte** F platform ticket; **Bahnstrecke** F railway (BRIT) *od* railroad (US) line; **Bahnübergang** M level (BRIT) *od* grade (US) crossing; **beschrankter Bahnübergang** crossing with gates; **unbeschrankter Bahnübergang** unguarded crossing; **Bahnwärter** M signalman
Bahrain [ba'raɪn] (**-s**) NT Bahrain
Bahre ['ba:rə] (**-, -n**) F stretcher
Baiser [bɛ'ze:] (**-s, -s**) NT meringue
Baisse ['bɛ:sə] (**-, -n**) F (*Börse*) fall; (*plötzlich*) slump
Bajonett [bajo'nɛt] (**-(e)s, -e**) NT bayonet
Bakelit® [bake'li:t] (**-s**) NT Bakelite®
Bakterien [bak'te:riən] PL bacteria *pl*
Balance [ba'lã:sə] (**-, -n**) F balance, equilibrium
balancieren VT, VI to balance
bald [balt] ADV (*zeitlich*) soon; (*beinahe*) almost; **~ ... ~ ...** now ... now ...; **~ darauf** soon afterwards; **bis ~!** see you soon
baldig ['baldɪç] ADJ early, speedy
baldmöglichst ADV as soon as possible
Baldrian ['baldria:n] (**-s, -e**) M valerian
Balearen [bale'a:rən] PL: **die ~** the Balearics *pl*
Balg [balk] (**-(e)s, Bälger**) (*pej, umg*) M OD NT (*Kind*) brat
balgen ['balgən] VR: **sich ~ (um)** to scrap (over)
Balkan ['balka:n] M: **der ~** the Balkans *pl*
Balken ['balkən] (**-s, -**) M beam; (*Tragbalken*) girder; (*Stützbalken*) prop
Balkon [bal'kõ:] (**-s, -s** *od* **-e**) M balcony; (*Theat*) (dress) circle
Ball [bal] (**-(e)s, Bälle**) M ball; (*Tanz*) dance, ball
Ballade [ba'la:də] (**-, -n**) F ballad
Ballast ['balast] (**-(e)s, -e**) M ballast; (*fig*) weight, burden; **Ballaststoffe** PL (*Med*) roughage *sing*
ballen VT (*formen*) to make into a ball; (*Faust*) to clench ▸ VR to build up; (*Menschen*) to gather
Ballen ['balən] (**-s, -**) M bale; (*Anat*) ball
ballern ['balərn] (*umg*) VI to shoot, to fire
Ballett [ba'lɛt] (**-(e)s, -e**) NT ballet; **Balletttänzer(in)** M(F) ballet dancer
Ballistik [ba'lɪstɪk] F ballistics *sing*
Balljunge M ball boy
Ballkleid NT evening dress
Ballon [ba'lõ:] (**-s, -s** *od* **-e**) M balloon
Ballspiel NT ball game
Ballung ['balʊŋ] F concentration; (*von Energie*) build-up
Ballungs- ZW: **Ballungsgebiet** NT, **Ballungsraum** M conurbation; **Ballungszentrum** NT centre (BRIT) *od* center (US: *of population, industry etc*)
Balsam ['balza:m] (**-s, -e**) M balsam; (*fig*) balm
Balte ['baltə] (**-n, -n**) M Balt; **er ist ~** he comes from the Baltic
Baltikum ['baltikʊm] (**-s**) NT: **das ~** the Baltic States *pl*
Baltin ['baltɪn] F *siehe* **Balte**
baltisch ADJ Baltic *attrib*
Balz [balts] (**-, -en**) F (*Paarungsspiel*) courtship display; (*Paarungszeit*) mating season
Bambus ['bambʊs] (**-ses, -se**) M bamboo; **Bambusrohr** NT bamboo cane
Bambussprossen PL bamboo shoots *pl*
Bammel ['baməl] (**-s**) (*umg*) M: **(einen) ~ vor jdm/etw haben** to be scared of sb/sth
banal [ba'na:l] ADJ banal
Banalität [banali'tɛ:t] F banality
Banane [ba'na:nə] (**-, -n**) F banana
Bananenschale F banana skin
Bananenstecker M jack plug
Banause [ba'naʊzə] (**-n, -n**) M philistine
band *etc* [bant] VB *siehe* **binden**
Band¹ [bant] (**-(e)s, Bände**) M (*Buchband*) volume; **das spricht Bände** that speaks volumes
Band² (**-(e)s, Bänder**) NT (*Stoffband*) ribbon, tape; (*Fließband*) production line; (*Fassband*) hoop; (*Zielband, Tonband*) tape; (*Anat*) ligament; **etw auf ~ aufnehmen** to tape sth; **am laufenden ~** (*umg*) non-stop
Band³ (**-(e)s, -e**) NT (*Freundschaftsband etc*) bond
Band⁴ [bɛnt] (**-, -s**) F band, group
Bandage [ban'da:ʒə] (**-, -n**) F bandage
bandagieren VT to bandage
Bandbreite F (*von Meinungen etc*) range
Bande ['bandə] (**-, -n**) F band; (*Straßenbande*) gang
bändigen ['bɛndɪgən] VT (*Tier*) to tame; (*Trieb, Leidenschaft*) to control, to restrain
Bandit [ban'di:t] (**-en, -en**) M bandit
Band- ZW: **Bandmaß** NT tape measure; **Bandnudeln** PL tagliatelle *pl*; **Bandsäge** F band saw; **Bandscheibe** F (*Anat*) disc; **Bandscheibenschaden** M slipped disc; **Bandwurm** M tapeworm
bange ['baŋə] ADJ scared; (*besorgt*) anxious; **jdm wird es ~** sb is becoming scared; **jdm B~ machen** to scare sb; **Bangemacher** (**-s, -**) M scaremonger
bangen VI: **um jdn/etw ~** to be anxious *od* worried about sb/sth
Bangkok ['baŋkɔk] (**-s**) NT Bangkok
Bangladesch [baŋgla'dɛʃ] (**-s**) NT Bangladesh
Banjo ['banjo, 'bɛndʒo] (**-s, -s**) NT banjo
Bank¹ [baŋk] (**-, Bänke**) F (*Sitzbank*) bench; (*Sandbank etc*) (sand)bank, (sand)bar; **etw auf die lange ~ schieben** (*umg*) to put sth off
Bank² (**-, -en**) F (*Geldbank*) bank; **bei der ~** at the bank; **Geld auf der ~ haben** to have money in the bank; **Bankanweisung** F banker's order; **Bankautomat** M cash dispenser; **Bankbeamte(r)** M bank clerk; **Bankeinlage** F (bank) deposit
Bankett [baŋ'kɛt] (**-(e)s, -e**) NT (*Essen*) banquet; (*Straßenrand*) verge (BRIT), shoulder (US)
Bank- ZW: **Bankfach** NT (*Schließfach*) safe-deposit box; **Bankgebühr** F bank charge; **Bankgeheimnis** NT confidentiality in banking

Bankier [baŋki'e:] (**-s, -s**) M banker
Bank- zW: **Bankkarte** F bank card; **Bankkonto** NT bank account; **Bankleitzahl** F bank code number; **Banknote** F banknote; **Bankraub** M bank robbery
bankrott [baŋ'krɔt] ADJ bankrupt; **Bankrott** (**-(e)s, -e**) M bankruptcy; **Bankrott machen** to go bankrupt; **den Bankrott anmelden** *od* **erklären** to declare o.s. bankrupt; **Bankrotterklärung** F (*lit*) declaration of bankruptcy; (*fig: umg*) declaration of failure
Bank- zW: **Banküberfall** M bank raid; **Bankverbindung** F (*Kontonummer etc*) banking *od* account details *pl*
Bann [ban] (**-(e)s, -e**) M (*Hist*) ban; (*Kirchenbann*) excommunication; (*fig: Zauber*) spell; **bannen** VT (*Geister*) to exorcize; (*Gefahr*) to avert; (*bezaubern*) to enchant; (*Hist*) to banish
Banner (**-s, -**) NT banner, flag
bar ADJ +*gen* (*unbedeckt*) bare; (*frei von*) lacking (in); (*offenkundig*) utter, sheer; **bares Geld** cash; **etw (in) ~ bezahlen** to pay sth (in) cash; **etw für bare Münze nehmen** (*fig*) to take sth at face value; **~ aller Hoffnung** (*liter*) devoid of hope, completely without hope
Bar [ba:r] (**-, -s**) F bar
Bär [bɛ:r] (**-en, -en**) M bear; **jdm einen Bären aufbinden** (*umg*) to have sb on
Baracke [ba'rakə] (**-, -n**) F hut
barbarisch [bar'ba:rɪʃ] ADJ barbaric, barbarous
Barbestand M money in hand
Bardame F barmaid
Bärenhunger (*umg*) M: **einen ~ haben** to be famished
bärenstark (*umg*) ADJ strapping, strong as an ox; (*fig*) terrific
barfuß ADJ barefoot
barg *etc* [bark] VB *siehe* **bergen**
Bargeld NT cash, ready money
bargeldlos ADJ non-cash; **bargeldloser Zahlungsverkehr** non-cash *od* credit transactions *pl*
barhäuptig ADJ bareheaded
Barhocker M bar stool
Bariton ['ba:ritɔn] M baritone
Barkauf M cash purchase
Barkeeper ['ba:rki:pər] (**-s, -**) M barman, bartender
Barkredit M cash loan
Barmann (**-(e)s**, *pl* **-männer**) M barman
barmherzig [barm'hɛrtsɪç] ADJ merciful, compassionate; **Barmherzigkeit** F mercy, compassion
Barock [ba'rɔk] (**-s** *od* **-**) NT OD M baroque
Barometer [baro'me:tər] (**-s, -**) NT barometer; **das ~ steht auf Sturm** (*fig*) there's a storm brewing
Baron [ba'ro:n] (**-s, -e**) M baron
Baronesse [baro'nɛsə] (**-, -n**) F baroness
Baronin F baroness
Barren ['barən] (**-s, -**) M parallel bars *pl*; (*Goldbarren*) ingot
Barriere [bari'ɛ:rə] (**-, -n**) F barrier
Barrikade [bari'ka:də] (**-, -n**) F barricade
barsch [barʃ] ADJ brusque, gruff; **jdn ~ anfahren** to snap at sb
Barsch [barʃ] (**-(e)s, -e**) M perch
Barschaft F ready money
Barscheck M open *od* uncrossed cheque (BRIT), open check (*US*)
barst *etc* [barst] VB *siehe* **bersten**
Bart [ba:rt] (**-(e)s, Bärte**) M beard; (*Schlüsselbart*) bit
bärtig ['bɛ:rtɪç] ADJ bearded
Barvermögen NT liquid assets *pl*
Barzahlung F cash payment
Basar [ba'za:r] (**-s, -e**) M bazaar
Base ['ba:zə] (**-, -n**) F (*Chem*) base; (*Cousine*) cousin
Baseballmütze ['be:sbo:lmʏtsə] F baseball cap
Basel ['ba:zəl] (**-s**) NT Basle
Basen PL *von* **Base; Basis**
basieren [ba'zi:rən] VT to base ▶ VI to be based
Basilikum [ba'zi:likʊm] (**-s**) NT basil
Basis ['ba:zɪs] (**-**, *pl* **Basen**) F basis; (*Archit, Mil, Math*) base; **~ und Überbau** (*Pol, Soziologie*) foundation and superstructure; **die ~** (*umg*) the grass roots
basisch ['ba:zɪʃ] ADJ (*Chem*) alkaline
Basisgruppe F action group
Baske ['baskə] (**-n, -n**) M Basque
Baskenland NT Basque region
Baskenmütze F beret
Basketball ['ba:skətbal] M basketball
Baskin F Basque
Bass [bas] (**-es, Bässe**) M bass
Bassin [ba'sɛ̃:] (**-s, -s**) NT pool
Bassist [ba'sɪst] M bass
Bassschlüssel M bass clef
Bassstimme F bass voice
Bast [bast] (**-(e)s, -e**) M raffia
basta ['basta] INTERJ: **(und damit) ~!** (and) that's that!
basteln ['bastəln] VT to make ▶ VI to do handicrafts; **an etw** *dat* **~** (*an etw herumbasteln*) to tinker with sth
Bastler ['bastlər] (**-s, -**) M do-it-yourselfer; (*handwerklich*) handicrafts enthusiast
bat *etc* [ba:t] VB *siehe* **bitten**
BAT M ABK (= *Bundesangestelltentarif*) *German salary scale for employees*
Bataillon [batal'jo:n] (**-s, -e**) NT battalion
Batist [ba'tɪst] (**-(e)s, -e**) M batiste
Batterie [batə'ri:] F battery
Bau [baʊ] (**-(e)s**) M (*Bauen*) building, construction; (*Aufbau*) structure; (*Körperbau*) frame; (*Baustelle*) building site; (*pl Baue: Tierbau*) hole, burrow; (*: Min*) working(s); (*pl Bauten: Gebäude*) building; **sich im ~ befinden** to be under construction; **Bauarbeiten** PL building *od* construction work *sing*; (*Straßenbau*) roadworks *pl* (BRIT), roadwork *sing* (*US*); **Bauarbeiter** M building worker
Bauch [baʊx] (**-(e)s, Bäuche**) M belly; (*Anat*) stomach, abdomen; **sich** *dat* **(vor Lachen) den ~ halten** (*umg*) to split one's sides (laughing);

b

mit etw auf den ~ fallen (*umg*) to come a cropper with sth; **Bauchansatz** M beginning of a paunch; **Bauchfell** NT peritoneum
bauchig ADJ bulging
Bauch- zW: **Bauchlandung** F: **eine Bauchlandung machen** (*fig*) to experience a failure, to flop; **Bauchmuskel** M abdominal muscle; **Bauchnabel** M navel, belly-button (*umg*); **Bauchredner** M ventriloquist; **Bauchschmerzen** PL stomachache *sing*; **Bauchspeicheldrüse** F pancreas; **Bauchtanz** M belly dancing; (*einzelner Tanz*) belly dance; **Bauchweh** NT stomachache
Baudrate [baʊtˈraːtə] F (*Comput*) baud rate
bauen [ˈbaʊən] VT to build; (*Tech*) to construct; (*umg: verursachen: Unfall*) to cause ▶ VI to build; **auf jdn/etw ~** to depend *od* count upon sb/sth; **da hast du Mist gebaut** (*umg*) you really messed that up
Bauer[1] [ˈbaʊər] (**-n** *od* **-s, -n**) M farmer; (*Schach*) pawn
Bauer[2] (**-s, -**) NT OD M (*Vogelbauer*) cage
Bäuerchen [ˈbɔʏərçən] NT (*Kindersprache*) burp
Bäuerin [ˈbɔʏərɪn] F farmer; (*Frau des Bauern*) farmer's wife
bäuerlich ADJ rustic
Bauern- zW: **Bauernbrot** NT black bread; **Bauernfängerei** F deception, confidence trick(s); **Bauernfrühstück** NT bacon and potato omelette (BRIT) *od* omelet (US); **Bauernhaus** NT farmhouse; **Bauernhof** M farm; **Bauernschaft** F farming community; **Bauernschläue** F native cunning, craftiness, shrewdness; **baufällig** ADJ dilapidated; **Baufälligkeit** F dilapidation
Bau- zW: **Baufirma** F construction firm; **Bauführer** M site foreman; **Baugelände** NT building site; **Baugenehmigung** F building permit; **Baugerüst** NT scaffolding; **Bauherr** M client (*of construction firm*); **Bauingenieur** M civil engineer
Bauj. ABK = **Baujahr**
Bau- zW: **Baujahr** NT year of construction; (*von Auto*) year of manufacture; **Baukasten** M box of bricks; **Bauklötzchen** NT (building) block; **Baukosten** PL construction costs *pl*; **Bauland** NT building land; **Bauleute** PL building workers *pl*; **baulich** ADJ structural; **Baulöwe** M building speculator; **Baulücke** F undeveloped building plot
Baum [baʊm] (**-(e)s,** *pl* **Bäume**) M tree; **heute könnte ich Bäume ausreißen** I feel full of energy today
Baumarkt M DIY superstore
baumeln [ˈbaʊməln] VI to dangle
bäumen [ˈbɔʏmən] VR to rear (up)
Baum- zW: **Baumgrenze** F tree line; **Baumschule** F nursery; **Baumstamm** M tree trunk; **Baumstumpf** M tree stump; **Baumwolle** F cotton
Bau- zW: **Bauplan** M architect's plan; **Bauplatz** M building site; **Bausachverständige(r)** F(M) quantity surveyor; **Bausatz** M construction kit
Bausch [baʊʃ] (**-(e)s,** *pl* **Bäusche**) M (*Wattebausch*) ball, wad; **in ~ und Bogen** (*fig*) lock, stock, and barrel
bauschen VT, VI, VR to puff out
bauschig ADJ baggy, wide
bausparen VI UNTR to save with a building society (BRIT) *od* a building and loan association (US)
Bau- zW: **Bausparkasse** F building society (BRIT), building and loan association (US); **Bausparvertrag** M savings contract with a building society (BRIT) *od* building and loan association (US); **Baustein** M building stone, freestone; (*Spielzeug*) brick; (*fig*) element; **Baustelle** F building site; (*bei Straßenbau*) roadworks *pl* (BRIT), roadwork (US); **Baustil** M architectural style; **bautechnisch** ADJ in accordance with building *od* construction methods; **Bauteil** NT prefabricated part (of building); **Bauten** PL *von* **Bau**; **Bauunternehmer** M contractor, builder; **Bauweise** F (method of) construction; **Bauwerk** NT building; **Bauzaun** M hoarding
b. a. W. ABK (= *bis auf Weiteres*) until further notice
Bayer(in) [ˈbaɪər(ɪn)] (**-n, -n**) M(F) Bavarian
bayerisch, bayrisch ADJ Bavarian
Bayern NT Bavaria
Bazillus [baˈtsɪlʊs] (**-,** *pl* **Bazillen**) M bacillus
Bd. ABK (= *Band*) vol.
Bde. ABK (= *Bände*) vols.
beabsichtigen [bəˈlapzɪçtɪgən] VT to intend
beachten [bəˈlaxtən] VT to take note of; (*Vorschrift*) to obey; (*Vorfahrt*) to observe
beachtenswert ADJ noteworthy
beachtlich ADJ considerable
Beachtung F notice, attention, observation; **jdm keine ~ schenken** to take no notice of sb
Beamte(r) [bəˈlamtə(r)] (**-n, -n**) M official; (*Staatsbeamte*) civil servant; (*Bankbeamte etc*) employee
Beamtenlaufbahn F: **die ~ einschlagen** to enter the civil service
Beamtenverhältnis NT: **im ~ stehen** to be a civil servant
beamtet ADJ (*form*) appointed on a permanent basis (*by the state*)
Beamtin F *siehe* **Beamte(r)**
beängstigend [bəˈlɛŋstɪgənt] ADJ alarming
beanspruchen [bəˈlanʃprʊxən] VT to claim; (*Zeit, Platz*) to take up, to occupy; **jdn ~** to take up sb's time; **etw stark ~** to put sth under a lot of stress
beanstanden [bəˈlanʃtandən] VT to complain about, to object to; (*Rechnung*) to query
Beanstandung F complaint
beantragen [bəˈlantraːgən] VT to apply for, to ask for
beantworten [bəˈlantvɔrtən] VT to answer
Beantwortung F reply
bearbeiten [bəˈlarbaɪtən] VT to work; (*Material*) to process; (*Thema*) to deal with; (*Land*) to cultivate; (*Chem*) to treat; (*Buch*) to revise; (*umg: beeinflussen wollen*) to work on

Bearbeitung F processing; (*von Land*) cultivation; (*Chem*) treatment; (*von Buch*) revision; **die ~ meines Antrags hat lange gedauert** it took a long time to deal with my claim
Bearbeitungsgebühr F handling charge
beatmen [bə'la:tmən] VT: **jdn künstlich ~** to give sb artificial respiration
Beatmung [bə'la:tmʊŋ] F respiration
beaufsichtigen [bə'laufzɪçtɪgən] VT to supervise
Beaufsichtigung F supervision
beauftragen [bə'lauftra:gən] VT to instruct; **jdn mit etw ~** to entrust sb with sth
Beauftragte(r) F(M) representative
bebauen [bə'baʊən] VT to build on; (*Agr*) to cultivate
beben ['be:bən] VI to tremble, to shake; **Beben (-s -)** NT earthquake
bebildern [bə'bɪldərn] VT to illustrate
Becher ['bɛçər] **(-s, -)** M mug; (*ohne Henkel*) tumbler; (*für Joghurt*) pot
bechern ['bɛçərn] (*umg*) VI (*trinken*) to have a few (drinks)
Becken ['bɛkən] **(-s, -)** NT basin; (*Mus*) cymbal; (*Anat*) pelvis
bedacht ADJ thoughtful, careful; **auf etw** *akk* **~ sein** to be concerned about sth
Bedacht [bə'daxt] M: **mit ~** (*vorsichtig*) prudently, carefully; (*absichtlich*) deliberately
bedächtig [bə'dɛçtɪç] ADJ (*umsichtig*) thoughtful, reflective; (*langsam*) slow, deliberate
bedanken [bə'daŋkən] VR: **sich (bei jdm) ~** to say thank you (to sb); **ich bedanke mich herzlich** thank you very much
Bedarf [bə'darf] **(-(e)s)** M need; (*Bedarfsmenge*) requirements *pl*; (*Comm*) demand; **alles für den häuslichen ~** all household requirements; **je nach ~** according to demand; **bei ~** if necessary; **~ an etw** *dat* **haben** to be in need of sth
Bedarfs- ZW: **Bedarfsartikel** M requisite; **Bedarfsdeckung** F satisfaction of sb's needs; **Bedarfsfall** M case of need; **Bedarfshaltestelle** F request stop
bedauerlich [bə'daʊərlɪç] ADJ regrettable
bedauern [bə'daʊərn] VT to be sorry for; (*bemitleiden*) to pity; **wir ~ Ihnen mitteilen zu müssen …** we regret to have to inform you …; **Bedauern (-s)** NT regret
bedauernswert ADJ (*Zustände*) regrettable; (*Mensch*) pitiable, unfortunate
bedecken [bə'dɛkən] VT to cover
bedeckt ADJ covered; (*Himmel*) overcast
bedenken [bə'dɛŋkən] *unreg* VT to think over, to consider; **ich gebe zu ~, dass …** (*geh*) I would ask you to consider that …; **Bedenken (-s, -)** NT (*Überlegen*) consideration; (*Zweifel*) doubt; (*Skrupel*) scruples *pl*; **mir kommen Bedenken** I am having second thoughts
bedenklich ADJ doubtful; (*bedrohlich*) dangerous, risky
Bedenkzeit F time to consider; **zwei Tage ~** two days to think about it
bedeuten [bə'dɔʏtən] VT to mean; (*wichtig sein*) to be of importance; **das bedeutet nichts Gutes** that means trouble
bedeutend ADJ important; (*beträchtlich*) considerable
bedeutsam ADJ significant; (*vielsagend*) meaningful
Bedeutung F meaning; (*Wichtigkeit*) importance
bedeutungslos ADJ insignificant, unimportant
bedeutungsvoll ADJ momentous, significant
bedienen [bə'di:nən] VT to serve; (*Maschine*) to work, to operate ▶ VR (*beim Essen*) to help o.s.; (*gebrauchen*): **sich jds/einer Sache ~** to make use of sb/sth; **werden Sie schon bedient?** are you being served?; **damit sind Sie sehr gut bedient** that should serve you very well; **ich bin bedient!** (*umg*) I've had enough
Bedienung F service; (*Kellner etc*) waiter/waitress; (*Zuschlag*) service (charge); (*von Maschinen*) operation
Bedienungsanleitung F operating instructions *pl*
bedingen [bə'dɪŋən] VT (*voraussetzen*) to demand, to involve; (*verursachen*) to cause, to occasion
bedingt ADJ limited; (*Straferlass*) conditional; (*Reflex*) conditioned; **(nur) ~ gelten** to be (only) partially valid; **~ geeignet** suitable up to a point
Bedingung F condition; (*Voraussetzung*) stipulation; **mit** *od* **unter der ~, dass …** on condition that …; **zu günstigen Bedingungen** (*Comm*) on favourable (BRIT) *od* favorable (US) terms
Bedingungsform F (*Gram*) conditional
bedingungslos ADJ unconditional
bedrängen [bə'drɛŋən] VT to pester, to harass
Bedrängnis [bə'drɛŋnɪs] F (*seelisch*) distress, torment
Bedrängung F trouble
bedrohen [bə'dro:ən] VT to threaten
bedrohlich ADJ ominous, threatening
Bedrohung F threat, menace
bedrucken [bə'drʊkən] VT to print on
bedrücken [bədrʏkən] VT to oppress, to trouble
bedürfen [bə'dʏrfən] *unreg* VI *+gen* (*geh*) to need, to require; **ohne dass es eines Hinweises bedurft hätte, …** without having to be asked …
Bedürfnis [bə'dʏrfnɪs] **(-ses, -se)** NT need; **das ~ nach etw haben** to need sth; **Bedürfnisanstalt** F (*form*) public convenience (BRIT), comfort station (US); **bedürfnislos** ADJ frugal, modest
bedürftig ADJ in need, poor, needy
Beefsteak ['bi:fste:k] **(-s, -s)** NT steak; **deutsches ~** hamburger
beehren [bə'le:rən] VT (*geh*) to honour (BRIT), to honor (US); **wir ~ uns …** we have pleasure in …
beeilen [bə'laɪlən] VR to hurry
beeindrucken [bə'laɪndrʊkən] VT to impress, to make an impression on
beeinflussen [bə'laɪnflʊsən] VT to influence
Beeinflussung F influence

beeinträchtigen [bə'laıntrɛçtıgən] VT to affect adversely; (*Sehvermögen*) to impair; (*Freiheit*) to infringe upon
beenden [bə'lɛndən], **beendigen** [bə'lɛndıgən] VT to end, to finish, to terminate
Beendung, Beendigung F end(ing), finish(ing)
beengen [bə'lɛŋən] VT to cramp; (*fig*) to hamper, to inhibit; **beengende Kleidung** restricting clothing
beengt ADJ cramped; (*fig*) stifled
beerben [bə'lɛrbən] VT to inherit from
beerdigen [bə'le:rdıgən] VT to bury
Beerdigung F funeral, burial
Beerdigungsunternehmer M undertaker
Beere ['be:rə] (**-, -n**) F berry; (*Traubenbeere*) grape
Beerenauslese F *wine made from specially selected grapes*
Beet [be:t] (**-(e)s, -e**) NT (*Blumenbeet*) bed
befähigen [bə'fɛ:ıgən] VT to enable
befähigt ADJ (*begabt*) talented; (*fähig*): **~ (für)** capable (of)
Befähigung F capability; (*Begabung*) talent, aptitude; **die ~ zum Richteramt** the qualifications to become a judge
befahl *etc* [bə'fa:l] VB *siehe* **befehlen**
befahrbar [bə'fa:rba:r] ADJ passable; (*Naut*) navigable; **nicht ~ sein** (*Straße, Weg*) to be closed (to traffic); (*wegen Schnee etc*) to be impassable
befahren [bə'fa:rən] *unreg* VT (*Straße*) to use; (*Pass*) to drive over; (*Naut*) to navigate ▶ ADJ: **stark/wenig ~** busy/quiet
befallen [bə'falən] *unreg* VT to come over
befangen [bə'faŋən] ADJ (*schüchtern*) shy, self-conscious; (*voreingenommen*) bias(s)ed; **Befangenheit** F shyness; (*Voreingenommenheit*) bias
befassen [bə'fasən] VR to concern o.s.
Befehl [bə'fe:l] (**-(e)s, -e**) M command, order; (*Comput*) command; **auf ~ handeln** to act under orders; **zu ~, Herr Hauptmann!** (*Mil*) yes, sir; **den ~ haben** *od* **führen (über** *+akk*) to be in command (of)
befehlen *unreg* VT to order ▶ VI to give orders; **jdm etw ~** to order sb to do sth; **du hast mir gar nichts zu ~** I won't take orders from you
befehligen VT to be in command of
Befehls- zW: **Befehlsempfänger** M subordinate; **Befehlsform** F (*Gram*) imperative; **Befehlshaber** (**-s, -**) M commanding officer; **Befehlsnotstand** M (*Jur*) obligation to obey orders; **Befehlsverweigerung** F insubordination
befestigen [bə'fɛstıgən] VT to fasten; (*stärken*) to strengthen; (*Mil*) to fortify; **~ an** *+dat* to fasten to
Befestigung F fastening; (*Stärkung*) strengthening; (*Mil*) fortification
Befestigungsanlage F fortification
befeuchten [bə'fɔʏçtən] VT to damp(en), to moisten
befinden [bə'fındən] *unreg* VR to be; (*sich fühlen*) to feel ▶ VT: **jdn/etw für** *od* **als etw ~** to deem sb/sth to be sth ▶ VI: **~ (über** *+akk*) to decide (on), to adjudicate (on)
Befinden (**-s**) NT health, condition; (*Meinung*) view, opinion
beflecken [bə'flɛkən] VT (*lit*) to stain; (*fig geh: Ruf, Ehre*) to besmirch
befliegen [bə'fli:gən] *unreg* VT (*Strecke*) to fly
beflügeln [bə'fly:gəln] VT (*geh*) to inspire
befohlen [bə'fo:lən] PP *von* **befehlen**
befolgen [bə'fɔlgən] VT to comply with, to follow
befördern [bə'fœrdərn] VT (*senden*) to transport, to send; (*beruflich*) to promote; **etw mit der Post/per Bahn ~** to send sth by post/by rail
Beförderung F transport; (*beruflich*) promotion
Beförderungskosten PL transport costs *pl*
befragen [bə'fra:gən] VT to question; (*um Stellungnahme bitten*): **~ (über** *+akk*) to consult (about)
Befragung F poll
befreien [bə'fraıən] VT to set free; (*erlassen*) to exempt
Befreier(in) (**-s, -**) M(F) liberator
befreit ADJ (*erleichtert*) relieved
Befreiung F liberation, release; (*Erlassen*) exemption
Befreiungs- zW: **Befreiungsbewegung** F liberation movement; **Befreiungskampf** M struggle for liberation; **Befreiungsversuch** M escape attempt
befremden [bə'frɛmdən] VT to surprise; (*unangenehm*) to disturb; **Befremden** (**-s**) NT surprise, astonishment
befreunden [bə'frɔʏndən] VR to make friends; (*mit Idee etc*) to acquaint o.s.
befreundet ADJ friendly; **wir sind schon lange (miteinander) ~** we have been friends for a long time
befriedigen [bə'fri:dıgən] VT to satisfy
befriedigend ADJ satisfactory
Befriedigung F satisfaction, gratification
befristet [bə'frıstət] ADJ limited; (*Arbeitsverhältnis, Anstellung*) temporary
befruchten [bə'frʊxtən] VT to fertilize; (*fig*) to stimulate
Befruchtung F: **künstliche ~** artificial insemination
Befugnis [bə'fu:knıs] (**-, -se**) F authorization, powers *pl*
befugt ADJ authorized, entitled
befühlen [bə'fy:lən] VT to feel, to touch
Befund [bə'fʊnt] (**-(e)s, -e**) M findings *pl*; (*Med*) diagnosis; **ohne ~** (*Med*) (results) negative
befürchten [bə'fʏrçtən] VT to fear
Befürchtung F fear, apprehension
befürworten [bə'fy:rvɔrtən] VT to support, to speak in favour (*BRIT*) *od* favor (*US*) of
Befürworter(in) (**-s, -**) M(F) supporter, advocate
Befürwortung F support(ing), favouring (*BRIT*), favoring (*US*)

begabt [bə'ga:pt] ADJ gifted
Begabung [bə'ga:bʊŋ] F talent, gift
begann *etc* [bə'gan] VB *siehe* **beginnen**
begatten [bə'gatən] VR to mate ▶ VT to mate *od* pair (with)
begeben [bə'ge:bən] *unreg* VR (*gehen*) to proceed; (*geschehen*) to occur; **sich ~ nach** *od* **zu** to proceed to(wards); **sich in ärztliche Behandlung ~** to undergo medical treatment; **sich in Gefahr ~** to expose o.s. to danger; **Begebenheit** F occurrence
begegnen [bə'ge:gnən] VI: **jdm ~** to meet sb; (*behandeln*) to treat; **Blicke ~ sich** eyes meet
Begegnung F meeting; (*Sport*) match
begehen [bə'ge:ən] *unreg* VT (*Straftat*) to commit; (*Weg etc*) to use, to negotiate; (*geh: feiern*) to celebrate
begehren [bə'ge:rən] VT to desire
begehrenswert ADJ desirable
begehrt ADJ in demand; (*Junggeselle*) eligible
begeistern [bə'gaɪstərn] VT to fill with enthusiasm; (*inspirieren*) to inspire ▶ VR: **sich für etw ~** to get enthusiastic about sth; **er ist für nichts zu ~** he's not interested in doing anything
begeistert ADJ enthusiastic
Begeisterung F enthusiasm
Begierde [bə'gi:rdə] (**-, -n**) F desire, passion
begierig [bə'gi:rɪç] ADJ eager, keen; (*voll Verlangen*) hungry, greedy
begießen [bə'gi:sən] *unreg* VT to water; (*mit Fett: Braten etc*) to baste; (*mit Alkohol*) to drink to
Beginn [bə'gɪn] (**-(e)s**) M beginning; **zu ~** at the beginning
beginnen *unreg* VT, VI to start, to begin
beglaubigen [bə'glaʊbɪgən] VT to countersign; (*Abschrift*) to authenticate; (*Echtheit, Übersetzung*) to certify
Beglaubigung F certification
Beglaubigungsschreiben NT credentials *pl*
begleichen [bə'glaɪçən] *unreg* VT to settle, to pay; **mit Ihnen habe ich noch eine Rechnung zu ~** (*fig*) I've a score to settle with you
begleiten [bə'glaɪtən] VT to accompany; (*Mil*) to escort
Begleiter(in) (**-s, -**) M(F) companion; (*zum Schutz*) escort; (*Mus*) accompanist
Begleit- ZW: **Begleiterscheinung** F side effect; **Begleitmusik** F accompaniment; **Begleitpapiere** PL (*Comm*) accompanying documents *pl*; **Begleitperson** F plus-one; **sie war ihre Begleitperson auf der Party** she was her plus-one for the party; **Begleitschiff** NT escort vessel; **Begleitschreiben** NT covering letter; **Begleitumstände** PL attendant circumstances
Begleitung F company; (*Mil*) escort; (*Mus*) accompaniment
beglücken [bə'glʏkən] VT to make happy, to delight
beglückwünschen [bə'glʏkvʏnʃən] VT: **~ (zu)** to congratulate (on)
begnadet [bə'gna:dət] ADJ gifted
begnadigen [bə'gna:dɪgən] VT to pardon
Begnadigung F pardon
begnügen [bə'gny:gən] VR: **sich ~ mit** to be satisfied with, to content o.s. with
Begonie [bə'go:niə] F begonia
begonnen [bə'gɔnən] PP *von* **beginnen**
begossen [bə'gɔsən] PP *von* **begießen** ▶ ADJ: **er stand da wie ein begossener Pudel** (*umg*) he looked so sheepish
begraben [bə'gra:bən] *unreg* VT to bury; (*aufgeben: Hoffnung*) to abandon; (*beenden: Streit etc*) to end; **dort möchte ich nicht ~ sein** (*umg*) I wouldn't like to be stuck in that hole
Begräbnis [bə'grɛ:pnɪs] (**-ses, -se**) NT burial, funeral
begradigen [bə'gra:dɪgən] VT to straighten (out)
begreifen [bə'graɪfən] *unreg* VT to understand, to comprehend
begreiflich [bə'graɪflɪç] ADJ understandable; **ich kann mich ihm nicht ~ machen** I can't make myself clear to him
begrenzen [bə'grɛntsən] VT (*beschränken*): **~ (auf** +*akk*) to restrict (to), to limit (to)
Begrenztheit [bə'grɛntsthaɪt] F limitation, restriction; (*fig*) narrowness
Begrenzung F boundary; (*fig*) restriction
Begriff [bə'grɪf] (**-(e)s, -e**) M concept, idea; **im ~ sein, etw zu tun** to be about to do sth; **sein Name ist mir ein/kein ~** his name means something/doesn't mean anything to me; **du machst dir keinen ~ (davon)** you've no idea; **für meine Begriffe** in my opinion; **schwer von ~** (*umg*) slow on the uptake
Begriffsbestimmung F definition
begriffsstutzig ADJ slow-witted, dense
begrub *etc* [bə'gru:p] VB *siehe* **begraben**
begründen [bə'grʏndən] VT (*Gründe geben*) to justify; **etw näher ~** to give specific reasons for sth
Begründer(in) (**-s, -**) M(F) founder
begründet ADJ well-founded, justified; **sachlich ~** founded on fact
Begründung F justification, reason
begrünen [bə'gry:nən] VT to plant with greenery
begrüßen [bə'gry:sən] VT to greet, to welcome
begrüßenswert ADJ welcome
Begrüßung F greeting, welcome
begünstigen [bə'gʏnstɪgən] VT (*Person*) to favour (BRIT), to favor (US); (*Sache*) to further, to promote
Begünstigte(r) F(M) beneficiary
begutachten [bə'gu:tlaxtən] VT to assess; (*umg: ansehen*) to have a look at
begütert [bə'gy:tərt] ADJ wealthy, well-to-do
begütigend ADJ (*Worte etc*) soothing; **~ auf jdn einreden** to calm sb down
behaart [bə'ha:rt] ADJ hairy
behäbig [bə'hɛ:bɪç] ADJ (*dick*) portly, stout; (*geruhsam*) comfortable
behaftet [bə'haftət] ADJ: **mit etw ~ sein** to be afflicted by sth

behagen [bəˈhaːgən] VI: **das behagt ihm nicht** he does not like it; **Behagen (-s)** NT comfort, ease; **mit Behagen essen** to eat with relish
behaglich [bəˈhaːklɪç] ADJ comfortable, cosy; **Behaglichkeit** F comfort, cosiness
behält [bəˈhɛlt] VB *siehe* **behalten**
behalten [bəˈhaltən] *unreg* VT to keep, to retain; (*im Gedächtnis*) to remember; **~ Sie (doch) Platz!** please don't get up!
Behälter [bəˈhɛltər] **(-s, -)** M container, receptacle
behämmert [bəˈhɛmərt] (*umg*) ADJ screwy, crazy
behandeln [bəˈhandəln] VT to treat; (*Thema*) to deal with; (*Maschine*) to handle; **der behandelnde Arzt** the doctor in attendance
Behändigkeit [bəˈhɛndɪçkaɪt] F agility, quickness
Behandlung F treatment; (*von Maschine*) handling
behängen [bəˈhɛŋən] VT to decorate
beharren [bəˈharən] VI: **auf etw** *dat* **~** to stick *od* keep to sth
beharrlich [bəˈharlɪç] ADJ (*ausdauernd*) steadfast, unwavering; (*hartnäckig*) tenacious, dogged; **Beharrlichkeit** F steadfastness; (*Hartnäckigkeit*) tenacity
behaupten [bəˈhaʊptən] VT to claim, to assert, to maintain; (*sein Recht*) to defend ▶ VR to assert o.s.; **von jdm ~, dass …** to say (of sb) that …; **sich auf dem Markt ~** to establish itself on the market
Behauptung F claim, assertion
Behausung [bəˈhaʊzʊŋ] F dwelling, abode; (*armselig*) hovel
beheben [bəˈheːbən] *unreg* VT (*beseitigen*) to remove; (*Missstände*) to remedy; (*Schaden*) to repair; (*Störung*) to clear
beheimatet [bəˈhaɪmaːtət] ADJ: **~ (in** *+dat***)** domiciled (at/in); (*Tier, Pflanze*) native (to)
beheizen [bəˈhaɪtsən] VT to heat
Behelf [bəˈhɛlf] **(-(e)s, -e)** M expedient, makeshift; **behelfen** *unreg* VR: **sich mit etw behelfen** to make do with sth
behelfsmäßig ADJ improvised, makeshift; (*vorübergehend*) temporary
behelligen [bəˈhɛlɪgən] VT to trouble, to bother
Behendigkeit [bəˈhɛndɪçkaɪt] F *siehe* **Behändigkeit**
beherbergen [bəˈhɛrbɛrgən] VT (*lit, fig*) to house
beherrschen [bəˈhɛrʃən] VT (*Volk*) to rule, to govern; (*Situation*) to control; (*Sprache, Gefühle*) to master ▶ VR to control o.s.
beherrscht ADJ controlled; **Beherrschtheit** F self-control
Beherrschung F rule; (*von Situation*) control; (*von Sprache, Gefühl*) mastery; **die ~ verlieren** to lose one's temper
beherzigen [bəˈhɛrtsɪgən] VT to take to heart
beherzt ADJ spirited, brave
behielt *etc* [bəˈhiːlt] VB *siehe* **behalten**
behilflich [bəˈhɪlflɪç] ADJ helpful; **jdm ~ sein (bei)** to help sb (with)
behindern [bəˈhɪndərn] VT to hinder, to impede
Behinderte(r) F(M) disabled person
behindertengerecht ADJ suitable for disabled people
Behinderung F hindrance; (*Körperbehinderung*) handicap
Behörde [bəˈhøːrdə] **(-, -n)** F authorities *pl*; (*Amtsgebäude*) office(s *pl*)
behördlich [bəˈhøːrtlɪç] ADJ official
behüten [bəˈhyːtən] VT to guard; **jdn vor etw** *dat* **~** to preserve sb from sth
behütet ADJ (*Jugend etc*) sheltered
behutsam [bəˈhuːtzaːm] ADJ cautious, careful; **man muss es ihr ~ beibringen** it will have to be broken to her gently; **Behutsamkeit** F caution, carefulness

SCHLÜSSELWORT

bei [baɪ] PRÄP *+dat* **1** (*nahe bei*) near; (*zum Aufenthalt*) at, with; (*unter, zwischen*) among; **bei München** near Munich; **bei uns** at our place; **beim Friseur** at the hairdresser's; **bei seinen Eltern wohnen** to live with one's parents; **bei einer Firma arbeiten** to work for a firm; **etw bei sich haben** to have sth on one; **jdn bei sich haben** to have sb with one; **bei Goethe** in Goethe; **beim Militär** in the army
2 (*zeitlich*) at, on; (*während*) during; (*Zustand, Umstand*) in; **bei Nacht** at night; **bei Nebel** in fog; **bei Regen** if it rains; **bei solcher Hitze** in such heat; **bei meiner Ankunft** on my arrival; **bei der Arbeit** when I'm *etc* working; **beim Fahren** while driving; **bei offenem Fenster schlafen** to sleep with the window open; **bei Feuer Scheibe einschlagen** in case of fire break glass; **bei seinem Talent** with his talent

beibehalten [ˈbaɪbəhaltən] *unreg* VT to keep, to retain
Beibehaltung F keeping, retaining
Beiblatt [ˈbaɪblat] NT supplement
beibringen [ˈbaɪbrɪŋən] *unreg* VT (*Beweis, Zeugen*) to bring forward; (*Gründe*) to adduce; **jdm etw ~** (*zufügen*) to inflict sth on sb; (*zu verstehen geben*) to make sb understand sth; (*lehren*) to teach sb sth
Beichte [ˈbaɪçtə] F confession
beichten VT to confess ▶ VI to go to confession
Beichtgeheimnis NT secret of the confessional
Beichtstuhl M confessional
beide [ˈbaɪdə] PRON, ADJ both; **meine beiden Brüder** my two brothers, both my brothers; **die ersten beiden** the first two; **wir ~** we two; **einer von beiden** one of the two; **alles beides** both (of them); **~ Mal** both times
beider- ZW: **beiderlei** ADJ *unver* of both; **beiderseitig** ADJ mutual, reciprocal; **beiderseits** ADV mutually ▶ PRÄP *+gen* on both sides of
beidhändig [ˈbaɪthɛndɪç] ADJ ambidextrous
beidrehen [ˈbaɪdreːən] VI to heave to

beidseitig [ˈbaɪtzaɪtɪç] ADJ (*auf beiden Seiten*) on both sides
beieinander [baɪlaɪˈnandər] ADV together; **gut ~ sein** (*umg*: *gesundheitlich*) to be in good shape; (: *geistig*) to be all there
Beifahrer(in) [ˈbaɪfa:rər(ɪn)] (**-s, -**) M(F) passenger; **Beifahrerairbag** M (*Aut*) passenger airbag; **Beifahrersitz** M passenger seat
Beifall [ˈbaɪfal] (**-(e)s**) M applause; (*Zustimmung*) approval; **~ heischend** fishing for applause/approval
beifällig [ˈbaɪfɛlɪç] ADJ approving; (*Kommentar*) favourable (BRIT), favorable (US)
Beifilm [ˈbaɪfɪlm] M supporting film
beifügen [ˈbaɪfy:gən] VT to enclose
Beigabe [ˈbaɪga:bə] F addition
beige [ˈbe:ʒ] ADJ beige
beigeben [ˈbaɪge:bən] *unreg* VT (*zufügen*) to add; (*mitgeben*) to give ▶ VI: **klein ~** (*nachgeben*) to climb down
Beigeschmack [ˈbaɪgeʃmak] M aftertaste
Beihilfe [ˈbaɪhɪlfə] F aid, assistance; (*Studienbeihilfe*) grant; (*Jur*) aiding and abetting; **wegen ~ zum Mord** (*Jur*) because of being an accessory to the murder
beikommen [ˈbaɪkɔmən] *unreg* VI *+dat* to get at; (*einem Problem*) to deal with
Beil [baɪl] (**-(e)s, -e**) NT axe (BRIT), ax (US), hatchet
Beilage [ˈbaɪla:gə] F (*Buchbeilage etc*) supplement; (*Koch*) accompanying vegetables; (*getrennt serviert*) side dish
beiläufig [ˈbaɪlɔʏfɪç] ADJ casual, incidental ▶ ADV casually, by the way
beilegen [ˈbaɪle:gən] VT (*hinzufügen*) to enclose, to add; (*beimessen*) to attribute, to ascribe; (*Streit*) to settle
beileibe [baɪˈlaɪbə] ADV: **~ nicht** by no means
Beileid [ˈbaɪlaɪt] NT condolence, sympathy; **herzliches ~** deepest sympathy
beiliegend [ˈbaɪli:gənt] ADJ (*Comm*) enclosed
beim [baɪm] = **bei dem**
beimessen [ˈbaɪmɛsən] *unreg* VT to attribute, to ascribe
Bein [baɪn] (**-(e)s, -e**) NT leg; **jdm ein ~ stellen** (*lit, fig*) to trip sb up; **wir sollten uns auf die Beine machen** (*umg*) we ought to be making tracks; **jdm Beine machen** (*umg*: *antreiben*) to make sb get a move on; **die Beine in die Hand nehmen** (*umg*) to take to one's heels; **sich** *dat* **die Beine in den Bauch stehen** (*umg*) to stand about until one is fit to drop; **etw auf die Beine stellen** (*fig*) to get sth off the ground
beinah [baɪˈna:], **beinahe** [baɪˈna:ə] ADV almost, nearly
Beinbruch M fracture of the leg; **das ist kein ~** (*fig*: *umg*) it could be worse
beinhalten [bəˈɪnhaltən] VT to contain
beipflichten [ˈbaɪpflɪçtən] VI: **jdm/etw ~** to agree with sb/sth
Beiprogramm [ˈbaɪprogram] NT supporting programme (BRIT) *od* program (US)
Beirat [ˈbaɪra:t] M advisory council; (*Elternbeirat*) parents' council
beirren [bəˈɪrən] VT to confuse, to muddle; **sich nicht ~ lassen** not to let o.s. be confused
Beirut [baɪˈru:t] (**-s**) NT Beirut
beisammen [baɪˈzamən] ADV together; **beisammenhaben** *unreg* VT: **er hat (sie) nicht alle beisammen** (*umg*) he's not all there; **Beisammensein** (**-s**) NT get-together
Beischlaf [ˈbaɪʃla:f] M (*Jur*) sexual intercourse
Beisein [ˈbaɪzaɪn] (**-s**) NT presence
beiseite [baɪˈzaɪtə] ADV to one side, to aside; (*stehen*) on one side, aside; **Spaß ~!** joking apart!; **beiseitelegen** VT (*sparen*) to put by; **beiseiteschaffen** VT to get rid of
beisetzen [ˈbaɪzɛtsən] VT to bury
Beisetzung F funeral
Beisitzer(in) [ˈbaɪzɪtsər(ɪn)] (**-s, -**) M(F) (*Jur*) assessor; (*bei Prüfung*) observer
Beispiel [ˈbaɪʃpi:l] (**-(e)s, -e**) NT example; **mit gutem ~ vorangehen** to set a good example; **sich** *dat* **an jdm ein ~ nehmen** to take sb as an example; **zum ~** for example; **beispielhaft** ADJ exemplary; **beispiellos** ADJ unprecedented
beispielsweise ADV for instance, for example
beispringen [ˈbaɪʃprɪŋən] *unreg* VI *+dat* to come to the aid of
beißen [ˈbaɪsən] *unreg* VT, VI to bite; (*stechen*: *Rauch, Säure*) to burn ▶ VR (*Farben*) to clash
beißend ADJ biting, caustic; (*Geruch*) pungent, sharp; (*fig*) sarcastic
Beißzange [ˈbaɪstsaŋgə] F pliers *pl*
Beistand [ˈbaɪʃtant] (**-(e)s, Beistände**) M support, help; (*Jur*) adviser; **jdm ~ leisten** to give sb assistance/one's support
beistehen [ˈbaɪʃte:ən] *unreg* VI: **jdm ~** to stand by sb
Beistelltisch [ˈbaɪʃtɛltɪʃ] M occasional table
beisteuern [ˈbaɪʃtɔʏərn] VT to contribute
beistimmen [ˈbaɪʃtɪmən] VI *+dat* to agree with
Beistrich [ˈbaɪʃtrɪç] M comma
Beitrag [ˈbaɪtra:k] (**-(e)s, Beiträge**) M contribution; (*Zahlung*) fee, subscription; (*Versicherungsbeitrag*) premium; **einen ~ zu etw leisten** to make a contribution to sth
beitragen [ˈbaɪtra:gən] *unreg* VT, VI: **~ (zu)** to contribute (to); (*mithelfen*) to help (with)
Beitrags- ZW: **beitragsfinanziert** ADJ financed by fees/contributions; **beitragsfrei** ADJ non-contributory; **beitragspflichtig** ADJ contributory; **beitragspflichtig sein** (*Mensch*) to have to pay contributions; **Beitragszahler(in)** M(F) contributor
beitreten [ˈbaɪtre:tən] *unreg* VI *+dat* to join
Beitritt [ˈbaɪtrɪt] M joining
Beitrittserklärung F declaration of membership
Beitrittsland NT (*zu EU etc*) acceding country
Beiwagen [ˈbaɪva:gən] M (*Motorradbeiwagen*) sidecar; (*Straßenbahnbeiwagen*) extra carriage
beiwohnen [ˈbaɪvo:nən] VI (*geh*): **einer Sache** *dat* **~** to attend *od* be present at sth
Beiwort [ˈbaɪvɔrt] NT adjective
Beize [ˈbaɪtsə] (**-, -n**) F (*Holzbeize*) stain; (*Koch*) marinade

beizeiten [baɪ'tsaɪtən] ADV in time
bejahen [bə'ja:ən] VT (*Frage*) to say yes to, to answer in the affirmative; (*gutheißen*) to agree with
bejahrt [bə'ja:rt] ADJ elderly, advanced in years
bejammern [bə'jamərn] VT to lament, to bewail
bejammernswert ADJ lamentable
bekakeln [bə'ka:kəln] (*umg*) VT to discuss
bekam *etc* [bə'kam] VB *siehe* **bekommen**
bekämpfen [bə'kɛmpfən] VT (*Gegner*) to fight; (*Seuche*) to combat ▸ VR to fight
Bekämpfung F: ~ *+gen* fight (against), struggle (against)
bekannt [bə'kant] ADJ (well-)known; (*nicht fremd*) familiar; **~ geben** to announce publicly; **mit jdm ~ sein** to know sb; **~ machen** to announce; **jdn mit jdm ~ machen** to introduce sb to sb; **sich mit etw ~ machen** to familiarize o.s. with sth; **das ist mir ~** I know that; **es/sie kommt mir ~ vor** it/she seems familiar; **durch etw ~ werden** to become famous because of sth
Bekannte(r) F(M) friend; (*entfernter*) acquaintance
Bekanntenkreis M circle of friends
bekanntermaßen ADV as is known
bekannt- ZW: **Bekanntgabe** F announcement; **Bekanntheitsgrad** M degree of fame; **bekanntlich** ADV as is well known, as you know; **Bekanntmachung** F publication; (*Anschlag etc*) announcement; **Bekanntschaft** F acquaintance
bekehren [bə'ke:rən] VT to convert ▸ VR to be *od* become converted
Bekehrung F conversion
bekennen [bə'kɛnən] *unreg* VT to confess; (*Glauben*) to profess ▸ VR: **sich zu jdm/etw ~** to declare one's support for sb/sth; **Farbe ~** (*umg*) to show where one stands
Bekenntnis [bə'kɛntnɪs] (**-ses, -se**) NT admission, confession; (*Religion*) confession, denomination; **ein ~ zur Demokratie ablegen** to declare one's belief in democracy; **Bekenntnisschule** F denominational school
beklagen [bə'kla:gən] VT to deplore, to lament ▸ VR to complain
beklagenswert ADJ lamentable, pathetic; (*Mensch*) pitiful; (*Zustand*) deplorable; (*Unfall*) terrible
beklatschen [bə'klatʃən] VT to applaud, to clap
bekleben [bə'kle:bən] VT: **etw mit Bildern ~** to stick pictures onto sth
bekleckern [bə'klɛkərn] (*umg*) VT to stain
bekleiden [bə'klaɪdən] VT to clothe; (*Amt*) to occupy, to fill
Bekleidung F clothing; (*form: eines Amtes*) tenure
Bekleidungsindustrie F clothing industry, rag trade (*umg*)
beklemmen [bə'klɛmən] VT to oppress
Beklemmung F oppressiveness; (*Gefühl der Angst*) feeling of apprehension
beklommen [bə'klɔmən] ADJ anxious, uneasy; **Beklommenheit** F anxiety, uneasiness
bekloppt [bə'klɔpt] (*umg*) ADJ (*Mensch*) crazy; (*: Sache*) lousy
beknackt [bə'knakt] (*umg*) ADJ = **bekloppt**
beknien [bə'kni:ən] (*umg*) VT (*jdn*) to beg
bekommen [bə'kɔmən] *unreg* VT to get, to receive; (*Kind*) to have; (*Zug*) to catch, to get ▸ VI: **jdm ~** to agree with sb; **es mit jdm zu tun ~** to get into trouble with sb; **wohl bekomms!** your health!
bekömmlich [bə'kœmlɪç] ADJ easily digestible
beköstigen [bə'kœstɪgən] VT to cater for
bekräftigen [bə'krɛftɪgən] VT to confirm, to corroborate
Bekräftigung F corroboration
bekreuzigen [bə'krɔʏtsɪgən] VR to cross o.s.
bekritteln [bə'krɪtəln] VT to criticize, to pick holes in
bekümmern [bə'kʏmərn] VT to worry, to trouble
bekunden [bə'kʊndən] VT (*sagen*) to state; (*zeigen*) to show
belächeln [bə'lɛçəln] VT to laugh at
beladen [bə'la:dən] *unreg* VT to load
Belag [bə'la:k] (**-(e)s, Beläge**) M covering, coating; (*Brotbelag*) spread; (*auf Pizza, Brot*) topping; (*auf Tortenboden, zwischen Brotscheiben*) filling; (*Zahnbelag*) tartar; (*auf Zunge*) fur; (*Bremsbelag*) lining
belagern [bə'la:gərn] VT to besiege
Belagerung F siege
Belagerungszustand M state of siege
belämmert [bəlɛmt] (*umg*) ADJ sheepish
Belang [bə'laŋ] (**-(e)s**) M importance
Belange PL interests *pl*, concerns *pl*
belangen VT (*Jur*) to take to court
belanglos ADJ trivial, unimportant
Belanglosigkeit F triviality
belassen [bə'lasən] *unreg* VT (*in Zustand, Glauben*) to leave; (*in Stellung*) to retain; **es dabei ~** to leave it at that
Belastbarkeit F (*von Brücke, Aufzug*) load-bearing capacity; (*von Menschen, Nerven*) ability to take stress
belasten [bə'lastən] VT (*lit*) to burden; (*fig: bedrücken*) to trouble, to worry; (*Comm: Konto*) to debit; (*Jur*) to incriminate ▸ VR to weigh o.s. down; (*Jur*) to incriminate o.s.; **etw (mit einer Hypothek) ~** to mortgage sth
belastend ADJ (*Jur*) incriminating
belästigen [bə'lɛstɪgən] VT to annoy, to pester; (*sexuell*) to harass
Belästigung F annoyance, pestering; (*körperlich*) molesting; **sexuelle ~** sexual harassment
Belastung [bə'lastʊŋ] F (*lit*) load; (*fig: Sorge etc*) weight; (*Comm*) charge, debit(ing); (*mit Hypothek*): **~** *+gen* mortgage (on); (*Jur*) incriminating evidence
Belastungs- ZW: **Belastungsmaterial** NT (*Jur*) incriminating evidence; **Belastungsprobe** F capacity test; (*fig*) test; **Belastungszeuge** M witness for the prosecution

belaubt [bə'laʊpt] ADJ: **dicht ~ sein** to have thick foliage
belaufen [bə'laʊfən] *unreg* VR: **sich ~ auf** *+akk* to amount to
belauschen [bə'laʊʃən] VT to eavesdrop on
beleben [bə'le:bən] VT (*anregen*) to liven up; (*Konjunktur, jds Hoffnungen*) to stimulate
belebt [bə'le:pt] ADJ (*Straße*) crowded
Beleg [bə'le:k] (**-(e)s, -e**) M (*Comm*) receipt; (*Beweis*) documentary evidence, proof; (*Beispiel*) example
belegen [bə'le:gən] VT to cover; (*Kuchen, Brot*) to spread; (*Platz*) to reserve, to book; (*Kurs, Vorlesung*) to register for; (*beweisen*) to verify, to prove
Belegschaft F personnel, staff
belegt ADJ (*Zunge*) furred; (*Stimme*) hoarse; (*Zimmer*) occupied; **belegte Brote** open sandwiches
belehren [bə'le:rən] VT to instruct, to teach; **jdn eines Besseren ~** to teach sb better; **er ist nicht zu ~** he won't be told
Belehrung F instruction
beleibt [bə'laɪpt] ADJ stout, corpulent
beleidigen [bə'laɪdɪgən] VT to insult; (*kränken*) to offend
beleidigt ADJ insulted; (*gekränkt*) offended; **die beleidigte Leberwurst spielen** (*umg*) to be in a huff
Beleidigung F insult; (*Jur*) slander; (*: schriftlich*) libel
beleihen [bə'laɪən] *unreg* VT (*Comm*) to lend money on
belemmert [bə'lɛmərt] (*umg*) ADJ *siehe* **belämmert**
belesen [bə'le:zən] ADJ well-read
beleuchten [bə'lɔʏçtən] VT to light, to illuminate; (*fig*) to throw light on
Beleuchter(in) (**-s, -**) M(F) lighting technician
Beleuchtung F lighting, illumination
beleumdet [bə'lɔʏmdət] ADJ: **gut/schlecht ~ sein** to have a good/bad reputation
beleumundet [bə'lɔʏmʊndət] ADJ = **beleumdet**
Belgien ['bɛlgiən] (**-s**) NT Belgium
Belgier(in) (**-s, -**) M(F) Belgian
belgisch ADJ Belgian
Belgrad ['bɛlgra:t] (**-s**) NT Belgrade
belichten [bə'lɪçtən] VT to expose
Belichtung F exposure
Belichtungsmesser M exposure meter
belieben VI UNPERS (*geh*): **wie es Ihnen beliebt** as you wish
Belieben [bə'li:bən] NT: **(ganz) nach ~** (just) as you wish
beliebig [bə'li:bɪç] ADJ any you like, as you like; **~ viel** as much as you like; **in beliebiger Reihenfolge** in any order whatever; **ein beliebiges Thema** any subject you like *od* want
beliebt [bə'li:pt] ADJ popular; **sich bei jdm ~ machen** to make o.s. popular with sb; **Beliebtheit** F popularity
beliefern [bə'li:fərn] VT to supply
Belize [bɛ'li:z] (**-s**) NT Belize
bellen ['bɛlən] VI to bark
Belletristik [bɛle'trɪstɪk] F fiction and poetry
belohnen [bə'lo:nən] VT to reward
Belohnung F reward
Belüftung [bə'lʏftʊŋ] F ventilation
belügen [bə'ly:gən] *unreg* VT to lie to, to deceive
belustigen [bə'lʊstɪgən] VT to amuse
Belustigung F amusement
bemächtigen [bə'mɛçtɪgən] VR: **sich einer Sache** *gen* **~** to take possession of sth, to seize sth
bemalen [bə'ma:lən] VT to paint ▶ VR (*pej: schminken*) to put on one's war paint (*umg*)
bemängeln [bə'mɛŋəln] VT to criticize
bemannen [bə'manən] VT to man
Bemannung F manning; (*Naut, Aviat etc*) crew
bemänteln [bə'mɛntəln] VT to cloak, to hide
bemerkbar ADJ perceptible, noticeable; **sich ~ machen** (*Person*) to make *od* get o.s. noticed; (*Unruhe*) to become noticeable
bemerken [bə'mɛrkən] VT (*wahrnehmen*) to notice, to observe; (*sagen*) to say, to mention; **nebenbei bemerkt** by the way
bemerkenswert ADJ remarkable, noteworthy
Bemerkung F remark, comment; (*schriftlich*) comment, note
bemitleiden [bə'mɪtlaɪdən] VT to pity
bemittelt [bə'mɪtəlt] ADJ well-to-do, well-off
bemühen [bə'my:ən] VR to make an effort; **sich um eine Stelle ~** to try to get a job
bemüht ADJ: **(darum) ~ sein, etw zu tun** to endeavour (BRIT) *od* endeavor (*US*) *od* be at pains to do sth
Bemühung F trouble, pains *pl*, effort
bemüßigt [bə'my:sɪçt] ADJ: **sich ~ fühlen/ sehen** (*geh*) to feel called upon
bemuttern [bə'mʊtərn] VT to mother
benachbart [bə'naxba:rt] ADJ neighbouring (BRIT), neighboring (*US*)
benachrichtigen [bə'na:xrɪçtɪgən] VT to inform
Benachrichtigung F notification
benachteiligen [bə'na:xtaɪlɪgən] VT to (put at a) disadvantage, to victimize
benehmen [bə'ne:mən] *unreg* VR to behave; **Benehmen** (**-s**) NT behaviour (BRIT), behavior (*US*); **kein Benehmen haben** not to know how to behave
beneiden [bə'naɪdən] VT to envy; **jdn um etw ~** to envy sb sth
beneidenswert ADJ enviable
Beneluxländer ['be:nelʊkslɛndər] PL Benelux (countries *pl*)
Beneluxstaaten PL Benelux (countries *pl*)
benennen [bə'nɛnən] *unreg* VT to name
Bengel ['bɛŋəl] (**-s, -**) M (little) rascal *od* rogue
Benimm [bə'nɪm] (**-s**) (*umg*) M manners *pl*
Benin [be'ni:n] (**-s**) NT Benin
benommen [bə'nɔmən] ADJ dazed
benoten [bə'no:tən] VT to mark
benötigen [bə'nø:tɪgən] VT to need
benutzen [bə'nʊtsən] VT to use
benützen [bə'nʏtsən] VT to use

b

Benutzer(in) (**-s**, **-**) M(F) user; **benutzerdefiniert** ADJ (*Comput*) user-defined; **benutzerfreundlich** ADJ user-friendly; **Benutzerkonto** NT (*Comput*) user account; **Benutzername** M (*Comput*) username; **Benutzeroberfläche** F (*Comput*) user/system interface; **Benutzerunterstützung** F (*bes Comput*) help desk
Benutzung F utilization, use; **jdm etw zur ~ überlassen** to put sth at sb's disposal
Benzin [bɛnt'si:n] (**-s**, **-e**) NT (*Aut*) petrol (BRIT), gas(oline) (*US*); **Benzineinspritzanlage** F (*Aut*) fuel injection system; **Benzinkanister** M petrol (BRIT) *od* gas (*US*) can; **Benzintank** M petrol (BRIT) *od* gas (*US*) tank; **Benzinuhr** F petrol (BRIT) *od* gas (*US*) gauge
beobachten [bə'lo:baxtən] VT to observe
Beobachter(in) (**-s**, **-**) M(F) observer; (*eines Unfalls*) witness; (*Presse, TV*) correspondent
Beobachtung F observation
beordern [bə'lɔrdərn] VT: **jdn zu sich ~** to send for sb
bepacken [bə'pakən] VT to load, to pack
bepflanzen [bə'pflantsən] VT to plant
bequatschen [bə'kvatʃən] (*umg*) VT (*überreden*) to persuade; **etw ~** to talk sth over
bequem [bə'kve:m] ADJ comfortable; (*Ausrede*) convenient; (*Person*) lazy, indolent; **machen Sie es sich ~** make yourself at home
bequemen [bə'kve:mən] VR: **sich ~, etw zu tun** to condescend to do sth
Bequemlichkeit F convenience, comfort; (*Faulheit*) laziness, indolence
Ber. ABK = **Bericht**; **Beruf**
berät [bə'rɛ:t] VB *siehe* **beraten**
beraten [bə'ra:tən] *unreg* VT to advise; (*besprechen*) to discuss, to debate ▸ VR to consult; **gut/schlecht ~ sein** to be well/ill advised; **sich ~ lassen** to get advice
beratend ADJ consultative; **jdm ~ zur Seite stehen** to act in an advisory capacity to sb
Berater(in) (**-s**, **-**) M(F) adviser; **Beratervertrag** M consultancy contract
beratschlagen [bə'ra:tʃla:gən] VI to deliberate, to confer ▸ VT to deliberate on, to confer about
Beratung F advice; (*Besprechung*) consultation
Beratungsstelle F advice centre (BRIT) *od* center (*US*)
berauben [bə'raʊbən] VT to rob
berauschen [bə'raʊʃən] VT (*lit, fig*) to intoxicate
berauschend ADJ: **das war nicht sehr ~** (*ironisch*) that wasn't very exciting
berechenbar [bə'rɛçənba:r] ADJ calculable; (*Verhalten*) predictable
berechnen [bə'rɛçnən] VT to calculate; (*Comm: anrechnen*) to charge
berechnend ADJ (*Mensch*) calculating, scheming
Berechnung F calculation; (*Comm*) charge
berechtigen [bə'rɛçtɪgən] VT to entitle; (*bevollmächtigen*) to authorize; (*fig*) to justify
berechtigt [bə'rɛçtɪçt] ADJ justifiable, justified
Berechtigung F authorization; (*fig*) justification
bereden [bə're:dən] VT (*besprechen*) to discuss; (*überreden*) to persuade ▸ VR to discuss
beredt [bə're:t] ADJ eloquent
Bereich [bə'raɪç] (**-(e)s**, **-e**) M (*Bezirk*) area; (*Ressort, Gebiet*) sphere; **im ~ des Möglichen liegen** to be within the bounds of possibility
bereichern [bə'raɪçərn] VT to enrich ▸ VR to get rich; **sich auf Kosten anderer ~** to feather one's nest at the expense of other people
Bereifung [bə'raɪfʊŋ] F (set of) tyres (BRIT) *od* tires (*US*) *pl*; (*Vorgang*) fitting with tyres (BRIT) *od* tires (*US*)
bereinigen [bə'raɪnɪgən] VT to settle
bereisen [bə'raɪzən] VT to travel through; (*Comm: Gebiet*) to travel, to cover
bereit [bə'raɪt] ADJ ready, prepared; **zu etw ~ sein** to be ready for sth; **sich ~ erklären** to declare o.s. willing; **(sich) ~ machen** to prepare, to get ready
bereiten VT to prepare, to make ready; (*Kummer, Freude*) to cause; **einer Sache** *dat* **ein Ende ~** to put an end to sth
bereit- ZW: **bereithalten** *unreg* VT to keep in readiness; **bereitlegen** VT to lay out; **bereitmachen** VT, VR *siehe* **bereit**
bereits ADV already
bereit- ZW: **Bereitschaft** F readiness; (*Polizei*) alert; **in Bereitschaft sein** to be on the alert *od* on stand-by; **Bereitschaftsarzt** M doctor on call; (*im Krankenhaus*) duty doctor; **Bereitschaftsdienst** M emergency service; **bereitstehen** *unreg* VI (*Person*) to be prepared; (*Ding*) to be ready; **bereitstellen** VT (*Kisten, Pakete etc*) to put ready; (*Geld etc*) to make available; (*Truppen, Maschinen*) to put at the ready
Bereitung F preparation
bereitwillig ADJ willing, ready; **Bereitwilligkeit** F willingness, readiness
bereuen [bə'rɔʏən] VT to regret
Berg [bɛrk] (**-(e)s**, **-e**) M mountain; (*kleiner*) hill; **mit etw hinterm ~ halten** (*fig*) to keep quiet about sth; **über alle Berge sein** to be miles away; **da stehen einem ja die Haare zu Berge** it's enough to make your hair stand on end; **bergab** ADV downhill; **bergan** ADV uphill; **Bergarbeiter** M miner; **bergauf** ADV uphill; **Bergbahn** F mountain railway (BRIT) *od* railroad (*US*); **Bergbau** M mining
bergen ['bɛrgən] *unreg* VT (*retten*) to rescue; (*Ladung*) to salvage; (*enthalten*) to contain
Bergführer M mountain guide
Berggipfel M mountain top, peak, summit
bergig ['bɛrgɪç] ADJ mountainous, hilly
Berg- ZW: **Bergkamm** M crest, ridge; **Bergkette** F mountain range; **Bergkristall** M rock crystal; **Bergmann** (**-(e)s**, *pl* **Bergleute**) M miner; **Bergnot** F: **in Bergnot sein/geraten** to be in/get into difficulties while climbing; **Bergpredigt** F (*Rel*) Sermon on the Mount; **Bergrettungsdienst** M mountain rescue service; **Bergrutsch** M landslide; **Bergschuh** M

walking boot; **Bergsteigen** NT mountaineering; **Bergsteiger(in)** M(F) mountaineer, climber; **Berg-und-Tal-Bahn** F big dipper, roller-coaster
Bergung ['bɛrgʊŋ] F *(von Menschen)* rescue; *(von Material)* recovery; *(Naut)* salvage
Bergwacht F mountain rescue service
Bergwerk NT mine
Bericht [bə'rɪçt] **(-(e)s, -e)** M report, account; **berichten** VT, VI to report; **Berichterstatter (-s, -)** M reporter, (newspaper) correspondent; **Berichterstattung** F reporting
berichtigen [bə'rɪçtɪgən] VT to correct
Berichtigung F correction
berieseln [bə'ri:zəln] VT to spray with water
Berieselung F watering; **die dauernde ~ mit Musik ...** *(fig)* the constant stream of music ...
Berieselungsanlage F sprinkler (system)
Beringmeer ['be:rɪŋme:r] NT Bering Sea
beritten [bə'rɪtən] ADJ mounted
Berlin [bɛr'li:n] **(-s)** NT Berlin
Berliner[1] ADJ *attrib* Berlin
Berliner[2] **(-s, -)** M *(Person)* Berliner; *(Koch)* jam doughnut
Berlinerin F Berliner
berlinerisch *(umg)* ADJ *(Dialekt)* Berlin *attrib*
Bermudadreieck [bɛr'mu:dadraɪlɛk] NT Bermuda triangle
Bermudainseln [bɛr'mu:dalɪnzəln] PL Bermuda *pl*
Bern [bɛrn] **(-s)** NT Berne
Bernhardiner [bɛrnhar'di:nər] **(-s, -)** M Saint Bernard (dog)
Bernstein ['bɛrnʃtaɪn] M amber
bersten ['bɛrstən] *unreg* VI to burst, to split
berüchtigt [bə'rʏçtɪçt] ADJ notorious, infamous
berücksichtigen [bə'rʏkzɪçtɪgən] VT to consider, to bear in mind
Berücksichtigung F consideration; **in** *od* **unter ~ der Tatsache, dass ...** in view of the fact that ...
Beruf [bə'ru:f] **(-(e)s, -e)** M occupation, profession; *(Gewerbe)* trade; **was sind Sie von ~?** what is your occupation *etc*?, what do you do for a living?; **seinen ~ verfehlt haben** to have missed one's vocation
berufen *unreg* VT *(in Amt)*: **jdn in etw** *akk* **~** to appoint sb to sth ▸ VR: **sich auf jdn/etw ~** to refer *od* appeal to sb/sth ▸ ADJ competent, qualified; *(ausersehen)*: **zu etw ~ sein** to have a vocation for sth
beruflich ADJ professional; **er ist ~ viel unterwegs** he is away a lot on business
Berufs- zW: **Berufsakademie** F college of advanced vocational studies; **Berufsausbildung** F vocational *od* professional training; **berufsbedingt** ADJ occupational; **Berufsberater** M careers adviser; **Berufsberatung** F vocational guidance; **Berufsbezeichnung** F job description; **Berufseinsteiger(in)** M(F) first-time employee; **Berufserfahrung** F (professional) experience; **Berufsfeuerwehr** F fire service; **Berufsgeheimnis** NT professional secret; **Berufskrankheit** F occupational disease; **Berufskriminalität** F professional crime; **Berufsleben** NT professional life; **im Berufsleben stehen** to be working *od* in employment; **berufsmäßig** ADJ professional; **Berufsperspektive** F job *od* career prospects *pl*; **Berufsrisiko** NT occupational hazard; **Berufsschule** F vocational *od* trade school; **Berufssoldat** M professional soldier, regular; **Berufssportler** M professional (sportsman); **berufstätig** ADJ employed; **berufsunfähig** ADJ unable to work (at one's profession); **Berufsunfall** M occupational accident; **Berufsverbot** NT: **jdm Berufsverbot erteilen** to ban sb from his/her profession; *(einem Arzt, Anwalt)* to strike sb off; **Berufsverkehr** M commuter traffic; **Berufswahl** F choice of a job
Berufung F vocation, calling; *(Ernennung)* appointment; *(Jur)* appeal; **~ einlegen** to appeal; **unter ~ auf etw** *akk (form)* with reference to sth
Berufungsgericht NT appeal court, court of appeal
beruhen [bə'ru:ən] VI: **auf etw** *dat* **~** to be based on sth; **etw auf sich ~ lassen** to leave sth at that; **das beruht auf Gegenseitigkeit** the feeling is mutual
beruhigen [bə'ru:ɪgən] VT to calm, to pacify, to soothe ▸ VR *(Mensch)* to calm (o.s.) down; *(Situation)* to calm down
beruhigend ADJ *(Gefühl, Wissen)* reassuring; *(Worte)* comforting; *(Mittel)* tranquillizing
Beruhigung F reassurance; *(der Nerven)* calming; **zu jds ~** to reassure sb
Beruhigungsmittel NT sedative
Beruhigungspille F tranquillizer
berühmt [bə'ry:mt] ADJ famous; **das war nicht ~** *(umg)* it was nothing to write home about; **berühmt-berüchtigt** ADJ infamous, notorious; **Berühmtheit** F *(Ruf)* fame; *(Mensch)* celebrity
berühren [bə'ry:rən] VT to touch; *(gefühlsmäßig bewegen)* to affect; *(flüchtig erwähnen)* to mention, to touch on ▸ VR to meet, to touch; **von etw peinlich berührt sein** to be embarrassed by sth
Berührung F contact
Berührungsbildschirm M *(Tech)* touch screen
berührungsempfindlich ADJ touch-sensitive
Berührungspunkt M point of contact
bes. ABK (= *besonders*) esp
besagen [bə'za:gən] VT to mean
besagt ADJ *(form: Tag etc)* in question
besaiten [bə'zaɪtən] VT: **neu ~** *(Instrument)* to restring
besänftigen [bə'zɛnftɪgən] VT to soothe, to calm
besänftigend ADJ soothing
Besänftigung F soothing, calming
besaß *etc* [bə'za:s] VB *siehe* **besitzen**
besät [bə'zɛ:t] ADJ covered; *(mit Blättern etc)* strewn

b

Besatz [bəˈzats] (**-es, Besätze**) M trimming, edging
Besatzung F garrison; (*Naut, Aviat*) crew
Besatzungsmacht F occupying power
Besatzungszone F occupied zone
besaufen [bəˈzaʊfən] *unreg* (*umg*) VR to get drunk *od* stoned
beschädigen [bəˈʃɛːdɪgən] VT to damage
Beschädigung F damage; (*Stelle*) damaged spot
beschaffen [bəˈʃafən] VT to get, to acquire ▶ ADJ constituted; **so ~ sein wie ...** to be the same as ...; **Beschaffenheit** F constitution, nature; **je nach Beschaffenheit der Lage** according to the situation
Beschaffung F acquisition
beschäftigen [bəˈʃɛftɪgən] VT to occupy; (*beruflich*) to employ; (*innerlich*): **jdn ~** to be on sb's mind ▶ VR to occupy *od* concern o.s.
beschäftigt ADJ busy, occupied; (*angestellt*): **(bei einer Firma) ~** employed (by a firm)
Beschäftigung F (*Beruf*) employment; (*Tätigkeit*) occupation; (*geistige Beschäftigung*) preoccupation; **einer ~ nachgehen** (*form*) to be employed
Beschäftigungsgesellschaft F *regional job creation scheme in areas with high unemployment*
Beschäftigungsprogramm NT employment scheme
Beschäftigungstherapie F occupational therapy
beschämen [bəˈʃɛːmən] VT to put to shame
beschämend ADJ shameful; (*Hilfsbereitschaft*) shaming
beschämt ADJ ashamed
beschatten [bəˈʃatən] VT to shade; (*Verdächtige*) to shadow
beschaulich [bəˈʃaʊlɪç] ADJ contemplative; (*Leben, Abend*) quiet, tranquil
Bescheid [bəˈʃaɪt] (**-(e)s, -e**) M information; (*Weisung*) directions *pl*; **~ wissen (über** *+akk*) to be well-informed (about); **ich weiß ~** I know; **jdm ~ geben** *od* **sagen** to let sb know; **jdm ordentlich ~ sagen** (*umg*) to tell sb where to go
bescheiden [bəˈʃaɪdən] *unreg* VR to content o.s. ▶ VT: **etw abschlägig ~** (*form*) to turn sth down ▶ ADJ modest; **Bescheidenheit** F modesty
bescheinen [bəˈʃaɪnən] *unreg* VT to shine on
bescheinigen [bəˈʃaɪnɪgən] VT to certify; (*bestätigen*) to acknowledge; **hiermit wird bescheinigt, dass ...** this is to certify that ...
Bescheinigung F certificate; (*Quittung*) receipt
bescheißen [bəˈʃaɪsən] *unreg* (*umg!*) VT to cheat
beschenken [bəˈʃɛŋkən] VT to give presents to
bescheren [bəˈʃeːrən] VT: **jdm etw ~** to give sb sth as a present; **jdn ~** to give presents to sb
Bescherung F giving of presents; (*umg*) mess; **da haben wir die ~!** (*umg*) what did I tell you!
bescheuert [bəˈʃɔʏərt] (*umg*) ADJ stupid
beschichten [bəˈʃɪçtən] VT (*Tech*) to coat, to cover
beschießen [bəˈʃiːsən] *unreg* VT to shoot *od* fire at
beschildern [bəˈʃɪldərn] VT to signpost
beschimpfen [bəˈʃɪmpfən] VT to abuse
Beschimpfung F abuse, insult
beschirmen [bəˈʃɪrmən] VT (*geh: beschützen*) to shield
beschiss *etc* VB *siehe* **bescheißen**
Beschiss [bəˈʃɪs] (**-es**) (*umg*) M: **das ist ~** that is a cheat
beschissen PP *von* **bescheißen** ▶ ADJ (*umg!*) bloody awful, lousy
Beschlag [bəˈʃlaːk] (**-(e)s, Beschläge**) M (*Metallband*) fitting; (*auf Fenster*) condensation; (*auf Metall*) tarnish; (*Politur*) finish; (*Hufeisen*) horseshoe; **jdn/etw in ~ nehmen** *od* **mit ~ belegen** to monopolize sb/sth
beschlagen [bəˈʃlaːgən] *unreg* VT to cover; (*Pferd*) to shoe; (*Fenster, Metall*) to cover ▶ VI, VR (*Fenster etc*) to mist over; **~ sein (in** *od* **auf** *+dat*) to be well versed (in)
beschlagnahmen VT to seize, to confiscate
Beschlagnahmung F confiscation
beschleunigen [bəˈʃlɔʏnɪgən] VT to accelerate, to speed up ▶ VI (*Aut*) to accelerate
Beschleunigung F acceleration
beschließen [bəˈʃliːsən] *unreg* VT to decide on; (*beenden*) to end, to close
beschlossen [bəˈʃlɔsən] PP *von* **beschließen** ▶ ADJ (*entschieden*) decided, agreed; **das ist beschlossene Sache** that's been settled
Beschluss [bəˈʃlʊs] (**-es, Beschlüsse**) M decision, conclusion; (*Ende*) close, end; **einen ~ fassen** to pass a resolution
beschlussfähig ADJ: **~ sein** to have a quorum
Beschlusslage F policy position
beschmieren [bəˈʃmiːrən] VT (*Wand*) to bedaub
beschmutzen [bəˈʃmʊtsən] VT to dirty, to soil
beschneiden [bəˈʃnaɪdən] *unreg* VT to cut; (*stutzen*) to trim; (*: Strauch*) to prune; (*Rel*) to circumcise
beschnuppern [bəˈʃnʊpərn] VR (*Hunde*) to sniff each other; (*fig: umg*) to size each other up
beschönigen [bəˈʃøːnɪgən] VT to gloss over; **beschönigender Ausdruck** euphemism
beschränken [bəˈʃrɛŋkən] VT to limit, to restrict (auf *+akk* to) ▶ VR: **sich ~ auf** *+akk* to limit *od* restrict o.s. to
beschrankt [bəˈʃraŋkt] ADJ (*Bahnübergang*) with barrier
beschränkt [bəˈʃrɛŋkt] ADJ confined, narrow; (*Mensch*) limited, narrow-minded; (*pej: geistig*) dim; **Gesellschaft mit beschränkter Haftung** limited company (BRIT), corporation (US); **Beschränktheit** F narrowness
Beschränkung F limitation
beschreiben [bəˈʃraɪbən] *unreg* VT to describe; (*Papier*) to write on
Beschreibung F description
beschrieb *etc* [bəˈʃriːp] VB *siehe* **beschreiben**
beschrieben [bəˈʃriːbən] PP *von* **beschreiben**
beschriften [bəˈʃrɪftən] VT to mark, to label
Beschriftung F lettering
beschuldigen [bəˈʃʊldɪgən] VT to accuse
Beschuldigung F accusation
beschummeln [bəˈʃʊməln] (*umg*) VT, VI to cheat

Beschuss [bəˈʃʊs] M: **jdn/etw unter ~ nehmen** (*Mil*) to (start to) bombard *od* shell sb/sth; (*fig*) to attack sb/sth; **unter ~ geraten** (*lit, fig*) to come into the firing line
beschützen [bəˈʃʏtsən] VT: **~ (vor** *+dat*) to protect (from)
Beschützer(in) (**-s, -**) M(F) protector
Beschützung F protection
beschwatzen [bəˈʃvatsən] (*umg*) VT (*überreden*) to talk over
Beschwerde [bəˈʃveːrdə] (**-, -n**) F complaint; (*Mühe*) hardship; (*Industrie*) grievance; **Beschwerden** PL (*Leiden*) trouble; **~ einlegen** (*form*) to lodge a complaint; **beschwerdefrei** ADJ fit and healthy; **Beschwerdefrist** F (*Jur*) *period of time during which an appeal may be lodged*
beschweren [bəˈʃveːrən] VT to weight down; (*fig*) to burden ▶ VR to complain
beschwerlich ADJ tiring, exhausting
beschwichtigen [bəˈʃvɪçtɪgən] VT to soothe, to pacify
Beschwichtigung F soothing, calming
beschwindeln [bəˈʃvɪndəln] VT (*betrügen*) to cheat; (*belügen*) to fib to
beschwingt [bəˈʃvɪŋt] ADJ cheery, in high spirits
beschwipst [bəˈʃvɪpst] ADJ tipsy
beschwören [bəˈʃvøːrən] *unreg* VT (*Aussage*) to swear to; (*anflehen*) to implore; (*Geister*) to conjure up
beseelen [bəˈzeːlən] VT to inspire
besehen [bəˈzeːən] *unreg* VT to look at; **genau ~** to examine closely
beseitigen [bəˈzaɪtɪgən] VT to remove
Beseitigung F removal
Besen [ˈbeːzən] (**-s, -**) M broom; (*pej, umg: Frau*) old bag; **ich fresse einen ~, wenn das stimmt** (*umg*) if that's right, I'll eat my hat; **Besenstiel** M broomstick
besessen [bəˈzɛsən] ADJ possessed; (*von einer Idee etc*): **~ (von)** obsessed (with)
besetzen [bəˈzɛtsən] VT (*Haus, Land*) to occupy; (*Platz*) to take, to fill; (*Posten*) to fill; (*Rolle*) to cast; (*mit Edelsteinen*) to set
besetzt ADJ full; (*Tel*) engaged, busy; (*Platz*) taken; (*WC*) engaged; **Besetztzeichen** NT engaged tone (BRIT), busy signal (US)
Besetzung F occupation; (*von Stelle*) filling; (*von Rolle*) casting; (*die Schauspieler*) cast; **zweite ~** (*Theat*) understudy
besichtigen [bəˈzɪçtɪgən] VT to visit, to look at
Besichtigung F visit
besiedeln VT: **dicht/dünn besiedelt** densely/thinly populated
Besiedelung [bəˈziːdəlʊŋ], **Besiedelung** [bəˈziːdlʊŋ] F population
besiegeln [bəˈziːgəln] VT to seal
besiegen [bəˈziːgən] VT to defeat, to overcome
Besiegte(r) [bəˈziːktə(r)] F(M) loser
besinnen [bəˈzɪnən] *unreg* VR (*nachdenken*) to think, to reflect; (*erinnern*) to remember; **sich anders ~** to change one's mind
besinnlich ADJ contemplative
Besinnung F consciousness; **bei/ohne ~ sein** to be conscious/unconscious; **zur ~ kommen** to recover consciousness; (*fig*) to come to one's senses
besinnungslos ADJ unconscious; (*fig*) blind
Besitz [bəˈzɪts] (**-es**) M possession; (*Eigentum*) property; **Besitzanspruch** M claim of ownership; (*Jur*) title; **besitzanzeigend** ADJ (*Gram*) possessive
besitzen *unreg* VT to possess, to own; (*Eigenschaft*) to have
Besitzer(in) (**-s, -**) M(F) owner, proprietor
Besitz- ZW: **Besitzergreifung** F seizure; **Besitznahme** F seizure; **Besitztum** NT (*Grundbesitz*) estate(s *pl*), property; **Besitzurkunde** F title deeds *pl*
besoffen [bəˈzɔfən] (*umg*) ADJ sozzled
besohlen [bəˈzoːlən] VT to sole
Besoldung [bəˈzɔldʊŋ] F salary, pay
besondere(r, s) [bəˈzɔndərə(r, s)] ADJ special; (*eigen*) particular; (*gesondert*) separate; (*eigentümlich*) peculiar; **nichts Besonderes** nothing special
Besonderheit F peculiarity
besonders ADV especially, particularly; (*getrennt*) separately; **das Essen/der Film war nicht ~** the food/film was nothing special *od* out of the ordinary; **wie gehts dir? — nicht ~** how are you? — not too hot
besonnen [bəˈzɔnən] ADJ sensible, level-headed; **Besonnenheit** F level-headedness
besorgen [bəˈzɔrgən] VT (*beschaffen*) to acquire; (*kaufen*) to purchase; (*erledigen: Geschäfte*) to deal with; (*sich kümmern um*) to take care of; **es jdm ~** (*umg*) to sort sb out
Besorgnis (**-, -se**) F anxiety, concern; **besorgniserregend** ADJ alarming, worrying
besorgt [bəˈzɔrkt] ADJ anxious, worried; **Besorgtheit** F anxiety, worry
Besorgung F acquisition; (*Kauf*) purchase; (*Einkauf*): **Besorgungen machen** to do some shopping
bespannen [bəˈʃpanən] VT (*mit Saiten, Fäden*) to string
bespielbar ADJ (*Rasen etc*) playable
bespielen [bəˈʃpiːlən] VT (*Tonband, Kassette*) to make a recording on
bespitzeln [bəˈʃpɪtsəln] VT to spy on
besprechen [bəˈʃprɛçən] *unreg* VT to discuss; (*Tonband etc*) to record, to speak onto; (*Buch*) to review ▶ VR to discuss, to consult
Besprechung F meeting, discussion; (*von Buch*) review
bespringen [bəˈʃprɪŋən] *unreg* VT (*Tier*) to mount, to cover
bespritzen [bəˈʃprɪtsən] VT to spray; (*beschmutzen*) to spatter
besser [ˈbɛsər] ADJ better; **nur ein besserer …** just a glorified …; **bessere Leute** a better class of people; **es geht ihm ~** he feels better; **~ gesagt** or rather; *siehe auch* **besserstehen**
bessern VT to make better, to improve ▶ VR to improve; (*Mensch*) to reform

b

besserstehen *unreg* VR (*umg*) to be better off
Besserung F improvement; **auf dem Weg(e) der ~ sein** to be getting better, to be improving; **gute ~!** get well soon!
Besserwisser(in) (**-s, -**) M(F) know-all (BRIT), know-it-all (US)
bestand *etc* VB *siehe* **bestehen**
Bestand [bə'ʃtant] (**-(e)s, Bestände**) M (*Fortbestehen*) duration, continuance; (*Kassenbestand*) amount, balance; (*Vorrat*) stock; **eiserner ~** iron rations *pl*; **~ haben, von ~ sein** to last long, to endure
bestanden PP *von* **bestehen** ▶ ADJ: **nach bestandener Prüfung** after passing the exam
beständig [bə'ʃtɛndɪç] ADJ (*ausdauernd*) constant (*auch fig*); (*Wetter*) settled; (*Stoffe*) resistant; (*Klagen etc*) continual
Bestandsaufnahme F stocktaking
Bestandsüberwachung F stock control, inventory control
Bestandteil M part, component; (*Zutat*) ingredient; **sich in seine Bestandteile auflösen** to fall to pieces
bestärken [bə'ʃtɛrkən] VT: **jdn in etw** *dat* **~** to strengthen *od* confirm sb in sth
bestätigen [bə'ʃtɛːtɪgən] VT to confirm; (*anerkennen*) to acknowledge; **jdn (im Amt) ~** to confirm sb's appointment
Bestätigung F confirmation; (*Anerkennung*) acknowledgement
bestatten [bə'ʃtatən] VT to bury
Bestatter (**-s, -**) M undertaker
Bestattung F funeral
Bestattungsinstitut NT undertaker's (BRIT), mortician's (US)
bestäuben [bə'ʃtɔʏbən] VT to powder, to dust; (*Pflanze*) to pollinate
beste(r, s) ['bɛstə(r, s)] ADJ best; **sie singt am besten** she sings best; **so ist es am besten** it's best that way; **am besten gehst du gleich** you'd better go at once; **jdn zum Besten haben** to pull sb's leg; **einen Witz** *etc* **zum Besten geben** to tell a joke *etc*; **aufs B~** in the best possible way; **zu jds Besten** for the benefit of sb; **es steht nicht zum Besten** it does not look too promising
bestechen [bə'ʃtɛçən] *unreg* VT to bribe ▶ VI (*Eindruck machen*): **(durch etw) ~** to be impressive (because of sth)
bestechend ADJ (*Schönheit, Eindruck*) captivating; (*Angebot*) tempting
bestechlich ADJ corruptible; **Bestechlichkeit** F corruptibility
Bestechung F bribery, corruption
Bestechungsgelder PL bribe *sing*
Bestechungsversuch M attempted bribery
Besteck [bə'ʃtɛk] (**-(e)s, -e**) NT knife, fork and spoon, cutlery; (*Med*) set of instruments; **Besteckkasten** M cutlery canteen
bestehen [bə'ʃteːən] *unreg* VI to exist; (*andauern*) to last ▶ VT (*Probe, Prüfung*) to pass; (*Kampf*) to win; **~ bleiben** to last, to endure; (*Frage, Hoffnung*) to remain; **die Schwierigkeit/das Problem besteht darin, dass ...** the difficulty/problem lies in the fact that ..., the difficulty/problem is that ...; **~ auf** *+dat* to insist on; **~ aus** to consist of; **Bestehen** NT: **seit Bestehen der Firma** ever since the firm came into existence *od* has existed
bestehlen [bə'ʃteːlən] *unreg* VT to rob
besteigen [bə'ʃtaɪgən] *unreg* VT to climb, to ascend; (*Pferd*) to mount; (*Thron*) to ascend
Bestellbuch NT order book
bestellen [bə'ʃtɛlən] VT to order; (*kommen lassen*) to arrange to see; (*nominieren*) to name; (*Acker*) to cultivate; (*Grüße, Auftrag*) to pass on; **wie bestellt und nicht abgeholt** (*hum: umg*) like orphan Annie; **er hat nicht viel/nichts zu ~** he doesn't have much/any say here; **ich bin für 10 Uhr bestellt** I have an appointment for *od* at 10 o'clock; **es ist schlecht um ihn bestellt** (*fig*) he is in a bad way
Bestell- ZW: **Bestellformular** NT purchase order; **Bestellnummer** F order number; **Bestellschein** M order coupon
Bestellung F (*Comm*) order; (*Bestellen*) ordering; (*Ernennung*) nomination, appointment
bestenfalls ['bɛstən'fals] ADV at best
bestens ['bɛstəns] ADV very well
besteuern [bə'ʃtɔʏərn] VT to tax
bestialisch [bɛsti'aːlɪʃ] (*umg*) ADJ awful, beastly
besticken [bə'ʃtɪkən] VT to embroider
Bestie ['bɛstiə] F (*lit, fig*) beast
bestimmen [bə'ʃtɪmən] VT (*Regeln*) to lay down; (*Tag, Ort*) to fix; (*prägen*) to characterize; (*ausersehen*) to mean; (*ernennen*) to appoint; (*definieren*) to define; (*veranlassen*) to induce ▶ VI: **du hast hier nicht zu ~** you don't make the decisions here; **er kann über sein Geld allein ~** it is up to him what he does with his money
bestimmend ADJ (*Faktor, Einfluss*) determining, decisive
bestimmt ADJ (*entschlossen*) firm; (*gewiss*) certain, definite; (*Artikel*) definite ▶ ADV (*gewiss*) definitely, for sure; **suchen Sie etwas Bestimmtes?** are you looking for anything in particular?; **Bestimmtheit** F certainty; **in** *od* **mit aller Bestimmtheit** quite categorically
Bestimmung F (*Verordnung*) regulation; (*Festsetzen*) determining; (*Verwendungszweck*) purpose; (*Schicksal*) fate; (*Definition*) definition
Bestimmungs- ZW: **Bestimmungsbahnhof** M (*Eisenb*) destination; **bestimmungsgemäß** ADJ as agreed; **Bestimmungshafen** M (port of) destination; **Bestimmungsort** M destination
Bestleistung F best performance
bestmöglich ADJ best possible
Best.-Nr. ABK = **Bestellnummer**
bestrafen [bə'ʃtraːfən] VT to punish
Bestrafung F punishment
bestrahlen [bə'ʃtraːlən] VT to shine on; (*Med*) to treat with X-rays
Bestrahlung F (*Med*) X-ray treatment, radiotherapy
Bestreben [bə'ʃtreːbən] (**-s**) NT endeavour (BRIT), endeavor (US), effort

bestrebt [bəˈʃtreːpt] ADJ: **~ sein, etw zu tun** to endeavour (BRIT) *od* endeavor (US) to do sth
Bestrebung [bəˈʃtreːbʊŋ] F = **Bestreben**
bestreichen [bəˈʃtraɪçən] *unreg* VT (*Brot*) to spread
bestreiken [bəˈʃtraɪkən] VT (*Industrie*) to black; **die Fabrik wird zur Zeit bestreikt** there's a strike on in the factory at the moment
bestreiten [bəˈʃtraɪtən] *unreg* VT (*abstreiten*) to dispute; (*finanzieren*) to pay for, to finance; **er hat das ganze Gespräch allein bestritten** he did all the talking
bestreuen [bəˈʃtrɔʏən] VT to sprinkle, to dust; (*Straße*) to (spread with) grit
Bestseller [ˈbɛstsɛlər] (**-s, -**) M best-seller
bestürmen [bəˈʃtʏrmən] VT (*mit Fragen, Bitten etc*) to overwhelm, to swamp
bestürzen [bəˈʃtʏrtsən] VT to dismay
bestürzt ADJ dismayed
Bestürzung F consternation
Bestzeit F (*bes Sport*) best time
Besuch [bəˈzuːx] (**-(e)s, -e**) M visit; (*Person*) visitor; **einen ~ bei jdm machen** to pay sb a visit *od* call; **~ haben** to have visitors; **bei jdm auf** *od* **zu ~ sein** to be visiting sb
besuchen VT to visit; (*Sch etc*) to attend; **gut besucht** well-attended
Besucher(in) (**-s, -**) M(F) visitor, guest
Besuchserlaubnis F permission to visit
Besuchszeit F visiting hours *pl*
besudeln [bəˈzuːdəln] VT (*Wände*) to smear; (*fig: Namen, Ehre*) to sully
betagt [bəˈtaːkt] ADJ aged
betasten [bəˈtastən] VT to touch, to feel
betätigen [bəˈtɛːtɪgən] VT (*bedienen*) to work, to operate ▸ VR to involve o.s.; **sich politisch ~** to be involved in politics; **sich als etw ~** to work as sth
Betätigung F activity; (*beruflich*) occupation; (*Tech*) operation
betäuben [bəˈtɔʏbən] VT to stun; (*fig: Gewissen*) to still; (*Med*) to anaesthetize (BRIT), to anesthetize (US); **ein betäubender Duft** an overpowering smell
Betäubung F (*Narkose*): **örtliche ~** local anaesthetic (BRIT) *od* anesthetic (US)
Betäubungsmittel NT anaesthetic (BRIT), anesthetic (US)
Bete [ˈbeːtə] (**-, -n**) F: **Rote ~** beetroot (BRIT), beet (US)
beteiligen [bəˈtaɪlɪgən] VR: **sich (an etw** *dat***) ~** to take part (in sth), to participate (in sth); (*an Geschäft: finanziell*) to have a share (in sth) ▸ VT: **jdn (an etw** *dat***) ~** to give sb a share *od* interest (in sth); **sich an den Unkosten ~** to contribute to the expenses
Beteiligung F participation; (*Anteil*) share, interest; (*Besucherzahl*) attendance
Beteiligungsgesellschaft F associated company
beten [ˈbeːtən] VI to pray ▸ VT (*Rosenkranz*) to say
beteuern [bəˈtɔʏərn] VT to assert; (*Unschuld*) to protest; **jdm etw ~** to assure sb of sth
Beteuerung F assertion; (*von Unschuld*) protestation; (*Versicherung*) assurance
Beton [beˈtõː] (**-s, -s**) M concrete
betonen [bəˈtoːnən] VT to stress
betonieren [betoˈniːrən] VT to concrete
Betonmischmaschine F concrete mixer
betont [bəˈtoːnt] ADJ (*Höflichkeit*) emphatic, deliberate; (*Kühle, Sachlichkeit*) pointed
Betonung F stress, emphasis
betören [bəˈtøːrən] VT to beguile
betr. ABK (= *betreffend, betreffs*) re
Betr. ABK = **Betreff**
Betracht [bəˈtraxt] M: **in ~ kommen** to be concerned *od* relevant; **nicht in ~ kommen** to be out of the question; **etw in ~ ziehen** to consider sth; **außer ~ bleiben** not to be considered
betrachten VT to look at; (*fig*) to consider, to look at
Betrachter(in) (**-s, -**) M(F) onlooker
beträchtlich [bəˈtrɛçtlɪç] ADJ considerable
Betrachtung F (*Ansehen*) examination; (*Erwägung*) consideration; **über etw** *akk* **Betrachtungen anstellen** to reflect on *od* contemplate sth
betraf *etc* [bəˈtraːf] VB *siehe* **betreffen**
Betrag [bəˈtraːk] (**-(e)s, Beträge**) M amount, sum; **~ erhalten** (*Comm*) sum received
betragen [bəˈtraːgən] *unreg* VT to amount to ▸ VR to behave
Betragen (**-s**) NT behaviour (BRIT), behavior (US); (*bes in Zeugnis*) conduct
beträgt [bəˈtrɛːkt] VB *siehe* **betragen**
betrat *etc* [bəˈtraːt] VB *siehe* **betreten**
betrauen [bəˈtraʊən] VT: **jdn mit etw ~** to entrust sb with sth
betrauern [bəˈtraʊərn] VT to mourn
beträufeln [bəˈtrɔʏfəln] VT: **den Fisch mit Zitrone ~** to sprinkle lemon juice on the fish
Betreff M: **~: Ihr Schreiben vom ...** re *od* reference your letter of ...
betreffen [bəˈtrɛfən] *unreg* VT to concern, to affect; **was mich betrifft** as for me
betreffend ADJ relevant, in question
betreffs [bəˈtrɛfs] PRÄP +*gen* concerning, regarding
betreiben [bəˈtraɪbən] *unreg* VT (*ausüben*) to practise (BRIT), to practice (US); (*Politik*) to follow; (*Studien*) to pursue; (*vorantreiben*) to push ahead; (*Tech: antreiben*) to drive; **auf jds B~** *akk* **hin** (*form*) at sb's instigation
Betreiberfirma [bəˈtraɪbərfɪrma] F operating company
betreten [bəˈtreːtən] *unreg* VT to enter; (*Bühne etc*) to step onto ▸ ADJ embarrassed; **„B~ verboten"** "keep off/out"
betreuen [bəˈtrɔʏən] VT to look after
Betreuer(in) (**-s, -**) M(F) carer; (*Kinderbetreuer*) child-minder
Betreuung F: **er wurde mit der ~ der Gruppe beauftragt** he was put in charge of the group
betrieb *etc* [bəˈtriːp] VB *siehe* **betreiben**

Betrieb (**-(e)s, -e**) M (*Firma*) firm, concern; (*Anlage*) plant; (*Tätigkeit*) operation; (*Treiben*) bustle; (*Verkehr*) traffic; **außer ~ sein** to be out of order; **in ~ sein** to be in operation; **eine Maschine in/außer ~ setzen** to start a machine up/stop a machine; **eine Maschine/Fabrik in ~ nehmen** to put a machine/factory into operation; **in den Geschäften herrscht großer ~** the shops are very busy; **er hält den ganzen ~ auf** (*umg*) he's holding everything up
betrieben [bə'tri:bən] PP *von* **betreiben**
betrieblich ADJ company *attrib* ▸ ADV (*regeln*) within the company
Betriebs- ZW: **Betriebsanleitung** F operating instructions *pl*; **Betriebsausflug** M firm's outing; **Betriebsausgaben** PL revenue expenditure *sing*; **betriebsbereit** ADJ operational; **betriebseigen** ADJ company *attrib*; **Betriebsergebnis** NT trading *od* operating result; **Betriebserlaubnis** F operating permission/licence (BRIT) *od* license (*US*); **betriebsfähig** ADJ in working order; **Betriebsferien** PL company holidays *pl* (BRIT) *od* vacation *sing* (*US*); **Betriebsführung** F management; **Betriebsgeheimnis** NT trade secret; **Betriebskapital** NT capital employed; **Betriebsklima** NT (working) atmosphere; **Betriebskosten** PL running costs; **Betriebsleitung** F management; **Betriebsrat** M workers' council; **Betriebsrente** F company pension; **betriebssicher** ADJ safe, reliable; **Betriebsstoff** M fuel; **Betriebsstörung** F breakdown; **Betriebssystem** NT (*Comput*) operating system; **Betriebsunfall** M industrial accident; **Betriebswirt** M management expert; **Betriebswirtschaft** F business management
betrifft [bə'trɪft] VB *siehe* **betreffen**
betrinken [bə'trɪŋkən] *unreg* VR to get drunk
betritt [bə'trɪt] VB *siehe* **betreten**
betroffen [bə'trɔfən] PP *von* **betreffen** ▸ ADJ (*bestürzt*) amazed, perplexed; **von etw ~ werden** *od* **sein** to be affected by sth
betrüben [bə'try:bən] VT to grieve
betrübt [bə'try:pt] ADJ sorrowful, grieved
betrug *etc* [bə'tru:k] VB *siehe* **betragen**
Betrug (**-(e)s**) M deception; (*Jur*) fraud
betrügen [bə'try:gən] *unreg* VT to cheat; (*Jur*) to defraud; (*Ehepartner*) to be unfaithful to ▸ VR to deceive o.s.
Betrüger(in) (**-s, -**) M(F) cheat, deceiver
betrügerisch ADJ deceitful; (*Jur*) fraudulent; **in betrügerischer Absicht** with intent to defraud
betrunken [bə'trʊŋkən] ADJ drunk
Betrunkene(r) F(M) drunk
Bett [bɛt] (**-(e)s, -en**) NT bed; **im ~** in bed; **ins** *od* **zu ~ gehen** to go to bed; **Bettbezug** M duvet cover; **Bettdecke** F blanket; (*Daunenbettdecke*) quilt; (*Überwurf*) bedspread
bettelarm ['bɛtəl|arm] ADJ very poor, destitute
Bettelei [bɛtə'laɪ] F begging
Bettelmönch M mendicant *od* begging monk
betteln VI to beg
betten VT to make a bed for
Bett- ZW: **Betthupferl** (SÜDD) NT bedtime sweet; **bettlägerig** ADJ bedridden; **Bettlaken** NT sheet; **Bettlektüre** F bedtime reading
Bettler(in) ['bɛtlər(ɪn)] (**-s, -**) M(F) beggar
Bett- ZW: **Bettnässer** (**-s, -**) M bedwetter; **Bettschwere** (*umg*) F: **die nötige Bettschwere haben/bekommen** to be/get tired enough to sleep; **Betttuch** NT sheet; **Bettvorleger** M bedside rug; **Bettwäsche** F, **Bettzeug** NT bedclothes *pl*, bedding
betucht [bə'tu:xt] (*umg*) ADJ well-to-do
betulich [bə'tu:lɪç] ADJ (*übertrieben besorgt*) fussing *attrib*; (*Redeweise*) twee
betupfen [bə'tʊpfən] VT to dab; (*Med*) to swab
Beugehaft ['bɔʏgəhaft] F (*Jur*) coercive detention
beugen ['bɔʏgən] VT to bend; (*Gram*) to inflect ▸ VR *+dat* (*sich fügen*) to bow (to)
Beule ['bɔʏlə] (**-, -n**) F bump
beunruhigen [bə'|ʊnru:ɪgən] VT to disturb, to alarm ▸ VR to become worried
Beunruhigung F worry, alarm
beurkunden [bə'|u:rkʊndən] VT to attest, to verify
beurlauben [bə'|u:rlaʊbən] VT to give leave *od* holiday to (BRIT), to grant vacation to (*US*); **beurlaubt sein** to have leave of absence; (*suspendiert sein*) to have been relieved of one's duties
beurteilen [bə'|ʊrtaɪlən] VT to judge; (*Buch etc*) to review
Beurteilung F judgement; (*von Buch etc*) review; (*Note*) mark
Beute ['bɔʏtə] (**-**) F booty, loot; (*von Raubtieren etc*) prey
Beutel (**-s, -**) M bag; (*Geldbeutel*) purse; (*Tabaksbeutel*) pouch
bevölkern [bə'fœlkərn] VT to populate
Bevölkerung F population
Bevölkerungs- ZW: **Bevölkerungsexplosion** F population explosion; **Bevölkerungsschicht** F social stratum; **Bevölkerungsstatistik** F vital statistics *pl*
bevollmächtigen [bə'fɔlmɛçtɪgən] VT to authorize
Bevollmächtigte(r) F(M) authorized agent
Bevollmächtigung F authorization
bevor [bə'fo:r] KONJ before; **bevormunden** VT UNTR to dominate; **bevorstehen** *unreg* VI (*Schwierigkeiten*) to lie ahead; (*Gefahr*) to be imminent; **(jdm) bevorstehen** to be in store (for sb); **bevorstehend** ADJ imminent, approaching; **bevorzugen** VT UNTR to prefer; **bevorzugt** [bə'fo:rtsu:kt] ADV: **etw bevorzugt abfertigen** *etc* to give sth priority; **Bevorzugung** F preference
bewachen [bə'vaxən] VT to watch, to guard
bewachsen [bə'vaksən] ADJ overgrown
Bewachung F (*Bewachen*) guarding; (*Leute*) guard, watch
bewaffnen [bə'vafnən] VT to arm

Bewaffnung F (*Vorgang*) arming; (*Ausrüstung*) armament, arms *pl*
bewahren [bəˈvaːrən] VT to keep; **jdn vor jdm/etw ~** to save sb from sb/sth; **(Gott) bewahre!** (*umg*) heaven *od* God forbid!
bewähren [bəˈvɛːrən] VR to prove o.s.; (*Maschine*) to prove its worth
bewahrheiten [bəˈvaːrhaɪtən] VR to come true
bewährt ADJ reliable
Bewährung F (*Jur*) probation; **ein Jahr Gefängnis mit ~** a suspended sentence of one year with probation
Bewährungs- ZW: **Bewährungsfrist** F (period of) probation; **Bewährungshelfer** M probation officer; **Bewährungsprobe** F: **etw einer Bewährungsprobe** *dat* **unterziehen** to put sth to the test
bewaldet [bəˈvaldət] ADJ wooded
bewältigen [bəˈvɛltɪgən] VT to overcome; (*Arbeit*) to finish; (*Portion*) to manage; (*Schwierigkeiten*) to cope with
bewandert [bəˈvandərt] ADJ expert, knowledgeable
Bewandtnis [bəˈvantnɪs] F: **damit hat es folgende ~** the fact of the matter is this
bewarb *etc* [bəˈvarp] VB *siehe* **bewerben**
bewässern [bəˈvɛsərn] VT to irrigate
Bewässerung F irrigation
bewegen [bəˈveːgən] VT, VR to move; **der Preis bewegt sich um die 50 Euro** the price is about 50 euros; **jdn zu etw ~** to induce sb to do sth
Beweggrund M motive
beweglich ADJ movable, mobile; (*flink*) quick
bewegt [bəˈveːkt] ADJ (*Leben*) eventful; (*Meer*) rough; (*ergriffen*) touched
Bewegung F movement, motion; (*innere*) emotion; (*körperlich*) exercise; **sich** *dat* **~ machen** to take exercise
Bewegungs- ZW: **Bewegungsfreiheit** F freedom of movement; (*fig*) freedom of action; **bewegungslos** ADJ motionless; **Bewegungsmelder (-s, -)** M sensor (*which reacts to movement*)
Beweis [bəˈvaɪs] **(-es, -e)** M proof; (*Zeichen*) sign; **Beweisaufnahme** F (*Jur*) taking *od* hearing of evidence; **beweisbar** ADJ provable
beweisen *unreg* VT to prove; (*zeigen*) to show; **was zu ~ war** QED
Beweis- ZW: **Beweisführung** F reasoning; (*Jur*) presentation of one's case; **Beweiskraft** F weight, conclusiveness; **beweiskräftig** ADJ convincing, conclusive; **Beweislast** F (*Jur*) onus, burden of proof; **Beweismittel** NT evidence; **Beweisnot** F (*Jur*) lack of evidence; **Beweisstück** NT exhibit
bewenden [bəˈvɛndən] VI: **etw dabei ~ lassen** to leave sth at that
bewerben [bəˈvɛrbən] *unreg* VR: **sich ~ (um)** to apply (for)
Bewerber(in) (-s, -) M(F) applicant
Bewerbung F application
Bewerbungsfrist F application deadline
Bewerbungsmappe F, **Bewerbungsunterlagen** PL application documents *pl*
bewerkstelligen [bəˈvɛrkʃtɛlɪgən] VT to manage, to accomplish
bewerten [bəˈveːrtən] VT to assess
bewies *etc* [bəˈviːs] VB *siehe* **beweisen**
bewiesen [bəˈviːzən] PP *von* **beweisen**
bewilligen [bəˈvɪlɪgən] VT to grant, to allow
Bewilligung F granting
bewirbt [bəˈvɪrpt] VB *siehe* **bewerben**
bewirken [bəˈvɪrkən] VT to cause, to bring about
bewirten [bəˈvɪrtən] VT to entertain
bewirtschaften [bəˈvɪrtʃaftən] VT to manage
Bewirtung F hospitality; **die ~ so vieler Gäste** catering for so many guests
bewog *etc* [bəˈvoːk] VB *siehe* **bewegen**
bewogen [bəˈvoːgən] PP *von* **bewegen**
bewohnbar ADJ inhabitable
bewohnen [bəˈvoːnən] VT to inhabit, to live in
Bewohner(in) (-s, -) M(F) inhabitant; (*von Haus*) resident
bewölkt [bəˈvœlkt] ADJ cloudy, overcast
Bewölkung F clouds *pl*
Bewölkungsauflockerung F break-up of the cloud
beworben [bəˈvɔrbən] PP *von* **bewerben**
Bewunderer(in) (-s, -) M(F) admirer
bewundern [bəˈvʊndərn] VT to admire
bewundernswert ADJ admirable, wonderful
Bewunderung F admiration
bewusst [bəˈvʊst] ADJ conscious; (*absichtlich*) deliberate; **jdm etw ~ machen** to make sb conscious of sth; **sich** *dat* **etw ~ machen** to realize sth; **sich** *dat* **einer Sache** *gen* **~ sein** to be aware of sth; **bewusstlos** ADJ unconscious; **Bewusstlosigkeit** F unconsciousness; **bis zur Bewusstlosigkeit** (*umg*) ad nauseam; **Bewusstsein** NT consciousness; **bei Bewusstsein** conscious; **im Bewusstsein, dass ...** in the knowledge that ...
Bewusstseins- ZW: **Bewusstseinsbildung** F (*Pol*) shaping of political ideas; **bewusstseinserweiternd** ADJ: **bewusstseinserweiternde Drogen** mind-expanding drugs; **Bewusstseinserweiterung** F consciousness raising
bez. ABK (= *bezüglich*) re.
Bez. ABK = **Bezirk**
bezahlen [bəˈtsaːlən] VT to pay (for); **es macht sich bezahlt** it will pay
Bezahlfernsehen NT pay TV
Bezahlschranke F (*Comput*) paywall
Bezahlung F payment; **ohne/gegen** *od* **für ~** without/for payment
bezaubern [bəˈtsaʊbərn] VT to enchant, to charm
bezeichnen [bəˈtsaɪçnən] VT (*kennzeichnen*) to mark; (*nennen*) to call; (*beschreiben*) to describe; (*zeigen*) to show, to indicate
bezeichnend ADJ: **~ (für)** characteristic (of), typical (of)

Bezeichnung F (*Zeichen*) mark, sign; (*Beschreibung*) description; (*Ausdruck*) expression, term
bezeugen [bəˈtsɔʏgən] VT to testify to
bezichtigen [bəˈtsɪçtɪgən] VT +*gen* to accuse (of)
Bezichtigung F accusation
beziehen [bəˈtsiːən] *unreg* VT (*mit Überzug*) to cover; (*Haus, Position*) to move into; (*Standpunkt*) to take up; (*erhalten*) to receive; (*Zeitung*) to subscribe to, to take ▸ VR (*Himmel*) to cloud over; **die Betten frisch ~** to change the beds; **etw auf jdn/etw ~** to relate sth to sb/sth; **sich ~ auf** +*akk* to refer to
Beziehung F (*Verbindung*) connection; (*Zusammenhang*) relation; (*Verhältnis*) relationship; (*Hinsicht*) respect; **diplomatische Beziehungen** diplomatic relations; **seine Beziehungen spielen lassen** to pull strings; **in jeder ~** in every respect; **Beziehungen haben** (*vorteilhaft*) to have connections *od* contacts
Beziehungskiste (*umg*) F relationship
beziehungsweise ADV or; (*genauer gesagt*) that is, or rather; (*im anderen Fall*) and ... respectively
beziffern [bəˈtsɪfərn] VT (*angeben*): **~ auf** +*akk od* **mit** to estimate at
Bezirk [bəˈtsɪrk] (**-(e)s, -e**) M district
bezirzen [bəˈtsɪrtsən] (*umg*) VT to bewitch
bezogen [bəˈtsoːgən] PP *von* **beziehen**
Bezogene(r) [bəˈtsoːgənə(r)] F(M) (*von Scheck etc*) drawee
Bezug [bəˈtsuːk] (**-(e)s, Bezüge**) M (*Hülle*) covering; (*Comm*) ordering; (*Gehalt*) income, salary; (*Beziehung*): **~ (zu)** relationship (to); **in ~ auf** +*akk* with reference to; **mit** *od* **unter ~ auf** +*akk* regarding; (*form*) with reference to; **~ nehmen auf** +*akk* to refer to
bezüglich [bəˈtsyːklɪç] PRÄP +*gen* concerning, referring to ▸ ADJ concerning; (*Gram*) relative
Bezugnahme F: **~ (auf** +*akk*) reference (to)
Bezugs- ZW: **Bezugsperson** F: **die wichtigste Bezugsperson des Kleinkindes** the person to whom the small child relates most closely; **Bezugspreis** M retail price; **Bezugsquelle** F source of supply
bezuschussen [bəˈtsuːʃʊsən] VT to subsidize
bezwecken [bəˈtsvɛkən] VT to aim at
bezweifeln [bəˈtsvaɪfəln] VT to doubt
bezwingen [bəˈtsvɪŋən] *unreg* VT to conquer; (*Feind*) to defeat, to overcome
bezwungen [bəˈtsvʊŋən] PP *von* **bezwingen**
Bf. ABK = **Bahnhof**; **Brief**
BfA (-) F ABK (= *Bundesversicherungsanstalt für Angestellte*) *Federal insurance company for employees*
BfV (-) NT ABK (= *Bundesamt für Verfassungsschutz*) *Federal Office for Protection of the Constitution*
BG (-) F ABK (= *Berufsgenossenschaft*) *professional association*
BGB (-) NT ABK (= *Bürgerliches Gesetzbuch*) *siehe* **bürgerlich**
BGH (-) M ABK (= *Bundesgerichtshof*) *Federal Supreme Court*
BGS (-) M ABK = **Bundesgrenzschutz**
BH (**-s, -(s)**) M ABK (= *Büstenhalter*) bra
Bhf. ABK = **Bahnhof**
BI F ABK = **Bürgerinitiative**
Biathlon [ˈbiːatlɔn] (**-s, -s**) NT biathlon
bibbern [ˈbɪbərn] (*umg*) VI (*vor Kälte*) to shiver
Bibel [ˈbiːbəl] (**-, -n**) F Bible
bibelfest ADJ well versed in the Bible
Biber [ˈbiːbər] (**-s, -**) M beaver
Biberbettuch NT flannelette sheet
Bibliografie [bibliograˈfiː] F bibliography
Bibliothek [biblioˈteːk] (**-, -en**) F (*auch Comput*) library
Bibliothekar(in) [biblioteˈkaːr(ɪn)] (**-s, -e**) M(F) librarian
biblisch [ˈbiːblɪʃ] ADJ biblical
bieder [ˈbiːdər] ADJ upright, worthy; (*pej*) conventional; (*Kleid etc*) plain
Biedermann (**-(e)s**, *pl* **-männer**) (*pej*) M (*geh*) petty bourgeois
biegbar [ˈbiːkbaːr] ADJ flexible
Biege F: **die ~ machen** (*umg*) to buzz off, to split
biegen [ˈbiːgən] *unreg* VT, VR to bend ▸ VI to turn; **sich vor Lachen ~** (*fig*) to double up with laughter; **auf B~ oder Brechen** (*umg*) by hook or by crook
biegsam [ˈbiːkzaːm] ADJ supple
Biegung F bend, curve
Biene [ˈbiːnə] (**-, -n**) F bee; (*veraltet: umg: Mädchen*) bird (BRIT), chick (*bes US*)
Bienen- ZW: **Bienenhonig** M honey; **Bienenkorb** M beehive; **Bienenstich** M (*Koch*) *sugar-and-almond coated cake filled with custard or cream*; **Bienenstock** M beehive; **Bienenwachs** NT beeswax
Bier [biːr] (**-(e)s, -e**) NT beer; **zwei ~, bitte!** two beers, please; **Bierbauch** (*umg*) M beer belly; **Bierbrauer** M brewer; **Bierdeckel** M beer mat; **Bierfilz** M beer mat; **Biergarten** M beer garden; **Bierkrug** M beer mug; **Bierschinken** M ham sausage; **Bierseidel** NT beer mug; **Bierwurst** F ham sausage; **Bierzelt** NT beer tent
Biest [biːst] (**-(e)s, -er**) (*pej, umg*) NT (*Mensch*) (little) wretch; (*Frau*) bitch (*umg!*)
biestig ADJ beastly
bieten [ˈbiːtən] *unreg* VT to offer; (*bei Versteigerung*) to bid ▸ VR (*Gelegenheit*): **sich jdm ~** to present itself to sb; **sich** *dat* **etw ~ lassen** to put up with sth
Bigamie [bigaˈmiː] F bigamy
Bikini [biˈkiːni] (**-s, -s**) M bikini
Bilanz [biˈlants] F balance; (*fig*) outcome; **eine ~ aufstellen** to draw up a balance sheet; **~ ziehen (aus)** to take stock (of); **Bilanzprüfer** M auditor
bilateral [ˈbiːlateraːl] ADJ bilateral; **bilateraler Handel** bilateral trade; **bilaterales Abkommen** bilateral agreement
Bild [bɪlt] (**-(e)s, -er**) NT (*lit, fig*) picture; (*Foto*) photo; (*Spiegelbild*) reflection; (*fig: Vorstellung*) image, picture; **ein ~ machen** to take a photo *od* picture; **im Bilde sein (über** +*akk*) to be in the picture (about); **Bildauflösung** F (*TV*,

Comput) resolution; **Bildband** M illustrated book; **Bildbericht** M pictorial report; **Bildbeschreibung** F (*Sch*) description of a picture; **Bilddatei** F picture file

bilden ['bɪldən] VT to form; (*erziehen*) to educate; (*ausmachen*) to constitute ▸ VR to arise; (*durch Lesen etc*) to improve one's mind; (*erziehen*) to educate o.s.

bildend ADJ: **die bildende Kunst** art

Bilderbuch NT picture book

Bilderrahmen M picture frame

Bild- zW: **Bildfläche** F screen; (*fig*) scene; **von der Bildfläche verschwinden** (*fig: umg*) to disappear (from the scene); **bildhaft** ADJ (*Sprache*) vivid; **Bildhauer** M sculptor; **bildhübsch** ADJ lovely, pretty as a picture; **bildlich** ADJ figurative; **sich** *dat* **etw bildlich vorstellen** to picture sth in one's mind's eye

Bildnis ['bɪltnɪs] NT (*liter*) portrait

Bild- zW: **Bildplatte** F videodisc; **Bildröhre** F (*TV*) cathode ray tube; **Bildschirm** M (*TV, Comput*) screen; **Bildschirmgerät** NT (*Comput*) visual display unit, VDU; **Bildschirmschoner** (**-s, -**) M (*Comput*) screen saver; **Bildschirmtext** M teletext, ≈ Ceefax®, ≈ Oracle®; **bildschön** ADJ lovely; **Bildtelefon** NT videophone

Bildung ['bɪldʊŋ] F formation; (*Wissen, Benehmen*) education

Bildungs- zW: **Bildungsgang** M school (and university/college) career; **Bildungsgut** NT cultural heritage; **Bildungslücke** F gap in one's education; **Bildungspolitik** F educational policy; **Bildungsroman** M (*Liter*) Bildungsroman, *novel relating hero's intellectual/spiritual development*; **Bildungsurlaub** M educational holiday; **Bildungsweg** M: **auf dem zweiten Bildungsweg** through night school/the Open University *etc*; **Bildungswesen** NT education system

Bildweite F (*Phot*) distance

Bildzuschrift F reply enclosing photograph

Billard ['bɪljart] (**-s, -e**) NT billiards *sing*; **Billardball** M billiard ball; **Billardkugel** F billiard ball

billig ['bɪlɪç] ADJ cheap; (*gerecht*) fair, reasonable; **billige Handelsflagge** flag of convenience; **billiges Geld** cheap/easy money

billigen ['bɪlɪgən] VT to approve of; **etw stillschweigend ~** to condone sth

billigerweise ADV (*veraltet*) in all fairness, reasonably

Billig- zW: **Billigflieger** M budget *od* low-cost airline; **Billigflug** M cheap flight; **Billigladen** M discount store; **Billigpreis** M low price; **Billigprodukt** NT low-price product

Billigung F approval

Billion [bɪli'o:n] F billion (BRIT), trillion (US)

bimmeln ['bɪməln] VI to tinkle

Bimsstein ['bɪmsʃtaɪn] M pumice stone

bin [bɪn] VB *siehe* **sein**

binär [bi'nɛ:r] ADJ binary; **Binärzahl** F binary number

Binde ['bɪndə] (**-, -n**) F bandage; (*Armbinde*) band; (*Med*) sanitary towel (BRIT) *od* napkin (US); **sich** *dat* **einen hinter die ~ gießen** *od* **kippen** (*umg*) to put a few drinks away

Binde- zW: **Bindeglied** NT connecting link; **Bindehautentzündung** F conjunctivitis; **Bindemittel** NT binder

binden *unreg* VT to bind, to tie ▸ VR (*sich verpflichten*): **sich ~ (an** *+akk*) to commit o.s. (to)

bindend ADJ binding; (*Zusage*) definite; **~ für** binding on

Bindestrich M hyphen

Bindewort NT conjunction

Bindfaden M string; **es regnet Bindfäden** (*umg*) it's sheeting down

Bindung F bond, tie; (*Ski*) binding

binnen ['bɪnən] PRÄP (*+dat od gen*) within; **Binnenhafen** M inland harbour (BRIT) *od* harbor (US); **Binnenhandel** M internal trade; **Binnenmarkt** M home market; **Europäischer Binnenmarkt** single European market; **Binnennachfrage** F domestic demand

Binse ['bɪnzə] (**-, -n**) F rush, reed; **in die Binsen gehen** (*fig: umg*) to be a wash-out

Binsenwahrheit F truism

Bio- [bio-] zW bio-, organic

Biodiesel ['biodi:zəl] (**--s, -**) M biodiesel

Biografie [biogra'fi:] F biography

Biokraftstoff ['biokraftʃtɔf] M biofuel

Bioladen ['biola:dən] M health food shop (BRIT) *od* store (US)

> A **Bioladen** is a shop which specializes in selling environmentally-friendly products such as phosphate-free washing powders, recycled paper and organically-grown vegetables.

Biologe [bio'lo:gə] (**-n, -n**) M biologist

Biologie [biolo'gi:] F biology

Biologin F biologist

biologisch [bio'lo:gɪʃ] ADJ biological; (*Anbau*) organic; **biologische Vielfalt** biodiversity; **biologische Uhr** biological clock

Bio- [bio-] zW: **Biosphäre** F biosphere; **Biotechnik** [bio'tɛçnɪk] F biotechnology; **Bioterrorismus** M bioterrorism; **Biotreibstoff** ['bi:otraipʃtɔf] M biofuel

birgt [bɪrkt] VB *siehe* **bergen**

Birke ['bɪrkə] (**-, -n**) F birch

Birma ['bɪrma] (**-s**) NT Burma

Birnbaum M pear tree

Birne ['bɪrnə] (**-, -n**) F pear; (*Elek*) (light) bulb

birst [bɪrst] VB *siehe* **bersten**

SCHLÜSSELWORT

bis [bɪs] PRÄP *+akk*, ADV **1** (*zeitlich*) till, until; (*bis spätestens*) by; **Sie haben bis Dienstag Zeit** you have until *od* till Tuesday; **bis zum Wochenende** up to *od* until the weekend; (*spätestens*) by the weekend; **bis Dienstag muss es fertig sein** it must be ready by Tuesday; **bis wann ist das fertig?** when will that be finished?; **bis auf Weiteres** until further notice; **bis in die Nacht** into the

night; **bis bald!/gleich!** see you later/soon
2 (*räumlich*) (up) to; **ich fahre bis Köln** I'm going as far as Cologne; **bis an unser Grundstück** (right *od* up) to our plot; **bis hierher** this far; **bis zur Straße kommen** to get as far as the road
3 (*bei Zahlen, Angaben*) up to; **bis zu** up to; **Gefängnis bis zu 8 Jahren** a maximum of 8 years' imprisonment
4: **bis auf etw** *akk* (*außer*) except sth; (*einschließlich*) including sth
▸ KONJ **1** (*mit Zahlen*) to; **10 bis 20** 10 to 20
2 (*zeitlich*) till, until; **bis es dunkel wird** till *od* until it gets dark; **von ... bis ...** from ... to ...

Bisamratte ['bi:zamratə] F muskrat (beaver)
Bischof ['bɪʃɔf] (**-s, Bischöfe**) M bishop
bischöflich ['bɪʃø:flɪç] ADJ episcopal
bisexuell [bizɛksu'ɛl] ADJ bisexual
bisher [bɪs'he:r] ADV till now, hitherto
bisherig [bɪs'he:rɪç] ADJ till now
Biskaya [bɪs'ka:ya] F: **Golf von ~** Bay of Biscay
Biskuit [bɪs'kvi:t] (**-(e)s, -s** *od* **-e**) M OD NT biscuit; **Biskuitgebäck** NT sponge cake(s); **Biskuitteig** M sponge mixture
bislang [bɪs'laŋ] ADV hitherto
biss*etc* [bɪs] VB *siehe* **beißen**
Biss (**-es, -e**) M bite
bisschen ['bɪsçən] ADJ: **ein ~** a bit of ▸ ADV: **ein ~** a bit; **kein ~** not at all; **ein ~ Salz/Liebe** a bit of salt/love; **ich habe kein ~ Hunger** I'm not a bit hungry
Bissen ['bɪsən] (**-s, -**) M bite, morsel; **sich** *dat* **jeden ~ vom** *od* **am Munde absparen** to watch every penny one spends
bissig ['bɪsɪç] ADJ (*Hund*) snappy; (*gefährlich*) vicious; (*Bemerkung*) cutting, biting; **„Vorsicht, bissiger Hund"** "beware of the dog"
bist [bɪst] VB *siehe* **sein**
Bistum ['bɪstu:m] NT bishopric
bisweilen [bɪs'vaɪlən] ADV at times, occasionally
Bit [bɪt] (**-(s), -(s)**) NT (*Comput*) bit
Bittbrief M petition
bitte INTERJ please; (*als Antwort auf Dank*) you're welcome; **wie ~?** (I beg your) pardon?; **~ schön!** it was a pleasure; **~ schön?** (*in Geschäft*) can I help you?; **na ~!** there you are!
Bitte ['bɪtə] (**-, -n**) F request; **auf seine ~ hin** at his request
bitten*unreg* VT to ask ▸ VI (*einladen*): **ich lasse ~** would you ask him/her *etc* to come in now?; **~ um** to ask for; **aber ich bitte dich!** not at all; **ich bitte darum** (*form*) if you wouldn't mind; **ich muss doch (sehr) ~!** well I must say!
bittend ADJ pleading, imploring
bitter ['bɪtər] ADJ bitter; (*Schokolade*) plain; **etw ~ nötig haben** to be in dire need of sth; **bitterböse** ADJ very angry; **bitterernst** ADJ: **damit ist es mir bitterernst** I am deadly serious *od* in deadly earnest; **Bitterkeit** F bitterness; **bitterlich** ADJ bitter ▸ ADV bitterly
Bittsteller(in) (**-s, -**) M(F) petitioner
Biwak ['bi:vak] (**-s, -s** *od* **-e**) NT bivouac

Bj. ABK = **Baujahr**
Blabla [bla:'bla:] (**-s**) (*umg*) NT waffle
blähen ['blɛ:ən] VT, VR to swell, to blow out ▸ VI (*Speisen*) to cause flatulence *od* wind
Blähungen PL (*Med*) wind *sing*
blamabel [bla'ma:bəl] ADJ disgraceful
Blamage [bla'ma:ʒə] (**-, -n**) F disgrace
blamieren [bla'mi:rən] VR to make a fool of o.s., to disgrace o.s. ▸ VT to let down, to disgrace
blank [blaŋk] ADJ bright; (*unbedeckt*) bare; (*sauber*) clean, polished; (*umg: ohne Geld*) broke; (*offensichtlich*) blatant
blanko ['blaŋko] ADV blank; **Blankoscheck** M blank cheque (BRIT) *od* check (US); **Blankovollmacht** F carte blanche
Bläschen ['blɛ:sçən] NT bubble; (*Med*) small blister
Blase ['bla:zə] (**-, -n**) F bubble; (*Med*) blister; (*Anat*) bladder
Blasebalg M bellows *pl*
blasen*unreg* VT, VI to blow; **zum Aufbruch ~** (*fig*) to say it's time to go
Blasenentzündung F cystitis
Bläser(in) ['blɛ:zər(ɪn)] (**-s, -**) M(F) (*Mus*) wind player; **die ~** the wind (section)
blasiert [bla'zi:rt] (*pej*) ADJ (*geh*) blasé
Blas- ZW: **Blasinstrument** NT wind instrument; **Blaskapelle** F brass band; **Blasmusik** F brass band music
blass [blas] ADJ pale; (*Ausdruck*) weak, insipid; (*fig: Ahnung, Vorstellung*) faint, vague; **~ vor Neid werden** to go green with envy
Blässe ['blɛsə] (**-**) F paleness, pallor
Blatt [blat] (**-(e)s, Blätter**) NT leaf; (*von Papier*) sheet; (*Zeitung*) newspaper; (*Karten*) hand; **vom ~ singen/spielen** to sight-read; **kein ~ vor den Mund nehmen** not to mince one's words
blättern ['blɛtərn] VI: **in etw** *dat* **~** to leaf through sth
Blätterteig M flaky *od* puff pastry
Blattlaus F greenfly, aphid
blau [blaʊ] ADJ blue; (*umg*) drunk, stoned; (*Koch*) boiled; (*Auge*) black; **blauer Fleck** bruise; **mit einem blauen Auge davonkommen** (*fig*) to get off lightly; **blauer Brief** (*Sch*) *letter telling parents a child may have to repeat a year*; **er wird sein blaues Wunder erleben** (*umg*) he won't know what's hit him; **blauäugig** ADJ blue-eyed; **Blaubeere** F bilberry
Blaue NT: **Fahrt ins ~** mystery tour; **das ~ vom Himmel (herunter) lügen** (*umg*) to tell a pack of lies
blau- ZW: **Blauhelm** (*umg*) M UN Soldier; **Blaukraut** NT red cabbage; **Blaulicht** NT flashing blue light; **blaumachen** (*umg*) VI to skive off work; **Blaupause** F blueprint; **Blausäure** F prussic acid; **Blaustrumpf** M (*fig*) bluestocking
Blech [blɛç] (**-(e)s, -e**) NT tin, sheet metal; (*Backblech*) baking tray; **~ reden** (*umg*) to talk rubbish *od* nonsense; **Blechbläser** PL the brass (section); **Blechbüchse** F tin, can; **Blechdose** F tin, can

blechen (*umg*) VT, VI to pay
Blechschaden M (*Aut*) damage to bodywork
Blechtrommel F tin drum
blecken ['blɛkən] VT: **die Zähne ~** to bare *od* show one's teeth
Blei [blaɪ] (**-(e)s, -e**) NT lead
Bleibe (**-, -n**) F roof over one's head
bleiben *unreg* VI to stay, to remain; **bitte, ~ Sie doch sitzen** please don't get up; **wo bleibst du so lange?** (*umg*) what's keeping you?; **das bleibt unter uns** (*fig*) that's (just) between ourselves; **~ lassen** (*aufgeben*) to give up; **etw ~ lassen** (*unterlassen*) to give sth a miss
bleich [blaɪç] ADJ faded, pale; **bleichen** VT to bleach; **Bleichgesicht** (*umg*) NT (*blasser Mensch*) pasty-face
bleiern ADJ leaden
Blei- ZW: **bleifrei** ADJ (*Benzin*) unleaded; **Bleigießen** NT *New Year's Eve fortune-telling using lead shapes*; **bleihaltig** ADJ (*Benzin*) leaded; **bleihaltig sein** to contain lead; **Bleistift** M pencil; **Bleistiftabsatz** M stiletto heel (BRIT), spike heel (US); **Bleistiftspitzer** M pencil sharpener; **Bleivergiftung** F lead poisoning
Blende ['blɛndə] (**-, -n**) F (*Phot*) aperture; (*: Einstellungsposition*) f-stop
blenden VT to blind, to dazzle; (*fig*) to hoodwink
blendend (*umg*) ADJ grand; **~ aussehen** to look smashing
Blender (**-s, -**) M con-man
blendfrei ['blɛntfraɪ] ADJ (*Glas*) non-reflective
Blick [blɪk] (**-(e)s, -e**) M (*kurz*) glance, glimpse; (*Anschauen*) look, gaze; (*Aussicht*) view; **Liebe auf den ersten ~** love at first sight; **den ~ senken** to look down; **den bösen ~ haben** to have the evil eye; **einen (guten) ~ für etw haben** to have an eye for sth; **mit einem ~** at a glance
blicken VI to look; **das lässt tief ~** that's very revealing; **sich ~ lassen** to put in an appearance
Blick- ZW: **Blickfang** M eye-catcher; **Blickfeld** NT range of vision (*auch fig*); **Blickkontakt** M visual contact; **Blickpunkt** M: **im Blickpunkt der Öffentlichkeit stehen** to be in the public eye
blieb *etc* [bli:p] VB *siehe* **bleiben**
blies *etc* [bli:s] VB *siehe* **blasen**
blind [blɪnt] ADJ blind; (*Glas etc*) dull; (*Alarm*) false; **blinder Passagier** stowaway
Blinddarm M appendix; **Blinddarmentzündung** F appendicitis
Blindekuh ['blɪndəku:] F: **~ spielen** to play blind man's buff
Blindenhund M guide dog
Blindenschrift F braille
Blind- ZW: **Blindgänger** M (*Mil, fig*) dud; **Blindheit** F blindness; **mit Blindheit geschlagen sein** (*fig*) to be blind; **blindlings** ADV blindly; **Blindschleiche** F slow worm; **blindschreiben** *unreg* VI to touch-type
blinken ['blɪŋkən] VI to twinkle, to sparkle; (*Licht*) to flash, to signal; (*Aut*) to indicate ▸ VT to flash, to signal
Blinker (**-s, -**) M (*Aut*) indicator
Blinklicht NT (*Aut*) indicator
blinzeln ['blɪntsəln] VI to blink, to wink
Blitz [blɪts] (**-es, -e**) M (flash of) lightning; (*Phot*) flash; **wie ein ~ aus heiterem Himmel** (*fig*) like a bolt from the blue; **Blitzableiter** M lightning conductor; (*fig*) vent *od* safety valve for feelings; **blitzen** VI (*aufleuchten*) to glint, to shine; **es blitzt** (*Met*) there's a flash of lightning; **Blitzgerät** NT (*Phot*) flash(gun); **Blitzlicht** NT flashlight; **blitzsauber** ADJ spick and span; **blitzschnell** ADJ, ADV as quick as a flash; **Blitzwürfel** M (*Phot*) flashcube
Block [blɔk] (**-(e)s, Blöcke**) M (*lit, fig*) block; (*von Papier*) pad; (*Pol: Staatenblock*) bloc; (*Fraktion*) faction
Blockade [blɔ'ka:də] (**-, -n**) F blockade
Block- ZW: **Blockbuchstabe** M block letter *od* capital; **Blockflöte** F recorder; **blockfrei** ADJ (*Pol*) non-aligned; **Blockhaus** NT log cabin; **Blockhütte** F log cabin
blockieren [blɔ'ki:rən] VT to block ▸ VI (*Räder*) to jam
Block- ZW: **Blockschokolade** F cooking chocolate; **Blockschrift** F block letters *pl*; **Blockstunde** F double period
blöd [blø:t] ADJ silly, stupid
blödeln ['blø:dəln] (*umg*) VI to fool around
Blödheit F stupidity
Blödian ['blø:dian] (**-(e)s, -e**) (*umg*) M idiot
blöd- ZW: **Blödmann** (**-(e)s,** *pl* **-männer**) (*umg*) M idiot; **Blödsinn** M nonsense; **blödsinnig** ADJ silly, idiotic
Blog (**-s, -s**) NT (*Comput*) blog; **bloggen** VI to blog; **Blogging** NT blogging
Blogosphäre ['blɔgosfɛ:rə] (**--, --n**) F blogosphere
blöken ['blø:kən] VI (*Schaf*) to bleat
blond [blɔnt] ADJ blond; (*Frau*) blonde
Blondine [blɔn'di:nə] F blonde

SCHLÜSSELWORT

bloß [blo:s] ADJ **1** (*unbedeckt*) bare; (*nackt*) naked; **mit der bloßen Hand** with one's bare hand; **mit bloßem Auge** with the naked eye
2 (*alleinig: nur*) mere; **der bloße Gedanke** the very thought; **bloßer Neid** sheer envy
▸ ADV only, merely; **lass das bloß!** just don't do that!; **wie ist das bloß passiert?** how on earth did that happen?

Blöße ['blø:sə] (**-, -n**) F bareness; (*Nacktheit*) nakedness; (*fig*) weakness; **sich** *dat* **eine ~ geben** (*fig*) to lay o.s. open to attack
bloßlegen VT to expose
bloßstellen VT to show up
blühen ['bly:ən] VI (*lit*) to bloom, to be in bloom; (*fig*) to flourish; (*umg: bevorstehen*): **(jdm) ~** to be in store (for sb)
blühend ADJ: **wie das blühende Leben aussehen** to look the very picture of health

Blume ['blu:mə] (**-, -n**) F flower; (*von Wein*) bouquet; **jdm etw durch die ~ sagen** to say sth in a roundabout way to sb

Blumen- ZW: **Blumenbeet** NT flower bed; **Blumengeschäft** NT flower shop, florist's; **Blumenkasten** M window box; **Blumenkohl** M cauliflower; **Blumenstrauß** M bouquet, bunch of flowers; **Blumentopf** M flowerpot; **Blumenzwiebel** F bulb

Bluse ['blu:zə] (**-, -n**) F blouse

Blut [blu:t] (**-(e)s**) NT (*lit, fig*) blood; **(nur) ruhig ~** keep your shirt on (*umg*); **jdn/sich bis aufs ~ bekämpfen** to fight sb/fight bitterly; **~ stillend** styptic; **blutarm** ADJ anaemic (BRIT), anemic (US); (*fig*) penniless; **Blutbahn** F bloodstream; **Blutbank** F blood bank; **blutbefleckt** ADJ bloodstained; **Blutbild** NT blood count; **Blutbuche** F copper beech; **Blutdruck** M blood pressure

Blüte ['bly:tə] (**-, -n**) F blossom; (*fig*) prime

Blutegel ['blu:tle:gəl] M leech

bluten VI to bleed

Blütenstaub M pollen

Bluter (**-s, -**) M (*Med*) haemophiliac (BRIT), hemophiliac (US)

Bluterguss M haemorrhage (BRIT), hemorrhage (US); (*auf Haut*) bruise

Blütezeit F flowering period; (*fig*) prime

Blutgerinnsel NT blood clot

Blutgruppe F blood group

blutig ADJ bloody; (*umg: Anfänger*) absolute; (*: Ernst*) deadly; **blutjung** ADJ very young

Blut- ZW: **Blutkonserve** F unit *od* pint of stored blood; **Blutkörperchen** NT blood corpuscle; **Blutprobe** F blood sample; **blutrünstig** ADJ bloodthirsty; **Blutschande** F incest; **Blutsenkung** F (*Med*): **eine Blutsenkung machen** to test the sedimentation rate of the blood; **Blutspender** M blood donor; **blutstillend** ADJ styptic; **Blutsturz** M haemorrhage (BRIT), hemorrhage (US)

blutsverwandt ADJ related by blood

Bluttransfusion F, **Blutübertragung** F blood transfusion

Blutung F bleeding, haemorrhage (BRIT), hemorrhage (US)

Blut- ZW: **blutunterlaufen** ADJ suffused with blood; (*Augen*) bloodshot; **Blutvergießen** NT bloodshed; **Blutvergiftung** F blood poisoning; **Blutwurst** F black pudding; **Blutzuckerspiegel** M blood sugar level

BLZ ABK = **Bankleitzahl**

BMX-Rad NT BMX

BND (**-s, -**) M ABK = **Bundesnachrichtendienst**

Bö (**-, -en**) F squall

Boccia ['bɔtʃa] NT OD F bowls *sing*

Bock [bɔk] (**-(e)s, Böcke**) M buck, ram; (*Gestell*) trestle, support; (*Sport*) buck; **alter ~** (*umg*) old goat; **den ~ zum Gärtner machen** (*fig*) to choose the worst possible person for the job; **einen ~ schießen** (*fig: umg*) to (make a) boob; **~ haben, etw zu tun** (*umg: Lust*) to fancy doing sth

Bockbier NT bock (beer) (*type of strong beer*)

bocken ['bɔkən] (*umg*) VI (*Auto, Mensch*) to play up

Bocksbeutel M *wide, rounded (dumpy) bottle containing Franconian wine*

Bockshorn NT: **sich von jdm ins ~ jagen lassen** to let sb upset one

Bocksprung M leapfrog; (*Sport*) vault

Bockwurst F bockwurst (*large frankfurter*)

Boden ['bo:dən] (**-s, Böden**) M ground; (*Fußboden*) floor; (*Meeresboden, Fassboden*) bottom; (*Speicher*) attic; **den ~ unter den Füßen verlieren** (*lit*) to lose one's footing; (*fig: in Diskussion*) to get out of one's depth; **ich hätte (vor Scham) im ~ versinken können** (*fig*) I was so ashamed, I wished the ground would swallow me up; **am ~ zerstört sein** (*umg*) to be shattered; **etw aus dem ~ stampfen** (*fig*) to conjure sth up out of nothing; (*Häuser*) to build overnight; **auf dem ~ der Tatsachen bleiben** (*fig: Grundlage*) to stick to the facts; **zu ~ fallen** to fall to the ground; **festen ~ unter den Füßen haben** to be on firm ground, to be on terra firma; **Bodenkontrolle** F (*Raumfahrt*) ground control; **bodenlos** ADJ bottomless; (*umg*) incredible; **Bodenpersonal** NT (*Aviat*) ground personnel *pl*, ground staff; **Bodensatz** M dregs *pl*, sediment; **Bodenschätze** PL mineral wealth *sing*

Bodensee ['bo:dənze:] M: **der ~** Lake Constance

Bodenturnen NT floor exercises *pl*

Böe (**-, -n**) F squall

bog *etc* [bo:k] VB *siehe* **biegen**

Bogen ['bo:gən] (**-s, -**) M (*Biegung*) curve; (*Archit*) arch; (*Waffe, Mus*) bow; (*Papier*) sheet; **den ~ heraushaben** (*umg*) to have got the hang of it; **einen großen ~ um jdn/etw machen** (*meiden*) to give sb/sth a wide berth; **jdn in hohem ~ hinauswerfen** (*umg*) to fling sb out; **Bogengang** M arcade; **Bogenschütze** M archer

Bohle ['bo:lə] (**-, -n**) F plank

Böhme ['bø:mə] (**-n, -n**) M Bohemian

Böhmen (**-s**) NT Bohemia

Böhmin F Bohemian woman

böhmisch ['bø:mɪʃ] ADJ Bohemian; **das sind für mich böhmische Dörfer** (*umg*) that's all Greek to me

Bohne ['bo:nə] (**-, -n**) F bean; **blaue ~** (*umg*) bullet; **nicht die ~** not one little bit

Bohnen- ZW: **Bohnenkaffee** M real coffee; **Bohnensprosse** F bean sprout; **Bohnenstange** F (*fig: umg*) beanpole; **Bohnenstroh** NT: **dumm wie Bohnenstroh** (*umg*) (as) thick as two (short) planks

bohnern VT to wax, to polish

Bohnerwachs NT floor polish

bohren ['bo:rən] VT to bore; (*Loch*) to drill ▸ VI to drill; (*fig: drängen*) to keep on; (*peinigen: Schmerz, Zweifel etc*) to gnaw; **nach Öl/Wasser ~** drill for oil/water; **in der Nase ~** to pick one's nose

Bohrer (**-s, -**) M drill

Bohr- ZW: **Bohrinsel** F oil rig; **Bohrmaschine** F drill; **Bohrturm** M derrick

Boiler ['bɔʏlər] (**-s, -**) M water heater

b

Boje ['bo:jə] (**-, -n**) F buoy
Bolivianer(in) [bolivi'a:nər(ɪn)] (**-s, -**) M(F) Bolivian
Bolivien [bo'li:viən] NT Bolivia
bolivisch [bo'li:vɪʃ] ADJ Bolivian
Bollwerk ['bɔlvɛrk] NT (*lit, fig*) bulwark
Bolschewismus [bɔlʃe'vɪsmʊs] (-) M Bolshevism
Bolzen ['bɔltsən] (**-s, -**) M bolt
bombardieren [bɔmbar'di:rən] VT to bombard; (*aus der Luft*) to bomb
Bombe ['bɔmbə] (-, **-n**) F bomb; **wie eine ~ einschlagen** to come as a (real) bombshell
Bomben- zW: **Bombenalarm** M bomb scare; **Bombenangriff** M bombing raid; **Bombenanschlag** M bomb attack; **Bombenerfolg** (*umg*) M huge success; **Bombengeschäft** (*umg*) NT: **ein Bombengeschäft machen** to do a roaring trade; **bombensicher** (*umg*) ADJ dead certain
bombig (*umg*) ADJ great, super
Bon [bɔŋ] (**-s, -s**) M voucher; (*Kassenzettel*) receipt
Bonbon [bõ'bõ:] (**-s, -s**) NT sweet (BRIT), candy (US)
Bonus ['bo:nʊs] (**-** *od* **-ses, -se** *od* **Boni**) M bonus
Bonusmeile F bonus mile
Bonuszahlung F bonus payment
Bonze ['bɔntsə] (**-n, -n**) M big shot (*umg*)
Bonzenviertel (*umg*) NT posh quarter (*of town*)
Boot [bo:t] (**-(e)s, -e**) NT boat
Bord [bɔrt] (**-(e)s, -e**) M (*Aviat, Naut*) board ▶ NT (*Brett*) shelf; **an ~** on board; **an ~ gehen** (*Schiff*) to go on board; (*Flugzeug*) to board; **über ~ gehen** to go overboard; (*fig*) to go by the board
Bordell [bɔr'dɛl] (**-s, -e**) NT brothel
Bordfunkanlage F radio
Bordstein M kerb(stone) (BRIT), curb(stone) (US)
borgen ['bɔrgən] VT to borrow; **jdm etw ~** to lend sb sth; **sich** *dat* **etw ~** to borrow sth
Borneo ['bɔrneo] (**-s**) NT Borneo
borniert [bɔr'ni:rt] ADJ narrow-minded
Börse ['bœ:rzə] (**-, -n**) F stock exchange; (*Geldbörse*) purse
Börsen- zW: **Börsenmakler** M stockbroker; **börsennotiert** ADJ: **börsennotierte Firma** listed company; **Börsennotierung** F quotation (on the stock exchange)
Borste ['bɔrstə] (**-, -n**) F bristle
Borte ['bɔrtə] (**-, -n**) F edging; (*Band*) trimming
bös [bø:s] ADJ = **böse**; **bösartig** ADJ malicious; (*Med*) malignant
Böschung ['bœʃʊŋ] F slope; (*Uferböschung etc*) embankment
böse ['bø:zə] ADJ bad, evil; (*zornig*) angry; **das war nicht ~ gemeint** I/he *etc* didn't mean it nastily; **bist du mir ~?** are you angry with me?
Bösewicht (*umg*) M baddy
boshaft ['bo:shaft] ADJ malicious, spiteful
Bosheit F malice, spite
Bosnien ['bɔsniən] (**-s**) NT Bosnia
Bosnien-Herzegowina ['bɔsniənhɛrtsə'go:vi:na] (**-s**) NT Bosnia-Herzegovina
Bosnier(in) (**-s, -**) M(F) Bosnian
bosnisch ADJ Bosnian
Boss [bɔs] (**-es, -e**) (*umg*) M boss
böswillig ['bø:svɪlɪç] ADJ malicious
bot *etc* [bo:t] VB *siehe* **bieten**
Botanik [bo'ta:nɪk] F botany
botanisch [bo'ta:nɪʃ] ADJ botanical; **botanischer Garten** botanical gardens *pl*
Bote ['bo:tə] (**-n, -n**) M messenger
Botengang M errand
Botenjunge M errand boy
Botin ['bo:tɪn] F messenger
Botschaft F message, news; (*Pol*) embassy; **die Frohe ~** the Gospel; **Botschafter** (**-s, -**) M ambassador
Botswana [bɔ'tsva:na] (**-s**) NT Botswana
Bottich ['bɔtɪç] (**-(e)s, -e**) M vat, tub
Bouillon [bʊ'ljõ:] (**-, -s**) F consommé
Boulevard- [bulə'va:r] zW: **Boulevardblatt** (*umg*) NT tabloid; **Boulevardpresse** F tabloid press; **Boulevardstück** NT light play/comedy
Boutique [bu'ti:k] (**-, -n**) F boutique
Bowle ['bo:lə] (**-, -n**) F punch
Bowlingbahn ['bo:lɪŋba:n] F bowling alley
Box [bɔks] F (*Behälter*) box; (*Lautsprecherbox*) speaker
boxen VI to box
Boxer (**-s, -**) M boxer
Boxhandschuh M boxing glove
Boxkampf M boxing match
Boykott [bɔʏ'kɔt] (**-(e)s, -s**) M boycott
boykottieren [bɔʏkɔ'ti:rən] VT to boycott
BR ABK (= *Bayerischer Rundfunk*) *German radio station*
brach *etc* [bra:x] VB *siehe* **brechen**
brachial [braxi'a:l] ADJ: **mit brachialer Gewalt** by brute force
brachliegen ['bra:xli:gən] *unreg* VI (*lit, fig*) to lie fallow
brachte *etc* ['braxtə] VB *siehe* **bringen**
Branche ['brã:ʃə] (**-, -n**) F line of business
Branchenführer(in) M(F) market leader
Branchenverzeichnis NT trade directory
Brand [brant] (**-(e)s, Brände**) M fire; (*Med*) gangrene
Brandanschlag M arson attack
branden ['brandən] VI to surge; (*Meer*) to break
Brandenburg ['brandənbʊrk] (**-s**) NT Brandenburg
Brandherd M source of the fire
brandmarken VT to brand; (*fig*) to stigmatize
brandneu (*umg*) ADJ brand-new
Brand- zW: **Brandsalbe** F ointment for burns; **Brandsatz** M incendiary device; **Brandstifter** M arsonist, fire-raiser; **Brandstiftung** F arson
Brandung F surf
Brandwunde F burn
brannte *etc* ['brantə] VB *siehe* **brennen**
Branntwein ['brantvaɪn] M brandy; **Branntweinsteuer** F tax on spirits
Brasilianer(in) [brazili'a:nər(ɪn)] (**-s, -**) M(F) Brazilian
brasilianisch ADJ Brazilian
Brasilien [bra'zi:liən] NT Brazil
brät [brɛt] VB *siehe* **braten**

Bratapfel M baked apple
braten ['bra:tən] *unreg* VT to roast; (*in Pfanne*) to fry; **Braten** (-**s**, -) M roast, joint; **den Braten riechen** (*umg*) to smell a rat, to suss something
Brat- zW: **Brathähnchen** NT roast chicken; **Brathendl** NT (SÜDD, ÖSTERR) roast chicken; **Brathuhn** NT roast chicken; **Bratkartoffeln** PL fried/roast potatoes *pl*; **Bratpfanne** F frying pan; **Bratrost** M grill
Bratsche ['bra:tʃə] (-, **-n**) F viola
Bratspieß M spit
Bratwurst F grilled sausage
Brauch [braʊx] (**-(e)s**, *pl* **Bräuche**) M custom
brauchbar ADJ usable, serviceable; (*Person*) capable
brauchen VT (*bedürfen*) to need; (*müssen*) to have to; (*verwenden*) to use; **wie lange braucht man, um ...?** how long does it take to ...?; **das braucht seine Zeit** it takes time; **du brauchst es nur zu sagen** you only need to say
Brauchtum NT customs *pl*, traditions *pl*
Braue ['braʊə] (-, **-n**) F brow
brauen ['braʊən] VT to brew
Brauerei [braʊə'raɪ] F brewery
braun [braʊn] ADJ brown; (*von Sonne*) tanned; **~ gebrannt** tanned; (*pej*) Nazi
Bräune ['brɔʏnə] (-, **-n**) F brownness; (*Sonnenbräune*) tan
bräunen VT to make brown; (*Sonne*) to tan
Braunkohle F brown coal
Braunschweig ['braʊnʃvaɪk] (**-s**) NT Brunswick
Brause ['braʊzə] (-, **-n**) F shower; (*von Gießkanne*) rose; (*Getränk*) lemonade
brausen VI to roar; (*auch vr: duschen*) to take a shower
Brausepulver NT lemonade powder
Brausetablette F lemonade tablet
Braut [braʊt] (-, *pl* **Bräute**) F bride; (*Verlobte*) fiancée
Bräutigam ['brɔʏtɪgam] (**-s**, **-e**) M bridegroom; (*Verlobter*) fiancé
Braut- zW: **Brautjungfer** F bridesmaid; **Brautkleid** NT wedding dress; **Brautpaar** NT bride and bridegroom, bridal pair
brav [bra:f] ADJ (*artig*) good; (*ehrenhaft*) worthy, honest; (*bieder: Frisur, Kleid*) plain; **sei schön ~!** be a good boy/girl
bravo [bra:vo] INTERJ well done
BRD (-) F ABK (= *Bundesrepublik Deutschland*) FRG; **die alte ~** former West Germany

> **BRD** (Bundesrepublik Deutschland) is the official name for the Federal Republic of Germany. It comprises 16 **Länder** (see **Land**). It was the name given to the former West Germany as opposed to East Germany (the **DDR**). The two Germanies were reunited on 3rd October 1990.

Brechbohne F French bean
Brecheisen NT crowbar
brechen *unreg* VT, VI to break; (*Licht*) to refract; (*speien*) to vomit; **die Ehe ~** to commit adultery; **mir bricht das Herz** it breaks my heart; **brechend voll sein** to be full to bursting
Brechmittel NT: **er/das ist das reinste ~** (*umg*) he/it makes me feel ill
Brechreiz M nausea
Brechung F (*des Lichts*) refraction
Brei [braɪ] (**-(e)s**, **-e**) M (*Masse*) pulp; (*Koch*) gruel; (*Haferbrei*) porridge (BRIT), oatmeal (US); (*für Kinder, Kranke*) mash; **um den heißen ~ herumreden** (*umg*) to beat about the bush
breit [braɪt] ADJ broad; (*bei Maßangabe*) wide ▸ ADV: **ein ~ gefächertes Angebot** a wide range; **die breite Masse** the masses *pl*; **Breitband** NT (*Comput*) broadband; **Breitbandanschluss** M (*Comput*) broadband connection; **breitbeinig** ADJ with one's legs apart
Breite (-, **-n**) F breadth; (*bei Maßangabe*) width; (*Geog*) latitude
breiten VT: **etw über etw** *akk* **~** to spread sth over sth
Breitengrad M degree of latitude
Breitensport M popular sport
breit- zW: **breitmachen** *unreg* (*umg*) VR to spread o.s. out; **breitschlagen** *unreg* (*umg*) VT: **sich breitschlagen lassen** to let o.s. be talked round; **breitschulterig, breitschultrig** ADJ broad-shouldered; **breittreten** *unreg* (*umg*) VT to go on about; **Breitwandfilm** M wide-screen film
Bremen ['bre:mən] (**-s**) NT Bremen
Bremsbelag M brake lining
Bremse ['brɛmzə] (-, **-n**) F brake; (*Zool*) horsefly
bremsen VI to brake, to apply the brakes ▸ VT (*Auto*) to brake; (*fig*) to slow down ▸ VR: **ich kann mich ~** (*umg*) not likely!
Brems- zW: **Bremsflüssigkeit** F brake fluid; **Bremslicht** NT brake light; **Bremspedal** NT brake pedal; **Bremsschuh** M brake shoe; **Bremsspur** F tyre (BRIT) *od* tire (US) marks *pl*; **Bremsweg** M braking distance
brennbar ADJ inflammable; **leicht ~** highly inflammable
Brennelement NT fuel element
brennen ['brɛnən] *unreg* VI to burn, to be on fire; (*Licht, Kerze etc*) to burn ▸ VT (*Holz etc*) to burn; (*Ziegel, Ton*) to fire; (*Kaffee*) to roast; (*Branntwein*) to distil; **es brennt!** fire!; **wo brennts denn?** (*fig: umg*) what's the panic?; **darauf ~, etw zu tun** to be dying to do sth
Brenn- zW: **Brennmaterial** NT fuel; **Brennnessel** F nettle; **Brennofen** M kiln; **Brennpunkt** M (*Math, Optik*) focus; **Brennspiritus** M methylated spirits *pl*; **Brennstab** M fuel rod; **Brennstoff** M liquid fuel
brenzlig ['brɛntslɪç] ADJ smelling of burning, burnt; (*fig*) precarious
Bresche ['brɛʃə] (-, **-n**) F: **in die ~ springen** (*fig*) to step into the breach
Bretagne [bre'tanjə] F: **die** ~ Brittany
Bretone [bre'to:nə] (**-n**, **-n**) M Breton
Bretonin [bre'to:nɪn] F Breton
Brett [brɛt] (**-(e)s**, **-er**) NT board, plank; (*Bord*) shelf; (*Spielbrett*) board; **Bretter** PL (*Ski*) skis *pl*; (*Theat*) boards *pl*; **Schwarzes ~** notice board; **er hat ein ~ vor dem Kopf** (*umg*) he's really thick

brettern (*umg*) VI to speed
Bretterzaun M wooden fence
Brettspiel NT board game
Brezel ['bre:tsəl] (**-, -n**) F pretzel
bricht [brɪçt] VB *siehe* **brechen**
Brief [bri:f] (**-(e)s, -e**) M letter; **Briefbeschwerer** (**-s, -**) M paperweight; **Briefdrucksache** F circular; **Brieffreund(in)** M(F) pen friend, pen-pal; **Briefkasten** M letter box; (*Comput*) mailbox; **Briefkopf** M letterhead; **brieflich** ADJ, ADV by letter; **Briefmarke** F postage stamp; **Brieföffner** M letter opener; **Briefpapier** NT notepaper; **Briefqualität** F (*Comput*) letter quality; **Brieftasche** F wallet; **Brieftaube** F carrier pigeon; **Briefträger** M postman; **Briefumschlag** M envelope; **Briefwahl** F postal vote; **Briefwechsel** M correspondence
briet *etc* [bri:t] VB *siehe* **braten**
Brigade [bri'ga:də] (-, **-n**) F (*Mil*) brigade; (*DDR*) (work) team *od* group
Brikett [bri'kɛt] (**-s, -s**) NT briquette
brillant [brɪl'jant] ADJ (*fig*) sparkling, brilliant; **Brillant** (**-en, -en**) M brilliant, diamond
Brille ['brɪlə] (**-, -n**) F spectacles *pl*; (*Schutzbrille*) goggles *pl*; (*Toilettenbrille*) (toilet) seat
Brillenschlange F (*hum*) four-eyes
Brillenträger(in) M(F): **er ist ~** he wears glasses
bringen ['brɪŋən] *unreg* VT to bring; (*mitnehmen, begleiten*) to take; (*einbringen: Profit*) to bring in; (*veröffentlichen*) to publish; (*Theat, Film*) to show; (*Rundf, TV*) to broadcast; (*in einen Zustand versetzen*) to get; (*umg: tun können*) to manage; **jdn dazu ~, etw zu tun** to make sb do sth; **jdn zum Lachen/Weinen ~** to make sb laugh/cry; **es weit ~** to do very well, to get far; **jdn nach Hause ~** to take sb home; **jdn um etw ~** to make sb lose sth; **jdn auf eine Idee ~** to give sb an idea
brisant [bri'zant] ADJ (*fig*) controversial
Brisanz [bri'zants] F (*fig*) controversial nature
Brise ['bri:zə] (**-, -n**) F breeze
Brite ['bri:tə] (**-n, -n**) M Briton, Britisher (*US*); **die Briten** the British
Britin F Briton, Britisher (*US*)
britisch ['bri:tɪʃ] ADJ British; **die Britischen Inseln** the British Isles
bröckelig ['brœkəlɪç] ADJ crumbly
Brocken ['brɔkən] (**-s, -**) M piece, bit; (*Felsbrocken*) lump of rock; **ein paar ~ Spanisch** a smattering of Spanish; **ein harter ~** (*umg*) a tough nut to crack
brodeln ['bro:dəln] VI to bubble
Brokat [bro'ka:t] (**-(e)s, -e**) M brocade
Brokkoli ['brɔkoli] PL broccoli
Brombeere ['brɔmbe:rə] F blackberry, bramble (BRIT)
bronchial [brɔnçi'a:l] ADJ bronchial
Bronchien ['brɔnçiən] PL bronchial tubes *pl*
Bronchitis [brɔn'çi:tɪs] (-, **-tiden**) F bronchitis
Bronze ['brõ:sə] (**-, -n**) F bronze
Brosame ['bro:za:mə] (**-, -n**) F crumb
Brosche ['brɔʃə] (**-, -n**) F brooch
Broschüre [brɔ'ʃy:rə] (**-, -n**) F pamphlet

Brot [bro:t] (**-(e)s, -e**) NT bread; (*Brotlaib*) loaf; **das ist ein hartes ~** (*fig*) that's a hard way to earn one's living
Brötchen ['brø:tçən] NT roll; **kleine ~ backen** (*fig*) to set one's sights lower; **Brötchengeber** M (*hum*) employer, provider (*hum*)
brotlos ['bro:tlo:s] ADJ (*Person*) unemployed; (*Arbeit etc*) unprofitable
Brotzeit (SÜDD) F (*Pause*) ≈ tea break
browsen ['brauzən] VI (*Comput*) to browse
Browser ['brauzər] (**-s, -**) M (*Comput*) browser
BRT ABK (= *Bruttoregistertonne*) GRT
Bruch [brʊx] (**-(e)s, Brüche**) M breakage; (*zerbrochene Stelle*) break; (*fig*) split, breach; (*Med: Eingeweidebruch*) rupture, hernia; (*Beinbruch etc*) fracture; (*Math*) fraction; **zu ~ gehen** to get broken; **sich einen ~ heben** to rupture o.s.; **Bruchbude** (*umg*) F shack
brüchig ['brʏçɪç] ADJ brittle, fragile
Bruch- zW: **Bruchlandung** F crash landing; **Bruchschaden** M breakage; **Bruchstelle** F break; (*von Knochen*) fracture; **Bruchstrich** M (*Math*) line; **Bruchstück** NT fragment; **Bruchteil** M fraction
Brücke ['brʏkə] (**-, -n**) F bridge; (*Teppich*) rug; (*Turnen*) crab
Bruder ['bru:dər] (**-s, Brüder**) M brother; **unter Brüdern** (*umg*) between friends
brüderlich ADJ brotherly; **Brüderlichkeit** F fraternity
Brudermord M fratricide
Brüderschaft F brotherhood, fellowship; **~ trinken** to agree to use the familiar "du" (*over a drink*)
Brühe ['bry:ə] (**-, -n**) F broth, stock; (*pej*) muck
brühwarm ['bry:'varm] (*umg*) ADJ: **er hat das sofort ~ weitererzählt** he promptly spread it around
Brühwürfel M stock cube (BRIT), bouillon cube (*US*)
brüllen ['brʏlən] VI to bellow, to roar
Brummbär M grumbler
brummeln ['brʊməln] VT, VI to mumble
brummen VI (*Bär, Mensch etc*) to growl; (*Insekt, Radio*) to buzz; (*Motor*) to roar; (*murren*) to grumble ▸ VT to growl; **jdm brummt der Kopf** sb's head is buzzing
Brummer ['brʊmər] (**-s, -**) (*umg*) M (*Lastwagen*) juggernaut
brummig (*umg*) ADJ grumpy
Brummschädel (*umg*) M thick head
brünett [brʏ'nɛt] ADJ brunette, brown-haired
Brunnen ['brʊnən] (**-s, -**) M fountain; (*tief*) well; (*natürlich*) spring; **Brunnenkresse** F watercress
Brunst [brʊnst] F (*von männlichen Tieren*) rut; (*von weiblichen Tieren*) heat; **Brunstzeit** F rutting season
brüsk [brʏsk] ADJ abrupt, brusque
brüskieren [brʏs'ki:rən] VT to snub
Brüssel ['brʏsəl] (**-s**) NT Brussels
Brust [brʊst] (**-, Brüste**) F breast; (*Männerbrust*) chest; **einem Kind die ~ geben** to breast-feed (BRIT) *od* nurse (*US*) a baby

brüsten ['brʏstən] VR to boast
Brust- zW: **Brustfellentzündung** F pleurisy; **Brustkasten** M chest; **Brustkorb** M (*Anat*) thorax; **Brustschwimmen** NT breast-stroke; **Brustton** M: **im Brustton der Überzeugung** in a tone of utter conviction
Brüstung ['brʏstʊŋ] F parapet
Brustwarze F nipple
Brut [bru:t] (-, -en) F brood; (*Brüten*) hatching
brutal [bru'ta:l] ADJ brutal; **Brutalität** F brutality
Brutapparat M incubator
brüten ['bry:tən] VI (*auch fig*) to brood; **brütende Hitze** oppressive *od* stifling heat
Brüter (-s, -) M (*Tech*): **Schneller ~** fast-breeder (reactor)
Brutkasten M incubator
Brutstätte F +*gen* (*lit, fig*) breeding ground (for)
brutto ['brʊto] ADV gross; **Bruttoeinkommen** NT gross salary; **Bruttogehalt** NT gross salary; **Bruttogewicht** NT gross weight; **Bruttogewinn** M gross profit; **Bruttoinlandsprodukt** NT gross domestic product; **Bruttolohn** M gross wages *pl*; **Bruttosozialprodukt** NT gross national product
brutzeln ['brʊtsəln] (*umg*) VI to sizzle away ▶ VT to fry (up)
Btx ABK = **Bildschirmtext**
Bub [bu:p] (-en, -en) M boy, lad
Bube ['bu:bə] (-n, -n) M (*Schurke*) rogue; (*Karten*) jack
Bubikopf M bobbed hair
Buch [bu:x] (-(e)s, Bücher) NT book; (*Comm*) account book; **er redet wie ein ~** (*umg*) he never stops talking; **ein ~ mit sieben Siegeln** (*fig*) a closed book; **über etw** *akk* **~ führen** to keep a record of sth; **zu ~(e) schlagen** to make a significant difference, to tip the balance; **Buchbinder** M bookbinder; **Buchdrucker** M printer
Buche (-, -n) F beech tree
buchen VT to book; (*Betrag*) to enter; **etw als Erfolg ~** to put sth down as a success
Bücherbord ['by:çər-] NT bookshelf
Bücherbrett NT bookshelf
Bücherei [by:çə'raɪ] F library
Bücherregal NT bookshelves *pl*, bookcase
Bücherschrank M bookcase
Bücherwurm (*umg*) M bookworm
Buchfink ['bu:xfɪŋk] M chaffinch
Buch- zW: **Buchführung** F book-keeping, accounting; **Buchhalter(in)** (-s, -) M(F) accountant; **Buchhandel** M book trade; **im Buchhandel erhältlich** available in bookshops; **Buchhändler(in)** M(F) bookseller; **Buchhandlung** F bookshop; **Buchprüfung** F audit; **Buchrücken** M spine
Büchse ['bʏksə] (-, -n) F tin, can; (*Holzbüchse*) box; (*Gewehr*) rifle
Büchsenfleisch NT tinned meat
Büchsenöffner M tin *od* can opener
Buchstabe (-ns, -n) M letter (of the alphabet)
buchstabieren [bu:xʃta'bi:rən] VT to spell
buchstäblich ['bu:xʃtɛ:plɪç] ADJ literal
Buchstütze F book end
Bucht ['bʊxt] (-, -en) F bay
Buchung ['bu:xʊŋ] F booking; (*Comm*) entry
Buchweizen M buckwheat
Buchwert M book value
Buckel ['bʊkəl] (-s, -) M hump; **er kann mir den ~ runterrutschen** (*umg*) he can (go and) take a running jump
buckeln (*pej*) VI to bow and scrape
bücken ['bʏkən] VR to bend; **sich nach etw ~** to bend down *od* stoop to pick sth up
Bückling ['bʏklɪŋ] M (*Fisch*) kipper; (*Verbeugung*) bow
Budapest ['bu:dapɛst] (-s) NT Budapest
buddeln ['bʊdəln] (*umg*) VI to dig
Buddhismus [bʊ'dɪsmʊs] (-) M Buddhism
Bude ['bu:də] (-, -n) F booth, stall; (*umg*) digs *pl* (BRIT) *od* place (*US*); **jdm die ~ einrennen** (*umg*) to pester sb; **Leben in die ~ bringen** to liven up the place
Budget [bʏ'dʒe:] (-s, -s) NT budget
Büfett [bʏ'fɛt] (-s, -s) NT (*Anrichte*) sideboard; (*Geschirrschrank*) dresser; **kaltes ~** cold buffet
Büffel ['bʏfəl] (-s, -) M buffalo
büffeln ['bʏfəln] (*umg*) VI to swot, to cram ▶ VT (*Lernstoff*) to swot up
Bug [bu:k] (-(e)s, -e) M (*Naut*) bow; (*Aviat*) nose
Bügel ['by:gəl] (-s, -) M (*Kleiderbügel*) hanger; (*Steigbügel*) stirrup; (*Brillenbügel*) arm; **Bügelbrett** NT ironing board; **Bügeleisen** NT iron; **Bügelfalte** F crease; **bügelfrei** ADJ non-iron; (*Hemd*) drip-dry
bügeln VT, VI to iron
Buhmann ['bu:man] (*umg*) M bogeyman
Bühne ['by:nə] (-, -n) F stage
Bühnenbild NT set, scenery
Buhruf ['bu:ru:f] M boo
buk *etc* [bu:k] VB (*veraltet*) *siehe* **backen**
Bukarest ['bu:karɛst] (-s) NT Bucharest
Bulette [bu'lɛtə] F meatball
Bulgare [bʊl'ga:rə] (-n, -n) M Bulgarian
Bulgarien (-s) NT Bulgaria
Bulgarin F Bulgarian
bulgarisch ADJ Bulgarian
Bulimie [bʊli'mi:] F (*Med*) bulimia
Bull- zW: **Bullauge** NT (*Naut*) porthole; **Bulldogge** F bulldog; **Bulldozer** ['bʊldo:zər] (-s, -) M bulldozer
Bulle (-n, -n) M bull; **die Bullen** (*pej, umg*) the fuzz *sing*, the cops
Bullenhitze (*umg*) F sweltering heat
Bummel ['bʊməl] (-s, -) M stroll; (*Schaufensterbummel*) window-shopping (expedition)
Bummelant [bʊmə'lant] M slowcoach
Bummelei [bʊmə'laɪ] F wandering; (*Trödelei*) dawdling; (*Faulenzen*) skiving
bummeln VI to wander, to stroll; (*trödeln*) to dawdle; (*faulenzen*) to skive (BRIT), to loaf around
Bummelstreik M go-slow (BRIT), slowdown (*US*)
Bummelzug M slow train

Bummler(in) ['bʊmlər(ɪn)] **(-s, -)** M(F) *(langsamer Mensch)* dawdler (BRIT), slowpoke (US); *(Faulenzer)* idler, loafer
bumsen ['bʊmzən] VI *(schlagen)* to thump; *(prallen, stoßen)* to bump, to bang; *(umg: koitieren)* to bonk, to have it off (BRIT)
Bund[1] [bʊnt] **(-(e)s, Bünde)** M *(Freundschaftsbund etc)* bond; *(Organisation)* union; *(Pol)* confederacy; *(Hosenbund, Rockbund)* waistband; **den ~ fürs Leben schließen** to take the marriage vows
Bund[2] [bʊnt] **(-(e)s, -e)** NT bunch; *(Strohbund)* bundle
Bündchen ['bʏntçən] NT ribbing; *(Ärmelbündchen)* cuff
Bündel **(-s, -)** NT bundle, bale
bündeln VT to bundle
Bundes- ['bʊndəs] IN ZW Federal; **Bundesagentur** F: **Bundesagentur für Arbeit** ≈ Department of Employment; **Bundesbahn** F: **die Deutsche Bundesbahn** German Federal Railways *pl*; **Bundesbank** F Federal Bank, Bundesbank; **Bundesbürger** M German citizen; *(vor 1990)* West German citizen; **Bundesgebiet** NT Federal territory; **Bundesgerichtshof** M Federal Supreme Court; **Bundesgrenzschutz** M Federal Border Guard; **Bundeshauptstadt** F Federal capital; **Bundeshaushalt** M *(Pol)* National Budget; **Bundeskanzler** M Federal Chancellor; *see note*

> The **Bundeskanzler**, head of the German government, is elected for 4 years and determines government guidelines. He/She is formally proposed by the **Bundespräsident** but needs a majority in parliament to be elected to office.

Bundes- ZW: **Bundesland** NT state, Land; **Bundesliga** F *(Sport)* national league; **Bundesministerium** NT Federal Ministry; **Bundesnachrichtendienst** M Federal Intelligence Service; **Bundespost** F *(früher)*: **die (Deutsche) Bundespost** the (German) Federal Post (Office); **Bundespräsident(in)** M(F) President; *see note*

> The **Bundespräsident** is the head of state of the Federal Republic of Germany who is elected every 5 years by the members of the **Bundestag** and by delegates of the Landtage (regional parliaments). His/Her role is that of a figurehead who represents Germany at home and abroad. He/She can only be elected twice.

Bundesrat M *(in Deutschland)* Upper House (of the German Parliament); *(in der Schweiz)* Council of Ministers; *see note*

> The **Bundesrat** is the Upper House of the German Parliament whose 68 members are not elected but determined by the parliaments of the individual **Länder**. Its most important function is the approval of federal laws which concern jurisdiction of the Länder. It can raise objections to all other laws but can be outvoted by the **Bundestag**.

Bundes- ZW: **Bundesrechnungshof** M Federal Audit Office; **Bundesregierung** F Federal Government; **Bundesrepublik** F Federal Republic; **Bundesrepublik Deutschland** Federal Republic of Germany; **Bundesstaat** M Federal state; **Bundesstraße** F Federal Highway, main road; **Bundestag** M Lower House (of the German Parliament); *see note*

> The **Bundestag** is the Lower House of the German Parliament, elected by the people. There are 646 MPs, half of them elected directly from the first vote (**Erststimme**), and half from the regional list of parliamentary candidates resulting from the second vote (**Zweitstimme**), and giving proportional representation to the parties. The Bundestag exercises parliamentary control over the government.

Bundes- ZW: **Bundestagsabgeordnete(r)** F(M) member of the German Parliament; **Bundestagswahl** F (Federal) parliamentary elections *pl*; **Bundesverfassungsgericht** NT Federal Constitutional Court; **Bundeswehr** F German Armed Forces *pl*; *see note*

> The **Bundeswehr** is the name for the German armed forces. It was established in 1955, first of all for volunteers, but since 1956 there has been compulsory military service for all able-bodied young men of 18 (see **Wehrdienst**). In peacetime the Defence Minister is the head of the Bundeswehr, but in wartime, the **Bundeskanzler** takes over. The Bundeswehr comes under the jurisdiction of NATO.

Bundfaltenhose F pleated trousers *pl*
Bundhose F knee breeches *pl*
bündig ['bʏndɪç] ADJ *(kurz)* concise
Bündnis ['bʏntnɪs] **(-ses, -se)** NT alliance
Bunker ['bʊŋkər] **(-s, -)** M bunker; *(Luftschutzbunker)* air-raid shelter
bunt [bʊnt] ADJ coloured (BRIT), colored (US); *(gemischt)* mixed; **jdm wird es zu ~** it's getting too much for sb; **Buntstift** M coloured (BRIT) *od* colored (US) pencil, crayon
Bürde ['bʏrdə] **(-, -n)** F *(lit, fig)* burden
Burg [bʊrk] **(-, -en)** F castle, fort
Bürge ['bʏrgə] **(-n, -n)** M guarantor
bürgen VI to vouch; **für jdn ~** *(fig)* to vouch for sb; *(Fin)* to stand surety for sb
Bürger(in) **(-s, -)** M(F) citizen; **bürgerfreundlich** ADJ citizen-friendly; **Bürgerinitiative** F citizen's initiative; **Bürgerkrieg** M civil war; **bürgerlich** ADJ *(Rechte)* civil; *(Klasse)* middle-class; *(pej)* bourgeois; **bürgerliches Gesetzbuch** Civil Code; **Bürgermeister** M mayor; **Bürgerrecht** NT civil rights *pl*; **Bürgerrechtler(in)** M(F) civil rights campaigner; **Bürgerschaft** F population, citizens *pl*; **Bürgerschaftswahl** F metropolitan council election; **Bürgerschreck** M bogey of the middle classes; **Bürgersteig** M pavement (BRIT), sidewalk (US); **Bürgertum** NT citizens *pl*; **Bürgerversicherung** F citizens' insurance; **Bürgerwehr** F vigilantes *pl*

Burgfriede, Burgfrieden M (*fig*) truce
Bürgin F guarantor
Bürgschaft F surety; **~ leisten** to give security
Burgund [bʊrˈgʊnt] (**-(s)**) NT Burgundy
Burgunder (**-s, -**) M (*Wein*) burgundy
Büro [byˈro:] (**-s, -s**) NT office; **Büroangestellte(r)** F(M) office worker; **Büroklammer** F paper clip; **Bürokraft** F (office) clerk
Bürokrat [byroˈkra:t] (**-en, -en**) M bureaucrat
Bürokratie [byrokraˈti:] F bureaucracy
bürokratisch ADJ bureaucratic
Bürokratismus M red tape
Büroschluss M office closing time
Büroturm M office tower
Bursch [ˈbʊrʃ(ə)] (**-en, -en**) M = **Bursche**
Bursche (**-n, -n**) M lad, fellow; (*Diener*) servant
Burschenschaft F student fraternity
burschikos [bʊrʃiˈko:s] ADJ (*jungenhaft*) (tom)boyish; (*unbekümmert*) casual
Bürste [ˈbʏrstə] (**-, -n**) F brush
bürsten VT to brush
Bus [bʊs] (**-ses, -se**) M bus
Busbahnhof M bus station
Busch [bʊʃ] (**-(e)s, Büsche**) M bush, shrub; **bei jdm auf den ~ klopfen** (*umg*) to sound sb out
Büschel [ˈbʏʃəl] (**-s, -**) NT tuft
buschig ADJ bushy
Busen [ˈbu:zən] (**-s, -**) M bosom; (*Meerbusen*) inlet, bay; **Busenfreund(in)** M(F) bosom friend
Busfahrer(in) M, F bus driver
Bushaltestelle F bus stop
Buslinie F bus route
Bussard [ˈbʊsart] (**-s, -e**) M buzzard
Buße [ˈbu:sə] (**-, -n**) F atonement, penance; (*Geld*) fine
büßen [ˈby:sən] VI to do penance, to atone ▸ VT to atone for
Bußgeld NT fine
Buß- und Bettag M day of prayer and repentance
Büste [ˈbʏstə] (**-, -n**) F bust
Büstenhalter M bra
Butan [buˈta:n] (**-s**) NT butane
Büttenrede [ˈbʏtənre:də] F carnival speech
Butter [ˈbʊtər] (**-**) F butter; **alles (ist) in ~** (*umg*) everything is fine *od* hunky-dory; **Butterberg** (*umg*) M butter mountain; **Butterblume** F buttercup; **Butterbrot** NT (piece of) bread and butter; **Butterbrotpapier** NT greaseproof paper; **Buttercremetorte** F gateau with buttercream filling; **Butterdose** F butter dish; **Butterkeks** M ≈ Rich Tea® biscuit; **Buttermilch** F buttermilk; **butterweich** ADJ soft as butter; (*fig: umg*) soft
Butzen [ˈbʊtsən] (**-s, -**) M core
BVG NT ABK (= *Betriebsverfassungsgesetz*) ≈ Industrial Relations Act; = **Bundesverfassungsgericht**
b. w. ABK (= *bitte wenden*) p.t.o
Byte [baɪt] (**-s, -s**) NT (*Comput*) byte
Bz. ABK = **Bezirk**
bzgl. ABK (= *bezüglich*) re.
bzw. ABK = **beziehungsweise**

Cc

C[1], c [tseː] NT C, c; **C wie Cäsar** ≈ C for Charlie
C[2] ABK (= *Celsius*) C
ca. [ka] ABK (= *circa*) approx.
Cabriolet [kabrio'leː] (**-s, -s**) NT (*Aut*) convertible
Café [ka'feː] (**-s, -s**) NT café
Cafeteria [kafete'riːa] (**-, -s**) F cafeteria
cal ABK (= *Kalorie*) cal
Calais [ka'lɛː] (**-'**) NT: **die Straße von ~** the Straits of Dover
Callcenter ['kɔːlsɛntər] NT call centre (BRIT), call center (US)
Camcorder (**-s, -**) M camcorder
campen ['kɛmpən] VI to camp
Camper(in) (**-s, -**) M(F) camper
Camping ['kɛmpɪŋ] (**-s**) NT camping; **Campingbus** M camper; **Campingplatz** M camp(ing) site
Caravan ['karavan] (**-s, -s**) M caravan
Cargo ['kargo] (**-s, -s**) M (*Comm*) cargo
Cäsium ['tsɛːziʊm] NT caesium (BRIT), cesium (US)
ccm ABK (= *Kubikzentimeter*) cm^3
CD F ABK (= *Compact Disc*) CD; **CD-Brenner** M CD burner; **CD-ROM** (**-, -s**) F CD-ROM; **CD-Spieler** M CD player
CDU [tseːdeː'luː] (**-**) F ABK (= *Christlich-Demokratische Union (Deutschlands)*) Christian Democratic Union; *see note*

> The **CDU** (Christlich-Demokratische Union) is a Christian and conservative political party founded in 1945. It operates in all the **Länder** apart from Bavaria where its sister party the **CSU** is active. In the **Bundestag** the two parties form a coalition. It is the second largest party in Germany after the **SPD**, the Social Democratic Party.

Celli PL *von* **Cello**
Cellist(in) [tʃɛ'lɪst(ɪn)] M(F) cellist
Cello ['tʃɛlo] (**-s, -s** *od* **Celli**) NT cello
Celsius ['tsɛlziʊs] M Celsius
Cent [(t)sɛnt] (**-(s), -(s)**) M cent
ces [tsɛs] (**-, -**) NT (*Mus*) C flat
Ces [tsɛs] (**-, -**) NT (*Mus*) C flat
Ceylon ['tsaɪlɔn] (**-s**) NT Ceylon
Chamäleon [ka'mɛːleɔn] (**-s, -s**) NT chameleon
Champagner [ʃam'panjər] (**-s, -**) M champagne
Champignon ['ʃampɪnjõ] (**-s, -s**) M button mushroom
Chance ['ʃãːs(ə)] (**-, -n**) F chance, opportunity
chancengleich ADJ with equal opportunities
Chancengleichheit F equality of opportunity
Chaos ['kaːɔs] (**-**) NT chaos
Chaot(in) [ka'oːt(ɪn)] (**-en, -en**) M(F) (*Pol: pej*) anarchist (*pej*); (*umg*) disorganized person, scatterbrain
chaotisch [ka'oːtɪʃ] ADJ chaotic
Charakter [ka'raktər] (**-s, -e**) M character; **charakterfest** ADJ of firm character
charakterisieren [karakteri'ziːrən] VT to characterize
Charakteristik [karakte'rɪstɪk] F characterization
charakteristisch [karakte'rɪstɪʃ] ADJ: **~ (für)** characteristic (of), typical (of); **charakterlos** ADJ unprincipled
Charakter- ZW: **Charakterlosigkeit** F lack of principle; **Charakterschwäche** F weakness of character; **Charakterstärke** F strength of character; **Charakterzug** M characteristic, trait
charmant [ʃar'mant] ADJ charming
Charme [ʃarm] (**-s**) M charm
Charta ['karta] (**-, -s**) F charter
Charterflug ['tʃartərfluːk] M charter flight
Chartermaschine ['tʃartərmaʃiːnə] F charter plane
chartern ['tʃartərn] VT to charter
Chassis [ʃa'siː] (**-, -**) NT chassis
Chat [tʃɛt] (**-s, -s**) M (*Comput*) chat; **Chatroom** ['tʃɛtruːm] M (*Comput*) chatroom
chatten ['tʃɛtən] VI (*Comput*) to chat
Chauffeur [ʃɔ'føːr] M chauffeur
Chaussee [ʃo'seː] (**-, -n**) F (*veraltet*) high road
Chauvi ['ʃovi] (**-s, -s**) (*umg*) M male chauvinist
Chauvinismus [ʃovi'nɪsmʊs] M chauvinism
Chauvinist [ʃovi'nɪst] M chauvinist
checken ['tʃɛkən] VT (*überprüfen*) to check; (*umg: verstehen*) to get
Chef(in) [ʃɛf(ɪn)] (**-s, -s**) M(F) head; (*umg*) boss; **Chefarzt** M senior consultant; **Chefetage** F executive floor; **Chefredakteur** M editor-in-chief; **Chefsekretärin** F personal assistant/secretary; **Chefvisite** F (*Med*) consultant's round
Chemie [çe'miː] (**-**) F chemistry; **Chemiefaser** F man-made fibre (BRIT) *od* fiber (US)

Chemikalie [çemi'ka:liə] F chemical

Chemiker(in) ['çe:mikər(ɪn)] (**-s, -**) M(F) (industrial) chemist

chemisch ['çe:mɪʃ] ADJ chemical; **chemische Reinigung** dry cleaning

Chemotherapie [çemotera'pi:] F chemotherapy

chic [ʃɪk] ADJ *unver* stylish, chic

Chicorée [ʃiko're:] (**-s**) M OD F chicory

Chiffre ['ʃɪfrə] (**-, -n**) F (*Geheimzeichen*) cipher; (*in Zeitung*) box number

Chiffriermaschine [ʃɪ'fri:rmaʃi:nə] F cipher machine

Chile ['tʃi:le] (**-s**) NT Chile

Chilene [tʃi'le:nə] (**-n, -n**) M Chilean

Chilenin [tʃi'le:nɪn] F Chilean

chilenisch ADJ Chilean

Chili ['tʃi:lɪ] (**-s, -s**) M chilli

China ['çi:na] (**-s**) NT China

Chinakohl M Chinese leaves *pl*

Chinese [çi'ne:zə] (**-n, -n**) M Chinaman, Chinese

Chinesin F Chinese woman

chinesisch ADJ Chinese

Chinin [çi'ni:n] (**-s**) NT quinine

Chipkarte ['tʃɪpkartə] F smart card

Chips [tʃɪps] PL crisps *pl* (BRIT), chips *pl* (*US*)

Chirurg(in) [çi'rʊrg(ɪn)] (**-en, -en**) M(F) surgeon

Chirurgie [çirʊr'gi:] F surgery

chirurgisch ADJ surgical; **ein chirurgischer Eingriff** surgery

Chlor [klo:r] (**-s**) NT chlorine

Chloroform [kloro'fɔrm] (**-s**) NT chloroform

chloroformieren [klorofor'mi:rən] VT to chloroform

Chlorophyll [kloro'fʏl] (**-s**) NT chlorophyll

Cholera ['ko:lera] (**-**) F cholera

Choleriker(in) [ko'le:rikər(ɪn)] (**-s, -**) M(F) hot-tempered person

cholerisch [ko'le:rɪʃ] ADJ choleric

Cholesterin [kolɛste'ri:n] (**-s**) NT cholesterol; **Cholesterinspiegel** [kolɛste'ri:nʃpigəl] M cholesterol level

Chor [ko:r] (**-(e)s, Chöre**) M choir; (*Musikstück, Theat*) chorus

Choral [ko'ra:l] (**-s, -äle**) M chorale

Choreograf(in) [koreo'gra:f(ɪn)] (**-en, -en**) M(F) choreographer

Choreografie [koreogra'fi:] F choreography

Chorgestühl NT choir stalls *pl*

Chorknabe M choirboy

Chose ['ʃo:zə] (**-, -n**) (*umg*) F (*Angelegenheit*) thing

Chr. ABK = **Christus; Chronik**

Christ [krɪst] (**-en, -en**) M Christian; **Christbaum** M Christmas tree

Christenheit F Christendom

Christentum (**-s**) NT Christianity

Christin F Christian

Christkind NT ≈ Father Christmas; (*Jesus*) baby Jesus

christlich ADJ Christian; **Christlicher Verein Junger Männer** Young Men's Christian Association

Christus (**Christi**) M Christ; **Christi Himmelfahrt** Ascension Day

Chrom [kro:m] (**-s**) NT chrome; (*Chem*) chromium

Chromosom [kromo'zo:m] (**-s, -en**) NT (*Biol*) chromosome

Chronik ['kro:nɪk] F chronicle

chronisch ADJ chronic

Chronologie [kronolo'gi:] F chronology

chronologisch ADJ chronological

Chrysantheme [kryzan'te:mə] (**-, -n**) F chrysanthemum

CIA ['si:aɪ'eɪ] (**-**) F OD M ABK (= *Central Intelligence Agency*) CIA

circa ['tsɪrka] ADV (round) about

cis [tsɪs] (**-, -**) NT (*Mus*) C sharp

Cis [tsɪs] (**-, -**) NT (*Mus*) C sharp

City ['sɪti] (**-, -s**) F city centre (BRIT); **in der ~** in the city centre (BRIT), downtown (*US*); **die ~ von Berlin** the (city) centre of Berlin (BRIT), downtown Berlin (*US*)

clean [kli:n] ADJ (*Drogen: umg*) off drugs

clever ['klɛvər] ADJ clever; (*gerissen*) crafty

Clique ['klɪkə] (**-, -n**) F set, crowd

Clou [klu:] (**-s, -s**) M (*von Geschichte*) (whole) point; (*von Show*) highlight, high spot

Cloud Computing [klaʊtkəm'pju:tɪŋ] NT Cloud Computing

Clown [klaʊn] (**-s, -s**) M clown

Club [klʊp] (**-s, -s**) M club

cm ABK (= *Zentimeter*) cm.

CO_2-neutral [tse:|o'tsvaɪnɔʏtra:l] ADJ carbon neutral

COBOL ['ko:bɔl] NT COBOL

Cockpit ['kɔkpɪt] (**-s, -s**) NT cockpit

Cocktail ['kɔkte:l] (**-s, -s**) M cocktail

Code [ko:t] (**-s, -s**) M code

Cola ['ko:la] (**-(s), -s**) NT OD F Coke®

Collier [kɔli'e:] (**-s, -s**) NT necklet, necklace

Comicheft ['kɔmɪkhɛft] NT comic

Computer [kɔm'pju:tər] (**-s, -**) M computer; **computergesteuert** ADJ computer-controlled; **computergestützt** ADJ computer-based; **computergestütztes Design** computer-aided design; **Computergrafik** F computer graphics *pl*; **Computerkriminalität** F computer crime; **Computerspiel** NT computer game; **Computerspieler(in)** M(F) (*Comput*) gamer; **Computertechnik** F computer technology; **Computervirus** M computer virus

Conférencier [kõferãsi'e:] (**-s, -s**) M compère

Container [kɔn'te:nər] (**-s, -**) M container; **Containerschiff** NT container ship

Contergankind [kɔntɛr'gankɪnt] (*umg*) NT thalidomide child

Cookie ['kʊki] (**-s, -s**) NT (*Comput*) cookie

cool [ku:l] (*umg*) ADJ (*gefasst*) cool

Cord [kɔrt] (**-(e)s, -e** *od* **-s**) M corduroy

Cornichon [kɔrni'ʃõ:] (**-s, -s**) NT gherkin

Couch [kaʊtʃ] (**-, -es** *od* **-en**) F couch; **Couchgarnitur** ['kaʊtʃgarni'tu:r] F three-piece suite

Couleur [ku'lø:r] (**-s, -s**) F (*geh*) kind, sort
Coupé [ku'pe:] (**-s, -s**) NT (*Aut*) coupé, sports version
Coupon [ku'põ:, ku'pɔŋ] (**-s, -s**) M coupon, voucher; (*Stoffcoupon*) length of cloth
Courage [ku'ra:ʒə] (-) F courage
Cousin [ku'zɛ̃:] (**-s, -s**) M cousin
Cousine [ku'zi:nə] (**-, -n**) F cousin
Crack [krɛk] (-) NT (*Droge*) crack
Creme [krɛ:m] (**-, -s**) F (*lit, fig*) cream; (*Schuhcreme*) polish; (*Koch*) mousse; **cremefarben** ADJ cream(-coloured (BRIT) *od* -colored (US))
cremig ['kre:mıç] ADJ creamy
Crux [krʊks] (-) F = **Krux**
CSU [tse:lɛs'lu:] (-) F ABK (= *Christlich-Soziale Union*) Christian Social Union; *see note*

The **CSU** (Christlich-Soziale Union) is a party founded in 1945 in Bavaria. Like its sister party the **CDU** it is a Christian, right-wing party.

CT-Scanner [tse:'te:skenər] M CT scanner
Curriculum [kʊ'ri:kulʊm] (**-s, -cula**) NT (*geh*) curriculum
Curry ['kari] (**-s**) M OD NT curry powder; (*indisches Gericht*) curry; **Currypulver** ['karipʊlfər] NT curry powder; **Currywurst** F curried sausage
Cursor ['kø:rsər] (**-s**) M (*Comput*) cursor; **Cursortaste** F cursor key
Cutter(in) ['katər(ın)] (**-s, -**) M(F) (*Film*) editor
CVJM [tse:faʊjɔt'lɛm] (-) M ABK (= *Christlicher Verein Junger Männer*) YMCA
Cybermobbing ['saıbərmɔbıŋ] (**--s, -**) NT cyberbullying

C

D, d [deː] NT D, d; **D wie Dora** ≈ D for David, ≈ D for Dog (US)
D. ABK = **Doktor**: *der evangelischen Theologie*

SCHLÜSSELWORT

da [daː] ADV **1** (*örtlich*) there; (*hier*) here; **da draußen** out there; **da sein** to be there; **ein Arzt, der immer für seine Patienten da ist** a doctor who always has time for his patients; **da bin ich** here I am; **da hast du dein Geld** (there you are,) there's your money; **da, wo** where; **ist noch Milch da?** is there any milk left?
2 (*zeitlich*) then; (*folglich*) so; **es war niemand im Zimmer, da habe ich ...** there was nobody in the room, so I ...
3: **da haben wir Glück gehabt** we were lucky there; **was gibts denn da zu lachen?** what's so funny about that?; **da kann man nichts machen** nothing can be done about it
▶ KONJ (*weil*) as, since

d. Ä. ABK (= *der Ältere*) Sen., sen.
DAAD (-) M ABK (= *Deutscher Akademischer Austauschdienst*) *German Academic Exchange Service*
dabehalten *unreg* VT to keep
dabei [da'baɪ] ADV (*räumlich*) close to it; (*noch dazu*) besides; (*zusammen mit*) with them/it *etc*; (*zeitlich*) during this; (*obwohl, doch*) but, however; **~ sein** (*anwesend*) to be present; (*beteiligt*) to be involved; **ich bin ~!** count me in!; **was ist schon ~?** what of it?; **es ist doch nichts ~, wenn ...** it doesn't matter if ...; **bleiben wir ~** let's leave it at that; **es soll nicht ~ bleiben** this isn't the end of it; **es bleibt ~** that's settled; **das Dumme/Schwierige ~** the stupid/difficult part of it; **er war gerade ~ zu gehen** he was just leaving; **hast du ~ etwas gelernt?** did you learn anything from it?; **~ darf man nicht vergessen, dass ...** it shouldn't be forgotten that ...; **die ~ entstehenden Kosten** the expenses arising from this; **es kommt doch nichts ~ heraus** nothing will come of it; **ich finde gar nichts ~** I don't see any harm in it; **dabeistehen** *unreg* VI to stand around
Dach [dax] (**-(e)s, Dächer**) NT roof; **unter ~ und Fach sein** (*abgeschlossen*) to be in the bag (*umg*); (*Vertrag, Geschäft*) to be signed and sealed; (*in Sicherheit*) to be safe; **jdm eins aufs ~ geben** (*umg: ausschimpfen*) to give sb a (good) talking to; **Dachboden** M attic, loft; **Dachdecker** (**-s, -**) M slater, tiler; **Dachfenster** NT skylight; (*ausgestellt*) dormer window; **Dachfirst** M ridge of the roof; **Dachgepäckträger** M (*Aut*) roof rack; **Dachgeschoss** NT attic storey (BRIT) *od* story (US); (*oberster Stock*) top floor *od* storey (BRIT) *od* story (US); **Dachluke** F skylight; **Dachpappe** F roofing felt; **Dachrinne** F gutter
Dachs [daks] (**-es, -e**) M badger
Dachschaden (*umg*) M: **einen ~ haben** to have a screw loose
dachte *etc* ['daxtə] VB *siehe* **denken**
Dach- ZW: **Dachterrasse** F roof terrace; **Dachverband** M umbrella organization; **Dachziegel** M roof tile
Dackel ['dakəl] (**-s, -**) M dachshund
dadurch [da'dʊrç] ADV (*räumlich*) through it; (*durch diesen Umstand*) thereby, in that way; (*deshalb*) because of that, for that reason ▶ KONJ: **~, dass** because
dafür [da'fyːr] ADV for it; (*anstatt*) instead; (*zum Ausgleich*): **in Latein ist er schlecht, ~ kann er gut Fußball spielen** he's bad at Latin but he makes up for it at football; **er ist bekannt ~** he is well-known for that; **was bekomme ich ~?** what will I get for it?; **~ ist er immer zu haben** he never says no to that; **~ bin ich ja hier** that's what I'm here for; **er kann nichts ~ (, dass ...)** he can't help it (that ...); **Dafürhalten** (**-s**) NT (*geh*): **nach meinem Dafürhalten** in my opinion
DAG F ABK (= *Deutsche Angestellten-Gewerkschaft*) *Clerical and Administrative Workers' Union*
dagegen [da'geːgən] ADV against it; (*im Vergleich damit*) in comparison with it; (*bei Tausch*) for it ▶ KONJ however; **haben Sie etwas ~, wenn ich rauche?** do you mind if I smoke?; **ich habe nichts ~** I don't mind; **ich war ~** I was against it; **ich hätte nichts ~ (einzuwenden)** that's okay by me; **~ kann man nichts tun** one can't do anything about it; **dagegenhalten** *unreg* VT (*vergleichen*) to compare with it; (*entgegnen*) to put forward as an objection
daheim [da'haɪm] ADV at home; **bei uns ~** back home; **Daheim** (**-s**) NT home

daher [da'he:r] ADV (*räumlich*) from there; (*Ursache*) from that ▸ KONJ (*deshalb*) that's why; **das kommt ~, dass ...** that is because ...; **~ kommt er auch** that's where he comes from too; **~ die Schwierigkeiten** that's what is causing the difficulties; **dahergelaufen** ADJ: **jeder dahergelaufene Kerl** any Tom, Dick or Harry; **daherreden** VI to talk away ▸ VT to say without thinking

dahin [da'hɪn] ADV (*räumlich*) there; (*zeitlich*) then; (*vergangen*) gone; **bis ~** (*zeitlich*) till then; (*örtlich*) up to there; **ist es noch weit bis ~?** is there still far to go?; **~ gehend** on this matter; **das tendiert ~** it is tending towards that; **er bringt es noch ~, dass ich ...** he'll make me ...; **dahingegen** KONJ on the other hand; **dahingehen** *unreg* VI (*Zeit*) to pass; **dahingestellt** ADV: **dahingestellt bleiben** to remain to be seen; **etw dahingestellt sein lassen** to leave sth open *od* undecided; **dahinschleppen** VR (*lit: sich fortbewegen*) to drag o.s. along; (*fig: Verhandlungen, Zeit*) to drag on; **dahinschmelzen** VI to be enthralled

dahinten [da'hɪntən] ADV over there

dahinter [da'hɪntər] ADV behind it; **sich ~ klemmen** *od* **knien** (*umg*) to put one's back into it

dahinterkommen VI to find out

dahinvegetieren [da'hɪnvege'ti:rən] VI to vegetate

Dahlie ['da:liə] (**-, -n**) F dahlia

DAK (**-**) F ABK (= *Deutsche Angestellten-Krankenkasse*) *health insurance company for employees*

Dakar ['dakar] (**-s**) NT Dakar

dalassen ['da:lasən] *unreg* VT to leave (behind)

dalli ['dali] (*umg*) ADV: **~, ~!** on (BRIT) *od* at (US) the double!

damalig ['da:ma:lɪç] ADJ of that time, then

damals ['da:ma:ls] ADV at that time, then

Damaskus [da'maskʊs] NT Damascus

Damast [da'mast] (**-(e)s, -e**) M damask

Dame ['da:mə] (**-, -n**) F lady; (*Schach, Karten*) queen; (*Spiel*) draughts (BRIT), checkers (US)

Damen- ZW: **Damenbesuch** M lady visitor *od* visitors; **Damenbinde** F sanitary towel (BRIT) *od* napkin (US); **damenhaft** ADJ ladylike; **Damensattel** M: **im Damensattel reiten** to ride side-saddle; **Damenwahl** F ladies' excuse-me

Damespiel NT draughts (BRIT), checkers (US)

damit [da'mɪt] ADV with it; (*begründend*) by that ▸ KONJ in order that *od* to; **was meint er ~?** what does he mean by that?; **was soll ich ~?** what am I meant to do with that?; **muss er denn immer wieder ~ ankommen?** must he keep on about it?; **was ist ~?** what about it?; **genug ~!** that's enough!; **~ basta!** and that's that!; **~ eilt es nicht** there's no hurry

dämlich ['dɛ:mlɪç] (*umg*) ADJ silly, stupid

Damm [dam] (**-(e)s, Dämme**) M dyke (BRIT), dike (US); (*Staudamm*) dam; (*Hafendamm*) mole; (*Bahndamm, Straßendamm*) embankment

dämmen ['dɛmən] VT (*Wasser*) to dam up; (*Schmerzen*) to keep back

dämmerig ADJ dim, faint

Dämmerlicht NT twilight; (*abends*) dusk; (*Halbdunkel*) half-light

dämmern ['dɛmərn] VI (*Tag*) to dawn; (*Abend*) to fall; **es dämmerte ihm, dass ...** (*umg*) it dawned on him that ...

Dämmerung F twilight; (*Morgendämmerung*) dawn; (*Abenddämmerung*) dusk

Dämmerzustand M (*Halbschlaf*) dozy state; (*Bewusstseinstrübung*) semi-conscious state

Dämmung F insulation

Dämon ['dɛ:mɔn] (**-s, -en**) M demon

dämonisch [dɛ'mo:nɪʃ] ADJ demonic

Dampf [dampf] (**-(e)s, Dämpfe**) M steam; (*Dunst*) vapour (BRIT), vapor (US); **jdm ~ machen** (*umg*) to make sb get a move on; **~ ablassen** (*lit, fig*) to let off steam; **dampfen** VI to steam

dämpfen ['dɛmpfən] VT (*Koch*) to steam; (*bügeln*) to iron with a damp cloth; (*mit Dampfbügeleisen*) to steam iron; (*fig*) to dampen, to subdue

Dampfer ['dampfər] (**-s, -**) M steamer; **auf dem falschen ~ sein** (*fig*) to have got the wrong idea

Dämpfer (**-s, -**) M (*Mus: bei Klavier*) damper; (*bei Geige, Trompete*) mute; **er hat einen ~ bekommen** (*fig*) it dampened his spirits

Dampf- ZW: **Dampfkochtopf** M pressure cooker; **Dampfmaschine** F steam engine; **Dampfschiff** NT steamship; **Dampfwalze** F steamroller

Damwild ['damvɪlt] NT fallow deer

danach [da'na:x] ADV after that; (*zeitlich*) afterwards; (*gemäß*) accordingly; (*laut diesem*) according to which *od* that; **mir war nicht ~ (zumute)** I didn't feel like it; **er griff schnell ~** he grabbed at it; **~ kann man nicht gehen** you can't go by that; **er sieht ~ aus** he looks it

Däne ['dɛ:nə] (**-n, -n**) M Dane, Danish man/boy

daneben [da'ne:bən] ADV beside it; (*im Vergleich*) in comparison; **~ sein** (*umg: verwirrt sein*) to be completely confused; **danebenbenehmen** *unreg* VR to misbehave; **danebengehen** *unreg* VI to miss; (*Plan*) to fail; **danebengreifen** *unreg* VI to miss; (*fig: mit Schätzung etc*) to be wide of the mark

Dänemark ['dɛ:nəmark] (**-s**) NT Denmark

Dänin ['dɛ:nɪn] F Dane, Danish woman *od* girl

dänisch ADJ Danish

dank PRÄP (*+dat od gen*) thanks to

Dank [daŋk] (**-(e)s**) M thanks *pl*; **vielen** *od* **schönen ~** many thanks; **jdm ~ sagen** to thank sb; **mit (bestem) ~ zurück!** many thanks for the loan

dankbar ADJ grateful; (*Aufgabe*) rewarding; (*haltbar*) hard-wearing; **Dankbarkeit** F gratitude

danke INTERJ thank you, thanks; **~ schön (o sehr)** thank you very much

danken VI *+dat* to thank; **nichts zu ~!** don't mention it; **dankend erhalten/ablehnen** to receive/decline with thanks

dankenswert ADJ (*Arbeit*) worthwhile; (*Aufgabe*) rewarding; (*Bemühung*) kind

Dank- ZW: **Dankgottesdienst** M service of thanksgiving; **danksagen** VI to express one's thanks; **Dankschreiben** NT letter of thanks
dann [dan] ADV then; **~ und wann** now and then; **~ eben nicht** well, in that case (there's no more to be said); **erst ~, wenn ...** only when ...; **~ erst recht nicht!** in that case no way (*umg*)
dannen ['danən] ADV: **von ~** (*liter*: *weg*) away
daran [da'ran] ADV on it; (*stoßen*) against it; **es liegt ~, dass ...** the cause of it is that ...; **gut/schlecht ~ sein** to be well/badly off; **das Beste/Dümmste ~** the best/stupidest thing about it; **ich war nahe ~, zu ...** I was on the point of ...; **im Anschluss ~** (*zeitlich*: *danach anschließend*) following that *od* this; **wir können nichts ~ machen** we can't do anything about it; **es ist nichts ~** (*ist nicht fundiert*) there's nothing in it; (*ist nichts Besonderes*) it's nothing special; **er ist ~ gestorben** he died from *od* of it; **darangehen** *unreg* VI to start; **daranmachen** (*umg*) VR: **sich daranmachen, etw zu tun** to set about doing sth; **daransetzen** VT to stake; **er hat alles darangesetzt, von Glasgow wegzukommen** he has done his utmost to get away from Glasgow
darauf [da'raʊf] ADV (*räumlich*) on it; (*zielgerichtet*) towards it; (*danach*) afterwards; **~ folgend** following; **es kommt ganz ~ an, ob ...** it depends whether ...; **seine Behauptungen stützen sich ~, dass ...** his claims are based on the supposition that ...; **wie kommst du ~?** what makes you think that?; **die Tage ~** the days following *od* thereafter; **am Tag ~** the next day; **darauffolgend** ADJ (*Tag, Jahr*) next, following; **daraufhin** ADV (*im Hinblick darauf*) in this respect; (*aus diesem Grund*) as a result; **wir müssen es daraufhin prüfen, ob ...** we must test it to see whether ...; **drauflegen** VT to lay *od* put on top
daraus [da'raʊs] ADV from it; **was ist ~ geworden?** what became of it?; **~ geht hervor, dass ...** this means that ...
darbieten ['da:rbi:tən] VT (*vortragen*: *Lehrstoff*) to present ▸ VR to present itself
Darbietung F performance
Dardanellen [darda'nɛlən] PL Dardanelles *pl*
Daressalam [darɛsa'la:m] NT Dar-es-Salaam
darf [darf] VB *siehe* **dürfen**
darin [da'rɪn] ADV in (there), in it; **der Unterschied liegt ~, dass ...** the difference is that ...
darlegen ['da:rle:gən] VT to explain, to expound, to set forth
Darlegung F explanation
Darlehen, Darlehn (**-s, -**) NT loan
Darm [darm] (**-(e)s, Därme**) M intestine; (*Wurstdarm*) skin; **Darmausgang** M anus; **Darmgrippe** F gastric influenza; **Darmsaite** F gut string
darstellen ['da:rʃtɛlən] VT (*abbilden, bedeuten*) to represent; (*Theat*) to act; (*beschreiben*) to describe ▸ VR to appear to be
Darsteller(in) (**-s, -**) M(F) actor, actress
darstellerisch ADJ: **eine darstellerische Höchstleistung** a magnificent piece of acting
Darstellung F portrayal, depiction
darüber [da'ry:bər] ADV (*räumlich*) over/above it; (*fahren*) over it; (*mehr*) more; (*währenddessen*) meanwhile; (*sprechen, streiten*) about it; **~ hinweg sein** (*fig*) to have got over it; **~ hinaus** over and above that; **~ geht nichts** there's nothing like it; **seine Gedanken ~** his thoughts about *od* on it; **~ liegen** (*fig*) to be higher
darum [da'rʊm] ADV (*räumlich*) round it ▸ KONJ that's why; **~ herum** round about (it); **er bittet ~** he is pleading for it; **es geht ~, dass ...** the thing is that ...; **~ geht es mir/geht es mir nicht** that's my point/that's not the point for me; **er würde viel ~ geben, wenn ...** he would give a lot to ...; *siehe auch* **drum**
darunter [da'rʊntər] ADV (*räumlich*) under it; (*dazwischen*) among them; (*weniger*) less; **ein Stockwerk ~** one floor below (it); **was verstehen Sie ~?** what do you understand by that?; **~ kann ich mir nichts vorstellen** that doesn't mean anything to me; **~ fallen** to be included; **~ mischen** (*Mehl*) to mix in; **sich ~ mischen** to mingle; **~ setzen** (*Unterschrift*) to put to it; **darunterfallen** VI to be included
das [das] PRON that ▸ DEF ART the; **~ heißt** that is; **~ und ~** such and such; *siehe auch* **der**
Dasein ['da:zaɪn] (**-s**) NT (*Leben*) life; (*Anwesenheit*) presence; (*Bestehen*) existence
da sein *unreg* VI *siehe* **da**
Daseinsberechtigung F right to exist
Daseinskampf M struggle for survival
dasjenige ['dasje:nɪgə] PRON *siehe* **derjenige**
dass [das] KONJ that
dasselbe [das'zɛlbə] NT PRON the same
dastehen ['da:ʃte:ən] *unreg* VI to stand there; (*fig*): **gut/schlecht ~** to be in a good/bad position; **allein ~** to be on one's own
Dat. ABK = **Dativ**
Datei [da'taɪ] F (*Comput*) file; **Dateimanager** M file manager; **Dateiname** M file name; **Dateiverwaltung** F file management
Daten ['da:tən] PL (*Comput*) data; (*Angaben*) data *pl*, particulars; *siehe auch* **Datum**; **Datenabgleich** M data comparison; **Datenaustausch** M (*Comput*) file sharing; **Datenautobahn** F information (super)highway; **Datenbank** F database; **Datendiebstahl** M (*Wirts, Comput*) data theft; **Datenerfassung** F data capture; **Datenleitung** F data line; **Datenmissbrauch** M misuse of data; **Datenmüll** M (*aus dem Internet*) Internet buildup; (*auf Festplatte*) hard disk clutter; **Datennetz** NT data network; **Datensatz** M record; **Datenschutz** M data protection; **Datensichtgerät** NT visual display unit, VDU; **Datenträger** M data carrier; **Datenübertragung** F data transmission; **Datenverarbeitung** F data processing;

Datenverarbeitungsanlage F data processing equipment, DP equipment
datieren [da'ti:rən] VT to date
Dativ ['da:ti:f] (**-s, -e**) M dative; **Dativobjekt** NT (*Gram*) indirect object
dato ['da:to] ADV: **bis ~** (*Comm umg*) to date
Dattel ['datəl] (**-, -n**) F date
Datum ['da:tʊm] (**-s, Daten**) NT date; **das heutige ~** today's date
Datumsgrenze F (*Geog*) (international) date line
Dauer ['daʊər] (**-, -n**) F duration; (*gewisse Zeitspanne*) length; (*Bestand, Fortbestehen*) permanence; **es war nur von kurzer ~** it didn't last long; **auf die ~** in the long run; (*auf längere Zeit*) indefinitely; **Dauerauftrag** M standing order; **dauerhaft** ADJ lasting, durable; **Dauerhaftigkeit** F durability; **Dauerkarte** F season ticket; **Dauerlauf** M long-distance run
dauern VI to last; **es hat sehr lang gedauert, bis er …** it took him a long time to …; **wie lange dauert es denn noch?** how much longer will it be?
dauernd ADJ constant ▸ ADV always, constantly; **er lachte ~** he kept laughing
Dauer- ZW: **Dauerobst** NT fruit suitable for storing; **Dauerredner** (*pej*) M long-winded speaker; **Dauerregen** M continuous rain; **Dauerschlaf** M prolonged sleep; **Dauerstellung** F permanent position; **Dauerwelle** F perm, permanent wave; **Dauerwurst** F German salami; **Dauerzustand** M permanent condition
Daumen ['daʊmən] (**-s, -**) M thumb; **jdm die ~ drücken** *od* **halten** to keep one's fingers crossed for sb; **über den ~ peilen** to guess roughly; **Daumenlutscher** M thumb-sucker
Daune ['daʊnə] (**-, -n**) F down
Daunendecke F down duvet
davon [da'fɔn] ADV of it; (*räumlich*) away; (*weg von*) away from it; (*Grund*) because of it; (*mit Passiv*) by it; **das kommt ~!** that's what you get; **~ abgesehen** apart from that; **wenn wir einmal ~ absehen, dass …** if for once we overlook the fact that …; **~ sprechen/wissen** to talk/know of *od* about it; **was habe ich ~?** what's the point?; **~ betroffen werden** to be affected by it; **davongehen** *unreg* VI to leave, to go away; **davonkommen** *unreg* VI to escape; **davonlassen** *unreg* VT: **die Finger davonlassen** (*umg*) to keep one's hands *od* fingers off (it); **davonlaufen** *unreg* VI to run away; **davonmachen** VR to make off; **davontragen** *unreg* VT to carry off; (*Verletzung*) to receive
davor [da'fo:r] ADV (*räumlich*) in front of it; (*zeitlich*) before (that); **~ warnen** to warn about it
dazu [da'tsu:] ADV (*legen, stellen*) by it; (*essen*) with it; **und ~ noch** and in addition; **ein Beispiel/seine Gedanken ~** one example for/his thoughts on this; **wie komme ich denn ~?** why should I?; **… aber ich bin nicht ~ gekommen** … but I didn't get around to it; **das Recht ~** the right to do it; **~ bereit sein, etw zu tun** to be prepared to do sth; **~ fähig sein** to be capable of it; **sich ~ äußern** to say something on it; **dazugehören** VI to belong to it; **das gehört dazu** (*versteht sich von selbst*) it's all part of it; **es gehört schon einiges dazu, das zu tun** it takes a lot to do that; **dazugehörig** ADJ appropriate; **dazukommen** *unreg* VI (*Ereignisse*) to happen too; (*an einen Ort*) to come along; **kommt noch etwas dazu?** will there be anything else?; **dazulernen** VT: **schon wieder was dazugelernt!** you learn something (new) every day!; **dazumal** ['da:tsuma:l] ADV in those days; **dazutun** *unreg* VT to add; **er hat es ohne dein Dazutun geschafft** he managed it without your doing *etc* anything
dazwischen [da'tsvɪʃən] ADV in between; (*zusammen mit*) among them; **der Unterschied ~** the difference between them; **dazwischenfahren** *unreg* VI (*eingreifen*) to intervene; **dazwischenfunken** (*umg*) VI (*eingreifen*) to put one's oar in; **dazwischenkommen** *unreg* VI (*hineingeraten*) to get caught in it; **es ist etwas dazwischengekommen** something (has) cropped up; **dazwischenreden** VI (*unterbrechen*) to interrupt; (*sich einmischen*) to interfere; **dazwischentreten** *unreg* VI to intervene
DB F ABK (= *Deutsche Bahn*) *German railways*
DBP F ABK (*früher*) = **Deutsche Bundespost**
DDR (-) F ABK (*früher*: = *Deutsche Demokratische Republik*) GDR

> The **DDR** (Deutsche Demokratische Republik) was the name by which the former Communist German Democratic Republic was known. It was founded in 1949 from the Soviet-occupied zone. After the building of the Berlin Wall in 1961 it was virtually sealed off from the West until mass demonstrations and demands for reform forced the opening of the borders in 1989. It then merged in 1990 with the **BRD**.

DDT® NT ABK DDT
Dealer(in) ['di:lər(ɪn)] (**-s, -**) (*umg*) M(F) pusher
Debatte [de'batə] (**-, -n**) F debate; **das steht hier nicht zur ~** that's not the issue
debattieren [deba'ti:rən] VT to debate
Debet ['de:bɛt] (**-s, -s**) NT (*Fin*) debits *pl*
Debüt [de'by:] (**-s, -s**) NT debut
dechiffrieren [deʃɪ'fri:rən] VT to decode; (*Text*) to decipher
Deck [dɛk] (**-(e)s, -s** *od* **-e**) NT deck; **an ~ gehen** to go on deck
Deckbett NT feather quilt
Deckblatt NT (*Schutzblatt*) cover
Decke (**-, -n**) F cover; (*Bettdecke*) blanket; (*Tischdecke*) tablecloth; (*Zimmerdecke*) ceiling; **unter einer ~ stecken** to be hand in glove; **an die ~ gehen** to hit the roof; **mir fällt die ~ auf den Kopf** (*fig*) I feel really claustrophobic
Deckel (**-s, -**) M lid; **du kriegst gleich eins auf den ~** (*umg*) you're going to catch it
Deckelung F capping

decken VT to cover; *(Tisch)* to lay, to set ▶ VR: **sich ~** *(Interessen)* to coincide; *(Aussagen)* to correspond; **mein Bedarf ist gedeckt** I have all I need; *(fig)* I've had enough; **sich an einen gedeckten Tisch setzen** *(fig)* to be handed everything on a plate
Deckmantel M: **unter dem ~ von** under the guise of
Deckname M assumed name
Deckung F *(das Schützen)* covering; *(Schutz)* cover; *(Sport)* defence (BRIT), defense (US); *(Übereinstimmen)* agreement; **zur ~ seiner Schulden** to meet his debts
deckungsgleich ADJ congruent
Decoder M *(TV)* decoder
de facto [de: 'fakto] ADV de facto
defekt ADJ faulty
Defekt [de'fɛkt] (**-(e)s, -e**) M fault, defect
defensiv [defɛn'si:f] ADJ defensive
Defensive F: **jdn in die ~ drängen** to force sb onto the defensive
definieren [defi'ni:rən] VT to define
Definition [definitsi'o:n] F definition
definitiv [defini'ti:f] ADJ definite
Defizit ['de:fitsɪt] (**-s, -e**) NT deficit
defizitär [defitsi'tɛ:r] ADJ: **eine defizitäre Haushaltspolitik führen** to follow an economic policy which can only lead to deficit
Deflation [deflatsi'o:n] F *(Wirts)* deflation
deflationär [deflatsio'nɛ:r] ADJ deflationary
deftig ['dɛftɪç] ADJ *(Preise)* steep; *(Witz)* coarse; **ein deftiges Essen** a good solid meal
Degen ['de:gən] (**-s, -**) M sword
degenerieren [degene'ri:rən] VI to degenerate
degradieren [degra'di:rən] VT to degrade
dehnbar ['de:nba:r] ADJ elastic; *(fig: Begriff)* loose; **Dehnbarkeit** F elasticity; *(von Begriff)* looseness
dehnen VT, VR to stretch
Dehnung F stretching
Deich [daɪç] (**-(e)s, -e**) M dyke (BRIT), dike (US)
Deichsel ['daɪksəl] (**-, -n**) F shaft
deichseln VT *(fig: umg)* to wangle
dein [daɪn] PRON your; *(adjektivisch)*: **herzliche Grüße, Deine Elke** with best wishes, yours *od* *(herzlicher)* love, Elke
deine(r, s) POSS PRON yours
deiner GEN *von* **du** ▶ PRON of you
deinerseits ADV on your part
deinesgleichen PRON people like you
deinetwegen ['daɪnət've:gən] ADV *(für dich)* for your sake; *(wegen dir)* on your account
deinetwillen ['daɪnət'vɪlən] ADV: **um ~** = **deinetwegen**
deinige PRON: **der/die/das D~** yours
deinstallieren [delɪnsta'li:rən] VT *(Programm)* to uninstall
dekadent [deka'dɛnt] ADJ decadent
Dekadenz F decadence
Dekan [de'ka:n] (**-s, -e**) M dean
deklassieren [dekla'si:rən] VT *(Soziologie: herabsetzen)* to downgrade; *(Sport: übertreffen)* to outclass
Deklination [deklinatsi'o:n] F declension
deklinieren [dekli'ni:rən] VT to decline
Dekolleté, Dekolletee [dekɔl'te:] (**-s, -s**) NT low neckline
dekomprimieren VT *(Comput)* to decompress
Dekor [de'ko:r] (**-s, -s** *od* **-e**) M OD NT decoration
Dekorateur(in) [dekora'tø:r(ɪn)] M(F) window dresser
Dekoration [dekoratsi'o:n] F decoration; *(in Laden)* window dressing
dekorativ [dekora'ti:f] ADJ decorative
dekorieren [deko'ri:rən] VT to decorate; *(Schaufenster)* to dress
Dekostoff ['de:koʃtɔf] M *(Textil)* furnishing fabric
Dekret [de'kre:t] (**-(e)s, -e**) NT decree
Delegation [delegatsi'o:n] F delegation
delegieren [dele'gi:rən] VT: **~ (an** *+akk***)** to delegate (to)
Delegierte(r) F(M) delegate
Delfin [dɛl'fi:n] (**-s, -e**) M dolphin
Delfinschwimmen NT butterfly (stroke)
Delhi ['de:lɪ] (**-s**) NT Delhi
delikat [deli'ka:t] ADJ *(zart, heikel)* delicate; *(köstlich)* delicious
Delikatesse [delika'tɛsə] (**-, -n**) F delicacy
Delikatessengeschäft NT delicatessen (shop)
Delikt [de'lɪkt] (**-(e)s, -e**) NT *(Jur)* offence (BRIT), offense (US)
Delinquent [delɪŋ'kvɛnt] M *(geh)* offender
Delirium [de'li:riʊm] NT: **im ~ sein** to be delirious; *(umg: betrunken)* to be paralytic
Delle ['dɛlə] (**-, -n**) *(umg)* F dent
Delphin [dɛl'fi:n] (**-s, -e**) M = **Delfin**
Delta ['dɛlta] (**-s, -s**) NT delta
dem [de(:)m] ART *dat von* **der**; **das**; **wie ~ auch sei** be that as it may
Demagoge [dema'go:gə] (**-n, -n**) M demagogue
Demarkationslinie [demarkatsi'o:nzli:niə] F demarcation line
Dementi [de'mɛnti] (**-s, -s**) NT denial
dementieren [demɛn'ti:rən] VT to deny
dem- ZW: **dementsprechend** ADJ appropriate ▶ ADV correspondingly; *(demnach)* accordingly; **demgemäß** ADV accordingly; **demnach** ADV accordingly; **demnächst** ADV shortly
Demo ['de:mo] (**-s, -s**) *(umg)* F demo
Demografie [demogra'fi:] F demography
Demokrat(in) [demo'kra:t(ɪn)] (**-en, -en**) M(F) democrat
Demokratie [demokra'ti:] F democracy; **Demokratieverständnis** NT understanding of (the meaning of) democracy
demokratisch ADJ democratic
demokratisieren [demokrati'zi:rən] VT to democratize
demolieren [demo'li:rən] VT to demolish
Demonstrant(in) [demɔn'strant(ɪn)] M(F) demonstrator
Demonstration [demɔnstratsi'o:n] F demonstration
demonstrativ [demɔnstra'ti:f] ADJ demonstrative; *(Protest)* pointed

demonstrieren [demɔn'stri:rən] VT, VI to demonstrate
Demontage [demɔn'ta:ʒə] (**-, -n**) F (*lit, fig*) dismantling
demontieren [demɔn'ti:rən] VT (*lit, fig*) to dismantle; (*Räder*) to take off
demoralisieren [demorali'zi:rən] VT to demoralize
Demoskopie [demosko'pi:] F public opinion research
demselben DAT *von* **derselbe**; **dasselbe**
Demut ['de:mu:t] (-) F humility
demütig ['de:my:tɪç] ADJ humble
demütigen ['de:my:tɪgən] VT to humiliate
Demütigung F humiliation
demzufolge ['de:mtsu'fɔlgə] ADV accordingly
den [de(:)n] ART *akk von* **der**
denen ['de:nən] PRON *dat pl von* **der**; **die**; **das**
Denk- ZW: **Denkanstoß** M: **jdm Denkanstöße geben** to give sb food for thought; **Denkart** F mentality; **denkbar** ADJ conceivable ▸ ADV: **denkbar einfach** extremely simple
denken ['dɛŋkən] *unreg* VI to think ▸ VT: **für jdn/etw gedacht sein** to be intended *od* meant for sb/sth ▸ VR (*vorstellen*): **das kann ich mir ~** I can imagine; (*beabsichtigen*): **sich** *dat* **etw bei etw ~** to mean sth by sth; **wo ~ Sie hin!** what an idea!; **ich denke schon** I think so; **an jdn/etw ~** to think of sb/sth; **daran ist gar nicht zu ~** that's (quite) out of the question; **ich denke nicht daran, das zu tun** there's no way I'm going to do that (*umg*)
Denken (**-s**) NT thinking
Denker(in) (**-s, -**) M(F) thinker; **das Volk der Dichter und ~** the nation of poets and philosophers
Denk- ZW: **Denkfähigkeit** F intelligence; **denkfaul** ADJ mentally lazy; **Denkfehler** M logical error; **Denkhorizont** M mental horizon
Denkmal (**-s, Denkmäler**) NT monument; **Denkmalschutz** M: **etw unter Denkmalschutz stellen** to classify sth as a historical monument
Denk- ZW: **Denkpause** F: **eine Denkpause einlegen** to have a break to think things over; **Denkschrift** F memorandum; **Denkvermögen** NT intellectual capacity; **denkwürdig** ADJ memorable; **Denkzettel** M: **jdm einen Denkzettel verpassen** to teach sb a lesson
denn [dɛn] KONJ for; (*konzessiv*): **es sei ~, (dass)** unless ▸ ADV then; (*nach Komparativ*) than
dennoch ['dɛnnɔx] KONJ nevertheless ▸ ADV: **und ~, ...** and yet ...
denselben AKK *von* **derselbe** ▸ DAT *von* **dieselben**
Denunziant(in) [denʊntsi'ant(ɪn)] M(F) informer
denunzieren [denʊn'tsi:rən] VT to inform against
Deo [de:o] (**-s, -s**), **Deodorant** (**-s, -s**) NT deodorant; **Deoroller** ['de:orɔlər] M roll-on deodorant; **Deospray** ['de:ospreɪ] NT OD M deodorant spray
Depesche [de'pɛʃə] (**-, -n**) F dispatch
deplatziert [depla'tsi:rt] ADJ out of place
Deponent(in) [depo'nɛnt(ɪn)] M(F) depositor
Deponie F dump, disposal site
deponieren [depo'ni:rən] VT (*Comm*) to deposit
deportieren [depɔr'ti:rən] VT to deport
Depot [de'po:] (**-s, -s**) NT warehouse; (*Busdepot, Eisenb*) depot; (*Bankdepot*) strongroom (BRIT), safe (*US*)
Depp [dɛp] (**-en, -en**) M (*Dialekt: pej*) twit
Depression [depresi'o:n] F depression
depressiv ADJ depressive; (*Fin*) depressed
deprimieren [depri'mi:rən] VT to depress

SCHLÜSSELWORT

der [de(:)r] (*f* **die**, *nt* **das**, *gen* **des**, **der**, **des**, *dat* **dem**, **der**, **dem**, *akk* **den**) DEF ART the; **der Rhein** the Rhine; **der Klaus** (*umg*) Klaus; **die Frau** (*im Allgemeinen*) women; **der Tod/das Leben** death/life; **der Fuß des Berges** the foot of the hill; **gib es der Frau** give it to the woman; **er hat sich** *dat* **die Hand verletzt** he has hurt his hand
▸ REL PRON (*bei Menschen*) who, that; (*bei Tieren, Sachen*) which, that; **der Mann, den ich gesehen habe** the man who *od* whom *od* that I saw
▸ DEMON PRON he/she/it; (*jener, dieser*) that; (*pl*) those; **der/die war es** it was him/her; **der mit der Brille** the one with the glasses; **ich will den (da)** I want that one

derart ['de:r'a:rt] ADV (*Art und Weise*) in such a way; (*Ausmaß: vor adj*) so; (*: vor vb*) so much
derartig ADJ such, this sort of
derb [dɛrp] ADJ sturdy; (*Kost*) solid; (*grob*) coarse; **Derbheit** F sturdiness; (*von Kost*) solidity; (*Grobheit*) coarseness
deren ['de:rən] REL PRON (*gen sing von die*) whose; (*von Sachen*) of which; (*gen pl von der, die, das*) whose, of whom
derentwillen ['de:rənt'vɪlən] ADV: **um ~** (*rel*) for whose sake; (*von Sachen*) for the sake of which
dergestalt ADV (*geh*): **~, dass ...** in such a way that ...
der- ZW: **dergleichen** PRON such; (*substantivisch*): **er tat nichts dergleichen** he did nothing of the kind; **und dergleichen (mehr)** and suchlike; **derjenige** PRON he/she/it; (*rel*) the one (who); (*von Sachen*) that (which); **dermaßen** ADV to such an extent, so; **derselbe** M PRON the same; **derweil, derweilen** ADV in the meantime; **derzeit** ADV (*jetzt*) at present, at the moment; **derzeitig** ADJ present, current; (*damalig*) then
des [dɛs] ART GEN *von* **der**
Des [dɛs] (-) NT (*Mus: auch*: **des**) D flat
Deserteur [dezɛr'tø:r] M deserter
desertieren [dezɛr'ti:rən] VI to desert
desgl. ABK = **desgleichen**
desgleichen ['dɛs'glaɪçən] PRON the same
deshalb ['dɛs'halp] ADV, KONJ therefore, that's why
Design [di'zaɪn] (**-s, -s**) NT design

designiert [dezi'gni:rt] ADJ *attrib*: **der designierte Vorsitzende/Nachfolger** the chairman designate/prospective successor
Desinfektion [dezɪnfɛktsi'o:n] F disinfection
Desinfektionsmittel NT disinfectant
desinfizieren [dezɪnfi'tsi:rən] VT to disinfect
Desinteresse [dɛslɪntə'rɛsə] **(-s)** NT: **~ (an** *+dat***)** lack of interest (in)
desinteressiert [dɛslɪntərɛ'si:rt] ADJ uninterested
desselben GEN *von* **derselbe; dasselbe**
dessen ['dɛsən] PRON *gen von* **der; das**; **~ ungeachtet** nevertheless, regardless
Dessert [dɛ'sɛ:r] **(-s, -s)** NT dessert
Dessin [dɛ'sɛ̃:] **(-s, -s)** NT (*Textil*) pattern, design
Destillation [dɛstɪlatsi'o:n] F distillation
destillieren [dɛstɪ'li:rən] VT to distil
desto ['dɛsto] ADV all *od* so much the; **~ besser** all the better
destruktiv [destrʊk'ti:f] ADJ destructive
deswegen ['dɛs've:gən] KONJ therefore, hence
Detail [de'taɪ] **(-s, -s)** NT detail
detaillieren [deta'ji:rən] VT to specify, to give details of
Detektiv [detɛk'ti:f] **(-s, -e)** M detective; **Detektivroman** M detective novel
Detektor [de'tɛktɔr] M (*Tech*) detector
Detonation [detonatsi'o:n] F explosion, blast
Deut M: **(um) keinen ~** not one iota *od* jot
deuten ['dɔytən] VT to interpret; (*Zukunft*) to read ▸ VI: **~ (auf** *+akk***)** to point (to *od* at)
deutlich ADJ clear; (*Unterschied*) distinct; **jdm etw ~ zu verstehen geben** to make sth perfectly clear *od* plain to sb; **Deutlichkeit** F clarity; (*von Unterschied*) distinctness
deutsch [dɔʏtʃ] ADJ German; **deutsche Schrift** Gothic script; **auf D~** in German; **auf gut D~ (gesagt)** (*fig: umg*) ≈ in plain English; **Deutsche Demokratische Republik** (*Hist*) German Democratic Republic
Deutsche(r) F(M): **er ist ~** he is (a) German
Deutschland NT Germany; **Deutschlandlied** NT *German national anthem*; **Deutschlandpolitik** F home *od* domestic policy; (*von fremdem Staat*) policy towards Germany
deutschsprachig ADJ (*Bevölkerung, Gebiete*) German-speaking; (*Zeitung, Ausgabe*) German-language; (*Literatur*) German
deutschstämmig ADJ of German origin
Deutung F interpretation
Devise [de'vi:zə] **(-, -n)** F motto, device; **Devisen** PL (*Fin*) foreign currency *od* exchange
Devisenausgleich M foreign exchange offset
Devisenkontrolle F exchange control
Dez. ABK (= *Dezember*) Dec.
Dezember [de'tsɛmbər] **(-(s), -)** M December; *siehe auch* **September**
dezent [de'tsɛnt] ADJ discreet
Dezentralisation [detsɛntralizatsi'o:n] F decentralization
Dezernat [detsɛr'na:t] **(-(e)s, -e)** NT (*Verwaltung*) department
Dezibel [detsi'bɛl] **(-s, -)** NT decibel
dezidiert [detsi'di:rt] ADJ firm, determined
dezimal [detsi'ma:l] ADJ decimal; **Dezimalbruch** M decimal (fraction); **Dezimalsystem** NT decimal system
dezimieren [detsi'mi:rən] VT (*fig*) to decimate ▸ VR to be decimated
DFB M ABK (= *Deutscher Fußball-Bund*) *German Football Association*
DFG F ABK (= *Deutsche Forschungsgemeinschaft*) *German Research Council*
DGB M ABK (= *Deutscher Gewerkschaftsbund*) ≈ TUC
dgl. ABK = **dergleichen**
d. h. ABK (= *das heißt*) i.e.
Di. ABK = **Dienstag**
Dia ['di:a] **(-s, -s)** NT slide
Diabetes [dia'be:tɛs] **(-, -)** M (*Med*) diabetes
Diabetiker(in) [dia'be:tikər(ɪn)] **(-s, -)** M(F) diabetic
Diagnose [dia'gno:zə] **(-, -n)** F diagnosis
diagnostizieren [diagnɔsti'tsi:rən] VT, VI (*Med, fig*) to diagnose
diagonal [diago'na:l] ADJ diagonal
Diagonale (-, -n) F diagonal
Diagramm [dia'gram] NT diagram
Diakonie [diako'ni:] F (*Rel*) social welfare work
Dialekt [dia'lɛkt] **(-(e)s, -e)** M dialect; **Dialektausdruck** M dialect expression *od* word; **dialektfrei** ADJ without an accent
dialektisch ADJ dialectal; (*Logik*) dialectical
Dialog [dia'lo:k] **(-(e)s, -e)** M dialogue
Diamant [dia'mant] M diamond
Diapositiv [diapozi'ti:f] **(-s, -e)** NT (*Phot*) slide, transparency
Diaprojektor M slide projector
Diät [di'ɛ:t] (-) F diet; **Diäten** PL (*Pol*) allowance *sing*; **~ essen** to eat according to a diet; **(nach einer) ~ leben** to be on a special diet
Diavortrag M slide show
dich [dɪç] AKK *von* **du** ▸ PRON you ▸ REFL PRON yourself
dicht [dɪçt] ADJ dense; (*Nebel*) thick; (*Gewebe*) close; (*undurchlässig*) (water)tight; (*fig*) concise; (*umg: zu*) shut, closed ▸ ADV: **~ an/bei** close to; **er ist nicht ganz ~** (*umg*) he's crackers; **~ machen** to make watertight/airtight; **~ hintereinander** right behind one another; **~ bevölkert** densely *od* heavily populated; *siehe auch* **dichtmachen**
Dichte (-, -n) F density; (*von Nebel*) thickness; (*von Gewebe*) closeness; (*Undurchlässigkeit*) (water)tightness; (*fig*) conciseness
dichten VT (*dicht machen*) to make watertight; (*versiegeln*) to seal; (*Naut*) to caulk; (*Liter*) to compose, to write ▸ VI (*Liter*) to compose, to write
Dichter(in) (-s, -) M(F) poet; (*Autor*) writer; **dichterisch** ADJ poetical; **dichterische Freiheit** poetic licence (BRIT) *od* license (US)
dichthalten *unreg* (*umg*) VI to keep one's mouth shut
dichtmachen (*umg*) VT (*Geschäft*) to wind up ▸ VI (*Person*) to close one's mind; *siehe auch* **dicht**

Dichtung F (*Tech*) washer; (*Aut*) gasket; (*Gedichte*) poetry; (*Prosa*) (piece of) writing; **~ und Wahrheit** (*fig*) fact and fantasy
dick [dɪk] ADJ thick; (*fett*) fat; **durch ~ und dünn** through thick and thin; **Dickdarm** M (*Anat*) colon
Dicke (-, -n) F thickness; (*von Mensch*) fatness
dickfellig ADJ thick-skinned
dickflüssig ADJ viscous
Dickicht (-s, -e) NT thicket
dick- ZW: **Dickkopf** M mule; **Dickmilch** F soured milk; **Dickschädel** M = **Dickkopf**
die [di:] DEF ART the; *siehe auch* **der**
Dieb(in) [di:p, 'di:bɪn] (-(e)s, -e) M(F) thief; **haltet den ~!** stop thief!; **diebisch** ADJ thieving; (*umg*) immense; **Diebstahl** M theft; **diebstahlsicher** ADJ theft-proof
diejenige ['di:je:nɪgə] PRON *siehe* **derjenige**
Diele ['di:lə] (-, -n) F (*Brett*) board; (*Flur*) hall, lobby; (*Eisdiele*) ice-cream parlour (BRIT) *od* parlor (US)
dienen ['di:nən] VI: **(jdm) ~** to serve (sb); **womit kann ich Ihnen ~?** what can I do for you?; (*in Geschäft*) can I help you?
Diener (-s, -) M servant; (*umg: Verbeugung*) bow; **Dienerin** F (maid)servant
dienern VI (*fig*): **~ (vor** *+dat*) to bow and scrape (to)
Dienerschaft F servants *pl*
dienlich ADJ useful, helpful
Dienst [di:nst] (-(e)s, -e) M service; (*Arbeit, Arbeitszeit*) work; **~ am Kunden** customer service; **jdm zu Diensten stehen** to be at sb's disposal; **außer ~** retired; **~ haben** to be on duty; **~ habend** = **diensthabend**; **~ tuend** = **diensttuend**; **der öffentliche ~** the civil service
Dienstag M Tuesday; **am ~** on Tuesday; **~ in acht Tagen** *od* **in einer Woche** a week on Tuesday, Tuesday week; **~ vor einer Woche** *od* **acht Tagen** a week (ago) last Tuesday
dienstags ADV on Tuesdays
Dienst- ZW: **Dienstalter** NT length of service; **dienstbeflissen** ADJ zealous; **Dienstbote** M servant; **Dienstboteneingang** M tradesmen's *od* service entrance; **diensteifrig** ADJ zealous; **dienstfrei** ADJ off duty; **Dienstgebrauch** M (*Mil, Verwaltung*): **nur für den Dienstgebrauch** for official use only; **Dienstgeheimnis** NT professional secret; **Dienstgespräch** NT business call; **Dienstgrad** M rank; **diensthabend** ADJ (*Arzt, Offizier*) on duty; **Dienstleistung** F service; **Dienstleistungsbereich** M service sector *od* industry; **Dienstleistungsbetrieb** M service industry business; **Dienstleistungsgewerbe** NT service industries *pl*; **Dienstleistungssektor** M service sector *od* industry; **dienstlich** ADJ official; (*Angelegenheiten*) business *attrib*; **Dienstmädchen** NT domestic servant; **Dienstplan** M duty rota; **Dienstreise** F business trip; **Dienststelle** F office; **diensttuend** ADJ on duty; **Dienstvorschrift** F service regulations *pl*; **Dienstwagen** M (*von Beamten*) official car; **Dienstweg** M official channels *pl*; **Dienstzeit** F office hours *pl*; (*Mil*) period of service
diesbezüglich ADJ (*Frage*) on this matter
diese(r, s) PRON this (one) ▸ ADJ this; **~ Nacht** tonight
Diesel ['di:zəl] (-s) M (*Kraftstoff*) diesel fuel
dieselbe [di:'zɛlbə] F PRON the same
dieselben [di:'zɛlbən] PL PRON the same
Dieselöl ['di:zəlø:l] NT diesel oil
diesig ADJ drizzly
dies- ZW: **diesjährig** ADJ this year's; **diesmal** ADV this time; **diesseits** PRÄP *+gen* on this side; **Diesseits** (-) NT this life
Dietrich ['di:trɪç] (-s, -e) M picklock
Diffamierungskampagne [dɪfa'mi:rʊŋskampanjə] F smear campaign
differential *etc* [dɪferɛntsi'a:l] ADJ = **differenzial** *usw*
Differenz [dɪfe'rɛnts] F difference; **Differenzbetrag** M difference, balance
differenzial [dɪferɛntsi'a:l] ADJ differential; **Differenzialgetriebe** NT differential gear; **Differenzialrechnung** F differential calculus
differenzieren [dɪferɛn'tsi:rən] VT to make distinctions in ▸ VI: **~ (bei)** to make distinctions (in)
differenziert ADJ complex
diffus [dɪ'fu:s] ADJ (*Gedanken etc*) confused
digital ADJ digital
Digitalanzeige F digital display
Digital- [digi'ta:l-] ZW: **Digitalfernsehen** NT digital TV; **Digitalkamera** F digital camera; **Digitalrechner** M digital computer; **Digitaluhr** F digital watch
Diktafon, Diktaphon [dɪkta'fo:n] NT dictaphone®
Diktat [dɪk'ta:t] (-(e)s, -e) NT dictation; (*fig: Gebot*) dictate; (*Pol*) diktat, dictate
Diktator [dɪk'ta:tɔr] M dictator; **diktatorisch** [-a'to:rɪʃ] ADJ dictatorial
Diktatur [dɪkta'tu:r] F dictatorship
diktieren [dɪk'ti:rən] VT to dictate
Diktion [dɪktsi'o:n] F style
Dilemma [di'lɛma] (-s, -s *od* -ta) NT dilemma
Dilettant [dilɛ'tant] M dilettante, amateur; **dilettantisch** ADJ dilettante
Dimension [dimɛnzi'o:n] F dimension
DIN F ABK (= *Deutsche Industrie-Norm*) *German Industrial Standard*; **~ A4** A4
Ding [dɪŋ] (-(e)s, -e) NT thing; (*Objekt*) object; **das ist ein ~ der Unmöglichkeit** that is totally impossible; **guter Dinge sein** to be in good spirits; **so wie die Dinge liegen, nach Lage der Dinge** as things are; **es müsste nicht mit rechten Dingen zugehen, wenn ...** it would be more than a little strange if ...; **ein krummes ~ drehen** to commit a crime; **dingfest** ADJ: **jdn dingfest machen** to arrest sb; **dinglich** ADJ real, concrete
Dings (-) (*umg*) NT thingummyjig (BRIT)
Dingsbums ['dɪŋsbʊms] (-) (*umg*) NT thingummybob (BRIT)

d

Dingsda (-) (*umg*) NT thingummyjig (BRIT)
Dinosaurier [dino'zaʊriər] M dinosaur
Diözese [diø'tse:zə] (-, **-n**) F diocese
Diphtherie [dɪfte'ri:] F diphtheria
Dipl.-Ing. ABK = **Diplom-Ingenieur**
Diplom [di'plo:m] (**-(e)s, -e**) NT diploma; (*Hochschulabschluss*) degree; **Diplomarbeit** F dissertation
Diplomat [diplo'ma:t] (**-en, -en**) M diplomat
Diplomatie [diploma'ti:] F diplomacy
diplomatisch [diplo'ma:tɪʃ] ADJ diplomatic
Diplom-Ingenieur M academically qualified engineer
dir [di:r] DAT *von* **du** ▶ PRON (to) you
direkt [di'rɛkt] ADJ direct; **~ fragen** to ask outright *od* straight out
Direktflug M direct flight
Direktion [dirɛktsi'o:n] F management; (*Büro*) manager's office
Direktmandat NT (*Pol*) direct mandate
Direktor(in) M(F) director; (*von Hochschule*) principal; (*von Schule*) principal, head (teacher) (BRIT)
Direktorium [direk'to:riʊm] NT board of directors
Direktübertragung F live broadcast
Direktverkauf M direct selling
Dirigent(in) [diri'gɛnt(ɪn)] M(F) conductor
dirigieren [diri'gi:rən] VT to direct; (*Mus*) to conduct
Dirne ['dɪrnə] (-, **-n**) F prostitute
dis [dɪs] (-, -) NT (*Mus*) D sharp
Dis [dɪs] (-, -) NT (*Mus*) D sharp
Disco ['dɪsko] (-, **-s**) F disco
Disharmonie [dɪsharmo'ni:] F (*lit, fig*) discord
Diskette [dɪs'kɛtə] F disk, diskette
Diskettenlaufwerk NT disk drive
Disko ['dɪsko] (-, **-s**) F disco
Diskont [dɪs'kɔnt] (**-s, -e**) M discount; **Diskontsatz** M rate of discount
Diskothek [dɪsko'te:k] (-, **-en**) F disco(theque)
diskreditieren [dɪskredi'ti:rən] VT (*geh*) to discredit
Diskrepanz [dɪskre'pants] F discrepancy
diskret [dɪs'kre:t] ADJ discreet
Diskretion [dɪskretsi'o:n] F discretion; **strengste ~ wahren** to preserve the strictest confidence
diskriminieren [dɪskrimi'ni:rən] VT to discriminate against
Diskriminierung F: **~ (von)** discrimination (against)
Diskussion [dɪskʊsi'o:n] F discussion; **zur ~ stehen** to be under discussion
Diskussionsbeitrag M contribution to the discussion
Diskuswerfen ['dɪskʊsvɛrfən] NT throwing the discus
diskutabel [dɪsku'ta:bəl] ADJ debatable
diskutieren [dɪsku'ti:rən] VT, VI to discuss; **darüber lässt sich ~** that sounds like something we could talk about
disponieren [dɪspo'ni:rən] VI (*geh: planen*) to make arrangements
Disposition [dɪspozitsi'o:n] F (*geh: Verfügung*): **jdm zur** *od* **zu jds ~ stehen** to be at sb's disposal
disqualifizieren [dɪskvalifi'tsi:rən] VT to disqualify
dissen ['dɪsən] (*umg*) VT to slag off (BRIT), to diss (*bes US*)
Dissertation [dɪsɛrtatsi'o:n] F dissertation; (*Doktorarbeit*) doctoral thesis
Dissident(in) [dɪsi'dɛnt(ɪn)] M(F) dissident
Distanz [dɪs'tants] F distance; (*fig: Abstand, Entfernung*) detachment; (*Zurückhaltung*) reserve
distanzieren [dɪstan'tsi:rən] VR: **sich von jdm/etw ~** to dissociate o.s. from sb/sth
distanziert ADJ (*Verhalten*) distant
Distel ['dɪstəl] (-, **-n**) F thistle
Disziplin [dɪstsi'pli:n] (-, **-en**) F discipline
Disziplinarverfahren [dɪstsipli'narfɛrfa:rən] NT disciplinary proceedings *pl*
dito ['di:to] ADV (*hum, Comm*) ditto
Diva ['di:va] (-, **-s**) F star; (*Film*) screen goddess
divers [di'vɛrs] ADJ various
Diverses PL sundries *pl*; **„~"** "miscellaneous"
Dividende [divi'dɛndə] (-, **-n**) F dividend
dividieren [divi'di:rən] VT: **~ (durch)** to divide (by)
d. J. ABK (= *der Jüngere*) jun.
Djakarta [dʒa'karta] NT Jakarta
DJH NT ABK (= *Deutsches Jugendherbergswerk*) *German Youth Hostel Association*
DKP F ABK (= *Deutsche Kommunistische Partei*) *German Communist Party*
DLV M ABK (= *Deutscher Leichtathletik-Verband*) *German track and field association*
DM F ABK (*Hist:* = *Deutsche Mark*) DM
d. M. ABK (= *dieses Monats*) inst.
D-Mark ['de:mark] (-, -) F (*Hist*) deutschmark
DNS F ABK (= *Desoxyribo(se)nukleinsäure*) DNA
Do. ABK = **Donnerstag**

SCHLÜSSELWORT

doch [dɔx] ADV **1** (*dennoch*) after all; (*sowieso*) anyway; **er kam doch noch** he came after all; **du weißt es ja doch besser** you know more about it (than I do) anyway; **es war doch ganz interessant** it was actually quite interesting; **und doch, …** and yet …
2 (*als bejahende Antwort*) yes I do/it does *etc*; **das ist nicht wahr — doch!** that's not true — yes it is!
3 (*auffordernd*): **komm doch** do come; **lass ihn doch** just leave him; **nicht doch!** oh no!
4: **sie ist doch noch so jung** but she's still so young; **Sie wissen doch, wie das ist** you know how it is(, don't you?); **wenn doch** if only
▶ KONJ (*aber*) but; (*trotzdem*) all the same; **und doch hat er es getan** but still he did it

Docht [dɔxt] (**-(e)s, -e**) M wick
Dock [dɔk] (**-s, -s** *od* **-e**) NT dock; **Dockgebühren** PL dock dues *pl*

Dogge ['dɔgə] (-, **-n**) F bulldog; **Deutsche ~** Great Dane
Dogma ['dɔgma] (**-s, -men**) NT dogma
dogmatisch [dɔ'gma:tɪʃ] ADJ dogmatic
Dohle ['do:lə] (-, **-n**) F jackdaw
Doktor ['dɔktɔr] (**-s, -en**) M doctor; **den ~ machen** (*umg*) to do a doctorate *od* Ph.D.
Doktorand(in) [dɔktɔ'rant (-dɪn)] (**-en, -en**) M(F) Ph.D. student
Doktor- zW: **Doktorarbeit** F doctoral thesis; **Doktortitel** M doctorate; **Doktorvater** M supervisor
doktrinär [dɔktri'nɛ:r] ADJ doctrinal; (*stur*) doctrinaire
Dokument [doku'mɛnt] NT document
Dokumentar- zW: **Dokumentarbericht** M documentary; **Dokumentarfilm** M documentary (film); **dokumentarisch** ADJ documentary; **Dokumentarspiel** NT docudrama
Dokumentationszentrum NT documentation centre (BRIT) *od* center (US)
dokumentieren [dokumɛn'ti:rən] VT to document; (*fig: zu erkennen geben*) to reveal, to show
Dolch [dɔlç] (**-(e)s, -e**) M dagger; **Dolchstoß** M (*bes fig*) stab
dolmetschen ['dɔlmɛtʃən] VT, VI to interpret
Dolmetscher(in) (**-s, -**) M(F) interpreter
Dolomiten [dolo'mi:tən] PL (*Geog*): **die ~** the Dolomites *pl*
Dom [do:m] (**-(e)s, -e**) M cathedral
Domäne [do'mɛ:nə] (-, **-n**) F (*fig*) domain, province
dominieren [domi'ni:rən] VT to dominate ▶ VI to predominate
Dominikanische Republik [domini'ka:nɪʃərepu'bli:k] F Dominican Republic
Dompfaff ['do:mpfaf] (**-en, -en**) M bullfinch
Dompteur [dɔmp'tø:r] M (*Zirkus*) trainer
Dompteuse [dɔmp'tø:zə] F (*Zirkus*) trainer
Donau ['do:naʊ] F: **die ~** the Danube
Döner ['dø:nər] (**-s, -**), **Döner Kebab** (**-(s), -s**) M doner kebab
Donner ['dɔnər] (**-s, -**) M thunder; **wie vom ~ gerührt** (*fig*) thunderstruck
donnern VI UNPERS to thunder ▶ VT (*umg*) to slam, to crash
Donnerschlag M thunderclap
Donnerstag M Thursday; *siehe auch* **Dienstag**
Donnerwetter NT thunderstorm; (*fig*) dressing-down ▶ INTERJ good heavens!; (*anerkennend*) my word!
doof [do:f] (*umg*) ADJ daft, stupid
dopen ['do:pən] VT to dope
Doping ['do:pɪŋ] (**-s**) NT doping; **Dopingkontrolle** F (*Sport*) dope check
Doppel ['dɔpəl] (**-s, -**) NT duplicate; (*Sport*) doubles; **Doppelband** M (*von doppeltem Umfang*) double-sized volume; (*zwei Bände*) two volumes *pl*; **Doppelbett** NT double bed; **doppelbödig** ADJ (*fig*) ambiguous; **doppeldeutig** ADJ ambiguous; **Doppelfenster** NT double glazing; **Doppelgänger(in)** (**-s, -**) M(F) double; **doppelklicken** VI to double-click; **Doppelkorn** M *type of schnapps*; **Doppelpunkt** M colon; **doppelseitig** ADJ (*auch Comput: Diskette*) double-sided; (*Lungenentzündung*) double; **doppelseitige Anzeige** double-page advertisement; **doppelsinnig** ADJ ambiguous; **Doppelstecker** M two-way adaptor; **Doppelstunde** F (*Sch*) double period
doppelt ADJ double; (*Comm: Buchführung*) double-entry; (*Staatsbürgerschaft*) dual ▶ ADV: **die Karte habe ich ~** I have two of these cards; **~ gemoppelt** (*umg*) saying the same thing twice over; **in doppelter Ausführung** in duplicate
Doppel- zW: **Doppelverdiener** PL two-income family; **Doppelzentner** M 100 kilograms; **Doppelzimmer** NT double room
Dorf [dɔrf] (**-(e)s, Dörfer**) NT village; **Dorfbewohner** M villager
dörflich ['dœrflɪç] ADJ village *attrib*
Dorn[1] [dɔrn] (**-(e)s, -en**) M (*Bot*) thorn; **das ist mir ein ~ im Auge** (*fig*) it's a thorn in my flesh
Dorn[2] [dɔrn] (**-(e)s, -e**) M (*Schnallendorn*) tongue, pin
dornig ADJ thorny
Dornröschen NT Sleeping Beauty
dörren ['dœrən] VT to dry
Dörrobst ['dœro:pst] NT dried fruit
dort [dɔrt] ADV there; **~ drüben** over there; **dorther** ADV from there; **dorthin** ADV (to) there
dortig ADJ of that place, there
Dose ['do:zə] (-, **-n**) F box; (*Blechdose*) tin, can; **in Dosen** (*Konserven*) canned, tinned (BRIT)
Dosen PL *von* **Dose**; **Dosis**
dösen ['dø:zən] (*umg*) VI to doze
Dosen- zW: **Dosenbier** NT canned beer; **Dosenöffner** M tin (BRIT) *od* can opener; **Dosenpfand** NT deposit on drink cans; (*allgemein: Einwegpfand*) deposit on drink cans and disposable bottles
dosieren [do'zi:rən] VT (*lit, fig*) to measure out
Dosis ['do:zɪs] (-, **Dosen**) F dose
Dotierung [do'ti:rʊŋ] F endowment; (*von Posten*) remuneration
Dotter ['dɔtər] (**-s, -**) M egg yolk
Double ['du:bəl] (**-s, -s**) NT (*Film etc*) stand-in
Download ['daunlo:d] M (*Comput*) download
downloaden ['daunlo:dən] VTI (*Comput*) to download
Downsyndrom NT *no pl* (*Med*) Down's Syndrome
Doz. ABK = **Dozent(in)**
Dozent(in) [do'tsɛnt(ɪn)] (**-en, -en**) M(F): **~ (für)** lecturer (in), professor (of) (US)
dpa (-) F ABK (= *Deutsche Presse-Agentur*) *German Press Agency*
Dr. ABK = **Doktor**
Drache ['draxə] (**-n, -n**) M (*Tier*) dragon
Drachen (**-s, -**) M kite; **einen ~ steigen lassen** to fly a kite; **drachenfliegen** VI to hang-glide; **Drachenfliegen** NT (*Sport*) hang-gliding
Dragee, Dragée [dra'ʒe:] (**-s, -s**) NT (*Pharm*) dragee, sugar-coated pill

Draht [draːt] (**-(e)s, Drähte**) M wire; **auf ~ sein** to be on the ball; **Drahtesel** M (*hum*) trusty bicycle; **Drahtgitter** NT wire grating; **drahtlos** ADJ wireless; **Drahtseil** NT cable; **Nerven wie Drahtseile** (*umg*) nerves of steel; **Drahtseilbahn** F cable railway; **Drahtzange** F pliers *pl*; **Drahtzieher(in)** M(F) (*fig*) wire-puller

drall [dral] ADJ strapping; (*Frau*) buxom

Drall M (*fig: Hang*) tendency; **einen ~ nach links haben** (*Aut*) to pull to the left

Drama ['draːma] (**-s, Dramen**) NT drama

Dramatiker(in) [dra'maːtikər(ɪn)] (**-s, -**) M(F) dramatist

dramatisch [dra'maːtɪʃ] ADJ dramatic

Dramaturg(in) [drama'tʊrk (-gɪn)] (**-en, -en**) M(F) artistic director; (*TV*) drama producer

dran [dran] (*umg*) ADV (*an der Reihe*): **jetzt bist du ~** it's your turn now; **früh/spät ~ sein** to be early/late; **ich weiß nicht, wie ich (bei ihm) ~ bin** I don't know where I stand (with him); *siehe auch* **daran**; **dranbleiben** *unreg* (*umg*) VI to stay close; (*am Apparat*) to hang on

drang *etc* [draŋ] VB *siehe* **dringen**

Drang (**-(e)s, Dränge**) M (*Trieb*) urge, yearning; (*Druck*) pressure; **~ nach** urge *od* yearning for

drängeln ['drɛŋəln] VT, VI to push, to jostle

drängen ['drɛŋən] VT (*schieben*) to push, to press; (*antreiben*) to urge ▶ VI (*eilig sein*) to be urgent; (*Zeit*) to press; **auf etw** *akk* **~** to press for sth

drangsalieren [draŋza'liːrən] VT to pester, to plague

dranhalten (*umg*) VR to get a move on

drankommen (*umg*) *unreg* VI (*an die Reihe kommen*) to have one's turn; (*Sch: beim Melden*) to be called; (*Frage, Aufgabe etc*) to come up

drannehmen (*umg*) *unreg* VT (*Schüler*) to ask

drastisch ['drastɪʃ] ADJ drastic

drauf [draʊf] (*umg*) ADV: **~ und dran sein, etw zu tun** to be on the point of doing sth; **gut/schlecht ~ sein** to be in a good/bad mood; *siehe auch* **darauf**; **Draufgänger** (**-s, -**) M daredevil; **draufgehen** *unreg* VI (*verbraucht werden*) to be used up; (*kaputtgehen*) to be smashed up; **draufhaben** (*umg*) VT *unreg*: **etw draufhaben** (*können*) to be able to do sth just like that; (*Kenntnisse*) to be well up on sth; **draufzahlen** VI (*fig: Einbußen erleiden*) to pay the price

draußen ['draʊsən] ADV outside, out-of-doors

Drechsler(in) ['drɛkslər(ɪn)] (**-s, -**) M(F) (wood) turner

Dreck [drɛk] (**-(e)s**) M mud, dirt; **~ am Stecken haben** (*fig*) to have a skeleton in the cupboard; **das geht ihn einen ~ an** (*umg*) that's none of his business

dreckig ADJ dirty, filthy; **es geht mir ~** (*umg*) I'm in a bad way

Dreckskerl (*umg!*) M dirty swine (*umg!*)

Dreh [dreː] M: **den ~ raushaben** *od* **weghaben** (*umg*) to have got the hang of it

Dreh- zW: **Drehachse** F axis of rotation; **Dreharbeiten** PL (*Film*) shooting *sing*; **Drehbank** F lathe; **drehbar** ADJ revolving; **Drehbuch** NT (*Film*) script

drehen VT to turn, to rotate; (*Zigaretten*) to roll; (*Film*) to shoot ▶ VI to turn, to rotate ▶ VR to turn; (*handeln von*): **sich um etw ~** to be about sth; **ein Ding ~** (*umg*) to play a prank

Dreher(in) (**-s, -**) M(F) lathe operator

Dreh- zW: **Drehorgel** F barrel organ; **Drehort** M (*Film*) location; **Drehscheibe** F (*Eisenb*) turntable; **Drehtür** F revolving door

Drehung F (*Rotation*) rotation; (*Umdrehung, Wendung*) turn

Dreh- zW: **Drehwurm** (*umg*) M: **einen Drehwurm haben/bekommen** to be/become dizzy; **Drehzahl** F rate of revolution; **Drehzahlmesser** M rev(olution) counter

drei [draɪ] NUM three; **~ viertel** three quarters; **aller guten Dinge sind ~!** (*Sprichwort*) all good things come in threes!; (*nach zwei missglückten Versuchen*) third time lucky!; **Dreieck** NT triangle; **dreieckig** ADJ triangular; **Dreiecksverhältnis** NT eternal triangle; **dreieinhalb** NUM three and a half; **Dreieinigkeit** [-'laɪnɪçkaɪt] F Trinity

dreierlei ADJ *unver* of three kinds

drei- zW: **dreifach** ADJ triple, treble ▶ ADV three times; **die dreifache Menge** three times the amount; **Dreifaltigkeit** F trinity; **Dreifuß** M tripod; (*Schemel*) three-legged stool; **Dreigangschaltung** F three-speed gear; **dreihundert** NUM three hundred; **Dreikäsehoch** (*umg*) M tiny tot; **Dreikönigsfest** NT Epiphany; **dreimal** ADV three times, thrice; **dreimalig** ADJ three times

dreinblicken ['draɪnblɪkən] VI: **traurig** *etc* **~** to look sad *etc*

dreinreden ['draɪnreːdən] VI: **jdm ~** (*dazwischenreden*) to interrupt sb; (*sich einmischen*) to interfere with sb

Dreirad NT tricycle

Dreisprung M triple jump

dreißig ['draɪsɪç] NUM thirty

dreist [draɪst] ADJ bold, audacious

Dreistigkeit F boldness, audacity

drei- zW: **Dreiviertelstunde** F three-quarters of an hour; **Dreivierteltakt** M: **im Dreivierteltakt** in three-four time; **dreizehn** NUM thirteen; **jetzt schlägts dreizehn!** (*umg*) that's a bit much

dreschen ['drɛʃən] *unreg* VT to thresh; **Skat ~** (*umg*) to play skat

Dresden ['dreːsdən] (**-s**) NT Dresden

dressieren [drɛ'siːrən] VT to train

Dressur [drɛ'suːr] F training; (*für Dressurreiten*) dressage

Dr. h. c. ABK (= *Doktor honoris causa*) honorary doctor

driften ['drɪftən] VI (*Naut, fig*) to drift

Drillbohrer M light drill

drillen ['drɪlən] VT (*bohren*) to drill, to bore; (*Mil*) to drill; (*fig*) to train; **auf etw** *akk* **gedrillt sein** (*fig: umg*) to be practised (BRIT) *od* practiced (US) at doing sth

Drilling M triplet

drin [drɪn] (*umg*) ADV: **bis jetzt ist noch alles ~** everything is still quite open; *siehe auch* **darin**

dringen ['drɪŋən] *unreg* VI (*Wasser, Licht, Kälte*): **~ (durch/in** *+akk*) to penetrate (through/into); **auf etw** *akk* **~** to insist on sth; **in jdn ~** (*geh*) to entreat sb

dringend ['drɪŋənt] ADJ urgent; **~ empfehlen** to recommend strongly

dringlich ['drɪŋlɪç] ADJ = **dringend**

Dringlichkeit F urgency

Dringlichkeitsstufe F priority; **~ 1** top priority

drinnen ['drɪnən] ADV inside, indoors

drinstecken ['drɪnʃtɛkən] (*umg*) VI: **da steckt eine Menge Arbeit drin** a lot of work has gone into it

drischt [drɪʃt] VB *siehe* **dreschen**

dritt ADV: **wir kommen zu ~** three of us are coming together

dritte(r, s) ADJ third; **die D~ Welt** Third World; **3. Juni** 3(rd) June; (*gesprochen*) the third of June; **am 3. Juni** on 3(rd) June, on June 3(rd); (*gesprochen*) on the third of June; **München, den 3. Juni** Munich, June 3(rd); **im Beisein Dritter** in the presence of a third party

Drittel (**-s, -**) NT third

drittens ADV thirdly

drittklassig ADJ third-rate, third-class

Dr. jur. ABK (= *Doktor der Rechtswissenschaften*) ≈ L.L.D.

DRK (**-**) NT ABK (= *Deutsches Rotes Kreuz*) ≈ R.C.

Dr. med. ABK (= *Doktor der Medizin*) ≈ M.D.

droben ['dro:bən] ADV above, up there

Droge ['dro:gə] (**-, -n**) F drug

dröge ['drøgə] (NORDD) ADJ boring

Drogen- ZW: **drogenabhängig** ADJ addicted to drugs; **Drogenentzug** (**-(e)s**) M detox (*umg*), detoxification; (*from drugs*) withdrawal; **Drogenhändler(in)** M(F) peddler, pusher; **drogensüchtig** ADJ addicted to drugs

Drogerie [drogə'ri:] F chemist's shop (BRIT), drugstore (US)

> The **Drogerie** as opposed to the **Apotheke** sells medicines not requiring a prescription. It tends to be cheaper and also sells cosmetics, perfume and toiletries.

Drogeriemarkt M discount chemist's (BRIT) *od* drugstore (US)

Drogist(in) [dro'gɪst(ɪn)] M(F) pharmacist, chemist (BRIT)

Drohbrief M threatening letter

drohen ['dro:ən] VI: **(jdm) ~** to threaten (sb)

Drohgebärde F (*lit, fig*) threatening gesture

Drohne ['dro:nə] (**-, -n**) F drone

dröhnen ['drø:nən] VI (*Motor*) to roar; (*Stimme, Musik*) to ring, to resound

Drohung ['dro:ʊŋ] F threat

drollig ['drɔlɪç] ADJ droll

Drops [drɔps] (**-, -**) M OD NT fruit drop

drosch *etc* [drɔʃ] VB *siehe* **dreschen**

Droschke ['drɔʃkə] (**-, -n**) F cab

Droschkenkutscher M cabman

Drossel ['drɔsəl] (**-, -n**) F thrush

drosseln ['drɔsəln] VT (*Motor etc*) to throttle; (*Heizung*) to turn down; (*Strom, Tempo, Produktion etc*) to cut down

Dr. phil. ABK (= *Doktor der Geisteswissenschaften*) ≈ Ph.D.

Dr. theol. ABK (= *Doktor der Theologie*) ≈ D.D.

drüben ['dry:bən] ADV over there, on the other side

drüber ['dry:bər] (*umg*) ADV = **darüber**

Druck [drʊk] (**-(e)s, -e**) M (*Zwang, Phys*) pressure; (*Typ: Vorgang*) printing; (*: Produkt*) print; (*fig: Belastung*) burden, weight; **~ hinter etw** *akk* **machen** to put some pressure on sth; **Druckbuchstabe** M block letter; **in Druckbuchstaben schreiben** to print

Drückeberger ['drʏkəbɛrgər] (**-s, -**) M shirker, dodger

drucken ['drʊkən] VT, VI (*Typ, Comput*) to print

drücken ['drʏkən] VT (*Knopf, Hand*) to press; (*zu eng sein*) to pinch; (*fig: Preise*) to keep down; (*: belasten*) to oppress, to weigh down ▶ VI to press ▶ VR: **sich vor etw** *dat* **~** to get out of (doing) sth; **jdm etw in die Hand ~** to press sth into sb's hand

drückend ADJ oppressive; (*Last, Steuern*) heavy; (*Armut*) grinding; (*Wetter, Hitze*) oppressive, close

Drucker (**-s, -**) M printer

Drücker (**-s, -**) M button; (*Türdrücker*) handle; (*Gewehrdrücker*) trigger; **am ~ sein** *od* **sitzen** (*fig: umg*) to be the key person; **auf den letzten ~** (*fig: umg*) at the last minute

Druckerei [drʊkə'raɪ] F printing works, press

Druckerschwärze F printer's ink

Druck- ZW: **Druckfahne** F galley(-proof); **Druckfehler** M misprint; **Druckknopf** M press stud (BRIT), snap fastener; **Druckkopf** M printhead; **Druckluft** F compressed air; **Druckmittel** NT leverage; **druckreif** ADJ ready for printing, passed for press; (*fig*) polished; **Drucksache** F printed matter; **Druckschrift** F block letters *pl*; (*gedrucktes Werk*) pamphlet; **Drucktaste** F push button; **Druckwelle** F shock wave

drum [drʊm] (*umg*) ADV around; **mit allem D~ und Dran** with all the bits and pieces *pl*; (*Mahlzeit*) with all the trimmings *pl*

Drumherum NT trappings *pl*

drunten ['drʊntən] ADV below, down there

Drüse ['dry:zə] (**-, -n**) F gland

DSB (**-**) M ABK (= *Deutscher Sportbund*) *German Sports Association*

Dschungel ['dʒʊŋəl] (**-s, -**) M jungle

DSD NT ABK (= *Duales System Deutschland*) *German waste collection and recycling service*

> The **DSD** (Duales System Deutschland) is a scheme introduced in Germany for separating domestic refuse into two types so as to reduce environmental damage. Normal refuse is disposed of in the usual way by burning or dumping at land-fill sites; packets and containers with a green spot (**Grüner Punkt**) imprinted on them are kept separate and are then collected for recycling.

dt. ABK = **deutsch**

DTC (-) M ABK (= *Deutscher Touring Automobil Club*) *German motoring organization*
DTP (-) NT ABK (= *Desktop publishing*) DTP
Dtzd. ABK (= *Dutzend*) doz.
du [du:] PRON you; **mit jdm per du sein** to be on familiar terms with sb; **Du** NT: **jdm das Du anbieten** to suggest that sb uses "du", to suggest that sb uses the familiar form of address
Dübel ['dy:bəl] (**-s, -**) M plug; (*Holzdübel*) dowel
dübeln ['dy:bəln] VT, VI to plug
Dublin ['dablɪn] NT Dublin
ducken ['dʊkən] VT (*Kopf*) to duck; (*fig*) to take down a peg or two ▶ VR to duck
Duckmäuser ['dʊkmɔʏzər] (**-s, -**) M yes-man
Dudelsack ['du:dəlzak] M bagpipes *pl*
Duell [du'ɛl] (**-s, -e**) NT duel
Duett [du'ɛt] (**-(e)s, -e**) NT duet
Duft [dʊft] (**-(e)s, Düfte**) M scent, odour (BRIT), odor (US); **duften** VI to be fragrant; **es duftet nach ...** it smells of ...
duftig ADJ (*Stoff, Kleid*) delicate, diaphanous; (*Muster*) fine
Duftnote F (*von Parfüm*) scent
dulden ['dʊldən] VT to suffer; (*zulassen*) to tolerate ▶ VI to suffer
duldsam ADJ tolerant
dumm [dʊm] ADJ stupid; **das wird mir zu ~** that's just too much; **der Dumme sein** to be the loser; **der dumme August** (*umg*) the clown; **du willst mich wohl für ~ verkaufen** you must think I'm stupid; **sich ~ und dämlich reden** (*umg*) to talk till one is blue in the face; **so etwas Dummes** how stupid; (*ärgerlich*) what a nuisance; **dummdreist** ADJ impudent
dummerweise ADV stupidly
Dummheit F stupidity; (*Tat*) blunder, stupid mistake
Dummkopf M blockhead
dumpf [dʊmpf] ADJ (*Ton*) hollow, dull; (*Luft*) close; (*Erinnerung, Schmerz*) vague; **Dumpfheit** F hollowness, dullness; (*von Luft*) closeness; (*von Erinnerung*) vagueness
dumpfig ADJ musty
Dumpingpreis ['dampɪŋprais] M give-away price
Düne ['dy:nə] (**-, -n**) F dune
Dung [dʊŋ] (**-(e)s**) M manure
düngen ['dʏŋən] VT to fertilize
Dünger (**-s, -**) M fertilizer; (*Dung*) manure
dunkel ['dʊŋkəl] ADJ dark; (*Stimme*) deep; (*Ahnung*) vague; (*rätselhaft*) obscure; (*verdächtig*) dubious, shady; **im Dunkeln tappen** (*fig*) to grope in the dark
Dünkel ['dʏŋkəl] (**-s**) M self-conceit; **dünkelhaft** ADJ conceited
Dunkelheit F darkness; (*fig*) obscurity; **bei Einbruch der ~** at nightfall
Dunkelkammer F (*Phot*) dark room
dunkeln VI UNPERS to grow dark
Dunkelziffer F estimated number of unnotified cases
dünn [dʏn] ADJ thin ▶ ADV: **~ gesät** scarce; **Dünndarm** M small intestine; **dünnflüssig** ADJ watery, thin; **Dünnheit** F thinness; **Dünnschiss** (*umg*) M the runs
Dunst [dʊnst] (**-es, Dünste**) M vapour (BRIT), vapor (US); (*Wetter*) haze; **Dunstabzugshaube** F extractor hood
dünsten ['dʏnstən] VT to steam
Dunstglocke F haze; (*Smog*) pall of smog
dunstig ['dʊnstɪç] ADJ vaporous; (*Wetter*) hazy, misty
düpieren [dy'pi:rən] VT to dupe
Duplikat [dupli'ka:t] (**-(e)s, -e**) NT duplicate
Dur [du:r] (**-, -**) NT (*Mus*) major

SCHLÜSSELWORT

durch [dʊrç] PRÄP +*akk* **1** (*hindurch*) through; **durch den Urwald** through the jungle; **durch die ganze Welt reisen** to travel all over the world
2 (*mittels*) through, by (means of); (*aufgrund*) due to, owing to; **Tod durch Herzschlag/den Strang** death from a heart attack/by hanging; **durch die Post** by post; **durch seine Bemühungen** through his efforts
▶ ADJ **1** (*hindurch*) through; **die ganze Nacht durch** all through the night; **den Sommer durch** during the summer; **8 Uhr durch** past 8 o'clock; **durch und durch** completely; **das geht mir durch und durch** that goes right through me
2 (*Koch: umg: durchgebraten*) done; **(gut) durch** well-done

durcharbeiten VT, VI to work through ▶ VR: **sich durch etw ~** to work one's way through sth
durchatmen VI to breathe deeply
durchaus [dʊrç'aʊs] ADV completely; (*unbedingt*) definitely; **~ nicht** (*in verneinten Sätzen: als Verstärkung*) by no means; (*: als Antwort*) not at all; **das lässt sich ~ machen** that sounds feasible; **ich bin ~ Ihrer Meinung** I quite *od* absolutely agree with you
durchbeißen *unreg* VT to bite through ▶ VR (*fig*) to battle on
durchblättern VT to leaf through
Durchblick ['dʊrçblɪk] M view; (*fig*) comprehension; **den ~ haben** (*fig: umg*) to know what's what
durchblicken VI to look through; (*umg: verstehen*): **(bei etw) ~** to understand (sth); **etw ~ lassen** (*fig*) to hint at sth
Durchblutung [dʊrç'blu:tʊŋ] F circulation (of blood)
durchbohren VT UNTR to bore through, to pierce
durchboxen ['dʊrçbɔksən] VR (*fig: umg*): **sich (durch etw) ~** to fight one's way through (sth)
durchbrechen[1] ['dʊrçbrɛçən] *unreg* VT, VI to break
durchbrechen[2] [dʊrç'brɛçən] *unreg* VT UNTR (*Schranken*) to break through
durchbrennen *unreg* VI (*Draht, Sicherung*) to burn through; (*umg*) to run away

durchbringen *unreg* VT to get through; (*Geld*) to squander ▸ VR to make a living
Durchbruch ['dʊrçbrʊx] M (*Öffnung*) opening; (*Mil*) breach; (*von Gefühlen etc*) eruption; (*der Zähne*) cutting; (*fig*) breakthrough; **zum ~ kommen** to break through
durchdacht [dʊrç'daxt] ADJ well thought-out
durchdenken *unreg* VT UNTR to think out
durch- ZW: **durchdiskutieren** VT to talk over, to discuss; **durchdrängen** VR to force one's way through; **durchdrehen** VT (*Fleisch*) to mince ▸ VI (*umg*) to crack up
durchdringen[1] ['dʊrçdrɪŋən] *unreg* VI to penetrate, to get through
durchdringen[2] [dʊrç'drɪŋən] *unreg* VT UNTR to penetrate
durchdringend ADJ piercing; (*Kälte, Wind*) biting; (*Geruch*) pungent
durchdrücken ['dʊrçdrʏkən] VT (*durch Presse*) to press through; (*Creme, Teig*) to pipe; (*fig: Gesetz, Reformen etc*) to push through; (*seinen Willen*) to get; (*Knie, Kreuz etc*) to straighten
durcheinander [dʊrçlaɪ'nandər] ADV in a mess, in confusion; (*verwirrt*) confused; **Durcheinander (-s)** NT (*Verwirrung*) confusion; (*Unordnung*) mess; **durcheinanderbringen** VT to mess up; (*verwirren*) to confuse; **durcheinanderreden** VI to talk at the same time; **durcheinandertrinken** VI to mix one's drinks; **durcheinanderwerfen** VT to muddle up; **durchfahren** *unreg* VI: **er ist bei Rot durchgefahren** he jumped the lights ▸ VT: **die Nacht durchfahren** to travel through the night
durch- ZW: **Durchfahrt** F transit; (*Verkehr*) thoroughfare; **Durchfahrt bitte freihalten!** please keep access free; **Durchfahrt verboten!** no through road; **Durchfall** M (*Med*) diarrhoea (BRIT), diarrhea (US); **durchfallen** *unreg* VI to fall through; (*in Prüfung*) to fail; **durchfinden** *unreg* VR to find one's way through; **durchfliegen** *unreg* (*umg*) VI (*in Prüfung*): **(durch etw** *od* **in etw** *dat*) **durchfliegen** to fail (sth); **Durchflug** M: **Passagiere auf dem Durchflug** transit passengers
durchforschen VT UNTR to explore
durchforsten [dʊrç'fɔrstən] VT UNTR (*fig: Akten etc*) to go through
durchfragen VR to find one's way by asking
durchfressen *unreg* VR to eat one's way through
durchführbar ADJ feasible, practicable
durchführen ['dʊrçfy:rən] VT to carry out; (*Gesetz*) to implement; (*Kursus*) to run
Durchführung F execution, performance
Durchgang ['dʊrçgaŋ] M passage(way); (*bei Produktion, Versuch*) run; (*Sport*) round; (*bei Wahl*) ballot; **~ verboten** no thoroughfare
durchgängig ['dʊrçgɛŋɪç] ADJ universal, general
Durchgangs- ZW: **Durchgangshandel** M transit trade; **Durchgangslager** NT transit camp; **Durchgangsstadium** NT transitory stage; **Durchgangsverkehr** M through traffic
durchgeben ['dʊrçge:bən] *unreg* VT (*Rundf, TV: Hinweis, Wetter*) to give; (*Lottozahlen*) to announce
durchgefroren ['dʊrçgəfro:rən] ADJ (*See*) completely frozen; (*Mensch*) frozen stiff
durchgehen ['dʊrçge:ən] *unreg* VT (*behandeln*) to go over *od* through ▸ VI to go through; (*ausreißen: Pferd*) to break loose; (*Mensch*) to run away; **mein Temperament ging mit mir durch** my temper got the better of me; **jdm etw ~ lassen** to let sb get away with sth
durchgehend ADJ (*Zug*) through; (*Öffnungszeiten*) continuous
durchgeschwitzt ['dʊrçgəʃvɪtst] ADJ soaked in sweat
durch- ZW: **durchgreifen** *unreg* VI to take strong action; **durchhalten** *unreg* VI to last out ▸ VT to keep up; **Durchhaltevermögen** NT staying power; **durchhängen** *unreg* VI (*lit, fig*) to sag; **durchhecheln** (*umg*) VT to gossip about; **durchkommen** *unreg* VI to get through; (*überleben*) to pull through
durchkreuzen VT UNTR to thwart, to frustrate
durchlassen *unreg* VT (*Person*) to let through; (*Wasser*) to let in
durchlässig ADJ leaky
Durchlaucht ['dʊrçlaʊxt] **(-, -en)** F: **(Euer) ~** Your Highness
Durchlauf ['dʊrçlaʊf] M (*Comput*) run
durchlaufen *unreg* VT UNTR (*Schule, Phase*) to go through
Durchlauferhitzer (-s, -) M continuous-flow water heater
Durchlaufzeit F (*Comput*) length of the run
durch- ZW: **durchleben** VT UNTR (*Zeit*) to live *od* go through; (*Jugend, Gefühl*) to experience; **durchlesen** *unreg* VT to read through; **durchleuchten** VT UNTR to X-ray; **durchlöchern** VT UNTR to perforate; (*mit Löchern*) to punch holes in; (*mit Kugeln*) to riddle; **durchmachen** VT to go through; **die Nacht durchmachen** to make a night of it
Durchmarsch M march through
Durchmesser (-s, -) M diameter
durchnässen VT UNTR to soak (through)
durch- ZW: **durchnehmen** *unreg* VT to go over; **durchnummerieren** VT to number consecutively; **durchorganisieren** VT to organize down to the last detail; **durchpausen** VT to trace; **durchpeitschen** VT (*lit*) to whip soundly; (*fig: Gesetzentwurf, Reform*) to force through
durchqueren [dʊrç'kve:rən] VT UNTR to cross
durch- ZW: **durchrechnen** VT to calculate; **durchregnen** VI UNPERS: **es regnet durchs Dach durch** the rain is coming through the roof; **Durchreiche (-, -n)** F (serving) hatch, pass-through (US); **Durchreise** F transit; **auf der Durchreise** passing through; (*Güter*) in transit; **Durchreisevisum** NT transit visa; **durchringen** *unreg* VR to make up one's mind finally; **durchrosten** VI to rust through; **durchrutschen** VI: **(durch etw)**

d

durchrutschen (*lit*) to slip through (sth); (*bei Prüfung*) to scrape through (sth)
durchs [dʊrçs] = **durch das**
Durchsage ['dʊrçza:gə] F intercom *od* radio announcement
Durchsatz ['dʊrçzats] M (*Produktion, Comput*) throughput
durchschauen[1] ['dʊrçʃauən] VT, VI (*lit*) to look *od* see through
durchschauen[2] [dʊrç'ʃauən] VT UNTR (*Person, Lüge*) to see through
durchscheinen ['dʊrçʃaɪnən] *unreg* VI to shine through
durchscheinend ADJ translucent
durchschlafen ['dʊrçʃla:fən] *unreg* VI to sleep through
Durchschlag ['dʊrçʃla:k] M (*Doppel*) carbon copy; (*Sieb*) strainer
durchschlagen *unreg* VT (*entzweischlagen*) to split (in two); (*sieben*) to sieve ▸ VI (*zum Vorschein kommen*) to emerge, to come out ▸ VR to get by
durchschlagend ADJ resounding; **(eine) durchschlagende Wirkung haben** to be totally effective
Durchschlagpapier NT flimsy; (*Kohlepapier*) carbon paper
Durchschlagskraft F (*von Geschoss*) penetration; (*fig: von Argument*) decisiveness
durch- ZW: **durchschlängeln** VR (*durch etw: Mensch*) to thread one's way through; **durchschlüpfen** VI to slip through; **durchschneiden** *unreg* VT to cut through
Durchschnitt ['dʊrçʃnɪt] M (*Mittelwert*) average; **über/unter dem ~** above/below average; **im ~** on average; **durchschnittlich** ADJ average ▸ ADV on average; **durchschnittlich begabt/groß** *etc* of average ability/height *etc*
Durchschnitts- ZW: **Durchschnittsgeschwindigkeit** F average speed; **Durchschnittsmensch** M average man, man in the street; **Durchschnittswert** M average
durch- ZW: **Durchschrift** F copy; **Durchschuss** M (*Loch*) bullet hole; **durchschwimmen** *unreg* VT UNTR to swim across; **durchsegeln** (*umg*) VI (*nicht bestehen*): **durch** *od* **bei etw durchsegeln** to fail *od* flunk (*umg*) (sth); **durchsehen** *unreg* VT to look through
durchsetzen[1] ['dʊrçzɛtsən] VT to enforce ▸ VR (*Erfolg haben*) to succeed; (*sich behaupten*) to get one's way; **seinen Kopf ~** to get one's own way
durchsetzen[2] [dʊrç'zɛtsən] VT UNTR to mix
Durchsicht ['dʊrçzɪçt] F looking through, checking
durchsichtig ADJ transparent; **Durchsichtigkeit** F transparency
durch- ZW: **durchsickern** VI to seep through; (*fig*) to leak out; **durchsieben** VT to sieve; **durchsitzen** *unreg* VT (*Sessel etc*) to wear out (the seat of); **durchspielen** VT to go *od* run through; **durchsprechen** *unreg* VT to talk over; **durchstehen** *unreg* VT to live through; **Durchstehvermögen** NT endurance, staying power; **durchstellen** VT (*Tel*) to put through; **durchstöbern** [-'ʃtø:bərn] VT UNTR to ransack, to search through; **durchstoßen** *unreg* VT, VI to break through (*auch Mil*); **durchstreichen** *unreg* VT to cross out; **durchstylen** VT to ponce up (*umg*); **durchsuchen** VT UNTR to search; **Durchsuchung** F search; **Durchsuchungsbefehl** M search warrant; **durchtrainieren** VT (*Sportler, Körper*): **gut durchtrainiert** in superb condition; **durchtränken** VT UNTR to soak; **durchtreten** *unreg* VT (*Pedal*) to step on; (*Starter*) to kick; **durchtrieben** ADJ cunning, wily; **durchwachsen** ADJ (*lit: Speck*) streaky; (*fig: mittelmäßig*) so-so
Durchwahl ['dʊrçva:l] F (*Tel*) direct dialling; (*bei Firma*) extension
durch- ZW: **durchweg** ADV throughout, completely; **durchwursteln** (*umg*) VR to muddle through; **durchzählen** VT to count ▸ VI to count *od* number off; **durchzechen** VT UNTR: **eine durchzechte Nacht** a night of drinking; **durchziehen** *unreg* VT (*Faden*) to draw through ▸ VI to pass through; **eine Sache durchziehen** to finish off sth; **durchzucken** VT UNTR to shoot *od* flash through; **Durchzug** M (*Luft*) draught (BRIT), draft (US); (*von Truppen, Vögeln*) passage; **durchzwängen** VT, VR to squeeze *od* force through

SCHLÜSSELWORT

dürfen ['dʏrfən] *unreg* VI **1** (*Erlaubnis haben*) to be allowed to; **ich darf das** I'm allowed to (do that); **darf ich?** may I?; **darf ich ins Kino?** can *od* may I go to the cinema?; **es darf geraucht werden** you may smoke
2 (*in Verneinungen*): **er darf das nicht** he's not allowed to (do that); **das darf nicht geschehen** that must not happen; **da darf sie sich nicht wundern** that shouldn't surprise her; **das darf doch nicht wahr sein!** that can't be true!
3 (*in Höflichkeitsformeln*): **darf ich Sie bitten, das zu tun?** may *od* could I ask you to do that?; **wir freuen uns, Ihnen mitteilen zu dürfen** we are pleased to be able to tell you; **was darf es sein?** what can I get for you?
4 (*können*): **das dürfen Sie mir glauben** you can believe me
5 (*Möglichkeit*): **das dürfte genug sein** that should be enough; **es dürfte Ihnen bekannt sein, dass ...** as you will probably know ...

durfte *etc* ['dʊrftə] VB *siehe* **dürfen**
dürftig ['dʏrftɪç] ADJ (*ärmlich*) needy, poor; (*unzulänglich*) inadequate
dürr [dʏr] ADJ dried-up; (*Land*) arid; (*mager*) skinny
Dürre (-, -n) F aridity; (*Zeit*) drought
Durst [dʊrst] (-(e)s) M thirst; **~ haben** to be thirsty; **einen über den ~ getrunken haben** (*umg*) to have had one too many
durstig ADJ thirsty

Durststrecke F hard times *pl*
Dusche ['dʊʃə] (**-, -n**) F shower; **das war eine kalte ~** (*fig*) that really brought him/her *etc* down with a bump
duschen VI, VR to have a shower
Duschgel NT shower gel
Duschgelegenheit F shower facilities *pl*
Düse ['dy:zə] (**-, -n**) F nozzle; (*Flugzeugdüse*) jet
Dusel ['du:zəl] (*umg*) M: **da hat er (einen) ~ gehabt** he was lucky
Düsen- zW: **Düsenantrieb** M jet propulsion; **Düsenflugzeug** NT jet (plane); **Düsenjäger** M jet fighter
Dussel ['dʊsəl] (**-s, -**) (*umg*) M twit, berk
Düsseldorf ['dʏsəldɔrf] NT Dusseldorf
dusselig ['dʊsəlɪç], **dusslig** ['dʊslɪç] (*umg*) ADJ stupid
düster ['dy:stər] ADJ dark; (*Gedanken, Zukunft*) gloomy; **Düsterkeit** F darkness, gloom; (*von Gedanken*) gloominess
Dutzend ['dʊtsənt] (**-s, -e**) NT dozen; **~(e) Mal** a dozen times; **Dutzendware** (*pej*) F (cheap) mass-produced item; **dutzendweise** ADV by the dozen
duzen ['du:tsən] VT to address with the familiar "du" form ▶ VR to address each other with the familiar "du" form; *see note*

> There are two different forms of address in German: du and Sie. **Duzen** means addressing someone as "du" and **siezen** means addressing someone as "Sie". "Du" is used to address children, family and close friends. Students almost always use "du" to each other. "Sie" is used for all grown-ups and older teenagers.

Duzfreund M good friend
DVD (**-, -s**) F ABK (= *Digital Versatile Disc*) DVD
Dynamik [dy'na:mɪk] F (*Phys*) dynamics; (*fig: Schwung*) momentum; (*von Mensch*) dynamism
dynamisch [dy'na:mɪʃ] ADJ (*lit, fig*) dynamic; (*rentendynamisch*) index-linked
Dynamit [dyna'mi:t] (**-s**) NT dynamite
Dynamo [dy'na:mo] (**-s, -s**) M dynamo
dz ABK = **Doppelzentner**
D-Zug ['de:tsu:k] M through train; **ein alter Mann ist doch kein ~** (*umg*) I am going as fast as I can

d

Ee

E¹, e [eː] NT E, e; **E wie Emil** ≈ E for Edward, ≈ E for Easy (*US*)
E² [eː] ABK = **Eilzug**; **Europastraße**
Ebbe ['ɛbə] (-, -**n**) F low tide; **~ und Flut** ebb and flow
eben ['eːbən] ADJ level; (*glatt*) smooth ▶ ADV just; (*bestätigend*) exactly; **das ist ~ so** that's just the way it is; **mein Bleistift war doch ~ noch da** my pencil was there (just) a minute ago; **~ deswegen** just because of that
Ebenbild NT: **das genaue ~ seines Vaters** the spitting image of his father
ebenbürtig ADJ: **jdm ~ sein** to be sb's peer
Ebene (-, -**n**) F plain; (*Math, Phys*) plane; (*fig*) level
eben- ZW: **ebenerdig** ADJ at ground level; **ebenfalls** ADV likewise; **Ebenheit** F levelness; (*Glätte*) smoothness; **Ebenholz** NT ebony; **ebenso** ADV just as; **ebenso gut** just as well; **ebenso oft** just as often; **ebenso viel** just as much; **ebenso weit** just as far; **ebenso wenig** just as little
Eber ['eːbər] (-**s**, -) M boar
Eberesche F mountain ash, rowan
ebnen ['eːbnən] VT to level; **jdm den Weg ~** (*fig*) to smooth the way for sb
E-Book-Reader ['iːbʊkriːdər] M e-reader, eReader
Echo ['ɛço] (-**s**, -**s**) NT echo; **(bei jdm) ein lebhaftes ~ finden** (*fig*) to meet with a lively response (from sb)
Echolot ['ɛçoloːt] NT (*Naut*) echo-sounder, sonar
Echse ['ɛksə] (-, -**n**) F (*Zool*) lizard
echt [ɛçt] ADJ genuine; (*typisch*) typical; **ich hab ~ keine Zeit** (*umg*) I really don't have any time; **Echtheit** F genuineness
Eckball ['ɛkbal] M corner (kick)
Ecke ['ɛkə] (-, -**n**) F corner; (*Math*) angle; **gleich um die ~** just around the corner; **an allen Ecken und Enden sparen** (*umg*) to pinch and scrape; **jdn um die ~ bringen** (*umg*) to bump sb off; **mit jdm um ein paar Ecken herum verwandt sein** (*umg*) to be distantly related to sb, to be sb's second cousin twice removed (*hum*)
eckig ADJ angular
Eckzahn M eye tooth
Eckzins M (*Fin*) minimum lending rate
Ecstasy ['ɛkstəsɪ] NT (*Droge*) ecstasy
Ecuador [ekua'doːr] (-**s**) NT Ecuador
edel ['eːdəl] ADJ noble; **Edelganove** M gentleman criminal; **Edelgas** NT rare gas; **Edelmetall** NT rare metal; **Edelstein** M precious stone
Edinburg, Edinburgh ['eːdɪnbʊrk] NT Edinburgh
EDV (-) F ABK (= *elektronische Datenverarbeitung*) EDP
EEG (-) NT ABK (= *Elektroenzephalogramm*) EEG
Efeu ['eːfɔʏ] (-**s**) M ivy
Effeff [ɛf'lɛf] (-) (*umg*) NT: **etw aus dem ~ können** to be able to do sth standing on one's head
Effekt [ɛ'fɛkt] (-**(e)s**, -**e**) M effect
Effekten [ɛ'fɛktən] PL stocks *pl*; **Effektenbörse** F Stock Exchange
Effekthascherei [ɛfɛkthaʃə'raɪ] F sensationalism
effektiv [ɛfɛk'tiːf] ADJ effective, actual
Effet [ɛ'feː] (-**s**) M spin
EG (-) F ABK (= *Europäische Gemeinschaft*) EC
egal [e'gaːl] ADJ all the same; **das ist mir ganz ~** it's all the same to me
egalitär [egali'tɛːr] ADJ (*geh*) egalitarian
Egge ['ɛgə] (-, -**n**) F (*Agr*) harrow
Egoismus [ego'ɪsmʊs] M selfishness, egoism
Egoist(in) M(F) egoist; **egoistisch** ADJ selfish, egoistic
egozentrisch [ego'tsɛntrɪʃ] ADJ egocentric, self-centred (BRIT), self-centered (*US*)
eh [eː] ADV: **seit eh und je** for ages, since the year dot (*umg*); **ich komme eh nicht dazu** I won't get around to it anyway
e. h. ABK = **ehrenhalber**
ehe KONJ before
Ehe ['eːə] (-, -**n**) F marriage; **die ~ eingehen** (*form*) to enter into matrimony; **sie leben in wilder ~** (*veraltet*) they are living in sin; **Ehebrecher** (-**s**, -) M adulterer; **Ehebrecherin** F adulteress; **Ehebruch** M adultery; **Ehefrau** F wife; **Eheleute** PL married couple *pl*; **ehelich** ADJ matrimonial; (*Kind*) legitimate
ehemalig ADJ former
ehemals ADV formerly
Ehe- ZW: **Ehemann** M married man; (*Partner*)

husband; **Ehepaar** NT married couple; **Ehepartner** M husband; **Ehepartnerin** F wife
eher ['e:ər] ADV *(früher)* sooner; *(lieber)* rather, sooner; *(mehr)* more; **nicht ~ als** not before; **umso ~, als** the more so because
Ehe- zW: **Ehering** M wedding ring; **Ehescheidung** F divorce; **Eheschließung** F marriage; **Ehestand** M: **in den Ehestand treten** *(form)* to enter into matrimony
eheste(r, s) ['e:əstə(r, s)] ADJ *(früheste)* first, earliest; **am ehesten** *(am liebsten)* soonest; *(meist)* most; *(am wahrscheinlichsten)* most probably
Ehevermittlung F *(Büro)* marriage bureau
Eheversprechen NT *(Jur)* promise to marry
ehrbar ['e:rba:r] ADJ honourable (BRIT), honorable (US), respectable
Ehre (-, -n) F honour (BRIT), honor (US); **etw in Ehren halten** to treasure *od* cherish sth
ehren VT to honour (BRIT), to honor (US)
Ehren- zW: **ehrenamtlich** ADJ honorary; **Ehrenbürgerrecht** NT: **die Stadt verlieh ihr das Ehrenbürgerrecht** she was given the freedom of the city; **Ehrengast** M guest of honour (BRIT) *od* honor (US); **ehrenhaft** ADJ honourable (BRIT), honorable (US); **ehrenhalber** ADV: **er wurde ehrenhalber zum Vorsitzenden auf Lebenszeit ernannt** he was made honorary president for life; **Ehrenmann** M man of honour (BRIT) *od* honor (US); **Ehrenmitglied** NT honorary member; **Ehrenplatz** M place of honour (BRIT) *od* honor (US); **Ehrenrechte** PL civic rights *pl*; **ehrenrührig** ADJ defamatory; **Ehrenrunde** F lap of honour (BRIT) *od* honor (US); **Ehrensache** F point of honour (BRIT) *od* honor (US); **Ehrensache!** *(umg)* you can count on me; **Ehrentag** M *(Geburtstag)* birthday; *(großer Tag)* big day; **ehrenvoll** ADJ honourable (BRIT), honorable (US); **Ehrenwort** NT word of honour (BRIT) *od* honor (US); **ich gebe dir mein Ehrenwort** I give you my word
Ehr- zW: **ehrerbietig** ADJ respectful; **Ehrfurcht** F awe, deep respect; **Ehrfurcht gebietend** awesome; *(Stimme)* authoritative; **Ehrgefühl** NT sense of honour (BRIT) *od* honor (US); **Ehrgeiz** M ambition; **ehrgeizig** ADJ ambitious; **ehrlich** ADJ honest; **ehrlich verdientes Geld** hard-earned money; **ehrlich gesagt ...** quite frankly *od* honestly ...; **Ehrlichkeit** F honesty; **ehrlos** ADJ dishonourable (BRIT), dishonorable (US)
Ehrung F honour(ing) (BRIT), honor(ing) (US)
ehrwürdig ADJ venerable
ei INTERJ well, well; *(beschwichtigend)* now, now
Ei [aɪ] **(-(e)s, -er)** NT egg; **Eier** PL *(umg!: Hoden)* balls *pl* *(umg!)*; **jdn wie ein rohes Ei behandeln** *(fig)* to handle sb with kid gloves; **wie aus dem Ei gepellt aussehen** *(umg)* to look spruce
Eibe ['aɪbə] **(-, -n)** F *(Bot)* yew
Eichamt ['aɪçlamt] NT Office of Weights and Measures
Eiche **(-, -n)** F oak (tree)
Eichel **(-, -n)** F acorn; *(Karten)* club; *(Anat)* glans
eichen VT to calibrate
Eichhörnchen NT squirrel
Eichmaß NT standard
Eichung F standardization
Eid ['aɪt] **(-(e)s, -e)** M oath; **eine Erklärung an Eides statt abgeben** *(Jur)* to make a solemn declaration
Eidechse ['aɪdɛksə] **(-, -n)** F lizard
eidesstattlich ADJ: **eidesstattliche Erklärung** affidavit
Eid- zW: **Eidgenosse** M Swiss; **Eidgenossenschaft** F: **Schweizerische Eidgenossenschaft** Swiss Confederation; **eidlich** ADJ (sworn) upon oath
Eidotter NT egg yolk
Eier- zW: **Eierbecher** M egg cup; **Eierkuchen** M pancake; *(Omelett)* omelette (BRIT), omelet (US); **Eierlikör** M advocaat
eiern ['aɪərn] *(umg)* VI to wobble
Eier- zW: **Eierschale** F eggshell; **Eierstock** M ovary; **Eieruhr** F egg timer
Eifel ['aɪfəl] (-) F Eifel (Mountains)
Eifer ['aɪfər] **(-s)** M zeal, enthusiasm; **mit großem ~ bei der Sache sein** to put one's heart into it; **im ~ des Gefechts** *(fig)* in the heat of the moment; **Eifersucht** F jealousy; **eifersüchtig** ADJ: **eifersüchtig (auf** *+akk***)** jealous (of)
eifrig ['aɪfrɪç] ADJ zealous, enthusiastic
Eigelb ['aɪgɛlp] **(-(e)s, -e** *od* **-)** NT egg yolk
eigen ['aɪgən] ADJ own; *(eigenartig)* peculiar; *(ordentlich)* particular; *(übergenau)* fussy; **ich möchte kurz in eigener Sache sprechen** I would like to say something on my own account; **mit dem ihm eigenen Lächeln** with that smile peculiar to him; **sich** *dat* **etw zu ~ machen** to make sth one's own; **Eigenart** F *(Besonderheit)* peculiarity; *(Eigenschaft)* characteristic; **eigenartig** ADJ peculiar; **Eigenbau** M: **er fährt ein Fahrrad Marke Eigenbau** *(hum: umg)* he rides a home-made bike; **Eigenbedarf** M one's own requirements *pl*; **Eigenbrötler(in)** (-s, -) M(F) loner, lone wolf; *(komischer Kauz)* oddball *(umg)*; **Eigengewicht** NT dead weight; **eigenhändig** ADJ with one's own hand; **Eigenheim** NT owner-occupied house; **Eigenheit** F peculiarity; **Eigeninitiative** F initiative of one's own; **Eigenkapital** NT personal capital; *(von Firma)* company capital; **Eigenlob** NT self-praise; **eigenmächtig** ADJ high-handed; *(eigenverantwortlich)* taken/done *etc* on one's own authority; *(unbefugt)* unauthorized; **Eigenname** M proper name; **Eigennutz** M self-interest
eigens ADV expressly, on purpose
eigen- zW: **Eigenschaft** F quality; *(Chem, Phys)* property; *(Merkmal)* characteristic; **Eigenschaftswort** NT adjective; **Eigensinn** M obstinacy; **eigensinnig** ADJ obstinate; **eigenständig** ADJ independent; **Eigenständigkeit** F independence

eigentlich ADJ actual, real ▶ ADV actually, really; **was willst du ~ hier?** what do you want here anyway?
eigen- ZW: **Eigentor** NT own goal; **Eigentum** NT property; **Eigentümer(in)** (**-s, -**) M(F) owner, proprietor; **eigentümlich** ADJ peculiar; **Eigentümlichkeit** F peculiarity
Eigentumsdelikt NT (*Jur: Diebstahl*) theft
Eigentumswohnung F freehold flat
Eigenvorsorge F private provision (*for retirement etc*)
eigenwillig ADJ with a mind of one's own
eignen ['aɪgnən] VR to be suited
Eignung F suitability
Eignungsprüfung F aptitude test
Eignungstest (**-(e)s, -s** *od* **-e**) M aptitude test
Eilbote M courier; **per** *od* **durch Eilboten** express
Eilbrief M express letter
Eile (-) F haste; **es hat keine ~** there's no hurry
Eileiter ['aɪlaɪtər] M (*Anat*) Fallopian tube
eilen VI (*Mensch*) to hurry; (*dringend sein*) to be urgent
eilends ADV hastily
Eilgut NT express goods *pl*, fast freight (*US*)
eilig ADJ hasty, hurried; (*dringlich*) urgent; **es ~ haben** to be in a hurry
Eil- ZW: **Eiltempo** NT: **etw im Eiltempo machen** to do sth in a rush; **Eilzug** M fast stopping train; **Eilzustellung** F special delivery
Eimer ['aɪmər] (**-s, -**) M bucket, pail; **im ~ sein** (*umg*) to be up the spout
ein(e) ['aɪn(ə)] NUM one ▶ INDEF ART a, an ▶ ADV: **nicht ~ noch aus wissen** not to know what to do; **E~/Aus** (*an Geräten*) on/off; **er ist ihr E~ und Alles** he means everything to her; **er geht bei uns ~ und aus** he is always round at our place
einander [aɪ'nandər] PRON one another, each other
einarbeiten ['aɪn|arbaɪtən] VR: **sich (in etw** *akk*) **~** to familiarize o.s. (with sth)
Einarbeitungszeit F training period
einarmig ['aɪn|armɪç] ADJ one-armed
einäschern ['aɪn|ɛʃərn] VT (*Leichnam*) to cremate; (*Stadt etc*) to reduce to ashes
einatmen ['aɪn|a:tmən] VT, VI to inhale, to breathe in
einäugig ['aɪn|ɔʏgɪç] ADJ one-eyed
Einbahnstraße ['aɪnba:nʃtrasə] F one-way street
Einband ['aɪnbant] M binding, cover
einbändig ['aɪnbɛndɪç] ADJ one-volume
einbauen ['aɪnbaʊən] VT to build in; (*Motor*) to install, to fit
Einbau- ZW: **Einbauküche** F (fully-)fitted kitchen; **Einbaumöbel** PL built-in furniture *sing*; **Einbauschrank** M fitted cupboard
einbegriffen ['aɪnbəgrɪfən] ADJ included, inclusive
einbehalten ['aɪnbəhaltən] *unreg* VT to keep back
einberufen *unreg* VT to convene; (*Mil*) to call up (BRIT), to draft (*US*)
Einberufung F convocation; (*Mil*) call-up (BRIT), draft (*US*)
Einberufungsbefehl M, **Einberufungsbescheid** M (*Mil*) call-up (BRIT) *od* draft (*US*) papers *pl*
einbetten ['aɪnbɛtən] VT to embed
Einbettzimmer NT single room
einbeziehen ['aɪnbətsi:ən] *unreg* VT to include
einbiegen ['aɪnbi:gən] *unreg* VI to turn
einbilden ['aɪnbɪldən] VR: **sich** *dat* **etw ~** to imagine sth; **sich** *dat* **viel auf etw** *akk* **~** (*stolz sein*) to be conceited about sth
Einbildung F imagination; (*Dünkel*) conceit
Einbildungskraft F imagination
einbinden ['aɪnbɪndən] *unreg* VT to bind (up)
einbläuen ['aɪnblɔʏən] (*umg*) VT: **jdm etw ~** to hammer sth into sb
einblenden ['aɪnblɛndən] VT to fade in
Einblick ['aɪnblɪk] M insight; **~ in die Akten nehmen** to examine the files; **jdm ~ in etw** *akk* **gewähren** to allow sb to look at sth
einbrechen ['aɪnbrɛçən] *unreg* VI (*einstürzen*) to fall in; (*Einbruch verüben*) to break in; **bei einbrechender Dunkelheit** at nightfall
Einbrecher (**-s, -**) M burglar
einbringen ['aɪnbrɪŋən] *unreg* VT to bring in; (*Geld, Vorteil*) to yield; (*mitbringen*) to contribute; **das bringt nichts ein** (*fig*) it's not worth it
einbrocken ['aɪnbrɔkən] (*umg*) VT: **jdm/sich etwas ~** to land sb/o.s. in it
Einbruch ['aɪnbrʊx] M (*Hauseinbruch*) break-in, burglary; (*des Winters*) onset; (*Einsturz, Fin*) collapse; (*Mil: in Front*) breakthrough; **bei ~ der Nacht** at nightfall
einbruchssicher ADJ burglar-proof
Einbuchtung ['aɪnbʊxtʊŋ] F indentation; (*Bucht*) inlet, bay
einbürgern ['aɪnbʏrgərn] VT to naturalize ▶ VR to become adopted; **das hat sich so eingebürgert** that's become a custom
Einbürgerung F naturalization
Einbuße ['aɪnbu:sə] F loss, forfeiture
einbüßen ['aɪnby:sən] VT to lose, to forfeit
einchecken ['aɪntʃɛkən] VT, VI to check in
eincremen ['aɪnkre:mən] VT to put cream on
eindämmen ['aɪndɛmən] VT (*Fluss*) to dam; (*fig*) to check, to contain
eindecken ['aɪndɛkən] VR: **sich ~ (mit)** to lay in stocks (of) ▶ VT (*umg: überhäufen*): **mit Arbeit eingedeckt sein** to be inundated with work
eindeutig ['aɪndɔʏtɪç] ADJ unequivocal
eindeutschen ['aɪndɔʏtʃən] VT (*Fremdwort*) to Germanize
eindösen ['aɪndø:zən] (*umg*) VI to doze off
eindringen ['aɪndrɪŋən] *unreg* VI: **~ (in** *+akk*) to force one's way in(to); (*in Haus*) to break in(to); (*in Land*) to invade; (*Gas, Wasser*) to penetrate; **auf jdn ~** (*mit Bitten*) to pester sb
eindringlich ADJ forcible, urgent; **ich habe ihn ~ gebeten ...** I urged him ...
Eindringling M intruder
Eindruck ['aɪndrʊk] M impression

eindrücken ['aındrʏkən] VT to press in
eindrucksfähig ADJ impressionable
eindrucksvoll ADJ impressive
eine(r, s) PRON one; *(jemand)* someone; **wie kann einer nur so dumm sein!** how could anybody be so stupid!; **es kam eines zum anderen** it was (just) one thing after another; **sich** *dat* **einen genehmigen** *(umg)* to have a quick one
einebnen ['aınle:bnən] VT *(lit)* to level (off); *(fig)* to level out
Einehe ['aınle:ə] F monogamy
eineiig ['aınlaııç] ADJ *(Zwillinge)* identical
eineinhalb ['aınlaın'halp] NUM one and a half
einengen ['aınlɛŋən] VT to confine, to restrict
Einer ['aınər] (-) M *(Math)* unit; *(Ruderboot)* single scull
einerlei ADJ *(gleichartig)* the same kind of; **es ist mir ~** it is all the same to me; **Einerlei** ['aınər'laı] **(-s)** NT monotony
einerseits ADV on the one hand
einfach ['aınfax] ADJ simple; *(nicht mehrfach)* single ▸ ADV simply; **Einfachheit** F simplicity
einfädeln ['aınfɛ:dəln] VT *(Nadel)* to thread; *(fig)* to contrive
einfahren ['aınfa:rən] *unreg* VT to bring in; *(Barriere)* to knock down; *(Auto)* to run in ▸ VI to drive in; *(Zug)* to pull in; *(Min)* to go down
Einfahrt F *(Vorgang)* driving in; *(von Zug)* pulling in; *(Min)* descent; *(Ort)* entrance; *(von Autobahn)* slip road (BRIT), entrance ramp (US)
Einfall ['aınfal] M *(Idee)* idea, notion; *(Lichteinfall)* incidence; *(Mil)* raid
einfallen *unreg* VI *(einstürzen)* to fall in, to collapse; *(Licht)* to fall; *(Mil)* to raid; *(einstimmen)*: **~ (in** *+akk***)** to join in (with); **etw fällt jdm ein** sth occurs to sb; **das fällt mir gar nicht ein!** I wouldn't dream of it; **sich** *dat* **etwas ~ lassen** to have a good idea; **dabei fällt mir mein Onkel ein, der ...** that reminds me of my uncle who ...; **es fällt mir jetzt nicht ein** I can't think of it *od* it won't come to me at the moment; **was fällt Ihnen ein!** what do you think you're doing?
einfallslos ADJ unimaginative
einfallsreich ADJ imaginative
einfältig ['aınfɛltıç] ADJ simple(-minded)
Einfaltspinsel ['aınfaltspınzəl] *(umg)* M simpleton
Einfamilienhaus [aınfa'mi:liənhaʊs] NT detached house
einfangen ['aınfaŋən] *unreg* VT to catch
einfarbig ['aınfarbıç] ADJ all one colour (BRIT) *od* color (US); *(Stoff etc)* self-coloured (BRIT), self-colored (US)
einfassen ['aınfasən] VT *(Edelstein)* to set; *(Beet, Stoff)* to edge
Einfassung F setting; *(von Beet, Stoff)* border
einfetten ['aınfɛtən] VT to grease
einfinden ['aınfındən] *unreg* VR to come, to turn up
einfliegen ['aınfli:gən] *unreg* VT to fly in
einfließen ['aınfli:sən] *unreg* VI to flow in
einflößen ['aınflø:sən] VT: **jdm etw ~** *(lit)* to give sb sth; *(fig)* to instil sth into sb
Einfluss ['aınflʊs] M influence; **~ nehmen** to bring an influence to bear; **Einflussbereich** M sphere of influence; **einflussreich** ADJ influential
einflüstern ['aınflʏstərn] VT: **jdm etw ~** to whisper sth to sb; *(fig)* to insinuate sth to sb
einförmig ['aınfœrmıç] ADJ uniform; *(eintönig)* monotonous; **Einförmigkeit** F uniformity; *(Eintönigkeit)* monotony
einfrieren ['aınfri:rən] *unreg* VI to freeze (in) ▸ VT to freeze; *(Pol: Beziehungen)* to suspend
einfügen ['aınfy:gən] VT to fit in; *(zusätzlich)* to add; *(Comput)* to insert
einfühlen ['aınfy:lən] VR: **sich in jdn ~** to empathize with sb
einfühlsam ['aınfy:lza:m] ADJ sensitive
Einfühlungsvermögen NT empathy; **mit großem ~** with a great deal of sensitivity
Einfuhr ['aınfu:r] (-) F import; **Einfuhrartikel** M imported article
einführen ['aınfy:rən] VT to bring in; *(Mensch, Sitten)* to introduce; *(Ware)* to import; **jdn in sein Amt ~** to install sb (in office)
Einfuhr- ZW: **Einfuhrgenehmigung** F import permit; **Einfuhrkontingent** NT import quota; **Einfuhrsperre** F ban on imports; **Einfuhrstopp** M ban on imports
Einführung F introduction
Einführungspreis M introductory price
Einfuhrzoll M import duty
einfüllen ['aınfʏlən] VT to pour in
Eingabe ['aınga:bə] F petition; *(Dateneingabe)* input; **~/Ausgabe** *(Comput)* input/output
Eingang ['aıngaŋ] M entrance; *(Comm: Ankunft)* arrival; *(Sendung)* post; **wir bestätigen den ~ Ihres Schreibens vom ...** we acknowledge receipt of your letter of the ...
eingängig ['aıngɛŋıç] ADJ catchy
eingangs ADV at the outset ▸ PRÄP *+gen* at the outset of
Eingangs- ZW: **Eingangsbestätigung** F acknowledgement of receipt; **Eingangshalle** F entrance hall; **Eingangsstempel** M *(Comm)* receipt stamp
eingeben ['aınge:bən] *unreg* VT *(Arznei)* to give; *(Daten etc)* to enter; *(Gedanken)* to inspire
eingebettet ['aıngəbɛtət] ADJ: **in** *od* **zwischen Hügeln ~** nestling among the hills
eingebildet ['aıngəbıldət] ADJ imaginary; *(eitel)* conceited; **eingebildeter Kranker** hypochondriac
Eingeborene(r) ['aıngəbo:rənə(r)] F(M) native
Eingebung F inspiration
eingedenk ['aıngədɛŋk] PRÄP *+gen* bearing in mind
eingefahren ['aıngəfa:rən] ADJ *(Verhaltensweise)* well-worn
eingefallen ['aıngəfalən] ADJ *(Gesicht)* gaunt
eingefleischt ['aıngəflaıʃt] ADJ inveterate; **eingefleischter Junggeselle** confirmed bachelor

e

eingefroren ['aɪngəfro:rən] ADJ frozen
eingehen ['aɪnge:ən] *unreg* VI (*Aufnahme finden*) to come in; (*Sendung, Geld*) to be received; (*Tier, Pflanze*) to die; (*Firma*) to fold; (*schrumpfen*) to shrink ▸ VT (*abmachen*) to enter into; (*Wette*) to make; **auf etw** *akk* **~** to go into sth; **auf jdn ~** to respond to sb; **jdm ~** (*verständlich sein*) to be comprehensible to sb; **auf einen Vorschlag/Plan ~** (*zustimmen*) to go along with a suggestion/plan; **bei dieser Hitze/Kälte geht man ja ein!** (*umg*) this heat/cold is just too much!
eingehend ADJ in-depth, thorough
eingekeilt ['aɪngəkaɪlt] ADJ hemmed in; (*fig*) trapped
eingekesselt ['aɪngəkɛsəlt] ADJ: **~ sein** to be encircled *od* surrounded
Eingemachte(s) ['aɪngəma:xtə(s)] NT preserves *pl*
eingemeinden ['aɪngəmaɪndən] VT to incorporate
eingenommen ['aɪngənɔmən] ADJ: **~ (von)** fond (of), partial (to); **~ (gegen)** prejudiced (against)
eingeschnappt ['aɪngəʃnapt] (*umg*) ADJ cross; **~ sein** to be in a huff
eingeschrieben ['aɪngəʃri:bən] ADJ registered
eingeschworen ['aɪngəʃvo:rən] ADJ confirmed; (*Gemeinschaft*) close
eingesessen ['aɪngəzɛsən] ADJ old-established
eingespannt ['aɪngəʃpant] ADJ busy
eingespielt ['aɪngəʃpi:lt] ADJ: **aufeinander ~ sein** to be in tune with each other
Eingeständnis ['aɪngəʃtɛntnɪs] NT admission, confession
eingestehen ['aɪngəʃte:ən] *unreg* VT to confess
eingestellt ['aɪngəʃtɛlt] ADJ: **ich bin im Moment nicht auf Besuch ~** I'm not prepared for visitors
eingetragen ['aɪngətra:gən] ADJ (*Comm*) registered; **eingetragener Gesellschaftssitz** registered office; **eingetragenes Warenzeichen** registered trademark
Eingeweide ['aɪngəvaɪdə] (**-s, -**) NT innards *pl*, intestines *pl*
Eingeweihte(r) ['aɪngəvaɪtə(r)] F(M) initiate
eingewöhnen ['aɪngəvø:nən] VR: **sich ~ (in** *+dat*) to settle down (in)
eingezahlt ['aɪngətsa:lt] ADJ: **eingezahltes Kapital** paid-up capital
eingießen ['aɪngi:sən] *unreg* VT to pour (out)
eingleisig ['aɪnglaɪzɪç] ADJ single-track; **er denkt sehr ~** (*fig*) he's completely single-minded
eingliedern ['aɪngli:dərn] VT: **~ (in** *+akk*) to integrate (into) ▸ VR: **sich ~ (in** *+akk*) to integrate o.s. (into)
eingraben ['aɪngra:bən] *unreg* VT to dig in ▸ VR to dig o.s. in; **dieses Erlebnis hat sich seinem Gedächtnis eingegraben** this experience has engraved itself on his memory
eingreifen ['aɪngraɪfən] *unreg* VI to intervene, to interfere; (*Zahnrad*) to mesh
Eingreiftruppe F (*Mil*) strike force
eingrenzen ['aɪngrɛntsən] VT to enclose; (*fig: Problem*) to delimit
Eingriff ['aɪngrɪf] M intervention, interference; (*Operation*) operation
einhaken ['aɪnha:kən] VT to hook in ▸ VR: **sich bei jdm ~** to link arms with sb ▸ VI (*sich einmischen*) to intervene
Einhalt ['aɪnhalt] M: **~ gebieten** *+dat* to put a stop to
einhalten *unreg* VT (*Regel*) to keep ▸ VI to stop
einhämmern ['aɪnhɛmərn] VT: **jdm etw ~** (*fig*) to hammer sth into sb
einhandeln ['aɪnhandəln] VT: **etw gegen** *od* **für etw ~** to trade sth for sth
einhändig ['aɪnhɛndɪç] ADJ one-handed
einhändigen ['aɪnhɛndɪgən] VT to hand in
einhängen ['aɪnhɛŋən] VT to hang; (*Telefon: auch vi*) to hang up; **sich bei jdm ~** to link arms with sb
einheimisch ['aɪnhaɪmɪʃ] ADJ native
Einheimische(r) F(M) local
einheimsen (*umg*) VT to bring home
einheiraten ['aɪnhaɪra:tən] VI: **in einen Betrieb ~** to marry into a business
Einheit ['aɪnhaɪt] F unity; (*Maß, Mil*) unit; **eine geschlossene ~ bilden** to form an integrated whole; **einheitlich** ADJ uniform
Einheits- ZW: **Einheitsfront** F (*Pol*) united front; **Einheitsliste** F (*Pol*) single *od* unified list of candidates; **Einheitspreis** M uniform price
einheizen ['aɪnhaɪtsən] VI: **jdm (tüchtig) ~** (*umg: die Meinung sagen*) to make things hot for sb
einhellig ['aɪnhɛlɪç] ADJ unanimous ▸ ADV unanimously
einholen ['aɪnho:lən] VT (*Tau*) to haul in; (*Fahne, Segel*) to lower; (*Vorsprung aufholen*) to catch up with; (*Verspätung*) to make up; (*Rat, Erlaubnis*) to ask ▸ VI (*einkaufen*) to buy, to shop
Einhorn ['aɪnhɔrn] NT unicorn
einhüllen ['aɪnhʏlən] VT to wrap up
einhundert ['aɪn'hʊndərt] NUM one hundred
einig ['aɪnɪç] ADJ (*vereint*) united; **sich** *dat* **~ sein** to be in agreement; **~ werden** to agree
einige(r, s) ADJ, PRON some ▸ PL some; (*mehrere*) several; **mit Ausnahme einiger weniger** with a few exceptions; **vor einigen Tagen** the other day, a few days ago; **dazu ist noch einiges zu sagen** there are still one or two things to say about that; **~ Mal** a few times
einigen VT to unite ▸ VR: **sich (auf etw** *akk*) **~** to agree (on sth)
einigermaßen ADV somewhat; (*leidlich*) reasonably
einiges PRON *siehe* **einige(r,s)**
einiggehen *unreg* VI to agree
Einigkeit F unity; (*Übereinstimmung*) agreement
Einigung F agreement; (*Vereinigung*) unification
einimpfen ['aɪnlɪmpfən] VT: **jdm etw ~** to inoculate sb with sth; (*fig*) to impress sth upon sb
einjagen ['aɪnja:gən] VT: **jdm Furcht/einen Schrecken ~** to give sb a fright

einjährig ['aɪnjɛːrɪç] ADJ of *od* for one year; (*Alter*) one-year-old; (*Pflanze*) annual
einkalkulieren ['aɪnkalkuliːrən] VT to take into account, to allow for
einkassieren ['aɪnkasiːrən] VT (*Geld, Schulden*) to collect
Einkauf ['aɪnkaʊf] M purchase; (*Comm: Abteilung*) purchasing (department)
einkaufen VT to buy ▸ VI to shop; **~ gehen** to go shopping
Einkäufer(in) ['aɪnkɔʏfər(ɪn)] M(F) (*Comm*) buyer
Einkaufs- ZW: **Einkaufsbummel** M: **einen Einkaufsbummel machen** to go on a shopping spree; **Einkaufskorb** M shopping basket; **Einkaufsleiter(in)** M(F) (*Comm*) chief buyer; **Einkaufsnetz** NT string bag; **Einkaufspreis** M cost price, wholesale price; **Einkaufstasche** F, **Einkaufstüte** F shopping bag; **Einkaufswagen** M trolley (BRIT), cart (*US*); **Einkaufszentrum** NT shopping centre (BRIT) *od* mall (*US*)
einkehren ['aɪnkeːrən] VI (*geh: Ruhe, Frühling*) to come; **in einem Gasthof ~** to (make a) stop at an inn
einkerben ['aɪnkɛrbən] VT to notch
einklagen ['aɪnklaːgən] VT (*Schulden*) to sue for (the recovery of)
einklammern ['aɪnklamərn] VT to put in brackets, to bracket
Einklang ['aɪnklaŋ] M harmony
einkleiden ['aɪnklaɪdən] VT to clothe; (*fig*) to express
einklemmen ['aɪnklɛmən] VT to jam
einknicken ['aɪnknɪkən] VT to bend in; (*Papier*) to fold ▸ VI (*Knie*) to give way
einkochen ['aɪnkɔxən] VT to boil down; (*Obst*) to preserve, to bottle
Einkommen ['aɪnkɔmən] (**-s, -**) NT income
einkommensschwach ADJ low-income *attrib*
einkommensstark ADJ high-income *attrib*
Einkommenssteuer, Einkommensteuer F income tax; **Einkommenssteuererklärung, Einkommensteuererklärung** F income tax return
Einkommensverhältnisse PL (level of) income *sing*
einkreisen ['aɪnkraɪzən] VT to encircle
einkriegen ['aɪnkriːgən] (*umg*) VR: **sie konnte sich gar nicht mehr darüber ~, dass ...** she couldn't get over the fact that ...
Einkünfte ['aɪnkʏnftə] PL income *sing*, revenue *sing*
einladen ['aɪnlaːdən] *unreg* VT (*Person*) to invite; (*Gegenstände*) to load; **jdn ins Kino ~** to take sb to the cinema
Einladung F invitation
Einlage ['aɪnlaːgə] F (*Programmeinlage*) interlude; (*Spareinlage*) deposit; (*Fin: Kapitaleinlage*) investment; (*Schuheinlage*) insole; (*Fußstütze*) support; (*Zahneinlage*) temporary filling; (*Koch*) *noodles, vegetables etc (in clear soup)*
einlagern ['aɪnlaːgərn] VT to store
Einlass ['aɪnlas] (**-es, Einlässe**) M admission; **jdm ~ gewähren** to admit sb
einlassen *unreg* VT to let in; (*einsetzen*) to set in ▸ VR: **sich mit jdm/auf etw** *akk* **~** to get involved with sb/sth; **sich auf einen Kompromiss ~** to agree to a compromise; **ich lasse mich auf keine Diskussion ein** I'm not having any discussion about it
Einlauf ['aɪnlaʊf] M arrival; (*von Pferden*) finish; (*Med*) enema
einlaufen *unreg* VI to arrive, to come in; (*Sport*) to finish; (*Wasser*) to run in; (*Stoff*) to shrink ▸ VT (*Schuhe*) to break in ▸ VR (*Sport*) to warm up; (*Motor, Maschine*) to run in; **jdm das Haus ~** to invade sb's house; **in den Hafen ~** to enter the harbour
einläuten ['aɪnlɔʏtən] VT (*neues Jahr*) to ring in; (*Sport: Runde*) to sound the bell for
einleben ['aɪnleːbən] VR to settle down
Einlegearbeit F inlay
einlegen ['aɪnleːgən] VT (*einfügen: Blatt, Sohle*) to insert; (*Koch*) to pickle; (*in Holz etc*) to inlay; (*Geld*) to deposit; (*Pause*) to have; (*Protest*) to make; (*Veto*) to use; (*Berufung*) to lodge; **ein gutes Wort bei jdm ~** to put in a good word with sb
Einlegesohle F insole
einleiten ['aɪnlaɪtən] VT to introduce, to start; (*Geburt*) to induce
Einleitung F introduction; (*von Geburt*) induction
einlenken ['aɪnlɛŋkən] VI (*fig*) to yield, to give way
einlesen ['aɪnleːzən] *unreg* VR: **sich in ein Gebiet ~** to get into a subject ▸ VT: **etw in etw** *+akk* **~** (*Daten*) to feed sth into sth
einleuchten ['aɪnlɔʏçtən] VI: **(jdm) ~** to be clear *od* evident (to sb)
einleuchtend ADJ clear
einliefern ['aɪnliːfərn] VT: **~ (in** *+akk***)** to take (into); **jdn ins Krankenhaus ~** to admit sb to hospital
Einlieferungsschein M certificate of posting
einlochen ['aɪnlɔxən] (*umg*) VT (*einsperren*) to lock up
einloggen ['aɪnlɔgən] VI (*Comput*) to log on *od* in
einlösen ['aɪnløːzən] VT (*Scheck*) to cash; (*Schuldschein, Pfand*) to redeem; (*Versprechen*) to keep
einmachen ['aɪnmaxən] VT to preserve
Einmachglas NT bottling jar
einmal ['aɪnmaːl] ADV once; (*erstens*) first of all, firstly; (*später*) one day; **nehmen wir ~ an** just let's suppose; **noch ~** once more; **nicht ~** not even; **auf ~** all at once; **es war ~** once upon a time there was/were; **~ ist keinmal** (*Sprichwort*) once doesn't count; **waren Sie schon ~ in Rom?** have you ever been to Rome?
Einmaleins NT multiplication tables *pl*; (*fig*) ABC, basics *pl*
einmalig ADJ unique; (*einmal geschehend*) single; (*prima*) fantastic
Einmalzahlung F one-off payment

Einmannbetrieb M one-man business
Einmannbus M one-man-operated bus
Einmarsch ['aɪnmarʃ] M entry; (*Mil*) invasion
einmarschieren VI to march in
einmengen ['aɪnmɛŋən] VR: **sich (in etw** *+akk*) **~** to interfere (with sth)
einmieten ['aɪnmi:tən] VR: **sich bei jdm ~** to take lodgings with sb
einmischen ['aɪnmɪʃən] VR: **sich (in etw** *+akk*) **~** to interfere (with sth)
einmotten ['aɪnmɔtən] VT (*Kleider etc*) to put in mothballs
einmünden ['aɪnmʏndən] VI: **~ in** *+akk* (*subj: Fluss*) to flow *od* run into, to join; (*Straße: in Platz*) to run into; (*: in andere Straße*) to run into, to join
einmütig ['aɪnmy:tɪç] ADJ unanimous
einnähen ['aɪnnɛ:ən] VT (*enger machen*) to take in
Einnahme ['aɪnna:mə] (-, -n) F (*Geld*) takings *pl*, revenue; (*von Medizin*) taking; (*Mil*) capture, taking; **Einnahmen und Ausgaben** income and expenditure; **Einnahmeausfall** F (*Wirts*) drop in takings *od* revenue; (*von Staat*) revenue shortfall; **Einnahmequelle** F source of income
einnehmen ['aɪnne:mən] *unreg* VT to take; (*Stellung, Raum*) to take up; **~ für/gegen** to persuade in favour of/against
einnehmend ADJ charming
einnicken ['aɪnnɪkən] VI to nod off
einnisten ['aɪnnɪstən] VR to nest; (*fig*) to settle o.s.
Einöde ['aɪnlø:də] (-, -n) F desert, wilderness
einordnen ['aɪnlɔrdnən] VT to arrange, to fit in ▶ VR to adapt; (*Aut*) to get in(to) lane
einpacken ['aɪnpakən] VT to pack (up)
einparken ['aɪnparkən] VT, VI to park
einpauken ['aɪnpaʊkən] (*umg*) VT: **jdm etw ~** to drum sth into sb
einpendeln ['aɪnpɛndəln] VR to even out
einpennen ['aɪnpɛnən] (*umg*) VI to drop off
einpferchen ['aɪnpfɛrçən] VT to pen in; (*fig*) to coop up
einpflanzen ['aɪnpflantsən] VT to plant; (*Med*) to implant
einplanen ['aɪnpla:nən] VT to plan for
einprägen ['aɪnprɛ:gən] VT to impress, to imprint; (*beibringen*): **jdm etw ~** to impress sth on sb; **sich** *dat* **etw ~** to memorize sth
einprägsam ['aɪnprɛ:kza:m] ADJ easy to remember; (*Melodie*) catchy
einprogrammieren ['aɪnprograми:rən] VT (*Comput*) to feed in
einprügeln ['aɪnpry:gəln] (*umg*) VT: **jdm etw ~** to din sth into sb
einquartieren ['aɪnkvarti:rən] VT (*Mil*) to billet; **Gäste bei Freunden ~** to put visitors up with friends
einrahmen ['aɪnra:mən] VT to frame
einrasten ['aɪnrastən] VI to engage
einräumen ['aɪnrɔʏmən] VT (*ordnend*) to put away; (*überlassen: Platz*) to give up; (*zugestehen*) to admit, to concede
einrechnen ['aɪnrɛçnən] VT to include; (*berücksichtigen*) to take into account
einreden ['aɪnre:dən] VT: **jdm/sich etw ~** to talk sb/o.s. into believing sth ▶ VI: **auf jdn ~** to keep on and on at sb
Einreibemittel NT liniment
einreiben ['aɪnraɪbən] *unreg* VT to rub in
einreichen ['aɪnraɪçən] VT to hand in; (*Antrag*) to submit
einreihen ['aɪnraɪən] VT (*einordnen, einfügen*) to put in; (*klassifizieren*) to classify ▶ VR (*Auto*) to get in lane; **etw in etw** *akk* **~** to put sth into sth
Einreise ['aɪnraɪzə] F entry; **Einreisebestimmungen** PL entry regulations *pl*; **Einreiseerlaubnis** F entry permit; **Einreisegenehmigung** F entry permit
einreisen ['aɪnraɪzən] VI: **in ein Land ~** to enter a country
Einreiseverbot NT refusal of entry
Einreisevisum NT entry visa
einreißen ['aɪnraɪsən] *unreg* VT (*Papier*) to tear; (*Gebäude*) to pull down ▶ VI to tear; (*Gewohnheit werden*) to catch on
einrenken ['aɪnrɛŋkən] VT (*Gelenk, Knie*) to put back in place; (*fig: umg*) to sort out ▶ VR (*fig: umg*) to sort itself out
einrichten ['aɪnrɪçtən] VT (*Haus*) to furnish; (*schaffen*) to establish, to set up; (*arrangieren*) to arrange; (*möglich machen*) to manage ▶ VR (*in Haus*) to furnish one's house; **sich ~ (auf** *+akk*) (*sich vorbereiten*) to prepare o.s. (for); (*sich anpassen*) to adapt (to)
Einrichtung F (*Wohnungseinrichtung*) furnishings *pl*; (*öffentliche Anstalt*) organization; (*Dienste*) service; (*Laboreinrichtung etc*) equipment; (*Gewohnheit*): **zur ständigen ~ werden** to become an institution
Einrichtungsgegenstand M item of furniture
einrosten ['aɪnrɔstən] VI to get rusty
einrücken ['aɪnrʏkən] VI (*Mil: Soldat*) to join up; (*: in Land*) to move in ▶ VT (*Anzeige*) to insert; (*Zeile, Text*) to indent
eins NUM one; **es ist mir alles ~** it's all one to me; **~ zu ~** (*Sport*) one all; **~ a** (*umg*) first-rate; **Eins** [aɪns] (-, -en) F one
einsalzen ['aɪnzaltsən] VT to salt
einsam ['aɪnza:m] ADJ lonely, solitary; **einsame Klasse/Spitze** (*umg: hervorragend*) absolutely fantastic; **Einsamkeit** F loneliness, solitude
einsammeln ['aɪnzaməln] VT to collect
Einsatz ['aɪnzats] M (*Teil*) insert; (*an Kleid*) insertion; (*Tischeinsatz*) leaf; (*Verwendung*) use, employment; (*Spieleinsatz*) stake; (*Risiko*) risk; (*Mil*) operation; (*Mus*) entry; **im ~** in action; **etw unter ~ seines Lebens tun** to risk one's life to do sth; **Einsatzbefehl** M order to go into action; **einsatzbereit** ADJ ready for action; **Einsatzkommando** NT (*Mil*) task force
einschalten ['aɪnʃaltən] VT (*Elek*) to switch on; (*einfügen*) to insert; (*Pause*) to make; (*Aut: Gang*) to engage; (*Anwalt*) to bring in ▶ VR (*dazwischentreten*) to intervene
Einschaltquote F (*TV*) viewing figures *pl*
einschärfen ['aɪnʃɛrfən] VT: **jdm etw ~** to impress sth on sb

einschätzen ['aɪnʃɛtsən] VT to estimate, to assess ▶ VR to rate o.s.
einschenken ['aɪnʃɛŋkən] VT to pour out
einscheren ['aɪnʃe:rən] VI to get back (into lane)
einschicken ['aɪnʃɪkən] VT to send in
einschieben ['aɪnʃi:bən] *unreg* VT to push in; (*zusätzlich*) to insert; **eine Pause ~** to have a break
einschiffen ['aɪnʃɪfən] VT to ship ▶ VR to embark, to go on board
einschl. ABK (= *einschließlich*) inc.
einschlafen ['aɪnʃla:fən] *unreg* VI to fall asleep, to go to sleep; (*fig: Freundschaft*) to peter out
einschläfern ['aɪnʃlɛ:fərn] VT (*schläfrig machen*) to make sleepy; (*Gewissen*) to soothe; (*narkotisieren*) to give a soporific to; (*töten: Tier*) to put to sleep
einschläfernd ADJ (*Med*) soporific; (*langweilig*) boring; (*Stimme*) lulling
Einschlag ['aɪnʃla:k] M impact; (*Aut*) lock; (*fig: Beimischung*) touch, hint
einschlagen ['aɪnʃla:gən] *unreg* VT to knock in; (*Fenster*) to smash, to break; (*Zähne, Schädel*) to smash in; (*Steuer*) to turn; (*kürzer machen*) to take up; (*Ware*) to pack, to wrap up; (*Weg, Richtung*) to take ▶ VI to hit; (*Blitz*) to strike; (*sich einigen*) to agree; (*Anklang finden*) to work, to succeed; **es muss irgendwo eingeschlagen haben** something must have been struck by lightning; **gut ~** (*umg*) to go down well, to be a big hit; **auf jdn ~** to hit sb
einschlägig ['aɪnʃlɛ:gɪç] ADJ relevant; **er ist ~ vorbestraft** (*Jur*) he has a previous conviction for a similar offence
einschleichen ['aɪnʃlaɪçən] *unreg* VR (*in Haus, fig: Fehler*) to creep in, to steal in; (*in Vertrauen*) to worm one's way in
einschleppen ['aɪnʃlɛpən] VT (*fig: Krankheit etc*) to bring in
einschleusen ['aɪnʃlɔyzən] VT: **~ (in** *+akk*) to smuggle in(to)
einschließen ['aɪnʃli:sən] *unreg* VT (*Kind*) to lock in; (*Häftling*) to lock up; (*Gegenstand*) to lock away; (*Bergleute*) to cut off; (*umgeben*) to surround; (*Mil*) to encircle; (*fig*) to include, to comprise ▶ VR to lock o.s. in
einschließlich ADV inclusive ▶ PRÄP *+gen* inclusive of, including
einschmeicheln ['aɪnʃmaɪçəln] VR: **sich (bei jdm) ~** to ingratiate o.s. (with sb)
einschmuggeln ['aɪnʃmʊgəln] VT: **~ (in** *+akk*) to smuggle in(to)
einschnappen ['aɪnʃnapən] VI (*Tür*) to click to; (*fig*) to be touchy; **eingeschnappt sein** to be in a huff
einschneidend ['aɪnʃnaɪdənt] ADJ incisive
einschneien ['aɪnʃnaɪən] VI: **eingeschneit sein** to be snowed in
Einschnitt ['aɪnʃnɪt] M (*Med*) incision; (*im Tal, Gebirge*) cleft; (*im Leben*) decisive point
einschnüren ['aɪnʃny:rən] VT (*einengen*) to cut into; **dieser Kragen schnürt mir den Hals ein** this collar is strangling me
einschränken ['aɪnʃrɛŋkən] VT to limit, to restrict; (*Kosten*) to cut down, to reduce ▶ VR to cut down (on expenditure); **einschränkend möchte ich sagen, dass …** I'd like to qualify that by saying …
einschränkend ADJ restrictive
Einschränkung F restriction, limitation; (*von Kosten*) reduction; (*von Behauptung*) qualification
Einschreibbrief, Einschreibebrief M registered (BRIT) *od* certified (US) letter
einschreiben ['aɪnʃraɪbən] *unreg* VT to write in; (*Post*) to send by registered (BRIT) *od* certified (US) mail ▶ VR to register; (*Univ*) to enrol; **Einschreiben** NT registered (BRIT) *od* certified (US) letter
einschreiten ['aɪnʃraɪtən] *unreg* VI to step in, to intervene; **~ gegen** to take action against
Einschub ['aɪnʃu:p] (**-(e)s, Einschübe**) M insertion
einschüchtern ['aɪnʃʏçtərn] VT to intimidate
Einschüchterung ['aɪnʃʏçtərʊŋ] F intimidation
einschulen ['aɪnʃu:lən] VT: **eingeschult werden** (*Kind*) to start school
einschweißen ['aɪnʃvaɪsən] VT (*in Plastik*) to shrink-wrap; (*Tech*): **etw in etw** *akk* **~** to weld sth into sth
einschwenken ['aɪnʃvɛŋkən] VI: **~ (in** *+akk*) to turn *od* swing in(to)
einsehen ['aɪnze:ən] *unreg* VT (*prüfen*) to inspect; (*Fehler etc*) to recognize; (*verstehen*) to see; **das sehe ich nicht ein** I don't see why; **Einsehen (-s)** NT understanding; **ein Einsehen haben** to show understanding
einseifen ['aɪnzaɪfən] VT to soap, to lather; (*fig: umg*) to take in, to con
einseitig ['aɪnzaɪtɪç] ADJ one-sided; (*Pol*) unilateral; (*Ernährung*) unbalanced; (*Diskette*) single-sided; **Einseitigkeit** F one-sidedness
einsenden ['aɪnzɛndən] *unreg* VT to send in
Einsender(in) (**-s, -**) M(F) sender, contributor
Einsendeschluss M closing date (for entries)
Einsendung F sending in
einsetzen ['aɪnzɛtsən] VT to put (in); (*in Amt*) to appoint, to install; (*Geld*) to stake; (*verwenden*) to use; (*Mil*) to employ ▶ VI (*beginnen*) to set in; (*Mus*) to enter, to come in ▶ VR to work hard; **sich für jdn/etw ~** to support sb/sth; **ich werde mich dafür ~, dass …** I will do what I can to see that …
Einsicht ['aɪnzɪçt] F insight; (*in Akten*) look, inspection; **zu der ~ kommen, dass …** to come to the conclusion that …
einsichtig ADJ (*Mensch*) judicious; **jdm etw ~ machen** to make sb understand *od* see sth
Einsichtnahme (**-, -n**) F (*form*) perusal; **„zur ~"** "for attention"
einsichtslos ADJ unreasonable
einsichtsvoll ADJ understanding
Einsiedler ['aɪnzi:dlər] (**-s, -**) M hermit
einsilbig ['aɪnzɪlbɪç] ADJ (*lit, fig*) monosyllabic; **Einsilbigkeit** F (*fig*) taciturnity

einsinken ['aɪnzɪŋkən] *unreg* VI to sink in
Einsitzer ['aɪnzɪtsər] **(-s, -)** M single-seater
einspannen ['aɪnʃpanən] VT (*Werkstück, Papier*) to put (in), to insert; (*Pferde*) to harness; (*umg: Person*) to rope in; **jdn für seine Zwecke ~** to use sb for one's own ends
einsparen ['aɪnʃpa:rən] VT to save, to economize on; (*Kosten*) to cut down on; (*Posten*) to eliminate
Einsparung F saving
einspeichern ['aɪnʃpaɪçərn] VT: **etw (in etw** *+akk*) **~** (*Comput*) to feed sth in(to sth)
einsperren ['aɪnʃpɛrən] VT to lock up
einspielen ['aɪnʃpi:lən] VR (*Sport*) to warm up ▸ VT (*Film: Geld*) to bring in; (*Instrument*) to play in; **sich aufeinander ~** to become attuned to each other; **gut eingespielt** running smoothly
einsprachig ['aɪnʃpra:xɪç] ADJ monolingual
einspringen ['aɪnʃprɪŋən] *unreg* VI (*aushelfen*) to stand in; (*mit Geld*) to help out
einspritzen ['aɪnʃprɪtsən] VT to inject
Einspritzmotor M (*Aut*) injection engine
Einspruch ['aɪnʃprʊx] M protest, objection; **~ einlegen** (*Jur*) to file an objection
Einspruchsfrist F (*Jur*) period for filing an objection
Einspruchsrecht NT veto
einspurig ['aɪnʃpu:rɪç] ADJ single-lane; (*Eisenb*) single-track
einst [aɪnst] ADV once; (*zukünftig*) one *od* some day
Einstand ['aɪnʃtant] M (*Tennis*) deuce; (*Antritt*) entrance (to office); **er hat gestern seinen ~ gegeben** yesterday he celebrated starting his new job
einstechen ['aɪnʃtɛçən] *unreg* VT to pierce
einstecken ['aɪnʃtɛkən] VT to stick in, to insert; (*Brief*) to post, to mail (*US*); (*Elek: Stecker*) to plug in; (*Geld*) to pocket; (*mitnehmen*) to take; (*überlegen sein*) to put in the shade; (*hinnehmen*) to swallow
einstehen ['aɪnʃte:ən] *unreg* VI: **für jdn ~** to vouch for sb; **für etw ~** to guarantee sth, to vouch for sth; (*Ersatz leisten*) to make good sth
einsteigen ['aɪnʃtaɪgən] *unreg* VI to get in *od* on; (*in Schiff*) to go on board; (*sich beteiligen*) to come in; (*hineinklettern*) to climb in; **~!** (*Eisenb etc*) all aboard!
Einsteiger (-s, -) (*umg*) M beginner
einstellbar ADJ adjustable
einstellen ['aɪnʃtɛlən] VT (*in Firma*) to employ, to take on; (*aufhören*) to stop; (*Geräte*) to adjust; (*Kamera etc*) to focus; (*Sender, Radio*) to tune in to; (*unterstellen*) to put ▸ VI to take on staff/workers ▸ VR (*anfangen*) to set in; (*kommen*) to arrive; **Zahlungen ~** to suspend payment; **etw auf etw** *akk* **~** to adjust sth to sth; (*Kamera etc*) to focus sth on sth; **sich auf jdn/etw ~** to adapt to sb/prepare o.s. for sth
einstellig ADJ (*Zahl*) single-digit
Einstellplatz M (*auf Hof*) carport; (*in Großgarage*) (covered) parking space
Einstellung F (*Aufhören*) suspension, cessation; (*von Gerät*) adjustment; (*von Kamera etc*) focusing; (*von Arbeiter etc*) appointment; (*Haltung*) attitude
Einstellungsgespräch NT interview
Einstellungsstopp M halt in recruitment
Einstieg ['aɪnʃti:k] **(-(e)s, -e)** M entry; (*fig*) approach; (*von Bus, Bahn*) door; **kein ~** exit only
einstig ['aɪnstɪç] ADJ former
einstimmen ['aɪnʃtɪmən] VI to join in ▸ VT (*Mus*) to tune; (*in Stimmung bringen*) to put in the mood
einstimmig ADJ unanimous; (*Mus*) for one voice; **Einstimmigkeit** F unanimity
einstmalig ADJ former
einstmals ADV once, formerly
einstöckig ['aɪnʃtœkɪç] ADJ two-storeyed (*BRIT*), two-storied (*US*)
einstöpseln ['aɪnʃtœpsəln] VT: **etw (in etw** *+akk*) **~** (*Elek*) to plug sth in(to sth)
einstudieren ['aɪnʃtudi:rən] VT to study, to rehearse
einstufen ['aɪnʃtu:fən] VT to classify
Einstufung F: **nach seiner ~ in eine höhere Gehaltsklasse** after he was put on a higher salary grade
einstündig ['aɪnʃtʏndɪç] ADJ one-hour *attrib*
einstürmen ['aɪnʃtʏrmən] VI: **auf jdn ~** to rush at sb; (*Eindrücke*) to overwhelm sb
Einsturz ['aɪnʃtʊrts] M collapse
einstürzen ['aɪnʃtʏrtsən] VI to fall in, to collapse; **auf jdn ~** (*fig*) to overwhelm sb
Einsturzgefahr F danger of collapse
einstweilen ADV meanwhile; (*vorläufig*) temporarily, for the time being
einstweilig ADJ temporary; **einstweilige Verfügung** (*Jur*) temporary *od* interim injunction
eintägig ['aɪntɛ:gɪç] ADJ one-day
Eintagsfliege ['aɪnta:ksfli:gə] F (*Zool*) mayfly; (*fig*) nine-day wonder
eintauchen ['aɪntaʊxən] VT to immerse, to dip in ▸ VI to dive
eintauschen ['aɪntaʊʃən] VT to exchange
eintausend ['aɪn'taʊzənt] NUM one thousand
einteilen ['aɪntaɪlən] VT (*in Teile*) to divide (up); (*Menschen*) to assign
einteilig ADJ one-piece
eintönig ['aɪntø:nɪç] ADJ monotonous; **Eintönigkeit** F monotony
Eintopf ['aɪntɔpf] M stew
Eintopfgericht ['aɪntɔpfgərɪçt] NT stew
Eintracht ['aɪntraxt] **(-)** F concord, harmony
einträchtig ['aɪntrɛçtɪç] ADJ harmonious
Eintrag ['aɪntra:k] **(-(e)s, Einträge)** M entry; **amtlicher ~** entry in the register
eintragen ['aɪntra:gən] *unreg* VT (*in Buch*) to enter; (*Profit*) to yield ▸ VR to put one's name down; **jdm etw ~** to bring sb sth
einträglich ['aɪntrɛ:klɪç] ADJ profitable
Eintragung F: **~ (in** *+akk*) entry (in)
eintreffen ['aɪntrɛfən] *unreg* VI to happen; (*ankommen*) to arrive; (*fig: wahr werden*) to come true

eintreiben ['aɪntraɪbən] *unreg* VT (*Geldbeträge*) to collect
eintreten ['aɪntre:tən] *unreg* VI (*hineingehen*) to enter; (*sich ereignen*) to occur ▶ VT (*Tür*) to kick open; **in etw** *akk* **~** to enter sth; (*in Klub, Partei*) to join sth; **für jdn/etw ~** to stand up for sb/sth
eintrichtern ['aɪntrɪçtərn] (*umg*) VT: **jdm etw ~** to drum sth into sb
Eintritt ['aɪntrɪt] M (*Betreten*) entrance; (*in Klub etc*) joining; **~ frei** admission free; **„~ verboten"** "no admittance"; **bei ~ der Dunkelheit** at nightfall
Eintritts- ZW: **Eintrittsgeld** NT admission charge; **Eintrittskarte** F (admission) ticket; **Eintrittspreis** M admission charge
eintrocknen ['aɪntrɔknən] VI to dry up
eintrudeln ['aɪntru:dəln] (*umg*) VI to drift in
eintunken ['aɪntʊŋkən] VT (*Brot*): **etw in etw** *akk* **~** to dunk sth in sth
einüben ['aɪnly:bən] VT to practise (BRIT), to practice (*US*), to drill
einverleiben ['aɪnfɛrlaɪbən] VT to incorporate; (*Gebiet*) to annex; **sich** *dat* **etw ~** (*fig: geistig*) to assimilate sth
Einvernehmen ['aɪnfɛrne:mən] **(-s, -)** NT agreement, understanding
einverstanden ['aɪnfɛrʃtandən] INTERJ agreed ▶ ADJ: **~ sein** to agree, to be agreed; **sich mit etw ~ erklären** to give one's agreement to sth
Einverständnis ['aɪnfɛrʃtɛntnɪs] **(-ses)** NT understanding; (*gleiche Meinung*) agreement; **im ~ mit jdm handeln** to act with sb's consent
Einwand ['aɪnvant] **(-(e)s, Einwände)** M objection; **einen ~ erheben** to raise an objection
Einwanderer ['aɪnvandərər] M immigrant
Einwanderin F immigrant
einwandern VI to immigrate
Einwanderung F immigration
einwandfrei ADJ perfect; **etw ~ beweisen** to prove sth beyond doubt
einwärts ['aɪnvɛrts] ADV inwards
Einwegflasche ['aɪnve:gflaʃə] F non-returnable bottle
Einwegpfand NT deposit on non-returnables
Einwegspritze F disposable (hypodermic) syringe
einweichen ['aɪnvaɪçən] VT to soak
einweihen ['aɪnvaɪən] VT (*Kirche*) to consecrate; (*Brücke*) to open; (*Gebäude*) to inaugurate; (*Person*): **in etw** *akk* **~** to initiate in sth; **er ist eingeweiht** (*fig*) he knows all about it
Einweihung F consecration; (*von Brücke*) opening; (*von Gebäude*) inauguration; (*von Person*) initiation
einweisen ['aɪnvaɪzən] *unreg* VT (*in Amt*) to install; (*in Arbeit*) to introduce; (*in Anstalt*) to send; (*in Krankenhaus*): **~ (in** *+akk***)** to admit (to)
Einweisung F installation; (*in Arbeit*) introduction; (*in Anstalt*) sending
einwenden ['aɪnvɛndən] *unreg* VT: **etwas ~ gegen** to object to, to oppose
einwerfen ['aɪnvɛrfən] *unreg* VT to throw in; (*Brief*) to post; (*Geld*) to put in, to insert; (*Fenster*) to smash; (*äußern*) to interpose
einwickeln ['aɪnvɪkəln] VT to wrap up; (*fig: umg*) to outsmart
einwilligen ['aɪnvɪlɪgən] VI: **(in etw** *akk***) ~** to consent (to sth), to agree (to sth)
Einwilligung F consent
einwirken ['aɪnvɪrkən] VI: **auf jdn/etw ~** to influence sb/sth
Einwirkung F influence
Einwohner(in) ['aɪnvo:nər(ɪn)] **(-s, -)** M(F) inhabitant; **Einwohnermeldeamt** NT registration office; **sich beim Einwohnermeldeamt (an)melden** ≈ to register with the police; **Einwohnerschaft** F population, inhabitants *pl*
Einwurf ['aɪnvʊrf] M (*Öffnung*) slot; (*Einwand*) objection; (*Sport*) throw-in
Einzahl ['aɪntsa:l] F singular
einzahlen VT to pay in
Einzahlung F payment; (*auf Sparkonto*) deposit
einzäunen ['aɪntsɔynən] VT to fence in
einzeichnen ['aɪntsaɪçnən] VT to draw in
Einzel ['aɪntsəl] **(-s, -)** NT (*Tennis*) singles *pl*
Einzel- ZW: **Einzelaufstellung** F (*Comm*) itemized list; **Einzelbett** NT single bed; **Einzelblattzuführung** F sheet feed; **Einzelfall** M single instance, individual case; **Einzelgänger(in)** M(F) loner; **Einzelhaft** F solitary confinement; **Einzelhandel** M retail trade; **im Einzelhandel erhältlich** available retail; **Einzelhandelsgeschäft** NT retail outlet; **Einzelhandelspreis** M retail price; **Einzelhändler** M retailer; **Einzelheit** F particular, detail; **Einzelkind** NT only child
Einzeller ['aɪntsɛlər] **(-s, -)** M (*Biol*) single-celled organism
einzeln ADJ single; (*von Paar*) odd ▶ ADV singly; **~ angeben** to specify; **Einzelne** some (people), a few (people); **der/die Einzelne** the individual; **das Einzelne** the particular; **ins Einzelne gehen** to go into detail(s); **etw im Einzelnen besprechen** to discuss sth in detail; **~ aufführen** to list separately *od* individually; **bitte ~ eintreten** please come in one (person) at a time
Einzelteil NT individual part; (*Ersatzteil*) spare part; **etw in seine Einzelteile zerlegen** to take sth to pieces, to dismantle sth
Einzelzimmer NT single room
einziehen ['aɪntsi:ən] *unreg* VT to draw in, to take in; (*Kopf*) to duck; (*Fühler, Antenne, Fahrgestell*) to retract; (*Steuern, Erkundigungen*) to collect; (*Mil*) to call up, to draft (*US*); (*aus dem Verkehr ziehen*) to withdraw; (*konfiszieren*) to confiscate ▶ VI to move in; (*Friede, Ruhe*) to come; (*Flüssigkeit*): **~ (in** *+akk***)** to soak in(to)
einzig ['aɪntsɪç] ADJ only; (*ohnegleichen*) unique ▶ ADV: **~ und allein** solely; **das Einzige** the only thing; **der/die Einzige** the only one; **kein einziges Mal** not once, not one single time; **kein Einziger** nobody, not a single person; **einzigartig** ADJ unique

Einzug ['aɪntsu:k] M entry, moving in
Einzugsauftrag M (*Fin*) direct debit
Einzugsbereich M catchment area
Einzugsverfahren NT (*Fin*) direct debit
Eis [aɪs] (**-es, -**) NT ice; (*Speiseeis*) ice cream; **~ am Stiel** ice lolly (BRIT), popsicle® (*US*); **Eisbahn** F ice *od* skating rink; **Eisbär** M polar bear; **Eisbecher** M sundae; **Eisbein** NT pork knuckle; **Eisberg** M iceberg; **Eisbergsalat** M iceberg lettuce; **Eisbeutel** M ice pack; **Eiscafé** NT ice-cream parlour (BRIT) *od* parlor (*US*)
Eischnee ['aɪʃne:] M (*Koch*) beaten white of egg
Eisdecke F sheet of ice
Eisdiele F ice-cream parlour (BRIT) *od* parlor (*US*)
Eisen ['aɪzən] (**-s, -**) NT iron; **zum alten ~ gehören** (*fig*) to be on the scrap heap
Eisenbahn F railway, railroad (*US*); **es ist (aller)höchste ~** (*umg*) it's high time; **Eisenbahner** (**-s, -**) M railwayman, railway employee, railroader (*US*); **Eisenbahnnetz** NT rail network; **Eisenbahnschaffner** M railway guard, (railroad) conductor (*US*); **Eisenbahnüberführung** F footbridge; **Eisenbahnübergang** M level crossing, grade crossing (*US*); **Eisenbahnwagen** M railway *od* railroad (*US*) carriage; **Eisenbahnwaggon, Eisenbahnwagon** M (*Güterwagen*) goods wagon
Eisen- ZW: **Eisenerz** NT iron ore; **eisenhaltig** ADJ containing iron; **Eisenmangel** M iron deficiency; **Eisenwarenhandlung** F ironmonger's (BRIT), hardware store (*US*)
eisern ['aɪzərn] ADJ iron; (*Gesundheit*) robust; (*Energie*) unrelenting; (*Reserve*) emergency; **der Eiserne Vorhang** the Iron Curtain; **in etw *dat* ~ sein** to be adamant about sth; **er ist ~ bei seinem Entschluss geblieben** he stuck firmly to his decision
Eis- ZW: **Eisfach** NT freezer compartment, icebox; **eisfrei** ADJ clear of ice; **eisgekühlt** ADJ chilled; **Eishockey** NT ice hockey
eisig ['aɪzɪç] ADJ icy
Eis- ZW: **Eiskaffee** M iced coffee; **eiskalt** ADJ icy cold; **Eiskunstlauf** M figure skating; **Eislaufen** NT ice-skating; **Eisläufer** M ice-skater; **Eismeer** NT: **Nördliches/Südliches Eismeer** Arctic/Antarctic Ocean; **Eispickel** M ice-axe (BRIT), ice-ax (*US*)
Eisprung ['aɪʃprʊŋ] M ovulation
Eis- ZW: **Eisschießen** NT ≈ curling; **Eisscholle** F ice floe; **Eisschrank** M fridge, icebox (*US*); **Eisstadion** NT ice *od* skating rink; **Eiswürfel** M ice cube; **Eiszapfen** M icicle; **Eiszeit** F Ice Age
eitel ['aɪtəl] ADJ vain; **Eitelkeit** F vanity
Eiter ['aɪtər] (**-s**) M pus
eiterig ADJ suppurating
eitern VI to suppurate
Ei- ZW: **Eiweiß** (**-es, -e**) NT white of an egg; (*Chem*) protein; **Eiweißgehalt** M protein content; **Eizelle** F ovum
EKD F ABK (= *Evangelische Kirche in Deutschland*) *German Protestant Church*
Ekel[1] ['e:kəl] (**-s**) M nausea, disgust; **vor jdm/etw einen ~ haben** to loathe sb/sth
Ekel[2] ['e:kəl] (**-s, -**) (*umg*) NT (*Mensch*) nauseating person
ekelerregend ADJ nauseating, disgusting
ekelhaft ADJ, **ekelig** ADJ nauseating, disgusting
ekeln VT to disgust ▶ VR: **sich vor etw** *dat* **~** to be disgusted at sth; **es ekelt ihn** he is disgusted
EKG (**-**) NT ABK (= *Elektrokardiogramm*) ECG
Eklat [e'kla:] (**-s**) M (*geh: Aufsehen*) sensation
eklig ADJ nauseating, disgusting
Ekstase [ɛk'sta:zə] (**-, -n**) F ecstasy; **jdn in ~ versetzen** to send sb into ecstasies
Ekzem [ɛk'tse:m] (**-s, -e**) NT (*Med*) eczema
Elan [e'lã:] (**-s**) M élan
elastisch [e'lastɪʃ] ADJ elastic
Elastizität [elastitsi'tɛ:t] F elasticity
Elbe ['ɛlbə] F (*Fluss*) Elbe
Elch [ɛlç] (**-(e)s, -e**) M elk
Elefant [ele'fant] M elephant; **wie ein ~ im Porzellanladen** (*umg*) like a bull in a china shop
elegant [ele'gant] ADJ elegant
Eleganz [ele'gants] F elegance
Elektrifizierung [elɛktrifi'tsi:rʊŋ] F electrification
Elektriker [e'lɛktrikər] (**-s, -**) M electrician
elektrisch [e'lɛktrɪʃ] ADJ electric
elektrisieren [elɛktri'zi:rən] VT (*lit, fig*) to electrify; (*Mensch*) to give an electric shock to ▶ VR to get an electric shock
Elektrizität [elɛktritsi'tɛ:t] F electricity
Elektrizitätswerk NT electric power station
Elektroartikel [e'lɛktro|artɪkəl] M electrical appliance
Elektroauto NT electric car
Elektrode [elɛk'tro:də] (**-, -n**) F electrode
Elektro- ZW: **Elektrogerät** NT electrical appliance; **Elektroherd** M electric cooker; **Elektrokardiogramm** NT (*Med*) electrocardiogram
Elektrolyse [elektro'ly:zə] (**-, -n**) F electrolysis
Elektromotor M electric motor
Elektron [e'lɛktrɔn] (**-s, -en**) NT electron
Elektronengehirn, Elektronenhirn NT electronic brain
Elektronenrechner M computer
Elektronik [elɛk'tro:nɪk] F electronics *sing*; (*Teile*) electronics *pl*
elektronisch ADJ electronic; **elektronische Post** electronic mail
Elektro- ZW: **Elektrorasierer** (**-s, -**) M electric razor; **Elektroschock** M (*Med*) electric shock, electroshock; **Elektrotechniker** M electrician; (*Ingenieur*) electrical engineer
Element [ele'mɛnt] (**-s, -e**) NT element; (*Elek*) cell, battery
elementar [elemɛn'ta:r] ADJ elementary; (*naturhaft*) elemental; **Elementarteilchen** NT (*Phys*) elementary particle
elend ADJ miserable; **mir ist ganz ~** I feel really awful; **Elend** ['e:lɛnt] (**-(e)s**) NT misery; **da kann man das heulende Elend kriegen** (*umg*) it's enough to make you scream

elendiglich ['e:lɛndɪklɪç] ADV miserably; **~ zugrunde gehen** to come to a wretched end
Elendsviertel NT slum
elf [ɛlf] NUM eleven; **Elf (-, en)** F (*Sport*) eleven
Elfe (-, **-n**) F elf
Elfenbein NT ivory; **Elfenbeinküste** F Ivory Coast
Elfmeter M (*Sport*) penalty (kick)
Elfmeterschießen NT (*Sport*) penalty shoot-out
eliminieren [elimi'ni:rən] VT to eliminate
elitär [eli'tɛ:r] ADJ elitist ▸ ADV in an elitist fashion
Elite [e'li:tə] (-, **-n**) F elite
Elixier [elɪ'ksi:r] (**-s, -e**) NT elixir
Ellbogen M = **Ellenbogen**
Elle ['ɛlə] (-, **-n**) F ell; (*Maß*) ≈ yard
Ellenbogen M elbow; **die ~ gebrauchen** (*umg*) to be pushy; **Ellenbogenfreiheit** F (*fig*) elbow room; **Ellenbogengesellschaft** F dog-eat-dog society
Ellipse [ɛ'lɪpsə] (-, **-n**) F ellipse
E-Lok ['e:lɔk] (-) F ABK (= *elektrische Lokomotive*) electric locomotive *od* engine
Elsass ['ɛlzas] NT: **das ~** Alsace
Elsässer ['ɛlzɛsər] ADJ Alsatian
Elsässer(in) (**-s**, -) M(F) Alsatian, inhabitant of Alsace
elsässisch ADJ Alsatian
Elster ['ɛlstər] (-, **-n**) F magpie
elterlich ADJ parental
Eltern ['ɛltərn] PL parents *pl*; **nicht von schlechten ~ sein** (*umg*) to be quite something; **Elternabend** M (*Sch*) parents' evening; **Elternhaus** NT home; **elternlos** ADJ orphaned; **Elternsprechtag** M open day (for parents); **Elternteil** M parent
Email [e'ma:j] (**-s, -s**) NT enamel
E-Mail ['i:me:l] (-, **-s**) F Email, email; **E-Mail-Adresse** F Email address
e-mailen ['i:me:lən] VT to email
emaillieren [ema'ji:rən] VT to enamel
Emanze (-, **-n**) (*pej*) F women's libber (*umg*)
Emanzipation [emantsipatsi'o:n] F emancipation
emanzipieren [emantsi'pi:rən] VT to emancipate
Embargo [ɛm'bargo] (**-s, -s**) NT embargo
Embryo ['ɛmbryo] (**-s, -s** *od* **-nen**) M embryo
Embryonenforschung F embryo research
Emigrant(in) [emi'grant(ɪn)] M(F) emigrant
Emigration [emigratsi'o:n] F emigration
emigrieren [emi'gri:rən] VI to emigrate
Emissionen PL emissions *pl*
emissionsarm [emɪsi'o:nsarm] ADJ low in emissions
Emissionsgutschrift F carbon credit
Emissionshandel M emissions trading
Emissionskurs M (*Aktien*) issued price
EMNID M ABK (= *Erforschung, Meinung, Nachrichten, Informationsdienst*) *opinion poll organization*
emotional [emotsio'na:l] ADJ emotional; (*Ausdrucksweise*) emotive
emotionsgeladen [emotsi'o:nsgəla:dən] ADJ emotionally-charged
Empf. ABK = **Empfänger(in)**
empfahl *etc* [ɛm'pfa:l] VB *siehe* **empfehlen**
empfand *etc* [ɛm'pfant] VB *siehe* **empfinden**
Empfang [ɛm'pfaŋ] (**-(e)s, Empfänge**) M reception; (*Erhalten*) receipt; **in ~ nehmen** to receive; **(zahlbar) nach** *od* **bei ~** *+gen* (payable) on receipt (of)
empfangen *unreg* VT to receive ▸ VI (*schwanger werden*) to conceive
Empfänger(in) [ɛm'pfɛŋər(ɪn)] (**-s**, -) M(F) receiver; (*Comm*) addressee, consignee; **~ unbekannt** (*auf Briefen*) not known at this address
empfänglich ADJ receptive, susceptible
Empfängnis (-, **-se**) F conception; **empfängnisverhütend** ADJ: **empfängnisverhütende Mittel** contraceptives *pl*; **Empfängnisverhütung** F contraception
Empfangs- ZW: **Empfangsbestätigung** F (acknowledgement of) receipt; **Empfangschef** M (*von Hotel*) head porter; **Empfangsdame** F receptionist; **Empfangsschein** M receipt; **Empfangsstörung** F (*Rundf, TV*) interference; **Empfangszimmer** NT reception room
empfehlen [ɛm'pfe:lən] *unreg* VT to recommend ▸ VR to take one's leave
empfehlenswert ADJ recommendable
Empfehlung F recommendation; **auf ~ von** on the recommendation of
Empfehlungsschreiben NT letter of recommendation
empfiehlt [ɛm'pfi:lt] VB *siehe* **empfehlen**
empfinden [ɛm'pfɪndən] *unreg* VT to feel; **etw als Beleidigung ~** to find sth insulting; **Empfinden (-s)** NT: **meinem Empfinden nach** to my mind
empfindlich ADJ sensitive; (*Stelle*) sore; (*reizbar*) touchy; **deine Kritik hat ihn ~ getroffen** your criticism cut him to the quick; **Empfindlichkeit** F sensitiveness; (*Reizbarkeit*) touchiness
empfindsam ADJ sentimental; (*Mensch*) sensitive
Empfindung F feeling, sentiment
empfindungslos ADJ unfeeling, insensitive
empfing *etc* [ɛm'pfɪŋ] VB *siehe* **empfangen**
empfohlen [ɛm'pfo:lən] PP *von* **empfehlen** ▸ ADJ: **empfohlener Einzelhandelspreis** recommended retail price
empfunden [ɛm'pfʊndən] PP *von* **empfinden**
empor [ɛm'po:r] ADV up, upwards
emporarbeiten VR (*geh*) to work one's way up
Empore [ɛm'po:rə] (-, **-n**) F (*Archit*) gallery
empören [ɛm'pø:rən] VT to make indignant; (*schockieren*) to shock ▸ VR to become indignant
empörend ADJ outrageous
emporkommen *unreg* VI to rise; (*vorankommen*) to succeed
Emporkömmling M upstart, parvenu
empört ADJ: **~ (über** *+akk***)** indignant (at), outraged (at)

e

Empörung F indignation
emsig ['ɛmzɪç] ADJ diligent, busy
End- ['ɛnt] IN ZW final; **Endauswertung** F final analysis; **Endbahnhof** M terminus; **Endbetrag** M final amount
Ende ['ɛndə] (**-s, -n**) NT end; **am ~** at the end; (*schließlich*) in the end; **am ~ sein** to be at the end of one's tether; **~ Dezember** at the end of December; **zu ~ sein** to be finished; **zu ~ gehen** to come to an end; **zu ~ führen** to finish (off); **letzten Endes** in the end, at the end of the day; **ein böses ~ nehmen** to come to a bad end; **ich bin mit meiner Weisheit am ~** I'm at my wits' end; **er wohnt am ~ der Welt** (*umg*) he lives at the back of beyond
Endeffekt M: **im ~** (*umg*) when it comes down to it
enden VI to end
Endergebnis NT final result
endgültig ADJ final, definite
Endivie [ɛn'di:viə] F endive
End- ZW: **Endkunde** M end customer *od* consumer; **Endlager** NT permanent waste disposal site; **Endlagerung** F permanent disposal; **endlich** ADJ final; (*Math*) finite ▶ ADV finally; **endlich!** at last!; **hör endlich damit auf!** will you stop that!; **endlos** ADJ endless; **Endlospapier** NT continuous paper; **Endprodukt** NT end *od* final product; **Endspiel** NT final(s); **Endspurt** M (*Sport*) final spurt; **Endstation** F terminus
Endung F ending
Endverbraucher M consumer, end-user
Energie [enɛr'gi:] F energy; **Energieaufwand** M energy expenditure; **Energiebedarf** M energy requirement; **Energieeinsparung** F energy saving; **Energiegetränk** NT energy drink; **Energiegewinnung** F generation of energy; **energielos** ADJ lacking in energy, weak; **Energiequelle** F source of energy; **Energieverbrauch** M energy consumption; **Energieversorgung** F supply of energy; **Energiewirtschaft** F energy industry
energisch [e'nɛrgɪʃ] ADJ energetic; **~ durchgreifen** to take vigorous *od* firm action
eng [ɛŋ] ADJ narrow; (*Kleidung*) tight; (*fig: Horizont*) narrow, limited; (*Freundschaft, Verhältnis*) close; **~ an etw** *dat* close to sth; **in die engere Wahl kommen** to be short-listed (BRIT)
Engadin ['ɛŋgadi:n] (**-s**) NT: **das ~** the Engadine
Engagement [ãgaʒə'mã:] (**-s, -s**) NT engagement; (*Verpflichtung*) commitment
engagieren [ãga'ʒi:rən] VT to engage ▶ VR to commit o.s.; **ein engagierter Schriftsteller** a committed writer
Enge ['ɛŋə] (**-, -n**) F (*lit, fig*) narrowness; (*Landenge*) defile; (*Meerenge*) straits *pl*; **jdn in die ~ treiben** to drive sb into a corner
Engel ['ɛŋəl] (**-s, -**) M angel; **engelhaft** ADJ angelic; **Engelmacher(in)** (**-s, -**) (*umg*) M(F) backstreet abortionist
Engelsgeduld F: **sie hat eine ~** she has the patience of a saint
Engelszungen PL: **(wie) mit ~ reden** to use all one's own powers of persuasion
engherzig ADJ petty
engl. ABK = **englisch**
England ['ɛŋlant] NT England
Engländer ['ɛŋlɛndər] (**-s, -**) M Englishman; (*Junge*) English boy; **die Engländer** PL the English, the Britishers (US)
Engländerin F Englishwoman; (*Mädchen*) English girl
englisch ['ɛŋlɪʃ] ADJ English
engmaschig ['ɛŋmaʃɪç] ADJ close-meshed
Engpass M defile, pass; (*fig: Verkehr*) bottleneck
en gros [ã'gro] ADV wholesale
engstirnig ['ɛŋʃtɪrnɪç] ADJ narrow-minded
Enkel ['ɛŋkəl] (**-s, -**) M grandson; **Enkelin** F granddaughter; **Enkelkind** NT grandchild
en masse [ã'mas] ADV en masse
enorm [e'nɔrm] ADJ enormous; (*umg: herrlich, kolossal*) tremendous
en passant [ãpa'sã] ADV en passant, in passing
Ensemble [ã'sãbəl] (**-s, -s**) NT ensemble
entarten [ɛnt'la:rten] VI to degenerate
entbehren [ɛnt'be:rən] VT to do without, to dispense with
entbehrlich ADJ superfluous
Entbehrung F privation; **Entbehrungen auf sich** *akk* **nehmen** to make sacrifices
entbinden [ɛnt'bɪndən] *unreg* VT *+gen* to release (from); (*Med*) to deliver ▶ VI (*Med*) to give birth
Entbindung F release; (*Med*) delivery, birth
Entbindungsheim NT maternity hospital
Entbindungsstation F maternity ward
entblößen [ɛnt'blø:sən] VT to denude, to uncover; (*berauben*): **einer Sache** *gen* **entblößt** deprived of sth
entbrennen [ɛnt'brɛnən] *unreg* VI (*liter: Kampf, Streit*) to flare up; (*: Liebe*) to be aroused
entdecken [ɛnt'dɛkən] VT to discover; **jdm etw ~** to disclose sth to sb
Entdecker(in) (**-s, -**) M(F) discoverer
Entdeckung F discovery
Ente ['ɛntə] (**-, -n**) F duck; (*fig*) canard, false report; (*Aut*) Citroën 2CV, deux-chevaux
entehren [ɛnt'le:rən] VT to dishonour (BRIT), to dishonor (US), to disgrace
enteignen [ɛnt'laɪgnən] VT to expropriate; (*Besitzer*) to dispossess
enteisen [ɛnt'laɪzən] VT to de-ice; (*Kühlschrank*) to defrost
enterben [ɛnt'lɛrbən] VT to disinherit
Enterhaken ['ɛntərha:kən] M grappling iron *od* hook
entfachen [ɛnt'faxən] VT to kindle
entfallen [ɛnt'falən] *unreg* VI to drop, to fall; (*wegfallen*) to be dropped; **jdm ~** (*vergessen*) to slip sb's memory; **auf jdn ~** to be allotted to sb
entfalten [ɛnt'faltən] VT to unfold; (*Talente*) to develop ▶ VR to open; (*Mensch*) to develop one's potential
Entfaltung F unfolding; (*von Talenten*) development

entfernen [ɛnt'fɛrnən] VT to remove; (*hinauswerfen*) to expel ▶ VR to go away, to retire, to withdraw
entfernt ADJ distant ▶ ADV: **nicht im Entferntesten!** not in the slightest!; **weit davon ~ sein, etw zu tun** to be far from doing sth
Entfernung F distance; (*Wegschaffen*) removal; **unerlaubte ~ von der Truppe** absence without leave
Entfernungsmesser M (*Phot*) rangefinder
entfesseln [ɛnt'fɛsəln] VT (*fig*) to arouse
entfetten [ɛnt'fɛtən] VT to take the fat from
entflammen [ɛnt'flamən] VT (*fig*) to (a)rouse ▶ VI to burst into flames; (*fig: Streit*) to flare up; (*: Leidenschaft*) to be (a)roused *od* inflamed
entfremden [ɛnt'frɛmdən] VT to estrange, to alienate
Entfremdung F estrangement, alienation
entfreunden [ɛnt'frɔʏndən] VT (*Internet*) to unfriend
entfrosten [ɛnt'frɔstən] VT to defrost
Entfroster (-s, -) M (*Aut*) defroster
entführen [ɛnt'fy:rən] VT to abduct, to kidnap; (*Flugzeug*) to hijack
Entführer (-s, -) M kidnapper (BRIT), kidnaper (US); (*Flugzeugentführer*) hijacker
Entführung F abduction, kidnapping (BRIT), kidnaping (US); (*von Flugzeug*) hijacking
entgegen [ɛnt'ge:gən] PRÄP *+dat* contrary to, against ▶ ADV towards; **entgegenbringen** *unreg* VT to bring; (*fig*): **jdm etw entgegenbringen** to show sb sth; **entgegengehen** *unreg* VI *+dat* to go to meet, to go towards; **Schwierigkeiten entgegengehen** to be heading for difficulties; **entgegengesetzt** ADJ opposite; (*widersprechend*) opposed; **entgegenhalten** *unreg* VT (*fig*): **einer Sache** *dat* **entgegenhalten, dass ...** to object to sth that ...; **entgegenkommen** *unreg* VI *+dat* to come towards, to approach; (*fig*): **jdm entgegenkommen** to accommodate sb; **das kommt unseren Plänen sehr entgegen** that fits in very well with our plans; **Entgegenkommen** NT obligingness; **entgegenkommend** ADJ obliging; **entgegenlaufen** *unreg* VI *+dat* to run towards *od* to meet; (*fig*) to run counter to; **Entgegennahme** F (*form: Empfang*) receipt; (*Annahme*) acceptance; **entgegennehmen** *unreg* VT to receive, to accept; **entgegensehen** *unreg* VI *+dat* to await; **entgegensetzen** VT to oppose; **dem habe ich entgegenzusetzen, dass ...** against that I'd like to say that ...; **jdm/etw Widerstand entgegensetzen** to put up resistance to sb/sth; **entgegenstehen** *unreg* VI: **dem steht nichts entgegen** there's no objection to that; **entgegentreten** *unreg* VI *+dat* (*lit*) to step up to; (*fig*) to oppose, to counter; **entgegenwirken** VI *+dat* to counteract
entgegnen [ɛnt'ge:gnən] VT to reply, to retort
Entgegnung F reply, retort
entgehen [ɛnt'ge:ən] *unreg* VI (*fig*): **jdm ~** to escape sb's notice; **sich** *dat* **etw ~ lassen** to miss sth
entgeistert [ɛnt'gaɪstərt] ADJ thunderstruck
Entgelt [ɛnt'gɛlt] **(-(e)s, -e)** NT remuneration
entgelten *unreg* VT: **jdm etw ~** to repay sb for sth
entgiften [ɛnt'gɪftən] VI to detox (*umg*), to detoxify
Entgiftung F detox (*umg*), detoxification
entgleisen [ɛnt'glaɪzən] VI (*Eisenb*) to be derailed; (*fig: Person*) to misbehave; **~ lassen** to derail
Entgleisung F derailment; (*fig*) faux pas, gaffe
entgleiten [ɛnt'glaɪtən] *unreg* VI: **jdm ~** to slip from sb's hand
entgräten [ɛnt'grɛ:tən] VT to fillet, to bone
Enthaarungsmittel [ɛnt'ha:rʊŋsmɪtəl] NT depilatory
enthält [ɛnt'hɛlt] VB *siehe* **enthalten**
enthalten [ɛnt'haltən] *unreg* VT to contain ▶ VR *+gen* to abstain from, to refrain from; **sich (der Stimme) ~** to abstain
enthaltsam [ɛnt'haltza:m] ADJ abstinent, abstemious; **Enthaltsamkeit** F abstinence
enthärten [ɛnt'hɛrtən] VT (*Wasser*) to soften; (*Metall*) to anneal
enthaupten [ɛnt'haʊptən] VT to decapitate; (*als Hinrichtung*) to behead
enthäuten [ɛnt'hɔʏtən] VT to skin
entheben [ɛnt'he:bən] *unreg* VT: **jdn einer Sache** *gen* **~** to relieve sb of sth
enthemmen [ɛnt'hɛmən] VT: **jdn ~** to free sb from his/her inhibitions
enthielt *etc* [ɛnt'hi:lt] VB *siehe* **enthalten**
enthüllen [ɛnt'hʏlən] VT to reveal, to unveil
Enthüllung F revelation; (*von Skandal*) exposure
Enthusiasmus [ɛntuzi'asmʊs] M enthusiasm
entjungfern [ɛnt'jʊŋfərn] VT to deflower
entkalken [ɛnt'kalkən] VT to decalcify
entkernen [ɛnt'kɛrnən] VT (*Kernobst*) to core; (*Steinobst*) to stone
entkleiden [ɛnt'klaɪdən] VT, VR (*geh*) to undress
entkommen [ɛnt'kɔmən] *unreg* VI to get away, to escape; **jdm/etw** *od* **aus etw ~** to get away *od* escape from sb/sth
entkorken [ɛnt'kɔrkən] VT to uncork
entkräften [ɛnt'krɛftən] VT to weaken, to exhaust; (*Argument*) to refute
entkrampfen [ɛnt'krampfən] VT (*fig*) to relax, to ease
entladen [ɛnt'la:dən] *unreg* VT to unload; (*Elek*) to discharge ▶ VR (*Gewehr, Elek*) to discharge; (*Ärger etc*) to vent itself
entlang [ɛnt'laŋ] PRÄP (*+akk od dat*) along ▶ ADV along; **~ dem Fluss, den Fluss ~** along the river; **hier ~** this way; **entlanggehen** *unreg* VI to walk along
entlarven [ɛnt'larfən] VT to unmask, to expose
entlassen [ɛnt'lasən] *unreg* VT to discharge; (*Arbeiter*) to dismiss; (*nach Stellenabbau*) to make redundant
entlässt [ɛnt'lɛst] VB *siehe* **entlassen**
Entlassung F discharge; (*von Arbeiter*) dismissal; **es gab 20 Entlassungen** there were 20 redundancies

Entlassungswelle F wave of redundancies *od* job losses
Entlassungszeugnis NT (*Sch*) school-leaving certificate
entlasten [ɛnt'lastən] VT to relieve; (*Arbeit abnehmen*) to take some of the load off; (*Angeklagte*) to exonerate; (*Konto*) to clear
Entlastung F relief; (*Comm*) crediting
Entlastungszeuge M defence (BRIT) *od* defense (US) witness
Entlastungszug M relief train
entledigen [ɛnt'le:dɪgən] VR: **sich jds/einer Sache ~** to rid o.s. of sb/sth
entleeren [ɛnt'le:rən] VT to empty; (*Darm*) to evacuate
entlegen [ɛnt'le:gən] ADJ remote
entließ *etc* [ɛnt'li:s] VB *siehe* **entlassen**
entlocken [ɛnt'lɔkən] VT: **jdm etw ~** to elicit sth from sb
entlohnen VT to pay; (*fig*) to reward
entlüften [ɛnt'lʏftən] VT to ventilate
entmachten [ɛnt'maxtən] VT to deprive of power
entmenscht [ɛnt'mɛnʃt] ADJ inhuman, bestial
entmilitarisiert [ɛntmilitari'zi:rt] ADJ demilitarized
entmündigen [ɛnt'mʏndɪgən] VT to certify; (*Jur*) to (legally) incapacitate, to declare incapable of managing one's own affairs
entmutigen [ɛnt'mu:tɪgən] VT to discourage
Entnahme [ɛnt'na:mə] (**-, -n**) F removal, withdrawal
Entnazifizierung [ɛntnatsifi'tsi:rʊŋ] F denazification
entnehmen [ɛnt'ne:mən] *unreg* VT *+dat* to take out of, to take from; (*folgern*) to infer from; **wie ich Ihren Worten entnehme, …** I gather from what you say that …
entpuppen [ɛnt'pʊpən] VR (*fig*) to reveal o.s., to turn out; **sich als etw ~** to turn out to be sth
entrahmen [ɛnt'ra:mən] VT to skim
entreißen [ɛnt'raɪsən] *unreg* VT: **jdm etw ~** to snatch sth (away) from sb
entrichten [ɛnt'rɪçtən] VT (*form*) to pay
entrosten [ɛnt'rɔstən] VT to derust
entrüsten [ɛnt'rʏstən] VT to incense, to outrage ▸ VR to be filled with indignation
entrüstet ADJ indignant, outraged
Entrüstung F indignation
Entsafter [ɛnt'zaftər] (**-s, -**) M juice extractor
entsagen [ɛnt'za:gən] VI *+dat* to renounce
entschädigen [ɛnt'ʃɛ:dɪgən] VT to compensate
Entschädigung F compensation
entschärfen [ɛnt'ʃɛrfən] VT to defuse; (*Kritik*) to tone down
Entscheid [ɛnt'ʃaɪt] (**-(e)s, -e**) M (*form*) decision
entscheiden *unreg* VT, VI, VR to decide; **darüber habe ich nicht zu ~** that is not for me to decide; **sich für jdn/etw ~** to decide in favour of sb/sth
entscheidend ADJ decisive; (*Stimme*) casting; **das Entscheidende** the decisive *od* deciding factor
Entscheidung F decision; **wie ist die ~ ausgefallen?** which way did the decision go?
Entscheidungs- ZW: **Entscheidungsbefugnis** F decision-making powers *pl*; **entscheidungsfähig** ADJ capable of deciding; **Entscheidungsspiel** NT play-off; **Entscheidungsträger** M decision-maker
entschied *etc* [ɛnt'ʃi:t] VB *siehe* **entscheiden**
entschieden [ɛnt'ʃi:dən] PP *von* **entscheiden** ▸ ADJ decided; (*entschlossen*) resolute; **das geht ~ zu weit** that's definitely going too far; **Entschiedenheit** F firmness, determination
entschlacken [ɛnt'ʃlakən] VT (*Med: Körper*) to purify
entschließen [ɛnt'ʃli:sən] *unreg* VR to decide; **sich zu nichts ~ können** to be unable to make up one's mind; **kurz entschlossen** straight away
Entschließungsantrag M (*Pol*) resolution proposal
entschloss *etc* [ɛnt'ʃlɔs] VB *siehe* **entschließen**
entschlossen [ɛnt'ʃlɔsən] PP *von* **entschließen** ▸ ADJ determined, resolute; **Entschlossenheit** F determination
entschlüpfen [ɛnt'ʃlʏpfən] VI to escape, to slip away; (*fig: Wort etc*) to slip out
Entschluss [ɛnt'ʃlʊs] M decision; **aus eigenem ~ handeln** to act on one's own initiative; **es ist mein fester ~** it is my firm intention
entschlüsseln [ɛnt'ʃlʏsəln] VT to decipher; to decode
entschlussfreudig ADJ decisive
Entschlusskraft F determination, decisiveness
entschuldbar [ɛnt'ʃʊltba:r] ADJ excusable
entschuldigen [ɛnt'ʃʊldɪgən] VT to excuse ▸ VR to apologize ▸ VI: **~ Sie (bitte)!** excuse me; (*Verzeihung*) sorry; **jdn bei jdm ~** to make sb's excuses *od* apologies to sb; **sich ~ lassen** to send one's apologies
entschuldigend ADJ apologetic
Entschuldigung F apology; (*Grund*) excuse; **jdn um ~ bitten** to apologize to sb; **~!** excuse me; (*Verzeihung*) sorry
entschwefeln [ɛnt'ʃve:fəln] VT to desulphurize
Entschwefelungsanlage F desulphurization plant
entschwinden [ɛnt'ʃvɪndən] *unreg* VI to disappear
entsetzen [ɛnt'zɛtsən] VT to horrify ▸ VR to be horrified *od* appalled; **Entsetzen** (**-s**) NT horror, dismay
entsetzlich ADJ dreadful, appalling
entsetzt ADJ horrified
entsichern [ɛnt'zɪçərn] VT to release the safety catch of
entsinnen [ɛnt'zɪnən] *unreg* VR *+gen* to remember
entsorgen [ɛnt'zɔrgən] VT: **eine Stadt ~** to dispose of a town's refuse and sewage
Entsorgung F waste disposal; (*von Chemikalien*) disposal
entspannen [ɛnt'ʃpanən] VT, VR (*Körper*) to relax; (*Pol: Lage*) to ease

Entspannung F relaxation, rest; (*Pol*) détente
Entspannungspolitik F policy of détente
Entspannungsübungen PL relaxation exercises *pl*
entspr. ABK = **entsprechend**
entsprach *etc* [ɛntˈʃpraːx] VB *siehe* **entsprechen**
entsprechen [ɛntˈʃprɛçən] *unreg* VI +*dat* to correspond to; (*Anforderungen, Wünschen*) to meet, to comply with
entsprechend ADJ appropriate ▶ ADV accordingly ▶ PRÄP +*dat*: **er wird seiner Leistung ~ bezahlt** he is paid according to output
entspricht [ɛntˈʃprɪçt] VB *siehe* **entsprechen**
entspringen [ɛntˈʃprɪŋən] *unreg* VI +*dat* to spring (from)
entsprochen [ɛntˈʃprɔxən] PP *von* **entsprechen**
entstaatlichen [ɛntˈʃtaːtlɪçən] VT to denationalize
entstammen [ɛntˈʃtamən] VI +*dat* to stem *od* come from
entstand *etc* [ɛntˈʃtant] VB *siehe* **entstehen**
entstanden [ɛntˈʃtandən] PP *von* **entstehen**
entstehen [ɛntˈʃteːən] *unreg* VI: **~ (aus** *od* **durch)** to arise (from), to result (from); **wir wollen nicht den Eindruck ~ lassen, …** we don't want to give rise to the impression that …; **für entstehenden** *od* **entstandenen Schaden** for damages incurred
Entstehung F genesis, origin
entstellen [ɛntˈʃtɛlən] VT to disfigure; (*Wahrheit*) to distort
Entstellung F disfigurement; (*von Wahrheit*) distortion
entstören [ɛntˈʃtøːrən] VT (*Rundf*) to eliminate interference from; (*Aut*) to suppress
enttäuschen [ɛntˈtɔʏʃən] VT to disappoint
Enttäuschung F disappointment
entwachsen [ɛntˈvaksən] *unreg* VI +*dat* to outgrow, to grow out of; (*geh: herauswachsen aus*) to spring from
entwaffnen [ɛntˈvafnən] VT (*lit, fig*) to disarm
entwaffnend ADJ disarming
Entwarnung [ɛntˈvarnʊŋ] F all clear (signal)
entwässern [ɛntˈvɛsərn] VT to drain
Entwässerung F drainage
entweder [ɛntˈveːdər] KONJ either; **~ … oder …** either … or …
entweichen [ɛntˈvaɪçən] *unreg* VI to escape
entweihen [ɛntˈvaɪən] *unreg* VT to desecrate
entwenden [ɛntˈvɛndən] *unreg* VT to purloin, to steal
entwerfen [ɛntˈvɛrfən] *unreg* VT (*Zeichnung*) to sketch; (*Modell*) to design; (*Vortrag, Gesetz etc*) to draft
entwerten [ɛntˈveːrtən] VT to devalue; (*stempeln*) to cancel
Entwerter (-s, -) M (ticket-)cancelling (BRIT) *od* canceling (US) machine
entwickeln [ɛntˈvɪkəln] VT to develop (*auch Phot*); (*Mut, Energie*) to show, to display ▶ VR to develop
Entwickler (-s, -) M developer
Entwicklung [ɛntˈvɪklʊŋ] F development; (*Phot*) developing; **in der ~** at the development stage; (*Jugendliche etc*) still developing
Entwicklungs- ZW: **Entwicklungsabschnitt** M stage of development; **Entwicklungshelfer(in)** M(F) VSO worker (BRIT), Peace Corps worker (US); **Entwicklungshilfe** F aid for developing countries; **Entwicklungsjahre** PL adolescence *sing*; **Entwicklungsland** NT developing country; **Entwicklungszeit** F period of development; (*Phot*) developing time
entwirren [ɛntˈvɪrən] VT to disentangle
entwischen [ɛntˈvɪʃən] VI to escape
entwöhnen [ɛntˈvøːnən] VT to wean; (*Süchtige*): **(einer Sache** *dat od* **von etw) ~** to cure (of sth)
Entwöhnung F weaning; (*von Sucht*) cure, curing
entwürdigend [ɛntˈvʏrdɪgənt] ADJ degrading
Entwurf [ɛntˈvʊrf] M outline, design; (*Vertragsentwurf, Konzept*) draft
entwurzeln [ɛntˈvʊrtsəln] VT to uproot
entziehen [ɛntˈtsiːən] *unreg* VT +*dat* to withdraw (from), to take away (from); (*Flüssigkeit*) to draw (from), to extract (from) ▶ VR +*dat* to escape (from); (*jds Kenntnis*) to be outside *od* beyond; (*der Pflicht*) to shirk (from); **sich jds Blicken ~** to be hidden from sight
Entziehung F withdrawal
Entziehungsanstalt F drug addiction/alcoholism treatment centre (BRIT) *od* center (US)
Entziehungskur F treatment for drug addiction/alcoholism
entziffern [ɛntˈtsɪfərn] VT to decipher; (*Funkspruch*) to decode
entzücken [ɛntˈtsʏkən] VT to delight; **Entzücken (-s)** NT delight
entzückend ADJ delightful, charming
Entzug [ɛntˈtsuːk] (-**(e)s**) M (*einer Lizenz etc, Med*) withdrawal
Entzugserscheinung F withdrawal symptom
entzündbar ADJ: **leicht ~** highly inflammable; (*fig*) easily roused
entzünden [ɛntˈtsʏndən] VT to light, to set light to; (*fig, Med*) to inflame; (*Streit*) to spark off ▶ VR (*lit, fig*) to catch fire; (*Streit*) to start; (*Med*) to become inflamed
Entzündung F (*Med*) inflammation
entzwei [ɛntˈtsvaɪ] ADV in two; (*kaputt*) broken; **entzweibrechen** *unreg* VT, VI to break in two
entzweien VT to set at odds ▶ VR to fall out
entzweigehen *unreg* VI to break (in two)
Enzian [ˈɛntsiaːn] (**-s, -e**) M gentian
Enzyklika [ɛnˈtsyːklika] (**-, -liken**) F (*Rel*) encyclical
Enzyklopädie [ɛntsyklopɛˈdiː] F encyclop(a)edia
Enzym [ɛnˈtsyːm] (**-s, -e**) NT enzyme
Epen PL *von* **Epos**
Epidemie [epideˈmiː] F epidemic
Epilepsie [epilɛˈpsiː] F epilepsy
episch [ˈeːpɪʃ] ADJ epic
Episode [epiˈzoːdə] (**-, -n**) F episode

Epoche [e'pɔxə] (**-, -n**) F epoch; **epochemachend** ADJ epoch-making
Epos ['e:pɔs] (**-, Epen**) NT epic (poem)
Equipe [e'kɪp] (**-, -n**) F team
er [e:r] PRON he; (*Sache*) it
erachten [ɛr'|axtən] VT (*geh*): **~ für** *od* **als** to consider (to be); **meines Erachtens** in my opinion
erarbeiten [ɛr'|arbaɪtən] VT to work for, to acquire; (*Theorie*) to work out
Erbanlage ['ɛrp|anla:gə] F hereditary factor(*s pl*)
erbarmen [ɛr'barmən] VR *+gen* to have pity *od* mercy (on) ▶ VT: **er sieht zum E~ aus** he's a pitiful sight; **Herr, erbarme dich (unser)!** Lord, have mercy (upon us)!; **Erbarmen (-s)** NT pity
erbärmlich [ɛr'bɛrmlɪç] ADJ wretched, pitiful; **Erbärmlichkeit** F wretchedness
Erbarmungs- zW: **erbarmungslos** ADJ pitiless, merciless; **erbarmungsvoll** ADJ compassionate; **erbarmungswürdig** ADJ pitiable, wretched
erbauen [ɛr'baʊən] VT to build, to erect; (*fig*) to edify; **er ist von meinem Plan nicht besonders erbaut** (*umg*) he isn't particularly enthusiastic about my plan
Erbauer (-s, -) M builder
erbaulich ADJ edifying
Erbauung F construction; (*fig*) edification
erbberechtigt ADJ entitled to inherit
erbbiologisch ADJ: **erbbiologisches Gutachten** (*Jur*) blood test (*to establish paternity*)
Erbe[1] ['ɛrbə] (**-n, -n**) M heir; **jdn zum** *od* **als Erben einsetzen** to make sb one's/sb's heir
Erbe[2] ['ɛrbə] (**-s**) NT inheritance; (*fig*) heritage
erben VT to inherit; (*umg: geschenkt bekommen*) to get, to be given
erbeuten [ɛr'bɔʏtən] VT to carry off; (*Mil*) to capture
Erb- zW: **Erbfaktor** M gene; **Erbfehler** M hereditary defect; **Erbfeind** M traditional *od* arch enemy; **Erbfolge** F (line of) succession
Erbin F heiress
erbitten [ɛr'bɪtən] *unreg* VT to ask for, request
erbittern [ɛr'bɪtərn] VT to embitter; (*erzürnen*) to incense
erbittert [ɛr'bɪtərt] ADJ (*Kampf*) fierce, bitter
erblassen [ɛr'blasən] VI to (turn) pale
Erblasser(in) ['ɛrblasər(ɪn)] (**-s, -**) M(F) (*Jur*) *person who leaves an inheritance*
erbleichen [ɛr'blaɪçən] *unreg* VI to (turn) pale
erblich ['ɛrplɪç] ADJ hereditary; **er/sie ist ~ (vor)belastet** it runs in the family
erblichen PP *von* **erbleichen**
erblicken [ɛr'blɪkən] VT to see; (*erspähen*) to catch sight of
erblinden [ɛr'blɪndən] VI to go blind
Erbmasse ['ɛrpmasə] F estate; (*Biol*) genotype
erbosen [ɛr'bo:zən] VT (*geh*) to anger ▶ VR to grow angry
erbrechen [ɛr'brɛçən] *unreg* VT, VR to vomit
Erbrecht NT hereditary right; (*Gesetze*) law of inheritance
Erbschaft F inheritance, legacy
Erbschaftssteuer F estate *od* death duties *pl*
Erbschleicher(in) ['ɛrpʃlaɪçər(ɪn)] (**-s, -**) M(F) legacy-hunter
Erbse ['ɛrpsə] (**-, -n**) F pea
Erb- zW: **Erbstück** NT heirloom; **Erbsünde** F (*Rel*) original sin; **Erbteil** NT inherited trait; (*Jur*) (portion of) inheritance
Erd- zW: **Erdachse** F earth's axis; **Erdapfel** (ÖSTERR) M potato; **Erdatmosphäre** F earth's atmosphere; **Erdbahn** F orbit of the earth; **Erdbeben** NT earthquake; **Erdbeere** F strawberry; **Erdboden** M ground; **etw dem Erdboden gleichmachen** to level sth, to raze sth to the ground
Erde (**-, -n**) F earth; **zu ebener ~** at ground level; **auf der ganzen ~** all over the world; **du wirst mich noch unter die ~ bringen** (*umg*) you'll be the death of me yet
erden VT (*Elek*) to earth
erdenkbar [ɛr'dɛŋkba:r] ADJ conceivable; **sich** *dat* **alle erdenkbare Mühe geben** to take the greatest (possible) pains
erdenklich [ɛr'dɛŋklɪç] ADJ = **erdenkbar**
Erdg. ABK = **Erdgeschoss**
Erd- zW: **Erdgas** NT natural gas; **Erdgeschoss** NT ground floor (BRIT), first floor (US); **Erdkunde** F geography; **Erdnuss** F peanut; **Erdoberfläche** F surface of the earth; **Erdöl** NT (mineral) oil; **Erdölfeld** NT oilfield; **Erdölindustrie** F oil industry; **Erdreich** NT soil, earth
erdreisten [ɛr'draɪstən] VR to dare, to have the audacity (*to do sth*)
erdrosseln [ɛr'drɔsəln] VT to strangle, to throttle
erdrücken [ɛr'drʏkən] VT to crush; **erdrückende Übermacht/erdrückendes Beweismaterial** overwhelming superiority/evidence
Erd- zW: **Erdrutsch** M landslide; **Erdstoß** M (seismic) shock; **Erdteil** M continent
erdulden [ɛr'dʊldən] VT to endure, to suffer
E-Reader ['i:'ri:də[r]] M e-reader, eReader
ereifern [ɛr'|aɪfərn] VR to get excited
ereignen [ɛr'|aɪgnən] VR to happen
Ereignis [ɛr'|aɪgnɪs] (**-ses, -se**) NT event; **ereignislos** ADJ uneventful; **ereignisreich** ADJ eventful
Eremit [ere'mi:t] (**-en, -en**) M hermit
erfahren [ɛr'fa:rən] *unreg* VT to learn, to find out; (*erleben*) to experience ▶ ADJ experienced
Erfahrung F experience; **Erfahrungen sammeln** to gain experience; **etw in ~ bringen** to learn *od* find out sth
Erfahrungsaustausch M exchange of experiences
erfahrungsgemäß ADV according to experience
erfand *etc* [ɛr'fant] VB *siehe* **erfinden**
erfassen [ɛr'fasən] VT to seize; (*fig: einbeziehen*) to include, to register; (*verstehen*) to grasp
erfinden [ɛr'fɪndən] *unreg* VT to invent; **frei erfunden** completely fictitious

Erfinder(in) (**-s, -**) M(F) inventor; **erfinderisch** ADJ inventive
Erfindung F invention
Erfindungsgabe F inventiveness
Erfolg [ɛr'fɔlk] (**-(e)s, -e**) M success; (*Folge*) result; **~ versprechend** promising; **viel ~!** good luck!
erfolgen [ɛr'fɔlgən] VI to follow; (*sich ergeben*) to result; (*stattfinden*) to take place; (*Zahlung*) to be effected; **nach erfolgter Zahlung** when payment has been made
Erfolg- ZW: **erfolglos** ADJ unsuccessful; **Erfolglosigkeit** F lack of success; **erfolgreich** ADJ successful
Erfolgserlebnis NT feeling of success, sense of achievement
erfolgversprechend ADJ *siehe* **Erfolg**
erforderlich ADJ requisite, necessary
erfordern [ɛr'fɔrdərn] VT to require, to demand
Erfordernis (**-ses, -se**) NT requirement, prerequisite
erforschen [ɛr'fɔrʃən] VT (*Land*) to explore; (*Problem*) to investigate; (*Gewissen*) to search
Erforscher(in) (**-s, -**) M(F) explorer; (*Ermittler*) investigator
Erforschung F exploration; (*von Problem*) investigation; (*von Gewissen*) searching
erfragen [ɛr'fra:gən] VT to inquire, to ascertain
erfreuen [ɛr'frɔʏən] VR: **sich ~ an** *+dat* to enjoy ▸ VT to delight; **sich einer Sache** *gen* **~** (*geh*) to enjoy sth; **sehr erfreut!** (*form: bei Vorstellung*) pleased to meet you!
erfreulich [ɛr'frɔʏlɪç] ADJ pleasing, gratifying
erfreulicherweise ADV happily, luckily
erfrieren [ɛr'fri:rən] *unreg* VI to freeze (to death); (*Glieder*) to get frostbitten; (*Pflanzen*) to be killed by frost
erfrischen [ɛr'frɪʃən] VT to refresh
Erfrischung F refreshment
Erfrischungsraum M snack bar, cafeteria
erfüllen [ɛr'fʏlən] VT (*Raum etc*) to fill; (*fig: Bitte etc*) to fulfil (BRIT), to fulfill (US) ▸ VR to come true; **ein erfülltes Leben** a full life
Erfüllung F: **in ~ gehen** to be fulfilled
erfunden [ɛr'fʊndən] PP *von* **erfinden**
ergab *etc* [ɛr'ga:p] VB *siehe* **ergeben**
ergänzen [ɛr'gɛntsən] VT to supplement, to complete ▸ VR to complement one another
Ergänzung F completion; (*Zusatz*) supplement
ergattern [ɛr'gatərn] (*umg*) VT to get hold of, to hunt up
ergaunern [ɛr'gaʊnərn] (*umg*) VT: **sich** *dat* **etw ~** to get hold of sth by underhand methods
ergeben [ɛr'ge:bən] *unreg* VT (*Betrag*) to come to; (*zum Ergebnis haben*) to result in ▸ VR to surrender; (*folgen*) to result ▸ ADJ devoted; (*demütig*) humble; **sich einer Sache** *dat* **~** (*sich hingeben*) to give o.s. up to sth, to yield to sth; **es ergab sich, dass unsere Befürchtungen ...** it turned out that our fears ...; **dem Trunk ~** addicted to drink;
Ergebenheit F devotion; (*Demut*) humility
Ergebnis [ɛr'ge:pnɪs] (**-ses, -se**) NT result; **zu einem ~ kommen** to come to *od* reach a conclusion; **ergebnislos** ADJ without result, fruitless; **ergebnislos bleiben** *od* **verlaufen** to come to nothing
ergehen [ɛr'ge:ən] *unreg* VI (*form*) to be issued, to go out ▸ VI UNPERS: **es ergeht ihm gut/schlecht** he's faring *od* getting on well/badly ▸ VR: **sich in etw** *dat* **~** to indulge in sth; **etw über sich** *akk* **~ lassen** to put up with sth; **sich (in langen Reden) über ein Thema ~** (*fig*) to hold forth at length on sth
ergiebig [ɛr'gi:bɪç] ADJ productive
ergo ['ɛrgo] KONJ therefore, ergo (*liter, hum*)
Ergonomie [ɛrgono'mi:] F ergonomics *pl*
ergötzen [ɛr'gœtsən] VT to amuse, to delight
ergrauen [ɛr'graʊən] VI to turn *od* go grey (BRIT) *od* gray (US)
ergreifen [ɛr'graɪfən] *unreg* VT (*lit, fig*) to seize; (*Beruf*) to take up; (*Maßnahmen*) to resort to; (*rühren*) to move; **er ergriff das Wort** he began to speak
ergreifend ADJ moving, affecting
ergriff *etc* [ɛr'grɪf] VB *siehe* **ergreifen**
ergriffen PP *von* **ergreifen** ▸ ADJ deeply moved
Ergriffenheit F emotion
ergründen [ɛr'grʏndən] VT (*Sinn etc*) to fathom; (*Ursache, Motive*) to discover
Erguss [ɛr'gʊs] (**-es, Ergüsse**) M discharge; (*fig*) outpouring, effusion
erhaben [ɛr'ha:bən] ADJ (*lit*) raised, embossed; (*fig*) exalted, lofty; **über etw** *akk* **~ sein** to be above sth
Erhalt M: **bei** *od* **nach ~** on receipt
erhält [ɛr'hɛlt] VB *siehe* **erhalten**
erhalten [ɛr'haltən] *unreg* VT to receive; (*bewahren*) to preserve, to maintain; **das Wort ~** to receive permission to speak; **jdn am Leben ~** to keep sb alive; **gut ~** in good condition
erhältlich [ɛr'hɛltlɪç] ADJ obtainable, available
Erhaltung F maintenance, preservation
erhängen [ɛr'hɛŋən] VT, VR to hang
erhärten [ɛr'hɛrtən] VT to harden; (*These*) to substantiate, to corroborate
erhaschen [ɛr'haʃən] VT to catch
erheben [ɛr'he:bən] *unreg* VT to raise; (*Protest, Forderungen*) to make; (*Fakten*) to ascertain ▸ VR to rise (up); **sich über etw** *akk* **~** to rise above sth
erheblich [ɛr'he:plɪç] ADJ considerable
erheitern [ɛr'haɪtərn] VT to amuse, to cheer (up)
Erheiterung F exhilaration; **zur allgemeinen ~** to everybody's amusement
erhellen [ɛr'hɛlən] VT (*lit, fig*) to illuminate; (*Geheimnis*) to shed light on ▸ VR (*Fenster*) to light up; (*Himmel, Miene*) to brighten (up); (*Gesicht*) to brighten up
erhielt *etc* [ɛr'hi:lt] VB *siehe* **erhalten**
erhitzen [ɛr'hɪtsən] VT to heat ▸ VR to heat up; (*fig*) to become heated *od* aroused
erhoffen [ɛr'hɔfən] VT to hope for; **was erhoffst du dir davon?** what do you hope to gain from it?

e

erhöhen [ɛr'hø:ən] VT to raise; (*verstärken*) to increase; **erhöhte Temperatur haben** to have a temperature
Erhöhung F (*Gehalt*) increment
erholen [ɛr'ho:lən] VR to recover; (*entspannen*) to have a rest; (*fig: Preise, Aktien*) to rally, to pick up
erholsam ADJ restful
Erholung F recovery; (*Entspannung*) relaxation, rest
erholungsbedürftig ADJ in need of a rest, run-down
Erholungsgebiet NT holiday (BRIT) *od* vacation (*US*) area
Erholungsheim NT convalescent home
erhören [ɛr'hø:rən] VT (*Gebet etc*) to hear; (*Bitte etc*) to yield to
Erika ['e:rika] (-, **Eriken**) F heather
erinnern [ɛr'|ɪnərn] VT: ~ (**an** *+akk*) to remind (of) ▸ VR: **sich (an etw** *akk*) ~ to remember (sth)
Erinnerung F memory; (*Andenken*) souvenir; (*Mahnung*) reminder; **Erinnerungen** PL (*Lebenserinnerung*) reminiscences *pl*; (*Liter*) memoirs *pl*; **jdn/etw in guter ~ behalten** to have pleasant memories of sb/sth
Erinnerungsschreiben NT (*Comm*) reminder
Erinnerungstafel F commemorative plaque
Eritrea [eri'tre:a] (**-s**) NT Eritrea
erkalten [ɛr'kaltən] VI to go cold, to cool (down)
erkälten [ɛr'kɛltən] VR to catch cold; **sich** *dat* **die Blase** ~ to catch a chill in one's bladder
erkältet ADJ with a cold; ~ **sein** to have a cold
Erkältung F cold
erkämpfen [ɛr'kɛmpfən] VT to win, to secure
erkannt [ɛr'kant] PP *von* **erkennen**
erkannte *etc* VB *siehe* **erkennen**
erkennbar ADJ recognizable
erkennen [ɛr'kɛnən] *unreg* VT to recognize; (*sehen, verstehen*) to see; **jdm zu ~ geben, dass ...** to give sb to understand that ...
erkenntlich ADJ: **sich ~ zeigen** to show one's appreciation; **Erkenntlichkeit** F gratitude; (*Geschenk*) token of one's gratitude
Erkenntnis (**-, -se**) F knowledge; (*das Erkennen*) recognition; (*Einsicht*) insight; **zur ~ kommen** to realize
Erkennung F recognition
Erkennungsdienst M police records department
Erkennungsmarke F identity disc
Erker ['ɛrkər] (**-s, -**) M bay; **Erkerfenster** NT bay window
erklärbar ADJ explicable
erklären [ɛr'klɛ:rən] VT to explain; (*Rücktritt*) to announce; (*Politiker, Pressesprecher etc*) to say; **ich kann mir nicht ~, warum ...** I can't understand why ...
erklärlich ADJ explicable; (*verständlich*) understandable
erklärt ADJ *attrib* (*Gegner etc*) professed, avowed; (*Favorit, Liebling*) acknowledged
Erklärung F explanation; (*Aussage*) declaration
erklecklich [ɛr'klɛklɪç] ADJ considerable
erklimmen [ɛr'klɪmən] *unreg* VT to climb to
erklingen [ɛr'klɪŋən] *unreg* VI to resound, to ring out
erklomm *etc* [ɛr'klɔm] VB *siehe* **erklimmen**
erklommen PP *von* **erklimmen**
erkranken [ɛr'kraŋkən] VI: ~ (**an** *+dat*) to be taken ill (with); (*Organ, Pflanze, Tier*) to become diseased (with)
Erkrankung F illness
erkunden [ɛr'kʊndən] VT to find out, to ascertain; (*bes Mil*) to reconnoitre (BRIT), to reconnoiter (*US*)
erkundigen VR: **sich ~ (nach)** to inquire (about); **ich werde mich** ~ I'll find out
Erkundigung F inquiry; **Erkundigungen einholen** to make inquiries
Erkundung F (*Mil*) reconnaissance, scouting
erlahmen [ɛr'la:mən] VI to tire; (*nachlassen*) to flag, to wane
erlangen [ɛr'laŋən] VT to attain, to achieve
Erlass [ɛr'las] (**-es, -e**) M decree; (*Aufhebung*) remission
erlassen *unreg* VT (*Verfügung*) to issue; (*Gesetz*) to enact; (*Strafe*) to remit; **jdm etw** ~ to release sb from sth
erlauben [ɛr'laʊbən] VT to allow, to permit ▸ VR: **sich** *dat* **etw** ~ (*Zigarette, Pause*) to permit o.s. sth; (*Bemerkung, Verschlag*) to venture sth; (*sich leisten*) to afford sth; **jdm etw** ~ to allow *od* permit sb (to do) sth; **~ Sie?** may I?; **~ Sie mal!** do you mind!; **was ~ Sie sich (eigentlich)!** how dare you!
Erlaubnis [ɛr'laʊpnɪs] (**-, -se**) F permission
erläutern [ɛr'lɔʏtərn] VT to explain
Erläuterung F explanation; **zur** ~ in explanation
Erle ['ɛrlə] (**-, -n**) F alder
erleben [ɛr'le:bən] VT to experience; (*Zeit*) to live through; (*miterleben*) to witness; (*noch miterleben*) to live to see; **so wütend habe ich ihn noch nie erlebt** I've never seen *od* known him so furious
Erlebnis [ɛr'le:pnɪs] (**-ses, -se**) NT experience
erledigen [ɛr'le:dɪgən] VT to take care of, to deal with; (*Antrag etc*) to process; (*umg: erschöpfen*) to wear out; (*ruinieren*) to finish; (*umbringen*) to do in ▸ VR: **das hat sich erledigt** that's all settled; **das ist erledigt** that's taken care of, that's been done; **ich habe noch einiges in der Stadt zu** ~ I've still got a few things to do in town
erledigt (*umg*) ADJ (*erschöpft*) shattered, done in; (*ruiniert*) finished, ruined
erlegen [ɛr'le:gən] VT to kill
erleichtern [ɛr'laɪçtərn] VT to make easier; (*fig: Last*) to lighten; (*lindern, beruhigen*) to relieve
erleichtert ADJ relieved; **~ aufatmen** to breathe a sigh of relief
Erleichterung F facilitation; (*von Last*) lightening; (*Linderung*) relief
erleiden [ɛr'laɪdən] *unreg* VT to suffer, to endure
erlernbar ADJ learnable
erlernen [ɛr'lɛrnən] VT to learn, to acquire
erlesen [ɛr'le:zən] ADJ select, choice

erleuchten [ɛr'lɔʏçtən] VT to illuminate; (*fig*) to inspire
Erleuchtung F (*Einfall*) inspiration
erliegen [ɛr'li:gən] *unreg* VI +*dat* (*lit, fig*) to succumb to; (*einem Irrtum*) to be the victim of; **zum E~ kommen** to come to a standstill
erlischt [ɛr'lɪʃt] VB *siehe* **erlöschen**
erlogen [ɛr'lo:gən] ADJ untrue, made-up
Erlös [ɛr'lø:s] **(-es, -e)** M proceeds *pl*
erlosch *etc* [ɛr'lɔʃ] VB *siehe* **erlöschen**
erlöschen [ɛr'lœʃən] *unreg* VI (*Feuer*) to go out; (*Interesse*) to cease, to die; (*Vertrag, Recht*) to expire; **ein erloschener Vulkan** an extinct volcano
erlösen [ɛr'lø:zən] VT to redeem, to save
Erlöser (-s, -) M (*Rel*) Redeemer; (*Befreier*) saviour (BRIT), savior (US)
Erlösung F release; (*Rel*) redemption
ermächtigen [ɛr'mɛçtɪgən] VT to authorize, to empower
Ermächtigung F authorization
ermahnen [ɛr'ma:nən] VT to admonish, to exhort
Ermahnung F admonition, exhortation
Ermangelung [ɛr'maŋəlʊŋ], **Ermanglung** [ɛr'maŋlʊŋ] F: **in Ermang(e)lung** +*gen* because of the lack of
ermäßigen [ɛr'mɛsɪgən] VT to reduce
Ermäßigung F reduction
ermessen [ɛr'mɛsən] *unreg* VT to estimate, to gauge; **Ermessen (-s)** NT estimation; **in jds Ermessen** *dat* **liegen** to lie within sb's discretion; **nach meinem Ermessen** in my judgement
Ermessensfrage F matter of discretion
ermitteln [ɛr'mɪtəln] VT to determine; (*Täter*) to trace ▶ VI: **gegen jdn ~** to investigate sb
Ermittlung [ɛr'mɪtlʊŋ] F determination; (*Polizeiermittlung*) investigation; **Ermittlungen anstellen (über** +*akk*) to make inquiries (about)
Ermittlungsverfahren NT (*Jur*) preliminary proceedings *pl*
ermöglichen [ɛr'mø:klɪçən] VT +*dat* to make possible (for)
ermorden [ɛr'mɔrdən] VT to murder
Ermordung F murder
ermüden [ɛr'my:dən] VT to tire; (*Tech*) to fatigue ▶ VI to tire
ermüdend ADJ tiring; (*fig*) wearisome
Ermüdung F fatigue
Ermüdungserscheinung F sign of fatigue
ermuntern [ɛr'mʊntərn] VT to rouse; (*ermutigen*) to encourage; (*beleben*) to liven up; (*aufmuntern*) to cheer up
ermutigen [ɛr'mu:tɪgən] VT to encourage
ernähren [ɛr'nɛ:rən] VT to feed, to nourish; (*Familie*) to support ▶ VR to support o.s., to earn a living; **sich ~ von** to live on
Ernährer(in) (-s, -) M(F) breadwinner
Ernährung F nourishment; (*Med*) nutrition; (*Unterhalt*) maintenance
ernennen [ɛr'nɛnən] *unreg* VT to appoint
Ernennung F appointment
erneuern [ɛr'nɔʏərn] VT to renew; (*restaurieren*) to restore; (*renovieren*) to renovate
Erneuerung F renewal; (*Restaurierung*) restoration; (*Renovierung*) renovation
erneut ADJ renewed, fresh ▶ ADV once more
erniedrigen [ɛr'ni:drɪgən] VT to humiliate, to degrade
ernst ADJ serious ▶ ADV: **es steht ~ um ihn** things don't look too good for him; **~ gemeint** meant in earnest, serious; **Ernst** [ɛrnst] **(-es)** M seriousness; **das ist mein Ernst** I'm quite serious; **im Ernst** in earnest; **Ernst machen mit etw** to put sth into practice; **Ernstfall** M emergency; **ernsthaft** ADJ serious; **Ernsthaftigkeit** F seriousness; **ernstlich** ADJ serious
Ernte ['ɛrntə] **(-, -n)** F harvest; **Erntedankfest** NT harvest festival (BRIT), Thanksgiving (Day) (US)
ernten VT to harvest; (*Lob etc*) to earn
ernüchtern [ɛr'nʏçtərn] VT to sober up; (*fig*) to bring down to earth
Ernüchterung F sobering up; (*fig*) disillusionment
Eroberer [ɛr'lobərər] **(-s, -)** M conqueror
erobern VT to conquer
Eroberung F conquest
eröffnen [ɛr'lœfnən] VT to open ▶ VR to present itself; **jdm etw ~** (*geh*) to disclose sth to sb
Eröffnung F opening
Eröffnungsansprache F inaugural *od* opening address
Eröffnungsfeier F opening ceremony
erogen [ero'ge:n] ADJ erogenous
erörtern [ɛr'lœrtərn] VT to discuss (in detail)
Erörterung F discussion
Erotik [e'ro:tɪk] F eroticism
erotisch ADJ erotic
Erpel ['ɛrpəl] **(-, -)** M drake
erpicht [ɛr'pɪçt] ADJ: **~ (auf** +*akk*) keen (on)
erpressen [ɛr'prɛsən] VT (*Geld etc*) to extort; (*jdn*) to blackmail
Erpresser (-s, -) M blackmailer
Erpressung F blackmail; (*von Geld*) extortion
erproben [ɛr'pro:bən] VT to test; **erprobt** tried and tested
erraten [ɛr'ra:tən] *unreg* VT to guess
errechnen [ɛr'rɛçnən] VT to calculate, to work out
erregbar [ɛr're:kba:r] ADJ excitable; (*reizbar*) irritable; **Erregbarkeit** F excitability; (*Reizbarkeit*) irritability
erregen [ɛr're:gən] VT to excite; (*sexuell*) to arouse; (*ärgern*) to infuriate; (*hervorrufen*) to arouse, to provoke ▶ VR to get excited *od* worked up
Erreger (-s, -) M causative agent
Erregtheit F excitement; (*Beunruhigung*) agitation
Erregung F excitement; (*sexuell*) arousal
erreichbar ADJ accessible, within reach

e

erreichen [ɛr'raɪçən] VT to reach; (*Zweck*) to achieve; (*Zug*) to catch; **wann kann ich Sie morgen ~?** when can I get in touch with you tomorrow?; **vom Bahnhof leicht zu ~** within easy reach of the station

errichten [ɛr'rɪçtən] VT to erect, to put up; (*gründen*) to establish, to set up

erringen [ɛr'rɪŋən] *unreg* VT to gain, to win

erröten [ɛr'rø:tən] VI to blush, to flush

Errungenschaft [ɛr'rʊŋənʃaft] F achievement; (*umg: Anschaffung*) acquisition

Ersatz [ɛr'zats] (**-es**) M substitute; (*von Mitarbeiter etc*) replacement; (*Schadenersatz*) compensation; (*Mil*) reinforcements *pl*; **als ~ für jdn einspringen** to stand in for sb; **Ersatzbefriedigung** F vicarious satisfaction; **Ersatzdienst** M (*Mil*) alternative service; **Ersatzkasse** F private health insurance; **Ersatzmann** M replacement; (*Sport*) substitute; **Ersatzmutter** F substitute mother; **ersatzpflichtig** ADJ liable to pay compensation; **Ersatzreifen** M (*Aut*) spare tyre (BRIT) *od* tire (US); **Ersatzteil** NT spare (part); **ersatzweise** ADV as an alternative

ersaufen [ɛr'zaʊfən] *unreg* (*umg*) VI to drown

ersäufen [ɛr'zɔʏfən] VT to drown

erschaffen [ɛr'ʃafən] *unreg* VT to create

erscheinen [ɛr'ʃaɪnən] *unreg* VI to appear

Erscheinung F appearance; (*Geist*) apparition; (*Gegebenheit*) phenomenon; (*Gestalt*) figure; **in ~ treten** (*Merkmale*) to appear; (*Gefühle*) to show themselves

Erscheinungsform F manifestation

Erscheinungsjahr NT (*von Buch*) year of publication

erschien *etc* [ɛr'ʃi:n] VB *siehe* **erscheinen**

erschienen PP *von* **erscheinen**

erschießen [ɛr'ʃi:sən] *unreg* VT to shoot (dead)

erschlaffen [ɛr'ʃlafən] VI to go limp; (*Mensch*) to become exhausted

erschlagen [ɛr'ʃla:gən] *unreg* VT to strike dead ▸ ADJ (*umg: todmüde*) worn out, dead beat (*umg*)

erschleichen [ɛr'ʃlaɪçən] *unreg* VT to obtain by stealth *od* dubious methods

erschließen [ɛr'ʃli:sən] *unreg* VT (*Gebiet, Absatzmarkt*) to develop, to open up; (*Bodenschätze*) to tap

erschlossen [ɛr'ʃlɔsən] ADJ (*Gebiet*) developed

erschöpfen [ɛr'ʃœpfən] VT to exhaust

erschöpfend ADJ exhaustive, thorough

erschöpft ADJ exhausted

Erschöpfung F exhaustion

erschossen [ɛr'ʃɔsən] (*umg*) ADJ: **(völlig) ~ sein** to be whacked, to be dead (beat)

erschrak *etc* [ɛr'ʃra:k] VB *siehe* **erschrecken²**

erschrecken¹ [ɛr'ʃrɛkən] VT to startle, to frighten

erschrecken² [ɛr'ʃrɛkən] *unreg* VI to be frightened *od* startled

erschreckend ADJ alarming, frightening

erschrickt [ɛr'ʃrɪkt] VB *siehe* **erschrecken²**

erschrocken [ɛr'ʃrɔkən] PP *von* **erschrecken²** ▸ ADJ frightened, startled

erschüttern [ɛr'ʃʏtərn] VT to shake; (*ergreifen*) to move deeply; **ihn kann nichts ~** he always keeps his cool (*umg*)

erschütternd ADJ shattering

Erschütterung F (*des Bodens*) tremor; (*tiefe Ergriffenheit*) shock

erschweren [ɛr'ʃve:rən] VT to complicate; **erschwerende Umstände** (*Jur*) aggravating circumstances; **es kommt noch erschwerend hinzu, dass …** to compound matters …

erschwindeln [ɛr'ʃvɪndəln] VT to obtain by fraud

erschwinglich ADJ affordable

ersehen [ɛr'ze:ən] *unreg* VT: **aus etw ~, dass …** to gather from sth that …

ersehnt [ɛr'ze:nt] ADJ longed-for

ersetzbar ADJ replaceable

ersetzen [ɛr'zɛtsən] VT to replace; **jdm Unkosten** *etc* **~** to pay sb's expenses *etc*

ersichtlich [ɛr'zɪçtlɪç] ADJ evident, obvious

ersparen [ɛr'ʃpa:rən] VT (*Ärger etc*) to spare; (*Geld*) to save; **ihr blieb auch nichts erspart** she was spared nothing

Ersparnis (**-, -se**) F saving

ersprießlich [ɛr'ʃpri:slɪç] ADJ profitable, useful; (*angenehm*) pleasant

SCHLÜSSELWORT

erst [e:rst] ADV **1** first; **mach erst (ein)mal die Arbeit fertig** finish your work first; **wenn du das erst (ein)mal hinter dir hast** once you've got that behind you

2 (*nicht früher als, nur*) only; (*nicht bis*) not till; **erst gestern** only yesterday; **erst morgen** not until tomorrow; **erst als** only when, not until; **wir fahren erst später** we're not going until later; **er ist (gerade) erst angekommen** he's only just arrived

3: **wäre er doch erst zurück!** if only he were back!; **da fange ich erst gar nicht an** I simply won't bother to begin; **jetzt erst recht!** that just makes me all the more determined; **da gings erst richtig los** then things really got going

erstarren [ɛr'ʃtarən] VI to stiffen; (*vor Furcht*) to grow rigid; (*Materie*) to solidify

erstatten [ɛr'ʃtatən] VT (*Unkosten*) to refund; **Anzeige gegen jdn ~** to report sb; **Bericht ~** to make a report

Erstattung F (*von Unkosten*) reimbursement

Erstaufführung ['e:rstlaʊffy:rʊŋ] F first performance

erstaunen [ɛr'ʃtaʊnən] VT to astonish ▸ VI to be astonished; **Erstaunen** (**-s**) NT astonishment

erstaunlich ADJ astonishing

Erstausgabe F first edition

erstbeste(r, s) ADJ first that comes along

erste(r, s) ADJ first; **als Erstes** first of all; **in erster Linie** first and foremost; **fürs E~** for the time being; **E~ Hilfe** first aid; **das ~ Mal** the first time

erstechen [ɛr'ʃtɛçən] *unreg* VT to stab (to death)

erstehen [ɛrˈʃteːən] *unreg* VT to buy ▸ VI to (a)rise
ersteigen [ɛrˈʃtaɪgən] *unreg* VT to climb, to ascend
ersteigern [ɛrˈʃtaɪgərn] VT to buy at an auction
erstellen [ɛrˈʃtɛlən] VT to erect, to build
erstens ADV firstly, in the first place
erstere(r, s) PRON (the) former; **der/die/das E~** the former
ersticken [ɛrˈʃtɪkən] VT (*lit, fig*) to stifle; (*Mensch*) to suffocate; (*Flammen*) to smother ▸ VI (*Mensch*) to suffocate; (*Feuer*) to be smothered; **mit erstickter Stimme** in a choked voice; **in Arbeit ~** to be snowed under with work
Erstickung F suffocation; **erstklassig** ADJ first-class
erst- zW: **Erstkommunion** F first communion; **erstmalig** ADJ first; **erstmals** ADV for the first time; **erstrangig** ADJ first-rate
erstrebenswert [ɛrˈʃtreːbənsveːrt] ADJ desirable, worthwhile
erstrecken [ɛrˈʃtrɛkən] VR to extend, to stretch
Erststimme F first vote

> The **Erststimme** and **Zweitstimme** (first and second vote) system is used to elect MPs to the **Bundestag**. Each elector is given two votes. The first is to choose a candidate in his constituency; the candidate with the most votes is elected MP. The second is to choose a party. All the second votes in each **Land** are counted and a proportionate number of MPs from each party is sent to the **Bundestag**.

Ersttagsbrief M first-day cover
Ersttagsstempel M first-day (date) stamp
erstunken [ɛrˈʃtʊŋkən] ADJ: **das ist ~ und erlogen** (*umg*) that's a pack of lies
Erstwähler (**-s, -**) M first-time voter
ersuchen [ɛrˈzuːxən] VT to request
ertappen [ɛrˈtapən] VT to catch, to detect
erteilen [ɛrˈtaɪlən] VT to give
ertönen [ɛrˈtøːnən] VI to sound, to ring out
Ertrag [ɛrˈtraːk] (**-(e)s, Erträge**) M yield; (*Gewinn*) proceeds *pl*
ertragen *unreg* VT to bear, to stand
erträglich [ɛrˈtrɛːklɪç] ADJ tolerable, bearable
ertragreich ADJ (*Geschäft*) profitable, lucrative
ertrank *etc* [ɛrˈtraŋk] VB *siehe* **ertrinken**
ertränken [ɛrˈtrɛŋkən] VT to drown
erträumen [ɛrˈtrɔymən] VT: **sich** *dat* **etw ~** to dream of sth, to imagine sth
ertrinken [ɛrˈtrɪŋkən] *unreg* VI to drown; **Ertrinken** (**-s**) NT drowning
ertrunken [ɛrˈtrʊŋkən] PP *von* **ertrinken**
erübrigen [ɛrˈlyːbrɪgən] VT to spare ▸ VR to be unnecessary
erwachen [ɛrˈvaxən] VI to awake; **ein böses E~** (*fig*) a rude awakening
erwachsen [ɛrˈvaksən] ADJ grown-up ▸ VI *unreg*: **daraus erwuchsen ihm Unannehmlichkeiten** that caused him some trouble
Erwachsene(r) F(M) adult
Erwachsenenbildung F adult education
erwägen [ɛrˈvɛːgən] *unreg* VT to consider
Erwägung F consideration; **etw in ~ ziehen** to take sth into consideration
erwähnen [ɛrˈvɛːnən] VT to mention
erwähnenswert ADJ worth mentioning
Erwähnung F mention
erwarb *etc* [ɛrˈvarp] VB *siehe* **erwerben**
erwärmen [ɛrˈvɛrmən] VT to warm, to heat ▸ VR to get warm, to warm up; **sich ~ für** to warm to
erwarten [ɛrˈvartən] VT to expect; (*warten auf*) to wait for; **etw kaum ~ können** to hardly be able to wait for sth
Erwartung F expectation; **in ~ Ihrer baldigen Antwort** (*form*) in anticipation of your early reply
erwartungsgemäß ADV as expected
erwartungsvoll ADJ expectant
erwecken [ɛrˈvɛkən] VT to rouse, to awake; **den Anschein ~** to give the impression; **etw zu neuem Leben ~** to resurrect sth
erwehren [ɛrˈveːrən] VR +*gen* (*geh*) to fend off, to ward off; (*des Lachens etc*) to refrain from
erweichen [ɛrˈvaɪçən] VT to soften; **sich nicht ~ lassen** to be unmoved
erweisen [ɛrˈvaɪzən] *unreg* VT to prove ▸ VR: **sich ~ als** to prove to be; **jdm einen Gefallen/Dienst ~** to do sb a favour/service; **sich jdm gegenüber dankbar ~** to show one's gratitude to sb
erweitern [ɛrˈvaɪtərn] VT, VR to widen, to enlarge; (*Geschäft*) to expand; (*Med*) to dilate; (*fig: Kenntnisse*) to broaden; (*Macht*) to extend
Erweiterung F expansion
Erwerb [ɛrˈvɛrp] (**-(e)s, -e**) M acquisition; (*Beruf*) trade
erwerben [ɛrˈvɛrbən] *unreg* VT to acquire; **er hat sich** *dat* **große Verdienste um die Firma erworben** he has done great service for the firm
Erwerbs- zW: **erwerbsfähig** ADJ (*form*) capable of gainful employment; **Erwerbsgesellschaft** F acquisitive society; **erwerbslos** ADJ unemployed; **Erwerbsquelle** F source of income; **erwerbstätig** ADJ (gainfully) employed; **erwerbsunfähig** ADJ unable to work
erwidern [ɛrˈviːdərn] VT to reply; (*vergelten*) to return
Erwiderung F: **in ~ Ihres Schreibens vom ...** (*form*) in reply to your letter of the ...
erwiesen [ɛrˈviːzən] ADJ proven
erwirbt [ɛrˈvɪrpt] VB *siehe* **erwerben**
erwirtschaften [ɛrˈvɪrtʃaftən] VT (*Gewinn etc*) to make by good management
erwischen [ɛrˈvɪʃən] (*umg*) VT to catch, to get; **ihn hats erwischt!** (*umg: verliebt*) he's got it bad; (*: krank*) he's got it; **kalt ~** (*umg*) to catch off-balance
erworben [ɛrˈvɔrbən] PP *von* **erwerben**
erwünscht [ɛrˈvʏnʃt] ADJ desired
erwürgen [ɛrˈvʏrgən] VT to strangle
Erz [eːrts] (**-es, -e**) NT ore
erzählen [ɛrˈtsɛːlən] VT, VI to tell; **dem werd ich was ~!** (*umg*) I'll have something to say to him; **erzählende Dichtung** narrative fiction

Erzähler(in) (**-s, -**) M(F) narrator
Erzählung F story, tale
Erzbischof M archbishop
Erzengel M archangel
erzeugen [ɛr'tsɔʏgən] VT to produce; (*Strom*) to generate
Erzeuger (**-s, -**) M producer; **Erzeugerpreis** M manufacturer's price
Erzeugnis (**-ses, -se**) NT product, produce
Erzeugung F production; (*von Strom*) generation
Erzfeind M arch enemy
erziehbar ADJ: **ein Heim für schwer erziehbare Kinder** a home for difficult children
erziehen [ɛr'tsi:ən] *unreg* VT to bring up; (*bilden*) to educate, to train
Erzieher(in) (**-s, -**) M(F) educator; (*in Kindergarten*) nursery school teacher
Erziehung F bringing up; (*Bildung*) education
Erziehungs- zW: **Erziehungsberechtigte(r)** F(M) parent, legal guardian; **Erziehungsgeld** NT payment for new parents; **Erziehungsheim** NT community home; **Erziehungsurlaub** M leave for a new parent
erzielen [ɛr'tsi:lən] VT to achieve, to obtain; (*Tor*) to score
erzkonservativ ['ɛrtskɔnzɛrva'ti:f] ADJ ultraconservative
erzog *etc* [ɛr'tso:k] VB *siehe* **erziehen**
erzogen [ɛr'tso:gən] PP *von* **erziehen**
erzürnen [ɛr'tsʏrnən] VT (*geh*) to anger, to incense
erzwingen [ɛr'tsvɪŋən] *unreg* VT to force, to obtain by force
es [ɛs] *nom, akk* PRON it; (*Baby, Tier*) he/she
Es [ɛs] (-) NT (*Mus: Dur*) E flat
Esche ['ɛʃə] (**-, -n**) F ash
Esel ['e:zəl] (**-s, -**) M donkey, ass; **ich ~!** (*umg*) silly me!
Eselsbrücke F (*Gedächtnishilfe*) mnemonic, aide-mémoire
Eselsohr NT dog-ear
Eskalation [ɛskalatsi'o:n] F escalation
eskalieren [ɛska'li:rən] VT, VI to escalate
Eskimo ['ɛskimo] (**-s, -s**) M eskimo
Eskorte [ɛs'kɔrtə] (**-, -n**) F (*Mil*) escort
eskortieren [ɛskɔr'ti:rən] VT (*geh*) to escort
Espenlaub ['ɛspənlaʊp] NT: **zittern wie ~** to shake like a leaf
essbar ['ɛsba:r] ADJ eatable, edible
Essecke F dining area
essen ['ɛsən] *unreg* VT, VI to eat; **~ gehen** (*auswärts*) to eat out; **~ Sie gern Äpfel?** do you like apples?; **Essen** (**-s, -**) NT (*Mahlzeit*) meal; (*Nahrung*) food; **Essen auf Rädern** meals on wheels
Essens- zW: **Essensausgabe** F serving of meals; (*Stelle*) serving counter; **Essensmarke** F meal voucher; **Essenszeit** F mealtime
Essgeschirr NT dinner service
Essig ['ɛsɪç] (**-s, -e**) M vinegar; **damit ist es ~** (*umg*) it's all off; **Essiggurke** F gherkin
Esskastanie F sweet chestnut
Essl. ABK (= *Esslöffel*) tbsp.
Ess- zW: **Esslöffel** M tablespoon; **Esstisch** M dining table; **Esswaren** PL foodstuffs *pl*; **Esszimmer** NT dining room
Establishment [ɪs'tæblɪʃmənt] (**-s, -s**) NT establishment
Este ['e:stə] (**-n, -n**) M, **Estin** F Estonian
Estland ['e:stlant] NT Estonia
estnisch ['e:stnɪʃ] ADJ Estonian
Estragon ['ɛstragɔn] (**-s**) M tarragon
Estrich ['ɛstrɪç] (**-s, -e**) M stone/clay *etc* floor
etablieren [eta'bli:rən] VR to establish o.s.; (*Comm*) to set up
Etage [e'ta:ʒə] (**-, -n**) F floor, storey (BRIT), story (US)
Etagenbett NT bunk bed
Etagenwohnung F flat (BRIT), apartment (US)
Etappe [e'tapə] (**-, -n**) F stage
etappenweise ADV step by step, stage by stage
Etat [e'ta:] (**-s, -s**) M budget; **Etatjahr** NT financial year; **Etatposten** M budget item
etc ABK (= *et cetera*) etc.
etepetete [e:təpe'te:tə] (*umg*) ADJ fussy
Ethik ['e:tɪk] F ethics *sing*
ethisch ['e:tɪʃ] ADJ ethical
ethnisch ['ɛtnɪʃ] ADJ ethnic; **ethnische Säuberung** ethnic cleansing
Etikett [eti'kɛt] (**-(e)s, -e**) NT (*lit, fig*) label
Etikette F etiquette, manners *pl*
Etikettenschwindel M (*Pol*): **es ist reinster ~, wenn ...** it is just playing *od* juggling with names if ...
etikettieren [etikɛ'ti:rən] VT to label
etliche(r, s) ['ɛtlɪçə(r, s)] ADJ quite a lot of ▸ PRON *pl* some, quite a few; **etliches** quite a lot
Etüde [e'ty:də] (**-, -n**) F (*Mus*) étude
Etui [ɛt'vi:] (**-s, -s**) NT case
etwa ['ɛtva] ADV (*ungefähr*) about; (*vielleicht*) perhaps; (*beispielsweise*) for instance; (*entrüstet, erstaunt*): **hast du ~ schon wieder kein Geld dabei?** don't tell me you haven't got any money again! ▸ ADV (*zur Bestätigung*): **Sie kommen doch, oder ~ nicht?** you are coming, aren't you?; **nicht ~** by no means; **willst du ~ schon gehen?** (surely) you don't want to go already?
etwaig ['ɛtvaɪç] ADJ possible
etwas PRON something; (*fragend, verneinend*) anything; (*ein wenig*) a little ▸ ADV a little; **er kann ~** he's good; **Etwas** NT: **das gewisse Etwas** that certain something
Etymologie [etymolo'gi:] F etymology
EU [e:'lu:] (-) F ABK (= *Europäische Union*) EU
euch [ɔʏç] PRON (*akk von ihr*) you; (*dat von ihr*) (to/for) you ▸ REFL PRON yourselves
euer ['ɔʏər] PRON *gen von* **ihr** ▸ ADJ your
EU-Erweiterung [e:'lu:-] F enlargement of the EU
EU-Kommissar(in) [e:'lu:-] M(F) EU commissioner
EU-Kommission [e:'lu:-] F EU commission
Eule ['ɔʏlə] (**-, -n**) F owl
EU-Osterweiterung [e:'lu:-] F eastward expansion of the EU

Euphemismus [ɔʏfe'mɪsmʊs] M euphemism
Eurasien [ɔʏ'ra:ziən] NT Eurasia
Euratom [ɔʏra'to:m] F ABK (= *Europäische Atomgemeinschaft*) Euratom
eure(r, s) ['ɔʏrə(r, s)] PRON yours
eurerseits ADV on your part
euresgleichen PRON people like you
euretwegen ['ɔʏrət'vegən] ADV (*für euch*) for your sakes; (*wegen euch*) on your account
euretwillen ['ɔʏrət'vɪlən] ADV: **um ~** = **euretwegen**
eurige PRON: **der/die/das E~** (*geh*) yours
Euro ['ɔʏro] (**-, -s**) M (*Fin*) euro
Eurocent M euro cent
Eurokrat [ɔʏro'kra:t] (**-en, -en**) M eurocrat
Europa [ɔʏ'ro:pa] (**-s**) NT Europe
Europäer(in) [ɔʏro'pɛ:ər(ɪn)] (**-s, -**) M(F) European
europäisch ADJ European; **das Europäische Parlament** the European Parliament; **Europäische Union** European Union; **Europäische (Wirtschafts)gemeinschaft** European (Economic) Community, Common Market
Europa- ZW: **Europameister** M European champion; **Europaparlament** NT European Parliament; **Europarat** M Council of Europe; **Europastraße** F Euroroute
Euter ['ɔʏtər] (**-s, -**) NT udder
Euthanasie [ɔʏtana'zi:] F euthanasia
EU-Verfassung [e:'|u:-] F EU constitution
ev. ABK = **evangelisch**
E.V., e.V. ABK (= *eingetragener Verein*) registered association
evakuieren [evaku'i:rən] VT to evacuate
evangelisch [evaŋ'ge:lɪʃ] ADJ Protestant
Evangelium [evaŋ'ge:liʊm] NT Gospel
Evaskostüm NT: **im ~** in her birthday suit
eventuell [evɛntu'ɛl] ADJ possible ▸ ADV possibly, perhaps
Evolution [evolutsi'o:n] F evolution
Evolutionstheorie F theory of evolution
evtl. ABK = **eventuell**
EWG [e:ve:'ge:] (-) F ABK (*früher: = Europäische Wirtschaftsgemeinschaft*) EEC
ewig ['e:vɪç] ADJ eternal ▸ ADV: **auf ~** forever; **ich habe Sie ~ lange nicht gesehen** (*umg*) I haven't seen you for ages; **Ewigkeit** F eternity; **bis in alle Ewigkeit** forever
EWS (-) NT ABK (= *Europäisches Währungssystem*) EMS
EWU (-) F ABK (= *Europäische Währungsunion*) EMU
ex [ɛks] (*umg*) ADV: **etw ex trinken** to drink sth down in one
Ex [ɛks] MF ex
exakt [ɛ'ksakt] ADJ exact
exaltiert [ɛksal'ti:rt] ADJ exaggerated, effusive
Examen [ɛ'ksa:mən] (**-s, -** *od* **Examina**) NT examination
Examensarbeit F dissertation
Exekutionskommando [ɛksekutsi'o:nskɔmando] NT firing squad
Exekutive [ɛkseku'ti:və] F executive
Exempel [ɛ'ksɛmpəl] (**-s, -**) NT example; **die Probe aufs ~ machen** to put it to the test
Exemplar [ɛksɛm'pla:r] (**-s, -e**) NT specimen; (*Buchexemplar*) copy; **exemplarisch** ADJ exemplary
exerzieren [ɛksɛr'tsi:rən] VI to drill
Exhibitionist [ɛkshibitsio'nɪst] M exhibitionist
Exil [ɛ'ksi:l] (**-s, -e**) NT exile
existentiell [ɛksɪstɛntsi'ɛl] ADJ = **existenziell**
Existenz [ɛksɪs'tɛnts] F existence; (*Unterhalt*) livelihood, living; (*pej: Mensch*) character; **Existenzberechtigung** F right to exist; **Existenzgrundlage** F basis of one's livelihood
existenziell [ɛksɪstɛntsi'ɛl] ADJ: **von existenzieller Bedeutung** of vital significance
Existenzkampf M struggle for existence
Existenzminimum (**-s, -ma**) NT subsistence level
existieren [ɛksɪs'ti:rən] VI to exist
exkl. ABK = **exklusive**
exklusiv [ɛksklu'zi:f] ADJ exclusive; **Exklusivbericht** M (*Presse*) exclusive report
exklusive [ɛksklu'zi:və] PRÄP +*gen* exclusive of, not including ▸ ADV exclusive of, excluding
Exkursion [ɛkskʊrzi'o:n] F (study) trip
Exmatrikulation [ɛksmatrikulatsi'o:n] F (*Univ*): **bei seiner ~** when he left university
exorzieren [ɛksɔr'tsi:rən] VT to exorcize
exotisch [ɛ'kso:tɪʃ] ADJ exotic
expandieren [ɛkspan'di:rən] VI (*Wirts*) to expand
Expansion [ɛkspanzi'o:n] F expansion
expansiv [ɛkspan'zi:f] ADJ expansionist; (*Wirtschaftszweige*) expanding
Expedition [ɛkspeditsi'o:n] F expedition; (*Comm*) forwarding department
Experiment [ɛksperi'mɛnt] NT experiment
experimentell [ɛksperimɛn'tɛl] ADJ experimental
experimentieren [ɛksperimɛn'ti:rən] VI to experiment
Experte [ɛks'pɛrtə] (**-n, -n**) M expert, specialist; **Expertenkommission** F think tank; **Expertenmeinung** F expert opinion
Expertin [ɛks'pɛrtɪn] F expert, specialist
explodieren [ɛksplo'di:rən] VI to explode
Explosion [ɛksplozi'o:n] F explosion
explosiv [ɛksplo'zi:f] ADJ explosive
Exponent [ɛkspo'nɛnt] M exponent
exponieren [ɛkspo'ni:rən] VT: **an exponierter Stelle stehen** to be in an exposed position
Export [ɛks'pɔrt] (**-(e)s, -e**) M export
Exportartikel M export
Exporteur [ɛkspɔr'tø:r] M exporter
Exporthandel M export trade
Exporthaus NT export house
exportieren [ɛkspɔr'ti:rən] VT to export
Exportkaufmann M exporter
Exportland NT exporting country
Exportvertreter M export agent
Exportwirtschaft F export business *od* sector

Expressgut [ɛks'prɛsgut] NT express goods *pl od* freight
Expressionismus [ɛksprɛsio'nɪsmʊs] M expressionism
Expresszug M express (train)
extra ['ɛkstra] ADJ *unver* (*umg: gesondert*) separate; (*besondere*) extra ▶ ADV (*gesondert*) separately; (*speziell*) specially; (*absichtlich*) on purpose; (*vor Adjektiven, zusätzlich*) extra; **Extra (-s, -s)** NT extra; **Extraausgabe** F special edition; **Extrablatt** NT special edition
Extrakt [ɛks'trakt] **(-(e)s, -e)** M extract
Extratour F (*fig: umg*): **sich** *dat* **Extratouren leisten** to do one's own thing
extravagant [ɛkstrava'gant] ADJ extravagant; (*Kleidung*) flamboyant
Extrawurst (*umg*) F (*Sonderwunsch*): **er will immer eine ~ (gebraten haben)** he always wants something different
extrem ADJ extreme; **Extrem** [ɛks'tre:m] **(-s, -e)** NT extreme; **Extremfall** M extreme (case)
Extremist(in) M(F) extremist
Extremistenerlass [ɛkstre'mɪstənlɛrlas] M *law(s) governing extremism*
extremistisch [ɛkstre'mɪstɪʃ] ADJ (*Pol*) extremist
Extremitäten [ɛkstremi'tɛ:tən] PL extremities *pl*
extrovertiert [ɛkstrovɛr'ti:rt] ADJ extrovert
Exzellenz [ɛkstsɛ'lɛnts] F excellency
exzentrisch [ɛks'tsɛntrɪʃ] ADJ eccentric
Exzess [ɛks'tsɛs] **(-es, -e)** M excess

F¹, f [ef] (**-, -**) NT F, f; **F wie Friedrich** ≈ F for Frederick, ≈ F for Fox (*US*); **nach Schema F** (*umg*) in the usual old way

f² ABK (= *feminin*) fem.

Fa. ABK (= *Firma*) co.

Fabel ['fa:bəl] (**-, -n**) F fable; **fabelhaft** ADJ fabulous, marvellous (BRIT), marvelous (*US*)

Fabrik [fa'bri:k] F factory; **Fabrikanlage** F plant; (*Gelände*) factory premises *pl*

Fabrikant [fabri:'kant] M (*Hersteller*) manufacturer; (*Besitzer*) industrialist

Fabrikarbeiter(in) M(F) factory worker

Fabrikat [fabri:'ka:t] (**-(e)s, -e**) NT product; (*Marke*) make

Fabrikation [fabri:katsi'o:n] F manufacture, production

Fabrikbesitzer M factory owner

Fabrikgelände NT factory site

fabrizieren [fabri'tsi:rən] VT (*geistiges Produkt*) to produce; (*Geschichte*) to concoct, to fabricate

Facebook® ['feɪsbʊk] NT Facebook®

Fach [fax] (**-(e)s, Fächer**) NT compartment; (*in Schrank, Regal etc*) shelf; (*Sachgebiet*) subject; **ein Mann/eine Frau vom ~** an expert; **Facharbeiter** M skilled worker; **Facharzt** M (medical) specialist; **Fachausdruck** M technical term; **Fachbereich** M (special) field; (*Univ*) school, faculty; **Fachbuch** NT reference book

Fächer ['fɛçər] (**-s, -**) M fan

Fach- ZW: **Fachfrau** F expert; **Fachgebiet** NT (special) field; **Fachgeschäft** NT specialist shop (BRIT) *od* store (*US*); **Fachhändler** M stockist; **Fachhochschule** F college; **Fachidiot** (*umg*) M narrow-minded specialist; **Fachkraft** F qualified employee; **Fachkräftemangel** M lack of skilled *od* qualified personnel; **Fachkreise** PL: **in Fachkreisen** among experts; **fachkundig** ADJ expert, specialist; **Fachlehrer** M specialist subject teacher; **fachlich** ADJ technical; (*beruflich*) professional; **Fachmann** (**-(e)s, *pl* Fachleute**) M expert; **fachmännisch** ADJ professional; **Fachrichtung** F subject area; **Fachschule** F technical college; **fachsimpeln** VI to talk shop; **fachspezifisch** ADJ technical; **Fachverband** M trade association; **Fachwelt** F profession; **Fachwerk** NT timber frame; **Fachwerkhaus** NT half-timbered house

Fackel ['fakəl] (**-, -n**) F torch

fackeln (*umg*) VI to dither

Fackelzug M torchlight procession

fad, fade ADJ insipid; (*langweilig*) dull; (*Essen*) tasteless

Faden ['fa:dən] (**-s, Fäden**) M thread; **der rote ~** (*fig*) the central theme; **alle Fäden laufen hier zusammen** this is the nerve centre (BRIT) *od* center (*US*) of the whole thing; **Fadennudeln** PL vermicelli *sing*; **fadenscheinig** ADJ (*lit, fig*) threadbare

Fagott [fa'gɔt] (**-(e)s, -e**) NT bassoon

fähig ['fɛ:ɪç] ADJ: **~ (zu** *od* **+*gen*)** able (to); (*imstande*) capable (of); **zu allem ~ sein** to be capable of anything; **Fähigkeit** F ability

Fähnchen ['fɛ:nçən] NT pennon, streamer

fahnden ['fa:ndən] VI: **~ nach** to search for

Fahndung F search

Fahndungsliste F list of wanted criminals, wanted list

Fahne ['fa:nə] (**-, -n**) F flag; **mit fliegenden Fahnen zu jdm/etw überlaufen** to go over to sb/sth; **eine ~ haben** (*umg*) to smell of drink

Fahnenflucht F desertion

Fahrausweis M (*form*) ticket

Fahrbahn F carriageway (BRIT), roadway

fahrbar ADJ: **fahrbarer Untersatz** (*hum*) wheels *pl*

Fähre ['fɛ:rə] (**-, -n**) F ferry

fahren ['fa:rən] *unreg* VT to drive; (*Rad*) to ride; (*befördern*) to drive, to take; (*Rennen*) to drive in ▶ VI (*sich bewegen*) to go; (*Schiff*) to sail; (*abfahren*) to leave; **mit dem Auto/Zug ~** to go *od* travel by car/train; **mit dem Aufzug ~** to take the lift, to ride the elevator (*US*); **links/rechts ~** to drive on the left/right; **gegen einen Baum ~** to drive *od* go into a tree; **die U-Bahn fährt alle fünf Minuten** the underground goes *od* runs every five minutes; **mit der Hand ~ über** *+akk* to pass one's hand over; **(bei etw) gut/schlecht ~** (*zurechtkommen*) to do well/badly (with sth); **was ist (denn) in dich gefahren?** what's got (BRIT) *od* gotten (*US*) into you?; **einen ~ lassen** (*umg*) to fart (*umg!*)

fahrend ADJ: **fahrendes Volk** travelling people

Fahrer(in) ['fa:rər(ɪn)] (**-s, -**) M(F) driver; **Fahrerflucht** F hit-and-run driving

Fahr- zW: **Fahrgast** M passenger; **Fahrgeld** NT fare; **Fahrgelegenheit** F transport; **Fahrgestell** NT chassis; (*Aviat*) undercarriage

fahrig ['fa:rɪç] ADJ nervous; (*unkonzentriert*) distracted

Fahr- zW: **Fahrkarte** F ticket; **Fahrkartenausgabe** F ticket office; **Fahrkartenautomat** M ticket machine; **Fahrkartenschalter** M ticket office

fahrlässig ADJ negligent; **fahrlässige Tötung** manslaughter; **Fahrlässigkeit** F negligence

Fahr- zW: **Fahrlehrer** M driving instructor; **Fahrplan** M timetable; **fahrplanmäßig** ADJ (*Eisenb*) scheduled; **Fahrpraxis** F driving experience; **Fahrpreis** M fare; **Fahrprüfung** F driving test; **Fahrrad** NT bicycle; **Fahrradweg** M cycle path; **Fahrrinne** F (*Naut*) shipping channel, fairway; **Fahrschein** M ticket; **Fahrscheinautomat** M ticket machine; **Fahrschule** F driving school; **Fahrschüler** M learner (driver); **Fahrspur** F lane; **Fahrstreifen** M lane; **Fahrstuhl** M lift (BRIT), elevator (US); **Fahrstunde** F driving lesson

Fahrt [fa:rt] (**-, -en**) F journey; (*kurz*) trip; (*Aut*) drive; (*Geschwindigkeit*) speed; **gute ~!** safe journey!; **volle ~ voraus!** (*Naut*) full speed ahead!

fährt [fɛ:rt] VB *siehe* **fahren**

fahrtauglich ['fa:rtaʊklɪç] ADJ fit to drive

Fährte ['fɛ:rtə] (**-, -n**) F track, trail; **jdn auf eine falsche ~ locken** (*fig*) to put sb off the scent

Fahrtenschreiber M tachograph

Fahrtkosten PL travelling expenses *pl*

Fahrtrichtung F course, direction

Fahr- zW: **fahrtüchtig** ['fa:rtʏçtɪç] ADJ fit to drive; (*Fahrzeug*) roadworthy; **Fahrverhalten** NT (*von Fahrer*) behaviour (BRIT) *od* behavior (US) behind the wheel; (*von Wagen*) road performance; **Fahrzeug** NT vehicle; **Fahrzeughalter** (**-s, -**) M owner of a vehicle; **Fahrzeugpapiere** PL vehicle documents *pl*

Faible ['fɛ:bl] (**-s, -s**) NT (*geh*) liking; (*Schwäche*) weakness; (*Vorliebe*) penchant

fair [fɛ:r] ADJ fair

Fäkalien [fɛ'ka:liən] PL faeces *pl*

Faksimile [fak'zi:mile] (**-s, -s**) NT facsimile

faktisch ['faktɪʃ] ADJ actual

Faktor M factor

Faktum (**-s, -ten**) NT fact

fakturieren [faktu'ri:rən] VT (*Comm*) to invoice

Fakultät [fakʊl'tɛ:t] F faculty

Falke ['falkə] (**-n, -n**) M falcon

Falklandinseln ['falklant'ɪnzəln] PL Falkland Islands, Falklands

Fall [fal] (**-(e)s, Fälle**) M (*Sturz*) fall; (*Sachverhalt, Jur, Gram*) case; **auf jeden ~, auf alle Fälle** in any case; (*bestimmt*) definitely; **gesetzt den ~** assuming (that); **jds ~ sein** (*umg*) to be sb's cup of tea; **klarer ~!** (*umg*) sure thing!, you bet!; **das mache ich auf keinen ~** there's no way I'm going to do that

Falle (**-, -n**) F trap; (*umg: Bett*) bed; **jdm eine ~ stellen** to set a trap for sb

fallen *unreg* VI to fall; (*im Krieg*) to fall, to be killed; **etw ~ lassen** to drop sth; (*Bemerkung*) to make sth; (*Plan*) to abandon sth, to drop sth

fällen ['fɛlən] VT (*Baum*) to fell; (*Urteil*) to pass

fällig ['fɛlɪç] ADJ due; (*Wechsel*) mature(d); **längst ~** long overdue; **Fälligkeit** F (*Comm*) maturity

Fallobst NT fallen fruit, windfall

falls ADV in case, if

Fall- zW: **Fallschirm** M parachute; **Fallschirmjäger** M paratrooper; **Fallschirmspringer(in)** M(F) parachutist; **Fallschirmtruppe** F paratroops *pl*; **Fallstrick** M (*fig*) trap, snare; **Fallstudie** F case study

fällt [fɛlt] VB *siehe* **fallen**

Falltür F trap door

fallweise ADJ from case to case

falsch [falʃ] ADJ false; (*unrichtig*) wrong; **ein falsches Spiel (mit jdm) treiben** to play (sb) false; **etw ~ verstehen** to misunderstand sth, to get sth wrong; *siehe auch* **falschliegen**

fälschen ['fɛlʃən] VT to forge

Fälscher(in) (**-s, -**) M(F) forger

Falschfahrer(in) M(F) *person driving the wrong way on the motorway*

Falschgeld NT counterfeit money

Falschheit F falsity, falseness; (*Unrichtigkeit*) wrongness

fälschlich ADJ false

fälschlicherweise ADV mistakenly

falschliegen *unreg* VI to be wrong; **~ bei/mit** to be wrong about/in

Falschmeldung F (*Presse*) false report

Fälschung F forgery

fälschungssicher ADJ forgery-proof

Faltblatt NT leaflet; (*in Zeitschrift etc*) insert

Fältchen ['fɛltçən] NT crease, wrinkle

Falte ['faltə] (**-, -n**) F (*Knick*) fold, crease; (*Hautfalte*) wrinkle; (*Rockfalte*) pleat

falten VT to fold; (*Stirn*) to wrinkle

faltenlos ADJ without folds; (*Haut*) without wrinkles

Faltenrock M pleated skirt

Falter ['faltər] (**-s, -**) M (*Tagfalter*) butterfly; (*Nachtfalter*) moth

faltig ['faltɪç] ADJ (*Haut*) wrinkled; (*Rock usw*) creased

falzen ['faltsən] VT (*Papierbogen*) to fold

Fam. ABK = **Familie**

familiär [famili'ɛ:r] ADJ familiar

Familie [fa'mi:liə] F family; **~ Otto Francke** (*als Anschrift*) Mr & Mrs Otto Francke and family; **zur ~ gehören** to be one of the family

Familien- zW: **Familienanschluss** M: **Unterkunft mit Familienanschluss** *accommodation where one is treated as one of the family*; **Familienkreis** M family circle; **Familienmitglied** NT member of the family; **Familienname** M surname; **Familienpackung** F family(-size) pack; **Familienplanung** F family planning; **Familienstand** M marital status; **Familienunternehmen** NT family business; **Familienvater** M head of the

family; **Familienverhältnisse** PL family circumstances *pl*
Fanatiker(in) [fa'na:tikər(ɪn)] (**-s, -**) M(F) fanatic
fanatisch ADJ fanatical
Fanatismus [fana'tɪsmʊs] M fanaticism
fand *etc* [fant] VB *siehe* **finden**
Fang [faŋ] (**-(e)s, Fänge**) M catch; (*Jagen*) hunting; (*Kralle*) talon, claw
fangen *unreg* VT to catch ▸ VR to get caught; (*Flugzeug*) to level out; (*Mensch: nicht fallen*) to steady o.s.; (*fig*) to compose o.s.; (*in Leistung*) to get back on form
Fangfrage F catch *od* trick question
Fanggründe PL fishing grounds *pl*
fängt [fɛŋkt] VB *siehe* **fangen**
Fantasie [fanta'zi:] F imagination; **in seiner ~** in his mind; **Fantasiegebilde** NT (*Einbildung*) figment of the imagination; **fantasielos** ADJ unimaginative
fantasieren [fanta'zi:ren] VI to fantasize; (*Med*) to be delirious
fantasievoll ADJ imaginative
Fantast [fan'tast] (**-en, -en**) M dreamer
fantastisch ADJ fantastic
Farb- ZW: **Farbabzug** M coloured (BRIT) *od* colored (US) print; **Farbaufnahme** F colour (BRIT) *od* color (US) photograph; **Farbband** NT typewriter ribbon; **Farbdrucker** M colour printer
Farbe ['fa:rbə] (**-, -n**) F colour (BRIT), color (US); (*zum Malen etc*) paint; (*Stofffarbe*) dye; (*Karten*) suit
farbecht ['farplɛçt] ADJ colourfast (BRIT), colorfast (US)
färben ['fɛrbən] VT to colour (BRIT), to color (US); (*Stoff, Haar*) to dye
farben- ZW: **farbenblind** ADJ colour-blind (BRIT), color-blind (US); **farbenfroh** ADJ colourful (BRIT), colorful (US); **farbenprächtig** ADJ colourful (BRIT), colorful (US)
Farbfernsehen NT colour (BRIT) *od* color (US) television
Farbfilm M colour (BRIT) *od* color (US) film
Farbfoto NT colour (BRIT) *od* color (US) photo
farbig ADJ coloured (BRIT), colored (US)
Farbige(r) F(M) coloured (BRIT) *od* colored (US) person
Farb- ZW: **Farbkasten** M paintbox; **farblos** ADJ colourless (BRIT), colorless (US); **Farbstift** M coloured (BRIT) *od* colored (US) pencil; **Farbstoff** M dye; (*Lebensmittelfarbstoff*) (artificial) colouring (BRIT) *od* coloring (US); **Farbton** M hue, tone
Färbung ['fɛrbʊŋ] F colouring (BRIT), coloring (US); (*Tendenz*) bias
Farn [farn] (**-(e)s, -e**) M fern; (*Adlerfarn*) bracken
Farnkraut [farn] NT = **Farn**
Färöer [fɛ'rø:ər] PL Faeroe Islands *pl*
Fasan [fa'za:n] (**-(e)s, -e(n)**) M pheasant
Fasching ['faʃɪŋ] (**-s, -e** *od* **-s**) M carnival
Faschismus [fa'ʃɪsmʊs] M fascism
Faschist(in) M(F) fascist
faschistisch [fa'ʃɪstɪʃ] ADJ fascist
faseln ['fa:zəln] VI to talk nonsense, to drivel
Faser ['fa:zər] (**-, -n**) F fibre
Fass [fas] (**-es, Fässer**) NT vat, barrel; (*für Öl*) drum; **Bier vom ~** draught beer; **ein ~ ohne Boden** (*fig*) a bottomless pit
Fassade [fa'sa:də] F (*lit, fig*) façade
fassbar ADJ comprehensible
Fassbier NT draught beer
fassen ['fasən] VT (*ergreifen*) to grasp, to take; (*inhaltlich*) to hold; (*Entschluss etc*) to take; (*verstehen*) to understand; (*Ring etc*) to set; (*formulieren*) to formulate, to phrase ▸ VR to calm down; **nicht zu ~** unbelievable; *siehe auch* **kurzfassen**
fasslich ['faslɪç] ADJ comprehensible
Fasson [fa'sõ:] (**-, -s**) F style; (*Art und Weise*) way; **aus der ~ geraten** (*lit*) to lose its shape
Fassung ['fasʊŋ] F (*Umrahmung*) mounting; (*Lampenfassung*) socket; (*Wortlaut*) version; (*Beherrschung*) composure; **jdn aus der ~ bringen** to upset sb; **völlig außer ~ geraten** to lose all self-control
fassungslos ADJ speechless
Fassungsvermögen NT capacity; (*Verständnis*) comprehension
fast [fast] ADV almost, nearly; **~ nie** hardly ever
fasten ['fastən] VI to fast; **Fasten** (**-s**) NT fasting; **Fastenzeit** F Lent
Fastnacht F Shrovetide carnival
faszinieren [fastsi'ni:rən] VT to fascinate
fatal [fa'ta:l] ADJ fatal; (*peinlich*) embarrassing
fauchen ['faʊxən] VT, VI to hiss
faul [faʊl] ADJ rotten; (*Person*) lazy; (*Ausreden*) lame; **daran ist etwas ~** there's something fishy about it
faulen VI to rot
faulenzen ['faulɛntsən] VI to idle
Faulenzer(in) (**-s, -**) M(F) idler, loafer
Faulheit F laziness
faulig ADJ putrid
Fäulnis ['fɔʏlnɪs] (**-**) F decay, putrefaction
Faulpelz (*umg*) M lazybones *sing*
Faust ['faʊst] (**-, Fäuste**) F fist; **das passt wie die ~ aufs Auge** (*passt nicht*) it's all wrong; **auf eigene ~** (*fig*) on one's own initiative
Fäustchen ['fɔʏstçən] NT: **sich** *dat* **ins ~ lachen** to laugh up one's sleeve
faustdick (*umg*) ADJ: **er hat es ~ hinter den Ohren** he's a crafty one
Fausthandschuh M mitten
Faustregel F rule of thumb
Favorit(in) [favo'ri:t(ɪn)] (**-en, -en**) M(F) favourite (BRIT), favorite (US)
Fax [faks] (**-, -e**) NT fax; **faxen** VT to fax
Faxen ['faksən] PL: **~ machen** to fool around
Fazit ['fa:tsɪt] (**-s, -s** *od* **-e**) NT: **wenn wir aus diesen vier Jahren das ~ ziehen** if we take stock of these four years
FCKW (**-s, -s**) M ABK (= *Fluorchlorkohlenwasserstoff*) CFC
FdH (*umg*) ABK (= *Friss die Hälfte*) eat less

f

FDP, F.D.P. F ABK (= *Freie Demokratische Partei*) Free Democratic Party

> The **FDP** (Freie Demokratische Partei) was founded in 1948 and is Germany's centre party. It is a liberal party which has formed governing coalitions with both the **SPD** and the **CDU/CSU** at times, both in the regions and in the **Bundestag**.

Feb. ABK (= *Februar*) Feb.

Februar ['fe:brua:r] **(-(s), -e)** (*pl selten*) M February; *siehe auch* **September**

fechten ['fɛçtən] *unreg* VI to fence

Feder ['fe:dər] **(-, -n)** F feather; (*Schreibfeder*) pen nib; (*Tech*) spring; **in den Federn liegen** (*umg*) to be/stay in bed; **Federball** M shuttlecock; **Federballspiel** NT badminton; **Federbett** NT continental quilt; **federführend** ADJ (*Behörde*): **federführend (für)** in overall charge (of); **Federhalter** M pen; **federleicht** ADJ light as a feather; **Federlesen** NT: **nicht viel Federlesens mit jdm/etw machen** to make short work of sb/sth

federn VI (*nachgeben*) to be springy; (*sich bewegen*) to bounce ▶ VT to spring

Federung F suspension

Federvieh NT poultry

Federweiße(r) M new wine

Federzeichnung F pen-and-ink drawing

Fee [fe:] **(-, -n)** F fairy

feenhaft ['fe:ənhaft] ADJ (*liter*) fairylike

Fegefeuer ['fe:gəfɔʏər] NT purgatory

fegen ['fe:gən] VT to sweep

fehl [fe:l] ADJ: **~ am Platz** *od* **Ort** out of place; **Fehlanzeige** (*umg*) F dead loss

fehlen VI to be wanting *od* missing; (*abwesend sein*) to be absent ▶ VI UNPERS: **es fehlte nicht viel und ich hätte ihn verprügelt** I almost hit him; **etw fehlt jdm** sb lacks sth; **du fehlst mir** I miss you; **was fehlt ihm?** what's wrong with him?; **der/das hat mir gerade noch gefehlt!** (*ironisch*) he/that was all I needed; **weit gefehlt!** (*fig*) you're way out! (*umg*); (*ganz im Gegenteil*) far from it!; **mir ~ die Worte** words fail me; **wo fehlt es?** what's the trouble?, what's up? (*umg*)

Fehlentscheidung F wrong decision

Fehlentwicklung F mistake

Fehler (-s, -) M mistake, error; (*Mangel, Schwäche*) fault; **ihr ist ein ~ unterlaufen** she's made a mistake; **Fehlerbeseitigung** F (*Comput*) debugging; **fehlerfrei** ADJ without any mistakes; (*ohne Mängel*) faultless; **fehlerhaft** ADJ incorrect; (*mangelhaft*) faulty; **fehlerlos** ADJ = **fehlerfrei**; **Fehlermeldung** F (*Comput*) error message; **Fehlersuchprogramm** NT (*Comput*) debugger

fehl- ZW: **Fehlgeburt** F miscarriage; **fehlgehen** *unreg* VI to go astray; **Fehlgriff** M blunder; **Fehlkonstruktion** F: **eine Fehlkonstruktion sein** to be badly designed; **Fehlleistung** F: **freudsche Fehlleistung** Freudian slip; **Fehlschlag** M failure; **fehlschlagen** *unreg* VI to fail; **Fehlschluss** M wrong conclusion; **Fehlstart** M (*Sport*) false start; **Fehltritt** M false move; (*fig*) blunder, slip; (*: Affäre*) indiscretion; **Fehlurteil** NT miscarriage of justice; **Fehlzündung** F (*Aut*) misfire, backfire

Feier ['faɪər] **(-, -n)** F celebration; **Feierabend** M *end of the working day*; **Feierabend haben** to finish work; **nach Feierabend** after work; **jetzt ist Feierabend!** that's enough!

feierlich ADJ solemn; **das ist ja nicht mehr ~** (*umg*) that's beyond a joke; **Feierlichkeit** F solemnity; **Feierlichkeiten** PL festivities *pl*

feiern VT, VI to celebrate

Feiertag M holiday

feig ADJ cowardly

feige ADJ cowardly

Feige ['faɪgə] **(-, -n)** F fig

Feigheit F cowardice

Feigling M coward

Feile ['faɪlə] **(-, -n)** F file

feilen VT, VI to file

feilschen ['faɪlʃən] VI to haggle

fein [faɪn] ADJ fine; (*vornehm*) refined; (*Gehör etc*) keen; **~!** great!; **er ist ~ raus** (*umg*) he's sitting pretty; **sich ~ machen** to get all dressed up

Feind(in) [faɪnt, 'faɪndɪn] **(-(e)s, -e)** M(F) enemy; **Feindbild** NT concept of an/the enemy; **feindlich** ADJ hostile; **Feindschaft** F enmity; **feindselig** ADJ hostile; **Feindseligkeit** F hostility

Fein- ZW: **feinfühlend** ADJ sensitive; **feinfühlig** ADJ sensitive; **Feingefühl** NT delicacy, tact; **Feinheit** F fineness; (*Vornehmheit*) refinement; (*von Gehör*) keenness; **Feinkost (-)** F delicacies *pl*; **Feinkostgeschäft** NT delicatessen (shop), deli; **Feinschmecker (-s, -)** M gourmet; **Feinstaub** M particulate matter; **Feinwaschmittel** NT mild(-action) detergent

feist [faɪst] ADJ fat

feixen ['faɪksən] (*umg*) VI to smirk

Feld [fɛlt] **(-(e)s, -er)** NT field; (*Schach*) square; (*Sport*) pitch; **Argumente ins ~ führen** to bring arguments to bear; **das ~ räumen** (*fig*) to bow out; **Feldarbeit** F (*Agr*) work in the fields; (*Geog etc*) fieldwork; **Feldblume** F wild flower; **Feldherr** M commander; **Feldjäger** PL (*Mil*) the military police; **Feldlazarett** NT (*Mil*) field hospital; **Feldsalat** M lamb's lettuce; **Feldstecher** M (pair of) binoculars *pl od* field glasses *pl*

Feld-Wald-und-Wiesen- (*umg*) IN ZW common-or-garden

Feld- ZW: **Feldwebel (-s, -)** M sergeant; **Feldweg** M path; **Feldzug** M (*lit, fig*) campaign

Felge ['fɛlgə] **(-, -n)** F (wheel) rim

Felgenbremse F caliper brake

Fell [fɛl] **(-(e)s, -e)** NT fur; (*von Schaf*) fleece; (*von toten Tieren*) skin; **ein dickes ~ haben** to be thick-skinned, to have a thick skin; **ihm sind die Felle weggeschwommen** (*fig*) all his hopes were dashed

Fels [fɛls] **(-en, -en)** M, **Felsen** ['fɛlzən] **(-s, -)** M rock; (*Klippe*) cliff; **felsenfest** ADJ firm

felsig ADJ rocky

Felsspalte F crevice
Felsvorsprung M ledge
feminin [femi'ni:n] ADJ feminine; (*pej*) effeminate
Feministin [femi'nɪstɪn] F feminist
Fenchel ['fɛnçəl] (**-s**) M fennel
Fenster ['fɛnstər] (**-s, -**) NT window; **weg vom ~** (*umg*) out of the game, finished; **Fensterbrett** NT windowsill; **Fensterladen** M shutter; **Fensterleder** NT chamois, shammy (leather); **Fensterplatz** M window seat; **Fensterputzer** (**-s, -**) M window cleaner; **Fensterscheibe** F windowpane; **Fenstersims** M windowsill
Ferien ['fe:riən] PL holidays *pl*, vacation (*US*); **die großen ~** the summer holidays (BRIT), the long vacation (*US Univ*); **~ haben** to be on holiday; **Ferienhaus** NT holiday home; **Ferienkurs** M holiday course; **Ferienlager** NT holiday camp (BRIT), vacation camp (*US*); (*für Kinder im Sommer*) summer camp; **Ferienreise** F holiday; **Ferienwohnung** F holiday flat (BRIT), vacation apartment (*US*); **Ferienzeit** F holiday period
Ferkel ['fɛrkəl] (**-s, -**) NT piglet
fern [fɛrn] ADJ, ADV far-off, distant; **~ von hier** a long way (away) from here; *siehe auch* **fernhalten**; **fernliegen**; **Fernamt** NT (*Tel*) exchange; **Fernbedienung** F remote control; **fernbleiben** *unreg* VI: **fernbleiben (von** *od* **+*dat*)** to stay away (from)
Ferne (**-, -n**) F distance
ferner ADJ, ADV further; (*weiterhin*) in future; **unter „~ liefen" rangieren** (*umg*) to be an also-ran
fern- zW: **Fernfahrer** M long-distance lorry (BRIT) *od* truck driver; **Fernflug** M long-distance flight; **Ferngespräch** NT long-distance call (BRIT), toll call (*US*); **ferngesteuert** ADJ remote-controlled; (*Rakete*) guided; **Fernglas** NT binoculars *pl*; **fernhalten** *unreg* VT to keep away; **Fernkopie** F fax; **Fernkopierer** M fax machine; **Fernkurs, Fernkursus** M correspondence course; **Fernlenkung** F remote control; **Fernlicht** NT (*Aut*): **mit Fernlicht fahren** to drive on full beam; **fernliegen** *unreg* VI: **jdm fernliegen** to be far from sb's mind
Fernmelde- IN zW telecommunications; (*Mil*) signals
fern- zW: **Fernost** M **aus/in Fernost** from/in the Far East; **fernöstlich** ADJ Far Eastern *attrib*; **Fernrohr** NT telescope; **Fernschreiben** NT telex; **Fernschreiber** M teleprinter; **fernschriftlich** ADJ by telex
Fernsehapparat M television (set)
Fernsehduell NT TV duel *od* debate
fernsehen ['fɛrnze:ən] *unreg* VI to watch television; **Fernsehen** (**-s**) NT television; **im Fernsehen** on television
Fernseher (**-s, -**) M television (set)
Fernseh- zW: **Fernsehgebühr** F television licence (BRIT) *od* license (*US*) fee; **Fernsehgerät** NT television set; **Fernsehprogramm** NT (*Kanal*) channel, station (*US*); (*Sendung*) programme (BRIT), program (*US*); (*Fernsehzeitschrift*) (television) programme (BRIT) *od* program (*US*) guide; **Fernsehsendung** F television programme (BRIT) *od* program (*US*); **Fernsehüberwachungsanlage** F closed-circuit television; **Fernsehzuschauer** M (television) viewer
Fern- zW: **Fernsprecher** M telephone; **Fernsprechzelle** F telephone box (BRIT) *od* booth (*US*); **Fernsteuerung** F remote control; **Fernstraße** F major road; **Fernstudium** NT multimedia course, ≈ Open University course (BRIT); *see note*

> **Fernstudium** is a distance-learning degree course where students do not go to university but receive their tuition by letter, television or radio programmes. There is no personal contact between student and lecturer. The first Fernstudium was founded in 1974. Students are free to practise their career or to bring up a family at the same time as studying.

Fernverkehr M long-distance traffic
Fernweh NT wanderlust
Ferse ['fɛrzə] (**-, -n**) F heel
Fersengeld NT: **~ geben** to take to one's heels
fertig ['fɛrtɪç] ADJ (*bereit*) ready; (*beendet*) finished; (*gebrauchsfertig*) ready-made; **~ ausgebildet** fully qualified; **mit jdm/etw ~ werden** to cope with sb/sth; **mit den Nerven ~ sein** to be at the end of one's tether; **~ bringen** *od* **machen** (*beenden*) to finish; **sich ~ machen** to get ready; **~ essen/lesen** to finish eating/reading; **Fertigbau** M prefab(ricated house); **fertigbringen** *unreg* VT (*fähig sein*) to manage, to be capable of; (*beenden*) to finish
fertigen ['fɛrtɪgən] VT to manufacture
Fertig- zW: **Fertiggericht** NT ready-to-serve meal; **Fertighaus** NT prefab(ricated house); **Fertigkeit** F skill; **fertigmachen** (*umg*) VT (*Person*) to finish; (*körperlich*) to exhaust; (*moralisch*) to get down; *siehe auch* **fertig**; **fertigstellen** VT to complete
Fertigung F production
Fertigungs- IN zW production; **Fertigungsstraße** F production line
Fertigware F finished product
fertigwerden *unreg* VI *siehe* **fertig**
fesch [fɛʃ] (*umg*) ADJ (*modisch*) smart; (*hübsch*) attractive
Fessel ['fɛsəl] (**-, -n**) F fetter
fesseln VT to bind; (*mit Fesseln*) to fetter; (*fig*) to grip; **ans Bett gefesselt** (*fig*) confined to bed
fesselnd ADJ gripping
fest ADJ firm; (*Nahrung*) solid; (*Gehalt*) regular; (*Gewebe, Schuhe*) strong, sturdy; (*Freund(in)*) steady ▸ ADV (*schlafen*) soundly; **~ angestellt** employed on a permanent basis; **~ entschlossen sein** to be absolutely determined; **~ umrissen** clearcut; **feste Kosten** (*Comm*) fixed costs *pl*

Fest [fɛst] (**-(e)s, -e**) NT (*Feier*) celebration; (*Party*) party; **man soll die Feste feiern wie sie fallen** (*Sprichwort*) make hay while the sun shines
Festbeleuchtung F illumination
festbinden *unreg* VT to tie, to fasten
festbleiben *unreg* VI to stand firm
Festessen NT banquet
festfahren *unreg* VR to get stuck
Festgeldkonto NT time-deposit account
festhalten *unreg* VT to seize, to hold fast; (*Ereignis*) to record ▶ VR: **sich ~ (an** *+dat*) to hold on (to)
festigen VT to strengthen
Festigkeit F strength
fest- ZW: **festklammern** VR: **sich festklammern (an** *+dat*) to cling on (to); **festklemmen** VT to wedge fast; **Festkomma** NT (*Comput*) fixed point; **Festland** NT mainland; **festlegen** VT to fix ▶ VR to commit o.s.; **jdn auf etw** *akk* **festlegen** (*festnageln*) to tie sb (down) to sth; (*verpflichten*) to commit sb to sth
festlich ADJ festive
fest- ZW: **festliegen** *unreg* VI (*Fin: Geld*) to be tied up; **festmachen** VT to fasten; (*Termin etc*) to fix; **festnageln** VT: **jdn festnageln (auf** *+akk*) (*fig: umg*) to pin sb down (to); **Festnahme (-, -n)** F capture; **festnehmen** *unreg* VT to capture, to arrest; **Festnetz** NT (*Tel*) landline; **Festnetztelefon** NT fixed-line phone; **Festplatte** F (*Comput*) hard disk; **Festpreis** M (*Comm*) fixed price
Festrede F speech, address
festschnallen VT to strap down ▶ VR to fasten one's seat belt
festsetzen VT to fix, to settle
Festspiel NT festival
fest- ZW: **feststehen** *unreg* VI to be certain; **feststellbar** ADJ (*herauszufinden*) ascertainable; **feststellen** VT to establish; (*sagen*) to remark; (*Tech*) to lock (fast); **Feststellung** F: **die Feststellung machen, dass ...** to realize that ...; (*bemerken*) to remark *od* observe that ...
Festtag M holiday
Festung F fortress
festverzinslich ADJ fixed-interest *attrib*
Festwertspeicher M (*Comput*) read-only memory
Festzelt NT marquee
Fete ['fe:tə] (**-, -n**) F party
fett ADJ fat; (*Essen etc*) greasy; **~ gedruckt** bold-type
Fett [fɛt] (**-(e)s, -e**) NT fat, grease; **fettarm** ADJ low fat; **fetten** VT to grease; **Fettfleck** M grease spot *od* stain; **fettfrei** ADJ fat-free; **Fettgehalt** M fat content; **fettig** ADJ greasy, fatty; **Fettnäpfchen** NT: **ins Fettnäpfchen treten** to put one's foot in it; **Fettpolster** NT (*hum: umg*): **Fettpolster haben** to be well-padded
Fetzen ['fɛtsən] (**-s, -**) M scrap; **..., dass die ~ fliegen** (*umg*) ... like mad
feucht [fɔʏçt] ADJ damp; (*Luft*) humid; **feuchtfröhlich** ADJ (*hum*) boozy
Feuchtigkeit F dampness; (*von Luft*) humidity
Feuchtigkeitscreme F moisturizer
feudal [fɔy'da:l] ADJ (*Pol, Hist*) feudal; (*umg*) plush
Feuer ['fɔʏər] (**-s, -**) NT fire; (*fig: Schwung*) spirit; **für jdn durchs ~ gehen** to go through fire and water for sb; **~ und Flamme (für etw) sein** (*umg*) to be dead keen (on sth); **~ für etw/jdn fangen** (*fig*) to develop a great interest in sth/sb; **haben Sie ~?** have you got a light?; **Feueralarm** M fire alarm; **Feuereifer** M zeal; **feuerfest** ADJ fireproof; **Feuergefahr** F danger of fire; **bei Feuergefahr** in the event of fire; **feuergefährlich** ADJ inflammable; **Feuerleiter** F fire escape ladder; **Feuerlöscher (-s, -)** M fire extinguisher; **Feuermelder (-s, -)** M fire alarm
feuern VT, VI (*lit, fig*) to fire
Feuer- ZW: **feuerpolizeilich** ADJ (*Bestimmungen*) laid down by the fire authorities; **Feuerprobe** F acid test; **feuerrot** ADJ fiery red
Feuersbrunst F (*geh*) conflagration
Feuer- ZW: **Feuerschlucker** M fire-eater; **Feuerschutz** M (*Vorbeugung*) fire prevention; (*Mil: Deckung*) covering fire; **feuersicher** ADJ fireproof; **Feuerstein** M flint; **Feuerstelle** F fireplace; **Feuertreppe** F fire escape; **Feuerversicherung** F fire insurance; **Feuerwaffe** F firearm; **Feuerwehr** F fire brigade; **Feuerwehrauto** NT fire engine; **Feuerwehrfrau** F firewoman, fire fighter; **Feuerwehrmann** M fireman, fire fighter; **Feuerwerk** NT fireworks *pl*; **Feuerwerkskörper** M firework; **Feuerzangenbowle** F *red wine punch containing rum which has been flamed off*; **Feuerzeug** NT (cigarette) lighter
Feuilleton [fœjə'tõ:] (**-s, -s**) NT (*Presse*) feature section; (*Artikel*) feature (article)
feurig ['fɔʏrɪç] ADJ fiery
Fiche [fi:ʃ] (**-s, -s**) M OD NT (micro)fiche
ficht [fɪçt] VB *siehe* **fechten**
Fichte ['fɪçtə] (**-, -n**) F spruce
ficken ['fɪkən] (*umg!*) VT, VI to fuck (*umg!*)
fickerig ['fɪkərɪç], **fickrig** ['fɪkrɪç] (*umg*) ADJ fidgety
fidel [fi'de:l] (*umg*) ADJ jolly
Fidschi-Inseln, Fidschiinseln ['fɪdʒiɪnzəln] PL Fiji Islands
Fieber ['fi:bər] (**-s, -**) NT fever, temperature; (*Krankheit*) fever; **~ haben** to have a temperature; **fieberhaft** ADJ feverish; **Fiebermesser** M thermometer; **Fieberthermometer** NT thermometer
fiel *etc* [fi:l] VB *siehe* **fallen**
fies [fi:s] (*umg*) ADJ nasty
Figur [fi'gu:r] (**-, -en**) F figure; (*Schachfigur*) chessman, chess piece; **eine gute/schlechte/traurige ~ abgeben** to cut a good/poor/sorry figure
fiktiv [fɪk'ti:f] ADJ fictitious

Filet [fi'le:] (**-s, -s**) NT (*Koch*) fillet; (*Rinderfilet*) fillet steak; (*zum Braten*) piece of sirloin *od* tenderloin (*US*)
Filiale [fili'a:lə] (**-, -n**) F (*Comm*) branch
Filipino [fili'pi:no] (**-s, -s**) M Filipino
Film [fɪlm] (**-(e)s, -e**) M film, movie (*bes US*); **da ist bei mir der ~ gerissen** (*umg*) I had a mental blackout; **Filmaufnahme** F shooting
Filmemacher(in) M(F) film-maker
filmen VT, VI to film
Film- ZW: **Filmfestspiele** PL film festival *sing*; **Filmkamera** F cine-camera; **Filmriss** (*umg*) M mental blackout; **Filmschauspieler(in)** M(F) film *od* movie (*bes US*) actor, film *od* movie actress; **Filmverleih** M film distributors *pl*; **Filmvorführgerät** NT cine-projector
Filter ['fɪltər] (**-s, -**) M filter; **Filterkaffee** M filter *od* drip (*US*) coffee; **Filtermundstück** NT filter tip
filtern VT to filter
Filterpapier NT filter paper
Filterzigarette F tipped cigarette
Filz [fɪlts] (**-es, -e**) M felt
filzen VT (*umg*) to frisk ▶ VI (*Wolle*) to mat
Filzstift M felt-tip (pen)
Fimmel ['fɪməl] (**-s, -**) (*umg*) M: **du hast wohl einen ~!** you're crazy!
Finale [fi'na:lə] (**-s, -(s)**) NT finale; (*Sport*) final(s *pl*)
Finanz [fi'nants] F finance; **Finanzen** PL finances *pl*; **das übersteigt meine Finanzen** that's beyond my means; **Finanzamt** NT ≈ Inland Revenue Office (BRIT), ≈ Internal Revenue Office (*US*); **Finanzbeamte(r)** F(M) revenue officer; **Finanzdienstleister(in)** M(F) (*Bank etc*) financial services provider
finanziell [finantsi'ɛl] ADJ financial
finanzieren [finan'tsi:rən] VT to finance, to fund
Finanzierung F financing, funding
Finanz- ZW: **Finanzminister** M ≈ Chancellor of the Exchequer (BRIT), Minister of Finance; **finanzschwach** ADJ financially weak; **Finanzwesen** NT financial system; **Finanzwirtschaft** F public finances *pl*
finden ['fɪndən] *unreg* VT to find; (*meinen*) to think ▶ VR to be (found); (*sich fassen*) to compose o.s. ▶ VI: **ich finde schon allein hinaus** I can see myself out; **ich finde es gut/schlecht** I like/don't like it; **ich finde nichts dabei, wenn ...** I don't see what's wrong if ...; **das wird sich ~** things will work out
Finder(in) (**-s, -**) M(F) finder; **Finderlohn** M reward (for the finder)
findig ADJ resourceful
fing *etc* [fɪŋ] VB *siehe* **fangen**
Finger ['fɪŋər] (**-s, -**) M finger; **mit Fingern auf jdn zeigen** (*fig*) to look askance at sb; **das kann sich jeder an den (fünf) Fingern abzählen** (*umg*) it sticks out a mile; **sich** *dat* **etw aus den Fingern saugen** to conjure sth up; **lange ~ machen** (*umg*) to be light-fingered; **Fingerabdruck** M fingerprint; **Fingerhandschuh** M glove; **Fingerhut** M thimble; (*Bot*) foxglove; **Fingernagel** M fingernail; **Fingerring** M ring; **Fingerspitze** F fingertip; **Fingerspitzengefühl** NT sensitivity; **Fingerzeig** (**-(e)s, -e**) M hint, pointer
fingieren [fɪŋ'gi:rən] VT to feign
fingiert ADJ made-up, fictitious
Fink ['fɪŋk] (**-en, -en**) M finch
Finne ['fɪnə] (**-n, -n**) M Finn
Finnin ['fɪnɪn] F Finn
finnisch ADJ Finnish
Finnland NT Finland
finster ['fɪnstər] ADJ dark, gloomy; (*verdächtig*) dubious; (*verdrossen*) grim; (*Gedanke*) dark; **jdn ~ ansehen** to give sb a black look; **Finsternis** (**-**) F darkness, gloom
Finte ['fɪntə] (**-, -n**) F feint, trick
Firlefanz ['fɪrləfants] (*umg*) M (*Kram*) frippery; (*Albernheit*): **mach keinen ~** don't clown around
firm [fɪrm] ADJ well-up
Firma (**-, -men**) F firm; **die ~ dankt** (*hum*) much obliged (to you)
Firmen- ZW: **Firmeninhaber** M proprietor (*of firm*); **Firmenregister** NT register of companies; **Firmenschild** NT (shop) sign; **Firmenübernahme** F takeover; **Firmenwagen** M company car; **Firmenzeichen** NT trademark
Firmung F (*Rel*) confirmation
Firnis ['fɪrnɪs] (**-ses, -se**) M varnish
Fis [fɪs] (**-, -**) NT (*Mus*) F sharp
Fisch [fɪʃ] (**-(e)s, -e**) M fish; **Fische** PL (*Astrol*) Pisces *sing*; **das sind kleine Fische** (*fig: umg*) that's child's play; **Fischbestand** M fish population
fischen VT, VI to fish
Fischer (**-s, -**) M fisherman
Fischerei [fɪʃə'raɪ] F fishing, fishery
Fisch- ZW: **Fischfang** M fishing; **Fischgeschäft** NT fishmonger's (shop); **Fischgräte** F fishbone; **Fischgründe** PL fishing grounds *pl*, fisheries *pl*; **Fischstäbchen** NT fish finger (BRIT), fish stick (*US*); **Fischzucht** F fish-farming; **Fischzug** M catch of fish
Fisimatenten [fizima'tɛntən] (*umg*) PL (*Ausflüchte*) excuses *pl*; (*Umstände*) fuss *sing*
Fiskus ['fɪskʊs] M (*fig: Staatskasse*) Treasury
fit [fɪt] ADJ fit
Fitness ['fɪtnəs] NT fitness
Fitnesscenter (**-s, -**) NT fitness centre
Fitnesstrainer(in) M(F) fitness trainer, personal trainer
Fittich ['fɪtɪç] (**-(e)s, -e**) M (*liter*): **jdn unter seine Fittiche nehmen** (*hum*) to take sb under one's wing
fix [fɪks] ADJ (*flink*) quick; (*Person*) alert, smart; **fixe Idee** obsession, idée fixe; **~ und fertig** finished; (*erschöpft*) done in; **jdn ~ und fertig machen** (*nervös machen*) to drive sb mad
fixen (*umg*) VI (*Drogen spritzen*) to fix
Fixer(in) ['fɪksər(ɪn)] (*umg*) M(F) junkie (*umg*); **Fixerstube** (*umg*) F junkies' centre (*umg*)

fixieren [fɪ'ksi:rən] VT to fix; (*anstarren*) to stare at; **er ist zu stark auf seine Mutter fixiert** (*Psych*) he has a mother fixation
Fixkosten PL (*Comm*) fixed costs *pl*
FKK ABK = **Freikörperkultur**
flach [flax] ADJ flat; (*Gefäß*) shallow; **auf dem flachen Land** in the middle of the country; **Flachbildschirm** M flat screen
Fläche ['flɛçə] (-, **-n**) F area; (*Oberfläche*) surface
Flächeninhalt M surface area
Flach- zW: **flachfallen** *unreg* (*umg*) VI to fall through; **Flachheit** F flatness; (*von Gefäß*) shallowness; **Flachland** NT lowland; **flachliegen** *unreg* (*umg*) VI to be laid up; **Flachmann** (**-(e)s**, *pl* **-männer**) (*umg*) M hip flask
flachsen ['flaksən] (*umg*) VI to kid around
flackern ['flakərn] VI to flare, to flicker
Fladen ['fla:dən] (**-s, -**) M (*Koch*) round flat dough-cake; (*umg: Kuhfladen*) cowpat
Flagge ['flagə] (-, **-n**) F flag; **~ zeigen** (*fig*) to nail one's colours to the mast
flaggen VI to fly flags *od* a flag
flagrant [fla'grant] ADJ flagrant; **in flagranti** red-handed
Flak [flak] (**-s, -**) F (= *Flug(zeug)abwehrkanone*) anti-aircraft gun; (*Einheit*) anti-aircraft unit
flambieren [flam'bi:rən] VT (*Koch*) to flambé
Flame ['fla:mə] (**-n, -n**) M Fleming
Flämin ['flɛ:mɪn] F Fleming
flämisch ['flɛ:mɪʃ] ADJ Flemish
Flamme ['flamə] (-, **-n**) F flame; **in Flammen stehen/aufgehen** to be in/go up in flames
Flandern ['flandərn] NT Flanders *sing*
Flanell [fla'nɛl] (**-s, -e**) M flannel
Flanke ['flaŋkə] (-, **-n**) F flank; (*Sport: Seite*) wing
Flasche ['flaʃə] (-, **-n**) F bottle; (*umg: Versager*) wash-out; **zur ~ greifen** (*fig*) to hit the bottle
Flaschen- zW: **Flaschenbier** NT bottled beer; **Flaschenöffner** M bottle opener; **Flaschenpfand** NT deposit; **Flaschenwein** M bottled wine; **Flaschenzug** M pulley
flatterhaft ADJ flighty, fickle
flattern ['flatərn] VI to flutter
flau [flaʊ] ADJ (*Brise, Comm*) slack; **jdm ist ~ (im Magen)** sb feels queasy
Flaum [flaʊm] (**-(e)s**) M (*Feder*) down
flauschig ['flaʊʃɪç] ADJ fluffy
Flausen ['flaʊzən] PL silly ideas *pl*; (*Ausflüchte*) weak excuses *pl*
Flaute ['flaʊtə] (-, **-n**) F calm; (*Comm*) recession
Flechte ['flɛçtə] (-, **-n**) F (*Med*) dry scab; (*Bot*) lichen
flechten *unreg* VT to plait; (*Kranz*) to twine
Fleck [flɛk] (**-(e)s, -e**) M (*Schmutzfleck*) stain; (*Farbfleck*) patch; (*Stelle*) spot; **nicht vom ~ kommen** (*lit, fig*) not to get any further; **sich nicht vom ~ rühren** not to budge; **vom ~ weg** straight away
Fleckchen NT: **ein schönes ~ (Erde)** a lovely little spot
Flecken (**-s, -**) M = **Fleck**; **fleckenlos** ADJ spotless; **Fleckenmittel** NT stain remover; **Fleckenwasser** NT stain remover
fleckig ADJ marked; (*schmutzig*) stained
Fledermaus ['fle:dərmaʊs] F bat
Flegel ['fle:gəl] (**-s, -**) M flail; (*Person*) lout; **flegelhaft** ADJ loutish, unmannerly; **Flegeljahre** PL adolescence *sing*
flegeln VR to loll, to sprawl
flehen ['fle:ən] VI (*geh*) to implore
flehentlich ADJ imploring
Fleisch ['flaɪʃ] (**-(e)s**) NT flesh; (*Essen*) meat; **sich** *dat, akk* **ins eigene ~ schneiden** to cut off one's nose to spite one's face (*Sprichwort*); **es ist mir in ~ und Blut übergegangen** it has become second nature to me; **Fleischbrühe** F meat stock
Fleischer (**-s, -**) M butcher
Fleischerei [flaɪʃə'raɪ] F butcher's (shop)
fleischig ADJ fleshy
Fleisch- zW: **Fleischkäse** M meat loaf; **fleischlich** ADJ carnal; **Fleischpastete** F meat pie; **Fleischsalat** M diced meat salad with mayonnaise; **Fleischtomate** F beef tomato; **Fleischvergiftung** F food poisoning (*from meat*); **Fleischwolf** M mincer; **Fleischwunde** F flesh wound; **Fleischwurst** F pork sausage
Fleiß ['flaɪs] (**-es**) M diligence, industry; **ohne ~ kein Preis** (*Sprichwort*) success never comes easily
fleißig ADJ diligent, industrious; **~ studieren/ arbeiten** to study/work hard
flektieren [flɛk'ti:rən] VT to inflect
flennen ['flɛnən] (*umg*) VI to cry, to blubber
fletschen ['flɛtʃən] VT (*Zähne*) to show
Fleurop® ['flɔyrɔp] F ≈ Interflora®
flexibel [flɛ'ksi:bəl] ADJ flexible
Flexibilität [flɛksibili'tɛ:t] F flexibility
flicht [flɪçt] VB *siehe* **flechten**
flicken VT to mend
Flicken ['flɪkən] (**-s, -**) M patch
Flickschusterei ['flɪkʃu:stəraɪ] F: **das ist ~** that's a patch-up job
Flieder ['fli:dər] (**-s, -**) M lilac
Fliege ['fli:gə] (-, **-n**) F fly; (*Schlips*) bow tie; **zwei Fliegen mit einer Klappe schlagen** (*Sprichwort*) to kill two birds with one stone; **ihn stört die ~ an der Wand** every little thing irritates him
fliegen *unreg* VT, VI to fly; **auf jdn/etw ~** (*umg*) to be mad about sb/sth; **aus der Kurve ~** to skid off the bend; **aus der Firma ~** (*umg*) to get the sack
fliegend ADJ *attrib* flying; **fliegende Hitze** hot flushes *pl*
Fliegengewicht NT (*Sport, fig*) flyweight
Fliegenklatsche ['fli:gənklatʃə] F fly-swat
Fliegenpilz M fly agaric
Flieger (**-s, -**) M flier, airman; **Fliegeralarm** M air-raid warning
fliehen ['fli:ən] *unreg* VI to flee
Fliehkraft ['fli:kraft] F centrifugal force
Fliese ['fli:zə] (-, **-n**) F tile
Fließband ['fli:sbant] NT assembly *od* production line; **am ~ arbeiten** to work on the assembly *od* production line; **Fließbandarbeit** F

production-line work; **Fließbandproduktion** F assembly-line production
fließen *unreg* VI to flow
fließend ADJ flowing; (*Rede, Deutsch*) fluent; (*Übergang*) smooth; **~es Wasser** running water
Fließ- ZW: **Fließheck** NT fastback; **Fließkomma** NT (*Comput*) ≈ floating point; **Fließpapier** NT blotting paper (BRIT), fleece paper (US)
Flimmerkasten (*umg*) M (*Fernsehen*) box
Flimmerkiste (*umg*) F (*Fernsehen*) box
flimmern ['flɪmərn] VI to glimmer; **es flimmert mir vor den Augen** my head's swimming
flink [flɪŋk] ADJ nimble, lively; **mit etw ~ bei der Hand sein** to be quick (off the mark) with sth; **Flinkheit** F nimbleness, liveliness
Flinte ['flɪntə] (-, -n) F shotgun; **die ~ ins Korn werfen** to throw in the sponge
Flirt [flœrt] (-s, -s) M flirtation; **einen ~ (mit jdm) haben** flirt (with sb)
flirten ['flɪrtən] VI to flirt
Flittchen (*pej, umg*) NT floozy
Flitter (-s, -) M (*Flitterschmuck*) sequins *pl*
Flitterwochen PL honeymoon *sing*
flitzen ['flɪtsən] VI to flit
Flitzer (-s, -) (*umg*) M (*Auto*) sporty car
floaten ['flo:tən] VT, VI (*Fin*) to float
flocht *etc* [flɔxt] VB *siehe* **flechten**
Flocke ['flɔkə] (-, -n) F flake
flockig ADJ flaky
flog *etc* [flo:k] VB *siehe* **fliegen**
floh *etc* VB *siehe* **fliehen**
Floh [flo:] (-(e)s, Flöhe) M flea; **jdm einen ~ ins Ohr setzen** (*umg*) to put an idea into sb's head
Flohmarkt M flea market
Flora ['flo:ra] (-, -ren) F flora
Florenz [flo'rɛnts] NT Florence
florieren [flo'ri:rən] VI to flourish
Florist(in) M(F) florist
Floskel ['flɔskəl] (-, -n) F set phrase; **floskelhaft** ADJ cliché-ridden, stereotyped
floss *etc* [flɔs] VB *siehe* **fließen**
Floß [flo:s] (-es, Flöße) NT raft
Flosse ['flɔsə] (-, -n) F fin; (*Taucherflosse*) flipper; (*umg: Hand*) paw
Flöte ['flø:tə] (-, -n) F flute; (*Blockflöte*) recorder
flöten gehen ['flø:tənge:ən] (*umg*) VI *unreg* to go for a burton
Flötist(in) [flø'tɪst(ɪn)] M(F) flautist, flutist (*bes US*)
flott [flɔt] ADJ lively; (*elegant*) smart; (*Naut*) afloat
Flotte (-, -n) F fleet
Flottenstützpunkt M naval base
flottmachen VT (*Schiff*) to float off; (*Auto, Fahrrad etc*) to put back on the road
Flöz [flø:ts] (-es, -e) NT layer, seam
Fluch [flu:x] (-(e)s, Flüche) M curse; **fluchen** VI to curse, to swear
Flucht [flʊxt] (-, -en) F flight; (*Fensterflucht*) row; (*Reihe*) range; (*Zimmerflucht*) suite; (*geglückt*) flight, escape; **jdn/etw in die ~ schlagen** to put sb/sth to flight
fluchtartig ADJ hasty
flüchten ['flʏçtən] VI to flee ▸ VR to take refuge
Fluchthilfe F: **~ leisten** to aid an escape
flüchtig ADJ fugitive; (*Chem*) volatile; (*oberflächlich*) cursory; (*eilig*) fleeting; **flüchtiger Speicher** (*Comput*) volatile memory; **jdn ~ kennen** to have met sb briefly; **Flüchtigkeit** F transitoriness; (*Chem*) volatility; (*Oberflächlichkeit*) cursoriness; **Flüchtigkeitsfehler** M careless slip
Flüchtling M refugee
Flüchtlingslager NT refugee camp
Flucht- ZW: **Fluchtversuch** M escape attempt; **Fluchtweg** M escape route
Flug [flu:k] (-(e)s, Flüge) M flight; **im ~** airborne, in flight; **wie im ~(e)** (*fig*) in a flash; **Flugabwehr** F anti-aircraft defence; **Flugbahn** F flight path; (*Kreisbahn*) orbit; **Flugbegleiter(in)** M(F) (*Aviat*) flight attendant; **Flugblatt** NT pamphlet
Flügel ['fly:gəl] (-s, -) M wing; (*Mus*) grand piano; **Flügeltür** F double door
flugfähig ADJ able to fly; (*Flugzeug: in Ordnung*) airworthy
Fluggast M airline passenger
flügge ['flʏgə] ADJ (fully-)fledged; **~ werden** (*lit*) to be able to fly; (*fig*) to leave the nest
Flug- ZW: **Fluggeschwindigkeit** F flying *od* air speed; **Fluggesellschaft** F airline (company); **Flughafen** M airport; **Flughöhe** F altitude (of flight); **Flugkarte** F airline ticket; **Fluglotse** M air traffic *od* flight controller; **Flugplan** M flight schedule; **Flugplatz** M airport; (*klein*) airfield; **Flugreise** F flight
flugs [flʊks] ADV speedily
Flug- ZW: **Flugsand** M drifting sand; **Flugschein** M (*von Pilot*) pilot's licence (BRIT) *od* license (US); **Flugschreiber** M flight recorder; **Flugschrift** F pamphlet; **Flugsteig** M gate; **Flugstrecke** F air route; **Flugticket** NT plane ticket; **Flugverkehr** M air traffic; **Flugwesen** NT aviation
Flugzeug (-(e)s, -e) NT plane, aeroplane (BRIT), airplane (US); **Flugzeugentführung** F hijacking of a plane; **Flugzeughalle** F hangar; **Flugzeugträger** M aircraft carrier
fluktuieren [flʊktu'i:rən] VI to fluctuate
Flunder ['flʊndər] (-, -n) F flounder
flunkern ['flʊŋkərn] VI to fib, to tell stories
Fluor ['flu:ɔr] (-s) NT fluorine
Flur[1] [flu:r] (-(e)s, -e) M hall; (*Treppenflur*) staircase
Flur[2] [flu:r] (-, -en) F (*geh*) open fields *pl*; **allein auf weiter ~ stehen** (*fig*) to be out on a limb
Fluss [flʊs] (-es, Flüsse) M river; (*Fließen*) flow; **im ~ sein** (*fig*) to be in a state of flux; **etw in ~** *akk* **bringen** to get sth moving; **flussab, flussabwärts** ADV downstream; **flussauf, flussaufwärts** ADV upstream; **Flussdiagramm** NT flow chart
flüssig ['flʏsɪç] ADJ liquid; (*Stil*) flowing; **flüssiges Vermögen** (*Comm*) liquid assets *pl*;

f

Flüssigkeit F liquid; (*Zustand*) liquidity; **flüssigmachen** VT (*Geld*) to make available
Flussmündung F estuary
Flusspferd NT hippopotamus
flüstern ['flʏstərn] VT, VI to whisper
Flüsterpropaganda F whispering campaign
Flut [flu:t] (-, **-en**) F (*lit, fig*) flood; (*Gezeiten*) high tide; **fluten** VI to flood; **Flutlicht** NT floodlight
flutschen ['flʊtʃən] (*umg*) VI (*rutschen*) to slide; (*funktionieren*) to go well
Flutwelle F tidal wave
fl.W. ABK (= *fließendes Wasser*) running water
focht *etc* [fɔxt] VB *siehe* **fechten**
föderativ [fødera'ti:f] ADJ federal
Fohlen ['fo:lən] (**-s**, **-**) NT foal
Föhn [fø:n] (**-(e)s**, **-e**) M foehn, *warm dry alpine wind*; (*Haartrockner*) hairdryer
föhnen VT to blow-dry
Föhre ['fø:rə] (**-**, **-n**) F Scots pine
Folge ['fɔlgə] (**-**, **-n**) F series, sequence; (*Fortsetzung*) instalment (BRIT), installment (US); (*TV, Rundf*) episode; (*Auswirkung*) result; **in rascher ~** in quick succession; **etw zur ~ haben** to result in sth; **Folgen haben** to have consequences; **einer Sache** *dat* **~ leisten** to comply with sth; **Folgeerscheinung** F result, consequence
folgen VI *+dat* to follow ▶ VI (*gehorchen*) to obey; **jdm ~ können** (*fig*) to follow *od* understand sb; **daraus folgt, dass …** it follows from this that …
folgend ADJ following; **im Folgenden** in the following; (*schriftlich*) below
folgendermaßen ['fɔlgəndər'ma:sən] ADV as follows, in the following way
folgenreich ADJ momentous
folgenschwer ADJ momentous
folgerichtig ADJ logical
folgern VT: **~ (aus)** to conclude (from)
Folgerung F conclusion
folgewidrig ADJ illogical
folglich ['fɔlklɪç] ADV consequently
folgsam ['fɔlkza:m] ADJ obedient
Folie ['fo:liə] (**-**, **-n**) F foil
Folienschweißgerät NT shrink-wrap machine
Folklore ['fɔlklo:ər] (**-**) F folklore
Folter ['fɔltər] (**-**, **-n**) F torture; (*Gerät*) rack; **jdn auf die ~ spannen** (*fig*) to keep sb on tenterhooks
foltern VT to torture
Fön® [fø:n] (**-(e)s**, **-e**) M hairdryer
Fonds [fõ:] (**-**, **-**) M (*lit, fig*) fund; (*Fin: Schuldverschreibung*) government bond; **Fondsmanager(in)** [fõ:-] M(F) fund manager
fönen VT *siehe* **föhnen**
Fono-, fono- IN ZW = **Phono-, phono-**
Fontäne [fɔn'tɛ:nə] (**-**, **-n**) F fountain
foppen ['fɔpən] VT to tease
forcieren [fɔr'si:rən] VT to push; (*Tempo*) to force; (*Konsum, Produktion*) to push *od* force up
Förderband ['fœrdərbant] NT conveyor belt
Förderer (**-s**, **-**) M patron
Fördergebiet NT development area
Förderin F patroness
Förderkorb M pit cage
Förderleistung F (*Min*) output
förderlich ADJ beneficial
fordern ['fɔrdərn] VT to demand; (*fig: kosten: Opfer*) to claim; (*: herausfordern*) to challenge
fördern ['fœrdərn] VT to promote; (*unterstützen*) to help; (*Kohle*) to extract; (*finanziell: Projekt*) to sponsor; (*jds Talent, Neigung*) to encourage, to foster
Förderplattform F production platform
Förderstufe F (*Sch*) *first stage of secondary school where abilities are judged*
Förderturm M (*Min*) winding tower; (*auf Bohrstelle*) derrick
Forderung ['fɔrdərʊŋ] F demand
Förderung ['fœrdərʊŋ] F promotion; (*Unterstützung*) help; (*von Kohle*) extraction
Forelle [fo'rɛlə] F trout
Form [fɔrm] (**-**, **-en**) F shape; (*Gestaltung*) form; (*Gussform*) mould; (*Backform*) baking tin; **in ~ von** in the shape of; **in ~ sein** to be in good form *od* shape; **die ~ wahren** to observe the proprieties; **in aller ~** formally
formal [fɔr'ma:l] ADJ formal; (*Besitzer, Grund*) technical
formalisieren [fɔrmali'zi:rən] VT to formalize
Formalität [fɔrmalɪ'tɛ:t] F formality; **alle Formalitäten erledigen** to go through all the formalities
Format [fɔr'ma:t] (**-(e)s**, **-e**) NT format; (*fig*) quality
formatieren [fɔrma'ti:rən] VT (*Text, Diskette*) to format
Formation [fɔrmatsi'o:n] F formation
formbar ADJ malleable
Formblatt NT form
Formel (**-**, **-n**) F formula; (*von Eid etc*) wording; (*Floskel*) set phrase; **formelhaft** ADJ (*Sprache, Stil*) stereotyped
formell [fɔr'mɛl] ADJ formal
formen VT to form, to shape
Formfehler M faux pas, gaffe; (*Jur*) irregularity
Formfleisch NT pressed meat
formieren [fɔr'mi:rən] VT to form ▶ VR to form up
förmlich ['fœrmlɪç] ADJ formal; (*umg*) real; **Förmlichkeit** F formality
formlos ADJ shapeless; (*Benehmen etc*) informal; (*Antrag*) unaccompanied by a form *od* any forms
Formsache F formality
Formular [fɔrmu'la:r] (**-s**, **-e**) NT form
formulieren [fɔrmu'li:rən] VT to formulate
Formulierung F wording
formvollendet ADJ perfect; (*Vase etc*) perfectly formed
forsch [fɔrʃ] ADJ energetic, vigorous
forschen [fɔrʃən] VI to search; (*wissenschaftlich*) to (do) research; **~ nach** to search for
forschend ADJ searching
Forscher (**-s**, **-**) M research scientist; (*Naturforscher*) explorer

Forschung ['fɔrʃʊŋ] F research; **~ und Lehre** research and teaching; **~ und Entwicklung** research and development
Forschungsreise F scientific expedition
Forst [fɔrst] (**-(e)s, -e**) M forest; **Forstarbeiter** M forestry worker
Förster ['fœrstər] (**-s, -**) M forester; (*für Wild*) gamekeeper
Forstwesen NT forestry
Forstwirtschaft F forestry
fort [fɔrt] ADV away; (*verschwunden*) gone; (*vorwärts*) on; **und so ~** and so on; **in einem ~** incessantly; **fortbestehen** *unreg* VI to continue to exist; **fortbewegen** VT, VR to move away; **fortbilden** VR to continue one's education; **Fortbildung** F further education; **fortbleiben** *unreg* VI to stay away; **fortbringen** *unreg* VT to take away; **Fortdauer** F continuance; **fortdauernd** ADJ continuing; (*in der Vergangenheit*) continued ▸ ADV constantly, continuously; **fortfahren** *unreg* VI to depart; (*fortsetzen*) to go on, to continue; **fortführen** VT to continue, to carry on; **Fortgang** M (*Verlauf*) progress; (*Weggang*): **Fortgang (aus)** departure (from); **fortgehen** *unreg* VI to go away; **fortgeschritten** ADJ advanced; **fortkommen** *unreg* VI to get on; (*wegkommen*) to get away; **fortkönnen** *unreg* VI to be able to get away; **fortlassen** VT (*auslassen*) to leave out, to omit; (*weggehen lassen*): **jdn fortlassen** to let sb go; **fortlaufend** ADJ: **fortlaufend nummeriert** consecutively numbered; **fortmüssen** *unreg* VI to have to go; **fortpflanzen** VR to reproduce; **Fortpflanzung** F reproduction
FORTRAN ['fɔrtran] NT FORTRAN
Forts. ABK = **Fortsetzung**
fortschaffen VT to remove
fortschreiten *unreg* VI to advance
Fortschritt ['fɔrtʃrɪt] M advance; **Fortschritte machen** to make progress; **dem ~ dienen** to further progress; **fortschrittlich** ADJ progressive
fortschrittsgläubig ADJ believing in progress
fort- ZW: **fortsetzen** VT to continue; **Fortsetzung** F continuation; (*folgender Teil*) instalment (BRIT), installment (US); **Fortsetzung folgt** to be continued; **Fortsetzungsroman** M serialized novel; **fortwährend** ADJ incessant, continual; **fortwirken** VI to continue to have an effect; **fortziehen** *unreg* VT to pull away ▸ VI to move on; (*umziehen*) to move away
Foto ['fo:to] (**-s, -s**) NT photo(graph); **ein ~ machen** to take a photo(graph); **Fotoalbum** NT photograph album; **Fotoapparat** M camera; **Fotograf(in)** (**-en, -en**) M(F) photographer; **Fotografie** F photography; (*Bild*) photograph; **fotografieren** VT to photograph ▸ VI to take photographs; **Fotohandy** NT camera phone; **Fotokopie** F photocopy; **fotokopieren** VT to photocopy; **Fotokopierer** M photocopier; **Fotokopiergerät** NT photocopier
Foul [faʊl] (**-s, -s**) NT foul
Foyer [foa'je:] (**-s, -s**) NT foyer; (*in Hotel*) lobby, foyer
FPÖ (**-**) F ABK (= *Freiheitliche Partei Österreichs*) Austrian Freedom Party
Fr. ABK (= *Frau*) Mrs, Ms
Fracht [fraxt] (**-, -en**) F freight; (*Naut*) cargo; (*Preis*) carriage; **~ zahlt Empfänger** (*Comm*) carriage forward; **Frachtbrief** M consignment note, waybill
Frachter (**-s, -**) M freighter
Fracht- ZW: **frachtfrei** ADJ (*Comm*) carriage paid *od* free; **Frachtgut** NT freight; **Frachtkosten** PL (*Comm*) freight charges *pl*
Frack [frak] (**-(e)s, Fräcke**) M tails *pl*, tail coat
Frage ['fra:gə] (**-, -n**) F question; **jdm eine ~ stellen** to ask sb a question, to put a question to sb; **das ist gar keine ~, das steht außer ~** there's no question about it; *siehe auch* **infrage**; **Fragebogen** M questionnaire
fragen VT, VI to ask ▸ VR to wonder; **nach Arbeit/Post ~** to ask whether there is/was any work/mail; **da fragst du mich zu viel** (*umg*) I really couldn't say; **nach** *od* **wegen** (*umg*) **jdm ~** to ask for sb; (*nach jds Befinden*) to ask after sb; **ohne lange zu ~** without asking a lot of questions
Fragerei [fra:gə'raɪ] F questions *pl*
Fragestunde F (*Parl*) question time
Fragezeichen NT question mark
fraglich ADJ questionable, doubtful; (*betreffend*) in question
fraglos ADV unquestionably
Fragment [fra'gmɛnt] NT fragment
fragmentarisch [fragmɛn'ta:rɪʃ] ADJ fragmentary
fragwürdig ['fra:kvʏrdɪç] ADJ questionable, dubious
Fraktion [fraktsi'o:n] F parliamentary party
Fraktionsvorsitzende(r) F(M) (*Pol*) party whip
Fraktionszwang M requirement to obey the party whip
Franchisekette ['frɛnʃaɪskɛtə] F franchise chain
frank [fraŋk] ADJ frank, candid
Franken[1] ['fraŋkən] NT Franconia
Franken[2] ['fraŋkən] (**-, -**) M: **(Schweizer) ~** (Swiss) Franc
Frankfurt ['fraŋkfʊrt] (**-s**) NT Frankfurt
Frankfurter(in) M(F) native of Frankfurt ▸ ADJ Frankfurt; **Frankfurter Würstchen** PL frankfurters
frankieren [fraŋ'ki:rən] VT to stamp, to frank
Frankiermaschine F franking machine
fränkisch ['fraŋkɪʃ] ADJ Franconian
franko ADV carriage paid; (*Post*) post-paid
Frankreich ['fraŋkraɪç] (**-s**) NT France
Franse ['franzə] (**-, -n**) F fringe
fransen VI to fray
franz. ABK = **französisch**
Franzbranntwein M alcoholic liniment
Franzose [fran'tso:zə] (**-n, -n**) M Frenchman; (*Junge*) French boy

Französin [fran'tsøːzɪn] F Frenchwoman; (*Mädchen*) French girl
französisch ADJ French; **französisches Bett** double bed
Fräse ['frɛːzə] (**-, -n**) F (*Werkzeug*) milling cutter; (*für Holz*) moulding cutter
fraß *etc* [fraːs] VB *siehe* **fressen**
Fraß (**-es, -e**) (*pej, umg*) M (*Essen*) muck
Fratze ['fratsə] (**-, -n**) F grimace; **eine ~ schneiden** to pull *od* make a face
Frau [fraʊ] (**-, -en**) F woman; (*Ehefrau*) wife; (*Anrede*) Mrs, Ms; **~ Doktor** Doctor
Frauen- zW: **Frauenarzt** M gynaecologist (BRIT), gynecologist (US); **Frauenbewegung** F feminist movement; **frauenfeindlich** ADJ anti-women, misogynous; **Frauenhaus** NT women's refuge; **Frauenquote** F recommended proportion of women (employed); **Frauenrechtlerin** F feminist; **Frauenzentrum** NT women's advice centre; **Frauenzimmer** (*pej*) NT female, broad (US)
Fräulein ['frɔʏlaɪn] NT young lady; (*Anrede*) Miss; (*Verkäuferin*) assistant (BRIT), sales clerk (US); (*Kellnerin*) waitress
fraulich ['fraʊlɪç] ADJ womanly
frech [frɛç] ADJ cheeky, impudent; **~ wie Oskar sein** (*umg*) to be a little monkey; **Frechdachs** M cheeky monkey; **Frechheit** F cheek, impudence; **sich** *dat* **(einige) Frechheiten erlauben** to be a bit cheeky (*bes* BRIT) *od* fresh (*bes* US)
Fregatte [fre'gatə] (**-, -n**) F frigate
frei [fraɪ] ADJ free; (*Stelle*) vacant; (*Mitarbeiter*) freelance; (*Geld*) available; (*unbekleidet*) bare; **aus freien Stücken** *od* **freiem Willen** of one's own free will; **~ nach ...** based on ...; **für etw freie Fahrt geben** (*fig*) to give sth the go-ahead; **der Film ist ~ ab 16 (Jahren)** the film may be seen by people of 16 years (of age) and over; **unter freiem Himmel** in the open (air); **morgen/Mittwoch ist ~** tomorrow/Wednesday is a holiday; **„Zimmer ~"** "vacancies"; **auf freier Strecke** (*Eisenb*) between stations; (*Aut*) on the road; **freier Wettbewerb** fair/open competition; **~ Haus** (*Comm*) carriage paid; **~ Schiff** (*Comm*) free on board; **freie Marktwirtschaft** free market economy; **von etw ~ sein** to be free of sth; **im Freien** in the open air; **~ halten** (*Ausfahrt etc*) to keep free; **~ sprechen** to talk without notes; **Freibad** NT open-air swimming pool; **freibekommen** *unreg* VT: **jdn/einen Tag freibekommen** to get sb freed/get a day off; **freiberuflich** ADJ self-employed; **Freibetrag** M tax allowance
Freier (**-s, -**) M suitor
Frei- zW: **Freiexemplar** NT free copy; **freigeben** *unreg* VT: **etw zum Verkauf freigeben** to allow sth to be sold on the open market; **freigebig** ADJ generous; **Freigebigkeit** F generosity; **Freihafen** M free port; **freihalten** *unreg* VT (*bezahlen*) to pay for; *siehe auch* **frei**; **Freihandel** M free trade; **Freihandelszone** F free trade area; **freihändig** ADV (*fahren*) with no hands
Freiheit F freedom; **sich** *dat* **die ~ nehmen, etw zu tun** to take the liberty of doing sth; **freiheitlich** ADJ liberal; (*Verfassung*) based on the principle of liberty; (*Demokratie*) free
Freiheits- zW: **Freiheitsberaubung** F (*Jur*) wrongful deprivation of personal liberty; **Freiheitsdrang** M urge/desire for freedom; **Freiheitskampf** M fight for freedom; **Freiheitskämpfer(in)** M(F) freedom fighter; **Freiheitsrechte** PL civil liberties *pl*; **Freiheitsstrafe** F prison sentence
frei- zW: **freiheraus** ADV frankly; **Freikarte** F free ticket; **freikaufen** VT: **jdn/sich freikaufen** to buy sb's/one's freedom; **freikommen** *unreg* VI to get free; **Freikörperkultur** F nudism; **freilassen** *unreg* VT to (set) free; **Freilauf** M freewheeling; **freilaufend** ADJ (*Hühner*) free-range; **freilegen** VT to expose; **freilich** ADV certainly, admittedly; **ja freilich!** yes of course; **Freilichtbühne** F open-air theatre; **freimachen** VT (*Post*) to frank ▸ VR to arrange to be free; **Tage freimachen** to take days off; **sich freimachen** (*beim Arzt*) to take one's clothes off, to strip; **Freimaurer** M Mason, Freemason
freimütig ['fraɪmyːtɪç] ADJ frank, honest
Frei- zW: **freinehmen** VT: **sich** *dat* **einen Tag freinehmen** to take a day off; **Freiraum** M: **Freiraum (zu)** (*fig*) freedom (for); **freischaffend** ADJ *attrib* freelance; **Freischaltcode** M (*Tel*) connecting *od* enabling code; **Freischärler** (**-s, -**) M guerrilla; **freischwimmen** VR (*fig*) to learn to stand on one's own two feet; **freisetzen** VT (*Energien*) to release; **freisinnig** ADJ liberal; **Freisprechanlage** F hands-free (headset); (*im Auto*) hands-free (car kit); **freisprechen** *unreg* VT: **freisprechen (von)** to acquit (of); **Freispruch** M acquittal; **freistehen** *unreg* VI: **es steht dir frei, das zu tun** you are free to do so; **das steht Ihnen völlig frei** that is completely up to you; **freistellen** VT: **jdm etw freistellen** to leave sth (up) to sb; **Freistoß** M free kick; **Freistunde** F free hour; (*Sch*) free period
Freitag M Friday; *siehe auch* **Dienstag**
freitags ADV on Fridays
Frei- zW: **Freitod** M suicide; **Freiübungen** PL (physical) exercises *pl*; **Freiumschlag** M reply-paid envelope; **Freiwild** NT (*fig*) fair game; **freiwillig** ADJ voluntary; **Freiwillige(r)** F(M) volunteer; **Freizeichen** NT (*Tel*) ringing tone; **Freizeit** F spare *od* free time; **Freizeitgestaltung** F organization of one's leisure time; **Freizeitpark** M leisure park; **freizügig** ADJ liberal, broad-minded; (*mit Geld*) generous
fremd [frɛmt] ADJ (*unvertraut*) strange; (*ausländisch*) foreign; (*nicht eigen*) someone else's; **etw ist jdm ~** sth is foreign to sb; **ich bin hier ~** I'm a stranger here; **sich ~ fühlen** to feel like a stranger; **fremdartig** ADJ strange; **Fremde** (**-**) F (*liter*): **die Fremde** foreign parts *pl*

Fremde(r) F(M) stranger; (*Ausländer*) foreigner
Fremden- zW: **Fremdenführer** M (tourist) guide; (*Buch*) guide (book); **Fremdenlegion** F foreign legion; **Fremdenverkehr** M tourism; **Fremdenverkehrsamt** NT tourist information office; **Fremdenzimmer** NT guest room; **fremdgehen** *unreg* (*umg*) VI to be unfaithful
fremd- zW: **Fremdkapital** NT loan capital; **Fremdkörper** M foreign body; **fremdländisch** ADJ foreign; **Fremdling** M stranger; **Fremdsprache** F foreign language; **Fremdsprachenkorrespondentin** F bilingual secretary; **fremdsprachig** ADJ *attrib* foreign-language; **Fremdwort** NT foreign word
frenetisch [fre'ne:tɪʃ] ADJ frenetic
Frequenz [fre'kvɛnts] F (*Rundf*) frequency
Fresse (-, **-n**) (*umg!*) F (*Mund*) gob; (*Gesicht*) mug
fressen ['frɛsən] *unreg* VT, VI to eat ▶ VR: **sich satt ~** to gorge o.s.; **einen Narren an jdm/etw gefressen haben** to dote on sb/sth
Freude ['frɔydə] (-, **-n**) F joy, delight; **~ an etw** *dat* **haben** to get *od* derive pleasure from sth; **jdm eine ~ machen** *od* **bereiten** to make sb happy
Freudenhaus NT (*veraltet*) house of ill repute
Freudentanz M: **einen ~ aufführen** to dance with joy
freudestrahlend ADJ beaming with delight
freudig ADJ joyful, happy
freudlos ADJ joyless
freuen ['frɔyən] VT UNPERS to make happy *od* pleased ▶ VR to be glad *od* happy; **sich auf etw** *akk* **~** to look forward to sth; **sich über etw** *akk* **~** to be pleased about sth; **sich zu früh ~** to get one's hopes up too soon
Freund ['frɔynt] (**-(e)s, -e**) M friend; (*Liebhaber*) boyfriend; **ich bin kein ~ von so etwas** I'm not one for that sort of thing; **Freundin** F friend; (*Liebhaberin*) girlfriend; **freundlich** ADJ kind, friendly; **bitte recht freundlich!** smile please!; **würden Sie bitte so freundlich sein und das tun?** would you be so kind as to do that?; **freundlicherweise** ADV kindly; **Freundlichkeit** F friendliness, kindness; **Freundschaft** F friendship; **freundschaftlich** ADJ friendly
Frevel ['fre:fəl] (**-s, -**) M: **~ (an** *+dat*) crime *od* offence (against); **frevelhaft** ADJ wicked
Frieden ['fri:dən] (**-s, -**) M peace; **im ~** in peacetime; **~ schließen** to make one's peace; (*Pol*) to make peace; **um des lieben Friedens willen** (*umg*) for the sake of peace and quiet; **ich traue dem ~ nicht** (*umg*) something (fishy) is going on
Friedens- zW: **Friedensbewegung** F peace movement; **Friedensrichter** M justice of the peace; **Friedensschluss** M peace agreement; **Friedenstruppe** F peace-keeping force; **Friedensverhandlungen** PL peace negotiations *pl*; **Friedensvertrag** M peace treaty; **Friedenszeit** F peacetime
fried- zW: **friedfertig** ADJ peaceable; **Friedhof** M cemetery; **friedlich** ADJ peaceful; **etw auf friedlichem Wege lösen** to solve sth by peaceful means
frieren ['fri:rən] *unreg* VI to freeze ▶ VT UNPERS to freeze ▶ VI UNPERS: **heute Nacht hat es gefroren** it was below freezing last night; **ich friere, es friert mich** I am freezing, I'm cold; **wie ein Schneider ~** (*umg*) to be *od* get frozen to the marrow
Fries [fri:s] (**-es, -e**) M (*Archit*) frieze
Friese ['fri:zə] (**-n, -n**) M Fri(e)sian
Friesin ['fri:zɪn] F Fri(e)sian
frigid, frigide ADJ frigid
Frikadelle [frika'dɛlə] F meatball
frisch [frɪʃ] ADJ fresh; (*lebhaft*) lively; **~ gestrichen!** wet paint!; **sich ~ machen** to freshen (o.s.) up; **jdn auf frischer Tat ertappen** to catch sb red-handed *od* in the act
Frische (-) F freshness; (*Lebhaftigkeit*) liveliness; **in alter ~** (*umg*) as always
Frischhaltebeutel M airtight bag
Frischhaltefolie F clingfilm
Frischkäse M cream cheese
frischweg ADV (*munter*) straight out
Friseur [fri'zø:r] M hairdresser
Friseuse [fri'zø:zə] F hairdresser
frisieren [fri'zi:rən] VT (*Haar*) to do; (*fig: Abrechnung*) to fiddle, to doctor ▶ VR to do one's hair; **jdn ~, jdm das Haar ~** to do sb's hair
Frisiersalon M hairdressing salon
Frisiertisch M dressing table
Frisör [fri'zø:r] (**-s, -e**) M = **Friseur**
frisst [frɪst] VB *siehe* **fressen**
Frist [frɪst] (**-, -en**) F period; (*Termin*) deadline; **eine ~ einhalten/verstreichen lassen** to meet a deadline/let a deadline pass; (*bei Rechnung*) to pay/not to pay within the period stipulated; **jdm eine ~ von vier Tagen geben** to give sb four days' grace
fristen VT (*Dasein*) to lead; (*kümmerlich*) to eke out
Fristenlösung F abortion law (*permitting abortion in the first three months*)
fristgerecht ADJ within the period stipulated
fristlos ADJ (*Entlassung*) instant
Frisur [fri'zu:r] F hairdo, hairstyle
Fritteuse [fri'tø:zə] (**-, -n**) F chip pan (BRIT), deep fat fryer
frittieren [fri'ti:rən] VT to deep fry
frivol [fri'vo:l] ADJ frivolous
Frl. ABK (= *Fräulein*) Miss
froh [fro:] ADJ happy, cheerful; **ich bin ~, dass …** I'm glad that …
fröhlich ['frø:lɪç] ADJ merry, happy; **Fröhlichkeit** F merriment, gaiety
frohlocken VI (*geh*) to rejoice; (*pej*) to gloat
Frohsinn M cheerfulness
fromm [frɔm] ADJ pious, good; (*Wunsch*) idle
Frömmelei [frœmə'laɪ] F false piety
Frömmigkeit F piety
frönen ['frø:nən] VI *+dat* to indulge in
Fronleichnam [fro:n'laɪçna:m] (**-(e)s**) M Corpus Christi
Front [frɔnt] (**-, -en**) F front; **klare Fronten schaffen** (*fig*) to clarify the position

frontal [frɔn'ta:l] ADJ frontal; **Frontalangriff** M frontal attack

fror *etc* [fro:r] VB *siehe* **frieren**

Frosch [frɔʃ] (**-(e)s, Frösche**) M frog; (*Feuerwerk*) squib; **sei kein ~!** (*umg*) be a sport!; **Froschmann** M frogman; **Froschperspektive** F: **etw aus der Froschperspektive sehen** to get a worm's-eye view of sth; **Froschschenkel** M frog's leg

Frost [frɔst] (**-(e)s, Fröste**) M frost; **frostbeständig** ADJ frost-resistant; **Frostbeule** F chilblain

frösteln ['frœstəln] VI to shiver

frostig ADJ frosty

Frostschutzmittel NT anti-freeze

Frottee, Frotté [frɔ'te:] (**-(s), -s**) NT OD M towelling

frottieren [frɔ'ti:rən] VT to rub, to towel

Frottierhandtuch NT towel

Frottiertuch NT towel

frotzeln ['frɔtsəln] (*umg*) VT, VI to tease

Frucht [frʊxt] (**-, Früchte**) F (*lit, fig*) fruit; (*Getreide*) corn; (*Embryo*) foetus; **fruchtbar** ADJ fruitful, fertile; **Fruchtbarkeit** F fertility; **Fruchtbecher** M fruit sundae

Früchtchen ['fryçtçən] (*umg*) NT (*Tunichtgut*) good-for-nothing

Fruchteis NT fruit-flavoured ice-cream

fruchten VI to be of use

fruchtlos ADJ fruitless

Fruchtsaft M fruit juice

früh [fry:] ADJ, ADV early; **heute ~** this morning; **von ~ auf** from an early age; **Frühaufsteher** (**-s, -**) M early riser; **Frühdienst** M: **Frühdienst haben** to be on early shift

Frühe (**-**) F early morning; **in aller ~** at the crack of dawn

früher ADJ earlier; (*ehemalig*) former ▶ ADV formerly; **~ war das anders** that used to be different; **~ oder später** sooner or later

frühestens ADV at the earliest

Frühgeburt F premature birth; (*Kind*) premature baby

Frühjahr NT spring

Frühjahrsmüdigkeit F springtime lethargy

Frühjahrsputz M spring-cleaning

Frühling M spring; **im ~** in spring

Frühlingsrolle F spring roll

früh- ZW: **frühreif** ADJ precocious; **Frührentner** M *person who has retired early*; **Frühschicht** F early shift; **Frühschoppen** M morning/lunchtime drink; **Frühsport** M early morning exercise; **Frühstück** NT breakfast; **frühstücken** VI to (have) breakfast; **Frühwarnsystem** NT early warning system; **frühzeitig** ADJ early; (*vorzeitig*) premature

Frust (**-(e)s**) (*umg*) M frustration

frustrieren [frʊs'tri:rən] VT to frustrate

frz. ABK = **französisch**

FSV ABK (= *Fußball-Sportverein*) F.C.

FU (**-**) F ABK (= *Freie Universität Berlin*) *Berlin University*

Fuchs [fʊks] (**-es, Füchse**) M fox

fuchsen (*umg*) VT to rile, to annoy ▶ VR to be annoyed

Füchsin ['fʏksɪn] F vixen

fuchsteufelswild ADJ hopping mad

Fuchtel ['fʊxtl] (**-, -n**) F (*fig: umg*): **unter jds ~** under sb's control *od* thumb

fuchteln ['fʊxtəln] VI to gesticulate wildly

Fuge ['fu:gə] (**-, -n**) F joint; (*Mus*) fugue

fügen ['fy:gən] VT to place, to join ▶ VR UNPERS to happen ▶ VR: **sich ~ (in** *+akk*) to be obedient (to); (*anpassen*) to adapt o.s. (to)

fügsam ['fy:kza:m] ADJ obedient

fühlbar ADJ perceptible, noticeable

fühlen ['fy:lən] VT, VI, VR to feel

Fühler (**-s, -**) M feeler

Fühlung F: **mit jdm in ~ bleiben/stehen** to stay/be in contact *od* touch with sb

fuhr *etc* [fu:r] VB *siehe* **fahren**

Fuhre (**-, -n**) F (*Ladung*) load

führen ['fy:rən] VT to lead; (*Geschäft*) to run; (*Name*) to bear; (*Buch*) to keep; (*im Angebot haben*) to stock ▶ VI to lead ▶ VR to behave; **was führt Sie zu mir?** (*form*) what brings you to me?; **Geld/seine Papiere bei sich ~** (*form*) to carry money/one's papers on one's person; **das führt zu nichts** that will come to nothing

Führer(in) ['fy:rər(ɪn)] (**-s, -**) M(F) leader; (*Fremdenführer*) guide; **Führerhaus** NT cab; **Führerschein** M driving licence (BRIT), driver's license (*US*); **den Führerschein machen** (*Aut*) to learn to drive; (*die Prüfung ablegen*) to take one's (driving) test; **Führerscheinentzug** M disqualification from driving

Fuhrmann ['fu:rman] (**-(e)s,** *pl* **-leute**) M carter

Führung ['fy:rʊŋ] F leadership; (*eines Unternehmens*) management; (*Mil*) command; (*Benehmen*) conduct; (*Museumsführung*) conducted tour

Führungs- ZW: **Führungskraft** F executive; **Führungsstab** M (*Mil*) command; (*Comm*) top management; **Führungsstil** M management style; **Führungszeugnis** NT certificate of good conduct

Fuhrunternehmen NT haulage business

Fuhrwerk NT cart

Fülle ['fʏlə] (**-**) F wealth, abundance

füllen VT to fill; (*Koch*) to stuff ▶ VR to fill (up)

Füllen (**-s, -**) NT foal

Füller (**-s, -**) M fountain pen

Füllfederhalter M fountain pen

Füllgewicht NT (*Comm*) weight at time of packing; (*auf Dosen*) net weight

füllig ['fʏlɪç] ADJ (*Mensch*) corpulent, portly; (*Figur*) ample

Füllung F filling; (*Holzfüllung*) panel

fummeln ['fʊməln] (*umg*) VI to fumble

Fund [fʊnt] (**-(e)s, -e**) M find

Fundament [fʊnda'mɛnt] NT foundation

fundamental ADJ fundamental

Fundamentalismus M fundamentalism

Fundbüro NT lost property office, lost and found (*US*)

Fundgrube F (*fig*) treasure trove

fundieren [fʊn'diːrən] VT to back up
fundiert ADJ sound
fündig ['fʏndɪç] ADJ (*Min*) rich; **~ werden** to make a strike; (*fig*) to strike it lucky
Fundsachen PL lost property *sing*
fünf [fʏnf] NUM five; **seine ~ Sinne beisammen haben** to have all one's wits about one; **~(e) gerade sein lassen** (*umg*) to turn a blind eye; **fünfhundert** NUM five hundred; **fünfjährig** ADJ (*Frist, Plan*) five-year; (*Kind*) five-year-old; **Fünfkampf** M pentathlon
Fünfprozentklausel F (*Parl*) *clause debarring parties with less than 5% of the vote from Parliament; see note*

The **Fünfprozentklausel** is a rule in German Federal elections whereby only those parties who collect at least 5% of the second vote (**Zweitstimme**) receive a parliamentary seat. This is to avoid the parliament being made up of a large number of very small parties which, in the Weimar Republic, led to political instability.

Fünftagewoche F five-day week
fünfte(r, s) ADJ fifth
Fünftel (-**s**, -) NT fifth
fünfzehn NUM fifteen
fünfzig NUM fifty
fungieren [fʊŋ'giːrən] VI to function; (*Person*) to act
Funk [fʊŋk] (-**s**) M radio, wireless (BRIT *old*); **Funkausstellung** F radio and television exhibition
Funke (-**ns**, -**n**) M (*lit, fig*) spark
funkeln VI to sparkle
funkelnagelneu (*umg*) ADJ brand-new
funken VT to radio
Funken (-**s**, -) M = **Funke**
Funker (-**s**, -) M radio operator
Funk- zW: **Funkgerät** NT radio set; **Funkhaus** NT broadcasting centre; **Funkkolleg** NT educational radio broadcasts *pl*; **Funkrufempfänger** M (*Tel*) pager, paging device; **Funkspot** M advertisement on the radio; **Funksprechgerät** NT radio telephone; **Funkspruch** M radio signal; **Funkstation** F radio station; **Funkstille** F (*fig*) ominous silence; **Funkstreife** F police radio patrol; **Funktaxi** NT radio taxi; **Funktelefon** NT cell phone; **Funktelefonnetz** NT radio telephone network
Funktion [fʊŋktsi'oːn] F function; **in ~ treten/sein** to come into/be in operation
Funktionär(in) [fʊŋktsio'nɛːr(ɪn)] (-**s**, -**e**) M(F) functionary, official
funktionieren [fʊŋktsio'niːrən] VI to work, to function
Funktions- zW: **Funktionsbekleidung** F functional wear; **funktionsfähig** ADJ working; **Funktionstaste** F (*Comput*) function key; **funktionstüchtig** ADJ in working order
Funzel [funtsəl] (-, -**n**) (*umg*) F dim lamp
für [fyːr] PRÄP +*akk* for; **was ~ ein ...?** what kind *od* sort of ...?; **fürs Erste** for the moment; **was Sie da sagen, hat etwas ~ sich** there's something in what you're saying; **Tag ~ Tag** day after day; **Schritt ~ Schritt** step by step; **das F~ und Wider** the pros and cons *pl*; **Fürbitte** F intercession
Furche ['fʊrçə] (-, -**n**) F furrow
furchen VT to furrow
Furcht [fʊrçt] (-) F fear; **furchtbar** ADJ terrible, awful
fürchten ['fʏrçtən] VT to be afraid of, to fear ▸ VR: **sich ~ (vor** +*dat*) to be afraid (of)
fürchterlich ADJ awful
furchtlos ADJ fearless
furchtsam ADJ timorous
füreinander [fyːr|aɪ'nandər] ADV for each other
Furie ['fuːriə] (-, -**n**) F (*Mythologie*) fury; (*fig*) hellcat
Furnier [fʊr'niːr] (-**s**, -**e**) NT veneer
Furore [fu'roːrə] NT OD F: **~ machen** (*umg*) to cause a sensation
fürs [fyːrs] = **für das**
Fürsorge ['fyːrzɔrgə] F care; (*Sozialfürsorge*) welfare; **von der ~ leben** to live on social security (BRIT) *od* welfare (*US*); **Fürsorgeamt** NT welfare office
Fürsorger(in) (-**s**, -) M(F) welfare worker
Fürsorgeunterstützung F social security (BRIT), welfare benefit (*US*)
fürsorglich ADJ caring
Fürsprache F recommendation; (*um Gnade*) intercession
Fürsprecher M advocate
Fürst [fʏrst] (-**en**, -**en**) M prince
Fürstentum NT principality
Fürstin F princess
fürstlich ADJ princely
Furt [fʊrt] (-, -**en**) F ford
Furunkel [fu'rʊŋkəl] (-**s**, -) NT OD M boil
Fürwort ['fyːrvɔrt] NT pronoun
furzen ['fʊrtsən] (*umg!*) VI to fart (*umg!*)
Fusion [fuzi'oːn] F amalgamation; (*von Unternehmen*) merger; (*von Atomkernen, Zellen*) fusion
fusionieren [fuzio'niːrən] VT to amalgamate
Fuß [fuːs] (-**es**, **Füße**) M foot; (*von Glas, Säule etc*) base; (*von Möbel*) leg; **zu ~** on foot; **zu ~ gehen** to walk; **bei ~!** heel!; **jdm etw vor die Füße werfen** (*lit*) to throw sth at sb; (*fig*) to tell sb to keep sth; **(festen) ~ fassen** (*lit, fig*) to gain a foothold; (*sich niederlassen*) to settle down; **mit jdm auf gutem ~ stehen** to be on good terms with sb; **auf großem ~ leben** to live the high life
Fußball M football; **Fußballmannschaft** F football (BRIT) *od* soccer team; **Fußballplatz** M football pitch; **Fußballspiel** NT football match; **Fußballspieler** M footballer (BRIT), football player (*US*); **Fußballtoto** M OD NT football pools *pl*
Fußboden M floor; **Fußbodenheizung** F underfloor heating
Fußbremse F (*Aut*) foot brake

fusselig ['fʊsəlɪç] ADJ: **sich** *dat* **den Mund ~ reden** (*umg*) to talk till one is blue in the face
fusseln ['fʊsəln] VI (*Stoff, Kleid etc*) to go bobbly (*umg*)
fußen VI: **~ auf** *+dat* to rest on, to be based on
Fuß- ZW: **Fußende** NT foot; **Fußgänger(in)** (**-s, -**) M(F) pedestrian; **Fußgängerüberführung** F pedestrian bridge; **Fußgängerüberweg** M pedestrian crossing (BRIT), crosswalk (US); **Fußgängerzone** F pedestrian precinct; **Fußleiste** F skirting board (BRIT), baseboard (US); **Fußnagel** M toenail; **Fußnote** F footnote; **Fußpfleger** M chiropodist; **Fußpilz** M (*Med*) athlete's foot; **Fußspur** F footprint; **Fußstapfen** (**-s, -**) M: **in jds Fußstapfen treten** (*fig*) to follow in sb's footsteps; **Fußtritt** M kick; (*Spur*) footstep; **Fußvolk** NT (*fig*): **das Fußvolk** the rank and file; **Fußweg** M footpath
futsch [fʊtʃ] (*umg*) ADJ (*weg*) gone, vanished
Futter ['fʊtər] (**-s, -**) NT fodder, feed; (*Stoff*) lining
Futteral [fʊtə'ra:l] (**-s, -e**) NT case
futtern ['fʊtərn] VI (*hum: umg*) to stuff o.s. ▶ VT to scoff
füttern ['fʏtərn] VT to feed; (*Kleidung*) to line; **„F~ verboten"** "do not feed the animals"
Futur [fu'tu:r] (**-s, -e**) NT future

Gg

G, g¹ [ge:] NT G, g; **G wie Gustav** ≈ G for George
g² ABK (ÖSTERR) = **Groschen**; (= *Gramm*) g
G-8 F ABK (*Pol: = Group of Eight*) G8
G-20 F ABK (*Pol: = Group of Twenty*) G20
gab *etc* [ga:p] VB *siehe* **geben**
Gabe ['ga:bə] (-, -n) F gift
Gabel ['ga:bəl] (-, -n) F fork; (*Tel*) rest, cradle; **Gabelfrühstück** NT mid-morning light lunch; **gabeln** VR to fork; **Gabelstapler** (-s, -) M fork-lift truck; **Gabelung** F fork
Gabentisch ['ga:bəntɪʃ] M *table for Christmas or birthday presents*
Gabun [ga'bu:n] NT Gabon
gackern ['gakərn] VI to cackle
Gag [gɛk] (-s, -s) M (*Filmgag*) gag; (*Werbegag*) gimmick
Gage ['ga:ʒə] (-, -n) F fee
gähnen ['gɛ:nən] VI to yawn; **gähnende Leere** total emptiness
GAL (-) F ABK (= *Grün-Alternative Liste*) *electoral pact of Greens and alternative parties*
Gala ['gala] (-) F formal dress
galant [ga'lant] ADJ gallant, courteous
Galavorstellung F (*Theat*) gala performance
Galerie [galə'ri:] F gallery
Galgen ['galgən] (-s, -) M gallows *pl*; **Galgenfrist** F respite; **Galgenhumor** M macabre humour (BRIT) *od* humor (*US*); **Galgenstrick** (*umg*) M, **Galgenvogel** (*umg*) M gallows bird
Galionsfigur [gali'o:nsfigu:r] F figurehead
gälisch ['gɛ:lɪʃ] ADJ Gaelic
Galle ['galə] (-, -n) F gall; (*Organ*) gall bladder; **jdm kommt die ~ hoch** sb's blood begins to boil
Galopp [ga'lɔp] (-s, -s *od* -e) M gallop; **im ~** (*lit*) at a gallop; (*fig*) at top speed
galoppieren [galɔ'pi:rən] VI to gallop
galt *etc* [galt] VB *siehe* **gelten**
galvanisieren [galvani'zi:rən] VT to galvanize
Gamasche [ga'maʃə] (-, -n) F gaiter; (*kurz*) spat
Gameboy® ['ge:mbɔʏ] M (*Comput*) games console
Gamer(in) ['ge:mər(ɪn)] (-s, -) M(F) (*Comput*) gamer
Gameshow ['ge:mʃo:] F game show
Gammastrahlen ['gamaʃtra:lən] PL gamma rays *pl*
gammelig ['gaməlɪç], **gammlig** ['gamlɪç] (*umg*) ADJ (*Kleidung*) tatty
gammeln ['gaməln] (*umg*) VI to loaf about
Gammler(in) ['gamlər(ɪn)] (-s, -) M(F) dropout
Gämse ['gɛmzə] (-, -n) F chamois
gang ADJ: **~ und gäbe** usual, normal
Gang¹ [gaŋ] (-(e)s, Gänge) M walk; (*Botengang*) errand; (*Gangart*) gait; (*Abschnitt eines Vorgangs*) operation; (*Essensgang, Ablauf*) course; (*Flur etc*) corridor; (*Durchgang*) passage; (*Aut, Tech*) gear; (*in Kirche, Theat, Aviat*) aisle; **den ersten ~ einlegen** to engage first (gear); **einen ~ machen/tun** to go on an errand/for a walk; **den ~ nach Canossa antreten** (*fig*) to eat humble pie; **seinen gewohnten ~ gehen** (*fig*) to run its usual course; **in ~ bringen** to start up; (*fig*) to get off the ground; **in ~ sein** to be in operation; (*fig*) to be under way
Gang² [gɛŋ] (-, -s) F gang
Gangart F way of walking, walk, gait; (*von Pferd*) gait; **eine härtere ~ einschlagen** (*fig*) to apply harder tactics
gangbar ADJ passable; (*Methode*) practicable
Gängelband ['gɛŋəlbant] NT: **jdn am ~ halten** (*fig*) to spoon-feed sb
gängeln VT to spoonfeed; **jdn ~** to treat sb like a child
gängig ['gɛŋɪç] ADJ common, current; (*Ware*) in demand, selling well
Gangschaltung F gears *pl*
Gangway ['gæŋweɪ] F (*Naut*) gangway; (*Aviat*) steps *pl*
Ganove [ga'no:və] (-n, -n) (*umg*) M crook
Gans [gans] (-, Gänse) F goose
Gänse- zW: **Gänseblümchen** NT daisy; **Gänsebraten** M roast goose; **Gänsefüßchen** (*umg*) PL inverted commas *pl* (BRIT), quotes *pl*; **Gänsehaut** F goose pimples *pl*; **Gänsemarsch** M: **im Gänsemarsch** in single file
Gänserich (-s, -e) M gander
ganz [gants] ADJ whole; (*vollständig*) complete ▸ ADV quite; (*völlig*) completely; (*sehr*) really; (*genau*) exactly; **~ Europa** all Europe; **im (Großen und) Ganzen genommen** on the whole, all in all; **etw wieder ~ machen** to mend sth; **sein ganzes Geld** all his money; **~ gewiss!** absolutely!; **ein ~ klein wenig** just a tiny bit; **das mag ich ~ besonders gern(e)** I'm particularly fond of that; **sie ist ~ die Mutter** she's just *od* exactly like her mother; **~ und gar nicht** not at all

Ganze(s) NT: **es geht ums ~** everything's at stake; **aufs ~ gehen** to go for the lot
Ganzheitsmethode ['gantshaɪtsmeto:də] F (*Sch*) look-and-say method
gänzlich ['gɛntslɪç] ADJ complete, entire ▸ ADV completely, entirely
ganztägig ['gantstɛ:gɪç] ADJ all-day *attrib*
ganztags ADV (*arbeiten*) full time; **Ganztagsschule** F all-day school; **Ganztagsstelle** F full-time job
gar [ga:r] ADJ cooked, done ▸ ADV quite; **~ nicht/nichts/keiner** not/nothing/nobody at all; **~ nicht schlecht** not bad at all; **~ kein Grund** no reason whatsoever *od* at all; **er wäre ~ zu gern noch länger geblieben** he would really have liked to stay longer
Garage [ga'ra:ʒə] (**-, -n**) F garage
Garantie [garan'ti:] F guarantee; **das fällt noch unter die ~** that's covered by the guarantee
garantieren VT to guarantee
garantiert ADV guaranteed; (*umg*) I bet
Garantieschein M guarantee
Garaus ['ga:raus] (*umg*) M: **jdm den ~ machen** to do sb in
Garbe ['garbə] (**-, -n**) F sheaf; (*Mil*) burst of fire
Garde ['gardə] (**-, -n**) F guard(s); **die alte ~** the old guard
Garderobe [gardə'ro:bə] (**-, -n**) F wardrobe; (*Abgabe*) cloakroom (BRIT), checkroom (US); (*Kleiderablage*) hall stand; (*Theat*: *Umkleideraum*) dressing room
Garderobenfrau F cloakroom attendant
Garderobenständer M hall stand
Gardine [gar'di:nə] (**-, -n**) F curtain
Gardinenpredigt (*umg*) F: **jdm eine ~ halten** to give sb a talking-to
Gardinenstange F curtain rail; (*zum Ziehen*) curtain rod
garen ['ga:rən] VT, VI (*Koch*) to cook
gären ['gɛ:rən] *unreg* VI to ferment
Garn [garn] (**-(e)s, -e**) NT thread; (*Häkelgarn, fig*) yarn
Garnele [gar'ne:lə] (**-, -n**) F shrimp, prawn
garnieren [gar'ni:rən] VT to decorate; (*Speisen*) to garnish
Garnison [garni'zo:n] (**-, -en**) F garrison
Garnitur [garni'tu:r] F (*Satz*) set; (*Unterwäsche*) set of (matching) underwear; **erste ~** (*fig*) top rank; **zweite ~** second rate
garstig ['garstɪç] ADJ nasty, horrid
Garten ['gartən] (**-s, Gärten**) M garden; **Gartenarbeit** F gardening; **Gartenbau** M horticulture; **Gartenfest** NT garden party; **Gartengerät** NT gardening tool; **Gartenhaus** NT summerhouse; **Gartenkresse** F cress; **Gartenlaube** F (*Gartenhäuschen*) summerhouse; **Gartenlokal** NT beer garden; **Gartenschere** F pruning shears *pl*; **Gartentür** F garden gate; **Gartenzaun** M garden fence; **Gartenzwerg** M garden gnome; (*pej, umg*) squirt
Gärtner(in) ['gɛrtnər(ɪn)] (**-s, -**) M(F) gardener
Gärtnerei [gɛrtnə'raɪ] F nursery; (*Gemüsegärtnerei*) market garden (BRIT), truck farm (US)
gärtnern VI to garden
Gärung ['gɛ:rʊŋ] F fermentation
Gas [ga:s] (**-es, -e**) NT gas; **~ geben** (*Aut*) to accelerate, to step on the gas
Gascogne [gas'kɔnjə] F Gascony
Gas- zW: **Gasflasche** F bottle of gas, gas canister; **gasförmig** ADJ gaseous; **Gashahn** M gas tap; **Gasheizung** F gas heating; **Gasherd** M gas cooker; **Gaskocher** M gas cooker; **Gasleitung** F gas pipeline; **Gasmaske** F gas mask; **Gaspedal** NT accelerator, gas pedal (US); **Gaspistole** F gas pistol
Gasse ['gasə] (**-, -n**) F lane, alley
Gassenhauer (**-s, -**) (*veraltet*: *umg*) M popular melody
Gassenjunge M street urchin
Gast [gast] (**-es, Gäste**) M guest; **bei jdm zu ~ sein** to be sb's guest(s); **Gastarbeiter** M foreign worker
Gäste- zW: **Gästebett** NT spare bed; **Gästebuch** NT visitors' book; **Gästezimmer** NT guest room
Gast- zW: **gastfreundlich** ADJ hospitable; **Gastfreundlichkeit** F hospitality; **Gastfreundschaft** F hospitality; **Gastgeber(in)** (**-s, -**) M(F) host(ess); **Gasthaus** NT hotel, inn; **Gasthof** M hotel, inn; **Gasthörer(in)** M(F) (*Univ*) observer, auditor (US)
gastieren [gas'ti:rən] VI (*Theat*) to (appear as a) guest
Gast- zW: **Gastland** NT host country; **gastlich** ADJ hospitable; **Gastlichkeit** F hospitality; **Gastrolle** F (*Theat*) guest role; **eine Gastrolle spielen** to make a guest appearance
Gastronomie [gastrono'mi:] F (*form*: *Gaststättengewerbe*) catering trade
gastronomisch [gastro'no:mɪʃ] ADJ gastronomic(al)
Gast- zW: **Gastspiel** NT (*Sport*) away game; **ein Gastspiel geben** (*Theat*) to give a guest performance; (*fig*) to put in a brief appearance; **Gaststätte** F restaurant; (*Trinklokal*) pub; **Gastwirt** M innkeeper; **Gastwirtschaft** F hotel, inn; **Gastzimmer** NT guest room
Gas- zW: **Gasvergiftung** F gas poisoning; **Gasversorgung** F (*System*) gas supply; **Gaswerk** NT gasworks *sing od pl*; **Gaszähler** M gas meter
Gatte ['gatə] (**-n, -n**) M (*form*) husband, spouse; **die Gatten** husband and wife
Gatter ['gatər] (**-s, -**) NT grating; (*Tür*) gate
Gattin F (*form*) wife, spouse
Gattung ['gatʊŋ] F (*Biol*) genus; (*Sorte*) kind
GAU [gaʊ] M ABK (= *größter anzunehmender Unfall*) MCA, maximum credible accident
Gaudi ['gaʊdi] (SÜDD, ÖSTERR *umg*) NT OD F fun
Gaukler ['gaʊklər] (**-s, -**) M (*liter*) travelling entertainer; (*Zauberkünstler*) conjurer, magician
Gaul [gaʊl] (**-(e)s, Gäule**) (*pej*) M nag
Gaumen ['gaʊmən] (**-s, -**) M palate
Gauner ['gaʊnər] (**-s, -**) M rogue
Gaunerei [gaʊnə'raɪ] F swindle
Gaunersprache F underworld jargon

Gaze ['ga:zə] (**-, -n**) F gauze
Geäst [gəl'ɛst] NT branches *pl*
geb. ABK = **geboren**
Gebäck [gə'bɛk] (**-(e)s, -e**) NT (*Kekse*) biscuits *pl* (BRIT), cookies *pl* (*US*); (*Teilchen*) pastries *pl*
gebacken [gə'bakən] PP *von* **backen**
Gebälk [gə'bɛlk] (**-(e)s**) NT timberwork
gebannt [gə'bant] ADJ spellbound
gebar *etc* [gə'ba:r] VB *siehe* **gebären**
Gebärde [gə'bɛ:rdə] (**-, -n**) F gesture
gebärden VR to behave
Gebaren [gə'ba:rən] (**-s**) NT behaviour (BRIT), behavior (*US*); (*Geschäftsgebaren*) conduct
gebären [gə'bɛ:rən] *unreg* VT to give birth to
Gebärmutter F uterus, womb
Gebäude [gə'bɔydə] (**-s, -**) NT building; **Gebäudekomplex** M (building) complex; **Gebäudereinigung** F (*das Reinigen*) commercial cleaning; (*Firma*) cleaning contractors *pl*
Gebein [gə'baɪn] (**-(e)s, -e**) NT bones *pl*
Gebell [gə'bɛl] (**-(e)s**) NT barking
geben ['ge:bən] *unreg* VT, VI to give; (*Karten*) to deal ▶ VT UNPERS: **es gibt** there is/are; (*zukünftig*) there will be ▶ VR (*sich verhalten*) to behave, to act; (*aufhören*) to abate; **jdm etw ~** to give sb sth *od* sth to sb; **in die Post ~** to post; **das gibt keinen Sinn** that doesn't make sense; **er gibt Englisch** he teaches English; **viel/nicht viel auf etw** *akk* **~** to set great store/not much store by sth; **etw von sich ~** (*Laute etc*) to utter; **ein Wort gab das andere** one angry word led to another; **ein gutes Beispiel ~** to set a good example; **~ Sie mir bitte Herrn Braun** (*Tel*) can I speak to Mr Braun please?; **ein Auto in Reparatur ~** to have a car repaired; **was gibts?** what's the matter?, what's up?; **was gibts zum Mittagessen?** what's for lunch?; **das gibts doch nicht!** that's impossible!; **sich geschlagen ~** to admit defeat; **das wird sich schon ~** that'll soon sort itself out
Geberkonferenz [ge:bər-] F (*Pol*) donor conference
Gebet [gə'be:t] (**-(e)s, -e**) NT prayer; **jdn ins ~ nehmen** (*fig*) to take sb to task
gebeten [gə'be:tən] PP *von* **bitten**
gebeugt [gə'bɔykt] ADJ (*Haltung*) stooped; (*Kopf*) bowed; (*Schultern*) sloping
gebiert [gə'bi:rt] VB *siehe* **gebären**
Gebiet [gə'bi:t] (**-(e)s, -e**) NT area; (*Hoheitsgebiet*) territory; (*fig*) field
gebieten *unreg* VT to command, to demand
Gebieter (**-s, -**) M master; (*Herrscher*) ruler; **Gebieterin** F mistress; **gebieterisch** ADJ imperious
Gebietshoheit F territorial sovereignty
Gebilde [gə'bɪldə] (**-s, -**) NT object, structure
gebildet ADJ cultured, educated
Gebimmel [gə'bɪməl] (**-s**) NT (continual) ringing
Gebirge [gə'bɪrgə] (**-s, -**) NT mountains *pl*
gebirgig ADJ mountainous
Gebirgs- ZW: **Gebirgsbahn** F *railway crossing a mountain range*; **Gebirgskette** F, **Gebirgszug** M mountain range
Gebiss [gə'bɪs] (**-es, -e**) NT teeth *pl*; (*künstlich*) dentures *pl*
gebissen PP *von* **beißen**
Gebläse [gə'blɛ:zə] (**-s, -**) NT fan, blower
geblasen [gə'bla:zən] PP *von* **blasen**
geblichen [gə'blɪçən] PP *von* **bleichen**
geblieben [gə'bli:bən] PP *von* **bleiben**
geblümt [gə'bly:mt] ADJ flowered; (*Stil*) flowery
Geblüt [gə'bly:t] (**-(e)s**) NT blood, race
gebogen [gə'bo:gən] PP *von* **biegen**
geboren [gə'bo:rən] PP *von* **gebären** ▶ ADJ born; **wo sind Sie ~?** where were you born?; **Andrea Jordan, geborene Christian** Andrea Jordan, née Christian
geborgen [gə'bɔrgən] PP *von* **bergen** ▶ ADJ secure, safe
geborsten [gə'bɔrstən] PP *von* **bersten**
gebot *etc* [gə'bo:t] VB *siehe* **gebieten**
Gebot (**-(e)s, -e**) NT (*Gesetz*) law; (*Rel*) commandment; (*bei Auktion*) bid; **das ~ der Stunde** the needs of the moment
geboten [gə'bo:tən] PP *von* **bieten; gebieten** ▶ ADJ (*geh*: *ratsam*) advisable; (: *notwendig*) necessary; (: *dringend geboten*) imperative
Gebr. ABK (= *Gebrüder*) Bros., bros.
gebracht [gə'braxt] PP *von* **bringen**
gebrannt [gə'brant] PP *von* **brennen** ▶ ADJ: **ein gebranntes Kind scheut das Feuer** (*Sprichwort*) once bitten twice shy (*Sprichwort*)
gebraten [gə'bra:tən] PP *von* **braten**
Gebräu [gə'brɔy] (**-(e)s, -e**) NT brew, concoction
Gebrauch [gə'braʊx] (**-(e)s, Gebräuche**) M use; (*Sitte*) custom; **zum äußerlichen/ innerlichen ~** for external use/to be taken internally
gebrauchen VT to use; **er/das ist zu nichts zu ~** he's/that's (of) no use to anybody
gebräuchlich [gə'brɔyçlɪç] ADJ usual, customary
Gebrauchs- ZW: **Gebrauchsanweisung** F directions *pl* for use; **Gebrauchsartikel** M article of everyday use; **gebrauchsfertig** ADJ ready for use; **Gebrauchsgegenstand** M commodity
gebraucht [gə'braʊxt] ADJ used, second-hand; **Gebrauchtwagen** M second-hand *od* used car
gebrechlich [gə'brɛçlɪç] ADJ frail; **Gebrechlichkeit** F frailty
gebrochen [gə'brɔxən] PP *von* **brechen**
Gebrüder [gə'bry:dər] PL brothers *pl*
Gebrüll [gə'brʏl] (**-(e)s**) NT (*von Mensch*) yelling; (*von Löwe*) roar
gebückt [gə'bʏkt] ADJ: **eine gebückte Haltung** a stoop
Gebühr [gə'by:r] (**-, -en**) F charge; (*Postgebühr*) postage *no pl*; (*Maut*) toll; (*Honorar*) fee; **zu ermäßigter ~** at a reduced rate; **~ (be)zahlt Empfänger** postage to be paid by addressee; **nach ~** suitably; **über ~** excessively
gebühren VI (*geh*): **jdm ~** to be sb's due *od* due to sb ▶ VR to be fitting
gebührend ADJ (*verdient*) due; (*angemessen*) suitable

g

Gebühren- zW: **Gebühreneinheit** F (*Tel*) tariff unit; **Gebührenerlass** M remission of fees; **Gebührenermäßigung** F reduction of fees; **gebührenfrei** ADJ free of charge; **Gebührenmanager** M tariff meter; **gebührenpflichtig** ADJ subject to charges; **gebührenpflichtige Verwarnung** (*Jur*) fine; **gebührenpflichtige Straße** toll road

gebunden [gəˈbʊndən] PP *von* **binden** ▶ ADJ: **vertraglich ~ sein** to be bound by contract

Geburt [gəˈbu:rt] (-, **-en**) F birth; **das war eine schwere ~!** (*fig: umg*) that took some doing

Geburten- zW: **Geburtenkontrolle** F birth control; **Geburtenregelung** F birth control; **Geburtenrückgang** M drop in the birth rate; **geburtenschwach** ADJ (*Jahrgang*) with a low birth rate; **Geburtenziffer** F birth rate

gebürtig [gəˈbʏrtɪç] ADJ born in, native of; **gebürtige Schweizerin** native of Switzerland, Swiss-born woman

Geburts- zW: **Geburtsanzeige** F birth notice; **Geburtsdatum** NT date of birth; **Geburtsfehler** M congenital defect; **Geburtshelfer** M (*Arzt*) obstetrician; **Geburtshelferin** F (*Ärztin*) obstetrician; (*Hebamme*) midwife; **Geburtshilfe** F (*als Fach*) obstetrics *sing*; (*von Hebamme*) midwifery; **Geburtsjahr** NT year of birth; **Geburtsort** M birthplace; **Geburtstag** M birthday; **herzlichen Glückwunsch zum Geburtstag!** happy birthday!, many happy returns (of the day)!; **Geburtsurkunde** F birth certificate

Gebüsch [gəˈbʏʃ] (**-(e)s, -e**) NT bushes *pl*

gedacht [gəˈdaxt] PP *von* **denken**; **gedenken**

gedachte *etc* VB *siehe* **gedenken**

Gedächtnis [gəˈdɛçtnɪs] (**-ses, -se**) NT memory; **wenn mich mein ~ nicht trügt** if my memory serves me right; **Gedächtnisfeier** F commemoration; **Gedächtnishilfe** F memory aid, mnemonic; **Gedächtnisschwund** M loss of memory; **Gedächtnisverlust** M amnesia

gedämpft [gəˈdɛmpft] ADJ (*Geräusch*) muffled; (*Farben, Instrument, Stimmung*) muted; (*Licht, Freude*) subdued

Gedanke [gəˈdaŋkə] (**-ns, -n**) M thought; (*Idee, Plan, Einfall*) idea; (*Konzept*) concept; **sich über etw** *akk* **Gedanken machen** to think about sth; **jdn auf andere Gedanken bringen** to make sb think about other things; **etw ganz in Gedanken** *dat* **tun** to do sth without thinking; **auf einen Gedanken kommen** to have *od* get an idea

Gedanken- zW: **Gedankenaustausch** M exchange of ideas; **Gedankenfreiheit** F freedom of thought; **gedankenlos** ADJ thoughtless; **Gedankenlosigkeit** F thoughtlessness; **Gedankensprung** M mental leap; **Gedankenstrich** M dash; **Gedankenübertragung** F thought transference, telepathy; **gedankenverloren** ADJ lost in thought; **gedankenvoll** ADJ thoughtful

Gedärme [gəˈdɛrmə] PL intestines *pl*

Gedeck [gəˈdɛk] (**-(e)s, -e**) NT cover(ing); (*Menü*) set meal; **ein ~ auflegen** to lay a place

gedeckt ADJ (*Farbe*) muted

Gedeih M: **auf ~ und Verderb** for better or for worse

gedeihen [gəˈdaɪən] *unreg* VI to thrive, to prosper; **die Sache ist so weit gediehen, dass ...** the matter has reached the point *od* stage where ...

gedenken [gəˈdɛŋkən] *unreg* VI *+gen* (*geh: denken an*) to remember; (*beabsichtigen*) to intend; **Gedenken** NT: **zum Gedenken an jdn** in memory *od* remembrance of sb

Gedenk- zW: **Gedenkfeier** F commemoration; **Gedenkminute** F minute's silence; **Gedenkstätte** F memorial; **Gedenktag** M remembrance day

Gedicht [gəˈdɪçt] (**-(e)s, -e**) NT poem

gediegen [gəˈdi:gən] ADJ (good) quality; (*Mensch*) reliable; (*rechtschaffen*) honest; **Gediegenheit** F quality; (*von Mensch*) reliability; (*Rechtschaffenheit*) honesty

gedieh *etc* [gəˈdi:] VB *siehe* **gedeihen**

gediehen PP *von* **gedeihen**

gedr. ABK = **gedruckt**

Gedränge [gəˈdrɛŋə] (**-s**) NT crush, crowd; **ins ~ kommen** (*fig*) to get into difficulties

gedrängt ADJ compressed; **~ voll** packed

gedroschen [gəˈdrɔʃən] PP *von* **dreschen**

gedruckt [gəˈdrʊkt] ADJ printed; **lügen wie ~** (*umg*) to lie left, right and centre

gedrungen [gəˈdrʊŋən] PP *von* **dringen** ▶ ADJ thickset, stocky

Geduld [gəˈdʊlt] (-) F patience; **mir reißt die ~, ich verliere die ~** my patience is wearing thin, I'm losing my patience

gedulden [gəˈdʊldən] VR to be patient

geduldig ADJ patient

Geduldsprobe F trial of (one's) patience

gedungen [gəˈdʊŋən] (*pej*) ADJ (*geh: Mörder*) hired

gedunsen [gəˈdʊnzən] ADJ bloated

gedurft [gəˈdʊrft] PP *von* **dürfen**

geehrt [gəˈle:rt] ADJ: **Sehr geehrte Damen und Herren!** Ladies and Gentlemen!; **Sehr geehrter Herr Young** Dear Mr Young

geeignet [gəˈlaɪgnət] ADJ suitable; **im geeigneten Augenblick** at the right moment

Gefahr [gəˈfa:r] (-, **-en**) F danger; **~ laufen, etw zu tun** to run the risk of doing sth; **auf eigene ~** at one's own risk; **außer ~** (*nicht gefährdet*) not in danger; (*nicht mehr gefährdet*) out of danger; (*Patienten*) off the danger list

gefährden [gəˈfɛ:rdən] VT to endanger

gefahren [gəˈfa:rən] PP *von* **fahren**

Gefahren- zW: **Gefahrenquelle** F source of danger; **Gefahrenschwelle** F threshold of danger; **Gefahrenstelle** F danger spot; **Gefahrenzulage** F danger money

gefährlich [gəˈfɛ:rlɪç] ADJ dangerous

Gefährte [gəˈfɛ:rtə] (**-n, -n**) M companion

Gefährtin [gəˈfɛ:rtɪn] F companion

Gefälle [gəˈfɛlə] (**-s, -**) NT (*von Land, Straße*) slope; (*Neigungsgrad*) gradient; **starkes ~!** steep hill

gefallen PP *von* **fallen**; **gefallen** ▸ VI (*unreg*): **jdm ~** to please sb; **er/es gefällt mir** I like him/it; **das gefällt mir an ihm** that's one thing I like about him; **sich** *dat* **etw ~ lassen** to put up with sth
Gefallen¹ [gəˈfalən] (**-s, -**) M favour; **jdm einen ~ tun** to do sb a favour; **jdm etw zu ~ tun** to do sth to please sb
Gefallen² [gəˈfalən] (**-s**) NT pleasure; **an etw** *dat* **~ finden** to derive pleasure from sth; **an jdm ~ finden** to take to sb
Gefallene(r) M soldier killed in action
gefällig [gəˈfɛlɪç] ADJ (*hilfsbereit*) obliging; (*erfreulich*) pleasant; **sonst noch etwas ~?** (*veraltet, ironisch*) will there be anything else?; **Gefälligkeit** F favour (BRIT), favor (US); (*Hilfsbereitschaft*) helpfulness; **etw aus Gefälligkeit tun** to do sth as a favour (BRIT) *od* favor (US)
gefälligst (*umg*) ADV kindly; **sei ~ still!** will you kindly keep your mouth shut!
gefällt [gəˈfɛlt] VB *siehe* **gefallen**
gefangen [gəˈfaŋən] PP *von* **fangen** ▸ ADJ captured; (*fig*) captivated; **~ halten** to keep prisoner; **~ nehmen** to capture
Gefangene(r) F(M) prisoner, captive
Gefangenenlager NT prisoner-of-war camp
Gefangen- zW: **Gefangennahme** (**-, -n**) F capture; **Gefangenschaft** F captivity
Gefängnis [gəˈfɛŋnɪs] (**-ses, -se**) NT prison; **zwei Jahre ~ bekommen** to get two years' imprisonment; **Gefängnisstrafe** F prison sentence; **Gefängniswärter** M prison warder (BRIT) *od* guard
gefärbt [gəˈfɛrpt] ADJ (*fig: Bericht*) biased; (*Lebensmittel*) coloured (BRIT), colored (US)
Gefasel [gəˈfa:zəl] (**-s**) NT twaddle, drivel
Gefäß [gəˈfɛ:s] (**-es, -e**) NT vessel (*auch Anat*), container
gefasst [gəˈfast] ADJ composed, calm; **auf etw** *akk* **~ sein** to be prepared *od* ready for sth; **er kann sich auf etwas ~ machen** (*umg*) I'll give him something to think about
Gefecht [gəˈfɛçt] (**-(e)s, -e**) NT fight; (*Mil*) engagement; **jdn/etw außer ~ setzen** (*lit, fig*) to put sb/sth out of action
gefedert [gəˈfe:dərt] ADJ (*Matratze*) sprung
gefeiert [gəˈfaɪərt] ADJ celebrated
gefeit [gəˈfaɪt] ADJ: **gegen etw ~ sein** to be immune to sth
gefestigt [gəˈfɛstɪçt] ADJ (*Charakter*) steadfast
Gefieder [gəˈfi:dər] (**-s, -**) NT plumage, feathers *pl*
gefiedert ADJ feathered
gefiel *etc* [gəˈfi:l] VB *siehe* **gefallen**
Geflecht [gəˈflɛçt] (**-(e)s, -e**) NT (*lit, fig*) network
gefleckt [gəˈflɛkt] ADJ spotted; (*Blume, Vogel*) speckled
Geflimmer [gəˈflɪmər] (**-s**) NT shimmering; (*Film, TV*) flicker(ing)
geflissentlich [gəˈflɪsəntlɪç] ADJ intentional ▸ ADV intentionally
geflochten [gəˈflɔxtən] PP *von* **flechten**
geflogen [gəˈflo:gən] PP *von* **fliegen**
geflohen [gəˈflo:ən] PP *von* **fliehen**
geflossen [gəˈflɔsən] PP *von* **fließen**
Geflügel [gəˈfly:gəl] (**-s**) NT poultry
Geflügelpest F poultry plague
geflügelt ADJ: **geflügelte Worte** familiar quotations
Geflüster [gəˈflʏstər] (**-s**) NT whispering
gefochten [gəˈfɔxtən] PP *von* **fechten**
Gefolge [gəˈfɔlgə] (**-s, -**) NT retinue
Gefolgschaft [gəˈfɔlkʃaft] F following
Gefolgsmann (**-(e)s**, *pl* **-leute**) M follower
gefragt [geˈfra:kt] ADJ in demand
gefräßig [gəˈfrɛ:sɪç] ADJ voracious
Gefreite(r) [gəˈfraɪtə(r)] M (*Mil*) lance corporal (BRIT), private first class (US); (*Naut*) able seaman (BRIT), seaman apprentice (US); (*Aviat*) aircraftman (BRIT), airman first class (US)
gefressen [gəˈfrɛsən] PP *von* **fressen** ▸ ADJ: **den hab(e) ich ~** (*umg*) I'm sick of him
gefrieren [gəˈfri:rən] *unreg* VI to freeze
Gefrier- zW: **Gefrierfach** NT freezer compartment; **Gefrierfleisch** NT frozen meat; **gefriergetrocknet** ADJ freeze-dried; **Gefrierpunkt** M freezing point; **Gefrierschrank** M (upright) freezer; **Gefrierschutzmittel** NT antifreeze; **Gefriertruhe** F deep-freeze
gefror *etc* [gəˈfro:r] VB *siehe* **gefrieren**
gefroren PP *von* **frieren**; **gefrieren**
Gefüge [gəˈfy:gə] (**-s, -**) NT structure
gefügig ADJ submissive; (*gehorsam*) obedient
Gefühl [gəˈfy:l] (**-(e)s, -e**) NT feeling; **etw im ~ haben** to have a feel for sth; **gefühllos** ADJ unfeeling; (*Glieder*) numb
Gefühls- zW: **gefühlsbetont** ADJ emotional; **Gefühlsduselei** [-du:zəˈlaɪ] (*pej*) F mawkishness; **Gefühlsleben** NT emotional life; **gefühlsmäßig** ADJ instinctive; **Gefühlsmensch** M emotional person
gefühlvoll ADJ (*empfindsam*) sensitive; (*ausdrucksvoll*) expressive; (*liebevoll*) loving
gefüllt [gəˈfʏlt] ADJ (*Koch*) stuffed; (*Pralinen*) with soft centres
gefunden [gəˈfʊndən] PP *von* **finden** ▸ ADJ: **das war ein gefundenes Fressen für ihn** that was handing it to him on a plate
gegangen [gəˈgaŋən] PP *von* **gehen**
gegeben [gəˈge:bən] PP *von* **geben** ▸ ADJ given; **zu gegebener Zeit** in due course
gegebenenfalls [gəˈge:bənənfals] ADV if need be

SCHLÜSSELWORT

gegen [ˈge:gən] PRÄP +*akk* **1** against; **nichts gegen jdn haben** to have nothing against sb; **X gegen Y** (*Sport, Jur*) X versus Y; **ein Mittel gegen Schnupfen** something for colds
2 (*in Richtung auf*) towards; **gegen Osten** to(wards) the east; **gegen Abend** towards evening; **gegen einen Baum fahren** to drive into a tree
3 (*ungefähr*) round about; **gegen 3 Uhr** around 3 o'clock

g

4 (*gegenüber*) towards; **gerecht gegen alle** fair to all
5 (*im Austausch für*) for; **gegen bar** for cash; **gegen Quittung** against a receipt
6 (*verglichen mit*) compared with

Gegen- zW: **Gegenangriff** M counter-attack; **Gegenbesuch** M return visit; **Gegenbeweis** M counter-evidence
Gegend ['ge:gənt] (**-, -en**) F area, district
Gegen- zW: **Gegendarstellung** F (*Presse*) reply; **gegeneinander** ADV against one another; **Gegenfahrbahn** F opposite carriageway; **gegenfinanzieren** VT to counterfinance; **Gegenfinanzierung** F *financing of state expenditure by means of cuts, tax increases etc*; **Gegenfrage** F counterquestion; **Gegengewicht** NT counterbalance; **Gegengift** NT antidote; **Gegenkandidat** M rival candidate; **gegenläufig** ADJ contrary; **Gegenleistung** F service in return; **Gegenlichtaufnahme** F back lit photograph; **Gegenliebe** F requited love; (*fig: Zustimmung*) approval; **Gegenmaßnahme** F countermeasure; **Gegenmittel** NT: **Gegenmittel (gegen)** (*Med*) antidote (to); **Gegenprobe** F cross-check
Gegensatz (**-es, Gegensätze**) M contrast; **im ~ zu** in contrast to; **Gegensätze überbrücken** to overcome differences
gegensätzlich ADJ contrary, opposite; (*widersprüchlich*) contradictory
Gegen- zW: **Gegenschlag** M counter-attack; **Gegenseite** F opposite side; (*Rückseite*) reverse; **gegenseitig** ADJ mutual, reciprocal; **sich gegenseitig helfen** to help each other; **in gegenseitigem Einverständnis** by mutual agreement; **Gegenseitigkeit** F reciprocity; **Gegenspieler** M opponent; **Gegensprechanlage** F (two-way) intercom; **Gegenstand** M object; **gegenständlich** ADJ objective, concrete; (*Kunst*) representational; **gegenstandslos** ADJ (*überflüssig*) irrelevant; (*grundlos*) groundless; **Gegenstimme** F vote against; **Gegenstoß** M counterblow; **Gegenstück** NT counterpart; **Gegenteil** NT opposite; **im Gegenteil** on the contrary; **das Gegenteil bewirken** to have the opposite effect; (*Mensch*) to achieve the exact opposite; **ganz im Gegenteil** quite the reverse; **ins Gegenteil umschlagen** to swing to the other extreme; **gegenteilig** ADJ opposite, contrary; **ich habe nichts Gegenteiliges gehört** I've heard nothing to the contrary
gegenüber [ge:gən'|y:bər] PRÄP +*dat* opposite; (*zu*) to(wards); (*in Bezug auf*) with regard to; (*im Vergleich zu*) in comparison with; (*angesichts*) in the face of ▶ ADV opposite; **mir ~ hat er das nicht geäußert** he didn't say that to me; **Gegenüber** (**-s, -**) NT person opposite; (*bei Kampf*) opponent; (*bei Diskussion*) opposite number; **gegenüberliegen** *unreg* VR to face each other; **gegenüberstehen** *unreg* VI +*dat* to face; (*Problem*) to be faced with ▶ VR to be opposed (to each other); **gegenüberstellen** VT to confront; (*fig*) to contrast; **Gegenüberstellung** F confrontation; (*fig*) contrast; (: *Vergleich*) comparison; **gegenübertreten** *unreg* VI +*dat* to face
Gegen- zW: **Gegenveranstaltung** F counter-meeting; **Gegenverkehr** M oncoming traffic; **Gegenvorschlag** M counterproposal
Gegenwart ['ge:gənvart] F present; **in ~ von** in the presence of
gegenwärtig ADJ present ▶ ADV at present; **das ist mir nicht mehr ~** that has slipped my mind
gegenwartsbezogen ADJ (*Roman etc*) relevant to present times
Gegen- zW: **Gegenwert** M equivalent; **Gegenwind** M headwind; **Gegenwirkung** F reaction; **gegenzeichnen** VT to countersign; **Gegenzug** M countermove; (*Eisenb*) corresponding train in the other direction
gegessen [gə'gɛsən] PP *von* **essen**
geglichen [gə'glɪçən] PP *von* **gleichen**
gegliedert [gə'gli:dərt] ADJ jointed; (*fig*) structured
geglitten [gə'glɪtən] PP *von* **gleiten**
geglommen [gə'glɔmən] PP *von* **glimmen**
geglückt [gə'glʏkt] ADJ (*Feier*) successful; (*Überraschung*) real
Gegner(in) ['ge:gnər(ɪn)] (**-s, -**) M(F) opponent; **gegnerisch** ADJ opposing; **Gegnerschaft** F opposition
gegolten [gə'gɔltən] PP *von* **gelten**
gegoren [gə'go:rən] PP *von* **gären**
gegossen [gə'gɔsən] PP *von* **gießen**
gegr. ABK (= *gegründet*) estab.
gegraben [gə'gra:bən] PP *von* **graben**
gegriffen [gə'grɪfən] PP *von* **greifen**
Gehabe [gə'ha:bə] (**-s**) (*umg*) NT affected behaviour (BRIT) *od* behavior (US)
gehabt [gə'ha:pt] PP *von* **haben**
Gehackte(s) [ge'haktə(s)] NT mince(d meat) (BRIT), ground meat (US)
Gehalt[1] [gə'halt] (**-(e)s, -e**) M content
Gehalt[2] [gə'halt] (**-(e)s, Gehälter**) NT salary
gehalten [gə'haltən] PP *von* **halten** ▶ ADJ: **~ sein, etw zu tun** (*form*) to be required to do sth
Gehalts- zW: **Gehaltsabrechnung** F salary statement; **Gehaltsempfänger** M salary earner; **Gehaltserhöhung** F salary increase; **Gehaltsklasse** F salary bracket; **Gehaltskonto** NT current account (BRIT), checking account (US); **Gehaltszulage** F salary increment
gehaltvoll [gə'haltfɔl] ADJ (*Speise, Buch*) substantial
gehandicapt, gehandikapt [gə'hɛndikɛpt] ADJ handicapped
gehangen [gə'haŋən] PP *von* **hängen**
geharnischt [gə'harnɪʃt] ADJ (*fig*) forceful, sharp
gehässig [gə'hɛsɪç] ADJ spiteful, nasty; **Gehässigkeit** F spite(fulness)
gehäuft [gə'hɔʏft] ADJ (*Löffel*) heaped
Gehäuse [gə'hɔʏzə] (**-s, -**) NT case; (*Radiogehäuse, Uhrgehäuse*) casing; (*von Apfel etc*) core

gehbehindert ['ge:behındərt] ADJ disabled
Gehege [gə'he:gə] (**-s, -**) NT enclosure, preserve; **jdm ins ~ kommen** (*fig*) to poach on sb's preserve
geheim [gə'haım] ADJ secret; (*Dokumente*) classified; **streng ~** top secret; **~ halten** to keep secret; **Geheimdienst** M secret service, intelligence service; **Geheimfach** NT secret compartment
Geheimnis (**-ses, -se**) NT secret; (*rätselhaftes Geheimnis*) mystery; **Geheimniskrämer** M mystery-monger; **geheimnisvoll** ADJ mysterious
Geheim- zW: **Geheimnummer** F (*Tel*) secret number; (*von Kreditkarte*) PIN number; **Geheimpolizei** F secret police; **Geheimrat** M privy councillor; **Geheimratsecken** PL: **er hat Geheimratsecken** he is going bald at the temples; **Geheimschrift** F code, secret writing; **Geheimtipp** M (personal) tip
Geheiß [gə'haıs] (**-es**) NT (*geh*) command; **auf jds ~** *akk* at sb's bidding
geheißen [gə'haısən] PP *von* **heißen**
gehemmt [gə'hɛmt] ADJ inhibited
gehen ['ge:ən] *unreg* VI (*auch Auto, Uhr*) to go; (*zu Fuß gehen*) to walk; (*funktionieren*) to work; (*Teig*) to rise ▶ VT to go; (*zu Fuß*) to walk ▶ VI UNPERS: **wie geht es dir?** how are you *od* things?; **~ nach** (*Fenster*) to face; **in sich** *akk* **~** to think things over; **nach etw ~** (*urteilen*) to go by sth; **sich ~ lassen** to lose one's self-control; (*nachlässig sein*) to let o.s. go; **wie viele Leute ~ in deinen Wagen?** how many people can you get in your car?; **nichts geht über** *+akk* **...** there's nothing to beat ..., there's nothing better than ...; **schwimmen/schlafen ~** to go swimming/to bed; **in die Tausende ~** to run into (the) thousands; **wie geht es dir?** how are you *od* things?; **mir/ihm geht es gut** I'm/he's (doing) fine; **geht das?** is that possible?; **gehts noch?** can you manage?; **es geht** not too bad, O.K.; **das geht nicht** that's not on; **es geht um etw** it concerns sth, it's about sth; **lass es dir gut ~** look after yourself, take care of yourself; **so geht das, das geht so** that/this is how it's done; **darum geht es (mir) nicht** that's not the point; (*spielt keine Rolle*) that's not important to me; **morgen geht es nicht** tomorrow's no good; **wenn es nach mir ginge** ... if it were *od* was up to me ...
gehetzt [gə'hɛtst] ADJ harassed
geheuer [gə'hɔʏər] ADJ: **nicht ~** eerie; (*fragwürdig*) dubious
Geheul [gə'hɔʏl] (**-(e)s**) NT howling
Gehilfe [gə'hılfə] (**-n, -n**) M assistant
Gehilfin [gə'hılfın] F assistant
Gehirn [gə'hırn] (**-(e)s, -e**) NT brain; **Gehirnerschütterung** F concussion; **Gehirnschlag** M stroke; **Gehirnwäsche** F brainwashing
gehoben [gə'ho:bən] PP *von* **heben** ▶ ADJ: **gehobener Dienst** *professional and executive levels of the civil service*
geholfen [gə'hɔlfən] PP *von* **helfen**
Gehör [gə'hø:r] (**-(e)s**) NT hearing; **musikalisches ~** ear; **absolutes ~** perfect pitch; **~ finden** to gain a hearing; **jdm ~ schenken** to give sb a hearing
gehorchen [gə'hɔrçən] VI *+dat* to obey
gehören [gə'hø:rən] VI to belong ▶ VR UNPERS to be right *od* proper; **das gehört sich nicht** it's not done; **wem gehört das Buch?** whose book is this?; **das gehört nicht zur Sache** that's irrelevant; **dazu gehört (schon) einiges** *od* **etwas** that takes some doing (*umg*); **er gehört ins Bett** he should be in bed
gehörig ADJ proper; **~ zu** *od +dat* (*geh*) belonging to
gehörlos ADJ (*form*) deaf
gehorsam [gə'ho:rza:m] ADJ obedient; **Gehorsam** (**-s**) M obedience
Gehörsinn M sense of hearing
Gehsteig ['ge:ʃtaık] M, **Gehweg** ['ge:vɛk] M pavement (BRIT), sidewalk (US)
Geier ['gaıər] (**-s, -**) M vulture; **weiß der ~!** (*umg*) God knows
geifern ['gaıfərn] VI to slaver; (*fig*) to be bursting with venom
Geige ['gaıgə] (**-, -n**) F violin; **die erste/zweite ~ spielen** (*lit*) to play first/second violin; (*fig*) to call the tune/play second fiddle
Geiger(in) (**-s, -**) M(F) violinist
Geigerzähler M geiger counter
geil [gaıl] ADJ randy (BRIT), horny (US); (*pej: lüstern*) lecherous; (*umg: gut*) fantastic
Geisel ['gaızəl] (**-, -n**) F hostage; **Geiselnahme** (**-**) F taking of hostages
Geißel ['gaısəl] (**-, -n**) F scourge, whip
geißeln VT to scourge
Geist [gaıst] (**-(e)s, -er**) M spirit; (*Gespenst*) ghost; (*Verstand*) mind; **von allen guten Geistern verlassen sein** (*umg*) to have taken leave of one's senses; **hier scheiden sich die Geister** this is the parting of the ways; **den** *od* **seinen ~ aufgeben** to give up the ghost
Geister- zW: **Geisterfahrer** (*umg*) M ghost-driver (US), *person driving in the wrong direction*; **geisterhaft** ADJ ghostly; **Geisterhand** F: **wie von Geisterhand** as if by magic
Geistes- zW: **geistesabwesend** ADJ absent-minded; **Geistesakrobat** M mental acrobat; **Geistesblitz** M brain wave; **Geistesgegenwart** F presence of mind; **geistesgegenwärtig** ADJ quick-witted; **geistesgestört** ADJ mentally disturbed; (*stärker*) (mentally) deranged; **Geisteshaltung** F mental attitude; **geisteskrank** ADJ mentally ill; **Geisteskranke(r)** F(M) mentally ill person; **Geisteskrankheit** F mental illness; **Geistesstörung** F mental disturbance; **Geistesverfassung** F frame of mind; **Geisteswissenschaften** PL arts (subjects) *pl*; **Geisteszustand** M state of mind; **jdn auf seinen Geisteszustand untersuchen** to give sb a psychiatric examination

geistig ADJ intellectual; (*Psych*) mental; (*Getränke*) alcoholic; **~ behindert** mentally handicapped; **~-seelisch** mental and spiritual
geistlich ADJ spiritual; (*religiös*) religious; **Geistliche(r)** M clergyman; **Geistlichkeit** F clergy
geist- ZW: **geistlos** ADJ uninspired, dull; **geistreich** ADJ intelligent; (*witzig*) witty; **geisttötend** ADJ soul-destroying; **geistvoll** ADJ intellectual; (*weise*) wise
Geiz [gaɪts] (**-es**) M miserliness, meanness; **geizen** VI to be miserly; **Geizhals** M miser
geizig ADJ miserly, mean
Geizkragen M miser
gekannt [gə'kant] PP *von* **kennen**
Gekicher [gə'kɪçər] (**-s**) NT giggling
Geklapper [gə'klapər] (**-s**) NT rattling
Geklimper [gə'klɪmpər] (**-s**) (*umg*) NT (*Klaviergeklimper*) tinkling; (*: stümperhaft*) plonking; (*von Geld*) jingling
geklungen [gə'klʊŋən] PP *von* **klingen**
geknickt [gə'knɪkt] ADJ (*fig*) dejected
gekniffen [gə'knɪfən] PP *von* **kneifen**
gekommen [gə'kɔmən] PP *von* **kommen**
gekonnt [gə'kɔnt] PP *von* **können** ▶ ADJ skilful (BRIT), skillful (*US*)
Gekritzel [gə'krɪtsəl] (**-s**) NT scrawl, scribble
gekrochen [gə'krɔxən] PP *von* **kriechen**
gekünstelt [ge'kʏnstəlt] ADJ artificial; (*Sprache, Benehmen*) affected
Gel [ge:l] (**-s, -e**) NT gel
Gelaber [gə'la:bər], **Gelabere** [gə'la:bərə] (**-s**) (*umg*) NT prattle
Gelächter [gə'lɛçtər] (**-s, -**) NT laughter; **in ~ ausbrechen** to burst out laughing
gelackmeiert [gə'lakmaɪərt] (*umg*) ADJ conned
geladen [ge'la:dən] PP *von* **laden** ▶ ADJ loaded; (*Elek*) live; (*fig*) furious
Gelage [gə'la:gə] (**-s, -**) NT feast, banquet
gelagert [gə'la:gərt] ADJ: **in anders/ähnlich gelagerten Fällen** in different/similar cases
gelähmt [gə'lɛ:mt] ADJ paralysed
Gelände [gə'lɛndə] (**-s, -**) NT land, terrain; (*von Fabrik, Sportgelände*) grounds *pl*; (*Baugelände*) site; **Geländefahrzeug** NT cross-country vehicle; **geländegängig** ADJ able to go cross-country; **Geländelauf** M cross-country race
Geländer [gə'lɛndər] (**-s, -**) NT railing; (*Treppengeländer*) banister(s)
Geländewagen M off-road vehicle, four-by-four
gelang *etc* VB *siehe* **gelingen**
gelangen [gə'laŋən] VI: **~ an** *+akk od* **zu** to reach; (*erwerben*) to attain; **in jds Besitz** *akk* **~** to come into sb's possession; **in die richtigen/falschen Hände ~** to fall into the right/wrong hands
gelangweilt ADJ bored
gelassen [gə'lasən] PP *von* **lassen** ▶ ADJ calm; (*gefasst*) composed; **Gelassenheit** F calmness; (*Fassung*) composure
Gelatine [ʒela'ti:nə] F gelatine
gelaufen [gə'laʊfən] PP *von* **laufen**
geläufig [gə'lɔʏfɪç] ADJ (*üblich*) common; **das ist mir nicht ~** I'm not familiar with that; **Geläufigkeit** F commonness; (*Vertrautheit*) familiarity
gelaunt [gə'laʊnt] ADJ: **schlecht/gut ~** in a bad/good mood; **wie ist er ~?** what sort of mood is he in?
Geläut [gə'lɔʏt] (**-(e)s**) NT ringing; (*Läutwerk*) chime
Geläute (**-s**) NT ringing
gelb [gɛlp] ADJ yellow; (*Ampellicht*) amber (BRIT), yellow (*US*); **Gelbe Seiten** Yellow Pages; **gelblich** ADJ yellowish
Gelbsucht F jaundice
Geld [gɛlt] (**-(e)s, -er**) NT money; **etw zu ~ machen** to sell sth off; **er hat ~ wie Heu** (*umg*) he's stinking rich; **am ~ hängen** *od* **kleben** to be tight with money; **staatliche/öffentliche Gelder** state/public funds *pl od* money; **Geldadel** M: **der Geldadel** the moneyed aristocracy; (*hum: die Reichen*) the rich; **Geldanlage** F investment; **Geldautomat** M cash dispenser; **Geldautomatenkarte** F cash card; **Geldbeutel** M purse; **Geldbörse** F purse; **Geldbuße** F fine; **Geldeinwurf** M slot; **Geldgeber** (**-s, -**) M financial backer; **geldgierig** ADJ avaricious; **Geldinstitut** NT financial institution; **Geldmittel** PL capital *sing*, means *pl*; **Geldquelle** F source of income; **Geldschein** M banknote; **Geldschrank** M safe, strongbox; **Geldstrafe** F fine; **Geldstück** NT coin; **Geldverlegenheit** F: **in Geldverlegenheit sein/kommen** to be/run short of money; **Geldverleiher** M moneylender; **Geldwäsche** F money-laundering; **Geldwechsel** M exchange (of money); **„Geldwechsel"** "bureau de change"; **Geldwert** M cash value; (*Fin: Kaufkraft*) currency value
geleckt [gə'lɛkt] ADJ: **wie ~ aussehen** to be neat and tidy
Gelee [ʒe'le:] (**-s, -s**) NT OD M jelly
gelegen [gə'le:gən] PP *von* **liegen** ▶ ADJ situated; (*passend*) convenient, opportune; **etw kommt jdm ~** sth is convenient for sb; **mir ist viel/nichts daran ~** (*wichtig*) it matters a great deal/doesn't matter to me
Gelegenheit [gə'le:gənhaɪt] F opportunity; (*Anlass*) occasion; **bei ~** some time (or other); **bei jeder ~** at every opportunity
Gelegenheits- ZW: **Gelegenheitsarbeit** F casual work; **Gelegenheitsarbeiter** M casual worker; **Gelegenheitskauf** M bargain
gelegentlich [gə'le:gəntlɪç] ADJ occasional ▶ ADV occasionally; (*bei Gelegenheit*) some time (or other) ▶ PRÄP *+gen* on the occasion of
gelehrig [gə'le:rɪç] ADJ quick to learn
gelehrt ADJ learned; **Gelehrte(r)** F(M) scholar; **Gelehrtheit** F scholarliness
Geleise [gə'laɪzə] (**-s, -**) NT = **Gleis**
Geleit [gə'laɪt] (**-(e)s, -e**) NT escort; **freies** *od* **sicheres ~** safe conduct; **geleiten** VT to escort; **Geleitschutz** M escort
Gelenk [gə'lɛŋk] (**-(e)s, -e**) NT joint

gelenkig ADJ supple
gelernt [gəˈlɛrnt] ADJ skilled
gelesen [gəˈleːzən] PP *von* **lesen**
Geliebte F sweetheart; (*Liebhaberin*) mistress
Geliebte(r) M sweetheart; (*Liebhaber*) lover
geliefert [gəˈliːfərt] ADJ: **ich bin ~** (*umg*) I've had it
geliehen [gəˈliːən] PP *von* **leihen**
gelind [gəˈlɪnt] ADJ = **gelinde**
gelinde [gəˈlɪndə] ADJ (*geh*) mild; **~ gesagt** to put it mildly
gelingen [gəˈlɪŋən] *unreg* VI to succeed; **die Arbeit gelingt mir nicht** I'm not doing very well with this work; **es ist mir gelungen, etw zu tun** I succeeded in doing sth; **Gelingen** NT (*geh: Glück*) success; (*: erfolgreiches Ergebnis*) successful outcome
gelitten [gəˈlɪtən] PP *von* **leiden**
gellen [ˈgɛlən] VI to shrill
gellend ADJ shrill, piercing
geloben [gəˈloːbən] VT, VI to vow, to swear; **das Gelobte Land** (*Rel*) the Promised Land
gelogen [gəˈloːgən] PP *von* **lügen**
gelten [ˈgɛltən] *unreg* VT (*wert sein*) to be worth ▶ VI (*gültig sein*) to be valid; (*erlaubt sein*) to be allowed ▶ VB UNPERS (*geh*): **es gilt, etw zu tun** it is necessary to do sth; **was gilt die Wette?** do you want a bet?; **das gilt nicht!** that doesn't count!; (*nicht erlaubt*) that's not allowed; **etw gilt bei jdm viel/wenig** sb values sth highly/doesn't value sth very highly; **jdm viel/wenig ~** to mean a lot/not mean much to sb; **jdm ~** (*gemünzt sein auf*) to be meant for *od* aimed at sb; **etw ~ lassen** to accept sth; **für diesmal lasse ichs ~** I'll let it go this time; **als** *od* **für etw ~** to be considered to be sth; **jdm** *od* **für jdn ~** (*betreffen*) to apply to sb
geltend ADJ (*Preise*) current; (*Gesetz*) in force; (*Meinung*) prevailing; **etw ~ machen** to assert sth; **sich ~ machen** to make itself/o.s. felt; **einen Einwand ~ machen** to raise an objection
Geltung [ˈgɛltʊŋ] F: **~ haben** to have validity; **sich/etw** *dat* **~ verschaffen** to establish o.s./sth; **etw zur ~ bringen** to show sth to its best advantage; **zur ~ kommen** to be seen/heard *etc* to its best advantage
Geltungsbedürfnis NT desire for admiration
geltungssüchtig ADJ craving admiration
Gelübde [gəˈlʏpdə] (**-s, -**) NT vow
gelungen [gəˈlʊŋən] PP *von* **gelingen** ▶ ADJ successful
Gem. ABK = **Gemeinde**
gemächlich [gəˈmɛːçlɪç] ADJ leisurely
gemacht [gəˈmaːxt] ADJ (*gewollt, gekünstelt*) false, contrived; **ein gemachter Mann sein** to be made
Gemahl [gəˈmaːl] (**-(e)s, -e**) M (*geh, form*) spouse, husband
gemahlen [gəˈmaːlən] PP *von* **mahlen**
Gemahlin F (*geh, form*) spouse, wife
Gemälde [gəˈmɛːldə] (**-s, -**) NT picture, painting
gemasert [gəˈmaːzərt] ADJ (*Holz*) grained
gemäß [gəˈmɛːs] PRÄP +*dat* in accordance with ▶ ADJ +*dat* appropriate to
gemäßigt ADJ moderate; (*Klima*) temperate
Gemauschel [gəˈmaʊʃəl] (**-s**) (*umg*) NT scheming
Gemecker [gəˈmɛkər] (**-s**) NT (*von Ziegen*) bleating; (*umg: Nörgelei*) moaning
gemein [gəˈmaɪn] ADJ common; (*niederträchtig*) mean; **etw ~ haben (mit)** to have sth in common (with)
Gemeinde [gəˈmaɪndə] (**-, -n**) F district; (*Bewohner*) community; (*Pfarrgemeinde*) parish; (*Kirchengemeinde*) congregation; **Gemeindeabgaben** PL rates and local taxes *pl*; **Gemeindebau** M (ÖSTERR) subsidized housing; (*Gebäude*) subsidized house; **Gemeindeordnung** F by(e) laws *pl*, ordinances *pl* (US); **Gemeinderat** M district council; (*Mitglied*) district councillor; **Gemeindeschwester** F district nurse (BRIT); **Gemeindesteuer** F local rates *pl*; **Gemeindeverwaltung** F local administration; **Gemeindevorstand** M local council; **Gemeindewahl** F local election
Gemein- ZW: **Gemeineigentum** NT common property; **gemeingefährlich** ADJ dangerous to the public; **Gemeingut** NT public property; **Gemeinheit** F (*Niedertracht*) meanness; **das war eine Gemeinheit** that was a mean thing to do/to say; **gemeinhin** ADV generally; **Gemeinkosten** PL overheads *pl*; **Gemeinnutz** M public good; **gemeinnützig** ADJ of benefit to the public; (*wohltätig*) charitable; **Gemeinplatz** M commonplace, platitude; **gemeinsam** ADJ joint, common (*auch Math*) ▶ ADV together; **gemeinsame Sache mit jdm machen** to be in cahoots with sb; **der Gemeinsame Markt** the Common Market; **gemeinsames Konto** joint account; **etw gemeinsam haben** to have sth in common; **Gemeinsamkeit** F common ground; **Gemeinschaft** F community; **in Gemeinschaft mit** jointly *od* together with; **eheliche Gemeinschaft** (*Jur*) matrimony; **Gemeinschaft Unabhängiger Staaten** Commonwealth of Independent States; **gemeinschaftlich** ADJ = **gemeinsam**; **Gemeinschaftsantenne** F party aerial (BRIT) *od* antenna (US); **Gemeinschaftsarbeit** F teamwork; **Gemeinschaftsbesitz** M collective ownership; **Gemeinschaftserziehung** F coeducation; **Gemeinschaftskunde** F social studies *pl*; **Gemeinschaftsraum** M common room; **Gemeinschaftswährung** F common *od* single currency; (*innerhalb der EU*) single European currency; **Gemeinsinn** M public spirit; **gemeinverständlich** ADJ generally comprehensible; **Gemeinwesen** NT community; **Gemeinwohl** NT common good
Gemenge [gəˈmɛŋə] (**-s, -**) NT mixture; (*Handgemenge*) scuffle
gemessen [gəˈmɛsən] PP *von* **messen** ▶ ADJ measured
Gemetzel [gəˈmɛtsəl] (**-s, -**) NT slaughter, carnage
gemieden [gəˈmiːdən] PP *von* **meiden**
Gemisch [gəˈmɪʃ] (**-es, -e**) NT mixture
gemischt ADJ mixed

gemocht [gə'mɔxt] PP *von* **mögen**
gemolken [gə'mɔlkən] PP *von* **melken**
Gemse ['gɛmzə] (**-, -n**) F *siehe* **Gämse**
Gemunkel [gə'mʊŋkəl] (**-s**) NT gossip
Gemurmel [gə'mʊrməl] (**-s**) NT murmur(ing)
Gemüse [gə'my:zə] (**-s, -**) NT vegetables *pl*; **Gemüsegarten** M vegetable garden; **Gemüsehändler** M greengrocer (BRIT), vegetable dealer (US); **Gemüseplatte** F (*Koch*): **eine Gemüseplatte** assorted vegetables
gemusst [gə'mʊst] PP *von* **müssen**
gemustert [gə'mʊstərt] ADJ patterned
Gemüt [gə'my:t] (**-(e)s, -er**) NT disposition, nature; (*fig: Mensch*) person; **sich** *dat* **etw zu Gemüte führen** (*umg*) to indulge in sth; **die Gemüter erregen** to arouse strong feelings; **wir müssen warten, bis sich die Gemüter beruhigt haben** we must wait until feelings have cooled down
gemütlich ADJ comfortable, cosy; (*Person*) good-natured; **wir verbrachten einen gemütlichen Abend** we spent a very pleasant evening; **Gemütlichkeit** F comfortableness, cosiness; (*von Person*) amiability
Gemüts- ZW: **Gemütsbewegung** F emotion; **gemütskrank** ADJ emotionally disturbed; **Gemütsmensch** M sentimental person; **Gemütsruhe** F composure; **in aller Gemütsruhe** (*umg*) (as) cool as a cucumber; (*gemächlich*) at a leisurely pace; **Gemütszustand** M state of mind
gemütvoll ADJ warm, tender
Gen [ge:n] (**-s, -e**) NT gene
gen. ABK (= *genannt*) named, called
Gen. ABK = **Genossenschaft**; (= *Genitiv*) gen.
genannt [gə'nant] PP *von* **nennen**
genas *etc* [gə'na:s] VB *siehe* **genesen**
genau [gə'naʊ] ADJ exact, precise ▶ ADV exactly, precisely; **etw ~ nehmen** to take sth seriously; **~ genommen** strictly speaking; **Genaueres** further details *pl*; **etw ~ wissen** to know sth for certain; **~ auf die Minute, auf die Minute ~** exactly on time
Genauigkeit F exactness, accuracy
genauso [gə'naʊzo:] ADV exactly the same (way); **~ gut/viel/viele Leute** just as well/ much/many people (wie as)
genehm [gə'ne:m] ADJ agreeable, acceptable
genehmigen VT to approve, to authorize; **sich** *dat* **etw ~** to indulge in sth
Genehmigung F approval, authorization
geneigt [gə'naɪkt] ADJ (*geh*) well-disposed, willing; **~ sein, etw zu tun** to be inclined to do sth
Genera PL *von* **Genus**
General [gene'ra:l] (**-s, -e** *od* **Generäle**) M general; **Generaldirektor** M chairman (BRIT), president (US); **Generalkonsulat** NT consulate general; **Generalprobe** F dress rehearsal; **Generalsekretär** M secretary-general; **Generalstabskarte** F ordnance survey map; **Generalstreik** M general strike; **generalüberholen** VT to overhaul thoroughly; **Generalvertretung** F sole agency
Generation [generatsi'o:n] F generation
Generationskonflikt M generation gap
Generator [gene'ra:tɔr] M generator, dynamo
generell [genə'rɛl] ADJ general
genesen [ge'ne:zən] *unreg* VI (*geh*) to convalesce, to recover
Genesende(r) F(M) convalescent
Genesung F recovery, convalescence
Genetik [ge'ne:tɪk] F genetics
genetisch [ge'ne:tɪʃ] ADJ genetic
Genf ['gɛnf] (**-s**) NT Geneva
Genfer ADJ *attrib*: **der ~ See** Lake Geneva; **die ~ Konvention** the Geneva Convention
genial [geni'a:l] ADJ brilliant
Genialität [geniali'tɛ:t] F brilliance, genius
Genick [gə'nɪk] (**-(e)s, -e**) NT (back of the) neck; **jdm/etw das ~ brechen** (*fig*) to finish sb/sth; **Genickstarre** F stiff neck
Genie [ʒe'ni:] (**-s, -s**) NT genius
genieren [ʒe'ni:rən] VR to be embarrassed ▶ VT to bother; **geniert es Sie, wenn …?** do you mind if …?
genießbar ADJ edible; (*trinkbar*) drinkable
genießen [gə'ni:sən] *unreg* VT to enjoy; (*essen*) to eat; (*trinken*) to drink; **er ist heute nicht zu ~** (*umg*) he is unbearable today
Genießer(in) (**-s, -**) M(F) connoisseur; (*des Lebens*) pleasure-lover; **genießerisch** ADJ appreciative ▶ ADV with relish
Genitalien [geni'ta:liən] PL genitals *pl*
Genitiv ['ge:niti:f] M genitive
Genmais M GM maize
genmanipuliert ADJ genetically modified
Genom ['ge:no:m] (**--s, --e**) NT genome
genommen [gə'nɔmən] PP *von* **nehmen**
genoss *etc* [gə'nɔs] VB *siehe* **genießen**
Genosse [gə'nɔsə] (**-n, -n**) M comrade (*bes Pol*), companion
genossen PP *von* **genießen**
Genossenschaft F cooperative (association)
Genossin [gə'nɔsɪn] F comrade (*bes Pol*), companion
genötigt [gə'nø:tɪçt] ADJ: **sich ~ sehen, etw zu tun** to feel obliged to do sth
Genre [ʒã:rə] (**-s, -s**) NT genre
Gent [gɛnt] (**-s**) NT Ghent
Gentechnik F, **Gentechnologie** F genetic engineering
Genua ['ge:nua] (**-s**) NT Genoa
genug [gə'nu:k] ADV enough; **jetzt ist(s) aber ~!** that's enough!
Genüge [gə'ny:gə] F: **jdm/etw ~ tun** *od* **leisten** to satisfy sb/sth; **etw zur ~ kennen** to know sth well enough; (*abwertender*) to know sth only too well
genügen VI to be enough; (*den Anforderungen etc*) to satisfy; **jdm ~** to be enough for sb
genügend ADJ enough, sufficient; (*befriedigend*) satisfactory
genügsam [gə'ny:kza:m] ADJ modest, easily satisfied; **Genügsamkeit** F moderation
Genugtuung [gə'nu:ktu:ʊŋ] F satisfaction
Genus ['ge:nʊs] (**-, Genera**) NT (*Gram*) gender

Genuss [gəˈnʊs] (**-es, Genüsse**) M pleasure; (*Zusichnehmen*) consumption; **etw mit ~ essen** to eat sth with relish; **in den ~ von etw kommen** to receive the benefit of sth
genüsslich [gəˈnʏslɪç] ADV with relish
Genussmittel PL (semi-)luxury items *pl*
geöffnet [gəˈœfnət] ADJ open
Geograf [geoˈgraːf] (**-en, -en**) M geographer
Geografie [geograˈfiː] F geography
Geografin F geographer
geografisch ADJ geographical
Geologe [geoˈloːgə] (**-n, -n**) M geologist
Geologie [geoloːˈgiː] F geology
Geologin F geologist
Geometrie [geomeˈtriː] F geometry
geordnet [gəˈɔrdnət] ADJ: **in geordneten Verhältnissen leben** to live a well-ordered life
Georgien [geˈɔrgiən] (**-s**) NT Georgia
Gepäck [gəˈpɛk] (**-(e)s**) NT luggage (BRIT), baggage; **mit leichtem ~ reisen** to travel light; **Gepäckabfertigung** F luggage (BRIT) *od* baggage desk/office; **Gepäckablage** F luggage (BRIT) *od* baggage rack; **Gepäckannahme** F (*Bahnhof*) luggage (BRIT) *od* baggage office; (*Flughafen*) luggage (BRIT) *od* baggage check-in; **Gepäckaufbewahrung** F left-luggage office (BRIT), baggage check (*US*); **Gepäckausgabe** F (*Bahnhof*) luggage (BRIT) *od* baggage office; (*Flughafen*) baggage reclaim; **Gepäckkontrolle** F luggage (BRIT) *od* baggage check; **Gepäcknetz** NT luggage (BRIT) *od* baggage rack; **Gepäckschein** M luggage (BRIT) *od* baggage ticket; **Gepäckstück** NT piece of luggage (BRIT) *od* baggage; **Gepäckträger** M porter; (*Fahrrad*) carrier; **Gepäckwagen** M luggage van (BRIT), baggage car (*US*)
Gepard [ˈgeːpart] (**-(e)s, -e**) M cheetah
gepfeffert [gəˈpfɛfərt] (*umg*) ADJ (*Preise*) steep; (*Fragen, Prüfung*) tough; (*Kritik*) biting
gepfiffen [gəˈpfɪfən] PP *von* **pfeifen**
gepflegt [gəˈpfleːkt] ADJ well-groomed; (*Park etc*) well looked after; (*Atmosphäre*) sophisticated; (*Ausdrucksweise, Sprache*) cultured
Gepflogenheit [gəˈpfloːgənhaɪt] F (*geh*) custom
Geplapper [gəˈplapər] (**-s**) NT chatter
Geplauder [gəˈplaʊdər] (**-s**) NT chat(ting)
Gepolter [gəˈpɔltər] (**-s**) NT din
gepr. ABK (= *geprüft*) tested
gepriesen [gəˈpriːzən] PP *von* **preisen**
gequält [gəˈkvɛːlt] ADJ (*Lächeln*) forced; (*Miene, Ausdruck*) pained; (*Gesang, Stimme*) strained
Gequatsche [gəˈkvatʃə] (**-s**) (*pej, umg*) NT gabbing; (*Blödsinn*) twaddle
gequollen [gəˈkvɔlən] PP *von* **quellen**

SCHLÜSSELWORT

gerade [gəˈraːdə] ADJ straight; (*aufrecht*) upright; **eine gerade Zahl** an even number
▶ ADV **1** (*genau*) just, exactly; (: *speziell*) especially; **gerade deshalb** that's just *od* exactly why; **das ist es ja gerade!** that's just it; **gerade du** you especially; **warum gerade ich?** why me (of all people)?; **jetzt gerade nicht!** not now!; **gerade neben** right next to; **nicht gerade schön** not exactly beautiful; **gerade biegen** to straighten out; **gerade stehen** (*aufrecht*) to stand up straight
2 (*eben, soeben*) just; **er wollte gerade aufstehen** he was just about to get up; **da wir gerade von Geld sprechen ...** talking of money ...; **gerade erst** only just; **gerade noch** (only) just

Gerade [gəˈraːdə] (**-n, -n**) F straight line
gerade- ZW: **geradeaus** ADV straight ahead; **geradebiegen** *unreg* VT (*fig*) to straighten out; **geradeheraus** ADV straight out, bluntly
gerädert [gəˈrɛːdərt] ADJ: **wie ~ sein, sich wie ~ fühlen** to be *od* feel (absolutely) whacked (*umg*)
geradeso ADV just so; **~ dumm** *etc* just as stupid *etc*; **~ wie** just as
geradestehen *unreg* VI: **für jdn/etw ~** (*fig*) to answer *od* be answerable for sb/sth
geradezu ADV (*beinahe*) virtually, almost
geradlinig ADJ straight
gerammelt [gəˈraməlt] ADV: **~ voll** (*umg*) (jam-)packed
Geranie [gɛˈraːniə] F geranium
gerannt [gəˈrant] PP *von* **rennen**
gerät [gəˈrɛːt] VB *siehe* **geraten**
Gerät [gəˈrɛːt] (**-(e)s, -e**) NT device; (*Apparat*) gadget; (*elektrisches Gerät*) appliance; (*Werkzeug*) tool; (*Sport*) apparatus; (*Zubehör*) equipment *no pl*
geraten [gəˈraːtən] *unreg* PP *von* **raten**; **geraten** ▶ VI (*gedeihen*) to thrive; (*gelingen*): **(jdm) ~** to turn out well (for sb); (*zufällig gelangen*): **~ in** *+akk* to get into; **gut/schlecht ~** to turn out well/badly; **an jdn ~** to come across sb; **an den Richtigen/Falschen ~** to come to the right/wrong person; **in Angst ~** to get frightened; **nach jdm ~** to take after sb
Geräteturnen NT apparatus gymnastics
Geratewohl [gəraːtəˈvoːl] NT: **aufs ~** on the off chance; (*bei Wahl*) at random
geraum [gəˈraʊm] ADJ: **seit geraumer Zeit** for some considerable time
geräumig [gəˈrɔʏmɪç] ADJ roomy
Geräusch [gəˈrɔʏʃ] (**-(e)s, -e**) NT sound; (*unangenehm*) noise; **geräuscharm** ADJ quiet; **Geräuschkulisse** F background noise; (*Film, Rundf, TV*) sound effects *pl*; **geräuschlos** ADJ silent; **Geräuschpegel** M sound level; **geräuschvoll** ADJ noisy
gerben [ˈgɛrbən] VT to tan
Gerber (**-s, -**) M tanner
Gerberei [gɛrbəˈraɪ] F tannery
gerecht [gəˈrɛçt] ADJ just, fair; **jdm/etw ~ werden** to do justice to sb/sth; **gerechtfertigt** ADJ justified
Gerechtigkeit F justice, fairness
Gerechtigkeits- ZW: **Gerechtigkeitsfanatiker** M justice fanatic; **Gerechtigkeitsgefühl** NT sense of justice; **Gerechtigkeitssinn** M sense of justice

Gerede [gə're:də] **(-s)** NT talk; (*Klatsch*) gossip
geregelt [gə're:gəlt] ADJ (*Arbeit, Mahlzeiten*) regular; (*Leben*) well-ordered
gereizt [gə'raɪtst] ADJ irritable; **Gereiztheit** F irritation
Gericht [gə'rɪçt] **(-(e)s, -e)** NT court; (*Essen*) dish; **jdn/einen Fall vor ~ bringen** to take sb/a case to court; **mit jdm ins ~ gehen** (*fig*) to judge sb harshly; **über jdn zu ~ sitzen** to sit in judgement on sb; **das Jüngste ~** the Last Judgement; **gerichtlich** ADJ judicial, legal ▸ ADV judicially, legally; **ein gerichtliches Nachspiel haben** to finish up in court; **gerichtlich gegen jdn vorgehen** to take legal proceedings against sb
Gerichts- zW: **Gerichtsakten** PL court records *pl*; **Gerichtsbarkeit** F jurisdiction; **Gerichtshof** M court (of law); **Gerichtskosten** PL (legal) costs *pl*; **gerichtsmedizinisch** ADJ forensic medical *attrib*; **Gerichtssaal** M courtroom; **Gerichtsstand** M court of jurisdiction; **Gerichtsverfahren** NT legal proceedings *pl*; **Gerichtsverhandlung** F court proceedings *pl*; **Gerichtsvollzieher** M bailiff
gerieben [gə'ri:bən] PP *von* **reiben** ▸ ADJ grated; (*umg: schlau*) smart, wily
geriet *etc* [gə'ri:t] VB *siehe* **geraten**
gering [gə'rɪŋ] ADJ slight, small; (*niedrig*) low; (*Zeit*) short ▸ ADV: **~ achten** to think little of; **geringfügig** ADJ slight, trivial; **geringfügig Beschäftigte** ≈ part-time workers *pl*; **geringschätzig** ADJ disparaging; **Geringschätzung** F disdain
geringste(r, s) ADJ slightest, least; **nicht im Geringsten** not in the least *od* slightest
Geringverdiener(in) M(F) low-income earner
gerinnen [gə'rɪnən] *unreg* VI to congeal; (*Blut*) to clot; (*Milch*) to curdle
Gerinnsel [gə'rɪnzəl] **(-s, -)** NT clot
Gerippe [gə'rɪpə] **(-s, -)** NT skeleton
gerissen [gə'rɪsən] PP *von* **reißen** ▸ ADJ wily, smart
geritten [gə'rɪtən] PP *von* **reiten**
geritzt [gə'rɪtst] (*umg*) ADJ: **die Sache ist ~** everything's fixed up *od* settled
Germanist(in) [gɛrma'nɪst(ɪn)] M(F) Germanist, German specialist; (*Student*) German student
Germanistik F German (studies *pl*)
gern [gɛrn] ADV willingly, gladly; **(aber) ~!** of course!; **~ mögen** to like; **etw ~ tun** to like doing sth; **~ geschehen!** you're welcome!, not at all!; **ein ~ gesehener Gast** a welcome visitor; **ich hätte** *od* **möchte ~ ...** I would like ...; *siehe auch* **gernhaben**
gerne ['gɛrnə] ADV = **gern**; **Gernegroß (-, -e)** M show-off; **gernhaben** *unreg* VT to like; **du kannst mich mal gernhaben!** (*umg*) (you can) go to hell!
gerochen [gə'rɔxən] PP *von* **riechen**
Geröll [gə'rœl] **(-(e)s, -e)** NT scree
geronnen [gə'rɔnən] PP *von* **rinnen**; **gerinnen**
Gerste ['gɛrstə] **(-, -n)** F barley
Gerstenkorn NT (*im Auge*) stye
Gerte ['gɛrtə] **(-, -n)** F switch, rod
gertenschlank ADJ willowy
Geruch [gə'rʊx] **(-(e)s, Gerüche)** M smell, odour (BRIT), odor (US); **geruchlos** ADJ odourless (BRIT), odorless (US)
Geruchssinn M sense of smell
Gerücht [gə'rʏçt] **(-(e)s, -e)** NT rumour (BRIT), rumor (US)
geruchtilgend ADJ deodorant
gerufen [gə'ru:fən] PP *von* **rufen**
geruhen [gə'ru:ən] VI to deign
geruhsam [gə'ru:za:m] ADJ peaceful; (*Spaziergang etc*) leisurely
Gerümpel [gə'rʏmpəl] **(-s)** NT junk
gerungen [gə'rʊŋən] PP *von* **ringen**
Gerüst [gə'rʏst] **(-(e)s, -e)** NT (*Baugerüst*) scaffold(ing); (*fig*) framework
Ges. ABK (= *Gesellschaft*) Co., co.
gesalzen [gə'zaltsən] PP *von* **salzen** ▸ ADJ (*fig: umg: Preis, Rechnung*) steep, stiff
gesamt [gə'zamt] ADJ whole, entire; (*Kosten*) total; (*Werke*) complete; **im Gesamten** all in all; **Gesamtauflage** F gross circulation; **Gesamtausgabe** F complete edition; **Gesamtbetrag** M total (amount); **gesamtdeutsch** ADJ all-German; **Gesamteindruck** M general impression; **Gesamtheit** F totality, whole
Gesamthochschule F polytechnic (BRIT); *see note*

> A **Gesamthochschule** is an institution combining several different kinds of higher education organizations e.g. a university, teacher training college and institute of applied science. Students can study for various degrees within the same subject area and it is easier to change course than it is in an individual institution.

Gesamt- zW: **Gesamtmasse** F (*Comm*) total assets *pl*; **Gesamtnachfrage** F (*Comm*) composite demand; **Gesamtschaden** M total damage
Gesamtschule F ≈ comprehensive school; *see note*

> The **Gesamtschule** is a comprehensive school teaching pupils who have different aims. Traditionally pupils would go to one of three different schools, the **Gymnasium**, **Realschule** or **Hauptschule**, depending on ability. The Gesamtschule seeks to avoid the elitist element prevalent in many Gymnasien, but in Germany these schools are still very controversial. Many parents still prefer the traditional system.

Gesamtwertung F (*Sport*) overall placings *pl*
gesandt PP *von* **senden²**
Gesandte(r) [gə'zantə(r)] F(M) envoy
Gesandtschaft [gə'zantʃaft] F legation
Gesang [gə'zaŋ] **(-(e)s, Gesänge)** M song; (*Singen*) singing; **Gesangbuch** NT (*Rel*) hymn book
Gesäß [gə'zɛ:s] **(-es, -e)** NT seat, bottom

gesättigt [gəˈzɛtɪçt] ADJ (*Chem*) saturated
gesch. ABK (= *geschieden*) div.
Geschädigte(r) [gəˈʃɛːdɪçtə(r)] F(M) victim
geschaffen [gəˈʃafən] PP *von* **schaffen²**
Geschäft [gəˈʃɛft] (**-(e)s, -e**) NT business; (*Laden*) shop; (*Geschäftsabschluss*) deal; **mit jdm ins ~ kommen** to do business with sb; **dabei hat er ein ~ gemacht** he made a profit by it; **im ~** at work; (*im Laden*) in the shop; **sein ~ verrichten** to do one's business (*euph*)
Geschäftemacher M wheeler-dealer
geschäftig ADJ active, busy; (*pej*) officious
geschäftlich ADJ commercial ▶ ADV on business; **~ unterwegs** away on business
Geschäfts- zW: **Geschäftsabschluss** M business deal *od* transaction; **Geschäftsaufgabe** F closure of a/the business; **Geschäftsauflösung** F closure of a/the business; **Geschäftsbedingungen** PL terms of business; **Geschäftsbereich** M (*Parl*) responsibilities *pl*; **Minister ohne Geschäftsbereich** minister without portfolio; **Geschäftsbericht** M financial report; **Geschäftsbeziehungen** PL business relations; **Geschäftscomputer** M business computer; **Geschäftsessen** NT business lunch; **Geschäftsführer** M manager; (*von Klub*) secretary; **Geschäftsgeheimnis** NT trade secret; **Geschäftsinhaber** M owner; **Geschäftsjahr** NT financial year; **Geschäftslage** F business conditions *pl*; **Geschäftsleitung** F management; **Geschäftsmann** (**-(e)s**, *pl* **-leute**) M businessman; **geschäftsmäßig** ADJ businesslike; **Geschäftsordnung** F standing orders *pl*; **eine Frage zur Geschäftsordnung** a question on a point of order; **Geschäftspartner** M partner; **Geschäftsreise** F business trip; **Geschäftsschluss** M closing time; **Geschäftssinn** M business sense; **Geschäftsstelle** F office(s *pl*), place of business; **geschäftstüchtig** ADJ business-minded; **Geschäftsviertel** NT shopping centre (BRIT) *od* center (US); (*Banken etc*) business quarter, commercial district; **Geschäftswagen** M company car; **Geschäftswesen** NT business; **Geschäftszeit** F business hours *pl*; **Geschäftszweig** M branch (of a business)
geschah *etc* [gəˈʃaː] VB *siehe* **geschehen**
geschehen [gəˈʃeːən] *unreg* VI to happen; **das geschieht ihm (ganz) recht** it serves him (jolly well (*umg*)) right; **was soll mit ihm/ damit ~?** what is to be done with him/it?; **es war um ihn ~** that was the end of him
gescheit [gəˈʃaɪt] ADJ clever; (*vernünftig*) sensible
Geschenk [gəˈʃɛŋk] (**-(e)s, -e**) NT present, gift; **Geschenkartikel** M gift; **Geschenkgutschein** M gift voucher; **Geschenkpackung** F gift pack; **Geschenkpapier** NT gift-wrapping paper, giftwrap; **Geschenksendung** F gift parcel
Geschichte [gəˈʃɪçtə] (**-, -n**) F story; (*Sache*) affair; (*Historie*) history
Geschichtenerzähler M storyteller
geschichtlich ADJ historical; (*bedeutungsvoll*) historic
Geschichtsfälschung F falsification of history
Geschichtsschreiber M historian
Geschick [gəˈʃɪk] (**-(e)s, -e**) NT skill; (*geh: Schicksal*) fate
Geschicklichkeit F skill, dexterity
Geschicklichkeitsspiel NT game of skill
geschickt ADJ skilful (BRIT), skillful (US); (*taktisch*) clever; (*beweglich*) agile
geschieden [gəˈʃiːdən] PP *von* **scheiden** ▶ ADJ divorced
geschieht [gəˈʃiːt] VB *siehe* **geschehen**
geschienen [gəˈʃiːnən] PP *von* **scheinen**
Geschirr [gəˈʃɪr] (**-(e)s, -e**) NT crockery; (*Küchengeschirr*) pots and pans *pl*; (*Pferdegeschirr*) harness; **Geschirrspülmaschine** F dishwasher; **Geschirrspülmittel** NT washing-up liquid (BRIT), dishwashing liquid (US); **Geschirrtuch** NT tea towel (BRIT), dishtowel (US)
geschissen [gəˈʃɪsən] PP *von* **scheißen**
geschlafen [gəˈʃlaːfən] PP *von* **schlafen**
geschlagen [gəˈʃlaːgən] PP *von* **schlagen**
geschlaucht [gəˈʃlaʊxt] ADV: **~ sein** (*umg*) to be exhausted *od* knackered
Geschlecht [gəˈʃlɛçt] (**-(e)s, -er**) NT sex; (*Gram*) gender; (*Gattung*) race; (*Abstammung*) lineage; **geschlechtlich** ADJ sexual
Geschlechts- zW: **Geschlechtskrankheit** F sexually-transmitted disease; **geschlechtsreif** ADJ sexually mature; **geschlechtsspezifisch** ADJ (*Soziologie*) sex-specific; **Geschlechtsteil** NT OD M genitals *pl*; **Geschlechtsverkehr** M sexual intercourse; **Geschlechtswort** NT (*Gram*) article
geschlichen [gəˈʃlɪçən] PP *von* **schleichen**
geschliffen [gəˈʃlɪfən] PP *von* **schleifen²**
geschlossen [gəˈʃlɔsən] PP *von* **schließen** ▶ ADJ closed ▶ ADV: **~ hinter jdm stehen** to stand solidly behind sb; **geschlossene Ortschaft** built-up area; **geschlossene Gesellschaft** (*Fest*) private party
geschlungen [gəˈʃlʊŋən] PP *von* **schlingen**
Geschmack [gəˈʃmak] (**-(e)s, Geschmäcke**) M taste; **nach jds ~** to sb's taste; **~ an etw** *dat* **finden** to (come to) like sth; **je nach ~** to one's own taste; **er hat einen guten ~** (*fig*) he has good taste; **geschmacklos** ADJ tasteless; (*fig*) in bad taste
Geschmacks- zW: **Geschmackssache** F matter of taste; **Geschmackssinn** M sense of taste; **Geschmacksverirrung** F: **unter Geschmacksverirrung leiden** (*ironisch*) to have no taste
geschmackvoll ADJ tasteful
Geschmeide [gəˈʃmaɪdə] (**-s, -**) NT jewellery (BRIT), jewelry (US)
geschmeidig ADJ supple; (*formbar*) malleable
Geschmeiß NT vermin *pl*
Geschmiere [gəˈʃmiːrə] (**-s**) NT scrawl; (*Bild*) daub
geschmissen [gəˈʃmɪsən] PP *von* **schmeißen**
geschmolzen [gəˈʃmɔltsən] PP *von* **schmelzen**

Geschnetzelte(s) [gəˈʃnɛtsəltə(s)] NT (*Koch*) *meat cut into strips and stewed to produce a thick sauce*
geschnitten [gəˈʃnɪtən] PP *von* **schneiden**
geschoben [gəˈʃo:bən] PP *von* **schieben**
geschollen [gəˈʃɔlən] PP *von* **schallen**
gescholten [gəˈʃɔltən] PP *von* **schelten**
Geschöpf [gəˈʃœpf] (**-(e)s, -e**) NT creature
geschoren [gəˈʃo:rən] PP *von* **scheren**
Geschoss [gəˈʃɔs] (**-es, -e**) NT, (ÖSTERR) **Geschoß** [gəˈʃo:s] (**-es, -e**) NT (*Mil*) projectile; (*Rakete*) missile; (*Stockwerk*) floor
geschossen [gəˈʃɔsən] PP *von* **schießen**
geschraubt [gəˈʃraʊpt] ADJ stilted, artificial
Geschrei [gəˈʃraɪ] (**-s**) NT cries *pl*, shouting; (*fig: Aufheben*) noise, fuss
geschrieben [gəˈʃri:bən] PP *von* **schreiben**
geschrien [gəˈʃri:n] PP *von* **schreien**
geschritten [gəˈʃrɪtən] PP *von* **schreiten**
geschunden [gəˈʃʊndən] PP *von* **schinden**
Geschütz [gəˈʃʏts] (**-es, -e**) NT gun, piece of artillery; **ein schweres ~ auffahren** (*fig*) to bring out the big guns; **Geschützfeuer** NT artillery fire, gunfire
geschützt ADJ protected; (*Winkel, Ecke*) sheltered
Geschw. ABK = **Geschwister**
Geschwader [gəˈʃva:dər] (**-s, -**) NT (*Naut*) squadron; (*Aviat*) group
Geschwafel [gəˈʃva:fəl] (**-s**) NT silly talk
Geschwätz [gəˈʃvɛts] (**-es**) NT chatter; (*Klatsch*) gossip
geschwätzig ADJ talkative; **Geschwätzigkeit** F talkativeness
geschweige [gəˈʃvaɪgə] ADV: **~ (denn)** let alone, not to mention
geschwiegen [gəˈʃvi:gən] PP *von* **schweigen**
geschwind [gəˈʃvɪnt] ADJ quick, swift
Geschwindigkeit [gəˈʃvɪndɪçkaɪt] F speed, velocity
Geschwindigkeits- ZW: **Geschwindigkeitsbegrenzung** F, **Geschwindigkeitsbeschränkung** F speed limit; **Geschwindigkeitsmesser** M (*Aut*) speedometer; **Geschwindigkeitsüberschreitung** F speeding
Geschwister [gəˈʃvɪstər] PL brothers and sisters *pl*
geschwollen [gəˈʃvɔlən] PP *von* **schwellen** ▸ ADJ pompous
geschwommen [gəˈʃvɔmən] PP *von* **schwimmen**
geschworen [gəˈʃvo:rən] PP *von* **schwören**
Geschworene(r) F(M) juror; **die Geschworenen** PL the jury
Geschwulst [gəˈʃvʊlst] (**-, Geschwülste**) F growth, tumour
geschwunden [gəˈʃvʊndən] PP *von* **schwinden**
geschwungen [gəˈʃvʊŋən] PP *von* **schwingen** ▸ ADJ curved
Geschwür [gəˈʃvy:r] (**-(e)s, -e**) NT ulcer; (*Furunkel*) boil
gesehen [gəˈze:ən] PP *von* **sehen**
Geselle [gəˈzɛlə] (**-n, -n**) M fellow; (*Handwerksgeselle*) journeyman
gesellen VR: **sich zu jdm ~** to join sb
Gesellenbrief M articles *pl*
Gesellenprüfung F examination to become a journeyman
gesellig ADJ sociable; **geselliges Beisammensein** get-together; **Geselligkeit** F sociability
Gesellschaft F society; (*Begleitung, Comm*) company; (*Abendgesellschaft etc*) party; (*pej*) crowd (*umg*); (*Kreis von Menschen*) group of people; **in schlechte ~ geraten** to get into bad company; **geschlossene ~** private party; **jdm ~ leisten** to keep sb company
Gesellschafter(in) (**-s, -**) M(F) shareholder; (*Partner*) partner
gesellschaftlich ADJ social
Gesellschafts- ZW: **Gesellschaftsanzug** M evening dress; **gesellschaftsfähig** ADJ socially acceptable; **Gesellschaftsordnung** F social structure; **Gesellschaftsreise** F group tour; **Gesellschaftsschicht** F social stratum; **Gesellschaftssystem** NT social system
gesessen [gəˈzɛsən] PP *von* **sitzen**
Gesetz [gəˈzɛts] (**-es, -e**) NT law; (*Parl*) act; (*Satzung, Regel*) rule; **vor dem ~** in (the eyes of the) law; **nach dem ~** under the law; **das oberste ~ (der Wirtschaft** *etc*) the golden rule (of industry *etc*); **Gesetzblatt** NT law gazette; **Gesetzbuch** NT statute book; **Gesetzentwurf** M bill
Gesetzeshüter M (*ironisch*) guardian of the law
Gesetzesvorlage F bill
Gesetz- ZW: **gesetzgebend** ADJ legislative; **Gesetzgeber** (**-s, -**) M legislator; **Gesetzgebung** F legislation; **gesetzlich** ADJ legal, lawful; **Gesetzlichkeit** F legality, lawfulness; **gesetzlos** ADJ lawless; **gesetzmäßig** ADJ lawful
gesetzt ADJ (*Mensch*) sedate ▸ KONJ: **~ den Fall ...** assuming (that) ...
gesetzwidrig ADJ illegal; (*unrechtmäßig*) unlawful
ges. gesch. ABK (= *gesetzlich geschützt*) reg.
Gesicht [gəˈzɪçt] (**-(e)s, -er**) NT face; **das Zweite ~** second sight; **das ist mir nie zu ~ gekommen** I've never laid eyes on that; **jdn zu ~ bekommen** to clap eyes on sb; **jdm etw ins ~ sagen** to tell sb sth to his face; **sein wahres ~ zeigen** to show (o.s. in) one's true colours; **jdm wie aus dem ~ geschnitten sein** to be the spitting image of sb
Gesichts- ZW: **Gesichtsausdruck** M (facial) expression; **Gesichtscreme** F face cream; **Gesichtsfarbe** F complexion; **Gesichtspackung** F face pack; **Gesichtspunkt** M point of view; **Gesichtswasser** NT face lotion; **Gesichtszüge** PL features *pl*
Gesindel [gəˈzɪndəl] (**-s**) NT rabble
gesinnt [gəˈzɪnt] ADJ disposed, minded
Gesinnung [gəˈzɪnʊŋ] F disposition; (*Ansicht*) views *pl*
Gesinnungs- ZW: **Gesinnungsgenosse** M like-minded person; **Gesinnungslosigkeit** F lack of conviction; **Gesinnungsschnüffelei**

(*pej*) F: **Gesinnungsschnüffelei betreiben** to pry into people's political convictions; **Gesinnungswandel** M change of opinion
gesittet [gəˈzɪtət] ADJ well-mannered
gesoffen [gəˈzɔfən] PP *von* **saufen**
gesogen [gəˈzoːgən] PP *von* **saugen**
gesollt [gəˈzɔlt] PP *von* **sollen**
gesondert [gəˈzɔndərt] ADJ separate
gesonnen [gəˈzɔnən] PP *von* **sinnen**
gespalten [gəˈʃpaltən] ADJ (*Bewusstsein*) split; (*Lippe*) cleft
Gespann [gəˈʃpan] (**-(e)s, -e**) NT team; (*umg*) couple
gespannt ADJ tense, strained; (*neugierig*) curious; (*begierig*) eager; **ich bin ~, ob** I wonder if *od* whether; **auf etw/jdn ~ sein** to look forward to sth/to meeting sb; **ich bin ~ wie ein Flitzebogen** (*hum: umg*) I'm on tenterhooks
Gespenst [gəˈʃpɛnst] (**-(e)s, -er**) NT ghost; (*fig: Gefahr*) spectre (BRIT), specter (US); **Gespenster sehen** (*fig: umg*) to imagine things
gespensterhaft, gespenstisch ADJ ghostly
gespielt [gəˈʃpiːlt] ADJ feigned
gespien [gəʃpiːn] PP *von* **speien**
gesponnen [gəʃpɔnən] PP *von* **spinnen**
Gespött [gəˈʃpœt] (**-(e)s**) NT mockery; **zum ~ werden** to become a laughing stock
Gespräch [gəˈʃprɛːç] (**-(e)s, -e**) NT conversation; (*Diskussion*) discussion; (*Anruf*) call; **zum ~ werden** to become a topic of conversation; **ein ~ unter vier Augen** a confidential *od* private talk; **mit jdm ins ~ kommen** to get into conversation with sb; (*fig*) to establish a dialogue with sb
gesprächig ADJ talkative; **Gesprächigkeit** F talkativeness
Gesprächs- ZW: **Gesprächseinheit** F (*Tel*) unit; **Gesprächsgegenstand** M topic; **Gesprächspartner** M: **mein Gesprächspartner bei den Verhandlungen** my opposite number at the talks; **Gesprächsstoff** M topics *pl*; **Gesprächsthema** NT subject *od* topic (of conversation)
gesprochen [gəˈʃprɔxən] PP *von* **sprechen**
gesprossen [gəˈʃprɔsən] PP *von* **sprießen**
gesprungen [gəˈʃprʊŋən] PP *von* **springen**
Gespür [gəˈʃpyːr] (**-s**) NT feeling
gest. ABK (= *gestorben*) dec.
Gestalt [gəˈʃtalt] (**-, -en**) F form, shape; (*Person*) figure; (*Liter: pej: Mensch*) character; **in ~ von** in the form of; **~ annehmen** to take shape
gestalten VT (*formen*) to shape, to form; (*organisieren*) to arrange, to organize ▶ VR: **sich ~ (zu)** to turn out (to be); **etw interessanter** *etc* **~** to make sth more interesting *etc*
Gestaltung F formation; (*Organisation*) organization
gestanden [gəʃtandən] PP *von* **stehen; gestehen**
geständig [gəˈʃtɛndɪç] ADJ: **~ sein** to have confessed
Geständnis [gəˈʃtɛntnɪs] (**-ses, -se**) NT confession
Gestank [gəˈʃtaŋk] (**-(e)s**) M stench
gestatten [gəˈʃtatən] VT to permit, to allow; **~ Sie?** may I?; **sich** *dat* **~, etw zu tun** to take the liberty of doing sth
Geste [ˈgɛstə] (**-, -n**) F gesture
Gesteck [gəˈʃtɛk] (**-(e)s, -e**) NT flower arrangement
gestehen [gəˈʃteːən] *unreg* VT to confess; **offen gestanden** quite frankly
Gestein [gəˈʃtaɪn] (**-(e)s, -e**) NT rock
Gestell [gəˈʃtɛl] (**-(e)s, -e**) NT stand; (*Regal*) shelf; (*Bettgestell, Brillengestell*) frame
gestellt ADJ (*unecht*) posed
gestern [ˈgɛstərn] ADV yesterday; **~ Abend/Morgen** yesterday evening/morning; **er ist nicht von ~** (*umg*) he wasn't born yesterday
gestiefelt [gəˈʃtiːfəlt] ADJ: **der Gestiefelte Kater** Puss-in-Boots
gestiegen [gəˈʃtiːgən] PP *von* **steigen**
Gestik (**-**) F gestures *pl*
gestikulieren [gɛstikuˈliːrən] VI to gesticulate
Gestirn [gəˈʃtɪrn] (**-(e)s, -e**) NT star
gestoben [gəˈʃtoːbən] PP *von* **stieben**
Gestöber [gəˈʃtøːbər] (**-s, -**) NT flurry; (*länger*) blizzard
gestochen [gəˈʃtɔxən] PP *von* **stechen** ▶ ADJ (*Handschrift*) clear, neat
gestohlen [gəˈʃtoːlən] PP *von* **stehlen** ▶ ADJ: **der/das kann mir ~ bleiben** (*umg*) he/it can go hang
gestorben [gəˈʃtɔrbən] PP *von* **sterben**
gestört [gəˈʃtøːrt] ADJ disturbed; (*Rundfunkempfang*) poor, with a lot of interference
gestoßen [gəˈʃtoːsən] PP *von* **stoßen**
Gestotter [gəˈʃtɔtər] (**-s**) NT stuttering, stammering
Gesträuch [gəˈʃtrɔʏç] (**-(e)s, -e**) NT shrubbery, bushes *pl*
gestreift [gəˈʃtraɪft] ADJ striped
gestrichen [gəˈʃtrɪçən] PP *von* **streichen** ▶ ADJ: **~ voll** (*genau voll*) level; (*sehr voll*) full to the brim; **ein gestrichener Teelöffel voll** a level teaspoon(ful)
gestrig [ˈgɛstrɪç] ADJ yesterday's
gestritten [gəˈʃtrɪtən] PP *von* **streiten**
Gestrüpp [gəˈʃtrʏp] (**-(e)s, -e**) NT undergrowth
gestunken [gəˈʃtʊŋkən] PP *von* **stinken**
Gestüt [gəˈʃtyːt] (**-(e)s, -e**) NT stud farm
Gesuch [gəˈzuːx] (**-(e)s, -e**) NT petition; (*Antrag*) application
gesucht ADJ (*begehrt*) sought after
gesund [gəˈzʊnt] ADJ healthy; **wieder ~ werden** to get better; **~ und munter** hale and hearty; **Gesundheit** F health; (*Sportlichkeit, fig*) healthiness; **Gesundheit!** bless you!; **bei guter Gesundheit** in good health; **gesundheitlich** ADJ health *attrib*, physical ▶ ADV physically; **wie geht es Ihnen gesundheitlich?** how's your health?
Gesundheits- ZW: **Gesundheitsamt** NT public health department; **Gesundheitsapostel** M (*ironisch*) health freak (*umg*); **Gesundheitsfarm** F

health farm; **Gesundheitsfürsorge** F health care; **Gesundheitsreform** F health service reforms *pl*; **Gesundheitsrisiko** NT health hazard; **gesundheitsschädlich** ADJ unhealthy; **Gesundheitssystem** NT health (care) system; **Gesundheitswesen** NT health service; **Gesundheitszeugnis** NT health certificate; **Gesundheitszustand** M state of health

gesundschreiben VT *unreg*: **jdn ~** to certify sb (as) fit

gesungen [gəˈzʊŋən] PP *von* **singen**

gesunken [gəˈzʊŋkən] PP *von* **sinken**

getan [gəˈta:n] PP *von* **tun** ▶ ADJ: **nach getaner Arbeit** when the day's work is done

Getier [gəˈti:ər] (**-(e)s, -e**) NT (*Tiere, bes Insekten*) creatures *pl*; (*einzelnes*) creature

Getöse [gəˈtø:zə] (**-s**) NT din, racket

getragen [gəˈtra:gən] PP *von* **tragen**

Getränk [gəˈtrɛŋk] (**-(e)s, -e**) NT drink

Getränkeautomat M drinks machine *od* dispenser

Getränkekarte F (*in Café*) list of beverages; (*in Restaurant*) wine list

getrauen [gəˈtraʊən] VR to dare

Getreide [gəˈtraɪdə] (**-s, -**) NT cereal, grain; **Getreidespeicher** M granary

getrennt [gəˈtrɛnt] ADJ separate; **~ leben** to be separated, to live apart; **~ zahlen** to pay separately

getreten [gəˈtre:tən] PP *von* **treten**

getreu [gəˈtrɔʏ] ADJ faithful

Getriebe [gəˈtri:bə] (**-s, -**) NT (*Leute*) bustle; (*Aut*) gearbox

getrieben PP *von* **treiben**

Getriebeöl NT transmission oil

getroffen [gəˈtrɔfən] PP *von* **treffen**

getrogen [gəˈtro:gən] PP *von* **trügen**

getrost [gəˈtro:st] ADV confidently; **~ sterben** to die in peace; **du kannst dich ~ auf ihn verlassen** you need have no fears about relying on him

getrunken [gəˈtrʊŋkən] PP *von* **trinken**

Getto [ˈgɛto] (**-s, -s**) NT ghetto

Gettoblaster [ˈgɛtobla:stər] (**-s, -s**) M ghettoblaster

Getue [gəˈtu:ə] (**-s**) NT fuss

Getümmel [gəˈtʏməl] (**-s**) NT turmoil

geübt [gəˈy:pt] ADJ experienced

GEW (**-**) F ABK (= *Gewerkschaft Erziehung und Wissenschaft*) *union of employees in education and science*

Gew. ABK = **Gewerkschaft**

Gewächs [gəˈvɛks] (**-es, -e**) NT growth; (*Pflanze*) plant

gewachsen [gəˈvaksən] PP *von* **wachsen²** ▶ ADJ: **jdm/etw ~ sein** to be sb's equal/equal to sth

Gewächshaus NT greenhouse

gewagt [gəˈva:kt] ADJ daring, risky

gewählt [gəˈvɛ:lt] ADJ (*Sprache*) refined, elegant

gewahr [gəˈva:r] ADJ: **eine** *od* **einer Sache** *gen* **~ werden** to become aware of sth

Gewähr [gəˈvɛ:r] (**-**) F guarantee; **keine ~ übernehmen für** to accept no responsibility for; **die Angabe erfolgt ohne ~** this information is supplied without liability

gewähren VT to grant; (*geben*) to provide; **jdn ~ lassen** not to stop sb

gewährleisten VT to guarantee

Gewährleistungspflicht F warranty obligation

Gewahrsam [gəˈva:rza:m] (**-s, -e**) M safekeeping; (*Polizeigewahrsam*) custody

Gewährsmann M informant, source

Gewährung F granting

Gewalt [gəˈvalt] (**-, -en**) F power; (*große Kraft*) force; (*Gewalttaten*) violence; **mit aller ~** with all one's might; **die ausübende/gesetzgebende/richterliche ~** the executive/legislature/judiciary; **elterliche ~** parental authority; **höhere ~** acts/an act of God; **Gewaltanwendung** F use of force

Gewaltenteilung F separation of powers

Gewaltherrschaft F tyranny

gewaltig ADJ tremendous; (*Irrtum*) huge; **sich ~ irren** to be very much mistaken

Gewalt- ZW: **gewaltlos** ADJ non-violent ▶ ADV without force/violence; **Gewaltmarsch** M forced march; **Gewaltmonopol** NT monopoly on the use of force; **gewaltsam** ADJ forcible; **gewalttätig** ADJ violent; **Gewaltverbrechen** NT crime of violence; **Gewaltverzicht** M non-aggression

Gewand [gəˈvant] (**-(e)s, Gewänder**) NT garment

gewandt [gəˈvant] PP *von* **wenden** ▶ ADJ deft, skilful (BRIT), skillful (US); (*erfahren*) experienced; **Gewandtheit** F dexterity, skill

gewann *etc* [gəˈvan] VB *siehe* **gewinnen**

gewaschen [gəˈvaʃən] PP *von* **waschen**

Gewässer [gəˈvɛsər] (**-s, -**) NT waters *pl*

Gewebe [gəˈve:bə] (**-s, -**) NT (*Stoff*) fabric; (*Biol*) tissue

Gewehr [gəˈve:r] (**-(e)s, -e**) NT (*Flinte*) rifle; (*Schrotbüchse*) shotgun; **Gewehrlauf** M rifle barrel; (*von Schrotbüchse*) barrel of a shotgun

Geweih [gəˈvaɪ] (**-(e)s, -e**) NT antlers *pl*

Gewerbe [gəˈvɛrbə] (**-s, -**) NT trade, occupation; **Handel und ~** trade and industry; **fahrendes ~** mobile trade; *siehe auch* **gewerbetreibend**; **Gewerbeaufsichtsamt** NT ≈ factory inspectorate; **Gewerbegebiet** NT industrial estate (BRIT) *od* park (US); **Gewerbepark** M trading estate, business park; **Gewerbeschein** M trading licence; **Gewerbeschule** F technical school

gewerbetreibend ADJ carrying on a trade

gewerblich ADJ industrial

gewerbsmäßig ADJ professional

Gewerbszweig M line of trade

Gewerkschaft [gəˈvɛrkʃaft] F trade *od* labor (US) union

Gewerkschafter(in), Gewerkschaftler(in) M(F) trade *od* labor (US) unionist

gewerkschaftlich ADJ: **wir haben uns ~ organisiert** we organized ourselves into a union

Gewerkschaftsbund M federation of trade *od* labor (US) unions, ≈ Trades Union Congress (BRIT), ≈ Federation of Labor (US)
gewesen [gə'veːzən] PP *von* **sein**
gewichen [gə'vɪçən] PP *von* **weichen**
Gewicht [gə'vɪçt] **(-(e)s, -e)** NT weight; (*fig*) importance
gewichten VT to evaluate
Gewichtheben (-s) NT (*Sport*) weight-lifting
gewichtig ADJ weighty
Gewichtsklasse F (*Sport*) weight (category)
gewieft [gə'viːft] (*umg*) ADJ shrewd, cunning
gewiesen [gə'viːzən] PP *von* **weisen**
gewillt [gə'vɪlt] ADJ willing, prepared
Gewimmel [gə'vɪməl] **(-s)** NT swarm; (*Menge*) crush
Gewinde [gə'vɪndə] **(-s, -)** NT (*Kranz*) wreath; (*von Schraube*) thread
Gewinn [gə'vɪn] **(-(e)s, -e)** M profit; (*bei Spiel*) winnings *pl*; **~ bringend** profitable; **etw mit ~ verkaufen** to sell sth at a profit; **aus etw ~ schlagen** (*umg*) to make a profit out of sth; **Gewinnanteil** M (*Comm*) dividend; **Gewinnausschüttung** F prize draw; **Gewinnbeteiligung** F profit-sharing; **gewinnbringend** ADJ profitable; **Gewinnchancen** PL (*beim Wetten*) odds *pl*; **Gewinneinbruch** M slump in profits
gewinnen *unreg* VT to win; (*erwerben*) to gain; (*Kohle, Öl*) to extract ▶ VI to win; (*profitieren*) to gain; **jdn (für etw) ~** to win sb over (to sth); **an etw** *dat* **~** to gain in sth
gewinnend ADJ winning, attractive
Gewinner(in) (-s, -) M(F) winner
Gewinn- ZW: **Gewinnmitnahme** F profit-taking; **Gewinnnummer** F winning number; **Gewinnspanne** F profit margin; **Gewinnsucht** F love of gain; **Gewinn- und Verlustrechnung** F profit and loss account
Gewinnung F (*von Kohle etc*) mining; (*von Zucker etc*) extraction
Gewinnwarnung F (*Comm*) profit warning
Gewirr [gə'vɪr] **(-(e)s, -e)** NT tangle; (*von Straßen*) maze
gewiss [gə'vɪs] ADJ certain ▶ ADV certainly; **in gewissem Maße** to a certain extent
Gewissen [gə'vɪsən] **(-s, -)** NT conscience; **ein gutes/schlechtes ~ haben** to have a clear/bad conscience; **jdm ins ~ reden** to have a serious talk with sb; **gewissenhaft** ADJ conscientious; **Gewissenhaftigkeit** F conscientiousness; **gewissenlos** ADJ unscrupulous
Gewissens- ZW: **Gewissensbisse** PL pangs of conscience *pl*, qualms *pl*; **Gewissensfrage** F matter of conscience; **Gewissensfreiheit** F freedom of conscience; **Gewissenskonflikt** M moral conflict
gewissermaßen [gəvɪsər'maːsən] ADV more or less, in a way
Gewissheit F certainty; **sich** *dat* **~ verschaffen** to find out for certain
gewisslich ADV surely
Gewitter [gə'vɪtər] **(-s, -)** NT thunderstorm
gewittern VI UNPERS: **es gewittert** there's a thunderstorm
gewitterschwül ADJ sultry and thundery
Gewitterwolke F thundercloud; (*fig: umg*) storm cloud
gewitzt [gə'vɪtst] ADJ shrewd, cunning
gewoben [gə'voːbən] PP *von* **weben**
gewogen [gə'voːgən] PP *von* **wiegen²** ▶ ADJ *+dat* well-disposed (towards)
gewöhnen [gə'vøːnən] VT: **jdn an etw** *akk* **~** to accustom sb to sth; (*erziehen zu*) to teach sb sth ▶ VR: **sich an etw** *akk* **~** to get used *od* accustomed to sth
Gewohnheit [gə'voːnhaɪt] F habit; (*Brauch*) custom; **aus ~** from habit; **zur ~ werden** to become a habit; **sich** *dat* **etw zur ~ machen** to make a habit of sth
Gewohnheits- IN ZW habitual; **Gewohnheitsmensch** M creature of habit; **Gewohnheitsrecht** NT common law; **Gewohnheitstier** (*umg*) NT creature of habit
gewöhnlich [gə'vøːnlɪç] ADJ usual; (*durchschnittlich*) ordinary; (*pej*) common; **wie ~** as usual
gewohnt [gə'voːnt] ADJ usual; **etw ~ sein** to be used to sth
Gewöhnung F: **~ (an** *+akk*) getting accustomed (to); (*das Angewöhnen*) training (in)
gewollt [gə'vɔlt] PP *von* **wollen** ▶ ADJ forced, artificial
gewonnen [gə'vɔnən] PP *von* **gewinnen**
geworben [gə'vɔrbən] PP *von* **werben**
geworden [gə'vɔrdən] PP *von* **werden**
geworfen [gə'vɔrfən] PP *von* **werfen**
gewrungen [gə'vrʊŋən] PP *von* **wringen**
Gewühl [gə'vyːl] **(-(e)s)** NT throng
gewunden [gə'vʊndən] PP *von* **winden**
gewunken [gə'vʊŋkən] PP *von* **winken**
Gewürz [gə'vʏrts] **(-es, -e)** NT spice; (*Pfeffer, Salz*) seasoning; **Gewürzgurke** F pickled gherkin; **Gewürznelke** F clove
gewusst [gə'vʊst] PP *von* **wissen**
gez. ABK (= *gezeichnet*) signed
gezackt [gə'tsakt] ADJ (*Fels*) jagged; (*Blatt*) serrated
gezähnt [gə'tsɛːnt] ADJ serrated, toothed
gezeichnet [gə'tsaɪçnət] ADJ marked
Gezeiten [gə'tsaɪtən] PL tides *pl*
Gezeter [gə'tseːtər] **(-s)** NT nagging
gezielt [gə'tsiːlt] ADJ (*Frage, Maßnahme*) specific; (*Hilfe*) well-directed; (*Kritik*) pointed
geziemen [gə'tsiːmən] VR UNPERS to be fitting
geziemend ADJ proper
geziert [gə'tsiːrt] ADJ affected; **Geziertheit** F affectation
gezogen [gə'tsoːgən] PP *von* **ziehen**
Gezwitscher [gə'tsvɪtʃər] **(-s)** NT twitter(ing), chirping
gezwungen [gə'tsvʊŋən] PP *von* **zwingen** ▶ ADJ forced; (*Atmosphäre*) strained
gezwungenermaßen ADV of necessity; **etw ~ tun** to be forced to do sth, to do sth of necessity
GG ABK = **Grundgesetz**

ggf. ABK = **gegebenenfalls**
Ghetto ['gɛto] (**-s, -s**) NT = **Getto**
Gibraltar [gi'braltar] (**-s**) NT Gibraltar
gibst [gi:pst] VB *siehe* **geben**
gibt VB *siehe* **geben**
Gicht [gɪçt] (**-**) F gout; **gichtisch** ADJ gouty
Giebel ['gi:bəl] (**-s, -**) M gable; **Giebeldach** NT gable(d) roof; **Giebelfenster** NT gable window
Gier [gi:r] (**-**) F greed
gierig ADJ greedy
Gießbach M torrent
gießen ['gi:sən] *unreg* VT to pour; (*Blumen*) to water; (*Metall*) to cast; (*Wachs*) to mould ▶ VI UNPERS: **es gießt in Strömen** it's pouring down
Gießerei [gi:sə'raɪ] F foundry
Gießkanne F watering can
Gift [gɪft] (**-(e)s, -e**) NT poison; **das ist ~ für ihn** (*umg*) that is very bad for him; **darauf kannst du ~ nehmen** (*umg*) you can bet your life on it; **giftgrün** ADJ bilious green
giftig ADJ poisonous; (*fig: boshaft*) venomous
Giftler(in) ['gɪftlər] M(F) (ÖSTERR *umg*) junkie
Gift- ZW: **Giftmüll** M toxic waste; **Giftpilz** M poisonous toadstool; **Giftstoff** M toxic substance; **Giftwolke** F poisonous cloud; **Giftzahn** M fang; **Giftzwerg** (*umg*) M spiteful little devil
Gigabyte ['gɪgabaɪt] NT (*Comput*) gigabyte
Gilde ['gɪldə] (**-, -n**) F guild
gilt [gɪlt] VB *siehe* **gelten**
ging *etc* [gɪŋ] VB *siehe* **gehen**
Ginseng ['gɪnzɛŋ] (**-s, -s**) M ginseng
Ginster ['gɪnstər] (**-s, -**) M broom
Gipfel ['gɪpfəl] (**-s, -**) M summit, peak; (*fig*) height; **das ist der ~!** (*umg*) that's the limit!; **Gipfelkonferenz** F (*Pol*) summit conference
gipfeln VI to culminate
Gipfeltreffen NT summit (meeting)
Gips [gɪps] (**-es, -e**) M plaster; (*Med*) plaster (of Paris); **Gipsabdruck** M plaster cast; **Gipsbein** (*umg*) NT leg in plaster; **gipsen** VT to plaster; **Gipsfigur** F plaster figure; **Gipsverband** M plaster (cast)
Giraffe [gi'rafə] (**-, -n**) F giraffe
Girlande [gɪr'landə] (**-, -n**) F garland
Giro ['ʒi:ro] (**-s, -s**) NT giro; **Girokonto** NT current account (BRIT), checking account (US)
girren ['gɪrən] VI to coo
Gis [gɪs] (**-, -**) NT (*Mus*) G sharp
Gischt [gɪʃt] (**-(e)s, -e**) M OD F spray, foam
Gitarre [gi'tarə] (**-, -n**) F guitar
Gitter ['gɪtər] (**-s, -**) NT grating, bars *pl*; (*für Pflanzen*) trellis; (*Zaun*) railing(s); **Gitterbett** NT cot (BRIT), crib (US); **Gitterfenster** NT barred window; **Gitterzaun** M railing(s)
Glacéhandschuh, Glaceehandschuh [gla'se:hantʃu:] M kid glove
Gladiole [gladi'o:lə] (**-, -n**) F gladiolus
Glanz [glants] (**-es**) M shine, lustre (BRIT), luster (US); (*fig*) splendour (BRIT), splendor (US); **Glanzabzug** M (*Phot*) glossy *od* gloss print
glänzen ['glɛntsən] VI to shine (*auch fig*), to gleam
glänzend ADJ shining; (*fig*) brilliant; **wir haben uns ~ amüsiert** we had a marvellous *od* great time
Glanz- ZW: **Glanzlack** M gloss (paint); **Glanzleistung** F brilliant achievement; **glanzlos** ADJ dull; **Glanzstück** NT pièce de résistance; **Glanzzeit** F heyday
Glas [gla:s] (**-es, Gläser**) NT glass; (*Brillenglas*) lens *sing*; **zwei ~ Wein** two glasses of wine; **Glasbläser** M glass blower; **Glaser** (**-s, -**) M glazier; **Glasfaser** F fibreglass (BRIT), fiberglass (US); **Glasfaserkabel** NT optical fibre (BRIT) *od* fiber (US) cable
Glasgow ['gla:sgoʊ] NT Glasgow
glasieren [gla'zi:rən] VT to glaze
glasig ADJ glassy; (*Zwiebeln*) transparent
glasklar ADJ crystal clear
Glasscheibe F pane
Glassplitter M splinter of glass
Glasur [gla'zu:r] F glaze; (*Koch*) icing, frosting (*bes US*)
glatt [glat] ADJ smooth; (*rutschig*) slippery; (*Absage*) flat; (*Lüge*) downright; (*Haar*) straight; (*Med: Bruch*) clean; (*pej: allzu gewandt*) smooth, slick ▶ ADV: **~ rasiert** (*Mann, Kinn*) clean-shaven **~ streichen** to smooth out; *siehe auch* **glattgehen**
Glätte ['glɛtə] (**-, -n**) F smoothness; (*Schlüpfrigkeit*) slipperiness
Glatteis NT (black) ice; **„Vorsicht ~!"** "danger, black ice!"; **jdn aufs ~ führen** (*fig*) to take sb for a ride
Glätteisen NT hair straighteners *pl*
glätten VT to smooth out
glattgehen *unreg* VI to go smoothly
Glatze ['glatsə] (**-, -n**) F bald head; **eine ~ bekommen** to go bald
glatzköpfig ADJ bald
Glaube ['glaʊbə] (**-ns, -n**) M: **~ (an** *+akk***)** faith (in); (*Überzeugung*) belief (in); **den Glauben an jdn/etw verlieren** to lose faith in sb/sth
glauben VT, VI to believe; (*meinen*) to think; **jdm ~** to believe sb; **~ an** *+akk* to believe in; **jdm (etw) aufs Wort ~** to take sb's word (for sth); **wers glaubt, wird selig** (*ironisch*) a likely story
Glaubens- ZW: **Glaubensbekenntnis** NT creed; **Glaubensfreiheit** F religious freedom; **Glaubensgemeinschaft** F religious sect; (*christliche*) denomination
glaubhaft ['glaʊbhaft] ADJ credible; **jdm etw ~ machen** to satisfy sb of sth
Glaubhaftigkeit F credibility
gläubig ['glɔʏbɪç] ADJ (*Rel*) devout; (*vertrauensvoll*) trustful; **Gläubige(r)** F(M) believer; **die Gläubigen** PL the faithful
Gläubiger(in) (**-s, -**) M(F) creditor
glaubwürdig ['glaʊbvʏrdɪç] ADJ credible; (*Mensch*) trustworthy; **Glaubwürdigkeit** F credibility; (*von Mensch*) trustworthiness
gleich [glaɪç] ADJ equal; (*identisch*) (the) same, identical ▶ ADV equally; (*sofort*) straight away; (*bald*) in a minute; (*räumlich*): **~ hinter dem Haus** just behind the house; (*zeitlich*): **~ am Anfang** at the very beginning; **es ist mir ~**

it's all the same to me; **zu gleichen Teilen** in equal parts; **das gleiche, aber nicht dasselbe Auto** a similar car, but not the same one; **ganz ~ wer/was** *etc* no matter who/what *etc*; **2 mal 2 ~ 4** 2 times 2 is *od* equals 4; **bis ~!** see you soon!; **wie war doch ~ Ihr Name?** what was your name again?; **es ist ~ drei Uhr** it's very nearly three o'clock; **~ gesinnt** like-minded; **~ lautend** identical; **sie sind ~ groß** they are the same size; **~ nach/an** right after/at; **gleichaltrig** ADJ of the same age; **gleichartig** ADJ similar; **gleichbedeutend** ADJ synonymous; **gleichberechtigt** ADJ with equal rights; **Gleichberechtigung** F equal rights *pl*; **gleichbleibend** ADJ constant; **bei gleichbleibendem Gehalt** when one's salary stays the same

gleichen *unreg* VI: **jdm/etw ~** to be like sb/sth ▶ VR to be alike

gleichermaßen ADV equally

gleich- ZW: **gleichfalls** ADV likewise; **danke gleichfalls!** the same to you; **Gleichförmigkeit** F uniformity; **gleichgestellt** ADJ: **rechtlich gleichgestellt** equal in law; **Gleichgewicht** NT equilibrium, balance; **jdm aus dem Gleichgewicht bringen** to throw sb off balance; **gleichgültig** ADJ indifferent; (*unbedeutend*) unimportant; **Gleichgültigkeit** F indifference; **Gleichheit** F equality; (*Identität*) identity; (*Industrie*) parity; **Gleichheitsprinzip** NT principle of equality; **Gleichheitszeichen** NT (*Math*) equals sign; **gleichkommen** *unreg* VI +*dat* to be equal to; **gleichlautend** ADJ identical; **Gleichmacherei** F egalitarianism, levelling down (*pej*); **gleichmäßig** ADJ even, equal; **Gleichmut** M equanimity

Gleichnis (**-ses, -se**) NT parable

gleich- ZW: **gleichrangig** ADJ (*Probleme etc*) equally important; **gleichrangig (mit)** (*Beamte etc*) equal in rank (to), at the same level (as); **gleichsam** ADV as it were; **gleichschalten** (*pej*) VT to bring into line; **Gleichschritt** M: **im Gleichschritt, marsch!** forward march!; **gleichsehen** *unreg* VI: **jdm gleichsehen** to be *od* look like sb; **gleichstellen** VT (*rechtlich etc*) to treat as equal; **Gleichstrom** M (*Elek*) direct current; **gleichtun** *unreg* VI: **es jdm gleichtun** to match sb

Gleichung F equation

gleich- ZW: **gleichviel** ADV no matter; **gleichwertig** ADJ of the same value; (*Leistung, Qualität*) equal; (*Gegner*) evenly matched; **gleichwohl** ADV (*geh*) nevertheless; **gleichzeitig** ADJ simultaneous

Gleis [glaɪs] (**-es, -e**) NT track, rails *pl*; (*am Bahnhof*) platform (BRIT), track (US)

gleißend ['glaɪsənt] ADJ glistening, gleaming

gleiten *unreg* VI to glide; (*rutschen*) to slide

gleitend ['glaɪtənt] ADJ: **gleitende Arbeitszeit** flexible working hours *pl*, flex(i)time

Gleit- ZW: **Gleitflug** M glide; **Gleitklausel** F (*Comm*) escalator clause; **Gleitkomma** NT floating point; **Gleitzeit** F flex(i)time

Gletscher ['glɛtʃər] (**-s, -**) M glacier; **Gletscherspalte** F crevasse

glich *etc* [glɪç] VB *siehe* **gleichen**

Glied [gli:t] (**-(e)s, -er**) NT member; (*Arm, Bein*) limb; (*Penis*) penis; (*von Kette*) link; (*Mil*) rank(s); **der Schreck steckt ihr noch in den Gliedern** she is still shaking with the shock

gliedern VT to organize, to structure

Gliederreißen NT rheumatic pains *pl*

Gliederschmerz M rheumatic pains *pl*

Gliederung F structure, organization

Gliedmaßen PL limbs *pl*

glimmen ['glɪmən] *unreg* VI to glow

Glimmer (**-s, -**) M (*Mineral*) mica

Glimmstängel (*umg*) M fag (BRIT), butt (US)

glimpflich ['glɪmpflɪç] ADJ mild, lenient; **~ davonkommen** to get off lightly

glitschig ['glɪtʃɪç] (*umg*) ADJ slippery, slippy

glitt *etc* [glɪt] VB *siehe* **gleiten**

glitzern ['glɪtsərn] VI to glitter; (*Stern*) to twinkle

global [glo'ba:l] ADJ (*weltweit*) global, worldwide; (*ungefähr, pauschal*) general

Globalisierung [globalɪ'zi:rʊŋ] F globalization; **Globalisierungsfalle** F globalization trap

Globus ['glo:bʊs] (**-** *od* **-ses, Globen** *od* **-se**) M globe

Glöckchen ['glœkçən] NT (little) bell

Glocke ['glɔkə] (**-, -n**) F bell; **etw an die große ~ hängen** (*fig*) to shout sth from the rooftops

Glocken- ZW: **Glockengeläut** NT peal of bells; **Glockenschlag** M stroke (of the bell); (*von Uhr*) chime; **Glockenspiel** NT chime(s); (*Mus*) glockenspiel; **Glockenturm** M belfry, bell-tower

glomm *etc* [glɔm] VB *siehe* **glimmen**

Glorie ['glo:riə] F glory; (*von Heiligen*) halo

glorreich ['glo:rraɪç] ADJ glorious

Glossar [glɔ'sa:r] (**-s, -e**) NT glossary

Glosse ['glɔsə] (**-, -n**) F comment

Glotze (**-, -n**) (*umg*) F gogglebox (BRIT), TV set

glotzen ['glɔtsən] (*umg*) VI to stare

Glück [glʏk] (**-(e)s**) NT luck, fortune; (*Freude*) happiness; **~ haben** to be lucky; **viel ~** good luck; **zum ~** fortunately; **ein ~!** how lucky!, what a stroke of luck!; **auf gut ~** (*aufs Geratewohl*) on the off-chance; (*unvorbereitet*) trusting to luck; (*wahllos*) at random; **sie weiß noch nichts von ihrem ~** (*ironisch*) she doesn't know anything about it yet; **er kann von ~ sagen, dass …** he can count himself lucky that …; **Glückauf** NT: **„Glückauf"** (*Bergleute*) (cry of) "good luck"

Glucke (**-, -n**) F (*Bruthenne*) broody hen; (*mit Jungen*) mother hen

glücken VI to succeed; **es glückte ihm, es zu bekommen** he succeeded in getting it

gluckern ['glʊkərn] VI to glug

glücklich ADJ fortunate; (*froh*) happy ▶ ADV happily; (*umg: endlich, zu guter Letzt*) finally, eventually

glücklicherweise ADV fortunately

glücklos ADJ luckless

g

Glücksbringer (**-s, -**) M lucky charm
glückselig [glYk'ze:lıç] ADJ blissful
Glücks- zW: **Glücksfall** M stroke of luck; **Glückskind** NT lucky person; **Glückspilz** M lucky beggar (*umg*); **Glückssache** F matter of luck; **Glücksspiel** NT game of chance; **Glücksstern** M lucky star; **Glückssträhne** F lucky streak
glückstrahlend ADJ radiant (with happiness)
Glückszahl F lucky number
Glückwunsch M: **~ (zu)** congratulations *pl* (on), best wishes *pl* (on)
Glühbirne F light bulb
glühen ['gly:ən] VI to glow
glühend ADJ glowing; (*heiß glühend: Metall*) red-hot; (*Hitze*) blazing; (*fig: leidenschaftlich*) ardent; (*: Hass*) burning; (*Wangen*) flushed, burning
Glüh- zW: **Glühfaden** M (*Elek*) filament; **Glühwein** M mulled wine; **Glühwürmchen** NT glow-worm
Glut [glu:t] (**-, -en**) F (*Röte*) glow; (*Feuersglut*) fire; (*Hitze*) heat; (*fig*) ardour (BRIT), ardor (*US*)
GmbH (**-, -s**) F ABK (= *Gesellschaft mit beschränkter Haftung*) ≈ Ltd. (BRIT), plc (BRIT), Inc. (*US*)
Gnade ['gna:də] (**-, -n**) F (*Gunst*) favour (BRIT), favor (*US*); (*Erbarmen*) mercy; (*Milde*) clemency; **~ vor Recht ergehen lassen** to temper justice with mercy
gnaden VI: **(dann) gnade dir Gott!** (then) God help you *od* heaven have mercy on you!
Gnaden- zW: **Gnadenbrot** NT: **jdm/einem Tier das Gnadenbrot geben** to keep sb/an animal in his/her/its old age; **Gnadenfrist** F reprieve; **Gnadengesuch** NT petition for clemency; **gnadenlos** ADJ merciless; **Gnadenstoß** M coup de grâce
gnädig ['gnɛ:dıç] ADJ gracious; (*voll Erbarmen*) merciful; **gnädige Frau** (*form*) madam, ma'am
Gockel ['gɔkəl] (**-s, -**) M (*bes SÜDD*) cock
Gold [gɔlt] (**-(e)s**) NT gold; **nicht mit ~ zu bezahlen** *od* **aufzuwiegen sein** to be worth one's weight in gold; **golden** ADJ golden; **goldene Worte** words of wisdom; **der Tanz ums Goldene Kalb** (*fig*) the worship of Mammon; **Goldfisch** M goldfish; **Goldgrube** F gold mine; **Goldhamster** M (golden) hamster
goldig ['gɔldıç] ADJ (*fig: umg*) sweet, cute
Gold- zW: **Goldmedaille** F gold medal; **Goldregen** M laburnum; (*fig*) riches *pl*; **goldrichtig** (*umg*) ADJ dead right; **Goldschnitt** M gilt edging; **Goldstandard** M gold standard; **Goldstück** NT piece of gold; (*fig: umg*) treasure; **Goldwaage** F: **jedes Wort auf die Goldwaage legen** (*fig*) to weigh one's words; **Goldwährung** F gold standard
Golf[1] [gɔlf] (**-(e)s, -e**) M gulf; **der (Persische) ~** the Gulf
Golf[2] [gɔlf] (**-s**) NT golf; **Golfplatz** M golf course; **Golfschläger** M golf club; **Golfspieler** M golfer
Golfstaaten PL: **die ~** the Gulf States *pl*
Golfstrom M (*Geog*) Gulf Stream
Gondel ['gɔndəl] (**-, -n**) F gondola; (*von Seilbahn*) cable car
gondeln (*umg*) VI: **durch die Welt ~** to go globetrotting
Gong [gɔŋ] (**-s, -s**) M gong; (*bei Boxkampf etc*) bell
gönnen ['gœnən] VT: **jdm etw ~** not to begrudge sb sth; **sich** *dat* **etw ~** to allow o.s. sth
Gönner (**-s, -**) M patron; **gönnerhaft** ADJ patronizing; **Gönnerin** F patroness; **Gönnermiene** F patronizing air
googeln ['gu:gəln] VT to google
Google® ['gu:gəl] NT Google®
gor *etc* [go:r] VB *siehe* **gären**
Gorilla [go'rıla] (**-s, -s**) M gorilla; (*umg: Leibwächter*) heavy
goss *etc* [gɔs] VB *siehe* **gießen**
Gosse ['gɔsə] (**-, -n**) F gutter
Gote ['go:tə] (**-n, -n**) M Goth
Gotik ['go:tık] F (*Kunst*) Gothic (style); (*Epoche*) Gothic period
Gotin ['go:tın] F Goth
Gott [gɔt] (**-es, Götter**) M god; (*als Name*) God; **um Gottes Willen!** for heaven's sake!; **~ sei Dank!** thank God!; **grüß ~!** (*bes* SÜDD, ÖSTERR) hello, good morning/afternoon/evening; **den lieben ~ einen guten Mann sein lassen** (*umg*) to take things as they come; **ein Bild für die Götter** (*hum: umg*) a sight for sore eyes; **das wissen die Götter** (*umg*) God (only) knows; **über ~ und die Welt reden** (*fig*) to talk about everything under the sun; **wie ~ in Frankreich leben** (*umg*) to be in clover
Götterspeise F (*Koch*) jelly (BRIT), jello (*US*)
Gottes- zW: **Gottesdienst** M service; **gottesfürchtig** ADJ god-fearing; **Gotteshaus** NT place of worship; **Gotteskrieger(in)** M(F) religious terrorist; **Gotteslästerung** F blasphemy
Gottheit F deity
Göttin ['gœtın] F goddess
göttlich ADJ divine
Gott- zW: **gottlob** INTERJ thank heavens!; **gottlos** ADJ godless; **gottverdammt** ADJ goddamn(ed); **gottverlassen** ADJ godforsaken; **Gottvertrauen** NT trust in God
Götze ['gœtsə] (**-n, -n**) M idol
Grab [gra:p] (**-(e)s, Gräber**) NT grave
grabbeln ['grabəln] (NORDD *umg*) VT to rummage
graben *unreg* VT to dig
Graben ['gra:bən] (**-s, Gräben**) M ditch; (*Mil*) trench
Grabesstille F (*liter*) deathly hush
Grab- zW: **Grabmal** NT monument; (*Grabstein*) gravestone; **Grabrede** F funeral oration; **Grabstein** M gravestone
gräbt VB *siehe* **graben**
Gracht [graxt] (**-, -en**) F canal
Grad [gra:t] (**-(e)s, -e**) M degree; **im höchsten ~(e)** extremely; **Verbrennungen ersten Grades** (*Med*) first-degree burns; **bis zu einem gewissen ~** up to a certain extent; **Gradeinteilung** F graduation; **gradlinig** ADJ straight; **gradweise** ADV gradually
Graf [gra:f] (**-en, -en**) M count, earl (BRIT)

Grafik ['gra:fɪk] (**-, -en**) F (*Illustration*) diagram; (*Comput, Tech*) graphics; (*Kunst*) graphic arts *pl*
Grafiker(in) ['gra:fɪkər(ɪn)] (**-s, -**) M(F) graphic artist; (*Illustrator*) illustrator
Grafikkarte F (*Comput*) graphics card
Grafikprogramm NT (*Comput*) graphics software
Gräfin ['grɛ:fɪn] F countess
grafisch ['gra:fɪʃ] ADJ graphic; **grafische Darstellung** graph
Grafschaft F county
Grahambrot ['gra:hambro:t] NT type of wholemeal (BRIT) *od* whole-wheat (*US*) bread
Gralshüter ['gra:lzhy:tər] (**-s, -**) M (*fig*) guardian
Gram [gra:m] (**-(e)s**) M (*geh*) grief, sorrow
grämen ['grɛ:mən] VR to grieve; **sich zu Tode ~** to die of grief *od* sorrow
Gramm [gram] (**-s, -e**) NT gram(me)
Grammatik [gra'matɪk] F grammar
grammatisch ADJ grammatical
Grammofon, Grammophon [gramo'fo:n] (**-s, -e**) NT gramophone
Granat [gra'na:t] (**-(e)s, -e**) M (*Stein*) garnet; **Granatapfel** M pomegranate
Granate (**-, -n**) F (*Mil*) shell; (*Handgranate*) grenade
grandios [gran'dio:s] ADJ magnificent, superb
Granit [gra'ni:t] (**-s, -e**) M granite; **auf ~ beißen (bei …)** to bang one's head against a brick wall (with …)
grantig ['grantɪç] (*umg*) ADJ grumpy
Graphik ['gra:fɪk] = **Grafik**
grapschen ['grapʃən] (*umg*) VT, VI to grab; **(sich *dat*) etw ~** to grab sth
Gras [gra:s] (**-es, Gräser**) NT grass; (*auch umg: Marihuana*) grass; **über etw *akk* ~ wachsen lassen** (*fig*) to let the dust settle on sth; **grasen** VI to graze; **Grashalm** M blade of grass
grasig ADJ grassy
Grasnarbe F turf
grassieren [gra'si:rən] VI to be rampant, to rage
grässlich ['grɛslɪç] ADJ horrible
Grat [gra:t] (**-(e)s, -e**) M ridge
Gräte ['grɛ:tə] (**-, -n**) F fish-bone
Gratifikation [gratifikatsi'o:n] F bonus
gratis ['gra:tɪs] ADJ, ADV free (of charge); **Gratisprobe** F free sample
Grätsche ['grɛ:tʃə] (**-, -n**) F (*Sport*) straddle
Gratulant(in) [gratu'lant(ɪn)] M(F) well-wisher
Gratulation [gratulatsi'o:n] F congratulation(s)
gratulieren [gratu'li:rən] VI: **jdm (zu etw) ~** to congratulate sb (on sth); **(ich) gratuliere!** congratulations!
Gratwanderung F (*fig*) tightrope walk
grau [graʊ] ADJ grey (BRIT), gray (*US*); **der graue Alltag** drab reality; **~ meliert** grey-flecked (BRIT), gray-flecked (*US*); **Graubrot** NT = **Mischbrot**
Gräuel ['grɔʏəl] (**-s, -**) M horror; (*Gräueltat*) atrocity; **etw ist jdm ein ~** sb loathes sth; **Gräuelpropaganda** F atrocity propaganda; **Gräueltat** F atrocity

grauen VI (*Tag*) to dawn ▶ VI UNPERS: **es graut jdm vor etw** sb dreads sth, sb is afraid of sth ▶ VR: **sich ~ vor** to dread
Grauen (**-s**) NT horror
grauenhaft, grauenvoll ADJ horrible
grauhaarig ADJ grey-haired (BRIT), gray-haired (*US*)
gräulich ['grɔʏlɪç] ADJ horrible
Graupelregen ['graupəlre:gən] M sleet
Graupelschauer M sleet
Graupen ['graʊpən] PL pearl barley *sing*
grausam ['graʊza:m] ADJ cruel; **Grausamkeit** F cruelty
grausen VB = **grauen**
Grausen ['graʊzən] (**-s**) NT horror; **da kann man das kalte ~ kriegen** (*umg*) it's enough to give you the creeps
Grauzone F (*fig*) grey (BRIT) *od* gray (*US*) area
gravieren [gra'vi:rən] VT to engrave
gravierend ADJ grave
Grazie ['gra:tsiə] F grace
graziös [gratsi'ø:s] ADJ graceful
Greencard, Green Card ['gri:nka:əd] (**-, -s**) F green card
greifbar ADJ tangible, concrete; **in greifbarer Nähe** within reach
greifen ['graɪfən] *unreg* VT (*nehmen*) to grasp; (*grapschen*) to seize, to grab ▶ VI (*nicht rutschen, einrasten*) to grip; **nach etw ~** to reach for sth; **um sich ~** (*fig*) to spread; **zu etw ~** (*fig*) to turn to sth; **diese Zahl ist zu niedrig gegriffen** (*fig*) this figure is too low; **aus dem Leben gegriffen** taken from life
Greifer (**-s, -**) M (*Tech*) grab
Greifvogel M bird of prey
Greis [graɪs] (**-es, -e**) M old man
Greisenalter NT old age
greisenhaft ADJ very old
Greisin ['graɪzɪn] F old woman
grell [grɛl] ADJ harsh
Gremium ['gre:miʊm] NT body; (*Ausschuss*) committee
Grenadier [grena'di:ər] (**-s, -e**) M (*Mil: Infanterist*) infantryman
Grenzbeamte(r) M frontier official
Grenze (**-, -n**) F border; (*zwischen Grundstücken, fig*) boundary; (*Staatsgrenze*) frontier; (*Schranke*) limit; **über die ~ gehen/fahren** to cross the border; **hart an der ~ des Erlaubten** bordering on the limits of what is permitted
grenzen VI: **~ an** *+akk* to border on
grenzenlos ADJ boundless
Grenz- ZW: **Grenzfall** M borderline case; **Grenzgänger** M (*Arbeiter*) international commuter (*across a local border*); **Grenzgebiet** NT (*lit, fig*) border area; **Grenzkosten** PL marginal cost *sing*; **Grenzlinie** F boundary; **Grenzübergang** M frontier crossing; **Grenzwert** M limit; **Grenzzwischenfall** M border incident
Gretchenfrage ['gre:tçənfra:gə] F (*fig*) crunch question, sixty-four-thousand-dollar question (*umg*)

Greuel *etc* ['grɔʏəl] *siehe* **Gräuel**
greulich ['grɔʏlɪç] *siehe* **gräulich**
Grieche ['gri:çə] (**-n, -n**) M Greek
Griechenland NT Greece
Griechin ['gri:çɪn] F Greek
griechisch ADJ Greek
griesgrämig ['gri:sgrɛ:mɪç] ADJ grumpy
Grieß [gri:s] (**-es, -e**) M (*Koch*) semolina; **Grießbrei** M cooked semolina
griff *etc* VB *siehe* **greifen**
Griff [grɪf] (**-(e)s, -e**) M grip; (*Vorrichtung*) handle; (*das Greifen*): **der ~ nach etw** reaching for sth; **jdn/etw in den ~ bekommen** (*fig*) to gain control of sb/sth; **etw in den ~ bekommen** (*geistig*) to get a grasp of sth
griffbereit ADJ handy
Griffel ['grɪfəl] (**-s, -**) M slate pencil; (*Bot*) style
griffig ['grɪfɪç] ADJ (*Fahrbahn etc*) that has a good grip; (*fig: Ausdruck*) useful, handy
Grill [grɪl] (**-s, -s**) M grill; (*Aut*) grille
Grille ['grɪlə] (**-, -n**) F cricket; (*fig*) whim
grillen VT to grill
Grimasse [gri'masə] (**-, -n**) F grimace; **Grimassen schneiden** to make faces
grimmig ADJ furious; (*heftig*) fierce, severe
grinsen ['grɪnzən] VI to grin; (*höhnisch*) to smirk
Grippe ['grɪpə] (**-, -n**) F influenza, flu
Grips [grɪps] (**-es, -e**) (*umg*) M sense
grob [gro:p] ADJ coarse, gross; (*Fehler, Verstoß*) gross; (*brutal, derb*) rough; (*unhöflich*) ill-mannered; **~ geschätzt** at a rough estimate; **Grobheit** F coarseness; (*Beschimpfung*) coarse expression
Grobian ['gro:bia:n] (**-s, -e**) M ruffian
grobknochig ADJ large-boned
groggy ['grɔgɪ] ADJ (*Boxen*) groggy; (*umg: erschöpft*) bushed
grölen ['grø:lən] (*pej*) VT, VI to bawl
Groll [grɔl] (**-(e)s**) M resentment; **grollen** VI (*Donner*) to rumble; **grollen (mit** *od* *+dat***)** to bear ill will (towards)
Grönland ['grø:nlant] (**-s**) NT Greenland
Grönländer(in) (**-s, -**) M(F) Greenlander
Groschen ['grɔʃən] (**-s, -**) (*umg*) M 10-pfennig piece; (ÖSTERR) groschen; (*fig*) penny, cent (*US*); **Groschenroman** (*pej*) M cheap *od* dime (*US*) novel
groß [gro:s] ADJ big, large; (*hoch*) tall; (*Freude, Werk*) great ▸ ADV greatly; **im Großen und Ganzen** on the whole; **wie ~ bist du?** how tall are you?; **die Großen** (*Erwachsene*) the grown-ups; **mit etw ~ geworden sein** to have grown up with sth; **die Großen Seen** the Great Lakes *pl*; **großen Hunger haben** to be very hungry; **große Mode sein** to be all the fashion; **~ angelegt** large-scale, on a large scale; **~ und breit** (*fig: umg*) at great *od* enormous length; *siehe auch* **großschreiben**; **Großabnehmer** M (*Comm*) bulk buyer; **Großalarm** M red alert; **großartig** ADJ great, splendid; **Großaufnahme** F (*Film*) close-up; **Großbritannien** (**-s**) NT (Great) Britain; **Großbuchstabe** M capital (letter)
Größe ['grø:sə] (**-, -n**) F size; (*Länge*) height; (*fig*) greatness; **eine unbekannte ~** (*lit, fig*) an unknown quantity
Groß- zW: **Großeinkauf** M bulk purchase; **Großeinsatz** M: **Großeinsatz der Polizei** *etc* large-scale operation by the police *etc*; **Großeltern** PL grandparents *pl*
Größenordnung F scale; (*Größe*) magnitude; (*Math*) order (of magnitude)
großenteils ADV for the most part
Größen- zW: **Größenunterschied** M difference in size; **Größenwahn** M, **Größenwahnsinn** M megalomania, delusions *pl* of grandeur
Groß- zW: **Großformat** NT large size; **Großhandel** M wholesale trade; **Großhandelspreisindex** M wholesale-price index; **Großhändler** M wholesaler; **großherzig** ADJ generous; **Großhirn** NT cerebrum; **Großindustrielle(r)** F(M) major industrialist; **großkotzig** (*umg*) ADJ show-offish, bragging; **Großkundgebung** F mass rally; **Großmacht** F great power; **Großmarkt** M hypermarket; **Großmaul** M braggart; **Großmut** (-) F magnanimity; **großmütig** ADJ magnanimous; **Großmutter** F grandmother; **Großraum** M: **der Großraum München** the Munich area *od* conurbation, Greater Munich; **Großraumbüro** NT open-plan office; **Großrechner** M mainframe; **Großreinemachen** NT thorough cleaning, ≈ spring cleaning; **großschreiben** *unreg* VT: **ein Wort großschreiben** to write a word with a capital; **großgeschrieben werden** (*umg*) to be stressed; **Großschreibung** F capitalization; **großspurig** ADJ pompous; **Großstadt** F city
größte(r, s) [grø:stə(r, s)] ADJ *superl von* **groß**
größtenteils ADV for the most part
Groß- zW: **Großtuer** (**-s, -**) M boaster; **großtun** *unreg* VI to boast; **Großvater** M grandfather; **Großverbraucher** M (*Comm*) heavy user; **Großverdiener** M big earner; **Großwild** NT big game; **großziehen** *unreg* VT to raise; **großzügig** ADJ generous; (*Planung*) on a large scale
grotesk [gro'tɛsk] ADJ grotesque
Grotte ['grɔtə] (**-, -n**) F grotto
grub *etc* [gru:p] VB *siehe* **graben**
Grübchen ['gry:pçən] NT dimple
Grube ['gru:bə] (**-, -n**) F pit; (*Bergwerk*) mine
grübeln ['gry:bəln] VI to brood
Grubenarbeiter M miner
Grubengas NT firedamp
Grübler ['gry:blər] (**-s, -**) M brooder; **grüblerisch** ADJ brooding, pensive
Gruft [gruft] (**-, Grüfte**) F tomb, vault
grün [gry:n] ADJ green; (*ökologisch*) green; (*Pol*): **die Grünen** the Greens; **grüner Salat** lettuce; **grüne Bohnen** French beans; **grüne Minna** (*umg*) Black Maria (BRIT), paddy wagon (*US*); **grüne Welle** phased traffic lights; **grüne Versicherungskarte** (*Aut*) green card; **sich ~ und blau** *od* **gelb ärgern** (*umg*) to be furious; **auf keinen grünen Zweig kommen** (*fig: umg*) to get nowhere; **jdm grünes Licht geben** to give sb the green light; **Grünanlage** F park

Grund [grʊnt] (**-(e)s, Gründe**) M ground; (*von See, Gefäß*) bottom; (*fig*) reason; **von ~ auf** entirely, completely; **aus gesundheitlichen** *etc* **Gründen** for health *etc* reasons; **im Grunde genommen** basically; **ich habe ~ zu der Annahme, dass ...** I have reason to believe that ...; **einer Sache** *dat* **auf den ~ gehen** (*fig*) to get to the bottom of sth; **in ~ und Boden** (*fig*) utterly, thoroughly; *siehe auch* **aufgrund**; **zugrunde**; **Grundausbildung** F basic training; **Grundbedeutung** F basic meaning; **Grundbedingung** F fundamental condition; **Grundbegriff** M basic concept; **Grundbesitz** M land(ed property), real estate; **Grundbuch** NT land register; **grundehrlich** ADJ thoroughly honest

gründen [ˈgrʏndən] VT to found ▸ VR: **sich ~ auf** +*akk* to be based on; **~ auf** +*akk* to base on

Gründer(in) (**-s, -**) M(F) founder

Grund- zW: **grundfalsch** ADJ utterly wrong; **Grundgebühr** F basic charge; **Grundgedanke** M basic idea; **Grundgesetz** NT constitution

Grundierung [grʊnˈdiːrʊŋ] F (*Farbe*) primer

Grund- zW: **Grundkapital** NT nominal capital; **Grundkurs** M basic course; **Grundlage** F foundation; **jeder Grundlage** *gen* **entbehren** to be completely unfounded; **grundlegend** ADJ fundamental

gründlich ADJ thorough; **jdm ~ die Meinung sagen** to give sb a piece of one's mind

Grund- zW: **grundlos** ADJ (*fig*) groundless; **Grundmauer** F foundation wall; **Grundnahrungsmittel** NT basic food(stuff)

Gründonnerstag M Maundy Thursday

Grund- zW: **Grundordnung** F: **die freiheitlich-demokratische Grundordnung** (*Pol*) *the German constitution based on democratic liberty*; **Grundrechenart** F basic arithmetical operation; **Grundrecht** NT basic *od* constitutional right; **Grundregel** F basic *od* ground rule; **Grundriss** M plan; (*fig*) outline; **Grundsatz** M principle; **grundsätzlich** ADJ fundamental; (*Frage*) of principle ▸ ADV fundamentally; (*prinzipiell*) on principle; **das ist grundsätzlich verboten** it is absolutely forbidden; **Grundsatzurteil** NT *judgement that establishes a principle*

Grundschule F primary (BRIT) *od* elementary school

> The **Grundschule** is a primary school which children attend for 4 years from the age of 6 to 10. There are no formal examinations in the Grundschule but parents receive a report on their child's progress twice a year. Many children attend a **Kindergarten** from 3-6 years before going to the Grundschule, but no formal instruction takes place in the Kindergarten.

Grund- zW: **Grundsicherung** F (*Wirts*) guaranteed minimum income; **Grundstein** M foundation stone; **Grundsteuer** F rates *pl*; **Grundstück** NT plot (of land); (*Anwesen*) estate; **Grundstücksmakler** M estate agent (BRIT), realtor (US); **Grundstufe** F first stage; (*Sch*) ≈ junior (BRIT) *od* grade (US) school

Gründung F foundation

Gründungsurkunde F (*Comm*) certificate of incorporation

Gründungsversammlung F (*Aktiengesellschaft*) statutory meeting

Grund- zW: **grundverschieden** ADJ utterly different; **Grundwasser** NT ground water; **Grundwasserspiegel** M water table, ground-water level; **Grundzug** M characteristic; **etw in seinen Grundzügen darstellen** to outline (the essentials of) sth

Grüne (**-n**) NT: **im Grünen** in the open air; **ins ~ fahren** to go to the country

Grüne(r) F(M) (*Pol*) Ecologist, Green; **die Grünen** PL (*als Partei*) the Greens; *see note*

> Die **Grünen** is the name given to the Green or ecological party in Germany which was founded in 1980. Since 1993 they have been allied with the originally East German party, Bündnis 90.

> The **Grüner Punkt** is the green spot symbol which appears on packaging, indicating that the packaging should not be thrown into the normal household refuse but kept separate to be recycled through the **DSD** system. The recycling is financed by licences bought by the manufacturer from the DSD and the cost of this is often passed on to the consumer.

Grün- zW: **Grünkohl** M kale; **Grünschnabel** M greenhorn; **Grünspan** M verdigris; **Grünstreifen** M central reservation

grunzen [ˈgrʊntsən] VI to grunt

Gruppe [ˈgrʊpə] (**-, -n**) F group

Gruppen- zW: **Gruppenarbeit** F teamwork; **Gruppendynamik** F group dynamics *pl*; **Gruppentherapie** F group therapy; **gruppenweise** ADV in groups

gruppieren [grʊˈpiːrən] VT, VR to group

Gruselfilm M horror film

gruselig ADJ creepy

gruseln [ˈgruːzəln] VI UNPERS: **es gruselt jdm vor etw** sth gives sb the creeps ▸ VR to have the creeps

Gruß [gruːs] (**-es, Grüße**) M greeting; (*Mil*) salute; **viele Grüße** best wishes; **Grüße an** +*akk* regards to; **einen (schönen) ~ an Ihre Frau!** (*geh*) my regards to your wife; **mit freundlichen Grüßen** (*als Briefformel*) Yours sincerely

grüßen [ˈgryːsən] VT to greet; (*Mil*) to salute; **jdn von jdm ~** to give sb sb's regards; **jdn ~ lassen** to send sb one's regards

Grütze [ˈgrʏtsə] (**-, -n**) F (*Brei*) gruel; **rote ~** (type of) red fruit jelly

Guatemala [guateˈmaːla] (**-s**) NT Guatemala

Guayana [guaˈjaːna] (**-s**) NT Guyana

gucken [ˈgʊkən] VI to look

Guckloch NT peephole

Guinea [giˈneːa] (**-s**) NT Guinea

Gulasch ['gu:laʃ] (**-(e)s, -e**) NT goulash; **Gulaschkanone** F (*Mil: umg*) field kitchen

gültig ['gʏltɪç] ADJ valid; **~ werden** to become valid; (*Gesetz, Vertrag*) to come into effect; (*Münze*) to become legal tender; **Gültigkeit** F validity; **Gültigkeitsdauer** F period of validity

Gummi ['gʊmi] (**-s, -s**) NT OD M rubber; (*Gummiharze*) gum; (*umg: Kondom*) rubber, Durex®; (*Gummiband*) rubber *od* elastic band; (*Hosengummi*) elastic; **Gummiband** NT rubber *od* elastic band; **Gummibärchen** NT jelly baby; **Gummigeschoss** NT rubber bullet; **Gummiknüppel** M rubber truncheon; **Gummiparagraf** M ambiguous *od* meaningless law *od* statute; **Gummistiefel** M rubber boot, wellington (boot) (BRIT); **Gummistrumpf** M elastic stocking; **Gummizelle** F padded cell

Gunst [gʊnst] (**-**) F favour (BRIT), favor (US); *siehe auch* **zugunsten**

günstig ['gʏnstɪç] ADJ favourable (BRIT), favorable (US); (*Angebot, Preis etc*) reasonable, good; **bei günstiger Witterung** weather permitting; **im günstigsten Fall(e)** with luck

Gurgel ['gʊrgəl] (**-, -n**) F throat

gurgeln VI to gurgle; (*im Rachen*) to gargle

Gurke ['gʊrkə] (**-, -n**) F cucumber; **saure ~** pickled cucumber, gherkin

Gurt [gʊrt] (**-(e)s, -e**) M belt

Gurtanlegepflicht F (*form*) *obligation to wear a safety belt in vehicles*

Gürtel ['gʏrtəl] (**-s, -**) M belt; (*Geog*) zone; **Gürtelreifen** M radial tyre; **Gürtelrose** F shingles *sing od pl*

GUS [ge:lu:'lɛs] F ABK (= *Gemeinschaft Unabhängiger Staaten*) CIS

Guss [gʊs] (**-es, Güsse**) M casting; (*Regenguss*) downpour; (*Koch*) glazing; **Gusseisen** NT cast iron

SCHLÜSSELWORT

gut ADJ good; **das ist gut gegen** *od* **für** (*umg*) **Husten** it's good for coughs; **sei so gut (und) gib mir das** would you mind giving me that; **dafür ist er sich zu gut** he wouldn't stoop to that sort of thing; **das ist ja alles gut und schön, aber ...** that's all very well but ...; **du bist gut!** (*umg*) you're a fine one!; **alles Gute** all the best; **also gut** all right then
▸ ADV well; **gut gehen** to work, to come off; **es geht jdm gut** sb's doing fine; **das ist noch einmal gut gegangen** it turned out all right; **gut gehend** thriving; **gut gelaunt** cheerful, in a good mood; **gut gemeint** well meant; **du hast es gut!** you've got it made!; **gut situiert** well-off; **gut unterrichtet** well-informed; **gut, aber ...** OK, but ...; **(na) gut, ich komme** all right, I'll come; **gut drei Stunden** a good three hours; **das kann gut sein** that may well be; **gut und gern** easily; **lass es gut sein** that'll do; *siehe auch* **guttun**

Gut [gu:t] (**-(e)s, Güter**) NT (*Besitz*) possession; (*Landgut*) estate; **Güter** PL (*Waren*) goods *pl*

Gut- zW: **Gutachten** (**-s, -**) NT report; **Gutachter** (**-s, -**) M expert; **Gutachterkommission** F quango; **gutartig** ADJ good-natured; (*Med*) benign; **gutbürgerlich** ADJ (*Küche*) (good) plain; **Gutdünken** NT: **nach Gutdünken** at one's discretion

Güte ['gy:tə] (**-**) F goodness, kindness; (*Qualität*) quality; **ach du liebe** *od* **meine ~!** (*umg*) goodness me!; **Güteklasse** F (*Comm*) grade; **Güteklasseneinteilung** F (*Comm*) grading

Güter- zW: **Güterabfertigung** F (*Eisenb*) goods office; **Güterbahnhof** M goods station; **Gütertrennung** F (*Jur*) separation of property; **Güterverkehr** M freight traffic; **Güterwagen** M goods waggon (BRIT), freight car (US); **Güterzug** M goods train (BRIT), freight train (US)

Gütesiegel NT (*Comm*) stamp of quality

gut- zW: **gutgläubig** ADJ trusting; **guthaben** *unreg* VT: **30 Euro (bei jdm) guthaben** to be in credit (with sb) to the tune of 30 euros; **Guthaben** (**-s**) NT credit; **gutheißen** *unreg* VT to approve (of); **gutherzig** ADJ kind(-hearted)

gütig ['gy:tɪç] ADJ kind

gütlich ['gy:tlɪç] ADJ amicable

gut- zW: **gutmachen** VT (*in Ordnung bringen: Fehler*) to put right, to correct; (*Schaden*) to make good; **gutmütig** ADJ good-natured; **Gutmütigkeit** F good nature

Gutsbesitzer(in) M(F) landowner

Gut- zW: **Gutschein** M voucher; **gutschreiben** *unreg* VT to credit; **Gutschrift** F credit

Gutsherr M squire

Gutshof M estate

guttun *unreg* VI: **jdm ~** to do sb good

Gutverdienende(r) F(M) high-income earner

gutwillig ADJ willing

GV-Lebensmittel [ge:'faʊle:bənsmɪtəl] PL (= *gentechnisch veränderte Lebensmittel*) GM foods

GV-Pflanze [ge:'faʊpflantsə] F (= *gentechnisch veränderte Pflanze*) GM crop

Gymnasiallehrer(in) [gʏmnazi'a:lle:rər(ɪn)] M(F) ≈ grammar school teacher (BRIT), high school teacher (US)

Gymnasium [gʏm'na:ziʊm] NT ≈ grammar school (BRIT), high school (US)

> The **Gymnasium** is a selective secondary school. There are nine years of study at a Gymnasium leading to the **Abitur** which gives access to higher education. Pupils who successfully complete six years automatically gain the **mittlere Reife**.

Gymnastik [gʏm'nastɪk] F exercises *pl*, keep-fit; **~ machen** to do keep-fit (exercises)/gymnastics

Gynäkologe [gynɛko'lo:gə] (**-n, -n**) M, **Gynäkologin** F gynaecologist (BRIT), gynecologist (US)

H, h [haː] NT H, h; **H wie Heinrich** ≈ H for Harry, ≈ H for How (*US*); (*Mus*) B

ha ABK = **Hektar**

Haag [haːk] (**-s**) M: **Den ~** The Hague

Haar [haːr] (**-(e)s, -e**) NT hair; **um ein ~** nearly; **Haare auf den Zähnen haben** to be a tough customer; **sich die Haare raufen** (*umg*) to tear one's hair; **sich** *dat* **in die Haare kriegen** (*umg*) to quarrel; **das ist an den Haaren herbeigezogen** that's rather far-fetched; **Haaransatz** M hairline; **Haarbürste** F hairbrush

haaren VI, VR to lose hair

Haaresbreite F: **um ~** by a hair's-breadth

Haarfestiger (**-s, -**) M setting lotion

haargenau ADV precisely

Haarglätter M hair straighteners *pl*

haarig ADJ hairy; (*fig*) nasty

Haar- ZW: **Haarklammer** F, **Haarklemme** F hair grip (BRIT), barrette (*US*); **haarklein** ADV in minute detail; **haarlos** ADJ hairless; **Haarnadel** F hairpin; **haarscharf** ADV (*beobachten*) very sharply; (*verfehlen*) by a hair's breadth; **Haarschnitt** M haircut; **Haarschopf** M head of hair; **Haarsieb** NT fine sieve; **Haarspalterei** F hair-splitting; **Haarspange** F hair slide; **haarsträubend** ADJ hair-raising; **Haarteil** NT hairpiece; **Haartrockner** (**-s, -**) M hairdryer; **Haarwaschmittel** NT shampoo

Hab [haːp] NT: **~ und Gut** possessions *pl*, belongings *pl*, worldly goods *pl*

Habe ['haːbə] (**-**) F property

haben ['haːbən] *unreg* VT, HILFSVERB to have ▶ VR UNPERS: **und damit hat es sich** (*umg*) and that's that; **Hunger/Angst ~** to be hungry/ afraid; **da hast du 10 Euro** there's 10 euros; **die habens (ja)** (*umg*) they can afford it; **Ferien ~** to be on holiday; **es am Herzen ~** (*umg*) to have heart trouble; **sie ist noch zu ~** (*umg: nicht verheiratet*) she's still single; **für etw zu ~ sein** to be keen on sth; **sie werden schon merken, was sie an ihm ~** they'll see how valuable he is; **haste was, biste was** (*Sprichwort*) money brings status; **wie gehabt!** some things don't change; **das hast du jetzt davon** now see what's happened; **woher hast du das?** where did you get that from?; **was hast du denn?** what's the matter (with you)?; **ich habe zu tun** I'm busy

Haben (**-s, -**) NT (*Comm*) credit

Habenseite F (*Comm*) credit side

Habgier F avarice

habgierig ADJ avaricious

habhaft ADJ: **jds/einer Sache ~ werden** (*geh*) to get hold of sb/sth

Habicht ['haːbɪçt] (**-(e)s, -e**) M hawk

Habilitation [habilitatsi'oːn] F (*Lehrberechtigung*) postdoctoral lecturing qualification

Habseligkeiten ['haːpzeːlɪçkaɪtən] PL belongings *pl*

Habsucht ['haːpzʊxt] F greed

Hachse ['haksə] (**-, -n**) F (*Koch*) knuckle

Hackbraten M meat loaf

Hackbrett NT chopping board; (*Mus*) dulcimer

Hacke ['hakə] (**-, -n**) F hoe; (*Ferse*) heel

hacken VT to hack, to chop; (*Erde*) to hoe

Hacker ['hakər] (**-s, -**) M (*Comput*) hacker

Hackfleisch NT mince, minced meat, ground meat (*US*)

Hackordnung F (*lit, fig*) pecking order

Häcksel ['hɛksəl] (**-s**) M OD NT chopped straw, chaff

hadern ['haːdərn] VI (*geh*): **~ mit** to quarrel with; (*unzufrieden sein*) to be at odds with

Hafen ['haːfən] (**-s, Häfen**) M harbour, harbor (*US*), port; (*fig*) haven; **Hafenanlagen** PL docks *pl*; **Hafenarbeiter** M docker; **Hafendamm** M jetty, mole; **Hafengebühren** PL harbo(u)r dues *pl*; **Hafenstadt** F port

Hafer ['haːfər] (**-s, -**) M oats *pl*; **ihn sticht der ~** (*umg*) he is feeling his oats; **Haferbrei** M porridge (BRIT), oatmeal (*US*); **Haferflocken** PL rolled oats *pl* (BRIT), oatmeal (*US*); **Haferschleim** M gruel

Haff [haf] (**-s, -s** *od* **-e**) NT lagoon

Haft [haft] (**-**) F custody; **Haftanstalt** F detention centre (BRIT) *od* center (*US*); **haftbar** ADJ liable, responsible; **Haftbefehl** M warrant (for arrest); **einen Haftbefehl gegen jdn ausstellen** to issue a warrant for sb's arrest

haften VI to stick, to cling; **~ für** to be liable *od* responsible for; **für Garderobe kann nicht gehaftet werden** all articles are left at owner's risk; **~ bleiben (an** *+dat***)** to stick (to)

Häftling ['hɛftlɪŋ] M prisoner
Haft- zW: **Haftnotiz** F Post-it®; **Haftpflicht** F liability; **Haftpflichtversicherung** F third party insurance; **Haftrichter** M magistrate
Haftschalen PL contact lenses *pl*
Haftung F liability
Hagebutte ['ha:gəbʊtə] (**-, -n**) F rose hip
Hagedorn M hawthorn
Hagel ['ha:gəl] (**-s**) M hail; **Hagelkorn** NT hailstone; (*Med*) eye cyst
hageln VI UNPERS to hail
Hagelschauer M (short) hailstorm
hager ['ha:gər] ADJ gaunt
Häher ['hɛ:ər] (**-s, -**) M jay
Hahn [ha:n] (**-(e)s, Hähne**) M cock; (*Wasserhahn*) tap, faucet (*US*); (*Abzug*) trigger; **~ im Korb sein** (*umg*) to be cock of the walk; **danach kräht kein ~ mehr** (*umg*) no one cares two hoots about that any more
Hähnchen ['hɛ:nçən] NT cockerel; (*Koch*) chicken
Hai ['haɪ] (**-(e)s, -e**), **Haifisch** ['haɪfɪʃ] M shark
Haiti [ha'i:ti] (**-s**) NT Haiti
Häkchen ['hɛ:kçən] NT small hook
Häkelarbeit F crochet work
häkeln ['hɛ:kəln] VT to crochet
Häkelnadel F crochet hook
Haken ['ha:kən] (**-s, -**) M hook; (*fig*) catch; **einen ~ schlagen** to dart sideways; **Hakenkreuz** NT swastika; **Hakennase** F hooked nose
halb [halp] ADJ half ▸ ADV (*beinahe*) almost; **~ eins** half past twelve; **~ offen** half-open; **ein halbes Dutzend** half a dozen; **nichts Halbes und nichts Ganzes** neither one thing nor the other; **(noch) ein halbes Kind sein** to be scarcely more than a child; **das ist ~ so schlimm** it's not as bad as all that; **mit jdm halbe-halbe machen** (*umg*) to go halves with sb
halb- zW: **Halbblut** NT (*Tier*) crossbreed; **Halbbruder** M half-brother; **Halbdunkel** NT semi-darkness
halber ['halbər] PRÄP +*gen* (*wegen*) on account of; (*für*) for the sake of
Halb- zW: **halbfett** ADJ medium fat; **Halbfinale** NT semi-final; **Halbheit** F half-measure; **halbherzig** ADJ half-hearted
halbieren [hal'bi:rən] VT to halve
Halb- zW: **Halbinsel** F peninsula; **Halbjahr** NT half-year; **halbjährlich** ADJ half-yearly; **Halbkreis** M semicircle; **Halbkugel** F hemisphere; **halblang** ADJ: **nun mach mal halblang!** (*umg*) now wait a minute!; **halblaut** ADV in an undertone; **Halbleiter** M (*Phys*) semiconductor; **halbmast** ADV at half-mast; **Halbmond** M half-moon; (*fig*) crescent; **Halbpension** F half-board (BRIT), European plan (*US*); **Halbschuh** M shoe; **Halbschwester** F half-sister; **halbseiden** ADJ (*lit*) fifty per cent silk; (*fig: Dame*) fast; (*: homosexuell*) gay; **halbseitig** ADJ (*Anzeige*) half-page; **halbseitig gelähmt** paralyzed on one side; **Halbstarke(r)** F(M) hooligan, rowdy; **halbtags** ADV: **halbtags arbeiten** to work part-time; **Halbtagsarbeit** F part-time work; **Halbtagskraft** F part-time worker; **Halbton** M half-tone; (*Mus*) semitone; **halbtrocken** ADJ medium-dry; **Halbwaise** F *child/person who has lost one parent*; **halbwegs** ADV (*leidlich*) reasonably; **halbwegs besser** more or less better; **Halbwelt** F demimonde; **Halbwertzeit** F half-life; **Halbwüchsige(r)** F(M) adolescent; **Halbzeit** F (*Sport*) half; (*Pause*) half-time
Halde ['haldə] F tip; (*Schlackenhalde*) slag heap
half *etc* [half] VB *siehe* **helfen**
Hälfte ['hɛlftə] (**-, -n**) F half; **um die ~ steigen** to increase by half
Halfter[1] ['halftər] (**-s, -**) M OD NT (*für Tiere*) halter
Halfter[2] ['halftər] (**-, -n** *od* **-s, -**) NT OD F (*Pistolenhalfter*) holster
Hall [hal] (**-(e)s, -e**) M sound
Halle ['halə] (**-, -n**) F hall; (*Aviat*) hangar
hallen VI to echo, to resound
Hallen- IN zW indoor; **Hallenbad** NT indoor swimming pool
hallo [ha'lo:] INTERJ hello
Halluzination [halutsinatsi'o:n] F hallucination
Halm ['halm] (**-(e)s, -e**) M blade, stalk
Hals [hals] (**-es, Hälse**) M neck; (*Kehle*) throat; **sich** *dat* **nach jdm/etw den ~ verrenken** (*umg*) to crane one's neck to see sb/sth; **jdm um den ~ fallen** to fling one's arms around sb's neck; **aus vollem ~(e)** at the top of one's voice; **~ über Kopf** in a rush; **jdn auf dem** *od* **am ~ haben** (*umg*) to be lumbered *od* saddled with sb; **das hängt mir zum ~ raus** (*umg*) I'm sick and tired of it; **sie hat es in den falschen ~ bekommen** (*falsch verstehen*) she took it wrongly; **Halsabschneider** (*pej, umg*) M shark; **Halsband** NT (*Hundehalsband*) collar; **halsbrecherisch** ADJ (*Tempo*) breakneck; (*Fahrt*) hair-raising; **Halskette** F necklace; **Halskrause** F ruff; **Hals-Nasen-Ohren-Arzt** M ear, nose and throat specialist; **Halsschlagader** F carotid artery; **Halsschmerzen** PL sore throat *sing*; **halsstarrig** ADJ stubborn, obstinate; **Halstuch** NT scarf; **Hals- und Beinbruch** INTERJ good luck; **Halsweh** NT sore throat; **Halswirbel** M cervical vertebra
Halt [halt] (**-(e)s, -e**) M stop; (*fester Halt*) hold; (*innerer Halt*) stability; **~!** stop!, halt!; **~ machen** to stop
hält [hɛlt] VB *siehe* **halten**; **haltbar** ADJ durable; (*Lebensmittel*) non-perishable; (*Mil, fig*) tenable; **haltbar bis 6.11.** use by 6 Nov.
Halt- zW: **Haltbarkeit** F durability; (*Mil, fig*) tenability; (*von Lebensmitteln*) shelf life; **Haltbarkeitsdatum** NT best-before date
halten ['haltən] *unreg* VT to keep; (*festhalten*) to hold ▸ VI to hold; (*frisch bleiben*) to keep; (*stoppen*) to stop ▸ VR (*frisch bleiben*) to keep; (*sich behaupten*) to hold out; **den Mund ~** (*umg*) to keep one's mouth shut; **~ für** to regard as; **~ von** to think of; **das kannst du ~ wie du willst** that's

completely up to you; **der Film hält nicht, was er verspricht** the film doesn't live up to expectations; **davon halt(e) ich nichts** I don't think much of it; **zu jdm ~** to stand *od* stick by sb; **an sich** *akk* **~** to restrain o.s.; **auf sich** *akk* **~** (*auf Äußeres achten*) to take a pride in o.s.; **er hat sich gut gehalten** (*umg*) he's well-preserved; **sich an ein Versprechen ~** to keep a promise; **sich rechts/links ~** to keep to the right/left

Halter ['haltər] (**-s, -**) M (*Halterung*) holder

Haltestelle F stop

Halteverbot NT: **absolutes ~** no stopping; **eingeschränktes ~** no waiting; **hier ist ~** you cannot stop here

haltlos ADJ unstable

Haltlosigkeit F instability

haltmachen VI to stop

Haltung F posture; (*fig*) attitude; (*Selbstbeherrschung*) composure; **~ bewahren** to keep one's composure

Halunke [ha'lʊŋkə] (**-n, -n**) M rascal

Hamburg ['hambʊrk] (**-s**) NT Hamburg

Hamburger (**-s, -**) M (*Koch*) burger, hamburger

Hamburger(in) (**-s, -**) M(F) native of Hamburg

Hameln ['ha:məln] NT Hamelin

hämisch ['hɛ:mɪʃ] ADJ malicious

Hammel ['haməl] (**-s, -**) M wether; **Hammelfleisch** NT mutton; **Hammelkeule** F leg of mutton

Hammelsprung M (*Parl*) division

Hammer ['hamər] (**-s, Hämmer**) M hammer; **das ist ein ~!** (*umg: unerhört*) that's absurd!

hämmern ['hɛmərn] VT, VI to hammer

Hammondorgel ['hæməndlɔrgəl] F electric organ

Hämorrhoiden [hɛmɔro'i:dən], **Hämorriden** [hɛmɔ'ri:dən] PL piles *pl*, haemorrhoids *pl* (BRIT), hemorrhoids *pl* (US)

Hampelmann ['hampəlman] M (*lit, fig*) puppet

Hamster ['hamstər] (**-s, -**) M hamster

Hamsterei [hamstə'raɪ] F hoarding

Hamsterer (**-s, -**) M hoarder

hamstern VI to hoard

Hand [hant] (**-, Hände**) F hand; **etw zur ~ haben** to have sth to hand; (*Ausrede, Erklärung*) to have sth ready; **jdm zur ~ gehen** to lend sb a helping hand; **jdm die ~ geben** to shake hands with sb; **jdn bei der ~ nehmen** to take sb by the hand; **zu Händen von jdm** for the attention of sb; **in festen Händen sein** to be spoken for; **die ~ für jdn ins Feuer legen** to vouch for sb; **hinter vorgehaltener ~** on the quiet; **~ aufs Herz** cross your heart; **jdn auf Händen tragen** to cherish sb; **bei etw die** *od* **seine ~ im Spiel haben** to have a hand in sth; **eine ~ wäscht die andere** (*Sprichwort*) if you scratch my back I'll scratch yours; **das hat weder ~ noch Fuß** that doesn't make sense; **das liegt auf der ~** (*umg*) that's obvious; **unter der ~** secretly; (*verkaufen*) privately; *siehe auch* **anhand**; **Handarbeit** F manual work; (*Nadelarbeit*) needlework; **Handarbeiter** M manual worker; **Handball** M handball; **Handbesen** M brush; **Handbetrieb** M: **mit Handbetrieb** hand-operated; **Handbewegung** F gesture; **Handbibliothek** F (*in Bibliothek*) reference section; (*auf Schreibtisch*) reference books *pl*; **Handbremse** F handbrake; **Handbuch** NT handbook, manual

Händedruck M handshake

Händeklatschen NT clapping, applause

Handel[1] ['handəl] (**-s**) M trade; (*Geschäft*) transaction; **im ~ sein** to be on the market; **(mit jdm) ~ treiben** to trade (with sb); **etw in den ~ bringen/aus dem ~ ziehen** to put sth on/take sth off the market

Handel[2] (**-s, Händel**) M quarrel

handeln ['handəln] VI to trade; (*tätig werden*) to act ▶ VR UNPERS: **sich ~ um** to be a question of, to be about; **~ von** to be about; **ich lasse mit mir ~** I'm open to persuasion; (*in Bezug auf Preis*) I'm open to offers

Handeln (**-s**) NT action

handelnd ADJ: **die handelnden Personen in einem Drama** the characters in a drama

Handels- ZW: **Handelsbank** F merchant bank (BRIT), commercial bank; **Handelsbilanz** F balance of trade; **aktive/passive Handelsbilanz** balance of trade surplus/deficit; **Handelsdelegation** F trade mission; **handelseinig** ADJ: **mit jdm handelseinig werden** to conclude a deal with sb; **Handelsgesellschaft** F commercial company; **Handelskammer** F chamber of commerce; **Handelsklasse** F grade; **Handelsmarine** F merchant navy; **Handelsmarke** F trade name; **Handelsname** M trade name; **Handelsrecht** NT commercial law; **Handelsregister** NT register of companies; **Handelsreisende(r)** F(M) = **Handlungsreisende(r)**; **Handelssanktionen** PL trade sanctions *pl*; **Handelsschule** F business school; **Handelsspanne** F gross margin, mark-up; **Handelssperre** F trade embargo; **handelsüblich** ADJ customary; **Handelsvertreter** M sales representative; **Handelsvertretung** F trade mission; **Handelsware** F commodity

händeringend ['hɛndərɪŋənd] ADV wringing one's hands; (*fig*) imploringly

Hand- ZW: **Handfeger** (**-s, -**) M brush; **Handfertigkeit** F dexterity; **handfest** ADJ hefty; **Handfläche** F palm *od* flat (of one's hand); **handgearbeitet** ADJ handmade; **Handgelenk** NT wrist; **aus dem Handgelenk** (*umg: ohne Mühe*) effortlessly; (*: improvisiert*) off the cuff; **Handgemenge** NT scuffle; **Handgepäck** NT hand baggage *od* luggage; **handgeschrieben** ADJ handwritten; **Handgranate** F hand grenade; **handgreiflich** ADJ palpable; **handgreiflich werden** to become violent; **Handgriff** M flick of the wrist; **Handhabe** F: **ich habe gegen ihn keine Handhabe** (*fig*) I have no hold on him; **handhaben** *unreg* VT UNTR to handle; **Handkarren** M handcart; **Handkäse** M

h

strong-smelling, round German cheese; **Handkuss** M kiss on the hand; **Handlanger** (**-s, -**) M odd-job man, handyman; (*fig: Untergeordneter*) dogsbody
Händler ['hɛndlər] (**-s, -**) M trader, dealer
handlich ['hantlɪç] ADJ handy
Handlung ['handlʊŋ] F action; (*Tat*) act; (*in Buch*) plot; (*Geschäft*) shop
Handlungs- zW: **Handlungsablauf** M plot; **Handlungsbevollmächtigte(r)** F(M) authorized agent; **handlungsfähig** ADJ (*Regierung*) able to act; (*Jur*) empowered to act; **Handlungsfreiheit** F freedom of action; **handlungsorientiert** ADJ action-orientated; **Handlungsreisende(r)** F(M) commercial traveller (BRIT), traveling salesman (US); **Handlungsvollmacht** F proxy; **Handlungsweise** F manner of dealing
Hand- zW: **Handpflege** F manicure; **Handschelle** F handcuff; **Handschlag** M handshake; **keinen Handschlag tun** not to do a stroke (of work); **Handschrift** F handwriting; (*Text*) manuscript; **handschriftlich** ADJ handwritten ▸ ADV (*korrigieren, einfügen*) by hand; **Handschuh** M glove; **Handschuhfach** NT (*Aut*) glove compartment; **Handtasche** F handbag (BRIT), pocket book (US), purse (US); **Handtuch** NT towel; **Handumdrehen** NT: **im Handumdrehen** (*fig*) in the twinkling of an eye
Handwerk NT trade; (*Kunsthandwerk*) craft; **jdm das ~ legen** (*fig*) to put a stop to sb's game
Handwerker (**-s, -**) M workman; (*Kunsthandwerker*) craftsman, artisan
Handwerkskammer F trade corporation
Handwerkszeug NT tools *pl*
Handwörterbuch NT concise dictionary
Handy ['hɛndi] (**-s, -s**) NT (*Tel*) mobile (phone) (BRIT), cellphone (US)
Handzeichen NT signal; (*Geste*) sign; (*bei Abstimmung*) show of hands
Handzettel M leaflet, handbill
Hanf [hanf] (**-(e)s**) M hemp
Hang [haŋ] (**-(e)s, Hänge**) M inclination; (*Abhang*) slope
Hänge- ['hɛŋə] IN ZW hanging; **Hängebrücke** F suspension bridge; **Hängematte** F hammock
hängen *unreg* VI to hang ▸ VT: **~ (an** *+akk*) to hang (on(to)); **an jdm ~** (*fig*) to be attached to sb; **~ bleiben** to be caught; (*fig*) to remain, to stick; **~ bleiben an** *+dat* to catch *od* get caught on; **es bleibt ja doch alles an mir ~** (*fig: umg*) in the end it's all down to me anyhow; **~ lassen** (*vergessen*) to leave behind; **sich ~ lassen** to let o.s. go; **den Kopf ~ lassen** (*fig*) to be downcast; **die ganze Sache hängt an ihm** it all depends on him; **sich ~ an** *+akk* to hang on to, to cling to
Hängen ['hɛŋən] NT: **mit ~ und Würgen** (*umg*) by the skin of one's teeth
hängend ADJ: **mit hängender Zunge kam er angelaufen** (*fig*) he came running up panting
Hängeschloss NT padlock
Hanglage F: **in ~** situated on a slope
Hannover [ha'no:fər] (**-s**) NT Hanover
Hannoveraner(in) [hanovə'ra:nər(ɪn)] (**-s, -**) M(F) Hanoverian
hänseln ['hɛnzəln] VT to tease
Hansestadt ['hanzəʃtat] F Hanseatic *od* Hanse town
Hanswurst [hans'vʊrst] (**-(e)s, -e** *od* **-würste**) M clown
Hantel ['hantəl] (**-, -n**) F (*Sport*) dumb-bell
hantieren [han'ti:rən] VI to work, to be busy; **mit etw ~** to handle sth
hapern ['ha:pərn] VI UNPERS: **es hapert an etw** *dat* there is a lack of sth
Happen ['hapən] (**-s, -**) M mouthful
happig ['hapɪç] (*umg*) ADJ steep
Hardware ['ha:dwɛə] (**-, -s**) F hardware
Harfe ['harfə] (**-, -n**) F harp
Harke ['harkə] (**-, -n**) F rake
harken VT, VI to rake
harmlos ['harmlo:s] ADJ harmless
Harmlosigkeit F harmlessness
Harmonie [harmo'ni:] F harmony
harmonieren VI to harmonize
Harmonika [har'mo:nika] (**-, -s**) F (*Ziehharmonika*) concertina
harmonisch [har'mo:nɪʃ] ADJ harmonious
Harmonium [har'mo:niʊm] (**-s, -nien** *od* **-s**) NT harmonium
Harn ['harn] (**-(e)s, -e**) M urine; **Harnblase** F bladder
Harnisch ['harnɪʃ] (**-(e)s, -e**) M armour, armor (US); **jdn in ~ bringen** to infuriate sb; **in ~ geraten** to become angry
Harpune [har'pu:nə] (**-, -n**) F harpoon
harren ['harən] VI: **~ auf** *+akk* to wait for
Harsch [harʃ] (**-(e)s**) M frozen snow
harschig ADJ (*Schnee*) frozen
hart [hart] ADJ hard; (*fig*) harsh ▸ ADV: **das ist ~ an der Grenze** that's almost going too far; **harte Währung** hard currency; **~ bleiben** to stand firm; **~ gekocht** hard-boiled; **~ gesotten** (*Ei*) hard-boiled; **es geht ~ auf ~** it's a tough fight
Härte ['hɛrtə] (**-, -n**) F hardness; (*fig*) harshness; **soziale Härten** social hardships; **Härtefall** M case of hardship; (*umg: Mensch*) hardship case; **Härteklausel** F hardship clause
härten VT, VR to harden
hart- zW: **Hartfaserplatte** F hardboard, fiberboard (US); **hartgesotten** ADJ (*Kerl*) tough, hard-boiled; **hartherzig** ADJ hard-hearted; **hartnäckig** ADJ stubborn; **Hartnäckigkeit** F stubbornness
Harz[1] [ha:rts] (**-es, -e**) NT resin
Harz[2] (**-es**) M (*Geog*) Harz Mountains *pl*
Haschee [ha'ʃe:] (**-s, -s**) NT hash
haschen ['haʃən] VT to catch, to snatch ▸ VI (*umg*) to smoke hash
Haschisch ['haʃɪʃ] (**-**) NT hashish
Hase ['ha:zə] (**-n, -n**) M hare; **falscher ~** (*Koch*) meat loaf; **wissen, wie der ~ läuft** (*fig: umg*) to know which way the wind blows; **mein**

Name ist ~(, ich weiß von nichts) I don't know anything about anything
Haselnuss ['ha:zəlnʊs] F hazelnut
Hasenfuß M coward
Hasenscharte F harelip
Hashtag ['hæʃtæg] NT (*bes auf Twitter*) hash tag
Haspel (-, **-n**) F reel, bobbin; (*Winde*) winch
Hass [has] (**-es**) M hate, hatred; **einen ~ (auf jdn) haben** (*umg: Wut*) to be really mad (with sb)
hassen ['hasən] VT to hate; **etw ~ wie die Pest** (*umg*) to detest sth
hassenswert ADJ hateful
hässlich ['hɛslıç] ADJ ugly; (*gemein*) nasty; **Hässlichkeit** F ugliness; (*Gemeinheit*) nastiness
Hassliebe F love-hate relationship
hast VB *siehe* **haben**
Hast [hast] (-) F haste
hasten VI, VR to rush
hastig ADJ hasty
hat [hat] VB *siehe* **haben**
hätscheln ['hɛtʃəln] VT to pamper; (*zärtlich*) to cuddle
hatte *etc* ['hatə] VB *siehe* **haben**
hätte *etc* ['hɛtə] VB *siehe* **haben**
Haube ['haʊbə] (-, **-n**) F hood; (*Mütze*) cap; (*Aut*) bonnet (BRIT), hood (US); **unter der ~ sein/unter die ~ kommen** (*hum*) to be/get married
Hauch [haʊx] (**-(e)s, -e**) M breath; (*Lufthauch*) breeze; (*fig*) trace; **hauchdünn** ADJ extremely thin; (*Scheiben*) wafer-thin; (*fig: Mehrheit*) extremely narrow; **hauchen** VI to breathe; **hauchfein** ADJ very fine
Haue ['haʊə] (-, **-n**) F hoe; (*Pickel*) pick; (*umg*) hiding
hauen *unreg* VT to hew, to cut; (*umg*) to thrash
Hauer ['haʊər] (**-s, -**) M (*Min*) face-worker
Häufchen ['hɔʏfçən] NT: **ein ~ Unglück** *od* **Elend** a picture of misery
Haufen ['haʊfən] (**-s, -**) M heap; (*Leute*) crowd; **ein ~ (Bücher)** (*umg*) loads *od* a lot (of books); **auf einem ~** in one heap; **etw über den ~ werfen** (*umg: verwerfen*) to chuck sth out; **jdn über den ~ rennen** *od* **fahren** *etc* (*umg*) to knock sb down
häufen ['hɔʏfən] VT to pile up ▶ VR to accumulate
haufenweise ADV in heaps; (*scharenweise*) in droves; **etw ~ haben** to have piles of sth
häufig ['hɔʏfıç] ADJ frequent ▶ ADV frequently; **Häufigkeit** F frequency
Haupt [haʊpt] (**-(e)s, Häupter**) NT head; (*Oberhaupt*) chief ▶ IN ZW main; **Hauptakteur** M (*lit, fig*) leading light; (*pej*) main figure; **Hauptaktionär** M major shareholder; **Hauptbahnhof** M central station; **hauptberuflich** ADV as one's main occupation; **Hauptbuch** NT (*Comm*) ledger; **Hauptdarsteller(in)** M(F) leading actor, leading actress; **Haupteingang** M main entrance; **Hauptfach** NT (*Sch, Univ*) main subject, major (US); **etw im Hauptfach studieren** to study sth as one's main subject, to major in sth (US); **Hauptfilm** M main film; **Hauptgericht** NT main course; **Hauptgeschäftsstelle** F head office; **Hauptgeschäftszeit** F peak (shopping) period; **Hauptgewinn** M first prize; **einer der Hauptgewinne** one of the main prizes; **Hauptleitung** F mains *pl*
Häuptling ['hɔʏptlıŋ] M chief(tain)
Haupt- ZW: **Hauptmahlzeit** F main meal; **Hauptmann** (**-(e)s**, *pl* **-leute**) M (*Mil*) captain; **Hauptnahrungsmittel** NT staple food; **Hauptperson** F (*im Roman usw*) main character; (*fig*) central figure; **Hauptpostamt** NT main post office; **Hauptquartier** NT headquarters *pl*; **Hauptrolle** F leading part; **Hauptsache** F main thing; **in der Hauptsache** in the main, mainly; **hauptsächlich** ADJ chief ▶ ADV chiefly; **Hauptsaison** F peak *od* high season; **Hauptsatz** M main clause; **Hauptschlagader** F aorta; **Hauptschlüssel** M master key
Hauptschule F ≈ secondary modern (school) (BRIT), junior high (school) (US); *see note*

> The **Hauptschule** is a non-selective school which pupils attend after the **Grundschule**. They complete five years of study and most go on to do some training in a practical subject or trade.

Haupt- ZW: **Hauptsendezeit** F (*TV*) prime time; **Hauptstadt** F capital; **Hauptstraße** F main street; **Hauptverkehrsstraße** F (*in Stadt*) main street; (*Durchgangsstraße*) main thoroughfare; (*zwischen Städten*) main highway, trunk road (BRIT); **Hauptverkehrszeit** F rush hour; **Hauptversammlung** F general meeting; **Hauptwohnsitz** M main place of residence; **Hauptwort** NT noun
hau ruck ['hau 'rʊk] INTERJ heave-ho
Haus [haʊs] (**-es, Häuser**) NT house; **nach Hause** home; **zu Hause** at home; **fühl dich wie zu Hause!** make yourself at home!; **ein Freund des Hauses** a friend of the family; **~ halten** (*sparen*) to economize; **wir liefern frei ~** (*Comm*) we offer free delivery; **das erste ~ am Platze** (*Hotel*) the best hotel in town; **Hausangestellte** F domestic servant; **Hausarbeit** F housework; (*Sch*) homework; **Hausarrest** M (*im Internat*) detention; (*Jur*) house arrest; **Hausarzt** M family doctor; **Hausaufgabe** F (*Sch*) homework; **Hausbesetzung** F squat; **Hausbesitzer** M house-owner; **Hausbesuch** M home visit; (*von Arzt*) house call
Häuschen ['hɔʏsçən] NT: **ganz aus dem ~ sein** (*fig: umg*) to be out of one's mind (with excitement/fear *etc*)
Haus- ZW: **Hausdurchsuchung** F police raid; **Hausdurchsuchungsbefehl** M search warrant; **Hauseigentümer** M house-owner
hausen ['haʊzən] VI to live (in poverty); (*pej*) to wreak havoc
Häuser- ZW: **Häuserblock** M block (of houses); **Häusermakler** M estate agent (BRIT), real estate

agent (*US*); **Häuserreihe** F, **Häuserzeile** F row of houses; (*aneinandergebaut*) terrace (BRIT)

Haus- zW: **Hausflur** M hall; **Hausfrau** F housewife; **Hausfreund** M family friend; (*umg*) lover; **Hausfriedensbruch** M (*Jur*) trespass (*in sb's house*); **Hausgebrauch** M: **für den Hausgebrauch** (*Gerät*) for domestic *od* household use; **hausgemacht** ADJ home-made; **Hausgemeinschaft** F household (community); **Haushalt** M household; (*Pol*) budget; **haushalten** *unreg* VI (*old*) to keep house; (*sparen*) to economize; **Haushälterin** F housekeeper

Haushalts- zW: **Haushaltsauflösung** F dissolution of the household; **Haushaltsbuch** NT housekeeping book; **Haushaltsdebatte** F (*Parl*) budget debate; **Haushaltsgeld** NT housekeeping (money); **Haushaltsgerät** NT domestic appliance; **Haushaltshilfe** F domestic *od* home help; **Haushaltsjahr** NT (*Pol, Wirts*) financial *od* fiscal year; **Haushaltsperiode** F budget period; **Haushaltsplan** M budget

Haus- zW: **Haushaltung** F housekeeping; **Hausherr** M host; (*Vermieter*) landlord; **haushoch** ADV: **haushoch verlieren** to lose by a mile

hausieren [haʊ'zi:rən] VI to peddle

Hausierer (**-s, -**) M pedlar (BRIT), peddler (*US*)

hausintern ['hausǀɪntɛrn] ADJ internal company *attrib*

häuslich ['hɔyslɪç] ADJ domestic; **sich irgendwo ~ einrichten** *od* **niederlassen** to settle in somewhere; **Häuslichkeit** F domesticity

Hausmacherart ['hausmaxərǀa:rt] F: **Wurst** *etc* **nach ~** home-made-style sausage *etc*

Haus- zW: **Hausmann** (**-(e)s,** *pl* **-männer**) M (*den Haushalt versorgender Mann*) househusband; **Hausmarke** F (*eigene Marke*) own brand; (*bevorzugte Marke*) favourite (BRIT) *od* favorite (*US*) brand; **Hausmeister** M caretaker, janitor; **Hausmittel** NT household remedy; **Hausnummer** F house number; **Hausordnung** F house rules *pl*; **Hausputz** M house cleaning; **Hausratversicherung** F (household) contents insurance; **Hausschlüssel** M front-door key; **Hausschuh** M slipper; **Hausschwamm** M dry rot

Hausse ['ho:sə] (**-, -n**) F (*Wirts*) boom; (*Börse*) bull market; **~ an** *+dat* boom in

Haus- zW: **Haussegen** M: **bei ihnen hängt der Haussegen schief** (*hum*) they're a bit short on domestic bliss; **Hausstand** M: **einen Hausstand gründen** to set up house *od* home; **Haussuchung** F = **Hausdurchsuchung**; **Haussuchungsbefehl** M = **Hausdurchsuchungsbefehl**; **Haustier** NT domestic animal; **Haustür** F front door; **Hausverbot** NT: **jdm Hausverbot erteilen** to ban sb from the house; **Hausverwalter** M property manager; **Hausverwaltung** F property management; **Hauswirt** M landlord; **Hauswirtschaft** F domestic science; **Haus-zu-haus-Verkauf** M door-to-door selling

Haut [haʊt] (**-, Häute**) F skin; (*Tierhaut*) hide; **mit ~ und Haar(en)** (*umg*) completely; **aus der ~ fahren** (*umg*) to go through the roof; **Hautarzt** M skin specialist, dermatologist; **Hautcreme** F skin cream

häuten ['hɔytən] VT to skin ▸ VR to shed one's skin

hauteng ADJ skintight

Hautfarbe F complexion

Hautkrebs M (*Med*) skin cancer

Havanna [ha'vana] (**-s**) NT Havana

Havel ['ha:fəl] (**-**) F (*Fluss*) Havel

Haxe ['haksə] (**-, -n**) F = **Hachse**

Hbf. ABK = **Hauptbahnhof**

H-Bombe ['ha:bɔmbə] F ABK H-bomb

HDTV ABK (= *high definition television*) HDTV

Hebamme ['he:pǀamə] F midwife

Hebel ['he:bəl] (**-s, -**) M lever; **alle ~ in Bewegung setzen** (*umg*) to move heaven and earth; **am längeren ~ sitzen** (*umg*) to have the whip hand

heben ['he:bən] *unreg* VT to raise, to lift; (*steigern*) to increase; **einen ~ gehen** (*umg*) to go for a drink

Hebräer(in) [he'brɛ:ər(ɪn)] (**-s, -**) M(F) Hebrew

hebräisch [he'brɛ:ɪʃ] ADJ Hebrew

Hebriden [he'bri:dən] PL: **die ~** the Hebrides *pl*

hecheln ['hɛçəln] VI (*Hund*) to pant

Hecht [hɛçt] (**-(e)s, -e**) M pike; **Hechtsprung** M (*beim Schwimmen*) racing dive; (*beim Turnen*) forward dive; (*Fussball*: *umg*) dive

Heck [hɛk] (**-(e)s, -e**) NT stern; (*von Auto*) rear

Hecke ['hɛkə] (**-, -n**) F hedge

Heckenrose F dog rose

Heckenschütze M sniper

Heck- zW: **Heckfenster** NT (*Aut*) rear window; **Heckklappe** F tailgate; **Heckmotor** M rear engine; **Heckscheibe** F rear window

heda ['he:da] INTERJ hey there

Heer [he:r] (**-(e)s, -e**) NT army

Hefe ['he:fə] (**-, -n**) F yeast

Heft ['hɛft] (**-(e)s, -e**) NT exercise book; (*Zeitschrift*) number; (*von Messer*) haft; **jdm das ~ aus der Hand nehmen** (*fig*) to seize control *od* power from sb

Heftchen NT (*Fahrkartenheftchen*) book of tickets; (*Briefmarkenheftchen*) book of stamps

heften VT: **~ (an** *+akk*) to fasten (to); (*nähen*) to tack (on (to)); (*mit Heftmaschine*) to staple *od* fasten (to) ▸ VR: **sich an jds Fersen** *od* **Sohlen ~** (*fig*) to dog sb's heels

Hefter (**-s, -**) M folder

heftig ADJ fierce, violent; **Heftigkeit** F fierceness, violence

Heft- zW: **Heftklammer** F staple; **Heftmaschine** F stapling machine; **Heftpflaster** NT sticking plaster; **Heftzwecke** F drawing pin (BRIT), thumb tack (*US*)

hegen ['he:gən] VT to nurse; (*fig*) to harbour (BRIT), to harbor (*US*), to foster

Hehl [he:l] M OD NT: **kein(en) ~ aus etw machen** to make no secret of sth
Hehler (-s, -) M receiver (of stolen goods), fence
Heide¹ ['haɪdə] **(-, -n)** F heath, moor; (*Heidekraut*) heather
Heide² ['haɪdə] **(-n, -n)** M heathen, pagan
Heidekraut NT heather
Heidelbeere F bilberry
Heiden- zW: **Heidenangst** (*umg*) F: **eine Heidenangst vor etw/jdm haben** to be scared stiff of sth/sb; **Heidenarbeit** (*umg*) F real slog; **heidenmäßig** (*umg*) ADJ terrific; **Heidentum** NT paganism
Heidin F heathen, pagan
heidnisch ['haɪdnɪʃ] ADJ heathen, pagan
heikel ['haɪkəl] ADJ awkward, thorny; (*wählerisch*) fussy
heil ADJ in one piece, intact; **mit heiler Haut davonkommen** to escape unscathed; **die heile Welt** an ideal world (*without problems etc*)
Heil [haɪl] **(-(e)s)** NT well-being; (*Seelenheil*) salvation ▸ INTERJ hail; **Ski/Petri ~!** good skiing/fishing!
Heiland (-(e)s, -e) M saviour (BRIT), savior (US)
Heil- zW: **Heilanstalt** F nursing home; (*für Sucht- oder Geisteskranke*) home; **Heilbad** NT (*Bad*) medicinal bath; (*Ort*) spa; **heilbar** ADJ curable
Heilbutt ['haɪlbʊt] **(-s, -e)** M halibut
heilen VT to cure ▸ VI to heal; **als geheilt entlassen werden** to be discharged with a clean bill of health
heilfroh ADJ very relieved
Heilgymnastin F physiotherapist
heilig ['haɪlɪç] ADJ holy; **jdm ~ sein** (*lit, fig*) to be sacred to sb; **die Heilige Schrift** the Holy Scriptures *pl*; **es ist mein heiliger Ernst** I am deadly serious; *siehe auch* **heiligsprechen**; **Heiligabend** M Christmas Eve
Heilige(r) F(M) saint
heiligen VT to sanctify, to hallow; **der Zweck heiligt die Mittel** the end justifies the means
Heiligenschein M halo
Heiligkeit F holiness
heiligsprechen *unreg* VT to canonize
Heiligtum NT shrine; (*Gegenstand*) relic
Heilkunde F medicine
heillos ADJ unholy; (*Schreck*) terrible
Heil- zW: **Heilmittel** NT remedy; **Heilpraktiker(in) (-s, -)** M(F) non-medical practitioner; **heilsam** ADJ (*fig*) salutary
Heilsarmee F Salvation Army
Heilung F cure
heim [haɪm] ADV home
Heim (-(e)s, -e) NT home; (*Wohnheim*) hostel
Heimarbeit F (*Industrie*) homework, outwork
Heimat ['haɪma:t] **(-, -en)** F home (town/country *etc*); **Heimatfilm** M *sentimental film in idealized regional setting*; **Heimatkunde** F (*Sch*) local history; **Heimatland** NT homeland; **heimatlich** ADJ native, home *attrib*; (*Gefühle*) nostalgic; **heimatlos** ADJ homeless; **Heimatmuseum** NT local history museum; **Heimatort** M home town *od* area; **Heimatvertriebene(r)** F(M) displaced person
heimbegleiten VT to accompany home
Heimchen NT: **~ (am Herd)** (*pej*: *Frau*) housewife
Heimcomputer M home computer
heimelig ['haɪməlɪç] ADJ homely
Heim- zW: **heimfahren** *unreg* VI to drive *od* go home; **Heimfahrt** F journey home; **Heimgang** M return home; (*Tod*) decease; **heimgehen** *unreg* VI to go home; (*sterben*) to pass away; **heimisch** ADJ (*gebürtig*) native; **sich heimisch fühlen** to feel at home; **Heimkehr** F homecoming; **heimkehren** VI to return home; **Heimkind** NT *child brought up in a home*; **heimkommen** *unreg* VI to come home; **Heimleiter** M warden of a home/hostel
heimlich ADJ secret ▸ ADV: **~, still und leise** (*umg*) quietly, on the quiet; **Heimlichkeit** F secrecy; **Heimlichtuerei** F secrecy
Heim- zW: **Heimreise** F journey home; **Heimspiel** NT home game; **heimsuchen** VT to afflict; (*Geist*) to haunt; **heimtückisch** ADJ malicious; **heimwärts** ADV homewards; **Heimweg** M way home; **Heimweh** NT homesickness; **Heimweh haben** to be homesick; **Heimwerker** M DIY enthusiast; **heimzahlen** VT: **jdm etw heimzahlen** to pay back sb for sth
Heini ['haɪni] **(-s, -s)** M: **blöder ~** (*umg*) silly idiot
Heirat ['haɪra:t] **(-, -en)** F marriage; **heiraten** VT, VI to marry
Heirats- zW: **Heiratsantrag** M proposal (of marriage); **Heiratsanzeige** F (*Annonce*) advertisement for a marriage partner; **Heiratsschwindler** M *person who makes a marriage proposal under false pretences*; **Heiratsurkunde** F marriage certificate
heiser ['haɪzər] ADJ hoarse; **Heiserkeit** F hoarseness
heiß [haɪs] ADJ hot; (*Thema*) hotly disputed; (*Diskussion, Kampf*) heated, fierce; (*Begierde, Liebe, Wunsch*) burning; **mir ist ~** I'm hot; **es wird nichts so ~ gegessen, wie es gekocht wird** (*Sprichwort*) things are never as bad as they seem; **heißer Draht** hot line; **heißes Eisen** (*fig*: *umg*) hot potato; **heißes Geld** hot money; **~ ersehnt** longed for; **~ umstritten** hotly debated; **jdn/etw ~ und innig lieben** to love sb/sth madly; **heißblütig** ADJ hot-blooded
heißen ['haɪsən] *unreg* VI to be called; (*bedeuten*) to mean ▸ VT to command; (*nennen*) to name ▸ VI UNPERS: **es heißt hier ...** it says here ...; **es heißt, dass ...** they say that ...; **wie ~ Sie?** what's your name?; **... und wie sie alle ~ ...** and the rest of them; **das will schon etwas ~** that's quite something; **jdn willkommen ~** to bid sb welcome; **das heißt** that is; (*mit anderen Worten*) that is to say
Heiß- zW: **Heißhunger** M ravenous hunger; **heißlaufen** *unreg* VI, VR to overheat; **Heißluft** F hot air; **Heißwasserbereiter** M water heater
heiter ['haɪtər] ADJ cheerful; (*Wetter*) bright; **aus heiterem Himmel** (*fig*) out of the blue;

Heiterkeit F cheerfulness; (*Belustigung*) amusement
heizbar ADJ heated; (*Raum*) with heating; **leicht ~** easily heated
Heizdecke F electric blanket
heizen VT to heat
Heizer (**-s, -**) M stoker
Heiz- ZW: **Heizgerät** NT heater; **Heizkissen** M (*Med*) heated pad; **Heizkörper** M radiator; **Heizöl** NT fuel oil; **Heizsonne** F electric fire
Heizung F heating
Heizungsanlage F heating system
Hektar [hɛk'ta:r] (**-s, -e**) NT OD M hectare
Hektik ['hɛktɪk] F hectic rush; (*von Leben etc*) hectic pace
hektisch ['hɛktɪʃ] ADJ hectic
Hektoliter [hɛkto'li:tər] M OD NT hectolitre (BRIT), hectoliter (US)
Held [hɛlt] (**-en, -en**) M hero; **heldenhaft** ['hɛldənhaft] ADJ heroic; **Heldin** F heroine
helfen ['hɛlfən] *unreg* VI to help; (*nützen*) to be of use ▸ VB UNPERS: **es hilft nichts, du musst ...** it's no use, you'll have to ...; **jdm (bei etw) ~** to help sb (with sth); **sich** *dat* **zu ~ wissen** to be resourceful; **er weiß sich** *dat* **nicht mehr zu ~** he's at his wits' end
Helfer(in) (**-s, -**) M(F) helper, assistant
Helfershelfer M accomplice
Helgoland ['helgolant] (**-s**) NT Heligoland
hell [hɛl] ADJ clear; (*Licht, Himmel*) bright; (*Farbe*) light; **helles Bier** ≈ lager; **von etw ~ begeistert sein** to be very enthusiastic about sth; **es wird ~** it's getting light; **hellblau** ADJ light blue; **hellblond** ADJ ash-blond
Helle (**-**) F clearness; (*von Licht, Himmel*) brightness
Heller (**-s, -**) M (*Hist*) farthing; **auf ~ und Pfennig** (down) to the last penny
hellhörig ADJ keen of hearing; (*Wand*) poorly soundproofed
hellicht ['hɛlɪçt] ADJ *siehe* **helllicht**
Helligkeit F clearness; (*von Licht, Himmel*) brightness; (*von Farbe*) lightness
helllicht ['hɛllɪçt] ADJ: **am helllichten Tage** in broad daylight
hell- ZW: **Hellraumprojektor** M (SCHWEIZ) overhead projector; **hellsehen** VI: **hellsehen können** to be clairvoyant; **Hellseher(in)** M(F) clairvoyant; **hellwach** ADJ wide-awake
Helm ['hɛlm] (**-(e)s, -e**) M helmet
Helsinki ['hɛlzɪŋki] (**-s**) NT Helsinki
Hemd [hɛmt] (**-(e)s, -en**) NT shirt; (*Unterhemd*) vest; **Hemdbluse** F blouse
Hemdenknopf M shirt button
hemdsärmelig ADJ shirt-sleeved; (*fig: umg: salopp*) pally; (*Ausdrucksweise*) casual
Hemisphäre [hemi'sfɛ:rə] F hemisphere
hemmen ['hɛmən] VT to check, to hold up; **gehemmt sein** to be inhibited
Hemmschuh M (*fig*) impediment
Hemmung F check; (*Psych*) inhibition; (*Bedenken*) scruple
hemmungslos ADJ unrestrained, without restraint
Hengst [hɛŋst] (**-es, -e**) M stallion
Henkel ['hɛŋkəl] (**-s, -**) M handle; **Henkelkrug** M jug; **Henkelmann** (*umg*) M (*Gefäß*) canteen
henken ['hɛŋkən] VT to hang
Henker (**-s, -**) M hangman
Henne ['hɛnə] (**-, -n**) F hen
Hepatitis [hepa'ti:tɪs] (**-, Hepatitiden**) F hepatitis

SCHLÜSSELWORT

her [he:r] ADV **1** (*Richtung*): **komm her zu mir** come here (to me); **von England her** from England; **von weit her** from a long way away; **her damit!** hand it over!; **wo bist du her?** where do you come from?; **wo hat er das her?** where did he get that from?; **hinter jdm/etw her sein** to be after sb/sth
2 (*Blickpunkt*): **von der Form her** as far as the form is concerned
3 (*zeitlich*): **das ist 5 Jahre her** that was 5 years ago; **ich kenne ihn von früher her** I know him from before

herab [hɛ'rap] ADV down, downward(s); **herabhängen** *unreg* VI to hang down; **herablassen** *unreg* VT to let down ▸ VR to condescend; **herablassend** ADJ condescending; **Herablassung** F condescension; **herabsehen** *unreg* VI: **herabsehen (auf** +*akk*) to look down (on); **herabsetzen** VT to lower, to reduce; (*fig*) to belittle, to disparage; **zu stark herabgesetzten Preisen** at greatly reduced prices; **Herabsetzung** F reduction; (*fig*) disparagement; **herabstufen** VT to downgrade; **herabstürzen** VI to fall off; (*Felsbrocken*) to fall down; **von etw herabstürzen** to fall off sth; **herabwürdigen** VT to belittle, to disparage
heran [hɛ'ran] ADV: **näher ~!** come closer!; **~ zu mir!** come up to me!; **heranbilden** VT to train; **heranbringen** *unreg* VT: **heranbringen (an** +*akk*) to bring up (to); **heranfahren** *unreg* VI: **heranfahren (an** +*akk*) to drive up (to); **herangehen** *unreg* VI: **an etw** *akk* **herangehen** (*an Problem, Aufgabe*) to tackle sth; **herankommen** *unreg* VI: **(an jdn/etw) herankommen** to approach (sb/sth), to come near ((to) sb/sth); **er lässt alle Probleme an sich herankommen** he always adopts a wait-and-see attitude; **heranmachen** VR: **sich an jdn heranmachen** to make up to sb; (*umg*) to approach sb; **heranwachsen** *unreg* VI to grow up; **Heranwachsende(r)** F(M) adolescent; **heranwinken** VT to beckon over; (*Taxi*) to hail; **heranziehen** *unreg* VT to pull nearer; (*aufziehen*) to raise; (*ausbilden*) to train; (*zu Hilfe holen*) to call in; (*Literatur*) to consult; **etw zum Vergleich heranziehen** to use sth by way of comparison; **jdn zu etw heranziehen** to call upon sb to help in sth
herauf [hɛ'raʊf] ADV up, upward(s), up here; **heraufbeschwören** *unreg* VT to conjure up, to

evoke; **heraufbringen** *unreg* VT to bring up; **heraufsetzen** VT to increase; **heraufziehen** *unreg* VT to draw *od* pull up ▸ VI to approach; (*Sturm*) to gather

heraus [hɛˈraʊs] ADV out; **nach vorn ~ wohnen** to live at the front (of the house); **aus dem Gröbsten ~ sein** to be over the worst; **~ mit der Sprache!** out with it!; **herausarbeiten** VT to work out; **herausbekommen** *unreg* VT to get out; (*fig*) to find *od* figure out; (*Wechselgeld*) to get back; **herausbringen** *unreg* VT to bring out; (*Geheimnis*) to elicit; **jdn/etw ganz groß herausbringen** (*umg*) to give sb/sth a big build-up; **aus ihm war kein Wort herauszubringen** they couldn't get a single word out of him; **herausfinden** *unreg* VT to find out; **herausfordern** VT to challenge; (*provozieren*) to provoke; **Herausforderung** F challenge; (*Provokation*) provocation; **herausgeben** *unreg* VT to give up, to surrender; (*Geld*) to give back; (*Buch*) to edit; (*veröffentlichen*) to publish ▸ VI (*Wechselgeld geben*): **können Sie (mir) herausgeben?** can you give me change?; **Herausgeber (-s, -)** M editor; (*Verleger*) publisher; **herausgehen** *unreg* VI: **aus sich herausgehen** to come out of one's shell; **heraushalten** *unreg* VR: **sich aus etw heraushalten** to keep out of sth; **heraushängen** *unreg* VT, VI to hang out; **herausholen** VT: **herausholen (aus)** to get out (of); **heraushören** VT (*wahrnehmen*) to hear; (*fühlen*): **heraushören (aus)** to detect (in); **herauskehren** VT (*fig*): **den Vorgesetzten herauskehren** to act the boss; **herauskommen** *unreg* VI to come out; **dabei kommt nichts heraus** nothing will come of it; **er kam aus dem Staunen nicht heraus** he couldn't get over his astonishment; **es kommt auf dasselbe heraus** it comes (down) to the same thing; **herausnehmen** *unreg* VT to take out; **sich** *dat* **Freiheiten herausnehmen** to take liberties; **Sie nehmen sich zu viel heraus** you're going too far; **herausputzen** VT: **sich herausputzen** to get dressed up; **herausreden** VR to talk one's way out of it (*umg*); **herausreißen** *unreg* VT to tear out; (*Zahn, Baum*) to pull out; **herausrücken** VT (*Geld*) to fork out, to hand over; **mit etw herausrücken** (*fig*) to come out with sth; **herausrutschen** VI to slip out; **herausschlagen** *unreg* VT to knock out; (*fig*) to obtain; **herausstellen** VR: **sich herausstellen (als)** to turn out (to be); **das muss sich erst herausstellen** that remains to be seen; **herausstrecken** VT to stick out; **heraussuchen** VT: **sich** *dat* **jdn/etw heraussuchen** to pick out sb/sth; **heraustreten** *unreg* VI: **heraustreten (aus)** to come out (of); **herauswachsen** *unreg* VI: **herauswachsen aus** to grow out of; **herauswinden** *unreg* VR (*fig*): **sich aus etw herauswinden** to wriggle out of sth; **herauswollen** VI: **nicht mit etw herauswollen** (*umg: sagen wollen*) to not want to come out with sth; **herausziehen** *unreg* VT to pull out, to extract

herb [hɛrp] ADJ (slightly) bitter, acid; (*Wein*) dry; (*fig: schmerzlich*) bitter; (*: streng*) stern, austere

herbei [hɛrˈbaɪ] ADV (over) here; **herbeiführen** VT to bring about; **herbeischaffen** VT to procure; **herbeisehnen** VT to long for

herbemühen [ˈheːrbəmyːən] VR to take the trouble to come

Herberge [ˈhɛrbɛrɡə] **(-, -n)** F (*Jugendherberge etc*) hostel

Herbergseltern PL (youth hostel) wardens *pl*

Herbergsmutter F warden

Herbergsvater M warden

herbitten *unreg* VT to ask to come (here)

herbringen *unreg* VT to bring here

Herbst [hɛrpst] **(-(e)s, -e)** M autumn, fall (*US*); **im ~** in autumn, in the fall (*US*); **herbstlich** ADJ autumnal

Herd [heːrt] **(-(e)s, -e)** M cooker; (*fig, Med*) focus, centre (BRIT), center (*US*)

Herde [ˈheːrdə] **(-, -n)** F herd; (*Schafherde*) flock

Herdentrieb M (*lit, fig: pej*) herd instinct

Herdplatte F (*von Elektroherd*) hotplate

herein [hɛˈraɪn] ADV in (here), here; **~!** come in!; **hereinbitten** *unreg* VT to ask in; **hereinbrechen** *unreg* VI to set in; **hereinbringen** *unreg* VT to bring in; **hereindürfen** *unreg* VI to have permission to enter; **Hereinfall** M letdown; **hereinfallen** *unreg* VI to be caught, to be taken in; **hereinfallen auf** *+akk* to fall for; **hereinkommen** *unreg* VI to come in; **hereinlassen** *unreg* VT to admit; **hereinlegen** VT: **jdn hereinlegen** to take sb in; **hereinplatzen** VI to burst in; **hereinschneien** (*umg*) VI to drop in; **hereinspazieren** VI: **hereinspaziert!** come right in!

her- ZW: **Herfahrt** F journey here; **herfallen** *unreg* VI: **herfallen über** *+akk* to fall upon; **Hergang** M course of events, circumstances *pl*; **hergeben** *unreg* VT to give, to hand (over); **sich zu etw hergeben** to lend one's name to sth; **das Thema gibt viel/nichts her** there's a lot/nothing to this topic; **hergebracht** ADJ: **in hergebrachter Weise** in the traditional way; **hergehen** *unreg* VI: **hinter jdm hergehen** to follow sb; **es geht hoch her** there are a lot of goings-on; **herhaben** *unreg* (*umg*) VT: **wo hat er das her?** where did he get that from?; **herhalten** *unreg* VT to hold out; **herhalten müssen** (*umg*) to have to suffer; **herhören** VI to listen; **hör mal her!** listen here!

Hering [ˈheːrɪŋ] **(-s, -e)** M herring; (*Zeltpflock*) (tent) peg

herkommen *unreg* VI to come; **komm mal her!** come here!

herkömmlich ADJ traditional

Herkunft (-, -künfte) F origin

Herkunftsland NT (*Comm*) country of origin

her- ZW: **herlaufen** *unreg* VI: **herlaufen hinter** *+dat* to run after; **herleiten** VR to derive; **hermachen** VR: **sich hermachen über** *+akk* to

h

set about *od* upon ▶ VT (*umg*): **viel hermachen** to look impressive
Hermelin [hɛrmə'li:n] (**-s, -e**) M OD NT ermine
hermetisch [hɛr'me:tɪʃ] ADJ hermetic; **~ abgeriegelt** completely sealed off
her- ZW: **hernach** ADV afterwards; **hernehmen** *unreg* VT: **wo soll ich das hernehmen?** where am I supposed to get that from?; **hernieder** ADV down
Heroin [hero'i:n] (**-s**) NT heroin; **heroinsüchtig** ADJ addicted to heroin; **Heroinsüchtige(r)** F(M) heroin addict
heroisch [he'ro:ɪʃ] ADJ heroic
Herold ['he:rɔlt] (**-(e)s, -e**) M herald
Herpes ['hɛrpɛs] (**-**) M (*Med*) herpes
Herr [hɛr] (**-(e)n, -en**) M master; (*Mann*) gentleman; (*adliger, Rel*) Lord; (*vor Namen*) Mr; **mein ~!** sir!; **meine Herren!** gentlemen!; **Lieber ~ A, Sehr geehrter ~ A** (*in Brief*) Dear Mr A; **„Herren"** (*Toilette*) "gentlemen" (BRIT), "men's room" (US); **die Herren der Schöpfung** (*hum: Männer*) the gentlemen
Herrchen (*umg*) NT (*von Hund*) master
Herren- ZW: **Herrenbekanntschaft** F gentleman friend; **Herrenbekleidung** F menswear; **Herrenbesuch** M gentleman visitor *od* visitors; **Herrendoppel** NT men's doubles; **Herreneinzel** NT men's singles; **Herrenhaus** NT mansion; **herrenlos** ADJ ownerless; **Herrenmagazin** NT men's magazine
Herrgott M: **~ noch mal!** (*umg*) damn it all!
Herrgottsfrühe F: **in aller ~** (*umg*) at the crack of dawn
herrichten ['he:rrɪçtən] VT to prepare
Herrin F mistress
herrisch ADJ domineering
herrje [hɛr'je:] INTERJ goodness gracious!
herrjemine [hɛr'je:mine] INTERJ goodness gracious!
herrlich ADJ marvellous (BRIT), marvelous (US), splendid; **Herrlichkeit** F splendour (BRIT), splendor (US), magnificence
Herrschaft F power, rule; (*Herr und Herrin*) master and mistress; **meine Herrschaften!** ladies and gentlemen!
herrschen ['hɛrʃən] VI to rule; (*bestehen*) to prevail, to be; **hier ~ ja Zustände!** things are in a pretty state round here!
Herrscher(in) (**-s, -**) M(F) ruler
Herrschsucht F domineeringness
her- ZW: **herrühren** VI to arise, to originate; **hersagen** VT to recite; **hersehen** *unreg* VI: **hinter jdm/etw hersehen** to follow sb/sth with one's eyes
her sein *siehe* **her**
her- ZW: **herstammen** VI to descend *od* come from; **herstellen** VT to make, to manufacture; (*zustande bringen*) to establish; **Hersteller** (**-s, -**) M manufacturer; **Herstellung** F manufacture; **Herstellungskosten** PL manufacturing costs *pl*; **hertragen** *unreg* VT: **etw hinter jdm hertragen** to carry sth behind sb
herüber [hɛ'ry:bər] ADV over (here), across
herum [hɛ'rʊm] ADV about, (a)round; **um etw ~** around sth; **herumärgern** VR: **sich herumärgern (mit)** to get annoyed (with); **herumblättern** VI: **herumblättern in** *+dat* to browse *od* flick through; **herumdoktern** (*umg*) VI to fiddle *od* tinker about; **herumdrehen** VT: **jdm das Wort im Mund herumdrehen** to twist sb's words; **herumdrücken** VR (*vermeiden*): **sich um etw herumdrücken** to dodge sth; **herumfahren** *unreg* VI to travel around; (*mit Auto*) to drive around; (*sich rasch umdrehen*) to spin (a)round; **herumführen** VT to show around; **herumgammeln** (*umg*) VI to bum around; **herumgehen** *unreg* VI (*herumspazieren*) to walk about; **um etw herumgehen** to walk *od* go round sth; **etw herumgehen lassen** to circulate sth; **herumhacken** VI (*fig: umg*): **auf jdm herumhacken** to pick on sb; **herumirren** VI to wander about; **herumkommen** *unreg* (*umg*) VI: **um etw herumkommen** to get out of sth; **er ist viel herumgekommen** he has been around a lot; **herumkriegen** VT to bring *od* talk round; **herumlungern** VI to lounge about; (*umg*) to hang around; **herumquälen** VR: **sich mit Rheuma herumquälen** to be plagued by rheumatism; **herumreißen** *unreg* VT to swing around (hard); **herumschlagen** *unreg* VR: **sich mit etw herumschlagen** (*umg*) to tussle with sth; **herumschleppen** VT: **etw mit sich herumschleppen** (*Sorge, Problem*) to be troubled by sth; (*Krankheit*) to have sth; **herumsprechen** *unreg* VR to get around, to be spread; **herumstochern** (*umg*) VI: **im Essen herumstochern** to pick at one's food; **herumtreiben** *unreg* VI, VR to drift about; **Herumtreiber(in)** (**-s, -**) (*pej*) M(F) tramp; **herumziehen** *unreg* VI, VR to wander about
herunter [hɛ'rʊntər] ADV downward(s), down (there); **mit den Nerven/der Gesundheit ~ sein** (*umg*) to be at the end of one's tether/be run-down; **herunterbrechen** *unreg* VT (*Zahlen, Kalkulation*) to break down; **herunterfahren** *unreg* VTI (*Comput, Tech*) to shut down; **heruntergekommen** ADJ run-down; **herunterhandeln** VT (*Preis*) to beat down; **herunterhängen** *unreg* VI to hang down; **herunterholen** VT to bring down; **herunterkommen** *unreg* VI to come down; (*fig*) to come down in the world; **herunterladbar** ADJ (*Comput*) downloadable; **herunterladen** *unreg* VT (*Comput*) to download; **herunterleiern** (*umg*) VT to reel off; **heruntermachen** VT to take down; (*schlechtmachen*) to run down, to knock; **herunterputzen** (*umg*) VT: **jdn herunterputzen** to tear sb off a strip; **herunterspielen** VT to play down; **herunterwirtschaften** (*umg*) VT to bring to the brink of ruin
hervor [hɛr'fo:r] ADV out, forth; **hervorbrechen** *unreg* VI to burst forth, to break out; **hervorbringen** *unreg* VT to produce; (*Wort*) to utter; **hervorgehen** *unreg* VI to emerge, to

result; **daraus geht hervor, dass ...** from this it follows that ...; **hervorheben** *unreg* VT to stress; (*als Kontrast*) to set off; **hervorragend** ADJ excellent; (*lit*) projecting; **hervorrufen** *unreg* VT to cause, to give rise to; **hervorstechen** *unreg* VI (*lit, fig*) to stand out; **hervorstoßen** *unreg* VT (*Worte*) to gasp (out); **hervortreten** *unreg* VI to come out; **hervortun** *unreg* VR to distinguish o.s.; (*umg: sich wichtigtun*) to show off; **sich mit etw hervortun** to show off sth

Herz [hɛrts] (**-ens, -en**) NT heart; (*Karten: Farbe*) hearts *pl*; **mit ganzem Herzen** wholeheartedly; **etw auf dem Herzen haben** to have sth on one's mind; **sich** *dat* **etw zu Herzen nehmen** to take sth to heart; **du sprichst mir aus dem Herzen** that's just what I feel; **es liegt mir am Herzen** I am very concerned about it; **seinem Herzen Luft machen** to give vent to one's feelings; **sein ~ an jdn/etw hängen** to commit o.s. heart and soul to sb/sth; **ein ~ und eine Seele sein** to be the best of friends; **jdn/etw auf ~ und Nieren prüfen** to examine sb/sth very thoroughly; **Herzanfall** M heart attack; **Herzbeschwerden** PL heart trouble *sing*

herzen VT to caress, to embrace

Herzenslust F: **nach ~** to one's heart's content

Herz- ZW: **herzergreifend** ADJ heart-rending; **herzerweichend** ADJ heartrending; **Herzfehler** M heart defect; **herzhaft** ADJ hearty

herziehen ['he:rtsi:ən] VI: **über jdn/etw ~** (*umg*) to pull sb/sth to pieces (*fig*)

Herz- ZW: **Herzinfarkt** M heart attack; **Herzklappe** F (heart) valve; **Herzklopfen** NT palpitations *pl*; **herzkrank** ADJ suffering from a heart condition

herzlich ADJ cordial ▸ ADV (*sehr*): **~ gern!** with the greatest of pleasure!; **herzlichen Glückwunsch** congratulations *pl*; **herzliche Grüße** best wishes; **Herzlichkeit** F cordiality

herzlos ADJ heartless; **Herzlosigkeit** F heartlessness

Herzog ['hɛrtso:k] (**-(e)s, Herzöge**) M duke; **Herzogin** F duchess; **herzoglich** ADJ ducal; **Herzogtum** NT duchy

Herz- ZW: **Herzschlag** M heartbeat; (*Med*) heart attack; **Herzschrittmacher** M pacemaker; **herzzerreißend** ADJ heartrending

Hesse ['hɛsə] (**-n, -n**) M Hessian

Hessen ['hɛsən] (**-s**) NT Hesse

Hessin F Hessian

hessisch ADJ Hessian

heterogen [hetero'ge:n] ADJ heterogeneous

heterosexuell [heterozɛksu'ɛl] ADJ heterosexual

Hetze ['hɛtsə] F (*Eile*) rush

hetzen VT to hunt; (*verfolgen*) to chase ▸ VI (*eilen*) to rush; **jdn/etw auf jdn/etw ~** to set sb/sth on sb/sth; **~ gegen** to stir up feeling against; **~ zu** to agitate for

Hetzerei [hɛtsə'raɪ] F agitation; (*Eile*) rush

Hetzkampagne ['hɛtskampanjə] F smear campaign

Heu [hɔʏ] (**-(e)s**) NT hay; **Heuboden** M hayloft

Heuchelei [hɔʏçə'laɪ] F hypocrisy

heucheln ['hɔʏçəln] VT to pretend, to feign ▸ VI to be hypocritical

Heuchler(in) [hɔʏçlər(ɪn)] (**-s, -**) M(F) hypocrite; **heuchlerisch** ADJ hypocritical

heuer ADV this year

Heuer ['hɔʏər] (**-, -n**) F (*Naut*) pay

heuern ['hɔʏərn] VT to sign on, to hire

Heugabel F pitchfork

Heuhaufen M haystack

heulen ['hɔʏlən] VI to howl; (*weinen*) to cry; **das heulende Elend bekommen** to get the blues

heurig ['hɔʏrɪç] ADJ this year's

Heuschnupfen M hay fever

Heuschrecke F grasshopper; (*in heißen Ländern*) locust

heute ['hɔʏtə] ADV today; **~ Abend/früh** this evening/morning; **~ Morgen** this morning; **~ in einer Woche** a week today, today week; **von ~ auf morgen** (*fig: plötzlich*) overnight, from one day to the next; **das H~** today

heutig ['hɔʏtɪç] ADJ today's; **unser heutiges Schreiben** (*Comm*) our letter of today('s date)

heutzutage ['hɔʏttsuta:gə] ADV nowadays

Hexe ['hɛksə] (**-, -n**) F witch

hexen VI to practise witchcraft; **ich kann doch nicht ~** I can't work miracles

Hexen- ZW: **Hexenhäuschen** NT gingerbread house; **Hexenkessel** M (*lit, fig*) cauldron; **Hexenmeister** M wizard; **Hexenschuss** M lumbago

Hexerei [hɛksə'raɪ] F witchcraft

HG F ABK = **Handelsgesellschaft**

hg. ABK (= *herausgegeben*) ed.

Hg. ABK (= *Herausgeber*) ed.

HGB (**-**) NT ABK (= *Handelsgesetzbuch*) *statutes of commercial law*

hieb *etc* [hi:p] VB (*veraltet*) *siehe* **hauen**

Hieb (**-(e)s, -e**) M blow; (*Wunde*) cut, gash; (*Stichelei*) cutting remark; **Hiebe bekommen** to get a thrashing

hieb- und stichfest ADJ (*fig*) watertight

hielt *etc* [hi:lt] VB *siehe* **halten**

hier [hi:r] ADV here; **~ spricht Dr. Müller** (*Tel*) this is Dr Müller (speaking); **er ist von ~** he's a local (man); *siehe auch* **hierbehalten**; **hierbleiben**; **hierlassen**

Hierarchie [hierar'çi:] F hierarchy

hier- ZW: **hierauf** ADV thereupon; (*danach*) after that; **hieraus** ADV: **hieraus folgt, dass ...** from this it follows that ...; **hierbehalten** *unreg* VT to keep here; **hierbei** ADV (*bei dieser Gelegenheit*) on this occasion; **hierbleiben** *unreg* VI to stay here; **hierdurch** ADV by this means; (*örtlich*) through here; **hierher** ADV this way, here; **hierher gehören** to belong here; (*fig: relevant sein*) to be relevant; **hierlassen** *unreg* VT to leave here; **hiermit** ADV hereby; **hiermit erkläre ich ...** (*form*) I hereby declare ...; **hiernach** ADV hereafter; **hiervon** ADV about this, hereof; **hiervon abgesehen** apart from this; **hierzu** ADV (*dafür*) for this; (*dazu*) with this; (*außerdem*) in addition

to this, to moreover; (*zu diesem Punkt*) about this; **hierzulande, hier zu Lande** ADV in this country
hiesig ['hi:zɪç] ADJ of this place, local
hieß *etc* [hi:s] VB *siehe* **heißen**
Hi-Fi-Anlage ['haifianla:gə] F hi-fi set *od* system
Hightechindustrie ['haɪtɛkɪndʊs'tri:] F high tech *od* hi-tech industry
Hilfe ['hɪlfə] (**-, -n**) F help; (*für Notleidende*) aid; **Erste ~** first aid; **jdm ~ leisten** to help sb; **~!** help!; **Hilfeleistung** F: **unterlassene Hilfeleistung** (*Jur*) denial of assistance; **Hilfestellung** F (*Sport, fig*) support
Hilf- zW: **hilflos** ADJ helpless; **Hilflosigkeit** F helplessness; **hilfreich** ADJ helpful
Hilfs- zW: **Hilfsaktion** F relief action, relief measures *pl*; **Hilfsarbeiter** M labourer (BRIT), laborer (US); **hilfsbedürftig** ADJ needy; **hilfsbereit** ADJ ready to help; **Hilfskraft** F assistant, helper; **Hilfsmittel** NT aid; **Hilfsschule** F school for backward children; **Hilfszeitwort** NT auxiliary verb
hilft [hɪlft] VB *siehe* **helfen**
Himalaja [hi'ma:laja] (**-s**) M: **der ~** the Himalayas *pl*
Himbeere ['hɪmbe:rə] (**-, -n**) F raspberry
Himmel ['hɪməl] (**-s, -**) M sky; (*Rel*) heaven; **um Himmels willen** (*umg*) for Heaven's sake; **zwischen ~ und Erde** in midair; **himmelangst** ADJ: **es ist mir himmelangst** I'm scared to death; **Himmelbett** NT four-poster bed; **himmelblau** ADJ sky-blue
Himmelfahrt F Ascension
Himmelfahrtskommando NT (*Mil: umg*) suicide squad; (*Unternehmen*) suicide mission
Himmelreich NT (*Rel*) Kingdom of Heaven
himmelschreiend ADJ outrageous
Himmelsrichtung F direction; **die vier Himmelsrichtungen** the four points of the compass
himmelweit ADJ: **ein himmelweiter Unterschied** a world of difference
himmlisch ['hɪmlɪʃ] ADJ heavenly

SCHLÜSSELWORT

hin [hɪn] ADV **1** (*Richtung*): **hin und zurück** there and back; **einmal London hin und zurück** a return to London (BRIT), a roundtrip ticket to London (US); **hin und her** to and fro; **etw hin und her überlegen** to turn sth over and over in one's mind; **bis zur Mauer hin** up to the wall; **wo ist er hin?** where has he gone?; **nichts wie hin!** (*umg*) let's go then!; **nach außen hin** (*fig*) outwardly; **Geld hin, Geld her** money or no money
2 (*auf ... hin*): **auf meine Bitte hin** at my request; **auf seinen Rat hin** on the basis of his advice; **auf meinen Brief hin** on the strength of my letter
3: **hin sein** (*umg*) (*kaputt sein*) to have had it; (*Ruhe*) to be gone; **mein Glück ist hin** my happiness has gone; **hin und wieder** (every) now and again

hinab [hɪ'nap] ADV down; **hinabgehen** *unreg* VI to go down; **hinabsehen** *unreg* VI to look down
hinarbeiten ['hɪnarbaɪtən] VI: **auf etw** *akk* **~** (*auf Ziel*) to work towards sth
hinauf [hɪ'naʊf] ADV up; **hinaufarbeiten** VR to work one's way up; **hinaufsteigen** *unreg* VI to climb
hinaus [hɪ'naʊs] ADV out; **hinten/vorn ~** at the back/front; **darüber ~** over and above this; **auf Jahre ~** for years to come; **hinausbefördern** VT to kick *od* throw out; **hinausfliegen** *unreg* (*umg*) VI to be kicked out; **hinausführen** VI: **über etw** *akk* **hinausführen** (*lit, fig*) to go beyond sth; **hinausgehen** *unreg* VI to go out; **hinausgehen über** +*akk* to exceed; **hinauslaufen** *unreg* VI to run out; **hinauslaufen auf** +*akk* to come to, to amount to; **hinausschieben** *unreg* VT to put off, to postpone; **hinausschießen** *unreg* VI: **über das Ziel hinausschießen** (*fig*) to overshoot the mark; **hinauswachsen** *unreg* VI: **er wuchs über sich selbst hinaus** he surpassed himself; **hinauswerfen** *unreg* VT to throw out; **hinauswollen** VI to want to go out; **hoch hinauswollen** to aim high; **hinauswollen auf** +*akk* to drive at, to get at; **hinausziehen** *unreg* VT to draw out ▶ VR to be protracted; **hinauszögern** VT to delay, to put off ▶ VR to be delayed, to be put off
hinbekommen *unreg* (*umg*) VT: **das hast du gut ~** you've made a good job of it
hinblättern (*umg*) VT (*Geld*) to fork out
Hinblick ['hɪnblɪk] M: **in** *od* **im ~ auf** +*akk* in view of
hinderlich ['hɪndərlɪç] ADJ awkward; **jds Karriere** *dat* **~ sein** to be a hindrance to sb's career
hindern VT to hinder, to hamper; **jdn an etw** *dat* **~** to prevent sb from doing sth
Hindernis (**-ses, -se**) NT obstacle; **Hindernislauf** M, **Hindernisrennen** NT steeplechase
Hinderungsgrund M obstacle
hindeuten ['hɪndɔʏtən] VI: **~ auf** +*akk* to point to
Hinduismus [hɪndu'ɪsmʊs] M Hinduism
hindurch [hɪn'dʊrç] ADV through; (*quer durch*) across; (*zeitlich*) over
hindürfen [hɪn'dʏrfən] *unreg* VI: **~ (zu)** to be allowed to go (to)
hinein [hɪ'naɪn] ADV in; **bis tief in die Nacht ~** well into the night; **hineinfallen** *unreg* VI to fall in; **hineinfallen in** +*akk* to fall into; **hineinfinden** *unreg* VR (*fig: sich vertraut machen*) to find one's feet; (*sich abfinden*) to come to terms with it; **hineingehen** *unreg* VI to go in; **hineingehen in** +*akk* to go into, to enter; **hineingeraten** *unreg* VI: **hineingeraten in** +*akk* to get into; **hineinknien** VR (*fig: umg*): **sich in etw** *akk* **hineinknien** to get into sth; **hineinlesen** *unreg* VT: **etw in etw** *akk* **hineinlesen** to read sth into sth; **hineinpassen** VI to fit in; **hineinpassen in** +*akk* to fit into; **hineinprügeln** VT: **etw in jdn hineinprügeln** to cudgel sth into sb; **hineinreden** VI: **jdm hineinreden** to interfere in sb's affairs;

hineinstecken VT: **Geld/Arbeit in etw** *akk* **hineinstecken** to put money/some work into sth; **hineinsteigern** VR to get worked up; **hineinversetzen** VR: **sich in jdn hineinversetzen** to put o.s. in sb's position; **hineinziehen** *unreg* VT: **hineinziehen (in** *+akk***)** to pull in (to); **jdn in etw hineinziehen** (*in Konflikt, Gespräch*) to draw sb into sth; **hinfahren** *unreg* VI to go; (*mit Auto*) to drive ▸ VT to take; (*mit Auto*) to drive

hin- ZW: **Hinfahrt** F journey there; **hinfallen** *unreg* VI to fall down; **hinfällig** ADJ frail, decrepit; (*Regel etc*) unnecessary; **hinfliegen** *unreg* VI to fly there; (*umg: hinfallen*) to fall over; **Hinflug** M outward flight

hing *etc* [hɪŋ] VB *siehe* **hängen**

hin- ZW: **Hingabe** F devotion; **mit Hingabe tanzen/singen** *etc* (*fig*) to dance/sing *etc* with abandon; **hingeben** *unreg* VR *+dat* to give o.s. up to, to devote o.s. to; **hingebungsvoll** [ˈhɪngeːbʊŋsfɔl] ADV (*begeistert*) with abandon; (*lauschen*) raptly

hingegen [hɪnˈgeːgən] KONJ however

hin- ZW: **hingehen** *unreg* VI to go; (*Zeit*) to pass; **gehst du auch hin?** are you going too?; **hingerissen** ADJ: **hingerissen sein** to be enraptured; **hin- und hergerissen sein** (*fig*) to be torn; **ich bin ganz hin- und hergerissen** (*ironisch*) that's absolutely great; **hinhalten** *unreg* VT to hold out; (*warten lassen*) to put off, to stall; **Hinhaltetaktik** F stalling *od* delaying tactics *pl*

hinhauen [ˈhɪnhaʊən] *unreg* (*umg*) VI (*klappen*) to work; (*ausreichen*) to do

hinhören [ˈhɪnhøːrən] VI to listen

hinken [ˈhɪŋkən] VI to limp; (*Vergleich*) to be unconvincing

hinknien VR to kneel down; **hinkommen** *unreg* (*umg*) VI (*auskommen*) to manage; (: *ausreichen, stimmen*) to be right; **hinlänglich** ADJ adequate ▸ ADV adequately

hin- ZW: **hinlegen** VT to put down ▸ VR to lie down; **sich der Länge nach hinlegen** (*umg*) to fall flat; **hinnehmen** *unreg* VT (*fig*) to put up with, to take; **hinreichen** VI to be adequate ▸ VT: **jdm etw hinreichen** to hand sb sth; **hinreichend** ADJ adequate; (*genug*) sufficient; **Hinreise** F journey out; **hinreißen** *unreg* VT to carry away, to enrapture; **sich hinreißen lassen, etw zu tun** to get carried away and do sth; **hinreißend** ADJ (*Landschaft, Anblick*) enchanting; (*Schönheit, Mensch*) captivating; **hinrichten** VT to execute; **Hinrichtung** F execution; **hinsehen** *unreg* VI: **bei genauerem Hinsehen** on closer inspection

hin sein [ˈhɪnzaɪn] *siehe* **hin**

hin- ZW: **hinsetzen** VR to sit down; **Hinsicht** F: **in mancher** *od* **gewisser Hinsicht** in some respects *od* ways; **hinsichtlich** PRÄP *+gen* with regard to; **hinsollen** (*umg*) VI: **wo soll ich/das Buch hin?** where do I/does the book go?; **Hinspiel** NT (*Sport*) first leg; **hinstellen** VT to put (down) ▸ VR to place o.s.

hintanstellen [hɪntˈlanʃtɛlən] VT (*fig*) to ignore

hinten [ˈhɪntən] ADV behind; (*rückwärtig*) at the back; **~ und vorn** (*fig: betrügen*) left, right and centre; **das reicht ~ und vorn nicht** that's nowhere near enough; **hintendran** (*umg*) ADV at the back; **hintenherum** ADV round the back; (*fig*) secretly

hinter [ˈhɪntər] PRÄP (*+dat od akk*) behind; (: *nach*) after; **~ jdm her sein** to be after sb; **~ die Wahrheit kommen** to get to the truth; **sich ~ jdn stellen** (*fig*) to support sb; **etw ~ sich** *dat* **haben** (*zurückgelegt haben*) to have got through sth; **sie hat viel ~ sich** she has been through a lot; **Hinterachse** F rear axle; **Hinterbänkler (-s, -)** M (*Pol: pej*) backbencher; **Hinterbein** NT hind leg; **sich auf die Hinterbeine stellen** to get tough; **Hinterbliebene(r)** F(M) surviving relative; **hinterdrein** ADV afterwards

hintere(r, s) ADJ rear, back

hinter- ZW: **hintereinander** ADV one after the other; **zwei Tage hintereinander** two days running; **Hintereingang** M rear entrance; **hinterfotzig** (*umg*) ADJ underhanded; **hinterfragen** VT UNTR to analyse; **Hintergedanke** M ulterior motive; **hintergehen** *unreg* VT UNTR to deceive; **Hintergrund** M background; **hintergründig** ADJ cryptic, enigmatic; **Hintergrundprogramm** NT (*Comput*) background program; **Hinterhalt** M ambush; **etw im Hinterhalt haben** to have sth in reserve; **hinterhältig** ADJ underhand, sneaky; **hinterher** ADV afterwards, after; **er ist hinterher, dass ...** (*fig*) he sees to it that ...; **Hinterhof** M back yard; **Hinterkopf** M back of one's head; **Hinterland** NT hinterland; **hinterlassen** *unreg* VT UNTR to leave; **Hinterlassenschaft** F (testator's) estate; **hinterlegen** VT UNTR to deposit; **Hinterlegungsstelle** F depository; **Hinterlist** F cunning, trickery; (*Handlung*) trick, dodge; **hinterlistig** ADJ cunning, crafty; **Hintermann** (**-(e)s**, *pl* **-männer**) M person behind; **die Hintermänner des Skandals** the men behind the scandal

Hintern [ˈhɪntərn] (**-s, -**) (*umg*) M bottom, backside; **jdm den ~ versohlen** to smack sb's bottom

hinter- ZW: **Hinterrad** NT back wheel; **Hinterradantrieb** M (*Aut*) rear-wheel drive; **hinterrücks** ADV from behind; **Hinterteil** NT behind; **Hintertreffen** NT: **ins Hintertreffen kommen** to lose ground; **hintertreiben** *unreg* VT UNTR to prevent, to frustrate; **Hintertreppe** F back stairs *pl*; **Hintertür** F back door; (*fig: Ausweg*) escape, loophole; **Hinterwäldler (-s, -)** (*umg*) M backwoodsman, hillbilly (*bes US*); **hinterziehen** *unreg* VT UNTR (*Steuern*) to evade (paying)

hintun [ˈhɪntuːn] *unreg* (*umg*) VT: **ich weiß nicht, wo ich ihn ~ soll** (*fig*) I can't (quite) place him

hinüber [hɪˈnyːbər] ADV across, over; **hinübergehen** *unreg* VI to go over *od* across

hinunter [hɪˈnʊntər] ADV down; **hinunterbringen** *unreg* VT to take down; **hinunterschlucken** VT (*lit, fig*) to swallow; **hinunterspülen** VT to flush away; (*Essen, Tablette*) to wash down; (*fig: Ärger*) to soothe; **hinuntersteigen** *unreg* VI to descend
Hinweg [ˈhɪnveːk] M journey out
hinweg- [hɪnˈvɛk] zW: **hinweggehen** *unreg* VI: **über etw** *akk* **hinweggehen** (*fig*) to pass over sth; **hinweghelfen** *unreg* VI: **jdm über etw** *akk* **hinweghelfen** to help sb to get over sth; **hinwegkommen** *unreg* VI (*fig*): **über etw** *akk* **hinwegkommen** to get over sth; **hinwegsehen** *unreg* VI: **darüber hinwegsehen, dass ...** to overlook the fact that ...; **hinwegsetzen** VR: **sich hinwegsetzen über** *+akk* to disregard
Hinweis [ˈhɪnvaɪs] (**-es, -e**) M (*Andeutung*) hint; (*Anweisung*) instruction; (*Verweis*) reference; **sachdienliche Hinweise** relevant information
hinweisen *unreg* VI: **~ auf** *+akk* to point to; (*verweisen*) to refer to; **darauf ~, dass ...** to point out that ...; (*anzeigen*) to indicate that ...
Hinweisschild NT sign
Hinweistafel F sign
hinwerfen *unreg* VT to throw down; **eine hingeworfene Bemerkung** a casual remark
hinwirken VI: **auf etw** *akk* **~** to work towards sth
Hinz [hɪnts] M: **~ und Kunz** (*umg*) every Tom, Dick and Harry
hinziehen *unreg* VR (*fig*) to drag on
hinzielen VI: **~ auf** *+akk* to aim at
hinzu [hɪnˈtsuː] ADV in addition; **hinzufügen** VT to add; **Hinzufügung** F: **unter Hinzufügung von etw** (*form*) by adding sth; **hinzukommen** *unreg* VI: **es kommt noch hinzu, dass ...** there is also the fact that ...; **hinzuziehen** *unreg* VT to consult
Hiobsbotschaft [ˈhiːɔpsboːtʃaft] F bad news
Hirn [hɪrn] (**-(e)s, -e**) NT brain(s); **Hirngespinst** (**-(e)s, -e**) NT fantasy; **Hirnhautentzündung** F (*Med*) meningitis; **hirntot** ADJ braindead; **hirnverbrannt** ADJ (*umg*) harebrained
Hirsch [hɪrʃ] (**-(e)s, -e**) M stag
Hirse [ˈhɪrzə] (**-, -n**) F millet
Hirt [ˈhɪrt] (**-en, -en**), **Hirte** (**-n, -n**) M herdsman; (*Schafhirt, fig*) shepherd
Hirtin F herdswoman; (*Schafhirtin*) shepherdess
hissen [ˈhɪsən] VT to hoist
Historiker [hɪsˈtoːrikər] (**-s, -**) M historian
historisch [hɪsˈtoːrɪʃ] ADJ historical
Hit [hɪt] (**-s, -s**) (*umg*) M (*Mus, fig*) hit; **Hitparade** F hit parade
Hitze [ˈhɪtsə] (**-**) F heat; **hitzebeständig** ADJ heat-resistant; **Hitzefrei** (**-**) NT: **Hitzefrei haben** *to have time off school/work because of excessive heat*; **Hitzewelle** F heat wave
hitzig ADJ hot-tempered; (*Debatte*) heated
Hitz- zW: **Hitzkopf** M hothead; **hitzköpfig** ADJ fiery, hot-headed; **Hitzschlag** M heatstroke
HIV-negativ ADJ HIV-negative
HIV-positiv ADJ HIV-positive
hl. ABK = **heilig**
H-Milch [ˈhaːmɪlç] F long-life milk, UHT milk
HNO-Arzt M ENT specialist
hob *etc* [hoːp] VB *siehe* **heben**
Hobby [ˈhɔbi] (**-s, -s**) NT hobby
Hobel [ˈhoːbəl] (**-s, -**) M plane; **Hobelbank** F carpenter's bench
hobeln VT, VI to plane
Hobelspäne PL wood shavings *pl*
hoch [hoːx] (*attrib* **hohe(r, s)**) ADJ high ▶ ADV: **~ achten** to respect; **~ begabt** = **hochbegabt**; **~ dotiert** highly paid; **~ entwickelt** (*Kultur, Land*) highly developed; (*Geräte, Methoden*) sophisticated; **wenn es ~ kommt** (*umg*) at (the) most, at the outside; **das ist mir zu ~** (*umg*) that's above my head; **ein hohes Tier** (*umg*) a big fish; **es ging ~ her** (*umg*) we/they *etc* had a whale of a time; **~ und heilig versprechen** to promise faithfully; **4 ~ 5** 4 to the power of 5; *siehe auch* **hochempfindlich**; **hochgestellt**
Hoch (**-s, -s**) NT (*Ruf*) cheer; (*Met, fig*) high
hoch- zW: **Hochachtung** F respect, esteem; **mit vorzüglicher Hochachtung** (*form: Briefschluss*) yours faithfully; **hochachtungsvoll** ADV yours faithfully; **hochaktuell** ADJ highly topical; **Hochamt** NT high mass; **hocharbeiten** VR to work one's way up; **hochbegabt** ADJ extremely gifted; **hochbetagt** ADJ very old, aged; **Hochbetrieb** M intense activity; (*Comm*) peak time; **Hochbetrieb haben** to be at one's *od* its busiest; **hochbringen** *unreg* VT to bring up; **Hochburg** F stronghold; **Hochdeutsch** NT High German; **Hochdruck** M high pressure; **Hochebene** F plateau; **hochempfindlich** ADJ highly sensitive; (*Film*) high-speed; **hocherfreut** ADJ highly delighted; **hochfahren** *unreg* VI (*erschreckt*) to jump; (*Comput, Tech*) to start up; **hochfliegend** ADJ ambitious; (*fig*) high-flown; **Hochform** F top form; **Hochgebirge** NT high mountains *pl*; **Hochgefühl** NT elation; **hochgehen** *unreg* (*umg*) VI (*explodieren*) to blow up; (*Bombe*) to go off; **Hochgenuss** M great *od* special treat; (*großes Vergnügen*) great pleasure; **hochgeschlossen** ADJ (*Kleid etc*) high-necked; **Hochgeschwindigkeitszug** M high-speed train; **hochgestellt** ADJ (*fig: Persönlichkeit*) high-ranking; **Hochglanz** M high polish; (*Phot*) gloss; **hochgradig** ADJ intense, extreme; **hochhalten** *unreg* VT to hold up; (*fig*) to uphold, to cherish; **Hochhaus** NT multi-storey building; **hochheben** *unreg* VT to lift (up); **hochkant** ADV: **jdn hochkant hinauswerfen** (*fig: umg*) to chuck sb out on his/her ear; **hochkommen** *unreg* VI (*nach oben*) to come up; (*fig: gesund werden*) to get back on one's feet; (*beruflich, gesellschaftlich*) to come up in the world; **Hochkonjunktur** F boom; **hochkrempeln** VT to roll up; **hochladen** *unreg* VT (*Comput*) to upload; **Hochland** NT highlands *pl*; **hochleben** VI: **jdn hochleben lassen** to give sb three cheers; **Hochleistungssport** M competitive sport; **hochmodern** ADJ very modern, ultra-modern; **Hochmut** M pride; **hochmütig** ADJ proud, haughty; **hochnäsig** ADJ stuck-up, snooty;

hochnehmen *unreg* VT to pick up; **jdn hochnehmen** (*umg: verspotten*) to pull sb's leg; **Hochofen** M blast furnace; **Hochrechnung** F projected result; **Hochsaison** F high season; **Hochschätzung** F high esteem
Hochschulabschluss M degree
Hochschulbildung F higher education
Hochschule F college; (*Universität*) university
Hochschulreife F: **er hat (die) ~** ≈ he's got his A-levels (BRIT), he's graduated from high school (US)
hoch- ZW: **hochschwanger** ADJ heavily pregnant, well advanced in pregnancy; **Hochseefischerei** F deep-sea fishing; **Hochsitz** M (*Jagd*) (raised) hide; **Hochsommer** M middle of summer; **Hochspannung** F high tension; (*Elek*) high voltage; **hochspielen** VT (*fig*) to blow up; **Hochsprache** F standard language; **hochspringen** *unreg* VI to jump up; **Hochsprung** M high jump
höchst [hø:çst] ADV highly, extremely
Hochstapler ['ho:xsta:plər] (**-s, -**) M swindler
höchste(r, s) ADJ highest; (*äußerste*) extreme; **die ~ Instanz** (*Jur*) the supreme court of appeal
höchstens ADV at the most
Höchstform F (*Sport*) top form
Höchstgeschwindigkeit F maximum speed
Höchstgrenze F upper limit
Hochstimmung F high spirits *pl*
Höchst- ZW: **Höchstleistung** F best performance; (*bei Produktion*) maximum output; **höchstpersönlich** ADV personally, in person; **Höchstpreis** M maximum price; **Höchststand** M peak; **höchstwahrscheinlich** ADV most probably
Hoch- ZW: **Hochtechnologie** F high technology; **hochtechnologisch** ADJ high-tech; **Hochtemperaturreaktor** M high-temperature reactor; **Hochtour** F: **auf Hochtouren laufen** *od* **arbeiten** to be working flat out; **hochtrabend** ADJ pompous; **Hoch- und Tiefbau** M structural and civil engineering; **Hochverrat** M high treason; **Hochwasser** NT high water; (*Überschwemmung*) floods *pl*; **hochwertig** ADJ high-class, first-rate; **Hochwürden** M Reverend; **Hochzahl** F (*Math*) exponent
Hochzeit ['hɔxtsaɪt] (**-, -en**) F wedding; **man kann nicht auf zwei Hochzeiten tanzen** (*Sprichwort*) you can't have your cake and eat it
Hochzeitsreise F honeymoon
Hochzeitstag M wedding day; (*Jahrestag*) wedding anniversary
hochziehen *unreg* VT (*Rollladen, Hose*) to pull up; (*Brauen*) to raise
Hocke ['hɔkə] (**-, -n**) F squatting position; (*beim Turnen*) squat vault; (*beim Skilaufen*) crouch
hocken ['hɔkən] VI, VR to squat, to crouch
Hocker (**-s, -**) M stool
Höcker ['hœkər] (**-s, -**) M hump
Hockey ['hɔki] (**-s**) NT hockey
Hoden ['ho:dən] (**-s, -**) M testicle
Hodensack M scrotum
Hof [ho:f] (**-(e)s, Höfe**) M (*Hinterhof*) yard; (*Bauernhof*) farm; (*Königshof*) court; **einem Mädchen den ~ machen** (*veraltet*) to court a girl
hoffen ['hɔfən] VI: **~ (auf** *+akk*) to hope (for)
hoffentlich ADV I hope, hopefully
Hoffnung ['hɔfnʊŋ] F hope; **jdm Hoffnungen machen** to raise sb's hopes; **sich** *dat* **Hoffnungen machen** to have hopes; **sich** *dat* **keine Hoffnungen machen** not to hold out any hope(s)
Hoffnungs- ZW: **hoffnungslos** ADJ hopeless; **Hoffnungslosigkeit** F hopelessness; **Hoffnungsschimmer** M glimmer of hope; **hoffnungsvoll** ADJ hopeful
höflich ['hø:flɪç] ADJ courteous, polite; **Höflichkeit** F courtesy, politeness
hohe(r, s) ['ho:ə(r, s)] ADJ *siehe* **hoch**
Höhe ['hø:ə] (**-, -n**) F height; (*Anhöhe*) hill; **nicht auf der ~ sein** (*fig: umg*) to feel below par; **ein Scheck in ~ von ...** a cheque (BRIT) *od* check (US) for the amount of ...; **das ist doch die ~** (*fig: umg*) that's the limit; **er geht immer gleich in die ~** (*umg*) he always flares up; **auf der ~ der Zeit sein** to be up-to-date
Hoheit ['ho:haɪt] F (*Pol*) sovereignty; (*Titel*) Highness
Hoheits- ZW: **Hoheitsgebiet** NT sovereign territory; **Hoheitsgewalt** F (national) jurisdiction; **Hoheitsgewässer** NT territorial waters *pl*; **Hoheitszeichen** NT national emblem
Höhen- ZW: **Höhenangabe** F altitude reading; (*auf Karte*) height marking; **Höhenflug** M: **geistiger Höhenflug** intellectual flight; **Höhenlage** F altitude; **Höhenluft** F mountain air; **Höhenmesser** M altimeter; **Höhensonne** F sun lamp; **Höhenunterschied** M difference in altitude; **Höhenzug** M mountain chain
Höhepunkt M climax; (*des Lebens*) high point
höher ADJ, ADV higher
hohl [ho:l] ADJ hollow; (*umg: dumm*) hollow(-headed)
Höhle ['hø:lə] (**-, -n**) F cave; (*Loch*) hole; (*Mundhöhle*) cavity; (*fig, Zool*) den
Hohl- ZW: **Hohlheit** F hollowness; **Hohlkreuz** NT (*Med*) hollow back; **Hohlmaß** NT measure of volume; **Hohlraum** M hollow space; (*Gebäude*) cavity; **Hohlsaum** M hemstitch; **Hohlspiegel** M concave mirror
Hohn [ho:n] (**-(e)s**) M scorn; **das ist der reinste ~** it's sheer mockery
höhnen ['hø:nən] VT to taunt, to scoff at
höhnisch ADJ scornful, taunting
Hokuspokus [ho:kʊs'po:kʊs] (-) M (*Zauberformel*) hey presto; (*fig: Täuschung*) hocus-pocus
hold [hɔlt] ADJ charming, sweet
holen ['ho:lən] VT to get, to fetch; (*Atem*) to take; **jdn/etw ~ lassen** to send for sb/sth; **sich** *dat* **eine Erkältung ~** to catch a cold
Holland ['hɔlant] (**-s**) NT Holland
Holländer ['hɔlɛndər] (**-s, -**) M Dutchman
Holländerin F Dutchwoman, Dutch girl
holländisch ADJ Dutch

Hölle ['hœlə] (-, -n) F hell; **ich werde ihm die ~ heißmachen** (*umg*) I'll give him hell
Höllenangst F: **eine ~ haben** to be scared to death
Höllenlärm M infernal noise (*umg*)
höllisch ['hœlɪʃ] ADJ hellish, infernal
Hologramm [holo'gram] (-s, -e) NT hologram
holperig ['hɔlpərɪç] ADJ rough, bumpy
holpern ['hɔlpərn] VI to jolt
Holunder [ho'lʊndər] (-s, -) M elder
Holz [hɔlts] (-es, Hölzer) NT wood; **aus ~** made of wood, wooden; **aus einem anderen/demselben ~ geschnitzt sein** (*fig*) to be cast in a different/the same mould; **gut ~!** (*Kegeln*) have a good game!; **Holzbläser** M woodwind player
hölzern ['hœltsərn] ADJ (*lit, fig*) wooden
Holz- ZW: **Holzfäller** (-s, -) M lumberjack, woodcutter; **Holzfaserplatte** F (wood) fibreboard (BRIT) *od* fiberboard (US); **holzfrei** ADJ (*Papier*) wood-free
holzig ADJ woody
Holz- ZW: **Holzklotz** M wooden block; **Holzkohle** F charcoal; **Holzkopf** M (*fig: umg*) blockhead, numbskull; **Holzscheit** NT log; **Holzschuh** M clog; **Holzweg** M (*fig*) wrong track; **Holzwolle** F fine wood shavings *pl*; **Holzwurm** M woodworm
Homecomputer ['hoʊmkɔm'pju:tər] (-s, -) M home computer
Homepage ['hoʊm'pa:gə] NT (*Comput*) home page
Homo-Ehe ['ho:mole:ə] (*umg*) F gay marriage
homogen [homo'ge:n] ADJ homogenous
Homöopath [homøo'pa:t] (-en, -en) M homeopath
Homöopathie [homøopa'ti:] F homeopathy, homeopathic medicine
homosexuell [homozɛksu'ɛl] ADJ homosexual
Honduras [hɔn'du:ras] (-) NT Honduras
Hongkong [hɔŋ'kɔŋ] (-s) NT Hong Kong
Honig ['ho:nɪç] (-s, -e) M honey; **Honiglecken** NT (*fig*): **das ist kein Honiglecken** it's no picnic; **Honigmelone** F honeydew melon; **Honigwabe** F honeycomb
Honorar [hono'ra:r] (-s, -e) NT fee
Honoratioren [honoratsi'o:rən] PL dignitaries
honorieren [hono'ri:rən] VT to remunerate; (*Scheck*) to honour (BRIT), to honor (US)
Hopfen ['hɔpfən] (-s, -) M hops *pl*; **bei ihm ist ~ und Malz verloren** (*umg*) he's a dead loss
hoppla ['hɔpla] INTERJ whoops
hopsen ['hɔpsən] VI to hop
hörbar ADJ audible
horch [hɔrç] INTERJ listen
horchen VI to listen; (*pej*) to eavesdrop
Horcher (-s, -) M listener; (*pej*) eavesdropper
Horde ['hɔrdə] (-, -n) F horde
hören ['hø:rən] VT, VI to hear; **auf jdn/etw ~** to listen to sb/sth; **ich lasse von mir ~** I'll be in touch; **etwas/nichts von sich ~ lassen** to get/not to get in touch; **Hören** NT: **es verging ihm Hören und Sehen** (*umg*) he didn't know whether he was coming or going
Hörensagen NT: **vom ~** from hearsay
Hörer (-s, -) M (*Rundf*) listener; (*Univ*) student; (*Telefonhörer*) receiver
Hörfunk M radio
Hörgerät NT hearing aid
hörig ['hø:rɪç] ADJ: **sie ist ihm (sexuell) ~** he has (sexual) power over her
Horizont [hori'tsɔnt] (-(e)s, -e) M horizon; **das geht über meinen ~** (*fig*) that is beyond me
horizontal [horitsɔ'ta:l] ADJ horizontal
Hormon [hɔr'mo:n] (-s, -e) NT hormone
Hörmuschel F (*Tel*) earpiece
Horn [hɔrn] (-(e)s, Hörner) NT horn; **ins gleiche** *od* **in jds ~ blasen** to chime in; **sich** *dat* **die Hörner abstoßen** (*umg*) to sow one's wild oats; **Hornbrille** F horn-rimmed spectacles *pl*
Hörnchen ['hœrnçən] NT (*Gebäck*) croissant
Hornhaut F hard skin; (*des Auges*) cornea
Hornisse [hɔr'nɪsə] (-, -n) F hornet
Hornochs, Hornochse M (*fig: umg*) blockhead, idiot
Horoskop [horo'sko:p] (-s, -e) NT horoscope
Hör- ZW: **Hörrohr** NT ear trumpet; (*Med*) stethoscope; **Hörsaal** M lecture room; **Hörspiel** NT radio play
Hort [hɔrt] (-(e)s, -e) M hoard; (*Sch*) nursery school; **horten** VT to hoard
Hörweite F: **in/außer ~** within/out of hearing *od* earshot
Hose ['ho:ze] (-, -n) F trousers *pl*, pants *pl* (US); **in die ~ gehen** (*umg*) to be a complete flop
Hosen- ZW: **Hosenanzug** M trouser suit, pantsuit (US); **Hosenboden** M: **sich auf den Hosenboden setzen** (*umg*) to get stuck in; **Hosenrock** M culottes *pl*; **Hosentasche** F trouser pocket; **Hosenträger** PL braces *pl* (BRIT), suspenders *pl* (US)
Hostie ['hɔstiə] F (*Rel*) host
Hotel [ho'tɛl] (-s, -s) NT hotel; **Hotelfach** NT hotel management; **Hotel garni** NT bed and breakfast hotel
Hotelier [hotɛli'e:] (-s, -s) M hotelier
Hotelkette F hotel chain
Hotelzimmer NT hotel room
Hotspot ['hɔtspɔt] M (wireless) hotspot
Hr. ABK (= *Herr*) Mr
hrsg. ABK (= *herausgegeben*) ed.
Hrsg. ABK (= *Herausgeber*) ed.
HTML ABK (= *Hyper Text Markup Language*) HTML
Hub [hu:p] (-(e)s, Hübe) M lift; (*Tech*) stroke
hüben ['hy:bən] ADV on this side, over here; **~ und drüben** on both sides
Hubraum M (*Aut*) cubic capacity
hübsch [hypʃ] ADJ pretty, nice; **immer ~ langsam!** (*umg*) nice and easy
Hubschrauber (-s, -) M helicopter
Hucke ['hʊkə] (-, -n) F: **jdm die ~ vollhauen** (*umg*) to give sb a good hiding
huckepack ['hʊkəpak] ADV piggy-back, pick-a-back
hudeln ['hu:dəln] VI to be sloppy

Huf ['hu:f] (**-(e)s, -e**) M hoof; **Hufeisen** NT horseshoe; **Hufnagel** M horseshoe nail
Hüfte ['hyftə] (**-, -n**) F hip
Hüftgürtel M girdle
Hüfthalter M girdle
Hüfthose F hip huggers *pl*
Huftier NT hoofed animal, ungulate
Hügel ['hy:gəl] (**-s, -**) M hill
hügelig, hüglig ADJ hilly
Huhn [hu:n] (**-(e)s, Hühner**) NT hen; (*Koch*) chicken; **da lachen ja die Hühner** (*umg*) it's enough to make a cat laugh; **er sah aus wie ein gerupftes ~** (*umg*) he looked as if he'd been dragged through a hedge backwards
Hühnchen ['hy:nçən] NT young chicken; **mit jdm ein ~ zu rupfen haben** (*umg*) to have a bone to pick with sb
Hühner- ZW: **Hühnerauge** NT corn; **Hühnerbrühe** F chicken broth; **Hühnerklein** NT (*Koch*) chicken trimmings *pl*
Huld [hʊlt] (-) F favour (BRIT), favor (US)
huldigen ['hʊldɪgən] VI: **jdm ~** to pay homage to sb
Huldigung F homage
Hülle ['hʏlə] (**-, -n**) F cover(ing); (*Zellophanhülle*) wrapping; **in ~ und Fülle** galore; **die Hüllen fallen lassen** (*fig*) to strip off
hüllen VT: **~ (in** *+akk*) to cover (with); (*in Zellophan*) to wrap (in)
Hülse ['hʏlzə] (**-, -n**) F husk, shell
Hülsenfrucht F pulse
human [hu'ma:n] ADJ humane
humanistisch [huma'nɪstɪʃ] ADJ: **humanistisches Gymnasium** *secondary school with bias on Latin and Greek*
humanitär [humani'tɛ:r] ADJ humanitarian
Humanität F humanity
Humanmedizin F (human) medicine
Hummel ['hʊməl] (**-, -n**) F bumblebee
Hummer ['hʊmər] (**-s, -**) M lobster
Humor [hu'mo:r] (**-s, -e**) M humour (BRIT), humor (US); **~ haben** to have a sense of humo(u)r; **Humorist(in)** M(F) humorist; **humoristisch** ADJ humorous; **humorlos** ADJ humourless; **humorvoll** ADJ humorous
humpeln ['hʊmpəln] VI to hobble
Humpen ['hʊmpən] (**-s, -**) M tankard
Humus ['hu:mʊs] (-) M humus
Hund [hʊnt] (**-(e)s, -e**) M dog; **auf den ~ kommen, vor die Hunde gehen** (*fig*: *umg*) to go to the dogs; **Hunde, die bellen, beißen nicht** (*Sprichwort*) empty vessels make most noise (*Sprichwort*); **er ist bekannt wie ein bunter ~** (*umg*) everybody knows him
Hunde- ZW: **hundeelend** (*umg*) ADJ: **mir ist hundeelend** I feel lousy; **Hundehütte** F (dog) kennel; **Hundekuchen** M dog biscuit; **Hundemarke** F dog licence disc, dog tag (US); **hundemüde** (*umg*) ADJ dog-tired
hundert ['hʊndərt] NUM hundred; **Hundert** (**-s, -e**) NT hundred; **Hunderte von Menschen** hundreds of people
Hunderter (**-s, -**) M hundred; (*umg*: *Geldschein*) hundred (euro/pound/dollar *etc* note)
hundert- ZW: **Hundertjahrfeier** F centenary; **Hundertmeterlauf** M (*Sport*): **der/ein Hundertmeterlauf** the/a hundred metres (BRIT) *od* meters (US) *sing*; **hundertprozentig** ADJ, ADV one hundred per cent
hundertste(r, s) ADJ hundredth; **von Hundertsten ins Tausendste kommen** (*fig*) to get carried away
Hundesteuer F dog licence (BRIT) *od* license (US) fee
Hundewetter (*umg*) NT filthy weather
Hündin ['hʏndɪn] F bitch
Hüne ['hy:nə] (**-n, -n**) M: **ein ~ von Mensch** a giant of a man
Hünengrab NT megalithic tomb
Hunger ['hʊŋər] (**-s**) M hunger; **~ haben** to be hungry; **ich sterbe vor ~** (*umg*) I'm starving; **Hungerlohn** M starvation wages *pl*
hungern VI to starve
Hungersnot F famine
Hungerstreik M hunger strike
Hungertuch NT: **am ~ nagen** (*fig*) to be starving
hungrig ['hʊŋrɪç] ADJ hungry
Hunsrück ['hʊnsrʏk] M Hunsruck (Mountains *pl*)
Hupe ['hu:pə] (**-, -n**) F horn
hupen VI to hoot, to sound one's horn
Hüpfburg F bouncy castle®
hupfen ['hu:pfən] VI to hop, to jump; **das ist gehupft wie gesprungen** (*umg*) it's six of one and half a dozen of the other
hüpfen ['hʏpfən] VI to hop, to jump
Hupkonzert (*umg*) NT hooting (of car horns)
Hürde ['hʏrdə] (**-, -n**) F hurdle; (*für Schafe*) pen
Hürdenlauf M hurdling
Hure ['hu:rə] (**-, -n**) F whore
Hurensohn (*pej, umg!*) M bastard (*umg!*), son of a bitch (*umg!*)
hurra [hʊ'ra:] INTERJ hooray, hurrah
hurtig ['hʊrtɪç] ADJ brisk, quick ▶ ADV briskly, quickly
huschen ['hʊʃən] VI to flit, to scurry
husten VI to cough; **auf etw** *akk* **~** (*umg*) not to give a damn for sth
Husten ['hu:stən] (**-s**) M cough; **Hustenanfall** M coughing fit; **Hustenbonbon** M OD NT cough drop; **Hustensaft** M cough mixture
Hut[1] [hu:t] (**-(e)s, Hüte**) M hat; **unter einen ~ bringen** (*umg*) to reconcile; (*Termine etc*) to fit in
Hut[2] [hu:t] (-) F care; **auf der ~ sein** to be on one's guard
hüten ['hy:tən] VT to guard ▶ VR to watch out; **das Bett/Haus ~** to stay in bed/indoors; **sich ~ zu** to take care not to; **sich ~ vor** *+dat* to beware of; **ich werde mich ~!** not likely!
Hutschnur F: **das geht mir über die ~** (*umg*) that's going too far
Hütte ['hʏtə] (**-, -n**) F hut; (*Holzhütte, Blockhütte*) cabin; (*Eisenhütte*) forge; (*umg*: *Wohnung*) pad; (*Tech*: *Hüttenwerk*) iron and steel works
Hüttenindustrie F iron and steel industry
Hüttenkäse M cottage cheese

h

Hüttenwerk NT iron and steel works
hutzelig ['hʊtsəlɪç] ADJ shrivelled
Hyäne [hy'ɛ:nə] (**-, -n**) F hyena
Hyazinthe [hya'tsɪntə] (**-, -n**) F hyacinth
Hydrant [hy'drant] M hydrant
hydraulisch [hy'draʊlɪʃ] ADJ hydraulic
Hydrierung [hy'dri:rʊŋ] F hydrogenation
Hygiene [hygi'e:nə] (-) F hygiene
hygienisch [hygi'e:nɪʃ] ADJ hygienic
Hymne ['hʏmnə] (**-, -n**) F hymn, anthem
hyper- ['hypɛr] PRÄF hyper-; **Hyperlink** ['haɪpərlɪŋk] (**-s, -s**) M hyperlink
Hypnose [hʏp'no:zə] (**-, -n**) F hypnosis
hypnotisch ADJ hypnotic
Hypnotiseur [hʏpnoti'zø:r] M hypnotist
hypnotisieren [hʏpnoti'zi:rən] VT to hypnotize
Hypotenuse [hypote'nu:zə] (**-, -n**) F hypotenuse
Hypothek [hypo'te:k] (**-, -en**) F mortgage; **eine ~ aufnehmen** to raise a mortgage; **etw mit einer ~ belasten** to mortgage sth
Hypothese [hypo'te:zə] (**-, -n**) F hypothesis
hypothetisch [hypo'te:tɪʃ] ADJ hypothetical
Hysterie [hyste'ri:] F hysteria
hysterisch [hʏs'te:rɪʃ] ADJ hysterical; **einen hysterischen Anfall bekommen** (*fig*) to have hysterics

I i

I, i [iː] NT I, i; **I wie Ida** ≈ I for Isaac, ≈ I for Item (*US*); **das Tüpfelchen auf dem i** (*fig*) the final touch
i. ABK = **in; im**
i. A. ABK (= *im Auftrag*) p.p.
iberisch [i'beːrɪʃ] ADJ Iberian; **die Iberische Halbinsel** the Iberian Peninsula
IC (-) M ABK = **Intercityzug**
ICE M ABK (= *Intercityexpresszug*) *German high-speed train*
ich [ɪç] PRON I; **~ bins!** it's me!; **Ich** (**-(s), -(s)**) NT self; (*Psych*) ego; **Ichform** F first person; **Ichroman** M novel in the first person
ideal ADJ ideal; **Idealfall** M: **im Idealfall** ideally
Idealismus [idea'lɪsmʊs] M idealism
Idealist(in) M(F) idealist
idealistisch ADJ idealistic
Idealvorstellung F ideal
Idee [i'deː] (**-, -n**) F idea; (*ein wenig*) shade, trifle; **jdn auf die ~ bringen, etw zu tun** to give sb the idea of doing sth
ideell [ide'ɛl] ADJ ideal
identifizieren [idɛntifi'tsiːrən] VT to identify
identisch [i'dɛntɪʃ] ADJ identical
Identität [idɛnti'tɛːt] F identity
Identitätsdiebstahl [idɛnti'tɛːtsdiːpʃtaːl] M identity theft
Ideologe [ideo'loːgə] (**-n, -n**) M ideologist
Ideologie [ideolo'giː] F ideology
Ideologin [ideo'loːgɪn] F ideologist
ideologisch [ideo'loːgɪʃ] ADJ ideological
idiomatisch [idio'maːtɪʃ] ADJ idiomatic
Idiot [idi'oːt] (**-en, -en**) M idiot
Idiotenhügel M (*hum: umg*) beginners' *od* nursery slope
idiotensicher (*umg*) ADJ foolproof
Idiotin F idiot
idiotisch ADJ idiotic
Idol [i'doːl] (**-s, -e**) NT idol
idyllisch [i'dʏlɪʃ] ADJ idyllic
IG ABK (= *Industriegewerkschaft*) *industrial trade union*
IGB (-) M ABK (= *Internationaler Gewerkschaftsbund*) International Trades Union Congress
Igel ['iːgəl] (**-s, -**) M hedgehog
igitt [i'gɪt], **igittigitt** [i'gɪti'gɪt] INTERJ ugh!
Iglu ['iːglu] (**-s, -s**) M OD NT igloo
Ignorant [ɪgno'rant] (**-en, -en**) M ignoramus
ignorieren [ɪgno'riːrən] VT to ignore
IHK F ABK = **Industrie- und Handelskammer**
ihm [iːm] PRON *dat von* **er**; **es** (to) him, (to) it; **es ist ~ nicht gut** he doesn't feel well
ihn [iːn] PRON *akk von* **er** him; (*bei Tieren, Dingen*) it
ihnen ['iːnən] PRON *dat pl von* **sie** (to) them; (*nach Präpositionen*) them
Ihnen PRON *dat von* **Sie** (to) you; (*nach Präpositionen*) you

SCHLÜSSELWORT

ihr [iːr] PRON **1** (*nom pl*) you; **ihr seid es** it's you
2 (*dat von sie*) (to) her; (: *bei Tieren, Dingen*) (to) it; **gib es ihr** give it to her; **er steht neben ihr** he is standing beside her
▸ POSS PRON **1** (*sing*) her; (: *bei Tieren, Dingen*) its; **ihr Mann** her husband
2 (*pl*) their; **die Bäume und ihre Blätter** the trees and their leaves

Ihr POSS PRON your
ihre(r, s) POSS PRON hers; (*eines Tieres*) its; (*von mehreren*) theirs; **sie taten das I~** (*geh*) they did their bit
Ihre(r, s) POSS PRON yours; **tun Sie das ~** (*geh*) you do your bit
ihrer ['iːrər] PRON *gen von* **sie** of her; (*pl*) of them
Ihrer PRON *gen von* **Sie** of you
ihrerseits ADV for her/their part
Ihrerseits ADV for your part
ihresgleichen PRON people like her/them; (*von Dingen*) others like it; **eine Frechheit, die ~ sucht!** an incredible cheek!
ihretwegen ADV (*für sie*) for her/its/their sake; (*wegen ihr, ihnen*) on her/its/their account; **sie sagte, ~ könnten wir gehen** she said that, as far as she was concerned, we could go
ihretwillen ADV: **um ~** for her/its/their sake
ihrige ['iːrɪgə] PRON: **der/die/das ~** *od* **I~** hers; (*von Sache*) its; (*pl*) theirs
i. J. ABK (= *im Jahre*) in (the year)
Ikone [i'koːnə] (**-, -n**) F icon
IKRK NT ABK (= *Internationales Komitee vom Roten Kreuz*) ICRC
illegal ['ɪlegaːl] ADJ illegal
illegitim ['ɪlegitiːm] ADJ illegitimate
Illusion [ɪluzi'oːn] F illusion; **sich** *dat* **Illusionen machen** to delude o.s.
illusorisch [ɪlu'zoːrɪʃ] ADJ illusory

Illustration [ɪlʊstratsi'o:n] F illustration
illustrieren [ɪlʊs'tri:rən] VT to illustrate
Illustrierte (**-n, -n**) F picture magazine
Iltis ['ɪltɪs] (**-ses, -se**) M polecat
im [ɪm] PRÄP = **in dem**; **im Bett** in bed; **im Fernsehen** on TV; **im Radio** on the radio; **etw im Liegen/Stehen tun** do sth lying down/standing up
IM (**-s**) NT ABK (= *instant messaging*) IM
Image ['ɪmɪtʃ] (**-(s), -s**) NT image; **Imagekampagne** ['ɪmɪtʃkampanjə] F image-building campaign; **Imagepflege** ['ɪmɪtʃpfle:gə] (*umg*) F image-building; **Imageschaden** F damage to one's image
imaginär [imagi'nɛ:r] ADJ imaginary
Imbiss ['ɪmbɪs] (**-es, -e**) M snack; **Imbisshalle** F snack bar; **Imbissstand** M, **Imbissstube** F snack bar
Imissionswert [imisi'o:nsve:rt] M pollution count
imitieren [imi'ti:rən] VT to imitate
Imker ['ɪmkər] (**-s, -**) M beekeeper
immanent [ɪma'nɛnt] ADJ inherent, intrinsic
Immatrikulation [ɪmatrikulatsi'o:n] F (*Univ*) registration
immatrikulieren [ɪmatriku'li:rən] VI, VR to register
immer ['ɪmər] ADV always; **~ wieder** again and again; **etw ~ wieder tun** to keep on doing sth; **~ noch** still; **~ noch nicht** still not; **für ~** forever; **~ wenn ich ...** every time I ...; **~ schöner** more and more beautiful; **~ trauriger** sadder and sadder; **was/wer (auch) ~** whatever/whoever; **immerhin** ADV all the same; **immerzu** ADV all the time
Immigrant(in) [ɪmi'grant(ɪn)] M(F) immigrant
Immobilien [ɪmo'bi:liən] PL real property (BRIT), real estate (US); (*in Zeitungsannoncen*) property *sing*
Immobilienhändler, Immobilienmakler M estate agent (BRIT), realtor (US)
immun [ɪ'mu:n] ADJ immune
immunisieren [ɪmuni'zi:rən] VT to immunize
Immunität [ɪmu:ni'tɛ:t] F immunity
Immunschwäche F immunodeficiency
Immunsystem NT immune system
imperativ ['ɪmperati:f] ADJ: **imperatives Mandat** imperative mandate
Imperativ (**-s, -e**) M imperative
Imperfekt ['ɪmpɛrfɛkt] (**-s, -e**) NT imperfect (tense)
Imperialismus [ɪmperia'lɪsmʊs] M imperialism
Imperialist [ɪmperia'lɪst] M imperialist; **imperialistisch** ADJ imperialistic
impfen ['ɪmpfən] VT to vaccinate
Impf- ZW: **Impfpass** M vaccination card; **Impfschutz** M protection given by vaccination; **Impfstoff** M vaccine; **Impfung** F vaccination; **Impfzwang** M compulsory vaccination
implizieren [ɪmpli'tsi:rən] VT to imply
imponieren [ɪmpo'ni:rən] VI +*dat* to impress
Import [ɪm'pɔrt] (**-(e)s, -e**) M import
Importeur [ɪmpɔr'tø:r] (**-s, -e**) M importer
importieren [ɪmpɔr'ti:rən] VT to import
imposant [ɪmpo'zant] ADJ imposing
impotent ['ɪmpotɛnt] ADJ impotent
Impotenz ['ɪmpotɛnts] F impotence
imprägnieren [ɪmprɛ'gni:rən] VT to (water)proof
Impressionismus [ɪmprɛsio'nɪsmʊs] M impressionism
Impressum [ɪm'prɛsʊm] (**-s, -ssen**) NT imprint
Improvisation [ɪmprovizatsi'o:n] F improvisation
improvisieren [ɪmprovi'zi:rən] VT, VI to improvise
Impuls [ɪm'pʊls] (**-es, -e**) M impulse; **etw aus einem ~ heraus tun** to do sth on impulse
impulsiv [ɪmpʊl'zi:f] ADJ impulsive
imstande, im Stande [ɪm'ʃtandə] ADJ: **~ sein** to be in a position; (*fähig*) to be able; **er ist zu allem ~** he's capable of anything

SCHLÜSSELWORT

in [ɪn] PRÄP +*akk* **1** (*räumlich: wohin*) in, into; **in die Stadt** into town; **in die Schule gehen** to go to school; **in die Hunderte gehen** to run into (the) hundreds
2 (*zeitlich*): **bis ins 20. Jahrhundert** into *od* up to the 20th century
▸ PRÄP +*dat* **1** (*räumlich: wo*) in; **in der Stadt** in town; **in der Schule sein** to be at school; **es in sich haben** (*umg: Text*) to be tough; (*: Drink*) to have quite a kick
2 (*zeitlich: wann*): **in diesem Jahr** this year; (*in jenem Jahr*) in that year; **heute in zwei Wochen** two weeks today

inaktiv ['ɪn|akti:f] ADJ inactive; (*Mitglied*) non-active
Inangriffnahme [ɪn'langrɪfna:mə] (**-, -n**) F (*form*) commencement
Inanspruchnahme [ɪn'lanʃprʊxna:mə] (**-, -n**) F: **~** (*+gen*) demands *pl* (on); **im Falle einer ~ der Arbeitslosenunterstützung** (*form*) where unemployment benefit has been sought
inbegr. ABK (= *inbegriffen*) enc.
Inbegriff ['ɪnbəgrɪf] M embodiment, personification
inbegriffen ADV included
Inbetriebnahme [ɪnbə'tri:pna:mə] (**-, -n**) F (*form*) commissioning; (*von Gebäude, U-Bahn etc*) inauguration
inbrünstig ['ɪnbrʏnstɪç] ADJ ardent
indem [ɪn'de:m] KONJ while; **~ man etw macht** (*dadurch*) by doing sth
Inder(in) ['ɪndər(ɪn)] (**-s, -**) M(F) Indian
indes [ɪn'dɛs], **indessen** [ɪn'dɛsən] ADV meanwhile ▸ KONJ while
Index ['ɪndɛks] (**-(es), -e** *od* **Indizes**) M: **auf dem ~ stehen** (*fig*) to be banned; **Indexzahl** F index number
Indianer(in) [ɪndi'a:nər(ɪn)] (**-s, -**) M(F) (Red *od* American) Indian
indianisch ADJ (Red *od* American) Indian

Indien ['ɪndiən] (**-s**) NT India
indigniert [ɪndɪ'gni:rt] ADJ indignant
Indikation [ɪndikatsi'o:n] F: **medizinische/soziale ~** medical/social grounds *pl* for the termination of pregnancy
Indikativ ['ɪndikati:f] (**-s, -e**) M indicative
indirekt ['ɪndirɛkt] ADJ indirect; **indirekte Steuer** indirect tax
indisch ['ɪndɪʃ] ADJ Indian; **Indischer Ozean** Indian Ocean
indiskret ['ɪndɪskre:t] ADJ indiscreet
Indiskretion [ɪndɪskretsi'o:n] F indiscretion
indiskutabel ['ɪndɪskuta:bəl] ADJ out of the question
indisponiert ['ɪndɪsponi:rt] ADJ (*geh*) indisposed
Individualist [ɪndividua'lɪst] M individualist
Individualität [ɪndividuali'tɛt] F individuality
Individualtourismus M individual tourism
individuell [ɪndividu'ɛl] ADJ individual; **etw ~ gestalten** to give sth a personal note; **etw ~ anpassen** to customize sth
Individuum [ɪndi'vi:duʊm] (**-s, -duen**) NT individual
Indiz [ɪn'di:ts] (**-es, -ien**) NT (*Jur*) clue; **~ (für)** sign (of)
Indizes ['ɪnditse:z] PL *von* **Index**
Indizienbeweis M circumstantial evidence
indizieren [ɪndi'tsi:rən] VT, VI (*Comput*) to index
Indochina ['ɪndo'çi:na] (**-s**) NT Indochina
indogermanisch ['ɪndogɛr'ma:nɪʃ] ADJ Indo-Germanic, Indo-European
indoktrinieren [ɪndɔktri'ni:rən] VT to indoctrinate
Indonesien [ɪndo'ne:ziən] (**-s**) NT Indonesia
Indonesier(in) (**-s, -**) M(F) Indonesian
indonesisch [ɪndo'ne:zɪʃ] ADJ Indonesian
Indossament [ɪndɔsa'mɛnt] NT (*Comm*) endorsement
Indossant [ɪndɔ'sant] M endorser
Indossat [ɪndɔ'sa:t] (**-en, -en**) M endorsee
indossieren VT to endorse
industrialisieren [ɪndʊstriali'zi:rən] VT to industrialize
Industrialisierung F industrialization
Industrie [ɪndʊs'tri:] F industry; **in der ~ arbeiten** to be in industry; **Industriegebiet** NT industrial area; **Industriegelände** NT industrial *od* trading estate; **Industriekaufmann** M industrial manager
industriell [ɪndʊstri'ɛl] ADJ industrial; **industrielle Revolution** industrial revolution
Industrielle(r) F(M) industrialist
Industrie- zW: **Industriestaat** M industrial nation; **Industrie- und Handelskammer** F chamber of industry and commerce; **Industriezone** F (*bes* ÖSTERR, SCHWEIZ) industrial zone; **Industriezweig** M branch of industry
ineinander [ɪn|aɪ'nandər] ADV in(to) one another *od* each other; **~ übergehen** to merge (into each other)
ineinandergreifen *unreg* VI (*lit*) to interlock; (*Zahnräder*) to mesh; (*fig: Ereignisse etc*) to overlap
Infanterie [ɪnfantə'ri:] F infantry
Infarkt [ɪn'farkt] (**-(e)s, -e**) M coronary (thrombosis)
Infektion [ɪnfɛktsi'o:n] F infection
Infektionsherd M focus of infection
Infektionskrankheit F infectious disease
Infinitiv ['ɪnfiniti:f] (**-s, -e**) M infinitive
infizieren [ɪnfi'tsi:rən] VT to infect ▸ VR: **sich (bei jdm) ~** to be infected (by sb)
in flagranti [ɪn fla'granti] ADV in the act, red-handed
Inflation [ɪnflatsi'o:n] F inflation
inflationär [ɪnflatsio'nɛ:r] ADJ inflationary
inflationsbereinigt ADJ inflation-adjusted
Inflationsrate F rate of inflation
inflatorisch [ɪnfla'to:rɪʃ] ADJ inflationary
Info ['ɪnfo] (**-s, -s**) (*umg*) NT (information) leaflet
Infobrief ['ɪnfo-] M info letter
infolge [ɪn'fɔlgə] PRÄP +*gen* as a result of, owing to; **infolgedessen** ADV consequently
Informatik [ɪnfɔr'ma:tɪk] F information studies *pl*
Informatiker(in) (**-s, -**) M(F) computer scientist
Information [ɪnfɔrmatsi'o:n] F information *no pl*; **Informationen** PL (*Comput*) data; **zu Ihrer ~** for your information
Informationsabruf M (*Comput*) information retrieval
Informationsgesellschaft F information society
Informationstechnik F information technology
informativ [ɪnfɔrma'ti:f] ADJ informative
informieren [ɪnfɔr'mi:rən] VT: **~ (über** +*akk*) to inform (about) ▸ VR: **sich ~ (über** +*akk*) to find out (about)
Infotelefon NT information line
infrage, in Frage [ɪn'fra:gə] ADV: **etw ~ stellen** to question sth; **~ kommend** possible; (*Bewerber*) worth considering; **nicht ~ kommen** to be out of the question
Infrastruktur ['ɪnfraʃtrʊktu:r] F infrastructure
Infusion [ɪnfuzi'o:n] F infusion
Ing. ABK = **Ingenieur**
Ingenieur [ɪnʒeni'ø:r] M engineer; **Ingenieurschule** F school of engineering
Ingwer ['ɪŋvər] (**-s**) M ginger
Inh. ABK (= *Inhaber(in)*) prop.; (= *Inhalt*) cont.
Inhaber(in) ['ɪnha:bər(ɪn)] (**-s, -**) M(F) owner; (*Comm*) proprietor; (*Hausinhaber*) occupier; (*Lizenzinhaber*) licensee, holder; (*Fin*) bearer
inhaftieren [ɪnhaf'ti:rən] VT to take into custody
inhalieren [ɪnha'li:rən] VT, VI to inhale
Inhalt ['ɪnhalt] (**-(e)s, -e**) M contents *pl*; (*eines Buchs etc*) content; (*Math: Flächen*) area; (*: Rauminhalt*) volume; **inhaltlich** ADJ as regards content
Inhalts- zW: **Inhaltsangabe** F summary; **inhaltslos** ADJ empty; **inhaltsreich** ADJ full; **Inhaltsverzeichnis** NT table of contents; (*Comput*) directory
inhuman ['ɪnhuma:n] ADJ inhuman

initialisieren [initsia:li'zi:rən] VT (*Comput*) to initialize
Initialisierung F (*Comput*) initialization
Initiative [initsia'ti:və] F initiative; **die ~ ergreifen** to take the initiative
Initiator(in) [initsi'a:tɔr, -'to:rɪn] M(F) (*geh*) initiator
Injektion [ɪnjɛktsi'o:n] F injection
injizieren [ɪnji'tsi:rən] VT to inject; **jdm etw ~** to inject sb with sth
Inka ['ɪŋka] (**-(s)**, **-s**) F(M) Inca
Inkaufnahme [ɪn'kaʊfna:mə] F (*form*): **unter ~ finanzieller Verluste** accepting the inevitable financial losses
inkl. ABK (= *inklusive*) inc.
inklusive [ɪnklu'zi:və] PRÄP +*gen* inclusive of ▶ ADV inclusive
Inklusivpreis M all-in rate
inkognito [ɪn'kɔgnito] ADV incognito
inkonsequent ['ɪnkɔnzekvɛnt] ADJ inconsistent
inkorrekt ['ɪnkɔrɛkt] ADJ incorrect
Inkrafttreten [ɪn'krafttre:tən] (**-s**) NT coming into force
Inkubationszeit [ɪnkubatsi'o:nstsaɪt] F (*Med*) incubation period
Inland ['ɪnlant] (**-(e)s**) NT (*Geog*) inland; (*Pol, Comm*) home (country); **im ~ und Ausland** at home and abroad
Inlandflug M domestic flight
Inlandsporto NT inland postage
inmitten [ɪn'mɪtən] PRÄP +*gen* in the middle of; **~ von** amongst
innehaben ['ɪnəha:bən] *unreg* VT to hold
innehalten ['ɪnəhaltən] *unreg* VI to pause, to stop
innen ['ɪnən] ADV inside; **nach ~** inwards; **von ~** from the inside; **Innenarchitekt** M interior designer; **Innenaufnahme** F indoor photograph; **Innenbahn** F (*Sport*) inside lane; **Innendienst** M: **im Innendienst sein** to work in the office; **Inneneinrichtung** F (interior) furnishings *pl*; **Innenleben** NT (*seelisch*) emotional life; (*umg*: *körperlich*) insides *pl*; **Innenminister** M minister of the interior, Home Secretary (BRIT); **Innenpolitik** F domestic policy; **innenpolitisch** ADJ relating to domestic policy, domestic; **Innenspiegel** M rearview mirror; **Innenstadt** F town *od* city centre (BRIT) *od* center (US)
innerbetrieblich ADJ in-house; **etw ~ regeln** to settle sth within the company
innerdeutsch ADJ: **innerdeutsche(r) Handel** domestic trade in Germany
innere(r, s) ADJ inner; (*im Körper, inländisch*) internal
Innere(s) NT inside; (*Mitte*) centre (BRIT), center (US); (*fig*) heart
Innereien [ɪnə'raɪən] PL innards *pl*
inner- ZW: **innerhalb** PRÄP +*gen*, ADV within; (*räumlich*) inside; **innerlich** ADJ internal; (*geistig*) inward; **Innerlichkeit** F (*Liter*) inwardness; **innerparteilich** ADJ: **innerparteiliche Demokratie** democracy (with)in the party structure
innerste(r, s) ADJ innermost
Innerste(s) NT heart; **bis ins ~ getroffen** hurt to the quick
innewohnen ['ɪnəvo:nən] VI +*dat* (*geh*) to be inherent in
innig ['ɪnɪç] ADJ profound; (*Freundschaft*) intimate; **mein innigster Wunsch** my dearest wish
Innovation [ɪnovatsi'o:n] F innovation
Innovationsschub [ɪnovatsi'o:nsʃu:p] F surge of innovations
innovativ [ɪnova'ti:f] ADJ innovative
Innung ['ɪnʊŋ] F (trade) guild; **du blamierst die ganze ~** (*hum*: *umg*) you are letting the whole side down
inoffiziell ['ɪnlofitsiɛl] ADJ unofficial
ins [ɪns] = **in das**
Insasse ['ɪnzasə] (**-n**, **-n**) M, **Insassin** F (*einer Anstalt*) inmate; (*Aut*) passenger
insbesondere [ɪnsbə'zɔndərə] ADV (e)specially
Inschrift ['ɪnʃrɪft] F inscription
Insekt [ɪn'zɛkt] (**-(e)s**, **-en**) NT insect
Insektenvertilgungsmittel NT insecticide
Insel ['ɪnzəl] (**-**, **-n**) F island
Inserat [ɪnze'ra:t] (**-(e)s**, **-e**) NT advertisement
Inserent [ɪnze'rɛnt] M advertiser
inserieren [ɪnze'ri:rən] VT, VI to advertise
insgeheim [ɪnsgə'haɪm] ADV secretly
insgesamt [ɪnsgə'zamt] ADV altogether, all in all
Insiderhandel ['ɪnsaɪdər-] M insider dealing *od* trading
Insidertipp ['ɪnsaɪdər-] M insider tip
insofern [ɪnzo'fɛrn] ADV in this respect ▶ KONJ if; (*deshalb*) (and) so; **~ als** in so far as
insolvent ['ɪnzɔlvɛnt] ADJ bankrupt, insolvent
Insolvenz ['ɪnzɔlvɛnts] F (*Comm*) insolvency; **Insolvenzantrag** M application for insolvency proceedings; **Insolvenzverfahren** NT insolvency proceedings *pl*; **Insolvenzverwalter(in)** M(F) official receiver
insoweit ADV, KONJ = **insofern**
in spe [ɪn'ʃpe:] (*umg*) ADJ: **unser Schwiegersohn ~** our son-in-law to be, our future son-in-law
Inspektion [ɪnspɛktsi'o:n] F inspection; (*Aut*) service
Inspektor(in) [ɪn'spɛktɔr, -'to:rɪn] (**-s**, **-en**) M(F) inspector
Inspiration [ɪnspiratsi'o:n] F inspiration
inspirieren [ɪnspi'ri:rən] VT to inspire; **sich von etw ~ lassen** to get one's inspiration from sth
inspizieren [ɪnspi'tsi:rən] VT to inspect
Installateur [ɪnstala'tø:r] M plumber; (*Elektroinstallateur*) electrician
installieren [ɪnsta'li:rən] VT to install (*auch fig, Comput*)
Instandhaltung [ɪn'ʃtanthaltʊŋ] F maintenance
inständig [ɪn'ʃtɛndɪç] ADJ urgent; **~ bitten** to beg
Instandsetzung F overhaul; (*eines Gebäudes*) restoration
Instant Messaging ['ɪnstənt'mɛsɪdʒɪŋ] (**-**) NT instant messaging

Instanz [ɪnˈstants] F authority; (*Jur*) court; **Verhandlung in erster/zweiter ~** first/second court case
Instanzenweg M official channels *pl*
Instinkt [ɪnˈstɪŋkt] (**-(e)s, -e**) M instinct
instinktiv [ɪnstɪŋkˈtiːf] ADJ instinctive
Institut [ɪnstiˈtuːt] (**-(e)s, -e**) NT institute
Institution [ɪnstitutsiˈoːn] F institution
Instrument [ɪnstruˈmɛnt] NT instrument
Insulin [ɪnzuˈliːn] (**-s**) NT insulin
inszenieren [ɪnstseˈniːrən] VT to direct; (*fig*) to stage-manage
Inszenierung F production
intakt [ɪnˈtakt] ADJ intact
Integralrechnung [ɪnteˈgraːlrɛçnʊŋ] F integral calculus
Integration [ɪntegratsiˈoːn] F integration
integrieren [ɪnteˈgriːrən] VT to integrate; **integrierte Gesamtschule** comprehensive school (Brit)
Integrität [ɪntegriˈtɛːt] F integrity
Intellekt [ɪntɛˈlɛkt] (**-(e)s**) M intellect
intellektuell [ɪntɛlɛktuˈɛl] ADJ intellectual
Intellektuelle(r) F(M) intellectual
intelligent [ɪnteliˈgɛnt] ADJ intelligent
Intelligenz [ɪnteliˈgɛnts] F intelligence; (*Leute*) intelligentsia *pl*; **Intelligenzquotient** M IQ, intelligence quotient
Intendant [ɪntɛnˈdant] M director
Intensität [ɪntɛnziˈtɛːt] F intensity
intensiv [ɪntɛnˈziːf] ADJ intensive
intensivieren [ɪntɛnziˈviːrən] VT to intensify
Intensivkurs M crash course
Intensivstation F intensive care unit
interaktiv ADJ (*Comput*) interactive
Intercityzug [ɪntərˈsɪtitsuːk] M inter-city train
interessant [ɪnterɛˈsant] ADJ interesting; **sich ~ machen** to attract attention
interessanterweise ADV interestingly enough
Interesse [ɪnteˈrɛsə] (**-s, -n**) NT interest; **~ haben an** *+dat* to be interested in
Interessengebiet NT field of interest
Interessengegensatz M clash of interests
Interessent(in) [ɪnterɛˈsɛnt(ɪn)] M(F) interested party; **es haben sich mehrere Interessenten gemeldet** several people have shown interest
Interessenvertretung F representation of interests; (*Personen*) group representing (one's) interests
interessieren [ɪnterɛˈsiːrən] VT: **jdn (für etw** *od* **an etw** *dat*) **~** to interest sb (in sth) ▶ VR: **sich ~ für** to be interested in
interessiert ADJ: **politisch ~** interested in politics
Interkontinentalrakete [ɪntərkɔntinɛnˈtaːlrakeːtə] F intercontinental missile
interkulturell ADJ intercultural
intern [ɪnˈtɛrn] ADJ internal
Internat [ɪntɛrˈnaːt] (**-(e)s, -e**) NT boarding school
international [ɪntɛrnatsioˈnaːl] ADJ international
Internatsschüler(in) M(F) boarder
Internet [ˈɪntɛrnɛt] (**-s**) NT internet; **im ~** on the internet; **im ~ surfen** to surf the net; **ins ~ stellen** to post on the internet; **Internetanbieter(in)** M(F) internet provider; **Internetangriff** M cyber attack; **Internetanschluss** M internet connection; **Internetauktion** F internet auction; **internetbasiert** ADJ internet-based; **internetbasierte Anwendung** internet-based application; **Internetcafé** NT internet café; **Internethandel** M e-commerce; **Internethändler(in)** M(F) online trader *od* dealer; **Internethandy** NT mobile phone with internet access, smartphone; **Internetportal** NT web *od* internet portal; **Internetseite** F web page; **Internetsicherheit** F cybersecurity; **Internetzugang** M internet access
internieren [ɪntɛrˈniːrən] VT to intern
Internierungslager NT internment camp
Internist(in) M(F) internist
Interpol [ˈɪntərpoːl] (**-**) F ABK (= *Internationale Polizei*) Interpol
Interpret [ɪntərˈpreːt] (**-en, -en**) M: **Lieder verschiedener Interpreten** songs by various singers
Interpretation [ɪntərpretatsiˈoːn] F interpretation
interpretieren [ɪntɛrpreˈtiːrən] VT to interpret
Interpretin F *siehe* **Interpret**
Interpunktion [ɪntɛrpʊŋktsiˈoːn] F punctuation
Intervall [ɪntɛrˈval] (**-s, -e**) NT interval
intervenieren [ɪntɛrveˈniːrən] VI to intervene
Interview [ɪntərˈvjuː] (**-s, -s**) NT interview; **interviewen** [-ˈvjuːən] VT to interview
intim [ɪnˈtiːm] ADJ intimate; **Intimbereich** M (*Anat*) genital area
Intimität [ɪntimiˈtɛːt] F intimacy
Intimsphäre F: **jds ~ verletzen** to invade sb's privacy
intolerant [ˈɪntolerant] ADJ intolerant
intransitiv [ˈɪntranzitiːf] ADJ (*Gram*) intransitive
Intrige [ɪnˈtriːgə] (**-, -n**) F intrigue, plot
intrinsisch [ɪnˈtrɪnzɪʃ] ADJ: **intrinsischer Wert** intrinsic value
introvertiert [ɪntrovɛrˈtiːrt] ADJ: **~ sein** to be an introvert
intuitiv [ɪntuiˈtiːf] ADJ intuitive
intus [ˈɪntʊs] ADJ: **etw ~ haben** (*umg: Wissen*) to have got sth into one's head; (*Essen, Trinken*) to have got sth down one (*umg*)
Invalide [ɪnvaˈliːdə] (**-n, -n**) M disabled person, invalid
Invalidenrente F disability pension
Invasion [ɪnvaziˈoːn] F invasion
Inventar [ɪnvɛnˈtaːr] (**-s, -e**) NT inventory; (*Comm*) assets and liabilities *pl*
Inventur [ɪnvɛnˈtuːr] F stocktaking; **~ machen** to stocktake
investieren [ɪnvɛsˈtiːrən] VT to invest
investiert ADJ: **investiertes Kapital** capital employed

Investition [ɪnvɛstitsi'o:n] F investment
Investitionszulage F investment grant
Investmentgesellschaft [ɪn'vɛstməntgəzɛlʃaft] F unit trust
inwiefern [ɪnvi'fɛrn] ADV how far, to what extent
inwieweit [ɪnvi'vaɪt] ADV how far, to what extent
Inzest [ɪn'tsɛst] **(-(e)s, -e)** M incest *no pl*
inzwischen [ɪn'tsvɪʃən] ADV meanwhile
IOK NT ABK (= *Internationales Olympisches Komitee*) IOC
Ion [i'o:n] **(-s, -en)** NT ion
ionisch [i'o:nɪʃ] ADJ Ionian; **Ionisches Meer** Ionian Sea
IP ABK (*Comput: = Internet Protocol*) IP
iPad® [aɪpaet], **I-Pad** NT iPad®
iPhone® [aifo:n], **I-Phone** NT iPhone®
IQ M ABK (= *Intelligenzquotient*) IQ
i. R. ABK (= *im Ruhestand*) retd
IRA F ABK (= *Irisch-Republikanische Armee*) IRA
Irak [i'ra:k] **(-s)** M: **(der) ~** Iraq
Iraker(in) **(-s, -)** M(F) Iraqi
irakisch ADJ Iraqi
Iran [i'ra:n] **(-s)** M: **(der) ~** Iran
Iraner(in) **(-s, -)** M(F) Iranian
iranisch ADJ Iranian
irdisch ['ɪrdɪʃ] ADJ earthly; **den Weg alles Irdischen gehen** to go the way of all flesh
Ire ['i:rə] **(-n, -n)** M Irishman; (*Junge*) Irish boy; **die Iren** the Irish
irgend ['ɪrgənt] ADV at all; **wenn ~ möglich** if at all possible; **wann/was/wer ~** whenever/whatever/whoever; **irgendein(e, s)** ADJ some, any; **haben Sie (sonst) noch irgendeinen Wunsch?** is there anything else you would like?; **irgendeine(r, s)** PRON (*Person*) somebody; (*Ding*) something; (*fragend, verneinend*) anybody/anything; **ich will nicht bloß irgendein(e)s** I don't want any old one; **irgendeinmal** ADV sometime or other; (*fragend*) ever; **irgendetwas** PRON something; (*fragend, verneinend*) anything; **irgendjemand** PRON somebody; (*fragend, verneinend*) anybody; **irgendwann** ADV sometime; **irgendwer** (*umg*) PRON somebody; (*fragend, verneinend*) anybody; **irgendwie** ADV somehow; **irgendwo** ADV somewhere (BRIT), someplace (*US*); (*fragend, verneinend, bedingend*) anywhere (BRIT), any place (*US*); **irgendwohin** ADV somewhere (BRIT), someplace (*US*); (*fragend, verneinend, bedingend*) anywhere (BRIT), any place (*US*)
Irin ['i:rɪn] F Irishwoman; (*Mädchen*) Irish girl
Iris ['i:rɪs] **(-, -)** F iris
irisch ADJ Irish; **Irische See** Irish Sea
IRK NT ABK (= *Internationales Rotes Kreuz*) IRC
Irland ['ɪrlant] **(-s)** NT Ireland; (*Republik Irland*) Eire
Irländer ['ɪrlɛndər(ɪn)] **(-s, -)** M = **Ire**; **Irländerin** F = **Irin**
Ironie [iro'ni:] F irony
ironisch [i'ro:nɪʃ] ADJ ironic(al)
irre ['ɪrə] ADJ crazy, mad; **~ gut** (*umg*) way out (*umg*); **Irre(r)** F(M) lunatic; **irreführen** VT to mislead; **Irreführung** F fraud
irrelevant ['ɪrelevant] ADJ: **~ (für)** irrelevant (for *od* to)
irremachen VT to confuse
irren VI to be mistaken; (*umherirren*) to wander, to stray ▶ VR to be mistaken; **jeder kann sich mal ~** anyone can make a mistake; **Irrenanstalt** F (*veraltet*) lunatic asylum; **Irrenhaus** NT: **hier geht es zu wie im Irrenhaus** (*umg*) this place is an absolute madhouse
Irrfahrt ['ɪrfa:rt] F wandering
irrig ['ɪrɪç] ADJ incorrect, wrong
irritieren [ɪri'ti:rən] VT (*verwirren*) to confuse, to muddle; (*ärgern*) to irritate
Irr- ZW: **Irrlicht** NT will-o'-the-wisp; **Irrsinn** M madness; **so ein Irrsinn, das zu tun!** what a crazy thing to do!; **irrsinnig** ADJ mad, crazy; (*umg*) terrific; **irrsinnig komisch** incredibly funny; **Irrtum** **(-s, -tümer)** M mistake, error; **im Irrtum sein** to be wrong *od* mistaken; **Irrtum!** wrong!; **irrtümlich** ADJ mistaken
ISBN F ABK (= *Internationale Standardbuchnummer*) ISBN
Ischias ['ɪʃias] **(-)** M OD NT sciatica
ISDN-Anlage [i:lɛsde:'lɛn-] M (*Tel*) ISDN connection
Islam ['ɪslam] **(-s)** M Islam
islamisch [ɪs'la:mɪʃ] ADJ Islamic
Island ['i:slant] **(-s)** NT Iceland
Isländer(in) ['i:slɛndər(ɪn)] **(-s, -)** M(F) Icelander
isländisch ADJ Icelandic
Isolation [izolatsi'o:n] F isolation; (*Elek*) insulation; (*von Häftlingen*) solitary confinement
Isolator [izo'la:tɔr] M insulator
Isolierband NT insulating tape
isolieren [izo'li:rən] VT to isolate; (*Elek*) to insulate
Isolierstation F (*Med*) isolation ward
Isolierung F isolation; (*Elek*) insulation
Israel ['ɪsrae:l] **(-s)** NT Israel
Israeli[1] [ɪsra'e:li] **(-(s), -s)** M Israeli
Israeli[2] [ɪsra'e:li] **(-, -(s))** F Israeli
israelisch ADJ Israeli
isst [ɪst] VB *siehe* **essen**
ist [ɪst] VB *siehe* **sein**
Istanbul ['ɪstambu:l] **(-s)** NT Istanbul
Istbestand M (*Geld*) cash in hand; (*Waren*) actual stock
Italien [i'ta:liən] **(-s)** NT Italy
Italiener(in) [itali'e:nər(ɪn)] **(-s, -)** M(F) Italian
italienisch ADJ Italian; **die italienische Schweiz** Italian-speaking Switzerland
i. V. ABK (= *in Vertretung*) on behalf of; (= *in Vollmacht*) by proxy
IWF M ABK (= *Internationaler Währungsfonds*) IMF

Jj

, j [jɔt] NT J, j; **J wie Julius** ≈ J for Jack, ≈ J for Jig (*US*)

SCHLÜSSELWORT

a [ja:] ADV **1** yes; **haben Sie das gesehen? — ja** did you see it? — yes(, I did); **ich glaube ja** (yes) I think so; **zu allem Ja und Amen sagen** (*umg*) to accept everything without question
2 (*fragend*) really; **ich habe gekündigt — ja?** I've quit — have you?; **du kommst, ja?** you're coming, aren't you?
3: **sei ja vorsichtig** do be careful; **Sie wissen ja, dass ...** as you know, ...; **tu das ja nicht!** don't do that!; **sie ist ja erst fünf** (after all) she's only five; **Sie wissen ja, wie das so ist** you know how it is; **ich habe es ja gewusst** I just knew it; **ja, also ...** well you see ...

acht [jaxt] **(-, -en)** F yacht
acke ['jakə] **(-, -n)** F jacket; (*Wolljacke*) cardigan
acketkrone ['dʒɛ'kɪtkro:nə] F (*Zahnkrone*) jacket crown
ackett [ʒa'kɛt] **(-s, -s** *od* **-e)** NT jacket
agd [ja:kt] **(-, -en)** F hunt; (*Jagen*) hunting; **Jagdbeute** F kill; **Jagdflugzeug** NT fighter; **Jagdgewehr** NT sporting gun; **Jagdhund** M hunting dog; **Jagdschein** M hunting licence (BRIT) *od* license (*US*); **Jagdwurst** F smoked sausage
agen ['ja:gən] VI to hunt; (*eilen*) to race ▶ VT to hunt; (*wegjagen*) to drive (off); (*verfolgen*) to chase; **mit diesem Essen kannst du mich ~** (*umg*) I wouldn't touch that food with a barge pole (BRIT) *od* ten-foot pole (*US*)
äger ['jɛ:gər] **(-s, -)** M hunter; **Jägerin** F huntress, huntswoman; **Jägerlatein** (*umg*) NT hunters' tales *pl*; **Jägerschnitzel** NT (*Koch*) *cutlet served with mushroom sauce*
äh [jɛ:] ADJ abrupt, sudden; (*steil*) steep, precipitous; **jählings** ADV abruptly
ahr [ja:r] **(-(e)s, -e)** NT year; **im ~(e) 1066** in (the year) 1066; **die Sechzigerjahre** *od* **sechziger Jahre** the sixties *pl*; **mit dreißig Jahren** at the age of thirty; **in den besten Jahren sein** to be in the prime of (one's) life; **nach ~ und Tag** after (many) years; **zwischen den Jahren** (*umg*) between Christmas and New Year; **jahraus** ADV: **jahraus, jahrein** year in, year out; **Jahrbuch** NT annual, year book
jahrelang ADV for years
Jahres- ZW: **Jahresabonnement** NT annual subscription; **Jahresabschluss** M end of the year; (*Comm*) annual statement of account; **Jahresbeitrag** M annual subscription; **Jahresbericht** M annual report; **Jahreshauptversammlung** F (*Comm*) annual general meeting, AGM; **Jahreskarte** F annual season ticket; **Jahrestag** M anniversary; **Jahresumsatz** M (*Comm*) yearly turnover; **Jahreswechsel** M turn of the year; **Jahreszahl** F date, year; **Jahreszeit** F season
Jahr- ZW: **Jahrgang** M age group; (*von Wein*) vintage; **er ist Jahrgang 1950** he was born in 1950; **Jahrhundert** NT century; **Jahrhundertfeier** F centenary; **Jahrhundertwende** F turn of the century
jährlich ['jɛ:rlɪç] ADJ, ADV yearly; **zweimal ~** twice a year
Jahr- ZW: **Jahrmarkt** M fair; **Jahrtausend** NT millennium; **Jahrzehnt** NT decade
Jähzorn ['jɛ:tsɔrn] M hot temper
jähzornig ADJ hot-tempered
Jalousie [ʒalu'zi:] F venetian blind
Jamaika [ja'maɪka] **(-s)** NT Jamaica
Jammer ['jamər] **(-s)** M misery; **es ist ein ~, dass ...** it is a crying shame that ...
jämmerlich ['jɛmərlɪç] ADJ wretched, pathetic; **Jämmerlichkeit** F wretchedness
jammern VI to wail ▶ VT UNPERS: **es jammert mich** it makes me feel sorry
jammerschade ADJ: **es ist ~** it is a crying shame
Jan. ABK (= *Januar*) Jan.
Januar ['janua:r] **(-s, -e)** (*pl selten*) M January; *siehe auch* **September**
Japan ['ja:pan] **(-s)** NT Japan
Japaner(in) [ja'pa:nər(ɪn)] **(-s, -)** M(F) Japanese
japanisch ADJ Japanese
Jargon [ʒar'gõ:] **(-s, -s)** M jargon
Jasager ['ja:za:gər] **(-s, -)** (*pej*) M yes man
Jastimme F vote in favour (BRIT) *od* favor (*US*) (of)
jäten ['jɛ:tən] VT, VI to weed
Jauche ['jaʊxə] F liquid manure; **Jauchegrube** F cesspool, cesspit
jauchzen ['jaʊxtsən] VI to rejoice, to shout (with joy)

Jauchzer (**-s, -**) M shout of joy
jaulen ['jaʊlən] VI to howl
Jause ['jaʊzə] (ÖSTERR) F snack
jawohl ADV yes (of course)
Jawort NT consent; **jdm das ~ geben** to consent to marry sb; (*bei Trauung*) to say "I do"
Jazz [dʒæz] (-) M jazz; **Jazzkeller** M jazz club

SCHLÜSSELWORT

je [je:] ADV **1** (*jemals*) ever; **hast du so was je gesehen?** did you ever see anything like it?
2 (*jeweils*) every, each; **sie zahlten je 15 Euro** they paid 15 euros each
▶ KONJ **1**: **je nach** depending on; **je nachdem** it depends; **je nachdem, ob ...** depending on whether ...
2: **je eher, desto** *od* **umso besser** the sooner the better; **je länger, je lieber** the longer the better

Jeans [dʒi:nz] PL jeans *pl*; **Jeansanzug** M denim suit
jede(r, s) ['je:də(r, s)] ADJ (*einzeln*) each; (*von zweien*) either; (*jede von allen*) every ▶ INDEF PRON (*einzeln*) each (one); (*jede(r) von allen*) everyone, everybody; **ohne ~ Anstrengung** without any effort; **jeder Zweite** every other (one); **jedes Mal** every time, each time
jedenfalls ADV in any case
jedermann PRON everyone; **das ist nicht jedermanns Sache** it's not everyone's cup of tea
jederzeit ADV at any time
jedoch [je'dɔx] ADV however
jeher ['je:he:r] ADV: **von ~** all along
jein [jaɪn] ADV (*hum*) yes no
jemals ['je:ma:ls] ADV ever
jemand ['je:mant] INDEF PRON someone, somebody; (*bei Fragen, bedingenden Sätzen, Negation*) anyone, anybody
Jemen ['je:mən] (**-s**) M Yemen
Jemenit(in) [jeme'ni:t(ɪn)] (**-en, -en**) M(F) Yemeni
jemenitisch ADJ Yemeni
Jenaer Glas® ['je:naərgla:s] NT heatproof glass, ≈ Pyrex®
jene(r, s) ['je:nə(r, s)] ADJ that; (*pl*) those ▶ PRON that one; (*pl*) those; (*der Vorherige, die Vorherigen*) the former
jenseits ['je:nzaɪts] ADV on the other side ▶ PRÄP +*gen* on the other side of, beyond; **Jenseits** NT: **das Jenseits** the hereafter, the beyond; **jdn ins Jenseits befördern** (*umg*) to send sb to kingdom come
Jesus ['je:zʊs] (**Jesu**) M Jesus; **~ Christus** Jesus Christ
jetten ['dʒɛtən] (*umg*) VI to jet (*umg*)
jetzig ['jɛtsɪç] ADJ present
jetzt [jɛtst] ADV now; **~ gleich** right now; **bis ~** so far, up to now; **von ~ an** from now on
jeweilig ADJ respective; **die jeweilige Regierung** the government of the day
jeweils ADV: **~ zwei zusammen** two at a time; **zu ~ 10 Euro** at 10 euros each; **~ das Erste** the first each time; **~ am Monatsletzten** on the last day of each month
Jg. ABK = **Jahrgang**
Jh. ABK (= *Jahrhundert*) cent.
jiddisch ['jɪdɪʃ] ADJ Yiddish
Job [dʒɔp] (**-s, -s**) (*umg*) M job
jobben ['dʒɔbən] (*umg*) VI to work, to have a job
Jobcenter ['dʒɔpsɛntər] NT job centre (BRIT) *od* center (US)
Jobmaschine ['dʒɔp-] F (*umg*) job-creation machine
Joch [jɔx] (**-(e)s, -e**) NT yoke
Jochbein NT cheekbone
Jockey, Jockei ['dʒɔke] (**-s, -s**) M jockey
Jod [jo:t] (**-(e)s**) NT iodine
jodeln ['jo:dəln] VI to yodel
joggen ['dʒɔgən] VI to jog
Jogging ['dʒɔgɪŋ] (**-s**) NT jogging; **Jogginganzug** M jogging suit, tracksuit
Joghurt, Jogurt ['jo:gʊrt] (**-s, -s**) M OD NT yog(h)urt
Johannisbeere [jo'hanɪsbe:rə] F: **Rote ~** redcurrant; **Schwarze ~** blackcurrant
johlen ['jo:lən] VI to yell
Joint [dʒɔɪnt] (**-s, -s**) (*umg*) M joint
Joint Venture ['dʒɔɪntventʃəʳ] (**-, -s**) NT joint venture
Jolle ['jɔlə] (**-, -n**) F dinghy
Jongleur [ʒõ'glø:r] (**-s, -e**) M juggler
jonglieren [ʒõ'gli:rən] VI to juggle
Joppe ['jɔpə] (**-, -n**) F jacket
Jordanien [jɔr'da:niən] (**-s**) NT Jordan
Jordanier(in) (**-s, -**) M(F) Jordanian
jordanisch ADJ Jordanian
Journalismus [ʒʊrna'lɪsmʊs] M journalism
Journalist(in) [ʒʊrna'lɪst(ɪn)] M(F) journalist; **journalistisch** ADJ journalistic
Jubel ['ju:bəl] (**-s**) M rejoicing; **~, Trubel, Heiterkeit** laughter and merriment; **Jubeljahr** NT: **alle Jubeljahre (einmal)** (*umg*) once in a blue moon
jubeln VI to rejoice
Jubilar(in) [jubi'la:r(ɪn)] (**-s, -e**) M(F) *person celebrating an anniversary*
Jubiläum [jubi'lɛ:ʊm] (**-s, Jubiläen**) NT jubilee; (*Jahrestag*) anniversary
jucken ['jʊkən] VI to itch ▶ VT: **es juckt mich am Arm** my arm is itching; **das juckt mich** that's itchy; **das juckt mich doch nicht** (*umg*) I don't care
Juckpulver NT itching powder
Juckreiz M itch
Judaslohn ['ju:daslo:n] M (*liter*) blood money
Jude ['ju:də] (**-n, -n**) M Jew
Juden- zW: **Judenstern** M star of David; **Judentum** (**-s**) NT (*die Juden*) Jewry; **Judenverfolgung** F persecution of the Jews
Jüdin ['jy:dɪn] F Jewess
jüdisch ADJ Jewish
Judo ['ju:do] (**-(s)**) NT judo
Jugend ['ju:gənt] (-) F youth; **Jugendamt** NT youth welfare department; **jugendfrei** ADJ suitable for young people; (*Film*) U(-certificate)

G (*US*); **Jugendherberge** F youth hostel; **Jugendhilfe** F youth welfare scheme; **Jugendkriminalität** F juvenile crime; **jugendlich** ADJ youthful; **Jugendliche(r)** F(M) teenager, young person; **Jugendliebe** F (*Geliebte(r)*) love of one's youth; **Jugendrichter** M juvenile court judge; **Jugendschutz** M protection of children and young people; **Jugendstil** M (*Kunst*) Art Nouveau; **Jugendstrafanstalt** F youth custody centre (BRIT); **Jugendsünde** F youthful misdeed; **Jugendzentrum** NT youth centre (BRIT) *od* center (*US*)

Jugoslawe [jugo'sla:və] (**-n**, **-n**) M Yugoslav

Jugoslawien [jugo'sla:viən] (**-s**) NT Yugoslavia

Jugoslawin [jugo'sla:vɪn] F Yugoslav

jugoslawisch ADJ Yugoslav(ian)

Juli ['ju:li] (**-(s)**, **-s**) (*pl selten*) M July; *siehe auch* **September**

jun. ABK (= *junior*) jun.

jung [jʊŋ] ADJ young

Junge (**-n**, **-n**) M boy, lad ▶ NT young animal; (*pl*) young *pl*

jünger ADJ younger

Jünger ['jʏŋər] (**-s**, **-**) M disciple

Jungfer (**-**, **-n**) F: **alte** ~ old maid

Jungfernfahrt F maiden voyage

Jung- ZW: **Jungfrau** F virgin; (*Astrol*) Virgo; **Junggeselle** M bachelor; **Junggesellin** F bachelor girl; (*älter*) single woman

Jüngling ['jʏŋlɪŋ] M youth

Jungsozialist M (*Pol*) Young Socialist

jüngst [jʏŋst] ADV lately, recently

jüngste(r, s) ADJ youngest; (*neueste*) latest; **das J~ Gericht** the Last Judgement; **der J~ Tag** Doomsday, the Day of Judgement

Jungwähler(in) M(F) young voter

Juni ['ju:ni] (**-(s)**, **-s**) (*pl selten*) M June; *siehe auch* **September**

Junior ['ju:niɔr] (**-s**, **-en**) M junior

Junta ['xʊnta] (**-**, **-ten**) F (*Pol*) junta

jur. ABK = **juristisch**

Jura ['ju:ra] NO ART (*Univ*) law

Jurist(in) [ju'rɪst(ɪn)] M(F) jurist, lawyer; (*Student*) law student; **juristisch** ADJ legal

Juso ['ju:zo] (**-s**, **-s**) M ABK = **Jungsozialist**

just [jʊst] ADV just

Justiz [jʊs'ti:ts] (**-**) F justice; **Justizbeamte(r)** M judicial officer; **Justizirrtum** M miscarriage of justice; **Justizminister** M minister of justice; **Justizmord** M judicial murder

Juwel [ju've:l] (**-s**, **-en**) M OD NT jewel

Juwelier [juve'li:r] (**-s**, **-e**) M jeweller (BRIT), jeweler (*US*); **Juweliergeschäft** NT jeweller's (BRIT) *od* jeweler's (*US*) (shop)

Jux [jʊks] (**-es**, **-e**) M joke, lark; **etw aus ~ tun/sagen** (*umg*) to do/say sth in fun

jwd [jɔtve:'de:] ADV (*hum*) in the back of beyond

K, k [ka:] NT K, k; **K wie Kaufmann** ≈ K for King

Kabarett [kaba'rɛt] (**-s, -e** *od* **-s**) NT cabaret; **Kabarettist(in)** [kabarɛ'tɪst(ɪn)] M(F) cabaret artiste

Kabel ['ka:bəl] (**-s, -**) NT (*Elek*) wire; (*stark*) cable; **Kabelanschluss** M: **Kabelanschluss haben** to have cable television; **Kabelfernsehen** NT cable television

Kabeljau ['ka:bəljaʊ] (**-s, -e** *od* **-s**) M cod

kabellos ADJ wireless

kabeln VT, VI to cable

Kabelsalat (*umg*) M tangle of cable

Kabine [ka'bi:nə] F cabin; (*Zelle*) cubicle

Kabinett [kabi'nɛt] (**-s, -e**) NT (*Pol*) cabinet; (*kleines Zimmer*) small room ▶ M *high-quality German white wine*

Kabriolett [kabrio'lɛt] (**-s, -s**) NT (*Aut*) convertible

Kachel ['kaxəl] (**-, -n**) F tile

kacheln VT to tile

Kachelofen M tiled stove

Kacke ['kakə] (**-, -n**) (*umg!*) F crap (*umg!*)

Kadaver [ka'da:vər] (**-s, -**) M carcass

Kader ['ka:dər] (**-s, -**) M (*Mil, Pol*) cadre; (*Sport*) squad; (*DDR, Schweiz: Fachleute*) group of specialists; **Kaderschmiede** F (*Pol: umg*) *institution for the training of cadre personnel*

Kadett [ka'dɛt] (**-en, -en**) M cadet

Käfer ['kɛ:fər] (**-s, -**) M beetle

Kaff [kaf] (**-s, -s**) (*umg*) NT dump, hole

Kaffee ['kafe] (**-s, -s**) M coffee; **zwei ~, bitte!** two coffees, please; **das ist kalter ~** (*umg*) that's old hat; **Kaffeekanne** F coffeepot; **Kaffeeklatsch** M, **Kaffeekränzchen** NT coffee circle; **Kaffeelöffel** M coffee spoon; **Kaffeemaschine** F coffee maker; **Kaffeemühle** F coffee grinder; **Kaffeesatz** M coffee grounds *pl*; **Kaffeetante** F (*hum*) coffee addict; (*in Café*) old biddy; **Kaffeetasse** F coffee cup; **Kaffeewärmer** M cosy (*for coffeepot*)

Käfig ['kɛ:fɪç] (**-s, -e**) M cage

kahl [ka:l] ADJ (*Mensch, Kopf*) bald; (*Baum, Wand*) bare; **~ fressen** to strip bare; **~ geschoren** shaven, shorn; **Kahlheit** F baldness; **kahlköpfig** ADJ bald-headed; **Kahlschlag** M (*in Wald*) clearing

Kahn [ka:n] (**-(e)s, Kähne**) M boat, barge

Kai [kaɪ] (**-s, -e** *od* **-s**) M quay

Kairo ['kaɪro] (**-s**) NT Cairo

Kaiser ['kaɪzər] (**-s, -**) M emperor; **Kaiserin** F empress; **kaiserlich** ADJ imperial; **Kaiserreich** NT empire; **Kaiserschmarren** ['kaizərʃmarən] M (*Koch*) *sugared, cut-up pancake with raisins*; **Kaiserschnitt** M (*Med*) Caesarean (BRIT) *od* Cesarean (US) (section)

Kajak ['ka:jak] (**-s, -s**) M OD NT kayak; **Kajakfahren** NT kayaking

Kajüte [ka'jy:tə] (**-, -n**) F cabin

Kakao [ka'ka:o] (**-s, -s**) M cocoa; **jdn durch den ~ ziehen** (*umg: veralbern*) to make fun of sb; (*: boshaft reden*) to run sb down

Kakerlake [ka:kər'la:kə] (**-, -n**) F cockroach

Kaktee [kak'te:ə] (**-, -n**) F cactus

Kaktus ['kaktʊs] (**-, -se**) M cactus

Kalabrien [ka'la:briən] (**-s**) NT Calabria

Kalauer ['ka:laʊər] (**-s, -**) M corny joke; (*Wortspiel*) corny pun

Kalb [kalp] (**-(e)s, Kälber**) NT calf; **kalben** ['kalbən] VI to calve; **Kalbfleisch** NT veal

Kalbsleder NT calf(skin)

Kalender [ka'lɛndər] (**-s, -**) M calendar; (*Taschenkalender*) diary

Kali ['ka:li] (**-s, -s**) NT potash

Kaliber [ka'li:bər] (**-s, -**) NT (*lit, fig*) calibre (BRIT), caliber (US)

Kalifornien [kali'fɔrniən] (**-s**) NT California

Kalk [kalk] (**-(e)s, -e**) M lime; (*Biol*) calcium; **Kalkstein** M limestone

Kalkül [kal'ky:l] (**-s, -e**) M OD NT (*geh*) calculation

Kalkulation [kalkulatsi'o:n] F calculation

Kalkulator [kalku'la:tɔr] M cost accountant

kalkulieren [kalku'li:rən] VT to calculate

kalkuliert ADJ: **kalkuliertes Risiko** calculated risk

Kalkutta [kal'kʊta] (**-s**) NT Calcutta

Kalorie [kalo'ri:] (**-, -n**) F calorie

kalorienarm ADJ low-calorie

kalt [kalt] ADJ cold; **mir ist (es) ~** I am cold; **kalte Platte** cold meat; **der Kalte Krieg** the Cold War; **etw ~ stellen** to chill, to put sth to chill; **die Wohnung kostet ~ 500 Euro** the flat costs 500 euros without heating; **~ bleiben** to be unmoved; **~ lächelnd** (*ironisch*) cool as you please; **kaltblütig** ADJ cold-blooded; (*ruhig*) cool; **Kaltblütigkeit** F cold-bloodedness; (*Ruhe*) coolness

Kälte ['kɛltə] (-) F coldness; (*Wetter*) cold; **Kälteeinbruch** M cold spell; **Kältegrad** M degree of frost *od* below zero; **Kältewelle** F cold spell

kalt- zW: **kaltherzig** ADJ cold-hearted; **kaltmachen** (*umg*) VT to do in; **Kaltmiete** F rent exclusive of heating; **Kaltschale** F (*Koch*) *cold sweet soup*; **kaltschnäuzig** ADJ cold, unfeeling; **kaltstellen** VT (*fig*) to leave out in the cold

Kalzium ['kaltsiʊm] (**-s**) NT calcium

kam *etc* [ka:m] VB *siehe* **kommen**

Kambodscha [kam'bɔdʒa] NT Cambodia

Kamel [ka'me:l] (**-(e)s, -e**) NT camel

Kamera ['kamera] (**-, -s**) F camera

Kamerad(in) [kamə'ra:t, -'ra:dɪn] (**-en, -en**) M(F) comrade, friend; **Kameradschaft** F comradeship; **kameradschaftlich** ADJ comradely

Kamera- zW: **Kameraführung** F camera work; **Kamerahandy** NT camera phone; **Kameramann** (**-(e)s**, *pl* **-männer**) M cameraman; **Kamerarekorder** M camcorder; **Kameratelefon** NT camera phone

Kamerun ['kaməru:n] (**-s**) NT Cameroon

Kamille [ka'mɪlə] (**-, -n**) F camomile

Kamillentee M camomile tea

Kamin [ka'mi:n] (**-s, -e**) M (*außen*) chimney; (*innen*) fireside; (*Feuerstelle*) fireplace; **Kaminfeger** (**-s, -**) M chimney sweep; **Kaminkehrer** (**-s, -**) M chimney sweep

Kamm [kam] (**-(e)s, Kämme**) M comb; (*Bergkamm*) ridge; (*Hahnenkamm*) crest; **alle/alles über einen ~ scheren** (*fig*) to lump everyone/everything together

kämmen ['kɛmən] VT to comb

Kammer ['kamər] (**-, -n**) F chamber; (*Zimmer*) small bedroom; **Kammerdiener** M valet; **Kammerjäger** M (*Schädlingsbekämpfer*) pest controller; **Kammermusik** F chamber music; **Kammerzofe** F chambermaid

Kammstück NT (*Koch*) shoulder

Kampagne [kam'panjə] (**-, -n**) F campaign

Kampf [kampf] (**-(e)s, Kämpfe**) M fight, battle; (*Wettbewerb*) contest; (*fig: Anstrengung*) struggle; **jdm/etw den ~ ansagen** (*fig*) to declare war on sb/sth; **kampfbereit** ADJ ready for action

kämpfen ['kɛmpfən] VI to fight; **ich habe lange mit mir ~ müssen, ehe …** I had a long battle with myself before …

Kampfer ['kampfər] (**-s**) M camphor

Kämpfer(in) (**-s, -**) M(F) fighter, combatant

Kampf- zW: **Kampfflugzeug** NT fighter (aircraft); **Kampfgeist** M fighting spirit; **Kampfhandlung** F action; **Kampfkunst** F martial arts *pl*; **kampflos** ADJ without a fight; **kampflustig** ADJ pugnacious; **Kampfplatz** M battlefield; (*Sport*) arena, stadium; **Kampfrichter** M (*Sport*) referee; **Kampfsport** M martial art

Kampuchea [kampʊ'tʃe:a] (**-s**) NT Kampuchea

Kanada ['kanada] (**-s**) NT Canada

Kanadier(in) [ka'na:diər(ɪn)] (**-s, -**) M(F) Canadian

kanadisch [ka'na:dɪʃ] ADJ Canadian

Kanal [ka'na:l] (**-s, Kanäle**) M (*Fluss*) canal; (*Rinne*) channel; (*für Abfluss*) drain; **der ~** (*auch*: **der Ärmelkanal**) the (English) Channel

Kanalinseln PL Channel Islands *pl*

Kanalisation [kanalizatsi'o:n] F sewage system

kanalisieren [kanali'zi:rən] VT to provide with a sewage system; (*fig: Energie etc*) to channel

Kanaltunnel M Channel Tunnel

Kanarienvogel [ka'na:riənfo:gəl] M canary

Kanarische Inseln [ka'na:rɪʃə'ɪnzəln] PL Canary Islands *pl*, Canaries *pl*

Kandare [kan'da:rə] (**-, -n**) F: **jdn an die ~ nehmen** (*fig*) to take sb in hand

Kandidat(in) [kandi'da:t(ɪn)] (**-en, -en**) M(F) candidate; **jdn als Kandidaten aufstellen** to nominate sb

Kandidatur [kandida'tu:r] F candidature, candidacy

kandidieren [kandi'di:rən] VI (*Pol*) to stand, to run

kandiert [kan'di:rt] ADJ (*Frucht*) candied

Kandis ['kandɪs] (**-**), **Kandiszucker** ['kandɪstsʊkər] M rock candy

Känguru ['kɛŋguru] (**-s, -s**) NT kangaroo

Kaninchen [ka'ni:nçən] NT rabbit

Kanister [ka'nɪstər] (**-s, -**) M can, canister

kann [kan] VB *siehe* **können**

Kännchen ['kɛnçən] NT pot; (*für Milch*) jug

Kanne ['kanə] (**-, -n**) F (*Krug*) jug; (*Kaffeekanne*) pot; (*Milchkanne*) churn; (*Gießkanne*) watering can

Kannibale [kani'ba:lə] (**-n, -n**) M cannibal

kannte *etc* ['kantə] VB *siehe* **kennen**

Kanon ['ka:nɔn] (**-s, -s**) M canon

Kanone [ka'no:nə] (**-, -n**) F gun; (*Hist*) cannon; (*fig: Mensch*) ace; **das ist unter aller ~** (*umg*) that defies description

Kanonenfutter (*umg*) NT cannon fodder

Kant. ABK = **Kanton**

Kantate [kan'ta:tə] (**-, -n**) F cantata

Kante ['kantə] (**-, -n**) F edge; **Geld auf die hohe ~ legen** (*umg*) to put money by

kantig ['kantɪç] ADJ (*Holz*) edged; (*Gesicht*) angular

Kantine [kan'ti:nə] F canteen

Kanton [kan'to:n] (**-s, -e**) M canton

Kantor ['kantɔr] M choirmaster

Kanu ['ka:nu] (**-s, -s**) NT canoe

Kanzel ['kantsəl] (**-, -n**) F pulpit; (*Aviat*) cockpit

Kanzlei [kants'laɪ] F chancery; (*Büro*) chambers *pl*

Kanzler(in) ['kantslər] (**-s, -**) M(F) chancellor

Kanzlerkandidatur F candidacy for the chancellorship

Kap [kap] (**-s, -s**) NT cape; **das ~ der guten Hoffnung** the Cape of Good Hope

Kapazität [kapatsi'tɛ:t] F capacity; (*Fachmann*) authority

Kapelle [ka'pɛlə] F (*Gebäude*) chapel; (*Mus*) band

Kapellmeister(in) M(F) director of music; (*Mil, von Tanzkapelle etc*) bandmaster, bandleader

Kaper ['ka:pər] (**-, -n**) F caper

kapern VT to capture
kapieren [ka'pi:rən] (*umg*) VT, VI to understand
Kapital [kapi'ta:l] (**-s, -e** *od* **-ien**) NT capital; **aus etw ~ schlagen** (*pej: lit, fig*) to make capital out of sth; **Kapitalanlage** F investment; **Kapitalaufwand** M capital expenditure; **Kapitalertrag** M capital gains *pl*; **Kapitalertragssteuer** F capital gains tax; **Kapitalflucht** F flight of capital; **Kapitalgesellschaft** F (*Comm*) joint-stock company; **Kapitalgüter** PL capital goods *pl*; **kapitalintensiv** ADJ capital-intensive
Kapitalismus [kapita'lɪsmʊs] M capitalism
Kapitalist [kapita'lɪst] M capitalist
kapitalistisch ADJ capitalist
Kapital- ZW: **kapitalkräftig** ADJ wealthy; **Kapitalmarkt** M money market; **kapitalschwach** ADJ financially weak; **kapitalstark** ADJ financially strong; **Kapitalverbrechen** NT serious crime; (*mit Todesstrafe*) capital crime
Kapitän [kapi'tɛ:n] (**-s, -e**) M captain
Kapitel [ka'pɪtəl] (**-s, -**) NT chapter; **ein trauriges ~** (*Angelegenheit*) a sad story
Kapitulation [kapitulatsi'o:n] F capitulation
kapitulieren [kapitu'li:rən] VI to capitulate
Kaplan [ka'pla:n] (**-s, Kapläne**) M chaplain
Kappe ['kapə] (**-, -n**) F cap; (*Kapuze*) hood; **das nehme ich auf meine ~** (*fig: umg*) I'll take the responsibility for that
kappen VT to cut
Kapsel ['kapsəl] (**-, -n**) F capsule
Kapstadt ['kapʃtat] NT Cape Town
kaputt [ka'pʊt] (*umg*) ADJ smashed, broken; (*Person*) exhausted, knackered; **etw ~ machen/schlagen** to break/smash sth; **der Fernseher ist ~** the TV's not working; **ein kaputter Typ** a bum; *siehe auch* **kaputtmachen**; **kaputtgehen** *unreg* VI to break; (*Schuhe*) to fall apart; (*Firma*) to go bust; (*Stoff*) to wear out; (*sterben*) to cop it (*umg*); **kaputtlachen** VR to laugh o.s. silly; **kaputtmachen** VT to break; (*Mensch*) to exhaust, to wear out; **kaputtschlagen** *unreg* VT to smash
Kapuze [ka'pu:tsə] (**-, -n**) F hood
Karabiner [kara'bi:nər] (**-s, -**) M (*Gewehr*) carbine
Karacho [ka'raxo] (**-s**) NT: **mit ~** (*umg*) hell for leather
Karaffe [ka'rafə] (**-, -n**) F carafe; (*geschliffen*) decanter
Karambolage [karambo'la:ʒə] (**-, -n**) F (*Zusammenstoß*) crash
Karamell [kara'mɛl] (**-s**) M caramel; **Karamellbonbon** M OD NT toffee
Karat [ka'ra:t] (**-(e)s, -e**) NT carat
Karate (**-s**) NT karate
Karawane [kara'va:nə] (**-, -n**) F caravan
Kardinal [kardi'na:l] (**-s, Kardinäle**) M cardinal; **Kardinalfehler** M cardinal error; **Kardinalzahl** F cardinal number
Karenzzeit [ka'rɛntstsaɪt] F waiting period
Karfreitag [ka:r'fraɪta:k] M Good Friday
karg [kark] ADJ scanty, poor; (*Mahlzeit*) meagre (BRIT), meager (US); **etw ~ bemessen** to be mean with sth; **Kargheit** F poverty, scantiness; (*von Mahlzeit*) meagreness (BRIT), meagerness (US)
kärglich ['kɛrklɪç] ADJ poor, scanty
Kargo ['kargo] (**-s, -s**) M (*Comm*) cargo
Karibik [ka'ri:bɪk] (-) F: **die ~** the Caribbean
karibisch ADJ Caribbean; **das Karibische Meer** the Caribbean Sea
kariert [ka'ri:rt] ADJ (*Stoff*) checked (BRIT), checkered (US); (*Papier*) squared; **~ reden** (*umg*) to talk rubbish *od* nonsense
Karies ['ka:riɛs] (-) F caries
Karikatur [karika'tu:r] F caricature; **Karikaturist(in)** [karikatu:'rɪst(ɪn)] M(F) cartoonist
karikieren [kari'ki:rən] VT to caricature
karitativ [karita'ti:f] ADJ charitable
Karneval ['karnəval] (**-s, -e** *od* **-s**) M carnival; *see note*

> **Karneval** is the name given to the days immediately before Lent when people gather to sing, dance, eat, drink and generally make merry before the fasting begins. **Rosenmontag**, the day before Shrove Tuesday, is the most important day of Karneval on the Rhine. Most firms take a day's holiday on that day to enjoy the parades and revelry. In South Germany Karneval is called "Fasching".

Karnickel [kar'nɪkəl] (**-s, -**) (*umg*) NT rabbit
Kärnten ['kɛrntən] (**-s**) NT Carinthia
Karo ['ka:ro] (**-s, -s**) NT square; (*Karten*) diamonds; **Karoass** NT ace of diamonds
Karosse [ka'rɔsə] (**-, -n**) F coach, carriage
Karosserie [karɔsə'ri:] F (*Aut*) body(work)
Karotte [ka'rɔtə] (**-, -n**) F carrot
Karpaten [kar'pa:tən] PL Carpathians *pl*
Karpfen ['karpfən] (**-s, -**) M carp
Karre ['karə] (**-, -n**) F = **Karren**
Karree [ka:'re:] (**-s, -s**) NT: **einmal ums ~ gehen** (*umg*) to walk around the block
karren ['karən] VT to cart, to transport; **Karren** (**-s, -**) M cart, barrow; **den Karren aus dem Dreck ziehen** (*umg*) to get things sorted out
Karriere [kari'ɛ:rə] (**-, -n**) F career; **~ machen** to get on, to get to the top; **Karrieremacher(in)** M(F) careerist
Karsamstag [ka:r'zamsta:k] M Easter Saturday
Karst [karst] (**-s, -e**) M (*Geog, Geol*) karst, *barren landscape*
Karte ['kartə] (**-, -n**) F card; (*Landkarte*) map; (*Speisekarte*) menu; (*Eintrittskarte, Fahrkarte*) ticket; **Karten spielen** to play cards; **mit offenen Karten spielen** (*fig*) to put one's cards on the table; **alles auf eine ~ setzen** to put all one's eggs in one basket
Kartei [kar'taɪ] F card index; **Karteikarte** F index card; **Karteileiche** (*umg*) F sleeping *od* non-active member; **Karteischrank** M filing cabinet

Kartell [kar'tɛl] (**-s, -e**) NT cartel; **Kartellamt** NT monopolies commission; **Kartellgesetzgebung** F anti-trust legislation
Karten- ZW: **Kartenhaus** NT (*lit, fig*) house of cards; **Kartenlegen** NT fortune-telling (*using cards*); **Kartenspiel** NT card game; (*Karten*) pack (BRIT) *od* deck (*US*) of cards; **Kartentelefon** NT cardphone; **Kartenvorverkauf** M advance sale of tickets
Kartoffel [kar'tɔfəl] (-, **-n**) F potato; **Kartoffelbrei** M mashed potatoes *pl*; **Kartoffelchips** PL potato crisps *pl* (BRIT), potato chips *pl* (*US*); **Kartoffelpuffer** M potato cake (*made from grated potatoes*); **Kartoffelpüree** NT mashed potatoes *pl*; **Kartoffelsalat** M potato salad
Karton [kar'tõ:] (**-s, -s**) M cardboard; (*Schachtel*) cardboard box
kartoniert [karto'ni:rt] ADJ hardback
Karussell [karʊ'sɛl] (**-s, -s**) NT roundabout (BRIT), merry-go-round
Karwoche ['ka:rvɔxə] F Holy Week
Karzinom [kartsi'no:m] (**-s, -e**) NT (*Med*) carcinoma
Kasachstan [kazaxs'ta:n] (**-s**) NT (*Geog*) Kazakhstan
Kaschemme [ka'ʃɛmə] (-, **-n**) F dive
kaschieren [ka'ʃi:rən] VT to conceal, to cover up
Kaschmir ['kaʃmi:r] (**-s**) NT (*Stoff*) Kashmir
Käse ['kɛ:zə] (**-s, -**) M cheese; (*umg: Unsinn*) rubbish, twaddle; **Käseblatt** (*umg*) NT (local) rag; **Käseglocke** F cheese cover; **Käsekuchen** M cheesecake
Kaserne [ka'zɛrnə] (-, **-n**) F barracks *pl*
Kasernenhof M parade ground
käsig ['kɛ:zɪç] ADJ (*fig: umg: Gesicht, Haut*) pasty, pale; (*vor Schreck*) white; (*lit*) cheesy
Kasino [ka'zi:no] (**-s, -s**) NT club; (*Mil*) officers' mess; (*Spielkasino*) casino
Kaskoversicherung ['kaskofɛrzɪçərʊŋ] F (*Aut: Teilkaskoversicherung*) ≈ third party, fire and theft insurance; (*: Vollkaskoversicherung*) fully comprehensive insurance
Kasper ['kaspər] (**-s, -**) M Punch; (*fig*) clown
Kasperletheater ['kaspərlətea:tər], **Kasperltheater** ['kaspərltea:tər] NT Punch and Judy (show)
Kaspisches Meer ['kaspɪʃəs'me:r] NT Caspian Sea
Kasse ['kasə] (-, **-n**) F (*Geldkasten*) cashbox; (*in Geschäft*) till, cash register; (*Kinokasse, Theaterkasse etc*) box office; (*Krankenkasse*) health insurance; (*Sparkasse*) savings bank; **die ~ führen** to be in charge of the money; **jdn zur ~ bitten** to ask sb to pay up; **~ machen** to count the money; **getrennte ~ führen** to pay separately; **an der ~** (*in Geschäft*) at the (cash) desk; **gut bei ~ sein** to be in the money
Kasseler ['kasələr] (**-s, -**) NT *lightly smoked pork loin*
Kassen- ZW: **Kassenarzt** M ≈ National Health doctor (BRIT), ≈ panel doctor (*US*); **Kassenbestand** M cash balance; **Kassenbon** M receipt; **Kassenführer** M (*Comm*) cashier; **Kassenpatient** M ≈ National Health patient (BRIT); **Kassenprüfung** F audit; **Kassenschlager** (*umg*) M (*Theat etc*) box-office hit; (*Ware*) big seller; **Kassensturz** M: **Kassensturz machen** to check one's money; **Kassenwart** M (*von Klub etc*) treasurer; **Kassenzettel** M sales slip
Kasserolle [kasə'rɔlə] (-, **-n**) F casserole
Kassette [ka'sɛtə] F small box; (*Tonband, Phot*) cassette; (*Comput*) cartridge, cassette; (*Bücherkassette*) case
Kassettenrekorder (**-s, -**) M cassette recorder
Kassiber [ka'si:bər] (**-s, -**) M (*in Gefängnis*) secret message
kassieren [ka'si:rən] VT (*Gelder etc*) to collect; (*umg: wegnehmen*) to take (away) ▸ VI: **darf ich ~?** would you like to pay now?
Kassierer(in) [ka'si:rər(ɪn)] (**-s, -**) M(F) cashier; (*von Klub*) treasurer
Kastanie [kas'ta:niə] F chestnut
Kastanienbaum M chestnut tree
Kästchen ['kɛstçən] NT small box, casket
Kaste ['kastə] (-, **-n**) F caste
Kasten ['kastən] (**-s, Kästen**) M box (*auch Sport*), case; (*Truhe*) chest; **er hat was auf dem ~** (*umg*) he's brainy; **Kastenform** F (*Koch*) (square) baking tin (BRIT) *od* pan (*US*); **Kastenwagen** M van
kastrieren [kas'tri:rən] VT to castrate
Kat (**-, -s**) M ABK (*Aut*) = **Katalysator**
katalanisch [kata'la:nɪʃ] ADJ Catalan
Katalog [kata'lo:k] (**-(e)s, -e**) M catalogue (BRIT), catalog (*US*)
katalogisieren [katalogi'zi:rən] VT to catalogue (BRIT), to catalog (*US*)
Katalysator [kataly'za:tɔr] M (*lit, fig*) catalyst; (*Aut*) catalytic converter; **~-Auto** vehicle fitted with a catalytic converter
Katapult [kata'pʊlt] (**-(e)s, -e**) M OD NT catapult
katapultieren [katapʊl'ti:rən] VT to catapult ▸ VR to catapult o.s.; (*Pilot*) to eject
Katar ['ka:tar] NT Qatar
Katarrh, Katarr [ka'tar] (**-s, -e**) M catarrh
Katasteramt [ka'tastəramt] NT land registry
katastrophal [katastro'fa:l] ADJ catastrophic
Katastrophe [kata'stro:fə] (-, **-n**) F catastrophe, disaster
Katastrophen- ZW: **Katastrophenalarm** M emergency alert; **Katastrophengebiet** NT disaster area; **Katastrophenmedizin** F medical treatment in disasters; **Katastrophenmeldung** F news of a/the catastrophe; **Katastrophenschutz** M disaster control
Katechismus [katɛ'çɪsmʊs] M catechism
Kategorie [katego'ri:] F category
kategorisch [kate'go:rɪʃ] ADJ categorical
kategorisieren [kategori'zi:rən] VT to categorize
Kater ['ka:tər] (**-s, -**) M tomcat; (*umg*) hangover; **Katerfrühstück** NT *breakfast (of pickled herring etc) to cure a hangover*
kath. ABK = **katholisch**

Katheder [ka'te:dər] (**-s, -**) NT (*Sch*) teacher's desk; (*Univ*) lectern
Kathedrale [kate'dra:lə] (**-, -n**) F cathedral
Katheter [ka'te:tər] (**-s, -**) M (*Med*) catheter
Kathode [ka'to:də] (**-, -n**) F cathode
Katholik(in) [kato'li:k(ɪn)] (**-en, -en**) M(F) Catholic
katholisch [ka'to:lɪʃ] ADJ Catholic
Katholizismus [katoli'tsɪsmʊs] M Catholicism
Katode [ka'to:də] (**-, -n**) F = **Kathode**
katzbuckeln ['katsbʊkəln] (*pej, umg*) VI to bow and scrape
Kätzchen ['kɛtsçən] NT kitten
Katze ['katsə] (**-, -n**) F cat; **die ~ im Sack kaufen** to buy a pig in a poke; **für die Katz** (*umg*) in vain, for nothing
Katzen- ZW: **Katzenauge** NT cat's-eye (BRIT); (*am Fahrrad*) rear light; **Katzenjammer** (*umg*) M hangover; **Katzenmusik** F (*fig*) caterwauling; **Katzensprung** (*umg*) M stone's throw, short distance; **Katzentür** F cat flap; **Katzenwäsche** F a lick and a promise
Kauderwelsch ['kaʊdərvɛlʃ] (**-(s)**) NT jargon; (*umg*) double Dutch (BRIT)
kauen ['kaʊən] VT, VI to chew
kauern ['kaʊərn] VI to crouch
Kauf [kaʊf] (**-(e)s, Käufe**) M purchase, buy; (*Kaufen*) buying; **ein guter ~** a bargain; **etw in ~ nehmen** to put up with sth
kaufen VT to buy; **dafür kann ich mir nichts ~** (*ironisch*) what use is that to me!
Käufer(in) ['kɔʏfər(ɪn)] (**-s, -**) M(F) buyer
Käuferverhalten NT buying habits *pl*
Kauf- ZW: **Kauffrau** F businesswoman; (*Einzelhandelskauffrau*) shopkeeper; **kauffreudig** ADJ consumerist; **Kaufhaus** NT department store; **Kaufkraft** F purchasing power; **Kaufladen** M shop, store
käuflich ['kɔʏflɪç] ADJ purchasable, for sale; (*pej*) venal ▶ ADV: **~ erwerben** to purchase
Kauf- ZW: **Kauflust** F desire to buy things; (*Börse*) buying; **kauflustig** ADJ interested in buying; **Kaufmann** (**-(e)s,** *pl* **-leute**) M businessman; (*Einzelhandelskaufmann*) shopkeeper; **kaufmännisch** ADJ commercial; **kaufmännischer Angestellter** clerk; **Kaufpreis** M purchase price; **kaufsüchtig** ADJ: **kaufsüchtig sein** to be a shopaholic (*umg*); **Kaufvertrag** M bill of sale; **Kaufwillige(r)** F(M) potential buyer; **Kaufzurückhaltung** F consumer reticence; **Kaufzwang** M: **kein/ohne Kaufzwang** no/without obligation
Kaugummi ['kaʊgʊmi] M chewing gum
Kaukasus ['kaʊkazʊs] M: **der ~** the Caucasus
Kaulquappe ['kaʊlkvapə] (**-, -n**) F tadpole
kaum [kaʊm] ADV hardly, scarcely; **wohl ~, ich glaube ~** I hardly think so
Kausalzusammenhang [kaʊ'za:ltsuzamənhaŋ] M causal connection
Kaution [kaʊtsi'o:n] F deposit; (*Jur*) bail
Kautschuk ['kaʊtʃʊk] (**-s, -e**) M India rubber
Kauz [kaʊts] (**-es, Käuze**) M owl; (*fig*) queer fellow
Kavalier [kava'li:r] (**-s, -e**) M gentleman
Kavaliersdelikt NT peccadillo
Kavallerie [kavalə'ri:] F cavalry
Kavallerist [kavalə'rɪst] M cavalryman
Kaviar ['ka:viar] M caviar
KB NT ABK (= *Kilobyte*) KB, kbyte
Kcal ABK (= *Kilokalorie*) kcal
keck [kɛk] ADJ daring, bold; **Keckheit** F daring, boldness
Kegel ['ke:gəl] (**-s, -**) M skittle; (*Math*) cone; **Kegelbahn** F skittle alley, bowling alley; **kegelförmig** ADJ conical
kegeln VI to play skittles
Kehle ['ke:lə] (**-, -n**) F throat; **er hat das in die falsche ~ bekommen** (*lit*) it went down the wrong way; (*fig*) he took it the wrong way; **aus voller ~** at the top of one's voice
Kehl- ZW: **Kehlkopf** M larynx; **Kehlkopfkrebs** M cancer of the throat; **Kehllaut** M guttural
Kehre ['ke:rə] (**-, -n**) F turn(ing), bend
kehren VT, VI (*wenden*) to turn; (*mit Besen*) to sweep; **sich an etw** *dat* **nicht ~** not to heed sth; **in sich** *akk* **gekehrt** (*versunken*) pensive; (*verschlossen*) introspective, introverted
Kehricht (**-s**) M sweepings *pl*
Kehr- ZW: **Kehrmaschine** F sweeper; **Kehrreim** M refrain; **Kehrseite** F reverse, other side; (*ungünstig*) wrong *od* bad side; **die Kehrseite der Medaille** the other side of the coin
kehrtmachen VI to turn about, to about-turn
Kehrtwendung F about-turn
keifen ['kaɪfən] VI to scold, to nag
Keil [kaɪl] (**-(e)s, -e**) M wedge; (*Mil*) arrowhead; **keilen** VT to wedge ▶ VR to fight
Keilerei [kaɪlə'raɪ] (*umg*) F punch-up
Keilriemen M (*Aut*) fan belt
Keim [kaɪm] (**-(e)s, -e**) M bud; (*Med, fig*) germ; **etw im ~ ersticken** to nip sth in the bud
keimen VI to germinate
Keim- ZW: **keimfrei** ADJ sterile; **keimtötend** ADJ antiseptic, germicidal; **Keimzelle** F (*fig*) nucleus
kein [kaɪn], **keine** ['kaɪnə] PRON none ▶ ADJ no, not any; **keine schlechte Idee** not a bad idea; **keine Stunde/drei Monate** (*nicht einmal*) less than an hour/three months
keine(r, s) INDEF PRON no one, nobody; (*von Gegenstand*) none; **keiner von ihnen** none of them
keinerlei ['kaɪnər'laɪ] ADJ *attrib* no ... whatever
keinesfalls ADV on no account
keineswegs ADV by no means
keinmal ADV not once
Keks [ke:ks] (**-es, -e**) M OD NT biscuit (BRIT), cookie (US)
Kelch [kɛlç] (**-(e)s, -e**) M cup, goblet, chalice
Kelle ['kɛlə] (**-, -n**) F ladle; (*Maurerkelle*) trowel
Keller ['kɛlər] (**-s, -**) M cellar; (*Geschoss*) basement; **Kellerassel** (**-, -n**) F woodlouse
Kellerei [kɛlə'raɪ] F wine cellars *pl*; (*Firma*) wine producer
Kellergeschoss NT basement

Kellerwohnung F basement flat (BRIT) *od* apartment (US)
Kellner(in) ['kɛlnər(ɪn)] **(-s, -)** M(F) waiter, waitress
kellnern *(umg)* VI to work as a waiter/waitress (BRIT), to wait on tables (US)
Kelte ['kɛltə] **(-n, -n)** M Celt
Kelter (-, **-n**) F winepress; *(Obstkelter)* press
keltern ['kɛltərn] VT to press
Keltin ['kɛltɪn] F (female) Celt
keltisch ADJ Celtic
Kenia ['ke:nia] **(-s)** NT Kenya
kennen ['kɛnən] *unreg* VT to know; **~ Sie sich schon?** do you know each other (already)?; **kennst du mich noch?** do you remember me?
kennenlernen VT to get to know ▸ VR to get to know each other; *(zum ersten Mal)* to meet
Kenner(in) **(-s, -)** M(F): **~ (von** *od* **+gen)** connoisseur (of); *(Experte)* expert (on)
Kennkarte F identity card
kenntlich ADJ distinguishable, discernible; **etw ~ machen** to mark sth
Kenntnis **(-, -se)** F knowledge *no pl*; **etw zur ~ nehmen** to note sth; **von etw ~ nehmen** to take notice of sth; **jdn in ~ setzen** to inform sb; **über Kenntnisse von etw verfügen** to be knowledgeable about sth
Kenn- ZW: **Kennwort** NT *(Chiffre)* code name; *(Losungswort)* password, code word; **Kennzeichen** NT mark, characteristic; **(amtliches/polizeiliches) Kennzeichen** *(Aut)* number plate (BRIT), license plate (US); **kennzeichnen** VT UNTR to characterize; **kennzeichnenderweise** ADV characteristically; **Kennziffer** F (code) number; *(Comm)* reference number
kentern ['kɛntərn] VI to capsize
Keramik [ke'ra:mɪk] **(-, -en)** F ceramics *pl*, pottery; *(Gegenstand)* piece of ceramic work *od* pottery
Kerbe ['kɛrbə] **(-, -n)** F notch, groove
Kerbel **(-s, -)** M chervil
kerben VT to notch
Kerbholz NT: **etw auf dem ~ haben** to have done sth wrong
Kerker ['kɛrkər] **(-s, -)** M prison
Kerl [kɛrl] **(-s, -e)** *(umg)* M chap, bloke (BRIT), guy; **du gemeiner ~!** you swine!
Kern [kɛrn] **(-(e)s, -e)** M *(Obstkern)* pip, stone; *(Nusskern)* kernel; *(Atomkern)* nucleus; *(fig)* heart, core; **Kernenergie** F nuclear energy; **Kernfach** NT *(Sch)* core subject; **Kernfamilie** F nuclear family; **Kernforschung** F nuclear research; **Kernfrage** F central issue; **Kernfusion** F nuclear fusion; **Kerngehäuse** NT core; **kerngesund** ADJ thoroughly healthy, fit as a fiddle
kernig ADJ robust; *(Ausspruch)* pithy
Kern- ZW: **Kernkompetenz** F core competence; **Kernkraft** F nuclear power; **Kernkraftwerk** NT nuclear power station; **Kernland** F heartland; **kernlos** ADJ seedless, pipless; **Kernphysik** F nuclear physics *sing*; **Kernreaktion** F nuclear reaction; **Kernreaktor** M nuclear reactor; **Kernschmelze** F meltdown; **Kernseife** F washing soap; **Kernspaltung** F nuclear fission; **Kernstück** NT *(fig)* main item; *(von Theorie etc)* central part, core; **Kernwaffen** PL nuclear weapons *pl*; **kernwaffenfrei** ADJ nuclear-free; **Kernzeit** F core time
Kerze ['kɛrtsə] **(-, -n)** F candle; *(Zündkerze)* plug; **kerzengerade** ADJ straight as a die
Kerzen- ZW: **Kerzenhalter** M candlestick; **Kerzenständer** M candleholder
kess [kɛs] ADJ saucy
Kessel ['kɛsəl] **(-s, -)** M kettle; *(von Lokomotive etc)* boiler; *(Mulde)* basin; *(Geog)* depression; *(Mil)* encirclement; **Kesselstein** M scale, fur (BRIT); **Kesseltreiben** NT *(fig)* witch-hunt
Ketchup ['kɛtʃʊp], **Ketschup** **(-(s), -s)** M OD NT ketchup
Kette ['kɛtə] **(-, -n)** F chain; *(Halskette)* necklace; **jdn an die ~ legen** *(fig)* to tie sb down
ketten VT to chain
Ketten- ZW: **Kettenfahrzeug** NT tracked vehicle; **Kettenhund** M watchdog; **Kettenkarussell** NT merry-go-round *(with gondolas on chains)*; **Kettenladen** M chain store; **Kettenrauchen** NT chain smoking; **Kettenreaktion** F chain reaction
Ketzer(in) ['kɛtsər(ɪn)] **(-s, -)** M(F) heretic; **Ketzerei** [kɛtsə'raɪ] F heresy; **ketzerisch** ADJ heretical
keuchen ['kɔʏçən] VI to pant, to gasp
Keuchhusten M whooping cough
Keule ['kɔʏlə] **(-, -n)** F club; *(Koch)* leg
Keulung ['kɔʏlʊŋ] F cull, culling
keusch [kɔʏʃ] ADJ chaste; **Keuschheit** F chastity
kfm. ABK = **kaufmännisch**
Kfm. ABK = **Kaufmann**
Kfz **(-(s), -(s))** F ABK = **Kraftfahrzeug**
kg ABK (= *Kilogramm*) kg
KG **(-, -s)** F ABK = **Kommanditgesellschaft**
kHz ABK (= *Kilohertz*) kHz
Kibbuz [kɪ'bu:ts] (-, **Kibbuzim** *od* **-e**) M kibbutz
Kichererbse ['kɪçərlɛrpsə] F chick pea
kichern ['kɪçərn] VI to giggle
kicken ['kɪkən] VT, VI *(Fußball)* to kick
kidnappen ['kɪtnɛpən] VT to kidnap
Kidnapper(in) **(-s, -)** M(F) kidnapper
Kiebitz ['ki:bɪts] **(-es, -e)** M peewit
Kiefer[1] ['ki:fər] **(-s, -)** M jaw
Kiefer[2] ['ki:fər] **(-, -n)** F pine
Kiefernholz NT pine(wood)
Kiefernzapfen M pine cone
Kieferorthopäde M orthodontist
Kieker ['ki:kər] **(-s, -)** M: **jdn auf dem ~ haben** *(umg)* to have it in for sb
Kiel [ki:l] **(-(e)s, -e)** M *(Federkiel)* quill; *(Naut)* keel; **Kielwasser** NT wake
Kieme ['ki:mə] **(-, -n)** F gill
Kies [ki:s] **(-es, -e)** M gravel; *(umg: Geld)* money, dough
Kiesel ['ki:zəl] **(-s, -)** M pebble; **Kieselstein** M pebble
Kiesgrube F gravel pit

Kiesweg M gravel path
Kiew ['ki:ɛf] (**-s**) NT Kiev
kiffen ['kɪfən] (*umg*) VT to smoke pot *od* grass
Kilimandscharo [kiliman'dʒa:ro] (**-s**) M Kilimanjaro
Killer ['kɪlər(ɪn)] (**-s, -**) (*umg*) M killer, murderer; (*gedungener*) hit man; **Killerin** (*umg*) F killer, female murderer, murderess
Kilo ['ki:lo] (**-s, -(s)**) NT kilo; **Kilobyte** [kilo'baɪt] NT (*Comput*) kilobyte; **Kilogramm** [kilo'gram] NT kilogram
Kilometer [kilo'me:tər] M kilometre (BRIT), kilometer (*US*); **Kilometerfresser** (*umg*) M long-haul driver; **Kilometergeld** NT ≈ mileage (allowance); **Kilometerstand** M ≈ mileage; **Kilometerstein** M ≈ milestone; **Kilometerzähler** M ≈ mileometer
Kilowatt [kilo'vat] NT kilowatt
Kimme ['kɪmə] (**-, -n**) F notch; (*Gewehr*) back sight
Kind [kɪnt] (**-(e)s, -er**) NT child; **sich freuen wie ein ~** to be as pleased as Punch; **sie bekommt ein ~** she's having a baby; **mit ~ und Kegel** (*hum: umg*) with the whole family; **von ~ auf** from childhood
Kinderarzt M paediatrician (BRIT), pediatrician (*US*)
Kinderbetreuung F childcare
Kinderbett NT cot (BRIT), crib (*US*)
Kinderei [kɪndə'raɪ] F childishness
Kindererziehung F bringing up of children; (*durch Schule*) education of children
kinderfeindlich ADJ anti-children; (*Architektur, Planung*) not catering for children
Kinderfreibetrag M child allowance
Kindergarten M nursery school

> A **Kindergarten** is a nursery school for children aged between 3 and 6 years. The children sing, play and do handicrafts. They are not taught the three Rs at this stage. Most Kindergartens are financed by the town or the church and not by the state. Parents pay a monthly contribution towards the cost.

Kinder- zW: **Kindergärtner(in)** M(F) nursery-school teacher; **Kindergeld** NT child benefit (BRIT); **Kinderheim** NT children's home; **Kinderkrankheit** F childhood illness; **Kinderkrippe** F crèche (BRIT), daycare center (*US*); **Kinderladen** M (alternative) playgroup; **Kinderlähmung** F polio(myelitis); **kinderleicht** ADJ childishly easy; **kinderlieb** ADJ fond of children; **Kinderlied** NT nursery rhyme; **kinderlos** ADJ childless; **Kindermädchen** NT nursemaid; **Kinderpflegerin** F child minder; **kinderreich** ADJ with a lot of children; **Kinderschuh** M: **es steckt noch in den Kinderschuhen** (*fig*) it's still in its infancy; **kindersicher** ADJ childproof; **Kindersicherung** F childproof safety catch; (*an Flasche*) childproof cap; **Kinderspiel** NT child's play; **ein Kinderspiel sein** to be a doddle; **Kinderstube** F: **eine gute Kinderstube haben** to be well-mannered; **Kindertagesstätte** F day-nursery; **Kinderteller** M children's dish; **Kinderwagen** M pram (BRIT), baby carriage (*US*); **Kinderzimmer** NT child's/children's room; (*für Kleinkinder*) nursery
Kindes- zW: **Kindesalter** NT infancy; **Kindesbeine** PL: **von Kindesbeinen an** from early childhood; **Kindesmisshandlung** F child abuse
Kind- zW: **kindgemäß** ADJ suitable for a child *od* children; **Kindheit** F childhood; **kindisch** ADJ childish
Kindle® [kɪndl] M Kindle®
kindlich ADJ childlike
kindsköpfig ADJ childish
Kinkerlitzchen ['kɪŋkərlɪtsçən] (*umg*) PL knick-knacks *pl*
Kinn [kɪn] (**-(e)s, -e**) NT chin; **Kinnhaken** M (*Boxen*) uppercut; **Kinnlade** F jaw
Kino ['ki:no] (**-s, -s**) NT cinema (BRIT), movies (*US*); **Kinobesucher** M, **Kinogänger** M cinema-goer (BRIT), movie-goer (*US*); **Kinoprogramm** NT film programme (BRIT), movie program (*US*)
Kiosk [ki'ɔsk] (**-(e)s, -e**) M kiosk
Kippe ['kɪpə] (**-, -n**) F (*umg*) cigarette end; **auf der ~ stehen** (*fig*) to be touch and go
kippen VI to topple over, to overturn ▶ VT to tilt
Kipper ['kɪpər] (**-s, -**) M (*Aut*) tipper, dump(er) truck
Kippschalter M rocker switch
Kirche ['kɪrçə] (**-, -n**) F church
Kirchen- zW: **Kirchenchor** M church choir; **Kirchendiener** M churchwarden; **Kirchenfest** NT church festival; **Kirchenlied** NT hymn; **Kirchenschiff** NT (*Längsschiff*) nave; (*Querschiff*) transept; **Kirchensteuer** F church tax; **Kirchentag** M church congress
Kirch- zW: **Kirchgänger(in)** (**-s, -**) M(F) churchgoer; **Kirchhof** M churchyard; **kirchlich** ADJ ecclesiastical; **Kirchturm** M church tower, steeple; **Kirchweih** F fair, kermis (*US*)
Kirgistan ['kɪrgista:n] (**-s**) NT (*Geog*) Kirghizia
Kirmes ['kɪrmɛs] (**-, -sen**) F (*Dialekt*) fair, kermis (*US*)
Kirschbaum ['kɪrʃbaʊm] M cherry tree; (*Holz*) cherry (wood)
Kirsche ['kɪrʃə] (**-, -n**) F cherry; **mit ihm ist nicht gut Kirschen essen** (*fig*) it's best not to tangle with him
Kirschtomate F cherry tomato
Kirschtorte F: **Schwarzwälder ~** Black Forest Gateau
Kirschwasser NT kirsch
Kissen ['kɪsən] (**-s, -**) NT cushion; (*Kopfkissen*) pillow; **Kissenbezug** M pillow case
Kiste ['kɪstə] (**-, -n**) F box; (*Truhe*) chest; (*umg: Bett*) sack; (*: Fernsehen*) box (BRIT), tube (*US*)
Kita ['kɪta] F ABK = **Kindertagesstätte**
Kitsch [kɪtʃ] (**-(e)s**) M trash
kitschig ADJ trashy
Kitt [kɪt] (**-(e)s, -e**) M putty
Kittchen (*umg*) NT clink

Kittel (**-s, -**) M overall; *(von Arzt, Laborant etc)* (white) coat
kitten VT to putty; *(fig)* to patch up
Kitz [kɪts] (**-es, -e**) NT kid; *(Rehkitz)* fawn
kitzelig ['kɪtsəlɪç] ADJ *(lit, fig)* ticklish
kitzeln VT, VI to tickle
Kiwi ['ki:vi] (**-, -s**) F kiwi fruit
KKW (**-, -s**) NT ABK = **Kernkraftwerk**
Kl. ABK (= *Klasse*) cl.
Klacks [klaks] (**-es, -e**) *(umg)* M *(von Kartoffelbrei, Sahne)* dollop; *(von Senf, Farbe etc)* blob
Kladde ['kladə] (**-, -n**) F rough book; *(Block)* scribbling pad
klaffen ['klafən] VI to gape
kläffen ['klɛfən] VI to yelp
Klage ['kla:gə] (**-, -n**) F complaint; *(Jur)* action; **eine ~ gegen jdn einreichen** *od* **erheben** to institute proceedings against sb; **Klagelied** NT: **ein Klagelied über jdn/etw anstimmen** *(fig)* to complain about sb/sth; **Klagemauer** F: **die Klagemauer** the Wailing Wall
klagen VI *(wehklagen)* to lament, to wail; *(sich beschweren)* to complain; *(Jur)* to take legal action; **jdm sein Leid/seine Not ~** to pour out one's sorrow/distress to sb
Kläger(in) ['klɛ:gər(ɪn)] (**-s, -**) M(F) *(Jur: im Zivilrecht)* plaintiff; *(: im Strafrecht)* prosecuting party; *(: in Scheidung)* petitioner
Klageschrift F *(Jur)* charge; *(bei Scheidung)* petition
kläglich ['klɛ:klɪç] ADJ wretched
Klamauk [kla'maʊk] (**-s**) *(umg)* M *(Alberei)* tomfoolery; *(im Theater)* slapstick
klamm ADJ *(Finger)* numb; *(feucht)* damp
Klamm [klam] (**-, -en**) F ravine
Klammer ['klamər] (**-, -n**) F clamp; *(in Text)* bracket; *(Büroklammer)* clip; *(Wäscheklammer)* peg (BRIT), pin *(US)*; *(Zahnklammer)* brace; **~ auf/zu** open/close brackets; **Klammeraffe** M *(umg)* at-sign, @
klammern VR: **sich ~ an** *+akk* to cling to
klammheimlich [klam'haɪmlɪç] *(umg)* ADJ secret ▸ ADV on the quiet
Klamotte [kla'mɔtə] (**-, -n**) F *(pej: Film etc)* rubbishy old film *etc*; **Klamotten** PL *(umg: Kleider)* clothes *pl*; *(: Zeug)* stuff
Klampfe ['klampfə] (**-, -n**) *(umg)* F guitar
klang *etc* [klaŋ] VB *siehe* **klingen**
Klang (**-(e)s, Klänge**) M sound
klangvoll ADJ sonorous
Klappbett NT folding bed
Klappe ['klapə] (**-, -n**) F valve; *(an Oboe etc)* key; *(Film)* clapperboard; *(Ofenklappe)* damper; *(umg: Mund)* trap; **die ~ halten** to shut one's trap
klappen VI *(Geräusch)* to click; *(Sitz etc)* to tip ▸ VT to tip ▸ VI UNPERS to work; **hat es mit den Karten/dem Job geklappt?** did you get the tickets/job O.K.?
Klappentext M blurb
Klapper ['klapər] (**-, -n**) F rattle
klapperig ADJ run-down, worn-out
klappern VI to clatter, to rattle
Klapperschlange F rattlesnake
Klapperstorch M stork; **er glaubt noch an den ~** he still thinks babies are found under the gooseberry bush
Klapp- ZW: **Klappmesser** NT jackknife; **Klapprad** NT collapsible *od* folding bicycle; **Klappstuhl** M folding chair; **Klapptisch** M folding table
Klaps [klaps] (**-es, -e**) M slap; **einen ~ haben** *(umg)* to have a screw loose; **klapsen** VT to slap
klar [kla:r] ADJ clear; *(Naut)* ready to sail; *(Mil)* ready for action; **bei klarem Verstand sein** to be in full possession of one's faculties; **sich** *dat* **im Klaren sein über** *+akk* to be clear about; **ins Klare kommen** to get clear; **~ sehen** to see clearly; **sich** *dat* **über etw** *akk* **~ werden** to get sth clear in one's mind; **alles ~?** everything okay?
Kläranlage F sewage plant; *(von Fabrik)* purification plant
Klare(r) *(umg)* M schnapps
klären VT *(Flüssigkeit)* to purify; *(Probleme)* to clarify ▸ VR to clear (itself) up
Klarheit F clarity; **sich** *dat* **~ über etw** *akk* **verschaffen** to get sth straight
Klarinette [klari'nɛtə] F clarinet
klar- ZW: **klarkommen** *unreg (umg)* VI: **mit jdm/etw klarkommen** to be able to cope with sb/sth; **klarlegen** VT to clear up, to explain; **klarmachen** VT *(Schiff)* to get ready for sea; **jdm etw klarmachen** to make sth clear to sb; **Klarsichtfolie** F transparent film; **klarstellen** VT to clarify; **Klartext** M: **im Klartext** in clear; *(fig: umg)* ≈ in plain English
Klärung ['klɛ:rʊŋ] F purification; *(von Problem)* clarification
Klärungsbedarf M need for clarification
klasse *(umg)* ADJ smashing
Klasse ['klasə] (**-, -n**) F class; *(Sch)* class, form; *(auch:* **Steuerklasse***)* bracket; *(Güterklasse)* grade
Klassen- ZW: **Klassenarbeit** F test; **Klassenbewusstsein** NT class-consciousness; **Klassenbuch** NT *(Sch)* (class) register; **Klassengesellschaft** F class society; **Klassenkamerad(in)** M(F) classmate; **Klassenkampf** M class conflict; **Klassenlehrer(in)** M(F) class teacher; **klassenlos** ADJ classless; **Klassensprecher(in)** M(F) class spokesperson; **Klassenziel** NT: **das Klassenziel nicht erreichen** *(Sch)* not to reach the required standard (for the year); *(fig)* not to make the grade; **Klassenzimmer** NT classroom
klassifizieren [klasifi'tsi:rən] VT to classify
Klassifizierung F classification
Klassik ['klasɪk] F *(Zeit)* classical period; *(Stil)* classicism; **Klassiker** (**-s, -**) M classic
klassisch ADJ *(lit, fig)* classical
Klassizismus [klasi'tsɪsmʊs] M classicism
Klatsch [klatʃ] (**-(e)s, -e**) M smack, crack; *(Gerede)* gossip; **Klatschbase** F gossip(monger)
klatschen VI *(tratschen)* to gossip; *(Beifall spenden)* to applaud, to clap ▸ VT: **(jdm) Beifall ~** to applaud *od* clap (sb)
Klatsch- ZW: **klatschnass** ADJ soaking wet;

Klatschspalte F gossip column; **Klatschtante** (*pej, umg*) F gossip(monger)
klauben ['klaubən] VT to pick
Klaue ['klauə] (-, **-n**) F claw; (*umg: Schrift*) scrawl
klauen VT to claw; (*umg*) to pinch
Klause ['klauzə] (-, **-n**) F cell; (*von Mönch*) hermitage
Klausel ['klauzəl] (-, **-n**) F clause; (*Vorbehalt*) proviso
Klausur [klau'zu:r] F seclusion; **Klausurarbeit** F examination paper
Klaviatur [klavia'tu:r] F keyboard
Klavier [kla'vi:r] (**-s, -e**) NT piano; **Klavierauszug** M piano score
Klebeband NT adhesive tape
Klebemittel NT glue
kleben ['kle:bən] VT, VI: **~ (an** *+akk***)** to stick (to); **jdm eine ~** (*umg*) to belt sb one
Klebezettel M gummed label
klebrig ADJ sticky
Klebstoff M glue
Klebstreifen M adhesive tape
kleckern ['klɛkərn] VI to slobber
Klecks [klɛks] (**-es, -e**) M blot, stain; **klecksen** VI to blot; (*pej*) to daub
Klee [kle:] (**-s**) M clover; **jdn/etw über den grünen ~ loben** (*fig*) to praise sb/sth to the skies; **Kleeblatt** NT cloverleaf; (*fig*) trio
Kleid [klait] (**-(e)s, -er**) NT garment; (*Frauenkleid*) dress; **Kleider** PL clothes *pl*
kleiden ['klaidən] VT to clothe, to dress ▶ VR to dress; **jdn ~** to suit sb
Kleider- ZW: **Kleiderbügel** M coat hanger; **Kleiderbürste** F clothes brush; **Kleiderschrank** M wardrobe; **Kleiderständer** M coat-stand
kleidsam ADJ becoming
Kleidung F clothing
Kleidungsstück NT garment
Kleie ['klaiə] (-, **-n**) F bran
klein [klain] ADJ little, small; **haben Sie es nicht kleiner?** haven't you got anything smaller?; **ein kleines Bier, ein Kleines** (*umg*) ≈ half a pint, ≈ a half; **von ~ an** *od* **auf** (*von Kindheit an*) from childhood; (*von Anfang an*) from the very beginning; **das kleinere Übel** the lesser evil; **sein Vater war (ein) kleiner Beamter** his father was a minor civil servant; **~ anfangen** to start off in a small way; **~ geschrieben werden** (*umg*) to count for (very) little; **~ hacken** to chop up; **~ schneiden** to chop up; **Kleinanzeige** F small ad (BRIT), want ad (*US*); **Kleinanzeigen** PL classified advertising *sing*; **Kleinarbeit** F: **in zäher/mühseliger Kleinarbeit** with rigorous/painstaking attention to detail; **Kleinasien** NT Asia Minor; **Kleinbürgertum** NT petite bourgeoisie; **Kleinbus** M minibus
Kleine(r) F(M) little one
klein- ZW: **Kleinfamilie** F small family, nuclear family (*Soziologie*); **Kleinformat** NT small size; **im Kleinformat** small-scale; **Kleingedruckte(s)** NT small print; **Kleingeld** NT small change; **das nötige Kleingeld haben** (*fig*) to have the wherewithal (*umg*); **kleingläubig** ADJ of little faith; **kleinhacken** VT to chop up; **Kleinholz** NT firewood; **Kleinholz aus jdm machen** to make mincemeat of sb
Kleinigkeit F trifle; **wegen** *od* **bei jeder ~** for the slightest reason; **eine ~ essen** to have a bite to eat
klein- ZW: **kleinkariert** ADJ: **kleinkariert denken** to think small; **Kleinkind** NT infant; **Kleinkram** M details *pl*; **Kleinkredit** M personal loan; **kleinkriegen** (*umg*) VT (*gefügig machen*) to bring into line; (*unterkriegen*) to get down; (*körperlich*) to tire out; **kleinlaut** ADJ dejected, quiet; **kleinlich** ADJ petty, paltry; **Kleinlichkeit** F pettiness, paltriness; **kleinmütig** ADJ fainthearted
Kleinod ['klaino:t] (**-s, -odien**) NT gem; (*fig*) treasure
klein- ZW: **Kleinrechner** M minicomputer; **kleinschneiden** *unreg* VT to chop up; **kleinschreiben** *unreg* VT: **ein Wort kleinschreiben** to write a word with a small initial letter; **Kleinschreibung** F use of small initial letters; **Kleinstadt** F small town; **kleinstädtisch** ADJ provincial
kleinstmöglich ADJ smallest possible
Kleinwagen M small car
Kleister ['klaistər] (**-s, -**) M paste
kleistern VT to paste
Klemme ['klɛmə] (-, **-n**) F clip; (*Med*) clamp; (*fig*) jam; **in der ~ sitzen** *od* **sein** (*fig: umg*) to be in a fix
klemmen VT (*festhalten*) to jam; (*quetschen*) to pinch, to nip ▶ VR to catch o.s.; (*sich hineinzwängen*) to squeeze o.s. ▶ VI (*Tür*) to stick, to jam; **sich hinter jdn/etw ~** to get on to sb/get down to sth
Klempner ['klɛmpnər] (**-s, -**) M plumber
Kleptomanie [klɛptoma'ni:] F kleptomania
Kleriker ['kle:rikər] (**-s, -**) M cleric
Klerus ['kle:rus] (-) M clergy
Klette ['klɛtə] (-, **-n**) F burr; **sich wie eine ~ an jdn hängen** to cling to sb like a limpet
Kletterer ['klɛtərər] (**-s, -**) M climber
Klettergerüst NT climbing frame
klettern VI to climb
Kletterpflanze F creeper
Kletterseil NT climbing rope
Klettverschluss M Velcro® fastener
klicken ['klikən] VI to click
Klient(in) [kli'ɛnt(in)] M(F) client
Klima ['kli:ma] (**-s, -s** *od* **-te**) NT climate; **Klimaanlage** F air conditioning; **Klimakompensation** (-, **-en**) F carbon offset
Klimaschutz M climate protection; **Klimaschutzabkommen** NT agreement on climate change
klimatisieren [kli:mati'zi:rən] VT to air-condition
klimatisiert ADJ air-conditioned
Klimawandel M climate change
Klimawechsel M change of air
Klimbim [klim'bim] (**-s**) (*umg*) M odds and ends *pl*

klimpern ['klɪmpərn] VI to tinkle; (*auf Gitarre*) to strum
Klinge ['klɪŋə] (**-, -n**) F blade, sword; **jdn über die ~ springen lassen** (*fig: umg*) to allow sb to run into trouble
Klingel ['klɪŋəl] (**-, -n**) F bell; **Klingelbeutel** M collection bag; **Klingelknopf** M bell push
klingeln VI to ring; **es hat geklingelt** (*an Tür*) somebody just rang the doorbell, the doorbell just rang
Klingelton M ringtone
klingen ['klɪŋən] *unreg* VI to sound; (*Gläser*) to clink
Klinik ['kli:nɪk] F clinic
klinisch ['kli:nɪʃ] ADJ clinical
Klinke ['klɪŋkə] (**-, -n**) F handle
Klinker ['klɪŋkər] (**-s, -**) M clinker
Klippe ['klɪpə] (**-, -n**) F cliff; (*im Meer*) reef; (*fig*) hurdle
klippenreich ADJ rocky
klipp und klar ['klɪplʊntkla:r] ADJ clear and concise
Klips [klɪps] (**-es, -e**) M clip; (*Ohrklips*) earring
klirren ['klɪrən] VI to clank, to jangle; (*Gläser*) to clink; **klirrende Kälte** biting cold
Klischee [klɪ'ʃe:] (**-s, -s**) NT (*Druckplatte*) plate, block; (*fig*) cliché; **Klischeevorstellung** F stereotyped idea
Klitoris ['kli:torɪs] (**-, -**) F clitoris
Klo [klo:] (**-s, -s**) (*umg*) NT loo (BRIT), john (US)
Kloake [klo'a:kə] (**-, -n**) F sewer
klobig ['klo:bɪç] ADJ clumsy
Klon [klo:n] (**-s, -e**) M clone
Klonschaf NT cloned sheep
Klopapier (*umg*) NT toilet paper
klopfen ['klɔpfən] VI to knock; (*Herz*) to thump ▶ VT to beat; **es klopft** somebody's knocking; **jdm auf die Finger ~** (*lit, fig*) to give sb a rap on the knuckles; **jdm auf die Schulter ~** to tap sb on the shoulder
Klopfer (**-s, -**) M (*Teppichklopfer*) beater; (*Türklopfer*) knocker
Klöppel ['klœpəl] (**-s, -**) M (*von Glocke*) clapper
klöppeln VI to make lace
Klops [klɔps] (**-es, -e**) M meatball
Klosett [klo'zɛt] (**-s, -e** *od* **-s**) NT lavatory, toilet; **Klosettbrille** F toilet seat; **Klosettpapier** NT toilet paper
Kloß [klo:s] (**-es, Klöße**) M (*Erdkloß*) clod; (*im Hals*) lump; (*Koch*) dumpling
Kloster ['klo:stər] (**-s, Klöster**) NT (*Männerkloster*) monastery; (*Frauenkloster*) convent; **ins ~ gehen** to become a monk/nun
klösterlich ['klø:stərlɪç] ADJ monastic; (*von Frauenkloster*) convent
Klotz [klɔts] (**-es, Klötze**) M log; (*Hackklotz*) block; **jdm ein ~ am Bein sein** (*fig*) to be a millstone round sb's neck
Klub [klʊp] (**-s, -s**) M club; **Klubjacke** F blazer; **Klubsessel** M easy chair
Kluft [klʊft] (**-, Klüfte**) F cleft, gap; (*Geog*) chasm; (*Uniform*) uniform; (*umg: Kleidung*) gear
klug [klu:k] ADJ clever, intelligent; **ich werde daraus nicht ~** I can't make head or tail of it; **Klugheit** F cleverness, intelligence; **Klugscheißer** (*umg*) M smart-ass
Klümpchen ['klʏmpçən] NT clot, blob
klumpen ['klʊmpən] VI to go lumpy, to clot
Klumpen (**-s, -**) M (*Koch*) lump; (*Erdklumpen*) clod; (*Blutklumpen*) clot; (*Goldklumpen*) nugget
Klumpfuß ['klʊmpfu:s] M club foot
Klüngel ['klʏŋəl] (**-s, -**) (*umg*) M (*Clique*) clique
Klunker ['klʊŋkər] (**-s, -**) (*umg*) M (*Schmuck*) rock(*s pl*)
km ABK (= *Kilometer*) km
km/h ABK (= *Kilometer pro Stunde*) km/h
knabbern ['knabərn] VT, VI to nibble; **an etw** *dat* **~** (*fig: umg*) to puzzle over sth
Knabe ['kna:bə] (**-n, -n**) M boy
knabenhaft ADJ boyish
Knäckebrot ['knɛkəbro:t] NT crispbread
knacken ['knakən] VI (*lit, fig*) to crack ▶ VT (*umg: Auto*) to break into
knackfrisch (*umg*) ADJ oven-fresh, crispy-fresh
knackig ADJ crisp
Knacks [knaks] (**-es, -e**) M: **einen ~ weghaben** (*umg*) to be uptight about sth
Knackwurst F *type of frankfurter*
Knall [knal] (**-(e)s, -e**) M bang; (*Peitschenknall*) crack; **~ auf Fall** (*umg*) just like that; **einen ~ haben** (*umg*) to be crazy *od* crackers; **Knallbonbon** NT cracker; **Knalleffekt** M surprise effect, spectacular effect; **knallen** VI to bang; (*Peitsche*) to crack ▶ VT: **jdm eine knallen** (*umg*) to clout sb; **Knallfrosch** M jumping jack; **knallhart** (*umg*) ADJ really hard; (*Worte*) hard-hitting; (*Film*) brutal; (*Porno*) hard-core; **Knallkopf** (*umg*) M dickhead; **knallrot** ADJ bright red
knapp [knap] ADJ tight; (*Geld*) scarce; (*kurz*) short; (*Mehrheit, Sieg*) narrow; (*Sprache*) concise; **~ zwei Stunden** just under two hours; **meine Zeit ist ~ bemessen** I am short of time; **mit knapper Not** only just; *siehe auch* **knapphalten**
Knappe (**-n, -n**) M (*Edelmann*) young knight
knapphalten *unreg* VT: **jdn (mit etw) ~** to keep sb short (of sth)
Knappheit F tightness; (*von Geld*) scarcity; (*von Sprache*) conciseness
Knarre ['knarə] (**-, -n**) (*umg*) F (*Gewehr*) shooter
knarren VI to creak
Knast [knast] (**-(e)s**) (*umg*) M clink, can (US)
Knatsch [kna:tʃ] (**-es**) (*umg*) M trouble
knattern ['knatərn] VI to rattle; (*Maschinengewehr*) to chatter
Knäuel ['knɔʏəl] (**-s, -**) M OD NT (*Wollknäuel*) ball; (*Menschenknäuel*) knot
Knauf [knaʊf] (**-(e)s, Knäufe**) M knob; (*Schwertknauf*) pommel
Knauser ['knaʊzər] (**-s, -**) M miser
knauserig ADJ miserly
knausern VI to be mean
knautschen ['knaʊtʃən] VT, VI to crumple
Knebel ['kne:bəl] (**-s, -**) M gag
knebeln VT to gag; (*Naut*) to fasten

Knecht [knɛçt] (**-(e)s, -e**) M servant; (*auf Bauernhof*) farm labourer (BRIT) *od* laborer (US)
knechten VT to enslave
Knechtschaft F servitude
kneifen ['knaɪfən] *unreg* VT to pinch ▸ VI to pinch; (*sich drücken*) to back out; **vor etw** *dat* **~** to dodge sth
Kneifzange F pliers *pl*; (*kleine*) pincers *pl*
Kneipe ['knaɪpə] (**-, -n**) (*umg*) F pub (BRIT), bar, saloon (US)
Kneippkur ['knaɪpku:r] F Kneipp cure, *type of hydropathic treatment combined with diet, rest etc*
Knete ['kne:tə] (*umg*) F (*Geld*) dough
kneten VT to knead; (*Wachs*) to mould (BRIT), to mold (US)
Knetgummi M OD NT Plasticine®
Knetmasse F Plasticine®
Knick [knɪk] (**-(e)s, -e**) M (*Sprung*) crack; (*Kurve*) bend; (*Falte*) fold
knicken VT, VI (*springen*) to crack; (*brechen*) to break; (*Papier*) to fold; **„nicht ~!“** “do not bend”; **geknickt sein** to be downcast
Knicks [knɪks] (**-es, -e**) M curts(e)y; **knicksen** VI to curts(e)y
Knie [kni:] (**-s, -**) NT knee; **in die ~ gehen** to kneel; (*fig*) to be brought to one's knees; **Kniebeuge** (**-, -n**) F knee bend; **Kniefall** M genuflection; **Kniegelenk** NT knee joint; **Kniekehle** F back of the knee
knien VI to kneel ▸ VR: **sich in die Arbeit ~** (*fig*) to get down to (one's) work
Kniescheibe F kneecap
Kniestrumpf M knee-length sock
kniff *etc* [knɪf] VB *siehe* **kneifen**
Kniff (**-(e)s, -e**) M (*Zwicken*) pinch; (*Falte*) fold; (*fig*) trick, knack
kniffelig ADJ tricky
knipsen ['knɪpsən] VT (*Fahrkarte*) to punch; (*Phot*) to take a snap of, to snap ▸ VI (*Phot*) to take snaps/a snap
Knirps [knɪrps] (**-es, -e**) M little chap; **er hat einen neuen ~® gekauft** he has bought a new Knirps® (*folding umbrella*)
knirschen ['knɪrʃən] VI to crunch; **mit den Zähnen ~** to grind one's teeth
knistern ['knɪstərn] VI to crackle; (*Papier, Seide*) to rustle
Knitterfalte F crease
knitterfrei ADJ non-crease
knittern VI to crease
knobeln ['kno:bəln] VI (*würfeln*) to play dice; (*um eine Entscheidung*) to toss for it
Knoblauch ['kno:plaʊx] (**-(e)s**) M garlic; **Knoblauchbrot** NT garlic bread; **Knoblauchzehe** F clove of garlic
Knöchel ['knœçəl] (**-s, -**) M knuckle; (*Fußknöchel*) ankle
Knochen ['knɔxən] (**-s, -**) M bone; **Knochenarbeit** (*umg*) F hard work; **Knochenbau** M bone structure; **Knochenbruch** M fracture; **Knochengerüst** NT skeleton; **Knochenmark** NT bone marrow
knöchern ['knœçərn] ADJ bone
knochig ['knɔxɪç] ADJ bony
Knödel ['knø:dəl] (**-s, -**) M dumpling
Knolle ['knɔlə] (**-, -n**) F bulb
Knopf [knɔpf] (**-(e)s, Knöpfe**) M button; **Knopfdruck** M: **auf Knopfdruck** at the touch of a button
knöpfen ['knœpfən] VT to button
Knopfloch NT buttonhole
Knorpel ['knɔrpəl] (**-s, -**) M cartilage, gristle
knorpelig ADJ gristly
knorrig ['knɔrɪç] ADJ gnarled, knotted
Knospe ['knɔspə] (**-, -n**) F bud
knospen VI to bud
knoten ['kno:tən] VT to knot; **Knoten** (**-s, -**) M knot; (*Haar*) bun; (*Bot*) node; (*Med*) lump
Knotenpunkt M junction
knuffen ['knʊfən] (*umg*) VT to cuff
Knüller ['knʏlər] (**-s, -**) (*umg*) M hit; (*Reportage*) scoop
knüpfen ['knʏpfən] VT to tie; (*Teppich*) to knot; (*Freundschaft*) to form
Knüppel ['knʏpəl] (**-s, -**) M cudgel; (*Polizeiknüppel*) baton, truncheon; (*Aviat*) (joy)stick; **jdm ~ zwischen die Beine werfen** (*fig*) to put a spoke in sb's wheel; **knüppeldick** (*umg*) ADJ very thick; (*fig*) thick and fast; **Knüppelschaltung** F (*Aut*) floor-mounted gear change
knurren ['knʊrən] VI (*Hund*) to snarl, to growl; (*Magen*) to rumble; (*Mensch*) to mutter
knusprig ['knʊsprɪç] ADJ crisp; (*Keks*) crunchy
knutschen ['knu:tʃən] (*umg*) VT to snog with ▸ VI, VR to snog
k. o. ADJ (*Sport*) knocked out; (*fig: umg*) whacked
Koalition [koalitsi'o:n] F coalition
Koalitionsabsprache F coalition agreement
koalitionsfähig F in a position to form a coalition
Kobalt ['ko:balt] (**-s**) NT cobalt
Kobold ['ko:bɔlt] (**-(e)s, -e**) M imp
Kobra ['ko:bra] (**-, -s**) F cobra
Koch [kɔx] (**-(e)s, Köche**) M cook; **Kochbuch** NT cookery book, cookbook; **kochecht** ADJ (*Farbe*) fast
kochen VI to cook; (*Wasser*) to boil ▸ VT (*Essen*) to cook; (*Kaffee, Tee*) to make; **er kochte vor Wut** (*umg*) he was seething; **etw auf kleiner Flamme ~** to simmer sth over a low heat
Kocher (**-s, -**) M stove, cooker
Köcher ['kœçər] (**-s, -**) M quiver
Kochgelegenheit F cooking facilities *pl*
Köchin ['kœçɪn] F cook
Koch- ZW: **Kochkunst** F cooking; **Kochlöffel** M kitchen spoon; **Kochnische** F kitchenette; **Kochplatte** F hotplate; **Kochrezept** NT recipe; **Kochsalz** NT cooking salt; **Kochtopf** M saucepan, pot; **Kochwäsche** F washing that can be boiled
Kode [ko:t] (**-s, -s**) M code
Köder ['kø:dər] (**-s, -**) M bait, lure
ködern VT to lure, to entice
Koexistenz [koɛksɪs'tɛnts] F coexistence
Koffein [kɔfe'i:n] (**-s**) NT caffeine; **koffeinfrei** ADJ decaffeinated

Koffer ['kɔfər] (**-s, -**) M suitcase; (*Schrankkoffer*) trunk; **die ~ packen** (*lit, fig*) to pack one's bags; **Kofferkuli** M (luggage) trolley (BRIT), cart (*US*); **Kofferradio** NT portable radio; **Kofferraum** M (*Aut*) boot (BRIT), trunk (*US*)
Kognak ['kɔnjak] (**-s, -s**) M brandy, cognac
kognitiv [kɔgni'ti:f] ADJ cognitive
Kohl [ko:l] (**-(e)s, -e**) M cabbage
Kohldampf (*umg*) M: **~ haben** to be famished
Kohle ['ko:lə] (**-, -n**) F coal; (*Holzkohle*) charcoal; (*Chem*) carbon; (*umg: Geld*): **die Kohlen stimmen** the money's right; **Kohlehydrat** (**-(e)s, -e**) NT carbohydrate, (*umg*) carb; **Kohlekraftwerk** NT coal-fired power station
kohlen ['ko:lən] (*umg*) VI to tell white lies
Kohlen- ZW: **Kohlenbergwerk** NT coal mine, pit, colliery (BRIT); **Kohlendioxid** (**-(e)s, -e**) NT carbon dioxide; **Kohlengrube** F coal mine, pit; **Kohlenhändler** M coal merchant, coalman; **Kohlenhydrat** (**-(e)s, -e**) NT = **Kohlehydrat**; **Kohlensäure** F carbon dioxide; **ein Getränk ohne Kohlensäure** a non-fizzy *od* still drink; **Kohlenstoff** M carbon
Kohlepapier NT carbon paper
Köhler ['kø:lər] (**-s, -**) M charcoal burner
Kohlestift M charcoal pencil
Kohlezeichnung F charcoal drawing
Kohl- ZW: **kohlpechrabenschwarz, kohlrabenschwarz** ADJ (*Haar*) jet-black; (*Nacht*) pitch-black; **Kohlrübe** F turnip; **kohlschwarz** ADJ coal-black
Koitus ['ko:itʊs] (**-, -** *od* **-se**) M coitus
Koje ['ko:jə] (**-, -n**) F cabin; (*Bett*) bunk
Kokain [koka'i:n] (**-s**) NT cocaine
kokett [ko'kɛt] ADJ coquettish, flirtatious
kokettieren [kokɛ'ti:rən] VI to flirt
Kokosnuss ['ko:kɔsnʊs] F coconut
Koks [ko:ks] (**-es, -e**) M coke
Kolben ['kɔlbən] (**-s, -**) M (*Gewehrkolben*) butt; (*Keule*) club; (*Chem*) flask; (*Tech*) piston; (*Maiskolben*) cob
Kolchose [kɔl'ço:zə] (**-, -n**) F collective farm
Kolik ['ko:lɪk] F colic, gripe
Kollaborateur(in) [kɔlabora'tø:r(ɪn)] M(F) (*Pol*) collaborator
Kollaps [kɔ'laps] (**-es, -e**) M collapse
Kolleg [kɔl'e:k] (**-s, -s** *od* **-ien**) NT lecture course
Kollege [kɔ'le:gə] (**-n, -n**) M colleague
kollegial [kɔlegi'a:l] ADJ cooperative
Kollegin [kɔ'le:gɪn] F colleague
Kollegium NT board; (*Sch*) staff
Kollekte [kɔ'lɛktə] (**-, -n**) F (*Rel*) collection
Kollektion [kɔlɛktsi'o:n] F collection; (*Sortiment*) range
kollektiv [kɔlɛk'ti:f] ADJ collective
Koller ['kɔlər] (**-s, -**) (*umg*) M (*Anfall*) funny mood; (*Wutanfall*) rage; (*Tropenkoller, Gefängniskoller*) madness
kollidieren [kɔli'di:rən] VI to collide; (*zeitlich*) to clash
Kollier [kɔli'e:] (**-s, -s**) NT = **Collier**
Kollision [kɔlizi'o:n] F collision; (*zeitlich*) clash
Kollisionskurs M: **auf ~ gehen** (*fig*) to be heading for trouble
Köln [kœln] (**-s**) NT Cologne
Kölnischwasser NT eau de Cologne
kolonial [koloni'a:l] ADJ colonial; **Kolonialmacht** F colonial power; **Kolonialwarenhändler** M grocer
Kolonie [kolo'ni:] F colony
kolonisieren [koloni'zi:rən] VT to colonize
Kolonist(in) [kolo'nɪst(ɪn)] M(F) colonist
Kolonne [ko'lɔnə] (**-, -n**) F column; (*von Fahrzeugen*) convoy
Koloss [ko'lɔs] (**-es, -e**) M colossus
kolossal [kolɔ'sa:l] ADJ colossal
Kolumbianer(in) [kolʊmbi'a:nər(ɪn)] M(F) Columbian
kolumbianisch ADJ Columbian
Kolumbien [ko'lʊmbiən] (**-s**) NT Columbia
Koma ['ko:ma] (**-s, -s** *od* **-ta**) NT (*Med*) coma
Kombi ['kɔmbi] (**-s, -s**) M (*Aut*) estate (car) (BRIT), station wagon (*US*)
Kombination [kɔmbinatsi'o:n] F combination; (*Vermutung*) conjecture; (*Hemdhose*) combinations *pl*; (*Aviat*) flying suit
Kombinationsschloss NT combination lock
kombinieren [kɔmbi'ni:rən] VT to combine ▶ VI to deduce, to work out; (*vermuten*) to guess
Kombiwagen M (*Aut*) estate (car) (BRIT), station wagon (*US*)
Kombizange F (pair of) pliers
Komet [ko'me:t] (**-en, -en**) M comet
kometenhaft ADJ (*fig: Aufstieg*) meteoric
Komfort [kɔm'fo:r] (**-s**) M luxury; (*von Möbel etc*) comfort; (*von Wohnung*) amenities *pl*; (*von Auto*) luxury features *pl*; (*von Gerät*) extras *pl*
komfortabel [kɔmfɔr'ta:bəl] ADJ comfortable
Komik ['ko:mɪk] F humour (BRIT), humor (*US*), comedy; **Komiker** (**-s, -**) M comedian
komisch ['ko:mɪʃ] ADJ funny; **mir ist so ~** (*umg*) I feel funny *od* strange *od* odd; **komischerweise** ['ko:mɪʃər'vaɪzə] ADV funnily enough
Komitee [komi'te:] (**-s, -s**) NT committee
Komm. ABK (= *Kommission*) comm.
Komma ['kɔma] (**-s, -s** *od* **-ta**) NT comma; (*Math*) decimal point; **fünf ~ drei** five point three
Kommandant [kɔman'dant] M commander, commanding officer
Kommandeur [kɔman'dø:r] M commanding officer
kommandieren [kɔman'di:rən] VT to command ▶ VI to command; (*Befehle geben*) to give orders
Kommanditgesellschaft [kɔman'di:tgəzɛlʃaft] F limited partnership
Kommando [kɔ'mando] (**-s, -s**) NT command, order; (*Truppe*) detachment, squad; **auf ~** to order; **Kommandobrücke** F (*Naut*) bridge; **Kommandowirtschaft** F command economy
kommen ['kɔmən] *unreg* VI to come; (*näher kommen*) to approach; (*passieren*) to happen; (*gelangen, geraten*) to get; (*Blumen, Zähne, Tränen etc*) to appear; (*in die Schule, ins Gefängnis etc*) to go ▶ VI UNPERS: **es kam eins zum anderen** one

thing led to another; **~ lassen** to send for; **in Bewegung ~** to start moving; **jdn besuchen ~** to come and visit sb; **das kommt davon!** see what happens?; **du kommst mir gerade recht** *(ironisch)* you're just what I need; **das kommt in den Schrank** that goes in the cupboard; **an etw** *akk* **~** *(berühren)* to touch sth; *(sich verschaffen)* to get hold of sth; **auf etw** *akk* **~** *(sich erinnern)* to think of sth; *(sprechen über)* to get onto sth; **was kommt diese Woche im Kino?** what's on at the cinema this week?; **das kommt auf die Rechnung** that goes onto the bill; **hinter etw** *akk* **~** *(herausfinden)* to find sth out; **zu sich ~** to come round *od* to; **zu etw ~** *(bekommen)* to acquire sth; *(Zeit dazu finden)* to get round to sth; **um etw ~** to lose sth; **nichts auf jdn/etw ~ lassen** to have nothing said against sb/sth; **jdm frech ~** to get cheeky with sb; **auf jeden vierten kommt ein Platz** there's one place to every fourth person; **mit einem Anliegen ~** to have a request (to make); **wer kommt zuerst?** who's first?; **wer zuerst kommt, mahlt zuerst** *(Sprichwort)* first come first served; **unter ein Auto ~** to be run over by a car; **das kommt zusammen auf 20 Euro** that comes to 20 euros altogether; **und so kam es, dass ...** and that is how it happened that ...; **daher kommt es, dass ...** that's why ...

Kommen (-**s**) NT coming

kommend ADJ *(Jahr, Woche, Generation)* coming; *(Ereignisse, Mode)* future; *(Trend)* upcoming; **(am) kommenden Montag** next Monday

Kommentar [kɔmɛn'taːr] M commentary; **kein ~** no comment; **kommentarlos** ADJ without comment

Kommentator [kɔmɛn'taːtɔr] M *(TV)* commentator

kommentieren [kɔmɛn'tiːrən] VT to comment on; **kommentierte Ausgabe** annotated edition

kommerziell [kɔmɛrtsi'ɛl] ADJ commercial

Kommilitone [kɔmili'toːnə] (-**n**, -**n**) M, **Kommilitonin** F fellow student

Kommiss [kɔ'mɪs] (-**es**) M (life in the) army

Kommissar [kɔmɪ'saːr] M police inspector

Kommissbrot NT army bread

Kommission [kɔmɪsi'oːn] F *(Comm)* commission; *(Ausschuss)* committee; **in ~ geben** to give (to a dealer) for sale on commission

Kommode [kɔ'moːdə] (-, -**n**) F (chest of) drawers

kommunal [kɔmu'naːl] ADJ local; *(von Stadt)* municipal; **Kommunalabgaben** PL local rates and taxes *pl*; **Kommunalpolitik** F local government politics; **Kommunalverwaltung** F local government; **Kommunalwahlen** PL local (government) elections *pl*

Kommune [kɔ'muːnə] (-, -**n**) F commune

Kommunikation [kɔmunɪkatsi'oːn] F communication

Kommunikator(in) [kɔmuni'kaːtɔr, -'toːrɪn] M(F) communicator

Kommunikee [kɔmyni'keː] (-**s**, -**s**) NT = **Kommuniqué**

Kommunion [kɔmuni'oːn] F communion

Kommuniqué [kɔmyni'keː] (-**s**, -**s**) NT communiqué

Kommunismus [kɔmu'nɪsmʊs] M communism

Kommunist(in) [kɔmu'nɪst(ɪn)] M(F) communist; **kommunistisch** ADJ communist

kommunizieren [kɔmuni'tsiːrən] VI to communicate; *(Eccl)* to receive communion

Komödiant [komødi'ant] M comedian; **Komödiantin** F comedienne

Komödie [ko'møːdiə] F comedy; **~ spielen** *(fig)* to put on an act

Kompagnon [kɔmpan'jõː] (-**s**, -**s**) M *(Comm)* partner

kompakt [kɔm'pakt] ADJ compact

Kompaktanlage F *(Rundf)* audio system

Kompanie [kɔmpa'niː] F company

Komparativ ['kɔmparatiːf] (-**s**, -**e**) M comparative

Kompass ['kɔmpas] (-**es**, -**e**) M compass

kompatibel [kɔmpa'tiːbəl] ADJ *(auch Comput)* compatible

Kompatibilität [kɔmpatibili'tɛːt] F *(auch Comput)* compatibility

kompensieren [kɔmpɛn'ziːrən] VT to compensate for, to offset

kompetent [kɔmpe'tɛnt] ADJ competent

Kompetenz F competence, authority; **Kompetenzstreitigkeiten** PL dispute over respective areas of responsibility; **Kompetenzverteilung** F distribution of powers; **Kompetenzzentrum** F competence centre (BRIT) *od* center (US)

komplett [kɔm'plɛt] ADJ complete

komplex [kɔm'plɛks] ADJ complex; **Komplex** (-**es**, -**e**) M complex

Komplikation [kɔmplikatsi'oːn] F complication

Kompliment [kɔmpli'mɛnt] NT compliment

Komplize [kɔm'pliːtsə] (-**n**, -**n**) M accomplice

komplizieren [kɔmpli'tsiːrən] VT to complicate

kompliziert ADJ complicated; *(Med: Bruch)* compound

Komplizin [kɔm'pliːtsɪn] F accomplice

Komplott [kɔm'plɔt] (-**(e)s**, -**e**) NT plot

komponieren [kɔmpo'niːrən] VT to compose

Komponist(in) [kɔmpo'nɪst(ɪn)] M(F) composer

Komposition [kɔmpozitsi'oːn] F composition

Kompost [kɔm'pɔst] (-**(e)s**, -**e**) M compost; **Komposthaufen** M compost heap

Kompott [kɔm'pɔt] (-**(e)s**, -**e**) NT stewed fruit

Kompresse [kɔm'prɛsə] (-, -**n**) F compress

Kompressor [kɔm'prɛsɔr] M compressor

Kompromiss [kɔmpro'mɪs] (-**es**, -**e**) M compromise; **einen ~ schließen** to compromise; **kompromissbereit** ADJ willing to compromise; **Kompromisslösung** F compromise solution

kompromittieren [kɔmpromɪ'tiːrən] VT to compromise

Kondensation [kɔndɛnzatsi'oːn] F condensation

Kondensator [kɔndɛn'zaːtɔr] M condenser

kondensieren [kɔndɛn'zi:rən] VT to condense
Kondensmilch F condensed milk
Kondensstreifen M vapour (BRIT) *od* vapor (US) trail
Kondition [kɔnditsi'o:n] F condition, shape; (*Durchhaltevermögen*) stamina
Konditionalsatz [kɔnditsio'na:lzats] M conditional clause
Konditionstraining NT fitness training
Konditor [kɔn'di:tɔr] M pastry-cook
Konditorei [kɔndito'raɪ] F cake shop; (*mit Café*) café
kondolieren [kɔndo'li:rən] VI: **jdm ~** to condole with sb, to offer sb one's condolences
Kondom [kɔn'do:m] (**-s, -e**) M OD NT condom
Konfektion [kɔnfɛktsi'o:n] F (production of) ready-to-wear *od* off-the-peg clothing
Konfektionsgröße F clothes size
Konfektionskleidung F ready-to-wear *od* off-the-peg clothing
Konferenz [kɔnfe'rɛnts] F conference; (*Besprechung*) meeting; **Konferenzschaltung** F (*Tel*) conference circuit; (*Rundf, TV*) television *od* radio link-up
konferieren [kɔnfe'ri:rən] VI to confer; (*Sitzung abhelten*) to have a meeting
Konfession [kɔnfɛsi'o:n] F religion; (*christlich*) denomination; **konfessionell** [-'nɛl] ADJ denominational
Konfessions- ZW: **konfessionsgebunden** ADJ denominational; **konfessionslos** ADJ non-denominational; **Konfessionsschule** F denominational school
Konfetti [kɔn'fɛti] (**-(s)**) NT confetti
Konfiguration [kɔnfiguratsi'o:n] F (*Comput*) configuration
Konfirmand(in) [kɔnfɪr'mant, -'mandɪn] M(F) candidate for confirmation
Konfirmation [kɔnfɪrmatsi'o:n] F (*Eccl*) confirmation
konfirmieren [kɔnfɪr'mi:rən] VT to confirm
konfiszieren [kɔnfɪs'tsi:rən] VT to confiscate
Konfitüre [kɔnfi'ty:rə] (**-, -n**) F jam
Konflikt [kɔn'flɪkt] (**-(e)s, -e**) M conflict; **Konfliktherd** M (*Pol*) centre (BRIT) *od* center (US) of conflict; **Konfliktstoff** M cause of conflict
konform [kɔn'fɔrm] ADJ concurring; **~ gehen** to be in agreement
Konfrontation [kɔnfrɔntatsi'o:n] F confrontation
konfrontieren [kɔnfrɔn'ti:rən] VT to confront
konfus [kɔn'fu:s] ADJ confused
Kongo ['kɔŋgo] (**-(s)**) M Congo
Kongress [kɔn'grɛs] (**-es, -e**) M congress
Kongruenz [kɔŋgru'ɛnts] F agreement, congruence
König ['kø:nɪç] (**-(e)s, -e**) M king
Königin ['kø:nɪgɪn] F queen
königlich ADJ royal ▶ ADV: **sich ~ amüsieren** (*umg*) to have the time of one's life
Königreich NT kingdom
Königtum ['kø:nɪçtu:m] (**-(e)s, -tümer**) NT kingship; (*Reich*) kingdom

konisch ['ko:nɪʃ] ADJ conical
Konj. ABK (= *Konjunktiv*) conj.
Konjugation [kɔnjugatsi'o:n] F conjugation
konjugieren [kɔnju'gi:rən] VT to conjugate
Konjunktion [kɔnjʊŋktsi'o:n] F conjunction
Konjunktiv ['kɔnjʊŋkti:f] (**-s, -e**) M subjunctive
Konjunktur [kɔnjʊŋk'tu:r] F economic situation; (*Hochkonjunktur*) boom; **steigende/ fallende ~** upward/downward economic trend; **Konjunkturbarometer** NT economic indicators *pl*; **Konjunktureinbruch** NT economic slump; **Konjunkturklima** NT economic climate; **Konjunkturloch** NT temporary economic dip; **Konjunkturpolitik** F *policies aimed at preventing economic fluctuations*
konkav [kɔn'ka:f] ADJ concave
konkret [kɔn'kre:t] ADJ concrete
Konkurrent(in) [kɔnkʊ'rɛnt(ɪn)] M(F) competitor
Konkurrenz [kɔnkʊ'rɛnts] F competition; **jdm ~ machen** (*Comm, fig*) to compete with sb; **konkurrenzfähig** ADJ competitive; **Konkurrenzkampf** M competition; (*umg*) rat race
konkurrieren [kɔnkʊ'ri:rən] VI to compete
Konkurs [kɔn'kʊrs] (**-es, -e**) M bankruptcy; **in ~ gehen** to go into receivership; **~ machen** (*umg*) to go bankrupt; **Konkursverfahren** NT bankruptcy proceedings *pl*; **Konkursverwalter** M receiver; (*von Gläubigern bevollmächtigt*) trustee

SCHLÜSSELWORT

können ['kœnən] (*pt* **konnte**, *pp* **gekonnt** *od* (*als Hilfsverb*) **können**) VT, VI **1** to be able to; **ich kann es machen** I can do it, I am able to do it; **ich kann es nicht machen** I can't do it, I'm not able to do it; **ich kann nicht …** I can't …, I cannot …; **was können Sie?** what can you do?; **ich kann nicht mehr** I can't go on; **ich kann nichts dafür** I can't help it; **du kannst mich (mal)!** (*umg*) get lost!
2 (*wissen, beherrschen*) to know; **können Sie Deutsch?** can you speak German?; **er kann gut Englisch** he speaks English well; **sie kann keine Mathematik** she can't do mathematics
3 (*dürfen*) to be allowed to; **kann ich gehen?** can I go?; **könnte ich …?** could I …?; **kann ich mit?** (*umg*) can I come with you?
4 (*möglich sein*): **Sie könnten recht haben** you may be right; **das kann sein** that's possible; **kann sein** maybe

Können (**-s**) NT ability
Könner (**-s, -**) M expert
Konnossement [kɔnɔsə'mɛnt] NT (*Export*) bill of lading
konnte *etc* ['kɔntə] VB *siehe* **können**
konsequent [kɔnze'kvɛnt] ADJ consistent; **ein Ziel ~ verfolgen** to pursue an objective single-mindedly
Konsequenz [kɔnze'kvɛnts] F consistency; (*Folgerung*) conclusion; **die Konsequenzen**

tragen to take the consequences; **(aus etw) die Konsequenzen ziehen** to take the appropriate steps
konservativ [kɔnzɛrva'ti:f] ADJ conservative
Konservatorium [kɔnzɛrva'to:riʊm] NT academy of music, conservatory
Konserve [kɔn'zɛrvə] (-, -n) F tinned (*BRIT*) *od* canned food
Konservenbüchse F, **Konservendose** F tin (*BRIT*), can
konservieren [kɔnzɛr'vi:rən] VT to preserve
Konservierung F preservation
Konservierungsmittel NT, **Konservierungsstoff** M preservative
Konsole [kɔnzo:lə] F games console
konsolidiert [kɔnzoli'di:rt] ADJ consolidated
Konsolidierung F consolidation
Konsonant [kɔnzo'nant] M consonant
Konsortium [kɔn'zɔrtsiʊm] NT consortium, syndicate
konspirativ [kɔnspira'ti:f] ADJ: **konspirative Wohnung** conspirators' hideaway
konstant [kɔn'stant] ADJ constant
Konstellation [kɔnstɛlatsi'o:n] F constellation; (*fig*) line-up; (*von Faktoren etc*) combination
Konstitution [kɔnstitutsi'o:n] F constitution
konstitutionell [kɔnstitutsio'nɛl] ADJ constitutional
konstruieren [kɔnstru'i:rən] VT to construct
Konstrukteur(in) [kɔnstrʊk'tø:r(ɪn)] M(F) designer
Konstruktion [kɔnstrʊktsi'on] F construction
Konstruktionsfehler M (*im Entwurf*) design fault; (*im Aufbau*) structural defect
konstruktiv [kɔnstrʊk'ti:f] ADJ constructive
Konsul ['kɔnzʊl] (-s, -n) M consul
Konsulat [kɔnzʊ'la:t] (-(e)s, -e) NT consulate
konsultieren [kɔnzʊl'ti:rən] VT to consult
Konsum[1] [kɔn'zu:m] (-s) M consumption
Konsum[2] ['kɔnzu:m] (-s, -s) M (*Genossenschaft*) cooperative society; (*Laden*) cooperative store, co-op (*umg*)
Konsumartikel M consumer article
Konsument [kɔnzu'mɛnt] M consumer
konsumfreudig F consumption-oriented, consumerist
Konsumgesellschaft F consumer society
konsumieren [kɔnzu'mi:rən] VT to consume
Konsumtempel M temple of consumerism
Konsumterror M pressures *pl* of a materialistic society
Konsumzwang M compulsion to buy
Kontakt [kɔn'takt] (-(e)s, -e) M contact; **mit jdm ~ aufnehmen** to get in touch with sb; **Kontaktanzeige** F lonely hearts ad; **kontaktarm** ADJ unsociable; **kontaktfreudig** ADJ sociable
kontaktieren [kɔntak'ti:rən] VT to contact
Kontakt- ZW: **Kontaktlinsen** PL contact lenses *pl*; **Kontaktmann** (-(e)s, *pl* -männer) M (*Agent*) contact; **Kontaktsperre** F ban on visits and letters (*to a prisoner*)
Konterfei ['kɔntərfaɪ] (-s, -s) NT likeness, portrait
kontern ['kɔntərn] VT, VI to counter
Konterrevolution ['kɔntərrevolutsio:n] F counter-revolution
Kontinent [kɔnti'nɛnt] M continent
Kontingent [kɔntɪŋ'gɛnt] (-(e)s, -e) NT quota; (*Truppenkontingent*) contingent
kontinuierlich [kɔntinu'i:rlɪç] ADJ continuous
Kontinuität [kɔntinui'tɛ:t] F continuity
Konto ['kɔnto] (-s, Konten) NT account; **das geht auf mein ~** (*umg*: *ich bin schuldig*) I am to blame for this; (*ich zahle*) this is on me (*umg*); **Kontoauszug** M statement (of account); **Kontoinhaber(in)** M(F) account holder; **Kontonummer** F account number
Kontor [kɔn'to:r] (-s, -e) NT office
Kontorist(in) [kɔnto'rɪst(ɪn)] M(F) clerk, office worker
Kontostand M bank balance
kontra ['kɔntra] PRÄP +*akk* against; (*Jur*) versus
Kontra (-s, -s) NT (*Karten*) double; **jdm ~ geben** (*fig*) to contradict sb
Kontrabass M double bass
Kontrahent [-'hɛnt] M contracting party; (*Gegner*) opponent
Kontrapunkt M counterpoint
Kontrast [kɔn'trast] (-(e)s, -e) M contrast
Kontrollabschnitt M (*Comm*) counterfoil, stub
Kontrollampe [kɔn'trɔllampə] F *siehe* **Kontrolllampe**
Kontrolle [kɔn'trɔlə] (-, -n) F control, supervision; (*Passkontrolle*) passport control
Kontrolleur [kɔntrɔ'lø:r] M inspector
kontrollieren [kɔntrɔ'li:rən] VT to control, to supervise; (*nachprüfen*) to check
Kontrolllampe [kɔn'trɔllampə] F pilot lamp; (*Aut*: *für Ölstand etc*) warning light
Kontrollturm M control tower
Kontroverse [kɔntro'vɛrzə] (-, -n) F controversy
Kontur [kɔn'tu:r] F contour
Konvention [kɔnvɛntsi'o:n] F convention
Konventionalstrafe [kɔnvɛntsio'na:lʃtra:fə] F penalty *od* fine (*for breach of contract*)
konventionell [kɔnvɛntsio'nɛl] ADJ conventional
Konversation [kɔnvɛrzatsi'o:n] F conversation
Konversationslexikon NT encyclopaedia
konvex [kɔn'vɛks] ADJ convex
Konvoi ['kɔnvɔʏ] (-s, -s) M convoy
Konzentrat [kɔntsɛn'tra:t] (-s, -e) NT concentrate
Konzentration [kɔntsɛntratsi'o:n] F concentration
Konzentrationsfähigkeit F power of concentration
Konzentrationslager NT concentration camp
konzentrieren [kɔntsɛn'tri:rən] VT, VR to concentrate
konzentriert ADJ concentrated ▶ ADV (*zuhören, arbeiten*) intently
Konzept [kɔn'tsɛpt] (-(e)s, -e) NT rough draft; (*Plan, Programm*) plan; (*Begriff, Vorstellung*)

concept; **jdn aus dem ~ bringen** to confuse sb; **Konzeptpapier** NT rough paper
Konzern [kɔn'tsɛrn] (**-s, -e**) M combine
Konzert [kɔn'tsɛrt] (**-(e)s, -e**) NT concert; (*Stück*) concerto; **Konzertsaal** M concert hall
Konzession [kɔntsɛsi'o:n] F licence (BRIT), license (US); (*Zugeständnis*) concession; **die ~ entziehen** *+dat* (*Comm*) to disenfranchise
Konzessionär [kɔntsɛsio'nɛ:r] (**-s, -e**) M concessionaire
konzessionieren [kɔntsɛsio'ni:rən] VT to license
Konzil [kɔn'tsi:l] (**-s, -e** *od* **-ien**) NT council
konzipieren [kɔntsi'pi:rən] VT to conceive; (*entwerfen*) to design
kooperativ [ko|opera'ti:f] ADJ cooperative
kooperieren [ko|ope'ri:rən] VI to cooperate
koordinieren [ko|ɔrdi'ni:rən] VT to coordinate
Kopenhagen [ko:pən'ha:gən] (**-s**) NT Copenhagen
Kopf [kɔpf] (**-(e)s, Köpfe**) M head; **~ hoch!** chin up!; **~ an ~** shoulder to shoulder; (*Sport*) neck and neck; **pro ~** per person *od* head; **~ oder Zahl?** heads or tails?; **jdm den ~ waschen** (*fig: umg*) to give sb a piece of one's mind; **jdm über den ~ wachsen** (*lit*) to outgrow sb; (*fig: Sorgen etc*) to be more than sb can cope with; **jdn vor den ~ stoßen** to antagonize sb; **sich** *dat* **an den ~ fassen** (*fig*) to be speechless; **sich** *dat* **über etw** *akk* **den ~ zerbrechen** to rack one's brains over sth; **sich** *dat* **etw durch den ~ gehen lassen** to think about sth; **sich** *dat* **etw aus dem ~ schlagen** to put sth out of one's mind; **... und wenn du dich auf den ~ stellst!** (*umg*) ... no matter what you say/do!; **er ist nicht auf den ~ gefallen** he's no fool; **Kopfbahnhof** M terminus station; **Kopfbedeckung** F headgear
Köpfchen ['kœpfçən] NT: **~ haben** to be brainy
köpfen ['kœpfən] VT to behead; (*Baum*) to lop; (*Ei*) to take the top off; (*Ball*) to head
Kopf- ZW: **Kopfende** NT head; **Kopfhaut** F scalp; **Kopfhörer** M headphone; **Kopfkissen** NT pillow; **kopflastig** ADJ (*fig*) completely rational; **kopflos** ADJ panic-stricken; **Kopflosigkeit** F panic; **kopfrechnen** VI to do mental arithmetic; **Kopfsalat** M lettuce; **kopfscheu** ADJ: **jdn kopfscheu machen** to intimidate sb; **Kopfschmerzen** PL headache *sing*; **Kopfsprung** M header, dive; **Kopfstand** M headstand; **Kopfsteinpflaster** NT: **eine Straße mit Kopfsteinpflaster** a cobbled street; **Kopfstütze** F headrest; (*im Auto*) head restraint; **Kopftuch** NT headscarf; **kopfüber** ADV head-first; **Kopfweh** NT headache; **Kopfzerbrechen** NT: **jdm Kopfzerbrechen machen** to give sb a lot of headaches
Kopie [ko'pi:] F copy
kopieren [ko'pi:rən] VT to copy
Kopierer (**-s, -**) M (photo)copier
Kopilot(in) ['ko:pilo:t(ɪn)] M(F) co-pilot
Koppel[1] ['kɔpəl] (**-, -n**) F (*Weide*) enclosure
Koppel[2] ['kɔpəl] (**-s, -**) NT (*Gürtel*) belt
koppeln VT to couple
Koppelung F coupling
Koppelungsmanöver NT docking manoeuvre (BRIT) *od* maneuver (US)
Koralle [ko'ralə] (**-, -n**) F coral
Korallenkette F coral necklace
Korallenriff NT coral reef
Koran [ko'ra:n] (**-s**) M (*Rel*) Koran
Korb [kɔrp] (**-(e)s, Körbe**) M basket; **jdm einen ~ geben** (*fig*) to turn sb down; **Korbball** M basketball
Körbchen ['kœrpçən] NT (*von Büstenhalter*) cup
Korbstuhl M wicker chair
Kord [kɔrt] (**-(e)s, -e** *od* **-s**) M = **Cord**
Kordel ['kɔrdəl] (**-, -n**) F cord, string
Korea [ko're:a] (**-s**) NT Korea
Koreaner(in) (**-s, -**) M(F) Korean
Korfu ['kɔrfu] (**-s**) NT Corfu
Korinthe [ko'rɪntə] (**-, -n**) F currant
Korinthenkacker [ko'rɪntənkakər] (**-s, -**) (*umg*) M fusspot, hair-splitter
Kork [kɔrk] (**-(e)s, -e**) M cork
Korken (**-s, -**) M stopper, cork; **Korkenzieher** (**-s, -**) M corkscrew
Korn[1] [kɔrn] (**-(e)s, Körner**) NT corn, grain
Korn[2] [kɔrn] (**-(e)s, -e**) NT (*Gewehr*) sight; **etw aufs ~ nehmen** (*fig: umg*) to hit out at sth
Korn[3] [kɔrn] (**-, -s**) M (*Kornbranntwein*) corn schnapps
Kornblume F cornflower
Körnchen ['kœrnçən] NT grain, granule
körnig ['kœrniç] ADJ granular, grainy
Kornkammer F granary
Körnung ['kœrnʊŋ] F (*Tech*) grain size; (*Phot*) granularity
Körper ['kœrper] (**-s, -**) M body; **Körperbau** M build; **körperbehindert** ADJ disabled; **Körpergeruch** M body odour (BRIT) *od* odor (US); **Körpergewicht** NT weight; **Körpergröße** F height; **Körperhaltung** F carriage, deportment; **körperlich** ADJ physical; **körperliche Arbeit** manual work; **Körperpflege** F personal hygiene; **Körperschaft** F corporation; **Körperschaft des öffentlichen Rechts** public corporation *od* body; **Körperschaftssteuer** F corporation tax; **Körpersprache** F body language; **Körperteil** M part of the body; **Körperverletzung** F (*Jur*): **schwere Körperverletzung** grievous bodily harm
Korps [ko:r] (**-, -**) NT (*Mil*) corps; (*Univ*) students' club
korpulent [kɔrpu'lɛnt] ADJ corpulent
korrekt [kɔ'rɛkt] ADJ correct; **Korrektheit** F correctness
Korrektor(in) [kɔ'rɛktɔr, -'to:rɪn] (**-s, -**) M(F) proofreader
Korrektur [kɔrɛk'tu:r] F (*eines Textes*) proofreading; (*Text*) proof; (*Sch*) marking, correction; **(bei etw) ~ lesen** to proofread (sth); **Korrekturfahne** F (*Typ*) proof
Korrespondent(in) [kɔrɛspɔn'dɛnt(ɪn)] M(F) correspondent

K

Korrespondenz [kɔrɛspɔn'dɛnts] F correspondence; **Korrespondenzqualität** F (*Drucker*) letter quality
korrespondieren [kɔrɛspɔn'di:rən] VI to correspond
Korridor ['kɔrido:r] (**-s, -e**) M corridor
korrigieren [kɔri'gi:rən] VT to correct; (*Meinung, Einstellung*) to change
Korrosion [kɔrozi'o:n] F corrosion
Korrosionsschutz M corrosion protection
korrumpieren [kɔrʊm'pi:rən] VT (*auch Comput*) to corrupt
korrupt [kɔ'rʊpt] ADJ corrupt
Korruption [kɔrʊptsi'o:n] F corruption
Korsett [kɔr'zɛt] (**-(e)s, -e**) NT corset
Korsika ['kɔrzika] (**-s**) NT Corsica
Koseform ['ko:zəfɔrm] F pet form
kosen VT to caress ▸ VI to bill and coo
Kosename M pet name
Kosewort NT term of endearment
Kosmetik [kɔs'me:tɪk] F cosmetics *pl*
Kosmetikerin F beautician
Kosmetikkoffer M vanity case
kosmetisch ADJ cosmetic; (*Chirurgie*) plastic
kosmisch ['kɔsmɪʃ] ADJ cosmic
Kosmonaut [kɔsmo'naʊt] (**-en, -en**) M cosmonaut
Kosmopolit [kɔsmopo'li:t] (**-en, -en**) M cosmopolitan; **kosmopolitisch** [-po'li:tiʃ] ADJ cosmopolitan
Kosmos ['kɔsmɔs] (**-**) M cosmos
Kost [kɔst] (**-**) F (*Nahrung*) food; (*Verpflegung*) board; **~ und Logis** board and lodging
kostbar ADJ precious; (*teuer*) costly, expensive; **Kostbarkeit** F preciousness; (*Kostspieligkeit*) costliness, expensiveness; (*Wertstück*) treasure
kosten VT to cost; (*versuchen*) to taste ▸ VI to taste; **koste es, was es wolle** whatever the cost
Kosten PL cost(s); (*Ausgaben*) expenses *pl*; **auf ~ von** at the expense of; **auf seine ~ kommen** (*fig*) to get one's money's worth
Kosten- ZW: **Kostenanschlag** M estimate; **kostendeckend** ADJ cost-effective; **Kostenerstattung** F reimbursement of expenses; **Kostenkontrolle** F cost control; **kostenlos** ADJ free (of charge); **Kosten-Nutzen-Analyse** F cost-benefit analysis; **kostenpflichtig** ADJ: **ein Auto kostenpflichtig abschleppen** to tow away a car at the owner's expense; **Kostenstelle** F (*Comm*) cost centre (BRIT) *od* center (*US*); **Kostenvoranschlag** M (costs) estimate
Kostgeld NT board
köstlich ['kœstlɪç] ADJ precious; (*Essen*) delicious; (*Einfall*) delightful; **sich ~ amüsieren** to have a marvellous time
Kostprobe F taste; (*fig*) sample
kostspielig ADJ expensive
Kostüm [kɔs'ty:m] (**-s, -e**) NT costume; (*Damenkostüm*) suit; **Kostümfest** NT fancy-dress party
kostümieren [kɔsty'mi:rən] VT, VR to dress up
Kostümprobe F (*Theat*) dress rehearsal
Kostümverleih M costume agency
Kot [ko:t] (**-(e)s**) M excrement
Kotelett [kotə'lɛt] (**-(e)s, -e** *od* **-s**) NT cutlet, chop
Koteletten PL sideboards *pl* (BRIT), sideburns *pl* (*US*)
Köter ['kø:tər] (**-s, -**) M cur
Kotflügel M (*Aut*) wing
kotzen ['kɔtsən] (*umg!*) VI to puke (*umg!*), to throw up; **das ist zum K~** it makes you sick
KP (**-, -s**) F ABK (= *Kommunistische Partei*) C.P.
KPÖ (**-**) F ABK (= *Kommunistische Partei Österreichs*) Austrian Communist Party
Kr. ABK = **Kreis**
Krabbe ['krabə] (**-, -n**) F shrimp
krabbeln VI to crawl
Krach [krax] (**-(e)s, -s** *od* **-e**) M crash; (*andauernd*) noise; (*umg: Streit*) quarrel, argument; **~ schlagen** to make a fuss; **krachen** VI to crash; (*beim Brechen*) to crack ▸ VR (*umg*) to argue, to quarrel
krächzen ['krɛçtsən] VI to croak
Kräcker ['krɛkər] (**-s, -**) M (*Koch*) cracker
kraft [kraft] PRÄP +*gen* by virtue of
Kraft (**-, Kräfte**) F strength; (*von Stimme, fig*) power, force; (*Arbeitskraft*) worker; **mit vereinten Kräften werden wir ...** if we combine our efforts we will ...; **nach (besten) Kräften** to the best of one's abilities; **außer ~ sein** (*Jur: Geltung*) to be no longer in force; **in ~ treten** to come into effect
Kraft- ZW: **Kraftaufwand** M effort; **Kraftausdruck** M swearword; **Kraftbrühe** F beef tea
Kräfteverhältnis ['krɛftəfɛrhɛltnɪs] NT (*Pol*) balance of power; (*von Mannschaften etc*) relative strength
Kraftfahrer M motor driver
Kraftfahrzeug NT motor vehicle; **Kraftfahrzeugbrief** M (*Aut*) logbook (BRIT), motor-vehicle registration certificate (*US*); **Kraftfahrzeugschein** M (*Aut*) car licence (BRIT) *od* license (*US*); **Kraftfahrzeugsteuer** F ≈ road tax
kräftig ['krɛftɪç] ADJ strong; (*Suppe, Essen*) nourishing; **kräftigen** ['krɛftɪgən] VT to strengthen
Kraft- ZW: **kraftlos** ADJ weak; (*machtlos*) powerless; (*Jur*) invalid; **Kraftmeierei** (*umg*) F *showing off of physical strength*; **Kraftprobe** F trial of strength; **Kraftrad** NT motorcycle; **Kraftstoff** M fuel; **Krafttraining** NT weight training; **kraftvoll** ADJ vigorous; **Kraftwagen** M motor vehicle; **Kraftwerk** NT power station; **Kraftwerker** M power station worker
Kragen ['kra:gən] (**-s, -**) M collar; **da ist mir der ~ geplatzt** (*umg*) I blew my top; **es geht ihm an den ~** (*umg*) he's in for it; **Kragenweite** F collar size; **das ist nicht meine Kragenweite** (*fig: umg*) that's not my cup of tea
Krähe ['krɛ:ə] (**-, -n**) F crow
krähen VI to crow
krakeelen [kra'ke:lən] (*umg*) VI to make a din

krakelig ['kra:kəlɪç] (*umg*) ADJ (*Schrift*) scrawly, spidery
Kralle ['kralə] (-, -n) F claw; (*Vogelkralle*) talon
krallen VT to clutch; (*krampfhaft*) to claw
Kram [kra:m] (-(e)s) M stuff, rubbish; **den ~ hinschmeißen** (*umg*) to chuck the whole thing; **kramen** VI to rummage; **Kramladen** (*pej*) M small shop
Krampf [krampf] (-(e)s, Krämpfe) M cramp; (*zuckend*) spasm; (*Unsinn*) rubbish; **Krampfader** F varicose vein; **krampfhaft** ADJ convulsive; (*fig: Versuche*) desperate
Kran [kra:n] (-(e)s, Kräne) M crane; (*Wasserkran*) tap (BRIT), faucet (US)
Kranich ['kra:nɪç] (-s, -e) M (*Zool*) crane
krank [kraŋk] ADJ ill, sick; **das macht mich ~!** (*umg*) it gets on my nerves!, it drives me round the bend!; **sich ~ stellen** to pretend to be ill, to malinger
Kranke(r) F(M) sick person, invalid; (*Patient*) patient
kränkeln ['krɛŋkəln] VI to be in bad health
kranken ['kraŋkən] VI: **an etw** *dat* **~** (*fig*) to suffer from sth
kränken ['krɛŋkən] VT to hurt
Kranken- zW: **Krankenbericht** M medical report; **Krankenbesuch** M visit to a sick person; **Krankengeld** NT sick pay; **Krankengeschichte** F medical history; **Krankengymnastik** F physiotherapy; **Krankenhaus** NT hospital; **Krankenkasse** F health insurance; **Krankenpfleger** M orderly; (*mit Schwesternausbildung*) male nurse; **Krankenpflegerin** F nurse; **Krankenschein** M medical insurance certificate; **Krankenschwester** F nurse; **Krankenversicherung** F health insurance; **Krankenwagen** M ambulance
krankfeiern (*umg*) VI to be off sick; (*vortäuschend*) to skive (BRIT)
krankhaft ADJ diseased; (*Angst etc*) morbid; **sein Geiz ist schon ~** his meanness is almost pathological
Krankheit F illness; (*chronisch*) disease; **nach langer schwerer ~** after a long serious illness
Krankheitserreger M disease-causing agent
kränklich ['krɛŋklɪç] ADJ sickly
krankmelden VR to let one's boss *etc* know that one is ill; (*telefonisch*) to phone in sick; (*bes Mil*) to report sick
krankschreiben *unreg* VT to give sb a medical certificate; (*bes Mil*) to put sb on the sick list
Kränkung F insult, offence (BRIT), offense (US)
Kranz [krants] (-es, Kränze) M wreath, garland
Kränzchen ['krɛntsçən] NT small wreath; (*fig: Kaffeekränzchen*) coffee circle
Krapfen ['krapfən] (-s, -) M fritter; (*Berliner*) doughnut (BRIT), donut (US)
krass [kras] ADJ crass; (*Unterschied*) extreme
Krater ['kra:tər] (-s, -) M crater
Kratzbürste ['kratsbʏrstə] F (*fig*) crosspatch
Krätze ['krɛtsə] F (*Med*) scabies *sing*
kratzen ['kratsən] VT, VI to scratch; (*abkratzen*): **etw von etw ~** to scrape sth off sth
Kratzer (-s, -) M scratch; (*Werkzeug*) scraper
Kraul [kraʊl] (-s) NT (*auch:* **Kraulschwimmen**) crawl; **kraulen** VI (*schwimmen*) to do the crawl ▶ VT (*streicheln*) to tickle
kraus [kraʊs] ADJ crinkly; (*Haar*) frizzy; (*Stirn*) wrinkled
Krause ['kraʊzə] (-, -n) F frill, ruffle
kräuseln ['krɔʏzəln] VT (*Haar*) to make frizzy; (*Stoff*) to gather; (*Stirn*) to wrinkle ▶ VR (*Haar*) to go frizzy; (*Stirn*) to wrinkle; (*Wasser*) to ripple
Kraut [kraʊt] (-(e)s, Kräuter) NT plant; (*Gewürz*) herb; (*Gemüse*) cabbage; **dagegen ist kein ~ gewachsen** (*fig*) there's nothing anyone can do about that; **ins ~ schießen** (*lit*) to run to seed; (*fig*) to get out of control; **wie ~ und Rüben** (*umg*) extremely untidy
Kräuterbutter F herb butter
Kräutertee ['krɔytərte:] M herb tea
Krautsalat M coleslaw
Krawall [kra'val] (-s, -e) M row, uproar
Krawatte [kra'vatə] (-, -n) F tie
kreativ [krea'ti:f] ADJ creative
Kreativität [kreativi'tɛ:t] F creativity
Kreatur [krea'tu:r] F creature
Krebs [kre:ps] (-es, -e) M crab; (*Med*) cancer; (*Astrol*) Cancer; **krebserregend** ADJ carcinogenic; **krebskrank** ADJ suffering from cancer; **krebskrank sein** to have cancer; **Krebskranke(r)** F(M) cancer victim; (*Patient*) cancer patient; **krebsrot** ADJ red as a lobster
Kredit [kre'di:t] (-(e)s, -e) M credit; (*Darlehen*) loan; (*fig*) standing; **Kreditdrosselung** F credit squeeze; **kreditfähig** ADJ creditworthy; **Kreditgrenze** F credit limit; **Kredithai** (*umg*) M loan-shark; **Kreditkarte** F credit card; **Kreditkonto** NT credit account; **Kreditpolitik** F lending policy; **kreditwürdig** ADJ creditworthy; **Kreditwürdigkeit** F creditworthiness, credit status
Kreide ['kraɪdə] (-, -n) F chalk; **bei jdm (tief) in der ~ stehen** to be (deep) in debt to sb; **kreidebleich** ADJ as white as a sheet
Kreis [kraɪs] (-es, -e) M circle; (*Stadtkreis etc*) district; **im ~ gehen** (*lit, fig*) to go round in circles; **(weite) Kreise ziehen** (*fig*) to have (wide) repercussions; **weite Kreise der Bevölkerung** wide sections of the population; **eine Feier im kleinen Kreise** a celebration for a few close friends and relatives
kreischen ['kraɪʃən] VI to shriek, to screech
Kreisel ['kraɪzəl] (-s, -) M top; (*Verkehrskreisel*) roundabout (BRIT), traffic circle (US)
kreisen ['kraɪzən] VI to spin; (*fig: Gedanken, Gespräch*): **~ um** to revolve around
Kreis- zW: **kreisförmig** ADJ circular; **Kreislauf** M (*Med*) circulation; (*fig: der Natur etc*) cycle; **Kreislaufkollaps** M circulatory collapse; **Kreislaufstörungen** PL circulation trouble *sing*; **Kreissäge** F circular saw
Kreißsaal ['kraɪsza:l] M delivery room
Kreisstadt F ≈ county town

Kreisverkehr M roundabout (*BRIT*), traffic circle (*US*)
Krematorium [krema'to:riʊm] NT crematorium
Kreml ['kre:ml] (**-s**) M: **der ~** the Kremlin
Krempe ['krɛmpə] (**-, -n**) F brim
Krempel (**-s**) (*umg*) M rubbish
krepieren [kre'pi:rən] (*umg*) VI (*sterben*) to die, to kick the bucket
Krepp [krɛp] (**-s, -s** *od* **-e**) M crêpe
Krepppapier NT crêpe paper
Kreppsohle F crêpe sole
Kresse ['krɛsə] (**-, -n**) F cress
Kreta ['kre:ta] (**-s**) NT Crete
Kreter(in) [kre:tər(ɪn)] (**-s, -**) M(F) Cretan
kretisch ADJ Cretan
kreuz [krɔʏts] ADJ: **~ und quer** all over
Kreuz (**-es, -e**) NT cross; (*Anat*) small of the back; (*Karten*) clubs; (*Mus*) sharp; (*Autobahnkreuz*) intersection; **zu Kreuze kriechen** (*fig*) to eat humble pie, to eat crow (*US*); **jdn aufs ~ legen** to throw sb on his back; (*fig: umg*) to take sb for a ride
kreuzen VT to cross ▶ VR to cross; (*Meinungen etc*) to clash ▶ VI (*Naut*) to cruise; **die Arme ~** to fold one's arms
Kreuzer (**-s, -**) M (*Schiff*) cruiser
Kreuz- zW: **Kreuzfahrt** F cruise; **Kreuzfeuer** NT (*fig*): **im Kreuzfeuer stehen** to be caught in the crossfire; **Kreuzgang** M cloisters *pl*
kreuzigen VT to crucify
Kreuzigung F crucifixion
Kreuzotter F adder
Kreuzschmerzen PL backache *sing*
Kreuzung F (*Verkehrskreuzung*) crossing, junction; (*Züchtung*) cross
Kreuz- zW: **kreuzunglücklich** ADJ absolutely miserable; **Kreuzverhör** NT cross-examination; **ins Kreuzverhör nehmen** to cross-examine; **Kreuzweg** M crossroads; (*Rel*) Way of the Cross; **Kreuzworträtsel** NT crossword puzzle; **Kreuzzeichen** NT sign of the cross; **Kreuzzug** M crusade
kribbelig ['krɪbəlɪç], **kribblig** ['krɪblɪç] (*umg*) ADJ fidgety; (*kribbelnd*) tingly
kribbeln ['krɪbəln] VI (*jucken*) to itch; (*prickeln*) to tingle
kriechen ['kri:çən] *unreg* VI to crawl, to creep; (*pej*) to grovel, to crawl
Kriecher (**-s, -**) M crawler
kriecherisch ADJ grovelling (*BRIT*), groveling (*US*)
Kriechspur F crawler lane (*BRIT*)
Kriechtier NT reptile
Krieg [kri:k] (**-(e)s, -e**) M war; **~ führen (mit** *od* **gegen)** to wage war (on)
kriegen ['kri:gən] (*umg*) VT to get; (*erwischen*) to catch
Krieger (**-s, -**) M warrior; **Kriegerdenkmal** NT war memorial; **kriegerisch** ADJ warlike
Kriegführung F warfare
Kriegs- zW: **Kriegsbeil** NT: **das Kriegsbeil begraben** (*fig*) to bury the hatchet; **Kriegsbemalung** F war paint; **Kriegsdienstverweigerer** M conscientious objector; **Kriegserklärung** F declaration of war; **Kriegsfuß** M: **mit jdm/etw auf Kriegsfuß stehen** to be at loggerheads with sb/not to get on with sth; **Kriegsgefangene(r)** F(M) prisoner of war; **Kriegsgefangenschaft** F captivity; **Kriegsgericht** NT court-martial; **Kriegsrat** M council of war; **Kriegsrecht** NT (*Mil*) martial law; **Kriegsschauplatz** M theatre (*BRIT*) *od* theater (*US*) of war; **Kriegsschiff** NT warship; **Kriegsschuld** F war guilt; **Kriegsverbrecher** M war criminal; **Kriegsversehrte(r)** F(M) person disabled in the war; **Kriegszustand** M state of war
Krim [krɪm] F: **die ~** the Crimea
Krimi ['kri:mi] (**-s, -s**) (*umg*) M thriller
kriminal [krimi'na:l] ADJ criminal; **Kriminalbeamte(r)** M detective; **Kriminalfilm** M crime thriller *od* movie (*bes US*)
Kriminalität [kriminali'tɛ:t] F criminality
Kriminalpolizei F ≈ Criminal Investigation Department (*BRIT*), ≈ Federal Bureau of Investigation (*US*)
Kriminalroman M detective story
kriminell [kri:mi'nɛl] ADJ criminal
Kriminelle(r) F(M) criminal
Krimskrams ['krɪmskrams] (**-es**) (*umg*) M odds and ends *pl*
Kringel ['krɪŋəl] (**-s, -**) M (*der Schrift*) squiggle; (*Koch*) ring
kringelig ADJ: **sich ~ lachen** (*umg*) to kill o.s. laughing
Kripo ['kri:po] (**-, -s**) F ABK (= *Kriminalpolizei*) ≈ CID (*BRIT*), ≈ FBI (*US*)
Krippe ['krɪpə] (**-, -n**) F manger, crib; (*Kinderkrippe*) crèche
Krippenspiel NT nativity play
Krippentod M cot death
Krise ['kri:zə] (**-, -n**) F crisis
kriseln VI: **es kriselt** there's a crisis looming, there is trouble brewing
Krisen- zW: **krisenfest** ADJ stable; **Krisenherd** M flash point, trouble spot; **Krisenstab** M action *od* crisis committee
Kristall[1] [krɪs'tal] (**-s, -e**) M crystal
Kristall[2] (**-s**) NT (*Glas*) crystal; **Kristallzucker** M refined sugar crystals *pl*
Kriterium [kri'te:riʊm] NT criterion
Kritik [kri'ti:k] F criticism; (*Zeitungskritik*) review, write-up; **an jdm/etw ~ üben** to criticize sb/sth; **unter aller ~ sein** (*umg*) to be beneath contempt
Kritiker(in) ['kri:tikər(ɪn)] (**-s, -**) M(F) critic
kritiklos ADJ uncritical
kritisch ['kri:tɪʃ] ADJ critical
kritisieren [kriti'zi:rən] VT, VI to criticize
kritteln ['krɪtəln] VI to find fault, to carp
kritzeln ['krɪtsəln] VT, VI to scribble, to scrawl
Kroate [kro'a:tə] (**-n, -n**) M Croat
Kroatien [kro'a:tsiən] (**-s**) NT Croatia
Kroatin F Croat
kroatisch ADJ Croatian
kroch *etc* [krɔx] VB *siehe* **kriechen**

Krokodil [kroko'di:l] **(-s, -e)** NT crocodile
Krokodilstränen PL crocodile tears *pl*
Krokus ['kro:kʊs] (-, - *od* **-se**) M crocus
Krone ['kro:nə] (-, **-n**) F crown; (*Baumkrone*) top; **einen in der ~ haben** (*umg*) to be tipsy
krönen ['krø:nən] VT to crown
Kron- ZW: **Kronkorken** M bottle top; **Kronleuchter** M chandelier; **Kronprinz** M crown prince
Krönung ['krø:nʊŋ] F coronation
Kronzeuge M (*Jur*) person who turns Queen's/ King's (BRIT) *od* State's (*US*) evidence; (*Hauptzeuge*) principal witness
Kropf [krɔpf] **(-(e)s, Kröpfe)** M (*Med*) goitre (BRIT), goiter (*US*); (*von Vogel*) crop
Krösus ['krø:zʊs] **(-ses, -se)** M: **ich bin doch kein ~** (*umg*) I'm not made of money
Kröte ['krø:tə] (-, **-n**) F toad; **Kröten** PL (*umg: Geld*) pennies *pl*
Krs. ABK = **Kreis**
Krücke ['krʏkə] (-, **-n**) F crutch
Krug [kru:k] **(-(e)s, Krüge)** M jug; (*Bierkrug*) mug
Krümel ['kry:məl] **(-s, -)** M crumb
krümeln VT, VI to crumble
krumm [krʊm] ADJ (*lit, fig*) crooked; (*kurvig*) curved; **keinen Finger ~ machen** (*umg*) not to lift a finger; **ein krummes Ding drehen** (*umg*) to do something crooked; **krummbeinig** ADJ bandy-legged
krümmen ['krʏm:ən] VT to bend ▶ VR to bend, to curve
krummlachen (*umg*) VR to laugh o.s. silly; **sich krumm- und schieflachen** to fall about laughing
krummnehmen *unreg* (*umg*) VT: **jdm etw ~** (*umg*) to take sth amiss
Krümmung F bend, curve
Krüppel ['krʏpəl] **(-s, -)** M cripple
Kruste ['krʊstə] (-, **-n**) F crust
Krux [krʊks] (-) F (*Schwierigkeit*) trouble, problem
Kruzifix [krutsi'fɪks] **(-es, -e)** NT crucifix
Kt. ABK = **Kanton**
Kto. ABK (= *Konto*) a/c
Kuba ['ku:ba] **(-s)** NT Cuba
Kubaner(in) [ku'ba:nər(ɪn)] **(-s, -)** M(F) Cuban
kubanisch [ku'ba:nɪʃ] ADJ Cuban
Kübel ['ky:bəl] **(-s, -)** M tub; (*Eimer*) pail
Kubik- [ku'bi:k] IN ZW cubic; **Kubikmeter** M cubic metre (BRIT) *od* meter (*US*)
Küche ['kʏçə] (-, **-n**) F kitchen; (*Kochen*) cooking, cuisine
Kuchen ['ku:xən] **(-s, -)** M cake; **Kuchenblech** NT baking tray; **Kuchenform** F baking tin (BRIT) *od* pan (*US*); **Kuchengabel** F pastry fork
Küchen- ZW: **Küchengerät** NT kitchen utensil; (*elektrisch*) kitchen appliance; **Küchenherd** M cooker, stove; **Küchenmaschine** F food processor; **Küchenmesser** NT kitchen knife; **Küchenpapier** NT kitchen roll; **Küchenschabe** F cockroach; **Küchenschrank** M kitchen cabinet
Kuchenteig M cake mixture
Kuckuck ['kʊkʊk] **(-s, -e)** M cuckoo; (*umg: Siegel des Gerichtsvollziehers*) bailiff's seal (*for distraint of goods*); **das weiß der ~** heaven (only) knows
Kuckucksuhr F cuckoo clock
Kuddelmuddel ['kʊdəlmʊdəl] **(-s)** (*umg*) M OD NT mess
Kufe ['ku:fə] (-, **-n**) F (*Fasskufe*) vat; (*Schlittenkufe*) runner; (*Aviat*) skid
Kugel ['ku:gəl] (-, **-n**) F ball; (*Math*) sphere; (*Mil*) bullet; (*Erdkugel*) globe; (*Sport*) shot; **eine ruhige ~ schieben** (*umg*) to have a cushy number; **kugelförmig** ADJ spherical; **Kugelkopf** M (*Schreibmaschine*) golf ball; **Kugelkopfschreibmaschine** F golf-ball typewriter; **Kugellager** NT ball bearing
kugeln VT to roll; (*Sport*) to bowl ▶ VR (*vor Lachen*) to double up
Kugel- ZW: **kugelrund** ADJ (*Gegenstand*) round; (*umg: Person*) tubby; **Kugelschreiber** M ball-point (pen), Biro®; **kugelsicher** ADJ bulletproof; **Kugelstoßen (-s)** NT shot put
Kuh [ku:] (-, **Kühe**) F cow; **Kuhdorf** (*pej, umg*) NT one-horse town; **Kuhhandel** (*pej, umg*) M horse-trading; **Kuhhaut** F: **das geht auf keine Kuhhaut** (*fig: umg*) that's absolutely incredible
kühl [ky:l] ADJ (*lit, fig*) cool; **Kühlanlage** F refrigeration plant
Kühle (-) F coolness
kühlen VT to cool
Kühler (-s, -) M (*Aut*) radiator; **Kühlerhaube** F (*Aut*) bonnet (BRIT), hood (*US*)
Kühl- ZW: **Kühlflüssigkeit** F coolant; **Kühlhaus** NT cold-storage depot; **Kühlraum** M cold-storage chamber; **Kühlschrank** M refrigerator; **Kühltasche** F cool bag; **Kühltruhe** F freezer
Kühlung F cooling
Kühlwagen M (*Lastwagen, Eisenb*) refrigerator van
Kühlwasser NT coolant
kühn [ky:n] ADJ bold, daring; **Kühnheit** F boldness
Kuhstall M cow-shed
k. u. k. ABK (= *kaiserlich und königlich*) imperial and royal
Küken ['ky:kən] **(-s, -)** NT chicken; (*umg: Nesthäkchen*) baby of the family
kulant [ku'lant] ADJ obliging
Kulanz [ku'lants] F accommodating attitude, generousness
Kuli ['ku:li] **(-s, -s)** M coolie; (*umg: Kugelschreiber*) Biro®
kulinarisch [kuli'na:rɪʃ] ADJ culinary
Kulisse [ku'lɪsə] (-, **-n**) F scene
Kulissenschieber(in) M(F) stagehand
Kulleraugen ['kʊləraʊgən] (*umg*) PL wide eyes *pl*
kullern ['kʊlərn] VI to roll
Kult [kʊlt] **(-(e)s, -e)** M worship, cult; **mit etw ~ treiben** to make a cult out of sth
kultivieren [kʊlti'vi:rən] VT to cultivate
kultiviert ADJ cultivated, refined
Kultstätte F place of worship
Kultstatus M: **~ haben/genießen** to have/ enjoy cult status

Kultur [kʊl'tuːr] F culture; (*Lebensform*) civilization; (*des Bodens*) cultivation; **Kulturbanause** (*umg*) M philistine, low-brow; **Kulturbetrieb** M culture industry; **Kulturbeutel** M toilet bag (BRIT), washbag
kulturell [kʊltu'rɛl] ADJ cultural
Kulturfilm M documentary film
Kulturhauptstadt F: **Europäische ~** European City of Culture
Kulturteil M (*von Zeitung*) arts section
Kultusminister ['kʊltʊsminɪstər] M minister of education and the arts
Kümmel ['kʏməl] (**-s, -**) M caraway seed; (*Branntwein*) kümmel
Kummer ['kʊmər] (**-s**) M grief, sorrow
kümmerlich ['kʏmərlɪç] ADJ miserable, wretched
kümmern VR: **sich um jdn ~** to look after sb ▸ VT to concern; **sich um etw ~** to see to sth; **das kümmert mich nicht** that doesn't worry me
Kumpan(in) [kʊm'paːn(ɪn)] (**-s, -e**) M(F) mate; (*pej*) accomplice
Kumpel ['kʊmpəl] (**-s, -**) (*umg*) M mate
kündbar ['kʏntbaːr] ADJ redeemable, recallable; (*Vertrag*) terminable
Kunde[1] ['kʊndə] (**-n, -n**) M customer
Kunde[2] ['kʊndə] (**-, -n**) F (*Botschaft*) news
Kunden- ZW: **Kundenberatung** F customer advisory service; **Kundendienst** M after-sales service; **Kundenfang** (*pej*) M: **auf Kundenfang sein** to be touting for customers; **Kundenfänger** M tout (*umg*); **Kundenkonto** NT charge account; **Kundenkreis** M customers *pl*, clientele; **kundenorientiert** M customer-oriented; **Kundenservice** F customer service; **Kundenwerbung** F publicity (*aimed at attracting custom or customers*)
Kund- ZW: **Kundgabe** F announcement; **kundgeben** *unreg* VT to announce; **Kundgebung** F announcement; (*Versammlung*) rally
kundig ADJ expert, experienced
kündigen ['kʏndɪgən] VI to give in one's notice ▸ VT to cancel; **jdm ~** to give sb his notice; **zum 1. April ~** to give one's notice for April 1st; (*Mieter*) to give notice for April 1st; (*bei Mitgliedschaft*) to cancel one's membership as of April 1st; **(jdm) die Stellung ~** to give (sb) notice; **sie hat ihm die Freundschaft gekündigt** she has broken off their friendship
Kündigung F notice
Kündigungsfrist F period of notice
Kündigungsschutz M protection against wrongful dismissal
Kundin F customer
Kundschaft F customers *pl*, clientele
Kundschafter (**-s, -**) M spy; (*Mil*) scout
künftig ['kʏnftɪç] ADJ future ▸ ADV in future
Kunst [kʊnst] (**-, Künste**) F (*auch Sch*) art; (*Können*) skill; **das ist doch keine ~** it's easy; **mit seiner ~ am Ende sein** to be at one's wits' end; **das ist eine brotlose ~** there's no money in that; **Kunstakademie** F academy of art; **Kunstdruck** M art print; **Kunstdünger** M artificial manure; **Kunsterziehung** F (*Sch*) art; **Kunstfaser** F synthetic fibre (BRIT) *od* fiber (US); **Kunstfehler** M professional error; (*weniger ernst*) slip; **Kunstfertigkeit** F skilfulness (BRIT), skillfulness (US); **Kunstflieger** M stunt flyer; **kunstgerecht** ADJ skilful (BRIT), skillful (US); **Kunstgeschichte** F history of art; **Kunstgewerbe** NT arts and crafts *pl*; **Kunstgriff** M trick, knack; **Kunsthändler** M art dealer; **Kunstharz** NT artificial resin; **Kunstleder** NT artificial leather
Künstler(in) ['kʏnstlər(ɪn)] (**-s, -**) M(F) artist; **künstlerisch** ADJ artistic; **Künstlername** M pseudonym; (*von Schauspieler*) stage name; **Künstlerpech** (*umg*) NT hard luck
künstlich ['kʏnstlɪç] ADJ artificial; **künstliche Intelligenz** (*Comput*) artificial intelligence; **sich ~ aufregen** (*umg*) to get all worked up about nothing
Kunst- ZW: **Kunstsammler** M art collector; **Kunstseide** F artificial silk; **Kunststoff** M synthetic material; **Kunststopfen** (**-s**) NT invisible mending; **Kunststück** NT trick; **das ist kein Kunststück** (*fig*) there's nothing to it; **Kunstturnen** NT gymnastics *sing*; **kunstvoll** ADJ artistic; **Kunstwerk** NT work of art
kunterbunt ['kʊntərbʊnt] ADJ higgledy-piggledy
Kupee [ku'peː] (**-s, -s**) NT = **Coupé**
Kupfer ['kʊpfər] (**-s, -**) NT copper; **Kupfergeld** NT coppers *pl*
kupfern ADJ copper ▸ VT (*fig: umg*) to plagiarize, to copy, to imitate
Kupferstich M copperplate engraving
Kupon [ku'põː] (**-s, -s**) M = **Coupon**
Kuppe ['kʊpə] (**-, -n**) F (*Bergkuppe*) top; (*Fingerkuppe*) tip
Kuppel (**-, -n**) F cupola, dome
Kuppelei [kʊpə'laɪ] F (*Jur*) procuring
kuppeln VI (*Jur*) to procure; (*Aut*) to operate *od* use the clutch ▸ VT to join
Kuppler ['kʊplər] (**-s, -**) M procurer; **Kupplerin** F procuress
Kupplung F (*auch Tech*) coupling; (*Aut etc*) clutch; **die ~ (durch)treten** to disengage the clutch
Kur [kuːr] (**-, -en**) F (course of) treatment; (*im Kurort*) (health) cure; (*Schlankheitskur*) diet; **eine ~ machen** to take a cure (in a health resort)
Kür [kyːr] (**-, -en**) F (*Sport*) free exercises *pl*
Kuratorium [kura'toːriʊm] NT (*Vereinigung*) committee
Kurbel ['kʊrbəl] (**-, -n**) F crank, winder; (*Aut*) starting handle; **Kurbelwelle** F crankshaft
Kürbis ['kʏrbɪs] (**-ses, -se**) M pumpkin; (*exotisch*) gourd
Kurde ['kʊrdə] (**-n, -n**) M, **Kurdin** F Kurd
Kurfürst ['kuːrfʏrst] M Elector, electoral prince
Kurgast M visitor (to a health resort)
Kurier [ku'riːr] (**-s, -e**) M courier, messenger
kurieren [ku'riːrən] VT to cure
kurios [kuri'oːs] ADJ curious, odd
Kuriosität [kuriozi'tɛːt] F curiosity

Kur- ZW: **Kurkonzert** NT concert (*at a health resort*); **Kurort** M health resort; **Kurpfuscher** M quack

Kurs [kʊrs] **(-es, -e)** M course; (*Fin*) rate; **hoch im ~ stehen** (*fig*) to be highly thought of; **einen ~ besuchen** *od* **mitmachen** to attend a class; **harter/weicher ~** (*Pol*) hard/soft line; **Kursänderung** F (*lit, fig*) change of course; **Kursbuch** NT timetable

Kürschner(in) ['kʏrʃnər(ɪn)] **(-s, -)** M(F) furrier

kursieren [kʊr'zi:rən] VI to circulate

kursiv ADV in italics

Kursnotierung F quotation

Kursus ['kʊrzʊs] (-, **Kurse**) M course

Kurswagen M (*Eisenb*) through carriage

Kurswert M (*Fin*) market value

Kurtaxe F spa tax (*paid by visitors*)

Kurve ['kʊrvə] **(-, -n)** F curve; (*Straßenkurve*) bend; (*statistisch, Fieberkurve etc*) graph; **die ~ nicht kriegen** (*umg*) not to get around to it

kurvenreich ADJ: **„kurvenreiche Strecke"** "bends"

kurvig ADJ (*Straße*) bendy

kurz [kʊrts] ADJ short ▶ ADV: **~ und bündig** concisely; **zu ~ kommen** to come off badly; **den Kürzeren ziehen** to get the worst of it; **~ und gut** in short; **über ~ oder lang** sooner or later; **eine Sache ~ abtun** to dismiss sth out of hand; **~ gefasst** concise; **darf ich mal ~ stören?** could I just interrupt for a moment?; *siehe auch* **kurzfassen**; **kurzhalten**; **kurztreten**

Kurzarbeit F short-time work; *see note*

> **Kurzarbeit** is the term used to describe a shorter working week made necessary by a lack of work. It has been introduced in recent years as a preferable alternative to redundancy. It has to be approved by the Arbeitsamt, the job centre, which pays some compensation to the worker for loss of pay.

kurzärmelig, kurzärmlig ADJ short-sleeved

kurzatmig ADJ (*fig*) feeble, lame; (*Med*) short-winded

Kürze ['kʏrtsə] **(-, -n)** F shortness, brevity

kürzen VT to cut short; (*in der Länge*) to shorten; (*Gehalt*) to reduce

kurzerhand ['kʊrtsər'hant] ADV without further ado; (*entlassen*) on the spot

kurz- ZW: **kurzfassen** VR to be brief; **Kurzfassung** F shortened version; **kurzfristig** ADJ short-term; **kurzfristige Verbindlichkeiten** current liabilities *pl*; **Kurzgeschichte** F short story; **kurzhalten** *unreg* VT to keep short; **kurzlebig** ADJ short-lived

kürzlich ['kʏrtslɪç] ADV lately, recently

Kurz- ZW: **Kurzmeldung** F news flash; **Kurzparker** M short-stay parker; **Kurzschluss** M (*Elek*) short circuit; **Kurzschlusshandlung** F (*fig*) rash action; **Kurzschrift** F shorthand; **kurzsichtig** ADJ short-sighted; **Kurzstrecken-** IN ZW short-range; **Kurzstreckenläufer(in)** M(F) sprinter; **kurztreten** *unreg* VI (*fig: umg*) to go easy; **kurzum** ADV in a word

Kürzung F cutback

Kurz- ZW: **Kurzurlaub** M short holiday (BRIT), short vacation (*US*); **Kurzwaren** PL haberdashery (BRIT), notions *pl* (*US*); **Kurzwelle** F short wave

kuschelig ADJ cuddly

kuscheln ['kʊʃəln] VR to snuggle up

kuschen ['kʊʃən] VI, VR (*Hund etc*) to get down; (*fig*) to knuckle under

Kusine [ku'zi:nə] F cousin

Kuss [kʊs] **(-es, Küsse)** M kiss

küssen ['kʏsən] VT, VR to kiss

Küste ['kʏstə] **(-, -n)** F coast, shore

Küsten- ZW: **Küstengewässer** PL coastal waters *pl*; **Küstenschiff** NT coaster; **Küstenwache** F coastguard (station)

Küster ['kʏstər] **(-s, -)** M sexton, verger

Kutsche ['kʊtʃə] **(-, -n)** F coach, carriage

Kutscher (-s, -) M coachman

kutschieren [kʊ'tʃi:rən] VI: **durch die Gegend ~** (*umg*) to drive around

Kutte ['kʊtə] **(-, -n)** F cowl

Kuvert [ku'vɛrt] **(-s, -e** *od* **-s)** NT envelope; (*Gedeck*) cover

Kuwait [ku'vaɪt] **(-s)** NT Kuwait

KV ABK (*Mus*) = **Köchelverzeichnis**; **KV 280** K. (number) 280

kW ABK (= *Kilowatt*) kW

KW ABK (= *Kurzwelle*) SW

Kybernetik [kybɛr'ne:tɪk] F cybernetics *sing*

kybernetisch [kybɛr'ne:tɪʃ] ADJ cybernetic

KZ (-s, -s) NT ABK = **Konzentrationslager**

k

L

L, l¹ [ɛl] NT L, l; **L wie Ludwig** ≈ L for Lucy, ≈ L for Love (*US*)
l² [ɛl] ABK (= *Liter*) l
laben ['la:bən] VT to refresh ▶ VR to refresh o.s.; (*fig*): **sich an etw** *dat* ~ to relish sth
labern ['la:bərn] (*umg*) VI to prattle (on) ▶ VT to talk
labil [la'bi:l] ADJ (*physisch: Gesundheit*) delicate; (*: Kreislauf*) poor; (*psychisch*) unstable
Labor [la'bo:r] (**-s, -e** *od* **-s**) NT laboratory, lab
Laborant(in) [labo'rant(ɪn)] M(F) lab(oratory) assistant
Laboratorium [labora'to:riʊm] NT lab(oratory)
Labyrinth [laby'rɪnt] (**-s, -e**) NT labyrinth
Lache ['laxə] (**-, -n**) F (*Wasser*) pool, puddle; (*umg: Gelächter*) laugh
lächeln ['lɛçəln] VI to smile; **Lächeln (-s)** NT smile
lachen ['laxən] VI to laugh; **mir ist nicht zum L~ (zumute)** I'm in no laughing mood; **dass ich nicht lache!** (*umg*) don't make me laugh!; **das wäre doch gelacht** it would be ridiculous; **Lachen** NT: **dir wird das Lachen schon noch vergehen!** you'll soon be laughing on the other side of your face
Lacher (-s, -) M: **die ~ auf seiner Seite haben** to have the last laugh
lächerlich ['lɛçərlɪç] ADJ ridiculous; **Lächerlichkeit** F absurdity
Lach- ZW: **Lachgas** NT laughing gas; **lachhaft** ADJ laughable; **Lachkrampf** M: **einen Lachkrampf bekommen** to go into fits of laughter
Lachs [laks] (**-es, -e**) M salmon
Lachsalve ['laxzalvə] F burst *od* roar of laughter
Lachsschinken M *smoked, rolled fillet of ham*
Lack [lak] (**-(e)s, -e**) M lacquer, varnish; (*von Auto*) paint
lackieren [la'ki:rən] VT to varnish; (*Auto*) to spray
Lackierer [la'ki:rər] (**-s, -**) M varnisher
Lackleder NT patent leather
Lackmus ['lakmʊs] (**-**) M OD NT litmus
Lade ['la:də] (**-, -n**) F box, chest; **Ladebaum** M derrick; **Ladefähigkeit** F load capacity; **Ladefläche** F load area; **Ladegerät** NT (battery) charger; **Ladegewicht** NT tonnage; **Ladehemmung** F: **das Gewehr hat Ladehemmung** the gun is jammed
laden ['la:dən] *unreg* VT (*Lasten, Comput*) to load; (*Handy etc*) to charge; (*Jur*) to summon; (*einladen*) to invite; **eine schwere Schuld auf sich** *akk* **~** to place o.s. under a heavy burden of guilt
Laden ['la:dən] (**-s, Läden**) M shop; (*Fensterladen*) shutter; (*umg: Betrieb*) outfit; **der ~ läuft** (*umg*) business is good
Laden- ZW: **Ladenaufsicht** F shopwalker (BRIT), floorwalker (*US*); **Ladenbesitzer** M shopkeeper; **Ladendieb** M shoplifter; **Ladendiebstahl** M shoplifting; **Ladenhüter (-s, -)** M unsaleable item; **Ladenöffnungszeit** F shop opening hours *pl*; **Ladenpreis** M retail price; **Ladenschluss** M, **Ladenschlusszeit** F closing time; **Ladentisch** M counter
Laderampe F loading ramp
Laderaum M (*Naut*) hold
lädieren [lɛ'di:rən] VT to damage
lädt [lɛ:t] VB *siehe* **laden**
Ladung ['la:dʊŋ] F (*Last*) load; (*Naut, Aviat*) cargo; (*Beladen*) loading; (*Jur*) summons; (*Einladung*) invitation; (*Sprengladung*) charge
lag *etc* [la:k] VB *siehe* **liegen**
Lage ['la:gə] (**-, -n**) F position, situation; (*Schicht*) layer; **in der ~ sein** to be in a position; **eine gute/ruhige ~ haben** to be in a good/peaceful location; **Herr der ~ sein** to be in control of the situation; **Lagebericht** M report; (*Mil*) situation report; **Lagebeurteilung** F situation assessment
lagenweise ADV in layers
Lager ['la:gər] (**-s, -**) NT camp; (*Comm*) warehouse; (*Schlaflager*) bed; (*von Tier*) lair; (*Tech*) bearing; **etw auf ~ haben** to have sth in stock; **Lagerarbeiter** M storehand; **Lagerbestand** M stocks *pl*; **Lagerfeuer** NT camp fire; **Lagergeld** NT storage (charges *pl*); **Lagerhaus** NT warehouse, store
Lagerist(in) [la:gə'rɪst(ɪn)] M(F) storeman, storewoman
lagern ['la:gərn] VI (*Dinge*) to be stored; (*Menschen*) to camp; (*auch vr: rasten*) to lie down ▶ VT to store; (*betten*) to lay down; (*Maschine*) to bed
Lager- ZW: **Lagerraum** M storeroom; (*in Geschäft*) stockroom; **Lagerschuppen** M store shed; **Lagerstätte** F resting place
Lagerung F storage

Lagune [la'gu:nə] (**-, -n**) F lagoon
lahm [la:m] ADJ lame; (*umg: langsam, langweilig*) dreary, dull; (*Geschäftsgang*) slow, sluggish; **eine lahme Ente sein** (*umg*) to have no zip; *siehe auch* **lähmen**; **lahmarschig** ['la:m|arʃıç] (*umg*) ADJ bloody *od* damn (*umg!*) slow
lahmen VI to be lame, to limp
lähmen ['lɛ:mən], **lahmlegen** VT to paralyse (BRIT), to paralyze (*US*)
Lähmung F paralysis
Lahn [la:n] (-) F (*Fluss*) Lahn
Laib [laıp] (**-s, -e**) M loaf
Laich [laıç] (**-(e)s, -e**) M spawn; **laichen** VI to spawn
Laie ['laıə] (**-n, -n**) M layman; (*fig, Theat*) amateur
laienhaft ADJ amateurish
Lakai [la'kaı] (**-en, -en**) M lackey
Laken ['la:kən] (**-s, -**) NT sheet
Lakritze [la'krıtsə] (**-, -n**) F liquorice
lala ['la'la] (*umg*) ADV: **so ~** so-so, not too bad
lallen ['lalən] VT, VI to slur; (*Baby*) to babble
Lama ['la:ma] (**-s, -s**) NT llama
Lamelle [la'mɛlə] F lamella; (*Elek*) lamina; (*Tech*) plate
lamentieren [lamɛn'ti:rən] VI to lament
Lametta [la'mɛta] (**-s**) NT tinsel
Lamm [lam] (**-(e)s, Lämmer**) NT lamb; **Lammfell** NT lambskin; **lammfromm** ADJ like a lamb; **Lammwolle** F lambswool
Lampe ['lampə] (-, **-n**) F lamp
Lampenfieber NT stage fright
Lampenschirm M lampshade
Lampion [lampi'õ:] (**-s, -s**) M Chinese lantern
Land [lant] (**-(e)s, Länder**) NT land; (*Nation, nicht Stadt*) country; (*Bundesland*) state; **auf dem ~(e)** in the country; **an ~ gehen** to go ashore; **endlich sehe ich ~** (*fig*) at last I can see the light at the end of the tunnel; **einen Auftrag an ~ ziehen** (*umg*) to land an order; **aus aller Herren Länder** from all over the world; *siehe auch* **hierzulande**; *see note*

> A **Land** (plural **Länder**) is a member state of the **BRD**. There are 16 **Länder**, namely Baden-Württemberg, Bayern, Berlin, Brandenburg, Bremen, Hamburg, Hessen, Mecklenburg-Vorpommern, Niedersachsen, Nordrhein-Westfalen, Rheinland-Pfalz, Saarland, Sachsen, Sachsen-Anhalt, Schleswig-Holstein and Thüringen. Each Land has its own parliament and constitution.

Landarbeiter M farm *od* agricultural worker
Landbesitz M landed property
Landbesitzer M landowner
Landebahn F runway
Landeerlaubnis F permission to land
landeinwärts [lant'laınvɛrts] ADV inland
landen ['landən] VT, VI to land; **mit deinen Komplimenten kannst du bei mir nicht ~** your compliments won't get you anywhere with me
Ländereien [lɛndə'raıən] PL estates *pl*
Länderspiel NT international (match)
Landes- zW: **Landesfarben** PL national colours *pl* (BRIT) *od* colors *pl* (*US*); **Landesgrenze** F (national) frontier; (*von Bundesland*) state boundary; **Landesinnere(s)** NT inland region; **Landeskind** NT *native of a German state*; **Landeskunde** F regional studies *pl*; **Landestracht** F national costume; **landesüblich** ADJ customary; **Landesverrat** M high treason; **Landesverweisung** F banishment; **Landeswährung** F national currency; **landesweit** ADJ countrywide
Landeverbot NT refusal of permission to land
Land- zW: **Landflucht** F emigration to the cities; **Landgut** NT estate; **Landhaus** NT country house; **Landkarte** F map; **Landkreis** M administrative region; **landläufig** ADJ customary
ländlich ['lɛntlıç] ADJ rural
Land- zW: **Landrat** M *head of administration of a Landkreis*; **Landschaft** F countryside; (*Kunst*) landscape; **die politische Landschaft** the political scene; **landschaftlich** ADJ scenic; (*Besonderheiten*) regional
Landsmann (**-(e)s**, *pl* **-leute**) M compatriot, fellow countryman
Landsmännin F compatriot, fellow countrywoman
Land- zW: **Landstraße** F country road; **Landstreicher** (**-s, -**) M tramp; **Landstrich** M region; **Landtag** M (*Pol*) regional parliament
Landung ['landʊŋ] F landing
Landungs- zW: **Landungsboot** NT landing craft; **Landungsbrücke** F jetty, pier; **Landungsstelle** F landing place
Landurlaub M shore leave
Landvermesser M surveyor
landw. ABK (= *landwirtschaftlich*) agricultural
Land- zW: **Landwirt** M farmer; **Landwirtschaft** F agriculture; **Landwirtschaft betreiben** to farm; **landwirtschaftlich** ADJ agricultural; **Landzunge** F spit
lang [laŋ] ADJ long; (*umg: Mensch*) tall ▶ ADV: **~ anhaltender Beifall** prolonged applause; **~ ersehnt** longed-for; **hier wird mir die Zeit nicht ~** I won't get bored here; **er machte ein langes Gesicht** his face fell; **den ganzen Tag ~** all day long; **die Straße ~** along the street; **~ und breit** at great length; **langatmig** ADJ long-winded
lange ADV for a long time; (*dauern, brauchen*) a long time; **ich bleibe nicht ~** I won't stay long; **~ nicht so ...** not nearly as ...; **wenn der das schafft, kannst du das schon ~** if he can do it, you can do it easily
Länge ['lɛŋə] (**-, -n**) F length; (*Geog*) longitude; **etw der ~ nach falten** to fold sth lengthways; **etw in die ~ ziehen** to drag sth out (*umg*); **der ~ nach hinfallen** to fall flat (on one's face)
langen ['laŋən] VI (*ausreichen*) to do, to suffice; (*fassen*): **~ nach** to reach for; **es langt mir** I've had enough; **jdm eine ~** (*umg*) to give sb a clip on the ear
Längengrad M longitude

Längenmaß NT linear measure
Langeweile F boredom
lang- zW: **langfristig** ADJ long-term ▶ ADV in the long term; (*planen*) for the long term; **langfristige Verbindlichkeiten** long-term liabilities *pl*; **langjährig** ADJ (*Freundschaft, Gewohnheit*) long-standing; (*Erfahrung, Verhandlungen*) many years of; (*Mitarbeiter*) of many years' standing; **Langlauf** M (*Ski*) cross-country skiing; **langlebig** ADJ long-lived; **langlebige Gebrauchsgüter** consumer durables *pl*
länglich ADJ longish
Langmut F forbearance, patience
langmütig ADJ forbearing
längs [lɛŋs] PRÄP (*+gen od dat*) along ▶ ADV lengthways
langsam ADJ slow; **immer schön ~!** (*umg*) easy does it!; **ich muss jetzt ~ gehen** I must be getting on my way; **~ (aber sicher) reicht es mir** I've just about had enough; **Langsamkeit** F slowness
Langschläfer M late riser
Langspielplatte F long-playing record
längsseit, längsseits ADV alongside ▶ PRÄP *+gen* alongside
längst [lɛŋst] ADV: **das ist ~ fertig** that was finished a long time ago, that has been finished for a long time
längste(r, s) ADJ longest
Langstrecken- IN ZW long-distance; **Langstreckenflug** M long-haul flight; **Langstreckenflugzeug** NT long-range aircraft
Languste [laŋ'gʊstə] (**-, -n**) F crayfish, crawfish (*US*)
lang- zW: **langweilen** VT UNTR to bore ▶ VR UNTR to be *od* get bored; **Langweiler** (**-s, -**) M bore; **langweilig** ADJ boring, tedious; **Langwelle** F long wave; **langwierig** ADJ lengthy, long-drawn-out
Lanze ['lantsə] (**-, -n**) F lance
Lanzette [lan'tsɛtə] F lancet
Laos ['la:ɔs] (**-**) NT Laos
Laote [la'o:tə] (**-n, -n**) M, **Laotin** F Laotian
laotisch [la'o:tɪʃ] ADJ Laotian
lapidar [lapi'da:r] ADJ terse, pithy
Lappalie [la'pa:liə] F trifle
Lappe ['lapə] (**-n, -n**) M Lapp, Laplander
Lappen (**-s, -**) M cloth, rag; (*Anat*) lobe; **jdm durch die ~ gehen** (*umg*) to slip through sb's fingers
läppern ['lɛpərn] (*umg*) VR UNPERS: **es läppert sich zusammen** it (all) mounts up
Lappin ['lapɪn] F Lapp, Laplander
läppisch ['lɛpɪʃ] ADJ silly; (*Summe*) ridiculous
Lappland ['laplant] (**-s**) NT Lapland
Lappländer(in) ['laplɛndər(ɪn)] (**-s, -**) M(F) Lapp, Laplander
lappländisch ADJ Lapp
Lapsus ['lapsʊs] (**-, -**) M slip
Laptop ['lɛptɔp] (**-s, -s**) M laptop
Lärche ['lɛrçə] (**-, -n**) F larch
Lärm [lɛrm] (**-(e)s**) M noise; **Lärmbelästigung** F noise nuisance; **Lärmemission** F noise emission; (*stärker*) noise pollution; **lärmen** VI to be noisy, to make a noise
Larve ['larfə] (**-, -n**) F mask; (*Biol*) larva
las *etc* [la:s] VB *siehe* **lesen**
Lasagne [la'zanjə] PL lasagne *sing*
lasch [laʃ] ADJ slack; (*Geschmack*) tasteless
Lasche ['laʃə] (**-, -n**) F flap; (*Schuhlasche*) tongue; (*Eisenb*) fishplate
Laser ['le:zər] (**-s, -**) M laser; **Laserdrucker** M laser printer

SCHLÜSSELWORT

lassen ['lasən] (*pt* **ließ**, *pp* **gelassen** *od* (*als Hilfsverb*) **lassen**) VT **1** (*unterlassen*) to stop; (*: momentan*) to leave; **lass das (sein)!** don't (do it)!; (*hör auf*) stop it!; **lass mich!** leave me alone!; **lassen wir das!** let's leave it; **er kann das Trinken nicht lassen** he can't stop drinking; **tu, was du nicht lassen kannst!** if you must, you must!
2 (*zurücklassen*) to leave; **etw lassen, wie es ist** to leave sth (just) as it is
3 (*erlauben*) to let, to allow; **lass ihn doch** let him; **jdn ins Haus lassen** to let sb into the house; **das muss man ihr lassen** (*zugestehen*) you've got to grant her that
▶ VI: **lass mal, ich mache das schon** leave it, I'll do it
▶ HILFSVERB **1** (*veranlassen*): **etw machen lassen** to have *od* get sth done; **jdn etw machen lassen** to get sb to do sth; (*durch Befehl usw*) to make sb do sth; **er ließ mich warten** he kept me waiting; **mein Vater wollte mich studieren lassen** my father wanted me to study; **sich** *dat* **etw schicken lassen** to have sth sent (to one)
2 (*zulassen*): **jdn etw wissen lassen** to let sb know sth; **das Licht brennen lassen** to leave the light on; **einen Bart wachsen lassen** to grow a beard; **lass es dir gut gehen!** take care of yourself!
3: **lass uns gehen** let's go
▶ VR: **das lässt sich machen** that can be done; **es lässt sich schwer sagen** it's difficult to say

lässig ['lɛsɪç] ADJ casual; **Lässigkeit** F casualness
lässlich ['lɛslɪç] ADJ pardonable, venial
lässt [lɛst] VB *siehe* **lassen**
Last [last] (**-, -en**) F load; (*Traglast*) burden; (*Naut, Aviat*) cargo; (*meist pl: Gebühr*) charge; **jdm zur ~ fallen** to be a burden to sb; **Lastauto** NT lorry (BRIT), truck
lasten VI: **~ auf** *+dat* to weigh on
Lastenaufzug M hoist, goods lift (BRIT) *od* elevator (*US*)
Lastenausgleichsgesetz NT *law on financial compensation for losses suffered in WWII*
Laster ['lastər] (**-s, -**) NT vice ▶ M (*umg*) lorry (BRIT), truck
Lästerer ['lɛstərər] (**-s, -**) M mocker; (*Gotteslästerer*) blasphemer
lasterhaft ADJ immoral

lästerlich ADJ scandalous
lästern ['lɛstərn] VT, VI (*Gott*) to blaspheme; (*schlecht sprechen*) to mock; **über jdn/etw ~** to make nasty remarks about sb/sth
Lästerung F jibe; (*Gotteslästerung*) blasphemy
lästig ['lɛstɪç] ADJ troublesome, tiresome; **(jdm) ~ werden** to become a nuisance (to sb); (*zum Ärgernis werden*) to get annoying (to sb)
Last- zW: **Lastkahn** M barge; **Lastkraftwagen** M heavy goods vehicle; **Lastschrift** F debiting; (*Eintrag*) debit item; **Lasttier** NT beast of burden; **Lastträger** M porter; **Lastwagen** M lorry (BRIT), truck; **Lastzug** M truck and trailer
Latein [la'taɪn] (**-s**) NT Latin; **mit seinem ~ am Ende sein** (*fig*) to be stumped (*umg*); **Lateinamerika** NT Latin America; **lateinamerikanisch** ADJ Latin-American; **lateinisch** ADJ Latin
latent [la'tɛnt] ADJ latent
Laterne [la'tɛrnə] (**-, -n**) F lantern; (*Straßenlaterne*) lamp, light
Laternenpfahl M lamppost
Latinum [la'ti:nʊm] (**-s**) NT: **kleines/großes ~** ≈ Latin O-/A-level exams (BRIT)
Latrine [la'tri:nə] F latrine
Latsche ['latʃə] (**-, -n**) F dwarf pine
latschen (*umg*) VI (*gehen*) to wander, to go; (*lässig*) to slouch
Latschen ['la:tʃən] (*umg*) M (*Hausschuh*) slipper; (*pej: Schuh*) worn-out shoe
Latte ['latə] (**-, -n**) F lath; (*Sport*) goalpost; (*quer*) crossbar
Lattenzaun M lattice fence
Latz [lats] (**-es, Lätze**) M bib; (*Hosenlatz*) front flap
Lätzchen ['lɛtsçən] NT bib
Latzhose F dungarees *pl*
lau [laʊ] ADJ (*Nacht*) balmy; (*Wasser*) lukewarm; (*fig: Haltung*) half-hearted
Laub [laʊp] (**-(e)s**) NT foliage; **Laubbaum** M deciduous tree
Laube ['laʊbə] (**-, -n**) F arbour (BRIT), arbor (US); (*Gartenhäuschen*) summerhouse
Laub- zW: **Laubfrosch** M tree frog; **Laubsäge** F fretsaw; **Laubwald** M deciduous forest
Lauch [laʊx] (**-(e)s, -e**) M leek
Lauer ['laʊər] F: **auf der ~ sein** *od* **liegen** to lie in wait
lauern VI to lie in wait; (*Gefahr*) to lurk
Lauf [laʊf] (**-(e)s, Läufe**) M run; (*Wettlauf*) race; (*Entwicklung, Astron*) course; (*Gewehrlauf*) barrel; **im Laufe des Gesprächs** during the conversation; **sie ließ ihren Gefühlen freien ~** she gave way to her feelings; **einer Sache** *dat* **ihren ~ lassen** to let sth take its course; **Laufbahn** F career; **eine Laufbahn einschlagen** to embark on a career; **Laufbursche** M errand boy
laufen ['laʊfən] *unreg* VI to run; (*umg: gehen*) to walk; (*Uhr*) to go; (*funktionieren*) to work; (*Elektrogerät: eingeschaltet sein*) to be on; (*gezeigt werden: Film, Stück*) to be on; (*Bewerbung, Antrag*) to be under consideration ▶ VT to run; **es lief mir eiskalt über den Rücken** a chill ran up my spine; **ihm läuft die Nase** he's got a runny nose; **~ lassen** (*Person*) to let go; **die Dinge ~ lassen** to let things slide; **die Sache ist gelaufen** (*umg*) it's in the bag; **das Auto läuft auf meinen Namen** the car is in my name; **Ski/Schlittschuh/Rollschuh** *etc* **~** to ski/skate/rollerskate *etc*
laufend ADJ running; (*Monat, Ausgaben*) current; **auf dem Laufenden sein/halten** to be/keep up to date; **am laufenden Band** (*fig*) continuously; **laufende Nummer** serial number; (*von Konto*) number; **laufende Kosten** running costs *pl*
Läufer ['lɔʏfər] (**-s, -**) M (*Teppich*) rug; (*Sport*) runner; (*Fußball*) half-back; (*Schach*) bishop
Lauferei [laʊfə'raɪ] (*umg*) F running about
Läuferin F (*Sport*) runner
Lauf- zW: **lauffähig** ADJ (*Comput*): **das Programm ist unter Windows lauffähig** the program can be run under Windows; **Lauffeuer** NT: **sich wie ein Lauffeuer verbreiten** to spread like wildfire; **Laufkundschaft** F passing trade; **Laufmasche** F run, ladder (BRIT); **Laufpass** M: **jdm den Laufpass geben** (*umg*) to give sb his/her marching orders; **Laufschritt** M: **im Laufschritt** at a run; **Laufstall** M playpen; **Laufsteg** M catwalk
läuft [lɔʏft] VB *siehe* **laufen**
Lauf- zW: **Laufwerk** NT running gear; (*Comput*) drive; **Laufzeit** F (*von Wechsel, Vertrag*) period of validity; (*von Maschine*) life; **Laufzettel** M circular
Lauge ['laʊgə] (**-, -n**) F soapy water; (*Chem*) alkaline solution
Laune ['laʊnə] (**-, -n**) F mood, humour (BRIT), humor (US); (*Einfall*) caprice; (*schlechte Laune*) temper
launenhaft ADJ capricious, changeable
launisch ADJ moody
Laus [laʊs] (**-, Läuse**) F louse; **ihm ist (wohl) eine ~ über die Leber gelaufen** (*umg*) something's biting him; **Lausbub** M rascal, imp
Lauschangriff M: **~ (gegen)** bugging operation (on)
lauschen ['laʊʃən] VI to listen; (*heimlich*) to eavesdrop
Lauscher(in) (**-s, -**) M(F) eavesdropper
lauschig ['laʊʃɪç] ADJ snug
Lausejunge (*umg*) M little devil; (*wohlwollend*) rascal
lausen ['laʊzən] VT to delouse
lausig ['laʊzɪç] (*umg*) ADJ lousy; (*Kälte*) perishing ▶ ADV awfully
laut [laʊt] ADJ loud ▶ ADV loudly; (*lesen*) aloud ▶ PRÄP (*+gen od dat*) according to
Laut (**-(e)s, -e**) M sound
Laute ['laʊtə] (**-, -n**) F lute
lauten ['laʊtən] VI to say; (*Urteil*) to be
läuten ['lɔʏtən] VT, VI to ring, to sound; **er hat davon (etwas) ~ hören** (*umg*) he has heard something about it

lauter ['laʊtər] ADJ (*Wasser*) clear, pure; (*Wahrheit, Charakter*) honest ▶ ADJ unver (*Freude, Dummheit etc*) sheer ▶ ADV (*nur*) nothing but, only; **Lauterkeit** F purity; (*von Charakter*) honesty, integrity

läutern ['lɔʏtərn] VT to purify

Läuterung F purification

laut- ZW: **lauthals** ADV at the top of one's voice; **lautlos** ADJ noiseless, silent; **lautmalend** ADJ onomatopoeic; **Lautschrift** F phonetics *pl*; **Lautsprecher** M loudspeaker; **Lautsprecheranlage** F: **öffentliche Lautsprecheranlage** public-address *od* PA system; **Lautsprecherwagen** M loudspeaker van; **lautstark** ADJ vociferous; **Lautstärke** F (*Rundf*) volume

lauwarm ['laʊvarm] ADJ (*lit, fig*) lukewarm

Lava ['la:va] (**-, Laven**) F lava

Lavendel [la'vɛndəl] (**-s, -**) M lavender

Lawine [la'vi:nə] F avalanche

Lawinengefahr F danger of avalanches

lax [laks] ADJ lax

Layout, Lay-out ['le:laʊt] (**-s, -s**) NT layout

Lazarett [latsa'rɛt] (**-(e)s, -e**) NT (*Mil*) hospital, infirmary

Ldkrs. ABK = **Landkreis**

leasen ['li:zən] VT to lease

Leasing ['li:zɪŋ] (**-s, -s**) NT (*Comm*) leasing

Lebehoch NT three cheers *pl*

Lebemann (**-(e)s**, *pl* **-männer**) M man about town

leben VT, VI to live

Leben ['le:bən] (**-s, -**) NT life; **am ~ sein/bleiben** to be/stay alive; **ums ~ kommen** to die; **etw ins ~ rufen** to bring sth into being; **seines Lebens nicht mehr sicher sein** to fear for one's life; **etw für sein ~ gern tun** to love doing sth

lebend ADJ living; **lebendes Inventar** livestock

lebendig [le'bɛndɪç] ADJ living, alive; (*lebhaft*) lively; **Lebendigkeit** F liveliness

Lebens- ZW: **Lebensabend** M old age; **Lebensalter** NT age; **Lebensanschauung** F philosophy of life; **Lebensart** F way of life; **lebensbejahend** ADJ positive; **Lebensdauer** F life (span); (*von Maschine*) life; **Lebenserfahrung** F experience of life; **Lebenserwartung** F life expectancy; **lebensfähig** ADJ able to live; **lebensfroh** ADJ full of the joys of life; **Lebensgefahr** F: **Lebensgefahr!** danger!; **in Lebensgefahr** critically *od* dangerously ill; **lebensgefährlich** ADJ dangerous; (*Krankheit, Verletzung*) critical; **Lebensgefährte** M, **Lebensgefährtin** F partner; **Lebensgröße** F: **in Lebensgröße** life-size(d); **Lebenshaltungskosten** PL cost of living *sing*; **Lebensinhalt** M purpose in life; **Lebensjahr** NT year of life; **Lebenskünstler** M master in the art of living; **Lebenslage** F situation in life; **lebenslänglich** ADJ (*Strafe*) for life; **lebenslänglich bekommen** to get life; **Lebenslauf** M curriculum vitae (BRIT), CV (BRIT), resumé (*US*); **lebenslustig** ADJ cheerful, lively; **Lebensmittel** PL food *sing*; **Lebensmittelgeschäft** NT grocer's; **Lebensmittelvergiftung** F food poisoning; **lebensmüde** ADJ tired of life; **Lebenspartnerschaft** F long-term relationship; **eingetragene Lebenspartnerschaft** registered *or* civil (BRIT) partnership; **Lebensqualität** F quality of life; **Lebensraum** M (*Pol*) Lebensraum; (*Biol*) biosphere; **Lebensretter** M lifesaver; **Lebensstandard** M standard of living; **Lebensstellung** F permanent post; **Lebensstil** M life style; **Lebensunterhalt** M livelihood; **Lebensversicherung** F life insurance; **Lebenswandel** M way of life; **Lebensweise** F way of life, habits *pl*; **Lebensweisheit** F maxim; (*Lebenserfahrung*) wisdom; **Lebenswichtig** ADJ vital; **Lebenszeichen** NT sign of life; **Lebenszeit** F lifetime; **Beamter auf Lebenszeit** permanent civil servant

Leber ['le:bər] (**-, -n**) F liver; **frei** *od* **frisch von der ~ weg reden** (*umg*) to speak out frankly; **Leberfleck** M mole; **Leberkäse** M ≈ meat loaf; **Leberpastete** F liver pâté; **Lebertran** M cod-liver oil; **Leberwurst** F liver sausage

Lebewesen NT creature

Lebewohl NT farewell, goodbye

leb- ZW: **lebhaft** ADJ lively, vivacious; **Lebhaftigkeit** F liveliness, vivacity; **Lebkuchen** M gingerbread; **leblos** ADJ lifeless; **Lebtag** M (*fig*): **das werde ich mein Lebtag nicht vergessen** I'll never forget that as long as I live; **Lebzeiten** PL: **zu jds Lebzeiten** (*Leben*) in sb's lifetime

lechzen ['lɛçtsən] VI: **nach etw ~** to long for sth

leck [lɛk] ADJ leaky, leaking; **Leck** (**-(e)s, -e**) NT leak

lecken[1] VI (*Loch haben*) to leak

lecken[2] VT, VI (*schlecken*) to lick

lecker ['lɛkər] ADJ delicious, tasty; **Leckerbissen** M dainty morsel; **Leckermaul** NT: **ein Leckermaul sein** to enjoy one's food

led. ABK = **ledig**

Leder ['le:dər] (**-s, -**) NT leather; (*umg: Fußball*) ball; **Lederhose** F leather trousers *pl*; (*von Tracht*) leather shorts *pl*

ledern ADJ leather

Lederwaren PL leather goods *pl*

ledig ['le:dɪç] ADJ single; **einer Sache** *gen* **~ sein** to be free of sth; **lediglich** ADV merely, solely

leer [le:r] ADJ empty; (*Blick*) vacant; **~ gefegt** (*Straße*) deserted; **~ stehend** empty

Leere (-) F emptiness; **(eine) gähnende ~** a gaping void

leeren VT to empty ▶ VR to (become) empty

Leer- ZW: **Leergewicht** NT unladen weight; **Leergut** NT empties *pl*; **Leerlauf** M (*Aut*) neutral; **Leertaste** F (*Schreibmaschine*) space-bar

Leerung F emptying; (*Post*) collection

legal [le'ga:l] ADJ legal, lawful

legalisieren [legali'zi:rən] VT to legalize

Legalität [legali'tɛ:t] F legality; **(etwas) außerhalb der ~** (*euph*) (slightly) outside the law

Legasthenie [legaste'ni:] F dyslexia
Legastheniker(in) [legas'te:nikər(ɪn)] (**-s, -**) M(F) dyslexic
Legebatterie F laying battery
legen ['le:gən] VT to lay, to put, to place; (*Ei*) to lay ▸ VR to lie down; (*fig*) to subside; **sich ins Bett ~** to go to bed
Legende [le'gɛndə] (**-, -n**) F legend
leger [le'ʒɛ:r] ADJ casual
legieren [le'gi:rən] VT to alloy
Legierung F alloy
Legislative [legɪsla'ti:və] F legislature
Legislaturperiode [legɪsla'tu:rperio:də] F parliamentary (BRIT) *od* congressional (*US*) term
legitim [legi'ti:m] ADJ legitimate
Legitimation [legiti:matsi'o:n] F legitimation
legitimieren [legiti:'mi:rən] VT to legitimate ▸ VR to prove one's identity
Legitimität [legitimi'tɛ:t] F legitimacy
Lehm [le:m] (**-(e)s, -e**) M loam
lehmig ADJ loamy
Lehne ['le:nə] (**-, -n**) F arm; (*Rückenlehne*) back
lehnen VT, VR to lean
Lehnstuhl M armchair
Lehr- ZW: **Lehramt** NT teaching profession; **Lehrbefähigung** F teaching qualification; **Lehrbrief** M indentures *pl*; **Lehrbuch** NT textbook
Lehre ['le:rə] (**-, -n**) F teaching, doctrine; (*beruflich*) apprenticeship; (*moralisch*) lesson; (*Tech*) gauge; **bei jdm in die ~ gehen** to serve one's apprenticeship with sb
lehren VT to teach
Lehrer(in) (**-s, -**) M(F) teacher; **Lehrerausbildung** F teacher training; **Lehrerkollegium** NT teaching staff; **Lehrerzimmer** NT staff room
Lehr- ZW: **Lehrgang** M course; **Lehrgeld** NT: **Lehrgeld für etw zahlen müssen** (*fig*) to pay dearly for sth; **Lehrjahre** PL apprenticeship *sing*; **Lehrkraft** F (*form*) teacher; **Lehrling** M trainee; (*in Handwerksberuf*) apprentice; **Lehrmittel** NT teaching aid; **Lehrplan** M syllabus; **Lehrprobe** F demonstration lesson, crit (*umg*); **lehrreich** ADJ instructive; **Lehrsatz** M proposition; **Lehrstelle** F apprenticeship; **Lehrstuhl** M chair; **Lehrzeit** F apprenticeship
Leib [laɪp] (**-(e)s, -er**) M body; **halt ihn mir vom ~!** keep him away from me!; **etw am eigenen ~(e) spüren** to experience sth for o.s.
leiben ['laɪbən] VI: **wie er leibt und lebt** to a T (*umg*)
Leibes- ZW: **Leibeserziehung** F physical education; **Leibeskräfte** PL: **aus Leibeskräften schreien** *etc* to shout *etc* with all one's might; **Leibesübung** F physical exercise; **Leibesvisitation** F body search
Leib- ZW: **Leibgericht** NT favourite (BRIT) *od* favorite (*US*) meal; **leibhaftig** ADJ personified; (*Teufel*) incarnate; **leiblich** ADJ bodily; (*Vater etc*) natural; **Leibrente** F life annuity; **Leibwache** F bodyguard
Leiche ['laɪçə] (**-, -n**) F corpse; **er geht über Leichen** (*umg*) he'd stick at nothing
Leichen- ZW: **Leichenbeschauer** (**-s, -**) M doctor conducting a post-mortem; **Leichenhalle** F mortuary; **Leichenhemd** NT shroud; **Leichenträger** M bearer; **Leichenwagen** M hearse
Leichnam ['laɪçna:m] (**-(e)s, -e**) M corpse
leicht [laɪçt] ADJ light; (*einfach*) easy ▸ ADV: **~ zerbrechlich** very fragile; **es sich** *dat* **~ machen** to make things easy for o.s.; (*nicht gewissenhaft sein*) to take the easy way out; **~ verletzt** slightly injured; **nichts leichter als das!** nothing (could be) simpler!; *siehe auch* **leichtfallen**; **leichtnehmen**; **Leichtathletik** F athletics *sing*; **leichtfallen** *unreg* VI: **jdm leichtfallen** to be easy for sb; **leichtfertig** ADJ thoughtless; **leichtgläubig** ADJ gullible, credulous; **Leichtgläubigkeit** F gullibility, credulity; **leichthin** ADV lightly
Leichtigkeit F easiness; **mit ~** with ease
leicht- ZW: **leichtlebig** ADJ easy-going; **Leichtmatrose** M ordinary seaman; **Leichtmetall** NT light alloy; **leichtnehmen** *unreg* VT to take lightly; **Leichtsinn** M carelessness; **sträflicher Leichtsinn** criminal negligence; **leichtsinnig** ADJ careless
leid ADJ: **etw ~ haben** *od* **sein** to be tired of sth; *siehe auch* **leidtun**
Leid [laɪt] (**-(e)s**) NT grief, sorrow; **jdm sein ~ klagen** to tell sb one's troubles
leiden ['laɪdən] *unreg* VT to suffer; (*erlauben*) to permit ▸ VI to suffer; **jdn/etw nicht ~ können** not to be able to stand sb/sth; **Leiden** (**-s, -**) NT suffering; (*Krankheit*) complaint
Leidenschaft F passion; **leidenschaftlich** ADJ passionate
Leidens- ZW: **Leidensgenosse** M, **Leidensgenossin** F fellow sufferer; **Leidensgeschichte** F: **die Leidensgeschichte (Christi)** (*Rel*) Christ's Passion
leider ['laɪdər] ADV unfortunately; **ja, ~** yes, I'm afraid so; **~ nicht** I'm afraid not
leidig ['laɪdɪç] ADJ miserable, tiresome
leidlich [laɪtlɪç] ADJ tolerable ▸ ADV tolerably
Leidtragende(r) F(M) bereaved; (*Benachteiligter*) one who suffers
leidtun *unreg* VI: **es tut mir/ihm leid** I am/he is sorry; **er/das tut mir leid** I am sorry for him/about it; **sie kann einem ~** you can't help feeling sorry for her
Leidwesen NT: **zu jds ~** to sb's dismay
Leier ['laɪər] (**-, -n**) F lyre; (*fig*) old story
Leierkasten M barrel organ
leiern VT (*Kurbel*) to turn; (*umg: Gedicht*) to rattle off ▸ VI (*drehen*): **~ an** +*dat* to crank
Leih- ZW: **Leiharbeit** F subcontracted labour; **Leiharbeiter(in)** M(F) subcontracted worker; **Leihbibliothek** F, **Leihbücherei** F lending library
leihen ['laɪən] *unreg* VT to lend; **sich** *dat* **etw ~** to borrow sth

Leih- zW: **Leihgabe** F loan; **Leihgebühr** F hire charge; **Leihhaus** NT pawnshop; **Leihmutter** F surrogate mother; **Leihschein** M pawn ticket; (*in der Bibliothek*) borrowing slip; **Leihunternehmen** NT hire service; (*Arbeitsmarkt*) temp service; **Leihwagen** M hired car (BRIT), rental car (*US*); **leihweise** ADV on loan

Leim [laɪm] (**-(e)s, -e**) M glue; **jdm auf den ~ gehen** to be taken in by sb; **leimen** VT to glue

Leine ['laɪnə] (-, **-n**) F cord; (*für Wäsche*) line; (*Hundeleine*) leash, lead; **~ ziehen** (*umg*) to clear out

leinen ADJ linen

Leinen (**-s, -**) NT linen; (*grob, segeltuchartig*) canvas; (*als Bucheinband*) cloth

Lein- zW: **Leinsamen** M linseed; **Leintuch** NT linen cloth; (*Bettuch*) sheet; **Leinwand** F (*Kunst*) canvas; (*Film*) screen

leise ['laɪzə] ADJ quiet; (*sanft*) soft, gentle; **mit leiser Stimme** in a low voice; **nicht die leiseste Ahnung haben** not to have the slightest (idea)

Leisetreter (*pej, umg*) M pussyfoot(er)

Leiste ['laɪstə] (-, **-n**) F ledge; (*Zierleiste*) strip; (*Anat*) groin

leisten ['laɪstən] VT (*Arbeit*) to do; (*Gesellschaft*) to keep; (*Ersatz*) to supply; (*vollbringen*) to achieve; **sich** *dat* **etw ~** to allow o.s. sth; (*sich gönnen*) to treat o.s. to sth; **sich** *dat* **etw ~ können** to be able to afford sth

Leistenbruch M (*Med*) hernia, rupture

Leistung F performance; (*gute*) achievement; (*eines Motors*) power; (*von Krankenkasse etc*) benefit; (*Zahlung*) payment

Leistungs- zW: **Leistungsabfall** M (*in Bezug auf Qualität*) drop in performance; (*in Bezug auf Quantität*) drop in productivity; **Leistungsbeurteilung** F performance appraisal; **Leistungsdruck** M pressure; **leistungsfähig** ADJ efficient; **Leistungsfähigkeit** F efficiency; **Leistungsgesellschaft** F meritocracy; **Leistungskurs** M (*Sch*) set; **Leistungskürzung** F reduction of benefit; **leistungsorientiert** ADJ performance-orientated; **Leistungsprinzip** NT achievement principle; **Leistungssport** M competitive sport; **Leistungszulage** F productivity bonus

Leitartikel M leader

Leitbild NT model

leiten ['laɪtən] VT to lead; (*Firma*) to manage; (*in eine Richtung*) to direct; (*Elek*) to conduct; **sich von jdm/etw ~ lassen** (*lit, fig*) to (let o.s.) be guided by sb/sth

leitend ADJ leading; (*Gedanke, Idee*) dominant; (*Stellung, Position*) managerial; (*Ingenieur, Beamter*) in charge; (*Phys*) conductive; **leitender Angestellter** executive

Leiter[1] ['laɪtər] (**-s, -**) M leader, head; (*Elek*) conductor

Leiter[2] ['laɪtər] (-, **-n**) F ladder

Leiterin F leader, head

Leiterplatte F (*Comput*) circuit board

Leit- zW: **Leitfaden** M guide; **Leitfähigkeit** F conductivity; **Leitgedanke** M central idea; **Leitmotiv** NT leitmotiv; **Leitplanke** F crash barrier; **Leitspruch** M motto

Leitung F (*Führung*) direction; (*Film, Theat etc*) production; (*von Firma*) management; (*Wasserleitung*) pipe; (*Kabel*) cable; (*Tel*) line; **eine lange ~ haben** to be slow on the uptake; **da ist jemand in der ~** (*umg*) there's somebody else on the line

Leitungs- zW: **Leitungsdraht** M wire; **Leitungsmast** M telegraph pole; **Leitungsrohr** NT pipe; **Leitungswasser** NT tap water

Leitwerk NT (*Aviat*) tail unit

Leitzins M (*Fin*) base rate

Lektion [lɛktsi'o:n] F lesson; **jdm eine ~ erteilen** (*fig*) to teach sb a lesson

Lektor(in) ['lɛktɔr, lɛk'to:rɪn] M(F) (*Univ*) lector; (*Verlag*) editor

Lektüre [lɛk'ty:rə] (-, **-n**) F (*Lesen*) reading; (*Lesestoff*) reading matter

Lende ['lɛndə] (-, **-n**) F loin

Lendenbraten M roast sirloin

Lendenstück NT fillet

lenkbar ['lɛŋkba:r] ADJ (*Fahrzeug*) steerable; (*Kind*) manageable

lenken VT to steer; (*Kind*) to guide; (*Gespräch*) to lead; **~ auf** *+akk* (*Blick, Aufmerksamkeit*) to direct at; (*Verdacht*) to throw on(to); (*auf sich*) to draw onto

Lenker M (*von Fahrrad, Motorrad*) handlebars *pl*

Lenkrad NT steering wheel

Lenkstange F handlebars *pl*

Lenkung F steering; (*Führung*) direction

Lenz [lɛnts] (**-es, -e**) M (*liter*) spring; **sich** *dat* **einen (faulen) ~ machen** (*umg*) to laze about, to swing the lead

Leopard [leo'part] (**-en, -en**) M leopard

Lepra ['le:pra] (-) F leprosy; **Leprakranke(r)** F(M) leper

Lerche ['lɛrçə] (-, **-n**) F lark

lernbegierig ADJ eager to learn

lernbehindert ADJ educationally handicapped (BRIT) *od* handicaped (*US*)

lernen VT, VI to learn; **er lernt bei der Firma Braun** he's training at Braun's

Lernhilfe F educational aid

lesbar ['le:sba:r] ADJ legible

Lesbierin ['lɛsbiərɪn] F lesbian

lesbisch ADJ lesbian

Lese ['le:zə] (-, **-n**) F (*Weinlese*) harvest

Lesebuch NT reading book, reader

lesen *unreg* VT to read; (*ernten*) to gather, to pick ▶ VI to read; **~/schreiben** (*Comput*) to read/write

Leser(in) (**-s, -**) M(F) reader

Leseratte ['le:zəratə] (*umg*) F bookworm

Leser- zW: **Leserbrief** M reader's letter; **„Leserbriefe"** "letters to the editor"; **Leserkreis** M readership; **leserlich** ADJ legible

Lese- zW: **Lesesaal** M reading room; **Lesestoff** M reading material; **Lesezeichen** NT bookmark; **Lesezirkel** M magazine club

Lesotho [le'zo:to] (**-s**) NT Lesotho

Lesung ['le:zʊŋ] F (*Parl*) reading; (*Eccl*) lesson
lethargisch [le'targɪʃ] ADJ (*Med, fig*) lethargic
Lette ['lɛtə] (**-n, -n**) M, **Lettin** F Latvian
lettisch ADJ Latvian
Lettland ['lɛtlant] (**-s**) NT Latvia
Letzt F: **zu guter ~** finally, in the end
letzte(r, s) ['lɛtstə(r, s)] ADJ last; (*neueste*) latest; **der L~ Wille** the last will and testament; **bis zum Letzten** to the utmost; **zum letzten Mal** for the last time; **in letzter Zeit** recently
Letzte(s) NT: **das ist ja das ~!** (*umg*) that really is the limit!
letztens ADV lately
letztere(r, s) ADJ the latter
letztlich ADV in the end
Leuchte ['lɔyçtə] (**-, -n**) F lamp, light; (*umg: Mensch*) genius
leuchten VI to shine, to gleam
Leuchter (**-s, -**) M candlestick
Leucht- ZW: **Leuchtfarbe** F fluorescent colour (BRIT) *od* color (US); **Leuchtfeuer** NT beacon; **Leuchtkäfer** M glow-worm; **Leuchtkugel** F flare; **Leuchtpistole** F flare pistol; **Leuchtrakete** F flare; **Leuchtreklame** F neon sign; **Leuchtröhre** F strip light; **Leuchtturm** M lighthouse; **Leuchtzifferblatt** NT luminous dial
leugnen ['lɔygnən] VT, VI to deny
Leugnung F denial
Leukämie [lɔykɛ'mi:] F leukaemia (BRIT), leukemia (US)
Leukoplast® [lɔyko'plast] (**-(e)s, -e**) NT Elastoplast®
Leumund ['lɔymʊnt] (**-(e)s, -e**) M reputation
Leumundszeugnis NT character reference
Leute ['lɔytə] PL people *pl*; **kleine ~** (*fig*) ordinary people; **etw unter die ~ bringen** (*umg: Gerücht etc*) to spread sth around
Leutnant ['lɔytnant] (**-s, -s** *od* **-e**) M lieutenant
leutselig ['lɔytze:lɪç] ADJ affable; **Leutseligkeit** F affability
Leviten [le'vi:tən] PL: **jdm die ~ lesen** (*umg*) to haul sb over the coals
lexikalisch [lɛksi'ka:lɪʃ] ADJ lexical
Lexikografie [lɛksikogra'fi:] F lexicography
Lexikon ['lɛksikɔn] (**-s, Lexiken** *od* **Lexika**) NT encyclopaedia (BRIT), encyclopedia (US); (*Wörterbuch*) dictionary
lfd. ABK = **laufend**
Libanese [liba'ne:zə] (**-n, -n**) M, **Libanesin** F Lebanese
libanesisch ADJ Lebanese
Libanon ['li:banɔn] (**-s**) M: **der ~** the Lebanon
Libelle [li'bɛlə] (**-, -n**) F dragonfly; (*Tech*) spirit level
liberal [libe'ra:l] ADJ liberal
Liberale(r) F(M) (*Pol*) Liberal
Liberalisierung [liberali'zi:rʊŋ] F liberalization
Liberalismus [libera'lɪsmʊs] M liberalism
Liberia [li'be:ria] (**-s**) NT Liberia
Liberianer(in) [liberi'a:nər(ɪn)] (**-s, -**) M(F) Liberian
liberianisch ADJ Liberian
Libero ['li:bero] (**-s, -s**) M (*Fussball*) sweeper
Libyen ['li:byən] (**-s**) NT Libya
Libyer(in) (**-s, -**) M(F) Libyan
libysch ADJ Libyan
licht ADJ light, bright
Licht [lɪçt] (**-(e)s, -er**) NT light; **~ machen** (*anschalten*) to turn on a light; (*anzünden*) to light a candle *etc*; **mir geht ein ~ auf** it's dawned on me; **jdn hinters ~ führen** (*fig*) to lead sb up the garden path
Licht- ZW: **Lichtbild** NT photograph; (*Dia*) slide; **Lichtblick** M cheering prospect; **lichtempfindlich** ADJ sensitive to light
lichten ['lɪçtən] VT to clear; (*Anker*) to weigh ▸ VR (*Nebel*) to clear; (*Haar*) to thin
lichterloh ['lɪçtər'lo:] ADV: **~ brennen** to blaze
Licht- ZW: **Lichtgeschwindigkeit** F speed of light; **Lichtgriffel** M (*Comput*) light pen; **Lichthupe** F: **die Lichthupe betätigen** to flash one's lights; **Lichtjahr** NT light year; **Lichtmaschine** F dynamo; **Lichtmess** (**-**) F Candlemas; **Lichtpause** F photocopy; (*bei Blaupausverfahren*) blueprint; **Lichtschalter** M light switch; **lichtscheu** ADJ averse to light; (*fig: Gesindel*) shady; **Lichtschutzfaktor** M sun protection factor, SPF
Lichtung F clearing, glade
Lid [li:t] (**-(e)s, -er**) NT eyelid; **Lidschatten** M eyeshadow
lieb [li:p] ADJ dear; **(viele) liebe Grüße, Deine Silvia** love, Silvia; **Liebe Anna, lieber Klaus! ...** Dear Anna and Klaus, ...; **am liebsten lese ich Kriminalromane** best of all I like detective novels; **den lieben langen Tag** (*umg*) all the livelong day; **sich bei jdm ~ Kind machen** (*pej*) to suck up to sb (*umg*); **~ gewinnen** to get fond of; **~ haben** to love; (*weniger stark*) to be (very) fond of
liebäugeln ['li:plɔygəln] VI UNTR: **mit dem Gedanken ~, etw zu tun** to toy with the idea of doing sth
Liebe ['li:bə] (**-, -n**) F love; **liebebedürftig** ADJ: **liebebedürftig sein** to need love
Liebelei F flirtation
lieben ['li:bən] VT to love; (*weniger stark*) to like; **etw liebend gern tun** to love to do sth
liebens- ZW: **liebenswert** ADJ loveable; **liebenswürdig** ADJ kind; **liebenswürdigerweise** ADV kindly; **Liebenswürdigkeit** F kindness
lieber ['li:bər] ADV rather, preferably; **ich gehe ~ nicht** I'd rather not go; **ich trinke ~ Wein als Bier** I prefer wine to beer; **bleib ~ im Bett** you'd better stay in bed
Liebes- ZW: **Liebesbrief** M love letter; **Liebesdienst** M good turn; **Liebeskummer** M: **Liebeskummer haben** to be lovesick; **Liebespaar** NT courting couple, lovers *pl*; **Liebesroman** M romantic novel
liebevoll ADJ loving
lieb- ZW: **Liebhaber(in)** (**-s, -**) M(F) lover; (*Sammler*) collector; **Liebhaberei** F hobby; **liebkosen** VT UNTR to caress; **lieblich** ADJ lovely, charming; (*Duft, Wein*) sweet

Liebling M darling
Lieblings- IN ZW favourite (BRIT), favorite (US)
lieblos ADJ unloving
Liebschaft F love affair
liebste(r, s) ADJ favourite
Liechtenstein ['lɪçtənʃtaɪn] (**-s**) NT Liechtenstein
Lied [li:t] (**-(e)s, -er**) NT song; (*Eccl*) hymn; **davon kann ich ein ~ singen** (*fig*) I could tell you a thing or two about that (*umg*)
Liederbuch NT songbook; (*Rel*) hymn book
liederlich ['li:dərlɪç] ADJ slovenly; (*Lebenswandel*) loose, immoral; **Liederlichkeit** F slovenliness; (*von Lebenswandel*) immorality
lief *etc* [li:f] VB *siehe* **laufen**
Lieferant [li:fə'rant] M supplier
Lieferanteneingang M tradesmen's entrance; (*von Warenhaus etc*) goods entrance
lieferbar ADJ (*vorrätig*) available
Lieferbedingungen PL terms of delivery
Lieferfrist F delivery period
liefern ['li:fərn] VT to deliver; (*versorgen mit*) to supply; (*Beweis*) to produce
Lieferschein M delivery note
Liefertermin M delivery date
Lieferung F delivery; (*Versorgung*) supply
Lieferwagen M (delivery) van, panel truck (US)
Lieferzeit F delivery period; **~ 6 Monate** delivery six months
Liege ['li:gə] (-, **-n**) F bed; (*Campingliege*) camp bed (BRIT), cot (US); **Liegegeld** NT (*Hafen, Flughafen*) demurrage
liegen ['li:gən] *unreg* VI to lie; (*sich befinden*) to be (situated); **mir liegt nichts/viel daran** it doesn't matter to me/it matters a lot to me; **es liegt bei Ihnen, ob …** it rests with you whether …; **Sprachen ~ mir nicht** languages are not my line; **woran liegt es?** what's the cause?; **so, wie die Dinge jetzt ~** as things stand at the moment; **an mir soll es nicht ~, wenn die Sache schiefgeht** it won't be my fault if things go wrong; **~ bleiben** (*Person*) to stay in bed; (*nicht aufstehen*) to stay lying down; (*Ding*) to be left (behind); (*nicht ausgeführt werden*) to be left (undone); **~ lassen** (*vergessen*) to leave behind; **Liegenschaft** F real estate
Liege- ZW: **Liegeplatz** M (*auf Schiff, in Zug etc*) berth; (*Ankerplatz*) moorings *pl*; **Liegesitz** M (*Aut*) reclining seat; **Liegestuhl** M deck chair; **Liegestütz** M (*Sport*) press-up (BRIT), push-up (US); **Liegewagen** M (*Eisenb*) couchette car; **Liegewiese** F lawn (*for sunbathing*)
lieh *etc* [li:] VB *siehe* **leihen**
ließ *etc* [li:s] VB *siehe* **lassen**
liest [li:st] VB *siehe* **lesen**
Lift [lɪft] (**-(e)s, -e** *od* **-s**) M lift
Liga ['li:ga] (-, **Ligen**) F (*Sport*) league
light [laɪt] ADJ (*Cola*) diet; (*fettarm*) low-fat; (*kalorienarm*) low-calorie; (*Zigaretten*) mild
liieren [li'i:rən] VT: **liiert sein** (*Firmen etc*) to be working together; (*ein Verhältnis haben*) to have a relationship
Likör [li'kø:r] (**-s, -e**) M liqueur
lila ['li:la] ADJ *unver* purple; **Lila** (**-s, -s**) NT (*Farbe*) purple
Lilie ['li:liə] F lily
Liliputaner(in) [lilipu'ta:nər(ɪn)] (**-s, -**) M(F) midget
Limit ['lɪmɪt] (**-s, -s** *od* **-e**) NT limit; (*Fin*) ceiling
Limonade [limo'na:də] (-, **-n**) F lemonade
Limousine [limu'zi:nə] (-, **-n**) F saloon (car) (BRIT), sedan (US); (*umg*) limo
lind [lɪnt] ADJ gentle, mild
Linde ['lɪndə] (-, **-n**) F lime tree, linden
lindern ['lɪndərn] VT to alleviate, to soothe
Linderung F alleviation
lindgrün ADJ lime green
Lineal [line'a:l] (**-s, -e**) NT ruler
linear [line'a:r] ADJ linear
Linguist(in) [lɪŋgu'ɪst(ɪn)] M(F) linguist
Linguistik F linguistics *sing*
Linie ['li:niə] F line; **in erster ~** first and foremost; **auf die ~ achten** to watch one's figure; **fahren Sie mit der ~ 2** take the number 2 (bus *etc*)
Linien- ZW: **Linienblatt** NT ruled sheet; **Linienbus** M service bus; **Linienflug** M scheduled flight; **Linienrichter** M (*Sport*) linesman; **linientreu** ADJ loyal to the (party) line
linieren [li'ni:rən], **liniieren** [lini'i:rən] VT to line
Link [lɪŋk] (**-s, -s**) M (*Comput*) link
linke(r, s) ADJ left; **~ Masche** purl
Linke ['lɪŋkə] (-, **-n**) F left side; (*linke Hand*) left hand; (*Pol*) left
Linke(r) F(M) (*Pol*) left-winger, leftie (*pej*)
linkisch ADJ awkward, gauche
links ADV (on the) left, to the left; **~ von mir** on *od* to my left; **~ von der Mitte** left of centre; **jdn ~ liegen lassen** (*fig: umg*) to ignore sb; **das mache ich mit ~** (*umg*) I can do that with my eyes shut; **Linksabbieger** M motorist/vehicle turning left; **Linksaußen** (**-s, -**) M (*Sport*) outside left; **Linkshänder(in)** (**-s, -**) M(F) left-handed person; **Linkskurve** F left-hand bend; **linkslastig** ADJ: **linkslastig sein** to list *od* lean to the left; **linksradikal** ADJ (*Pol*) radically left-wing; **Linksrutsch** M (*Pol*) swing to the left; **Linkssteuerung** F (*Aut*) left-hand drive; **Linksverkehr** M driving on the left
Linse ['lɪnzə] (-, **-n**) F lentil; (*optisch*) lens
linsen (*umg*) VI to peek
Lippe ['lɪpə] (-, **-n**) F lip
Lippenbekenntnis NT lip service
Lippenstift M lipstick
liquid [lik'vi:t], **liquide** [lik'vi:də] ADJ (*Firma*) solvent
Liquidation [likvidatsi'o:n] F liquidation
Liquidationswert M break-up value
Liquidator [likvi'da:tɔr] M liquidator
liquidieren [likvi'di:rən] VT to liquidate
Liquidität [likvidi'tɛ:t] F liquidity
lispeln ['lɪspəln] VI to lisp
Lissabon ['lɪsabɔn] NT Lisbon
List [lɪst] (-, **-en**) F cunning; (*Plan*) trick, ruse; **mit ~ und Tücke** (*umg*) with a lot of coaxing

Liste ['lɪstə] (-, **-n**) F list
Listenplatz M (*Pol*) place on the party list
Listenpreis M list price
listig ADJ cunning, sly
Litanei [lita'naɪ] F litany
Litauen ['li:taʊən] (**-s**) NT Lithuania
Litauer(in) (**-s**, -) M(F) Lithuanian
litauisch ADJ Lithuanian
Liter ['li:tər] (**-s**, -) M OD NT litre (BRIT), liter (*US*)
literarisch [lɪte'ra:rɪʃ] ADJ literary
Literatur [lɪtera'tu:r] F literature; **Literaturpreis** M award *od* prize for literature; **Literaturwissenschaft** F literary studies *pl*
literweise ['li:tərvaɪzə] ADV (*lit*) by the litre (BRIT) *od* liter (*US*); (*fig*) by the gallon
Litfaßsäule ['lɪtfaszɔʏlə] F advertising (BRIT) *od* advertizing (*US*) pillar
Lithografie [litogra'fi:] F lithography
Litschi ['lɪtʃi] (-, **-s**) F lychee, litchi
litt *etc* [lɪt] VB *siehe* **leiden**
Liturgie [litʊr'gi:] F liturgy
liturgisch [li'tʊrgɪʃ] ADJ liturgical
Litze ['lɪtsə] (-, **-n**) F braid; (*Elek*) flex
live [laɪf] ADJ, ADV (*Rundf, TV*) live
Livree [li'vre:] (-, **-n**) F livery
Lizenz [li'tsɛnts] F licence (BRIT), license (*US*); **Lizenzausgabe** F licensed edition; **Lizenzgebühr** F licence fee; (*im Verlagswesen*) royalty
Lkw, LKW (**-(s)**, **-(s)**) M ABK = **Lastkraftwagen**
Lkw-Maut, LKW-Maut F toll for trucks
l. M. ABK (= *laufenden Monats*) inst.
Lob [lo:p] (**-(e)s**) NT praise
Lobby ['lɔbi] (-, **-s**) F lobby
loben ['lo:bən] VT to praise; **das lob ich mir** that's what I like (to see/hear *etc*)
lobenswert ADJ praiseworthy
löblich ['lø:plɪç] ADJ praiseworthy, laudable
Loblied NT: **ein ~ auf jdn/etw singen** to sing sb's/sth's praises
Lobrede F eulogy
Loch [lɔx] (**-(e)s, Löcher**) NT hole; **lochen** VT to punch holes in; **Locher** (**-s**, -) M punch
löcherig ['lœçərɪç] ADJ full of holes
löchern (*umg*) VT: **jdn ~** to pester sb with questions
Loch- zW: **Lochkarte** F punch card; **Lochstreifen** M punch tape; **Lochzange** F punch
Locke ['lɔkə] (-, **-n**) F lock, curl
locken VT to entice; (*Haare*) to curl
lockend ADJ tempting
Lockenwickler (**-s**, -) M curler
locker ['lɔkər] ADJ loose; (*Kuchen, Schaum*) light; (*Haltung*) relaxed; (*Person*) easy-going; **lockerlassen** *unreg* VI: **nicht lockerlassen** not to let up
lockern VT to loosen ▸ VR (*Atmosphäre*) to get more relaxed
Lockerungsübung F loosening-up exercise; (*zum Warmwerden*) limbering-up exercise
lockig ['lɔkɪç] ADJ curly
Lockmittel NT lure
Lockruf M call
Lockung F enticement
Lockvogel M decoy, bait; **Lockvogelangebot** NT (*Comm*) loss leader
Lodenmantel ['lo:dənmantəl] M thick woollen coat
lodern ['lo:dərn] VI to blaze
Löffel ['lœfəl] (**-s**, -) M spoon
löffeln VT to spoon
löffelweise ADV by the spoonful
log *etc* [lo:k] VB *siehe* **lügen**
Logarithmentafel [loga'rɪtməntaːfəl] F log(arithm) tables *pl*
Logarithmus [loga'rɪtmʊs] M logarithm
Loge ['lo:ʒə] (-, **-n**) F (*Theat*) box; (*Freimaurerloge*) (masonic) lodge; (*Pförtnerloge*) office
logieren [lo'ʒi:rən] VI to lodge, to stay
Logik ['lo:gɪk] F logic
Logis [lo'ʒi:] (-, -) NT: **Kost und ~** board and lodging
logisch ['lo:gɪʃ] ADJ logical; (*umg: selbstverständlich*): **gehst du auch hin? — ~** are you going too? — of course
logo ['logo] (*umg*) INTERJ obvious!
Logopäde [logo'pɛ:də] (**-n**, **-n**) M speech therapist
Logopädin [logo'pɛ:dɪn] F speech therapist
Lohn [lo:n] (**-(e)s, Löhne**) M reward; (*Arbeitslohn*) pay, wages *pl*; **Lohnabrechnung** F wages slip; **Lohnausfall** M loss of earnings; **Lohnbüro** NT wages office; **Lohndiktat** NT wage dictate; **Lohndumping** NT wage dumping; **Lohnempfänger** M wage earner
lohnen ['lo:nən] VT (*liter*): **jdm etw ~** to reward sb for sth ▸ VR UNPERS to be worth it
lohnend ADJ worthwhile
Lohn- zW: **Lohnerhöhung** F wage increase, pay rise; **Lohnforderung** F wage claim; **Lohnfortzahlung** F continued payment of wages; **Lohnfortzahlungsgesetz** NT *law on continued payment of wages*; **Lohngefälle** NT wage differential; **Lohnkosten** PL labour (BRIT) *od* labor (*US*) costs; **Lohnpolitik** F wages policy; **Lohnrunde** F pay round; **Lohnsteuer** F income tax; **Lohnsteuerjahresausgleich** M income tax return; **Lohnsteuerkarte** F (income) tax card; **Lohnstopp** M pay freeze; **Lohnstreifen** M pay slip; **Lohntüte** F pay packet
Lok [lɔk] (-, **-s**) F ABK (= *Lokomotive*) loco (*umg*)
lokal [lo'ka:l] ADJ local
Lokal (**-(e)s, -e**) NT pub(lic house) (BRIT), bar
Lokalblatt (*umg*) NT local paper
lokalisieren [loka:li'zi:rən] VT to localize
Lokalisierung F localization
Lokalität [lokali'tɛ:t] F locality; (*Raum*) premises *pl*
Lokal- zW: **Lokalpresse** F local press; **Lokalteil** M (*Zeitung*) local section; **Lokaltermin** M (*Jur*) visit to the scene of the crime
Lokomotive [lokomo'ti:və] (-, **-n**) F locomotive
Lokomotivführer M engine driver (BRIT), engineer (*US*)
lol ABK (*Internet, Tel*) lol, laugh out loud

L

Lombardei [lɔmbar'daɪ] F Lombardy
London ['lɔndɔn] (**-s**) NT London
Londoner ADJ *attrib* London
Londoner(in) (**-s, -**) M(F) Londoner
Lorbeer ['lɔrbe:r] (**-s, -en**) M (*lit, fig*) laurel; **Lorbeerblatt** NT (*Koch*) bay leaf
Lore ['lo:rə] (**-, -n**) F (*Min*) truck
los ADJ loose ▸ ADV: **~!** go on!; **etw ~ sein** to be rid of sth; **was ist ~?** what's the matter?; **dort ist nichts/viel ~** there's nothing/a lot going on there; **ich bin mein ganzes Geld ~** (*umg*) I'm cleaned out; **irgendwas ist mit ihm ~** there's something wrong with him; **wir wollen früh ~** we want to be off early; **nichts wie ~!** let's get going
Los [lo:s] (**-es, -e**) NT (*Schicksal*) lot, fate; (*in Lotterie*) lottery ticket; **das große ~ ziehen** (*lit, fig*) to hit the jackpot; **etw durch das ~ entscheiden** to decide sth by drawing lots
losbinden *unreg* VT to untie
losbrechen *unreg* VI (*Sturm, Gewitter*) to break
Löschblatt ['lœʃblat] NT sheet of blotting paper
löschen ['lœʃən] VT (*Feuer, Licht*) to put out, to extinguish; (*Durst*) to quench; (*Comm*) to cancel; (*Tonband*) to erase; (*Fracht*) to unload; (*Comput*) to delete; (*Tinte*) to blot ▸ VI (*Feuerwehr*) to put out a fire; (*Papier*) to blot
Lösch- zW: **Löschfahrzeug** NT fire engine; **Löschgerät** NT fire extinguisher; **Löschpapier** NT blotting paper; **Löschtaste** F (*Comput*) delete key
Löschung F extinguishing; (*Comm*) cancellation; (*Fracht*) unloading
lose ['lo:zə] ADJ loose
Lösegeld NT ransom
losen ['lo:zən] VI to draw lots
lösen ['lø:zən] VT to loosen; (*Handbremse*) to release; (*Husten, Krampf*) to ease; (*Rätsel etc*) to solve; (*Verlobung*) to call off; (*Chem*) to dissolve; (*Partnerschaft*) to break up; (*Fahrkarte*) to buy ▸ VR (*aufgehen*) to come loose; (*Schuss*) to go off; (*Zucker etc*) to dissolve; (*Problem, Schwierigkeit*) to (re)solve itself
los- zW: **losfahren** *unreg* VI to leave; **losgehen** *unreg* VI to set out; (*anfangen*) to start; (*Bombe*) to go off; **jetzt gehts los!** here we go!; **nach hinten losgehen** (*umg*) to backfire; **auf jdn losgehen** to go for sb; **loskaufen** VT (*Gefangene, Geiseln*) to pay ransom for; **loskommen** *unreg* VI (*sich befreien*) to free o.s.; **von etw loskommen** to get away from sth; **loslassen** *unreg* VT (*Seil etc*) to let go of; **der Gedanke lässt mich nicht mehr los** the thought haunts me; **loslaufen** *unreg* VI to run off; **loslegen** (*umg*) VI: **nun leg mal los und erzähl(e) ...** now come on and tell me/us ...
löslich ['lø:slɪç] ADJ soluble; **Löslichkeit** F solubility
loslösen VT to free ▸ VR: **sich (von etw) ~** to detach o.s. (from sth)
losmachen VT to loosen; (*Boot*) to unmoor ▸ VR to get free
Losnummer F ticket number
los- zW: **lossagen** VR: **sich von jdm/etw lossagen** to renounce sb/sth; **losschießen** *unreg* VI: **schieß los!** (*fig: umg*) fire away!; **losschrauben** VT to unscrew; **lossprechen** *unreg* VT to absolve; **losstürzen** VI: **auf jdn/etw losstürzen** to pounce on sb/sth
Losung ['lo:zʊŋ] F watchword, slogan
Lösung ['lø:zʊŋ] F (*Lockermachen*) loosening; (*eines Rätsels, Chem*) solution
Lösungsmittel NT solvent
loswerden *unreg* VT to get rid of
losziehen *unreg* VI (*sich aufmachen*) to set out; **gegen jdn ~** (*fig*) to run sb down
Lot [lo:t] (**-(e)s, -e**) NT plumbline; (*Math*) perpendicular; **im ~** vertical; (*fig*) on an even keel; **die Sache ist wieder im ~** things have been straightened out; **loten** VT to plumb, to sound
löten ['lø:tən] VT to solder
Lothringen ['lo:trɪŋən] (**-s**) NT Lorraine
Lötkolben M soldering iron
Lotse ['lo:tsə] (**-n, -n**) M pilot; (*Aviat*) air traffic controller
lotsen VT to pilot; (*umg*) to lure
Lotterie [lɔtə'ri:] F lottery
Lotterleben ['lɔtərle:bən] (*umg*) NT dissolute life
Lotto ['lɔto] (**-s, -s**) NT ≈ National Lottery
Lottozahlen PL winning Lotto numbers *pl*
Löwe ['lø:və] (**-n, -n**) M lion; (*Astrol*) Leo
Löwen- zW: **Löwenanteil** M lion's share; **Löwenmaul** NT, **Löwenmäulchen** NT antirrhinum, snapdragon; **Löwenzahn** M dandelion
Löwin ['lø:vɪn] F lioness
loyal [loa'ja:l] ADJ loyal
Loyalität [loajali'tɛ:t] F loyalty
LP (**-, -s**) F ABK (= *Langspielplatte*) LP
LSD (**-(s)**) NT ABK (= *Lysergsäurediäthylamid*) LSD
lt. ABK = **laut**
Luchs [lʊks] (**-es, -e**) M lynx
Lücke ['lʏkə] (**-, -n**) F gap; (*Gesetzeslücke*) loophole; (*in Versorgung*) break
Lücken- zW: **Lückenbüßer** (**-s, -**) M stopgap; **lückenhaft** ADJ full of gaps; (*Versorgung*) deficient; **lückenlos** ADJ complete
lud *etc* [lu:t] VB *siehe* **laden**
Luder ['lu:dər] (**-s, -**) (*pej*) NT (*Frau*) hussy; (*bedauernswert*) poor wretch
Luft [lʊft] (**-, Lüfte**) F air; (*Atem*) breath; **die ~ anhalten** (*lit*) to hold one's breath; **seinem Herzen ~ machen** to get everything off one's chest; **in der ~ liegen** to be in the air; **dicke ~** (*umg*) a bad atmosphere; **(frische) ~ schnappen** (*umg*) to get some fresh air; **in die ~ fliegen** (*umg*) to explode; **diese Behauptung ist aus der ~ gegriffen** this statement is (a) pure invention; **die ~ ist rein** (*umg*) the coast is clear; **jdn an die (frische) ~ setzen** (*umg*) to show sb the door; **er ist ~ für mich** I'm not speaking to him; **jdn wie ~ behandeln** to ignore sb; **Luftangriff** M air raid; **Luftaufnahme** F aerial photo; **Luftballon** M

balloon; **Luftblase** F air bubble; **Luftbrücke** F airlift; **luftdicht** ADJ airtight; **Luftdruck** M atmospheric pressure; **luftdurchlässig** ADJ pervious to air

lüften ['lʏftən] VT to air; (*Hut*) to lift, to raise; (*Geheimnis*) to reveal ▶ VI to let some air in

Luft- zW: **Luftfahrt** F aviation; **Luftfeuchtigkeit** F humidity; **Luftfracht** F air cargo; **luftgekühlt** ADJ air-cooled; **Luftgewehr** NT air rifle

luftig ADJ (*Ort*) breezy; (*Raum*) airy; (*Kleider*) summery

Luft- zW: **Luftkissenboot** NT, **Luftkissenfahrzeug** NT hovercraft; **Luftkrieg** M war in the air, aerial warfare; **Luftkurort** M health resort; **luftleer** ADJ: **luftleerer Raum** vacuum; **Luftlinie** F: **in der Luftlinie** as the crow flies; **Luftloch** NT air hole; (*Aviat*) air pocket; **Luftmatratze** F Lilo® (BRIT), air mattress; **Luftpirat** M hijacker; **Luftpost** F airmail; **Luftpumpe** F (*für Fahrrad*) (bicycle) pump; **Luftraum** M air space; **Luftröhre** F (*Anat*) windpipe; **Luftschlange** F streamer; **Luftschloss** NT (*fig*) castle in the air; **Luftschutz** M anti-aircraft defence (BRIT) *od* defense (US); **Luftschutzbunker** M, **Luftschutzkeller** M air-raid shelter; **Luftsprung** M (*fig*): **einen Luftsprung machen** to jump for joy

Lüftung ['lʏftʊŋ] F ventilation

Luft- zW: **Luftveränderung** F change of air; **Luftverkehr** M air traffic; **Luftverschmutzung** F air pollution; **Luftwaffe** F air force; **Luftweg** M: **etw auf dem Luftweg befördern** to transport sth by air; **Luftzufuhr** F air supply; **Luftzug** M draught (BRIT), draft (US)

Lüge ['ly:gə] (-, **-n**) F lie; **jdn/etw Lügen strafen** to give the lie to sb/sth

lügen ['ly:gən] *unreg* VI to lie; **wie gedruckt ~** (*umg*) to lie like mad

Lügendetektor ['ly:gəndetɛktɔr] M lie detector

Lügner(in) (**-s, -**) M(F) liar

Luke ['lu:kə] (-, **-n**) F hatch; (*Dachluke*) skylight

lukrativ [lukra'ti:f] ADJ lucrative

Lümmel ['lʏməl] (**-s, -**) M lout

lümmeln VR to lounge (about)

Lump [lʊmp] (**-en, -en**) M scamp, rascal

lumpen ['lʊmpən] VT: **sich nicht ~ lassen** not to be mean

Lumpen (**-s, -**) M rag

Lumpensammler M rag and bone man

lumpig ['lʊmpɪç] ADJ shabby; **lumpige 10 Euro** (*umg*) 10 measly euros

Lüneburger Heide ['ly:nəbʊrgər 'haɪdə] F Lüneburg Heath

Lunge ['lʊŋə] (-, **-n**) F lung

Lungen- zW: **Lungenentzündung** F pneumonia; **lungenkrank** ADJ suffering from a lung disease; **Lungenkrankheit** F lung disease

lungern ['lʊŋərn] VI to hang about

Lunte ['lʊntə] (-, **-n**) F fuse; **~ riechen** to smell a rat

Lupe ['lu:pə] (-, **-n**) F magnifying glass; **unter die ~ nehmen** (*fig*) to scrutinize

lupenrein ADJ (*lit: Edelstein*) flawless

Lupine [lu'pi:nə] F lupin

Lurch [lʊrç] (**-(e)s, -e**) M amphibian

Lust [lʊst] (-, **Lüste**) F joy, delight; (*Neigung*) desire; (*sexuell*) lust (*pej*); **~ haben zu** *od* **auf etw** *akk*/**etw zu tun** to feel like sth/doing sth; **hast du ~?** how about it?; **er hat die ~ daran verloren** he has lost all interest in it; **je nach ~ und Laune** just depending on how I *od* you *etc* feel; **lustbetont** ADJ pleasure-orientated

lüstern ['lʏstərn] ADJ lustful, lecherous

Lustgefühl NT pleasurable feeling

Lustgewinn M pleasure

lustig ['lʊstɪç] ADJ (*komisch*) amusing, funny; (*fröhlich*) cheerful; **sich über jdn/etw ~ machen** to make fun of sb/sth

Lüstling M lecher

Lust- zW: **lustlos** ADJ unenthusiastic; **Lustmord** M sex(ual) murder; **Lustprinzip** NT (*Psych*) pleasure principle; **Lustspiel** NT comedy; **lustwandeln** VI to stroll about

luth. ABK = **lutherisch**

Lutheraner(in) [lʊtə'ra:nər(ɪn)] M(F) Lutheran

lutherisch ['lʊtərɪʃ] ADJ Lutheran

lutschen ['lʊtʃən] VT, VI to suck; **am Daumen ~** to suck one's thumb

Lutscher (**-s, -**) M lollipop

Luxemburg ['lʊksəmbʊrk] (**-s**) NT Luxembourg

Luxemburger(in) ['lʊksəmbʊrgər(ɪn)] (**-s, -**) M(F) citizen of Luxembourg, Luxembourger

luxemburgisch ADJ Luxembourgian

luxuriös [lʊksuri'ø:s] ADJ luxurious

Luxus ['lʊksʊs] (-) M luxury; **Luxusartikel** PL luxury goods *pl*; **Luxusausführung** F de luxe model; **Luxusdampfer** M luxury cruise ship; **Luxushotel** NT luxury hotel; **Luxussteuer** F tax on luxuries

LVA (-) F ABK (= *Landesversicherungsanstalt*) *county insurance company*

LW ABK (= *Langwelle*) LW

Lycra ['ly:kra] (**-(s)**) *no pl* NT Lycra®

Lymphe ['lʏmfə] (-, **-n**) F lymph

Lymphknoten M lymph(atic) gland

lynchen ['lʏnçən] VT to lynch

Lynchjustiz F lynch law

Lyrik ['ly:rɪk] F lyric poetry; **Lyriker(in)** (**-s, -**) M(F) lyric poet

lyrisch ['ly:rɪʃ] ADJ lyrical

Mm

M, m[1] [ɛm] NT M, m; **M wie Martha** ≈ M for Mary, ≈ M for Mike (*US*)
m[2] ABK (= *Meter*) m; (= *männlich*) m.
M. ABK = **Monat**
MA. ABK = **Mittelalter**
Maat [maːt] (**-s, -e** *od* **-en**) M (*Naut*) (ship's) mate
Machart F make
machbar ADJ feasible
Machbarkeitsstudie F feasibility study
Mache (-) (*umg*) F show, sham; **jdn in der ~ haben** to be having a go at sb

SCHLÜSSELWORT

machen ['maxən] VT **1** to do; **was machst du da?** what are you doing there?; **das ist nicht zu machen** that can't be done; **was machen Sie (beruflich)?** what do you do for a living?; **mach, dass du hier verschwindest!** (you just) get out of here!; **mit mir kann mans ja machen!** (*umg*) the things I put up with!; **das lässt er nicht mit sich machen** he won't stand for that; **eine Prüfung machen** to take an exam
2 (*herstellen*) to make; **das Radio leiser machen** to turn the radio down; **aus Holz gemacht** made of wood; **das Essen machen** to get the meal; **Schluss machen** to finish (off)
3 (*verursachen: bewirken*) to make; **jdm Angst machen** to make sb afraid; **das macht die Kälte** it's the cold that does that
4 (*ausmachen*) to matter; **das macht nichts** that doesn't matter; **die Kälte macht mir nichts** I don't mind the cold
5 (*kosten, ergeben*) to be; **3 und 5 macht 8** 3 and 5 is *od* are 8; **was** *od* **wie viel macht das?** how much does that come to?
6: **was macht die Arbeit?** how's the work going?; **was macht dein Bruder?** how is your brother doing?; **das Auto machen lassen** to have the car done; **machs gut!** take care!; (*viel Glück*) good luck!
▶ VI: **mach schnell!** hurry up!; **mach schon!** come on!; **jetzt macht sie auf große Dame** (*umg*) she's playing the lady now; **lass mich mal machen** (*umg*) let me do it; (*ich bringe das in Ordnung*) I'll deal with it; **groß/klein machen** (*umg: Notdurft*) to do a big/little job; **sich** *dat* **in die Hose machen** to wet o.s.; **ins Bett machen** to wet one's bed; **das macht müde** it makes you tired; **in etw** *dat* **machen** to be *od* deal in sth
▶ VR to come along (nicely); **sich an etw** *akk* **machen** to set about sth; **sich verständlich machen** to make o.s. understood; **sich** *dat* **viel aus jdm/etw machen** to like sb/sth; **mach dir nichts daraus** don't let it bother you; **sich auf den Weg machen** to get going; **sich an etw** *akk* **machen** to set about sth

Machenschaften PL wheelings and dealings *pl*
Macher (**-s, -**) (*umg*) M man of action
Macho (**-s, -s**) (*umg*) M macho type
Macho ['matʃo] (*umg*) ADJ macho
Macht [maxt] (**-, Mächte**) F power; **mit aller ~** with all one's might; **an der ~ sein** to be in power; **alles in unserer ~ Stehende** everything in our power; **Machtergreifung** F seizure of power; **Machthaber** (**-s, -**) M ruler
mächtig ['mɛçtɪç] ADJ powerful, mighty; (*umg: ungeheuer*) enormous
Macht- ZW: **machtlos** ADJ powerless; **Machtprobe** F trial of strength; **Machtstellung** F position of power; **Machtwort** NT: **ein Machtwort sprechen** to lay down the law
Machwerk NT work; (*schlechte Arbeit*) botched job
Macke ['makə] (**-, -n**) (*umg*) F (*Tick, Knall*) quirk; (*Fehler*) fault
Macker (**-s, -**) (*umg*) M fellow, guy
MAD (**-**) M ABK (= *Militärischer Abschirmdienst*) ≈ MI5 (BRIT), ≈ CIA (*US*)
Madagaskar [mada'gaskar] (**-s**) NT Madagascar
Mädchen ['mɛːtçən] NT girl; **ein ~ für alles** (*umg*) a dogsbody; (*im Büro etc*) a girl Friday; **mädchenhaft** ADJ girlish; **Mädchenname** M maiden name
Made ['maːdə] (**-, -n**) F maggot
Madeira[1] [ma'deːra] (**-s**) NT (*Geog*) Madeira
Madeira[2] (**-s, -s**) M (*Wein*) Madeira
Mädel ['mɛːdl] (**-s, -(s)**) NT (*Dialekt*) lass, girl
madig ['maːdɪç] ADJ maggoty; **madigmachen** VT: **jdm etw madigmachen** to spoil sth for sb
Madrid [ma'drɪt] (**-s**) NT Madrid
mag [maːk] VB *siehe* **mögen**
Mag. ABK = **Magister**

Magazin [maga'tsi:n] (**-s, -e**) NT (*Zeitschrift, am Gewehr*) magazine; (*Lager*) storeroom; (*Bibliotheksmagazin*) stockroom
Magd [ma:kt] (-, **Mägde**) F maid(servant)
Magen ['ma:gən] (**-s, -** *od* **Mägen**) M stomach; **jdm auf den ~ schlagen** (*umg*) to upset sb's stomach; (*fig*) to upset sb; **sich** *dat* **den ~ verderben** to upset one's stomach
Magenband ['ma:gənbant] (**--(e)s, - -bänder**) NT gastric band; **Magenbeschwerden** PL stomach trouble *sing*; **Magenbitter** M bitters *pl*; **Magengeschwür** NT stomach ulcer; **Magenschmerzen** PL stomach-ache *sing*; **Magenverstimmung** F stomach upset
mager ['ma:gər] ADJ lean; (*dünn*) thin; (*Käse, Joghurt*) low-fat; **Magerkeit** F leanness; (*Dünnheit*) thinness; **Magermilch** F skimmed milk; **Magerquark** M low-fat soft cheese; **Magersucht** F (*Med*) anorexia; **magersüchtig** ADJ anorexic
Magie [ma'gi:] F magic
Magier ['ma:giər] (**-s, -**) M magician
magisch ['ma:gɪʃ] ADJ magical
Magister [ma'gɪstər] (**-s, -**) M (*Univ*) M.A., Master of Arts
Magistrat [magɪs'tra:t] (**-(e)s, -e**) M municipal authorities *pl*
Magnat [ma'gna:t] (**-en, -en**) M magnate
Magnet [ma'gne:t] (**-s** *od* **-en, -en**) M magnet; **Magnetbahn** F magnetic railway; **Magnetband** NT (*Comput*) magnetic tape; **magnetisch** ADJ magnetic
magnetisieren [magneti'zi:rən] VT to magnetize
Magnetnadel F magnetic needle
Magnettafel F magnetic board
Mahagoni [maha'go:ni] (**-s**) NT mahogany
Mähdrescher (**-s, -**) M combine (harvester)
mähen ['mɛ:ən] VT, VI to mow
Mahl [ma:l] (**-(e)s, -e**) NT meal
mahlen *unreg* VT to grind
Mahlstein M grindstone
Mahlzeit F meal ▸ INTERJ enjoy your meal!
Mahnbrief M reminder
Mähne ['mɛ:nə] (**-, -n**) F mane
mahnen ['ma:nən] VT to remind; (*warnend*) to warn; (*wegen Schuld*) to demand payment from; **jdn zur Eile/Geduld** *etc* **~** (*auffordern*) to urge sb to hurry/be patient *etc*
Mahn- ZW: **Mahngebühr** F reminder fee; **Mahnmal** NT memorial; **Mahnschreiben** NT reminder
Mahnung F admonition, warning; (*Mahnbrief*) reminder
Mähre ['mɛ:rə] (**-, -n**) F mare
Mähren ['mɛ:rən] (**-s**) NT Moravia
Mai [maɪ] (**-(e)s, -e**) (*pl selten*) M May; *siehe auch* **September**; **Maibaum** M maypole; **Maibowle** F white wine punch (*flavoured with woodruff*); **Maiglöckchen** NT lily of the valley; **Maikäfer** M cockchafer
Mail [me:l] (**-, -s**) F (*Comput*) email
Mailand ['maɪlant] (**-s**) NT Milan
mailen ['me:lən] VI, VT to email
Main [maɪn] (**-(e)s**) M (*Fluss*) Main
Mais [maɪs] (**-es, -e**) M maize, corn (*US*); **Maiskolben** M corncob
Majestät [majɛs'tɛ:t] F majesty
majestätisch ADJ majestic
Majestätsbeleidigung F lese-majesty
Majonäse [majɔ'nɛ:zə] (**-, -n**) F mayonnaise
Major [ma'jo:r] (**-s, -e**) M (*Mil*) major; (*Aviat*) squadron leader
Majoran [majo'ra:n] (**-s, -e**) M marjoram
makaber [ma'ka:bər] ADJ macabre
Makedonien [make'do:niən] (**-s**) NT Macedonia
makedonisch ADJ Macedonian
Makel ['ma:kəl] (**-s, -**) M blemish; (*moralisch*) stain; **ohne ~** flawless; **makellos** ADJ immaculate, spotless
mäkeln ['mɛ:kəln] VI to find fault
Make-up [me:k'lap] (**-s, -s**) NT make-up; (*flüssig*) foundation
Makkaroni [maka'ro:ni] PL macaroni *sing*
Makler ['ma:klər] (**-s, -**) M broker; (*Grundstücksmakler*) estate agent (BRIT), realtor (*US*); **Maklergebühr** F broker's commission, brokerage
Makrele [ma'kre:lə] (**-, -n**) F mackerel
Makro- IN ZW macro-
Makrone [ma'kro:nə] (**-, -n**) F macaroon
Makroökonomie F macroeconomics *sing*
mal ADV times
Mal [ma:l] (**-(e)s, -e**) NT (*Markierung*) mark; (*Zeitpunkt*) time; **ein für alle ~** once and for all; **mit einem ~(e)** all of a sudden; **das erste ~** the first time; **jedes ~** every time, each time; **zum letzten ~** for the last time; **ein paar ~** a few times
-mal SUFF -times
Malaie [ma'laɪə] (**-n, -n**) M, **Malaiin** F Malay
malaiisch ADJ Malayan
Malawi [ma'la:vi] (**-s**) NT Malawi
Malaysia [ma'laɪzia] (**-s**) NT Malaysia
Malaysier(in) (**-s, -**) M(F) Malaysian
malaysisch ADJ Malaysian
Malediven [male'di:vən] PL: **die ~** the Maldive Islands
malen VT, VI to paint
Maler (**-s, -**) M painter
Malerei [ma:lə'raɪ] F painting
malerisch ADJ picturesque
Malkasten M paintbox
Mallorca [ma'jɔrka, ma'lɔrka] (**-s**) NT Majorca
Mallorquiner(in) [majɔr'ki:nər(ɪn), malɔr'ki:nər(ɪn)] (**-s, -**) M(F) Majorcan
mallorquinisch ADJ Majorcan
malnehmen *unreg* VT, VI to multiply
Malta ['malta] (**-s**) NT Malta
Malteser(in) [mal'te:zər(ɪn)] (**-s, -**) M(F) Maltese
Malteser-Hilfsdienst M ≈ St. John's Ambulance Brigade (BRIT)
maltesisch ADJ Maltese
malträtieren [maltrɛ'ti:rən] VT to ill-treat, to maltreat
Malware ['mælwɛ:ər] F (*Comput*) malware

m

Malz [malts] (**-es**) NT malt; **Malzbonbon** M OD NT cough drop; **Malzkaffee** M *coffee substitute made from malt barley*
Mama ['mama:] (-, **-s**) (*umg*) F mum(my) (BRIT), mom(my) (US)
Mami ['mami] (-, **-s**) F = **Mama**
Mammografie [mamɔgra'fi:] F (*Med*) mammography
Mammut ['mamʊt] (**-s**, **-e** *od* **-s**) NT mammoth ▶ IN ZW mammoth, giant; **Mammutanlagen** PL (*Industrie*) mammoth plants
mampfen ['mampfən] (*umg*) VT, VI to munch, to chomp
man [man] PRON one, you, people *pl*; **~ hat mir gesagt ...** I was told ...; **wie schreibt ~ das?** how do you spell that?
managen ['mɛnɪdʒən] VT to manage; **ich manage das schon!** (*umg*) I'll fix it somehow!
Manager(in) (**-s**, **-**) M(F) manager
manch [manç] PRON: **~ ein(e) ...** many a ...; **~ eine(r)** many a person
manche(r, s) ADJ many a; (*pl*) a number of ▶ PRON some
mancherlei [mançər'laɪ] ADJ *unver* various ▶ PRON a variety of things
manchmal ADV sometimes
Mandant(in) [man'dant(ɪn)] M(F) (*Jur*) client
Mandarine [manda'ri:nə] F mandarin, tangerine
Mandat [man'da:t] (**-(e)s**, **-e**) NT mandate; **sein ~ niederlegen** (*Parl*) to resign one's seat
Mandel ['mandəl] (-, **-n**) F almond; (*Anat*) tonsil; **Mandelentzündung** F tonsillitis
Mandschurei [mandʒu'raɪ] (-) F: **die ~** Manchuria
Manege [ma'nɛ:ʒə] (-, **-n**) F ring, arena
Mangel[1] ['maŋəl] (-, **-n**) F mangle; **durch die ~ drehen** (*fig: umg*) to put through it; (*Prüfling etc*) to put through the mill
Mangel[2] ['maŋəl] (**-s**, **Mängel**) M lack; (*Knappheit*) shortage; (*Fehler*) defect, fault; **~ an** *+dat* shortage of
Mängelbericht ['mɛŋəlbərɪçt] M list of faults
Mangelerscheinung F deficiency symptom
mangelhaft ADJ poor; (*fehlerhaft*) defective, faulty; (*Schulnote*) unsatisfactory
mangeln VI UNPERS: **es mangelt jdm an etw** *dat* sb lacks sth ▶ VT (*Wäsche*) to mangle
mangels PRÄP *+gen* for lack of
Mangelware F scarce commodity
Manie [ma'ni:] F mania
Manier [ma'ni:r] (-) F manner; (*Stil*) style; (*pej*) mannerism
Manieren PL manners *pl*; (*pej*) mannerisms *pl*
manieriert [mani'ri:rt] ADJ mannered, affected
manierlich ADJ well-mannered
Manifest [mani'fɛst] (**-es**, **-e**) NT manifesto
Maniküre [mani'ky:rə] (-, **-n**) F manicure
maniküren VT to manicure
Manipulation [manipulatsi'o:n] F manipulation; (*Trick*) manoeuvre (BRIT), maneuver (US)
manipulieren [manipu'li:rən] VT to manipulate
Manko ['maŋko] (**-s**, **-s**) NT deficiency; (*Comm*) deficit
Mann [man] (**-(e)s**, **Männer**) M man; (*Ehemann*) husband; (*Naut*) hand; **pro ~** per head; **mit ~ und Maus untergehen** to go down with all hands; (*Passagierschiff*) to go down with no survivors; **seinen ~ stehen** to hold one's own; **etw an den ~ bringen** (*umg*) to get rid of sth; **einen kleinen ~ im Ohr haben** (*hum: umg*) to be crazy
Männchen ['mɛnçən] NT little man; (*Tier*) male; **~ machen** (*Hund*) to (sit up and) beg
Mannequin [manə'kɛ̃:] (**-s**, **-s**) NT fashion model
Männersache ['mɛnərzaxə] F (*Angelegenheit*) man's business; (*Arbeit*) man's job
mannigfaltig ['manıçfaltıç] ADJ various, varied; **Mannigfaltigkeit** F variety
männlich ['mɛnlıç] ADJ (*Biol*) male; (*fig, Gram*) masculine
Mannsbild NT (*veraltet: pej*) fellow
Mannschaft F (*Sport, fig*) team; (*Naut, Aviat*) crew; (*Mil*) other ranks *pl*
Mannschaftsgeist M team spirit
Mannsleute (*umg*) PL menfolk *pl*
Mannweib (*pej*) NT mannish woman
Manometer [mano'me:tər] NT (*Tech*) pressure gauge; **~!** (*umg*) wow!
Manöver [ma'nø:vər] (**-s**, **-**) NT manoeuvre (BRIT), maneuver (US)
manövrieren [manø'vri:rən] VT, VI to manoeuvre (BRIT), to maneuver (US)
Mansarde [man'zardə] (-, **-n**) F attic
Manschette [man'ʃɛtə] F cuff; (*Papiermanschette*) paper frill; (*Tech*) sleeve
Manschettenknopf M cufflink
Mantel ['mantəl] (**-s**, **Mäntel**) M coat; (*Tech*) casing, jacket; **Manteltarif** M general terms of employment; **Manteltarifvertrag** M general agreement on conditions of employment
Manuskript [manu'skrɪpt] (**-(e)s**, **-e**) NT manuscript
Mappe ['mapə] (-, **-n**) F briefcase; (*Aktenmappe*) folder
Marathonlauf ['ma:ratɔnlaʊf] M marathon
Märchen ['mɛ:rçən] NT fairy tale; **märchenhaft** ADJ fabulous; **Märchenprinz** M prince charming
Marder ['mardər] (**-s**, **-**) M marten
Margarine [marga'ri:nə] F margarine
Marge ['marʒə] (-, **-n**) F (*Comm*) margin
Maria [ma'ri:a] (-) F Mary
Marienbild NT picture of the Virgin Mary
Marienkäfer M ladybird
Marihuana [marihu'a:na] (**-s**) NT marijuana
Marinade [mari'na:də] (-, **-n**) F (*Koch*) marinade; (*Soße*) mayonnaise-based sauce
Marine [ma'ri:nə] F navy; **marineblau** ADJ navy-blue
marinieren [mari'ni:rən] VT to marinate
Marionette [mario'nɛtə] F puppet
Mark[1] [mark] (-, -) F (*Hist: Geld*) mark

Mark² [mark] (**-(e)s**) NT (*Knochenmark*) marrow; **jdn bis ins ~ treffen** (*fig*) to cut sb to the quick; **jdm durch ~ und Bein gehen** to go right through sb
markant [mar'kant] ADJ striking
Marke ['markə] (**-, -n**) F mark; (*Warensorte*) brand; (*Fabrikat*) make; (*Rabattmarke, Briefmarke*) stamp; (*Essen(s)marke*) luncheon voucher; (*aus Metall etc*) token, disc
Marken- ZW: **Markenartikel** M proprietary article; **markenbewusst** ADJ brand conscious; **Markenbutter** F best quality butter; **Markenkleidung** F designer clothes; **Markenzeichen** NT trademark
Marketing ['markətɪŋ] (**-s**) NT marketing
markieren [mar'ki:rən] VT to mark; (*umg*) to act ▸ VI (*umg*) to act it
Markierung F marking
markig ['markɪç] ADJ (*fig*) pithy
Markise [mar'ki:zə] (**-, -n**) F awning
Markstück NT (*Hist*) one-mark piece
Markt [markt] (**-(e)s, Märkte**) M market; **auf den ~ bringen** to launch; **Marktanalyse** F market analysis; **Marktanteil** M market share; **marktfähig** ADJ marketable; **Marktforschung** F market research; **marktgängig** ADJ marketable; **marktgerecht** ADJ geared to market requirements; **Markthalle** F covered market; **Marktlücke** F gap in the market; **Marktmacht** F market power; **Marktplatz** M market place; **Marktpotenzial, Marktpotential** NT market potential; **Marktpreis** M market price; **Marktwert** M market value; **Marktwirtschaft** F market economy; **marktwirtschaftlich** ADJ free enterprise
Marmelade [marmə'la:də] (**-, -n**) F jam
Marmor ['marmɔr] (**-s, -e**) M marble
marmorieren [marmo'ri:rən] VT to marble
Marmorkuchen M marble cake
marmorn ADJ marble
Marokkaner(in) [marɔ'ka:nər(ɪn)] (**-s, -**) M(F) Moroccan
marokkanisch ADJ Moroccan
Marokko [ma'rɔko] (**-s**) NT Morocco
Marone [ma'ro:nə] (**-, -n**) F chestnut
Marotte [ma'rɔtə] (**-, -n**) F fad, quirk
Marsch¹ [marʃ] (**-, -en**) F marsh
Marsch² (**-(e)s, Märsche**) M march; **jdm den ~ blasen** (*umg*) to give sb a rocket; **marsch** *interj* march; **marsch ins Bett!** off to bed with you!
Marschbefehl M marching orders *pl*
marschbereit ADJ ready to move
marschieren [mar'ʃi:rən] VI to march
Marschverpflegung F rations *pl*; (*Mil*) field rations *pl*
Marseille [mar'sɛ:j] (**-s**) NT Marseilles
Marsmensch ['marsmɛnʃ] M Martian
Marter ['martər] (**-, -n**) F torment
martern VT to torture
Martinshorn ['marti:nshɔrn] NT siren (*of police etc*)
Märtyrer(in) ['mɛrtyrər(ɪn)] (**-s, -**) M(F) martyr
Martyrium [mar'ty:riʊm] NT (*fig*) ordeal
Marxismus [mar'ksɪsmʊs] M Marxism
März [mɛrts] (**-(es), -e**) (*pl selten*) M March; *siehe auch* **September**
Marzipan [martsi'pa:n] (**-s, -e**) NT marzipan
Masche ['maʃə] (**-, -n**) F mesh; (*Strickmasche*) stitch; **das ist die neueste ~** that's the latest dodge; **durch die Maschen schlüpfen** to slip through the net
Maschendraht M wire mesh
maschenfest ADJ runproof
Maschine [ma'ʃi:nə] F machine; (*Motor*) engine; **~ schreiben** to type
maschinell [maʃi'nɛl] ADJ machine(-), mechanical
Maschinen- ZW: **Maschinenausfallzeit** F machine downtime; **Maschinenbau** M mechanical engineering; **Maschinenbauer** M mechanical engineer; **Maschinenführer** M machinist; **maschinengeschrieben** ADJ typewritten; **Maschinengewehr** NT machine gun; **maschinenlesbar** ADJ (*Comput*) machine-readable; **Maschinenpistole** F submachine gun; **Maschinenraum** M plant room; (*Naut*) engine room; **Maschinensaal** M machine shop; **Maschinenschaden** M mechanical fault; **Maschinenschlosser** M fitter; **Maschinenschrift** F typescript; **Maschinensprache** F (*Comput*) machine language
Maschinerie [maʃinə'ri:] F (*fig*) machinery
Maschinist(in) [maʃi'nɪst(ɪn)] M(F) engineer
Maser ['ma:zər] (**-, -n**) F grain
Masern PL (*Med*) measles *sing*
Maserung F grain(ing)
Maske ['maskə] (**-, -n**) F mask
Maskenball M fancy-dress ball
Maskenbildner(in) M(F) make-up artist
Maskerade [maskə'ra:də] F masquerade
maskieren [mas'ki:rən] VT to mask; (*verkleiden*) to dress up ▸ VR to disguise o.s.; (*verkleiden*) to dress up
Maskottchen [mas'kɔtçən] NT (lucky) mascot
Maskulinum [masku'li:nʊm] (**-s, Maskulina**) NT (*Gram*) masculine noun
Masochist [mazɔ'xɪst] (**-en, -en**) M masochist
maß *etc* VB *siehe* **messen**
Maß¹ [ma:s] (**-es, -e**) NT measure; (*Mäßigung*) moderation; (*Grad*) degree, extent; **über alle Maßen** (*liter*) extremely, beyond measure; **~ halten** = **maßhalten**; **mit zweierlei ~ messen** (*fig*) to operate a double standard; **sich** *dat* **etw nach ~ anfertigen lassen** to have sth made to measure *od* order (*US*); **in besonderem Maße** especially; **das ~ ist voll** (*fig*) that's enough (of that)
Maß² (**-, -(e)**) F litre (BRIT) *od* liter (*US*) of beer
Massage [ma'sa:ʒə] (**-, -n**) F massage
Massaker [ma'sa:kər] (**-s, -**) NT massacre
Maßanzug M made-to-measure suit
Maßarbeit F (*fig*) neat piece of work
Masse ['masə] (**-, -n**) F mass; **eine ganze ~** (*umg*) a great deal

Maßeinheit F unit of measurement
Massen- zW: **Massenartikel** M mass-produced article; **Massenblatt** NT tabloid; **Massengrab** NT mass grave; **massenhaft** ADJ masses of; **Massenmedien** PL mass media *pl*; **Massenproduktion** F mass production; **Massenveranstaltung** F mass meeting; **Massenvernichtungswaffen** PL weapons of mass destruction; **Massenware** F mass-produced article; **massenweise** ADV in huge numbers
Masseur [ma'sø:r] M masseur
Masseurin [ma'sø:rɪn] F masseuse
Maß- zW: **maßgebend** ADJ authoritative; **maßgebende Kreise** influential circles; **maßgeblich** ADJ definitive; **maßgeschneidert** ADJ (*Anzug*) made-to-measure, made-to-order (*US*), custom *attrib* (*US*); **maßhalten** *unreg* VI to exercise moderation
massieren [ma'si:rən] VT to massage; (*Mil*) to mass
massig ['masɪç] ADJ massive; (*umg*) a massive amount of
mäßig ['mɛ:sɪç] ADJ moderate; **mäßigen** ['mɛ:sɪgən] VT to restrain, to moderate; **sein Tempo mäßigen** to slacken one's pace; **Mäßigkeit** F moderation
massiv [ma'si:f] ADJ solid; (*fig*) massive; **~ werden** (*umg*) to turn nasty; **Massiv (-s, -e)** NT massif
Maß- zW: **Maßkrug** M tankard; **maßlos** ADJ (*Verschwendung, Essen, Trinken*) excessive, immoderate; (*Enttäuschung, Ärger etc*) extreme; **Maßnahme (-, -n)** F measure, step; **maßregeln** VT UNTR to reprimand
Maßstab M rule, measure; (*fig*) standard; (*Geog*) scale; **als ~ dienen** to serve as a model
maßstabgetreu, maßstabsgetreu ADJ (true) to scale
maßvoll ADJ moderate
Mast [mast] **(-(e)s, -e(n))** M mast; (*Elek*) pylon
Mastdarm M rectum
mästen ['mɛstən] VT to fatten
masturbieren [mastʊr'bi:rən] VI to masturbate
Material [materi'a:l] **(-s, -ien)** NT material; (*Arbeitsmaterial*) materials *pl*; **Materialfehler** M material defect
Materialismus [materia'lɪsmʊs] M materialism
Materialist(in) M(F) materialist; **materialistisch** ADJ materialistic
Materialkosten PL cost *sing* of materials
Materialprüfung F material(s) control
Materie [ma'te:riə] F matter, substance
materiell [materi'ɛl] ADJ material
Mathe ['matə] **(-)** F (*Sch: umg*) maths (*Brit*), math (*US*)
Mathematik [matema'ti:k] F mathematics *sing*; **Mathematiker(in)** [mate'ma:tɪkər(ɪn)] **(-s, -)** M(F) mathematician
mathematisch [mate'ma:tɪʃ] ADJ mathematical
Matjeshering ['matjəshe:rɪŋ] (*umg*) M salted young herring
Matratze [ma'tratsə] **(-, -n)** F mattress
Matrixdrucker M dot-matrix printer
Matrixzeichen NT matrix character
Matrize [ma'tri:tsə] **(-, -n)** F matrix; (*zum Abziehen*) stencil
Matrose [ma'tro:zə] **(-n, -n)** M sailor
Matsch [matʃ] **(-(e)s)** M mud; (*Schneematsch*) slush
matschig ADJ muddy; (*Schnee*) slushy
matt [mat] ADJ weak; (*glanzlos*) dull; (*Phot*) matt; (*Schach*) mate; **jdn ~ setzen** (*lit*) to checkmate sb; *siehe auch* **mattsetzen**; **Matt (-s, -s)** NT (*Schach*) checkmate
Matte ['matə] **(-, -n)** F mat; **auf der ~ stehen** (*am Arbeitsplatz etc*) to be in
Mattigkeit F weakness; (*Glanzlosigkeit*) dullness
Mattscheibe F (*TV*) screen; **~ haben** (*umg*) to be not quite with it
mattsetzen VT (*fig*) to checkmate
Matura [ma'tu:ra] **(-)** (Österr, Schweiz) F *Austrian school-leaving examination*, ≈ A-levels (*Brit*), ≈ High School Diploma (*US*)
Mätzchen ['mɛtsçən] (*umg*) NT antics *pl*; **~ machen** to fool around
mau [maʊ] (*umg*) ADJ poor, bad
Mauer ['maʊər] **(-, -n)** F wall; **Mauerblümchen** (*umg*) NT (*fig*) wallflower
mauern VI to build, to lay bricks ▸ VT to build
Mauer- zW: **Mauerschwalbe** F swift; **Mauersegler** M swift; **Mauerwerk** NT brickwork; (*Stein*) masonry
Maul [maʊl] **(-(e)s, Mäuler)** NT mouth; **ein loses** *od* **lockeres ~ haben** (*umg: frech sein*) to be an impudent so-and-so; (*: indiskret sein*) to be a blabbermouth; **halts ~!** (*umg*) shut your face! (*umg!*); **darüber werden sich die Leute das ~ zerreißen** (*umg*) that will start people's tongues wagging; **dem Volk** *od* **den Leuten aufs ~ schauen** (*umg*) to listen to what ordinary people say; **maulen** (*umg*) VI to grumble; **Maulesel** M mule; **Maulkorb** M muzzle; **Maulsperre** F lockjaw; **Maultier** NT mule; **Maul- und Klauenseuche** F (*Tiere*) foot-and-mouth disease
Maulwurf M mole
Maulwurfshaufen M molehill
Maurer ['maʊrər] **(-s, -)** M bricklayer; **pünktlich wie die ~** (*hum*) super-punctual
Mauretanien [maʊrə'ta:niən] **(-s)** NT Mauritania
Maus [maʊs] **(-, Mäuse)** F (*auch Comput*) mouse; **Mäuse** PL (*umg: Geld*) bread *sing*, dough *sing*
mauscheln ['maʊʃəln] (*umg*) VT, VI (*manipulieren*) to fiddle
mäuschenstill ['mɔʏsçən'ʃtɪl] ADJ very quiet
Mausefalle F mousetrap
mausen VT (*umg*) to pinch ▸ VI to catch mice
mausern VR to moult (*Brit*), to molt (*US*)
mausetot ADJ stone dead
mausgesteuert ADJ (*Comput*) mouse-driven
Mausklick [maʊsklɪk] NT (*Comput*) (mouse) click
Maustaste F mouse key *od* button

Maut [maʊt] (-, **-en**) F toll; **Mautsystem** NT toll system
max. ABK (= *maximal*) max.
maximal [maksi'ma:l] ADJ maximum
Maxime [ma'ksi:mə] (-, **-n**) F maxim
maximieren [maksi'mi:rən] VT to maximize
Maximierung F (*Wirts*) maximization
Maximum ['maksimʊm] (**-s, Maxima**) NT maximum
Mayonnaise [majɔ'nɛ:zə] (-, **-n**) F mayonnaise
Mazedonien [matse'do:niən] (**-s**) NT Macedonia
Mäzen [mɛ'tse:n] (**-s, -e**) M (*gen*) patron, sponsor
MdB NT ABK (= *Mitglied des Bundestages*) *member of the Bundestag*, ≈ MP
MdL NT ABK (= *Mitglied des Landtages*) *member of the Landtag*
m. E. ABK (= *meines Erachtens*) in my opinion
Mechanik [me'ça:nɪk] F mechanics *sing*; (*Getriebe*) mechanics *pl*; **Mechaniker** (**-s, -**) M mechanic, engineer
mechanisch ADJ mechanical
Mechanisierung F mechanization
Mechanismus [meça'nɪsmʊs] M mechanism
meckern ['mɛkərn] VI to bleat; (*umg*) to moan
Mecklenburg ['me:klənbʊrk] (**-s**) NT Mecklenburg
Mecklenburg-Vorpommern (**-s**) NT (state of) Mecklenburg-Vorpommern
Medaille [me'daljə] (-, **-n**) F medal
Medaillon [medal'jõ:] (**-s, -s**) NT (*Schmuck*) locket
Medien ['me:diən] PL media *pl*; **Medienbericht** M (*meist pl*) media report; **Medienberichten zufolge** according to reports in the media; **Medienforschung** F media research; **Mediengesellschaft** F media society; **Medienmogul** M media mogul; **medienübergreifend** ADJ cross-media *attrib*; **Medienvielfalt** F mixture of media
Medikament [medika'mɛnt] NT medicine
Meditation [meditatsi'o:n] F meditation
meditieren [medi'ti:rən] VI to meditate
Medium ['me:diʊm] NT medium
Medizin [medi'tsi:n] (-, **-en**) F medicine
Mediziner(in) (**-s, -**) M(F) doctor; (*Univ*) medic (*umg*)
medizinisch ADJ medical; **~-technische Assistentin** medical assistant
Meer [me:r] (**-(e)s, -e**) NT sea; **am ~(e)** by the sea; **ans ~ fahren** to go to the sea(side); **Meerbusen** M bay, gulf; **Meerenge** F straits *pl*
Meeres- ZW: **Meeresfrüchte** PL seafood; **Meeresklima** NT maritime climate; **Meeresspiegel** M sea level
Meer- ZW: **Meerjungfrau** F mermaid; **Meerrettich** M horseradish; **Meerschweinchen** NT guinea pig; **Meerwasser** NT sea water
Mega-, mega- [mɛga-] IN ZW mega-; **Megabyte** [mega'baɪt] NT megabyte; **Megafon, Megaphon** [mega'fo:n] (**-s, -e**) NT megaphone; **Megawatt** [mɛga'vat] NT megawatt
Mehl [m'e:l] (**-(e)s, -e**) NT flour
mehlig ADJ floury
Mehlschwitze F (*Koch*) roux
mehr [me:r] ADV more; **nie ~** never again, nevermore (*liter*); **es war niemand ~ da** there was no one left; **nicht ~ lange** not much longer; **Mehraufwand** M additional expenditure; **Mehrbelastung** F excess load; (*fig*) additional burden; **mehrdeutig** ADJ ambiguous
mehrere INDEF PRON several; (*verschiedene*) various; **mehreres** several things
mehrfach ADJ multiple; (*wiederholt*) repeated
Mehrheit F majority
Mehrheitsprinzip NT principle of majority rule
Mehrheitswahlrecht NT first-past-the-post voting system
mehr- ZW: **mehrjährig** ADJ *attrib* of several years; **Mehrkosten** PL additional costs *pl*; **mehrmalig** ADJ repeated; **mehrmals** ADV repeatedly; **Mehrparteiensystem** NT multi-party system; **Mehrplatzsystem** NT (*Comput*) multi-user system; **Mehrprogrammbetrieb** M (*Comput*) multiprogramming; **mehrsprachig** ADJ multilingual; **mehrstimmig** ADJ for several voices; **mehrstimmig singen** to harmonize; **Mehrwegflasche** F returnable bottle; **Mehrwertsteuer** F value added tax, VAT; **Mehrzahl** F majority; (*Gram*) plural
Mehrzweck- IN ZW multipurpose
meiden ['maɪdən] *unreg* VT to avoid
Meile ['maɪlə] (-, **-n**) F mile; **das riecht man drei Meilen gegen den Wind** (*umg*) you can smell that a mile off
Meilenstein M milestone
meilenweit ADJ for miles
mein [maɪn] PRON my
meine(r, s) POSS PRON mine
Meineid ['maɪnlaɪt] M perjury
meinen ['maɪnən] VT to think; (*sagen*) to say; (*sagen wollen*) to mean ▶ VI to think; **wie Sie ~!** as you wish; **damit bin ich gemeint** that refers to me; **das will ich ~** I should think so
meiner GEN *von* **ich** ▶ PRON of me
meinerseits ADV for my part
meinesgleichen ['maɪnəs'glaɪçən] PRON people like me
meinetwegen ['maɪnət've:gən] ADV (*für mich*) for my sake; (*wegen mir*) on my account; (*von mir aus*) as far as I'm concerned; (*ich habe nichts dagegen*) I don't care *od* mind
meinetwillen ['maɪnət'vɪlən] ADV: **um ~** = **meinetwegen**
meinige PRON: **der/die/das ~** *od* **M~** mine
meins [maɪns] PRON mine
Meinung ['maɪnʊŋ] F opinion; **meiner ~ nach** in my opinion; **einer ~ sein** to think the same; **jdm die ~ sagen** to give sb a piece of one's mind
Meinungs- ZW: **Meinungsaustausch** M exchange of views; **Meinungsbildungsprozess** F opinion-forming process; **Meinungsforscher(in)** M(F) pollster; **Meinungsforschungsinstitut** NT opinion research institute; **Meinungsfreiheit** F

m

freedom of speech; **Meinungsumfrage** F opinion poll; **Meinungsverschiedenheit** F difference of opinion

Meise ['maɪzə] (**-, -n**) F tit(mouse); **eine ~ haben** (*umg*) to be crackers

Meißel ['maɪsəl] (**-s, -**) M chisel

meißeln VT to chisel

meist [maɪst] ADJ most ▶ ADV mostly; **Meistbegünstigungsklausel** F (*Comm*) most-favoured-nation clause; **meistbietend** ADJ: **meistbietend versteigern** to sell to the highest bidder

meiste(r, s) PRON (*adjektivisch*) most; **die meisten Leute** most people; **die ~ Zeit** most of the time; **das ~ davon** most of it; **die meisten von ihnen** most of them; (*substantivisch*) most of them; **am meisten** (the) most

meistens ADV mostly

Meister ['maɪstər] (**-s, -**) M master; (*Sport*) champion; **seinen ~ machen** to take one's master craftsman's diploma; **es ist noch kein ~ vom Himmel gefallen** (*Sprichwort*) no one is born an expert; **Meisterbrief** M master craftsman's diploma; **meisterhaft** ADJ masterly

Meisterin F (*auf einem Gebiet*) master, expert; (*Sport*) (woman) champion

meistern VT to master; **sein Leben ~** to come to grips with one's life

Meister- zW: **Meisterschaft** F mastery; (*Sport*) championship; **Meisterstück** NT masterpiece; **Meisterwerk** NT masterpiece

meistgekauft ADJ *attrib* best-selling

Mekka ['mɛka] (**-s, -s**) NT (*Geog, fig*) Mecca

Melancholie [melaŋko'li:] F melancholy

melancholisch [melaŋ'ko:lɪʃ] ADJ melancholy

Meldebehörde F registration authorities *pl*

Meldefrist F registration period

melden VT to report; (*registrieren*) to register ▶ VR to report; (*registrieren lassen*) to register; (*Sch*) to put one's hand up; (*freiwillig*) to volunteer; (*auf etw, am Telefon*) to answer; **nichts zu ~ haben** (*umg*) to have no say; **wen darf ich ~?** who shall I say (is here)?; **sich auf eine Anzeige ~** to answer an advertisement; **es meldet sich niemand** there's no answer; **sich zu Wort ~** to ask to speak

Meldepflicht F obligation to register with the police

Meldestelle F registration office

Meldung ['mɛldʊŋ] F announcement; (*Bericht*) report; (*Comput*) message

meliert [me'li:rt] ADJ mottled, speckled

melken ['mɛlkən] *unreg* VT to milk

Melodie [melo'di:] F melody, tune

melodisch [me'lo:dɪʃ] ADJ melodious, tuneful

melodramatisch [melodra'ma:tɪʃ] ADJ (*auch fig*) melodramatic

Melone [me'lo:nə] (**-, -n**) F melon; (*Hut*) bowler (hat)

Membran [mem'bra:n] (**-, -en**) F (*Tech*) diaphragm; (*Anat*) membrane

Memme ['mɛmə] (**-, -n**) (*umg*) F cissy, yellow-belly

Memoiren [memo'a:rən] PL memoirs *pl*

Menge ['mɛŋə] (**-, -n**) F quantity; (*Menschenmenge*) crowd; (*große Anzahl*) lot (of); **jede ~** (*umg*) masses *pl*, loads *pl*

mengen VT to mix ▶ VR: **sich ~ in** +*akk* to meddle with

Mengen- zW: **Mengeneinkauf** M bulk buying; **Mengenlehre** F (*Math*) set theory; **Mengenrabatt** M bulk discount

Menorca [me'nɔrka] (**-s**) NT Menorca

Mensa ['mɛnza] (**-, -s** *od* **Mensen**) F (*Univ*) refectory (BRIT), commons (US)

Mensch [mɛnʃ] (**-en, -en**) M human being, man; (*Person*) person; **kein ~** nobody; **ich bin auch nur ein ~!** I'm only human; **~ ärgere dich nicht** *nt* (*Spiel*) ludo

Menschen- zW: **Menschenalter** NT generation; **Menschenfeind** M misanthrope; **menschenfreundlich** ADJ philanthropical; **Menschengedenken** NT: **der kälteste Winter seit Menschengedenken** the coldest winter in living memory; **Menschenhandel** M slave trade; (*Jur*) trafficking in human beings; **Menschenkenner** M judge of human nature; **Menschenkenntnis** F knowledge of human nature; **menschenleer** ADJ deserted; **Menschenliebe** F philanthropy; **Menschenmasse** F crowd (of people); **Menschenmenge** F crowd (of people); **menschenmöglich** ADJ humanly possible; **Menschenrechte** PL human rights *pl*; **menschenscheu** ADJ shy; **Menschenschlag** (*umg*) M kind of people; **Menschenseele** F: **keine Menschenseele** (*fig*) not a soul

Menschenskind INTERJ good heavens!

Menschen- zW: **menschenunwürdig** ADJ degrading; **Menschenverachtung** F contempt for human beings *od* of mankind; **Menschenverstand** M: **gesunder Menschenverstand** common sense; **Menschenwürde** F human dignity; **menschenwürdig** ADJ (*Behandlung*) humane; (*Unterkunft*) fit for human habitation

Mensch- zW: **Menschheit** F humanity, mankind; **menschlich** ADJ human; (*human*) humane; **Menschlichkeit** F humanity

Menstruation [mɛnstruatsi'o:n] F menstruation

Mentalität [mɛntali'tɛ:t] F mentality

Menü [me'ny:] (**-s, -s**) NT (*auch Comput*) menu; **Menüführung** F (*Comput*) menu assistance; **menügesteuert** ADJ (*Comput*) menu-driven; **Menüleiste** F (*Comput*) menu bar

Merkblatt NT instruction sheet *od* leaflet

merken ['mɛrkən] VT to notice; **sich** *dat* **etw ~** to remember sth; **sich** *dat* **eine Autonummer ~** to make a (mental) note of a licence (BRIT) *od* license (US) number

merklich ADJ noticeable

Merkmal NT sign, characteristic

merkwürdig ADJ odd

meschugge [me'ʃʊgə] (*umg*) ADJ nuts, meshuga (US)

Mess- zW: **Messband** NT tape measure; **messbar** ADJ measurable; **Messbecher** M measuring cup

Messbuch NT missal

Messdiener M (*Rel*) server, acolyte (*form*)

Messe ['mɛsə] (-, -n) F fair; (*Eccl*) mass; (*Mil*) mess; **auf der ~** at the fair; **Messegelände** NT exhibition centre (BRIT) *od* center (*US*)

messen *unreg* VT to measure ▶ VR to compete

Messer (-s, -) NT knife; **auf des Messers Schneide stehen** (*fig*) to hang in the balance; **jdm ins offene ~ laufen** (*fig*) to walk into a trap; **messerscharf** ADJ (*fig*): **messerscharf schließen** to conclude with incredible logic (*ironisch*); **Messerspitze** F knife point; (*in Rezept*) pinch; **Messerstecherei** F knife fight

Messestadt F (town with an) exhibition centre (BRIT) *od* center (*US*)

Messestand M exhibition stand

Messgerät NT measuring device, gauge

Messgewand NT chasuble

Messing ['mɛsɪŋ] (-s) NT brass

Messstab M (*Aut*: *Ölmessstab etc*) dipstick

Messung F (*das Messen*) measuring; (*von Blutdruck*) taking; (*Messergebnis*) measurement

Messwert M measurement; (*Ableseergebnis*) reading

Metall [me'tal] (-s, -e) NT metal; **die ~ verarbeitende Industrie** the metal-processing industry; **metallen** ADJ metallic; **metallisch** ADJ metallic

Metallurgie [metalʊr'gi:] F metallurgy

Metapher [me'tafər] (-, -n) F metaphor

metaphorisch [meta'fo:rɪʃ] ADJ metaphorical

Metaphysik [metafy'zi:k] F metaphysics *sing*

Metastase [meta'sta:zə] (-, -n) F (*Med*) secondary growth

Meteor [mete'o:r] (-s, -e) M meteor

Meteorologe [meteoro'lo:gə] (-n, -n) M meteorologist

Meter ['me:tər] (-s, -) M OD NT metre (BRIT), meter (*US*); **in 500 ~ Höhe** at a height of 500 metres; **Metermaß** NT tape measure; **Meterware** F (*Textil*) piece goods

Methode [me'to:də] (-, -n) F method

Methodik [me'to:dɪk] F methodology

methodisch [me'to:dɪʃ] ADJ methodical

Metier [meti'e:] (-s, -s) NT (*hum*) job, profession

metrisch ['me:trɪʃ] ADJ metric, metrical

Metropole [metro'po:lə] (-, -n) F metropolis

Mettwurst ['mɛtvʊrst] F (smoked) sausage

Metzger ['mɛtsgər] (-s, -) M butcher

Metzgerei [mɛtsgə'raɪ] F butcher's (shop)

Meuchelmord ['mɔʏçəlmɔrt] M assassination

Meute ['mɔʏtə] (-, -n) F pack

Meuterei [mɔʏtə'raɪ] F mutiny

meutern VI to mutiny

Mexikaner(in) [mɛksi'ka:nər(ɪn)] (-s, -) M(F) Mexican

mexikanisch ADJ Mexican

Mexiko ['mɛksiko] (-s) NT Mexico

MEZ ABK (= *mitteleuropäische Zeit*) C.E.T.

MfG ABK (= *mit freundlichen Grüßen*) (with) best wishes

MFG ABK = **Mitfahrgelegenheit**

mg ABK (= *Milligramm*) mg

MG (-(s), -(s)) NT ABK = **Maschinengewehr**

mhd. ABK (= *mittelhochdeutsch*) MHG

MHz ABK (= *Megahertz*) MHz

Mi. ABK = **Mittwoch**

miauen [mi'aʊən] VI to miaow

mich [mɪç] AKK *von* **ich** ▶ PRON me; (*reflexiv*) myself

mickerig ['mɪkərɪç], **mickrig** ['mɪkrɪç] (*umg*) ADJ pathetic; (*altes Männchen*) puny

mied *etc* [mi:t] VB *siehe* **meiden**

Miederwaren ['mi:dərva:rən] PL corsetry *sing*

Mief [mi:f] (-s) (*umg*) M fug; (*muffig*) stale air; (*Gestank*) stink, pong (BRIT)

miefig (*umg*) ADJ smelly, pongy (BRIT)

Miene ['mi:nə] (-, -n) F look, expression; **gute ~ zum bösen Spiel machen** to grin and bear it

Mienenspiel NT facial expressions *pl*

mies [mi:s] (*umg*) ADJ lousy

Miese ['mi:zə] (*umg*) PL: **in den Miesen sein** to be in the red

Miesmacher(in) (*umg*) M(F) killjoy

Mietauto NT hired car (BRIT), rental car (*US*)

Miete ['mi:tə] (-, -n) F rent; **zur ~ wohnen** to live in rented accommodation *od* accommodations (*US*)

mieten VT to rent; (*Auto*) to hire (BRIT), to rent

Mieter(in) (-s, -) M(F) tenant; **Mieterschutz** M rent control

Mietshaus NT tenement, block of flats (BRIT) *od* apartments (*US*)

Miet- zW: **Mietverhältnis** NT tenancy; **Mietvertrag** M tenancy agreement; **Mietwagen** M = **Mietauto**; **Mietwucher** M the charging of exorbitant rent(s)

Mieze ['mi:tsə] (-, -n) (*umg*) F (*Katze*) pussy; (*Mädchen*) chick, bird (BRIT)

Migräne [mi'grɛ:nə] (-, -n) F migraine

migrieren [mi'gri:rən] VI to migrate

Mikado [mi'ka:do] (-s) NT (*Spiel*) pick-a-stick

Mikro- ['mi:kro] IN ZW micro-

Mikrobe [mi'kro:bə] (-, -n) F microbe

Mikroblog ['mi:kroblɔg] NT microblog

Mikro- zW: **Mikrochip** M microchip; **Mikrocomputer** M microcomputer; **Mikrofiche** M OD NT microfiche; **Mikrofilm** M microfilm

Mikrofon [mikro'fo:n] (-s, e) NT microphone

Mikroökonomie F microeconomics *pl*

Mikrophon [mikro'fo:n] (-s, -e) NT microphone

Mikroprozessor (-s, -oren) M microprocessor

Mikroskop [mikro'sko:p] (-s, -e) NT microscope; **mikroskopisch** ADJ microscopic

Mikrowelle ['mi:krovɛlə] F microwave

Mikrowellenherd M microwave (oven)

Milbe ['mɪlbə] (-, -n) F mite

Milch [mɪlç] (-) F milk; (*Fischmilch*) milt, roe; **Milchdrüse** F mammary gland; **Milchglas** NT frosted glass

milchig ADJ milky

Milch- zW: **Milchkaffee** M white coffee; **Milchmixgetränk** NT milk shake; **Milchpulver**

m

NT powdered milk; **Milchreis** M rice pudding; **Milchstraße** F Milky Way; **Milchtüte** F milk carton; **Milchzahn** M milk tooth
mild [mɪlt] ADJ mild; (*Richter*) lenient; (*freundlich*) kind, charitable
Milde ['mɪldə] (-, **-n**) F mildness; (*von Richter*) leniency
mildern VT to mitigate, to soften; (*Schmerz*) to alleviate; **mildernde Umstände** extenuating circumstances
Milieu [mili'øː] (**-s, -s**) NT background, environment; **milieugeschädigt** ADJ maladjusted
militant [mili'tant] ADJ militant
Militär [mili'tɛːr] (**-s**) NT military, army; **Militärdienst** M military service; **Militäreinsatz** M use of troops; (*Kampfhandlung*) military action; **Militärgericht** NT military court; **militärisch** ADJ military
Militarismus [milita'rɪsmʊs] M militarism
militaristisch ADJ militaristic
Militärpflicht F (compulsory) military service
Mill. ABK (= *Million(en)*) m
Milli- IN ZW milli-
Milliardär(in) [mɪliar'dɛːr(ɪn)] (**-s, -e**) M(F) multimillionaire
Milliarde [mɪli'ardə] (-, **-n**) F billion; **Milliardengrab** NT (*fig*) money burner, white elephant
Millimeter M millimetre (BRIT), millimeter (US); **Millimeterpapier** NT graph paper
Million [mɪli'oːn] (-, **-en**) F million
Millionär(in) [mɪlio'nɛːr(ɪn)] (**-s, -e**) M(F) millionaire
millionenschwer (*umg*) ADJ worth a few million
Milz [mɪlts] (-, **-en**) F spleen
Mimik ['miːmɪk] F facial expression(s)
Mimose [mi'moːzə] (-, **-n**) F mimosa; (*fig*) sensitive person
minder ['mɪndər] ADJ inferior ▸ ADV less; **minderbegabt** ADJ less able; **minderbemittelt** ADJ: **geistig minderbemittelt** (*ironisch*) intellectually challenged
Minderheit F minority
Minderheitsbeteiligung F (*Aktien*) minority interest
Minderheitsregierung F minority government
minderjährig ADJ minor; **Minderjährige(r)** F(M) minor; **Minderjährigkeit** F minority
mindern VT, VR to decrease, to diminish
minderqualifiziert ADJ less qualified; **Minderqualifizierte(r)** F(M) less qualified person
Minderung F decrease
minder- ZW: **minderwertig** ADJ inferior; **Minderwertigkeitsgefühl** NT inferiority complex; **Minderwertigkeitskomplex** M inferiority complex
Mindestalter NT minimum age
Mindestbetrag M minimum amount
mindeste(r, s) ADJ least
mindestens ADV at least
Mindest- ZW: **Mindesthaltbarkeitsdatum** NT best-before date, sell-by date (BRIT); **Mindestlohn** M minimum wage; **Mindestmaß** NT minimum; **Mindeststand** M (*Comm*) minimum stock; **Mindeststudiendauer** NT (ÖSTERR) minimum length of study; **Mindestumtausch** M minimum obligatory exchange
Mine ['miːnə] (-, **-n**) F mine; (*Bleistiftmine*) lead; (*Kugelschreibermine*) refill
Minenfeld NT minefield
Minensuchboot NT minesweeper
Mineral [mine'raːl] (**-s, -e** *od* **-ien**) NT mineral; **mineralisch** ADJ mineral; **Mineralölsteuer** F tax on oil and petrol (BRIT) *od* gasoline (US); **Mineralwasser** NT mineral water
Miniatur [minia'tuːr] F miniature
Minigolf ['mɪnigɔlf] NT miniature golf
minimal [mini'maːl] ADJ minimal
Minimum ['miːnimʊm] (**-s, Minima**) NT minimum
Minirock ['mɪnirɔk] M miniskirt
Minister(in) [mi'nɪstər(ɪn)] (**-s, -**) M(F) (*Pol*) minister
ministeriell [minɪsteri'ɛl] ADJ ministerial
Ministerium [minɪs'teːriʊm] NT ministry
Ministerpräsident(in) M(F) prime minister
Minna ['mɪna] F: **jdn zur ~ machen** (*umg*) to give sb a piece of one's mind
minus ['miːnʊs] ADV minus; **Minus** (-, **-**) NT deficit; **Minuspol** M negative pole; **Minuszeichen** NT minus sign
Minute [mi'nuːtə] (-, **-n**) F minute; **auf die ~ (genau** *od* **pünktlich)** (right) on the dot
Minutenzeiger M minute hand
Mio. ABK (= *Million(en)*) m
mir [miːr] DAT *von* **ich** ▸ PRON (to) me; **ein Freund von ~** a friend of mine; **von ~ aus!** I don't mind; **wie du ~, so ich dir** (*Sprichwort*) tit for tat (*umg*); (*als Drohung*) I'll get my own back; **~ nichts, dir nichts** just like that
Mirabelle [mira'bɛlə] F mirabelle, *small yellow plum*
Misch- ZW: **Mischbatterie** F mixer tap; **Mischbrot** NT *bread made from more than one kind of flour*; **Mischehe** F mixed marriage
mischen VT to mix; (*Comput: Datei, Text*) to merge; (*Karten*) to shuffle ▸ VI (*Karten*) to shuffle
Misch- ZW: **Mischfinanzierung** M (*Wirts*) mixed financing; **Mischkonzern** M conglomerate; **Mischling** M half-caste; **Mischmasch** (*umg*) M hotchpotch; (*Essen*) concoction; **Mischpult** NT (*Rundf, TV*) mixing panel
Mischung F mixture
Mischwald M mixed (deciduous and coniferous) woodland
miserabel [mizə'raːbəl] (*umg*) ADJ lousy; (*Gesundheit*) wretched; (*Benehmen*) dreadful
Misere [mi'zeːrə] (-, **-n**) F (*von Leuten, Wirtschaft etc*) plight; (*von Hunger, Krieg etc*) misery, miseries *pl*

Miss- zW: **missachten** VT UNTR to disregard; **Missachtung** F disregard; **Missbehagen** NT uneasiness; (*Missfallen*) discontent; **Missbildung** F deformity; **missbilligen** VT UNTR to disapprove of; **Missbilligung** F disapproval; **Missbrauch** M abuse; (*falscher Gebrauch*) misuse; **missbrauchen** VT UNTR to abuse; (*falsch gebrauchen*) to misuse; (*vergewaltigen*) to assault; **jdn zu** *od* **für etw missbrauchen** to use sb for *od* to do sth; **missdeuten** VT UNTR to misinterpret

missen VT to do without; (*Erfahrung*) to miss

Misserfolg M failure

Missernte F crop failure

Missetat ['mɪsəta:t] F misdeed

Missetäter M criminal; (*umg*) scoundrel

Miss- zW: **missfallen** *unreg* VI UNTR: **jdm missfallen** to displease sb; **Missfallen (-s)** NT displeasure; **Missgeburt** F freak; (*fig*) failure; **Missgeschick** NT misfortune; **missglücken** VI UNTR to fail; **jdm missglückt etw** sb does not succeed with sth; **missgönnen** VT UNTR: **jdm etw missgönnen** to (be)grudge sb sth; **Missgriff** M mistake; **Missgunst** F envy; **missgünstig** ADJ envious; **misshandeln** VT UNTR to ill-treat; **Misshandlung** F ill-treatment; **Misshelligkeit** F: **Misshelligkeiten haben** to be at variance

Mission [mɪsi'o:n] F mission

Missionar(in) [mɪsio'na:r(ɪn)] M(F) missionary

Missklang M discord

Misskredit M discredit

misslang *etc* [mɪs'laŋ] VB *siehe* **misslingen**

missliebig ADJ unpopular

misslingen [mɪs'lɪŋən] *unreg* VI UNTR to fail; **Misslingen (-s)** NT failure

misslungen [mɪs'lʊŋən] PP *von* **misslingen**

Miss- zW: **Missmut** M bad temper; **missmutig** ADJ cross; **missraten** *unreg* VI UNTR to turn out badly ▶ ADJ ill-bred; **Missstand** M deplorable state of affairs; **Missstimmung** F discord; (*Missmut*) ill feeling

misst VB *siehe* **messen**

Miss- zW: **misstrauen** VI UNTR to mistrust; **Misstrauen (-s)** NT: **Misstrauen (gegenüber)** distrust (of), suspicion (of); **Misstrauensantrag** M (*Pol*) motion of no confidence; **Misstrauensvotum** NT (*Pol*) vote of no confidence; **misstrauisch** ADJ distrustful, suspicious; **Missverhältnis** NT disproportion; **missverständlich** ADJ unclear; **Missverständnis** NT misunderstanding; **missverstehen** *unreg* VT UNTR to misunderstand

Misswahl ['mɪsva:l] F beauty contest

Misswirtschaft F mismanagement

Mist [mɪst] **(-(e)s)** M dung; (*umg*) rubbish; **~!** (*umg*) blast!; **das ist nicht auf seinem ~ gewachsen** (*umg*) he didn't think that up himself

Mistel (-, -n) F mistletoe

Mist- zW: **Mistgabel** F pitchfork (*used for shifting manure*); **Misthaufen** M dungheap; **Miststück** (*umg!*) NT, **Mistvieh** (*umg!*) NT (*Mann*) bastard (*umg!*); (*Frau*) bitch (*umg!*)

mit [mɪt] PRÄP *+dat* with; (*mittels*) by ▶ ADV along, too; **~ der Bahn** by train; **~ dem nächsten Flugzeug/Bus kommen** to come on the next plane/bus; **~ Bleistift schreiben** to write in pencil; **~ Verlust** at a loss; **er ist ~ der Beste in der Gruppe** he is among the best in the group; **wie wärs ~ einem Bier?** (*umg*) how about a beer?; **~ 10 Jahren** at the age of 10; **wollen Sie ~?** do you want to come along?

Mitarbeit ['mɪt|arbaɪt] F cooperation; **mitarbeiten** VI: **mitarbeiten (an** *+dat***)** to cooperate (on), to collaborate (on)

Mitarbeiter(in) M(F) (*an Projekt*) collaborator; (*Kollege*) colleague; (*Angestellter*) member of staff ▶ PL staff; **Mitarbeiterstab** M staff

mit- zW: **mitbekommen** *unreg* VT to get *od* be given; (*umg: hören*) to hear; (*verstehen*) to get; **mitbestimmen** VI: **(bei etw) mitbestimmen** to have a say (in sth) ▶ VT to have an influence on; **Mitbestimmung** F participation in decision-making; (*Pol*) determination; **Mitbewohner(in)** M(F) (*in Wohnung*) flatmate (BRIT), roommate (US); **mitbringen** *unreg* VT to bring along; **Mitbringsel** ['mɪtbrɪŋzəl] **(-s, -)** NT (*Geschenk*) small present; (*Andenken*) souvenir; **Mitbürger(in)** M(F) fellow citizen; **mitdenken** *unreg* VI to follow; **du hast ja mitgedacht!** good thinking!; **mitdürfen** *unreg* VI: **wir durften nicht mit** we weren't allowed to go along; **Miteigentümer** M joint owner

miteinander [mɪt|aɪ'nandər] ADV together, with one another

miterleben VT to see, to witness

Mitesser ['mɪt|ɛsər] **(-s, -)** M blackhead

mit- zW: **mitfahren** *unreg* VI: **(mit jdm) mitfahren** to go (with sb); (*auf Reise auch*) to go *od* travel (with sb); **Mitfahrerzentrale** F agency for arranging lifts; **Mitfahrgelegenheit** F lift; **mitfühlen** VI: **mit jdm/etw mitfühlen** to sympathize with sb/sth; **mitfühlend** ADJ sympathetic; **mitführen** VT (*Papiere, Ware etc*) to carry (with one); (*Fluss*) to carry along; **mitgeben** *unreg* VT to give; **Mitgefühl** NT sympathy; **mitgehen** *unreg* VI to go *od* come along; **etw mitgehen lassen** (*umg*) to pinch sth; **mitgenommen** ADJ done in, in a bad way; **Mitgift** F dowry

Mitglied ['mɪtgli:t] NT member

Mitgliedsbeitrag M membership fee, subscription

Mitgliedschaft F membership

mit- zW: **mithaben** *unreg* VT: **etw mithaben** to have sth (with one); **mithalten** *unreg* VI to keep up; **mithelfen** VI *unreg* to help, to lend a hand; **bei etw mithelfen** to help with sth; **mithilfe** PRÄP *+gen*: **mithilfe von** with the help of; **Mithilfe** F help, assistance; **mithören** VT to listen in to; **mitkommen** *unreg* VI to come along; (*verstehen*) to keep up, to follow; **Mitläufer** M hanger-on; (*Pol*) fellow traveller

Mitleid NT sympathy; (*Erbarmen*) compassion

Mitleidenschaft F: **in ~ ziehen** to affect

mitleidig ADJ sympathetic

m

mitleidslos ADJ pitiless, merciless
mit- zW: **mitmachen** VT to join in, to take part in; (*umg: einverstanden sein*): **da macht mein Chef nicht mit** my boss won't go along with that; **Mitmensch** M fellow man; **mitmischen** (*umg*) VI (*sich beteiligen*): **mitmischen (in** *+dat od* **bei)** to be involved (in); (*sich einmischen*) to interfere (in); **mitnehmen** *unreg* VT to take along *od* away; (*anstrengen*) to wear out, to exhaust; **mitgenommen aussehen** to look the worse for wear; **mitreden** VI (*Meinung äußern*): **(bei etw) mitreden** to join in (sth); (*mitbestimmen*) to have a say (in sth) ▸ VT: **Sie haben hier nichts mitzureden** this is none of your concern; **mitreißen** VT *unreg* to sweep away; (*fig: begeistern*) to carry away; **mitreißend** ADJ (*Rhythmus*) infectious; (*Reden*) rousing; (*Film, Fußballspiel*) thrilling, exciting
mitsamt [mɪt'zamt] PRÄP *+dat* together with
mitschneiden VT *unreg* to record
Mitschnitt ['mɪtʃnɪt] **(-(e)s, -e)** M recording
mitschreiben *unreg* VT to write *od* take down ▸ VI to take notes
Mitschuld F complicity
mitschuldig ADJ: **~ (an** *+dat***)** implicated (in); (*an Unfall*) partly responsible (for)
Mitschuldige(r) F(M) accomplice
mit- zW: **Mitschüler(in)** M(F) schoolmate; **mitspielen** VI to join in, to take part; (*in Mannschaft*) to play; **er hat ihr übel** *od* **hart mitgespielt** (*Schaden zufügen*) he has treated her badly; **Mitspieler(in)** M(F) partner; **Mitspracherecht** NT voice, say
Mittag ['mɪta:k] **(-(e)s, -e)** M midday, noon, lunchtime; **morgen ~** tomorrow at lunchtime *od* noon; **~ machen** to take one's lunch hour; **(zu) ~ essen** to have lunch; **Mittagessen** NT lunch, dinner
mittags ADV at lunchtime *od* noon
Mittags- zW: **Mittagspause** F lunch break; **Mittagsruhe** F period of quiet (after lunch); (*in Geschäft*) midday closing; **Mittagsschlaf** M early afternoon nap, siesta; **Mittagszeit** F: **während** *od* **in der Mittagszeit** at lunchtime
Mittäter(in) ['mɪttɛ:tər(ɪn)] M(F) accomplice
Mitte ['mɪtə] **(-, -n)** F middle; **sie ist ~ zwanzig** she's in her mid-twenties; **aus unserer ~** from our midst
mitteilen ['mɪttaɪlən] VT: **jdm etw ~** to inform sb of sth, to communicate sth to sb ▸ VR: **sich (jdm) ~** to communicate (with sb)
mitteilsam ADJ communicative
Mitteilung F communication; **jdm (eine) ~ von etw machen** (*form*) to inform sb of sth; (*bekannt geben*) to announce sth to sb
Mitteilungsbedürfnis NT need to talk to other people
Mittel ['mɪtəl] **(-s, -)** NT means; (*Methode*) method; (*Math*) average; (*Med*) medicine; **kein ~ unversucht lassen** to try everything; **als letztes ~** as a last resort; **ein ~ zum Zweck** a means to an end; **Mittelalter** NT Middle Ages *pl*; **mittelalterlich** ADJ medieval; **Mittelamerika** NT Central America (and the Caribbean); **mittelamerikanisch** ADJ Central American; **mittelbar** ADJ indirect; **Mittelding** NT (*Mischung*) cross; **Mitteleuropa** NT Central Europe; **Mitteleuropäer(in)** M(F) Central European; **mitteleuropäisch** ADJ Central European; **Mittelfeld** NT midfield; **Mittelfinger** M middle finger; **mittelfristig** ADJ (*Finanzplanung, Kredite*) medium-term; **Mittelgebirge** NT low mountain range; **mittelgroß** ADJ medium-sized; **mittellos** ADJ without means; **Mittelmaß** NT: **das (gesunde) Mittelmaß** the happy medium; **mittelmäßig** ADJ mediocre, middling; **Mittelmäßigkeit** F mediocrity; **Mittelmeer** NT Mediterranean (Sea); **mittelprächtig** ADJ not bad; **Mittelpunkt** M centre (BRIT), center (US); **im Mittelpunkt stehen** to be centre-stage
mittels PRÄP *+gen* by means of
Mittelschicht F middle class
Mittelsmann (-(e)s, *pl* **Mittelsmänner** *od* **Mittelsleute)** M intermediary
Mittel- zW: **Mittelstand** M middle class; **Mittelstreckenrakete** F medium-range missile; **Mittelstreifen** M central reservation (BRIT), median strip (US); **Mittelstufe** F (*Sch*) middle school (BRIT), junior high (US); **Mittelstürmer** M centre forward; **Mittelweg** M middle course; **Mittelwelle** F (*Rundf*) medium wave; **Mittelwert** M average value, mean
mitten ['mɪtən] ADV in the middle; **~ auf der Straße/in der Nacht** in the middle of the street/night; **mittendrin** ADV (right) in the middle of it; **mittendurch** ADV (right) through the middle
Mitternacht ['mɪtərnaxt] F midnight
mittlere(r, s) ['mɪtlərə(r, s)] ADJ middle; (*durchschnittlich*) medium, average; **der M~ Osten** the Middle East; **mittleres Management** middle management; **~ Reife** *see note*

> The **mittlere Reife** is the standard certificate achieved at a **Realschule** on successful completion of 6 years' education there. If a pupil at a **Realschule** attains good results in several subjects he or she is allowed to enter the 11th class of a **Gymnasium** to study for the **Abitur**.

mittlerweile ['mɪtlər'vaɪlə] ADV meanwhile
Mittwoch ['mɪtvɔx] **(-(e)s, -e)** M Wednesday; *siehe auch* **Dienstag**
mittwochs ADV on Wednesdays
mitunter [mɪt'ʊntər] ADV occasionally, sometimes
mit- zW: **mitverantwortlich** ADJ also responsible; **mitverdienen** VI to (go out to) work as well; **Mitverfasser** M co-author; **Mitverschulden** NT contributory negligence; **mitwirken** VI: **(bei etw) mitwirken** to contribute (to sth); (*Theat*) to take part (in sth); **Mitwirkende(r)** F(M): **die Mitwirkenden** (*Theat*) the cast; **Mitwirkung** F contribution; (*Theat*) participation; **unter Mitwirkung von**

with the help of; **Mitwisser (-s, -)** M: **Mitwisser (einer Sache** *gen*) **sein** to be in the know (about sth); **jdn zum Mitwisser machen** to tell sb (all) about it
Mixer ['mɪksər] (**-s, -**) M (*Barmixer*) cocktail waiter; (*Küchenmixer*) blender; (*Rührmaschine, Rundf, TV*) mixer
ml ABK (= *Milliliter*) ml
mm ABK (= *Millimeter*) mm
MMS® M (= *Multimedia Messaging Service*) MMS
Mnemonik [mne'mo:nɪk] F mnemonic
Mo. ABK = **Montag**
mobben ['mɔbən] VT to bully (at work)
Mobbing ['mɔbɪŋ] (**-s**) NT workplace bullying
Möbel ['mø:bəl] (**-s, -**) NT (piece of) furniture; **Möbelpacker** M removal man (BRIT), (furniture) mover (US); **Möbelwagen** M furniture *od* removal van (BRIT), moving van (US)
mobil [mo'bi:l] ADJ mobile; (*Internet, Tel*): **mobile Internetnutzung** mobile internet use; **mobiles Internet** mobile web; (*Mil*) mobilized
Mobilfunk M cellular telephone service; **Mobilfunkmast** M (*Tel*) mobile phone mast (BRIT), cell tower (US); **Mobilfunknetz** NT cellular network
Mobiliar [mobili'a:r] (**-s, -e**) NT movable assets *pl*
mobilisieren [mobili'zi:rən] VT (*Mil*) to mobilize
Mobilmachung F mobilization
Mobiltelefon NT (*Tel*) mobile phone
möbl. ABK = **möbliert**
möblieren [mø'bli:rən] VT to furnish; **möbliert wohnen** to live in furnished accommodation
mochte *etc* ['mɔxtə] VB *siehe* **mögen**
Möchtegern- ['mœçtəgɛrn] IN ZW (*ironisch*) would-be
Modalität [modali'tɛ:t] F (*von Plan, Vertrag etc*) arrangement
Mode ['mo:də] (**-, -n**) F fashion; **Modefarbe** F in colour (BRIT) *od* color (US); **Modeheft** NT fashion magazine; **Modejournal** NT fashion magazine
Modell [mo'dɛl] (**-s, -e**) NT model; **Modelleisenbahn** F model railway; (*als Spielzeug*) train set; **Modellfall** M textbook case
modellieren [modɛ'li:rən] VT to model
Modellversuch M (*bes Sch*) pilot scheme
Modem ['mo:dɛm] (**-s, -s**) NT (*Comput*) modem
Modenschau F fashion show
Modepapst M high priest of fashion
Moder ['mo:dər] (**-s**) M mustiness; (*Schimmel*) mildew
moderat [mode'ra:t] ADJ moderate
Moderator(in) [mode'ra:tɔr, -a'to:rɪn] M(F) presenter
moderieren [mode'ri:rən] VT, VI (*Rundf, TV*) to present
modern [mo'dɛrn] ADJ modern; (*modisch*) fashionable
modernisieren [modɛrni'zi:rən] VT to modernize
Mode- ZW: **Modeschmuck** M fashion jewellery (BRIT) *od* jewelry (US); **Modeschöpfer(in)** M(F) fashion designer; **Modewort** NT fashionable word
modifizieren [modifi'tsi:rən] VT to modify
modisch ['mo:dɪʃ] ADJ fashionable
Modul ['mo:dʊl] (**-s, -n**) NT (*Comput*) module
Modus ['mo:dʊs] (**-, Modi**) M way; (*Gram*) mood; (*Comput*) mode
Mofa ['mo:fa] (**-s, -s**) NT (= *Motorfahrrad*) small moped
Mogadischu [moga'dɪʃu] (**-s**) NT Mogadishu
mogeln ['mo:gəln] (*umg*) VI to cheat

SCHLÜSSELWORT

mögen ['mø:gən] (*pt* **mochte**, *pp* **gemocht** *od* (*als Hilfsverb*) **mögen**) VT, VI to like; **magst du/mögen Sie ihn?** do you like him?; **ich möchte ...** I would like ..., I'd like ...; **er möchte in die Stadt** he'd like to go into town; **ich möchte nicht, dass du ...** I wouldn't like you to ...; **ich mag nicht mehr** I've had enough; (*bin am Ende*) I can't take any more; **man möchte meinen, dass ...** you would think that ...
▶ HILFSVERB to like to; (*wollen*) to want; **möchtest du etwas essen?** would you like something to eat?; **sie mag nicht bleiben** she doesn't want to stay; **das mag wohl sein** that may very well be; **was mag das heißen?** what might that mean?; **Sie möchten zu Hause anrufen** could you please call home?

möglich ['mø:klɪç] ADJ possible; **er tat sein Möglichstes** he did his utmost
möglicherweise ADV possibly
Möglichkeit F possibility; **nach ~** if possible
möglichst ADV as ... as possible
Mohammedaner(in) [mohame'da:nər(ɪn)] (**-s, -**) M(F) Mohammedan, Muslim
Mohikaner [mohi'ka:nər] (**-s, -**) M: **der letzte ~** (*hum: umg*) the very last one
Mohn [mo:n] (**-(e)s, -e**) M (*Mohnblume*) poppy; (*Mohnsamen*) poppy seed
Möhre ['mø:rə] (**-, -n**) F carrot
Mohrenkopf ['mo:rənkɔpf] M *chocolate-covered marshmallow*
Mohrrübe F carrot
mokieren [mo'ki:rən] VR: **sich über etw** *akk* **~** to make fun of sth
Mokka ['mɔka] (**-s**) M mocha, *strong coffee*
Moldau ['mɔldaʊ] F: **die ~** the Vltava
Moldawien [mɔl'da:viən] (**-s**) NT Moldavia
moldawisch ADJ Moldavian
Mole ['mo:lə] (**-, -n**) F (*Naut*) mole
Molekül [mole'ky:l] (**-s, -e**) NT molecule
molk *etc* [mɔlk] VB *siehe* **melken**
Molkerei [mɔlkə'raɪ] F dairy; **Molkereibutter** F blended butter
Moll [mɔl] (**-, -**) NT (*Mus*) minor (key)
mollig ADJ cosy; (*dicklich*) plump
Molotowcocktail ['mo:lotɔfkɔkte:l] M Molotov cocktail
Moment [mo'mɛnt] (**-(e)s, -e**) M moment
▶ NT factor, element; **im ~** at the moment; **~ mal!** just a minute!; **im ersten ~** for a moment

m

momentan [momɛn'ta:n] ADJ momentary ▶ ADV at the moment
Monaco [mo'nako, 'mo:nako] (**-s**) NT Monaco
Monarch [mo'narç] (**-en, -en**) M monarch
Monarchie [monar'çi:] F monarchy
Monat ['mo:nat] (**-(e)s, -e**) M month; **sie ist im sechsten ~ (schwanger)** she's five months pregnant; **was verdient er im ~?** how much does he earn a month?
monatelang ADV for months
monatlich ADJ monthly
Monats- zW: **Monatsblutung** F menstrual period; **Monatskarte** F monthly ticket; **Monatsrate** F monthly instalment (BRIT) *od* installment (US)
Mönch [mœnç] (**-(e)s, -e**) M monk
Mond [mo:nt] (**-(e)s, -e**) M moon; **auf** *od* **hinter dem ~ leben** (*umg*) to be behind the times; **Mondfähre** F lunar (excursion) module; **Mondfinsternis** F eclipse of the moon; **mondhell** ADJ moonlit; **Mondlandung** F moon landing; **Mondschein** M moonlight; **Mondsonde** F moon probe
Monegasse [mone'gasə] (**-n, -n**) M Monegasque
Monegassin [mone'gasɪn] F Monegasque
monegassisch ADJ Monegasque
Monetarismus [moneta'rɪsmʊs] M (*Wirts*) monetarism
Monetarist M monetarist
Moneten [mo'ne:tən] (*umg*) PL (*Geld*) bread *sing*, dough *sing*
Mongole [mɔŋ'go:lə] (**-n, -n**) M Mongolian, Mongol
Mongolei [mɔŋgo'laɪ] F: **die ~** Mongolia
Mongolin F Mongolian, Mongol
mongolisch [mɔŋ'go:lɪʃ] ADJ Mongolian
mongoloid [mɔŋgolo'i:t] ADJ (*Med*) mongoloid
monieren [mo'ni:rən] VT to complain about ▶ VI to complain
Monitor ['mo:nitɔr] M (*Bildschirm*) monitor
Mono- [mono] IN zW mono
monogam [mono'ga:m] ADJ monogamous
Monogamie [monoga'mi:] F monogamy
Monolog [mono'lo:k] (**-s, -e**) M monologue
Monopol (**-s, -e**) NT monopoly
monopolisieren [monopoli'zi:rən] VT to monopolize
Monopolstellung F monopoly
monoton [mono'to:n] ADJ monotonous
Monotonie [monoto'ni:] F monotony
Monstrum ['mɔnstrʊm] (**-s, Monstren**) NT (*lit, fig*) monster; **ein ~ von einem/einer ...** a hulking great ...
Monsun [mɔn'zu:n] (**-s, -e**) M monsoon
Montag ['mo:nta:k] (**-(e)s, -e**) M Monday; *siehe auch* **Dienstag**
Montage [mɔn'ta:ʒə] (**-, -n**) F (*Phot etc*) montage; (*Tech*) assembly; (*Einbauen*) fitting
montags ADV on Mondays
Montanindustrie [mɔn'ta:nɪndʊstri:] F coal and steel industry
Montblanc [mõ'blã:] M Mont Blanc
Monte Carlo ['mɔntə 'karlo] (**-s**) NT Monte Carlo
Montenegro [mɔnte'ne:gro] (**-s**) NT Montenegro
Monteur [mɔn'tø:r] M fitter, assembly man
montieren [mɔn'ti:rən] VT to assemble, to set up
Montur [mɔn'tu:r] (*umg*) F (*Spezialkleidung*) gear, rig-out
Monument [monu'mɛnt] NT monument
monumental [monumɛn'ta:l] ADJ monumental
Moor [mo:r] (**-(e)s, -e**) NT moor; **Moorbad** NT mud bath
Moos [mo:s] (**-es, -e**) NT moss
Moped ['mo:pɛt] (**-s, -s**) NT moped
Mops [mɔps] (**-es, Möpse**) M (*Hund*) pug
Moral [mo'ra:l] (**-, -en**) F morality; (*einer Geschichte*) moral; (*Disziplin: von Volk, Soldaten*) morale; **Moralapostel** M upholder of moral standards; **moralisch** ADJ moral; **einen** *od* **den Moralischen haben** (*umg*) to have (a fit of) the blues
Moräne [mo'rɛ:nə] (**-, -n**) F moraine
Morast [mo'rast] (**-(e)s, -e**) M morass, mire
morastig ADJ boggy
Mord [mɔrt] (**-(e)s, -e**) M murder; **dann gibt es ~ und Totschlag** (*umg*) there'll be hell to pay; **Mordanschlag** M murder attempt
Mörder ['mœrdər] (**-s, -**) M murderer
Mörderin F murderess
mörderisch ADJ (*fig: schrecklich*) dreadful, terrible; (*Preise*) exorbitant; (*Konkurrenzkampf*) cut-throat ▶ ADV (*umg: entsetzlich*) dreadfully, terribly
Mordkommission F murder squad
Mords- zW: **Mordsding** (*umg*) NT whopper; **Mordsglück** (*umg*) NT amazing luck; **Mordskerl** (*umg*) M (*verwegen*) hell of a guy; **mordsmäßig** (*umg*) ADJ terrific, enormous; **Mordsschreck** (*umg*) M terrible fright
Mord- zW: **Mordverdacht** M suspicion of murder; **Mordversuch** M murder attempt; **Mordwaffe** F murder weapon
morgen ['mɔrgən] ADV tomorrow; **bis ~!** see you tomorrow!; **~ in acht Tagen** a week (from) tomorrow; **~ um diese Zeit** this time tomorrow; **~ früh** tomorrow morning; **Morgen** (**-s, -**) M morning; (*Maß*) ≈ acre; **am Morgen** in the morning; **guten Morgen!** good morning!
Morgen- zW: **Morgengrauen** NT dawn, daybreak; **Morgenmantel** M dressing gown; **Morgenrock** M dressing gown; **Morgenrot** NT, **Morgenröte** F dawn
morgens ADV in the morning; **von ~ bis abends** from morning to night
Morgenstunde F: **Morgenstund(e) hat Gold im Mund(e)** (*Sprichwort*) the early bird catches the worm (*Sprichwort*)
morgig ['mɔrgɪç] ADJ tomorrow's; **der morgige Tag** tomorrow
Morphium ['mɔrfiʊm] NT morphine

morsch [mɔrʃ] ADJ rotten
Morsealphabet ['mɔrzəlalfabe:t] NT Morse code
morsen VI to send a message by Morse code
Mörser ['mœrzər] **(-s, -)** M mortar (*auch Mil*)
Mörtel ['mœrtəl] **(-s, -)** M mortar
Mosaik [moza'i:k] **(-s, -en** *od* **-e)** NT mosaic
Mosambik [mosam'bi:k] **(-s)** NT Mozambique
Moschee [mɔ'ʃe:] **(-, -n)** F mosque
Mosel[1] ['mo:zəl] F (*Geog*) Moselle
Mosel[2] **(-s, -)** M (*auch*: **Moselwein**) Moselle (wine)
mosern ['mo:zərn] (*umg*) VI to gripe, to bellyache
Moskau ['mɔskaʊ] **(-s)** NT Moscow
Moskauer ADJ Moscow *attrib*
Moskauer(in) **(-s, -)** M(F) Muscovite
Moskito [mɔs'ki:to] **(-s, -s)** M mosquito
Moslem ['mɔslɛm] **(-s, -s)** M Muslim
moslemisch [mɔs'le:mɪʃ] ADJ Muslim
Most [mɔst] **(-(e)s, -e)** M (unfermented) fruit juice; (*Apfelwein*) cider
Motel [mo'tɛl] **(-s, -s)** NT motel
Motiv [mo'ti:f] **(-s, -e)** NT motive; (*Mus*) theme
Motivation [motivatsi'o:n] F motivation
motivieren [moti'vi:rən] VT to motivate
Motivierung F motivation
Motor ['mo:tɔr] **(-s, -en)** M engine; (*bes Elek*) motor; **Motorboot** NT motorboat
Motorenöl NT engine oil
Motorhaube F (*Aut*) bonnet (BRIT), hood (US)
motorisch ADJ (*Physiologie*) motor *attrib*
motorisieren [motori'zi:rən] VT to motorize
Motor- ZW: **Motorrad** NT motorcycle; **Motorradfahrer** M motorcyclist; **Motorroller** M motor scooter; **Motorschaden** M engine trouble *od* failure; **Motorsport** M motor sport
Motte ['mɔtə] **(-, -n)** F moth
Motten- ZW: **mottenfest** ADJ mothproof; **Mottenkiste** F: **etw aus der Mottenkiste hervorholen** (*fig*) to dig sth out; **Mottenkugel** F mothball
Motto ['mɔto] **(-s, -s)** NT motto
motzen ['mɔtsən] (*umg*) VI to grouse, to beef
Mountainbike NT mountain bike
Möwe ['mø:və] **(-, -n)** F seagull
MP (-) F ABK = **Maschinenpistole**
MP3 ABK (*Comput*) MP3
MP3-Spieler M (*Comput*) MP3 player
Mrd. ABK = **Milliarde**
MS ABK (= *Motorschiff*) motor vessel, MV; (= *multiple Sklerose*) MS
MTA **(-, -s)** F ABK (= *medizinisch-technische Assistentin*) medical assistant
mtl. ABK = **monatlich**
Mucke ['mʊkə] **(-, -n)** F (*meist pl*) caprice; (*von Ding*) snag, bug; **seine Mucken haben** to be temperamental
Mücke ['mʏkə] **(-, -n)** F midge, gnat; **aus einer ~ einen Elefanten machen** (*umg*) to make a mountain out of a molehill
Muckefuck ['mʊkəfʊk] **(-s)** (*umg*) M coffee substitute
mucken VI: **ohne zu ~** without a murmur
Mückenstich M midge *od* gnat bite
Mucks [mʊks] **(-es, e)** M: **keinen ~ sagen** not to make a sound; (*nicht widersprechen*) not to say a word
mucksen (*umg*) VR to budge; (*Laut geben*) to open one's mouth
mucksmäuschenstill ['mʊks'mɔʏsçənʃtɪl] (*umg*) ADJ (as) quiet as a mouse
müde ['my:də] ADJ tired; **nicht ~ werden, etw zu tun** never to tire of doing something
Müdigkeit ['my:dɪçkaɪt] F tiredness; **nur keine ~ vorschützen!** (*umg*) don't (you) tell me you're tired!
Muff [mʊf] **(-(e)s, -e)** M (*Handwärmer*) muff
Muffel **(-s, -)** (*umg*) M killjoy, sourpuss
muffig ADJ (*Luft*) musty
Mühe ['my:ə] **(-, -n)** F trouble, pains *pl*; **mit Müh(e) und Not** with great difficulty; **sich** *dat* **~ geben** to go to a lot of trouble; **mühelos** ADJ effortless, easy
muhen ['mu:ən] VI to low, to moo
mühevoll ADJ laborious, arduous
Mühle ['my:lə] **(-, -n)** F mill; (*Kaffeemühle*) grinder; (*Mühlespiel*) nine men's morris
Mühlrad NT millwheel
Mühlstein M millstone
Mühsal **(-, -e)** F tribulation
mühsam ADJ arduous, troublesome ▶ ADV with difficulty
mühselig ADJ arduous, laborious
Mulatte [mu'latə] **(-, -n)** M mulatto
Mulattin F mulatto
Mulde ['mʊldə] **(-, -n)** F hollow, depression
Mull [mʊl] **(-(e)s, -e)** M thin muslin
Müll [mʏl] **(-(e)s)** M refuse, rubbish, garbage (US); **Müllabfuhr** F refuse *od* garbage (US) collection; (*Leute*) dustmen *pl* (BRIT), garbage collectors *pl* (US); **Müllabladeplatz** M rubbish dump; **Müllbeutel** M bin liner (BRIT), trashcan liner (US)
Mullbinde F gauze bandage
Müll- ZW: **Müllcontainer** M waste container; **Mülldeponie** F waste disposal site, rubbish (BRIT) *od* garbage (US) dump; **Mülleimer** M rubbish bin (BRIT), garbage can (US)
Müller **(-s, -)** M miller
Müll- ZW: **Müllhalde** F, **Müllhaufen** M rubbish *od* garbage (US) heap; **Müllmann** **(-(e)s,** *pl* **Müllmänner)** (*umg*) M dustman (BRIT), garbage collector (US); **Müllsack** M rubbish *od* garbage (US) bag; **Müllschlucker** M waste (BRIT) *od* garbage (US) disposal unit; **Mülltonne** F dustbin (BRIT), trashcan (US); **Mülltrennung** F *sorting and collecting household waste according to type of material*; **Müllverbrennung** F rubbish *od* garbage (US) incineration; **Müllverbrennungsanlage** F incinerator, incinerating plant; **Müllwagen** M dustcart (BRIT), garbage truck (US)
mulmig ['mʊlmɪç] ADJ rotten; (*umg*) uncomfortable; **jdm ist ~** sb feels funny
Multi ['mʊlti] **(-s, -s)** (*umg*) M multinational (organization)

m

multi- IN ZW multi; **multikulturell** ADJ multicultural; **multilateral** ADJ: **multilateraler Handel** multilateral trade; **multinational** ADJ multinational; **multinationaler Konzern** multinational organization
multiple Sklerose [mʊl'ti:plə skle'ro:zə] F multiple sclerosis
multiplizieren [mʊltipli'tsi:rən] VT to multiply
Mumie ['mu:miə] F (*Leiche*) mummy
Mumm [mʊm] (**-s**) (*umg*) M gumption, nerve
Mumps [mʊmps] (-) M OD F mumps *sing*
München ['mʏnçən] NT Munich
Münchener, Münchner(in) (**-s, -**) M(F) person from Munich
Mund [mʊnt] (**-(e)s, Münder**) M mouth; **den ~ aufmachen** (*fig: seine Meinung sagen*) to speak up; **sie ist nicht auf den ~ gefallen** (*umg*) she's never at a loss for words; **halt den ~!** shut up; **Mundart** F dialect
Mündel ['mʏndəl] (**-s, -**) NT (*Jur*) ward
münden ['mʏndən] VI: **in etw** *akk* **~** to flow into sth
Mund- ZW: **mundfaul** ADJ uncommunicative; **mundgerecht** ADJ bite-sized; **Mundgeruch** M bad breath; **Mundharmonika** F mouth organ
mündig ['mʏndıç] ADJ of age; **Mündigkeit** F majority
mündlich ['mʏntlıç] ADJ oral; **mündliche Prüfung** oral (exam); **mündliche Verhandlung** (*Jur*) hearing; **alles Weitere ~!** let's talk about it more when I see you
Mund- ZW: **Mundraub** M (*Jur*) theft of food for personal consumption; **Mundstück** NT mouthpiece; (*von Zigarette*) tip; **mundtot** ADJ: **jdn mundtot machen** to muzzle sb
Mündung ['mʏndʊŋ] F estuary; (*von Fluss, Rohr etc*) mouth; (*Gewehrmündung*) muzzle
Mund- ZW: **Mundwasser** NT mouthwash; **Mundwerk** NT: **ein großes Mundwerk haben** to have a big mouth; **Mundwinkel** M corner of the mouth; **Mund-zu-mund-Beatmung** F mouth-to-mouth resuscitation
Munition [munitsi'o:n] F ammunition
Munitionslager NT ammunition dump
munkeln ['mʊŋkəln] VI to whisper, to mutter; **man munkelt, dass …** there's a rumour (BRIT) *od* rumor (US) that …
Münster ['mʏnstər] (**-s, -**) NT minster
munter ['mʊntər] ADJ lively; (*wach*) awake; (*aufgestanden*) up and about; **Munterkeit** F liveliness
Münzanstalt F mint
Münzautomat M slot machine
Münze ['mʏntsə] (**-, -n**) F coin
münzen VT to coin, to mint; **auf jdn gemünzt sein** to be aimed at sb
Münzfernsprecher ['mʏntsfɛrnʃprɛçər] M callbox (BRIT), pay phone (US)
Münzwechsler M change machine
mürb ['mʏrb], **mürbe** ['mʏrbə] ADJ (*Gestein*) crumbly; (*Holz*) rotten; (*Gebäck*) crisp; **jdn ~(e) machen** to wear sb down
Mürbeteig, Mürbteig M shortcrust pastry
Murmel ['mʊrməl] (**-, -n**) F marble
murmeln VT, VI to murmur, to mutter
Murmeltier ['mʊrməlti:r] NT marmot; **schlafen wie ein ~** to sleep like a log
murren ['mʊrən] VI to grumble, to grouse
mürrisch ['mʏrıʃ] ADJ sullen
Mus [mu:s] (**-es, -e**) NT purée
Muschel ['mʊʃəl] (**-, -n**) F mussel; (*Muschelschale*) shell; (*Telefonmuschel*) receiver
Muse ['mu:zə] (**-, -n**) F muse
Museum [mu'ze:ʊm] (**-s, Museen**) NT museum
museumsreif ADJ: **~ sein** to be almost a museum piece
Musik [mu'zi:k] F music; (*Kapelle*) band
musikalisch [muzi:'ka:lıʃ] ADJ musical
Musikbox F jukebox
Musiker(in) ['mu:zikər(ın)] (**-s, -**) M(F) musician
Musik- ZW: **Musikhochschule** F music school; **Musikinstrument** NT musical instrument; **Musikkapelle** F band; **Musikstück** NT piece of music; **Musikstunde** F music lesson
musisch ['mu:zıʃ] ADJ artistic
musizieren [muzi'tsi:rən] VI to make music
Muskat [mʊs'ka:t] (**-(e)s, -e**) M nutmeg
Muskel ['mʊskəl] (**-s, -n**) M muscle; **Muskeldystrophie** F muscular dystrophy; **Muskelkater** M: **einen Muskelkater haben** to be stiff; **Muskelpaket** (*umg*) NT muscleman; **Muskelzerrung** F pulled muscle
Muskulatur [mʊskula'tu:r] F muscular system
muskulös [mʊsku'lø:s] ADJ muscular
Müsli ['my:sli] (**-s, -**) NT muesli
Muslim ['mʊslım] (**-s, -s**) M, **Muslimin** [mʊs'li:mın] F Muslim
muss VB *siehe* **müssen**
Muss [mʊs] (-) NT necessity, must
Muße ['mu:sə] (-) F leisure

SCHLÜSSELWORT

müssen ['mʏsən] (*pt* **musste**, *pp* **gemusst**: *od (als Hilfsverb)* **müssen**) VI **1** (*Zwang*) must (*nur im Präsens*), to have to; **ich muss es tun** I must do it, I have to do it; **ich musste es tun** I had to do it; **er muss es nicht tun** he doesn't have to do it; **muss ich?** must I?, do I have to?; **wann müsst ihr zur Schule?** when do you have to go to school?; **der Brief muss heute noch zur Post** the letter must be posted (BRIT) *od* mailed (US) today; **er hat gehen müssen** he (has) had to go; **muss das sein?** is that really necessary?; **wenn es (unbedingt) sein muss** if it's absolutely necessary; **ich muss mal** (*umg*) I need to go to the loo (BRIT) *od* bathroom (US)
2 (*sollen*): **das musst du nicht tun!** you oughtn't to *od* shouldn't do that; **das müsstest du eigentlich wissen** you ought to *od* you should know that; **Sie hätten ihn fragen müssen** you should have asked him
3: **es muss geregnet haben** it must have rained; **es muss nicht wahr sein** it needn't be true

Mussheirat (*umg*) F shotgun wedding
müßig ['my:sıç] ADJ idle; **Müßiggang** M idleness
musst [mʊst] VB *siehe* **müssen**
musste *etc* ['mʊstə] VB *siehe* **müssen**
Muster ['mʊstər] (**-s, -**) NT model; (*Dessin*) pattern; (*Probe*) sample; **~ ohne Wert** free sample; **Musterbeispiel** NT classic example; **mustergültig** ADJ exemplary; **musterhaft** ADJ exemplary
mustern VT (*betrachten, Mil*) to examine; (*Truppen*) to inspect
Musterprozess M test case
Musterschüler M model pupil
Musterung F (*von Stoff*) pattern; (*Mil*) inspection
Mut [mu:t] M courage; **nur ~!** cheer up!; **jdm ~ machen** to encourage sb; **~ fassen** to pluck up courage
mutig ADJ courageous
mutlos ADJ discouraged, despondent
mutmaßen VT UNTR to conjecture ▶ VI UNTR to conjecture
mutmaßlich ['mu:tma:slıç] ADJ presumed ▶ ADV probably
Mutprobe F test of courage
Mutter[1] ['mʊtər] (**-, -n**) F (*Schraubenmutter*) nut
Mutter[2] ['mʊtər] (**-, Mütter**) F mother; **Mutterfreuden** PL the joys *pl* of motherhood; **Muttergesellschaft** F (*Comm*) parent company; **Mutterkuchen** M (*Anat*) placenta; **Mutterland** NT mother country; **Mutterleib** M womb
mütterlich ['mʏtərlıç] ADJ motherly
mütterlicherseits ADV on the mother's side
Mutter- ZW: **Mutterliebe** F motherly love; **Muttermal** NT birthmark; **Muttermilch** F mother's milk
Mutterschaft F motherhood
Mutterschaftsgeld NT maternity benefit
Mutterschaftsurlaub M maternity leave
Mutter- ZW: **Mutterschutz** M maternity regulations *pl*; **mutterseelenallein** ADJ all alone; **Muttersprache** F native language; **Muttertag** M Mother's Day
Mutti (**-, -s**) (*umg*) F mum(my) (BRIT), mom(my) (*US*)
mutwillig ['mu:tvılıç] ADJ deliberate
Mütze ['mʏtsə] (**-, -n**) F cap
MV F ABK (= *Mitgliederversammlung*) general meeting
MW ABK (= *Mittelwelle*) MW
MwSt, Mw.-St. ABK (= *Mehrwertsteuer*) VAT
mysteriös [mʏsteri'ø:s] ADJ mysterious
Mystik ['mʏstık] F mysticism
Mystiker(in) (**-s, -**) M(F) mystic
mystisch ['mʏstıʃ] ADJ mystical; (*rätselhaft*) mysterious
Mythologie [mytolo'gi:] F mythology
Mythos ['my:tɔs] (**-, Mythen**) M myth

m

Nn

N¹, n [ɛn] NT N, n; **N wie Nordpol** ≈ N for Nellie, ≈ N for Nan (*US*)
N² [ɛn] ABK (= *Norden*) N
na [na] INTERJ well; **na gut** (*umg*) all right, OK; **na also!** (well,) there you are (then)!; **na so was!** well, I never!; **na und?** so what?
Nabel ['na:bəl] (**-s, -**) M navel; **der ~ der Welt** (*fig*) the hub of the universe; **Nabelschnur** F umbilical cord

SCHLÜSSELWORT

nach [na:x] PRÄP +*dat* **1** (*örtlich*) to; **nach Berlin** to Berlin; **nach links/rechts** (to the) left/right; **nach oben/hinten** up/back; **er ist schon nach London abgefahren** he has already left for London
2 (*zeitlich*) after; **einer nach dem anderen** one after the other; **nach Ihnen!** after you!; **zehn (Minuten) nach drei** ten (minutes) past *od* after (*US*) three
3 (*gemäß*) according to; **nach dem Gesetz** according to the law; **die Uhr nach dem Radio stellen** to put a clock right by the radio; **ihrer Sprache nach (zu urteilen)** judging by her language; **dem Namen nach** judging by his/her name; **nach allem, was ich weiß** as far as I know
▸ ADV: **ihm nach!** after him!; **nach und nach** gradually, little by little; **nach wie vor** still

nachäffen ['na:x|ɛfən] VT to ape
nachahmen ['na:x|a:mən] VT to imitate
nachahmenswert ADJ exemplary
Nachahmung F imitation; **etw zur ~ empfehlen** to recommend sth as an example
Nachbar(in) ['naxba:r(ɪn)] (**-s, -n**) M(F) neighbour (*Brit*), neighbor (*US*); **Nachbarhaus** NT: **im Nachbarhaus** next door; **nachbarlich** ADJ neighbourly (*Brit*), neighborly (*US*); **Nachbarschaft** F neighbourhood (*Brit*), neighborhood (*US*); **Nachbarstaat** M neighbouring (*Brit*) *od* neighboring (*US*) state
nach- zW: **Nachbehandlung** F (*Med*) follow-up treatment; **nachbestellen** VT to order again; **Nachbestellung** F (*Comm*) repeat order; **nachbeten** (*pej, umg*) VT to repeat parrot-fashion; **nachbezahlen** VT to pay; (*später*) to pay later; **nachbilden** VT to copy; **Nachbildung** F imitation, copy; **nachblicken** VI to look *od* gaze after; **nachdatieren** VT to postdate
nachdem [na:x'de:m] KONJ after; (*weil*) since; **je ~ (ob)** it depends (whether)
nach- zW: **nachdenken** *unreg* VI: **über etw** *akk* **nachdenken** to think about sth; **darüber darf man gar nicht nachdenken** it doesn't bear thinking about; **Nachdenken** NT reflection, meditation; **nachdenklich** ADJ thoughtful, pensive; **nachdenklich gestimmt sein** to be in a thoughtful mood
Nachdruck ['na:xdrʊk] M emphasis; (*Typ*) reprint, reproduction; **besonderen ~ darauf legen, dass ...** to stress *od* emphasize particularly that ...
nachdrücklich ['na:xdrʏklɪç] ADJ emphatic; **~ auf etw** *dat* **bestehen** to insist firmly (up)on sth
nacheifern ['na:x|aɪfərn] VI: **jdm ~** to emulate sb
nacheinander [na:x|aɪ'nandər] ADV one after the other; **kurz ~** shortly after each other; **drei Tage ~** three days running, three days on the trot (*umg*)
nachempfinden ['na:x|ɛmpfɪndən] *unreg* VT: **jdm etw ~** to feel sth with sb
nacherzählen ['na:x|ɛrtsɛ:lən] VT to retell
Nacherzählung F reproduction (of a story)
Nachf. ABK = **Nachfolger(in)**
Nachfahr ['na:xfa:r] (**-en, -en**) M descendant
Nachfolge ['na:xfɔlgə] F succession; **die/jds ~ antreten** to succeed/succeed sb
nachfolgen VI (*lit*): **jdm/etw ~** to follow sb/sth
nachfolgend ADJ following
Nachfolger(in) (**-s, -**) M(F) successor
nachforschen VT, VI to investigate
Nachforschung F investigation; **Nachforschungen anstellen** to make enquiries
Nachfrage ['na:xfra:gə] F inquiry; (*Comm*) demand; **es besteht eine rege ~** (*Comm*) there is a great demand; **danke der ~** (*form*) thank you for your concern; (*umg*) nice of you to ask; **nachfragemäßig** ADJ according to demand
nachfragen VI to inquire
nach- zW: **nachfühlen** VT = **nachempfinden**; **nachfüllen** VT to refill; **nachgeben** *unreg* VI to give way, to yield

Nachgebühr F surcharge; (*Post*) excess postage
Nachgeburt F afterbirth
nachgehen ['na:xge:ən] *unreg* VI *+dat* to follow; (*erforschen*) to inquire (into); (*Uhr*) to be slow; **einer geregelten Arbeit ~** to have a steady job
Nachgeschmack ['na:xgəʃmak] M aftertaste
nachgiebig ['na:xgi:bɪç] ADJ soft, accommodating; **Nachgiebigkeit** F softness
nachgrübeln ['na:xgry:bəln] VI: **über etw** *akk* **~** to think about sth; (*sich Gedanken machen*) to ponder on sth
nachgucken ['na:xgʊkən] VT, VI = **nachsehen**
nachhaken ['na:xha:kən] (*umg*) VI to dig deeper
Nachhall ['na:xhal] M resonance
nachhallen VI to resound
nachhaltig ['na:xhaltɪç] ADJ lasting; (*Widerstand*) persistent
nachhängen ['na:xhɛŋən] *unreg* VI: **seinen Erinnerungen ~** to lose o.s. in one's memories
nachhause ADV home
Nachhauseweg [na:x'haʊzəve:k] M way home
nachhelfen ['na:xhɛlfən] *unreg* VI: **jdm ~** to help *od* assist sb; **er hat dem Glück ein bisschen nachgeholfen** he engineered himself a little luck
nachher [na:x'he:r] ADV afterwards; **bis ~** see you later!
Nachhilfe ['na:xhɪlfə] F (*auch*: **Nachhilfeunterricht**) extra (private) tuition
Nachhinein ['na:xhɪnaɪn] ADV: **im ~** afterwards; (*rückblickend*) in retrospect
Nachholbedarf M: **einen ~ an etw** *dat* **haben** to have a lot of sth to catch up on
nachholen ['na:xho:lən] VT to catch up with; (*Versäumtes*) to make up for
Nachkomme ['na:xkɔmə] (**-n, -n**) M descendant
nachkommen *unreg* VI to follow; (*einer Verpflichtung*) to fulfil; **Sie können Ihr Gepäck ~ lassen** you can have your luggage sent on (after)
Nachkommenschaft F descendants *pl*
Nachkriegs- ['na:xkri:ks] IN ZW postwar; **Nachkriegszeit** F postwar period
Nach- ZW: **Nachlass (-es, -lässe)** M (*Comm*) discount, rebate; (*Erbe*) estate; **nachlassen** *unreg* VT (*Strafe*) to remit; (*Summe*) to take off; (*Schulden*) to cancel ▸ VI to decrease, to ease off; (*Sturm*) to die down; (*schlechter werden*) to deteriorate; **er hat nachgelassen** he has got worse; **nachlässig** ADJ negligent, careless; **Nachlässigkeit** F negligence, carelessness; **Nachlasssteuer** F death duty; **Nachlassverwalter** M executor
nachlaufen ['na:xlaʊfən] *unreg* VI: **jdm ~** to run after *od* chase sb
nachliefern ['na:xli:fərn] VT (*später liefern*) to deliver at a later date; (*zuzüglich liefern*) to make a further delivery of
nachlösen ['na:xløːzən] VI to pay on the train/ when one gets off; (*zur Weiterfahrt*) to pay the extra
nachm. ABK (= *nachmittags*) p.m.
nachmachen ['na:xmaxən] VT to imitate, to copy; (*fälschen*) to counterfeit; **jdm etw ~** to copy sth from sb; **das soll erst mal einer ~!** I'd like to see anyone else do that!
Nachmieter(in) ['na:xmi:tər(ɪn)] M(F): **wir müssen einen ~ finden** we have to find someone to take over the flat *etc*
Nachmittag ['na:xmɪta:k] M afternoon; **am ~** in the afternoon; **gestern/heute ~** yesterday/ this afternoon
nachmittags ADV in the afternoon
Nachmittagsvorstellung F matinée (performance)
Nachn. ABK = **Nachnahme**
Nachnahme (-, -n) F cash on delivery (*Brit*), collect on delivery (*US*); **per ~** C.O.D.
Nachname M surname
Nachporto NT excess postage
nachprüfbar ['na:xpry:fba:r] ADJ verifiable
nachprüfen ['na:xpry:fən] VT to check, to verify
nachrechnen ['na:xrɛçnən] VT to check
Nachrede ['na:xre:də] F: **üble ~** (*Jur*) defamation of character
nachreichen ['na:xraɪçən] VT to hand in later
Nachricht ['na:xrɪçt] (**-, -en**) F (piece of) news *sing*; (*Mitteilung*) message
Nachrichten PL news *sing*; **Nachrichtenagentur** F news agency; **Nachrichtendienst** M (*Mil*) intelligence service; **Nachrichtensatellit** M (tele)communications satellite; **Nachrichtensperre** F news blackout; **Nachrichtensprecher(in)** M(F) newsreader; **Nachrichtentechnik** F telecommunications *sing*
nachrücken ['na:xrʏkən] VI to move up
Nachruf ['na:xru:f] M obituary (notice)
nachrüsten ['na:xrʏstən] VT (*Kraftwerk etc*) to modernize; (*Auto etc*) to refit; (*Waffen*) to keep up to date ▸ VI (*Mil*) to deploy new arms
nachsagen ['na:xza:gən] VT to repeat; **jdm etw ~** to say sth of sb; **das lasse ich mir nicht ~!** I'm not having that said of me!
Nachsaison ['na:xzɛzõ:] F off season
nachschenken ['na:xʃɛŋkən] VT, VI: **darf ich Ihnen noch (etwas) ~?** may I top up your glass?
nachschicken ['na:xʃɪkən] VT to forward
nachschlagen ['na:xʃla:gən] *unreg* VT to look up ▸ VI: **jdm ~** to take after sb
Nachschlagewerk NT reference book
Nachschlüssel M master key
nachschmeißen ['na:xʃmaɪsən] *unreg* (*umg*) VT: **das ist ja nachgeschmissen!** it's a real bargain!
Nachschrift ['na:xʃrɪft] F postscript
Nachschub ['na:xʃu:p] M supplies *pl*; (*Truppen*) reinforcements *pl*
nachsehen ['na:xze:ən] *unreg* VT (*prüfen*) to check ▸ VI (*erforschen*) to look and see; **jdm etw ~** to forgive sb sth; **jdm ~** to gaze after sb
Nachsehen NT: **das ~ haben** to be left empty-handed

n

nachsenden ['na:xzɛndən] *unreg* VT to send on, to forward
Nachsicht ['na:xzɪçt] (-) F indulgence, leniency
nachsichtig ADJ indulgent, lenient
Nachsilbe ['na:xzɪlbə] F suffix
nachsitzen ['na:xzɪtsən] *unreg* VI (*Sch*) to be kept in
Nachsorge ['na:xzɔrgə] F (*Med*) aftercare
Nachspann ['na:xʃpan] M credits *pl*
Nachspeise ['na:xʃpaɪzə] F dessert, sweet (BRIT)
Nachspiel ['na:xʃpi:l] NT epilogue; (*fig*) sequel
nachspionieren ['na:xʃpioni:rən] (*umg*) VI: **jdm ~** to spy on sb
nachsprechen ['na:xʃprɛçən] *unreg* VT: **(jdm) ~** to repeat (after sb)
nächst [nɛ:çst] PRÄP +*dat* (*räumlich*) next to; (*außer*) apart from; **nächstbeste(r, s)** ADJ: **der nächstbeste Zug/Job** the first train/job that comes along
nächste(r, s) ADJ next; (*nächstgelegen*) nearest; **aus nächster Nähe** from close by; (*betrachten*) at close quarters; **Ende nächsten Monats** at the end of next month; **am nächsten Tag** (the) next day; **bei nächster Gelegenheit** at the earliest opportunity; **in nächster Zeit** some time soon; **der ~ Angehörige** the next of kin
Nächste(r, s) F(M) neighbour (BRIT), neighbor (US)
nachstehen ['na:xʃte:ən] *unreg* VI: **jdm in nichts ~** to be sb's equal in every way
nachstehend ADJ *attrib* following
nachstellen ['na:xʃtɛlən] VI: **jdm ~** to follow sb; (*aufdringlich umwerben*) to pester sb
Nächstenliebe F love for one's fellow men
nächstens ADV shortly, soon
nächstliegend ADJ (*lit*) nearest; (*fig*) obvious
nächstmöglich ADJ next possible
nachsuchen ['na:xzu:xən] VI: **um etw ~** to ask *od* apply for sth
Nacht [naxt] (**-, Nächte**) F night; **gute ~!** good night!; **heute ~** tonight; **in der ~** at night; **in der ~ auf Dienstag** during Monday night; **in der ~ vom 12. zum 13. April** during the night of April 12th to 13th; **über ~** (*auch fig*) overnight; **bei ~ und Nebel** (*umg*) at dead of night; **sich** *dat* **die ~ um die Ohren schlagen** (*umg*) to stay up all night; (*mit Feiern, arbeiten*) to make a night of it
Nachtdienst M night duty
Nachteil ['na:xtaɪl] M disadvantage; **im ~ sein** to be at a disadvantage
nachteilig ADJ disadvantageous
Nachtfalter M moth
Nachthemd NT (*Damennachthemd*) nightdress (BRIT), nightgown; (*Herrennachthemd*) nightshirt
Nachtigall ['naxtɪgal] (**-, -en**) F nightingale
Nachtisch ['na:xtɪʃ] M dessert, sweet (BRIT)
Nachtklub M night club
Nachtleben NT night life
nächtlich ['nɛçtlɪç] ADJ nightly
Nacht- zW: **Nachtlokal** NT night club; **Nachtmensch** ['naxtmɛnʃ] M night person; **Nachtportier** M night porter

nach- zW: **Nachtrag** ['na:xtra:k] (**-(e)s, -träge**) M supplement; **nachtragen** *unreg* VT (*zufügen*) to add; **jdm etw nachtragen** to carry sth after sb; (*fig*) to hold sth against sb; **nachtragend** ADJ resentful; **nachträglich** ADJ later, subsequent; (*zusätzlich*) additional ▶ ADV later, subsequently; (*zusätzlich*) additionally; **nachtrauern** VI: **jdm/etw nachtrauern** to mourn the loss of sb/sth
Nachtruhe ['naxtru:ə] F sleep
nachts ADV by night
Nachtschicht F night shift
Nachtschwester F night nurse
nachtsüber ADV during the night
Nacht- zW: **Nachttarif** M off-peak tariff; **Nachttisch** M bedside table; **Nachttopf** M chamber pot; **Nachtwache** F night watch; (*im Krankenhaus*) night duty; **Nachtwächter** M night watchman; **Nachtzug** M night train
Nach- zW: **Nachuntersuchung** F checkup; **nachvollziehen** *unreg* VT to understand, to comprehend; **nachwachsen** *unreg* VI to grow again; **Nachwahl** F ≈ by-election (*bes* BRIT); **Nachwehen** PL afterpains *pl*; (*fig*) aftereffects *pl*; **nachweinen** VI +*dat* to mourn ▶ VT: **dieser Sache** *dat* **weine ich keine Träne nach** I won't shed any tears over that
Nachweis ['na:xvaɪs] (**-es, -e**) M proof; **den ~ für etw erbringen** *od* **liefern** to furnish proof of sth; **nachweisbar** ADJ provable, demonstrable; **nachweisen** ['na:xvaɪzən] *unreg* VT to prove; **jdm etw nachweisen** to point sth out to sb; **nachweislich** ADJ evident, demonstrable
nach- zW: **Nachwelt** F: **die Nachwelt** posterity; **nachwinken** VI: **jdm nachwinken** to wave after sb; **nachwirken** VI to have aftereffects; **Nachwirkung** F aftereffect; **Nachwort** NT appendix; **Nachwuchs** M offspring; (*beruflich etc*) new recruits *pl*; **nachzahlen** VT, VI to pay extra; **nachzählen** VT to count again; **Nachzahlung** F additional payment; (*zurückdatiert*) back pay
nachziehen ['na:xtsi:ən] *unreg* VT (*Linie*) to go over; (*Lippen*) to paint; (*Augenbrauen*) to pencil in; (*hinterherziehen*): **etw ~** to drag sth behind one
Nachzügler (**-s, -**) M straggler
Nackedei ['nakədaɪ] (**-(e)s, -e** *od* **-s**) M (*hum: umg: Kind*) little bare monkey
Nacken ['nakən] (**-s, -**) M nape of the neck; **jdm im ~ sitzen** (*umg*) to breathe down sb's neck
nackt [nakt] ADJ naked; (*Tatsachen*) plain, bare; **Nacktheit** F nakedness; **Nacktkultur** F nudism
Nadel ['na:dəl] (**-, -n**) F needle; (*Stecknadel*) pin; **Nadelbaum** M conifer; **Nadelkissen** NT pincushion; **Nadelöhr** NT eye of a needle; **Nadelwald** M coniferous forest
Nagel ['na:gəl] (**-s, Nägel**) M nail; **sich** *dat* **etw unter den ~ reißen** (*umg*) to pinch sth; **etw an den ~ hängen** (*fig*) to chuck sth in (*umg*); **Nägel mit Köpfen machen** (*umg*) to do the job properly; **Nagelbürste** F nailbrush;

Nagelfeile F nailfile; **Nagelhaut** F cuticle; **Nagellack** M nail varnish (BRIT) *od* polish; **Nagellackentferner** (**-s, -**) M nail polish remover
nageln VT, VI to nail
nagelneu ADJ brand-new
Nagelschere F nail scissors *pl*
nagen ['na:gən] VT, VI to gnaw
Nagetier ['na:gəti:r] NT rodent
nah ADJ = **nahe**
Nahaufnahme F close-up
nahe ADJ (*räumlich*) near(by); (*Verwandte*) near, close; (*Freunde*) close; (*zeitlich*) near, close ▸ ADV: **von nah und fern** from near and far ▸ PRÄP *+dat* near (to), close to; **von Nahem** at close quarters; **der N~ Osten** the Middle East; **jdm ~ kommen** to get close to sb; **~ liegend** obvious; **~ stehend** close; **jdm zu ~ treten** (*fig*) to offend sb; **mit jdm ~ verwandt sein** to be closely related to sb; **die nähere Umgebung** the immediate area; *siehe auch* **naheliegen**; **nahestehen**
Nahe F (*Fluss*) Nahe
Nähe ['nɛ:ə] (**-**) F nearness, proximity; (*Umgebung*) vicinity; **in der ~** close by; **aus der ~** from close to
nahebei ADV nearby
nahebringen *unreg* VT (*fig*): **jdm etw ~** to bring sth home to sb
nahegehen *unreg* VI (*fig*): **jdm ~** to grieve sb
nahelegen VT (*fig*): **jdm etw ~** to suggest sth to sb
naheliegen *unreg* VI (*fig*) to be obvious; **der Verdacht liegt nahe, dass ...** it seems reasonable to suspect that ...
nahen VI, VR to approach, to draw near
nähen ['nɛ:ən] VT, VI to sew
näher ADJ nearer; (*Erklärung, Erkundigung*) more detailed ▸ ADV nearer; (*genauer*) in greater detail; **~ kommen** to get closer; **ich kenne ihn nicht ~** I don't know him well
Nähere(s) NT details *pl*, particulars *pl*
Näherei [nɛ:ə'raɪ] F sewing, needlework
Naherholungsgebiet NT recreational area (*close to a centre of population*)
Näherin F seamstress
nähern VR to approach
Näherungswert M approximate value
nahestehen *unreg* VI (*fig*): **jdm ~** to be close to sb; **einer Sache ~** to sympathize with sth
nahezu ADV nearly
Nähgarn NT thread
Nahkampf M hand-to-hand fighting
Nähkasten M workbox, sewing basket
nahm *etc* [na:m] VB *siehe* **nehmen**
Nähmaschine F sewing machine
Nähnadel F (sewing) needle
Nahost [na:'ɔst] M: **aus ~** from the Middle East
Nährboden M (*lit*) fertile soil; (*fig*) breeding ground
nähren ['nɛ:rən] VT to feed ▸ VR (*Person*) to feed o.s.; (*Tier*) to feed; **er sieht gut genährt aus** he looks well fed
Nährgehalt ['nɛ:rgəhalt] M nutritional value
nahrhaft ['na:rhaft] ADJ (*Essen*) nourishing
Nährstoffe PL nutrients *pl*
Nahrung ['na:rʊŋ] F food; (*fig*) sustenance
Nahrungs- ZW: **Nahrungsaufnahme** F: **die Nahrungsaufnahme verweigern** to refuse food; **Nahrungskette** F food chain; **Nahrungsmittel** NT food(stuff); **Nahrungsmittelindustrie** F food industry; **Nahrungssuche** F search for food
Nährwert M nutritional value
Naht [na:t] (**-, Nähte**) F seam; (*Med*) suture; (*Tech*) join; **aus allen Nähten platzen** (*umg*) to be bursting at the seams; **nahtlos** ADJ seamless; **nahtlos ineinander übergehen** to follow without a gap
Nahverkehr M local traffic
Nahverkehrszug M local train
Nähzeug NT sewing kit, sewing things *pl*
Nahziel NT immediate objective
naiv [na'i:f] ADJ naïve
Naivität [naivi'tɛ:t] F naïveté, naïvety
Name ['na:mə] (**-ns, -n**) M name; **im Namen von** on behalf of; **dem Namen nach müsste sie Deutsche sein** judging by her name she must be German; **die Dinge beim Namen nennen** (*fig*) to call a spade a spade; **ich kenne das Stück nur dem Namen nach** I've heard of the play but that's all
namens ADV by the name of
Namensänderung F change of name
Namenstag M name day, saint's day

> In Catholic areas of Germany the **Namenstag** is often a more important celebration than a birthday. It is the day dedicated to the saint after whom a person is called, and on that day the person receives presents and invites relatives and friends round to celebrate.

namentlich ['na:məntlɪç] ADJ by name ▸ ADV particularly, especially
namhaft ['na:mhaft] ADJ (*berühmt*) famed, renowned; (*beträchtlich*) considerable; **~ machen** to name, to identify
Namibia [na'mi:bia] (**-s**) NT Namibia
nämlich ['nɛ:mlɪç] ADV that is to say, namely; (*denn*) since; **der/die/das Nämliche** the same
nannte *etc* ['nantə] VB *siehe* **nennen**
nanu [na'nu:] INTERJ well I never!
Napalm ['na:palm] (**-s**) NT napalm
Napf [napf] (**-(e)s, Näpfe**) M bowl, dish; **Napfkuchen** M ≈ ring-shaped pound cake
Narbe ['narbə] (**-, -n**) F scar
narbig ['narbɪç] ADJ scarred
Narkose [nar'ko:zə] (**-, -n**) F anaesthetic (BRIT), anesthetic (US)
Narr [nar] (**-en, -en**) M fool; **jdn zum Narren halten** to make a fool of sb; **narren** VT to fool
Narrenfreiheit F: **sie hat bei ihm ~** he gives her (a) free rein
narrensicher ADJ foolproof
Narrheit F foolishness
Närrin ['nɛrɪn] F fool

n

närrisch ADJ foolish, crazy; **die närrischen Tage** *Fasching and the period leading up to it*
Narzisse [nar'tsɪsə] (-, -**n**) F narcissus
narzisstisch [nar'tsɪstɪʃ] ADJ narcissistic
NASA ['na:za] (-) F ABK (= *National Aeronautics and Space Administration*) NASA
naschen ['naʃən] VT to nibble; (*heimlich*) to eat secretly ▸ VI to nibble sweet things; **~ von** *od* **an** *+dat* to nibble at
naschhaft ADJ sweet-toothed
Nase ['na:zə] (-, -**n**) F nose; **sich** *dat* **die ~ putzen** to wipe one's nose; (*sich schnäuzen*) to blow one's nose; **jdm auf der ~ herumtanzen** (*umg*) to play sb up; **jdm etw vor der ~ wegschnappen** (*umg*) to just beat sb to sth; **die ~ voll haben** (*umg*) to have had enough; **jdm etw auf die ~ binden** (*umg*) to tell sb all about sth; **(immer) der ~ nachgehen** (*umg*) to follow one's nose; **jdn an der ~ herumführen** (*als Täuschung*) to lead sb by the nose; (*als Scherz*) to pull sb's leg
Nasen- zW: **Nasenbluten** (-**s**) NT nosebleed; **Nasenloch** NT nostril; **Nasenrücken** M bridge of the nose; **Nasentropfen** PL nose drops *pl*
naseweis ADJ pert, cheeky; (*neugierig*) nosey
Nashorn ['na:shɔrn] NT rhinoceros
nass [nas] ADJ wet
Nassauer ['nasaʊər] (-**s**, -) (*umg*) M scrounger
Nässe ['nɛsə] (-) F wetness
nässen VT to wet
nasskalt ADJ wet and cold
Nassrasur F wet shave
Nation [natsi'o:n] F nation
national [natsio'na:l] ADJ national; **Nationalelf** F international (football) team; **Nationalfeiertag** M national holiday; **Nationalhymne** F national anthem
nationalisieren [natsiona:li'zi:rən] VT to nationalize
Nationalisierung F nationalization
Nationalismus [natsiona:'lɪsmʊs] M nationalism
nationalistisch [natsiona:'lɪstɪʃ] ADJ nationalistic
Nationalität [natsionali'tɛ:t] F nationality
National- zW: **Nationalmannschaft** F national team; **Nationalsozialismus** M National Socialism; **Nationalsozialist** M National Socialist; **Nationalspieler(in)** M(F) international (player)
NATO, Nato ['na:to] (-) F ABK: **die ~** NATO
Natrium ['na:triʊm] (-**s**) NT sodium
Natron ['na:trɔn] (-**s**) NT soda
Natter ['natər] (-, -**n**) F adder
Natur [na'tu:r] F nature; (*körperlich*) constitution; (*freies Land*) countryside; **das geht gegen meine ~** it goes against the grain
Naturalien [natu'ra:liən] PL natural produce *sing*; **in ~** in kind
Naturalismus [natu:ra'lɪsmʊs] M naturalism
Naturell [natu'rɛl] (-**s**, -**e**) NT temperament, disposition
Natur- zW: **Naturerscheinung** F natural phenomenon *od* event; **naturfarben** ADJ natural-coloured (BRIT) *od* -colored (US); **Naturforscher** M natural scientist; **Naturfreak** (-**s**, -**s**) (*umg*) M back-to-nature freak; **naturgemäß** ADJ natural; **Naturgeschichte** F natural history; **Naturgesetz** NT law of nature; **naturgetreu** ADJ true to life; **Naturheilverfahren** NT natural cure; **Naturkatastrophe** F natural disaster; **Naturkostladen** M health food shop; **Naturkunde** F natural history; **Naturlehrpfad** M nature trail
natürlich [na'ty:rlɪç] ADJ natural ▸ ADV naturally; (*selbstverständlich*) of course; **eines natürlichen Todes sterben** to die of natural causes
natürlicherweise [na'ty:rlɪçər'vaɪzə] ADV naturally, of course
Natürlichkeit F naturalness
Natur- zW: **Naturprodukt** NT natural product; **naturrein** ADJ natural, pure; **Naturschutz** M: **unter Naturschutz stehen** to be legally protected; **Naturschutzgebiet** NT nature reserve (BRIT), national park (US); **Naturtalent** NT natural prodigy; **naturverbunden** ADJ nature-loving; **Naturwissenschaft** F natural science; **Naturwissenschaftler** M scientist; **Naturzustand** M natural state
Nautik ['naʊtɪk] F nautical science, navigation
nautisch ['naʊtɪʃ] ADJ nautical
Navelorange ['na:vəlorã:ʒə] F navel orange
Navigation [navigatsi'o:n] F navigation
Navigations- zW: **Navigationsfehler** M navigational error; **Navigationsinstrumente** PL navigation instruments *pl*; **Navigationssystem** NT (*Aut*) navigation system
Nazi ['na:tsi] (-**s**, -**s**) M Nazi
NB ABK (= *nota bene*) NB
n. Br. ABK (= *nördlicher Breite*) northern latitude
NC M ABK (= *numerus clausus*) *siehe* **Numerus**
Nchf. ABK = **Nachfolger(in)**
n. Chr. ABK (= *nach Christus*) A.D.
NDR (-) M ABK (= *Norddeutscher Rundfunk*) North German Radio
Neapel [ne'a:pəl] (-**s**) NT Naples
Neapolitaner(in) [neapoli'ta:nər(ɪn)] (-**s**, -) M(F) Neapolitan
neapolitanisch [neapoli'ta:nɪʃ] ADJ Neapolitan
Nebel ['ne:bəl] (-**s**, -) M fog, mist
nebelig ADJ foggy, misty
Nebel- zW: **Nebelleuchte** F (*Aut*) rear fog-light; **Nebelscheinwerfer** M fog-lamp; **Nebelschlussleuchte** F (*Aut*) rear fog-light
neben ['ne:bən] PRÄP *+akk* next to ▸ PRÄP *+dat* next to; (*außer*) apart from, besides; **nebenan** [ne:bən'an] ADV next door; **Nebenanschluss** M (*Tel*) extension; **Nebenausgaben** PL incidental expenses *pl*; **nebenbei** [ne:bən'baɪ] ADV at the same time; (*außerdem*) additionally; (*beiläufig*) incidentally; **nebenbei bemerkt** *od* **gesagt** by the way, incidentally; **Nebenberuf** M second occupation; **er ist im Nebenberuf ...** he has a second job as a ...; **Nebenbeschäftigung** F

sideline; (*Zweitberuf*) extra job; **Nebenbuhler(in)** (**-s, -**) M(F) rival; **nebeneinander** [ne:bənaɪ'nandər] ADV side by side; **nebeneinanderlegen** VT to put next to each other; **Nebeneingang** M side entrance; **Nebeneinkünfte** PL, **Nebeneinnahmen** PL supplementary income *sing*; **Nebenerscheinung** F side effect; **Nebenfach** NT subsidiary subject; **Nebenfluss** M tributary; **Nebengeräusch** NT (*Rundf*) atmospherics *pl*, interference; **Nebenhandlung** F (*Liter*) subplot; **nebenher** [ne:bən'he:r] ADV (*zusätzlich*) besides; (*gleichzeitig*) at the same time; (*daneben*) alongside; **nebenherfahren** *unreg* VI to drive alongside; **Nebenkläger** M (*Jur*) joint plaintiff; **Nebenkosten** PL extra charges *pl*, extras *pl*; **Nebenmann** (**-(e)s**, *pl* **-männer**) M: **Ihr Nebenmann** the person next to you; **Nebenprodukt** NT by-product; **Nebenrolle** F minor part; **Nebensache** F trifle, side issue; **nebensächlich** ADJ minor, peripheral; **Nebensaison** F low season; **Nebensatz** M (*Gram*) subordinate clause; **nebenstehend** ADJ: **nebenstehende Abbildung** illustration opposite; **Nebenstraße** F side street; **Nebenstrecke** F (*Eisenb*) branch *od* local line; **Nebenverdienst** M secondary income; **Nebenzimmer** NT adjoining room

neblig ['ne:blɪç] ADJ = **nebelig**

nebst [ne:pst] PRÄP *+dat* together with

Necessaire [nesɛ'sɛ:r] (**-s, -s**) NT (*Nähnecessaire*) needlework box; (*Nagelnecessaire*) manicure case

Neckar ['nɛkar] (**-s**) M (*Fluss*) Neckar

necken ['nɛkən] VT to tease

Neckerei [nɛkə'raɪ] F teasing

neckisch ADJ coy; (*Einfall, Lied*) amusing

nee [ne:] (*umg*) ADV no, nope

Neffe ['nɛfə] (**-n, -n**) M nephew

negativ ['ne:gati:f] ADJ negative; **Negativ** (**-s, -e**) NT (*Phot*) negative

Neger ['ne:gər] (**-s, -**) (*pej*) M negro (*pej*); **Negerin** (*pej*) F negress (*pej*); **Negerkuss** M *chocolate-covered marshmallow*

negieren [ne'gi:rən] VT (*bestreiten*) to deny; (*verneinen*) to negate

nehmen ['ne:mən] *unreg* VT, VI to take; **etw zu sich ~** to take sth, to partake of sth (*liter*); **jdm etw ~** to take sth (away) from sb; **sich ernst ~** to take o.s. seriously; **~ Sie sich doch bitte** help yourself; **man nehme ...** (*Koch*) take ...; **wie mans nimmt** depending on your point of view; **die Mauer nimmt einem die ganze Sicht** the wall blocks the whole view; **er ließ es sich** *dat* **nicht ~, es persönlich zu tun** he insisted on doing it himself

Nehrung ['ne:rʊŋ] F (*Geog*) spit (of land)

Neid [naɪt] (**-(e)s**) M envy

Neider ['naɪdər] (**-s, -**) M envier

Neidhammel (*umg*) M envious person

neidisch ADJ envious, jealous

Neige (**-, -n**) F (*geh: Ende*): **die Vorräte gehen zur ~** the provisions are fast becoming exhausted

neigen ['naɪgən] VT to incline, to lean; (*Kopf*) to bow ▶ VI: **zu etw ~** to tend towards sth

Neigung F (*des Geländes*) slope; (*Tendenz*) tendency, inclination; (*Vorliebe*) liking; (*Zuneigung*) affection

Neigungswinkel M angle of inclination

nein [naɪn] ADV no

Nektarine [nɛkta'ri:nə] F nectarine

Nelke ['nɛlkə] (**-, -n**) F carnation, pink; (*Gewürznelke*) clove

nennen ['nɛnən] *unreg* VT to name; (*mit Namen*) to call; **das nenne ich Mut!** that's what I call courage!

nennenswert ADJ worth mentioning

Nenner (**-s, -**) M denominator; **etw auf einen ~ bringen** (*lit, fig*) to reduce sth to a common denominator

Nennung F naming

Nennwert M nominal value; (*Comm*) par

neokonservativ ADJ neo-conservative, neo-con (*umg*)

neoliberal ADJ neo-liberal, neo-lib (*umg*)

Neon ['ne:ɔn] (**-s**) NT neon

Neonazi [neo'na:tsi] M Neonazi

Neon- ZW: **Neonlicht** NT neon light; **Neonreklame** F neon sign; **Neonröhre** F neon tube

Nepal ['ne:pal] (**-s**) NT Nepal

Nepp [nɛp] (**-s**) (*umg*) M: **der reinste ~** daylight robbery, a rip-off

Nerv [nɛrf] (**-s, -en**) M nerve; **die Nerven sind mit ihm durchgegangen** he lost control, he snapped (*umg*); **jdm auf die Nerven gehen** to get on sb's nerves

nerven (*umg*) VT: **jdn ~** to get on sb's nerves

Nerven- ZW: **nervenaufreibend** ADJ nerve-racking; **Nervenbündel** NT bundle of nerves; **Nervengas** NT (*Mil*) nerve gas; **Nervenheilanstalt** F mental hospital; **Nervenklinik** F psychiatric clinic; **nervenkrank** ADJ mentally ill; **Nervensäge** (*umg*) F pain (in the neck); **Nervenschwäche** F neurasthenia; **Nervensystem** NT nervous system; **Nervenzusammenbruch** M nervous breakdown

nervig ['nɛrvɪç] (*umg*) ADJ exasperating, annoying

nervös [nɛr'vø:s] ADJ nervous

Nervosität [nɛrvozi'tɛ:t] F nervousness

nervtötend ADJ nerve-racking; (*Arbeit*) soul-destroying

Nerz [nɛrts] (**-es, -e**) M mink

Nessel ['nɛsəl] (**-, -n**) F nettle; **sich in die Nesseln setzen** (*fig: umg*) to put o.s. in a spot

Nessessär [nesɛ'sɛ:r] (**-s, -s**) NT = **Necessaire**

Nest [nɛst] (**-(e)s, -er**) NT nest; (*umg: Ort*) dump; (*fig: Bett*) bed; (*: Schlupfwinkel*) hide-out, lair; **da hat er sich ins warme ~ gesetzt** (*umg*) he's got it made; **Nestbeschmutzung** (*pej*) F running-down (*umg*) *od* denigration (of one's family/country)

nesteln VI: **an etw** *+dat* **~** to fumble *od* fiddle about with sth

Nesthäkchen ['nɛsthɛːkçən] NT baby of the family
Netiquette [netɪ'kɛtə] (-) F (*Internet*) Netiquette
nett [nɛt] ADJ nice; **sei so ~ und räum auf!** would you mind clearing up?
netterweise ['nɛtər'vaɪzə] ADV kindly
netto ADV net; **Nettoeinkommen** NT net income; **Nettogewicht** NT net weight; **Nettogewinn** M net profit; **Nettogewinnspanne** F net margin; **Nettolohn** M take-home pay; **Nettozahler** M (*Land etc*) net contributor
Netz [nɛts] (**-es, -e**) NT net; (*Gepäcknetz*) rack; (*Einkaufsnetz*) string bag; (*Spinnennetz*) web; (*System, Comput*) network; (*Stromnetz*) mains *sing od pl*; **das soziale ~** the social security network; **jdm ins ~ gehen** (*fig*) to fall into sb's trap; **Netzanbieter** M (*Comput*) Internet provider; **Netzanschluss** M mains connection; **Netzbetreiber** M (*Comput*) Internet provider; **Netzcomputer** M network computer; **Netzhaut** F retina; **Netzkarte** F season ticket; **Netzplantechnik** F network analysis; **Netzspannung** F mains voltage; **netzunabhängig** ADJ off-grid; **Netzwerk** NT (*Comput*) network; **Netzwerken** NT (social) networking; **Netzzugang** M (*Comput*) network access
neu [nɔʏ] ADJ new; (*Sprache, Geschichte*) modern; **der/die Neue** the new person, the newcomer; **seit Neuestem** (since) recently; **~ schreiben** to rewrite, to write again; **auf ein Neues!** (*Aufmunterung*) let's try again; **was gibts Neues?** (*umg*) what's the latest?; **von Neuem** (*von vorn*) from the beginning; (*wieder*) again; **sich ~ einkleiden** to buy o.s. a new set of clothes; **~ eröffnet** newly-opened; (*wieder geöffnet*) reopened; **Neuankömmling** M newcomer; **Neuanschaffung** F new purchase *od* acquisition; **neuartig** ADJ new kind of; **Neuauflage** F new edition; **Neuausgabe** F new edition; **Neubau** (**-(e)s, -ten**) M new building; **Neubauwohnung** F newly-built flat; **Neubearbeitung** F revised edition; (*das Neubearbeiten*) revision, reworking; **Neudruck** M reprint; **Neuemission** F (*Aktien*) new issue
neuerdings ADV (*kürzlich*) (since) recently; (*von Neuem*) again
Neuerscheinung F (*Buch*) new publication; (*CD*) new release
Neuerung F innovation, new departure
Neufassung F revised version
Neufundland [nɔʏ'fʊntlant] NT Newfoundland; **Neufundländer(in)** (**-s, -**) M(F) Newfoundlander; **neufundländisch** ADJ Newfoundland *attrib*
neugeboren ADJ newborn; **sich wie ~ fühlen** to feel (like) a new man/woman
Neugier F curiosity
Neugierde (-) F: **aus ~** out of curiosity
neugierig ADJ curious
Neuguinea [nɔʏgi'neːa] (**-s**) NT New Guinea
Neuheit F novelty; (*neuartige Ware*) new thing
Neuigkeit F news *sing*
neu- zW: **Neujahr** NT New Year; **Neuland** NT virgin land; (*fig*) new ground; **neulich** ADV recently, the other day; **Neuling** M novice; **neumodisch** ADJ fashionable; (*pej*) newfangled; **Neumond** M new moon
neun [nɔʏn] NUM nine; **Neun** (**-, -en**) F nine; **ach du grüne Neune!** (*umg*) well I'm blowed!
neunmalklug ADJ (*ironisch*) smart-aleck *attrib*
neunzehn NUM nineteen
neunzig NUM ninety
Neuregelung, Neureglung F adjustment
neureich ADJ nouveau riche; **Neureiche(r)** F(M) nouveau riche
Neurologe [nɔʏro'loːgə] M, **Neurologin** F neurologist
Neurologie [nɔʏrolo'giː] F neurology
neurologisch [nɔʏro'loːgɪʃ] ADJ neurological
Neurose [nɔʏ'roːzə] (**-, -n**) F neurosis
Neurotiker(in) [nɔʏ'roːtikər(ɪn)] (**-s, -**) M(F) neurotic
neurotisch ADJ neurotic
Neu- zW: **Neuschnee** M fresh snow; **Neuseeland** [nɔʏ'zeːlant] NT New Zealand; **Neuseeländer(in)** (**-s, -**) M(F) New Zealander; **neuseeländisch** ADJ New Zealand *attrib*; **neusprachlich** ADJ: **neusprachliches Gymnasium** grammar school (BRIT) *od* high school (*bes US*) stressing modern languages
neutral [nɔʏ'traːl] ADJ neutral
neutralisieren [nɔʏtrali'ziːrən] VT to neutralize
Neutralität [nɔʏtrali'tɛːt] F neutrality
Neutron ['nɔʏtrɔn] (**-s, -en**) NT neutron
Neutrum ['nɔʏtrʊm] (**-s, Neutra** *od* **Neutren**) NT neuter
Neu- zW: **Neuwert** M purchase price; **neuwertig** ADJ as new; **Neuzeit** F modern age; **neuzeitlich** ADJ modern, recent
N. H. ABK (= *Normalhöhenpunkt*) normal peak (level)
nhd. ABK (= *neuhochdeutsch*) NHG
Nicaragua [nika'raːgua] (**-s**) NT Nicaragua; **Nicaraguaner(in)** [nikaragu'aːnər(ɪn)] (**-s, -**) M(F) Nicaraguan; **nicaraguanisch** [nikaragu'aːnɪʃ] ADJ Nicaraguan

SCHLÜSSELWORT

nicht [nɪçt] ADV **1** (*Verneinung*) not; **er ist es nicht** it's not him, it isn't him; **nicht rostend** stainless; **er raucht nicht** (*gerade*) he isn't smoking; (*gewöhnlich*) he doesn't smoke; **ich kann das nicht — ich auch nicht** I can't do it — neither *od* nor can I; **es regnet nicht mehr** it's not raining any more; **nicht mehr als** no more than
2 (*Bitte, Verbot*): **nicht!** don't!, no!; **nicht berühren!** do not touch!; **nicht doch!** don't!
3 (*rhetorisch*): **du bist müde, nicht (wahr)?** you're tired, aren't you?; **das ist schön, nicht (wahr)?** it's nice, isn't it?
4: **was du nicht sagst!** the things you say!
▶ PRÄF non-

Nicht- zW: **Nichtachtung** F disregard; **Nichtanerkennung** F repudiation; **Nichtangriffspakt** M non-aggression pact
Nichte ['nɪçtə] (-, -n) F niece
Nicht- zW: **Nichteinhaltung** F +gen non-compliance (with); **Nichteinmischung** F (*Pol*) nonintervention; **Nichtgefallen** NT: **bei Nichtgefallen (zurück)** if not satisfied (return)
nichtig ['nɪçtɪç] ADJ (*ungültig*) null, void; (*wertlos*) futile; **Nichtigkeit** F nullity, invalidity; (*Sinnlosigkeit*) futility
Nichtraucher M nonsmoker; **ich bin ~** I don't smoke
nichts [nɪçts] PRON nothing; **~ ahnend** unsuspecting; **~ sagend** meaningless; **~ als** nothing but; **~ da!** (*ausgeschlossen*) nothing doing (*umg*); **~ wie raus/hin** *etc* (*umg*) let's get out/over there *etc* (on the double); **für ~ und wieder ~** for nothing at all; **ich habe ~ gesagt** I didn't say anything; **Nichts (-s)** NT nothingness; (*pej: Person*) nonentity
Nichtschwimmer (-s, -) M nonswimmer
nichts- zW: **nichtsdestotrotz** ADV notwithstanding (*form*), nonetheless; **nichtsdestoweniger** ADV nevertheless; **Nichtsnutz (-es, -e)** M good-for-nothing; **nichtsnutzig** ADJ worthless, useless; **nichtssagend** ADJ meaningless; **Nichtstun (-s)** NT idleness
Nichtzutreffende(s) NT: **~ (bitte) streichen** (please) delete as applicable
Nick ['nɪk] (-s) M username
Nickel ['nɪkəl] (-s) NT nickel; **Nickelbrille** F metal-rimmed glasses *pl*
nicken ['nɪkən] VI to nod
Nickerchen ['nɪkərçən] NT nap; **ein ~ machen** (*umg*) to have forty winks
Nicki ['nɪki] (-s, -s) M velours pullover
Nickname (-ns, -n) M username
nie [ni:] ADV never; **~ wieder** *od* **mehr** never again; **~ und nimmer** never ever; **fast ~** hardly ever
nieder ['ni:dər] ADJ low; (*gering*) inferior ▶ ADV down; **niederdeutsch** ADJ (*Ling*) Low-German; **Niedergang** M decline; **niedergedrückt** ADJ depressed; **niedergehen** *unreg* VI to descend; (*Aviat*) to come down; (*Regen*) to fall; (*Boxer*) to go down; **niedergeschlagen** ADJ depressed, dejected; **Niedergeschlagenheit** F depression, dejection; **Niederkunft** F (*veraltet*) delivery, giving birth; **Niederlage** F defeat
Niederlande ['ni:dərlandə] PL: **die ~** the Netherlands *pl*
Niederländer(in) ['ni:dərlɛndər(ɪn)] (-s, -) M(F) Dutchman, Dutchwoman
niederländisch ADJ Dutch, Netherlands *attrib*
nieder- zW: **niederlassen** *unreg* VR (*sich setzen*) to sit down; (*an Ort*) to settle (down); (*Arzt, Rechtsanwalt*) to set up in practice; **Niederlassung** F settlement; (*Comm*) branch; **niederlegen** VT to lay down; (*Arbeit*) to stop; (*Amt*) to resign; **niedermachen** VT to mow down; **Niederösterreich** NT Lower Austria; **Niederrhein** M Lower Rhine; **niederrheinisch** ADJ Lower Rhine *attrib*; **Niedersachsen** NT Lower Saxony; **Niederschlag** M (*Chem*) precipitate; (*Bodensatz*) sediment; (*Met*) precipitation (*geh*), rainfall; (*Boxen*) knockdown; **radioaktiver Niederschlag** (radioactive) fallout; **niederschlagen** *unreg* VT (*Gegner*) to beat down; (*Gegenstand*) to knock down; (*Augen*) to lower; (*Jur: Prozess*) to dismiss; (*Aufstand*) to put down ▶ VR (*Chem*) to precipitate; **sich in etw** *dat* **niederschlagen** (*Erfahrungen etc*) to find expression in sth; **niederschlagsfrei** ['ni:dərʃla:ksfraɪ] ADJ dry, without precipitation (*form*); **niederschmetternd** ADJ (*Nachricht, Ergebnis*) shattering; **niederschreiben** *unreg* VT to write down; **Niederschrift** F transcription; **niedertourig** ADJ (*Motor*) low-revving; **niederträchtig** ADJ base, mean; **Niederträchtigkeit** F despicable *od* malicious behaviour
Niederung F (*Geog*) depression
niederwalzen ['ni:dərvaltsən] VT: **jdn/etw ~** (*umg*) to mow sb/sth down
niederwerfen ['ni:dərvɛrfən] *unreg* VT to throw down; (*fig*) to overcome; (*Aufstand*) to suppress
niedlich ['ni:tlɪç] ADJ sweet, nice, cute
niedrig ['ni:drɪç] ADJ low; (*Stand*) lowly, humble; (*Gesinnung*) mean
Niedriglohnsektor M low-wage sector
niemals ['ni:ma:ls] ADV never
niemand ['ni:mant] PRON nobody, no-one; **ich habe niemanden gesehen** I haven't seen anyone
Niemandsland ['ni:mantslant] NT no-man's-land
Niere ['ni:rə] (-, -n) F kidney; **künstliche ~** kidney machine
Nierenentzündung F kidney infection
nieseln ['ni:zəln] VI to drizzle
Nieselregen M drizzle
niesen ['ni:zən] VI to sneeze
Niespulver NT sneezing powder
Niet [ni:t] (-(e)s, -e) M (*Tech*) rivet
Niete ['ni:tə] (-, -n) F (*Tech*) rivet; (*Los*) blank; (*Reinfall*) flop; (*Mensch*) failure
nieten VT to rivet
Nietenhose F (pair of) studded jeans *pl*
niet- und nagelfest (*umg*) ADJ nailed down
Niger[1] ['ni:gər] (-s) NT (*Staat*) Niger
Niger[2] ['ni:gər] (-s) M (*Fluss*) Niger
Nigeria [ni'ge:ria] (-s) NT Nigeria; **Nigerianer(in)** [nigeri'a:nər(ɪn)] M(F) Nigerian; **nigerianisch** [nige:ri'a:nɪʃ] ADJ Nigerian
Nihilismus [nihi'lɪsmʊs] M nihilism
Nihilist [nihi'lɪst] M nihilist; **nihilistisch** ADJ nihilistic
Nikolaus ['ni:kolaʊs] (-, -e *od hum* **-läuse**) M ≈ Santa Claus, ≈ Father Christmas
Nikosia [niko'zi:a] (-s) NT Nicosia
Nikotin [niko'ti:n] (-s) NT nicotine; **nikotinarm** ADJ low-nicotine

Nil [ni:l] (**-s**) M Nile; **Nilpferd** NT hippopotamus
Nimbus ['nɪmbʊs] (**-, -se**) M (*Heiligenschein*) halo; (*fig*) aura
nimmersatt ['nɪmərzat] ADJ insatiable; **Nimmersatt** (**-(e)s, -e**) M glutton
Nimmerwiedersehen (*umg*) NT: **auf ~!** I never want to see you again
nimmt [nɪmt] VB *siehe* **nehmen**
nippen ['nɪpən] VT, VI to sip
Nippes ['nɪpəs] PL knick-knacks *pl*, bric-a-brac *sing*
Nippsachen ['nɪpzaxən] PL knick-knacks *pl*
nirgends ['nɪrgənts] ADV nowhere; **überall und ~** here, there and everywhere
nirgendwo ['nɪrgəntvo] ADV = **nirgends**
nirgendwohin ADV nowhere
Nische ['ni:ʃə] (**-, -n**) F niche
nisten ['nɪstən] VI to nest
Nitrat [ni'tra:t] (**-(e)s, -e**) NT nitrate
Niveau [ni'vo:] (**-s, -s**) NT level; **diese Schule hat ein hohes ~** this school has high standards; **unter meinem ~** beneath me
Nivellierung [nivɛ'li:rʊŋ] F (*Ausgleichung*) levelling out
nix [nɪks] (*umg*) PRON = **nichts**
Nixe ['nɪksə] (**-, -n**) F water nymph
Nizza ['nɪtsa] (**-s**) NT Nice
n. J. ABK (= *nächsten Jahres*) next year
n. M. ABK (= *nächsten Monats*) next month
NN ABK (= *Normalnull*) m.s.l.
N. N. ABK = **NN**
NO ABK (= *Nordost*) NE
no. ABK (= *netto*) net
nobel ['no:bəl] ADJ (*großzügig*) generous; (*elegant*) posh (*umg*)
Nobelpreis [no'bɛlpraɪs] M Nobel prize; **Nobelpreisträger(in)** M(F) Nobel prize winner

SCHLÜSSELWORT

noch [nɔx] ADV **1** (*weiterhin*) still; **noch nicht** not yet; **noch nie** never (yet); **noch immer** *od* **immer noch** still; **bleiben Sie doch noch** stay a bit longer; **ich gehe kaum noch aus** I hardly go out any more
2 (*in Zukunft*) still, yet; (*: irgendwann einmal*) one day; **das kann noch passieren** that might still happen; **er wird noch kommen** he'll come (yet); **das wirst du noch bereuen** you'll come to regret it (one day)
3 (*nicht später als*): **noch vor einer Woche** only a week ago; **noch am selben Tag** the very same day; **noch im 19. Jahrhundert** as late as the 19th century; **noch heute** today
4 (*zusätzlich*): **wer war noch da?** who else was there?; **noch (ein)mal** once more, again; **noch dreimal** three more times; **noch einer** another one; **und es regnete auch noch** and on top of that it was raining
5 (*bei Vergleichen*): **noch größer** even bigger; **das ist noch besser** that's better still; **und wenn es noch so schwer ist** however hard it is
6: **Geld noch und noch** heaps (and heaps) of money; **sie hat noch und noch versucht, ...** she tried again and again to ...
▶ KONJ: **weder A noch B** neither A nor B

nochmal, nochmals ADV once more, again
nochmalig ADJ repeated
Nockenwelle ['nɔkənvɛlə] F camshaft
NOK NT ABK (= *Nationales Olympisches Komitee*) National Olympic Committee
Nom. ABK = **Nominativ**
Nominalwert [nomi'na:lve:rt] M (*Fin*) nominal *od* par value
Nominativ ['no:minati:f] (**-s, -e**) M nominative
nominell [nomi'nɛl] ADJ nominal
nominieren [nomi'ni:rən] VT to nominate
Nonne ['nɔnə] (**-, -n**) F nun
Nonnenkloster NT convent
Nonplusultra [nɔnplʊs'ʊltra] (**-s**) NT ultimate
Non-Profit-Unternehmen, Nonprofitunternehmen [nɔn'prɔfit-] NT non-profit company
Nord [nɔrt] (**-s**) M north; **Nordafrika** ['nɔrt'la:frika] NT North Africa; **Nordamerika** NT North America; **nordamerikanisch** ['nɔrt|ameri'ka:nɪʃ] ADJ North American
nordd. ABK = **norddeutsch**
norddeutsch ADJ North German
Norddeutschland NT North(ern) Germany
Norden ['nɔrdən] M north
Nord- ZW: **Nordengland** NT the North of England; **Nordeuropa** NT Northern Europe; **Nordirland** NT Northern Ireland, Ulster; **nordisch** ADJ northern; (*Völker, Sprache*) Nordic; **nordische Kombination** (*Ski*) nordic combination; **Nordkap** NT North Cape; **Nordkorea** ['nɔrtko're:a] NT North Korea
nördlich ['nœrtlɪç] ADJ northerly, northern ▶ PRÄP *+gen* (to the) north of; **der nördliche Polarkreis** the Arctic Circle; **Nördliches Eismeer** Arctic Ocean; **~ von** north of
Nord- ZW: **Nordlicht** NT northern lights *pl*, aurora borealis; **Nord-Ostsee-Kanal** M Kiel Canal; **Nordpol** M North Pole; **Nordpolargebiet** NT Arctic (Zone)
Nordrhein-Westfalen ['nɔrtraɪnvɛst'fa:lən] (**-s**) NT North Rhine-Westphalia
Nordsee F North Sea
nordwärts ADV northwards
Nörgelei [nœrgə'laɪ] F grumbling
nörgeln VI to grumble
Nörgler(in) (**-s, -**) M(F) grumbler
Norm [nɔrm] (**-, -en**) F norm; (*Leistungssoll*) quota; (*Größenvorschrift*) standard (specification)
normal [nɔr'ma:l] ADJ normal; **bist du noch ~?** (*umg*) have you gone mad?; **Normalbenzin** NT regular (petrol (BRIT) *od* gas (*US*))
normalerweise ADV normally
Normalfall M: **im ~** normally
Normalgewicht NT normal weight; (*genormt*) standard weight
normalisieren [nɔrmali'zi:rən] VT to normalize ▶ VR to return to normal
Normalzeit F (*Geog*) standard time
Normandie [nɔrman'di:] F Normandy

normen VT to standardize
Norwegen ['nɔrve:gən] (**-s**) NT Norway
Norweger(in) (**-s, -**) M(F) Norwegian
norwegisch ADJ Norwegian
Nostalgie [nɔstal'gi:] F nostalgia
Not [no:t] (**-, Nöte**) F need; (*Armut*) poverty; (*Mangel*) want; (*Mühe*) trouble; (*Zwang*) necessity; **~ leidend** needy; **zur ~** if necessary; (*gerade noch*) just about; **wenn ~ am Mann ist** if you/they *etc* are short (*umg*); (*im Notfall*) in an emergency; **er hat seine liebe ~ mit ihr/damit** he really has problems with her/it; **in seiner ~** in his hour of need
Notar(in) [no'ta:r(ɪn)] (**-s, -e**) M(F) notary; **notariell** ADJ notarial; **notariell beglaubigt** attested by a notary
Not- zW: **Notarzt** M emergency doctor; **Notaufnahme** F A&E casualty (BRIT), emergency room (US); **Notausgang** M emergency exit, fire exit; **Notbehelf** M stopgap; **Notbremse** F emergency brake; **Notdienst** M: **Notdienst haben** (*Apotheke*) to be open 24 hours; (*Arzt*) to be on call; **notdürftig** ADJ scanty; (*behelfsmäßig*) makeshift; **sich notdürftig verständigen können** to be able to communicate to some extent
Note ['no:tə] (**-, -n**) F note; (*Sch*) mark (BRIT), grade (US); **Noten** PL (*Mus*) music *sing*; **eine persönliche ~** a personal touch
Noten- zW: **Notenbank** F issuing bank; **Notenblatt** NT sheet of music; **Notenschlüssel** M clef; **Notenständer** M music stand
Not- zW: **Notfall** M (case of) emergency; **notfalls** ADV if need be; **notgedrungen** ADJ necessary, unavoidable; **etw notgedrungen machen** to be forced to do sth; **Notgroschen** ['no:tgrɔʃən] M nest egg
notieren [no'ti:rən] VT to note; (*Comm*) to quote
Notierung F (*Comm*) quotation
nötig ['nø:tɪç] ADJ necessary ▶ ADV (*dringend*): **etw ~ brauchen** to need sth urgently; **etw ~ haben** to need sth; **das habe ich nicht ~!** I can do without that!
nötigen VT to compel, to force; **nötigenfalls** ADV if necessary
Nötigung F compulsion, coercion (*JUR*)
Notiz [no'ti:ts] (**-, -en**) F note; (*Zeitungsnotiz*) item; **~ nehmen** to take notice; **Notizblock** M notepad; **Notizbuch** NT notebook; **Notizzettel** M piece of paper
Not- zW: **Notlage** F crisis, emergency; **notlanden** VI to make a forced *od* emergency landing; **Notlandung** F forced *od* emergency landing; **Notlösung** F temporary solution; **Notlüge** F white lie
notorisch [no'to:rɪʃ] ADJ notorious
Not- zW: **Notruf** M emergency call; **Notrufsäule** F emergency telephone; **notschlachten** VT (*Tiere*) to destroy; **Notstand** M state of emergency; **Notstandsgebiet** NT (*wirtschaftlich*) depressed area; (*bei Katastrophen*) disaster area; **Notstandsgesetz** NT emergency law; **Notunterkunft** F emergency accommodation; **Notverband** M emergency dressing; **Notwehr** (**-**) F self-defence; **notwendig** ADJ necessary; **Notwendigkeit** F necessity; **Notzucht** F rape
Nov. ABK (= *November*) Nov.
Novelle [no'vɛlə] (**-, -n**) F novella; (*Jur*) amendment
November [no'vɛmbər] (**-(s), -**) M November; *siehe auch* **September**
Novum ['no:vʊm] (**-s, Nova**) NT novelty
NPD (**-**) F ABK (= *Nationaldemokratische Partei Deutschlands*) National Democratic Party
Nr. ABK (= *Nummer*) no.
NRW ABK = **Nordrhein-Westfalen**
NS ABK = **Nachschrift**; **Nationalsozialismus**
NS- IN zW Nazi
N. T. ABK (= *Neues Testament*) N.T.
Nu [nu:] M: **im Nu** in an instant
Nuance [ny'ã:sə] (**-, -n**) F nuance; (*Kleinigkeit*) shade
nüchtern ['nʏçtərn] ADJ sober; (*Magen*) empty; (*Urteil*) prudent; **Nüchternheit** F sobriety
Nudel ['nu:dəl] (**-, -n**) F noodle; (*umg: Mensch: dick*) dumpling; (*: komisch*) character; **Nudeln** *pl* pasta *sing*; **Nudelholz** NT rolling pin
Nugat ['nu:gat] (**-s, -s**) M OD NT nougat
nuklear [nukle'a:r] ADJ *attrib* nuclear
null [nʊl] NUM zero; **~ Fehler** no mistakes; **~ Uhr** midnight; **in ~ Komma nichts** (*umg*) in less than no time; **die Stunde ~** the new starting point; **gleich ~ sein** to be absolutely nil; **~ und nichtig** null and void; **Null** (**-, -en**) F nought, zero; (*pej: Mensch*) dead loss; **nullachtfünfzehn** (*umg*) ADJ run-of-the-mill; **Nulldiät** F starvation diet; **Nulllösung** F (*Pol*) zero option; **Nullpunkt** M zero; **auf dem Nullpunkt** at zero; **Nulltarif** M (*für Verkehrsmittel*) free travel; **zum Nulltarif** free of charge
numerieren [nume'ri:rən] VT *siehe* **nummerieren**
numerisch [nu'me:rɪʃ] ADJ numerical; **numerisches Tastenfeld** (*Comput*) numeric pad
Numerus ['nu:merʊs] (**-, Numeri**) M (*Gram*) number; **~ clausus** (*Univ*) restricted entry
Nummer ['nʊmər] (**-, -n**) F number; **auf ~ sicher gehen** (*umg*) to play (it) safe
nummerieren [nume'ri:rən] VT to number
Nummern- zW: **Nummernkonto** NT numbered bank account; **Nummernscheibe** F telephone dial; **Nummernschild** NT (*Aut*) number *od* license (*US*) plate
nun [nu:n] ADV now ▶ INTERJ well; **es ist ~ mal so** that's the way it is
nur [nu:r] ADV just, only; **nicht ~ ..., sondern auch ...** not only ... but also ...; **alle, ~ ich nicht** everyone but me; **ich hab das ~ so gesagt** I was just talking
Nürnberg ['nʏrnbɛrk] (**-s**) NT Nuremberg
nuscheln ['nʊʃəln] (*umg*) VT, VI to mutter, to mumble

n

Nuss [nʊs] **(-, Nüsse)** F nut; **eine doofe ~** (*umg*) a stupid twit; **eine harte ~** a hard nut (to crack); **Nussbaum** M walnut tree; **Nussknacker (-s, -)** M nutcracker
Nüster ['ny:stər] **(-, -n)** F nostril
Nutte ['nʊtə] **(-, -n)** F tart (BRIT), hooker (US)
nutz [nʊts] ADJ = **nütze**; **nutzbar** ADJ: **nutzbar machen** to utilize; **Nutzbarmachung** F utilization; **nutzbringend** ADJ profitable; **etw nutzbringend anwenden** to use sth to good effect, to put sth to good use
nütze ['nʏtsə] ADJ: **zu nichts ~ sein** to be useless
nutzen VI to be of use ▸ VT: **(zu etw) ~** to use (for sth); **was nutzt es?** what's the use?, what use is it?; **Nutzen (-s)** M usefulness; (*Gewinn*) profit; **von Nutzen** useful
nützen VT, VI = **nutzen**
Nutz- ZW: **Nutzfahrzeug** NT *farm od military vehicle etc*; (*Comm*) commercial vehicle; **Nutzfläche** F us(e)able floor space; (*Agr*) productive land; **Nutzlast** F maximum load, payload
nützlich ['nʏtslɪç] ADJ useful; **Nützlichkeit** F usefulness
Nutz- ZW: **nutzlos** ADJ useless; (*unnötig*) needless; **Nutzlosigkeit** F uselessness; **Nutznießer (-s, -)** M beneficiary
Nutzung F (*Gebrauch*) use; (*das Ausnutzen*) exploitation
NW ABK (= *Nordwest*) NW
Nylon ['naɪlɔn] **(-s)** NT nylon
Nymphe ['nʏmfə] **(-, -n)** F nymph

Oo

O[1], o [oː] NT O, o; **O wie Otto** ≈ O for Olive, ≈ O for Oboe (*US*)
O[2] [oː] ABK (= *Osten*) E
o. Ä. ABK (= *oder Ähnliche(s)*) or similar
Oase [oˈaːzə] (**-, -n**) F oasis
ob [ɔp] KONJ if, whether; **ob das wohl wahr ist?** can that be true?; **ob ich (nicht) lieber gehe?** maybe I'd better go; **(so) tun als ob** (*umg*) to pretend; **und ob!** you bet!
OB (**-s, -s**) M ABK = **Oberbürgermeister**
Obacht [ˈoːbaxt] F: **~ geben** to pay attention
Obdach [ˈɔpdax] (**-(e)s**) NT shelter, lodging; **obdachlos** ADJ homeless; **Obdachlose(r)** F(M) homeless person; **Obdachlosenasyl** NT hostel *od* shelter for the homeless; **Obdachlosenheim** NT = **Obdachlosenasyl**
Obduktion [ɔpdʊktsiˈoːn] F postmortem
obduzieren [ɔpduˈtsiːrən] VT to do a postmortem on
O-Beine [ˈoːbaɪnə] PL bow *od* bandy legs *pl*
oben [ˈoːbən] ADV above; (*in Haus*) upstairs; (*am oberen Ende*) at the top; **~ erwähnt, ~ genannt** above-mentioned; **nach ~** up; **von ~** down; **siehe ~** see above; **ganz ~** right at the top; **~ ohne** topless; **die Abbildung ~ links** *od* **links ~** the illustration in the top left-hand corner; **jdn von ~ herab behandeln** to treat sb condescendingly; **jdn von ~ bis unten ansehen** to look sb up and down; **Befehl von ~** orders from above; **die da ~** (*umg: die Vorgesetzten*) the powers that be; **obenan** ADV at the top; **obenauf** ADV up above, on the top ▸ ADJ (*munter*) in form; **obendrein** ADV into the bargain; **obenhin** ADV cursorily, superficially
Ober [ˈoːbər] (**-s, -**) M waiter
Ober- ZW: **Oberarm** M upper arm; **Oberarzt** M senior physician; **Oberaufsicht** F supervision; **Oberbayern** NT Upper Bavaria; **Oberbefehl** M supreme command; **Oberbefehlshaber** M commander-in-chief; **Oberbegriff** M generic term; **Oberbekleidung** F outer clothing; **Oberbett** NT quilt; **Oberbürgermeister** M lord mayor; **Oberdeck** NT upper *od* top deck
obere(r, s) ADJ upper; **die Oberen** the bosses; (*Eccl*) the superiors; **die oberen Zehntausend** (*umg*) high society
Ober- ZW: **Oberfläche** F surface; **oberflächlich** ADJ superficial; **bei oberflächlicher Betrachtung** at a quick glance; **jdn (nur) oberflächlich kennen** to know sb (only) slightly; **Obergeschoss** NT upper storey *od* story (*US*); **im zweiten Obergeschoss** on the second floor (*Brit*), on the third floor (*US*); **oberhalb** ADV above ▸ PRÄP *+gen* above; **Oberhand** F (*fig*): **die Oberhand gewinnen (über** *+akk*) to get the upper hand (over); **Oberhaupt** NT head, chief; **Oberhaus** NT (*in Großbritannien*) upper house, House of Lords; **Oberhemd** NT shirt; **Oberherrschaft** F supremacy, sovereignty
Oberin F matron; (*Eccl*) Mother Superior
Ober- ZW: **oberirdisch** ADJ above ground; (*Leitung*) overhead; **Oberitalien** NT Northern Italy; **Oberkellner** M head waiter; **Oberkiefer** M upper jaw; **Oberkommando** NT supreme command; **Oberkörper** M upper part of body; **Oberlauf** M: **am Oberlauf des Rheins** in the upper reaches of the Rhine; **Oberleitung** F (*Elek*) overhead cable; **Oberlicht** NT skylight; **Oberlippe** F upper lip; **Oberösterreich** NT Upper Austria; **Oberprima** F (*früher*) *final year of German secondary school*; **Oberschenkel** M thigh; **Oberschicht** F upper classes *pl*; **Oberschule** F grammar school (*Brit*), high school (*US*); **Oberschwester** F (*Med*) matron; **Oberseite** F top (side); **Obersekunda** F (*früher*) *seventh year of German secondary school*
Oberst [ˈoːbərst] (**-en** *od* **-s, -en** *od* **-e**) M colonel
oberste(r, s) ADJ very top, topmost
Ober- ZW: **Oberstübchen** (*umg*) NT: **er ist nicht ganz richtig im Oberstübchen** he's not quite right up top; **Oberstufe** F upper school; **Oberteil** NT top; **Obertertia** F (*früher*) *fifth year of German secondary school*; **Oberwasser** NT: **Oberwasser haben/bekommen** to be/get on top (of things)
obgleich [ɔpˈglaɪç] KONJ although
Obhut [ˈɔphuːt] (**-**) F care, protection; **in jds ~ dat sein** to be in sb's care
obig [ˈoːbɪç] ADJ above
Objekt [ɔpˈjɛkt] (**-(e)s, -e**) NT object
objektiv [ɔpjɛkˈtiːf] ADJ objective
Objektiv (**-s, -e**) NT lens
Objektivität [ɔpjɛktiviˈtɛːt] F objectivity
Oblate [oˈblaːtə] (**-, -n**) F (*Gebäck*) wafer; (*Eccl*) host

obligatorisch [obliga'to:rɪʃ] ADJ compulsory, obligatory
Oboe [o'bo:ə] (-, **-n**) F oboe
Obrigkeit ['o:brɪçkaɪt] F (*Behörden*) authorities *pl*, administration; (*Regierung*) government
Obrigkeitsdenken NT acceptance of authority
obschon [ɔp'ʃo:n] KONJ although
Observatorium [ɔpzɛrva'to:riʊm] NT observatory
obskur [ɔps'ku:r] ADJ obscure; (*verdächtig*) dubious
Obst [o:pst] (**-(e)s**) NT fruit; **Obstbau** M fruit-growing; **Obstbaum** M fruit tree; **Obstgarten** M orchard; **Obsthändler** M fruiterer (BRIT), fruit merchant; **Obstkuchen** M fruit tart; **Obstsaft** M fruit juice; **Obstsalat** M fruit salad
obszön [ɔps'tsø:n] ADJ obscene
Obszönität [ɔpstøni'tɛ:t] F obscenity
Obus ['o:bʊs] (**-ses, -se**) (*umg*) M trolleybus
obwohl [ɔp'vo:l] KONJ although
Ochse ['ɔksə] (**-n, -n**) M ox; (*umg: Dummkopf*) twit; **er stand da wie der ~ vorm Berg** (*umg*) he stood there utterly bewildered
ochsen (*umg*) VT, VI to cram, to swot (BRIT)
Ochsenschwanzsuppe F oxtail soup
Ochsenzunge F ox tongue
Ocker ['ɔkər] (**-s, -**) M OD NT ochre (BRIT), ocher (US)
öd [ø:t] ADJ = **öde**
öde ADJ (*Land*) waste, barren; (*fig*) dull; **~ und leer** dreary and desolate
Öde (-, **-n**) F desert, waste(land); (*fig*) tedium
oder ['o:dər] KONJ or; **entweder ... ~** either ... or; **du kommst doch, ~?** you're coming, aren't you?
Ofen ['o:fən] (**-s, Öfen**) M oven; (*Heizofen*) fire, heater; (*Kohleofen*) stove; (*Hochofen*) furnace; (*Herd*) cooker, stove; **jetzt ist der ~ aus** (*umg*) that does it!; **Ofenrohr** NT stovepipe
offen ['ɔfən] ADJ open; (*aufrichtig*) frank; (*Stelle*) vacant; (*Bein*) ulcerated; (*Haare*) loose; **offener Wein** wine by the carafe *od* glass; **auf offener Strecke** (*Straße*) on the open road; (*Eisenb*) between stations; **Tag der offenen Tür** open day (BRIT), open house (US); **offene Handelsgesellschaft** (*Comm*) general *od* ordinary (US) partnership; **~ bleiben** (*Fenster*) to stay open; **~ halten** to keep open; **~ lassen** to leave open; **~ stehen** to be open; **seine Meinung ~ sagen** to speak one's mind; **ein offenes Wort mit jdm reden** to have a frank talk with sb; **~ gesagt** to be honest; *siehe auch* **offenbleiben**; **offenstehen**
offenbar ADJ obvious; (*vermutlich*) apparently
offenbaren [ɔfən'ba:rən] VT to reveal, to manifest
Offenbarung F (*Rel*) revelation
Offenbarungseid M (*Jur*) oath of disclosure
Offen- ZW: **offenbleiben** *unreg* VI (*fig: Frage, Entscheidung*) to remain open; *siehe auch* **offen**; **Offenheit** F candour (BRIT), candor (US), frankness; **offenherzig** ADJ candid, frank; (*hum: Kleid*) revealing; **Offenherzigkeit** F frankness; **offenkundig** ADJ well-known; (*klar*) evident; **offensichtlich** ADJ evident, obvious
offensiv [ɔfɛn'zi:f] ADJ offensive
Offensive (-, **-n**) F offensive
offenstehen *unreg* VI (*fig: Rechnung*) to be unpaid; **es steht Ihnen offen, es zu tun** you are at liberty to do it; **die (ganze) Welt steht ihm offen** he has the (whole) world at his feet; *siehe auch* **offen**
öffentlich ['œfəntlɪç] ADJ public; **die öffentliche Hand** (central/local) government; **Anstalt des öffentlichen Rechts** public institution; **Ausgaben der öffentlichen Hand** public spending *sing*
Öffentlichkeit F (*Leute*) public; (*einer Versammlung etc*) public nature; **in aller ~** in public; **an die ~ dringen** to reach the public ear; **unter Ausschluss der ~** in secret; (*Jur*) in camera
Öffentlichkeitsarbeit F public relations work
öffentlich-rechtlich ADJ *attrib* (under) public law
offerieren [ɔfe'ri:rən] VT to offer
Offerte [ɔ'fɛrtə] (-, **-n**) F offer
offiziell [ɔfitsi'ɛl] ADJ official
Offizier [ɔfi'tsi:r] (**-s, -e**) M officer
Offizierskasino NT officers' mess
öffnen ['œfnən] VT, VR to open; **jdm die Tür ~** to open the door for sb
Öffner ['œfnər] (**-s, -**) M opener
Öffnung ['œfnʊŋ] F opening
Öffnungsklausel F (*Jur*) escape clause; (*fig: Schlupfloch*) loophole
Öffnungszeiten PL opening times *pl*
Offsetdruck ['ɔfsɛtdrʊk] M offset (printing)
oft [ɔft] ADV often
öfter ['œftər] ADV more often *od* frequently; **des Öfteren** quite frequently; **~ mal was Neues** (*umg*) variety is the spice of life (*Sprichwort*)
öfters ADV often, frequently
oftmals ADV often, frequently
o. G. ABK (= *ohne Gewähr*) without liability
OHG F ABK (= *offene Handelsgesellschaft*) *siehe* **offen**
ohne ['o:nə] PRÄP +*akk*, KONJ without; **das ist nicht ~** (*umg*) it's not bad; **~ Weiteres** without a second thought; (*sofort*) immediately; **das kann man nicht ~ Weiteres voraussetzen** you can't just assume that automatically; **ohnedies** ADV anyway; **ohneeinander** [o:nəlaɪ'nandər] ADV without each other; **ohnegleichen** ADJ unsurpassed, without equal; **ohnehin** ADV anyway, in any case; **es ist ohnehin schon spät** it's late enough already
Ohnmacht ['o:nmaxt] F faint; (*fig*) impotence; **in ~ fallen** to faint
ohnmächtig ['o:nmɛçtɪç] ADJ in a faint, unconscious; (*fig*) weak, impotent; **sie ist ~** she has fainted; **ohnmächtige Wut, ohnmächtiger Zorn** helpless rage; **einer Sache** *dat* **~ gegenüberstehen** to be helpless in the face of sth
Ohr [o:r] (**-(e)s, -en**) NT ear; (*Gehör*) hearing; **sich aufs ~ legen** *od* **hauen** (*umg*) to kip down;

jdm die Ohren lang ziehen (*umg*) to tweak sb's ear(s); **jdm in den Ohren liegen** to keep on at sb; **jdn übers ~ hauen** (*umg*) to pull a fast one on sb; **auf dem ~ bin ich taub** (*fig*) nothing doing (*umg*); **schreib es dir hinter die Ohren** (*umg*) will you (finally) get that into your (thick) head!; **bis über die** *od* **beide Ohren verliebt sein** to be head over heels in love; **viel um die Ohren haben** (*umg*) to have a lot on (one's plate); **halt die Ohren steif!** keep a stiff upper lip!
Öhr [øːr] (**-(e)s, -e**) NT eye
Ohren- zW: **Ohrenarzt** M ear specialist; **ohrenbetäubend** ADJ deafening; **Ohrensausen** NT (*Med*) buzzing in one's ears; **Ohrenschmalz** NT earwax; **Ohrenschmerzen** PL earache *sing*; **Ohrenschützer** (**-s, -**) M earmuff
Ohr- zW: **Ohrfeige** F slap on the face; (*als Strafe*) box on the ears; **ohrfeigen** VT UNTR: **jdn ohrfeigen** to slap sb's face; (*als Strafe*) to box sb's ears; **ich könnte mich selbst ohrfeigen, dass ich das gemacht habe** I could kick myself for doing that; **Ohrläppchen** NT ear lobe; **Ohrringe** PL earrings *pl*; **Ohrwurm** M earwig; (*Mus*) catchy tune
o. J. ABK (= *ohne Jahr*) no year given
okkupieren [ɔku'piːrən] VT to occupy
Öko- ['øko-] IN ZW eco-, ecological; **Ökofonds** ['øːkofõː] M eco-fund, green fund; **Ökoladen** ['øːkolaːdən] M wholefood shop
Ökologie [økolo'giː] F ecology
ökologisch [øko'loːgɪʃ] ADJ ecological, environmental
Ökonometrie [økonome'triː] F econometrics *pl*
Ökonomie [økono'miː] F economy; (*als Wissenschaft*) economics *sing*
ökonomisch [øko'noːmɪʃ] ADJ economical
Ökopax [øko'paks] (**-en, -e**) (*umg*) M environmentalist
Ökostrom ['øːkoʃtroːm] M green electricity
Ökosystem ['øːkozʏsteːm] NT ecosystem
Okt. ABK (= *Oktober*) Oct.
Oktan [ɔk'taːn] (**-s, -e**) NT octane; **Oktanzahl** F octane rating
Oktave [ɔk'taːvə] (**-, -n**) F octave
Oktober [ɔk'toːbər] (**-(s), -**) M October; *siehe auch* **September**
Oktoberfest NT; *see note*

> The annual October beer festival, the **Oktoberfest**, takes place in Munich on a huge field where beer tents, roller coasters and many other amusements are set up. People sit at long wooden tables, drink beer from enormous litre beer mugs, eat pretzels and listen to brass bands. It is a great attraction for tourists and locals alike.

ökumenisch [øku'meːnɪʃ] ADJ ecumenical
Öl [øːl] (**-(e)s, -e**) NT oil; **auf Öl stoßen** to strike oil
Öl- zW: **Ölbaum** M olive tree; **ölen** VT to oil; (*Tech*) to lubricate; **wie ein geölter Blitz** (*umg*) like greased lightning; **Ölfarbe** F oil paint; **Ölfeld** NT oilfield; **Ölfilm** M film of oil; **Ölgemälde** NT oil painting; **Ölheizung** F oil-fired central heating
ölig ADJ oily
Oligopol [oligo'poːl] (**-s, -e**) NT oligopoly
oliv [o'liːf] ADJ olive-green
Olive [o'liːvə] (**-, -n**) F olive
Olivenöl NT olive oil
Öljacke F oilskin jacket
oll [ɔl] (*umg*) ADJ old; **das sind olle Kamellen** that's old hat
Öl- zW: **Ölmessstab** M dipstick; **Ölpest** F oil pollution; **Ölplattform** F oil rig; **Ölsardine** F sardine; **Ölscheich** M oil sheik; **Ölstand** M oil level; **Ölstandanzeiger** M (*Aut*) oil level indicator; **Öltanker** M oil tanker; **Ölteppich** M oil slick
Ölung F oiling; (*Eccl*) anointment; **die Letzte ~** Extreme Unction
Ölwanne F (*Aut*) sump (BRIT), oil pan (*US*)
Ölwechsel M oil change
Olymp [o'lʏmp] (**-s**) M (*Berg*) Mount Olympus
Olympiade [olʏmpi'aːdə] (**-, -n**) F Olympic Games *pl*
Olympiasieger(in) [o'lʏmpiaziːgər(ɪn)] M(F) Olympic champion
olympisch [o'lʏmpɪʃ] ADJ Olympic
Ölzeug NT oilskins *pl*
Oma ['oːma] (**-, -s**) (*umg*) F granny
Oman [o'maːn] (**-s**) NT Oman
Omelett [ɔm(ə)'lɛt] (**-(e)s, -s**) NT omelette (BRIT), omelet (*US*)
Omelette [ɔm(ə)'lɛt] F = **Omelett**
Omen ['oːmɛn] (**-s, -** *od* **Omina**) NT omen
Omnibus ['ɔmnibʊs] M (omni)bus
Onanie [ona'niː] F masturbation
onanieren VI to masturbate
ondulieren [ɔndu'liːrən] VT, VI to crimp
Onkel ['ɔŋkəl] (**-s, -**) M uncle
online ['ɔnlaɪn] ADJ (*Comput*) on-line
Onlineauktion F on-line auction
Onlinedienst M (*Comput*) on-line service
OP M ABK = **Operationssaal**
Opa ['oːpa] (**-s, -s**) (*umg*) M grandpa
Opal [o'paːl] (**-s, -e**) M opal
Oper ['oːpər] (**-, -n**) F opera; (*Opernhaus*) opera house
Operation [operatsi'oːn] F operation
Operationssaal M operating theatre (BRIT) *od* theater (*US*)
operativ [opəra'tiːf] ADV (*Med*): **eine Geschwulst ~ entfernen** to remove a growth by surgery
Operette [ope'rɛtə] F operetta
operieren [ope'riːrən] VT, VI to operate; **sich ~ lassen** to have an operation
Opern- zW: **Opernglas** NT opera glasses *pl*; **Opernhaus** NT opera house; **Opernsänger(in)** M(F) opera singer
Opfer ['ɔpfər] (**-s, -**) NT sacrifice; (*Mensch*) victim; **Opferbereitschaft** F readiness to make sacrifices
opfern VT to sacrifice
Opferstock M (*Eccl*) offertory box

Opferung F sacrifice; (*Eccl*) offertory
Opium ['o:piʊm] (**-s**) NT opium
opponieren [ɔpo'ni:rən] VI: **gegen jdn/etw ~** to oppose sb/sth
opportun [ɔpɔr'tu:n] ADJ opportune; **Opportunismus** [-'nɪsmʊs] M opportunism; **Opportunist(in)** [-'nɪst(ɪn)] M(F) opportunist
Opposition [ɔpozitsi'o:n] F opposition
oppositionell [ɔpozitsio:'nɛl] ADJ opposing
Oppositionsführer M leader of the opposition
optieren [ɔp'ti:rən] VI (*Pol: form*): **~ für** to opt for
Optik ['ɔptɪk] F optics *sing*
Optiker(in) (**-s, -**) M(F) optician
optimal [ɔpti'ma:l] ADJ optimal, optimum
Optimismus [ɔpti'mɪsmʊs] M optimism
Optimist(in) [ɔpti'mɪst(ɪn)] M(F) optimist; **optimistisch** ADJ optimistic
optisch ['ɔptɪʃ] ADJ optical; **optische Täuschung** optical illusion
Orakel [o'ra:kəl] (**-s, -**) NT oracle
orange ADJ orange
Orange [o'rã:ʒə] (**-, -n**) F orange
Orangeade [orã'ʒa:də] (**-, -n**) F orangeade
Orangeat [orã'ʒa:t] (**-s, -e**) NT candied peel
Orangen- ZW: **Orangenmarmelade** F marmalade; **Orangensaft** M orange juice; **Orangenschale** F orange peel
Oratorium [ora'to:riʊm] NT (*Mus*) oratorio
Orchester [ɔr'kɛstər] (**-s, -**) NT orchestra
Orchidee [ɔrçi'de:ə] (**-, -n**) F orchid
Orden ['ɔrdən] (**-s, -**) M (*Eccl*) order; (*Mil*) decoration
Ordensgemeinschaft F religious order
Ordensschwester F nun
ordentlich ['ɔrdəntlɪç] ADJ (*anständig*) decent, respectable; (*geordnet*) tidy, neat; (*umg: annehmbar*) not bad; (*: tüchtig*) real, proper; (*Leistung*) reasonable; **ordentliches Mitglied** full member; **ordentlicher Professor** (full) professor; **eine ordentliche Tracht Prügel** a proper hiding; **~ arbeiten** to be a thorough and precise worker; **Ordentlichkeit** F respectability; (*von Zimmer etc*) tidiness
Order (**-, -s** *od* **-n**) F (*Comm: Auftrag*) order
ordern VT (*Comm*) to order
Ordinalzahl [ɔrdi'na:ltsa:l] F ordinal number
ordinär [ɔrdi'nɛ:r] ADJ common, vulgar
Ordinarius [ɔrdi'na:riʊs] (**-, Ordinarien**) M (*Univ*): **~ (für)** professor (of)
ordnen ['ɔrdnən] VT to order, to put in order
Ordner (**-s, -**) M steward; (*Comm*) file
Ordnung F order; (*Ordnen*) ordering; (*Geordnetsein*) tidiness; **geht in ~** (*umg*) that's all right *od* OK (*umg*); **~ schaffen, für ~ sorgen** to put things in order, to tidy things up; **jdn zur ~ rufen** to call sb to order; **bei ihm muss alles seine ~ haben** (*räumlich*) he has to have everything in its proper place; (*zeitlich*) he has to do everything according to a fixed schedule; **das Kind braucht seine ~** the child needs a routine
Ordnungs- ZW: **Ordnungsamt** NT ≈ town clerk's office; **ordnungsgemäß** ADJ proper, according to the rules; **ordnungshalber** ADV as a matter of form; **Ordnungsliebe** F tidiness, orderliness; **Ordnungsstrafe** F fine; **ordnungswidrig** ADJ contrary to the rules, irregular; **Ordnungswidrigkeit** F infringement (*of law or rule*); **Ordnungszahl** F ordinal number
ORF (-) M ABK = **Österreichischer Rundfunk**
Organ [ɔr'ga:n] (**-s, -e**) NT organ; (*Stimme*) voice
Organisation [ɔrganizatsi'o:n] F organization
Organisationstalent NT organizing ability; (*Person*) good organizer
Organisator [ɔrgani'za:tɔr] M organizer
organisch [ɔr'ga:nɪʃ] ADJ organic; (*Erkrankung, Leiden*) physical
organisieren [ɔrgani'zi:rən] VT to organize, to arrange; (*umg: beschaffen*) to acquire ▸ VR to organize
Organismus [ɔrga'nɪsmʊs] M organism
Organist [ɔrga'nɪst] M organist
Organspender M donor (of an organ)
Organspenderausweis M donor card
Organverpflanzung F transplantation (of an organ)
Orgasmus [ɔr'gasmʊs] M orgasm
Orgel ['ɔrgəl] (**-, -n**) F organ; **Orgelpfeife** F organ pipe; **wie die Orgelpfeifen stehen** to stand in order of height
Orgie ['ɔrgiə] F orgy
Orient ['o:riɛnt] (**-s**) M Orient, east; **der Vordere ~** the Near East
Orientale [o:riɛn'ta:lə] (**-n, -n**) M Oriental
Orientalin [o:riɛn'ta:lɪn] F Oriental
orientalisch ADJ oriental
orientieren [o:riɛn'ti:rən] VT (*örtlich*) to locate; (*fig*) to inform ▸ VR to find one's way *od* bearings; (*fig*) to inform o.s.
Orientierung [o:riɛn'ti:rʊŋ] F orientation; (*fig*) information; **die ~ verlieren** to lose one's bearings
Orientierungssinn M sense of direction
Orientierungsstufe M; *see note*

> The **Orientierungsstufe** is the name given to the first two years spent in a **Realschule** or **Gymnasium**, during which a child is assessed as to his or her suitability for the school. At the end of the two years it may be decided to transfer the child to a school more suited to his or her ability.

original [origi'na:l] ADJ original; **~ Meißener Porzellan** genuine Meissen porcelain; **Original** (**-s, -e**) NT original; (*Mensch*) character; **Originalausgabe** F first edition; **Originalfassung** F original version
Originalität [originali'tɛ:t] F originality
Originalübertragung F live broadcast
originell [origi'nɛl] ADJ original; (*komisch*) witty
Orkan [ɔr'ka:n] (**-(e)s, -e**) M hurricane; **orkanartig** ADJ (*Wind*) gale-force; (*Beifall*) thunderous
Orkneyinseln ['ɔ:knɪlɪnzəln] PL Orkney Islands *pl*, Orkneys *pl*
Ornament [ɔrna'mɛnt] NT decoration, ornament

ornamental [ɔrnamɛn'ta:l] ADJ decorative, ornamental
Ornithologe [ɔrnito'lo:gə] (**-n, -n**) M ornithologist
Ornithologin [ɔrnito'lo:gɪn] F ornithologist
Ort[1] [ɔrt] (**-(e)s, -e**) M place; **an ~ und Stelle** on the spot; **am ~** in the place; **am angegebenen ~** in the place quoted, loc. cit.; **~ der Handlung** (*Theat*) scene of the action; **das ist höheren ~(e)s entschieden worden** (*hum: form*) the decision came from above
Ort[2] [ɔrt] (**-(e)s, Örter**) M: **vor ~** at the (coal) face; (*auch fig*) on the spot
Örtchen ['œrtçən] (*umg*) NT loo (BRIT), john (*US*)
orten VT to locate
orthodox [ɔrto'dɔks] ADJ orthodox
Orthografie [ɔrtogra'fi:] F spelling, orthography
orthografisch [ɔrto'gra:fɪʃ] ADJ orthographic
Orthopäde [ɔrto'pɛ:də] (**-n, -n**) M orthopaedic (BRIT) *od* orthopedic (*US*) specialist, orthopaedist (BRIT), orthopedist (*US*)
Orthopädie [ɔrtopɛ'di:] F orthopaedics *sing* (BRIT), orthopedics *sing* (*US*)
orthopädisch ADJ orthopaedic (BRIT), orthopedic (*US*)
örtlich ['œrtlɪç] ADJ local; **jdn ~ betäuben** to give sb a local anaesthetic (BRIT) *od* anesthetic (*US*); **Örtlichkeit** F locality; **sich mit den Örtlichkeiten vertraut machen** to get to know the place
Ortsangabe F (name of the) town; **ohne ~** (*Buch*) no place of publication indicated
ortsansässig ADJ local
Ortschaft F village, small town; **geschlossene ~** built-up area
Orts- zW: **ortsfremd** ADJ nonlocal; **Ortsfremde(r)** F(M) stranger; **Ortsgespräch** NT local (phone) call; **Ortsgruppe** F local branch *od* group; **Ortskenntnis** F: **(gute) Ortskenntnisse haben** to know one's way around (well); **Ortskrankenkasse** F: **Allgemeine Ortskrankenkasse** *compulsory medical insurance scheme*; **ortskundig** ADJ familiar with the place; **ortskundig sein** to know one's way around; **Ortsname** M place name; **Ortsnetz** NT (*Tel*) local telephone exchange area; **Ortsnetzkennzahl** F (*Tel*) dialling (BRIT) *od* area (*US*) code; **Ortsschild** NT place name sign; **Ortssinn** M sense of direction; **Ortstarif** M local rate; **Ortsvorschriften** PL by(e)-laws *pl*; **Ortszeit** F local time; **Ortszuschlag** M (local) weighting allowance
Ortung F locating
öS. ABK = **österreichischer Schilling**
Öse ['ø:zə] (**-, -n**) F loop; (*an Kleidung*) eye
Oslo ['ɔslo] (**-s**) NT Oslo
Ossi ['ɔsi] (**-s, -s**) (*umg*) M East German

> **Ossi** is a colloquial and rather derogatory word used to describe a German from the former **DDR**.

öst. ABK (= *österreichisch*) Aust.
Ost- zW: **Ostafrika** NT East Africa; **ostdeutsch** ADJ East German; **Ostdeutsche(r)** F(M) East German; **Ostdeutschland** NT (*Pol: früher*) East Germany; (*Geog*) Eastern Germany
Osten (**-s**) M east; **der Ferne ~** the Far East; **der Nahe ~** the Middle East, the Near East
ostentativ [ɔstɛnta'ti:f] ADJ pointed, ostentatious
Oster- zW: **Osterei** NT Easter egg; **Osterfest** NT Easter; **Osterglocke** F daffodil; **Osterhase** M Easter bunny; **Osterinsel** F Easter Island; **Ostermarsch** M Easter demonstration; **Ostermontag** M Easter Monday
Ostern (**-s, -**) NT Easter; **frohe** *od* **fröhliche ~!** Happy Easter!; **zu ~** at Easter
Österreich ['ø:stəraɪç] (**-s**) NT Austria
Österreicher(in) (**-s, -**) M(F) Austrian
österreichisch ADJ Austrian
Ostersonntag M Easter Day *od* Sunday
Osteuropa NT East(ern) Europe
osteuropäisch ADJ East European
östlich ['œstlɪç] ADJ eastern, easterly
Östrogen [œstro'ge:n] (**-s, -e**) NT oestrogen (BRIT), estrogen (*US*)
Ost- zW: **Ostsee** F Baltic Sea; **ostwärts** ADV eastwards; **Ostwind** M east wind
oszillieren [ɔstsɪ'li:rən] VI to oscillate
Otter[1] ['ɔtər] (**-s, -**) M otter
Otter[2] ['ɔtər] (**-, -n**) F (*Schlange*) adder
ÖTV (**-**) F ABK (= *Gewerkschaft öffentliche Dienste, Transport und Verkehr*) ≈ Transport and General Workers' Union
outen ['aʊtən] VT to out
Ouvertüre [uvɛr'ty:rə] (**-, -n**) F overture
oval [o'va:l] ADJ oval
Ovation [ovatsi'o:n] F ovation
Overall ['oʊvərɔ:l] (**-s, -s**) M (*Schutzanzug*) overalls *pl*
ÖVP (**-**) F ABK (= *Österreichische Volkspartei*) Austrian People's Party
Ovulation [ovulatsi'o:n] F ovulation
Oxid, Oxyd [ɔ'ksy:t] (**-(e)s, -e**) NT oxide
oxidieren, oxydieren [ɔksy'di:rən] VT, VI to oxidize
Oxidierung, Oxydierung F oxidization
Ozean ['o:tsea:n] (**-s, -e**) M ocean; **Ozeandampfer** M (ocean-going) liner
Ozeanien [otse'a:niən] (**-s**) NT Oceania
ozeanisch [otse'a:nɪʃ] ADJ oceanic; (*Sprachen*) Oceanic
Ozeanriese (*umg*) M ocean liner
Ozon [o'tso:n] (**-s**) NT ozone; **Ozonloch** NT hole in the ozone layer; **Ozonschicht** F ozone layer; **Ozonwerte** PL ozone levels *pl*

Pp

P, p [pe:] NT P, p; **P wie Peter** ≈ P for Peter
P. ABK = **Pastor**; **Pater**
paar ADJ *unver*: **ein ~** a few; **ein ~ Mal** a few times; **ein ~ Äpfel** some apples; *siehe auch* **paarmal**
Paar [pa:r] (**-(e)s, -e**) NT pair; (*Liebespaar*) couple
paaren VT, VR (*Tiere*) to mate, to pair
Paar- ZW: **Paarhufer** PL (*Zool*) cloven-hoofed animals *pl*; **Paarlauf** M pair skating; **paarmal** ADV: **ein paarmal** a few times
Paarung F combination; (*von Tieren*) mating
paarweise ADV in pairs
Pacht [paxt] (**-, -en**) F lease; (*Entgelt*) rent; **pachten** VT to lease; **du hast das Sofa doch nicht für dich gepachtet** (*umg*) don't hog the sofa
Pächter(in) ['pɛçtər(ɪn)] (**-s, -**) M(F) leaseholder, tenant
Pachtvertrag M lease
Pack¹ [pak] (**-(e)s, -e** *od* **Päcke**) M bundle, pack
Pack² [pak] (**-(e)s**) (*pej*) NT mob, rabble
Päckchen ['pɛkçən] NT small package; (*Zigaretten*) packet; (*Postpäckchen*) small parcel
Packeis NT pack ice
packen VT, VI (*auch Comput*) to pack; (*fassen*) to grasp, to seize; (*umg: schaffen*) to manage; (*fig: fesseln*) to grip; **~ wirs!** (*umg: gehen*) let's go; **Packen** (**-s, -**) M bundle; (*fig: Menge*) heaps (of)
Packer(in) (**-s, -**) M(F) packer
Packesel M pack mule; (*fig*) packhorse
Packpapier NT brown paper, wrapping paper
Packung F packet; (*Pralinenpackung*) box; (*Med*) compress
Packungsbeilage F package insert, patient information leaflet
Packzettel M (*Comm*) packing slip
Pädagoge [pɛda'go:gə] (**-n, -n**) M educationalist
Pädagogik F education
Pädagogin [pɛda'go:gɪn] F educationalist
pädagogisch ADJ educational, pedagogical; **pädagogische Hochschule** college of education
Paddel ['padəl] (**-s, -**) NT paddle; **Paddelboot** NT canoe
paddeln VI to paddle
pädophil [pɛdo'fi:l] ADJ paedophile (BRIT), pedophile (US)
Pädophilie [pɛdofɪ'li:] F paedophilia (BRIT), pedophilia (US)
paffen ['pafən] VT, VI to puff
Page ['pa:ʒə] (**-n, -n**) M page(boy)
Pagenkopf M pageboy cut
paginieren [pagi'ni:rən] VT to paginate
Paginierung F pagination
Paillette [paɪ'jɛtə] F sequin
Paket [pa'ke:t] (**-(e)s, -e**) NT packet; (*Postpaket*) parcel; **Paketannahme** F parcels office; **Paketausgabe** F parcels office; **Paketkarte** F dispatch note; **Paketpost** F parcel post; **Paketschalter** M parcels counter
Pakistan ['pa:kɪsta:n] (**-s**) NT Pakistan
Pakistaner(in) [pakɪs'ta:nər(ɪn)] (**-s, -**) M(F) Pakistani
Pakistani [pakɪs'ta:ni] (**-(s), -(s)**) M Pakistani
pakistanisch ADJ Pakistani
Pakt [pakt] (**-(e)s, -e**) M pact
Paläontologie [palɛɔntolo'gi:] F palaeontology (BRIT), paleontology (US)
Palast [pa'last] (**-es, Paläste**) M palace
Palästina [palɛ'sti:na] (**-s**) NT Palestine
Palästinenser(in) [palɛsti'nɛnzər(ɪn)] (**-s, -**) M(F) Palestinian
palästinensisch ADJ Palestinian
Palaver [pa'la:vər] (**-s, -**) NT (*auch fig: umg*) palaver
Palette [pa'lɛtə] F palette; (*fig*) range; (*Ladepalette*) pallet
Palme ['palmə] (**-, -n**) F palm (tree); **jdn auf die ~ bringen** (*umg*) to make sb see red
Palmsonntag M Palm Sunday
Pampelmuse ['pampəlmu:zə] (**-, -n**) F grapefruit
pampig ['pampɪç] (*umg*) ADJ (*frech*) fresh
Panama ['panama] (**-s**) NT Panama; **Panamakanal** M Panama Canal
Pandemie [pande'mi:] F pandemic
Panflöte ['pa:nflø:tə] F panpipes *pl*, Pan's pipes *pl*
panieren [pa'ni:rən] VT (*Koch*) to coat with egg and breadcrumbs
Paniermehl [pa'ni:rme:l] NT breadcrumbs *pl*
Panik ['pa:nɪk] F panic; **nur keine ~!** don't panic!; **in ~ ausbrechen** to panic; **Panikkäufe** PL panic buying *sing*; **Panikmache** (*umg*) F panicmongering
panisch ['pa:nɪʃ] ADJ panic-stricken

Panne ['panə] (-, **-n**) F (*Aut etc*) breakdown; (*Missgeschick*) slip; **uns ist eine ~ passiert** we've boobed (BRIT *umg*) *od* goofed (*US umg*)
Pannendienst M breakdown service
Pannenhilfe F breakdown service
Panorama [pano'ra:ma] (**-s, -men**) NT panorama
panschen ['panʃən] VI to splash about ▸ VT to water down
Panther, Panter ['pantər] (**-s, -**) M panther
Pantoffel [pan'tɔfəl] (**-s, -n**) M slipper; **Pantoffelheld** (*umg*) M henpecked husband
Pantomime [panto'mi:mə] (**-, -n**) F mime
Panzer ['pantsər] (**-s, -**) M (*Platte*) armour (BRIT) *od* armor (*US*) plate; (*Fahrzeug*) tank; (*fig*) shield; **Panzerfaust** F bazooka; **Panzerglas** NT bulletproof glass; **Panzergrenadier** M armoured (BRIT) *od* armored (*US*) infantryman
panzern VT to armour (BRIT) *od* armor (*US*) plate ▸ VR (*fig*) to arm o.s.
Panzerschrank M strongbox
Panzerwagen M armoured (BRIT) *od* armored (*US*) car
Papa [pa'pa:] (**-s, -s**) (*umg*) M dad(dy), pa
Papagei [papa:'gaɪ] (**-s, -en**) M parrot
Papier [pa'pi:r] (**-s, -e**) NT paper; (*Wertpapier*) share; **Papiere** PL (identity) papers *pl*; (*Urkunden*) documents *pl*; **seine Papiere bekommen** (*entlassen werden*) to get one's cards; **Papierfabrik** F paper mill; **Papiergeld** NT paper money; **Papierkorb** M wastepaper basket; (*Comput*) recycle bin; **Papierkram** (*umg*) M bumf (BRIT *umg*); **Papierkrieg** M red tape; **Papiertüte** F paper bag; **Papiervorschub** M (*Drucker*) paper advance
Pappbecher M paper cup
Pappdeckel (**-, -n**) M cardboard
Pappe ['papə] F cardboard; **das ist nicht von ~** (*umg*) that is really something
Pappeinband M pasteboard
Pappel (**-, -n**) F poplar
pappen (*umg*) VT, VI to stick
Pappenheimer PL: **ich kenne meine ~** (*umg*) I know you lot/that lot (inside out)
Pappenstiel (*umg*) M: **keinen ~ wert sein** not to be worth a thing; **für einen ~ bekommen** to get for a song
papperlapapp [papərla'pap] INTERJ rubbish!
pappig ADJ sticky
Pappkarton M cardboard box
Pappmaschee, Pappmaché [papma'ʃe:] (**-s, -s**) NT papier-mâché
Pappteller M paper plate
Paprika ['paprika] (**-s, -s**) M (*Gewürz*) paprika; (*Paprikaschote*) pepper; **Paprikaschote** F pepper; **gefüllte Paprikaschoten** stuffed peppers
Papst [pa:pst] (**-(e)s, Päpste**) M pope
päpstlich ['pɛ:pstlɪç] ADJ papal; **päpstlicher als der Papst sein** to be more Catholic than the Pope
Parabel [pa'ra:bəl] (**-, -n**) F parable; (*Math*) parabola
Parabolantenne [para'bo:llantɛnə] F (*TV*) satellite dish
Parade [pa'ra:də] (**-, -n**) F (*Mil*) parade, review; (*Sport*) parry; **Paradebeispiel** NT prime example; **Parademarsch** M march past; **Paradeschritt** M goose step
Paradies [para'di:s] (**-es, -e**) NT paradise; **paradiesisch** ADJ heavenly
paradox ADJ paradoxical; **Paradox** [para'dɔks] (**-es, -e**) NT paradox
Paraffin [para'fi:n] (**-s, -e**) NT (*Chem: Paraffinöl*) paraffin (BRIT), kerosene (*US*); (*Paraffinwachs*) paraffin wax
Paragraf [para'gra:f] (**-en, -en**) M paragraph; (*Jur*) section
Paragrafenreiter (*umg*) M pedant
Paraguay [paragu'a:i] (**-s**) NT Paraguay
Paraguayer(in) [para'gua:jər(ɪn)] (**-s, -**) M(F) Paraguayan
paraguayisch ADJ Paraguayan
parallel [para'le:l] ADJ parallel; **~ schalten** (*Elek*) to connect in parallel
Parallele (**-, -n**) F parallel
Parameter [pa'ra:metər] M parameter
paramilitärisch [paramili'tɛ:rɪʃ] ADJ paramilitary
Paranuss ['pa:ranʊs] F Brazil nut
paraphieren [para'fi:rən] VT (*Vertrag*) to initial
Parasit [para'zi:t] (**-en, -en**) M (*lit, fig*) parasite
parat [pa'ra:t] ADJ ready
Pärchen ['pɛ:rçən] NT couple
Parcours [par'ku:r] (**-, -**) M showjumping course; (*Sportart*) showjumping
Pardon [par'dõ:] (**-s**) (*umg*) M OD NT: **~!** (*Verzeihung*) sorry!; **kein ~ kennen** to be ruthless
Parfüm [par'fy:m] (**-s, -s** *od* **-e**) NT perfume
Parfümerie [parfymə'ri:] F perfumery
Parfümflasche F scent bottle
parfümieren [parfy'mi:rən] VT to scent, to perfume
parieren [pa'ri:rən] VT to parry ▸ VI (*umg*) to obey
Paris [pa'ri:s] (**-**) NT Paris
Pariser [pa'ri:zər] (**-s, -**) M Parisian; (*umg: Kondom*) condom, rubber (*US*) ▸ ADJ *attrib* Parisian, Paris *attrib*
Pariserin F Parisian
Parität [pari'tɛ:t] F parity; **paritätisch** ADJ: **paritätische Mitbestimmung** equal representation
Pariwert ['pa:rive:rt] M par value, parity
Park [park] (**-s, -s**) M park
Parka ['parka] (**-(s), -s**) M parka
Park-and-Ride ['parkənd'raɪd] NT park and ride
Parkanlage F park; (*um Gebäude*) grounds *pl*
Parkbank F park bench
Parkbucht F parking bay
parken VT, VI to park; **„P~ verboten!"** "No Parking"
Parkett [par'kɛt] (**-(e)s, -e**) NT parquet (floor); (*Theat*) stalls *pl* (BRIT), orchestra (*US*); **Parketthandel** M (*Fin*) floor trading

Park- ZW: **Parkhaus** NT multistorey car park; **Parklücke** F parking space; **Parkplatz** M car park, parking lot (*US*); (*Parklücke*) parking place; **Parkscheibe** F parking disc; **Parkuhr** F parking meter; **Parkverbot** NT parking ban
Parlament [parla'mɛnt] NT parliament
Parlamentarier [parlamɛn'ta:riər] (**-s, -**) M parliamentarian
parlamentarisch ADJ parliamentary
Parlaments- ZW: **Parlamentsausschuss** M parliamentary committee; **Parlamentsbeschluss** M vote of parliament; **Parlamentsferien** PL recess *sing*; **Parlamentsmitglied** NT Member of Parliament (BRIT), Congressman (*US*); **Parlamentssitzung** F sitting (of parliament)
Parodie [paro'di:] F parody
parodieren VT to parody
Parodontose [parodɔn'to:zə] (**-, -n**) F shrinking gums *pl*
Parole [pa'ro:lə] (**-, -n**) F password; (*Wahlspruch*) motto
Partei [par'taɪ] F party; (*im Mietshaus*) tenant, party (*form*); **für jdn ~ ergreifen** to take sb's side; **Parteibuch** NT party membership book; **Parteiführung** F party leadership; **Parteigenosse** M party member; **parteiisch** ADJ partial, bias(s)ed; **parteilich** ADJ party *attrib*; **Parteilinie** F party line; **parteilos** ADJ neutral; **Parteinahme** (**-, -n**) F partisanship; **parteipolitisch** ADJ party political; **Parteiprogramm** NT (party) manifesto; **Parteitag** M party conference; **Parteivorsitzende(r)** F(M) party leader
Parterre [par'tɛr] (**-s, -s**) NT ground floor (BRIT), first floor (*US*); (*Theat*) stalls *pl* (BRIT), orchestra (*US*)
Partie [par'ti:] F part; (*Spiel*) game; (*Ausflug*) outing; (*Mann, Frau*) catch; (*Comm*) lot; **mit von der ~ sein** to join in
partiell [partsi'ɛl] ADJ partial
Partikel [par'ti:kəl] (**-, -n**) F particle
Partisan(in) [parti'za:n(ɪn)] (**-s** *od* **-en, -en**) M(F) partisan
Partitur [parti'tu:r] F (*Mus*) score
Partizip [parti'tsi:p] (**-s, -ien**) NT participle; **~ Präsens/Perfekt** (*Gram*) present/past participle
Partner(in) ['partnər(ɪn)] (**-s, -**) M(F) partner; **Partnerschaft** F partnership; (*Städtepartnerschaft*) twinning; **eingetragene Partnerschaft** civil partnership; **partnerschaftlich** ADJ as partners; **Partnerstadt** F twin town (BRIT)
partout [par'tu:] ADV: **er will ~ ins Kino gehen** he insists on going to the cinema
Party ['pa:rti] (**-, -s**) F party
Parzelle [par'tsɛlə] F plot, lot
Pascha ['paʃa] (**-s, -s**) M: **wie ein ~** like Lord Muck (BRIT *umg*)
Pass [pas] (**-es, Pässe**) M pass; (*Ausweis*) passport
passabel [pa'sa:bəl] ADJ passable, reasonable
Passage [pa'sa:ʒə] (**-, -n**) F passage; (*Ladenstraße*) arcade
Passagier [pasa'ʒi:r] (**-s, -e**) M passenger; **Passagierdampfer** M passenger steamer; **Passagierflugzeug** NT airliner
Passah ['pasa], **Passahfest** ['pasafɛst] NT (Feast of the) Passover
Passamt NT passport office
Passant(in) [pa'sant(ɪn)] M(F) passer-by
Passbild NT passport photo(graph)
passé, passee [pa'se:] ADJ: **diese Mode ist längst ~** this fashion went out long ago
passen ['pasən] VI to fit; (*auf Frage, Karten*) to pass; **~ zu** (*Farbe etc*) to go with; **Sonntag passt uns nicht** Sunday is no good for us; **die Schuhe ~ (mir) gut** the shoes are a good fit (for me); **zu jdm ~** (*Mensch*) to suit sb; **das passt mir nicht** that doesn't suit me; **er passt nicht zu dir** he's not right for you; **das könnte dir so ~!** (*umg*) you'd like that, wouldn't you?
passend ADJ suitable; (*zusammenpassend*) matching; (*angebracht*) fitting; (*Zeit*) convenient; **haben Sie es ~?** (*Geld*) have you got the right money?
Passfoto NT passport photo(graph)
passierbar [pa'si:rba:r] ADJ passable; (*Fluss, Kanal*) negotiable
passieren VT to pass; (*durch Sieb*) to strain ▸ VI (*Hilfsverb sein*) to happen; **es ist ein Unfall passiert** there has been an accident
Passierschein M pass, permit
Passion [pasi'o:n] F passion
passioniert [pasio:'ni:rt] ADJ enthusiastic, passionate
Passionsfrucht F passion fruit
Passionsspiel NT Passion Play
Passionszeit F Passiontide
passiv ['pasi:f] ADJ passive; **passives Rauchen** passive smoking; **Passiv** (**-s, -e**) NT passive
Passiva [pa'si:va] PL (*Comm*) liabilities *pl*
Passivität [pasivi'tɛ:t] F passiveness
Passivposten M (*Comm*) debit entry
Pass- ZW: **Passkontrolle** F passport control; **Passstelle** F passport office; **Passstraße** F (mountain) pass; **Passwort** NT password; **Passzwang** M requirement to carry a passport
Paste ['pastə] (**-, -n**) F paste
Pastell [pas'tɛl] (**-(e)s, -e**) NT pastel; **Pastellfarbe** F pastel colour (BRIT) *od* color (*US*); **pastellfarben** ADJ pastel-colo(u)red
Pastete [pas'te:tə] (**-, -n**) F pie; (*Pastetchen*) vol-au-vent; (*: ungefüllt*) vol-au-vent case
pasteurisieren [pastøri'zi:rən] VT to pasteurize
Pastor ['pastɔr] M minister; (*anglikanisch*) vicar
Pate ['pa:tə] (**-n, -n**) M godfather; **bei etw ~ gestanden haben** (*fig*) to be the force behind sth
Patenkind NT godchild
Patenstadt F twin town (BRIT)
patent [pa'tɛnt] ADJ clever
Patent (**-(e)s, -e**) NT patent; (*Mil*) commission; **etw als** *od* **zum ~ anmelden** to apply for a patent on sth
Patentamt NT patent office
patentieren [patɛn'ti:rən] VT to patent

Patent- ZW: **Patentinhaber** M patentee; **Patentlösung** F (*fig*) patent remedy; **Patentschutz** M patent right; **Patenturkunde** F letters patent *pl*

Pater ['pa:tər] (**-s, -** *od* **Patres**) M Father

Paternoster [patər'nɔstər] (**-s, -**) M (*Aufzug*) paternoster

pathetisch [pa'te:tɪʃ] ADJ emotional

Pathologe [pato'lo:gə] (**-n, -n**) M pathologist

Pathologin [pato'lo:gɪn] F pathologist

pathologisch ADJ pathological

Pathos ['pa:tɔs] (**-**) NT pathos

Patience [pasi'ã:s] (**-, -n**) F: **Patiencen legen** to play patience

Patient(in) [patsi'ɛnt(ɪn)] M(F) patient

Patientenverfügung [patsi'ɛntənfɛrfy:gʊŋ] F living will

Patin ['pa:tɪn] F godmother

Patriarch [patri'arç] (**-en, -en**) M patriarch

patriarchalisch [patriar'ça:lɪʃ] ADJ patriarchal

Patriot(in) [patri'o:t(ɪn)] (**-en, -en**) M(F) patriot; **patriotisch** ADJ patriotic

Patriotismus [patrio:'tɪsmʊs] M patriotism

Patron [pa'tro:n] (**-s, -e**) M patron; (*Eccl*) patron saint

Patrone (**-, -n**) F cartridge

Patronenhülse F cartridge case

Patronin F patroness; (*Eccl*) patron saint

Patrouille [pa'trʊljə] (**-, -n**) F patrol

patrouillieren [patrʊl'ji:rən] VI to patrol

patsch [patʃ] INTERJ splash!

Patsche (**-, -n**) (*umg*) F (*Händchen*) paw; (*Fliegenpatsche*) swat; (*Feuerpatsche*) beater; (*Bedrängnis*) mess, jam

patschen VI to smack, to slap; (*im Wasser*) to splash

patschnass ADJ soaking wet

Patt [pat] (**-s, -s**) NT (*lit, fig*) stalemate

patzen ['patsən] (*umg*) VI to boob (BRIT), to goof (US)

patzig ['patsɪç] (*umg*) ADJ cheeky, saucy

Pauke ['paʊkə] (**-, -n**) F kettledrum; **auf die ~ hauen** to live it up; **mit Pauken und Trompeten durchfallen** (*umg*) to fail dismally

pauken VT, VI (*Sch*) to swot (BRIT), to cram

Pauker (**-s, -**) (*umg*) M teacher

pausbäckig ['paʊsbɛkɪç] ADJ chubby-cheeked

pauschal [paʊ'ʃa:l] ADJ (*Kosten*) inclusive; (*einheitlich*) flat-rate *attrib*; (*Urteil*) sweeping; **die Werkstatt berechnet ~ pro Inspektion 130 Euro** the garage has a flat rate of 130 euros per service

Pauschale (**-, -n**) F flat rate; (*vorläufig geschätzter Betrag*) estimated amount

Pauschal- ZW: **Pauschalgebühr** F flat rate; **Pauschalpreis** M flat rate; (*für Hotel, Reise*) all-inclusive price; **Pauschalreise** F package tour; **Pauschalsumme** F lump sum; **Pauschalversicherung** F comprehensive insurance

Pause ['paʊzə] (**-, -n**) F break; (*Theat*) interval; (*das Innehalten*) pause; (*Mus*) rest; (*Kopie*) tracing

pausen VT to trace

Pausen- ZW: **Pausenbrot** NT sandwich (*to eat at break*); **Pausenhof** M playground, schoolyard (*US*); **pausenlos** ADJ nonstop; **Pausenzeichen** NT (*Rundf*) call sign; (*Mus*) rest

pausieren [paʊ'si:rən] VI to make a break

Pauspapier ['paʊspapi:r] NT tracing paper

Pavian ['pa:via:n] (**-s, -e**) M baboon

Paybackkarte ['pe:bɛkkartə] F loyalty card

Pay-per-Click ['pe:pərklɪk] (**-s**) NT pay-per-click

Pay-TV ['pe:ti:vi:] NT pay-per-view television, pay TV

Pazifik [pa'tsi:fɪk] (**-s**) M Pacific

pazifisch ADJ Pacific; **der Pazifische Ozean** the Pacific (Ocean)

Pazifist(in) [patsi'fɪst(ɪn)] M(F) pacifist; **pazifistisch** ADJ pacifist

PC M ABK (= *Personal Computer*) PC

PDA M ABK (*Comput: = personal digital assistant*) PDA

PDS F ABK (= *Partei des Demokratischen Sozialismus*) *German Socialist Party*

> The **PDS** (Partei des Demokratischen Sozialismus) was founded in 1989 as the successor of the SED, the former East German Communist Party. Its aims are the establishment of a democratic socialist society and to hold a position in the German political scene left of the **SPD**.

Pech [pɛç] (**-s, -e**) NT pitch; (*fig*) bad luck; **~ haben** to be unlucky; **die beiden halten zusammen wie ~ und Schwefel** (*umg*) the two are inseparable; **~ gehabt!** tough! (*umg*); **pechschwarz** ADJ pitch-black; **Pechsträhne** (*umg*) F unlucky patch; **Pechvogel** (*umg*) M unlucky person

Pedal [pe'da:l] (**-s, -e**) NT pedal; **in die Pedale treten** to pedal (hard)

Pedant [pe'dant] M pedant

Pedanterie [pedantə'ri:] F pedantry

pedantisch ADJ pedantic

Peddigrohr ['pɛdɪçro:r] NT cane

Pediküre [pedi'ky:rə] (**-, -n**) F (*Fußpflege*) pedicure; (*Fußpflegerin*) chiropodist

Pegel ['pe:gəl] (**-s, -**) M water gauge; (*Geräuschpegel*) noise level; **Pegelstand** M water level

peilen ['paɪlən] VT to get a fix on; **die Lage ~** (*umg*) to see how the land lies

Pein [paɪn] (**-**) F agony, suffering

peinigen VT to torture; (*plagen*) to torment

peinlich ADJ (*unangenehm*) embarrassing, awkward, painful; (*genau*) painstaking; **in seinem Zimmer herrschte peinliche Ordnung** his room was meticulously tidy; **er vermied es peinlichst, davon zu sprechen** he was at pains not to talk about it; **es war mir sehr ~** I was totally embarrassed; **Peinlichkeit** F painfulness, awkwardness; (*Genauigkeit*) scrupulousness

Peitsche ['paɪtʃə] (**-, -n**) F whip

peitschen VT to whip; (*Regen*) to lash

Peitschenhieb M lash

Pekinese [peki'ne:zə] (**-n, -n**) M Pekinese, peke (*umg*)

P

Peking ['pe:kɪŋ] **(-s)** NT Peking
Pelikan ['pe:lika:n] **(-s, -e)** M pelican
Pelle ['pɛlə] (-, **-n**) F skin; **der Chef sitzt mir auf der ~** (*umg*) I've got the boss on my back
pellen VT to skin, to peel
Pellkartoffeln PL jacket potatoes *pl*
Pelz [pɛlts] **(-es, -e)** M fur
Pendel ['pɛndəl] **(-s, -)** NT pendulum
pendeln VI (*schwingen*) to swing (to and fro); (*Zug, Fähre etc*) to shuttle; (*Mensch*) to commute; (*fig*) to fluctuate
Pendelverkehr M shuttle service; (*Berufsverkehr*) commuter traffic
Pendler(in) ['pɛndlər(ɪn)] **(-s, -)** M(F) commuter
penetrant [pene'trant] ADJ sharp; (*Person*) pushing; **das schmeckt/riecht ~ nach Knoblauch** it has a very strong taste/smell of garlic
penibel [pe'ni:bəl] ADJ pernickety (BRIT *umg*), persnickety (*US umg*), precise
Penis ['pe:nɪs] (-, **-se**) M penis
Pennbruder ['pɛnbru:dər] (*umg*) M tramp (BRIT), hobo (*US*)
Penne (-, **-n**) (*umg*) F (*Sch*) school
pennen (*umg*) VI to kip
Penner (**-s**, -) (*pej, umg*) M tramp (BRIT), hobo (*US*)
Pension [pɛnzi'o:n] F (*Geld*) pension; (*Ruhestand*) retirement; (*für Gäste*) boarding house, guesthouse; **halbe/volle ~** half/full board; **in ~ gehen** to retire
Pensionär(in) [pɛnzio'nɛ:r(ɪn)] **(-s, -e)** M(F) pensioner
Pensionat **(-(e)s, -e)** NT boarding school
pensionieren [pɛnzio'ni:rən] VT to pension (off); **sich ~ lassen** to retire
pensioniert ADJ retired
Pensionierung F retirement
Pensions- ZW: **pensionsberechtigt** ADJ entitled to a pension; **Pensionsfonds** M pension fund; **Pensionsgast** M boarder, paying guest; **pensionsreif** (*umg*) ADJ ready for retirement
Pensum ['pɛnzʊm] **(-s, Pensen)** NT quota; (*Sch*) curriculum
Peperoni [pepe'ro:ni] (-, -) F chilli
per [pɛr] PRÄP +*akk* by, per; (*pro*) per; (*bis*) by; **~ Adresse** (*Comm*) care of, c/o; **mit jdm ~ du sein** (*umg*) to be on first-name terms with sb
perfekt [pɛr'fɛkt] ADJ perfect; (*abgemacht*) settled; **die Sache ~ machen** to clinch the deal; **der Vertrag ist ~** the contract is all settled
Perfekt ['pɛrfɛkt] **(-(e)s, -e)** NT perfect
perfektionieren [pɛrfɛktsio'ni:rən] VT to perfect
Perfektionismus [pɛrfɛktsio'nɪsmʊs] M perfectionism
perforieren [pɛrfo'ri:rən] VT to perforate
Pergament [pɛrga'mɛnt] NT parchment; **Pergamentpapier** NT greaseproof paper (BRIT), wax(ed) paper (*US*)
Pergola ['pɛrgola] (-, **Pergolen**) F pergola, arbour (BRIT), arbor (*US*)
Periode [peri'o:də] (-, **-n**) F period; **0,33 ~** 0.33 recurring
periodisch [peri'o:dɪʃ] ADJ periodic; (*dezimal*) recurring
Peripherie [perife'ri:] F periphery; (*um Stadt*) outskirts *pl*; (*Math*) circumference; **Peripheriegerät** NT (*Comput*) peripheral
Perle ['pɛrlə] (-, **-n**) F (*lit, fig*) pearl; (*Glasperle, Holzperle, Tropfen*) bead; (*veraltet: umg: Hausgehilfin*) maid
perlen VI to sparkle; (*Tropfen*) to trickle
Perlenkette F pearl necklace
Perlhuhn NT guinea fowl
Perlmutt ['pɛrlmʊt] **(-s)** NT mother-of-pearl
Perlon® ['pɛrlɔn] **(-s)** NT ≈ nylon
Perlwein M sparkling wine
perplex [pɛr'plɛks] ADJ dumbfounded
Perser ['pɛrzər] **(-s, -)** M (*Person*) Persian; (*umg: Teppich*) Persian carpet
Perserin F Persian
Persianer [pɛrzi'a:nər] **(-s, -)** M Persian lamb (coat)
Persien ['pɛrziən] **(-s)** NT Persia
Persiflage [pɛrzi'fla:ʒə] (-, **-n**) F: **~ (+*gen od* auf +*akk*)** pastiche (of), satire (on)
persisch ADJ Persian; **Persischer Golf** Persian Gulf
Person [pɛr'zo:n] (-, **-en**) F person; (*pej: Frau*) female; **sie ist Köchin und Haushälterin in einer ~** she is cook and housekeeper rolled into one; **ich für meine ~** personally I
Personal [pɛrzo'na:l] **(-s)** NT personnel; (*Bedienung*) servants *pl*; **Personalabbau** M staff cuts *pl*; **Personalakte** F personal file; **Personalangaben** PL particulars *pl*; **Personalausweis** M identity card; **Personalbogen** M personal record; **Personalbüro** NT personnel (department); **Personalchef** M personnel manager; **Personal Computer** M personal computer
Personalien [pɛrzo'na:liən] PL particulars *pl*
Personalität [pɛrzonali'tɛ:t] F personality
Personal- ZW: **Personalkosten** PL staff costs; **Personalmangel** M staff shortage; **Personalpronomen** NT personal pronoun; **Personalreduzierung** F staff reduction
personell [pɛrzo'nɛl] ADJ staff *attrib*; **personelle Veränderungen** changes in personnel
Personen- ZW: **Personenaufzug** M lift, elevator (*US*); **Personenbeschreibung** F (personal) description; **Personengedächtnis** NT memory for faces; **Personengesellschaft** F partnership; **Personenkraftwagen** M private motorcar, automobile (*US*); **Personenkreis** M group of people; **Personenkult** M personality cult; **Personennahverkehr** M: **öffentlicher Personennahverkehr** local public transport; **Personenschaden** M injury to persons; **Personenverkehr** M passenger services *pl*; **Personenwaage** F scales *pl*; **Personenzug** M passenger train; (*Nahzug*) stopping train
personifizieren [pɛrzonifi'tsi:rən] VT to personify
persönlich [pɛr'zø:nlɪç] ADJ personal ▶ ADV personally; (*erscheinen*) in person; (*auf Briefen*)

private (and confidential); **~ haften** (*Comm*) to be personally liable; **Persönlichkeit** F personality; **Persönlichkeiten des öffentlichen Lebens** public figures
Perspektive [pɛrspɛk'ti:və] F perspective; **das eröffnet ganz neue Perspektiven für uns** that opens new horizons for us
Pers. Ref. ABK (= *Persönlicher Referent*) personal representative
Peru [pe'ru:] (**-s**) NT Peru
Peruaner(in) [peru'a:nər(ɪn)] (**-s, -**) M(F) Peruvian
peruanisch ADJ Peruvian
Perücke [pe'rʏkə] (**-, -n**) F wig
pervers [pɛr'vɛrs] ADJ perverse
Perversität [pɛrvɛrzi'tɛ:t] F perversity
Pessar [pe'sa:r] (**-s, -e**) NT pessary; (*zur Empfängnisverhütung*) cap, diaphragm
Pessimismus [pɛsi'mɪsmʊs] M pessimism
Pessimist(in) [pɛsi'mɪst(ɪn)] M(F) pessimist; **pessimistisch** ADJ pessimistic
Pest [pɛst] (-) F plague; **jdn/etw wie die ~ hassen** (*umg*) to loathe (and detest) sb/sth
Petersilie [petər'zi:liə] F parsley
Petrochemie [petro:çe'mi:] F petrochemistry
Petrodollar [petro'dɔlar] M petrodollar
Petroleum [pe'tro:leʊm] (**-s**) NT paraffin (BRIT), kerosene (*US*)
petzen ['pɛtsən] (*umg*) VI to tell tales; **er petzt immer** he always tells
Pf. (*Hist*) ABK = **Pfennig**
Pfad [pfa:t] (**-(e)s, -e**) M path; **Pfadfinder** M Boy Scout; **er ist bei den Pfadfindern** he's in the (Boy) Scouts; **Pfadfinderin** F Girl Guide
Pfaffe ['pfafə] (**-n, -n**) (*pej*) M cleric, parson
Pfahl [pfa:l] (**-(e)s, Pfähle**) M post, stake; **Pfahlbau** M pile dwelling
Pfalz [pfalts] (**-, -en**) F (*Geog*) Palatinate
Pfälzer(in) ['pfɛltsər(ɪn)] (**-s, -**) M(F) person from the Palatinate
pfälzisch ADJ Palatine, of the (Rhineland) Palatinate
Pfand [pfant] (**-(e)s, Pfänder**) NT pledge, security; (*Flaschenpfand*) deposit; (*im Spiel*) forfeit; (*fig: der Liebe etc*) pledge; **Pfandbrief** M bond
pfänden ['pfɛndən] VT to seize, to impound
Pfänderspiel NT game of forfeits
Pfand- ZW: **Pfandflasche** F returnable bottle; **Pfandhaus** NT pawnshop; **Pfandleiher** (**-s, -**) M pawnbroker; **Pfandrecht** NT lien; **Pfandschein** M pawn ticket
Pfändung ['pfɛndʊŋ] F seizure, distraint (*form*)
Pfanne ['pfanə] (**-, -n**) F (frying) pan; **jdn in die ~ hauen** (*umg*) to tear a strip off sb
Pfannkuchen M pancake; (*Berliner*) doughnut (BRIT), donut (*US*)
Pfarrei [pfar'raɪ] F parish
Pfarrer (**-s, -**) M priest; (*evangelisch*) vicar; (*von Freikirchen*) minister
Pfarrhaus NT vicarage
Pfau [pfaʊ] (**-(e)s, -en**) M peacock
Pfauenauge NT peacock butterfly
Pfd. ABK (= *Pfund*) ≈ lb.
Pfeffer ['pfɛfər] (**-s, -**) M pepper; **er soll bleiben, wo der ~ wächst!** (*umg*) he can take a running jump; **Pfefferkorn** NT peppercorn; **Pfefferkuchen** M gingerbread; **Pfefferminz** (**-es, -e**) NT peppermint; **Pfefferminze** F peppermint (plant); **Pfeffermühle** F pepper mill
pfeffern VT to pepper; (*umg: werfen*) to fling; **gepfefferte Preise/Witze** steep prices/spicy jokes
Pfeife ['pfaɪfə] (**-, -n**) F whistle; (*Tabakpfeife, Orgelpfeife*) pipe; **nach jds ~ tanzen** to dance to sb's tune
pfeifen *unreg* VT, VI to whistle; **auf dem letzten Loch ~** (*umg: erschöpft sein*) to be on one's last legs; (*: finanziell*) to be on one's beam ends; **ich pfeif(e) drauf!** (*umg*) I don't give a damn!; **Pfeifenstopfer** M tamper
Pfeifer (**-s, -**) M piper
Pfeifkonzert NT catcalls *pl*
Pfeil [pfaɪl] (**-(e)s, -e**) M arrow
Pfeiler ['pfaɪlər] (**-s, -**) M pillar, prop; (*Brückenpfeiler*) pier
Pfeiltaste F (*Comput*) arrow key
Pfennig ['pfɛnɪç] (**-(e)s, -e**) M (*Hist*) pfennig (*one hundredth of a mark*); **Pfennigabsatz** M stiletto heel; **Pfennigfuchser** (**-s, -**) (*umg*) M skinflint
pferchen ['pfɛrçən] VT to cram, to pack
Pferd [pfe:rt] (**-(e)s, -e**) NT horse; **wie ein ~ arbeiten** (*umg*) to work like a Trojan; **mit ihm kann man Pferde stehlen** (*umg*) he's a great sport; **auf das falsche/richtige ~ setzen** (*lit, fig*) to back the wrong/right horse
Pferde- ZW: **Pferdeäpfel** PL horse droppings *pl od* dung *sing*; **Pferdefuß** M: **die Sache hat aber einen Pferdefuß** there's just one snag; **Pferderennen** NT horse-race; (*Sportart*) horse-racing; **Pferdeschwanz** M (*Frisur*) ponytail; **Pferdestall** M stable; **Pferdestärke** F horsepower
pfiff *etc* [pfɪf] VB *siehe* **pfeifen**
Pfiff (**-(e)s, -e**) M whistle; (*Kniff*) trick
Pfifferling ['pfɪfərlɪŋ] M chanterelle; **keinen ~ wert** not worth a thing
pfiffig ADJ smart
Pfingsten ['pfɪŋstən] (**-, -**) NT Whitsun
Pfingstrose F peony
Pfingstsonntag M Whit Sunday, Pentecost (*Rel*)
Pfirsich ['pfɪrzɪç] (**-s, -e**) M peach
Pflanze ['pflantsə] (**-, -n**) F plant
pflanzen VT to plant ▶ VR (*umg*) to plonk o.s.
Pflanzenfett NT vegetable fat
Pflanzenschutzmittel NT pesticide
pflanzlich ADJ vegetable
Pflanzung F plantation
Pflaster ['pflastər] (**-s, -**) NT plaster; (*Straßenpflaster*) pavement (BRIT), sidewalk (*US*); **ein teures ~** (*umg*) a pricey place; **ein heißes ~** a dangerous *od* unsafe place; **pflastermüde** ADJ dead on one's feet
pflastern VT to pave
Pflasterstein M paving stone

P

Pflaume ['pflaʊmə] (-, **-n**) F plum; (*umg: Mensch*) twit (BRIT)
Pflaumenmus NT plum jam
Pflege ['pfle:gə] (-, **-n**) F care; (*von Idee*) cultivation; (*Krankenpflege*) nursing; **jdn/etw in ~ nehmen** to look after sb/sth; **in ~ sein** (*Kind*) to be fostered out; **pflegebedürftig** ADJ needing care; **Pflegeeltern** PL foster parents *pl*; **Pflegefall** M case for nursing; **Pflegegeld** NT (*für Pflegekinder*) boarding-out allowance; (*für Kranke*) attendance allowance; **Pflegeheim** NT nursing home; **Pflegekind** NT foster child; **pflegeleicht** ADJ easy-care; **Pflegemutter** F foster mother
pflegen VT to look after; (*Kranke*) to nurse; (*Beziehungen*) to foster ▶ VI (*gewöhnlich tun*): **sie pflegte zu sagen** she used to say
Pfleger (-s, -) M (*im Krankenhaus*) orderly; (*voll qualifiziert*) male nurse; **Pflegerin** F nurse
Pflegesatz M hospital and nursing charges *pl*
Pflegevater M foster father
Pflegeversicherung F geriatric care insurance
Pflicht [pflɪçt] (-, **-en**) F duty; (*Sport*) compulsory section; **Rechte und Pflichten** rights and responsibilities; **pflichtbewusst** ADJ conscientious; **Pflichtbewusstsein** NT sense of duty; **Pflichtfach** NT (*Sch*) compulsory subject; **Pflichtgefühl** NT sense of duty; **pflichtgemäß** ADJ dutiful; **pflichtvergessen** ADJ irresponsible; **Pflichtversicherung** F compulsory insurance
Pflock [pflɔk] (**-(e)s, Pflöcke**) M peg; (*für Tiere*) stake
pflog *etc* [pflo:k] VB (*veraltet*) *siehe* **pflegen**
pflücken ['pflʏkən] VT to pick
Pflug [pflu:k] (**-(e)s, Pflüge**) M plough (BRIT), plow (US)
pflügen ['pfly:gən] VT to plough (BRIT), to plow (US)
Pflugschar F ploughshare (BRIT), plowshare (US)
Pforte ['pfɔrtə] (-, **-n**) F (*Tor*) gate
Pförtner ['pfœrtnər] (**-s, -**) M porter, doorkeeper, doorman
Pförtnerin F doorkeeper, porter
Pfosten ['pfɔstən] (**-s, -**) M post; (*senkrechter Balken*) upright
Pfote ['pfo:tə] (-, **-n**) F paw; (*umg: Schrift*) scrawl
Pfropf [pfrɔpf] (**-(e)s, -e**) M (*Flaschenpfropf*) stopper; (*Blutpfropf*) clot
pfropfen VT (*stopfen*) to cram; (*Baum*) to graft; **gepfropft voll** crammed full
Pfropfen (**-s, -**) M = **Pfropf**
pfui [pfʊɪ] INTERJ ugh!; (*na na*) tut tut!; (*Buhruf*) boo!; **~ Teufel!** (*umg*) ugh!, yuck!
Pfund [pfʊnt] (**-(e)s, -e**) NT (*Gewicht, Fin*) pound; **das ~ sinkt** sterling *od* the pound is falling
pfundig (*umg*) ADJ great
Pfundskerl ['pfʊntskɛrl] (*umg*) M great guy
pfundweise ADV by the pound
pfuschen ['pfʊʃən] VI to bungle; (*einen Fehler machen*) to slip up
Pfuscher(in) ['pfʊʃər(ɪn)] (**-s, -**) (*umg*) M(F) sloppy worker; (*Kurpfuscher*) quack
Pfuscherei [pfʊʃə'raɪ] (*umg*) F sloppy work; (*Kurpfuscherei*) quackery
Pfütze ['pfʏtsə] (-, **-n**) F puddle
PH (**-, -s**) F ABK = **pädagogische Hochschule**
Phänomen [fɛno'me:n] (**-s, -e**) NT phenomenon; **phänomenal** [-'na:l] ADJ phenomenal
Phantasie [fanta'zi:] = **Fantasie**
phantasieren [fanta'zi:rən] VI = **fantasieren**
phantasievoll ADJ = **fantasievoll**
Phantast [fan'tast] (**-en, -en**) M = **Fantast**
phantastisch ADJ = **fantastisch**
Phantom [fan'to:m] (**-s, -e**) NT (*Trugbild*) phantom; **einem ~ nachjagen** (*fig*) to tilt at windmills; **Phantombild** NT Identikit® picture
Pharisäer [fari'zɛ:ər] (**-s, -**) M (*lit, fig*) pharisee
Pharmazeut(in) [farma'tsɔʏt(ɪn)] (**-en, -en**) M(F) pharmacist
pharmazeutisch ADJ pharmaceutical
Pharmazie F pharmacy, pharmaceutics *sing*
Phase ['fa:zə] (-, **-n**) F phase
Philanthrop [filan'tro:p] (**-en, -en**) M philanthropist; **philanthropisch** ADJ philanthropic
Philatelist(in) [filate'lɪst(ɪn)] (**-en, -en**) M(F) philatelist
Philharmoniker [fɪlhar'mo:nikər] (**-s, -**) M: **die ~** the philharmonic (orchestra) *sing*
Philippine [fɪlɪ'pi:nə] (**-n, -n**) M Filipino
Philippinen PL Philippines *pl*, Philippine Islands *pl*
Philippinin F Filipino
philippinisch ADJ Filipino
Philologe [filo'lo:gə] (**-n, -n**) M philologist
Philologie [filolo'gi:] F philology
Philologin F philologist
Philosoph(in) [filo'zo:f(ɪn)] (**-en, -en**) M(F) philosopher
Philosophie [filozo'fi:] F philosophy
philosophieren [filozo'fi:rən] VI: **~ (über** *+akk*) to philosophize (about)
philosophisch ADJ philosophical
Phlegma ['flɛgma] (**-s**) NT lethargy
phlegmatisch [flɛ'gma:tɪʃ] ADJ lethargic
Phobie [fo'bi:] F: **~ (vor** *+dat*) phobia (about)
Phonetik [fo'ne:tɪk] F phonetics *sing*
phonetisch ADJ phonetic
Phonotypistin [fonoty'pɪstɪn] F audiotypist
Phosphat [fɔs'fa:t] (**-(e)s, -e**) NT phosphate
Phosphor ['fɔsfɔr] (**-s**) M phosphorus
phosphoreszieren [fɔsforɛs'tsi:rən] VT to phosphoresce
Photo ['fo:to] = **Foto**
Photoshop® ['fo:toʃɔp] NT Photoshop®
Phrase ['fra:zə] (-, **-n**) F phrase; (*pej*) hollow phrase; **Phrasen dreschen** (*umg*) to churn out one cliché after another
pH-Wert [pe:'ha:ve:rt] M pH value
Physik [fy'zi:k] F physics *sing*
physikalisch [fyzi'ka:lɪʃ] ADJ of physics
Physiker(in) ['fy:zikər(ɪn)] (**-s, -**) M(F) physicist
Physikum ['fy:zikʊm] (**-s**) NT (*Univ*) *preliminary examination in medicine*

Physiologe [fyzio'lo:gə] (**-n, -n**) M physiologist
Physiologie [fyziolo'gi:] F physiology
Physiologin F physiologist
physisch ['fy:zɪʃ] ADJ physical
Pianist(in) [pia'nɪst(ɪn)] M(F) pianist
Piccolo ['pɪkolo] (**-s, -s**) M trainee waiter; (*auch*: **Piccoloflasche**) *quarter bottle of champagne*; (*Mus: auch*: **Piccoloflöte**) piccolo
picheln ['pɪçəln] (*umg*) VI to booze
Pickel ['pɪkəl] (**-s, -**) M pimple; (*Werkzeug*) pickaxe; (*Bergpickel*) ice axe
pickelig, picklig ADJ pimply
picken ['pɪkən] VT to peck ▶VI: **~ (nach)** to peck (at)
Picknick ['pɪknɪk] (**-s, -e** *od* **-s**) NT picnic; **~ machen** to have a picnic
piekfein ['pi:k'faɪn] (*umg*) ADJ posh
Piemont [pie'mɔnt] (**-s**) NT Piedmont
piepen ['pi:pən] VI to chirp; (*Funkgerät etc*) to bleep; **bei dir piepts wohl!** (*umg*) are you off your head?; **es war zum P~!** (*umg*) it was a scream!
piepsen ['pi:psən] VI to chirp
Piepser (*umg*) M pager, paging device
Piepsstimme F squeaky voice
Piepton M bleep
Pier [pi:ər] (**-s, -s** *od* **-e**) M jetty, pier
piercen ['pi:rsən] VT: **sich die Nase ~ lassen** to have one's nose pierced
Piercing ['pi:rsɪŋ] (**-s**) NT (body) piercing
piesacken ['pi:zakən] (*umg*) VT to torment
Pietät [pie'tɛ:t] F piety; (*Ehrfurcht*) reverence; **pietätlos** ADJ impious, irreverent
Pigment [pɪg'mɛnt] (**-(e)s, -e**) NT pigment
Pik [pi:k] (**-s, -s**) NT (*Karten*) spades; **einen ~ auf jdn haben** (*umg*) to have it in for sb
pikant [pi'kant] ADJ spicy, piquant; (*anzüglich*) suggestive
Pike (**-, -n**) F: **etw von der ~ auf lernen** (*fig*) to learn sth from the bottom up
pikiert [pi'ki:rt] ADJ offended
Pikkolo ['pɪkolo] (**-s, -s**) M = **Piccolo**
Piktogramm [pɪkto'gram] NT pictogram
Pilger(in) ['pɪlgər(ɪn)] (**-s, -**) M(F) pilgrim; **Pilgerfahrt** F pilgrimage
pilgern VI to make a pilgrimage; (*umg: gehen*) to wend one's way
Pille ['pɪlə] (**-, -n**) F pill
Pilot(in) [pi'lo:t(ɪn)] (**-en, -en**) M(F) pilot; **Pilotenschein** M pilot's licence (BRIT) *od* license (*US*)
Pils [pɪls] (**-, -**) NT Pilsner (lager)
Pilsener [pɪlzənər], **Pilsner** [pɪlznər] (**-s, -**) NT Pilsner (lager)
Pilz [pɪlts] (**-es, -e**) M (*essbar*) mushroom; (*giftig*) toadstool; (*Med*) fungus; **wie Pilze aus dem Boden schießen** (*fig*) to mushroom; **Pilzkrankheit** F fungal disease
Pimmel ['pɪməl] (**-s, -**) (*umg*) M (*Penis*) willie
pingelig ['pɪŋəlɪç] (*umg*) ADJ fussy
Pinguin ['pɪŋgui:n] (**-s, -e**) M penguin
Pinie ['pi:niə] F pine
Pinkel (**-s, -**) (*umg*) M: **ein feiner** *od* **vornehmer ~** a swell, Lord Muck (BRIT *umg*)
pinkeln ['pɪŋkəln] (*umg*) VI to pee
Pinnwand ['pɪnvant] F pinboard
Pinsel ['pɪnzəl] (**-s, -**) M paintbrush
pinseln (*umg*) VT, VI to paint; (*pej: malen*) to daub
Pinte ['pɪntə] (**-, -n**) (*umg*) F (*Lokal*) boozer (BRIT)
Pinzette [pɪn'tsɛtə] F tweezers *pl*
Pionier [pio'ni:r] (**-s, -e**) M pioneer; (*Mil*) sapper, engineer; **Pionierarbeit** F pioneering work; **Pionierunternehmen** NT pioneer company
Pipi [pi'pi:] (**-s, -s**) NT OD M (*Kindersprache*) wee(-wee)
Pirat [pi'ra:t] (**-en, -en**) M pirate
Piratensender M pirate radio station
Pirsch [pɪrʃ] (**-**) F stalking
PISA-Studie ['pi:za-] F (*Sch*) PISA study
pissen ['pɪsən] (*umg!*) VI to (have a) piss (*umg!*); (*regnen*) to piss down (*umg!*)
Pistazie [pɪs'ta:tsiə] (**-, -n**) F pistachio
Piste ['pɪstə] (**-, -n**) F (*Ski*) run, piste; (*Aviat*) runway
Pistole [pɪs'to:lə] (**-, -n**) F pistol; **wie aus der ~ geschossen** (*fig*) like a shot; **jdm die ~ auf die Brust setzen** (*fig*) to hold a pistol to sb's head
pitschenass ['pɪtʃə'nas], **pitschnass** ['pɪtʃ'nas] (*umg*) ADJ soaking (wet)
Pixel ['pɪksəl] (**-s**) NT (*Comput*) pixel
Pizza ['pɪtsa] (**-, -s**) F pizza
PKW, Pkw (**-(s), -(s)**) M ABK = **Personenkraftwagen**
Pl. ABK (= *Plural*) pl.; (= *Platz*) Sq.
Plackerei [plakə'raɪ] F drudgery
plädieren [plɛ'di:rən] VI to plead
Plädoyer [plɛdoa'je:] (**-s, -s**) NT speech for the defence; (*fig*) plea
Plage ['pla:gə] (**-, -n**) F plague; (*Mühe*) nuisance; **Plagegeist** M pest, nuisance
plagen VT to torment ▶VR to toil, to slave
Plagiat [plagi'a:t] (**-(e)s, -e**) NT plagiarism
Plakat [pla'ka:t] (**-(e)s, -e**) NT poster; (*aus Pappe*) placard
plakativ [plaka'ti:f] ADJ striking, bold
Plakatwand F hoarding, billboard (*US*)
Plakette [pla'kɛtə] (**-, -n**) F (*Abzeichen*) badge; (*Münze*) commemorative coin; (*an Wänden*) plaque
Plan [pla:n] (**-(e)s, Pläne**) M plan; (*Karte*) map; **Pläne schmieden** to make plans; **nach ~ verlaufen** to go according to plan; **jdn auf den ~ rufen** (*fig*) to bring sb into the arena
Plane (**-, -n**) F tarpaulin
planen VT to plan; (*Mord etc*) to plot
Planer(in) (**-s, -**) M(F) planner
Planet [pla'ne:t] (**-en, -en**) M planet
Planetenbahn F orbit (of a planet)
planieren [pla'ni:rən] VT to level off
Planierraupe F bulldozer
Planke ['plaŋkə] (**-, -n**) F plank
Plänkelei [plɛŋkə'laɪ] F skirmish(ing)
plänkeln ['plɛŋkəln] VI to skirmish
Plankton ['plaŋktɔn] (**-s**) NT plankton
planlos ADJ (*Vorgehen*) unsystematic; (*Umherlaufen*) aimless

P

planmäßig ADJ according to plan; (*methodisch*) systematic; (*Eisenb*) scheduled
Planschbecken, Plantschbecken ['planʃbɛkən] NT paddling pool
planschen VI to splash
Plansoll NT output target
Planstelle F post
Plantage [plan'ta:ʒə] (**-, -n**) F plantation
plantschen VI to splash
Planung F planning
Planwagen M covered wagon
Planwirtschaft F planned economy
Plappermaul (*umg*) NT (*Kind*) chatterbox
plappern ['plapərn] VI to chatter
plärren ['plɛrən] VI (*Mensch*) to cry, to whine; (*Radio*) to blare
Plasma ['plasma] (**-s, Plasmen**) NT plasma
Plastik[1] ['plastɪk] F sculpture
Plastik[2] ['plastɪk] (**-s**) NT (*Kunststoff*) plastic; **Plastikfolie** F plastic film; **Plastikgeschoss** NT plastic bullet; **Plastiktüte** F plastic bag
Plastilin [plasti'li:n] (**-s**) NT Plasticine®
plastisch ['plastɪʃ] ADJ plastic; **stell dir das ~ vor!** just picture it!
Platane [pla'ta:nə] (**-, -n**) F plane (tree)
Platin ['pla:ti:n] (**-s**) NT platinum
Platitüde [plati'ty:də] (**-, -n**) F platitude
platonisch [pla'to:nɪʃ] ADJ platonic
platsch [platʃ] INTERJ splash!
platschen VI to splash
plätschern ['plɛtʃərn] VI to babble
platschnass ADJ drenched
platt [plat] ADJ flat; (*umg: überrascht*) flabbergasted; (*fig: geistlos*) flat, boring; **einen Platten haben** to have a flat (*umg*), to have a flat tyre (BRIT) *od* tire (US)
plattdeutsch ADJ Low German
Platte (**-, -n**) F (*Speisenplatte, Phot, Tech*) plate; (*Steinplatte*) flag; (*Kachel*) tile; (*Schallplatte*) record; **kalte ~** cold dish; **die ~ kenne ich schon** (*umg*) I've heard all that before
Plätteisen NT iron
plätten VT, VI to iron
Platten- ZW: **Plattenleger** (**-s, -**) M paver; **Plattenspieler** M record player; **Plattenteller** M turntable
Plattform F platform; (*fig: Grundlage*) basis
Plattfuß M flat foot; (*Reifen*) flat tyre (BRIT) *od* tire (US)
Plattitüde [plati'ty:də] (**-, -n**) F platitude
Platz [plats] (**-es, Plätze**) M place; (*Sitzplatz*) seat; (*Raum*) space, room; (*in Stadt*) square; (*Sportplatz*) playing field; **~ machen** to get out of the way; **~ nehmen** to take a seat; **jdm ~ machen** to make room for sb; **~ sparend** space-saving; **auf ~ zwei** in second place; **fehl am Platze sein** to be out of place; **seinen ~ behaupten** to stand one's ground; **das erste Hotel am ~** the best hotel in town; **auf die Plätze, fertig, los!** (*beim Sport*) on your marks, get set, go!; **einen Spieler vom ~ stellen** *od* **verweisen** (*Sport*) to send a player off; **Platzangst** F (*Med*) agoraphobia; (*umg*) claustrophobia; **Platzangst haben/bekommen** (*umg*) to feel/ get claustrophobic; **Platzanweiser** (**-s, -**) M usher; **Platzanweiserin** F usherette
Plätzchen ['plɛtsçən] NT spot; (*Gebäck*) biscuit
platzen VI (*Hilfsverb sein*) to burst; (*Bombe*) to explode; (*Naht, Hose, Haut*) to split; (*umg: scheitern: Geschäft*) to fall through; (*: Freundschaft*) to break up; (*: Theorie, Verschwörung*) to collapse; (*: Wechsel*) to bounce; **vor Wut ~** (*umg*) to be bursting with anger
platzieren [pla'tsi:rən] VT to place ▶ VR (*Sport*) to be placed; (*Tennis*) to be seeded; (*umg: sich setzen, stellen*) to plant o.s.
Platz- ZW: **Platzkarte** F seat reservation; **Platzkonzert** NT open-air concert; **Platzmangel** M lack of space; **Platzpatrone** F blank cartridge; **Platzregen** M downpour; **platzsparend** ADJ space-saving; **Platzverweis** M sending-off; **Platzwart** M (*Sport*) groundsman (BRIT), groundskeeper (US); **Platzwunde** F cut
Plauderei [plaʊdə'raɪ] F chat, conversation
plaudern ['plaʊdərn] VI to chat, to talk
Plausch [plaʊʃ] (**-(e)s, -e**) (*umg*) M chat
plausibel [plaʊ'zi:bəl] ADJ plausible
Play-back, Playback ['pleɪbæk] (**-s, -s**) NT (*Verfahren: Schallplatte*) double-tracking; (*TV*) miming
plazieren [pla'tsi:rən] VT *siehe* **platzieren**
Plebejer(in) [ple'be:jər(ɪn)] (**-s, -**) M(F) plebeian
plebejisch [ple'be:jɪʃ] ADJ plebeian
pleite ['plaɪtə] (*umg*) ADJ broke; **Pleite** (**-, -n**) F bankruptcy; (*umg: Reinfall*) flop; **Pleite machen** to go bust
Pleitegeier (*umg*) M (*drohende Pleite*) vulture; (*Bankrotteur*) bankrupt
plemplem [plɛm'plɛm] (*umg*) ADJ nuts
Plenarsitzung [ple'na:rzɪtsʊŋ] F plenary session
Plenum ['ple:nʊm] (**-s, Plenen**) NT plenum
Pleuelstange ['plɔʏəlʃtaŋə] F connecting rod
Plissee [plɪ'se:] (**-s, -s**) NT pleat
Plombe ['plɔmbə] (**-, -n**) F lead seal; (*Zahnplombe*) filling
plombieren [plɔm'bi:rən] VT to seal; (*Zahn*) to fill
Plotter ['plɔtər] (**-s, -s**) M (*Comput*) plotter
plötzlich ['plœtslɪç] ADJ sudden ▶ ADV suddenly; **plötzlicher Kindstod** sudden infant death syndrome
Pluderhose ['plu:dərho:zə] F harem trousers *pl*
plump [plʊmp] ADJ clumsy; (*Hände*) coarse; (*Körper*) shapeless; **plumpe Annäherungsversuche** very obvious advances
plumpsen (*umg*) VI to plump down, to fall
Plumpsklo, Plumpsklosett (*umg*) NT earth closet
Plunder ['plʊndər] (**-s**) M junk, rubbish
Plundergebäck NT flaky pastry
plündern ['plʏndərn] VT to plunder; (*Stadt*) to sack ▶ VI to plunder
Plünderung ['plʏndərʊŋ] F plundering, sack, pillage

Plural ['plu:ra:l] (**-s, -e**) M plural; **im ~ stehen** to be (in the) plural
pluralistisch [plura'lıstıʃ] ADJ pluralistic
plus [plʊs] ADV plus; **mit ~ minus null abschließen** (*Comm*) to break even; **Plus** (**-, -**) NT plus; (*Fin*) profit; (*Vorteil*) advantage
Plüsch [ply:ʃ] (**-(e)s, -e**) M plush; **Plüschtier** NT ≈ soft toy
Plus- ZW: **Pluspol** M (*Elek*) positive pole; **Pluspunkt** M (*Sport*) point; (*fig*) point in sb's favour; **Plusquamperfekt** NT pluperfect
Plutonium [plu'to:niʊm] (**-s**) NT plutonium
PLZ ABK = **Postleitzahl**
Pneu [pnɔʏ] (**-s, -s**) M ABK (= *Pneumatik*) tyre (BRIT), tire (US)
Po [po:] (**-s, -s**) (*umg*) M bum (BRIT), fanny (US)
Pöbel ['pø:bəl] (**-s**) M mob, rabble
Pöbelei [pø:bə'laı] F vulgarity
pöbelhaft ADJ low, vulgar
pochen ['pɔxən] VI to knock; (*Herz*) to pound; **auf etw** *akk* **~** (*fig*) to insist on sth
Pocken ['pɔkən] PL smallpox *sing*
Pockenimpfung, Pockenschutzimpfung F smallpox vaccination
Podcast ['pɔtka:st] (**-s, -s**) M podcast
Podest [po'dɛst] (**-(e)s, -e**) NT OD M (*Sockel, fig*) pedestal; (*Podium*) platform
Podium ['po:diʊm] NT podium
Podiumsdiskussion F panel discussion
Poesie [poe'zi:] F poetry
Poet [po'e:t] (**-en, -en**) M poet; **poetisch** ADJ poetic
pofen ['po:fən] (*umg*) VI to kip (BRIT), to doss
Pointe [po'ɛ̃:tə] (**-, -n**) F point; (*eines Witzes*) punch line
pointiert [poɛ̃'ti:rt] ADJ trenchant, pithy
Pokal [po'ka:l] (**-s, -e**) M goblet; (*Sport*) cup; **Pokalspiel** NT cup tie
Pökelfleisch ['pø:kəlflaıʃ] NT salt meat
pökeln VT (*Fleisch, Fisch*) to pickle, to salt
Poker ['po:kər] (**-s**) NT poker
pokern ['po:kərn] VI to play poker
Pol [po:l] (**-s, -e**) M pole; **der ruhende ~** (*fig*) the calming influence
pol. ABK = **politisch; polizeilich**
polar [po'la:r] ADJ polar
polarisieren [polari'zi:rən] VT, VR to polarize
Polarkreis M polar circle; **nördlicher/ südlicher ~** Arctic/Antarctic Circle
Polarstern M Pole Star
Pole ['po:lə] (**-n, -n**) M Pole
Polemik [po'le:mık] F polemics *sing*
polemisch ADJ polemical
polemisieren [polemi'zi:rən] VI to polemicize
Polen ['po:lən] (**-s**) NT Poland
Polente (**-**) (*veraltet: umg*) F cops *pl*
Police [po'li:s(ə)] (**-, -n**) F insurance policy
Polier [po'li:r] (**-s, -e**) M foreman
polieren VT to polish
Poliklinik [poli'kli:nık] F outpatients (department) *sing*
Polin F Pole, Polish woman
Politesse [poli'tɛsə] (**-, -n**) F (*Frau*) ≈ traffic warden (BRIT)
Politik [poli'ti:k] F politics *sing*; (*eine bestimmte*) policy; **in die ~ gehen** to go into politics; **eine ~ verfolgen** to pursue a policy
Politiker(in) [po'li:tikər(ın)] (**-s, -**) M(F) politician
politisch [po'li:tıʃ] ADJ political
politisieren [politi'zi:rən] VI to talk politics ▶ VT to politicize; **jdn ~** to make sb politically aware
Politur [poli'tu:r] F polish
Polizei [poli'tsaı] F police; **Polizeiaufsicht** F: **unter Polizeiaufsicht stehen** to have to report regularly to the police; **Polizeibeamte(r)** M police officer; **polizeilich** ADJ police *attrib*; **sich polizeilich melden** to register with the police; **polizeiliches Führungszeugnis** *certificate of "no criminal record" issued by the police*; **Polizeipräsidium** NT police headquarters *pl*; **Polizeirevier** NT police station; **Polizeispitzel** M police spy, informer; **Polizeistaat** M police state; **Polizeistreife** F police patrol; **Polizeistunde** F closing time; **Polizeiwache** F police station; **polizeiwidrig** ADJ illegal
Polizist(in) [poli'tsıst(ın)] (**-en, -en**) M(F) policeman/-woman
Pollen ['pɔlən] (**-s, -**) M pollen; **Pollenflug** M pollen count
poln. ABK = **polnisch**
polnisch ['pɔlnıʃ] ADJ Polish
Polohemd ['po:lohɛmt] NT polo shirt
Polster ['pɔlstər] (**-s, -**) NT cushion; (*Polsterung*) upholstery; (*in Kleidung*) padding; (*fig: Geld*) reserves *pl*; **Polsterer** (**-s, -**) M upholsterer
polstern VT (*Möbel*) to upholster; (*Kleidung*) to pad; **sie ist gut gepolstert** (*umg*) she's well padded; (*umg: finanziell*) she's not short of the odd penny
Polsterung F upholstery
Polterabend ['pɔltəra:bənt] M *party on the eve of a wedding*
poltern VI (*Krach machen*) to crash; (*schimpfen*) to rant
Polyester [poly'ɛstər] (**-s, -**) M polyester
Polygamie [polyga'mi:] F polygamy
Polynesien [poly'ne:ziən] (**-s**) NT Polynesia
Polynesier(in) [poly'ne:ziər(ın)] (**-s, -**) M(F) Polynesian
polynesisch ADJ Polynesian
Polyp [po'ly:p] (**-en, -en**) M polyp; (*umg*) cop; **Polypen** PL (*Med*) adenoids *pl*
Polytechnikum [poly'tɛçnikʊm] (**-s, Polytechnika**) NT polytechnic, poly (*umg*)
Pomade [po'ma:də] F pomade
Pommern ['pɔmərn] (**-s**) NT Pomerania
Pommes frites [pɔm'frıt] PL chips *pl* (BRIT), French fried potatoes *pl* (BRIT), French fries *pl* (US)
Pomp [pɔmp] (**-(e)s**) M pomp
pompös [pɔm'pø:s] ADJ grandiose
Pontius ['pɔntsiʊs] M: **von ~ zu Pilatus** from pillar to post
Pony ['pɔni] (**-s, -s**) M (*Frisur*) fringe (BRIT), bangs *pl* (US) ▶ NT (*Pferd*) pony
Pop [pɔp] (**-s**) M (*Mus*) pop; (*Kunst*) pop art

P

Popelin [popə'li:n] (**-s, -e**) M poplin
Popeline (**-, -n**) F poplin
Popkonzert NT pop concert
Popmusik F pop music
Popo [po'po:] (**-s, -s**) (*umg*) M bottom, bum (BRIT)
populär [popu'lɛ:r] ADJ popular
Popularität [populari'tɛ:t] F popularity
populärwissenschaftlich ADJ popular science
Pop-up ['pɔpap], **Popup** NT (*Comput, Wirts*) pop-up
Pore ['po:rə] (**-, -n**) F pore
Porno ['pɔrno] (**-s**, *no pl*) (*umg*) M porn
Pornografie [pɔrnogra'fi:] F pornography
pornografisch [pɔrno'gra:fɪʃ] ADJ pornographic
porös [po'rø:s] ADJ porous
Porree ['pɔre] (**-s, -s**) M leek
Portal [pɔr'ta:l] (**-s, -e**) NT portal
Portefeuille [pɔrt(ə)'fø:j] (**-s, -s**) NT (*Pol, Fin*) portfolio
Portemonnaie [pɔrtmɔ'nɛ:] (**-s, -s**) NT purse
Portier [pɔrti'e:] (**-s, -s**) M porter; (*Pförtner*) porter, doorkeeper, doorman
Portion [pɔrtsi'o:n] F portion, helping; (*umg: Anteil*) amount; **eine halbe ~** (*fig: umg: Person*) a half-pint; **eine ~ Kaffee** a pot of coffee
Portmonee [pɔrtmɔ'nɛ:] (**-s, -s**) NT purse
Porto ['pɔrto] (**-s, -s** *od* **Porti**) NT postage; **~ zahlt Empfänger** postage paid; **portofrei** ADJ post-free, (postage) prepaid
Porträt [pɔr'trɛ:] (**-s, -s**) NT portrait
porträtieren [pɔrtrɛ'ti:rən] VT to paint (a portrait of); (*fig*) to portray
Portugal ['pɔrtugal] (**-s**) NT Portugal
Portugiese [pɔrtu'gi:zə] (**-n, -n**) M Portuguese
Portugiesin F Portuguese
portugiesisch ADJ Portuguese
Portwein ['pɔrtvaɪn] M port
Porzellan [pɔrtsɛ'la:n] (**-s, -e**) NT china, porcelain; (*Geschirr*) china
Posaune [po'zaʊnə] (**-, -n**) F trombone
Pose ['po:zə] (**-, -n**) F pose
posieren [po'zi:rən] VI to pose
Position [pozitsi'o:n] F position; (*Comm: auf Liste*) item
Positionslichter PL navigation lights *pl*
Positionspapier NT position paper
positiv ['po:ziti:f] ADJ positive; **~ zu etw stehen** to be in favour (BRIT) *od* favor (US) of sth; **Positiv** (**-s, -e**) NT (*Phot*) positive
Positur [pozi'tu:r] F posture, attitude; **sich in ~ setzen** *od* **stellen** to adopt a posture
Posse ['pɔsə] (**-, -n**) F farce
possessiv ['pɔsɛsi:f] ADJ possessive; **Possessiv** (**-s, -e**) NT possessive pronoun; **Possessivpronomen** (**-s, -e**) NT possessive pronoun
possierlich [pɔ'si:rlɪç] ADJ funny
Post [pɔst] (**-, -en**) F post (office); (*Briefe*) post, mail; **ist ~ für mich da?** are there any letters for me?; **mit getrennter ~** under separate cover; **etw auf die ~ geben** to post (BRIT) *od* mail sth; **auf die** *od* **zur ~ gehen** to go to the post office
Postamt NT post office
Postanweisung F postal order (BRIT), money order
Postbote M postman (BRIT), mailman (US)
posten ['po:stən] VT (*auf Forum, Blog*) to post
Posten (**-s, -**) M post, position; (*Comm*) item; (*: Warenmenge*) quantity, lot; (*auf Liste*) entry; (*Mil*) sentry; (*Streikposten*) picket; **~ beziehen** to take up one's post; **nicht ganz auf dem ~ sein** (*nicht gesund sein*) to be off-colour (BRIT) *od* off-color (US)
Poster ['po:stər] (**-s, -(s)**) NT poster
Postf. ABK (= *Postfach*) PO Box
Post- zW: **Postfach** NT post office box; **Postkarte** F postcard; **postlagernd** ADV poste restante; **Postleitzahl** F postcode (BRIT), zip code (US)
postmodern [pɔstmo'dɛrn] ADJ postmodern
Post- zW: **Postscheckkonto** NT Post Office Giro account (BRIT); **Postsparbuch** NT post office savings book (BRIT); **Postsparkasse** F post office savings bank; **Poststempel** M postmark; **postwendend** ADV by return (of post); **Postwertzeichen** NT (*form*) postage stamp; **Postwurfsendung** F direct mail advertising
potent [po'tɛnt] ADJ potent; (*fig*) high-powered
Potential [potɛntsi'a:l] (**-s, -e**) NT = **Potenzial**
potentiell [potɛntsi'ɛl] ADJ = **potenziell**
Potenz [po'tɛnts] F power; (*eines Mannes*) potency
Potenzial [potɛntsi'a:l] (**-s, -e**) NT potential
potenziell [potɛntsi'ɛl] ADJ potential
potenzieren [potɛn'tsi:rən] VT (*Math*) to raise to the power of
Potpourri ['pɔtpʊri] (**-s, -s**) NT: **~ (aus)** (*Mus*) medley (of); (*fig*) assortment (of)
Pott [pɔt] (**-(e)s, Pötte**) (*umg*) M pot; **potthässlich** (*umg*) ADJ ugly as sin
pp., ppa. ABK (= *per procura*) p.p.
Präambel [prɛ'lambəl] (**-, -n**) F +*gen* preamble (to)
Pracht [praxt] (**-**) F splendour (BRIT), splendor (US), magnificence; **es ist eine wahre ~** it's (really) marvellous; **Prachtexemplar** NT beauty (*umg*); (*fig: Mensch*) fine specimen
prächtig ['prɛçtɪç] ADJ splendid
Prachtstück NT showpiece
prachtvoll ADJ splendid, magnificent
prädestinieren [prɛdɛsti'ni:rən] VT to predestine
Prädikat [prɛdi'ka:t] (**-(e)s, -e**) NT title; (*Gram*) predicate; (*Zensur*) distinction; **Wein mit ~** special quality wine
Prag [pra:k] (**-s**) NT Prague
prägen ['prɛ:gən] VT to stamp; (*Münze*) to mint; (*Ausdruck*) to coin; (*Charakter*) to form; (*kennzeichnen: Stadtbild*) to characterize; **das Erlebnis prägte ihn** the experience left its mark on him
prägend ADJ having a forming *od* shaping influence
pragmatisch [pra'gma:tɪʃ] ADJ pragmatic
prägnant [prɛ'gnant] ADJ concise, terse

Prägnanz F conciseness, terseness
Prägung ['prɛ:gʊŋ] F minting; (*von Charakter*) forming; (*Eigenart*) character, stamp
prahlen ['pra:lən] VI to boast, to brag
Prahlerei [pra:lə'raɪ] F boasting
prahlerisch ADJ boastful
Praktik ['praktɪk] F practice
praktikabel [praktɪ'ka:bəl] ADJ practicable
Praktikant(in) [praktɪ'kant(ɪn)] M(F) trainee
Praktikum (**-s, Praktika** *od* **Praktiken**) NT practical training
praktisch ['praktɪʃ] ADJ practical, handy; **praktischer Arzt** general practitioner; **praktisches Beispiel** concrete example
praktizieren [prakti'tsi:rən] VT, VI to practise (BRIT), to practice (US)
Praline [pra'li:nə] F chocolate
prall [pral] ADJ firmly rounded; (*Segel*) taut; (*Arme*) plump; (*Sonne*) blazing
prallen VI to bounce, to rebound; (*Sonne*) to blaze
prallvoll ADJ full to bursting; (*Brieftasche*) bulging
Prämie ['prɛ:miə] F premium; (*Belohnung*) award, prize
prämienbegünstigt ADJ with benefit of premiums
prämiensparen VI to save in a bonus scheme
prämieren [prɛ'mi:rən] VT to give an award to
Pranger ['praŋər] (**-s, -**) M (*Hist*) pillory; **jdn an den ~ stellen** (*fig*) to pillory sb
Pranke ['praŋkə] (**-, -n**) F (*Tierpranke: umg: Hand*) paw
Präparat [prɛpa'ra:t] (**-(e)s, -e**) NT (*Biol*) preparation; (*Med*) medicine
präparieren VT (*konservieren*) to preserve; (*Med: zerlegen*) to dissect
Präposition [prɛpozitsi'o:n] F preposition
Prärie [prɛ'ri:] F prairie
Präs. ABK = **Präsens; Präsident**
Präsens ['prɛ:zɛns] (**-**) NT present tense
präsent ADJ: **etw ~ haben** to have sth at hand
präsentieren [prɛzɛn'ti:rən] VT to present
Präsenzbibliothek F reference library
Präservativ [prɛzɛrva'ti:f] (**-s, -e**) NT condom, sheath
Präsident(in) [prɛzi'dɛnt(ɪn)] M(F) president; **Präsidentschaft** F presidency; **Präsidentschaftskandidat** M presidential candidate
Präsidium [prɛ'zi:diʊm] NT presidency, chairmanship; (*Polizeipräsidium*) police headquarters *pl*
prasseln ['prasəln] VI (*Feuer*) to crackle; (*Hagel*) to drum; (*Wörter*) to rain down
prassen ['prasən] VI to live it up
Präteritum [prɛ'te:ritʊm] (**-s, Präterita**) NT preterite
Pratze ['pratsə] (**-, -n**) F paw
Präventiv- [prɛvɛn'ti:f] IN ZW preventive
Praxis ['praksɪs] (**-, Praxen**) F practice; (*Erfahrung*) experience; (*Behandlungsraum*) surgery; (*von Anwalt*) office; **die ~ sieht anders aus** the reality is different; **ein Beispiel aus der ~** an example from real life; **Praxisgebühr** F *surgery surcharge*
Präzedenzfall [prɛtse:'dɛntsfal] M precedent
präzise [prɛ'tsi:zə] ADJ precise
Präzision [prɛtsizi'o:n] F precision
PR-Chef M PR officer
predigen ['pre:dɪgən] VT, VI to preach
Prediger (**-s, -**) M preacher
Predigt ['pre:dɪçt] (**-, -en**) F sermon
Preis [praɪs] (**-es, -e**) M price; (*Siegespreis*) prize; (*Auszeichnung*) award; **um keinen ~** not at any price; **um jeden ~** at all costs; **Preisangebot** NT quotation; **Preisausschreiben** NT competition; **Preisbindung** F price-fixing; **Preisbrecher** M (*Firma*) undercutter
Preiselbeere F cranberry
preisempfindlich ADJ price-sensitive
preisen [praɪzən] *unreg* VT to praise; **sich glücklich ~** (*geh*) to count o.s. lucky
Preis- ZW: **Preisentwicklung** F price trend; **Preiserhöhung** F price increase; **Preisfrage** F question of price; (*Wettbewerb*) prize question
preisgeben *unreg* VT to abandon; (*opfern*) to sacrifice; (*zeigen*) to expose
Preis- ZW: **Preisgefälle** NT price gap; **preisgekrönt** ADJ prizewinning; **Preisgericht** NT jury; **preisgünstig** ADJ inexpensive; **Preisindex** M price index; **Preiskrieg** M price war; **Preislage** F price range; **preislich** ADJ price *attrib*, in price; **Preisliste** F price list, tariff; **Preisnachlass** M discount; **Preisschild** NT price tag; **Preisspanne** F price range; **Preissturz** M slump; **Preisträger** M prizewinner; **preiswert** ADJ inexpensive
prekär [pre'kɛ:r] ADJ precarious
Prellbock [prɛlbɔk] M buffers *pl*
prellen VT to bruise; (*fig*) to cheat, to swindle
Prellung F bruise
Premiere [prəmi'ɛ:rə] (**-, -n**) F premiere
Premierminister(in) [prəmɪ'e:mɪnɪstər(ɪn)] M(F) prime minister, premier
Prepaidhandy ['pri:pe:thɛndɪ] NT prepaid mobile (BRIT), prepaid cell phone (US)
Presse ['prɛsə] (**-, -n**) F press; **Presseagentur** F press *od* news agency; **Presseausweis** M press pass; **Presseerklärung** F press release; **Pressefreiheit** F freedom of the press; **Pressekonferenz** F press conference; **Pressemeldung** F press report
pressen VT to press
Presse- ZW: **Pressesprecher(in)** M(F) spokesperson, press officer; **Pressestelle** F press office; **Presseverlautbarung** F press release
pressieren [prɛ'si:rən] VI to be in a hurry; **es pressiert** it's urgent
Pressluft ['prɛslʊft] F compressed air; **Pressluftbohrer** M pneumatic drill
Prestige [prɛs'ti:ʒə] (**-s**) NT prestige; **Prestigeverlust** M loss of prestige
Preuße ['prɔʏsə] (**-n, -n**) M Prussian
Preußen (**-s**) NT Prussia
Preußin F Prussian

P

preußisch ADJ Prussian
prickeln ['prɪkəln] VI to tingle; (*kitzeln*) to tickle; (*Bläschen bilden*) to sparkle, to bubble ▶ VT to tickle
pries *etc* [pri:s] VB *siehe* **preisen**
Priester ['pri:stər] (**-s, -**) M priest
Priesterin F priestess
Priesterweihe F ordination (to the priesthood)
prima ADJ *unver* first-class, excellent
Prima ['pri:ma] (**-, Primen**) F (*früher*) *eighth and ninth year of German secondary school*
primär [pri'mɛ:r] ADJ primary; **Primärdaten** PL primary data *pl*
Primel ['pri:məl] (**-, -n**) F primrose
primitiv [primi'ti:f] ADJ primitive
Primzahl ['pri:mtsa:l] F prime (number)
Prinz [prɪnts] (**-en, -en**) M prince
Prinzessin [prɪn'tsɛsɪn] F princess
Prinzip [prɪn'tsi:p] (**-s, -ien**) NT principle; **aus ~** on principle; **im ~** in principle
prinzipiell [prɪntsi'piɛl] ADJ on principle
prinzipienlos ADJ unprincipled
Priorität [priori'tɛ:t] F priority; **Prioritäten** PL (*Comm*) preference shares *pl*, preferred stock *sing* (*US*); **Prioritäten setzen** to establish one's priorities
Prise ['pri:zə] (**-, -n**) F pinch
Prisma ['prɪsma] (**-s, Prismen**) NT prism
privat [pri'va:t] ADJ private; **jdn ~ sprechen** to speak to sb in private; **Privatbesitz** M private property; **Privatdozent** M outside lecturer; **Privatfernsehen** NT commercial television; **Privatgespräch** NT private conversation; (*am Telefon*) private call
privatisieren [privati'zi:rən] VT to privatize
Privatschule F private school
Privatvorsorge F (*fürs Alter*) private pension scheme; (*für Gesundheit*) health insurance scheme
Privatwirtschaft F private sector
Privileg [privi'le:k] (**-(e)s, -ien**) NT privilege
pro PRÄP +*akk* per; **~ Stück** each, apiece
Pro [pro:] (**-**) NT pro
Probe ['pro:bə] (**-, -n**) F test; (*Teststück*) sample; (*Theat*) rehearsal; **jdn auf die ~ stellen** to put sb to the test; **er ist auf ~ angestellt** he's employed for a probationary period; **zur ~** to try out; **Probebohrung** F (*Öl*) exploration well; **Probeexemplar** NT specimen copy; **Probefahrt** F test drive; **Probelauf** M trial run
proben VT to try; (*Theat*) to rehearse
Probe- zW: **Probestück** NT specimen; **probeweise** ADV on approval; **Probezeit** F probation period
probieren [pro'bi:rən] VT to try; (*Wein, Speise*) to taste, to sample ▶ VI to try; (*Wein, Speise*) to taste
Problem [pro'ble:m] (**-s, -e**) NT problem; **vor einem ~ stehen** to be faced with a problem
Problematik [proble:'ma:tɪk] F problem
problematisch [proble:'ma:tɪʃ] ADJ problematic
problemlos ADJ problem-free
Problemstellung F way of looking at a problem
Produkt [pro'dʊkt] (**-(e)s, -e**) NT product; (*Agr*) produce *no pl*
Produktentwicklung F product development
Produktion [produktsi'o:n] F production
Produktionsleiter M production manager
Produktionsstätte F (*Halle*) shop floor
produktiv [prodʊk'ti:f] ADJ productive
Produktivität [produktivi'tɛ:t] F productivity
Produzent [produ'tsɛnt] M manufacturer; (*Film*) producer
produzieren [produ'tsi:rən] VT to produce ▶ VR to show off
Prof. [prof] ABK (= *Professor*) Prof
profan [pro'fa:n] ADJ (*weltlich*) secular, profane; (*gewöhnlich*) mundane
professionell [profɛsio'nɛl] ADJ professional
Professor(in) [pro'fɛsɔr, profɛ'so:rɪn] M(F) professor; (ÖSTERR: *Gymnasiallehrer*) grammar school teacher (BRIT), high school teacher (*US*)
Professur [profɛ'su:r] F: **~ (für)** chair (of)
Profi ['pro:fi] (**-s, -s**) M ABK (= *Professional*) pro
Profil [pro'fi:l] (**-s, -e**) NT profile; (*fig*) image; (*Querschnitt*) cross section; (*Längsschnitt*) vertical section; (*von Reifen, Schuhsohle*) tread
profilieren [profi'li:rən] VR to create an image for o.s.
Profilsohle F sole with a tread
Profit [pro'fi:t] (**-(e)s, -e**) M profit
profitgeil ADJ (*umg*) profit-greedy
profitieren [profi'ti:rən] VI: **~ (von)** to profit (from)
Profitmacherei (*umg*) F profiteering
pro forma ADV as a matter of form
Pro-forma-Rechnung F pro forma invoice
Prognose [pro'gno:zə] (**-, -n**) F prediction, prognosis
Programm [pro'gram] (**-s, -e**) NT programme (BRIT), program (*US*); (*Comput*) program; (*TV: Sender*) channel; (*Kollektion*) range; **nach ~** as planned; **Programmfehler** M (*Comput*) bug; **programmgemäß** ADJ according to plan; **Programmhinweis** M (*Rundf, TV*) programme (BRIT) *od* program (*US*) announcement
programmieren [progra'mi:rən] VT to programme (BRIT), to program (*US*); (*Comput*) to program; **auf etw** *akk* **programmiert sein** (*fig*) to be geared to sth
Programmierer(in) (**-s, -**) M(F) programmer
Programmiersprache F (*Comput*) programming language
Programmierung F (*Comput*) programming
Programmkino NT arts *od* repertory (*US*) cinema
Programmvorschau F preview; (*Film*) trailer
progressiv [progrɛ'si:f] ADJ progressive
Projekt [pro'jɛkt] (**-(e)s, -e**) NT project
Projektleiter(in) M(F) project manager(ess)
Projektor [pro'jɛktɔr] M projector
projizieren [proji'tsi:rən] VT to project
proklamieren [prokla'mi:rən] VT to proclaim
Pro-Kopf-Einkommen NT per capita income
Prokura [pro'ku:ra] (**-, Prokuren**) F (*form*) power of attorney
Prokurist(in) [proku'rɪst(ɪn)] M(F) attorney
Prolet [pro'le:t] (**-en, -en**) M prole, pleb

Proletariat [proletari'a:t] (**-(e)s, -e**) NT proletariat
Proletarier [prole'ta:riər] (**-s, -**) M proletarian
Prolog [pro'lo:k] (**-(e)s, -e**) M prologue
Promenade [promə'na:də] (**-, -n**) F promenade
Promenadenmischung F (*hum*) mongrel
Promille [pro'mɪle] (**-(s), -**) (*umg*) NT alcohol level; **Promillegrenze** F legal (alcohol) limit
prominent [promi'nɛnt] ADJ prominent
Prominenz [promi'nɛnts] F VIPs *pl*
Promoter [pro'mo:tər] (**-s, -**) M promoter
Promotion [promotsi'o:n] F doctorate, Ph.D.
promovieren [promo'vi:rən] VI to receive a doctorate *etc*
prompt [prɔmpt] ADJ prompt
Pronomen [pro'no:mɛn] (**-s, -**) NT pronoun
Propaganda [propa'ganda] (**-**) F propaganda
propagieren [propa'gi:rən] VT to propagate
Propangas [pro'pa:nga:s] NT propane gas
Propeller [pro'pɛlər] (**-s, -**) M propeller
proper ['prɔpər] (*umg*) ADJ neat, tidy
Prophet(in) [pro'fe:t(ɪn)] (**-en, -en**) M(F) prophet(ess)
prophezeien [profe'tsaɪən] VT to prophesy
Prophezeiung F prophecy
prophylaktisch [profy'laktɪʃ] ADJ prophylactic (*form*), preventive
Proportion [propɔrtsi'o:n] F proportion
proportional [propɔrtsio'na:l] ADJ proportional; **Proportionalschrift** F (*Comput*) proportional printing
proportioniert [propɔrtsio'ni:rt] ADJ: **gut/schlecht ~** well/badly proportioned
Proporz [pro'pɔrts] (**-es, -e**) M proportional representation
Prosa ['pro:za] (**-**) F prose
prosaisch [pro'za:ɪʃ] ADJ prosaic
prosit ['pro:zɪt] INTERJ cheers!; **~ Neujahr!** happy New Year!
Prospekt [pro'spɛkt] (**-(e)s, -e**) M leaflet, brochure
prost [pro:st] INTERJ cheers!
Prostata ['prɔstata] (**-**) F prostate gland
Prostituierte [prostitu'i:rtə] (**-n, -n**) F prostitute
Prostitution [prostitutsi'o:n] F prostitution
prot. [prot] ABK = **protestantisch**
Protektionismus [protɛktsio'nɪsmʊs] M protectionism
Protektorat [protɛkto'ra:t] (**-(e)s, -e**) NT (*Schirmherrschaft*) patronage; (*Schutzgebiet*) protectorate
Protest [pro'tɛst] (**-(e)s, -e**) M protest
Protestant(in) [protɛs'tant(ɪn)] M(F) Protestant; **protestantisch** ADJ Protestant
Protestbewegung F protest movement
protestieren [protɛs'ti:rən] VI to protest
Protestkundgebung F (protest) rally
Protestpartei F protest party
Prothese [pro'te:zə] (**-, -n**) F artificial limb; (*Zahnprothese*) dentures *pl*
Protokoll [proto'kɔl] (**-s, -e**) NT register; (*Niederschrift*) record; (*von Sitzung*) minutes *pl*; (*diplomatisch*) protocol; (*Polizeiprotokoll*) statement; (*Strafzettel*) ticket; **(das) ~ führen** (*bei Sitzung*) to take the minutes; (*bei Gericht*) to make a transcript of the proceedings; **etw zu ~ geben** to have sth put on record; (*bei Polizei*) to say sth in one's statement; **Protokollführer** M secretary; (*Jur*) clerk (of the court)
protokollieren [protokɔ'li:rən] VT to take down; (*Bemerkung*) to enter in the minutes
Proton ['pro:tɔn] (**-s, -en**) NT proton
Prototyp M prototype
Protz ['prɔts] (**-es, -e**) M swank; **protzen** VI to show off
protzig ADJ ostentatious
Proviant [provi'ant] (**-s, -e**) M provisions *pl*, supplies *pl*
Provinz [pro'vɪnts] (**-, -en**) F province; **das ist finsterste ~** (*pej*) it's a cultural backwater
provinziell [provɪn'tsiɛl] ADJ provincial
Provision [provizi'o:n] F (*Comm*) commission
provisorisch [provi'zo:rɪʃ] ADJ provisional
Provisorium [provi'zo:riʊm] (**-s, -ien**) NT provisional arrangement
Provokation [provokatsi'o:n] F provocation
provokativ [provoka'ti:f] ADJ provocative, provoking
provokatorisch [provoka'to:rɪʃ] ADJ provocative, provoking
provozieren [provo'tsi:rən] VT to provoke
Proz. ABK (= *Prozent*) pc
Prozedur [protse'du:r] F procedure; (*pej*) carry-on; **die ~ beim Zahnarzt** the ordeal at the dentist's
Prozent [pro'tsɛnt] (**-(e)s, -e**) NT per cent, percentage; **Prozentrechnung** F percentage calculation; **Prozentsatz** M percentage
prozentual [protsɛntu'a:l] ADJ percentage *attrib*
Prozess [pro'tsɛs] (**-es, -e**) M trial, case; (*Vorgang*) process; **es zum ~ kommen lassen** to go to court; **mit jdm/etw kurzen ~ machen** (*fig: umg*) to make short work of sb/sth; **Prozessanwalt** M barrister, counsel; **Prozessführung** F handling of a case
prozessieren [protsɛ'si:rən] VI: **~ (mit)** to bring an action (against), to go to law (with *od* against)
Prozession [protsɛsi'o:n] F procession
Prozesskosten PL (legal) costs *pl*
prüde ['pry:də] ADJ prudish
Prüderie [pry:də'ri:] F prudery
prüfen ['pry:fən] VT to examine, to test; (*nachprüfen*) to check; (*erwägen*) to consider; (*Geschäftsbücher*) to audit; (*mustern*) to scrutinize
Prüfer(in) (**-s, -**) M(F) examiner
Prüfling M examinee
Prüfstein M touchstone
Prüfung F (*Sch, Univ*) examination, exam; (*Überprüfung*) checking; **eine ~ machen** to take *od* sit (BRIT) an exam(ination); **durch eine ~ fallen** to fail an exam(ination)
Prüfungs- ZW: **Prüfungsausschuss** M examining board; **Prüfungskommission** F examining board; **Prüfungsordnung** F exam(ination) regulations *pl*

Prügel ['pry:gəl] (**-s, -**) M cudgel ▶ PL beating *sing*
Prügelei [pry:gə'laɪ] F fight
Prügelknabe M scapegoat
prügeln VT to beat ▶ VR to fight
Prügelstrafe F corporal punishment
Prunk [prʊŋk] (**-(e)s**) M pomp, show; **prunkvoll** ADJ splendid, magnificent
prusten ['pru:stən] (*umg*) VI to snort
PS ABK (= *Pferdestärke*) hp; (= *Postskript(um)*) PS
Psalm [psalm] (**-s, -en**) M psalm
pseudo- [psɔʏdo] IN ZW pseudo
Pseudonym [psɔʏdo'ny:m] (**-s, -e**) NT pseudonym
Psychiater [psy'çia:tər] (**-s, -**) M psychiatrist
Psychiatrie [psyçia'tri:] F psychiatry
psychiatrisch [psy'çia:trɪʃ] ADJ psychiatric; **psychiatrische Klinik** mental *od* psychiatric hospital
psychisch ['psy:çɪʃ] ADJ psychological; **~ gestört** emotionally *od* psychologically disturbed
Psychoanalyse [psyçoana'ly:zə] F psychoanalysis
Psychologe [psyço'lo:gə] (**-n, -n**) M psychologist
Psychologie F psychology
Psychologin F psychologist
psychologisch ADJ psychological
Psychopharmaka PL mind-affecting drugs *pl*, psychotropic drugs *pl*; **psychosomatisch** ADJ psychosomatic; **Psychoterror** M psychological intimidation
Psychotherapie F psychotherapy
PTT (SCHWEIZ) ABK (= *Post, Telefon, Telegraf*) *postal and telecommunication services*
Pubertät [pubɛr'tɛ:t] F puberty
publik [pu'bli:k] ADJ: **~ werden** to become public knowledge
Publikum ['pu:blikʊm] (**-s**) NT audience; (*Sport*) crowd; **das ~ in dieser Bar ist sehr gemischt** you get a very mixed group of people using this bar
Publikumserfolg M popular success
Publikumsverkehr M: **„heute kein ~“** “closed today for public business”
publizieren [publi'tsi:rən] VT to publish
Pudding ['pʊdɪŋ] (**-s, -e** *od* **-s**) M blancmange; **Puddingpulver** NT custard powder
Pudel ['pu:dəl] (**-s, -**) M poodle; **das also ist des Pudels Kern** (*fig*) that's what it's really all about
pudelwohl (*umg*) ADJ: **sich ~ fühlen** to feel on top of the world
Puder ['pu:dər] (**-s, -**) M powder; **Puderdose** F powder compact
pudern VT to powder
Puderzucker M icing sugar (BRIT), confectioner's sugar (US)
Puerto Ricaner(in) [puɛrtori'ka:nər(ɪn)] (**-s, -**) M(F) Puerto Rican
puerto-ricanisch ADJ Puerto Rican
Puerto Rico [pu'ɛrto'ri:ko] (**-s**) NT Puerto Rico
Puff[1] [pʊf] (**-(e)s, -e**) M (*Wäschepuff*) linen basket; (*Sitzpuff*) pouf
Puff[2] (**-(e)s, Püffe**) (*umg*) M (*Stoß*) push
Puff[3] (**-s, -s**) (*umg*) M OD NT (*Bordell*) brothel
Puffer (**-s, -**) M (*auch Comput*) buffer; **Pufferspeicher** M (*Comput*) cache; **Pufferstaat** M buffer state; **Pufferzone** F buffer zone
Puffreis M puffed rice
Pulle ['pʊlə] (**-, -n**) (*umg*) F bottle; **volle ~ fahren** (*umg*) to drive flat out
Pulli ['pʊli] (**-s, -s**) (*umg*) M sweater, jumper (BRIT)
Pullover [pʊ'lo:vər] (**-s, -**) M sweater, jumper (BRIT)
Pullunder [pʊ'lʊndər] (**-s, -**) M slipover
Puls [pʊls] (**-es, -e**) M pulse; **Pulsader** F artery; **sich** *dat* **die Pulsader(n) aufschneiden** to slash one's wrists
pulsieren [pʊl'zi:rən] VI to throb, to pulsate
Pult [pʊlt] (**-(e)s, -e**) NT desk
Pulver ['pʊlfər] (**-s, -**) NT powder; **Pulverfass** NT powder keg; **(wie) auf einem Pulverfass sitzen** (*fig*) to be sitting on (top of) a volcano
pulverig ADJ powdery
pulverisieren [pʊlveri'zi:rən] VT to pulverize
Pulverkaffee M instant coffee
Pulverschnee M powdery snow
pummelig ['pʊməlɪç] ADJ chubby
Pump (**-(e)s**) (*umg*) M: **auf ~ kaufen** to buy on tick (BRIT) *od* credit
Pumpe ['pʊmpə] (**-, -n**) F pump; (*umg: Herz*) ticker
pumpen VT to pump; (*umg*) to lend; (*: entleihen*) to borrow
Pumphose F knickerbockers *pl*
puncto ['pʊŋkto] PRÄP +*gen*: **in ~ X** where X is concerned
Punkt [pʊŋkt] (**-(e)s, -e**) M point; (*bei Muster*) dot; (*Satzzeichen*) full stop, period (*bes US*); **~ 12 Uhr** at 12 o'clock on the dot; **nun mach aber mal einen ~!** (*umg*) come off it!; **punktgleich** ADJ (*Sport*) level
punktieren [pʊŋk'ti:rən] VT to dot; (*Med*) to aspirate
pünktlich ['pʏŋktlɪç] ADJ punctual; **Pünktlichkeit** F punctuality
Punkt- ZW: **Punktmatrix** F dot matrix; **Punktrichter** M (*Sport*) judge; **Punktsieg** M victory on points; **Punktwertung** F points system; **Punktzahl** F score
Punsch [pʊnʃ] (**-(e)s, -e**) M (hot) punch
Pupille [pu'pɪlə] (**-, -n**) F (*im Auge*) pupil
Puppe ['pʊpə] (**-, -n**) F doll; (*Marionette*) puppet; (*Insektenpuppe*) pupa, chrysalis; (*Schaufensterpuppe, Übungspuppe*) dummy; (*umg: Mädchen*) doll, bird (*bes* BRIT)
Puppen- ZW: **Puppenhaus** NT doll's house, dollhouse (US); **Puppenspieler** M puppeteer; **Puppenstube** F (single-room) doll's house *od* dollhouse (US); **Puppentheater** NT puppet theatre (BRIT) *od* theater (US); **Puppenwagen** M doll's pram
pupsen ['pu:psən] (*umg*) VI to make a rude noise/smell
pur [pu:r] ADJ pure; (*völlig*) sheer; (*Whisky*) neat
Püree [py're:] (**-s, -s**) NT purée; (*Kartoffelpüree*) mashed potatoes *pl*
Purpur ['pʊrpʊr] (**-s**) M crimson

Purzelbaum ['pʊrtsəlbaʊm] M somersault
purzeln VI to tumble
Puste ['pu:stə] (-) (*umg*) F puff; (*fig*) steam
Pusteblume (*umg*) F dandelion
Pustel ['pʊstəl] (-, **-n**) F pustule
pusten ['pu:stən] (*umg*) VI to puff
Pute ['pu:tə] (-, **-n**) F turkey hen
Puter (**-s**, -) M turkey cock; **puterrot** ADJ scarlet
Putsch [pʊtʃ] (**-(e)s**, **-e**) M revolt, putsch; **putschen** VI to revolt; **Putschist** M rebel; **Putschversuch** M attempted coup (d'état)
Putte ['pʊtə] (-, **-n**) F (*Kunst*) cherub
Putz [pʊts] (**-es**) M (*Mörtel*) plaster, roughcast; **eine Mauer mit ~ verkleiden** to roughcast a wall
putzen VT to clean; (*Nase*) to wipe, to blow ▶ VR to clean o.s.; (*veraltet: sich schmücken*) to dress o.s. up; **sich** *dat* **die Zähne ~** to brush one's teeth
Putzfrau F cleaning lady, charwoman (BRIT)
putzig ADJ quaint, funny
Putzlappen M cloth
putzmunter (*umg*) ADJ full of beans
Putz- ZW: **Putztag** M cleaning day; **Putzteufel** (*umg*) M maniac for housework; **Putzzeug** NT cleaning things *pl*
Puzzle ['pasəl] (**-s**, **-s**) NT jigsaw (puzzle)
PVC [pe:fau'tse:] (**-(s)**) NT ABK PVC
Pygmäe [pʏ'gmɛ:ə] (**-n**, **-n**) M Pygmy
Pyjama [pi'dʒa:ma] (**-s**, **-s**) M pyjamas *pl* (BRIT), pajamas *pl* (US)
Pyramide [pyra'mi:də] (-, **-n**) F pyramid
Pyrenäen [pyre'nɛ:ən] PL: **die ~** the Pyrenees *pl*
Python ['py:tɔn] (**-s**, **-s**) M python; **Pythonschlange** F python

P

Qq

Q, q [ku:] NT Q, q; **Q wie Quelle** ≈ Q for Queen
qcm ABK (= *Quadratzentimeter*) cm^2
qkm ABK (= *Quadratkilometer*) km^2
qm ABK (= *Quadratmeter*) m^2
quabbelig ['kvabəlıç], **quabblig** ['kvablıç] ADJ wobbly; (*Frosch*) slimy
Quacksalber ['kvakzalbər] (**-s, -**) M quack (doctor)
Quader ['kva:dər] (**-s, -**) M square stone block; (*Math*) cuboid
Quadrat [kva'dra:t] (**-(e)s, -e**) NT square; **quadratisch** ADJ square; **Quadratlatschen** PL (*hum: umg: Schuhe*) clodhoppers *pl*; **Quadratmeter** M square metre (BRIT) *od* meter (*US*)
quadrieren [kva'dri:rən] VT to square
quaken ['kva:kən] VI to croak; (*Ente*) to quack
quäken ['kvɛ:kən] VI to screech
quäkend ADJ screeching
Quäker(in) (**-s, -**) M(F) Quaker
Qual [kva:l] (**-, -en**) F pain, agony; (*seelisch*) anguish; **er machte ihr das Leben zur ~** he made her life a misery
quälen ['kvɛ:lən] VT to torment ▸ VR (*sich abmühen*) to struggle; (*geistig*) to torment o.s.; **quälende Ungewissheit** agonizing uncertainty
Quälerei [kvɛ:lə'raı] F torture, torment
Quälgeist (*umg*) M pest
Qualifikation [kvalifikatsi'o:n] F qualification
qualifizieren [kvalifi'tsi:rən] VT to qualify; (*einstufen*) to label ▸ VR to qualify
qualifiziert ADJ (*Arbeiter, Nachwuchs*) qualified; (*Arbeit*) professional; (*Pol: Mehrheit*) requisite
Qualität [kvali'tɛ:t] F quality; **von ausgezeichneter ~** (of) top quality
qualitativ [kvalita'ti:f] ADJ qualitative
Qualitätskontrolle F quality control
Qualitätsstandard M quality standard
Qualitätsware F article of high quality
Qualle ['kvalə] (**-, -n**) F jellyfish
Qualm [kvalm] (**-(e)s**) M thick smoke
qualmen VT, VI to smoke
qualvoll ['kva:lfɔl] ADJ painful; (*Schmerzen*) excruciating, agonizing
Quantensprung M quantum leap
Quantentheorie ['kvantənteori:] F quantum theory
Quantität [kvanti'tɛ:t] F quantity
quantitativ [kvantita'ti:f] ADJ quantitative
Quantum ['kvantʊm] (**-s, Quanten**) NT quantity, amount
Quarantäne [karan'tɛ:nə] (**-, -n**) F quarantine
Quark[1] [kvark] (**-s**) M curd cheese, quark; (*umg*) rubbish
Quark[2] [kvark] (**-s, -s**) NT (*Phys*) quark
Quarta ['kvarta] (**-, Quarten**) F (*früher*) *third year of German secondary school*
Quartal [kvar'ta:l] (**-s, -e**) NT quarter (year); **Kündigung zum ~** quarterly notice date
Quartett [kvar'tɛt] (**-(e)s, -e**) NT (*Mus*) quartet; (*Karten*) set of four cards; (*: Spiel*) ≈ happy families
Quartier [kvar'ti:r] (**-s, -e**) NT accommodation (BRIT), accommodations *pl* (*US*); (*Mil*) quarters *pl*; (*Stadtquartier*) district
Quarz [kva:rts] (**-es, -e**) M quartz
quasi ['kva:zi] ADV virtually ▸ PRÄF quasi
quasseln ['kvasəln] (*umg*) VI to natter
Quaste ['kvastə] (**-, -n**) F (*Troddel*) tassel; (*von Pinsel*) bristles *pl*
Quästur [kvɛs'tu:r] F (*Univ*) bursary
Quatsch [kvatʃ] (*umg*) (**-es**) M rubbish, hogwash; **hört doch endlich auf mit dem ~!** stop being so stupid!; **~ machen** to mess about
quatschen VI to chat, to natter
Quatschkopf (*umg*) M (*pej: Schwätzer*) windbag; (*: Dummkopf*) twit (BRIT)
Quecksilber ['kvɛkzılbər] NT mercury
Quelle ['kvɛlə] (**-, -n**) F spring; (*eines Flusses, Comput*) source; **an der ~ sitzen** (*fig*) to be well placed; **aus zuverlässiger ~** from a reliable source
quellen VI (*hervorquellen*) to pour *od* gush forth; (*schwellen*) to swell
Quellenangabe F reference
Quellsprache F source language
Quengelei [kvɛŋə'laı] (*umg*) F whining
quengelig (*umg*) ADJ whining
quengeln (*umg*) VI to whine
quer [kve:r] ADV crossways, diagonally; (*rechtwinklig*) at right angles; **~ gestreift** horizontally striped; **~ auf dem Bett** across the bed; *siehe auch* **querlegen**; **Querbalken** M crossbeam; **Querdenker** M maverick
Quere ['kve:rə] (**-**) F: **jdm in die ~ kommen** to cross sb's path

quer- ZW: **querfeldein** ADV across country; **Querfeldeinrennen** NT cross-country; (*mit Motorrädern*) motocross; (*Radrennen*) cyclo-cross; **Querflöte** F flute; **Querformat** NT oblong format; **Querkopf** M awkward customer; **querlegen** VR (*fig: umg*) to be awkward; **Querschiff** NT transept; **Querschläger** (*umg*) M ricochet; **Querschnitt** M cross section; **querschnittsgelähmt** ADJ paraplegic, paralysed below the waist; **Querschnittslähmung** F paraplegia; **Querstraße** F intersecting road; **Querstrich** M (horizontal) stroke *od* line; **Quersumme** F (*Math*) sum of digits of a number; **Quertreiber** (**-s, -**) M obstructionist

Querulant(in) [kveru'lant(ɪn)] (**-en, -en**) M(F) grumbler

Querverbindung F connection, link

Querverweis M cross-reference

quetschen ['kvɛtʃən] VT to squash, to crush; (*Med*) to bruise ▶ VR (*sich klemmen*) to be caught; (*sich zwängen*) to squeeze (o.s.)

Quetschung F bruise, contusion (*form*)

Queue [kø:] (**-s, -s**) NT (*Billiard*) cue

quicklebendig ['kvɪkle'bɛndɪc] (*umg*) ADJ (*Kind*) lively, active; (*ältere Person*) spry

quieken ['kvi:kən] VI to squeak

quietschen ['kvi:tʃən] VI to squeak; (*Bremsen*) to screech

quietschvergnügt ['kvi:tʃfɛrgny:kt] (*umg*) ADJ happy as a sandboy

quillt [kvɪlt] VB *siehe* **quellen**

Quinta ['kvɪnta] (**-, Quinten**) F (*früher*) *second year in German secondary school*

Quintessenz ['kvɪntɛsɛnts] F quintessence

Quintett [kvɪn'tɛt] (**-(e)s, -e**) NT quintet

Quirl [kvɪrl] (**-(e)s, -e**) M whisk

quirlig ['kvɪrlɪç] ADJ lively, frisky

quitt [kvɪt] ADJ quits, even

Quitte (**-, -n**) F quince

quittieren [kvɪ'ti:rən] VT to give a receipt for; (*Dienst*) to leave

Quittung F receipt; **er hat seine ~ bekommen** he's paid the penalty *od* price

Quiz [kvɪs] (**-, -**) NT quiz

quoll *etc* [kvɔl] VB *siehe* **quellen**

Quote ['kvo:tə] (**-, -n**) F proportion; (*Rate*) rate

Quotenbringer M (*TV: umg*) ratings booster

Quotenregelung F quota system (*for ensuring adequate representation of women*)

Quotierung [kvo'ti:rʊŋ] F (*Comm*) quotation

Rr

R¹, r NT R, r; **R wie Richard** ≈ R for Robert, ≈ R for Roger (*US*)
R², r ABK (= *Radius*) r.
r. ABK (= *rechts*) r.
Rabatt [ra'bat] **(-(e)s, -e)** M discount
Rabatte (-, **-n**) F flower bed, border
Rabattmarke F trading stamp
Rabatz [ra'bats] **(-es)** (*umg*) M row, din
Rabe ['ra:bə] (**-n, -n**) M raven
Rabenmutter F bad mother
rabenschwarz ADJ pitch-black
rabiat [rabi'a:t] ADJ furious
Rache ['raxə] (-) F revenge, vengeance
Rachen (**-s, -**) M throat
rächen ['rɛçən] VT to avenge, to revenge ▸ VR to take (one's) revenge; **das wird sich** ~ you'll pay for that
Rachitis [ra'xi:tɪs] (-) F rickets *sing*
Rachsucht F vindictiveness
rachsüchtig ADJ vindictive
Racker ['rakər] (**-s, -**) M rascal, scamp
Rad [ra:t] (**-(e)s, Räder**) NT wheel; (*Fahrrad*) bike; ~ **fahren** to cycle; **unter die Räder kommen** (*umg*) to fall into bad ways; **das fünfte ~ am Wagen sein** (*umg*) to be in the way
Radar ['ra:da:r] (**-s**) M OD NT radar; **Radarfalle** F speed trap; **Radarkontrolle** F radar-controlled speed check
Radau [ra'daʊ] (**-s**) (*umg*) M row; ~ **machen** to kick up a row; (*Unruhe stiften*) to cause trouble
Raddampfer M paddle steamer
radebrechen ['ra:dəbrɛçən] VI UNTR: **Deutsch** *etc* ~ to speak broken German *etc*
radeln VI (*Hilfsverb sein*) to cycle
Rädelsführer ['rɛ:dəlsfy:rər] (**-s, -**) M ringleader
Rad- ZW: **Radfahrer** M cyclist; (*pej, umg*) crawler; **Radfahrweg** M cycle track *od* path
radieren [ra'di:rən] VT to rub out, to erase; (*Kunst*) to etch
Radiergummi M rubber (BRIT), eraser (*bes US*)
Radierung F etching
Radieschen [ra'di:sçən] NT radish
radikal [radi'ka:l] ADJ radical; ~ **gegen etw vorgehen** to take radical steps against sth
Radikale(r) F(M) radical
Radikalisierung [radikali'zi:rʊŋ] F radicalization
Radikalkur (*umg*) F drastic remedy
Radio ['ra:dio] (**-s, -s**) NT radio, wireless (*bes* BRIT); **im** ~ on the radio; **radioaktiv** ADJ radioactive; **radioaktiver Niederschlag** (radioactive) fallout; **Radioaktivität** F radioactivity; **Radioapparat** M radio (set); **Radiorekorder** M radio-cassette recorder; **Radiosender** M radio station; **Radiowecker** M radio alarm (clock)
Radium ['ra:diʊm] (**-s**) NT radium
Radius ['ra:diʊs] (**-, Radien**) M radius
Radkappe F (*Aut*) hub cap
Radler(in) (**-s, -**) M(F) cyclist
Rad- ZW: **Radrennbahn** F cycling (race)track; **Radrennen** NT cycle race; (*Sportart*) cycle racing; **Radsport** M cycling; **Radweg** M cycle track *od* path
RAF (-) F ABK (= *Rote Armee Fraktion*) Red Army Faction
raffen ['rafən] VT to snatch, to pick up; (*Stoff*) to gather (up); (*Geld*) to pile up, to rake in; (*umg: verstehen*) to catch on to
Raffgier F greed, avarice
Raffinade [rafi'na:də] F refined sugar
Raffinesse [rafi'nɛsə] (-) F (*Feinheit*) refinement; (*Schlauheit*) cunning
raffinieren [rafi'ni:rən] VT to refine
raffiniert ADJ crafty, cunning; (*Zucker*) refined
Rage ['ra:ʒə] (-) F (*Wut*) rage, fury
ragen ['ra:gən] VI to tower, to rise
Rahm [ra:m] (**-s**) M cream
rahmen VT to frame; **Rahmen** (**-s, -**) M frame(work); **aus dem Rahmen fallen** to go too far; **im Rahmen des Möglichen** within the bounds of possibility; **Rahmenhandlung** F (*Liter*) background story; **Rahmenplan** M outline plan; **Rahmenrichtlinien** PL guidelines *pl*
rahmig ADJ creamy
räkeln ['rɛ:kln] VR = **rekeln**
Rakete [ra'ke:tə] (-, **-n**) F rocket; **ferngelenkte** ~ guided missile
Raketenstützpunkt M missile base
Rallye ['rali] (-, **-s**) F rally
rammdösig ['ramdø:zɪç] (*umg*) ADJ giddy, dizzy
rammen ['ramən] VT to ram
Rampe ['rampə] (-, **-n**) F ramp
Rampenlicht NT (*Theat*) footlights *pl*; **sie möchte immer im ~ stehen** (*fig*) she always wants to be in the limelight

ramponieren [rampo'ni:rən] (*umg*) VT to damage
Ramsch [ramʃ] **(-(e)s, -e)** M junk
ran [ran] (*umg*) ADV = **heran**
Rand [rant] **(-(e)s, Ränder)** M edge; (*von Brille, Tasse etc*) rim; (*Hutrand*) brim; (*auf Papier*) margin; (*Schmutzrand, unter Augen*) ring; (*fig*) verge, brink; **außer ~ und Band** wild; **am Rande bemerkt** mentioned in passing; **am Rande der Stadt** on the outskirts of the town; **etw am Rande miterleben** to experience sth from the sidelines
randalieren [randa'li:rən] VI to (go on the) rampage
Randalierer(in) **(-s, -)** M(F) hooligan
Rand- zW: **Randbemerkung** F marginal note; (*fig*) odd comment; **Randerscheinung** F unimportant side effect, marginal phenomenon; **Randfigur** F minor figure; **Randgebiet** NT (*Geog*) fringe; (*Pol*) border territory; (*fig*) subsidiary; **Randstreifen** M (*der Straße*) verge (BRIT), berm (US); (*der Autobahn*) hard shoulder (BRIT), shoulder (US); **randvoll** ADJ full to the brim
rang *etc* [raŋ] VB *siehe* **ringen**
Rang **(-(e)s, Ränge)** M rank; (*Stand*) standing; (*Wert*) quality; (*Theat*) circle; **ein Mann ohne ~ und Namen** a man without any standing; **erster/zweiter ~** dress/upper circle
Rangabzeichen NT badge of rank
Rangälteste(r) M senior officer
rangeln ['raŋəln] (*umg*) VI to scrap; (*um Posten*): **~ (um)** to wrangle (for)
Rangfolge F order of rank (*bes Mil*)
Rangierbahnhof [rã'ʒi:rba:nho:f] M marshalling yard
rangieren VT (*Eisenb*) to shunt, to switch (US) ▶ VI to rank, to be classed
Rangiergleis NT siding
Rangliste F (*Sport*) ranking list, rankings *pl*
Rangordnung F hierarchy; (*Mil*) rank
Rangunterschied M social distinction; (*Mil*) difference in rank
rank [raŋk] ADJ: **~ und schlank** (*liter*) slender and supple
Ranke ['raŋkə] **(-, -n)** F tendril, shoot
Ränke ['rɛŋkə] PL intrigues *pl*
ranken ['raŋkən] VR to trail, to grow; **sich um etw ~** to twine around sth
Ränkeschmied M (*liter*) intriguer
ränkevoll ADJ scheming
ranklotzen ['ranklɔtsən] (*umg*) VI to put one's nose to the grindstone
ranlassen *unreg* (*umg*) VT: **jdn ~** to let sb have a go
rann *etc* [ran] VB *siehe* **rinnen**
rannte *etc* ['rantə] VB *siehe* **rennen**
Ranzen ['rantsən] **(-s, -)** M satchel; (*umg: Bauch*) belly, gut
ranzig ['rantsɪç] ADJ rancid
Rap [rɛp] **(-(s), -s)** M (*Mus*) rap
Rappe ['rapə] **(-n, -n)** M black horse
Rappel ['rapəl] **(-s, -)** (*umg*) M (*Fimmel*) craze; (*Wutanfall*): **einen ~ kriegen** to throw a fit
rappen ['rɛpən] VI (*Mus*) to rap
Rappen ['rapən] **(-s, -)** (SCHWEIZ) M (*Geld*) centime, rappen
Rapper(in) ['rɛpər] **(-s, -)** M(F) (*Mus*) rapper
Raps [raps] **(-es, -e)** M (*Bot*) rape; **Rapsöl** NT rapeseed oil
rar [ra:r] ADJ rare; *siehe auch* **rarmachen**
Rarität [rari'tɛ:t] F rarity; (*Sammelobjekt*) curio
rarmachen (*umg*) VR to stay away
rasant [ra'zant] ADJ quick, rapid
rasch [raʃ] ADJ quick
rascheln VI to rustle
rasen ['ra:zən] VI to rave; (*sich schnell bewegen*) to race
Rasen **(-s, -)** M grass; (*gepflegt*) lawn
rasend ADJ furious; **rasende Kopfschmerzen** a splitting headache
Rasen- zW: **Rasenmäher** **(-s, -)** M lawnmower; **Rasenmähmaschine** F lawnmower; **Rasenplatz** M lawn; **Rasensprenger** M (lawn) sprinkler
Raserei [ra:zə'raɪ] F raving, ranting; (*Schnelle*) reckless speeding
Rasier- zW: **Rasierapparat** M shaver; **Rasiercreme** F shaving cream; **rasieren** VT, VR to shave; **Rasierklinge** F razor blade; **Rasiermesser** NT razor; **Rasierpinsel** M shaving brush; **Rasierseife** F shaving soap *od* stick; **Rasierwasser** NT aftershave
raspeln ['raspəln] VT to grate; (*Holz*) to rasp
Rasse ['rasə] **(-, -n)** F race; (*Tierrasse*) breed; **Rassehund** M thoroughbred dog
Rassel **(-, -n)** F rattle
rasseln VI to rattle, to clatter
Rassenhass M race *od* racial hatred
Rassentrennung F racial segregation
rassig ['rasɪç] ADJ (*Pferd, Auto*) sleek; (*Frau*) vivacious; (*Wein*) spirited, lively
Rassismus [ra'sɪsmʊs] **(-)** M racialism, racism
Rassist(in) [ra'sɪst(ɪn)] M(F) racist
rassistisch [ra'sɪstɪʃ] ADJ racialist, racist
Rast [rast] **(-, -en)** F rest; **rasten** VI to rest
Raster ['rastər] **(-s, -)** M (*Archit*) grid; (*Phot: Gitter*) screen; (*TV*) raster; (*fig*) framework
Rast- zW: **Rasthaus** NT (*Aut*) service area, services *pl*; **Rasthof** M (motorway) motel; (*mit Tankstelle*) service area (*with a motel*); **rastlos** ADJ tireless; (*unruhig*) restless; **Rastplatz** M (*Aut*) lay-by (BRIT); **Raststätte** F service area, services *pl*
Rasur [ra'zu:r] F shave; (*das Rasieren*) shaving
Rat [ra:t] **(-(e)s, -schläge)** M (piece of) advice; **jdm mit ~ und Tat zur Seite stehen** to support sb in (both) word and deed; **um ~ fragen** to ask for advice; **(sich *dat*) keinen ~ wissen** not to know what to do; *siehe auch* **zurate**
rät [rɛ:t] VB *siehe* **raten**
Rate **(-, -n)** F instalment (BRIT), installment (US); **auf Raten kaufen** to buy on hire purchase (BRIT) *od* on the installment plan (US); **in Raten zahlen** to pay in instalments (BRIT) *od* installments (US)

r

raten *unreg* VT, VI to guess; (*empfehlen*): **jdm ~** to advise sb; **dreimal darfst du ~** I'll give you three guesses (*auch ironisch*)
ratenweise ADV by instalments (BRIT) *od* installments (*US*)
Ratenzahlung F hire purchase (BRIT), installment plan (*US*)
Ratespiel NT guessing game; (*TV*) quiz; (: *Beruferaten etc*) panel game
Ratgeber (**-s, -**) M adviser
Rathaus NT town hall; (*einer Großstadt*) city hall (*bes US*)
ratifizieren [ratifi'tsi:rən] VT to ratify
Ratifizierung F ratification
Ration [ratsi'o:n] F ration
rational [ratsio'na:l] ADJ rational
rationalisieren [ratsionali'zi:rən] VT to rationalize
rationell [ratsio'nɛl] ADJ efficient
rationieren [ratsio'ni:rən] VT to ration
ratlos ADJ at a loss, helpless
Ratlosigkeit F helplessness
rätoromanisch [rɛtoro'ma:nɪʃ] ADJ Rhaetian
ratsam ADJ advisable
Ratschlag M (piece of) advice
Rätsel ['rɛ:tsəl] (**-s, -**) NT puzzle; (*Worträtsel*) riddle; **vor einem ~ stehen** to be baffled; **rätselhaft** ADJ mysterious; **es ist mir rätselhaft** it's a mystery to me; **rätseln** VI to puzzle; **Rätselraten** NT guessing game
Ratsherr M councillor (BRIT), councilor (*US*)
Ratskeller M town-hall restaurant
Ratte ['ratə] (**-, -n**) F rat
Rattenfänger (**-s, -**) M rat-catcher
rattern ['ratərn] VI to rattle, to clatter
rau [raʊ] ADJ rough, coarse; (*Wetter*) harsh; **in rauen Mengen** (*umg*) by the ton, galore
Raub [raʊp] (**-(e)s**) M robbery; (*Beute*) loot, booty; **Raubbau** M overexploitation; **Raubdruck** M pirate(d) edition
raubeinig ADJ rough-and-ready
rauben ['raʊbən] VT to rob; (*jdn*) to kidnap, to abduct
Räuber ['rɔʏbər] (**-s, -**) M robber; **räuberisch** ADJ thieving
Raub- ZW: **Raubfisch** M predatory fish; **raubgierig** ADJ rapacious; **Raubkassette** F pirate cassette; **Raubkopie** F pirate copy; **Raubmord** M robbery with murder; **Raubtier** NT predator; **Raubüberfall** M robbery with violence; **Raubvogel** M bird of prey
Rauch [raʊx] (**-(e)s**) M smoke; **Rauchabzug** M smoke outlet
rauchen VT, VI to smoke; **mir raucht der Kopf** (*fig*) my head's spinning; **„R~ verboten"** "no smoking"
Raucher(in) (**-s, -**) M(F) smoker; **Raucherabteil** NT (*Eisenb*) smoking compartment
Räucherlachs M smoked salmon
räuchern ['rɔʏçərn] VT to smoke, to cure
Räucherspeck M ≈ smoked bacon
Räucherstäbchen NT joss stick
Rauch- ZW: **Rauchfahne** F smoke trail; **Rauchfang** M chimney hood; **Rauchfleisch** NT smoked meat
rauchig ADJ smoky
Rauchschwaden PL drifts of smoke *pl*
räudig ['rɔʏdɪç] ADJ mangy
rauf [raʊf] (*umg*) ADV = **herauf**; **hinauf**
Raufasertapete F woodchip paper
Raufbold (**-(e)s, -e**) M thug, hooligan
raufen VT (*Haare*) to pull out ▶ VI, VR to fight
Rauferei [raʊfə'raɪ] F brawl, fight
rauflustig ADJ ready for a fight, pugnacious
rauh *siehe* **rau**
rauhaarig ADJ wire-haired
Raum [raʊm] (**-(e)s, Räume**) M space; (*Zimmer, Platz*) room; (*Gebiet*) area; **~ sparend** space-saving; **eine Frage im ~ stehen lassen** to leave a question unresolved; **Raumausstatter(in)** M(F) interior decorator
räumen ['rɔʏmən] VT to clear; (*Wohnung, Platz*) to vacate, to move out of; (*verlassen: Gebäude, Gebiet*) to evacuate; (*wegbringen*) to shift, to move; (*in Schrank etc*) to put away
Raum- ZW: **Raumfähre** F space shuttle; **Raumfahrer** M astronaut; (*sowjetisch*) cosmonaut; **Raumfahrt** F space travel
Räumfahrzeug ['rɔʏmfa:rtsɔʏk] NT bulldozer; (*für Schnee*) snow-clearer
Rauminhalt M cubic capacity, volume
Raumkapsel F space capsule
räumlich ['rɔʏmlɪç] ADJ spatial; **Räumlichkeiten** PL premises *pl*
Raum- ZW: **Raummangel** M lack of space; **Raummaß** NT unit of volume; **Raummeter** M cubic metre (BRIT) *od* meter (*US*); **Raumnot** F shortage of space; **Raumordnung** F environmental planning; **Raumpflegerin** F cleaner; **Raumschiff** NT spaceship; **Raumschifffahrt** F space travel; **Raumstation** F space station; **Raumtransporter** M space shuttle
Räumung ['rɔʏmʊŋ] F clearing (away); (*von Haus etc*) vacating; (*wegen Gefahr*) evacuation; (*unter Zwang*) eviction
Räumungs- ZW: **Räumungsbefehl** M eviction order; **Räumungsklage** F action for eviction; **Räumungsverkauf** M clearance sale
raunen ['raʊnən] VT, VI to whisper
Raupe ['raʊpə] (**-, -n**) F caterpillar; (*Raupenkette*) (caterpillar) track
Raupenschlepper M caterpillar tractor
Raureif ['raʊraɪf] M hoarfrost
raus [raʊs] (*umg*) ADV = **heraus**; **hinaus**
Rausch [raʊʃ] (**-(e)**, *pl* **Räusche**) M intoxication; **einen ~ haben** to be drunk
rauschen VI (*Wasser*) to rush; (*Baum*) to rustle; (*Radio etc*) to hiss; (*Mensch*) to sweep, to sail
rauschend ADJ (*Beifall*) thunderous; (*Fest*) sumptuous
Rauschgift NT drug; **Rauschgifthandel** M drug traffic; **Rauschgifthändler(in)** M(F) drug trafficker; **Rauschgiftsüchtige(r)** F(M) drug addict

rausfliegen *unreg* (*umg*) VI to be chucked out
räuspern ['rɔʏspərn] VR to clear one's throat
Rausschmeißer ['raʊsʃmaɪsər] (**-s, -**) (*umg*) M bouncer
Raute ['raʊtə] (**-, -n**) F diamond; (*Math*) rhombus
rautenförmig ADJ rhombic
Razzia ['ratsia] (**-, Razzien**) F raid
Reagenzglas [rea'gɛntsglaːs] NT test tube
reagieren [rea'giːrən] VI: **~** (**auf** *+akk*) to react (to)
Reaktion [reaktsi'oːn] F reaction
reaktionär [reaktsio'nɛːr] ADJ reactionary
Reaktionsfähigkeit F reactions *pl*
Reaktionsgeschwindigkeit F speed of reaction
Reaktor [re'aktɔr] M reactor; **Reaktorkern** M reactor core; **Reaktorunglück** NT nuclear accident
real [re'aːl] ADJ real, material; **Realeinkommen** NT real income
realisierbar [reali'ziːrbaːr] ADJ practicable, feasible
Realismus [rea'lɪsmʊs] M realism
Realist(in) [rea'lɪst(ɪn)] M(F) realist; **realistisch** ADJ realistic
Realität [reali'tɛːt] F reality; **Realitäten** PL (*Gegebenheiten*) facts *pl*
realitätsfremd ADJ out of touch with reality
Realpolitik F political realism
Realschule F ≈ middle school (BRIT), junior high school (US)

> The **Realschule** is one of the choices of secondary schools available to a German schoolchild after the **Grundschule**. At the end of six years' schooling in the Realschule pupils gain the **mittlere Reife** and usually go on to some kind of training or to a college of further education.

Realzeit F real time
Rebe ['reːbə] (**-, -n**) F vine
Rebell(in) [re'bɛl(ɪn)] (**-en, -en**) M(F) rebel
rebellieren [rebɛ'liːrən] VI to rebel
Rebellion [rebɛli'oːn] F rebellion
rebellisch [re'bɛlɪʃ] ADJ rebellious
Rebensaft M wine
Reb- [rɛp] ZW: **Rebhuhn** NT partridge; **Reblaus** F vine pest; **Rebstock** M vine
rechen VT, VI to rake; **Rechen** ['rɛçən] (**-s, -**) M rake
Rechen- ZW: **Rechenaufgabe** F sum, mathematical problem; **Rechenfehler** M miscalculation; **Rechenmaschine** F adding machine
Rechenschaft F account; **jdm über etw** *akk* **~ ablegen** to account to sb for sth; **jdn zur ~ ziehen (für)** to call sb to account (for *od* over); **jdm ~ schulden** to be accountable to sb
Rechenschaftsbericht M report
Rechenschieber M slide rule
Rechenzentrum NT computer centre (BRIT) *od* center (US)
recherchieren [reʃɛr'ʃiːrən] VT, VI to investigate
rechnen ['rɛçnən] VT, VI to calculate; (*veranschlagen*) to estimate, to reckon ▶ VR to pay off; **jdn/etw zu etw ~** to count sb/sth among sth; **~ mit** to reckon with; **~ auf** *+akk* to count on
Rechnen NT arithmetic; (*bes Sch*) sums *pl*
Rechner (**-s, -**) M calculator; (*Comput*) computer; **rechnerfern** ADJ (*Comput*) remote; **rechnerisch** ADJ arithmetical
Rechnung F calculation(s); (*Comm*) bill (BRIT), check (US); **auf eigene ~** on one's own account; **(jdm) etw in ~ stellen** to charge (sb) for sth; **jdm/etw ~ tragen** to take sb/sth into account
Rechnungs- ZW: **Rechnungsbuch** NT account book; **Rechnungshof** M ≈ Auditor-General's office (BRIT), audit division (US); **Rechnungsjahr** NT financial year; **Rechnungsprüfer** M auditor; **Rechnungsprüfung** F audit(ing)
recht [rɛçt] ADJ right ▶ ADV (*vor Adjektiv*) really, quite; **das ist mir ~** that suits me; **jetzt erst ~** now more than ever; **alles, was ~ ist** (*empört*) fair's fair; (*anerkennend*) you can't deny it; **es geschieht ihm ~** it serves him right; **nach dem Rechten sehen** to see that everything's O.K.; **~ haben** to be right; **jdm ~ geben** to agree with sb, to admit that sb is right; **du kommst gerade ~, um ...** you're just in time to ...; **gehe ich ~ in der Annahme, dass ...?** am I correct in assuming that ...?; **~ herzlichen Dank** thank you very much indeed
Recht (**-(e)s, -e**) NT right; (*Jur*) law; **~ sprechen** to administer justice; **mit** *od* **zu ~** rightly, justly; **von Rechts wegen** by rights; **zu seinem ~ kommen** (*lit*) to gain one's rights; (*fig*) to come into one's own; **gleiches ~ für alle!** equal rights for all!
Rechte F right (hand); (*Pol*) Right
rechte(r, s) ADJ right; (*Pol*) right-wing
Rechte(s) NT right thing; **etwas/nichts ~** something/nothing proper
recht- ZW: **Rechteck** (**-(e)s, -e**) NT rectangle; **rechteckig** ADJ rectangular; **rechtfertigen** VT UNTR to justify ▶ VR UNTR to justify o.s.; **Rechtfertigung** F justification; **rechthaberisch** ADJ dogmatic; **rechtlich** ADJ legal, lawful; **rechtlich nicht zulässig** not permissible in law, illegal; **rechtmäßig** ADJ legal, lawful
rechts [rɛçts] ADV on *od* to the right; **~ von** to the right of; **~ stehen** *od* **sein** (*Pol*) to be right-wing; **~ stricken** to knit (plain); **Rechtsabbieger** (**-s, -**) M: **die Spur für Rechtsabbieger** the right-hand turn-off lane; **Rechtsanspruch** M: **einen Rechtsanspruch auf etw** *akk* **haben** to be legally entitled to sth; **Rechtsanwalt** M, **Rechtsanwältin** F lawyer, barrister; **Rechtsaußen** (**-, -**) M (*Sport*) outside right; **Rechtsbeistand** M legal adviser
rechtschaffen ADJ upright
Rechtschreibung F spelling
Rechts- ZW: **Rechtsdrehung** F clockwise rotation; **Rechtsextremismus** M right-wing

r

extremism; **Rechtsextremist** M right-wing extremist; **Rechtsfall** M (law) case; **Rechtsfrage** F legal question; **rechtsgültig** ADJ legally valid; **Rechtshänder(in)** (**-s, -**) M(F) right-handed person; **rechtskräftig** ADJ valid, legal; **Rechtskurve** F right-hand bend; **Rechtslage** F legal position; **rechtslastig** ADJ listing to the right; (*fig*) leaning to the right; **Rechtspflege** F administration of justice; **Rechtspfleger** M *official with certain judicial powers*

Rechtsprechung ['rɛçtʃprɛçʊŋ] F (*Gerichtsbarkeit*) jurisdiction; (*richterliche Tätigkeit*) dispensation of justice; **rechtsradikal** ADJ (*Pol*) extreme right-wing

Rechts- ZW: **Rechtsschutz** M legal protection; **Rechtsspruch** M verdict; **Rechtsstaat** M state under the rule of law; **Rechtsstreit** M lawsuit; **Rechtstitel** M title; **rechtsverbindlich** ADJ legally binding; **Rechtsverkehr** M driving on the right; **Rechtsweg** M: **der Rechtsweg ist ausgeschlossen** ≈ the judges' decision is final; **rechtswidrig** ADJ illegal; **Rechtswissenschaft** F jurisprudence

rechtwinklig ADJ right-angled

rechtzeitig ADJ timely ▶ ADV in time

Reck [rɛk] (**-(e)s, -e**) NT horizontal bar

recken VT, VR to stretch

recycelbar [ri:'saɪkəlba:r] ADJ recyclable

recyceln [ri:'saɪkəln] VT to recycle

Recycling [ri'saɪklɪŋ] (**-s**) NT recycling; **Recyclingpapier** NT recycled paper

Red. ABK = **Redaktion**; (= *Redakteur(in)*) ed

Redakteur(in) [redak'tø:r(ɪn)] M(F) editor

Redaktion [redaktsi'o:n] F editing; (*Leute*) editorial staff; (*Büro*) editorial office(s *pl*)

Redaktionsschluss M time of going to press; (*Einsendeschluss*) copy deadline

Rede ['re:də] (**-, -n**) F speech; (*Gespräch*) talk; **jdn zur ~ stellen** to take sb to task; **eine ~ halten** to make a speech; **das ist nicht der ~ wert** it's not worth mentioning; **davon kann keine ~ sein** it's out of the question; **Redefreiheit** F freedom of speech; **redegewandt** ADJ eloquent

reden VI to talk, to speak ▶ VT to say; (*Unsinn etc*) to talk; **(viel) von sich ~ machen** to become (very much) a talking point; **darüber lässt sich ~** that's a possibility; (*über Preis, Bedingungen*) I think we could discuss that; **er lässt mit sich ~** he could be persuaded; (*in Bezug auf Preis*) he's open to offers; (*gesprächsbereit*) he's open to discussion

Reden (**-s**) NT talking, speech

Redensart F set phrase

Redeschwall M torrent of words

Redewendung F expression, idiom

redlich ['re:tlɪç] ADJ honest; **Redlichkeit** F honesty

Redner(in) (**-s, -**) M(F) speaker, orator

redselig ['re:tze:lɪç] ADJ talkative, loquacious; **Redseligkeit** F talkativeness, loquacity

redundant [redʊn'dant] ADJ redundant

Redundanz [redʊn'dants] (**-**) F redundancy

reduzieren [redu'tsi:rən] VT to reduce

Reduzierung F reduction

Reede ['re:də] (**-, -n**) F protected anchorage

Reeder (**-s, -**) M shipowner

Reederei [re:də'raɪ] F shipping line *od* firm

reell [re'ɛl] ADJ fair, honest; (*Preis*) fair; (*Comm: Geschäft*) sound; (*Math*) real

Reetdach ['re:tdax] NT thatched roof

Ref. ABK = **Referendar(in)**; **Referent(in)**

Referat [refe'ra:t] (**-(e)s, -e**) NT report; (*Vortrag*) paper; (*Gebiet*) section; (*Verwaltung: Ressort*) department; **ein ~ halten (über** *+akk*) to give a paper (on)

Referendar(in) [referen'dar(ɪn)] M(F) trainee (in civil service); (*Studienreferendar*) trainee teacher; (*Gerichtsreferendar*) articled clerk

Referendum [refe'rɛndʊm] (**-s, Referenden**) NT referendum

Referent(in) [refe'rɛnt(ɪn)] M(F) speaker; (*Berichterstatter*) reporter; (*Sachbearbeiter*) expert

Referenz [refe'rɛnts] F reference

referieren [refe'ri:rən] VI: **~ über** *+akk* to speak *od* talk on

reflektieren [reflek'ti:rən] VT, VI to reflect; **~ auf** *+akk* to be interested in

Reflex [re'flɛks] (**-es, -e**) M reflex; **Reflexbewegung** F reflex action

reflexiv [reflɛ'ksi:f] ADJ (*Gram*) reflexive

Reform [re'fɔrm] (**-, -en**) F reform

Reformation [refɔrmatsi'o:n] F reformation

Reformator [refɔr'ma:tɔr] M reformer; **reformatorisch** ADJ reformatory, reforming

reform- ZW: **reformbedürftig** ADJ in need of reform; **reformfreudig** ADJ avid for reform; **Reformhaus** NT health food shop

reformieren [refɔr'mi:rən] VT to reform

Refrain [rə'frɛ̃:] (**-s, -s**) M refrain, chorus

Reg. ABK (= *Regierungs-*) gov.; (= *Register*) reg

Regal [re'ga:l] (**-s, -e**) NT (book)shelves *pl*, bookcase; (*Typ*) stand, rack

Regatta [re'gata] (**-, Regatten**) F regatta

Reg.-Bez. ABK = **Regierungsbezirk**

rege ['re:gə] ADJ lively, active; (*Geschäft*) brisk

Regel ['re:gəl] (**-, -n**) F rule; (*Med*) period; **in der ~** as a rule; **nach allen Regeln der Kunst** (*fig*) thoroughly; **sich** *dat* **etw zur ~ machen** to make a habit of sth; **regellos** ADJ irregular, unsystematic; **regelmäßig** ADJ regular; **Regelmäßigkeit** F regularity

regeln VT to regulate, to control; (*Angelegenheit*) to settle ▶ VR: **sich von selbst ~** to take care of itself; **gesetzlich geregelt sein** to be laid down by law

regelrecht ADJ proper, thorough

Regelung F regulation; (*von Angelegenheit*) settlement

regelwidrig ADJ irregular, against the rules

regen ['re:gən] VT to move ▶ VR to move, to stir

Regen (**-s, -**) M rain; **vom ~ in die Traufe kommen** (*Sprichwort*) to jump out of the frying pan into the fire (*Sprichwort*)

Regenbogen M rainbow; **Regenbogenhaut** F (*Anat*) iris; **Regenbogenpresse** F trashy magazines *pl*

regenerieren [regene'ri:rən] VR (*Biol*) to regenerate; (*fig*) to revitalize *od* regenerate o.s. *od* itself; (*nach Anstrengung, Schock etc*) to recover
Regen- zW: **Regenguss** M downpour; **Regenmantel** M raincoat, mac(kintosh); **Regenmenge** F rainfall; **Regenschauer** M shower (of rain); **Regenschirm** M umbrella
Regent(in) [re'gɛnt(ɪn)] M(F) regent
Regentag M rainy day
Regentropfen M raindrop
Regentschaft F regency
Regen- zW: **Regenwald** M (*Geog*) rain forest; **Regenwetter** NT: **er macht ein Gesicht wie drei** *od* **sieben Tage Regenwetter** (*umg*) he's got a face as long as a month of Sundays; **Regenwurm** M earthworm; **Regenzeit** F rainy season, rains *pl*
Regie [re'ʒi:] F (*Film etc*) direction; (*Theat*) production; **unter der ~ von** directed *od* produced by; **Regieanweisung** F (stage) direction
regieren [re'gi:rən] VT, VI to govern, to rule
Regierung F government; (*Monarchie*) reign; **an die ~ kommen** to come to power
Regierungs- zW: **Regierungsbezirk** M ≈ county (BRIT, US), ≈ region (SCOT); **Regierungserklärung** F inaugural speech; (*in Großbritannien*) Queen's/King's Speech; **Regierungsmannschaft** F government team; **Regierungssprecher** M government spokesman; **Regierungsvorlage** F government bill; **Regierungswechsel** M change of government; **Regierungszeit** F period in government; (*von König*) reign
Regiment [regi'mɛnt] (**-s, -er**) NT regiment
Region [regi'o:n] F region
Regionalplanung [regio'na:lpla:nʊŋ] F regional planning
Regionalprogramm NT (*Rundf, TV*) regional programme (BRIT) *od* program (US)
Regisseur(in) [reʒɪ'sø:r(ɪn)] M(F) director; (*Theat*) (stage) producer
Register [re'gɪstər] (**-s, -**) NT register; (*in Buch*) table of contents, index; **alle ~ ziehen** (*fig*) to pull out all the stops; **Registerführer** M registrar
Registratur [regɪstra'tu:r] F registry, records office
registrieren [regɪs'tri:rən] VT to register; (*umg: zur Kenntnis nehmen*) to note
Registrierkasse F cash register
Regler ['re:glər] (**-s, -**) M regulator, governor
reglos ['re:klo:s] ADJ motionless
regnen ['re:gnən] VI UNPERS to rain ▶ VT UNPERS: **es regnet Glückwünsche** congratulations are pouring in; **es regnet in Strömen** it's pouring (with rain)
regnerisch ADJ rainy
Regress [re'grɛs] (**-es, -e**) M (*Jur*) recourse, redress; **Regressanspruch** M (*Jur*) claim for compensation
regsam ['re:kza:m] ADJ active
regulär [regu'lɛ:r] ADJ regular
regulieren [regu'li:rən] VT to regulate; (*Comm*) to settle; **sich von selbst ~** to be self-regulating
Regulierungsbehörde [regu'li:rʊŋsbəhø:rdə] F regulatory body *od* authority
Regung ['re:gʊŋ] F motion; (*Gefühl*) feeling, impulse
regungslos ADJ motionless
Reh [re:] (**-(e)s, -e**) NT deer; (*weiblich*) roe deer
rehabilitieren [rehabili'ti:rən] VT to rehabilitate; (*Ruf, Ehre*) to vindicate ▶ VR to rehabilitate (*form*) *od* vindicate o.s.
Rehabilitierung F rehabilitation
Reh- zW: **Rehbock** M roebuck; **Rehbraten** M roast venison; **Rehkalb** NT fawn; **Rehkitz** NT fawn
Reibach ['raɪbax] (**-s**) M: **einen ~ machen** (*umg*) to make a killing
Reibe ['raɪbə] (**-, -n**) F grater
Reibeisen ['raɪplaɪzən] NT grater
Reibekuchen M (*Koch*) ≈ potato waffle
reiben *unreg* VT to rub; (*Koch*) to grate
Reiberei [raɪbə'raɪ] F friction *no pl*
Reibfläche F rough surface
Reibung F friction
reibungslos ADJ smooth; **~ verlaufen** to go off smoothly
reich ADJ rich ▶ ADV: **eine ~ ausgestattete Bibliothek** a well-stocked library
Reich [raɪç] (**-(e)s, -e**) NT empire; (*von König*) kingdom; (*fig*) realm; **das Dritte ~** the Third Reich
reichen VI to reach; (*genügen*) to be enough *od* sufficient ▶ VT to hold out; (*geben*) to pass, to hand; (*anbieten*) to offer; **so weit das Auge reicht** as far as the eye can see; **jdm ~** (*genügen*) to be enough *od* sufficient for sb; **mir reichts!** I've had enough!
reich- zW: **reichhaltig** ADJ ample, rich; **reichlich** ADJ ample; **reichlich Zeit** plenty of time; **Reichtum** (**-s, -tümer**) M wealth; **Reichweite** F range; **jd ist in Reichweite** sb is nearby
reif [raɪf] ADJ ripe; (*Mensch, Urteil*) mature; **für etw ~ sein** (*umg*) to be ready for sth
Reif[1] (**-(e)s**) M hoarfrost
Reif[2] (**-(e)s, -e**) M (*Ring*) ring, hoop
Reife (**-**) F ripeness; (*von Mensch*) maturity; **mittlere ~** (*Sch*) *first public examination in secondary school*, ≈ O-Levels *pl* (BRIT)
reifen VI to mature; (*Obst*) to ripen
Reifen (**-s, -**) M ring, hoop; (*Fahrzeugreifen*) tyre (BRIT), tire (US)
Reifen- zW: **Reifendruck** M tyre (BRIT) *od* tire (US) pressure; **Reifenpanne** F puncture, flat; **Reifenprofil** NT tyre (BRIT) *od* tire (US) tread; **Reifenschaden** M puncture, flat
Reifeprüfung F school-leaving exam
Reifezeugnis NT school-leaving certificate
reiflich ['raɪflɪç] ADJ thorough, careful
Reihe ['raɪə] (**-, -n**) F row; (*von Tagen etc: umg: Anzahl*) series *sing*; **eine ganze ~ (von)** (*unbestimmte Anzahl*) a whole lot (of); **der ~ nach** one after the other; **er ist an der ~** it's his turn; **an die ~ kommen** to have one's turn; **außer**

der ~ out of turn; (*ausnahmsweise*) out of the usual way of things; **aus der ~ tanzen** (*fig: umg*) to be different; (*gegen Konventionen verstoßen*) to step out of line; **ich kriege heute nichts auf die ~** I can't get my act together today
reihen VT to set in a row; (*aneinanderreihen*) to arrange in series; (*Perlen*) to string
Reihen- ZW: **Reihenfolge** F sequence; **alphabetische Reihenfolge** alphabetical order; **Reihenhaus** NT terraced (BRIT) *od* row (US) house; **Reihenuntersuchung** F mass screening; **reihenweise** ADV (*in Reihen*) in rows; (*fig: in großer Anzahl*) by the dozen
Reiher (**-s, -**) M heron
reihum [raɪ'ʊm] ADV: **etw ~ gehen lassen** to pass sth around
Reim [raɪm] (**-(e)s, -e**) M rhyme; **sich** *dat* **einen ~ auf etw** *akk* **machen** (*umg*) to make sense of sth; **reimen** VT to rhyme
rein[1] [raɪn] (*umg*) ADV = **herein**; **hinein**
rein[2] [raɪn] ADJ pure; (*sauber*) clean ▶ ADV purely; **~ waschen** to clear o.s.; **das ist die reinste Freude/der reinste Hohn** *etc* it's pure *od* sheer joy/mockery *etc*; **etw ins Reine schreiben** to make a fair copy of sth; **etw ins Reine bringen** to clear sth up; **reinen Tisch machen** (*fig*) to get things straight; **~ unmöglich** (*umg: ganz, völlig*) absolutely impossible
Rein- IN ZW (*Comm*) net(t)
Reinemachefrau F cleaning lady, charwoman (BRIT)
reineweg (*umg*) ADV completely, absolutely
rein- ZW: **Reinfall** (*umg*) M let-down; (*Misserfolg*) flop; **reinfallen** VI: **auf jdn/etw reinfallen** to be taken in by sb/sth; **Reingewinn** M net profit; **Reinheit** F purity; (*Sauberkeit*) cleanness
reinigen ['raɪnɪgən] VT to clean; (*Wasser*) to purify
Reiniger (**-s, -**) M cleaner
Reinigung F cleaning; (*von Wasser*) purification; (*Geschäft*) cleaner's; **chemische ~** dry-cleaning; (*Geschäft*) dry-cleaner's
Reinigungsmittel NT cleansing agent; **reinlich** ADJ clean
rein- ZW: **Reinlichkeit** F cleanliness; **Reinmachefrau** F = **Reinemachefrau**; **reinrassig** ADJ pedigree; **reinreiten** *unreg* VT: **jdn reinreiten** to get sb into a mess; **Reinschrift** F fair copy; **Reinvermögen** NT net assets *pl*
reinweg (*umg*) ADV = **reineweg**
Reis[1] [raɪs] (**-es, -e**) M rice
Reis[2] [raɪs] (**-es, -er**) NT twig, sprig
Reise ['raɪzə] (**-, -n**) F journey; (*Schiffsreise*) voyage; **Reisen** PL travels *pl*; **gute ~!** bon voyage!, have a good journey!; **auf Reisen sein** to be away (travelling (BRIT) *od* traveling (US)); **er ist viel auf Reisen** he does a lot of travelling (BRIT) *od* traveling (US); **Reiseandenken** NT souvenir; **Reiseapotheke** F first-aid kit; **Reisebericht** M account of one's journey; (*Buch*) travel story; (*Film*) travelogue (BRIT), travelog (US); **Reisebüro** NT travel agency; **Reisediplomatie** F shuttle diplomacy; **Reiseerleichterungen** PL easing *sing* of travel restrictions; **reisefertig** ADJ ready to start; **Reisefieber** NT (*fig*) travel nerves *pl*; **Reiseführer** M guide(book); (*Mensch*) (travel) guide; **Reisegepäck** NT luggage; **Reisegesellschaft** F party of travellers (BRIT) *od* travelers (US); **Reisegruppe** F tourist party; (*mit Reisebus*) coach party; **Reisekosten** PL travelling (BRIT) *od* traveling (US) expenses *pl*; **Reiseleiter** M courier; **Reiselektüre** F reading for the journey; **Reiselust** F wanderlust
reisen VI to travel; **~ nach** to go to
Reisende(r) F(M) traveller (BRIT), traveler (US)
Reise- ZW: **Reisepass** M passport; **Reisepläne** PL plans *pl* for a *od* the journey; **Reiseproviant** M provisions *pl* for the journey; **Reiseroute** F itinerary; **Reisescheck** M traveller's cheque (BRIT), traveler's check (US); **Reiseschreibmaschine** F portable typewriter; **Reisetasche** F travelling (BRIT) *od* traveling (US) bag *od* case; **Reisethrombose** F deep vein thrombosis, economy-class syndrome (*umg*); **Reiseveranstalter** M tour operator; **Reiseverkehr** M tourist *od* holiday traffic; **Reiseversicherung** F travel insurance; **Reisewetter** NT holiday weather; **Reiseziel** NT destination
Reisig ['raɪzɪç] (**-s**) NT brushwood
Reißaus M: **~ nehmen** to run away, to flee
Reißbrett NT drawing board; **Reißbrettstift** M drawing pin (BRIT), thumbtack (US)
reißen ['raɪsən] *unreg* VT, VI to tear; (*ziehen*) to pull, to drag; **etw an sich ~** to snatch sth up; (*fig*) to take sth over; **sich um etw ~** to scramble for sth; **wenn alle Stricke ~** (*fig: umg*) if the worst comes to the worst; **einen Witz ~** to crack a joke; *siehe auch* **hingerissen**
Reißen NT (*Gewichtheben: Disziplin*) snatch; (*umg: Gliederreißen*) ache
reißend ADJ (*Fluss*) torrential; (*Comm*) rapid; **reißenden Absatz finden** to sell like hot cakes (*umg*)
Reißer (**-s, -**) (*umg*) M thriller; **reißerisch** ADJ sensational
Reiß- ZW: **Reißleine** F (*Aviat*) ripcord; **Reißnagel** M drawing pin (BRIT), thumbtack (US); **Reißschiene** F T-square; **Reißverschluss** M zip (fastener) (BRIT), zipper (US); **Reißwolf** M shredder; **durch den Reißwolf geben** (*Dokumente*) to shred; **Reißzeug** NT geometry set; **Reißzwecke** F = **Reißnagel**
reiten ['raɪtən] *unreg* VT, VI to ride
Reiter (**-s, -**) M rider; (*Mil*) cavalryman, trooper
Reiterei [raɪtə'raɪ] F cavalry
Reiterin F rider
Reit- ZW: **Reithose** F riding breeches *pl*; **Reitpferd** NT saddle horse; **Reitschule** F riding school; **Reitstiefel** M riding boot; **Reitturnier** NT horse show; **Reitweg** M bridle path; **Reitzeug** NT riding outfit
Reiz [raɪts] (**-es, -e**) M stimulus; (*angenehm*) charm; (*Verlockung*) attraction

reizbar ADJ irritable; **Reizbarkeit** F irritability
reizen VT to stimulate; (*unangenehm*) to irritate; (*verlocken*) to appeal to, to attract; (*Karten*) to bid ▶ VI: **zum Widerspruch ~** to invite contradiction
reizend ADJ charming
Reiz- ZW: **Reizgas** NT tear gas, CS gas; **Reizhusten** M chesty cough; **reizlos** ADJ unattractive; **reizvoll** ADJ attractive; **Reizwäsche** F sexy underwear; **Reizwort** NT emotive word
rekapitulieren [rekapitu'li:rən] VT to recapitulate
rekeln ['re:kəln] VR to stretch out; (*lümmeln*) to lounge *od* loll about
Reklamation [reklamatsi'o:n] F complaint
Reklame [re'kla:mə] (-, -n) F advertising; (*Anzeige*) advertisement; **mit etw ~ machen** (*pej*) to show off about sth; **für etw ~ machen** to advertise sth; **Reklametrommel** F: **die Reklametrommel für jdn/etw rühren** (*umg*) to beat the (big) drum for sb/sth; **Reklamewand** F notice (BRIT) *od* bulletin (US) board
reklamieren [rekla'mi:rən] VI to complain ▶ VT to complain about; (*zurückfordern*) to reclaim
rekonstruieren [rekɔnstru'i:rən] VT to reconstruct
Rekonvaleszenz [rekɔnvalɛs'tsɛnts] F convalescence
Rekord [re'kɔrt] (-(e)s, -e) M record; **Rekordleistung** F record performance
Rekrut [re'kru:t] (-en, -en) M recruit
rekrutieren [rekru'ti:rən] VT to recruit ▶ VR to be recruited
Rektor ['rɛktɔr] M (*Univ*) rector, vice-chancellor; (*Sch*) head teacher (BRIT), principal (US)
Rektorat [rɛktɔ'rat] (-(e)s, -e) NT (*Univ*) rectorate, vice-chancellorship; (*Sch*) headship (BRIT), principalship (US); (*Zimmer*) rector's *etc* office
Rektorin [rɛk'to:rɪn] F (*Sch*) head teacher (BRIT), principal (US)
Rel. ABK (= *Religion*) rel.
Relais [rə'lɛ:] (-, -) NT relay
Relation [relatsi'o:n] F relation
relativ [rela'ti:f] ADJ relative ▶ ADV relatively
Relativität [relativi'tɛ:t] F relativity
Relativpronomen NT (*Gram*) relative pronoun
relaxen [ri'lɛksən] VI to relax, to chill out
relevant [rele'vant] ADJ relevant
Relevanz F relevance
Relief [reli'ɛf] (-s, -s) NT relief
Religion [religi'o:n] F religion
Religions- ZW: **Religionsfreiheit** F freedom of worship; **Religionslehre** F religious education; **Religionsunterricht** M religious education
religiös [religi'ø:s] ADJ religious
Relikt [re'lɪkt] (-(e)s, -e) NT relic
Reling ['re:lɪŋ] (-, -s) F (*Naut*) rail
Reliquie [re'li:kviə] F relic
Reminiszenz [reminɪs'tsɛnts] F reminiscence, recollection

Remis [rə'mi:] (-, - *od* -en) NT (*Schach, Sport*) draw
Remittende [remɪ'tɛndə] (-, -n) F (*Comm*) return
Remittent M (*Fin*) payee
remittieren VT (*Comm: Waren*) to return; (*Geld*) to remit
Remmidemmi ['rɛmi'dɛmi] (-s) (*umg*) NT (*Krach*) row, rumpus; (*Trubel*) rave-up
Remoulade [remu'la:də] (-, -n) F remoulade
rempeln ['rɛmpəln] (*umg*) VT to jostle, to elbow; (*Sport*) to barge into; (*foulen*) to push
Ren [re:n, rɛn] (-s, -s *od* -e) NT reindeer
Renaissance [rənɛ'sã:s] (-, -n) F (*Hist*) Renaissance; (*fig*) revival, rebirth
Rendezvous [rãde'vu:] (-, -) NT rendezvous
Rendite [rɛn'di:tə] (-, -n) F (*Fin*) yield, return on capital
Rennbahn F racecourse; (*Aut*) circuit, racetrack
rennen ['rɛnən] *unreg* VT, VI to run, to race; **um die Wette ~** to have a race; **Rennen** (-s, -) NT running; (*Wettbewerb*) race; **das Rennen machen** (*lit, fig*) to win (the race)
Renner (-s, -) (*umg*) M winner, worldbeater
Renn- ZW: **Rennfahrer** M racing driver (BRIT), race car driver (US); **Rennpferd** NT racehorse; **Rennplatz** M racecourse; **Rennrad** NT racing cycle; **Rennsport** M racing; **Rennwagen** M racing car (BRIT), race car (US)
renommiert [renɔ'mi:rt] ADJ: **~ (wegen)** renowned (for), famous (for)
renovieren [reno'vi:rən] VT to renovate
Renovierung F renovation
rentabel [rɛn'ta:bəl] ADJ profitable, lucrative
Rentabilität [rɛntabili'tɛ:t] F profitability
Rente ['rɛntə] (-, -n) F pension
Renten- ZW: **Rentenbasis** F annuity basis; **Rentenempfänger** M pensioner; **Rentenpapier** NT (*Fin*) fixed-interest security; **Rentenversicherung** F pension scheme; **Rentenversicherungsträger** M pension provider
Rentier ['rɛnti:r] NT reindeer
rentieren [rɛn'ti:rən] VI, VR to pay, to be profitable; **das rentiert (sich) nicht** it's not worth it
Rentner(in) ['rɛntnər(ɪn)] (-s, -) M(F) pensioner
Reparation [reparatsi'o:n] F reparation
Reparatur [repara'tu:r] F repair; **etw in ~ geben** to have sth repaired; **reparaturbedürftig** ADJ in need of repair; **Reparaturwerkstatt** F repair shop; (*Aut*) garage
reparieren [repa'ri:rən] VT to repair
Repertoire [repɛrto'a:r] (-s, -s) NT repertoire
Reportage [repɔr'ta:ʒə] (-, -n) F report
Reporter(in) [re'pɔrtər(ɪn)] (-s, -) M(F) reporter, commentator
Repräsentant(in) [reprɛzɛn'tant(ɪn)] M(F) representative
repräsentativ [reprɛzɛnta'ti:f] ADJ representative; (*Geschenk etc*) prestigious; **die repräsentativen Pflichten eines Botschafters** the social duties of an ambassador

repräsentieren [reprɛzɛn'ti:rən] VT to represent ▸ VI to perform official duties
Repressalien [reprɛ'sa:liən] PL reprisals *pl*
reprivatisieren [reprivati'zi:rən] VT to denationalize
Reprivatisierung F denationalization
Reproduktion [reprodʊktsi'o:n] F reproduction
reproduzieren [reprodu'tsi:rən] VT to reproduce
Reptil [rɛp'ti:l] (**-s, -ien**) NT reptile
Republik [repu'bli:k] F republic
Republikaner [republi'ka:nər] (**-s, -**) M republican
republikanisch ADJ republican
Requisiten PL (*Theat*) props *pl*, properties *pl* (*form*)
Reservat [rezɛr'va:t] (**-(e)s, -e**) NT reservation
Reserve [re'zɛrvə] (**-, -n**) F reserve; **jdn aus der ~ locken** to bring sb out of his/her shell; **Reserverad** NT (*Aut*) spare wheel; **Reservespieler** M reserve; **Reservetank** M reserve tank
reservieren [rezɛr'vi:rən] VT to reserve
reserviert ADJ (*Platz, Mensch*) reserved
Reservist [rezɛr'vɪst] M reservist
Reservoir [rezɛrvo'a:r] (**-s, -e**) NT reservoir
Residenz [rezi'dɛnts] F residence, seat
residieren [rezi'di:rən] VI to reside
Resignation [rezɪgnatsi'o:n] F resignation
resignieren [rezɪ'gni:rən] VI to resign
resolut [rezo'lu:t] ADJ resolute
Resolution [rezolutsi'o:n] F resolution; (*Bittschrift*) petition
Resonanz [rezo'nants] F (*lit, fig*) resonance; **Resonanzboden** M sounding board; **Resonanzkasten** M soundbox
Resopal® [rezo'pa:l] (**-s**) NT Formica®
resozialisieren [rezotsiali'zi:rən] VT to rehabilitate
Resozialisierung F rehabilitation
Respekt [rɛ'spɛkt] (**-(e)s**) M respect; (*Angst*) fear; **bei allem ~ (vor jdm/etw)** with all due respect (to sb/for sth)
respektabel [rɛspɛk'ta:bəl] ADJ respectable
respektieren [rɛspɛk'ti:rən] VT to respect
respektlos ADJ disrespectful
Respektsperson F person commanding respect
respektvoll ADJ respectful
Ressentiment [rɛsãti'mã:] (**-s, -s**) NT resentment
Ressort [rɛ'so:r] (**-s, -s**) NT department; **in das ~ von jdm fallen** (*lit, fig*) to be sb's department
Ressourcen [rɛ'sʊrsən] PL resources *pl*
Rest [rɛst] (**-(e)s, -e**) M remainder, rest; (*Überrest*) remains *pl*; **Reste** PL (*Comm*) remnants *pl*; **das hat mir den ~ gegeben** (*umg*) that finished me off
Restaurant [rɛsto'rã:] (**-s, -s**) NT restaurant
Restauration [restaʊratsi'o:n] F restoration
restaurieren [restaʊ'ri:rən] VT to restore
Restaurierung F restoration
Rest- ZW: **Restbetrag** M remainder, outstanding sum; **Restlaufzeit** F (*Wirts*) unexpired term; **restlich** ADJ remaining; **restlos** ADJ complete; **Restmüll** M non-recyclable waste; **Restposten** M (*Comm*) remaining stock
Resultat [rezʊl'ta:t] (**-(e)s, -e**) NT result
Retorte [re'tɔrtə] (**-, -n**) F retort; **aus der ~** (*umg*) synthetic
Retortenbaby NT test-tube baby
retour [re'tu:r] ADV (*veraltet*) back
Retouren PL (*Waren*) returns *pl*
retten ['rɛtən] VT to save, to rescue ▸ VR to escape; **bist du noch zu ~?** (*umg*) are you out of your mind?; **sich vor etw** *dat* **nicht mehr ~ können** (*fig*) to be swamped with sth
Retter(in) (**-s, -**) M(F) rescuer, saviour (BRIT), savior (*US*)
Rettich ['rɛtɪç] (**-s, -e**) M radish
Rettung F rescue; (*Hilfe*) help; **seine letzte ~** his last hope
Rettungs- ZW: **Rettungsaktion** F rescue operation; (*für Banken, Unternehmen etc*) bailout; **Rettungsboot** NT lifeboat; **Rettungsdienst** M rescue service; **Rettungsgürtel** M = **Rettungsring**; **Rettungshubschrauber** M rescue helicopter; **rettungslos** ADJ hopeless; **Rettungsring** M lifebelt, life preserver (*US*); **Rettungsschwimmer** M lifesaver; (*am Strand*) lifeguard; **Rettungswagen** M ambulance
Return-Taste [ri'tø:rntastə] F (*Comput*) return key
retuschieren [retʊ'ʃi:rən] VT (*Phot*) to retouch
Reue ['rɔʏə] (**-**) F remorse; (*Bedauern*) regret
reuen VT: **es reut ihn** he regrets it, he is sorry about it
reuig ['rɔʏɪç] ADJ penitent
reumütig ADJ remorseful; (*Sünder*) contrite
Reuse ['rɔʏzə] (**-, -n**) F fish trap
Revanche [re'vã:ʃ(ə)] (**-, -n**) F revenge; (*Sport*) return match
revanchieren [revã'ʃi:rən] VR (*sich rächen*) to get one's own back, to have one's revenge; (*erwidern*) to reciprocate, to return the compliment
Revers [re've:r] (**-, -**) M OD NT lapel
revidieren [revi'di:rən] VT to revise; (*Comm*) to audit
Revier [re'vi:r] (**-s, -e**) NT district; (*Min: Kohlenrevier*) (coal)mine; (*Jagdrevier*) preserve; (*Polizeirevier*) police station, station house (*US*); (*Dienstbereich*) beat (BRIT), precinct (*US*); (*Mil*) sick bay
Revision [revizi'o:n] F revision; (*Comm*) auditing; (*Jur*) appeal
Revisionsverhandlung F appeal hearing
Revisor [re'vi:zɔr] (**-s, -en**) M (*Comm*) auditor
Revolte [re'vɔltə] (**-, -n**) F revolt
Revolution [revolutsi'o:n] F revolution
revolutionär [revolutsio'nɛ:r] ADJ revolutionary
Revolutionär(in) [revolutsio'nɛ:r(ɪn)] (**-s, -e**) M(F) revolutionary
revolutionieren [revolutsio'ni:rən] VT to revolutionize

Revoluzzer [revo'lʊtsər] (**-s, -**) (*pej*) M would-be revolutionary
Revolver [re'vɔlvər] (**-s, -**) M revolver
Revue [rə'vy:] (-, **-n**) F: **etw ~ passieren lassen** (*fig*) to pass sth in review
Reykjavik ['raɪkjavi:k] (**-s**) NT Reykjavik
Rezensent [retsɛn'zɛnt] M reviewer, critic
rezensieren [retsɛn'zi:rən] VT to review
Rezension F review
Rezept [re'tsɛpt] (**-(e)s, -e**) NT (*Koch*) recipe; (*Med*) prescription
Rezeption [retsɛptsi'o:n] F (*von Hotel: Empfang*) reception
rezeptpflichtig ADJ available only on prescription
Rezession [retsɛsi'o:n] F (*Fin*) recession
rezitieren [retsi'ti:rən] VT to recite
R-Gespräch ['ɛrgəʃprɛ:ç] NT (*Tel*) reverse charge call (BRIT), collect call (US)
rh ABK (= *Rhesus(faktor) negativ*) Rh negative
Rh ABK (= *Rhesus(faktor) positiv*) Rh positive
Rhabarber [ra'barbər] (**-s**) M rhubarb
Rhein [raɪn] (**-(e)s**) M Rhine
rhein. ABK = **rheinisch**
Rheingau M *wine-growing area along the Rhine*
Rheinhessen NT *wine-growing area along the Rhine*
rheinisch ADJ *attrib* Rhenish, Rhineland
Rheinland NT Rhineland
Rheinländer(in) M(F) Rhinelander
Rheinland-Pfalz NT Rhineland-Palatinate
Rhesusfaktor ['re:zusfaktɔr] M rhesus factor
Rhetorik [re'to:rɪk] F rhetoric
rhetorisch [re'to:rɪʃ] ADJ rhetorical
Rheuma ['rɔyma] (**-s**) NT rheumatism
Rheumatismus [rɔyma'tɪsmʊs] M rheumatism
Rhinozeros [ri'no:tserɔs] (- *od* **-ses, -se**) NT rhinoceros; (*umg: Dummkopf*) fool
Rhld. ABK = **Rheinland**
Rhodesien [ro'de:ziən] (**-s**) NT Rhodesia
Rhodos ['ro:dɔs] (-) NT Rhodes
rhythmisch ['rytmɪʃ] ADJ rhythmical
Rhythmus M rhythm
RIAS ['ri:as] (-) M ABK (= *Rundfunk im amerikanischen Sektor (Berlin)*) *broadcasting station in the former American sector of Berlin*
Richtantenne ['rɪçtlantɛnə] (-, **-n**) F directional aerial (*bes* BRIT) *od* antenna
richten ['rɪçtən] VT to direct; (*Waffe*) to aim; (*einstellen*) to adjust; (*instand setzen*) to repair; (*zurechtmachen*) to prepare, to get ready; (*adressieren: Briefe, Anfragen*) to address; (*Bitten, Forderungen*) to make; (*in Ordnung bringen*) to do, to fix; (*bestrafen*) to pass judgement on ▸ VR: **sich ~ nach** to go by; **~ an** +*akk* to direct at; (*fig*) to direct to; (*Briefe etc*) to address to; (*Bitten etc*) to make to; **~ auf** +*akk* to aim at; **wir ~ uns ganz nach unseren Kunden** we are guided entirely by our customers' wishes
Richter(in) (**-s, -**) M(F) judge; **sich zum ~ machen** (*fig*) to set (o.s.) up in judgement;
richterlich ADJ judicial
Richtgeschwindigkeit F recommended speed
richtig ADJ right, correct; (*echt*) proper ▸ ADV correctly, right; (*umg: sehr*) really; **der/die Richtige** the right one *od* person; **das Richtige** the right thing; **die Uhr geht ~** the clock is right; **Richtigkeit** F correctness; **das hat schon seine Richtigkeit** it's right enough; **richtigstellen** VT to correct; **Richtigstellung** F correction, rectification
Richt- ZW: **Richtlinie** F guideline; **Richtpreis** M recommended price; **Richtschnur** F (*fig: Grundsatz*) guiding principle
Richtung F direction; (*Tendenz*) tendency, orientation; **in jeder ~** each way
Richtungsstreit M (*Pol*) factional dispute
Richtungstaste F arrow key
richtungweisend ADJ: **~ sein** to point the way (ahead)
rieb *etc* [ri:p] VB *siehe* **reiben**
riechen ['ri:çən] *unreg* VT, VI to smell; **an etw** *dat* **~** to smell sth; **es riecht nach Gas** there's a smell of gas; **ich kann das/ihn nicht ~** (*umg*) I can't stand it/him; **das konnte ich doch nicht ~!** (*umg*) how was I (supposed) to know?
Riecher (**-s, -**) M: **einen guten** *od* **den richtigen ~ für etw haben** (*umg*) to have a nose for sth
Ried [ri:t] (**-(e)s, -e**) NT reed; (*Moor*) marsh
rief *etc* [ri:f] VB *siehe* **rufen**
Riege ['ri:gə] (-, **-n**) F team, squad
Riegel ['ri:gəl] (**-s, -**) M bolt, bar; **einer Sache** *dat* **einen ~ vorschieben** (*fig*) to clamp down on sth
Riemen ['ri:mən] (**-s, -**) M strap; (*Gürtel, Tech*) belt; (*Naut*) oar; **sich am ~ reißen** (*fig: umg*) to get a grip on o.s.; **Riemenantrieb** M belt drive
Riese ['ri:zə] (**-n, -n**) M giant
rieseln VI to trickle; (*Schnee*) to fall gently
Riesen- ZW: **Riesenerfolg** M enormous success; **Riesengebirge** NT (*Geog*) Sudeten Mountains *pl*; **riesengroß** ADJ, **riesenhaft** ADJ colossal, gigantic, huge; **Riesenrad** NT big *od* Ferris wheel; **Riesenschritt** M: **sich mit Riesenschritten nähern** (*fig*) to be drawing on apace; **Riesenslalom** M (*Ski*) giant slalom
riesig ['ri:zɪç] ADJ enormous, huge, vast
Riesin F giantess
riet *etc* [ri:t] VB *siehe* **raten**
Riff [rɪf] (**-(e)s, -e**) NT reef
rigoros [rigo'ro:s] ADJ rigorous
Rille ['rɪlə] (-, **-n**) F groove
Rind [rɪnt] (**-(e)s, -er**) NT cow; (*Bulle*) bull; (*Koch*) beef; **Rinder** PL cattle *pl*; **vom ~** beef
Rinde ['rɪndə] (-, **-n**) F rind; (*Baumrinde*) bark; (*Brotrinde*) crust
Rinderbraten M roast beef
Rinderwahn ['rɪndərva:n] M mad cow disease
Rindfleisch NT beef
Rindvieh NT cattle *pl*; (*umg*) blockhead, stupid oaf
Ring [rɪŋ] (**-(e)s, -e**) M ring; **Ringbuch** NT ring binder
ringeln ['rɪŋəln] VT (*Pflanze*) to (en)twine; (*Schwanz etc*) to curl ▸ VR to go curly, to curl; (*Rauch*) to curl up(wards)
Ringelnatter F grass snake

r

Ringeltaube F wood pigeon
ringen *unreg* VI to wrestle; **nach** *od* **um etw ~** (*streben*) to struggle for sth; **Ringen (-s)** NT wrestling
Ringer (-s, -) M wrestler
Ring- zW: **Ringfinger** M ring finger; **ringförmig** ADJ ring-shaped; **Ringkampf** M wrestling bout; **Ringrichter** M referee
rings ADV: **~ um** round; **ringsherum** ADV round about
Ringstraße F ring road
ringsum [rɪŋs'ʊm], **ringsumher** ['rɪŋsʊm'he:r] ADV (*rundherum*) round about; (*überall*) all round
Rinne ['rɪnə] (-, **-n**) F gutter, drain
rinnen *unreg* VI to run, to trickle
Rinnsal (-s, -e) NT trickle of water
Rinnstein M gutter
Rippchen ['rɪpçən] NT small rib; (*Koch*) cutlet
Rippe ['rɪpə] (-, **-n**) F rib
Rippen- zW: **Rippenfellentzündung** F pleurisy; **Rippenspeer** M OD NT (*Koch*): **Kasseler Rippenspeer** *slightly cured pork spare rib*; **Rippenstoß** M dig in the ribs
Risiko ['ri:ziko] (**-s, -s** *od* **Risiken**) NT risk; **risikobehaftet** ADJ fraught with risk; **Risikoinvestition** F sunk cost
riskant [rɪs'kant] ADJ risky, hazardous
riskieren [rɪs'ki:rən] VT to risk
riss *etc* [rɪs] VB *siehe* **reißen**
Riss (-es, -e) M tear; (*in Mauer, Tasse etc*) crack; (*in Haut*) scratch; (*Tech*) design
rissig ['rɪsɪç] ADJ torn; (*Mauer*) cracked; (*Haut*) scratched
ritt *etc* [rɪt] VB *siehe* **reiten**
Ritt (-(e)s, -e) M ride
Ritter (-s, -) M knight; **jdn zum ~ schlagen** to knight sb; **arme ~** *pl* (*Koch*) *sweet French toast, made with bread soaked in milk*; **ritterlich** ADJ chivalrous; **Ritterschlag** M knighting; **Rittertum (-s)** NT chivalry; **Ritterzeit** F age of chivalry
rittlings ADV astride
Ritual [ritu'a:l] (**-s, -e** *od* **-ien**) NT (*lit, fig*) ritual
rituell [ritu'ɛl] ADJ ritual
Ritus ['ri:tʊs] (-, **Riten**) M rite
Ritze ['rɪtsə] (-, **-n**) F crack, chink
ritzen VT to scratch; **die Sache ist geritzt** (*umg*) it's all fixed up
Rivale [ri'va:lə] (**-n, -n**) M, **Rivalin** F rival
rivalisieren [rivali'zi:rən] VI: **mit jdm ~** to compete with sb
Rivalität [rivali'tɛ:t] F rivalry
Riviera [rivi'e:ra] (-) F Riviera
Rizinusöl ['ri:tsinʊsløːl] NT castor oil
r.-k. ABK (= *römisch-katholisch*) R.C.
Robbe ['rɔbə] (-, **-n**) F seal
robben ['rɔbən] VI (*Hilfsverb sein: auch Mil*) to crawl (*using elbows*)
Robbenfang M seal hunting
Robe ['ro:bə] (-, **-n**) F robe
Roboter ['rɔbɔtər] (**-s, -**) M robot; **Robotertechnik** F robotics *sing*
Robotik ['rɔbɔtɪk] F robotics *sing*
robust [ro'bʊst] ADJ (*Mensch, Gesundheit*) robust; (*Material*) tough
roch *etc* [rɔx] VB *siehe* **riechen**
Rochade [rɔ'xa:də] (-, **-n**) F (*Schach*): **die kleine/große ~** castling king's side/queen's side
röcheln ['rœçəln] VI to wheeze; (*Sterbender*) to give the death rattle
Rock[1] [rɔk] (**-(e)s, Röcke**) M skirt; (*Jackett*) jacket; (*Uniformrock*) tunic
Rock[2] [rɔk] (**-(s), -(s)**) M (*Mus*) rock; **Rockmusik** F rock music
Rockzipfel M: **an Mutters ~ hängen** (*umg*) to cling to (one's) mother's skirts
Rodel ['ro:dəl] (**-s, -**) M toboggan; **Rodelbahn** F toboggan run
rodeln VI to toboggan
roden ['ro:dən] VT, VI to clear
Rogen ['ro:gən] (**-s, -**) M roe
Roggen ['rɔgən] (**-s, -**) M rye; **Roggenbrot** NT rye bread; (*Vollkornbrot*) black bread
roh [ro:] ADJ raw; (*Mensch*) coarse, crude; **rohe Gewalt** brute force; **Rohbau** M shell of a building; **Roheisen** NT pig iron; **Rohfassung** rough draft; **Rohkost** F raw fruit and vegetables *pl*; **Rohling** M ruffian; **Rohmaterial** NT raw material; **Rohöl** NT crude oil
Rohr [ro:r] (**-(e)s, -e**) NT pipe, tube; (*Bot*) cane; (*Schilf*) reed; (*Gewehrrohr*) barrel; **Rohrbruch** M burst pipe
Röhre ['rø:rə] (-, **-n**) F tube, pipe; (*Rundf etc*) valve; (*Backröhre*) oven
Rohr- zW: **Rohrgeflecht** NT wickerwork; **Rohrleger (-s, -)** M plumber; **Rohrleitung** F pipeline; **Rohrpost** F pneumatic post; **Rohrspatz** M: **schimpfen wie ein Rohrspatz** (*umg*) to curse and swear; **Rohrstock** M cane; **Rohrstuhl** M basket chair; **Rohrzucker** M cane sugar
Rohseide F raw silk
Rohstoff M raw material
Rokoko ['rɔkoko] (**-s**) NT rococo
Rolladen M *siehe* **Rollladen**
Rollbahn F (*Aviat*) runway
Rollbrett NT skateboard
Rolle ['rɔlə] (-, **-n**) F roll; (*Theat, Soziologie*) role; (*Garnrolle etc*) reel, spool; (*Walze*) roller; (*Wäscherolle*) mangle, wringer; **bei** *od* **in etw** *dat* **eine ~ spielen** to play a part in sth; **aus der ~ fallen** (*fig*) to forget o.s.; **keine ~ spielen** not to matter
rollen VI to roll; (*Aviat*) to taxi ▶ VT to roll; (*Wäsche*) to mangle, to put through the wringer; **den Stein ins R~ bringen** (*fig*) to start the ball rolling
Rollen- zW: **Rollenbesetzung** F (*Theat*) cast; **Rollenkonflikt** M (*Psych*) role conflict; **Rollenspiel** NT role-play; **Rollentausch** M exchange of roles; (*Soziologie*) role reversal
Roller (-s, -) M scooter; (*Welle*) roller
Roll- zW: **Rollfeld** NT runway; **Rollkragen** M roll *od* polo neck; **Rollladen** M shutter; **Rollmops** M pickled herring
Rollo ['rɔlo] (**-, -s**) NT (roller) blind

Roll- zW: **Rollschrank** M roll-fronted cupboard; **Rollschuh** M roller skate; **Rollschuhlaufen** NT roller skating; **Rollsplitt** M grit; **Rollstuhl** M wheelchair; **Rolltreppe** F escalator
Rom [ro:m] (**-s**) NT Rome; **das sind Zustände wie im alten ~** (*umg: unmoralisch*) it's disgraceful; (*: primitiv*) it's medieval (*umg*)
röm. ABK = **römisch**
Roman [ro'ma:n] (**-s, -e**) M novel; **(jdm) einen ganzen ~ erzählen** (*umg*) to give (sb) a long rigmarole; **Romanheft** NT pulp novel
romanisch ADJ (*Volk, Sprache*) Romance; (*Kunst*) Romanesque
Romanistik [roma'nɪstɪk] F (*Univ*) Romance languages and literature
Romanschreiber M novelist
Romanschriftsteller M novelist
Romantik [ro'mantɪk] F romanticism
Romantiker(in) (**-s, -**) M(F) romanticist
romantisch ADJ romantic
Romanze [ro'mantsə] (**-, -n**) F romance
Römer ['rø:mər] (**-s, -**) M wineglass; (*Mensch*) Roman; **Römertopf**® M (*Koch*) ≈ (chicken) brick
römisch ['rø:mɪʃ] ADJ Roman; **römisch-katholisch** ADJ Roman Catholic
röm.-kath. ABK (= *römisch-katholisch*) R.C.
Rommé, Rommee [rɔ'me:] (**-s, -s**) NT rummy
röntgen ['rœntgən] VT to X-ray; **Röntgenaufnahme** F X-ray; **Röntgenbild** NT X-ray; **Röntgenstrahlen** PL X-rays *pl*
rosa ['ro:za] ADJ *unver* pink, rose(-coloured)
Rose ['ro:zə] (**-, -n**) F rose
Rosé [ro'ze:] (**-s, -s**) M rosé
Rosenkohl M Brussels sprouts *pl*
Rosenkranz M rosary
Rosenmontag M Monday of Shrovetide; *siehe auch* **Karneval**
Rosette [ro'zɛtə] F rosette
rosig ['ro:zɪç] ADJ rosy
Rosine [ro'zi:nə] F raisin; **(große) Rosinen im Kopf haben** (*umg*) to have big ideas
Rosmarin ['ro:smari:n] (**-s**) M rosemary
Ross [rɔs] (**-es, -e**) NT horse, steed; **auf dem hohen ~ sitzen** (*fig*) to be on one's high horse; **Rosskastanie** F horse chestnut; **Rosskur** (*umg*) F kill-or-cure remedy
Rost [rɔst] (**-(e)s, -e**) M rust; (*Gitter*) grill, gridiron; (*Bettrost*) springs *pl*; **Rostbraten** M roast(ed) meat, roast; **Rostbratwurst** F grilled *od* barbecued sausage
rosten VI to rust
rösten ['rø:stən] VT to roast; (*Brot*) to toast
rostfrei ADJ (*Stahl*) stainless
rostig ADJ rusty
Röstkartoffeln PL fried potatoes *pl*
Rostschutz M rustproofing
rot [ro:t] ADJ red; **~ werden, einen roten Kopf bekommen** to blush, to go red; **die Rote Armee** the Red Army; **das Rote Kreuz** the Red Cross; **das Rote Meer** the Red Sea
Rotation [rotatsi'o:n] F rotation
rot- zW: **rotbäckig** ADJ red-cheeked; **Rotbarsch** M rosefish; **rotblond** ADJ strawberry blond
Röte ['rø:tə] (**-**) F redness
Röteln PL German measles *sing*
röten VT, VR to redden
rothaarig ADJ red-haired
rotieren [ro'ti:rən] VI to rotate
Rot- zW: **Rotkäppchen** NT Little Red Riding Hood; **Rotkehlchen** NT robin; **Rotkohl** M red cabbage; **Rotkraut** NT red cabbage; **rotsehen** (*umg*) *unreg* VI to see red, to become angry; **Rotstift** M red pencil; **Rotwein** M red wine
Rotz [rɔts] (**-es, -e**) (*umg*) M snot; **rotzfrech** (*umg*) ADJ cocky; **rotznäsig** (*umg*) ADJ snotty-nosed
Rouge [ru:ʒ] (**-s, -s**) NT rouge
Roulade [ru'la:də] (**-, -n**) F (*Koch*) beef olive
Roulette, Roulett [ru'lɛt] (**-s, -s**) NT roulette
Route ['ru:tə] (**-, -n**) F route
Routine [ru'ti:nə] F experience; (*Gewohnheit*) routine
routiniert [ruti'ni:ərt] ADJ experienced
Rowdy ['raʊdɪ] (**-s, -s**) M hooligan; (*zerstörerisch*) vandal; (*lärmend*) rowdy (type)
Ruanda [ru'anda] NT Rwanda
ruandisch ADJ Rwandan
rubbeln ['rʊbəln] (*umg*) VT, VI to rub
Rübe ['ry:bə] (**-, -n**) F turnip; **Gelbe ~** carrot; **Rote ~** beetroot (BRIT), beet (US)
Rübenzucker M beet sugar
Rubin [ru'bi:n] (**-s, -e**) M ruby
Rubrik [ru'bri:k] F heading; (*Spalte*) column
ruck ADV: **das geht ~, zuck** it won't take a second
Ruck [rʊk] (**-(e)s, -e**) M jerk, jolt; **sich** *dat* **einen ~ geben** (*fig: umg*) to make an effort
Rückantwort F reply, answer; **um ~ wird gebeten** please reply
ruckartig ADJ: **er stand ~ auf** he shot to his feet
Rück- zW: **Rückbesinnung** F recollection; **rückbezüglich** ADJ reflexive; **Rückblende** F flashback; **rückblenden** VI to flash back; **Rückblick** M: **im Rückblick auf etw** *akk* looking back on sth; **rückblickend** ADJ retrospective ▸ ADV in retrospect; **rückdatieren** VT to backdate
rücken VT, VI to move
Rücken (**-s, -**) M back; (*Bergrücken*) ridge; **jdm in den ~ fallen** (*fig*) to stab sb in the back; **Rückendeckung** F backing; **Rückenlage** F supine position; **Rückenlehne** F back (of chair); **Rückenmark** NT spinal cord; **Rückenschmerzen** PL backache *sing*; **Rückenschwimmen** NT backstroke; **Rückenstärkung** F (*fig*) moral support; **Rückenwind** M following wind
Rück- zW: **Rückerstattung** F refund; **Rückfahrkarte** F return ticket (BRIT), round-trip ticket (US); **Rückfahrt** F return journey; **Rückfall** M relapse; **rückfällig** ADJ relapsed; **rückfällig werden** to relapse; **Rückflug** M return flight; **Rückfrage** F question; **nach Rückfrage bei der zuständigen Behörde …** after checking this with the appropriate authority …;

r

rückfragen VI to inquire; (*nachprüfen*) to check; **Rückführung** F (*von Menschen*) repatriation, return; **Rückgabe** F return; **gegen Rückgabe** (+*gen*) on return (of); **Rückgang** M decline, fall; **rückgängig** ADJ: **etw rückgängig machen** (*widerrufen*) to undo sth; (*Bestellung*) to cancel sth; **Rückgewinnung** F recovery; (*von Land, Gebiet*) reclaiming; (*aus verbrauchten Stoffen*) recycling
Rückgrat NT spine, backbone
Rück- zW: **Rückgriff** M recourse; **Rückhalt** M backing; (*Einschränkung*) reserve; **rückhaltlos** ADJ unreserved; **Rückhand** F (*Sport*) backhand; **rückkaufbar** ADJ redeemable; **Rückkehr** (**-, -en**) F return; **Rückkoppelung** F feedback; **Rücklage** F reserve, savings *pl*; **Rücklauf** M reverse running; (*beim Tonband*) rewind; (*von Maschinenteil*) return travel; **rückläufig** ADJ declining, falling; **eine rückläufige Entwicklung** a decline; **Rücklicht** NT rear light; **rücklings** ADV from behind; (*rückwärts*) backwards; **Rückmeldung** F (*Univ*) reregistration; **Rücknahme** (**-, -n**) F taking back; **Rückporto** NT return postage; **Rückreise** F return journey; (*Naut*) home voyage; **Rückruf** M recall
Rucksack [ˈrʊkzak] M rucksack
Rück- zW: **Rückschau** F reflection; **rückschauend** ADJ = **rückblickend**; **Rückschlag** M setback; **Rückschluss** M conclusion; **Rückschritt** M retrogression; **rückschrittlich** ADJ reactionary; (*Entwicklung*) retrograde; **Rückseite** F back; (*hinterer Teil*) rear; (*von Münze etc*) reverse; **siehe Rückseite** see over(leaf); **rücksetzen** VT (*Comput*) to reset
Rücksicht F consideration; **~ nehmen auf** +*akk* to show consideration for; **Rücksichtnahme** F consideration
rücksichtslos ADJ inconsiderate; (*Fahren*) reckless; (*unbarmherzig*) ruthless
Rücksichtslosigkeit F lack of consideration; (*beim Fahren*) recklessness; (*Unbarmherzigkeit*) ruthlessness
rücksichtsvoll ADJ considerate
Rück- zW: **Rücksitz** M back seat; **Rückspiegel** M (*Aut*) rear-view mirror; **Rückspiel** NT return match; **Rücksprache** F further discussion *od* talk; **Rücksprache mit jdm nehmen** to confer with sb; **Rückstand** M arrears *pl*; (*Verzug*) delay; **im Rückstand sein mit** (*Arbeit, Miete*) to be behind with; **rückständig** ADJ backward, out-of-date; (*Zahlungen*) in arrears; **Rückstau** M (*Aut*) tailback (BRIT), line of cars; **Rückstoß** M recoil; **Rückstrahler** (**-s, -**) M rear reflector; **Rückstrom** M (*von Menschen, Fahrzeugen*) return; **Rücktaste** F (*an Schreibmaschine*) backspace key; **Rücktritt** M resignation; **Rücktrittbremse** F backpedal brake; **Rücktrittsklausel** F (*Vertrag*) escape clause; **Rückvergütung** F repayment; (*Comm*) refund; **rückversichern** VT, VI to reinsure ▶ VR to check (up *od* back); **Rückversicherung** F reinsurance; **rückwärtig** ADJ rear; **rückwärts** ADV backward(s), back; **Rückwärtsgang** M (*Aut*) reverse gear; **im Rückwärtsgang fahren** to reverse; **Rückweg** M return journey, way back; **rückwirkend** ADJ retroactive; **Rückwirkung** F repercussion; **eine Zahlung mit Rückwirkung vom ...** a payment backdated to ...; **eine Gesetzesänderung mit Rückwirkung vom ...** an amendment made retrospective to ...; **Rückzahlung** F repayment; **Rückzieher** (*umg*) M: **einen Rückzieher machen** to back out; **Rückzug** M retreat; **Rückzugsgefecht** NT (*Mil, fig*) rearguard action
rüde [ˈryːdə] ADJ blunt, gruff
Rüde (**-n, -n**) M male dog
Rudel [ˈruːdəl] (**-s, -**) NT pack; (*von Hirschen*) herd
Ruder [ˈruːdər] (**-s, -**) NT oar; (*Steuer*) rudder; **das ~ fest in der Hand haben** (*fig*) to be in control of the situation; **Ruderboot** NT rowing boat; **Ruderer** (**-s, -**) M rower, oarsman
rudern VT, VI to row; **mit den Armen ~** (*fig*) to flail one's arms about
Ruf [ruːf] (**-(e)s, -e**) M call, cry; (*Ansehen*) reputation; (*Univ: Berufung*) offer of a chair
rufen *unreg* VT, VI to call; (*ausrufen*) to cry; **um Hilfe ~** to call for help; **das kommt mir wie gerufen** that's just what I needed
Rüffel [ˈrʏfəl] (**-s, -**) (*umg*) M telling-off, ticking-off
Ruf- zW: **Rufmord** M character assassination; **Rufname** M usual (first) name; **Rufnummer** F (tele)phone number; **Rufsäule** F (*für Taxi*) telephone; (*an Autobahn*) emergency telephone; **Rufzeichen** NT (*Rundf*) call sign; (*Tel*) ringing tone
Rüge [ˈryːgə] (**-, -n**) F reprimand, rebuke
rügen VT to reprimand
Ruhe [ˈruːə] (**-**) F rest; (*Ungestörtheit*) peace, quiet; (*Gelassenheit, Stille*) calm; (*Schweigen*) silence; **~!** be quiet!, silence!; **angenehme ~!** sleep well!; **~ bewahren** to stay cool *od* calm; **das lässt ihm keine ~** he can't stop thinking about it; **sich zur ~ setzen** to retire; **die ~ weghaben** (*umg*) to be unflappable; **immer mit der ~** (*umg*) don't panic; **lass mich in ~!** leave me alone; **die letzte ~ finden** (*liter*) to be laid to rest; **Ruhelage** F (*von Mensch*) reclining position; (*Med: bei Bruch*) immobile position; **ruhelos** ADJ restless
ruhen VI to rest; (*Verkehr*) to cease; (*Arbeit*) to stop, to cease; (*Waffen*) to be laid down; (*begraben sein*) to lie, to be buried
Ruhe- zW: **Ruhepause** F break; **Ruheplatz** M resting place; **Ruhestand** M retirement; **Ruhestätte** F: **letzte Ruhestätte** final resting place; **Ruhestörung** F breach of the peace; **Ruhetag** M closing day
ruhig [ˈruːɪç] ADJ quiet; (*bewegungslos*) still; (*Hand*) steady; (*gelassen, friedlich*) calm; (*Gewissen*) clear; **tu das ~** feel free to do that; **etw ~ mit ansehen** (*gleichgültig*) to stand by and watch sth; **du könntest ~ mal etwas für mich tun!** it's about time you did something for me!
Ruhm [ruːm] (**-(e)s**) M fame, glory
rühmen [ˈryːmən] VT to praise ▶ VR to boast

rühmlich ADJ praiseworthy; (*Ausnahme*) notable
ruhmlos ADJ inglorious
ruhmreich ADJ glorious
Ruhr [ru:r] (-) F dysentery
Rührei ['ry:rlaɪ] NT scrambled egg
rühren VT (*lit, fig*) to move, to stir (*auch Koch*) ▸ VR (*lit, fig*) to move, to stir ▸ VI: **~ von** to come *od* stem from; **~ an** *+akk* to touch; (*fig*) to touch on
rührend ADJ touching, moving; **das ist ~ von Ihnen** that is sweet of you
Ruhrgebiet NT Ruhr (area)
rührig ADJ active, lively
rührselig ADJ sentimental, emotional
Rührung F emotion
Ruin [ru'i:n] (**-s**) M ruin; **vor dem ~ stehen** to be on the brink *od* verge of ruin
Ruine (**-, -n**) F (*lit, fig*) ruin
ruinieren [rui'ni:rən] VT to ruin
rülpsen ['rʏlpsən] VI to burp, to belch
rum (*umg*) ADV = **herum**
Rum [rʊm] (**-s, -s**) M rum
Rumäne [ru'mɛ:nə] (**-n, -n**) M Romanian
Rumänien (**-s**) NT Romania
Rumänin F Romanian
rumänisch ADJ Romanian
rumfuhrwerken ['rʊmfu:rvɛrkən] (*umg*) VT to bustle around
Rummel ['rʊməl] (**-s**) (*umg*) M (*Trubel*) hustle and bustle; (*Jahrmarkt*) fair; (*Medienrummel*) hype; **Rummelplatz** M fairground, fair
rumoren [ru'mo:rən] VI to be noisy, to make a noise
Rumpelkammer ['rʊmpəlkamər] F junk room
rumpeln VI to rumble; (*holpern*) to jolt
Rumpf [rʊmpf] (**-(e)s, Rümpfe**) M trunk, torso; (*Aviat*) fuselage; (*Naut*) hull
rümpfen ['rʏmpfən] VT (*Nase*) to turn up
Rumtopf M *soft fruit in rum*
rund [rʊnt] ADJ round ▸ ADV (*etwa*) around; **~ um etw** round sth; **jetzt gehts ~** (*umg*) this is where the fun starts; **wenn er das erfährt, gehts ~** (*umg*) there'll be a to-do when he finds out; **Rundbogen** M Norman *od* Romanesque arch; **Rundbrief** M circular
Runde ['rʊndə] (**-, -n**) F round; (*in Rennen*) lap; (*Gesellschaft*) circle; **die ~ machen** to do the rounds; (*herumgegeben werden*) to be passed round; **über die Runden kommen** (*Sport, fig*) to pull through; **eine ~ spendieren** *od* **schmeißen** (*umg*: *Getränke*) to stand a round
runden VT to make round ▸ VR (*fig*) to take shape
rund- ZW: **runderneuert** ADJ (*Reifen*) remoulded (BRIT), remolded (US); **Rundfahrt** F (round) trip; **Rundfrage** F: **Rundfrage (unter** *+dat*) survey (of)
Rundfunk ['rʊntfʊŋk] (**-(e)s**) M broadcasting; (*bes Hörfunk*) radio; (*Rundfunkanstalt*) broadcasting corporation; **im ~** on the radio; **Rundfunkanstalt** F broadcasting corporation; **Rundfunkempfang** M reception; **Rundfunkgebühr** F licence (BRIT), license (US); **Rundfunkgerät** NT radio set; **Rundfunksendung** F broadcast, radio programme (BRIT) *od* program (US)
Rund- ZW: **Rundgang** M (*Spaziergang*) walk; (*von Wachmann*) rounds *pl*; (*von Briefträger etc*) round; (*zur Besichtigung*): **Rundgang (durch)** tour (of); **rundheraus** ADV straight out, bluntly; **rundherum** ADV all round; (*fig*: *umg*: *völlig*) totally; **rundlich** ADJ plump, rounded; **Rundreise** F round trip; **Rundschreiben** NT (*Comm*) circular; **rundum** ADV all around; (*fig*) completely
Rundung F curve, roundness
rundweg ADV straight out
runter ['rʊntər] (*umg*) ADV = **herunter**; **hinunter**; **runterwürgen** (*umg*) VT (*Ärger*) to swallow
Runzel ['rʊntsəl] (**-, -n**) F wrinkle
runzelig, runzlig ADJ wrinkled
runzeln VT to wrinkle; **die Stirn ~** to frown
Rüpel ['ry:pəl] (**-s, -**) M lout; **rüpelhaft** ADJ loutish
rupfen ['rʊpfən] VT to pluck
Rupfen (**-s, -**) M sackcloth
ruppig ['rʊpɪç] ADJ rough, gruff
Rüsche ['ry:ʃə] (**-, -n**) F frill
Ruß [ru:s] (**-es**) M soot
Russe ['rʊsə] (**-n, -n**) M Russian
Rüssel ['rʏsəl] (**-s, -**) M snout; (*Elefantenrüssel*) trunk
rußen VI to smoke; (*Ofen*) to be sooty
rußig ADJ sooty
Russin F Russian
russisch ADJ Russian; **russische Eier** (*Koch*) egg(s) mayonnaise
Russland (**-s**) NT Russia
rüsten ['rʏstən] VT, VI, VR to prepare; (*Mil*) to arm
rüstig ['rʏstɪç] ADJ sprightly, vigorous; **Rüstigkeit** F sprightliness, vigour (BRIT), vigor (US)
rustikal [rʊsti'ka:l] ADJ: **sich ~ einrichten** to furnish one's home in a rustic style
Rüstung ['rʏstʊŋ] F preparation; (*Mil*) arming; (*Ritterrüstung*) armour (BRIT), armor (US); (*Waffen etc*) armaments *pl*
Rüstungs- ZW: **Rüstungsgegner** M opponent of the arms race; **Rüstungsindustrie** F armaments industry; **Rüstungskontrolle** F arms control; **Rüstungswettlauf** M arms race
Rüstzeug NT tools *pl*; (*fig*) capacity
Rute ['ru:tə] (**-, -n**) F rod, switch
Rutsch [rʊtʃ] (**-(e)s, -e**) M slide; (*Erdrutsch*) landslide; **guten ~!** (*umg*) have a good New Year!; **Rutschbahn** F slide
rutschen VI to slide; (*ausrutschen*) to slip; **auf dem Stuhl hin und her ~** to fidget around on one's chair
rutschfest ADJ non-slip
rutschig ADJ slippery
rütteln ['rʏtəln] VT, VI to shake, to jolt; **daran ist nicht zu ~** (*fig*: *umg*: *an Grundsätzen*) there's no doubt about that
Rüttelschwelle F (*Aut*) rumble strips *pl*

r

Ss

S¹, s¹ [ɛs] NT S, s; **S wie Samuel** ≈ S for Sugar
s.² ABK (= *Sekunde*) sec.; (= *siehe*) see, vid.
S² [ɛs] ABK (= *Süden*) S; (= *Seite*) p; (= *Schilling*) S
SA (-) F ABK (= *Sturmabteilung*) SA
Sa. ABK = **Samstag**
s. a. ABK (= *siehe auch*) see also
Saal [za:l] (**-(e)s, Säle**) M hall; (*für Sitzungen etc*) room
Saarland ['za:rlant] (**-s**) NT Saarland
Saat [za:t] (**-, -en**) F seed; (*Pflanzen*) crop; (*Säen*) sowing; **Saatgut** NT seed(s *pl*)
Sabbat ['zabat] (**-s, -e**) M sabbath
sabbern ['zabərn] (*umg*) VI to dribble
Säbel ['zɛ:bəl] (**-s, -**) M sabre (BRIT), saber (US); **Säbelrasseln** NT sabre-rattling
Sabotage [zabo'ta:ʒə] (**-, -n**) F sabotage
sabotieren [zabo'ti:rən] VT to sabotage
Saccharin, Sacharin [zaxa'ri:n] (**-s**) NT saccharin
Sachanlagen ['zaxlanla:gən] PL tangible assets *pl*
Sachbearbeiter(in) M(F): **~ (für)** (*Beamter*) official in charge (of)
Sachbuch NT non-fiction book
sachdienlich ADJ relevant, helpful
Sache ['zaxə] (**-, -n**) F thing; (*Angelegenheit*) affair, business; (*Frage*) matter; (*Pflicht*) task; (*Thema*) subject; (*Jur*) case; (*Aufgabe*) job; (*Ideal*) cause; (*umg: km/h*): **mit 60/100 Sachen** ≈ at 40/60 (mph); **ich habe mir die ~ anders vorgestellt** I had imagined things differently; **er versteht seine ~** he knows what he's doing; **das ist so eine ~** (*umg*) it's a bit tricky; **mach keine Sachen!** (*umg*) don't be daft!; **bei der ~ bleiben** (*bei Diskussion*) to keep to the point; **bei der ~ sein** to be with it (*umg*); **das ist ~ der Polizei** this is a matter for the police; **zur ~** to the point; **das ist eine runde ~** that is well-balanced *od* rounded-off
Sachertorte ['zaxərtɔrtə] F *rich chocolate cake*, sachertorte
Sach- zW: **sachgemäß** ADJ appropriate, suitable; **Sachkenntnis** F (*in Bezug auf Wissensgebiet*) knowledge of the/his *etc* subject; (*in Bezug auf Sachlage*) knowledge of the facts; **sachkundig** ADJ (well-)informed; **sich sachkundig machen** to inform oneself; **Sachlage** F situation, state of affairs; **Sachleistung** F payment in kind; **sachlich** ADJ matter-of-fact; (*Kritik etc*) objective; (*Irrtum, Angabe*) factual; **bleiben Sie bitte sachlich** don't get carried away (*umg*); (*nicht persönlich werden*) please stay objective
sächlich ['zɛxlɪç] ADJ neuter
Sachregister NT subject index
Sachschaden M material damage
Sachse ['zaksə] (**-n, -n**) M Saxon
Sachsen (**-s**) NT Saxony; **Sachsen-Anhalt** (**-s**) NT Saxony Anhalt
Sächsin ['zɛksɪn] F Saxon
sächsisch ['zɛksɪʃ] ADJ Saxon
sacht, sachte ADV softly, gently
Sach- zW: **Sachverhalt** (**-(e)s, -e**) M facts *pl* (of the case); **sachverständig** ADJ (*Urteil*) expert; (*Publikum*) informed; **Sachverständige(r)** F(M) expert; **Sachzwang** M force of circumstances
Sack [zak] (**-(e)s, Säcke**) M sack; (*aus Papier, Plastik*) bag; (*Anat, Zool*) sac; (*umg!: Hoden*) balls *pl* (*umg!*); (*: Kerl, Bursche*) bastard (*umg!*); **mit ~ und Pack** (*umg*) with bag and baggage
sacken VI to sag, to sink
Sackgasse F cul-de-sac, dead-end street (US)
Sackhüpfen NT sack race
Sadismus [za'dɪsmʊs] M sadism
Sadist(in) [za'dɪst(ɪn)] M(F) sadist; **sadistisch** ADJ sadistic
Sadomasochismus [zadomazɔ'xɪsmʊs] M sadomasochism
säen ['zɛ:ən] VT, VI to sow; **dünn gesät** (*fig*) thin on the ground, few and far between
Safari [za'fa:ri] (**-, -s**) F safari
Safe [ze:f] (**-s, -s**) M OD NT safe
Saft [zaft] (**-(e)s, Säfte**) M juice; (*Bot*) sap; **ohne ~ und Kraft** (*fig*) wishy-washy (*umg*), effete
saftig ADJ juicy; (*Grün*) lush; (*umg: Rechnung, Ohrfeige*) hefty; (*Brief, Antwort*) hard-hitting
Saftladen (*pej, umg*) M rum joint
saftlos ADJ dry
Sage ['za:gə] (**-, -n**) F saga
Säge ['zɛ:gə] (**-, -n**) F saw; **Sägeblatt** NT saw blade; **Sägemehl** NT sawdust
sagen ['za:gən] VT, VI: **(jdm etw) ~** to say (sth to sb), to tell (sb sth); **unter uns gesagt** between you and me (and the gatepost (*hum umg*)); **lass dir das gesagt sein** take it from me; **das hat nichts zu ~** that doesn't mean anything; **sagt dir der Name etwas?** does the name mean

anything to you?; **das ist nicht gesagt** that's by no means certain; **sage und schreibe** (whether you) believe it or not
sägen VT, VI to saw; (*hum: umg: schnarchen*) to snore, to saw wood (*US*)
sagenhaft ADJ legendary; (*umg*) great, smashing
sagenumwoben ADJ legendary
Sägespäne PL wood shavings *pl*
Sägewerk NT sawmill
sah *etc* [za:] VB *siehe* **sehen**
Sahara [za'ha:ra] F Sahara (Desert)
Sahne ['za:nə] (-) F cream
Saison [zɛ'zõ:] (-, -s) F season
saisonal [zɛzo'na:l] ADJ seasonal
Saisonarbeiter M seasonal worker
saisonbedingt ADJ seasonal
Saite ['zaɪtə] (-, -n) F string; **andere Saiten aufziehen** (*umg*) to get tough
Saiteninstrument NT string(ed) instrument
Sakko ['zako] (-s, -s) M OD NT jacket
Sakrament [zakra'mɛnt] NT sacrament
Sakristei [zakrɪs'taɪ] F sacristy
Salami [za'la:mi] (-, -s) F salami
Salat [za'la:t] (-(e)s, -e) M salad; (*Kopfsalat*) lettuce; **da haben wir den ~!** (*umg*) now we're in a fine mess!; **Salatbesteck** NT salad servers *pl*; **Salatplatte** F salad; **Salatsoße** F salad dressing
Salbe ['zalbə] (-, -n) F ointment
Salbei ['zalbaɪ] (-s) M sage
salben VT to anoint
Salbung F anointing
salbungsvoll ADJ unctuous
saldieren [zal'di:rən] VT (*Comm*) to balance
Saldo ['zaldo] (-s, **Salden**) M balance; **Saldoübertrag** M balance brought *od* carried forward; **Saldovortrag** M balance brought *od* carried forward
Säle ['zɛ:lə] PL *von* **Saal**
Salmiak [zalmi'ak] (-s) M sal ammoniac; **Salmiakgeist** M liquid ammonia
Salmonellen [zalmo'nɛlən] PL salmonellae *pl*
Salon [za'lɔŋ, za'lõ:] (-s, -s) M salon; **Salonlöwe** M lounge lizard
salopp [za'lɔp] ADJ (*Kleidung*) casual; (*Manieren*) slovenly; (*Sprache*) slangy
Salpeter [zal'pe:tər] (-s) M saltpetre (BRIT), saltpeter (*US*); **Salpetersäure** F nitric acid
Salto ['zalto] (-s, -s *od* **Salti**) M somersault
Salut [za'lu:t] (-(e)s, -e) M salute
salutieren [zalu'ti:rən] VI to salute
Salve ['zalvə] (-, -n) F salvo
Salz [zalts] (-es, -e) NT salt; **salzarm** ADJ (*Koch*) low-salt; **Salzbergwerk** NT salt mine
salzen *unreg* VT to salt
salzig ADJ salty
Salz- ZW: **Salzkartoffeln** PL boiled potatoes *pl*; **Salzsäule** F: **zur Salzsäule erstarren** (*fig*) to stand rooted to the spot; **Salzsäure** F hydrochloric acid; **Salzstange** F pretzel stick; **Salzstreuer** M salt cellar; **Salzwasser** NT salt water
Sambia ['zambia] (-s) NT Zambia
sambisch ADJ Zambian
Samen ['za:mən] (-s, -) M seed; (*Anat*) sperm; **Samenbank** F sperm bank; **Samenhandlung** F seed shop
sämig ['zɛ:mɪç] ADJ thick, creamy
Sammel- ZW: **Sammelanschluss** M (*Tel*) private (branch) exchange; (*von Privathäusern*) party line; **Sammelantrag** M composite motion; **Sammelband** M anthology; **Sammelbecken** NT reservoir; (*fig*): **Sammelbecken (von)** melting pot (for); **Sammelbegriff** M collective term; **Sammelbestellung** F collective order; **Sammelbüchse** F collecting tin; **Sammelmappe** F folder
sammeln VT to collect ▶ VR to assemble, to gather; (*sich konzentrieren*) to collect one's thoughts
Sammelname M collective term
Sammelnummer F (*Tel*) private exchange number, switchboard number
Sammelsurium [zaməl'zu:riʊm] NT hotchpotch (BRIT), hodgepodge (*US*)
Sammler(in) (-s, -) M(F) collector
Sammlung ['zamlʊŋ] F collection; (*Konzentration*) composure
Samstag ['zamsta:k] M Saturday; *siehe auch* **Dienstag**
samstags ADV (on) Saturdays
samt [zamt] PRÄP +*dat* (along) with, together with; **~ und sonders** each and every one (of them); **Samt** (-(e)s, -e) M velvet; **in Samt und Seide** (*liter*) in silks and satins
Samthandschuh M: **jdn mit Samthandschuhen anfassen** (*umg*) to handle sb with kid gloves
sämtlich ['zɛmtlɪç] ADJ (*alle*) all (the); (*vollständig*) complete; **Schillers sämtliche Werke** the complete works of Schiller
Sanatorium [zana'to:riʊm] NT sanatorium (BRIT), sanitarium (*US*)
Sand [zant] (-(e)s, -e) M sand; **das/die gibts wie ~ am Meer** (*umg*) there are piles of it/heaps of them; **im Sande verlaufen** to peter out
Sandale [zan'da:lə] (-, -n) F sandal
Sandbank F sandbank
Sandelholz ['zandəlhɔlts] (-es) NT sandalwood
sandig ['zandɪç] ADJ sandy
Sand- ZW: **Sandkasten** M sandpit; **Sandkastenspiele** PL (*Mil*) sand-table exercises *pl*; (*fig*) tactical manoeuvrings *pl* (BRIT) *od* maneuverings *pl* (*US*); **Sandkuchen** M Madeira cake; **Sandmann** M, **Sandmännchen** NT (*in Geschichten*) sandman; **Sandpapier** NT sandpaper; **Sandstein** M sandstone; **sandstrahlen** VT, VI UNTR to sandblast; **Sandstrand** M sandy beach
sandte *etc* ['zantə] VB *siehe* **senden²**
Sanduhr F hourglass; (*Eieruhr*) egg timer
sanft [zanft] ADJ soft, gentle; **sanftmütig** ADJ gentle, meek
sang *etc* [zaŋ] VB *siehe* **singen**
Sänger(in) ['zɛŋər(ɪn)] (-s, -) M(F) singer

S

sang- und klanglos (*umg*) ADV without any ado, quietly
Sani ['zani] (**-s, -s**) (*umg*) M = **Sanitäter**
sanieren [za'niːrən] VT to redevelop; (*Betrieb*) to make financially sound; (*Haus*) to renovate ▶ VR to line one's pockets; (*Unternehmen*) to become financially sound
Sanierung F redevelopment; (*von Haus*) renovation
sanitär [zani'tɛːr] ADJ sanitary; **sanitäre Anlagen** sanitation *sing*
Sanitäter [zani'tɛːtər] (**-s, -**) M first-aid attendant; (*in Krankenwagen*) ambulance man; (*Mil*) (medical) orderly
Sanitätsauto NT ambulance
sank *etc* [zaŋk] VB *siehe* **sinken**
Sanktion [zaŋktsi'oːn] F sanction
sanktionieren [zaŋktsio'niːrən] VT to sanction
sann *etc* [zan] VB *siehe* **sinnen**
Saphir ['zaːfiːr] (**-s, -e**) M sapphire
Sarde ['zardə] (**-n, -n**) M Sardinian
Sardelle [zar'dɛlə] F anchovy
Sardine [zar'diːnə] F sardine
Sardinien [zar'diːniən] (**-s**) NT Sardinia
Sardinier(in) (**-s, -**) M(F) Sardinian
sardinisch ADJ Sardinian
sardisch ADJ Sardinian
Sarg [zark] (**-(e)s, Särge**) M coffin; **Sargnagel** (*umg*) M (*Zigarette*) coffin nail
Sarkasmus [zar'kasmʊs] M sarcasm
sarkastisch [zar'kastɪʃ] ADJ sarcastic
SARS, Sars [zars] ABK (= *Schweres Akutes Respiratorisches Syndrom*) SARS
saß *etc* [zas] VB *siehe* **sitzen**
Satan ['zaːtan] (**-s, -e**) M Satan; (*fig*) devil
Satansbraten M (*hum: umg*) young devil
Satellit [zatɛ'liːt] (**-en, -en**) M satellite
Satelliten- ZW: **Satellitenantenne** F satellite dish; **Satellitenfernsehen** NT satellite television; **Satellitenfoto** NT satellite picture; **Satellitenschüssel** F satellite dish; **Satellitenstation** F space station
Satin [za'tɛ̃ː] (**-s, -s**) M satin
Satire [za'tiːrə] (**-, -n**) F: **~ (auf** *+akk***)** satire (on)
Satiriker [za'tiːrikər] (**-s, -**) M satirist
satirisch [za'tiːrɪʃ] ADJ satirical
satt [zat] ADJ full; (*Farbe*) rich, deep; (*blasiert, übersättigt*) well-fed; (*selbstgefällig*) smug; **jdn/etw ~ sein** to be fed-up with sb/sth; **sich ~ essen** to eat one's fill; **~ machen** to be filling; *siehe auch* **satthaben**; **satthören**; **sattsehen**
Sattel ['zatəl] (**-s, Sättel**) M saddle; (*Berg*) ridge; **sattelfest** ADJ (*fig*) proficient
satteln VT to saddle
Sattelschlepper M articulated lorry (BRIT), artic (BRIT *umg*), semitrailer (US), semi (US *umg*)
Satteltasche F saddlebag; (*Gepäcktasche am Fahrrad*) pannier
satthaben *unreg* VT: **jdn/etw ~** to be fed up with sb/sth
satthören VR: **sich ~ an** *+dat* to hear enough of
sättigen ['zɛtɪgən] VT to satisfy; (*Chem*) to saturate
Sattler (**-s, -**) M saddler; (*Polsterer*) upholsterer
sattsehen *unreg* VT: **sich ~ an** *+dat* to see enough of
Satz [zats] (**-es, Sätze**) M (*Gram*) sentence; (*Nebensatz, Adverbialsatz*) clause; (*Theorem*) theorem; (*der gesetzte Text*) type; (*Mus*) movement; (*Comput*) record; (*Briefmarken, Zusammengehöriges, Tennis*) set; (*Kaffeesatz*) grounds *pl*; (*Bodensatz*) dregs *pl*; (*Spesensatz*) allowance; (*Comm*) rate; (*Sprung*) jump; **Satzbau** M sentence construction; **Satzgegenstand** M (*Gram*) subject; **Satzlehre** F syntax; **Satzteil** M constituent (of a sentence)
Satzung F statute, rule; (*Firma*) (memorandum and) articles of association
satzungsgemäß ADJ statutory
Satzzeichen NT punctuation mark
Sau [zaʊ] (**-, Säue**) F sow; (*umg*) dirty pig; **die ~ rauslassen** (*fig: umg*) to let it all hang out
sauber ['zaʊbər] ADJ clean; (*anständig*) honest, upstanding; (*umg: großartig*) fantastic, great; (*: ironisch*) fine; **~ sein** (*Kind*) to be (potty-)trained; (*Hund etc*) to be house-trained; **~ halten** to keep clean; **~ machen** to clean; **Sauberkeit** F cleanness; (*einer Person*) cleanliness
säuberlich ['zɔʏbərlɪç] ADV neatly
säubern VT to clean; (*Pol etc*) to purge
Säuberung F cleaning; (*Pol etc*) purge
Säuberungsaktion F cleaning-up operation; (*Pol*) purge
saublöd (*umg*) ADJ bloody (BRIT) *od* damn (*umg!*) stupid
Saubohne F broad bean
Sauce ['zoːsə] (**-, -n**) F = **Soße**
Sauciere [zosi'eːrə] (**-, -n**) F sauce boat
Saudi- [zaʊdi-] ZW: **Saudi-Araber(in)** M(F) Saudi; **Saudi-Arabien (-s)** NT Saudi Arabia; **saudi-arabisch** ADJ Saudi(-Arabian)
sauer ['zaʊər] ADJ sour; (*Chem*) acid; (*umg*) cross; **saurer Regen** acid rain; **~ werden** (*Milch, Sahne*) to go sour, to turn; **jdm das Leben ~ machen** to make sb's life a misery; **Sauerbraten** M *braised beef (marinaded in vinegar)*, sauerbraten (US)
Sauerei [zaʊə'raɪ] (*umg*) F rotten state of affairs, scandal; (*Schmutz etc*) mess; (*Unanständigkeit*) obscenity
Sauerkirsche F sour cherry
Sauerkraut (**-(e)s**) NT sauerkraut, pickled cabbage
säuerlich ['zɔʏərlɪç] ADJ sourish, tart
Sauer- ZW: **Sauermilch** F sour milk; **Sauerstoff** M oxygen; **Sauerstoffgerät** NT breathing apparatus; **Sauerteig** M leaven
saufen ['zaʊfən] *unreg* (*umg*) VT, VI to drink, to booze; **wie ein Loch ~** (*umg*) to drink like a fish
Säufer(in) ['zɔʏfər(ɪn)] (**-s, -**) (*umg*) M(F) boozer, drunkard
Sauferei [zaʊfə'raɪ] F drinking, boozing; (*Saufgelage*) booze-up
Saufgelage (*pej, umg*) NT drinking bout, booze-up
säuft [zɔʏft] VB *siehe* **saufen**

saugen ['zaʊgən] *unreg* VT, VI to suck
säugen ['zɔʏgən] VT to suckle
Sauger ['zaʊgər] (**-s, -**) M dummy (BRIT), pacifier (US); (*auf Flasche*) teat; (*Staubsauger*) vacuum cleaner, Hoover® (BRIT)
Säugetier NT mammal
saugfähig ADJ absorbent
Säugling M infant, baby
Säuglingsschwester F infant nurse
Sau- zW: **Sauhaufen** (*umg*) M bunch of layabouts; **saukalt** (*umg*) ADJ bloody (BRIT) *od* damn (*umg!*) cold; **Sauklaue** (*umg*) F scrawl
Säule ['zɔʏlə] (**-, -n**) F column, pillar
Säulengang M arcade
Saum [zaʊm] (**-(e)s, Säume**) M hem; (*Naht*) seam
saumäßig (*umg*) ADJ lousy ▶ ADV lousily
säumen ['zɔʏmən] VT to hem ▶ VI to delay, to hesitate
säumig ['zɔʏmɪç] ADJ (*geh: Schuldner*) defaulting; (*Zahlung*) outstanding, overdue
Sauna ['zaʊna] (**-, -s**) F sauna
Säure ['zɔʏrə] (**-, -n**) F acid; (*Geschmack*) sourness, acidity; **säurebeständig** ADJ acid-proof
Saure-Gurken-Zeit (**-**) F (*hum: umg*) bad time *od* period; (*in den Medien*) silly season
säurehaltig ADJ acidic
Saurier ['zaʊriər] (**-s, -**) M dinosaur
Saus [zaʊs] (**-es**) M: **in ~ und Braus leben** to live like a lord
säuseln ['zɔʏzəln] VI to murmur; (*Blätter*) to rustle ▶ VT to murmur
sausen ['zaʊzən] VI to blow; (*umg: eilen*) to rush; (*Ohren*) to buzz; **etw ~ lassen** (*umg*) not to bother with sth
Sau- zW: **Saustall** (*umg*) M pigsty; **Sauwetter** (*umg*) NT bloody (BRIT) *od* damn (*umg!*) awful weather; **sauwohl** (*umg*) ADJ: **ich fühle mich sauwohl** I feel bloody (BRIT *umg!*) *od* really good
Saxofon, Saxophon [zakso'fo:n] (**-s, -e**) NT saxophone
SB ABK = **Selbstbedienung**
S-Bahn F ABK (= *Schnellbahn*) *high-speed suburban railway or railroad (US)*
SBB ABK (= *Schweizerische Bundesbahnen*) Swiss Railways
s. Br. ABK (= *südlicher Breite*) southern latitude
scannen ['skɛnən] VT to scan
Scanner ['skɛnər] (**-s, -**) M scanner
Schabe ['ʃa:bə] (**-, -n**) F cockroach
schaben VT to scrape
Schaber (**-s, -**) M scraper
Schabernack (**-(e)s, -e**) M trick, prank
schäbig ['ʃɛ:bɪç] ADJ shabby; (*Mensch*) mean; **Schäbigkeit** F shabbiness
Schablone [ʃa'blo:nə] (**-, -n**) F stencil; (*Muster*) pattern; (*fig*) convention
schablonenhaft ADJ stereotyped, conventional
Schach [ʃax] (**-s, -s**) NT chess; (*Stellung*) check; **im ~ stehen** to be in check; **jdn in ~ halten** (*fig*) to stall sb; **Schachbrett** NT chessboard
schachern (*pej*) VI: **um etw ~** to haggle over sth
Schach- zW: **Schachfigur** F chessman; **schachmatt** ADJ checkmate; **jdn schachmatt setzen** (*lit*) to (check)mate sb; (*fig*) to snooker sb (*umg*); **Schachpartie** F game of chess; **Schachspiel** NT game of chess
Schacht [ʃaxt] (**-(e)s, Schächte**) M shaft
Schachtel (**-, -n**) F box; (*pej: Frau*) bag, cow (BRIT); **Schachtelsatz** M complicated *od* multi-clause sentence
Schachzug M (*auch fig*) move
schade ['ʃa:də] ADJ a pity *od* shame ▶ INTERJ (what a) pity *od* shame; **sich** *dat* **für etw zu ~ sein** to consider o.s. too good for sth; **um sie ist es nicht ~** she's no great loss
Schädel ['ʃɛ:dəl] (**-s, -**) M skull; **einen dicken ~ haben** (*fig: umg*) to be stubborn; **Schädelbruch** M fractured skull
schaden ['ʃa:dən] VI +*dat* to hurt; **einer Sache ~** to damage sth; **das schadet nichts** it won't do any harm
Schaden (**-s, Schäden**) M damage; (*Verletzung*) injury; (*Nachteil*) disadvantage; **zu ~ kommen** to suffer; (*physisch*) to be injured; **jdm ~ zufügen** to harm sb
Schaden- zW: **Schadenersatz** M compensation, damages *pl*; **Schadenersatz leisten** to pay compensation; **Schadenersatzanspruch** M claim for compensation; **schadenersatzpflichtig** ADJ liable for damages; **Schadenfreiheitsrabatt** M (*Versicherung*) no-claim(s) bonus; **Schadenfreude** F malicious delight; **schadenfroh** ADJ gloating
schadhaft ['ʃa:thaft] ADJ faulty, damaged
schädigen ['ʃɛdɪgən] VT to damage; (*Person*) to do harm to, to harm
Schädigung F damage; (*von Person*) harm
schädlich ADJ: **~ (für)** harmful (to); **Schädlichkeit** F harmfulness
Schädling M pest
Schädlingsbekämpfungsmittel NT pesticide
schadlos ['ʃa:tlos] ADJ: **sich ~ halten an** +*dat* to take advantage of
Schadprogramm ['ʃa:tprogram] NT (*Comput*) malware
Schadstoff (**-(e)s, -e**) M pollutant; **schadstoffarm** ADJ low in pollutants; **schadstoffhaltig** ADJ containing pollutants
Schaf [ʃa:f] (**-(e)s, -e**) NT sheep; (*umg: Dummkopf*) twit (BRIT), dope; **Schafbock** M ram
Schäfchen ['ʃɛ:fçən] NT lamb; **sein ~ ins Trockene bringen** (*Sprichwort*) to see o.s. all right (*umg*); **Schäfchenwolken** PL cirrus clouds *pl*
Schäfer ['ʃɛ:fər] (**-s, -**) M shepherd; **Schäferhund** M Alsatian (dog) (BRIT), German shepherd (dog) (US); **Schäferin** F shepherdess
schaffen[1] *unreg* VT to create; (*Platz*) to make; **sich** *dat* **etw ~** to get o.s. sth; **dafür ist er wie geschaffen** he's just made for it
schaffen[2] ['ʃafən] VT (*erreichen*) to manage, to do; (*erledigen*) to finish; (*Prüfung*) to pass; (*transportieren*) to take ▶ VI (*tun*) to do; (*umg: arbeiten*) to work; **das ist nicht zu ~** that can't

S

be done; **das hat mich geschafft** it took it out of me; (*nervlich*) it got on top of me; **ich habe damit nichts zu ~** that has nothing to do with me; **jdm (schwer) zu ~ machen** (*zusetzen*) to cause sb (a lot of) trouble; (*bekümmern*) to worry sb (a lot); **sich** *dat* **an etw** *dat* **zu ~ machen** to busy o.s. with sth
Schaffen ['ʃafən] (**-s**) NT (creative) activity
Schaffensdrang M energy; (*von Künstler*) creative urge
Schaffenskraft F creativity
Schaffner(in) ['ʃafnər(ɪn)] (**-s, -**) M(F) (*Busschaffner*) conductor, conductress; (*Eisenb*) guard (BRIT), conductor (US)
Schaffung F creation
Schafskäse M sheep's *od* ewe's milk cheese
Schaft [ʃaft] (**-(e)s, Schäfte**) M shaft; (*von Gewehr*) stock; (*von Stiefel*) leg; (*Bot*) stalk; (*von Baum*) tree trunk; **Schaftstiefel** M high boot
Schakal [ʃa'ka:l] (**-s, -e**) M jackal
Schäker(in) ['ʃɛ:kər(ɪn)] (**-s, -**) M(F) flirt; (*Witzbold*) joker
schäkern VI to flirt; (*Witze machen*) to joke
schal ADJ (*Getränk*) flat; (*fig*) insipid
Schal [ʃa:l] (**-s, -s** *od* **-e**) M scarf
Schälchen ['ʃɛ:lçən] NT bowl
Schale ['ʃa:lə] (**-, -n**) F skin; (*abgeschält*) peel; (*Nussschale, Muschelschale, Eierschale*) shell; (*Geschirr*) dish, bowl; **sich in ~ werfen** (*umg*) to get dressed up
schälen ['ʃɛ:lən] VT to peel; (*Nuss*) to shell ▶ VR to peel
Schalk [ʃalk] (**-s, -e** *od* **Schälke**) M (*veraltet*) joker
Schall [ʃal] (**-(e)s, -e**) M sound; **Name ist ~ und Rauch** what's in a name?; **schalldämmend** ADJ sound-deadening; **Schalldämpfer** M (*Aut*) silencer (BRIT), muffler (US); **schalldicht** ADJ soundproof
schallen VI to (re)sound
schallend ADJ resounding, loud
Schall- ZW: **Schallgeschwindigkeit** F speed of sound; **Schallgrenze** F sound barrier; **Schallmauer** F sound barrier; **Schallplatte** F record
schalt *etc* [ʃalt] VB *siehe* **schelten**
Schaltbild NT circuit diagram
Schaltbrett NT switchboard
schalten ['ʃaltən] VT to switch, to turn ▶ VI (*Aut*) to change (gear); (*umg: begreifen*) to catch on; (*reagieren*) to react; **in Reihe/parallel ~** (*Elek*) to connect in series/in parallel; **~ und walten** to do as one pleases
Schalter (**-s, -**) M counter; (*an Gerät*) switch; **Schalterbeamte(r)** M counter clerk; **Schalterstunden** PL hours of business *pl*
Schalt- ZW: **Schaltfläche** F (*Comput*) button; **Schalthebel** M switch; (*Aut*) gear lever (BRIT), gearshift (US); **Schaltjahr** NT leap year; **Schaltknüppel** M (*Aut*) gear lever (BRIT), gearshift (US); (*Aviat, Comput*) joystick; **Schaltkreis** M (switching) circuit; **Schaltplan** M circuit diagram; **Schaltpult** NT control desk; **Schaltstelle** F (*fig*) coordinating point; **Schaltuhr** F time switch
Schaltung F switching; (*Elek*) circuit; (*Aut*) gear change
Scham [ʃa:m] (**-**) F shame; (*Schamgefühl*) modesty; (*Organe*) private parts *pl*
schämen ['ʃɛ:mən] VR to be ashamed
Scham- ZW: **Schamgefühl** NT sense of shame; **Schamhaare** PL pubic hair *sing*; **schamhaft** ADJ modest; (*verlegen*) bashful; **Schamlippen** PL labia *pl*, lips *pl* of the vulva; **schamlos** ADJ shameless; (*unanständig*) indecent; (*Lüge*) brazen, barefaced
Schampus ['ʃampʊs] (**-,** *no pl*) (*umg*) M champagne, champers (BRIT)
Schande ['ʃandə] (**-**) F disgrace; **zu meiner ~ muss ich gestehen, dass ...** to my shame I have to admit that ...
schänden ['ʃɛndən] VT to violate
Schandfleck ['ʃantflɛk] M: **er war der ~ der Familie** he was the disgrace of his family
schändlich ['ʃɛntlɪç] ADJ disgraceful, shameful; **Schändlichkeit** F disgracefulness, shamefulness
Schandtat (*umg*) F escapade, shenanigan
Schändung F violation, defilement
Schänke ['ʃɛŋkə] (**-, -n**) F = **Schenke**
Schank- ZW: **Schankerlaubnis** F, **Schankkonzession** F (publican's) licence (BRIT), excise license (US); **Schanktisch** M bar
Schanze ['ʃantsə] (**-, -n**) F (*Mil*) fieldwork, earthworks *pl*; (*Sprungschanze*) ski jump
Schar [ʃa:r] (**-, -en**) F band, company; (*Vögel*) flock; (*Menge*) crowd; **in Scharen** in droves
Scharade [ʃa'ra:də] (**-, -n**) F charade
scharen VR to assemble, to rally
scharenweise ADV in droves
scharf [ʃarf] ADJ sharp; (*Verstand, Augen*) keen; (*Kälte, Wind*) biting; (*Protest*) fierce; (*Ton*) piercing, shrill; (*Essen*) hot, spicy; (*Munition*) live; (*Maßnahmen*) severe; (*Bewachung*) close, tight; (*Geruch, Geschmack*) pungent, acrid; (*umg: geil*) randy (BRIT), horny; (*Film*) sexy, blue *attrib*; **~ nachdenken** to think hard; **~ aufpassen/zuhören** to pay close attention/listen closely; **etw ~ einstellen** (*Bild, Diaprojektor etc*) to bring sth into focus; **mit scharfem Blick** (*fig*) with penetrating insight; **auf etw** *akk* **~ sein** (*umg*) to be keen on sth; **scharfe Sachen** (*umg*) hard stuff
Scharfblick M (*fig*) penetration
Schärfe ['ʃɛrfə] (**-, -n**) F sharpness; (*Strenge*) rigour (BRIT), rigor (US); (*an Kamera, Fernsehen*) focus
schärfen VT to sharpen
Schärfentiefe F (*Phot*) depth of focus
Scharf- ZW: **scharfmachen** (*umg*) VT to stir up; **Scharfrichter** M executioner; **Scharfschießen** NT shooting with live ammunition; **Scharfschütze** M marksman, sharpshooter; **Scharfsinn** M astuteness, shrewdness; **scharfsinnig** ADJ astute, shrewd
Scharlach ['ʃarlax] (**-s, -e**) M scarlet; (*Krankheit*)

scarlet fever; **Scharlachfieber** NT scarlet fever
Scharlatan ['ʃarlatan] (**-s, -e**) M charlatan
Scharmützel [ʃar'mʏtsəl] (**-s, -**) NT skirmish
Scharnier [ʃar'ni:r] (**-s, -e**) NT hinge
Schärpe ['ʃɛrpə] (**-, -n**) F sash
scharren ['ʃarən] VT, VI to scrape, to scratch
Scharte ['ʃartə] (**-, -n**) F notch, nick; (*Berg*) wind gap
schartig ['ʃartɪç] ADJ jagged
Schaschlik ['ʃaʃlɪk] (**-s, -s**) M OD NT (shish) kebab
Schatten ['ʃatən] (**-s, -**) M shadow; (*schattige Stelle*) shade; **jdn/etw in den ~ stellen** (*fig*) to put sb/sth in the shade; **Schattenbild** NT silhouette; **schattenhaft** ADJ shadowy
Schattenmorelle (**-, -n**) F morello cherry
Schatten- ZW: **Schattenriss** M silhouette; **Schattenseite** F shady side; (*von Planeten*) dark side; (*fig: Nachteil*) drawback; **Schattenwirtschaft** F black economy
schattieren [ʃa'ti:rən] VT, VI to shade
Schattierung F shading
schattig ['ʃatɪç] ADJ shady
Schatulle [ʃa'tʊlə] (**-, -n**) F casket; (*Geldschatulle*) coffer
Schatz [ʃats] (**-es, Schätze**) M treasure; (*Person*) darling; **Schatzamt** NT treasury
schätzbar ['ʃɛtsba:r] ADJ assessable
Schätzchen NT darling, love
schätzen VT (*abschätzen*) to estimate; (*Gegenstand*) to value; (*würdigen*) to value, to esteem; (*vermuten*) to reckon; **etw zu ~ wissen** to appreciate sth; **sich glücklich ~** to consider o.s. lucky; **~ lernen** to learn to appreciate
Schatzkammer F treasure chamber *od* vault
Schatzmeister M treasurer
Schätzung F estimate; (*das Schätzen*) estimation; (*Würdigung*) valuation; **nach meiner ~ ...** I reckon that ...
schätzungsweise ADV (*ungefähr*) approximately; (*so vermutet man*) it is thought
Schätzwert M estimated value
Schau [ʃaʊ] (**-**) F show; (*Ausstellung*) display, exhibition; **etw zur ~ stellen** to make a show of sth, to show sth off; **eine ~ abziehen** (*umg*) to put on a show; **Schaubild** NT diagram
Schauder ['ʃaʊdər] (**-s, -**) M shudder; (*wegen Kälte*) shiver; **schauderhaft** ADJ horrible
schaudern VI to shudder; (*wegen Kälte*) to shiver
schauen ['ʃaʊən] VI to look; **da schau her!** well, well!
Schauer ['ʃaʊər] (**-s, -**) M (*Regenschauer*) shower; (*Schreck*) shudder; **Schauergeschichte** F horror story; **schauerlich** ADJ horrific, spine-chilling; **Schauermärchen** (*umg*) NT horror story
Schaufel ['ʃaʊfəl] (**-, -n**) F shovel; (*Kehrichtschaufel*) dustpan; (*von Turbine*) vane; (*Naut*) paddle; (*Tech*) scoop
schaufeln VT to shovel; (*Grab, Grube*) to dig ▶ VI to shovel
Schaufenster NT shop window; **Schaufensterauslage** F window display; **Schaufensterbummel** M window-shopping (expedition); **Schaufensterdekorateur(in)** M(F) window dresser; **Schaufensterpuppe** F display dummy
Schaugeschäft NT show business
Schaukasten M showcase
Schaukel ['ʃaʊkəl] (**-, -n**) F swing
schaukeln VI to swing, to rock ▶ VT to rock; **wir werden das Kind *od* das schon ~** (*fig: umg*) we'll manage it
Schaukelpferd NT rocking horse
Schaukelstuhl M rocking chair
Schaulustige(r) ['ʃaʊlʊstɪgə(r)] F(M) onlooker
Schaum [ʃaʊm] (**-(e)s, Schäume**) M foam; (*Seifenschaum*) lather; (*von Getränken*) froth; (*von Bier*) head; **Schaumbad** NT bubble bath
schäumen ['ʃɔymən] VI to foam
Schaumgummi M foam (rubber)
schaumig ADJ frothy, foamy
Schaum- ZW: **Schaumkrone** F whitecap; **Schaumschläger** M (*fig*) windbag; **Schaumschlägerei** F (*fig: umg*) hot air; **Schaumstoff** M foam material; **Schaumwein** M sparkling wine
Schauplatz M scene
Schauprozess M show trial
schaurig ADJ horrific, dreadful
Schauspiel NT spectacle; (*Theat*) play
Schauspieler(in) M(F) actor, actress
schauspielerisch ADJ (*Können, Leistung*) acting
schauspielern VI UNTR to act
Schauspielhaus NT playhouse, theatre (BRIT), theater (US)
Schauspielschule F drama school
Schausteller ['ʃaʊʃtɛlər] (**-s, -**) M *person who owns or runs a fairground ride/sideshow etc*
Scheck [ʃɛk] (**-s, -s**) M cheque (BRIT), check (US); **Scheckbuch** NT, **Scheckheft** NT cheque book (BRIT), check book (US)
scheckig ADJ dappled, piebald
Scheckkarte F cheque (BRIT) *od* check (US) card, banker's card
scheel [ʃe:l] (*umg*) ADJ dirty; **jdn ~ ansehen** to give sb a dirty look
scheffeln ['ʃɛfəln] VT to amass
Scheibe ['ʃaɪbə] (**-, -n**) F disc (BRIT), disk (US); (*Brot etc*) slice; (*Glasscheibe*) pane; (*Mil*) target; (*Eishockey*) puck; (*Töpferscheibe*) wheel; (*umg: Schallplatte*) disc (BRIT), disk (US); **von ihm könntest du dir eine ~ abschneiden** (*fig: umg*) you could take a leaf out of his book
Scheiben- ZW: **Scheibenbremse** F (*Aut*) disc brake; **Scheibenkleister** INTERJ (*euph: umg*) sugar!; **Scheibenwaschanlage** F (*Aut*) windscreen (BRIT) *od* windshield (US) washers *pl*; **Scheibenwischer** M (*Aut*) windscreen (BRIT) *od* windshield (US) wiper
Scheich [ʃaɪç] (**-s, -e** *od* **-s**) M sheik(h)
Scheide ['ʃaɪdə] (**-, -n**) F sheath; (*Anat*) vagina
scheiden *unreg* VT to separate; (*Ehe*) to dissolve ▶ VI to depart; (*sich trennen*) to part ▶ VR (*Wege*) to divide; (*Meinungen*) to diverge; **sich ~ lassen** to get a divorce; **von dem Moment an waren wir (zwei) geschiedene Leute** (*umg*) after that it was the parting of the ways for us; **aus dem**

S

Leben ~ to depart this life
Scheideweg M (*fig*) crossroads *sing*
Scheidung F (*Ehescheidung*) divorce; **die ~ einreichen** to file a petition for divorce
Scheidungsgrund M grounds *pl* for divorce
Scheidungsklage F divorce suit
Schein [ʃaɪn] (**-(e)s, -e**) M light; (*Anschein*) appearance; (*Geldschein*) (bank)note; (*Bescheinigung*) certificate; **den ~ wahren** to keep up appearances; **etw zum ~ tun** to pretend to do sth, to make a pretence (BRIT) *od* pretense (*US*) of doing sth; **scheinbar** ADJ apparent
scheinen *unreg* VI to shine; (*Anschein haben*) to seem
Schein- ZW: **scheinheilig** ADJ hypocritical; **Scheintod** M apparent death; **Scheinwerfer** (**-s, -**) M floodlight; (*Theat*) spotlight; (*Suchscheinwerfer*) searchlight; (*Aut*) headlight
Scheiß [ʃaɪs] (-, *no pl*) (*umg*) M bullshit (*umg!*)
Scheiß- ['ʃaɪs-] (*umg*) IN ZW bloody (BRIT *umg!*); **Scheißdreck** (*umg!*) M shit (*umg!*), crap (*umg!*); **das geht dich einen Scheißdreck an** it's got bugger-all to do with you (*umg!*)
Scheiße ['ʃaɪsə] (-) (*umg!*) F shit (*umg!*)
scheißegal (*umg!*) ADJ: **das ist mir doch ~!** I don't give a shit (*umg!*)
scheißen (*umg!*) VI to shit (*umg!*)
scheißfreundlich (*pej, umg*) ADJ as nice as pie (*ironisch*)
Scheißkerl (*umg!*) M bastard (*umg!*), son-of-a-bitch (*US umg!*)
Scheit [ʃaɪt] (**-(e)s, -e** *od* **-er**) NT log
Scheitel ['ʃaɪtəl] (**-s, -**) M top; (*Haar*) parting (BRIT), part (*US*)
scheiteln VT to part
Scheitelpunkt M zenith, apex
Scheiterhaufen ['ʃaɪtərhaʊfən] M (funeral) pyre; (*Hist: zur Hinrichtung*) stake
scheitern ['ʃaɪtərn] VI to fail
Schelle ['ʃɛlə] (**-, -n**) F small bell
schellen VI to ring; **es hat geschellt** the bell has gone
Schellfisch ['ʃɛlfɪʃ] M haddock
Schelm [ʃɛlm] (**-(e)s, -e**) M rogue
Schelmenroman M picaresque novel
schelmisch ADJ mischievous, roguish
Schelte ['ʃɛltə] (**-, -n**) F scolding
schelten *unreg* VT to scold
Schema ['ʃe:ma] (**-s, -s** *od* **-ta**) NT scheme, plan; (*Darstellung*) schema; **nach ~ F** quite mechanically
schematisch [ʃe'ma:tɪʃ] ADJ schematic; (*pej*) mechanical
Schemel ['ʃe:məl] (**-s, -**) M (foot)stool
schemenhaft ADJ shadowy
Schenke (**-, -n**) F tavern, inn
Schenkel ['ʃɛŋkəl] (**-s, -**) M thigh; (*Math: von Winkel*) side
schenken ['ʃɛŋkən] VT (*lit, fig*) to give; (*Getränk*) to pour; **ich möchte nichts geschenkt haben!** (*lit*) I don't want any presents!; (*fig: bevorzugt werden*) I don't want any special treatment!; **sich** *dat* **etw ~** (*umg*) to skip sth; **jdm etw ~** (*erlassen*) to let sb off sth; **ihm ist nie etwas geschenkt worden** (*fig*) he never had it easy; **das ist geschenkt!** (*billig*) that's a giveaway!; (*nichts wert*) that's worthless!
Schenkung F gift
Schenkungsurkunde F deed of gift
scheppern ['ʃɛpərn] (*umg*) VI to clatter
Scherbe ['ʃɛrbə] (**-, -n**) F broken piece, fragment; (*archäologisch*) potsherd
Schere ['ʃe:rə] (**-, -n**) F scissors *pl*; (*groß*) shears *pl*; (*Zool*) pincer; (*von Hummer, Krebs etc*) pincer, claw; **eine ~** a pair of scissors
scheren *unreg* VT to cut; (*Schaf*) to shear; (*stören*) to bother ▶ VR (*sich kümmern*) to care; **scher dich (zum Teufel)!** get lost!
Scherenschleifer (**-s, -**) M knife grinder
Scherenschnitt M silhouette
Schererei [ʃe:rə'raɪ] (*umg*) F bother, trouble
Scherflein ['ʃɛrflaɪn] NT mite, bit
Scherz [ʃɛrts] (**-es, -e**) M joke; **scherzen** VI to joke; (*albern*) to banter; **Scherzfrage** F conundrum; **scherzhaft** ADJ joking, jocular
scheu [ʃɔʏ] ADJ shy
Scheu [ʃɔʏ] (-) F shyness; (*Ehrfurcht*) awe; (*Angst*): **~ (vor** *+dat*) fear (of)
Scheuche (**-, -n**) F scarecrow
scheuchen ['ʃɔʏçən] VT to scare (off)
scheuen VR: **sich ~ vor** *+dat* to be afraid of, to shrink from ▶ VT to shun ▶ VI (*Pferd*) to shy; **weder Mühe noch Kosten ~** to spare neither trouble nor expense
Scheuer ['ʃɔʏər] (**-, -n**) F barn
Scheuer- ZW: **Scheuerbürste** F scrubbing brush; **Scheuerlappen** M floorcloth (BRIT), scrubbing rag (*US*); **Scheuerleiste** F skirting board
scheuern VT to scour; (*mit Bürste*) to scrub ▶ VR: **sich** *akk* **(wund) ~** to chafe o.s.; **jdm eine ~** (*umg*) to clout sb one
Scheuklappe F blinker
Scheune ['ʃɔʏnə] (**-, -n**) F barn
Scheunendrescher (**-s, -**) M: **er frisst wie ein ~** (*umg*) he eats like a horse
Scheusal ['ʃɔʏza:l] (**-s, -e**) NT monster
scheußlich ['ʃɔʏslɪç] ADJ dreadful, frightful; **Scheußlichkeit** F dreadfulness
Schi [ʃi:] M = **Ski**
Schicht [ʃɪçt] (**-, -en**) F layer; (*Klasse*) class, level; (*in Fabrik etc*) shift; **Schichtarbeit** F shift work
schichten VT to layer, to stack
Schichtwechsel M change of shifts
schick [ʃɪk] ADJ = **chic**
schicken VT to send ▶ VR: **sich ~ (in** *+akk*) to resign o.s. (to) ▶ VB UNPERS (*anständig sein*) to be fitting
Schickeria [ʃɪkə'ri:a] F (*ironisch*) in-people *pl*
Schicki ['ʃɪkɪ], **Schickimicki** ['ʃɪkɪ'mɪkɪ] (**-s, -s**) (*umg*) M trendy
schicklich ADJ proper, fitting
Schicksal (**-s, -e**) NT fate
schicksalhaft ADJ fateful
Schicksalsschlag M great misfortune, blow

Schickse ['ʃɪksə] (**-, -n**) (*umg*) F floozy, shiksa (*US*)
Schiebedach NT (*Aut*) sunroof, sunshine roof
schieben ['ʃi:bən] *unreg* VT (*auch Drogen*) to push; (*Schuld*) to put; (*umg: handeln mit*) to traffic in; **die Schuld auf jdn ~** to put the blame on (to) sb; **etw vor sich** *dat* **her ~** (*fig*) to put sth off
Schieber (**-s, -**) M slide; (*Besteckteil*) pusher; (*Person*) profiteer; (*umg: Schwarzhändler*) black marketeer; (*: Waffenschieber*) gunrunner; (*: Drogenschieber*) pusher
Schiebetür F sliding door
Schieblehre F (*Math*) calliper (BRIT) *od* caliper (*US*) rule
Schiebung F fiddle; **das war doch ~** (*umg*) that was rigged *od* a fix
schied *etc* [ʃi:t] VB *siehe* **scheiden**
Schieds- zW: **Schiedsgericht** NT court of arbitration; **Schiedsmann** (**-(e)s,** *pl* **-männer**) M arbitrator; **Schiedsrichter** M referee, umpire; (*Schlichter*) arbitrator; **schiedsrichtern** VI UNTR to referee, to umpire; (*schlichten*) to arbitrate; **Schiedsspruch** M (arbitration) award; **Schiedsverfahren** NT arbitration
schief [ʃi:f] ADJ crooked; (*Ebene*) sloping; (*Turm*) leaning; (*Winkel*) oblique; (*Blick*) wry; (*Vergleich*) distorted ▶ ADV crookedly; (*ansehen*) askance; **auf die schiefe Bahn geraten** (*fig*) to leave the straight and narrow; **etw ~ stellen** to slope sth; *siehe auch* **schiefliegen**
Schiefer ['ʃi:fər] (**-s, -**) M slate; **Schieferdach** NT slate roof; **Schiefertafel** F (child's) slate
schiefgehen (*umg*) *unreg* VI to go wrong; **es wird schon ~!** (*hum*) it'll be OK
schieflachen (*umg*) VR to kill o.s. laughing
schiefliegen (*umg*) *unreg* VI to be wrong, to be on the wrong track (*umg*)
schielen ['ʃi:lən] VI to squint; **nach etw ~** (*fig*) to eye sth up
schien *etc* [ʃi:n] VB *siehe* **scheinen**
Schienbein NT shinbone
Schiene ['ʃi:nə] F rail; (*Med*) splint
schienen VT to put in splints
Schienenbus M railcar
Schienenstrang M (*Eisenb etc*) (section of) track
schier [ʃi:r] ADJ pure; (*fig*) sheer ▶ ADV nearly, almost
Schießbude F shooting gallery
Schießbudenfigur (*umg*) F clown, ludicrous figure
schießen ['ʃi:sən] *unreg* VI to shoot; (*Salat etc*) to run to seed ▶ VT to shoot; (*Ball*) to kick; (*Tor*) to score; (*Geschoss*) to fire; **~ auf** *+akk* to shoot at; **aus dem Boden ~** (*lit, fig*) to spring *od* sprout up; **jdm durch den Kopf ~** (*fig*) to flash through sb's mind
Schießerei [ʃi:sə'raɪ] F shoot-out, gun battle
Schieß- zW: **Schießgewehr** NT (*hum*) gun; **Schießhund** M: **wie ein Schießhund aufpassen** (*umg*) to watch like a hawk; **Schießplatz** M firing range; **Schießpulver** NT gunpowder; **Schießscharte** F embrasure; **Schießstand** M rifle *od* shooting range

Schiff [ʃɪf] (**-(e)s, -e**) NT ship, vessel; (*Kirchenschiff*) nave
Schiffahrt F *siehe* **Schifffahrt**
Schiff- zW: **schiffbar** ADJ navigable; **Schiffbau** M shipbuilding; **Schiffbruch** M shipwreck; **Schiffbruch erleiden** (*lit*) to be shipwrecked; (*fig*) to fail; (*Unternehmen*) to founder; **schiffbrüchig** ADJ shipwrecked
Schiffchen NT small boat; (*Weben*) shuttle; (*Mütze*) forage cap
Schiffer (**-s, -**) M boatman, sailor; (*von Lastkahn*) bargee
Schiff- zW: **Schifffahrt** F shipping; (*Reise*) voyage; **Schifffahrtslinie** F shipping route; **Schiffschaukel** F swing boat
Schiffs- zW: **Schiffsjunge** M cabin boy; **Schiffskörper** M hull; **Schiffsladung** F cargo, shipload; **Schiffsplanke** F gangplank; **Schiffsschraube** F ship's propeller
Schiit [ʃi:it] (**-en, -en**) M Shiite; **schiitisch** ADJ Shiite
Schikane [ʃi'ka:nə] (**-, -n**) F harassment; (*von Mitschülern*) bullying; **mit allen Schikanen** with all the trimmings; **das hat er aus reiner ~ gemacht** he did it out of sheer bloody-mindedness
schikanieren [ʃika'ni:rən] VT to harass; (*Ehepartner*) to mess around; (*Mitschüler*) to bully
schikanös [ʃika'nø:s] ADJ (*Mensch*) bloody-minded; (*Maßnahme etc*) harassing
Schild[1] [ʃɪlt] (**-(e)s, -e**) M shield; (*Mützenschild*) peak, visor; **etwas im Schilde führen** to be up to something
Schild[2] [ʃɪlt] (**-(e)s, -er**) NT sign; (*Namensschild*) nameplate; (*an Monument, Haus, Grab*) plaque; (*Etikett*) label
Schildbürger M duffer, blockhead
Schilddrüse F thyroid gland
schildern ['ʃɪldərn] VT to describe; (*Menschen etc*) to portray; (*skizzieren*) to outline
Schilderung F description; (*von Menschen etc*) portrayal
Schildkröte F tortoise; (*Wasserschildkröte*) turtle
Schildkrötensuppe F turtle soup
Schilf [ʃɪlf] (**-(e)s, -e**) NT, **Schilfrohr** NT (*Pflanze*) reed; (*Material*) reeds *pl*, rushes *pl*
Schillerlocke ['ʃɪlərlɔkə] F (*Gebäck*) cream horn; (*Räucherfisch*) *strip of smoked rock salmon*
schillern ['ʃɪlərn] VI to shimmer
schillernd ADJ iridescent; (*fig: Charakter*) enigmatic
Schilling ['ʃɪlɪŋ] (**-s, -** *od* (*Schillingstücke*) **-e**) (ÖSTERR) M schilling
schilt [ʃɪlt] VB *siehe* **schelten**
Schimmel ['ʃɪməl] (**-s, -**) M mould (BRIT), mold (*US*); (*Pferd*) white horse
schimmelig ADJ mouldy (BRIT), moldy (*US*)
schimmeln VI to go mouldy (BRIT) *od* moldy (*US*)
Schimmer ['ʃɪmər] (**-s**) M glimmer; **keinen (blassen) ~ von etw haben** (*umg*) not to have the slightest idea about sth
schimmern VI to glimmer; (*Seide, Perlen*) to shimmer

S

schimmlig ADJ = **schimmelig**
Schimpanse [ʃɪm'panzə] (**-n, -n**) M chimpanzee
Schimpf [ʃɪmpf] (**-(e)s, -e**) M disgrace; **mit ~ und Schande** in disgrace
schimpfen VI (*sich beklagen*) to grumble; (*fluchen*) to curse; **mit jdm ~** to tell sb off
Schimpfkanonade F barrage of abuse
Schimpfwort NT term of abuse
Schindel ['ʃɪndəl] (**-, -n**) F shingle
schinden ['ʃɪndən] *unreg* VT to maltreat, to drive too hard ▸ VR: **sich ~ (mit)** to sweat and strain (at), to toil away (at); **Eindruck ~** (*umg*) to create an impression
Schinder (**-s, -**) M knacker; (*fig*) slave driver
Schinderei [ʃɪndə'raɪ] F grind, drudgery
Schindluder ['ʃɪntlu:dər] NT: **mit etw ~ treiben** to muck *od* mess sth about; (*Vorrecht*) to abuse sth
Schinken ['ʃɪŋkən] (**-s, -**) M ham; (*gekocht und geräuchert*) gammon; (*pej, umg: Theaterstück etc*) hackneyed and clichéd play *etc*; **Schinkenspeck** M bacon
Schippe ['ʃɪpə] (**-, -n**) F shovel; **jdn auf die ~ nehmen** (*fig: umg*) to pull sb's leg
schippen VT to shovel
Schirm [ʃɪrm] (**-(e)s, -e**) M (*Regenschirm*) umbrella; (*Sonnenschirm*) parasol, sunshade; (*Wandschirm, Bildschirm*) screen; (*Lampenschirm*) (lamp)shade; (*Mützenschirm*) peak; (*Pilzschirm*) cap; **Schirmbildaufnahme** F X-ray; **Schirmherr(in)** M(F) patron(ess); **Schirmherrschaft** F patronage; **Schirmmütze** F peaked cap; **Schirmständer** M umbrella stand
schiss *etc* [ʃɪs] VB *siehe* **scheißen**
Schiss M: **~ haben** (*umg*) to be shit scared (*umg!*)
schizophren [ʃitso'fre:n] ADJ schizophrenic
Schizophrenie [ʃitsofre'ni:] F schizophrenia
schlabbern ['ʃlabərn] (*umg*) VT, VI to slurp
Schlacht [ʃlaxt] (**-, -en**) F battle
schlachten VT to slaughter, to kill
Schlachtenbummler (*umg*) M visiting football fan
Schlachter (**-s, -**) M butcher
Schlacht- zW: **Schlachtfeld** NT battlefield; **Schlachtfest** NT *country feast at which freshly slaughtered meat is served*; **Schlachthaus** NT, **Schlachthof** M slaughterhouse, abattoir (BRIT); **Schlachtopfer** NT sacrifice; (*Mensch*) human sacrifice; **Schlachtplan** M battle plan; (*fig*) plan of action; **Schlachtruf** M battle cry, war cry; **Schlachtschiff** NT battleship; **Schlachtvieh** NT animals *pl* kept for meat
Schlacke ['ʃlakə] (**-, -n**) F slag
schlackern (*umg*) VI to tremble; (*Kleidung*) to hang loosely, to be baggy; **mit den Ohren ~** (*fig*) to be (left) speechless
Schlaf [ʃla:f] (**-(e)s**) M sleep; **um seinen ~ kommen** *od* **gebracht werden** to lose sleep; **Schlafanzug** M pyjamas *pl* (BRIT), pajamas *pl* (US)
Schläfchen ['ʃlɛ:fçən] NT nap
Schläfe (**-, -n**) F (*Anat*) temple
schlafen *unreg* VI to sleep; (*umg: nicht aufpassen*) to be asleep; **~ gehen** to go to bed; **bei jdm ~** to stay overnight with sb; **Schlafengehen** NT going to bed
Schlafenszeit F bedtime
Schläfer(in) ['ʃlɛ:fər(ɪn)] (**-s, -**) M(F) sleeper
schlaff [ʃlaf] ADJ slack; (*Haut*) loose; (*Muskeln*) flabby; (*energielos*) limp; (*erschöpft*) exhausted; **Schlaffheit** F slackness; (*von Haut*) looseness; (*von Muskeln*) flabbiness; (*Energielosigkeit*) limpness; (*Erschöpfung*) exhaustion
Schlafgelegenheit F place to sleep
Schlafittchen [ʃla'fɪtçən] (*umg*) NT: **jdn am** *od* **beim ~ nehmen** to take sb by the scruff of the neck
Schlaf- zW: **Schlafkrankheit** F sleeping sickness; **Schlaflied** NT lullaby; **schlaflos** ADJ sleepless; **Schlaflosigkeit** F sleeplessness, insomnia; **Schlafmittel** NT sleeping drug; (*fig, ironisch*) soporific; **Schlafmütze** (*umg*) F dope
schläfrig ['ʃlɛ:frɪç] ADJ sleepy
Schlaf- zW: **Schlafrock** M dressing gown; **Apfel im Schlafrock** baked apple in puff pastry; **Schlafsaal** M dormitory; **Schlafsack** M sleeping bag
schläft [ʃlɛ:ft] VB *siehe* **schlafen**
Schlaf- zW: **Schlaftablette** F sleeping pill; **schlaftrunken** ADJ drowsy, half-asleep; **Schlafwagen** M sleeping car, sleeper; **schlafwandeln** VI UNTR to sleepwalk; **Schlafwandler(in)** (**-s, -**) M(F) sleepwalker; **Schlafzimmer** NT bedroom
Schlag [ʃla:k] (**-(e)s, Schläge**) M (*lit, fig*) blow; (*auch Med*) stroke; (*Pulsschlag, Herzschlag*) beat; (*Elek*) shock; (*Blitzschlag*) bolt, stroke; (*Glockenschlag*) chime; (*Autotür*) car door; (*umg: Portion*) helping; (*: Art*) kind, type; **Schläge** PL (*Tracht Prügel*) beating *sing*; **~ acht Uhr** (*umg*) on the stroke of eight; **mit einem ~** all at once; **~ auf ~** in rapid succession; **die haben keinen ~ getan** (*umg*) they haven't done a stroke (of work); **ich dachte, mich trifft der ~** (*umg*) I was thunderstruck; **vom gleichen ~ sein** to be cast in the same mould (BRIT) *od* mold (US); (*pej*) to be tarred with the same brush; **ein ~ ins Wasser** (*umg*) a wash-out; **Schlagabtausch** M (*Boxen*) exchange of blows; (*fig*) (verbal) exchange; **Schlagader** F artery; **Schlaganfall** M stroke; **schlagartig** ADJ sudden, without warning; **Schlagbaum** M barrier; **Schlagbohrer** M percussion drill
Schlägel ['ʃlɛ:gl] (**-s, -**) M drumstick; (*Hammer*) hammer
schlagen ['ʃla:gən] *unreg* VT to strike, to hit; (*wiederholt schlagen, besiegen*) to beat; (*Glocke*) to ring; (*Stunde*) to strike; (*Kreis, Bogen*) to describe; (*Purzelbaum*) to do; (*Sahne*) to whip; (*Schlacht*) to fight; (*einwickeln*) to wrap ▸ VI to strike, to hit; (*Herz*) to beat; (*Glocke*) to ring ▸ VR to fight; **um sich ~** to lash out; **ein Ei in die Pfanne ~** to crack an egg into the pan; **eine geschlagene Stunde** a full hour; **na ja, ehe ich mich ~ lasse!** (*hum: umg*) I suppose you could twist my

arm; **nach jdm ~** (*fig*) to take after sb; **sich gut ~** (*fig*) to do well; **sich nach links/Norden ~** to strike out to the left/(for the) north; **sich auf jds Seite** *akk* **~** to side with sb; (*die Fronten wechseln*) to go over to sb

schlagend ADJ (*Beweis*) convincing; **schlagende Wetter** (*Min*) firedamp

Schlager ['ʃla:gər] (**-s, -**) M (*Mus, fig*) hit

Schläger ['ʃlɛ:gər] (**-s, -**) M brawler; (*Sport*) bat; (*Tennis etc*) racket; (*Golf*) club; (*Hockeyschläger*) hockey stick

Schlägerei [ʃlɛ:gə'raɪ] F fight, punch-up

Schlagersänger M pop singer

Schlägertyp (*umg*) M thug

Schlag- ZW: **schlagfertig** ADJ quick-witted; **Schlagfertigkeit** F ready wit, quickness of repartee; **Schlaginstrument** NT percussion instrument; **Schlagkraft** F (*lit, fig*) power; (*Mil*) strike power; (*Boxen*) punch(ing power); **schlagkräftig** ADJ powerful; (*Beweise*) clear-cut; **Schlagloch** NT pothole; **Schlagobers** (**-, -**) (ÖSTERR) NT, **Schlagrahm** M, **Schlagsahne** F whipped cream; **Schlagseite** F (*Naut*) list; **Schlagstock** M (*form*) truncheon (BRIT), nightstick (*US*)

schlägt [ʃlɛ:kt] VB *siehe* **schlagen**

Schlag- ZW: **Schlagwort** NT slogan, catch phrase; **Schlagzeile** F headline; **Schlagzeilen machen** (*umg*) to hit the headlines; **Schlagzeug** NT drums *pl*; (*in Orchester*) percussion; **Schlagzeuger** (**-s, -**) M drummer; (*in Orchester*) percussionist

schlaksig ['ʃla:ksɪç] (*umg*) ADJ gangling, gawky

Schlamassel [ʃla'masəl] (**-s, -**) (*umg*) M mess

Schlamm [ʃlam] (**-(e)s, -e**) M mud

schlammig ADJ muddy

Schlampe ['ʃlampə] (**-, -n**) (*umg*) F slattern, slut

schlampen (*umg*) VI to be sloppy

Schlamperei [ʃlampə'raɪ] (*umg*) F disorder, untidiness; (*schlechte Arbeit*) sloppy work

schlampig (*umg*) ADJ slovenly, sloppy

schlang *etc* [ʃlaŋ] VB *siehe* **schlingen**

Schlange ['ʃlaŋə] (**-, -n**) F snake; (*Menschenschlange*) queue (BRIT), line (*US*); **~ stehen** to (form a) queue (BRIT), to stand in line (*US*); **eine falsche ~** a snake in the grass

schlängeln ['ʃlɛŋəln] VR to twist, to wind; (*Fluss*) to meander

Schlangen- ZW: **Schlangenbiss** M snake bite; **Schlangengift** NT snake venom; **Schlangenlinie** F wavy line

schlank [ʃlaŋk] ADJ slim, slender; **Schlankheit** F slimness, slenderness; **Schlankheitskur** F diet

schlapp [ʃlap] ADJ limp; (*locker*) slack; (*umg: energielos*) listless; (*nach Krankheit etc*) run-down

Schlappe (**-, -n**) (*umg*) F setback

Schlappen (**-s, -**) (*umg*) M slipper

schlapp- ZW: **Schlappheit** F limpness; (*Lockerheit*) slackness; **Schlapphut** M slouch hat; **schlappmachen** (*umg*) VI to wilt, to droop; **Schlappschwanz** (*pej, umg*) M weakling, softy

Schlaraffenland [ʃla'rafənlant] NT land of milk and honey

schlau [ʃlaʊ] ADJ crafty, cunning; **ich werde nicht ~ aus ihm** I don't know what to make of him; **Schlauberger** (**-s, -**) (*umg*) M clever Dick

Schlauch [ʃlaʊx] (**-(e)s, Schläuche**) M hose; (*in Reifen*) inner tube; (*umg: Anstrengung*) grind; **auf dem ~ stehen** (*umg*) to be in a jam *od* fix; **Schlauchboot** NT rubber dinghy

schlauchen (*umg*) VT to tell on, to exhaust

schlauchlos ADJ (*Reifen*) tubeless

Schläue ['ʃlɔʏə] (**-**) F cunning

Schlaufe ['ʃlaʊfə] (**-, -n**) F loop; (*Aufhänger*) hanger

Schlauheit F cunning

Schlaukopf M clever Dick

Schlawiner [ʃla'vi:nər] (**-s, -**) M (*hum: umg*) villain, rogue

schlecht [ʃlɛçt] ADJ bad; (*ungenießbar*) bad, off (BRIT) ▶ ADV: **es geht ihm ~** he's having a hard time; (*gesundheitlich*) he's not feeling well; (*finanziell*) he's pretty hard up; **heute geht es ~** today is not very convenient; **er kann ~ Nein sagen** he finds it hard to say no, he can't say no; **jdm ist ~** sb feels sick *od* ill; **~ und recht** after a fashion; **auf jdn ~ zu sprechen sein** not to have a good word to say for sb; **er hat nicht ~ gestaunt** (*umg*) he wasn't half surprised; *siehe auch* **schlechtmachen**

schlechterdings ADV simply

Schlecht- ZW: **Schlechtheit** F badness; **schlechthin** ADV simply; **der Dramatiker schlechthin** THE playwright

Schlechtigkeit F badness; (*Tat*) bad deed

schlechtmachen VT to run down, to denigrate

schlecken ['ʃlɛkən] VT, VI to lick

Schlegel ['ʃle:gəl] (**-s, -**) M (*Koch*) leg; *siehe auch* **Schlägel**

schleichen ['ʃlaɪçən] *unreg* VI to creep, to crawl

schleichend ADJ creeping; (*Krankheit, Gift*) insidious

Schleichweg M: **auf Schleichwegen** (*fig*) on the quiet

Schleichwerbung F: **eine ~** a plug

Schleie ['ʃlaɪə] (**-, -n**) F tench

Schleier ['ʃlaɪər] (**-s, -**) M veil; **Schleiereule** F barn owl; **schleierhaft** (*umg*) ADJ: **jdm schleierhaft sein** to be a mystery to sb

Schleife ['ʃlaɪfə] (**-, -n**) F (*auch Comput*) loop; (*Band*) bow; (*Kranzschleife*) ribbon

schleifen[1] VT (*ziehen, schleppen*) to drag; (*Mil: Festung*) to raze ▶ VI to drag; **die Kupplung ~ lassen** (*Aut*) to slip the clutch

schleifen[2] *unreg* VT (*schärfen*) to grind; (*Edelstein*) to cut; (*Mil: Soldaten*) to drill

Schleifmaschine F sander; (*in Fabrik*) grinding machine

Schleifstein M grindstone

Schleim [ʃlaɪm] (**-(e)s, -e**) M slime; (*Med*) mucus; (*Koch*) gruel; **Schleimhaut** F mucous membrane

schleimig ADJ slimy

schlemmen ['ʃlɛmən] VI to feast

Schlemmer(in) (**-s, -**) M(F) gourmet, bon vivant

S

Schlemmerei [ʃlɛmə'raɪ] F feasting
schlendern ['ʃlɛndərn] VI to stroll
Schlendrian ['ʃlɛndria:n] (**-(e)s**) M sloppy way of working
Schlenker ['ʃlɛŋkər] (**-s, -**) M swerve
schlenkern VT, VI to swing, to dangle
Schleppe ['ʃlɛpə] (**-, -n**) F train
schleppen VT to drag; (*Auto, Schiff*) to tow; (*tragen*) to lug
schleppend ADJ dragging; (*Bedienung, Abfertigung*) sluggish, slow
Schlepper (**-s, -**) M tractor; (*Schiff*) tug
Schleppkahn M (canal) barge
Schlepptau NT towrope; **jdn ins ~ nehmen** (*fig*) to take sb in tow
Schlesien ['ʃle:ziən] (**-s**) NT Silesia
Schlesier(in) (**-s, -**) M(F) Silesian
schlesisch ADJ Silesian
Schleswig-Holstein ['ʃle:svɪç'hɔlʃtaɪn] (**-s**) NT Schleswig-Holstein
Schleuder ['ʃlɔʏdər] (**-, -n**) F catapult; (*Wäscheschleuder*) spin-dryer; (*Zentrifuge*) centrifuge; **Schleuderhonig** M extracted honey
schleudern VT to hurl; (*Wäsche*) to spin-dry ▶ VI (*Aut*) to skid; **ins S~ kommen** (*Aut*) to go into a skid; (*fig: umg*) to run into trouble
Schleuder- ZW: **Schleuderpreis** M give-away price; **Schleudersitz** M (*Aviat*) ejector seat; (*fig*) hot seat; **Schleuderware** F cut-price (BRIT) *od* cut-rate (*US*) goods *pl*
schleunig ['ʃlɔʏnɪç] ADJ prompt, speedy; (*Schritte*) quick
schleunigst ADV straight away
Schleuse ['ʃlɔʏzə] (**-, -n**) F lock; (*Schleusentor*) sluice
schleusen VT (*Schiffe*) to pass through a lock, to lock; (*Wasser*) to channel; (*Menschen*) to filter; (*fig: heimlich*) to smuggle
schlich *etc* [ʃlɪç] VB *siehe* **schleichen**
Schlich (**-(e)s, -e**) M dodge, trick; **jdm auf die Schliche kommen** to get wise to sb
schlicht [ʃlɪçt] ADJ simple, plain
schlichten VT to smooth; (*beilegen*) to settle; (*Streit: vermitteln*) to mediate, to arbitrate
Schlichter(in) (**-s, -**) M(F) mediator, arbitrator
Schlichtheit F simplicity, plainness
Schlichtung F settlement; (*Vermittlung*) arbitration
Schlick [ʃlɪk] (**-(e)s, -e**) M mud; (*Ölschlick*) slick
schlief *etc* [ʃli:f] VB *siehe* **schlafen**
Schließe ['ʃli:sə] (**-, -n**) F fastener
schließen ['ʃli:sən] *unreg* VT to close, to shut; (*beenden*) to close; (*Freundschaft, Bündnis, Ehe*) to enter into; (*Comput: Datei*) to close; (*folgern*): **~ (aus)** to infer (from) ▶ VI, VR to close, to shut; **auf etw** *akk* **~ lassen** to suggest sth; **jdn/etw in sein Herz ~** to take sb/sth to one's heart; **etw in sich ~** to include sth; **„geschlossen"** "closed"
Schließfach NT locker
schließlich ADV finally; (*schließlich doch*) after all
schliff *etc* [ʃlɪf] VB *siehe* **schleifen²**
Schliff (**-(e)s, -e**) M cut(ting); (*fig*) polish; **einer Sache den letzten ~ geben** (*fig*) to put the finishing touch(es) to sth
schlimm [ʃlɪm] ADJ bad; **das war ~** that was terrible; **das ist halb so ~!** that's not so bad!; **schlimmer** ADJ worse; **schlimmste(r, s)** ADJ worst
schlimmstenfalls ADV at (the) worst
Schlinge ['ʃlɪŋə] (**-, -n**) F loop; (*an Galgen*) noose; (*Falle*) snare; (*Med*) sling
Schlingel (**-s, -**) M rascal
schlingen *unreg* VT to wind ▶ VI (*essen*) to bolt one's food, to gobble
schlingern VI to roll
Schlingpflanze F creeper
Schlips [ʃlɪps] (**-es, -e**) M tie, necktie (*US*); **sich auf den ~ getreten fühlen** (*fig: umg*) to feel offended
Schlitten ['ʃlɪtən] (**-s, -**) M sledge, sled; (*Pferdeschlitten*) sleigh; **mit jdm ~ fahren** (*umg*) to give sb a rough time; **Schlittenbahn** F toboggan run; **Schlittenfahren** (**-s**) NT tobogganing
schlittern ['ʃlɪtərn] VI to slide; (*Wagen*) to skid
Schlittschuh ['ʃlɪtʃu:] M skate; **~ laufen** to skate; **Schlittschuhbahn** F skating rink; **Schlittschuhläufer** M skater
Schlitz [ʃlɪts] (**-es, -e**) M slit; (*für Münze*) slot; (*Hosenschlitz*) flies *pl*; **schlitzäugig** ADJ slant-eyed; **schlitzen** VT to slit; **Schlitzohr** NT (*fig*) sly fox
schlohweiß ['ʃlo:'vaɪs] ADJ snow-white
Schlokal NT gourmet restaurant
schloss [ʃlɔs] VB *siehe* **schließen**
Schloss (**-es, -Schlösser**) NT lock, padlock; (*an Schmuck etc*) clasp; (*Bau*) castle; (*Palast*) palace; **ins ~ fallen** to lock (itself)
Schlosser ['ʃlɔsər] (**-s, -**) M (*Autoschlosser*) fitter; (*für Schlüssel etc*) locksmith
Schlosserei [slɔsə'raɪ] F metal(working) shop
Schlosshund M: **heulen wie ein ~** to howl one's head off
Schlot [ʃlo:t] (**-(e)s, -e**) M chimney; (*Naut*) funnel
schlottern ['ʃlɔtərn] VI to shake; (*vor Angst*) to tremble; (*Kleidung*) to be baggy
Schlucht [ʃlʊxt] (**-, -en**) F gorge, ravine
schluchzen ['ʃlʊxtsən] VI to sob
Schluck [ʃlʊk] (**-(e)s, -e**) M swallow; (*größer*) gulp; (*kleiner*) sip; (*ein bisschen*) drop
Schluckauf (**-s**) M hiccups *pl*
schlucken VT to swallow; (*umg: Alkohol, Benzin*) to guzzle; (*: verschlingen*) to swallow up ▶ VI to swallow
Schlucker (**-s, -**) (*umg*) M: **armer ~** poor devil
Schluckimpfung F oral vaccination
schluderig ['ʃlu:dərɪç], **schludrig** ['ʃlu:drɪç] (*umg*) ADJ slipshod
schludern ['ʃlu:dərn] (*umg*) VI to do slipshod work
schlug *etc* [ʃlu:k] VB *siehe* **schlagen**
Schlummer ['ʃlʊmər] (**-s**) M slumber
schlummern VI to slumber

Schlund [ʃlʊnt] (**-(e)s, Schlünde**) M gullet; (*fig*) jaw
schlüpfen [ˈʃlʏpfən] VI to slip; (*Vogel etc*) to hatch (out)
Schlüpfer [ˈʃlʏpfər] (**-s, -**) M panties *pl*, knickers *pl*
Schlupfloch [ˈʃlʊpflɔx] NT hole; (*Versteck*) hide-out; (*fig*) loophole
schlüpfrig [ˈʃlʏpfrɪç] ADJ slippery; (*fig*) lewd; **Schlüpfrigkeit** F slipperiness; (*fig*) lewdness
Schlupfwinkel M hiding place; (*fig*) quiet corner
schlurfen [ˈʃlʊrfən] VI to shuffle
schlürfen [ˈʃlʏrfən] VT, VI to slurp
Schluss [ʃlʊs] (**-es, -Schlüsse**) M end; (*Schlussfolgerung*) conclusion; **am ~** at the end; **~ für heute!** that'll do for today; **~ jetzt!** that's enough now!; **~ machen mit** to finish with
Schlüssel [ˈʃlʏsəl] (**-s, -**) M (*lit, fig*) key; (*Schraubschlüssel*) spanner, wrench; (*Mus*) clef; **Schlüsselbein** NT collarbone; **Schlüsselblume** F cowslip, primrose; **Schlüsselbund** M bunch of keys; **Schlüsselerlebnis** NT (*Psych*) crucial experience; **Schlüsselkind** NT latchkey child; **Schlüsselloch** NT keyhole; **Schlüsselposition** F key position; **Schlüsselwort** NT safe combination; (*Comput*) keyword
Schlussfolgerung F conclusion, inference
Schlussformel F (*in Brief*) closing formula; (*bei Vertrag*) final clause
schlüssig [ˈʃlʏsɪç] ADJ conclusive; **sich** *dat* **(über etw** *akk***) ~ sein** to have made up one's mind (about sth)
Schluss- zW: **Schlusslicht** NT rear light (BRIT), taillight (US); (*fig*) tail ender; **Schlussstrich** M (*fig*) final stroke; **einen Schlussstrich unter etw** *akk* **ziehen** to consider sth finished; **Schlussverkauf** M clearance sale; **Schlusswort** NT concluding words *pl*
Schmach [ʃma:x] (**-**) F disgrace, ignominy
schmachten [ˈʃmaxtən] VI to languish; **nach jdm ~** to pine for sb
schmächtig [ˈʃmɛçtɪç] ADJ slight
schmachvoll ADJ ignominious, humiliating
schmackhaft [ˈʃmakhaft] ADJ tasty; **jdm etw ~ machen** (*fig*) to make sth palatable to sb
schmähen [ˈʃmɛ:ən] VT to abuse, to revile
schmählich ADJ ignominious, shameful
Schmähung F abuse
schmal [ʃma:l] ADJ narrow; (*Person, Buch etc*) slender, slim; (*karg*) meagre (BRIT), meager (US); **schmalbrüstig** ADJ narrow-chested
schmälern [ˈʃmɛ:lərn] VT to diminish; (*fig*) to belittle
Schmalfilm M cine (BRIT) *od* movie (US) film
Schmalspur F narrow gauge
Schmalspur- (*pej*) IN ZW small-time
Schmalz [ʃmalts] (**-es, -e**) NT dripping; (*Schweineschmalz*) lard; (*fig*) sentiment, schmaltz
schmalzig ADJ (*fig*) schmaltzy, slushy
schmarotzen [ʃmaˈrɔtsən] VI (*Biol*) to be parasitic; (*fig*) to sponge
Schmarotzer (**-s, -**) M (*auch fig*) parasite
Schmarren [ˈʃmarən] (**-s, -**) M (ÖSTERR) small pieces of pancake; (*fig*) rubbish, tripe
schmatzen [ˈʃmatsən] VI to eat noisily
Schmaus [ʃmaʊs] (**-es, Schmäuse**) M feast; **schmausen** VI to feast
schmecken [ˈʃmɛkən] VT, VI to taste; **es schmeckt ihm** he likes it; **schmeckt es Ihnen?** is it good?, are you enjoying your food *od* meal?; **das schmeckt nach mehr!** (*umg*) it's very moreish (*hum*); **es sich ~ lassen** to tuck in
Schmeichelei [ʃmaɪçəˈlaɪ] F flattery
schmeichelhaft [ˈʃmaɪçəlhaft] ADJ flattering
schmeicheln VI: **jdm ~** to flatter sb
Schmeichler(in) (**-s, -**) M(F) flatterer
schmeißen [ˈʃmaɪsən] *unreg* (*umg*) VT to throw, to chuck; (*spendieren*): **eine Runde** *od* **Lage ~** to stand a round
Schmeißfliege F bluebottle
Schmelz [ʃmɛlts] (**-es, -e**) M enamel; (*Glasur*) glaze; (*von Stimme*) melodiousness; **schmelzbar** ADJ fusible
schmelzen *unreg* VT to melt; (Erz) to smelt ▸ VI to melt
Schmelz- zW: **Schmelzhütte** F smelting works *pl*; **Schmelzkäse** M cheese spread; (*in Scheiben*) processed cheese; **Schmelzofen** M melting furnace; (*für Erze*) smelting furnace; **Schmelzpunkt** M melting point; **Schmelztiegel** M (*lit, fig*) melting pot; **Schmelzwasser** NT melted snow
Schmerbauch [ˈʃme:rbaʊx] (*umg*) M paunch, potbelly
Schmerz [ʃmɛrts] (**-es, -en**) M pain; (*Trauer*) grief *no pl*; **Schmerzen haben** to be in pain; **schmerzempfindlich** ADJ sensitive to pain
schmerzen VT, VI to hurt
Schmerzensgeld NT compensation
Schmerz- zW: **schmerzhaft** ADJ painful; **schmerzlich** ADJ painful; **schmerzlindernd** ADJ pain-relieving; **schmerzlos** ADJ painless; **Schmerzmittel** NT painkiller, analgesic; **schmerzstillend** ADJ pain-killing, analgesic; **Schmerztablette** F pain-killing tablet
Schmetterling [ˈʃmɛtərlɪŋ] M butterfly
Schmetterlingsstil M (*Schwimmen*) butterfly stroke
schmettern [ˈʃmɛtərn] VT to smash; (*Melodie*) to sing loudly, to bellow out ▸ VI to smash (*Sport*); (*Trompete*) to blare
Schmied [ʃmi:t] (**-(e)s, -e**) M blacksmith
Schmiede [ˈʃmi:də] (**-, -n**) F smithy, forge; **Schmiedeeisen** NT wrought iron
schmieden VT to forge; (*Pläne*) to devise, to concoct
schmiegen [ˈʃmi:gən] VT to press, to nestle ▸ VR: **sich ~ an** +*akk* to cuddle up to, to nestle up to
schmiegsam [ˈʃmi:kza:m] ADJ flexible, pliable
Schmiere [ˈʃmi:rə] F grease; (*Theat*) greasepaint, make-up; (*pej: schlechtes Theater*) fleapit; **~ stehen** (*umg*) to be the look-out
schmieren VT to smear; (*ölen*) to lubricate, to grease; (*bestechen*) to bribe ▸ VI (*schreiben*) to

S

scrawl; **es läuft wie geschmiert** it's going like clockwork; **jdm eine ~** (*umg*) to clout sb one
Schmierenkomödiant (*pej*) M ham (actor)
Schmier- ZW: **Schmierfett** NT grease; **Schmierfink** M messy person; **Schmiergeld** NT bribe; **Schmierheft** NT jotter
schmierig ADJ greasy
Schmiermittel NT lubricant
Schmierseife F soft soap
schmilzt [ʃmɪltst] VB *siehe* **schmelzen**
Schminke ['ʃmɪŋkə] (**-, -n**) F make-up
schminken VT, VR to make up
schmirgeln ['ʃmɪrgəln] VT to sand (down)
Schmirgelpapier (**-s**) NT emery paper
schmiss *etc* [ʃmɪs] VB *siehe* **schmeißen**
Schmiss (**-es, -e**) M (*Narbe*) duelling (BRIT) *od* dueling (US) scar; (*veraltet: Schwung*) dash, élan
Schmöker ['ʃmø:kər] (**-s, -**) (*umg*) M (trashy) old book
schmökern VI to bury o.s. in a book; (*umg*) to browse
schmollen ['ʃmɔlən] VI to pout; (*gekränkt*) to sulk
schmollend ADJ sulky
Schmollmund M pout
schmolz *etc* [ʃmɔlts] VB *siehe* **schmelzen**
Schmorbraten M stewed *od* braised meat
schmoren ['ʃmo:rən] VT to braise
Schmu [ʃmu:] (**-s**) (*umg*) M cheating
Schmuck [ʃmʊk] (**-(e)s, -e**) M jewellery (BRIT), jewelry (US); (*Verzierung*) decoration
schmücken ['ʃmʏkən] VT to decorate
Schmuck- ZW: **schmucklos** ADJ unadorned, plain; **Schmucklosigkeit** F simplicity; **Schmucksachen** PL jewels *pl*, jewellery *sing* (BRIT), jewelry *sing* (US); **Schmuckstück** NT (*Ring etc*) piece of jewellery (BRIT) *od* jewelry (US); (*fig: Prachtstück*) gem
schmuddelig ['ʃmʊdəlɪç], **schmuddlig** ['ʃmʊdlɪç] ADJ messy; (*schmutzig*) dirty; (*schmierig, unsauber*) filthy
Schmuggel ['ʃmʊgəl] (**-s**) M smuggling
schmuggeln VT, VI to smuggle
Schmuggelware F contraband
Schmuggler(in) (**-s, -**) M(F) smuggler
schmunzeln ['ʃmʊntsəln] VI to smile benignly
schmusen ['ʃmu:zən] (*umg*) VI (*zärtlich sein*) to cuddle; **mit jdm ~** to cuddle sb
Schmutz [ʃmʊts] (**-es**) M dirt; (*fig*) filth; **schmutzen** VI to get dirty; **Schmutzfink** M filthy creature; **Schmutzfleck** M stain
schmutzig ADJ dirty; **schmutzige Wäsche waschen** (*fig*) to wash one's dirty linen in public
Schnabel ['ʃna:bəl] (**-s, Schnäbel**) M beak, bill; (*Ausguss*) spout; (*umg: Mund*) mouth; **reden, wie einem der ~ gewachsen ist** to say exactly what comes into one's head; (*unaffektiert*) to talk naturally
schnacken ['ʃnakən] (NORDD *umg*) VI to chat
Schnake ['ʃna:kə] (**-, -n**) F crane fly; (*Stechmücke*) gnat
Schnalle ['ʃnalə] (**-, -n**) F buckle; (*an Handtasche, Buch*) clasp
schnallen VT to buckle
schnalzen ['ʃnaltsən] VI to snap; (*mit Zunge*) to click
Schnäppchen ['ʃnɛpçən] (*umg*) NT bargain, snip
schnappen ['ʃnapən] VT to grab, to catch; (*umg: ergreifen*) to snatch ▸ VI to snap
Schnappschloss NT spring lock
Schnappschuss M (*Phot*) snapshot
Schnaps [ʃnaps] (**-es, Schnäpse**) M schnapps; (*umg: Branntwein*) spirits *pl*; **Schnapsidee** (*umg*) F crackpot idea; **Schnapsleiche** (*umg*) F drunk
schnarchen ['ʃnarçən] VI to snore
schnattern ['ʃnatərn] VI to chatter; (*zittern*) to shiver
schnauben ['ʃnaʊbən] VI to snort ▸ VR to blow one's nose
schnaufen ['ʃnaʊfən] VI to puff, to pant
Schnaufer (**-s, -**) (*umg*) M breath
Schnauzbart ['ʃnaʊtsba:rt] M moustache (BRIT), mustache (US)
Schnauze (**-, -n**) F snout, muzzle; (*Ausguss*) spout; (*umg*) gob; **auf die ~ fallen** (*fig*) to come a cropper (*umg*); **etw frei nach ~ machen** to do sth any old how
schnäuzen ['ʃnɔʏtsn] VR to blow one's nose
Schnecke ['ʃnɛkə] (**-, -n**) F snail; (*Nacktschnecke*) slug; (*Koch: Gebäck*) ≈ Chelsea bun; **jdn zur ~ machen** (*umg*) to give sb a real bawling out
Schneckenhaus NT snail's shell
Schneckentempo (*umg*) NT: **im ~** at a snail's pace
Schnee [ʃne:] (**-s**) M snow; (*Eischnee*) beaten egg white; **~ von gestern** old hat; **Schneeball** M snowball; **Schneebesen** M (*Koch*) whisk; **Schneefall** M snowfall; **Schneeflocke** F snowflake; **Schneegestöber** NT snowstorm; **Schneeglöckchen** NT snowdrop; **Schneegrenze** F snowline; **Schneekette** F (*Aut*) snow chain; **Schneekönig** M: **sich freuen wie ein Schneekönig** to be as pleased as Punch; **Schneemann** M snowman; **Schneepflug** M snowplough (BRIT), snowplow (US); **Schneeregen** M sleet; **Schneeschmelze** F thaw; **Schneetreiben** NT driving snow; **Schneewehe** F snowdrift; **Schneewittchen** NT Snow White
Schneid [ʃnaɪt] (**-(e)s**) (*umg*) M pluck
Schneidbrenner (**-s, -**) M (*Tech*) oxyacetylene cutter
Schneide ['ʃnaɪdə] (**-, -n**) F edge; (*Klinge*) blade
schneiden *unreg* VT to cut; (*Film, Tonband*) to edit; (*kreuzen*) to cross, to intersect ▸ VR to cut o.s.; (*umg: sich täuschen*): **da hat er sich aber geschnitten!** he's very much mistaken; **die Luft ist zum S~** (*fig: umg*) the air is very bad
schneidend ADJ cutting
Schneider (**-s, -**) M tailor; **frieren wie ein ~** (*umg*) to be frozen to the marrow; **aus dem ~ sein** (*fig*) to be out of the woods
Schneiderei [ʃnaɪdə'raɪ] F tailor's shop; (*einer Schneiderin*) dressmaker's shop
Schneiderin F dressmaker
schneidern VT to make ▸ VI to be a tailor

Schneidersitz (**-es**) M: **im ~ sitzen** to sit cross-legged
Schneidezahn M incisor
schneidig ADJ dashing; (*mutig*) plucky
schneien ['ʃnaɪən] VI to snow; **jdm ins Haus ~** (*umg: Besuch*) to drop in on sb; (: *Rechnung, Brief*) to come in the post (BRIT) *od* mail (US)
Schneise ['ʃnaɪzə] (**-, -n**) F (*Waldschneise*) clearing
schnell [ʃnɛl] ADJ quick, fast ▶ ADV quick(ly), fast; **das ging ~** that was quick; **mach ~!** hurry up; **Schnellboot** NT speedboat
Schnelle (**-**) F: **etw auf die ~ machen** to do sth in a rush
schnellen VI to shoot
Schnellgericht NT (*Jur*) summary court; (*Koch*) convenience food
Schnellhefter M loose-leaf binder
Schnelligkeit F speed
Schnell- ZW: **Schnellimbiss** M (*Essen*) (quick) snack; (*Raum*) snack bar; **Schnellkochtopf** M (*Dampfkochtopf*) pressure cooker; **Schnellreinigung** F express cleaner's
schnellstens ADV as quickly as possible
Schnellstraße F expressway
Schnellzug M fast *od* express train
schneuzen ['ʃnɔʏtsən] VR *siehe* **schnäuzen**
Schnickschnack ['ʃnɪkʃnak] (**-(e)s**) (*umg*) M twaddle
Schnippchen ['ʃnɪpçən] NT: **jdm ein ~ schlagen** to play a trick on sb
schnippeln ['ʃnɪpəln] (*umg*) VT to snip; (*mit Messer*) to hack ▶ VI: **~ an** *+dat* to snip at; (*mit Messer*) to hack at
schnippen ['ʃnɪpən] VI: **mit den Fingern ~** to snap one's fingers
schnippisch ['ʃnɪpɪʃ] ADJ sharp-tongued
Schnipsel ['ʃnɪpsəl] (**-s, -**) (*umg*) M OD NT scrap; (*Papierschnipsel*) scrap of paper
schnitt *etc* [ʃnɪt] VB *siehe* **schneiden**
Schnitt (**-(e)s, -e**) M cut(ting); (*Schnittpunkt*) intersection; (*Querschnitt*) (cross) section; (*Durchschnitt*) average; (*Schnittmuster*) pattern; (*Ernte*) crop; (*an Buch*) edge; (*umg: Gewinn*) profit; **~: L. Schwarz** (*Film*) Editor: L. Schwarz; **im ~** on average
Schnittblumen PL cut flowers *pl*
Schnittbohnen PL French *od* green beans *pl*
Schnitte (**-, -n**) F slice; (*belegt*) sandwich
schnittfest ADJ (*Tomaten*) firm
Schnittfläche F section
schnittig ['ʃnɪtɪç] ADJ smart; (*Auto, Formen*) stylish
Schnitt- ZW: **Schnittlauch** M chive; **Schnittmuster** NT pattern; **Schnittpunkt** M (point of) intersection; **Schnittstelle** F (*Comput*) interface; **Schnittwunde** F cut
Schnitzarbeit F wood carving
Schnitzel (**-s, -**) NT scrap; (*Koch*) escalope; **Schnitzeljagd** F paperchase
schnitzen ['ʃnɪtsən] VT to carve
Schnitzer (**-s, -**) M carver; (*umg*) blunder
Schnitzerei [ʃnɪtsə'raɪ] F wood carving
schnodderig ['ʃnɔdərɪç] (*umg*) ADJ snotty
schnöde ['ʃnøːdə] ADJ base, mean
Schnorchel ['ʃnɔrçəl] (**-s, -**) M snorkel
schnorcheln VI to go snorkelling
Schnörkel ['ʃnœrkəl] (**-s, -**) M flourish; (*Archit*) scroll
schnorren ['ʃnɔrən] VT, VI to cadge (BRIT)
Schnorrer (**-s, -**) (*umg*) M cadger (BRIT)
Schnösel ['ʃnøːzəl] (**-s, -**) (*umg*) M snotty(-nosed) little upstart
schnuckelig ['ʃnʊkəlɪç] (*umg*) ADJ (*gemütlich*) snug, cosy; (*Person*) sweet
schnüffeln ['ʃnʏfəln] VI to sniff; (*fig: umg: spionieren*) to snoop around; **Schnüffeln** NT (*von Klebstoff etc*) glue-sniffing *etc*
Schnüffler(in) (**-s, -**) M(F) snooper
Schnuller ['ʃnʊlər] (**-s, -**) M dummy (BRIT), pacifier (US)
Schnulze ['ʃnʊltsə] (**-, -n**) (*umg*) F schmaltzy film/book/song
Schnupfen ['ʃnʊpfən] (**-s, -**) M cold
Schnupftabak M snuff
schnuppe ['ʃnʊpə] (*umg*) ADJ: **jdm ~ sein** to be all the same to sb
schnuppern ['ʃnʊpərn] VI to sniff
Schnur [ʃnuːr] (**-, Schnüre**) F string; (*Kordel*) cord; (*Elek*) flex
Schnürchen ['ʃnyːrçən] NT: **es läuft** *od* **klappt (alles) wie am ~** everything's going like clockwork
schnüren ['ʃnyːrən] VT to tie
schnurgerade ADJ straight (as a die *od* an arrow)
schnurlos ADJ (*Telefon*) cordless
Schnurrbart ['ʃnʊrbaːrt] M moustache (BRIT), mustache (US)
schnurren ['ʃnʊrən] VI to purr; (*Kreisel*) to hum
Schnürschuh M lace-up (shoe)
Schnürsenkel M shoelace
schnurstracks ADV straight (away); **~ auf jdn/etw zugehen** to make a beeline for sb/sth (*umg*)
schob *etc* [ʃoːp] VB *siehe* **schieben**
Schock [ʃɔk] (**-(e)s, -e**) M shock; **unter ~ stehen** to be in (a state of) shock
schocken (*umg*) VT to shock
Schocker (**-s, -**) (*umg*) M shocking film/novel, shocker
schockieren VT to shock, to outrage
Schöffe ['ʃœfə] (**-n, -n**) M lay magistrate
Schöffengericht NT magistrates' court
Schöffin F lay magistrate
Schokolade [ʃoko'laːdə] (**-, -n**) F chocolate
Schokoriegel M chocolate bar
scholl *etc* [ʃɔl] VB *siehe* **schallen**
Scholle ['ʃɔlə] (**-, -n**) F clod; (*Eisscholle*) ice floe; (*Fisch*) plaice
Scholli ['ʃɔli] (*umg*) M: **mein lieber ~!** (*drohend*) now look here!

SCHLÜSSELWORT

schon [ʃoːn] ADV **1** (*bereits*) already; **er ist schon da** he's there/here already, he's already there/here; **ist er schon da?** is he there/here yet?; **warst du schon einmal dort?** have you ever been there?; **ich war schon einmal dort** I've

S

been there before; **das war schon immer so** that has always been the case; **hast du schon gehört?** have you heard?; **schon 1920** as early as 1920; **schon vor 100 Jahren** as far back as 100 years ago; **er wollte schon die Hoffnung aufgeben, als ...** he was just about to give up hope when ...; **wartest du schon lange?** have you been waiting (for) long?; **wie schon so oft** as so often (before); **was, schon wieder?** what – again?

2 (*bestimmt*) all right; **du wirst schon sehen** you'll see (all right); **das wird schon noch gut gehen** that should turn out OK (in the end)

3 (*bloß*) just; **allein schon das Gefühl ...** just the very feeling ...; **schon der Gedanke** the mere *od* very thought; **wenn ich das schon höre** I only have to hear that

4 (*einschränkend*): **ja schon, aber ...** yes (well), but ...

5: **das ist schon möglich** that's quite possible; **schon gut** OK; **du weißt schon** you know; **komm schon** come on; **hör schon auf damit!** will you stop that!; **was macht das schon, wenn ...?** what does it matter if ...?; **und wenn schon!** (*umg*) so what?

schön [ʃøːn] ADJ beautiful; (*Mann*) handsome; (*nett*) nice ▶ ADV: **sich ganz ~ ärgern** to be very angry; **da hast du etwas Schönes angerichtet** you've made a fine *od* nice mess; **sich ~ machen** to make o.s. look nice; **schöne Grüße** best wishes; **schönen Dank** (many) thanks; **~ weich/warm** nice and soft/warm

schonen [ˈʃoːnən] VT to look after; (*jds Nerven*) to spare; (*Gegner, Kind*) to be easy on; (*Teppich, Füße*) to save ▶ VR to take it easy

schonend ADJ careful, gentle; **jdm etw ~ beibringen** to break sth to sb gently

Schoner [ˈʃoːnər] (**-s, -**) M (*Naut*) schooner; (*Sesselschoner*) cover

Schönfärberei F (*fig*) glossing things over

Schonfrist F period of grace

Schöngeist M cultured person, aesthete (BRIT), esthete (US)

Schönheit F beauty

Schönheits- ZW: **Schönheitsfehler** M blemish, flaw; **Schönheitsoperation** F cosmetic surgery; **Schönheitswettbewerb** M beauty contest

Schonkost (**-**) F light diet

Schönschrift F: **in ~** in one's best (hand)writing

schöntun *unreg* VI: **jdm ~** (*schmeicheln*) to flatter *od* soft-soap sb, to play up to sb

Schonung F good care; (*Nachsicht*) consideration; (*Forst*) plantation of young trees

schonungslos ADJ ruthless, harsh

Schonzeit F close season

Schopf [ʃɔpf] (**-(e)s, Schöpfe**) M: **eine Gelegenheit beim ~ ergreifen** *od* **fassen** to seize *od* grasp an opportunity with both hands

schöpfen [ˈʃœpfən] VT to scoop; (*Suppe*) to ladle; (*Mut*) to summon up; (*Luft*) to breathe in; (*Hoffnung*) to find

Schöpfer (**-s, -**) M creator; (*Gott*) Creator; (*umg: Schöpfkelle*) ladle; **schöpferisch** ADJ creative

Schöpfkelle F ladle

Schöpflöffel M skimmer, scoop

Schöpfung F creation

Schoppen [ˈʃɔpən] (**-s, -**) M (*Glas Wein*) glass of wine; **Schoppenwein** M wine by the glass

schor *etc* [ʃoːr] VB *siehe* **scheren**

Schorf [ʃɔrf] (**-(e)s, -e**) M scab

Schorle [ˈʃɔrlə] (**-, -n**) F spritzer, *wine and soda water or lemonade*

Schornstein [ˈʃɔrnʃtaɪn] M chimney; (*Naut*) funnel; **Schornsteinfeger** (**-s, -**) M chimney sweep

Schose [ˈʃoːzə] (**-, -n**) F = **Chose**

schoss [ʃɔs] VB *siehe* **schießen**

Schoß (**-es, -Schöße**) M lap; (*Rockschoß*) coat tail; **im Schoße der Familie** in the bosom of one's family

Schoßhund M lapdog

Schössling [ˈʃœslɪŋ] M (*Bot*) shoot

Schote [ˈʃoːtə] (**-, -n**) F pod

Schotte [ˈʃɔtə] (**-n, -n**) M Scot, Scotsman

Schottenrock [ˈʃɔtənrɔk] M kilt; (*für Frauen*) tartan skirt

Schotter [ˈʃɔtər] (**-s**) M gravel; (*im Straßenbau*) road metal; (*Eisenb*) ballast

Schottin [ˈʃɔtɪn] F Scot, Scotswoman

schottisch [ˈʃɔtɪʃ] ADJ Scottish, Scots; **das schottische Hochland** the Scottish Highlands *pl*

Schottland (**-s**) NT Scotland

schraffieren [ʃraˈfiːrən] VT to hatch

schräg [ʃrɛːk] ADJ slanting; (*schief, geneigt*) sloping; (*nicht gerade od parallel*) oblique ▶ ADV: **~ gedruckt** in italics; **etw ~ stellen** to put sth at an angle; **~ gegenüber** diagonally opposite

Schräge [ˈʃrɛːgə] (**-, -n**) F slant

Schräg- ZW: **Schrägkante** F bevelled (BRIT) *od* beveled (US) edge; **Schrägschrift** F italics *pl*; **Schrägstreifen** M bias binding; **Schrägstrich** M oblique stroke

Schramme [ˈʃramə] (**-, -n**) F scratch

schrammen VT to scratch

Schrank [ʃraŋk] (**-(e)s, Schränke**) M cupboard (BRIT), closet (US); (*Kleiderschrank*) wardrobe

Schranke (**-, -n**) F barrier; (*fig: Grenze*) limit; (*: Hindernis*) barrier; **jdn in seine Schranken (ver)weisen** (*fig*) to put sb in his place

schrankenlos ADJ boundless; (*zügellos*) unrestrained

Schrankenwärter M (*Eisenb*) level-crossing (BRIT) *od* grade-crossing (US) attendant

Schrankkoffer M wardrobe trunk

Schrankwand F wall unit

Schraube [ˈʃraʊbə] (**-, -n**) F screw

schrauben VT to screw; **etw in die Höhe ~** (*fig: Preise, Rekorde*) to push sth up; (*: Ansprüche*) to raise sth

Schrauben- ZW: **Schraubendreher** (**-s, -**) M screwdriver; **Schraubenschlüssel** M spanner (BRIT), wrench (US); **Schraubenzieher** (**-s, -**) M screwdriver

Schraubstock ['ʃraupʃtɔk] M (*Tech*) vice (BRIT), vise (US)
Schraubverschluss M screw top, screw cap
Schrebergarten ['ʃre:bərgartən] M allotment (BRIT)
Schreck [ʃrɛk] (**-(e)s, -e**) M fright; **o ~ lass nach!** (*hum: umg*) for goodness' sake!
schrecken VT to frighten, to scare ▶ VI: **aus dem Schlaf ~** to be startled out of one's sleep; **Schrecken** (**-s, -**) M terror; (*Schreck*) fright
schreckensbleich ADJ as white as a sheet *od* ghost
Schreckensherrschaft F (reign of) terror
Schreck- zW: **Schreckgespenst** NT nightmare; **schreckhaft** ADJ jumpy, easily frightened; **schrecklich** ADJ terrible, dreadful; **schrecklich gerne!** (*umg*) I'd absolutely love to; **Schreckschraube** (*pej, umg*) F (old) battle-axe; **Schreckschuss** M shot fired in the air; **Schrecksekunde** F moment of shock
Schrei [ʃraɪ] (**-(e)s, -e**) M scream; (*Ruf*) shout; **der letzte ~** (*umg*) the latest thing, all the rage
Schreibbedarf M writing materials *pl*, stationery
Schreibblock M writing pad
schreiben ['ʃraɪbən] *unreg* VT to write; (*mit Schreibmaschine*) to type out; (*berichten: Zeitung etc*) to say; (*buchstabieren*) to spell ▶ VI to write; (*mit Schreibmaschine*) to type; (*in Zeitung etc*) to say; (*buchstabieren*) to spell ▶ VR: **wie schreibt sich das?** how is that spelt?; **Schreiben** (**-s, -**) NT letter, communication
Schreiber(in) (**-s, -**) M(F) writer; (*Büroschreiber*) clerk
Schreib- zW: **schreibfaul** ADJ lazy about writing letters; **Schreibfehler** M spelling mistake; **Schreibkraft** F typist; **Schreibmaschine** F typewriter; **Schreibpapier** NT notepaper; **Schreibschrift** F running handwriting; (*Typ*) script; **Schreibschutz** M (*Comput*) write-protect; **Schreibstube** F orderly room; **Schreibtisch** M desk; **Schreibtischtäter** M wire *od* string puller
Schreibung F spelling
Schreib- zW: **Schreibunterlage** F pad; **Schreibwaren** PL stationery *sing*; **Schreibwarengeschäft** NT stationer's (shop) (BRIT), stationery store (US); **Schreibweise** F spelling; (*Stil*) style; **schreibwütig** ADJ crazy about writing; **Schreibzentrale** F typing pool; **Schreibzeug** NT writing materials *pl*
schreien ['ʃraɪən] *unreg* VT, VI to scream; (*rufen*) to shout; **es war zum S~** (*umg*) it was a scream *od* a hoot; **nach etw ~** (*fig*) to cry out for sth
schreiend ADJ (*fig*) glaring; (: *Farbe*) loud
Schreihals (*umg*) M (*Baby*) bawler; (*Unruhestifter*) noisy troublemaker
Schreikrampf M screaming fit
Schreiner ['ʃraɪnər] (**-s, -**) M joiner; (*Zimmermann*) carpenter; (*Möbelschreiner*) cabinetmaker
Schreinerei [ʃraɪnə'raɪ] F joiner's workshop
schreiten ['ʃraɪtən] *unreg* VI to stride
schrie *etc* [ʃri:] VB *siehe* **schreien**
schrieb *etc* [ʃri:p] VB *siehe* **schreiben**
Schrieb (**-(e)s, -e**) (*umg*) M missive (*hum*)
Schrift [ʃrɪft] (**-, -en**) F writing; (*Handschrift*) handwriting; (*Schriftart*) script; (*Typ*) typeface; (*Buch*) work; **Schriftart** F (*Handschrift*) script; (*Typ*) typeface; **Schriftbild** NT script; (*Comput*) typeface; **Schriftdeutsch** NT written German; **Schrifterkennung** F optical character recognition, OCR; **Schriftführer** M secretary; **schriftlich** ADJ written ▶ ADV in writing; **das kann ich Ihnen schriftlich geben** (*fig: umg*) I can tell you that for free; **Schriftprobe** F (*Handschrift*) specimen of one's handwriting; **Schriftsatz** M (*Typ*) fount (BRIT), font (US); **Schriftsetzer** M compositor; **Schriftsprache** F written language
Schriftsteller(in) (**-s, -**) M(F) writer; **schriftstellerisch** ADJ literary
Schrift- zW: **Schriftstück** NT document; **Schriftverkehr** M correspondence; **Schriftwechsel** M correspondence
schrill [ʃrɪl] ADJ shrill; **schrillen** VI (*Stimme*) to sound shrilly; (*Telefon*) to ring shrilly
schritt *etc* [ʃrɪt] VB *siehe* **schreiten**
Schritt (**-(e)s, -e**) M step; (*Gangart*) walk; (*Tempo*) pace; (*von Hose*) crotch, crutch (BRIT); **auf ~ und Tritt** (*lit, fig*) wherever *od* everywhere one goes; **„~ fahren"** "dead slow"; **mit zehn Schritten Abstand** at a distance of ten paces; **den ersten ~ tun** (*fig*) to make the first move; (*etw beginnen*) to take the first step; **Schritte gegen etw unternehmen** to take steps against sth
Schritt- zW: **Schrittmacher** M pacemaker; **Schritttempo** NT: **im Schritttempo** at a walking pace; **schrittweise** ADV gradually, little by little
schroff [ʃrɔf] ADJ steep; (*zackig*) jagged; (*fig*) brusque; (*ungeduldig*) abrupt
schröpfen ['ʃrœpfən] VT (*fig*) to fleece
Schrot [ʃro:t] (**-(e)s, -e**) M OD NT (*Blei*) (small) shot; (*Getreide*) coarsely ground grain, groats *pl*; **Schrotflinte** F shotgun
Schrott [ʃrɔt] (**-(e)s, -e**) M scrap metal; (*fig*) rubbish; **ein Auto zu ~ fahren** to write off a car; **Schrotthändler** M scrap merchant; **Schrotthaufen** M scrap heap; **schrottreif** ADJ ready for the scrap heap; **Schrottwert** M scrap value
schrubben ['ʃrubən] VT to scrub
Schrubber (**-s, -**) M scrubbing brush
Schrulle ['ʃrulə] (**-, -n**) F eccentricity, quirk
schrullig ADJ cranky
schrumpfen ['ʃrumpfən] VI (*Hilfsverb sein*) to shrink; (*Apfel*) to shrivel; (*Leber, Niere*) to atrophy
Schub [ʃu:p] (**-(e)s, Schübe**) M (*Stoß*) push, shove; (*Gruppe, Anzahl*) batch; **Schubfach** NT drawer; **Schubkarren** M wheelbarrow; **Schublade** F drawer
Schubs [ʃu:ps] (**-es, -e**) (*umg*) M shove, push; **schubsen** (*umg*) VT, VI to shove, to push
schüchtern ['ʃʏçtərn] ADJ shy; **Schüchternheit** F shyness
schuf *etc* [ʃu:f] VB *siehe* **schaffen²**

S

Schuft [ʃʊft] (**-(e)s, -e**) M scoundrel
schuften (*umg*) VI to graft, to slave away
Schuh [ʃu:] (**-(e)s, -e**) M shoe; **jdm etw in die Schuhe schieben** (*fig: umg*) to put the blame for sth on sb; **wo drückt der ~?** (*fig*) what's troubling you?; **Schuhband** NT shoelace; **Schuhcreme** F shoe polish; **Schuhgröße** F shoe size; **Schuhlöffel** M shoehorn; **Schuhmacher** M shoemaker; **Schuhwerk** NT footwear
Schukosteckdose® ['ʃʊkoʃtɛkdo:zə] F safety socket
Schukostecker® M safety plug
Schul- zW: **Schulaufgaben** PL homework *sing*; **Schulbank** F: **die Schulbank drücken** (*umg*) to go to school; **Schulbehörde** F education authority; **Schulbesuch** M school attendance; **Schulbuch** NT schoolbook; **Schulbuchverlag** M educational publisher
schuld ADJ: **~ sein (an** *+dat***)** to be to blame (for); **er ist ~** it's his fault
Schuld [ʃʊlt] (**-, -en**) F guilt; (*Fin*) debt; (*Verschulden*) fault; **~ haben (an** *+dat***)** to be to blame (for); **jdm (die) ~ geben, jdm die ~ zuschieben** to blame sb; **ich bin mir keiner ~ bewusst** I'm not aware of having done anything wrong; **~ und Sühne** crime and punishment; **ich stehe tief in seiner ~** (*fig*) I'm deeply indebted to him; **Schulden haben** to be in debt; **Schulden machen** to run up debts; *siehe auch* **zuschulden**
schuldbewusst ADJ (*Mensch*) feeling guilty; (*Miene*) guilty
schulden ['ʃʊldən] VT to owe
schuldenfrei ADJ free from debt
Schuldgefühl NT feeling of guilt
schuldhaft ADJ (*Jur*) culpable
Schuldienst (**-(e)s**) M (school)teaching
schuldig ADJ guilty; (*gebührend*) due; **an etw** *dat* **~ sein** to be guilty of sth; **jdm etw ~ sein** *od* **bleiben** to owe sb sth; **jdn ~ sprechen** to find sb guilty; **~ geschieden sein** to be the guilty party in a divorce; **Schuldigkeit** F duty
schuldlos ADJ innocent, blameless
Schuldner(in) (**-s, -**) M(F) debtor
Schuld- zW: **Schuldprinzip** NT (*Jur*) principle of the guilty party; **Schuldschein** M promissory note, IOU; **Schuldspruch** M verdict of guilty
Schule ['ʃu:lə] (**-, -n**) F school; **auf** *od* **in der ~** at school; **in die ~ kommen/gehen** to start school/go to school; **~ machen** (*fig*) to become the accepted thing
schulen VT to train, to school
Schüler(in) ['ʃy:lər(ɪn)] (**-s, -**) M(F) pupil; **Schülerausweis** M (school) student card; **Schülerlotse** M *pupil acting as a road-crossing warden*; **Schülermitverwaltung** F school *od* student council
Schul- zW: **Schulferien** PL school holidays *pl* (BRIT) *od* vacation *sing* (US); **Schulfernsehen** NT schools' *od* educational television; **schulfrei** ADJ: **die Kinder haben morgen schulfrei** the children don't have to go to school tomorrow; **Schulfreund(in)** M(F) schoolmate; **Schulfunk** M schools' broadcasts *pl*; **Schulgeld** NT school fees *pl*, tuition (US); **Schulheft** NT exercise book; **Schulhof** M playground, schoolyard
schulisch ['ʃu:lɪʃ] ADJ (*Leistungen, Probleme*) at school; (*Angelegenheiten*) school *attrib*
Schul- zW: **Schuljahr** NT school year; **Schuljunge** M schoolboy; **Schulkind** NT schoolchild; **Schulleiter** M headmaster (*bes* BRIT), principal; **Schulleiterin** F headmistress (*bes* BRIT), principal; **Schulmädchen** NT schoolgirl; **Schulmedizin** F orthodox medicine; **Schulpflicht** F compulsory school attendance; **schulpflichtig** ADJ of school age; **Schulreife** F: **die Schulreife haben** to be ready to go to school; **Schulschiff** NT (*Naut*) training ship; **Schulsprecher(in)** M(F) head boy/girl (BRIT); **Schulstunde** F period, lesson; **Schultasche** F school bag
Schulter ['ʃʊltər] (**-, -n**) F shoulder; **auf die leichte ~ nehmen** to take lightly; **Schulterblatt** NT shoulder blade
schultern VT to shoulder
Schultüte F *bag of sweets given to children on the first day at school*
Schulung F training; (*Veranstaltung*) training course
Schul- zW: **Schulverweigerer(in)** M(F) school refuser; **Schulweg** M way to school; **Schulwesen** NT educational system; **Schulzeugnis** NT school report
schummeln ['ʃʊməln] (*umg*) VI: **(bei etw) ~** to cheat (at sth)
schummerig ['ʃʊmərɪç], **schummrig** ['ʃʊmrɪç] ADJ (*Beleuchtung*) dim; (*Raum*) dimly-lit
schund [ʃʊnt] VB *siehe* **schinden**
Schund (**-(e)s**) M trash, garbage
Schundroman M trashy novel
Schupo ['ʃu:po] (**-s, -s**) M ABK (*veraltet: = Schutzpolizist*) cop
Schuppe ['ʃʊpə] (**-, -n**) F scale; **Schuppen** PL (*Haarschuppen*) dandruff
schuppen VT to scale ▶ VR to peel
Schuppen (**-s, -**) M shed; (*umg: übles Lokal*) dive; *siehe auch* **Schuppe**
schuppig ['ʃʊpɪç] ADJ scaly
Schur [ʃu:r] (**-, -en**) F shearing
Schüreisen NT poker
schüren ['ʃy:rən] VT to rake; (*fig*) to stir up
schürfen ['ʃʏrfən] VT, VI to scrape, to scratch; (*Min*) to prospect
Schürfung F abrasion; (*Min*) prospecting
Schürhaken M poker
Schurke ['ʃʊrkə] (**-n, -n**) M rogue
Schurwolle F: **„reine ~"** "pure new wool"
Schurz [ʃʊrts] (**-es, -e**) M apron
Schürze ['ʃʏrtsə] (**-, -n**) F apron
Schürzenjäger (*umg*) M philanderer, one for the girls
Schuss [ʃʊs] (**-es, -Schüsse**) M shot; (*Fussball*) kick; (*Spritzer: von Wein, Essig etc*) dash; (*Weben*) weft; **(gut) in ~ sein** (*umg*) to be in good shape *od* nick; (*Mensch*) to be in form; **etw in ~ halten** to keep sth in good shape; **weitab vom ~ sein**

(*fig: umg*) to be miles from where the action is; **der goldene ~** *a lethal dose of a drug*; **ein ~ in den Ofen** (*umg*) a complete waste of time, a failure; **Schussbereich** M effective range

Schüssel ['ʃʏsəl] (**-, -n**) F bowl, basin; (*Servierschüssel, umg: Satellitenschüssel*) dish; (*Waschschüssel*) basin

schusselig ['ʃʊsəlıç] (*umg*) ADJ (*zerstreut*) scatterbrained, muddle-headed (*umg*)

Schuss- zW: **Schusslinie** F line of fire; **Schussverletzung** F bullet wound; **Schusswaffe** F firearm; **Schusswaffengebrauch** M (*form*) use of firearms; **Schusswechsel** M exchange of shots; **Schussweite** F range (of fire)

Schuster ['ʃu:stər] (**-s, -**) M cobbler, shoemaker

Schutt [ʃʊt] (**-(e)s**) M rubbish; (*Bauschutt*) rubble; **„~ abladen verboten"** "no tipping"; **Schuttabladeplatz** M refuse dump

Schüttelfrost M shivering

schütteln ['ʃʏtəln] VT to shake ▶ VR to shake o.s.; **sich vor Kälte ~** to shiver with cold; **sich vor Ekel ~** to shudder with *od* in disgust

schütten ['ʃʏtən] VT to pour; (*Zucker, Kies etc*) to tip; (*verschütten*) to spill ▶ VI UNPERS to pour (down)

schütter ADJ (*Haare*) sparse, thin

Schutthalde F dump

Schutthaufen M heap of rubble

Schutz [ʃʊts] (**-es**) M protection; (*Unterschlupf*) shelter; **jdn in ~ nehmen** to stand up for sb; **Schutzanzug** M overalls *pl*; **schutzbedürftig** ADJ in need of protection; **Schutzbefohlene(r)** F(M) charge; **Schutzblech** NT mudguard; **Schutzbrief** M (international) travel cover; **Schutzbrille** F goggles *pl*

Schütze ['ʃʏtsə] (**-n, -n**) M gunman; (*Gewehrschütze*) rifleman; (*Scharfschütze, Sportschütze*) marksman; (*Astrol*) Sagittarius

schützen ['ʃʏtsən] VT to protect ▶ VR to protect o.s.; **(sich) ~ vor** *+dat od* **gegen** to protect (o.s.) from *od* against; **gesetzlich geschützt** registered; **urheberrechtlich geschützt** protected by copyright; **vor Nässe ~!** keep dry

Schützenfest NT *fair featuring shooting matches*

Schutzengel M guardian angel

Schützen- zW: **Schützengraben** M trench; **Schützenhilfe** F (*fig*) support; **Schützenverein** M shooting club

Schutz- zW: **Schutzgebiet** NT protectorate; (*Naturschutzgebiet*) reserve; **Schutzgebühr** F (token) fee; **Schutzhaft** F protective custody; **Schutzheilige(r)** F(M) patron saint; **Schutzhelm** M safety helmet; **Schutzimpfung** F immunization

Schützling ['ʃʏtslıŋ] M protégé; (*bes Kind*) charge

Schutz- zW: **schutzlos** ADJ defenceless (BRIT), defenseless (US); **Schutzmann** (*pl* **-(e)s, -leute** *od* **-männer**) M policeman; **Schutzmarke** F trademark; **Schutzmaßnahme** F precaution; **Schutzpatron** M patron saint; **Schutzschirm** M (*Tech*) protective screen; **Schutzumschlag** M (book) jacket; **Schutzverband** M (*Med*) protective bandage *od* dressing; **Schutzvorrichtung** F safety device

Schw. ABK = **Schwester**

schwabbelig ['ʃvab(ə)lıç] (*umg*) ADJ (*Körperteil*) flabby; (: *Gelee*) wobbly

Schwabe ['ʃva:bə] (**-n, -n**) M Swabian

Schwaben (**-s**) NT Swabia

Schwäbin ['ʃvɛ:bın] F Swabian

schwäbisch ['ʃvɛ:bıʃ] ADJ Swabian

schwach [ʃvax] ADJ weak, feeble; (*Gedächtnis, Gesundheit*) poor; (*Hoffnung*) faint; **~ werden** to weaken; **das ist ein schwaches Bild** (*umg*) **od eine schwache Leistung** (*umg*) that's a poor show; **ein schwacher Trost** cold *od* small comfort; **mach mich nicht ~!** (*umg*) don't say that!; **auf schwachen Beinen** *od* **Füßen stehen** (*fig*) to be on shaky ground; (*Theorie*) to be shaky

Schwäche ['ʃvɛçə] (**-, -n**) F weakness

schwächen VT to weaken

schwach- zW: **Schwachheit** F weakness; **Schwachkopf** (*umg*) M dimwit, idiot; **schwachköpfig** ADJ silly, daft (BRIT)

schwächlich ADJ weakly, delicate

Schwächling M weakling

Schwach- zW: **Schwachsinn** M (*Med*) mental deficiency, feeble-mindedness (*veraltet*); (*umg: Quatsch*) rubbish; (*fig: umg: unsinnige Tat*) idiocy; **schwachsinnig** ADJ mentally deficient; (*Idee*) idiotic; **Schwachstelle** F weak point; **Schwachstrom** M weak current

Schwächung ['ʃvɛçʊŋ] F weakening

Schwaden ['ʃva:dən] (**-s, -**) M cloud

schwafeln ['ʃva:fəln] (*umg*) VI to blather, to drivel; (*in einer Prüfung*) to waffle

Schwager ['ʃva:gər] (**-s, Schwäger**) M brother-in-law

Schwägerin ['ʃvɛ:gərın] F sister-in-law

Schwalbe ['ʃvalbə] (**-, -n**) F swallow

Schwall [ʃval] (**-(e)s, -e**) M surge; (*Worte*) flood, torrent

schwamm [ʃvam] VB *siehe* **schwimmen**

Schwamm (**-(e)s, Schwämme**) M sponge; (*Pilz*) fungus; **~ drüber!** (*umg*) (let's) forget it!

schwammig ADJ spongy; (*Gesicht*) puffy; (*vage: Begriff*) woolly (BRIT), wooly (US)

Schwan [ʃva:n] (**-(e)s, Schwäne**) M swan

schwand *etc* [ʃvant] VB *siehe* **schwinden**

schwanen VI UNPERS: **jdm schwant es** sb has a foreboding *od* forebodings; **jdm schwant etwas** sb senses something might happen

schwang *etc* [ʃvaŋ] VB *siehe* **schwingen**

schwanger ['ʃvaŋər] ADJ pregnant

schwängern ['ʃvɛŋərn] VT to make pregnant

Schwangerschaft F pregnancy

Schwangerschaftsabbruch M termination of pregnancy, abortion

Schwank [ʃvaŋk] (**-(e)s, Schwänke**) M funny story; (*Liter*) merry *od* comical tale; (*Theat*) farce

schwanken VI to sway; (*taumeln*) to stagger, to reel; (*Preise, Zahlen*) to fluctuate; (*zögern*) to hesitate; (*Überzeugung etc*) to begin to waver; **ins S~ kommen** (*Baum, Gebäude etc*) to start to

S

sway; (*Preise, Kurs etc*) to start to fluctuate *od* vary
Schwankung F fluctuation
Schwanz [ʃvants] (**-es, Schwänze**) M tail; (*umg!: Penis*) prick (*umg!*); **kein ~** (*umg*) not a (blessed) soul
schwänzen ['ʃvɛntsən] (*umg*) VT (*Stunde, Vorlesung*) to skip ▶ VI to play truant
Schwänzer ['ʃvɛntsər] (**-s, -**) (*umg*) M truant
schwappen ['ʃvapən] VI (*überschwappen*) to splash, to slosh
Schwarm [ʃvarm] (**-(e)s, Schwärme**) M swarm; (*umg*) heart-throb, idol
schwärmen ['ʃvɛrmən] VI to swarm; **~ für** to be mad *od* wild about
Schwärmerei [ʃvɛrmə'raɪ] F enthusiasm
schwärmerisch ADJ impassioned, effusive
Schwarte ['ʃvartə] (**-, -n**) F hard skin; (*Speckschwarte*) rind; (*umg: Buch*) tome (*hum*)
Schwartenmagen (**-s**) M (*Koch*) brawn
schwarz [ʃvarts] ADJ black; (*umg: ungesetzlich*) illicit; (*: katholisch*) Catholic, Papist (*pej*); (*Pol*) Christian Democrat; **ins Schwarze treffen** (*lit, fig*) to hit the bull's-eye; **das Schwarze Brett** the notice (BRIT) *od* bulletin (US) board; **schwarze Liste** blacklist; **schwarzes Loch** black hole; **das Schwarze Meer** the Black Sea; **Schwarzer Peter** (*Karten*) *children's card game*; **jdm den schwarzen Peter zuschieben** (*fig: die Verantwortung abschieben*) to pass the buck to sb (*umg*); **dort wählen alle ~** they all vote conservative there; **in den schwarzen Zahlen** in the black; *siehe auch* **schwarzmalen**; **Schwarzarbeit** F illicit work, moonlighting; **Schwarzarbeiter** M moonlighter; **schwarzärgern** VR to get extremely annoyed; **Schwarzbrot** NT (*Pumpernickel*) black bread, pumpernickel; (*braun*) brown rye bread
Schwarze(r) F(M) (*Neger*) black; (*umg: Katholik*) Papist; (*Pol: umg*) Christian Democrat
Schwärze ['ʃvɛrtsə] (**-, -n**) F blackness; (*Farbe*) blacking; (*Druckerschwärze*) printer's ink
schwärzen VT to blacken
Schwarz- ZW: **schwarzfahren** *unreg* VI to travel without paying; (*ohne Führerschein*) to drive without a licence (BRIT) *od* license (US); **Schwarzfahrer** M (*Bus etc*) fare dodger (*umg*); **Schwarzhandel** M black market (trade); **Schwarzhändler** M black-market operator; **schwarzhören** VI to listen to the radio without a licence (BRIT) *od* license (US)
schwärzlich ['ʃvɛrtslɪç] ADJ blackish, darkish
Schwarz- ZW: **schwarzmalen** VI to be pessimistic; **Schwarzmarkt** M black market; **schwarzsehen** VI *unreg* (*TV*) to watch TV without a licence (BRIT) *od* license (US); (*umg*) to see the gloomy side of things; **Schwarzseher** M pessimist; (*TV*) viewer without a licence (BRIT) *od* license (US); **Schwarzwald** M Black Forest; **Schwarzwälder Kirschtorte** F Black Forest gâteau; **Schwarzweiß-** IN ZW black and white; **schwarz-weiß, schwarzweiß** ADJ black and white
Schwatz [ʃvats] (**-es, -e**) M chat
schwatzen ['ʃvatsən] VI to chat; (*schnell, unaufhörlich*) to chatter; (*über belanglose Dinge*) to prattle; (*Unsinn reden*) to blether (*umg*)
schwätzen ['ʃvɛtsən] VI = **schwatzen**
Schwätzer(in) ['ʃvɛtsər(ɪn)] (**-s, -**) M(F) chatterbox; (*Schwafler*) gasbag (*umg*); (*Klatschbase*) gossip
schwatzhaft ADJ talkative, gossipy
Schwebe ['ʃve:bə] F: **in der ~** (*fig*) in abeyance; (*Jur, Comm*) pending
Schwebebahn F overhead railway (BRIT) *od* railroad (US)
Schwebebalken M (*Sport*) beam
schweben VI to drift, to float; (*hoch*) to soar; (*unentschieden sein*) to be in the balance; **es schwebte mir vor Augen** (*Bild*) I saw it in my mind's eye
schwebend ADJ (*Tech, Chem*) suspended; (*fig*) undecided, unresolved; **schwebendes Verfahren** (*Jur*) pending case
schwed. ABK = **schwedisch**
Schwede ['ʃve:də] (**-n, -n**) M Swede
Schweden (**-s**) NT Sweden
Schwedin ['ʃve:dɪn] F Swede
schwedisch ADJ Swedish
Schwefel ['ʃve:fəl] (**-s**) M sulphur (BRIT), sulfur (US); **Schwefeldioxid** NT sulphur dioxide
schwefelig ADJ sulphurous (BRIT), sulfurous (US)
Schwefelsäure F sulphuric (BRIT) *od* sulfuric (US) acid
Schweif [ʃvaɪf] (**-(e)s, -e**) M tail
schweifen VI to wander, to roam
Schweigegeld NT hush money
Schweigeminute F one minute('s) silence
schweigen ['ʃvaɪgən] *unreg* VI to be silent; (*still sein*) to keep quiet; **kannst du ~?** can you keep a secret?; **ganz zu ~ von ...** to say nothing of ...; **Schweigen** (**-s**) NT silence
schweigend ADJ silent
Schweigepflicht F pledge of secrecy; (*von Anwalt etc*) requirement of confidentiality
schweigsam ['ʃvaɪkza:m] ADJ silent; (*als Charaktereigenschaft*) taciturn; **Schweigsamkeit** F silence; (*als Charaktereigenschaft*) taciturnity
Schwein [ʃvaɪn] (**-(e)s, -e**) NT pig; (*fig: umg*) (good) luck; (*gemeiner Mensch*) swine; **kein ~** (*umg*) nobody, not a single person
Schweine- ZW: **Schweinebraten** M joint of pork; (*gekocht*) roast pork; **Schweinefleisch** NT pork; **Schweinegeld** (*umg*) NT: **ein Schweinegeld** a packet; **Schweinegrippe** F swine flu; **Schweinehund** (*umg*) M stinker, swine
Schweinerei [ʃvaɪnə'raɪ] F mess; (*Gemeinheit*) dirty trick; **so eine ~!** (*umg*) how disgusting!
Schweineschmalz NT dripping; (*als Kochfett*) lard
Schweinestall M pigsty
schweinisch ADJ filthy
Schweinsleder NT pigskin
Schweinsohr NT pig's ear; (*Gebäck*) (kidney-shaped) pastry

Schweiß [ʃvais] (**-es**) M sweat, perspiration; **Schweißband** NT sweatband
Schweißbrenner (**-s, -**) M (*Tech*) welding torch
schweißen VT, VI to weld
Schweißer (**-s, -**) M welder
Schweiß- zW: **Schweißfüße** PL sweaty feet *pl*; **Schweißnaht** F weld; **schweißnass** ADJ sweaty
Schweiz [ʃvaits] F: **die ~** Switzerland
schweiz. ABK = **schweizerisch**
Schweizer [ˈʃvaitsər] (**-s, -**) M Swiss ▸ ADJ *attrib* Swiss; **Schweizerdeutsch** NT Swiss German; **Schweizerin** F Swiss; **schweizerisch** ADJ Swiss
schwelen [ˈʃveːlən] VI to smoulder (BRIT), to smolder (US)
schwelgen [ˈʃvɛlgən] VI to indulge o.s.; **~ in** *+dat* to indulge in
Schwelle [ˈʃvɛlə] (**-, -n**) F (*auch fig*) threshold; (*Eisenb*) sleeper (BRIT), tie (US)
schwellen *unreg* VI to swell
Schwellenland NT threshold country
Schwellung F swelling
Schwemme [ˈʃvɛmə] F: **eine ~ an** *+dat* a glut of
schwemmen [ˈʃvɛmən] VT (*treiben: Sand etc*) to wash
Schwengel [ˈʃvɛŋəl] (**-s, -**) M pump handle; (*Glockenschwengel*) clapper
Schwenk [ʃvɛŋk] (**-(e)s, -s**) M (*Film*) pan, panning shot
Schwenkarm M swivel arm
schwenkbar ADJ swivel-mounted
schwenken VT to swing; (*Kamera*) to pan; (*Fahne*) to wave; (*Kartoffeln*) to toss; (*abspülen*) to rinse ▸ VI to turn, to swivel; (*Mil*) to wheel
Schwenkung F turn; (*Mil*) wheel
schwer [ʃveːr] ADJ heavy; (*schwierig*) difficult, hard; (*schlimm*) serious, bad ▸ ADV (*sehr*) very (much); (*verletzt etc*) seriously, badly; **~ erziehbar** maladjusted; **jdm/sich etw ~ machen** to make sth difficult for sb/o.s.; **~ verdaulich** indigestible; (*fig*) heavy; **~ verdient** (*Geld*) hard-earned; **~ verletzt** seriously *od* badly injured; **~ verwundet** seriously wounded; **~ erkältet sein** to have a heavy cold; **er lernt ~** he's a slow learner; **er ist ~ in Ordnung** (*umg*) he's a good bloke (BRIT) *od* guy; **~ hören** to be hard of hearing; *siehe auch* **schwerfallen**; **schwernehmen**; **schwertun**; **schwerwiegend**; **Schwerarbeiter** M labourer (BRIT), laborer (US); **Schwerbehinderte(r)** F(M), **Schwerbeschädigte(r)** F(M) (*veraltet*) severely handicapped person
Schwere (**-, -n**) F heaviness; (*Gewicht*) weight; (*Phys*) gravity; **schwerelos** ADJ weightless; **Schwerelosigkeit** F weightlessness
schwer- zW: **schwerfallen** *unreg* VI: **jdm schwerfallen** to be difficult for sb; **schwerfällig** ADJ (*auch Stil*) ponderous; (*Gang*) clumsy, awkward; (*Verstand*) slow; **Schwergewicht** NT heavyweight; (*fig*) emphasis; **schwergewichtig** ADJ heavyweight; **schwerhörig** ADJ hard of hearing; **Schwerindustrie** F heavy industry; **Schwerkraft** F gravity; **Schwerkranke(r)** F(M) person who is seriously ill; **schwerlich** ADV hardly; **Schwermetall** NT heavy metal; **schwermütig** ADJ melancholy; **schwernehmen** *unreg* VT to take to heart; **Schwerpunkt** M centre (BRIT) *od* center (US) of gravity; (*fig*) emphasis, crucial point; **Schwerpunktstreik** M pinpoint strike; **schwerreich** (*umg*) ADJ *attrib* stinking rich
Schwert [ʃveːrt] (**-(e)s, -er**) NT sword; **Schwertlilie** F iris
schwer- zW: **schwertun** *unreg* VR: **sich** *dat, akk* **schwertun** to have difficulties; **Schwerverbrecher** M criminal; **Schwerverletzte(r)** F(M) serious casualty; **schwerwiegend** ADJ weighty, important
Schwester [ˈʃvɛstər] (**-, -n**) F sister; (*Med*) nurse; **schwesterlich** ADJ sisterly
schwieg *etc* [ʃviːk] VB *siehe* **schweigen**
Schwieger- zW: **Schwiegereltern** PL parents-in-law *pl*; **Schwiegermutter** F mother-in-law; **Schwiegersohn** M son-in-law; **Schwiegertochter** F daughter-in-law; **Schwiegervater** M father-in-law
Schwiele [ˈʃviːlə] (**-, -n**) F callus
schwierig [ˈʃviːrɪç] ADJ difficult, hard; **Schwierigkeit** F difficulty; **in Schwierigkeiten kommen** to get into trouble; **Schwierigkeitsgrad** M degree of difficulty
schwillt [ʃvɪlt] VB *siehe* **schwellen**
Schwimmbad NT swimming baths *pl*
Schwimmbecken NT swimming pool
schwimmen *unreg* VI to swim; (*treiben, nicht sinken*) to float; (*fig: unsicher sein*) to be all at sea; **im Geld ~** (*umg*) to be rolling in money; **mir schwimmt es vor den Augen** I feel dizzy
Schwimmer (**-s, -**) M swimmer; (*Angeln*) float
Schwimmerin F swimmer
Schwimm- zW: **Schwimmflosse** F (*von Taucher*) flipper; **Schwimmhaut** F (*Ornithologie*) web; **Schwimmlehrer** M swimming instructor; **Schwimmsport** M swimming; **Schwimmweste** F life jacket
Schwindel [ˈʃvɪndəl] (**-s**) M dizziness; (*Betrug*) swindle, fraud; (*Zeug*) stuff; **in ~ erregender Höhe** at a dizzy height; **schwindelfrei** ADJ free from giddiness; **nicht schwindelfrei sein** to suffer from vertigo
schwindeln VI (*umg: lügen*) to fib; **mir schwindelt** I feel dizzy; **jdm schwindelt es** sb feels dizzy
schwinden [ˈʃvɪndən] *unreg* VI to disappear; (*Kräfte*) to fade, to fail; (*sich verringern*) to decrease
Schwindler (**-s, -**) M swindler; (*Hochstapler*) con man, fraud; (*Lügner*) liar
schwindlig ADJ dizzy; **mir ist ~** I feel dizzy
Schwindsucht F (*veraltet*) consumption
schwingen [ˈʃvɪŋən] *unreg* VT to swing; (*Waffe etc*) to brandish ▸ VI to swing; (*vibrieren*) to vibrate; (*klingen*) to sound
Schwinger (**-s, -**) M (*Boxen*) swing
Schwingtor NT up-and-over door
Schwingtür F swing door(s *pl*) (BRIT), swinging door(s *pl*) (US)
Schwingung F vibration; (*Phys*) oscillation

Schwips [ʃvɪps] (**-es, -e**) M: **einen ~ haben** to be tipsy
schwirren ['ʃvɪrən] VI to buzz
Schwitze ['ʃvɪtsə] (**-, -n**) F (*Koch*) roux
schwitzen VI to sweat, to perspire
schwofen ['ʃvo:fən] (*umg*) VI to dance
schwoll *etc* [ʃvɔl] VB *siehe* **schwellen**
schwören ['ʃvø:rən] *unreg* VT, VI to swear; **auf jdn/etw ~** (*fig*) to swear by sb/sth
schwul [ʃvu:l] (*umg*) ADJ gay, queer (*pej*)
schwül [ʃvy:l] ADJ sultry, close
Schwule(r) (*umg*) M gay, queer (*pej*), fag (*US pej*)
Schwüle (-) F sultriness, closeness
Schwulität [ʃvuli'tɛ:t] (*umg*) F trouble, difficulty
Schwulst [ʃvʊlst] (**-(e)s**) M bombast
schwülstig ['ʃvʏlstɪç] ADJ pompous
Schwund [ʃvʊnt] (**-(e)s**) M *+gen* decrease (in), decline (in), dwindling (of); (*Med*) atrophy; (*Schrumpfen*) shrinkage
Schwung [ʃvʊŋ] (**-(e)s, Schwünge**) M swing; (*Triebkraft*) momentum; (*fig: Energie*) verve, energy; (*umg: Menge*) batch; **in ~ sein** (*fig*) to be in full swing; **~ in die Sache bringen** (*umg*) to liven things up; **schwunghaft** ADJ brisk, lively; **Schwungrad** NT flywheel; **schwungvoll** ADJ vigorous
schwur *etc* [ʃvu:r] VB *siehe* **schwören**
Schwur (**-(e)s, Schwüre**) M oath
Schwurgericht NT court with a jury
scrollen ['skrɔlən] VI (*Comput*) to scroll
SDR (-) M ABK (= *Süddeutscher Rundfunk*) South German Radio
sechs [zɛks] NUM six; **Sechseck** NT hexagon; **sechshundert** NUM six hundred
sechste(r, s) ADJ sixth
Sechstel ['zɛkstəl] (**-s, -**) NT sixth
sechzehn ['zɛçtse:n] NUM sixteen
sechzig ['zɛçtsɪç] NUM sixty
See[1] [ze:] (**-, -n**) F sea; **an der ~** by the sea, at the seaside; **in ~ stechen** to put to sea; **auf hoher ~** on the high seas
See[2] [ze:] (**-s, -n**) M lake
See- ZW: **Seebad** NT seaside resort; **Seebär** M (*hum: umg*) seadog; (*Zool*) fur seal; **Seefahrt** F seafaring; (*Reise*) voyage; **seefest** ADJ (*Mensch*) not subject to seasickness; **Seegang** M (motion of the) sea; **Seegras** NT seaweed; **Seehund** M seal; **Seeigel** M sea urchin; **Seekarte** F chart; **seekrank** ADJ seasick; **Seekrankheit** F seasickness; **Seelachs** M rock salmon
Seele ['ze:lə] (**-, -n**) F soul; (*Mittelpunkt*) life and soul; **jdm aus der ~ sprechen** to express exactly what sb feels; **das liegt mir auf der ~** it weighs heavily on my mind; **eine ~ von Mensch** an absolute dear
Seelen- ZW: **Seelenamt** NT (*Rel*) requiem; **Seelenfriede, Seelenfrieden** M peace of mind; **Seelenheil** NT salvation of one's soul; (*fig*) spiritual welfare; **Seelenruhe** F: **in aller Seelenruhe** calmly; (*kaltblütig*) as cool as you please; **seelenruhig** ADV calmly
Seeleute ['ze:lɔʏtə] PL seamen *pl*
Seel- ZW: **seelisch** ADJ mental; (*Rel*) spiritual; (*Belastung*) emotional; **Seelsorge** F pastoral duties *pl*; **Seelsorger** (**-s, -**) M clergyman
See- ZW: **Seemacht** F naval power; **Seemann** (**-(e)s**, *pl* **-leute**) M seaman, sailor; **Seemeile** F nautical mile
Seengebiet ['ze:əngəbi:t] NT lakeland district
See- ZW: **Seenot** F: **in Seenot** (*Schiff etc*) in distress; **Seepferd** NT, **Seepferdchen** NT sea horse; **Seeräuber** M pirate; **Seerecht** NT maritime law; **Seerose** F waterlily; **Seestern** M starfish; **Seetang** M seaweed; **seetüchtig** ADJ seaworthy; **Seeversicherung** F marine insurance; **Seeweg** M sea route; **auf dem Seeweg** by sea; **Seezunge** F sole
Segel ['ze:gəl] (**-s, -**) NT sail; **mit vollen Segeln** under full sail *od* canvas; (*fig*) with gusto; **die ~ streichen** (*fig*) to give in; **Segelboot** NT yacht; **Segelfliegen** (**-s**) NT gliding; **Segelflieger** M glider pilot; **Segelflugzeug** NT glider
segeln VT, VI to sail; **durch eine Prüfung ~** (*umg*) to flop in an exam, to fail (in) an exam
Segel- ZW: **Segelschiff** NT sailing vessel; **Segelsport** M sailing; **Segeltuch** NT canvas
Segen ['ze:gən] (**-s, -**) M blessing
segensreich ADJ beneficial
Segler ['ze:glər] (**-s, -**) M sailor, yachtsman; (*Boot*) sailing boat
Seglerin F yachtswoman
segnen ['ze:gnən] VT to bless
sehen ['ze:ən] *unreg* VT, VI to see; (*in bestimmte Richtung*) to look; (*Fernsehsendung*) to watch; **sieht man das?** does it show?; **da sieht man(s) mal wieder!** that's typical!; **du siehst das nicht richtig** you've got it wrong; **so gesehen** looked at in this way; **sich ~ lassen** to put in an appearance, to appear; **das neue Rathaus kann sich ~ lassen** the new town hall is certainly something to be proud of; **siehe oben/unten** see above/below; **kann ich das mal ~?** can I have a look at it?; **da kann man mal ~** that just shows (you) *od* just goes to show (*umg*); **mal ~!** we'll see!; **darauf ~, dass ...** to make sure (that) ...; **jdn kommen ~** to see sb coming
sehenswert ADJ worth seeing
Sehenswürdigkeiten PL sights *pl* (of a town)
Seher (**-s, -**) M seer
Sehfehler M sight defect
Sehkraft F (eye)sight
Sehne ['ze:nə] (**-, -n**) F sinew; (*an Bogen*) string
sehnen VR: **sich ~ nach** to long *od* yearn for
Sehnenscheidenentzündung F (*Med*) tendinitis
Sehnerv M optic nerve
sehnig ADJ sinewy
sehnlich ADJ ardent
Sehnsucht F longing
sehnsüchtig ADJ longing; (*Erwartung*) eager
sehnsuchtsvoll ADV longingly, yearningly
sehr [ze:r] ADV (*vor adj, adv*) very; (*mit Verben*) a lot, (very) much; **zu ~** too much; **er ist ~ dafür/dagegen** he is all for it/very much against it;

wie ~ er sich auch bemühte ... however much he tried ...
Sehvermögen ['ze:fɛrmø:gən] **(-s)** NT powers *pl* of vision
seicht [zaɪçt] ADJ (*lit, fig*) shallow
seid [zaɪt] VB *siehe* **sein**
Seide ['zaɪdə] **(-, -n)** F silk
Seidel (-s, -) NT tankard, beer mug
seiden ADJ silk; **Seidenpapier** NT tissue paper
seidig ['zaɪdɪç] ADJ silky
Seife ['zaɪfə] **(-, -n)** F soap
Seifen- zW: **Seifenblase** F soap bubble; (*fig*) bubble; **Seifenlauge** F soapsuds *pl*; **Seifenoper** F soap (opera); **Seifenschale** F soap dish; **Seifenschaum** M lather
seifig ['zaɪfɪç] ADJ soapy
seihen ['zaɪən] VT to strain, to filter
Seil [zaɪl] **(-(e)s, -e)** NT rope; (*Kabel*) cable; **Seilbahn** F cable railway; **Seilhüpfen (-s)** NT skipping; **Seilspringen (-s)** NT skipping; **Seiltänzer(in)** M(F) tightrope walker; **Seilzug** M tackle

SCHLÜSSELWORT

sein [zaɪn] (*pt* **war**, *pp* **gewesen**) VI **1** to be; **ich bin** I am; **du bist** you are; **er/sie/es ist** he/she/it is; **wir sind/ihr seid/sie sind** we/you/they are; **wir waren** we were; **wir sind gewesen** we have been
2: **seien Sie nicht böse** don't be angry; **sei so gut und ...** be so kind as to ...; **das wäre gut** that would *od* that'd be a good thing; **wenn ich Sie wäre** if I were *od* was you; **das wärs** that's all, that's it; **morgen bin ich in Rom** tomorrow I'll *od* I will *od* I shall be in Rome; **waren Sie mal in Rom?** have you ever been to Rome?
3: **wie ist das zu verstehen?** how is that to be understood?; **er ist nicht zu ersetzen** he cannot be replaced; **mit ihr ist nicht zu reden** you can't talk to her
4: **mir ist kalt** I'm cold; **mir ist, als hätte ich ihn früher schon einmal gesehen** I've a feeling I've seen him before; **was ist?** what's the matter?, what is it?; **ist was?** is something the matter?; **es sei denn(, dass ...)** unless ...; **wie dem auch sei** be that as it may; **wie wäre es mit ...?** how *od* what about ...?; **etw sein lassen** (*aufhören*) to stop (doing) sth; (*nicht tun*) to drop sth, to leave sth; **lass das sein!** stop that!; **es ist an dir, zu ...** it's up to you to ...; **was sind Sie (beruflich)?** what do you do?; **das kann schon sein** that may well be
▸ PRON his; (*bei Dingen*) its

Sein (-s) NT: **~ oder Nichtsein** to be or not to be
seine(r, s) POSS PRON his; (*bei Tieren, Dingen*) its; **er ist gut ~ zwei Meter** (*umg*) he's a good two metres (BRIT) *od* meters (US); **die Seinen** (*geh*) his family, his people; **jedem das S~** to each his own
seiner GEN *von* **er**; **es** ▸ PRON of him; (*bei Tieren, Dingen*) of it
seinerseits ADV for his part
seinerzeit ADV in those days, formerly
seinesgleichen PRON people like him
seinetwegen ADV (*für ihn*) for his sake; (*wegen ihm*) on his account; (*von ihm aus*) as far as he is concerned
seinetwillen ADV: **um ~ = seinetwegen**
seinige PRON: **der/die/das ~** his
Seismograf [zaɪsmo'gra:f] **(-en, -en)** M seismograph
seit [zaɪt] PRÄP +*dat* since; (*Zeitdauer*) for, in (*bes US*) ▸ KONJ since; **er ist ~ einer Woche hier** he has been here for a week; **~ Langem** for a long time; **seitdem** ADV, KONJ since
Seite ['zaɪtə] **(-, -n)** F side; (*Buchseite*) page; (*Mil*) flank; **~ an ~** side by side; **jdm zur ~ stehen** (*fig*) to stand by sb's side; **jdn zur ~ nehmen** to take sb aside *od* on one side; **auf der einen ~ ..., auf der anderen (seite) ...** on the one hand ..., on the other (hand) ...; **einer Sache** *dat* **die beste ~ abgewinnen** to make the best *od* most of sth; *siehe auch* **aufseiten**; **vonseiten**
Seiten- zW: **Seitenairbag** M (*Aut*) side-impact airbag; **Seitenansicht** F side view; **Seitenhieb** M (*fig*) passing shot, dig; **seitenlang** ADJ several pages long, going on for pages; **Seitenruder** NT (*Aviat*) rudder
seitens PRÄP +*gen* on the part of
Seiten- zW: **Seitenschiff** NT aisle; **Seitensprung** M affair; **Seitenstechen** NT (a) stitch; **Seitenstraße** F side road; **Seitenstreifen** M (*der Straße*) verge (BRIT), berm (US); (*der Autobahn*) hard shoulder (BRIT), shoulder (US); **seitenverkehrt** ADJ the wrong way round; **Seitenwagen** M sidecar; **Seitenwind** M crosswind; **Seitenzahl** F page number; (*Gesamtzahl*) number of pages
seit- zW: **seither** [zaɪt'he:r] ADV, KONJ since (then); **seitlich** ADV on one/the side ▸ ADJ side *attrib*; **seitwärts** ADV sideways
sek, Sek. ABK (= *Sekunde*) sec.
Sekretär [zekre'tɛ:r] M secretary; (*Möbel*) bureau
Sekretariat [zekretari'a:t] **(-(e)s, -e)** NT secretary's office, secretariat
Sekretärin F secretary
Sekt [zɛkt] **(-(e)s, -e)** M sparkling wine
Sekte (-, -n) F sect
Sektor ['zɛktɔr] M sector; (*Sachgebiet*) field
Sekunda [ze'kʊnda] (-, **Sekunden**) F (*Sch: früher: Untersekunda/Obersekunda*) *sixth/seventh year of German secondary school*
sekundär [zekʊn'dɛ:r] ADJ secondary; **Sekundärliteratur** F secondary literature
Sekunde [ze'kʊndə] **(-, -n)** F second
Sekunden- zW: **Sekundenkleber** M superglue; **Sekundenschnelle** F: **in Sekundenschnelle** in a matter of seconds; **Sekundenzeiger** M second hand
sel. ABK = **selig**
selber ['zɛlbər] DEMON PRON = **selbst**; **Selbermachen** NT do-it-yourself, DIY (BRIT); (*von Kleidern etc*) making one's own

S

SCHLÜSSELWORT

selbst [zɛlpst] PRON **1**: **ich/er/wir selbst** I myself/he himself/we ourselves; **sie ist die Tugend selbst** she's virtue itself; **er braut sein Bier selbst** he brews his own beer; **das muss er selbst wissen** it's up to him; **wie gehts? — gut, und selbst?** how are things? — fine, and yourself?
2 (*ohne Hilfe*) alone, on my/his/one's *etc* own; **von selbst** by itself; **er kam von selbst** he came of his own accord; **selbst ist der Mann/die Frau!** self-reliance is the name of the game (*umg*); **selbst gemacht** home-made; **selbst gestrickt** hand-knitted; (*umg: Methode etc*) homespun, amateurish; **selbst verdientes Geld** money one has earned o.s.
▶ ADV even; **selbst wenn** even if; **selbst Gott** even God (himself)

Selbst [zɛlpst] (-) NT self
Selbstachtung F self-respect
selbständig *etc* ['zɛlpʃtɛndıç] ADJ = **selbstständig** *usw*
Selbst- zW: **Selbstanzeige** F: **Selbstanzeige erstatten** to come forward oneself; **der Dieb hat Selbstanzeige erstattet** the thief has come forward; **Selbstauslöser** M (*Phot*) delayed-action shutter release; **Selbstbedienung** F self-service; **Selbstbedienungsmentalität** F self-service mentality; **Selbstbefriedigung** F masturbation; (*fig*) self-gratification; **Selbstbeherrschung** F self-control; **Selbstbestätigung** F self-affirmation; **selbstbewusst** ADJ self-confident; (*selbstsicher*) self-assured; **Selbstbewusstsein** NT self-confidence; **Selbstbildnis** NT self-portrait; **Selbsterhaltung** F self-preservation; **Selbsterkenntnis** F self-knowledge; **Selbstfahrer** M (*Aut*): **Autovermietung für Selbstfahrer** self-drive car hire (BRIT) *od* rental; **selbstgefällig** ADJ smug, self-satisfied; **selbstgerecht** ADJ self-righteous; **Selbstgespräch** NT conversation with o.s.; **selbstgewiss** ADJ confident; **selbstherrlich** ADJ high-handed; (*selbstgerecht*) self-satisfied; **Selbsthilfe** F self-help; **zur Selbsthilfe greifen** to take matters into one's own hands; **selbstklebend** ADJ self-adhesive; **Selbstkostenpreis** M cost price; **selbstlos** ADJ unselfish, selfless; **Selbstmord** M suicide; **Selbstmordanschlag** M suicide attack; **Selbstmordattentat** NT suicide bombing; **Selbstmordattentäter(in)** M(F) suicide bomber; **Selbstmörder(in)** M(F) (*Person*) suicide; **selbstmörderisch** ADJ suicidal; **selbstsicher** ADJ self-assured; **Selbstsicherheit** F self-assurance; **selbstständig** ['zɛlpstʃtɛndıç] ADJ independent; (*arbeitend*) self-employed; **sich selbstständig machen** (*beruflich*) to set up on one's own, to start one's own business; **Selbstständigkeit** F independence; **Selbststudium** NT private study; **selbstsüchtig** ADJ selfish; **selbsttätig** ADJ automatic; **Selbstüberwindung** F willpower; **selbstvergessen** ADJ absent-minded; (*Blick*) faraway; **selbstverschuldet** ADJ: **wenn der Unfall selbstverschuldet ist** if there is personal responsibility for the accident; **Selbstversorger** M: **Selbstversorger sein** to be self-sufficient *od* self-reliant; **Urlaub für Selbstversorger** self-catering holiday
selbstverständlich ADJ obvious ▶ ADV naturally; **ich halte das für ~** I take that for granted
Selbstverständlichkeit F (*Unbefangenheit*) naturalness; (*natürliche Voraussetzung*) matter of course
Selbst- zW: **Selbstverständnis** NT: **nach seinem eigenen Selbstverständnis** as he sees himself; **Selbstverteidigung** F self-defence (BRIT), self-defense (US); **Selbstvertrauen** NT self-confidence; **Selbstverwaltung** F autonomy, self-government; **Selbstwählferndienst** M (*Tel*) automatic dialling service, subscriber trunk dialling (BRIT), STD (BRIT), direct distance dialing (US); **Selbstwertgefühl** NT feeling of one's own worth *od* value, self-esteem; **selbstzufrieden** ADJ self-satisfied; **Selbstzweck** M end in itself
selig ['ze:lıç] ADJ happy, blissful; (*Rel*) blessed; (*tot*) late; **Seligkeit** F bliss
Sellerie ['zɛləri:] (**-s**, **-(s)** *od* **-**, **-n**) M OD F celery
selten ['zɛltən] ADJ rare ▶ ADV seldom, rarely; **Seltenheit** F rarity; **Seltenheitswert** (**-(e)s**) M rarity value
Selterswasser ['zɛltərsvasər] NT soda water
seltsam ['zɛltza:m] ADJ curious, strange
seltsamerweise ADV curiously, strangely
Seltsamkeit F strangeness
Semester [ze'mɛstər] (**-s**, **-**) NT semester; **ein älteres ~** a senior student
Semi- [zemi] IN ZW semi-
Semikolon [-'ko:lɔn] (**-s**, **-s**) NT semicolon
Seminar [zemi'na:r] (**-s**, **-e**) NT seminary; (*Kurs*) seminar; (*Univ: Ort*) department building
semitisch [ze'mi:tıʃ] ADJ Semitic
Semmel ['zɛməl] (**-**, **-n**) F roll; **Semmelbrösel, Semmelbröseln** PL breadcrumbs *pl*; **Semmelknödel** (SÜDD, ÖSTERR) M bread dumpling
sen. ABK (= *senior*) sen.
Senat [ze'na:t] (**-(e)s**, **-e**) M senate
Sendebereich M transmission range
Sendefolge F (*Serie*) series
senden[1] *unreg* VT to send
senden[2] VT, VI (*Rundf*, *TV*) to transmit, to broadcast
Sendenetz NT network
Sendepause F (*Rundf*, *TV*) interval
Sender (**-s**, **-**) M station; (*Anlage*) transmitter
Sende- zW: **Sendereihe** F series (of broadcasts); **Sendeschluss** M (*Rundf*, *TV*) closedown; **Sendestation** F transmitting station; **Sendestelle** F transmitting station; **Sendezeit** F broadcasting time, air time

Sendung ['zɛndʊŋ] F consignment; (*Aufgabe*) mission; (*Rundf, TV*) transmission; (*Programm*) programme (BRIT), program (US)
Senegal ['ze:negal] **(-s)** NT Senegal
Senf [zɛnf] **(-(e)s, -e)** M mustard; **seinen ~ dazugeben** (*umg*) to put one's oar in; **Senfkorn** NT mustard seed
sengen ['zɛŋən] VT to singe ▶ VI to scorch
senil [ze'ni:l] (*pej*) ADJ senile
Senior ['ze:niɔr] **(-s, -en)** M (*Rentner*) senior citizen; (*Geschäftspartner*) senior partner
Seniorenpass [zeni'o:rənpas] M senior citizen's travel pass (BRIT)
Senkblei ['zɛŋkblaɪ] NT plumb
Senke **(-, -n)** F depression
Senkel **(-s, -)** M (shoe)lace
senken VT to lower; (*Kopf*) to bow; (*Tech*) to sink ▶ VR to sink; (*Stimme*) to drop
Senk- ZW: **Senkfuß** M flat foot; **Senkgrube** F cesspit; **senkrecht** ADJ vertical, perpendicular; **Senkrechte** F perpendicular; **Senkrechtstarter** M (*Aviat*) vertical takeoff plane; (*fig: Person*) high-flier
Senner(in) ['zɛnər(ɪn)] **(-s, -)** M(F) (Alpine) dairyman, dairymaid
Sensation [zenzatsi'o:n] F sensation
sensationell [zɛnzatsio'nɛl] ADJ sensational
Sensationsblatt NT sensational paper
Sensationssucht F sensationalism
Sense ['zɛnzə] **(-, -n)** F scythe; **dann ist ~!** (*umg*) that's the end!
sensibel [zɛn'zi:bəl] ADJ sensitive
sensibilisieren [zɛnzibili'zi:rən] VT to sensitize
Sensibilität [zɛnzibili'tɛ:t] F sensitivity
sentimental [zɛntimɛn'ta:l] ADJ sentimental
Sentimentalität [zɛntimɛntali'tɛ:t] F sentimentality
separat [zepa'ra:t] ADJ separate; (*Wohnung, Zimmer*) self-contained
Sept. ABK (= *September*) Sept.
September [zɛp'tɛmbər] **(-(s), -)** M September; **im ~** in September; **im Monat ~** in the month of September; **heute ist der zweite ~** today is the second of September *od* September second (US); (*geschrieben*) today is 2nd September; **in diesem ~** this September; **Anfang/Ende/Mitte ~** at the beginning/end/in the middle of September
septisch ['zɛptɪʃ] ADJ septic
sequentiell [zekvɛntsi'ɛl] ADJ = **sequenziell**
Sequenz [ze'kvɛnts] F sequence
sequenziell [zekvɛntsi'ɛl] ADJ (*Comput*) sequential; **sequenzieller Zugriff** sequential access
Serbe ['zɛrbə] **(-n, -n)** M Serbian
Serbien **(-s)** NT Serbia; **~ und Montenegro** Serbia and Montenegro
Serbin F Serbian
serbisch ADJ Serbian
Serbokroatisch(e) NT Serbo-Croat
Serie ['ze:riə] F series
seriell [zeri'ɛl] ADJ (*Comput*) serial; **serielle Daten** serial data *pl*; **serieller Anschluss** serial port; **serieller Drucker** serial printer
Serien- ZW: **Serienanfertigung** F, **Serienherstellung** F series production; **serienmäßig** ADJ (*Ausstattung*) standard; (*Herstellung*) series *attrib* ▶ ADV (*herstellen*) in series; **Seriennummer** F serial number; **serienweise** ADV in series
seriös [zeri'ø:s] ADJ serious; (*anständig*) respectable
Serpentine [zɛrpɛn'ti:nə] F hairpin (bend)
Serum ['ze:rʊm] **(-s, Seren)** NT serum
Service[1] [zɛr'vi:s] **(-(s), -)** NT (*Gläserservice*) set; (*Geschirr*) service
Service[2] ['sə:vɪs] **(-, -s)** M (*Comm, Sport*) service
servieren [zɛr'vi:rən] VT, VI to serve
Serviererin [zɛr'vi:rərɪn] F waitress
Servierwagen M trolley
Serviette [zɛrvi'ɛtə] F napkin, serviette
Servolenkung F power steering
Servomotor M servo motor
Servus ['zɛrvʊs] (ÖSTERR, SÜDD) INTERJ hello; (*beim Abschied*) goodbye, so long (*umg*)
Sesam ['ze:zam] **(-s, -s)** M sesame
Sessel ['zɛsəl] **(-s, -)** M armchair; **Sessellift** M chairlift
sesshaft ['zɛshaft] ADJ settled; (*ansässig*) resident
Set [zɛt] **(-s, -s)** NT OD M set; (*Deckchen*) tablemat
setzen ['zɛtsən] VT to put, to place, to set; (*Baum etc*) to plant; (*Segel, Typ*) to set ▶ VR (*Platz nehmen*) to sit down; (*Kaffee, Tee*) to settle ▶ VI to leap; (*wetten*) to bet; (*Typ*) to set; **jdm ein Denkmal ~** to build a monument to sb; **sich zu jdm ~** to sit with sb
Setzer ['zɛtsər] **(-s, -)** M (*Typ*) typesetter
Setzerei [zɛtsə'raɪ] F caseroom; (*Firma*) typesetting firm
Setz- ZW: **Setzkasten** M (*Typ*) case; (*an Wand*) ornament shelf; **Setzling** M young plant; **Setzmaschine** F (*Typ*) typesetting machine
Seuche ['zɔʏçə] **(-, -n)** F epidemic
Seuchengebiet NT infected area
seufzen ['zɔʏftsən] VT, VI to sigh
Seufzer ['zɔʏftsər] **(-s, -)** M sigh
Sex [zɛks] **(-(es))** M sex
Sexta ['zɛksta] **(-, Sexten)** F (*früher*) *first year of German secondary school*
Sexualerziehung [zɛksu'a:lɛrtsi:ʊŋ] F sex education
Sexualität [zɛksuali'tɛ:t] F sex, sexuality
Sexual- ZW: **Sexualkunde** [zɛksu'a:lkʊndə] F sex education; **Sexualleben** NT sex life; **Sexualobjekt** NT sex object
sexuell [zɛksu'ɛl] ADJ sexual
Seychellen [ze'ʃɛlən] PL Seychelles *pl*
sezieren [ze'tsi:rən] VT to dissect
SFB **(-)** M ABK (= *Sender Freies Berlin*) Radio Free Berlin
Sfr, sFr. ABK (= *Schweizer Franken*) sfr
Shampoo [ʃam'pu:] **(-s, -s)** NT shampoo
Shetlandinseln ['ʃɛtlantlɪnzəln] PL Shetland, Shetland Isles *pl*
Shorts [ʃo:rts] PL shorts *pl*
Showmaster ['ʃoʊma:stər] **(-s, -)** M compère, MC

S

siamesisch [zia'me:zɪʃ] ADJ: **siamesische Zwillinge** Siamese twins
Siamkatze F Siamese (cat)
Sibirien [zi'bi:riən] (**-s**) NT Siberia
sibirisch ADJ Siberian

SCHLÜSSELWORT

sich [zɪç] PRON **1** (*akk*): **er/sie/es ... sich** he/she/it ... himself/herself/itself; **sie** *pl*/**man ... sich** they/one ...themselves/oneself; **Sie ... sich** you ... yourself/yourselves *pl*; **sich wiederholen** to repeat oneself/itself
2 (*dat*): **er/sie/es ... sich** he/she/it ... to himself/herself/itself; **sie** *pl*/**man ... sich** they/one ... to themselves/oneself; **Sie ... sich** you ... to yourself/yourselves *pl*; **sie hat sich einen Pullover gekauft** she bought herself a jumper; **sich die Haare waschen** to wash one's hair
3 (*mit Präposition*): **haben Sie Ihren Ausweis bei sich?** do you have your pass on you?; **er hat nichts bei sich** he's got nothing on him; **sie bleiben gern unter sich** they keep themselves to themselves
4 (*einander*) each other, one another; **sie bekämpfen sich** they fight each other *od* one another
5: **dieses Auto fährt sich gut** this car drives well; **hier sitzt es sich gut** it's good to sit here

Sichel ['zɪçəl] (**-, -n**) F sickle; (*Mondsichel*) crescent
sicher ['zɪçər] ADJ safe; (*gewiss*) certain; (*Hand, Job*) steady; (*zuverlässig*) secure, reliable; (*selbstsicher*) confident; (*Stellung*) secure ▶ ADV (*natürlich*): **du hast dich ~ verrechnet** you must have counted wrongly; **vor jdm/etw ~ sein** to be safe from sb/sth; **sich** *dat* **einer Sache/jds ~ sein** to be sure of sth/sb; **~ ist ~** you can't be too sure
sichergehen *unreg* VI to make sure
Sicherheit ['zɪçərhaɪt] F safety; (*auch Fin*) security; (*Gewissheit*) certainty; (*Selbstsicherheit*) confidence; **die öffentliche ~** public security; **~ im Straßenverkehr** road safety; **~ leisten** (*Comm*) to offer security
Sicherheits- ZW: **Sicherheitsabstand** M safe distance; **Sicherheitsbestimmungen** PL safety regulations *pl*; (*betrieblich, Pol etc*) security controls *pl*; **Sicherheitseinrichtungen** PL security equipment *sing*, security devices *pl*; **Sicherheitsglas** NT safety glass; **Sicherheitsgurt** M seat belt; **sicherheitshalber** ADV to be on the safe side; **Sicherheitsnadel** F safety pin; **Sicherheitsrat** M Security Council; **Sicherheitsschloss** NT safety lock; **Sicherheitsspanne** F (*Comm*) margin of safety; **Sicherheitsverschluss** M safety clasp; **Sicherheitsvorkehrung** F safety precaution
sicherlich ADV certainly, surely
sichern VT to secure; (*schützen*) to protect; (*Bergsteiger etc*) to belay; (*Waffe*) to put the safety catch on; (*Comput: Daten*) to back up; **jdm/sich etw ~** to secure sth for sb/for o.s.
sicherstellen VT to impound; (*garantieren*) to guarantee
Sicherung F (*Sichern*) securing; (*Vorrichtung*) safety device; (*an Waffen*) safety catch; (*Elek*) fuse; **da ist (bei) ihm die ~ durchgebrannt** (*fig: umg*) he blew a fuse
Sicherungskopie F backup copy
Sicht [zɪçt] (-) F sight; (*Aussicht*) view; (*Sehweite*) visibility; **auf** *od* **nach ~** (*Fin*) at sight; **auf lange ~** on a long-term basis; **sichtbar** ADJ visible; **Sichtbarkeit** F visibility
sichten VT to sight; (*auswählen*) to sort out; (*ordnen*) to sift through
Sicht- ZW: **sichtlich** ADJ evident, obvious; **Sichtverhältnisse** PL visibility *sing*; **Sichtvermerk** M visa; **Sichtweite** F visibility; **außer Sichtweite** out of sight
sickern ['zɪkərn] VI (*Hilfsverb sein*) to seep; (*in Tropfen*) to drip
sie PRON (*sing: nom*) she; (*: akk*) her; (*pl: nom*) they; (*: akk*) them
Sie [zi:] *nom, akk* PRON you
Sieb [zi:p] (**-(e)s, -e**) NT sieve; (*Koch*) strainer; (*Gemüsesieb*) colander
sieben[1] ['zi:bən] VT to sieve, to sift; (*Flüssigkeit*) to strain ▶ VI: **bei der Prüfung wird stark gesiebt** (*fig: umg*) the exam will weed a lot of people out
sieben[2] ['zi:bən] NUM seven; **Siebengebirge** NT: **das Siebengebirge** the Seven Mountains *pl* (*near Bonn*); **siebenhundert** NUM seven hundred; **Siebenmeter** M (*Sport*) penalty; **Siebensachen** PL belongings *pl*; **Siebenschläfer** M (*Zool*) dormouse
siebte(r, s) ['zi:ptə(r, s)] ADJ seventh
Siebtel (**-s, -**) NT seventh
siebzehn ['zi:ptse:n] NUM seventeen
siebzig ['zi:ptsɪç] NUM seventy
siedeln ['zi:dəln] VI to settle
sieden ['zi:dən] VT, VI to boil
Siedepunkt M boiling point
Siedler (**-s, -**) M settler
Siedlung F settlement; (*Häusersiedlung*) housing estate (BRIT) *od* development (*US*)
Sieg [zi:k] (**-(e)s, -e**) M victory
Siegel ['zi:gəl] (**-s, -**) NT seal; **Siegellack** M sealing wax; **Siegelring** M signet ring
siegen ['zi:gən] VI to be victorious; (*Sport*) to win; **über jdn/etw ~** (*fig*) to triumph over sb/sth; (*in Wettkampf*) to beat sb/sth
Sieger(in) (**-s, -**) M(F) victor; (*Sport etc*) winner; **Siegerehrung** F (*Sport*) presentation ceremony
siegessicher ADJ sure of victory
Siegeszug M triumphal procession
siegreich ADJ victorious
siehe ['zi:ə] IMPERATIV see; (*siehe da*) behold
siehst [zi:st], **sieht** [zi:t] VB *siehe* **sehen**
Siel [zi:l] (**-(e)s, -e**) NT OD M (*Schleuse*) sluice; (*Abwasserkanal*) sewer
siezen ['zi:tsən] VT to address as "Sie"; *siehe auch* **duzen**
Signal [zɪ'gna:l] (**-s, -e**) NT signal; **Signalanlage** F signals *pl*, set of signals

signalisieren [zɪgnali'zi:rən] VT (*lit, fig*) to signal
Signatur [zɪgna'tu:r] F signature; (*Bibliothekssignatur*) shelf mark
Silbe ['zɪlbə] (**-, -n**) F syllable; **er hat es mit keiner ~ erwähnt** he didn't say a word about it
Silber ['zɪlbər] (**-s**) NT silver; **Silberbergwerk** NT silver mine; **Silberblick** M: **einen Silberblick haben** to have a slight squint; **Silberhochzeit** F silver wedding; **Silbermedaille** F silver medal
silbern ADJ silver
Silberpapier NT silver paper
Silhouette [zilu'ɛtə] F silhouette
Silikon [zili'ko:n] (**-s, -e**) NT silicone; **Silikonchip** M silicon chip
Silo ['zi:lo] (**-s, -s**) NT OD M silo
Silvester [zɪl'vɛstər] (**-s, -**) M OD NT New Year's Eve, Hogmanay (SCOT); *see note*

Silvester is the German name for New Year's Eve. Although not an official holiday, most businesses close early and shops shut at midday. Most Germans celebrate in the evening and at midnight they let off fireworks and rockets; the revelry usually lasts until the early hours of the morning.

Simbabwe [zɪm'ba:bvə] (**-s**) NT Zimbabwe
SIM-Karte ['zɪm-] F SIM card
simpel ['zɪmpəl] ADJ simple; **Simpel** (**-s, -**) (*umg*) M simpleton
Sims [zɪms] (**-es, -e**) NT OD M (*Kaminsims*) mantelpiece; (*Fenstersims*) (window)sill
simsen ['zɪmsən] (*umg*) VTI to text
Simulant(in) [zimu'lant(ɪn)] (**-en, -en**) M(F) malingerer
simulieren [zimu'li:rən] VT to simulate; (*vortäuschen*) to feign ▸ VI to feign illness
simultan [zimʊl'ta:n] ADJ simultaneous; **Simultandolmetscher** M simultaneous interpreter
sind [zɪnt] VB *siehe* **sein**
Sinfonie [zɪnfo'ni:] F symphony
Singapur ['zɪŋgapu:r] (**-s**) NT Singapore
singen ['zɪŋən] *unreg* VT, VI to sing
Single[1] ['sɪŋgəl] (**-s, -s**) M (*Alleinlebender*) single person
Single[2] ['sɪŋgəl] (**-, -s**) F (*Mus*) single
Singsang M (*Gesang*) monotonous singing
Singstimme F vocal part
Singular ['zɪŋgula:r] M singular
Singvogel ['zɪŋfo:gəl] M songbird
sinken ['zɪŋkən] *unreg* VI to sink; (*Boden, Gebäude*) to subside; (*Fundament*) to settle; (*Preise etc*) to fall, to go down; **den Mut/die Hoffnung ~ lassen** to lose courage/hope
Sinn [zɪn] (**-(e)s, -e**) M mind; (*Wahrnehmungssinn*) sense; (*Bedeutung*) sense, meaning; **im Sinne des Gesetzes** according to the spirit of the law; **~ für etw** sense of sth; **im Sinne des Verstorbenen** in accordance with the wishes of the deceased; **von Sinnen sein** to be out of one's mind; **das ist nicht der ~ der Sache** that is not the point; **~ machen** to make sense; **das hat keinen ~** there is no point in that; **Sinnbild** NT symbol; **sinnbildlich** ADJ symbolic
sinnen *unreg* VI to ponder; **auf etw** *akk* **~** to contemplate sth; **über etw** *akk* **~** to reflect on sth
Sinnenmensch M sensualist
Sinnes- ZW: **Sinnesorgan** NT sense organ; **Sinnestäuschung** F illusion; **Sinneswandel** M change of mind
sinngemäß ADJ faithful; (*Wiedergabe*) in one's own words
sinnig ADJ apt; (*ironisch*) clever; **sinnlich** ADJ sensual, sensuous; (*Wahrnehmung*) sensory
Sinn- ZW: **Sinnlichkeit** F sensuality; **sinnlos** ADJ senseless; (*zwecklos*) pointless; (*bedeutungslos*) meaningless; **sinnlos betrunken** blind drunk; **Sinnlosigkeit** F senselessness, meaninglessness; **sinnverwandt** ADJ synonymous; **sinnvoll** ADJ meaningful; (*vernünftig*) sensible
Sinologe [zino'lo:gə] (**-n, -n**) M Sinologist
Sinologie F Sinology
Sinologin F Sinologist
Sintflut ['zɪntflu:t] F Flood; **nach uns die ~** (*umg*) it doesn't matter what happens after we've gone; **sintflutartig** ADJ: **sintflutartige Regenfälle** torrential rain *sing*
Sinus ['zi:nʊs] (**-, -** *od* **-se**) M (*Anat*) sinus; (*Math*) sine
Siphon [zi'fõ:] (**-s, -s**) M siphon
Sippe ['zɪpə] (**-, -n**) F (extended) family; (*umg: Verwandtschaft*) clan
Sippschaft ['zɪpʃaft] (*pej*) F tribe; (*Bande*) gang
Sirene [zi're:nə] (**-, -n**) F siren
Sirup ['zi:rʊp] (**-s, -e**) M syrup
Sit-in [sɪt'|ɪn] (**-(s), -s**) NT: **ein ~ machen** to stage a sit-in
Sitte ['zɪtə] (**-, -n**) F custom; **Sitten** PL morals *pl*; **was sind denn das für Sitten?** what sort of way is that to behave?
Sitten- ZW: **Sittenpolizei** F vice squad; **Sittenstrolch** (*umg*) M sex fiend; **Sittenwächter** M (*ironisch*) guardian of public morals; **sittenwidrig** ADJ (*form*) immoral
Sittich ['zɪtɪç] (**-(e)s, -e**) M parakeet
Sitt- ZW: **sittlich** ADJ moral; **Sittlichkeit** F morality; **Sittlichkeitsverbrechen** NT sex offence (BRIT) *od* offense (US); **sittsam** ADJ modest, demure
Situation [zituatsi'o:n] F situation
situiert [zitu'i:rt] ADJ: **gut ~ sein** to be well off
Sitz [zɪts] (**-es, -e**) M seat; (*von Firma, Verwaltung*) headquarters *pl*; **der Anzug hat einen guten ~** the suit sits well
sitzen *unreg* VI to sit; (*Bemerkung, Schlag*) to strike home; (*Gelerntes*) to have sunk in; (*umg: im Gefängnis sitzen*) to be inside; **locker ~** to be loose; **einen ~ haben** (*umg*) to have had one too many; **er sitzt im Kultusministerium** (*umg: sein*) he's in the Ministry of Education; **~ bleiben** to remain seated; (*Sch*) to have to repeat a year; **auf etw** *dat* **~ bleiben** to be lumbered with sth; **~ lassen** (*Sch*) to keep down a year; (*Mädchen*) to jilt; (*Wartenden*) to stand up; **etw auf sich** *dat* **~ lassen** to take sth lying down

S

sitzend ADJ (*Tätigkeit*) sedentary
Sitz- zW: **Sitzfleisch** (*umg*) NT: **Sitzfleisch haben** to be able to sit still; **Sitzgelegenheit** F seats *pl*; **Sitzordnung** F seating plan; **Sitzplatz** M seat; **Sitzstreik** M sit-down strike
Sitzung F meeting
Sizilianer(in) [zitsili'a:nər(ɪn)] (**-s, -**) M(F) Sicilian
sizilianisch ADJ Sicilian
Sizilien [zi'tsi:liən] (**-s**) NT Sicily
Skala ['ska:la] (**-, Skalen**) F scale; (*fig*) range
Skalpell [skal'pɛl] (**-s, -e**) NT scalpel
skalpieren [skal'pi:rən] VT to scalp
Skandal [skan'da:l] (**-s, -e**) M scandal
skandalös [skanda'lø:s] ADJ scandalous
Skandinavien [skandi'na:viən] (**-s**) NT Scandinavia
Skandinavier(in) (**-s, -**) M(F) Scandinavian
skandinavisch ADJ Scandinavian
Skat [ska:t] (**-(e)s, -e** *od* **-s**) M (*Karten*) skat
Skateboard ['ske:tbɔ:rd] (**-s, -s**) NT skateboard; **skateboarden** VI to skateboard
Skelett [ske'lɛt] (**-(e)s, -e**) NT skeleton
Skepsis ['skɛpsɪs] (**-**) F scepticism (BRIT), skepticism (*US*)
skeptisch ['skɛptɪʃ] ADJ sceptical (BRIT), skeptical (*US*)
Ski [ʃi:] (**-s, -er**) M ski; **~ laufen** *od* **fahren** to ski; **Skifahrer** M skier; **Skihütte** F ski hut; **Skiläufer** M skier; **Skilehrer** M ski instructor; **Skilift** M ski lift; **Skipiste** F ski run; **Skispringen** NT ski jumping; **Skistiefel** M ski boot; **Skistock** M ski pole
Skizze ['skɪtsə] (**-, -n**) F sketch
skizzieren [skɪ'tsi:rən] VT to sketch; (*fig: Plan etc*) to outline ▸ VI to sketch
Sklave ['skla:və] (**-n, -n**) M slave
Sklaventreiber (**-s, -**) (*pej*) M slave-driver
Sklaverei [skla:və'raɪ] F slavery
Sklavin F slave
sklavisch ADJ slavish
Skonto ['skɔnto] (**-s, -s**) NT OD M discount
Skorbut [skɔr'bu:t] (**-(e)s**) M scurvy
Skorpion [skɔrpi'o:n] (**-s, -e**) M scorpion; (*Astrol*) Scorpio
Skrupel ['skru:pəl] (**-s, -**) M scruple; **skrupellos** ADJ unscrupulous
Skulptur [skʊlp'tu:r] F sculpture
skurril [skʊ'ri:l] ADJ (*geh*) droll, comical
Skype® [skaɪp] (*Internet, Tel*) NT Skype®
skypen ['skaɪpən] (*Internet, Tel*) VT to skype
Slalom ['sla:lɔm] (**-s, -s**) M slalom
Slawe ['sla:və] (**-n, -n**) M Slav
Slawin F Slav
slawisch ADJ Slavonic, Slavic
Slip [slɪp] (**-s, -s**) M (pair of) briefs *pl*
Slowake [slo'va:kə] (**-n, -n**) M Slovak
Slowakei [slova'kaɪ] F Slovakia
Slowakin F Slovak; **slowakisch** ADJ Slovakian; **Slowakisch** [slo'va:kɪʃ] NT (*Ling*) Slovak
Slowenien [slo've:niən] (**-s**) NT Slovenia
slowenisch ADJ Slovenian
Smaragd [sma'rakt] (**-(e)s, -e**) M emerald
Smoking ['smo:kɪŋ] (**-s, -s**) M dinner jacket (BRIT), tuxedo (*US*)
SMS (**-, -**) F ABK (= *Short Message Service*) text message; **jdm eine ~ schicken** to send sb a text; **SMS-Nachricht** F text message
SMV (**-, -s**) F ABK = **Schülermitverwaltung**
Snob [snɔp] (**-s, -s**) M snob
Snowboard (**-s, -s**) NT snowboard; **snowboarden** VI to snowboard

SCHLÜSSELWORT

so [zo:] ADV **1** (*so sehr*) so; **so groß/schön** *etc* so big/nice *etc*; **so groß/schön wie …** as big/nice as …; **das hat ihn so geärgert, dass …** that annoyed him so much that …
2 (*auf diese Weise*) like this; **so genannt** so-called; **mach es nicht so** don't do it like that; **so oder so** (in) one way or the other; **… oder so** something (like that); **und so weiter** and so on; **so viel (wie)** as much as; **rede nicht so viel** don't talk so much; **so weit sein** to be ready; **so weit wie** *od* **als möglich** as far as possible; **ich bin so weit zufrieden** by and large I'm quite satisfied; **es ist bald so weit** it's nearly time; **so wenig (wie)** no more (than), not any more (than); **so wenig wie möglich** as little as possible; **so ein …** such a …; **so einer wie ich** somebody like me; **so (et)was** something like this/that; **na so was!** well I never!; **das ist gut so** that's fine; **sie ist nun einmal so** that's just the way she is; **das habe ich nur so gesagt** I didn't really mean it
3 (*umg: umsonst*): **ich habe es so bekommen** I got it for nothing
4 (*als Füllwort: nicht übersetzt*): **so mancher** a number of people *pl*
▸ KONJ: **so wie es jetzt ist** as things are at the moment; *siehe auch* **sodass**
▸ INTERJ: **so?** really?; **so, das wärs** right, that's it then

SO ABK (= *Südost(en)*) SE
So. ABK = **Sonntag**
s. o. ABK (= *siehe oben*) see above
sobald [zo'balt] KONJ as soon as
Söckchen [zœkçən] NT ankle sock
Socke ['zɔkə] (**-, -n**) F sock; **sich auf die Socken machen** (*umg*) to get going
Sockel ['zɔkəl] (**-s, -**) M pedestal, base
sodass [zo'das] KONJ so that
Sodawasser ['zo:davasər] NT soda water
Sodbrennen ['zo:tbrɛnən] (**-s**) NT heartburn
Sodomie [zodo'mi:] F bestiality
soeben [zo'le:bən] ADV just (now)
Sofa ['zo:fa] (**-s, -s**) NT sofa
Sofabett NT sofa bed, bed settee
sofern [zo'fɛrn] KONJ if, provided (that)
soff *etc* [zɔf] VB *siehe* **saufen**
sofort [zo'fɔrt] ADV immediately, at once; **(ich) komme ~!** (I'm) just coming!; **Soforthilfe** F emergency relief *od* aid; **Soforthilfegesetz** NT law on emergency aid
sofortig ADJ immediate

Sofortmaßnahme F immediate measure
Sofortnachricht [zo'fɔrtnaːxrɪçt] F instant message
Softeis ['sɔftlaɪs] (**-es**) NT soft ice-cream
Softie ['zɔftiː] (**-s, -s**) (*umg*) M softy
Software ['zɔftwɛːər] (**-, -s**) F software; **softwarekompatibel** ADJ software compatible; **Softwarepaket** NT software package
sog *etc* [zoːk] VB *siehe* **saugen**
Sog (**-(e)s, -e**) M suction; (*von Strudel*) vortex; (*fig*) maelstrom
sog. ABK = **sogenannt**
sogar [zo'gaːr] ADV even
sogenannt ['zoːgənant] ADJ *attrib* so-called
sogleich [zo'glaɪç] ADV straight away, at once
Sogwirkung F suction; (*fig*) knock-on effect
Sohle ['zoːlə] (**-, -n**) F (*Fußsohle*) sole; (*Talsohle etc*) bottom; (*Min*) level; **auf leisen Sohlen** (*fig*) softly, noiselessly
Sohn [zoːn] (**-(e)s, Söhne**) M son
Soja ['zoːja] (**-, Sojen**) F soya; **Sojasoße** F soy *od* soya sauce; **Sojasprossen** PL bean sprouts *pl*
solang, solange KONJ as *od* so long as
Solar- [zo'laːr] IN ZW solar; **Solarenergie** F solar energy
Solarium [zo'laːriʊm] NT solarium
Solbad ['zoːlbaːt] NT saltwater bath
solch [zɔlç] ADJ *unver* such
solche(r, s) ADJ such; **ein solcher Mensch** such a person
Sold [zɔlt] (**-(e)s, -e**) M pay
Soldat [zɔl'daːt] (**-en, -en**) M soldier; **soldatisch** ADJ soldierly
Söldner ['zœldnər] (**-s, -**) M mercenary
Sole ['zoːlə] (**-, -n**) F brine, salt water
Solei ['zoːlaɪ] NT pickled egg
Soli ['zoːli] PL *von* **Solo**
solid [zo'liːd], **solide** [zo'liːdə] ADJ solid; (*Arbeit, Wissen*) sound; (*Leben, Person*) staid, respectable
solidarisch [zoli'daːrɪʃ] ADJ in *od* with solidarity; **sich ~ erklären** to declare one's solidarity
solidarisieren [zolidari'ziːrən] VR: **sich ~ mit** to show (one's) solidarity with
Solidarität [zolidari'tɛːt] F solidarity
Solidaritätsstreik M sympathy strike
Solist(in) [zo'lɪst(ɪn)] M(F) (*Mus*) soloist
soll VB *siehe* **sollen**
Soll [zɔl] (**-(s), -(s)**) NT (*Fin*) debit (side); (*Arbeitsmenge*) quota, target; **~ und Haben** debit and credit

SCHLÜSSELWORT

sollen ['zɔlən] (*pt* **sollte**, *pp* **gesollt**, (*als Hilfsverb*) **sollen**) HILFSVERB **1** (*Pflicht, Befehl*) be supposed to; **du hättest nicht gehen sollen** you shouldn't have gone, you oughtn't to have gone; **er sollte eigentlich morgen kommen** he was supposed to come tomorrow; **soll ich?** shall I?; **soll ich dir helfen?** shall I help you?; **sag ihm, er soll warten** tell him he's to wait; **was soll ich machen?** what should I do?; **mir soll es gleich sein** it's all the same to me; **er sollte sie nie wiedersehen** he was never to see her again
2 (*Vermutung*): **sie soll verheiratet sein** she's said to be married; **was soll das heißen?** what's that supposed to mean?; **man sollte glauben, dass ...** you would think that ...; **sollte das passieren, ...** if that should happen ...
▸ VT, VI: **was soll das?** what's all this about *od* in aid of?; **das sollst du nicht** you shouldn't do that; **was solls?** what the hell!

sollte *etc* ['zɔltə] VB *siehe* **sollen**
solo ADV (*Mus*) solo; (*fig: umg*) on one's own, alone
Solo ['zoːlo] (**-s, -s** *od* **Soli**) NT solo
solvent [zɔl'vɛnt] ADJ (*Fin*) solvent
Solvenz [zɔl'vɛnts] F (*Fin*) solvency
Somalia [zo'maːlia] (**-s**) NT Somalia
somit [zo'mɪt] KONJ and so, therefore
Sommer ['zɔmər] (**-s, -**) M summer; **~ wie Winter** all year round; **Sommerferien** PL summer holidays *pl* (BRIT) *od* vacation *sing* (US); (*Jur, Parl*) summer recess *sing*; **sommerlich** ADJ summer *attrib*; (*sommerartig*) summery; **Sommerloch** NT silly season; **Sommerreifen** M normal tyre (BRIT) *od* tire (US); **Sommerschlussverkauf** M summer sale; **Sommersemester** NT (*Univ*) summer semester (*bes US*), ≈ summer term (BRIT); **Sommersprossen** PL freckles *pl*; **Sommerzeit** F summertime
Sonate [zo'naːtə] (**-, -n**) F sonata
Sonde ['zɔndə] (**-, -n**) F probe
Sonder- ['zɔndər] IN ZW special; **Sonderanfertigung** F special model; **Sonderangebot** NT special offer; **Sonderausgabe** F special edition; **sonderbar** ADJ strange, odd; **Sonderbeauftragte(r)** F(M) (*Pol*) special emissary; **Sonderbeitrag** M (special) feature; **Sonderfahrt** F special trip; **Sonderfall** M special case; **sondergleichen** ADJ *unver* without parallel, unparalleled; **eine Frechheit sondergleichen** the height of cheek; **sonderlich** ADJ particular; (*außergewöhnlich*) remarkable; (*eigenartig*) peculiar; **Sonderling** M eccentric; **Sondermarke** F special issue (stamp); **Sondermüll** M dangerous waste
sondern KONJ but ▸ VT to separate; **nicht nur ..., ~ auch** not only ..., but also
Sonder- ZW: **Sonderpreis** M special price; **Sonderregelung** F special provision; **Sonderschule** F special school; **Sondervergünstigungen** PL perquisites *pl*, perks *pl* (*bes* BRIT); **Sonderwünsche** PL special requests *pl*; **Sonderzug** M special train
sondieren [zɔn'diːrən] VT to suss out; (*Gelände*) to scout out
Sonett [zo'nɛt] (**-(e)s, -e**) NT sonnet
Sonnabend ['zɔnlaːbənt] M Saturday; *siehe auch* **Dienstag**

S

Sonne ['zɔnə] (**-, -n**) F sun; **an die ~ gehen** to go out in the sun
sonnen VR to sun o.s.; **sich in etw** *dat* **~** (*fig*) to bask in sth
Sonnen- zW: **Sonnenaufgang** M sunrise; **sonnenbaden** VI to sunbathe; **Sonnenblume** F sunflower; **Sonnenbrand** M sunburn; **Sonnenbrille** F sunglasses *pl*; **Sonnencreme** F suntan lotion; **Sonnenenergie** F solar energy; **Sonnenfinsternis** F solar eclipse; **Sonnenfleck** M sunspot; **sonnengebräunt** ADJ suntanned; **sonnenklar** ADJ crystal-clear; **Sonnenkollektor** M solar panel; **Sonnenkraftwerk** NT solar power station; **Sonnenmilch** F suntan lotion; **Sonnenöl** NT suntan oil; **Sonnenschein** M sunshine; **Sonnenschirm** M sunshade; **Sonnenschutzmittel** NT sunscreen; **Sonnenstich** M sunstroke; **du hast wohl einen Sonnenstich!** (*hum: umg*) you must have been out in the sun too long!; **Sonnensystem** NT solar system; **Sonnenuhr** F sundial; **Sonnenuntergang** M sunset; **Sonnenwende** F solstice
sonnig ['zɔnɪç] ADJ sunny
Sonntag ['zɔnta:k] M Sunday; *siehe auch* **Dienstag**
sonntäglich ADJ *attrib*: **~ gekleidet** dressed in one's Sunday best
sonntags ADV (on) Sundays
Sonntagsdienst M: **~ haben** (*Apotheke*) to be open on Sundays
Sonntagsfahrer (*pej*) M Sunday driver
sonst [zɔnst] ADV otherwise; (*mit pron, in Fragen*) else; (*zu anderer Zeit*) at other times; (*gewöhnlich*) usually, normally ▸ KONJ otherwise; **er denkt, er ist ~ wer** (*umg*) he thinks he's somebody special; **~ gehts dir gut?** (*ironisch: umg*) are you feeling okay?; **wenn ich Ihnen ~ noch behilflich sein kann** if I can help you in any other way; **~ noch etwas?** anything else?; **~ nichts** nothing else; **~ jemand** (*umg*) anybody (at all); **da kann ja ~ was passieren** (*umg*) anything could happen; **~ wo** (*umg*) somewhere else; **~ woher** (*umg*) from somewhere else; **~ wohin** (*umg*) somewhere else
sonstig ADJ other; **„Sonstiges"** "other"
sooft [zo'ɔft] KONJ whenever
Sopran [zo'pra:n] (**-s, -e**) M soprano (voice)
Sopranistin [zopra'nɪstɪn] F soprano (singer)
Sorge ['zɔrgə] (-, **-n**) F care, worry; **dafür ~ tragen, dass ...** (*geh*) to see to it that ...
sorgen VI: **für jdn ~** to look after sb ▸ VR: **sich ~ (um)** to worry (about); **für etw ~** to take care of *od* see to sth; **dafür ~, dass ...** to see to it that ...; **dafür ist gesorgt** that's taken care of
Sorgen- zW: **sorgenfrei** ADJ carefree; **Sorgenkind** NT problem child; **sorgenvoll** ADJ troubled, worried
Sorgerecht (**-(e)s**) NT custody (of a child)
Sorgfalt ['zɔrkfalt] (-) F care(fulness); **viel ~ auf etw** *akk* **verwenden** to take a lot of care over sth
sorgfältig ADJ careful
sorglos ADJ careless; (*ohne Sorgen*) carefree
sorgsam ADJ careful
Sorte ['zɔrtə] (**-, -n**) F sort; (*Warensorte*) brand; **Sorten** PL (*Fin*) foreign currency *sing*
sortieren [zɔr'ti:rən] VT to sort (out); (*Comput*) to sort
Sortiermaschine F sorting machine
Sortiment [zɔrti'mɛnt] NT assortment
SOS [ɛslo:'lɛs] NT ABK SOS
sosehr [zo'ze:r] KONJ as much as
soso [zo'zo:] INTERJ: **~!** I see!; (*erstaunt*) well, well!; (*drohend*) well!
Soße ['zo:sə] (**-, -n**) F sauce; (*Bratensoße*) gravy
Souffleur [zu'flø:r] M prompter
Souffleuse [zu'flø:zə] F prompter
soufflieren [zu'fli:rən] VT, VI to prompt
soundso ['zo:lʊnt'zo:] ADV: **~ lange** for such and such a time
soundsovielte(r, s) ADJ: **am Soundsovielten** (*Datum*) on such and such a date
Souterrain [zutɛ'rɛ̃:] (**-s, -s**) NT basement
Souvenir [zuvə'ni:r] (**-s, -s**) NT souvenir
souverän [zuvə'rɛ:n] ADJ sovereign; (*überlegen*) superior; (*fig*) supremely good
soviel [zo'fi:l] KONJ as far as
soweit [zo'vaɪt] KONJ as far as
sowenig [zo've:nɪç] KONJ however little
sowie [zo'vi:] KONJ (*sobald*) as soon as; (*ebenso*) as well as
sowieso [zovi'zo:] ADV anyway
Sowjetbürger M (*früher*) Soviet citizen
sowjetisch [zɔ'vjɛtɪʃ] ADJ (*früher*) Soviet
Sowjet- zW: **Sowjetrepublik** F Soviet Republic; **Sowjetrusse** M Soviet Russian; **Sowjetunion** F Soviet Union
sowohl [zo'vo:l] KONJ: **~ ... als** *od* **wie auch ...** both ... and ...
soz. ABK = **sozial; sozialistisch**
sozial [zotsi'a:l] ADJ social; **~ eingestellt** public-spirited; **~ verträglich** socially acceptable; **sozialer Wohnungsbau** public-sector housing (programme); **soziales Netzwerk** social networking site; **soziale Medien** social media; **Sozialabbau** M public-spending cuts *pl*; **Sozialabgaben** PL National Insurance contributions *pl* (BRIT), Social Security contributions *pl* (US); **Sozialamt** NT (social) welfare office; **Sozialarbeiter** M social worker; **Sozialberuf** M caring profession; **Sozialdemokrat** M social democrat; **Sozialhilfe** F welfare (aid)
Sozialisation [zotsializatsi'o:n] F (*Psych, Soziologie*) socialization
sozialisieren [zotsiali'zi:rən] VT to socialize
Sozialismus [zotsia'lɪsmʊs] M socialism
Sozialist(in) [zotsia'lɪst(ɪn)] M(F) socialist
sozialistisch ADJ socialist
Sozial- zW: **Sozialkunde** F social studies *sing*; **Sozialleistungen** PL social security contributions (*from the state and employer*); **Sozialplan** M redundancy payments scheme; **Sozialpolitik** F social welfare policy; **Sozialprodukt** NT (gross *od* net) national product; **Sozialstaat** M welfare state;

Sozialversicherung F national insurance (BRIT), social security (US); **sozialverträglich** ADJ *siehe* **sozial**; **Sozialwohnung** F ≈ council flat (BRIT), state-subsidized apartment; *see note*

A **Sozialwohnung** is a council house or flat let at a fairly low rent to people on low income. They are built from public funds. People applying for a **Sozialwohnung** have to prove their entitlement.

Soziologe [zotsio'lo:gə] (**-n, -n**) M sociologist
Soziologie [zotsiolo'gi:] F sociology
Soziologin [zotsio'lo:gɪn] F sociologist
soziologisch [zotsio'lo:gɪʃ] ADJ sociological
Sozius ['zo:tsiʊs] (**-, -se**) M (*Comm*) partner; (*Motorrad*) pillion rider; **Soziussitz** M pillion (seat)
sozusagen [zotsu'za:gən] ADV so to speak
Spachtel ['ʃpaxtəl] (**-s, -**) M spatula
spachteln VT (*Mauerfugen, Ritzen*) to fill (in) ▸ VI (*umg: essen*) to tuck in
Spagat [ʃpa'ga:t] (**-s, -e**) M OD NT splits *pl*
Spaghetti, Spagetti [ʃpa'gɛti] PL spaghetti *sing*
spähen ['ʃpɛ:ən] VI to peep, to peek
Spalier [ʃpa'li:r] (**-s, -e**) NT (*Gerüst*) trellis; (*Leute*) guard of honour (BRIT) *od* honor (US); **~ stehen, ein ~ bilden** to form a guard of honour (BRIT) *od* honor (US)
Spalt [ʃpalt] (**-(e)s, -e**) M crack; (*Türspalt*) chink; (*fig: Kluft*) split
Spalte (**-, -n**) F crack, fissure; (*Gletscherspalte*) crevasse; (*in Text*) column
spalten VT, VR (*lit, fig*) to split
Spaltung F splitting
Spam [spɛm] (**-s, -s**) NT (*Comput*) spam
Spamfilter ['spɛmfɪltər] M spam filter *od* blocker
spammen ['spɛmən] VT, VI to spam
Span [ʃpa:n] (**-(e)s, Späne**) M shaving
Spanferkel NT sucking pig
Spange ['ʃpaŋə] (**-, -n**) F clasp; (*Haarspange*) hair slide; (*Schnalle*) buckle; (*Armspange*) bangle
Spaniel ['ʃpa:niəl] (**-s, -s**) M spaniel
Spanien ['ʃpa:niən] (**-s**) NT Spain
Spanier(in) (**-s, -**) M(F) Spaniard
spanisch ADJ Spanish; **das kommt mir ~ vor** (*umg*) that seems odd to me; **spanische Wand** (folding) screen
spann [ʃpan] VB *siehe* **spinnen**
Spann (**-(e)s, -e**) M instep
Spannbeton (**-s**) M prestressed concrete
Spanne (**-, -n**) F (*Zeitspanne*) space; (*Differenz*) gap; *siehe auch* **Spann**
spannen VT (*straffen*) to tighten, to tauten; (*befestigen*) to brace ▸ VI to be tight
spannend ADJ exciting, gripping; **machs nicht so ~!** (*umg*) don't keep me *etc* in suspense!
Spanner (**-s, -**) (*umg*) M (*Voyeur*) peeping Tom
Spannkraft F elasticity; (*fig*) energy
Spannung F tension; (*Elek*) voltage; (*fig*) suspense; (*unangenehm*) tension
Spannungsgebiet NT (*Pol*) flashpoint, area of tension
Spannungsprüfer M voltage detector
Spannweite F (*von Flügeln, Aviat*) (wing)span
Spanplatte F chipboard
Sparbuch NT savings book
Sparbüchse F moneybox
sparen ['ʃpa:rən] VT, VI to save; **sich** *dat* **etw ~** to save o.s. sth; (*Bemerkung*) to keep sth to o.s.; **mit etw ~** to be sparing with sth; **an etw** *dat* **~** to economize on sth
Sparer(in) (**-s, -**) M(F) (*bei Bank etc*) saver
Sparflamme F low flame; **auf ~** (*fig: umg*) just ticking over
Spargel ['ʃpargəl] (**-s, -**) M asparagus
Spar- zW: **Spargroschen** M nest egg; **Sparkasse** F savings bank; **Sparkonto** NT savings account
spärlich ['ʃpɛ:rlɪç] ADJ meagre (BRIT), meager (US); (*Bekleidung*) scanty; (*Beleuchtung*) poor
Spar- zW: **Sparmaßnahme** F economy measure; **Sparpackung** F economy size; **sparsam** ADJ economical, thrifty; **sparsam im Verbrauch** economical; **Sparsamkeit** F thrift, economizing; **Sparschwein** NT piggy bank
Sparte ['ʃpartə] (**-, -n**) F field; (*Comm*) line of business; (*Presse*) column
Sparvertrag M savings agreement
Spaß [ʃpa:s] (**-es, Späße**) M joke; (*Freude*) fun; **~ muss sein** there's no harm in a joke; **jdm ~ machen** to be fun (for sb); **viel ~!** have fun!; **spaßen** VI to joke; **mit ihm ist nicht zu spaßen** you can't take liberties with him
spaßeshalber ADV for the fun of it
spaßig ADJ funny, droll
Spaß- zW: **Spaßmacher** M joker, funny man; **Spaßverderber** (**-s, -**) M spoilsport; **Spaßvogel** M joker
Spastiker(in) ['ʃpastikər(ɪn)] M(F) (*Med*) spastic
spät [ʃpɛ:t] ADJ, ADV late; **heute Abend wird es ~** it'll be a late night tonight
Spaten ['ʃpa:tən] (**-s, -**) M spade; **Spatenstich** M: **den ersten Spatenstich tun** to turn the first sod
Spätentwickler M late developer
später ADJ, ADV later; **an ~ denken** to think of the future; **bis ~!** see you later!
spätestens ADV at the latest
Spatz [ʃpats] (**-en, -en**) M sparrow
spazieren [ʃpa'tsi:rən] VI (*Hilfsverb sein*) to stroll; **~ fahren** to go for a drive; **~ gehen** to go for a walk
Spazier- zW: **Spaziergang** M walk; **einen Spaziergang machen** to go for a walk; **Spaziergänger(in)** M(F) stroller; **Spazierstock** M walking stick; **Spazierweg** M path, walk
SPD (**-**) F ABK (= *Sozialdemokratische Partei Deutschlands*) German Social Democratic Party; *see note*

The **SPD** (Sozialdemokratische Partei Deutschlands), the German Social Democratic Party, was newly formed in 1945. It is the largest political party in Germany.

Specht [ʃpɛçt] (**-(e)s, -e**) M woodpecker
Speck [ʃpɛk] (**-(e)s, -e**) M bacon; **mit ~ fängt man Mäuse** (*Sprichwort*) you need a sprat to

S

catch a mackerel; **ran an den ~** (*umg*) let's get stuck in
Spediteur [ʃpedi'tø:r] M carrier; (*Möbelspediteur*) furniture remover
Spedition [ʃpeditsi'o:n] F carriage; (*Speditionsfirma*) road haulage contractor; (*Umzugsfirma*) removal (BRIT) *od* moving (US) firm
Speer [ʃpe:r] (**-(e)s, -e**) M spear; (*Sport*) javelin; **Speerwerfen** NT: **das Speerwerfen** throwing the javelin
Speiche ['ʃpaɪçə] (**-, -n**) F spoke
Speichel ['ʃpaɪçəl] (**-s**) M saliva, spit, spittle; **Speichellecker** (*pej, umg*) M bootlicker
Speicher ['ʃpaɪçər] (**-s, -**) M storehouse; (*Dachspeicher*) attic, loft; (*Kornspeicher*) granary; (*Wasserspeicher*) tank; (*Tech*) store; (*Comput*) memory; **Speicherauszug** M (*Comput*) dump; **Speicherkarte** F memory card; **speichern** VT (*auch Comput*) to store; (*sichern*) to save
speien ['ʃpaɪən] *unreg* VT, VI to spit; (*erbrechen*) to vomit; (*Vulkan*) to spew
Speise ['ʃpaɪzə] (**-, -n**) F food; (*Gericht*) dish; **kalte und warme Speisen** hot and cold meals; **Speiseeis** NT ice-cream; **Speisefett** NT cooking fat; **Speisekammer** F larder, pantry; **Speisekarte** F menu
speisen VT to eat ▸ VI to dine
Speise- ZW: **Speiseöl** NT salad oil; (*zum Braten*) cooking oil; **Speiseröhre** F (*Anat*) gullet, oesophagus (BRIT), esophagus (US); **Speisesaal** M dining room; **Speisewagen** M dining car; **Speisezettel** M menu
Spektakel [ʃpɛk'ta:kəl] (**-s, -**) M (*umg: Lärm*) row ▸ NT spectacle
spektakulär [ʃpɛktaku'lɛ:r] ADJ spectacular
Spektrum ['ʃpɛktrʊm] (**-s, -tren**) NT spectrum
Spekulant(in) [ʃpeku'lant(ɪn)] M(F) speculator
Spekulation [ʃpekulatsi'o:n] F speculation
Spekulatius [ʃpeku'la:tsiʊs] (**-, -**) M spiced biscuit (BRIT) *od* cookie (US)
spekulieren [ʃpeku'li:rən] VI (*fig*) to speculate; **auf etw** *akk* ~ to have hopes of sth
Spelunke [ʃpe'lʊŋkə] (**-, -n**) F dive
spendabel [ʃpɛn'da:bəl] (*umg*) ADJ generous, open-handed
Spende ['ʃpɛndə] (**-, -n**) F donation
spenden VT to donate, to give; **Spendenkonto** NT donations account; **Spendenwaschanlage** F donation-laundering organization
Spender(in) (**-s, -**) M(F) donator; (*Med*) donor
spendieren [ʃpɛn'di:rən] VT to pay for, to buy; **jdm etw** ~ to treat sb to sth, to stand sb sth
Sperling ['ʃpɛrlɪŋ] M sparrow
Sperma ['spɛrma] (**-s, Spermen**) NT sperm
sperrangelweit ['ʃpɛr'laŋəl'vaɪt] ADJ wide-open
Sperrbezirk M no-go area
Sperre (**-, -n**) F barrier; (*Verbot*) ban; (*Polizeisperre*) roadblock
sperren ['ʃpɛrən] VT to block; (*Comm: Konto*) to freeze; (*Comput: Daten*) to disable; (*Sport*) to suspend, to bar; (*: vom Ball*) to obstruct; (*einschließen*) to lock; (*verbieten*) to ban ▸ VR to baulk, to jibe
Sperr- ZW: **Sperrfeuer** NT (*Mil, fig*) barrage; **Sperrfrist** F (*auch Jur*) waiting period; (*Sport*) (period of) suspension; **Sperrgebiet** NT prohibited area; **Sperrgut** NT bulky freight; **Sperrholz** NT plywood
sperrig ADJ bulky
Sperr- ZW: **Sperrkonto** NT blocked account; **Sperrsitz** M (*Theat*) stalls *pl* (BRIT), orchestra (US); **Sperrstunde** F closing time; **Sperrzeit** F closing time; **Sperrzone** F exclusion zone
Spesen ['ʃpe:zən] PL expenses *pl*; **Spesenabrechnung** F expense account
Spessart ['ʃpɛsart] (**-s**) M Spessart (Mountains *pl*)
Spezi ['ʃpe:tsi] (**-s, -s**) (*umg*) M pal, mate (BRIT)
Spezial- [ʃpetsi'a:l] IN ZW special; **Spezialausbildung** F specialized training
spezialisieren [ʃpetsiali'zi:rən] VR to specialize
Spezialisierung F specialization
Spezialist(in) [ʃpetsia'lɪst(ɪn)] M(F): **~ (für)** specialist (in)
Spezialität [ʃpetsiali'tɛ:t] F speciality (BRIT), specialty (US)
speziell [ʃpetsi'ɛl] ADJ special ▸ ADV especially
Spezifikation [ʃpetsifikatsi'o:n] F specification
spezifisch [ʃpe'tsi:fɪʃ] ADJ specific
Sphäre ['sfɛ:rə] (**-, -n**) F sphere
spicken ['ʃpɪkən] VT to lard ▸ VI (*Sch*) to copy, to crib
Spickzettel M (*Sch: umg*) crib
spie *etc* [ʃpi:] VB *siehe* **speien**
Spiegel ['ʃpi:gəl] (**-s, -**) M mirror; (*Wasserspiegel*) level; (*Mil*) tab; **Spiegelbild** NT reflection; **spiegelbildlich** ADJ reversed
Spiegelei ['ʃpi:gəllaɪ] NT fried egg
spiegeln VT to mirror, to reflect ▸ VR to be reflected ▸ VI to gleam; (*widerspiegeln*) to be reflective
Spiegelreflexkamera F reflex camera
Spiegelschrift F mirror writing
Spiegelung F reflection
spiegelverkehrt ADJ in mirror image
Spiel [ʃpi:l] (**-(e)s, -e**) NT game; (*Schauspiel*) play; (*Tätigkeit*) play(ing); (*Karten*) pack (BRIT), deck (US); (*Tech*) (free) play; **leichtes ~ (bei** *od* **mit jdm) haben** to have an easy job of it (with sb); **die Hand** *od* **Finger im ~ haben** to have a hand in affairs; **jdn/etw aus dem ~ lassen** to leave sb/sth out of it; **auf dem ~(e) stehen** to be at stake; **Spielautomat** M gambling machine; (*zum Geldgewinnen*) slot machine, fruit machine (BRIT); **Spielbank** F casino; **Spieldose** F musical box (BRIT), music box (US)
spielen VT, VI to play; (*um Geld*) to gamble; (*Theat*) to perform, to act; **was wird hier gespielt?** (*umg*) what's going on here?
spielend ADV easily
Spieler(in) (**-s, -**) M(F) player; (*um Geld*) gambler
Spielerei [ʃpi:lə'raɪ] F (*Kinderspiel*) child's play
spielerisch ADJ playful; (*Leichtigkeit*) effortless; **spielerisches Können** skill as a player; (*Theat*) acting ability

Spiel- zW: **Spielfeld** NT pitch, field; **Spielfilm** M feature film; **Spielgeld** NT (*Einsatz*) stake; (*unechtes Geld*) toy money; **Spielkarte** F playing card; **Spielkasino** NT casino; **Spielkonsole** F games console; **Spielmannszug** M (brass) band; **Spielplan** M (*Theat*) programme (BRIT), program (*US*); **Spielplatz** M playground; **Spielraum** M room to manoeuvre (BRIT) *od* maneuver (*US*), scope; **Spielregel** F (*lit, fig*) rule of the game; **Spielsachen** PL toys *pl*; **Spielshow** F gameshow; **Spielstand** M score; **Spielstraße** F play street; **Spielsucht** F addiction to gambling; **Spielverderber** (**-s, -**) M spoilsport; **Spielwaren** PL toys *pl*; **Spielzeit** F (*Saison*) season; (*Spieldauer*) playing time; **Spielzeug** NT toy; (*Spielsachen*) toys *pl*

Spieß [ʃpi:s] (**-es, -e**) M spear; (*Bratspieß*) spit; (*Mil: umg*) sarge; **den ~ umdrehen** (*fig*) to turn the tables; **wie am ~(e) schreien** (*umg*) to squeal like a stuck pig; **Spießbraten** M joint roasted on a spit

Spießbürger (**-s, -**) M bourgeois

Spießer (**-s, -**) M bourgeois

Spikes [spaɪks] PL (*Sport*) spikes *pl*; (*Aut*) studs *pl*; **Spikesreifen** M studded tyre (BRIT) *od* tire (*US*)

Spinat [ʃpi'na:t] (**-(e)s, -e**) M spinach

Spind [ʃpɪnt] (**-(e)s, -e**) M OD NT locker

spindeldürr ['ʃpɪndəl'dʏr] (*pej*) ADJ spindly, thin as a rake

Spinne ['ʃpɪnə] (**-, -n**) F spider; **spinnefeind** (*umg*) ADJ: **sich** *od* **einander** *dat* **spinnefeind sein** to be deadly enemies

spinnen *unreg* VT to spin ▸ VI (*umg*) to talk rubbish; (*verrückt*) to be crazy *od* mad; **du spinnst!** you must be mad; **ich denk ich spinne** (*umg*) I don't believe it

Spinnengewebe NT cobweb

Spinner(in) (**-s, -**) M(F) (*fig: umg*) screwball, crackpot

Spinnerei [ʃpɪnə'raɪ] F spinning mill

Spinn- zW: **Spinngewebe** NT cobweb; **Spinnrad** NT spinning wheel; **Spinnwebe** F cobweb

Spion [ʃpi'o:n] (**-s, -e**) M spy; (*in Tür*) spyhole

Spionage [ʃpio'na:ʒə] (**-**) F espionage; **Spionageabwehr** F counterintelligence; **Spionagesatellit** M spy satellite; **Spionagesoftware** [ʃpio'na:ʒəzɔftwɛ:ər] F (*Comput*) spyware

spionieren [ʃpio'ni:rən] VI to spy

Spionin F (woman) spy

Spirale [ʃpi'ra:lə] (**-, -n**) F spiral; (*Med*) coil

Spirituosen [ʃpiritu'o:zən] PL spirits *pl*

Spiritus ['ʃpi:ritʊs] (**-, -se**) M (methylated) spirits *pl*; **Spirituskocher** M spirit stove

spitz ADJ pointed; (*Winkel*) acute; (*fig: Zunge*) sharp; (*: Bemerkung*) caustic

Spitz [ʃpɪts] (**-es, -e**) M (*Hund*) spitz

Spitz- zW: **spitzbekommen** *unreg* VT: **etw spitzbekommen** (*umg*) to get wise to sth; **Spitzbogen** M pointed arch; **Spitzbube** M rogue

spitze ADJ *unver* (*umg: prima*) great

Spitze (**-, -n**) F point, tip; (*Bergspitze*) peak; (*Bemerkung*) taunt; (*fig: Stichelei*) dig; (*erster Platz*) lead, top; (*meist pl: Gewebe*) lace; **etw auf die ~ treiben** to carry sth too far

Spitzel (**-s, -**) M police informer

spitzen VT to sharpen; (*Lippen, Mund*) to purse; (*lit, fig: Ohren*) to prick up

Spitzen- IN zW top; **Spitzenleistung** F top performance; **Spitzenlohn** M top wages *pl*; **Spitzenmarke** F brand leader; **spitzenmäßig** ADJ really great; **Spitzenposition** F leading position; **Spitzenreiter** M (*Sport*) leader; (*fig: Kandidat*) front runner; (*Ware*) top seller; (*Schlager*) number one; **Spitzensportler** M top-class sportsman; **Spitzenverband** M leading organization; **Spitzenverdiener(in)** M(F) top earner

Spitzer (**-s, -**) M sharpener

spitzfindig ADJ (over)subtle

Spitzmaus F shrew

Spitzname M nickname

Spleen [ʃpli:n] (**-s, -e** *od* **-s**) M (*Angewohnheit*) crazy habit; (*Idee*) crazy idea; (*Fimmel*) obsession

Splitt [ʃplɪt] (**-s, -e**) M stone chippings *pl*; (*Streumittel*) grit

Splitter (**-s, -**) M splinter; **Splittergruppe** F (*Pol*) splinter group; **splitternackt** ADJ stark naked

SPÖ (**-**) F ABK (= *Sozialistische Partei Österreichs*) Austrian Socialist Party

sponsern ['ʃpɔnzərn] VT to sponsor

Sponsor ['ʃpɔnzɔr] (**-s, -en**) M sponsor

spontan [ʃpɔn'ta:n] ADJ spontaneous

sporadisch [ʃpo'ra:dɪʃ] ADJ sporadic

Sporen ['ʃpo:rən] PL (*auch Bot, Zool*) spurs *pl*

Sport [ʃpɔrt] (**-(e)s, -e**) M sport; (*fig*) hobby; **treiben Sie ~?** do you do any sport?; **Sportabzeichen** NT sports certificate; **Sportartikel** PL sports equipment *sing*; **Sportfest** NT sports gala; (*Sch*) sports day (BRIT); **Sportgeist** M sportsmanship; **Sportgetränk** ['ʃpɔrtgətrɛŋk] NT sports drink; **Sporthalle** F sports hall; **Sportklub** M sports club; **Sportlehrer** M games *od* P.E. teacher

Sportler(in) (**-s, -**) M(F) sportsman, sportswoman

sportlich ADJ sporting; (*Mensch*) sporty; (*durchtrainiert*) athletic; (*Kleidung*) smart but casual

Sport- zW: **Sportmedizin** F sports medicine; **Sportplatz** M playing *od* sports field; **Sportschuh** M sports shoe; (*sportlicher Schuh*) casual shoe

Sportsfreund M (*fig: umg*) buddy

Sport- zW: **Sportverein** M sports club; **Sportwagen** M sports car; **Sportzeug** NT sports gear

Spot [spɔt] (**-s, -s**) M commercial, advertisement

Spott [ʃpɔt] (**-(e)s**) M mockery, ridicule; **spottbillig** ADJ dirt-cheap; **spotten** VI to mock; **spotten über** +*akk* to mock (at), to ridicule; **das spottet jeder Beschreibung** that simply defies description

spöttisch ['ʃpœtɪʃ] ADJ mocking

Spottpreis M ridiculously low price

S

sprach [ʃpra:x] VB *siehe* **sprechen**
sprachbegabt ADJ good at languages
Sprache (-, -n) F language; **heraus mit der ~!** (*umg*) come on, out with it!; **zur ~ kommen** to be mentioned; **in französischer ~** in French
Sprachenschule F language school
Sprach- zW: **Sprachfehler** M speech defect; **Sprachfertigkeit** F fluency; **Sprachführer** M phrase book; **Sprachgebrauch** M (linguistic) usage; **Sprachgefühl** NT feeling for language; **Sprachkenntnisse** PL: **mit englischen Sprachkenntnissen** with a knowledge of English; **Sprachkurs** M language course; **Sprachlabor** NT language laboratory; **sprachlich** ADJ linguistic; **sprachlos** ADJ speechless; **Sprachrohr** NT megaphone; (*fig*) mouthpiece; **Sprachstörung** F speech disorder; **Sprachwissenschaft** F linguistics *sing*
sprang [ʃpraŋ] VB *siehe* **springen**
Spray [spre:] (-s, -s) M OD NT spray; **Spraydose** F aerosol (can), spray
sprayen VT, VI to spray
Sprechanlage F intercom
Sprechblase F speech balloon
sprechen [ˈʃprɛçən] *unreg* VI to speak, to talk ▸ VT to say; (*Sprache*) to speak; (*Person*) to speak to; **mit jdm ~** to speak *od* talk to sb; **das spricht für ihn** that's a point in his favour; **frei ~** to extemporize; **nicht gut auf jdn zu ~ sein** to be on bad terms with sb; **es spricht vieles dafür, dass ...** there is every reason to believe that ...; **hier spricht man Spanisch** Spanish spoken; **wir ~ uns noch!** you haven't heard the last of this!
Sprecher(in) (-s, -) M(F) speaker; (*für Gruppe*) spokesman, spokeswoman; (*Rundf, TV*) announcer
Sprech- zW: **Sprechfunkgerät** NT radio telephone; **Sprechrolle** F speaking part; **Sprechstunde** F consultation (hour); (*von Arzt*) (doctor's) surgery (BRIT); **Sprechstundenhilfe** F (doctor's) receptionist; **Sprechzimmer** NT consulting room, surgery (BRIT)
spreizen [ˈʃpraɪtsən] VT to spread ▸ VR to put on airs
Sprengarbeiten PL blasting operations *pl*
sprengen [ˈʃprɛŋən] VT to sprinkle; (*mit Sprengstoff*) to blow up; (*Gestein*) to blast; (*Versammlung*) to break up
Spreng- zW: **Sprengkopf** M warhead; **Sprengladung** F explosive charge; **Sprengsatz** M explosive device; **Sprengstoff** M explosive(s *pl*); **Sprengstoffanschlag** M bomb attack
Spreu [ʃprɔʏ] (-) F chaff
spricht [ʃprɪçt] VB *siehe* **sprechen**
Sprichwort NT proverb
sprichwörtlich ADJ proverbial
sprießen [ˈʃpri:sən] VI (*aus der Erde*) to spring up; (*Knospen*) to shoot
Springbrunnen M fountain
springen [ˈʃprɪŋən] *unreg* VI to jump, to leap; (*Glas*) to crack; (*mit Kopfsprung*) to dive; **etw ~ lassen** (*umg*) to fork out sth
springend ADJ: **der springende Punkt** the crucial point
Springer (-s, -) M jumper; (*Schach*) knight
Springreiten NT show jumping
Springseil NT skipping rope
Sprinkler [ˈʃprɪŋklər] (-s, -) M sprinkler
Sprit [ʃprɪt] (-(e)s, -e) (*umg*) M petrol (BRIT), gas(oline) (US), fuel
Spritzbeutel M icing bag
Spritze [ˈʃprɪtsə] (-, -n) F syringe; (*Injektion*) injection; (*an Schlauch*) nozzle
spritzen VT to spray; (*Wein*) to dilute with soda water/lemonade; (*Med*) to inject ▸ VI to splash; (*heißes Fett*) to spit; (*herausspritzen*) to spurt; (*aus einer Tube etc*) to squirt; (*Med*) to give injections
Spritzer (-s, -) M (*Farbspritzer, Wasserspritzer*) splash
Spritzpistole F spray gun
Spritztour (*umg*) F spin
spröde [ˈʃprø:də] ADJ brittle; (*Person*) reserved; (*Haut*) rough
spross *etc* [ʃprɔs] VB *siehe* **sprießen**
Spross (-es, -e) M shoot
Sprosse [ˈʃprɔsə] (-, -n) F rung
Sprossenwand F (*Sport*) wall bars *pl*
Sprössling [ˈʃprœslɪŋ] M offspring *no pl*
Spruch [ʃprʊx] (-(e)s, **Sprüche**) M saying, maxim; (*Jur*) judgement; **Sprüche klopfen** (*umg*) to talk fancy; **Spruchband** NT banner
Sprüchemacher [ˈʃprʏçəmaxər] (*umg*) M patter-merchant
spruchreif ADJ: **die Sache ist noch nicht ~** it's not definite yet
Sprudel [ˈʃpru:dəl] (-s, -) M mineral water; (*süß*) lemonade
sprudeln VI to bubble
Sprüh- zW: **Sprühdose** F aerosol (can); **sprühen** VI to spray; (*fig*) to sparkle ▸ VT to spray; **Sprühregen** M drizzle
Sprung [ʃprʊŋ] (-(e)s, **Sprünge**) M jump; (*schwungvoll, fig: Gedankensprung*) leap; (*Riss*) crack; **immer auf dem ~ sein** (*umg*) to be always on the go; **jdm auf die Sprünge helfen** (*wohlwollend*) to give sb a (helping) hand; **auf einen ~ bei jdm vorbeikommen** (*umg*) to drop in to see sb; **damit kann man keine großen Sprünge machen** (*umg*) you can't exactly live it up on that; **Sprungbrett** NT springboard; **Sprungfeder** F spring; **sprunghaft** ADJ erratic; (*Aufstieg*) rapid; **Sprungschanze** F ski jump; **Sprungturm** M diving platform
Spucke [ˈʃpʊkə] (-) F spit
spucken VT, VI to spit; **in die Hände ~** (*fig*) to roll up one's sleeves
Spucknapf M spittoon
Spucktüte F sickbag
Spuk [ʃpu:k] (-(e)s, -e) M haunting; (*fig*) nightmare; **spuken** VI to haunt; **hier spukt es** this place is haunted
Spülbecken [ˈʃpy:lbɛkən] NT sink
Spule [ˈʃpu:lə] (-, -n) F spool; (*Elek*) coil
Spüle [ˈʃpy:lə] (-, -n) F (kitchen) sink

spülen VT to rinse; (*Geschirr*) to wash, to do; (*Toilette*) to flush ▶ VI to rinse; (*Geschirr*) to wash up (BRIT), to do the dishes; (*Toilette*) to flush; **etw an Land ~** to wash sth ashore

Spül- ZW: **Spülmaschine** F dishwasher; **Spülmittel** NT washing-up liquid (BRIT), dish-washing liquid; **Spülstein** M sink

Spülung F rinsing; (*Wasserspülung*) flush; (*Med*) irrigation

Spund [ʃpʊnt] (**-(e)s, -e**) M: **junger ~** (*veraltet: umg*) young pup

Spur [ʃpu:r] (**-, -en**) F trace; (*Fußspur, Radspur, Tonbandspur*) track; (*Fährte*) trail; (*Fahrspur*) lane; **jdm auf die ~ kommen** to get onto sb; **(seine) Spuren hinterlassen** (*fig*) to leave its mark; **keine ~** (*umg*) not/nothing at all

spürbar ADJ noticeable, perceptible

spuren (*umg*) VI to obey; (*sich fügen*) to toe the line

spüren ['ʃpy:rən] VT to feel; **etw zu ~ bekommen** (*lit*) to feel sth; (*fig*) to feel the (full) force of sth

Spurenelement NT trace element

Spurensicherung F securing of evidence

Spürhund M tracker dog; (*fig*) sleuth

spurlos ADV without (a) trace; **~ an jdm vorübergehen** to have no effect on sb

Spurt [ʃpʊrt] (**-(e)s, -s** *od* **-e**) M spurt

spurten VI (*Hilfsverb sein: Sport*) to spurt; (*umg: rennen*) to sprint

sputen ['ʃpu:tən] VR to make haste

Spyware ['spaɪwɛ:ər] F (*Comput*) spyware

Squash [skvɔʃ] (-) NT (*Sport*) squash

SS (-) F ABK (= *Schutzstaffel*) SS ▶ NT ABK = **Sommersemester**

s. S. ABK (= *siehe Seite*) see p.

SSV ABK = **Sommerschlussverkauf**

st ABK (= *Stunde*) h.

St. ABK = **Stück**; (= *Stunde*) h.; (= *Sankt*) St

Staat [ʃta:t] (**-(e)s, -en**) M state; (*Prunk*) show; (*Kleidung*) finery; **mit etw ~ machen** to show off *od* parade sth

staatenlos ADJ stateless

staatl. ABK = **staatlich**

staatlich ADJ state *attrib*; (*staatseigen*) state-run ▶ ADV: **~ geprüft** state-certified

Staats- ZW: **Staatsaffäre** F (*lit*) affair of state; (*fig*) major operation; **Staatsangehörige(r)** F(M) national; **Staatsangehörigkeit** F nationality; **Staatsanleihe** F government bond; **Staatsanwalt** M public prosecutor; **Staatsbürger** M citizen; **Staatsbürgerschaft** F nationality; **doppelte Staatsbürgerschaft** dual nationality; **Staatsdienst** M civil service; **staatseigen** ADJ state-owned; **Staatseigentum** NT public ownership; **Staatsexamen** NT (*Univ*) degree; **staatsfeindlich** ADJ subversive; **Staatsgeheimnis** NT (*lit, fig hum*) state secret; **Staatshaushalt** M budget; **Staatskosten** PL public expenses *pl*; **Staatsmann (-(e)s,** *pl* **-männer)** M statesman; **staatsmännisch** ADJ statesmanlike; **Staatsoberhaupt** NT head of state; **Staatsschuld** F (*Fin*) national debt; **Staatssekretär** M secretary of state; **Staatsstreich** M coup (d'état); **Staatsverschuldung** F national debt

Stab [ʃta:p] (**-(e)s, Stäbe**) M rod; (*für Stabhochsprung*) pole; (*für Staffellauf*) baton; (*Gitterstab*) bar; (*Menschen*) staff; (*von Experten*) panel

Stäbchen ['ʃtɛ:pçən] NT (*Essstäbchen*) chopstick

Stabhochsprung M pole vault

stabil [ʃta'bi:l] ADJ stable; (*Möbel*) sturdy

Stabilisator [ʃtabili'za:tɔr] M stabilizer

stabilisieren [ʃtabili'zi:rən] VT to stabilize

Stabilisierung F stabilization

Stabilität [ʃtabili'tɛ:t] F stability

Stabreim M alliteration

Stabsarzt M (*Mil*) captain in the medical corps

stach *etc* [ʃta:x] VB *siehe* **stechen**

Stachel ['ʃtaxəl] (**-s, -n**) M spike; (*von Tier*) spine; (*von Insekten*) sting; **Stachelbeere** F gooseberry; **Stacheldraht** M barbed wire

stachelig, stachlig ADJ prickly

Stachelschwein NT porcupine

Stadion ['ʃta:diɔn] (**-s, Stadien**) NT stadium

Stadium ['ʃta:diʊm] NT stage, phase

Stadt [ʃtat] (-, **Städte**) F town; (*Großstadt*) city; (*Stadtverwaltung*) (town/city) council; **Stadtbad** NT municipal swimming baths *pl*; **stadtbekannt** ADJ known all over town; **Stadtbezirk** M municipal district

Städtchen ['ʃtɛ:tçən] NT small town

Städtebau (**-(e)s**) M town planning

Städter(in) (**-s, -**) M(F) town/city dweller, townie

Stadtgespräch NT: **(das) ~ sein** to be the talk of the town

Stadtguerilla F urban guerrilla

städtisch ADJ municipal; (*nicht ländlich*) urban

Stadt- ZW: **Stadtkasse** F town/city treasury; **Stadtkern** M = **Stadtzentrum**; **Stadtkreis** M town/city borough; **Stadtmauer** F city wall(s *pl*); **Stadtmitte** F town/city centre (BRIT) *od* center (US); **Stadtpark** M municipal park; **Stadtplan** M street map; **Stadtrand** M outskirts *pl*; **Stadtrat** M (*Behörde*) (town/city) council; **Stadtrundfahrt** F city tour; **Stadtstreicher** M street vagrant; **Stadtstreicherin** F bag lady; **Stadtteil** M district, part of town; **Stadtverwaltung** F (*Behörde*) municipal authority; **Stadtviertel** M district *od* part of a town; **Stadtzentrum** NT town/city centre (BRIT) *od* center (US)

Staffel ['ʃtafəl] (-, **-n**) F rung; (*Sport*) relay (team); (*Aviat*) squadron

Staffelei [ʃtafə'laɪ] F easel

Staffellauf M relay race

staffeln VT to graduate

Staffelung F graduation

Stagnation [ʃtagnatsi'o:n] F stagnation

stagnieren [ʃta'gni:rən] VI to stagnate

stahl *etc* [ʃta:l] VB *siehe* **stehlen**

Stahl (**-(e)s, Stähle**) M steel

Stahlhelm M steel helmet

stak *etc* [ʃta:k] VB *siehe* **stecken**

Stall [ʃtal] (**-(e)s, Ställe**) M stable; (*Kaninchenstall*) hutch; (*Schweinestall*) sty; (*Hühnerstall*) henhouse
Stallung F stables *pl*
Stamm [ʃtam] (**-(e)s, Stämme**) M (*Baumstamm*) trunk; (*Menschenstamm*) tribe; (*Gram*) stem; (*Bakterienstamm*) strain; **Stammaktie** F ordinary share, common stock (*US*); **Stammbaum** M family tree; (*von Tier*) pedigree; **Stammbuch** NT *book of family events with legal documents*
stammeln VT, VI to stammer
stammen VI: **~ von** *od* **aus** to come from
Stamm- ZW: **Stammform** F base form; **Stammgast** M regular (customer); **Stammhalter** M son and heir
stämmig [ˈʃtɛmɪç] ADJ sturdy; (*Mensch*) stocky; **Stämmigkeit** F sturdiness; (*von Mensch*) stockiness
Stamm- ZW: **Stammkapital** NT (*Fin*) ordinary share *od* common stock (*US*) capital; **Stammkunde** M, **Stammkundin** F regular (customer); **Stammlokal** NT favourite (*Brit*) *od* favorite (*US*) café/restaurant *etc*; (*Kneipe*) local (*Brit*); **Stammplatz** M usual seat; **Stammtisch** M (*Tisch in Gasthaus*) *table reserved for the regulars*; **Stammzelle** F stem cell; **embryonale Stammzellen** embryonic stem cells
stampfen [ˈʃtampfən] VI to stamp; (*stapfen*) to tramp ▶ VT (*mit Stampfer*) to mash
Stampfer (**-s, -**) M (*Stampfgerät*) masher
stand [ʃtant] VB *siehe* **stehen**
Stand (**-(e)s, Stände**) M position; (*Wasserstand, Benzinstand etc*) level; (*Zählerstand etc*) reading; (*Stehen*) standing position; (*Zustand*) state; (*Spielstand*) score; (*Messestand etc*) stand; (*Klasse*) class; (*Beruf*) profession; **bei jdm** *od* **gegen jdn einen schweren ~ haben** (*fig*) to have a hard time of it with sb; **etw auf den neuesten ~ bringen** to bring sth up to date; *siehe auch* **außerstande**; **imstande**; **zustande**
Standard [ˈʃtandart] (**-s, -s**) M standard; **Standardausführung** F standard design
standardisieren [ʃtandardiˈziːrən] VT to standardize
Standarte (**-, -n**) F (*Mil, Pol*) standard
Standbild NT statue
Ständchen [ˈʃtɛntçən] NT serenade
Ständer (**-s, -**) M stand
Standes- ZW: **Standesamt** NT registry office (*Brit*), city/county clerk's office (*US*); **standesamtlich** ADJ: **standesamtliche Trauung** registry office wedding (*Brit*), civil marriage ceremony; **Standesbeamte(r)** M registrar; **Standesbewusstsein** NT status consciousness; **Standesdünkel** M snobbery; **standesgemäß** ADJ, ADV according to one's social position; **Standesunterschied** M social difference
Stand- ZW: **standfest** ADJ (*Tisch, Leiter*) stable, steady; (*fig*) steadfast; **standhaft** ADJ steadfast; **Standhaftigkeit** F steadfastness; **standhalten** *unreg* VI: **(jdm/etw) standhalten** to stand firm (against sb/sth), to resist (sb/sth)
ständig [ˈʃtɛndɪç] ADJ permanent; (*ununterbrochen*) constant, continual
Stand- ZW: **Standlicht** NT sidelights *pl* (*Brit*), parking lights *pl* (*US*); **Standort** M location; (*Mil*) garrison; **Standpauke** (*umg*) F: **jdm eine Standpauke halten** to give sb a lecture; **Standpunkt** M standpoint; **standrechtlich** ADJ: **standrechtlich erschießen** to put before a firing squad; **Standspur** F (*Aut*) hard shoulder (*Brit*), berm (*US*)
Stange [ˈʃtaŋə] (**-, -n**) F stick; (*Stab*) pole; (*Querstange*) bar; (*Zigaretten*) carton; **von der ~** (*Comm*) off the peg (*Brit*) *od* rack (*US*); **eine ~ Geld** quite a packet; **jdm die ~ halten** (*umg*) to stick up for sb; **bei der ~ bleiben** (*umg*) to stick at *od* to sth
Stängel [ˈʃtɛŋl] (**-s, -**) M stalk; **vom ~ fallen** (*umg: überrascht sein*) to be staggered
Stangenbohne F runner bean
Stangenbrot NT French bread; (*Laib*) French stick (loaf)
stank [ʃtaŋk] VB *siehe* **stinken**
stänkern [ˈʃtɛŋkərn] (*umg*) VI to stir things up
Stanniol [ʃtaniˈoːl] (**-s, -e**) NT tinfoil
Stanze [ˈʃtantsə] (**-, -n**) F stanza; (*Tech*) stamp
stanzen VT to stamp; (*Löcher*) to punch
Stapel [ˈʃtaːpəl] (**-s, -**) M pile; (*Naut*) stocks *pl*; **Stapellauf** M launch
stapeln VT to pile (up)
Stapelverarbeitung F (*Comput*) batch processing
stapfen [ˈʃtapfən] VI to trudge, to plod
Star[1] [ʃtaːr] (**-(e)s, -e**) M starling; **grauer/grüner ~** (*Med*) cataract/glaucoma
Star[2] [ʃtaːr] (**-s, -s**) M (*Filmstar etc*) star
starb [ʃtarp] VB *siehe* **sterben**
stark [ʃtark] ADJ strong; (*heftig, groß*) heavy; (*Maßangabe*) thick; (*umg: hervorragend*) great ▶ ADV very; (*beschädigt etc*) badly; (*vergrößert, verkleinert*) greatly; **das ist ein starkes Stück!** (*umg*) that's a bit much!; **er ist ~ erkältet** he has a bad cold; *siehe auch* **starkmachen**
Stärke [ˈʃtɛrkə] (**-, -n**) F strength (*auch fig*); (*Größe*) heaviness; (*bei Maßangaben*) thickness; (*von Mannschaft*) size; (*Wäschestärke, Koch*) starch; **Stärkemehl** NT (*Koch*) thickening agent
stärken VT (*lit, fig*) to strengthen; (*Wäsche*) to starch; (*Selbstbewusstsein*) to boost; (*Gesundheit*) to improve; (*erfrischen*) to fortify ▶ VI to be fortifying; **stärkendes Mittel** tonic
starkmachen VR: **sich für etw ~** (*umg*) to stand up for sth
Starkstrom M high-voltage current
Stärkung [ˈʃtɛrkʊŋ] F strengthening; (*Essen*) refreshment
Stärkungsmittel NT tonic
starr [ʃtar] ADJ stiff; (*unnachgiebig*) rigid; (*Blick*) staring
starren VI to stare; **~ vor** *+dat od* **von** (*voll von*) to be covered in; (*Waffen*) to be bristling with; **vor sich** *akk* **hin ~** to stare straight ahead
starr- ZW: **Starrheit** F rigidity; **starrköpfig** ADJ stubborn; **Starrsinn** M obstinacy

Start [ʃtart] (**-(e)s, -e**) M start; (*Aviat*) takeoff; **Startautomatik** F (*Aut*) automatic choke; **Startbahn** F runway; **starten** VI to start; (*Aviat*) to take off ▶ VT to start; **Starter** (**-s, -**) M starter; **Starterlaubnis** F takeoff clearance; **Starthilfe** F (*Aviat*) rocket-assisted takeoff; (*fig*) initial aid; **jdm Starthilfe geben** to help sb get off the ground; **Starthilfekabel** NT jump leads *pl* (BRIT), jumper cables *pl* (*US*); **startklar** ADJ (*Aviat*) clear for takeoff; (*Sport*) ready to start; **Startkommando** NT (*Sport*) starting signal; **Startzeichen** NT start signal

Stasi [ˈʃtaːzi] (-) (*umg*) F ABK (*früher*: = *Staatssicherheitsdienst der DDR*) Stasi; *see note*

> **Stasi**, an abbreviation of Staatssicherheitsdienst, the **DDR** secret service, was founded in 1950 and disbanded in 1989. The Stasi organized an extensive spy network of full-time and part-time workers who often held positions of trust in both the **DDR** and the **BRD**. They held personal files on 6 million people.

Station [ʃtatsiˈoːn] F station; (*Krankenstation*) hospital ward; (*Haltestelle*) stop; **~ machen** to stop off

stationär [ʃtatsioˈnɛːr] ADJ stationary; (*Med*) in-patient *attrib*

stationieren [ʃtatsioˈniːrən] VT to station; (*Atomwaffen etc*) to deploy

Stations- ZW: **Stationsarzt** M ward doctor; **Stationsärztin** F ward doctor; **Stationsvorsteher** M (*Eisenb*) stationmaster

statisch [ˈʃtaːtɪʃ] ADJ static

Statist(in) [ʃtaˈtɪst(ɪn)] M(F) (*Film*) extra; (*Theat*) supernumerary

Statistik F statistic; (*Wissenschaft*) statistics *sing*

Statistiker(in) (**-s, -**) M(F) statistician

statistisch ADJ statistical

Stativ [ʃtaˈtiːf] (**-s, -e**) NT tripod

statt KONJ instead of ▶ PRÄP (*+dat od gen*) instead of

stattdessen ADV instead

Stätte [ˈʃtɛtə] (**-, -n**) F place

statt- ZW: **stattfinden** *unreg* VI to take place; **statthaft** ADJ admissible; **Statthalter** M governor; **stattlich** ADJ imposing, handsome; (*Bursche*) strapping; (*Sammlung*) impressive; (*Familie*) large; (*Summe*) handsome

Statue [ˈʃtaːtuə] (**-, -n**) F statue

Statur [ʃtaˈtuːr] F build

Status [ˈʃtaːtʊs] (**-, -**) M status; **Statussymbol** NT status symbol

Statuten [ʃtaˈtuːtən] PL by(e)-law(s *pl*)

Stau [ʃtaʊ] (**-(e)s, -e**) M blockage; (*Verkehrsstau*) (traffic) jam

Staub [ʃtaʊp] (**-(e)s**) M dust; **~ saugen** to vacuum; **~ wischen** to dust; **sich aus dem ~ machen** (*umg*) to clear off

stauben [ˈʃtaʊbən] VI to be dusty

Staubfaden M (*Bot*) stamen

staubig [ˈʃtaʊbɪç] ADJ dusty

Staub- ZW: **Staublappen** M duster; **Staublunge** F (*Med*) dust on the lung; **staubsaugen** (*pp* **staubgesaugt**) VI UNTR to vacuum; **Staubsauger** M vacuum cleaner; **Staubtuch** NT duster

Staudamm M dam

Staude [ˈʃtaʊdə] (**-, -n**) F shrub

stauen [ˈʃtaʊən] VT (*Wasser*) to dam up; (*Blut*) to stop the flow of ▶ VR (*Wasser*) to become dammed up; (*Verkehr, Med*) to become congested; (*Menschen*) to collect together; (*Gefühle*) to build up

staunen [ˈʃtaʊnən] VI to be astonished; **da kann man nur noch ~** it's just amazing; **Staunen** (**-s**) NT amazement

Stausee [ˈʃtaʊzeː] M reservoir, artificial lake

Stauung [ˈʃtaʊʊŋ] F (*von Wasser*) damming-up; (*von Blut, Verkehr*) congestion

Std. ABK (= *Stunde*) h.

stdl. ABK = **stündlich**

Steak [ʃteːk] (**-s, -s**) NT steak

stechen *unreg* VT (*mit Nadel etc*) to prick; (*mit Messer*) to stab; (*mit Finger*) to poke; (*Biene etc*) to sting; (*Mücke*) to bite; (*Karten*) to take; (*Kunst*) to engrave; (*Torf, Spargel*) to cut ▶ VI (*Sonne*) to beat down; (*mit Stechkarte*) to clock in ▶ VR: **sich** *akk, dat* **in den Finger ~** to prick one's finger; **es sticht** it is prickly; **in See ~** to put to sea

Stechen [ˈʃtɛçən] (**-s, -**) NT (*Sport*) play-off; (*Springreiten*) jump-off; (*Schmerz*) sharp pain

stechend ADJ piercing, stabbing; (*Geruch*) pungent

Stech- ZW: **Stechginster** M gorse; **Stechkarte** F clocking-in card; **Stechmücke** F gnat; **Stechpalme** F holly; **Stechuhr** F time clock

Steck- ZW: **Steckbrief** M "wanted" poster; **steckbrieflich** ADV: **steckbrieflich gesucht werden** to be wanted; **Steckdose** F (wall) socket

stecken [ˈʃtɛkən] VT to put; (*einführen*) to insert; (*Nadel*) to stick; (*Pflanzen*) to plant; (*beim Nähen*) to pin ▶ VI (*auch unreg*) to be; (*festsitzen*) to be stuck; (*Nadeln*) to stick; **etw in etw** *akk* **~** (*umg*: *Geld, Mühe*) to put sth into sth; (*: Zeit*) to devote sth to sth; **der Schlüssel steckt** the key is in the lock; **wo steckt er?** where has he got to?; **zeigen, was in einem steckt** to show what one is made of; **~ bleiben** to get stuck; **~ lassen** to leave in

Steckenpferd NT hobbyhorse

Stecker (**-s, -**) M (*Elek*) plug

Steck- ZW: **Stecknadel** F pin; **Steckrübe** F swede, turnip; **Steckschlüssel** M box spanner (BRIT) *od* wrench (*US*); **Steckzwiebel** F bulb

Steg [ʃteːk] (**-(e)s, -e**) M small bridge; (*Anlegesteg*) landing stage

Stegreif M: **aus dem ~** just like that

Stehaufmännchen [ˈʃteːlaʊfmɛnçən] NT (*Spielzeug*) tumbler

stehen [ˈʃteːən] *unreg* VI to stand; (*sich befinden*) to be; (*in Zeitung*) to say; (*angehalten haben*) to have stopped ▶ VI UNPERS: **es steht schlecht um …** things are bad for … ▶ VR: **sich gut/schlecht ~** to be well-off/badly off; **zu jdm/etw ~** to stand

S

by sb/sth; **jdm ~** to suit sb; **ich tue, was in meinen Kräften steht** I'll do everything I can; **es steht 2:1 für München** the score is 2-1 to Munich; **mit dem Dativ ~** (*Gram*) to take the dative; **auf Betrug steht eine Gefängnisstrafe** the penalty for fraud is imprisonment; **wie ~ Sie dazu?** what are your views on that?; **wie stehts?** how are things?; (*Sport*) what's the score?; **wie steht es damit?** how about it?; **~ bleiben** (*Uhr*) to stop; (*Zeit*) to stand still; (*Auto, Zug*) to stand; (*Fehler*) to stay as it is; (*Verkehr, Produktion etc*) to come to a standstill *od* stop; **~ lassen** to leave; (*Bart*) to grow; **alles ~ und liegen lassen** to drop everything

stehend ADJ *attrib* (*Fahrzeug*) stationary; (*Gewässer*) stagnant; (*ständig: Heer*) regular

Stehlampe F standard lamp (BRIT), floor lamp (US)

stehlen ['ʃteːlən] *unreg* VT to steal

Stehplatz M: **ein ~ kostet 15 Euro** a standing ticket costs 15 euros

Stehvermögen NT staying power, stamina

Steiermark ['ʃtaɪrmark] F: **die ~** Styria

steif [ʃtaɪf] ADJ stiff; **~ und fest auf etw** *dat* **beharren** to insist stubbornly on sth

Steifftier® ['ʃtaɪftiːr] NT *soft toy animal*

Steifheit F stiffness

Steigbügel ['ʃtaɪkbyːgəl] M stirrup

Steigeisen NT crampon

steigen *unreg* VI to rise; (*klettern*) to climb ▶ VT (*Treppen, Stufen*) to climb (up); **das Blut stieg ihm in den Kopf** the blood rushed to his head; **~ in** *+akk***/auf** *+akk* to get in/on

Steiger (**-s, -**) M (*Min*) pit foreman

steigern VT to raise; (*Gram*) to compare ▶ VI (*Auktion*) to bid ▶ VR to increase

Steigerung F raising; (*Gram*) comparison

Steigung F incline, gradient, rise

steil [ʃtaɪl] ADJ steep; **Steilhang** M steep slope; **Steilpass** M (*Sport*) through ball

Stein [ʃtaɪn] (**-(e)s, -e**) M stone; (*in Uhr*) jewel; **mir fällt ein ~ vom Herzen!** (*fig*) that's a load off my mind!; **bei jdm einen ~ im Brett haben** (*fig: umg*) to be well in with sb; **jdm Steine in den Weg legen** to make things difficult for sb; **Steinadler** M golden eagle; **steinalt** ADJ ancient; **Steinbock** M (*Astrol*) Capricorn; **Steinbruch** M quarry

steinern ADJ (made of) stone; (*fig*) stony

Stein- zW: **Steinerweichen** NT: **zum Steinerweichen weinen** to cry heartbreakingly; **Steingarten** M rockery; **Steingut** NT stoneware; **steinhart** ADJ hard as stone

steinig ADJ stony

steinigen VT to stone

Stein- zW: **Steinkohle** F mineral coal; **Steinmetz** (**-es, -e**) M stonemason; **steinreich** (*umg*) ADJ stinking rich; **Steinschlag** M: **„Achtung Steinschlag"** "danger – falling rocks"; **Steinwurf** M (*fig*) stone's throw; **Steinzeit** F Stone Age

Steiß [ʃtaɪs] (**-es, -e**) M rump; **Steißbein** NT (*Anat*) coccyx

Stelle ['ʃtɛlə] (**-, -n**) F place; (*Arbeit*) post, job; (*Amt*) office; (*Abschnitt*) passage; (*Textstelle, bes beim Zitieren*) reference; **drei Stellen hinter dem Komma** (*Math*) three decimal places; **eine freie** *od* **offene ~** a vacancy; **an dieser ~** in this place, here; **ich an deiner ~** if I were you; **an anderer ~** elsewhere; **nicht von der ~ kommen** not to make any progress; **auf der ~** (*fig: sofort*) on the spot; *siehe auch* **anstelle**

stellen VT to put; (*Uhr etc*) to set; (*zur Verfügung stellen*) to supply; (*fassen: Dieb*) to apprehend; (*Antrag, Forderung*) to make; (*Aufnahme*) to pose; (*arrangieren: Szene*) to arrange ▶ VR (*sich aufstellen*) to stand; (*sich einfinden*) to present o.s.; (*bei Polizei*) to give o.s. up; (*vorgeben*) to pretend (to be); **das Radio lauter/leiser ~** to turn the radio up/down; **auf sich** *akk* **selbst gestellt sein** (*fig*) to have to fend for o.s.; **sich hinter jdn/etw ~** (*fig*) to support sb/sth; **sich einer Herausforderung ~** to take up a challenge; **sich zu etw ~** to have an opinion of sth

Stellen- zW: **Stellenangebot** NT job offer; (*in Zeitung*): **„Stellenangebote"** "vacancies"; **Stellenanzeige** F job advertisement *od* ad (*umg*); **Stellengesuch** NT application for a post; **„Stellengesuche"** "situations wanted"; **Stellenmarkt** M job market; (*in Zeitung*) appointments section; **Stellennachweis** M employment agency; **Stellenvermittlung** F employment agency; **stellenweise** ADV in places; **Stellenwert** M (*fig*) status; **einen hohen Stellenwert haben** to play an important role

Stellung F position; (*Mil*) line; **~ nehmen zu** to comment on

Stellungnahme F comment

stellungslos ADJ unemployed

stellv. ABK = **stellvertretend**

Stell- zW: **stellvertretend** ADJ deputy *attrib*, acting *attrib*; **Stellvertreter** M representative; (*von Amts wegen*) deputy; **Stellwerk** NT (*Eisenb*) signal box

Stelze ['ʃtɛltsə] (**-, -n**) F stilt

stelzen (*umg*) VI to stalk

Stemmbogen M (*Ski*) stem turn

Stemmeisen NT crowbar

stemmen ['ʃtɛmən] VT to lift (up); (*drücken*) to press; **sich ~ gegen** (*fig*) to resist, to oppose

Stempel ['ʃtɛmpəl] (**-s, -**) M stamp; (*Poststempel*) postmark; (*Tech: Prägestempel*) die; (*Bot*) pistil; **Stempelgebühr** F stamp duty; **Stempelkissen** NT inkpad

stempeln VT to stamp; (*Briefmarke*) to cancel ▶ VI (*umg: Stempeluhr betätigen*) to clock in/out; **~ gehen** (*umg*) to be *od* go on the dole (BRIT) *od* on welfare (US)

Stengel ['ʃtɛŋəl] (**-s, -**) M *siehe* **Stängel**

Steno ['ʃteno] (*umg*) F shorthand; **Stenograf(in)** [-graːf(ɪn)] M(F) (*im Büro*) shorthand secretary; **Stenografie** [-gra'fiː] F shorthand; **stenografieren** [-gra'fiːrən] VT, VI to write (in)

shorthand; **Stenogramm** [-'gram] NT text in shorthand; **Stenotypist(in)** [-ty'pɪst(ɪn)] M(F) shorthand typist (BRIT), stenographer (US)
Steppdecke F quilt
Steppe (-, -n) F steppe
steppen ['ʃtɛpən] VT to stitch ▸ VI to tap-dance
Stepptanz M tap-dance
Sterbe- zW: **Sterbebett** NT deathbed; **Sterbefall** M death; **Sterbehilfe** F euthanasia; **Sterbekasse** F death benefit fund
sterben ['ʃtɛrbən] *unreg* VI to die; **an einer Krankheit/Verletzung ~** to die of an illness/ from an injury; **er ist für mich gestorben** (*fig: umg*) he might as well be dead
Sterben NT: **im ~ liegen** to be dying
sterbenslangweilig (*umg*) ADJ deadly boring
Sterbenswörtchen (*umg*) NT: **er hat kein ~ gesagt** he didn't say a word
Sterbeurkunde F death certificate
sterblich ['ʃtɛrplɪç] ADJ mortal; **Sterblichkeit** F mortality; **Sterblichkeitsziffer** F death rate
stereo- ['ste:reo] IN zW stereo(-); **Stereoanlage** F stereo unit; **stereotyp** ADJ stereotyped
steril [ʃte'ri:l] ADJ sterile
sterilisieren [ʃterili'zi:rən] VT to sterilize
Sterilisierung F sterilization
Stern [ʃtɛrn] (**-(e)s, -e**) M star; **das steht (noch) in den Sternen** (*fig*) it's in the lap of the gods; **Sternbild** NT constellation; **Sternchen** NT asterisk; **Sternenbanner** NT Stars and Stripes *sing*; **sternhagelvoll** (*umg*) ADJ legless; **Sternschnuppe** (-, -n) F meteor, falling star; **Sternstunde** F historic moment; **Sternwarte** F observatory; **Sternzeichen** NT (*Astrol*) sign of the zodiac
stet [ʃte:t] ADJ steady
Stethoskop [ʃteto'sko:p] (**-(e)s, -e**) NT stethoscope
stetig ADJ constant, continual; (*Math: Funktion*) continuous
stets ADV continually, always
Steuer[1] ['ʃtɔyər] (**-s, -**) NT (*Naut*) helm; (*Steuerruder*) rudder; (*Aut*) steering wheel; **am ~ sitzen** (*Aut*) to be at the wheel; (*Aviat*) to be at the controls
Steuer[2] (**-, -n**) F tax
Steuer- zW: **Steuerbefreiung** F tax exemption; **steuerbegünstigt** ADJ (*Investitionen, Hypothek*) tax-deductible; (*Waren*) taxed at a lower rate; **Steuerberater(in)** M(F) tax consultant; **Steuerbescheid** M tax assessment; **Steuerbord** NT starboard; **Steuererhöhung** F tax increase; **Steuererklärung** F tax return; **steuerfrei** ADJ tax-free; **Steuerfreibetrag** M tax allowance; **Steuerhinterziehung** F tax evasion; **Steuerjahr** NT fiscal *od* tax year; **Steuerkarte** F tax notice; **Steuerklasse** F tax group; **Steuerknüppel** M control column; (*Aviat, Comput*) joystick; **steuerlich** ADJ tax *attrib*; **Steuermann** (**-(e)s,** *pl* **-männer** *od* **-leute**) M helmsman
steuern VT to steer; (*Flugzeug*) to pilot; (*Entwicklung, Tonstärke*) to control ▸ VI to steer; (*in Flugzeug etc*) to be at the controls; (*bei Entwicklung etc*) to be in control
Steuer- zW: **Steuernummer** F ≈ National Insurance Number (BRIT), ≈ Social Security Number (US); **Steuerparadies** NT tax haven; **steuerpflichtig** ADJ taxable; (*Person*) liable to pay tax; **Steuerprogression** F progressive taxation; **Steuerprüfung** F tax inspector's investigation; **Steuerrad** NT steering wheel; **Steuerrückvergütung** F tax rebate; **Steuersenkung** F tax cut
Steuerung F steering (*auch Aut*); (*von Flugzeug*) piloting; (*von Entwicklung*) control; (*Vorrichtung*) controls *pl*; **automatische ~** (*Aviat*) autopilot; (*Tech*) automatic steering (device)
Steuer- zW: **Steuervergünstigung** F tax relief; **Steuerzahler** M taxpayer; **Steuerzuschlag** M additional tax
Steward ['stju:ərt] (**-s, -s**) M steward
Stewardess ['stju:ərdɛs] (**-, -en**) F stewardess
StGB (**-s**) NT ABK = **Strafgesetzbuch**
stibitzen [ʃti'bɪtsən] (*umg*) VT to pilfer, to pinch (*umg*)
Stich [ʃtɪç] (**-(e)s, -e**) M (*Insektenstich*) sting; (*Messerstich*) stab; (*beim Nähen*) stitch; (*Färbung*) tinge; (*Karten*) trick; (*Kunst*) engraving; (*fig*) pang; **ein ~ ins Rote** a tinge of red; **einen ~ haben** (*umg: Esswaren*) to be bad *od* off (BRIT); (*: Mensch: verrückt sein*) to be nuts; **jdn im ~ lassen** to leave sb in the lurch
Stichel (**-s, -**) M engraving tool, style
Stichelei [ʃtɪçə'laɪ] F jibe, taunt
sticheln VI (*fig*) to jibe; (*pej, umg*) to make snide remarks
Stich- zW: **Stichflamme** F tongue of flame; **stichhaltig** ADJ valid; (*Beweis*) conclusive; **Stichprobe** F spot check
sticht [ʃtɪçt] VB *siehe* **stechen**
Stichtag M qualifying date
Stichwahl F final ballot
Stichwort NT (*pl* **-worte**) cue; (*für Vortrag*) note; (*pl* **-wörter**: *in Wörterbuch*) headword; **Stichwortkatalog** M classified catalogue (BRIT) *od* catalog (US); **Stichwortverzeichnis** NT index
Stichwunde F stab wound
sticken ['ʃtɪkən] VT, VI to embroider
Stickerei [ʃtɪkə'raɪ] F embroidery
stickig ADJ stuffy, close
Stickstoff (**-(e)s**) M nitrogen
stieben ['ʃti:bən] VI (*geh: sprühen*) to fly
Stief- ['ʃti:f] IN zW step-
Stiefel ['ʃti:fəl] (**-s, -**) M boot; (*Trinkgefäß*) *large boot-shaped beer glass*
Stief- zW: **Stiefkind** NT stepchild; (*fig*) Cinderella; **Stiefmutter** F stepmother; **Stiefmütterchen** NT pansy; **stiefmütterlich** ADJ (*fig*): **jdn/etw stiefmütterlich behandeln** to pay little attention to sb/sth; **Stiefvater** M stepfather
stieg [ʃti:k] VB *siehe* **steigen**
Stiege ['ʃti:gə] (**-, -n**) F staircase
Stieglitz ['ʃti:glɪts] (**-es, -e**) M goldfinch
stiehlt [ʃti:lt] VB *siehe* **stehlen**

S

Stiel [ʃti:l] (**-(e)s, -e**) M handle; (*Bot*) stalk
Stielaugen PL (*fig: umg*): **er machte ~** his eyes (nearly) popped out of his head
stier [ʃti:ɾ] ADJ staring, fixed
Stier (**-(e)s, -e**) M bull; (*Astrol*) Taurus
stieren VI to stare
Stierkampf M bullfight
stieß [ʃti:s] VB *siehe* **stoßen**
Stift [ʃtɪft] (**-(e)s, -e**) M peg; (*Nagel*) tack; (*Buntstift*) crayon; (*Bleistift*) pencil; (*umg: Lehrling*) apprentice (boy)
stiften VT to found; (*Unruhe*) to cause; (*spenden*) to contribute; **~ gehen** to hop it
Stifter(in) (**-s, -**) M(F) founder
Stiftung F donation; (*Organisation*) foundation
Stiftzahn M post crown
Stil [ʃti:l] (**-(e)s, -e**) M style; (*Eigenart*) way, manner; **Stilblüte** F howler; **Stilbruch** M stylistic incongruity
stilistisch [ʃti'lɪstɪʃ] ADJ stylistic
still [ʃtɪl] ADJ quiet; (*unbewegt*) still; (*heimlich*) secret; **ich dachte mir im Stillen** I thought to myself; **er ist ein stilles Wasser** he's a deep one; **stiller Teilhaber** (*Comm*) sleeping (BRIT) *od* silent (US) partner; **der Stille Ozean** the Pacific (Ocean); **~ stehen** (*unbewegt*) to stand still
Stille (**-, -n**) F quietness; (*Unbewegtheit*) stillness; **in aller ~** quietly
Stilleben NT *siehe* **Stillleben**
Stillegung F *siehe* **Stilllegung**
stillen VT to stop; (*befriedigen*) to satisfy; (*Säugling*) to breast-feed
still- ZW: **stillgestanden** INTERJ attention!; **Stillhalteabkommen** NT (*Fin, fig*) moratorium; **stillhalten** *unreg* VI to keep still; **Stillleben** NT still life; **stilllegen** VT to close down; **Stilllegung** F (*Betrieb*) shut-down, closure; **stillliegen** *unreg* VI (*außer Betrieb sein*) to be shut down; (*lahmgelegt sein*) to be at a standstill; **stillschweigen** *unreg* VI to be silent; **Stillschweigen** NT silence; **stillschweigend** ADJ silent; (*Einverständnis*) tacit ▶ ADV silently; (*mit Einverständnis*) tacitly; **Stillstand** M standstill; **stillstehen** *unreg* VI to stand still
Stilmöbel PL reproduction *od* (*antik*) period furniture *sing*
stilvoll ADJ stylish
Stimm- ZW: **Stimmabgabe** F voting; **Stimmbänder** PL vocal cords *pl*; **stimmberechtigt** ADJ entitled to vote; **Stimmbruch** M: **er ist im Stimmbruch** his voice is breaking
Stimme ['ʃtɪmə] (**-, -n**) F voice; (*Wahlstimme*) vote; (*Mus: Rolle*) part; **mit leiser/lauter ~** in a soft/loud voice; **seine ~ abgeben** to vote
stimmen VI (*richtig sein*) to be right; (*wählen*) to vote ▶ VT (*Instrument*) to tune; **stimmt so!** (*beim Bezahlen*) keep the change; **für/gegen etw ~** to vote for/against sth; **jdn traurig ~** to make sb feel sad
Stimmen- ZW: **Stimmengewirr** NT babble of voices; **Stimmengleichheit** F tied vote; **Stimmenmehrheit** F majority (of votes)
Stimm- ZW: **Stimmenthaltung** F abstention; **Stimmgabel** F tuning fork; **stimmhaft** ADJ voiced
stimmig ADJ harmonious
Stimm- ZW: **stimmlos** ADJ (*Ling*) unvoiced; **Stimmrecht** NT right to vote; **stimmrechtslos** ADJ: **stimmrechtslose Aktien** "A" shares
Stimmung F mood; (*Atmosphäre*) atmosphere; (*Moral*) morale; **in ~ kommen** to liven up; **~ gegen/für jdn/etw machen** to stir up (public) opinion against/in favour of sb/sth
Stimmungs- ZW: **Stimmungskanone** (*umg*) F life and soul of the party; **Stimmungsmache** (*pej*) F cheap propaganda; **stimmungsvoll** ADJ (*Atmosphäre*) enjoyable; (*Gedicht*) full of atmosphere
Stimmzettel M ballot paper
stinken ['ʃtɪŋkən] *unreg* VI to stink; **die Sache stinkt mir** (*umg*) I'm fed-up to the back teeth (with it)
Stink- ZW: **stinkfaul** (*umg*) ADJ bone-lazy; **stinklangweilig** (*umg*) ADJ deadly boring; **Stinktier** NT skunk; **Stinkwut** (*umg*) F: **eine Stinkwut (auf jdn) haben** to be livid (with sb)
Stipendium [ʃti'pɛndiʊm] NT grant; (*als Auszeichnung*) scholarship
Stippvisite ['ʃtɪpvi'zi:tə] (*umg*) F flying visit
stirbt [ʃtɪrpt] VB *siehe* **sterben**
Stirn [ʃtɪrn] (**-, -en**) F forehead, brow; (*Frechheit*) impudence; **die ~ haben zu ...** to have the nerve to ...; **Stirnband** NT headband; **Stirnhöhle** F sinus; **Stirnrunzeln** (**-s**) NT frown
stob*etc* [ʃto:p] VB *siehe* **stieben**
stöbern ['ʃtøbərn] VI to rummage
stochern ['stɔxərn] VI to poke (about)
Stock[1] [ʃtɔk] (**-(e)s, Stöcke**) M stick; (*Rohrstock*) cane; (*Zeigestock*) pointer; (*Bot*) stock; **über ~ und Stein** up hill and down dale
Stock[2] [ʃtɔk] (**-(e)s, -** *od* **-werke**) M storey (BRIT), story (US); **im ersten ~** on the first (BRIT) *od* second (US) floor
stock- IN ZW (*vor adj: umg*) completely
Stöckelschuh ['ʃtœkəlʃu:] M stiletto-heeled shoe
stocken VI to stop, to pause; (*Arbeit, Entwicklung*) to make no progress; (*im Satz*) to break off; (*Verkehr*) to be held up
stockend ADJ halting
stockfinster (*umg*) ADJ pitch-dark
Stockholm ['ʃtɔkhɔlm] (**-s**) NT Stockholm
stocksauer (*umg*) ADJ pissed-off (*umg!*)
stocktaub ADJ stone-deaf
Stockung F stoppage
Stockwerk NT storey (BRIT), story (US), floor
Stoff [ʃtɔf] (**-(e)s, -e**) M (*Gewebe*) material, cloth; (*Materie*) matter; (*von Buch etc*) subject (matter); (*umg: Rauschgift*) dope
Stoffel (**-s, -**) (*pej, umg*) M lout, boor
stofflich ADJ with regard to subject matter
Stoff- ZW: **Stoffrest** M remnant; **Stofftier** NT soft toy; **Stoffwechsel** M metabolism
stöhnen ['ʃtø:nən] VI to groan

stoisch ['ʃto:ɪʃ] ADJ stoical
Stola ['ʃto:la] (-, **Stolen**) F stole
Stollen ['ʃtɔlən] (-s, -) M (*Min*) gallery; (*Koch*) stollen, *cake eaten at Christmas*; (*von Schuhen*) stud
stolpern ['ʃtɔlpərn] VI to stumble, to trip; (*fig: zu Fall kommen*) to come a cropper (*umg*)
stolz [ʃtɔlts] ADJ proud; (*imposant: Bauwerk*) majestic; (*ironisch: Preis*) princely; **Stolz** (-es) M pride
stolzieren [ʃtɔl'tsi:rən] VI to strut
stopfen ['ʃtɔpfən] VT (*hineinstopfen*) to stuff; (*nähen*) to darn ▶ VI (*Med*) to cause constipation; **jdm das Maul ~** (*umg*) to silence sb
Stopfgarn NT darning thread
Stopp [ʃtɔp] (-s, -s) M stop, halt; (*Lohnstopp*) freeze
Stoppel ['ʃtɔpəl] (-, -n) F stubble
stoppen VT to stop; (*mit Uhr*) to time ▶ VI to stop
Stoppschild NT stop sign
Stoppuhr F stopwatch
Stöpsel ['ʃtœpsəl] (-s, -) M plug; (*für Flaschen*) stopper
Stör [ʃtø:r] (-(e)s, -e) M sturgeon
Störaktion F disruptive action
störanfällig ADJ susceptible to interference *od* breakdown
Storch [ʃtɔrç] (-(e)s, **Störche**) M stork
Store [sto:r] (-s, -s) M net curtain
stören ['ʃtø:rən] VT to disturb; (*behindern, Rundf*) to interfere with ▶ VR: **sich an etw** *dat* **~** to let sth bother one ▶ VI to get in the way; **was mich an ihm/daran stört** what I don't like about him/it; **stört es Sie, wenn ich rauche?** do you mind if I smoke?; **ich möchte nicht ~** I don't want to be in the way
störend ADJ disturbing, annoying
Störenfried (-(e)s, -e) M troublemaker
Störfall M (*in Kraftwerk etc*) malfunction, accident
stornieren [ʃtɔr'ni:rən] VT (*Comm: Auftrag*) to cancel; (*: Buchungsfehler*) to reverse
Storno ['ʃtɔrno] (-s) M OD NT (*Comm: von Buchungsfehler*) reversal; (*: von Auftrag*) cancellation (BRIT), cancelation (US)
störrisch ['ʃtœrɪʃ] ADJ stubborn, perverse
Störsender M jammer, jamming transmitter
Störung F disturbance; (*Rundf*) interference; (*Tech*) fault; (*Med*) disorder
Störungsstelle F (*Tel*) faults service
Stoß [ʃto:s] (-es, **Stöße**) M (*Schub*) push; (*leicht*) poke; (*Schlag*) blow; (*mit Schwert*) thrust; (*mit Ellbogen*) nudge; (*mit Fuß*) kick; (*Erdstoß*) shock; (*Haufen*) pile; **seinem Herzen einen ~ geben** to pluck up courage; **Stoßdämpfer** M shock absorber
Stößel ['ʃtø:səl] (-s, -) M pestle; (*Aut: Ventilstößel*) tappet
stoßen *unreg* VT (*mit Druck*) to shove, to push; (*mit Schlag*) to knock, to bump; (*mit Ellbogen*) to nudge; (*mit Fuß*) to kick; (*mit Schwert*) to thrust; (*anstoßen: Kopf etc*) to bump; (*zerkleinern*) to pulverize ▶ VR to get a knock ▶ VI: **~ an** *od* **auf** *+akk* to bump into; (*finden*) to come across; (*angrenzen*) to be next to; **sich ~ an** *+dat* (*fig*) to take exception to; **zu jdm ~** to meet up with sb
Stoßgebet NT quick prayer
Stoßstange F (*Aut*) bumper
stößt [ʃtø:st] VB *siehe* **stoßen**
Stoß- ZW: **Stoßverkehr** M rush-hour traffic; **Stoßzahn** M tusk; **Stoßzeit** F (*im Verkehr*) rush hour; (*in Geschäft etc*) peak period
Stotterer (-s, -) M stutterer
Stotterin F stutterer
stottern ['ʃtɔtərn] VT, VI to stutter
Stövchen ['ʃtø:fçən] NT (teapot- *etc*) warmer
StPO ABK = **Strafprozessordnung**
Str. ABK (= *Straße*) St.
stracks [ʃtraks] ADV straight
Straf- ZW: **Strafanstalt** F penal institution; **Strafarbeit** F (*Sch*) lines *pl*, punishment exercise; **Strafbank** F (*Sport*) penalty bench; **strafbar** ADJ punishable; **sich strafbar machen** to commit an offence (BRIT) *od* offense (US); **Strafbarkeit** F criminal nature
Strafe ['ʃtra:fə] (-, -n) F punishment; (*Jur*) penalty; (*Gefängnisstrafe*) sentence; (*Geldstrafe*) fine; **... bei ~ verboten** ... forbidden; **100 Dollar ~ zahlen** to pay a $100 fine; **er hat seine ~ weg** (*umg*) he's had his punishment
strafen VT, VI to punish; **mit etw gestraft sein** to be cursed with sth
strafend ADJ *attrib* punitive; (*Blick*) reproachful
straff [ʃtraf] ADJ tight; (*streng*) strict; (*Stil etc*) concise; (*Haltung*) erect
straffällig ['ʃtra:ffɛlɪç] ADJ: **~ werden** to commit a criminal offence (BRIT) *od* offense (US)
straffen VT to tighten
Straf- ZW: **straffrei** ADJ: **straffrei ausgehen** to go unpunished; **Strafgefangene(r)** F(M) prisoner, convict; **Strafgesetzbuch** NT penal code; **Strafkolonie** F penal colony
sträflich ['ʃtrɛ:flɪç] ADJ criminal ▶ ADV (*vernachlässigen etc*) criminally
Sträfling M convict
Straf- ZW: **Strafmandat** NT ticket; **Strafmaß** NT sentence; **strafmildernd** ADJ mitigating; **Strafporto** NT excess postage (charge); **Strafpredigt** F severe lecture; **Strafprozessordnung** F code of criminal procedure; **Strafraum** M (*Sport*) penalty area; **Strafrecht** NT criminal law; **strafrechtlich** ADJ criminal; **Strafstoß** M (*Sport*) penalty (kick); **Straftat** F punishable act; **strafversetzen** VT UNTR (*Beamte*) to transfer for disciplinary reasons; **Strafvollzug** M penal system; **Strafzettel** (*umg*) M ticket
Strahl [ʃtra:l] (-(e)s, -en) M ray, beam; (*Wasserstrahl*) jet
strahlen VI (*Kernreaktor*) to radiate; (*Sonne, Licht*) to shine; (*fig*) to beam
Strahlenbehandlung F radiotherapy
Strahlenbelastung F (effects of) radiation
strahlend ADJ (*Wetter*) glorious; (*Lächeln, Schönheit*) radiant
Strahlen- ZW: **Strahlendosis** F radiation dose; **strahlengeschädigt** ADJ suffering from

S

radiation damage; **Strahlenopfer** NT victim of radiation; **Strahlenschutz** M radiation protection; **Strahlentherapie** F radiotherapy
Strahlung F radiation
Strähnchen ['ʃtrɛːnçən] PL strands (of hair); (*gefärbt*) highlights
Strähne ['strɛːnə] (-, **-n**) F strand
strähnig ADJ (*Haar*) straggly
stramm [ʃtram] ADJ tight; (*Haltung*) erect; (*Mensch*) robust; **strammstehen** *unreg* VI (*Mil*) to stand to attention
Strampelhöschen NT rompers *pl*
strampeln ['ʃtrampəln] VI to kick (about), to fidget
Strand [ʃtrant] (**-(e)s, Strände**) M shore; (*Meeresstrand*) beach; **am ~** on the beach; **Strandbad** NT open-air swimming pool; (*Badeort*) bathing resort
stranden ['ʃtrandən] VI to run aground; (*fig: Mensch*) to fail
Strandgut NT flotsam and jetsam
Strandkorb M beach chair
Strang [ʃtraŋ] (**-(e)s, Stränge**) M (*Nervenstrang, Muskelstrang*) cord; (*Schienenstrang*) track; **über die Stränge schlagen** to run riot (*umg*); **an einem ~ ziehen** (*fig*) to act in concert
strangulieren [ʃtraŋgu'liːrən] VT to strangle
Strapaze [ʃtra'paːtsə] (-, **-n**) F strain
strapazieren [ʃtrapa'tsiːrən] VT (*Material*) to be hard on, to punish; (*jdn*) to be a strain on; (*erschöpfen*) to wear out, to exhaust
strapazierfähig ADJ hard-wearing
strapaziös [ʃtrapatsi'øːs] ADJ exhausting, tough
Straßburg ['ʃtraːsbʊrk] (**-s**) NT Strasbourg
Straße ['ʃtraːsə] (-, **-n**) F road; (*in Stadt, Dorf*) street; **auf der ~** in the street; **auf der ~ liegen** (*fig: umg*) to be out of work; **auf die ~ gesetzt werden** (*umg*) to be turned out (onto the streets)
Straßen- ZW: **Straßenbahn** F tram (BRIT), streetcar (US); **Straßenbau** M roadworks *pl* (BRIT), roadwork *sing* (US); **Straßenbeleuchtung** F street lighting; **Straßencafé** NT pavement café (BRIT), sidewalk café (US); **Straßenfeger** (**-s, -**) M roadsweeper; **Straßenglätte** F slippery road surface; **Straßenjunge** (*pej*) M street urchin; **Straßenkarte** F road map; **Straßenkehrer** (**-s, -**) M roadsweeper; **Straßenkind** NT child of the streets; **Straßenkreuzer** (*umg*) M limousine; **Straßenmädchen** NT streetwalker; **Straßenrand** M roadside; **Straßensperre** F roadblock; **Straßenüberführung** F footbridge; **Straßenverkehr** M road traffic; **Straßenverkehrsordnung** F Highway Code (BRIT); **Straßenzustandsbericht** M road report
Stratege [ʃtra'teːgə] (**-n, -n**) M strategist
Strategie [ʃtrate'giː] F strategy
strategisch ADJ strategic
Stratosphäre [ʃtrato'sfɛːrə] (**-**) F stratosphere
sträuben ['ʃtrɔʏbən] VT to ruffle ▶ VR to bristle; (*Mensch*): **sich (gegen etw) ~** to resist (sth)
Strauch [ʃtraʊx] (**-(e)s, Sträucher**) M bush, shrub
straucheln ['ʃtraʊxəln] VI to stumble, to stagger
Strauchtomate F vine-ripened tomato
Strauß[1] [ʃtraʊs] (**-es, Sträuße**) M (*Blumenstrauß*) bouquet, bunch
Strauß[2] [ʃtraʊs] (**-es, -e**) M ostrich
Strebe ['ʃtreːbə] (-, **-n**) F strut
Strebebalken M buttress
streben VI to strive, to endeavour (BRIT), to endeavor (US); **~ nach** to strive for; **~ zu** *od* **nach** (*sich bewegen*) to make for
Strebepfeiler M buttress
Streber (**-s, -**) M (*pej*) pushy person; (*Sch*) swot (BRIT)
strebsam ADJ industrious; **Strebsamkeit** F industry
Strecke ['ʃtrɛkə] (-, **-n**) F stretch; (*Entfernung*) distance; (*Eisenb, Math*) line; **auf der ~ Paris-Brüssel** on the way from Paris to Brussels; **auf der ~ bleiben** (*fig*) to fall by the wayside; **zur ~ bringen** (*Jagd*) to bag
strecken VT to stretch; (*Waffen*) to lay down; (*Koch*) to eke out ▶ VR to stretch (o.s.)
streckenweise ADV in parts
Streich [ʃtraɪç] (**-(e)s, -e**) M trick, prank; (*Hieb*) blow; **jdm einen ~ spielen** (*Person*) to play a trick on sb
streicheln VT to stroke
streichen *unreg* VT (*berühren*) to stroke; (*auftragen*) to spread; (*anmalen*) to paint; (*durchstreichen*) to delete; (*nicht genehmigen*) to cancel; (*Schulden*) to write off; (*Zuschuss etc*) to cut ▶ VI (*berühren*) to brush past; (*schleichen*) to prowl; **etw glatt ~** to smooth sth (out)
Streicher PL (*Mus*) strings *pl*
Streich- ZW: **Streichholz** NT match; **Streichholzschachtel** F matchbox; **Streichinstrument** NT string(ed) instrument; **Streichkäse** M cheese spread
Streifband NT wrapper; **Streifbandzeitung** F *newspaper sent at printed paper rate*
Streife (-, **-n**) F patrol
streifen ['ʃtraɪfən] VT (*leicht berühren*) to brush against, to graze; (*Blick*) to skim over; (*Thema, Problem*) to touch on; (*abstreifen*) to take off ▶ VI (*gehen*) to roam
Streifen (**-s, -**) M (*Linie*) stripe; (*Stück*) strip; (*Film*) film
Streifendienst M patrol duty
Streifenwagen M patrol car
Streifschuss M graze, grazing shot
Streifzug M scouting trip; (*Bummel*) expedition; (*fig: kurzer Überblick*): **~ (durch)** brief survey (of)
Streik [ʃtraɪk] (**-(e)s, -s**) M strike; **in den ~ treten** to come out on strike, to strike; **Streikbrecher** M blackleg (BRIT), strikebreaker; **streiken** VI to strike; **der Computer streikt** the computer's packed up (*umg*), the computer's on the blink (*umg*); **da streike ich** (*umg*) I refuse!; **Streikkasse** F strike fund; **Streikmaßnahmen** PL industrial action *sing*; **Streikposten** M (peaceful) picket
Streit [ʃtraɪt] (**-(e)s, -e**) M argument; (*Auseinandersetzung*) dispute

streiten *unreg* VI, VR to argue; (*sich auseinandersetzen*) to dispute; **darüber lässt sich** ~ that's debatable
Streitfrage F point at issue
Streitgespräch NT debate
streitig ADJ: **jdm etw ~ machen** to dispute sb's right to sth; **Streitigkeiten** PL quarrel *sing*, dispute *sing*
Streit- zW: **Streitkräfte** PL (*Mil*) armed forces *pl*; **streitlustig** ADJ quarrelsome; **Streitpunkt** M contentious issue; **Streitsucht** F quarrelsomeness
streng [ʃtrɛŋ] ADJ severe; (*Lehrer, Maßnahme*) strict; (*Geruch etc*) sharp; ~ **geheim** top-secret; ~ **genommen** strictly speaking; ~ **verboten!** strictly prohibited
Strenge (-) F severity; (*von Lehrer, Maßnahme*) strictness; (*von Geruch etc*) sharpness
strenggläubig ADJ strict
strengstens ADV strictly
Stress [ʃtrɛs] (**-es, -e**) M stress
stressen VT to put under stress
stressfrei ADJ without stress
stressig ADJ stressful
Streu [ʃtrɔʏ] (-, **-en**) F litter, bed of straw
streuen VT to strew, to scatter, to spread ▶ VI (*mit Streupulver*) to grit; (*mit Salz*) to put down salt
Streuer (**-s, -**) M shaker; (*Salzstreuer*) cellar; (*Pfefferstreuer*) pot
Streufahrzeug NT gritter (BRIT), sander
streunen VI to roam about; (*Hund, Katze*) to stray
Streupulver (**-s**) NT grit *od* sand for road
Streuselkuchen [ˈʃtrɔʏzəlku:xən] M *cake with crumble topping*
Streuung F dispersion; (*Statistik*) mean variation; (*Phys*) scattering
strich [ʃtrɪç] VB *siehe* **streichen**
Strich (**-(e)s, -e**) M (*Linie*) line; (*Federstrich, Pinselstrich*) stroke; (*von Geweben*) nap; (*von Fell*) pile; (*Querstrich*) dash; (*Schrägstrich*) oblique, slash (*bes US*); **einen ~ machen durch** (*lit*) to cross out; (*fig*) to foil; **jdm einen ~ durch die Rechnung machen** to thwart *od* foil sb's plans; **einen ~ unter etw** *akk* **machen** (*fig*) to forget sth; **nach ~ und Faden** (*umg*) good and proper; **auf den ~ gehen** (*umg*) to walk the streets; **jdm gegen den ~ gehen** to rub sb up the wrong way
Strichcode M bar code (BRIT), universal product code (US)
Stricheinteilung F calibration
stricheln [ˈʃtrɪçəln] VT: **eine gestrichelte Linie** a broken line
Strich- zW: **Strichjunge** (*umg*) M male prostitute; **Strichkode** M = **Strichcode**; **Strichmädchen** NT streetwalker; **Strichpunkt** M semicolon; **strichweise** ADV here and there; **strichweise Regen** (*Met*) rain in places
Strick [ʃtrɪk] (**-(e)s, -e**) M rope; **jdm aus etw einen ~ drehen** to use sth against sb
stricken VT, VI to knit
Strick- zW: **Strickjacke** F cardigan; **Strickleiter** F rope ladder; **Stricknadel** F knitting needle; **Strickwaren** PL knitwear *sing*
striegeln [ˈʃtri:gəln] (*umg*) VR to spruce o.s. up
Strieme [ˈʃtri:mə] (-, **-n**) F weal
strikt [strɪkt] ADJ strict
Strippe [ˈʃtrɪpə] (-, **-n**) F (*Tel: umg*): **jdn an der ~ haben** to have sb on the line
Stripper(in) (**-s, -**) M(F) stripper
stritt [ʃtrɪt] VB *siehe* **streiten**
strittig [ˈʃtrɪtɪç] ADJ disputed, in dispute
Stroh [ʃtro:] (**-(e)s**) NT straw; **Strohblume** F everlasting flower; **Strohdach** NT thatched roof; **strohdumm** (*umg*) ADJ thick; **Strohfeuer** NT: **ein Strohfeuer sein** (*fig*) to be a passing fancy; **Strohhalm** M (drinking) straw; **Strohmann** (**-(e)s**, *pl* **-männer**) M (*Comm*) dummy; **Strohwitwe** F grass widow; **Strohwitwer** M grass widower
Strolch [ʃtrɔlç] (**-(e)s, -e**) (*pej*) M rogue, rascal
Strom [ʃtro:m] (**-(e)s, Ströme**) M river; (*fig*) stream; (*Elek*) current; **unter ~ stehen** (*Elek*) to be live; (*fig*) to be excited; **der Wein floss in Strömen** the wine flowed like water; **in Strömen regnen** to be pouring with rain; **stromabwärts** ADV downstream; **Stromanschluss** M: **Stromanschluss haben** to be connected to the electricity mains; **stromaufwärts** ADV upstream; **Stromausfall** M power failure
strömen [ˈʃtrø:mən] VI to stream, to pour
Strom- zW: **Stromkabel** NT electric cable; **Stromkreis** M (electrical) circuit; **stromlinienförmig** ADJ streamlined; **Stromnetz** NT power supply system; **Stromrechnung** F electricity bill; **Stromschnelle** F rapids *pl*; **Stromsperre** F power cut; **Stromstärke** F amperage
Strömung [ˈʃtrø:mʊŋ] F current
Stromverbrauch M power consumption
Stromzähler M electricity meter
Strophe [ˈʃtro:fə] (-, **-n**) F verse
strotzen [ˈʃtrɔtsən] VI: ~ **vor** *+dat od* **von** to abound in, to be full of
Strudel [ˈʃtru:dəl] (**-s, -**) M whirlpool, vortex; (*Koch*) strudel
strudeln VI to swirl, to eddy
Struktur [ʃtrʊkˈtu:r] F structure
strukturell [ʃtrʊktuˈrɛl] ADJ structural
strukturieren [ʃtrʊktuˈri:rən] VT to structure
Strumpf [ʃtrʊmpf] (**-(e)s, Strümpfe**) M stocking; **Strumpfband** NT garter; **Strumpfhalter** M suspender (BRIT), garter (US); **Strumpfhose** F (pair of) tights *pl* (BRIT) *od* pantihose *pl* (US)
Strunk [ʃtrʊŋk] (**-(e)s, Strünke**) M stump
struppig [ˈʃtrʊpɪç] ADJ shaggy, unkempt
Stube [ˈʃtu:bə] (-, **-n**) F room; **die gute ~** (*veraltet*) the parlour (BRIT) *od* parlor (US)
Stuben- zW: **Stubenarrest** M confinement to one's room; (*Mil*) confinement to quarters; **Stubenfliege** F (common) housefly; **Stubenhocker** (*umg*) M stay-at-home; **stubenrein** ADJ house-trained
Stuck [ʃtʊk] (**-(e)s**) M stucco

S

Stück [ʃtʏk] (**-(e)s, -e**) NT piece; (*etwas*) bit; (*Theat*) play; **am ~** in one piece; **das ist ein starkes ~!** (*umg*) that's a bit much!; **große Stücke auf jdn halten** to think highly of sb; **Stückarbeit** F piecework
Stuckateur [ʃtʊka'tøːr] M (ornamental) plasterer
Stück- zW: **Stückgut** NT (*Eisenb*) parcel service; **Stückkosten** PL unit cost *sing*; **Stücklohn** M piecework rates *pl*; **stückweise** ADV bit by bit, piecemeal; (*Comm*) individually; **Stückwerk** NT bits and pieces *pl*
Student(in) [ʃtu'dɛnt(ɪn)] M(F) student
Studenten- zW: **Studentenausweis** M student card; **Studentenfutter** NT nuts and raisins *pl*; **Studentenwerk** NT student administration; **Studentenwohnheim** NT hall of residence (BRIT), dormitory (US)
studentisch ADJ student *attrib*
Studie ['ʃtuːdiə] F study
Studien- zW: **Studienberatung** F course guidance service; **Studienbuch** NT (*Univ*) *book in which the courses one has attended are entered*; **Studienfahrt** F study trip; **Studienplatz** M university place; **Studienrat** M, **Studienrätin** F teacher at a secondary (BRIT) *od* high (US) school; **Studienreform** F university course reform; **Studienzeitverkürzung** F shortening of the course of studies
studieren [ʃtu'diːrən] VT, VI to study; **bei jdm ~** to study under sb
Studio ['ʃtuːdio] (**-s, -s**) NT studio
Studium ['ʃtuːdiʊm] NT studies *pl*
Stufe ['ʃtuːfə] (**-, -n**) F step; (*Entwicklungsstufe*) stage; (*Niveau*) level
Stufen- zW: **Stufenheck** NT (*Aut*) notchback; **Stufenleiter** F (*fig*) ladder; **stufenlos** ADJ (*Tech*) infinitely variable; **stufenlos verstellbar** continuously adjustable; **Stufenplan** M graduated plan; **Stufenschnitt** M (*Frisur*) layered cut; **stufenweise** ADV gradually
Stuhl [ʃtuːl] (**-(e)s, Stühle**) M chair; **zwischen zwei Stühlen sitzen** (*fig*) to fall between two stools
Stuhlgang M bowel movement
Stukkateur [ʃtʊka'tøːr] M *siehe* **Stuckateur**
stülpen ['ʃtʏlpən] VT (*bedecken*) to put; **etw über etw** *akk* **~** to put sth over sth; **den Kragen nach oben ~** to turn up one's collar
stumm [ʃtʊm] ADJ silent; (*Med*) dumb
Stummel (**-s, -**) M stump; (*Zigarettenstummel*) stub
Stummfilm M silent film (BRIT) *od* movie (US)
Stümper(in) ['ʃtʏmpər(ɪn)] (**-s, -**) M(F) incompetent, duffer; **stümperhaft** ADJ bungling, incompetent
stümpern (*umg*) VI to bungle
stumpf ADJ blunt; (*teilnahmslos, glanzlos*) dull; (*Winkel*) obtuse
Stumpf [ʃtʊmpf] (**-(e)s, Stümpfe**) M stump; **etw mit ~ und Stiel ausrotten** to eradicate sth root and branch
Stumpfsinn (**-(e)s**) M tediousness
stumpfsinnig ADJ dull
Stunde ['ʃtʊndə] (**-, -n**) F hour; (*Augenblick, Zeitpunkt*) time; (*Sch*) lesson, period (BRIT); **~ um ~** hour after hour; **80 Kilometer in der ~** ≈ 50 miles per hour
stunden VT: **jdm etw ~** to give sb time to pay sth
Stunden- zW: **Stundengeschwindigkeit** F average speed (per hour); **Stundenkilometer** PL kilometres (BRIT) *od* kilometers (US) per hour; **stundenlang** ADJ for hours; **Stundenlohn** M hourly wage; **Stundenplan** M timetable; **stundenweise** ADV by the hour; (*stündlich*) every hour
stündlich ['ʃtʏntlɪç] ADJ hourly
Stunk [ʃtʊŋk] (**-s**, *no pl*) M: **~ machen** (*umg*) to kick up a stink
stupide [ʃtu'piːdə] ADJ mindless
Stups [ʃtʊps] (**-es, -e**) (*umg*) M push
stupsen VT to nudge
Stupsnase F snub nose
stur [ʃtuːr] ADJ obstinate, stubborn; (*Nein, Arbeiten*) dogged; **er fuhr ~ geradeaus** he just carried straight on; **sich ~ stellen, auf ~ stellen** (*umg*) to dig one's heels in; **ein sturer Bock** (*umg*) a pig-headed fellow
Sturm [ʃtʊrm] (**-(e)s, Stürme**) M storm; (*Wind*) gale; (*Mil etc*) attack, assault; **~ läuten** to keep one's finger on the doorbell; **gegen etw ~ laufen** (*fig*) to be up in arms against sth
stürmen ['ʃtʏrmən] VI (*Wind*) to blow hard, to rage; (*rennen*) to storm ▶ VT (*Mil, fig*) to storm ▶ VI UNPERS: **es stürmt** there's a gale blowing
Stürmer (**-s, -**) M (*Sport*) forward
sturmfrei ADJ (*Mil*) unassailable; **eine sturmfreie Bude** (*umg*) a room free from disturbance
stürmisch ADJ stormy; (*fig*) tempestuous; (*Entwicklung*) rapid; (*Liebhaber*) passionate; (*Beifall*) tumultuous; **nicht so ~** take it easy
Sturm- zW: **Sturmschritt** M (*Mil, fig*): **im Sturmschritt** at the double; **Sturmwarnung** F gale warning; **Sturmwind** M gale
Sturz [ʃtʊrts] (**-es, Stürze**) M fall; (*Pol*) overthrow; (*in Temperatur, Preis*) drop
stürzen ['ʃtʏrtsən] VT (*werfen*) to hurl; (*Pol*) to overthrow; (*umkehren*) to overturn ▶ VR to rush; (*hineinstürzen*) to plunge ▶ VI to fall; (*Aviat*) to dive; (*rennen*) to dash; **jdn ins Unglück ~** to bring disaster upon sb; **„nicht ~"** "this side up"; **sich auf jdn/etw ~** to pounce on sb/sth; **sich in Unkosten ~** to go to great expense
Sturzflug M nose dive
Sturzhelm M crash helmet
Stuss [ʃtʊs] (**-es**) (*umg*) M nonsense, rubbish
Stute ['ʃtuːtə] (**-, -n**) F mare
Stuttgart ['ʃtʊtgart] (**-s**) NT Stuttgart
Stützbalken M brace, joist
Stütze ['ʃtʏtsə] (**-, -n**) F support; (*Hilfe*) help; **die Stützen der Gesellschaft** the pillars of society
stutzen ['ʃtʊtsən] VT to trim; (*Ohr, Schwanz*) to dock; (*Flügel*) to clip ▶ VI to hesitate; (*argwöhnisch werden*) to become suspicious

stützen VT (*lit, fig*) to support; (*Ellbogen etc*) to prop up ▸ VR: **sich auf jdn/etw ~** (*lit*) to lean on sb/sth; (*Beweise, Theorie*) to be based on sb/sth
stutzig ADJ perplexed, puzzled; (*misstrauisch*) suspicious
Stützmauer F supporting wall
Stützpunkt M point of support; (*von Hebel*) fulcrum; (*Mil, fig*) base
Stützungskäufe PL (*Fin*) support buying *sing*
StVO ABK = **Straßenverkehrsordnung**
stylen ['staılən] VT to style; (*Wohnung*) to design
Styling ['stailıŋ] (**-s**, *no pl*) NT styling
Styropor® [ʃtyro'po:r] (**-s**) NT (expanded) polystyrene
s. u. ABK (= *siehe unten*) see below
Suaheli [zua'he:li] (**-(s)**) NT Swahili
Subjekt [zʊp'jɛkt] (**-(e)s, -e**) NT subject; (*pej: Mensch*) character (*umg*)
subjektiv [zʊpjɛk'ti:f] ADJ subjective
Subjektivität [zʊpjɛktivi'tɛ:t] F subjectivity
Subkultur ['zʊpkʊltu:r] F subculture
sublimieren [zubli'mi:rən] VT (*Chem, Psych*) to sublimate
Submissionsangebot [zʊpmısi'o:nslangəbo:t] NT sealed-bid tender
Subprime-Hypothek ['sabpraım-hypo'te:k] (**-, -en**) F subprime mortgage
Subroutine ['zʊpruti:nə] F (*Comput*) subroutine
Subskription [zʊpskrıptsi'o:n] F subscription
Substantiv ['zʊpstanti:f] (**-s, -e**) NT noun
Substanz [zʊp'stants] F substance; **von der ~ zehren** to live on one's capital
subtil [zʊp'ti:l] ADJ subtle
subtrahieren [zʊptra'hi:rən] VT to subtract
subtropisch ['zʊptro:pıʃ] ADJ subtropical
Subunternehmer M subcontractor
Subvention [zʊpvɛntsi'o:n] F subsidy
subventionieren [zʊpvɛntsio'ni:rən] VT to subsidize
subversiv [zʊpvɛr'zi:f] ADJ subversive
Suchaktion F search
Suchdienst M missing persons tracing service
Suche (**-, -n**) F search
suchen ['zu:xən] VT to look for, to seek; (*versuchen*) to try ▸ VI to seek, to search; **du hast hier nichts zu ~** you have no business being here; **nach Worten ~** to search for words; (*sprachlos sein*) to be at a loss for words; **such!** (*zu Hund*) seek!, find!; **~ und ersetzen** (*Comput*) search and replace
Sucher (**-s, -**) M seeker, searcher; (*Phot*) viewfinder
Suchmaschine F (*Comput*) search engine
Suchmeldung F missing *od* wanted person announcement
Suchscheinwerfer M searchlight
Sucht [zʊxt] (**-, Süchte**) F mania; (*Med*) addiction; **Suchtdroge** F addictive drug; **suchterzeugend** ADJ addictive
süchtig ['zyçtıç] ADJ addicted
Süchtige(r) F(M) addict
Süd [zy:t] (**-(e)s**) M south; **Südafrika** NT South Africa; **Südamerika** NT South America
Sudan [zu'da:n] (**-s**) M: **der ~** the Sudan
Sudanese [zuda'ne:zə] (**-n, -n**) M Sudanese
Sudanesin F Sudanese
südd. ABK = **süddeutsch**
süddeutsch ADJ South German
Süddeutschland NT South(ern) Germany
Süden ['zy:dən] (**-s**) M south
Süd- ZW: **Südeuropa** NT Southern Europe; **Südfrüchte** PL Mediterranean fruit; **Südkorea** NT South Korea; **südländisch** ADJ southern; (*italienisch, spanisch etc*) Latin; **südlich** ADJ southern; **südlich von** (to the) south of; **Südostasien** NT South-East Asia; **Südpol** M South Pole; **Südpolarmeer** NT Antarctic Ocean; **Südsee** F South Seas *pl*, South Pacific; **Südtirol** NT South Tyrol; **südwärts** ADV southwards; **Südwestafrika** NT South West Africa, Namibia
Sueskanal ['zu:ɛskana:l] (**-s**) M Suez Canal
Suff [zʊf] M: **etw im ~ sagen** (*umg*) to say sth while under the influence
süffig ['zyfıç] ADJ (*Wein*) very drinkable
süffisant [zyfi'zant] ADJ smug
suggerieren [zʊge'ri:rən] VT to suggest
Suggestivfrage [zʊgɛs'ti:ffra:gə] F leading question
suhlen ['zu:lən] VR (*lit, fig*) to wallow
Sühne ['zy:nə] (**-, -n**) F atonement, expiation
sühnen VT to atone for, to expiate
Sühnetermin M (*Jur*) conciliatory hearing
Suite ['svi:tə] F suite
Sulfat [zʊl'fa:t] (**-(e)s, -e**) NT sulphate (BRIT), sulfate (US)
Sultan ['zʊltan] (**-s, -e**) M sultan
Sultanine [zʊlta'ni:nə] F sultana
Sülze ['zyltsə] (**-, -n**) F brawn (BRIT), headcheese (US); (*Aspik*) aspic
summarisch [zʊ'ma:rıʃ] ADJ summary
Sümmchen ['zymçən] NT: **ein hübsches ~** a tidy sum
Summe (**-, -n**) F sum; (*Gesamtsumme*) total
summen VI to buzz ▸ VT (*Lied*) to hum
Summer (**-s, -**) M buzzer
summieren [zʊ'mi:rən] VT to add up ▸ VR to mount up
Sumpf [zʊmpf] (**-(e)s, Sümpfe**) M swamp, marsh
sumpfig ADJ marshy
Sund [zʊnt] (**-(e)s, -e**) M sound, straits *pl*
Sünde ['zyndə] (**-, -n**) F sin
Sünden- ZW: **Sündenbock** M (*fig*) scapegoat; **Sündenfall** M (*Rel*) Fall; **Sündenregister** NT (*fig*) list of sins
Sünder(in) (**-s, -**) M(F) sinner
sündhaft ADJ (*lit*) sinful; (*fig: umg: Preise*) wicked
sündigen ['zyndıgən] VI to sin; (*hum*) to indulge; **~ an** *+dat* to sin against
super (*umg*) ADJ super ▸ ADV incredibly well
Super ['zu:pər] (**-s**) NT (*Benzin*) four-star (petrol) (BRIT), premium (US)
Superlativ ['zu:pərlati:f] (**-s, -e**) M superlative
Supermarkt M supermarket
Superstar M superstar

S

Suppe ['zʊpə] (-, **-n**) F soup; (*mit Einlage*) broth; (*klare Brühe*) bouillon; (*fig: umg: Nebel*) peasouper (BRIT), pea soup (US); **jdm die ~ versalzen** (*umg*) to put a spoke in sb's wheel
Suppen- ZW: **Suppenfleisch** NT meat for making soup; **Suppengrün** NT *herbs and vegetables for making soup*; **Suppenkasper** (*umg*) M poor eater; **Suppenteller** M soup plate
Surfbrett ['zø:rfbrɛt] NT surfboard
surfen ['zø:rfən] VI to surf
Surfer(in) M(F) surfer
Surrealismus [zʊrea'lɪsmʊs] M surrealism
surren ['zʊrən] VI to buzz; (*Insekt*) to hum
Surrogat [zʊro'ga:t] (**-(e)s, -e**) NT substitute, surrogate
suspekt [zʊs'pɛkt] ADJ suspect
suspendieren [zʊspɛn'di:rən] VT: **~ (von)** to suspend (from)
Suspendierung F suspension
süß [zy:s] ADJ sweet
Süße (-) F sweetness
süßen VT to sweeten
Süßholz NT: **~ raspeln** (*fig*) to turn on the blarney
Süßigkeit F sweetness; (*Bonbon etc*) sweet (BRIT), candy (US); **süßlich** ADJ sweetish; (*fig*) sugary
süß- ZW: **süßsauer** ADJ sweet-and-sour; (*fig: gezwungen: Lächeln*) forced; (*Gurken etc*) pickled; (*Miene*) artificially friendly; **Süßspeise** F pudding, sweet (BRIT); **Süßstoff** M sweetener; **Süßwaren** PL confectionery *sing*; **Süßwasser** NT fresh water
SV (-) M ABK = **Sportverein**
SW ABK (= *Südwest(en)*) SW
Swasiland ['sva:zilant] (**-s**) NT Swaziland
SWF (-) M ABK (*früher: = Südwestfunk*) *South West German Radio*
Sylvester [zyl'vɛstər] (**-s, -**) NT = **Silvester**
Symbol [zym'bo:l] (**-s, -e**) NT symbol
Symbolik F symbolism
symbolisch ADJ symbolic(al)
symbolisieren [zymboli'zi:rən] VT to symbolize
Symbolleiste F (*Comput*) toolbar
Symmetrie [zyme'tri:] F symmetry; **Symmetrieachse** F symmetric axis
symmetrisch [zy'me:trɪʃ] ADJ symmetrical
Sympathie [zympa'ti:] F liking; (*Mitgefühl*) sympathy; **er hat sich** *dat* **alle ~(n) verscherzt** he has turned everyone against him; **Sympathiekundgebung** F demonstration of support; **Sympathiestreik** M sympathy strike
Sympathisant(in) M(F) sympathizer
sympathisch [zym'pa:tɪʃ] ADJ likeable, congenial; **er ist mir ~** I like him
sympathisieren [zympati'zi:rən] VI to sympathize
Symphonie [zymfo'ni:] F symphony
Symptom [zymp'to:m] (**-s, -e**) NT symptom
symptomatisch [zympto'ma:tɪʃ] ADJ symptomatic
Synagoge [zyna'go:gə] (-, **-n**) F synagogue
synchron [zyn'kro:n] ADJ synchronous; **Synchrongetriebe** NT synchromesh gearbox (BRIT) *od* transmission (US)
synchronisieren [zynkroni'zi:rən] VT to synchronize; (*Film*) to dub
Synchronschwimmen NT synchronized swimming
Syndikat [zyndi'ka:t] (**-(e)s, -e**) NT combine, syndicate
Syndrom [zyn'dro:m] (**-s, -e**) NT syndrome
Synkope [zyn'ko:pə] (-, **-n**) F (*Mus*) syncopation
Synode [zy'no:də] (-, **-n**) F (*Rel*) synod
synonym ADJ synonymous; **Synonym** [zyno'ny:m] (**-s, -e**) NT synonym
Syntax ['zyntaks] (-, **-en**) F syntax
Synthese [zyn'te:zə] (-, **-n**) F synthesis
synthetisch ADJ synthetic
Syphilis ['zy:filɪs] (-) F syphilis
Syrer(in) ['zy:rər(ɪn)] (**-s, -**) M(F) Syrian
Syrien (**-s**) NT Syria
syrisch ADJ Syrian
System [zys'te:m] (**-s, -e**) NT system; **Systemanalyse** F systems analysis; **Systemanalytiker(in)** M(F) systems analyst
Systematik F system
systematisch [zyste'ma:tɪʃ] ADJ systematic
systematisieren [zystemati'zi:rən] VT to systematize
System- ZW: **Systemkritiker** M critic of the system; **Systemplatte** F (*Comput*) system disk; **Systemsteuerung** F (*Comput*) control panel; **Systemvoraussetzung** F (*meist pl*) system requirement; **Systemzwang** M obligation to conform (to the system)
Szenarium [stse'na:riʊm] NT scenario
Szene ['stse:nə] (-, **-n**) F scene; **sich in der ~ auskennen** (*umg*) to know the scene; **sich in ~ setzen** to play to the gallery
Szenenwechsel M scene change
Szenerie [stsenə'ri:] F scenery

Tt

T¹, t [teː] NT T, t; **T wie Theodor** ≈ T for Tommy
t² ABK (= *Tonne*) t
Tabak ['taːbak] **(-s, -e)** M tobacco; **Tabakladen** M tobacconist's (BRIT), tobacco store (*US*)
tabellarisch [tabɛ'laːrɪʃ] ADJ tabular
Tabelle (-, -n) F table
Tabellenführer M (*Sport*) top of the table, league leader
Tabernakel [tabɛr'naːkəl] **(-s, -)** NT tabernacle
Tabl. ABK = **Tablette**
Tablett (-(e)s, -s *od* **-e)** NT tray
Tablette [ta'blɛtə] **(-, -n)** F tablet, pill
Tabu [ta'buː] **(-s, -s)** NT taboo
tabuisieren [tabui'ziːrən] VT to make taboo
Tabulator [tabu'laːtɔr] M tabulator, tab (*umg*)
tabulieren VT to tab
Tacho ['taxo] **(-s, -s)** (*umg*) M speedo (BRIT)
Tachometer [taxo'meːtər] **(-s, -)** M (*Aut*) speedometer
Tadel ['taːdəl] **(-s, -)** M censure, scolding; (*Fehler*) fault; (*Makel*) blemish; **tadellos** ADJ faultless, irreproachable
tadeln VT to scold
tadelnswert ADJ blameworthy
Tadschikistan [ta'dʒiːkistaːn] **(-s)** NT Tajikistan
Tafel ['taːfəl] **(-, -n)** F (*form: festlicher Speisetisch, Math*) table; (*Festmahl*) meal; (*Anschlagtafel*) board; (*Wandtafel*) blackboard; (*Schiefertafel*) slate; (*Gedenktafel*) plaque; (*Illustration*) plate; (*Schalttafel*) panel; (*Schokoladentafel etc*) bar; **tafelfertig** ADJ ready to serve
täfeln ['tɛːfəln] VT to panel
Tafelöl NT cooking oil; (*Salatöl*) salad oil
Täfelung F panelling (BRIT), paneling (*US*)
Tafelwasser NT table water
Tafelwein M table wine
Taft [taft] **(-(e)s, -e)** M taffeta
Tag [taːk] **(-(e)s, -e)** M day; (*Tageslicht*) daylight; **am ~** during the day; **für** *od* **auf ein paar Tage** for a few days; **eines Tages** one day; **in den ~ hinein leben** to take each day as it comes; **bei ~(e)** (*ankommen*) while it's light; (*arbeiten, reisen*) during the day; **unter Tage** (*Min*) underground; **über Tage** (*Min*) on the surface; **an den ~ kommen** to come to light; **er legte großes Interesse an den ~** he showed great interest; **auf den ~ (genau)** to the day; **auf seine alten Tage** at his age; **guten ~!** good morning/afternoon!; *siehe auch* **zutage**; **tagaus** ADV: **tagaus, tagein** day in, day out; **Tagdienst** M day duty
Tage- ZW: **Tagebau** M (*Min*) open-cast mining; **Tagebuch** NT diary; **Tagedieb** M idler; **Tagegeld** NT daily allowance; **tagelang** ADV for days
tagen VI to sit, to meet ▶ VI UNPERS: **es tagt** dawn is breaking
Tages- ZW: **Tagesablauf** M daily routine; **Tagesanbruch** M dawn; **Tagesausflug** M day trip; **Tagescreme** F day cream; **Tagesdecke** F bedspread; **Tagesfahrt** F day trip; **Tageskarte** F (*Eintrittskarte*) day ticket; (*Speisekarte*) menu of the day; **Tageskasse** F (*Comm*) day's takings *pl*; (*Theat*) box office; **Tageslicht** NT daylight; **Tagesmutter** F child minder; **Tagesordnung** F agenda; **an der Tagesordnung sein** (*fig*) to be the order of the day; **Tagesrückfahrkarte** F day return (ticket); **Tagessatz** M daily rate; **Tagesschau** F (*TV*) television news (programme (BRIT) *od* program (*US*)); **Tagesstätte** F day nursery (BRIT), daycare center (*US*); **Tageswert** M (*Fin*) present value; **Tageszeit** F time of day; **zu jeder Tages- und Nachtzeit** at all hours of the day and night; **Tageszeitung** F daily (paper)
tägl. ABK = **täglich**
täglich ['tɛːklɪç] ADJ, ADV daily; **einmal ~** once a day
tags [taːks] ADV: **~ darauf** *od* **danach** the next *od* following day; **tagsüber** ADV during the day
tagtäglich ADJ daily ▶ ADV every (single) day
Tagung F conference
Tagungsort M venue (of a conference)
Tahiti [ta'hiːti] **(-s)** NT Tahiti
Taifun [taɪ'fuːn] **(-s, -e)** M typhoon
Taille ['taljə] **(-, -n)** F waist
tailliert [ta'jiːrt] ADJ waisted, gathered at the waist
Taiwan ['taɪvan] **(-s)** NT Taiwan
Takel ['taːkəl] **(-s, -)** NT tackle
takeln ['taːkəln] VT to rig
Takt [takt] **(-(e)s, -e)** M tact; (*Mus*) time; **Taktgefühl** NT tact
Taktik F tactics *pl*
Taktiker(in) M(F) tactician
taktisch ADJ tactical

Takt- zW: **taktlos** ADJ tactless; **Taktlosigkeit** F tactlessness; **Taktstock** M (conductor's) baton; **Taktstrich** M (*Mus*) bar (line); **taktvoll** ADJ tactful

Tal [ta:l] (**-(e)s, Täler**) NT valley

Talar [ta'la:r] (**-s, -e**) M (*Jur*) robe; (*Univ*) gown

Talbrücke F bridge over a valley

Talent [ta'lɛnt] (**-(e)s, -e**) NT talent

talentiert [talɛn'ti:rt] ADJ talented, gifted

Talfahrt F descent; (*fig*) decline

Talg [talk] (**-(e)s, -e**) M tallow

Talgdrüse F sebaceous gland

Talisman ['ta:lɪsman] (**-s, -e**) M talisman

Tal- zW: **Talsohle** F bottom of a valley; **Talsperre** F dam; **talwärts** ADV down to the valley

Tamburin [tambu'ri:n] (**-s, -e**) NT tambourine

Tamile [ta'mi:lə] (**-n, -n**) M, **Tamilin** F Tamil

tamilisch ADJ Tamil

Tampon ['tampɔn] (**-s, -s**) M tampon

Tamtam [tam'tam] (**-s, -s**) NT (*Mus*) tomtom; (*umg: Wirbel*) fuss, ballyhoo; (*Lärm*) din

Tang [taŋ] (**-(e)s, -e**) M seaweed

Tangente [taŋ'gɛntə] (**-, -n**) F tangent

Tanger ['taŋər] (**-s**) NT Tangier(s)

tangieren [taŋ'gi:rən] VT (*Problem*) to touch on; (*fig*) to affect

Tank [taŋk] (**-s, -s**) M tank

tanken VT (*Wagen etc*) to fill up with petrol (BRIT) *od* gas (*US*); (*Benzin etc*) to fill up with; (*Aviat*) to (re)fuel; (*umg: frische Luft, neue Kräfte*) to get ▶ VI to fill up (with petrol (BRIT) *od* gas (*US*)); (*Aviat*) to (re)fuel

Tanker (**-s, -**) M tanker

Tank- zW: **Tanklaster** M tanker; **Tankschiff** NT tanker; **Tankstelle** F petrol (BRIT) *od* gas (*US*) station; **Tankuhr** F fuel gauge; **Tankverschluss** M fuel cap; **Tankwart** M petrol pump (BRIT) *od* gas station (*US*) attendant

Tanne ['tanə] (**-, -n**) F fir

Tannenbaum M fir tree

Tannenzapfen M fir cone

Tansania [tan'za:nia] (**-s**) NT Tanzania

Tante ['tantə] (**-, -n**) F aunt; **Tante-Emma-Laden** (*umg*) M corner shop

Tantieme [tãti'e:mə] (**-, -n**) F fee; (*für Künstler etc*) royalty

Tanz [tants] (**-es, Tänze**) M dance

tänzeln ['tɛntsəln] VI to dance along

tanzen VT, VI to dance

Tänzer(in) (**-s, -**) M(F) dancer

Tanz- zW: **Tanzfläche** F dance floor; **Tanzlokal** NT café/restaurant with dancing; **Tanzschule** F dancing school

Tapet [ta'pe:t] (*umg*) NT: **etw aufs ~ bringen** to bring sth up

Tapete [ta'pe:tə] (**-, -n**) F wallpaper

Tapetenwechsel M (*fig*) change of scenery

tapezieren [tape'tsi:rən] VT to (wall)paper

Tapezierer (**-s, -**) M (interior) decorator

tapfer ['tapfər] ADJ brave; **sich ~ schlagen** (*umg*) to put on a brave show; **Tapferkeit** F courage, bravery

tappen ['tapən] VI to walk uncertainly *od* clumsily; **im Dunkeln ~** (*fig*) to grope in the dark

täppisch ['tɛpɪʃ] ADJ clumsy

Tara ['ta:ra] (**-, Taren**) F tare

Tarantel [ta'rantəl] (**-, -n**) F tarantula; **wie von der ~ gestochen** as if stung by a bee

Tarif [ta'ri:f] (**-s, -e**) M tariff, (scale of) fares/charges; **nach/über/unter ~ bezahlen** to pay according to/above/below the (union) rate(s); **Tarifautonomie** F free collective bargaining; **Tarifgruppe** F grade; **tariflich** ADJ agreed, union; **Tariflohn** M standard wage rate; **Tarifordnung** F wage *od* salary scale; **Tarifpartner** M: **die Tarifpartner** union and management; **Tarifvereinbarung** F labour (BRIT) *od* labor (*US*) agreement; **Tarifverhandlungen** PL collective bargaining *sing*; **Tarifvertrag** M pay agreement

tarnen ['tarnən] VT to camouflage; (*Person, Absicht*) to disguise

Tarnfarbe F camouflage paint

Tarnmanöver NT (*lit, fig*) feint, covering ploy

Tarnung F camouflaging; (*von Person, Absicht*) disguising

Tarock [ta'rɔk] (**-s, s**) M OD NT tarot

Tasche ['taʃə] (**-, -n**) F bag; (*Hosentasche*) pocket; (*Handtasche*) handbag; **in die eigene ~ wirtschaften** to line one's own pockets; **jdm auf der ~ liegen** (*umg*) to live off sb

Taschen- zW: **Taschenbuch** NT paperback; **Taschendieb** M pickpocket; **Taschengeld** NT pocket money; **Taschenlampe** F (electric) torch, flashlight (*US*); **Taschenmesser** NT penknife; **Taschenrechner** M pocket calculator; **Taschenspieler** M conjurer; **Taschentuch** NT handkerchief

Tasmanien [tas'ma:niən] (**-s**) NT Tasmania

Tasse ['tasə] (**-, -n**) F cup; **er hat nicht alle Tassen im Schrank** (*umg*) he's not all there

Tastatur [tasta'tu:r] F keyboard

Taste ['tastə] (**-, -n**) F button; (*von Klavier, Computer*) key

tasten VT to feel, to touch; (*drücken*) to press ▶ VI to feel, to grope ▶ VR to feel one's way

Tastentelefon NT push-button telephone

Tastsinn M sense of touch

tat *etc* [ta:t] VB *siehe* **tun**

Tat (**-, -en**) F act, deed, action; **in der ~** indeed, as a matter of fact; **etw in die ~ umsetzen** to put sth into action

Tatbestand M facts *pl* of the case

Tatendrang M energy

tatenlos ADJ inactive

Täter(in) ['tɛ:tər(ɪn)] (**-s, -**) M(F) perpetrator, culprit; **Täterschaft** F guilt

tätig ADJ active; **tätiger Teilhaber** active partner; **in einer Firma ~ sein** to work for a firm

tätigen VT (*Comm*) to conclude; (*geh: Einkäufe, Anruf*) to make

Tätigkeit F activity; (*Beruf*) occupation

Tätigkeitsbereich M field of activity

tatkräftig ADJ energetic; (*Hilfe*) active
tätlich ADJ violent; **Tätlichkeit** F violence; **es kam zu Tätlichkeiten** there were violent scenes
Tatort (-(e)s, -e) M scene of the crime
tätowieren [tɛto'vi:rən] VT to tattoo
Tätowierung F tattooing; (*Ergebnis*) tattoo
Tatsache F fact; **jdn vor vollendete Tatsachen stellen** to present sb with a fait accompli
Tatsachenbericht M documentary (report)
tatsächlich ADJ actual ▶ ADV really
tatverdächtig ADJ suspected
Tatze ['tatsə] (-, -n) F paw
Tau[1] [taʊ] (-(e)s, -e) NT rope
Tau[2] (-(e)s) M dew
taub [taʊp] ADJ deaf; (*Nuss*) hollow; **sich ~ stellen** to pretend not to hear
Taube ['taʊbə] (-, -n) F (*Zool*) pigeon; (*fig*) dove
Taubenschlag M dovecote; **hier geht es zu wie im ~** (*fig: umg*) it's like Waterloo Station here (BRIT), it's like Grand Central Station here (US)
Taubheit F deafness
taubstumm ADJ deaf-mute
tauchen ['taʊxən] VT to dip ▶ VI to dive; (*Naut*) to submerge
Taucher (-s, -) M diver; **Taucheranzug** M diving suit
Tauchsieder (-s, -) M portable immersion heater
Tauchstation F: **auf ~ gehen** (*U-Boot*) to dive
tauen ['taʊən] VT, VI to thaw ▶ VI UNPERS: **es taut** it's thawing
Taufbecken NT font
Taufe ['taʊfə] (-, -n) F baptism
taufen VT to baptize; (*nennen*) to christen
Tauf- ZW: **Taufname** M Christian name; **Taufpate** M godfather; **Taufpatin** F godmother; **Taufschein** M certificate of baptism
taugen ['taʊgən] VI to be of use; **~ für** to do *od* be good for; **nicht ~** to be no good *od* useless
Taugenichts (-es, -e) M good-for-nothing
tauglich ['taʊklɪç] ADJ suitable; (*Mil*) fit (for service); **Tauglichkeit** F suitability; (*Mil*) fitness
Taumel ['taʊməl] (-s) M dizziness; (*fig*) frenzy
taumelig ADJ giddy, reeling
taumeln VI to reel, to stagger
Taunus ['taʊnʊs] (-) M Taunus (Mountains *pl*)
Tausch [taʊʃ] (-(e)s, -e) M exchange; **einen guten/schlechten ~ machen** to get a good/bad deal
tauschen VT to exchange, to swap ▶ VI: **ich möchte nicht mit ihm ~** I wouldn't like to be in his place
täuschen ['tɔʏʃən] VT to deceive ▶ VI to be deceptive ▶ VR to be wrong; **wenn mich nicht alles täuscht** unless I'm completely wrong
täuschend ADJ deceptive
Tauschhandel M barter
Täuschung F deception; (*optisch*) illusion
Täuschungsmanöver NT (*Sport*) feint; (*fig*) ploy
tausend ['taʊzənt] NUM a *od* one thousand; **Tausend** (-, -en) F (*Zahl*) thousand
Tausender (-s, -) M (*Geldschein*) thousand
Tausendfüßler (-s, -) M centipede
Tausendstel (-s, -) NT (*Bruchteil*) thousandth
Tau- ZW: **Tautropfen** M dew drop; **Tauwetter** NT thaw; **Tauziehen** NT tug-of-war
Taxe ['taksə] (-, -n) F taxi, cab
Taxi ['taksi] (-(s), -(s)) NT taxi, cab
taxieren [ta'ksi:rən] VT (*Preis, Wert*) to estimate; (*Haus, Gemälde*) to value; (*mustern*) to look up and down
Taxi- ZW: **Taxifahrer** M taxi driver; **Taxistand** M taxi rank (BRIT) *od* stand (US)
Tb, Tbc F ABK (= *Tuberkulose*) TB
Teamarbeit ['ti:mǀarbaɪt] F teamwork
Technik ['tɛçnɪk] F technology; (*Methode, Kunstfertigkeit*) technique
Techniker(in) (-s -) M(F) technician
technisch ADJ technical; **technische Hochschule** ≈ polytechnic
Technologie [tɛçnolo'gi:] F technology
technologisch [tɛçno'lo:gɪʃ] ADJ technological
Techtelmechtel [tɛçtəl'mɛçtəl] (-s, -) (*umg*) NT (*Liebschaft*) affair, carry-on
Tee [te:] (-s, -s) M tea
TEE ABK (= *Trans-Europ-Express*) Trans-Europe-Express
Tee- ZW: **Teebeutel** M tea bag; **Teekanne** F teapot; **Teelicht** NT night-light; **Teelöffel** M teaspoon; **Teemischung** F blend of tea
Teer [te:r] (-(e)s, -e) M tar; **teeren** VT to tar
Teesieb NT tea strainer
Teetasse F teacup
Teewagen M tea trolley
Teflon® ['tɛflo:n] (-s) NT Teflon®
Teheran ['te:həra:n] (-s) NT Teheran
Teich [taɪç] (-(e)s, -e) M pond
Teig [taɪk] (-(e)s, -e) M dough
teigig ['taɪgɪç] ADJ doughy
Teigwaren PL pasta *sing*
Teil [taɪl] (-(e)s, -e) M OD NT part; (*Anteil*) share ▶ NT part; (*Bestandteil*) component; (*Ersatzteil*) spare (part); **zum ~** partly; **ich für mein(en) ~ ...** I, for my part ...; **sich** *dat* **sein ~ denken** (*umg*) to draw one's own conclusions; **er hat sein(en) ~ dazu beigetragen** he did his bit *od* share; **teilbar** ADJ divisible; **Teilbetrag** M instalment (BRIT), installment (US); **Teilchen** NT (atomic) particle
teilen VT to divide; (*mit jdm*) to share ▶ VR to divide; (*in Gruppen*) to split up
Teil- ZW: **teilentrahmt** ADJ semi-skimmed; **Teilgebiet** NT (*Bereich*) branch; (*räumlich*) area; **teilhaben** *unreg* VI: **an etw** *dat* **teilhaben** to share in sth; **Teilhaber** (-s, -) M partner; **Teilkaskoversicherung** F third party, fire and theft insurance
Teilnahme (-, -n) F participation; (*Mitleid*) sympathy; **jdm seine herzliche ~ aussprechen** to offer sb one's heartfelt sympathy
teilnahmslos ADJ disinterested, apathetic
teilnehmen *unreg* VI: **an etw** *dat* **~** to take part in sth
Teilnehmer(in) (-s, -) M(F) participant

teils ADV partly
Teilschaden M partial loss
Teilstrecke F stage; (*von Straße*) stretch; (*bei Bus etc*) fare stage
Teilung F division
teilweise ADV partially, in part
Teil- ZW: **Teilzahlung** F payment by instalments (BRIT) *od* installments (US); **Teilzeitarbeit** F part-time job *od* work; **Teilzeitbasis** F: **auf Teilzeitbasis arbeiten** to work part-time; **Teilzeitmodell** NT part-time working arrangements
Teint [tɛ̃:] (**-s, -s**) M complexion
Telearbeit ['te:learbaɪt] F teleworking
Telebanking ['te:lebɛŋkɪŋ] (**-s**) NT telebanking
Telebrief ['te:lebri:f] M facsimile, fax
Telefax ['te:lefaks] (**-**) NT telefax
Telefon [tele'fo:n] (**-s, -e**) NT (tele)phone; **ans ~ gehen** to answer the phone; **Telefonamt** NT telephone exchange; **Telefonanruf** M (tele)phone call
Telefonat [telefo'na:t] (**-(e)s, -e**) NT (tele)phone call
Telefon- ZW: **Telefonbuch** NT (tele)phone directory; **Telefongebühr** F call charge; (*Grundgebühr*) (tele)phone rental; **Telefongespräch** NT (tele)phone call; **Telefonhäuschen** (*umg*) NT = **Telefonzelle**
telefonieren [telefo'ni:rən] VI to (tele)phone; **bei jdm ~** to use sb's phone; **mit jdm ~** to speak to sb on the phone
telefonisch [tele'fo:nɪʃ] ADJ telephone; (*Benachrichtigung*) by telephone; **ich bin ~ zu erreichen** I can be reached by phone
Telefonist(in) [telefo'nɪst(ɪn)] M(F) telephonist
Telefon- ZW: **Telefonkarte** F phone card; **Telefonnummer** F (tele)phone number; **Telefonrechnung** F phone bill; **Telefonseelsorge** F: **die Telefonseelsorge** ≈ the Samaritans; **Telefonverbindung** F telephone connection; **Telefonzelle** F telephone box (BRIT) *od* booth (US), callbox (BRIT); **Telefonzentrale** F telephone exchange
Telegraf [tele'gra:f] (**-en, -en**) M telegraph
Telegrafenleitung F telegraph line
Telegrafenmast M telegraph pole
Telegrafie [telegra'fi:] F telegraphy
telegrafieren [telegra'fi:rən] VT, VI to telegraph, to cable, to wire
telegrafisch [tele'gra:fɪʃ] ADJ telegraphic; **jdm ~ Geld überweisen** to cable sb money
Telegramm [tele'gram] (**-s, -e**) NT telegram, cable; **Telegrammadresse** F telegraphic address; **Telegrammformular** NT telegram form
Telekolleg ['te:ləkɔle:k] NT ≈ Open University (BRIT)
Teleobjektiv ['te:ləlɔpjɛkti:f] NT telephoto lens
Telepathie [telepa'ti:] F telepathy
telepathisch [tele'pa:tɪʃ] ADJ telepathic
Teleskop [tele'sko:p] (**-s, -e**) NT telescope
Telespiel NT video game
Telex ['te:lɛks] (**-, -(e)**) NT telex
Teller ['tɛlər] (**-s, -**) M plate
Tempel ['tɛmpəl] (**-s, -**) M temple
Temperafarbe ['tɛmperafarbə] F distemper
Temperament [tɛmpera'mɛnt] NT temperament; (*Schwung*) vivacity, vitality; **sein ~ ist mit ihm durchgegangen** he went over the top; **temperamentlos** ADJ spiritless; **temperamentvoll** ADJ high-spirited, lively
Temperatur [tɛmpera'tu:r] F temperature; **erhöhte ~ haben** to have a temperature
Tempo[1] ['tɛmpo] (**-s, -s**) NT speed, pace; **~!** get a move on!
Tempo[2] ['tɛmpo] (**-s, Tempi**) NT (*Mus*) tempo; **das ~ angeben** (*fig*) to set the pace; **Tempolimit** NT speed limit
temporär [tɛmpo'rɛ:r] ADJ temporary
Tempotaschentuch® NT paper handkerchief
Tendenz [tɛn'dɛnts] F tendency; (*Absicht*) intention
tendenziell [tɛndɛntsi'ɛl] ADJ: **nur tendenzielle Unterschiede** merely differences in emphasis
tendenziös [tɛndɛntsi'ø:s] ADJ bias(s)ed, tendentious
tendieren [tɛn'di:rən] VI: **zu etw ~** to show a tendency to(wards) sth, to incline to(wards) sth
Teneriffa [tene'rɪfa] (**-s**) NT Tenerife
Tenne ['tɛnə] (**-, -n**) F threshing floor
Tennis ['tɛnɪs] (**-**) NT tennis; **Tennisplatz** M tennis court; **Tennisschläger** M tennis racket; **Tennisspieler** M tennis player
Tenor [te'no:r] (**-s, Tenöre**) M tenor
Teppich ['tɛpɪç] (**-s, -e**) M carpet; **Teppichboden** M wall-to-wall carpeting; **Teppichkehrmaschine** F carpet sweeper; **Teppichklopfer** M carpet beater
Termin [tɛr'mi:n] (**-s, -e**) M (*Zeitpunkt*) date; (*Frist*) deadline; (*Arzttermin etc*) appointment; (*Jur: Verhandlung*) hearing; **sich** *dat* **einen ~ geben lassen** to make an appointment; **termingerecht** ADJ on schedule
terminieren [tɛrmi'ni:rən] VT (*befristen*) to limit; (*festsetzen*) to set a date for
Terminkalender M diary, appointments book
Terminologie [tɛrminolo'gi:] F terminology
Termite [tɛr'mi:tə] (**-, -n**) F termite
Terpentin [tɛrpɛn'ti:n] (**-s, -e**) NT turpentine, turps *sing*
Terrain [tɛ'rɛ̃:] (**-s, -s**) NT land, terrain; (*fig*) territory; **das ~ sondieren** (*Mil*) to reconnoitre the terrain; (*fig*) to see how the land lies
Terrasse [tɛ'rasə] (**-, -n**) F terrace
Terrine [tɛ'ri:nə] F tureen
territorial [tɛritori'a:l] ADJ territorial
Territorium [tɛri'to:riʊm] NT territory
Terror ['tɛrɔr] (**-s**) M terror; (*Terrorherrschaft*) reign of terror; **blanker ~** sheer terror; **Terroranschlag** M terrorist attack
terrorisieren [tɛrori'zi:rən] VT to terrorize
Terrorismus [tɛro'rɪsmʊs] M terrorism
Terrorismusbekämpfung [tɛro'rɪsmʊsbəkɛmpfʊŋ] F counterterrorism

Terrorist(in) M(F) terrorist
terroristisch ADJ terrorist *attrib*
Terrornetz(werk) NT terrorist network
Terrororganisation F terrorist organization
Terrorzelle F terrorist cell
Tertia ['tɛrtsia] (-, **Tertien**) F (*Sch: früher: Untertertia/Obertertia*) *fourth/fifth year of German secondary school*
Terz [tɛrts] (-, **-en**) F (*Mus*) third
Terzett [tɛr'tsɛt] (**-(e)s, -e**) NT (*Mus*) trio
Tesafilm® ['te:zafɪlm] M Sellotape® (BRIT), Scotch tape® (*US*)
Test [tɛst] (**-s, -s**) M test
Testament [tɛsta'mɛnt] NT will, testament; (*Rel*) Testament; **Altes/Neues ~** Old/New Testament
testamentarisch [tɛstamɛn'ta:rɪʃ] ADJ testamentary
Testamentsvollstrecker(in) (**-s, -**) M(F) executor (of a will)
Testat [tɛs'ta:t] (**-(e)s, -e**) NT certificate
Testator [tɛs'ta:tɔr] M testator
Test- ZW: **Testbild** NT (*TV*) test card; **testen** VT to test; **Testfall** M test case; **Testperson** F subject (of a test); **Teststoppabkommen** NT nuclear test ban agreement
Tetanus ['te:tanʊs] (-) M tetanus; **Tetanusimpfung** F (anti-)tetanus injection
teuer ['tɔʏər] ADJ dear, expensive; **teures Geld** good money; **das wird ihn ~ zu stehen kommen** (*fig*) that will cost him dear
Teuerung F increase in prices
Teuerungszulage F cost-of-living bonus
Teufel ['tɔʏfəl] (**-s, -**) M devil; **den ~ an die Wand malen** (*schwarzmalen*) to imagine the worst; (*Unheil heraufbeschwören*) to tempt fate *od* providence; **in Teufels Küche kommen** to get into a mess; **jdn zum ~ jagen** (*umg*) to send sb packing
Teufelei [tɔʏfə'laɪ] F devilment
Teufels- ZW: **Teufelsaustreibung** F exorcism; **Teufelsbrut** (*umg*) F devil's brood; **Teufelskreis** M vicious circle
teuflisch ['tɔʏflɪʃ] ADJ fiendish, diabolic
Text [tɛkst] (**-(e)s, -e**) M text; (*Liedertext*) words *pl*; (*: von Schlager*) lyrics *pl*; **Textdichter** M songwriter; **texten** VI to write the words
textil [tɛks'ti:l] ADJ textile; **Textilbranche** F textile trade
Textilien PL textiles *pl*
Textilindustrie F textile industry
Textilwaren PL textiles *pl*
Text- ZW: **Textnachrichten** PL (*Tel*) text messaging; **Textstelle** F passage; **Textverarbeitung** F word processing; **Textverarbeitungssystem** NT word processor
TH (**-, -s**) F ABK (= *technische Hochschule*) *siehe* **technisch**
Thailand ['taɪlant] (**-s**) NT Thailand
Thailänder(in) ['taɪlɛndər(ɪn)] (**-s, -**) M(F) Thai
Theater [te'a:tər] (**-s, -**) NT theatre (BRIT), theater (*US*); (*umg*) fuss; **(ein) ~ machen** to make a (big) fuss; **~ spielen** to act; (*fig*) to put on an act; **Theaterbesucher** M playgoer; **Theaterkasse** F box office; **Theaterstück** NT (stage) play
theatralisch [tea'tra:lɪʃ] ADJ theatrical
Theke ['te:kə] (**-, -n**) F (*Schanktisch*) bar; (*Ladentisch*) counter
Thema ['te:ma] (**-s, Themen** *od* **-ta**) NT topic, subject; (*Leitgedanke, Mus*) theme; **beim ~ bleiben/vom ~ abschweifen** to stick to/wander off the subject
thematisch [te'ma:tɪʃ] ADJ thematic
Themenkreis M topic
Themenpark M theme park
Themse ['tɛmzə] F: **die ~** the Thames
Theologe [teo'lo:gə] (**-n, -n**) M theologian
Theologie [teolo'gi:] F theology
Theologin F theologian
theologisch [teo'lo:gɪʃ] ADJ theological
Theoretiker(in) [teo're:tikər(ɪn)] (**-s, -**) M(F) theorist
theoretisch ADJ theoretical; **~ gesehen** in theory, theoretically
Theorie [teo'ri:] F theory
Therapeut [tera'pɔʏt] (**-en, -en**) M therapist
therapeutisch ADJ therapeutic
Therapie [tera'pi:] F therapy
Thermalbad [tɛr'ma:lba:t] NT thermal bath; (*Badeort*) thermal spa
Thermalquelle F thermal spring
Thermometer [tɛrmo'me:tər] (**-s, -**) NT thermometer
Thermosflasche® ['tɛrmɔsflaʃə] F Thermos® flask
Thermostat [tɛrmo'sta:t] (**-(e)s** *od* **-en, -e(n)**) M thermostat
These ['te:zə] (**-, -n**) F thesis
Thrombose [trɔm'bo:sə] (**-, -n**) F thrombosis
Thron [tro:n] (**-(e)s, -e**) M throne; **Thronbesteigung** F accession (to the throne)
thronen VI to sit enthroned; (*fig*) to sit in state
Thronerbe M heir to the throne
Thronfolge F succession (to the throne)
Thunfisch ['tu:nfɪʃ] M tuna (fish)
Thüringen ['ty:rɪŋən] (**-s**) NT Thuringia
Thymian ['ty:mia:n] (**-s, -e**) M thyme
Tibet ['ti:bɛt] (**-s**) NT Tibet
Tick [tɪk] (**-(e)s, -s**) M tic; (*Eigenart*) quirk; (*Fimmel*) craze
ticken VI to tick; **nicht richtig ~** (*umg*) to be off one's rocker
Ticket ['tɪkət] (**-s, -s**) NT ticket
tief [ti:f] ADJ deep; (*tiefsinnig*) profound; (*Ausschnitt, Ton*) low; **tiefer Teller** soup plate; **~ greifend** far-reaching; **~ schürfend** profound; **bis ~ in die Nacht hinein** late into the night; **Tief** (**-s, -s**) NT (*Met*) low; (*seelisch*) depression; **Tiefbau** M civil engineering (*at or below ground level*); **Tiefdruck** M (*Met*) low pressure
Tiefe (**-, -n**) F depth
Tiefebene ['ti:fle:bənə] F plain
Tiefenpsychologie F depth psychology
Tiefenschärfe F (*Phot*) depth of focus
tief- ZW: **tiefernst** ADJ very grave *od* solemn;

t

Tiefflug M low-level *od* low-altitude flight; **Tiefgang** M (*Naut*) draught (BRIT), draft (*US*); (*geistig*) depth; **Tiefgarage** F underground car park (BRIT) *od* parking lot (*US*); **tiefgekühlt** ADJ frozen; **Tiefkühlfach** NT freezer compartment; **Tiefkühlkost** F frozen food; **Tiefkühltruhe** F freezer, deep freeze (*US*); **Tieflader (-s, -)** M low-loader; **Tiefland** NT lowlands *pl*; **Tiefparterre** F basement; **Tiefpunkt** M low point; (*fig*) low ebb; **Tiefschlag** M (*Boxen, fig*) blow below the belt; **Tiefsee** F deep parts of the sea; **Tiefsinn** M profundity; **tiefsinnig** ADJ profound; (*umg*) melancholy; **Tiefstand** M low level; **tiefstapeln** VI to be overmodest; **Tiefstart** M (*Sport*) crouch start

Tiefstwert M minimum *od* lowest value

Tiegel ['ti:gəl] **(-s, -)** M saucepan; (*Chem*) crucible

Tier [ti:r] **(-(e)s, -e)** NT animal; **Tierarzt** M, **Tierärztin** F vet(erinary surgeon) (BRIT), veterinarian (*US*); **Tierfreund** M animal lover; **Tiergarten** M zoo, zoological gardens *pl*; **Tierhandlung** F pet shop (BRIT) *od* store (*US*); **tierisch** ADJ animal *attrib*; **tierisch ernst** deadly serious; **ich hatte tierisch Angst** I was dead scared; **Tierkreis** M zodiac; **Tierkunde** F zoology; **tierlieb** ADJ, **tierliebend** ADJ fond of animals; **Tierpark** M zoo; **Tierquälerei** F cruelty to animals; **Tierreich** NT animal kingdom; **Tierschutz** M protection of animals; **Tierschützer(in) (-s, -)** M(F) animal rights campaigner; **Tierschutzverein** M society for the prevention of cruelty to animals; **Tierversuch** M animal experiment; **Tierwelt** F animal kingdom

Tiger ['ti:gər] **(-s, -)** M tiger; **Tigerin** F tigress

tilgen ['tɪlgən] VT to erase; (*Sünden*) to expiate; (*Schulden*) to pay off

Tilgung F erasing, blotting out; (*von Sünden*) expiation; (*von Schulden*) repayment

Tilgungsfonds M (*Comm*) sinking fund

tingeln ['tɪŋəln] (*umg*) VI to appear in small night clubs

Tinktur [tɪŋk'tu:r] F tincture

Tinte ['tɪntə] **(-, -n)** F ink

Tinten- ZW: **Tintenfass** NT inkwell; **Tintenfisch** M cuttlefish; (*achtarmig*) octopus; **Tintenfleck** M ink stain *od* blot; **Tintenstift** M indelible pencil; **Tintenstrahldrucker** M ink-jet printer

Tipp [tɪp] **(-s, -s)** M (*Sport, Börse*) tip; (*Andeutung*) hint; (*an Polizei*) tip-off

Tippelbruder (*umg*) M tramp, gentleman of the road (BRIT), hobo (*US*)

tippen ['tɪpən] VI to tap, to touch; (*umg: schreiben*) to type; (*im Lotto etc*) to bet ▶ VT to type; (*Lottozahlen etc*) to bet; **auf jdn ~** (*umg: raten*) to tip sb, to put one's money on sb (*fig*)

Tippfehler (*umg*) M typing error

Tippse (-, -n) (*umg*) F typist

tipptopp ['tɪp'tɔp] (*umg*) ADJ tiptop

Tippzettel M (pools) coupon

Tirade [ti'ra:də] **(-, -n)** F tirade

Tirol [ti'ro:l] **(-s)** NT the Tyrol

Tiroler(in) (-s, -) M(F) Tyrolese, Tyrolean

tirolerisch ADJ Tyrolese, Tyrolean

Tisch [tɪʃ] **(-(e)s, -e)** M table; **bitte zu ~!** lunch *od* dinner is served; **bei ~** at table; **vor/nach ~** before/after eating; **unter den ~ fallen** (*fig*) to be dropped; **Tischdecke** F tablecloth

Tischler (-s, -) M carpenter, joiner

Tischlerei [tɪʃlə'raɪ] F joiner's workshop; (*Arbeit*) carpentry, joinery

Tischlerhandwerk NT cabinetmaking

tischlern VI to do carpentry *etc*

Tisch- ZW: **Tischnachbar** M neighbour (BRIT) *od* neighbor (*US*) (at table); **Tischrechner** M desk calculator; **Tischrede** F after-dinner speech; **Tischtennis** NT table tennis; **Tischtuch** NT tablecloth

Titel ['ti:təl] **(-s, -)** M title; **Titelanwärter** M (*Sport*) challenger; **Titelbild** NT cover (picture); (*von Buch*) frontispiece; **Titelgeschichte** F headline story; **Titelrolle** F title role; **Titelseite** F cover; (*Buchtitel*) title page; **Titelverteidiger** M defending champion, title holder

Titte ['tɪtə] **(-, -n)** (*umg*) F (*weibliche Brust*) boob, tit (*umg*)

titulieren [titu'li:rən] VT to entitle; (*anreden*) to address

tja [tja] INTERJ well!

Toast [to:st] **(-(e)s, -s** *od* **-e)** M toast

toasten VI to drink a toast ▶ VT (*Brot*) to toast; **auf jdn ~** to toast sb, to drink a toast to sb

Toaster (-s, -) M toaster

toben ['to:bən] VI to rage; (*Kinder*) to romp about

tob- ZW: **Tobsucht** F raving madness; **tobsüchtig** ADJ maniacal; **Tobsuchtsanfall** M maniacal fit

Tochter ['tɔxtər] **(-, Töchter)** F daughter; **Tochtergesellschaft** F subsidiary (company)

Tod [to:t] **(-(e)s, -e)** M death; **zu Tode betrübt sein** to be in the depths of despair; **eines natürlichen/gewaltsamen Todes sterben** to die of natural causes/die a violent death; **todernst** (*umg*) ADJ deadly serious ▶ ADV in dead earnest

Todes- ZW: **Todesangst** F mortal fear; **Todesängste ausstehen** (*umg*) to be scared to death; **Todesanzeige** F obituary (notice); **Todesfall** M death; **Todeskampf** M death throes *pl*; **Todesopfer** NT death, casualty, fatality; **Todesqualen** PL: **Todesqualen ausstehen** (*fig*) to suffer agonies; **Todesstoß** M deathblow; **Todesstrafe** F death penalty; **Todestag** M anniversary of death; **Todesursache** F cause of death; **Todesurteil** NT death sentence; **Todesverachtung** F utter disgust

Todfeind M deadly *od* mortal enemy

todkrank ADJ dangerously ill

tödlich ['tø:tlɪç] ADJ fatal; (*Gift*) deadly, lethal

tod- ZW: **todmüde** ADJ dead tired; **todschick** (*umg*) ADJ smart, classy; **todsicher** (*umg*) ADJ absolutely *od* dead certain; **Todsünde** F deadly sin; **todtraurig** ADJ extremely sad

Tofu ['to:fu] **(-(s))** M tofu

Togo ['to:go] (**-s**) NT Togo
Toilette [toa'lɛtə] F toilet, lavatory (BRIT), john (US); (*Frisiertisch*) dressing table; (*Kleidung*) outfit; **auf die ~ gehen/auf der ~ sein** to go to/be in the toilet
Toiletten- zW: **Toilettenartikel** PL toiletries *pl*, toilet articles *pl*; **Toilettenpapier** NT toilet paper; **Toilettentisch** M dressing table
toi, toi, toi ['tɔy'tɔy'tɔy] (*umg*) INTERJ good luck; (*unberufen*) touch wood
Tokio ['to:kjo] (**-s**) NT Tokyo
tolerant [tole'rant] ADJ tolerant
Toleranz F tolerance
tolerieren [tole'ri:rən] VT to tolerate
toll [tɔl] ADJ mad; (*Treiben*) wild; (*umg*) terrific
tollen VI to romp
toll- zW: **Tollheit** F madness, wildness; **Tollkirsche** F deadly nightshade; **tollkühn** ADJ daring; **Tollwut** F rabies
Tölpel ['tœlpəl] (**-s, -**) M oaf, clod
Tomate [to'ma:tə] (**-, -n**) F tomato; **du treulose ~!** (*umg*) you're a fine friend!
Tomatenmark (**-(e)s**) NT tomato purée
Tombola ['tɔmbola] (**-, -s** *od* **Tombolen**) F tombola
Ton[1] [to:n] (**-(e)s, -e**) M (*Erde*) clay
Ton[2] [to:n] (**-(e)s, Töne**) M (*Laut*) sound; (*Mus*) note; (*Redeweise*) tone; (*Farbton, Nuance*) shade; (*Betonung*) stress; **keinen ~ herausbringen** not to be able to say a word; **den ~ angeben** (*Mus*) to give an A; (*fig: Mensch*) to set the tone; **Tonabnehmer** M pick-up; **tonangebend** ADJ leading; **Tonarm** M pick-up arm; **Tonart** F (musical) key; **Tonband** NT tape; **Tonbandaufnahme** F tape recording
Tonbandgerät NT tape recorder
tönen ['tø:nən] VI to sound ▶ VT to shade; (*Haare*) to tint
Toner ['to:nər] (**-s, -**) M toner; **Tonerkassette** F toner cartridge
tönern ['tø:nərn] ADJ clay
Ton- zW: **Tonfall** M intonation; **Tonfilm** M sound film; **Tonhöhe** F pitch
Tonika ['to:nika] (**-, -iken**) F (*Mus*) tonic
Tonikum (**-s, -ika**) NT (*Med*) tonic
Ton- zW: **Toningenieur** M sound engineer; **Tonkopf** M recording head; **Tonkünstler** M musician; **Tonleiter** F (*Mus*) scale; **tonlos** ADJ soundless
Tonne ['tɔnə] (**-, -n**) F barrel; (*Maß*) ton
Ton- zW: **Tonspur** F soundtrack; **Tontaube** F clay pigeon; **Tonwaren** PL pottery *sing*, earthenware *sing*
Topf [tɔpf] (**-(e)s, Töpfe**) M pot; **alles in einen ~ werfen** (*fig*) to lump everything together; **Topfblume** F pot plant
Töpfer(in) ['tœpfər(ɪn)] (**-s, -**) M(F) potter
Töpferei [tœpfə'raɪ] F (*Töpferware*) pottery; (*Werkstatt*) pottery, potter's workshop
töpfern VI to do pottery
Töpferscheibe F potter's wheel
topfit ['tɔp'fɪt] ADJ in top form
Topflappen M ovencloth
topografisch [topo'gra:fɪʃ] ADJ topographic
topp [tɔp] INTERJ O.K.
Tor[1] [to:r] (**-en, -en**) M fool
Tor[2] (**-(e)s, -e**) NT gate; (*Sport*) goal; **Torbogen** M archway; **Toreinfahrt** F entrance gate
Toresschluss M: **(kurz) vor ~** right at the last minute
Torf [tɔrf] (**-(e)s**) M peat; **Torfstechen** NT peat-cutting
Torheit F foolishness; (*törichte Handlung*) foolish deed
Torhüter (**-s, -**) M goalkeeper
töricht ['tøːrɪçt] ADJ foolish
torkeln ['tɔrkəln] VI to stagger, to reel
torpedieren [tɔrpe'di:rən] VT (*lit, fig*) to torpedo
Torpedo [tɔr'pe:do] (**-s, -s**) M torpedo
Torschlusspanik ['to:rʃlʊspa:nɪk] (*umg*) F (*von Unverheirateten*) *fear of being left on the shelf*
Torschütze M, **Torschützin** F (goal) scorer
Torte ['tɔrtə] (**-, -n**) F cake; (*Obsttorte*) flan, tart
Tortenguss M glaze
Tortenheber M cake slice
Tortur [tɔr'tu:r] F ordeal
Torverhältnis NT goal average
Torwart (**-(e)s, -e**) M goalkeeper
tosen ['to:zən] VI to roar
Toskana [tɔs'ka:na] F Tuscany
tot [to:t] ADJ dead; **er war auf der Stelle ~** he died instantly; **~ geboren** stillborn; **sich ~ stellen** to pretend to be dead; **der tote Winkel** the blind spot; **einen toten Punkt haben** to be at one's lowest; **das Tote Meer** the Dead Sea
total [to'ta:l] ADJ total; **Totalausverkauf** M clearance sale
totalitär [tɔtali'tɛ:r] ADJ totalitarian
Totaloperation F extirpation; (*von Gebärmutter*) hysterectomy
Totalschaden M (*Aut*) complete write-off
totarbeiten VR to work o.s. to death
totärgern (*umg*) VR to get really annoyed
Tote(r) F(M) dead person
töten ['tøtən] VT, VI to kill
Toten- zW: **Totenbett** NT deathbed; **totenblass** ADJ deathly pale, white as a sheet; **Totengräber** (**-s, -**) M gravedigger; **Totenhemd** NT shroud; **Totenkopf** M skull; **Totenmesse** F requiem mass; **Totenschein** M death certificate; **Totenstille** F deathly silence; **Totentanz** M danse macabre; **Totenwache** F wake
tot- zW: **totfahren** *unreg* VT to run over; **totkriegen** (*umg*) VT: **nicht totzukriegen sein** to go on for ever; **totlachen** (*umg*) VR to laugh one's head off
Toto ['to:to] (**-s, -s**) M OD NT ≈ pools *pl*; **Totoschein** M ≈ pools coupon
tot- zW: **totsagen** VT: **jdn totsagen** to say that sb is dead; **Totschlag** M (*Jur*) manslaughter, second degree murder (US); **totschlagen** *unreg* VT (*lit, fig*) to kill; **Totschläger** M (*Waffe*) cosh (BRIT), blackjack (US); **totschweigen** *unreg* VT to hush up; **tottreten** *unreg* VT to trample to death

Tötung ['tøːtʊŋ] F killing
Touchscreen ['tatʃskriːn] M (*Tech*) touch screen; **Touchscreen-Handy** NT (*Tech*) touch screen mobile; **Touchscreen-Technologie** F (*Tech*) touch screen technology
Toupet [tu'peː] (**-s, -s**) NT toupee
toupieren [tu'piːrən] VT to backcomb
Tour [tuːr] (**-, -en**) F tour, trip; (*Umdrehung*) revolution; (*Verhaltensart*) way; **auf Touren kommen** (*Aut*) to reach top speed; (*fig*) to get into top gear; **auf vollen Touren laufen** (*lit*) to run at full speed; (*fig*) to be in full swing; **auf die krumme ~** by dishonest means; **in einer ~** incessantly
Tourenzahl F number of revolutions
Tourenzähler M rev counter
Tourismus [tu'rɪsmʊs] M tourism
Tourist(in) M(F) tourist
Touristenklasse F tourist class
Touristik [tu'rɪstɪk] F tourism
touristisch ADJ tourist *attrib*
Tournee [tʊr'neː] (-, **-s** *od* **-n**) F (*Theat etc*) tour; **auf ~ gehen** to go on tour
Trab [traːp] (**-(e)s**) M trot; **auf ~ sein** (*umg*) to be on the go
Trabant [tra'bant] M satellite
Trabantenstadt F satellite town
traben ['traːbən] VI to trot
Tracht [traxt] (**-, -en**) F (*Kleidung*) costume, dress; **eine ~ Prügel** a sound thrashing
trachten VI to strive, to endeavour (BRIT), to endeavor (US); **danach ~, etw zu tun** to strive to do sth; **jdm nach dem Leben ~** to seek to kill sb
trächtig ['trɛçtɪç] ADJ (*Tier*) pregnant
Tradition [traditsi'oːn] F tradition
traditionell [traditsioː'nɛl] ADJ traditional
traf *etc* [traːf] VB *siehe* **treffen**
Tragbahre F stretcher
tragbar ADJ (*Gerät*) portable; (*Kleidung*) wearable; (*erträglich*) bearable
träge ['trɛːgə] ADJ sluggish, slow; (*Phys*) inert
tragen ['traːgən] *unreg* VT to carry; (*Kleidung, Brille*) to wear; (*Namen, Früchte*) to bear; (*erdulden*) to endure ▸ VI (*schwanger sein*) to be pregnant; (*Eis*) to hold; **schwer an etw** *dat* **~** (*lit*) to have a job carrying sth; (*fig*) to find sth hard to bear; **zum T~ kommen** to come to fruition; (*nützlich werden*) to come in useful
tragend ADJ (*Säule, Bauteil*) load-bearing; (*Idee, Motiv*) fundamental
Träger ['trɛːgər] (**-s, -**) M carrier; (*von Kleidung*) wearer; (*von Namen*) bearer; (*Ordensträger*) holder; (*an Kleidung*) (shoulder) strap; (*Körperschaft etc*) sponsor; (*Holzträger, Betonträger*) (supporting) beam; (*Stahlträger, Eisenträger*) girder; (*Tech: Stütze von Brücken etc*) support
Trägerin F (*Person*) *siehe* **Träger**
Träger- ZW: **Trägerkleid** NT pinafore dress (BRIT), jumper (US); **Trägerrakete** F launch vehicle; **Trägerrock** M skirt with shoulder straps
Tragetasche F carrier bag (BRIT), carry-all (US)
Trag- ZW: **Tragfähigkeit** F load-bearing capacity; **Tragfläche** F (*Aviat*) wing; **Tragflügelboot** NT hydrofoil
Trägheit ['trɛːkhaɪt] F laziness; (*Phys*) inertia
Tragik ['traːgɪk] F tragedy
tragikomisch [tragi'koːmɪʃ] ADJ tragi-comic
tragisch ADJ tragic; **etw ~ nehmen** (*umg*) to take sth to heart
Traglast F load
Tragödie [tra'gøːdiə] F tragedy
trägt [trɛːkt] VB *siehe* **tragen**
Tragweite F range; (*fig*) scope; **von großer ~ sein** to have far-reaching consequences
Tragwerk NT wing assembly
Trainer(in) ['trɛːnər(ɪn)] (**-s, -**) M(F) (*Sport*) trainer, coach; (*Fussball*) manager
trainieren [trɛ'niːrən] VT to train; (*Übung*) to practise (BRIT), to practice (US) ▸ VI to train; **Fußball ~** to do football practice
Training (**-s, -s**) NT training
Trainingsanzug M track suit
Trakt [trakt] (**-(e)s, -e**) M (*Gebäudeteil*) section; (*Flügel*) wing
Traktat [trak'taːt] (**-(e)s, -e**) M OD NT (*Abhandlung*) treatise; (*Flugschrift, religiöse Schrift*) tract
traktieren (*umg*) VT (*schlecht behandeln*) to maltreat; (*quälen*) to torment
Traktor ['traktɔr] M tractor; (*von Drucker*) tractor feed
trällern ['trɛlərn] VT, VI to warble; (*Vogel*) to trill, to warble
trampeln ['trampəln] VT to trample; (*abschütteln*) to stamp ▸ VI to stamp
Trampelpfad M track, path
Trampeltier NT (*Zool*) (Bactrian) camel; (*fig: umg*) clumsy oaf
trampen ['trɛmpən] VI to hitchhike
Tramper(in) [trɛmpər(ɪn)] (**-s, -**) M(F) hitchhiker
Trampolin [trampo'liːn] (**-s, -e**) NT trampoline
Tranchierbesteck NT pair of carvers, carvers *pl*
tranchieren [trã'ʃiːrən] VT to carve
Träne ['trɛːnə] (**-, -n**) F tear
tränen VI to water
Tränengas NT tear gas
tranig ['traːnɪç] (*umg*) ADJ slow, sluggish
trank *etc* [traŋk] VB *siehe* **trinken**
Tränke ['trɛŋkə] (**-, -n**) F watering place
tränken VT (*nass machen*) to soak; (*Tiere*) to water
Transaktion [trans|aktsi'oːn] F transaction
Transchierbesteck NT = **Tranchierbesteck**
transchieren VT = **tranchieren**
Transformator [transfɔr'maːtɔr] M transformer
Transfusion [transfuzi'oːn] F transfusion
Transistor [tran'zistɔr] M transistor
transitiv ['tranzitiːf] ADJ transitive
Transitverkehr [tran'ziːtfɛrkeːr] M transit traffic
transparent [transpa'rɛnt] ADJ transparent; **Transparent** (**-(e)s, -e**) NT (*Bild*) transparency; (*Spruchband*) banner
transpirieren [transpi'riːrən] VI to perspire

Transplantation [transplantatsi'o:n] F transplantation; (*Hauttransplantation*) graft(ing)
Transport [trans'pɔrt] (**-(e)s, -e**) M transport; (*Fracht*) consignment, shipment; **transportfähig** ADJ moveable
transportieren [transpɔr'ti:rən] VT to transport
Transport- ZW: **Transportkosten** PL transport charges *pl*, carriage *sing*; **Transportmittel** NT means *sing* of transport; **Transportunternehmen** NT carrier
transsexuell [transzɛksu'ɛl] ADJ transsexual
transusig ['tra:nzu:ziç] (*umg*) ADJ sluggish
Transvestit [transvɛs'ti:t] (**-en, -en**) M transvestite
Trapez [tra'pe:ts] (**-es, -e**) NT trapeze; (*Math*) trapezium
Trara [tra'ra:] (**-s**) NT: **mit viel ~ (um)** (*fig: umg*) with a great hullabaloo (about)
trat *etc* [tra:t] VB *siehe* **treten**
Tratsch [tra:tʃ] (**-(e)s**) (*umg*) M gossip
tratschen ['tra:tʃən] (*umg*) VI to gossip
Tratte ['tratə] (**-, -n**) F (*Fin*) draft
Traube ['traʊbə] (**-, -n**) F grape; (*ganze Frucht*) bunch (of grapes)
Traubenlese F grape harvest
Traubenzucker M glucose
trauen ['traʊən] VI *+dat* to trust ▸ VR to dare ▸ VT to marry; **jdm/etw ~** to trust sb/sth
Trauer ['traʊər] (**-**) F sorrow; (*für Verstorbenen*) mourning; **Trauerfall** M death, bereavement; **Trauerfeier** F funeral service; **Trauerflor** (**-s, -e**) M black ribbon; **Trauergemeinde** F mourners *pl*; **Trauermarsch** M funeral march
trauern VI to mourn; **um jdn ~** to mourn (for) sb
Trauer- ZW: **Trauerrand** M black border; **Trauerspiel** NT tragedy; **Trauerweide** F weeping willow
Traufe ['traʊfə] (**-, -n**) F eaves *pl*
träufeln ['trɔʏfəln] VT, VI to drip
traulich ['traʊliç] ADJ cosy, intimate
Traum [traʊm] (**-(e)s, Träume**) M dream; **aus der ~!** it's all over!
Trauma (**-s, -men**) NT trauma
traumatisieren [traʊmati'zi:rən] VT to traumatize
Traumbild NT vision
Traumdeutung F interpretation of dreams
träumen ['trɔʏmən] VT, VI to dream; **das hätte ich mir nicht ~ lassen** I'd never have thought it possible
Träumer(in) (**-s, -**) M(F) dreamer
Träumerei [trɔʏmə'raɪ] F dreaming
träumerisch ADJ dreamy
traumhaft ADJ dreamlike; (*fig*) wonderful
Traumtänzer M dreamer
traurig ['traʊriç] ADJ sad; **Traurigkeit** F sadness
Trauring M wedding ring
Trauschein M marriage certificate
Trauung F wedding ceremony
Trauzeuge M witness (to a marriage)

treffen ['trɛfən] *unreg* VT to strike, to hit; (*Bemerkung*) to hurt; (*begegnen*) to meet; (*Entscheidung etc*) to make; (*Maßnahmen*) to take ▸ VI to hit ▸ VR to meet; **er hat es gut getroffen** he did well; **er fühlte sich getroffen** he took it personally; **~ auf** *+akk* to come across, to meet; **es traf sich, dass ...** it so happened that ...; **es trifft sich gut** it's convenient
Treffen (**-s, -**) NT meeting
treffend ADJ pertinent, apposite
Treffer (**-s, -**) M hit; (*Tor*) goal; (*Los*) winner
trefflich ADJ excellent
Treffpunkt M meeting place
Treibeis NT drift ice
treiben ['traɪbən] *unreg* VT to drive; (*Studien etc*) to pursue; (*Sport*) to do, to go in for ▸ VI (*Schiff etc*) to drift; (*Pflanzen*) to sprout; (*Koch: aufgehen*) to rise; (*Medikamente*) to be diuretic; **die treibende Kraft** (*fig*) the driving force; **Handel mit etw/jdm ~** to trade in sth/with sb; **es zu weit ~** to go too far; **Unsinn ~** to fool around;
Treiben (**-s**) NT activity
Treiber (**-s, -**) M (*Comput*) driver
Treib- ZW: **Treibgut** NT flotsam and jetsam; **Treibhaus** NT greenhouse; **Treibhauseffekt** M greenhouse effect; **Treibhausgas** NT greenhouse gas; **Treibjagd** F shoot (*in which game is sent up*); (*fig*) witchhunt; **Treibsand** M quicksand; **Treibstoff** M fuel
Trend [trɛnt] (**-s, -s**) M trend; **Trendwende** F new trend
trennbar ADJ separable
trennen ['trɛnən] VT to separate; (*teilen*) to divide ▸ VR to separate; **sich ~ von** to part with
Trennschärfe F (*Rundf*) selectivity
Trennung F separation
Trennungsstrich M hyphen
Trennwand F partition (wall)
treppab ADV downstairs
treppauf ADV upstairs
Treppe ['trɛpə] (**-, -n**) F stairs *pl*, staircase; (*im Freien*) steps *pl*; **eine ~** a staircase, a flight of stairs *od* steps; **sie wohnt zwei Treppen hoch/höher** she lives two flights up/higher up
Treppengeländer NT banister
Treppenhaus NT staircase
Tresen ['tre:zən] (**-s, -**) M (*Theke*) bar; (*Ladentisch*) counter
Tresor [tre'zo:r] (**-s, -e**) M safe
Tretboot NT pedal boat, pedalo
treten ['tre:tən] *unreg* VI to step; (*Tränen, Schweiß*) to appear ▸ VT (*mit Fußtritt*) to kick; (*niedertreten*) to tread, to trample; **~ nach** to kick at; **~ in** *+akk* to step in(to); **in Verbindung ~** to get in contact; **in Erscheinung ~** to appear; **der Fluss trat über die Ufer** the river overflowed its banks; **in Streik ~** to go on strike
Treter ['tre:tər] (*umg*) PL (*Schuhe*) casual shoes *pl*
Tretmine F (*Mil*) (anti-personnel) mine
Tretmühle F (*fig*) daily grind
treu [trɔʏ] ADJ faithful, true; (*Kunde, Fan*) loyal; **treudoof** (*umg*) ADJ naïve

t

Treue (-) F faithfulness; *(von Kunde, Fan)* loyalty
Treuhand *(umg)* F, **Treuhandanstalt** F trustee organization *(overseeing the privatization of former GDR state-owned firms)*; *see note*

> The **Treuhandanstalt** is a now defunct organization set up in 1990 to take over the nationally-owned companies of the former **DDR**, to break them down into smaller units and to privatize them. It was based in Berlin and had nine branches. Many companies were closed down by the Treuhandanstalt because of their outdated equipment and inability to compete with the western firms. This resulted in a rise in unemployment.

Treuhänder (-s, -) M trustee
Treuhandgesellschaft F trust company
treu- zW: **treuherzig** ADJ innocent; **treulich** ADV faithfully; **treulos** ADJ faithless; **treulos an jdm handeln** to fail sb
Triathlon ['tri:atlɔn] (-s, -s) NT triathlon
Tribüne [tri'by:nə] (-, -n) F grandstand; *(Rednertribüne)* platform
Tribut [tri'bu:t] (-(e)s, -e) M tribute
Trichter ['trɪçtər] (-s, -) M funnel; *(Bombentrichter)* crater
Trick [trɪk] (-s, -e *od* -s) M trick; **Trickfilm** M cartoon
trieb *etc* [tri:p] VB *siehe* **treiben**
Trieb (-(e)s, -e) M urge, drive; *(Neigung)* inclination; *(Bot)* shoot
Trieb- zW: **Triebfeder** F *(fig)* motivating force; **triebhaft** ADJ impulsive; **Triebkraft** F *(fig)* drive; **Triebtäter** M sex offender; **Triebwagen** M *(Eisenb)* railcar; **Triebwerk** NT engine
triefen ['tri:fən] VI to drip
trifft [trɪft] VB *siehe* **treffen**
triftig ['trɪftɪç] ADJ convincing; *(Grund etc)* good
Trigonometrie [trigonome'tri:] F trigonometry
Trikot [tri'ko:] (-s, -s) NT vest; *(Sport)* shirt ▶ M *(Gewebe)* tricot
Triller ['trɪlər] (-s, -) M *(Mus)* trill
trillern VI to trill, to warble
Trillerpfeife F whistle
Trilogie [trilo'gi:] F trilogy
Trimester [tri'mɛstər] (-s, -) NT term
Trimm-Aktion F keep-fit campaign
Trimm-dich-Pfad M keep-fit trail
trimmen VT *(Hund)* to trim; *(umg: Mensch, Tier)* to teach, to train ▶ VR to keep fit
trinkbar ADJ drinkable
trinken ['trɪŋkən] *unreg* VT, VI to drink
Trinker(in) (-s, -) M(F) drinker
Trink- zW: **trinkfest** ADJ: **ich bin nicht sehr trinkfest** I can't hold my drink very well; **Trinkgeld** NT tip; **Trinkhalle** F *(Kiosk)* refreshment kiosk; **Trinkhalm** M (drinking) straw; **Trinkmilch** F milk; **Trinkspruch** M toast; **Trinkwasser** NT drinking water
Trio ['tri:o] (-s, -s) NT trio
trippeln ['trɪpəln] VI to toddle
Tripper ['trɪpər] (-s, -) M gonorrhoea (BRIT), gonorrhea (US)
trist [trɪst] ADJ dreary, dismal; *(Farbe)* dull
tritt [trɪt] VB *siehe* **treten**
Tritt (-(e)s, -e) M step; *(Fußtritt)* kick
Trittbrett NT *(Eisenb)* step; *(Aut)* running board
Trittleiter F stepladder
Triumph [tri'ʊmf] (-(e)s, -e) M triumph; **Triumphbogen** M triumphal arch
triumphieren [triʊm'fi:rən] VI to triumph; *(jubeln)* to exult
trivial [trivi'a:l] ADJ trivial; **Trivialliteratur** F light fiction
trocken ['trɔkən] ADJ dry; **sich ~ rasieren** to use an electric razor; **Trockenautomat** M tumble dryer; **Trockendock** NT dry dock; **Trockeneis** NT dry ice; **Trockenelement** NT dry cell; **Trockenhaube** F hair-dryer; **Trockenheit** F dryness; **trockenlegen** VT *(Sumpf)* to drain; *(Kind)* to put a clean nappy (BRIT) *od* diaper (US) on; **Trockenmilch** F dried milk; **Trockenzeit** F *(Jahreszeit)* dry season
trocknen VT, VI to dry
Trockner (-s, -) M dryer
Troddel ['trɔdəl] (-, -n) F tassel
Trödel ['trø:dəl] (-s) *(umg)* M junk; **Trödelmarkt** M flea market
trödeln *(umg)* VI to dawdle
Trödler (-s, -) M secondhand dealer
trog *etc* [tro:k] VB *siehe* **trügen**
Trog (-(e)s, Tröge) M trough
trollen ['trɔlən] *(umg)* VR to push off
Trommel ['trɔməl] (-, -n) F drum; **die ~ rühren** *(fig: umg)* to drum up support; **Trommelfell** NT eardrum; **Trommelfeuer** NT drumfire, heavy barrage
trommeln VT, VI to drum
Trommelrevolver M revolver
Trommelwaschmaschine F tumble-action washing machine
Trommler(in) ['trɔmlər(ɪn)] (-s, -) M(F) drummer
Trompete [trɔm'pe:tə] (-, -n) F trumpet
Trompeter (-s, -) M trumpeter
Tropen ['tro:pən] PL tropics *pl*; **tropenbeständig** ADJ suitable for the tropics; **Tropenhelm** M topee, sun helmet
Tropf[1] [trɔpf] (-(e)s, Tröpfe) *(umg)* M rogue; **armer ~** poor devil
Tropf[2] (-(e)s) *(umg)* M *(Med: Infusion)* drip *(umg)*; **am ~ hängen** to be on a drip
tröpfeln ['trœpfəln] VI to drip, to trickle
tropfen VT, VI to drip ▶ VI UNPERS: **es tropft** a few raindrops are falling
Tropfen (-s, -) M drop; **ein guter** *od* **edler ~** a good wine; **ein ~ auf den heißen Stein** *(fig: umg)* a drop in the ocean
tropfenweise ADV in drops
tropfnass ADJ dripping wet
Tropfsteinhöhle F stalactite cave
Trophäe [tro'fɛ:ə] (-, -n) F trophy
tropisch ['tro:pɪʃ] ADJ tropical
Trost [tro:st] (-es) M consolation, comfort; **trostbedürftig** ADJ in need of consolation

trösten ['trø:stən] VT to console, to comfort
Tröster(in) (**-s, -**) M(F) comfort(er)
tröstlich ADJ comforting
trost- ZW: **trostlos** ADJ bleak; (*Verhältnisse*) wretched; **Trostpflaster** NT (*fig*) consolation; **Trostpreis** M consolation prize; **trostreich** ADJ comforting
Tröstung ['trø:stʊŋ] F comfort, consolation
Trott [trɔt] (**-(e)s, -e**) M trot; (*Routine*) routine
Trottel (**-s, -**) (*umg*) M fool, dope
trotten VI to trot
Trottoir [trɔto'a:r] (**-s, -s** *od* **-e**) NT (*veraltet*) pavement (BRIT), sidewalk (US)
trotz [trɔts] PRÄP (*+gen od dat*) in spite of
Trotz (**-es**) M pig-headedness; **etw aus ~ tun** to do sth just to show them; **jdm zum ~** in defiance of sb
Trotzalter NT obstinate phase
trotzdem ADV nevertheless ▶ KONJ although
trotzen VI *+dat* to defy; (*der Kälte, dem Klima etc*) to withstand; (*der Gefahr*) to brave; (*trotzig sein*) to be awkward
trotzig ADJ defiant; (*Kind*) difficult, awkward
Trotzkopf M obstinate child
Trotzreaktion F fit of pique
trüb [try:p] ADJ dull; (*Flüssigkeit, Glas*) cloudy; (*fig*) gloomy; **trübe Tasse** (*umg*) drip
Trubel ['tru:bəl] (**-s**) M hurly-burly
trüben ['try:bən] VT to cloud ▶ VR to become clouded
Trübheit F dullness; (*von Flüssigkeit, Glas*) cloudiness; (*fig*) gloom
Trübsal (**-, -e**) F distress; **~ blasen** (*umg*) to mope
trüb- ZW: **trübselig** ADJ sad, melancholy; **Trübsinn** M depression; **trübsinnig** ADJ depressed, gloomy
trudeln ['tru:dəln] VI (*Aviat*) to (go into a) spin
Trüffel ['trʏfəl] (**-, -n**) F truffle
trug *etc* [tru:k] VB *siehe* **tragen**
Trug (**-(e)s**) M (*liter*) deception; (*der Sinne*) illusion
trügen ['try:gən] *unreg* VT to deceive ▶ VI to be deceptive; **wenn mich nicht alles trügt** unless I am very much mistaken
trügerisch ADJ deceptive
Trugschluss ['tru:gʃlʊs] M false conclusion
Truhe ['tru:ə] (**-, -n**) F chest
Trümmer ['trʏmər] PL wreckage *sing*; (*Bautrümmer*) ruins *pl*; **Trümmerfeld** NT expanse of rubble *od* ruins; (*fig*) scene of devastation; **Trümmerfrauen** PL *(German) women who cleared away the rubble after the war*; **Trümmerhaufen** M heap of rubble
Trumpf [trʊmpf] (**-(e)s, Trümpfe**) M (*lit, fig*) trump; **trumpfen** VT, VI to trump
Trunk [trʊŋk] (**-(e)s, Trünke**) M drink
trunken ADJ intoxicated; **Trunkenbold** (**-(e)s, -e**) M drunkard; **Trunkenheit** F intoxication; **Trunkenheit am Steuer** drink-driving
Trunksucht F alcoholism
Trupp [trʊp] (**-s, -s**) M troop
Truppe (**-, -n**) F troop; (*Waffengattung*) force; (*Schauspieltruppe*) troupe; **nicht von der schnellen ~ sein** (*umg*) to be slow
Truppen PL troops *pl*; **Truppenabbau** M cutback in troop numbers; **Truppenführer** M (military) commander; **Truppenteil** M unit; **Truppenübungsplatz** M training area
Trust [trast] (**-(e)s, -e** *od* **-s**) M trust
Truthahn ['tru:tha:n] M turkey
Tschad [tʃat] (**-s**) M: **der ~** Chad
Tscheche ['tʃɛçə] (**-n, -n**) M, **Tschechin** F Czech
Tschechien (**-s**) NT Czech Republic
tschechisch ADJ Czech; **die Tschechische Republik** the Czech Republic
Tschechoslowakei [tʃɛçoslova:'kai] F (*Hist*): **die ~** Czechoslovakia
tschüs [tʃʏs] (*umg*) INTERJ cheerio (BRIT), so long (US)
T-Shirt ['ti:ʃø:t] (**-s, -s**) NT T-shirt
TU (**-**) F ABK (= *technische Universität*) ≈ polytechnic
Tuba ['tu:ba] (**-, Tuben**) F (*Mus*) tuba
Tube ['tu:bə] (**-, -n**) F tube
Tuberkulose [tubɛrku'lo:zə] (**-, -n**) F tuberculosis
Tuch [tu:x] (**-(e)s, Tücher**) NT cloth; (*Halstuch*) scarf; (*Kopftuch*) (head)scarf; (*Handtuch*) towel; **Tuchfühlung** F physical contact
tüchtig ['tʏçtɪç] ADJ efficient; (*fähig*) able, capable; (*umg: kräftig*) good, sound; **etwas Tüchtiges lernen/werden** (*umg*) to get a proper training/job; **Tüchtigkeit** F efficiency; (*Fähigkeit*) ability
Tücke ['tʏkə] (**-, -n**) F (*Arglist*) malice; (*Trick*) trick; (*Schwierigkeit*) difficulty, problem; **seine Tücken haben** to be temperamental
tückisch ADJ treacherous; (*böswillig*) malicious
tüfteln ['tʏftəln] (*umg*) VI to puzzle; (*basteln*) to fiddle about
Tugend ['tu:gənt] (**-, -en**) F virtue; **tugendhaft** ADJ virtuous
Tüll [tʏl] (**-s, -e**) M tulle
Tülle (**-, -n**) F spout
Tulpe ['tʊlpə] (**-, -n**) F tulip
tummeln ['tʊməln] VR to romp (about); (*sich beeilen*) to hurry
Tummelplatz M play area; (*fig*) hotbed
Tumor ['tu:mɔr] (**-s, -e**) M tumour (BRIT), tumor (US)
Tümpel ['tʏmpəl] (**-s, -**) M pond
Tumult [tu'mʊlt] (**-(e)s, -e**) M tumult
tun [tu:n] *unreg* VT (*machen*) to do; (*legen*) to put ▶ VI to act ▶ VR: **es tut sich etwas/viel** something/a lot is happening; **jdm etw ~** to do sth to sb; **etw tut es auch** sth will do; **das tut nichts** that doesn't matter; **das tut nichts zur Sache** that's neither here nor there; **du kannst ~ und lassen, was du willst** you can do as you please; **so ~, als ob** to act as if; **zu ~ haben** (*beschäftigt sein*) to be busy, to have things *od* something to do
Tünche ['tʏnçə] (**-, -n**) F whitewash
tünchen VT to whitewash
Tunesien [tu'ne:ziən] (**-s**) NT Tunisia
Tunesier(in) (**-s, -**) M(F) Tunisian
tunesisch ADJ Tunisian
Tunfisch M = **Thunfisch**
Tunke ['tʊŋkə] (**-, -n**) F sauce

t

tunken VT to dip, to dunk
tunlichst ['tu:nlıçst] ADV if at all possible; **~ bald** as soon as possible
Tunnel ['tʊnəl] (**-s, -s** *od* **-**) M tunnel
Tunte ['tʊntə] (**-, -n**) (*pej, umg*) F fairy (*pej*)
Tüpfel ['tʏpfəl] (**-s, -**) M dot; **Tüpfelchen** NT (small) dot
tüpfeln ['tʏpfəln] VT to dab
tupfen ['tʊpfən] VT to dab; (*mit Farbe*) to dot; **Tupfen** (**-s, -**) M dot, spot
Tupfer (**-s, -**) M swab
Tür [ty:r] (**-, -en**) F door; **an die ~ gehen** to answer the door; **zwischen ~ und Angel** in passing; **Weihnachten steht vor der ~** (*fig*) Christmas is just around the corner; **mit der ~ ins Haus fallen** (*umg*) to blurt it *od* things out; **Türangel** F (door) hinge
Turbine [tʊr'bi:nə] F turbine
turbulent [tʊrbu'lɛnt] ADJ turbulent
Türke ['tʏrkə] (**-n, -n**) M Turk
Türkei [tʏr'kaı] F: **die ~** Turkey
Türkin F Turk
türkis ADJ turquoise; **Türkis** [tʏr'ki:s] (**-es, -e**) M turquoise
türkisch ADJ Turkish
Türklinke F door handle
Turm [tʊrm] (**-(e)s, Türme**) M tower; (*Kirchturm*) steeple; (*Sprungturm*) diving platform; (*Schach*) castle, rook
türmen ['tʏrmən] VR to tower up ▸ VT to heap up ▸ VI (*umg*) to scarper, to bolt
Turmuhr F clock (on a tower); (*Kirchturmuhr*) church clock
Turnanzug M gym costume
turnen ['tʊrnən] VI to do gymnastic exercises; (*herumklettern*) to climb about; (*Kind*) to romp ▸ VT to perform; **Turnen** (**-s**) NT gymnastics *sing*; (*Sch*) physical education, P.E.
Turner(in) (**-s, -**) M(F) gymnast
Turnhalle F gym(nasium)
Turnhose F gym shorts *pl*
Turnier [tʊr'ni:r] (**-s, -e**) NT tournament
Turn- ZW: **Turnlehrer(in)** M(F) gym *od* PE teacher; **Turnschuh** M gym shoe; **Turnstunde** F gym *od* PE lesson
Turnus ['tʊrnʊs] (**-, -se**) M rota; **im ~** in rotation
Turnverein M gymnastics club
Turnzeug NT gym kit
Türöffner M buzzer
turteln ['tʊrtəln] (*umg*) VI to bill and coo; (*fig*) to whisper sweet nothings
Tusch [tʊʃ] (**-(e)s, -e**) M (*Mus*) flourish
Tusche ['tʊʃə] (**-, -n**) F Indian ink
tuscheln ['tʊʃəln] VT, VI to whisper
Tuschkasten M paintbox
Tussi ['tʊsı] (**-, -s**) (*umg*) F (*Frau, Freundin*) bird (BRIT), chick (US)
tust [tu:st] VB *siehe* **tun**
tut [tu:t] VB *siehe* **tun**
Tüte ['ty:tə] (**-, -n**) F bag; **in die ~ blasen** (*umg*) to be breathalyzed; **das kommt nicht in die ~!** (*umg*) no way!
tuten ['tu:tən] VI (*Aut*) to hoot (BRIT), to honk (US); **von T~ und Blasen keine Ahnung haben** (*umg*) not to have a clue
TÜV [tʏf] M ABK (= *Technischer Überwachungs-Verein*) ≈ MOT (BRIT); **durch den ~ kommen** (*Aut*) to pass its test *od* MOT (BRIT); *see note*

> The **TÜV** (Technischer Überwachungsverein) is the organization responsible for checking the safety of machinery, particularly vehicles. Cars over three years old have to be examined every two years for their safety and for their exhaust emissions. The TÜV is the German equivalent of the MOT.

TV (**-**) NT ABK (= *Television*) TV ▸ M ABK = **Turnverein**
Twen [tvɛn] (**-(s), -s**) M *person in his/her twenties*
Twitter® ['tvıtər] NT Twitter®
twittern ['tvıtərn] VI (*auf Twitter*) to tweet
Typ [ty:p] (**-s, -en**) M type; (*Mann*) guy, bloke
Type (**-, -n**) F (*Typ*) type
Typenrad NT (*Drucker*) daisywheel; **Typenraddrucker** M daisywheel printer
Typhus ['ty:fʊs] (**-**) M typhoid (fever)
typisch ['ty:pıʃ] ADJ: **~ (für)** typical (of)
Tyrann [ty'ran] (**-en, -en**) M(F) tyrant
Tyrannei [tyra'naı] F tyranny
Tyrannin F tyrant
tyrannisch ADJ tyrannical
tyrannisieren [tyrani'zi:rən] VT to tyrannize
tyrrhenisch [ty're:nıʃ] ADJ Tyrrhenian; **Tyrrhenisches Meer** Tyrrhenian Sea

Uu

U, u [uː] NT U, u; **U wie Ulrich** ≈ U for Uncle
u. ABK = **und**
u. a. ABK (= *und andere(s)*) and others; (= *unter anderem*) amongst other things
u. Ä. ABK (= *und Ähnliche(s)*) and similar
u. A. w. g. ABK (= *um Antwort wird gebeten*) R.S.V.P.
U-Bahn [ˈuːbaːn] F ABK (= *Untergrundbahn*) underground (BRIT), subway (US)
übel [ˈyːbəl] ADJ bad; **jdm ist ~** sb feels sick; **~ gelaunt** bad-tempered, sullen; **jdm eine Bemerkung** *etc* **~ nehmen** to be offended at sb's remark *etc*; *siehe auch* **übelwollend**; **Übel** (**-s, -**) NT evil; (*Krankheit*) disease; **zu allem Übel …** to make matters worse …; **Übelkeit** F nausea; **Übelstand** M bad state of affairs; **Übeltäter** M wrongdoer; **übelwollend** ADJ malevolent
üben [ˈyːbən] VT, VI, VR to practise (BRIT), to practice (US); (*Gedächtnis, Muskeln*) to exercise; **Kritik an etw** *dat* **~** to criticize sth

SCHLÜSSELWORT

über [ˈyːbər] PRÄP +*dat* **1** (*räumlich*) over, above; **zwei Grad über null** two degrees above zero
2 (*zeitlich*) over; **über der Arbeit einschlafen** to fall asleep over one's work
▸ PRÄP +*akk* **1** (*räumlich*) over; (*hoch über*) above; (*quer über*) across; **er lachte über das ganze Gesicht** he was beaming all over his face; **Macht über jdn haben** to have power over sb
2 (*zeitlich*) over; **über Weihnachten** over Christmas; **über kurz oder lang** sooner or later
3 (*auf dem Wege*) via; **nach Köln über Aachen** to Cologne via Aachen; **ich habe es über die Auskunft erfahren** I found out from information
4 (*betreffend*) about; **ein Buch über …** a book about *od* on …; **über jdn/etw lachen** to laugh about *od* at sb/sth; **ein Scheck über 200 Euro** a cheque for 200 euros
5: **Fehler über Fehler** mistake after mistake
▸ ADV **1** (*mehr als*) over, more than; **Kinder über 12 Jahren** children over *od* above 12 years of age; **sie liebt ihn über alles** she loves him more than anything
2: **über und über** over and over; **den ganzen Tag/die ganze Zeit über** all day long/all the time; **jdm in etw** *dat* **über sein** to be superior to sb in sth

überall [yːbərˈal] ADV everywhere; **überallhin** ADV everywhere
überaltert [yːbərˈaltərt] ADJ obsolete
Überangebot [ˈyːbərangəboːt] NT: **~ (an** +*dat***)** surplus (of)
überanstrengen [yːbərˈanʃtrɛŋən] VT UNTR to overexert ▸ VR UNTR to overexert o.s.
überantworten [yːbərˈantvɔrtən] VT UNTR to hand over, to deliver (up)
überarbeiten [yːbərˈarbaɪtən] VT UNTR to revise, to rework ▸ VR UNTR to overwork (o.s.)
überaus [ˈyːbəraʊs] ADV exceedingly
überbacken [yːbərˈbakən] *unreg* VT UNTR to put in the oven/under the grill
Überbau [ˈyːbərbaʊ] M (*Gebäude, Philosophie*) superstructure
überbeanspruchen [ˈyːbərbəlanʃpruxən] VT UNTR (*Menschen, Körper, Maschine*) to overtax
überbelichten [ˈyːbərbəlɪçtən] VT UNTR (*Phot*) to overexpose
Überbesetzung [ˈyːbərbəzɛtsʊŋ] F overmanning
überbewerten [ˈyːbərbəveːrtən] VT UNTR (*fig*) to overrate; (*Äußerungen*) to attach too much importance to
überbieten [yːbərˈbiːtən] *unreg* VT UNTR to outbid; (*übertreffen*) to surpass; (*Rekord*) to break ▸ VR UNTR: **sich in etw** *dat* **(gegenseitig) ~** to vie with each other in sth
Überbleibsel [ˈyːbərblaɪpsəl] (**-s, -**) NT residue, remainder
Überblick [ˈyːbərblɪk] M view; (*fig: Darstellung*) survey, overview; (*Fähigkeit*): **~ (über** +*akk***)** overall view (of), grasp (of); **den ~ verlieren** to lose track (of things); **sich** *dat* **einen ~ verschaffen** to get a general idea
überblicken [yːbərˈblɪkən] VT UNTR to survey; (*fig*) to see; (*: Lage etc*) to grasp
überbringen [yːbərˈbrɪŋən] *unreg* VT UNTR to deliver, to hand over
Überbringer (**-s, -**) M bearer
Überbringung F delivery
überbrücken [yːbərˈbrʏkən] VT UNTR to bridge
Überbrückung F: **100 Euro zur ~** 100 euros to tide me/him *etc* over

Überbrückungskredit M bridging loan
überbuchen ['y:bərbu:xən] VT to overbook
überdauern [y:bər'daʊərn] VT UNTR to outlast
überdenken [y:bər'dɛŋkən] *unreg* VT UNTR to think over
überdies [y:bər'di:s] ADV besides
überdimensional ['y:bərdimɛnziona:l] ADJ oversize
Überdosis ['y:bərdo:zɪs] F overdose, OD (*umg*); (*zu große Zumessung*) excessive amount
überdrehen [y:bər'dre:ən] VT UNTR (*Uhr etc*) to overwind
überdreht ADJ: **~ sein** (*fig*) to be hyped up, to be overexcited
Überdruck ['y:bərdrʊk] M (*Tech*) excess pressure
Überdruss ['y:bərdrʊs] (**-es**) M weariness; **bis zum ~** ad nauseam
überdrüssig ['y:bərdrʏsɪç] ADJ *+gen* tired of, sick of
überdurchschnittlich ['y:bərdʊrçʃnɪtlɪç] ADJ above-average ▶ ADV exceptionally
übereifrig ['y:bər|aɪfrɪç] ADJ overzealous
übereignen [y:bər'|aɪgnən] VT UNTR: **jdm etw ~** (*geh*) to make sth over to sb
übereilen [y:bər'|aɪlən] VT UNTR to hurry
übereilt ADJ (over)hasty
übereinander [y:bər|aɪ'nandər] ADV one upon the other; (*sprechen*) about each other
übereinanderschlagen *unreg* VT (*Arme*) to fold; (*Beine*) to cross
übereinkommen [y:bər'|aɪnkɔmən] *unreg* VI to agree
Übereinkunft [y:bər'|aɪnkʊnft] (-, **-künfte**) F agreement
übereinstimmen [y:bər'|aɪnʃtɪmən] VI to agree; (*Angaben, Messwerte etc*) to tally; (*mit Tatsachen*) to fit
Übereinstimmung F agreement
überempfindlich ['y:bər|ɛmpfɪntlɪç] ADJ hypersensitive
überfahren¹ ['y:bərfa:rən] *unreg* VT to take across ▶ VI to cross, to go across
überfahren² [y:bər'fa:rən] *unreg* VT UNTR (*Aut*) to run over; (*fig*) to walk all over
Überfahrt ['y:bərfa:rt] F crossing
Überfall ['y:bərfal] M (*Banküberfall, Mil*) raid; (*auf jdn*) assault
überfallen [y:bər'falən] *unreg* VT UNTR to attack; (*Bank*) to raid; (*besuchen*) to drop in on, to descend (up)on
überfällig ['y:bərfɛlɪç] ADJ overdue
Überfallkommando NT flying squad
überfliegen [y:bər'fli:gən] *unreg* VT UNTR to fly over, to overfly; (*Buch*) to skim through
Überflieger M (*fig*) high-flier
überflügeln [y:bər'fly:gəln] VT UNTR to outdo
Überfluss ['y:bərflʊs] M: **~ (an** *+dat*) (super)abundance (of), excess (of); **zu allem** *od* **zum ~** (*unnötigerweise*) superfluously; (*obendrein*) to crown it all (*umg*); **Überflussgesellschaft** F affluent society
überflüssig ['y:bərflʏsɪç] ADJ superfluous
überfluten [y:bər'flu:tən] VT UNTR (*lit*) to flood; (*fig*) to flood, to inundate
überfordern [y:bər'fɔrdərn] VT UNTR to demand too much of; (*Kräfte etc*) to overtax
überfragt [y:bər'fra:kt] ADJ: **da bin ich ~** there you've got me, you've got me there
überführen¹ ['y:bərfy:rən] VT to transfer; (*Leiche etc*) to transport
überführen² [y:bər'fy:rən] VT UNTR (*Täter*) to have convicted
Überführung F transfer; (*von Leiche etc*) transport; (*von Täter*) conviction; (*Brücke*) bridge, overpass
überfüllt [y:bər'fʏlt] ADJ overcrowded; (*Kurs*) oversubscribed
Übergabe ['y:bərga:bə] F handing over; (*Mil*) surrender
Übergang ['y:bərgaŋ] M crossing; (*Wandel, Überleitung*) transition
Übergangs- ZW: **Übergangserscheinung** F transitory phenomenon; **Übergangsfinanzierung** F (*Fin*) accommodation; **übergangslos** ADJ without a transition; **Übergangslösung** F provisional solution, stopgap; **Übergangsstadium** NT state of transition; **Übergangszeit** F transitional period
übergeben [y:bər'ge:bən] *unreg* VT UNTR to hand over; (*Mil*) to surrender ▶ VR UNTR to be sick; **dem Verkehr ~** to open to traffic
übergehen¹ ['y:bərge:ən] *unreg* VI (*Besitz*) to pass; (*zum Feind etc*) to go over, to defect; (*überwechseln*) **(zu etw) ~** to go on (to sth); **~ in** *+akk* to turn into
übergehen² [y:bər'ge:ən] *unreg* VT UNTR to pass over, to omit
übergeordnet ['y:bərgə|ɔrdnət] ADJ (*Behörde*) higher
Übergepäck ['y:bərgəpɛk] NT excess baggage
übergeschnappt ['y:bərgəʃnapt] (*umg*) ADJ crazy
Übergewicht ['y:bərgəvɪçt] NT excess weight; (*fig*) preponderance
übergießen [y:bər'gi:sən] *unreg* VT UNTR to pour over; (*Braten*) to baste
überglücklich ['y:bərglʏklɪç] ADJ overjoyed
übergreifen ['y:bərgraɪfən] *unreg* VI: **~ (auf** *+akk*) (*auf Rechte etc*) to encroach (on); (*Feuer, Streik, Krankheit etc*) to spread (to); **ineinander ~** to overlap
übergroß ['y:bərgro:s] ADJ outsize, huge
Übergröße ['y:bərgrø:sə] F oversize
überhaben ['y:bərha:bən] *unreg* (*umg*) VT to be fed up with
überhandnehmen [y:bər'hant-] *unreg* VI to gain the ascendancy
überhängen ['y:bərhɛŋən] *unreg* VI to overhang
überhäufen [y:bər'hɔʏfən] VT UNTR: **jdn mit Geschenken/Vorwürfen ~** to heap presents/reproaches on sb
überhaupt [y:bər'haʊpt] ADV at all; (*im Allgemeinen*) in general; (*besonders*) especially; **~ nicht** not at all; **wer sind Sie ~?** who do you think you are?
überheblich [y:bər'he:plɪç] ADJ arrogant; **Überheblichkeit** F arrogance

überhöht [y:bər'hø:t] ADJ (*Forderungen, Preise*) exorbitant, excessive
überholen [y:bər'ho:lən] VT UNTR to overtake; (*Tech*) to overhaul
Überholspur F overtaking lane
überholt ADJ out-of-date, obsolete
Überholverbot [y:bər'ho:lfɛrbo:t] NT overtaking (BRIT) *od* passing ban
überhören [y:bər'hø:rən] VT UNTR to not hear; (*absichtlich*) to ignore; **das möchte ich überhört haben!** (I'll pretend) I didn't hear that!
Über-Ich, Überich ['y:bərlıç] (-**s**) NT superego
überirdisch ['y:bərlırdıʃ] ADJ supernatural, unearthly
überkapitalisieren ['y:bərkapitali'zi:rən] VT UNTR to overcapitalize
überkochen ['y:bərkɔxən] VI to boil over
überkompensieren ['y:bərkɔmpɛnzi:rən] VT UNTR to overcompensate for
überladen [y:bər'ladən] *unreg* VT UNTR to overload ▶ ADJ (*fig*) cluttered
überlassen [y:bər'lasən] *unreg* VT UNTR: **jdm etw** ~ to leave sth to sb ▶ VR UNTR: **sich einer Sache** *dat* ~ to give o.s. over to sth; **das bleibt Ihnen** ~ that's up to you; **jdn sich** *dat* **selbst** ~ to leave sb to his/her own devices
überlasten [y:bər'lastən] VT UNTR to overload; (*jdn*) to overtax
überlaufen[1] ['y:bərlaufən] *unreg* VI (*Flüssigkeit*) to flow over; (*zum Feind etc*) to go over, to defect
überlaufen[2] [y:bər'laufən] *unreg* VT UNTR (*Schauer etc*) to come over ▶ ADJ overcrowded; ~ **sein** to be inundated *od* besieged
Überläufer ['y:bərlɔyfər] M deserter
überleben [y:bər'le:bən] VT UNTR to survive
Überlebende(r) F(M) survivor
überlebensgroß ADJ larger-than-life
überlegen [y:bər'le:gən] VT UNTR to consider ▶ ADJ superior; **ich habe es mir anders** *od* **noch einmal überlegt** I've changed my mind; **Überlegenheit** F superiority
Überlegung F consideration, deliberation
überleiten ['y:bərlaitən] VT (*Abschnitt etc*): ~ **in** *+akk* to link up with
überlesen [y:bər'le:zən] *unreg* VT UNTR (*übersehen*) to overlook, to miss
überliefern [y:bər'li:fərn] VT UNTR to hand down, to transmit
Überlieferung F tradition; **schriftliche Überlieferungen** (written) records
überlisten [y:bər'lıstən] VT UNTR to outwit
überm ['y:bərm] = **über dem**
Übermacht ['y:bərmaxt] F superior force, superiority
übermächtig ['y:bərmɛçtıç] ADJ superior (in strength); (*Gefühl etc*) overwhelming
übermannen [y:bər'manən] VT UNTR to overcome
Übermaß ['ybərma:s] NT: ~ **(an** *+dat***)** excess (of)
übermäßig ['y:bərmɛ:sıç] ADJ excessive
Übermensch ['y:bərmɛnʃ] M superman; **übermenschlich** ADJ superhuman
übermitteln [y:bər'mıtəln] VT UNTR to convey
übermorgen ['y:bərmɔrgən] ADV the day after tomorrow
Übermüdung [y:bər'my:dʊŋ] F overtiredness
Übermut ['y:bərmu:t] M exuberance
übermütig ['y:bərmy:tıç] ADJ exuberant, high-spirited; ~ **werden** to get overconfident
übernächste(r, s) ['y:bərnɛ:çstə(r, s)] ADJ next ... but one; ~ **Woche** the week after next
übernachten [y:bər'naxtən] VI UNTR: **(bei jdm)** ~ to spend the night (at sb's place)
übernächtigt [y:bər'nɛçtıçt] ADJ sleepy, tired
Übernachtung F: ~ **mit Frühstück** bed and breakfast
Übernahme ['y:bərna:mə] (-, -**n**) F taking over *od* on; (*von Verantwortung*) acceptance; **Übernahmeangebot** NT takeover bid
übernatürlich ['y:bərnaty:rlıç] ADJ supernatural
übernehmen [y:bər'ne:mən] *unreg* VT UNTR to take on, to accept; (*Amt, Geschäft*) to take over ▶ VR UNTR to take on too much; (*sich überanstrengen*) to overdo it
überparteilich ['y:bərpartailıç] ADJ (*Zeitung*) independent; (*Amt, Präsident etc*) above party politics
überprüfen [y:bər'pry:fən] VT UNTR to examine, to check; (*Pol*: *jdn*) to screen
Überprüfung F examination
überqueren [y:bər'kve:rən] VT UNTR to cross
überragen [y:bər'ra:gən] VT UNTR to tower above; (*fig*) to surpass
überragend ADJ outstanding; (*Bedeutung*) paramount
überraschen [y:bər'raʃən] VT UNTR to surprise
Überraschung F surprise
überreden [y:bər're:dən] VT UNTR to persuade; **jdn zu etw** ~ to talk sb into sth
Überredungskunst F powers *pl* of persuasion
überregional ['y:bərregiona:l] ADJ national; (*Zeitung, Sender*) nationwide
überreichen [y:bər'raiçən] VT UNTR to hand over; (*feierlich*) to present
überreichlich ADJ (more than) ample
überreizt [y:bər'raitst] ADJ overwrought
Überreste ['y:bərrɛstə] PL remains *pl*, remnants *pl*
überrumpeln [y:bər'rʊmpəln] VT UNTR to take by surprise; (*umg*: *überwältigen*) to overpower
überrunden [y:bər'rʊndən] VT UNTR (*Sport*) to lap
übers ['y:bərs] = **über das**
übersättigen [y:bər'zɛtıgən] VT UNTR to satiate
Überschall- ['y:bərʃal] IN ZW supersonic; **Überschallflugzeug** NT supersonic jet; **Überschallgeschwindigkeit** F supersonic speed
überschatten [y:bər'ʃatən] VT UNTR to overshadow
überschätzen [y:bər'ʃɛtsən] VT UNTR, VR UNTR to overestimate
überschaubar [y:bər'ʃauba:r] ADJ (*Plan*) easily comprehensible, clear

überschäumen ['y:bɐrʃɔymən] VI to froth over; (*fig*) to bubble over
überschlafen [y:bɐr'ʃla:fən] *unreg* VT UNTR (*Problem*) to sleep on
Überschlag ['y:bɐrʃla:k] M (*Fin*) estimate; (*Sport*) somersault
überschlagen¹ [y:bɐr'ʃla:gən] *unreg* VT UNTR (*berechnen*) to estimate; (*auslassen*: *Seite*) to omit ▸ VR UNTR to somersault; (*Stimme*) to crack; (*Aviat*) to loop the loop ▸ ADJ lukewarm, tepid
überschlagen² ['y:bɐrʃla:gən] *unreg* VT (*Beine*) to cross; (*Arme*) to fold ▸ VI (*Hilfsverb sein*: *Wellen*) to break; (: *Funken*) to flash over; **in etw** *akk* **~** (*Stimmung etc*) to turn into sth
überschnappen ['y:bɐrʃnapən] VI (*Stimme*) to crack; (*umg*: *Mensch*) to flip one's lid
überschneiden [y:bɐr'ʃnaɪdən] *unreg* VR UNTR (*lit, fig*) to overlap; (*Linien*) to intersect; (*Termine*) to clash
überschreiben [y:bɐr'ʃraɪbən] *unreg* VT UNTR to provide with a heading; (*Comput*) to overwrite; **jdm etw ~** to transfer *od* make over sth to sb
überschreiten [y:bɐr'ʃraɪtən] *unreg* VT UNTR to cross over; (*fig*) to exceed; (*verletzen*) to transgress
Überschrift ['y:bɐrʃrɪft] F heading, title
überschuldet [y:bɐr'ʃʊldət] ADJ heavily in debt; (*Grundstück*) heavily mortgaged
Überschuss ['y:bɐrʃʊs] M: **~ (an** *+dat***)** surplus (of)
überschüssig ['y:bɐrʃʏsɪç] ADJ surplus, excess
überschütten [y:bɐr'ʃʏtən] VT UNTR: **jdn/etw mit etw ~** (*lit*) to pour sth over sb/sth; **jdn mit etw ~** (*fig*) to shower sb with sth
Überschwang ['y:bɐrʃvaŋ] M exuberance
überschwänglich ['y:bɐrʃvɛŋlɪç] ADJ effusive; **Überschwänglichkeit** F effusion
überschwappen ['y:bɐrʃvapən] VI to splash over
überschwemmen [y:bɐr'ʃvɛmən] VT UNTR to flood
Überschwemmung F flood
überschwenglich ['y:bɐrʃvɛŋlɪç] ADJ *siehe* **überschwänglich**
Übersee ['y:bɐrze:] F: **nach/in ~** overseas
überseeisch ADJ overseas
übersehbar [y:bɐr'ze:ba:r] ADJ (*fig*: *Folgen, Zusammenhänge etc*) clear; (*Kosten, Dauer etc*) assessable
übersehen [y:bɐr'ze:ən] *unreg* VT UNTR to look (out) over; (*fig*: *Folgen*) to see, to get an overall view of; (: *nicht beachten*) to overlook
übersenden [y:bɐr'zɛndən] *unreg* VT UNTR to send, to forward
übersetzen¹ [y:bɐr'zɛtsən] VT UNTR, VI UNTR to translate
übersetzen² ['y:bɐrzɛtsən] VI (*Hilfsverb sein*) to cross
Übersetzer(in) [y:bɐr'zɛtsɐr(ɪn)] **(-s, -)** M(F) translator
Übersetzung [y:bɐr'zɛtsʊŋ] F translation; (*Tech*) gear ratio
Übersicht ['y:bɐrzɪçt] F overall view; (*Darstellung*) survey; **die ~ verlieren** to lose track; **übersichtlich** ADJ clear; (*Gelände*) open; **Übersichtlichkeit** F clarity, lucidity
übersiedeln¹ ['y:bɐrzi:dəln] VI to move
übersiedeln² [y:bɐr'zi:dəln] VI UNTR to move
überspannen [y:bɐr'ʃpanən] VT UNTR (*zu sehr spannen*) to overstretch; (*überdecken*) to cover
überspannt ADJ eccentric; (*Idee*) wild, crazy; **Überspanntheit** F eccentricity
überspielen [y:bɐr'ʃpi:lən] VT UNTR (*verbergen*) to cover (up); (*übertragen*: *Aufnahme*) to transfer
überspitzt [y:bɐr'ʃpɪtst] ADJ exaggerated
überspringen [y:bɐr'ʃprɪŋən] *unreg* VT UNTR to jump over; (*fig*) to skip
übersprudeln ['y:bɐrʃpru:dəln] VI to bubble over
überstehen¹ [y:bɐr'ʃte:ən] *unreg* VT UNTR to overcome, to get over; (*Winter etc*) to survive, to get through
überstehen² ['y:bɐrʃte:ən] *unreg* VI to project
übersteigen [y:bɐr'ʃtaɪgən] *unreg* VT UNTR to climb over; (*fig*) to exceed
übersteigert [y:bɐr'ʃtaɪgɐrt] ADJ excessive
überstimmen [y:bɐr'ʃtɪmən] VT UNTR to outvote
überstrapazieren ['y:bɐrʃtrapatsi:rən] VT UNTR to wear out ▸ VR to wear o.s. out
überstreifen ['y:bɐrʃtraɪfən] VT: **(sich** *dat***) etw ~** to slip sth on
überströmen¹ [y:bɐr'ʃtrø:mən] VT UNTR: **von Blut überströmt sein** to be streaming with blood
überströmen² ['y:bɐrʃtrø:mən] VI (*lit, fig*): **~ (vor** *+dat***)** to overflow (with)
Überstunden ['y:bɐrʃtʊndən] PL overtime *sing*
überstürzen [y:bɐr'ʃtʏrtsən] VT UNTR to rush ▸ VR UNTR to follow (one another) in rapid succession
überstürzt ADJ (over)hasty
übertariflich ['y:bɐrtariflɪç] ADJ, ADV above the agreed *od* union rate
übertölpeln [y:bɐr'tœlpln] VT UNTR to dupe
übertönen [y:bɐr'tø:nən] VT UNTR to drown (out)
Übertrag ['y:bɐrtra:k] **(-(e)s, -träge)** M (*Comm*) amount brought forward
übertragbar [y:bɐr'tra:kba:r] ADJ transferable; (*Med*) infectious
übertragen [y:bɐr'tra:gən] *unreg* VT UNTR to transfer; (*Rundf*) to broadcast; (*anwenden*: *Methode*) to apply; (*übersetzen*) to render; (*Krankheit*) to transmit ▸ VR UNTR to spread ▸ ADJ figurative; **~ auf** *+akk* to transfer to; (*Methode*) to apply to; **sich ~ auf** *+akk* to spread to; **jdm etw ~** to assign sth to sb; (*Verantwortung etc*) to give sb sth *od* sth to sb
Übertragung F transference; (*Rundf*) broadcast; (*Übersetzung*) rendering; (*von Krankheit, Daten*) transmission
übertreffen [y:bɐr'trɛfən] *unreg* VT UNTR to surpass
übertreiben [y:bɐr'traɪbən] *unreg* VT UNTR to exaggerate; **man kann es auch ~** you can overdo things
Übertreibung F exaggeration

übertreten[1] [y:bər'tre:tən] *unreg* VT UNTR to cross; (*Gebot etc*) to break
übertreten[2] ['y:bərtre:tən] *unreg* VI (*über Linie, Gebiet*) to step (over); (*Sport*) to overstep; (*zu anderem Glauben*) to be converted; **~ (in** +*akk*) (*Pol*) to go over (to)
Übertretung [y:bər'tre:tʊŋ] F violation, transgression
übertrieben [y:bər'tri:bən] ADJ exaggerated, excessive
Übertritt ['y:bərtrɪt] M (*zu anderem Glauben*) conversion; (*bes zu anderer Partei*) defection
übertrumpfen [y:bər'trʊmpfən] VT UNTR to outdo; (*Karten*) to overtrump
übertünchen [y:bər'tʏnçən] VT UNTR to whitewash; (*fig*) to cover up, to whitewash
übervölkert [y:bər'fœlkərt] ADJ overpopulated
übervoll ['y:bərfɔl] ADJ overfull
übervorteilen [y:bər'fɔrtaɪlən] VT UNTR to dupe, to cheat
überwachen [y:bər'vaxən] VT UNTR to supervise; (*Verdächtigen*) to keep under surveillance
Überwachung F supervision; (*von Verdächtigen*) surveillance
Überwachungskamera [y:bər'vaxʊŋskamera] (-, **-s**) F CCTV camera
überwältigen [y:bər'vɛltɪgən] VT UNTR to overpower
überwältigend ADJ overwhelming
überwechseln ['y:bərvɛksəln] VI: **~ (in** +*akk*) to move (to); (*zu Partei etc*): **~ (zu)** to go over (to)
überweisen [y:bər'vaɪzən] *unreg* VT UNTR to transfer; (*Patienten*) to refer
Überweisung F transfer; (*von Patient*) referral
überwerfen[1] ['y:bərvɛrfən] *unreg* VT (*Kleidungsstück*) to put on; (*sehr rasch*) to throw on
überwerfen[2] [y:bər'vɛrfən] *unreg* VR UNTR: **sich (mit jdm) ~** to fall out (with sb)
überwiegen [y:bər'vi:gən] *unreg* VI UNTR to predominate
überwiegend ADJ predominant
überwinden [y:bər'vɪndən] *unreg* VT UNTR to overcome ▸ VR UNTR: **sich ~, etw zu tun** to make an effort to do sth, to bring o.s. to do sth
Überwindung F overcoming; (*Selbstüberwindung*) effort of will
überwintern [y:bər'vɪntərn] VI UNTR to (spend the) winter; (*umg: Winterschlaf halten*) to hibernate
Überwurf ['y:bərvʊrf] M wrap
Überzahl ['y:bərtsa:l] F superior numbers *pl*, superiority; **in der ~ sein** to be numerically superior
überzählig ['y:bərtsɛ:lɪç] ADJ surplus
überzeugen [y:bər'tsɔʏgən] VT UNTR to convince
überzeugend ADJ convincing
überzeugt ADJ *attrib* (*Anhänger etc*) dedicated; (*Vegetarier*) strict; (*Christ, Moslem*) devout
Überzeugung F conviction; **zu der ~ gelangen, dass ...** to become convinced that ...
Überzeugungskraft F power of persuasion
überziehen[1] ['y:bərtsi:ən] *unreg* VT to put on
überziehen[2] [y:bər'tsi:ən] *unreg* VT UNTR to cover; (*Konto*) to overdraw; (*Redezeit etc*) to overrun ▸ VR UNTR (*Himmel*) to cloud over; **ein Bett frisch ~** to change a bed, to change the sheets (on a bed)
Überziehungskredit M overdraft
überzüchten [y:bər'tsʏçtən] VT UNTR to overbreed
Überzug ['y:bərtsu:k] M cover; (*Belag*) coating
üblich ['y:plɪç] ADJ usual; **allgemein ~ sein** to be common practice
U-Boot ['u:bo:t] NT U-boat, submarine
übrig ['y:brɪç] ADJ remaining; **die Übrigen** the others; **das Übrige** the rest; **im Übrigen** besides; **~ bleiben** to remain, to be left (over); **~ lassen** to leave (over); **einiges/viel zu wünschen ~ lassen** (*umg*) to leave something/a lot to be desired; *siehe auch* **übrighaben**
übrigens ['y:brɪgəns] ADV besides; (*nebenbei bemerkt*) by the way
übrighaben *unreg* VI: **für jdn etwas ~** (*umg*) to be fond of sb
Übung ['y:bʊŋ] F practice; (*Turnübung, Aufgabe etc*) exercise; **~ macht den Meister** (*Sprichwort*) practice makes perfect
Übungsarbeit F (*Sch*) mock test
Übungsplatz M training ground; (*Mil*) drill ground
u. d. M. ABK (= *unter dem Meeresspiegel*) below sea level
ü. d. M. ABK (= *über dem Meeresspiegel*) above sea level
u. E. ABK (= *unseres Erachtens*) in our opinion
Ufer ['u:fər] (**-s, -**) NT bank; (*Meeresufer*) shore; **Uferbefestigung** F embankment
uferlos ADJ endless; (*grenzenlos*) boundless; **ins Uferlose gehen** (*Kosten*) to go up and up; (*Debatte etc*) to go on forever
UFO, Ufo ['u:fo] (**-(s), -s**) NT ABK (= *unbekanntes Flugobjekt*) UFO, ufo
Uganda [u'ganda] (**-s**) NT Uganda
Ugander(in) (**-s, -**) M(F) Ugandan
ugandisch ADJ Ugandan
U-Haft ['u:haft] F ABK = **Untersuchungshaft**
Uhr [u:r] (**-, -en**) F clock; (*Armbanduhr*) watch; **wie viel ~ ist es?** what time is it?; **um wie viel ~?** at what time?; **1 ~** 1 o'clock; **20 ~** 8 o'clock, 20.00 (twenty hundred) hours; **Uhrband** NT watchstrap; **Uhrkette** F watch chain; **Uhrmacher** M watchmaker; **Uhrwerk** NT (*auch fig*) clockwork mechanism; **Uhrzeiger** M hand; **Uhrzeigersinn** M: **im Uhrzeigersinn** clockwise; **entgegen dem Uhrzeigersinn** anticlockwise (BRIT), counterclockwise (*US*); **Uhrzeit** F time (of day)
Uhu ['u:hu] (**-s, -s**) M eagle owl
Ukraine [ukra'i:nə] F Ukraine
Ukrainer(in) [ukra'i:nər(ɪn)] (**-s, -**) M(F) Ukrainian
ukrainisch ADJ Ukrainian
UKW ABK (= *Ultrakurzwelle*) VHF
Ulk [ʊlk] (**-s, -e**) M lark

ulkig ['ʊlkɪç] ADJ funny
Ulme ['ʊlmə] (**-, -n**) F elm
Ulster ['ʊlstər] (**-s**) NT Ulster
Ultimatum [ʊlti'maːtʊm] (**-s, Ultimaten**) NT ultimatum; **jdm ein ~ stellen** to give sb an ultimatum
Ultra- ZW: **Ultrakurzwelle** F very high frequency; **Ultraleichtflugzeug** NT microlight; **Ultraschall** M (*Phys*) ultrasound; **ultraviolett** ADJ ultraviolet

SCHLÜSSELWORT

um [ʊm] PRÄP +*akk* **1** (*um herum*) (a)round; **um Weihnachten** around Christmas; **er schlug um sich** he hit about him
2 (*mit Zeitangabe*) at; **um acht (Uhr)** at eight (o'clock)
3 (*mit Größenangabe*) by; **etw um 4 cm kürzen** to shorten sth by 4 cm; **um 10% teurer** 10% more expensive; **um vieles besser** better by far; **um nichts besser** not in the least bit better; *siehe* **umso**
4: **der Kampf um den Titel** the battle for the title; **um Geld spielen** to play for money; **es geht um das Prinzip** it's a question of principle; **Stunde um Stunde** hour after hour; **Auge um Auge** an eye for an eye
▸ PRÄP +*gen*: **um ... willen** for the sake of ...; **um Gottes willen** for goodness *od* (*stärker*) God's sake
▸ KONJ: **um ... zu** (in order) to ...; **zu klug, um zu ...** too clever to ...; *siehe auch* **umso**
▸ ADV **1** (*ungefähr*) about; **um (die) 30 Leute** about *od* around 30 people
2 (*vorbei*): **die zwei Stunden sind um** the two hours are up

umadressieren ['ʊm|adrɛsiːrən] VT to readdress
umändern ['ʊm|ɛndərn] VT to alter
Umänderung F alteration
umarbeiten ['ʊm|arbaɪtən] VT to remodel; (*Buch etc*) to revise, to rework
umarmen [ʊm'|armən] VT UNTR to embrace
Umbau ['ʊmbaʊ] (**-(e)s, -e** *od* **-ten**) M reconstruction, alteration(s *pl*)
umbauen ['ʊmbaʊən] VT to rebuild, to reconstruct
umbenennen ['ʊmbənɛnən] *unreg* VT to rename
umbesetzen ['ʊmbəzɛtsən] VT (*Theat*) to recast; (*Mannschaft*) to change; (*Posten, Stelle*) to find someone else for
umbiegen ['ʊmbiːgən] *unreg* VT to bend (over)
umbilden ['ʊmbɪldən] VT to reorganize; (*Pol: Kabinett*) to reshuffle
umbinden[1] ['ʊmbɪndən] *unreg* VT (*Krawatte etc*) to put on
umbinden[2] [ʊm'bɪndən] *unreg* VT UNTR: **etw mit etw ~** to tie sth round sth
umblättern ['ʊmblɛtərn] VT to turn over
umblicken ['ʊmblɪkən] VR to look around
umbringen ['ʊmbrɪŋən] *unreg* VT to kill
Umbruch ['ʊmbrʊx] M radical change; (*Typ*) make-up (into page)
umbuchen ['ʊmbuːxən] VI to change one's reservation *od* flight *etc* ▸ VT to change
umdenken ['ʊmdɛŋkən] *unreg* VI to adjust one's views
umdisponieren ['ʊmdɪsponiːrən] VI UNTR to change one's plans
umdrängen [ʊm'drɛŋən] VT UNTR to crowd round
umdrehen ['ʊmdreːən] VT to turn (round); (*Hals*) to wring ▸ VR to turn (round); **jdm den Arm ~** to twist sb's arm
Umdrehung F turn; (*Phys*) revolution, rotation
umeinander [ʊm|aɪ'nandər] ADV round one another; (*füreinander*) for one another
umerziehen ['ʊm|ɛrtsiːən] *unreg* VT (*Pol: euph*): **jdn (zu etw) ~** to re-educate sb (to become sth)
umfahren[1] ['ʊmfaːrən] *unreg* VT to run over
umfahren[2] [ʊm'faːrən] *unreg* VT UNTR to drive round; (*die Welt*) to sail round
umfallen ['ʊmfalən] *unreg* VI to fall down *od* over; (*fig: umg: nachgeben*) to give in
Umfang ['ʊmfaŋ] M extent; (*von Buch*) size; (*Reichweite*) range; (*Fläche*) area; (*Math*) circumference; **in großem ~** on a large scale; **umfangreich** ADJ extensive; (*Buch etc*) voluminous
umfassen [ʊm'fasən] VT UNTR to embrace; (*umgeben*) to surround; (*enthalten*) to include
umfassend ADJ comprehensive; (*umfangreich*) extensive
Umfeld ['ʊmfɛlt] NT environment; **zum ~ von etw gehören** to be associated with sth
umformatieren ['ʊmfɔrmatiːrən] VT (*Comput*) to reformat
umformen ['ʊmfɔrmən] VI to transform
Umformer (**-s, -**) M (*Elek*) converter
umformulieren ['ʊmfɔrmuliːrən] VT to redraft
Umfrage ['ʊmfraːgə] F poll; **~ halten** to ask around
umfüllen ['ʊmfʏlən] VT to transfer; (*Wein*) to decant
umfunktionieren ['ʊmfʊŋktsioniːrən] VT to convert
Umgang ['ʊmgaŋ] M company; (*mit jdm*) dealings *pl*; (*Behandlung*) dealing
umgänglich ['ʊmgɛŋlɪç] ADJ sociable
Umgangs- ZW: **Umgangsformen** PL manners *pl*; **Umgangssprache** F colloquial language; **umgangssprachlich** ADJ colloquial
umgeben [ʊm'geːbən] *unreg* VT UNTR to surround
Umgebung F surroundings *pl*; (*Milieu*) environment; (*Personen*) people in one's circle; **in der näheren/weiteren ~ Münchens** on the outskirts/in the environs of Munich
umgehen[1] ['ʊmgeːən] *unreg* VI to go (a)round; **im Schlosse ~** to haunt the castle; **mit jdm/etw ~ können** to know how to handle sb/sth; **mit jdm grob** *etc* **~** to treat sb roughly *etc*; **mit Geld sparsam ~** to be careful with one's money
umgehen[2] [ʊm'geːən] *unreg* VT UNTR to bypass; (*Mil*) to outflank; (*Gesetz, Vorschrift etc*) to circumvent; (*vermeiden*) to avoid

umgehend ADJ immediate
Umgehung F bypassing; (*Mil*) outflanking; (*von Gesetz, Vorschrift etc*) circumvention; (*Vermeidung*) avoidance
Umgehungsstraße F bypass
umgekehrt ['ʊmgəke:rt] ADJ reverse(d); (*gegenteilig*) opposite ▸ ADV the other way around; **und ~** and vice versa
umgestalten ['ʊmgəʃtaltən] VT to alter; (*reorganisieren*) to reorganize; (*umordnen*) to rearrange
umgewöhnen ['ʊmgəvø:nən] VR to readapt
umgraben ['ʊmgra:bən] *unreg* VT to dig up
umgruppieren ['ʊmgrʊpi:rən] VT to regroup
Umhang ['ʊmhaŋ] M wrap, cape
umhängen ['ʊmhɛŋən] VT (*Bild*) to hang somewhere else; **jdm etw ~** to put sth on sb
Umhängetasche F shoulder bag
umhauen ['ʊmhaʊən] VT to fell; (*fig*) to bowl over
umher [ʊm'he:r] ADV about, around; **umhergehen** *unreg* VI to walk about; **umherirren** VI to wander around; (*Blick, Augen*) to roam about; **umherreisen** VI to travel about; **umherschweifen** VI to roam about; **umherziehen** *unreg* VI to wander from place to place
umhinkönnen [ʊm'hɪnkœnən] *unreg* VI: **ich kann nicht umhin, das zu tun** I can't help doing it
umhören ['ʊmhø:rən] VR to ask around
umkämpfen [ʊm'kɛmpfən] VT UNTR (*Entscheidung*) to dispute; (*Wahlkreis, Sieg*) to contest
Umkehr ['ʊmke:r] (-) F turning back; (*Änderung*) change
umkehren VI to turn back; (*fig*) to change one's ways ▸ VT to turn round, to reverse; (*Tasche etc*) to turn inside out; (*Gefäß etc*) to turn upside down
umkippen ['ʊmkɪpən] VT to tip over ▸ VI to overturn; (*umg: ohnmächtig werden*) to keel over; (*fig: Meinung ändern*) to change one's mind
umklammern [ʊm'klamərn] VT UNTR (*mit Händen*) to clasp; (*festhalten*) to cling to
umklappen ['ʊmklapən] VT to fold down
Umkleidekabine ['ʊmklaɪdəkabi:nə] F changing cubicle (BRIT), dressing room (US)
Umkleideraum ['ʊmklaɪdəraʊm] M changing room; (*US Theat*) dressing room
umknicken ['ʊmknɪkən] VT (*Ast*) to snap; (*Papier*) to fold (over) ▸ VI: **mit dem Fuß ~** to twist one's ankle
umkommen ['ʊmkɔmən] *unreg* VI to die, to perish; (*Lebensmittel*) to go bad
Umkreis ['ʊmkraɪs] M neighbourhood (BRIT), neighborhood (US); **im ~ von** within a radius of
umkreisen [ʊm'kraɪzən] VT UNTR to circle (round); (*Satellit*) to orbit
umkrempeln ['ʊmkrɛmpəln] VT to turn up; (*mehrmals*) to roll up; (*umg: Betrieb*) to shake up
umladen ['ʊmla:dən] *unreg* VT to transfer, to reload
Umlage ['ʊmla:gə] F share of the costs
Umlauf M (*Geldumlauf*) circulation; (*von Gestirn*) revolution; (*Schreiben*) circular; **in ~ bringen** to circulate; **Umlaufbahn** F orbit
umlaufen ['ʊmlaʊfən] *unreg* VI to circulate
Umlaufkapital NT working capital
Umlaufvermögen NT current assets *pl*
Umlaut ['ʊmlaʊt] M umlaut
umlegen ['ʊmle:gən] VT to put on; (*verlegen*) to move, to shift; (*Kosten*) to share out; (*umkippen*) to tip over; (*umg: töten*) to bump off
umleiten ['ʊmlaɪtən] VT to divert
Umleitung F diversion
umlernen ['ʊmlɛrnən] VI to learn something new; (*fig*) to adjust one's views
umliegend ['ʊmli:gənt] ADJ surrounding
ummelden ['ʊmmɛldən] VT, VR: **jdn/sich ~** to notify (the police of) a change in sb's/one's address
Umnachtung [ʊm'naxtʊŋ] F mental derangement
umorganisieren ['ʊmlɔrganizi:rən] VT to reorganize
umpflanzen ['ʊmpflantsən] VT to transplant
umquartieren ['ʊmkvarti:rən] VT to move; (*Truppen*) to requarter
umrahmen [ʊm'ra:mən] VT UNTR to frame
umranden [ʊm'randən] VT UNTR to border, to edge
umräumen ['ʊmrɔʏmən] VT (*anders anordnen*) to rearrange ▸ VI to rearrange things, to move things around
umrechnen ['ʊmrɛçnən] VT to convert
Umrechnung F conversion
Umrechnungskurs M rate of exchange
umreißen [ʊm'raɪsən] *unreg* VT UNTR to outline
umrennen ['ʊmrɛnən] *unreg* VT to (run into and) knock down
umringen [ʊm'rɪŋən] VT UNTR to surround
Umriss ['ʊmrɪs] M outline
umrühren ['ʊmry:rən] VT, VI to stir
umrüsten ['ʊmrʏstən] VT (*Tech*) to adapt; (*Mil*) to re-equip; **~ auf** *+akk* to adapt to
ums [ʊms] = **um das**
umsatteln ['ʊmzatəln] (*umg*) VI to change one's occupation, to switch jobs
Umsatz ['ʊmzats] M turnover; **Umsatzbeteiligung** F commission; **Umsatzeinbuße** F loss of profit; **Umsatzsteuer** F turnover tax
umschalten ['ʊmʃaltən] VT to switch ▸ VI to push/pull a lever; (*auf anderen Sender*): **~ (auf** *+akk*) to change over (to); (*Aut*): **~ in** *+akk* to change (BRIT) *od* shift into; **„wir schalten jetzt um nach Hamburg"** "and now we go over to Hamburg"
Umschalttaste F shift key
Umschau F look(ing) round; **~ halten nach** to look around for
umschauen ['ʊmʃaʊən] VR to look round
Umschlag ['ʊmʃla:k] M cover; (*Buchumschlag*) jacket, cover; (*Med*) compress; (*Briefumschlag*) envelope; (*Gütermenge*) volume of traffic;

U

(*Wechsel*) change; (*von Hose*) turn-up (BRIT), cuff (*US*)

umschlagen ['ʊmʃla:gən] *unreg* VI to change; (*Naut*) to capsize ▸ VT to knock over; (*Ärmel*) to turn up; (*Seite*) to turn over; (*Waren*) to transfer

Umschlag- ZW: **Umschlaghafen** M port of transshipment; **Umschlagplatz** M (*Comm*) distribution centre (BRIT) *od* center (*US*); **Umschlagseite** F cover page

umschlingen [ʊm'ʃlɪŋən] *unreg* VT UNTR (*Pflanze*) to twine around; (*jdn*) to embrace

umschreiben[1] ['ʊmʃraɪbən] *unreg* VT (*neu umschreiben*) to rewrite; (*übertragen*) to transfer; **~ auf** *+akk* to transfer to

umschreiben[2] [ʊm'ʃraɪbən] *unreg* VT UNTR to paraphrase; (*abgrenzen*) to circumscribe, to define

Umschuldung ['ʊmʃʊldʊŋ] F rescheduling (of debts)

umschulen ['ʊmʃu:lən] VT to retrain; (*Kind*) to send to another school

umschwärmen [ʊm'ʃvɛrmən] VT UNTR to swarm round; (*fig*) to surround, to idolize

Umschweife ['ʊmʃvaɪfə] PL: **ohne ~** without beating about the bush, straight out

umschwenken ['ʊmʃvɛnkən] VI (*Kran*) to swing out; (*fig*) to do an about-turn (BRIT) *od* about-face (*US*); (*Wind*) to veer

Umschwung ['ʊmʃvʊŋ] M (*Gymnastik*) circle; (*fig: ins Gegenteil*) change (around)

umsegeln [ʊm'ze:gəln] VT UNTR to sail around; (*Erde*) to circumnavigate

umsehen ['ʊmze:ən] *unreg* VR to look around *od* about; (*suchen*): **sich ~ (nach)** to look out (for); **ich möchte mich nur mal ~** (*in Geschäft*) I'm just looking

umseitig ['ʊmzaɪtɪç] ADV overleaf

umsetzen ['ʊmzɛtsən] VT (*Waren*) to turn over ▸ VR (*Schüler*) to change places; **etw in die Tat ~** to translate sth into action

Umsicht ['ʊmzɪçt] F prudence, caution

umsichtig ADJ prudent, cautious

umsiedeln ['ʊmzi:dəln] VT to resettle

Umsiedler(in) (**-s, -**) M(F) resettler

umso ['ʊmzo] KONJ: **~ besser/schlimmer** so much the better/worse; **~ mehr, als …** all the more considering …

umsonst [ʊm'zɔnst] ADV in vain; (*gratis*) for nothing

umspringen ['ʊmʃprɪŋən] *unreg* VI to change; **mit jdm ~** to treat sb badly

Umstand ['ʊmʃtant] M circumstance; **Umstände** PL (*fig: Schwierigkeiten*) fuss *sing*; **in anderen Umständen sein** to be pregnant; **Umstände machen** to go to a lot of trouble; **den Umständen entsprechend** much as one would expect (under the circumstances); **die näheren Umstände** further details; **unter Umständen** possibly; **mildernde Umstände** (*Jur*) extenuating circumstances

umständehalber ADV owing to circumstances

umständlich ['ʊmʃtɛntlɪç] ADJ (*Methode*) cumbersome, complicated; (*Ausdrucksweise, Erklärung*) long-winded; (*ungeschickt*) ponderous; **etw ~ machen** to make heavy weather of (doing) sth

Umstandskleid NT maternity dress

Umstandswort NT adverb

umstehend ['ʊmʃte:ənt] ADJ *attrib* (*umseitig*) overleaf; **die Umstehenden** *pl* the bystanders *pl*

Umsteigekarte F transfer ticket

umsteigen ['ʊmʃtaɪgən] *unreg* VI (*Eisenb*) to change; (*fig: umg*): **~ (auf** *+akk***)** to change over (to), to switch (over) (to)

umstellen[1] ['ʊmʃtɛlən] VT (*an anderen Ort*) to change round, to rearrange; (*Tech*) to convert ▸ VR: **sich ~ (auf** *+akk***)** to adapt o.s. (to)

umstellen[2] [ʊm'ʃtɛlən] VT UNTR to surround

Umstellung F change; (*Umgewöhnung*) adjustment; (*Tech*) conversion

umstimmen ['ʊmʃtɪmən] VT (*Mus*) to retune; **jdn ~** to make sb change his mind

umstoßen ['ʊmʃto:sən] *unreg* VT (*lit*) to overturn; (*Plan etc*) to change, to upset

umstritten [ʊm'ʃtrɪtən] ADJ disputed; (*fraglich*) controversial

Umsturz ['ʊmʃtʊrts] M overthrow

umstürzen ['ʊmʃtʏrtsən] VT (*umwerfen*) to overturn ▸ VI to collapse, to fall down; (*Wagen*) to overturn

umstürzlerisch ADJ revolutionary

Umtausch ['ʊmtaʊʃ] M exchange; **diese Waren sind vom ~ ausgeschlossen** these goods cannot be exchanged

umtauschen VT to exchange

Umtriebe ['ʊmtri:bə] PL machinations *pl*, intrigues *pl*

umtun ['ʊmtu:n] *unreg* VR: **sich nach etw ~** to look for sth

umverteilen ['ʊmfɛrtaɪlən] VT to redistribute

umwälzend ['ʊmvɛltsənt] ADJ (*fig*) radical; (*Veränderungen*) sweeping; (*Ereignisse*) revolutionary

Umwälzung F (*fig*) radical change

umwandeln ['ʊmvandəln] VT to change, to convert; (*Elek*) to transform

umwechseln ['ʊmvɛksəln] VT to change

Umweg ['ʊmve:k] M detour; (*fig*) roundabout way

Umwelt ['ʊmvɛlt] F environment; **Umweltallergie** F environmental allergy; **Umweltauto** (*umg*) NT environment-friendly vehicle; **Umweltbelastung** F environmental pollution; **umweltbewusst** ADJ environmentally aware; **Umweltbewusstsein** NT environmental awareness; **umweltfreundlich** ADJ environment-friendly; **umweltfreundliche Technologie** clean technology; **Umweltkrankheit** F environmental illness; **Umweltkriminalität** F crimes *pl* against the environment; **Umweltministerium** NT Ministry of the Environment; **umweltschädlich** ADJ harmful to the environment; **Umweltschutz** M environmental protection; **Umweltschützer** (**-s, -**) M environmentalist; **Umweltsteuer** F

green tax; **Umweltverschmutzung** F pollution (of the environment); **umweltverträglich** ADJ not harmful to the environment; **Umweltverträglichkeit** F ecofriendliness
umwenden ['ʊmvɛndən] *unreg* VT, VR to turn (round)
umwerben [ʊm'vɛrbən] *unreg* VT UNTR to court, to woo
umwerfen ['ʊmvɛrfən] *unreg* VT (*lit*) to upset, to overturn; (*Mantel*) to throw on; (*fig: erschüttern*) to upset, to throw
umwerfend (*umg*) ADJ fantastic
umziehen ['ʊmtsi:ən] *unreg* VT, VR to change ▶ VI to move
umzingeln [ʊm'tsɪŋəln] VT UNTR to surround, to encircle
Umzug ['ʊmtsu:k] M procession; (*Wohnungsumzug*) move, removal
UN PL ABK (= *United Nations*): **die UN** the UN *sing*
un- ZW: **unabänderlich** ADJ irreversible, unalterable; **~ feststehen** to be absolutely certain; **unabdingbar** ADJ indispensable, essential; (*Recht*) inalienable; **unabhängig** ADJ independent; **Unabhängigkeit** F independence; **unabkömmlich** ADJ indispensable; **zur Zeit unabkömmlich** not free at the moment; **unablässig** ADJ incessant, constant; **unabsehbar** ADJ immeasurable; (*Folgen*) unforeseeable; (*Kosten*) incalculable; **unabsichtlich** ADJ unintentional; **unabwendbar** ADJ inevitable
unachtsam ['ʊnlaxtza:m] ADJ careless; **Unachtsamkeit** F carelessness
un- ZW: **unanfechtbar** ADJ indisputable; **unangebracht** ADJ uncalled-for; **unangefochten** ADJ unchallenged; (*Testament, Wahlkandidat, Urteil*) uncontested; **unangemeldet** ADJ unannounced; (*Besucher*) unexpected; **unangemessen** ADJ inadequate; **unangenehm** ADJ unpleasant; (*peinlich*) embarrassing; **unangepasst** ADJ nonconformist; **Unannehmlichkeit** F inconvenience; **Unannehmlichkeiten** PL trouble *sing*; **unansehnlich** ADJ unsightly; **unanständig** ADJ indecent, improper; **Unanständigkeit** F indecency, impropriety; **unantastbar** ADJ inviolable, sacrosanct
unappetitlich ['ʊnlapeti:tlɪç] ADJ unsavoury (BRIT), unsavory (US)
Unart ['ʊnla:rt] F bad manners *pl*; (*Angewohnheit*) bad habit
unartig ADJ naughty, badly behaved
un- ZW: **unaufdringlich** ADJ unobtrusive; (*Parfüm*) discreet; (*Mensch*) unassuming; **unauffällig** ADJ unobtrusive; (*Kleidung*) inconspicuous; **unauffindbar** ADJ not to be found; **unaufgefordert** ADJ unsolicited ▶ ADV unasked, spontaneously; **unaufgefordert zugesandte Manuskripte** unsolicited manuscripts; **unaufhaltsam** ADJ irresistible; **unaufhörlich** ADJ incessant, continuous; **unaufmerksam** ADJ inattentive; **unaufrichtig** ADJ insincere
un- ZW: **unausbleiblich** ADJ inevitable, unavoidable; **unausgeglichen** ADJ volatile; **unausgegoren** ADJ immature; (*Idee, Plan*) half-baked; **unausgesetzt** ADJ incessant, constant; **unausgewogen** ADJ unbalanced; **unaussprechlich** ADJ inexpressible; **unausstehlich** ADJ intolerable; **unausweichlich** ADJ inescapable, ineluctable
unbändig ['ʊnbɛndɪç] ADJ extreme, excessive
unbarmherzig ['ʊnbarmhɛrtsɪç] ADJ pitiless, merciless
unbeabsichtigt ['ʊnbəlapzɪçtɪçt] ADJ unintentional
unbeachtet ['ʊnbəlaxtət] ADJ unnoticed; (*Warnung*) ignored
unbedacht ['ʊnbədaxt] ADJ rash
unbedarft ['ʊnbədarft] (*umg*) ADJ clueless
unbedenklich ['ʊnbədɛŋklɪç] ADJ unhesitating; (*Plan*) unobjectionable ▶ ADV without hesitation
unbedeutend ['ʊnbədɔʏtənt] ADJ insignificant, unimportant; (*Fehler*) slight
unbedingt ['ʊnbədɪŋt] ADJ unconditional ▶ ADV absolutely; **musst du ~ gehen?** do you really have to go?; **nicht ~** not necessarily
unbefangen ['ʊnbəfaŋən] ADJ impartial, unprejudiced; (*ohne Hemmungen*) uninhibited; **Unbefangenheit** F impartiality; (*Hemmungslosigkeit*) uninhibitedness
unbefriedigend ['ʊnbəfri:dɪgənd] ADJ unsatisfactory
unbefriedigt ['ʊnbəfri:dɪçt] ADJ unsatisfied; (*unzufrieden*) dissatisfied; (*unerfüllt*) unfulfilled
unbefristet ['ʊnbəfrɪstət] ADJ permanent
unbefugt ['ʊnbəfu:kt] ADJ unauthorized; **Unbefugten ist der Eintritt verboten** no admittance to unauthorized persons
unbegabt ['ʊnbəga:pt] ADJ untalented
unbegreiflich [ʊnbə'graɪflɪç] ADJ inconceivable
unbegrenzt ['ʊnbəgrɛntst] ADJ unlimited
unbegründet ['ʊnbəgryndət] ADJ unfounded
Unbehagen ['ʊnbəha:gən] NT discomfort
unbehaglich ['ʊnbəha:klɪç] ADJ uncomfortable; (*Gefühl*) uneasy
unbeherrscht ['ʊnbəhɛrʃt] ADJ uncontrolled; (*Mensch*) lacking self-control
unbeholfen ['ʊnbəhɔlfən] ADJ awkward, clumsy; **Unbeholfenheit** F awkwardness, clumsiness
unbeirrt ['ʊnbəlɪrt] ADJ imperturbable
unbekannt ['ʊnbəkant] ADJ unknown; **unbekannte Größe** (*Math, fig*) unknown quantity
unbekannterweise ADV: **grüß(e) sie ~ von mir** give her my regards although I don't know her
unbekümmert ['ʊnbəkʏmərt] ADJ unconcerned
unbelehrbar [ʊnbə'le:rba:r] ADJ fixed in one's views; (*Rassist etc*) dyed-in-the-wool *attrib*
unbeliebt ['ʊnbəli:pt] ADJ unpopular; **Unbeliebtheit** F unpopularity
unbemannt ['ʊnbəmant] ADJ (*Raumflug*) unmanned; (*Flugzeug*) pilotless
unbemerkt ['ʊnbəmɛrkt] ADJ unnoticed

u

unbenommen [ʊnbəˈnɔmən] ADJ (*form*): **es bleibt** *od* **ist Ihnen ~, zu …** you are at liberty to …
unbequem [ˈʊnbəkveːm] ADJ (*Stuhl*) uncomfortable; (*Mensch*) bothersome; (*Regelung*) inconvenient
unberechenbar [ʊnbəˈrɛçənbaːr] ADJ incalculable; (*Mensch, Verhalten*) unpredictable
unberechtigt [ˈʊnbərɛçtɪçt] ADJ unjustified; (*nicht erlaubt*) unauthorized
unberücksichtigt [ʊnbəˈrʏkzɪçtɪçt] ADJ: **etw ~ lassen** not to consider sth
unberufen [ʊnbəˈruːfən] INTERJ touch wood!
unberührt [ˈʊnbəryːrt] ADJ untouched; (*Natur*) unspoiled; **sie ist noch ~** she is still a virgin
unbeschadet [ʊnbəˈʃaːdət] PRÄP +*gen* (*form*) regardless of
unbescheiden [ˈʊnbəʃaɪdən] ADJ presumptuous
unbescholten [ˈʊnbəʃɔltən] ADJ respectable; (*Ruf*) spotless
unbeschrankt [ˈʊnbəʃraŋkt] ADJ (*Bahnübergang*) unguarded
unbeschränkt [ʊnbəˈʃrɛŋkt] ADJ unlimited
unbeschreiblich [ʊnbəˈʃraɪplɪç] ADJ indescribable
unbeschwert [ˈʊnbəʃveːrt] ADJ (*sorgenfrei*) carefree; (*Melodien*) light
unbesehen [ʊnbəˈzeːən] ADV indiscriminately; (*ohne es anzusehen*) without looking at it
unbesonnen [ˈʊnbəzɔnən] ADJ unwise, rash, imprudent
unbesorgt [ˈʊnbəzɔrkt] ADJ unconcerned; **Sie können ganz ~ sein** you can set your mind at rest
unbespielt [ˈʊnbəʃpiːlt] ADJ (*Kassette*) blank
unbest. ABK = **unbestimmt**
unbeständig [ˈʊnbəʃtɛndɪç] ADJ (*Mensch*) inconstant; (*Wetter*) unsettled; (*Lage*) unstable
unbestechlich [ʊnbəˈʃtɛçlɪç] ADJ incorruptible
unbestimmt [ˈʊnbəʃtɪmt] ADJ indefinite; (*Zukunft*) uncertain; **Unbestimmtheit** F vagueness
unbestritten [ˈʊnbəʃtrɪtən] ADJ undisputed
unbeteiligt [ʊnbəˈtaɪlɪçt] ADJ unconcerned; (*uninteressiert*) indifferent
unbeugsam [ˈʊnbɔykzaːm] ADJ stubborn, inflexible; (*Wille*) unbending
unbewacht [ˈʊnbəvaxt] ADJ unguarded, unwatched
unbewaffnet [ˈʊnbəvafnət] ADJ unarmed
unbeweglich [ˈʊnbəveːklɪç] ADJ immovable
unbewegt ADJ motionless; (*fig: unberührt*) unmoved
unbewohnt [ˈʊnbəvoːnt] ADJ (*Gegend*) uninhabited; (*Haus*) unoccupied
unbewusst [ˈʊnbəvʊst] ADJ unconscious
unbezahlbar [ʊnbəˈtsaːlbaːr] ADJ prohibitively expensive; (*fig*) priceless; (*nützlich*) invaluable
unbezahlt [ˈʊnbətsaːlt] ADJ unpaid
unblutig [ˈʊnbluːtɪç] ADJ bloodless
unbrauchbar [ˈʊnbraʊxbaːr] ADJ (*nutzlos*) useless; (*Gerät*) unusable; **Unbrauchbarkeit** F uselessness
unbürokratisch [ˈʊnbyrokratɪʃ] ADJ without any red tape
und [ʊnt] KONJ and; **~ so weiter** and so on; **na ~?** so what?
Undank [ˈʊndaŋk] M ingratitude; **undankbar** ADJ ungrateful; (*Aufgabe*) thankless; **Undankbarkeit** F ingratitude
undefinierbar [ʊndefiˈniːrbaːr] ADJ indefinable
undenkbar [ʊnˈdɛŋkbaːr] ADJ inconceivable
undeutlich [ˈʊndɔytlɪç] ADJ indistinct; (*Schrift*) illegible; (*Ausdrucksweise*) unclear
undicht [ˈʊndɪçt] ADJ leaky
undifferenziert [ˈʊndɪfərɛntsiːrt] ADJ simplistic
Unding [ˈʊndɪŋ] NT absurdity
unduldsam [ˈʊnduldsaːm] ADJ intolerant
un- ZW: **undurchdringlich** ADJ (*Urwald*) impenetrable; (*Gesicht*) inscrutable; **undurchführbar** ADJ impracticable; **undurchlässig** ADJ impervious; (*wasserundurchlässig*) waterproof, impermeable; **undurchschaubar** ADJ inscrutable; **undurchsichtig** ADJ opaque; (*Motive*) obscure; (*fig: pej: Mensch, Methoden*) devious
uneben [ˈʊnleːbən] ADJ uneven
unecht [ˈʊnlɛçt] ADJ artificial; (*Schmuck etc*) fake; (*pej: Freundschaft, Lächeln*) false
unehelich [ˈʊnleːəlɪç] ADJ illegitimate
uneigennützig [ˈʊnlaɪgənnʏtsɪç] ADJ unselfish
uneinbringlich [ʊnlaɪnˈbrɪŋlɪç] ADJ: **uneinbringliche Forderungen** (*Comm*) bad debts *pl*
uneingeschränkt [ˈʊnlaɪngəʃrɛŋkt] ADJ absolute, total; (*Rechte, Handel*) unrestricted; (*Zustimmung*) unqualified
uneinig [ˈʊnlaɪnɪç] ADJ divided; **~ sein** to disagree; **Uneinigkeit** F discord, dissension
uneinnehmbar [ʊnlaɪnˈneːmbaːr] ADJ impregnable
uneins [ˈʊnlaɪns] ADJ at variance, at odds
unempfänglich [ˈʊnlɛmpfɛŋlɪç] ADJ: **~ (für)** not susceptible (to)
unempfindlich [ˈʊnlɛmpfɪntlɪç] ADJ insensitive; **Unempfindlichkeit** F insensitivity
unendlich [ʊnˈlɛntlɪç] ADJ infinite ▶ ADV endlessly; (*fig: sehr*) terribly; **Unendlichkeit** F infinity
un- ZW: **unentbehrlich** ADJ indispensable; **unentgeltlich** ADJ free (of charge); **unentschieden** ADJ undecided; **unentschieden enden** (*Sport*) to end in a draw; **unentschlossen** ADJ undecided; (*entschlusslos*) irresolute; **unentwegt** ADJ unswerving; (*unaufhörlich*) incessant
un- ZW: **unerbittlich** ADJ unyielding, inexorable; **unerfahren** ADJ inexperienced; **unerfreulich** ADJ unpleasant; **Unerfreuliches** (*schlechte Nachrichten*) bad news *sing*; (*Übles*) bad things *pl*; **unerfüllt** ADJ unfulfilled; **unergiebig** ADJ (*Quelle, Thema*) unproductive; (*Ernte, Nachschlagewerk*) poor; **unergründlich** ADJ unfathomable; **unerheblich** ADJ unimportant; **unerhört** ADJ unheard-of; (*unverschämt*) outrageous; (*Bitte*)

unanswered; **unerlässlich** ADJ indispensable; **unerlaubt** ADJ unauthorized; **unerledigt** ADJ unfinished; (*Post*) unanswered; (*Rechnung*) outstanding; (*schwebend*) pending; **unermesslich** ADJ immeasurable, immense; **unermüdlich** ADJ indefatigable; **unersättlich** ADJ insatiable; **unerschlossen** ADJ (*Land*) undeveloped; (*Boden*) unexploited; (*Vorkommen, Markt*) untapped; **unerschöpflich** ADJ inexhaustible; **unerschrocken** ADJ intrepid, courageous; **unerschütterlich** ADJ unshakeable; **unerschwinglich** ADJ (*Preis*) prohibitive; **unersetzlich** ADJ irreplaceable; **unerträglich** ADJ unbearable; (*Frechheit*) insufferable; **unerwartet** ADJ unexpected; **unerwünscht** ADJ undesirable, unwelcome; **unerzogen** ADJ ill-bred, rude

unfähig ['ʊnfɛːɪç] ADJ incapable; (*untüchtig*) incompetent; **zu etw ~ sein** to be incapable of sth; **Unfähigkeit** F inability; (*Untüchtigkeit*) incompetence

unfair ['ʊnfɛːr] ADJ unfair

Unfall ['ʊnfal] M accident; **Unfallflucht** F hit-and-run (driving); **Unfallopfer** NT casualty; **Unfallstation** F emergency ward; **Unfallstelle** F scene of the accident; **Unfallversicherung** F accident insurance; **Unfallwagen** M *car involved in an accident*; (*umg*: *Rettungswagen*) ambulance

unfassbar [ʊn'fasbaːr] ADJ inconceivable

unfehlbar [ʊn'feːlbaːr] ADJ infallible ▸ ADV without fail; **Unfehlbarkeit** F infallibility

unfertig ['ʊnfɛrtɪç] ADJ unfinished, incomplete; (*Mensch*) immature

unflätig ['ʊnflɛːtɪç] ADJ rude

unfolgsam ['ʊnfɔlkzaːm] ADJ disobedient

unförmig ['ʊnfœrmɪç] ADJ (*formlos*) shapeless; (*groß*) cumbersome; (*Füße, Nase*) unshapely

unfrankiert ['ʊnfraŋkiːrt] ADJ unfranked

unfrei ['ʊnfraɪ] ADJ not free

unfreiwillig ADJ involuntary

unfreundlich ['ʊnfrɔʏntlɪç] ADJ unfriendly; **Unfreundlichkeit** F unfriendliness

Unfriede ['ʊnfriːdə], **Unfrieden** ['ʊnfriːdən] M dissension, strife

unfruchtbar ['ʊnfrʊxtbaːr] ADJ infertile; (*Gespräche*) fruitless; **Unfruchtbarkeit** F infertility; (*von Gesprächen*) fruitlessness

Unfug ['ʊnfuːk] (**-s**) M (*Benehmen*) mischief; (*Unsinn*) nonsense; **grober ~** (*Jur*) gross misconduct

Ungar(in) ['ʊŋgar(ɪn)] (**-n, -n**) M(F) Hungarian; **ungarisch** ADJ Hungarian

Ungarn (**-s**) NT Hungary

ungeachtet ['ʊngəlaxtət] PRÄP *+gen* notwithstanding

ungeahndet ['ʊngəlaːndət] ADJ (*Jur*) unpunished

ungeahnt ['ʊngəlaːnt] ADJ unsuspected, undreamt-of

ungebeten ['ʊngəbeːtən] ADJ uninvited

ungebildet ['ʊngəbɪldət] ADJ uncultured; (*ohne Bildung*) uneducated

ungeboren ['ʊngəboːrən] ADJ unborn

ungebräuchlich ['ʊngəbrɔʏçlɪç] ADJ unusual, uncommon

ungebraucht ['ʊngəbraʊxt] ADJ unused

ungebührlich ['ʊngəbyːrlɪç] ADJ: **sich ~ aufregen** to get unduly excited

ungebunden ['ʊngəbʊndən] ADJ (*Buch*) unbound; (*Leben*) (fancy-)free; (*ohne festen Partner*) unattached; (*Pol*) independent

ungedeckt ['ʊngədɛkt] ADJ (*schutzlos*) unprotected; (*Scheck*) uncovered

Ungeduld ['ʊngədʊlt] F impatience

ungeduldig ['ʊngədʊldɪç] ADJ impatient

ungeeignet ['ʊngəlaɪgnət] ADJ unsuitable

ungefähr ['ʊngəfɛːr] ADJ rough, approximate ▸ ADV roughly, approximately; **so ~** more or less; **~ 10 Kilometer** about 10 kilometres; **das kommt nicht von ~** that's hardly surprising

ungefährlich ['ʊngəfɛːrlɪç] ADJ not dangerous, harmless

ungehalten ['ʊngəhaltən] ADJ indignant

ungeheuer ['ʊngəhɔʏər] ADJ huge ▸ ADV (*umg*) enormously; **Ungeheuer** (**-s, -**) NT monster; **ungeheuerlich** [ʊngə'hɔʏərlɪç] ADJ monstrous

ungehindert ['ʊngəhɪndərt] ADJ unimpeded

ungehobelt ['ʊngəhoːbəlt] ADJ (*fig*) uncouth

ungehörig ['ʊngəhøːrɪç] ADJ impertinent, improper; **Ungehörigkeit** F impertinence

ungehorsam ['ʊngəhoːrzaːm] ADJ disobedient; **Ungehorsam** M disobedience

ungeklärt ['ʊngəklɛːrt] ADJ not cleared up; (*Rätsel*) unsolved; (*Abwasser*) untreated

ungekürzt ['ʊngəkʏrtst] ADJ not shortened; (*Film*) uncut

ungeladen ['ʊngəlaːdən] ADJ not loaded; (*Elek*) uncharged; (*Gast*) uninvited

ungelegen ['ʊngəleːgən] ADJ inconvenient; **komme ich (Ihnen) ~?** is this an inconvenient time for you?

ungelernt ['ʊngəlɛrnt] ADJ unskilled

ungelogen ['ʊngəloːgən] ADV really, honestly

ungemein ['ʊngəmaɪn] ADJ immense

ungemütlich ['ʊngəmyːtlɪç] ADJ uncomfortable; (*Person*) disagreeable; **er kann ~ werden** he can get nasty

ungenau ['ʊngənaʊ] ADJ inaccurate

Ungenauigkeit F inaccuracy

ungeniert ['ʊnʒeniːrt] ADJ free and easy; (*bedenkenlos, taktlos*) uninhibited ▸ ADV without embarrassment, freely

ungenießbar ['ʊngəniːsbaːr] ADJ inedible; (*nicht zu trinken*) undrinkable; (*umg*) unbearable

ungenügend ['ʊngənyːgənt] ADJ insufficient, inadequate; (*Sch*) unsatisfactory

ungenutzt ['ʊngənʊtst] ADJ: **eine Chance ~ lassen** to miss an opportunity

ungepflegt ['ʊngəpfleːkt] ADJ (*Garten etc*) untended; (*Person*) unkempt; (*Hände*) neglected

ungerade ['ʊngəraːdə] ADJ odd, uneven (*US*)

ungerecht ['ʊngərɛçt] ADJ unjust

ungerechtfertigt ADJ unjustified

Ungerechtigkeit F unfairness, injustice

ungeregelt ['ʊngəreːgəlt] ADJ irregular

ungereimt ['ʊngəraɪmt] ADJ (*Verse*) unrhymed; (*fig*) inconsistent
ungern ['ʊngɛrn] ADV unwillingly, reluctantly
ungerufen ['ʊngəru:fən] ADJ without being called
ungeschehen ['ʊngəʃe:ən] ADJ: **~ machen** to undo
Ungeschicklichkeit ['ʊngəʃɪklɪçkaɪt] F clumsiness
ungeschickt ADJ awkward, clumsy
ungeschliffen ['ʊngəʃlɪfən] ADJ (*Edelstein*) uncut; (*Messer etc*) blunt; (*fig: Benehmen*) uncouth
ungeschmälert ['ʊngəʃmɛ:lərt] ADJ undiminished
ungeschminkt ['ʊngəʃmɪŋkt] ADJ without make-up; (*fig*) unvarnished
ungeschoren ['ʊngəʃo:rən] ADJ: **jdn ~ lassen** (*umg*) to spare sb; (*ungestraft*) to let sb off
ungesetzlich ['ʊngəzɛtslɪç] ADJ illegal
ungestempelt ['ʊngəʃtɛmpəlt] ADJ (*Briefmarke*) unfranked, mint
ungestört ['ʊngəʃtø:rt] ADJ undisturbed
ungestraft ['ʊngəʃtra:ft] ADV with impunity
ungestüm ['ʊngəʃty:m] ADJ impetuous; **Ungestüm** (**-(e)s**) NT impetuosity
ungesund ['ʊngəzʊnt] ADJ unhealthy
ungetrübt ['ʊngətry:pt] ADJ clear; (*fig*) untroubled; (*Freude*) unalloyed
Ungetüm ['ʊngəty:m] (**-(e)s, -e**) NT monster
ungeübt ['ʊngəly:pt] ADJ unpractised (BRIT), unpracticed (US); (*Mensch*) out of practice
ungewiss ['ʊngəvɪs] ADJ uncertain; **Ungewissheit** F uncertainty
ungewöhnlich ['ʊngəvø:nlɪç] ADJ unusual
ungewohnt ['ʊngəvo:nt] ADJ unusual
ungewollt ['ʊngəvɔlt] ADJ unintentional
Ungeziefer ['ʊngətsi:fər] (**-s**) NT vermin *pl*
ungezogen ['ʊngətso:gən] ADJ rude, impertinent; **Ungezogenheit** F rudeness, impertinence
ungezwungen ['ʊngətsvʊŋən] ADJ natural, unconstrained
ungläubig ['ʊnglɔʏbɪç] ADJ unbelieving; **ein ungläubiger Thomas** a doubting Thomas; **die Ungläubigen** the infidel(s *pl*)
unglaublich [ʊn'glaʊplɪç] ADJ incredible
unglaubwürdig ['ʊnglaʊpvʏrdɪç] ADJ untrustworthy, unreliable; (*Geschichte*) improbable; **sich ~ machen** to lose credibility
ungleich ['ʊnglaɪç] ADJ dissimilar; (*Mittel, Waffen*) unequal ▸ ADV incomparably; **ungleichartig** ADJ different; **Ungleichbehandlung** F (*von Frauen, Ausländern*) unequal treatment; **Ungleichheit** F dissimilarity; (*von Mitteln, Waffen*) inequality; **ungleichmäßig** ADJ uneven; (*Atemzüge, Gesichtszüge, Puls*) irregular
Unglück ['ʊnglʏk] NT misfortune; (*Pech*) bad luck; (*Unglücksfall*) calamity, disaster; (*Verkehrsunglück*) accident; **zu allem ~** to make matters worse; **unglücklich** ADJ unhappy; (*erfolglos*) unlucky; (*unerfreulich*) unfortunate; **unglücklicherweise** ADV unfortunately; **unglückselig** ADJ calamitous; (*Person*) unfortunate
Unglücksfall M accident, mishap
Unglücksrabe (*umg*) M unlucky thing
Ungnade ['ʊngna:də] F: **bei jdm in ~ fallen** to fall out of favour (BRIT) *od* favor (US) with sb
ungültig ['ʊngʏltɪç] ADJ invalid; **etw für ~ erklären** to declare sth null and void; **Ungültigkeit** F invalidity
ungünstig ['ʊngʏnstɪç] ADJ unfavourable (BRIT), unfavorable (US); (*Termin*) inconvenient; (*Augenblick, Wetter*) bad; (*nicht preiswert*) expensive
ungut ['ʊngu:t] ADJ (*Gefühl*) uneasy; **nichts für ~!** no offence!
unhaltbar ['ʊnhaltba:r] ADJ untenable
unhandlich ['ʊnhantlɪç] ADJ unwieldy
Unheil ['ʊnhaɪl] NT evil; (*Unglück*) misfortune; **~ anrichten** to cause mischief; **~ bringend** fatal, fateful
unheilbar [un'haɪlbar] ADJ incurable; **~ krank** terminally ill
unheilvoll ADJ disastrous
unheimlich ['ʊnhaɪmlɪç] ADJ weird, uncanny ▸ ADV (*umg*) tremendously; **das/er ist mir ~** it/he gives me the creeps (*umg*)
unhöflich ['ʊnhø:flɪç] ADJ impolite; **Unhöflichkeit** F impoliteness
unhörbar [ʊn'hø:rba:r] ADJ silent; (*Frequenzen*) inaudible
unhygienisch ['ʊnhygie:nɪʃ] ADJ unhygienic
uni ['yni:] ADJ self-coloured (BRIT), self-colored (US)
Uni ['ʊni] (**-, -s**) (*umg*) F university
Uniform [uni'fɔrm] (**-, -en**) F uniform
uniformiert [unifɔr'mi:rt] ADJ uniformed
Unikum ['u:nɪkʊm] (**-s, -s** *od* **Unika**) (*umg*) NT real character
uninteressant ['ʊnlɪnterɛsant] ADJ uninteresting
uninteressiert ['ʊnlɪntərɛ'si:rt] ADJ: **~ (an** *+dat*) uninterested (in), not interested (in)
Union [uni'o:n] F union
Unionsparteien PL (*Pol*) CDU and CSU parties *pl*
universal [univɛr'za:l] ADJ universal
universell [univɛr'zɛl] ADJ universal
Universität [univɛrzi'tɛ:t] F university; **auf die ~ gehen, die ~ besuchen** to go to university
Universum [uni'vɛrzʊm] (**-s**) NT universe
unkenntlich ['ʊnkɛntlɪç] ADJ unrecognizable; **Unkenntlichkeit** F: **bis zur Unkenntlichkeit** beyond recognition
Unkenntnis ['ʊnkɛntnɪs] F ignorance
unklar ['ʊnkla:r] ADJ unclear; **im Unklaren sein über** *+akk* to be in the dark about; **Unklarheit** F unclarity; (*Unentschiedenheit*) uncertainty
unklug ['ʊnklu:k] ADJ unwise
unkompliziert ['ʊnkɔmplitsi:rt] ADJ straightforward, uncomplicated
unkontrolliert ['ʊnkɔntrɔli:rt] ADJ unchecked
unkonzentriert ['ʊnkɔntsɛntri:rt] ADJ lacking in concentration
Unkosten ['ʊnkɔstən] PL expense(s *pl*); **sich in ~ stürzen** (*umg*) to go to a lot of expense

Unkraut ['ʊnkraʊt] NT weeds *pl*; (*einzelne Pflanze*) weed; **~ vergeht nicht** (*Sprichwort*) it would take more than that to finish me/him *etc* off; **Unkrautvertilgungsmittel** NT weedkiller
unlängst ['ʊnlɛŋst] ADV not long ago
unlauter ['ʊnlaʊtər] ADJ unfair
unleserlich ['ʊnle:zərlɪç] ADJ illegible
unleugbar ['ʊnlɔʏkba:r] ADJ undeniable, indisputable
unlogisch ['ʊnlo:gɪʃ] ADJ illogical
unlösbar [ʊn'lø:sbar] ADJ insoluble
unlöslich [ʊn'lø:slɪç] ADJ insoluble
Unlust ['ʊnlʊst] F lack of enthusiasm
unlustig ADJ unenthusiastic ▶ ADV without enthusiasm
unmännlich ['ʊnmɛnlɪç] ADJ unmanly
Unmasse ['ʊnmasə] (*umg*) F load
unmäßig ['ʊnmɛ:sɪç] ADJ immoderate
Unmenge ['ʊnmɛŋə] F tremendous number, vast number
Unmensch ['ʊnmɛnʃ] M ogre, brute; **unmenschlich** ADJ inhuman, brutal; (*ungeheuer*) awful
unmerklich [ʊn'mɛrklɪç] ADJ imperceptible
unmissverständlich ['ʊnmɪsfɛrʃtɛntlɪç] ADJ unmistakable
unmittelbar ['ʊnmɪtəlba:r] ADJ immediate; **unmittelbarer Kostenaufwand** direct expense
unmöbliert ['ʊnmøbli:rt] ADJ unfurnished
unmöglich ['ʊnmø:klɪç] ADJ impossible; **ich kann es ~ tun** I can't possibly do it; **~ aussehen** (*umg*) to look ridiculous; **Unmöglichkeit** F impossibility
unmoralisch ['ʊnmora:lɪʃ] ADJ immoral
unmotiviert ['ʊnmotivi:rt] ADJ unmotivated
unmündig ['ʊnmʏndɪç] ADJ (*minderjährig*) underage
Unmut ['ʊnmu:t] M ill humour (BRIT) *od* humor (*US*)
unnachahmlich ['ʊnna:x|a:mlɪç] ADJ inimitable
unnachgiebig ['ʊnna:xgi:bɪç] ADJ unyielding
unnahbar [ʊn'na:ba:r] ADJ unapproachable
unnatürlich ['ʊnnaty:rlɪç] ADJ unnatural
unnormal ['ʊnnɔrma:l] ADJ abnormal
unnötig ['ʊnnø:tɪç] ADJ unnecessary
unnötigerweise ADV unnecessarily
unnütz ['ʊnnʏts] ADJ useless
UNO ['u:no] F ABK (= *United Nations Organization*): **die ~** the UN
unordentlich ['ʊn|ɔrdəntlɪç] ADJ untidy
Unordnung ['ʊn|ɔrdnʊŋ] F disorder; (*Durcheinander*) mess
unorganisiert ['ʊn|ɔrganizi:rt] ADJ disorganized
unparteiisch ['ʊnpartaɪɪʃ] ADJ impartial
Unparteiische(r) F(M) umpire; (*Fussball*) referee
unpassend ['ʊnpasənt] ADJ inappropriate; (*Zeit*) inopportune
unpässlich ['ʊnpɛslɪç] ADJ unwell
unpersönlich ['ʊnpɛrzø:nlɪç] ADJ impersonal
unpolitisch ['ʊnpoli:tɪʃ] ADJ apolitical
unpraktisch ['ʊnpraktɪʃ] ADJ impractical, unpractical
unproduktiv ['ʊnprodʊkti:f] ADJ unproductive
unproportioniert ['ʊnproportsioni:rt] ADJ out of proportion
unpünktlich ['ʊnpʏŋktlɪç] ADJ unpunctual
unqualifiziert ['ʊnkvalifitsi:rt] ADJ unqualified; (*Äußerung*) incompetent
unrasiert ['ʊnrazi:rt] ADJ unshaven
Unrat ['ʊnra:t] (**-(e)s**) M (*geh*) refuse; (*fig*) filth
unrationell ['ʊnratsionɛl] ADJ inefficient
unrecht ['ʊnrɛçt] ADJ wrong; **das ist mir gar nicht so ~** I don't really mind; **~ haben** to be wrong; **Unrecht** NT wrong; **zu Unrecht** wrongly; **nicht zu Unrecht** not without good reason; **im Unrecht sein** to be wrong
unrechtmäßig ADJ unlawful, illegal
unredlich ['ʊnre:tlɪç] ADJ dishonest; **Unredlichkeit** F dishonesty
unreell ['ʊnreɛl] ADJ unfair; (*unredlich*) dishonest; (*Preis*) unreasonable
unregelmäßig ['ʊnre:gəlmɛ:sɪç] ADJ irregular; **Unregelmäßigkeit** F irregularity
unreif ['ʊnraɪf] ADJ (*Obst*) unripe; (*fig*) immature
Unreife F immaturity
unrein ['ʊnraɪn] ADJ not clean; (*Ton, Gedanken, Taten*) impure; (*Atem, Haut*) bad
unrentabel ['ʊnrɛnta:bəl] ADJ unprofitable
unrichtig ['ʊnrɪçtɪç] ADJ incorrect, wrong
Unruh ['ʊnru:] (**-, -en**) F (*von Uhr*) balance
Unruhe (**-, -n**) F unrest; **Unruheherd** M trouble spot; **Unruhestifter** M troublemaker
unruhig ADJ restless; (*nervös*) fidgety; (*belebt*) noisy; (*Schlaf*) fitful; (*Zeit etc, Meer*) troubled
unrühmlich ['ʊnry:mlɪç] ADJ inglorious
uns [ʊns] PRON *akk, dat von* **wir** us; (*reflexiv*) ourselves
unsachgemäß ['ʊnzaxgəmɛ:s] ADJ improper
unsachlich ['ʊnzaxlɪç] ADJ not to the point, irrelevant; (*persönlich*) personal
unsagbar [ʊn'za:kba:r] ADJ indescribable
unsäglich [ʊn'zɛ:klɪç] ADJ indescribable
unsanft ['ʊnzanft] ADJ rough
unsauber ['ʊnzaʊbər] ADJ (*schmutzig*) dirty; (*fig*) crooked; (*: Klang*) impure
unschädlich ['ʊnʃɛ:tlɪç] ADJ harmless; **jdn/etw ~ machen** to render sb/sth harmless
unscharf ['ʊnʃarf] ADJ indistinct; (*Bild etc*) out of focus, blurred
unschätzbar [ʊn'ʃɛtsba:r] ADJ incalculable; (*Hilfe*) invaluable
unscheinbar ['ʊnʃaɪnba:r] ADJ insignificant; (*Aussehen, Haus etc*) unprepossessing
unschlagbar [ʊn'ʃla:kba:r] ADJ invincible
unschlüssig ['ʊnʃlʏsɪç] ADJ undecided
unschön ['ʊnʃø:n] ADJ unsightly; (*lit, fig: Szene*) ugly; (*Vorfall*) unpleasant
Unschuld ['ʊnʃʊlt] F innocence
unschuldig ['ʊnʃʊldɪç] ADJ innocent
Unschuldsmiene F innocent expression
unschwer ['ʊnʃve:r] ADV easily, without difficulty

U

unselbstständig ['ʊnzɛlpstʃtɛndɪç], **unselbständig** ['ʊnzɛlpʃtɛndɪç] ADJ dependent, over-reliant on others
unselig ['ʊnze:lɪç] ADJ unfortunate; *(verhängnisvoll)* ill-fated
unser ['ʊnzər] POSS PRON our ▶ PRON *gen von* **wir** of us
unsere(r, s) POSS PRON ours; **wir tun das U~** *(geh)* we are doing our bit
unsereiner PRON the likes of us
unsereins PRON the likes of us
unsererseits ['ʊnzərər'zaɪts] ADV on our part
unseresgleichen PRON the likes of us
unserige(r, s) POSS PRON: **der/die/das U~** ours
unseriös ['ʊnzeriø:s] ADJ *(unehrlich)* not straight, untrustworthy
unserseits ['ʊnzər'zaɪts] ADV = **unsererseits**
unsertwegen ['ʊnzərt've:gən] ADV *(für uns)* for our sake; *(wegen uns)* on our account
unsertwillen ['ʊnzərt'vɪlən] ADV: **um ~** = **unsertwegen**
unsicher ['ʊnzɪçər] ADJ uncertain; *(Mensch)* insecure; **die Gegend ~ machen** *(fig: umg)* to knock about the district; **Unsicherheit** F uncertainty; *(von Mensch)* insecurity
unsichtbar ['ʊnzɪçtba:r] ADJ invisible; **Unsichtbarkeit** F invisibility
Unsinn ['ʊnzɪn] M nonsense
unsinnig ADJ nonsensical
Unsitte ['ʊnzɪtə] F deplorable habit
unsittlich ['ʊnzɪtlɪç] ADJ indecent; **Unsittlichkeit** F indecency
unsolide ['ʊnzoli:də] ADJ *(Mensch, Leben)* loose; *(Firma)* unreliable
unsozial ['ʊnzotsia:l] ADJ *(Verhalten)* antisocial; *(Politik)* unsocial
unsportlich ['ʊnʃpɔrtlɪç] ADJ not sporty; *(Verhalten)* unsporting
unsre *etc* ['ʊnzrə] POSS PRON = **unsere(r, s)** *usw*; *siehe auch* **unser**
unsrige(r, s) ['ʊnzrɪgə(r, s)] POSS PRON = **unserige(r, s)**
unsterblich ['ʊnʃtɛrplɪç] ADJ immortal; **Unsterblichkeit** F immortality
unstet ['ʊnʃte:t] ADJ *(Mensch)* restless; *(wankelmütig)* changeable; *(Leben)* unsettled
Unstimmigkeit ['ʊnʃtɪmɪçkaɪt] F inconsistency; *(Streit)* disagreement
Unsumme ['ʊnzʊmə] F vast sum
unsympathisch ['ʊnzʏmpa:tɪʃ] ADJ unpleasant; **er ist mir ~** I don't like him
untadelig ['ʊnta:dəlɪç], **untadlig** ['ʊnta:dlɪç] ADJ impeccable; *(Mensch)* beyond reproach
Untat ['ʊnta:t] F atrocity
untätig ['ʊntɛ:tɪç] ADJ idle
untauglich ['ʊntaʊklɪç] ADJ unsuitable; *(Mil)* unfit; **Untauglichkeit** F unsuitability; *(Mil)* unfitness
unteilbar [ʊn'taɪlba:r] ADJ indivisible
unten ['ʊntən] ADV below; *(im Haus)* downstairs; *(an der Treppe etc)* at the bottom; **~ genannt** undermentioned; **siehe ~** see below; **nach ~** down; **~ am Berg** *etc* at the bottom of the mountain *etc*; **er ist bei mir ~ durch** *(umg)* I'm through with him; **untenan** ADV *(am unteren Ende)* at the far end; *(lit, fig)* at the bottom

SCHLÜSSELWORT

unter ['ʊntər] PRÄP *+dat* **1** *(räumlich)* under; *(drunter)* underneath, below
2 *(zwischen)* among(st); **sie waren unter sich** they were by themselves; **einer unter ihnen** one of them; **unter anderem** among other things; **unter der Hand** secretly; *(verkaufen)* privately
▶ PRÄP *+akk* under, below
▶ ADV *(weniger als)* under; **Mädchen unter 18 Jahren** girls under *od* less than 18 (years of age)

Unter- zW: **Unterabteilung** F subdivision; **Unterarm** M forearm; **unterbelegt** ADJ *(Kurs)* under-subscribed; *(Hotel etc)* not full
unterbelichten ['ʊntərbəlɪçtən] VT UNTR *(Phot)* to underexpose
Unterbeschäftigung ['ʊntərbəʃɛ:ftɪgʊŋ] F underemployment
unterbesetzt ['ʊntərbəzɛtst] ADJ understaffed
Unterbewusstsein ['ʊntərbəvʊstzaɪn] NT subconscious
unterbezahlt ['ʊntərbətsa:lt] ADJ underpaid
unterbieten [ʊntər'bi:tən] *unreg* VT UNTR *(Comm)* to undercut; *(fig)* to surpass
unterbinden [ʊntər'bɪndən] *unreg* VT UNTR to stop, to call a halt to
unterbleiben [ʊntər'blaɪbən] *unreg* VI UNTR *(aufhören)* to stop; *(versäumt werden)* to be omitted
Unterbodenschutz [ʊntər'bo:dənʃʊts] M *(Aut)* underseal
unterbrechen [ʊntər'brɛçən] *unreg* VT UNTR to interrupt
Unterbrechung F interruption
unterbreiten [ʊntər'braɪtən] VT UNTR *(Plan)* to present
unterbringen ['ʊntərbrɪŋən] *unreg* VT *(in Koffer)* to stow; *(in Zeitung)* to place; *(Person: in Hotel etc)* to accommodate, to put up; (: *beruflich*): **~ (bei)** to fix up (with)
unterbuttern ['ʊntərbʊtərn] *(umg)* VT *(zuschießen)* to throw in; *(unterdrücken)* to ride roughshod over
unterdessen [ʊntər'dɛsən] ADV meanwhile
Unterdruck ['ʊntərdrʊk] M *(Tech)* below atmospheric pressure
unterdrücken [ʊntər'drʏkən] VT UNTR to suppress; *(Leute)* to oppress
untere(r, s) ['ʊntərə(r, s)] ADJ lower
untereinander [ʊntər|aɪ'nandər] ADV *(gegenseitig)* each other; *(miteinander)* among themselves *etc*
unterentwickelt ['ʊntər|ɛntvɪkəlt] ADJ underdeveloped
unterernährt ['ʊntər|ɛrnɛ:rt] ADJ undernourished
Unterernährung F malnutrition
Unterfangen [ʊntər'faŋən] NT undertaking

Unterführung [ʊntərˈfyːrʊŋ] F subway, underpass
Untergang [ˈʊntərgaŋ] M (down)fall, decline; (*Naut*) sinking; (*von Gestirn*) setting; **dem ~ geweiht sein** to be doomed
untergeben [ʊntərˈgeːbən] ADJ subordinate
Untergebene(r) F(M) subordinate
untergehen [ˈʊntərgeːən] *unreg* VI to go down; (*Sonne*) to set, to go down; (*Staat*) to fall; (*Volk*) to perish; (*Welt*) to come to an end; (*im Lärm*) to be drowned
untergeordnet [ˈʊntərgəlɔrdnət] ADJ (*Dienststelle*) subordinate; (*Bedeutung*) secondary
Untergeschoss [ˈʊntərgəʃɔs] NT basement
Untergewicht [ˈʊntərgəvɪçt] NT: **(10 Kilo) ~ haben** to be (10 kilos) underweight
untergliedern [ʊntərˈgliːdərn] VT UNTR to subdivide
untergraben [ʊntərˈgraːbən] *unreg* VT UNTR to undermine
Untergrund [ˈʊntərgrʊnt] M foundation; (*Pol*) underground; **Untergrundbahn** F underground (BRIT), subway (*US*); **Untergrundbewegung** F underground (movement)
unterhaken [ˈʊntərhaːkən] VR: **sich bei jdm ~** to link arms with sb
unterhalb [ˈʊntərhalp] PRÄP *+gen* below ▸ ADV below; **~ von** below
Unterhalt [ˈʊntərhalt] M maintenance; **seinen ~ verdienen** to earn one's living
unterhalten [ʊntərˈhaltən] *unreg* VT UNTR to maintain; (*belustigen*) to entertain; (*versorgen*) to support; (*Geschäft, Kfz*) to run; (*Konto*) to have ▸ VR UNTR to talk; (*sich belustigen*) to enjoy o.s.
unterhaltend, unterhaltsam [ʊntərˈhaltzaːm] ADJ entertaining
Unterhaltskosten PL maintenance costs *pl*
Unterhaltszahlung F maintenance payment
Unterhaltung F maintenance; (*Belustigung*) entertainment, amusement; (*Gespräch*) talk
Unterhaltungskosten PL running costs *pl*
Unterhaltungsmusik F light music
Unterhändler [ˈʊntərhɛntlər] M negotiator
Unterhaus [ˈʊntərhaus] NT House of Commons (BRIT), House of Representatives (*US*), Lower House
Unterhemd [ˈʊntərhɛmt] NT vest (BRIT), undershirt (*US*)
unterhöhlen [ʊntərˈhøːlən] VT UNTR (*lit, fig*) to undermine
Unterholz [ˈʊntərhɔlts] NT undergrowth
Unterhose [ˈʊntərhoːzə] F underpants *pl*
unterirdisch [ˈʊntərlɪrdɪʃ] ADJ underground
unterjubeln [ˈʊntərjubəln] (*umg*) VT: **jdm etw ~** to palm sth off on sb
unterkapitalisiert [ˈʊntərkapitaliˈziːrt] ADJ undercapitalized
unterkellern [ʊntərˈkɛlərn] VT UNTR to build with a cellar
Unterkiefer [ˈʊntərkiːfər] M lower jaw
unterkommen [ˈʊntərkɔmən] *unreg* VI to find shelter; (*Stelle finden*) to find work; **das ist mir noch nie untergekommen** I've never met with that; **bei jdm ~** to stay at sb's (place)
unterkriegen [ˈʊntərkriːgən] (*umg*) VT: **sich nicht ~ lassen** not to let things get one down
unterkühlt [ʊntərˈkyːlt] ADJ (*Körper*) affected by hypothermia; (*fig: Mensch, Atmosphäre*) cool
Unterkunft [ˈʊntərkʊnft] (-, **-künfte**) F accommodation (BRIT), accommodations *pl* (*US*); **~ und Verpflegung** board and lodging
Unterlage [ˈʊntərlaːgə] F foundation; (*Beleg*) document; (*Schreibunterlage etc*) pad
unterlassen [ʊntərˈlasən] *unreg* VT UNTR (*versäumen*) to fail to do; (*sich enthalten*) to refrain from
unterlaufen [ʊntərˈlaʊfən] *unreg* VI UNTR to happen ▸ ADJ: **mit Blut ~** suffused with blood; (*Augen*) bloodshot; **mir ist ein Fehler ~** I made a mistake
unterlegen[1] [ˈʊntərleːgən] VT to lay *od* put under
unterlegen[2] [ʊntərˈleːgən] ADJ inferior; (*besiegt*) defeated
Unterleib [ˈʊntərlaɪp] M abdomen
unterliegen [ʊntərˈliːgən] *unreg* VI UNTR *+dat* to be defeated *od* overcome (by); (*unterworfen sein*) to be subject (to)
Unterlippe [ˈʊntərlɪpə] F bottom *od* lower lip
unterm = **unter dem**
untermalen [ʊntərˈmaːlən] VT UNTR (*mit Musik*) to provide with background music
Untermalung F: **musikalische ~** background music
untermauern [ʊntərˈmauərn] VT UNTR (*Gebäude, fig*) to underpin
Untermiete [ˈʊntərmiːtə] F subtenancy; **bei jdm zur ~ wohnen** to rent a room from sb
Untermieter(in) M(F) lodger
untern = **unter den**
unternehmen [ʊntərˈneːmən] *unreg* VT UNTR to do; (*durchführen*) to undertake; (*Versuch, Reise*) to make; **Unternehmen** (**-s, -**) NT undertaking, enterprise (*auch Comm*); (*Firma*) business
unternehmend ADJ enterprising, daring
Unternehmensberater M management consultant
Unternehmensplanung F corporate planning, management planning
Unternehmer(in) [ʊntərˈneːmər(ɪn)] (**-s, -**) M(F) (business) employer; (*alten Stils*) entrepreneur; **Unternehmerverband** M employers' association
Unternehmungsgeist M spirit of enterprise
unternehmungslustig ADJ enterprising
Unteroffizier [ˈʊntərlɔfɪtsiːr] M noncommissioned officer, NCO
unterordnen [ˈʊntərlɔrdnən] VT: **~** (*+dat*) to subordinate (to)
Unterordnung F subordination
Unterprima [ˈʊntərpriːma] F (*früher*) *eighth year of German secondary school*
Unterprogramm [ˈʊntərprogram] NT (*Comput*) subroutine
Unterredung [ʊntərˈreːdʊŋ] F discussion, talk

Unterricht [ˈʊntərrɪçt] (**-(e)s**) M teaching; (*Stunden*) lessons *pl*; **jdm ~ (in etw** *dat***) geben** to teach sb (sth)
unterrichten [ʊntərˈrɪçtən] VT UNTR to instruct; (*Sch*) to teach ▶ VR UNTR: **sich ~ (über** *+akk*) to inform o.s. (about), to obtain information (about)
Unterrichts- ZW: **Unterrichtsgegenstand** M topic, subject; **Unterrichtsmethode** F teaching method; **Unterrichtsstoff** M teaching material; **Unterrichtsstunde** F lesson; **Unterrichtszwecke** PL: **zu Unterrichtszwecken** for teaching purposes
Unterrock [ˈʊntərrɔk] M petticoat, slip
unters = **unter das**
untersagen [ʊntərˈza:gən] VT UNTR to forbid; **jdm etw ~** to forbid sb to do sth
Untersatz [ˈʊntərzats] M mat; (*für Blumentöpfe etc*) base
unterschätzen [ʊntərˈʃɛtsən] VT UNTR to underestimate
unterscheiden [ʊntərˈʃaɪdən] *unreg* VT UNTR to distinguish ▶ VR UNTR to differ
Unterscheidung F (*Unterschied*) distinction; (*Unterscheiden*) differentiation
Unterschenkel [ˈʊntərʃɛŋkəl] M lower leg
Unterschicht [ˈʊntərʃɪçt] F lower class
unterschieben [ˈʊntərʃi:bən] *unreg* VT (*fig*): **jdm etw ~** to foist sth on sb
Unterschied [ˈʊntərʃi:t] (**-(e)s, -e**) M difference, distinction; **im ~ zu** as distinct from; **unterschiedlich** ADJ varying, differing; (*diskriminierend*) discriminatory
unterschiedslos ADV indiscriminately
unterschlagen [ʊntərˈʃlagən] *unreg* VT UNTR to embezzle; (*verheimlichen*) to suppress
Unterschlagung F embezzlement; (*von Briefen, Beweis*) withholding
Unterschlupf [ˈʊntərʃlʊpf] (**-(e)s, -schlüpfe**) M refuge
unterschlüpfen [ˈʊntərʃlʏpfən] (*umg*) VI to take cover *od* shelter; (*Versteck finden*): **(bei jdm) ~** to hide out (at sb's) (*umg*)
unterschreiben [ʊntərˈʃraɪbən] *unreg* VT UNTR to sign
Unterschrift [ˈʊntərʃrɪft] F signature; (*Bildunterschrift*) caption
unterschwellig [ˈʊntərʃvɛlɪç] ADJ subliminal
Unterseeboot [ˈʊntərze:bo:t] NT submarine
Unterseite [ˈʊntərzaɪtə] F underside
Untersekunda [ˈʊntərzekunda] F (*früher*) *sixth year of German secondary school*
Untersetzer [ˈʊntərzɛtsər] M tablemat; (*für Gläser*) coaster
untersetzt [ʊntərˈzɛtst] ADJ stocky
unterste(r, s) [ˈʊntərstə(r, s)] ADJ lowest, bottom
unterstehen¹ [ʊntərˈʃte:ən] *unreg* VI UNTR *+dat* to be under ▶ VR UNTR to dare
unterstehen² [ˈʊntərʃte:ən] *unreg* VI to shelter
unterstellen¹ [ʊntərˈʃtɛlən] VT UNTR to subordinate; (*fig*) to impute; **jdm/etw unterstellt sein** to be under sb/sth; (*in Firma*) to report to sb/sth
unterstellen² [ˈʊntərʃtɛlən] VT (*Auto*) to garage, to park ▶ VR to take shelter
Unterstellung F (*falsche Behauptung*) misrepresentation; (*Andeutung*) insinuation
unterstreichen [ʊntərˈʃtraɪçən] *unreg* VT UNTR (*lit, fig*) to underline
Unterstufe [ˈʊntərʃtu:fə] F lower grade
unterstützen [ʊntərˈʃtʏtsən] VT UNTR to support
Unterstützung F support, assistance
untersuchen [ʊntərˈzu:xən] VT UNTR (*Med*) to examine; (*Polizei*) to investigate; **sich ärztlich ~ lassen** to have a medical (*BRIT*) *od* physical (*US*) (examination), have a check-up
Untersuchung F examination; (*polizeilich*) investigation, inquiry
Untersuchungs- ZW: **Untersuchungsausschuss** M committee of inquiry; **Untersuchungsergebnis** NT (*Jur*) findings *pl*; (*Med*) result of an examination; **Untersuchungshaft** F custody; **in Untersuchungshaft sein** to be remanded in custody; **Untersuchungsrichter** M examining magistrate
Untertagebau [ʊntərˈta:gəbau] M underground mining
Untertan [ˈʊntərta:n] (**-s, -en**) M subject
untertänig [ˈʊntərtɛ:nɪç] ADJ submissive, humble
Untertasse [ˈʊntərtasə] F saucer
untertauchen [ˈʊntərtauxən] VI to dive; (*fig*) to disappear, to go underground
Unterteil [ˈʊntərtaɪl] NT OD M lower part, bottom
unterteilen [ʊntərˈtaɪlən] VT UNTR to divide up
Untertertia [ˈʊntərtɛrtsia] F (*früher*) *fourth year of German secondary school*
Untertitel [ˈʊntərti:təl] M subtitle; (*für Bild*) caption
unterwandern [ʊntərˈvandərn] VT UNTR to infiltrate
Unterwäsche [ˈʊntərvɛʃə] F underwear
unterwegs [ʊntərˈve:ks] ADV on the way; (*auf Reisen*) away
unterweisen [ʊntərˈvaɪzən] *unreg* VT UNTR to instruct
Unterwelt [ˈʊntərvɛlt] F (*lit, fig*) underworld
unterwerfen [ʊntərˈvɛrfən] *unreg* VT UNTR to subject; (*Volk*) to subjugate ▶ VR UNTR to submit
unterwürfig [ʊntərˈvʏrfɪç] ADJ obsequious
unterzeichnen [ʊntərˈtsaɪçnən] VT UNTR to sign
Unterzeichner M signatory
unterziehen [ʊntərˈtsi:ən] *unreg* VT UNTR *+dat* to subject ▶ VR UNTR *+dat* to undergo; (*einer Prüfung*) to take
Untiefe [ˈʊnti:fə] F shallow
Untier [ˈʊnti:r] NT monster
untragbar [ʊnˈtra:kba:r] ADJ intolerable, unbearable
untreu [ˈʊntrɔʏ] ADJ unfaithful; **sich** *dat* **selbst ~ werden** to be untrue to o.s.
Untreue F unfaithfulness

untröstlich [ʊnˈtrøːstlɪç] ADJ inconsolable
Untugend [ˈʊntuːgənt] F vice; (*Angewohnheit*) bad habit
un- zW: **unüberbrückbar** ADJ (*fig: Gegensätze etc*) irreconcilable; (*Kluft*) unbridgeable; **unüberlegt** ADJ ill-considered ▸ ADV without thinking; **unübersehbar** ADJ (*Schaden etc*) incalculable; (*Menge*) vast, immense; (*auffällig: Fehler etc*) obvious; **unübersichtlich** ADJ (*Gelände*) broken; (*Kurve*) blind; (*System, Plan*) confused; **unübertroffen** ADJ unsurpassed
un- zW: **unumgänglich** ADJ indispensable, vital; **unumstößlich** ADJ (*Tatsache*) incontrovertible; (*Entschluss*) irrevocable; **unumstritten** ADJ undisputed; **unumwunden** [-ʊmˈvʊndən] ADJ candid ▸ ADV straight out
ununterbrochen [ˈʊnlʊntərbrɔxən] ADJ uninterrupted
un- zW: **unveränderlich** ADJ unchangeable; **unverantwortlich** ADJ irresponsible; (*unentschuldbar*) inexcusable; **unverarbeitet** ADJ (*lit, fig*) raw; **unveräußerlich** [-fɛrˈɔʏsərlich] ADJ inalienable; (*Besitz*) unmarketable; **unverbesserlich** ADJ incorrigible; **unverbindlich** ADJ not binding; (*Antwort*) noncommittal ▸ ADV (*Comm*) without obligation; **unverbleit** [-fɛrblaɪt] ADJ (*Benzin*) unleaded; **unverblümt** [-fɛrˈblyːmt] ADJ plain, blunt ▸ ADV plainly, bluntly; **unverdaulich** ADJ indigestible; **unverdorben** ADJ unspoilt; **unverdrossen** ADJ undeterred; (*unermüdlich*) untiring; **unvereinbar** ADJ incompatible; **unverfälscht** [-fɛrfɛlʃt] ADJ (*auch fig*) unadulterated; (*Dialekt*) pure; (*Natürlichkeit*) unaffected; **unverfänglich** ADJ harmless; **unverfroren** ADJ impudent; **unvergänglich** ADJ immortal; (*Eindruck, Erinnerung*) everlasting; **unvergesslich** ADJ unforgettable; **unvergleichlich** ADJ unique, incomparable; **unverhältnismäßig** ADV disproportionately; (*übermäßig*) excessively; **unverheiratet** ADJ unmarried; **unverhofft** ADJ unexpected; **unverhohlen** [-fɛrhoːlən] ADJ open, unconcealed; **unverkäuflich** ADJ: **„unverkäuflich"** "not for sale"; **unverkennbar** ADJ unmistakable; **unverletzlich** ADJ (*fig: Rechte*) inviolable; (*lit*) invulnerable; **unverletzt** ADJ uninjured; **unvermeidlich** ADJ unavoidable; **unvermittelt** ADJ (*plötzlich*) sudden, unexpected; **Unvermögen** NT inability; **unvermutet** ADJ unexpected; **unvernünftig** ADJ foolish; **unverrichtet** ADJ: **unverrichteter Dinge** empty-handed; **unverschämt** ADJ impudent; **Unverschämtheit** F impudence, insolence; **unverschuldet** ADJ occurring through no fault of one's own; **unversehens** ADV all of a sudden; **unversehrt** [-fɛrzeːrt] ADJ uninjured; **unversöhnlich** ADJ irreconcilable; **Unverstand** M lack of judgement; (*Torheit*) folly; **unverständlich** ADJ unintelligible; **unversucht** ADJ: **nichts unversucht lassen** to try everything; **unverträglich** ADJ quarrelsome; (*Meinungen, Med*) incompatible; (*Essen*) indigestible; **unverwechselbar** ADJ unmistakable, distinctive; **unverwüstlich** ADJ indestructible; (*Mensch*) irrepressible; **unverzeihlich** ADJ unpardonable; **unverzinslich** ADJ interest-free; **unverzüglich** [-fɛrˈtsyːklɪç] ADJ immediate; **unvollendet** ADJ unfinished; **unvollkommen** ADJ imperfect; **unvollständig** ADJ incomplete; **unvorbereitet** ADJ unprepared; **unvoreingenommen** ADJ unbiased; **unvorhergesehen** ADJ unforeseen; **unvorsichtig** ADJ careless, imprudent; **unvorstellbar** ADJ inconceivable; **unvorteilhaft** ADJ disadvantageous
unwahr [ˈʊnvaːr] ADJ untrue; **unwahrhaftig** ADJ untruthful; **Unwahrheit** F untruth; **die Unwahrheit sagen** not to tell the truth; **unwahrscheinlich** ADJ improbable, unlikely ▸ ADV (*umg*) incredibly; **Unwahrscheinlichkeit** F improbability, unlikelihood
unwegsam [ˈʊnveːkzaːm] ADJ (*Gelände etc*) rough
unweigerlich [ʊnˈvaɪgərlɪç] ADJ unquestioning ▸ ADV without fail
unweit [ˈʊnvaɪt] PRÄP +*gen* not far from ▸ ADV not far
Unwesen [ˈʊnveːzən] NT nuisance; (*Unfug*) mischief; **sein ~ treiben** to wreak havoc; (*Mörder etc*) to be at large
unwesentlich ADJ inessential, unimportant; **~ besser** marginally better
Unwetter [ˈʊnvɛtər] NT thunderstorm
unwichtig [ˈʊnvɪçtɪç] ADJ unimportant
un- zW: **unwiderlegbar** ADJ irrefutable; **unwiderruflich** ADJ irrevocable; **unwiderstehlich** [-viːdərˈʃteːlɪç] ADJ irresistible
unwiederbringlich [ʊnviːdərˈbrɪŋlɪç] ADJ (*geh*) irretrievable
Unwille [ˈʊnvɪlə], **Unwillen** [ˈʊnvɪlən] M indignation
unwillig ADJ indignant; (*widerwillig*) reluctant
unwillkürlich [ˈʊnvɪlkyːrlɪç] ADJ involuntary ▸ ADV instinctively; (*lachen*) involuntarily
unwirklich [ˈʊnvɪrklɪç] ADJ unreal
unwirksam [ˈʊnvɪrkzaːm] ADJ ineffective
unwirsch [ˈʊnvɪrʃ] ADJ cross, surly
unwirtlich [ˈʊnvɪrtlɪç] ADJ inhospitable
unwirtschaftlich [ˈʊnvɪrtʃaftlɪç] ADJ uneconomical
unwissend [ˈʊnvɪsənt] ADJ ignorant
Unwissenheit F ignorance
unwissenschaftlich ADJ unscientific
unwissentlich ADV unwittingly, unknowingly
unwohl [ˈʊnvoːl] ADJ unwell, ill; **Unwohlsein** (**-s**) NT indisposition
unwürdig [ˈʊnvʏrdɪç] ADJ unworthy
Unzahl [ˈʊntsaːl] F: **eine ~ von …** a whole host of …
unzählig [ʊnˈtsɛːlɪç] ADJ innumerable, countless
unzeitgemäß [ˈʊntsaɪtgəmɛːs] ADJ (*altmodisch*) old-fashioned
un- zW: **unzerbrechlich** ADJ unbreakable; **unzerreißbar** ADJ untearable; **unzerstörbar** ADJ indestructible; **unzertrennlich** ADJ inseparable

u

Unzucht ['ʊntsʊxt] F sexual offence
unzüchtig ['ʊntsʏçtɪç] ADJ immoral
un- zW: **unzufrieden** ADJ dissatisfied; **Unzufriedenheit** F discontent; **unzugänglich** ADJ (*Gegend*) inaccessible; (*Mensch*) inapproachable; **unzulänglich** ADJ inadequate; **unzulässig** ADJ inadmissible; **unzumutbar** ADJ unreasonable; **unzurechnungsfähig** ADJ irresponsible; **jdn für unzurechnungsfähig erklären lassen** (*Jur*) to have sb certified (insane); **unzusammenhängend** ADJ disconnected; (*Äußerung*) incoherent; **unzustellbar** ADJ: **falls unzustellbar, bitte an Absender zurück** if undelivered, please return to sender; **unzutreffend** ADJ incorrect; **„Unzutreffendes bitte streichen"** "delete as applicable"; **unzuverlässig** ADJ unreliable
unzweckmäßig ['ʊntsvɛkmɛːsɪç] ADJ (*nicht ratsam*) inadvisable; (*unpraktisch*) impractical; (*ungeeignet*) unsuitable
unzweideutig ['ʊntsvaɪdɔʏtɪç] ADJ unambiguous
unzweifelhaft ['ʊntsvaɪfəlhaft] ADJ indubitable
üppig ['ʏpɪç] ADJ (*Frau*) curvaceous; (*Essen*) sumptuous, lavish; (*Vegetation*) luxuriant, lush; (*Haar*) thick
Ur- ['uːr] IN ZW original
Urabstimmung ['uːrlapʃtɪmʊŋ] F ballot
Ural [u'raːl] (**-s**) M: **der ~** the Ural mountains *pl*, the Urals *pl*; **Uralgebirge** NT Ural mountains
uralt ['uːrlalt] ADJ ancient, very old
Uran [u'raːn] (**-s**) NT uranium
Uraufführung F premiere
urbar ADJ: **die Wüste/Land ~ machen** to reclaim the desert/cultivate land
Urdu ['ʊrdu] (-) NT Urdu
Ur- zW: **Ureinwohner** M original inhabitant; **Ureltern** PL ancestors *pl*; **Urenkel(in)** M(F) great-grandchild; **Urfassung** F original version; **Urgroßmutter** F great-grandmother; **Urgroßvater** M great-grandfather
Urheber (**-s, -**) M originator; (*Autor*) author; **Urheberrecht** NT: **Urheberrecht (an** *+dat*) copyright (on); **urheberrechtlich** ADV: **urheberrechtlich geschützt** copyright
urig ['uːrɪç] (*umg*) ADJ (*Mensch, Atmosphäre*) earthy
Urin [u'riːn] (**-s, -e**) M urine
urkomisch ADJ incredibly funny
Urkunde F document; (*Kaufurkunde*) deed
urkundlich ['uːrkʊntlɪç] ADJ documentary
URL F ABK (= *uniform resource locator*) URL
urladen ['uːrlaːdən] VT UNTR (*Comput*) to boot
Urlader M (*Comput*) bootstrap
Urlaub ['uːrlaʊp] (**-(e)s, -e**) M holiday(*s pl*) (BRIT), vacation (*US*); (*Mil etc*) leave; **in ~ fahren** to go on holiday (BRIT) *od* vacation (*US*); **Urlauber** (**-s, -**) M holiday-maker (BRIT), vacationer (*US*)
Urlaubs- zW: **Urlaubsgeld** NT holiday (BRIT) *od* vacation (*US*) money; **Urlaubsort** M holiday (BRIT) *od* vacation (*US*) resort; **urlaubsreif** ADJ in need of a holiday (BRIT) *od* vacation (*US*)
Urmensch M primitive man
Urne ['ʊrnə] (**-, -n**) F urn; **zur ~ gehen** to go to the polls
urplötzlich ['uːr'plœtslɪç] (*umg*) ADV all of a sudden
Ursache ['uːrzaxə] F cause; **keine ~!** (*auf Dank*) don't mention it, you're welcome; (*auf Entschuldigung*) that's all right
ursächlich ['uːrzɛçlɪç] ADJ causal
Urschrei ['uːrʃraɪ] M (*Psych*) primal scream
Ursprung ['uːrʃprʊŋ] M origin, source; (*von Fluss*) source
ursprünglich ['uːrʃprʏŋlɪç] ADJ original ▶ ADV originally
Ursprungsland NT (*Comm*) country of origin
Ursprungszeugnis NT certificate of origin
Urteil ['ʊrtaɪl] (**-s, -e**) NT opinion; (*Jur*) sentence, judgement; **sich** *dat* **ein ~ über etw** *akk* **erlauben** to pass judgement on sth; **ein ~ über etw** *akk* **fällen** to pass judgement on sth; **urteilen** VI to judge
Urteilsbegründung F (*Jur*) opinion
Urteilsspruch M sentence; (*von Geschworenen*) verdict
Uruguay [uru'guaːi] (**-s**) NT Uruguay
Uruguayer(in) (**-s, -**) M(F) Uruguayan
uruguayisch ADJ Uruguayan
Ur- zW: **Urwald** M jungle; **urwüchsig** ADJ natural; (*Landschaft*) unspoilt; (*Humor*) earthy; **Urzeit** F prehistoric times *pl*
USA [uː'ɛs'laː] PL ABK: **die ~** the USA *sing*
USB ABK (= *universal serial bus*) USB
Usbekistan [ʊs'beːkistaːn] (**-s**) NT Uzbekistan
USB-Stick [uːlɛs'beːstɪk] M (*Comput*) flash drive
USBV [uːlɛsbeː'faʊ] F ABK (= *unbekannte Spreng- und Brandvorrichtung*) IED
usw. ABK (= *und so weiter*) etc.
Utensilien [utɛn'ziːliən] PL utensils *pl*
Utopie [uto'piː] F pipe dream
utopisch [u'toːpɪʃ] ADJ utopian
u. U. ABK (= *unter Umständen*) possibly
UV ABK (= *ultraviolett*) U.V.
u. v. a. ABK (= *und viele(s) andere*) and much/many more
u. v. a. m. ABK (= *und viele(s) andere mehr*) and much/many more
u. W. ABK (= *unseres Wissens*) to our knowledge
Ü-Wagen M (*Rundf, TV*) outside broadcast vehicle
uzen ['uːtsən] (*umg*) VT, VI to tease, to kid
u. zw. ABK = **und zwar**

V¹, v [faʊ] NT V, v; **V wie Viktor** ≈ V for Victor
V² [faʊ] ABK (= *Volt*) v
VAE PL ABK (= *Vereinigte Arabische Emirate*) UAE
vag, vage ADJ vague
Vagina [va'gi:na] (-, **Vaginen**) F vagina
Vakuum ['va:kuʊm] (**-s, Vakua** *od* **Vakuen**) NT vacuum; **vakuumverpackt** ADJ vacuum-packed
Vandalismus [vanda'lɪsmʊs] M vandalism
Vanille [va'nɪljə] (-) F vanilla; **Vanillezucker** M vanilla sugar
Vanillinzucker M vanilla sugar
variabel [vari'a:bəl] ADJ: **variable Kosten** variable costs
Variable [vari'a:blə] (**-, -n**) F variable
Variante [vari'antə] (**-, -n**) F: **~ (zu)** variant (on)
Variation [variatsi'o:n] F variation
variieren [vari'i:rən] VT, VI to vary
Vase ['va:zə] (**-, -n**) F vase
Vater ['fa:tər] (**-s, Väter**) M father; **~ Staat** (*umg*) the State; **Vaterland** NT native country; (*bes Deutschland*) Fatherland; **Vaterlandsliebe** F patriotism
väterlich ['fɛ:tərlɪç] ADJ fatherly
väterlicherseits ADV on the father's side
Vaterschaft F paternity
Vaterschaftsklage F paternity suit
Vaterstelle F: **~ bei jdm vertreten** to take the place of sb's father
Vatertag M Father's Day
Vaterunser (**-s, -**) NT Lord's Prayer
Vati ['fa:ti] (**-s, -s**) (*umg*) M dad(dy)
Vatikan [vati'ka:n] (**-s**) M Vatican
V-Ausschnitt ['faʊlaʊsʃnɪt] M V-neck
VB ABK (= *Verhandlungsbasis*) o.i.r.o.
v. Chr. ABK (= *vor Christus*) B.C.
Veganer(in) [ve'ga:nər(ɪn)] (**-s, -**) M(F) vegan
Vegetarier(in) [vege'ta:riər(ɪn)] (**-s, -**) M(F) vegetarian
vegetarisch ADJ vegetarian
Vegetation [vegetatsi'o:n] F vegetation
vegetativ [vegeta'ti:f] ADJ (*Biol*) vegetative; (*Med*) autonomic
vegetieren [vege'ti:rən] VI to vegetate; (*kärglich leben*) to eke out a bare existence
Vehikel [ve'hi:kəl] (**-s, -**) (*pej, umg*) NT boneshaker
Veilchen ['faɪlçən] NT violet; (*umg: blaues Auge*) shiner, black eye
Velours (**-, -**) NT suede; **Veloursleder** NT suede
Vene ['ve:nə] (**-, -n**) F vein
Venedig [ve'ne:dɪç] (**-s**) NT Venice
Venezianer(in) [venetsi'a:nər(ɪn)] (**-s, -**) M(F) Venetian
venezianisch [venetsi'a:nɪʃ] ADJ Venetian
Venezolaner(in) [venetso'la:nər(ɪn)] (**-s, -**) M(F) Venezuelan
venezolanisch ADJ Venezuelan
Venezuela [venetsu'e:la] (**-s**) NT Venezuela
Ventil [vɛn'ti:l] (**-s, -e**) NT valve
Ventilator [vɛnti'la:tɔr] M ventilator
verabreden [fɛr'lapre:dən] VT to arrange; (*Termin*) to agree upon ▸ VR to arrange to meet; **sich (mit jdm) ~** to arrange to meet (sb); **schon verabredet sein** to have a prior engagement (*form*), to have something else on
Verabredung F arrangement; (*Treffen*) appointment; **ich habe eine ~** I'm meeting somebody
verabreichen [fɛr'lapraɪçən] VT (*Tracht Prügel etc*) to give; (*Arznei*) to administer (*form*)
verabscheuen [fɛr'lapʃɔyən] VT to detest, to abhor
verabschieden [fɛr'lapʃi:dən] VT (*Gäste*) to say goodbye to; (*entlassen*) to discharge; (*Gesetz*) to pass ▸ VR: **sich ~ (von)** to take one's leave (of)
Verabschiedung F (*von Beamten etc*) discharge; (*von Gesetz*) passing
verachten [fɛr'laxtən] VT to despise; **nicht zu ~** (*umg*) not to be scoffed at
verächtlich [fɛr'lɛçtlɪç] ADJ contemptuous; (*verachtenswert*) contemptible; **jdn ~ machen** to run sb down
Verachtung F contempt; **jdn mit ~ strafen** to treat sb with contempt
veralbern [fɛr'lalbərn] (*umg*) VT to make fun of
verallgemeinern [fɛrlalgə'maɪnərn] VT to generalize
Verallgemeinerung F generalization
veralten [fɛr'laltən] VI to become obsolete *od* out-of-date
Veranda [ve'randa] (**-, Veranden**) F veranda
veränderlich [fɛr'lɛndərlɪç] ADJ variable; (*Wetter*) changeable; **Veränderlichkeit** F variability; (*von Wetter*) changeability
verändern VT, VR to change

Veränderung F change; **eine berufliche ~** a change of job
verängstigen [fɛr'lɛŋstɪgən] VT (*erschrecken*) to frighten; (*einschüchtern*) to intimidate
verankern [fɛr'laŋkərn] VT (*Naut, Tech*) to anchor; (*fig*): **~ (in** *+dat***)** to embed (in)
veranlagen [fɛr'lanla:gən] VT: **etw ~ (mit)** to assess sth (at)
veranlagt ADJ: **praktisch ~ sein** to be practically-minded; **zu** *od* **für etw ~ sein** to be cut out for sth
Veranlagung F disposition, aptitude
veranlassen [fɛr'lanlasən] VT to cause; **Maßnahmen ~** to take measures; **sich veranlasst sehen** to feel prompted; **etw ~** to arrange for sth; (*befehlen*) to order sth
Veranlassung F cause; (*Motiv*) motive; **auf jds ~** *akk* **(hin)** at sb's instigation
veranschaulichen [fɛr'lanʃaʊlıçən] VT to illustrate
veranschlagen [fɛr'lanʃla:gən] VT to estimate
veranstalten [fɛr'lanʃtaltən] VT to organize, to arrange
Veranstalter(in) (**-s, -**) M(F) organizer; (*Comm: von Konzerten etc*) promoter
Veranstaltung F (*Veranstalten*) organizing; (*Veranstaltetes*) event; (*feierlich, öffentlich*) function
verantworten [fɛr'lantvɔrtən] VT to accept responsibility for; (*Folgen etc*) to answer for ▸ VR to justify o.s.; **etw vor jdm ~** to answer to sb for sth
verantwortlich ADJ responsible
Verantwortung F responsibility; **jdn zur ~ ziehen** to call sb to account
verantwortungs- ZW: **verantwortungsbewusst** ADJ responsible; **Verantwortungsgefühl** NT sense of responsibility; **verantwortungslos** ADJ irresponsible; **verantwortungsvoll** ADJ responsible
verarbeiten [fɛr'larbaɪtən] VT to process; (*geistig*) to assimilate; (*Erlebnis etc*) to digest; **etw zu etw ~** to make sth into sth; **verarbeitende Industrie** processing industries *pl*
verarbeitet ADJ: **gut ~** (*Kleid etc*) well finished
Verarbeitung F processing; (*geistig*) assimilation
verärgern [fɛr'lɛrgərn] VT to annoy
verarmen [fɛr'larmən] VI (*lit, fig*) to become impoverished
verarschen [fɛr'larʃən] (*umg!*) VT: **jdn ~** to take the mickey out of sb
verarzten [fɛr'la:rtstən] VT to fix up (*umg*)
verausgaben [fɛr'laʊsga:bən] VR to run out of money; (*fig*) to exhaust o.s.
veräußern [fɛr'lɔʏsərn] VT (*form: verkaufen*) to dispose of
Verb [vɛrp] (**-s, -en**) NT verb
Verb. ABK (= *Verband*) assoc.
verband *etc* VB *siehe* **verbinden**
Verband [fɛr'bant] (**-(e)s, Verbände**) M (*Med*) bandage, dressing; (*Bund*) association, society; (*Mil*) unit; **Verbandkasten, Verbandskasten** M medicine chest, first-aid box; **Verbandpäckchen, Verbandspäckchen** NT gauze bandage; **Verbandstoff** M bandage, dressing material; **Verbandzeug** NT bandage, dressing material
verbannen [fɛr'banən] VT to banish
Verbannung F exile
verbarrikadieren [fɛrbarika'di:rən] VT to barricade ▸ VR to barricade o.s. in
verbauen [fɛr'baʊən] VT: **sich** *dat* **alle Chancen ~** to spoil one's chances
verbergen [fɛr'bɛrgən] *unreg* VT, VR: **(sich) ~ (vor** *+dat***)** to hide (from)
verbessern [fɛr'bɛsərn] VT to improve; (*berichtigen*) to correct ▸ VR to improve; (*sich korrigieren*) to correct o.s.
verbessert ADJ improved; **eine neue, verbesserte Auflage** a new revised edition
Verbesserung F improvement; (*Korrektur*) correction
verbeugen [fɛr'bɔʏgən] VR to bow
Verbeugung F bow
verbiegen [fɛr'bi:gən] *unreg* VI to bend
verbiestert [fɛr'bi:stərt] (*umg*) ADJ crotchety
verbieten [fɛr'bi:tən] *unreg* VT to forbid; (*amtlich*) to prohibit; (*Zeitung, Partei*) to ban; **jdm etw ~** to forbid sb to do sth
verbilligen [fɛr'bılıgən] VT to reduce (the price of) ▸ VR to become cheaper, to go down
verbinden [fɛr'bındən] *unreg* VT to connect; (*kombinieren*) to combine; (*Med*) to bandage ▸ VR to combine (*auch Chem*), to join (together); **jdm die Augen ~** to blindfold sb
verbindlich [fɛr'bıntlıç] ADJ binding; (*freundlich*) obliging; **~ zusagen** to accept definitely; **Verbindlichkeit** F obligation; (*Höflichkeit*) civility; **Verbindlichkeiten** PL (*Jur*) obligations *pl*; (*Comm*) liabilities *pl*
Verbindung F connection; (*Zusammensetzung*) combination; (*Chem*) compound; (*Univ*) club; (*Tel: Anschluss*) line; **mit jdm in ~ stehen** to be in touch *od* contact with sb; **~ mit jdm aufnehmen** to contact sb
Verbindungsmann (*pl* **-(e)s, -männer** *od* **-leute**) M intermediary; (*Agent*) contact
verbissen [fɛr'bısən] ADJ grim; (*Kampf*) dogged; **Verbissenheit** F grimness; (*von Kampf*) doggedness
verbitten [fɛr'bıtən] *unreg* VT: **sich** *dat* **etw ~** not to tolerate sth, not to stand for sth
verbittern [fɛr'bıtərn] VT to embitter ▸ VI to get bitter
verblassen [fɛr'blasən] VI to fade
Verbleib [fɛr'blaɪp] (**-(e)s**) M whereabouts
verbleiben [fɛr'blaɪbən] *unreg* VI to remain; **wir sind so verblieben, dass wir ...** we agreed to ...
verbleit [fɛr'blaɪt] ADJ leaded
Verblendung [fɛr'blɛndʊŋ] F (*fig*) delusion
verblöden [fɛr'blø:dən] VI (*Hilfsverb sein*) to get stupid

verblüffen [fɛrˈblʏfən] VT to amaze; (*verwirren*) to baffle
Verblüffung F stupefaction
verblühen [fɛrˈbly:ən] VI to wither, to fade
verbluten [fɛrˈblu:tən] VI to bleed to death
verbohren [fɛrˈbo:rən] (*umg*) VR: **sich in etw** *akk* ~ to become obsessed with sth
verbohrt ADJ (*Haltung*) stubborn, obstinate
verborgen [fɛrˈbɔrgən] ADJ hidden; **verborgene Mängel** latent defects *pl*
Verbot [fɛrˈbo:t] (**-(e)s, -e**) NT prohibition, ban
verboten ADJ forbidden; **Rauchen ~!** no smoking; **er sah ~ aus** (*umg*) he looked a real sight
verbotenerweise ADV though it is forbidden
Verbotsschild NT prohibitory sign
verbrämen [fɛrˈbrɛ:mən] VT (*fig*) to gloss over; (*Kritik*): ~ (**mit**) to veil (in)
Verbrauch [fɛrˈbraʊx] (**-(e)s**) M consumption
verbrauchen VT to use up; **der Wagen verbraucht 10 Liter Benzin auf 100 km** the car does 10 kms to the litre (BRIT) *od* liter (US)
Verbraucher(in) (**-s, -**) M(F) consumer; **Verbrauchermarkt** M hypermarket; **verbrauchernah** ADJ consumer-friendly; **Verbraucherschutz** M consumer protection; **Verbraucherverband** M consumer council
Verbrauchsgüter PL consumer goods *pl*
verbraucht ADJ used up, finished; (*Luft*) stale; (*Mensch*) worn-out
Verbrechen (**-s, -**) NT crime
Verbrecher(in) (**-s, -**) M(F) criminal; **verbrecherisch** ADJ criminal; **Verbrecherkartei** F file of offenders, ≈ rogues' gallery; **Verbrechertum** (**-s**) NT criminality
verbreiten [fɛrˈbraɪtən] VT to spread; (*Licht*) to shed; (*Wärme, Ruhe*) to radiate ▸ VR to spread; **eine (weit) verbreitete Ansicht** a widely held opinion; **sich über etw** *akk* ~ to expound on sth
verbreitern [fɛrˈbraɪtərn] VT to broaden
Verbreitung F spread(ing); (*von Licht*) shedding; (*von Wärme, Ruhe*) radiation
verbrennbar ADJ combustible
verbrennen [fɛrˈbrɛnən] *unreg* VT to burn; (*Leiche*) to cremate; (*versengen*) to scorch; (*Haar*) to singe; (*verbrühen*) to scald
Verbrennung F burning; (*in Motor*) combustion; (*von Leiche*) cremation
Verbrennungsanlage F incineration plant
Verbrennungsmotor M internal-combustion engine
verbriefen [fɛrˈbri:fən] VT to document
verbringen [fɛrˈbrɪŋən] *unreg* VT to spend
Verbrüderung [fɛrˈbry:dərʊŋ] F fraternization
verbrühen [fɛrˈbry:ən] VT to scald
verbuchen [fɛrˈbu:xən] VT (*Fin*) to register; (*Erfolg*) to enjoy; (*Misserfolg*) to suffer
verbummeln [fɛrˈbʊməln] (*umg*) VT (*verlieren*) to lose; (*Zeit*) to waste, to fritter away; (*Verabredung*) to miss
verbunden [fɛrˈbʊndən] ADJ connected; **jdm ~ sein** to be obliged *od* indebted to sb; **ich/er** *etc* **war falsch ~** (*Tel*) it was a wrong number
verbünden [fɛrˈbʏndən] VR to form an alliance
Verbundenheit F bond, relationship
Verbündete(r) F(M) ally
Verbundglas [fɛrˈbʊntgla:s] NT laminated glass
verbürgen [fɛrˈbʏrgən] VR: **sich ~ für** to vouch for; **ein verbürgtes Recht** an established right
verbüßen [fɛrˈby:sən] VT: **eine Strafe ~** to serve a sentence
verchromt [fɛrˈkro:mt] ADJ chromium-plated
Verdacht [fɛrˈdaxt] (**-(e)s**) M suspicion; **~ schöpfen (gegen jdn)** to become suspicious (of sb); **jdn in ~ haben** to suspect sb; **es besteht ~ auf Krebs** *akk* cancer is suspected
verdächtig ADJ suspicious
verdächtigen [fɛrˈdɛçtɪgən] VT to suspect
Verdächtigung F suspicion
verdammen [fɛrˈdamən] VT to damn, to condemn
Verdammnis (-) F perdition, damnation
verdammt (*umg*) ADJ, ADV damned; **~ noch mal!** bloody hell (*umg!*), damn (*umg!*)
verdampfen [fɛrˈdampfən] VT, VI (*vi Hilfsverb sein*) to vaporize; (*Koch*) to boil away
verdanken [fɛrˈdaŋkən] VT: **jdm etw ~** to owe sb sth
verdarb *etc* [fɛrˈdarp] VB *siehe* **verderben**
verdattert [fɛrˈdatərt] (*umg*) ADJ, ADV flabbergasted
verdauen [fɛrˈdaʊən] VT (*lit, fig*) to digest ▸ VI (*lit*) to digest
verdaulich [fɛrˈdaʊlɪç] ADJ digestible; **das ist schwer ~** that is hard to digest
Verdauung F digestion
Verdauungsspaziergang M constitutional
Verdauungsstörung F indigestion
Verdeck [fɛrˈdɛk] (**-(e)s, -e**) NT (*Aut*) soft top; (*Naut*) deck
verdecken VT to cover (up); (*verbergen*) to hide
verdenken [fɛrˈdɛŋkən] *unreg* VT: **jdm etw ~** to blame sb for sth, to hold sth against sb
verderben [fɛrˈdɛrbən] *unreg* VT to spoil; (*schädigen*) to ruin; (*moralisch*) to corrupt ▸ VI (*Essen*) to spoil, to rot; (*Mensch*) to go to the bad; **es mit jdm ~** to get into sb's bad books
Verderben (**-s**) NT ruin
verderblich ADJ (*Einfluss*) pernicious; (*Lebensmittel*) perishable
verderbt ADJ (*veraltet*) depraved; **Verderbtheit** F depravity
verdeutlichen [fɛrˈdɔʏtlɪçən] VT to make clear
verdichten [fɛrˈdɪçtən] VT (*Phys, fig*) to compress ▸ VR to thicken; (*Verdacht, Eindruck*) to deepen
verdienen [fɛrˈdi:nən] VT to earn; (*moralisch*) to deserve ▸ VI (*Gewinn machen*): **~ (an** +*dat*) to make (a profit) (on)
Verdienst [fɛrˈdi:nst] (**-(e)s, -e**) M earnings *pl* ▸ NT merit; (*Dank*) credit; (*Leistung*): **~ (um)** service (to), contribution (to); **verdienstvoll** ADJ commendable
verdient [fɛrˈdi:nt] ADJ well-earned; (*Person*) of outstanding merit; (*Lohn, Strafe*) rightful; **sich um etw ~ machen** to do a lot for sth

V

verdirbst [fɛrˈdɪrpst] VB *siehe* **verderben**
verdirbt [fɛrˈdɪrpt] VB *siehe* **verderben**
verdonnern [fɛrˈdɔnərn] (*umg*) VT (*zu Haft etc*): **~ (zu)** to sentence (to); **jdn zu etw ~** to order sb to do sth
verdoppeln [fɛrˈdɔpəln] VT to double
Verdoppelung, Verdopplung F doubling
verdorben [fɛrˈdɔrbən] PP *von* **verderben** ▶ ADJ spoilt; (*geschädigt*) ruined; (*moralisch*) corrupt
verdorren [fɛrˈdɔrən] VI to wither
verdrängen [fɛrˈdrɛŋən] VT to oust; (*auch Phys*) to displace; (*Psych*) to repress
Verdrängung F displacement; (*Psych*) repression
verdrehen [fɛrˈdre:ən] VT (*lit, fig*) to twist; (*Augen*) to roll; **jdm den Kopf ~** (*fig*) to turn sb's head
verdreht (*umg*) ADJ crazy; (*Bericht*) confused
verdreifachen [fɛrˈdraɪfaxən] VT to treble
verdrießen [fɛrˈdri:sən] *unreg* VT to annoy
verdrießlich [fɛrˈdri:slɪç] ADJ peevish, annoyed
verdross *etc* [fɛrˈdrɔs] VB *siehe* **verdrießen**
verdrossen [fɛrˈdrɔsən] PP *von* **verdrießen** ▶ ADJ cross, sulky
verdrücken [fɛrˈdrʏkən] (*umg*) VT to put away, to eat ▶ VR to disappear
Verdruss [fɛrˈdrʊs] (**-es, -e**) M frustration; **zu jds ~** to sb's annoyance
verduften [fɛrˈdʊftən] VI to evaporate; (*umg*) to disappear
verdummen [fɛrˈdʊmən] VT to make stupid ▶ VI to grow stupid
verdunkeln [fɛrˈdʊŋkəln] VT to darken; (*fig*) to obscure ▶ VR to darken
Verdunkelung, Verdunklung F blackout; (*fig*) obscuring
verdünnen [fɛrˈdʏnən] VT to dilute
Verdünner (**-s, -**) M thinner
verdünnisieren [fɛrdʏniˈzi:rən] (*umg*) VR to make o.s. scarce
verdunsten [fɛrˈdʊnstən] VI to evaporate
verdursten [fɛrˈdʊrstən] VI to die of thirst
verdutzt [fɛrˈdʊtst] ADJ nonplussed (BRIT), nonplused (US), taken aback
verebben [fɛrˈlɛbən] VI to subside
veredeln [fɛrˈle:dəln] VT (*Metalle, Erdöl*) to refine; (*Fasern*) to finish; (*Bot*) to graft
verehren [fɛrˈle:rən] VT to venerate, to worship (*auch Rel*); **jdm etw ~** to present sb with sth
Verehrer(in) (**-s, -**) M(F) admirer, worshipper (BRIT), worshiper (US)
verehrt ADJ esteemed; **(sehr) verehrte Anwesende/verehrtes Publikum** Ladies and Gentlemen
Verehrung F respect; (*Rel*) worship
vereidigen [fɛrˈlaɪdɪgən] VT to put on oath; **jdn auf etw** *akk* **~** to make sb swear on sth
Vereidigung F swearing in
Verein [fɛrˈlaɪn] (**-(e)s, -e**) M club, association; **ein wohltätiger ~** a charity
vereinbar ADJ compatible
vereinbaren [fɛrˈlaɪnba:rən] VT to agree upon
Vereinbarkeit F compatibility
Vereinbarung F agreement
vereinfachen [fɛrˈlaɪnfaxən] VT to simplify
Vereinfachung F simplification
vereinheitlichen [fɛrˈlaɪnhaɪtlɪçən] VT to standardize
vereinigen [fɛrˈlaɪnɪgən] VT, VR to unite
vereinigt ADJ united; **Vereinigte Arabische Emirate** PL United Arab Emirates; **Vereinigtes Königreich** NT United Kingdom; **Vereinigte Staaten** PL United States
Vereinigung F union; (*Verein*) association
vereinnahmen [fɛrˈlaɪnna:mən] VT (*geh*) to take; **jdn ~** (*fig*) to make demands on sb
vereinsamen [fɛrˈlaɪnza:mən] VI to become lonely
vereint [fɛrˈlaɪnt] ADJ united; **Vereinte Nationen** PL United Nations
vereinzelt [fɛrˈlaɪntsəlt] ADJ isolated
vereisen [fɛrˈlaɪzən] VI to freeze, to ice over ▶ VT (*Med*) to freeze
vereiteln [fɛrˈlaɪtəln] VT to frustrate
vereitern [fɛrˈlaɪtərn] VI to suppurate, to fester
Verelendung [fɛrˈle:lɛndʊŋ] F impoverishment
verenden [fɛrˈlɛndən] VI to perish, to die
verengen [fɛrˈlɛŋən] VR to narrow
vererben [fɛrˈlɛrbən] VT to bequeath; (*Biol*) to transmit ▶ VR to be hereditary
vererblich [fɛrˈlɛrplɪç] ADJ hereditary
Vererbung F bequeathing; (*Biol*) transmission; **das ist ~** (*umg*) it's hereditary
verewigen [fɛrˈle:vɪgən] VT to immortalize ▶ VR (*umg*) to leave one's name
Verf. ABK = **Verfasser**
verfahren [fɛrˈfa:rən] *unreg* VI to act ▶ VR to get lost ▶ ADJ tangled; **~ mit** to deal with
Verfahren (**-s, -**) NT procedure; (*Tech*) process; (*Jur*) proceedings *pl*
Verfahrenstechnik F (*Methode*) process
Verfahrensweise F procedure
Verfall [fɛrˈfal] (**-(e)s**) M decline; (*von Haus*) dilapidation; (*Fin*) expiry
verfallen *unreg* VI to decline; (*Haus*) to be falling down; (*Fin*) to lapse ▶ ADJ (*Gebäude*) dilapidated, ruined; (*Karten, Briefmarken*) invalid; (*Strafe*) lapsed; (*Pass*) expired; **~ in** *+akk* to lapse into; **~ auf** *+akk* to hit upon; **einem Laster ~ sein** to be addicted to a vice; **jdm völlig ~ sein** to be completely under sb's spell
Verfallsdatum NT expiry date; (*der Haltbarkeit*) best-before date
verfänglich [fɛrˈfɛŋlɪç] ADJ awkward, tricky; (*Aussage, Beweismaterial etc*) incriminating; (*gefährlich*) dangerous
verfärben [fɛrˈfɛrbən] VR to change colour (BRIT) *od* color (US)
verfassen [fɛrˈfasən] VT to write; (*Gesetz, Urkunde*) to draw up
Verfasser(in) (**-s, -**) M(F) author, writer
Verfassung F constitution (*auch Pol*); (*körperlich*) state of health; (*seelisch*) state of mind; **sie ist in guter/schlechter ~** she is in good/bad shape
Verfassungs- ZW: **verfassungsfeindlich** ADJ anticonstitutional; **Verfassungsgericht** NT

constitutional court; **verfassungsmäßig** ADJ constitutional; **Verfassungsschutz** M (*Aufgabe*) defence of the constitution; (*Amt*) *office responsible for defending the constitution*; **Verfassungsschützer(in)** M(F) defender of the constitution; **verfassungswidrig** ADJ unconstitutional

verfaulen [fɛr'faulən] VI to rot

verfechten [fɛr'fɛçtən] *unreg* VT to defend; (*Lehre*) to advocate

Verfechter(in) [fɛr'fɛçtər(ɪn)] (**-s, -**) M(F) champion

verfehlen [fɛr'fe:lən] VT to miss; **das Thema ~** to be completely off the subject

verfehlt ADJ unsuccessful; (*unangebracht*) inappropriate; **etw für ~ halten** to regard sth as mistaken

Verfehlung F (*Vergehen*) misdemeanour (BRIT), misdemeanor (US); (*Sünde*) transgression

verfeinern [fɛr'faɪnərn] VT to refine

Verfettung [fɛr'fɛtʊŋ] F (*von Organ, Muskeln*) fatty degeneration

verfeuern [fɛr'fɔʏərn] VT to burn; (*Munition*) to fire; (*umg*) to use up

verfilmen [fɛr'fɪlmən] VT to film, to make a film of

Verfilmung F film (version)

Verfilzung [fɛr'fɪltsʊŋ] F (*fig: von Firmen, Parteien*) entanglements *pl*

verflachen [fɛr'flaxən] VI to flatten out; (*fig: Diskussion*) to become superficial

verfliegen [fɛr'fli:gən] *unreg* VI to evaporate; (*Zeit*) to pass, to fly ▶ VR to stray (past)

verflixt [fɛr'flɪkst] (*umg*) ADJ, ADV darned

verflossen [fɛr'flɔsən] ADJ past, former

verfluchen [fɛr'flu:xən] VT to curse

verflüchtigen [fɛr'flʏçtɪgən] VR to evaporate; (*Geruch*) to fade

verflüssigen [fɛr'flʏsɪgən] VR to become liquid

verfolgen [fɛr'fɔlgən] VT to pursue; (*gerichtlich*) to prosecute; (*grausam, bes Pol*) to persecute

Verfolger(in) (**-s, -**) M(F) pursuer

Verfolgte(r) F(M) (*politisch*) victim of persecution

Verfolgung F pursuit; (*Pol*) persecution; **strafrechtliche ~** prosecution

Verfolgungswahn M persecution mania

verfrachten [fɛr'fraxtən] VT to ship

verfremden [fɛr'frɛmdən] VT to alienate, to distance

verfressen [fɛr'frɛsən] (*umg*) ADJ greedy

verfrüht [fɛr'fry:t] ADJ premature

verfügbar ADJ available

verfügen [fɛr'fy:gən] VT to direct, to order ▶ VR to proceed ▶ VI: **~ über** *+akk* to have at one's disposal; **über etw** *akk* **frei ~ können** to be able to do as one wants with sth

Verfügung F direction, order; (*Jur*) writ; **zur ~** at one's disposal; **jdm zur ~ stehen** to be available to sb

Verfügungsgewalt F (*Jur*) right of disposal

verführen [fɛr'fy:rən] VT to tempt; (*sexuell*) to seduce; (*die Jugend, das Volk etc*) to lead astray

Verführer M tempter; (*sexuell*) seducer

Verführerin F temptress; (*sexuell*) seductress

verführerisch ADJ seductive

Verführung F seduction; (*Versuchung*) temptation

Vergabe [fɛr'ga:bə] F (*von Arbeiten*) allocation; (*von Stipendium, Auftrag etc*) award

vergällen [fɛr'gɛlən] VT (*geh*): **jdm die Freude/das Leben ~** to spoil sb's fun/sour sb's life

vergaloppieren [fɛrgalɔ'pi:rən] (*umg*) VR (*sich irren*) to be on the wrong track

vergammeln [fɛr'gaməln] (*umg*) VI to go to seed; (*Nahrung*) to go off; (*Zeit*) to waste

vergangen [fɛr'gaŋən] ADJ past; **vergangene Woche** last week; **Vergangenheit** F past; **Vergangenheitsbewältigung** F coming to terms with the past

vergänglich [fɛr'gɛŋlɪç] ADJ transitory; **Vergänglichkeit** F transitoriness, impermanence

vergasen [fɛr'ga:zən] VT to gasify; (*töten*) to gas

Vergaser (**-s, -**) M (*Aut*) carburettor (BRIT), carburetor (US)

vergaß *etc* [fɛr'ga:s] VB *siehe* **vergessen**

vergeben [fɛr'ge:bən] *unreg* VT to forgive; (*weggeben*) to give away; (*fig: Chance*) to throw away; (*Auftrag, Preis*) to award; (*Studienplätze, Stellen*) to allocate; **jdm (etw) ~** to forgive sb (sth); **~ an** *+akk* to award to; (*Studienplatz, Stelle*) to allocate to; **~ sein** to be occupied; (*umg: Mädchen*) to be spoken for

vergebens ADV in vain

vergeblich [fɛr'ge:plɪç] ADV in vain ▶ ADJ vain, futile

Vergebung F forgiveness

vergegenwärtigen [fɛrge:gən'vɛrtɪgən] VR: **sich** *dat* **etw ~** to visualize sth; (*erinnern*) to recall sth

vergehen [fɛr'ge:ən] *unreg* VI to pass by *od* away ▶ VR to commit an offence (BRIT) *od* offense (US); **vor Angst ~** to be scared to death; **jdm vergeht etw** sb loses sth; **sich an jdm ~** to (sexually) assault sb; **Vergehen** (**-s, -**) NT offence (BRIT), offense (US)

vergeigen [fɛr'gaɪgən] (*umg*) VT to cock up

vergeistigt [fɛr'gaɪstɪçt] ADJ spiritual

vergelten [fɛr'gɛltən] *unreg* VT: **jdm etw ~** to pay sb back for sth, to repay sb for sth

Vergeltung F retaliation, reprisal

Vergeltungsmaßnahme F retaliatory measure

Vergeltungsschlag M (*Mil*) reprisal

vergesellschaften [fɛrgə'zɛlʃaftən] VT (*Pol*) to nationalize

vergessen [fɛr'gɛsən] *unreg* VT to forget; **Vergessenheit** F oblivion; **in Vergessenheit geraten** to fall into oblivion

vergesslich [fɛr'gɛslɪç] ADJ forgetful; **Vergesslichkeit** F forgetfulness

vergeuden [fɛr'gɔʏdən] VT to squander, to waste

vergewaltigen [fɛrgə'valtɪgən] VT to rape; (*fig*) to violate
Vergewaltigung F rape
vergewissern [fɛrgə'vɪsərn] VR to make sure; **sich einer Sache** *gen od* **über etw** *akk* **~** to make sure of sth
vergießen [fɛr'gi:sən] *unreg* VT to shed
vergiften [fɛr'gɪftən] VT to poison
Vergiftung F poisoning
vergilbt [fɛr'gɪlpt] ADJ yellowed
Vergissmeinnicht [fɛr'gɪsmaɪnnɪçt] **(-(e)s, -e)** NT forget-me-not
vergisst [fɛr'gɪst] VB *siehe* **vergessen**
vergittert [fɛr'gɪtərt] ADJ: **vergitterte Fenster** barred windows
verglasen [fɛr'gla:zən] VT to glaze
Vergleich [fɛr'glaɪç] **(-(e)s, -e)** M comparison; (*Jur*) settlement; **einen ~ schließen** (*Jur*) to reach a settlement; **in keinem ~ zu etw stehen** to be out of all proportion to sth; **im ~ mit** *od* **zu** compared with *od* to; **vergleichbar** ADJ comparable
vergleichen *unreg* VT to compare ▸ VR (*Jur*) to reach a settlement
vergleichsweise ADV comparatively
verglühen [fɛr'gly:ən] VI (*Feuer*) to die away; (*Draht*) to burn out; (*Raumkapsel, Meteor etc*) to burn up
vergnügen [fɛr'gny:gən] VR to enjoy *od* amuse o.s.; **Vergnügen (-s, -)** NT pleasure; **das war ein teures Vergnügen** (*umg*) that was an expensive bit of fun; **viel Vergnügen!** enjoy yourself!
vergnüglich ADJ enjoyable
vergnügt [fɛr'gny:kt] ADJ cheerful
Vergnügung F pleasure, amusement
Vergnügungs- ZW: **Vergnügungspark** M amusement park; **vergnügungssüchtig** ADJ pleasure-loving; **Vergnügungsviertel** NT entertainments district
vergolden [fɛr'gɔldən] VT to gild
vergönnen [fɛr'gœnən] VT to grant
vergöttern [fɛr'gœtərn] VT to idolize
vergraben [fɛr'gra:bən] *unreg* VT to bury
vergrämt [fɛr'grɛ:mt] ADJ (*Gesicht*) troubled
vergreifen [fɛr'graɪfən] *unreg* VR: **sich an jdm ~** to lay hands on sb; **sich an etw** *dat* **~** to misappropriate sth; **sich im Ton ~** to say the wrong thing
vergriffen [fɛr'grɪfən] ADJ (*Buch*) out of print; (*Ware*) out of stock
vergrößern [fɛr'grø:sərn] VT to enlarge; (*mengenmäßig*) to increase; (*Lupe*) to magnify
Vergrößerung F enlargement; (*von Menge*) increase; (*mit Lupe*) magnification
Vergrößerungsglas NT magnifying glass
vergünstigt ADJ (*Lage*) improved; (*Preis*) reduced
Vergünstigung [fɛr'gʏnstɪgʊŋ] F concession; (*Vorteil*) privilege
vergüten [fɛr'gy:tən] VT: **jdm etw ~** to compensate sb for sth; (*Arbeit, Leistung*) to pay sb for sth
Vergütung F compensation; (*von Arbeit, Leistung*) payment
verh. ABK = **verheiratet**
verhaften [fɛr'haftən] VT to arrest
Verhaftete(r) F(M) prisoner
Verhaftung F arrest
verhallen [fɛr'halən] VI to die away
verhalten [fɛr'haltən] *unreg* VR (*Sache*) to be, to stand; (*sich benehmen*) to behave; (*Math*) to be in proportion to ▸ VR UNPERS: **wie verhält es sich damit?** (*wie ist die Lage?*) how do things stand?; (*wie wird das gehandhabt?*) how do you go about it? ▸ ADJ restrained; **sich ruhig ~** to keep quiet; (*sich nicht bewegen*) to keep still; **wenn sich das so verhält ...** if that is the case ...; **Verhalten (-s)** NT behaviour (BRIT), behavior (US); **selbstverletzendes Verhalten** self-harm
Verhaltens- ZW: **Verhaltensforschung** F behavioural (BRIT) *od* behavioral (US) science; **verhaltensgestört** ADJ disturbed; **Verhaltensmaßregel** F rule of conduct
Verhältnis [fɛr'hɛltnɪs] **(-ses, -se)** NT relationship; (*Liebesverhältnis*) affair; (*Math*) proportion, ratio; (*Einstellung*): **~ (zu)** attitude (to); **Verhältnisse** PL (*Umstände*) conditions *pl*; **aus was für Verhältnissen kommt er?** what sort of background does he come from?; **für klare Verhältnisse sorgen, klare Verhältnisse schaffen** to get things straight; **über seine Verhältnisse leben** to live beyond one's means; **verhältnismäßig** ADJ relative, comparative ▸ ADV relatively, comparatively; **Verhältniswahl** F proportional representation; **Verhältniswahlrecht** NT (system of) proportional representation
verhandeln [fɛr'handəln] VI to negotiate; (*Jur*) to hold proceedings ▸ VT to discuss; (*Jur*) to hear; **über etw** *akk* **~** to negotiate sth *od* about sth
Verhandlung F negotiation; (*Jur*) proceedings *pl*; **Verhandlungen führen** to negotiate
Verhandlungspaket NT (*Comm*) package deal
Verhandlungstisch M negotiating table
verhangen [fɛr'haŋən] ADJ overcast
verhängen [fɛr'hɛŋən] VT (*fig*) to impose, to inflict
Verhängnis [fɛr'hɛŋnɪs] **(-ses, -se)** NT fate; **jdm zum ~ werden** to be sb's undoing; **verhängnisvoll** ADJ fatal, disastrous
verharmlosen [fɛr'harmlo:zən] VT to make light of, to play down
verharren [fɛr'harən] VI to remain; (*hartnäckig*) to persist
verhärten [fɛr'hɛrtən] VR to harden
verhaspeln [fɛr'haspəln] (*umg*) VR to get into a muddle *od* tangle
verhasst [fɛr'hast] ADJ odious, hateful
verhätscheln [fɛr'hɛ:tʃəln] VT to spoil, to pamper
Verhau [fɛr'haʊ] **(-(e)s, -e)** M (*zur Absperrung*) barrier; (*Käfig*) coop
verhauen *unreg* (*umg*) VT (*verprügeln*) to beat up; (*Prüfung etc*) to muff

verheben [fɛr'he:bən] *unreg* VR to hurt o.s. lifting sth
verheerend [fɛr'he:rənt] ADJ disastrous, devastating
verhehlen [fɛr'he:lən] VT to conceal
verheilen [fɛr'haɪlən] VI to heal
verheimlichen [fɛr'haɪmlɪçən] VT: **(jdm) etw ~** to keep sth secret (from sb)
verheiratet [fɛr'haɪra:tət] ADJ married
verheißen [fɛr'haɪsən] *unreg* VT: **jdm etw ~** to promise sb sth
verheißungsvoll ADJ promising
verheizen [fɛr'haɪtsən] VT to burn, to use as fuel
verhelfen [fɛr'hɛlfən] *unreg* VI: **jdm zu etw ~** to help sb to get sth
verherrlichen [fɛr'hɛrlɪçən] VT to glorify
verheult [fɛr'hɔʏlt] ADJ (*Augen, Gesicht*) puffy (*from crying*)
verhexen [fɛr'hɛksən] VT to bewitch; **es ist wie verhext** it's jinxed
verhindern [fɛr'hɪndərn] VT to prevent; **verhindert sein** to be unable to make it; **das lässt sich leider nicht ~** it can't be helped, unfortunately; **ein verhinderter Politiker** (*umg*) a would-be politician
Verhinderung F prevention
verhöhnen [fɛr'hø:nən] VT to mock, to sneer at
verhohnepipeln [fɛr'ho:nəpi:pəln] (*umg*) VT to send up (BRIT), to ridicule
verhökern [fɛr'hø:kərn] (*umg*) VT to turn into cash
Verhör [fɛr'hø:r] (**-(e)s, -e**) NT interrogation; (*gerichtlich*) (cross-)examination
verhören VT to interrogate; (*vor Gericht*) to (cross-)examine ▸ VR to mishear
verhüllen [fɛr'hʏlən] VT to veil; (*Haupt, Körperteil*) to cover
verhungern [fɛr'hʊŋərn] VI to starve, to die of hunger
verhunzen [fɛr'hʊntsən] (*umg*) VT to ruin
verhüten [fɛr'hy:tən] VT to prevent, to avert
Verhütung F prevention
Verhütungsmittel NT contraceptive
verifizieren [verifi'tsi:rən] VT to verify
verinnerlichen [fɛr'ɪnərlɪçən] VT to internalize
verirren [fɛr'ɪrən] VR to get lost, to lose one's way; (*fig*) to go astray; (*Tier, Kugel*) to stray
verjagen [fɛr'ja:gən] VT to drive away *od* out
verjähren [fɛr'jɛ:rən] VI to come under the statute of limitations; (*Anspruch*) to lapse
Verjährungsfrist F limitation period
verjubeln [fɛr'ju:bəln] (*umg*) VT (*Geld*) to blow
verjüngen [fɛr'jʏŋən] VT to rejuvenate ▸ VR to taper
verkabeln [fɛr'ka:bəln] VT (TV) to link up to the cable network
Verkabelung F (TV) linking up to the cable network
verkalken [fɛr'kalkən] VI to calcify; (*umg*) to become senile
verkalkulieren [fɛrkalku'li:rən] VR to miscalculate
verkannt [fɛr'kant] ADJ unappreciated
verkatert [fɛr'ka:tərt] (*umg*) ADJ hung over
Verkauf [fɛr'kaʊf] M sale; **zum ~ stehen** to be up for sale
verkaufen VT, VI to sell; **„zu ~"** "for sale"
Verkäufer(in) [fɛr'kɔʏfər(ɪn)] (**-s, -**) M(F) seller; (*im Außendienst*) salesman, saleswoman; (*in Laden*) shop assistant (BRIT), sales clerk (US)
verkäuflich [fɛr'kɔʏflɪç] ADJ saleable
Verkaufs- ZW: **Verkaufsabteilung** F sales department; **Verkaufsautomat** M slot machine; **Verkaufsbedingungen** PL (*Comm*) terms and conditions of sale; **Verkaufskampagne** F sales drive; **Verkaufsleiter** M sales manager; **verkaufsoffen** ADJ: **verkaufsoffener Samstag** *Saturday on which the shops are open all day*; **Verkaufsschlager** M big seller; **Verkaufsstelle** F outlet; **Verkaufstüchtigkeit** F salesmanship
Verkehr [fɛr'ke:r] (**-s, -e**) M traffic; (*Umgang, bes sexuell*) intercourse; (*Umlauf*) circulation; **aus dem ~ ziehen** to withdraw from service; **für den ~ freigeben** (*Straße etc*) to open to traffic; (*Transportmittel*) to bring into service
verkehren VI (*Fahrzeug*) to ply, to run ▸ VT, VR to turn, to transform; **~ mit** to associate with; **mit jdm brieflich** *od* **schriftlich ~** (*form*) to correspond with sb; **bei jdm ~** to visit sb regularly
Verkehrs- ZW: **Verkehrsampel** F traffic lights *pl*; **Verkehrsamt** NT tourist (information) office; **Verkehrsaufkommen** NT volume of traffic; **verkehrsberuhigt** ADJ traffic-calmed; **Verkehrsberuhigung** F traffic-calming; **Verkehrsbetriebe** PL transport services *pl*; **Verkehrsdelikt** NT traffic offence (BRIT) *od* violation (US); **Verkehrserziehung** F road safety training; **verkehrsgünstig** ADJ convenient; **Verkehrsinsel** F traffic island; **Verkehrsknotenpunkt** M traffic junction; **Verkehrsmittel** NT: **öffentliche/private Verkehrsmittel** public/private transport *sing*; **Verkehrsschild** NT road sign; **verkehrssicher** ADJ (*Fahrzeug*) roadworthy; **Verkehrssicherheit** F road safety; **Verkehrsstockung** F traffic jam, stoppage; **Verkehrssünder** (*umg*) M traffic offender; **Verkehrsteilnehmer** M road user; **verkehrstüchtig** ADJ (*Fahrzeug*) roadworthy; (*Mensch*) fit to drive; **Verkehrsunfall** M traffic accident; **Verkehrsverein** M tourist information office; **verkehrswidrig** ADJ contrary to traffic regulations; **Verkehrszeichen** NT road sign
verkehrt ADJ wrong; (*umgekehrt*) the wrong way round
verkennen [fɛr'kɛnən] *unreg* VT to misjudge; (*unterschätzen*) to underestimate
Verkettung [fɛr'kɛtʊŋ] F: **eine ~ unglücklicher Umstände** an unfortunate chain of events
verklagen [fɛr'kla:gən] VT to take to court
verklappen [fɛr'klapən] VT to dump (at sea)
verklären [fɛr'klɛ:rən] VT to transfigure; **verklärt lächeln** to smile radiantly

verklausulieren [fɛrklauzu'li:rən] VT (*Vertrag*) to hedge in with (restrictive) clauses
verkleben [fɛr'kle:bən] VT to glue up, to stick ▶ VI to stick together
verkleiden [fɛr'klaidən] VT to disguise; (*kostümieren*) to dress up; (*Schacht, Tunnel*) to line; (*vertäfeln*) to panel; (*Heizkörper*) to cover in ▶ VR to disguise o.s.; (*sich kostümieren*) to dress up
Verkleidung F disguise; (*Archit*) panelling (BRIT), paneling (US)
verkleinern [fɛr'klainərn] VT to make smaller, to reduce in size
verklemmt [fɛr'klɛmt] ADJ (*fig*) inhibited
verklickern [fɛr'klikərn] (*umg*) VT: **jdm etw ~** to make sth clear to sb
verklingen [fɛr'kliŋən] *unreg* VI to die away
verknacksen [fɛr'knaksən] (*umg*) VT: **sich** *dat* **den Fuß ~** to twist one's ankle
verknallen [fɛr'knalən] (*umg*) VR: **sich in jdn ~** to fall for sb
verkneifen [fɛr'knaifən] (*umg*) VT: **sich** *dat* **etw ~** to stop o.s. from doing sth; **ich konnte mir das Lachen nicht ~** I couldn't help laughing
verknöchert [fɛr'knœçərt] ADJ (*fig*) fossilized
verknüpfen [fɛr'knypfən] VT to tie (up), to knot; (*fig*) to connect
Verknüpfung F connection
verkochen [fɛr'kɔxən] VT, VI (*Flüssigkeit*) to boil away
verkohlen [fɛr'ko:lən] VI to carbonize ▶ VT to carbonize; (*umg*): **jdn ~** to have sb on
verkommen [fɛr'kɔmən] *unreg* VI to deteriorate, to decay; (*Mensch*) to go downhill, to come down in the world ▶ ADJ (*moralisch*) dissolute, depraved; **Verkommenheit** F depravity
verkorksen [fɛr'kɔrksən] (*umg*) VT to ruin, to mess up
verkörpern [fɛr'kœrpərn] VT to embody, to personify
verköstigen [fɛr'kœstigən] VT to feed
verkrachen [fɛr'kraxən] (*umg*) VR: **sich (mit jdm) ~** to fall out (with sb)
verkracht (*umg*) ADJ (*Leben*) ruined
verkraften [fɛr'kraftən] VT to cope with
verkrampfen [fɛr'krampfən] VR (*Muskeln*) to go tense
verkrampft [fɛr'krampft] ADJ (*fig*) tense
verkriechen [fɛr'kri:çən] *unreg* VR to creep away, to creep into a corner
verkrümeln [fɛr'kry:məln] (*umg*) VR to disappear
verkrümmt [fɛr'krymt] ADJ crooked
Verkrümmung F bend, warp; (*Anat*) curvature
verkrüppelt [fɛr'krypəlt] ADJ crippled
verkrustet [fɛr'krustət] ADJ encrusted
verkühlen [fɛr'ky:lən] VR to get a chill
verkümmern [fɛr'kymərn] VI to waste away; **emotionell/geistig ~** to become emotionally/intellectually stunted
verkünden [fɛr'kyndən] VT to proclaim; (*Urteil*) to pronounce
verkündigen [fɛr'kyndigən] VT to proclaim; (*ironisch*) to announce; (*Evangelium*) to preach
verkuppeln [fɛr'kupəln] VT: **jdn an jdn ~** (*Zuhälter*) to procure sb for sb
verkürzen [fɛr'kyrtsən] VT to shorten; (*Wort*) to abbreviate; **sich** *dat* **die Zeit ~** to while away the time; **verkürzte Arbeitszeit** shorter working hours *pl*
Verkürzung F shortening; (*von Wort*) abbreviation
Verl. ABK (= *Verlag*) publ.
verladen [fɛr'la:dən] *unreg* VT to load
Verlag [fɛr'la:k] **(-(e)s, -e)** M publishing firm
verlagern [fɛr'la:gərn] VT, VR (*lit, fig*) to shift
Verlagsanstalt F publishing firm
Verlagswesen NT publishing
verlangen [fɛr'laŋən] VT to demand; (*wollen*) to want; (*Preis*) to ask; (*Qualifikation*) to require; (*erwarten von*) to ask of; (*fragen nach*) to ask for ▶ VI: **~ nach** to ask for; **Sie werden am Telefon verlangt** you are wanted on the phone; **~ Sie Herrn X** ask for Mr X; **Verlangen (-s, -)** NT: **Verlangen (nach)** desire (for); **auf jds Verlangen** *akk* **(hin)** at sb's request
verlängern [fɛr'lɛŋərn] VT to extend; (*länger machen*) to lengthen; (*zeitlich*) to prolong; (*Pass, Abonnement etc*) to renew; **ein verlängertes Wochenende** a long weekend
Verlängerung F extension; (*Sport*) extra time; (*von Pass, Erlaubnis*) renewal
Verlängerungsschnur F extension cable
verlangsamen [fɛr'laŋza:mən] VT, VR to decelerate, to slow down
Verlass [fɛr'las] M: **auf ihn/das ist kein ~** he/it cannot be relied upon
verlassen [fɛr'lasən] *unreg* VT to leave ▶ VR: **sich ~ auf** *+akk* to depend on ▶ ADJ desolate; (*Mensch*) abandoned; **einsam und ~** so all alone; **Verlassenheit** F loneliness (BRIT), lonesomeness (US)
verlässlich [fɛr'lɛsliç] ADJ reliable
Verlauf [fɛr'lauf] M course; **einen guten/schlechten ~ nehmen** to go well/badly
verlaufen *unreg* VI (*zeitlich*) to pass; (*Farben*) to run ▶ VR to get lost; (*Menschenmenge*) to disperse
Verlautbarung F announcement
verlauten [fɛr'lautən] VI: **etw ~ lassen** to disclose sth; **wie verlautet** as reported
verleben [fɛr'le:bən] VT to spend
verlebt [fɛr'le:pt] ADJ dissipated, worn-out
verlegen [fɛr'le:gən] VT to move; (*verlieren*) to mislay; (*Kabel, Fliesen etc*) to lay; (*Buch*) to publish; (*verschieben*): **~ (auf** *+akk***)** to postpone (until) ▶ VR: **sich auf etw** *akk* **~** to resort to sth ▶ ADJ embarrassed; **nicht ~ um** never at a loss for; **Verlegenheit** F embarrassment; (*Situation*) difficulty, scrape
Verleger [fɛr'le:gər] **(-s, -)** M publisher
verleiden [fɛr'laidən] VT: **jdm etw ~** to put sb off sth
Verleih [fɛr'lai] **(-(e)s, -e)** M (*Firma*) hire service; (*das Verleihen*) renting (out), hiring (out) (BRIT); (*Filmverleih*) distribution
verleihen *unreg* VT: **etw (an jdn) ~** to lend sth (to sb), to lend (sb) sth; (*gegen Gebühr*) to rent sth

(out) (to sb), to hire sth (out) (to sb) (BRIT); (*Kraft, Anschein*) to confer sth (on sb), to bestow sth (on sb); (*Preis, Medaille*) to award sth (to sb), to award (sb) sth
Verleiher (**-s, -**) M hire (BRIT) *od* rental firm; (*von Filmen*) distributor; (*von Büchern*) lender
Verleihung F lending; (*von Kraft etc*) bestowal; (*von Preis*) award
verleiten [fɛrˈlaɪtən] VT to lead astray; **~ zu** to talk into, to tempt into
verlernen [fɛrˈlɛrnən] VT to forget, to unlearn
verlesen [fɛrˈleːzən] *unreg* VT to read out; (*aussondern*) to sort out ▸ VR to make a mistake in reading
verletzbar ADJ vulnerable
verletzen [fɛrˈlɛtsən] VT (*lit, fig*) to injure, to hurt; (*Gesetz etc*) to violate
verletzend ADJ (*fig: Worte*) hurtful
verletzlich ADJ vulnerable
Verletzte(r) F(M) injured person
Verletzung F injury; (*Verstoß*) violation, infringement
verleugnen [fɛrˈlɔʏgnən] VT to deny; (*Menschen*) to disown; **er lässt sich immer (vor ihr) ~** he always pretends not to be there (when she calls)
Verleugnung F denial
verleumden [fɛrˈlɔʏmdən] VT to slander; (*schriftlich*) to libel
verleumderisch ADJ slanderous; (*schriftlich*) libellous (BRIT), libelous (US)
Verleumdung F slander; (*schriftlich*) libel
verlieben VR: **sich ~ (in +*akk*)** to fall in love (with)
verliebt [fɛrˈliːpt] ADJ in love; **Verliebtheit** F being in love
verlieren [fɛrˈliːrən] *unreg* VT, VI to lose ▸ VR to get lost; (*verschwinden*) to disappear; **das/er hat hier nichts verloren** (*umg*) that/he has no business to be here
Verlierer(in) (**-s, -**) M(F) loser
Verlies [fɛrˈliːs] (**-es, -e**) NT dungeon
verloben [fɛrˈloːbən] VR: **sich ~ (mit)** to get engaged (to); **verlobt sein** to be engaged
Verlobte(r) [fɛrˈloːptə(r)] F(M): **mein ~** my fiancé; **meine ~** my fiancée
Verlobung F engagement
verlocken [fɛrˈlɔkən] VT to entice, to lure
verlockend ADJ (*Angebot, Idee*) tempting
Verlockung F temptation, attraction
verlogen [fɛrˈloːgən] ADJ untruthful; (*Komplimente, Versprechungen*) false; (*Moral, Gesellschaft*) hypocritical; **Verlogenheit** F untruthfulness
verlor *etc* [fɛrˈloːr] VB *siehe* **verlieren**
verloren PP *von* **verlieren** ▸ ADJ lost; (*Eier*) poached; **der verlorene Sohn** the prodigal son; **auf verlorenem Posten kämpfen** *od* **stehen** to be fighting a losing battle; **etw ~ geben** to give sth up for lost; **~ gehen** to get lost; **an ihm ist ein Sänger ~ gegangen** he would have made a (good) singer
verlöschen [fɛrˈlœʃən] VI (*Hilfsverb sein*) to go out; (*Inschrift, Farbe, Erinnerung*) to fade
verlosen [fɛrˈloːzən] VT to raffle (off), to draw lots for
Verlosung F raffle, lottery
verlottern [fɛrˈlɔtərn] (*umg*) VI to go to the dogs
verludern [fɛrˈluːdərn] (*umg*) VI to go to the dogs
Verlust [fɛrˈlʊst] (**-(e)s, -e**) M loss; (*Mil*) casualty; **mit ~ verkaufen** to sell at a loss;
Verlustanzeige F "lost" notice;
Verlustgeschäft NT: **das war ein Verlustgeschäft** I/he *etc* made a loss;
Verlustzeit F (*Industrie*) waiting time
vermachen [fɛrˈmaxən] VT to bequeath, to leave
Vermächtnis [fɛrˈmɛçtnɪs] (**-ses, -se**) NT legacy
vermählen [fɛrˈmɛːlən] VR to marry
Vermählung F wedding, marriage
vermarkten [fɛrˈmarktən] VT to market; (*fig: Persönlichkeit*) to promote
Vermarktung [fɛrˈmarktʊŋ] F marketing
vermasseln [fɛrˈmasəln] (*umg*) VT to mess up
vermehren [fɛrˈmeːrən] VT, VR to multiply; (*Menge*) to increase
Vermehrung F multiplying; (*von Menge*) increase
vermeiden [fɛrˈmaɪdən] *unreg* VT to avoid
vermeidlich ADJ avoidable
vermeintlich [fɛrˈmaɪntlɪç] ADJ supposed
vermengen [fɛrˈmɛŋən] VT to mix; (*fig*) to mix up, to confuse
Vermenschlichung [fɛrˈmɛnʃlɪçʊŋ] F humanization
Vermerk [fɛrˈmɛrk] (**-(e)s, -e**) M note; (*in Ausweis*) endorsement
vermerken VT to note
vermessen [fɛrˈmɛsən] *unreg* VT to survey ▸ VR (*falsch messen*) to measure incorrectly ▸ ADJ presumptuous, bold; **Vermessenheit** F presumptuousness
Vermessung F survey(ing)
Vermessungsamt NT land survey(ing) office
Vermessungsingenieur M land surveyor
vermiesen [fɛrˈmiːzən] (*umg*) VT to spoil
vermieten [fɛrˈmiːtən] VT to let (BRIT), to rent (out); (*Auto*) to hire out, to rent
Vermieter(in) (**-s, -**) M(F) landlord, landlady
Vermietung F letting, renting (out); (*von Autos*) hiring (out), rental
vermindern [fɛrˈmɪndərn] VT, VR to lessen, to decrease
Verminderung F reduction
verminen [fɛrˈmiːnən] VT to mine
vermischen [fɛrˈmɪʃən] VT, VR to mix; (*Teesorten etc*) to blend; **vermischte Schriften** miscellaneous writings
vermissen [fɛrˈmɪsən] VT to miss; **vermisst sein, als vermisst gemeldet sein** to be reported missing; **wir haben dich bei der Party vermisst** we didn't see you at the party
Vermisste(r) F(M) missing person
Vermisstenanzeige F missing persons report
vermitteln [fɛrˈmɪtəln] VI to mediate ▸ VT to arrange; (*Gespräch*) to connect; (*Stelle*) to find; (*Gefühl, Bild, Idee etc*) to convey; (*Wissen*) to

impart; **vermittelnde Worte** conciliatory words; **jdm etw ~** to help sb to obtain sth; (*Stelle*) to find sth for sb
Vermittler(in) [fɛrˈmɪtlər(ɪn)] (**-s, -**) M(F) (*Comm*) agent; (*Schlichter*) mediator
Vermittlung F procurement; (*Stellenvermittlung*) agency; (*Tel*) exchange; (*Schlichtung*) mediation
Vermittlungsgebühr F commission
vermögen [fɛrˈmøːgən] *unreg* VT to be capable of; **~ zu** to be able to; **Vermögen** (**-s, -**) NT wealth; (*Fähigkeit*) ability; **mein ganzes Vermögen besteht aus …** my entire assets consist of …; **ein Vermögen kosten** to cost a fortune
vermögend ADJ wealthy
Vermögens- ZW: **Vermögenssteuer** F property tax, wealth tax; **Vermögenswert** M asset; **vermögenswirksam** ADJ: **sein Geld vermögenswirksam anlegen** to invest one's money profitably; **vermögenswirksame Leistungen** *employers' contributions to tax-deductible savings scheme*
vermummen [fɛrˈmʊmən] VR to wrap up (warm); (*sich verkleiden*) to disguise
Vermummungsverbot (**-(e)s**) NT *law against disguising o.s. at demonstrations*
vermurksen [fɛrˈmʊrksən] (*umg*) VT to make a mess of
vermuten [fɛrˈmuːtən] VT to suppose; (*argwöhnen*) to suspect
vermutlich ADJ supposed, presumed ▸ ADV probably
Vermutung F supposition; (*Argwohn*) suspicion; **die ~ liegt nahe, dass …** there are grounds for assuming that …
vernachlässigen [fɛrˈnaːxlɛsɪgən] VT to neglect ▸ VR to neglect o.s. *od* one's appearance
Vernachlässigung F neglect
vernarben [fɛrˈnarbən] VI to heal up
vernarren [fɛrˈnarən] (*umg*) VR: **in jdn/etw vernarrt sein** to be crazy about sb/sth
vernaschen [fɛrˈnaʃən] VT (*Geld*) to spend on sweets; (*umg: Mädchen, Mann*) to make it with
vernehmen [fɛrˈneːmən] *unreg* VT to hear, to perceive; (*erfahren*) to learn; (*Jur*) to (cross-)examine; (*Polizei*) to question; **Vernehmen** NT: **dem Vernehmen nach** from what I/we *etc* hear
vernehmlich ADJ audible
Vernehmung F (cross-)examination
vernehmungsfähig ADJ in a condition to be (cross-)examined
verneigen [fɛrˈnaɪgən] VR to bow
verneinen [fɛrˈnaɪnən] VT (*Frage*) to answer in the negative; (*ablehnen*) to deny; (*Gram*) to negate
verneinend ADJ negative
Verneinung F negation
vernichten [fɛrˈnɪçtən] VT to destroy, to annihilate
vernichtend ADJ (*fig*) crushing; (*Blick*) withering; (*Kritik*) scathing
Vernichtung F destruction, annihilation
Vernichtungsschlag M devastating blow
verniedlichen [fɛrˈniːtlɪçən] VT to play down
Vernunft [fɛrˈnʊnft] (**-**) F reason; **~ annehmen** to see reason; **Vernunftehe** F, **Vernunftheirat** F marriage of convenience
vernünftig [fɛrˈnʏnftɪç] ADJ sensible, reasonable
Vernunftmensch M rational person
veröden [fɛrˈløːdən] VI to become desolate ▸ VT (*Med*) to remove
veröffentlichen [fɛrˈlœfəntlɪçən] VT to publish
Veröffentlichung F publication
verordnen [fɛrˈlɔrdnən] VT (*Med*) to prescribe
Verordnung F order, decree; (*Med*) prescription
verpachten [fɛrˈpaxtən] VT to lease (out)
verpacken [fɛrˈpakən] VT to pack; (*verbrauchergerecht*) to package; (*einwickeln*) to wrap
Verpackung F packaging; (*das Verpacken*) packing; (*ds Einwickeln*) wrapping
verpassen [fɛrˈpasən] VT to miss; **jdm eine Ohrfeige ~** (*umg*) to give sb a clip round the ear
verpatzen [fɛrˈpatsən] (*umg*) VT to spoil, to mess up
verpennen [fɛrˈpɛnən] (*umg*) VI, VR to oversleep
verpesten [fɛrˈpɛstən] VT to pollute
verpetzen [fɛrˈpɛtsən] (*umg*) VT: **jdn ~ (bei)** to tell on sb (to)
verpfänden [fɛrˈpfɛndən] VT to pawn; (*Jur*) to mortgage
verpfeifen [fɛrˈpfaɪfən] *unreg* (*umg*) VT: **jdn ~ (bei)** to grass on sb (to)
verpflanzen [fɛrˈpflantsən] VT to transplant
Verpflanzung F transplanting; (*Med*) transplant
verpflegen [fɛrˈpfleːgən] VT to feed, to cater for (BRIT)
Verpflegung F catering; (*Kost*) food; (*in Hotel*) board
verpflichten [fɛrˈpflɪçtən] VT to oblige, to bind; (*anstellen*) to engage ▸ VR to undertake; (*Mil*) to sign on ▸ VI to carry obligations; **jdm verpflichtet sein** to be under an obligation to sb; **sich zu etw ~** to commit o.s. to doing sth; **jdm zu Dank verpflichtet sein** to be obliged to sb
verpflichtend ADJ (*Zusage*) binding
Verpflichtung F obligation; (*Aufgabe*) duty
verpfuschen [fɛrˈpfʊʃən] (*umg*) VT to bungle, to make a mess of
verplanen [fɛrˈplaːnən] VT (*Zeit*) to book up; (*Geld*) to budget
verplappern [fɛrˈplapərn] (*umg*) VR to open one's big mouth
verplempern [fɛrˈplɛmpərn] (*umg*) VT to waste
verpönt [fɛrˈpøːnt] ADJ: **~ (bei)** frowned upon (by)
verprassen [fɛrˈprasən] VT to squander
verprügeln [fɛrˈpryːgəln] VT to beat up
verpuffen [fɛrˈpʊfən] VI to (go) pop; (*fig*) to fall flat
Verputz [fɛrˈpʊts] M plaster; (*Rauputz*) roughcast; **verputzen** VT to plaster; (*umg: Essen*) to put away

verqualmen [fɛr'kvalmən] VT (*Zimmer*) to fill with smoke
verquollen [fɛr'kvɔlən] ADJ swollen; (*Holz*) warped
verrammeln [fɛr'raməln] VT to barricade
Verrat [fɛr'ra:t] (**-(e)s**) M treachery; (*Pol*) treason; **~ an jdm üben** to betray sb
verraten *unreg* VT to betray; (*fig: erkennen lassen*) to show; (*Geheimnis*) to divulge ▶ VR to give o.s. away
Verräter(in) [fɛr'rɛ:tər(ɪn)] (**-s, -**) M(F) traitor, traitress; **verräterisch** ADJ treacherous
verrauchen [fɛr'rauxən] VI (*fig: Zorn*) to blow over
verrechnen [fɛr'rɛçnən] VT: **~ mit** to set off against ▶ VR to miscalculate
Verrechnung F: **nur zur ~** (*auf Scheck*) a/c payee only
Verrechnungsscheck M crossed cheque (BRIT)
verregnet [fɛr're:gnət] ADJ rainy, spoilt by rain
verreisen [fɛr'raɪzən] VI to go away (on a journey); **er ist geschäftlich verreist** he's away on business
verreißen [fɛr'raɪsən] *unreg* VT to pull to pieces
verrenken [fɛr'rɛŋkən] VT to contort; (*Med*) to dislocate; **sich** *dat* **den Knöchel ~** to sprain one's ankle
Verrenkung F contortion; (*Med*) dislocation
verrennen [fɛr'rɛnən] *unreg* VR: **sich in etw** *akk* **~** to get stuck on sth
verrichten [fɛr'rɪçtən] VT (*Arbeit*) to do, to perform
verriegeln [fɛr'ri:gəln] VT to bolt
verringern [fɛr'rɪŋərn] VT to reduce ▶ VR to decrease
Verringerung F reduction; (*Abnahme*) decrease
verrinnen [fɛr'rɪnən] *unreg* VI to run out *od* away; (*Zeit*) to elapse
Verriss [fɛr'rɪs] M slating review
verrohen [fɛr'ro:ən] VI to become brutalized
verrosten [fɛr'rɔstən] VI to rust
verrotten [fɛr'rɔtən] VI to rot
verrucht [fɛr'ru:xt] ADJ despicable; (*verrufen*) disreputable
verrücken [fɛr'rʏkən] VT to move, to shift
verrückt ADJ crazy, mad; **Verrückte(r)** F(M) lunatic; **Verrücktheit** F madness, lunacy
Verruf [fɛr'ru:f] M: **in ~ geraten/bringen** to fall/bring into disrepute
verrufen ADJ disreputable
verrutschen [fɛr'rʊtʃən] VI to slip
Vers [fɛrs] (**-es, -e**) M verse
versacken [fɛr'zakən] VI (*lit*) to sink; (*fig: umg: herunterkommen*) to go downhill; (*: lange zechen*) to get involved in a booze-up (BRIT) *od* a drinking spree
versagen [fɛr'za:gən] VT: **jdm/sich etw ~** to deny sb/o.s. sth ▶ VI to fail; **Versagen** (**-s**) NT failure; **menschliches Versagen** human error
Versager (**-s, -**) M failure
versalzen [fɛr'zaltsən] VT to put too much salt in; (*fig*) to spoil
versammeln [fɛr'zaməln] VT, VR to assemble, to gather
Versammlung F meeting, gathering
Versammlungsfreiheit F freedom of assembly
Versand [fɛr'zant] (**-(e)s**) M dispatch; (*Versandabteilung*) dispatch department; **Versandbahnhof** M dispatch station; **Versandhaus** NT mail-order firm; **Versandkosten** PL transport(ation) costs *pl*; **Versandweg** M: **auf dem Versandweg** by mail order
versäumen [fɛr'zɔʏmən] VT to miss; (*Pflicht*) to neglect; (*Zeit*) to lose; **es ~, etw zu tun** to fail to do sth
Versäumnis (**-ses, -se**) NT neglect; (*Unterlassung*) omission
verschachern [fɛr'ʃaxərn] (*umg*) VT to sell off
verschachtelt [fɛr'ʃaxtəlt] ADJ (*Satz*) complex
verschaffen [fɛr'ʃafən] VT: **jdm/sich etw ~** to get *od* procure sth for sb/o.s.
verschämt [fɛr'ʃɛ:mt] ADJ bashful
verschandeln [fɛr'ʃandəln] (*umg*) VT to spoil
verschanzen [fɛr'ʃantsən] VR: **sich hinter etw** *dat* **~** to dig in behind sth; (*fig*) to take refuge behind sth
verschärfen [fɛr'ʃɛrfən] VT to intensify; (*Lage*) to aggravate; (*strenger machen: Kontrollen, Gesetze*) to tighten up ▶ VR to intensify; (*Lage*) to become aggravated; (*Kontrolle, Gesetze*) to become tighter
Verschärfung F intensification; (*der Lage*) aggravation; (*von Kontrollen etc*) tightening
verscharren [fɛr'ʃarən] VT to bury
verschätzen [fɛr'ʃɛtsən] VR to miscalculate
verschenken [fɛr'ʃɛŋkən] VT to give away
verscherzen [fɛr'ʃɛrtsən] VT: **sich** *dat* **etw ~** to lose sth, to throw sth away
verscheuchen [fɛr'ʃɔʏçən] VT to frighten away
verschicken [fɛr'ʃɪkən] VT to send off; (*Sträfling*) to transport
verschieben [fɛr'ʃi:bən] *unreg* VT to shift; (*Eisenb*) to shunt; (*Termin*) to postpone; (*umg: Waren, Devisen*) to traffic in
Verschiebung F shift, displacement; (*Eisenb*) shunting; (*von Termin*) postponement
verschieden [fɛr'ʃi:dən] ADJ different; (*mehrere*) various; **das ist ganz ~** (*wird verschieden gehandhabt*) that varies, that just depends; **sie sind ~ groß** they are of different sizes; **verschiedenartig** ADJ various, of different kinds; **zwei so verschiedenartige ...** two such differing ...; **Verschiedene(r, s)** PRON (*Menschen*) various people; (*Dinge*) various things *pl*; **etwas Verschiedenes** something different; **Verschiedenheit** F difference
verschiedentlich ADV several times
verschiffen [fɛr'ʃɪfən] VT to ship; (*Sträfling*) to transport
verschimmeln [fɛr'ʃɪməln] VI (*Nahrungsmittel*) to go mouldy (BRIT) *od* moldy (US); (*Leder, Papier etc*) to become mildewed

V

verschlafen [fɛr'ʃla:fən] *unreg* VT to sleep through; (*fig: versäumen*) to miss ▶ VI, VR to oversleep ▶ ADJ sleepy
Verschlag [fɛr'ʃla:k] M shed
verschlagen [fɛr'ʃla:gən] *unreg* VT to board up; (*Tennis*) to hit out of play; (*Buchseite*) to lose ▶ ADJ cunning; **jdm den Atem ~** to take sb's breath away; **an einen Ort ~ werden** to wind up in a place
verschlampen [fɛr'ʃlampən] VI (*Hilfsverb sein: Mensch*) to go to seed (*umg*) ▶ VT to lose, to mislay
verschlechtern [fɛr'ʃlɛçtərn] VT to make worse ▶ VR to deteriorate, to get worse; (*gehaltlich*) to take a lower-paid job
Verschlechterung F deterioration
Verschleierung [fɛr'ʃlaɪərʊŋ] F veiling; (*fig*) concealment; (*Mil*) screening
Verschleierungstaktik F smoke-screen tactics *pl*
Verschleiß [fɛr'ʃlaɪs] (**-es, -e**) M wear and tear
verschleißen *unreg* VT, VI, VR to wear out
verschleppen [fɛr'ʃlɛpən] VT to carry off, to abduct; (*zeitlich*) to drag out, to delay; (*verbreiten: Seuche*) to spread
verschleudern [fɛr'ʃlɔydərn] VT to squander; (*Comm*) to sell dirt-cheap
verschließbar ADJ lockable
verschließen [fɛr'ʃli:sən] *unreg* VT to lock ▶ VR: **sich einer Sache** *dat* **~** to close one's mind to sth
verschlimmern [fɛr'ʃlɪmərn] VT to make worse, to aggravate ▶ VR to get worse, to deteriorate
Verschlimmerung F deterioration
verschlingen [fɛr'ʃlɪŋən] *unreg* VT to devour, to swallow up; (*Fäden*) to twist
verschliss *etc* [fɛr'ʃlɪs] VB *siehe* **verschleißen**
verschlissen [fɛr'ʃlɪsən] PP *von* **verschleißen** ▶ ADJ worn(-out)
verschlossen [fɛr'ʃlɔsən] ADJ locked; (*fig*) reserved; (*schweigsam*) tight-lipped; **Verschlossenheit** F reserve
verschlucken [fɛr'ʃlʊkən] VT to swallow ▶ VR to choke
Verschluss [fɛr'ʃlʊs] M lock; (*von Kleid etc*) fastener; (*Phot*) shutter; (*Stöpsel*) plug; **unter ~ halten** to keep under lock and key
verschlüsseln [fɛr'ʃlʏsəln] VT to encode, to encrypt
verschmachten [fɛr'ʃmaxtən] VI: **~ (vor** *+dat***)** to languish (for); **vor Durst ~** to be dying of thirst
verschmähen [fɛr'ʃmɛ:ən] VT to scorn
verschmelzen [fɛr'ʃmɛltsən] *unreg* VT, VI to merge, to blend
verschmerzen [fɛr'ʃmɛrtsən] VT to get over
verschmiert [fɛr'ʃmi:rt] ADJ (*Hände*) smeary; (*Schminke*) smudged
verschmitzt [fɛr'ʃmɪtst] ADJ mischievous
verschmutzen [fɛr'ʃmʊtsən] VT to soil; (*Umwelt*) to pollute
Verschmutzung F pollution
verschnaufen [fɛr'ʃnaʊfən] (*umg*) VI, VR to have a breather
verschneiden [fɛr'ʃnaɪdən] VT (*Whisky etc*) to blend
verschneit [fɛr'ʃnaɪt] ADJ covered in snow, snowed up
Verschnitt [fɛr'ʃnɪt] M (*von Whisky etc*) blend
verschnörkelt [fɛr'ʃnœrkəlt] ADJ ornate
verschnupft [fɛr'ʃnʊpft] (*umg*) ADJ: **~ sein** to have a cold; (*beleidigt*) to be peeved (*umg*)
verschnüren [fɛr'ʃny:rən] VT to tie up
verschollen [fɛr'ʃɔlən] ADJ lost, missing
verschonen [fɛr'ʃo:nən] VT: **jdn mit etw ~** to spare sb sth; **von etw verschont bleiben** to escape sth
verschönern [fɛr'ʃø:nərn] VT to decorate; (*verbessern*) to improve
verschossen [fɛr'ʃɔsən] ADJ: **~ sein** (*fig: umg*) to be in love
verschränken [fɛr'ʃrɛŋkən] VT to cross; (*Arme*) to fold
verschreckt [fɛr'ʃrɛkt] ADJ frightened, scared
verschreiben [fɛr'ʃraɪbən] *unreg* VT (*Papier*) to use up; (*Med*) to prescribe ▶ VR to make a mistake (in writing); **sich einer Sache** *dat* **~** to devote o.s. to sth
verschreibungspflichtig ADJ available only on prescription
verschrieen [fɛr'ʃri:ən], **verschrien** [fɛr'ʃri:n] ADJ notorious
verschroben [fɛr'ʃro:bən] ADJ eccentric, odd
verschrotten [fɛr'ʃrɔtən] VT to scrap
verschüchtert [fɛr'ʃʏçtərt] ADJ subdued, intimidated
verschulden [fɛr'ʃʊldən] VT to be guilty of ▶ VI (*in Schulden geraten*) to get into debt; **Verschulden** (**-s**) NT fault
verschuldet ADJ in debt
Verschuldung F debts *pl*
verschütten [fɛr'ʃʏtən] VT to spill; (*zuschütten*) to fill; (*unter Trümmer*) to bury
verschwand *etc* [fɛr'ʃvant] VB *siehe* **verschwinden**
verschweigen [fɛr'ʃvaɪgən] *unreg* VT to keep secret; **jdm etw ~** to keep sth from sb
verschwenden [fɛr'ʃvɛndən] VT to squander
Verschwender(in) (**-s, -**) M(F) spendthrift; **verschwenderisch** ADJ wasteful; (*Leben*) extravagant
Verschwendung F waste
verschwiegen [fɛr'ʃvi:gən] ADJ discreet; (*Ort*) secluded; **Verschwiegenheit** F discretion; (*von Ort*) seclusion; **zur Verschwiegenheit verpflichtet** bound to secrecy
verschwimmen [fɛr'ʃvɪmən] *unreg* VI to grow hazy, to become blurred
verschwinden [fɛr'ʃvɪndən] *unreg* VI to disappear, to vanish; **verschwinde!** clear off! (*umg*); **Verschwinden** (**-s**) NT disappearance
verschwindend ADJ (*Anzahl, Menge*) insignificant
verschwitzen [fɛr'ʃvɪtsən] VT to stain with sweat; (*umg*) to forget
verschwitzt ADJ (*Kleidung*) sweat-stained; (*Mensch*) sweaty

verschwommen [fɛrˈʃvɔmən] ADJ hazy, vague
verschworen [fɛrˈʃvoːrən] ADJ (*Gesellschaft*) sworn
verschwören [fɛrˈʃvøːrən] *unreg* VR to conspire, to plot
Verschwörer(in) (**-s, -**) M(F) conspirator
Verschwörung F conspiracy, plot
verschwunden [fɛrˈʃvʊndən] PP *von* **verschwinden** ▶ ADJ missing
versehen [fɛrˈzeːən] *unreg* VT to supply, to provide; (*Pflicht*) to carry out; (*Amt*) to fill; (*Haushalt*) to keep ▶ VR (*fig*) to make a mistake; **ehe er (es) sich ~ hatte ...** before he knew it ...; **Versehen** (**-s, -**) NT oversight; **aus Versehen** by mistake
versehentlich ADV by mistake
Versehrte(r) [fɛrˈzeːrtə(r)] F(M) disabled person
verselbstständigen [fɛrˈzɛlpstʃtɛndɪgən], **verselbständigen** [fɛrˈzɛlpʃtɛndɪgən] VR to become independent
versenden [fɛrˈzɛndən] *unreg* VT to send; (*Comm*) to forward
versengen [fɛrˈzɛŋən] VT to scorch; (*Feuer*) to singe; (*umg: verprügeln*) to wallop
versenken [fɛrˈzɛŋkən] VT to sink ▶ VR: **sich ~ in** *+akk* to become engrossed in
versessen [fɛrˈzɛsən] ADJ: **~ auf** *+akk* mad about, hellbent on
versetzen [fɛrˈzɛtsən] VT to transfer; (*verpfänden*) to pawn; (*umg: vergeblich warten lassen*) to stand up; (*nicht geradlinig anordnen*) to stagger; (*Sch: in höhere Klasse*) to move up ▶ VR: **sich in jdn** *od* **in jds Lage ~** to put o.s. in sb's place; **jdm einen Tritt/Schlag ~** to kick/hit sb; **etw mit etw ~** to mix sth with sth; **jdm einen Stich ~** (*fig*) to cut sb to the quick, to wound sb (deeply); **jdn in gute Laune ~** to put sb in a good mood
Versetzung F transfer; **seine ~ ist gefährdet** (*Sch*) he's in danger of having to repeat a year
verseuchen [fɛrˈzɔʏçən] VT to contaminate
Versicherer (**-s, -**) M insurer; (*bei Schiffen*) underwriter
versichern [fɛrˈzɪçərn] VT to insure; (*bestätigen*) to assure ▶ VR: **sich ~** *+gen* to make sure of
Versicherte(r) F(M) insured
Versicherung F insurance; (*Bestätigung*) assurance
Versicherungs- ZW: **Versicherungsbeitrag** M insurance premium; (*bei staatlicher Versicherung etc*) *social security contribution*; **Versicherungsgesellschaft** F insurance company; **Versicherungsnehmer** (**-s, -**) M (*form*) insured, policy holder; **Versicherungspolice** F insurance policy; **Versicherungsschutz** M insurance cover; **Versicherungssumme** F sum insured; **Versicherungsträger** M insurer
versickern [fɛrˈzɪkərn] VI to seep away; (*fig: Interesse etc*) to peter out
versiegeln [fɛrˈziːgəln] VT to seal (up)
versiegen [fɛrˈziːgən] VI to dry up
versiert [vɛrˈziːrt] ADJ: **in etw** *dat* **~ sein** to be experienced *od* well versed in sth
versilbert [fɛrˈzɪlbərt] ADJ silver-plated
versinken [fɛrˈzɪŋkən] *unreg* VI to sink; **ich hätte im Boden** *od* **vor Scham ~ mögen** I wished the ground would swallow me up
versinnbildlichen [fɛrˈzɪnbɪltlɪçən] VT to symbolize
Version [vɛrziˈoːn] F version
Versmaß [ˈfɛrsmaːs] NT metre (BRIT), meter (US)
versohlen [fɛrˈzoːlən] (*umg*) VT to belt
versöhnen [fɛrˈzøːnən] VT to reconcile ▶ VR to become reconciled
versöhnlich ADJ (*Ton, Worte*) conciliatory; (*Ende*) happy
Versöhnung F reconciliation
versonnen [fɛrˈzɔnən] ADJ (*Gesichtsausdruck*) pensive, thoughtful; (*träumerisch: Blick*) dreamy
versorgen [fɛrˈzɔrgən] VT to provide, to supply; (*Familie etc*) to look after ▶ VR to look after o.s.
Versorger(in) (**-s, -**) M(F) (*Ernährer*) provider, breadwinner; (*Belieferer*) supplier
Versorgung F provision; (*Unterhalt*) maintenance; (*Altersversorgung etc*) benefit, assistance
Versorgungs- ZW: **Versorgungsamt** NT pension office; **Versorgungsbetrieb** M public utility; **Versorgungsnetz** NT (*Wasserversorgung etc*) (supply) grid; (*von Waren*) supply network
verspannen [fɛrˈʃpanən] VR (*Muskeln*) to tense up
verspäten [fɛrˈʃpɛːtən] VR to be late
verspätet ADJ late
Verspätung F delay; **~ haben** to be late; **mit zwanzig Minuten ~** twenty minutes late
versperren [fɛrˈʃpɛrən] VT to bar, to obstruct
verspielen [fɛrˈʃpiːlən] VT, VI to lose; **(bei jdm) verspielt haben** to have had it (as far as sb is concerned)
verspielt [fɛrˈʃpiːlt] ADJ playful
versponnen [fɛrˈʃpɔnən] ADJ crackpot
verspotten [fɛrˈʃpɔtən] VT to ridicule, to scoff at
versprach *etc* [fɛrˈʃpraːx] VB *siehe* **versprechen**
versprechen [fɛrˈʃprɛçən] *unreg* VT to promise ▶ VR (*etwas Nichtgemeintes sagen*) to make a slip of the tongue; **sich** *dat* **etw von etw ~** to expect sth from sth; **Versprechen** (**-s, -**) NT promise
Versprecher (**-s, -**) (*umg*) M slip (of the tongue)
verspricht [fɛrˈʃprɪçt] VB *siehe* **versprechen**
verspüren [fɛrˈʃpyːrən] VT to feel, to be conscious of
verstaatlichen [fɛrˈʃtaːtlɪçən] VT to nationalize
verstaatlicht ADJ: **verstaatlichter Industriezweig** nationalized industry
Verstaatlichung F nationalization
verstand *etc* VB *siehe* **verstehen**
Verstand [fɛrˈʃtant] M intelligence; (*Intellekt*) mind; (*Fähigkeit zu denken*) reason; **den ~ verlieren** to go out of one's mind; **über jds ~** *akk* **gehen** to be beyond sb
verstanden [fɛrˈʃtandən] PP *von* **verstehen**
verstandesmäßig ADJ rational
verständig [fɛrˈʃtɛndɪç] ADJ sensible
verständigen [fɛrˈʃtɛndɪgən] VT to inform ▶ VR to communicate; (*sich einigen*) to come to an understanding

V

Verständigkeit F good sense
Verständigung F communication; (*Benachrichtigung*) informing; (*Einigung*) agreement
verständlich [fɛrˈʃtɛntlɪç] ADJ understandable, comprehensible; (*hörbar*) audible; **sich ~ machen** to make o.s. understood; (*sich klar ausdrücken*) to make o.s. clear
verständlicherweise ADV understandably (enough)
Verständlichkeit F clarity, intelligibility
Verständnis (-ses, -se) NT understanding; **für etw kein ~ haben** to have no understanding *od* sympathy for sth; (*für Kunst etc*) to have no appreciation of sth; **verständnislos** ADJ uncomprehending; **verständnisvoll** ADJ understanding, sympathetic
verstärken [fɛrˈʃtɛrkən] VT to strengthen; (*Ton*) to amplify; (*erhöhen*) to intensify ▶ VR to intensify
Verstärker (-s, -) M amplifier
Verstärkung F strengthening; (*Hilfe*) reinforcements *pl*; (*von Ton*) amplification
verstaubt [fɛrˈʃtaʊpt] ADJ dusty; (*fig: Ansichten*) fuddy-duddy (*umg*)
verstauchen [fɛrˈʃtaʊxən] VT to sprain
verstauen [fɛrˈʃtaʊən] VT to stow away
Versteck [fɛrˈʃtɛk] **(-(e)s, -e)** NT hiding (place)
verstecken VT, VR to hide
versteckt ADJ hidden; (*Tür*) concealed; (*fig: Lächeln, Blick*) furtive; (*Andeutung*) veiled
verstehen [fɛrˈʃteːən] *unreg* VT, VI to understand; (*können, beherrschen*) to know ▶ VR (*auskommen*) to get on; **das ist nicht wörtlich zu ~** that isn't to be taken literally; **das versteht sich von selbst** that goes without saying; **die Preise ~ sich einschließlich Lieferung** prices are inclusive of delivery; **sich auf etw** *akk* **~** to be an expert at sth
versteifen [fɛrˈʃtaɪfən] VT to stiffen, to brace ▶ VR (*fig*): **sich ~ auf** *+akk* to insist on
versteigen [fɛrˈʃtaɪgən] *unreg* VR: **sie hat sich zu der Behauptung verstiegen, dass …** she presumed to claim that …
versteigern [fɛrˈʃtaɪgərn] VT to auction
Versteigerung F auction
verstellbar ADJ adjustable, variable
verstellen [fɛrˈʃtɛlən] VT to move, to shift; (*Uhr*) to adjust; (*versperren*) to block; (*fig*) to disguise ▶ VR to pretend, to put on an act
Verstellung F pretence (BRIT), pretense (US)
versteuern [fɛrˈʃtɔʏərn] VT to pay tax on; **zu ~** taxable
verstiegen [fɛrˈʃtiːgən] ADJ exaggerated
verstimmt [fɛrˈʃtɪmt] ADJ out of tune; (*fig*) cross, put out; (*: Magen*) upset
Verstimmung F (*fig*) disgruntled state, peevishness
verstockt [fɛrˈʃtɔkt] ADJ stubborn; **Verstocktheit** F stubbornness
verstohlen [fɛrˈʃtoːlən] ADJ stealthy
verstopfen [fɛrˈʃtɔpfən] VT to block, to stop up; (*Med*) to constipate
Verstopfung F obstruction; (*Med*) constipation
verstorben [fɛrˈʃtɔrbən] ADJ deceased, late
Verstorbene(r) F(M) deceased
verstört [fɛrˈʃtøːrt] ADJ (*Mensch*) distraught
Verstoß [fɛrˈʃtoːs] M: **~ (gegen)** infringement (of), violation (of)
verstoßen *unreg* VT to disown, to reject ▶ VI: **~ gegen** to offend against
Verstrebung [fɛrˈʃtreːbʊŋ] F (*Strebebalken*) support(ing beam)
verstreichen [fɛrˈʃtraɪçən] *unreg* VT to spread ▶ VI to elapse; (*Zeit*) to pass (by); (*Frist*) to expire
verstreuen [fɛrˈʃtrɔʏən] VT to scatter (about)
verstricken [fɛrˈʃtrɪkən] VT (*fig*) to entangle, to ensnare ▶ VR: **sich ~ in** *+akk* to get entangled in
verströmen [fɛrˈʃtrøːmən] VT to exude
verstümmeln [fɛrˈʃtʏməln] VT to maim, to mutilate (*auch fig*)
verstummen [fɛrˈʃtʊmən] VI to go silent; (*Lärm*) to die away
Versuch [fɛrˈzuːx] **(-(e)s, -e)** M attempt; (*Chem etc*) experiment; **das käme auf einen ~ an** we'll have to have a try
versuchen VT to try; (*verlocken*) to tempt ▶ VR: **sich an etw** *dat* **~** to try one's hand at sth
Versuchs- ZW: **Versuchsanstalt** F research institute; **Versuchsbohrung** F experimental drilling; **Versuchskaninchen** NT guinea pig; **Versuchsobjekt** NT test object; (*fig: Mensch*) guinea pig; **Versuchsreihe** F series of experiments; **versuchsweise** ADV tentatively
Versuchung F temptation
versumpfen [fɛrˈzʊmpfən] VI (*Gebiet*) to become marshy; (*fig: umg*) to go to pot; (*lange zechen*) to get involved in a booze-up (BRIT) *od* drinking spree (US)
versündigen [fɛrˈzʏndɪgən] VR (*geh*): **sich an jdm/etw ~** to sin against sb/sth
versunken [fɛrˈzʊŋkən] ADJ sunken; **~ sein in** *+akk* to be absorbed *od* engrossed in; **Versunkenheit** F absorption
versüßen [fɛrˈzyːsən] VT: **jdm etw ~** (*fig*) to make sth more pleasant for sb
vertagen [fɛrˈtaːgən] VT, VI to adjourn
Vertagung F adjournment
vertauschen [fɛrˈtaʊʃən] VT to exchange; (*versehentlich*) to mix up; **vertauschte Rollen** reversed roles
verteidigen [fɛrˈtaɪdɪgən] VT to defend ▶ VR to defend o.s.; (*vor Gericht*) to conduct one's own defence (BRIT) *od* defense (US)
Verteidiger(in) (-s, -) M(F) defender; (*Anwalt*) defence (BRIT) *od* defense (US) lawyer
Verteidigung F defence (BRIT), defense (US)
Verteidigungsfähigkeit F ability to defend
Verteidigungsminister M Minister of Defence (BRIT), Defense Secretary (US)
verteilen [fɛrˈtaɪlən] VT to distribute; (*Rollen*) to assign; (*Salbe*) to spread
Verteiler (-s, -) M (*Comm, Aut*) distributor
Verteilung F distribution
Verteuerung [fɛrˈtɔʏərʊŋ] F increase in price
verteufeln [fɛrˈtɔʏfəln] VT to condemn

verteufelt (*umg*) ADJ awful, devilish ▶ ADV awfully, devilishly
vertiefen [fɛr'tiːfən] VT to deepen; (*Sch*) to consolidate ▶ VR: **sich in etw** *akk* **~** to become engrossed *od* absorbed in sth
Vertiefung F depression
vertikal [vɛrti'kaːl] ADJ vertical
vertilgen [fɛr'tɪlgən] VT to exterminate; (*umg*) to eat up, to consume
Vertilgungsmittel NT weedkiller; (*Insektenvertilgungsmittel*) pesticide
vertippen [fɛr'tɪpən] VR to make a typing mistake
vertonen [fɛr'toːnən] VT to set to music; (*Film etc*) to add a soundtrack to
vertrackt [fɛr'trakt] ADJ awkward, tricky, complex
Vertrag [fɛr'traːk] **(-(e)s, Verträge)** M contract, agreement; (*Pol*) treaty
vertragen [fɛr'traːgən] *unreg* VT to tolerate, to stand ▶ VR to get along; (*sich aussöhnen*) to become reconciled; **viel ~ können** (*umg: Alkohol*) to be able to hold one's drink; **sich mit etw ~** (*Nahrungsmittel, Farbe*) to go with sth; (*Aussage, Verhalten*) to be consistent with sth
vertraglich ADJ contractual
verträglich [fɛr'trɛːklɪç] ADJ good-natured; (*Speisen*) easily digested; (*Med*) easily tolerated; **Verträglichkeit** F good nature; (*von Speisen*) digestibility
Vertrags- ZW: **Vertragsbruch** M breach of contract; **vertragsbrüchig** ADJ in breach of contract; **vertragsfähig** ADJ (*Jur*) competent to contract; **vertragsmäßig** ADJ, ADV (as) stipulated, according to contract; **Vertragspartner** M party to a contract; **Vertragsspieler** M (*Sport*) player under contract; **vertragswidrig** ADJ, ADV contrary to contract
vertrauen [fɛr'traʊən] VI: **jdm ~** to trust sb; **~ auf** *+akk* to rely on; **Vertrauen (-s)** NT confidence; **jdn ins Vertrauen ziehen** to take sb into one's confidence; **Vertrauen zu jdm fassen** to gain confidence in sb; **vertrauenerweckend** ADJ inspiring trust
Vertrauens- ZW: **Vertrauensmann** (*pl* **-(e)s, -männer** *od* **-leute**) M intermediary; **Vertrauenssache** F (*vertrauliche Angelegenheit*) confidential matter; (*Frage des Vertrauens*) question of trust; **vertrauensselig** ADJ trusting; **vertrauensvoll** ADJ trustful; **Vertrauensvotum** NT (*Parl*) vote of confidence; **vertrauenswürdig** ADJ trustworthy
vertraulich [fɛr'traʊlɪç] ADJ familiar; (*geheim*) confidential; **Vertraulichkeit** F familiarity; (*von Geheimnis*) confidentiality
verträumt [fɛr'trɔʏmt] ADJ dreamy; (*Städtchen etc*) sleepy
vertraut [fɛr'traʊt] ADJ familiar; **sich mit dem Gedanken ~ machen, dass ...** to get used to the idea that ...
Vertraute(r) F(M) confidant(e), close friend
Vertrautheit F familiarity
vertreiben [fɛr'traɪbən] *unreg* VT to drive away; (*aus Land*) to expel; (*Comm*) to sell; (*Zeit*) to pass
Vertreibung F expulsion
vertretbar ADJ justifiable; (*Theorie, Argument*) tenable
vertreten [fɛr'treːtən] *unreg* VT to represent; (*Ansicht*) to hold, to advocate; (*ersetzen*) to replace; (*Kollegen*) to cover for; (*Comm*) to be the agent for; **sich** *dat* **die Beine ~** to stretch one's legs
Vertreter(in) **(-s, -)** M(F) representative; (*Verfechter*) advocate; (*Comm: Firma*) agent; **Vertreterprovision** F agent's commission
Vertretung F representation; (*Befürwortung*) advocacy; **die ~ übernehmen (für)** to stand in (for)
Vertretungsstunde F (*Sch*) cover lesson
Vertrieb [fɛr'triːp] **(-(e)s, -e)** M marketing; (*Abteilung*) sales department; **den ~ für eine Firma haben** to have the (selling) agency for a firm
Vertriebene(r) [fɛr'triːbənə(r)] F(M) exile
Vertriebskosten PL marketing costs *pl*
vertrocknen [fɛr'trɔknən] VI to dry up
vertrödeln [fɛr'trøːdəln] (*umg*) VT to fritter away
vertrösten [fɛr'trøːstən] VT to put off
vertun [fɛr'tuːn] *unreg* VT to waste ▶ VR (*umg*) to make a mistake
vertuschen [fɛr'tʊʃən] VT to hush *od* cover up
verübeln [fɛr'|yːbəln] VT: **jdm etw ~** to be cross *od* offended with sb on account of sth
verüben [fɛr'|yːbən] VT to commit
verulken [fɛr'|ʊlkən] (*umg*) VT to make fun of
verunglimpfen [fɛr'|ʊnglɪmpfən] VT to disparage
verunglücken [fɛr'|ʊnglʏkən] VI to have an accident; (*fig: umg: misslingen*) to go wrong; **tödlich ~** to be killed in an accident
Verunglückte(r) F(M) accident victim
verunreinigen [fɛr'|ʊnraɪnɪgən] VT to soil; (*Umwelt*) to pollute
verunsichern [fɛr'|ʊnzɪçərn] VT to rattle (*fig*)
verunstalten [fɛr'|ʊnʃtaltən] VT to disfigure; (*Gebäude etc*) to deface
veruntreuen [fɛr'|ʊntrɔʏən] VT to embezzle
verursachen [fɛr'|uːrzaxən] VT to cause
verurteilen [fɛr'|uːrtaɪlən] VT to condemn; (*zu Strafe*) to sentence; (*für schuldig befinden*): **jdn ~ (für)** to convict sb (of)
Verurteilung F condemnation; (*Jur*) sentence; (*Schuldspruch*) conviction
vervielfachen [fɛr'fiːlfaxən] VT to multiply
vervielfältigen [fɛr'fiːlfɛltɪgən] VT to duplicate, to copy
Vervielfältigung F duplication, copying
vervollkommnen [fɛr'fɔlkɔmnən] VT to perfect
vervollständigen [fɛr'fɔlʃtɛndɪgən] VT to complete
verw. ABK = **verwitwet**
verwachsen [fɛr'vaksən] ADJ (*Mensch*) deformed; (*verkümmert*) stunted; (*überwuchert*) overgrown

V

verwackeln [fɛr'vakəln] VT (*Foto*) to blur
verwählen [fɛr'vɛ:lən] VR (*Tel*) to dial the wrong number
verwahren [fɛr'va:rən] VT to keep (safe) ▶ VR to protest
verwahrlosen VI to become neglected; (*moralisch*) to go to the bad
verwahrlost ADJ neglected; (*moralisch*) wayward
Verwahrung F (*von Geld etc*) keeping; (*von Täter*) custody, detention; **jdn in ~ nehmen** to take sb into custody
verwaist [fɛr'vaɪst] ADJ orphaned
verwalten [fɛr'valtən] VT to manage; (*Behörde*) to administer
Verwalter(in) (**-s, -**) M(F) administrator; (*Vermögensverwalter*) trustee
Verwaltung F management; (*behördlich*) administration
Verwaltungs- ZW: **Verwaltungsapparat** M administrative machinery; **Verwaltungsbezirk** M administrative district; **Verwaltungsgericht** NT Administrative Court
verwandeln [fɛr'vandəln] VT to change, to transform ▶ VR to change
Verwandlung F change, transformation
verwandt [fɛr'vant] ADJ: ~ **(mit)** related (to); **geistig ~ sein** (*fig*) to be kindred spirits
Verwandte(r) F(M) relative, relation
Verwandtschaft F relationship; (*Menschen*) relatives *pl*, relations *pl*; (*fig*) affinity
verwarnen [fɛr'varnən] VT to caution
Verwarnung F caution
verwaschen [fɛr'vaʃən] ADJ faded; (*fig*) vague
verwässern [fɛr'vɛsərn] VT to dilute, to water down
verwechseln [fɛr'vɛksəln] VT: **~ mit** to confuse with; **zum V~ ähnlich** as like as two peas
Verwechslung F confusion, mixing up; **das muss eine ~ sein** there must be some mistake
verwegen [fɛr've:gən] ADJ daring, bold; **Verwegenheit** F daring, audacity, boldness
verwehren [fɛr've:rən] VT (*geh*): **jdm etw ~** to refuse *od* deny sb sth
Verwehung [fɛr've:ʊŋ] F (*Schneeverwehung*) snowdrift; (*Sandverwehung*) sanddrift
verweichlichen [fɛr'vaɪçlɪçən] VT to mollycoddle
verweichlicht ADJ effeminate, soft
verweigern [fɛr'vaɪgərn] VT: **jdm etw ~** to refuse sb sth; **den Gehorsam/die Aussage ~** to refuse to obey/testify
Verweigerung F refusal
verweilen [fɛr'vaɪlən] VI to stay; (*fig*): **~ bei** to dwell on
verweint [fɛr'vaɪnt] ADJ (*Augen*) swollen with tears *od* with crying; (*Gesicht*) tear-stained
Verweis [fɛr'vaɪs] (**-es, -e**) M reprimand, rebuke; (*Hinweis*) reference
verweisen [fɛr'vaɪzən] *unreg* VT to refer; **jdn auf etw** *akk*/**an jdn ~** (*hinweisen*) to refer sb to sth/sb; **jdn vom Platz** *od* **des Spielfeldes ~** (*Sport*) to send sb off; **jdn von der Schule ~** to expel sb (from school); **jdn des Landes ~** to deport sb
Verweisung F reference; (*Landesverweisung*) deportation
verwelken [fɛr'vɛlkən] VI to fade; (*Blumen*) to wilt
verweltlichen [fɛr'vɛltlɪçən] VT to secularize
verwendbar [fɛr'vɛndba:r] ADJ usable
verwenden [fɛr'vɛndən] *unreg* VT to use; (*Mühe, Zeit, Arbeit*) to spend ▶ VR to intercede
Verwendung F use
Verwendungsmöglichkeit F (possible) use
verwerfen [fɛr'vɛrfən] *unreg* VT to reject; (*Urteil*) to quash; (*kritisieren: Handlungsweise*) to condemn
verwerflich [fɛr'vɛrflɪç] ADJ reprehensible
verwertbar ADJ usable
verwerten [fɛr've:rtən] VT to utilize
Verwertung F utilization
verwesen [fɛr've:zən] VI to decay
Verwesung F decomposition
verwickeln [fɛr'vɪkəln] VT to tangle (up); (*fig*) to involve ▶ VR to get tangled (up); **jdn ~ in** +*akk* to involve sb in, to get sb involved in; **sich ~ in** +*akk* to get involved in
verwickelt ADJ involved
Verwicklung F entanglement, complication
verwildern [fɛr'vɪldərn] VI to run wild
verwildert ADJ wild; (*Garten*) overgrown; (*jds Aussehen*) unkempt
verwinden [fɛr'vɪndən] *unreg* VT to get over
verwirken [fɛr'vɪrkən] VT (*geh*) to forfeit
verwirklichen [fɛr'vɪrklɪçən] VT to realize, to put into effect
Verwirklichung F realization
verwirren [fɛr'vɪrən] VT to tangle (up); (*fig*) to confuse
Verwirrspiel NT confusing tactics *pl*
Verwirrung F confusion
verwischen [fɛr'vɪʃən] VT (*verschmieren*) to smudge; (*lit, fig: Spuren*) to cover over; (*fig: Erinnerungen*) to blur
verwittern [fɛr'vɪtərn] VI to weather
verwitwet [fɛr'vɪtvət] ADJ widowed
verwöhnen [fɛr'vø:nən] VT to spoil, to pamper
Verwöhnung F spoiling, pampering
verworfen [fɛr'vɔrfən] ADJ depraved; **Verworfenheit** F depravity
verworren [fɛr'vɔrən] ADJ confused
verwundbar [fɛr'vʊntba:r] ADJ vulnerable
verwunden [fɛr'vʊndən] VT to wound
verwunderlich [fɛr'vʊndərlɪç] ADJ surprising; (*stärker*) astonishing
verwundern VT to astonish ▶ VR: **sich ~ über** +*akk* to be astonished at
Verwunderung F astonishment
Verwundete(r) F(M) injured person; **die Verwundeten** the injured; (*Mil*) the wounded
Verwundung F wound, injury
verwünschen [fɛr'vʏnʃən] VT to curse
verwurzelt [fɛr'vʊrtsəlt] ADJ: **(fest) in etw** *dat* *od* **mit etw ~** (*fig*) deeply rooted in sth
verwüsten [fɛr'vy:stən] VT to devastate
Verwüstung F devastation
Verz. ABK = **Verzeichnis**
verzagen [fɛr'tsa:gən] VI to despair

verzagt [fɛr'tsa:kt] ADJ disheartened
verzählen [fɛr'tsɛ:lən] VR to miscount
verzahnen [fɛr'tsa:nən] VT to dovetail; (*Zahnräder*) to cut teeth in
verzapfen [fɛr'tsapfən] (*umg*) VT: **Unsinn ~** to talk nonsense
verzaubern [fɛr'tsaʊbərn] VT (*lit*) to cast a spell on; (*fig: jdn*) to enchant
verzehren [fɛr'tse:rən] VT to consume
verzeichnen [fɛr'tsaɪçnən] VT to list; (*Niederlage, Verlust*) to register
Verzeichnis (**-ses, -se**) NT list, catalogue (BRIT), catalog (US); (*in Buch*) index; (*Comput*) directory
verzeihen [fɛr'tsaɪən] *unreg* VT, VI to forgive; **jdm etw ~** to forgive sb (for) sth; **~ Sie!** excuse me!
verzeihlich ADJ pardonable
Verzeihung F forgiveness, pardon; **~!** sorry!; **~, ...** (*vor Frage etc*) excuse me, ...; **(jdn) um ~ bitten** to apologize (to sb)
verzerren [fɛr'tsɛrən] VT to distort; (*Sehne, Muskel*) to strain, to pull
verzetteln [fɛr'tsɛtəln] VR to waste a lot of time
Verzicht [fɛr'tsɪçt] (**-(e)s, -e**) M: **~ (auf** *+akk*) renunciation (of); **verzichten** VI: **verzichten auf** *+akk* to forego, to give up
verziehen [fɛr'tsi:ən] *unreg* VI (*Hilfsverb sein*) to move ▸ VT to put out of shape; (*Kind*) to spoil; (*Pflanzen*) to thin out ▸ VR to go out of shape; (*Gesicht*) to contort; (*verschwinden*) to disappear; **verzogen** (*Vermerk*) no longer at this address; **keine Miene ~** not to turn a hair; **das Gesicht ~** to pull a face
verzieren [fɛr'tsi:rən] VT to decorate
Verzierung F decoration
verzinsen [fɛr'tsɪnzən] VT to pay interest on
verzinslich ADJ: **(fest)~ sein** to yield (a fixed rate of) interest
verzogen [fɛr'tso:gən] ADJ (*Kind*) spoilt; *siehe auch* **verziehen**
verzögern [fɛr'tsø:gərn] VT to delay ▸ VR to be delayed
Verzögerung F delay
Verzögerungstaktik F delaying tactics *pl*
verzollen [fɛr'tsɔlən] VT to pay duty on; **haben Sie etwas zu ~?** have you anything to declare?
verzücken [fɛr'tsʏkən] VT to send into ecstasies, to enrapture
Verzug [fɛr'tsu:k] M delay; (*Fin*) arrears *pl*; **mit etw in ~ geraten** to fall behind with sth
verzweifeln [fɛr'tsvaɪfəln] VI to despair
verzweifelt ADJ desperate
Verzweiflung F despair
verzweigen [fɛr'tsvaɪgən] VR to branch out
verzwickt [fɛr'tsvɪkt] (*umg*) ADJ awkward, complicated
Vesper ['fɛspər] (**-, -n**) F vespers *pl*
Vesuv [ve'zu:f] (**-(s)**) M Vesuvius
Veto ['ve:to] (**-s, -s**) NT veto
Vetter ['fɛtər] (**-s, -n**) M cousin
vgl. ABK (= *vergleiche*) cf
v. H. ABK (= *vom Hundert*) pc

VHS (-) F ABK = **Volkshochschule**
Viadukt [via'dʊkt] (**-(e)s, -e**) M viaduct
Vibrator [vi'bra:tɔr] M vibrator
vibrieren [vi'bri:rən] VI to vibrate
Video ['vi:deo] (**-s, -s**) NT video; **Videoaufnahme** F video (recording); **Videokamera** F video camera; **Videorekorder** M video recorder; **Videospiel** NT video game; **Videotext** M teletext
Vieh [fi:] (**-(e)s**) NT cattle *pl*; (*Nutztiere*) livestock; (*umg: Tier*) animal; **viehisch** ADJ bestial; **Viehzucht** F (live)stock *od* cattle breeding
viel [fi:l] ADJ a lot of, much ▸ ADV a lot, much; **sehr ~** a great deal; **ziemlich ~** quite a lot; **noch (ein)mal so ~** (*Zeit etc*) as much (time *etc*) again; **einer zu ~** one too many; **viele Leute** a lot of people, many people; **~ zu wenig** much too little; **~ beschäftigt** very busy; **er geht ~ ins Kino** he goes a lot to the cinema; **~ besser** much better; **~ teurer** much more expensive; **~ zu ~** far too much; **in vielem** in many respects
vielerlei ADJ a great variety of
vielerorts ADV in many places; **vielfach** ADJ, ADV many times; **auf vielfachen Wunsch** at the request of many people
viel- ZW: **Vielfache(s)** NT (*Math*) multiple; **um ein Vielfaches** many times over; **Vielfalt** (-) F variety; **vielfältig** ADJ varied, many-sided; **Vielfraß** M glutton
vielleicht [fi'laɪçt] ADV perhaps; (*in Bitten*) by any chance; **du bist ~ ein Idiot!** (*umg*) you really are an idiot!
viel- ZW: **vielmal, vielmals** ADV many times; **danke vielmals** many thanks; **ich bitte vielmals um Entschuldigung!** I do apologize!; **vielmehr** ADV rather, on the contrary; **vielsagend** ADJ significant; **vielschichtig** ADJ (*fig*) complex; **vielseitig** ADJ many-sided; (*Ausbildung*) all-round *attrib*; (*Interessen*) varied; (*Mensch, Gerät*) versatile; **vielversprechend** ADJ promising; **Vielvölkerstaat** M multinational state
vier [fi:r] NUM four; **auf allen vieren** on all fours; **alle viere von sich strecken** (*umg*) to stretch out; **Vierbeiner** M (*hum*) four-legged friend; **Viereck** (**-(e)s, -e**) NT four-sided figure; (*Quadrat*) square; **viereckig** ADJ four-sided; (*quadratisch*) square; **vierhundert** NUM four hundred; **vierkant** ADJ, ADV (*Naut*) square; **vierköpfig** ADJ: **eine vierköpfige Familie** a family of four; **Viermächteabkommen** NT four-power agreement
viert ADJ: **wir gingen zu ~** four of us went
Viertaktmotor M four-stroke engine
vierte(r, s) ['fi:rtə(r, s)] ADJ fourth
vierteilen VT to quarter
Viertel ['fɪrtəl] (**-s, -**) NT quarter; (*Stadtviertel*) district; **~ vor/nach drei** a quarter to/past three; **ein ~ Leberwurst** a quarter of liver sausage; **Viertelfinale** NT quarter-finals *pl*; **Vierteljahr** NT three months *pl*, quarter (*Comm, Fin*); **Vierteljahresschrift** F quarterly;

vierteljährlich ADJ quarterly; **Viertelnote** F crotchet (BRIT), quarter note (*US*); **Viertelstunde** F quarter of an hour
vier- zW: **viertürig** ADJ four-door *attrib*; **Vierwaldstättersee** M Lake Lucerne; **vierzehn** ['fɪrtse:n] NUM fourteen; **in vierzehn Tagen** in a fortnight (BRIT), in two weeks (*US*); **vierzehntägig** ADJ fortnightly; **vierzehnte(r, s)** ADJ fourteenth
vierzig ['fɪrtsɪç] NUM forty; **Vierzigstundenwoche** F forty-hour week
Vierzimmerwohnung F four-room flat (BRIT) *od* apartment (*US*)
Vietnam [viɛt'nam] (**-s**) NT Vietnam
Vietnamese [viɛtna'me:zə] (**-n, -n**) M, **Vietnamesin** F Vietnamese
vietnamesisch ADJ Vietnamese
Vikar [vi'ka:r] (**-s, -e**) M curate
Villa ['vɪla] (**-, Villen**) F villa
Villenviertel NT (prosperous) residential area
violett [vio'lɛt] ADJ violet
Violinbogen M violin bow
Violine [vio'li:nə] (**-, -n**) F violin
Violinkonzert NT violin concerto
Violinschlüssel M treble clef
virtuell [vɪrtu'ɛl] ADJ (*Comput*) virtual; **virtuelle Realität** virtual reality
virtuos [vɪrtu'o:s] ADJ virtuoso *attrib*
Virtuose [vɪrtu'o:zə] (**-n, -n**) M virtuoso
Virtuosin [vɪrtu'o:zɪn] F virtuoso
Virtuosität [vɪrtuozi'tɛt] F virtuosity
Virus ['vi:rʊs] (**-, Viren**) M OD NT (*auch Comput*) virus
Virus- IN ZW viral: **Virusinfektion** F virus infection
Visage [vi'za:ʒə] (**-, -n**) (*pej*) F face, (ugly) mug (*umg*)
Visagist(in) [viza'ʒɪst(ɪn)] M(F) make-up artist
vis-à-vis, vis-a-vis [viza'vi:] ADV (*veraltet*): **~ (von)** opposite (to) ▸ PRÄP *+dat* opposite (to)
Visier [vi'zi:r] (**-s, -e**) NT gunsight; (*am Helm*) visor
Vision [vizi'o:n] F vision
Visite [vi'zi:tə] (**-, -n**) F (*Med*) visit
Visitenkarte F visiting card
visuell [vizu'ɛl] ADJ visual
Visum ['vi:zʊm] (**-s, Visa** *od* **Visen**) NT visa; **Visumzwang** M obligation to hold a visa
vital [vi'ta:l] ADJ lively, full of life; (*lebenswichtig*) vital
Vitamin [vita'mi:n] (**-s, -e**) NT vitamin; **Vitaminmangel** M vitamin deficiency
Vitrine [vi'tri:nə] (**-, -n**) F (*Schrank*) glass cabinet; (*Schaukasten*) showcase, display case
Vivisektion [vivizɛktsi'o:n] F vivisection
Vize ['fi:tsə] M (*umg*) number two; (*: Vizemeister*) runner-up ▸ IN ZW vice-
v. J. ABK (= *vorigen Jahres*) of the previous *od* last year
Vlies [fli:s] (**-es, -e**) NT fleece
v. M. ABK (= *vorigen Monats*) ult.
V-Mann M ABK = **Verbindungsmann; Vertrauensmann**
VN PL ABK (= *Vereinte Nationen*) UN
VO ABK = **Verordnung**
Vogel ['fo:gəl] (**-s, Vögel**) M bird; **einen ~ haben** (*umg*) to have bats in the belfry; **den ~ abschießen** (*umg*) to surpass everyone (*ironisch*); **Vogelbauer** NT birdcage; **Vogelbeerbaum** M rowan (tree); **Vogeldreck** M bird droppings *pl*; **Vogelperspektive** F bird's-eye view; **Vogelschau** F bird's-eye view; **Vogelscheuche** F scarecrow; **Vogelschutzgebiet** NT bird sanctuary; **Vogel-Strauß-Politik** F head-in-the-sand policy
Vogesen [vo'ge:zən] PL Vosges *pl*
Voicemail ['vɔisme:l] F (*Tel*) voice mail
Vokabel [vo'ka:bəl] (**-, -n**) F word
Vokabular [vokabu'la:r] (**-s, -e**) NT vocabulary
Vokal [vo'ka:l] (**-s, -e**) M vowel
Volk [fɔlk] (**-(e)s, Völker**) NT people; (*Nation*) nation; **etw unters ~ bringen** (*Nachricht*) to spread sth
Völker- zW: **Völkerbund** M League of Nations; **Völkerkunde** F ethnology; **Völkermord** M genocide; **Völkerrecht** NT international law; **völkerrechtlich** ADJ according to international law; **Völkerverständigung** F international understanding; **Völkerwanderung** F migration
Volks- zW: **Volksabstimmung** F referendum; **Volksarmee** F People's Army; **Volksbegehren** NT petition for a referendum; **Volksdeutsche(r)** F(M) *dekl wie adj* ethnic German; **volkseigen** ADJ (DDR) nationally-owned; **Volksfeind** M enemy of the people; **Volksfest** NT popular festival; (*Jahrmarkt*) fair
Volkshochschule F adult education centre (BRIT) *od* center (*US*)

> The **Volkshochschule** (VHS) is an institution which offers Adult Education classes. No set qualifications are necessary to attend. For a small fee adults can attend both vocational and non-vocational classes in the day-time or evening.

Volks- zW: **Volkslauf** M fun run; **Volkslied** NT folk song; **Volksmund** M vernacular; **Volkspolizei** F (DDR) People's Police; **Volksrepublik** F people's republic; **Volksschule** F ≈ primary school (BRIT), ≈ elementary school (*US*); **Volksseuche** F epidemic; **Volksstamm** M tribe; **Volksstück** NT folk play in dialect; **Volkstanz** M folk dance; **Volkstrauertag** M ≈ Remembrance Day (BRIT), ≈ Memorial Day (*US*); **volkstümlich** ADJ popular; **Volkswirtschaft** F national economy; (*Fach*) economics *sing*, political economy; **Volkswirtschaftler** M economist; **Volkszählung** F (national) census
voll [fɔl] ADJ full ▸ ADV fully; (*Tafel*) to cover (with writing); **jdn für ~ nehmen** (*umg*) to take sb seriously; **aus dem Vollen schöpfen** to draw on unlimited resources; **in voller Größe** (*Bild*) life-size(d); (*bei plötzlicher Erscheinung etc*) large as life; **~ sein** (*umg: satt*) to be full (up); (*: betrunken*) to be plastered; **~ und ganz**

completely; *siehe auch* **vollmachen**; **vollschreiben**; **volltanken**

vollauf [fɔl'laʊf] ADV amply; **~ zu tun haben** to have quite enough to do

voll- zW: **Vollbad** NT (proper) bath; **Vollbart** M full beard; **Vollbeschäftigung** F full employment; **Vollbesitz** M: **im Vollbesitz** *+gen* in full possession of; **Vollblut** NT thoroughbred; **vollblütig** ADJ full-blooded; **Vollbremsung** F emergency stop; **vollbringen** *unreg* VT UNTR to accomplish; **Volldampf** M (*Naut*): **mit Volldampf** at full steam; **vollenden** VT UNTR to finish, to complete; **vollendet** ADJ (*vollkommen*) perfect; (*Tänzer etc*) accomplished; **vollends** ADV completely; **Vollendung** F completion

voller ADJ fuller; **~ Flecken/Ideen** full of stains/ideas

Völlerei [fœlə'raɪ] F gluttony

Volleyball ['vɔlibal] **(-(e)s)** M volleyball

voll- zW: **vollfett** ADJ full-fat; **Vollgas** NT: **mit Vollgas** at full throttle; **Vollgas geben** to step on it

völlig ['fœlɪç] ADJ complete ▸ ADV completely

voll- zW: **volljährig** ADJ of age; **Vollkaskoversicherung** F fully comprehensive insurance; **vollkommen** ADJ perfect; (*völlig*) complete, absolute ▸ ADV completely; **Vollkommenheit** F perfection; **Vollkornbrot** NT wholemeal (*BRIT*) *od* whole-wheat (*US*) bread; **volllaufen** *unreg* VI: **etw volllaufen lassen** to fill sth up; **vollmachen** VT to fill (up); **Vollmacht** F authority, power of attorney; **Vollmatrose** M able-bodied seaman; **Vollmilch** F full-cream milk; **Vollmond** M full moon; **Vollnarkose** F general anaesthetic (*BRIT*) *od* anesthetic (*US*); **Vollpension** F full board; **vollschlank** ADJ plump, stout; **vollschreiben** *unreg* VT (*Heft, Seite*) to fill; **vollständig** ADJ complete; **vollstrecken** VT UNTR to execute; **volltanken** VT, VI to fill up; **Volltreffer** M (*lit, fig*) bull's-eye; **Vollversammlung** F general meeting; **Vollwaise** F orphan; **vollwertig** ADJ full *attrib*; (*Stellung*) equal; **Vollwertkost** F wholefoods *pl*; **vollzählig** ADJ complete; (*anwesend*) in full number; **vollziehen** *unreg* VT UNTR to carry out ▸ VR UNTR to happen; **Vollzug** M execution

Volontär(in) [volɔn'tɛːr(ɪn)] **(-s, -e)** M(F) trainee

Volt [vɔlt] (- *od* **-(e)s, -**) NT volt

Volumen [vo'luːmən] **(-s, -** *od* **Volumina)** NT volume

vom [fɔm] = **von dem**

SCHLÜSSELWORT

von [fɔn] PRÄP *+dat* **1** (*Ausgangspunkt*) from; **von ... bis** from ... to; **von morgens bis abends** from morning till night; **von ... nach ...** from ... to ...; **von ... an** from ...; **von ... aus** from ...; **von dort aus** from there; **etw von sich aus tun** to do sth of one's own accord; **von mir aus** (*umg*) if you like, I don't mind; **von wo/wann ...?** where/when ... from?

2 (*Ursache, im Passiv*) by; **ein Gedicht von Schiller** a poem by Schiller; **von etw müde** tired from sth

3 (*als Genitiv*) of; **ein Freund von mir** a friend of mine; **nett von dir** nice of you; **jeweils zwei von zehn** two out of every ten

4 (*über*) about; **er erzählte vom Urlaub** he talked about his holiday

5: **von wegen!** (*umg*) no way!

voneinander ADV from each other

vonseiten, von Seiten [vɔn'zaɪtn] PRÄP *+gen* on the part of

vonstattengehen [fɔn'ʃtatən-] *unreg* VI to proceed, to go

SCHLÜSSELWORT

vor [foːr] PRÄP *+dat* **1** (*räumlich*) in front of

2 (*zeitlich, Reihenfolge*) before; **ich war vor ihm da** I was there before him; **X kommt vor Y** X comes before Y; **vor zwei Tagen** two days ago; **5 (Minuten) vor 4** 5 (minutes) to 4; **vor Kurzem** a little while ago

3 (*Ursache*) with; **vor Wut/Liebe** with rage/love; **vor Hunger sterben** to die of hunger; **vor lauter Arbeit** because of work

4: **vor allem, vor allen Dingen** above all

▸ PRÄP *+akk* (*räumlich*) in front of; **vor sich hin summen** to hum to oneself

▸ ADV: **vor und zurück** backwards and forwards

Vor- zW: **Vorabdruck** M preprint; **Vorabend** M evening before, eve; **Vorahnung** F presentiment, premonition

voran [fo'ran] ADV before, ahead; **voranbringen** *unreg* VT to make progress with; **vorangehen** *unreg* VI to go ahead; **einer Sache** *dat* **vorangehen** to precede sth; **vorangehend** ADJ previous; **vorankommen** *unreg* VI to make progress, to come along

Voranschlag ['foːrlanʃlaːk] M estimate

voranstellen [fo'ranʃtɛlən] VT *+dat* to put in front (of); (*fig*) to give precedence (over)

Vorarbeiter ['foːrlarbaɪtər] M foreman

voraus [fo'raʊs] ADV ahead; (*zeitlich*) in advance; **jdm ~ sein** to be ahead of sb; **im V~** in advance; **vorausbezahlen** VT to pay in advance; **vorausgehen** *unreg* VI to go (on) ahead; (*fig*) to precede; **voraushaben** *unreg* VT: **jdm etw voraushaben** to have the edge on sb in sth; **Voraussage** F prediction; **voraussagen** VT to predict; **voraussehen** *unreg* VT to foresee; **voraussetzen** VT to assume; (*sicher annehmen*) to take for granted; (*erfordern: Kenntnisse, Geduld*) to require, to demand; **vorausgesetzt, dass ...** provided that ...; **Voraussetzung** F requirement, prerequisite; **unter der Voraussetzung, dass ...** on condition that ...; **Voraussicht** F foresight; **aller Voraussicht nach** in all probability; **in der Voraussicht, dass ...**

anticipating that ...; **voraussichtlich** ADV probably; **Vorauszahlung** F advance payment

Vorbau ['fo:rbaʊ] **(-(e)s, -ten)** M porch; (*Balkon*) balcony

vorbauen ['fo:rbaʊən] VT to build up in front ▶ VI *+dat* to take precautions (against)

Vorbedacht ['fo:rbədaxt] M: **mit/ohne ~** (*Überlegung*) with/without due consideration; (*Absicht*) intentionally/unintentionally

Vorbedingung ['fo:rbədɪŋʊŋ] F precondition

Vorbehalt ['fo:rbəhalt] M reservation, proviso; **unter dem ~, dass ...** with the reservation that ...

vorbehalten *unreg* VT: **sich/jdm etw ~** to reserve sth (for o.s.)/for sb; **alle Rechte ~** all rights reserved

vorbehaltlich PRÄP *+gen* (*form*) subject to

vorbehaltlos ADJ unconditional ▶ ADV unconditionally

vorbei [fɔr'baɪ] ADV by, past; **aus und ~** over and done with; **damit ist es nun ~** that's all over now; **vorbeibringen** *unreg* (*umg*) VT to drop off; **vorbeigehen** *unreg* VI to pass by, to go past; **vorbeikommen** *unreg* VI: **bei jdm vorbeikommen** to drop *od* call in on sb; **vorbeireden** VI: **an etw** *dat* **vorbeireden** to talk around sth

vorbelastet ['fo:rbəlastət] ADJ (*fig*) handicapped (BRIT), handicaped (US)

Vorbemerkung ['fo:rbəmɛrkʊŋ] F introductory remark

vorbereiten ['fo:rbəraɪtən] VT to prepare

Vorbereitung F preparation

vorbestellen ['fo:rbəʃtɛlən] VT to book (in advance), to reserve

Vorbestellung F advance booking

vorbestraft ['fo:rbəʃtraft] ADJ previously convicted, with a record

Vorbeugehaft F preventive custody

vorbeugen ['fo:rbɔygən] VT, VR to lean forward ▶ VI *+dat* to prevent

vorbeugend ADJ preventive

Vorbeugung F prevention; **zur ~ gegen** for the prevention of

Vorbild ['fo:rbɪlt] NT model; **sich** *dat* **jdn zum ~ nehmen** to model o.s. on sb; **vorbildlich** ADJ model, ideal

Vorbildung ['fo:rbɪldʊŋ] F educational background

Vorbote ['fo:rbo:tə] M (*fig*) herald

vorbringen ['fo:rbrɪŋən] *unreg* VT to voice; (*Meinung etc*) to advance, to state; (*umg: nach vorne*) to bring to the front

vordatieren ['fo:rdati:rən] VT (*Schreiben*) to postdate

Vorder- ZW: **Vorderachse** F front axle; **Vorderansicht** F front view; **Vorderasien** NT Near East

vordere(r, s) ADJ front

Vorder- ZW: **Vordergrund** M foreground; **im Vordergrund stehen** (*fig*) to be to the fore; **Vordergrundprogramm** NT (*Comput*) foreground program; **vorderhand** ADV for the present; **Vordermann** **(-(e)s,** *pl* **-männer)** M man in front; **jdn auf Vordermann bringen** (*umg*) to get sb to shape up; **Vorderseite** F front (side); **Vordersitz** M front seat

vorderste(r, s) ADJ front

vordrängen ['fo:rdrɛŋən] VR to push to the front

vordringen ['fo:rdrɪŋən] *unreg* VI: **bis zu jdm/etw ~** to get as far as sb/sth

vordringlich ADJ urgent

Vordruck ['fo:rdrʊk] M form

vorehelich ['fo:rle:əlɪç] ADJ premarital

voreilig ['fo:rlaɪlɪç] ADJ hasty, rash; **voreilige Schlüsse ziehen** to jump to conclusions

voreinander [fo:rlaɪ'nandər] ADV (*räumlich*) in front of each other; (*einander gegenüber*) face to face

voreingenommen ['fo:rlaɪngənɔmən] ADJ bias(s)ed; **Voreingenommenheit** F bias

voreingestellt ['fo:rlaɪngəʃtɛlt] ADJ: **voreingestellter Parameter** (*Comput*) default (parameter)

vorenthalten ['fo:rlɛnthaltən] *unreg* VT: **jdm etw ~** to withhold sth from sb

Vorentscheidung ['fo:rlɛntʃaɪdʊŋ] F preliminary decision

vorerst ['fo:rle:rst] ADV for the moment *od* present

Vorfahr ['fo:rfa:r] **(-en, -en)** M ancestor

vorfahren *unreg* VI to drive (on) ahead; (*vors Haus etc*) to drive up

Vorfahrt F (*Aut*) right of way; **„~ (be)achten"** "give way" (BRIT), "yield" (US)

Vorfahrts- ZW: **Vorfahrtsregel** F rule of right of way; **Vorfahrtsschild** NT "give way" (BRIT) *od* "yield" (US) sign; **Vorfahrtsstraße** F major road

Vorfall ['fo:rfal] M incident

vorfallen *unreg* VI to occur

Vorfeld ['fo:rfɛlt] NT (*fig*): **im ~ (+gen)** in the run-up (to)

Vorfilm ['fo:rfɪlm] M short

vorfinden ['fo:rfɪndən] *unreg* VT to find

Vorfreude ['fo:rfrɔydə] F anticipation

vorfühlen ['fo:rfy:lən] VI (*fig*) to put out feelers

vorführen ['fo:rfy:rən] VT to show, to display; (*Theaterstück, Kunststücke*): **(jdm) etw ~** to perform sth (to *od* in front of sb); **dem Gericht ~** to bring before the court

Vorgabe ['fo:rga:bə] F (*Sport*) handicap

Vorgang ['fo:rgaŋ] M (*Ereignis*) event; (*Ablauf*) course of events; (*Chem etc*) process

Vorgänger(in) ['fo:rgɛŋər(ɪn)] **(-s, -)** M(F) predecessor

vorgaukeln ['fo:rgaʊkəln] VT: **jdm etw ~** to lead sb to believe in sth

vorgeben ['fo:rge:bən] *unreg* VT to pretend, to use as a pretext; (*Sport*) to give an advantage *od* a start of

Vorgebirge ['fo:rgəbɪrgə] NT foothills *pl*

vorgefasst ['fo:rgəfast] ADJ preconceived

vorgefertigt ['fo:rgəfɛrtɪçt] ADJ prefabricated

Vorgefühl ['fo:rgəfy:l] NT anticipation; (*etwas Böses*) presentiment
vorgehen ['fo:rge:ən] *unreg* VI (*voraus*) to go (on) ahead; (*nach vorn*) to go forward; (*handeln*) to act, to proceed; (*Uhr*) to be fast; (*Vorrang haben*) to take precedence; (*passieren*) to go on
Vorgehen (-s) NT action
Vorgehensweise F proceedings *pl*
vorgerückt ['fo:rgərYkt] ADJ (*Stunde*) late; (*Alter*) advanced
Vorgeschichte ['fo:rgəʃɪçtə] F prehistory; (*von Fall, Krankheit*) past history
Vorgeschmack ['fo:rgəʃmak] M foretaste
Vorgesetzte(r) ['fo:rgəzɛtstə(r)] F(M) superior
vorgestern ['fo:rgɛstərn] ADV the day before yesterday; **von ~** (*fig*) antiquated
vorgreifen ['fo:rgraɪfən] *unreg* VI *+dat* to anticipate; **jdm ~** to forestall sb
vorhaben ['fo:rha:bən] *unreg* VT to intend; **hast du schon was vor?** have you got anything on?
Vorhaben (-s, -) NT intention
Vorhalle ['fo:rhalə] F (*Diele*) entrance hall; (*von Parlament*) lobby
vorhalten ['fo:rhaltən] *unreg* VT to hold *od* put up ▸ VI to last; **jdm etw ~** to reproach sb for sth
Vorhaltung F reproach
Vorhand ['fo:rhant] F forehand
vorhanden [fo:r'handən] ADJ existing; (*erhältlich*) available; **Vorhandensein (-s)** NT existence, presence
Vorhang ['fo:rhaŋ] M curtain
Vorhängeschloss ['fo:rhɛŋəʃlɔs] NT padlock
Vorhaut ['fo:rhaʊt] F (*Anat*) foreskin
vorher [fo:r'he:r] ADV before(hand); **zwei Tage ~** two days before; **vorherbestimmen** VT (*Schicksal*) to preordain; **vorhergehen** *unreg* VI to precede
vorherig [fo:r'he:rɪç] ADJ previous
Vorherrschaft ['fo:rhɛrʃaft] F predominance, supremacy
vorherrschen VI to predominate
vorher- ZW: **Vorhersage** F forecast; **vorhersagen** VT to forecast, to predict; **vorhersehbar** ADJ predictable; **vorhersehen** *unreg* VT to foresee
vorhin [fo:r'hɪn] ADV not long ago, just now
Vorhinein ['fo:rhɪnaɪn] ADV: **im ~** beforehand
Vorhof ['fo:rho:f] M forecourt
vorig ['fo:rɪç] ADJ previous, last
Vorjahr ['fo:rja:r] NT previous year, year before
vorjährig ['fo:rjɛ:rɪç] ADJ of the previous year
vorjammern ['fo:rjamərn] VT, VI: **jdm (etwas) ~** to moan to sb (about sth)
Vorkämpfer(in) ['fo:rkɛmpfər(ɪn)] M(F) pioneer
Vorkaufsrecht ['fo:rkaʊfsrɛçt] NT option to buy
Vorkehrung ['fo:rke:rʊŋ] F precaution
Vorkenntnis ['fo:rkɛntnɪs] F previous knowledge
vorknöpfen ['fo:rknœpfən] VT (*fig: umg*): **sich** *dat* **jdn ~** to take sb to task
vorkommen ['fo:rkɔmən] *unreg* VI to come forward; (*geschehen, sich finden*) to occur; (*scheinen*) to seem (to be); **so was soll ~!** that's life!; **sich** *dat* **dumm** *etc* **~** to feel stupid *etc*
Vorkommen NT occurrence; (*Min*) deposit
Vorkommnis ['fo:rkɔmnɪs] **(-ses, -se)** NT occurrence
Vorkriegs- ['fo:rkri:ks] IN ZW pre-war
vorladen ['fo:rla:dən] *unreg* VT (*bei Gericht*) to summons
Vorladung F summons
Vorlage ['fo:rla:gə] F model, pattern; (*das Vorlegen*) presentation; (*von Beweismaterial*) submission; (*Gesetzesvorlage*) bill; (*Sport*) pass
vorlassen ['fo:rlasən] *unreg* VT to admit; (*überholen lassen*) to let pass; (*vorgehen lassen*) to allow to go in front
Vorlauf ['fo:rlaʊf] M (preliminary) heat (*of running event*)
Vorläufer M forerunner
vorläufig ['fo:rlɔyfɪç] ADJ temporary; (*provisorisch*) provisional
vorlaut ['fo:rlaʊt] ADJ impertinent, cheeky
Vorleben ['fo:rle:bən] NT past (life)
vorlegen ['fo:rle:gən] VT to put in front, to present; (*Beweismaterial etc*) to produce, to submit; **jdm etw ~** to put sth before sb
Vorleger (-s, -) M mat
Vorleistung ['fo:rlaɪstʊŋ] F (*Fin: Vorausbezahlung*) advance (payment); (*Vorarbeit*) preliminary work; (*Pol*) prior concession
vorlesen ['fo:rle:zən] *unreg* VT to read (out)
Vorlesung F (*Univ*) lecture
Vorlesungsverzeichnis NT lecture timetable
vorletzte(r, s) ['fo:rlɛtstə(r, s)] ADJ last but one, penultimate
Vorliebe ['fo:rli:bə] F preference, special liking; **etw mit ~ tun** to particularly like doing sth
vorliebnehmen [fo:r'li:p-] *unreg* VI: **~ mit** to make do with
vorliegen ['fo:rli:gən] *unreg* VI to be (here); **etw liegt jdm vor** sb has sth; **etw liegt gegen jdn vor** sb is charged with sth
vorliegend ADJ present, at issue
vorm. ABK (= *vormittags*) a.m.; (= *vormals*) formerly
vormachen ['fo:rmaxən] VT: **jdm etw ~** to show sb how to do sth; **jdm etw ~** (*fig*) to fool sb; **mach mir doch nichts vor** don't try and fool me
Vormachtstellung ['fo:rmaxtʃtɛlʊŋ] F supremacy
vormals ['fo:rmals] ADV formerly
Vormarsch ['fo:rmarʃ] M advance
vormerken ['fo:rmɛrkən] VT to book; (*notieren*) to make note of; (*bei Bestellung*) to take an order for
Vormittag ['fo:rmɪta:k] M morning; **am ~** in the morning
vormittags ADV in the morning, before noon
Vormund ['fo:rmʊnt] **(-(e)s, -e** *od* **-münder)** M guardian
vorn [fɔrn] ADV in front; **von ~ anfangen** to start at the beginning; **nach ~** to the front; **er**

V

betrügt sie von ~ bis hinten he deceives her right, left and centre
Vorname ['fo:rna:mə] M first *od* Christian name
vornan [fɔrn'|an] ADV at the front
vorne ['fɔrnə] = **vorn**
vornehm ['fo:rne:m] ADJ distinguished; (*Manieren etc*) refined; (*Kleid*) elegant; **in vornehmen Kreisen** in polite society
vornehmen *unreg* VT (*fig*) to carry out; **sich** *dat* **etw ~** to start on sth; (*beschließen*) to decide to do sth; **sich** *dat* **zu viel ~** to take on too much; **sich** *dat* **jdn ~** to tell sb off
vornehmlich ADV chiefly, specially
vorneweg ['fɔrnəvɛk], **vornweg** ['fɔrnvɛk] ADV in front; (*als Erstes*) first
vornherein ['fɔrnhɛraɪn] ADV: **von ~** from the start
Vorort ['fo:r|ɔrt] M suburb; **Vorortzug** M commuter train
vorprogrammiert ['fo:rprogrami:rt] ADJ (*Erfolg, Antwort*) automatic
Vorrang ['fo:rraŋ] M precedence, priority
vorrangig ADJ of prime importance, primary
Vorrat ['fo:rra:t] M stock, supply; **solange der ~ reicht** (*Comm*) while stocks last
vorrätig ['fo:rrɛ:tɪç] ADJ in stock
Vorratskammer F store cupboard; (*für Lebensmittel*) larder
Vorraum M anteroom; (*Büro*) outer office
vorrechnen ['fo:rrɛçnən] VT: **jdm etw ~** to calculate sth for sb; (*als Kritik*) to point sth out to sb
Vorrecht ['fo:rrɛçt] NT privilege
Vorrede ['fo:rre:də] F introductory speech; (*Theat*) prologue (BRIT), prolog (US)
Vorrichtung ['fo:rrɪçtʊŋ] F device, gadget
vorrücken ['fo:rrʏkən] VI to advance ▸ VT to move forward
Vorruhestand ['fo:rru:əʃtant] M early retirement
Vorrunde ['fo:rrʊndə] F (*Sport*) preliminary round
Vors. ABK = **Vorsitzende(r)**
vorsagen ['fo:rza:gən] VT to recite; (*Sch: zuflüstern*) to tell secretly, to prompt
Vorsaison ['fo:rzɛzõ:] F early season, low season
Vorsatz ['fo:rzats] M intention; (*Jur*) intent; **einen ~ fassen** to make a resolution
vorsätzlich ['fo:rzɛtslɪç] ADJ intentional; (*Jur*) premeditated ▸ ADV intentionally
Vorschau ['fo:rʃaʊ] F (*Rundf, TV*) (programme (BRIT) *od* program (US)) preview; (*Film*) trailer
Vorschein ['fo:rʃaɪn] M: **zum ~ kommen** (*lit: sichtbar werden*) to appear; (*fig: entdeckt werden*) to come to light
vorschieben ['fo:rʃi:bən] *unreg* VT to push forward; (*vor etw*) to push across; (*fig*) to put forward as an excuse; **jdn ~** to use sb as a front
vorschießen ['fo:rʃi:sən] *unreg* (*umg*) VT: **jdm Geld ~** to advance sb money
Vorschlag ['fo:rʃla:k] M suggestion, proposal
vorschlagen ['fo:rʃla:gən] *unreg* VT to suggest, to propose
Vorschlaghammer M sledgehammer
vorschnell ['fo:rʃnɛl] ADJ hasty, too quick
vorschreiben ['fo:rʃraɪbən] *unreg* VT (*Dosis*) to prescribe; (*befehlen*) to specify; **(jdm) etw ~** (*lit*) to write sth out (for sb); **ich lasse mir nichts ~** I won't be dictated to
Vorschrift ['fo:rʃrɪft] F regulation(s *pl*), rule(s *pl*); (*Anweisungen*) instruction(s *pl*); **jdm Vorschriften machen** to give sb orders; **Dienst nach ~** work-to-rule (BRIT), slowdown (US)
vorschriftsmäßig ADV as per regulations/instructions
Vorschub ['fo:rʃu:p] M: **jdm/einer Sache ~ leisten** to encourage sb/sth
Vorschule ['fo:rʃu:lə] F nursery school
vorschulisch ['fo:rʃu:lɪʃ] ADJ preschool *attrib*
Vorschuss ['fo:rʃʊs] M advance
vorschützen ['fo:rʃʏtsən] VT to put forward as a pretext; (*Unwissenheit*) to plead
vorschweben ['fo:rʃve:bən] VI: **jdm schwebt etw vor** sb has sth in mind
vorsehen ['fo:rze:ən] *unreg* VT to provide for; (*planen*) to plan ▸ VR to take care, to be careful
Vorsehung F providence
vorsetzen ['fo:rzɛtsən] VT to move forward; (*davor setzen*): **~ vor** *+akk* to put in front of; (*anbieten*): **jdm etw ~** to offer sb sth
Vorsicht ['fo:rzɪçt] F caution, care; **~!** look out!, take care!; (*auf Schildern*) caution!, danger!; **~ Stufe!** mind the step!; **etw mit ~ genießen** (*umg*) to take sth with a pinch of salt
vorsichtig ADJ cautious, careful
vorsichtshalber ADV just in case
Vorsichtsmaßnahme F precaution
Vorsilbe ['fo:rzɪlbə] F prefix
vorsintflutlich ['fo:rzɪntflu:tlɪç] (*umg*) ADJ antiquated
Vorsitz ['fo:rzɪts] M chair(manship); **den ~ führen** to chair the meeting
Vorsitzende(r) F(M) chairman/-woman, chair(person)
Vorsorge ['fo:rzɔrgə] F precaution(s *pl*); (*Fürsorge*) provision(s *pl*)
vorsorgen VI: **~ für** to make provision(s *pl*) for
Vorsorgeuntersuchung ['fo:rzɔrgə|ʊntərzu:xʊŋ] F medical check-up
vorsorglich ['fo:rzɔrklɪç] ADV as a precaution
Vorspann ['vo:rʃpan] M (*Film, TV*) opening credits *pl*; (*Presse*) opening paragraph
vorspannen VT (*Pferde*) to harness
Vorspeise ['fo:rʃpaɪzə] F hors d'œuvre, starter
Vorspiegelung ['fo:rʃpi:gəlʊŋ] F: **das ist (eine) ~ falscher Tatsachen** it's all sham
Vorspiel ['fo:rʃpi:l] NT prelude; (*bei Geschlechtsverkehr*) foreplay
vorspielen VT: **jdm etw ~** (*Mus*) to play sth to sb; (*Theat*) to act sth to sb; (*fig*) to act out a sham of sth in front of sb
vorsprechen ['fo:rʃprɛçən] *unreg* VT to say out loud; (*vortragen*) to recite ▸ VI (*Theat*) to audition; **bei jdm ~** to call on sb

vorspringend ['fo:rʃprɪŋənt] ADJ projecting; (*Nase, Kinn*) prominent
Vorsprung ['fo:rʃprʊŋ] M projection; (*Felsvorsprung*) ledge; (*fig*) advantage, start
Vorstadt ['fo:rʃtat] F suburbs *pl*
Vorstand ['fo:rʃtant] M executive committee; (*Comm*) board (of directors); (*Person*) director; (*Leiter*) head
Vorstandssitzung F (*von Firma*) board meeting
Vorstandsvorsitzende(r) F(M) chairperson
vorstehen ['fo:rʃte:ən] *unreg* VI to project; **einer Sache** *dat* **~** (*fig*) to be the head of sth
Vorsteher(in) (**-s, -**) M(F) (*von Abteilung*) head; (*von Gefängnis*) governor; (*Bahnhofsvorsteher*) stationmaster
vorstellbar ADJ conceivable
vorstellen ['fo:rʃtɛlən] VT to put forward; (*vor etw*) to put in front; (*bekannt machen*) to introduce; (*darstellen*) to represent ▸ VR to introduce o.s.; (*bei Bewerbung*) to go for an interview; **sich** *dat* **etw ~** to imagine sth; **stell dir das nicht so einfach vor** don't think it's so easy
Vorstellung F (*Bekanntmachen*) introduction; (*Theat etc*) performance; (*Gedanke*) idea
Vorstellungsgespräch NT interview
Vorstellungsvermögen NT powers of imagination *pl*
Vorstoß ['fo:rʃto:s] M advance; (*fig: Versuch*) attempt
vorstoßen *unreg* VT, VI to push forward
Vorstrafe ['fo:rʃtra:fə] F previous conviction
vorstrecken ['fo:rʃtrɛkən] VT to stretch out; (*Geld*) to advance
Vorstufe ['fo:rʃtu:fə] F first step(s *pl*)
Vortag ['fo:rtak] M: **am ~ einer Sache** *gen* on the day before sth
Vortal ['fo:rta:l] NT (*Comput*) vortal
vortasten ['fo:rtastən] VR: **sich langsam zu etw ~** to approach sth carefully
vortäuschen ['fo:rtɔʏʃən] VT to pretend, to feign
Vortäuschung F: **unter ~ falscher Tatsachen** under false pretences (BRIT) *od* pretenses (US)
Vorteil ['fo:rtaɪl] (**-s, -e**) M: **~ (gegenüber)** advantage (over); **im ~ sein** to have the advantage; **die Vor- und Nachteile** the pros and cons; **vorteilhaft** ADJ advantageous; (*Kleider*) flattering; (*Geschäft*) lucrative
Vortr. ABK = **Vortrag**
Vortrag ['fo:rtra:k] (**-(e)s, Vorträge**) M talk, lecture; (*Vortragsart*) delivery; (*von Gedicht*) rendering; (*Comm*) balance carried forward; **einen ~ halten** to give a lecture *od* talk
vortragen ['fo:rtra:gən] *unreg* VT to carry forward (*auch Comm*); (*fig*) to recite; (*Rede*) to deliver; (*Lied*) to perform; (*Meinung etc*) to express
Vortragsabend M lecture evening; (*mit Musik*) recital; (*mit Gedichten*) poetry reading
Vortragsreihe F series of lectures
vortrefflich [fo:r'trɛflɪç] ADJ excellent
vortreten ['fo:rtre:tən] *unreg* VI to step forward; (*Augen etc*) to protrude
Vortritt ['fo:rtrɪt] M: **jdm den ~ lassen** (*lit, fig*) to let sb go first
vorüber [fo'ry:bər] ADV past, over; **vorübergehen** *unreg* VI to pass (by); **vorübergehen an** *+dat* (*fig*) to pass over; **vorübergehend** ADJ temporary, passing ▸ ADV temporarily, for the time being
Voruntersuchung ['fo:r|ʊntərzu:xʊŋ] F (*Med*) preliminary examination; (*Jur*) preliminary investigation
Vorurteil ['fo:r|ʊrtaɪl] NT prejudice
vorurteilsfrei ADJ unprejudiced, open-minded
Vorverkauf ['fo:rfɛrkaʊf] M advance booking
Vorverkaufsstelle F advance booking office
vorverlegen ['fo:rfɛrle:gən] VT (*Termin*) to bring forward
Vorw. ABK = **Vorwort**
vorwagen ['fo:rva:gən] VR to venture forward
Vorwahl ['fo:rva:l] F preliminary election; (*Tel*) dialling (BRIT) *od* area (US) code
Vorwand ['fo:rvant] (**-(e)s, Vorwände**) M pretext
Vorwarnung ['fo:rvarnʊŋ] F (advance) warning
vorwärts ['fo:rvɛrts] ADV forward; **~!** (*umg*) let's go!; (*Mil*) forward march!; *siehe auch* **vorwärtsgehen**; **vorwärtskommen**; **Vorwärtsgang** M (*Aut etc*) forward gear; **vorwärtsgehen** *unreg* VI to progress; **vorwärtskommen** *unreg* VI to get on, to make progress
Vorwäsche F prewash
Vorwaschgang M prewash
vorweg [fo:r'vɛk] ADV in advance; **Vorwegnahme** (**-, -n**) F anticipation; **vorwegnehmen** *unreg* VT to anticipate
vorweisen ['fo:rvaɪzən] *unreg* VT to show, to produce
vorwerfen ['fo:rvɛrfən] *unreg* VT: **jdm etw ~** to reproach sb for sth, to accuse sb of sth; **sich** *dat* **nichts vorzuwerfen haben** to have nothing to reproach o.s. with; **das wirft er mir heute noch vor** he still holds it against me; **Tieren/Gefangenen etw ~** (*lit*) to throw sth down for the animals/prisoners
vorwiegend ['fo:rvi:gənt] ADJ predominant ▸ ADV predominantly
vorwitzig ADJ saucy, cheeky
Vorwort ['fo:rvɔrt] (**-(e)s, -e**) NT preface
Vorwurf ['fo:rvʊrf] (**-(e)s, Vorwürfe**) M reproach; **jdm/sich Vorwürfe machen** to reproach sb/o.s.
vorwurfsvoll ADJ reproachful
Vorzeichen ['fo:rtsaɪçən] NT (*Omen*) omen; (*Med*) early symptom; (*Math*) sign
vorzeigen ['fo:rtsaɪgən] VT to show, to produce
Vorzeit ['fo:rtsaɪt] F prehistoric times *pl*
vorzeitig ADJ premature
vorziehen ['fo:rtsi:ən] *unreg* VT to pull forward; (*Gardinen*) to draw; (*zuerst behandeln, abfertigen*) to give priority to; (*lieber haben*) to prefer

V

Vorzimmer ['fo:rtsɪmər] NT anteroom; (*Büro*) outer office
Vorzug ['fo:rtsu:k] M preference; (*gute Eigenschaft*) merit, good quality; (*Vorteil*) advantage; (*Eisenb*) relief train; **einer Sache** *dat* **den ~ geben** (*form*) to prefer sth; (*Vorrang geben*) to give sth precedence
vorzüglich [fo:r'tsy:klɪç] ADJ excellent, first-rate
Vorzugsaktien PL preference shares (BRIT), preferred stock (*US*)
vorzugsweise ADV preferably; (*hauptsächlich*) chiefly
Votum ['vo:tʊm] (**-s, Voten**) NT vote
Voyeur [voa'jø:r] (**-s, -e**) M voyeur; **Voyeurismus** [voajø'rɪsmʊs] M voyeurism
v. T. ABK (= *vom Tausend*) per thousand
vulgär [vʊl'gɛ:r] ADJ vulgar
Vulkan [vʊl'ka:n] (**-s, -e**) M volcano; **Vulkanausbruch** M volcanic eruption
vulkanisieren [vʊlkani'zi:rən] VT to vulcanize
v. u. Z. ABK (= *vor unserer Zeitrechnung*) B.C.

W, w [ve:] NT W, w; **W wie Wilhelm** ≈ W for William

w. ABK = **wenden**; **werktags**; **westlich**; (= *weiblich*) f

W. ABK (= *West(en)*) W

Waage ['va:gə] (-, -n) F scales *pl*; (*Astrol*) Libra; **sich** *dat* **die ~ halten** (*fig*) to balance one another; **waagerecht** ADJ horizontal

Waagschale F (scale) pan; **(schwer) in die ~ fallen** (*fig*) to carry weight

wabbelig ['vabəlıç], **wabblig** ['vablıç] ADJ wobbly

Wabe ['va:bə] (-, -n) F honeycomb

wach [vax] ADJ awake; (*fig*) alert; **~ werden** to wake up

Wachablösung F changing of the guard; (*Mensch*) relief guard; (*fig: Regierungswechsel*) change of government

Wache (-, -n) F guard, watch; **~ halten** to keep watch; **~ stehen** *od* **schieben** (*umg*) to be on guard (duty)

wachen VI to be awake; (*Wache halten*) to keep watch; **bei jdm ~** to sit up with sb

wachhabend ADJ *attrib* duty

Wachhund M watchdog, guard dog; (*fig*) watchdog

Wacholder [va'xɔldər] (-s, -) M juniper

wachrütteln ['vaxrʏtəln] VT (*fig*) to (a)rouse

Wachs [vaks] (-es, -e) NT wax

wachsam ['vaxza:m] ADJ watchful, vigilant, alert; **Wachsamkeit** F vigilance

wachsen¹ *unreg* VI to grow

wachsen² VT (*Skier*) to wax

Wachsfigurenkabinett NT waxworks (exhibition)

Wachsmalstift, Wachsstift M wax crayon

wächst [vɛkst] VB *siehe* **wachsen²**

Wachstuch ['vakstu:x] NT oilcloth

Wachstum ['vakstu:m] (-s) NT growth

Wachstums- zW: **Wachstumsbranche** F growth industry; **Wachstumsgrenze** F limits of growth; **wachstumshemmend** ADJ growth-inhibiting; **Wachstumsrate** F growth rate; **Wachstumsschmerzen** PL growing pains; **Wachstumsstörung** F disturbance of growth

Wachtel ['vaxtəl] (-, -n) F quail

Wächter ['vɛçtər] (-s, -) M guard; (*Parkwächter*) warden, keeper; (*Museumswächter, Parkplatzwächter*) attendant

Wachtmeister M officer

Wachtposten M guard, sentry

Wachtturm, Wachturm M watchtower

Wach- und Schließgesellschaft F security corps

wackelig ADJ shaky, wobbly; **auf wackeligen Beinen stehen** to be wobbly on one's legs; (*fig*) to be unsteady

Wackelkontakt M loose connection

wackeln VI (*Stuhl*) to be wobbly; (*Zahn, Schraube*) to be loose; (*fig: Position*) to be shaky; **mit den Hüften/dem Schwanz ~** to wiggle one's hips/ wag its tail

wacker ['vakər] ADJ valiant, stout; **sich ~ schlagen** (*umg*) to put up a brave fight

wacklig ADJ = **wackelig**

Wade ['va:də] (-, -n) F (*Anat*) calf

Waffe ['vafə] (-, -n) F weapon; **jdn mit seinen eigenen Waffen schlagen** (*fig*) to beat sb at his own game

Waffel ['vafəl] (-, -n) F waffle; (*Eiswaffel*) wafer

Waffen- zW: **Waffengewalt** F: **mit Waffengewalt** by force of arms; **Waffenlager** NT (*von Armee*) ordnance depot; (*von Terroristen*) cache; **Waffenschein** M firearms *od* gun licence (BRIT), firearms license (US); **Waffenschmuggel** M gunrunning, arms smuggling; **Waffenstillstand** M armistice, truce

Wagemut ['va:gəmu:t] M daring

wagen VT to risk; **es ~, etw zu tun** to dare to do sth

Wagen ['va:gən] (-s, -) M vehicle; (*Auto*) car, automobile (US); (*Eisenb*) car, carriage (BRIT); (*Pferdewagen*) wag(g)on, cart

Wagen- zW: **Wagenführer** M driver; **Wagenheber** (-s, -) M jack; **Wagenpark** M fleet of cars; **Wagenrückholtaste** F (*Schreibmaschine*) carriage return (key); **Wagenrücklauf** M carriage return

Waggon [va'gõ:] (-s, -s) M wag(g)on; (*Güterwaggon*) goods van (BRIT), freight truck (US)

waghalsig ['va:khalzıç] ADJ foolhardy

Wagnis ['va:knıs] (-ses, -se) NT risk

Wagon (-s, -s) M = **Waggon**

Wahl [va:l] (**-, -en**) F choice; (*Pol*) election; **erste ~** (*Qualität*) top quality; (*Gemüse, Eier*) grade one; **zweite ~** (*Comm*) seconds *pl*; **aus freier ~** of one's own free choice; **wer die ~ hat, hat die Qual** (*Sprichwort*) he is *od* you are *etc* spoilt for choice; **die ~ fiel auf ihn** he was chosen; **sich zur ~ stellen** (*Pol etc*) to stand (BRIT) *od* run (for parliament *etc*)
wählbar ADJ eligible
Wahl- zW: **wahlberechtigt** ADJ entitled to vote; **Wahlbeteiligung** F poll, turnout; **Wahlbezirk** M (*Pol*) ward
wählen ['vɛ:lən] VT to choose; (*Pol*) to elect, to vote for; (*Tel*) to dial ▶ VI to choose; (*Pol*) to vote; (*Tel*) to dial
Wähler(in) (**-s, -**) M(F) voter; **Wählerabwanderung** F voter drift; **wählerisch** ADJ choosy; **Wählerschaft** F electorate
Wahl- zW: **Wahlfach** NT optional subject; **wahlfrei** ADJ: **wahlfreier Zugriff** (*Comput*) random access; **Wahlgang** M ballot; **Wahlgeschenk** NT *pre-election vote-catching gimmick*; **Wahlheimat** F country of adoption; **Wahlhelfer** M (*im Wahlkampf*) election assistant; (*bei der Wahl*) polling officer; **Wahlkabine** F polling booth; **Wahlkampf** M election campaign; **Wahlkreis** M constituency; **Wahlleiter** M returning officer; **Wahlliste** F electoral register; **Wahllokal** NT polling station; **wahllos** ADV at random; (*nicht wählerisch*) indiscriminately; **Wahlrecht** NT franchise; **allgemeines Wahlrecht** universal franchise; **das aktive Wahlrecht** the right to vote; **das passive Wahlrecht** eligibility (for political office); **Wahlspruch** M motto; **Wahlurne** F ballot box; **wahlweise** ADV alternatively
Wählzeichen NT (*Tel*) dialling tone (BRIT), dial tone (US)
Wahn [va:n] (**-(e)s**) M delusion; **Wahnsinn** M madness; **wahnsinnig** ADJ insane, mad ▶ ADV (*umg*) incredibly; **wahnwitzig** ADJ crazy *attrib* ▶ ADV terribly
wahr [va:r] ADJ true; **da ist (et)was Wahres dran** there's some truth in that; **das darf doch nicht ~ sein!** I don't believe it; **nicht ~?** that's right, isn't it?
wahren VT to maintain, to keep
währen ['vɛ:rən] VI to last
während PRÄP *+gen* during ▶ KONJ while; **währenddessen** ADV meanwhile
wahr- zW: **wahrhaben** *unreg* VT: **etw nicht wahrhaben wollen** to refuse to admit sth; **wahrhaft** ADV (*tatsächlich*) truly; **wahrhaftig** ADJ true, real ▶ ADV really
Wahrheit F truth; **die ~ sagen** to tell the truth
wahrheitsgetreu ADJ (*Bericht*) truthful; (*Darstellung*) faithful
wahrnehmen *unreg* VT to perceive; (*Frist*) to observe; (*Veränderungen etc*) to be aware of; (*Gelegenheit*) to take; (*Interessen, Rechte*) to look after
Wahrnehmung F perception; (*von Frist*) observing; (*von Veränderungen etc*) awareness; (*von Gelegenheit*) taking; (*von Interessen, Rechten*) looking after
wahrsagen VI to predict the future, to tell fortunes
Wahrsager M fortune-teller
wahrscheinlich [va:r'ʃaɪnlɪç] ADJ probable ▶ ADV probably; **Wahrscheinlichkeit** F probability; **aller Wahrscheinlichkeit nach** in all probability
Währung ['vɛ:rʊŋ] F currency
Währungs- zW: **Währungseinheit** F monetary unit; **Währungspolitik** F monetary policy; **Währungsraum** M currency area; **Währungsreserven** PL official reserves *pl*; **Währungsunion** F monetary union
Wahrzeichen NT (*Gebäude, Turm etc*) symbol; (*von Stadt, Verein*) emblem
Waise ['vaɪzə] (**-, -n**) F orphan
Waisen- zW: **Waisenhaus** NT orphanage; **Waisenkind** NT orphan; **Waisenknabe** M: **gegen dich ist er ein Waisenknabe** (*umg*) he's no match for you; **Waisenrente** F orphan's allowance
Wal [va:l] (**-(e)s, -e**) M whale
Wald [valt] (**-(e)s, Wälder**) M wood(s *pl*); (*groß*) forest; **Waldbrand** M forest fire
Wäldchen ['vɛltçən] NT copse, grove
Waldhorn NT (*Mus*) French horn
waldig ['valdɪç] ADJ wooded
Wald- zW: **Waldlehrpfad** M nature trail; **Waldmeister** M (*Bot*) woodruff; **Waldsterben** NT *loss of trees due to pollution*
Wald- und Wiesen- (*umg*) IN zW common-or-garden
Waldweg M woodland *od* forest path
Wales [weɪlz] NT Wales
Walfang ['va:lfaŋ] M whaling
Walfisch ['valfɪʃ] M whale
Waliser(in) [va'li:zər(ɪn)] (**-s, -**) M(F) Welshman, Welshwoman
walisisch ADJ Welsh
Walkman® ['wɔ:kman] (**-s, Walkmen**) M Walkman®, personal stereo
Wall [val] (**-(e)s, Wälle**) M embankment; (*Bollwerk*) rampart
wallfahren VI UNTR to go on a pilgrimage
Wallfahrer(in) M(F) pilgrim
Wallfahrt F pilgrimage
Wallis ['valɪs] (-) NT: **das ~** Valais
Wallone [va'lo:nə] (**-n, -n**) M, **Wallonin** F Walloon
Walnuss ['valnʊs] F walnut
Walross ['valrɔs] NT walrus
walten ['valtən] VI (*geh*): **Vernunft ~ lassen** to let reason prevail
Walzblech (**-(e)s**) NT sheet metal
Walze ['valtsə] (**-, -n**) F (*Gerät*) cylinder; (*Fahrzeug*) roller
walzen VT to roll (out)
wälzen ['vɛltsən] VT to roll (over); (*Bücher*) to hunt through; (*Probleme*) to deliberate on ▶ VR

to wallow; (*vor Schmerzen*) to roll about; (*im Bett*) to toss and turn
Walzer ['valtsər] (**-s, -**) M waltz
Wälzer ['vɛltsər] (**-s, -**) (*umg*) M tome
Wampe ['vampə] (-, **-n**) (*umg*) F paunch
wand *etc* [vant] VB *siehe* **winden**
Wand (-, **Wände**) F wall; (*Trennwand*) partition; (*Bergwand*) precipice; (*Felswand*) (rock) face; (*fig*) barrier; **weiß wie die ~** as white as a sheet; **jdn an die ~ spielen** to put sb in the shade; (*Sport*) to outplay sb
Wandel ['vandəl] (**-s**) M change; **wandelbar** ADJ changeable, variable
Wandelhalle F foyer
wandeln VT, VR to change ▶ VI (*gehen*) to walk
Wanderausstellung F touring exhibition
Wanderbühne F touring theatre (BRIT) *od* theater (US)
Wanderer (**-s, -**) M, **Wanderin** F hiker, rambler
Wanderkarte F hiker's map
Wanderlied NT hiking song
wandern VI to hike; (*Blick*) to wander; (*Gedanken*) to stray; (*umg: in den Papierkorb etc*) to land
Wanderpreis M challenge trophy
Wanderschaft F travelling (BRIT), traveling (US)
Wanderung F walk, hike; (*von Tieren, Völkern*) migration
Wanderweg M trail, (foot)path
Wandgemälde NT mural
Wandlung F change; (*völlige Umwandlung*) transformation; (*Rel*) transubstantiation
Wand- ZW: **Wandmalerei** F mural painting; **Wandschirm** M (folding) screen; **Wandschrank** M cupboard
wandte *etc* ['vantə] VB *siehe* **wenden**
Wandteppich M tapestry
Wandverkleidung F panelling
Wange ['vaŋə] (-, **-n**) F cheek
wankelmütig ['vaŋkəlmy:tıç] ADJ fickle, inconstant
wanken ['vankən] VI to stagger; (*fig*) to waver
wann [van] ADV when; **seit ~ bist/hast du ...?** how long have you been/have you had ...?
Wanne ['vanə] (-, **-n**) F tub
Wanze ['vantsə] (-, **-n**) F (*Abhörgerät, Zool*) bug
WAP NT ABK (*Comput: = Wireless Application Protocol*) WAP
WAP-Handy NT WAP phone
Wappen ['vapən] (**-s, -**) NT coat of arms, crest; **Wappenkunde** F heraldry
wappnen VR (*fig*) to prepare o.s.; **gewappnet sein** to be forearmed
war *etc* [va:r] VB *siehe* **sein**
warb *etc* [varp] VB *siehe* **werben**
Ware ['va:rə] (-, **-n**) F ware; **Waren** PL goods *pl*
wäre *etc* ['vɛ:rə] VB *siehe* **sein**
Waren- ZW: **Warenbestand** M stock; **Warenhaus** NT department store; **Warenlager** NT stock, store; **Warenmuster** NT sample; **Warenprobe** F sample; **Warenrückstände** PL backlog *sing*; **Warensendung** F trade sample (sent by post); **Warenzeichen** NT trademark
warf *etc* [varf] VB *siehe* **werfen**
warm [varm] ADJ warm; (*Essen*) hot; (*umg: homosexuell*) queer; **mir ist ~** I'm warm; **mit jdm ~ werden** (*umg*) to get close to sb; **~ laufen** (*Aut*) to warm up; *siehe auch* **warmhalten**
Wärme ['vɛrmə] (-, **-n**) F warmth; **10 Grad ~** 10 degrees above zero
wärmen VT, VR to warm (up), to heat (up) ▶ VI (*Kleidung, Sonne*) to be warm
Wärmflasche F hot-water bottle
warm- ZW: **Warmfront** F (*Met*) warm front; **warmhalten** *unreg* VT: **sich** *dat* **jdn warmhalten** (*fig*) to keep in with sb; **warmherzig** ADJ warm-hearted; **Warmwassertank** M hot-water tank
Warnblinkanlage F (*Aut*) hazard warning lights *pl*
Warndreieck NT warning triangle
warnen ['varnən] VT to warn
Warnstreik M token strike
Warnung F warning
Warschau ['varʃaʊ] (**-s**) NT Warsaw; **Warschauer Pakt** M Warsaw Pact
Warte (-, **-n**) F observation point; (*fig*) viewpoint
warten ['vartən] VI to wait ▶ VT (*Auto, Maschine*) to service; **~ auf** +*akk* to wait for; **auf sich ~ lassen** to take a long time; **warte mal!** wait a minute!; (*überlegend*) let me see; **mit dem Essen auf jdn ~** to wait for sb before eating
Wärter(in) ['vɛrtər(ın)] (**-s, -**) M(F) attendant
Wartesaal M (*Eisenb*) waiting room
Wartezimmer NT waiting room
Wartung F (*von Auto, Maschine*) servicing; **~ und Instandhaltung** maintenance
warum [va'rʊm] ADV why; **~ nicht gleich so!** that's better
Warze ['vartsə] (-, **-n**) F wart
was [vas] PRON what; (*umg: etwas*) something; **das, ~ ...** that which ...; **~ für ...?** what sort *od* kind of ...?; **alles, ~ er hat** everything he's got
Wasch- ZW: **Waschanlage** F (*für Autos*) car wash; **waschbar** ADJ washable; **Waschbecken** NT washbasin
Wäsche ['vɛʃə] (-, **-n**) F washing; (*Bettwäsche*) linen; (*Unterwäsche*) underwear; **in der ~** in the wash; **dumm aus der ~ gucken** (*umg*) to look stupid
waschecht ADJ (*Farbe*) fast; (*fig*) genuine
Wäsche- ZW: **Wäscheklammer** F clothes peg (BRIT), clothespin (US); **Wäschekorb** M dirty clothes basket; **Wäscheleine** F washing line (BRIT), clothes line (US)
waschen ['vaʃən] *unreg* VT, VI to wash ▶ VR to (have a) wash; **sich** *dat* **die Hände ~** to wash one's hands; **~ und legen** (*Haare*) to shampoo and set
Wäscherei [vɛʃə'raı] F laundry
Wäscheschleuder F spin-dryer
Wäschetrockner M tumble-drier
Wasch- ZW: **Waschgang** M stage of the washing programme (BRIT) *od* program (US); **Waschküche** F laundry room; **Waschlappen** M face cloth *od* flannel (BRIT), washcloth (US);

W

(*umg*) softy; **Waschmaschine** F washing machine; **Waschmittel** NT detergent; **Waschpulver** NT washing powder; **Waschsalon** M Launderette® (BRIT), Laundromat® (*US*); **Waschstraße** F car wash
wäscht [vɛʃt] VB *siehe* **waschen**
Waschtisch M washstand
Washington ['wɔʃɪŋtən] (**-s**) NT Washington
Wasser ['vasər] (**-s, -** *or* **Wässer**) NT (*no pl*) water; (*pl* **Wässer**) (*Flüssigkeit*) water; (*Med*) lotion; (*Parfüm*) cologne; (*Mineralwasser*) mineral water; **~ abstoßend** water-repellent; **dort wird auch nur mit ~ gekocht** (*fig*) they're no different from anybody else (there); **ins ~ fallen** (*fig*) to fall through; **mit allen Wassern gewaschen sein** (*umg*) to be a shrewd customer; **~ lassen** (*euph*) to pass water; **jdm das ~ abgraben** (*fig*) to take the bread from sb's mouth, to take away sb's livelihood
Wässerchen NT: **er sieht aus, als ob er kein ~ trüben könnte** he looks as if butter wouldn't melt in his mouth
Wasser- zW: **wasserdicht** ADJ watertight; (*Stoff, Uhr*) waterproof; **Wasserfall** M waterfall; **Wasserfarbe** F watercolour (BRIT), watercolor (*US*); **wassergekühlt** ADJ (*Aut*) water-cooled; **Wassergraben** M (*Sport*) water jump; (*um Burg*) moat; **Wasserhahn** M tap, faucet (*US*)
wässerig ['vɛsərɪç] ADJ watery
Wasser- zW: **Wasserkessel** M kettle; (*Tech*) boiler; **Wasserkraftwerk** NT hydroelectric power station; **Wasserleitung** F water pipe; (*Anlagen*) plumbing; **wasserlöslich** ADJ water-soluble; **Wassermann** M (*Astrol*) Aquarius; **Wassermelone** F water melon
wassern VI to land on the water
wässern ['vɛsərn] VT, VI to water
Wasser- zW: **Wasserscheide** F watershed; **wasserscheu** ADJ afraid of water; **Wasserschutzpolizei** F (*auf Flüssen*) river police; (*im Hafen*) harbour (BRIT) *od* harbor (*US*) police; (*auf der See*) coastguard service; **Wasserski** NT water-skiing; **Wasserspiegel** M (*Oberfläche*) surface of the water; (*Wasserstand*) water level; **Wassersport** M water sports *pl*; **Wasserstand** M water level; **Wasserstoff** M hydrogen; **Wasserstoffbombe** F hydrogen bomb; **Wasserverbrauch** M water consumption; **Wasserwaage** F spirit level; **Wasserwelle** F shampoo and set; **Wasserwerfer** (**-s, -**) M water cannon; **Wasserwerk** NT waterworks; **Wasserzeichen** NT watermark
waten ['va:tən] VI to wade
watscheln ['va:tʃəln] VI to waddle
Watt[1] [vat] (**-(e)s, -en**) NT (*Geog*) mud flats *pl*
Watt[2] (**-s, -**) NT (*Elek*) watt
Watte (**-, -n**) F cotton wool (BRIT), absorbent cotton (*US*)
Wattenmeer (**-(e)s**) NT mud flats *pl*
Wattestäbchen NT cotton(-wool) swab
wattieren [va'ti:rən] VT to pad
WC [ve:'tse:] (**-s, -s**) NT ABK (= *Wasserklosett*) WC
Web [wɛb] NT (*Comput*): **das ~** the Web; **im ~** on the Web
Webadresse F (*Comput*) web address
weben ['ve:bən] *unreg* VT to weave
Weber(in) (**-s, -**) M(F) weaver
Weberei [ve:bə'raɪ] F (*Betrieb*) weaving mill
Webinar ['wɛbina:r] NT (*Comput*) webinar
Webmail ['wɛbme:l] NT (*Comput*) webmail
Webpage ['wɛbpa:gə] NT web page
Webseite ['wɛbzaɪtə] F Web page, web site
Webstuhl ['ve:pʃtu:l] M loom
Wechsel ['vɛksəl] (**-s, -**) M change; (*Geldwechsel*) exchange; (*Comm*) bill of exchange; **Wechselbäder** PL alternating hot and cold baths *pl*; **Wechselbeziehung** F correlation; **Wechselforderungen** PL (*Comm*) bills receivable *pl*; **Wechselgeld** NT change; **wechselhaft** ADJ (*Wetter*) variable; **Wechselinhaber** M bearer; **Wechseljahre** PL change of life, menopause; **in die Wechseljahre kommen** to start the change; **Wechselkurs** M rate of exchange; **Wechselkursmechanismus** M Exchange Rate Mechanism, ERM
wechseln VT to change; (*Blicke*) to exchange ▶ VI to change; (*einander ablösen*) to alternate
wechselnd ADJ changing; (*Stimmungen*) changeable; (*Winde, Bewölkung*) variable
Wechsel- zW: **wechselseitig** ADJ reciprocal; **Wechselsprechanlage** F two-way intercom; **Wechselstrom** M alternating current; **Wechselstube** F currency exchange, bureau de change; **Wechselverbindlichkeiten** PL bills payable *pl*; **wechselweise** ADV alternately; **Wechselwirkung** F interaction
wecken ['vɛkən] VT to wake (up); (*fig*) to arouse; (*Bedarf*) to create; (*Erinnerungen*) to revive
Wecker (**-s, -**) M alarm clock; **jdm auf den ~ fallen** (*umg*) to get on sb's nerves
Weckglas® NT preserving jar
Weckruf M (*Tel*) alarm call
wedeln ['ve:dəln] VI (*mit Schwanz*) to wag; (*mit Fächer*) to fan; (*Ski*) to wedel
weder ['ve:dər] KONJ neither; **~ … noch …** neither … nor …
weg [vɛk] ADV away; (*los, ab*) off; **über etw** *akk* **~ sein** to be over sth; **er war schon ~** he had already left; **nichts wie** *od* **nur ~ von hier!** let's get out of here!; **~ damit!** (*mit Schere etc*) put it/them away!; **Finger ~!** hands off!
Weg [ve:k] (**-(e)s, -e**) M way; (*Pfad*) path; (*Route*) route; **sich auf den ~ machen** to be on one's way; **jdm aus dem ~ gehen** to keep out of sb's way; **jdm nicht über den ~ trauen** (*fig*) not to trust sb an inch; **den ~ des geringsten Widerstandes gehen** to follow the line of least resistance; **etw in die Wege leiten** to arrange sth; **jdm Steine in den ~ legen** (*fig*) to put obstacles in sb's way; *siehe auch* **zuwege**
wegbereitend ['ve:kbəraɪtənt] ADJ cutting-edge
Wegbereiter (**-s, -**) M pioneer
wegblasen *unreg* VT to blow away; **wie weggeblasen sein** (*fig*) to have vanished

wegbleiben *unreg* VI to stay away; **mir bleibt die Spucke weg!** *(umg)* I am absolutely flabbergasted!
wegen ['ve:gən] PRÄP *+gen od +dat* because of; **von ~!** you must be joking!
weg- ZW: **wegfahren** *unreg* VI to drive away; *(abfahren)* to leave; **Wegfahrsperre** F *(Aut)*: **(elektronische) Wegfahrsperre** (electronic) immobilizer; **wegfallen** *unreg* VI to be left out; *(Ferien, Bezahlung)* to be cancelled; *(aufhören)* to cease; **weggehen** *unreg* VI to go away, to leave; *(umg: Ware)* to sell; **weghören** VI to turn a deaf ear; **wegjagen** VT to chase away; **wegkommen** *unreg* VI: **(bei etw) gut/schlecht wegkommen** *(umg)* to come off well/badly (with sth); **weglassen** *unreg* VT to leave out; **weglaufen** *unreg* VI to run away *od* off; **das läuft (dir) nicht weg!** *(fig hum)* that can wait; **weglegen** VT to put aside; **wegmachen** *(umg)* VT to get rid of; **wegmüssen** *unreg (umg)* VI to have to go; **wegnehmen** *unreg* VT to take away
Wegrand ['ve:krant] M wayside
weg- ZW: **wegräumen** VT to clear away; **wegschaffen** VT to clear away; **wegschließen** *unreg* VT to lock away; **wegschmeißen** *unreg* VT to throw away; **wegschnappen** VT: **(jdm) etw wegschnappen** to snatch sth away (from sb); **wegstecken** VT to put away; *(umg: verkraften)* to cope with; **wegtreten** *unreg* VI *(Mil)*: **wegtreten!** dismiss!; **geistig weggetreten sein** *(umg: geistesabwesend)* to be away with the fairies; **wegtun** *unreg* VT to put away
wegweisend ['ve:gvaɪzənt] ADJ pioneering *attrib*, revolutionary
Wegweiser ['ve:gvaɪzər] (**-s, -**) M road sign, signpost; *(fig: Buch etc)* guide
Wegwerf- ['vɛkvɛrf] IN ZW disposable
weg- ZW: **wegwerfen** *unreg* VT to throw away; **wegwerfend** ADJ disparaging; **Wegwerfgesellschaft** F throw-away society; **wegwollen** *unreg* VI *(verreisen)* to want to go away; **wegziehen** *unreg* VI to move away
weh [ve:] ADJ sore
wehe INTERJ: **~, wenn du …** you'll regret it if you …; **~ dir!** you dare!
Wehe ['ve:ə] (**-, -n**) F drift
wehen VT, VI to blow; *(Fahnen)* to flutter
Wehen PL *(Med)* contractions *pl*; **in den ~ liegen** to be in labour (BRIT) *od* labor (US)
weh- ZW: **wehklagen** VI UNTR to wail; **wehleidig** ADJ oversensitive to pain; *(jammernd)* whiny, whining; **Wehmut** F melancholy; **wehmütig** ADJ melancholy
Wehr[1] [ve:r] (**-(e)s, -e**) NT weir
Wehr[2] [ve:r] (**-, -en**) F *(Feuerwehr)* fire brigade (BRIT) *od* department (US) ▶ IN ZW defence (BRIT), defense (US); **sich zur ~ setzen** to defend o.s.
wehren VR to defend o.s.
Wehr- ZW: **wehrlos** ADJ defenceless (BRIT), defenseless (US); **jdm wehrlos ausgeliefert sein** to be at sb's mercy; **Wehrmacht** F armed forces *pl*; **Wehrpflicht** F conscription; **wehrpflichtig** ADJ liable for military service; **Wehrübung** F reserve duty training exercise
wehtun ['ve:tu:n] *unreg* VT: **jdm/sich ~** to hurt sb/o.s.
Wehwehchen *(umg)* NT (minor) complaint
Weib [vaɪp] (**-(e)s, -er**) NT woman, female *(pej)*
Weibchen NT *(Ehefrau)* little woman; *(Zool)* female
weibisch ['vaɪbɪʃ] ADJ effeminate
weiblich ADJ feminine; *(Biol)* female
weich [vaɪç] ADJ soft; *(Ei)* soft-boiled; **weiche Währung** soft currency
Weiche (**-, -n**) F *(Eisenb)* points *pl*; **die Weichen stellen** *(lit)* to switch the points; *(fig)* to set the course
weichen *unreg* VI to yield, to give way; **(nicht) von jdm** *od* **von jds Seite ~** (not) to leave sb's side
Weichensteller (**-s, -**) M pointsman
weich- ZW: **Weichheit** F softness; **Weichkäse** M soft cheese; **weichlich** ADJ soft, namby-pamby; **Weichling** M wimp; **Weichspüler** (**-s, -**) M fabric conditioner; **Weichteile** PL soft parts *pl*; **Weichtier** NT mollusc (BRIT), mollusk (US)
Weide ['vaɪdə] (**-, -n**) F *(Baum)* willow; *(Gras)* pasture
weiden VI to graze ▶ VR: **sich an etw** *dat* **~** to delight in sth
Weidenkätzchen NT willow catkin
weidlich ['vaɪtlɪç] ADV thoroughly
weigern ['vaɪgərn] VR to refuse
Weigerung ['vaɪgərʊŋ] F refusal
Weihe ['vaɪə] (**-, -n**) F consecration; *(Priesterweihe)* ordination
weihen VT to consecrate; *(widmen)* to dedicate; **dem Untergang geweiht** *(liter)* doomed
Weiher (**-s, -**) M pond
weihnachten VI UNPERS: **es weihnachtet sehr** *(poetisch, ironisch)* Christmas is very much in evidence
Weihnachten (**-**) NT Christmas; **fröhliche ~!** happy *od* merry Christmas!
weihnachtlich ADJ Christmas(sy)
Weihnachts- ZW: **Weihnachtsabend** M Christmas Eve; **Weihnachtsbaum** M Christmas tree; **Weihnachtsferien** PL Christmas holidays *pl* (BRIT), Christmas vacation *sing* (US); **Weihnachtsgeld** NT Christmas bonus; **Weihnachtsgeschenk** NT Christmas present; **Weihnachtslied** NT Christmas carol; **Weihnachtsmann** M Father Christmas (BRIT), Santa Claus
Weihnachtsmarkt M Christmas fair; *see note*

> The **Weihnachtsmarkt** is a market held in most large towns in Germany in the weeks prior to Christmas. People visit it to buy presents, toys and Christmas decorations, and to enjoy the festive atmosphere. Food and drink associated with the Christmas festivities can also be eaten and drunk there, for example, gingerbread and mulled wine.

W

Weihnachtstag M: **(erster) ~** Christmas day; **zweiter ~** Boxing Day (BRIT)
Weihrauch M incense
Weihwasser NT holy water
weil [vaɪl] KONJ because
Weile ['vaɪlə] (-) F while, short time
Weiler ['vaɪlər] (**-s, -**) M hamlet
Weimarer Republik ['vaɪmarər repu'bli:k] F Weimar Republic
Wein [vaɪn] (**-(e)s, -e**) M wine; (*Pflanze*) vine; **jdm reinen ~ einschenken** (*fig*) to tell sb the truth; **Weinbau** M cultivation of vines; **Weinbauer** M wine-grower; **Weinbeere** F grape; **Weinberg** M vineyard; **Weinbergschnecke** F snail; **Weinbrand** M brandy
weinen VT, VI to cry; **das ist zum W~** it's enough to make you cry *od* weep
weinerlich ADJ tearful
Wein- zW: **Weingegend** F wine-growing area; **Weingeist** M (ethyl) alcohol; **Weinglas** NT wine glass; **Weingut** NT wine-growing estate; **Weinkarte** F wine list
Weinkrampf M crying fit
Wein- zW: **Weinlese** F vintage; **Weinprobe** F wine tasting; **Weinrebe** F vine; **weinrot** ADJ (*Farbe*) claret; **weinselig** ADJ merry with wine; **Weinstein** M tartar; **Weinstock** M vine; **Weinstube** F wine bar; **Weintraube** F grape
weise ['vaɪzə] ADJ wise
Weise (**-, -n**) F manner, way; (*Lied*) tune; **auf diese ~** in this way
Weise(r) F(M) wise man, wise woman, sage
weisen *unreg* VT to show; **etw (weit) von sich ~** (*fig*) to reject sth (emphatically)
Weisheit ['vaɪshaɪt] F wisdom
Weisheitszahn M wisdom tooth
weismachen ['vaɪsmaxən] VT: **er wollte uns ~, dass ...** he would have us believe that ...
weiß[1] [vaɪs] VB *siehe* **wissen**
weiß[2] ADJ white; **Weißblech** NT tin plate; **Weißbrot** NT white bread; **weißen** VT to whitewash; **Weißglut** F (*Tech*) incandescence; **jdn zur Weißglut bringen** (*fig*) to make sb see red; **Weißkohl** M (white) cabbage
Weißrussland NT B(y)elorussia
weißt [vaɪst] VB *siehe* **wissen**
Weiß- zW: **Weißwandtafel** F whiteboard; **interaktive Weißwandtafel** interactive whiteboard; **Weißwaren** PL linen *sing*; **Weißwein** M white wine; **Weißwurst** F veal sausage
Weisung ['vaɪzʊŋ] F instruction
weit [vaɪt] ADJ wide; (*Begriff*) broad; (*Reise, Wurf*) long ▸ ADV far; **~ blickend** far-seeing; **~ hergeholt** far-fetched; **~ reichend** (*fig*) far-reaching; **~ verbreitet** widespread; **~ verzweigt** = **weitverzweigt**; **in weiter Ferne** in the far distance; **wie ~ ist es ...?** how far is it ...?; **das geht zu ~** that's going too far; **~ und breit** for miles around; **~ gefehlt!** far from it!; **es so ~ bringen, dass ...** to bring it about that ...; **~ zurückliegen** to be far behind; **von Weitem** from a long way off; **weitab** ADV: **weitab von** far (away) from; **weitaus** ADV by far; **Weitblick** M (*fig*) far-sightedness; **weitblickend** ADJ far-seeing
Weite (**-, -n**) F width; (*Raum*) space; (*von Entfernung*) distance
weiten VT, VR to widen
weiter ['vaɪtər] ADJ wider; (*zusätzlich*) further ▸ ADV further; **wenn es ~ nichts ist, ...** well, if that's all (it is), ...; **das hat ~ nichts zu sagen** that doesn't really matter; **immer ~** on and on; (*Anweisung*) keep on (going); **und so ~** and so on; **~ nichts/niemand** nothing/nobody else; **weiterarbeiten** VI to go on working; **weiterbilden** VR to continue one's studies; **Weiterbildung** F further education
Weitere(s) NT further details *pl*; **bis auf ~** for the time being; **ohne ~** without further ado, just like that
weiter- zW: **weiterempfehlen** *unreg* VT to recommend (to others); **weitererzählen** VT (*Geheimnis*) to pass on; **Weiterfahrt** F continuation of the journey; **weiterführend** ADJ (*Schule*) secondary (BRIT), high (*US*); **weitergehen** *unreg* VI to go on; **weiterhin** ADV: **etw weiterhin tun** to go on doing sth; **weiterkommen** *unreg* VI: **nicht weiterkommen** (*fig*) to be bogged down; **weiterleiten** VT to pass on; **weitermachen** VT, VI to continue; **weiterreisen** VI to continue one's journey; **weitersagen** VT: **nicht weitersagen!** don't tell anyone!; **weitersehen** *unreg* VI: **dann sehen wir weiter** then we'll see; **weitertwittern** VI (*auf Twitter*) to retweet; **weiterverarbeiten** VT to process; **weiterwissen** *unreg* VI: **nicht (mehr) weiterwissen** (*verzweifelt sein*) to be at one's wits' end
weit- zW: **weitgehend** ADJ considerable ▸ ADV largely; **weithin** ADV widely; (*weitgehend*) to a large extent; **weitläufig** ADJ (*Gebäude*) spacious; (*Erklärung*) lengthy; (*Verwandter*) distant; **weitreichend** ADJ (*fig*) far-reaching; **weitschweifig** ADJ long-winded; **weitsichtig** ADJ (*lit*) long-sighted (BRIT), far-sighted (*US*); (*fig*) far-sighted; **Weitsprung** M long jump; **weitverbreitet** ADJ widespread; **weitverzweigt** ADJ (*Straßensystem*) extensive; **Weitwinkelobjektiv** NT (*Phot*) wide-angle lens
Weizen ['vaɪtsən] (**-s, -**) M wheat; **Weizenbier** NT *light, fizzy wheat beer*; **Weizenkeime** PL (*Koch*) wheatgerm *sing*
welch [vɛlç] PRON: **~ ein(e) ...** what a ...

SCHLÜSSELWORT

welche(r, s) INTERROG PRON which; **welcher von beiden?** which (one) of the two?; **welchen hast du genommen?** which (one) did you take?; **welche Freude!** what joy!
▸ INDEF PRON some; (*in Fragen*) any; **ich habe welche** I have some; **haben Sie welche?** do you have any?
▸ REL PRON (*bei Menschen*) who; (*bei Sachen*) which, that; **welche(r, s) auch immer** whoever/whichever/whatever

welk [vɛlk] ADJ withered; **welken** VI to wither
Wellblech NT corrugated iron
Welle ['vɛlə] (-, -n) F wave; (*Tech*) shaft; **(hohe) Wellen schlagen** (*fig*) to create (quite) a stir
Wellen- zW: **Wellenbereich** M waveband; **Wellenbrecher** M breakwater; **Wellengang** M: **starker Wellengang** heavy sea(s) *od* swell; **Wellenlänge** F (*lit, fig*) wavelength; **mit jdm auf einer Wellenlänge sein** (*fig*) to be on the same wavelength as sb; **Wellenlinie** F wavy line
Wellensittich M budgerigar
Wellpappe F corrugated cardboard
Welpe ['vɛlpə] (-n, -n) M pup, whelp; (*von Wolf etc*) cub
Welt [vɛlt] (-, -en) F world; **auf der ~** in the world; **aus der ~ schaffen** to eliminate; **in aller ~** all over the world; **vor aller ~** in front of everybody; **auf die ~ kommen** to be born; **Weltall** NT universe; **Weltanschauung** F philosophy of life; **weltberühmt** ADJ world-famous; **weltbewegend** ADJ world-shattering; **Weltbild** NT conception of the world; (*jds Ansichten*) philosophy
Weltenbummler(in) M(F) globetrotter
Weltergewicht ['vɛltərgəviçt] NT (*Sport*) welterweight
weltfremd ADJ unworldly
Weltgesundheitsorganisation F World Health Organization
Welt- zW: **weltgewandt** ADJ sophisticated; **Weltkirchenrat** M World Council of Churches; **Weltkrieg** M world war; **weltlich** ADJ worldly; (*nicht kirchlich*) secular; **Weltliteratur** F world literature; **Weltmacht** F world power; **weltmännisch** ADJ sophisticated; **Weltmeister** M world champion; **Weltmeisterschaft** F world *od* world's (US) championship; (*Fussball etc*) World Cup; **Weltrang** M: **von Weltrang** world-famous; **Weltraum** M space; **Weltraumforschung** F space research; **Weltraumstation** F space station; **Weltreise** F trip round the world; **Weltrekord** M world record; **Weltruf** M world-wide reputation; **Weltsicherheitsrat** M (*Pol*) United Nations Security Council; **Weltstadt** F metropolis; **Weltuntergang** M (*lit, fig*) end of the world; **weltweit** ADJ world-wide; **Weltwirtschaft** F world economy; **Weltwirtschaftskrise** F world economic crisis; **Weltwunder** NT wonder of the world
wem [ve:m] DAT *von* **wer** ▸ PRON to whom
wen [ve:n] AKK *von* **wer** ▸ PRON whom
Wende ['vɛndə] (-, -n) F turn; (*Veränderung*) change; **die ~** (*Pol*) (the) reunification (of Germany); **Wendekreis** M (*Geog*) tropic; (*Aut*) turning circle
Wendeltreppe F spiral staircase
wenden *unreg* VT, VI, VR to turn; **bitte ~!** please turn over; **sich an jdn ~** to go/come to sb
Wendepunkt M turning point
wendig ADJ (*lit, fig*) agile; (*Auto etc*) manoeuvrable (BRIT), maneuverable (US)
Wendung F turn; (*Redewendung*) idiom
wenig ['ve:nıç] ADJ, ADV little; **ein ~** a little; **er hat zu ~ Geld** he doesn't have enough money; **ein Exemplar zu ~** one copy too few
wenige ['ve:nıgə] PL few *pl*; **in wenigen Tagen** in (just) a few days
weniger ADJ less; (*mit pl*) fewer ▸ ADV less
Wenigkeit F trifle; **meine ~** (*umg*) little me
wenigste(r, s) ADJ least
wenigstens ADV at least
wenn [vɛn] KONJ if; (*zeitlich*) when; **~ auch …** even if …; **~ ich doch …** if only I …; **~ wir erst die neue Wohnung haben** once we get the new flat
Wenn NT: **ohne ~ und Aber** unequivocally
wennschon ADV: **na ~!** so what?; **~, dennschon!** in for a penny, in for a pound!
wer [ve:r] PRON who; **~ von euch?** which (one) of you?
Werbe- zW: **Werbeagentur** F advertising agency; **Werbeaktion** F advertising campaign; **Werbeantwort** F business reply card; **Werbebanner** NT banner; **Werbefernsehen** NT commercial television; **Werbefilm** M promotional film; **Werbegeschenk** NT promotional gift, freebie (*umg*); (*zu Gekauftem*) free gift; **Werbegrafiker(in)** M(F) commercial artist; **Werbekampagne** F advertising campaign
werben ['vɛrbən] *unreg* VT to win; (*Mitglied*) to recruit ▸ VI to advertise; **um jdn/etw ~** to try to win sb/sth; **für jdn/etw ~** to promote sb/sth
Werbe- zW: **Werbespot** M commercial; **Werbetexter (-s, -)** M copywriter; **Werbetrommel** F: **die Werbetrommel (für etw) rühren** (*umg*) to beat the big drum (for sth); **werbewirksam** ADJ: **werbewirksam sein** to be good publicity
Werbung F advertising; (*von Mitgliedern*) recruitment; (*TV etc: Werbeblock*) commercial break; **~ um jdn/etw** promotion of sb/sth
Werbungskosten PL professional *od* business expenses *pl*
Werdegang ['ve:rdəgaŋ] M development; (*beruflich*) career

SCHLÜSSELWORT

werden ['ve:rdən] (*pt* **wurde**, *pp* **geworden** *od* (*bei Passiv*) **worden**) VI to become; **was ist aus ihm/aus der Sache geworden?** what became of him/it?; **es ist nichts/gut geworden** it came to nothing/turned out well; **es wird Nacht/Tage** it's getting dark/light; **es wird bald ein Jahr, dass …** it's almost a year since …; **er wird am 8. Mai 36** he will be 36 on the 8th May; **mir wird kalt** I'm getting cold; **mir wird schlecht** I feel ill; **Erster werden** to come *od* be first; **das muss anders werden** that will have to change; **rot/zu Eis werden** to turn red/to ice; **was willst du (mal) werden?** what do you want to be?; **die Fotos sind gut geworden** the photos turned out well
▸ HILFSVERB **1** (*bei Futur*): **er wird es tun** he will

W

od he'll do it; **er wird das nicht tun** he will not *od* he won't do it; **es wird gleich regnen** it's going to rain any moment
2 (*bei Konjunktiv*): **ich würde ...** I would ...; **er würde gern ...** he would *od* he'd like to ...; **ich würde lieber ...** I would *od* I'd rather ...
3 (*bei Vermutung*): **sie wird in der Küche sein** she will be in the kitchen
4 (*bei Passiv*): **gebraucht werden** to be used; **er ist erschossen worden** he has *od* he's been shot; **mir wurde gesagt, dass ...** I was told that ...

werdend ADJ: **werdende Mutter** expectant mother
werfen ['vɛrfən] *unreg* VT to throw ▸ VI (*Tier*) to have its young; **„nicht ~"** "handle with care"
Werft [vɛrft] (-, **-en**) F shipyard; (*für Flugzeuge*) hangar
Werk [vɛrk] (**-(e)s, -e**) NT work; (*Tätigkeit*) job; (*Fabrik, Mechanismus*) works *pl*; **ans ~ gehen** to set to work; **das ist sein ~** this is his doing; **ab ~** (*Comm*) ex works
werkeln ['vɛrkəln] (*umg*) VI to potter about (BRIT), to putter around (*US*)
Werken (**-s**) NT (*Sch*) handicrafts *pl*
Werkschutz M works security service
Werksgelände NT factory premises *pl*
Werk- zW: **Werkstatt** (-, **-stätten**) F workshop; (*Aut*) garage; **Werkstoff** M material; **Werkstudent** M self-supporting student; **Werktag** M working day; **werktags** ADV on working days; **werktätig** ADJ working; **Werkzeug** NT tool; **Werkzeugkasten** M toolbox; **Werkzeugmaschine** F machine tool; **Werkzeugschrank** M tool chest
Wermut ['ve:rmu:t] (**-(e)s, -s**) M wormwood; (*Wein*) vermouth
Wermutstropfen M (*fig*) drop of bitterness
wert [ve:rt] ADJ worth; (*geschätzt*) dear; (*würdig*) worthy; **das ist nichts/viel ~** it's not worth anything/it's worth a lot; **das ist es/er mir ~** it's/he's worth that to me; **ein Auto ist viel ~** (*nützlich*) a car is very useful
Wert [ve:rt] (**-(e)s, -e**) M worth; (*Fin*) value; **~ legen auf** *+akk* to attach importance to; **es hat doch keinen ~** it's useless; **im Werte von** to the value of
Wertangabe F declaration of value
wertbeständig ADJ stable in value
werten VT to rate; (*beurteilen*) to judge; (*Sport: als gültig werten*) to allow; **~ als** to rate as; (*beurteilen*) to judge to be
Wert- zW: **Wertgegenstand** M article of value; **wertlos** ADJ worthless; **Wertlosigkeit** F worthlessness; **Wertmaßstab** M standard; **Wertpapier** NT security; **faule Wertpapiere** toxic asset(s); **Wertsteigerung** F appreciation; **Wertstoff** M recyclable waste
Wertung F (*Sport*) score
Wert- zW: **wertvoll** ADJ valuable; **Wertvorstellung** F moral concept; **Wertzuwachs** M appreciation

Wesen ['ve:zən] (**-s, -**) NT (*Geschöpf*) being; (*Natur, Character*) nature
wesentlich ADJ significant; (*beträchtlich*) considerable; **im Wesentlichen** essentially; (*im Großen*) in the main
weshalb [vɛs'halp] ADV why
Wespe ['vɛspə] (-, **-n**) F wasp
wessen ['vɛsən] GEN *von* **wer** ▸ PRON whose
Wessi ['vɛsɪ] (**-s, -s**) (*umg*) M West German; *see note*

> A **Wessi** is a colloquial and often derogatory word used to describe a German from the former West Germany. The expression "Besserwessi" is used by East Germans to describe a West German who is considered to be a know-all.

West- zW: **westdeutsch** ADJ West German; **Westdeutsche(r)** F(M) West German; **Westdeutschland** NT (*Pol: früher*) West Germany; (*Geog*) Western Germany
Weste ['vɛstə] (-, **-n**) F waistcoat, vest (*US*); **eine reine ~ haben** (*fig*) to have a clean slate
Westen (**-s**) M west
Westentasche F: **etw wie seine ~ kennen** (*umg*) to know sth like the back of one's hand
Westerwald ['vɛstərvalt] (**-s**) M Westerwald (Mountains *pl*)
Westeuropa NT Western Europe
westeuropäisch ['vɛst|ɔʏro'pɛ:ɪʃ] ADJ West(ern) European; **westeuropäische Zeit** Greenwich Mean Time
Westfale [vɛst'fa:lə] (**-n, -n**) M Westphalian
Westfalen (**-s**) NT Westphalia
Westfälin [vɛst'fɛ:lɪn] F Westphalian
westfälisch ADJ Westphalian
Westindien ['vɛst|ɪndiən] (**-s**) NT West Indies *pl*
westindisch ADJ West Indian; **die Westindischen Inseln** the West Indies
west- zW: **westlich** ADJ western ▸ ADV to the west; **Westmächte** PL (*Pol: früher*): **die Westmächte** the Western powers *pl*; **westwärts** ADV westwards
weswegen [vɛs've:gən] ADV why
wett [vɛt] ADJ even; **~ sein** to be quits
Wettbewerb M competition
Wettbewerbsbeschränkung F restraint of trade
wettbewerbsfähig ADJ competitive
Wettbüro NT betting office
Wette (-, **-n**) F bet, wager; **eine ~ abschließen** to make a bet; **um die ~ laufen** to run a race (with each other)
Wetteifer M rivalry
wetteifern VI UNTR: **mit jdm um etw ~** to compete with sb for sth
wetten ['vɛtən] VT, VI to bet; **ich wette mit dir um 50 Euro** I'll bet you 50 euros; **so haben wir nicht gewettet!** that's not part of the bargain!
Wetter ['vɛtər] (**-s, -**) NT weather; (*Min*) air; **Wetteramt** NT meteorological office; **Wetteraussichten** PL weather outlook *sing*; **Wetterbericht** M weather report; **Wetterdienst** M meteorological service;

wetterfest ADJ weatherproof; **wetterfühlig** ADJ sensitive to changes in the weather; **Wetterkarte** F weather chart; **Wetterlage** F (weather) situation
wettern ['vɛtərn] VI to curse and swear
Wetter- ZW: **Wetterumschlag** M sudden change in the weather; **Wettervorhersage** F weather forecast; **Wetterwarte** F weather station; **wetterwendisch** ADJ capricious
Wett- ZW: **Wettkampf** M contest; **Wettlauf** M race; **ein Wettlauf mit der Zeit** a race against time
wettmachen VT to make good
Wett- ZW: **Wettrennen** NT race; **Wettrüsten** NT arms race; **Wettspiel** NT match; **Wettstreit** M contest
wetzen ['vɛtsən] VT to sharpen ▸ VI (*umg*) to scoot
WEU F ABK (= *Westeuropäische Union*) WEU
WEZ ABK (= *westeuropäische Zeit*) GMT
WG ABK = **Wohngemeinschaft**
Whirlpool® ['vœrlpu:l] (**-s, -s**) M jacuzzi®
Whisky ['vɪski] (**-s, -s**) M whisky (BRIT), whiskey (US, IRELAND)
WHO (**-**) F ABK (= *World Health Organization*) WHO
wich *etc* [vɪç] VB *siehe* **weichen**
wichsen ['vɪksən] VT (*Schuhe*) to polish ▸ VI (*umg!: onanieren*) to jerk *od* toss off (*umg!*)
Wichser (*umg!*) M wanker (*umg!*)
Wicht [vɪçt] (**-(e)s, -e**) M titch; (*pej*) worthless creature
wichtig ADJ important; **sich selbst/etw (zu) ~ nehmen** to take o.s./sth (too) seriously; **Wichtigkeit** F importance; **Wichtigtuer(in)** (*pej*) M(F) pompous ass (*umg*)
Wicke ['vɪkə] (**-, -n**) F (*Bot*) vetch; (*Gartenwicke*) sweet pea
Wickelkleid NT wrap-around dress
wickeln ['vɪkəln] VT to wind; (*Haare*) to set; (*Kind*) to change; **da bist du schief gewickelt!** (*fig: umg*) you're very much mistaken; **jdn/etw in etw** *akk* **~** to wrap sb/sth in sth
Wickeltisch M baby's changing table
Widder ['vɪdər] (**-s, -**) M ram; (*Astrol*) Aries
wider ['vi:dər] PRÄP +*akk* against
widerfahren *unreg* VI UNTR: **jdm ~** to happen to sb
Widerhaken ['vi:dərha:kən] M barb
Widerhall ['vi:dərhal] M echo; **keinen ~ (bei jdm) finden** (*Interesse*) to meet with no response (from sb)
widerlegen VT UNTR to refute
widerlich ['vi:dərlɪç] ADJ disgusting, repulsive; **Widerlichkeit** F repulsiveness
widerrechtlich ADJ unlawful
Widerrede F contradiction; **keine ~!** don't argue!
Widerruf ['vi:dərru:f] M retraction; (*von Befehl*) countermanding; **bis auf ~** until revoked
widerrufen *unreg* VT UNTR to retract; (*Anordnung*) to revoke; (*Befehl*) to countermand
Widersacher(in) ['vi:dərzaxər(ɪn)] (**-s, -**) M(F) adversary
widersetzen VR UNTR: **sich jdm ~** to oppose sb; (*der Polizei*) to resist sb; **sich einer Sache ~** to oppose sth; (*einem Befehl*) to refuse to comply with sth
widerspenstig ['vi:dərʃpɛnstɪç] ADJ wilful (BRIT), willful (US); **Widerspenstigkeit** F wilfulness (BRIT), willfulness (US)
widerspiegeln ['vi:dərʃpi:gəln] VT to reflect
widersprechen *unreg* VI UNTR: **jdm ~** to contradict sb
widersprechend ADJ contradictory
Widerspruch ['vi:dərʃprux] M contradiction; **ein ~ in sich** a contradiction in terms
widersprüchlich ['vi:dərʃprʏçlɪç] ADJ contradictory, inconsistent
widerspruchslos ADV without arguing
Widerstand ['vi:dərʃtant] M resistance; **der Weg des geringsten Widerstandes** the line of least resistance; **jdm/etw ~ leisten** to resist sb/sth
Widerstands- ZW: **Widerstandsbewegung** F resistance (movement); **widerstandsfähig** ADJ resistant, tough; **widerstandslos** ADJ unresisting
widerstehen *unreg* VI UNTR: **jdm/etw ~** to withstand sb/sth
widerstreben VI UNTR: **es widerstrebt mir, so etwas zu tun** I am reluctant to do anything like that
widerstrebend ADJ reluctant; (*gegensätzlich*) conflicting
Wider- ZW: **Widerstreit** M conflict; **widerwärtig** ADJ nasty, horrid; **Widerwille** M: **Widerwille (gegen)** aversion (to); (*Abneigung*) distaste (for); (*Widerstreben*) reluctance; **widerwillig** ADJ unwilling, reluctant; **Widerworte** PL answering back *sing*
Widget ['vɪdʒɪt] NT (*Comput*) widget
widmen ['vɪtmən] VT to dedicate ▸ VR to devote o.s.
Widmung F dedication
widrig ['vi:drɪç] ADJ (*Umstände*) adverse; (*Mensch*) repulsive

SCHLÜSSELWORT

wie [vi:] ADV how; **wie groß/schnell?** how big/fast?; **wie viel** how much; **wie viele Menschen** how many people; **wie wärs?** how about it?; **wie wärs mit einem Whisky?** (*umg*) how about a whisky?; **wie nennt man das?** what is that called?; **wie ist er?** what's he like?; **wie gut du das kannst!** you're very good at it; **wie bitte?** pardon? (BRIT), pardon me? (US); (*entrüstet*) I beg your pardon!; **und wie!** and how!
▸ KONJ **1** (*bei Vergleichen*): **so schön wie ...** as beautiful as ...; **wie ich schon sagte** as I said; **wie noch nie** as never before; **wie du** like you; **singen wie ein ...** to sing like a ...; **wie (zum Beispiel)** such as (for example)
2 (*zeitlich*): **wie er das hörte, ging er** when he heard that he left; **er hörte, wie der Regen fiel** he heard the rain falling

wieder ['vi:dər] ADV again; **~ da sein** to be back (again); **gehst du schon ~?** are you off again?; **~ ein(e) ...** another ...; **das ist auch ~ wahr** that's true enough; **da sieht man mal ~ ...** it just shows ...
wieder- zW: **Wiederaufbau** [-'laufbau] M rebuilding; **wiederaufbereiten** VT to recycle; (*Atommüll*) to reprocess; **Wiederaufbereitungsanlage** F reprocessing plant; **Wiederaufnahme** [-'laufna:mə] F resumption; **wiederaufnehmen** *unreg* VT to resume; (*Gedanken, Hobby*) to take up again; (*Thema*) to revert to; (*Jur: Verfahren*) to reopen; **wiederaufrollen** VT (*Fall, Prozess*) to reopen; **wiederbekommen** *unreg* VT to get back; **wiederbeleben** *unreg* VT to revive; **wiederbeschreibbar** ADJ (*CD, DVD*) rewritable; **wiederbringen** *unreg* VT to bring back; **wiedererkennen** *unreg* VT to recognize; **Wiedererstattung** F reimbursement; **wiederfinden** *unreg* VT (*fig: Selbstachtung etc*) to regain
Wiedergabe F (*von Rede, Ereignis*) account; (*Wiederholung*) repetition; (*Darbietung*) performance; (*Reproduktion*) reproduction; **Wiedergabegerät** NT playback unit; **wiedergeben** *unreg* VT (*zurückgeben*) to return; (*Erzählung etc*) to repeat; (*Gefühle etc*) to convey
wieder- zW: **Wiedergeburt** F rebirth; **wiedergutmachen** VT to make up for; (*Fehler*) to put right; **Wiedergutmachung** F reparation; **wiederherstellen** VT (*Gesundheit, Gebäude, Ruhe*) to restore
wiederholen VT UNTR to repeat
wiederholt ADJ: **zum wiederholten Male** once again
Wiederholung F repetition
Wiederholungstäter(in) M(F) (*Jur*) second-time offender; (*mehrmalig*) persistent offender
wieder- zW: **Wiederhören** NT: **auf Wiederhören** (*Tel*) goodbye; **wiederkäuen** VI to ruminate ▶ VT to ruminate; (*fig: umg*) to go over again and again; **Wiederkehr** (-) F return; (*von Vorfall*) repetition, recurrence; **wiederkehrend** ADJ recurrent; **Wiederkunft** (-, **Wiederkünfte**) F return; **wiedersehen** *unreg* VT to see again; **auf Wiedersehen** goodbye; **wiederum** ADV again; (*seinerseits etc*) in turn; (*andererseits*) on the other hand; **wiedervereinigen** VT to reunite; **Wiedervereinigung** F reunification; **Wiederverkäufer** M distributor; **Wiederwahl** F re-election
Wiege ['vi:ge] (-, **-n**) F cradle
wiegen[1] VT (*schaukeln*) to rock; (*Kopf*) to shake
wiegen[2] *unreg* VT, VI to weigh; **schwer ~** (*fig*) to carry a lot of weight; (*Irrtum*) to be serious
wiehern ['vi:ərn] VI to neigh, to whinny
Wien [vi:n] (**-s**) NT Vienna
Wiener(in) (**-s, -**) M(F) Viennese ▶ ADJ *attrib* Viennese; **~ Schnitzel** Wiener schnitzel
wies *etc* [vi:s] VB *siehe* **weisen**
Wiese ['vi:zə] (-, **-n**) F meadow
Wiesel ['vi:zəl] (**-s, -**) NT weasel; **schnell** *od* **flink wie ein ~** quick as a flash
wieso [vi:'zo:] ADV why
wievielmal [vi:'fi:lma:l] ADV how often
wievielte(r, s) ADJ: **zum wievielten Mal?** how many times?; **den Wievielten haben wir?** what's the date?; **an wievielter Stelle?** in what place?; **der ~ Besucher war er?** how many visitors were there before him?
wieweit [vi:'vaɪt] ADV to what extent
Wi-Fi ['waɪfi, 'waɪfaɪ] NT Wi-Fi
Wiki ['vi:kɪ] NT (*Internet*) wiki
Wikinger ['vi:kɪŋər] (**-s, -**) M Viking
wild [vɪlt] ADJ wild; **wilder Streik** unofficial strike; **in wilder Ehe leben** (*veraltet, hum*) to live in sin; **~ entschlossen** (*umg*) dead set
Wild (**-(e)s**) NT game
Wild- zW: **Wildbahn** F: **in freier Wildbahn** in the wild; **Wildbret** NT game; (*von Rotwild*) venison; **Wilddieb** M poacher
Wilde(r) ['vɪldə(r)] F(M) savage
wildern ['vɪldərn] VI to poach
wild- zW: **Wildfang** M little rascal; **wildfremd** ['vɪlt'frɛmt] (*umg*) ADJ: **ein wildfremder Mensch** a complete *od* total stranger; **Wildheit** F wildness; **Wildleder** NT suede
Wildnis (-, **-se**) F wilderness
Wild- zW: **Wildpark** M game park; **Wildschwein** NT (wild) boar; **Wildwechsel** M: **„Wildwechsel"** "wild animals"; **Wildwestroman** M western
will [vɪl] VB *siehe* **wollen**
Wille ['vɪlə] (**-ns, -n**) M will; **jdm seinen Willen lassen** to let sb have his own way; **seinen eigenen Willen haben** to be self-willed
willen PRÄP +*gen*: **um ... ~** for the sake of ...
willenlos ADJ weak-willed
willens ADJ (*geh*): **~ sein** to be willing
willensstark ADJ strong-willed
willentlich ['vɪləntlɪç] ADJ wilful (BRIT), willful (US), deliberate
willig ADJ willing
willkommen [vɪl'kɔmən] ADJ welcome; **jdn ~ heißen** to welcome sb; **herzlich ~ (in** +*dat*) welcome (to); **Willkommen** (**-s, -**) NT welcome
willkürlich ADJ arbitrary; (*Bewegung*) voluntary
willst [vɪlst] VB *siehe* **wollen**
Wilna ['vɪlna] (**-s**) NT Vilnius
wimmeln ['vɪməln] VI: **~ (von)** to swarm (with)
wimmern ['vɪmərn] VI to whimper
Wimper ['vɪmpər] (-, **-n**) F eyelash; **ohne mit der ~ zu zucken** (*fig*) without batting an eyelid
Wimperntusche F mascara
Wind [vɪnt] (**-(e)s, -e**) M wind; **den Mantel** *od* **das Fähnchen nach dem ~ hängen** to trim one's sails to the wind; **etw in den ~ schlagen** to turn a deaf ear to sth
Windbeutel M cream puff; (*fig*) windbag
Winde ['vɪndə] (-, **-n**) F (*Tech*) winch, windlass; (*Bot*) bindweed
Windel ['vɪndəl] (-, **-n**) F nappy (BRIT), diaper (US)

windelweich ADJ: **jdn ~ schlagen** (*umg*) to beat the living daylights out of sb
winden[1] ['vɪndən] VI UNPERS to be windy
winden[2] *unreg* VT to wind; (*Kranz*) to weave; (*entwinden*) to twist ▸ VR to wind; (*Person*) to writhe; (*fig: ausweichen*) to try to wriggle out
Windenergie F wind power
Windeseile F: **sich in** *od* **mit ~ verbreiten** to spread like wildfire
Windhose F whirlwind
Windhund M greyhound; (*Mensch*) fly-by-night
windig ['vɪndɪç] ADJ windy; (*fig*) dubious
Wind- ZW: **Windjacke** F windcheater, windbreaker (*US*); **Windkanal** M (*Tech*) wind tunnel; **Windkraft** F wind power; **Windkraftanlage** F wind power station; **Windmühle** F windmill; **gegen Windmühlen (an)kämpfen** (*fig*) to tilt at windmills; **Windpark** M wind farm
Windpocken PL chickenpox *sing*
Wind- ZW: **Windrose** F (*Naut*) compass card; (*Met*) wind rose; **Windschatten** M lee; (*von Fahrzeugen*) slipstream; **Windschutzscheibe** F (*Aut*) windscreen (BRIT), windshield (*US*); **Windstärke** F wind force; **windstill** ADJ (*Tag*) windless; **es ist windstill** there's no wind; **Windstille** F calm; **Windstoß** M gust of wind; **Windsurfen** NT windsurfing
Windung F (*von Weg, Fluss etc*) meander; (*von Schlange, Spule*) coil; (*von Schraube*) thread
Wink [vɪŋk] **(-(e)s, -e)** M (*mit Kopf*) nod; (*mit Hand*) wave; (*Tipp, Hinweis*) hint; **ein ~ mit dem Zaunpfahl** a broad hint
Winkel ['vɪŋkəl] **(-s, -)** M (*Math*) angle; (*Gerät*) set square; (*in Raum*) corner; **Winkeladvokat** (*pej*) M incompetent lawyer; **Winkelmesser** M protractor; **Winkelzug** M: **mach keine Winkelzüge** stop evading the issue
winken ['vɪŋkən] VT, VI to wave; **dem Sieger winkt eine Reise nach Italien** the (lucky) winner will receive a trip to Italy
winseln ['vɪnzəln] VI to whine
Winter ['vɪntər] **(-s, -)** M winter; **Wintergarten** M conservatory; **winterlich** ADJ wintry; **Winterreifen** M winter tyre (BRIT) *od* tire (*US*); **Winterschlaf** M (*Zool*) hibernation; **Winterschlussverkauf** M winter sale; **Wintersemester** NT (*Univ*) winter semester (*bes US*), ≈ autumn term (BRIT); **Winterspiele** PL: **(Olympische) Winterspiele** Winter Olympics *pl*; **Wintersport** M winter sports *pl*
Winzer(in) ['vɪntsər(ɪn)] **(-s, -)** M(F) wine-grower
winzig ['vɪntsɪç] ADJ tiny
Wipfel ['vɪpfəl] **(-s, -)** M treetop
Wippe ['vɪpə] **(-, -n)** F seesaw
wir [vi:r] PRON we; **~ alle** all of us, we all; **~ nicht** not us
Wirbel ['vɪrbəl] **(-s, -)** M whirl, swirl; (*Trubel*) hurly-burly; (*Aufsehen*) fuss; (*Anat*) vertebra; **~ um jdn/etw machen** to make a fuss about sb/sth
wirbellos ADJ (*Zool*) invertebrate
wirbeln VI to whirl, to swirl
Wirbel- ZW: **Wirbelsäule** F spine; **Wirbeltier** NT vertebrate; **Wirbelwind** M whirlwind
wirbst VB *siehe* **werben**
wirbt [vɪrpt] VB *siehe* **werben**
wird [vɪrt] VB *siehe* **werden**
wirfst VB *siehe* **werfen**
wirft [vɪrft] VB *siehe* **werfen**
wirken ['vɪrkən] VI to have an effect; (*erfolgreich sein*) to work; (*scheinen*) to seem ▸ VT (*Wunder*) to work; **etw auf sich** *akk* **~ lassen** to take sth in
wirklich ['vɪrklɪç] ADJ real; **Wirklichkeit** F reality; **wirklichkeitsgetreu** ADJ realistic
wirksam ['vɪrkza:m] ADJ effective; **Wirksamkeit** F effectiveness
Wirkstoff M active substance
Wirkung ['vɪrkʊŋ] F effect
Wirkungs- ZW: **Wirkungsbereich** M field (of activity *od* interest *etc*); (*Domäne*) domain; **wirkungslos** ADJ ineffective; **wirkungslos bleiben** to have no effect; **wirkungsvoll** ADJ effective
wirr [vɪr] ADJ confused; (*unrealistisch*) wild; (*Haare etc*) tangled
Wirren PL disturbances *pl*
Wirrwarr ['vɪrvar] **(-s)** M disorder, chaos; (*von Stimmen*) hubbub; (*von Fäden, Haaren etc*) tangle
Wirsing ['vɪrzɪŋ], **Wirsingkohl** ['vɪrzɪŋko:l] **(-s)** M savoy cabbage
wirst [vɪrst] VB *siehe* **werden**
Wirt [vɪrt] **(-(e)s, -e)** M landlord
Wirtin F landlady
Wirtschaft ['vɪrtʃaft] F (*Gaststätte*) pub; (*Haushalt*) housekeeping; (*eines Landes*) economy; (*Geschäftsleben*) industry and commerce; (*umg: Durcheinander*) mess; **wirtschaften** VI (*sparsam sein*): **gut wirtschaften können** to be economical; **Wirtschafter** M (*Verwalter*) manager; **Wirtschafterin** F (*im Haushalt, Heim etc*) housekeeper; **wirtschaftlich** ADJ economical; (*Pol*) economic; **Wirtschaftlichkeit** F economy; (*von Betrieb*) viability
Wirtschafts- ZW: **Wirtschaftsgeld** NT housekeeping (money); **Wirtschaftsgeografie** F economic geography; **Wirtschaftshilfe** F economic aid; **Wirtschaftskrise** F economic crisis; **Wirtschaftsminister** M minister of economic affairs; **Wirtschaftsordnung** F economic system; **Wirtschaftspolitik** F economic policy; **Wirtschaftsprüfer** M chartered accountant (BRIT), certified public accountant (*US*); **Wirtschaftsspionage** F industrial espionage; **Wirtschaftswachstum** NT economic growth; **Wirtschaftswissenschaft** F economics *sing*; **Wirtschaftswunder** NT economic miracle; **Wirtschaftszweig** M branch of industry
Wirtshaus NT inn
Wisch [vɪʃ] **(-(e)s, -e)** M scrap of paper
wischen VT to wipe
Wischer **(-s, -)** M (*Aut*) wiper
Wischiwaschi [vɪʃi:'vaʃi:] **(-s)** (*pej, umg*) NT drivel

W

Wisent ['vi:zɛnt] (**-s, -e**) M bison
WiSo ['vɪzo] ABK (= *Wirtschafts- und Sozialwissenschaften*) economics and social sciences
wispern ['vɪspərn] VT, VI to whisper
wiss. ABK = **wissenschaftlich**
Wiss. ABK = **Wissenschaft**
Wissbegier ['vɪsbəgi:r], **Wissbegierde** ['vɪsbəgi:rdə] F thirst for knowledge
wissbegierig ADJ eager for knowledge
wissen ['vɪsən] *unreg* VT, VI to know; **woher weißt du das?** how do you know?; **von jdm/etw nichts ~ wollen** not to be interested in sb/sth; **sie hält sich für wer weiß wie klug** (*umg*) she doesn't half think she's clever; **gewusst wie/wo!** *etc* sheer brilliance!; **ich weiß seine Adresse nicht mehr** (*sich erinnern*) I can't remember his address; **Wissen (-s)** NT knowledge; **etw gegen (sein) besseres Wissen tun** to do sth against one's better judgement; **nach bestem Wissen und Gewissen** to the best of one's knowledge and belief
Wissenschaft ['vɪsənʃaft] F science
Wissenschaftler(in) (**-s, -**) M(F) scientist; (*Geisteswissenschaftler*) academic
wissenschaftlich ADJ scientific; **Wissenschaftlicher Assistent** assistant lecturer
wissenswert ADJ worth knowing
wissentlich ADJ knowing
wittern ['vɪtərn] VT to scent; (*fig*) to suspect
Witterung F weather; (*Geruch*) scent
Witwe ['vɪtvə] (**-, -n**) F widow
Witwer (**-s, -**) M widower
Witz [vɪts] (**-es, -e**) M joke; **mach keine Witze!** you're kidding!; **der ~ an der Sache ist, dass ...** the great thing about it is that ...; **Witzbold** (**-(e)s, -e**) M joker
witzeln VI to joke
witzig ADJ funny
witzlos (*umg*) ADJ (*unsinnig*) pointless, futile
WM (**-**) F ABK = **Weltmeisterschaft**
wo [vo:] ADV where; (*umg: irgendwo*) somewhere ▸ KONJ (*wenn*) if; **im Augenblick, wo ...** the moment (that) ...; **die Zeit, wo ...** the time when ...
woanders [vo:'landərs] ADV elsewhere
wob *etc* [vo:p] VB *siehe* **weben**
wobei [vo:'baɪ] ADV (*rel*) ... in/by/with which; (*interrog*) how; **~ mir gerade einfällt ...** which reminds me ...
Woche ['vɔxə] (**-, -n**) F week; **einmal die ~** once a week
Wochen- ZW: **Wochenbett** NT: **im ~ sterben** to die in childbirth; **Wochenende** NT weekend; **Wochenendhaus** NT weekend house; **Wochenkarte** F weekly ticket; **wochenlang** ADJ lasting weeks ▸ ADV for weeks; **Wochenmarkt** M weekly market; **Wochenschau** F newsreel; **Wochentag** M weekday
wöchentlich ['vœçəntlɪç] ADJ, ADV weekly
Wochenzeitung F weekly (paper)
Wöchnerin ['vœçnərɪn] F *woman who has recently given birth*
Wodka ['vɔtka] (**-s, -s**) M vodka
wodurch [vo'dʊrç] ADV (*rel*) through which; (*interrog*) what ... through
wofür [vo'fy:r] ADV (*rel*) for which; (*interrog*) what ... for
wog *etc* [vo:k] VB *siehe* **wiegen²**
Woge ['vo:gə] (**-, -n**) F wave
wogegen [vo'ge:gən] ADV (*rel*) against which; (*interrog*) what ... against
wogen VI to heave, to surge
woher [vo'he:r] ADV where ... from; **~ kommt es eigentlich, dass ...?** how is it that ...?
wohin [vo'hɪn] ADV where ... to; **~ man auch schaut** wherever you look
wohingegen KONJ whereas, while

SCHLÜSSELWORT

wohl [vo:l] ADV **1** well; (*behaglich*) at ease, comfortable; **sich wohl fühlen** *siehe* **wohlfühlen**; **wohl gemeint** = **wohlgemeint**; **bei dem Gedanken ist mir nicht wohl** I'm not very happy at the thought; **wohl oder übel** whether one likes it or not; **er weiß das sehr wohl** he knows that perfectly well
2 (*wahrscheinlich*) probably; (*vermutlich*) I suppose; (*gewiss*) certainly; (*vielleicht*) perhaps; **sie ist wohl zu Hause** she's probably at home; **sie wird wohl das Haus verkaufen** I suppose *od* presumably she's going to sell the house; **das ist doch wohl nicht dein Ernst!** surely you're not serious!; **das mag wohl sein** that may well be; **ob das wohl stimmt?** I wonder if that's true; *siehe auch* **wohltun**

Wohl (**-(e)s**) NT welfare; **zum ~!** cheers!
wohl- ZW: **wohlauf** [vo:l'laʊf] ADJ well, in good health; **Wohlbefinden** NT well-being; **Wohlbehagen** NT comfort; **wohlbehalten** ADJ safe and sound; **Wohlergehen** NT welfare; **Wohlfahrt** F welfare; **Wohlfahrtsstaat** M welfare state; **wohlfühlen** VR (*zufrieden*) to feel happy; (*gesundheitlich*) to feel well; **Wohlgefallen** NT: **sich in Wohlgefallen auflösen** (*hum: Gegenstände, Probleme*) to vanish into thin air; (*zerfallen*) to fall apart; **wohlgemeint** ADJ well-intentioned; **wohlgemerkt** ADV mark you; **wohlhabend** ADJ wealthy
wohlig ADJ contented; (*gemütlich*) comfortable
wohl- ZW: **Wohlklang** M melodious sound; **wohlmeinend** ADJ well-meaning; **wohlschmeckend** ADJ delicious; **Wohlstand** M prosperity; **Wohlstandsgesellschaft** F affluent society; **Wohltat** F (*Gefallen*) favour (BRIT), favor (US); (*gute Tat*) good deed; (*Erleichterung*) relief; **Wohltäter** M benefactor; **wohltätig** ADJ charitable; **Wohltätigkeit** F charity; **wohltuend** ADJ pleasant; **wohltun** *unreg* VI: **jdm wohltun** to do sb good; **wohlverdient** ADJ

(*Ruhe*) well-earned; (*Strafe*) well-deserved; **wohlweislich** ADV prudently; **Wohlwollen** (**-s**) NT good will; **wohlwollend** ADJ benevolent
Wohnanlage ['vo:n|anla:gə] F housing complex; (BRIT) housing estate; **bewachte ~** gated community
Wohnblock ['vo:nblɔk] (**-s, -s**) M block of flats (BRIT), apartment house (US)
wohnen ['vo:nən] VI to live
wohn- ZW: **Wohnfläche** F living space; **Wohngeld** NT housing benefit; **Wohngemeinschaft** F people sharing a flat (BRIT) *od* apartment (US); (*von Hippies*) commune; **wohnhaft** ADJ resident; **Wohnheim** NT (*für Studenten*) hall (of residence), dormitory (US); (*für Senioren*) home; (*bes für Arbeiter*) hostel; **Wohnkomfort** M: **mit sämtlichem Wohnkomfort** with all mod cons (BRIT); **wohnlich** ADJ comfortable; **Wohnmobil** NT motor caravan (BRIT), motor home (US); **Wohnort** M domicile; **Wohnsilo** NT concrete block of flats (BRIT) *od* apartment block (US); **Wohnsitz** M place of residence; **ohne festen Wohnsitz** of no fixed abode
Wohnung F house; (*Etagenwohnung*) flat (BRIT), apartment (US)
Wohnungs- ZW: **Wohnungsamt** NT housing office; **Wohnungsbau** M house-building; **Wohnungsmarkt** M housing market; **Wohnungsnot** F housing shortage
wohn- ZW: **Wohnviertel** NT residential area; **Wohnwagen** M caravan (BRIT), trailer (US); **Wohnzimmer** NT living room
wölben ['vœlbən] VT, VR to curve
Wölbung F curve
Wolf [vɔlf] (**-(e)s, Wölfe**) M wolf; (*Tech*) shredder; (*Fleischwolf*) mincer (BRIT), grinder (US)
Wölfin ['vœlfɪn] F she-wolf
Wolke ['vɔlkə] (**-, -n**) F cloud; **aus allen Wolken fallen** (*fig*) to be flabbergasted (*umg*)
Wolken- ZW: **Wolkenbruch** M cloudburst; **wolkenbruchartig** ADJ torrential; **Wolkenkratzer** M skyscraper; **Wolkenkuckucksheim** NT cloud-cuckoo-land (BRIT), cloudland (US); **wolkenlos** ADJ cloudless
wolkig ['vɔlkɪç] ADJ cloudy
Wolle ['vɔlə] (**-, -n**) F wool; **sich mit jdm in die ~ kriegen** (*fig: umg*) to start squabbling with sb

SCHLÜSSELWORT

wollen¹ ['vɔlən] (*pt* **wollte**, *pp* **gewollt** *od* (*als Hilfsverb*) **wollen**) VT, VI to want; **ich will nach Hause** I want to go home; **er will nicht** he doesn't want to; **sie wollte das nicht** she didn't want it; **wenn du willst** if you like; **ich will, dass du mir zuhörst** I want you to listen to me; **oh, das hab ich nicht gewollt** oh, I didn't mean to do that; **ich weiß nicht, was er will** (*verstehe ihn nicht*) I don't know what he's on about
▶ HILFSVERB: **er will ein Haus kaufen** he wants to buy a house; **ich wollte, ich wäre ...** I wish I were ...; **etw gerade tun wollen** to be just about to *od* going to do sth; **und so jemand** *od* **etwas will Lehrer sein!** (*umg*) and he calls himself a teacher!; **das will alles gut überlegt sein** that needs a lot of thought

wollen² ADJ woollen (BRIT), woolen (US)
Wollsachen PL wool(l)ens *pl*
wollüstig ['vɔlʏstɪç] ADJ lusty, sensual
wo- ZW: **womit** [vo'mɪt] ADV (*rel*) with which; (*interrog*) what ... with; **womit kann ich dienen?** what can I do for you?; **womöglich** [vo'mø:klɪç] ADV probably, I suppose; **wonach** [vo'na:x] ADV (*rel*) after/for which; (*interrog*) what ... after
Wonne ['vɔnə] (**-, -n**) F joy, bliss
woran [vo'ran] ADV (*rel*) on/at which; (*interrog*) what ... on/at; **~ denkst du?** what are you thinking of?; **~ liegt das?** what's the reason for it?
worauf [vo'raʊf] ADV (*rel*) on which; (*interrog*) what ... on; (*zeitlich*) whereupon; **~ wartest du?** what are you waiting for?; **~ du dich verlassen kannst** of that you can be sure
woraus [vo'raʊs] ADV (*rel*) from/out of which; (*interrog*) what ... from/out of; **~ ist das gemacht?** what is it made of?
worden ['vɔrdən] VB *siehe* **werden**
worin [vo'rɪn] ADV (*rel*) in which; (*interrog*) what ... in
Wort [vɔrt] (**-(e)s, Wörter** *od* **-e**) NT word; **jdn beim ~ nehmen** to take sb at his word; **ein ernstes ~ mit jdm reden** to have a serious talk with sb; **man kann sein eigenes ~ nicht (mehr) verstehen** you can't hear yourself speak; **jdm aufs ~ gehorchen** to obey sb's every word; **zu ~ kommen** to get a chance to speak; **mit anderen Worten** in other words; **jdm das ~ erteilen** to allow sb to speak; **Wortart** F (*Gram*) part of speech; **wortbrüchig** ADJ not true to one's word
Wörtchen NT: **da habe ich wohl ein ~ mitzureden** (*umg*) I think I have some say in that
Wörterbuch ['vœrtərbu:x] NT dictionary
Wort- ZW: **Wortfetzen** PL snatches *pl* of conversation; **Wortführer** M spokesman; **wortgetreu** ADJ true to one's word; (*Übersetzung*) literal; **wortgewaltig** ADJ eloquent; **wortkarg** ADJ taciturn; **Wortlaut** M wording; **im Wortlaut** verbatim
wörtlich ['vœrtlɪç] ADJ literal; **wortlos** ADJ mute
Wort- ZW: **Wortmeldung** F: **wenn es keine weiteren Wortmeldungen gibt, ...** if nobody else wishes to speak ...; **wortreich** ADJ wordy, verbose; **Wortschatz** M vocabulary; **Wortspiel** NT play on words, pun; **Wortwechsel** M dispute; **wortwörtlich** ADJ word-for-word
▶ ADV quite literally
worüber [vo'ry:bər] ADV (*rel*) over/about which; (*interrog*) what ... over/about; **~ redet sie?** what is she talking about?

W

worum [vo'rʊm] ADV (*rel*) about/round which; (*interrog*) what ... about/round; **~ handelt es sich?** what's it about?
worunter [vo'rʊntər] ADV (*rel*) under which; (*interrog*) what ... under; **~ leidet er?** what is he suffering from?
wo- ZW: **wovon** [vo'fɔn] ADV (*rel*) from which; (*interrog*) what ... from; **wovon redest du?** what are you talking about?; **wovor** [vo'fɔr] ADV (*rel*) in front of/before which; (*interrog*) in front of/before what; **wozu** [vo'tsu] ADV (*rel*) to/for which; (*interrog*) what ... for/to; (*warum*) why; **wozu soll das gut sein?** what's the point of that?
Wrack [vrak] (**-(e)s, -s**) NT wreck
wrang *etc* [vraŋ] VB *siehe* **wringen**
wringen ['vrɪŋən] *unreg* VT to wring
WS ABK = **Wintersemester**
WSV ABK = **Winterschlussverkauf**
Wucher ['vu:xər] (**-s**) M profiteering; **Wucherer** (**-s, -**) M, **Wucherin** F profiteer; **wucherisch** ADJ profiteering
wuchern VI (*Pflanzen*) to grow wild
Wucherpreis M exorbitant price
Wucherung F (*Med*) growth
wuchs *etc* VB *siehe* **wachsen²**
Wuchs [vu:ks] (**-es**) M (*Wachstum*) growth; (*Statur*) build
Wucht [vʊxt] (**-**) F force
wuchtig ADJ massive, solid
wühlen ['vy:lən] VI to scrabble; (*Tier*) to root; (*Maulwurf*) to burrow; (*umg: arbeiten*) to slave away ▸ VT to dig
Wühlmaus F vole
Wühltisch M (*in Kaufhaus*) bargain counter
Wulst [vʊlst] (**-es, Wülste**) M bulge; (*an Wunde*) swelling
wulstig ADJ bulging; (*Rand, Lippen*) thick
wund [vʊnt] ADJ sore; **sich** *dat* **die Füße ~ laufen** (*lit*) to get sore feet from walking; (*fig*) to walk one's legs off; **ein wunder Punkt** a sore point; **Wundbrand** M gangrene
Wunde ['vʊndə] (**-, -n**) F wound; **alte Wunden wieder aufreißen** (*fig*) to open up old wounds
Wunder (**-s, -**) NT miracle; **es ist kein ~** it's no wonder; **meine Eltern denken ~ was passiert ist** my parents think goodness knows what has happened; **wunderbar** ADJ wonderful, marvellous (BRIT), marvelous (US); **Wunderkerze** F sparkler; **Wunderkind** NT child prodigy; **wunderlich** ADJ odd, peculiar
wundern VT to surprise ▸ VR: **sich wundern über** +*akk* to be surprised at
Wunder- ZW: **wunderschön** ADJ beautiful; **Wundertüte** F lucky bag; **wundervoll** ADJ wonderful
Wundfieber (**-s**) NT traumatic fever
Wundstarrkrampf ['vʊntʃtarkrampf] M tetanus, lockjaw
Wunsch [vʊnʃ] (**-(e)s, Wünsche**) M wish; **haben Sie (sonst) noch einen ~?** (*beim Einkauf etc*) is there anything else you'd like?; **auf jds (besonderen/ausdrücklichen) ~ hin** at sb's (special/express) request; **Wunschdenken** NT wishful thinking
Wünschelrute ['vʏnʃəlru:tə] F divining rod
wünschen ['vʏnʃən] VT to wish ▸ VI: **zu ~/viel zu ~ übrig lassen** to leave something/a great deal to be desired; **sich** *dat* **etw ~** to want sth, to wish for sth; **was ~ Sie?** (*in Geschäft*) what can I do for you?; (*in Restaurant*) what would you like?
wünschenswert ADJ desirable
Wunsch- ZW: **Wunschkind** NT planned child; **Wunschkonzert** NT (*Rundf*) musical request programme (BRIT) *od* program (US); **wunschlos** ADJ: **wunschlos glücklich** perfectly happy; **Wunschtraum** M dream; (*unrealistisch*) pipe dream; **Wunschzettel** M list of things one would like
wurde *etc* ['vʊrdə] VB *siehe* **werden**
Würde ['vʏrdə] (**-, -n**) F dignity; (*Stellung*) honour (BRIT), honor (US); **unter aller ~ sein** to be beneath contempt
Würdenträger M dignitary
würdevoll ADJ dignified
würdig ['vʏrdɪç] ADJ worthy; (*würdevoll*) dignified
würdigen ['vʏrdɪgən] VT to appreciate; **etw zu ~ wissen** to appreciate sth; **jdn keines Blickes ~** not to so much as look at sb
Wurf [vʊrf] (**-(e)s, Würfe**) M throw; (*Junge*) litter
Würfel ['vʏrfəl] (**-s, -**) M dice; (*Math*) cube; **die ~ sind gefallen** the die is cast; **Würfelbecher** M (dice) cup
würfeln VI to throw (the dice); (*Würfel spielen*) to play dice ▸ VT (*Zahl*) to throw; (*Koch*) to dice
Würfelspiel NT game of dice
Würfelzucker M lump sugar
Wurf- ZW: **Wurfgeschoss** NT projectile; **Wurfsendung** F circular; **Wurfsendungen** PL (*Reklame*) junk mail
Würgegriff (**-(e)s**) M (*lit, fig*) stranglehold
würgen ['vʏrgən] VT, VI to choke; **mit Hängen und W~** by the skin of one's teeth
Wurm [vʊrm] (**-(e)s, Würmer**) M worm; **da steckt der ~ drin** (*fig: umg*) there's something wrong somewhere; (*verdächtig*) there's something fishy about it (*umg*)
wurmen (*umg*) VT to rile, to nettle
Wurmfortsatz M (*Med*) appendix
wurmig ADJ worm-eaten
wurmstichig ADJ worm-ridden
Wurst [vʊrst] (**-, Würste**) F sausage; **das ist mir ~** (*umg*) I don't care, I don't give a damn; **jetzt geht es um die ~** (*fig: umg*) the moment of truth has come
Würstchen ['vʏrstçən] NT frankfurter, hot dog sausage; **Würstchenbude** F, **Würstchenstand** M hot dog stall
Württemberg ['vʏrtəmbɛrk] NT Württemberg
Würze ['vʏrtsə] (**-, -n**) F seasoning
Wurzel ['vʊrtsəl] (**-, -n**) F root; **Wurzeln schlagen** (*lit*) to root; (*fig*) to put down roots; **die ~ aus 4 ist 2** (*Math*) the square root of 4 is 2
würzen VT to season; (*würzig machen*) to spice
würzig ADJ spicy

wusch *etc* [vu:ʃ] VB *siehe* **waschen**
wusste *etc* ['vʊstə] VB *siehe* **wissen**
Wust [vu:st] (**-(e)s**) (*umg*) M (*Durcheinander*) jumble; (*Menge*) pile
wüst [vy:st] ADJ untidy, messy; (*ausschweifend*) wild; (*öde*) waste; (*umg: heftig*) terrible; **jdn ~ beschimpfen** to use vile language to sb
Wüste (**-, -n**) F desert; **die ~ Gobi** the Gobi Desert; **jdn in die ~ schicken** (*fig*) to send sb packing
Wut [vu:t] (**-**) F rage, fury; **eine ~ (auf jdn/etw) haben** to be furious (with sb/sth); **Wutanfall** M fit of rage
wüten ['vy:tən] VI to rage
wütend ADJ furious, enraged
wutentbrannt ADJ furious, enraged
Wz ABK = **Warenzeichen**®

W

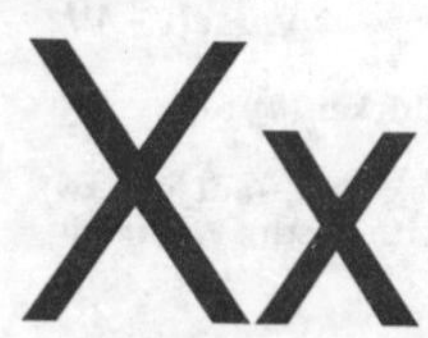

X, x [ɪks] NT X, x; **X wie Xanthippe** ≈ X for Xmas; **jdm ein X für ein U vormachen** to put one over on sb (*umg*)
X-Beine ['ɪksbaɪnə] PL knock-knees *pl*
x-beliebig [ɪksbə'li:bɪç] ADJ any (... whatever); **ein x-beliebiges Buch** any book (you like)
Xerografie [kserogra'fi:] F xerography
xerokopieren [kseroko'pi:rən] VT to xerox, to photocopy
x-fach ['ɪksfax] ADJ: **die x-fache Menge** (*Math*) n times the amount
x-mal ['ɪksma:l] ADV any number of times, umpteen times
XML ABK (*Comput*: = *extensible markup language*) XML
x-te ['ɪkstə] ADJ (*Math*: *umg*) nth; **zum x-ten Male** (*umg*) for the nth *od* umpteenth time
Xylofon, Xylophon [ksylo'fo:n] (**-s, -e**) NT xylophone

Y, y ['ʏpsilɔn] NT Y, y; **Y wie Ypsilon** ≈ Y for Yellow, ≈ Y for Yoke (*US*)
Yen [jɛn] **(-(s), -(s))** M yen
Yoga ['jo:ga] **(-(s))** M OD NT yoga
Ypsilon ['ʏpsilɔn] **(-(s), -s)** NT the letter Y

Zz

Z, z [tsɛt] NT Z, z; **Z wie Zacharias** ≈ Z for Zebra
Zack [tsak] M: **auf ~ sein** (*umg*) to be on the ball
Zacke ['tsakə] (**-, -n**) F point; (*Bergzacke*) jagged peak; (*Gabelzacke*) prong; (*Kammzacke*) tooth
zackig ['tsakɪç] ADJ jagged; (*umg*) smart; (*: Tempo*) brisk
zaghaft ['tsa:khaft] ADJ timid
Zaghaftigkeit F timidity
Zagreb ['za:grɛp] (**-s**) NT Zagreb
zäh [tsɛ:] ADJ tough; (*Mensch*) tenacious; (*Flüssigkeit*) thick; (*schleppend*) sluggish; **zähflüssig** ADJ viscous; (*Verkehr*) slow-moving
Zähigkeit F toughness; (*von Mensch*) tenacity
Zahl [tsa:l] (**-, -en**) F number
zahlbar ADJ payable
zahlen VT, VI to pay; **~ bitte!** the bill *od* check (*US*) please!
zählen ['tsɛ:lən] VT to count ▶ VI (*sich verlassen*): **~ auf** *+akk* to count on; **seine Tage sind gezählt** his days are numbered; **~ zu** to be numbered among
Zahlen- ZW: **Zahlenangabe** F figure; **Zahlenkombination** F combination of figures; **zahlenmäßig** ADJ numerical; **Zahlenschloss** NT combination lock
Zahler (**-s, -**) M payer
Zähler (**-s, -**) M (*Tech*) meter; (*Math*) numerator; **Zählerstand** M meter reading
Zahl- ZW: **Zahlgrenze** F fare stage; **Zahlkarte** F transfer form; **zahllos** ADJ countless; **Zahlmeister** M (*Naut*) purser; **zahlreich** ADJ numerous; **Zahltag** M payday
Zahlung F payment; **in ~ geben/nehmen** to give/take in part exchange
Zahlungs- ZW: **Zahlungsanweisung** F transfer order; **Zahlungsaufforderung** F request for payment; **zahlungsfähig** ADJ solvent; **Zahlungsmittel** NT means *sing* of payment; (*Münzen, Banknoten*) currency; **Zahlungsrückstände** PL arrears *pl*; **zahlungsunfähig** ADJ insolvent; **Zahlungsverzug** M default
Zahlwort NT numeral
zahm [tsa:m] ADJ tame
zähmen ['tsɛ:mən] VT to tame; (*fig*) to curb
Zahn [tsa:n] (**-(e)s, Zähne**) M tooth; **die dritten Zähne** (*umg*) false teeth *pl*; **einen ~ draufhaben** (*umg: Geschwindigkeit*) to be going like the clappers (*BRIT*) *od* like crazy (*US*); **jdm auf den ~ fühlen** (*fig*) to sound sb out; **einen ~ zulegen** (*fig*) to get a move on; **Zahnarzt** M, **Zahnärztin** F dentist; **Zahnbelag** M plaque; **Zahnbürste** F toothbrush; **Zahncreme** F toothpaste; **zahnen** VI to teethe; **Zahnersatz** M denture; **Zahnfäule** (-) F tooth decay, caries *sing*; **Zahnfleisch** NT gums *pl*; **auf dem Zahnfleisch gehen** (*fig: umg*) to be all in, to be at the end of one's tether; **zahnlos** ADJ toothless; **Zahnmedizin** F dentistry; **Zahnpasta** F, **Zahnpaste** F toothpaste; **Zahnrad** NT cog(wheel); **Zahnradbahn** F rack railway (*BRIT*) *od* railroad (*US*); **Zahnschmelz** M (tooth) enamel; **Zahnschmerzen** PL toothache *sing*; **Zahnseide** F dental floss; **Zahnspange** F brace; **Zahnstein** M tartar; **Zahnstocher** (**-s, -**) M toothpick; **Zahntechniker(in)** M(F) dental technician; **Zahnweh** NT toothache
Zaire [za'i:r] (**-s**) NT Zaire
Zange ['tsaŋə] (**-, -n**) F pliers *pl*; (*Zuckerzange etc*) tongs *pl*; (*Beißzange, Zool*) pincers *pl*; (*Med*) forceps *pl*; **jdn in die ~ nehmen** (*fig*) to put the screws on sb (*umg*)
Zangengeburt F forceps delivery
Zankapfel M bone of contention
zanken ['tsaŋkən] VI, VR to quarrel
zänkisch ['tsɛŋkɪʃ] ADJ quarrelsome
Zäpfchen ['tsɛpfçən] NT (*Anat*) uvula; (*Med*) suppository
zapfen VT to tap
Zapfen ['tsapfən] (**-s, -**) M plug; (*Bot*) cone; (*Eiszapfen*) icicle
Zapfenstreich M (*Mil*) tattoo
Zapfsäule F petrol (*BRIT*) *od* gas (*US*) pump
zappelig ['tsapəlɪç] ADJ wriggly; (*unruhig*) fidgety
zappeln ['tsapəln] VI to wriggle; (*unruhig*) to fidget; **jdn ~ lassen** (*fig: umg*) to keep sb in suspense
Zar [tsa:r] (**-en, -en**) M tzar, czar
zart [tsa:rt] ADJ (*weich, leise*) soft; (*Braten etc*) tender; (*empfindlich*) delicate; **zartbesaitet** ['tsa:rtbəzaɪtət] ADJ highly sensitive; **zartbitter** ADJ (*Schokolade*) plain (*BRIT*), bittersweet (*US*); **Zartgefühl** NT tact; **Zartheit** F softness; (*von Braten etc*) tenderness; (*Empfindlichkeit*) delicacy

zärtlich ['tsɛ:rtlɪç] ADJ tender, affectionate; **Zärtlichkeit** F tenderness; **Zärtlichkeiten** PL caresses *pl*
Zäsium ['tsɛ:zium] NT = **Cäsium**
Zäsur [tsɛ'zu:r] F caesura; (*fig*) break
Zauber ['tsaubər] (**-s, -**) M magic; (*Zauberbann*) spell; **fauler ~** (*umg*) humbug
Zauberei [tsaubə'raɪ] F magic
Zauberer (**-s, -**) M magician; (*Zauberkünstler*) conjurer
Zauber- ZW: **zauberhaft** ADJ magical, enchanting; **Zauberin** F magician; (*Zauberkünstlerin*) conjurer; **Zauberkünstler** M conjurer; **Zauberkunststück** NT conjuring trick; **Zaubermittel** NT magical cure; (*Trank*) magic potion
zaubern VI to conjure, to do magic
Zauberspruch M (magic) spell
Zauberstab M magic wand
zaudern ['tsaudərn] VI to hesitate
Zaum [tsaum] (**-(e)s, Zäume**) M bridle; **etw im ~ halten** to keep sth in check
Zaun [tsaun] (**-(e)s, Zäune**) M fence; **vom ~(e) brechen** (*fig*) to start; **Zaungast** M (*Person*) mere onlooker; **Zaunkönig** M wren
z. B. ABK (= *zum Beispiel*) e.g.
z. d. A. ABK (= *zu den Akten*) to be filed
ZDF NT (= *Zweites Deutsches Fernsehen*) *German television channel*

> The **ZDF** (Zweites Deutsches Fernsehen) is the second German television channel. It was founded in 1961 and is based in Mainz. It is financed by licence fees and advertising. About 40% of its transmissions are news and educational programmes.

Zebra ['tse:bra] (**-s, -s**) NT zebra; **Zebrastreifen** M pedestrian crossing (BRIT), crosswalk (US)
Zeche ['tsɛçə] (**-, -n**) F (*Rechnung*) bill, check (US); (*Bergbau*) mine
zechen VI to booze (*umg*)
Zechprellerei [tsɛçprɛlə'raɪ] F *skipping payment in restaurants etc*
Zecke ['tsɛkə] (**-, -n**) F tick
Zeder ['tse:dər] (**-, -n**) F cedar
Zeh [tse:] (**-s, -en**) M toe
Zehe ['tse:ə] (**-, -n**) F toe; (*Knoblauchzehe*) clove
Zehenspitze F: **auf Zehenspitzen** on tiptoe
zehn [tse:n] NUM ten
Zehnerpackung F packet of ten
Zehnfingersystem NT touch-typing method
Zehnkampf M (*Sport*) decathlon
zehnte(r, s) ADJ tenth
Zehntel (**-s, -**) NT tenth (part)
zehren ['tse:rən] VI: **an jdm/etw ~** (*an Mensch, Kraft*) to wear sb/sth out
Zeichen ['tsaɪçən] (**-s, -**) NT sign; (*Comput*) character; **jdm ein ~ geben** to give sb a signal; **unser/Ihr ~** (*Comm*) our/your reference; **Zeichenblock** M sketch pad; **Zeichencode** M (*Comput*) character code; **Zeichenerklärung** F key; (*auf Karten*) legend; **Zeichenfolge** F (*Comput*) string; **Zeichenkette** F (*Comput*) character string; **Zeichensatz** M (*Comput*) character set; **Zeichensetzung** F punctuation; **Zeichentrickfilm** M (animated) cartoon
zeichnen VT to draw; (*kennzeichnen*) to mark; (*unterzeichnen*) to sign ▸ VI to draw; (*unterzeichnen*) to sign
Zeichner(in) (**-s, -**) M(F) artist; **technischer ~** draughtsman (BRIT), draftsman (US)
Zeichnung F drawing; (*Markierung*) markings *pl*
zeichnungsberechtigt ADJ authorized to sign
Zeigefinger M index finger
zeigen ['tsaɪgən] VT to show ▸ VI to point ▸ VR to show o.s.; **~ auf** *+akk* to point to; **es wird sich ~** time will tell; **es zeigte sich, dass ...** it turned out that ...
Zeiger (**-s, -**) M pointer; (*Uhrzeiger*) hand
Zeile ['tsaɪlə] (**-, -n**) F line; (*Häuserzeile*) row
Zeilen- ZW: **Zeilenabstand** M line spacing; **Zeilenausrichtung** F justification; **Zeilendrucker** M line printer; **Zeilenumbruch** M (*Comput*) wraparound; **Zeilenvorschub** M (*Comput*) line feed
zeit [tsaɪt] PRÄP *+gen*: **~ meines Lebens** in my lifetime
Zeit (**-, -en**) F time; (*Gram*) tense; **sich** *dat* **~ lassen** to take one's time; **eine Stunde ~ haben** to have an hour (to spare); **sich** *dat* **für jdn/etw ~ nehmen** to devote time to sb/sth; **eine ~ lang** a while, a time; **von ~ zu ~** from time to time; **~ raubend** = **zeitraubend**; **in letzter ~** recently; **nach ~ bezahlt werden** to be paid by the hour; **zu der ~, als ...** (at the time) when ...; *siehe auch* **zurzeit**
Zeit- ZW: **Zeitalter** NT age; **Zeitansage** F (*Rundf*) time check; (*Tel*) speaking clock; **Zeitarbeit** F temporary work; **Zeitaufwand** M time (*needed for a task*); **Zeitbombe** F time bomb; **Zeitdruck** M: **unter Zeitdruck stehen** to be under pressure; **Zeitgeist** M spirit of the times; **zeitgemäß** ADJ in keeping with the times; **Zeitgenosse** M contemporary; **zeitgenössisch** ['tsaɪtgənœsɪʃ] ADJ contemporary
zeitig ADJ, ADV early
Zeit- ZW: **Zeitkarte** F season ticket; **zeitkritisch** ADJ (*Aufsatz*) commenting on contemporary issues; **zeitlebens** ADV all one's life; **zeitlich** ADJ temporal; (*Reihenfolge*) chronological ▸ ADV: **das kann sie zeitlich nicht einrichten** she can't find (the) time for that; **das Zeitliche segnen** (*euph*) to depart this life; **zeitlos** ADJ timeless; **Zeitlupe** F slow motion; **Zeitlupentempo** NT: **im Zeitlupentempo** at a snail's pace; **Zeitnot** F: **in Zeitnot geraten** to run short of time; **Zeitplan** M schedule; **Zeitpunkt** M moment, point in time; **Zeitraffer** (**-s**) M time-lapse photography; **zeitraubend** ADJ time-consuming; **Zeitraum** M period; **Zeitrechnung** F time, era; **nach/vor unserer Zeitrechnung** A.D./B.C.; **Zeitschrift** F magazine; (*wissenschaftlich*) periodical; **Zeittafel** F chronological table
Zeitung F newspaper
Zeitungs- ZW: **Zeitungsanzeige** F newspaper advertisement; **Zeitungsausschnitt** M press

cutting; **Zeitungshändler** M newsagent (BRIT), newsdealer (US); **Zeitungspapier** NT newsprint; **Zeitungsstand** M newsstand
Zeit- zW: **Zeitverschiebung** F time lag; **Zeitverschwendung** F waste of time; **Zeitvertreib** M pastime, diversion; **zum Zeitvertreib** to pass the time; **zeitweilig** ADJ temporary; **zeitweise** ADV for a time; **Zeitwort** NT verb; **Zeitzeichen** NT (*Rundf*) time signal; **Zeitzone** F time zone; **Zeitzünder** M time fuse
Zelle ['tsɛlə] (**-, -n**) F cell; (*Telefonzelle*) callbox (BRIT), booth
Zellkern M cell, nucleus
Zellophan [tsɛlo'fa:n] (**-s**) NT cellophane
Zellstoff M cellulose
Zelt [tsɛlt] (**-(e)s, -e**) NT tent; **seine Zelte aufschlagen/abbrechen** to settle down/pack one's bags; **Zeltbahn** F groundsheet; **zelten** VI to camp; **Zeltlager** NT camp; **Zeltplatz** M camp site
Zement [tse'mɛnt] (**-(e)s, -e**) M cement
zementieren [tsemɛn'ti:rən] VT to cement
Zementmaschine F cement mixer
Zenit [tse'ni:t] (**-(e)s**) M (*lit, fig*) zenith
zensieren [tsɛn'zi:rən] VT to censor; (*Sch*) to mark
Zensur [tsɛn'zu:r] F censorship; (*Sch*) mark
Zensus ['tsɛnzʊs] (**-, -**) M census
Zentimeter [tsɛnti'me:tər] M OD NT centimetre (BRIT), centimeter (US); **Zentimetermaß** NT (metric) tape measure
Zentner ['tsɛntnər] (**-s, -**) M hundredweight
zentral [tsɛn'tra:l] ADJ central
Zentrale (**-, -n**) F central office; (*Tel*) exchange
Zentraleinheit F (*Comput*) central processing unit
Zentralheizung F central heating
zentralisieren [tsɛntrali'zi:rən] VT to centralize
Zentralverriegelung F (*Aut*) central locking
Zentrifugalkraft [tsɛntrifu'ga:lkraft] F centrifugal force
Zentrifuge [tsɛntri'fu:gə] (**-, -n**) F centrifuge; (*für Wäsche*) spin-dryer
Zentrum ['tsɛntrʊm] (**-s, Zentren**) NT centre (BRIT), center (US)
Zepter ['tsɛptər] (**-s, -**) NT sceptre (BRIT), scepter (US)
zerbrechen *unreg* VT, VI to break
zerbrechlich ADJ fragile
zerbröckeln [tsɛr'brœkəln] VT, VI to crumble (to pieces)
zerdeppern [tsɛr'dɛpərn] VT to smash
zerdrücken VT to squash, to crush; (*Kartoffeln*) to mash
Zeremonie [tseremo'ni:] F ceremony
Zeremoniell [tseremoni'ɛl] (**-s, -e**) NT ceremonial
zerfahren ADJ scatterbrained, distracted
Zerfall M decay, disintegration; (*von Kultur, Gesundheit*) decline; **zerfallen** *unreg* VI to disintegrate, to decay; (*sich gliedern*): **zerfallen in** *+akk* to fall into
zerfetzen [tsɛr'fɛtsən] VT to tear to pieces
zerfleischen [tsɛr'flaɪʃən] VT to tear to pieces
zerfließen *unreg* VI to dissolve, to melt away
zerfressen *unreg* VT to eat away; (*Motten, Mäuse etc*) to eat
zergehen *unreg* VI to melt, to dissolve
zerkleinern [tsɛr'klaɪnərn] VT to reduce to small pieces
zerklüftet [tsɛr'klʏftət] ADJ: **tief zerklüftetes Gestein** deeply fissured rock
zerknirscht [tsɛr'knɪrʃt] ADJ overcome with remorse
zerknüllen [tsɛr'knʏlən] VT to crumple up
zerlaufen *unreg* VI to melt
zerlegbar [tsɛr'le:kba:r] ADJ able to be dismantled
zerlegen VT to take to pieces; (*Fleisch*) to carve; (*Satz*) to analyse
zerlumpt [tsɛr'lʊmpt] ADJ ragged
zermalmen [tsɛr'malmən] VT to crush
zermürben [tsɛr'mʏrbən] VT to wear down
zerpflücken VT (*lit, fig*) to pick to pieces
zerplatzen VI to burst
zerquetschen VT to squash
Zerrbild ['tsɛrbɪlt] NT (*fig*) caricature, distorted picture
zerreden VT (*Problem*) to flog to death
zerreiben *unreg* VT to grind down
zerreißen *unreg* VT to tear to pieces ▶ VI to tear, to rip
Zerreißprobe F (*lit*) pull test; (*fig*) real test
zerren ['tsɛrən] VT to drag ▶ VI: **~ (an** *+dat*) to tug (at)
zerrinnen *unreg* VI to melt away; (*Geld*) to disappear
zerrissen [tsɛr'rɪsən] PP *von* **zerreißen** ▶ ADJ torn, tattered; **Zerrissenheit** F tattered state; (*Pol*) disunion, discord; (*innere*) disintegration
Zerrspiegel ['tsɛrʃpi:gəl] M (*lit*) distorting mirror; (*fig*) travesty
Zerrung F: **eine ~** a pulled ligament/muscle
zerrütten [tsɛr'rʏtən] VT to wreck, to destroy
zerrüttet ADJ wrecked, shattered
Zerrüttungsprinzip NT (*bei Ehescheidung*) principle of irretrievable breakdown
zerschellen [tsɛr'ʃɛlən] VI (*Schiff, Flugzeug*) to be smashed to pieces
zerschießen *unreg* VT to shoot to pieces
zerschlagen *unreg* VT to shatter, to smash; (*fig: Opposition*) to crush; (*: Vereinigung*) to break up ▶ VR to fall through
zerschleißen [tsɛr'ʃlaɪsən] *unreg* VT, VI to wear out
zerschmelzen *unreg* VI to melt
zerschmettern *unreg* VT to shatter; (*Feind*) to crush ▶ VI to shatter
zerschneiden *unreg* VT to cut up
zersetzen VT, VR to decompose, to dissolve
zersetzend ADJ (*fig*) subversive
zersplittern [tsɛr'ʃplɪtərn] VT, VI to split (into pieces); (*Glas*) to shatter
zerspringen *unreg* VI to shatter ▶ VI (*fig*) to burst
zerstäuben [tsɛr'ʃtɔʏbən] VT to spray
Zerstäuber (**-s, -**) M atomizer

zerstören VT to destroy
Zerstörer (**-s, -**) M (*Naut*) destroyer
Zerstörung F destruction
Zerstörungswut F destructive mania
zerstoßen *unreg* VT to pound, to pulverize
zerstreiten *unreg* VR to fall out, to break up
zerstreuen VT to disperse, to scatter; (*Zweifel etc*) to dispel ▶ VR (*sich verteilen*) to scatter; (*Menge*) to disperse; (*sich ablenken*) to take one's mind off things
zerstreut ADJ scattered; (*Mensch*) absent-minded; **Zerstreutheit** F absent-mindedness
Zerstreuung F dispersion; (*Ablenkung*) diversion
zerstritten ADJ: **mit jdm ~ sein** to be on very bad terms with sb
zerstückeln [tsɛr'ʃtʏkəln] VT to cut into pieces
zerteilen VT to divide into parts
Zertifikat [tsɛrtifi'ka:t] (**-(e)s, -e**) NT certificate
zertreten *unreg* VT to crush underfoot
zertrümmern [tsɛr'trʏmərn] VT to shatter; (*Gebäude etc*) to demolish
zerwühlen VT to ruffle up, to tousle; (*Bett*) to rumple (up)
Zerwürfnis [tsɛr'vʏrfnɪs] (**-ses, -se**) NT dissension, quarrel
zerzausen [tsɛr'tsaʊzən] VT (*Haare*) to ruffle up, to tousle
zetern ['tse:tərn] (*pej*) VI to clamour (BRIT), to clamor (US); (*keifen*) to scold
Zettel ['tsɛtəl] (**-s, -**) M piece *od* slip of paper; (*Notizzettel*) note; (*Formular*) form; **„~ ankleben verboten"** "stick no bills"; **Zettelkasten** M card index (box); **Zettelwirtschaft** (*pej*) F: **eine Zettelwirtschaft haben** to have bits of paper everywhere
Zeug [tsɔʏk] (**-(e)s, -e**) (*umg*) NT stuff; (*Ausrüstung*) gear; **dummes ~** (stupid) nonsense; **das ~ haben zu** to have the makings of; **sich ins ~ legen** to put one's shoulder to the wheel; **was das ~ hält** for all one is worth; **jdm am ~ flicken** to find fault with sb
Zeuge ['tsɔʏgə] (**-n, -n**) M witness
zeugen VI to bear witness, to testify ▶ VT (*Kind*) to father; **es zeugt von ...** it testifies to ...
Zeugenaussage F evidence
Zeugenstand M witness box (BRIT) *od* stand (US)
Zeugin F witness
Zeugnis ['tsɔʏgnɪs] (**-ses, -se**) NT certificate; (*Sch*) report; (*Referenz*) reference; (*Aussage*) evidence, testimony; **~ geben von** to be evidence of, to testify to; **Zeugniskonferenz** F (*Sch*) *staff meeting to decide on marks etc*
Zeugung ['tsɔʏgʊŋ] F procreation
zeugungsunfähig ADJ sterile
ZH ABK = **Zentralheizung**
z. H., z. Hd. ABK (= *zu Händen*) att., attn.
Zicken ['tsɪkən] (*umg*) PL: **~ machen** to make trouble
zickig (*umg*) ADJ touchy, bitchy; (*albern*) silly; (*prüde*) prudish
Zickzack ['tsɪktsak] (**-(e)s, -e**) M zigzag
Ziege ['tsi:gə] (**-, -n**) F goat; (*pej, umg: Frau*) cow (!)
Ziegel ['tsi:gəl] (**-s, -**) M brick; (*Dachziegel*) tile
Ziegelei [tsi:gə'laɪ] F brickworks
Ziegelstein M brick
Ziegen- ZW: **Ziegenbock** M billy goat; **Ziegenkäse** M goat's cheese; **Ziegenleder** NT kid; **Ziegenpeter** M mumps *sing*
Ziehbrunnen M well
ziehen ['tsi:ən] *unreg* VT to draw; (*zerren*) to pull; (*Schach etc*) to move; (*züchten*) to rear ▶ VI to draw; (*umziehen, wandern*) to move; (*Rauch, Wolke etc*) to drift; (*reißen*) to pull ▶ VB UNPERS: **es zieht** there is a draught (BRIT) *od* draft (US), it's draughty (BRIT) *od* drafty (US) ▶ VR (*Gummi*) to stretch; (*Grenze etc*) to run; (*Gespräche*) to be drawn out; **etw nach sich ~** to lead to sth, to entail sth; **etw ins Lächerliche ~** to ridicule sth; **so was zieht bei mir nicht** I don't like that sort of thing; **den Tee ~ lassen** to let the tea stand; **zu jdm ~** to move in with sb; **mir ziehts im Rücken** my back hurts; **Ziehen** (**-s, -**) NT (*Schmerz*) ache; (*im Unterleib*) dragging pain
Ziehharmonika ['tsi:harmo:nika] F concertina
Ziehschwester ['tsi:ʃvɛstər] (**-, n**) F foster sister
Ziehung ['tsi:ʊŋ] F (*Losziehung*) drawing
Ziel [tsi:l] (**-(e)s, -e**) NT (*einer Reise*) destination; (*Sport*) finish; (*Mil*) target; (*Absicht*) goal, aim; **jdm/sich ein ~ stecken** to set sb/o.s. a goal; **am ~ sein** to be at one's destination; (*fig*) to have reached one's goal; **über das ~ hinausschießen** (*fig*) to overshoot the mark; **zielbewusst** ADJ purposeful; **zielen** VI: **zielen (auf** +*akk*) to aim (at); **Zielfernrohr** NT telescopic sight; **Zielfoto** NT (*Sport*) photo-finish, photograph; **Zielgruppe** F target group; **Ziellinie** F (*Sport*) finishing line; **ziellos** ADJ aimless; **Zielort** M destination; **Zielscheibe** F target; **zielstrebig** ADJ purposeful
ziemen ['tsi:mən] VR UNPERS (*geh*): **das ziemt sich nicht (für dich)** it is not proper (for you)
ziemlich ['tsi:mlɪç] ADJ *attrib* (*Anzahl*) fair ▶ ADV quite, pretty (*umg*); (*beinahe*) almost, nearly; **eine ziemliche Anstrengung** quite an effort; **~ lange** quite a long time; **~ fertig** almost *od* nearly ready
Zierde ['tsi:rdə] (**-, -n**) F ornament, decoration; (*Schmuckstück*) adornment
zieren ['tsi:rən] VR to act coy
Zierleiste F border; (*an Wand, Möbeln*) moulding (BRIT), molding (US); (*an Auto*) trim
zierlich ADJ dainty; **Zierlichkeit** F daintiness
Zierstrauch M flowering shrub
Ziffer ['tsɪfər] (**-, -n**) F figure, digit; **römische/arabische Ziffern** roman/arabic numerals; **Zifferblatt** NT dial, (clock *od* watch) face
zig [tsɪk] (*umg*) ADJ umpteen
Zigarette [tsiga'rɛtə] F cigarette
Zigaretten- ZW: **Zigarettenautomat** M cigarette machine; **Zigarettenpause** F break for a cigarette; **Zigarettenschachtel** F cigarette packet *od* pack (US); **Zigarettenspitze** F cigarette holder
Zigarillo [tsiga'rɪlo] (**-s, -s**) NT OD M cigarillo
Zigarre [tsi'garə] (**-, -n**) F cigar

Z

Zigeuner(in) [tsi'gɔʏnər(ɪn)] (**-s, -**) M(F) gipsy; **Zigeunerschnitzel** NT (*Koch*) *cutlet served in a spicy sauce with green and red peppers*; **Zigeunersprache** F Romany (language)
Zimmer ['tsɪmər] (**-s, -**) NT room; **Zimmerantenne** F indoor aerial; **Zimmerdecke** F ceiling; **Zimmerlautstärke** F reasonable volume; **Zimmermädchen** NT chambermaid; **Zimmermann** (**-(e)s**, *pl* **-leute**) M carpenter
zimmern VT to make from wood
Zimmer- ZW: **Zimmernachweis** M accommodation service; **Zimmerpflanze** F indoor plant; **Zimmervermittlung** F accommodation (BRIT) *od* accommodations (US) service
zimperlich ['tsɪmpərlɪç] ADJ squeamish; (*pingelig*) fussy, finicky
Zimt [tsɪmt] (**-(e)s, -e**) M cinnamon; **Zimtstange** F cinnamon stick
Zink [tsɪŋk] (**-(e)s**) NT zinc
Zinke (**-, -n**) F (*Gabelzinke*) prong; (*Kammzinke*) tooth
zinken VT (*Karten*) to mark
Zinken (**-s, -**) (*umg*) M (*Nase*) hooter
Zinksalbe F zinc ointment
Zinn [tsɪn] (**-(e)s**) NT (*Element*) tin; (*in Zinnwaren*) pewter; **Zinnbecher** M pewter tankard
zinnoberrot [tsɪ'no:bərrot] ADJ vermilion
Zinnsoldat M tin soldier
Zinnwaren PL pewter *sing*
Zins [tsɪns] (**-es, -en**) M interest
Zinseszins M compound interest
Zins- ZW: **Zinsfuß** M rate of interest; **zinslos** ADJ interest-free; **Zinssatz** M rate of interest; **Zinssteuer** F tax on interest
Zionismus [tsio'nɪsmʊs] M Zionism
Zipfel ['tsɪpfəl] (**-s, -**) M corner; (*von Land*) tip; (*Hemdzipfel*) tail; (*Wurstzipfel*) end; **Zipfelmütze** F pointed cap
zirka ['tsɪrka] ADV about, approximately
Zirkel ['tsɪrkəl] (**-s, -**) M circle; (*Math*) pair of compasses; **Zirkelkasten** M geometry set
zirkulieren [tsɪrku'li:rən] VI to circulate
Zirkus ['tsɪrkʊs] (**-, -se**) M circus; (*umg: Getue*) fuss, to-do
zirpen ['tsɪrpən] VI to chirp, to cheep
Zirrhose [tsɪ'ro:zə] (**-, -n**) F cirrhosis
zischeln ['tsɪʃəln] VT, VI to whisper
zischen ['tsɪʃən] VI to hiss; (*Limonade*) to fizz; (*Fett*) to sizzle
Zitat [tsi'ta:t] (**-(e)s, -e**) NT quotation, quote
zitieren [tsi'ti:rən] VT to quote; (*vorladen, rufen*): ~ (**vor** *+akk*) to summon (before)
Zitronat [tsitro'na:t] (**-(e)s, -e**) NT candied lemon peel
Zitrone [tsi'tro:nə] (**-, -n**) F lemon
Zitronen- ZW: **Zitronenlimonade** F lemonade; **Zitronensaft** M lemon juice; **Zitronensäure** F citric acid; **Zitronenscheibe** F lemon slice
zitterig ['tsɪtərɪç], **zittrig** ['tsɪtrɪç] ADJ shaky
zittern ['tsɪtərn] VI to tremble; **vor jdm ~** to be terrified of sb
Zitze ['tsɪtsə] (**-, -n**) F teat, dug
Zivi ['tsivi] (**-s, -s**) M ABK = **Zivildienstleistender**
zivil [tsi'vi:l] ADJ civilian; (*anständig*) civil; (*Preis*) moderate; **ziviler Ungehorsam** civil disobedience; **Zivil** (**-s**) NT plain clothes *pl*; (*Mil*) civilian clothing; **Zivilbevölkerung** F civilian population; **Zivilcourage** F courage of one's convictions
Zivildienst M (*früher*) *alternative service (for conscientious objectors)*

> Until the abolition of compulsory military service in 2011, a young German had to complete his 13 months' **Zivildienst** or community service if he had opted out of military service. In a way, this has now been replaced by the **Bundesfreiwilligendienst** or Federal Volunteer Service, which gives young men and women the opportunity to work as community volunteers for a year.

Zivildienstleistender M (*früher*) *conscientious objector doing alternative community service*
Zivilisation [tsivilizatsi'o:n] F civilization
Zivilisationserscheinung F phenomenon of civilization
Zivilisationskrankheit F disease of civilized man
zivilisieren [tsivili'zi:rən] VT to civilize
zivilisiert ADJ civilized
Zivilist [tsivi'lɪst] M civilian
Zivilrecht NT civil law
ZK (**-s, -s**) NT ABK (= *Zentralkomitee*) central committee
Zobel ['tso:bəl] (**-s, -**) M (*auch*: **Zobelpelz**) sable (fur)
zocken ['tsɔkən] VI (*umg*) to gamble
Zofe ['tso:fə] (**-, -n**) F lady's maid; (*von Königin*) lady-in-waiting
Zoff [tsɔf] (**-s**) M (*umg*) trouble
zog *etc* [tso:k] VB *siehe* **ziehen**
zögern ['tsø:gərn] VI to hesitate
Zölibat [tsøli'ba:t] (**-(e)s**) NT OD M celibacy
Zoll[1] [tsɔl] (**-(e)s, -**) M (*Maß*) inch
Zoll[2] (**-(e)s, Zölle**) M customs *pl*; (*Abgabe*) duty; **Zollabfertigung** F customs clearance; **Zollamt** NT customs office; **Zollbeamte(r)** M customs official; **Zollerklärung** F customs declaration; **zollfrei** ADJ duty-free; **Zollgutlager** NT bonded warehouse; **Zollkontrolle** F customs (check); **zollpflichtig** ADJ liable to duty, dutiable
Zollstock M inch rule
Zone ['tso:nə] (**-, -n**) F zone; (*von Fahrkarte*) fare stage
Zoo [tso:] (**-s, -s**) M zoo; **Zoohandlung** F pet shop
Zoologe [tsoo'lo:gə] (**-n, -n**) M zoologist
Zoologie F zoology
Zoologin F zoologist
zoologisch ADJ zoological
Zoom [zu:m] (**-s, -s**) NT zoom shot; (*Objektiv*) zoom lens
Zopf [tsɔpf] (**-(e)s, Zöpfe**) M plait, pigtail; **alter ~** antiquated custom
Zorn [tsɔrn] (**-(e)s**) M anger
zornig ADJ angry

Zote ['tso:tə] (**-, -n**) F smutty joke/remark
zottig ['tsɔtɪç] ADJ shaggy
ZPO ABK (= *Zivilprozessordnung*) ≈ General Practice Act (*US*)
z. T. ABK = **zum Teil**

SCHLÜSSELWORT

zu [tsu:] PRÄP +*dat* **1** (*örtlich*) to; **zum Bahnhof/Arzt gehen** to go to the station/doctor; **zur Schule/Kirche gehen** to go to school/church; **sollen wir zu Euch gehen?** shall we go to your place?; **sie sah zu ihm hin** she looked towards him; **zum Fenster herein** through the window; **zu meiner Linken** to *od* on my left
2 (*zeitlich*) at; **zu Ostern** at Easter; **bis zum 1. Mai** until May 1st; (*nicht später als*) by May 1st; **zu meiner Zeit** in my time
3 (*Zusatz*) with; **Wein zum Essen trinken** to drink wine with one's meal; **sich zu jdm setzen** to sit down beside sb; **setz dich doch zu uns** (come and) sit with us; **Anmerkungen zu etw** notes on sth
4 (*Zweck*) for; **Wasser zum Waschen** water for washing; **Papier zum Schreiben** paper to write on; **etw zum Geburtstag bekommen** to get sth for one's birthday; **es ist zu seinem Besten** it's for his own good
5 (*Veränderung*) into; **zu etw werden** to turn into sth; **jdn zu etw machen** to make sb (into) sth; **zu Asche verbrennen** to burn to ashes
6 (*mit Zahlen*): **3 zu 2** (*Sport*) 3-2; **das Stück zu 5 Euro** at 5 euros each; **zum ersten Mal** for the first time
7: **zu meiner Freude** *etc* to my joy *etc*; **zum Glück** luckily; **zu Fuß** on foot; **es ist zum Weinen** it's enough to make you cry
▸ KONJ to; **etw zu essen** sth to eat; **um besser sehen zu können** in order to see better; **ohne es zu wissen** without knowing it; **noch zu bezahlende Rechnungen** outstanding bills
▸ ADV **1** (*allzu*) too; **zu sehr** too much; **zu viel** too much; (*zu viele*) too many; **er kriegt zu viel** (*umg*) he gets annoyed; **zu wenig** too little; (*zu wenige*) too few
2 (*örtlich*) toward(s); **er kam auf mich zu** he came towards *od* up to me
3 (*geschlossen*) shut, closed; **die Geschäfte haben zu** the shops are closed; **zu sein** to be closed; **auf/zu** (*Wasserhahn etc*) on/off
4 (*umg*: *los*): **nur zu!** just keep at it!; **mach zu!** hurry up!

zuallererst ADV first of all
zuallerletzt ADV last of all
zubauen ['tsu:baʊən] VT (*Lücke*) to fill in; (*Platz, Gebäude*) to build up
Zubehör ['tsu:bəhø:r] (**-(e)s, -e**) NT accessories *pl*
Zuber ['tsu:bər] (**-s, -**) M tub
zubereiten ['tsu:bəraɪtən] VT to prepare
zubilligen ['tsu:bɪlɪgən] VT to grant
zubinden ['tsu:bɪndən] *unreg* VT to tie up; **jdm die Augen ~** to blindfold sb
zubleiben ['tsu:blaɪbən] *unreg* VI to stay shut
zubringen ['tsu:brɪŋən] *unreg* VT to spend; (*herbeibringen*) to bring, to take; (*umg*: *Tür*) to get shut
Zubringer (**-s, -**) M (*Tech*) feeder, conveyor; (*Verkehrsmittel*) shuttle; (*zum Flughafen*) airport bus; **Zubringerbus** M shuttle (bus); **Zubringerstraße** F slip road (*BRIT*), entrance ramp (*US*)
Zucchini [tsʊ'ki:ni:] PL courgettes *pl* (*BRIT*), zucchini(s) *pl* (*US*)
Zucht [tsʊxt] (**-, -en**) F (*von Tieren*) breeding; (*von Pflanzen*) cultivation; (*Rasse*) breed; (*Erziehung*) raising; (*Disziplin*) discipline; **Zuchtbulle** M breeding bull
züchten ['tsʏçtən] VT (*Tiere*) to breed; (*Pflanzen*) to cultivate, to grow
Züchter(in) (**-s, -**) M(F) breeder; (*von Pflanzen*) grower
Zuchthaus NT prison, penitentiary (*US*)
Zuchthengst M stallion, stud
züchtig ['tsʏçtɪç] ADJ modest, demure
züchtigen ['tsʏçtɪgən] VT to chastise
Züchtigung F chastisement; **körperliche ~** corporal punishment
Zuchtperle F cultured pearl
Züchtung F (*von Tieren*) breeding; (*von Pflanzen*) cultivation; (*Zuchtart*: *von Tier*) breed; (: *von Pflanze*) strain
zucken ['tsʊkən] VI to jerk, to twitch; (*Strahl etc*) to flicker; **mit den Schultern ~** to shrug (one's shoulders); **der Schmerz zuckte (mir) durch den ganzen Körper** the pain shot right through my body
zücken ['tsʏkən] VT (*Schwert*) to draw; (*Geldbeutel*) to pull out
Zucker ['tsʊkər] (**-s, -**) M sugar; (*Med*) diabetes; **~ haben** (*umg*) to be a diabetic; **Zuckerdose** F sugar bowl; **Zuckererbse** F mangetout (*BRIT*), sugar pea (*US*); **Zuckerguss** M icing; **Zuckerhut** M sugar loaf; **zuckerkrank** ADJ diabetic; **Zuckerkrankheit** F diabetes *sing*; **Zuckerlecken** NT: **das ist kein Zuckerlecken** it's no picnic
zuckern VT to sugar
Zucker- ZW: **Zuckerrohr** NT sugar cane; **Zuckerrübe** F sugar beet; **Zuckerspiegel** M (*Med*) (blood) sugar level; **zuckersüß** ADJ sugary; **Zuckerwatte** F candy floss (*BRIT*), cotton candy (*US*)
Zuckung F convulsion, spasm; (*leicht*) twitch
zudecken ['tsu:dɛkən] VT to cover (up); (*im Bett*) to tuck up *od* in
zudem [tsu'de:m] ADV in addition (to this)
zudrehen ['tsu:dre:ən] VT to turn off
zudringlich ['tsu:drɪŋlɪç] ADJ forward, pushy; (*Nachbar etc*) intrusive; **~ werden** to make advances; **Zudringlichkeit** F forwardness; (*von Nachbar etc*) intrusiveness
zudrücken ['tsu:drʏkən] VT to close; **jdm die Kehle ~** to throttle sb; **ein Auge ~** to turn a blind eye
zueinander [tsuaɪ'nandər] ADV to one other; (*in Verbverbindung*) together
zuerkennen ['tsu:ɛrkɛnən] *unreg* VT: **jdm etw ~**

Z

to award sth to sb, to award sb sth

zuerst [tsu'le:rst] ADV first; (*zu Anfang*) at first; **~ einmal** first of all

Zufahrt ['tsu:fa:rt] F access; (*Einfahrt*) drive(way); **„keine ~ zum Krankenhaus"** "no access to hospital"

Zufahrtsstraße F access road; (*von Autobahn etc*) slip road (BRIT), entrance ramp (US)

Zufall ['tsu:fal] M chance; (*Ereignis*) coincidence; **durch ~** by accident; **so ein ~!** what a coincidence!

zufallen *unreg* VI to close, to shut; (*Anteil, Aufgabe*): **jdm ~** to fall to sb

zufällig ['tsu:fɛlɪç] ADJ chance ▸ ADV by chance; (*in Frage*) by any chance

Zufallstreffer M fluke

zufassen ['tsu:fasən] VI (*zugreifen*) to take hold (of it *od* them); (*fig: schnell handeln*) to seize the opportunity; (*helfen*) to lend a hand

zufliegen ['tsu:fli:gən] *unreg* VI: **ihm fliegt alles nur so zu** (*fig*) everything comes so easily to him

Zuflucht ['tsu:flʊxt] F recourse; (*Ort*) refuge; **zu etw ~ nehmen** (*fig*) to resort to sth

Zufluchtsort M, **Zufluchtsstätte** F place of refuge

Zufluss ['tsu:flʊs] M (*Zufließen*) inflow, influx; (*Geog*) tributary; (*Comm*) supply

zufolge [tsu'fɔlgə] PRÄP +*dat*, +*gen* (*laut*) according to; (*aufgrund*) as a result of

zufrieden [tsu'fri:dən] ADJ content(ed); (*befriedigt*) satisfied; **er ist mit nichts ~** nothing pleases him; **zufriedengeben** *unreg* VR: **sich mit etw zufriedengeben** to be satisfied with sth; **Zufriedenheit** F contentedness; (*Befriedigtsein*) satisfaction; **zufriedenlassen** *unreg* VT: **lass mich damit zufrieden!** (*umg*) shut up about it!; **zufriedenstellen** VT to satisfy; **zufriedenstellend** ADJ satisfactory

zufrieren ['tsu:fri:rən] *unreg* VI to freeze up *od* over

zufügen ['tsu:fy:gən] VT to add; (*Leid etc*): **jdm etw ~** to cause sb sth

Zufuhr ['tsu:fu:r] (**-, -en**) F (*Herbeibringen*) supplying; (*Met*) influx; (*Mil*) supplies *pl*

zuführen ['tsu:fy:rən] VT (*bringen*) to bring; (*transportieren*) to convey; (*versorgen*) to supply ▸ VI: **auf etw** *akk* **~** to lead to sth

Zug [tsu:k] (**-(e)s, Züge**) M (*Eisenbahnzug*) train; (*Luftzug*) draught (BRIT), draft (US); (*Ziehen*) pull(ing); (*Gesichtszug*) feature; (*Schach etc*) move; (*Klingelzug*) pull; (*Schriftzug, beim Schwimmen*) stroke; (*Atemzug*) breath; (*Charakterzug*) trait; (*an Zigarette*) puff, pull, drag; (*Schluck*) gulp; (*Menschengruppe*) procession; (*von Vögeln*) migration; (*Mil*) platoon; **etw in vollen Zügen genießen** to enjoy sth to the full; **in den letzten Zügen liegen** (*umg*) to be at one's last gasp; **im ~(e)** +*gen* (*im Verlauf*) in the course of; **~ um ~** (*fig*) step by step; **zum ~(e) kommen** (*umg*) to get a look-in; **etw in groben Zügen darstellen** *od* **umreißen** to outline sth; **das war kein schöner ~ von dir** that wasn't nice of you

Zugabe ['tsu:ga:bə] F extra; (*in Konzert etc*) encore

Zugabteil NT train compartment

Zugang ['tsu:gaŋ] M entrance; (*Zutritt, fig*) access

zugänglich ['tsu:gɛŋlɪç] ADJ accessible; (*öffentliche Einrichtungen*) open; (*Mensch*) approachable

Zugangscode M (*Comput*) access code

Zugbegleiter M (*Eisenb*) guard (BRIT), conductor (US)

Zugbrücke F drawbridge

zugeben ['tsu:ge:bən] *unreg* VT (*beifügen*) to add, to throw in; (*zugestehen*) to admit; (*erlauben*) to permit; **zugegeben ...** granted ...

zugegebenermaßen ['tsu:gegə:bənər'ma:sən] ADV admittedly

zugegen [tsu'ge:gən] ADV (*geh*): **~ sein** to be present

zugehen ['tsu:ge:ən] *unreg* VI (*schließen*) to shut ▸ VI UNPERS (*sich ereignen*) to go on, to happen; **auf jdn/etw ~** to walk towards sb/sth; **dem Ende ~** to be finishing; **er geht schon auf die siebzig zu** he's getting on for seventy; **hier geht es nicht mit rechten Dingen zu** there's something odd going on here; **es ging lustig zu** we/they had a lot of fun; **dort geht es streng zu** it's strict there

Zugehörigkeit ['tsu:gəhø:rɪçkaɪt] F: **~ (zu)** membership (of), belonging (to)

Zugehörigkeitsgefühl NT feeling of belonging

zugeknöpft ['tsu:gəknœpft] (*umg*) ADJ reserved, stand-offish

Zügel ['tsy:gəl] (**-s, -**) M rein, reins *pl*; (*fig*) rein, curb; **die ~ locker lassen** to slacken one's hold on the reins; **die ~ locker lassen bei** (*fig*) to give free rein to

zugelassen ['tsu:gəlasən] ADJ authorized; (*Heilpraktiker*) registered; (*Kfz*) licensed

zügellos ADJ unrestrained; (*sexuell*) licentious

Zügellosigkeit F lack of restraint; (*sexuell*) licentiousness

zügeln VT to curb; (*Pferd*) to rein in

zugesellen VR: **sich jdm ~** to join sb, to join up with sb

Zugeständnis ['tsu:gəʃtɛntnɪs] (**-ses, -se**) NT concession; **Zugeständnisse machen** to make allowances

zugestehen *unreg* VT to admit; (*Rechte*) to concede

zugetan ['tsu:gəta:n] ADJ: **jdm/etw ~ sein** to be fond of sb/sth

Zugewinn (**-(e)s**) M (*Jur*) *property acquired during marriage*

Zugezogene(r) ['tsu:gətso:gənə(r)] F(M) newcomer

Zugführer M (*Eisenb*) chief guard (BRIT) *od* conductor (US); (*Mil*) platoon commander

zugig ADJ draughty (BRIT), drafty (US)

zügig ['tsy:gɪç] ADJ speedy, swift

zugkräftig ADJ (*fig*: *Werbetext*, *Titel*) eye-catching; (*Schauspieler*) crowd-pulling *attrib*, popular
zugleich [tsu'glaıç] ADV (*zur gleichen Zeit*) at the same time; (*ebenso*) both
Zugluft F draught (BRIT), draft (US)
Zugmaschine F traction engine, tractor
zugreifen ['tsu:graıfən] *unreg* VI to seize *od* grab it/them; (*helfen*) to help; (*beim Essen*) to help o.s.; **~ auf** *+akk* (*Comput*) to access
Zugriff ['tsu:grıf] M (*Comput*) access; **sich dem ~ der Polizei entziehen** (*fig*) to evade justice
zugrunde, zu Grunde [tsu'grʊndə] ADV: **~ gehen** to collapse; (*Mensch*) to perish; **er wird daran nicht ~ gehen** he'll survive; (*finanziell*) it won't ruin him; **einer Sache** *dat* **etw ~ legen** to base sth on sth; **einer Sache** *dat* **~ liegen** to be based on sth; **~ richten** to ruin, to destroy
zugunsten, zu Gunsten [tsu'gʊnstən] PRÄP *+gen*, *+dat*, in favour (BRIT) *od* favor (US) of
zugutehalten [tsu'gu:təhaltən] *unreg* VT: **jdm etw ~** to concede sth to sb
zugutekommen [tsu'gu:təkɔmən] *unreg* VT: **jdm ~** to be of assistance to sb
Zug- ZW: **Zugverbindung** F train connection; **Zugvogel** M migratory bird; **Zugzwang** M (*Schach*) zugzwang; **unter Zugzwang stehen** (*fig*) to be in a tight spot
zuhalten ['tsu:haltən] *unreg* VT to hold shut ▶ VI: **auf jdn/etw ~** to make for sb/sth; **sich** *dat* **die Nase ~** to hold one's nose
Zuhälter ['tsu:hɛltər] **(-s, -)** M pimp
zuhause [tsu'haʊzə] ADV at home
Zuhause (-s) NT home
Zuhilfenahme [tsu'hılfəna:mə] F: **unter ~ von** with the help of
zuhören ['tsu:hø:rən] VI to listen
Zuhörer (-s, -) M listener; **Zuhörerschaft** F audience
zujubeln ['tsu:ju:bəln] VI: **jdm ~** to cheer sb
zukehren ['tsu:ke:rən] VT (*zuwenden*) to turn
zuklappen ['tsu:klapən] VT (*Buch*, *Deckel*) to close ▶ VI (*Hilfsverb sein*: *Tür etc*) to click shut
zukleben ['tsu:kle:bən] VT to paste up
zukneifen ['tsu:knaıfən] VT (*Augen*) to screw up; (*Mund*) to shut tight(ly)
zuknöpfen ['tsu:knœpfən] VT to button (up), to fasten (up)
zukommen ['tsu:kɔmən] *unreg* VI to come up; **auf jdn ~** to come up to sb; **jdm ~** (*sich gehören*) to be fitting for sb; **diesem Treffen kommt große Bedeutung zu** this meeting is of the utmost importance; **jdm etw ~ lassen** to give sb sth; **die Dinge auf sich** *akk* **~ lassen** to take things as they come
Zukunft ['tsu:kʊnft] (-, *no pl*) F future
zukünftig ['tsu:kʏnftıç] ADJ future ▶ ADV in future; **mein zukünftiger Mann** my husband-to-be
Zukunfts- ZW: **Zukunftsaussichten** PL future prospects *pl*; **Zukunftsmusik** (*umg*) F wishful thinking; **Zukunftsroman** M science-fiction novel; **zukunftsträchtig** ADJ promising for the future; **zukunftsweisend** ADJ trend-setting
Zulage ['tsu:la:gə] F bonus
zulande [tsu'landə] ADV: **bei uns ~** in our country
zulangen ['tsu:laŋən] (*umg*) VI (*Dieb*, *beim Essen*) to help o.s.
zulassen ['tsu:lasən] *unreg* VT (*hereinlassen*) to admit; (*erlauben*) to permit; (*Auto*) to license; (*umg*: *nicht öffnen*) to keep shut
zulässig ['tsu:lɛsıç] ADJ permissible, permitted; **zulässige Höchstgeschwindigkeit** (upper) speed limit
Zulassung F (*amtlich*) authorization; (*von Kfz*) licensing; (*als praktizierender Arzt*) registration
Zulauf M: **großen ~ haben** (*Geschäft*) to be very popular
zulaufen ['tsu:laʊfən] *unreg* VI: **~ auf** *+akk* to run towards; **jdm ~** (*Tier*) to adopt sb; **spitz ~** to come to a point
zulegen ['tsu:le:gən] VT to add; (*Geld*) to put in; (*Tempo*) to accelerate, to quicken; (*schließen*) to cover over; **sich** *dat* **etw ~** (*umg*) to get oneself sth
zuleide [tsu'laıdə] ADJ: **jdm etw ~ tun** to harm sb
zuleiten ['tsu:laıtən] VT (*Wasser*) to supply; (*schicken*) to send
Zuleitung F (*Tech*) supply
zuletzt [tsu'lɛtst] ADV finally, at last; **wir blieben bis ~** we stayed to the very end; **nicht ~ wegen** not least because of
zuliebe [tsu'li:bə] ADV: **jdm ~** (in order) to please sb
Zulieferbetrieb ['tsu:li:fərbətri:p] M (*Comm*) supplier
zum [tsʊm] = **zu dem**; **~ dritten Mal** for the third time; **~ Scherz** as a joke; **~ Trinken** for drinking; **bis ~ 15. April** until 15th April; (*nicht später als*) by 15th April; **~ ersten Mal(e)** for the first time; **es ist ~ Weinen** it's enough to make you (want to) weep; **~ Glück** luckily
zumachen ['tsu:maxən] VT to shut; (*Kleidung*) to do up, to fasten ▶ VI to shut; (*umg*) to hurry up
zumal [tsu'ma:l] KONJ especially (as)
zumeist [tsu'maıst] ADV mostly
zumessen ['tsu:mɛsən] *unreg* VT *+dat* (*Zeit*) to allocate (for); (*Bedeutung*) to attach (to)
zumindest [tsu'mındəst] ADV at least
zumutbar ['tsu:mu:tba:r] ADJ reasonable
zumute [tsu'mu:tə] ADV: **wie ist ihm ~?** how does he feel?
zumuten ['tsu:mu:tən] VT: **(jdm) etw ~** to expect *od* ask sth (of sb); **sich** *dat* **zu viel ~** to take on too much
Zumutung F unreasonable expectation *od* demand; (*Unverschämtheit*) impertinence; **das ist eine ~!** that's a bit much!
zunächst [tsu'nɛ:çst] ADV first of all; **~ einmal** to start with
zunageln ['tsu:na:gəln] VT (*Fenster etc*) to nail up; (*Kiste etc*) to nail down
zunähen ['tsu:nɛ:ən] VT to sew up
Zunahme ['tsu:na:mə] **(-, -n)** F increase
Zuname ['tsu:na:mə] M surname

Z

zünden ['tsʏndən] VI (*Feuer*) to light, to ignite; (*Motor*) to fire; (*fig*) to kindle enthusiasm ▶ VT to ignite; (*Rakete*) to fire
zündend ADJ fiery
Zünder (**-s, -**) M fuse; (*Mil*) detonator
Zünd- ZW: **Zündholz** NT match; **Zündkabel** NT (*Aut*) plug lead; **Zündkerze** F (*Aut*) spark(ing) plug; **Zündplättchen** NT cap; **Zündschlüssel** M ignition key; **Zündschnur** F fuse wire; **Zündstoff** M fuel; (*fig*) dynamite
Zündung F ignition
zunehmen ['tsu:ne:mən] *unreg* VI to increase, to grow; (*Mensch*) to put on weight
zunehmend ADJ: **mit zunehmendem Alter** with advancing age
zuneigen ['tsu:naɪgən] VI to incline, to lean; **sich dem Ende ~** to draw to a close; **einer Auffassung ~** to incline towards a view; **jdm zugeneigt sein** to be attracted to sb
Zuneigung F affection
Zunft [tsʊnft] (**-, Zünfte**) F guild
zünftig ['tsʏnftɪç] ADJ (*Arbeit*) professional; (*umg: ordentlich*) proper, real
Zunge ['tsʊŋə] F tongue; (*Fisch*) sole; **böse Zungen behaupten, ...** malicious gossip has it ...
züngeln ['tsʏŋəln] VI (*Flammen*) to lick
Zungen- ZW: **Zungenbrecher** M tongue-twister; **zungenfertig** ADJ glib; **Zungenkuss** M French kiss
Zünglein ['tsʏŋlaɪn] NT: **das ~ an der Waage sein** (*fig*) to tip the scales
zunichtemachen [tsu'nɪçtəmaxən] VT to ruin, to destroy
zunichtewerden [tsu'nɪçtəve:rdən] *unreg* VI to come to nothing
zunutze [tsu'nʊtsə] ADV: **sich** *dat* **etw ~ machen** to make use of sth
zuoberst [tsu'|o:bərst] ADV at the top
zuordnen ['tsu:|ɔrdnən] VT to assign
zupacken ['tsu:pakən] (*umg*) VI (*zugreifen*) to make a grab for it; (*bei der Arbeit*) to get down to it; **mit ~** (*helfen*) to give me/them *etc* a hand
zupfen ['tsʊpfən] VT to pull, to pick, to pluck; (*Gitarre*) to pluck
zur [tsu:r] = **zu der**
zurate, zu Rate [tsu'ra:tə] ADV: **jdn ~ ziehen** to consult sb
zurechnungsfähig ['tsu:rɛçnʊŋsfɛ:ɪç] ADJ (*Jur*) responsible, of sound mind; **Zurechnungsfähigkeit** F responsibility, accountability
zurecht- ZW: **zurechtbiegen** *unreg* VT to bend into shape; (*fig*) to twist; **zurechtfinden** *unreg* VR to find one's way (about); **zurechtkommen** *unreg* VI (*rechtzeitig kommen*) to come in time; (*schaffen*) to cope; (*finanziell*) to manage; **zurechtlegen** VT to get ready; (*Ausrede etc*) to have ready; **zurechtmachen** VT to prepare ▶ VR to get ready; (*sich schminken*) to put on one's make-up; **zurechtweisen** *unreg* VT to reprimand; **Zurechtweisung** F reprimand, rebuff
zureden ['tsu:re:dən] VI: **jdm ~** to persuade sb, to urge sb
zureiten ['tsuraɪtən] *unreg* VT (*Pferd*) to break in
Zürich ['tsy:rɪç] (**-s**) NT Zurich
zurichten ['tsu:rɪçtən] VT (*Essen*) to prepare; (*beschädigen*) to batter, to bash up
zürnen ['tsʏrnən] VI: **jdm ~** to be angry with sb
zurück [tsu'rʏk] ADV back; (*mit Zahlungen*) behind; (*fig: zurückgeblieben: von Kind*) backward; **~!** get back!; **zurückbehalten** *unreg* VT to keep back; **er hat Schäden zurückbehalten** he suffered lasting damage; **zurückbekommen** *unreg* VT to get back; **zurückbezahlen** VT to repay, to pay back; **zurückbleiben** *unreg* VI (*Mensch*) to remain behind; (*nicht nachkommen*) to fall behind, to lag; (*Schaden*) to remain; **zurückbringen** *unreg* VT to bring back; **zurückdatieren** VT to backdate; **zurückdrängen** VT (*Gefühle*) to repress; (*Feind*) to push back; **zurückdrehen** VT to turn back; **zurückerobern** VT to reconquer; **zurückerstatten** VT to refund; **zurückfahren** *unreg* VI to travel back; (*vor Schreck*) to recoil ▶ VT to drive back; **zurückfallen** *unreg* VI to fall back; (*in Laster*) to relapse; (*in Leistungen*) to fall behind; (*an Besitzer*): **zurückfallen an** *+akk* to revert to; **zurückfinden** *unreg* VI to find one's way back; **zurückfordern** VT to demand back; **zurückführen** VT to lead back; **etw auf etw** *akk* **zurückführen** to trace sth back to sth; **zurückgeben** *unreg* VT to give back; (*antworten*) to retort with; **zurückgeblieben** ADJ retarded; **zurückgehen** *unreg* VI to go back; (*fallen*) to go down, to fall; (*zeitlich*): **zurückgehen (auf** *+akk*) to date back (to); **Waren zurückgehen lassen** to send back goods; **zurückgezogen** ADJ retired, withdrawn; **zurückgreifen** *unreg* VI: **zurückgreifen (auf** *+akk*) (*fig*) to fall back (upon); (*zeitlich*) to go back (to); **zurückhalten** *unreg* VT to hold back; (*Mensch*) to restrain; (*hindern*) to prevent ▶ VR (*reserviert sein*) to be reserved; (*im Essen*) to hold back; (*im Hintergrund bleiben*) to keep in the background; (*bei Verhandlung*) to keep a low profile; **zurückhaltend** ADJ reserved; **Zurückhaltung** F reserve; **zurückholen** VT to fetch back; (*Comput: Daten*) to retrieve; **zurückkehren** VI to return; **zurückkommen** *unreg* VI to come back; **auf etw** *akk* **zurückkommen** to return to sth; **zurücklassen** *unreg* VT to leave behind; **zurücklegen** VT to put back; (*Geld*) to put by; (*reservieren*) to keep back; (*Strecke*) to cover ▶ VR to lie back; **zurückliegen** *unreg* VI: **der Unfall liegt etwa eine Woche zurück** the accident was about a week ago; **zurücknehmen** *unreg* VT to take back; **zurückreichen** VI (*Tradition etc*): **zurückreichen (in** *+akk*) to go back (to); **zurückrufen** *unreg* VT, VI to call back; **etw ins Gedächtnis zurückrufen** to recall sth; **zurückschrauben** VT: **seine Ansprüche zurückschrauben** to lower one's sights; **zurückschrecken** VI: **zurückschrecken vor** *+dat* to shrink from; **vor nichts**

zurückschrecken to stop at nothing; **zurücksetzen** VT to put back; (*im Preis*) to reduce; (*benachteiligen*) to put at a disadvantage ▸ VI (*mit Fahrzeug*) to reverse, to back; **zurückstecken** VT to put back ▸ VI (*fig*) to moderate one's wishes; **zurückstellen** VT to put back, to replace; (*aufschieben*) to put off, to postpone; (*Mil*) to turn down; (*Interessen*) to defer; (*Ware*) to keep; **persönliche Interessen hinter etw** *dat* **zurückstellen** to put sth before one's personal interests; **zurückstoßen** *unreg* VT to repulse; **zurückstufen** VT to downgrade; **zurücktreten** *unreg* VI to step back; (*vom Amt*) to retire; (*von einem Vertrag etc*): **zurücktreten (von)** to withdraw (from); **gegenüber** *od* **hinter etw** *dat* **zurücktreten** to diminish in importance in view of sth; **bitte zurücktreten!** stand back, please!; **zurückverfolgen** VT (*fig*) to trace back; **zurückversetzen** VT (*in alten Zustand*): **zurückversetzen (in** *+akk***)** to restore (to) ▸ VR: **sich zurückversetzen (in** *+akk***)** to think back (to); **zurückweichen** *unreg* VI: **zurückweichen (vor** *+dat***)** to shrink back (from); **zurückweisen** *unreg* VT to turn down; (*Mensch*) to reject; **zurückwerfen** *unreg* VT (*Ball, Kopf*) to throw back; (*Strahlen, Schall*) to reflect; (*fig: Feind*) to repel; (*: wirtschaftlich*): **zurückwerfen (um)** to set back (by); **zurückzahlen** VT to pay back, to repay; **Zurückzahlung** F repayment; **zurückziehen** *unreg* VT to pull back; (*Angebot*) to withdraw ▸ VR to retire

Zuruf ['tsu:ru:f] M shout, cry

zurzeit [tsʊr'tsaɪt] ADV at the moment

zus. ABK = **zusammen**; **zusätzlich**

Zusage ['tsu:za:gə] F promise; (*Annahme*) consent

zusagen VT to promise ▸ VI to accept; **jdm etw auf den Kopf ~** (*umg*) to tell sb sth outright; **jdm ~** (*gefallen*) to appeal to *od* please sb

zusammen [tsu'zamən] ADV together; **Zusammenarbeit** F cooperation; **zusammenarbeiten** VI to cooperate; **Zusammenballung** F accumulation; **zusammenbauen** VT to assemble; **zusammenbeißen** *unreg* VT (*Zähne*) to clench; **zusammenbleiben** *unreg* VI to stay together; **zusammenbrauen** (*umg*) VT to concoct ▸ VR (*Gewitter, Unheil etc*) to be brewing; **zusammenbrechen** *unreg* VI (*Hilfsverb sein*) to collapse; (*Mensch*) to break down, to collapse; (*Verkehr etc*) to come to a standstill; **zusammenbringen** *unreg* VT to bring *od* get together; (*Geld*) to get; (*Sätze*) to put together; **Zusammenbruch** M collapse; (*Comput*) crash; **zusammenfahren** *unreg* VI to collide; (*erschrecken*) to start; **zusammenfallen** *unreg* VI (*einstürzen*) to collapse; (*Ereignisse*) to coincide; **zusammenfassen** VT to summarize; (*vereinigen*) to unite; **zusammenfassend** ADJ summarizing ▸ ADV to summarize; **Zusammenfassung** F summary, résumé; **zusammenfinden** *unreg* VI, VR to meet (together); **zusammenfließen** *unreg* VI to flow together, to meet; **Zusammenfluss** M confluence; **zusammenfügen** VT to join (together), to unite; **zusammenführen** VT to bring together; (*Familie*) to reunite; **zusammengehören** VI to belong together; (*Paar*) to match; **Zusammengehörigkeitsgefühl** NT sense of belonging; **zusammengesetzt** ADJ compound, composite; **zusammengewürfelt** ADJ motley; **zusammenhalten** *unreg* VT to hold together ▸ VI to hold together; (*Freunde, fig*) to stick together; **Zusammenhang** M connection; **im/aus dem Zusammenhang** in/out of context; **etw aus dem Zusammenhang reißen** to take sth out of its context; **zusammenhängen** *unreg* VI to be connected *od* linked; **zusammenhängend** ADJ (*Erzählung*) coherent; **zusammenhanglos, zusammenhangslos** ADJ incoherent; **zusammenklappbar** ADJ folding, collapsible; **zusammenklappen** VT (*Messer etc*) to fold ▸ VI (*umg: Mensch*) to flake out; **zusammenknüllen** VT to crumple up; **zusammenkommen** *unreg* VI to meet, to assemble; (*sich ereignen*) to occur at once *od* together; **zusammenkramen** VT to gather (together); **Zusammenkunft (-, -künfte)** F meeting; **zusammenlaufen** *unreg* VI to run *od* come together; (*Straßen, Flüsse etc*) to converge, to meet; (*Farben*) to run into one another; **zusammenlegen** VT to put together; (*stapeln*) to pile up; (*falten*) to fold; (*verbinden*) to combine, to unite; (*Termine, Feste*) to combine; (*Geld*) to collect ▸ VI (*Geld sammeln*) to club together; **zusammennehmen** *unreg* VT to summon up ▸ VR to pull o.s. together; **alles zusammengenommen** all in all; **zusammenpassen** VI to go well together, to match; **Zusammenprall** M (*lit*) collision; (*fig*) clash; **zusammenprallen** VI (*Hilfsverb sein*) to collide; **zusammenreimen** (*umg*) VT: **das kann ich mir nicht zusammenreimen** I can't make head nor tail of this; **zusammenreißen** *unreg* VR to pull o.s. together; **zusammenrotten** *unreg* (*pej*) VR to gang up; **zusammenschlagen** *unreg* VT (*jdn*) to beat up; (*Dinge*) to smash up; (*falten*) to fold; (*Hände*) to clap; (*Hacken*) to click; **zusammenschließen** *unreg* VT, VR to join (together); **Zusammenschluss** M amalgamation; **zusammenschmelzen** *unreg* VI (*verschmelzen*) to fuse; (*zerschmelzen*) to melt (away); (*Anzahl*) to dwindle; **zusammenschrecken** *unreg* VI to start; **zusammenschreiben** *unreg* VT to write together; (*Bericht*) to put together; **zusammenschrumpfen** VI (*Hilfsverb sein*) to shrink, to shrivel up; **Zusammensein (-s)** NT get-together; **zusammensetzen** VT to put together ▸ VR: **sich zusammensetzen aus** to consist of; **Zusammensetzung** F composition; **Zusammenspiel** NT teamwork; (*von Kräften etc*) interaction; **zusammenstellen** VT to put together; **Zusammenstellung** F list; (*Vorgang*) compilation; **Zusammenstoß** M collision; **zusammenstoßen** *unreg* VI (*Hilfsverb sein*) to

Z

collide; **zusammenströmen** VI (*Hilfsverb sein*: *Menschen*) to flock together; **zusammentragen** *unreg* VT to collect; **zusammentreffen** *unreg* VI (*Hilfsverb sein*) to coincide; (*Menschen*) to meet; **Zusammentreffen** NT meeting; (*Zufall*) coincidence; **zusammentreten** *unreg* VI (*Verein etc*) to meet; **zusammenwachsen** *unreg* VI to grow together; **zusammenwirken** VI to combine; **zusammenzählen** VT to add up; **zusammenziehen** *unreg* VT (*verengern*) to draw together; (*vereinigen*) to bring together; (*addieren*) to add up ▸ VI (*in Wohnung etc*) to move in together ▸ VR to shrink; (*sich bilden*) to form, to develop; **zusammenzucken** VI (*Hilfsverb sein*) to start

Zusatz ['tsu:zats] M addition; **Zusatzantrag** M (*Pol*) amendment; **Zusatzgerät** NT attachment

zusätzlich ['tsu:zɛtslɪç] ADJ additional ▸ ADV in addition

Zusatzmittel NT additive

Zusatzprogramm ['tsu:zatsprogram] NT (*Comput*) plug-in; Plug-in ▸ NT (*Comput*) plug-in

zuschauen ['tsu:ʃaʊən] VI to watch, to look on

Zuschauer (**-s, -**) M spectator ▸ PL (*Theat*) audience *sing*

zuschicken ['tsu:ʃɪkən] VT: **jdm etw ~** to send *od* forward sth to sb

zuschießen ['tsu:ʃi:sən] *unreg* VT to fire; (*Geld*) to put in ▸ VI: **~ auf** *+akk* to rush towards

Zuschlag ['tsu:ʃla:k] M extra charge; (*Erhöhung*) surcharge; (*Eisenb*) supplement

zuschlagen ['tsu:ʃla:gən] *unreg* VT (*Tür*) to slam; (*Ball*) to hit; (*bei Auktion*) to knock down; (*Steine etc*) to knock into shape ▸ VI (*Fenster, Tür*) to shut; (*Mensch*) to hit, to punch

zuschlagfrei ADJ (*Eisenb*) not subject to a supplement

zuschlagpflichtig ADJ subject to an extra charge; (*Eisenb*) subject to a supplement

Zuschlagskarte F (*Eisenb*) supplementary ticket

zuschließen ['tsu:ʃli:sən] *unreg* VT to lock (up)

zuschmeißen ['tsu:ʃmaɪsən] *unreg* (*umg*) VT to slam, to bang shut

zuschmieren ['tsu:ʃmi:rən] VT to smear over; (*Löcher*) to fill in

zuschneiden ['tsu:ʃnaɪdən] *unreg* VT to cut to size; (*Nähen*) to cut out; **auf etw** *akk* **zugeschnitten sein** (*fig*) to be geared to sth

zuschnüren ['tsu:ʃny:rən] VT to tie up; **die Angst schnürte ihm die Kehle zu** (*fig*) he was choked with fear

zuschrauben ['tsu:ʃraʊbən] VT to screw shut

zuschreiben ['tsu:ʃraɪbən] *unreg* VT (*fig*) to ascribe, to attribute; (*Comm*) to credit; **das hast du dir selbst zuzuschreiben** you've only got yourself to blame

Zuschrift ['tsu:ʃrɪft] F letter, reply

zuschulden, zu Schulden [tsu'ʃʊldən] ADV: **sich** *dat* **etw ~ kommen lassen** to make o.s. guilty of sth

Zuschuss ['tsu:ʃʊs] M subsidy

Zuschussbetrieb M loss-making concern

zuschütten ['tsu:ʃʏtən] VT to fill up

zusehen ['tsu:zɛ:ən] *unreg* VI to watch; (*dafür sorgen*) to take care; (*etw dulden*) to sit back (and watch); **jdm/etw ~** to watch sb/sth

zusehends ADV visibly

zu sein ['tsu:zaɪn] *siehe* **zu**

zusenden ['tsu:zɛndən] *unreg* VT to forward, to send on

zusetzen ['tsu:zɛtsən] VT (*beifügen*) to add; (*Geld*) to lose ▸ VI: **jdm ~** to harass sb; (*Krankheit*) to take a lot out of sb; (*unter Druck setzen*) to lean on sb (*umg*); (*schwer treffen*) to hit sb hard

zusichern ['tsu:zɪçərn] VT: **jdm etw ~** to assure sb of sth

Zusicherung F assurance

zusperren ['tsu:ʃpɛrən] VT to bar

zuspielen ['tsu:ʃpi:lən] VT, VI to pass; **jdm etw ~** to pass sth to sb; (*fig*) to pass sth on to sb; **etw der Presse ~** to leak sth to the press

zuspitzen ['tsu:ʃpɪtsən] VT to sharpen ▸ VR (*Lage*) to become critical

zusprechen ['tsu:ʃprɛçən] *unreg* VT (*zuerkennen*): **jdm etw ~** to award sb sth, to award sth to sb ▸ VI: **jdm ~** to speak to sb; **jdm Trost ~** to comfort sb; **dem Essen/Alkohol ~** to eat/drink a lot

Zuspruch ['tsu:ʃprʊx] M encouragement; (*Anklang*) popularity

Zustand ['tsu:ʃtant] M state, condition; **in gutem/schlechtem ~** in good/poor condition; (*Haus*) in good/bad repair; **Zustände bekommen** *od* **kriegen** (*umg*) to have a fit

zustande, zu Stande [tsu'ʃtandə] ADV: **~ bringen** to bring about; **~ kommen** to come about

zuständig ['tsu:ʃtɛndɪç] ADJ competent, responsible; **Zuständigkeit** F competence, responsibility; **Zuständigkeitsbereich** M area of responsibility

zustattenkommen [tsu'ʃtatənkɔmən] *unreg* VI: **jdm ~** (*geh*) to come in useful for sb

zustehen ['tsu:ʃte:ən] *unreg* VI: **jdm ~** to be sb's right

zusteigen ['tsu:ʃtaɪgən] *unreg* VI: **noch jemand zugestiegen?** (*in Zug*) any more tickets?

zustellen ['tsu:ʃtɛlən] VT (*verstellen*) to block; (*Post etc*) to send

Zustellung F delivery

zusteuern ['tsu:ʃtɔʏərn] VI: **auf etw** *akk* **~** to head for sth; (*beim Gespräch*) to steer towards sth ▸ VT (*beitragen*) to contribute

zustimmen ['tsu:ʃtɪmən] VI to agree

Zustimmung F agreement; (*Einwilligung*) consent; **allgemeine ~ finden** to meet with general approval

zustoßen ['tsu:ʃto:sən] *unreg* VI (*fig*): **jdm ~** to happen to sb

Zustrom ['tsu:ʃtro:m] M (*fig: Menschenmenge*) stream (of visitors *etc*); (*hineinströmend*) influx; (*Met*) inflow

zustürzen ['tsu:ʃtʏrtsən] VI: **auf jdn/etw ~** to rush up to sb/sth

zutage, zu Tage [tsu'ta:gə] ADV: **~ bringen** to bring to light; **~ treten** to come to light
Zutaten ['tsu:ta:tən] PL ingredients *pl*; (*fig*) accessories *pl*
zuteilen ['tsu:taɪlən] VT to allocate, to assign
zuteilwerden [tsu'taɪlve:rdən] *unreg* VI (*geh*): **jdm wird etw zuteil** sb is granted sth, sth is granted to sb
zutiefst [tsu'ti:fst] ADV deeply
zutragen ['tsu:tra:gən] *unreg* VT: **jdm etw ~** to bring sb sth, to bring sth to sb ▶ VT (*Klatsch*) to tell sb sth ▶ VR to happen
zuträglich ['tsu:trɛ:klɪç] ADJ beneficial
zutrauen ['tsu:traʊən] VT: **jdm etw ~** to credit sb with sth; **sich** *dat* **nichts ~** to have no confidence in o.s.; **jdm viel ~** to think a lot of sb; **jdm wenig ~** not to think much of sb; **Zutrauen (-s)** NT: **Zutrauen (zu)** trust (in); **zu jdm Zutrauen fassen** to begin to trust sb
zutraulich ADJ trusting; (*Tier*) friendly; **Zutraulichkeit** F trust
zutreffen ['tsu:trɛfən] *unreg* VI to be correct; (*gelten*) to apply
zutreffend ADJ (*richtig*) accurate; **Zutreffendes bitte unterstreichen** please underline where applicable
zutrinken ['tsu:trɪŋkən] *unreg* VI: **jdm ~** to drink to sb
Zutritt ['tsu:trɪt] M access; (*Einlass*) admittance; **kein ~, ~ verboten** no admittance
zutun ['tsu:tu:n] *unreg* VT to add; (*schließen*) to shut
Zutun (-s) NT assistance
zuunterst [tsu'ʊntərst] ADV right at the bottom
zuverlässig ['tsu:fɛrlɛsɪç] ADJ reliable; **Zuverlässigkeit** F reliability
Zuversicht ['tsu:fɛrzɪçt] (-) F confidence; **zuversichtlich** ADJ confident; **Zuversichtlichkeit** F confidence
zu viel [tsu'fi:l] *siehe* **zu**
zuvor [tsu'fo:r] ADV before, previously; (*zunächst*) first
zuvorderst [tsu'fɔrdərst] ADV right at the front
zuvorkommen *unreg* VI *+dat* to anticipate; (*Gefahr etc*) to forestall; **jdm ~** to beat sb to it
zuvorkommend ADJ courteous; (*gefällig*) obliging
Zuwachs ['tsu:vaks] **(-es)** M increase, growth; (*umg: Baby*) addition to the family
zuwachsen *unreg* VI to become overgrown; (*Wunde*) to heal (up)
Zuwachsrate F rate of increase
zuwandern ['tsu:vandərn] VI to immigrate
zuwege, zu Wege [tsu've:gə] ADV: **etw ~ bringen** to accomplish sth; **mit etw ~ kommen** to manage sth; **gut ~ sein** to be (doing) well
zuweilen [tsu'vaɪlən] ADV at times, now and then
zuweisen ['tsu:vaɪzən] *unreg* VT to assign, to allocate
zuwenden ['tsu:vɛndən] *unreg* VT *+dat* to turn towards ▶ VR *+dat* to turn to; (*sich widmen*) to devote o.s. to; **jdm seine Aufmerksamkeit ~** to give sb one's attention
Zuwendung F (*Geld*) financial contribution; (*Liebe*) love and care
zu wenig [tsu've:nɪç] *siehe* **zu**
zuwerfen ['tsu:vɛrfən] *unreg* VT: **jdm etw ~** to throw sth to sb, to throw sb sth
zuwider [tsu'vi:dər] ADV: **etw ist jdm ~** sb loathes sth, sb finds sth repugnant ▶ PRÄP *+dat* contrary to; **es ist mir ~** I hate *od* detest it; **zuwiderhandeln** VI *+dat* to act contrary to; **einem Gesetz zuwiderhandeln** to contravene a law; **Zuwiderhandlung** F contravention; **zuwiderlaufen** *unreg* VI: **einer Sache** *dat* **zuwiderlaufen** to run counter to sth
zuwinken VI: **jdm ~** to wave to sb
zuz. ABK = **zuzüglich**
zuzahlen ['tsu:tsa:lən] VT: **10 Euro ~** to pay another 10 euros
zuziehen ['tsu:tsi:ən] *unreg* VT (*schließen: Vorhang*) to draw, to close; (*herbeirufen: Experten*) to call in ▶ VI to move in, to come; **sich** *dat* **etw ~** (*Krankheit*) to catch sth; (*Zorn*) to incur sth; **sich** *dat* **eine Verletzung ~** (*form*) to sustain an injury
Zuzug ['tsu:tsuk] **(-(e)s)** M (*Zustrom*) influx; (*von Familie etc*): **~ nach** move to
zuzüglich ['tsu:tsy:klɪç] PRÄP *+gen* plus, with the addition of
zuzwinkern ['tsu:tsvɪnkərn] VI: **jdm ~** to wink at sb
ZVS F ABK (= *Zentralstelle für die Vergabe von Studienplätzen*) *central body organizing the granting of places at university*
zwang *etc* [tsvaŋ] VB *siehe* **zwingen**
Zwang (-(e)s, Zwänge) M compulsion; (*Gewalt*) coercion; **gesellschaftliche Zwänge** social constraints; **tu dir keinen ~ an** don't feel you have to be polite
zwängen ['tsvɛŋən] VT, VR to squeeze
Zwang- ZW: **zwanghaft** ADJ compulsive; **zwanglos** ADJ informal; **Zwanglosigkeit** F informality
Zwangs- ZW: **Zwangsabgabe** F (*Comm*) compulsory levy; **Zwangsarbeit** F forced labour (BRIT) *od* labor (*US*); **Zwangsernährung** F force-feeding; **Zwangsjacke** F straitjacket; **Zwangslage** F predicament, tight corner; **zwangsläufig** ADJ inevitable; **Zwangsmaßnahme** F compulsory measure; (*Pol*) sanction; **Zwangsvollstreckung** F execution; **Zwangsvorstellung** F (*Psych*) obsession; **zwangsweise** ADV compulsorily
zwanzig ['tsvantsɪç] NUM twenty
zwanzigste(r, s) ADJ twentieth
zwar [tsva:r] ADV to be sure, indeed; **das ist ~ …, aber …** that may be … but …; **und ~ in** fact, actually; **und ~ am Sonntag** on Sunday to be precise; **und ~ so schnell, dass …** in fact so quickly that …
Zweck [tsvɛk] **(-(e)s, -e)** M purpose, aim; **es hat keinen ~, darüber zu reden** there is no point (in) talking about it; **zweckdienlich** ADJ

practical; (*nützlich*) useful; **zweckdienliche Hinweise** (any) relevant information
Zwecke (-, -n) F hobnail; (*Heftzwecke*) drawing pin (BRIT), thumbtack (US)
Zweck- zW: **zweckentfremden** VT UNTR to use for another purpose; **Zweckentfremdung** F misuse; **zweckfrei** ADJ (*Forschung etc*) pure; **zwecklos** ADJ pointless; **zweckmäßig** ADJ suitable, appropriate; **Zweckmäßigkeit** F suitability
zwecks PRÄP +*gen* (*form*) for (the purpose of)
zweckwidrig ADJ unsuitable
zwei [tsvaɪ] NUM two; **Zweibettzimmer** NT twin-bedded room; **zweideutig** ADJ ambiguous; (*unanständig*) suggestive; **Zweidrittelmehrheit** F (*Parl*) two-thirds majority; **zweieiig** ADJ (*Zwillinge*) non-identical
zweierlei ['tsvaɪər'laɪ] ADJ two kinds *od* sorts of; **~ Stoff** two different kinds of material; **~ zu tun haben** to have two different things to do
zweifach ADJ double
Zweifel ['tsvaɪfəl] (-s, -) M doubt; **ich bin mir darüber im ~** I'm in two minds about it; **zweifelhaft** ADJ doubtful, dubious; **zweifellos** ADJ doubtless
zweifeln VI: **(an etw** *dat***) ~** to doubt (sth)
Zweifelsfall M: **im ~** in case of doubt
Zweifrontenkrieg M war(fare) on two fronts
Zweig [tsvaɪk] (-(e)s, -e) M branch; **Zweiggeschäft** NT (*Comm*) branch
zweigleisig ['tsvaɪglaɪzɪç] ADJ: **~ argumentieren** to argue along two different lines
Zweigstelle F branch (office)
zwei- zW: **zweihändig** ADJ two-handed; (*Mus*) for two hands; **Zweiheit** F duality; **zweihundert** NUM two hundred; **Zweikampf** M duel; **zweimal** ADV twice; **das lasse ich mir nicht zweimal sagen** I don't have to be told twice; **zweimotorig** ADJ twin-engined; **zweireihig** ADJ (*Anzug*) double-breasted; **Zweisamkeit** F togetherness; **zweischneidig** ADJ (*fig*) double-edged; **Zweisitzer** (-s, -) M two-seater; **zweisprachig** ADJ bilingual; **Zweispurgerät, Zweispurtonbandgerät** NT twin-track (tape) recorder; **zweispurig** ADJ (*Aut*) two-lane; **zweistellig** ADJ (*Zahl*) two-digit *attrib*, with two digits; **zweistimmig** ADJ for two voices
zweit [tsvaɪt] ADV: **zu ~** (*in Paaren*) in twos; **wir sind zu ~** there are two of us
Zweitaktmotor M two-stroke engine
zweitbeste(r, s) ADJ second best
zweite(r, s) ADJ second; **Bürger zweiter Klasse** second-class citizen(s *pl*)
zweiteilig ['tsvaɪtaɪlɪç] ADJ (*Buch, Film etc*) in two parts; (*Kleidung*) two-piece
zweitens ADV secondly
zweit- zW: **zweitgrößte(r, s)** ADJ second largest; **zweitklassig** ADJ second-class; **zweitletzte(r, s)** ADJ last but one, penultimate; **zweitrangig** ADJ second-rate; **Zweitschlüssel** M duplicate key; **Zweitstimme** F second vote; *siehe auch* **Erststimme**
zweitürig ['tsvaɪtyrɪç] ADJ two-door
Zweitwagen M second car
Zweitwohnung F second home
zweizeilig ADJ two-lined; (*Typ: Abstand*) double-spaced
Zweizimmerwohnung F two-room(ed) flat (BRIT) *od* apartment (US)
Zwerchfell ['tsvɛrçfɛl] NT diaphragm
Zwerg(in) [tsvɛrk, 'tsvɛrgɪn] (-(e)s, -e) M(F) dwarf; (*fig: Knirps*) midget; **Zwergschule** (*umg*) F village school
Zwetsche ['tsvɛtʃə] F, **Zwetschge** ['tsvɛtʃgə] (-, -n) F plum
Zwickel ['tsvɪkəl] (-s, -) M gusset
zwicken ['tsvɪkən] VT to pinch, to nip
Zwickmühle ['tsvɪkmy:lə] F: **in der ~ sitzen** (*fig*) to be in a dilemma
Zwieback ['tsvi:bak] (-(e)s, -e *od* -bäcke) M rusk
Zwiebel ['tsvi:bəl] (-, -n) F onion; (*Blumenzwiebel*) bulb; **zwiebelartig** ADJ bulbous; **Zwiebelturm** M (tower with an) onion dome
Zwie- zW: **Zwiegespräch** NT dialogue (BRIT), dialog (US); **Zwielicht** NT twilight; **ins Zwielicht geraten sein** (*fig*) to appear in an unfavourable (BRIT) *od* unfavorable (US) light; **zwielichtig** ADJ shady, dubious; **Zwiespalt** M conflict; (*zwischen Menschen*) rift, gulf; **zwiespältig** ADJ (*Gefühle*) conflicting; (*Charakter*) contradictory; **Zwietracht** F discord, dissension
Zwilling ['tsvɪlɪŋ] (-s, -e) M twin; **Zwillinge** PL (*Astrol*) Gemini
zwingen ['tsvɪŋən] *unreg* VT to force
zwingend ADJ (*Grund etc*) compelling; (*logisch notwendig*) necessary; (*Schluss, Beweis*) conclusive
Zwinger (-s, -) M (*Käfig*) cage; (*Hundezwinger*) run
zwinkern ['tsvɪŋkərn] VI to blink; (*absichtlich*) to wink
Zwirn [tsvɪrn] (-(e)s, -e) M thread
zwischen ['tsvɪʃən] PRÄP (+*akk od dat*) between; (*bei mehreren*) among; **Zwischenablage** F (*Comput*) clipboard; **Zwischenaufenthalt** M stopover; **Zwischenbemerkung** F (incidental) remark; **Zwischenbilanz** F (*Comm*) interim balance; **zwischenblenden** VT (*Film, Rundf, TV*) to insert; **Zwischending** NT cross; **Zwischendividende** F interim dividend; **zwischendurch** ADV in between; (*räumlich*) here and there; **Zwischenergebnis** NT intermediate result; **Zwischenfall** M incident; **Zwischenfrage** F question; **Zwischengröße** F in-between size; **Zwischenhandel** M wholesaling; **Zwischenhändler** M middleman, agent; **Zwischenlagerung** F temporary storage; **Zwischenlandung** F (*Aviat*) stopover; **Zwischenlösung** F temporary solution; **zwischenmahlzeit** F snack (*between meals*); **zwischenmenschlich** ADJ interpersonal; **Zwischenprüfung** F intermediate examination; **Zwischenraum** M gap, space;

Zwischenruf M interjection, interruption; **Zwischenrufe** PL heckling *sing*; **Zwischensaison** F low season; **Zwischenspeicher** M (*Comput*) buffer; **zwischenspeichern** VT (*Comput*) to buffer; **Zwischenspiel** NT (*Theat, fig*) interlude; (*Mus*) intermezzo; **zwischenstaatlich** ADJ interstate; (*international*) international; **Zwischenstation** F intermediate station; **Zwischenstecker** M (*Elek*) adapter; **Zwischenstück** NT connecting piece; **Zwischensumme** F subtotal; **Zwischenwand** F partition; **Zwischenzeit** F interval; **in der Zwischenzeit** in the interim, meanwhile; **Zwischenzeugnis** NT (*Sch*) interim report

Zwist [tsvɪst] (**-es, -e**) M dispute

zwitschern ['tsvɪtʃərn] VT, VI to twitter, to chirp; **einen ~** (*umg*) to have a drink

Zwitter ['tsvɪtər] (**-s, -**) M hermaphrodite

zwo [tsvo:] NUM (*Tel, Mil*) two

zwölf [tsvœlf] NUM twelve; **fünf Minuten vor ~** (*fig*) at the eleventh hour

Zwölffingerdarm (**-(e)s**) M duodenum

Zyankali [tsya:n'ka:li] (**-s**) NT (*Chem*) potassium cyanide

Zyklon [tsy'klo:n] (**-s, -e**) M cyclone

Zyklus ['tsy:klʊs] (**-, Zyklen**) M cycle

Zylinder [tsi'lɪndər] (**-s, -**) M cylinder; (*Hut*) top hat; **zylinderförmig** ADJ cylindrical

Zyniker(in) ['tsy:nikər(ɪn)] (**-s, -**) M(F) cynic

zynisch ['tsy:nɪʃ] ADJ cynical

Zynismus [tsy'nɪsmʊs] M cynicism

Zypern ['tsy:pərn] (**-s**) NT Cyprus

Zypresse [tsy'prɛsə] (**-, -n**) F (*Bot*) cypress

Zypriot(in) [tsypri'o:t(ɪn)] (**-en, -en**) M(F) Cypriot

zypriotisch ADJ Cypriot, Cyprian

zyprisch ['tsy:prɪʃ] ADJ Cypriot, Cyprian

Zyste ['tsʏstə] (**-, -n**) F cyst

z. Z., z. Zt. ABK = **zur Zeit**

zz., zzt. ABK = **zurzeit**

ENGLISH–GERMAN

ENGLISCH–DEUTSCH

A¹, a [eɪ] N *(letter)* A *nt*, a *nt*; *(Scol)* ≈ Eins *f*, sehr gut *nt*; **A for Andrew, A for Able** *(US)* ≈ A wie Anton; **A road** (BRIT *Aut*) Hauptverkehrsstraße *f*; **A shares** (BRIT *Stock Exchange*) stimmrechtslose Aktien *pl*

A² [eɪ] N *(Mus)* A *nt*, a *nt*

KEYWORD

a [ə] *(before vowel and silent h:* **an***)* INDEF ART **1** ein; *(before feminine noun)* eine; **a book** ein Buch; **a lamp** eine Lampe; **she's a doctor** sie ist Ärztin; **I haven't got a car** ich habe kein Auto; **a hundred/thousand** *etc* **pounds** einhundert/eintausend *etc* Pfund

2 *(in expressing ratios, prices etc)* pro; **3 a day/week** 3 pro Tag/Woche, 3 am Tag/in der Woche; **10 km an hour** 10 km pro Stunde

A2 (BRIT) N *(Scol) Mit „A2" wird das zweite Jahr der britischen Sekundarstufe II bezeichnet, in dem die übrigen drei Wahlpflichtfächer unterrichtet und am Ende des Schuljahres geprüft werden. Die Note für den „A level" setzt sich aus den Noten der Jahre „AS" und „A2" zusammen*

AA N ABBR (BRIT: = *Automobile Association*) *Autofahrerorganisation*, ≈ ADAC *m*; (US: = *Associate in Art*) *akademischer Grad für Geisteswissenschaftler*; (= *Alcoholics Anonymous*) Anonyme Alkoholiker *pl*, AA *pl*

AAA N ABBR (= *American Automobile Association*) *Autofahrerorganisation*, ≈ ADAC *m*; (BRIT: = *Amateur Athletics Association*) *Leichtathletikverband der Amateure*

A & E N ABBR (= *Accident and Emergency*): **~ department** Notfallstation *f*, Notaufnahme *f*

abaci ['æbəsaɪ] NPL *of* **abacus**

aback [ə'bæk] ADV: **to be taken ~** verblüfft sein

abacus ['æbəkəs] *(pl* **abaci***)* N Abakus *m*

abandon [ə'bændən] VT verlassen; *(child)* aussetzen; *(give up)* aufgeben ▶ N *(wild behaviour)*: **with ~** selbstvergessen; **to ~ ship** das Schiff verlassen

abandoned [ə'bændənd] ADJ verlassen; *(child)* ausgesetzt; *(unrestrained)* selbstvergessen

abase [ə'beɪs] VT: **to ~ o.s.** sich erniedrigen; **to ~ o.s. so far as to do sth** sich dazu erniedrigen, etw zu tun

abashed [ə'bæʃt] ADJ verlegen

abate [ə'beɪt] VI nachlassen, sich legen

abatement [ə'beɪtmənt] N: **noise ~ society** Gesellschaft *f* zur Lärmbekämpfung

abattoir ['æbətwɑːʳ] (BRIT) N Schlachthof *m*

abbey ['æbɪ] N Abtei *f*

abbot ['æbət] N Abt *m*

abbreviate [ə'briːvɪeɪt] VT abkürzen; *(essay etc)* kürzen

abbreviation [əbriːvɪ'eɪʃən] N Abkürzung *f*

ABC N ABBR (= *American Broadcasting Companies*) *Fernsehsender* ▶ N Abc *nt*

abdicate ['æbdɪkeɪt] VT verzichten auf *+acc* ▶ VI *(monarch)* abdanken

abdication [æbdɪ'keɪʃən] N Verzicht *m*; Abdankung *f*

abdomen ['æbdəmɛn] N Unterleib *m*

abdominal [æb'dɔmɪnl] ADJ *(pain etc)* Unterleibs-

abduct [æb'dʌkt] VT entführen

abduction [æb'dʌkʃən] N Entführung *f*

Aberdonian [æbə'dəunɪən] ADJ *(Geog)* Aberdeener *inv* ▶ N Aberdeener(in) *m(f)*

aberration [æbə'reɪʃən] N Anomalie *f*; **in a moment of mental ~** in einem Augenblick geistiger Verwirrung

abet [ə'bɛt] VT *see* **aid**

abeyance [ə'beɪəns] N: **in ~** *(law)* außer Kraft; *(matter)* ruhend

abhor [əb'hɔːʳ] VT verabscheuen

abhorrent [əb'hɔrənt] ADJ abscheulich

abide [ə'baɪd] VT: **I can't ~ it/him** ich kann es/ihn nicht ausstehen

▶ **abide by** VT FUS sich halten an *+acc*

abiding [ə'baɪdɪŋ] ADJ *(memory, impression)* bleibend

ability [ə'bɪlɪtɪ] N Fähigkeit *f*; **to the best of my ~** so gut ich es kann

abject ['æbdʒɛkt] ADJ *(poverty)* bitter; *(apology)* demütig; *(coward)* erbärmlich

ablaze [ə'bleɪz] ADJ in Flammen; **~ with light** hell erleuchtet

able ['eɪbl] ADJ fähig; **to be ~ to do sth** etw tun können

able-bodied ['eɪbl'bɔdɪd] ADJ kräftig; **~ seaman** (BRIT) Vollmatrose *m*

ablutions [ə'bluːʃənz] NPL Waschungen *pl*

ably ['eɪblɪ] ADV gekonnt

ABM N ABBR (= *antiballistic missile*) Anti-Raketen-Rakete *f*
abnormal [æb'nɔ:məl] ADJ abnorm; (*child*) anormal
abnormality [æbnɔ:'mælɪtɪ] N Abnormität *f*
aboard [ə'bɔ:d] ADV (*Naut, Aviat*) an Bord ▸ PREP an Bord *+gen*; **~ the train/bus** im Zug/Bus
abode [ə'bəud] N (*Law*): **of no fixed ~** ohne festen Wohnsitz
abolish [ə'bɔlɪʃ] VT abschaffen
abolition [æbə'lɪʃən] N Abschaffung *f*
abominable [ə'bɔmɪnəbl] ADJ scheußlich
abominably [ə'bɔmɪnəblɪ] ADV scheußlich
Aborigine [æbə'rɪdʒɪnɪ] N Ureinwohner(in) *m(f)* Australiens
abort [ə'bɔ:t] VT abtreiben; (*Med: miscarry*) fehlgebären; (*Comput*) abbrechen
abortion [ə'bɔ:ʃən] N Abtreibung *f*; (*miscarriage*) Fehlgeburt *f*; **to have an ~** abtreiben lassen
abortionist [ə'bɔ:ʃənɪst] N Abtreibungshelfer(in) *m(f)*
abortive [ə'bɔ:tɪv] ADJ misslungen
abound [ə'baund] VI im Überfluss vorhanden sein; **to ~ in** *or* **with** reich sein an *+dat*

KEYWORD

about [ə'baut] ADV **1** (*approximately*) etwa, ungefähr; **about a hundred/thousand** *etc* etwa hundert/tausend *etc*; **at about two o'clock** etwa um zwei Uhr; **I've just about finished** ich bin gerade fertig
2 (*referring to place*) herum; **to run/walk** *etc* **about** herumlaufen/-gehen *etc*; **is Paul about?** ist Paul da?
3: **to be about to do sth** im Begriff sein, etw zu tun; **he was about to cry** er fing fast an zu weinen; **she was about to leave/wash the dishes** sie wollte gerade gehen/das Geschirr spülen
▸ PREP **1** (*relating to*) über *+acc*; **what is it about?** worum geht es?; (*book etc*) wovon handelt es?; **we talked about it** wir haben darüber geredet; **what** *or* **how about going to the cinema?** wollen wir ins Kino gehen?
2 (*referring to place*) um ... herum; **to walk about the town** durch die Stadt gehen; **her clothes were scattered about the room** ihre Kleider waren über das ganze Zimmer verstreut

about-face [ə'baut'feɪs] (*US*) N = **about-turn**
about-turn [ə'baut'tə:n] (BRIT) N Kehrtwendung *f*
above [ə'bʌv] ADV oben; (*greater, more*) darüber ▸ PREP über *+dat*; **to cost ~ £10** mehr als £10 kosten; **mentioned ~** oben genannt; **he's not ~ a bit of blackmail** er ist sich *dat* nicht zu gut für eine kleine Erpressung; **~ all** vor allem
above board ADJ korrekt
abrasion [ə'breɪʒən] N Abschürfung *f*
abrasive [ə'breɪzɪv] ADJ (*substance*) Scheuer-; (*person, manner*) aggressiv
abreast [ə'brɛst] ADV nebeneinander; **three ~** zu dritt nebeneinander; **to keep ~ of** (*fig*) auf dem Laufenden bleiben mit
abridge [ə'brɪdʒ] VT kürzen
abroad [ə'brɔ:d] ADV (*be*) im Ausland; (*go*) ins Ausland; **there is a rumour ~ that ...** (*fig*) ein Gerücht geht um *or* kursiert, dass ...
abrupt [ə'brʌpt] ADJ abrupt; (*person, behaviour*) schroff
abruptly [ə'brʌptlɪ] ADV abrupt
abscess ['æbsɪs] N Abszess *m*
abscond [əb'skɔnd] VI: **to ~ with** sich davonmachen mit; **to ~ (from)** fliehen (aus)
abseil ['æbseɪl] VI sich abseilen
absence ['æbsəns] N Abwesenheit *f*; **in the ~ of** (*person*) in Abwesenheit *+gen*; (*thing*) in Ermangelung *+gen*
absent ['æbsənt] ADJ abwesend, nicht da ▸ VT [æb'sənt]: **to ~ o.s. from** fernbleiben *+dat*; **to be ~** fehlen; **to be ~ without leave** (*Mil*) sich unerlaubt von der Truppe entfernen
absentee [æbsən'ti:] N Abwesende(r) *f(m)*
absenteeism [æbsən'ti:ɪzəm] N (*from school*) Schwänzen *nt*; (*from work*) Nichterscheinen *nt* am Arbeitsplatz
absent-minded ['æbsənt'maɪndɪd] ADJ zerstreut
absent-mindedly ['æbsənt'maɪndɪdlɪ] ADV zerstreut; (*look*) abwesend
absent-mindedness ['æbsənt'maɪndɪdnɪs] N Zerstreutheit *f*
absolute ['æbsəlu:t] ADJ absolut; (*power*) uneingeschränkt
absolutely [æbsə'lu:tlɪ] ADV absolut; (*agree*) vollkommen; **~!** genau!
absolution [æbsə'lu:ʃən] N Lossprechung *f*
absolve [əb'zɔlv] VT: **to ~ sb (from)** jdn lossprechen (von); (*responsibility*) jdn entbinden (von)
absorb [əb'zɔ:b] VT aufnehmen (*also fig*); (*light, heat*) absorbieren; (*group, business*) übernehmen; **to be absorbed in a book** in ein Buch vertieft sein
absorbent [əb'zɔ:bənt] ADJ saugfähig
absorbent cotton (*US*) N Watte *f*
absorbing [əb'zɔ:bɪŋ] ADJ saugfähig; (*book, film, work etc*) fesselnd
absorption [əb'sɔ:pʃən] N Aufnahme *f*; Absorption *f*; Übernahme *f*; (*interest*) Faszination *f*
abstain [əb'steɪn] VI (*voting*) sich (der Stimme) enthalten; **to ~ (from)** (*eating, drinking etc*) sich enthalten (*+gen*)
abstemious [əb'sti:mɪəs] ADJ enthaltsam
abstention [əb'stɛnʃən] N (Stimm)enthaltung *f*
abstinence ['æbstɪnəns] N Enthaltsamkeit *f*
abstract ['æbstrækt] ADJ abstrakt ▸ N (*summary*) Zusammenfassung *f* ▸ VT [æb'strækt]: **to ~ sth (from)** (*summarize*) etw entnehmen (aus); (*remove*) etw entfernen (aus)
abstruse [æb'stru:s] ADJ abstrus
absurd [əb'sə:d] ADJ absurd
absurdity [əb'sə:dɪtɪ] N Absurdität *f*
ABTA ['æbtə] N ABBR (= *Association of British Travel Agents*) *Verband der Reiseveranstalter*
Abu Dhabi ['æbu:'dɑ:bɪ] N (*Geog*) Abu Dhabi *nt*

abundance [ə'bʌndəns] N Reichtum *m*; **an ~ of** eine Fülle von; **in ~** in Hülle und Fülle
abundant [ə'bʌndənt] ADJ reichlich
abundantly [ə'bʌndəntlɪ] ADV reichlich; **~ clear** völlig klar
abuse [ə'bju:s] N (*insults*) Beschimpfungen *pl*; (*ill-treatment*) Misshandlung *f*; (*misuse*) Missbrauch *m* ▶ VT [ə'bju:z] beschimpfen; misshandeln; missbrauchen; **to be open to ~** sich leicht missbrauchen lassen
abuser [ə'bju:zəʳ] N (*also*: **drug abuser**) *jd, der Drogen missbraucht*; (*also*: **child abuser**) *jd, der Kinder missbraucht oder misshandelt*
abusive [ə'bju:sɪv] ADJ beleidigend
abysmal [ə'bɪzməl] ADJ entsetzlich; (*ignorance etc*) grenzenlos
abysmally [ə'bɪzməlɪ] ADV entsetzlich; grenzenlos
abyss [ə'bɪs] N Abgrund *m*
AC ABBR = **alternating current**; (*US*: = *athletic club*) ≈ SV *m*
a/c ABBR (*Banking etc*) = **account**; (= *current account*) Girokonto *nt*
academic [ækə'dɛmɪk] ADJ akademisch (*also pej*); (*work*) wissenschaftlich; (*person*) intellektuell ▶ N Akademiker(in) *m(f)*
academic year N (*university year*) Universitätsjahr *nt*; (*school year*) Schuljahr *nt*
academy [ə'kædəmɪ] N Akademie *f*; (*school*) Hochschule *f*; **~ of music** Musikhochschule *f*; **military/naval ~** Militär-/Marineakademie *f*
ACAS ['eɪkæs] (BRIT) N ABBR (= *Advisory Conciliation and Arbitration Service*) *Schlichtungsstelle für Arbeitskonflikte*
accede [æk'si:d] VI: **to ~ to** zustimmen +*dat*
accelerate [æk'sɛləreɪt] VT beschleunigen ▶ VI (*Aut*) Gas geben
acceleration [æksɛlə'reɪʃən] N Beschleunigung *f*
accelerator [æk'sɛləreɪtəʳ] N Gaspedal *nt*
accent ['æksɛnt] N Akzent *m*; (*fig*: *emphasis, stress*) Betonung *f*; **to speak with an Irish ~** mit einem irischen Akzent sprechen; **to have a strong ~** einen starken Akzent haben
accentuate [æk'sɛntjueɪt] VT betonen; (*need, difference etc*) hervorheben
accept [ək'sɛpt] VT annehmen; (*fact, situation*) sich abfinden mit; (*risk*) in Kauf nehmen; (*responsibility*) übernehmen; (*blame*) auf sich *acc* nehmen
acceptable [ək'sɛptəbl] ADJ annehmbar
acceptance [ək'sɛptəns] N Annahme *f*; **to meet with general ~** allgemeine Anerkennung finden
access ['æksɛs] N Zugang *m* ▶ VT (*Comput*) zugreifen auf +*acc*; **the burglars gained ~ through a window** die Einbrecher gelangten durch ein Fenster hinein
accessible [æk'sɛsəbl] ADJ erreichbar; (*knowledge, art etc*) zugänglich
accession [æk'sɛʃən] N Antritt *m*; (*of monarch*) Thronbesteigung *f*; (*to library*) Neuanschaffung *f*
accessory [æk'sɛsərɪ] N Zubehörteil *nt*; (*Dress*) Accessoire *nt*; (*Law*): **~ to** Mitschuldige(r) *f(m)* an +*dat*; **accessories** NPL Zubehör *nt*; **toilet accessories** (BRIT) Toilettenartikel *pl*
access road N Zufahrt(sstraße) *f*
access time N (*Comput*) Zugriffszeit *f*
accident ['æksɪdənt] N Zufall *m*; (*mishap, disaster*) Unfall *m*; **to meet with** *or* **to have an ~** einen Unfall haben, verunglücken; **accidents at work** Arbeitsunfälle *pl*; **by ~** zufällig
accidental [æksɪ'dɛntl] ADJ zufällig; (*death, damage*) Unfall-
accidentally [æksɪ'dɛntəlɪ] ADV zufällig
accident insurance N Unfallversicherung *f*
accident-prone ['æksɪdənt'prəun] ADJ vom Pech verfolgt
accident risk N Unfallrisiko *f*
acclaim [ə'kleɪm] N Beifall *m* ▶ VT: **to be acclaimed for one's achievements** für seine Leistungen gefeiert werden
acclamation [æklə'meɪʃən] N Anerkennung *f*; (*applause*) Beifall *m*
acclimate [ə'klaɪmət] (US) VT = **acclimatize**
acclimatize [ə'klaɪmətaɪz], (US) **acclimate** [ə'klaɪmət] VT: **to become acclimatized** sich akklimatisieren; **to become acclimatized to** sich gewöhnen an +*acc*
accolade ['ækəleɪd] N (*fig*) Auszeichnung *f*
accommodate [ə'kɔmədeɪt] VT unterbringen; (*subj*: *car, hotel etc*) Platz bieten +*dat*; (*oblige, help*) entgegenkommen +*dat*; **to ~ one's plans to** seine Pläne anpassen an +*acc*
accommodating [ə'kɔmədeɪtɪŋ] ADJ entgegenkommend
accommodation [əkɔmə'deɪʃən] N Unterkunft *f*; **accommodations** NPL (US) Unterkunft *f*; **have you any ~?** haben Sie eine Unterkunft?; **"~ to let"** „Zimmer zu vermieten"; **they have ~ for 500** sie können 500 Personen unterbringen; **the hall has seating ~ for 600** (BRIT) in dem Saal können 600 Personen sitzen
accompaniment [ə'kʌmpənɪmənt] N Begleitung *f*
accompanist [ə'kʌmpənɪst] N Begleiter(in) *m(f)*
accompany [ə'kʌmpənɪ] VT begleiten
accomplice [ə'kʌmplɪs] N Komplize *m*, Komplizin *f*
accomplish [ə'kʌmplɪʃ] VT vollenden; (*achieve*) erreichen
accomplished [ə'kʌmplɪʃt] ADJ ausgezeichnet
accomplishment [ə'kʌmplɪʃmənt] N Vollendung *f*; (*achievement*) Leistung *f*; (*skill*: *gen pl*) Fähigkeit *f*
accord [ə'kɔ:d] N Übereinstimmung *f*; (*treaty*) Vertrag *m* ▶ VT gewähren; **of his own ~** freiwillig; **with one ~** geschlossen; **to be in ~** übereinstimmen
accordance [ə'kɔ:dəns] N: **in ~ with** in Übereinstimmung mit
according [ə'kɔ:dɪŋ] PREP: **~ to** zufolge +*dat*; **~ to plan** wie geplant
accordingly [ə'kɔ:dɪŋlɪ] ADV entsprechend; (*as a result*) folglich

accordion [əˈkɔːdɪən] N Akkordeon *nt*
accost [əˈkɔst] VT ansprechen
account [əˈkaunt] N (*Comm: bill*) Rechnung *f*; (*in bank, department store*) Konto *nt*; (*report*) Bericht *m*; **accounts** NPL (*Comm*) Buchhaltung *f*; (*Bookkeeping*) (Geschäfts)bücher *pl*; **"~ payee only"** (BRIT) „nur zur Verrechnung"; **to keep an ~ of** Buch führen über *+acc*; **to bring sb to ~ for sth/for having embezzled £50,000** jdn für etw/für die Unterschlagung von £50.000 zur Rechenschaft ziehen; **by all accounts** nach allem, was man hört; **of no ~** ohne Bedeutung; **on ~** auf Kredit; **to pay £5 on ~** eine Anzahlung von £5 leisten; **on no ~** auf keinen Fall; **on ~ of** wegen *+gen*; **to take into ~, take ~ of** berücksichtigen
▸ **account for** VT FUS erklären; (*expenditure*) Rechenschaft ablegen für; (*represent*) ausmachen; **all the children were accounted for** man wusste, wo alle Kinder waren; **four people are still not accounted for** vier Personen werden immer noch vermisst
accountability [əkauntəˈbɪlɪtɪ] N Verantwortlichkeit *f*
accountable [əˈkauntəbl] ADJ: **~ (to)** verantwortlich (gegenüber *+dat*); **to be held ~ for sth** für etw verantwortlich gemacht werden
accountancy [əˈkauntənsɪ] N Buchhaltung *f*
accountant [əˈkauntənt] N Buchhalter(in) *m(f)*
accounting [əˈkauntɪŋ] N Buchhaltung *f*
accounting period N Abrechnungszeitraum *m*
account number N Kontonummer *f*
accounts payable NPL Verbindlichkeiten *pl*
accounts receivable NPL Forderungen *pl*
accredited [əˈkrɛdɪtɪd] ADJ anerkannt
accretion [əˈkriːʃən] N Ablagerung *f*
accrue [əˈkruː] VI sich ansammeln; **to ~ to** zufließen *+dat*
accrued interest [əˈkruːd-] N aufgelaufene Zinsen *pl*
accumulate [əˈkjuːmjuleɪt] VT ansammeln ▸ VI sich ansammeln
accumulation [əkjuːmjuˈleɪʃən] N Ansammlung *f*
accuracy [ˈækjurəsɪ] N Genauigkeit *f*
accurate [ˈækjurɪt] ADJ genau
accurately [ˈækjurɪtlɪ] ADV genau; (*answer*) richtig
accusation [ækjuˈzeɪʃən] N Vorwurf *m*; (*instance*) Beschuldigung *f*; (*Law*) Anklage *f*
accusative [əˈkjuːzətɪv] N Akkusativ *m*
accuse [əˈkjuːz] VT: **to ~ sb (of sth)** jdn (einer Sache *gen*) beschuldigen; (*Law*) jdn (wegen etw *dat*) anklagen
accused [əˈkjuːzd] N (*Law*): **the ~** der/die Angeklagte
accuser [əˈkjuːzə^r] N Ankläger(in) *m(f)*
accusing [əˈkjuːzɪŋ] ADJ anklagend
accustom [əˈkʌstəm] VT gewöhnen; **to ~ o.s. to sth** sich an etw *acc* gewöhnen
accustomed [əˈkʌstəmd] ADJ gewohnt; (*in the habit*): **~ to** gewohnt an *+acc*
AC/DC ABBR (= *alternating current/direct current*) WS/GS
ACE [eɪs] N ABBR (= *American Council on Education*) *akademischer Verband für das Erziehungswesen*
ace [eɪs] N Ass *nt*
acerbic [əˈsəːbɪk] ADJ scharf
acetate [ˈæsɪteɪt] N Acetat *nt*
ache [eɪk] N Schmerz *m* ▸ VI schmerzen, wehtun; (*yearn*): **to ~ to do sth** sich danach sehnen, etw zu tun; **I've got (a) stomach ~** ich habe Magenschmerzen; **I'm aching all over** mir tut alles weh; **my head aches** mir tut der Kopf weh
achieve [əˈtʃiːv] VT (*aim, result*) erreichen; (*success*) erzielen; (*victory*) erringen
achievement [əˈtʃiːvmənt] N (*act of achieving*) Erreichen *nt*; (*success, feat*) Leistung *f*
Achilles heel [əˈkɪliːz-] N Achillesferse *f*
acid [ˈæsɪd] ADJ sauer ▸ N (*Chem*) Säure *f*; (*inf: LSD*) Acid *nt*
Acid House N Acid House *nt*, *elektronische Funk-Diskomusik*
acidic [əˈsɪdɪk] ADJ sauer
acidity [əˈsɪdɪtɪ] N Säure *f*
acid rain N saurer Regen *m*
acid test N (*fig*) Feuerprobe *f*
acknowledge [əkˈnɔlɪdʒ] VT (*also:* **acknowledge receipt of**) den Empfang *+gen* bestätigen; (*fact*) zugeben; (*situation*) zur Kenntnis nehmen; (*person*) grüßen
acknowledgement [əkˈnɔlɪdʒmənt] N Empfangsbestätigung *f*; **acknowledgements** NPL (*in book*) ≈ Danksagung *f*
ACLU N ABBR (= *American Civil Liberties Union*) *Bürgerrechtsverband*
acme [ˈækmɪ] N Gipfel *m*, Höhepunkt *m*
acne [ˈæknɪ] N Akne *f*
acorn [ˈeɪkɔːn] N Eichel *f*
acoustic [əˈkuːstɪk] ADJ akustisch
acoustic coupler N (*Comput*) Akustikkoppler *m*
acoustics [əˈkuːstɪks] N Akustik *f*
acoustic screen N Trennwand *f* zur Schalldämpfung
acquaint [əˈkweɪnt] VT: **to ~ sb with sth** jdn mit etw vertraut machen; **to be acquainted with** (*person*) bekannt sein mit; (*fact*) vertraut sein mit
acquaintance [əˈkweɪntəns] N Bekannte(r) *f(m)*; (*with person*) Bekanntschaft *f*; (*with subject*) Kenntnis *f*; **to make sb's ~** jds Bekanntschaft machen
acquiesce [ækwɪˈɛs] VI einwilligen; **to ~ (to)** (*demand, arrangement, request*) einwilligen (in *+acc*)
acquire [əˈkwaɪə^r] VT erwerben; (*interest*) entwickeln; (*habit*) annehmen
acquired [əˈkwaɪəd] ADJ erworben; **whisky is an ~ taste** man muss sich an Whisky erst gewöhnen
acquisition [ækwɪˈzɪʃən] N (*of skills*) Erwerb *m*; (*object*) Anschaffung *f*
acquisitive [əˈkwɪzɪtɪv] ADJ habgierig; **the ~ society** die Erwerbsgesellschaft
acquit [əˈkwɪt] VT freisprechen; **to ~ o.s. well** seine Sache gut machen

acquittal [əˈkwɪtl] N Freispruch *m*
acre [ˈeɪkəʳ] N Morgen *m*
acreage [ˈeɪkərɪdʒ] N Fläche *f*
acrid [ˈækrɪd] ADJ bitter; (*smoke, fig*) beißend
acrimonious [ækrɪˈməunɪəs] ADJ bitter; (*dispute*) erbittert
acrimony [ˈækrɪmənɪ] N Erbitterung *f*
acrobat [ˈækrəbæt] N Akrobat(in) *m(f)*
acrobatic [ækrəˈbætɪk] ADJ akrobatisch
acrobatics [ækrəˈbætɪks] NPL Akrobatik *f*
acronym [ˈækrənɪm] N Akronym *nt*
Acropolis [əˈkrɔpəlɪs] N: **the ~** (*Geog*) die Akropolis
across [əˈkrɔs] PREP über *+acc*; (*on the other side of*) auf der anderen Seite *+gen* ▶ ADV (*direction*) hinüber, herüber; (*measurement*) breit; **to take sb ~ the road** jdn über die Straße bringen; **a road ~ the wood** eine Straße durch den Wald; **the lake is 12 km ~** der See ist 12 km breit; **~ from** gegenüber *+dat*; **to get sth ~ (to sb)** (jdm) etw klarmachen
acrylic [əˈkrɪlɪk] ADJ (*acid, paint, blanket*) Acryl- ▶ N Acryl *nt*; **acrylics** NPL: **he paints in acrylics** er malt mit Acrylfarbe
ACT® N ABBR (= *American College Test*) *Eignungstest für Studienbewerber*
act [ækt] N Tat *f*; (*of play*) Akt *m*; (*in a show etc*) Nummer *f*; (*Law*) Gesetz *nt* ▶ VI handeln; (*behave*) sich verhalten; (*have effect*) wirken; (*Theat*) spielen ▶ VT spielen; **it's only an ~** es ist nur Schau; **~ of God** (*Law*) höhere Gewalt *f*; **to be in the ~ of doing sth** dabei sein, etw zu tun; **to catch sb in the ~** jdn auf frischer Tat ertappen; **to ~ the fool** (BRIT) herumalbern; **he is only acting** er tut (doch) nur so; **to ~ as** fungieren als; **it acts as a deterrent** es dient zur Abschreckung
▶ **act on** VT: **to ~ on sth** (*take action*) auf etw *+acc* hin handeln
▶ **act out** VT (*event*) durchspielen; (*fantasies*) zum Ausdruck bringen
acting [ˈæktɪŋ] ADJ stellvertretend ▶ N (*profession*) Schauspielkunst *f*; (*activity*) Spielen *nt*; **~ in my capacity as chairman …** in meiner Eigenschaft als Vorsitzender …
action [ˈækʃən] N Tat *f*; (*motion*) Bewegung *f*; (*Mil*) Kampf *m*, Gefecht *nt*; (*Law*) Klage *f* ▶ VT (*Comm*) in die Tat umsetzen; **to bring an ~ against sb** (*Law*) eine Klage gegen jdn anstrengen; **killed in ~** (*Mil*) gefallen; **out of ~** (*person*) nicht einsatzfähig; (*thing*) außer Betrieb; **to take ~** etwas unternehmen; **to put a plan into ~** einen Plan in die Tat umsetzen
action replay N (TV) Wiederholung *f*
activate [ˈæktɪveɪt] VT in Betrieb setzen; (*Chem, Phys*) aktivieren
active [ˈæktɪv] ADJ aktiv; (*volcano*) tätig; **to play an ~ part in sth** sich aktiv an etw *dat* beteiligen
active duty (US) N (*Mil*) Einsatz *m*
actively [ˈæktɪvlɪ] ADV aktiv; (*dislike*) offen
active partner N (*Comm*) aktiver Teilhaber *m*
active service (BRIT) N (*Mil*) Einsatz *m*
active suspension N (*Aut*) aktives *or* computergesteuertes Fahrwerk *nt*
activist [ˈæktɪvɪst] N Aktivist(in) *m(f)*
activity [ækˈtɪvɪtɪ] N Aktivität *f*; (*pastime, pursuit*) Betätigung *f*
activity holiday N Aktivurlaub *m*
actor [ˈæktəʳ] N Schauspieler *m*
actress [ˈæktrɪs] N Schauspielerin *f*
actual [ˈæktjuəl] ADJ wirklich; (*emphatic use*) eigentlich
actually [ˈæktjuəlɪ] ADV wirklich; (*in fact*) tatsächlich; (*even*) sogar
actuary [ˈæktjuərɪ] N Aktuar *m*
actuate [ˈæktjueɪt] VT auslösen
acuity [əˈkjuːɪtɪ] N Schärfe *f*
acumen [ˈækjumən] N Scharfsinn *m*; **business ~** Geschäftssinn *m*
acupuncture [ˈækjupʌŋktʃəʳ] N Akupunktur *f*
acute [əˈkjuːt] ADJ akut; (*anxiety*) heftig; (*mind*) scharf; (*person*) scharfsinnig; (*Math: angle*) spitz; (*Ling*): **~ accent** Akut *m*
AD ADV ABBR (= *Anno Domini*) n. Chr. ▶ N ABBR (*US Mil*) = **active duty**
ad [æd] (*inf*) N = **advertisement**
adage [ˈædɪdʒ] N Sprichwort *nt*
adamant [ˈædəmənt] ADJ: **to be ~ that …** darauf bestehen, dass …; **to be ~ about sth** auf etw *dat* bestehen
Adam's apple [ˈædəmz-] N Adamsapfel *m*
adapt [əˈdæpt] VT anpassen; (*novel etc*) bearbeiten ▶ VI: **to ~ (to)** sich anpassen (an *+acc*)
adaptability [ədæptəˈbɪlɪtɪ] N Anpassungsfähigkeit *f*
adaptable [əˈdæptəbl] ADJ anpassungsfähig; (*device*) vielseitig
adaptation [ædæpˈteɪʃən] N (*of novel etc*) Bearbeitung *f*; (*of machine etc*) Umstellung *f*
adapter [əˈdæptəʳ] N (*Elec*) Adapter *m*; (*: for several plugs*) Mehrfachsteckdose *f*
adaptor [əˈdæptəʳ] N = **adapter**
ADC N ABBR (*Mil*) = **aide-de-camp**; (US: = *Aid to Dependent Children*) *Beihilfe für sozialschwache Familien*
add [æd] VT hinzufügen; (*figures*: *also*: **add up**) zusammenzählen ▶ VI: **to ~ to** (*increase*) beitragen zu ▶ N (*Internet*): **thanks for the ~** danke fürs Adden *or* Hinzufügen
▶ **add on** VT (*amount*) dazurechnen; (*room*) anbauen
▶ **add up** VT (*figures*) zusammenzählen ▶ VI: **it doesn't ~ up** (*fig*) es ergibt keinen Sinn; **it doesn't ~ up to much** (*fig*) das ist nicht berühmt (*inf*)
addenda [əˈdɛndə] NPL *of* **addendum**
addendum [əˈdɛndəm] (*pl* **addenda**) N Nachtrag *m*
adder [ˈædəʳ] N Kreuzotter *f*, Viper *f*
addict [ˈædɪkt] N Süchtige(r) *f(m)*; (*enthusiast*) Anhänger(in) *m(f)*
addicted [əˈdɪktɪd] ADJ: **to be ~ to drugs/drink** drogensüchtig/alkoholsüchtig sein; **to be ~ to football** (*fig*) ohne Fußball nicht mehr leben können

a

addiction [ə'dɪkʃən] N Sucht *f*
addictive [ə'dɪktɪv] ADJ: **to be ~** (*drug*) süchtig machen; (*activity*) zur Sucht werden können
adding machine ['ædɪŋ-] N Addiermaschine *f*
Addis Ababa ['ædɪs'æbəbə] N (*Geog*) Addis Abeba *nt*
addition [ə'dɪʃən] N (*adding up*) Zusammenzählen *nt*; (*thing added*) Zusatz *m*; (*: to payment, bill*) Zuschlag *m*; (*: to building*) Anbau *m*; **in ~ (to)** zusätzlich (zu)
additional [ə'dɪʃənl] ADJ zusätzlich
additive ['ædɪtɪv] N Zusatz *m*
addled ['ædld] ADJ (BRIT: *egg*) faul; (*brain*) verwirrt
address [ə'drɛs] N Adresse *f*; (*speech*) Ansprache *f* ▸ VT adressieren; (*speak to: person*) ansprechen; (*: audience*) sprechen zu; **form of ~** (Form *f* der) Anrede *f*; **what form of ~ do you use for ...?** wie redet man ... an?; **absolute/relative ~** (*Comput*) absolute/relative Adresse; **to ~ (o.s. to)** (*problem*) sich befassen mit
address book N Adressbuch *nt*
addressee [ædrɛ'si:] N Empfänger(in) *m(f)*
Aden ['eɪdən] N (*Geog*): **Gulf of ~** Golf *m* von Aden
adenoids ['ædɪnɔɪdz] NPL Rachenmandeln *pl*
adept ['ædɛpt] ADJ: **to be ~ at** gut sein in *+dat*
adequacy ['ædɪkwəsɪ] N (*of resources*) Adäquatheit *f*; (*of performance, proposals etc*) Angemessenheit *f*
adequate ['ædɪkwɪt] ADJ ausreichend, adäquat; (*satisfactory*) angemessen
adequately ['ædɪkwɪtlɪ] ADV ausreichend; (*satisfactorily*) zufriedenstellend
adhere [əd'hɪə^r] VI: **to ~ to** haften an *+dat*; (*fig: abide by*) sich halten an *+acc*; (*: hold to*) festhalten an *+dat*
adhesion [əd'hi:ʒən] N Haften *nt*, Haftung *f*
adhesive [əd'hi:zɪv] ADJ klebend, Klebe- ▸ N Klebstoff *m*
adhesive tape N (BRIT) Klebstreifen *m*; (*US Med*) Heftpflaster *nt*
ad hoc [æd'hɔk] ADJ (*committee, decision*) Ad-hoc- ▸ ADV ad hoc
ad infinitum ['ædɪnfɪ'naɪtəm] ADV ad infinitum
adjacent [ə'dʒeɪsənt] ADJ: **~ to** neben *+dat*
adjective ['ædʒɛktɪv] N Adjektiv *nt*, Eigenschaftswort *nt*
adjoin [ə'dʒɔɪn] VT: **the hotel adjoining the station** das Hotel neben dem Bahnhof
adjoining [ə'dʒɔɪnɪŋ] ADJ benachbart, Neben-
adjourn [ə'dʒə:n] VT vertagen ▸ VI sich vertagen; **to ~ a meeting till the following week** eine Besprechung auf die nächste Woche vertagen; **they adjourned to the pub** (BRIT *inf*) sie begaben sich in die Kneipe
adjournment [ə'dʒə:nmənt] N Unterbrechung *f*
Adjt. ABBR (*Mil*) = **adjutant**
adjudicate [ə'dʒu:dɪkeɪt] VT (*contest*) Preisrichter sein bei; (*claim*) entscheiden ▸ VI entscheiden; **to ~ on** urteilen bei *+dat*
adjudication [ədʒu:dɪ'keɪʃən] N Entscheidung *f*
adjudicator [ə'dju:dɪkeɪtə^r] N Schiedsrichter(in) *m(f)*; (*in contest*) Preisrichter(in) *m(f)*
adjust [ə'dʒʌst] VT anpassen; (*change*) ändern; (*clothing*) zurechtrücken; (*machine etc*) einstellen; (*Insurance*) regulieren ▸ VI: **to ~ (to)** sich anpassen (an *+acc*)
adjustable [ə'dʒʌstəbl] ADJ verstellbar
adjuster [ə'dʒʌstə^r] N *see* **loss**
adjustment [ə'dʒʌstmənt] N Anpassung *f*; (*to machine*) Einstellung *f*
adjutant ['ædʒətənt] N Adjutant *m*
ad-lib [æd'lɪb] VI, VT improvisieren ▸ ADV: **ad lib** aus dem Stegreif
adman ['ædmæn] (*inf*) N (*irreg*) Werbefachmann *m*
admin ['ædmɪn] (*inf*) N = **administration**
administer [əd'mɪnɪstə^r] VT (*country, department*) verwalten; (*justice*) sprechen; (*oath*) abnehmen; (*Med: drug*) verabreichen
administration [ədmɪnɪs'treɪʃən] N (*management*) Verwaltung *f*; (*government*) Regierung *f*; **the A~** (*US*) die Regierung
administrative [əd'mɪnɪstrətɪv] ADJ (*department, reform etc*) Verwaltungs-
administrator [əd'mɪnɪstreɪtə^r] N Verwaltungsbeamte(r) *m*, Verwaltungsbeamtin *f*
admirable ['ædmərəbl] ADJ bewundernswert
admiral ['ædmərəl] N Admiral *m*
Admiralty ['ædmərəltɪ] (BRIT) N (*also*: **the Admiralty Board**) das Marineministerium
admiration [ædmə'reɪʃən] N Bewunderung *f*; **to have great ~ for sb/sth** jdn/etw sehr bewundern
admire [əd'maɪə^r] VT bewundern
admirer [əd'maɪərə^r] N (*suitor*) Verehrer *m*; (*fan*) Bewunderer *m*, Bewunderin *f*
admiring [əd'maɪərɪŋ] ADJ bewundernd
admissible [əd'mɪsəbl] ADJ (*evidence, as evidence*) zulässig
admission [əd'mɪʃən] N (*admittance*) Zutritt *m*; (*to exhibition, night club etc*) Einlass *m*; (*to club, hospital*) Aufnahme *f*; (*entry fee*) Eintritt(spreis) *m*; (*confession*) Geständnis *nt*; **"~ free", "free ~"** „Eintritt frei"; **by his own ~** nach eigenem Eingeständnis
admission charge, admission fee N Eintrittspreis *m*
admit [əd'mɪt] VT (*confess*) gestehen; (*permit to enter*) einlassen; (*to club, hospital*) aufnehmen; (*responsibility etc*) anerkennen; **"children not admitted"** „kein Zutritt für Kinder"; **this ticket admits two** diese Karte ist für zwei Personen; **I must ~ that ...** ich muss zugeben, dass ...; **to ~ defeat** sich geschlagen geben
▸ **admit of** VT FUS (*interpretation etc*) erlauben
▸ **admit to** VT FUS (*murder etc*) gestehen
admittance [əd'mɪtəns] N Zutritt *m*; **"no ~"** „kein Zutritt"
admittedly [əd'mɪtɪdlɪ] ADV zugegebenermaßen
admonish [əd'mɔnɪʃ] VT ermahnen
ad nauseam [æd'nɔ:sɪæm] ADV (*talk*) endlos; (*repeat*) bis zum Gehtnichtmehr (*inf*)

ado [ə'du:] N: **without (any) more ~** ohne weitere Umstände
adolescence [ædəu'lɛsns] N Jugend *f*
adolescent [ædəu'lɛsnt] ADJ heranwachsend; (*remark, behaviour*) pubertär ▶ N Jugendliche(r) *f*(*m*)
adopt [ə'dɔpt] VT adoptieren; (*Pol: candidate*) aufstellen; (*policy, attitude, accent*) annehmen
adopted [ə'dɔptɪd] ADJ (*child*) adoptiert
adoption [ə'dɔpʃən] N Adoption *f*; Aufstellung *f*; Annahme *f*
adoptive [ə'dɔptɪv] ADJ (*parents etc*) Adoptiv-; **~ country** Wahlheimat *f*
adorable [ə'dɔ:rəbl] ADJ entzückend
adoration [ædə'reɪʃən] N Verehrung *f*
adore [ə'dɔ:ʳ] VT (*person*) verehren; (*film, activity etc*) schwärmen für
adoring [ə'dɔ:rɪŋ] ADJ (*fans etc*) ihn/sie bewundernd; (*husband/wife*) sie/ihn innig liebend
adoringly [ə'dɔ:rɪŋlɪ] ADV bewundernd
adorn [ə'dɔ:n] VT schmücken
adornment [ə'dɔ:nmənt] N Schmuck *m*
ADP N ABBR = **automatic data processing**
adrenalin [ə'drɛnəlɪn] N Adrenalin *nt*; **it gets the ~ going** das bringt einen in Fahrt
Adriatic [eɪdrɪ'ætɪk] N: **the ~ (Sea)** (*Geog*) die Adria, das Adriatische Meer
adrift [ə'drɪft] ADV (*Naut*) treibend; (*fig*) ziellos; **to be ~** (*Naut*) treiben; **to come ~** (*boat*) sich losmachen; (*fastening etc*) sich lösen
adroit [ə'drɔɪt] ADJ gewandt
adroitly [ə'drɔɪtlɪ] ADV gewandt
ADSL ABBR (= *asymmetric digital subscriber line*) ADSL *nt*
ADT (US) ABBR (= *Atlantic Daylight Time*) *atlantische Sommerzeit*
adulation [ædju'leɪʃən] N Verherrlichung *f*
adult ['ædʌlt] N Erwachsene(r) *f*(*m*) ▶ ADJ erwachsen; (*animal*) ausgewachsen; (*literature etc*) für Erwachsene
adult education N Erwachsenenbildung *f*
adulterate [ə'dʌltəreɪt] VT verunreinigen; (*with water*) panschen
adulterer [ə'dʌltərəʳ] N Ehebrecher *m*
adulteress [ə'dʌltərɪs] N Ehebrecherin *f*
adultery [ə'dʌltərɪ] N Ehebruch *m*
adulthood ['ædʌlthud] N Erwachsenenalter *nt*
advance [əd'vɑ:ns] N (*movement*) Vorrücken *nt*; (*progress*) Fortschritt *m*; (*money*) Vorschuss *m* ▶ VT (*money*) vorschießen; (*theory, idea*) vorbringen ▶ VI (*move forward*) vorrücken; (*make progress*) Fortschritte machen ▶ ADJ: **~ booking** Vorverkauf *m*; **~ payment** Vorauszahlung *f*; **to make advances (to sb)** Annäherungsversuche (bei jdm) machen; **in ~** im Voraus; **to give sb ~ notice** jdm frühzeitig Bescheid sagen; **to give sb ~ warning** jdn vorwarnen
advanced [əd'vɑ:nst] ADJ (*Scol: studies*) für Fortgeschrittene; (*country*) fortgeschritten; (*child*) weit entwickelt; (*ideas*) fortschrittlich; **~ in years** in fortgeschrittenem Alter
Advanced Higher (Scot) N (*Scol*) *Mit „Advanced Higher" wird das Ausbildungsjahr nach „Higher" bezeichnet, dessen erfolgreicher Abschluss eine Hochschulzugangsberechtigung darstellt*
advancement [əd'vɑ:nsmənt] N (*improvement*) Förderung *f*; (*in job, rank*) Aufstieg *m*
advantage [əd'vɑ:ntɪdʒ] N Vorteil *m*; **to take ~ of** ausnutzen; (*opportunity*) nutzen; **it's to our ~ (to)** es ist für uns von Vorteil(, wenn wir)
advantageous [ædvən'teɪdʒəs] ADJ: **~ (to)** vorteilhaft (für), von Vorteil (für)
advent ['ædvənt] N (*of innovation*) Aufkommen *nt*; (*Rel*): **A~** Advent *m*
Advent calendar N Adventskalender *m*
adventure [əd'vɛntʃəʳ] N Abenteuer *nt*
adventure holiday N Abenteuerurlaub *m*
adventure playground N Abenteuerspielplatz *m*
adventurous [əd'vɛntʃərəs] ADJ abenteuerlustig; (*bold*) mutig
adverb ['ædvə:b] N Adverb *nt*
adversarial [ædvə'sɛərɪəl] ADJ konfliktreich
adversary ['ædvəsərɪ] N Widersacher(in) *m*(*f*)
adverse ['ædvə:s] ADJ ungünstig; **in ~ circumstances** unter widrigen Umständen; **~ to** ablehnend gegenüber *+dat*
adversity [əd'və:sɪtɪ] N Widrigkeit *f*
advert ['ædvə:t] (Brit) N = **advertisement**
advertise ['ædvətaɪz] VI (*Comm*) werben; (*in newspaper*) annoncieren, inserieren ▶ VT (*product, event*) werben für; (*job*) ausschreiben; **to ~ for** (*staff, accommodation etc*) (per Anzeige) suchen
advertisement [əd'və:tɪsmənt] N (*Comm*) Werbung *f*, Reklame *f*; (*in classified ads*) Anzeige *f*, Inserat *nt*
advertiser ['ædvətaɪzəʳ] N (*in newspaper*) Inserent(in) *m*(*f*); (*on television etc*) Firma, die im Fernsehen *etc* wirbt
advertising ['ædvətaɪzɪŋ] N Werbung *f*
advertising agency N Werbeagentur *f*
advertising campaign N Werbekampagne *f*
advice [əd'vaɪs] N Rat *m*; (*notification*) Benachrichtigung *f*, Avis *m or nt* (*Comm*); **a piece of ~** ein Rat(schlag); **to ask sb for ~** jdn um Rat fragen; **to take legal ~** einen Rechtsanwalt zurate ziehen
advice note (Brit) N (*Comm*) Avis *m or nt*
advisable [əd'vaɪzəbl] ADJ ratsam
advise [əd'vaɪz] VT (*person*) raten *+dat*; (*company etc*) beraten; **to ~ sb of sth** jdn von etw in Kenntnis setzen; **to ~ against sth** von etw abraten; **to ~ against doing sth** davon abraten, etw zu tun; **you would be well-/ill-advised to go** Sie wären gut/schlecht beraten, wenn Sie gingen
advisedly [əd'vaɪzɪdlɪ] ADV bewusst
adviser [əd'vaɪzəʳ] N Berater(in) *m*(*f*)
advisor [əd'vaɪzəʳ] N = **adviser**
advisory [əd'vaɪzərɪ] ADJ beratend, Beratungs-; **in an ~ capacity** in beratender Funktion
advocate ['ædvəkeɪt] VT befürworten ▶ N (*Law*) (Rechts)anwalt *m*, (Rechts)anwältin *f*; (*supporter, upholder*): **~ of** Befürworter(in) *m*(*f*) *+gen*; **to be an ~ of sth** etw befürworten

advt. ABBR = **advertisement**
AEA (BRIT) N ABBR (= *Atomic Energy Authority*) *britische Atomenergiebehörde*; (BRIT *Scol*: = *Advanced Extension Award*) *eine besondere Qualifikation für leistungsstarke Schüler des „A level"*
AEC (US) N ABBR (= *Atomic Energy Commission*) *amerikanische Atomenergiebehörde*
AEEU (BRIT) N ABBR (= *Amalgamated Engineering and Electrical Union*) *Gewerkschaft der Ingenieure und Elektriker*
Aegean [iːˈdʒiːən] N: **the ~ (Sea)** (*Geog*) die Ägäis, das Ägäische Meer
aegis [ˈiːdʒɪs] N: **under the ~ of** unter der Schirmherrschaft *+gen*
aeon [ˈiːən] N Äon *m*, Ewigkeit *f*
aerial [ˈɛərɪəl] N Antenne *f* ▶ ADJ (*view, bombardment etc*) Luft-
aero... [ˈɛərə(u)] PREF Luft-
aerobatics [ˈɛərəuˈbætɪks] NPL fliegerische Kunststücke *pl*
aerobics [ɛəˈrəubɪks] N Aerobic *nt*
aerodrome [ˈɛərədrəum] (BRIT) N Flugplatz *m*
aerodynamic [ˈɛərəudaɪˈnæmɪk] ADJ aerodynamisch
aeronautics [ɛərəˈnɔːtɪks] N Luftfahrt *f*, Aeronautik *f*
aeroplane [ˈɛərəpleɪn] (BRIT) N Flugzeug *nt*
aerosol [ˈɛərəsɔl] N Sprühdose *f*
aerospace industry [ˈɛərəuspeɪs-] N Raumfahrtindustrie *f*
aesthetic [iːsˈθɛtɪk] ADJ ästhetisch
aesthetically [iːsˈθɛtɪklɪ] ADV ästhetisch
afaik ABBR (*SMS*: = *as far as I know*) ≈ soweit ich weiß
afar [əˈfɑːʳ] ADV: **from ~** aus der Ferne
AFB (US) N ABBR (= *Air Force Base*) Luftwaffenstützpunkt *m*
affable [ˈæfəbl] ADJ umgänglich, freundlich
affair [əˈfɛəʳ] N Angelegenheit *f*; (*romance*: *also*: **love affair**) Verhältnis *nt*; **affairs** NPL Geschäfte *pl*
affect [əˈfɛkt] VT (*influence*) sich auswirken auf *+acc*; (*subj*: *disease*) befallen; (*move deeply*) bewegen; (*concern*) betreffen; (*feign*) vortäuschen; **to be affected by sth** von etw beeinflusst werden
affectation [æfɛkˈteɪʃən] N Affektiertheit *f*
affected [əˈfɛktɪd] ADJ affektiert
affection [əˈfɛkʃən] N Zuneigung *f*
affectionate [əˈfɛkʃənɪt] ADJ liebevoll, zärtlich; (*animal*) anhänglich
affectionately [əˈfɛkʃənɪtlɪ] ADV liebevoll, zärtlich
affidavit [æfɪˈdeɪvɪt] N (*Law*) eidesstattliche Erklärung *f*
affiliated [əˈfɪlɪeɪtɪd] ADJ angeschlossen
affinity [əˈfɪnɪtɪ] N: **to have an ~ with** *or* **for** sich verbunden fühlen mit; (*resemblance*): **to have an ~ with** verwandt sein mit
affirm [əˈfəːm] VT versichern; (*profess*) sich bekennen zu
affirmation [æfəˈmeɪʃən] N (*of facts*) Bestätigung *f*; (*of beliefs*) Bekenntnis *nt*
affirmative [əˈfəːmətɪv] ADJ bejahend ▶ N: **to reply in the ~** mit „Ja" antworten
affix [əˈfɪks] VT aufkleben
afflict [əˈflɪkt] VT quälen; (*misfortune*) heimsuchen
affliction [əˈflɪkʃən] N Leiden *nt*
affluence [ˈæfluəns] N Wohlstand *m*
affluent [ˈæfluənt] ADJ wohlhabend; **the ~ society** die Wohlstandsgesellschaft
afford [əˈfɔːd] VT sich *dat* leisten; (*time*) aufbringen; (*provide*) bieten; **can we ~ a car?** können wir uns ein Auto leisten?; **I can't ~ the time** ich habe einfach nicht die Zeit
affordable [əˈfɔːdəbl] ADJ erschwinglich
affray [əˈfreɪ] (BRIT) N Schlägerei *f*
affront [əˈfrʌnt] N Beleidigung *f*
affronted [əˈfrʌntɪd] ADJ beleidigt
Afghan [ˈæfgæn] ADJ afghanisch ▶ N Afghane *m*, Afghanin *f*
Afghanistan [æfˈgænɪstæn] N Afghanistan *nt*
afield [əˈfiːld] ADV: **far ~** weit fort; **from far ~** aus weiter Ferne
AFL-CIO N ABBR (= *American Federation of Labor and Congress of Industrial Organizations*) *amerikanischer Gewerkschafts-Dachverband*
afloat [əˈfləut] ADV auf dem Wasser ▶ ADJ: **to be ~** schwimmen; **to stay ~** sich über Wasser halten; **to keep/get a business ~** ein Geschäft über Wasser halten/auf die Beine stellen
afoot [əˈfut] ADV: **there is something ~** da ist etwas im Gang
aforementioned [əˈfɔːmɛnʃənd] ADJ oben erwähnt
aforesaid [əˈfɔːsɛd] ADJ = **aforementioned**
afraid [əˈfreɪd] ADJ ängstlich; **to be ~ of** Angst haben vor *+dat*; **to be ~ of doing sth** *or* **to do sth** Angst davor haben, etw zu tun; **to be ~ to** sich scheuen, ...; **I am ~ that ...** leider ...; **I am ~ so/not** leider ja/nein
afresh [əˈfrɛʃ] ADV von Neuem, neu
Africa [ˈæfrɪkə] N Afrika *nt*
African [ˈæfrɪkən] ADJ afrikanisch ▶ N Afrikaner(in) *m(f)*
African American, Afro-American [ˈæfrəuəˈmɛrɪkən] ADJ afro-amerikanisch ▶ N Afroamerikaner(in) *m(f)*
Afrikaans [æfrɪˈkɑːns] N Afrikaans *nt*
Afrikaner [æfrɪˈkɑːnəʳ] N Afrika(a)nder(in) *m(f)*
AFT (US) N ABBR (= *American Federation of Teachers*) *Lehrergewerkschaft*
aft [ɑːft] ADV (*be*) achtern; (*go*) nach achtern
after [ˈɑːftəʳ] PREP nach *+dat*; (*of place*) hinter *+dat* ▶ ADV danach ▶ CONJ nachdem; **~ dinner** nach dem Essen; **the day ~ tomorrow** übermorgen; **what are you ~?** was willst du; **who are you ~?** wen suchst du?; **the police are ~ him** die Polizei ist hinter ihm her; **to name sb ~ sb** jdn nach jdm nennen; **it's twenty ~ eight** (US) es ist zwanzig nach acht; **to ask ~ sb** nach jdm fragen; **~ all** schließlich; **~ you!** nach Ihnen!; **~ he left** nachdem er gegangen war; **~ having shaved** nachdem er sich rasiert hatte
afterbirth [ˈɑːftəbəːθ] N Nachgeburt *f*

aftercare ['ɑ:ftəkɛə^r] (BRIT) N Nachbehandlung *f*
aftereffects ['ɑ:ftərɪfɛkts] NPL Nachwirkungen *pl*
afterlife ['ɑ:ftəlaɪf] N Leben *nt* nach dem Tod
aftermath ['ɑ:ftəmɑ:θ] N Auswirkungen *pl*; **in the ~ of** nach *+dat*
afternoon ['ɑ:ftə'nu:n] N Nachmittag *m*
afternoon market N (*Econ*) Nachmittagsmarkt *m*
afterparty ['ɑ:ftəpɑ:tɪ] N anschließende Feier *f*
afters ['ɑ:ftəz] (BRIT *inf*) N Nachtisch *m*
after-sales service [ɑ:ftə'seɪlz-] (BRIT) N Kundendienst *m*
aftershave ['ɑ:ftəʃeɪv], **aftershave lotion** N Rasierwasser *nt*
aftershock ['ɑ:ftəʃɔk] N Nachbeben *nt*
aftersun ['ɑ:ftəsʌn] N After-Sun-Lotion *f*
aftertaste ['ɑ:ftəteɪst] N Nachgeschmack *m*
afterthought ['ɑ:ftəθɔ:t] N: **as an ~** nachträglich; **I had an ~** mir ist noch etwas eingefallen
afterwards ['ɑ:ftəwədz], (*US*) **afterward** ['ɑ:ftəwəd] ADV danach
again [ə'gɛn] ADV (*once more*) noch einmal; (*repeatedly*) wieder; **not him ~!** nicht schon wieder er!; **to do sth ~** etw noch einmal tun; **to begin ~** noch einmal anfangen; **to see ~** wiedersehen; **he's opened it ~** er hat es schon wieder geöffnet; **~ and ~** immer wieder; **now and ~** ab und zu, hin und wieder
against [ə'gɛnst] PREP gegen *+acc*; (*leaning on*) an *+acc*; (*compared to*) gegenüber *+dat*; **~ a blue background** vor einem blauen Hintergrund; **(as) ~** gegenüber *+dat*
age [eɪdʒ] N Alter *nt*; (*period*) Zeitalter *nt* ▸ VI altern, alt werden ▸ VT alt machen; **what ~ is he?** wie alt ist er?; **20 years of ~** 20 Jahre alt; **under ~** minderjährig; **to come of ~** mündig werden; **it's been ages since …** es ist ewig her, seit …
aged[1] [eɪdʒd] ADJ: **~ ten** zehn Jahre alt, zehnjährig
aged[2] ['eɪdʒɪd] NPL: **the ~** die Alten *pl*
age group N Altersgruppe *f*; **the 40 to 50 ~** die Gruppe der Vierzig- bis Fünfzigjährigen
ageing ['eɪdʒɪŋ] ADJ (*person, population*) alternd; (*thing*) älter werdend; (*system, technology*) veraltend
ageism ['eɪdʒɪzəm] N Diskriminierung *f* aufgrund des Alters
ageless ['eɪdʒlɪs] ADJ zeitlos
age limit N Altersgrenze *f*
agency ['eɪdʒənsɪ] N Agentur *f*; (*government body*) Behörde *f*; **through** *or* **by the ~ of** durch die Vermittlung von
agenda [ə'dʒɛndə] N Tagesordnung *f*
agent ['eɪdʒənt] N (*Comm*) Vertreter(in) *m(f)*; (*representative, spy*) Agent(in) *m(f)*; (*Chem*) Mittel *nt*; (*fig*) Kraft *f*
aggravate ['ægrəveɪt] VT verschlimmern; (*inf: annoy*) ärgern
aggravating ['ægrəveɪtɪŋ] (*inf*) ADJ ärgerlich
aggravation [ægrə'veɪʃən] (*inf*) N Ärger *m*
aggregate ['ægrɪgɪt] N Gesamtmenge *f* ▸ VT zusammenzählen; **on ~** (*Sport*) nach Toren
aggression [ə'grɛʃən] N Aggression *f*
aggressive [ə'grɛsɪv] ADJ aggressiv
aggressiveness [ə'grɛsɪvnɪs] N Aggressivität *f*
aggressor [ə'grɛsə^r] N Aggressor(in) *m(f)*, Angreifer(in) *m(f)*
aggrieved [ə'gri:vd] ADJ verärgert
aggro ['ægrəu] (BRIT *inf*) N (*hassle*) Ärger *m*, Theater *nt*; (*aggressive behaviour*) Aggressivität *f*
aghast [ə'gɑ:st] ADJ entsetzt
agile ['ædʒaɪl] ADJ beweglich, wendig
agility [ə'dʒɪlɪtɪ] N Beweglichkeit *f*, Wendigkeit *f*; (*of mind*) (geistige) Beweglichkeit *f*
agitate ['ædʒɪteɪt] VT aufregen; (*liquid: stir*) aufrühren; (*: shake*) schütteln ▸ VI: **to ~ for/against sth** für/gegen etw agitieren
agitated ['ædʒɪteɪtɪd] ADJ aufgeregt
agitator ['ædʒɪteɪtə^r] N Agitator(in) *m(f)*
AGM N ABBR (= *annual general meeting*) JHV *f*
agnostic [æg'nɔstɪk] N Agnostiker(in) *m(f)*
ago [ə'gəu] ADV: **two days ~** vor zwei Tagen; **not long ~** vor Kurzem; **as long ~ as 1980** schon 1980; **how long ~?** wie lange ist das her?
agog [ə'gɔg] ADJ gespannt
agonize ['ægənaɪz] VI: **to ~ over sth** sich *dat* den Kopf über etw *acc* zermartern
agonizing ['ægənaɪzɪŋ] ADJ qualvoll; (*pain etc*) quälend
agony ['ægənɪ] N (*pain*) Schmerz *m*; (*torment*) Qual *f*; **to be in ~** Qualen leiden
agony aunt (BRIT *inf*) N Briefkastentante *f*
agony column N Kummerkasten *m*
agree [ə'gri:] VT (*price, date*) vereinbaren ▸ VI übereinstimmen; (*consent*) zustimmen; **to ~ with sb** (*subj: person*) jdm zustimmen; (*: food*) jdm bekommen; **to ~ to sth** einer Sache *dat* zustimmen; **to ~ to do sth** sich bereit erklären, etw zu tun; **to ~ on sth** sich auf etw *acc* einigen; **to ~ that** (*admit*) zugeben, dass; **garlic doesn't ~ with me** Knoblauch vertrage ich nicht; **it was agreed that …** es wurde beschlossen, dass …; **they agreed on this** sie haben sich in diesem Punkt geeinigt; **they agreed on going** sie einigten sich darauf, zu gehen; **they agreed on a price** sie vereinbarten einen Preis
agreeable [ə'gri:əbl] ADJ angenehm; (*willing*) einverstanden; **are you ~ to this?** sind Sie hiermit einverstanden?
agreed [ə'gri:d] ADJ vereinbart; **to be ~** sich *dat* einig sein
agreement [ə'gri:mənt] N (*concurrence*) Übereinstimmung *f*; (*consent*) Zustimmung *f*; (*arrangement*) Abmachung *f*; (*contract*) Vertrag *m*; **to be in ~ (with sb)** (mit jdm) einer Meinung sein; **by mutual ~** in gegenseitigem Einverständnis
agricultural [ægrɪ'kʌltʃərəl] ADJ landwirtschaftlich; (*show*) Landwirtschafts-
agriculture ['ægrɪkʌltʃə^r] N Landwirtschaft *f*
aground [ə'graund] ADV: **to run ~** auf Grund laufen

ahead [ə'hɛd] ADV vor uns/ihnen *etc*; **~ of** (*in advance of*) vor *+dat*; **to be ~ of sb** (*in progress, ranking*) vor jdm liegen; **to be ~ of schedule** schneller als geplant vorankommen; **~ of time** zeitlich voraus; **to arrive ~ of time** zu früh ankommen; **go right** *or* **straight ~** gehen/fahren Sie geradeaus; **go ~!** (*fig*) machen Sie nur!, nur zu!; **they were (right) ~ of us** sie waren (genau) vor uns

AI N ABBR (= *Amnesty International*) AI *no art*; (*Comput*) = **artificial intelligence**

AID N ABBR (= *artificial insemination by donor*) *künstliche Besamung durch Samenspender*; (*US*: = *Agency for International Development*) *Abteilung zur Koordination von Entwicklungshilfe und Außenpolitik*

aid [eɪd] N Hilfe *f*; (*to less developed country*) Entwicklungshilfe *f*; (*device*) Hilfsmittel *nt* ▶ VT (*help*) helfen, unterstützen; **with the ~ of** mithilfe von; **in ~ of** zugunsten *+gen*; **to ~ and abet** Beihilfe leisten; *see also* **hearing aid**

aide [eɪd] N Berater(in) *m(f)*; (*Mil*) Adjutant *m*

aide-de-camp ['eɪddə'kɔŋ] N (*Mil*) Adjutant *m*

AIDS [eɪdz] N ABBR (= *acquired immune deficiency syndrome*) AIDS *nt*

AIH N ABBR (= *artificial insemination by husband*) *künstliche Besamung durch den Ehemann/Partner*

ailing ['eɪlɪŋ] ADJ kränklich; (*economy, industry etc*) krank

ailment ['eɪlmənt] N Leiden *nt*

aim [eɪm] VT: **to ~ at** (*gun, missile, camera*) richten auf *+acc*; (*blow*) zielen auf *+acc*; (*remark*) richten an *+acc* ▶ VI (*also*: **take aim**) zielen ▶ N (*objective*) Ziel *nt*; (*in shooting*) Zielsicherheit *f*; **to ~ at** zielen auf *+acc*; (*objective*) anstreben *+acc*; **to ~ to do sth** vorhaben, etw zu tun

aimless ['eɪmlɪs] ADJ ziellos

aimlessly ['eɪmlɪslɪ] ADV ziellos

ain't [eɪnt] (*inf*) = **am not; aren't; isn't**

air [ɛəʳ] N Luft *f*; (*tune*) Melodie *f*; (*appearance*) Auftreten *nt*; (*demeanour*) Haltung *f*; (*of house etc*) Atmosphäre *f* ▶ VT lüften; (*grievances, views*) Luft machen *+dat*; (*knowledge*) zur Schau stellen; (*ideas*) darlegen ▶ CPD Luft-; **into the ~** in die Luft; **by ~** mit dem Flugzeug; **to be on the ~** (*Radio, TV*: *programme*) gesendet werden; (: *station*) senden; (: *person*) auf Sendung sein

airbag ['ɛəbæg] N (*Aut*) Airbag *m*

air base N Luftwaffenstützpunkt *m*

air bed (BRIT) N Luftmatratze *f*

airborne ['ɛəbɔːn] ADJ in der Luft; (*plane, particles*) in der Luft befindlich; (*troops*) Luftlande-

air cargo N Luftfracht *f*

air-conditioned ['ɛəkən'dɪʃənd] ADJ klimatisiert

air conditioning N Klimaanlage *f*

air-cooled ['ɛəkuːld] ADJ (*engine*) luftgekühlt

aircraft ['ɛəkrɑːft] N INV Flugzeug *nt*

aircraft carrier N Flugzeugträger *m*

air cushion N Luftkissen *nt*

airfield ['ɛəfiːld] N Flugplatz *m*

Air Force N Luftwaffe *f*

air freight N Luftfracht *f*

air freshener N Raumspray *nt*

air gun N Luftgewehr *nt*

air hostess (BRIT) N Stewardess *f*

airily ['ɛərɪlɪ] ADV leichtfertig

airing ['ɛərɪŋ] N: **to give an ~ to** (*fig*: *ideas*) darlegen; (: *views*) Luft machen *+dat*

air letter (BRIT) N Luftpostbrief *m*

airlift ['ɛəlɪft] N Luftbrücke *f*

airline ['ɛəlaɪn] N Fluggesellschaft *f*

airliner ['ɛəlaɪnəʳ] N Verkehrsflugzeug *nt*

airlock ['ɛəlɔk] N (*in pipe etc*) Luftblase *f*; (*compartment*) Luftschleuse *f*

air mail N: **by ~** per *or* mit Luftpost

air mattress N Luftmatratze *f*

airplane ['ɛəpleɪn] (US) N Flugzeug *nt*

air pocket N Luftloch *nt*

airport ['ɛəpɔːt] N Flughafen *m*

air raid N Luftangriff *m*

air rifle N Luftgewehr *nt*

airsick ['ɛəsɪk] ADJ luftkrank

airspace ['ɛəspeɪs] N Luftraum *m*

airspeed ['ɛəspiːd] N Fluggeschwindigkeit *f*

airstrip ['ɛəstrɪp] N Start-und-Lande-Bahn *f*

air terminal N Terminal *m or nt*

airtight ['ɛətaɪt] ADJ luftdicht

airtime ['ɛətaɪm] N (*Radio, TV*) Sendezeit *f*

air-traffic control ['ɛətræfɪk-] N Flugsicherung *f*

air-traffic controller ['ɛətræfɪk-] N Fluglotse *m*

air waybill N Luftfrachtbrief *m*

airy ['ɛərɪ] ADJ luftig; (*casual*) lässig

aisle [aɪl] N Gang *m*; (*section of church*) Seitenschiff *nt*

aisle seat N Sitz *m* am Gang

ajar [ə'dʒɑːʳ] ADJ angelehnt

AK (US) ABBR (*Post*) = **Alaska**

a.k.a. ABBR (= *also known as*) alias

akin [ə'kɪn] ADJ: **~ to** ähnlich *+dat*

AL (US) ABBR (*Post*) = **Alabama**

ALA N ABBR (= *American Library Association*) *akademischer Verband für das Bibliothekswesen*

Ala. (US) ABBR (*Post*) = **Alabama**

alabaster ['æləbɑːstəʳ] N Alabaster *m*

à la carte ADV à la carte

alacrity [ə'lækrɪtɪ] N Bereitwilligkeit *f*; **with ~** ohne zu zögern

alarm [ə'lɑːm] N (*anxiety*) Besorgnis *f*; (*in shop, bank*) Alarmanlage *f* ▶ VT (*worry*) beunruhigen; (*frighten*) erschrecken

alarm call N Weckruf *m*

alarm clock N Wecker *m*

alarmed [ə'lɑːmd] ADJ beunruhigt; **don't be ~** erschrecken Sie nicht

alarming [ə'lɑːmɪŋ] ADJ (*worrying*) beunruhigend; (*frightening*) erschreckend

alarmingly [ə'lɑːmɪŋlɪ] ADV erschreckend

alarmist [ə'lɑːmɪst] N Panikmacher(in) *m(f)*

alas [ə'læs] EXCL leider

Alaska [ə'læskə] N Alaska *nt*

Albania [æl'beɪnɪə] N Albanien *nt*

Albanian [æl'beɪnɪən] ADJ albanisch ▶ N (*Ling*) Albanisch *nt*

albatross ['ælbətrɔs] N Albatros *m*

albeit [ɔːlˈbiːɪt] CONJ wenn auch
album [ˈælbəm] N Album *nt*
albumen [ˈælbjʊmɪn] N Albumen *nt*
alchemy [ˈælkɪmɪ] N Alchimie *f*, Alchemie *f*
alcohol [ˈælkəhɔl] N Alkohol *m*
alcohol-free [ˈælkəhɔlfriː] ADJ alkoholfrei
alcoholic [ælkəˈhɔlɪk] ADJ alkoholisch ▸ N Alkoholiker(in) *m(f)*
alcoholism [ˈælkəhɔlɪzəm] N Alkoholismus *m*
alcove [ˈælkəuv] N Alkoven *m*, Nische *f*
Ald. ABBR = **alderman**
alderman [ˈɔːldəmən] N *(irreg)* ≈ Stadtrat *m*
ale [eɪl] N Ale *nt*
alert [əˈləːt] ADJ aufmerksam ▸ N Alarm *m* ▸ VT alarmieren; **to be ~ to** *(danger, opportunity)* sich *dat* bewusst sein *+gen*; **to be on the ~** wachsam sein; **to ~ sb (to sth)** jdn (vor etw *dat*) warnen
Aleutian Islands [əˈluːʃən-] NPL Aleuten *pl*
A level (BRIT) N ≈ Abschluss *m* der Sekundarstufe 2, ≈ Abitur *nt*
Alexandria [ælɪgˈzɑːndrɪə] N Alexandria *nt*
alfresco [ælˈfrɛskəu] ADJ, ADV im Freien
algebra [ˈældʒɪbrə] N Algebra *f*
Algeria [ælˈdʒɪərɪə] N Algerien *nt*
Algerian [ælˈdʒɪərɪən] ADJ algerisch ▸ N Algerier(in) *m(f)*
Algiers [ælˈdʒɪəz] N Algier *nt*
algorithm [ˈælgərɪðəm] N Algorithmus *m*
alias [ˈeɪlɪəs] ADV alias ▸ N Deckname *m*
alibi [ˈælɪbaɪ] N Alibi *nt*
alien [ˈeɪlɪən] N Ausländer(in) *m(f)*; *(extraterrestrial)* außerirdisches Wesen *nt* ▸ ADJ: **~ (to)** fremd *(+dat)*
alienate [ˈeɪlɪəneɪt] VT entfremden; *(antagonize)* befremden
alienation [eɪlɪəˈneɪʃən] N Entfremdung *f*
alight [əˈlaɪt] ADJ brennend; *(eyes, expression)* leuchtend ▸ VI *(bird)* sich niederlassen; *(passenger)* aussteigen
align [əˈlaɪn] VT ausrichten
alignment [əˈlaɪnmənt] N Ausrichtung *f*; **it's out of ~ (with)** es ist nicht richtig ausgerichtet (nach)
alike [əˈlaɪk] ADJ ähnlich ▸ ADV *(similarly)* ähnlich; *(equally)* gleich; **to look ~** sich *dat* ähnlich sehen; **winter and summer ~** Sommer wie Winter
alimony [ˈælɪmənɪ] N Unterhalt *m*
alive [əˈlaɪv] ADJ *(living)* lebend; *(lively)* lebendig; *(active)* lebhaft; **~ with** erfüllt von; **to be ~ to sth** sich *dat* einer Sache *gen* bewusst sein
alkali [ˈælkəlaɪ] N Base *f*, Lauge *f*
alkaline [ˈælkəlaɪn] ADJ basisch, alkalisch

KEYWORD

all [ɔːl] ADJ alle(r, s); **all day/night** den ganzen Tag/die ganze Nacht (über); **all men are equal** alle Menschen sind gleich; **all five came** alle fünf kamen; **all the books** die ganzen Bücher, alle Bücher; **all the food** das ganze Essen; **all the time** die ganze Zeit (über); **all his life** sein ganzes Leben (lang)
▸ PRON **1** alles; **I ate it all, I ate all of it** ich habe alles gegessen; **all of us/the boys went** wir alle/alle Jungen gingen; **we all sat down** wir setzten uns alle; **is that all?** ist das alles?; *(in shop)* sonst noch etwas?
2 *(in phrases)*: **above all** vor allem; **after all** schließlich; **all in all** alles in allem
▸ ADV ganz; **all alone** ganz allein; **it's not as hard as all that** so schwer ist es nun auch wieder nicht; **all the more/the better** um so mehr/besser; **all but** *(all except for)* alle außer; *(almost)* fast; **the score is 2 all** der Spielstand ist 2 zu 2

allay [əˈleɪ] VT *(fears)* zerstreuen
all clear N Entwarnung *f*
allegation [ælɪˈgeɪʃən] N Behauptung *f*
allege [əˈlɛdʒ] VT behaupten; **he is alleged to have said that ...** er soll angeblich gesagt haben, dass ...
alleged [əˈlɛdʒd] ADJ angeblich
allegedly [əˈlɛdʒɪdlɪ] ADV angeblich
allegiance [əˈliːdʒəns] N Treue *f*
allegory [ˈælɪgərɪ] N Allegorie *f*
all-embracing [ˈɔːlɪmˈbreɪsɪŋ] ADJ (all)umfassend
allergic [əˈləːdʒɪk] ADJ *(rash, reaction)* allergisch; **~ to** *(person)* allergisch gegen
allergy [ˈælədʒɪ] N Allergie *f*
alleviate [əˈliːvɪeɪt] VT lindern
alley [ˈælɪ] N Gasse *f*
alleyway [ˈælɪweɪ] N Durchgang *m*
alliance [əˈlaɪəns] N Bündnis *nt*
allied [ˈælaɪd] ADJ verbündet, alliiert; *(products, industries)* verwandt
alligator [ˈælɪgeɪtə^r] N Alligator *m*
all-important [ˈɔːlɪmˈpɔːtənt] ADJ entscheidend, äußerst wichtig
all in (BRIT) ADV inklusive
all-in [ˈɔːlɪn] (BRIT) ADJ *(price)* Inklusiv-
all-in wrestling N *(esp Brit)* Freistilringen *nt*
alliteration [əlɪtəˈreɪʃən] N Alliteration *f*
all-night [ˈɔːlˈnaɪt] ADJ *(café, cinema)* die ganze Nacht geöffnet; *(party)* die ganze Nacht dauernd
allocate [ˈæləkeɪt] VT zuteilen
allocation [æləuˈkeɪʃən] N Verteilung *f*; *(of money, resources)* Zuteilung *f*
allot [əˈlɔt] VT: **to ~ (to)** zuteilen *(+dat)*; **in the allotted time** in der vorgesehenen Zeit
allotment [əˈlɔtmənt] N *(share)* Anteil *m*; *(garden)* Schrebergarten *m*
all-out [ˈɔːlaut] ADJ *(effort, dedication etc)* äußerste(r, s); *(strike)* total ▸ ADV: **all out** mit aller Kraft; **to go all out for** sein Letztes *or* Äußerstes geben für
allow [əˈlau] VT erlauben; *(behaviour)* zulassen; *(sum, time)* einplanen; *(claim, goal)* anerkennen; *(concede)*: **to ~ that** annehmen, dass; **to ~ sb to do sth** jdm erlauben, etw zu tun; **he is allowed to ...** er darf ...; **smoking is not allowed** Rauchen ist nicht gestattet; **we must ~ three days for the journey** wir müssen für die Reise drei Tage einplanen
▸ **allow for** VT FUS einplanen, berücksichtigen

allowance [əˈlauəns] N finanzielle Unterstützung *f*; (*welfare payment*) Beihilfe *f*; (*pocket money*) Taschengeld *nt*; (*tax allowance*) Freibetrag *m*; **to make allowances for** (*person*) Zugeständnisse machen für; (*thing*) berücksichtigen
alloy [ˈælɔɪ] N Legierung *f*
all right ADV (*well*) gut; (*correctly*) richtig; (*as answer*) okay, in Ordnung
all-rounder [ɔːlˈraundə^r] N Allrounder *m*; (*athlete etc*) Allroundsportler(in) *m(f)*
allspice [ˈɔːlspaɪs] N Piment *m or nt*
all-time [ˈɔːlˈtaɪm] ADJ aller Zeiten
allude [əˈluːd] VI: **to ~ to** anspielen auf *+acc*
alluring [əˈljuərɪŋ] ADJ verführerisch
allusion [əˈluːʒən] N Anspielung *f*
alluvium [əˈluːvɪəm] N Anschwemmung *f*
ally [ˈælaɪ] N Verbündete(r) *f(m)*; (*during wars*) Alliierte(r) *f(m)* ▶ VT: **to ~ o.s. with** sich verbünden mit
almighty [ɔːlˈmaɪtɪ] ADJ allmächtig; (*tremendous*) mächtig
almond [ˈɑːmənd] N Mandel *f*; (*tree*) Mandelbaum *m*
almost [ˈɔːlməust] ADV fast, beinahe; **he ~ fell** er wäre beinahe gefallen
alms [ɑːmz] NPL Almosen *pl*
aloft [əˈlɔft] ADV (*hold, carry*) empor
alone [əˈləun] ADJ, ADV allein; **to leave sb ~** jdn in Ruhe lassen; **to leave sth ~** die Finger von etw lassen; **let ~ …** geschweige denn …
along [əˈlɔŋ] PREP entlang *+acc* ▶ ADV: **is he coming ~ with us?** kommt er mit?; **he was hopping/limping ~** er hüpfte/humpelte daher; **~ with** (*together with*) zusammen mit; **all ~** (*all the time*) die ganze Zeit
alongside [əˈlɔŋˈsaɪd] PREP neben *+dat*; (*ship*) längsseits *+gen* ▶ ADV (*come*) nebendran; (*be*) daneben; **we brought our boat ~** wir brachten unser Boot heran; **a car drew up ~** ein Auto fuhr neben mich/ihn *etc* heran
aloof [əˈluːf] ADJ unnahbar ▶ ADV: **to stand ~** abseitsstehen
aloofness [əˈluːfnɪs] N Unnahbarkeit *f*
aloud [əˈlaud] ADV laut
alphabet [ˈælfəbɛt] N Alphabet *nt*
alphabetical [ælfəˈbɛtɪkl] ADJ alphabetisch; **in ~ order** in alphabetischer Reihenfolge
alphanumeric [ˈælfənjuːˈmɛrɪk] ADJ alphanumerisch
alpine [ˈælpaɪn] ADJ alpin, Alpen-
Alps [ælps] NPL: **the ~** die Alpen
already [ɔːlˈrɛdɪ] ADV schon
alright [ˈɔːlˈraɪt] (BRIT) ADV = **all right**
Alsace [ˈælsæs] N Elsass *nt*
Alsatian [ælˈseɪʃən] (BRIT) N (*dog*) Schäferhund *m*
also [ˈɔːlsəu] ADV (*too*) auch; (*moreover*) außerdem
altar [ˈɔltə^r] N Altar *m*
alter [ˈɔltə^r] VT ändern; (*clothes*) umändern ▶ VI sich (ver)ändern
alteration [ɔltəˈreɪʃən] N Änderung *f*; (*to clothes*) Umänderung *f*; (*to building*) Umbau *m*;
alterations NPL (*Sewing*) Änderungen *pl*; (*Archit*) Umbau *m*
altercation [ɔltəˈkeɪʃən] N Auseinandersetzung *f*
alternate ADJ [ɔlˈtəːnɪt] abwechselnd; (*US: alternative: plans etc*) Alternativ- ▶ VI [ˈɔltəneɪt]: **to ~ (with)** sich abwechseln (mit); **on ~ days** jeden zweiten Tag
alternately [ɔlˈtəːnɪtlɪ] ADV abwechselnd
alternating current [ˈɔltəːneɪtɪŋ-] N Wechselstrom *m*
alternative [ɔlˈtəːnətɪv] ADJ alternativ; (*solution etc*) Alternativ- ▶ N Alternative *f*
alternative energy N Alternativenergie *f*
alternatively [ɔlˈtəːnətɪvlɪ] ADV: **~ one could …** oder man könnte …
alternative medicine N Alternativmedizin *f*
alternative society N Alternativgesellschaft *f*
alternator [ˈɔltəːneɪtə^r] N (*Aut*) Lichtmaschine *f*
although [ɔːlˈðəu] CONJ obwohl
altitude [ˈæltɪtjuːd] N Höhe *f*
alto [ˈæltəu] N Alt *m*
altogether [ɔːltəˈgɛðə^r] ADV ganz; (*on the whole, in all*) im Ganzen, insgesamt; **how much is that ~?** was macht das zusammen?
altruism [ˈæltruɪzəm] N Altruismus *m*
altruistic [æltruˈɪstɪk] ADJ uneigennützig, altruistisch
aluminium [æljuˈmɪnɪəm], (US) **aluminum** [əˈluːmɪnəm] N Aluminium *nt*
always [ˈɔːlweɪz] ADV immer; **we can ~ …** (*if all else fails*) wir können ja auch …
Alzheimer's [ˈæltshaɪməz], **Alzheimer's disease** N (*Med*) Alzheimerkrankheit *f*
AM ABBR (= *amplitude modulation*) AM, ≈ MW ▶ N ABBR (BRIT: *in Wales*: *Pol*: = *Assembly Member*) Mitglied *nt* der walisischen Versammlung
am [æm] VB *see* **be**
a.m. ADV ABBR (= *ante meridiem*) morgens; (*later*) vormittags
AMA N ABBR (= *American Medical Association*) *Medizinerverband*
amalgam [əˈmælgəm] N Amalgam *nt*; (*fig*) Mischung *f*
amalgamate [əˈmælgəmeɪt] VI, VT fusionieren
amalgamation [əmælgəˈmeɪʃən] N Fusion *f*
amass [əˈmæs] VT anhäufen; (*evidence*) zusammentragen
amateur [ˈæmətə^r] N Amateur *m* ▶ ADJ (*Sport*) Amateur-; **~ dramatics** Laientheater *nt*
amateurish [ˈæmətərɪʃ] ADJ laienhaft; (*pej*) dilettantisch, stümperhaft
amaze [əˈmeɪz] VT erstaunen; **to be amazed (at)** erstaunt sein (über *+acc*)
amazement [əˈmeɪzmənt] N Erstaunen *nt*
amazing [əˈmeɪzɪŋ] ADJ erstaunlich; (*bargain, offer*) sensationell
amazingly [əˈmeɪzɪŋlɪ] ADV erstaunlich
Amazon [ˈæməzən] N (*river*) Amazonas *m*; **the ~ basin** das Amazonastiefland; **the ~ jungle** der Amazonas-Regenwald
Amazonian [æməˈzəunɪən] ADJ amazonisch
ambassador [æmˈbæsədə^r] N Botschafter(in) *m(f)*

amber [ˈæmbəʳ] N Bernstein *m*; **at ~** (BRIT: *traffic lights*) auf Gelb; (: *move off*) bei Gelb
ambidextrous [æmbɪˈdɛkstrəs] ADJ beidhändig
ambience [ˈæmbɪəns] N Atmosphäre *f*
ambiguity [æmbɪˈgjuɪtɪ] N Zweideutigkeit *f*; (*lack of clarity*) Unklarheit *f*
ambiguous [æmˈbɪgjuəs] ADJ zweideutig; (*not clear*) unklar
ambition [æmˈbɪʃən] N Ehrgeiz *m*; (*desire*) Ambition *f*; **to achieve one's ~** seine Ambitionen erfüllen
ambitious [æmˈbɪʃəs] ADJ ehrgeizig
ambivalence [æmˈbɪvələns] N Ambivalenz *f*
ambivalent [æmˈbɪvələnt] ADJ ambivalent
amble [ˈæmbl] VI schleudern
ambulance [ˈæmbjuləns] N Krankenwagen *m*
ambulanceman [ˈæmbjulənsmən] N (*irreg*) Sanitäter *m*
ambush [ˈæmbuʃ] N Hinterhalt *m*; (*attack*) Überfall *m* aus dem Hinterhalt ▶ VT (aus dem Hinterhalt) überfallen
ameba [əˈmiːbə] (*US*) N = **amoeba**
ameliorate [əˈmiːlɪəreɪt] VT verbessern
amen [ˈɑːˈmɛn] EXCL amen
amenable [əˈmiːnəbl] ADJ: **~ to** zugänglich *+dat*; (*to flattery etc*) empfänglich für; **~ to the law** dem Gesetz verantwortlich
amend [əˈmɛnd] VT ändern; (*habits, behaviour*) bessern
amendment [əˈmɛndmənt] N Änderung *f*; (*to law*) Amendement *nt*
amends [əˈmɛndz] NPL: **to make ~** es wiedergutmachen; **to make ~ for sth** etw wiedergutmachen
amenities [əˈmiːnɪtɪz] NPL *Einkaufs-, Unterhaltungs- und Transportmöglichkeiten*
amenity [əˈmiːnɪtɪ] N (Freizeit)einrichtung *f*
America [əˈmɛrɪkə] N Amerika *nt*
American [əˈmɛrɪkən] ADJ amerikanisch ▶ N Amerikaner(in) *m(f)*
Americanize [əˈmɛrɪkənaɪz] VT amerikanisieren
amethyst [ˈæmɪθɪst] N Amethyst *m*
Amex [ˈæmɛks] N ABBR (= *American Stock Exchange*) *US-Börse*; (= *American Express®*) *Kreditkarte*
amiable [ˈeɪmɪəbl] ADJ liebenswürdig
amiably [ˈeɪmɪəblɪ] ADV liebenswürdig
amicable [ˈæmɪkəbl] ADJ freundschaftlich; (*settlement*) gütlich
amicably [ˈæmɪkəblɪ] ADV (*part, discuss*) in aller Freundschaft; (*settle*) gütlich
amid [əˈmɪd], **amidst** [əˈmɪdst] PREP inmitten *+gen*
amiss [əˈmɪs] ADJ, ADV: **to take sth ~** etw übel nehmen; **there's something ~** da stimmt irgendetwas nicht
ammeter [ˈæmɪtəʳ] N Amperemeter *nt*
ammo [ˈæməu] (*inf*) N = **ammunition**
ammonia [əˈməunɪə] N Ammoniak *nt*
ammunition [æmjuˈnɪʃən] N Munition *f*
ammunition dump N Munitionslager *nt*
amnesia [æmˈniːzɪə] N Amnesie *f*, Gedächtnisschwund *m*
amnesty [ˈæmnɪstɪ] N Amnestie *f*; **to grant an ~ to** amnestieren
Amnesty International N Amnesty International *no art*
amoeba, (*US*) **ameba** [əˈmiːbə] N Amöbe *f*
amok [əˈmɔk] ADV: **to run ~** Amok laufen
among [əˈmʌŋ], **amongst** [əˈmʌŋst] PREP unter *+dat*
amoral [æˈmɔrəl] ADJ unmoralisch
amorous [ˈæmərəs] ADJ amourös
amorphous [əˈmɔːfəs] ADJ formlos, gestaltlos
amortization [əmɔːtaɪˈzeɪʃən] N Amortisation *f*
amount [əˈmaunt] N (*quantity*) Menge *f*; (*sum of money*) Betrag *m*; (*total*) Summe *f*; (*of bill etc*) Höhe *f* ▶ VI: **to ~ to** (*total*) sich belaufen auf *+acc*; (*be same as*) gleichkommen *+dat*; **the total ~** (*of money*) die Gesamtsumme
amp [ˈæmp], **ampère** [ˈæmpɛəʳ] N Ampere *nt*; **a 3 ~(ère) fuse** eine Sicherung von 3 Ampere; **a 13 ~(ère) plug** ein Stecker mit einer Sicherung von 13 Ampere
ampersand [ˈæmpəsænd] N Et-Zeichen *nt*, Und-Zeichen *nt*
amphetamine [æmˈfɛtəmiːn] N Amphetamin *nt*
amphibian [æmˈfɪbɪən] N Amphibie *f*
amphibious [æmˈfɪbɪəs] ADJ amphibisch; (*vehicle*) Amphibien-
amphitheatre, (*US*) **amphitheater** [ˈæmfɪθɪətəʳ] N Amphitheater *nt*
ample [ˈæmpl] ADJ (*large*) üppig; (*abundant*) reichlich; (*enough*) genügend; **this is ~** das ist reichlich; **to have ~ time/room** genügend Zeit/Platz haben
amplifier [ˈæmplɪfaɪəʳ] N Verstärker *m*
amplify [ˈæmplɪfaɪ] VT verstärken; (*expand: idea etc*) genauer ausführen
amply [ˈæmplɪ] ADV reichlich
ampoule, (*US*) **ampule** [ˈæmpuːl] N Ampulle *f*
amputate [ˈæmpjuteɪt] VT amputieren
amputation [æmpjuˈteɪʃən] N Amputation *f*
amputee [æmpjuˈtiː] N Amputierte(r) *f(m)*
Amsterdam [ˈæmstədæm] N Amsterdam *nt*
amt ABBR = **amount**
amuck [əˈmʌk] ADV = **amok**
amuse [əˈmjuːz] VT (*entertain*) unterhalten; (*make smile*) amüsieren, belustigen; **to ~ o.s. with sth/by doing sth** sich die Zeit mit etw vertreiben/damit vertreiben, etw zu tun; **to be amused at** sich amüsieren über *+acc*; **he was not amused** er fand das gar nicht komisch *or* zum Lachen
amusement [əˈmjuːzmənt] N (*mirth*) Vergnügen *nt*; (*pleasure*) Unterhaltung *f*; (*pastime*) Zeitvertreib *m*; **much to my ~** zu meiner großen Belustigung
amusement arcade N Spielhalle *f*
amusement park N Vergnügungspark *m*
amusing [əˈmjuːzɪŋ] ADJ amüsant, unterhaltsam
an [æn, ən] INDEF ART *see* **a**
ANA N ABBR (= *American Newspaper Association*) *amerikanischer Zeitungsverband*; (= *American Nurses Association*) *Verband amerikanischer Krankenschwestern und Krankenpfleger*

anachronism [ə'nækrənɪzəm] N Anachronismus *m*
anaemia, (*US*) **anemia** [ə'ni:mɪə] N Anämie *f*
anaemic, (*US*) **anemic** [ə'ni:mɪk] ADJ blutarm
anaesthetic, (*US*) **anesthetic** [ænɪs'θɛtɪk] N Betäubungsmittel *nt*; **under (the)** ~ unter Narkose; **local** ~ örtliche Betäubung *f*; **general** ~ Vollnarkose *f*
anaesthetist [æ'ni:sθɪtɪst] N Anästhesist(in) *m(f)*
anagram ['ænəgræm] N Anagramm *nt*
anal ['eɪnl] ADJ anal, Anal-
analgesic [ænæl'dʒi:sɪk] ADJ schmerzstillend ▸ N Schmerzmittel *nt*, schmerzstillendes Mittel *nt*
analogous [ə'næləgəs] ADJ: ~ **(to** *or* **with)** analog (zu)
analogue, (*US*) **analog** ['ænəlɔg] ADJ (*watch, computer*) Analog-
analogy [ə'nælədʒɪ] N Analogie *f*; **to draw an ~ between** eine Analogie herstellen zwischen *+dat*; **by** ~ durch einen Analogieschluss
analyse, (*US*) **analyze** ['ænəlaɪz] VT analysieren; (*Chem, Med*) untersuchen; (*person*) psychoanalytisch behandeln
analyses [ə'næləsi:z] NPL *of* **analysis**
analysis [ə'næləsɪs] (*pl* **analyses**) N Analyse *f*; Untersuchung *f*; Psychoanalyse *f*; **in the last ~** letzten Endes
analyst ['ænəlɪst] N Analytiker(in) *m(f)*; (*US*) Psychoanalytiker(in) *m(f)*
analytic [ænə'lɪtɪk], **analytical** [ænə'lɪtɪkəl] ADJ analytisch
analyze ['ænəlaɪz] (*US*) VT = **analyse**
anarchic [æ'nɑ:kɪk] ADJ anarchisch
anarchist ['ænəkɪst] ADJ anarchistisch ▸ N Anarchist(in) *m(f)*
anarchy ['ænəkɪ] N Anarchie *f*
anathema [ə'næθɪmə] N: **that is ~ to him** das ist ihm ein Gräuel
anatomical [ænə'tɔmɪkl] ADJ anatomisch
anatomy [ə'nætəmɪ] N Anatomie *f*; (*body*) Körper *m*
ANC N ABBR (= *African National Congress*) ANC *m*
ancestor ['ænsɪstə^r] N Vorfahr(in) *m(f)*
ancestral [æn'sɛstrəl] ADJ angestammt; **~ home** Stammsitz *m*
ancestry ['ænsɪstrɪ] N Abstammung *f*
anchor ['æŋkə^r] N Anker *m* ▸ VI (*also*: **to drop anchor**) ankern, vor Anker gehen ▸ VT (*fig*) verankern; **to ~ sth to** etw verankern in *+dat*; **to weigh ~** den Anker lichten
anchorage ['æŋkərɪdʒ] N Ankerplatz *m*
anchorman [æŋkəmæn] N (*irreg*) (*TV, Radio*) ≈ Moderator *m*
anchor store N (*attractive store*) ≈ Magnetbetrieb *m*
anchorwoman [æŋkəwʊmən] N (*irreg*) (*TV, Radio*) ≈ Moderatorin *f*
anchovy ['æntʃəvɪ] N Sardelle *f*, An(s)chovis *f*
ancient ['eɪnʃənt] ADJ alt; (*person, car*) uralt
ancient monument N historisches Denkmal *nt*
ancillary [æn'sɪlərɪ] ADJ Hilfs-
and [ænd] CONJ und; **~ so on** und so weiter; **try ~ come please** bitte versuche zu kommen; **better ~ better** immer besser
Andes ['ændi:z] NPL: **the ~** die Anden *pl*
Andorra [æn'dɔ:rə] N Andorra *nt*
anecdote ['ænɪkdəut] N Anekdote *f*
anemia *etc* [ə'ni:mɪə] (*US*) = **anaemia** *etc*
anemone [ə'nɛmənɪ] N (*Bot*) Anemone *f*, Buschwindröschen *nt*
anesthesiologist [ænɪsθi:zɪ'ɔlədʒɪst] N (*US*) Anästhesist(in) *m(f)*
anesthetic *etc* [ænɪs'θɛtɪk] (*US*) = **anaesthetic** *etc*
anew [ə'nju:] ADV von Neuem
angel ['eɪndʒəl] N Engel *m*
angel dust (*inf*) N *als halluzinogene Droge missbrauchtes Medikament*
angelic [æn'dʒɛlɪk] ADJ engelhaft
anger ['æŋgə^r] N Zorn *m* ▸ VT ärgern; (*enrage*) erzürnen; **red with ~** rot vor Wut
angina [æn'dʒaɪnə] N Angina pectoris *f*
angle ['æŋgl] N Winkel *m*; (*viewpoint*): **from their ~** von ihrem Standpunkt aus ▸ VI: **to ~ for** (*invitation*) aus sein auf *+acc*; (*compliments*) fischen nach ▸ VT: **to ~ sth towards** *or* **to** etw ausrichten auf *+acc*
angler ['æŋglə^r] N Angler(in) *m(f)*
Anglican ['æŋglɪkən] ADJ anglikanisch ▸ N Anglikaner(in) *m(f)*
anglicize ['æŋglɪsaɪz] VT anglisieren
angling ['æŋglɪŋ] N Angeln *nt*
Anglo- ['æŋgləu] PREF Anglo-, anglo-
Anglo-German ['æŋgləu'dʒə:mən] ADJ englisch-deutsch
Anglo-Saxon ['æŋgləu'sæksən] ADJ angelsächsisch ▸ N Angelsachse *m*, Angelsächsin *f*
Angola [æŋ'gəulə] N Angola *nt*
Angolan [æŋ'gəulən] ADJ angolanisch ▸ N Angolaner(in) *m(f)*
angrily ['æŋgrɪlɪ] ADV verärgert
angry ['æŋgrɪ] ADJ verärgert; (*wound*) entzündet; **to be ~ with sb** auf jdn böse sein; **to be ~ at sth** über etw *acc* verärgert sein; **to get ~** wütend werden; **to make sb ~** jdn wütend machen
anguish ['æŋgwɪʃ] N Qual *f*
anguished ['æŋgwɪʃt] ADJ gequält
angular ['æŋgjulə^r] ADJ eckig; (*features*) kantig
animal ['ænɪməl] N Tier *nt*; (*living creature*) Lebewesen *nt*; (*pej*: *person*) Bestie *f* ▸ ADJ tierhaft; (*attraction etc*) animalisch
animal spirits NPL Vitalität *f*
animate VT ['ænɪmeɪt] beleben ▸ ADJ ['ænɪmɪt] lebend
animated ['ænɪmeɪtɪd] ADJ lebhaft; (*film*) Zeichentrick-
animation [ænɪ'meɪʃən] N (*liveliness*) Lebhaftigkeit *f*; (*film*) Animation *f*
animosity [ænɪ'mɔsɪtɪ] N Feindseligkeit *f*
aniseed ['ænɪsi:d] N Anis *m*
Ankara ['æŋkərə] N Ankara *nt*
ankle ['æŋkl] N Knöchel *m*
ankle sock (BRIT) N Söckchen *nt*

annex, (BRIT) **annexe** ['ænɛks] N Anhang *m*; (*building*) Nebengebäude *nt*; (*extension*) Anbau *m* ▸ VT (*take over*) annektieren
annexation [ænɛk'seɪʃən] N Annexion *f*
annihilate [ə'naɪəleɪt] VT (*also fig*) vernichten
annihilation [ənaɪə'leɪʃən] N Vernichtung *f*
anniversary [ænɪ'və:sərɪ] N Jahrestag *m*
anno Domini ADV anno Domini, nach Christus
annotate ['ænəuteɪt] VT kommentieren
announce [ə'nauns] VT ankündigen; (*birth, death etc*) anzeigen; **he announced that he wasn't going** er verkündete, dass er nicht gehen würde
announcement [ə'naunsmənt] N Ankündigung *f*; (*official*) Bekanntmachung *f*; (*of birth, death etc*) Anzeige *f*; **I'd like to make an ~** ich möchte etwas bekannt geben
announcer [ə'naunsə[r]] N Ansager(in) *m(f)*
annoy [ə'nɔɪ] VT ärgern; **to be annoyed (at sth/ with sb)** sich (über etw/jdn) ärgern; **don't get annoyed!** reg dich nicht auf!
annoyance [ə'nɔɪəns] N Ärger *m*
annoying [ə'nɔɪɪŋ] ADJ ärgerlich; (*person, habit*) lästig
annual ['ænjuəl] ADJ jährlich; (*income*) Jahres- ▸ N (*Bot*) einjährige Pflanze *f*; (*book*) Jahresband *m*
annual general meeting (BRIT) N Jahreshauptversammlung *f*
annually ['ænjuəlɪ] ADV jährlich
annual report N Geschäftsbericht *m*
annuity [ə'nju:ɪtɪ] N Rente *f*; **life ~** Rente *f* auf Lebenszeit
annul [ə'nʌl] VT annullieren; (*law*) aufheben
annulment [ə'nʌlmənt] N Annullierung *f*; Aufhebung *f*
annum ['ænəm] N *see* **per**
Annunciation [ənʌnsɪ'eɪʃən] N Mariä Verkündigung *f*
anode ['ænəud] N Anode *f*
anodyne ['ænədaɪn] (*fig*) N Wohltat *f* ▸ ADJ schmerzlos
anoint [ə'nɔɪnt] VT salben
anomalous [ə'nɔmələs] ADJ anomal
anomaly [ə'nɔməlɪ] N Anomalie *f*
anon. [ə'nɔn] ABBR = **anonymous**
anonymity [ænə'nɪmɪtɪ] N Anonymität *f*
anonymous [ə'nɔnɪməs] ADJ anonym
anorak ['ænəræk] N Anorak *m*
anorexia [ænə'rɛksɪə] N Magersucht *f*, Anorexie *f*
anorexic [ænə'rɛksɪk] ADJ magersüchtig
another [ə'nʌðə[r]] PRON (*additional*) noch eine(r, s); (*different*) ein(e, r) andere(s) ▸ ADJ: **~ book** (*one more*) noch ein Buch; (*a different one*) ein anderes Buch; **~ drink?** noch etwas zu trinken?; **in ~ five years** in weiteren fünf Jahren; *see also* **one**
ANSI N ABBR (= *American National Standards Institution*) *amerikanischer Normenausschuss*
answer ['ɑ:nsə[r]] N Antwort *f*; (*to problem*) Lösung *f* ▸ VI antworten; (*Tel*) sich melden ▸ VT (*reply to: person*) antworten +*dat*; (*: letter, question*) beantworten; (*problem*) lösen; (*prayer*) erhören; **in ~ to your letter** in Beantwortung Ihres Schreibens; **to ~ the phone** ans Telefon gehen; **to ~ the bell** *or* **the door** die Tür aufmachen
▸ **answer back** VI widersprechen; (*child*) frech sein
▸ **answer for** VT FUS (*person*) verantwortlich sein für, sich verbürgen für
▸ **answer to** VT FUS (*description*) entsprechen +*dat*
answerable ['ɑ:nsərəbl] ADJ: **to be ~ to sb for sth** jdm gegenüber für etw verantwortlich sein; **I am ~ to no-one** ich brauche mich vor niemandem zu verantworten
answering machine ['ɑ:nsərɪŋ-] N Anrufbeantworter *m*
ant [ænt] N Ameise *f*
antagonism [æn'tægənɪzəm] N Feindseligkeit *f*, Antagonismus *m*
antagonist [æn'tægənɪst] N Gegner(in) *m(f)*, Antagonist(in) *m(f)*
antagonistic [æntægə'nɪstɪk] ADJ feindselig
antagonize [æn'tægənaɪz] VT gegen sich aufbringen
Antarctic [ænt'ɑ:ktɪk] N: **the ~** die Antarktis
Antarctica [ænt'ɑ:ktɪkə] N Antarktik *f*
Antarctic Circle N: **the ~** der südliche Polarkreis
Antarctic Ocean N: **the ~** das Südpolarmeer
ante ['æntɪ] N: **to up the ~** den Einsatz erhöhen
ante... ['æntɪ] PREF vor-
anteater ['ænti:tə[r]] N Ameisenbär *m*
antecedent [æntɪ'si:dənt] N Vorläufer *m*; (*of living creature*) Vorfahr *m*; **antecedents** NPL Herkunft *f*
antechamber ['æntɪtʃeɪmbə[r]] N Vorzimmer *nt*
antelope ['æntɪləup] N Antilope *f*
antenatal ['æntɪ'neɪtl] ADJ vor der Geburt, Schwangerschafts-
antenatal clinic N Sprechstunde *f* für werdende Mütter
antenna [æn'tɛnə] (*pl* **antennae**) N (*of insect*) Fühler *m*; (*Radio, TV*) Antenne *f*
antennae [æn'tɛni:] NPL *of* **antenna**
anteroom ['æntɪrum] N Vorzimmer *nt*
anthem ['ænθəm] N: **national ~** Nationalhymne *f*
ant hill N Ameisenhaufen *m*
anthology [æn'θɔlədʒɪ] N Anthologie *f*
anthropologist [ænθrə'pɔlədʒɪst] N Anthropologe *m*, Anthropologin *f*
anthropology [ænθrə'pɔlədʒɪ] N Anthropologie *f*
anti... ['æntɪ] PREF Anti-, anti-
anti-aircraft ['æntɪ'ɛəkrɑ:ft] ADJ (*gun, rocket*) Flugabwehr-
anti-aircraft defence N Luftverteidigung *f*
antiballistic ['æntɪbə'lɪstɪk] ADJ (*missile*) Anti-Raketen-
antibiotic ['æntɪbaɪ'ɔtɪk] N Antibiotikum *nt*
antibody ['æntɪbɔdɪ] N Antikörper *m*
anticipate [æn'tɪsɪpeɪt] VT erwarten; (*foresee*) vorhersehen; (*look forward to*) sich freuen auf +*acc*; (*forestall*) vorwegnehmen; **this is worse**

than I anticipated es ist schlimmer, als ich erwartet hatte; **as anticipated** wie erwartet
anticipation [æntɪsɪ'peɪʃən] N Erwartung *f*; (*eagerness*) Vorfreude *f*; **thanking you in ~** vielen Dank im Voraus
anticlimax ['æntɪ'klaɪmæks] N Enttäuschung *f*
anticlockwise ['æntɪ'klɔkwaɪz] (BRIT) ADV gegen den Uhrzeigersinn
antics ['æntɪks] NPL Mätzchen *pl*; (*of politicians etc*) Gehabe *nt*
anticyclone ['æntɪ'saɪkləun] N Hoch(druckgebiet) *nt*
antidote ['æntɪdəut] N Gegenmittel *nt*
antifreeze ['æntɪfri:z] N Frostschutzmittel *nt*
anti-globalist [æntɪ'gləubəlɪst], **anti-globalization protester** [æntɪgləublaɪ'zeɪʃn-] N Globalisierungsgegner(in) *m(f)*
antihistamine ['æntɪ'hɪstəmɪn] N Antihistamin *nt*
Antilles [æn'tɪli:z] NPL: **the ~** die Antillen *pl*
antipathy [æn'tɪpəθɪ] N Antipathie *f*, Abneigung *f*
antiperspirant ['æntɪ'pə:spɪrənt] N Antitranspirant *nt*
Antipodean [æntɪpə'di:ən] ADJ antipodisch
Antipodes [æn'tɪpədi:z] NPL: **the ~** Australien und Neuseeland *nt*
antiquarian [æntɪ'kwɛərɪən] N (*collector*) Antiquitätensammler(in) *m(f)*; (*seller*) Antiquitätenhändler(in) *m(f)* ▶ ADJ: **~ bookshop** Antiquariat *nt*
antiquated ['æntɪkweɪtɪd] ADJ antiquiert
antique [æn'ti:k] N Antiquität *f* ▶ ADJ antik
antique dealer N Antiquitätenhändler(in) *m(f)*
antique shop N Antiquitätenladen *m*
antiquity [æn'tɪkwɪtɪ] N (*period*) Antike *f*; **antiquities** NPL (*objects*) Altertümer *pl*
anti-Semitic ['æntɪsɪ'mɪtɪk] ADJ antisemitisch
anti-Semitism ['æntɪ'sɛmɪtɪzəm] N Antisemitismus *m*
antiseptic [æntɪ'sɛptɪk] N Antiseptikum *nt* ▶ ADJ antiseptisch
antisocial ['æntɪ'səuʃəl] ADJ unsozial; (*person*) ungesellig
antitank ['æntɪ'tæŋk] ADJ (*gun, fire*) Panzerabwehr-
antitheses [æn'tɪθɪsi:z] NPL *of* **antithesis**
antithesis [æn'tɪθɪsɪs] (*pl* **antitheses**) N Gegensatz *m*; **she's the ~ of a good cook** sie ist das genaue Gegenteil einer guten Köchin
antitrust ['æntɪ'trʌst] (US) ADJ: **~ legislation** Kartellgesetzgebung *f*
antiviral [æntɪ'vaɪərəl] ADJ (*Med*) antiviral
antivirus [æntɪ'vaɪrəs] ADJ (*Comput*) Antiviren-
antivirus software N Antivirensoftware *f*
antlers ['æntləz] NPL Geweih *nt*
Antwerp ['æntwə:p] N Antwerpen *nt*
anus ['eɪnəs] N After *m*
anvil ['ænvɪl] N Amboss *m*
anxiety [æŋ'zaɪətɪ] N (*worry*) Sorge *f*; (*Med*) Angstzustand *m*; (*eagerness*): **~ to do sth** Verlangen (danach), etw zu tun
anxious ['æŋkʃəs] ADJ (*worried*) besorgt; (*situation*) Angst einflößend; (*question, moments*) bang(e); (*keen*): **to be ~ to do sth** etw unbedingt tun wollen; **I'm very ~ about you** ich mache mir große Sorgen um dich
anxiously ['æŋkʃəslɪ] ADV besorgt

KEYWORD

any ['ɛnɪ] ADJ **1** (*in questions etc*): **have you any butter/children?** haben Sie Butter/Kinder?; **if there are any tickets left** falls noch Karten da sind
2 (*with negative*) kein(e); **I haven't any money/books** ich habe kein Geld/keine Bücher
3 (*no matter which*) irgendein(e); **choose any book you like** nehmen Sie irgendein Buch *or* ein beliebiges Buch
4 (*in phrases*): **in any case** in jedem Fall; **any day now** jeden Tag; **at any moment** jeden Moment; **at any rate** auf jeden Fall; **any time** (*at any moment*) jeden Moment; (*whenever*) jederzeit
▶ PRON **1** (*in questions etc*): **have you got any?** haben Sie welche?; **can any of you sing?** kann (irgend)einer von euch singen?
2 (*with negative*): **I haven't any (of them)** ich habe keine (davon)
3 (*no matter which one(s)*) egal welche; **take any of those books (you like)** nehmen Sie irgendwelche von diesen Büchern
▶ ADV **1** (*in questions etc*): **do you want any more soup/sandwiches?** möchtest du noch Suppe/Butterbrote?; **are you feeling any better?** geht es Ihnen etwas besser?
2 (*with negative*): **I can't hear him any more** ich kann ihn nicht mehr hören; **don't wait any longer** warte nicht noch länger

anybody ['ɛnɪbɔdɪ] PRON = **anyone**

KEYWORD

anyhow ['ɛnɪhau] ADV **1** (*at any rate*) sowieso, ohnehin; **I shall go anyhow** ich gehe auf jeden Fall
2 (*haphazard*): **do it anyhow you like** machen Sie es, wie Sie wollen

KEYWORD

anyone ['ɛnɪwʌn] PRON **1** (*in questions etc*) (irgend)jemand; **can you see anyone?** siehst du jemanden?
2 (*with negative*) keine(r); **I can't see anyone** ich kann keinen *or* niemanden sehen
3 (*no matter who*) jede(r); **anyone could do it** das kann jeder

anyplace ['ɛnɪpleɪs] (US) ADV = **anywhere**

KEYWORD

anything ['ɛnɪθɪŋ] PRON **1** (*in questions etc*) (irgend)etwas; **can you see anything?** kannst du etwas sehen?
2 (*with negative*) nichts; **I can't see anything** ich kann nichts sehen

3 (*no matter what*) irgendetwas; **you can say anything you like** du kannst sagen, was du willst; **anything between 15 and 20 pounds** (ungefähr) zwischen 15 und 20 Pfund

anytime ADV jederzeit

KEYWORD

anyway ['ɛnɪweɪ] ADV **1** (*at any rate*) sowieso, ohnehin; **I shall go anyway** ich gehe auf jeden Fall
2 (*besides*): **anyway, I can't come** jedenfalls kann ich nicht kommen; **why are you phoning, anyway?** warum rufst du überhaupt *or* eigentlich an?

KEYWORD

anywhere ['ɛnɪwɛəʳ] ADV **1** (*in questions etc*) irgendwo; **can you see him anywhere?** kannst du ihn irgendwo sehen?
2 (*with negative*) nirgendwo, nirgends; **I can't see him anywhere** ich kann ihn nirgendwo *or* nirgends sehen
3 (*no matter where*) irgendwo; **put the books down anywhere** legen Sie die Bücher irgendwohin

Anzac ['ænzæk] N ABBR = **Australia-New Zealand Army Corps**; (*soldier*) australischer/neuseeländischer Soldat *m*

Anzac Day, der 25 April, ist in Australien und Neuseeland ein Feiertag zum Gedenken an die Landung der australischen und neuseeländischen Truppen in Gallipoli im Ersten Weltkrieg (1915).

apace [ə'peɪs] ADV: **to continue ~** (*negotiations, preparations etc*) rasch vorangehen
apart [ə'pɑːt] ADV (*be*) entfernt; (*move*) auseinander; (*aside*) beiseite; (*separately*) getrennt; **10 miles ~** 10 Meilen voneinander entfernt; **a long way ~** weit auseinander; **they are living ~** sie leben getrennt; **with one's legs ~** mit gespreizten Beinen; **to take ~** auseinandernehmen; **~ from** (*excepting*) abgesehen von; (*in addition*) außerdem
apartheid [ə'pɑːteɪt] N Apartheid *f*
apartment [ə'pɑːtmənt] N (*US: flat*) Wohnung *f*; (*room*) Raum *m*, Zimmer *nt*
apartment block, (*US*) **apartment building** N Wohnblock *m*
apathetic [æpə'θɛtɪk] ADJ apathisch, teilnahmslos
apathy ['æpəθɪ] N Apathie *f*, Teilnahmslosigkeit *f*
APB (*US*) N ABBR (= *all points bulletin*) *polizeiliche Fahndung*
ape [eɪp] N (Menschen)affe *m* ▶ VT nachahmen
Apennines ['æpənaɪnz] NPL: **the ~** die Apenninen *pl*, der Appenin
apéritif N Aperitif *m*
APEX ['eɪpɛks] N ABBR (*Aviat, Rail: = advance purchase excursion*) APEX
apex ['eɪpɛks] N Spitze *f*
aphid ['æfɪd] N Blattlaus *f*
aphorism ['æfərɪzəm] N Aphorismus *m*
aphrodisiac [æfrəu'dɪzɪæk] ADJ aphrodisisch ▶ N Aphrodisiakum *nt*
apiece [ə'piːs] ADV (*each person*) pro Person; (*each thing*) pro Stück
aplomb [ə'plɔm] N Gelassenheit *f*
APO (*US*) N ABBR (= *Army Post Office*) *Poststelle der Armee*
apocalypse [ə'pɔkəlɪps] N Apokalypse *f*
apolitical [eɪpə'lɪtɪkl] ADJ apolitisch
apologetic [əpɔlə'dʒɛtɪk] ADJ entschuldigend; **to be very ~ (about sth)** sich (wegen etw *gen*) sehr entschuldigen
apologize [ə'pɔlədʒaɪz] VI: **to ~ (for sth to sb)** sich (für etw bei jdm) entschuldigen
apology [ə'pɔlədʒɪ] N Entschuldigung *f*; **to send one's apologies** sich entschuldigen lassen; **please accept my apologies** ich bitte um Verzeihung
apoplectic [æpə'plɛktɪk] ADJ (*Med*) apoplektisch; (*fig*): **to be ~ with rage** vor Wut fast platzen
apoplexy ['æpəplɛksɪ] N Schlaganfall *m*
apostle [ə'pɔsl] N Apostel *m*
apostrophe [ə'pɔstrəfɪ] N Apostroph *m*, Auslassungszeichen *nt*
apotheosis [əpɔθɪ'əusɪs] N Apotheose *f*
app [æp] N ABBR (*for mobile phone*) App *f*
appal [ə'pɔːl] VT entsetzen; **to be appalled by** entsetzt sein über *+acc*
Appalachian Mountains [æpə'leɪʃən-] NPL: **the ~** die Appalachen *pl*
appalling [ə'pɔːlɪŋ] ADJ entsetzlich; **she's an ~ cook** sie kann überhaupt nicht kochen
apparatus [æpə'reɪtəs] N Gerät *nt*; (*in gymnasium*) Geräte *pl*; (*of organization*) Apparat *m*; **a piece of ~** ein Gerät *nt*
apparel [ə'pærəl] (*US*) N Kleidung *f*
apparent [ə'pærənt] ADJ (*seeming*) scheinbar; (*obvious*) offensichtlich; **it is ~ that ...** es ist klar, dass ...
apparently [ə'pærəntlɪ] ADV anscheinend
apparition [æpə'rɪʃən] N Erscheinung *f*
appeal [ə'piːl] VI (*Law*) Berufung einlegen ▶ N (*Law*) Berufung *f*; (*plea*) Aufruf *m*; (*charm*) Reiz *m*; **to ~ (to sb) for** (jdn) bitten um; **to ~ to** (*be attractive to*) gefallen *+dat*; **it doesn't ~ to me** es reizt mich nicht; **right of ~** (*Law*) Berufungsrecht *nt*; **on ~** (*Law*) in der Berufung
appealing [ə'piːlɪŋ] ADJ ansprechend; (*touching*) rührend
appear [ə'pɪəʳ] VI erscheinen; (*seem*) scheinen; **to ~ on TV/in "Hamlet"** im Fernsehen/in „Hamlet" auftreten; **it would ~ that ...** anscheinend ...
appearance [ə'pɪərəns] N Erscheinen *nt*; (*look*) Aussehen *nt*; (*in public, on TV*) Auftritt *m*; **to put in** *or* **make an ~** sich sehen lassen; **in** *or* **by order of ~** (*Theat etc*) in der Reihenfolge ihres Auftritts; **to keep up appearances** den (äußeren) Schein wahren; **to all appearances** allem Anschein nach

appease [əˈpiːz] VT beschwichtigen
appeasement [əˈpiːzmənt] N Beschwichtigung *f*
append [əˈpɛnd] VT (*Comput*) anhängen
appendage [əˈpɛndɪdʒ] N Anhängsel *nt*
appendices [əˈpɛndɪsiːz] NPL *of* **appendix**
appendicitis [əpɛndɪˈsaɪtɪs] N Blinddarmentzündung *f*
appendix [əˈpɛndɪks] (*pl* **appendices**) N (*Anat*) Blinddarm *m*; (*to publication*) Anhang *m*; **to have one's ~ out** sich *dat* den Blinddarm herausnehmen lassen
appetite [ˈæpɪtaɪt] N Appetit *m*; (*fig*) Lust *f*; **that walk has given me an ~** von dem Spaziergang habe ich Appetit bekommen
appetizer [ˈæpɪtaɪzəʳ] N (*food*) Appetithappen *m*; (*drink*) appetitanregendes Getränk *nt*
appetizing [ˈæpɪtaɪzɪŋ] ADJ appetitanregend
applaud [əˈplɔːd] VI applaudieren, klatschen ▸ VT (*actor etc*) applaudieren *+dat*, Beifall spenden *or* klatschen *+dat*; (*action, attitude*) loben; (*decision*) begrüßen
applause [əˈplɔːz] N Applaus *m*, Beifall *m*
apple [ˈæpl] N Apfel *m*; **he's the ~ of her eye** er ist ihr Ein und Alles
apple crumble N *mit Streuseln bestreutes Apfeldessert*
apple juice N Apfelsaft *m*
apple pie N gedeckter Apfelkuchen *m*
apple puree, apple sauce N Apfelmus *nt*
apple tart N Apfelkuchen *m*
apple tree N Apfelbaum *m*
apple turnover N Apfeltasche *f*
appliance [əˈplaɪəns] N Gerät *nt*
applicable [əˈplɪkəbl] ADJ: **~ (to)** anwendbar (auf *+acc*); (*on official forms*) zutreffend (auf *+acc*); **the law is ~ from January** das Gesetz gilt ab Januar
applicant [ˈæplɪkənt] N Bewerber(in) *m(f)*
application [æplɪˈkeɪʃən] N (*for job*) Bewerbung *f*; (*for grant etc*) Antrag *m*; (*hard work*) Fleiß *m*; (*applying: of paint etc*) Auftragen *nt*; (*Comput*) Anwendung *f*; **on ~** auf Antrag
application form N (*for a job*) Bewerbungsformular *nt*; (*for a grant etc*) Antragsformular *nt*
application program N (*Comput*) Anwendungsprogramm *nt*
applications package N (*Comput*) Anwendungspaket *nt*
applied [əˈplaɪd] ADJ angewandt
apply [əˈplaɪ] VT anwenden; (*paint etc*) auftragen ▸ VI: **to ~ (to)** (*be applicable*) gelten (für); **to ~ the brakes** die Bremse betätigen, bremsen; **to ~ o.s. to sth** sich bei etw anstrengen; **to ~ to** (*ask*) sich wenden an *+acc*; **to ~ for** (*permit, grant*) beantragen; (*job*) sich bewerben um
appoint [əˈpɔɪnt] VT ernennen; (*date, place*) festlegen, festsetzen
appointed [əˈpɔɪntɪd] ADJ: **at the ~ time** zur festgesetzten Zeit
appointee [əpɔɪnˈtiː] N Ernannte(r) *f(m)*
appointment [əˈpɔɪntmənt] N Ernennung *f*; (*post*) Stelle *f*; (*arranged meeting*) Termin *m*; **to make an ~ (with sb)** einen Termin (mit jdm) vereinbaren; **by ~** nach Anmeldung, mit Voranmeldung
apportion [əˈpɔːʃən] VT aufteilen; (*blame*) zuweisen; **to ~ sth to sb** jdm etw zuteilen
apposition [æpəˈzɪʃən] N Apposition *f*, Beifügung *f*; **A is in ~ to B** A ist eine Apposition zu B
appraisal [əˈpreɪzl] N Beurteilung *f*
appraise [əˈpreɪz] VT beurteilen
appreciable [əˈpriːʃəbl] ADJ merklich, deutlich
appreciably [əˈpriːʃəblɪ] ADV merklich
appreciate [əˈpriːʃɪeɪt] VT (*like*) schätzen; (*be grateful for*) zu schätzen wissen; (*understand*) verstehen; (*be aware of*) sich *dat* bewusst sein *+gen* ▸ VI (*Comm: currency, shares*) im Wert steigen; **I ~ your help** ich weiß Ihre Hilfe zu schätzen
appreciation [əpriːʃɪˈeɪʃən] N (*enjoyment*) Wertschätzung *f*; (*understanding*) Verständnis *nt*; (*gratitude*) Dankbarkeit *f*; (*Comm: in value*) (Wert)steigerung *f*
appreciative [əˈpriːʃɪətɪv] ADJ dankbar; (*comment*) anerkennend
apprehend [æprɪˈhɛnd] VT (*arrest*) festnehmen; (*understand*) verstehen
apprehension [æprɪˈhɛnʃən] N (*fear*) Besorgnis *f*; (*arrest*) Festnahme *f*
apprehensive [æprɪˈhɛnsɪv] ADJ ängstlich; **to be ~ about sth** sich *dat* Gedanken *or* Sorgen um etw machen
apprentice [əˈprɛntɪs] N Lehrling *m*, Auszubildende(r) *f(m)* ▸ VT: **to be apprenticed to sb** bei jdm in der Lehre sein
apprenticeship [əˈprɛntɪsʃɪp] N Lehre *f*, Lehrzeit *f*; **to serve one's ~** seine Lehre machen
appro [ˈæprəu] (BRIT *inf*) ABBR (*Comm: = approval*): **on ~** zur Ansicht
approach [əˈprəutʃ] VI sich nähern; (*event*) nahen ▸ VT (*come to*) sich nähern *+dat*; (*ask, apply to: person*) herantreten an *+acc*, ansprechen; (*situation, problem*) herangehen an *+acc*, angehen ▸ N (*advance*) (Heran)nahen *nt*; (*access*) Zugang *m*; (*: for vehicles*) Zufahrt *f*; (*to problem etc*) Ansatz *m*; **to ~ sb about sth** jdn wegen etw ansprechen
approachable [əˈprəutʃəbl] ADJ (*person*) umgänglich; (*place*) zugänglich
approach road N Zufahrtsstraße *f*
approbation [æprəˈbeɪʃən] N Zustimmung *f*
appropriate ADJ [əˈprəuprɪɪt] (*apt*) angebracht; (*relevant*) entsprechend ▸ VT [əˈprəuprɪeɪt] sich *dat* aneignen; **it would not be ~ for me to comment** es wäre nicht angebracht, wenn ich mich dazu äußern würde
appropriately [əˈprəuprɪɪtlɪ] ADV entsprechend
appropriation [əprəuprɪˈeɪʃən] N Zuteilung *f*, Zuweisung *f*
approval [əˈpruːvəl] N (*approbation*) Zustimmung *f*, Billigung *f*; (*permission*)

Einverständnis *f*; **to meet with sb's ~** jds Zustimmung *or* Beifall finden; **on ~** (*Comm*) zur Probe

approve [ə'pru:v] VT billigen; (*motion, decision*) annehmen

▸ **approve of** VT FUS etwas halten von; **I don't ~ of it/him** ich halte nichts davon/von ihm

approved school [ə'pru:vd-] (BRIT) N Erziehungsheim *nt*

approvingly [ə'pru:vɪŋlɪ] ADV zustimmend

approx. ABBR = **approximately**

approximate ADJ [ə'prɔksɪmɪt] ungefähr ▸ VT, VI [ə'prɔksɪmeɪt]: **to ~ (to)** nahe kommen +*dat*

approximately [ə'prɔksɪmɪtlɪ] ADV ungefähr

approximation [ə'prɔksɪ'meɪʃən] N Annäherung *f*

APR N ABBR (= *annual(ized) percentage rate*) Jahreszinssatz *m*

Apr. ABBR = **April**

apricot ['eɪprɪkɔt] N Aprikose *f*

April ['eɪprəl] N April *m*; **~ fool!** April, April!; *see also* **July**

apron ['eɪprən] N Schürze *f*; (*Aviat*) Vorfeld *nt*

apse [æps] N Apsis *f*

apt [æpt] ADJ (*suitable*) passend, treffend; (*likely*): **to be ~ to do sth** dazu neigen, etw zu tun

Apt. ABBR = **apartment**

aptitude ['æptɪtju:d] N Begabung *f*

aptitude test N Eignungstest *m*

aptly ['æptlɪ] ADV passend, treffend

aqualung ['ækwəlʌŋ] N Tauchgerät *nt*

aquarium [ə'kwɛərɪəm] N Aquarium *nt*

Aquarius [ə'kwɛərɪəs] N Wassermann *m*; **to be ~** (ein) Wassermann sein

aquatic [ə'kwætɪk] ADJ (*plants etc*) Wasser-; (*life*) im Wasser

aqueduct ['ækwɪdʌkt] N Aquädukt *m or nt*

AR (US) ABBR (*Post*) = **Arkansas**

ARA (BRIT) N ABBR (= *Associate of the Royal Academy*) *Qualifikationsnachweis im künstlerischen Bereich*

Arab ['ærəb] ADJ arabisch ▸ N Araber(in) *m(f)*

Arabia [ə'reɪbɪə] N Arabien *nt*

Arabian [ə'reɪbɪən] ADJ arabisch

Arabian Desert N: **the ~** die Arabische Wüste

Arabian Sea N: **the ~** das Arabische Meer

Arabic ['ærəbɪk] ADJ arabisch ▸ N (*Ling*) Arabisch *nt*

arable ['ærəbl] ADJ (*land*) bebaubar; **~ farm** *Bauernhof, der ausschließlich Ackerbau betreibt*

ARAM (BRIT) N ABBR (= *Associate of the Royal Academy of Music*) *Qualifikationsnachweis in Musik*

arbiter ['ɑ:bɪtə[r]] N Vermittler *m*

arbitrary ['ɑ:bɪtrərɪ] ADJ willkürlich

arbitrate ['ɑ:bɪtreɪt] VI vermitteln

arbitration [ɑ:bɪ'treɪʃən] N Schlichtung *f*; **the dispute went to ~** der Streit wurde vor eine Schlichtungskommission gebracht

arbitrator ['ɑ:bɪtreɪtə[r]] N Vermittler(in) *m(f)*; (*Industry*) Schlichter(in) *m(f)*

ARC N ABBR (= *American Red Cross*) ≈ DRK *nt*

arc [ɑ:k] N Bogen *m*

arcade [ɑ:'keɪd] N Arkade *f*; (*shopping mall*) Passage *f*

arch [ɑ:tʃ] N Bogen *m*; (*of foot*) Gewölbe *nt* ▸ VT (*back*) krümmen ▸ ADJ schelmisch ▸ PREF Erz-

archaeological [ɑ:kɪə'lɔdʒɪkl] ADJ archäologisch

archaeologist [ɑ:kɪ'ɔlədʒɪst] N Archäologe *m*, Archäologin *f*

archaeology, (US) **archeology** [ɑ:kɪ'ɔlədʒɪ] N Archäologie *f*

archaic [ɑ:'keɪɪk] ADJ altertümlich; (*language*) veraltet, archaisch

archangel ['ɑ:keɪndʒəl] N Erzengel *m*

archbishop [ɑ:tʃ'bɪʃəp] N Erzbischof *m*

archenemy ['ɑ:tʃ'ɛnəmɪ] N Erzfeind(in) *m(f)*

archeology *etc* [ɑ:kɪ'ɔlədʒɪ] (US) = **archaeology** *etc*

archery ['ɑ:tʃərɪ] N Bogenschießen *nt*

archetypal ['ɑ:kɪtaɪpəl] ADJ (arche)typisch

archetype ['ɑ:kɪtaɪp] N Urbild *nt*, Urtyp *m*

archipelago [ɑ:kɪ'pɛlɪgəu] N Archipel *m*

architect ['ɑ:kɪtɛkt] N Architekt(in) *m(f)*

architectural [ɑ:kɪ'tɛktʃərəl] ADJ architektonisch

architecture ['ɑ:kɪtɛktʃə[r]] N Architektur *f*

archive file ['ɑ:kaɪv-] N (*Comput*) Archivdatei *f*

archives ['ɑ:kaɪvz] NPL Archiv *nt*

archivist ['ɑ:kɪvɪst] N Archivar(in) *m(f)*

archway ['ɑ:tʃweɪ] N Torbogen *m*

ARCM (BRIT) N ABBR (= *Associate of the Royal College of Music*) *Qualifikationsnachweis in Musik*

Arctic ['ɑ:ktɪk] ADJ arktisch ▸ N: **the ~** die Arktis

Arctic Circle N: **the ~** der nördliche Polarkreis

Arctic Ocean N: **the ~** das Nordpolarmeer

ardent ['ɑ:dənt] ADJ leidenschaftlich; (*admirer*) glühend

ardour, (US) **ardor** ['ɑ:də[r]] N Leidenschaft *f*

arduous ['ɑ:djuəs] ADJ mühsam

are [ɑ:[r]] VB *see* **be**

area ['ɛərɪə] N Gebiet *nt*; (*Geom etc*) Fläche *f*; (*dining area etc*) Bereich *m*; **in the London ~** im Raum London

area code (US) N Vorwahl(nummer) *f*

arena [ə'ri:nə] N Arena *f*

aren't [ɑ:nt] = **are not**

Argentina [ɑ:dʒən'ti:nə] N Argentinien *nt*

Argentinian [ɑ:dʒən'tɪnɪən] ADJ argentinisch ▸ N Argentinier(in) *m(f)*

arguable ['ɑ:gjuəbl] ADJ: **it is ~ whether ...** es ist (noch) die Frage, ob ...; **it is ~ that ...** man kann (wohl) sagen, dass ...

arguably ['ɑ:gjuəblɪ] ADV wohl; **it is ~ ...** es dürfte wohl ... sein

argue ['ɑ:gju:] VI (*quarrel*) sich streiten; (*reason*) diskutieren ▸ VT (*debate*) diskutieren, erörtern; **to ~ that ...** den Standpunkt vertreten, dass ...; **to ~ about sth** sich über etw *acc* streiten; **to ~ for/against sth** sich für/gegen etw aussprechen

argument ['ɑ:gjumənt] N (*reasons*) Argument *nt*; (*quarrel*) Streit *m*, Auseinandersetzung *f*; (*debate*) Diskussion *f*; **~ for/against** Argument für/gegen; **to have an ~** sich streiten

argumentative [ɑ:gju'mɛntətɪv] ADJ streitlustig

aria ['ɑ:rɪə] N Arie *f*

ARIBA [ə'ri:bə] (BRIT) N ABBR (= *Associate of the Royal Institute of British Architects*) *Qualifikationsnachweis in Architektur*
arid ['ærɪd] ADJ (*land*) dürr; (*subject*) trocken
aridity [ə'rɪdɪtɪ] N Dürre *f*, Trockenheit *f*
Aries ['ɛərɪz] N Widder *m*; **to be ~** (ein) Widder sein
arise [ə'raɪz] (*pt* **arose**, *pp* **arisen**) VI (*difficulty etc*) sich ergeben; (*question*) sich stellen; **to ~ from** sich ergeben aus, herrühren von; **should the need ~** falls es nötig wird
arisen [ə'rɪzn] PP *of* **arise**
aristocracy [ærɪs'tɔkrəsɪ] N Aristokratie *f*, Adel *m*
aristocrat ['ærɪstəkræt] N Aristokrat(in) *m(f)*, Ad(e)lige(r) *f(m)*
aristocratic [ærɪstə'krætɪk] ADJ aristokratisch, ad(e)lig
arithmetic [ə'rɪθmətɪk] N Rechnen *nt*; (*calculation*) Rechnung *f*
arithmetical [ærɪθ'mɛtɪkl] ADJ rechnerisch, arithmetisch
Ariz. (US) ABBR (*Post*) = **Arizona**
ark [ɑ:k] N: **Noah's A~** die Arche Noah
arm [ɑ:m] N Arm *m*; (*of clothing*) Ärmel *m*; (*of chair*) Armlehne *f*; (*of organization etc*) Zweig *m* ▶ VT bewaffnen; **arms** NPL (*weapons*) Waffen *pl*; (*Heraldry*) Wappen *nt*
armaments ['ɑ:məmənts] NPL (*weapons*) (Aus)rüstung *f*
armband ['ɑ:mbænd] N Armbinde *f*
armchair ['ɑ:mtʃɛə^r] N Sessel *m*, Lehnstuhl *m*
armed [ɑ:md] ADJ bewaffnet; **the ~ forces** die Streitkräfte *pl*
armed robbery N bewaffneter Raubüberfall *m*
Armenia [ɑ:'mi:nɪə] N Armenien *nt*
Armenian [ɑ:'mi:nɪən] ADJ armenisch ▶ N Armenier(in) *m(f)*; (*Ling*) Armenisch *nt*
armful ['ɑ:mful] N Armvoll *m*
armistice ['ɑ:mɪstɪs] N Waffenstillstand *m*
armour, (US) **armor** ['ɑ:mə^r] N (*Hist*) Rüstung *f*; (*also*: **armour-plating**) Panzerplatte *f*; (*Mil: tanks*) Panzerfahrzeuge *pl*
armoured car ['ɑ:məd-] N Panzerwagen *m*
armoury ['ɑ:mərɪ] N (*storeroom*) Waffenlager *nt*
armpit ['ɑ:mpɪt] N Achselhöhle *f*
armrest ['ɑ:mrɛst] N Armlehne *f*
arms control [ɑ:mz-] N Rüstungskontrolle *f*
arms race [ɑ:mz-] N: **the ~** das Wettrüsten
army ['ɑ:mɪ] N Armee *f*, Heer *nt*; (*fig: host*) Heer
aroma [ə'rəumə] N Aroma *nt*, Duft *m*
aromatherapy [ərəumə'θɛrəpɪ] N Aromatherapie *f*
aromatic [ærə'mætɪk] ADJ aromatisch, duftend
arose [ə'rəuz] PT *of* **arise**
around [ə'raund] ADV (*about*) herum; (*in the area*) in der Nähe ▶ PREP (*encircling*) um ... herum; (*near*) in der Nähe von; (*fig: about: dimensions*) etwa; (*: time*) gegen; (*: date*) um; **is he ~?** ist er da?; **~ £5** um die £5, etwa £5; **~ 3 o'clock** gegen 3 Uhr
arousal [ə'rauzəl] N (*sexual*) Erregung *f*; (*of feelings, interest*) Weckung *f*
arouse [ə'rauz] VT (*feelings, interest*) wecken
arpeggio [ɑ:'pɛdʒɪəu] N Arpeggio *nt*
arr. ABBR (= *arrival; arrives*) Ank.
arrange [ə'reɪndʒ] VT (*meeting etc*) vereinbaren; (*tour etc*) planen; (*books etc*) anordnen; (*flowers*) arrangieren; (*Mus*) arrangieren, bearbeiten ▶ VI: **we have arranged for a car to pick you up** wir haben veranlasst, dass Sie mit dem Auto abgeholt werden; **it was arranged that ...** es wurde vereinbart, dass ...; **to ~ to do sth** vereinbaren *or* ausmachen, etw zu tun
arrangement [ə'reɪndʒmənt] N (*agreement*) Vereinbarung *f*; (*layout*) Anordnung *f*; (*Mus*) Arrangement *nt*, Bearbeitung *f*; **arrangements** NPL Pläne *pl*; (*preparations*) Vorbereitungen *pl*; **to come to an ~ with sb** eine Regelung mit jdm treffen; **home deliveries by ~** nach Vereinbarung Lieferung ins Haus; **I'll make arrangements for you to be met** ich werde veranlassen, dass Sie abgeholt werden
arrant ['ærənt] ADJ (*coward, fool etc*) Erz-; (*nonsense*) total
array [ə'reɪ] N: **an ~ of** (*things*) eine Reihe von; (*people*) Aufgebot an *+dat*; (*Math, Comput*) (Daten)feld *nt*
arrears [ə'rɪəz] NPL Rückstand *m*; **to be in ~ with one's rent** mit seiner Miete im Rückstand sein
arrest [ə'rɛst] VT (*person*) verhaften; (*sb's attention*) erregen ▶ N Verhaftung *f*; **under ~** verhaftet
arresting [ə'rɛstɪŋ] ADJ (*fig*) atemberaubend
arrival [ə'raɪvl] N Ankunft *f*; (*Comm: of goods*) Sendung *f*; **new ~** (*person*) Neuankömmling *m*; (*baby*) Neugeborene(s) *nt*
arrivals N (*airport*) Ankunftshalle *f*
arrive [ə'raɪv] VI ankommen
▶ **arrive at** VT FUS (*fig: conclusion*) kommen zu; (*: situation*) es bringen zu
arrogance ['ærəgəns] N Arroganz *f*, Überheblichkeit *f*
arrogant ['ærəgənt] ADJ arrogant, überheblich
arrow ['ærəu] N Pfeil *m*
arse [ɑ:s] (BRIT *inf!*) N Arsch *m* (*inf!*)
arsenal ['ɑ:sɪnl] N Waffenlager *nt*; (*stockpile*) Arsenal *nt*
arsenic ['ɑ:snɪk] N Arsen *nt*
arson ['ɑ:sn] N Brandstiftung *f*
art [ɑ:t] N Kunst *f*; **Arts** NPL (*Scol*) Geisteswissenschaften *pl*; **work of ~** Kunstwerk *nt*
art and design (BRIT) N (*Scol*) ≈ Kunst und Design
arterial [ɑ:'tɪərɪəl] ADJ arteriell; **~ road** Fernverkehrsstraße *f*; **~ line** (*Rail*) Hauptstrecke *f*
artery ['ɑ:tərɪ] N Arterie *f*, Schlagader *f*; (*fig*) Verkehrsader *f*
artful ['ɑ:tful] ADJ raffiniert
art gallery N Kunstgalerie *f*
arthritic [ɑ:'θrɪtɪk] ADJ arthritisch
arthritis [ɑ:'θraɪtɪs] N Arthritis *f*

artichoke ['ɑːtɪtʃəuk] N (*also:* **globe artichoke**) Artischocke *f*; (*also:* **Jerusalem artichoke**) Topinambur *m*
article ['ɑːtɪkl] N Artikel *m*; (*object, item*) Gegenstand *m*; **articles** NPL (BRIT *Law*) (Rechts)referendarzeit *f*; **~ of clothing** Kleidungsstück *nt*
articles of association NPL (*Comm*) Gesellschaftsvertrag *m*
articulate ADJ [ɑː'tɪkjulɪt] (*speech, writing*) klar; (*speaker*) redegewandt ▸ VT [ɑː'tɪkjuleɪt] darlegen ▸ VI artikulieren; **to be ~** (*person*) sich gut ausdrücken können
articulated lorry [ɑː'tɪkjuleɪtɪd-] (BRIT) N Sattelschlepper *m*
artifice ['ɑːtɪfɪs] N List *f*
artificial [ɑːtɪ'fɪʃəl] ADJ künstlich; (*manner*) gekünstelt; **to be ~** (*person*) gekünstelt *or* unnatürlich wirken
artificial insemination N künstliche Besamung *f*
artificial intelligence N künstliche Intelligenz *f*
artificial respiration N künstliche Beatmung *f*
artillery [ɑː'tɪlərɪ] N Artillerie *f*
artisan ['ɑːtɪzæn] N Handwerker *m*
artist ['ɑːtɪst] N Künstler(in) *m(f)*
artistic [ɑː'tɪstɪk] ADJ künstlerisch
artistry ['ɑːtɪstrɪ] N künstlerisches Geschick *nt*
artless ['ɑːtlɪs] ADJ arglos
art school N Kunstakademie *f*, Kunsthochschule *f*
artwork ['ɑːtwəːk] N (*for advert etc, material for printing*) Druckvorlage *f*; (*in book*) Bildmaterial *nt*
ARV N ABBR (*Bible: = American Revised Version*) *amerikanische revidierte Bibelübersetzung*
AS (*US*) N ABBR (*= Associate in Science*) *akademischer Grad in Naturwissenschaften* ▸ ABBR (*Post*) = **American Samoa**

KEYWORD

as [æz] CONJ **1** (*referring to time*) als; **as the years went by** mit den Jahren; **he came in as I was leaving** als er hereinkam, ging ich gerade; **as from tomorrow** ab morgen
2 (*in comparisons*): **as big as** so groß wie; **twice as big as** zweimal so groß wie; **as much/many as** so viel/so viele wie; **as soon as** sobald; **much as I admire her ...** sosehr ich sie auch bewundere ...
3 (*since, because*) da, weil; **as you can't come I'll go without you** da du nicht mitkommen kannst, gehe ich ohne dich
4 (*referring to manner, way*) wie; **do as you wish** mach, was du willst; **as she said** wie sie sagte; **he gave it to me as a present** er gab es mir als Geschenk; **as it were** sozusagen
5 (*in the capacity of*) als; **he works as a driver** er arbeitet als Fahrer
6 (*concerning*): **as for** *or* **to that** was das betrifft *or* angeht
7: **as if** *or* **though** als ob; *see also* **long**; **such**; **well**

ASA N ABBR (*= American Standards Association*) *amerikanischer Normenausschuss*; (BRIT) = **Advertising Standards Authority**
a.s.a.p. ADV ABBR (*= as soon as possible*) baldmöglichst
asbestos [æz'bɛstəs] N Asbest *m*
ascend [ə'sɛnd] VT hinaufsteigen; (*throne*) besteigen
ascendancy [ə'sɛndənsɪ] N Vormachtstellung *f*; **~ over sb** Vorherrschaft *f* über jdn
ascendant [ə'sɛndənt] N: **to be in the ~** im Aufstieg begriffen sein
ascension [ə'sɛnʃən] N: **the A~** (*Rel*) die Himmelfahrt *f* (Christi)
Ascension Island N Ascension *nt*
ascent [ə'sɛnt] N Aufstieg *m*
ascertain [æsə'teɪn] VT feststellen
ascetic [ə'sɛtɪk] ADJ asketisch
asceticism [ə'sɛtɪsɪzəm] N Askese *f*
ASCII ['æskiː] N ABBR (*Comput: = American Standard Code for Information Interchange*) ASCII
ascribe [ə'skraɪb] VT: **to ~ sth to** etw zuschreiben *+dat*; (*cause*) etw zurückführen auf *+acc*
ASCU (*US*) N ABBR (*= Association of State Colleges and Universities*) *Verband staatlicher Bildungseinrichtungen*
ASEAN ['æsɪæn] N ABBR (*= Association of Southeast Asian Nations*) ASEAN *f* (*Gemeinschaft südostasiatischer Staaten*)
ASH [æʃ] (BRIT) N ABBR (*= Action on Smoking and Health*) *Antiraucherinitiative*
ash [æʃ] N Asche *f*; (*wood, tree*) Esche *f*
ashamed [ə'ʃeɪmd] ADJ beschämt; **to be ~ of** sich schämen für; **to be ~ of o.s. for having done sth** sich schämen, dass man etw getan hat
A shares NPL stimmrechtslose Aktien *pl*
ashen ['æʃən] ADJ (*face*) aschfahl
ashore [ə'ʃɔːʳ] ADV an Land
ashtray ['æʃtreɪ] N Aschenbecher *m*
Ash Wednesday N Aschermittwoch *m*
Asia ['eɪʃə] N Asien *nt*
Asia Minor N Kleinasien *nt*
Asian ['eɪʃən] ADJ asiatisch ▸ N Asiat(in) *m(f)*
Asiatic [eɪsɪ'ætɪk] ADJ asiatisch
aside [ə'saɪd] ADV zur Seite; (*take*) beiseite ▸ N beiseite gesprochene Worte *pl*; **to brush objections ~** Einwände beiseiteschieben
aside from PREP außer *+dat*
ask [ɑːsk] VT fragen; (*invite*) einladen; **to ~ sb to do sth** jdn bitten, etw zu tun; **to ~ (sb) sth** (jdn) etw fragen; **to ~ sb a question** jdm eine Frage stellen; **to ~ sb the time** jdn nach der Uhrzeit fragen; **to ~ sb about sth** jdn nach etw fragen; **to ~ sb out to dinner** jdn zum Essen einladen
▸ **ask after** VT FUS fragen nach
▸ **ask for** VT FUS bitten um; (*trouble*) haben wollen; **it's just asking for trouble/it** das kann ja nicht gut gehen
askance [ə'skɑːns] ADV: **to look ~ at sb** jdn misstrauisch ansehen; **to look ~ at sth** etw mit Misstrauen betrachten
askew [ə'skjuː] ADV schief
asking price ['ɑːskɪŋ-] N: **the ~** der geforderte Preis

asleep [ə'sli:p] ADJ schlafend; **to be ~** schlafen; **to fall ~** einschlafen
AS level N ABBR (= *Advanced Subsidiary level*) *Mit „AS level" wird das erste Jahr der Sekundarstufe II bezeichnet, nach dessen Abschluss Prüfungen in drei der ingesamt sechs für den „A level" benötigten Wahlpflichtfächern abgehalten werden*
asp [æsp] N Natter *f*
asparagus [əs'pærəgəs] N Spargel *m*
asparagus tips NPL Spargelspitzen *pl*
ASPCA N ABBR (= *American Society for the Prevention of Cruelty to Animals*) *Tierschutzverein*
aspect ['æspɛkt] N (*of subject*) Aspekt *m*; (*of building etc*) Lage *f*; (*quality, air*) Erscheinung *f*; **to have a south-westerly ~** nach Südwesten liegen
aspersions [əs'pə:ʃənz] NPL: **to cast ~ on** sich abfällig äußern über *+acc*
asphalt ['æsfælt] N Asphalt *m*
asphyxiate [æs'fɪksɪeɪt] VT ersticken
asphyxiation [æsfɪksɪ'eɪʃən] N Erstickung *f*
aspirate ['æspəreɪt] VT aspirieren, behauchen
aspirations [æspə'reɪʃənz] NPL Hoffnungen *pl*; **to have ~ to(wards) sth** etw anstreben
aspire [əs'paɪə^r] VI: **to ~ to** streben nach
aspirin ['æsprɪn] N Kopfschmerztablette *f*, Aspirin® *nt*
aspiring [əs'paɪərɪŋ] ADJ aufstrebend
ass [æs] N (*also fig*) Esel *m*; (*US inf!*) Arsch *m*
assail [ə'seɪl] VT angreifen; (*fig*): **to be assailed by doubts** von Zweifeln geplagt werden
assailant [ə'seɪlənt] N Angreifer(in) *m(f)*
assassin [ə'sæsɪn] N Attentäter(in) *m(f)*
assassinate [ə'sæsɪneɪt] VT ermorden, ein Attentat verüben auf *+acc*
assassination [əsæsɪ'neɪʃən] N Ermordung *f*, (geglücktes) Attentat *nt*
assault [ə'sɔ:lt] N Angriff *m* ▸ VT angreifen; (*sexually*) vergewaltigen; **~ and battery** (*Law*) Körperverletzung *f*
assemble [ə'sɛmbl] VT versammeln; (*car, machine*) montieren; (*furniture etc*) zusammenbauen ▸ VI sich versammeln
assembly [ə'sɛmblɪ] N Versammlung *f*; (*of car, machine*) Montage *f*; (*of furniture*) Zusammenbau *m*
assembly hall N Aula *f*
assembly language N (*Comput*) Assemblersprache *f*
assembly line N Fließband *nt*
assent [ə'sɛnt] N Zustimmung *f* ▸ VI: **to ~ (to)** zustimmen (*+dat*)
assert [ə'sə:t] VT behaupten; (*innocence*) beteuern; (*authority*) geltend machen; **to ~ o.s.** sich durchsetzen
assertion [ə'sə:ʃən] N Behauptung *f*
assertive [ə'sə:tɪv] ADJ (*person*) selbstbewusst; (*manner*) bestimmt
assess [ə'sɛs] VT (*situation*) einschätzen; (*abilities etc*) beurteilen; (*tax*) festsetzen; (*damages, property etc*) schätzen
assessment [ə'sɛsmənt] N Einschätzung *f*; Beurteilung *f*; Festsetzung *f*; Schätzung *f*
assessor [ə'sɛsə^r] N (*Law*) Gutachter(in) *m(f)*
asset ['æsɛt] N Vorteil *m*; (*person*) Stütze *f*; **assets** NPL (*property, funds*) Vermögen *nt*; (*Comm*) Aktiva *pl*
asset-stripping ['æsɛt'strɪpɪŋ] N (*Comm*) *Aufkauf von finanziell gefährdeten Firmen und anschließender Verkauf ihrer Vermögenswerte*
assiduous [ə'sɪdjuəs] ADJ gewissenhaft
assign [ə'saɪn] VT: **to ~ (to)** (*date*) zuweisen (*+dat*); (*task*) übertragen (*+dat*); (*person*) einteilen (für); (*cause*) zuschreiben (*+dat*); (*meaning*) zuordnen (*+dat*); **to ~ sb to do sth** jdn damit beauftragen, etw zu tun
assignment [ə'saɪnmənt] N Aufgabe *f*
assimilate [ə'sɪmɪleɪt] VT aufnehmen; (*immigrants*) integrieren
assimilation [əsɪmɪ'leɪʃən] N Aufnahme *f*; Integration *f*
assist [ə'sɪst] VT helfen; (*with money etc*) unterstützen
assistance [ə'sɪstəns] N Hilfe *f*; (*with money etc*) Unterstützung *f*
assistant [ə'sɪstənt] N Assistent(in) *m(f)*; (BRIT: *also*: **shop assistant**) Verkäufer(in) *m(f)*
assistant manager N stellvertretender Geschäftsführer *m*, stellvertretende Geschäftsführerin *f*
assistant referee N (*Sport*) Schiedsrichterassistent(in) *m(f)*
assisted living [ə'sɪstd-] N (*US*) betreutes Wohnen *nt*
associate ADJ [ə'səuʃɪɪt] (*director*) assoziiert; (*member, professor*) außerordentlich ▸ N [ə'səuʃɪɪt] (*at work*) Kollege *m*, Kollegin *f* ▸ VT [ə'səuʃɪeɪt] in Verbindung bringen ▸ VI: **to ~ with sb** mit jdm verkehren
associated company [ə'səuʃɪeɪtɪd-] N Partnerfirma *f*
association [əsəusɪ'eɪʃən] N (*group*) Verband *m*; (*involvement*) Verbindung *f*; (*Psych*) Assoziation *f*; **in ~ with** in Zusammenarbeit mit
association football N Fußball *m*
assorted [ə'sɔ:tɪd] ADJ gemischt; (*various*) diverse(r, s); **in ~ sizes** in verschiedenen Größen
assortment [ə'sɔ:tmənt] N Mischung *f*; (*of books, people etc*) Ansammlung *f*
Asst ABBR = **assistant**
assuage [ə'sweɪdʒ] VT (*grief, pain*) lindern; (*thirst, appetite*) stillen, befriedigen
assume [ə'sju:m] VT annehmen; (*responsibilities etc*) übernehmen
assumed name [ə'sju:md-] N Deckname *m*
assumption [ə'sʌmpʃən] N Annahme *f*; (*of power etc*) Übernahme *f*; **on the ~ that ...** vorausgesetzt, dass ...
assurance [ə'ʃuərəns] N Versicherung *f*; (*promise*) Zusicherung *f*; (*confidence*) Zuversicht *f*; **I can give you no assurances** ich kann Ihnen nichts versprechen
assure [ə'ʃuə^r] VT versichern; (*guarantee*) sichern
assured [ə'ʃuəd] N (BRIT) Versicherte(r) *f(m)* ▸ ADJ sicher

AST (US) ABBR (= *Atlantic Standard Time*) *Ortszeit in Ostkanada*
asterisk [ˈæstərɪsk] N Sternchen *nt*
astern [əˈstəːn] ADV achtern
asteroid [ˈæstərɔɪd] N Asteroid *m*
asthma [ˈæsmə] N Asthma *nt*
asthmatic [æsˈmætɪk] ADJ asthmatisch ▸ N Asthmatiker(in) *m(f)*
astigmatism [əˈstɪgmətɪzəm] N Astigmatismus *m*
astir [əˈstəːʳ] ADV: **to be ~** (*out of bed*) auf sein
astonish [əˈstɔnɪʃ] VT erstaunen
astonished [əˈstɔnɪʃt] ADJ erstaunt (at über)
astonishing [əˈstɔnɪʃɪŋ] ADJ erstaunlich; **I find it ~ that ...** es überrascht mich, dass ...
astonishingly [əˈstɔnɪʃɪŋlɪ] ADV erstaunlich; **~, ...** erstaunlicherweise ...
astonishment [əˈstɔnɪʃmənt] N Erstaunen *nt*
astound [əˈstaund] VT verblüffen, sehr erstaunen
astounded [əˈstaundɪd] ADJ (höchst) erstaunt
astounding [əˈstaundɪŋ] ADJ erstaunlich
astray [əˈstreɪ] ADV: **to go ~** (*letter*) verloren gehen; (*fig*) auf Abwege geraten; **to lead ~** auf Abwege bringen; **to go ~ in one's calculations** sich verrechnen
astride [əˈstraɪd] ADV (*sit, ride*) rittlings; (*stand*) breitbeinig ▸ PREP rittlings auf *+dat*; breitbeinig über *+dat*
astringent [əsˈtrɪndʒənt] ADJ adstringierend; (*fig: caustic*) ätzend, beißend ▸ N Adstringens *nt*
astrologer [əsˈtrɔlədʒəʳ] N Astrologe *m*, Astrologin *f*
astrology [əsˈtrɔlədʒɪ] N Astrologie *f*
astronaut [ˈæstrənɔːt] N Astronaut(in) *m(f)*
astronomer [əsˈtrɔnəməʳ] N Astronom(in) *m(f)*
astronomical [æstrəˈnɔmɪkl] ADJ (*also fig*) astronomisch
astronomy [əsˈtrɔnəmɪ] N Astronomie *f*
astrophysics [ˈæstrəuˈfɪzɪks] N Astrophysik *f*
astute [əsˈtjuːt] ADJ scharfsinnig; (*operator, behaviour*) geschickt
asunder [əˈsʌndəʳ] ADV: **to tear ~** auseinanderreißen
ASV N ABBR (*Bible:* = *American Standard Version*) *amerikanische Standard-Bibelübersetzung*
asylum [əˈsaɪləm] N Asyl *nt*; (*mental hospital*) psychiatrische Klinik *f*; **to seek political ~** um (politisches) Asyl bitten
asylum seeker N Asylbewerber(in) *m(f)*
asymmetrical [eɪsɪˈmɛtrɪkl] ADJ asymmetrisch

KEYWORD

at [æt] PREP **1** (*referring to position, direction*) an *+dat*, in *+dat*; **at the top** an der Spitze; **at home** zu Hause; **at school** in der Schule; **at the baker's** beim Bäcker; **to look at sth** auf etw *acc* blicken
2 (*referring to time*): **at four o'clock** um vier Uhr; **at night/dawn** bei Nacht/Tagesanbruch; **at Christmas** zu Weihnachten; **at times** zuweilen
3 (*referring to rates, speed etc*): **at £2 a kilo** zu £2 pro Kilo; **two at a time** zwei auf einmal; **at 50 km/h** mit 50 km/h
4 (*referring to activity*): **to be at work** (*in office etc*) auf der Arbeit sein; **to play at cowboys** Cowboy spielen; **to be good at sth** gut in etw *dat* sein
5 (*referring to cause*): **shocked/surprised/annoyed at sth** schockiert/überrascht/verärgert über etw *acc*; **I went at his suggestion** ich ging auf seinen Vorschlag hin
6: **not at all** (*in answer to question*) überhaupt nicht, ganz und gar nicht; (*in answer to thanks*) nichts zu danken, keine Ursache; **I'm not at all tired** ich bin überhaupt nicht müde; **anything at all** irgendetwas
7 (*@ symbol*) At-Zeichen *nt*

ate [eɪt] PT *of* **eat**
atheism [ˈeɪθɪɪzəm] N Atheismus *m*
atheist [ˈeɪθɪɪst] N Atheist(in) *m(f)*
Athenian [əˈθiːnɪən] ADJ Athener ▸ N Athener(in) *m(f)*
Athens [ˈæθɪnz] N Athen *nt*
athlete [ˈæθliːt] N Athlet(in) *m(f)*
athletic [æθˈlɛtɪk] ADJ sportlich; (*muscular*) athletisch
athletics [æθˈlɛtɪks] N Leichtathletik *f*
Atlantic [ətˈlæntɪk] ADJ atlantisch; (*coast etc*) Atlantik- ▸ N: **the ~ (Ocean)** der Atlantik
atlas [ˈætləs] N Atlas *m*
Atlas Mountains NPL: **the ~** der Atlas, das Atlasgebirge
ATM ABBR (= *automated teller machine*) Geldautomat *m*
atmosphere [ˈætməsfɪəʳ] N Atmosphäre *f*; (*air*) Luft *f*
atmospheric [ætməsˈfɛrɪk] ADJ atmosphärisch
atmospherics [ætməsˈfɛrɪks] NPL atmosphärische Störungen *pl*
atoll [ˈætɔl] N Atoll *nt*
atom [ˈætəm] N Atom *nt*
atom bomb, atomic bomb N Atombombe *f*
atomic [əˈtɔmɪk] ADJ atomar; (*energy, weapons*) Atom-
atomizer [ˈætəmaɪzəʳ] N Zerstäuber *m*
atone [əˈtəun] VI: **to ~ for** büßen für
atonement [əˈtəunmənt] N Buße *f*
A to Z® [ˈeɪtəˈzɛd] N Stadtplan *m*
ATP N ABBR (= *Association of Tennis Professionals*) *Tennis-Profiverband*
atrocious [əˈtrəuʃəs] ADJ grauenhaft
atrocity [əˈtrɔsɪtɪ] N Gräueltat *f*
atrophy [ˈætrəfɪ] N Schwund *m*, Atrophie *f* ▸ VT schwinden lassen ▸ VI schwinden, verkümmern
attach [əˈtætʃ] VT befestigen; (*document, letter*) anheften, beiheften; (*employee, troops*) zuteilen; (*importance etc*) beimessen; **to be attached to sb/sth** (*like*) an jdm/etw hängen; (*be connected with*) mit jdm/etw zu tun haben; **the attached letter** der beiliegende Brief; **to ~ a file to an email** eine Datei an eine E-Mail anhängen
attaché [əˈtæʃeɪ] N Attaché *m*

attaché case N Aktenkoffer *m*
attachment [ə'tætʃmənt] N (*tool*) Zubehörteil *nt*; (*love*): **~ (to sb)** Zuneigung *f* (zu jdm); (*to email*) Attachment *nt*, Anhang *m*
attack [ə'tæk] VT angreifen; (*subj: criminal*) überfallen; (*task, problem etc*) in Angriff nehmen ▶ N (*also fig*) Angriff *m*; (*on sb's life*) Anschlag *m*; (*of illness*) Anfall *m*; **heart ~** Herzanfall *m*, Herzinfarkt *m*
attacker [ə'tækə^r] N Angreifer(in) *m(f)*
attain [ə'teɪn] VT (*also:* **attain to**) erreichen; (*knowledge*) erlangen
attainments [ə'teɪnmənts] NPL Fähigkeiten *pl*
attempt [ə'tɛmpt] N Versuch *m* ▶ VT versuchen; **to make an ~ on sb's life** einen Anschlag auf jdn verüben
attempted [ə'tɛmptɪd] ADJ versucht; **~ murder/suicide** Mord-/Selbstmordversuch *m*; **~ theft** versuchter Diebstahl
attend [ə'tɛnd] VT besuchen; (*patient*) behandeln
▶ **attend to** VT FUS sich kümmern um; (*needs*) nachkommen *+dat*; (*customer*) bedienen
attendance [ə'tɛndəns] N Anwesenheit *f*; (*people present*) Besucherzahl *f*; (*Sport*) Zuschauerzahl *f*
attendant [ə'tɛndənt] N (*helper*) Begleiter(in) *m(f)*; (*in garage*) Tankwart *m*; (*in museum*) Aufseher(in) *m(f)* ▶ ADJ damit verbunden
attention [ə'tɛnʃən] N Aufmerksamkeit *f*; (*care*) Fürsorge *f* ▶ EXCL (*Mil*) Achtung!; **attentions** NPL (*acts of courtesy*) Aufmerksamkeiten *pl*; **for the ~ of ...** zu Händen von ...; **it has come to my ~ that ...** ich bin darauf aufmerksam geworden, dass ...; **to stand to** *or* **at ~** (*Mil*) stillstehen
attentive [ə'tɛntɪv] ADJ aufmerksam
attentively [ə'tɛntɪvlɪ] ADV aufmerksam
attenuate [ə'tɛnjueɪt] VT abschwächen ▶ VI schwächer werden
attest [ə'tɛst] VT, VI: **to ~ (to)** bezeugen
attic ['ætɪk] N Dachboden *m*
attire [ə'taɪə^r] N Kleidung *f*
attitude ['ætɪtju:d] N (*posture, manner*) Haltung *f*; (*mental*): **~ to** *or* **towards** Einstellung *f* zu
attorney [ə'tə:nɪ] N (*US: lawyer*) (Rechts)anwalt *m*, (Rechts)anwältin *f*; (*having proxy*) Bevollmächtigte(r) *f(m)*; **power of ~** Vollmacht *f*
Attorney General N (BRIT) ≈ Justizminister(in) *m(f)*; (*US*) ≈ Generalbundesanwalt *m*, ≈ Generalbundesanwältin *f*
attract [ə'trækt] VT (*draw*) anziehen; (*interest*) auf sich *acc* lenken; (*attention*) erregen
attraction [ə'trækʃən] N Anziehungskraft *f*; (*of house, city*) Reiz *m*; (*gen pl: amusements*) Attraktion *f*; (*fig*): **to feel an ~ towards sb/sth** sich von jdm/etw angezogen fühlen
attractive [ə'træktɪv] ADJ attraktiv; (*price, idea, offer*) verlockend, reizvoll
attribute N ['ætrɪbju:t] Eigenschaft *f* ▶ VT [ə'trɪbju:t]: **to ~ sth to** (*cause*) etw zurückführen auf *+acc*; (*poem, painting*) etw zuschreiben *+dat*; (*quality*) etw beimessen *+dat*
attribution [ætrɪ'bju:ʃən] N Zurückführung *f*; Zuschreibung *f*; Beimessung *f*
attrition [ə'trɪʃən] N: **war of ~** Zermürbungskrieg *m*
Atty. Gen. ABBR = **Attorney General**
ATV N ABBR (= *all-terrain vehicle*) Geländefahrzeug *nt*
atypical [eɪ'tɪpɪkl] ADJ atypisch
AU N ABBR = **African Union**
aubergine ['əubəʒi:n] N Aubergine *f*; (*colour*) Aubergine *nt*
auburn ['ɔ:bən] ADJ rotbraun
auction ['ɔ:kʃən] N (*also:* **sale by auction**) Versteigerung *f*, Auktion *f* ▶ VT versteigern
auctioneer [ɔ:kʃə'nɪə^r] N Versteigerer *m*
auction room N Auktionssaal *m*
audacious [ɔ:'deɪʃəs] ADJ wagemutig, kühn
audacity [ɔ:'dæsɪtɪ] N Kühnheit *f*, Verwegenheit *f*; (*pej: impudence*) Dreistigkeit *f*
audible ['ɔ:dɪbl] ADJ hörbar
audience ['ɔ:dɪəns] N Publikum *nt*; (*Radio*) Zuhörer *pl*; (*TV*) Zuschauer *pl*; (*with queen etc*) Audienz *f*
audiotypist ['ɔ:dɪəu'taɪpɪst] N Fonotypist(in) *m(f)*, Phonotypist(in) *m(f)*
audiovisual ['ɔ:dɪəu'vɪzjuəl] ADJ audiovisuell
audiovisual aid N audiovisuelles Lehrmittel *nt*
audit ['ɔ:dɪt] VT (*Comm*) prüfen ▶ N Buchprüfung *f*, Rechnungsprüfung *f*
audition [ɔ:'dɪʃən] N Vorsprechprobe *f* ▶ VI: **to ~ (for)** vorsprechen (für)
auditor ['ɔ:dɪtə^r] N Buchprüfer(in) *m(f)*, Rechnungsprüfer(in) *m(f)*
auditorium [ɔ:dɪ'tɔ:rɪəm] N (*building*) Auditorium *nt*; (*audience area*) Zuschauerraum *m*
Aug. ABBR = **August**
augment [ɔ:g'mɛnt] VT vermehren; (*income, diet*) verbessern
augur ['ɔ:gə^r] VI: **it augurs well** das ist ein gutes Zeichen *or* Omen
August ['ɔ:gəst] N August *m*; *see also* **July**
august [ɔ:'gʌst] ADJ erhaben
aunt [ɑ:nt] N Tante *f*
auntie ['ɑ:ntɪ] N DIMIN *of* **aunt**
aunty ['ɑ:ntɪ] N DIMIN *of* **aunt**
au pair ['əu'pɛə^r] N (*also:* **au pair girl**) Aupair(mädchen) *nt*, Au-pair(-Mädchen) *nt*
aura ['ɔ:rə] N Aura *f*
auspices ['ɔ:spɪsɪz] NPL: **under the ~ of** unter der Schirmherrschaft *+gen*
auspicious [ɔ:s'pɪʃəs] ADJ verheißungsvoll; (*opening, start*) vielversprechend
austere [ɔs'tɪə^r] ADJ streng; (*room, decoration*) schmucklos; (*person, lifestyle*) asketisch
austerity [ɔs'tɛrɪtɪ] N Strenge *f*; (*of room etc*) Schmucklosigkeit *f*; (*hardship*) Entbehrung *f*
Australasia [ɔ:strə'leɪzɪə] N Australien und Ozeanien *nt*
Australasian [ɔ:strə'leɪzɪən] ADJ ozeanisch, südwestpazifisch
Australia [ɔs'treɪlɪə] N Australien *nt*
Australian [ɔs'treɪlɪən] ADJ australisch ▶ N Australier(in) *m(f)*
Austria ['ɔstrɪə] N Österreich *nt*

Austrian ['ɔstrɪən] ADJ österreichisch ▸ N Österreicher(in) *m(f)*
AUT (BRIT) N ABBR (= *Association of University Teachers*) *Gewerkschaft der Universitätsdozenten*
authentic [ɔː'θɛntɪk] ADJ authentisch
authenticate [ɔː'θɛntɪkeɪt] VT beglaubigen
authenticity [ɔːθɛn'tɪsɪtɪ] N Echtheit *f*
author ['ɔːθə^r] N (*of text*) Verfasser(in) *m(f)*; (*profession*) Autor(in) *m(f)*, Schriftsteller(in) *m(f)*; (*creator*) Urheber(in) *m(f)*; (: *of plan*) Initiator(in) *m(f)*
authoritarian [ɔːθɔrɪ'tɛərɪən] ADJ autoritär
authoritative [ɔː'θɔrɪtətɪv] ADJ (*person, manner*) bestimmt, entschieden; (*source, account*) zuverlässig; (*study, treatise*) maßgeblich, maßgebend
authority [ɔː'θɔrɪtɪ] N Autorität *f*; (*government body*) Behörde *f*, Amt *nt*; (*official permission*) Genehmigung *f*; **the authorities** NPL (*ruling body*) die Behörden *pl*; **to have the ~ to do sth** befugt sein, etw zu tun
authorization [ɔːθəraɪ'zeɪʃən] N Genehmigung *f*
authorize ['ɔːθəraɪz] VT genehmigen; **to ~ sb to do sth** jdn ermächtigen, etw zu tun
authorized capital ['ɔːθəraɪzd-] N autorisiertes Aktienkapital *nt*
authorship ['ɔːθəʃɪp] N Autorschaft *f*, Verfasserschaft *f*
autistic [ɔː'tɪstɪk] ADJ autistisch
auto ['ɔːtəu] (US) N Auto *nt*, Wagen *m*
autobiographical ['ɔːtəbaɪə'græfɪkl] ADJ autobiografisch
autobiography [ɔːtəbaɪ'ɔgrəfɪ] N Autobiografie *f*
autocratic [ɔːtə'krætɪk] ADJ autokratisch
Autocue® ['ɔːtəukjuː] N Teleprompter *m*
autograph ['ɔːtəgrɑːf] N Autogramm *nt* ▸ VT signieren
autoimmune [ɔːtəuɪ'mjuːn] ADJ (*disease*) Autoimmun-
automat ['ɔːtəmæt] N Automat *m*; (US) Automatenrestaurant *nt*
automata [ɔː'tɔmətə] NPL *of* **automaton**
automate ['ɔːtəmeɪt] VT automatisieren
automatic [ɔːtə'mætɪk] ADJ automatisch ▸ N (*gun*) automatische Waffe; (*washing machine*) Waschautomat *m*; (*car*) Automatikwagen *m*
automatically [ɔːtə'mætɪklɪ] ADV automatisch
automatic data processing N automatische Datenverarbeitung *f*
automation [ɔːtə'meɪʃən] N Automatisierung *f*
automaton [ɔː'tɔmətən] (*pl* **automata**) N Roboter *m*
automobile ['ɔːtəməbiːl] (US) N Auto(mobil) *nt*
autonomous [ɔː'tɔnəməs] ADJ autonom
autonomy [ɔː'tɔnəmɪ] N Autonomie *f*
autopsy ['ɔːtɔpsɪ] N Autopsie *f*
autumn ['ɔːtəm] N Herbst *m*; **in ~** im Herbst
autumnal [ɔː'tʌmnəl] ADJ herbstlich
auxiliary [ɔːg'zɪlɪərɪ] ADJ (*tool, verb*) Hilfs- ▸ N (*assistant*) Hilfskraft *f*
AV N ABBR (*Bible*: = *Authorized Version*) *englische Bibelübersetzung von 1611* ▸ ABBR = **audiovisual**
avail [ə'veɪl] VT: **to ~ o.s. of** Gebrauch machen von ▸ N: **to no ~** vergeblich, erfolglos
availability [əveɪlə'bɪlɪtɪ] N Erhältlichkeit *f*; (*of staff*) Vorhandensein *nt*
available [ə'veɪləbl] ADJ erhältlich; (*person*: *unoccupied*) frei, abkömmlich; (: *unattached*) zu haben; (*time*) frei, verfügbar; **every ~ means** alle verfügbaren Mittel; **is the manager ~?** ist der Geschäftsführer zu sprechen?; **to make sth ~ to sb** jdm etw zur Verfügung stellen
avalanche ['ævəlɑːnʃ] N (*also fig*) Lawine *f*
avant-garde ['ævɑ̃ŋ'gɑːd] ADJ avantgardistisch
avarice ['ævərɪs] N Habsucht *f*
avaricious [ævə'rɪʃəs] ADJ habsüchtig
avdp. ABBR (= *avoirdupois*) *Handelsgewicht*
Ave ABBR = **avenue**
avenge [ə'vɛndʒ] VT rächen
avenue ['ævənjuː] N Straße *f*; (*drive*) Auffahrt *f*; (*means*) Weg *m*
average ['ævərɪdʒ] N Durchschnitt *m* ▸ ADJ durchschnittlich, Durchschnitts- ▸ VT (*reach an average of*) einen Durchschnitt erreichen von; **on ~** im Durchschnitt, durchschnittlich; **above/below (the) ~** über/unter dem Durchschnitt
▸ **average out** VI: **to ~ out at** durchschnittlich ausmachen
averse [ə'vəːs] ADJ: **to be ~ to sth/doing sth** eine Abneigung gegen etw haben/dagegen haben, etw zu tun; **I wouldn't be ~ to a drink** ich hätte nichts gegen einen Drink
aversion [ə'vəːʃən] N Abneigung *f*; **to have an ~ to sb/sth** eine Abneigung gegen jdn/etw haben
avert [ə'vəːt] VT (*prevent*) verhindern; (*ward off*) abwehren; (*turn away*) abwenden
avian flu ['eɪvɪən-] N Vogelgrippe *f*
aviary ['eɪvɪərɪ] N Vogelhaus *nt*
aviation [eɪvɪ'eɪʃən] N Luftfahrt *f*
avid ['ævɪd] ADJ begeistert, eifrig
avidly ['ævɪdlɪ] ADV begeistert, eifrig
avocado [ævə'kɑːdəu] (BRIT) N (*also*: **avocado pear**) Avocado *f*
avoid [ə'vɔɪd] VT (*person, obstacle*) ausweichen *+dat*; (*trouble*) vermeiden; (*danger*) meiden
avoidable [ə'vɔɪdəbl] ADJ vermeidbar
avoidance [ə'vɔɪdəns] N (*of tax*) Umgehung *f*; (*of issue*) Vermeidung *f*
avowed [ə'vaud] ADJ erklärt
AVP (US) N ABBR (= *assistant vice president*) *stellvertretender Vizepräsident*
avuncular [ə'vʌŋkjulə^r] ADJ onkelhaft
AWACS ['eɪwæks] N ABBR (= *airborne warning and control system*) AWACS
await [ə'weɪt] VT warten auf *+acc*; **awaiting attention/delivery** zur Bearbeitung/Lieferung bestimmt; **long awaited** lang ersehnt
awake [ə'weɪk] (*pt* **awoke**, *pp* **awoken** *or* **awaked**) ADJ wach ▸ VT wecken ▸ VI erwachen, aufwachen; **~ to** sich *dat* bewusst werden *+gen*
awakening [ə'weɪknɪŋ] N (*also fig*) Erwachen *nt*

a

award [ə'wɔ:d] N Preis *m*; (*for bravery*) Auszeichnung *f*; (*damages*) Entschädigung(ssumme) *f* ▶ VT (*prize*) verleihen; (*damages*) zusprechen
aware [ə'wɛə^r] ADJ: **~ (of)** bewusst (*+gen*); **to become ~ of** sich *dat* bewusst werden *+gen*; **to become ~ that ...** sich *dat* bewusst werden, dass ...; **politically/socially ~** politik-/sozialbewusst; **I am fully ~ that** es ist mir völlig klar *or* bewusst, dass
awareness [ə'wɛənɪs] N Bewusstsein *nt*; **to develop people's ~ of sth** den Menschen etw zu Bewusstsein bringen
awash [ə'wɔʃ] ADJ (*also fig*) überflutet
away [ə'weɪ] ADV weg, fort; (*position*) entfernt; **two kilometres ~** zwei Kilometer entfernt; **two hours ~ by car** zwei Autostunden entfernt; **the holiday was two weeks ~** es war noch zwei Wochen bis zum Urlaub; **he's ~ for a week** er ist eine Woche nicht da; **he's ~ in Milan** er ist in Mailand; **to take ~ (from)** (*remove*) entfernen (von); (*subtract*) abziehen (von); **to work/pedal** *etc* **~** unablässig arbeiten/strampeln *etc*; **to fade ~** (*colour, light*) verblassen; (*sound*) verhallen; (*enthusiasm*) schwinden
away game N Auswärtsspiel *nt*
awe [ɔ:] N Ehrfurcht *f*
awe-inspiring ['ɔ:ɪnspaɪərɪŋ] ADJ Ehrfurcht gebietend
awesome ['ɔ:səm] ADJ Ehrfurcht gebietend; (*fig, inf*) überwältigend
awe-struck ['ɔ:strʌk] ADJ von Ehrfurcht ergriffen
awful ['ɔ:fəl] ADJ furchtbar, schrecklich; **an ~ lot (of)** furchtbar viel(e)
awfully ['ɔ:fəlɪ] ADV furchtbar, schrecklich
awhile [ə'waɪl] ADV eine Weile
awkward ['ɔ:kwəd] ADJ (*clumsy*) unbeholfen; (*inconvenient, difficult*) ungünstig; (*embarrassing*) peinlich
awkwardness ['ɔ:kwədnɪs] N Unbeholfenheit *f*; Ungünstigkeit *f*; Peinlichkeit *f*
awl [ɔ:l] N Ahle *f*, Pfriem *m*
awning ['ɔ:nɪŋ] N (*of tent, caravan*) Vordach *nt*; (*of shop etc*) Markise *f*
awoke [ə'wəuk] PT *of* **awake**
awoken [ə'wəukən] PP *of* **awake**
AWOL ['eɪwɔl] ABBR (*Mil:* = *absent without leave*) *see* **absent**
awry [ə'raɪ] ADV: **to be ~** (*clothes*) schief sitzen; **to go ~** schiefgehen
axe, (US) ax [æks] N Axt *f*, Beil *nt* ▶ VT (*employee*) entlassen; (*project, jobs etc*) streichen; **to have an ~ to grind** (*fig*) ein persönliches Interesse haben
axes¹ ['æksɪz] NPL *of* **axe**
axes² ['æksi:z] NPL *of* **axis**
axiom ['æksɪəm] N Axiom *nt*, Grundsatz *m*
axiomatic [æksɪəu'mætɪk] ADJ axiomatisch
axis ['æksɪs] (*pl* **axes**) N Achse *f*
axle ['æksl] N (*also:* **axletree**) Achse *f*
aye [aɪ] EXCL (*yes*) ja ▶ N: **the ayes** die Jastimmen *pl*
AYH N ABBR (= *American Youth Hostels*) *Jugendherbergsverband*, ≈ DJHV *m*
AZ (US) ABBR (*Post*) = **Arizona**
azalea [ə'zeɪlɪə] N Azalee *f*
Azerbaijan [æzəbaɪ'dʒɑ:n] N Aserbaidschan *nt*
Azerbaijani [æzəbaɪ'dʒɑ:nɪ], **Azeri** [ə'zeərɪ] ADJ aserbaidschanisch ▶ N Aserbaidschaner(in) *m(f)*
Azores [ə'zɔ:z] NPL: **the ~** die Azoren *pl*
AZT N ABBR (= *azidothymidine*) AZT *nt*
Aztec ['æztɛk] ADJ aztekisch ▶ N Azteke *m*, Aztekin *f*
azure ['eɪʒə^r] ADJ azurblau, tiefblau

Bb

B¹, b [bi:] N (*letter*) B *nt*, b *nt*; (*Scol*) ≈ Zwei *f*, ≈ Gut *nt*; **B for Benjamin, B for Baker** (*US*) ≈ B wie Bertha; **B road** (BRIT) Landstraße *f*
B² [bi:] N (*Mus*) H *nt*, h *nt*
b. ABBR = **born**
BA N ABBR (= *Bachelor of Arts*) *see* **bachelor**; (= *British Academy*) *Verband zur Förderung der Künste und Geisteswissenschaften*
babble ['bæbl] VI schwatzen; (*baby*) plappern; (*brook*) plätschern ▸ N: **a ~ of voices** ein Stimmengewirr *nt*
babe [beɪb] N (*liter*) Kindlein *nt*; (*esp US*: *address*) Schätzchen *nt*; **~ in arms** Säugling *m*
baboon [bə'bu:n] N Pavian *m*
baby ['beɪbɪ] N Baby *nt*; (*US inf*: *darling*) Schatz *m*, Schätzchen *nt*
baby carriage (*US*) N Kinderwagen *m*
baby food N Babynahrung *f*
baby grand N (*also*: **baby grand piano**) Stutzflügel *m*
babyhood ['beɪbɪhud] N frühe Kindheit *f*
babyish ['beɪbɪɪʃ] ADJ kindlich
baby-minder ['beɪbɪ'maɪndəʳ] (BRIT) N Tagesmutter *f*
baby-sit ['beɪbɪsɪt] VI babysitten
baby-sitter ['beɪbɪsɪtəʳ] N Babysitter(in) *m(f)*
baby wipe N Ölpflegetuch *nt*
bachelor ['bætʃələʳ] N Junggeselle *m*; **B~ of Arts/Science (degree)** ≈ Magister *m* der philosophischen Fakultät/der Naturwissenschaften
bachelorhood ['bætʃələhud] N Junggesellentum *nt*
bachelor party (*US*) N Junggesellenparty *f*

> **Bachelor's Degree** ist der akademische Grad, den man nach drei- oder vierjährigem, erfolgreich abgeschlossenem Universitätsstudium erhält. Die am häufigsten verliehenen Grade sind **BA** (Bachelor of Arts = Magister der Geisteswissenschaften), **BSc** (Bachelor of Science = Magister der Naturwissenschaften), **BEd** (Bachelor of Education = Magister der Erziehungswissenschaften) und **LLB** (Bachelor of Laws = Magister der Rechtswissenschaften). Siehe auch **master's degree, doctorate.**

back [bæk] N Rücken *m*; (*of house, page*) Rückseite *f*; (*of chair*) (Rücken)lehne *f*; (*of train*) Ende *nt*; (*Football*) Verteidiger *m* ▸ VT (*candidate*: *also*: **back up**) unterstützen; (*horse*) setzen *or* wetten auf *+acc*; (*car*) zurücksetzen, zurückfahren ▸ VI (*person*: *also*: **back up**) rückwärtsgehen; (*car etc*) zurücksetzen, zurückfahren ▸ CPD (*payment, rent*) ausstehend ▸ ADV hinten; **in the ~ (of the car)** hinten (im Auto); **at the ~ of the book/crowd/audience** hinten im Buch/in der Menge/im Publikum; **~ to front** verkehrt herum; **to break the ~ of a job** (BRIT) mit einer Arbeit über den Berg sein; **to have one's ~ to the wall** (*fig*) in die Enge getrieben sein; **~ room** Hinterzimmer *nt*; **~ garden** Garten *m* (hinter dem Haus); **~ seat** (*Aut*) Rücksitz *m*; **to take a ~ seat** (*fig*) sich zurückhalten; **~ wheels** Hinterräder *pl*; **he's ~** er ist zurück *or* wieder da; **throw the ball ~** wirf den Ball zurück; **he called ~** er rief zurück; **he ran ~** er rannte zurück; **when will you be ~?** wann kommen Sie wieder?; **can I have it ~?** kann ich es zurückhaben *or* wiederhaben?
▸ **back away** VI sich zurückziehen
▸ **back down** VI nachgeben
▸ **back on to** VT FUS: **the house backs on to the golf course** das Haus grenzt hinten an den Golfplatz an
▸ **back out** VI (*of promise*) einen Rückzieher machen
▸ **back up** VT (*support*) unterstützen; (*Comput*) sichern
backache ['bækeɪk] N Rückenschmerzen *pl*

> **Back Bench** bezeichnet im britischen Unterhaus die am weitesten vom Mittelgang entfernten Bänke, im Gegensatz zur **front bench**. Auf diesen hinteren Bänken sitzen diejenigen Unterhausabgeordneten (auch backbenchers genannt), die kein Regierungsamt bzw. keine wichtige Stellung in der Opposition innehaben.

backbencher ['bæk'bentʃəʳ] (BRIT) N Abgeordnete(r) *f(m)* (*in den hinteren Reihen im britischen Parlament*), Hinterbänkler(in) *m(f)* (*pej*); *see also* **back bench**
backbiting ['bækbaɪtɪŋ] N Lästern *nt*
backbone ['bækbəun] N (*also fig*) Rückgrat *nt*
backchat ['bæktʃæt] (BRIT *inf*) N Widerrede *f*

backcloth ['bækklɔθ] (BRIT) N Hintergrund *m*
backcomb ['bækkəum] (BRIT) VT toupieren
backdate [bæk'deɪt] VT (zu)rückdatieren; **backdated pay rise** rückwirkend geltende Gehaltserhöhung *f*
back door N Hintertür *f*
backdrop ['bækdrɔp] N = **backcloth**
backer ['bækəʳ] N (*Comm*) Geldgeber *m*
backfire [bæk'faɪəʳ] VI (*Aut*) Fehlzündungen haben; (*plans*) ins Auge gehen
backgammon ['bækgæmən] N Backgammon *nt*
background ['bækgraund] N Hintergrund *m*; (*basic knowledge*) Grundkenntnisse *pl*; (*experience*) Erfahrung *f* ▸ CPD (*music*) Hintergrund-; **family** ~ Herkunft *f*; **~ noise** Geräuschkulisse *f*; **~ reading** vertiefende Lektüre *f*
backhand ['bækhænd] N (*Tennis*: *also*: **backhand stroke**) Rückhand *f*
backhanded ['bæk'hændɪd] ADJ (*fig*: *compliment*) zweifelhaft
backhander ['bæk'hændəʳ] (BRIT) N Schmiergeld *nt*
backing ['bækɪŋ] N (*Comm*, *fig*) Unterstützung *f*; (*Mus*) Begleitung *f*
backlash ['bæklæʃ] N (*fig*) Gegenreaktion *f*
backlog ['bæklɔg] N: **to have a ~ of work** mit der Arbeit im Rückstand sein
back number N alte Ausgabe *f or* Nummer *f*
backpack ['bækpæk] N Rucksack *m*
backpacker ['bækpækəʳ] N Rucksacktourist(in) *m(f)*
backpacking ['bækpækɪŋ] N Rucksacktourismus *m*
back pay N Nachzahlung *f*
back-pedal ['bækpɛdl] VI (*fig*) einen Rückzieher machen
back seat N Rücksitz *m*
back-seat driver ['bæksi:t-] N *Mitfahrer, der dem Fahrer dazwischenredet*
backside ['bæksaɪd] (*inf*) N Hintern *m*
backslash ['bækslæʃ] N Backslash *m*
backslide ['bækslaɪd] VI rückfällig werden
backspace ['bækspeɪs] VI (*in typing*) die Rücktaste betätigen
backstage [bæk'steɪdʒ] ADV (*Theat*) hinter den Kulissen; (: *in dressing-room area*) in der Garderobe
backstreet ['bækstri:t] N Seitenstraße *f* ▸ CPD: **~ abortionist** Engelmacher(in) *m(f)*
backstroke ['bækstrəuk] N Rückenschwimmen *nt*
backtrack ['bæktræk] VI (*fig*) einen Rückzieher machen
backup ['bækʌp] ADJ (*train, plane*) Entlastungs-; (*Comput*: *copy etc*) Sicherungs- ▸ N (*support*) Unterstützung *f*; (*Comput*: *also*: **backup disk, backup file**) Sicherungskopie *f*, Back-up *nt*
backward ['bækwəd] ADJ (*movement*) Rückwärts-; (*person*) zurückgeblieben; (*country*) rückständig; **~ and forward movement** Vor- und Zurückbewegung *f*; **~ step/glance** Blick *m*/Schritt *m* zurück
backwards ['bækwədz] ADV rückwärts; (*read*) von hinten nach vorne; (*fall*) nach hinten; (*in time*) zurück; **to know sth ~, to know sth ~ and forwards** (*US*) etw in- und auswendig kennen
backwater ['bækwɔ:təʳ] N (*fig*) Kaff *nt*
back yard N Hinterhof *m*
bacon ['beɪkən] N (Frühstücks)speck *m*, (Schinken)speck *m*
bacteria [bæk'tɪərɪə] NPL Bakterien *pl*
bacteriology [bæktɪərɪ'ɔlədʒɪ] N Bakteriologie *f*
bad [bæd] ADJ schlecht; (*naughty*) unartig, ungezogen; (*mistake, accident, injury*) schwer; **his ~ leg** sein schlimmes Bein; **to go ~** verderben, schlecht werden; **to have a ~ time of it** es schwer haben; **I feel ~ about it** es tut mir leid; **in ~ faith** mit böser Absicht
bad debt N uneinbringliche Forderung *f*
baddy ['bædɪ] (*inf*) N Bösewicht *m*
bade [bæd] PT *of* **bid**
badge [bædʒ] N Plakette *f*; (*stick-on*) Aufkleber *m*; (*fig*) Merkmal *nt*
badger ['bædʒəʳ] N Dachs *m* ▸ VT zusetzen *+dat*
bad hair day N (*inf*) Scheißtag *f*, Tag *m*, an dem alles schiefgeht
badly ['bædlɪ] ADV schlecht; **~ wounded** schwer verletzt; **he needs it ~** er braucht es dringend; **things are going ~** es sieht schlecht *or* nicht gut aus; **to be ~ off (for money)** wenig Geld haben
bad-mannered ['bæd'mænəd] ADJ ungezogen, unhöflich
badminton ['bædmɪntən] N Federball *m*
bad-tempered ['bæd'tɛmpəd] ADJ schlecht gelaunt; (*by nature*) übellaunig
baffle ['bæfl] VT verblüffen
baffling ['bæflɪŋ] ADJ rätselhaft, verwirrend
bag [bæg] N Tasche *f*; (*made of paper, plastic*) Tüte *f*; (*handbag*) (Hand)tasche *f*; (*satchel*) Schultasche *f*; (*case*) Reisetasche *f*; (*of hunter*) Jagdbeute *f*; (*pej*: *woman*) Schachtel *f*; **bags of** (*inf*: *lots of*) jede Menge; **to pack one's bags** die Koffer packen; **bags under the eyes** Ringe *pl* unter den Augen
bagful ['bægful] N: **a ~ of** eine Tasche/Tüte voll
baggage ['bægɪdʒ] N Gepäck *nt*
baggage allowance N Freigepäck *nt*
baggage car (*US*) N Gepäckwagen *m*
baggage (re)claim N Gepäckausgabe *f*
baggy ['bægɪ] ADJ weit; (*out of shape*) ausgebeult
Baghdad [bæg'dæd] N Bagdad *nt*
bag lady (*esp US*) N Stadtstreicherin *f*
bagpipes ['bægpaɪps] NPL Dudelsack *m*
bag-snatcher ['bægsnætʃəʳ] (BRIT) N Handtaschendieb(in) *m(f)*
Bahamas [bə'hɑ:məz] NPL: **the ~** die Bahamas *pl*, die Bahamainseln *pl*
Bahrain [bɑ:'reɪn] N Bahrain *nt*
bail [beɪl] N (*Law*: *payment*) Kaution *f*; (: *release*) Freilassung *f* gegen Kaution ▸ VT (*prisoner*) gegen Kaution freilassen; (*boat*: *also*: **bail out**) ausschöpfen; **to be on ~** gegen Kaution freigelassen sein; **to be released on ~** gegen Kaution freigelassen werden; *see also* **bale**
▸ **bail out** VT (*prisoner*) gegen Kaution freibekommen; (*firm, friend*) aus der Patsche helfen *+dat*

bailiff ['beɪlɪf] N (*Law: Brit*) Gerichtsvollzieher(in) *m(f)*; (*: US*) Gerichtsdiener(in) *m(f)*; (*Brit: factor*) (Guts)verwalter(in) *m(f)*
bailout ['beɪlaʊt] N Rettungsaktion *f*
bait [beɪt] N Köder *m* ▸ VT (*hook, trap*) mit einem Köder versehen; (*tease*) necken
baize [beɪz] N Flausch *m*; **green ~** Billardtuch *nt*
bake [beɪk] VT backen; (*clay etc*) brennen ▸ VI backen
baked beans [beɪkt-] NPL gebackene Bohnen *pl* (in Tomatensoße)
baked potato N in der Schale gebackene Kartoffel *f*
baker ['beɪkəʳ] N Bäcker(in) *m(f)*
baker's dozen N dreizehn (Stück)
bakery ['beɪkərɪ] N Bäckerei *f*
baking ['beɪkɪŋ] N Backen *nt*; (*batch*) Ofenladung *f* ▸ ADJ (*inf: hot*) wie im Backofen
baking powder N Backpulver *nt*
baking tin N Backform *f*
baking tray N Backblech *nt*
balaclava [bælə'klɑːvə] N (*also:* **balaclava helmet**) Kapuzenmütze *f*
balance ['bæləns] N (*equilibrium*) Gleichgewicht *nt*; (*Comm: sum*) Saldo *m*; (*remainder*) Restbetrag *m*; (*scales*) Waage *f* ▸ VT ausgleichen; (*Aut: wheels*) auswuchten; (*pros and cons*) (gegeneinander) abwägen; **on ~** alles in allem; **~ of trade/payments** Handels-/Zahlungsbilanz *f*; **~ carried forward** *or* **brought forward** (*Comm*) Saldovortrag *m*, Saldoübertrag *m*; **to ~ the books** (*Comm*) die Bilanz ziehen *or* machen
balanced ['bælənst] ADJ ausgeglichen; (*report*) ausgewogen
balance sheet N Bilanz *f*
balance wheel N Unruh *f*
balcony ['bælkənɪ] N Balkon *m*; (*in theatre*) oberster Rang *m*
bald [bɔːld] ADJ kahl; (*tyre*) abgefahren; (*statement*) knapp
baldness ['bɔːldnɪs] N Kahlheit *f*
bale [beɪl] N (*Agr*) Bündel *nt*; (*of papers etc*) Packen *m*
▸ **bale out** VI (*of a plane*) abspringen ▸ VT (*water*) schöpfen; (*boat*) ausschöpfen
Balearic Islands [bælɪ'ærɪk-] NPL: **the ~** die Balearen *pl*
baleful ['beɪlful] ADJ böse
balk [bɔːk] VI: **to ~ (at)** (*subj: person*) zurückschrecken (vor *+dat*); (*: horse*) scheuen (vor *+dat*)
Balkan ['bɔːlkən] ADJ (*countries etc*) Balkan- ▸ N: **the Balkans** der Balkan, die Balkanländer *pl*
ball [bɔːl] N Ball *m*; (*of wool, string*) Knäuel *m or nt*; **to set the ~ rolling** (*fig*) den Stein ins Rollen bringen; **to play ~ (with sb)** (*fig*) (mit jdm) mitspielen; **to be on the ~** (*fig: competent*) am Ball sein; (*: alert*) auf Draht *or* Zack sein; **the ~ is in their court** (*fig*) sie sind am Ball
ballad ['bæləd] N Ballade *f*
ballast ['bæləst] N Ballast *m*
ball bearing NPL Kugellager *nt*; (*individual ball*) Kugellagerkugel *f*
ball cock N Schwimmerhahn *m*
ballerina [bælə'riːnə] N Ballerina *f*
ballet ['bæleɪ] N Ballett *nt*
ballet dancer N Balletttänzer(in) *m(f)*
ballistic [bə'lɪstɪk] ADJ ballistisch
ballistic missile N Raketengeschoss *nt*
ballistics [bə'lɪstɪks] N Ballistik *f*
balloon [bə'luːn] N (Luft)ballon *m*; (*hot air balloon*) Heißluftballon *m*; (*in comic strip*) Sprechblase *f*
balloonist [bə'luːnɪst] N Ballonfahrer(in) *m(f)*
ballot ['bælət] N (geheime) Abstimmung *f*
ballot box N Wahlurne *f*
ballot paper N Stimmzettel *m*
ballpark ['bɔːlpɑːk] (*US*) N (*Sport*) Baseballstadion *nt*
ballpark figure (*inf*) N Richtzahl *f*
ballpoint ['bɔːlpɔɪnt], **ballpoint pen** N Kugelschreiber *m*
ballroom ['bɔːlrum] N Tanzsaal *m*
balls [bɔːlz] (*inf!*) NPL (*testicles*) Eier *pl* (*inf!*); (*courage*) Schneid *m*, Mumm *m* ▸ EXCL red keinen Scheiß! (*inf!*)
balm [bɑːm] N Balsam *m*
balmy ['bɑːmɪ] ADJ (*breeze*) sanft; (*air*) lau, lind; (*Brit inf*) = **barmy**
BALPA ['bælpə] N ABBR (= *British Airline Pilots' Association*) *Flugpilotengewerkschaft*
balsa ['bɔːlsə], **balsa wood** N Balsaholz *nt*
balsam ['bɔːlsəm] N Balsam *m*
Baltic ['bɔːltɪk] N: **the ~ (Sea)** die Ostsee
balustrade [bæləs'treɪd] N Balustrade *f*
bamboo [bæm'buː] N Bambus *m*
bamboozle [bæm'buːzl] (*inf*) VT hereinlegen; **to ~ sb into doing sth** jdn durch Tricks dazu bringen, etw zu tun
ban [bæn] N Verbot *nt* ▸ VT verbieten; **he was banned from driving** (*Brit*) ihm wurde Fahrverbot erteilt
banal [bə'nɑːl] ADJ banal
banana [bə'nɑːnə] N Banane *f*
band [bænd] N (*group*) Gruppe *f*, Schar *f*; (*Mus: jazz, rock etc*) Band *f*; (*: military etc*) (Musik)kapelle *f*; (*strip, range*) Band *nt*; (*stripe*) Streifen *m*
▸ **band together** VI sich zusammenschließen
bandage ['bændɪdʒ] N Verband *m* ▸ VT verbinden
Band-Aid® ['bændeɪd] (*US*) N Heftpflaster *nt*
B & B N ABBR = **bed and breakfast**
bandit ['bændɪt] N Bandit *m*
bandstand ['bændstænd] N Musikpavillion *m*
bandwagon ['bændwægən] N: **to jump on the ~** (*fig*) auf den fahrenden Zug aufspringen
bandy ['bændɪ] VT (*jokes*) sich erzählen; (*ideas*) diskutieren; (*insults*) sich an den Kopf werfen
▸ **bandy about** VT (*word, expression*) immer wieder gebrauchen; (*name*) immer wieder nennen
bandy-legged ['bændɪ'lɛgɪd] ADJ o-beinig
bane [beɪn] N: **it/he is the ~ of my life** das/er ist noch mal mein Ende

b

bang [bæŋ] N (*of door*) Knallen *nt*; (*of gun, exhaust*) Knall *m*; (*blow*) Schlag *m* ▸ EXCL peng ▸ VT (*door*) zuschlagen, zuknallen; (*one's head etc*) sich *dat* stoßen *+acc* ▸ VI knallen ▸ ADV: **to be ~ on time** (BRIT *inf*) auf die Sekunde pünktlich sein; **to ~ at the door** gegen die Tür hämmern; **to ~ into sth** sich an etw *dat* stoßen

banger ['bæŋəʳ] (BRIT *inf*) N (*car*: *also*: **old banger**) Klapperkiste *f*; (*sausage*) Würstchen *nt*; (*firework*) Knallkörper *m*

Bangkok [bæŋ'kɔk] N Bangkok *nt*

Bangladesh [bæŋglə'dɛʃ] N Bangladesch *nt*

bangle ['bæŋgl] N Armreif(en) *m*

bangs [bæŋz] (*US*) NPL (*fringe*) Pony *m*

banish ['bænɪʃ] VT verbannen

banister ['bænɪstəʳ] N, **banisters** ['bænɪstəz] NPL Geländer *nt*

banjo ['bændʒəu] (*pl* **banjoes** *or* **banjos**) N Banjo *nt*

bank [bæŋk] N Bank *f*; (*of river, lake*) Ufer *nt*; (*of earth*) Wall *m*; (*of switches*) Reihe *f* ▸ VI (*Aviat*) sich in die Kurve legen; (*Comm*): **they ~ with Pitt's** sie haben ihr Konto bei Pitt's

▸ **bank on** VT FUS sich verlassen auf *+acc*

bank account N Bankkonto *nt*

bank balance N Kontostand *m*

bank card N Scheckkarte *f*

bank charges (BRIT) NPL Kontoführungsgebühren *pl*

bank draft N Bankanweisung *f*

banker ['bæŋkəʳ] N Bankier *m*

banker's card (BRIT) N = **bank card**

banker's order (BRIT) N Dauerauftrag *m*

bank giro N Banküberweisung *f*

bank holiday (BRIT) N (öffentlicher) Feiertag *m*

> Als **bank holiday** wird in Großbritannien ein gesetzlicher Feiertag bezeichnet, an dem die Banken geschlossen sind. Die meisten dieser Feiertage, abgesehen von Weihnachten und Ostern, fallen auf Montage im Mai und August. An diesen langen Wochenenden (bank holiday weekends) fahren viele Briten in Urlaub, sodass dann auf den Straßen, Flughäfen und bei der Bahn sehr viel Betrieb ist.

banking ['bæŋkɪŋ] N Bankwesen *nt*

banking hours NPL Schalterstunden *pl*

bank loan N Bankkredit *m*

bank manager N Filialleiter(in) *m(f)* (einer Bank)

banknote ['bæŋknəut] N Geldschein *m*, Banknote *f*

bank rate N Diskontsatz *m*

bankrupt ['bæŋkrʌpt] ADJ bankrott ▸ N Bankrotteur(in) *m(f)*; **to go ~** Bankrott machen

bankruptcy ['bæŋkrʌptsɪ] N (*Comm, fig*) Bankrott *m*

bank statement N Kontoauszug *m*

banner ['bænəʳ] N Banner *nt*; (*in demonstration*) Spruchband *nt*

banner headline N Schlagzeile *f*

bannister ['bænɪstəʳ] N, **bannisters** ['bænɪstəz] NPL = **banister**

banns [bænz] NPL Aufgebot *nt*

banquet ['bæŋkwɪt] N Bankett *nt*

bantamweight ['bæntəmweɪt] N Bantamgewicht *nt*

banter ['bæntəʳ] N Geplänkel *nt*

BAOR N ABBR (= *British Army of the Rhine*) *britische Rheinarmee*

baptism ['bæptɪzəm] N Taufe *f*

Baptist ['bæptɪst] N Baptist(in) *m(f)*

baptize [bæp'taɪz] VT taufen

bar [bɑːʳ] N (*for drinking*) Lokal *nt*; (*counter*) Theke *f*; (*rod*) Stange *f*; (*on window etc*) (Gitter)stab *m*; (*slab*: *of chocolate*) Tafel *f*; (*fig*: *obstacle*) Hindernis *nt*; (*prohibition*) Verbot *nt*; (*Mus*) Takt *m* ▸ VT (*road*) blockieren, versperren; (*window*) verriegeln; (*person*) ausschließen; (*activity*) verbieten; **~ of soap** Stück *nt* Seife; **behind bars** hinter Gittern; **the B~** (*Law*) die Anwaltschaft; **~ none** ohne Ausnahme

Barbados [bɑː'beɪdɔs] N Barbados *nt*

barbaric [bɑː'bærɪk] ADJ barbarisch

barbarous ['bɑːbərəs] ADJ barbarisch

barbecue ['bɑːbɪkjuː] N Grill *m*; (*meal, party*) Barbecue *nt*

barbed wire ['bɑːbd-] N Stacheldraht *m*

barber ['bɑːbəʳ] N (Herren)friseur *m*

barbiturate [bɑː'bɪtjurɪt] N Schlafmittel *nt*, Barbiturat *nt*

Barcelona [bɑːsə'ləunə] N Barcelona *nt*

bar chart N Balkendiagramm *nt*

bar code N Strichcode *m*

bare [bɛəʳ] ADJ nackt; (*trees, countryside*) kahl; (*minimum*) absolut ▸ VT entblößen; (*teeth*) blecken; **the ~ essentials, the ~ necessities** das Allernotwendigste; **to ~ one's soul** sein Innerstes entblößen

bareback ['bɛəbæk] ADV ohne Sattel

barefaced ['bɛəfeɪst] ADJ (*fig*) unverfroren, schamlos

barefoot ['bɛəfut] ADJ barfüßig ▸ ADV barfuß

bareheaded [bɛə'hɛdɪd] ADJ barhäuptig ▸ ADV ohne Kopfbedeckung

barely ['bɛəlɪ] ADV kaum

Barents Sea ['bærənts-] N: **the ~** die Barentssee

bargain ['bɑːgɪn] N (*deal*) Geschäft *nt*; (*transaction*) Handel *m*; (*good offer*) Sonderangebot *nt*; (*good buy*) guter Kauf *m* ▸ VI: **to ~ (with sb)** (mit jdm) verhandeln; (*haggle*) (mit jdm) handeln; **into the ~** obendrein

▸ **bargain for** VT FUS: **he got more than he bargained for** er bekam mehr, als er erwartet hatte

bargaining ['bɑːgənɪŋ] N Verhandeln *nt*

bargaining position N Verhandlungsposition *f*

barge [bɑːdʒ] N Lastkahn *m*, Frachtkahn *m*

▸ **barge in** VI (*enter*) hereinplatzen; (*interrupt*) unterbrechen

▸ **barge into** VT FUS (*place*) hereinplatzen; (*person*) anrempeln

bargepole ['bɑːdʒpəul] N: **I wouldn't touch it with a ~** (*fig*) das würde ich nicht mal mit der Kneifzange anfassen

baritone ['bærɪtəun] N Bariton *m*
barium meal ['bɛərɪəm-] N Kontrastbrei *m*
bark [bɑ:k] N (*of tree*) Rinde *f*; (*of dog*) Bellen *nt* ▸ VI bellen; **she's barking up the wrong tree** (*fig*) sie ist auf dem Holzweg
barley ['bɑ:lɪ] N Gerste *f*
barley sugar N Malzbonbon *m or nt*
barmaid ['bɑ:meɪd] N Bardame *f*
barman ['bɑ:mən] N (*irreg*) Barmann *m*
barmy ['bɑ:mɪ] (BRIT *inf*) ADJ bekloppt
barn [bɑ:n] N Scheune *f*
barnacle ['bɑ:nəkl] N Rankenfußkrebs *m*
barn owl N Schleiereule *f*
barometer [bə'rɔmɪtə[r]] N Barometer *nt*
baron ['bærən] N Baron *m*; **industrial ~** Industriemagnat *m*; **press ~** Pressezar *m*
baroness ['bærənɪs] N (*baron's wife*) Baronin *f*; (*baron's daughter*) Baroness *f*, Baronesse *f*
baronet ['bærənɪt] N Baronet *m*
barracking ['bærəkɪŋ] N Buhrufe *pl*
barracks ['bærəks] NPL Kaserne *f*
barrage ['bærɑ:ʒ] N (*Mil*) Sperrfeuer *nt*; (*dam*) Staustufe *f*; (*fig: of criticism, questions etc*) Hagel *m*
barrel ['bærəl] N Fass *nt*; (*of oil*) Barrel *nt*; (*of gun*) Lauf *m*
barrel organ N Drehorgel *f*
barren ['bærən] ADJ unfruchtbar
barricade [bærɪ'keɪd] N Barrikade *f* ▸ VT (*road, entrance*) verbarrikadieren; **to ~ o.s. (in)** sich verbarrikadieren
barrier ['bærɪə[r]] N (*at frontier, entrance*) Schranke *f*; (BRIT: *also*: **crash barrier**) Leitplanke *f*; (*fig*) Barriere *f*; (: *to progress etc*) Hindernis *nt*
barrier cream (BRIT) N Hautschutzcreme *f*
barring ['bɑ:rɪŋ] PREP außer im Falle *+gen*
barrister ['bærɪstə[r]] (BRIT) N Rechtsanwalt *m*, Rechtsanwältin *f*

> **Barrister** oder **barrister-at-law** ist in England die Bezeichnung für einen Rechtsanwalt, der seine Klienten vor allem vor Gericht vertritt, im Gegensatz zum **solicitor**, der nicht vor Gericht auftritt, sondern einen **barrister** mit dieser Aufgabe beauftragt.

barrow ['bærəu] N Schubkarre *f*, Schubkarren *m*; (*cart*) Karren *m*
bar stool N Barhocker *m*
Bart. (BRIT) ABBR = **baronet**
bartender ['bɑ:tɛndə[r]] (US) N Barmann *m*
barter ['bɑ:tə[r]] N Tauschhandel *m* ▸ VT: **to ~ sth for sth** etw gegen etw tauschen
barter exchange N Tauschbörse *f*
base [beɪs] N (*of tree etc*) Fuß *m*; (*of cup, box etc*) Boden *m*; (*foundation*) Grundlage *f*; (*centre*) Stützpunkt *m*, Standort *m*; (*for organization*) Sitz *m* ▸ ADJ gemein, niederträchtig ▸ VT: **to ~ sth on** etw gründen *or* basieren auf *+acc*; **to be based at** (*troops*) stationiert sein in *+dat*; (*employee*) arbeiten in *+dat*; **I'm based in London** ich wohne in London; **a Paris-based firm** eine Firma mit Sitz in Paris; **coffee-based** auf Kaffeebasis
baseball ['beɪsbɔ:l] N Baseball *m*
baseboard ['beɪsbɔ:d] (US) N Fußleiste *f*
base camp N Basislager *nt*, Versorgungslager *nt*
Basel [bɑ:l] N = **Basle**
baseline ['beɪslaɪn] N (*Tennis*) Grundlinie *f*; (*fig: standard*) Ausgangspunkt *m*
basement ['beɪsmənt] N Keller *m*
base rate N Eckzins *m*, Leitzins *m*
bases[1] ['beɪsɪz] NPL *of* **base**
bases[2] ['beɪsi:z] NPL *of* **basis**
bash [bæʃ] (*inf*) VT schlagen, hauen ▸ N: **I'll have a ~ (at it)** (BRIT) ich probier's mal
▸ **bash up** VT (*car*) demolieren; (BRIT: *person*) vermöbeln
bashful ['bæʃful] ADJ schüchtern
bashing ['bæʃɪŋ] (*inf*) N Prügel *pl*; **Paki-/queer-~** Überfälle *pl* auf Pakistaner/Schwule
BASIC ['beɪsɪk] N (*Comput*) BASIC *nt*
basic ['beɪsɪk] ADJ (*method, needs etc*) Grund-; (*principles*) grundlegend; (*problem*) grundsätzlich; (*knowledge*) elementar; (*facilities*) primitiv
basically ['beɪsɪklɪ] ADV im Grunde
basic rate N Eingangssteuersatz *m*
basics ['beɪsɪks] NPL: **the ~** das Wesentliche
basil ['bæzl] N Basilikum *nt*
basin ['beɪsn] N Gefäß *nt*; (BRIT: *for food*) Schüssel *f*; (*also*: **wash basin**) (Wasch)becken *nt*; (*of river, lake*) Becken *nt*
basis ['beɪsɪs] (*pl* **bases**) N Basis *f*, Grundlage *f*; **on a part-time ~** stundenweise; **on a trial ~** zur Probe; **on the ~ of what you've said** aufgrund dessen, was Sie gesagt haben
bask [bɑ:sk] VI: **to ~ in the sun** sich sonnen
basket ['bɑ:skɪt] N Korb *m*; (*smaller*) Körbchen *nt*
basketball ['bɑ:skɪtbɔ:l] N Basketball *m*
basketball player N Basketballspieler(in) *m(f)*
Basle [bɑ:l] N Basel *nt*
basmati rice [bəz'mætɪ-] N Basmatireis *m*
Basque [bæsk] ADJ baskisch ▸ N Baske *m*, Baskin *f*
bass [beɪs] N Bass *m*
bass clef N Bassschlüssel *m*
bassoon [bə'su:n] N Fagott *nt*
bastard ['bɑ:stəd] N uneheliches Kind *nt*; (*inf!*) Arschloch *nt* (*inf!*)
baste [beɪst] VT (*Culin*) (mit Fett und Bratensaft) begießen; (*Sewing*) heften, reihen
bastion ['bæstɪən] N Bastion *f*
bat [bæt] N (*Zool*) Fledermaus *f*; (*for cricket, baseball etc*) Schlagholz *nt*; (BRIT: *for table tennis*) Schläger *m* ▸ VT: **he didn't ~ an eyelid** er hat nicht mit der Wimper gezuckt; **off one's own ~** auf eigene Faust
batch [bætʃ] N (*of bread*) Schub *m*; (*of letters, papers*) Stoß *m*, Stapel *m*; (*of applicants*) Gruppe *f*; (*of work*) Schwung *m*; (*of goods*) Ladung *f*, Sendung *f*
batch processing N (*Comput*) Stapelverarbeitung *f*
bated ['beɪtɪd] ADJ: **with ~ breath** mit angehaltenem Atem
bath [bɑ:θ] N Bad *nt*; (*bathtub*) (Bade)wanne *f* ▸ VT baden; **to have a ~** baden, ein Bad nehmen; *see also* **baths**

bathe [beɪð] VI, VT (*also fig*) baden
bather ['beɪðə^r] N Badende(r) *f*(*m*)
bathing ['beɪðɪŋ] N Baden *nt*
bathing cap N Bademütze *f*, Badekappe *f*
bathing costume, (*US*) **bathing suit** N Badeanzug *m*
bath mat N Badematte *f*, Badevorleger *m*
bathrobe ['bɑːθrəub] N Bademantel *m*
bathroom ['bɑːθrum] N Bad(ezimmer) *nt*
baths [bɑːðz] NPL (*also*: **swimming baths**) (Schwimm)bad *nt*
bath towel N Badetuch *nt*
bathtub ['bɑːθtʌb] N (Bade)wanne *f*
batman ['bætmən] N (*irreg*) (BRIT *Mil*) (Offiziers)bursche *m*
baton ['bætən] N (*Mus*) Taktstock *m*; (*Athletics*) Staffelholz *nt*; (*policeman's*) Schlagstock *m*
battalion [bə'tælɪən] N Bataillon *nt*
batten ['bætn] N Leiste *f*, Latte *f*; (*Naut*: *on sail*) Segellatte *f*
▸ **batten down** VT (*Naut*); **to ~ down the hatches** die Luken dicht machen
batter ['bætə^r] VT schlagen, misshandeln; (*subj*: *rain*) schlagen; (*wind*) rütteln ▸ N (*Culin*) Teig *m*; (*for frying*) (Ausback)teig *m*
battered ['bætəd] ADJ (*hat, pan*) verbeult; **~ wife** misshandelte Ehefrau; **~ child** misshandeltes Kind
battering ram ['bætərɪŋ-] N Rammbock *m*
battery ['bætərɪ] N Batterie *f*; (*of tests, reporters*) Reihe *f*
battery charger N (Batterie)ladegerät *nt*
battery farming N Batteriehaltung *f*
battle ['bætl] N (*Mil*) Schlacht *f*; (*fig*) Kampf *m* ▸ VI kämpfen; **that's half the ~** damit ist schon viel gewonnen; **it's a losing ~, we're fighting a losing ~** (*fig*) es ist ein aussichtsloser Kampf
battledress ['bætldrɛs] N Kampfanzug *m*
battlefield ['bætlfiːld] N Schlachtfeld *nt*
battlements ['bætlmənts] NPL Zinnen *pl*
battleship ['bætlʃɪp] N Schlachtschiff *nt*
batty ['bætɪ] (*inf*) ADJ verrückt
bauble ['bɔːbl] N Flitter *m*
baud [bɔːd] N (*Comput*) Baud *nt*
baud rate N (*Comput*) Baudrate *f*
baulk [bɔːk] VI = **balk**
bauxite ['bɔːksaɪt] N Bauxit *m*
Bavaria [bə'vɛərɪə] N Bayern *nt*
Bavarian [bə'vɛərɪən] ADJ bay(e)risch ▸ N Bayer(in) *m*(*f*)
bawdy ['bɔːdɪ] ADJ derb, obszön
bawl [bɔːl] VI brüllen, schreien
bay [beɪ] N Bucht *f*; (BRIT: *for parking*) Parkbucht *f*; (: *for loading*) Ladeplatz *m*; (*horse*) Braune(r) *m*; **to hold sb at ~** jdn in Schach halten
bay leaf N Lorbeerblatt *nt*
bayonet ['beɪənɪt] N Bajonett *nt*
bay tree N Lorbeerbaum *m*
bay window N Erkerfenster *nt*
bazaar [bə'zɑː^r] N Basar *m*
bazooka [bə'zuːkə] N Panzerfaust *f*
BB (BRIT) N ABBR (= *Boys' Brigade*) *Jugendorganisation für Jungen*
BBB (*US*) N ABBR (= *Better Business Bureau*) *amerikanische Verbraucherbehörde*
BBC N ABBR BBC *f*

> **BBC** (Abkürzung für British Broadcasting Corporation) ist die staatliche britische Rundfunk- und Fernsehanstalt. Die Fernsehsender BBC1 und BBC2 bieten beide ein umfangsreiches Fernsehprogramm, wobei BBC1 mehr Sendungen von allgemeinem Interesse wie z.B. leichte Unterhaltung, Sport, Aktuelles, Kinderprogramme und Außenübertragungen zeigt. BBC2 berücksichtigt Reisesendungen, Drama, Musik und internationale Filme. Die 5 landesweiten Radiosender bieten von Popmusik bis Kricket etwas für jeden Geschmack; dazu gibt es noch 37 regionale Radiosender. Der BBC World Service ist auf der ganzen Welt auf Englisch oder in einer von 35 anderen Sprachen zu empfangen. Finanziert wird die BBC vor allem durch Fernsehgebühren und ins Ausland verkaufte Sendungen. Obwohl die BBC dem Parlament gegenüber verantwortlich ist, werden die Sendungen nicht vom Staat kontrolliert.

BC ADV ABBR (= *before Christ*) v. Chr. ▸ ABBR (CANADA: = *British Columbia*) Britisch-Kolumbien *nt*
BCG N ABBR (= *bacille Calmette-Guérin*) BCG *m*
BD N ABBR (= *Bachelor of Divinity*) *akademischer Grad in Theologie*
B/D ABBR = **bank draft**
BDS N ABBR (= *Bachelor of Dental Surgery*) *akademischer Grad in Zahnmedizin*

KEYWORD

be [biː] (*pt* **was, were**, *pp* **been**) AUX VB **1** (*with present participle: forming continuous tenses*): **what are you doing?** was machst du?; **it is raining** es regnet; **are you working in Rome?** arbeiten Sie in Rom?
2 (*with pp: forming passives*) werden; **to be killed** getötet werden; **the box had been opened** die Kiste war geöffnet worden
3 (*in tag questions*): **he's good-looking, isn't he?** er sieht gut aus, nicht (wahr)?; **she's back again, is she?** sie ist wieder da, oder?
4 (*+ to + infinitive*): **the house is to be sold** das Haus soll verkauft werden; **he's not to open it** er darf es nicht öffnen
▸ VB + COMPLEMENT **1** sein; **I'm tired/English** ich bin müde/Engländer(in); **I'm hot/cold** mir ist heiß/kalt; **2 and 2 are 4** 2 und 2 ist *or* macht 4; **she's tall/pretty** sie ist groß/hübsch; **be careful/quiet** sei vorsichtig/ruhig
2 (*of health*): **how are you?** wie geht es Ihnen?
3 (*of age*): **how old are you?** wie alt bist du?; **I'm sixteen (years old)** ich bin sechzehn (Jahre alt)
4 (*cost*) kosten; **how much was the meal?** was hat das Essen gekostet?; **that'll be 5 pounds please** das macht 5 Pfund, bitte

▸ VI **1** (*exist, occur etc*) sein; **there is/are** es gibt; **is there a God?** gibt es einen Gott?; **be that as it may** wie dem auch sei; **so be it** gut (und schön) **2** (*referring to place*) sein, liegen; **Edinburgh is in Scotland** Edinburgh liegt *or* ist in Schottland; **I won't be here tomorrow** morgen bin ich nicht da
3 (*referring to movement*) sein; **where have you been?** wo warst du?
▸ IMPERS VB **1** (*referring to time, distance, weather*) sein; **it's 5 o'clock** es ist 5 Uhr; **it's 10 km to the village** es sind 10 km bis zum Dorf; **it's too hot/cold** es ist zu heiß/kalt
2 (*emphatic*): **it's only me** ich bins nur; **it's only the postman** es ist nur der Briefträger

B/E ABBR = **bill of exchange**
beach [bi:tʃ] N Strand *m* ▸ VT (*boat*) auf (den) Strand setzen
beach buggy N Strandbuggy *m*
beachcomber ['bi:tʃkəuməʳ] N Strandgutsammler *m*
beachwear ['bi:tʃwɛəʳ] N Strandkleidung *f*
beacon ['bi:kən] N Leuchtfeuer *nt*; (*marker*) Bake *f*; (*also*: **radio beacon**) Funkfeuer *nt*
bead [bi:d] N Perle *f*; **beads** NPL (*necklace*) Perlenkette *f*
beady ['bi:dɪ] ADJ: **~ eyes** Knopfaugen *pl*
beagle ['bi:gl] N Beagle *m*
beak [bi:k] N Schnabel *m*
beaker ['bi:kəʳ] N Becher *m*
beam [bi:m] N (*Archit*) Balken *m*; (*of light*) Strahl *m*; (*Radio*) Leitstrahl *m* ▸ VI (*smile*) strahlen ▸ VT ausstrahlen, senden; **to ~ at sb** jdn anstrahlen; **to drive on full** *or* **main** *or* **high ~** mit Fernlicht fahren
beaming ['bi:mɪŋ] ADJ strahlend
bean [bi:n] N Bohne *f*; **runner ~** Stangenbohne *f*; **broad ~** dicke Bohne; **coffee ~** Kaffeebohne *f*
beanpole ['bi:npəul] N (*lit, fig*) Bohnenstange *f*
beanshoots ['bi:nʃu:ts] NPL Sojabohnensprossen *pl*
beansprouts ['bi:nsprauts] NPL = **beanshoots**
bear [bɛəʳ] (*pt* **bore**, *pp* **borne**) N Bär *m*; (*Stock Exchange*) Baissier *m* ▸ VT tragen; (*tolerate, endure*) ertragen; (*examination*) standhalten *+dat*; (*traces, signs*) aufweisen, zeigen; (*Comm: interest*) tragen, bringen; (*produce: children*) gebären; (*: fruit*) tragen ▸ VI: **to ~ right/left** (*Aut*) sich rechts/links halten; **to ~ the responsibility of** die Verantwortung tragen für; **to ~ comparison with** einem Vergleich standhalten mit; **I can't ~ him** ich kann ihn nicht ausstehen; **to bring pressure to ~ on sb** Druck auf jdn ausüben
▸ **bear out** VT (*person, suspicions etc*) bestätigen
▸ **bear up** VI Haltung bewahren; **he bore up well** er hat sich gut gehalten
▸ **bear with** VT FUS Nachsicht haben mit; **~ with me a minute** bitte gedulden Sie sich einen Moment
bearable ['bɛərəbl] ADJ erträglich
beard [bɪəd] N Bart *m*
bearded ['bɪədɪd] ADJ bärtig
bearer ['bɛərəʳ] N (*of letter, news*) Überbringer(in) *m(f)*; (*of cheque, passport, title etc*) Inhaber(in) *m(f)*
bearing ['bɛərɪŋ] N (*posture*) Haltung *f*; (*air*) Auftreten *nt*; (*connection*) Bezug *m*; (*Tech*) Lager *nt*; **bearings** NPL (*also*: **ball bearings**) Kugellager *nt*; **to take a ~ with a compass** den Kompasskurs feststellen; **to get one's bearings** sich zurechtfinden
beast [bi:st] N (*animal*) Tier *nt*; (*inf: person*) Biest *nt*
beastly ['bi:stlɪ] ADJ scheußlich
beat [bi:t] (*pt* **~**, *pp* **beaten**) N (*of heart*) Schlag *m*; (*Mus*) Takt *m*; (*of policeman*) Revier *nt* ▸ VT schlagen; (*record*) brechen ▸ VI schlagen; **to ~ time** den Takt schlagen; **to ~ it** (*inf*) abhauen, verschwinden; **that beats everything** das ist doch wirklich der Gipfel *or* die Höhe; **to ~ about the bush** um den heißen Brei herumreden; **off the beaten track** abgelegen
▸ **beat down** VT (*door*) einschlagen; (*price*) herunterhandeln; (*seller*) einen niedrigeren Preis aushandeln mit ▸ VI (*rain*) herunterprasseln; (*sun*) herunterbrennen
▸ **beat off** VT (*attack, attacker*) abwehren
▸ **beat up** VT (*person*) zusammenschlagen; (*mixture, eggs*) schlagen
beater ['bi:təʳ] N (*for eggs, cream*) Schneebesen *m*
beating ['bi:tɪŋ] N Schläge *pl*, Prügel *pl*; **to take a ~** (*fig*) eine Schlappe einstecken
beat-up ['bi:t'ʌp] (*inf*) ADJ zerbeult, ramponiert
beautician [bju:'tɪʃən] N Kosmetiker(in) *m(f)*
beautiful ['bju:tɪful] ADJ schön
beautifully ['bju:tɪflɪ] ADV (*play, sing, drive etc*) hervorragend; (*quiet, empty etc*) schön
beautify ['bju:tɪfaɪ] VT verschönern
beauty ['bju:tɪ] N Schönheit *f*; (*fig: attraction*) Schöne *nt*; **the ~ of it is that ...** das Schöne daran ist, dass ...
beauty contest N Schönheitswettbewerb *m*
beauty queen N Schönheitskönigin *f*
beauty salon N Kosmetiksalon *m*
beauty sleep N (Schönheits)schlaf *m*
beauty spot (BRIT) N besonders schöner Ort *m*
beaver ['bi:vəʳ] N Biber *m*
becalmed [bɪ'kɑ:md] ADJ: **to be ~** (*sailing ship*) in eine Flaute geraten
became [bɪ'keɪm] PT *of* **become**
because [bɪ'kɔz] CONJ weil; **~ of** wegen *+gen or* (*inf*) *+dat*
beck [bɛk] N: **to be at sb's ~ and call** nach jds Pfeife tanzen
beckon ['bɛkən] VT (*also*: **beckon to**) winken ▸ VI locken
become [bɪ'kʌm] VI (*irreg: like* **come**) werden; **it became known that** es wurde bekannt, dass; **what has ~ of him?** was ist aus ihm geworden?
becoming [bɪ'kʌmɪŋ] ADJ (*behaviour*) schicklich; (*clothes*) kleidsam
BECTU ['bɛktu] (BRIT) N ABBR (= *Broadcasting, Entertainment, Cinematographic and Theatre Union*) *Gewerkschaft für Beschäftigte in der Unterhaltungsindustrie*
BEd N ABBR (= *Bachelor of Education*) *akademischer Grad im Erziehungswesen*

bed [bɛd] N Bett *nt*; (*of coal*) Flöz *nt*; (*of clay*) Schicht *f*; (*of river*) (Fluss)bett *nt*; (*of sea*) (Meeres)boden *m*, (Meeres)grund *m*; (*of flowers*) Beet *nt*; **to go to ~** ins *or* zu Bett gehen ▸ **bed down** VI sein Lager aufschlagen

bed and breakfast N (*place*) (Frühstücks)pension *f*; (*terms*) Übernachtung *f* mit Frühstück

> **Bed and breakfast** bedeutet „Übernachtung mit Frühstück", wobei sich dies in Großbritannien nicht auf Hotels, sondern auf kleinere Pensionen, Privathäuser und Bauernhöfe bezieht, wo man wesentlich preisgünstiger übernachten kann als in Hotels. Oft wird für **bed and breakfast**, auch **B & B** genannt, durch ein entsprechendes Schild im Garten oder an der Einfahrt geworben.

bedbug [ˈbɛdbʌg] N Wanze *f*

bedclothes [ˈbɛdkləuðz] NPL Bettzeug *nt*

bedding [ˈbɛdɪŋ] N Bettzeug *nt*

bedevil [bɪˈdɛvl] VT (*person*) heimsuchen; (*plans*) komplizieren; **to be bedevilled by misfortune/bad luck** vom Schicksal/Pech verfolgt sein

bedfellow [ˈbɛdfɛləu] N: **they are strange bedfellows** (*fig*) sie sind ein merkwürdiges Gespann

bedlam [ˈbɛdləm] N Chaos *nt*

bed linen N Bettwäsche *f*

bedpan [ˈbɛdpæn] N Bettpfanne *f*, Bettschüssel *f*

bedpost [ˈbɛdpəust] N Bettpfosten *m*

bedraggled [bɪˈdrægld] ADJ (*wet*) triefnass, tropfnass; (*dirty*) verdreckt

bedridden [ˈbɛdrɪdn] ADJ bettlägerig

bedrock [ˈbɛdrɔk] N (*fig*) Fundament *nt*; (*Geog*) Grundgebirge *nt*, Grundgestein *nt*

bedroom [ˈbɛdrum] N Schlafzimmer *nt*

Beds [bɛdz] (BRIT) ABBR (*Post*) = **Bedfordshire**

bed settee N Sofabett *nt*

bedside [ˈbɛdsaɪd] N: **at sb's ~** an jds Bett; **~ lamp** Nachttischlampe *f*; **~ book** Bettlektüre *f*

bedsit [ˈbɛdsɪt], **bedsitter** [ˈbɛdsɪtəʳ] N (BRIT) möbliertes Zimmer *nt*

bedspread [ˈbɛdsprɛd] N Tagesdecke *f*

bedtime [ˈbɛdtaɪm] N Schlafenszeit *f*; **it's ~** es ist Zeit, ins Bett zu gehen

bee [bi:] N Biene *f*; **to have a ~ in one's bonnet about cleanliness** einen Sauberkeitsfimmel *or* Sauberkeitstick haben

beech [bi:tʃ] N Buche *f*

beef [bi:f] N Rind(fleisch) *nt*; **roast ~** Rinderbraten *m* ▸ **beef up** (*inf*) VT aufmotzen; (*essay*) auswalzen

beefburger [ˈbi:fbə:gəʳ] N Hamburger *m*

beefeater [ˈbi:fi:təʳ] N Beefeater *m*

beehive [ˈbi:haɪv] N Bienenstock *m*

beekeeping [ˈbi:ki:pɪŋ] N Bienenzucht *f*, Imkerei *f*

beeline [ˈbi:laɪn] N: **to make a ~ for** schnurstracks zugehen auf *+acc*

been [bi:n] PP *of* **be**

beep [bi:p] (*inf*) N Tut(tut) *nt* ▸ VI tuten ▸ VT: **to ~ one's horn** hupen

beer [bɪəʳ] N Bier *nt*

beer belly (*inf*) N Bierbauch *m*

beer can N Bierdose *f*

beet [bi:t] N Rübe *f*; (*US*: *also*: **red beet**) Rote Bete *f*

beetle [ˈbi:tl] N Käfer *m*

beetroot [ˈbi:tru:t] (BRIT) N Rote Bete *f*

befall [bɪˈfɔ:l] VI (*irreg*: *like* **fall**) sich zutragen ▸ VT widerfahren *+dat*

befit [bɪˈfɪt] VT sich gehören für

before [bɪˈfɔ:ʳ] PREP vor *+dat*; (*with movement*) vor *+acc* ▸ CONJ bevor ▸ ADV (*time*) vorher; (*space*) davor; **~ going** bevor er/sie *etc* geht/ging; **~ she goes** bevor sie geht; **the week ~** die Woche davor; **I've never seen it ~** ich habe es noch nie gesehen

beforehand [bɪˈfɔ:hænd] ADV vorher

befriend [bɪˈfrɛnd] VT sich annehmen *+gen*

befuddled [bɪˈfʌdld] ADJ: **to be ~** verwirrt sein

beg [bɛg] VI betteln ▸ VT (*food, money*) betteln um; (*favour, forgiveness etc*) bitten um; **to ~ for** (*food etc*) betteln um; (*forgiveness, mercy etc*) bitten um; **to ~ sb to do sth** jdn bitten, etw zu tun; **I ~ your pardon** (*apologizing*) entschuldigen Sie bitte; (*not hearing*) (wie) bitte?; **to ~ the question** der Frage ausweichen; *see also* **pardon**

began [bɪˈgæn] PT *of* **begin**

beggar [ˈbɛgəʳ] N Bettler(in) *m(f)*

begin [bɪˈgɪn] (*pt* **began**, *pp* **begun**) VT, VI beginnen, anfangen; **to ~ doing** *or* **to do sth** anfangen, etw zu tun; **beginning (from) Monday** ab Montag; **I can't ~ to thank you** ich kann Ihnen gar nicht genug danken; **we'll have soup to ~ with** als Vorspeise hätten wir gern Suppe; **to ~ with, I'd like to know …** zunächst einmal möchte ich wissen, …

beginner [bɪˈgɪnəʳ] N Anfänger(in) *m(f)*

beginning [bɪˈgɪnɪŋ] N Anfang *m*; **right from the ~** von Anfang an

begrudge [bɪˈgrʌdʒ] VT: **to ~ sb sth** jdm etw missgönnen *or* nicht gönnen

beguile [bɪˈgaɪl] VT betören

beguiling [bɪˈgaɪlɪŋ] ADJ (*charming*) verführerisch; (*deluding*) betörend

begun [bɪˈgʌn] PP *of* **begin**

behalf [bɪˈhɑ:f] N: **on ~ of**, (*US*) **in ~ of** (*as representative of*) im Namen von; (*for benefit of*) zugunsten von; **on my/his ~** in meinem/seinem Namen; zu meinen/seinen Gunsten

behave [bɪˈheɪv] VI (*person*) sich verhalten, sich benehmen; (*thing*) funktionieren; (*also*: **behave o.s.**) sich benehmen

behaviour, (*US*) **behavior** [bɪˈheɪvjəʳ] N Verhalten *nt*; (*manner*) Benehmen *nt*

behead [bɪˈhɛd] VT enthaupten

beheld [bɪˈhɛld] PT, PP *of* **behold**

behind [bɪˈhaɪnd] PREP hinter ▸ ADV (*at/towards the back*) hinten ▸ N (*buttocks*) Hintern *m*, Hinterteil *nt*; **~ the scenes** (*fig*) hinter den Kulissen; **we're ~ them in technology** auf dem Gebiet der Technologie liegen wir hinter

ihnen zurück; **to be ~** (*schedule*) im Rückstand *or* Verzug sein; **to leave/stay ~** zurücklassen/-bleiben
behold [bɪ'həuld] VT (*irreg: like* **hold**) sehen, erblicken
beige [beɪʒ] ADJ beige
Beijing ['beɪ'dʒɪŋ] N Peking *nt*
being ['bi:ɪŋ] N (*creature*) (Lebe)wesen *nt*; (*existence*) Leben *nt*, (Da)sein *nt*; **to come into ~** entstehen
Beirut [beɪ'ru:t] N Beirut *nt*
Belarus [bɛlə'rus] N Weißrussland *nt*
Belarussian [bɛlə'rʌʃən] ADJ belarussisch, weißrussisch ▶ N Weißrusse *m*, Weißrussin *f*; (*Ling*) Weißrussisch *nt*
belated [bɪ'leɪtɪd] ADJ verspätet
belch [bɛltʃ] VI rülpsen ▶ VT (*smoke etc: also:* **belch out**) ausstoßen
beleaguered [bɪ'li:gɪd] ADJ (*city*) belagert; (*army*) eingekesselt; (*fig*) geplagt
Belfast ['bɛlfɑ:st] N Belfast *nt*
belfry ['bɛlfrɪ] N Glockenstube *f*
Belgian ['bɛldʒən] ADJ belgisch ▶ N Belgier(in) *m(f)*
Belgium ['bɛldʒəm] N Belgien *nt*
Belgrade [bɛl'greɪd] N Belgrad *nt*
belie [bɪ'laɪ] VT (*contradict*) im Widerspruch stehen zu; (*give false impression of*) hinwegtäuschen über *+acc*; (*disprove*) widerlegen, Lügen strafen
belief [bɪ'li:f] N Glaube *m*; (*opinion*) Überzeugung *f*; **it's beyond ~** es ist unglaublich *or* nicht zu glauben; **in the ~ that** im Glauben, dass
believable [bɪ'li:vəbl] ADJ glaubhaft
believe [bɪ'li:v] VT glauben ▶ VI (an Gott) glauben; **he is believed to be abroad** es heißt, dass er im Ausland ist; **to ~ in** (*God, ghosts*) glauben an *+acc*; (*method etc*) Vertrauen haben zu; **I don't ~ in corporal punishment** ich halte nicht viel von der Prügelstrafe
believer [bɪ'li:və^r] N (*in idea, activity*) Anhänger(in) *m(f)*; (*Rel*) Gläubige(r) *f(m)*; **she's a great ~ in healthy eating** sie ist sehr für eine gesunde Ernährung
belittle [bɪ'lɪtl] VT herabsetzen
Belize [bɛ'li:z] N Belize *nt*
bell [bɛl] N Glocke *f*; (*small*) Glöckchen *nt*, Schelle *f*; (*on door*) Klingel *f*; **that rings a ~** (*fig*) das kommt mir bekannt vor
bell-bottoms ['bɛlbɔtəmz] NPL Hose *f* mit Schlag
bellboy ['bɛlbɔɪ] (BRIT) N Page *m*, Hoteljunge *m*
bellhop ['bɛlhɔp] (US) N = **bellboy**
belligerence [bɪ'lɪdʒərəns] N Angriffslust *f*
belligerent [bɪ'lɪdʒərənt] ADJ angriffslustig
bellow ['bɛləu] VI, VT brüllen
bellows ['bɛləuz] NPL Blasebalg *m*
bell push (BRIT) N Klingel *f*
belly ['bɛlɪ] N Bauch *m*
bellyache ['bɛlɪeɪk] (*inf*) N Bauchschmerzen *pl* ▶ VI murren
bellybutton ['bɛlɪbʌtn] N Bauchnabel *m*
bellyful ['bɛlɪful] (*inf*) N: **I've had a ~ of that** davon habe ich die Nase voll
belong [bɪ'lɔŋ] VI: **to ~ to** (*person*) gehören *+dat*; (*club etc*) angehören *+dat*; **this book belongs here** dieses Buch gehört hierher
belongings [bɪ'lɔŋɪŋz] NPL Sachen *pl*, Habe *f*; **personal ~** persönlicher Besitz *m*, persönliches Eigentum *nt*
Belorussia [bɛleu'rʌʃə] N Weißrussland *nt*
Belorussian [bɛleu'rʌʃən] ADJ, N = **Belarussian**
beloved [bɪ'lʌvɪd] ADJ geliebt ▶ N Geliebte(r) *f(m)*
below [bɪ'ləu] PREP (*beneath*) unterhalb *+gen*; (*less than*) unter *+dat* ▶ ADV (*beneath*) unten; **see ~** siehe unten; **temperatures ~ normal** Temperaturen unter dem Durchschnitt
belt [bɛlt] N Gürtel *m*; (*Tech*) (Treib)riemen *m* ▶ VT schlagen ▶ VI (BRIT *inf*): **to ~ along** rasen; **to ~ down/into** hinunter-/hineinrasen; **industrial ~** Industriegebiet *nt*
▶ **belt out** VT (*song*) schmettern
▶ **belt up** (BRIT *inf*) VI den Mund *or* die Klappe halten
beltway ['bɛltweɪ] (US) N Umgehungsstraße *f*, Ringstraße *f*; (*motorway*) Umgehungsautobahn *f*
bemoan [bɪ'məun] VT beklagen
bemused [bɪ'mju:zd] ADJ verwirrt
bench [bɛntʃ] N Bank *f*; (*work bench*) Werkbank *f*; **the B~** (*Law: judges*) die Richter *pl*, der Richterstand
benchmark ['bɛntʃmɑ:k] N (*fig*) Maßstab *m*
bend [bɛnd] (*pt, pp* **bent**) VT (*leg, arm*) beugen; (*pipe*) biegen ▶ VI (*person*) sich beugen ▶ N (BRIT: *in road*) Kurve *f*; (*in pipe, river*) Biegung *f*; **bends** NPL (*Med*): **the bends** die Taucherkrankheit
▶ **bend down** VI sich bücken
▶ **bend over** VI sich bücken
beneath [bɪ'ni:θ] PREP unter *+dat* ▶ ADV darunter
benefactor ['bɛnɪfæktə^r] N Wohltäter *m*
benefactress ['bɛnɪfæktrɪs] N Wohltäterin *f*
beneficial [bɛnɪ'fɪʃəl] ADJ (*effect*) nützlich; (*influence*) vorteilhaft; **~ (to)** gut (für)
beneficiary [bɛnɪ'fɪʃərɪ] N (*Law*) Nutznießer(in) *m(f)*
benefit ['bɛnɪfɪt] N (*advantage*) Vorteil *m*; (*money*) Beihilfe *f*; (*also:* **benefit concert, benefit match**) Benefizveranstaltung *f* ▶ VT nützen *+dat*, zugutekommen *+dat* ▶ VI: **he'll ~ from it** er wird davon profitieren
Benelux ['bɛnɪlʌks] N die Beneluxstaaten *pl*
benevolent [bɪ'nɛvələnt] ADJ wohlwollend; (*organization*) Wohltätigkeits-
BEng N ABBR (= *Bachelor of Engineering*) *akademischer Grad für Ingenieure*
benign [bɪ'naɪn] ADJ gütig; (*Med*) gutartig
bent [bɛnt] PT, PP *of* **bend** ▶ N Neigung *f* ▶ ADJ (*wire, pipe*) gebogen; (*inf: dishonest*) korrupt; (*: pej: homosexual*) andersrum; **to be ~ on** entschlossen sein zu
bequeath [bɪ'kwi:ð] VT vermachen
bequest [bɪ'kwɛst] N Vermächtnis *nt*, Legat *nt*
bereaved [bɪ'ri:vd] ADJ leidtragend ▶ NPL: **the ~** die Hinterbliebenen *pl*

bereavement [bɪˈriːvmənt] N schmerzlicher Verlust *m*
bereft [bɪˈrɛft] ADJ: **~ of** beraubt *+gen*
beret [ˈbɛreɪ] N Baskenmütze *f*
Bering Sea [ˈbeɪrɪŋ-] N: **the ~** das Beringmeer
berk [bəːk] (*inf*) N Dussel *m*
Berks [bɑːks] (BRIT) ABBR (*Post*) = **Berkshire**
Berlin [bəːˈlɪn] N Berlin *nt*; **East/West ~** (*formerly*) Ost-/Westberlin *nt*
berm [bəːm] (*US*) N Seitenstreifen *m*
Bermuda [bəːˈmjuːdə] N Bermuda *nt*, die Bermudinseln *pl*
Bermuda shorts NPL Bermudashorts *pl*
Bern [bəːn] N Bern *nt*
berry [ˈbɛrɪ] N Beere *f*
berserk [bəˈsəːk] ADJ: **to go ~** wild werden
berth [bəːθ] N (*bed*) Bett *nt*; (*on ship*) Koje *f*; (*on train*) Schlafwagenbett *nt*; (*for ship*) Liegeplatz *m* ▶ VI anlegen; **to give sb a wide ~** (*fig*) einen großen Bogen um jdn machen
beseech [bɪˈsiːtʃ] (*pt, pp* **besought**) VT anflehen
beset [bɪˈsɛt] (*pt, pp* **~**) VT (*subj: difficulties*) bedrängen; (*: fears, doubts*) befallen; **~ with** (*problems, dangers etc*) voller *+dat*
beside [bɪˈsaɪd] PREP neben *+dat*; (*with movement*) neben *+acc*; **to be ~ o.s.** außer sich sein; **that's ~ the point** das hat damit nichts zu tun
besides [bɪˈsaɪdz] ADV außerdem ▶ PREP außer *+dat*
besiege [bɪˈsiːdʒ] VT belagern; (*fig*) belagern, bedrängen
besmirch [bɪˈsməːtʃ] VT besudeln
besotted [bɪˈsɔtɪd] (BRIT) ADJ: **~ with** vernarrt in *+acc*
besought [bɪˈsɔːt] PT, PP *of* **beseech**
bespectacled [bɪˈspɛktɪkld] ADJ bebrillt
bespoke [bɪˈspəuk] (BRIT) ADJ (*garment*) maßgeschneidert; (*suit*) Maß-; **~ tailor** Maßschneider *m*
best [bɛst] ADJ beste(r, s) ▶ ADV am besten ▶ N: **at ~** bestenfalls; **the ~ thing to do is …** das Beste ist …; **the ~ part of** der größte Teil *+gen*; **to make the ~ of sth** das Beste aus etw machen; **to do one's ~** sein Bestes tun; **to the ~ of my knowledge** meines Wissens; **to the ~ of my ability** so gut ich kann; **he's not exactly patient at the ~ of times** er ist schon normalerweise ziemlich ungeduldig
best-before date N Mindesthaltbarkeitsdatum *nt*
bestial [ˈbɛstɪəl] ADJ bestialisch
best man N (*irreg*) Trauzeuge *m* (*des Bräutigams*)
bestow [bɪˈstəu] VT schenken; **to ~ sth on sb** (*honour, praise*) jdm etw zuteilwerden lassen; (*title*) jdm etw verleihen
best seller N Bestseller *m*
bet [bɛt] (*pt, pp* **~** *or* **betted**) N Wette *f* ▶ VI wetten ▶ VT: **to ~ sb sth** mit jdm um etw wetten; **it's a safe ~** (*fig*) es ist so gut wie sicher; **to ~ money on sth** Geld auf etw *acc* setzen
Bethlehem [ˈbɛθlɪhɛm] N Bethlehem *nt*
betray [bɪˈtreɪ] VT verraten; (*trust, confidence*) missbrauchen
betrayal [bɪˈtreɪəl] N Verrat *m*
better [ˈbɛtəʳ] ADJ, ADV besser ▶ VT verbessern ▶ N: **to get the ~ of sb** jdn unterkriegen; (*curiosity*) über jdn siegen; **I had ~ go** ich gehe jetzt (wohl) besser; **you had ~ do it** tun Sie es lieber; **he thought ~ of it** er überlegte es sich *dat* anders; **to get ~** gesund werden; **that's ~!** so ist es besser!; **a change for the ~** eine Wendung zum Guten
better off ADJ (*wealthier*) bessergestellt; (*more comfortable etc*) besser dran; (*fig*): **you'd be ~ this way** so wäre es besser für Sie
betting [ˈbɛtɪŋ] N Wetten *nt*
betting shop (BRIT) N Wettbüro *nt*
between [bɪˈtwiːn] PREP zwischen *+dat*; (*with movement*) zwischen *+acc*; (*amongst*) unter *+acc or dat* ▶ ADV dazwischen; **the road ~ here and London** die Straße zwischen hier und London; **we only had £5 ~ us** wir hatten zusammen nur £5
bevel [ˈbɛvəl] N (*also*: **bevel edge**) abgeschrägte Kante *f*
bevelled [ˈbɛvəld] ADJ: **a ~ edge** eine Schrägkante, eine abgeschrägte Kante
beverage [ˈbɛvərɪdʒ] N Getränk *nt*
bevy [ˈbɛvɪ] N: **a ~ of** eine Schar *+gen*
bewail [bɪˈweɪl] VT beklagen
beware [bɪˈwɛəʳ] VI: **to ~ (of)** sich in Acht nehmen (vor *+dat*); **"~ of the dog"** „Vorsicht, bissiger Hund"
bewildered [bɪˈwɪldəd] ADJ verwirrt
bewildering [bɪˈwɪldrɪŋ] ADJ verwirrend
bewitching [bɪˈwɪtʃɪŋ] ADJ bezaubernd, hinreißend
beyond [bɪˈjɔnd] PREP (*in space*) jenseits *+gen*; (*exceeding*) über *+acc* … hinaus; (*after*) nach; (*above*) über *+dat* ▶ ADV (*in space*) dahinter; (*in time*) darüber hinaus; **it is ~ doubt** es steht außer Zweifel; **~ repair** nicht mehr zu reparieren; **it is ~ my understanding** es übersteigt mein Begriffsvermögen; **it's ~ me** das geht über meinen Verstand
b/f ABBR (*Comm*: = *brought forward*) Übertr.
BFPO N ABBR (= *British Forces Post Office*) *Postbehörde der britischen Armee*
bhp N ABBR (*Aut*: = *brake horsepower*) Bremsleistung *f*
bi… [baɪ] PREF Bi-, bi-
biannual [baɪˈænjuəl] ADJ zweimal jährlich
bias [ˈbaɪəs] N (*prejudice*) Vorurteil *nt*; (*preference*) Vorliebe *f*
biased, biassed [ˈbaɪəst] ADJ voreingenommen; **to be bias(s)ed against** voreingenommen sein gegen
biathlon [baɪˈæθlən] N Biathlon *nt*
bib [bɪb] N Latz *m*
Bible [ˈbaɪbl] N Bibel *f*
biblical [ˈbɪblɪkl] ADJ biblisch
bibliography [bɪblɪˈɔgrəfɪ] N Bibliografie *f*
bicarbonate of soda [baɪˈkɑːbənɪt-] N Natron *nt*
bicentenary [baɪsɛnˈtiːnərɪ] N Zweihundertjahrfeier *f*
bicentennial [baɪsɛnˈtɛnɪəl] (*US*) N = **bicentenary**

biceps ['baɪsɛps] N Bizeps *m*
bicker ['bɪkə^r] VI sich zanken
bickering ['bɪkərɪŋ] N Zankerei *f*
bicycle ['baɪsɪkl] N Fahrrad *nt*
bicycle path N (Fahr)radweg *m*
bicycle pump N Luftpumpe *f*
bicycle track N (Fahr)radweg *m*
bid [bɪd] (*pt* **bade** *or* **~**, *pp* **bidden** *or* **~**) N (*at auction*) Gebot *nt*; (*in tender*) Angebot *nt*; (*attempt*) Versuch *m* ▶ VI bieten; (*Cards*) bieten, reizen ▶ VT bieten; **to ~ sb good day** jdm einen Guten Tag wünschen
bidden ['bɪdn] PP *of* **bid**
bidder ['bɪdə^r] N: **the highest ~** der/die Höchstbietende *or* Meistbietende
bidding ['bɪdɪŋ] N Steigern *nt*, Bieten *nt*; (*order, command*): **to do sb's ~** tun, was jd einem sagt
bide [baɪd] VT: **to ~ one's time** den rechten Augenblick abwarten
bidet ['bi:deɪ] N Bidet *nt*
bidirectional ['baɪdɪ'rɛkʃənl] ADJ (*Comput*) bidirektional
biennial [baɪ'ɛnɪəl] ADJ zweijährlich ▶ N zweijährige Pflanze *f*
bifocals [baɪ'fəuklz] NPL Bifokalbrille *f*
big [bɪg] ADJ groß; **to do things in a ~ way** alles im großen Stil tun
bigamist ['bɪgəmɪst] N Bigamist(in) *m(f)*
bigamous ['bɪgəməs] ADJ bigamistisch
bigamy ['bɪgəmɪ] N Bigamie *f*
big end N (*Aut*) Pleuelfuß *m*, Schubstangenkopf *m*
biggish ['bɪgɪʃ] ADJ ziemlich groß
bigheaded ['bɪg'hɛdɪd] ADJ eingebildet
big-hearted ['bɪg'hɑ:tɪd] ADJ großherzig
bigot ['bɪgət] N Eiferer *m*; (*about religion*) bigotter Mensch *m*
bigoted ['bɪgətɪd] ADJ eifernd; bigott
bigotry ['bɪgətrɪ] N eifernde Borniertheit *f*; Bigotterie *f*
big toe N große Zehe *f*
big top N Zirkuszelt *nt*
big wheel N Riesenrad *nt*
bigwig ['bɪgwɪg] (*inf*) N hohes Tier *nt*
bike [baɪk] N (Fahr)rad *nt*; (*motorcycle*) Motorrad *nt*
bike lane N Fahrradspur *f*
bikini [bɪ'ki:nɪ] N Bikini *m*
bilateral [baɪ'lætərəl] ADJ bilateral
bile [baɪl] N Galle(nflüssigkeit) *f*; (*fig: invective*) Beschimpfungen *pl*
bilingual [baɪ'lɪŋgwəl] ADJ zweisprachig
bilious ['bɪlɪəs] ADJ unwohl; (*fig: colour*) widerlich; **he felt ~** ihm war schlecht *or* übel
bill [bɪl] N Rechnung *f*; (*Pol*) (Gesetz)entwurf *m*, (Gesetzes)vorlage *f*; (*US: banknote*) Banknote *f*, (Geld)schein *m*; (*of bird*) Schnabel *m* ▶ VT (*item*) in Rechnung stellen, berechnen; (*customer*) eine Rechnung ausstellen *+dat*; **"post no bills"** „Plakate ankleben verboten"; **on the ~** (*Theat*) auf dem Programm; **to fit** *or* **fill the ~** (*fig*) der/die/das Richtige sein; **~ of exchange** Wechsel *m*, Tratte *f*; **~ of fare** Speisekarte *f*; **~ of lading** Seefrachtbrief *m*, Konnossement *nt*; **~ of sale** Verkaufsurkunde *f*
billboard ['bɪlbɔ:d] N Reklametafel *f*
billet ['bɪlɪt] (*Mil*) N Quartier *nt* ▶ VT einquartieren
billfold ['bɪlfəuld] (*US*) N Brieftasche *f*
billiards ['bɪljədz] N Billard *nt*
billion ['bɪljən] N (BRIT) Billion *f*; (*US*) Milliarde *f*
billionaire [bɪljə'nɛə^r] N Milliardär(in) *m(f)*
billow ['bɪləu] N (*of smoke*) Schwaden *m* ▶ VI (*smoke*) in Schwaden aufsteigen; (*sail*) sich blähen
billy goat ['bɪlɪ-] N Ziegenbock *m*
bimbo ['bɪmbəu] (*inf, pej*) N (*woman*) Puppe *f*, Häschen *nt*
bin [bɪn] N (BRIT) Mülleimer *m*; (*container*) Behälter *m*
binary ['baɪnərɪ] ADJ binär
bind [baɪnd] (*pt, pp* **bound**) VT binden; (*tie together: hands and feet*) fesseln; (*constrain, oblige*) verpflichten ▶ N (*inf: nuisance*) Last *f*
▶ **bind over** VT rechtlich verpflichten
▶ **bind up** VT (*wound*) verbinden; **to be bound up in** sehr beschäftigt sein mit; **to be bound up with** verbunden *or* verknüpft sein mit
binder ['baɪndə^r] N (*file*) Hefter *m*; (*for magazines*) Mappe *f*
binding ['baɪndɪŋ] ADJ bindend, verbindlich ▶ N (*of book*) Einband *m*
binge [bɪndʒ] (*inf*) N: **to go on a ~** auf eine Sauftour gehen
bingo ['bɪŋgəu] N Bingo *nt*
bin liner N Müllbeutel *m*
binoculars [bɪ'nɔkjuləz] NPL Fernglas *nt*
biochemistry [baɪə'kɛmɪstrɪ] N Biochemie *f*
biodegradable ['baɪəudɪ'greɪdəbl] ADJ biologisch abbaubar
biodiesel ['baɪəudi:zl] N Biodiesel *m*
biodiversity ['baɪəudaɪ'və:sɪtɪ] N biologische Vielfalt *f*
biofuel ['baɪəu'fjuəl] N Biokraftstoff *m*
biographer [baɪ'ɔgrəfə^r] N Biograf(in) *m(f)*
biographic [baɪə'græfɪk], **biographical** [baɪə'græfɪkl] ADJ biografisch
biography [baɪ'ɔgrəfɪ] N Biografie *f*
biological [baɪə'lɔdʒɪkl] ADJ biologisch
biological clock N biologische Uhr *f*
biological waste N Bioabfall *m*
biologist [baɪ'ɔlədʒɪst] N Biologe *m*, Biologin *f*
biology [baɪ'ɔlədʒɪ] N Biologie *f*
biophysics ['baɪəu'fɪzɪks] N Biophysik *f*
biopic ['baɪəupɪk] N Filmbiografie *f*
biopsy ['baɪɔpsɪ] N Biopsie *f*
biosphere ['baɪəsfɪə^r] N Biosphäre *f*
biotechnology ['baɪəutɛk'nɔlədʒɪ] N Biotechnik *f*
biped ['baɪpɛd] N Zweifüßer *m*
birch [bə:tʃ] N Birke *f*
bird [bə:d] N Vogel *m*; (BRIT *inf: girl*) Biene *f*
bird of prey N Raubvogel *m*
bird's-eye view ['bə:dzaɪ-] N Vogelperspektive *f*; (*overview*) Überblick *m*

bird-watcher ['bəːdwɔtʃəʳ] N Vogelbeobachter(in) *m(f)*
Biro® ['baɪərəu] N Kugelschreiber *m*, Kuli *m (inf)*
birth [bəːθ] N Geburt *f*; **to give ~ to** *(subj: woman)* gebären, entbunden werden von; *(: animal)* werfen
birth certificate N Geburtsurkunde *f*
birth control N Geburtenkontrolle *f*, Geburtenregelung *f*
birthday ['bəːθdeɪ] N Geburtstag *m* ▶ CPD Geburtstags-; *see also* **happy**
birthmark ['bəːθmɑːk] N Muttermal *nt*
birthplace ['bəːθpleɪs] N Geburtsort *m*; *(house)* Geburtshaus *nt*; *(fig)* Entstehungsort *m*
birth rate N Geburtenrate *f*, Geburtenziffer *f*
Biscay ['bɪskeɪ] N: **the Bay of ~** der Golf von Biskaya
biscuit ['bɪskɪt] N (BRIT) Keks *m or nt*; (US) Brötchen *nt*
bisect [baɪ'sɛkt] VT halbieren
bisexual ['baɪ'sɛksjuəl] ADJ bisexuell ▶ N Bisexuelle(r) *f(m)*
bishop ['bɪʃəp] N *(Rel)* Bischof *m*; *(Chess)* Läufer *m*
bistro ['biːstrəu] N Bistro *nt*
bit [bɪt] PT *of* **bite** ▶ N *(piece)* Stück *nt*; *(of drill)* (Bohr)einsatz *m*, Bohrer *m*; *(of plane)* (Hobel)messer *nt*; *(Comput)* Bit *nt*; *(of horse)* Gebiss *nt*; (US): **two/four/six bits** 25/50/75 Cent(s); **a ~ of** ein bisschen; **a ~ mad** ein bisschen verrückt; **a ~ dangerous** etwas gefährlich; **~ by ~** nach und nach; **to come to bits** kaputtgehen; **bring all your bits and pieces** bringen Sie Ihre (Sieben)sachen mit; **to do one's ~** sein(en) Teil tun *or* beitragen
bitch [bɪtʃ] N *(dog)* Hündin *f*; *(inf!: woman)* Miststück *nt*
bite [baɪt] *(pt* **bit**, *pp* **bitten**) VT, VI beißen; *(subj: insect etc)* stechen ▶ N *(insect bite)* Stich *m*; *(mouthful)* Bissen *m*; **to ~ one's nails** an seinen Nägeln kauen; **let's have a ~ (to eat)** *(inf)* lasst uns eine Kleinigkeit essen
biting ['baɪtɪŋ] ADJ *(wind)* schneidend; *(wit)* scharf
bit part N kleine Nebenrolle *f*
bitten ['bɪtn] PP *of* **bite**
bitter ['bɪtəʳ] ADJ bitter; *(person)* verbittert; *(wind, weather)* bitterkalt, eisig; *(criticism)* scharf ▶ N (BRIT: *beer) halbdunkles obergäriges Bier*; **to the ~ end** bis zum bitteren Ende
bitterly ['bɪtəlɪ] ADV *(complain, weep)* bitterlich; *(oppose)* erbittert; *(criticize)* scharf; *(disappointed)* bitter; *(jealous)* sehr; **it's ~ cold** es ist bitterkalt
bitterness ['bɪtənɪs] N Bitterkeit *f*
bittersweet ['bɪtəswiːt] ADJ bittersüß
bitty ['bɪtɪ] (BRIT *inf*) ADJ zusammengestoppelt, zusammengestückelt
bitumen ['bɪtjumɪn] N Bitumen *nt*
bivouac ['bɪvuæk] N Biwak *nt*
bizarre [bɪ'zɑːʳ] ADJ bizarr
bk ABBR = **bank**; **book**
BL N ABBR *(= Bachelor of Law) akademischer Grad für Juristen*; *(= Bachelor of Letters) akademischer Grad für Literaturwissenschaftler*; *(US: = Bachelor of Literature) akademischer Grad für Literaturwissenschaftler*
B/L ABBR = **bill of lading**
blab [blæb] *(inf)* VI quatschen
black [blæk] ADJ schwarz ▶ VT (BRIT *Industry*) boykottieren ▶ N Schwarz *nt*; *(person)*: **B~** Schwarze(r) *f(m)*; **to give sb a ~ eye** jdm ein blaues Auge schlagen; **~ and blue** grün und blau; **there it is in ~ and white** *(fig)* da steht es schwarz auf weiß; **to be in the ~** in den schwarzen Zahlen sein
▶ **black out** VI *(faint)* ohnmächtig werden
black belt N (US) *Gebiet in den Südstaaten der USA, das vorwiegend von Schwarzen bewohnt wird*; *(Judo)* schwarzer Gürtel *m*
blackberry ['blækbərɪ] N Brombeere *f*
blackbird ['blækbəːd] N Amsel *f*
blackboard ['blækbɔːd] N Tafel *f*
black box N *(Aviat)* Flugschreiber *m*
black coffee N schwarzer Kaffee *m*
Black Country (BRIT) N: **the ~** *Industriegebiet in den englischen Midlands*
blackcurrant ['blæk'kʌrənt] N Johannisbeere *f*
black economy N: **the ~** die Schattenwirtschaft
blacken ['blækn] VT: **to ~ sb's name/ reputation** *(fig)* jdn verunglimpfen
Black Forest N: **the ~** der Schwarzwald
blackhead ['blækhɛd] N Mitesser *m*
black hole N schwarzes Loch *nt*
black ice N Glatteis *nt*
blackjack ['blækdʒæk] N *(Cards)* Siebzehnundvier *nt*; *(US: truncheon)* Schlagstock *m*
blackleg ['blæklɛg] (BRIT) N Streikbrecher(in) *m(f)*
blacklist ['blæklɪst] N schwarze Liste *f* ▶ VT auf die schwarze Liste setzen
blackmail ['blækmeɪl] N Erpressung *f* ▶ VT erpressen
blackmailer ['blækmeɪləʳ] N Erpresser(in) *m(f)*
black market N Schwarzmarkt *m*
blackout ['blækaut] N *(in wartime)* Verdunkelung *f*; *(power cut)* Stromausfall *m*; *(TV, Radio)* Ausfall *m*; *(faint)* Ohnmachtsanfall *m*
black pepper N schwarzer Pfeffer *m*
Black Sea N: **the ~** das Schwarze Meer
black sheep N *(fig)* schwarzes Schaf *nt*
blacksmith ['blæksmɪθ] N Schmied *m*
black spot N *(Aut)* Gefahrenstelle *f*; *(for unemployment etc) Gebiet, in dem ein Problem besonders ausgeprägt ist*
bladder ['blædəʳ] N Blase *f*
blade [bleɪd] N *(of knife etc)* Klinge *f*; *(of oar, propeller)* Blatt *nt*; **a ~ of grass** ein Grashalm *m*
Blairite ['blɛəraɪt] *(Pol)* ADJ blairistisch ▶ N Blair-Anhänger(in) *m(f)*
blame [bleɪm] N Schuld *f* ▶ VT: **to ~ sb for sth** jdm die Schuld an etw *dat* geben; **to be to ~** Schuld daran haben, schuld sein; **who's to ~?** wer hat Schuld *or* ist schuld?; **I'm not to ~** es ist nicht meine Schuld
blameless ['bleɪmlɪs] ADJ schuldlos
blanch [blɑːntʃ] VI blass werden ▶ VT *(Culin)* blanchieren
blancmange [blə'mɔnʒ] N Pudding *m*

bland [blænd] ADJ (*taste, food*) fade
blank [blæŋk] ADJ (*paper*) leer, unbeschrieben; (*look*) ausdruckslos ▸ N (*on form*) Lücke *f*; (*cartridge*) Platzpatrone *f*; **my mind was a ~** ich hatte ein Brett vor dem Kopf; **we drew a ~** (*fig*) wir hatten kein Glück
blank cheque N Blankoscheck *m*; **to give sb a ~ to do sth** (*fig*) jdm freie Hand geben, etw zu tun
blanket ['blæŋkɪt] N Decke *f* ▸ ADJ (*statement*) pauschal; (*agreement*) Pauschal-
blanket cover N umfassende Versicherung *f*
blare [blɛəʳ] VI (*brass band*) schmettern; (*horn*) tuten; (*radio*) plärren
▸ **blare out** VI (*radio, stereo*) plärren
blasé ['blɑ:zeɪ] ADJ blasiert
blaspheme [blæs'fi:m] VI Gott lästern
blasphemous ['blæsfɪməs] ADJ lästerlich, blasphemisch
blasphemy ['blæsfɪmɪ] N (Gottes)lästerung *f*, Blasphemie *f*
blast [blɑ:st] N (*of wind*) Windstoß *m*; (*of whistle*) Trillern *nt*; (*shock wave*) Druckwelle *f*; (*of air, steam*) Schwall *m*; (*of explosive*) Explosion *f* ▸ VT (*blow up*) sprengen ▸ EXCL (BRIT *inf*) verdammt!, so ein Mist!; **at full ~** (*play music*) mit voller Lautstärke; (*move, work*) auf Hochtouren
▸ **blast off** VI (*Space*) abheben, starten
blast furnace N Hochofen *m*
blastoff ['blɑ:stɔf] N (*Space*) Abschuss *m*
blatant ['bleɪtənt] ADJ offensichtlich
blatantly ['bleɪtəntlɪ] ADV (*lie*) unverfroren; **it's ~ obvious** es ist überdeutlich
blaze [bleɪz] N (*fire*) Feuer *nt*, Brand *m*; (*fig: of colour*) Farbenpracht *f*; (*: of glory*) Glanz *m* ▸ VI (*fire*) lodern; (*guns*) feuern; (*fig: eyes*) glühen ▸ VT: **to ~ a trail** (*fig*) den Weg bahnen; **in a ~ of publicity** mit viel Publicity
blazer ['bleɪzəʳ] N Blazer *m*
bleach [bli:tʃ] N (*also:* **household bleach**) ≈ Reinigungsmittel *nt* ▸ VT bleichen
bleached [bli:tʃt] ADJ gebleicht
bleachers ['bli:tʃəz] (US) NPL unüberdachte Zuschauertribüne *f*
bleak [bli:k] ADJ (*countryside*) öde; (*weather, situation*) trostlos; (*prospect*) trüb; (*expression, voice*) deprimiert
bleary-eyed ['blɪərɪ'aɪd] ADJ triefäugig
bleat [bli:t] VI (*goat*) meckern; (*sheep*) blöken ▸ N Meckern *nt*; Blöken *nt*
bled [blɛd] PT, PP *of* **bleed**
bleed [bli:d] (*pt, pp* **bled**) VI bluten; (*colour*) auslaufen ▸ VT (*brakes, radiator*) entlüften; **my nose is bleeding** ich habe Nasenbluten
bleep [bli:p] N Piepton *m* ▸ VI piepen ▸ VT (*doctor etc*) rufen, anpiepen (*inf*)
bleeper ['bli:pəʳ] N Piepser *m* (*inf*), Funkrufempfänger *m*
blemish ['blɛmɪʃ] N Makel *m*
blend [blɛnd] N Mischung *f* ▸ VT (*Culin*) mischen, mixen; (*colours, styles, flavours etc*) vermischen ▸ VI (*colours etc: also:* **blend in**) harmonieren
blender ['blɛndəʳ] N (*Culin*) Mixer *m*
bless [blɛs] (*pt, pp* **blessed** *or* **blest**) VT segnen; **to be blessed with** gesegnet sein mit; **~ you!** (*after sneeze*) Gesundheit!
blessed ['blɛsɪd] ADJ heilig; (*happy*) selig; **it rains every ~ day** (*inf*) es regnet aber auch jeden Tag
blessing ['blɛsɪŋ] N (*approval*) Zustimmung *f*; (*Rel, fig*) Segen *m*; **to count one's blessings** von Glück sagen können; **it was a ~ in disguise** es war schließlich doch ein Segen
blew [blu:] PT *of* **blow**
blight [blaɪt] VT zerstören; (*hopes*) vereiteln; (*life*) verderben ▸ N (*of plants*) Brand *m*
blimey ['blaɪmɪ] (BRIT *inf*) EXCL Mensch!
blind [blaɪnd] ADJ blind ▸ N (*for window*) Rollo *nt*, Rouleau *nt*; (*also:* **Venetian blind**) Jalousie *f* ▸ VT blind machen; (*dazzle*) blenden; (*deceive: with facts etc*) verblenden; **the blind** NPL (*blind people*) die Blinden *pl*; **to turn a ~ eye (on** *or* **to)** ein Auge zudrücken (bei); **to be ~ to sth** (*fig*) blind für etw sein
blind alley N (*fig*) Sackgasse *f*
blind corner (BRIT) N unübersichtliche Ecke *f*
blind date N Rendezvous *nt* mit einem/einer Unbekannten
blinders ['blaɪndəz] (US) NPL = **blinkers**
blindfold ['blaɪndfəuld] N Augenbinde *f* ▸ ADJ, ADV mit verbundenen Augen ▸ VT die Augen verbinden *+dat*
blinding ['blaɪndɪŋ] ADJ (*dazzling*) blendend; (*remarkable*) bemerkenswert
blindly ['blaɪndlɪ] ADV (*without seeing*) wie blind; (*without thinking*) blindlings
blindness ['blaɪndnɪs] N Blindheit *f*
blind spot N (*Aut*) toter Winkel *m*; (*fig: weak spot*) schwacher Punkt *m*
blink [blɪŋk] VI blinzeln; (*light*) blinken ▸ N: **the TV's on the ~** (*inf*) der Fernseher ist kaputt
blinkers ['blɪŋkəz] NPL Scheuklappen *pl*
blinking ['blɪŋkɪŋ] (BRIT *inf*) ADJ: **this ~ ...** diese(r, s) verflixte ...
blip [blɪp] N (*on radar screen*) leuchtender Punkt *m*; (*in a straight line*) Ausschlag *m*; (*fig*) (zeitweilige) Abweichung *f*
bliss [blɪs] N Glück *nt*, Seligkeit *f*
blissful ['blɪsful] ADJ (*event, day*) herrlich; (*smile*) selig; **a ~ sigh** ein wohliger Seufzer *m*; **in ~ ignorance** in herrlicher Ahnungslosigkeit
blissfully ['blɪsfəlɪ] ADV selig; **~ happy** überglücklich; **~ unaware of ...** ohne auch nur zu ahnen, dass ...
blister ['blɪstəʳ] N Blase *f* ▸ VI (*paint*) Blasen werfen
BLit, BLitt N ABBR (= *Bachelor of Literature; Bachelor of Letters*) *akademischer Grad für Literaturwissenschaftler*
blithely ['blaɪðlɪ] ADV (*unconcernedly*) unbekümmert, munter; (*joyfully*) fröhlich
blithering ['blɪðərɪŋ] (*inf*) ADJ: **this ~ idiot** dieser Trottel
blitz [blɪts] N (*Mil*) Luftangriff *m*; **to have a ~ on sth** (*fig*) einen Großangriff auf etw *acc* starten
blizzard ['blɪzəd] N Schneesturm *m*

bloated ['bləutɪd] ADJ aufgedunsen; *(full)* (über)satt
blob [blɔb] N Tropfen *m*; *(sth indistinct)* verschwommener Fleck *m*
bloc [blɔk] N Block *m*; **the Eastern ~** *(Hist)* der Ostblock
block [blɔk] N Block *m*; *(toy)* Bauklotz *m*; *(in pipes)* Verstopfung *f* ▸ VT blockieren; *(progress)* aufhalten; *(Comput)* blocken; **~ of flats** (BRIT) Wohnblock *m*; **3 blocks from here** 3 Blocks *or* Straßen weiter; **mental ~** geistige Sperre *f*, Mattscheibe *f* *(inf)*; **~ and tackle** Flaschenzug *m*
▸ **block up** VT, VI verstopfen
blockade [blɔ'keɪd] N Blockade *f* ▸ VT blockieren
blockage ['blɔkɪdʒ] N Verstopfung *f*
block booking N Gruppenbuchung *f*
blockbuster ['blɔkbʌstəʳ] N Knüller *m*
block capitals NPL Blockschrift *f*
blockhead ['blɔkhɛd] *(inf)* N Dummkopf *m*
block letters NPL Blockschrift *f*
block release (BRIT) N *blockweise Freistellung von Auszubildenden zur Weiterbildung*
block vote (BRIT) N Stimmenblock *m*
blog [blɔg] N *(Comput)* Blog *m*, Weblog *m* ▸ VI bloggen
blogger ['blɔgəʳ] N Blogger(in) *m(f)*
blogging ['blɔgɪŋ] N Blogging *nt*
blogosphere ['blɔgəsfɪəʳ] N Blogosphäre *f*
bloke [bləuk] (BRIT *inf*) N Typ *m*
blond, blonde [blɔnd] ADJ blond ▸ N: **~(e)** *(woman)* Blondine *f*
blood [blʌd] N Blut *nt*; **new ~** *(fig)* frisches Blut *nt*
blood bank N Blutbank *f*
blood bath N Blutbad *nt*
blood count N Blutbild *nt*
bloodcurdling ['blʌdkə:dlɪŋ] ADJ grauenerregend
blood donor N Blutspender(in) *m(f)*
blood group N Blutgruppe *f*
bloodhound ['blʌdhaund] N Bluthund *m*
bloodless ['blʌdlɪs] ADJ *(victory)* unblutig; *(pale)* blutleer
blood-letting ['blʌdlɛtɪŋ] N *(also fig)* Aderlass *m*
blood poisoning N Blutvergiftung *f*
blood pressure N Blutdruck *m*; **to have high/low ~** hohen/niedrigen Blutdruck haben
bloodshed ['blʌdʃɛd] N Blutvergießen *nt*
bloodshot ['blʌdʃɔt] ADJ *(eyes)* blutunterlaufen
blood sport N Jagdsport *m* *(und andere Sportarten, bei denen Tiere getötet werden)*
bloodstained ['blʌdsteɪnd] ADJ blutbefleckt
bloodstream ['blʌdstri:m] N Blut *nt*, Blutkreislauf *m*
blood test N Blutprobe *f*
bloodthirsty ['blʌdθə:stɪ] ADJ blutrünstig
blood transfusion N Blutübertragung *f*, (Blut)transfusion *f*
blood type N Blutgruppe *f*
blood vessel N Blutgefäß *nt*
bloody ['blʌdɪ] ADJ blutig; (BRIT *inf!*): **this ~ ...** diese(r, s) verdammte ...; **~ strong** *(inf!)* verdammt stark; **~ good** *(inf!)* echt gut
bloody-minded ['blʌdɪ'maɪndɪd] (BRIT *inf*) ADJ stur
bloom [blu:m] N Blüte *f* ▸ VI blühen; **to be in ~** in Blüte stehen
blooming ['blu:mɪŋ] (BRIT *inf*) ADJ: **this ~ ...** diese(r, s) verflixte ...
blossom ['blɔsəm] N Blüte *f* ▸ VI blühen; *(fig)*: **to ~ into** erblühen *or* aufblühen zu
blot [blɔt] N Klecks *m*; *(fig: on name etc)* Makel *m* ▸ VT *(liquid)* aufsaugen; *(make blot on)* beklecksen; **to be a ~ on the landscape** ein Schandfleck in der Landschaft sein; **to ~ one's copy book** *(fig)* sich unmöglich machen
▸ **blot out** VT *(view)* verdecken; *(memory)* auslöschen
blotchy ['blɔtʃɪ] ADJ fleckig
blotter ['blɔtəʳ] N (Tinten)löscher *m*
blotting paper ['blɔtɪŋ-] N Löschpapier *nt*
blotto ['blɔtəu] *(inf)* ADJ *(drunk)* sternhagelvoll
blouse [blauz] N Bluse *f*
blow [bləu] *(pt* **blew**, *pp* **blown**) N *(also fig)* Schlag *m* ▸ VI *(wind)* wehen; *(person)* blasen ▸ VT *(subj: wind)* wehen; *(instrument, whistle)* blasen; *(fuse)* durchbrennen lassen; **to come to blows** handgreiflich werden; **to ~ off course** *(ship)* vom Kurs abgetrieben werden; **to ~ one's nose** sich *dat* die Nase putzen; **to ~ a whistle** pfeifen
▸ **blow away** VT wegblasen ▸ VI wegfliegen
▸ **blow down** VT umwehen
▸ **blow off** VT wegwehen ▸ VI wegfliegen
▸ **blow out** VI ausgehen
▸ **blow over** VI sich legen
▸ **blow up** VI ausbrechen ▸ VT *(bridge)* in die Luft jagen; *(tyre)* aufblasen; *(Phot)* vergrößern
blow-dry ['bləudraɪ] VT föhnen ▸ N: **to have a ~** sich föhnen lassen
blowlamp ['bləulæmp] (BRIT) N Lötlampe *f*
blown [bləun] PP *of* **blow**
blowout ['bləʊaʊt] N Reifenpanne *f*; *(inf: big meal)* Schlemmerei *f*; *(of oil-well)* Ölausbruch *m*
blowtorch ['bləutɔ:tʃ] N = **blowlamp**
blow-up ['bləuʌp] N Vergrößerung *f*
blowzy ['blauzɪ] (BRIT) ADJ schlampig
BLS *(US)* N ABBR *(= Bureau of Labor Statistics) Amt für Arbeitsstatistik*
blubber ['blʌbəʳ] N Walfischspeck *m* ▸ VI *(pej)* heulen
bludgeon ['blʌdʒən] VT niederknüppeln; *(fig)*: **to ~ sb into doing sth** jdm so lange zusetzen, bis er etw tut
blue [blu:] ADJ blau; *(depressed)* deprimiert, niedergeschlagen ▸ N: **out of the ~** *(fig)* aus heiterem Himmel; **blues** N *(Mus)*: **the blues** der Blues; **~ film** Pornofilm *m*; **~ joke** schlüpfriger Witz *m*; **(only) once in a ~ moon** (nur) alle Jubeljahre einmal; **to have the blues** deprimiert *or* niedergeschlagen sein
blue baby N Baby *nt* mit angeborenem Herzfehler
bluebell ['blu:bɛl] N Glockenblume *f*
blueberry ['blu:bərɪ] N Blaubeere *f*
bluebottle ['blu:bɔtl] N Schmeißfliege *f*
blue cheese N Blauschimmelkäse *m*

blue-chip ['blu:tʃɪp] ADJ: **~ investment** sichere Geldanlage *f*
blue-collar worker ['blu:kɔlə^r-] N Arbeiter(in) *m(f)*
blue jeans NPL (Blue)jeans *pl*
blueprint ['blu:prɪnt] N (*fig*): **a ~ (for)** ein Plan *m* *or* Entwurf *m* (für)
bluff [blʌf] VI bluffen ▸ N Bluff *m*; (*cliff*) Klippe *f*; (*promontory*) Felsvorsprung *m*; **to call sb's ~** es darauf ankommen lassen
blunder ['blʌndə^r] N (dummer) Fehler *m* ▸ VI einen (dummen) Fehler machen; **to ~ into sb** mit jdm zusammenstoßen; **to ~ into sth** in etw *acc* (hinein)tappen
blunt [blʌnt] ADJ stumpf; (*person*) direkt; (*talk*) unverblümt ▸ VT stumpf machen; **~ instrument** (*Law*) stumpfer Gegenstand *m*
bluntly ['blʌntlɪ] ADV (*speak*) unverblümt
bluntness ['blʌntnɪs] N (*of person*) Direktheit *f*
blur [blə:^r] N (*shape*) verschwommener Fleck *m*; (*scene etc*) verschwommenes Bild *nt*; (*memory*) verschwommene Erinnerung *f* ▸ VT (*vision*) trüben; (*distinction*) verwischen
blurb [blə:b] N Informationsmaterial *nt*
blurred [blə:d] ADJ (*photograph, TV picture etc*) verschwommen; (*distinction*) verwischt
blurt out [blə:t-] VT herausplatzen mit
blush [blʌʃ] VI erröten ▸ N Röte *f*
blusher ['blʌʃə^r] N Rouge *nt*
bluster ['blʌstə^r] N Toben *nt*, Geschrei *nt* ▸ VI toben
blustering ['blʌstərɪŋ] ADJ polternd
blustery ['blʌstərɪ] ADJ stürmisch
Blvd ABBR = **boulevard**
BM N ABBR (= *British Museum*) Britisches Museum *nt*; (= *Bachelor of Medicine*) *akademischer Grad für Mediziner*
BMA N ABBR (= *British Medical Association*) *Dachverband der Ärzte*
BMJ N ABBR (= *British Medical Journal*) *vom BMA herausgegebene Zeitschrift*
BMus N ABBR (= *Bachelor of Music*) *akademischer Grad für Musikwissenschaftler*
BMX N ABBR (= *bicycle motocross*): **~ bike** BMX-Rad *nt*
bn ABBR = **billion**
BO N ABBR (*inf*: = *body odour*) Körpergeruch *m*; = **box office**
boar [bɔ:^r] N (*male pig*) Eber *m*; (*wild pig*) Keiler *m*
board [bɔ:d] N Brett *nt*; (*cardboard*) Pappe *f*; (*committee*) Ausschuss *m*; (*in firm*) Vorstand *m* ▸ VT (*ship*) an Bord +*gen* gehen; (*train*) einsteigen in +*acc*; **on ~** (*Naut, Aviat*) an Bord; **full/half ~** (BRIT) Voll-/Halbpension *f*; **~ and lodging** Unterkunft und Verpflegung *f*; **to go by the ~** (*fig*) unter den Tisch fallen; **above ~** (*fig*) korrekt; **across the ~** (*fig*) allgemein; (*criticize, reject*) pauschal
▸ **board up** VT mit Brettern vernageln
boarder ['bɔ:də^r] N Internatsschüler(in) *m(f)*
board game N Brettspiel *nt*
boarding card ['bɔ:dɪŋ-] N (*Aviat, Naut*) = **boarding pass**
boarding house ['bɔ:dɪŋ-] N Pension *f*
boarding party ['bɔ:dɪŋ-] N (*Naut*) Enterkommando *nt*
boarding pass ['bɔ:dɪŋ-] N Bordkarte *f*
boarding school ['bɔ:dɪŋ-] N Internat *nt*
board meeting N Vorstandssitzung *f*
boardroom ['bɔ:dru:m] N Sitzungssaal *m*
boardwalk ['bɔ:dwɔ:k] (*US*) N Holzsteg *m*
boast [bəust] VI prahlen ▸ VT (*fig: possess*) sich rühmen +*gen*, besitzen; **to ~ about** *or* **of** prahlen mit
boastful ['bəustful] ADJ prahlerisch
boastfulness ['bəustfulnɪs] N Prahlerei *f*
boat [bəut] N Boot *nt*; (*ship*) Schiff *nt*; **to go by ~** mit dem Schiff fahren; **to be in the same ~** (*fig*) in einem Boot *or* im gleichen Boot sitzen
boater ['bəutə^r] N steifer Strohhut *m*, Kreissäge *f* (*inf*)
boating ['bəutɪŋ] N Bootfahren *nt*
boat people NPL Bootsflüchtlinge *pl*
boatswain ['bəusn] N Bootsmann *m*
bob [bɔb] VI (*also*: **bob up and down**) sich auf und ab bewegen ▸ N (BRIT *inf*) = **shilling**
▸ **bob up** VI auftauchen
bobbin ['bɔbɪn] N Spule *f*
bobby ['bɔbɪ] (BRIT *inf*) N Bobby *m*, Polizist *m*
bobsleigh ['bɔbsleɪ] N Bob *m*
bode [bəud] VI: **to ~ well/ill (for)** ein gutes/ schlechtes Zeichen sein (für)
bodice ['bɔdɪs] N (*of dress*) Oberteil *nt*
bodily ['bɔdɪlɪ] ADJ körperlich; (*needs*) leiblich ▸ ADV (*lift, carry*) mit aller Kraft
body ['bɔdɪ] N Körper *m*; (*corpse*) Leiche *f*; (*main part*) Hauptteil *m*; (*of car*) Karosserie *f*; (*of plane*) Rumpf *m*; (*group*) Gruppe *f*; (*organization*) Organ *nt*; **ruling ~** amtierendes Organ; **in a ~** geschlossen; **a ~ of facts** Tatsachenmaterial *nt*
body blow N (*fig: setback*) schwerer Schlag *m*
body building N Bodybuilding *nt*
body double N (*Cine, TV*) *Double für Szenen, in denen Körperpartien in Nahaufnahme gezeigt werden*
bodyguard ['bɔdɪga:d] N (*group*) Leibwache *f*; (*one person*) Leibwächter *m*
body language N Körpersprache *f*
body repairs NPL Karosseriearbeiten *pl*
body search N Leibesvisitation *f*
body stocking N Body(stocking) *m*
bodywork ['bɔdɪwə:k] N Karosserie *f*
boffin ['bɔfɪn] (BRIT) N Fachidiot *m*
bog [bɔg] N Sumpf *m* ▸ VT: **to get bogged down** (*fig*) sich verzetteln
bogey ['bəugɪ] N Schreckgespenst *nt*; (*also*: **bogeyman**) Butzemann *m*, schwarzer Mann *m*
boggle ['bɔgl] VI: **the mind boggles** das ist nicht *or* kaum auszumalen
bogie ['bəugɪ] N Drehgestell *nt*; (*trolley*) Draisine *f*
Bogotá [bəugə'ta:] N Bogotá *nt*
bogus ['bəugəs] ADJ (*workman etc*) falsch; (*claim*) erfunden
Bohemia [bəu'hi:mɪə] N Böhmen *nt*
Bohemian [bəu'hi:mɪən] ADJ böhmisch ▸ N Böhme *m*, Böhmin *f*; (*also*: **bohemian**) Bohemien *m*

boil [bɔɪl] VT, VI kochen ▸ N (*Med*) Furunkel *m or nt*; **to come to the ~** (BRIT), **to come to a ~** (*US*) zu kochen anfangen
▸ **boil down to** VT FUS (*fig*) hinauslaufen auf *+acc*
▸ **boil over** VI überkochen
boiled egg [bɔɪld-] N gekochtes Ei *nt*
boiled potatoes [bɔɪld-] NPL Salzkartoffeln *pl*
boiler ['bɔɪləʳ] N Boiler *m*
boiler suit (BRIT) N Overall *m*
boiling ['bɔɪlɪŋ] ADJ: **I'm ~ (hot)** (*inf*) mir ist fürchterlich heiß; **it's ~** es ist eine Affenhitze (*inf*)
boiling point N Siedepunkt *m*
boil-in-the-bag [bɔɪlɪnðə'bæg] ADJ (*meals*) Kochbeutel-
boisterous ['bɔɪstərəs] ADJ ausgelassen
bold [bəuld] ADJ (*brave*) mutig; (*pej: cheeky*) dreist; (*pattern, colours*) kräftig
boldly ['bəuldlɪ] ADV mutig; dreist; kräftig
boldness ['bəuldnɪs] N Mut *m*; (*cheekiness*) Dreistigkeit *f*
bold type N Fettdruck *m*
Bolivia [bə'lɪvɪə] N Bolivien *nt*
Bolivian [bə'lɪvɪən] ADJ bolivisch, bolivianisch ▸ N Bolivier(in) *m(f)*, Bolivianer(in) *m(f)*
bollard ['bɔləd] (BRIT) N Poller *m*
Bollywood ['bɔlɪwud] N Bollywood *nt*
bolshy ['bɔlʃɪ] (BRIT *inf*) ADJ (*stroppy*) pampig
bolster ['bəulstəʳ] N Nackenrolle *f*
▸ **bolster up** VT stützen; (*case*) untermauern
bolt [bəult] N Riegel *m*; (*with nut*) Schraube *f*; (*of lightning*) Blitz(strahl) *m* ▸ VT (*door*) verriegeln; (*also:* **bolt together**) verschrauben; (*food*) hinunterschlingen ▸ VI (*run away: person*) weglaufen; (*: horse*) durchgehen ▸ ADV: **~ upright** kerzengerade; **a ~ from the blue** (*fig*) ein Blitz *m* aus heiterem Himmel
bomb [bɔm] N Bombe *f* ▸ VT bombardieren; (*plant bomb in or near*) einen Bombenanschlag verüben auf *+acc*
bombard [bɔm'bɑːd] VT (*also fig*) bombardieren
bombardment [bɔm'bɑːdmənt] N Bombardierung *f*, Bombardement *nt*
bombastic [bɔm'bæstɪk] ADJ bombastisch
bomb disposal N: **~ unit** Bombenräumkommando *nt*; **~ expert** Bombenräumexperte *m*, Bombenräumexpertin *f*
bomber ['bɔməʳ] N Bomber *m*; (*terrorist*) Bombenattentäter(in) *m(f)*
bombing ['bɔmɪŋ] N Bombenangriff *m*
bomb scare N Bombenalarm *m*
bombshell ['bɔmʃɛl] N (*fig: revelation*) Bombe *f*
bomb site N Trümmergrundstück *nt*
bona fide ['bəunə'faɪdɪ] ADJ echt; **~ offer** Angebot *nt* auf Treu und Glauben
bonanza [bə'nænzə] N (*Econ*) Boom *m*
bond [bɔnd] N Band *nt*, Bindung *f*; (*Fin*) festverzinsliches Wertpapier *nt*, Bond *m*
bondage ['bɔndɪdʒ] N Sklaverei *f*
bonded warehouse ['bɔndɪd-] N Zolllager *nt*
bone [bəun] N Knochen *m*; (*of fish*) Gräte *f* ▸ VT (*meat*) die Knochen herauslösen aus; (*fish*) entgräten; **I've got a ~ to pick with you** ich habe mit Ihnen (noch) ein Hühnchen zu rupfen
bone china N ≈ feines Porzellan *nt*
bone-dry ['bəun'draɪ] ADJ knochentrocken
bone idle ADJ stinkfaul
bone marrow N Knochenmark *nt*
boner ['bəunəʳ] (*US*) N Schnitzer *m*
bonfire ['bɔnfaɪəʳ] N Feuer *nt*
bonk [bɔŋk] (*inf*) VT, VI (*have sex (with)*) bumsen
bonkers ['bɔŋkəz] (BRIT *inf*) ADJ (*mad*) verrückt
Bonn [bɔn] N Bonn *nt*
bonnet ['bɔnɪt] N Haube *f*; (*for baby*) Häubchen *nt*; (BRIT: *of car*) Motorhaube *f*
bonny ['bɔnɪ] (SCOT, NORTHERN ENGLISH) ADJ schön, hübsch
bonus ['bəunəs] N Prämie *f*; (*on wages*) Zulage *f*; (*at Christmas*) Gratifikation *f*; (*fig: additional benefit*) Plus *nt*
bony ['bəunɪ] ADJ knochig; (*Med*) knöchern; (*tissue*) knochenartig; (*meat*) mit viel Knochen; (*fish*) mit viel Gräten
boo [buː] EXCL buh ▸ VT auspfeifen, ausbuhen
boob [buːb] (*inf*) N (*breast*) Brust *f*; (BRIT: *mistake*) Schnitzer *m*
booby prize ['buːbɪ-] N *Scherzpreis für den schlechtesten Teilnehmer*
booby trap ['buːbɪ-] N versteckte Bombe *f*; (*fig: joke etc*) *als Schabernack versteckt angebrachte Falle*
booby-trapped ['buːbɪtræpt] ADJ: **a ~ car** ein Auto *nt*, in dem eine Bombe versteckt ist
book [buk] N Buch *nt*; (*of stamps, tickets*) Heftchen *nt* ▸ VT bestellen; (*seat, room*) buchen, reservieren lassen; (*subj: traffic warden, policeman*) aufschreiben; (*: referee*) verwarnen; **books** NPL (*Comm: accounts*) Bücher *pl*; **to keep the books** die Bücher führen; **by the ~** nach Vorschrift; **to throw the ~ at sb** jdn nach allen Regeln der Kunst fertig machen
▸ **book in** (BRIT) VI sich eintragen
▸ **book up** VT: **all seats are booked up** es ist bis auf den letzten Platz ausverkauft; **the hotel is booked up** das Hotel ist ausgebucht
bookable ['bukəbl] ADJ: **all seats are ~** Karten für alle Plätze können vorbestellt werden
bookcase ['bukkeɪs] N Bücherregal *nt*
book ends NPL Bücherstützen *pl*
booking ['bukɪŋ] (BRIT) N Bestellung *f*; (*of seat, room*) Buchung *f*, Reservierung *f*
booking office (BRIT) N (*Rail*) Fahrkartenschalter *m*; (*Theat*) Vorverkaufsstelle *f*, Vorverkaufskasse *f*
book-keeping ['buk'kiːpɪŋ] N Buchhaltung *f*, Buchführung *f*
booklet ['buklɪt] N Broschüre *f*
bookmaker ['bukmeɪkəʳ] N Buchmacher *m*
bookmark ['bukmɑːk] N Lesezeichen *nt*; (*Comput*) Bookmark *nt* ▸ VT (*Comput*) ein Bookmark einrichten für, bookmarken
bookseller ['buksɛləʳ] N Buchhändler(in) *m(f)*
bookshelf ['bukʃɛlf] N Bücherbord *nt*;
bookshelves NPL Bücherregal *nt*
bookshop ['bukʃɔp] N Buchhandlung *f*

bookstall ['bukstɔ:l] N Bücher- und Zeitungskiosk *m*

book store N = **bookshop**

book token N Buchgutschein *m*

book value N Buchwert *m*, Bilanzwert *m*

bookworm ['bukwə:m] N (*fig*) Bücherwurm *m*

boom [bu:m] N Donnern *nt*, Dröhnen *nt*; (*in prices, population etc*) rapider Anstieg *m*; (*Econ*) Hochkonjunktur *f*; (*busy period*) Boom *m* ▶ VI (*guns*) donnern; (*thunder*) hallen; (*voice*) dröhnen; (*business*) florieren

boomerang ['bu:məræŋ] N Bumerang *m* ▶ VI (*fig*) einen Bumerangeffekt haben

boom town N Goldgräberstadt *f*

boon [bu:n] N Segen *m*

boorish ['buərɪʃ] ADJ rüpelhaft

boost [bu:st] N Auftrieb *m* ▶ VT (*confidence*) stärken; (*sales, economy etc*) ankurbeln; **to give a ~ to sb/sb's spirits** jdm Auftrieb geben

booster ['bu:stə^r] N (*Med*) Wiederholungsimpfung *f*; (TV) Zusatzgleichrichter *m*; (*Elec*) Puffersatz *m*; (*also*: **booster rocket**) Booster *m*, Startrakete *f*

booster seat N (*Aut*) Sitzerhöhung *f*

boot [bu:t] N Stiefel *m*; (*ankle boot*) hoher Schuh *m*; (BRIT: *of car*) Kofferraum *m* ▶ VT (*Comput*) laden; **... to ~** (*in addition*) obendrein ...; **to give sb the ~** (*inf*) jdn rauswerfen *or* rausschmeißen

booth [bu:ð] N (*at fair*) Bude *f*, Stand *m*; (*telephone booth*) Zelle *f*; (*voting booth*) Kabine *f*

bootleg ['bu:tlɛg] ADJ (*alcohol*) schwarzgebrannt; (*fuel*) schwarz hergestellt; (*tape etc*) schwarz mitgeschnitten

bootlegger ['bu:tlɛgə^r] N Bootlegger *m*, Schwarzhändler *m*

booty ['bu:tɪ] N Beute *f*

booze [bu:z] (*inf*) N Alkohol *m* ▶ VI saufen

boozer ['bu:zə^r] (*inf*) N (*person*) Säufer(in) *m(f)*; (BRIT: *pub*) Kneipe *f*

border ['bɔ:də^r] N Grenze *f*; (*for flowers*) Rabatte *f*; (*on cloth etc*) Bordüre *f* ▶ VT (*road*) säumen; (*another country*: *also*: **border on**) grenzen an *+acc*; **Borders** N: **the Borders** *das Grenzgebiet zwischen England und Schottland*
▶ **border on** VT FUS (*fig*) grenzen an *+acc*

borderline ['bɔ:dəlaɪn] N (*fig*): **on the ~** an der Grenze

borderline case N Grenzfall *m*

bore [bɔ:^r] PT *of* **bear** ▶ VT bohren; (*person*) langweilen ▶ N Langweiler *m*; (*of gun*) Kaliber *nt*; **to be bored** sich langweilen; **he's bored to tears** *or* **bored to death** *or* **bored stiff** er langweilt sich zu Tode

boredom ['bɔ:dəm] N Langeweile *f*; (*boring quality*) Langweiligkeit *f*

boring ['bɔ:rɪŋ] ADJ langweilig

born [bɔ:n] ADJ: **to be ~** geboren werden; **I was ~ in 1960** ich bin *or* wurde 1960 geboren; **~ blind** blind geboren, von Geburt (an) blind; **a ~ comedian** ein geborener Komiker

born-again [bɔ:nə'gɛn] ADJ wiedergeboren

borne [bɔ:n] PP *of* **bear**

Borneo ['bɔ:nɪəu] N Borneo *nt*

borough ['bʌrə] N Bezirk *m*, Stadtgemeinde *f*

borrow ['bɔrəu] VT: **to ~ sth** etw borgen, sich *dat* etw leihen; (*from library*) sich *dat* etw ausleihen; **may I ~ your car?** kann ich deinen Wagen leihen?

borrower ['bɔrəuə^r] N (*of loan etc*) Kreditnehmer(in) *m(f)*

borrowing ['bɔrəuɪŋ] N Kreditaufnahme *f*

borstal ['bɔ:stl] (BRIT) N (*formerly*) Besserungsanstalt *f*

Bosnia ['bɔznɪə] N Bosnien *nt*

Bosnia-Herzegovina ['bɔznɪəhɛrtsə'gəuvi:nə] N Bosnien-Herzegowina *nt*

Bosnian ['bɔznɪən] ADJ bosnisch ▶ N Bosnier(in) *m(f)*

bosom ['buzəm] N Busen *m*; (*fig*: *of family*) Schoß *m*

bosom friend N Busenfreund(in) *m(f)*

boss [bɔs] N Chef(in) *m(f)*; (*leader*) Boss *m* ▶ VT (*also*: **boss around, boss about**) herumkommandieren; **stop bossing everyone about!** hör auf mit dem ständigen Herumkommandieren!

bossy ['bɔsɪ] ADJ herrisch

bosun ['bəusn] N Bootsmann *m*

botanical [bə'tænɪkl] ADJ botanisch

botanist ['bɔtənɪst] N Botaniker(in) *m(f)*

botany ['bɔtənɪ] N Botanik *f*

botch [bɔtʃ] VT (*also*: **botch up**) verpfuschen

both [bəuθ] ADJ beide ▶ PRON beide; (*two different things*) beides ▶ ADV: **~ A and B** sowohl A als auch B; **~ (of them)** (alle) beide; **~ of us went, we ~ went** wir gingen beide; **they sell ~ the fabric and the finished curtains** sie verkaufen sowohl den Stoff als auch die fertigen Vorhänge

bother ['bɔðə^r] VT Sorgen machen *+dat*; (*disturb*) stören ▶ VI (*also*: **bother o.s.**) sich *dat* Sorgen *or* Gedanken machen ▶ N (*trouble*) Mühe *f*; (*nuisance*) Plage *f* ▶ EXCL Mist! (*inf*); **don't ~ phoning** du brauchst nicht anzurufen; **I'm sorry to ~ you** es tut mir leid, dass ich Sie belästigen muss; **I can't be bothered** ich habe keine Lust; **please don't ~** bitte machen Sie sich keine Umstände; **don't ~!** lass es!; **it is a ~ to have to shave every morning** es ist wirklich lästig, sich jeden Morgen rasieren zu müssen; **it's no ~** es ist kein Problem

Botswana [bɔt'swa:nə] N Botswana *nt*

bottle ['bɔtl] N Flasche *f*; (BRIT *inf*: *courage*) Mumm *m* ▶ VT in Flaschen abfüllen; (*fruit*) einmachen; **a ~ of wine/milk** eine Flasche Wein/Milch; **wine/milk ~** Wein-/Milchflasche *f*
▶ **bottle out** VI (*inf*) den Mut verlieren, aufgeben
▶ **bottle up** VT in sich *dat* aufstauen

bottle bank N Altglascontainer *m*

bottle-fed ['bɔtlfɛd] ADJ mit der Flasche ernährt

bottleneck ['bɔtlnɛk] N (*also fig*) Engpass *m*

bottle-opener ['bɔtləupnə^r] N Flaschenöffner *m*

bottom ['bɔtəm] N Boden *m*; *(buttocks)* Hintern *m*; *(of page, list)* Ende *nt*; *(of chair)* Sitz *m*; *(of mountain, tree)* Fuß *m* ▸ ADJ *(lower)* untere(r, s); *(last)* unterste(r, s); **at the ~ of** unten an/in *+dat*; **at the ~ of the page/list** unten auf der Seite/Liste; **to be at the ~ of the class** der/die Letzte in der Klasse sein; **to get to the ~ of sth** *(fig)* einer Sache *dat* auf den Grund kommen
bottomless ['bɔtəmlɪs] ADJ *(fig)* unerschöpflich
bottom line N *(of accounts)* Saldo *m*; *(fig)*: **that's the ~ (of it)** darauf läuft es im Endeffekt hinaus
botulism ['bɔtjulɪzəm] N Botulismus *m*, Nahrungsmittelvergiftung *f*
bough [bau] N Ast *m*
bought [bɔ:t] PT, PP *of* **buy**
boulder ['bəuldəʳ] N Felsblock *m*
boulevard ['bu:ləvɑ:d] N Boulevard *m*
bounce [bauns] VI (auf)springen; *(cheque)* platzen ▸ VT *(ball)* (auf)springen lassen; *(signal)* reflektieren ▸ N Aufprall *m*; **he's got plenty of ~** *(fig)* er hat viel Schwung
bouncer ['baunsəʳ] *(inf)* N Rausschmeißer *m*
bouncy castle ['baunsɪ-] N Hüpfburg *f*
bound [baund] PT, PP *of* **bind** ▸ N Sprung *m*; *(gen pl: limit)* Grenze *f* ▸ VI springen ▸ VT begrenzen ▸ ADJ: **~ by** gebunden durch; **to be ~ to do sth** *(obliged)* verpflichtet sein, etw zu tun; *(very likely)* etw bestimmt tun; **he's ~ to fail** es kann ihm ja gar nicht gelingen; **~ for** nach; **the area is out of bounds** das Betreten des Gebiets ist verboten
boundary ['baundrɪ] N Grenze *f*
boundless ['baundlɪs] ADJ grenzenlos
bountiful ['bauntɪful] ADJ großzügig; *(God)* gütig; *(supply)* reichlich
bounty ['bauntɪ] N Freigebigkeit *f*; *(reward)* Kopfgeld *nt*
bounty hunter N Kopfgeldjäger *m*
bouquet ['bukeɪ] N (Blumen)strauß *m*; *(of wine)* Bukett *nt*, Blume *f*
bourbon ['buəbən] *(US)* N *(also:* **bourbon whiskey***)* Bourbon *m*
bourgeois ['buəʒwɑ:] ADJ bürgerlich, spießig *(pej)* ▸ N Bürger(in) *m(f)*, Bourgeois *m*
bout [baut] N Anfall *m*; *(Boxing etc)* Kampf *m*
boutique [bu:'ti:k] N Boutique *f*
bow¹ [bəu] N Schleife *f*; *(weapon, Mus)* Bogen *m*
bow² [bau] N Verbeugung *f*; *(Naut: also:* **bows***)* Bug *m* ▸ VI sich verbeugen; *(yield)*: **to ~ to** *or* **before** sich beugen *+dat*; **to ~ to the inevitable** sich in das Unvermeidliche fügen
bowels ['bauəlz] NPL Darm *m*; *(of the earth etc)* Innere *nt*
bowl [bəul] N Schüssel *f*; *(shallower)* Schale *f*; *(ball)* Kugel *f*; *(of pipe)* Kopf *m*; *(US: stadium)* Stadion *nt* ▸ VI werfen
▸ **bowl over** VT *(fig)* überwältigen
bow-legged ['bəu'lɛgɪd] ADJ o-beinig
bowler ['bəuləʳ] N Werfer(in) *m(f)*; *(BRIT: also:* **bowler hat***)* Melone *f*
bowling ['bəulɪŋ] N Kegeln *nt*; *(on grass)* Bowling *nt*
bowling alley N Kegelbahn *f*
bowling green N Bowlingrasen *m*
bowls [bəulz] N Bowling *nt*
bow tie [bəu-] N Fliege *f*
box [bɔks] N Schachtel *f*; *(cardboard box)* Karton *m*; *(crate)* Kiste *f*; *(Theat)* Loge *f*; *(BRIT Aut) gelb schraffierter Kreuzungsbereich*; *(on form)* Feld *nt* ▸ VT (in eine Schachtel *etc*) verpacken; *(fighter)* boxen ▸ VI boxen; **to ~ sb's ears** jdm eine Ohrfeige geben
▸ **box in** VT einkeilen
▸ **box off** VT abtrennen
boxer ['bɔksəʳ] N *(person, dog)* Boxer *m*
boxers, boxer shorts NPL Boxershorts *pl*
box file N Sammelordner *m*
boxing ['bɔksɪŋ] N Boxen *nt*
Boxing Day *(BRIT)* N zweiter Weihnachts(feier)tag *m*

> **Boxing Day** ist ein Feiertag in Großbritannien. Wenn Weihnachten auf ein Wochenende fällt, wird der Feiertag am nächsten darauffolgenden Wochentag nachgeholt. Der Name geht auf einen alten Brauch zurück; früher erhielten Händler und Lieferanten an diesem Tag ein Geschenk, die sogenannte Christmas Box.

boxing gloves NPL Boxhandschuhe *pl*
boxing ring N Boxring *m*
box number N Chiffre *f*
box office N Kasse *f*
boxroom ['bɔksrum] N Abstellraum *m*
boy [bɔɪ] N Junge *m*
boycott ['bɔɪkɔt] N Boykott *m* ▸ VT boykottieren
boyfriend ['bɔɪfrɛnd] N Freund *m*
boyish ['bɔɪɪʃ] ADJ jungenhaft; *(woman)* knabenhaft
boy scout N Pfadfinder *m*
bp ABBR = **bishop**
bra [brɑ:] N BH *m*
brace [breɪs] N *(on teeth)* (Zahn)klammer *f*, (Zahn)spange *f*; *(tool)* (Hand)bohrer *m*; *(also:* **brace bracket***)* geschweifte Klammer *f* ▸ VT spannen; **braces** NPL *(BRIT)* Hosenträger *pl*; **to ~ o.s.** *(for weight)* sich stützen; *(for shock)* sich innerlich vorbereiten
bracelet ['breɪslɪt] N Armband *nt*
bracing ['breɪsɪŋ] ADJ belebend
bracken ['brækən] N Farn *m*
bracket ['brækɪt] N Träger *m*; *(group, range)* Gruppe *f*; *(also:* **round bracket***)* (runde) Klammer *f*; *(also:* **brace bracket***)* geschweifte Klammer *f*; *(also:* **square bracket***)* eckige Klammer *f* ▸ VT *(also:* **bracket together***)* zusammenfassen; *(word, phrase)* einklammern; **income ~** Einkommensgruppe *f*; **in brackets** in Klammern
brackish ['brækɪʃ] ADJ brackig
brag [bræg] VI prahlen
braid [breɪd] N Borte *f*; *(of hair)* Zopf *m*
Braille [breɪl] N Blindenschrift *f*, Brailleschrift *f*
brain [breɪn] N Gehirn *nt*; **brains** NPL *(Culin)* Hirn *nt*; *(intelligence)* Intelligenz *f*; **he's got brains** er hat Köpfchen *or* Grips

brainchild ['breɪntʃaɪld] N Geistesprodukt *nt*
braindead ['breɪndɛd] ADJ hirntot; (*inf*) hirnlos
brain drain N Abwanderung *f* von Wissenschaftlern, Braindrain *m*
brainless ['breɪnlɪs] ADJ dumm
brainstorm ['breɪnstɔ:m] N (*fig*) Anfall *m* geistiger Umnachtung; (*US*: *brain wave*) Geistesblitz *m*
brainwash ['breɪnwɔʃ] VT einer Gehirnwäsche *dat* unterziehen
brain wave N Geistesblitz *m*
brainy ['breɪnɪ] ADJ intelligent
braise [breɪz] VT schmoren
brake [breɪk] N Bremse *f* ▸ VI bremsen
brake fluid N Bremsflüssigkeit *f*
brake light N Bremslicht *nt*
brake pedal N Bremspedal *nt*
bramble ['bræmbl] N Brombeerstrauch *m*; (*fruit*) Brombeere *f*
bran [bræn] N Kleie *f*
branch [brɑ:ntʃ] N Ast *m*; (*of family, organization*) Zweig *m*; (*Comm*) Filiale *f*, Zweigstelle *f*; (*: bank, company etc*) Geschäftsstelle *f* ▸ VI sich gabeln
▸ **branch out** VI (*fig*): **to ~ out into** seinen (Geschäfts)bereich erweitern auf *+acc*
branch line N (*Rail*) Zweiglinie *f*, Nebenlinie *f*
branch manager N Zweigstellenleiter(in) *m(f)*, Filialleiter(in) *m(f)*
brand [brænd] N (*also*: **brand name**) Marke *f*; (*fig: type*) Art *f* ▸ VT mit einem Brandzeichen kennzeichnen; (*fig, pej*): **to ~ sb a communist** jdn als Kommunist brandmarken
brandish ['brændɪʃ] VT schwingen
brand name N Markenname *m*
brand-new ['brænd'nju:] ADJ nagelneu, brandneu
brandy ['brændɪ] N Weinbrand *m*
brash [bræʃ] ADJ dreist
Brasilia [brə'zɪlɪə] N Brasilia *nt*
brass [brɑ:s] N Messing *nt*; **the ~** (*Mus*) die Blechbläser *pl*
brass band N Blaskapelle *f*
brassière ['bræsɪə^r] N Büstenhalter *m*
brass tacks NPL: **to get down to ~** zur Sache kommen
brassy ['brɑ:sɪ] ADJ (*colour*) messingfarben; (*sound*) blechern; (*appearance, behaviour*) auffällig
brat [bræt] (*pej*) N Balg *m or nt*, Gör *nt*
bravado [brə'vɑ:dəu] N Draufgängertum *nt*
brave [breɪv] ADJ mutig; (*attempt, smile*) tapfer ▸ N (indianischer) Krieger *m* ▸ VT trotzen *+dat*
bravely ['breɪvlɪ] ADV mutig; tapfer
bravery ['breɪvərɪ] N Mut *m*; Tapferkeit *f*
bravo [brɑ:'vəu] EXCL bravo
brawl [brɔ:l] N Schlägerei *f* ▸ VI sich schlagen
brawn [brɔ:n] N Muskeln *pl*; (*meat*) Schweinskopfsülze *f*
brawny ['brɔ:nɪ] ADJ muskulös, kräftig
bray [breɪ] VI schreien ▸ N (Esels)schrei *m*
brazen ['breɪzn] ADJ unverschämt, dreist; (*lie*) schamlos ▸ VT: **to ~ it out** durchhalten
brazier ['breɪzɪə^r] N (*container*) Kohlenbecken *nt*
Brazil [brə'zɪl] N Brasilien *nt*
Brazilian [brə'zɪljən] ADJ brasilianisch ▸ N Brasilianer(in) *m(f)*
Brazil nut N Paranuss *f*
breach [bri:tʃ] VT (*defence*) durchbrechen; (*wall*) eine Bresche schlagen in *+acc* ▸ N (*gap*) Bresche *f*; (*estrangement*) Bruch *m*; (*breaking*): **~ of contract** Vertragsbruch *m*; **~ of the peace** öffentliche Ruhestörung *f*; **~ of trust** Vertrauensbruch *m*
bread [brɛd] N Brot *nt*; (*inf: money*) Moos *nt*, Kies *m*; **to earn one's daily ~** sein Brot verdienen; **to know which side one's ~ is buttered (on)** wissen, wo etwas zu holen ist
bread and butter N Butterbrot *nt*; (*fig*) Broterwerb *m*
bread bin (BRIT) N Brotkasten *m*
breadboard ['brɛdbɔ:d] N Brot(schneide)brett *nt*; (*Comput*) Leiterplatte *f*
bread box (*US*) N Brotkasten *m*
breadcrumbs ['brɛdkrʌmz] NPL Brotkrumen *pl*; (*Culin*) Paniermehl *nt*
breaded ADJ paniert
breadline ['brɛdlaɪn] N: **to be on the ~** nur das Allernotwendigste zum Leben haben
breadth [brɛtθ] N (*also fig*) Breite *f*
breadwinner ['brɛdwɪnə^r] N Ernährer(in) *m(f)*
break [breɪk] (*pt* **broke**, *pp* **broken**) VT zerbrechen; (*leg, arm*) sich *dat* brechen; (*promise, record*) brechen; (*law*) verstoßen gegen ▸ VI zerbrechen, kaputtgehen; (*storm*) losbrechen; (*weather*) umschlagen; (*dawn*) anbrechen; (*story, news*) bekannt werden ▸ N Pause *f*; (*gap*) Lücke *f*; (*fracture*) Bruch *m*; (*chance*) Chance *f*, Gelegenheit *f*; (*holiday*) Urlaub *m*; **to ~ the news to sb** es jdm sagen; **to ~ even** seine (Un)kosten decken; **to ~ with sb** mit jdm brechen, sich von jdm trennen; **to ~ free** *or* **loose** sich losreißen; **to take a ~** (eine) Pause machen; (*holiday*) Urlaub machen; **without a ~** ohne Unterbrechung *or* Pause, ununterbrochen; **a lucky ~** ein Durchbruch *m*
▸ **break down** VT (*figures, data*) aufschlüsseln; (*door etc*) einrennen ▸ VI (*car*) eine Panne haben; (*machine*) kaputtgehen; (*person, resistance*) zusammenbrechen; (*talks*) scheitern
▸ **break in** VT (*horse*) zureiten ▸ VI einbrechen; (*interrupt*) unterbrechen
▸ **break into** VT FUS einbrechen in *+acc*
▸ **break off** VI abbrechen ▸ VT (*talks*) abbrechen; (*engagement*) lösen
▸ **break open** VT, VI aufbrechen
▸ **break out** VI ausbrechen; **to ~ out in spots/a rash** Pickel/einen Ausschlag bekommen
▸ **break through** VI: **the sun broke through** die Sonne kam durch ▸ VT FUS durchbrechen
▸ **break up** VI (*ship*) zerbersten; (*crowd, meeting, partnership*) sich auflösen; (*marriage*) scheitern; (*friends*) sich trennen; (*Scol*) in die Ferien gehen ▸ VT zerbrechen; (*journey, fight etc*) unterbrechen; (*meeting*) auflösen; (*marriage*) zerstören
breakable ['breɪkəbl] ADJ zerbrechlich ▸ N: **breakables** zerbrechliche Ware *f*

b

breakage ['breɪkɪdʒ] N Bruch *m*; **to pay for breakages** für zerbrochene Ware *or* für Bruch bezahlen
breakaway ['breɪkəweɪ] ADJ (*group etc*) Splitter-
break dancing N Breakdance *m*
breakdown ['breɪkdaun] N (*Aut*) Panne *f*; (*in communications*) Zusammenbruch *m*; (*of marriage*) Scheitern *nt*; (*also*: **nervous breakdown**) (Nerven)zusammenbruch *m*; (*of statistics*) Aufschlüsselung *f*
breakdown service (BRIT) N Pannendienst *m*
breakdown van (BRIT) N Abschleppwagen *m*
breaker ['breɪkə^r] N (*wave*) Brecher *m*
breakeven ['breɪk'i:vn] CPD: **~ chart** Gewinnschwellendiagramm *nt*; **~ point** Gewinnschwelle *f*
breakfast ['brɛkfəst] N Frühstück *nt* ▸ VI frühstücken
breakfast cereal N Getreideflocken *pl*
break-in ['breɪkɪn] N Einbruch *m*
breaking and entering ['breɪkɪŋən'ɛntrɪŋ] N (*Law*) Einbruch *m*
breaking point ['breɪkɪŋ-] N (*fig*): **to reach ~** völlig am Ende sein
breakthrough ['breɪkθru:] N Durchbruch *m*
break-up ['breɪkʌp] N (*of partnership*) Auflösung *f*; (*of marriage*) Scheitern *nt*
break-up value N (*Comm*) Liquidationswert *m*
breakwater ['breɪkwɔ:tə^r] N Wellenbrecher *m*
breast [brɛst] N Brust *f*; (*of meat*) Brust *f*, Bruststück *nt*
breast-feed ['brɛstfi:d] VT, VI (*irreg: like* **feed**) stillen
breast pocket N Brusttasche *f*
breaststroke ['brɛststrəuk] N Brustschwimmen *nt*
breath [brɛθ] N Atem *m*; (*a breath*) Atemzug *m*; **to go out for a ~ of air** an die frische Luft gehen, frische Luft schnappen gehen; **out of ~** außer Atem, atemlos; **to get one's ~ back** wieder zu Atem kommen
breathalyse ['brɛθəlaɪz] VT blasen lassen (*inf*)
Breathalyser® ['brɛθəlaɪzə^r] N Promillemesser *m*
breathe [bri:ð] VT, VI atmen; **I won't ~ a word about it** ich werde kein Sterbenswörtchen darüber sagen
▸ **breathe in** VT, VI einatmen
▸ **breathe out** VT, VI ausatmen
breather ['bri:ðə^r] N Atempause *f*, Verschnaufpause *f*
breathing ['bri:ðɪŋ] N Atmung *f*
breathing space N (*fig*) Atempause *f*, Ruhepause *f*
breathless ['brɛθlɪs] ADJ atemlos, außer Atem; (*Med*) an Atemnot leidend; **I was ~ with excitement** die Aufregung verschlug mir den Atem
breathtaking ['brɛθteɪkɪŋ] ADJ atemberaubend
breath test N Atemalkoholtest *m*
bred [brɛd] PT, PP *of* **breed**
-bred SUFF: **well/ill~** gut/schlecht erzogen
breed [bri:d] (*pt, pp* **bred**) VT züchten; (*fig: give rise to*) erzeugen; (*: hate, suspicion*) hervorrufen ▸ VI Junge *pl* haben ▸ N Rasse *f*; (*type, class*) Art *f*
breeder ['bri:də^r] N Züchter(in) *m(f)*; (*also*: **breeder reactor**) Brutreaktor *m*, Brüter *m*
breeding ['bri:dɪŋ] N Erziehung *f*
breeding ground N (*also fig*) Brutstätte *f*
breeze [bri:z] N Brise *f*
breeze block (BRIT) N Ytong® *m*
breezy ['bri:zɪ] ADJ (*manner, tone*) munter; (*weather*) windig
Breton ['brɛtən] ADJ bretonisch ▸ N Bretone *m*, Bretonin *f*
brevity ['brɛvɪtɪ] N Kürze *f*
brew [bru:] VT (*tea*) aufbrühen, kochen; (*beer*) brauen ▸ VI (*tea*) ziehen; (*beer*) gären; (*storm, fig*) sich zusammenbrauen
brewer ['bru:ə^r] N Brauer *m*
brewery ['bru:ərɪ] N Brauerei *f*
briar ['braɪə^r] N Dornbusch *m*; (*wild rose*) wilde Rose *f*
bribe [braɪb] N Bestechungsgeld *nt* ▸ VT bestechen; **to ~ sb to do sth** jdn bestechen, damit er etw tut
bribery ['braɪbərɪ] N Bestechung *f*
bric-a-brac ['brɪkəbræk] N Nippes *pl*, Nippsachen *pl*
brick [brɪk] N Ziegelstein *m*, Backstein *m*; (*of ice cream*) Block *m*
bricklayer ['brɪkleɪə^r] N Maurer(in) *m(f)*
brickwork ['brɪkwə:k] N Mauerwerk *nt*
bridal ['braɪdl] ADJ (*gown, veil etc*) Braut-
bride [braɪd] N Braut *f*
bridegroom ['braɪdgru:m] N Bräutigam *m*
bridesmaid ['braɪdzmeɪd] N Brautjungfer *f*
bridge [brɪdʒ] N Brücke *f*; (*Naut*) (Kommando)brücke *f*; (*of nose*) Sattel *m*; (*Cards*) Bridge *nt* ▸ VT (*river*) eine Brücke schlagen *or* bauen über *+acc*; (*fig*) überbrücken
bridging loan ['brɪdʒɪŋ-] (BRIT) N Überbrückungskredit *m*
bridle ['braɪdl] N Zaum *m* ▸ VT aufzäumen ▸ VI: **to ~ (at)** sich entrüstet wehren (gegen)
bridle path N Reitweg *m*
brief [bri:f] ADJ kurz ▸ N (*Law*) Auftrag *m*; (*task*) Aufgabe *f* ▸ VT instruieren; (*Mil etc*): **to ~ sb (about)** jdn instruieren (über *+acc*); **briefs** NPL Slip *m*; **in ~ ...** kurz (gesagt) ...
briefcase ['bri:fkeɪs] N Aktentasche *f*
briefing ['bri:fɪŋ] N Briefing *nt*, Lagebespechung *f*
briefly ['bri:flɪ] ADV kurz; **to glimpse sth ~** einen flüchtigen Blick von etw erhaschen
Brig. ABBR = **brigadier**
brigade [brɪ'geɪd] N Brigade *f*
brigadier [brɪgə'dɪə^r] N Brigadegeneral *m*
bright [braɪt] ADJ (*light, room*) hell; (*weather*) heiter; (*clever*) intelligent; (*lively*) heiter, fröhlich; (*colour*) leuchtend; (*outlook, future*) glänzend; **to look on the ~ side** die Dinge von der positiven Seite betrachten
brighten ['braɪtn] VT (*also*: **brighten up**) aufheitern; (*event*) beleben ▸ VI (*weather, face:*

also: **brighten up**) sich aufheitern; (*person*) fröhlicher werden; (*prospects*) sich verbessern
brightly ['braɪtlɪ] ADV (*shine*) hell; (*smile*) fröhlich; (*talk*) heiter
brill [brɪl] (BRIT *inf*) ADJ toll
brilliance ['brɪljəns] N Strahlen *nt*; (*of person*) Genialität *f*, Brillanz *f*; (*of talent, skill*) Großartigkeit *f*
brilliant ['brɪljənt] ADJ strahlend; (*person, idea*) genial, brillant; (*career*) großartig; (*inf: holiday etc*) fantastisch
brilliantly ['brɪljəntlɪ] ADV strahlend; genial, brillant; großartig; fantastisch
brim [brɪm] N Rand *m*; (*of hat*) Krempe *f*
brimful ['brɪm'ful] ADJ: **~ (of)** randvoll (mit); (*fig*) voll (von)
brine [braɪn] N Lake *f*
bring [brɪŋ] (*pt, pp* **brought**) VT bringen; (*with you*) mitbringen; **to ~ sth to an end** etw zu Ende bringen; **I can't ~ myself to fire him** ich kann es nicht über mich bringen, ihn zu entlassen
▸ **bring about** VT herbeiführen
▸ **bring back** VT (*restore*) wiedereinführen; (*return*) zurückbringen
▸ **bring down** VT (*government*) zu Fall bringen; (*plane*) herunterholen; (*price*) senken
▸ **bring forward** VT (*meeting*) vorverlegen; (*proposal*) vorbringen; (*Bookkeeping*) übertragen
▸ **bring in** VT (*money*) (ein)bringen; (*include*) einbeziehen; (*person*) einschalten; (*legislation*) einbringen; (*verdict*) fällen
▸ **bring off** VT (*plan*) durchführen; (*deal*) zustande bringen
▸ **bring out** VT herausholen; (*meaning, book, album*) herausbringen
▸ **bring round** VT (*after faint*) wieder zu Bewusstsein bringen
▸ **bring up** VT heraufbringen; (*educate*) erziehen; (*question, subject*) zur Sprache bringen; (*food*) erbrechen
bring-and-buy sale N Basar *m* (*wo mitgebrachte Sachen verkauft werden*)
brink [brɪŋk] N Rand *m*; **on the ~ of doing sth** nahe daran, etw zu tun; **she was on the ~ of tears** sie war den Tränen nahe
brisk [brɪsk] ADJ (*abrupt: person, tone*) forsch; (*pace*) flott; (*trade*) lebhaft, rege; **to go for a ~ walk** einen ordentlichen Spaziergang machen; **business is ~** das Geschäft ist rege
bristle ['brɪsl] N Borste *f*; (*of beard*) Stoppel *f* ▸ VI zornig werden; **bristling with** strotzend von
bristly ['brɪslɪ] ADJ borstig; (*chin*) stoppelig
Brit [brɪt] (*inf*) N (= *British person*) Brite *m*, Britin *f*
Britain ['brɪtən] N (*also*: **Great Britain**) Großbritannien *nt*
British ['brɪtɪʃ] ADJ britisch ▸ NPL: **the ~** die Briten *pl*
British Isles NPL: **the ~** die Britischen Inseln
British Rail N *britische Eisenbahngesellschaft*
British Summer Time N britische Sommerzeit *f*
Briton ['brɪtən] N Brite *m*, Britin *f*
Brittany ['brɪtənɪ] N die Bretagne
brittle ['brɪtl] ADJ spröde; (*glass*) zerbrechlich; (*bones*) schwach
broach [brəutʃ] VT (*subject*) anschneiden
broad [brɔːd] ADJ breit; (*general*) allgemein; (*accent*) stark ▸ N (*US inf*) Frau *f*; **in ~ daylight** am helllichten Tag; **~ hint** deutlicher Wink *m*
broadband ['brɔːdbænd] (*Comput*) ADJ Breitband- ▸ N Breitband *nt*
broad bean N dicke Bohne *f*, Saubohne *f*
broadcast ['brɔːdkɑːst] (*pt, pp* **~**) N Sendung *f* ▸ VT, VI senden
broadcaster ['brɔːdkɑːstə^r] N (*Radio, TV*) Rundfunk-/Fernsehpersönlichkeit *f*
broadcasting ['brɔːdkɑːstɪŋ] N (*Radio*) Rundfunk *m*; (*TV*) Fernsehen *nt*
broadcasting station N (*Radio*) Rundfunkstation *f*; (*TV*) Fernsehstation *f*
broaden ['brɔːdn] VT erweitern ▸ VI breiter werden, sich verbreitern; **to ~ one's mind** seinen Horizont erweitern
broadly ['brɔːdlɪ] ADV (*in general terms*) in großen Zügen; **~ speaking** allgemein *or* generell gesagt
broad-minded ['brɔːd'maɪndɪd] ADJ tolerant
broadsheet ['brɔːdʃiːt] N (*newspaper*) *großformatige Zeitung*
broccoli ['brɔkəlɪ] N Brokkoli *pl*, Spargelkohl *m*
brochure ['brəuʃjuə^r] N Broschüre *f*
brogue [brəug] N Akzent *m*; (*shoe*) fester Schuh *m*
broil [brɔɪl] (*US*) VT grillen
broiler ['brɔɪlə^r] N Brathähnchen *nt*
broke [brəuk] PT *of* **break** ▸ ADJ (*inf*) pleite; **to go ~** pleitegehen
broken ['brəukn] PP *of* **break** ▸ ADJ zerbrochen; (*machine: also*: **broken down**) kaputt; (*promise, vow*) gebrochen; **a ~ leg** ein gebrochenes Bein; **a ~ marriage** eine gescheiterte Ehe; **a ~ home** zerrüttete Familienverhältnisse *pl*; **in ~ English/German** in gebrochenem Englisch/Deutsch
broken-down ['brəukn'daun] ADJ kaputt; (*house*) baufällig
brokenhearted [brəukn'hɑːtɪd] ADJ untröstlich
broker ['brəukə^r] N Makler(in) *m(f)*
brokerage ['brəukrɪdʒ] N (*commission*) Maklergebühr *f*; (*business*) Maklergeschäft *nt*
brolly ['brɔlɪ] (BRIT *inf*) N (Regen)schirm *m*
bronchitis [brɔŋ'kaɪtɪs] N Bronchitis *f*
bronze [brɔnz] N Bronze *f*
bronzed [brɔnzd] ADJ braun, (sonnen)gebräunt
brooch [brəutʃ] N Brosche *f*
brood [bruːd] N Brut *f* ▸ VI (*hen*) brüten; (*person*) grübeln
▸ **brood on** VT FUS nachgrübeln über +*acc*
▸ **brood over** VT FUS = **brood on**
broody ['bruːdɪ] ADJ (*person*) grüblerisch; (*hen*) brütig
brook [bruk] N Bach *m*
broom [brum] N Besen *m*; (*Bot*) Ginster *m*
broomstick ['brumstɪk] N Besenstiel *m*
bros., Bros. ABBR (*Comm*: = *brothers*) Gebr.
broth [brɔθ] N Suppe *f*, Fleischbrühe *f*

brothel ['brɔθl] N Bordell *nt*
brother ['brʌðəʳ] N Bruder *m*; (*in trade union, society etc*) Kollege *m*
brotherhood ['brʌðəhud] N Brüderlichkeit *f*
brother-in-law ['brʌðərɪn'lɔ:] N Schwager *m*
brotherly ['brʌðəlɪ] ADJ brüderlich
brought [brɔ:t] PT, PP *of* **bring**
brought forward ADJ (*Comm*) vorgetragen
brow [brau] N Stirn *f*; (*eyebrow*) (Augen)braue *f*; (*of hill*) (Berg)kuppe *f*
browbeat ['braubi:t] VT (*irreg: like* **beat**): **to ~ sb (into doing sth)** jdn (so) unter Druck setzen(, dass er etw tut)
brown [braun] ADJ braun ▶ N Braun *nt* ▶ VT (*Culin*) (an)bräunen; **to go ~** braun werden
brown bread N Graubrot *nt*, Mischbrot *nt*
Brownie ['braunɪ] N (*also*: **Brownie Guide**) Wichtel *m*
brownie ['braunɪ] (*US*) N *kleiner Schokoladenkuchen*
brown paper N Packpapier *nt*
brown rice N Naturreis *m*
brown sugar N brauner Zucker *m*
browse [brauz] VI (*in shop*) sich umsehen; (*animal*) weiden; (*: deer*) äsen ▶ VTI (*Comput*) browsen ▶ N: **to have a ~ (around)** sich umsehen; **to ~ through a book** in einem Buch schmökern
browser ['brauzəʳ] N (*Comput*) Browser *m*
bruise [bru:z] N blauer Fleck *m*, Bluterguss *m*; (*on fruit*) Druckstelle *f* ▶ VT (*arm, leg etc*) sich *dat* stoßen; (*person*) einen blauen Fleck schlagen; (*fruit*) beschädigen ▶ VI (*fruit*) eine Druckstelle bekommen; **to ~ one's arm** sich *dat* den Arm stoßen, sich *dat* einen blauen Fleck am Arm holen
bruising ['bru:zɪŋ] ADJ (*experience, encounter*) schmerzhaft ▶ N Quetschung *f*
Brum [brʌm] (BRIT *inf*) N ABBR = **Birmingham**
Brummie ['brʌmɪ] (*inf*) N *aus Birmingham stammende oder dort wohnhafte Person*, Birminghamer(in) *m(f)*
brunch [brʌntʃ] N Brunch *m*
brunette [bru:'nɛt] N Brünette *f*
brunt [brʌnt] N: **to bear the ~ of** die volle Wucht *+gen* tragen
brush [brʌʃ] N Bürste *f*; (*for painting, shaving etc*) Pinsel *m*; (*quarrel*) Auseinandersetzung *f* ▶ VT fegen; (*groom*) bürsten; (*teeth*) putzen; (*also*: **brush against**) streifen; **to have a ~ with sb** (*verbally*) sich mit jdm streiten; (*physically*) mit jdm aneinandergeraten; **to have a ~ with the police** mit der Polizei aneinandergeraten
▶ **brush aside** VT abtun
▶ **brush past** VT streifen
▶ **brush up** VT auffrischen
brushed [brʌʃt] ADJ (*steel, chrome etc*) gebürstet; (*denim etc*) aufgeraut; **~ nylon** Nylonvelours *m*
brushoff ['brʌʃɔf] (*inf*) N: **to give sb the ~** jdm eine Abfuhr erteilen
brushwood ['brʌʃwud] N Reisig *nt*
brusque [bru:sk] ADJ brüsk; (*tone*) schroff
Brussels ['brʌslz] N Brüssel *nt*
Brussels sprouts NPL Rosenkohl *m*
brutal ['bru:tl] ADJ brutal
brutality [bru:'tælɪtɪ] N Brutalität *f*
brutalize ['bru:təlaɪz] VT brutalisieren; (*ill-treat*) brutal behandeln
brute [bru:t] N brutaler Kerl *m*; (*animal*) Tier *nt* ▶ ADJ: **by ~ force** mit roher Gewalt
brutish ['bru:tɪʃ] ADJ tierisch
BS (*US*) N ABBR (= *Bachelor of Science*) *akademischer Grad für Naturwissenschaftler*
BSA N ABBR (= *Boy Scouts of America*) *amerikanische Pfadfinderorganisation*
BSc ABBR (= *Bachelor of Science*) *akademischer Grad für Naturwissenschaftler*
BSE N ABBR (= *bovine spongiform encephalopathy*) BSE *f*
BSI N ABBR (= *British Standards Institution*) *britischer Normenausschuss*
BST ABBR = **British Summer Time**
Bt (BRIT) ABBR = **baronet**
btu N ABBR (= *British thermal unit*) *britische Wärmeeinheit*
bubble ['bʌbl] N Blase *f* ▶ VI sprudeln; (*sparkle*) perlen; (*fig: person*) übersprudeln
bubble bath N Schaumbad *nt*
bubble gum N Bubblegum *m*
bubble-jet printer ['bʌbldʒɛt-] N Bubblejetdrucker *m*, Bubble-Jet-Drucker *m*
bubble pack N (Klar)sichtpackung *f*
bubbly ['bʌblɪ] ADJ (*person*) lebendig; (*liquid*) sprudelnd ▶ N (*inf: champagne*) Schampus *m*
Bucharest [bu:kə'rɛst] N Bukarest *nt*
buck [bʌk] N (*rabbit*) Rammler *m*; (*deer*) Bock *m*; (*US inf*) Dollar *m* ▶ VI bocken; **to pass the ~** die Verantwortung abschieben; **to pass the ~ to sb** jdm die Verantwortung zuschieben
▶ **buck up** VI (*cheer up*) aufleben ▶ VT: **to ~ one's ideas up** sich zusammenreißen
bucket ['bʌkɪt] N Eimer *m* ▶ VI (BRIT *inf*): **the rain is bucketing (down)** es gießt *or* schüttet (wie aus Kübeln)

> **Buckingham Palace** ist die offizielle Londoner Residenz der britischen Monarchen und liegt am St James Park. Der Palast wurde 1703 für den Herzog von Buckingham erbaut, 1762 von Georg III. gekauft, zwischen 1821 und 1836 von John Nash umgebaut und Anfang des 20. Jahrhunderts teilweise neu gestaltet. Teile des Buckingham Palace sind heute der Öffentlichkeit zugänglich.

buckle ['bʌkl] N Schnalle *f* ▶ VT zuschnallen; (*wheel*) verbiegen ▶ VI sich verbiegen
▶ **buckle down** VI sich dahinter klemmen; **to ~ down to sth** sich hinter etw *acc* klemmen
Bucks [bʌks] (BRIT) ABBR (*Post*) = **Buckinghamshire**
bud [bʌd] N Knospe *f* ▶ VI knospen, Knospen treiben
Budapest [bju:də'pɛst] N Budapest *nt*
Buddha ['budə] N Buddha *m*
Buddhism ['budɪzəm] N Buddhismus *m*
Buddhist ['budɪst] ADJ buddhistisch ▶ N Buddhist(in) *m(f)*

budding ['bʌdɪŋ] ADJ angehend
buddy ['bʌdɪ] (US) N Kumpel *m*
budge [bʌdʒ] VT (von der Stelle) bewegen; (*fig*) zum Nachgeben bewegen ▸ VI sich von der Stelle rühren; (*fig*) nachgeben
budgerigar ['bʌdʒərɪgɑːʳ] N Wellensittich *m*
budget ['bʌdʒɪt] N Budget *nt*, Etat *m*, Haushalt *m* ▸ VI Haus halten, haushalten, wirtschaften; **I'm on a tight ~** ich habe nicht viel Geld zur Verfügung; **she works out her ~ every month** sie macht (sich *dat*) jeden Monat einen Haushaltsplan; **to ~ for sth** etw kostenmäßig einplanen
budget airline N Billigflieger *m*
budgie ['bʌdʒɪ] N = **budgerigar**
Buenos Aires ['bweɪnɔs'aɪrɪz] N Buenos Aires *nt*
buff [bʌf] ADJ gelbbraun ▸ N (*inf*) Fan *m*
buffalo ['bʌfələu] (*pl* ~ *or* **buffaloes**) N (BRIT) Büffel *m*; (*US*) Bison *m*
buffer ['bʌfəʳ] N Puffer *m*; (*Comput*) Zwischenspeicher *m*, Pufferspeicher *m*; (*Rail*) Prellbock *m*; (*fig*) Polster *nt* ▸ VI (*Comput*) zwischenspeichern
buffering ['bʌfərɪŋ] N (*Comput*) Pufferung *f*
buffer state N Pufferstaat *m*
buffer zone N Pufferzone *f*
buffet[1] ['bufeɪ] (BRIT) N Büfett *nt*, Bahnhofsrestaurant *nt*; (*food*) kaltes Buffet *nt*
buffet[2] ['bʌfɪt] VT (*subj: sea*) hin und her werfen; (*: wind*) schütteln
buffet car (BRIT) N Speisewagen *m*
buffet lunch N Buffet *nt*
buffoon [bə'fuːn] N Clown *m*
bug [bʌg] N (*esp US*) Insekt *nt*; (*Comput: of program*) Programmfehler *m*; (*: of equipment*) Fehler *m*; (*fig: germ*) Bazillus *m*; (*hidden microphone*) Wanze *f* ▸ VT (*inf*) nerven; (*telephone etc*) abhören; (*room*) verwanzen; **I've got the travel ~** (*fig*) mich hat die Reiselust gepackt
bugbear ['bʌgbɛəʳ] N Schreckgespenst *nt*
bugger ['bʌgəʳ] (*inf!*) N Scheißkerl *m*, Arschloch *nt* ▸ VB: **~ off!** hau ab!; **~ (it)!** Scheiße!
buggy ['bʌgɪ] N (*for baby*) Sportwagen *m*
bugle ['bjuːgl] N Bügelhorn *nt*
build [bɪld] (*pt, pp* **built**) N Körperbau *m* ▸ VT bauen
▸ **build on** VT FUS (*fig*) aufbauen auf +*dat*
▸ **build up** VT aufbauen; (*production*) steigern; (*morale*) stärken; (*stocks*) anlegen; **don't ~ your hopes up too soon** mach dir nicht zu früh Hoffnungen
builder ['bɪldəʳ] N Bauunternehmer *m*
building ['bɪldɪŋ] N (*industry*) Bauindustrie *f*; (*construction*) Bau *m*; (*structure*) Gebäude *nt*, Bau
building contractor N Bauunternehmer *m*
building industry N Bauindustrie *f*
building site N Baustelle *f*
building society (BRIT) N Bausparkasse *f*
building trade N Baubranche *f or* -gewerbe *nt*
build-up ['bɪldʌp] N Ansammlung *f*; (*publicity*): **to give sb/sth a good ~** jdn/etw ganz groß herausbringen
built [bɪlt] PT, PP *of* **build** ▸ ADJ: **~-in** eingebaut, Einbau-; (*safeguards*) eingebaut; **well-~** gut gebaut
built-up area ['bɪltʌp-] N bebautes Gebiet *nt*
bulb [bʌlb] N (Blumen)zwiebel *f*; (*Elec*) (Glüh)birne *f*
bulbous ['bʌlbəs] ADJ knollig
Bulgaria [bʌl'gɛərɪə] N Bulgarien *nt*
Bulgarian [bʌl'gɛərɪən] ADJ bulgarisch ▸ N Bulgare *m*, Bulgarin *f*; (*Ling*) Bulgarisch *nt*
bulge [bʌldʒ] N Wölbung *f*; (*in birth rate, sales*) Zunahme *f* ▸ VI (*pocket*) prall gefüllt sein; (*cheeks*) voll sein; (*file*) (zum Bersten) voll sein; **to be bulging with** prall gefüllt sein mit
bulimia [bə'lɪmɪə] N Bulimie *f*
bulk [bʌlk] N (*of thing*) massige Form *f*; (*of person*) massige Gestalt *f*; **in ~** im Großen, en gros; **the ~ of** der Großteil +*gen*
bulk buying [-'baɪɪŋ] N Mengeneinkauf *m*, Großeinkauf *m*
bulk carrier N Bulkcarrier *m*
bulkhead ['bʌlkhɛd] N Schott *nt*
bulky ['bʌlkɪ] ADJ sperrig
bull [bul] N Stier *m*; (*male elephant or whale*) Bulle *m*; (*Stock Exchange*) Haussier *m*, Haussespekulant *m*; (*Rel*) Bulle *f*
bulldog ['buldɔg] N Bulldogge *f*
bulldoze ['buldəuz] VT mit Bulldozern wegräumen; (*building*) mit Bulldozern abreißen; **I was bulldozed into it** (*fig: inf*) ich wurde gezwungen *or* unter Druck gesetzt, es zu tun
bulldozer ['buldəuzəʳ] N Bulldozer *m*, Planierraupe *f*
bullet ['bulɪt] N Kugel *f*
bulletin ['bulɪtɪn] N (*TV etc*) Kurznachrichten *pl*; (*journal*) Bulletin *nt*
bulletin board N (*Comput*) Schwarzes Brett *nt*
bulletproof ['bulɪtpruːf] ADJ kugelsicher
bullfight ['bulfaɪt] N Stierkampf *m*
bullfighter ['bulfaɪtəʳ] N Stierkämpfer *m*
bullfighting ['bulfaɪtɪŋ] N Stierkampf *m*
bullion ['buljən] N: **gold/silver ~** Barrengold *nt*/-silber *nt*
bullock ['bulək] N Ochse *m*
bullring ['bulrɪŋ] N Stierkampfarena *f*
bull's-eye ['bulzaɪ] N (*on a target*): **the ~** der Scheibenmittelpunkt, das Schwarze
bullshit ['bulʃɪt] (*inf!*) N Scheiß *m*, Quatsch *m* ▸ VI Scheiß erzählen; **~!** Quatsch!
bully ['bulɪ] N Tyrann *m* ▸ VT tyrannisieren; (*frighten*) einschüchtern
bullying ['bulɪɪŋ] N Tyrannisieren *nt*
bum [bʌm] (*inf*) N Hintern *m*; (*esp US: good-for-nothing*) Rumtreiber *m*; (*tramp*) Penner *m*
▸ **bum around** (*inf*) VI herumgammeln
bumblebee ['bʌmblbiː] N Hummel *f*
bumf [bʌmf] (*inf*) N Papierkram *m*
bump [bʌmp] N Zusammenstoß *m*; (*jolt*) Erschütterung *f*; (*swelling*) Beule *f*; (*on road*) Unebenheit *f* ▸ VT stoßen; (*car*) eine Delle fahren in +*acc*
▸ **bump along** VI entlangholpern

b

▸ **bump into** VT FUS (*obstacle*) stoßen gegen; (*inf: person*) treffen
bumper ['bʌmpəʳ] N Stoßstange *f* ▸ ADJ: **~ crop, ~ harvest** Rekordernte *f*
bumper cars NPL Autoskooter *pl*
bumper sticker N Aufkleber *m*
bumph [bʌmf] N = **bumf**
bumptious ['bʌmpʃəs] ADJ wichtigtuerisch
bumpy ['bʌmpɪ] ADJ holperig; **it was a ~ flight/ride** während des Fluges/auf der Fahrt wurden wir tüchtig durchgerüttelt
bun [bʌn] N Brötchen *nt*; (*of hair*) Knoten *m*
bunch [bʌntʃ] N Strauß *m*; (*of keys*) Bund *m*; (*of bananas*) Büschel *nt*; (*of people*) Haufen *m*; **bunches** NPL (*in hair*) Zöpfe *pl*; **~ of grapes** Weintraube *f*
bundle ['bʌndl] N Bündel *nt* ▸ VT (*also*: **bundle up**) bündeln; (*put*): **to ~ sth into** etw stopfen *or* packen in *+acc*; **to ~ sb into** jdn schaffen in *+acc*
▸ **bundle off** VT schaffen
▸ **bundle out** VT herausschaffen
bun fight (BRIT *inf*) N Festivitäten *pl*; (*tea party*) Teegesellschaft *f*
bung [bʌŋ] N Spund *m*, Spundzapfen *m* ▸ VT (BRIT *inf*: *also*: **bung in**) schmeißen; (*also*: **bung up**) verstopfen; **my nose is bunged up** meine Nase ist verstopft
bungalow ['bʌŋgələu] N Bungalow *m*
bungee jumping ['bʌndʒiː'dʒʌmpɪŋ] N Bungeespringen *nt*
bungle ['bʌŋgl] VT verpfuschen
bunion ['bʌnjən] N entzündeter Ballen *m*
bunk [bʌŋk] N Bett *nt*, Koje *f*; **to do a ~** (*inf*) abhauen
▸ **bunk off** (*inf*) VI abhauen
bunk beds NPL Etagenbett *nt*
bunker ['bʌŋkəʳ] N Kohlenbunker *m*; (*Mil, Golf*) Bunker *m*
bunny ['bʌnɪ] N (*also*: **bunny rabbit**) Hase *m*, Häschen *nt*
bunny girl (BRIT) N Häschen *nt*
bunny hill (US) N (*Ski*) Anfängerhügel *m*
bunting ['bʌntɪŋ] N (*flags*) Wimpel *pl*, Fähnchen *pl*
buoy [bɔɪ] N Boje *f*
▸ **buoy up** VT (*fig*) Auftrieb geben *+dat*
buoyancy ['bɔɪənsɪ] N (*of ship, object*) Schwimmfähigkeit *f*
buoyant ['bɔɪənt] ADJ (*ship, object*) schwimmfähig; (*market*) fest; (*economy*) stabil; (*prices, currency*) fest, stabil; (*person, nature*) heiter
burden ['bəːdn] N Belastung *f*; (*load*) Last *f* ▸ VT: **to ~ sb with sth** jdn mit etw belasten; **to be a ~ to sb** jdm zur Last fallen
bureau ['bjuərəu] (*pl* **bureaux**) N (BRIT: *writing desk*) Sekretär *m*; (US: *chest of drawers*) Kommode *f*; (*office*) Büro *nt*
bureaucracy [bjuə'rɔkrəsɪ] N Bürokratie *f*
bureaucrat ['bjuərəkræt] N Bürokrat(in) *m(f)*
bureaucratic [bjuərə'krætɪk] ADJ bürokratisch
bureaux ['bjuərəuz] NPL *of* **bureau**
burgeon ['bəːdʒən] VI hervorsprießen
burger ['bəːgəʳ] (*inf*) N Hamburger *m*
burglar ['bəːgləʳ] N Einbrecher(in) *m(f)*
burglar alarm N Alarmanlage *f*
burglarize ['bəːgləraɪz] (US) VT einbrechen in *+acc*
burglary ['bəːglərɪ] N Einbruch *m*
burgle ['bəːgl] VT einbrechen in *+acc*
Burgundy ['bəːgəndɪ] N Burgund *nt*
burial ['bɛrɪəl] N Beerdigung *f*
burial ground N Begräbnisstätte *f*
burlesque [bəː'lɛsk] N (*parody*) Persiflage *f*; (US: *Theat*) Burleske *f*
burly ['bəːlɪ] ADJ kräftig, stämmig
Burma ['bəːmə] N Birma *nt*, Burma *nt*
Burmese [bəː'miːz] ADJ birmanisch, burmesisch ▸ N INV Birmane *m*, Burmese *m*, Birmanin *f*, Burmesin *f* ▸ N (*Ling*) Birmanisch *nt*, Burmesisch *nt*
burn [bəːn] (*pt, pp* **burned** *or* **burnt**) VT verbrennen; (*fuel*) als Brennstoff verwenden; (*food*) anbrennen lassen; (*house etc*) niederbrennen ▸ VI brennen; (*food*) anbrennen ▸ N Verbrennung *f*; **the cigarette burnt a hole in her dress** die Zigarette brannte ein Loch in ihr Kleid; **I've burnt myself!** ich habe mich verbrannt!
▸ **burn down** VT abbrennen
▸ **burn out** VT: **to ~ o.s. out** (*writer etc*) sich völlig verausgaben; **the fire burnt itself out** das Feuer brannte aus
burner ['bəːnəʳ] N Brenner *m*
burning ['bəːnɪŋ] ADJ brennend; (*sand, desert*) glühend heiß
burnish ['bəːnɪʃ] VT polieren

> **Burns' Night** ist der am 25. Januar begangene Gedenktag für den schottischen Dichter Robert Burns (1759–1796). Wo Schotten leben, sei es in Schottland oder im Ausland, wird dieser Tag mit einem Abendessen gefeiert, bei dem es als Hauptgericht **haggis** gibt, der mit Dudelsackbegleitung aufgetischt wird. Dazu isst man Steckrüben- und Kartoffelpüree und trinkt Whisky. Während des Essens werden Burns' Gedichte vorgelesen, seine Lieder gesungen, bestimmte Reden gehalten und Trinksprüche ausgegeben.

burnt [bəːnt] PT, PP *of* **burn**
burnt sugar (BRIT) N Karamell *m*
burp [bəːp] (*inf*) N Rülpser *m* ▸ VT (*baby*) aufstoßen lassen ▸ VI rülpsen
burrow ['bʌrəu] N Bau *m* ▸ VI graben; (*rummage*) wühlen
bursar ['bəːsəʳ] N Schatzmeister *m*, Finanzverwalter *m*
bursary ['bəːsərɪ] (BRIT) N Stipendium *nt*
burst [bəːst] (*pt, pp* **~**) VT zum Platzen bringen, platzen lassen ▸ VI platzen ▸ N Salve *f*; (*also*: **burst pipe**) (Rohr)bruch *m*; **the river has ~ its banks** der Fluss ist über die Ufer getreten; **to ~ into flames** in Flammen aufgehen; **to ~ into tears** in Tränen ausbrechen; **to ~ out laughing** in Lachen ausbrechen; **~ blood vessel** geplatzte Ader *f*; **to be bursting with** zum Bersten voll sein mit; (*pride*) fast platzen

vor *+dat*; **to ~ open** aufspringen; **a ~ of energy** ein Ausbruch *m* von Energie; **a ~ of enthusiasm** ein Begeisterungsausbruch *m*; **a ~ of speed** ein Spurt *m*; **~ of laughter** Lachsalve *f*; **~ of applause** Beifallssturm *m*
▶ **burst in on** VT FUS: **to ~ in on sb** bei jdm hereinplatzen
▶ **burst into** VT FUS (*into room*) platzen in *+acc*
▶ **burst out of** VT FUS (*of room*) stürmen *or* stürzen aus

bury ['bɛrɪ] VT begraben; (*at funeral*) beerdigen; **to ~ one's face in one's hands** das Gesicht in den Händen vergraben; **to ~ one's head in the sand** (*fig*) den Kopf in den Sand stecken; **to ~ the hatchet** (*fig*) das Kriegsbeil begraben

bus [bʌs] N (Auto)bus *m*, (Omni)bus *m*; (*double decker*) Doppeldecker *m* (*inf*)

bus boy (*US*) N Bedienungshilfe *f*

bush [buʃ] N Busch *m*, Strauch *m*; (*scrubland*) Busch; **to beat about the ~** um den heißen Brei herumreden

bushed [buʃt] (*inf*) ADJ (*exhausted*) groggy

bushel ['buʃl] N Scheffel *m*

bushfire N Buschfeuer *nt*

bushy ['buʃɪ] ADJ buschig

busily ['bɪzɪlɪ] ADV eifrig; **to be ~ doing sth** eifrig etw tun

business ['bɪznɪs] N (*matter*) Angelegenheit *f*; (*trading*) Geschäft *nt*; (*firm*) Firma *f*, Betrieb *m*; (*occupation*) Beruf *m*; **to be away on ~** geschäftlich unterwegs sein; **I'm here on ~** ich bin geschäftlich hier; **he's in the insurance/transport ~** er arbeitet in der Versicherungs-/Transportbranche; **to do ~ with sb** Geschäfte *pl* mit jdm machen; **it's my ~ to …** es ist meine Aufgabe, zu …; **it's none of my ~** es geht mich nichts an; **he means ~** er meint es ernst

business address N Geschäftsadresse *f*

business card N (Visiten)karte *f*

business class N (*Aviat*) Businessclass *f*

businesslike ['bɪznɪslaɪk] ADJ geschäftsmäßig

businessman ['bɪznɪsmən] N (*irreg*) Geschäftsmann *m*

business studies NPL Betriebswirtschaftslehre *f*

business trip N Geschäftsreise *f*

businesswoman ['bɪznɪswumən] N (*irreg*) Geschäftsfrau *f*

busker ['bʌskə^r] (BRIT) N Straßenmusikant(in) *m(f)*

bus lane (BRIT) N Busspur *f*

bus service N Busverbindung *f*

bus shelter N Wartehäuschen *nt*

bus station N Busbahnhof *m*

bus stop N Bushaltestelle *f*

bust [bʌst] N Busen *m*; (*measurement*) Oberweite *f*; (*sculpture*) Büste *f* ▶ ADJ (*inf*) kaputt ▶ VT (*inf*) verhaften; **to go ~** pleitegehen

bustle ['bʌsl] N Betrieb *m* ▶ VI eilig herumlaufen

bustling ['bʌslɪŋ] ADJ belebt

bust-up ['bʌstʌp] (BRIT *inf*) N Krach *m*

busty ['bʌstɪ] ADJ (*woman*) vollbusig

busy ['bɪzɪ] ADJ (*person*) beschäftigt; (*shop, street*) belebt; (*Tel: esp US*) besetzt ▶ VT: **to ~ o.s. with** sich beschäftigen mit; **he's a ~ man** er ist ein viel beschäftigter Mann; **he's ~** er hat (zurzeit) viel zu tun

busybody ['bɪzɪbɔdɪ] N: **to be a ~** sich ständig einmischen

busy signal (*US*) N (*Tel*) Besetztzeichen *nt*

KEYWORD

but [bʌt] CONJ **1** (*yet*) aber; **not blue but red** nicht blau, sondern rot; **he's not very bright, but he's hard-working** er ist nicht sehr intelligent, aber er ist fleißig
2 (*however*): **I'd love to come, but I'm busy** ich würde gern kommen, bin aber beschäftigt
3 (*showing disagreement, surprise etc*): **but that's far too expensive!** aber das ist viel zu teuer!; **but that's fantastic!** das ist doch toll!
▶ PREP (*apart from, except*) außer *+dat*; **nothing but trouble** nichts als Ärger; **no-one but him can do it** keiner außer ihm kann es machen; **but for you** wenn Sie nicht gewesen wären; **but for your help** ohne Ihre Hilfe; **I'll do anything but that** ich mache alles, nur nicht das; **the last house but one** das vorletzte Haus; **the next street but one** die übernächste Straße
▶ ADV (*just, only*) nur; **she's but a child** sie ist doch noch ein Kind; **I can but try** ich kann es ja versuchen

butane ['bju:teɪn] N (*also*: **butane gas**) Butan(gas) *nt*

butch [butʃ] (*inf*) ADJ maskulin

butcher ['butʃə^r] N Fleischer *m*, Metzger *m*; (*pej: murderer*) Schlächter *m* ▶ VT schlachten; (*prisoners etc*) abschlachten

butcher's ['butʃəz], **butcher's shop** N Fleischerei *f*, Metzgerei *f*

butler ['bʌtlə^r] N Butler *m*

butt [bʌt] N großes Fass *nt*, Tonne *f*; (*thick end*) dickes Ende *nt*; (*of gun*) Kolben *m*; (*of cigarette*) Kippe *f*; (BRIT *fig: target*) Zielscheibe *f*; (*US inf!*) Arsch *m* ▶ VT (*goat*) mit den Hörnern stoßen; (*person*) mit dem Kopf stoßen
▶ **butt in** VI sich einmischen, dazwischenfunken (*inf*)

butter ['bʌtə^r] N Butter *f* ▶ VT buttern

buttercup ['bʌtəkʌp] N Butterblume *f*

butter dish N Butterdose *f*

butterfingers ['bʌtəfɪŋgəz] (*inf*) N Schussel *m*

butterfly ['bʌtəflaɪ] N Schmetterling *m*; (*Swimming: also*: **butterfly stroke**) Schmetterlingsstil *m*, Butterfly *m*

buttocks ['bʌtəks] NPL Gesäß *nt*

button ['bʌtn] N Knopf *m*; (*US: badge*) Plakette *f* ▶ VT (*also*: **button up**) zuknöpfen ▶ VI geknöpft werden

buttonhole ['bʌtnhəul] N Knopfloch *nt*; (*flower*) Blume *f* im Knopfloch ▶ VT zu fassen bekommen, sich *dat* schnappen (*inf*)

buttress ['bʌtrɪs] N Strebepfeiler *m*

buxom [ˈbʌksəm] ADJ drall
buy [baɪ] (*pt, pp* **bought**) VT kaufen; (*company*) aufkaufen ▶ N Kauf *m*; **that was a good/bad ~** das war ein guter/schlechter Kauf; **to ~ sb sth** jdm etw kaufen; **to ~ sth from sb** etw bei jdm kaufen; (*from individual*) jdm etw abkaufen; **to ~ sb a drink** jdm einen ausgeben (*inf*)
▶ **buy back** VT zurückkaufen
▶ **buy in** (BRIT) VT einkaufen
▶ **buy into** (BRIT) VT FUS sich einkaufen in *+acc*
▶ **buy off** VT kaufen
▶ **buy out** VT (*partner*) auszahlen; (*business*) aufkaufen
▶ **buy up** VT aufkaufen
buyer [ˈbaɪəʳ] N Käufer(in) *m(f)*; (*Comm*) Einkäufer(in) *m(f)*
buyer's market [ˈbaɪəz-] N Käufermarkt *m*
buyout [ˈbaɪaʊt] N (*of firm: by workers, management*) Aufkauf *m*
buzz [bʌz] VI summen, brummen; (*saw*) kreischen ▶ VT rufen; (*with buzzer*) (mit dem Summer) rufen; (*Aviat: plane, building*) dicht vorbeifliegen an *+dat* ▶ N Summen *nt*, Brummen *nt*; (*inf*): **to give sb a ~** jdn anrufen; **my head is buzzing** mir schwirrt der Kopf
▶ **buzz off** (*inf*) VI abhauen
buzzard [ˈbʌzəd] N Bussard *m*
buzzer [ˈbʌzəʳ] N Summer *m*
buzz word (*inf*) N Modewort *nt*

KEYWORD

by [baɪ] PREP **1** (*referring to cause, agent*) von *+dat*, durch *+acc*; **killed by lightning** vom Blitz *or* durch einen Blitz getötet; **a painting by Picasso** ein Bild von Picasso
2 (*referring to method, manner, means*): **by bus/car/train** mit dem Bus/Auto/Zug; **to pay by cheque** mit *or* per Scheck bezahlen; **by saving hard, he was able to ...** indem er eisern sparte, konnte er ...
3 (*via, through*) über *+acc*; **we came by Dover** wir sind über Dover gekommen
4 (*close to*) bei *+dat*, an *+dat*; **the house by the river** das Haus am Fluss
5 (*past*) an ... *dat* vorbei; **she rushed by me** sie eilte an mir vorbei
6 (*not later than*) bis *+acc*; **by 4 o'clock** bis 4 Uhr; **by this time tomorrow** morgen um diese Zeit
7 (*amount*): **by the kilo/metre** kilo-/meterweise; **to be paid by the hour** stundenweise bezahlt werden
8 (*Math, measure*): **to divide by 3** durch 3 teilen; **to multiply by 3** mit 3 malnehmen; **it missed me by inches** es hat mich um Zentimeter verfehlt
9 (*according to*): **to play by the rules** sich an die Regeln halten; **it's all right by me** von mir aus ist es in Ordnung
10: **(all) by myself/himself** *etc* (ganz) allein
11: **by the way** übrigens
▶ ADV **1** *see* **go**; **pass**
2: **by and by** irgendwann
3: **by and large** im Großen und Ganzen

bye [baɪ], **bye-bye** [ˈbaɪˈbaɪ] EXCL (auf) Wiedersehen, tschüss (*inf*)
bye-law [ˈbaɪlɔː] N *see* **by-law**
by-election [ˈbaɪɪlɛkʃən] (BRIT) N Nachwahl *f*
Byelorussia [bjɛləuˈrʌʃə] N = **Belorussia**
Byelorussian [bjɛləuˈrʌʃən] ADJ, N = **Belarussian**
bygone [ˈbaɪgɔn] ADJ (längst) vergangen ▶ N: **let bygones be bygones** wir sollten die Vergangenheit ruhen lassen
by-law [ˈbaɪlɔː] N Verordnung *f*
bypass [ˈbaɪpɑːs] N Umgehungsstraße *f*; (*Med*) Bypassoperation *f* ▶ VT (*also fig*) umgehen
by-product [ˈbaɪprɔdʌkt] N Nebenprodukt *nt*
byre [ˈbaɪəʳ] (BRIT) N Kuhstall *m*
bystander [ˈbaɪstændəʳ] N Zuschauer(in) *m(f)*
byte [baɪt] N (*Comput*) Byte *nt*
byway [ˈbaɪweɪ] N Seitenweg *m*
byword [ˈbaɪwəːd] N: **to be a ~ for** der Inbegriff *+gen* sein, gleichbedeutend sein mit
by-your-leave [ˈbaɪjɔːˈliːv] N: **without so much as a ~** ohne auch nur (um Erlaubnis) zu fragen

Cc

C¹, c¹ [siː] N (*letter*) C *nt*, c *nt*; (*Scol*) ≈ Drei *f*, ≈ Befriedigend *nt*; **C for Charlie** ≈ C wie Cäsar
C² [siː] N (*Mus*) C *nt*, c *nt*
C³ [siː] ABBR = **Celsius; centigrade**
c² ABBR = **century**; (= *circa*) ca.; (*US etc*: = *cent(s)*) Cent
CA N ABBR (BRIT) = **chartered accountant** ▸ ABBR = **Central America**; (*US Post*) = **California**
ca. ABBR (= *circa*) ca.
C/A ABBR (*Comm*) = **capital account; credit account; current account**
CAA N ABBR (BRIT) = **Civil Aviation Authority**; (*US*: = *Civil Aeronautics Authority*) *Zivilluftfahrtbehörde*
CAB (BRIT) N ABBR = **Citizens' Advice Bureau**
cab [kæb] N Taxi *nt*; (*of truck, train etc*) Führerhaus *nt*; (*horse-drawn*) Droschke *f*
cabaret ['kæbəreɪ] N Kabarett *nt*
cabbage ['kæbɪdʒ] N Kohl *m*
cabbie, cabby ['kæbɪ] N Taxifahrer(in) *m(f)*
cab driver N Taxifahrer(in) *m(f)*
cabin ['kæbɪn] N Kabine *f*; (*house*) Hütte *f*
cabin cruiser N Kajütboot *nt*
cabinet ['kæbɪnɪt] N kleiner Schrank *m*; (*also*: **display cabinet**) Vitrine *f*; (*Pol*) Kabinett *nt*
cabinet-maker ['kæbɪnɪt'meɪkəʳ] N Möbeltischler *m*
cabinet minister N Mitglied *nt* des Kabinetts, Minister(in) *m(f)*
cable ['keɪbl] N Kabel *nt* ▸ VT kabeln
cable car N (Draht)seilbahn *f*
cablegram ['keɪblgræm] N (Übersee)telegramm *nt*, Kabel *nt*
cable railway N Seilbahn *f*
cable television N Kabelfernsehen *nt*
cable TV N = **cable television**
cache [kæʃ] N Versteck *nt*, geheimes Lager *nt*; **a ~ of food** ein geheimes Proviantlager
cackle ['kækl] VI (*person: laugh*) meckernd lachen; (*hen*) gackern
cacti ['kæktaɪ] NPL *of* **cactus**
cactus ['kæktəs] (*pl* **cacti**) N Kaktus *m*
CAD N ABBR (= *computer-aided design*) CAD *nt*
caddie, caddy ['kædɪ] N (*Golf*) Caddie *m*
cadence ['keɪdəns] N (*of voice*) Tonfall *m*
cadet [kə'dɛt] N Kadett *m*; **police ~** Polizeianwärter(in) *m(f)*
cadge [kædʒ] (*inf*) VT: **to ~ (from** *or* **off)** schnorren (bei *or* von +*dat*); **to ~ a lift with sb** von jdm mitgenommen werden
cadger ['kædʒəʳ] (BRIT *inf*) N Schnorrer(in) *m(f)*
cadre ['kædrɪ] N Kader *m*
Caesarean [siː'zɛərɪən] N: **~ (section)** Kaiserschnitt *m*
CAF (BRIT) ABBR (= *cost and freight*) cf
café ['kæfeɪ] N Café *nt*
cafeteria [kæfɪ'tɪərɪə] N Cafeteria *f*
caffeine, caffein ['kæfiːn] N Koffein *nt*
cage [keɪdʒ] N Käfig *m*; (*of lift*) Fahrkorb *m* ▸ VT einsperren
cagey ['keɪdʒɪ] (*inf*) ADJ vorsichtig; (*evasive*) ausweichend
cagoule [kə'guːl] N Regenjacke *f*
cahoots [kə'huːts] (*inf*) N: **to be in ~ with** unter einer Decke stecken mit
CAI N ABBR (= *computer-aided instruction*) CAI *nt*
Cairo ['kaɪərəu] N Kairo *nt*
cajole [kə'dʒəul] VT: **to ~ sb into doing sth** jdn bereden, etw zu tun
cake [keɪk] N Kuchen *m*; (*small*) Gebäckstück *nt*; (*of soap*) Stück *nt*; **it's a piece of ~** (*inf*) das ist ein Kinderspiel *or* ein Klacks; **he wants to have his ~ and eat it (too)** (*fig*) er will das eine, ohne das andere zu lassen
caked [keɪkt] ADJ: **~ with** (*mud, blood*) verkrustet mit
cake shop N Konditorei *f*
Cal. (*US*) ABBR (*Post*) = **California**
calamine lotion ['kæləmaɪn-] N Galmeilotion *f*
calamitous [kə'læmɪtəs] ADJ katastrophal
calamity [kə'læmɪtɪ] N Katastrophe *f*
calcium ['kælsɪəm] N Kalzium *nt*
calculate ['kælkjuleɪt] VT (*work out*) berechnen; (*estimate*) abschätzen
▸ **calculate on** VT FUS: **to ~ on sth** mit etw rechnen; **to ~ on doing sth** damit rechnen, etw zu tun
calculated ['kælkjuleɪtɪd] ADJ (*insult*) bewusst; (*action*) vorsätzlich; **a ~ risk** ein kalkuliertes Risiko
calculating ['kælkjuleɪtɪŋ] ADJ (*scheming*) berechnend
calculation [kælkju'leɪʃən] N Berechnung *f*; Abschätzung *f*; (*sum*) Rechnung *f*
calculator ['kælkjuleɪtəʳ] N Rechner *m*

calculus ['kælkjuləs] N Infinitesimalrechnung *f*; **integral/differential** ~ Integral-/ Differenzialrechnung *f*
calendar ['kæləndəʳ] N Kalender *m*; (*timetable, schedule*) (Termin)kalender *m*
calendar month N Kalendermonat *m*
calendar year N Kalenderjahr *nt*
calf [kɑːf] (*pl* **calves**) N Kalb *nt*; (*of elephant, seal etc*) Junge(s) *nt*; (*also*: **calfskin**) Kalb(s)leder *nt*; (*Anat*) Wade *f*
caliber ['kælɪbəʳ] (*US*) N = **calibre**
calibrate ['kælɪbreɪt] VT (*gun etc*) kalibrieren; (*scale of measuring instrument*) eichen
calibre, (*US*) **caliber** ['kælɪbəʳ] N Kaliber *nt*; (*of person*) Format *nt*
calico ['kælɪkəu] N (*Brit*) Kattun *m*, Kaliko *m*; (*US*) bedruckter Kattun
Calif. (*US*) ABBR (*Post*) = **California**
California [kælɪ'fɔːnɪə] N Kalifornien *nt*
calipers ['kælɪpəz] (*US*) NPL = **callipers**
call [kɔːl] VT (*name, consider*) nennen; (*shout out, summon*) rufen; (*Tel*) anrufen; (*witness, flight*) aufrufen; (*meeting*) einberufen; (*strike*) ausrufen ▶ VI rufen; (*Tel*) anrufen; (*visit*: *also*: **call in, call round**) vorbeigehen, vorbeikommen ▶ N Ruf *m*; (*Tel*) Anruf *m*; (*visit*) Besuch *m*; (*for a service etc*) Nachfrage *f*; (*for flight etc*) Aufruf *m*; (*fig*: *lure*) Ruf *m*, Verlockung *f*; **to be called** (*named*) heißen; **who is calling?** (*Tel*) wer spricht da bitte?; **London calling** (*Radio*) hier ist London; **please give me a ~ at 7** rufen Sie mich bitte um 7 an; **to make a ~** ein (Telefon)gespräch führen; **to pay a ~ on sb** jdn besuchen; **on ~** dienstbereit; **to be on ~** einsatzbereit sein; (*doctor etc*) Bereitschaftsdienst haben; **there's not much ~ for these items** es besteht keine große Nachfrage nach diesen Dingen
▶ **call at** VT FUS (*subj*: *ship*) anlaufen; (: *train*) halten in *+dat*
▶ **call back** VI (*return*) wiederkommen; (*Tel*) zurückrufen ▶ VT (*Tel*) zurückrufen
▶ **call for** VT FUS (*demand*) fordern; (*fetch*) abholen
▶ **call in** VT (*doctor, expert, police*) zurate ziehen; (*books, cars, stock etc*) aus dem Verkehr ziehen ▶ VI vorbeigehen, vorbeikommen
▶ **call off** VT absagen
▶ **call on** VT FUS besuchen; (*appeal to*) appellieren an *+acc*; **to ~ on sb to do sth** jdn bitten *or* auffordern, etw zu tun
▶ **call out** VI rufen ▶ VT rufen; (*police, troops*) alarmieren
▶ **call up** VT (*Mil*) einberufen; (*Tel*) anrufen
Callanetics® N SING Callanetics *f*
call box (*Brit*) N Telefonzelle *f*
call centre N Telefoncenter *nt*, Callcenter *nt*
caller ['kɔːləʳ] N Besucher(in) *m(f)*; (*Tel*) Anrufer(in) *m(f)*; **hold the line, ~!** (*Tel*) bitte bleiben Sie am Apparat!
caller ID N (*Tel*) Anruferkennung *m*; (*of email, text message*) Absenderkennung *m*
call girl N Callgirl *nt*
call-in ['kɔːlɪn] (*US*) N (*Radio, TV*) Phone-in *nt*
calling ['kɔːlɪŋ] N (*trade*) Beruf *m*; (*vocation*) Berufung *f*
calling card (*US*) N Visitenkarte *f*
callipers, (*US*) **calipers** ['kælɪpəz] NPL (*Math*) Tastzirkel *m*; (*Med*) Schiene *f*
callous ['kæləs] ADJ herzlos
callousness ['kæləsnɪs] N Herzlosigkeit *f*
callow ['kæləu] ADJ unreif
calm [kɑːm] ADJ ruhig; (*unworried*) gelassen ▶ N Ruhe *f* ▶ VT beruhigen; (*fears*) zerstreuen; (*grief*) lindern
▶ **calm down** VT beruhigen ▶ VI sich beruhigen
calmly ['kɑːmlɪ] ADV ruhig; gelassen
calmness ['kɑːmnɪs] N Ruhe *f*; Gelassenheit *f*
Calor gas® ['kæləʳ-] N Butangas *nt*
calorie ['kælərɪ] N Kalorie *f*; **low-~ product** kalorienarmes Produkt *nt*
calve [kɑːv] VI kalben
calves [kɑːvz] NPL *of* **calf**
CAM N ABBR (= *computer-aided manufacture*) CAM *nt*
camber ['kæmbəʳ] N Wölbung *f*
Cambodia [kæm'bəudɪə] N Kambodscha *nt*
Cambodian [kæm'bəudɪən] ADJ kambodschanisch ▶ N Kambodschaner(in) *m(f)*
Cambs (*Brit*) ABBR (*Post*) = **Cambridgeshire**
camcorder ['kæmkɔːdəʳ] N Camcorder *m*, Kamerarekorder *m*
came [keɪm] PT *of* **come**
camel ['kæməl] N Kamel *nt*
cameo ['kæmɪəu] N Kamee *f*; (*Theat, Liter*) Miniatur *f*
camera ['kæmərə] N (*Cine, Phot*) Kamera *f*; (*also*: **cine camera, movie camera**) Filmkamera *f*; **35 mm ~** Kleinbildkamera *f*; **in ~** (*Law*) unter Ausschluss der Öffentlichkeit
cameraman ['kæmərəmæn] N (*irreg*) Kameramann *m*
camera phone N Fotohandy *nt*
Cameroon [kæmə'ruːn] N Kamerun *nt*
Cameroun [kæmə'ruːn] N = **Cameroon**
camomile ['kæməumaɪl] N Kamille *f*
camouflage ['kæməflɑːʒ] N Tarnung *f* ▶ VT tarnen
camp [kæmp] N Lager *nt*; (*barracks*) Kaserne *f* ▶ VI zelten ▶ ADJ (*effeminate*) tuntenhaft (*inf*)
campaign [kæm'peɪn] N (*Mil*) Feldzug *m*; (*Pol etc*) Kampagne *f* ▶ VI kämpfen; **to ~ for/against** sich einsetzen für/gegen
campaigner [kæm'peɪnəʳ] N: **~ for** Befürworter(in) *m(f)* *+gen*; **~ against** Gegner(in) *m(f)* *+gen*
camp bed (*Brit*) N Campingliege *f*
camper ['kæmpəʳ] N (*person*) Camper *m*; (*vehicle*) Wohnmobil *nt*
camping ['kæmpɪŋ] N Camping *nt*; **to go ~** zelten gehen, campen
camping site, camp site N Campingplatz *m*
campus ['kæmpəs] N (*Univ*) Universitätsgelände *nt*, Campus *m*
camshaft ['kæmʃɑːft] N Nockenwelle *f*
can[1] [kæn] N Büchse *f*, Dose *f*; (*for oil, water*) Kanister *m* ▶ VT eindosen, in Büchsen *or* Dosen

einmachen; **a ~ of beer** eine Dose Bier; **he had to carry the ~** (BRIT *inf*) er musste die Sache ausbaden

KEYWORD

can² (*negative* **cannot, can't**, *conditional, pt* **could**) AUX VB **1** (*be able to, know how to*) können; **you can do it if you try** du kannst es, wenn du es nur versuchst; **I can't see you** ich kann dich nicht sehen; **I can swim/drive** ich kann schwimmen/Auto fahren; **can you speak English?** sprechen Sie Englisch?
2 (*may*) können, dürfen; **can I use your phone?** kann *or* darf ich Ihr Telefon benutzen?; **could I have a word with you?** könnte ich Sie mal sprechen?
3 (*expressing disbelief, puzzlement*): **it can't be true!** das darf doch nicht wahr sein!
4 (*expressing possibility, suggestion, etc*): **he could be in the library** er könnte in der Bibliothek sein

Canada ['kænədə] N Kanada *nt*
Canadian [kə'neɪdɪən] ADJ kanadisch ▶ N Kanadier(in) *m(f)*
canal [kə'næl] N (*also Anat*) Kanal *m*
Canaries [kə'nɛərɪz] NPL = **Canary Islands**
canary [kə'nɛərɪ] N Kanarienvogel *m*
Canary Islands [kə'nɛərɪ 'aɪləndz] NPL: **the ~** die Kanarischen Inseln *pl*
Canberra ['kænbərə] N Canberra *nt*
cancel ['kænsəl] VT absagen; (*reservation*) abbestellen; (*train, flight*) ausfallen lassen; (*contract*) annullieren; (*order*) stornieren; (*cross out*) durchstreichen; (*stamp*) entwerten; (*cheque*) ungültig machen
▶ **cancel out** VT aufheben; **they ~ each other out** sie heben sich gegenseitig auf
cancellation [kænsə'leɪʃən] N Absage *f*; (*of reservation*) Abbestellung *f*; (*of train, flight*) Ausfall *m*; (*Tourism*) Rücktritt *m*
cancer ['kænsəʳ] N (*Astrol*: *also*: **Cancer**) Krebs *m*; **to be C~** (ein) Krebs sein
cancerous ['kænsrəs] ADJ krebsartig
cancer patient N Krebskranke(r) *f(m)*
cancer research N Krebsforschung *f*
c and f (BRIT) ABBR (*Comm*: = *cost and freight*) cf
candid ['kændɪd] ADJ offen, ehrlich
candidacy ['kændɪdəsɪ] N Kandidatur *f*
candidate ['kændɪdeɪt] N Kandidat(in) *m(f)*; (*for job*) Bewerber(in) *m(f)*
candidature ['kændɪdətʃəʳ] (BRIT) N = **candidacy**
candied ['kændɪd] ADJ kandiert; **~ apple** (US) kandierter Apfel *m*
candle ['kændl] N Kerze *f*; (*of tallow*) Talglicht *nt*
candleholder ['kændlhəuldəʳ] N *see* **candlestick**
candlelight ['kændllaɪt] N: **by ~** bei Kerzenlicht
candlestick ['kændlstɪk] N Kerzenhalter *m*; (*bigger, ornate*) Kerzenleuchter *m*
candour, (US) **candor** ['kændəʳ] N Offenheit *f*
C & W N ABBR = **country and western**
candy ['kændɪ] N (*also*: **sugar-candy**) Kandis(zucker) *m*; (US) Bonbon *m or nt*
candyfloss ['kændɪflɔs] (BRIT) N Zuckerwatte *f*
candy store (US) N Süßwarenhandlung *f*
cane [keɪn] N Rohr *nt*; (*stick*) Stock *m*; (: *for walking*) (Spazier)stock *m* ▶ VT (BRIT *Scol*) mit dem Stock schlagen
canine ['keɪnaɪn] ADJ (*species*) Hunde-
canister ['kænɪstəʳ] N Dose *f*; (*pressurized container*) Sprühdose *f*; (*of gas, chemicals etc*) Kanister *m*
cannabis ['kænəbɪs] N Haschisch *nt*; (*also*: **cannabis plant**) Hanf *m*, Cannabis *m*
canned [kænd] ADJ Dosen-; (*inf*: *music*) aus der Konserve; (*US inf*: *worker*) entlassen, rausgeschmissen (*inf*)
cannibal ['kænɪbəl] N Kannibale *m*, Kannibalin *f*
cannibalism ['kænɪbəlɪzəm] N Kannibalismus *m*
cannibalization [kænɪbəlaɪ'zeɪʃn] N (*Econ*) Kannibalisierung *f*
cannon ['kænən] (*pl* **~** *or* **cannons**) N Kanone *f*
cannonball ['kænənbɔ:l] N Kanonenkugel *f*
cannon fodder N Kanonenfutter *nt*
cannot ['kænɔt] = **can not**
canny ['kænɪ] ADJ schlau
canoe [kə'nu:] N Kanu *nt*
canoeing [kə'nu:ɪŋ] N Kanusport *m*
canon ['kænən] N Kanon *m*; (*clergyman*) Kanoniker *m*, Kanonikus *m*
canonize ['kænənaɪz] VT kanonisieren, heiligsprechen
can-opener ['kænəupnəʳ] N Dosenöffner *m*, Büchsenöffner *m*
canopy ['kænəpɪ] N (*also fig*) Baldachin *m*
cant [kænt] N scheinheiliges Gerede *nt*
can't [kænt] = **can not**
Cantab. (BRIT) ABBR (*in degree titles*: = *Cantabrigiensis*) *der Universität Cambridge*
cantankerous [kæn'tæŋkərəs] ADJ mürrisch
canteen [kæn'ti:n] N (*in school, workplace*) Kantine *f*; (: *mobile*) Feldküche *f*; (BRIT: *of cutlery*) Besteckkasten *m*
canter ['kæntəʳ] VI leicht galoppieren, kantern ▶ N leichter Galopp *m*, Kanter *m*
cantilever ['kæntɪli:vəʳ] N Ausleger *m*
canvas ['kænvəs] N Leinwand *f*; (*painting*) Gemälde *nt*; (*Naut*) Segeltuch *nt*; **under ~** im Zelt
canvass ['kænvəs] VT (*opinions, views*) erforschen; (*person*) für seine Partei zu gewinnen suchen; (*place*) Wahlwerbung machen in +*dat* ▶ VI: **to ~ for ...** (*Pol*) um Stimmen für ... werben
canvasser ['kænvəsəʳ] N (*Pol*) Wahlhelfer(in) *m(f)*
canvassing ['kænvəsɪŋ] N (*Pol*) Wahlwerbung *f*
canyon ['kænjən] N Cañon *m*
CAP N ABBR (= *Common Agricultural Policy*) gemeinsame Agrarpolitik *f* der EG
cap [kæp] N Mütze *f*, Kappe *f*; (*of pen*) (Verschluss)kappe *f*; (*of bottle*) Verschluss *m*, Deckel *m*; (*contraceptive*: *also*: **Dutch cap**) Pessar *nt*; (*for toy gun*) Zündplättchen *nt*; (*for swimming*) Bademütze *f*, Badekappe *f*; (*Sport*) *Ehrenkappe, die Nationalspielern verliehen wird* ▶ VT (*outdo*)

überbieten; (*Sport*) für die Nationalmannschaft aufstellen; **capped with ...** mit ... obendrauf; **and to ~ it all, ...** und obendrein ...

capability [keɪpə'bɪlɪtɪ] N Fähigkeit *f*; (*Mil*) Potenzial *nt*

capable ['keɪpəbl] ADJ fähig; **to be ~ of doing sth** etw tun können, fähig sein, etw zu tun; **to be ~ of sth** (*interpretation etc*) etw zulassen

capacious [kə'peɪʃəs] ADJ geräumig

capacity [kə'pæsɪtɪ] N Fassungsvermögen *nt*; (*of lift etc*) Höchstlast *f*; (*capability*) Fähigkeit *f*; (*position, role*) Eigenschaft *f*; (*of factory*) Kapazität *f*; **filled to ~** randvoll; (*stadium etc*) bis auf den letzten Platz besetzt; **in his ~ as ...** in seiner Eigenschaft als ...; **this work is beyond my ~** zu dieser Arbeit bin ich nicht fähig; **in an advisory ~** in beratender Funktion; **to work at full ~** voll ausgelastet sein

cape [keɪp] N Kap *nt*; (*cloak*) Cape *nt*, Umhang *m*

Cape of Good Hope N: **the ~** das Kap der guten Hoffnung

caper ['keɪpə^r^] N (*Culin: usu pl*) Kaper *f*; (*prank*) Eskapade *f*, Kapriole *f*

Cape Town N Kapstadt *nt*

capita ['kæpɪtə] N *see* **per capita**

capital ['kæpɪtl] N (*also*: **capital city**) Hauptstadt *f*; (*money*) Kapital *nt*; (*also*: **capital letter**) Großbuchstabe *m*

capital account N Kapitalverkehrsbilanz *f*; (*of country*) Kapitalkonto *nt*

capital allowance N (Anlage)abschreibung *f*

capital assets NPL Kapitalvermögen *nt*

capital expenditure N Kapitalaufwendungen *pl*

capital gains tax N Kapitalertragssteuer *f*

capital goods NPL Investitionsgüter *pl*

capital-intensive ['kæpɪtlɪn'tɛnsɪv] ADJ kapitalintensiv

capitalism ['kæpɪtəlɪzəm] N Kapitalismus *m*

capitalist ['kæpɪtəlɪst] ADJ kapitalistisch ▶ N Kapitalist(in) *m(f)*

capitalize ['kæpɪtəlaɪz] VT (*Comm*) kapitalisieren ▶ VI: **to ~ on** Kapital schlagen aus

capital punishment N Todesstrafe *f*

capital transfer tax (BRIT) N Erbschafts- und Schenkungssteuer *f*

Capitol ['kæpɪtl] N: **the ~** das Kapitol

> **Capitol** ist das Gebäude in Washington auf dem Capitol Hill, in dem der Kongress der USA zusammentritt. Die Bezeichnung wird in vielen amerikanischen Bundesstaaten auch für das Parlamentsgebäude des jeweiligen Staates verwendet.

capitulate [kə'pɪtjuleɪt] VI kapitulieren

capitulation [kəpɪtju'leɪʃən] N Kapitulation *f*

capricious [kə'prɪʃəs] ADJ launisch

Capricorn ['kæprɪkɔ:n] N (*Astrol*) Steinbock *m*; **to be ~** (ein) Steinbock sein

caps. [kæps] ABBR (= *capital letters*) Großbuchstaben *pl*

capsize [kæp'saɪz] VT zum Kentern bringen ▶ VI kentern

capstan ['kæpstən] N Poller *m*

capsule ['kæpsju:l] N Kapsel *f*

Capt. ABBR (*Mil*) = **captain**

captain ['kæptɪn] N Kapitän *m*; (*of plane*) (Flug)kapitän *m*; (*in army*) Hauptmann *m* ▶ VT (*ship*) befehligen; (*team*) anführen

caption ['kæpʃən] N Bildunterschrift *f*

captivate ['kæptɪveɪt] VT fesseln

captive ['kæptɪv] ADJ gefangen ▶ N Gefangene(r) *f(m)*

captivity [kæp'tɪvɪtɪ] N Gefangenschaft *f*

captor ['kæptə^r^] N: **his captors** diejenigen, die ihn gefangen nahmen

capture ['kæptʃə^r^] VT (*animal*) (ein)fangen; (*person*) gefangen nehmen; (*town, country, share of market*) erobern; (*attention*) erregen; (*Comput*) erfassen ▶ N (*of animal*) Einfangen *nt*; (*of person*) Gefangennahme *f*; (*of town etc*) Eroberung *f*; (*also*: **data capture**) Erfassung *f*

car [kɑ:^r^] N Auto *nt*, Wagen *m*; (*Rail*) Wagen *m*; **by ~** mit dem Auto *or* Wagen

Caracas [kə'rækəs] N Caracas *nt*

carafe [kə'ræf] N Karaffe *f*

caramel ['kærəməl] N Karamelle *f*, Karamellbonbon *m or nt*; (*burnt sugar*) Karamell *m*

carat ['kærət] N Karat *nt*; **18 ~ gold** achtzehnkarätiges Gold

caravan ['kærəvæn] N (BRIT) Wohnwagen *m*; (*in desert*) Karawane *f*

caravan site (BRIT) N Campingplatz *m* für Wohnwagen

caraway seed ['kærəweɪ-] N Kümmel *m*

carb [kɑ:b] N ABBR (*inf*: = *carbohydrate*) Kohle(n)hydrat *nt*

carbohydrate [kɑ:bəu'haɪdreɪt] N Kohle(n)hydrat *nt*

carbolic acid [kɑ:'bɔlɪk-] N Karbolsäure *f*

car bomb N Autobombe *f*

carbon ['kɑ:bən] N Kohlenstoff *m*

carbonated ['kɑ:bəneɪtɪd] ADJ mit Kohlensäure (versetzt)

carbon copy N Durchschlag *m*

carbon credit N Emissionsgutschrift *f*

carbon dioxide N Kohlendioxid *nt*

carbon footprint N ökologischer Fußabdruck

carbon monoxide [mɔ'nɔksaɪd] N Kohlenmonoxid *nt*

carbon-neutral ADJ CO_2-neutral

carbon offset N Klimakompensation *f*

carbon paper N Kohlepapier *nt*

carbon ribbon N Kohlefarbband *nt*

car-boot sale N *auf einem Parkplatz stattfindender Flohmarkt mit dem Kofferraum als Auslage*

carburettor, (US) carburetor [kɑ:bju'rɛtə^r^] N Vergaser *m*

carcass ['kɑ:kəs] N Kadaver *m*

carcinogenic [kɑ:sɪnə'dʒɛnɪk] ADJ krebserregend, karzinogen

card [kɑ:d] N Karte *f*; (*material*) (dünne) Pappe *f*, Karton *m*; (*also*: **record card, index card**) (Kartei)karte *f*; (*also*: **membership card**) (Mitglieds)ausweis *m*; (*also*: **playing card**)

(Spiel)karte *f*; (*also*: **visiting card**) (Visiten)karte *f*; **to play cards** Karten spielen
cardamom ['kɑːdəməm] N Kardamom *m*
cardboard ['kɑːdbɔːd] N Pappe *f*
cardboard box N (Papp)karton *m*
card-carrying ['kɑːd'kærɪɪŋ] ADJ: **~ member** eingetragenes Mitglied *nt*
card game N Kartenspiel *nt*
cardiac ['kɑːdɪæk] ADJ (*failure, patient*) Herz-
cardigan ['kɑːdɪgən] N Strickjacke *f*
cardinal ['kɑːdɪnl] ADJ (*principle, importance*) Haupt- ▶ N Kardinal *m*; **~ number** Kardinalzahl *f*; **~ sin** Todsünde *f*
card index N Kartei *f*
cardphone N Kartentelefon *nt*
cardsharp ['kɑːdʃɑːp] N Falschspieler *m*
card vote (BRIT) N Abstimmung *f* durch Wahlmänner
CARE [kɛəʳ] N ABBR (= *Cooperative for American Relief Everywhere*) *karitative Organisation*
care [kɛəʳ] N (*attention*) Versorgung *f*; (*worry*) Sorge *f*; (*charge*) Obhut *f*, Fürsorge *f* ▶ VI: **to ~ about** sich kümmern um; **~ of** bei; **"handle with ~"** „Vorsicht, zerbrechlich"; **in sb's ~** in jds *dat* Obhut; **to take ~** aufpassen; **to take ~ to do sth** sich bemühen, etw zu tun; **to take ~ of** sich kümmern um; **the child has been taken into ~** das Kind ist in Pflege genommen worden; **would you ~ to/for ...?** möchten Sie gerne ...?; **I wouldn't ~ to do it** ich möchte es nicht gern tun; **I don't ~** es ist mir egal *or* gleichgültig; **I couldn't ~ less** es ist mir völlig egal *or* gleichgültig
▶ **care for** VT FUS (*look after*) sich kümmern um; (*like*) mögen
career [kə'rɪəʳ] N Karriere *f*; (*job, profession*) Beruf *m*; (*life*) Laufbahn *f* ▶ VI (*also*: **career along**) rasen
career girl N Karrierefrau *f*
careers officer [kə'rɪəz-], **careers adviser** N Berufsberater(in) *m(f)*
career woman N (*irreg*) Karrierefrau *f*
carefree ['kɛəfriː] ADJ sorglos
careful ['kɛəful] ADJ vorsichtig; (*thorough*) sorgfältig; **(be) ~!** Vorsicht!, pass auf!; **to be ~ with one's money** sein Geld gut zusammenhalten
carefully ['kɛəfəlɪ] ADV vorsichtig; (*methodically*) sorgfältig
careless ['kɛəlɪs] ADJ leichtsinnig; (*negligent*) nachlässig; (*remark*) gedankenlos
carelessly ['kɛəlɪslɪ] ADV leichtsinnig; nachlässig; gedankenlos
carelessness ['kɛəlɪsnɪs] N Leichtsinn *m*; Nachlässigkeit *f*; Gedankenlosigkeit *f*
carer ['kɛərəʳ] N Betreuer(in) *m(f)*, Pfleger(in) *m(f)*
caress [kə'rɛs] N Streicheln *nt* ▶ VT streicheln
caretaker ['kɛəteɪkəʳ] N Hausmeister(in) *m(f)*
caretaker government (BRIT) N geschäftsführende Regierung *f*
car ferry N Autofähre *f*
cargo ['kɑːgəu] (*pl* **cargoes**) N Fracht *f*, Ladung *f*
cargo boat N Frachter *m*, Frachtschiff *nt*
cargo plane N Transportflugzeug *nt*
car hire (BRIT) N Autovermietung *f*
Caribbean [kærɪ'biːən] ADJ karibisch ▶ N: **the ~ (Sea)** die Karibik, das Karibische Meer
caricature ['kærɪkətjuəʳ] N Karikatur *f*
caring ['kɛərɪŋ] ADJ liebevoll; (*society, organization*) sozial; (*behaviour*) fürsorglich
car insurance N Kraftfahrzeugversicherung *f*
carjacking N *Angriff durch Banditen, die gewaltsam in PKWs eindringen und den Wagen samt Insassen entführen*
carnage ['kɑːnɪdʒ] N (*Mil*) Blutbad *nt*, Gemetzel *nt*
carnal ['kɑːnl] ADJ fleischlich, sinnlich
carnation [kɑː'neɪʃən] N Nelke *f*
carnival ['kɑːnɪvl] N Karneval *m*; (*US: funfair*) Kirmes *f*
carnivorous [kɑː'nɪvərəs] ADJ fleischfressend
carol ['kærəl] N: **(Christmas) ~** Weihnachtslied *nt*
carouse [kə'rauz] VI zechen
carousel [kærə'sɛl] (*US*) N Karussell *nt*
carp [kɑːp] N Karpfen *m*
▶ **carp at** VT FUS herumnörgeln an +*dat*
car park N Parkplatz *m*; (*building*) Parkhaus *nt*
car-park ticket N Parkschein *m*
carpenter ['kɑːpɪntəʳ] N Zimmermann *m*
carpentry ['kɑːpɪntrɪ] N Zimmerhandwerk *nt*; (*school subject, hobby*) Tischlern *nt*
carpet ['kɑːpɪt] N (*also fig*) Teppich *m* ▶ VT (mit Teppichen/Teppichboden) auslegen; **fitted ~** (BRIT) Teppichboden *m*
carpet bombing N Flächenbombardierung *f*
carpet slippers NPL Pantoffeln *pl*
carpet-sweeper ['kɑːpɪtswiːpəʳ] N Teppichkehrer *m*
car phone N (*Tel*) Autotelefon *nt*
carport ['kɑːpɔːt] N Einstellplatz *m*
car rental N Autovermietung *f*
carriage ['kærɪdʒ] N (*Rail, of typewriter*) Wagen *m*; (*horse-drawn vehicle*) Kutsche *f*; (*of goods*) Beförderung *f*; (*transport costs*) Beförderungskosten *pl*; **~ forward** Fracht zahlt Empfänger; **~ free** frachtfrei; **~ paid** frei Haus
carriage return N (*on typewriter*) Wagenrücklauf *m*; (*Comput*) Return *nt*
carriageway ['kærɪdʒweɪ] (BRIT) N Fahrbahn *f*
carrier ['kærɪəʳ] N Spediteur *m*, Transportunternehmer *m*; (*Med*) Überträger *m*
carrier bag (BRIT) N Tragetasche *f*, Tragetüte *f*
carrier pigeon N Brieftaube *f*
carrion ['kærɪən] N Aas *nt*
carrot ['kærət] N Möhre *f*, Mohrrübe *f*, Karotte *f*; (*fig*) Köder *m*
carry ['kærɪ] VT tragen; (*transport*) transportieren; (*a motion, bill*) annehmen; (*responsibilities etc*) mit sich bringen; (*disease, virus*) übertragen ▶ VI (*sound*) tragen; **to get carried away** (*fig*) sich hinreißen lassen; **this loan carries 10% interest** dieses Darlehen wird mit 10% verzinst
▶ **carry forward** VT übertragen, vortragen

C

▸ **carry on** VI weitermachen; (*inf*: *make a fuss*) (ein) Theater machen ▸ VT fortführen; **to ~ on with sth** mit etw weitermachen; **to ~ on singing/eating** weitersingen/-essen
▸ **carry out** VT (*orders*) ausführen; (*investigation*) durchführen; (*idea*) in die Tat umsetzen; (*threat*) wahr machen
carrycot ['kærɪkɔt] (BRIT) N Babytragetasche *f*
carry-on ['kærɪ'ɔn] (*inf*) N Theater *nt*
cart [kɑːt] N Wagen *m*, Karren *m*; (*for passengers*) Wagen *m*; (*handcart*) (Hand)wagen *m* ▸ VT (*inf*) mit sich herumschleppen
carte blanche ['kɑːt'blɔŋʃ] N: **to give sb ~** jdm Carte blanche *or* (eine) Blankovollmacht geben
cartel [kɑː'tɛl] N Kartell *nt*
cartilage ['kɑːtɪlɪdʒ] N Knorpel *m*
cartographer [kɑː'tɔgrəfə^r] N Kartograf(in) *m(f)*
cartography [kɑː'tɔgrəfɪ] N Kartografie *f*
carton ['kɑːtən] N (Papp)karton *m*; (*of yogurt*) Becher *m*; (*of milk*) Tüte *f*; (*of cigarettes*) Stange *f*
cartoon [kɑː'tuːn] N (*drawing*) Karikatur *f*; (BRIT: *comic strip*) Cartoon *m*; (*Cine*) Zeichentrickfilm *m*
cartoonist [kɑː'tuːnɪst] N Karikaturist(in) *m(f)*
cartridge ['kɑːtrɪdʒ] N (*for gun, pen*) Patrone *f*; (*music tape, for camera*) Kassette *f*; (*of record-player*) Tonabnehmer *m*
cartwheel ['kɑːtwiːl] N Rad *nt*; **to turn a ~** Rad schlagen
carve [kɑːv] VT (*meat*) (ab)schneiden; (*wood*) schnitzen; (*stone*) meißeln; (*initials, design*) einritzen
▸ **carve up** VT (*land etc*) aufteilen; (*meat*) aufschneiden
carving ['kɑːvɪŋ] N Skulptur *f*; (*in wood etc*) Schnitzerei *f*
carving knife N Tran(s)chiermesser *nt*
car wash N Autowaschanlage *f*
Casablanca [kæsə'blæŋkə] N Casablanca *nt*
cascade [kæs'keɪd] N Wasserfall *m*, Kaskade *f*; (*of money*) Regen *m*; (*of hair*) wallende Fülle *f* ▸ VI (in Kaskaden) herabfallen; (*hair etc*) wallen; (*people*) strömen
case [keɪs] N Fall *m*; (*for spectacles etc*) Etui *nt*; (BRIT: *also*: **suitcase**) Koffer *m*; (*of wine, whisky etc*) Kiste *f*; (*Typ*): **lower/upper ~** klein-/großgeschrieben; **to have a good ~** gute Chancen haben, durchzukommen; **there's a strong ~ for reform** es spricht viel für eine Reform; **in ~ ...** falls ...; **in ~ of fire** bei Feuer; **in ~ of emergency** im Notfall; **in ~ he comes** falls er kommt; **in any ~** sowieso; **just in ~** für alle Fälle
case-hardened ['keɪshɑːdnd] ADJ (*fig*) abgebrüht (*inf*)
case history N (*Med*) Krankengeschichte *f*
case study N Fallstudie *f*
cash [kæʃ] N (Bar)geld *nt* ▸ VT (*cheque etc*) einlösen; **to pay (in) ~** bar bezahlen; **~ on delivery** per Nachnahme; **~ with order** zahlbar bei Bestellung
▸ **cash in** VT einlösen
▸ **cash in on** VT FUS Kapital schlagen aus
cash account N Kassenbuch *nt*
cash-and-carry [kæʃən'kærɪ] N Abholmarkt *m*
cash-book ['kæʃbuk] N Kassenkonto *nt*
cash box N (Geld)kassette *f*
cash card (BRIT) N (Geld)automatenkarte *f*
cash crop N zum Verkauf bestimmte Ernte *f*
cash desk (BRIT) N Kasse *f*
cash discount N Skonto *m or nt*
cash dispenser (BRIT) N Geldautomat *m*
cashew [kæ'ʃuː] N (*also*: **cashew nut**) Cashewnuss *f*
cash flow N Cashflow *m*
cashier [kæ'ʃɪə^r] N Kassierer(in) *m(f)*
cash machine N (BRIT) Geldautomat *m*
cashmere ['kæʃmɪə^r] N Kaschmir *m*
cash point N Geldautomat *m*
cash price N Bar(zahlungs)preis *m*
cash register N Registrierkasse *f*
cash sale N Barverkauf *m*
casing ['keɪsɪŋ] N Gehäuse *nt*
casino [kə'siːnəu] N Kasino *nt*
cask [kɑːsk] N Fass *nt*
casket ['kɑːskɪt] N Schatulle *f*; (*US*: *coffin*) Sarg *m*
Caspian Sea ['kæspɪən-] N: **the ~** das Kaspische Meer
casserole ['kæsərəul] N Auflauf *m*; (*pot, container*) Kasserolle *f*
cassette [kæ'sɛt] N Kassette *f*
cassette deck N Kassettendeck *nt*
cassette player N Kassettenrekorder *m*
cassette recorder N Kassettenrekorder *m*
cast [kɑːst] (*pt, pp* **~**) VT werfen; (*net, fishing-line*) auswerfen; (*metal, statue*) gießen ▸ VI die Angel auswerfen ▸ N (*Theat*) Besetzung *f*; (*mould*) (Guss)form *f*; (*also*: **plaster cast**) Gipsverband *m*; **to ~ sb as Hamlet** (*Theat*) die Rolle des Hamlet mit jdm besetzen; **to ~ one's vote** seine Stimme abgeben; **to ~ one's eyes over sth** einen Blick auf etw *acc* werfen; **to ~ aspersions on sb/sth** abfällige Bemerkungen über jdn/etw machen; **to ~ doubts on sth** etw in Zweifel ziehen; **to ~ a spell on sb/sth** jdn/etw verzaubern; **to ~ its skin** sich häuten
▸ **cast aside** VT fallen lassen
▸ **cast off** VI (*Naut*) losmachen; (*Knitting*) abketten ▸ VT abketten
▸ **cast on** VI, VT (*Knitting*) anschlagen, aufschlagen
castaway ['kɑːstəweɪ] N Schiffbrüchige(r) *f(m)*
caste [kɑːst] N Kaste *f*; (*system*) Kastenwesen *nt*
caster sugar ['kɑːstə-] (BRIT) N Raffinade *f*
casting vote ['kɑːstɪŋ-] (BRIT) N ausschlaggebende Stimme *f*
cast iron N Gusseisen *nt* ▸ ADJ: **cast-iron** (*fig*: *will*) eisern; (*: alibi, excuse etc*) hieb- und stichfest
castle ['kɑːsl] N Schloss *nt*; (*manor*) Herrenhaus *nt*; (*fortified*) Burg *f*; (*Chess*) Turm *m*
cast off N abgelegtes Kleidungsstück *nt*
castor ['kɑːstə^r] N Rolle *f*
castor oil N Rizinusöl *nt*
castrate [kæs'treɪt] VT kastrieren
casual ['kæʒjul] ADJ (*by chance*) zufällig; (*work etc*) Gelegenheits-; (*unconcerned*) lässig, gleichgültig; (*clothes*) leger; **~ wear** Freizeitkleidung *f*

casual labour N Gelegenheitsarbeit *f*
casually ['kæʒjulɪ] ADV lässig; *(glance)* beiläufig; *(dress)* leger; *(by chance)* zufällig
casualty ['kæʒjultɪ] N *(of war etc)* Opfer *nt*; *(someone injured)* Verletzte(r) *f(m)*; *(someone killed)* Tote(r) *f(m)*; *(Med)* Unfallstation *f*; **heavy casualties** *(Mil)* schwere Verluste *pl*
casualty ward (BRIT) N Unfallstation *f*
cat [kæt] N Katze *f*; *(lion etc)* (Raub)katze *f*
catacombs ['kætəku:mz] NPL Katakomben *pl*
catalogue, *(US)* **catalog** ['kætəlɔg] N Katalog *m* ▶ VT katalogisieren
catalyst ['kætəlɪst] N Katalysator *m*
catalytic converter [kætə'lɪtɪkkən'və:tə^r] N *(Aut)* Katalysator *m*
catapult ['kætəpʌlt] (BRIT) N Schleuder *f*; *(Mil)* Katapult *m or nt* ▶ VI geschleudert *or* katapultiert werden ▶ VT schleudern, katapultieren
cataract ['kætərækt] N *(Med)* grauer Star *m*
catarrh [kə'tɑ:^r] N Katarrh *m*
catastrophe [kə'tæstrəfɪ] N Katastrophe *f*
catastrophic [kætə'strɔfɪk] ADJ katastrophal
catcalls ['kætkɔ:lz] NPL Pfiffe und Buhrufe *pl*
catch [kætʃ] *(pt, pp* **caught***)* VT fangen; *(take: bus, train etc)* nehmen; *(arrest)* festnehmen; *(surprise)* erwischen, ertappen; *(breath)* holen; *(attention)* erregen; *(hit)* treffen; *(hear)* mitbekommen; *(illness)* sich *dat* zuziehen *or* holen; *(person: also:* **catch up***)* einholen ▶ VI *(fire)* (anfangen zu) brennen; *(become trapped)* hängen bleiben ▶ N Fang *m*; *(trick, hidden problem)* Haken *m*; *(of lock)* Riegel *m*; *(game)* Fangen *nt*; **to ~ sb's attention/eye** jdn auf sich *acc* aufmerksam machen; **to ~ fire** Feuer fangen; **to ~ sight of** erblicken
▶ **catch on** VI *(grow popular)* sich durchsetzen; **to ~ on (to sth)** (etw) kapieren
▶ **catch out** (BRIT) VT *(fig)* hereinlegen
▶ **catch up** VI *(fig: with person)* mitkommen; *(: on work)* aufholen ▶ VT: **to ~ sb up, to ~ up with sb** jdn einholen
catch-22 ['kætʃtwɛntɪ'tu:] N: **it's a ~ situation** es ist eine Zwickmühle
catching ['kætʃɪŋ] ADJ ansteckend
catchment area ['kætʃmənt-] (BRIT) N Einzugsgebiet *nt*
catch phrase N Schlagwort *nt*, Slogan *m*
catchy ['kætʃɪ] ADJ *(tune)* eingängig
catechism ['kætɪkɪzəm] N Katechismus *m*
categoric [kætɪ'gɔrɪk], **categorical** [kætɪ'gɔrɪkəl] ADJ kategorisch
categorize ['kætɪgəraɪz] VT kategorisieren
category ['kætɪgərɪ] N Kategorie *f*
cater ['keɪtə^r] VI: **to ~ (for)** die Speisen und Getränke liefern (für)
▶ **cater for** (BRIT) VT FUS *(needs, tastes)* gerecht werden *+dat*; *(readers, consumers)* eingestellt *or* ausgerichtet sein auf *+acc*
caterer ['keɪtərə^r] N Lieferant(in) *m(f)* von Speisen und Getränken; *(company)* Lieferfirma *f* für Speisen und Getränke
catering ['keɪtərɪŋ] N Gastronomie *f*
caterpillar ['kætəpɪlə^r] N Raupe *f* ▶ CPD *(vehicle)* Raupen-
caterpillar track N Raupenkette *f*, Gleiskette *f*
cat flap N Katzentür *f*
cathedral [kə'θi:drəl] N Kathedrale *f*, Dom *m*
cathode ['kæθəud] N Kat(h)ode *f*
cathode-ray tube [kæθəud'reɪ-] N Kat(h)odenstrahlröhre *f*
Catholic ['kæθəlɪk] ADJ katholisch ▶ N Katholik(in) *m(f)*
catholic ['kæθəlɪk] ADJ vielseitig
CAT scanner N ABBR *(Med: = computerized axial tomography scanner)* CAT-Scanner *m*
Catseye® ['kæts'aɪ] (BRIT) N *(Aut)* Katzenauge *nt*
catsup ['kætsəp] *(US)* N Ket(s)chup *m or nt*
cattle ['kætl] NPL Vieh *nt*
catty ['kætɪ] ADJ gehässig
catwalk ['kætwɔ:k] N Steg *m*; *(for models)* Laufsteg *m*
Caucasian [kɔ:'keɪzɪən] ADJ kaukasisch ▶ N Kaukasier(in) *m(f)*
Caucasus ['kɔ:kəsəs] N Kaukasus *m*
caucus ['kɔ:kəs] N *(group)* Gremium *nt*, Ausschuss *m*; *(US)* Parteiversammlung *f*

> **Caucus** bedeutet vor allem in den USA ein privates Treffen von Parteifunktionären, bei dem z. B. Kandidaten ausgewählt oder Grundsatzentscheidungen getroffen werden. Meist wird ein solches Treffen vor einer öffentlichen Parteiversammlung abgehalten. Der Begriff bezieht sich im weiteren Sinne auch auf den kleinen, aber mächtigen Kreis von Parteifunktionären, der beim caucus zusammentrifft.

caught [kɔ:t] PT, PP *of* **catch**
cauliflower ['kɔlɪflauə^r] N Blumenkohl *m*; **~ cheese** Blumenkohl in Käsesoße
cause [kɔ:z] N Ursache *f*; *(reason)* Grund *m*; *(aim)* Sache *f* ▶ VT verursachen; **there is no ~ for concern** es besteht kein Grund zur Sorge; **to ~ sth to be done** veranlassen, dass etw getan wird; **to ~ sb to do sth** jdn veranlassen, etw zu tun
causeway ['kɔ:zweɪ] N Damm *m*
caustic ['kɔ:stɪk] ADJ ätzend, kaustisch; *(remark)* bissig
cauterize ['kɔ:təraɪz] VT kauterisieren
caution ['kɔ:ʃən] N Vorsicht *f*; *(warning)* Warnung *f*; *(: Law)* Verwarnung *f* ▶ VT warnen; *(Law)* verwarnen
cautious ['kɔ:ʃəs] ADJ vorsichtig
cautiously ['kɔ:ʃəslɪ] ADV vorsichtig
cautiousness ['kɔ:ʃəsnɪs] N Vorsicht *f*
cavalier [kævə'lɪə^r] ADJ unbekümmert
cavalry ['kævəlrɪ] N Kavallerie *f*
cave [keɪv] N Höhle *f* ▶ VI: **to go caving** auf Höhlenexpedition(en) gehen
▶ **cave in** VI einstürzen; *(to demands)* nachgeben
caveman ['keɪvmæn] N *(irreg)* Höhlenmensch *m*
cavern ['kævən] N Höhle *f*
caviar, caviare ['kævɪɑ:^r] N Kaviar *m*
cavity ['kævɪtɪ] N Hohlraum *m*; *(in tooth)* Loch *nt*

cavity wall insulation N Schaumisolierung *f*
cavort [kə'vɔːt] VI tollen, toben
cayenne [keɪ'ɛn] N (*also*: **cayenne pepper**) Cayennepfeffer *m*
CB N ABBR (= *Citizens' Band (Radio)*) CB-Funk *m*
CBC N ABBR (= *Canadian Broadcasting Corporation*) *kanadische Rundfunkgesellschaft*
CBE (BRIT) N ABBR (= *Commander of (the Order of) the British Empire*) *britischer Ordenstitel*
CBI N ABBR (= *Confederation of British Industry*) *britischer Unternehmerverband*, ≈ BDI *m*
CBS (US) N ABBR (= *Columbia Broadcasting System*) *Rundfunkgesellschaft*
CC (BRIT) ABBR = **county council**
cc ABBR (= *cubic centimetre*) ccm; = **carbon copy**
CCTV N ABBR = **closed-circuit television**
CCTV camera N Überwachungskamera *f*
CCU (US) N ABBR (= *cardiac or coronary care unit*) *Intensivstation für Herzpatienten*
CD ABBR (= *compact disc*) CD *f*; **CD player** CD-Spieler *m*; (BRIT: = *Corps Diplomatique*) CD; (*Mil*: BRIT: = *Civil Defence (Corps)*) Zivilschutz *m*; (: US: = *Civil Defense*) Zivilschutz *m*
CDC (US) N ABBR (= *Center for Disease Control*) *Seuchenkontrollbehörde*
Cdr ABBR (*Mil*) = **commander**
CD-ROM N ABBR (= *compact disc read-only memory*) CD-ROM *f*
CDT (US) ABBR (= *Central Daylight Time*) *mittelamerikanische Sommerzeit*; (BRIT *Scol*: = *Craft, Design and Technology*) Arbeitslehre *f*
cease [siːs] VT beenden ▸ VI aufhören
ceasefire ['siːsfaɪəʳ] N Waffenruhe *f*
ceaseless ['siːslɪs] ADJ endlos, unaufhörlich
CED (US) N ABBR (= *Committee for Economic Development*) *Komitee für wirtschaftliche Entwicklung*
cedar ['siːdəʳ] N Zeder *f*; (*wood*) Zedernholz *nt*
cede [siːd] VT abtreten
cedilla [sɪ'dɪlə] N Cedille *f*
CEEB (US) N ABBR (= *College Entry Examination Board*) *akademische Zulassungsstelle*
ceilidh ['keɪlɪ] (SCOT) N *Fest mit Volksmusik, Gesang und Tanz*
ceiling ['siːlɪŋ] N Decke *f*; (*upper limit*) Obergrenze *f*, Höchstgrenze *f*
celebrate ['sɛlɪbreɪt] VT feiern; (*mass*) zelebrieren ▸ VI feiern
celebrated ['sɛlɪbreɪtɪd] ADJ gefeiert
celebration [sɛlɪ'breɪʃən] N Feier *f*
celebrity [sɪ'lɛbrɪtɪ] N berühmte Persönlichkeit *f*
celeriac [sə'lɛrɪæk] N (Knollen)sellerie *f*
celery ['sɛlərɪ] N (Stangen)sellerie *f*
celestial [sɪ'lɛstɪəl] ADJ himmlisch
celibacy ['sɛlɪbəsɪ] N Zölibat *m or nt*
cell [sɛl] N Zelle *f*
cellar ['sɛləʳ] N Keller *m*; (*for wine*) (Wein)keller *m*
cellist ['tʃɛlɪst] N Cellist(in) *m(f)*
cello ['tʃɛləu] N Cello *nt*
cellophane ['sɛləfeɪn] N Cellophan *nt*
cell phone N Handy *nt*, Mobiltelefon *nt*
cell tower N (*US Tel*) Mobilfunkmast *m*
cellular ['sɛljuləʳ] ADJ (*Biol*) zellular, Zell-; (*fabrics*) aus porösem Material
Celluloid® ['sɛljulɔɪd] N Zelluloid *nt*
cellulose ['sɛljuləus] N Zellulose *f*, Zellstoff *m*
Celsius ['sɛlsɪəs] ADJ (*scale*) Celsius-
Celt [kɛlt] N Kelte *m*, Keltin *f*
Celtic ['kɛltɪk] ADJ keltisch ▸ N (*Ling*) Keltisch *nt*
cement [sə'mɛnt] N Zement *m*; (*concrete*) Beton *m*; (*glue*) Klebstoff *m* ▸ VT zementieren; (*stick, glue*) kleben; (*fig*) festigen
cement mixer N Betonmischmaschine *f*
cemetery ['sɛmɪtrɪ] N Friedhof *m*
cenotaph ['sɛnətɑːf] N Ehrenmal *nt*
censor ['sɛnsəʳ] N Zensor(in) *m(f)* ▸ VT zensieren
censorship ['sɛnsəʃɪp] N Zensur *f*
censure ['sɛnʃəʳ] VT tadeln ▸ N Tadel *m*
census ['sɛnsəs] N Volkszählung *f*
cent [sɛnt] N Cent *m*; *see also* **per cent**
centenary [sɛn'tiːnərɪ] N hundertster Jahrestag *m*
centennial [sɛn'tɛnɪəl] (US) N = **centenary**
center *etc* ['sɛntəʳ] (US) = **centre** *etc*
centigrade ['sɛntɪgreɪd] ADJ (*scale*) Celsius-
centilitre, (US) **centiliter** ['sɛntɪliːtəʳ] N Zentiliter *m or nt*
centimetre, (US) **centimeter** ['sɛntɪmiːtəʳ] N Zentimeter *m or nt*
centipede ['sɛntɪpiːd] N Tausendfüßler *m*
central ['sɛntrəl] ADJ zentral; (*committee, government*) Zentral-; (*idea*) wesentlich
Central African Republic N Zentralafrikanische Republik *f*
Central America N Mittelamerika *nt*
central heating N Zentralheizung *f*
centralize ['sɛntrəlaɪz] VT zentralisieren
central processing unit N (*Comput*) Zentraleinheit *f*
central reservation (BRIT) N Mittelstreifen *m*
centre, (US) **center** ['sɛntəʳ] N Mitte *f*; (*health centre etc, town centre*) Zentrum *nt*; (*of attention, interest*) Mittelpunkt *m*; (*of action, belief etc*) Kern *m* ▸ VT zentrieren; (*ball*) zur Mitte spielen ▸ VI (*concentrate*): **to ~ on** sich konzentrieren auf *+acc*
centrefold, (US) **centerfold** ['sɛntəfəuld] N *doppelseitiges Bild in der Mitte einer Zeitschrift*
centre forward N Mittelstürmer(in) *m(f)*
centre half N Stopper(in) *m(f)*
centrepiece, (US) **centerpiece** ['sɛntəpiːs] N Tafelaufsatz *m*; (*fig*) Kernstück *nt*
centre spread (BRIT) N *Doppelseite in der Mitte einer Zeitschrift*
centre-stage [sɛntə'steɪdʒ] (*fig*) ADV: **to be ~** im Mittelpunkt stehen ▸ N: **to take centre stage** in den Mittelpunkt rücken
centrifugal [sɛn'trɪfjugl] ADJ (*force*) Zentrifugal-
centrifuge ['sɛntrɪfjuːʒ] N Zentrifuge *f*, Schleuder *f*
century ['sɛntjurɪ] N Jahrhundert *nt*; (*Cricket*) Hundert *f*; **in the twentieth ~** im zwanzigsten Jahrhundert
CEO N ABBR = **chief executive**
ceramic [sɪ'ræmɪk] ADJ keramisch; (*tiles*) Keramik-

ceramics [sɪ'ræmɪks] NPL Keramiken *pl*
cereal ['si:rɪəl] N Getreide *nt*; (*food*) Getreideflocken *pl* (*Cornflakes etc*)
cerebral ['sɛrɪbrəl] ADJ (*Med*) zerebral; (*intellectual*) geistig
ceremonial [sɛrɪ'məunɪəl] N Zeremoniell *nt* ▶ ADJ zeremoniell
ceremony ['sɛrɪmənɪ] N Zeremonie *f*; (*behaviour*) Förmlichkeit *f*; **to stand on ~** förmlich sein
cert [sə:t] (BRIT *inf*) N: **it's a dead ~** es ist todsicher
certain ['sə:tən] ADJ sicher; **a ~ Mr Smith** ein gewisser Herr Smith; **~ days/places** bestimmte Tage/Orte; **a ~ coldness** eine gewisse Kälte; **to make ~ of** sich vergewissern +*gen*; **for ~** ganz sicher, ganz genau
certainly ['sə:tənlɪ] ADV bestimmt; (*of course*) sicherlich; **~!** (aber) sicher!
certainty ['sə:təntɪ] N Sicherheit *f*; (*inevitability*) Gewissheit *f*
certificate [sə'tɪfɪkɪt] N Urkunde *f*; (*diploma*) Zeugnis *nt*
certified letter ['sə:tɪfaɪd-] (*US*) N Einschreibebrief *m*
certified mail ['sə:tɪfaɪd-] (*US*) N Einschreiben *nt*
certified public accountant ['sə:tɪfaɪd-] (*US*) N geprüfter Buchhalter *m*, geprüfte Buchhalterin *f*
certify ['sə:tɪfaɪ] VT bescheinigen; (*award a diploma to*) ein Zeugnis verleihen +*dat*; (*declare insane*) für unzurechnungsfähig erklären ▶ VI: **to ~ to** sich verbürgen für
cervical ['sə:vɪkl] ADJ: **~ cancer** Gebärmutterhalskrebs *m*; **~ smear** Abstrich *m*
cervix ['sə:vɪks] N Gebärmutterhals *m*
Cesarean [sɪ'zɛərɪən] (*US*) N = **Caesarean**
cessation [sə'seɪʃən] N (*of hostilities etc*) Einstellung *f*, Ende *nt*
cesspit ['sɛspɪt] N (*sewage tank*) Senkgrube *f*
CET ABBR (= *Central European Time*) MEZ
Ceylon [sɪ'lɔn] N Ceylon *nt*
cf. ABBR (= *compare*) vgl.
c/f ABBR (*Comm*: = *carried forward*) Übertr.
CFC N ABBR (= *chlorofluorocarbon*) FCKW *m*
CG (*US*) N ABBR = **coastguard**
cg ABBR (= *centigram*) cg
CH (BRIT) N ABBR (= *Companion of Honour*) *britischer Ordenstitel*
ch. ABBR (= *chapter*) Kap.
Chad [tʃæd] N Tschad *m*
chafe [tʃeɪf] VT (wund) reiben ▶ VI (*fig*): **to ~ against** sich ärgern über +*acc*
chaffinch ['tʃæfɪntʃ] N Buchfink *m*
chagrin ['ʃægrɪn] N Ärger *m*
chain [tʃeɪn] N Kette *f* ▶ VT (*also*: **chain up**: *prisoner*) anketten; (: *dog*) an die Kette legen
chain reaction N Kettenreaktion *f*
chain-smoke ['tʃeɪnsməuk] VI eine Zigarette nach der anderen rauchen
chain store N Kettenladen *m*
chair [tʃɛə^r] N Stuhl *m*; (*armchair*) Sessel *m*; (*of university*) Lehrstuhl *m*; (*of meeting, committee*) Vorsitz *m* ▶ VT den Vorsitz führen bei; **the ~** (*US*) der elektrische Stuhl
chair lift N Sessellift *m*
chairman ['tʃɛəmən] N (*irreg*) Vorsitzende(r) *f*(*m*); (BRIT: *of company*) Präsident *m*
chairperson ['tʃɛəpə:sn] N Vorsitzende(r) *f*(*m*)
chairwoman ['tʃɛəwumən] N (*irreg*) Vorsitzende *f*
chalet ['ʃæleɪ] N Chalet *nt*
chalice ['tʃælɪs] N Kelch *m*
chalk [tʃɔ:k] N Kalkstein *m*, Kreide *f*; (*for writing*) Kreide *f*
▶ **chalk up** VT aufschreiben, notieren; (*fig*: *success etc*) verbuchen
challenge ['tʃælɪndʒ] N (*of new job*) Anforderungen *pl*; (*of unknown etc*) Reiz *m*; (*to authority etc*) Infragestellung *f*; (*dare*) Herausforderung *f* ▶ VT herausfordern; (*authority, right, idea etc*) infrage stellen; **to ~ sb to do sth** jdn dazu auffordern, etw zu tun; **to ~ sb to a fight/game** jdn zu einem Kampf/Spiel herausfordern
challenger ['tʃælɪndʒə^r] N Herausforderer *m*, Herausforderin *f*
challenging ['tʃælɪndʒɪŋ] ADJ (*career, task*) anspruchsvoll; (*tone, look etc*) herausfordernd
chamber ['tʃeɪmbə^r] N Kammer *f*; (BRIT *Law*: *gen pl*: *of barristers*) Kanzlei *f*; (: *of judge*) Amtszimmer *nt*; **~ of commerce** Handelskammer *f*
chambermaid ['tʃeɪmbəmeɪd] N Zimmermädchen *nt*
chamber music N Kammermusik *f*
chamber pot N Nachttopf *m*
chameleon [kə'mi:lɪən] N Chamäleon *nt*
chamois ['ʃæmwɑ:] N Gämse *f*; (*cloth*) Ledertuch *nt*, Fensterleder *nt*
chamois leather ['ʃæmɪ-] N Ledertuch *nt*, Fensterleder *nt*
champagne [ʃæm'peɪn] N Champagner *m*
champers ['ʃæmpəz] (*inf*) N (*champagne*) Schampus *m*
champion ['tʃæmpɪən] N Meister(in) *m*(*f*); (*of cause, principle*) Verfechter(in) *m*(*f*); (*of person*) Fürsprecher(in) *m*(*f*) ▶ VT eintreten für, sich engagieren für
championship ['tʃæmpɪənʃɪp] N Meisterschaft *f*; (*title*) Titel *m*
chance [tʃɑ:ns] N (*hope*) Aussicht *f*; (*likelihood, possibility*) Möglichkeit *f*; (*opportunity*) Gelegenheit *f*; (*risk*) Risiko *nt* ▶ VT riskieren ▶ ADJ zufällig; **the chances are that ...** aller Wahrscheinlichkeit nach ..., wahrscheinlich ...; **there is little ~ of his coming** es ist unwahrscheinlich, dass er kommt; **to take a ~** es darauf ankommen lassen; **by ~** durch Zufall, zufällig; **it's the ~ of a lifetime** es ist eine einmalige Chance; **to ~ to do sth** zufällig etw tun; **to ~ it** es riskieren
▶ **chance (up)on** VT FUS (*person*) zufällig begegnen +*dat*, zufällig treffen; (*thing*) zufällig stoßen auf +*acc*
chancel ['tʃɑ:nsəl] N Altarraum *m*
chancellor ['tʃɑ:nsələ^r] N Kanzler *m*

C

Chancellor of the Exchequer (BRIT) N Schatzkanzler *m*, Finanzminister *m*
chancy ['tʃɑ:nsɪ] ADJ riskant
chandelier [ʃændə'lɪəʳ] N Kronleuchter *m*
change [tʃeɪndʒ] VT ändern; (*wheel, job, money, baby's nappy*) wechseln; (*bulb*) auswechseln; (*baby*) wickeln ▸ VI sich verändern; (*traffic lights*) umspringen ▸ N Veränderung *f*; (*difference*) Abwechslung *f*; (*of government, climate, job*) Wechsel *m*; (*coins*) Kleingeld *nt*; (*money returned*) Wechselgeld *nt*; **to ~ sb into** jdn verwandeln in *+acc*; **to ~ gear** (*Aut*) schalten; **to ~ one's mind** seine Meinung ändern, es sich *dat* anders überlegen; **to ~ hands** den Besitzer wechseln; **to ~ (trains/buses/planes** *etc*) umsteigen; **to ~ (one's clothes)** sich umziehen; **to ~ into** (*be transformed*) sich verwandeln in *+acc*; **she changed into an old skirt** sie zog einen alten Rock an; **a ~ of clothes** Kleidung *f* zum Wechseln; **~ of government/climate/job** Regierungs-/Klima-/Berufswechsel *m*; **small ~** Kleingeld *nt*; **to give sb ~ for** *or* **of £10** jdm £10 wechseln; **keep the ~** das stimmt so, der Rest ist für Sie; **for a ~** zur Abwechslung
changeable ['tʃeɪndʒəbl] ADJ (*weather*) wechselhaft, veränderlich; (*mood*) wechselnd; (*person*) unbeständig
change machine N (Geld)wechselautomat *m*
changeover ['tʃeɪndʒəuvəʳ] N Umstellung *f*
changing ['tʃeɪndʒɪŋ] ADJ sich verändernd
changing room (BRIT) N (Umkleide)kabine *f*; (*Sport*) Umkleideraum *m*
channel ['tʃænl] N (*TV*) Kanal *m*; (*of river, waterway*) (Fluss)bett *nt*; (*for boats*) Fahrrinne *f*; (*groove*) Rille *f*; (*fig: means*) Weg *m* ▸ VT leiten; (*fig*): **to ~ into** lenken auf *+acc*; **through the usual channels** auf dem üblichen Wege; **green ~** (*Customs*) „nichts zu verzollen"; **red ~** (*Customs*) „Waren zu verzollen"; **the (English) C~** der Ärmelkanal; **the C~ Islands** die Kanalinseln *pl*
channel-hopping ['tʃænlhɔpɪŋ] N (*TV*) ständiges Umschalten
Channel Tunnel N: **the ~** der Kanaltunnel
chant [tʃɑ:nt] N Sprechchor *m*; (*Rel*) Gesang *m* ▸ VT im (Sprech)chor rufen; (*Rel*) singen ▸ VI Sprechchöre anstimmen; (*Rel*) singen; **the demonstrators chanted their disapproval** die Demonstranten machten ihrem Unmut in Sprechchören Luft
chaos ['keɪɔs] N Chaos *nt*, Durcheinander *nt*
chaos theory N Chaostheorie *f*
chaotic [keɪ'ɔtɪk] ADJ chaotisch
chap [tʃæp] (BRIT *inf*) N Kerl *m*, Typ *m*; **old ~** alter Knabe *or* Junge
chapel ['tʃæpl] N Kapelle *f*; (BRIT: *non-conformist chapel*) Sektenkirche *f*; (: *of union*) *Betriebsgruppe innerhalb der Gewerkschaft der Drucker und Journalisten*
chaperone ['ʃæpərəun] N Anstandsdame *f* ▸ VT begleiten
chaplain ['tʃæplɪn] N Pfarrer(in) *m(f)*; (*Roman Catholic*) Kaplan *m*
chapped [tʃæpt] ADJ aufgesprungen, rau
chapter ['tʃæptəʳ] N Kapitel *nt*; **a ~ of accidents** eine Serie von Unfällen
char [tʃɑ:ʳ] VT verkohlen ▸ VI (BRIT) putzen gehen ▸ N (BRIT) = **charlady**
character ['kærɪktəʳ] N Charakter *m*; (*personality*) Persönlichkeit *f*; (*in novel, film*) Figur *f*, Gestalt *f*; (*eccentric*) Original *nt*; (*letter: also Comput*) Zeichen *nt*; **a person of good ~** ein guter Mensch
character code N (*Comput*) Zeichencode *m*
characteristic [kærɪktə'rɪstɪk] N Merkmal *nt* ▸ ADJ: **~ (of)** charakteristisch (für), typisch (für)
characterize ['kærɪktəraɪz] VT kennzeichnen, charakterisieren; (*describe the character of*): **to ~ (as)** beschreiben (als)
charade [ʃə'rɑ:d] N Scharade *f*
charcoal ['tʃɑ:kəul] N Holzkohle *f*; (*for drawing*) Kohle *f*, Kohlestift *m*
charge [tʃɑ:dʒ] N (*fee*) Gebühr *f*; (*accusation*) Anklage *f*; (*responsibility*) Verantwortung *f*; (*attack*) Angriff *m* ▸ VT (*customer*) berechnen *+dat*; (*sum*) berechnen; (*battery*) (auf)laden; (*gun*) laden; (*enemy*) angreifen; (*sb with task*) beauftragen ▸ VI angreifen; (*usu with: up, along etc*) stürmen; **charges** NPL Gebühren *pl*; **labour charges** Arbeitskosten *pl*; **to reverse the charges** (BRIT *Tel*) ein R-Gespräch führen; **is there a ~?** kostet das etwas?; **there's no ~** es ist umsonst, es kostet nichts; **at no extra ~** ohne Aufpreis; **free of ~** kostenlos, gratis; **to take ~ of** (*child*) sich kümmern um; (*company*) übernehmen; **to be in ~ of** die Verantwortung haben für; (*business*) leiten; **they charged us £10 for the meal** das Essen kostete £10; **how much do you ~?** was verlangen Sie?; **to ~ an expense (up) to sb's account** eine Ausgabe auf jds Rechnung *acc* setzen; **to ~ sb (with)** (*Law*) jdn anklagen (wegen)
charge account N Kunden(kredit)konto *nt*
charge card N Kundenkreditkarte *f*
chargé d'affaires N Chargé d'affaires *m*
charge hand (BRIT) N Vorarbeiter(in) *m(f)*
charger ['tʃɑ:dʒəʳ] N (*also*: **battery charger**) Ladegerät *nt*; (*warhorse*) (Schlacht)ross *nt*
chariot ['tʃærɪət] N (Streit)wagen *m*
charisma [kæ'rɪsmə] N Charisma *nt*
charitable ['tʃærɪtəbl] ADJ (*organization*) karitativ, Wohltätigkeits-; (*remark*) freundlich
charity ['tʃærɪtɪ] N (*organization*) karitative Organisation *f*, Wohltätigkeitsverein *m*; (*kindness, generosity*) Menschenfreundlichkeit *f*; (*money, gifts*) Almosen *nt*
charlady ['tʃɑ:leɪdɪ] N (BRIT) Putzfrau *f*, Reinemachefrau *f*
charlatan ['ʃɑ:lətən] N Scharlatan *m*
charm [tʃɑ:m] N Charme *m*; (*to bring good luck*) Talisman *m*; (*on bracelet etc*) Anhänger *m* ▸ VT bezaubern
charm bracelet N Armband *nt* mit Anhängern
charming ['tʃɑ:mɪŋ] ADJ reizend, charmant; (*place*) bezaubernd

chart [tʃɑ:t] N Schaubild *nt*, Diagramm *nt*; (*map*) Karte *f*; (*also*: **weather chart**) Wetterkarte *f* ▸ VT (*course*) planen; (*progress*) aufzeichnen; **charts** NPL (*hit parade*) Hitliste *f*
charter ['tʃɑ:təʳ] VT chartern ▸ N Charta *f*; (*of university, company*) Gründungsurkunde *f*; **on ~** gechartert
chartered accountant ['tʃɑ:təd-] (BRIT) N Wirtschaftsprüfer(in) *m(f)*
charter flight N Charterflug *m*
charwoman ['tʃɑ:wumən] N (*irreg*) Putzfrau *f*, Reinemachefrau *f*
chary ['tʃɛərɪ] ADJ: **to be ~ of doing sth** zögern, etw zu tun
chase [tʃeɪs] VT jagen, verfolgen; (*also*: **chase away**) wegjagen, vertreiben; (*business, job etc*) her sein hinter +*dat* (*inf*) ▸ N Verfolgungsjagd *f*
▸ **chase down** (US) VT = **chase up**
▸ **chase up** (BRIT) VT (*person*) rankriegen (*inf*); (*information*) ranschaffen (*inf*)
chasm ['kæzəm] N Kluft *f*
chassis ['ʃæsɪ] N Fahrgestell *nt*
chaste [tʃeɪst] ADJ keusch
chastened ['tʃeɪsnd] ADJ zur Einsicht gebracht
chastening ['tʃeɪsnɪŋ] ADJ ernüchternd
chastise [tʃæs'taɪz] VT (*scold*) schelten
chastity ['tʃæstɪtɪ] N Keuschheit *f*
chat [tʃæt] VI (*also*: **have a chat**) plaudern, sich unterhalten; (*Comput*) chatten ▸ N Plauderei *f*, Unterhaltung *f*; (*Comput*) Chat *m*
▸ **chat up** (BRIT *inf*) VT anmachen
chatline ['tʃætlaɪn] N *Telefondienst, der Anrufern die Teilnahme an einer Gesprächsrunde ermöglicht*
chatroom ['tʃætru:m] N (*Comput*) Chatroom *m*
chat show (BRIT) N Talkshow *f*
chattel ['tʃætl] N: **goods and chattels** *see* **good**
chatter ['tʃætəʳ] VI schwatzen; (*monkey*) schnattern; (*teeth*) klappern ▸ N Schwatzen *nt*; Schnattern *nt*; Klappern *nt*; **my teeth are chattering** mir klappern die Zähne
chatterbox ['tʃætəbɔks] (*inf*) N Quasselstrippe *f*
chattering classes ['tʃætərɪŋ'klɑ:sɪz] NPL: **the ~** die intellektuellen Schwätzer *pl*
chatty ['tʃætɪ] ADJ geschwätzig; (*letter*) im Plauderton
chauffeur ['ʃəufəʳ] N Chauffeur *m*, Fahrer *m*
chauvinism ['ʃəuvɪnɪzəm] N (*also*: **male chauvinism**) Chauvinismus *m*
chauvinist ['ʃəuvɪnɪst] N Chauvinist *m*
chauvinistic [ʃəuvɪ'nɪstɪk] ADJ chauvinistisch
ChE ABBR (= *chemical engineer*) *Titel für Chemotechniker*
cheap [tʃi:p] ADJ billig; (*reduced*) ermäßigt; (*poor quality*) billig, minderwertig; (*behaviour, joke*) ordinär ▸ ADV: **to buy/sell sth ~** etw billig kaufen/verkaufen
cheap day return N Tagesrückfahrkarte *f* (*zu einem günstigeren Tarif*)
cheapen ['tʃi:pn] VT entwürdigen
cheaper ['tʃi:pəʳ] ADJ billiger
cheaply ['tʃi:plɪ] ADV billig
cheat [tʃi:t] VI mogeln (*inf*), schummeln (*inf*) ▸ N Betrüger(in) *m(f)* ▸ VT: **to ~ sb (out of sth)** jdn (um etw) betrügen; **to ~ on sb** (*inf*) jdn betrügen
cheating ['tʃi:tɪŋ] N Mogeln *nt* (*inf*), Schummeln *nt* (*inf*)
Chechen ['tʃetʃen] ADJ tschetschenisch ▸ N Tschetschene *m*, Tschetschenin *f*
Chechnya ['tʃetʃnɪə] N Tschetschenien *nt*
check [tʃɛk] VT überprüfen; (*passport, ticket*) kontrollieren; (*facts*) nachprüfen; (*enemy, disease*) aufhalten; (*impulse*) unterdrücken; (*person*) zurückhalten ▸ VI nachprüfen ▸ N Kontrolle *f*; (*curb*) Beschränkung *f*; (US) = **cheque**; (: *bill*) Rechnung *f*; (*pattern*: *gen pl*) Karo(muster) *nt* ▸ ADJ kariert; **to ~ o.s.** sich beherrschen; **to ~ with sb** bei jdm nachfragen; **to keep a ~ on sb/sth** jdn/etw kontrollieren
▸ **check in** VI (*at hotel*) sich anmelden; (*at airport*) einchecken ▸ VT (*luggage*) abfertigen lassen
▸ **check off** VT abhaken
▸ **check out** VI (*of hotel*) abreisen ▸ VT (*luggage*) abfertigen; (*investigate*) überprüfen
▸ **check up** VI: **to ~ up on sth** etw überprüfen; **to ~ up on sb** Nachforschungen über jdn anstellen
checkered ['tʃɛkəd] (US) ADJ = **chequered**
checkers ['tʃɛkəz] (US) NPL Damespiel *nt*
check guarantee card (US) N Scheckkarte *f*
check-in ['tʃɛkɪn], **check-in desk** N (*at airport*) Abfertigung *f*, Abfertigungsschalter *m*
checking account ['tʃɛkɪŋ-] (US) N Girokonto *nt*
check list N Prüfliste *f*, Checkliste *f*
checkmate ['tʃɛkmeɪt] N Schachmatt *nt*
checkout ['tʃɛkaut] N Kasse *f*
checkpoint ['tʃɛkpɔɪnt] N Kontrollpunkt *m*
checkroom ['tʃɛkrum] (US) N (*left-luggage office*) Gepäckaufbewahrung *f*
checkup ['tʃɛkʌp] N Untersuchung *f*
cheddar ['tʃedəʳ] N Cheddarkäse *m*
cheek [tʃi:k] N Backe *f*; (*impudence*) Frechheit *f*; (*nerve*) Unverschämtheit *f*
cheekbone ['tʃi:kbəun] N Backenknochen *m*
cheeky ['tʃi:kɪ] ADJ frech
cheep [tʃi:p] VI (*bird*) piep(s)en ▸ N Piep(s) *m*, Piepser *m*
cheer [tʃɪəʳ] VT zujubeln +*dat*; (*gladden*) aufmuntern, aufheitern ▸ VI jubeln, Hurra rufen ▸ N (*gen pl*) Hurraruf *m*, Beifallsruf *m*; **cheers** NPL Hurrageschrei *nt*, Jubel *m*; **cheers!** prost!
▸ **cheer on** VT anspornen, anfeuern
▸ **cheer up** VI vergnügter *or* fröhlicher werden ▸ VT aufmuntern, aufheitern
cheerful ['tʃɪəful] ADJ fröhlich
cheerfulness ['tʃɪəfulnɪs] N Fröhlichkeit *f*
cheerio [tʃɪərɪ'əu] (BRIT) EXCL tschüss (*inf*)
cheerleader ['tʃɪəli:dəʳ] N *jd, der bei Sportveranstaltungen etc die Zuschauer zu Beifallsrufen anfeuert*
cheerless ['tʃɪəlɪs] ADJ freudlos, trüb; (*room*) trostlos
cheese [tʃi:z] N Käse *m*

cheeseboard ['tʃi:zbɔ:d] N Käsebrett *nt*; (*with cheese on it*) Käseplatte *f*
cheeseburger ['tʃi:zbə:gəʳ] N Cheeseburger *m*
cheesecake ['tʃi:zkeɪk] N Käsekuchen *m*
cheetah ['tʃi:tə] N Gepard *m*
chef [ʃɛf] N Küchenchef(in) *m(f)*
chemical ['kɛmɪkl] ADJ chemisch ▸ N Chemikalie *f*
chemical engineering N Chemotechnik *f*
chemist ['kɛmɪst] N (BRIT: *pharmacist*) Apotheker(in) *m(f)*; (*scientist*) Chemiker(in) *m(f)*
chemistry ['kɛmɪstrɪ] N Chemie *f*
chemist's ['kɛmɪsts], **chemist's shop** (BRIT) N Drogerie *f*; (*also*: **dispensing chemist's**) Apotheke *f*
chemotherapy [ki:məu'θɛrəpɪ] N Chemotherapie *f*
cheque [tʃɛk] (BRIT) N Scheck *m*; **to pay by ~** mit (einem) Scheck bezahlen
chequebook ['tʃɛkbuk] N Scheckbuch *nt*
cheque card (BRIT) N Scheckkarte *f*
chequered, (US) **checkered** ['tʃɛkəd] ADJ (*fig*) bewegt
cherish ['tʃɛrɪʃ] VT (*person*) liebevoll sorgen für; (*memory*) in Ehren halten; (*dream*) sich hingeben *+dat*; (*hope*) hegen
cheroot [ʃə'ru:t] N Stumpen *m*
cherry ['tʃɛrɪ] N Kirsche *f*; (*also*: **cherry tree**) Kirschbaum *m*
chervil ['tʃə:vɪl] N Kerbel *m*
Ches. (BRIT) ABBR (*Post*) = **Cheshire**
chess [tʃɛs] N Schach(spiel) *nt*
chessboard ['tʃɛsbɔ:d] N Schachbrett *nt*
chessman ['tʃɛsmən] N (*irreg*) Schachfigur *f*
chess player N Schachspieler(in) *m(f)*
chest [tʃɛst] N Brust *f*, Brustkorb *m*; (*box*) Kiste *f*, Truhe *f*; **to get sth off one's ~** (*inf*) sich *dat* etw von der Seele reden
chest measurement N Brustweite *f*, Brustumfang *m*
chestnut ['tʃɛsnʌt] N Kastanie *f* ▸ ADJ kastanienbraun
chest of drawers N Kommode *f*
chesty ['tʃɛstɪ] ADJ (*cough*) tief sitzend
chew [tʃu:] VT kauen
chewing gum ['tʃu:ɪŋ-] N Kaugummi *m*
chic [ʃi:k] ADJ chic *inv*, schick
chick [tʃɪk] N Küken *nt*; (*inf*: *girl*) Mieze *f*
chicken ['tʃɪkɪn] N Huhn *nt*; (*meat*) Hähnchen *nt*; (*inf*: *coward*) Feigling *m*
▸ **chicken out** (*inf*) VI: **to ~ out of doing sth** davor kneifen, etw zu tun
chicken feed N (*inf*: *money*) ein paar Pfennige *pl* (Hist); (*as salary*) ein Hungerlohn *m*
chickenpox ['tʃɪkɪnpɔks] N Windpocken *pl*
chickpea ['tʃɪkpi:] N Kichererbse *f*
chicory ['tʃɪkərɪ] N (*in coffee*) Zichorie *f*; (*salad vegetable*) Chicorée *m or f*
chide [tʃaɪd] VT: **to ~ sb (for)** jdn schelten (wegen)
chief [tʃi:f] N Häuptling *m*; (*of organization, department*) Leiter(in) *m(f)*, Chef(in) *m(f)* ▸ ADJ Haupt-, wichtigste(r, s)
chief constable (BRIT) N Polizeipräsident *m*, Polizeichef *m*
chief executive, (US) **chief executive officer** N Generaldirektor(in) *m(f)*
chiefly ['tʃi:flɪ] ADV hauptsächlich
Chief of Staff N Stabschef *m*
chiffon ['ʃɪfɔn] N Chiffon *m*
chilblain ['tʃɪlbleɪn] N Frostbeule *f*
child [tʃaɪld] (*pl* **children**) N Kind *nt*; **do you have any children?** haben Sie Kinder?
child benefit (BRIT) N Kindergeld *nt*
childbirth ['tʃaɪldbə:θ] N Geburt *f*, Entbindung *f*
childcare ['tʃaɪldkɛəʳ] N Kinderbetreuung *f*
childhood ['tʃaɪldhud] N Kindheit *f*
childish ['tʃaɪldɪʃ] ADJ kindisch
childless ['tʃaɪldlɪs] ADJ kinderlos
childlike ['tʃaɪldlaɪk] ADJ kindlich
child minder (BRIT) N Tagesmutter *f*
child prodigy N Wunderkind *nt*
children ['tʃɪldrən] NPL *of* **child**
children's home ['tʃɪldrənz-] N Kinderheim *nt*
child's play ['tʃaɪldz-] N: **it was ~** es war ein Kinderspiel
Chile ['tʃɪlɪ] N Chile *nt*
Chilean ['tʃɪlɪən] ADJ chilenisch ▸ N Chilene *m*, Chilenin *f*
chill [tʃɪl] N Kühle *f*; (*illness*) Erkältung *f* ▸ ADJ kühl; (*fig*: *reminder*) erschreckend ▸ VT kühlen; (*person*) frösteln *or* frieren lassen; **"serve chilled"** „gekühlt servieren"
chilli, (US) **chili** ['tʃɪlɪ] N Peperoni *pl*
chilling ['tʃɪlɪŋ] ADJ (*wind, morning*) eisig; (*fig*: *effect, prospect etc*) beängstigend
chill out (*inf*) VI sich entspannen, relaxen
chilly ['tʃɪlɪ] ADJ kühl; (*person, response, look*) kühl, frostig; **to feel ~** frösteln, frieren
chime [tʃaɪm] N Glockenspiel *nt* ▸ VI läuten
chimney ['tʃɪmnɪ] N Schornstein *m*
chimney sweep N Schornsteinfeger(in) *m(f)*
chimpanzee [tʃɪmpæn'zi:] N Schimpanse *m*
chin [tʃɪn] N Kinn *nt*
China ['tʃaɪnə] N China *nt*
china ['tʃaɪnə] N Porzellan *nt*
Chinese [tʃaɪ'ni:z] ADJ chinesisch ▸ N INV Chinese *m*, Chinesin *f*; (*Ling*) Chinesisch *nt*
chink [tʃɪŋk] N (*in door, wall etc*) Ritze *f*, Spalt *m*; (*of bottles etc*) Klirren *nt*
chintz [tʃɪnts] N Chintz *m*
chinwag ['tʃɪnwæg] (BRIT *inf*) N Schwatz *m*
chip [tʃɪp] N (*gen pl*) Pommes frites *pl*; (US: *also*: **potato chip**) Chip *m*; (*of wood*) Span *m*; (*of glass, stone*) Splitter *m*; (*in glass, cup etc*) abgestoßene Stelle *f*; (*in gambling*) Chip *m*, Spielmarke *f*; (*Comput*: *also*: **microchip**) Chip *m* ▸ VT (*cup, plate*) anschlagen; **when the chips are down** (*fig*) wenn es drauf ankommt
▸ **chip in** (*inf*) VI (*contribute*) etwas beisteuern; (*interrupt*) sich einschalten
chip and PIN N: **~ machine** Chip-und-Pin-Kartenlesegerät *nt*
chipboard ['tʃɪpbɔ:d] N Spanplatte *f*
chipmunk ['tʃɪpmʌŋk] N Backenhörnchen *nt*

chippings ['tʃɪpɪŋz] NPL: **loose ~** (*on road*) Schotter *m*

> **Chip shop**, auch „fish-and-chip shop", ist die traditionelle britische Imbissbude, in der vor allem frittierte Fischfilets und Pommes frites, aber auch andere einfache Mahlzeiten angeboten werden. Früher wurde das Essen zum Mitnehmen in Zeitungspapier verpackt. Manche chip shops haben auch einen Essraum.

chiropodist [kɪ'rɔpədɪst] (BRIT) N Fußpfleger(in) *m(f)*
chiropody [kɪ'rɔpədɪ] (BRIT) N Fußpflege *f*
chirp [tʃə:p] VI (*bird*) zwitschern; (*crickets*) zirpen
chirpy ['tʃə:pɪ] (*inf*) ADJ munter
chisel ['tʃɪzl] N (*for stone*) Meißel *m*; (*for wood*) Beitel *m*
chit [tʃɪt] N Zettel *m*
chitchat ['tʃɪttʃæt] N Plauderei *f*
chivalrous ['ʃɪvəlrəs] ADJ ritterlich
chivalry ['ʃɪvəlrɪ] N Ritterlichkeit *f*
chives [tʃaɪvz] NPL Schnittlauch *m*
chloride ['klɔ:raɪd] N Chlorid *nt*
chlorinate ['klɔrɪneɪt] VT chloren
chlorine ['klɔ:ri:n] N Chlor *nt*
chock [tʃɔk] N Bremskeil *m*, Bremsklotz *m*
chock-a-block ['tʃɔkə'blɔk] ADJ gerammelt voll
chock-full [tʃɔk'ful] ADJ = **chock-a-block**
chocolate ['tʃɔklɪt] N Schokolade *f*; (*drink*) Kakao *m*, Schokolade *f*; (*sweet*) Praline *f* ▶ CPD Schokoladen-
chocolate cake N Schokoladenkuchen *m*
choice [tʃɔɪs] N Auswahl *f*; (*option*) Möglichkeit *f*; (*preference*) Wahl *f* ▶ ADJ Qualitäts-, erstklassig; **I did it by** *or* **from ~** ich habe es mir so ausgesucht; **a wide ~** eine große Auswahl
choir ['kwaɪəʳ] N Chor *m*
choirboy ['kwaɪə'bɔɪ] N Chorknabe *m*
choke [tʃəuk] VI ersticken; (*with smoke, dust, anger etc*) keine Luft mehr bekommen ▶ VT erwürgen, erdrosseln ▶ N (*Aut*) Choke *m*, Starterklappe *f*; **to be choked (with)** verstopft sein (mit)
cholera ['kɔlərə] N Cholera *f*
cholesterol [kə'lɛstərɔl] N Cholesterin *nt*
chook [tʃuk] N (AUST, NZ *inf*) Huhn *nt*
choose [tʃu:z] (*pt* **chose**, *pp* **chosen**) VT (aus)wählen; (*profession, friend*) sich *dat* aussuchen ▶ VI: **to ~ between** wählen zwischen *+dat*, eine Wahl treffen zwischen *+dat*; **to ~ from** wählen aus *or* unter *+dat*, eine Wahl treffen aus *or* unter *+dat*; **to ~ to do sth** beschließen, etw zu tun
choosy ['tʃu:zɪ] ADJ wählerisch
chop [tʃɔp] VT (*wood*) hacken; (*vegetables, fruit, meat*: *also*: **chop up**) klein schneiden ▶ N Kotelett *nt*; **chops** NPL (*inf*: *of animal*) Maul *nt*; (*of person*) Mund *m*; **to get the ~** (BRIT *inf*: *project*) dem Rotstift zum Opfer fallen; (: *be sacked*) rausgeschmissen werden
▶ **chop down** VT (*tree*) fällen
chopper ['tʃɔpəʳ] (*inf*) N Hubschrauber *m*
choppy ['tʃɔpɪ] ADJ (*sea*) kabbelig, bewegt
chopsticks ['tʃɔpstɪks] NPL Stäbchen *pl*
choral ['kɔ:rəl] ADJ (*singing*) Chor-; (*society*) Gesang-
chord [kɔ:d] N Akkord *m*; (*Math*) Sehne *f*
chore [tʃɔ:ʳ] N Hausarbeit *f*; (*routine task*) lästige Routinearbeit *f*; **household chores** Hausarbeit
choreographer [kɔrɪ'ɔgrəfəʳ] N Choreograf(in) *m(f)*
choreography [kɔrɪ'ɔgrəfɪ] N Choreografie *f*
chorister ['kɔrɪstəʳ] N Chorsänger(in) *m(f)*
chortle ['tʃɔ:tl] VI glucksen
chorus ['kɔ:rəs] N Chor *m*; (*refrain*) Refrain *m*; (*of complaints*) Flut *f*
chose [tʃəuz] PT *of* **choose**
chosen ['tʃəuzn] PP *of* **choose**
chow [tʃau] N Chow-Chow *m*
chowder ['tʃaudəʳ] N (sämige) Fischsuppe *f*
Christ [kraɪst] N Christus *m*
christen ['krɪsn] VT taufen
christening ['krɪsnɪŋ] N Taufe *f*
Christian ['krɪstɪən] ADJ christlich ▶ N Christ(in) *m(f)*
Christianity [krɪstɪ'ænɪtɪ] N Christentum *nt*
Christian name N Vorname *m*
Christmas ['krɪsməs] N Weihnachten *nt*; **Happy** *or* **Merry ~!** frohe *or* fröhliche Weihnachten!
Christmas card N Weihnachtskarte *f*
Christmas Day N der erste Weihnachtstag
Christmas Eve N Heiligabend *m*
Christmas Island N Weihnachtsinsel *f*
Christmas pudding N Plumpudding *m*
Christmas tree N Weihnachtsbaum *m*, Christbaum *m*
chrome [krəum] N = **chromium**
chromium ['krəumɪəm] N Chrom *nt*; (*also*: **chromium plating**) Verchromung *f*
chromosome ['krəuməsəum] N Chromosom *nt*
chronic ['krɔnɪk] ADJ (*also fig*) chronisch; (*severe*) schlimm
chronicle ['krɔnɪkl] N Chronik *f*
chronological [krɔnə'lɔdʒɪkl] ADJ chronologisch
chrysanthemum [krɪ'sænθəməm] N Chrysantheme *f*
chubby ['tʃʌbɪ] ADJ pummelig; **~ cheeks** Pausbacken *pl*
chuck [tʃʌk] (*inf*) VT werfen, schmeißen; (BRIT: *also*: **chuck up, chuck in**: *job*) hinschmeißen; (: *person*) Schluss machen mit
▶ **chuck out** VT (*person*) rausschmeißen; (*rubbish etc*) wegschmeißen
▶ **chuck up** VI (*inf*) kotzen
chuckle ['tʃʌkl] VI leise in sich *acc* hineinlachen
chuffed [tʃʌft] (BRIT *inf*) ADJ vergnügt und zufrieden; (*flattered*) gebauchpinselt
chug [tʃʌg] VI (*also*: **chug along**) tuckern
chum [tʃʌm] N Kumpel *m*
chump [tʃʌmp] (*inf*) N Trottel *m*
chunk [tʃʌŋk] N großes Stück *nt*

C

chunky ['tʃʌŋkɪ] ADJ (*furniture etc*) klobig; (*person*) stämmig, untersetzt; (*knitwear*) dick
church [tʃə:tʃ] N Kirche *f*; **the C~ of England** die anglikanische Kirche
churchyard ['tʃə:tʃjɑ:d] N Friedhof *m*
churlish ['tʃə:lɪʃ] ADJ griesgrämig; (*behaviour*) ungehobelt
churn [tʃə:n] N Butterfass *nt*; (*also*: **milk churn**) Milchkanne *f*
▸ **churn out** VT am laufenden Band produzieren
chute [ʃu:t] N (*also*: **rubbish chute**) Müllschlucker *m*; (*for coal, parcels etc*) Rutsche *f*; (BRIT: *slide*) Rutschbahn *f*, Rutsche *f*
chutney ['tʃʌtnɪ] N Chutney *nt*
CIA (US) N ABBR (= *Central Intelligence Agency*) CIA *m or f*
cicada [sɪ'kɑ:də] N Zikade *f*
CID (BRIT) N ABBR = **Criminal Investigation Department**
cider ['saɪdə^r] N Apfelwein *m*
c.i.f., CIF ABBR (*Comm*: = *cost, insurance, and freight*) cif
cigar [sɪ'gɑ:^r] N Zigarre *f*
cigarette [sɪgə'rɛt] N Zigarette *f*
cigarette case N Zigarettenetui *nt*
cigarette end N Zigarettenstummel *m*
cigarette holder N Zigarettenspitze *f*
C in C ABBR (*Mil*) = **commander in chief**
cinch [sɪntʃ] (*inf*) N: **it's a ~** das ist ein Kinderspiel *or* ein Klacks
Cinderella [sɪndə'rɛlə] N Aschenputtel *nt*, Aschenbrödel *nt*
cinders ['sɪndəz] NPL Asche *f*
cine camera ['sɪnɪ-] (BRIT) N (Schmal)filmkamera *f*
cine film ['sɪnɪ-] (BRIT) N Schmalfilm *m*
cinema ['sɪnəmə] N Kino *nt*; (*film-making*) Film *m*
cine projector ['sɪnɪ-] (BRIT) N Filmprojektor *m*
cinnamon ['sɪnəmən] N Zimt *m*
cipher ['saɪfə^r] N (*code*) Chiffre *f*; (*fig*) Niemand *m*; **in ~** chiffriert
circa ['sə:kə] PREP circa
circle ['sə:kl] N Kreis *m*; (*in cinema, theatre*) Rang *m* ▸ VI kreisen ▸ VT kreisen um; (*surround*) umgeben
circuit ['sə:kɪt] N Runde *f*; (*Elec*) Stromkreis *m*; (*track*) Rennbahn *f*
circuit board N Platine *f*, Leiterplatte *f*
circuitous [sə:'kjuɪtəs] ADJ umständlich
circular ['sə:kjulə^r] ADJ rund; (*route*) Rund- ▸ N (*letter*) Rundschreiben *nt*, Rundbrief *m*; (*as advertisement*) Wurfsendung *f*; **~ argument** Zirkelschluss *m*
circulate ['sə:kjuleɪt] VI (*traffic*) fließen; (*blood, report*) zirkulieren; (*news, rumour*) kursieren, in Umlauf sein; (*person*) die Runde machen ▸ VT herumgehen *or* zirkulieren lassen
circulating capital [sə:kju'leɪtɪŋ-] N (*Comm*) flüssiges Kapital *nt*, Umlaufkapital *nt*
circulation [sə:kju'leɪʃən] N (*of traffic*) Fluss *m*; (*of air etc*) Zirkulation *f*; (*of newspaper*) Auflage *f*; (*Med*: *of blood*) Kreislauf *m*
circumcise ['sə:kəmsaɪz] VT beschneiden
circumference [sə'kʌmfərəns] N Umfang *m*; (*edge*) Rand *m*
circumflex ['sə:kəmflɛks] N (*also*: **circumflex accent**) Zirkumflex *m*
circumscribe ['sə:kəmskraɪb] VT (*Math*) einen Kreis umbeschreiben; (*fig*) eingrenzen
circumspect ['sə:kəmspɛkt] ADJ umsichtig
circumstances ['sə:kəmstənsɪz] NPL Umstände *pl*; (*financial condition*) (finanzielle) Verhältnisse *pl*; **in the ~** unter diesen Umständen; **under no ~** unter (gar) keinen Umständen, auf keinen Fall
circumstantial [sə:kəm'stænʃl] ADJ ausführlich; **~ evidence** Indizienbeweis *m*
circumvent [sə:kəm'vɛnt] VT umgehen
circus ['sə:kəs] N Zirkus *m*; (*in place names*: *also*: **Circus**) Platz *m*
cirrhosis [sɪ'rəusɪs] N (*also*: **cirrhosis of the liver**) Leberzirrhose *f*
CIS N ABBR (= *Commonwealth of Independent States*) GUS *f*
cissy ['sɪsɪ] N, ADJ *see* **sissy**
cistern ['sɪstən] N Zisterne *f*; (*of toilet*) Spülkasten *m*
citation [saɪ'teɪʃən] N Zitat *nt*; (US) Belobigung *f*; (*Law*) Vorladung *f* (vor Gericht)
cite [saɪt] VT zitieren; (*example*) anführen; (*Law*) vorladen
citizen ['sɪtɪzn] N Staatsbürger(in) *m(f)*; (*of town*) Bürger(in) *m(f)*
Citizens' Advice Bureau ['sɪtɪznz-] N ≈ Bürgerberatungsstelle *f*
citizenship ['sɪtɪznʃɪp] N Staatsbürgerschaft *f*; (BRIT *Scol*) Gesellschaftskunde *f*
citric acid ['sɪtrɪk-] N Zitronensäure *f*
citrus fruit ['sɪtrəs-] N Zitrusfrucht *f*
city ['sɪtɪ] N (Groß)stadt *f*; **the C~** (*Fin*) die City, das Londoner Banken- und Börsenviertel
city centre N Stadtzentrum *nt*, Innenstadt *f*
City Hall N Rathaus *nt*; (US: *municipal government*) Stadtverwaltung *f*
civic ['sɪvɪk] ADJ (*authorities etc*) Stadt-, städtisch; (*duties, pride*) Bürger-, bürgerlich
civic centre (BRIT) N Stadtverwaltung *f*
civil ['sɪvɪl] ADJ (*disturbances, rights*) Bürger-; (*liberties, law*) bürgerlich; (*polite*) höflich
Civil Aviation Authority (BRIT) N Behörde *f* für Zivilluftfahrt
civil ceremony N standesamtliche Hochzeit
civil defence N Zivilschutz *m*
civil disobedience N ziviler Ungehorsam *m*
civil engineer N Bauingenieur(in) *m(f)*
civil engineering N Hoch- und Tiefbau *m*
civilian [sɪ'vɪlɪən] ADJ (*population*) Zivil- ▸ N Zivilist *m*; **~ casualties** Verluste *pl* unter der Zivilbevölkerung
civilization [sɪvɪlaɪ'zeɪʃən] N Zivilisation *f*; (*a society*) Kultur *f*
civilized ['sɪvɪlaɪzd] ADJ zivilisiert; (*person*) kultiviert; (*place, experience*) gepflegt
civil law N Zivilrecht *nt*, bürgerliches Recht *nt*
civil liberties N (bürgerliche) Freiheitsrechte *pl*

civil partnership N eingetragene Partnerschaft
civil rights NPL Bürgerrechte *pl*
civil servant N (Staats)beamter *m*, (Staats)beamtin *f*
Civil Service N Beamtenschaft *f*
civil war N Bürgerkrieg *m*
civvies ['sɪvɪz] (*inf*) NPL Zivilklamotten *pl*
cl ABBR (= *centilitre*) cl
clad [klæd] ADJ: **~ (in)** gekleidet (in *+acc*)
claim [kleɪm] VT (*assert*) behaupten; (*responsibility*) übernehmen; (*credit*) in Anspruch nehmen; (*rights, inheritance*) Anspruch erheben auf *+acc*; (*expenses*) sich *dat* zurückerstatten lassen; (*compensation, damages*) verlangen ▸ VI (*for insurance*) Ansprüche geltend machen ▸ N (*assertion*) Behauptung *f*; (*for pension, wage rise, compensation*) Forderung *f*; (*right: to inheritance, land*) Anspruch *m*; (*for expenses*) Spesenabrechnung *f*; **(insurance) ~** (Versicherungs)anspruch *m*; **to put in a ~ for** beantragen
claimant ['kleɪmənt] N Antragsteller(in) *m(f)*
claim form N Antragsformular *nt*
clairvoyant [klɛə'vɔɪənt] N Hellseher(in) *m(f)*
clam [klæm] N Venusmuschel *f*
▸ **clam up** (*inf*) VI keinen Piep (mehr) sagen
clamber ['klæmbəʳ] VI klettern
clammy ['klæmɪ] ADJ feucht
clamour, (*US*) **clamor** ['klæməʳ] N Lärm *m*; (*protest*) Protest *m*, Aufschrei *m* ▸ VI: **to ~ for** schreien nach
clamp [klæmp] N Schraubzwinge *f*, Klemme *f* ▸ VT (*two things*) zusammenklemmen; (*one thing on another*) klemmen; (*wheel*) krallen
▸ **clamp down on** VT FUS rigoros vorgehen gegen
clampdown ['klæmpdaun] N: **~ (on)** hartes Durchgreifen *nt* (gegen)
clan [klæn] N Clan *m*
clandestine [klæn'dɛstɪn] ADJ geheim, Geheim-
clang [klæŋ] VI klappern; (*bell*) läuten ▸ N Klappern *nt*; Läuten *nt*
clanger ['klæŋəʳ] (BRIT *inf*) N Fauxpas *m*; **to drop a ~** ins Fettnäpfchen treten
clansman ['klænzmən] N (*irreg*) Clanmitglied *nt*
clap [klæp] VI (Beifall) klatschen ▸ VT: **to ~ (one's hands)** (in die Hände) klatschen ▸ N: **a ~ of thunder** ein Donnerschlag *m*
clapping ['klæpɪŋ] N Beifall *m*
claptrap ['klæptræp] (*inf*) N Geschwafel *nt*
claret ['klærət] N roter Bordeaux(wein) *m*
clarification [klærɪfɪ'keɪʃən] N Klärung *f*
clarify ['klærɪfaɪ] VT klären
clarinet [klærɪ'nɛt] N Klarinette *f*
clarity ['klærɪtɪ] N Klarheit *f*
clash [klæʃ] N (*fight*) Zusammenstoß *m*; (*disagreement*) Streit *m*, Auseinandersetzung *f*; (*of beliefs, ideas, views*) Konflikt *m*; (*of colours, styles, personalities*) Unverträglichkeit *f*; (*of events, dates, appointments*) Überschneidung *f*; (*noise*) Klirren *nt* ▸ VI (*fight*) zusammenstoßen; (*disagree*) sich streiten, eine Auseinandersetzung haben; (*beliefs, ideas, views*) aufeinanderprallen; (*colours*) sich beißen; (*styles, personalities*) nicht zusammenpassen; (*two events, dates, appointments*) sich überschneiden; (*make noise*) klirrend aneinanderschlagen
clasp [klɑːsp] N Griff *m*; (*embrace*) Umklammerung *f*; (*of necklace, bag*) Verschluss *m* ▸ VT (er)greifen; (*embrace*) umklammern
class [klɑːs] N Klasse *f*; (*lesson*) (Unterrichts)stunde *f* ▸ ADJ (*struggle, distinction*) Klassen- ▸ VT einordnen, einstufen
class-conscious ['klɑːs'kɔnʃəs] ADJ klassenbewusst, standesbewusst
class-consciousness ['klɑːs'kɔnʃəsnɪs] N Klassenbewusstsein *nt*, Standesbewusstsein *nt*
classic ['klæsɪk] ADJ klassisch ▸ N Klassiker *m*; (*race*) *bedeutendes Pferderennen für dreijährige Pferde*;
classics NPL (*Scol*) Altphilologie *f*
classical ['klæsɪkl] ADJ klassisch
classification [klæsɪfɪ'keɪʃən] N Klassifikation *f*; (*category*) Klasse *f*; (*system*) Einteilung *f*
classified ['klæsɪfaɪd] ADJ geheim
classified advertisement N Kleinanzeige *f*
classify ['klæsɪfaɪ] VT klassifizieren, (ein)ordnen
classless ['klɑːslɪs] ADJ: **~ society** klassenlose Gesellschaft *f*
classmate ['klɑːsmeɪt] N Klassenkamerad(in) *m(f)*
classroom ['klɑːsrum] N Klassenzimmer *nt*
classroom assistant N Assistenzlehrkraft *f*
classy ['klɑːsɪ] (*inf*) ADJ nobel, exklusiv; (*person*) todschick
clatter ['klætəʳ] N Klappern *nt*; (*of hooves*) Trappeln *nt* ▸ VI klappern; trappeln
clause [klɔːz] N (*Law*) Klausel *f*; (*Ling*) Satz *m*
claustrophobia [klɔːstrə'fəubɪə] N Klaustrophobie *f*, Platzangst *f*
claustrophobic [klɔːstrə'fəubɪk] ADJ (*place, situation*) beengend; (*person*): **to be/feel ~** Platzangst haben/bekommen
claw [klɔː] N Kralle *f*; (*of lobster*) Schere *f*, Zange *f*
▸ **claw at** VT FUS sich krallen an *+acc*
clay [kleɪ] N Ton *m*; (*soil*) Lehm *m*
clean [kliːn] ADJ sauber; (*fight*) fair; (*record, reputation*) einwandfrei; (*joke, story*) stubenrein, anständig; (*edge, fracture*) glatt ▸ VT sauber machen; (*car, hands, face etc*) waschen ▸ ADV: **he ~ forgot** er hat es glatt(weg) vergessen; **to have a ~ driving licence, to have a ~ driving record** (*US*) keine Strafpunkte haben; **to ~ one's teeth** (BRIT) sich *dat* die Zähne putzen; **the thief got ~ away** der Dieb konnte entkommen; **to come ~** (*inf*) auspacken
▸ **clean off** VT abwaschen, abwischen
▸ **clean out** VT gründlich sauber machen; (*inf: person*) ausnehmen
▸ **clean up** VT aufräumen; (*child*) sauber machen; (*fig*) für Ordnung sorgen in *+dat* ▸ VI aufräumen, sauber machen; (*inf: make profit*) absahnen
clean-cut ['kliːn'kʌt] ADJ gepflegt; (*situation*) klar

cleaner ['kli:nə^r] N Raumpfleger(in) *m(f)*; (*woman*) Putzfrau *f*; (*substance*) Reinigungsmittel *nt*, Putzmittel *nt*
cleaner's ['kli:nəz] N (*also*: **dry cleaner's**) Reinigung *f*
cleaning ['kli:nɪŋ] N Putzen *nt*
cleaning lady N Putzfrau *f*, Reinemachefrau *f*
cleanliness ['klɛnlɪnɪs] N Sauberkeit *f*, Reinlichkeit *f*
cleanly ['kli:nlɪ] ADV sauber
cleanse [klɛnz] VT (*purify*) läutern; (*face, cut*) reinigen
cleanser ['klɛnzə^r] N (*for face*) Reinigungscreme *f*, Reinigungsmilch *f*
clean-shaven ['kli:n'ʃeɪvn] ADJ glatt rasiert
cleansing department ['klɛnzɪŋ-] (BRIT) N ≈ Stadtreinigung *f*
clean sweep N: **to make a ~** (*Sport*) alle Preise einstecken
clean technology N umweltfreundliche Technologie *f*
clean-up ['kli:nʌp] N: **to give sth a ~** etw gründlich sauber machen
clear [klɪə^r] ADJ klar; (*footprint*) deutlich; (*photograph*) scharf; (*commitment*) eindeutig; (*glass, plastic*) durchsichtig; (*road, way, floor etc*) frei; (*conscience, skin*) rein ▸ VT (*room*) ausräumen; (*trees*) abholzen; (*weeds etc*) entfernen; (*slums etc, stock*) räumen; (*Law*) freisprechen; (*fence, wall*) überspringen; (*cheque*) verrechnen ▸ VI (*weather, sky*) aufklaren; (*fog, smoke*) sich auflösen; (*room etc*) sich leeren ▸ ADV: **to be ~ of the ground** den Boden nicht berühren ▸ N: **to be in the ~** (*out of debt*) schuldenfrei sein; (*free of suspicion*) von jedem Verdacht frei sein; (*out of danger*) außer Gefahr sein; **~ profit** Reingewinn *m*; **I have a ~ day tomorrow** (BRIT) ich habe morgen nichts vor; **to make o.s. ~** sich klar ausdrücken; **to make it ~ to sb that ...** es jdm (unmissverständlich) klarmachen, dass ...; **to ~ the table** den Tisch abräumen; **to ~ a space (for sth)** (für etw) Platz schaffen; **to ~ one's throat** sich räuspern; **to ~ a profit** einen Gewinn machen; **to keep ~ of sb** jdm aus dem Weg gehen; **to keep ~ of sth** etw meiden; **to keep ~ of trouble** allem Ärger aus dem Weg gehen
▸ **clear off** (*inf*) VI abhauen, verschwinden
▸ **clear up** VT aufräumen; (*mystery*) aufklären; (*problem*) lösen ▸ VI (*bad weather*) sich aufklären; (*illness*) sich bessern
clearance ['klɪərəns] N (*of slums*) Räumung *f*; (*of trees*) Abholzung *f*; (*permission*) Genehmigung *f*; (*free space*) lichte Höhe *f*
clear-cut ['klɪə'kʌt] ADJ klar
clearing ['klɪərɪŋ] N Lichtung *f*; (BRIT *Banking*) Clearing *nt*
clearing bank (BRIT) N Clearingbank *f*
clearing house N (*Comm*) Clearingstelle *f*
clearly ['klɪəlɪ] ADV klar; (*obviously*) eindeutig
clearway ['klɪəweɪ] (BRIT) N Straße *f* mit Halteverbot
cleavage ['kli:vɪdʒ] N (*of woman's breasts*) Dekolleté *nt*
cleaver ['kli:və^r] N Hackbeil *nt*
clef [klɛf] N (Noten)schlüssel *m*
cleft [klɛft] N Spalte *f*
cleft palate N (*Med*) Gaumenspalte *f*
clemency ['klɛmənsɪ] N Milde *f*
clement ['klɛmənt] ADJ mild
clench [klɛntʃ] VT (*fist*) ballen; (*teeth*) zusammenbeißen
clergy ['klə:dʒɪ] N Klerus *m*, Geistlichkeit *f*
clergyman ['klə:dʒɪmən] N (*irreg*) Geistliche(r) *m*
clerical ['klɛrɪkl] ADJ (*job, worker*) Büro-; (*error*) Schreib-; (*Rel*) geistlich
clerk [klɑ:k, (*US*) klə:rk] N (BRIT) Büroangestellte(r) *f(m)*; (*US: sales person*) Verkäufer(in) *m(f)*
Clerk of Court N Protokollführer(in) *m(f)*
clever ['klɛvə^r] ADJ klug; (*deft, crafty*) schlau, clever (*inf*); (*device, arrangement*) raffiniert
cleverly ['klɛvəlɪ] ADV geschickt
clew [klu:] (*US*) N = **clue**
cliché ['kli:ʃeɪ] N Klischee *nt*
click [klɪk] VI klicken ▸ VT: **to ~ one's tongue** mit der Zunge schnalzen; **to ~ one's heels** die Hacken zusammenschlagen
client ['klaɪənt] N Kunde *m*, Kundin *f*; (*of bank, lawyer*) Klient(in) *m(f)*; (*of restaurant*) Gast *m*
clientele [kli:ɑ̃:n'tɛl] N Kundschaft *f*
cliff [klɪf] N Kliff *nt*
cliffhanger ['klɪfhæŋə^r] N *spannungsgeladene Szene am Ende einer Filmepisode*, Cliffhanger *m*
climactic [klaɪ'mæktɪk] ADJ: **~ point** Höhepunkt *m*
climate ['klaɪmɪt] N Klima *nt*
climate change N Klimawandel *m*
climate conference N (*Pol*) Klimakonferenz *f*
climax ['klaɪmæks] N (*sexual*) Höhepunkt *m*
climb [klaɪm] VI klettern; (*plane, sun, prices, shares*) steigen ▸ VT (*stairs, ladder*) hochsteigen, hinaufsteigen; (*tree*) klettern auf *+acc*; (*hill*) steigen auf *+acc* ▸ N Aufstieg *m*; (*of prices etc*) Anstieg *m*; **to ~ over a wall/into a car** über eine Mauer/in ein Auto steigen *or* klettern
▸ **climb down** (BRIT) VI (*fig*) nachgeben
climb-down ['klaɪmdaun] N Nachgeben *nt*, Rückzieher *m* (*inf*)
climber ['klaɪmə^r] N Bergsteiger(in) *m(f)*; (*plant*) Kletterpflanze *f*
climbing ['klaɪmɪŋ] N Bergsteigen *nt*
clinch [klɪntʃ] VT (*deal*) perfekt machen; (*argument*) zum Abschluss bringen
clincher ['klɪntʃə^r] N ausschlaggebender Faktor *m*
cling [klɪŋ] (*pt, pp* **clung**) VI: **to ~ to** (*mother, support*) sich festklammern an *+dat*; (*idea, belief*) festhalten an *+dat*; (*subj: clothes, dress*) sich anschmiegen *+dat*
clingfilm ['klɪŋfɪlm], (*US*) **clingwrap** ['klɪŋræp] N Frischhaltefolie *f*
clinic ['klɪnɪk] N Klinik *f*; (*session*) Sprechstunde *f*; (*: Sport*) Trainingsstunde *f*
clinical ['klɪnɪkl] ADJ klinisch; (*fig*) nüchtern, kühl; (*: building, room*) steril
clink [klɪŋk] VI klirren

clip [klɪp] N (*also*: **paper clip**) Büroklammer *f*; (BRIT: *also*: **bulldog clip**) Klammer *f*; (*holding wire, hose etc*) Klemme *f*; (*for hair*) Spange *f*; (TV, *Cine*) Ausschnitt *m* ▸ VT festklemmen; (*also*: **clip together**) zusammenheften; (*cut*) schneiden
clippers ['klɪpəz] NPL (*for gardening*) Schere *f*; (*also*: **nail clippers**) Nagelzange *f*
clipping ['klɪpɪŋ] N (*from newspaper*) Ausschnitt *m*
clique [kli:k] N Clique *f*, Gruppe *f*
clitoris ['klɪtərɪs] N Klitoris *f*
cloak [kləuk] N Umhang *m* ▸ VT (*fig*) hüllen
cloakroom ['kləukrum] N Garderobe *f*; (BRIT: WC) Toilette *f*
clobber ['klɔbəʳ] (*inf*) N Klamotten *pl* ▸ VT (*hit*) hauen, schlagen; (*defeat*) in die Pfanne hauen
clock [klɔk] N Uhr *f*; **round the ~** rund um die Uhr; **30,000 on the ~** (BRIT *Aut*) ein Tachostand von 30.000; **to work against the ~** gegen die Uhr arbeiten
▸ **clock in** (BRIT) VI (den Arbeitsbeginn) stempeln *or* stechen
▸ **clock off** (BRIT) VI (das Arbeitsende) stempeln *or* stechen
▸ **clock on** (BRIT) VI = **clock in**
▸ **clock out** (BRIT) VI = **clock off**
▸ **clock up** VT (*miles*) fahren; (*hours*) arbeiten
clockwise ['klɔkwaɪz] ADV im Uhrzeigersinn
clockwork ['klɔkwə:k] N Uhrwerk *nt* ▸ ADJ aufziehbar, zum Aufziehen; **like ~** wie am Schnürchen
clog [klɔg] N Clog *m*; (*wooden*) Holzschuh *m* ▸ VT verstopfen ▸ VI (*also*: **clog up**) verstopfen
cloister ['klɔɪstəʳ] N Kreuzgang *m*
clone [kləun] N Klon *m*
close¹ [kləus] ADJ (*writing, friend, contact*) eng; (*texture*) dicht, fest; (*relative*) nahe; (*examination*) genau, gründlich; (*watch*) streng, scharf; (*contest*) knapp; (*weather*) schwül; (*room*) stickig ▸ ADV nahe; **~ (to)** nahe (*+gen*); **~ to** in der Nähe *+gen*; **~ by, ~ at hand** in der Nähe; **how ~ is Edinburgh to Glasgow?** wie weit ist Edinburgh von Glasgow entfernt?; **a ~ friend** ein guter *or* enger Freund; **to have a ~ shave** (*fig*) gerade noch davonkommen; **at ~ quarters** aus der Nähe
close² [kləuz] VT schließen, zumachen; (*sale, deal, case*) abschließen; (*speech*) schließen, beenden ▸ VI schließen, zumachen; (*door, lid*) sich schließen, zugehen; (*end*) aufhören ▸ N Ende *nt*, Schlus *m*; **to bring sth to a ~** etw beenden
▸ **close down** VI (*factory*) stillgelegt werden; (*magazine etc*) eingestellt werden
▸ **close in** VI (*night*) hereinbrechen; (*fog*) sich verdichten; **to ~ in on sb/sth** jdm/etw auf den Leib rücken; **the days are closing in** die Tage werden kürzer
▸ **close off** VT (*area*) abriegeln; (*road*) sperren
closed [kləuzd] ADJ geschlossen; (*road*) gesperrt
closed-circuit television ['kləuzd'sə:kɪt-] N Fernsehüberwachungsanlage *f*
closed shop N Betrieb *m* mit Gewerkschaftszwang
close-knit ['kləus'nɪt] ADJ eng zusammengewachsen
closely ['kləuslɪ] ADV (*examine, watch*) genau; (*connected*) eng; (*related*) nah(e); (*resemble*) sehr; **we are ~ related** wir sind nah verwandt; **a ~ guarded secret** ein streng gehütetes Geheimnis
close season ['kləus-] N Schonzeit *f*; (*Sport*) Sommerpause *f*
closet ['klɔzɪt] N Wandschrank *m*
close-up ['kləusʌp] N Nahaufnahme *f*
closing ['kləuzɪŋ] ADJ (*stages*) Schluss-; (*remarks*) abschließend; **closing price** N (*Stock Exchange*) Schlusskurs *m*, Schlussnotierung *f*; **closing time** (BRIT) N (*in pub*) Polizeistunde *f*, Sperrstunde *f*
closure ['kləuʒəʳ] N (*of factory*) Stilllegung *f*; (*of magazine*) Einstellung *f*; (*of road*) Sperrung *f*; (*of border*) Schließung *f*
clot [klɔt] N (*blood clot*) (Blut)gerinnsel *nt*; (*inf: idiot*) Trottel *m* ▸ VI gerinnen; (*external bleeding*) zum Stillstand kommen
cloth [klɔθ] N (*material*) Stoff *m*, Tuch *nt*; (*rag*) Lappen *m*; (BRIT: *also*: **teacloth**) (Spül)tuch *nt*; (*also*: **tablecloth**) Tischtuch *nt*, Tischdecke *f*
clothe [kləuð] VT anziehen, kleiden
clothes [kləuðz] NPL Kleidung *f*, Kleider *pl*; **to put one's ~ on** sich anziehen; **to take one's ~ off** sich ausziehen
clothes brush N Kleiderbürste *f*
clothesline ['kləuðzlaɪn] N Wäscheleine *f*
clothes peg, (*US*) **clothes pin** N Wäscheklammer *f*
clothing ['kləuðɪŋ] N = **clothes**
clotted cream ['klɔtɪd-] (BRIT) N *Sahne aus erhitzter Milch*
cloud [klaud] N Wolke *f* ▸ VT trüben; **every ~ has a silver lining** (*proverb*) auf Regen folgt Sonnenschein; **to ~ the issue** es unnötig kompliziert machen; (*deliberately*) die Angelegenheit verschleiern
▸ **cloud over** VI (*sky*) sich bewölken, sich bedecken; (*face, eyes*) sich verfinstern
cloudburst ['klaudbə:st] N Wolkenbruch *m*
cloud computing N Cloud Computing *nt*
cloud-cuckoo-land [klaud'kuku:lænd] (BRIT) N Wolkenkuckucksheim *nt*
cloudy ['klaudɪ] ADJ wolkig, bewölkt; (*liquid*) trüb
clout [klaut] VT schlagen, hauen ▸ N (*fig*) Schlagkraft *f*
clove [kləuv] N Gewürznelke *f*; **~ of garlic** Knoblauchzehe *f*
clover ['kləuvəʳ] N Klee *m*
cloverleaf ['kləuvəli:f] N Kleeblatt *nt*
clown [klaun] N Clown *m* ▸ VI (*also*: **clown about, clown around**) herumblödeln, herumkaspern
cloying ['klɔɪɪŋ] ADJ süßlich
club [klʌb] N Klub *m*, Verein *m*; (*weapon*) Keule *f*, Knüppel *m*; (*object*: *also*: **golf club**) Golfschläger *m* ▸ VT knüppeln ▸ VI: **to ~ together** zusammenlegen; **clubs** NPL (*Cards*) Kreuz *nt*
club car (*US*) N Speisewagen *m*

club class N Klubklasse *f*, Businessklasse *f*
clubhouse ['klʌbhaus] N Klubhaus *nt*
club soda (US) N (*soda water*) Sodawasser *nt*
cluck [klʌk] VI glucken
clue [klu:] N Hinweis *m*, Anhaltspunkt *m*; (*in crossword*) Frage *f*; **I haven't a ~** ich habe keine Ahnung
clued-up ['klu:dʌp], (US) **clued in** (*inf*) ADJ: **to be ~ on sth** über etw *acc* im Bilde sein
clueless ['klu:lɪs] ADJ ahnungslos, unbedarft
clump [klʌmp] N Gruppe *f*
clumsy ['klʌmzɪ] ADJ ungeschickt; (*object*) unförmig; (*effort, attempt*) plump
clung [klʌŋ] PT, PP *of* **cling**
cluster ['klʌstə^r] N Gruppe *f* ▸ VI (*people*) sich scharen; (*houses*) sich drängen
clutch [klʌtʃ] N Griff *m*; (*Aut*) Kupplung *f* ▸ VT (*purse, hand*) umklammern; (*stick*) sich festklammern an *+dat* ▸ VI: **to ~ at** sich klammern an *+acc*
clutter ['klʌtə^r] VT (*also*: **clutter up**: *room*) vollstopfen; (*: table*) vollstellen ▸ N Kram *m* (*inf*)
cm ABBR (= *centimetre*) cm
CNAA (BRIT) N ABBR (= *Council for National Academic Awards*) *Zentralstelle zur Vergabe von Qualifikationsnachweisen*
CND (BRIT) N ABBR (= *Campaign for Nuclear Disarmament*) *Organisation für atomare Abrüstung*
CO N ABBR = **commanding officer**; (BRIT: = *Commonwealth Office*) *Regierungsstelle für Angelegenheiten des Commonwealth* ▸ ABBR (*US Post*) = **Colorado**
Co. ABBR = **company**; **county**
c/o ABBR (= *care of*) bei, c/o
coach [kəutʃ] N (Reise)bus *m*; (*horse-drawn*) Kutsche *f*; (*of train*) Wagen *m*; (*Sport*) Trainer *m*; (*Scol*) Nachhilfelehrer(in) *m(f)* ▸ VT trainieren; (*student*) Nachhilfeunterricht geben *+dat*
coach trip N Busfahrt *f*
coagulate [kəu'ægjuleɪt] VI (*blood*) gerinnen; (*paint etc*) eindicken ▸ VT (*blood*) gerinnen lassen; (*paint*) dick werden lassen
coal [kəul] N Kohle *f*
coalface ['kəulfeɪs] N Streb *m*
coalfield ['kəulfi:ld] N Kohlenrevier *nt*
coalition [kəuə'lɪʃən] N (*Pol*) Koalition *f*; (*of pressure groups etc*) Zusammenschluss *m*
coalman ['kəulmən] N (*irreg*) Kohlenhändler *m*
coal merchant N = **coalman**
coal mine N Kohlenbergwerk *nt*, Zeche *f*
coal miner N Bergmann *m*, Kumpel *m* (*inf*)
coal mining N (Kohlen)bergbau *m*
coarse [kɔ:s] ADJ (*texture*) grob; (*vulgar*) gewöhnlich, derb; (*salt, sand etc*) grobkörnig
coast [kəust] N Küste *f* ▸ VI (im Leerlauf) fahren
coastal ['kəustl] ADJ Küsten-
coaster ['kəustə^r] N (*Naut*) Küstenfahrzeug *nt*; (*for glass*) Untersetzer *m*
coastguard ['kəustgɑ:d] N (*officer*) Küstenwächter *m*; (*service*) Küstenwacht *f*
coastline ['kəustlaɪn] N Küste *f*
coat [kəut] N Mantel *m*; (*of animal*) Fell *nt*; (*layer*) Schicht *f*; (*: of paint*) Anstrich *m* ▸ VT überziehen
coat hanger N Kleiderbügel *m*
coating ['kəutɪŋ] N (*of chocolate etc*) Überzug *m*; (*of dust etc*) Schicht *f*
coat of arms N Wappen *nt*
coauthor ['kəu'ɔ:θə^r] N Mitautor(in) *m(f)*, Mitverfasser(in) *m(f)*
coax [kəuks] VT (*person*) überreden
cob [kɔb] N *see* **corn**
cobbler ['kɔblə^r] N Schuster *m*
cobbles ['kɔblz] NPL Kopfsteinpflaster *nt*
cobblestones ['kɔblstəunz] NPL = **cobbles**
COBOL ['kəubɔl] N COBOL *nt*
cobra ['kəubrə] N Kobra *f*
cobweb ['kɔbwɛb] N Spinnennetz *nt*
cocaine [kə'keɪn] N Kokain *nt*
cock [kɔk] N Hahn *m*; (*male bird*) Männchen *nt* ▸ VT (*gun*) entsichern; **to ~ one's ears** (*fig*) die Ohren spitzen
cock-a-hoop [kɔkə'hu:p] ADJ ganz aus dem Häuschen
cockerel ['kɔkərl] N junger Hahn *m*
cock-eyed ['kɔkaɪd] ADJ (*fig*) verrückt, widersinnig
cockle ['kɔkl] N Herzmuschel *f*
cockney ['kɔknɪ] N Cockney *m*, echter Londoner *m*; (*Ling*) Cockney *nt*
cockpit ['kɔkpɪt] N Cockpit *nt*
cockroach ['kɔkrəutʃ] N Küchenschabe *f*, Kakerlak *m*
cocktail ['kɔkteɪl] N Cocktail *m*; **fruit ~** Obstsalat *m*; **prawn ~** Krabbencocktail *m*
cocktail cabinet N Hausbar *f*
cocktail party N Cocktailparty *f*
cocktail shaker [-'ʃeɪkə^r] N Mixbecher *m*
cock-up ['kɔkʌp] (*inf!*) N Schlamassel *m*
cocky ['kɔkɪ] ADJ großspurig
cocoa ['kəukəu] N Kakao *m*
coconut ['kəukənʌt] N Kokosnuss *f*
cocoon [kə'ku:n] N Puppe *f*, Kokon *m*; (*fig*) schützende Umgebung *f*
COD ABBR (BRIT) = **cash on delivery**; (US) = **collect on delivery**
cod [kɔd] N Kabeljau *m*
code [kəud] N (*cipher*) Chiffre *f*; (*also*: **dialling code**) Vorwahl *f*; (*also*: **post code**) Postleitzahl *f*; **~ of behaviour** Sittenkodex *m*; **~ of practice** Verfahrensregeln *pl*
codeine ['kəudi:n] N Codein *nt*
codger ['kɔdʒə^r] (*inf*) N: **old ~** komischer Kauz *m*
codicil ['kɔdɪsɪl] N (*Law*) Kodizill *nt*
codify ['kəudɪfaɪ] VT kodifizieren
cod-liver oil ['kɔdlɪvə-] N Lebertran *m*
co-driver ['kəu'draɪvə^r] N Beifahrer(in) *m(f)*
co-ed ['kəu'ɛd] (*Scol*) ADJ ABBR = **coeducational** ▸ N ABBR (*US: female pupil/student*) *Schülerin/Studentin an einer gemischten Schule/Universität*; (BRIT: *school*) gemischte Schule *f*
coeducational ['kəuɛdju'keɪʃənl] ADJ (*school*) Koedukations-, gemischt
coerce [kəu'ə:s] VT zwingen
coercion [kəu'ə:ʃən] N Zwang *m*
coexistence ['kəuɪg'zɪstəns] N Koexistenz *f*
C of C N ABBR = **chamber of commerce**

C of E ABBR = **Church of England**
coffee ['kɔfɪ] N Kaffee *m*; **black ~** schwarzer Kaffee *m*; **white ~** Kaffee mit Milch; **~ with cream** Kaffee mit Sahne
coffee bar (BRIT) N Café *nt*
coffee bean N Kaffeebohne *f*
coffee break N Kaffeepause *f*
coffee cake (US) N Kuchen *m* zum Kaffee
coffee cup N Kaffeetasse *f*
coffeepot ['kɔfɪpɔt] N Kaffeekanne *f*
coffee table N Couchtisch *m*
coffin ['kɔfɪn] N Sarg *m*
C of I ABBR (= *Church of Ireland*) *anglikanische Kirche Irlands*
C of S ABBR (= *Church of Scotland*) *presbyterianische Kirche in Schottland*
cog [kɔg] N (*wheel*) Zahnrad *nt*; (*tooth*) Zahn *m*
cogent ['kəudʒənt] ADJ stichhaltig, zwingend
cognac ['kɔnjæk] N Kognak *m*
cognitive ['kɔgnɪtɪv] ADJ kognitiv
cogwheel ['kɔgwi:l] N Zahnrad *nt*
cohabit [kəu'hæbɪt] VI (*formal*) in eheähnlicher Gemeinschaft leben; **to ~ (with sb)** (mit jdm) zusammenleben
coherent [kəu'hɪərənt] ADJ (*speech*) zusammenhängend; (*answer, theory*) schlüssig; (*person*) bei klarem Verstand
cohesion [kəu'hi:ʒən] N Geschlossenheit *f*
cohesive [kə'hi:sɪv] ADJ geschlossen
coil [kɔɪl] N Rolle *f*; (*one loop*) Windung *f*; (*of smoke*) Kringel *m*; (*Aut, Elec*) Spule *f*; (*contraceptive*) Spirale *f* ▸ VT aufrollen, aufwickeln
coin [kɔɪn] N Münze *f* ▸ VT prägen
coinage ['kɔɪnɪdʒ] N Münzen *pl*; (*Ling*) Prägung *f*
coin box (BRIT) N Münzfernsprecher *m*
coincide [kəuɪn'saɪd] VI (*events*) zusammenfallen; (*ideas, views*) übereinstimmen
coincidence [kəu'ɪnsɪdəns] N Zufall *m*
coin-operated ['kɔɪn'ɔpəreɪtɪd] ADJ Münz-
Coke® [kəuk] N Coca-Cola® *f or nt*, Coke® *nt*
coke [kəuk] N Koks *m*
Col. ABBR = **colonel**
COLA (US) N ABBR (= *cost of living adjustment*) *Anpassung der Löhne und Gehälter an steigende Lebenshaltungskosten*
colander ['kɔləndəʳ] N Durchschlag *m*
cold [kəuld] ADJ kalt; (*unemotional*) kalt, kühl ▸ N Kälte *f*; (*Med*) Erkältung *f*; **it's ~** es ist kalt; **to be/feel ~** (*person*) frieren; (*object*) kalt sein; **in ~ blood** kaltblütig; **to have ~ feet** (*fig*) kalte Füße bekommen; **to give sb the ~ shoulder** jdm die kalte Schulter zeigen; **to catch ~, to catch a ~** sich erkälten
cold-blooded ['kəuld'blʌdɪd] ADJ kaltblütig
cold calling N (*Comm: on phone*) unaufgeforderte Telefonwerbung; (*: visit*) unaufgeforderter Vertreterbesuch
cold cream N (halbfette) Feuchtigkeitscreme *f*
coldly ['kəuldlɪ] ADV kalt, kühl
cold-shoulder [kəuld'ʃəuldəʳ] VT die kalte Schulter zeigen *+dat*
cold sore N Bläschenausschlag *m*
cold sweat N: **to come out in a ~ (about sth)** (wegen etw) in kalten Schweiß ausbrechen
cold turkey N: **to do ~** Totalentzug machen
Cold War N: **the ~** der Kalte Krieg
coleslaw ['kəulslɔ:] N Krautsalat *m*
colic ['kɔlɪk] N Kolik *f*
colicky ['kɔlɪkɪ] ADJ: **to be ~** Kolik *f or* Leibschmerzen*pl* haben
collaborate [kə'læbəreɪt] VI zusammenarbeiten; (*with enemy*) kollaborieren
collaboration [kəlæbə'reɪʃən] N Zusammenarbeit *f*; Kollaboration *f*
collaborator [kə'læbəreɪtəʳ] N Mitarbeiter(in) *m(f)*; Kollaborateur(in) *m(f)*
collage [kɔ'lɑ:ʒ] N Collage *f*
collagen ['kɔlədʒən] N Kollagen *nt*
collapse [kə'læps] VI zusammenbrechen; (*building*) einstürzen; (*plans*) scheitern; (*government*) stürzen ▸ N Zusammenbruch *m*; Einsturz *m*; Scheitern *nt*; Sturz *m*
collapsible [kə'læpsəbl] ADJ Klapp-, zusammenklappbar
collar ['kɔləʳ] N Kragen *m*; (*of dog, cat*) Halsband *nt*; (*Tech*) Bund *m* ▸ VT (*inf*) schnappen
collarbone ['kɔləbəun] N Schlüsselbein *nt*
collate [kɔ'leɪt] VT vergleichen
collateral [kə'lætərl] N (*Comm*) (zusätzliche) Sicherheit *f*
collateral damage N (*Mil*) Schäden *pl* in Wohngebieten; (*: casualties*) Opfer *pl* unter der Zivilbevölkerung
collation [kə'leɪʃən] N Vergleich *m*; (*Culin*): **a cold ~** ein kalter Imbiss *m*
colleague ['kɔli:g] N Kollege *m*, Kollegin *f*
collect [kə'lɛkt] VT sammeln; (*mail*: BRIT: *fetch*) abholen; (*debts*) eintreiben; (*taxes*) einziehen ▸ VI sich ansammeln ▸ ADV (*US Tel*): **to call ~** ein R-Gespräch führen; **to ~ one's thoughts** seine Gedanken ordnen, sich sammeln; **~ on delivery** (*US Comm*) per Nachnahme
collected [kə'lɛktɪd] ADJ: **~ works** gesammelte Werke *pl*
collection [kə'lɛkʃən] N Sammlung *f*; (*from place, person, of mail*) Abholung *f*; (*in church*) Kollekte *f*
collective [kə'lɛktɪv] ADJ kollektiv, gemeinsam ▸ N Kollektiv *nt*; **~ farm** landwirtschaftliche Produktionsgenossenschaft *f*
collective bargaining N Tarifverhandlungen *pl*
collector [kə'lɛktəʳ] N Sammler(in) *m(f)*; (*of taxes etc*) Einnehmer(in) *m(f)*; (*of rent, cash*) Kassierer(in) *m(f)*; **~'s item** *or* **piece** Sammlerstück *nt*, Liebhaberstück *nt*
college ['kɔlɪdʒ] N College *nt*; (*of agriculture, technology*) Fachhochschule *f*; **to go to ~** studieren; **~ of education** pädagogische Hochschule *f*
collide [kə'laɪd] VI: **to ~ (with)** zusammenstoßen (mit); (*fig: clash*) eine heftige Auseinandersetzung haben (mit)
collie ['kɔlɪ] N Collie *m*
colliery ['kɔlɪərɪ] (BRIT) N (Kohlen)bergwerk *nt*, Zeche *f*

collision [kə'lɪʒən] N Zusammenstoß *m*; **to be on a ~ course** (*also fig*) auf Kollisionskurs sein
collision damage waiver N (*Insurance*) *Verzicht auf Haftungsbeschränkung bei Unfällen mit Mietwagen*
colloquial [kə'ləukwɪəl] ADJ umgangssprachlich
collusion [kə'lu:ʒən] N (geheime) Absprache *f*; **to be in ~ with** gemeinsame Sache machen mit
Colo. (US) ABBR (*Post*) = **Colorado**
Cologne [kə'ləun] N Köln *nt*
cologne [kə'ləun] N (*also*: **eau de cologne**) Kölnischwasser *nt*, Eau de Cologne *nt*
Colombia [kə'lɔmbɪə] N Kolumbien *nt*
Colombian [kə'lɔmbɪən] ADJ kolumbianisch ▶ N Kolumbianer(in) *m(f)*
colon ['kəulən] N Doppelpunkt *m*; (*Anat*) Dickdarm *m*
colonel ['kə:nl] N Oberst *m*
colonial [kə'ləunɪəl] ADJ Kolonial-
colonize ['kɔlənaɪz] VT kolonisieren
colony ['kɔlənɪ] N Kolonie *f*
color *etc* ['kʌlə[r]] (US) = **colour** *etc*
Colorado beetle [kɔlə'rɑ:dəu-] N Kartoffelkäfer *m*
colossal [kə'lɔsl] ADJ riesig, kolossal
colour, (US) **color** ['kʌlə[r]] N Farbe *f*; (*skin colour*) Hautfarbe *f*; (*of spectacle etc*) Atmosphäre *f* ▶ VT bemalen; (*with crayons*) ausmalen; (*dye*) färben; (*fig*) beeinflussen ▶ VI (*blush*) erröten, rot werden ▶ CPD Farb-; **colours** NPL (*of party, club etc*) Farben *pl*; **in ~** (*film*) in Farbe; (*illustrations*) bunt
▶ **colour in** VT ausmalen
colour bar N Rassenschranke *f*
colour-blind ['kʌləblaɪnd] ADJ farbenblind
coloured ['kʌləd] ADJ farbig; (*photo*) Farb-; (*illustration etc*) bunt
colour film N Farbfilm *m*
colourful ['kʌləful] ADJ bunt; (*account, story*) farbig, anschaulich; (*personality*) schillernd
colouring ['kʌlərɪŋ] N Gesichtsfarbe *f*, Teint *m*; (*in food*) Farbstoff *m*
colour scheme N Farbzusammenstellung *f*
colour supplement (BRIT) N Farbbeilage *f*, Magazin *nt*
colour television N Farbfernsehen *nt*; (*set*) Farbfernseher *m*
colt [kəult] N Hengstfohlen *nt*
column ['kɔləm] N Säule *f*; (*of people*) Kolonne *f*; (*of print*) Spalte *f*; (*gossip/sports column*) Kolumne *f*; **the editorial ~** der Leitartikel
columnist ['kɔləmnɪst] N Kolumnist(in) *m(f)*
coma ['kəumə] N Koma *nt*; **to be in a ~** im Koma liegen
comb [kəum] N Kamm *m* ▶ VT kämmen; (*area*) durchkämmen
combat ['kɔmbæt] N Kampf *m* ▶ VT bekämpfen
combination [kɔmbɪ'neɪʃən] N Kombination *f*
combination lock N Kombinationsschloss *nt*
combine VT [kəm'baɪn] verbinden ▶ VI sich zusammenschließen; (*Chem*) sich verbinden ▶ N ['kɔmbaɪn] Konzern *m*; (*Agr*) = **combine harvester**; **combined effort** vereintes Unternehmen
combine harvester N Mähdrescher *m*
combo ['kɔmbəu] N Combo *f*
combustible [kəm'bʌstɪbl] ADJ brennbar
combustion [kəm'bʌstʃən] N Verbrennung *f*

KEYWORD

come [kʌm] (*pt* **came**, *pp* **come**) VI **1** (*movement towards*) kommen; **come with me** kommen Sie mit mir; **to come running** angelaufen kommen; **coming!** ich komme!
2 (*arrive*) kommen; **they came to a river** sie kamen an einen Fluss; **to come home** nach Hause kommen
3 (*reach*): **to come to** kommen an *+acc*; **her hair came to her waist** ihr Haar reichte ihr bis zur Hüfte; **to come to a decision** zu einer Entscheidung kommen
4 (*occur*): **an idea came to me** mir kam eine Idee
5 (*be, become*) werden; **I've come to like him** mittlerweile mag ich ihn; **if it comes to it** wenn es darauf ankommt
▶ **come about** VI geschehen
▶ **come across** VT FUS (*find: person, thing*) stoßen auf *+acc* ▶ VI: **to come across well/badly** (*idea etc*) gut/schlecht ankommen; (*meaning*) gut/schlecht verstanden werden
▶ **come along** VI (*arrive*) daherkommen; (*make progress*) vorankommen; **come along!** komm schon!
▶ **come apart** VI (*break in pieces*) auseinandergehen
▶ **come away** VI (*leave*) weggehen; (*become detached*) abgehen
▶ **come back** VI (*return*) zurückkommen; **to come back into fashion** wieder in Mode kommen
▶ **come by** VT FUS (*acquire*) kommen zu
▶ **come down** VI (*price*) sinken, fallen; (*building: be demolished*) abgerissen werden; (*tree: during storm*) umstürzen
▶ **come forward** VI (*volunteer*) sich melden
▶ **come from** VT FUS kommen von, stammen aus; (*person*) kommen aus
▶ **come in** VI (*enter*) hereinkommen; (*report, news*) eintreffen; (*on deal etc*) sich beteiligen; **come in!** herein!
▶ **come in for** VT FUS (*criticism etc*) einstecken müssen
▶ **come into** VT FUS (*inherit: money*) erben; **to come into fashion** in Mode kommen; **money doesn't come into it** Geld hat nichts damit zu tun
▶ **come off** VI (*become detached: button, handle*) sich lösen; (*succeed: attempt, plan*) klappen ▶ VT FUS (*inf*): **come off it!** mach mal halblang!
▶ **come on** VI (*pupil, work, project*) vorankommen; (*lights etc*) angehen; **come on!** (*hurry up*) mach schon!; (*giving encouragement*) los!
▶ **come out** VI herauskommen; (*stain*)

herausgehen; **to come out (on strike)** in den Streik treten
▶ **come over** VT FUS: **I don't know what's come over him!** ich weiß nicht, was in ihn gefahren ist
▶ **come round** VI (*after faint, operation*) wieder zu sich kommen; (*visit*) vorbeikommen; (*agree*) zustimmen
▶ **come through** VI (*survive*) durchkommen; (*telephone call*) (durch)kommen ▶ VT FUS (*illness etc*) überstehen
▶ **come to** VI (*regain consciousness*) wieder zu sich kommen ▶ VT FUS (*add up to*): **how much does it come to?** was macht das zusammen?
▶ **come under** VT FUS (*heading*) kommen unter +*acc*; (*criticism, pressure, attack*) geraten unter +*acc*
▶ **come up** VI (*approach*) herankommen; (*sun*) aufgehen; (*problem*) auftauchen; (*event*) bevorstehen; (*in conversation*) genannt werden; **something's come up** etwas ist dazwischengekommen
▶ **come up against** VT FUS (*resistance, difficulties*) stoßen auf +*acc*
▶ **come upon** VT FUS (*find*) stoßen auf +*acc*
▶ **come up to** VT FUS: **the film didn't come up to our expectations** der Film entsprach nicht unseren Erwartungen; **it's coming up to 10 o'clock** es ist gleich 10 Uhr
▶ **come up with** VT FUS (*idea*) aufwarten mit; (*money*) aufbringen

comeback ['kʌmbæk] N (*of film star etc*) Comeback *nt*; (*reaction, response*) Reaktion *f*
comedian [kə'mi:dɪən] N Komiker *m*
comedienne [kəmi:dɪ'ɛn] N Komikerin *f*
comedown ['kʌmdaun] (*inf*) N Enttäuschung *f*; (*professional*) Abstieg *m*
comedy ['kɔmɪdɪ] N Komödie *f*; (*humour*) Witz *m*
comet ['kɔmɪt] N Komet *m*
comeuppance [kʌm'ʌpəns] N: **to get one's ~** die Quittung bekommen
comfort ['kʌmfət] N (*physical*) Behaglichkeit *f*; (*material*) Komfort *m*; (*solace, relief*) Trost *m* ▶ VT trösten; **comforts** NPL (*of home etc*) Komfort *m*, Annehmlichkeiten *pl*
comfortable ['kʌmfətəbl] ADJ bequem; (*room*) komfortabel; (*walk, climb etc*) geruhsam; (*income*) ausreichend; (*majority*) sicher; **to be ~** (*physically*) sich wohlfühlen; (*financially*) sehr angenehm leben; **the patient is ~** dem Patienten geht es den Umständen entsprechend gut; **I don't feel very ~ about it** mir ist nicht ganz wohl bei der Sache
comfortably ['kʌmfətəblɪ] ADV (*sit*) bequem; (*live*) angenehm
comforter ['kʌmfətə^r] (*US*) N Schnuller *m*
comfort shopping N Frustkauf *m*
comfort station (*US*) N öffentliche Toilette *f*
comic ['kɔmɪk] ADJ (*also*: **comical**) komisch ▶ N Komiker(in) *m(f)*; (BRIT: *magazine*) Comicheft *nt*
comical ['kɔmɪkl] ADJ komisch
comic strip N Comicstrip *m*

coming ['kʌmɪŋ] N Ankunft *f*, Kommen *nt* ▶ ADJ kommend; (*next*) nächste(r, s); **in the ~ weeks** in den nächsten Wochen
coming and going N, **comings and goings** NPL Kommen und Gehen *nt*
Comintern ['kɔmɪntə:n] N (*Pol*) Komintern *f*
comma ['kɔmə] N Komma *nt*
command [kə'mɑ:nd] N (*also Comput*) Befehl *m*; (*control, charge*) Führung *f*; (*Mil: authority*) Kommando *nt*, Befehlsgewalt *f*; (*mastery*) Beherrschung *f* ▶ VT (*troops*) befehligen, kommandieren; (*be able to get*) verfügen über +*acc*; (*deserve: respect, admiration etc*) verdient haben; **to be in ~ of** das Kommando *or* den (Ober)befehl haben über +*acc*; **to have ~ of** das Kommando haben über +*acc*; **to take ~ of** das Kommando übernehmen +*gen*; **to have at one's ~** verfügen über +*acc*; **to ~ sb to do sth** jdm befehlen, etw zu tun
commandant ['kɔməndænt] N Kommandant *m*
command economy N Kommandowirtschaft *f*
commandeer [kɔmən'dɪə^r] VT requirieren, beschlagnahmen; (*fig*) sich aneignen
commander [kə'mɑ:ndə^r] N Befehlshaber *m*, Kommandant *m*
commander in chief N Oberbefehlshaber *m*
commanding [kə'mɑ:ndɪŋ] ADJ (*appearance*) imposant; (*voice, tone*) gebieterisch; (*lead*) entscheidend; (*position*) vorherrschend
commanding officer N befehlshabender Offizier *m*
commandment [kə'mɑ:ndmənt] N Gebot *nt*
command module N Kommandokapsel *f*
commando [kə'mɑ:ndəu] N Kommando *nt*, Kommandotrupp *m*; (*soldier*) Angehörige(r) *m* eines Kommando(trupp)s
commemorate [kə'mɛməreɪt] VT gedenken +*gen*
commemoration [kəmɛmə'reɪʃən] N Gedenken *nt*
commemorative [kə'mɛmərətɪv] ADJ Gedenk-
commence [kə'mɛns] VT, VI beginnen
commend [kə'mɛnd] VT loben; **to ~ sth to sb** jdm etw empfehlen
commendable [kə'mɛndəbl] ADJ lobenswert
commendation [kɔmɛn'deɪʃən] N Auszeichnung *f*
commensurate [kə'mɛnʃərɪt] ADJ: **~ with** *or* **to** entsprechend +*dat*
comment ['kɔmɛnt] N Bemerkung *f*; (*on situation etc*) Kommentar *m* ▶ VI: **to ~ (on)** sich äußern (über +*acc or* zu); (*on situation etc*) einen Kommentar abgeben (zu); **"no ~"** „kein Kommentar!"; **to ~ that ...** bemerken, dass ...
commentary ['kɔməntərɪ] N Kommentar *m*; (*Sport*) Reportage *f*
commentator ['kɔmənteɪtə^r] N Kommentator(in) *m(f)*; (*Sport*) Reporter(in) *m(f)*
commerce ['kɔmə:s] N Handel *m*
commercial [kə'mə:ʃəl] ADJ kommerziell; (*organization*) Wirtschafts- ▶ N (*advertisement*) Werbespot *m*

commercial bank N Handelsbank *f*
commercial break N Werbung *f*
commercial college N Fachschule *f* für kaufmännische Berufe
commercialism [kəˈməːʃəlɪzəm] N Kommerzialisierung *f*
commercialize [kəˈməːʃəlaɪz] VT kommerzialisieren
commercialized [kəˈməːʃəlaɪzd] (*pej*) ADJ kommerzialisiert
commercial radio N kommerzielles Radio *nt*
commercial television N kommerzielles Fernsehen *nt*
commercial traveller N Handelsvertreter(in) *m(f)*
commercial vehicle N Lieferwagen *m*
commiserate [kəˈmɪzəreɪt] VI: **to ~ with sb** jdm sein Mitgefühl zeigen
commission [kəˈmɪʃən] N (*order for work*) Auftrag *m*; (*Comm*) Provision *f*; (*committee*) Kommission *f*; (*Mil*) Offizierspatent *nt* ▸ VT (*work of art*) in Auftrag geben; (*Mil*) (zum Offizier) ernennen; **out of ~** außer Betrieb; (*Naut*) nicht im Dienst; **I get 10% ~** ich bekomme 10% Provision; **~ of inquiry** Untersuchungsausschuss *m*, Untersuchungskommission *f*; **to ~ sb to do sth** jdn damit beauftragen, etw zu tun; **to ~ sth from sb** jdm etw in Auftrag geben
commissionaire [kəmɪʃəˈnɛəʳ] (BRIT) N Portier *m*
commissioner [kəˈmɪʃənəʳ] N Polizeipräsident *m*
commit [kəˈmɪt] VT (*crime*) begehen; (*money, resources*) einsetzen; (*to sb's care*) anvertrauen; **to ~ o.s.** sich festlegen; **to ~ o.s. to do sth** sich (dazu) verpflichten, etw zu tun; **to ~ suicide** Selbstmord begehen; **to ~ to writing** zu Papier bringen; **to ~ sb for trial** jdn einem Gericht überstellen
commitment [kəˈmɪtmənt] N Verpflichtung *f*; (*to ideology, system*) Engagement *nt*
committed [kəˈmɪtɪd] ADJ engagiert
committee [kəˈmɪtɪ] N Ausschuss *m*, Komitee *nt*; **to be on a ~** in einem Ausschuss *or* Komitee sein *or* sitzen
committee meeting N Ausschusssitzung *f*
commodity [kəˈmɔdɪtɪ] N Ware *f*; (*food*) Nahrungsmittel *nt*
common [ˈkɔmən] ADJ (*shared by all*) gemeinsam; (*good*) Gemein-; (*property*) Gemeinschafts-; (*usual, ordinary*) häufig; (*vulgar*) gewöhnlich ▸ N Gemeindeland *nt*; **the Commons** NPL (BRIT *Pol*) das Unterhaus; **in ~ use** allgemein gebräuchlich; **it's ~ knowledge that** es ist allgemein bekannt, dass; **to the ~ good** für das Gemeinwohl; **to have sth in ~ (with sb)** etw (mit jdm) gemein haben
common cold N Schnupfen *m*
common denominator N (*Math, fig*) gemeinsamer Nenner *m*
commoner [ˈkɔmənəʳ] N Bürgerliche(r) *f(m)*
common ground N (*fig*) gemeinsame Basis *f*
common land N Gemeindeland *nt*
common law N Gewohnheitsrecht *nt*
common-law [ˈkɔmənlɔː] ADJ: **she is his ~ wife** sie lebt mit ihm in eheähnlicher Gemeinschaft
commonly [ˈkɔmənlɪ] ADV häufig
Common Market N: **the ~** der Gemeinsame Markt
commonplace [ˈkɔmənpleɪs] ADJ alltäglich
common room N Aufenthaltsraum *m*, Tagesraum *m*
common sense N gesunder Menschenverstand *m*
Commonwealth [ˈkɔmənwɛlθ] (BRIT) N: **the ~** das Commonwealth

> Das **Commonwealth**, offiziell Commonwealth of Nations, ist ein lockerer Zusammenschluss aus souveränen Staaten, die früher unter britischer Regierung standen, und von Großbritannien abhängigen Gebieten. Die Mitgliedstaaten erkennen den britischen Monarchen als Oberhaupt des Commonwealth an. Bei der Commonwealth Conference, einem Treffen der Staatsoberhäupter der Commonwealthländer, werden Angelegenheiten von gemeinsamem Interesse diskutiert.

commotion [kəˈməuʃən] N Tumult *m*
communal [ˈkɔmjuːnl] ADJ gemeinsam, Gemeinschafts-; (*life*) Gemeinschafts-
commune N [ˈkɔmjuːn] Kommune *f* ▸ VI [kəˈmjuːn]: **to ~ with** Zwiesprache halten mit
communicate [kəˈmjuːnɪkeɪt] VT mitteilen; (*idea, feeling*) vermitteln ▸ VI: **to ~ (with)** (*by speech, gesture*) sich verständigen (mit); (*in writing*) in Verbindung *or* Kontakt stehen (mit)
communication [kəmjuːnɪˈkeɪʃən] N Kommunikation *f*; (*letter, call*) Mitteilung *f*
communication cord (BRIT) N Notbremse *f*
communications network [kəmjuːnɪˈkeɪʃənz-] N Kommunikationsnetz *nt*
communications satellite [kəmjuːnɪˈkeɪʃənz-] N Kommunikationssatellit *m*, Nachrichtensatellit *m*
communicative [kəˈmjuːnɪkətɪv] ADJ gesprächig, mitteilsam
communion [kəˈmjuːnɪən] N (*also*: **Holy Communion**: *Catholic*) Kommunion *f*; (: *Protestant*) Abendmahl *nt*
communiqué [kəˈmjuːnɪkeɪ] N Kommuniqué *nt*, (amtliche) Verlautbarung *f*
communism [ˈkɔmjunɪzəm] N Kommunismus *m*
communist [ˈkɔmjunɪst] ADJ kommunistisch ▸ N Kommunist(in) *m(f)*
community [kəˈmjuːnɪtɪ] N Gemeinschaft *f*; (*within larger group*) Bevölkerungsgruppe *f*
community centre N Gemeindezentrum *nt*
community charge (BRIT) N (*formerly*) Gemeindesteuer *f*
community chest (US) N Wohltätigkeitsfonds *m*, Hilfsfonds *m*
community health centre N Gemeinde-Ärztezentrum *nt*

community home (BRIT) N Erziehungsheim *nt*
community service N Sozialdienst *m*
community spirit N Gemeinschaftssinn *m*
commutation ticket [kɔmju'teɪʃən-] (US) N Zeitkarte *f*
commute [kə'mju:t] VI pendeln ▶ VT (*Law, Math*) umwandeln
commuter [kə'mju:tə^r] N Pendler(in) *m(f)*
compact ADJ [kəm'pækt] kompakt ▶ N ['kɔmpækt] (*also*: **powder compact**) Puderdose *f*
compact disc N Compact Disc *f*, CD *f*
compact disc player N CD-Spieler *m*
companion [kəm'pænjən] N Begleiter(in) *m(f)*
companionship [kəm'pænjənʃɪp] N Gesellschaft *f*
companionway [kəm'pænjənweɪ] N (*Naut*) Niedergang *m*
company ['kʌmpənɪ] N Firma *f*; (*Theat*) (Schauspiel)truppe *f*; (*Mil*) Kompanie *f*; (*companionship*) Gesellschaft *f*; **he's good ~** seine Gesellschaft ist angenehm; **to keep sb ~** jdm Gesellschaft leisten; **to part ~ with** sich trennen von; **Smith and C~** Smith & Co
company car N Firmenwagen *m*
company director N Direktor(in) *m(f)*, Firmenchef(in) *m(f)*
company secretary (BRIT) N ≈ Prokurist(in) *m(f)*
comparable ['kɔmpərəbl] ADJ vergleichbar
comparative [kəm'pærətɪv] ADJ relativ; (*study, literature*) vergleichend; (*Ling*) komparativ
comparatively [kəm'pærətɪvlɪ] ADV relativ
compare [kəm'pɛə^r] VT: **to ~ (with** *or* **to)** vergleichen (mit) ▶ VI: **to ~ (with)** sich vergleichen lassen (mit); **how do the prices ~?** wie lassen sich die Preise vergleichen?; **compared with** *or* **to** im Vergleich zu, verglichen mit
comparison [kəm'pærɪsn] N Vergleich *m*; **in ~ (with)** im Vergleich (zu)
compartment [kəm'pɑ:tmənt] N (*Rail*) Abteil *nt*; (*section*) Fach *nt*
compass ['kʌmpəs] N Kompass *m*; (*fig: scope*) Bereich *m*; **compasses** NPL (*also*: **pair of compasses**) Zirkel *m*; **within the ~ of** im Rahmen *or* Bereich *+gen*; **beyond the ~ of** über den Rahmen *or* Bereich *+gen* hinaus
compassion [kəm'pæʃən] N Mitgefühl *nt*
compassionate [kəm'pæʃənɪt] ADJ mitfühlend; **on ~ grounds** aus familiären Gründen
compassionate leave N (*esp Mil*) *Beurlaubung wegen Krankheit oder Trauerfall in der Familie*
compatibility [kəmpætɪ'bɪlɪtɪ] N Vereinbarkeit *f*; Zueinanderpassen *nt*; Kompatibilität *f*
compatible [kəm'pætɪbl] ADJ (*ideas etc*) vereinbar; (*people*) zueinanderpassend; (*Comput*) kompatibel
compel [kəm'pɛl] VT zwingen
compelling [kəm'pɛlɪŋ] ADJ zwingend
compendium [kəm'pɛndɪəm] N Kompendium *nt*
compensate ['kɔmpənseɪt] VT entschädigen ▶ VI: **to ~ for** (*loss*) ersetzen; (*disappointment, change etc*) (wieder) ausgleichen
compensation [kɔmpən'seɪʃən] N Entschädigung *f*; Ersatz *m*; Ausgleich *m*; (*money*) Schaden(s)ersatz *m*
compère ['kɔmpɛə^r] N Conférencier *m*
compete [kəm'pi:t] VI (*in contest, game*) teilnehmen; (*two theories, statements*) unvereinbar sein; **to ~ (with)** (*companies, rivals*) konkurrieren (mit)
competence ['kɔmpɪtəns] N Fähigkeit *f*
competent ['kɔmpɪtənt] ADJ fähig
competing [kəm'pi:tɪŋ] ADJ konkurrierend
competition [kɔmpɪ'tɪʃən] N Konkurrenz *f*; (*contest*) Wettbewerb *m*; **in ~ with** im Wettbewerb mit
competitive [kəm'pɛtɪtɪv] ADJ (*industry, society*) wettbewerbsbetont, wettbewerbsorientiert; (*person*) vom Konkurrenzdenken geprägt; (*price, product*) wettbewerbsfähig, konkurrenzfähig; (*sport*) (Wett)kampf-
competitive examination N (*for places*) Auswahlprüfung *f*; (*for prizes*) Wettbewerb *m*
competitor [kəm'pɛtɪtə^r] N Konkurrent(in) *m(f)*; (*participant*) Teilnehmer(in) *m(f)*
compilation [kɔmpɪ'leɪʃən] N Zusammenstellung *f*
compile [kəm'paɪl] VT zusammenstellen; (*book*) verfassen
complacency [kəm'pleɪsnsɪ] N Selbstzufriedenheit *f*, Selbstgefälligkeit *f*
complacent [kəm'pleɪsnt] ADJ selbstzufrieden, selbstgefällig
complain [kəm'pleɪn] VI (*protest*) sich beschweren; **to ~ (about)** sich beklagen (über *+acc*); **to ~ of** (*headache etc*) klagen über *+acc*
complaint [kəm'pleɪnt] N Klage *f*; (*in shop etc*) Beschwerde *f*; (*illness*) Beschwerden *pl*
complement ['kɔmplɪmənt] N Ergänzung *f*; (*esp ship's crew*) Besatzung *f* ▶ VT ergänzen; **to have a full ~ of ...** (*people*) die volle Stärke an ... *dat* haben; (*items*) die volle Zahl an ... *dat* haben
complementary [kɔmplɪ'mɛntərɪ] ADJ komplementär, einander ergänzend
complete [kəm'pli:t] ADJ (*total: silence*) vollkommen; (*: change*) völlig; (*: success*) voll; (*whole*) ganz; (*: set*) vollständig; (*: edition*) Gesamt-; (*finished*) fertig ▶ VT fertigstellen; (*task*) beenden; (*set, group etc*) vervollständigen; (*fill in*) ausfüllen; **it's a ~ disaster** es ist eine totale Katastrophe
completely [kəm'pli:tlɪ] ADV völlig, vollkommen
completion [kəm'pli:ʃən] N Fertigstellung *f*; (*of contract*) Abschluss *m*; **to be nearing ~** kurz vor dem Abschluss sein *or* stehen; **on ~ of the contract** bei Vertragsabschluss
complex ['kɔmplɛks] ADJ kompliziert ▶ N Komplex *m*
complexion [kəm'plɛkʃən] N Teint *m*, Gesichtsfarbe *f*; (*of event etc*) Charakter *m*; (*political, religious*) Anschauung *f*; **to put a**

different ~ on sth etw in einem anderen Licht erscheinen lassen

complexity [kəm'plɛksɪtɪ] N Kompliziertheit *f*

compliance [kəm'plaɪəns] N Fügsamkeit *f*; (*agreement*) Einverständnis *nt*; **~ with** Einverständnis mit, Zustimmung *f* zu; **in ~ with** gemäß *+dat*

compliant [kəm'plaɪənt] ADJ gefällig, entgegenkommend

complicate ['kɔmplɪkeɪt] VT komplizieren

complicated ['kɔmplɪkeɪtɪd] ADJ kompliziert

complication [kɔmplɪ'keɪʃən] N Komplikation *f*

complicity [kəm'plɪsɪtɪ] N Mittäterschaft *f*

compliment N ['kɔmplɪmənt] Kompliment *nt* ▶ VT ['kɔmplɪmɛnt] ein Kompliment/ Komplimente machen; **compliments** NPL (*regards*) Grüße *pl*; **to pay sb a ~** jdm ein Kompliment machen; **to ~ sb (on sth)** jdm Komplimente (wegen etw) machen; **to ~ sb on doing sth** jdm Komplimente machen, dass er/ sie etw getan hat

complimentary [kɔmplɪ'mɛntərɪ] ADJ schmeichelhaft; (*ticket, copy of book etc*) Frei-

compliments slip N Empfehlungszettel *m*

comply [kəm'plaɪ] VI: **to ~ with** (*law*) einhalten *+acc*; (*ruling*) sich richten nach

component [kəm'pəunənt] ADJ einzeln ▶ N Bestandteil *m*

compose [kəm'pəuz] VT (*music*) komponieren; (*poem*) verfassen; (*letter*) abfassen; **to be composed of** bestehen aus; **to ~ o.s.** sich sammeln

composed [kəm'pəuzd] ADJ ruhig, gelassen

composer [kəm'pəuzə^r] N Komponist(in) *m(f)*

composite ['kɔmpəzɪt] ADJ zusammengesetzt; (*Bot*) Korbblütler-; (*Math*) teilbar; (*Bot*): **~ plant** Korbblütler *m*

composition [kɔmpə'zɪʃən] N Zusammensetzung *f*; (*essay*) Aufsatz *m*; (*Mus*) Komposition *f*

compositor [kəm'pɔzɪtə^r] N (Schrift)setzer(in) *m(f)*

compos mentis ['kɔmpɔs 'mɛntɪs] ADJ zurechnungsfähig

compost ['kɔmpɔst] N Kompost *m*; (*also*: **potting compost**) Blumenerde *f*

composure [kəm'pəuʒə^r] N Fassung *f*, Beherrschung *f*

compound N ['kɔmpaund] (*Chem*) Verbindung *f*; (*enclosure*) umzäuntes Gebiet *or* Gelände *nt*; (*Ling*) Kompositum *nt* ▶ ADJ ['kɔmpaund] zusammengesetzt; (*eye*) Facetten- ▶ VT [kəm'paund] verschlimmern, vergrößern

compound fracture N komplizierter Bruch *m*

compound interest N Zinseszins *m*

comprehend [kɔmprɪ'hɛnd] VT begreifen, verstehen

comprehension [kɔmprɪ'hɛnʃən] N Verständnis *nt*

comprehensive [kɔmprɪ'hɛnsɪv] ADJ umfassend; (*insurance*) Vollkasko- ▶ N = **comprehensive school**

comprehensive school (BRIT) N Gesamtschule *f*

> **Comprehensive school** ist in Großbritannien eine nicht selektive, weiterführende Schule, an der alle Kinder aus einem Einzugsgebiet gemeinsam unterrichtet werden. An einer solchen Gesamtschule können alle Schulabschlüsse gemacht werden. Die meisten staatlichen Schulen in Großbritannien sind comprehensive schools.

compress VT [kəm'prɛs] (*information etc*) verdichten; (*air*) komprimieren; (*cotton, paper etc*) zusammenpressen ▶ N ['kɔmprɛs] (*Med*) Kompresse *f*

compressed air [kəm'prɛst-] N Druckluft *f*, Pressluft *f*

compression [kəm'prɛʃən] N Verdichtung *f*; Kompression *f*; Zusammenpressen *nt*

comprise [kəm'praɪz] VT (*also*: **be comprised of**) bestehen aus; (*constitute*) bilden, ausmachen

compromise ['kɔmprəmaɪz] N Kompromiss *m* ▶ VT (*beliefs, principles*) verraten; (*person*) kompromittieren ▶ VI Kompromisse schließen ▶ CPD (*solution etc*) Kompromiss-

compulsion [kəm'pʌlʃən] N Zwang *m*; (*force*) Druck *m*, Zwang *m*; **under ~** unter Druck *or* Zwang

compulsive [kəm'pʌlsɪv] ADJ zwanghaft; **it makes ~ viewing/reading** das muss man einfach sehen/lesen; **he's a ~ smoker** das Rauchen ist bei ihm zur Sucht geworden

compulsory [kəm'pʌlsərɪ] ADJ obligatorisch; (*retirement*) Zwangs-

compulsory purchase N Enteignung *f*

compunction [kəm'pʌŋkʃən] N Schuldgefühle *pl*, Gewissensbisse *pl*; **to have no ~ about doing sth** etw tun, ohne sich schuldig zu fühlen

computer [kəm'pju:tə^r] N Computer *m*, Rechner *m* ▶ CPD Computer-; **the process is done by ~** das Verfahren wird per Computer durchgeführt

computer game N Computerspiel *nt*

computerization [kəmpju:təraɪ'zeɪʃən] N Computerisierung *f*

computerize [kəm'pju:təraɪz] VT auf Computer umstellen; (*information*) computerisieren

computer literate ADJ: **to be ~** Computerkenntnisse haben

computer programmer N Programmierer(in) *m(f)*

computer programming N Programmieren *nt*

computer science N Informatik *f*

computer scientist N Informatiker(in) *m(f)*

computing [kəm'pju:tɪŋ] N Informatik *f*; (*activity*) Computerarbeit *f*

comrade ['kɔmrɪd] N Genosse *m*, Genossin *f*; (*friend*) Kamerad(in) *m(f)*

comradeship ['kɔmrɪdʃɪp] N Kameradschaft *f*

Comsat® ['kɔmsæt] N ABBR = **communications satellite**

con [kɔn] VT betrügen; (*cheat*) hereinlegen ▶ N Schwindel *m*; **to ~ sb into doing sth** jdn durch einen Trick dazu bringen, dass er/sie etw tut

concave ['kɔnkeɪv] ADJ konkav
conceal [kən'si:l] VT verbergen; (*information*) verheimlichen
concede [kən'si:d] VT zugeben ▶ VI nachgeben; (*admit defeat*) sich geschlagen geben; **to ~ defeat** sich geschlagen geben; **to ~ a point to sb** jdm in einem Punkt recht geben
conceit [kən'si:t] N Einbildung *f*
conceited [kən'si:tɪd] ADJ eingebildet
conceivable [kən'si:vəbl] ADJ denkbar, vorstellbar; **it is ~ that ...** es ist denkbar, dass ...
conceivably [kən'si:vəblɪ] ADV: **he may ~ be right** es ist durchaus denkbar, dass er recht hat
conceive [kən'si:v] VT (*child*) empfangen; (*plan*) kommen auf *+acc*; (*policy*) konzipieren ▶ VI empfangen; **to ~ of sth** sich *dat* etw vorstellen; **to ~ of doing sth** sich *dat* vorstellen, etw zu tun
concentrate ['kɔnsəntreɪt] VI sich konzentrieren ▶ VT konzentrieren
concentration [kɔnsən'treɪʃən] N Konzentration *f*
concentration camp N Konzentrationslager *nt*, KZ *nt*
concentric [kɔn'sɛntrɪk] ADJ konzentrisch
concept ['kɔnsɛpt] N Vorstellung *f*; (*principle*) Begriff *m*
conception [kən'sɛpʃən] N Vorstellung *f*; (*of child*) Empfängnis *f*
concern [kən'sə:n] N Angelegenheit *f*; (*anxiety, worry*) Sorge *f*; (*Comm*) Konzern *m* ▶ VT Sorgen machen *+dat*; (*involve*) angehen; (*relate to*) betreffen; **to be concerned (about)** sich *dat* Sorgen machen (um); **"to whom it may ~"** (*on certificate*) „Bestätigung"; (*on reference*) „Zeugnis"; **as far as I am concerned** was mich betrifft; **to be concerned with** sich interessieren für; **the department concerned** (*under discussion*) die betreffende Abteilung; (*involved*) die zuständige Abteilung
concerning [kən'sə:nɪŋ] PREP bezüglich *+gen*, hinsichtlich *+gen*
concert ['kɔnsət] N Konzert *nt*; **in ~** (*Mus*) live; (*activities, actions etc*) gemeinsam
concerted [kən'sə:tɪd] ADJ gemeinsam
concert hall N Konzerthalle *f*, Konzertsaal *m*
concertina [kɔnsə'ti:nə] N Konzertina *f* ▶ VI sich wie eine Ziehharmonika zusammenschieben
concerto [kən'tʃə:təu] N Konzert *nt*
concession [kən'sɛʃən] N Zugeständnis *nt*, Konzession *f*; (*Comm*) Konzession; **tax ~** Steuervergünstigung *f*
concessionaire [kənsɛʃə'nɛə[r]] N Konzessionär *m*
concessionary [kən'sɛʃənrɪ] ADJ ermäßigt
conciliation [kənsɪlɪ'eɪʃən] N Schlichtung *f*
conciliatory [kən'sɪlɪətrɪ] ADJ versöhnlich
concise [kən'saɪs] ADJ kurz gefasst, prägnant
conclave ['kɔnkleɪv] N Klausur *f*; (*Rel*) Konklave *f*
conclude [kən'klu:d] VT beenden, schließen; (*treaty, deal etc*) abschließen; (*decide*) schließen, folgern ▶ VI schließen; (*events*): **to ~ (with)** enden (mit); **"that," he concluded, "is why we did it"** „darum", schloss er, „haben wir es getan"; **I ~ that ...** ich komme zu dem Schluss, dass ...
concluding [kən'klu:dɪŋ] ADJ (*remarks etc*) abschließend, Schluss-
conclusion [kən'klu:ʒən] N Ende *nt*; Schluss *m*; Abschluss *m*; Folgerung *f*; **to come to the ~ that ...** zu dem Schluss kommen, dass ...
conclusive [kən'klu:sɪv] ADJ (*evidence*) schlüssig; (*defeat*) endgültig
concoct [kən'kɔkt] VT (*excuse etc*) sich *dat* ausdenken; (*meal, sauce*) improvisieren
concoction [kən'kɔkʃən] N Zusammenstellung *f*; (*drink*) Gebräu *nt*
concord ['kɔŋkɔ:d] N Eintracht *f*; (*treaty*) Vertrag *m*
concourse ['kɔŋkɔ:s] N (Eingangs)halle *f*; (*crowd*) Menge *f*
concrete ['kɔŋkri:t] N Beton *m* ▶ ADJ (*ceiling, block*) Beton-; (*proposal, idea*) konkret
concrete mixer N Betonmischmaschine *f*
concur [kən'kə:[r]] VI übereinstimmen; **to ~ with** beipflichten *+dat*
concurrently [kən'kʌrntlɪ] ADV gleichzeitig
concussion [kən'kʌʃən] N Gehirnerschütterung *f*
condemn [kən'dɛm] VT verurteilen; (*building*) für abbruchreif erklären
condemnation [kɔndɛm'neɪʃən] N Verurteilung *f*
condensation [kɔndɛn'seɪʃən] N Kondenswasser *nt*
condense [kən'dɛns] VI kondensieren, sich niederschlagen ▶ VT zusammenfassen
condensed milk [kən'dɛnst-] N Kondensmilch *f*, Büchsenmilch *f*
condescend [kɔndɪ'sɛnd] VI herablassend sein; **to ~ to do sth** sich dazu herablassen, etw zu tun
condescending [kɔndɪ'sɛndɪŋ] ADJ herablassend
condition [kən'dɪʃən] N Zustand *m*; (*requirement*) Bedingung *f*; (*illness*) Leiden *nt* ▶ VT konditionieren; (*hair*) in Form bringen; **conditions** NPL (*circumstances*) Verhältnisse *pl*; **in good/poor ~** (*person*) in guter/schlechter Verfassung; (*thing*) in gutem/schlechtem Zustand; **a heart ~** ein Herzleiden *nt*; **weather conditions** die Wetterlage; **on ~ that ...** unter der Bedingung, dass ...
conditional [kən'dɪʃənl] ADJ bedingt; **to be ~ upon** abhängen von
conditioner [kən'dɪʃənə[r]] N (*for hair*) Pflegespülung *f*; (*for fabrics*) Weichspüler *m*
condo ['kɔndəu] (*US inf*) N ABBR = **condominium**
condolences [kən'dəulənsɪz] NPL Beileid *nt*
condom ['kɔndəm] N Kondom *m or nt*
condominium [kɔndə'mɪnɪəm] (*US*) N Haus *nt* mit Eigentumswohnungen; (*rooms*) Eigentumswohnung *f*
condone [kən'dəun] VT gutheißen

conducive [kən'dju:sɪv] ADJ: **~ to** förderlich *+dat*
conduct N ['kɔndʌkt] Verhalten *nt* ▶ VT [kən'dʌkt] (*investigation etc*) durchführen; (*manage*) führen; (*orchestra, choir etc*) dirigieren; (*heat, electricity*) leiten; **to ~ o.s.** sich verhalten
conducted tour [kən'dʌktɪd-] N Führung *f*
conductor [kən'dʌktəʳ] N (*of orchestra*) Dirigent(in) *m(f)*; (*on bus*) Schaffner *m*; (*US: on train*) Zugführer(in) *m(f)*; (*Elec*) Leiter *m*
conductress [kən'dʌktrɪs] N (*on bus*) Schaffnerin *f*
conduit ['kɔndjuɪt] N (*Tech*) Leitungsrohr *nt*; (*Elec*) Isolierrohr *nt*
cone [kəun] N Kegel *m*; (*on road*) Leitkegel *m*; (*Bot*) Zapfen *m*; (*ice cream cornet*) (Eis)tüte *f*
confectioner [kən'fɛkʃənəʳ] N (*maker*) Süßwarenhersteller(in) *m(f)*; (*seller*) Süßwarenhändler(in) *m(f)*; (*of cakes*) Konditor(in) *m(f)*
confectioner's [kən'fɛkʃənəz], **confectioner's shop** N Süßwarenladen *m*; (*cake shop*) Konditorei *f*
confectionery [kən'fɛkʃənrɪ] N Süßwaren *pl*, Süßigkeiten *pl*; (*cakes*) Konditorwaren *pl*
confederate [kən'fɛdrɪt] ADJ verbündet ▶ N (*pej*) Komplize *m*, Komplizin *f*; (*US Hist*): **the Confederates** die Konföderierten *pl*
confederation [kənfɛdə'reɪʃən] N Bund *m*; (*Pol*) Bündnis *nt*; (*Comm*) Verband *m*
confer [kən'fə:ʳ] VT: **to ~ sth (on sb)** (jdm) etw verleihen ▶ VI sich beraten; **to ~ with sb about sth** sich mit jdm über etw *acc* beraten, etw mit jdm besprechen
conference ['kɔnfərəns] N Konferenz *f*; (*more informal*) Besprechung *f*; **to be in ~** in *or* bei einer Konferenz/Besprechung sein
conference room N Konferenzraum *m*; (*smaller*) Besprechungszimmer *nt*
confess [kən'fɛs] VT bekennen; (*sin*) beichten; (*crime*) zugeben, gestehen ▶ VI (*admit*) gestehen; **to ~ to sth** (*crime*) etw gestehen; (*weakness etc*) sich zu etw bekennen; **I must ~ that I didn't enjoy it at all** ich muss sagen, dass es mir überhaupt keinen Spaß gemacht hat
confession [kən'fɛʃən] N Geständnis *nt*; (*Rel*) Beichte *f*; **to make a ~** ein Geständnis ablegen
confessor [kən'fɛsəʳ] N Beichtvater *m*
confetti [kən'fɛtɪ] N Konfetti *nt*
confide [kən'faɪd] VI: **to ~ in** sich anvertrauen *+dat*
confidence ['kɔnfɪdns] N Vertrauen *nt*; (*self-assurance*) Selbstvertrauen *nt*; (*secret*) vertrauliche Mitteilung *f*, Geheimnis *nt*; **to have ~ in sb/sth** Vertrauen zu jdm/etw haben; **to have (every) ~ that ...** ganz zuversichtlich sein, dass ...; **motion of no ~** Misstrauensantrag *m*; **to tell sb sth in strict ~** jdm etw ganz im Vertrauen sagen; **in ~** vertraulich
confidence trick N Schwindel *m*
confident ['kɔnfɪdənt] ADJ (selbst)sicher; (*positive*) zuversichtlich
confidential [kɔnfɪ'dɛnʃəl] ADJ vertraulich; (*secretary*) Privat-
confidentiality [kɔnfɪdɛnʃɪ'ælɪtɪ] N Vertraulichkeit *f*
configuration [kənfɪgju'reɪʃən] N Anordnung *f*; (*Comput*) Konfiguration *f*
confine [kən'faɪn] VT (*shut up*) einsperren; **to ~ (to)** beschränken (auf *+acc*); **to ~ o.s. to sth** sich auf etw *acc* beschränken; **to ~ o.s. to doing sth** sich darauf beschränken, etw zu tun
confined [kən'faɪnd] ADJ begrenzt
confinement [kən'faɪnmənt] N Haft *f*
confines ['kɔnfaɪnz] NPL Grenzen *pl*; (*of situation*) Rahmen *m*
confirm [kən'fə:m] VT bestätigen; **to be confirmed** (*Rel*) konfirmiert werden
confirmation [kɔnfə'meɪʃən] N Bestätigung *f*; (*Rel*) Konfirmation *f*
confirmed [kən'fə:md] ADJ (*bachelor*) eingefleischt; (*teetotaller*) überzeugt
confiscate ['kɔnfɪskeɪt] VT beschlagnahmen, konfiszieren
confiscation [kɔnfɪs'keɪʃən] N Beschlagnahme *f*, Konfiszierung *f*
conflagration [kɔnflə'greɪʃən] N Feuersbrunst *f*
conflict N ['kɔnflɪkt] Konflikt *m*; (*fighting*) Zusammenstoß *m*, Kampf *m* ▶ VI [kən'flɪkt]: **to ~ (with)** im Widerspruch stehen (zu)
conflicting [kən'flɪktɪŋ] ADJ widersprüchlich
conform [kən'fɔ:m] VI sich anpassen; **to ~ to** entsprechen *+dat*
conformist [kən'fɔ:mɪst] N Konformist(in) *m(f)*
confound [kən'faund] VT verwirren; (*amaze*) verblüffen
confounded [kən'faundɪd] ADJ verdammt, verflixt (*inf*)
confront [kən'frʌnt] VT (*problems, task*) sich stellen *+dat*; (*enemy, danger*) gegenübertreten *+dat*
confrontation [kɔnfrən'teɪʃən] N Konfrontation *f*
confuse [kən'fju:z] VT verwirren; (*mix up*) verwechseln; (*complicate*) durcheinanderbringen
confused [kən'fju:zd] ADJ (*person*) verwirrt; (*situation*) verworren, konfus; **to get ~** konfus werden
confusing [kən'fju:zɪŋ] ADJ verwirrend
confusion [kən'fju:ʒən] N (*mix-up*) Verwechslung *f*; (*perplexity*) Verwirrung *f*; (*disorder*) Durcheinander *nt*
congeal [kən'dʒi:l] VI (*blood*) gerinnen; (*sauce, oil*) erstarren
congenial [kən'dʒi:nɪəl] ADJ ansprechend, sympathisch; (*atmosphere, place, work, company*) angenehm
congenital [kən'dʒɛnɪtl] ADJ angeboren
conger eel ['kɔngər-] N Seeaal *m*
congested [kən'dʒɛstɪd] ADJ (*road*) verstopft; (*area*) überfüllt; (*nose*) verstopft; **his lungs are ~** in seiner Lunge hat sich Blut angestaut
congestion [kən'dʒɛstʃən] N (*Med*) Blutstau *m*; (*of road*) Verstopfung *f*; (*of area*) Überfüllung *f*

congestion charge N City-Maut *f*
conglomerate [kən'glɔmərɪt] N (*Comm*) Konglomerat *nt*
conglomeration [kənglɔmə'reɪʃən] N Ansammlung *f*
Congo ['kɔŋgəu] N (*state*) Kongo *m*
congratulate [kən'grætjuleɪt] VT gratulieren; **to ~ sb (on sth)** jdm (zu etw) gratulieren
congratulations [kəngrætju'leɪʃənz] NPL Glückwunsch *m*, Glückwünsche *pl*; **~!** herzlichen Glückwunsch!; **~ on** Glückwünsche zu
congregate ['kɔŋgrɪgeɪt] VI sich versammeln
congregation [kɔŋgrɪ'geɪʃən] N Gemeinde *f*
congress ['kɔŋgrɛs] N Kongress *m*; (*US*): **C~** der Kongress

> Der **Congress** ist die nationale gesetzgebende Versammlung der USA, die in Washington im **Capitol** zusammentritt. Der Kongress besteht aus dem Repräsentantenhaus (435 Abgeordnete, entsprechend den Bevölkerungszahlen auf die einzelnen Bundesstaaten verteilt und jeweils für 2 Jahre gewählt) und dem Senat (100 Senatoren, 2 für jeden Bundesstaat, für 6 Jahre gewählt, wobei ein Drittel alle zwei Jahre neu gewählt wird). Sowohl die Abgeordneten als auch die Senatoren werden in direkter Wahl vom Volk gewählt.

congressman ['kɔŋgrɛsmən] (*US*) N (*irreg*) Kongressabgeordnete(r) *m*
congresswoman ['kɔŋgrɛswumən] (*US*) N (*irreg*) Kongressabgeordnete *f*
conical ['kɔnɪkl] ADJ kegelförmig, konisch
conifer ['kɔnɪfə^r] N Nadelbaum *m*
coniferous [kə'nɪfərəs] ADJ Nadel-
conjecture [kən'dʒɛktʃə^r] N Vermutung *f*, Mutmaßung *f* ▸ VI vermuten, mutmaßen
conjugal ['kɔndʒugl] ADJ ehelich
conjugate ['kɔndʒugeɪt] VT konjugieren
conjugation [kɔndʒə'geɪʃən] N Konjugation *f*
conjunction [kən'dʒʌŋkʃən] N Konjunktion *f*; **in ~ with** zusammen mit, in Verbindung mit
conjunctivitis [kəndʒʌŋktɪ'vaɪtɪs] N Bindehautentzündung *f*
conjure ['kʌndʒə^r] VI zaubern ▸ VT (*also fig*) hervorzaubern
▸ **conjure up** VT (*ghost, spirit*) beschwören; (*memories*) heraufbeschwören
conjurer ['kʌndʒərə^r] N Zauberer *m*, Zauberkünstler(in) *m(f)*
conjuring trick ['kʌndʒərɪŋ-] N Zaubertrick *m*, Zauberkunststück *nt*
conker ['kɔŋkə^r] (*Brit*) N (Ross)kastanie *f*
conk out [kɔŋk-] (*inf*) VI den Geist aufgeben
con man N Schwindler *m*
Conn. (*US*) ABBR (*Post*) = **Connecticut**
connect [kə'nɛkt] VT verbinden; (*Elec*) anschließen; (*Tel: caller*) verbinden; (*: subscriber*) anschließen; (*fig: associate*) in Zusammenhang bringen ▸ VI: **to ~ with** (*train, plane etc*) Anschluss haben an *+acc*; **to ~ sth to sth** etw mit einer Sache verbinden; **to be connected with** (*associated*) in einer Beziehung *or* in Verbindung stehen zu; (*have dealings with*) zu tun haben mit; **I am trying to ~ you** (*Tel*) ich versuche, Sie zu verbinden
connection [kə'nɛkʃən] N Verbindung *f*; (*Elec*) Kontakt *m*; (*train, plane etc, Tel: subscriber*) Anschluss *m*; (*fig: association*) Beziehung *f*, Zusammenhang *m*; **in ~ with** in Zusammenhang mit; **what is the ~ between them?** welche Verbindung besteht zwischen ihnen?; **business connections** Geschäftsbeziehungen *pl*; **to get/miss one's ~** seinen Anschluss erreichen/verpassen
connexion [kə'nɛkʃən] (*Brit*) N = **connection**
conning tower ['kɔnɪŋ-] N Kommandoturm *m*
connive [kə'naɪv] VI: **to ~ at** stillschweigend dulden
connoisseur [kɔnɪ'sə:^r] N Kenner(in) *m(f)*
connotation [kɔnə'teɪʃən] N Konnotation *f*
connubial [kə'nju:bɪəl] ADJ ehelich
conquer ['kɔŋkə^r] VT erobern; (*enemy, fear, feelings*) besiegen
conqueror ['kɔŋkərə^r] N Eroberer *m*
conquest ['kɔŋkwɛst] N Eroberung *f*
cons [kɔnz] NPL *see* **convenience**; **pro**
conscience ['kɔnʃəns] N Gewissen *nt*; **to have a guilty/clear ~** ein schlechtes/gutes Gewissen haben; **in all ~** allen Ernstes
conscientious [kɔnʃɪ'ɛnʃəs] ADJ gewissenhaft
conscientious objector N Wehrdienst- *or* Kriegsdienstverweigerer *m* (*aus Gewissensgründen*)
conscious ['kɔnʃəs] ADJ bewusst; (*awake*) bei Bewusstsein; **to become ~ of sth** sich *dat* einer Sache *gen* bewusst werden; **to become ~ that ...** sich *dat* bewusst werden, dass ...
consciousness ['kɔnʃəsnɪs] N Bewusstsein *nt*; **to lose ~** bewusstlos werden; **to regain ~** wieder zu sich kommen
conscript ['kɔnskrɪpt] N Wehrpflichtige(r) *m*
conscription [kən'skrɪpʃən] N Wehrpflicht *f*
consecrate ['kɔnsɪkreɪt] VT weihen
consecutive [kən'sɛkjutɪv] ADJ aufeinanderfolgend; **on three ~ occasions** dreimal hintereinander
consensus [kən'sɛnsəs] N Übereinstimmung *f*; **the ~ (of opinion)** die allgemeine Meinung
consent [kən'sɛnt] N Zustimmung *f* ▸ VI: **to ~ to** zustimmen *+dat*; **age of ~** Ehemündigkeitsalter *nt*; **by common ~** auf allgemeinen Wunsch
consenting [kən'sɛntɪŋ] ADJ: **between ~ adults** ≈ zwischen Erwachsenen
consequence ['kɔnsɪkwəns] N Folge *f*; **of ~** bedeutend, wichtig; **it's of little ~** es spielt kaum eine Rolle; **in ~** folglich
consequently ['kɔnsɪkwəntlɪ] ADV folglich
conservation [kɔnsə'veɪʃən] N Erhaltung *f*, Schutz *m*; (*of energy*) Sparen *nt*; (*also*: **nature conservation**) Umweltschutz *m*; (*of paintings, books*) Erhaltung *f*, Konservierung *f*; **energy ~** Energieeinsparung *f*
conservationist [kɔnsə'veɪʃnɪst] N Umweltschützer(in) *m(f)*

conservative [kən'sə:vətɪv] ADJ konservativ; (*cautious*) vorsichtig; (BRIT *Pol*): **C~** konservativ ▶ N (BRIT *Pol*): **C~** Konservative(r) *f(m)*
Conservative Party N: **the ~** die Konservative Partei *f*
conservatory [kən'sə:vətrɪ] N Wintergarten *m*; (*Mus*) Konservatorium *nt*
conserve [kən'sə:v] VT erhalten; (*supplies, energy*) sparen ▶ N Konfitüre *f*
consider [kən'sɪdə^r] VT (*study*) sich *dat* überlegen; (*take into account*) in Betracht ziehen; **to ~ that ...** der Meinung sein, dass ...; **to ~ sb/sth as ...** jdn/etw für ... halten; **to ~ doing sth** in Erwägung ziehen, etw zu tun; **they ~ themselves to be superior** sie halten sich für etwas Besseres; **she considered it a disaster** sie betrachtete es als eine Katastrophe; **~ yourself lucky** Sie können sich glücklich schätzen; **all things considered** alles in allem
considerable [kən'sɪdərəbl] ADJ beträchtlich
considerably [kən'sɪdərəblɪ] ADV beträchtlich; (*bigger, smaller etc*) um einiges
considerate [kən'sɪdərɪt] ADJ rücksichtsvoll
consideration [kənsɪdə'reɪʃən] N Überlegung *f*; (*factor*) Gesichtspunkt *m*, Faktor *m*; (*thoughtfulness*) Rücksicht *f*; (*reward*) Entgelt *nt*; **out of ~ for** aus Rücksicht auf *+acc*; **to be under ~** geprüft werden; **my first ~ is my family** ich denke zuerst an meine Familie
considered [kən'sɪdəd] ADJ: **~ opinion** ernsthafte Überzeugung *f*
considering [kən'sɪdərɪŋ] PREP in Anbetracht *+gen*; **~ (that)** wenn man bedenkt(, dass)
consign [kən'saɪn] VT: **to ~ to** (*object: to place*) verbannen in *+acc*; (*person: to sb's care*) anvertrauen *+dat*; (*: to poverty*) verurteilen zu; (*send*) versenden an *+acc*
consignment [kən'saɪnmənt] N Sendung *f*, Lieferung *f*
consignment note N Frachtbrief *m*
consist [kən'sɪst] VI: **to ~ of** bestehen aus
consistency [kən'sɪstənsɪ] N (*of actions etc*) Konsequenz *f*; (*of cream etc*) Konsistenz *f*, Dicke *f*
consistent [kən'sɪstənt] ADJ konsequent; (*argument, idea*) logisch, folgerichtig; **to be ~ with** entsprechen *+dat*
consolation [kɔnsə'leɪʃən] N Trost *m*
console VT [kən'səul] trösten ▶ N ['kɔnsəul] (*panel*) Schalttafel *f*
consolidate [kən'sɔlɪdeɪt] VT festigen
consols ['kɔnsɔlz] (BRIT) NPL (*Stock Exchange*) Konsols *pl*, konsolidierte Staatsanleihen *pl*
consommé [kən'sɔmeɪ] N Kraftbrühe *f*, Consommé *f*
consonant ['kɔnsənənt] N Konsonant *m*, Mitlaut *m*
consort N ['kɔnsɔ:t] Gemahl(in) *m(f)*, Gatte *m*, Gattin *f* ▶ VI [kən'sɔ:t]: **to ~ with sb** mit jdm verkehren; **prince ~** Prinzgemahl *m*
consortium [kən'sɔ:tɪəm] N Konsortium *nt*
conspicuous [kən'spɪkjuəs] ADJ auffallend; **to make o.s. ~** auffallen
conspiracy [kən'spɪrəsɪ] N Verschwörung *f*, Komplott *nt*
conspiratorial [kənspɪrə'tɔ:rɪəl] ADJ verschwörerisch
conspire [kən'spaɪə^r] VI sich verschwören; (*events*) zusammenkommen
constable ['kʌnstəbl] (BRIT) N Polizist *m*; **chief ~** Polizeipräsident *m*, Polizeichef *m*
constabulary [kən'stæbjulərɪ] (BRIT) N Polizei *f*
constant ['kɔnstənt] ADJ dauernd, ständig; (*fixed*) konstant, gleichbleibend
constantly ['kɔnstəntlɪ] ADV (an)dauernd, ständig
constellation [kɔnstə'leɪʃən] N Sternbild *nt*
consternation [kɔnstə'neɪʃən] N Bestürzung *f*
constipated ['kɔnstɪpeɪtɪd] ADJ: **to be ~** Verstopfung haben, verstopft sein
constipation [kɔnstɪ'peɪʃən] N Verstopfung *f*
constituency [kən'stɪtjuənsɪ] N (*Pol*) Wahlkreis *m*; (*electors*) Wähler *pl* (*eines Wahlkreises*)
constituency party N *Parteiorganisation in einem Wahlkreis*
constituent [kən'stɪtjuənt] N (*Pol*) Wähler(in) *m(f)*; (*component*) Bestandteil *m*
constitute ['kɔnstɪtju:t] VT (*represent*) darstellen; (*make up*) bilden, ausmachen
constitution [kɔnstɪ'tju:ʃən] N (*Pol*) Verfassung *f*; (*of club etc*) Satzung *f*; (*health*) Konstitution *f*, Gesundheit *f*; (*make-up*) Zusammensetzung *f*
constitutional [kɔnstɪ'tju:ʃənl] ADJ (*government*) verfassungsmäßig; (*reform etc*) Verfassungs-
constitutional monarchy N konstitutionelle Monarchie *f*
constrain [kən'streɪn] VT zwingen
constrained [kən'streɪnd] ADJ gezwungen
constraint [kən'streɪnt] N Beschränkung *f*, Einschränkung *f*; (*compulsion*) Zwang *m*; (*embarrassment*) Befangenheit *f*
constrict [kən'strɪkt] VT einschnüren; (*blood vessel*) verengen; (*limit, restrict*) einschränken
constriction [kən'strɪkʃən] N Einschränkung *f*; (*tightness*) Verengung *f*; (*squeezing*) Einschnürung *f*
construct [kən'strʌkt] VT bauen; (*machine*) konstruieren; (*theory, argument*) entwickeln
construction [kən'strʌkʃən] N Bau *m*; (*structure*) Konstruktion *f*; (*fig: interpretation*) Deutung *f*; **under ~** in *or* im Bau
construction industry N Bauindustrie *f*
constructive [kən'strʌktɪv] ADJ konstruktiv
construe [kən'stru:] VT auslegen, deuten
consul ['kɔnsl] N Konsul(in) *m(f)*
consulate ['kɔnsjulɪt] N Konsulat *nt*
consult [kən'sʌlt] VT (*doctor, lawyer*) konsultieren; (*friend*) sich beraten *or* besprechen mit; (*reference book*) nachschlagen in *+dat*; **to ~ sb (about sth)** jdn (wegen etw) fragen
consultancy [kən'sʌltənsɪ] N Beratungsbüro *nt or* -firma *f*; (*Med: job*) Facharztstelle *f*
consultant [kən'sʌltənt] N (*Med*) Facharzt *m*, Fachärztin *f*; (*other specialist*) Berater(in) *m(f)* ▶ CPD: **~ engineer** beratender Ingenieur *m*;

~ paediatrician Facharzt/-ärztin *m(f)* für Pädiatrie *or* Kinderheilkunde; **legal/management ~** Rechts-/Unternehmensberater *m*, Rechts-/Unternehmensberaterin *f*; **consultants** NPL Beratungsbüro *nt or* -firma *f*

consultation [kɔnsəl'teɪʃən] N (*Med, Law*) Konsultation *f*; (*discussion*) Beratung *f*, Besprechung *f*; **in ~ with** in gemeinsamer Beratung mit

consultative [kən'sʌltətɪv] ADJ beratend

consulting room [kən'sʌltɪŋ-] (BRIT) N Sprechzimmer *nt*

consume [kən'sju:m] VT (*food, drink*) zu sich nehmen, konsumieren; (*fuel, energy*) verbrauchen; (*time*) in Anspruch nehmen; (*subj: emotion*) verzehren; (*: fire*) vernichten

consumer [kən'sju:mə^r] N Verbraucher(in) *m(f)*

consumer credit N Verbraucherkredit *m*

consumer durables NPL (langlebige) Gebrauchsgüter *pl*

consumer goods NPL Konsumgüter *pl*

consumerism [kən'sju:mərɪzəm] N Verbraucherschutz *m*

consumer society N Konsumgesellschaft *f*

consumer watchdog N Verbraucherschutzorganisation *f*

consummate ['kɔnsʌmeɪt] VT (*marriage*) vollziehen; (*ambition etc*) erfüllen

consumption [kən'sʌmpʃən] N Verbrauch *m*; (*of food*) Verzehr *m*; (*of drinks, buying*) Konsum *m*; (*Med*) Schwindsucht *f*; **not fit for human ~** zum Verzehr ungeeignet

cont. ABBR (= *continued*) Forts.

contact ['kɔntækt] N Kontakt *m*; (*touch*) Berührung *f*; (*person*) Kontaktperson *f* ▶ VT sich in Verbindung setzen mit; **to be in ~ with sb/sth** mit jdm/etw in Verbindung *or* Kontakt stehen; (*touch*) jdn/etw berühren; **business contacts** Geschäftsverbindungen *pl*

contact lenses NPL Kontaktlinsen *pl*

contagious [kən'teɪdʒəs] ADJ ansteckend

contain [kən'teɪn] VT enthalten; (*growth, spread*) in Grenzen halten; (*feeling*) beherrschen; **to ~ o.s.** an sich *acc* halten

container [kən'teɪnə^r] N Behälter *m*; (*for shipping etc*) Container *m* ▶ CPD Container-

containerize [kən'teɪnəraɪz] VT in Container verpacken; (*port*) auf Container umstellen

container ship N Containerschiff *nt*

contaminate [kən'tæmɪneɪt] VT (*water, food*) verunreinigen; (*soil etc*) verseuchen

contamination [kəntæmɪ'neɪʃən] N Verunreinigung *f*; Verseuchung *f*

cont'd ABBR (= *continued*) Forts.

contemplate ['kɔntəmpleɪt] VT nachdenken über *+acc*; (*course of action*) in Erwägung ziehen; (*person, painting etc*) betrachten

contemplation [kɔntəm'pleɪʃən] N Betrachtung *f*

contemporary [kən'tɛmpərərɪ] ADJ zeitgenössisch; (*present-day*) modern ▶ N Altersgenosse *m*, Altersgenossin *f*; **Samuel Pepys and his contemporaries** Samuel Pepys und seine Zeitgenossen

contempt [kən'tɛmpt] N Verachtung *f*; **~ of court** (*Law*) Missachtung *f* (der Würde) des Gerichts, Ungebühr *f* vor Gericht; **to have ~ for sb/sth** jdn/etw verachten; **to hold sb in ~** jdn verachten

contemptible [kən'tɛmptəbl] ADJ verachtenswert

contemptuous [kən'tɛmptjuəs] ADJ verächtlich, geringschätzig

contend [kən'tɛnd] VT: **to ~ that ...** behaupten, dass ...; **to ~ with** fertig werden mit; **to ~ for** kämpfen um; **to have to ~ with** es zu tun haben mit; **he has a lot to ~ with** er hat viel um die Ohren

contender [kən'tɛndə^r] N (*Sport*) Wettkämpfer(in) *m(f)*; (*for title*) Anwärter(in) *m(f)*; (*Pol*) Kandidat(in) *m(f)*

content ADJ [kən'tɛnt] zufrieden ▶ VT [kən'tɛnt] zufriedenstellen ▶ N ['kɔntɛnt] Inhalt *m*; (*fat content, moisture content etc*) Gehalt *m*;

contents NPL Inhalt; **(table of) contents** Inhaltsverzeichnis *nt*; **to be ~ with** zufrieden sein mit; **to ~ o.s. with sth** sich mit etw zufriedengeben *or* begnügen; **to ~ o.s. with doing sth** sich damit zufriedengeben *or* begnügen, etw zu tun

contented [kən'tɛntɪd] ADJ zufrieden

contentedly [kən'tɛntɪdlɪ] ADV zufrieden

contention [kən'tɛnʃən] N Behauptung *f*; (*disagreement, argument*) Streit *m*; **bone of ~** Zankapfel *m*

contentious [kən'tɛnʃəs] ADJ strittig, umstritten

contentment [kən'tɛntmənt] N Zufriedenheit *f*

contest N ['kɔntɛst] (*competition*) Wettkampf *m*; (*for control, power etc*) Kampf *m* ▶ VT [kən'tɛst] (*election, competition*) teilnehmen an *+dat*; (*compete for*) kämpfen um; (*statement*) bestreiten; (*decision*) angreifen; (*Law*) anfechten

contestant [kən'tɛstənt] N (*in quiz*) Kandidat(in) *m(f)*; (*in competition*) Teilnehmer(in) *m(f)*; (*in fight*) Kämpfer(in) *m(f)*

context ['kɔntɛkst] N Zusammenhang *m*, Kontext *m*; **in ~** im Zusammenhang; **out of ~** aus dem Zusammenhang gerissen

continent ['kɔntɪnənt] N Kontinent *m*, Erdteil *m*; **the C~** (BRIT) (Kontinental)europa *nt*; **on the C~** in (Kontinental)europa, auf dem Kontinent

continental [kɔntɪ'nɛntl] ADJ kontinental; (*European*) europäisch ▶ N (BRIT) (Festlands)europäer(in) *m(f)*

continental breakfast N kleines Frühstück *nt*

continental quilt (BRIT) N Steppdecke *f*

contingency [kən'tɪndʒənsɪ] N möglicher Fall *m*, Eventualität *f*

contingency plan N Plan *m* für den Eventualfall

C

contingent [kən'tɪndʒənt] N Kontingent *nt* ▸ ADJ: **to be ~ upon** abhängen von
continual [kən'tɪnjuəl] ADJ ständig; (*process*) ununterbrochen
continually [kən'tɪnjuəlɪ] ADV ständig; ununterbrochen
continuation [kəntɪnju'eɪʃən] N Fortsetzung *f*; (*extension*) Weiterführung *f*
continue [kən'tɪnju:] VI weitermachen, andauern; (*performance, road*) weitergehen; (*person: talking*) fortfahren ▸ VT fortsetzen; **to ~ to do sth/doing sth** etw weiter tun; **"to be continued"** „Fortsetzung folgt"; **"continued on page 10"** „Fortsetzung auf Seite 10"
continuing education [kən'tɪnjuɪŋ-] N Erwachsenenbildung *f*
continuity [kɔntɪ'nju:ɪtɪ] N Kontinuität *f*; (*TV, Cine*) Anschluß *m* ▸ CPD (*TV*): **~ announcer** Ansager(in) *m(f)*; **~ studio** Ansagestudio *nt*
continuous [kən'tɪnjuəs] ADJ ununterbrochen; (*growth etc*) kontinuierlich; **~ form** (*Ling*) Verlaufsform *f*; **~ performance** (*Cine*) durchgehende Vorstellung *f*
continuously [kən'tɪnjuəslɪ] ADV dauernd, ständig; (*uninterruptedly*) ununterbrochen
continuous stationery N (*Comput*) Endlospapier *nt*
contort [kən'tɔ:t] VT (*body*) verrenken, verdrehen; (*face*) verziehen
contortion [kən'tɔ:ʃən] N Verrenkung *f*
contortionist [kən'tɔ:ʃənɪst] N Schlangenmensch *m*
contour ['kɔntuə[r]] N (*also:* **contour line**) Höhenlinie *f*; (*shape, outline: gen pl*) Kontur *f*, Umriss *m*
contraband ['kɔntrəbænd] N Schmuggelware *f* ▸ ADJ Schmuggel-
contraception [kɔntrə'sɛpʃən] N Empfängnisverhütung *f*
contraceptive [kɔntrə'sɛptɪv] ADJ empfängnisverhütend ▸ N Verhütungsmittel *nt*
contract N ['kɔntrækt] Vertrag *m* ▸ VI schrumpfen; (*metal, muscle*) sich zusammenziehen ▸ VT [kən'trækt] (*illness*) erkranken an *+dat* ▸ CPD vertraglich festgelegt; (*work*) Auftrags-; **~ of employment/service** Arbeitsvertrag *m*; **to ~ to do sth** (*Comm*) sich vertraglich verpflichten, etw zu tun
▸ **contract in** (*BRIT*) VI beitreten
▸ **contract out** (*BRIT*) VI austreten
contraction [kən'trækʃən] N Zusammenziehen *nt*; (*Ling*) Kontraktion *f*; (*Med*) Wehe *f*
contractor [kən'træktə[r]] N Auftragnehmer *m*; (*also:* **building contractor**) Bauunternehmer *m*
contractual [kən'træktʃuəl] ADJ vertraglich
contradict [kɔntrə'dɪkt] VT widersprechen *+dat*
contradiction [kɔntrə'dɪkʃən] N Widerspruch *m*; **to be in ~ with** im Widerspruch stehen zu; **a ~ in terms** ein Widerspruch in sich
contradictory [kɔntrə'dɪktərɪ] ADJ widersprüchlich
contralto [kən'træltəu] N (*Mus*) Altistin *f*; (*: voice*) Alt *m*
contraption [kən'træpʃən] (*pej*) N (*device*) Vorrichtung *f*; (*machine*) Gerät *nt*, Apparat *m*
contrary[1] ['kɔntrərɪ] ADJ entgegengesetzt; (*ideas, opinions*) gegensätzlich; (*unfavourable*) widrig ▸ N Gegenteil *nt*; **~ to what we thought** im Gegensatz zu dem, was wir dachten; **on the ~** im Gegenteil; **unless you hear to the ~** sofern Sie nichts Gegenteiliges hören
contrary[2] [kən'trɛərɪ] ADJ widerspenstig
contrast N ['kɔntrɑ:st] Gegensatz *m*, Kontrast *m* ▸ VT [kən'trɑ:st] vergleichen, gegenüberstellen; **in ~ to** *or* **with** im Gegensatz zu
contrasting [kən'trɑ:stɪŋ] ADJ (*colours*) kontrastierend; (*attitudes*) gegensätzlich
contravene [kɔntrə'vi:n] VT verstoßen gegen
contravention [kɔntrə'vɛnʃən] N Verstoß *m*; **to be in ~ of sth** gegen etw verstoßen
contribute [kən'trɪbju:t] VI beitragen ▸ VT: **to ~ £10/an article to** £10/einen Artikel beisteuern zu; **to ~ to** (*charity*) spenden für; (*newspaper*) schreiben für; (*discussion, problem etc*) beitragen zu
contribution [kɔntrɪ'bju:ʃən] N Beitrag *m*; (*donation*) Spende *f*
contributor [kən'trɪbjutə[r]] N (*to appeal*) Spender(in) *m(f)*; (*to newspaper*) Mitarbeiter(in) *m(f)*
contributory [kən'trɪbjutərɪ] ADJ: **a ~ cause** ein Faktor, der mit eine Rolle spielt; **it was a ~ factor in ...** es trug zu ... bei
contributory pension scheme (*BRIT*) N beitragspflichtige Rentenversicherung *f*
contrite ['kɔntraɪt] ADJ zerknirscht
contrivance [kən'traɪvəns] N (*scheme*) List *f*; (*device*) Vorrichtung *f*
contrive [kən'traɪv] VT (*meeting*) arrangieren ▸ VI: **to ~ to do sth** es fertigbringen, etw zu tun
control [kən'trəul] VT (*country*) regieren; (*organization*) leiten; (*machinery, process*) steuern; (*wages, prices*) kontrollieren; (*temper*) zügeln; (*disease, fire*) unter Kontrolle bringen ▸ N (*of country*) Kontrolle *f*; (*of organization*) Leitung *f*; (*of oneself, emotions*) Beherrschung *f*; (*Sci: also:* **control group**) Kontrollgruppe *f*; **controls** NPL (*of vehicle*) Steuerung *f*; (*on radio, television etc*) Bedienungsfeld *nt*; (*governmental*) Kontrolle *f*; **to ~ o.s.** sich beherrschen; **to take ~ of** die Kontrolle übernehmen über *+acc*; (*Comm*) übernehmen; **to be in ~ of** unter Kontrolle haben; (*in charge of*) unter sich *dat* haben; **out of/under ~** außer/unter Kontrolle; **everything is under ~** ich habe/wir haben *etc* die Sache im Griff (*inf*); **the car went out of ~** der Fahrer verlor die Kontrolle über den Wagen; **circumstances beyond our ~** unvorhersehbare Umstände
control key N (*Comput*) Controltaste *f*, Steuerungstaste *f*
controlled substance [kən'trəuld-] N veschreibungspflichtiges Medikament
controller [kən'trəulə[r]] N (*Radio, TV*) Intendant(in) *m(f)*

controlling interest [kən'trəulɪŋ-] N Mehrheitsanteil *m*
control panel N Schalttafel *f*; (*on television*) Bedienungsfeld *nt*
control point N Kontrollpunkt *m*, Kontrollstelle *f*
control room N (*Naut*) Kommandoraum *m*; (*Mil*) (Operations)zentrale *f*; (*Radio, TV*) Regieraum *m*
control tower N Kontrollturm *m*
control unit N (*Comput*) Steuereinheit *f*
controversial [kɔntrə'vəːʃl] ADJ umstritten, kontrovers
controversy ['kɔntrəvəːsɪ] N Streit *m*, Kontroverse *f*
conurbation [kɔnə'beɪʃən] N Ballungsgebiet *nt*, Ballungsraum *m*
convalesce [kɔnvə'lɛs] VI genesen
convalescence [kɔnvə'lɛsns] N Genesungszeit *f*
convalescent [kɔnvə'lɛsnt] ADJ (*leave etc*) Genesungs-, Kur- ▶ N Genesende(r) *f*(*m*)
convector [kən'vɛktəʳ] N Heizlüfter *m*
convene [kən'viːn] VT einberufen ▶ VI zusammentreten
convener [kən'viːnəʳ] N (*organizer*) Organisator(in) *m*(*f*); (*chairperson*) Vorsitzende(r) *f*(*m*)
convenience [kən'viːnɪəns] N Annehmlichkeit *f*; (*suitability*): **the ~ of this arrangement/location** diese günstige Vereinbarung/Lage; **I like the ~ of having a shower** mir gefällt, wie angenehm es ist, eine Dusche zu haben; **I like the ~ of living in the city** mir gefällt, wie praktisch es ist, in der Stadt zu wohnen; **at your ~** wann es Ihnen passt; **at your earliest ~** möglichst bald, baldmöglichst; **with all modern conveniences, with all mod cons** (BRIT) mit allem modernen Komfort; *see also* **public convenience**
convenience foods NPL Fertiggerichte *pl*
convenient [kən'viːnɪənt] ADJ günstig; (*handy*) praktisch; (*house etc*) günstig gelegen; **if it is ~ to you** wenn es Ihnen (so) passt, wenn es Ihnen keine Umstände macht
conveniently [kən'viːnɪəntlɪ] ADV (*happen*) günstigerweise; (*situated*) günstig
convenor [kən'viːnəʳ] N = **convener**
convent ['kɔnvənt] N Kloster *nt*
convention [kən'vɛnʃən] N Konvention *f*; (*conference*) Tagung *f*, Konferenz *f*; (*agreement*) Abkommen *nt*
conventional [kən'vɛnʃənl] ADJ konventionell
convent school N Klosterschule *f*
converge [kən'vəːdʒ] VI (*roads*) zusammenlaufen ▶ VI sich einander annähern; **to ~ on sb/a place** (*people*) von überallher zu jdm/an einen Ort strömen
conversant [kən'vəːsnt] ADJ: **to be ~ with** vertraut sein mit
conversation [kɔnvə'seɪʃən] N Gespräch *nt*, Unterhaltung *f*
conversational [kɔnvə'seɪʃənl] ADJ (*tone, style*) Unterhaltungs-; (*language*) gesprochen; **~ mode** (*Comput*) Dialogbetrieb *m*
conversationalist [kɔnvə'seɪʃnəlɪst] N Unterhalter(in) *m*(*f*), Gesprächspartner(in) *m*(*f*)
converse N ['kɔnvəːs] Gegenteil *nt* ▶ VI [kən'vəːs]: **to ~ (with sb) (about sth)** sich (mit jdm) (über etw) unterhalten
conversely [kɔn'vəːslɪ] ADV umgekehrt
conversion [kən'vəːʃən] N Umwandlung *f*; (*of weights etc*) Umrechnung *f*; (*Rel*) Bekehrung *f*; (BRIT: *of house*) Umbau *m*
conversion table N Umrechnungstabelle *f*
convert VT [kən'vəːt] umwandeln; (*person*) bekehren; (*building*) umbauen; (*vehicle*) umrüsten; (*Comm*) konvertieren; (*Rugby*) verwandeln ▶ N ['kɔnvəːt] Bekehrte(r) *f*(*m*)
convertible [kən'vəːtəbl] ADJ (*currency*) konvertierbar ▶ N (*Aut*) Kabriolett *nt*
convex ['kɔnvɛks] ADJ konvex
convey [kən'veɪ] VT (*information etc*) vermitteln; (*cargo, traveller*) befördern; (*thanks*) übermitteln
conveyance [kən'veɪəns] N Beförderung *f*, Spedition *f*; (*vehicle*) Gefährt *nt*
conveyancing [kən'veɪənsɪŋ] N (Eigentums)übertragung *f*
conveyor belt N Fließband *nt*
convict [*vt* kən'vɪkt, *n* 'kɔnvɪkt] VT verurteilen ▶ N Sträfling *m*
conviction [kən'vɪkʃən] N Überzeugung *f*; (*Law*) Verurteilung *f*
convince [kən'vɪns] VT überzeugen; **to ~ sb (of sth)** jdn (von etw) überzeugen; **to ~ sb that …** jdn davon überzeugen, dass …
convinced [kən'vɪnst] ADJ: **~ (of)** überzeugt (von); **~ that …** überzeugt davon, dass …
convincing [kən'vɪnsɪŋ] ADJ überzeugend
convincingly [kən'vɪnsɪŋlɪ] ADV überzeugend
convivial [kən'vɪvɪəl] ADJ freundlich; (*event*) gesellig
convoluted ['kɔnvəluːtɪd] ADJ verwickelt, kompliziert; (*shape*) gewunden
convoy ['kɔnvɔɪ] N Konvoi *m*
convulse [kən'vʌls] VT: **to be convulsed with laughter/pain** sich vor Lachen schütteln/Schmerzen krümmen
convulsion [kən'vʌlʃən] N Schüttelkrampf *m*
coo [kuː] VI gurren
cook [kuk] VT kochen, zubereiten ▶ VI (*person, food*) kochen; (*fry, roast*) braten; (*pie*) backen ▶ N Koch *m*, Köchin *f*
▶ **cook up** (*inf*) VT sich *dat* einfallen lassen, zurechtbasteln
cookbook ['kukbuk] N Kochbuch *nt*
cook-chill ['kuktʃɪl] ADJ durch rasches Kühlen haltbar gemacht
cooker ['kukəʳ] N Herd *m*
cookery ['kukərɪ] N Kochen *nt*, Kochkunst *f*
cookery book (BRIT) N = **cookbook**
cookie ['kukɪ] (*US*) N Keks *m or nt*, Plätzchen *nt*; (*Comput*) Cookie *nt*
cooking ['kukɪŋ] N Kochen *nt*; (*food*) Essen *nt* ▶ CPD Koch-; (*chocolate*) Block-
cookout ['kukaut] (*US*) N ≈ Grillparty *f*
cool [kuːl] ADJ kühl; (*dress, clothes*) leicht, luftig; (*person: calm*) besonnen; (*: unfriendly*) kühl ▶ VT

kühlen ▶ VI abkühlen; **it's ~** es ist kühl; **to keep sth ~** *or* **in a ~ place** etw kühl aufbewahren; **to keep one's ~** die Ruhe bewahren
▶ **cool down** VI abkühlen; (*fig*) sich beruhigen
coolant ['ku:lənt] N Kühlflüssigkeit *f*
cool box N Kühlbox *f*
cooler ['ku:ləʳ] (*US*) N = **cool box**
cooling ['ku:lɪŋ] ADJ (*drink, shower*) kühlend; (*feeling, emotion*) abkühlend
cooling tower N Kühlturm *m*
coolly ['ku:lɪ] ADV (*calmly*) besonnen, ruhig; (*in unfriendly way*) kühl
coolness ['ku:lnɪs] N Kühle *f*; Leichtigkeit *f*, Luftigkeit *f*; Besonnenheit *f*
coop [ku:p] N (*for rabbits*) Kaninchenstall *m*; (*for poultry*) Hühnerstall *m* ▶ VT: **to ~ up** (*fig*) einsperren
co-op ['kəuɔp] N ABBR (= *cooperative (society)*) Genossenschaft *f*
cooperate [kəu'ɔpəreɪt] VI zusammenarbeiten; (*assist*) mitmachen, kooperieren; **to ~ with sb** mit jdm zusammenarbeiten
cooperation [kəuɔpə'reɪʃən] N Zusammenarbeit *f*; Mitarbeit *f*, Kooperation *f*
cooperative [kəu'ɔpərətɪv] ADJ (*farm, business*) auf Genossenschaftsbasis; (*person*) kooperativ; (: *helpful*) hilfsbereit ▶ N Genossenschaft *f*, Kooperative *f*
coopt [kəu'ɔpt] VT: **to ~ sb onto a committee** jdn in ein Komitee hinzuwählen *or* kooptieren
coordinate VT [kəu'ɔ:dɪneɪt] koordinieren ▶ N [kəu'ɔ:dɪnɪt] (*Math*) Koordinate *f*; **coordinates** NPL (*clothes*) Kleidung *f* zum Kombinieren
coordination [kəuɔ:dɪ'neɪʃən] N Koordinierung *f*, Koordination *f*
co-ownership [kəu'əunəʃɪp] N Mitbesitz *m*
cop [kɔp] (*inf*) N Polizist(in) *m(f)*, Bulle *m* (*pej*)
cope [kəup] VI zurechtkommen; **to ~ with** fertig werden mit
Copenhagen ['kəupn'heɪgən] N Kopenhagen *nt*
copier ['kɔpɪəʳ] N (*also*: **photocopier**) Kopiergerät *nt*, Kopierer *m*
copilot ['kəupaɪlət] N Kopilot(in) *m(f)*
copious ['kəupɪəs] ADJ reichlich
copper ['kɔpəʳ] N Kupfer *nt*; (BRIT *inf*) Polizist(in) *m(f)*, Bulle *m* (*pej*); **coppers** NPL (*small change, coins*) Kleingeld *nt*
coppice ['kɔpɪs] N Wäldchen *nt*
copse [kɔps] N = **coppice**
copulate ['kɔpjuleɪt] VI kopulieren
copy ['kɔpɪ] N Kopie *f*; (*of book, record, newspaper*) Exemplar *nt*; (*for printing*) Artikel *m* ▶ VT (*person*) nachahmen; (*idea etc*) nachmachen; (*something written*) abschreiben; **this murder story will make good ~** (*Press*) aus diesem Mord kann man etwas machen
▶ **copy out** VT abschreiben
copycat ['kɔpɪkæt] (*pej*) N Nachahmer(in) *m(f)*
copyright ['kɔpɪraɪt] N Copyright *nt*, Urheberrecht *nt*; **~ reserved** urheberrechtlich geschützt
copy typist N Schreibkraft *f* (*die mit Textvorlagen arbeitet*)
copywriter ['kɔpɪraɪtəʳ] N Werbetexter(in) *m(f)*
coral ['kɔrəl] N Koralle *f*
coral reef N Korallenriff *nt*
Coral Sea N: **the ~** das Korallenmeer
cord [kɔ:d] N Schnur *f*; (*string*) Kordel *f*; (*Elec*) Kabel *nt*, Schnur *f*; (*fabric*) Cord(samt) *m*; **cords** NPL (*trousers*) Cordhosen *pl*
cordial ['kɔ:dɪəl] ADJ herzlich ▶ N (BRIT) Fruchtsaftkonzentrat *nt*
cordless ['kɔ:dlɪs] ADJ schnurlos
cordon ['kɔ:dn] N Kordon *m*, Absperrkette *f*
▶ **cordon off** VT (*area*) absperren, abriegeln; (*crowd*) mit einer Absperrkette zurückhalten
corduroy ['kɔ:dərɔɪ] N Cord(samt) *m*
CORE [kɔ:ʳ] (*US*) N ABBR (= *Congress of Racial Equality*) *Ausschuss für Rassengleichheit*
core [kɔ:ʳ] N Kern *m*; (*of fruit*) Kerngehäuse *nt* ▶ VT das Kerngehäuse ausschneiden aus; **rotten to the ~** durch und durch schlecht
core (business) activity N (*Econ*) Kerngeschäft *nt*
Corfu [kɔ:'fu:] N Korfu *nt*
coriander [kɔrɪ'ændəʳ] N Koriander *m*
cork [kɔ:k] N (*stopper*) Korken *m*; (*substance*) Kork *m*
corkage ['kɔ:kɪdʒ] N Korkengeld *nt*
corked [kɔ:kt] ADJ: **the wine is ~** der Wein schmeckt nach Kork
corkscrew ['kɔ:kskru:] N Korkenzieher *m*
corky ['kɔ:kɪ] (*US*) ADJ = **corked**
corm [kɔ:m] N Knolle *f*
cormorant ['kɔ:mərnt] N Kormoran *m*
corn [kɔ:n] N (BRIT) Getreide *nt*, Korn *nt*; (*US*) Mais *m*; (*on foot*) Hühnerauge *nt*; **~ on the cob** Maiskolben *m*
cornea ['kɔ:nɪə] N Hornhaut *f*
corned beef ['kɔ:nd-] N Corned Beef *nt*
corner ['kɔ:nəʳ] N Ecke *f*; (*bend*) Kurve *f* ▶ VT in die Enge treiben; (*Comm*: *market*) monopolisieren ▶ VI (*in car*) die Kurve nehmen; **to cut corners** (*fig*) das Verfahren abkürzen
corner flag N Eckfahne *f*
corner kick N Eckball *m*
cornerstone ['kɔ:nəstəun] N (*fig*) Grundstein *m*, Eckstein *m*
cornet ['kɔ:nɪt] N (*Mus*) Kornett *nt*; (BRIT: *for ice cream*) Eistüte *f*
cornflakes ['kɔ:nfleɪks] NPL Cornflakes *pl*
cornflour ['kɔ:nflauəʳ] (BRIT) N Stärkemehl *nt*
cornice ['kɔ:nɪs] N (Ge)sims *nt*
Cornish ['kɔ:nɪʃ] ADJ kornisch, aus Cornwall
corn oil N (Mais)keimöl *nt*
cornstarch ['kɔ:nstɑ:tʃ] (*US*) N = **cornflour**
cornucopia [kɔ:nju'kəupɪə] N Fülle *f*
Cornwall ['kɔ:nwəl] N Cornwall *nt*
corny ['kɔ:nɪ] (*inf*) ADJ (*joke*) blöd
corollary [kə'rɔlərɪ] N (logische) Folge *f*
coronary ['kɔrənərɪ] N (*also*: **coronary thrombosis**) Herzinfarkt *m*
coronation [kɔrə'neɪʃən] N Krönung *f*

coroner ['kɔrənəʳ] N *Beamter, der Todesfälle untersucht, die nicht eindeutig eine natürliche Ursache haben*
coronet ['kɔrənɪt] N Krone *f*
Corp. ABBR = **corporation**; (*Mil*) = **corporal**
corporal ['kɔ:pərl] N Stabsunteroffizier *m*
corporal punishment N Prügelstrafe *f*
corporate ['kɔ:pərɪt] ADJ (*organization*) körperschaftlich; (*action, effort, ownership*) gemeinschaftlich; (*finance*) Unternehmens-; (*image, identity*) Firmen-
corporate hospitality N *Empfänge, Diners etc auf Kosten der ausrichtenden Firma*
corporation [kɔ:pə'reɪʃən] N (*Comm*) Körperschaft *f*; (*of town*) Gemeinde *f*, Stadt *f*
corporation tax N Körperschaftssteuer *f*
corps [kɔ:ʳ] (*pl* ~) N Korps *nt*; **the press** ~ die Presse
corpse [kɔ:ps] N Leiche *f*
corpuscle ['kɔ:pʌsl] N Blutkörperchen *nt*
corral [kə'rɑ:l] N Korral *m*
correct [kə'rɛkt] ADJ richtig; (*proper*) korrekt ▸ VT korrigieren; (*mistake*) berichtigen, verbessern; **you are** ~ Sie haben recht
correction [kə'rɛkʃən] N Korrektur *f*; Berichtigung *f*, Verbesserung *f*
correctly [kə'rɛktlɪ] ADV richtig; korrekt
correlate ['kɔrɪleɪt] VT zueinander in Beziehung setzen ▸ VI: **to ~ with** in einer Beziehung stehen zu
correlation [kɔrɪ'leɪʃən] N Beziehung *f*, Zusammenhang *m*
correspond [kɔrɪs'pɔnd] VI: **to ~ (with)** (*write*) korrespondieren (mit); (*be in accordance*) übereinstimmen (mit); **to ~ to** (*be equivalent*) entsprechen +*dat*
correspondence [kɔrɪs'pɔndəns] N Korrespondenz *f*, Briefwechsel *m*; (*relationship*) Beziehung *f*
correspondence column N Leserbriefspalte *f*
correspondence course N Fernkurs *m*
correspondent [kɔrɪs'pɔndənt] N Korrespondent(in) *m(f)*
corresponding [kɔrɪs'pɔndɪŋ] ADJ entsprechend
corridor ['kɔrɪdɔ:ʳ] N Korridor *m*; (*in train*) Gang *m*
corroborate [kə'rɔbəreɪt] VT bestätigen
corrode [kə'rəud] VT zerfressen ▸ VI korrodieren
corrosion [kə'rəuʒən] N Korrosion *f*
corrosive [kə'rəuzɪv] ADJ korrosiv
corrugated ['kɔrəgeɪtɪd] ADJ (*roof*) gewellt; (*cardboard*) Well-
corrugated iron N Wellblech *nt*
corrupt [kə'rʌpt] ADJ korrupt; (*depraved*) verdorben ▸ VT korrumpieren; (*morally*) verderben; **~ practices** Korruption *f*
corruption [kə'rʌpʃən] N Korruption *f*
corset ['kɔ:sɪt] N Korsett *nt*; (*Med*) Stützkorsett *nt*
Corsica ['kɔ:sɪkə] N Korsika *nt*
Corsican ['kɔ:sɪkən] ADJ korsisch ▸ N Korse *m*, Korsin *f*
cortège [kɔ:'teɪʒ] N (*also*: **funeral cortège**) Leichenzug *m*
cortisone ['kɔ:tɪzəun] N Kortison *nt*
coruscating ['kɔrəskeɪtɪŋ] ADJ sprühend
cosh [kɔʃ] (BRIT) N Totschläger *m*
cosignatory ['kəu'sɪgnətərɪ] N Mitunterzeichner(in) *m(f)*
cosiness ['kəuzɪnɪs] N Gemütlichkeit *f*, Behaglichkeit *f*
cos lettuce ['kɔs-] N römischer Salat *m*
cosmetic [kɔz'mɛtɪk] N Kosmetikum *nt* ▸ ADJ kosmetisch; **~ surgery** (*Med*) kosmetische Chirurgie *f*
cosmic ['kɔzmɪk] ADJ kosmisch
cosmonaut ['kɔzmənɔ:t] N Kosmonaut(in) *m(f)*
cosmopolitan [kɔzmə'pɔlɪtn] ADJ kosmopolitisch
cosmos ['kɔzmɔs] N: **the ~** der Kosmos
cosset ['kɔsɪt] VT verwöhnen
cost [kɔst] (*pt, pp* ~) N Kosten *pl*; (*fig: loss, damage etc*) Preis *m* ▸ VT kosten; (*pt, pp* **costed**: *find out cost of*) veranschlagen; **costs** NPL (*Comm, Law*) Kosten *pl*; **the ~ of living** die Lebenshaltungskosten *pl*; **at all costs** um jeden Preis; **how much does it ~?** wie viel *or* was kostet es?; **it costs £5/too much** es kostet £5/ist zu teuer; **what will it ~ to have it repaired?** wie viel kostet die Reparatur?; **to ~ sb time/effort** jdn Zeit/Mühe kosten; **it ~ him his life/job** es kostete ihn das Leben/seine Stelle
cost accountant N Kostenbuchhalter(in) *m(f)*
co-star ['kəustɑ:ʳ] N einer der Hauptdarsteller *m*, eine der Hauptdarstellerinnen *f*; **she was Sean Connery's ~ in ...** sie spielte neben Sean Connery in ...
Costa Rica ['kɔstə'ri:kə] N Costa Rica *nt*
cost centre N Kostenstelle *f*
cost control N Kostenkontrolle *f*
cost-effective ['kɔstɪ'fɛktɪv] ADJ rentabel; (*Comm*) kostengünstig
cost-effectiveness ['kɔstɪ'fɛktɪvnɪs] N Rentabilität *f*
costing ['kɔstɪŋ] N Kalkulation *f*
costly ['kɔstlɪ] ADJ teuer, kostspielig; (*in time, effort*) aufwendig
cost-of-living ['kɔstəv'lɪvɪŋ] ADJ Lebenshaltungskosten-; (*index*) Lebenshaltungs-
cost price (BRIT) N Selbstkostenpreis *m*; **to sell/buy at ~** zum Selbstkostenpreis verkaufen/kaufen
costume ['kɔstju:m] N Kostüm *nt*; (BRIT: *also*: **swimming costume**) Badeanzug *m*
costume jewellery N Modeschmuck *m*
cosy, (US) **cozy** ['kəuzɪ] ADJ gemütlich, behaglich; (*bed, scarf, gloves*) warm; (*chat, evening*) gemütlich; **I'm very ~ here** ich fühle mich hier sehr wohl, ich finde es hier sehr gemütlich
cot [kɔt] N (BRIT) Kinderbett *nt*; (*US*: *campbed*) Feldbett *nt*
cot death N Krippentod *m*, plötzlicher Kindstod *m*

Cotswolds ['kɔtswəuldz] NPL: **the ~** die Cotswolds *pl*
cottage ['kɔtɪdʒ] N Cottage *nt*, Häuschen *nt*
cottage cheese N Hüttenkäse *m*
cottage industry N Heimindustrie *f*
cottage pie N *Hackfleisch mit Kartoffelbrei überbacken*
cotton ['kɔtn] N (*fabric*) Baumwollstoff *m*; (*plant*) Baumwollstrauch *m*; (*thread*) (Baumwoll)garn *nt* ▸ CPD (*dress etc*) Baumwoll-
▸ **cotton on** (*inf*) VI: **to ~ on** es kapieren *or* schnallen; **to ~ on to sth** etw kapieren *or* schnallen
cotton candy (US) N Zuckerwatte *f*
cotton wool (BRIT) N Watte *f*
couch [kautʃ] N Couch *f* ▸ VT formulieren
couchette [ku:'ʃɛt] N Liegewagen(platz) *m*
couch potato (*esp US inf*) N Dauerglotzer(in) *m(f)*
cough [kɔf] VI husten; (*engine*) stottern ▸ N Husten *m*
cough drop N Hustenpastille *f*
cough mixture N Hustensaft *m*
cough sweet N = **cough drop**
cough syrup N = **cough mixture**
could [kud] PT *of* **can²**
couldn't ['kudnt] = **could not**
council ['kaunsl] N Rat *m*; **city/town ~** Stadtrat *m*; **C~ of Europe** Europarat *m*
council estate (BRIT) N Siedlung *f* mit Sozialwohnungen
council house (BRIT) N Sozialwohnung *f*
council housing N sozialer Wohnungsbau *m*; (*accommodation*) Sozialwohnungen *pl*
councillor ['kaunslə^r] N Stadtrat *m*, Stadträtin *f*
council tax (BRIT) N Gemeindesteuer *f*
counsel ['kaunsl] N Rat(schlag) *m*; (*lawyer*) Rechtsanwalt *m*, Rechtsanwältin *f* ▸ VT beraten; **to ~ sth** etw raten *or* empfehlen; **to ~ sb to do sth** jdm raten *or* empfehlen, etw zu tun; **~ for the defence** Verteidiger(in) *m(f)*; **~ for the prosecution** Vertreter(in) *m(f)* der Anklage
counsellor ['kaunslə^r] N Berater(in) *m(f)*; (*US: lawyer*) Rechtsanwalt *m*, Rechtsanwältin *f*
count [kaunt] VT zählen; (*include*) mitrechnen, mitzählen ▸ VI zählen; (*be considered*) betrachtet *or* angesehen werden ▸ N Zählung *f*; (*level*) Zahl *f*; (*nobleman*) Graf *m*; **to ~ (up) to 10** bis 10 zählen; **not counting the children** die Kinder nicht mitgerechnet; **10 counting him** 10, wenn man ihn mitrechnet; **to ~ the cost of sth** die Folgen von etw abschätzen; **it counts for very little** es zählt nicht viel; **~ yourself lucky** Sie können sich glücklich schätzen; **to keep ~ of sth** die Übersicht über etw *acc* behalten; **blood ~** Blutbild *nt*; **cholesterol/alcohol ~** Cholesterin-/Alkoholspiegel *m*
▸ **count on** VT FUS rechnen mit; (*depend on*) sich verlassen auf *+acc*; **to ~ on doing sth** die feste Absicht haben, etw zu tun
▸ **count up** VT zusammenzählen, zusammenrechnen
countdown ['kauntdaun] N Countdown *m*
countenance ['kauntɪnəns] N Gesicht *nt* ▸ VT gutheißen
counter ['kauntə^r] N (*in shop*) Ladentisch *m*; (*in café*) Theke *f*; (*in bank, post office*) Schalter *m*; (*in game*) Spielmarke *f*; (*Tech*) Zähler *m* ▸ VT (*oppose: sth said, sth done*) begegnen *+dat*; (*blow*) kontern ▸ ADV: **~ to** gegen *+acc*; **to buy sth under the ~** (*fig*) etw unter dem Ladentisch bekommen; **to ~ sth with sth** auf etw *acc* mit etw antworten; **to ~ sth by doing sth** einer Sache damit begegnen, dass man etw tut
counteract ['kauntər'ækt] VT entgegenwirken *+dat*; (*effect*) neutralisieren
counterattack ['kauntərə'tæk] N Gegenangriff *m* ▸ VI einen Gegenangriff starten
counterbalance ['kauntə'bæləns] VT Gegengewicht *nt*
counterclockwise ['kauntə'klɔkwaɪz] ADV gegen den Uhrzeigersinn
counterespionage ['kauntər'ɛspɪənɑ:ʒ] N Gegenspionage *f*, Spionageabwehr *f*
counterfeit ['kauntəfɪt] N Fälschung *f* ▸ VT fälschen ▸ ADJ (*coin*) Falsch-
counterfoil ['kauntəfɔɪl] N Kontrollabschnitt *m*
counterintelligence ['kauntərɪn'tɛlɪdʒəns] N Gegenspionage *f*, Spionageabwehr *f*
countermand ['kauntəmɑ:nd] VT aufheben, widerrufen
countermeasure ['kauntəmɛʒə^r] N Gegenmaßnahme *f*
counteroffensive ['kauntərə'fɛnsɪv] N Gegenoffensive *f*
counterpane ['kauntəpeɪn] N Tagesdecke *f*
counterpart ['kauntəpɑ:t] N Gegenüber *nt*; (*of document etc*) Gegenstück *nt*, Pendant *nt*
counterproductive ['kauntəprə'dʌktɪv] ADJ widersinnig
counterproposal ['kauntəprə'pəuzl] N Gegenvorschlag *m*
countersign ['kauntəsaɪn] VT gegenzeichnen
countersink ['kauntəsɪŋk] VT senken
counterterrorism [kauntə'tɛrərɪzəm] N Terrorismusbekämpfung *f*
countess ['kauntɪs] N Gräfin *f*
countless ['kauntlɪs] ADJ unzählig, zahllos
countrified ['kʌntrɪfaɪd] ADJ ländlich
country ['kʌntrɪ] N Land *nt*; (*native land*) Heimatland *nt*; **in the ~** auf dem Land; **mountainous ~** gebirgige Landschaft *f*
country and western, country and western music N Country-und-Western-Musik *f*
country dancing (BRIT) N Volkstanz *m*
country house N Landhaus *nt*
countryman ['kʌntrɪmən] N (*irreg*) (*compatriot*) Landsmann *m*; (*country dweller*) Landmann *m*
countryside ['kʌntrɪsaɪd] N Land *nt*; (*scenery*) Landschaft *f*, Gegend *f*
country-wide ['kʌntrɪ'waɪd] ADJ, ADV landesweit
county ['kauntɪ] N (BRIT) Grafschaft *f*; (US) (Verwaltungs)bezirk *m*
county council (BRIT) N Gemeinderat *m* (*einer Grafschaft*)

county town (BRIT) N *Hauptstadt einer Grafschaft*
coup [ku:] (*pl* **coups**) N (*also*: **coup d'état**) Staatsstreich *m*, Coup d'Etat *m*; (*achievement*) Coup *m*
coupé [ku:'peɪ] N Coupé *nt*
couple ['kʌpl] N Paar *nt*; (*also*: **married couple**) Ehepaar *nt* ▶ VT verbinden; (*vehicles*) koppeln; **a ~ of** (*two*) zwei; (*a few*) ein paar
couplet ['kʌplɪt] N Verspaar *nt*
coupling ['kʌplɪŋ] N Kupplung *f*
coupon ['ku:pɔn] N Gutschein *m*; (*detachable form*) Abschnitt *m*; (*Comm*) Coupon *m*
courage ['kʌrɪdʒ] N Mut *m*
courageous [kə'reɪdʒəs] ADJ mutig
courgette [kuə'ʒɛt] (BRIT) N Zucchino *m*
courier ['kurɪə^r] N (*messenger*) Kurier(in) *m(f)*; (*for tourists*) Reiseleiter(in) *m(f)*
course [kɔ:s] N (*Scol*) Kurs(us) *m*; (*of ship*) Kurs *m*; (*of life, events, time etc, of river*) Lauf *m*; (*of argument*) Richtung *f*; (*part of meal*) Gang *m*; (*for golf*) Platz *m*; **of ~** natürlich; **of ~!** (aber) natürlich!, (aber) selbstverständlich!; **(no) of ~ not!** natürlich nicht!; **in the ~ of the next few days** während *or* im Laufe der nächsten paar Tage; **in due ~** zu gegebener Zeit; **~ (of action)** Vorgehensweise *f*; **the best ~ would be to ...** das Beste wäre es, zu ...; **we have no other ~ but to ...** es bleibt uns nichts anderes übrig, als zu ...; **~ of lectures** Vorlesungsreihe *f*; **~ of treatment** (*Med*) Behandlung *f*; **first/last ~** erster/letzter Gang, Vor-/Nachspeise *f*
court [kɔ:t] N Hof *m*; (*Law*) Gericht *nt*; (*for tennis, badminton etc*) Platz *m* ▶ VT den Hof machen *+dat*; (*favour, popularity*) werben um; (*death, disaster*) herausfordern; **out of ~** (*Law*) außergerichtlich; **to take to ~** (*Law*) verklagen, vor Gericht bringen
courteous ['kə:tɪəs] ADJ höflich
courtesan [kɔ:tɪ'zæn] N Kurtisane *f*
courtesy ['kə:təsɪ] N Höflichkeit *f*; **(by) ~ of** freundlicherweise zur Verfügung gestellt von
courtesy bus, courtesy coach N gebührenfreier Bus *m*
courtesy light N Innenleuchte *f*
court fine N Ordnungsgeld *nt*; **to issue/face a ~** ein Ordnungsgeld verhängen/zu zahlen haben
courthouse ['kɔ:thaus] (US) N Gerichtsgebäude *nt*
courtier ['kɔ:tɪə^r] N Höfling *m*
court martial (*pl* **courts martial**) N Militärgericht *nt*
court of appeal (*pl* **courts of appeal**) N Berufungsgericht *nt*
court of inquiry (*pl* **courts of inquiry**) N Untersuchungskommission *f*
court order N Gerichtsbeschluss *m*
courtroom ['kɔ:trum] N Gerichtssaal *m*
court shoe N Pumps *m*
courtyard ['kɔ:tjɑ:d] N Hof *m*
cousin ['kʌzn] N (*male*) Cousin *m*, Vetter *m*; (*female*) Cousine *f*; **first ~** Cousin(e) ersten Grades
cove [kəuv] N (kleine) Bucht *f*
covenant ['kʌvənənt] N Schwur *m* ▶ VT: **to ~ £200 per year to a charity** sich vertraglich verpflichten, £200 im Jahr für wohltätige Zwecke zu spenden
Coventry ['kɔvəntrɪ] N: **to send sb to ~** (*fig*) jdn schneiden (*inf*)
cover ['kʌvə^r] VT bedecken; (*distance*) zurücklegen; (*Insurance*) versichern; (*topic*) behandeln; (*include*) erfassen; (*Press*: *report on*) berichten über *+acc* ▶ N (*for furniture*) Bezug *m*; (*for typewriter, PC etc*) Hülle *f*; (*of book, magazine*) Umschlag *m*; (*shelter*) Schutz *m*; (*Insurance*) Versicherung *f*; (*fig*: *for illegal activities*) Tarnung *f*; **to be covered in** *or* **with** bedeckt sein mit; **£10 will ~ my expenses** £10 decken meine Unkosten; **to take ~** (*from rain*) sich unterstellen; **under ~** geschützt; **under ~ of darkness** im Schutz(e) der Dunkelheit; **under separate ~** getrennt
▶ **cover up** VT zudecken; (*fig*: *facts, feelings*) verheimlichen; (*: mistakes*) vertuschen ▶ VI (*fig*): **to ~ up for sb** jdn decken
coverage ['kʌvərɪdʒ] N Berichterstattung *f*; **television ~ of the conference** Fernsehberichte *pl* über die Konferenz; **to give full ~ to** ausführlich berichten über *+acc*
coveralls ['kʌvərɔ:lz] (US) NPL Overall *m*
cover charge N Kosten *pl* für ein Gedeck
covering ['kʌvərɪŋ] N Schicht *f*; (*of snow, dust etc*) Decke *f*
covering letter, (US) **cover letter** N Begleitbrief *m*
cover note N (*Insurance*) Deckungszusage *f*
cover price N Einzel(exemplar)preis *m*
covert ['kʌvət] ADJ versteckt; (*glance*) verstohlen
cover-up ['kʌvərʌp] N Vertuschung *f*, Verschleierung *f*
covet ['kʌvɪt] VT begehren
cow [kau] N (*animal, inf!*: *woman*) Kuh *f* ▶ CPD Kuh- ▶ VT einschüchtern
coward ['kauəd] N Feigling *m*
cowardice ['kauədɪs] N Feigheit *f*
cowardly ['kauədlɪ] ADJ feige
cowboy ['kaubɔɪ] N (*in US*) Cowboy *m*; (*pej*: *tradesman*) Pfuscher *m*
cow elephant N Elefantenkuh *f*
cower ['kauə^r] VI sich ducken; (*squatting*) kauern
cowshed ['kauʃɛd] N Kuhstall *m*
cowslip ['kauslɪp] N Schlüsselblume *f*
cox [kɔks] N ABBR = **coxswain**
coxswain ['kɔksn] N Steuermann *m*; (*of ship*) Boot(s)führer *m*
coy [kɔɪ] ADJ verschämt
coyote [kɔɪ'əutɪ] N Kojote *m*
cozy ['kəuzɪ] (US) ADJ = **cosy**
CP N ABBR (= *Communist Party*) KP *f*
cp. ABBR (= *compare*) vgl.
CPA (US) N ABBR = **certified public accountant**
CPI N ABBR (= *Consumer Price Index*) (Verbraucher)preisindex *m*
Cpl ABBR (*Mil*) = **corporal**
CP/M N ABBR (= *Control Program for Microprocessors*) CP/M *nt*

cps ABBR (*Comput, Typ:* = *characters per second*) cps, Zeichen *pl* pro Sekunde
CPSA (BRIT) N ABBR (= *Civil and Public Services Association*) *Gewerkschaft im öffentlichen Dienst*
CPU N ABBR (*Comput*) = **central processing unit**
cr. ABBR = **credit**; **creditor**
crab [kræb] N Krabbe *f*, Krebs *m*; (*meat*) Krabbe *f*
crab apple N Holzapfel *m*
crack [kræk] N (*noise*) Knall *m*; (*of wood breaking*) Knacks *m*; (*gap*) Spalte *f*; (*in bone, dish, glass*) Sprung *m*; (*in wall*) Riss *m*; (*joke*) Witz *m*; (*Drugs*) Crack *nt* ▶ VT (*whip*) knallen mit; (*twig*) knacken mit; (*dish, glass*) einen Sprung machen in *+acc*; (*bone*) anbrechen; (*nut, code*) knacken; (*wall*) rissig machen; (*problem*) lösen; (*joke*) reißen ▶ ADJ erstklassig; **to have a ~ at sth** (*inf*) etw mal probieren; **to ~ jokes** (*inf*) Witze reißen; **to get cracking** (*inf*) loslegen
▶ **crack down on** VT FUS hart durchgreifen gegen
▶ **crack up** VI durchdrehen, zusammenbrechen
crackdown ['krækdaun] N: **~ (on)** scharfes Durchgreifen *nt* (gegen)
cracked [krækt] (*inf*) ADJ übergeschnappt
cracker ['krækə^r] N (*biscuit*) Cracker *m*; (*also:* **Christmas cracker**) Knallbonbon *nt*; (*firework*) Knallkörper *m*, Kracher *m*; **a ~ of a ...** (BRIT *inf*) ein(e, r) tolle(s) ...; **he's crackers** (BRIT *inf*) er ist übergeschnappt
crackle ['krækl] VI (*fire*) knistern, prasseln; (*twig*) knacken
crackling ['kræklɪŋ] N (*of fire*) Knistern *nt*, Prasseln *nt*; (*of twig, on radio, telephone*) Knacken *nt*; (*of pork*) Kruste *f* (*des Schweinebratens*)
crackpot ['krækpɔt] (*inf*) N Spinner(in) *m(f)* ▶ ADJ verrückt
cradle ['kreɪdl] N Wiege *f* ▶ VT fest in den Armen halten
craft [krɑ:ft] N (*skill*) Geschicklichkeit *f*; (*art*) Kunsthandwerk *nt*; (*trade*) Handwerk *nt*; (*pl inv: boat*) Boot *nt*; (*: plane*) Flugzeug *nt*
craftsman ['krɑ:ftsmən] N (*irreg*) Handwerker *m*
craftsmanship ['krɑ:ftsmənʃɪp] N handwerkliche Ausführung *f*
crafty ['krɑ:ftɪ] ADJ schlau, clever
crag [kræg] N Fels *m*
craggy ['krægɪ] ADJ (*mountain*) zerklüftet; (*cliff*) felsig; (*face*) kantig
cram [kræm] VT vollstopfen ▶ VI pauken (*inf*), büffeln (*inf*); **to ~ with** vollstopfen mit; **to ~ sth into** etw hineinstopfen in *+acc*
cramming ['kræmɪŋ] N (*for exams*) Pauken *nt*, Büffeln *nt*
cramp [kræmp] N Krampf *m* ▶ VT hemmen
cramped [kræmpt] ADJ eng
crampon ['kræmpən] N Steigeisen *nt*
cranberry ['krænbərɪ] N Preiselbeere *f*
crane [kreɪn] N Kran *m*; (*bird*) Kranich *m* ▶ VT: **to ~ one's neck** den Hals recken ▶ VI: **to ~ forward** den Hals recken
crania ['kreɪnɪə] NPL *of* **cranium**
cranium ['kreɪnɪəm] (*pl* **crania**) N Schädel *m*
crank [kræŋk] N Spinner(in) *m(f)*; (*handle*) Kurbel *f*
crankshaft ['kræŋkʃɑ:ft] N Kurbelwelle *f*
cranky ['kræŋkɪ] ADJ verrückt
cranny ['krænɪ] N *see* **nook**
crap [kræp] (*inf!*) N Scheiße *f* (*inf!*) ▶ VI scheißen (*inf!*); **to have a ~** scheißen (*inf!*)
crappy ['kræpɪ] (*inf!*) ADJ beschissen (*inf!*)
crash [kræʃ] N (*noise*) Krachen *nt*; (*of car*) Unfall *m*; (*of plane etc*) Unglück *nt*; (*collision*) Zusammenstoß *m*; (*of stock market, business etc*) Zusammenbruch *m* ▶ VT (*car*) einen Unfall haben mit; (*plane etc*) abstürzen mit ▶ VI (*plane*) abstürzen; (*car*) einen Unfall haben; (*two cars*) zusammenstoßen; (*market*) zusammenbrechen; (*firm*) Pleite machen; **to ~ into** krachen *or* knallen gegen; **he crashed the car into a wall** er fuhr mit dem Auto gegen eine Mauer
crash barrier (BRIT) N Leitplanke *f*
crash course N Schnellkurs *m*, Intensivkurs *m*
crash helmet N Sturzhelm *m*
crash-landing ['kræʃlændɪŋ] N Bruchlandung *f*
crass [kræs] ADJ krass; (*behaviour*) unfein, derb
crate [kreɪt] N (*also inf*) Kiste *f*; (*for bottles*) Kasten *m*
crater ['kreɪtə^r] N Krater *m*
cravat [krə'væt] N Halstuch *nt*
crave [kreɪv] VT, VI: **to ~ (for)** sich sehnen nach
craven ['kreɪvən] ADJ feige
craving ['kreɪvɪŋ] N: **~ (for)** Verlangen *nt* (nach)
crawl [krɔ:l] VI kriechen; (*child*) krabbeln ▶ N (*Swimming*) Kraulstil *m*, Kraul(en) *nt*; **to ~ to sb** (*inf*) vor jdm kriechen; **to drive along at a ~** im Schneckentempo *or* Kriechtempo vorankommen
crawler lane (BRIT) N (*Aut*) Kriechspur *f*
crayfish ['kreɪfɪʃ] N INV (*freshwater*) Flusskrebs *m*; (*saltwater*) Languste *f*
crayon ['kreɪən] N Buntstift *m*
craze [kreɪz] N Fimmel *m*; **to be all the ~** große Mode sein
crazed [kreɪzd] ADJ wahnsinnig; (*pottery, glaze*) rissig
crazy ['kreɪzɪ] ADJ wahnsinnig, verrückt; **~ about sb/sth** (*inf*) verrückt *or* wild auf jdn/etw; **to go ~** wahnsinnig *or* verrückt werden
crazy paving (BRIT) N Mosaikpflaster *nt*
creak [kri:k] VI knarren
cream [kri:m] N Sahne *f*, Rahm *m* (SÜDD); (*artificial cream, cosmetic*) Creme *f*; (*élite*) Creme *f*, Elite *f* ▶ ADJ cremefarben; **whipped ~** Schlagsahne *f*
▶ **cream off** VT absahnen (*inf*)
cream cake N Sahnetorte *f*; (*small*) Sahnetörtchen *nt*
cream cheese N (Doppelrahm)frischkäse *m*
creamery ['kri:mərɪ] N (*shop*) Milchgeschäft *nt*; (*factory*) Molkerei *f*
creamy ['kri:mɪ] ADJ (*colour*) cremefarben; (*taste*) sahnig
crease [kri:s] N Falte *f*; (*in trousers*) Bügelfalte *f* ▶ VT zerknittern; (*forehead*) runzeln ▶ VI knittern; (*forehead*) sich runzeln
crease-resistant ['kri:srɪzɪstənt] ADJ knitterfrei

create [kriː'eɪt] VT schaffen; (*interest*) hervorrufen; (*problems*) verursachen; (*produce*) herstellen; (*design*) entwerfen, kreieren; (*impression, fuss*) machen
creation [kriː'eɪʃən] N Schaffung *f*; Hervorrufen *nt*; Verursachung *f*; Herstellung *f*; Entwurf *m*, Kreation *f*; (*Rel*) Schöpfung *f*
creative [kriː'eɪtɪv] ADJ kreativ, schöpferisch
creativity [kriːeɪ'tɪvɪtɪ] N Kreativität *f*
creator [kriː'eɪtəʳ] N Schöpfer(in) *m(f)*
creature ['kriːtʃəʳ] N Geschöpf *nt*; (*living animal*) Lebewesen *nt*
creature comforts [-'kʌmfəts] NPL Lebensgenüsse *pl*
crèche [krɛʃ] N (Kinder)krippe *f*; (*all day*) (Kinder)tagesstätte *f*
credence ['kriːdns] N: **to lend** *or* **give ~ to sth** etw glaubwürdig erscheinen lassen *or* machen
credentials [krɪ'dɛnʃlz] NPL Referenzen *pl*, Zeugnisse *pl*; (*papers of identity*) (Ausweis)papiere *pl*
credibility [krɛdɪ'bɪlɪtɪ] N Glaubwürdigkeit *f*
credible ['krɛdɪbl] ADJ glaubwürdig
credit ['krɛdɪt] N (*loan*) Kredit *m*; (*recognition*) Anerkennung *f*; (*Scol*) Schein *m* ▸ ADJ (*Comm: terms etc*) Kredit- ▸ VT (*Comm*) gutschreiben; (*believe: also:* **give credit to**) glauben; **credits** NPL (*Cine, TV: at beginning*) Vorspann *m*; (*: at end*) Nachspann *m*; **to be in ~** (*person*) Geld auf dem Konto haben; (*bank account*) im Haben sein; **on ~** auf Kredit; **it is to his ~ that …** es ehrt ihn, dass …; **to take the ~ for** das Verdienst in Anspruch nehmen für; **it does him ~** es spricht für ihn; **he's a ~ to his family** er macht seiner Familie Ehre; **to ~ sb with sth** (*fig*) jdm etw zuschreiben; **to ~ £5 to sb** jdm £5 gutschreiben
creditable ['krɛdɪtəbl] ADJ lobenswert, anerkennenswert
credit account N Kreditkonto *nt*
credit agency (BRIT) N Kreditauskunftei *f*
credit balance N Kontostand *m*
credit bureau (US) N = **credit agency**
credit card N Kreditkarte *f*
credit control N Kreditüberwachung *f*
credit crunch N Kreditklemme *f*
credit facilities NPL (*Comm*) Kreditmöglichkeiten *pl*
credit limit N Kreditgrenze *f*
credit note (BRIT) N Gutschrift *f*
creditor ['krɛdɪtəʳ] N Gläubiger *m*
credit transfer N Banküberweisung *f*
creditworthy ['krɛdɪt'wəːðɪ] ADJ kreditwürdig
credulity [krɪ'djuːlɪtɪ] N Leichtgläubigkeit *f*
creed [kriːd] N Glaubensbekenntnis *nt*
creek [kriːk] N (kleine) Bucht *f*; (*US: stream*) Bach *m*; **to be up the ~** (*inf*) in der Tinte sitzen
creel [kriːl] N (*also:* **lobster creel**) Hummer(fang)korb *m*
creep [kriːp] (*pt, pp* **crept**) VI schleichen; (*plant: horizontally*) kriechen; (*: vertically*) klettern ▸ N (*inf*) Kriecher *m*; **to ~ up on sb** sich an jdn heranschleichen; (*time etc*) langsam auf jdn zukommen; **he's a ~** er ist ein widerlicher *or* fieser Typ; **it gives me the creeps** davon kriege ich das kalte Grausen
creeper ['kriːpəʳ] N Kletterpflanze *f*
creepers ['kriːpəz] (*US*) NPL *Schuhe mit weichen Sohlen*
creepy ['kriːpɪ] ADJ gruselig; (*experience*) unheimlich, gruselig
creepy-crawly ['kriːpɪ'krɔːlɪ] (*inf*) N Krabbeltier *nt*
cremate [krɪ'meɪt] VT einäschern
cremation [krɪ'meɪʃən] N Einäscherung *f*, Kremation *f*
crematoria [krɛmə'tɔːrɪə] NPL *of* **crematorium**
crematorium [krɛmə'tɔːrɪəm] (*pl* **crematoria**) N Krematorium *nt*
creosote ['krɪəsəut] N Kreosot *nt*
crepe [kreɪp] N Krepp *m*; (*rubber*) Krepp(gummi) *m*
crepe bandage (BRIT) N elastische Binde *f*
crepe paper N Kreppapier *nt*
crepe sole N Kreppsohle *f*
crept [krɛpt] PT, PP *of* **creep**
crescendo [krɪ'ʃɛndəu] N Höhepunkt *m*; (*Mus*) Crescendo *nt*
crescent ['krɛsnt] N Halbmond *m*; (*street*) *halbkreisförmig verlaufende Straße*
cress [krɛs] N Kresse *f*
crest [krɛst] N (*of hill*) Kamm *m*; (*of bird*) Haube *f*; (*coat of arms*) Wappen *nt*
crestfallen ['krɛstfɔːlən] ADJ niedergeschlagen
Crete [kriːt] N Kreta *nt*
crevasse [krɪ'væs] N Gletscherspalte *f*
crevice ['krɛvɪs] N Spalte *f*
crew [kruː] N Besatzung *f*; (*TV, Cine*) Crew *f*; (*gang*) Bande *f*
crew cut N Bürstenschnitt *m*
crew neck N runder (Hals)ausschnitt *m*
crib [krɪb] N Kinderbett *nt*; (*Rel*) Krippe *f* ▸ VT (*inf: copy*) abschreiben
cribbage ['krɪbɪdʒ] N Cribbage *nt*
crib death (US) N = **cot death**
crick [krɪk] N Krampf *m*
cricket ['krɪkɪt] N Kricket *nt*; (*insect*) Grille *f*
cricketer ['krɪkɪtəʳ] N Kricketspieler(in) *m(f)*
crime [kraɪm] N (*no pl: illegal activities*) Verbrechen *pl*; (*illegal action, fig*) Verbrechen *nt*; **minor ~** kleinere Vergehen *pl*
crime wave N Verbrechenswelle *f*
criminal ['krɪmɪnl] N Kriminelle(r) *f(m)*, Verbrecher(in) *m(f)* ▸ ADJ kriminell; **C~ Investigation Department** Kriminalpolizei *f*
criminal code N Strafgesetzbuch *nt*
criminal profile N Täterprofil *nt*
crimp [krɪmp] VT kräuseln; (*hair*) wellen
crimson ['krɪmzn] ADJ purpurrot
cringe [krɪndʒ] VI (*in fear*) zurückweichen; (*in embarrassment*) zusammenzucken
crinkle ['krɪŋkl] VT (zer)knittern
cripple ['krɪpl] N Krüppel *m* ▸ VT zum Krüppel machen; (*ship, plane*) aktionsunfähig machen; (*production, exports*) lahmlegen, lähmen; **crippled with rheumatism** von Rheuma praktisch gelähmt

crippling ['krɪplɪŋ] ADJ (*disease*) schwer; (*taxation, debts*) erdrückend
crises ['kraɪsi:z] NPL *of* **crisis**
crisis ['kraɪsɪs] (*pl* **crises**) N Krise *f*
crisp [krɪsp] ADJ (*vegetables etc*) knackig; (*bacon etc*) knusprig; (*weather*) frisch; (*manner, tone, reply*) knapp
crisps [krɪsps] (BRIT) NPL Chips *pl*
crisscross ['krɪskrɔs] ADJ (*pattern*) Kreuz- ▶ VT kreuz und quer durchziehen
criteria [kraɪ'tɪərɪə] NPL *of* **criterion**
criterion [kraɪ'tɪərɪən] (*pl* **criteria**) N Kriterium *nt*
critic ['krɪtɪk] N Kritiker(in) *m(f)*
critical ['krɪtɪkl] ADJ kritisch; **to be ~ of sb/sth** jdn/etw kritisieren; **he is in a ~ condition** sein Zustand ist kritisch
critically ['krɪtɪklɪ] ADV kritisch; (*ill*) schwer
criticism ['krɪtɪsɪzəm] N Kritik *f*
criticize ['krɪtɪsaɪz] VT kritisieren
critique [krɪ'ti:k] N Kritik *f*
croak [krəuk] VI (*frog*) quaken; (*bird, person*) krächzen
Croat N Kroate *m*, Kroatin *f*; (*Ling*) Kroatisch *nt*
Croatia [krəu'eɪʃə] N Kroatien *nt*
Croatian [krəu'eɪʃən] ADJ kroatisch
crochet ['krəuʃeɪ] N (*activity*) Häkeln *nt*; (*result*) Häkelei *f*
crock [krɔk] N Topf *m*; (*inf: also:* **old crock**: *vehicle*) Kiste *f*; (*: person*) Wrack *nt*
crockery ['krɔkərɪ] N Geschirr *nt*
crocodile ['krɔkədaɪl] N Krokodil *nt*
crocus ['krəukəs] N Krokus *m*
croft [krɔft] (BRIT) N kleines Pachtgut *nt*
crofter ['krɔftəʳ] (BRIT) N Kleinpächter(in) *m(f)*
crone [krəun] N alte Hexe *f*
crony ['krəunɪ] (*inf, pej*) N Kumpan(in) *m(f)*
crook [kruk] N (*criminal*) Gauner *m*; (*of shepherd*) Hirtenstab *m*; (*of arm*) Beuge *f*
crooked ['krukɪd] ADJ krumm; (*dishonest*) unehrlich
crop [krɔp] N (Feld)frucht *f*; (*amount produced*) Ernte *f*; (*riding crop*) Reitpeitsche *f*; (*of bird*) Kropf *m* ▶ VT (*hair*) stutzen; (*subj: animal: grass*) abfressen
▶ **crop up** VI aufkommen
cropper ['krɔpəʳ] (*inf*) N: **to come a ~** hinfallen; (*fig: fail*) auf die Nase fallen
crop spraying [-'spreɪɪŋ] N Schädlingsbekämpfung *f* (*durch Besprühen*)
croquet ['krəukeɪ] (BRIT) N Krocket *nt*
croquette [krə'kɛt] N Krokette *f*
cross [krɔs] N Kreuz *nt*; (*Biol, Bot*) Kreuzung *f* ▶ VT (*street*) überqueren; (*room etc*) durchqueren; (*cheque*) zur Verrechnung ausstellen; (*arms*) verschränken; (*legs*) übereinanderschlagen; (*animal, plant*) kreuzen; (*thwart: person*) verärgern; (*: plan*) durchkreuzen ▶ ADJ ärgerlich, böse ▶ VI: **the boat crosses from ... to ...** das Schiff fährt von ... nach ...; **to ~ o.s.** sich bekreuzigen; **we have a crossed line** (BRIT) es ist jemand in der Leitung; **they've got their lines** *or* **wires crossed** (*fig*) sie reden aneinander vorbei; **to be/get ~ with sb (about sth)** mit jdm *or* auf jdn (wegen etw) böse sein/werden
▶ **cross out** VT streichen
▶ **cross over** VI hinübergehen
crossbar ['krɔsbɑ:ʳ] N (*Sport*) Querlatte *f*; (*of bicycle*) Stange *f*
crossbow N Armbrust *f*
crossbreed ['krɔsbri:d] N Kreuzung *f*
cross-Channel ferry ['krɔs'tʃænl-] N Kanalfähre *f*
crosscheck ['krɔstʃɛk] N Gegenprobe *f* ▶ VT überprüfen
cross-country ['krɔs'kʌntrɪ], **cross-country race** N Querfeldeinrennen *nt*
cross-dressing [krɔs'drɛsɪŋ] N (*transvestism*) Transvestismus *m*
cross-examination ['krɔsɪgzæmɪ'neɪʃən] N Kreuzverhör *nt*
cross-examine ['krɔsɪg'zæmɪn] VT ins Kreuzverhör nehmen
cross-eyed ['krɔsaɪd] ADJ schielend; **to be ~** schielen
crossfire ['krɔsfaɪəʳ] N Kreuzfeuer *nt*; **to get caught in the ~** (*also fig*) ins Kreuzfeuer geraten
crossing ['krɔsɪŋ] N Überfahrt *f*; (*also:* **pedestrian crossing**) Fußgängerüberweg *m*
crossing guard (US) N ≈ Schülerlotse *m*
crossing point N Übergangsstelle *f*
cross-purposes ['krɔs'pə:pəsɪz] NPL: **to be at ~ with sb** jdn missverstehen; **we're (talking) at ~** wir reden aneinander vorbei
cross-question ['krɔs'kwɛstʃən] VT ins Kreuzverhör nehmen
cross-reference ['krɔs'rɛfrəns] N (Quer)verweis *m*
crossroads ['krɔsrəudz] N Kreuzung *f*
cross section N Querschnitt *m*
crosswalk ['krɔswɔ:k] (US) N Fußgängerüberweg *m*
crosswind ['krɔswɪnd] N Seitenwind *m*
crosswise ['krɔswaɪz] ADV quer
crossword ['krɔswə:d] N (*also:* **crossword puzzle**) Kreuzworträtsel *nt*
crotch [krɔtʃ] N Unterleib *m*; (*of garment*) Schritt *m*
crotchet ['krɔtʃɪt] N Viertelnote *f*
crotchety ['krɔtʃɪtɪ] ADJ reizbar
crouch [krautʃ] VI kauern
croup [kru:p] N (*Med*) Krupp *m*
croupier ['kru:pɪəʳ] N Croupier *m*
crouton ['kru:tɔn] N Crouton *m*
crow [krəu] N (*bird*) Krähe *f*; (*of cock*) Krähen *nt* ▶ VI krähen; (*fig*) sich brüsten, angeben
crowbar ['krəubɑ:ʳ] N Brechstange *f*
crowd [kraud] N (Menschen)menge *f* ▶ VT (*room, stadium*) füllen ▶ VI: **to ~ round** sich herumdrängen; **crowds of people** Menschenmassen *pl*; **the/our ~** (*of friends*) die/unsere Clique *f*; **to ~ sb/sth in** jdn/etw hineinstopfen; **to ~ sb/sth into** jdn pferchen/etw stopfen in *+acc*; **to ~ in** sich hineindrängen
crowded ['kraudɪd] ADJ überfüllt; (*densely populated*) dicht besiedelt; **~ with** voll von

crowd scene N Massenszene *f*
crowdsource ['kraudsɔ:s] VT *Arbeitsprozesse auf freiwillige Nutzer auslagern*
crowdsourcing ['kraudsɔ:sɪŋ] N Auslagerung *f* (*von Arbeitsprozessen auf freiwillige Nutzer*), Crowdsourcing *nt*
crown [kraun] N (*also of tooth*) Krone *f*; (*of head*) Wirbel *m*; (*of hill*) Kuppe *f*; (*of hat*) Kopf *m* ▶ VT krönen; (*tooth*) überkronen; **the C~** die Krone; **and to ~ it all ...** (*fig*) und zur Krönung des Ganzen ...

> **Crown Court** ist ein Strafgericht, das in etwa 90 verschiedenen Städten in England und Wales zusammentritt. Schwere Verbrechen wie Mord, Totschlag, Vergewaltigung und Raub werden nur vor dem crown court unter Vorsitz eines Richters mit Geschworenen verhandelt.

crowning ['kraunɪŋ] ADJ krönend
crown jewels NPL Kronjuwelen *pl*
crown prince N Kronprinz *m*
crow's-feet ['krəuzfi:t] NPL Krähenfüße *pl*
crow's-nest ['krəuznɛst] N Krähennest *nt*, Mastkorb *m*
crucial ['kru:ʃl] ADJ (*decision*) äußerst wichtig; (*vote*) entscheidend; **~ to** äußerst wichtig für
crucifix ['kru:sɪfɪks] N Kruzifix *nt*
crucifixion [kru:sɪ'fɪkʃən] N Kreuzigung *f*
crucify ['kru:sɪfaɪ] VT kreuzigen; (*fig*) in der Luft zerreißen
crude [kru:d] ADJ (*oil, fibre*) Roh-; (*fig: basic*) primitiv; (*: vulgar*) ordinär ▶ N = **crude oil**
crude oil N Rohöl *nt*
cruel ['kruəl] ADJ grausam
cruelty ['kruəltɪ] N Grausamkeit *f*
cruet ['kru:ɪt] N Gewürzständer *m*
cruise [kru:z] N Kreuzfahrt *f* ▶ VI (*ship*) kreuzen; (*car*) (mit Dauergeschwindigkeit) fahren; (*aircraft*) (mit Reisegeschwindigkeit) fliegen; (*taxi*) gemächlich fahren
cruise missile N Marschflugkörper *m*
cruiser ['kru:zə^r] N Motorboot *nt*; (*warship*) Kreuzer *m*
cruising speed N Reisegeschwindigkeit *f*
crumb [krʌm] N Krümel *m*; (*fig: of information*) Brocken *m*; **a ~ of comfort** ein winziger Trost
crumble ['krʌmbl] VT (*bread*) zerbröckeln; (*biscuit etc*) zerkrümeln ▶ VI (*building, earth etc*) zerbröckeln; (*plaster*) abbröckeln; (*fig: opposition*) sich auflösen; (*: belief*) ins Wanken geraten
crumbly ['krʌmblɪ] ADJ krümelig
crummy ['krʌmɪ] (*inf*) ADJ mies
crumpet ['krʌmpɪt] N Teekuchen *m* (*zum Toasten*)
crumple ['krʌmpl] VT zerknittern
crunch [krʌntʃ] VT (*biscuit, apple etc*) knabbern; (*underfoot*) zertreten ▶ N: **the ~** der große Krach; **if it comes to the ~** wenn es wirklich dahin kommt; **when the ~ comes** wenn es hart auf hart geht
crunchy ['krʌntʃɪ] ADJ knusprig; (*apple etc*) knackig; (*gravel, snow etc*) knirschend
crusade [kru:'seɪd] N Feldzug *m* ▶ VI: **to ~ for/against sth** für/gegen etw zu Felde ziehen
crusader [kru:'seɪdə^r] N Kreuzritter *m*; (*fig*): **~ (for)** Apostel *m* (*+gen*)
crush [krʌʃ] N (*crowd*) Gedränge *nt* ▶ VT quetschen; (*grapes*) zerquetschen; (*paper, clothes*) zerknittern; (*garlic, ice*) (zer)stoßen; (*defeat*) niederschlagen; (*devastate*) vernichten; **to have a ~ on sb** (*love*) für jdn schwärmen; **lemon ~** Zitronensaftgetränk *nt*
crush barrier (BRIT) N Absperrung *f*
crushing ['krʌʃɪŋ] ADJ vernichtend
crust [krʌst] N Kruste *f*
crustacean [krʌs'teɪʃən] N Schalentier *nt*, Krustazee *f*
crusty ['krʌstɪ] ADJ knusprig
crutch [krʌtʃ] N Krücke *f*; (*support*) Stütze *f*; *see also* **crotch**
crux [krʌks] N Kern *m*
cry [kraɪ] VI weinen; (*also:* **cry out**) aufschreien ▶ N Schrei *m*; (*shout*) Ruf *m*; **what are you crying about?** warum weinst du?; **to ~ for help** um Hilfe rufen; **she had a good ~** sie hat sich (mal richtig) ausgeweint; **it's a far ~ from ...** (*fig*) das ist etwas ganz anderes als ...
▶ **cry off** (*inf*) VI absagen
crying ['kraɪɪŋ] ADJ (*fig: need*) dringend; **it's a ~ shame** es ist ein Jammer
crypt [krɪpt] N Krypta *f*
cryptic ['krɪptɪk] ADJ hintergründig, rätselhaft; (*clue*) verschlüsselt
crystal ['krɪstl] N Kristall *m*; (*glass*) Kristall(glas) *nt*
crystal clear ADJ glasklar
crystallize ['krɪstəlaɪz] VT (*opinion, thoughts*) (feste) Form geben *+dat* ▶ VI (*sugar etc*) kristallisieren; **crystallized fruits** (BRIT) kandierte Früchte *pl*
CSA N ABBR (= *Child Support Agency*) *Amt zur Regelung von Unterhaltszahlungen für Kinder*
CSC N ABBR (= *Civil Service Commission*) *Einstellungsbehörde für den öffentlichen Dienst*
CSE (BRIT) N ABBR (*formerly:* = *Certificate of Secondary Education*) *Schulabschlusszeugnis*, ≈ mittlere Reife *f*
CS gas (BRIT) N ≈ Tränengas *nt*
CST (US) ABBR (= *Central Standard Time*) *mittelamerikanische Standardzeit*
CT (US) ABBR (*Post*) = **Connecticut**
ct ABBR = **cent**; **court**
CTC (BRIT) N ABBR = **city technology college**
CT scanner N ABBR (*Med:* = *computerized tomography scanner*) CT-Scanner *m*
cu ['si:ju:] ABBR = **see you**; (*in text messages*) bis dann, bis später
cu. ABBR = **cubic**
cub [kʌb] N Junge(s) *nt*; (*also:* **cub scout**) Wölfling *m*
Cuba ['kju:bə] N Kuba *nt*
Cuban ['kju:bən] ADJ kubanisch ▶ N Kubaner(in) *m(f)*
cubbyhole ['kʌbɪhəul] N (*room*) Kabuff *nt*; (*space*) Eckchen *nt*
cube [kju:b] N Würfel *m*; (*Math: of number*) dritte Potenz *f* ▶ VT (*Math*) in die dritte Potenz erheben, hoch drei nehmen

cube farm N (*inf*) Großraumbüro *nt* (*mit Trennwänden*)
cube root N Kubikwurzel *f*
cubic ['kju:bɪk] ADJ (*volume*) Kubik-; **~ metre** *etc* Kubikmeter *m etc*
cubic capacity N Hubraum *m*
cubicle ['kju:bɪkl] N Kabine *f*; (*in hospital*) Bettnische *f*
cuckoo ['kuku:] N Kuckuck *m*
cuckoo clock N Kuckucksuhr *f*
cucumber ['kju:kʌmbəʳ] N Gurke *f*
cud [kʌd] N: **to chew the ~** (*animal*) wiederkäuen; (*fig: person*) vor sich *acc* hin grübeln
cuddle ['kʌdl] VT in den Arm nehmen, drücken ▸ VI schmusen
cuddly ['kʌdlɪ] ADJ (*person*) knuddelig (*inf*); **~ toy** Plüschtier *nt*
cudgel ['kʌdʒl] N Knüppel *m* ▸ VT: **to ~ one's brains** sich *dat* das (Ge)hirn zermartern
cue [kju:] N (*Sport*) Billardstock *m*, Queue *nt*; (*Theat: word*) Stichwort *nt*; (*: action*) (Einsatz)zeichen *nt*; (*Mus*) Einsatz *m*
cuff [kʌf] N (*of sleeve*) Manschette *f*; (*US: of trousers*) Aufschlag *m*; (*blow*) Klaps *m* ▸ VT einen Klaps geben *+dat*; **off the ~** aus dem Stegreif
cuff links NPL Manschettenknöpfe *pl*
cu. in. ABBR (= *cubic inches*) Kubikzoll
cuisine [kwɪ'zi:n] N Küche *f*
cul-de-sac ['kʌldəsæk] N Sackgasse *f*
culinary ['kʌlɪnərɪ] ADJ (*skill*) Koch-; (*delight*) kulinarisch
cull [kʌl] VT (zusammen)sammeln; (*animals*) ausmerzen ▸ N *Erlegen überschüssiger Tierbestände*
culminate ['kʌlmɪneɪt] VI: **to ~ in** gipfeln in *+dat*
culmination [kʌlmɪ'neɪʃən] N Höhepunkt *m*
culottes [kju:'lɔts] NPL Hosenrock *m*
culpable ['kʌlpəbl] ADJ schuldig
culprit ['kʌlprɪt] N Täter(in) *m(f)*
cult [kʌlt] N Kult *m*
cult figure N Kultfigur *f*
cultivate ['kʌltɪveɪt] VT (*land*) bebauen, landwirtschaftlich nutzen; (*crop*) anbauen; (*feeling*) entwickeln; (*person*) sich *dat* warm halten (*inf*), die Beziehung pflegen zu
cultivation [kʌltɪ'veɪʃən] N (*of land*) Bebauung *f*, landwirtschaftliche Nutzung *f*; (*of crop*) Anbau *m*
cultural ['kʌltʃərəl] ADJ kulturell
culture ['kʌltʃəʳ] N Kultur *f*
cultured ['kʌltʃəd] ADJ kultiviert; (*pearl*) Zucht-
cumbersome ['kʌmbəsəm] ADJ (*suitcase etc*) sperrig, unhandlich; (*piece of machinery*) schwer zu handhaben; (*clothing*) hinderlich; (*process*) umständlich
cumin ['kʌmɪn] N Kreuzkümmel *m*
cumulative ['kju:mjulətɪv] ADJ (*effect, result*) Gesamt-
cunning ['kʌnɪŋ] N Gerissenheit *f* ▸ ADJ gerissen; (*device, idea*) schlau
cunt [kʌnt] (*inf!*) N (*vagina*) Fotze *f* (*inf!*); (*term of abuse*) Arsch *m* (*inf!*)
cup [kʌp] N Tasse *f*; (*as prize*) Pokal *m*; (*of bra*) Körbchen *nt*; **a ~ of tea** eine Tasse Tee
cupboard ['kʌbəd] N Schrank *m*
cup final (BRIT) N Pokalendspiel *nt*
cupful ['kʌpful] N Tasse *f*
Cupid ['kju:pɪd] N Amor *m*; (*figurine*) Amorette *f*
cupidity [kju:'pɪdɪtɪ] N Begierde *f*, Gier *f*
cupola ['kju:pələ] N Kuppel *f*
cuppa ['kʌpə] (BRIT *inf*) N Tasse *f* Tee
cup tie (BRIT) N Pokalspiel *nt*
curable ['kjuərəbl] ADJ heilbar
curate ['kjuərɪt] N Vikar *m*
curator [kjuə'reɪtəʳ] N Kustos *m*
curb [kə:b] VT einschränken; (*person*) an die Kandare nehmen ▸ N Einschränkung *f*; (*US: kerb*) Bordstein *m*
curd cheese N Weißkäse *m*
curdle ['kə:dl] VI gerinnen
curds [kə:dz] NPL ≈ Quark *m*
cure [kjuəʳ] VT heilen; (*Culin: salt*) pökeln; (*: smoke*) räuchern; (*: dry*) trocknen; (*problem*) abhelfen *+dat* ▸ N (*remedy*) (Heil)mittel *nt*; (*treatment*) Heilverfahren *nt*; (*solution*) Abhilfe *f*; **to be cured of sth** von etw geheilt sein
cure-all ['kjuərɔ:l] N (*also fig*) Allheilmittel *nt*
curfew ['kə:fju:] N Ausgangssperre *f*; (*time*) Sperrstunde *f*
curio ['kjuərɪəu] N Kuriosität *f*
curiosity [kjuərɪ'ɔsɪtɪ] N Wissbegier(de) *f*; Neugier *f*; Merkwürdigkeit *f*
curious ['kjuərɪəs] ADJ (*interested*) wissbegierig; (*nosy*) neugierig; (*strange, unusual*) sonderbar, merkwürdig; **I'm ~ about him** ich bin gespannt auf ihn
curiously ['kjuərɪəslɪ] ADV neugierig; (*inquisitively*) wissbegierig; **~ enough, ...** merkwürdigerweise ...
curl [kə:l] N Locke *f*; (*of smoke etc*) Kringel *m* ▸ VT (*hair: loosely*) locken; (*: tightly*) kräuseln ▸ VI sich locken; sich kräuseln; (*smoke*) sich kringeln
▸ **curl up** VI sich zusammenrollen
curler ['kə:ləʳ] N Lockenwickler *m*; (*Sport*) Curlingspieler(in) *m(f)*
curlew ['kə:lu:] N Brachvogel *m*
curling ['kə:lɪŋ] N (*Sport*) Curling *nt*
curling tongs, (US) **curling irons** NPL Lockenschere *f*, Brennschere *f*
curly ['kə:lɪ] ADJ lockig; (*tightly curled*) kraus
currant ['kʌrnt] N Korinthe *f*; (*blackcurrant, redcurrant*) Johannisbeere *f*
currency ['kʌrnsɪ] N (*system*) Währung *f*; (*money*) Geld *nt*; **foreign ~** Devisen *pl*; **to gain ~** (*fig*) sich verbreiten, um sich greifen
current ['kʌrnt] N Strömung *f*; (*Elec*) Strom *m*; (*of opinion*) Tendenz *f*, Trend *m* ▸ ADJ gegenwärtig; (*expression*) gebräuchlich; (*idea, custom*) verbreitet; **direct/alternating ~** (*Elec*) Gleich-/Wechselstrom *m*; **the ~ issue of a magazine** die neueste *or* letzte Nummer einer Zeitschrift; **in ~ use** allgemein gebräuchlich
current account (BRIT) N Girokonto *nt*
current affairs NPL Tagespolitik *f*
current assets NPL (*Comm*) Umlaufvermögen *nt*
current liabilities NPL (*Comm*) kurzfristige Verbindlichkeiten *pl*
currently ['kʌrntlɪ] ADV zurzeit

curricula [kəˈrɪkjulə] NPL *of* **curriculum**
curriculum [kəˈrɪkjuləm] (*pl* **curriculums** *or* **curricula**) N Lehrplan *m*
curriculum vitae [-ˈviːtaɪ] N Lebenslauf *m*
curry [ˈkʌrɪ] N (*dish*) Currygericht *nt* ▸ VT: **to ~ favour with** sich einschmeicheln bei
curry powder N Curry *m or nt*, Currypulver *nt*
curse [kəːs] VI fluchen ▸ VT verfluchen ▸ N Fluch *m*
cursor [ˈkəːsəʳ] N (*Comput*) Cursor *m*
cursory [ˈkəːsərɪ] ADJ flüchtig; (*examination*) oberflächlich
curt [kəːt] ADJ knapp, kurz angebunden
curtail [kəːˈteɪl] VT einschränken; (*visit etc*) abkürzen
curtain [ˈkəːtn] N Vorhang *m*; (*net*) Gardine *f*; **to draw the curtains** (*together*) die Vorhänge zuziehen; (*apart*) die Vorhänge aufmachen
curtain call N (*Theat*) Vorhang *m*
curtsey, curtsy [ˈkəːtsɪ] VI knicksen ▸ N Knicks *m*
curvature [ˈkəːvətʃəʳ] N Krümmung *f*
curve [kəːv] N Bogen *m*; (*in the road*) Kurve *f* ▸ VI einen Bogen machen; (*surface, arch*) sich wölben ▸ VT biegen
curved [kəːvd] ADJ (*line*) gebogen; (*table legs etc*) geschwungen; (*surface, arch, sides of ship*) gewölbt
cushion [ˈkuʃən] N Kissen *nt* ▸ VT dämpfen; (*seat*) polstern
cushy [ˈkuʃɪ] (*inf*) ADJ: **a ~ job** ein gemütlicher *or* ruhiger Job; **to have a ~ time** eine ruhige Kugel schieben
custard [ˈkʌstəd] N (*for pouring*) Vanillesoße *f*
custard powder (BRIT) N Vanillesoßenpulver *nt*
custodial [kʌsˈtəudɪəl] ADJ: **~ sentence** Gefängnisstrafe *f*
custodian [kʌsˈtəudɪən] N Verwalter(in) *m(f)*; (*of museum etc*) Aufseher(in) *m(f)*, Wächter(in) *m(f)*
custody [ˈkʌstədɪ] N (*of child*) Vormundschaft *f*; (*for offenders*) (polizeilicher) Gewahrsam *m*, Haft *f*; **to take into ~** verhaften; **in the ~ of** unter der Obhut *+gen*; **the mother has ~ of the children** die Kinder sind der Mutter zugesprochen worden
custom [ˈkʌstəm] N Brauch *m*; (*habit*) (An)gewohnheit *f*; (*Law*) Gewohnheitsrecht *nt*; (*Comm*) Kundschaft *f*
customary [ˈkʌstəmərɪ] ADJ (*conventional*) üblich; (*habitual*) gewohnt; **it is ~ to do it** es ist üblich, es zu tun
custom-built [ˈkʌstəmˈbɪlt] ADJ speziell angefertigt
customer [ˈkʌstəməʳ] N Kunde *m*, Kundin *f*; **he's an awkward ~** (*inf*) er ist ein schwieriger Typ
customer profile N Kundenprofil *nt*
customize [ˈkʌstəmaɪz] VT individuell anpassen
customized [ˈkʌstəmaɪzd] ADJ individuell aufgemacht
custom-made [ˈkʌstəmˈmeɪd] ADJ (*shirt etc*) maßgefertigt, nach Maß; (*car etc*) speziell angefertigt
customs [ˈkʌstəmz] NPL Zoll *m*; **to go through ~** durch den Zoll gehen
Customs and Excise (BRIT) N die Zollbehörde *f*
customs duty N Zoll *m*
customs officer N Zollbeamte(r) *m*, Zollbeamtin *f*
cut [kʌt] (*pt, pp* **~**) VT schneiden; (*text, programme, spending*) kürzen; (*prices*) senken, heruntersetzen, herabsetzen; (*supply*) einschränken; (*cloth*) zuschneiden; (*road*) schlagen, hauen; (*inf: lecture, appointment*) schwänzen ▸ VI schneiden; (*lines*) sich schneiden ▸ N Schnitt *m*; (*in skin*) Schnittwunde *f*; (*in salary, spending etc*) Kürzung *f*; (*of meat*) Stück *nt*; (*of jewel*) Schnitt *m*, Schliff *m*; **to ~ a tooth** zahnen, einen Zahn bekommen; **to ~ one's finger/hand/knee** sich in den Finger/in die Hand/am Knie schneiden; **to get one's hair ~** sich *dat* die Haare schneiden lassen; **to ~ sth short** etw vorzeitig abbrechen; **to ~ sb dead** jdn wie Luft behandeln; **cold cuts** (*US*) Aufschnitt *m*; **power ~** Stromausfall *m*
▸ **cut back** VT (*plants*) zurückschneiden; (*production*) zurückschrauben; (*expenditure*) einschränken
▸ **cut down** VT (*tree*) fällen; (*consumption*) einschränken; **to ~ sb down to size** (*fig*) jdn auf seinen Platz verweisen
▸ **cut down on** VT FUS einschränken
▸ **cut in** VI (*Aut*) sich direkt vor ein anderes Auto setzen; **to ~ in (on)** (*conversation*) sich einschalten (in *+acc*)
▸ **cut off** VT abschneiden; (*supply*) sperren; (*Tel*) unterbrechen; **we've been ~ off** (*Tel*) wir sind unterbrochen worden
▸ **cut out** VT ausschneiden; (*an activity etc*) aufhören mit; (*remove*) herausschneiden
▸ **cut up** VT klein schneiden; **it really ~ me up** (*inf*) es hat mich ziemlich mitgenommen; **to feel ~ up about sth** (*inf*) betroffen über etw *acc* sein
cut and dried ADJ (*also*: **cut-and-dry**: *answer*) eindeutig; (: *solution*) einfach
cutaway [ˈkʌtəweɪ] N (*coat*) Cut(away) *m*; (*drawing*) Schnittdiagramm *nt*; (*model*) Schnittmodell *nt*; (*Cine, TV*) Schnitt *m*
cutback [ˈkʌtbæk] N Kürzung *f*
cute [kjuːt] ADJ süß, niedlich; (*clever*) schlau
cut glass N geschliffenes Glas *nt*
cuticle [ˈkjuːtɪkl] N Nagelhaut *f*; **~ remover** Nagelhautentferner *m*
cutlery [ˈkʌtlərɪ] N Besteck *nt*
cutlet [ˈkʌtlɪt] N Schnitzel *nt*; (*also*: **vegetable cutlet, nut cutlet**) Bratling *m*
cutoff [ˈkʌtɔf] N (*also*: **cutoff point**) Trennlinie *f*
cutoff switch N Ausschaltmechanismus *m*
cutout [ˈkʌtaut] N (*switch*) Unterbrecher *m*; (*shape*) Ausschneidemodell *nt*; (*paper figure*) Ausschneidepuppe *f*
cut-price [ˈkʌtˈpraɪs] ADJ (*goods*) heruntergesetzt; (*offer*) Billig-
cut-rate [ˈkʌtˈreɪt] (US) ADJ = **cut-price**

C

cut-throat ['kʌtθrəut] N Mörder(in) *m(f)* ▶ ADJ unbarmherzig, mörderisch
cutting ['kʌtɪŋ] ADJ (*edge, remark*) scharf ▶ N (BRIT: *from newspaper*) Ausschnitt *m*; (: *Rail*) Durchstich *m*; (*from plant*) Ableger *m*
cutting edge N (*fig*) Spitzenstellung *f*; **on the ~ (of)** an der Spitze *+gen*
cutting-edge [kʌtɪŋ'ɛdʒ] ADJ wegbereitend, innovativ
cuttlefish ['kʌtlfɪʃ] N Tintenfisch *m*
CV N ABBR = **curriculum vitae**
c.w.o. ABBR (*Comm*) = **cash with order**
cwt ABBR = **hundredweight**
cyanide ['saɪənaɪd] N Zyanid *nt*
cyber attack ['saɪbə-] N Internetangriff *m*
cyberbullying ['saɪbəbulɪɪŋ] N Cybermobbing *nt*
cybercafé ['saɪbəkæfeɪ] N Internetcafé *nt*
cybernetics [saɪbə'nɛtɪks] N Kybernetik *f*
cybersecurity [saɪbəsɪ'kjurɪtɪ] N Internetsicherheit *f*
cyberspace N Cyberspace *m*
cyclamen ['sɪkləmən] N Alpenveilchen *nt*
cycle ['saɪkl] N (*bicycle*) (Fahr)rad *nt*; (*series: of seasons, songs etc*) Zyklus *m*; (: *of events*) Gang *m*; (: *Tech*) Periode *f* ▶ VI Rad fahren
cycle lane, cycle path N (Fahr)radweg *m*
cycle race N Radrennen *nt*
cycle rack N Fahrradständer *m*
cycling ['saɪklɪŋ] N Radfahren *nt*; **to go on a ~ holiday** (BRIT) Urlaub mit dem Fahrrad machen
cyclist ['saɪklɪst] N (Fahr)radfahrer(in) *m(f)*
cyclone ['saɪkləun] N Zyklon *m*
cygnet ['sɪgnɪt] N Schwanjunge(s) *nt*
cylinder ['sɪlɪndə^r] N Zylinder *m*; (*of gas*) Gasflasche *f*
cylinder block N Zylinderblock *m*
cylinder head N Zylinderkopf *m*
cylinder-head gasket ['sɪlɪndəhɛd-] N Zylinderkopfdichtung *f*
cymbals ['sɪmblz] NPL (*Mus*) Becken *nt*
cynic ['sɪnɪk] N Zyniker(in) *m(f)*
cynical ['sɪnɪkl] ADJ zynisch
cynicism ['sɪnɪsɪzəm] N Zynismus *m*
cypress ['saɪprɪs] N Zypresse *f*
Cypriot ['sɪprɪət] ADJ zypriotisch, zyprisch ▶ N Zypriot(in) *m(f)*
Cyprus ['saɪprəs] N Zypern *nt*
cyst [sɪst] N Zyste *f*
cystitis [sɪs'taɪtɪs] N Blasenentzündung *f*, Zystitis *f*
CZ (*US*) N ABBR (= *Canal Zone*) *Bereich des Panamakanals*
czar [zɑː^r] N = **tsar**
Czech [tʃɛk] ADJ tschechisch ▶ N Tscheche *m*, Tschechin *f*; (*language*) Tschechisch *nt*; **the ~ Republic** die Tschechische Republik *f*
Czechoslovak [tʃɛkə'sləuvæk] (*Hist*) ADJ, N = **Czechoslovakian**
Czechoslovakia [tʃɛkəslə'vækɪə] N (*Hist*) die Tschechoslowakei *f*
Czechoslovakian [tʃɛkəslə'vækɪən] (*Hist*) ADJ tschechoslowakisch ▶ N Tschechoslowake *m*, Tschechoslowakin *f*

Dd

D¹, d¹ [diː] N *(letter)* D *nt*, d *nt*; **D for David, D for Dog** *(US)* ≈ D wie Dora
D² [diː] N *(Mus)* D *nt*, d *nt*
D³ [diː] *(US)* ABBR *(Pol)* = **Democrat; Democratic**
d² *(BRIT: formerly)* ABBR = **penny**
d. ABBR = **died; Henry Jones, d. 1754** Henry Jones, gest. 1754
DA *(US)* N ABBR = **district attorney**
dab [dæb] VT betupfen; *(paint, cream)* tupfen ▶ N Tupfer *m*; **to be a ~ hand at sth** gut in etw *dat* sein; **to be a ~ hand at doing sth** sich darauf verstehen, etw zu tun
▶ **dab at** VT betupfen
dabble ['dæbl] VI: **to ~ in** sich (nebenbei) beschäftigen mit
dachshund ['dækshund] N Dackel *m*
dad [dæd] *(inf)* N Papa *m*, Vati *m*
daddy ['dædɪ] *(inf)* N = **dad**
daddy-longlegs [dædɪ'lɔŋlɛgz] *(inf)* N Schnake *f*
daffodil ['dæfədɪl] N Osterglocke *f*, Narzisse *f*
daft [dɑːft] *(inf)* ADJ doof *(inf)*, blöd *(inf)*; **to be ~ about sb/sth** verrückt nach jdm/etw sein
dagger ['dægəʳ] N Dolch *m*; **to be at daggers drawn with sb** mit jdm auf Kriegsfuß stehen; **to look daggers at sb** jdn mit Blicken durchbohren
dahlia ['deɪljə] N Dahlie *f*
daily ['deɪlɪ] ADJ täglich; *(wages)* Tages- ▶ N *(paper)* Tageszeitung *f*; *(BRIT: also:* **daily help***)* Putzfrau *f* ▶ ADV täglich; **twice ~** zweimal täglich *or* am Tag
dainty ['deɪntɪ] ADJ zierlich
dairy ['dɛərɪ] N *(BRIT: shop)* Milchgeschäft *nt*; *(company)* Molkerei *f*; *(on farm)* Milchkammer *f* ▶ CPD Milch-; *(herd, industry, farming)* Milchvieh-
dairy farm N *auf Milchviehhaltung spezialisierter Bauernhof*
dairy products NPL Milchprodukte *pl*, Molkereiprodukte *pl*
dairy store *(US)* N Milchgeschäft *nt*
dais ['deɪɪs] N Podium *nt*
daisy ['deɪzɪ] N Gänseblümchen *nt*
daisywheel ['deɪzɪwiːl] N Typenrad *nt*
daisywheel printer N Typenraddrucker *m*
Dakar ['dækəʳ] N Dakar *nt*
dale [deɪl] *(BRIT)* N Tal *nt*
dally ['dælɪ] VI (herum)trödeln; **to ~ with** *(plan, idea)* spielen mit
dalmatian [dæl'meɪʃən] N Dalmatiner *m*
dam [dæm] N (Stau)damm *m*; *(reservoir)* Stausee *m* ▶ VT stauen
damage ['dæmɪdʒ] N Schaden *m* ▶ VT schaden *+dat*; *(spoil, break)* beschädigen; **damages** NPL *(Law)* Schaden(s)ersatz *m*; **~ to property** Sachbeschädigung *f*; **to pay £5,000 in damages** 5000 Pfund Schaden(s)ersatz (be)zahlen
damaging ['dæmɪdʒɪŋ] ADJ: **~ (to)** schädlich (für)
Damascus [də'mɑːskəs] N Damaskus *nt*
dame [deɪm] N Dame *f*; *(US inf)* Weib *nt*; *(Theat)* (komische) Alte *f (von einem Mann gespielt)*
damn [dæm] VT verfluchen; *(condemn)* verurteilen ▶ ADJ *(inf: also:* **damned***)* verdammt ▶ N *(inf)*: **I don't give a ~** das ist mir scheißegal *(inf!)*; **~ (it)!** verdammt (noch mal)!
damnable ['dæmnəbl] ADJ grässlich
damnation [dæm'neɪʃən] N Verdammnis *f* ▶ EXCL *(inf)* verdammt
damning ['dæmɪŋ] ADJ belastend
damp [dæmp] ADJ feucht ▶ N Feuchtigkeit *f* ▶ VT *(also:* **dampen***)* befeuchten, anfeuchten; *(enthusiasm etc)* dämpfen
dampcourse ['dæmpkɔːs] N Dämmschicht *f*
damper ['dæmpəʳ] N *(Mus)* Dämpfer *m*; *(of fire)* (Luft)klappe *f*; **to put a ~ on** *(fig)* einen Dämpfer aufsetzen *+dat*
dampness ['dæmpnɪs] N Feuchtigkeit *f*
damson ['dæmzən] N Damaszenerpflaume *f*
dance [dɑːns] N Tanz *m*; *(social event)* Tanz(abend) *m* ▶ VI tanzen; **to ~ about** (herum)tänzeln
dance hall N Tanzsaal *m*
dancer ['dɑːnsəʳ] N Tänzer(in) *m(f)*
dancing ['dɑːnsɪŋ] N Tanzen *nt* ▶ CPD *(teacher, school, class etc)* Tanz-
D and C N ABBR *(Med: = dilation and curettage)* Ausschabung *f*
dandelion ['dændɪlaɪən] N Löwenzahn *m*
dandruff ['dændrəf] N Schuppen *pl*
D and T *(BRIT)* N ABBR *(Scol)* = **Design and Technology**
dandy ['dændɪ] N Dandy *m* ▶ ADJ *(US inf)* prima
Dane [deɪn] N Däne *m*, Dänin *f*
danger ['deɪndʒəʳ] N Gefahr *f*; **there is ~ of fire/poisoning** es besteht Feuer-/Vergiftungsgefahr; **there is a ~ of sth**

happening es besteht die Gefahr, dass etw geschieht; **"~!"** „Achtung!"; **in ~** in Gefahr; **to be in ~ of doing sth** Gefahr laufen, etw zu tun; **out of ~** außer Gefahr
danger list N: **on the ~** in Lebensgefahr
dangerous ['deɪndʒrəs] ADJ gefährlich
dangerously ['deɪndʒrəslɪ] ADV gefährlich; (*close*) bedenklich; **~ ill** schwer krank
danger zone N Gefahrenzone *f*
dangle ['dæŋgl] VT baumeln lassen ▸ VI baumeln
Danish ['deɪnɪʃ] ADJ dänisch ▸ N (*Ling*) Dänisch *nt*
Danish pastry N Plundergebäck *nt*
dank [dæŋk] ADJ (unangenehm) feucht
Danube ['dænju:b] N: **the ~** die Donau
dapper ['dæpə^r] ADJ gepflegt
Dardanelles [dɑ:də'nɛlz] NPL: **the ~** die Dardanellen *pl*
dare [dɛə^r] VT: **to ~ sb to do sth** jdn dazu herausfordern, etw zu tun ▸ VI: **to ~ (to) do sth** es wagen, etw zu tun; **I daren't tell him** (BRIT) ich wage nicht, es ihm zu sagen; **I ~ say** ich nehme an
daredevil ['dɛədɛvl] N Draufgänger *m*
Dar-es-Salaam ['dɑ:rɛssə'lɑ:m] N Daressalam *nt*
daring ['dɛərɪŋ] ADJ kühn, verwegen; (*bold*) gewagt ▸ N Kühnheit *f*
dark [dɑ:k] ADJ dunkel; (*look*) finster ▸ N: **in the ~** im Dunkeln; **to be in the ~ about** (*fig*) keine Ahnung haben von; **after ~** nach Einbruch der Dunkelheit; **it is/is getting ~** es ist/wird dunkel; **~ chocolate** Zartbitterschokolade *f*
Dark Ages NPL: **the ~** das finstere Mittelalter
darken ['dɑ:kn] VT dunkel machen ▸ VI sich verdunkeln
dark glasses NPL Sonnenbrille *f*
dark horse N (*in competition*) Unbekannte(r) *f(m)* (mit Außenseiterchancen); (*quiet person*) stilles Wasser *nt*
darkly ['dɑ:klɪ] ADV finster
darkness ['dɑ:knɪs] N Dunkelheit *f*, Finsternis *f*
darkroom ['dɑ:krum] N Dunkelkammer *f*
darling ['dɑ:lɪŋ] ADJ lieb ▸ N Liebling *m*; **to be the ~ of** der Liebling *+gen* sein; **she is a ~** sie ist ein Schatz
darn [dɑ:n] VT stopfen
dart [dɑ:t] N (*in game*) (Wurf)pfeil *m*; (*in sewing*) Abnäher *m* ▸ VI: **to ~ towards** (*also*: **make a dart towards**) zustürzen auf *+acc*; **to ~ away/along** davon-/entlangflitzen
dartboard ['dɑ:tbɔ:d] N Dartscheibe *f*
darts [dɑ:ts] N Darts *nt*, Pfeilwurfspiel *nt*
dash [dæʃ] N (*sign*) Gedankenstrich *m*; (*rush*) Jagd *f* ▸ VT (*throw*) schleudern; (*hopes*) zunichtemachen ▸ VI: **to ~ towards** zustürzen auf *+acc*; **a ~ of ...** (*small quantity*) etwas ..., ein Schuss *m* ...; **to make a ~ for sth** auf etw *acc* zustürzen; **we'll have to make a ~ for it** wir müssen rennen, so schnell wir können
▸ **dash away** VI losstürzen
▸ **dash off** VI = **dash away**
dashboard ['dæʃbɔ:d] N Armaturenbrett *nt*
dashing ['dæʃɪŋ] ADJ flott
dastardly ['dæstədlɪ] ADJ niederträchtig
DAT N ABBR (= *digital audio tape*) DAT *nt*
data ['deɪtə] NPL Daten *pl*
data analysis N Datenanalyse *f*
database ['deɪtəbeɪs] N Datenbank *f*
data capture N Datenerfassung *f*
data processing N Datenverarbeitung *f*
data projector N Beamer *m*
data transmission N Datenübertragung *f*
date [deɪt] N Datum *nt*; (*with friend*) Verabredung *f*; (*fruit*) Dattel *f* ▸ VT datieren; (*person*) ausgehen mit; **what's the ~ today?** der Wievielte ist heute?; **~ of birth** Geburtsdatum *nt*; **closing ~** Einsendeschluss *m*; **to ~** bis heute; **out of ~** altmodisch; (*expired*) abgelaufen; **up to ~** auf dem neuesten Stand; **to bring up to ~** auf den neuesten Stand bringen; (*person*) über den neuesten Stand der Dinge informieren; **a letter dated 5 July** ein vom 5. Juli datierter Brief
dated ['deɪtɪd] ADJ altmodisch
dateline ['deɪtlaɪn] N (*Geog*) Datumsgrenze *f*; (*Press*) Datumszeile *f*
date rape N Vergewaltigung *f* einer/eines Bekannten (*mit der/dem der Täter eine Verabredung hatte*)
date stamp N Datumsstempel *m*
dative ['deɪtɪv] N Dativ *m*
daub [dɔ:b] VT schmieren; **to ~ with** beschmieren mit
daughter ['dɔ:tə^r] N Tochter *f*
daughter-in-law ['dɔ:tərɪnlɔ:] N Schwiegertochter *f*
daunt [dɔ:nt] VT entmutigen
daunting ['dɔ:ntɪŋ] ADJ entmutigend
dauntless ['dɔ:ntlɪs] ADJ unerschrocken, beherzt
dawdle ['dɔ:dl] VI trödeln; **to ~ over one's work** bei der Arbeit bummeln *or* trödeln
dawn [dɔ:n] N Tagesanbruch *m*, Morgengrauen *nt*; (*of period*) Anbruch *m* ▸ VI dämmern; (*fig*): **it dawned on him that ...** es dämmerte ihm, dass ...; **from ~ to dusk** von morgens bis abends
dawn chorus (BRIT) N Morgenkonzert *nt* der Vögel
day [deɪ] N Tag *m*; (*heyday*) Zeit *f*; **the ~ before/after** am Tag zuvor/danach; **the ~ after tomorrow** übermorgen; **the ~ before yesterday** vorgestern; **(on) the following ~** am Tag danach; **the ~ that ...** (am Tag,) als ...; **~ by ~** jeden Tag, täglich; **by ~** tagsüber; **paid by the ~** tageweise bezahlt; **to work an eight hour ~** einen Achtstundentag haben; **these days, in the present ~** heute, heutzutage
daybook ['deɪbuk] (BRIT) N Journal *nt*
dayboy ['deɪbɔɪ] N Externe(r) *m*
daybreak ['deɪbreɪk] N Tagesanbruch *m*
day-care centre ['deɪkɛə-] N (*for children*) (Kinder)tagesstätte *f*; (*for old people*) Altentagesstätte *f*
daydream ['deɪdri:m] VI (mit offenen Augen) träumen ▸ N Tagtraum *m*, Träumerei *f*

daygirl ['deɪgəːl] N Externe *f*
daylight ['deɪlaɪt] N Tageslicht *nt*
daylight robbery (*inf*) N Halsabschneiderei *f*
daylight-saving time ['deɪlaɪt'seɪvɪŋ-] (*US*) N Sommerzeit *f*
day release N: **to be on ~** tageweise (zur Weiterbildung) freigestellt sein
day return (BRIT) N Tagesrückfahrkarte *f*
day shift N Tagschicht *f*
daytime ['deɪtaɪm] N Tag *m*; **in the ~** tagsüber, bei Tage
day-to-day ['deɪtə'deɪ] ADJ täglich, Alltags-; **on a ~ basis** tageweise
day trader N (*Stock Exchange*) Day-Trader(in) *m(f)*, Tageshändler(in) *m(f)*
day trip N Tagesausflug *m*
day-tripper ['deɪ'trɪpə^r] N Tagesausflügler(in) *m(f)*
daze [deɪz] VT benommen machen ▸ N: **in a ~** ganz benommen
dazed [deɪzd] ADJ benommen
dazzle ['dæzl] VT blenden
dazzling ['dæzlɪŋ] ADJ (*light*) blendend; (*smile*) strahlend; (*career, achievements*) glänzend
DC ABBR = **direct current**
DCC N ABBR (= *digital compact cassette*) DCC *f*
DD N ABBR (= *Doctor of Divinity*) ≈ Dr. theol.
DD ABBR = **direct debit**
D-day ['di:deɪ] N der Tag X
DDS (*US*) N ABBR (= *Doctor of Dental Surgery*) ≈ Dr. med. dent.
DDT N ABBR (= *dichlorodiphenyltrichloroethane*) DDT *nt*
deacon ['di:kən] N Diakon *m*
dead [dɛd] ADJ tot; (*flowers*) verwelkt; (*numb*) abgestorben, taub; (*battery*) leer; (*place*) wie ausgestorben ▸ ADV total, völlig; (*directly, exactly*) genau ▸ NPL: **the ~** die Toten *pl*; **to shoot sb ~** jdn erschießen; **~ silence** Totenstille *f*; **in the ~ centre (of)** genau in der Mitte *+gen*; **the line has gone ~** (*Tel*) die Leitung ist tot; **~ on time** auf die Minute pünktlich; **~ tired** todmüde; **to stop ~** abrupt stehen bleiben
dead beat (*inf*) ADJ (*tired*) völlig kaputt
deaden ['dɛdn] VT (*blow*) abschwächen; (*pain*) mildern; (*sound*) dämpfen
dead end N Sackgasse *f*
dead-end ['dɛdɛnd] ADJ: **a ~ job** ein Job *m* ohne Aufstiegsmöglichkeiten
dead heat N: **to finish in a ~** unentschieden ausgehen
dead letter office N Amt *nt* für unzustellbare Briefe
deadline ['dɛdlaɪn] N (letzter) Termin *m*; **to work to a ~** auf einen Termin hinarbeiten
deadlock ['dɛdlɔk] N Stillstand *m*; **the meeting ended in ~** die Verhandlung war festgefahren
dead loss (*inf*) N: **to be a ~** ein hoffnungsloser Fall sein
deadly ['dɛdlɪ] ADJ tödlich ▸ ADV: **~ dull** todlangweilig
deadpan ['dɛdpæn] ADJ (*look*) unbewegt; (*tone*) trocken
Dead Sea N: **the ~** das Tote Meer
dead season N tote Saison *f*
deaf [dɛf] ADJ taub; (*partially*) schwerhörig; **to turn a ~ ear to sth** sich einer Sache *dat* gegenüber taub stellen
deaf aid (BRIT) N Hörgerät *nt*
deaf-and-dumb ['dɛfən'dʌm] ADJ taubstumm; **~ alphabet** Taubstummensprache *f*
deafen ['dɛfn] VT taub machen
deafening ['dɛfnɪŋ] ADJ ohrenbetäubend
deaf-mute ['dɛfmju:t] N Taubstumme(r) *f(m)*
deafness ['dɛfnɪs] N Taubheit *f*
deal [di:l] (*pt, pp* **dealt**) N Geschäft *nt*, Handel *m* ▸ VT (*blow*) versetzen; (*card*) geben, austeilen; **to strike a ~ with sb** ein Geschäft mit jdm abschließen; **it's a ~!** (*inf*) abgemacht!; **he got a fair/bad ~ from them** er ist von ihnen anständig/schlecht behandelt worden; **a good ~** (*a lot*) ziemlich viel; **a great ~ (of)** ziemlich viel
▸ **deal in** VT FUS handeln mit
▸ **deal with** VT FUS (*person*) sich kümmern um; (*problem*) sich befassen mit; (*successfully*) fertig werden mit; (*subject*) behandeln
dealer ['di:lə^r] N Händler(in) *m(f)*; (*in drugs*) Dealer *m*; (*Cards*) Kartengeber(in) *m(f)*
dealership ['di:ləʃɪp] N (Vertrags)händler *m*
dealings ['di:lɪŋz] NPL Geschäfte *pl*; (*relations*) Beziehungen *pl*
dealt [dɛlt] PT, PP *of* **deal**
dean [di:n] N Dekan *m*; (*US Scol: administrator*) *Schul- oder Collegeverwalter mit Beratungs- und Disziplinarfunktion*
dear [dɪə^r] ADJ lieb; (*expensive*) teuer ▸ N: **(my) ~** (mein) Liebling *m* ▸ EXCL: **~ me!** (ach) du liebe Zeit!; **D~ Sir/Madam** Sehr geehrte Damen und Herren; **D~ Mr/Mrs X** Sehr geehrter Herr/geehrte Frau X; (*less formal*) Lieber Herr/Liebe Frau X
dearly ['dɪəlɪ] ADV (*love*) von ganzem Herzen; (*pay*) teuer
dear money N (*Comm*) teures Geld *nt*
dearth [dəːθ] N: **a ~ of** ein Mangel *m* an *+dat*
death [dɛθ] N Tod *m*; (*fatality*) Tote(r) *f(m)*, Todesfall *m*
deathbed ['dɛθbɛd] N: **to be on one's ~** auf dem Sterbebett liegen
death certificate N Sterbeurkunde *f*, Totenschein *m*
deathly ['dɛθlɪ] ADJ (*silence*) eisig ▸ ADV (*pale etc*) toten-
death penalty N Todesstrafe *f*
death rate N Sterbeziffer *f*
death row [-rəu] (*US*) N Todestrakt *m*
death sentence N Todesurteil *nt*
death squad N Todeskommando *nt*
death toll N Zahl *f* der Todesopfer *or* Toten
deathtrap ['dɛθtræp] N Todesfalle *f*
deb [dɛb] (*inf*) N ABBR = **debutante**
debacle [deɪ'bɑ:kl] N Debakel *nt*
debar [dɪ'bɑ:^r] VT: **to ~ sb from doing sth** jdn davon ausschließen, etw zu tun; **to ~ sb from a club** jdn aus einem Klub ausschließen

debase [dɪ'beɪs] VT (*value, quality*) mindern, herabsetzen; (*person*) erniedrigen, entwürdigen
debatable [dɪ'beɪtəbl] ADJ fraglich
debate [dɪ'beɪt] N Debatte *f* ▸ VT debattieren über *+acc*; (*course of action*) überlegen ▸ VI: **to ~ whether** hin und her überlegen, ob
debauchery [dɪ'bɔːtʃərɪ] N Ausschweifungen *pl*
debenture [dɪ'bɛntʃə^r] N Schuldschein *m*
debilitate [dɪ'bɪlɪteɪt] VT schwächen
debilitating [dɪ'bɪlɪteɪtɪŋ] ADJ schwächend
debit ['dɛbɪt] N Schuldposten *m* ▸ VT: **to ~ a sum to sb/sb's account** jdn/jds Konto mit einer Summe belasten; *see also* **direct**
debit balance N Sollsaldo *nt*, Debetsaldo *nt*
debit card N Geldkarte *f*
debit note N Lastschriftanzeige *f*
debonair [dɛbə'nɛə^r] ADJ flott
debrief [diː'briːf] VT befragen
debriefing [diː'briːfɪŋ] N Befragung *f*
debris ['dɛbriː] N Trümmer *pl*, Schutt *m*
debt [dɛt] N Schuld *f*; (*state of owing money*) Schulden *pl*, Verschuldung *f*; **to be in ~** Schulden haben, verschuldet sein; **bad ~** uneinbringliche Forderung *f*
debt collector N Inkassobeauftragte(r) *f(m)*, Schuldeneintreiber(in) *m(f)*
debtor ['dɛtə^r] N Schuldner(in) *m(f)*
debug ['diː'bʌg] VT (*Comput*) Fehler beseitigen in *+dat*
debunk [diː'bʌŋk] VT (*myths, ideas*) bloßstellen; (*claim*) entlarven; (*person, institution*) vom Sockel stoßen
debut ['deɪbjuː] N Debüt *nt*
debutante ['dɛbjutænt] N Debütantin *f*
Dec. ABBR = **December**
decade ['dɛkeɪd] N Jahrzehnt *nt*
decadence ['dɛkədəns] N Dekadenz *f*
decadent ['dɛkədənt] ADJ dekadent
decaff ['diːkæf] N koffeinfreier Kaffee *m*
decaffeinated [dɪ'kæfɪneɪtɪd] ADJ koffeinfrei
decamp [dɪ'kæmp] (*inf*) VI verschwinden, sich aus dem Staub machen
decant [dɪ'kænt] VT umfüllen
decanter [dɪ'kæntə^r] N Karaffe *f*
decarbonize [diː'kɑːbənaɪz] VT entkohlen
decathlon [dɪ'kæθlən] N Zehnkampf *m*
decay [dɪ'keɪ] N Verfall *m*; (*of tooth*) Fäule *f* ▸ VI (*body*) verwesen; (*teeth*) faulen; (*leaves*) verrotten; (*fig: society etc*) verfallen
decease [dɪ'siːs] N (*Law*): **upon your ~** bei Ihrem Ableben
deceased [dɪ'siːst] N: **the ~** der/die Tote *or* Verstorbene
deceit [dɪ'siːt] N Betrug *m*
deceitful [dɪ'siːtful] ADJ betrügerisch
deceive [dɪ'siːv] VT täuschen; (*husband, wife etc*) betrügen; **to ~ o.s.** sich *dat* etwas vormachen
decelerate [diː'sɛləreɪt] VI (*car etc*) langsamer werden; (*driver*) die Geschwindigkeit herabsetzen
December [dɪ'sɛmbə^r] N Dezember *m*; *see also* **July**
decency ['diːsənsɪ] N (*propriety*) Anstand *m*; (*kindness*) Anständigkeit *f*
decent ['diːsənt] ADJ anständig; **we expect you to do the ~ thing** wir erwarten, dass Sie die Konsequenzen ziehen; **they were very ~ about it** sie haben sich sehr anständig verhalten; **that was very ~ of him** das war sehr anständig von ihm; **are you ~?** (*dressed*) hast du etwas an?
decently ['diːsəntlɪ] ADV anständig
decentralization ['diːsɛntrəlaɪ'zeɪʃən] N Dezentralisierung *f*
decentralize [diː'sɛntrəlaɪz] VT dezentralisieren
deception [dɪ'sɛpʃən] N Täuschung *f*, Betrug *m*
deceptive [dɪ'sɛptɪv] ADJ irreführend, täuschend
decibel ['dɛsɪbɛl] N Dezibel *nt*
decide [dɪ'saɪd] VT entscheiden; (*persuade*) veranlassen ▸ VI sich entscheiden; **to ~ to do sth/that** beschließen, etw zu tun/dass; **to ~ on sth** sich für etw entscheiden; **to ~ on/against doing sth** sich dafür/dagegen entscheiden, etw zu tun
decided [dɪ'saɪdɪd] ADJ entschieden; (*character*) entschlossen; (*difference*) deutlich
decidedly [dɪ'saɪdɪdlɪ] ADV entschieden; (*emphatically*) entschlossen
deciding [dɪ'saɪdɪŋ] ADJ entscheidend
deciduous [dɪ'sɪdjuəs] ADJ (*tree, woods*) Laub-
decimal ['dɛsɪməl] ADJ (*system, number*) Dezimal- ▸ N Dezimalzahl *f*; **to three ~ places** auf drei Dezimalstellen
decimalize ['dɛsɪməlaɪz] (BRIT) VT auf das Dezimalsystem umstellen
decimal point N Komma *nt*
decimate ['dɛsɪmeɪt] VT dezimieren
decipher [dɪ'saɪfə^r] VT entziffern
decision [dɪ'sɪʒən] N Entscheidung *f*; (*decisiveness*) Bestimmtheit *f*, Entschlossenheit *f*; **to make a ~** eine Entscheidung treffen
decisive [dɪ'saɪsɪv] ADJ (*action etc*) entscheidend; (*person*) entschlussfreudig; (*manner, reply*) bestimmt, entschlossen
deck [dɛk] N Deck *nt*; (*also:* **record deck**) Plattenspieler *m*; (*of cards*) Spiel *nt*; **to go up on ~** an Deck gehen; **below ~** unter Deck; **top ~** (*of bus*) Oberdeck *nt*; **cassette ~** Tapedeck *nt*
deck chair N Liegestuhl *m*
deck hand N Deckshelfer(in) *m(f)*
declaration [dɛklə'reɪʃən] N Erklärung *f*
declare [dɪ'klɛə^r] VT erklären; (*result*) bekannt geben, veröffentlichen; (*income etc*) angeben; (*goods at customs*) verzollen
declassify [diː'klæsɪfaɪ] VT freigeben
decline [dɪ'klaɪn] N Rückgang *m*; (*decay*) Verfall *m* ▸ VT ablehnen ▸ VI (*strength*) nachlassen; (*business*) zurückgehen; (*old person*) abbauen; **~ in/of** Rückgang *m +gen*; **~ in living standards** Sinken *nt* des Lebensstandards
declutch [diː'klʌtʃ] VI auskuppeln
decode [diː'kəud] VT entschlüsseln
decoder [diː'kəudə^r] N Decoder *m*
decompose [diːkəm'pəuz] VI (*organic matter*) sich zersetzen; (*corpse*) verwesen

decomposition [di:kɔmpə'zɪʃən] N Zersetzung *f*
decompression [di:kəm'prɛʃən] N Dekompression *f*, Druckverminderung *f*
decompression chamber N Dekompressionskammer *f*
decongestant [di:kən'dʒɛstənt] N (*Med*) abschwellendes Mittel *nt*; (: *drops*) Nasentropfen *pl*
decontaminate [di:kən'tæmɪneɪt] VT entgiften
decontrol [di:kən'trəul] VT freigeben
décor ['deɪkɔ:ʳ] N Ausstattung *f*; (*Theat*) Dekor *m or nt*
decorate ['dɛkəreɪt] VI: **to ~ (with)** verzieren (mit) ▸ VT (*tree, building*) schmücken (mit); (*room, house: from bare walls*) anstreichen und tapezieren; (: *redecorate*) renovieren
decoration [dɛkə'reɪʃən] N Verzierung *f*; (*on tree, building*) Schmuck *m*; (*act*) Verzieren *nt*; Schmücken *nt*; (An)streichen *nt*; Tapezieren *nt*; (*medal*) Auszeichnung *f*
decorative ['dɛkərətɪv] ADJ dekorativ
decorator ['dɛkəreɪtəʳ] N Maler(in) *m(f)*, Anstreicher(in) *m(f)*
decorum [dɪ'kɔ:rəm] N Anstand *m*
decoy ['di:kɔɪ] N Lockvogel *m*; (*object*) Köder *m*; **they used him as a ~ for the enemy** sie benutzten ihn dazu, den Feind anzulocken
decrease VT [di'kri:s] verringern, reduzieren ▸ VI abnehmen, zurückgehen ▸ N ['di:kri:s]: **~ (in)** Abnahme *f* (*+gen*), Rückgang *m* (*+gen*); **to be on the ~** abnehmen, zurückgehen
decreasing [di:'kri:sɪŋ] ADJ abnehmend, zurückgehend
decree [dɪ'kri:] N (*Admin, Law*) Verfügung *f*; (*Pol*) Erlass *m*; (*Rel*) Dekret *nt* ▸ VT: **to ~ (that)** verfügen(, dass), verordnen(, dass)
decree absolute N endgültiges Scheidungsurteil *nt*
decree nisi [-'naɪsaɪ] N vorläufiges Scheidungsurteil *nt*
decrepit [dɪ'krɛpɪt] ADJ (*shack*) baufällig; (*person*) klapprig (*inf*)
decry [dɪ'kraɪ] VT schlechtmachen
decrypt [di:'krɪpt] VT entschlüsseln
dedicate ['dɛdɪkeɪt] VT: **to ~ to** widmen *+dat*
dedicated ['dɛdɪkeɪtɪd] ADJ hingebungsvoll, engagiert; (*Comput*) dediziert; **~ word processor** dediziertes Textverarbeitungssystem *nt*
dedication [dɛdɪ'keɪʃən] N Hingabe *f*; (*in book, on radio*) Widmung *f*
deduce [dɪ'dju:s] VT: **to ~ (that)** schließen(, dass), folgern(, dass)
deduct [dɪ'dʌkt] VT abziehen; **to ~ sth (from)** etw abziehen (von); (*esp from wage etc*) etw einbehalten (von)
deduction [dɪ'dʌkʃən] N (*act of deducting*) Abzug *m*; (*act of deducing*) Folgerung *f*
deed [di:d] N Tat *f*; (*Law*) Urkunde *f*; **~ of covenant** Vertragsurkunde *f*
deem [di:m] VT (*formal*) erachten für, halten für; **to ~ it wise/helpful to do sth** es für klug/ hilfreich halten, etw zu tun
deep [di:p] ADJ tief ▸ ADV: **the spectators stood 20 ~** die Zuschauer standen in 20 Reihen hintereinander; **to be 4 metres ~** 4 Meter tief sein; **knee-~ in water** bis zu den Knien im Wasser; **he took a ~ breath** er holte tief Luft
deepen ['di:pn] VT vertiefen ▸ VI (*crisis*) sich verschärfen; (*mystery*) größer werden
deepfreeze ['di:p'fri:z] N Tiefkühltruhe *f*
deep-fry ['di:p'fraɪ] VT frittieren
deeply ['di:plɪ] ADV (*breathe*) tief; (*interested*) höchst; (*moved, grateful*) zutiefst
deep-rooted ['di:p'ru:tɪd] ADJ tief verwurzelt; (*habit*) fest eingefahren
deep-sea ['di:p'si:] CPD Tiefsee-; (*fishing*) Hochsee-
deep-seated ['di:p'si:tɪd] ADJ tief sitzend
deep-set ['di:psɛt] ADJ tief liegend
deer [dɪəʳ] N INV Reh *nt*; (*male*) Hirsch *m*; **(red) ~** Rotwild *nt*; **(roe) ~** Reh *nt*; **(fallow) ~** Damwild *nt*
deerskin ['dɪəskɪn] N Hirschleder *nt*, Rehleder *nt*
deerstalker ['dɪəstɔ:kəʳ] N ≈ Sherlock-Holmes-Mütze *f*
deface [dɪ'feɪs] VT (*with paint etc*) beschmieren; (*slash, tear*) zerstören
defamation [dɛfə'meɪʃən] N Diffamierung *f*, Verleumdung *f*
defamatory [dɪ'fæmətrɪ] ADJ diffamierend, verleumderisch
default [dɪ'fɔ:lt] N (*also*: **default value**) Voreinstellung *f* ▸ VI: **to ~ on a debt** einer Zahlungsverpflichtung nicht nachkommen; **to win by ~** kampflos gewinnen
defaulter [dɪ'fɔ:ltəʳ] N säumiger Zahler *m*, säumige Zahlerin *f*
default option N Voreinstellung *f*
defeat [dɪ'fi:t] VT besiegen, schlagen ▸ N (*failure*) Niederlage *f*; (*of enemy*): **~ (of)** Sieg *m* (über *+acc*)
defeatism [dɪ'fi:tɪzəm] N Defätismus *m*
defeatist [dɪ'fi:tɪst] ADJ defätistisch ▸ N Defätist(in) *m(f)*
defect N ['di:fɛkt] Fehler *m* ▸ VI [dɪ'fɛkt]: **to ~ to the enemy** zum Feind überlaufen; **physical/ mental ~** körperlicher/geistiger Schaden *m or* Defekt *m*; **to ~ to the West** sich in den Westen absetzen
defective [dɪ'fɛktɪv] ADJ fehlerhaft
defector [dɪ'fɛktəʳ] N Überläufer(in) *m(f)*
defence, (*US*) **defense** [dɪ'fɛns] N Verteidigung *f*; (*justification*) Rechtfertigung *f*; **in ~ of** zur Verteidigung *+gen*; **witness for the ~** Zeuge *m*/ Zeugin *f* der Verteidigung; **the Ministry of D~, the Department of Defense** (*US*) das Verteidigungsministerium
defenceless [dɪ'fɛnslɪs] ADJ schutzlos
defend [dɪ'fɛnd] VT verteidigen
defendant [dɪ'fɛndənt] N Angeklagte(r) *f(m)*; (*in civil case*) Beklagte(r) *f(m)*
defender [dɪ'fɛndəʳ] N Verteidiger(in) *m(f)*
defending champion [dɪ'fɛndɪŋ-] N (*Sport*) Titelverteidiger(in) *m(f)*
defending counsel [dɪ'fɛndɪŋ-] N Verteidiger(in) *m(f)*

defense [dɪˈfɛns] (*US*) N = **defence**
defensive [dɪˈfɛnsɪv] ADJ defensiv ▶ N: **on the ~** in der Defensive
defer [dɪˈfəːʳ] VT verschieben
deference [ˈdɛfərəns] N Achtung *f*, Respekt *m*; **out of** *or* **in ~ to** aus Rücksicht auf *+acc*
deferential [dɛfəˈrɛnʃəl] ADJ ehrerbietig, respektvoll
defiance [dɪˈfaɪəns] N Trotz *m*; **in ~ of sth** einer Sache *dat* zum Trotz, unter Missachtung einer Sache *gen*
defiant [dɪˈfaɪənt] ADJ trotzig; (*challenging*) herausfordernd
defiantly [dɪˈfaɪəntlɪ] ADV trotzig; herausfordernd
deficiency [dɪˈfɪʃənsɪ] N Mangel *m*; (*defect*) Unzulänglichkeit *f*; (*deficit*) Defizit *nt*
deficiency disease N Mangelkrankheit *f*
deficient [dɪˈfɪʃənt] ADJ: **sb/sth is ~ in sth** jdm/etw fehlt es an etw *dat*
deficit [ˈdɛfɪsɪt] N Defizit *nt*
defile [dɪˈfaɪl] VT (*memory*) beschmutzen; (*statue etc*) schänden ▶ N Hohlweg *m*
define [dɪˈfaɪn] VT (*limits, boundaries*) bestimmen, festlegen; (*word*) definieren
definite [ˈdɛfɪnɪt] ADJ definitiv; (*date etc*) fest; (*clear, obvious*) klar, eindeutig; (*certain*) bestimmt; **he was ~ about it** er war sich *dat* sehr sicher
definite article N bestimmter Artikel *m*
definitely [ˈdɛfɪnɪtlɪ] ADV bestimmt; (*decide*) fest, definitiv
definition [dɛfɪˈnɪʃən] N (*of word*) Definition *f*; (*of photograph etc*) Schärfe *f*
definitive [dɪˈfɪnɪtɪv] ADJ (*account*) definitiv; (*version*) maßgeblich
deflate [diːˈfleɪt] VT (*tyre, balloon*) die Luft ablassen aus; (*person*) einen Dämpfer versetzen *+dat*; (*Econ*) deflationieren
deflation [diːˈfleɪʃən] N Deflation *f*
deflationary [diːˈfleɪʃənrɪ] ADJ deflationistisch
deflect [dɪˈflɛkt] VT (*attention*) ablenken; (*criticism*) abwehren; (*shot*) abfälschen; (*light*) brechen, beugen
defog [ˈdiːˈfɔg] (*US*) VT von Beschlag freimachen
defogger [ˈdiːˈfɔgəʳ] (*US*) N Gebläse *nt*
deform [dɪˈfɔːm] VT deformieren, verunstalten
deformed [dɪˈfɔːmd] ADJ deformiert, missgebildet
deformity [dɪˈfɔːmɪtɪ] N Deformität *f*, Missbildung *f*
defraud [dɪˈfrɔːd] VT: **to ~ sb (of sth)** jdn (um etw) betrügen
defray [dɪˈfreɪ] VT: **to ~ sb's expenses** jds Unkosten tragen *or* übernehmen
defriend [diːˈfrɛnd] VT (*on social network*) entfreunden
defrost [diːˈfrɔst] VT (*fridge*) abtauen; (*windscreen*) entfrosten; (*food*) auftauen
defroster [diːˈfrɔstəʳ] (*US*) N (*Aut*) Gebläse *nt*
deft [dɛft] ADJ geschickt
defunct [dɪˈfʌŋkt] ADJ (*industry*) stillgelegt; (*organization*) nicht mehr bestehend
defuse [diːˈfjuːz] VT entschärfen
defy [dɪˈfaɪ] VT sich widersetzen *+dat*; (*challenge*) auffordern; **it defies description** es spottet jeder Beschreibung
degenerate VI [dɪˈdʒɛnəreɪt] degenerieren ▶ ADJ [dɪˈdʒɛnərɪt] degeneriert
degradation [dɛgrəˈdeɪʃən] N Erniedrigung *f*
degrade [dɪˈgreɪd] VT erniedrigen; (*reduce the quality of*) degradieren
degrading [dɪˈgreɪdɪŋ] ADJ erniedrigend
degree [dɪˈgriː] N Grad *m*; (*Scol*) akademischer Grad *m*; **10 degrees below (zero)** 10 Grad unter null; **6 degrees of frost** 6 Grad Kälte *or* unter null; **a considerable ~ of risk** ein gewisses Risiko; **a ~ in maths** ein Hochschulabschluss *m* in Mathematik; **by degrees** nach und nach; **to some ~, to a certain ~** einigermaßen, in gewissem Maße
dehydrated [diːhaɪˈdreɪtɪd] ADJ ausgetrocknet, dehydriert; (*milk, eggs*) pulverisiert, Trocken-
dehydration [diːhaɪˈdreɪʃən] N Austrocknung *f*, Dehydration *f*
de-ice [ˈdiːˈaɪs] VT enteisen
de-icer [ˈdiːˈaɪsəʳ] N Defroster *m*
deign [deɪn] VI: **to ~ to do sth** sich herablassen, etw zu tun
deity [ˈdiːɪtɪ] N Gottheit *f*
dejected [dɪˈdʒɛktɪd] ADJ niedergeschlagen, deprimiert
dejection [dɪˈdʒɛkʃən] N Niedergeschlagenheit *f*, Depression *f*
Del. (*US*) ABBR (*Post*) = **Delaware**
delay [dɪˈleɪ] VT (*decision, ceremony*) verschieben, aufschieben; (*person, plane, train*) aufhalten ▶ VI zögern ▶ N Verzögerung *f*; (*postponement*) Aufschub *m*; **to be delayed** (*person*) sich verspäten; (*departure etc*) verspätet sein; (*flight etc*) Verspätung haben; **without ~** unverzüglich
delayed-action [dɪˈleɪdˈækʃən] ADJ (*bomb, mine*) mit Zeitzünder; (*Phot*): **~ shutter release** Selbstauslöser *m*
delectable [dɪˈlɛktəbl] ADJ (*person*) reizend; (*food*) köstlich
delegate [ˈdɛlɪgɪt] N Delegierte(r) *f*(*m*) ▶ VT delegieren; **to ~ sth to sb** jdm mit etw beauftragen; **to ~ sb to do sth** jdn damit beauftragen, etw zu tun
delegation [dɛlɪˈgeɪʃən] N Delegation *f*; (*group*) Abordnung *f*, Delegation *f*
delete [dɪˈliːt] VT streichen; (*Comput*) löschen
Delhi [ˈdɛlɪ] N Delhi *nt*
deli [ˈdɛlɪ] N Feinkostgeschäft *nt*
deliberate ADJ [dɪˈlɪbərɪt] absichtlich; (*action, insult*) bewusst; (*slow*) bedächtig ▶ VI [dɪˈlɪbəreɪt] überlegen
deliberately [dɪˈlɪbərɪtlɪ] ADV absichtlich, bewusst; (*slowly*) bedächtig
deliberation [dɪlɪbəˈreɪʃən] N Überlegung *f*; (*usu pl: discussions*) Beratungen *pl*
delicacy [ˈdɛlɪkəsɪ] N Feinheit *f*, Zartheit *f*; (*of problem*) Delikatheit *f*; (*choice food*) Delikatesse *f*
delicate [ˈdɛlɪkɪt] ADJ fein; (*colour, health*) zart; (*approach*) feinfühlig; (*problem*) delikat, heikel

delicately ['dɛlɪkɪtlɪ] ADV zart, fein; (*act, express*) feinfühlig
delicatessen [dɛlɪkə'tɛsn] N Feinkostgeschäft *nt*
delicious [dɪ'lɪʃəs] ADJ köstlich; (*feeling, person*) herrlich
delight [dɪ'laɪt] N Freude *f* ▸ VT erfreuen; **sb takes (a) ~ in sth** etw bereitet jdm große Freude; **sb takes (a) ~ in doing sth** es bereitet jdm große Freude, etw zu tun; **to be the ~ of** die Freude +*gen* sein; **she was a ~ to interview** es war eine Freude, sie zu interviewen; **the delights of country life** die Freuden des Landlebens
delighted [dɪ'laɪtɪd] ADJ: ~ **(at** *or* **with)** erfreut (über +*acc*), entzückt (über +*acc*); **to be ~ to do sth** etw gern tun; **I'd be ~** ich würde mich sehr freuen
delightful [dɪ'laɪtful] ADJ reizend, wunderbar
delimit [di:'lɪmɪt] VT abgrenzen
delineate [dɪ'lɪnɪeɪt] VT (*fig*) beschreiben
delinquency [dɪ'lɪŋkwənsɪ] N Kriminalität *f*
delinquent [dɪ'lɪŋkwənt] ADJ straffällig ▸ N Delinquent(in) *m(f)*
delirious [dɪ'lɪrɪəs] ADJ: **to be ~** (*with fever*) im Delirium sein; (*with excitement*) im Taumel sein
delirium [dɪ'lɪrɪəm] N Delirium *nt*
deliver [dɪ'lɪvə^r] VT liefern; (*letters, papers*) zustellen; (*hand over*) übergeben; (*message*) überbringen; (*speech*) halten; (*blow*) versetzen; (*Med: baby*) zur Welt bringen; (*warning*) geben; (*ultimatum*) stellen; (*free*): **to ~ (from)** befreien (von); **to ~ the goods** (*fig*) halten, was man versprochen hat
deliverance [dɪ'lɪvrəns] N Befreiung *f*
delivery [dɪ'lɪvərɪ] N Lieferung *f*; (*of letters, papers*) Zustellung *f*; (*of speaker*) Vortrag *m*; (*Med*) Entbindung *f*; **to take ~ of sth** etw in Empfang nehmen
delivery note N Lieferschein *m*
delivery van, (*US*) **delivery truck** N Lieferwagen *m*
delouse ['di:'laus] VT entlausen
delta ['dɛltə] N Delta *nt*
delude [dɪ'lu:d] VT täuschen; **to ~ o.s.** sich *dat* etwas vormachen
deluge ['dɛlju:dʒ] N (*of rain*) Guss *m*; (*fig: of petitions, requests*) Flut *f*
delusion [dɪ'lu:ʒən] N Irrglaube *m*; **to have delusions of grandeur** größenwahnsinnig sein
de luxe [də'lʌks] ADJ (*hotel, model*) Luxus-
delve [dɛlv] VI: **to ~ into** (*subject*) sich eingehend befassen mit; (*cupboard, handbag*) tief greifen in +*acc*
Dem. (*US*) ABBR (*Pol*) = **Democrat; Democratic**
demagogue ['dɛməgɔg] N Demagoge *m*, Demagogin *f*
demand [dɪ'mɑ:nd] VT verlangen; (*rights*) fordern; (*need*) erfordern, verlangen ▸ N Verlangen *nt*; (*claim*) Forderung *f*; (*Econ*) Nachfrage *f*; **to ~ sth (from** *or* **of sb)** etw (von jdm) verlangen *or* fordern; **to be in ~** gefragt sein; **on ~** (*available*) auf Verlangen; (*payable*) bei Vorlage *or* Sicht
demand draft N Sichtwechsel *m*
demanding [dɪ'mɑ:ndɪŋ] ADJ anspruchsvoll; (*work, child*) anstrengend
demarcation [di:mɑ:'keɪʃən] N (*of area, tasks*) Abgrenzung *f*
demarcation dispute N Streit *m* um den Zuständigkeitsbereich
demean [dɪ'mi:n] VT: **to ~ o.s.** sich erniedrigen
demeanour, (*US*) **demeanor** [dɪ'mi:nə^r] N Benehmen *nt*, Auftreten *nt*
demented [dɪ'mɛntɪd] ADJ wahnsinnig
demerger [di:'mə:dʒə^r] N (*Comm*) Abspaltung *f*, Demerger *m*
demilitarized zone [di:'mɪlɪtəraɪzd-] N entmilitarisierte Zone *f*
demise [dɪ'maɪz] N Ende *nt*; (*death*) Tod *m*
demist [di:'mɪst] (BRIT) VT (*Aut: windscreen*) von Beschlag freimachen
demister [di:'mɪstə^r] (BRIT) N (*Aut*) Gebläse *nt*
demo ['dɛməu] (*inf*) N ABBR = **demonstration**
demob [di:'mɔb] (*inf*) VT = **demobilize**
demobilize [di:'məubɪlaɪz] VT aus dem Kriegsdienst entlassen, demobilisieren
democracy [dɪ'mɔkrəsɪ] N Demokratie *f*
democrat ['dɛməkræt] N Demokrat(in) *m(f)*
democratic [dɛmə'krætɪk] ADJ demokratisch
Democratic Party (*US*) N: **the ~** die Demokratische Partei
demography [dɪ'mɔgrəfɪ] N Demografie *f*
demolish [dɪ'mɔlɪʃ] VT abreißen, abbrechen; (*fig: argument*) widerlegen
demolition [dɛmə'lɪʃən] N Abriss *m*, Abbruch *m*; (*of argument*) Widerlegung *f*
demon ['di:mən] N Dämon *m* ▸ ADJ teuflisch gut
demonstrate ['dɛmənstreɪt] VT (*theory*) demonstrieren; (*skill*) zeigen, beweisen; (*appliance*) vorführen ▸ VI: **to ~ (for/against)** demonstrieren (für/gegen)
demonstration [dɛmən'streɪʃən] N Demonstration *f*; (*of gadget, machine etc*) Vorführung *f*; **to hold a ~** eine Demonstration veranstalten *or* durchführen
demonstrative [dɪ'mɔnstrətɪv] ADJ demonstrativ
demonstrator ['dɛmənstreɪtə^r] N Demonstrant(in) *m(f)*; (*sales person*) Vorführer(in) *m(f)*; (*car*) Vorführwagen *m*; (*computer etc*) Vorführgerät *nt*
demoralize [dɪ'mɔrəlaɪz] VT entmutigen
demote [dɪ'məut] VT zurückstufen; (*Mil*) degradieren
demotion [dɪ'məuʃən] N Zurückstufung *f*; (*Mil*) Degradierung *f*
demur [dɪ'mə:^r] (*form*) VI Einwände *pl* erheben ▸ N: **without ~** widerspruchslos; **they demurred at the suggestion** sie erhoben Einwände gegen den Vorschlag
demure [dɪ'mjuə^r] ADJ zurückhaltend; (*smile*) höflich; (*dress*) schlicht
demurrage [dɪ'mʌrɪdʒ] N Liegegeld *nt*
den [dɛn] N Höhle *f*; (*of fox*) Bau *m*; (*room*) Bude *f*
denationalization ['di:næʃnəlaɪ'zeɪʃən] N Privatisierung *f*

denationalize [diːˈnæʃnəlaɪz] VT privatisieren
denatured alcohol [diːˈneɪtʃəd-] *(US)* N vergällter Alkohol *m*
denial [dɪˈnaɪəl] N Leugnen *nt*; *(of rights)* Verweigerung *f*
denier [ˈdɛnɪə^r] N Denier *nt*
denigrate [ˈdɛnɪgreɪt] VT verunglimpfen
denim [ˈdɛnɪm] N Jeansstoff *m*; **denims** NPL (Blue) Jeans *pl*
denim jacket N Jeansjacke *f*
denizen [ˈdɛnɪzn] N Bewohner(in) *m(f)*; *(person in town)* Einwohner(in) *m(f)*; *(foreigner)* eingebürgerter Ausländer *m*, eingebürgerte Ausländerin *f*
Denmark [ˈdɛnmɑːk] N Dänemark *nt*
denomination [dɪnɔmɪˈneɪʃən] N *(of money)* Nennwert *m*; *(Rel)* Konfession *f*
denominator [dɪˈnɔmɪneɪtə^r] N Nenner *m*
denote [dɪˈnəut] VT *(indicate)* hindeuten auf *+acc*; *(represent)* bezeichnen
denounce [dɪˈnauns] VT *(person)* anprangern; *(action)* verurteilen
dense [dɛns] ADJ dicht; *(inf: person)* beschränkt
densely [ˈdɛnslɪ] ADV dicht
density [ˈdɛnsɪtɪ] N Dichte *f*; **single/double-~ disk** *(Comput)* Diskette *f* mit einfacher/ doppelter Dichte
dent [dɛnt] N Beule *f*; *(in pride, ego)* Knacks *m* ▸ VT *(also:* **make a dent in***)* einbeulen; *(pride, ego)* anknacksen
dental [ˈdɛntl] ADJ *(filling, hygiene etc)* Zahn-; *(treatment)* zahnärztlich
dental floss [-flɔs] N Zahnseide *f*
dental surgeon N Zahnarzt *m*, Zahnärztin *f*
dentifrice [ˈdɛntɪfrɪs] N Zahnpasta *f*
dentist [ˈdɛntɪst] N Zahnarzt *m*, Zahnärztin *f*; *(also:* **dentist's (surgery)***)* Zahnarzt *m*, Zahnarztpraxis *f*
dentistry [ˈdɛntɪstrɪ] N Zahnmedizin *f*
dentures [ˈdɛntʃəz] NPL Zahnprothese *f*; *(full)* Gebiss *nt*
denuded [diːˈnjuːdɪd] ADJ: **~ of** entblößt von
denunciation [dɪnʌnsɪˈeɪʃən] N *(of person)* Anprangerung *f*; *(of action)* Verurteilung *f*
deny [dɪˈnaɪ] VT leugnen; *(involvement)* abstreiten; *(permission, chance)* verweigern; *(country, religion etc)* verleugnen; **he denies having said it** er leugnet *or* bestreitet, das gesagt zu haben
deodorant [diːˈəudərənt] N Deodorant *nt*
depart [dɪˈpɑːt] VI *(visitor)* abreisen; *(: on foot)* weggehen; *(bus, train)* abfahren; *(plane)* abfliegen; **to ~ from** *(fig)* abweichen von
departed [dɪˈpɑːtɪd] ADJ: **the (dear) ~** der (liebe) Verstorbene *m*, die (liebe) Verstorbene *f*, die (lieben) Verstorbenen *pl*
department [dɪˈpɑːtmənt] N Abteilung *f*; *(Scol)* Fachbereich *m*; *(Pol)* Ministerium *nt*; **that's not my ~** *(fig)* dafür bin ich nicht zuständig; **D~ of State** *(US)* Außenministerium *nt*
departmental [diːpɑːtˈmɛntl] ADJ *(budget, costs)* der Abteilung; *(level)* Abteilungs-; **~ manager** Abteilungsleiter(in) *m(f)*
department store N Warenhaus *nt*
departure [dɪˈpɑːtʃə^r] N *(of visitor)* Abreise *f*; *(on foot, of employee etc)* Weggang *m*; *(of bus, train)* Abfahrt *f*; *(of plane)* Abflug *m*; *(fig)*: **~ from** Abweichen *nt* von; **a new ~** ein neuer Weg *m*
departure lounge N Abflughalle *f*
depend [dɪˈpɛnd] VI: **to ~ on** abhängen von; *(rely on, trust)* sich verlassen auf *+acc*; *(financially)* abhängig sein von, angewiesen sein auf *+acc*; **it depends** es kommt darauf an; **depending on the result ...** je nachdem, wie das Ergebnis ausfällt, ...
dependable [dɪˈpɛndəbl] ADJ zuverlässig
dependant [dɪˈpɛndənt] N abhängige(r) (Familien)angehörige(r) *f(m)*
dependence [dɪˈpɛndəns] N Abhängigkeit *f*
dependent [dɪˈpɛndənt] ADJ: **to be ~ on** *(person)* abhängig sein von, angewiesen sein auf *+acc*; *(decision)* abhängen von ▸ N = **dependant**
depict [dɪˈpɪkt] VT *(in picture)* darstellen; *(describe)* beschreiben
depilatory [dɪˈpɪlətrɪ] N *(also:* **depilatory cream***)* Enthaarungsmittel *nt*
depleted [dɪˈpliːtɪd] ADJ *(reserves)* aufgebraucht; *(stocks)* erschöpft
deplorable [dɪˈplɔːrəbl] ADJ bedauerlich
deplore [dɪˈplɔː^r] VT verurteilen
deploy [dɪˈplɔɪ] VT einsetzen
depopulate [diːˈpɔpjuleɪt] VT entvölkern
depopulation [ˈdiːpɔpjuˈleɪʃən] N Entvölkerung *f*
deport [dɪˈpɔːt] VT *(criminal)* deportieren; *(illegal immigrant)* abschieben
deportation [diːpɔːˈteɪʃən] N Deportation *f*; Abschiebung *f*
deportation order N Ausweisung *f*
deportee [diːpɔːˈtiː] N Deportierte(r) *f(m)*
deportment [dɪˈpɔːtmənt] N Benehmen *nt*
depose [dɪˈpəuz] VT absetzen
deposit [dɪˈpɔzɪt] N *(in account)* Guthaben *nt*; *(down payment)* Anzahlung *f*; *(for hired goods etc)* Sicherheit *f*, Kaution *f*; *(on bottle etc)* Pfand *nt*; *(Chem)* Ablagerung *f*; *(of ore, oil)* Lagerstätte *f* ▸ VT deponieren; *(subj: river: sand etc)* ablagern; **to put down a ~ of £50** eine Anzahlung von £50 machen
deposit account N Sparkonto *nt*
depositary [dɪˈpɔzɪtərɪ] N Treuhänder(in) *m(f)*
depositor [dɪˈpɔzɪtə^r] N Deponent(in) *m(f)*, Einzahler(in) *m(f)*
depository [dɪˈpɔzɪtərɪ] N *(person)* Treuhänder(in) *m(f)*; *(place)* Lager(haus) *nt*
depot [ˈdɛpəu] N Lager(haus) *nt*; *(for vehicles)* Depot *nt*; *(US: station)* Bahnhof *m*; *(: bus station)* Busbahnhof *m*
depraved [dɪˈpreɪvd] ADJ verworfen
depravity [dɪˈprævɪtɪ] N Verworfenheit *f*
deprecate [ˈdɛprɪkeɪt] VT missbilligen
deprecating [ˈdɛprɪkeɪtɪŋ] ADJ *(disapproving)* missbilligend; *(apologetic)* entschuldigend
depreciate [dɪˈpriːʃɪeɪt] VI an Wert verlieren; *(currency)* an Kaufkraft verlieren; *(value)* sinken
depreciation [dɪpriːʃɪˈeɪʃən] N Wertminderung *f*; Kaufkraftverlust *m*; Sinken *nt*

depress [dɪ'prɛs] VT deprimieren; (*price, wages*) drücken; (*press down*) herunterdrücken
depressant [dɪ'prɛsnt] N Beruhigungsmittel *nt*
depressed [dɪ'prɛst] ADJ deprimiert, niedergeschlagen; (*price*) gesunken; (*industry*) geschwächt; (*area*) Notstands-; **to get ~** deprimiert werden
depressing [dɪ'prɛsɪŋ] ADJ deprimierend
depression [dɪ'prɛʃən] N (*Psych*) Depressionen *pl*; (*Econ*) Wirtschaftskrise *f*; (*Met*) Tief(druckgebiet) *nt*; (*hollow*) Vertiefung *f*
deprivation [dɛprɪ'veɪʃən] N Entbehrung *f*, Not *f*; (*of freedom, rights etc*) Entzug *m*
deprive [dɪ'praɪv] VT: **to ~ sb of sth** (*liberty*) jdm etw entziehen; (*life*) jdm etw nehmen
deprived [dɪ'praɪvd] ADJ benachteiligt; (*area*) Not leidend
dept ABBR = **department**
depth [dɛpθ] N Tiefe *f*; **in the depths of** in den Tiefen *+gen*; **in the depths of despair** in tiefster Verzweiflung; **in the depths of winter** im tiefsten Winter; **at a ~ of 3 metres** in 3 Meter Tiefe; **to be out of one's ~** (*in water*) nicht mehr stehen können; (*fig*) überfordert sein; **to study sth in ~** etw gründlich *or* eingehend studieren
depth charge N Wasserbombe *f*
deputation [dɛpju'teɪʃən] N Abordnung *f*
deputize ['dɛpjutaɪz] VI: **to ~ for sb** jdn vertreten
deputy ['dɛpjutɪ] CPD stellvertretend ▸ N (Stell)vertreter(in) *m(f)*; (*Pol*) Abgeordnete(r) *f(m)*; (*US: also*: **deputy sheriff**) Hilfssheriff *m*; **~ head** (BRIT *Scol*) Konrektor(in) *m(f)*
derail [dɪ'reɪl] VT: **to be derailed** entgleisen
derailment [dɪ'reɪlmənt] N Entgleisung *f*
deranged [dɪ'reɪndʒd] ADJ: **to be mentally ~** geistesgestört sein
derby ['də:rbɪ] N Derby *nt*; (*US: hat*) Melone *f*
deregulate [dɪ'rɛgjuleɪt] VT staatliche Kontrollen aufheben bei
deregulation [dɪ'rɛgju'leɪʃən] N Aufhebung *f* staatlicher Kontrollen
derelict ['dɛrɪlɪkt] ADJ verfallen
deride [dɪ'raɪd] VT sich lustig machen über *+acc*
derision [dɪ'rɪʒən] N Hohn *m*, Spott *m*
derisive [dɪ'raɪsɪv] ADJ spöttisch
derisory [dɪ'raɪsərɪ] ADJ spöttisch; (*sum*) lächerlich
derivation [dɛrɪ'veɪʃən] N Ableitung *f*
derivative [dɪ'rɪvətɪv] N (*Ling*) Ableitung *f*; (*Chem*) Derivat *nt* ▸ ADJ nachahmend
derive [dɪ'raɪv] VT: **to ~ (from)** gewinnen (aus); (*benefit*) ziehen (aus) ▸ VI: **to ~ from** (*originate in*) sich herleiten *or* ableiten von; **to ~ pleasure from** Freude haben an *+dat*
dermatitis [də:mə'taɪtɪs] N Hautentzündung *f*, Dermatitis *f*
dermatology [də:mə'tɔlədʒɪ] N Dermatologie *f*
derogatory [dɪ'rɔgətərɪ] ADJ abfällig
derrick ['dɛrɪk] N (*on ship*) Derrickkran *m*; (*on well*) Bohrturm *m*
derv [də:v] (BRIT) N (*Aut*) Diesel(kraftstoff) *m*
desalination [di:sælɪ'neɪʃən] N Entsalzung *f*
descend [dɪ'sɛnd] VT hinuntergehen, hinuntersteigen; (*lift, vehicle*) hinunterfahren; (*road*) hinunterführen ▸ VI hinuntergehen; (*lift*) nach unten fahren; **to ~ from** abstammen von; **to ~ to** sich erniedrigen zu; **in descending order of importance** nach Wichtigkeit geordnet
▸ **descend on** VT FUS überfallen; (*subj: misfortune*) hereinbrechen über *+acc*; (*: gloom*) befallen; (*: silence*) sich senken auf *+acc*; **visitors descended (up)on us** der Besuch hat uns überfallen
descendant [dɪ'sɛndənt] N Nachkomme *m*
descent [dɪ'sɛnt] N Abstieg *m*; (*origin*) Abstammung *f*
describe [dɪs'kraɪb] VT beschreiben
description [dɪs'krɪpʃən] N Beschreibung *f*; (*sort*): **of every ~** aller Art
descriptive [dɪs'krɪptɪv] ADJ deskriptiv
desecrate ['dɛsɪkreɪt] VT schänden
desegregate [di:'sɛgrɪgeɪt] VT die Rassentrennung aufheben in *+dat*
desert N ['dɛzət] Wüste *f* ▸ VT [dɪ'zə:t] verlassen ▸ VI desertieren; *see also* **deserts**
deserter [dɪ'zə:tə[r]] N Deserteur *m*
desertion [dɪ'zə:ʃən] N Desertion *f*, Fahnenflucht *f*; (*Law*) böswilliges Verlassen *nt*
desert island N einsame *or* verlassene Insel *f*
deserts [dɪ'zə:ts] NPL: **to get one's just ~** bekommen, was man verdient
deserve [dɪ'zə:v] VT verdienen
deservedly [dɪ'zə:vɪdlɪ] ADV verdientermaßen
deserving [dɪ'zə:vɪŋ] ADJ verdienstvoll
desiccated ['dɛsɪkeɪtɪd] ADJ vertrocknet; (*coconut*) getrocknet
design [dɪ'zaɪn] N Design *nt*; (*process*) Entwurf *m*, Gestaltung *f*; (*sketch*) Entwurf *m*; (*layout, shape*) Form *f*; (*pattern*) Muster *nt*; (*of car*) Konstruktion *f*; (*intention*) Plan *m*, Absicht *f* ▸ VT entwerfen; **to have designs on** es abgesehen haben auf *+acc*; **well-designed** mit gutem Design
design and technology (BRIT) N (*Scol*) ≈ Design und Technologie
designate VT ['dɛzɪgneɪt] bestimmen, ernennen ▸ ADJ ['dɛzɪgnɪt] designiert
designation [dɛzɪg'neɪʃən] N Bezeichnung *f*
designer [dɪ'zaɪnə[r]] N Designer(in) *m(f)*; (*Tech*) Konstrukteur(in) *m(f)*; (*also*: **fashion designer**) Modeschöpfer(in) *m(f)* ▸ ADJ (*clothes etc*) Designer-
desirability [dɪzaɪərə'bɪlɪtɪ] N: **they discussed the ~ of the plan** sie besprachen, ob der Plan wünschenswert sei
desirable [dɪ'zaɪərəbl] ADJ (*proper*) wünschenswert; (*attractive*) reizvoll, attraktiv
desire [dɪ'zaɪə[r]] N Wunsch *m*; (*sexual*) Verlangen *nt*, Begehren *nt* ▸ VT wünschen; (*lust after*) begehren; **to ~ to do sth/that** wünschen, etw zu tun/dass
desirous [dɪ'zaɪərəs] ADJ: **to be ~ of doing sth** den Wunsch haben, etw zu tun

desist [dɪ'zɪst] VI: **to ~ (from)** absehen (von), Abstand nehmen (von)
desk [dɛsk] N Schreibtisch *m*; (*for pupil*) Pult *nt*; (*in hotel*) Empfang *m*; (*at airport*) Schalter *m*; (BRIT: *in shop, restaurant*) Kasse *f*
desk job N Bürojob *m*
desktop ['dɛsktɔp] N Arbeitsfläche *f*
desktop publishing N Desktop-Publishing *nt*
desolate ['dɛsəlɪt] ADJ trostlos
desolation [dɛsə'leɪʃən] N Trostlosigkeit *f*
despair [dɪs'pɛəʳ] N Verzweiflung *f* ▸ VI: **to ~ of** alle Hoffnung aufgeben auf *+acc*; **to be in ~** verzweifelt sein
despatch [dɪs'pætʃ] N, VT = **dispatch**
desperate ['dɛspərɪt] ADJ verzweifelt; (*shortage*) akut; (*criminal*) zum Äußersten entschlossen; **to be ~ for sth/to do sth** etw dringend brauchen/unbedingt tun wollen
desperately ['dɛspərɪtlɪ] ADV (*shout, struggle etc*) verzweifelt; (*ill*) schwer; (*unhappy etc*) äußerst
desperation [dɛspə'reɪʃən] N Verzweiflung *f*; **in (sheer) ~** aus (reiner) Verzweiflung
despicable [dɪs'pɪkəbl] ADJ (*action*) verabscheuungswürdig; (*person*) widerwärtig
despise [dɪs'paɪz] VT verachten
despite [dɪs'paɪt] PREP trotz *+gen*
despondent [dɪs'pɔndənt] ADJ niedergeschlagen, mutlos
despot ['dɛspɔt] N Despot *m*
dessert [dɪ'zə:t] N Nachtisch *m*, Dessert *nt*
dessertspoon [dɪ'zə:tspu:n] N Dessertlöffel *m*
destabilize [di:'steɪbɪlaɪz] VT destabilisieren
destination [dɛstɪ'neɪʃən] N (Reise)ziel *nt*; (*of mail*) Bestimmungsort *m*
destined ['dɛstɪnd] ADJ: **to be ~ to do sth** dazu bestimmt *or* ausersehen sein, etw zu tun; **to be ~ for** bestimmt *or* ausersehen sein für
destiny ['dɛstɪnɪ] N Schicksal *nt*
destitute ['dɛstɪtju:t] ADJ mittellos
destroy [dɪs'trɔɪ] VT zerstören; (*animal*) töten
destroyer [dɪs'trɔɪəʳ] N Zerstörer *m*
destruction [dɪs'trʌkʃən] N Zerstörung *f*
destructive [dɪs'trʌktɪv] ADJ zerstörerisch; (*child, criticism etc*) destruktiv
desultory ['dɛsəltərɪ] ADJ flüchtig; (*conversation*) zwanglos
detach [dɪ'tætʃ] VT (*remove*) entfernen; (*unclip*) abnehmen; (*unstick*) ablösen
detachable [dɪ'tætʃəbl] ADJ abnehmbar
detached [dɪ'tætʃt] ADJ distanziert; (*house*) frei stehend, Einzel-
detachment [dɪ'tætʃmənt] N Distanz *f*; (*Mil*) Sonderkommando *nt*
detail ['di:teɪl] N Einzelheit *f*; (*no pl: in picture, one's work etc*) Detail *nt*; (*trifle*) unwichtige Einzelheit ▸ VT (einzeln) aufführen; **in ~** in Einzelheiten; **to go into details** auf Einzelheiten eingehen, ins Detail gehen
detailed ['di:teɪld] ADJ detailliert, genau
detain [dɪ'teɪn] VT aufhalten; (*in captivity*) in Haft halten; (*in hospital*) festhalten
detainee [di:teɪ'ni:] N Häftling *m*
detect [dɪ'tɛkt] VT wahrnehmen; (*Med, Tech*) feststellen; (*Mil*) ausfindig machen
detection [dɪ'tɛkʃən] N Entdeckung *f*, Feststellung *f*; **crime ~** Ermittlungsarbeit *f*; **to escape ~** (*criminal*) nicht gefasst werden; (*mistake*) der Aufmerksamkeit *dat* entgehen
detective [dɪ'tɛktɪv] N Kriminalbeamte(r) *m*; **private ~** Privatdetektiv *m*
detective story N Kriminalgeschichte *f*, Detektivgeschichte *f*
detector [dɪ'tɛktəʳ] N Detektor *m*
détente [deɪ'tɑ:nt] N Entspannung *f*, Détente *f*
detention [dɪ'tɛnʃən] N (*arrest*) Festnahme *f*; (*captivity*) Haft *f*; (*Scol*) Nachsitzen *nt*
deter [dɪ'tə:ʳ] VT (*discourage*) abschrecken; (*dissuade*) abhalten
detergent [dɪ'tə:dʒənt] N Reinigungsmittel *nt*; (*for clothes*) Waschmittel *nt*; (*for dishes*) Spülmittel *nt*
deteriorate [dɪ'tɪərɪəreɪt] VI sich verschlechtern
deterioration [dɪtɪərɪə'reɪʃən] N Verschlechterung *f*
determination [dɪtə:mɪ'neɪʃən] N Entschlossenheit *f*; (*establishment*) Festsetzung *f*
determine [dɪ'tə:mɪn] VT (*facts*) feststellen; (*limits etc*) festlegen; **to ~ that** beschließen, dass; **to ~ to do sth** sich entschließen, etw zu tun
determined [dɪ'tə:mɪnd] ADJ entschlossen; (*quantity*) bestimmt; **to be ~ to do sth** (fest) entschlossen sein, etw zu tun
deterrence [dɪ'tɛrəns] N Abschreckung *f*
deterrent [dɪ'tɛrənt] N Abschreckungsmittel *nt*; **to act as a ~** als Abschreckung(smittel) dienen
detest [dɪ'tɛst] VT verabscheuen
detestable [dɪ'tɛstəbl] ADJ abscheulich, widerwärtig
detonate ['dɛtəneɪt] VI detonieren ▸ VT zur Explosion bringen
detonator ['dɛtəneɪtəʳ] N Sprengkapsel *f*
detour ['di:tuəʳ] N Umweg *m*; (*US Aut*) Umleitung *f*
detox ['di:tɔks] (*inf*) N (*from drugs*) Drogenentzug *m*; (*from alcohol etc*) Entgiftung *f* ▸ VI (*from drugs*) entziehen, Entzug machen; (*from alcohol etc*) entgiften
detoxification [di:tɔksɪfɪ'keɪʃən] N (*from drugs*) Drogenentzug *m*; (*from alcohol etc*) Entgiftung *f*
detoxify [di:'tɔksɪfaɪ] VI (*from drugs*) entziehen, Entzug machen; (*from alcohol etc*) entgiften
detract [dɪ'trækt] VI: **to ~ from** schmälern; (*effect*) beeinträchtigen
detractor [dɪ'træktəʳ] N Kritiker(in) *m(f)*
detriment ['dɛtrɪmənt] N: **to the ~ of** zum Schaden *+gen*; **without ~ to** ohne Schaden für
detrimental [dɛtrɪ'mɛntl] ADJ: **to be ~ to** schaden *+dat*
deuce [dju:s] N (*Tennis*) Einstand *m*
devaluation [dɪvælju'eɪʃən] N Abwertung *f*
devalue ['di:'vælju:] VT abwerten

devastate ['dɛvəsteɪt] VT verwüsten; (*fig: shock*): **to be devastated by** niedergeschmettert sein von
devastating ['dɛvəsteɪtɪŋ] ADJ verheerend; (*announcement, news*) niederschmetternd
devastation [dɛvəs'teɪʃən] N Verwüstung *f*
develop [dɪ'vɛləp] VT entwickeln; (*business*) erweitern, ausbauen; (*land, resource*) erschließen; (*disease*) bekommen ▸ VI sich entwickeln; (*facts*) an den Tag kommen; (*symptoms*) auftreten; **to ~ a taste for sth** Geschmack an etw finden; **the machine/car developed a fault/engine trouble** an dem Gerät/dem Wagen trat ein Defekt/ein Motorschaden auf; **to ~ into** sich entwickeln zu, werden
developer [dɪ'vɛləpə^r] N (*also:* **property developer**) *Bauunternehmer und Immobilienmakler*
developing country [dɪ'vɛləpɪŋ-] N Entwicklungsland *nt*
development [dɪ'vɛləpmənt] N Entwicklung *f*; (*of land*) Erschließung *f*
development area N Entwicklungsgebiet *nt*
deviant ['di:vɪənt] ADJ abweichend
deviate ['di:vɪeɪt] VI: **to ~ (from)** abweichen (von)
deviation [di:vɪ'eɪʃən] N Abweichung *f*
device [dɪ'vaɪs] N Gerät *nt*; (*ploy, stratagem*) Trick *m*; **explosive ~** Sprengkörper *m*
devil ['dɛvl] N Teufel *m*; **go on, be a ~!** nur zu, riskier mal was!; **talk of the ~!** wenn man vom Teufel spricht!
devilish ['dɛvlɪʃ] ADJ teuflisch
devil's advocate ['dɛvlz-] N Advocatus Diaboli *m*
devious ['di:vɪəs] ADJ (*person*) verschlagen; (*route, path*) gewunden
devise [dɪ'vaɪz] VT sich *dat* ausdenken; (*machine*) entwerfen
devoid [dɪ'vɔɪd] ADJ: **~ of** bar *+gen*, ohne *+acc*
devolution [di:və'lu:ʃən] N Dezentralisierung *f*
devolve [dɪ'vɔlv] VT übertragen ▸ VI: **to ~ (up)on** übergehen auf *+acc*
devote [dɪ'vəut] VT: **to ~ sth/o.s. to** etw/sich widmen *+dat*
devoted [dɪ'vəutɪd] ADJ treu; (*admirer*) eifrig; **to be ~ to sb** jdn innig lieben; **the book is ~ to politics** das Buch widmet sich ganz der Politik *dat*
devotee [dɛvəu'ti:] N (*fan*) Liebhaber(in) *m(f)*; (*Rel*) Anhänger(in) *m(f)*
devotion [dɪ'vəuʃən] N (*affection*) Ergebenheit *f*; (*dedication*) Hingabe *f*; (*Rel*) Andacht *f*
devour [dɪ'vauə^r] VT verschlingen
devout [dɪ'vaut] ADJ fromm
dew [dju:] N Tau *m*
dexterity [dɛks'tɛrɪtɪ] N Geschicklichkeit *f*; (*mental*) Gewandtheit *f*
dexterous, dextrous ['dɛkstrəs] ADJ geschickt
DfEE (BRIT) N ABBR (= *Department for Education and Employment*) ≈ Ministerium *nt* für Bildung und Arbeit
dg ABBR (= *decigram*) dg
DHSS (BRIT) N ABBR (*formerly:* = *Department of Health and Social Security*) *Ministerium für Gesundheit und Sozialfürsorge*
diabetes [daɪə'bi:ti:z] N Zuckerkrankheit *f*
diabetic [daɪə'bɛtɪk] ADJ zuckerkrank; (*chocolate, jam*) Diabetiker- ▸ N Diabetiker(in) *m(f)*
diabolical [daɪə'bɔlɪkl] (*inf*) ADJ schrecklich, fürchterlich
diaeresis [daɪ'ɛrɪsɪs] N Diärese *f*
diagnose [daɪəg'nəuz] VT diagnostizieren
diagnoses [daɪəg'nəusi:z] PL *of* **diagnosis**
diagnosis [daɪəg'nəusɪs] (*pl* **diagnoses**) N Diagnose *f*
diagonal [daɪ'ægənl] ADJ diagonal ▸ N Diagonale *f*
diagram ['daɪəgræm] N Diagramm *nt*, Schaubild *nt*
dial ['daɪəl] N Zifferblatt *nt*; (*on radio set*) Einstellskala *f*; (*of phone*) Wählscheibe *f* ▸ VT wählen; **to ~ a wrong number** sich verwählen; **can I ~ London direct?** kann ich nach London durchwählen?
dial. ABBR = **dialect**
dial code (US) N = **dialling code**
dialect ['daɪəlɛkt] N Dialekt *m*
dialling code ['daɪəlɪŋ-], (US) **dial code** N Vorwahl *f*
dialling tone, (US) **dial tone** N Amtszeichen *nt*
dialogue, (US) **dialog** ['daɪəlɔg] N Dialog *m*; (*conversation*) Gespräch *nt*, Dialog *m*
dial tone (US) N = **dialling tone**
dialysis [daɪ'ælɪsɪs] N Dialyse *f*
diameter [daɪ'æmɪtə^r] N Durchmesser *m*
diametrically [daɪə'mɛtrɪklɪ] ADV: **~ opposed (to)** diametral entgegengesetzt (*+dat*)
diamond ['daɪəmənd] N Diamant *m*; (*shape*) Raute *f*; **diamonds** NPL (*Cards*) Karo *nt*
diamond ring N Diamantring *m*
diaper ['daɪəpə^r] (US) N Windel *f*
diaphragm ['daɪəfræm] N Zwerchfell *nt*; (*contraceptive*) Pessar *nt*
diarrhoea, (US) **diarrhea** [daɪə'ri:ə] N Durchfall *m*
diary ['daɪərɪ] N (Termin)kalender *m*; (*daily account*) Tagebuch *nt*; **to keep a ~** Tagebuch führen
diatribe ['daɪətraɪb] N Schmährede *f*; (*written*) Schmähschrift *f*
dice [daɪs] N INV Würfel *m* ▸ VT in Würfel schneiden
diced [daɪst] ADJ in Würfel geschnitten
dicey ['daɪsɪ] (*inf*) ADJ riskant
dichotomy [daɪ'kɔtəmɪ] N Dichotomie *f*, Kluft *f*
dickhead ['dɪkhɛd] (*inf*) N Knallkopf *m*
Dictaphone® ['dɪktəfəun] N Diktafon *nt*, Diktiergerät *nt*
dictate [dɪk'teɪt] VT diktieren ▸ N Diktat *nt*; (*principle*): **the dictates of** die Gebote *+gen* ▸ VI: **to ~ to** diktieren *+dat*; **I won't be dictated to** ich lasse mir keine Vorschriften machen
dictation [dɪk'teɪʃən] N Diktat *nt*; **at ~ speed** im Diktiertempo
dictator [dɪk'teɪtə^r] N Diktator *m*

d

dictatorship [dɪk'teɪtəʃɪp] N Diktatur *f*
diction ['dɪkʃən] N Diktion *f*
dictionary ['dɪkʃənrɪ] N Wörterbuch *nt*
did [dɪd] PT *of* **do**
didactic [daɪ'dæktɪk] ADJ didaktisch
diddle ['dɪdl] (*inf*) VT übers Ohr hauen
didn't ['dɪdnt] = **did not**
die [daɪ] N (*pl: dice*) Würfel *m*; (*: dies*) Gussform *f* ▶ VI sterben; (*plant*) eingehen; (*fig: noise*) aufhören; (*: smile*) vergehen; (*engine*) stehen bleiben; **to ~ of** *or* **from** sterben an +*dat*; **to be dying** im Sterben liegen; **to be dying for sth** etw unbedingt brauchen; **to be dying to do sth** darauf brennen, etw zu tun
▶ **die away** VI (*sound*) schwächer werden; (*light*) nachlassen
▶ **die down** VI (*wind*) sich legen; (*fire*) herunterbrennen; (*excitement, noise*) nachlassen
▶ **die out** VI aussterben
die-hard ['daɪhɑːd] N Ewiggestrige(r) *f*(*m*)
diesel ['diːzl] N (*vehicle*) Diesel *m*; (*also:* **diesel oil**) Diesel(kraftstoff) *m*
diesel engine N Dieselmotor *m*
diet ['daɪət] N Ernährung *f*; (*Med*) Diät *f*; (*when slimming*) Schlankheitskur *f* ▶ VI (*also:* **be on a diet**) eine Schlankheitskur machen; **to live on a ~ of** sich ernähren von, leben von
dietician [daɪə'tɪʃən] N Diätassistent(in) *m*(*f*)
differ ['dɪfəʳ] VI (*be different*): **to ~ (from)** sich unterscheiden (von); (*disagree*): **to ~ (about)** anderer Meinung sein (über +*acc*); **to agree to ~** sich *dat* verschiedene Meinungen zugestehen
difference ['dɪfrəns] N Unterschied *m*; (*disagreement*) Differenz *f*, Auseinandersetzung *f*; **it makes no ~ to me** das ist mir egal *or* einerlei; **to settle one's differences** die Differenzen *or* Meinungsverschiedenheiten beilegen
different ['dɪfrənt] ADJ (*various people, things*) verschieden, unterschiedlich; **to be ~ (from)** anders sein (als)
differential [dɪfə'rɛnʃəl] N (*Math*) Differenzial *nt*; (BRIT: *in wages*) (Einkommens)unterschied *m*
differentiate [dɪfə'rɛnʃɪeɪt] VI: **to ~ (between)** unterscheiden (zwischen) ▶ VT: **to ~ A from B** A von B unterscheiden
differently ['dɪfrəntlɪ] ADV anders; (*shaped, designed*) verschieden, unterschiedlich
difficult ['dɪfɪkəlt] ADJ schwierig; (*task, problem*) schwer, schwierig; **~ to understand** schwer zu verstehen
difficulty ['dɪfɪkəltɪ] N Schwierigkeit *f*; **to be in/get into difficulties** in Schwierigkeiten sein/geraten
diffidence ['dɪfɪdəns] N Bescheidenheit *f*, Zurückhaltung *f*
diffident ['dɪfɪdənt] ADJ bescheiden, zurückhaltend
diffuse ADJ [dɪ'fjuːs] diffus ▶ VT [dɪ'fjuːz] verbreiten
dig [dɪg] (*pt, pp* **dug**) VT graben; (*garden*) umgraben ▶ N (*prod*) Stoß *m*; (*archaeological*) (Aus)grabung *f*; (*remark*) Seitenhiebdigital *m*, spitze Bemerkung *f*; **to ~ one's nails into sth** seine Nägel in etw *acc* krallen
▶ **dig in** VI (*fig: inf: eat*) reinhauen ▶ VT (*compost*) untergraben, eingraben; (*knife*) hineinstoßen; (*claw*) festkrallen; **to ~ one's heels in** (*fig*) sich auf die Hinterbeine stellen (*inf*)
▶ **dig into** VT FUS (*savings*) angreifen; (*snow, soil*) ein Loch graben in +*acc*; **to ~ into one's pockets for sth** in seinen Taschen nach etw suchen *or* wühlen
▶ **dig out** VT ausgraben
▶ **dig up** VT ausgraben
digest [daɪ'dʒɛst] VT verdauen ▶ N Digest *m or nt*, Auswahl *f*
digestible [dɪ'dʒɛstəbl] ADJ verdaulich
digestion [dɪ'dʒɛstʃən] N Verdauung *f*
digestive [dɪ'dʒɛstɪv] ADJ (*system, upsets*) Verdauungs- ▶ N *Keks aus Vollkornmehl*
digit ['dɪdʒɪt] N (*number*) Ziffer *f*; (*finger*) Finger *m*
digital ['dɪdʒɪtl] ADJ (*watch, display etc*) Digital-
digital camera N Digitalkamera *f*
digital computer N Digitalrechner *m*
digital projector N Beamer *m*
digital TV, digital television N Digitalfernsehen *nt*
dignified ['dɪgnɪfaɪd] ADJ würdevoll
dignitary ['dɪgnɪtərɪ] N Würdenträger(in) *m*(*f*)
dignity ['dɪgnɪtɪ] N Würde *f*
digress [daɪ'grɛs] VI: **to ~ (from)** abschweifen (von)
digression [daɪ'grɛʃən] N Abschweifung *f*
digs [dɪgz] (BRIT *inf*) NPL Bude *f*
dike [daɪk] N = **dyke**
dilapidated [dɪ'læpɪdeɪtɪd] ADJ verfallen
dilate [daɪ'leɪt] VI sich weiten ▶ VT weiten
dilatory ['dɪlətərɪ] ADJ langsam
dilemma [daɪ'lɛmə] N Dilemma *nt*; **to be in a ~** sich in einem Dilemma befinden, in der Klemme sitzen (*inf*)
diligence ['dɪlɪdʒəns] N Fleiß *m*
diligent ['dɪlɪdʒənt] ADJ fleißig; (*research*) sorgfältig, genau
dill [dɪl] N Dill *m*
dilly-dally ['dɪlɪ'dælɪ] VI trödeln
dilute [daɪ'luːt] VT verdünnen; (*belief, principle*) schwächen ▶ ADJ verdünnt
dim [dɪm] ADJ schwach; (*outline, figure*) undeutlich, verschwommen; (*room*) dämmerig; (*future*) düster; (*prospects*) schlecht; (*inf: person*) schwer von Begriff ▶ VT (*light*) dämpfen; (*US Aut*) abblenden; **to take a ~ view of sth** wenig *or* nicht viel von etw halten
dime [daɪm] (US) N Zehncentstück *nt*
dimension [daɪ'mɛnʃən] N (*aspect*) Dimension *f*; (*measurement*) Abmessung *f*, Maß *nt*; (*also pl: scale, size*) Ausmaß *nt*
-dimensional [dɪ'mɛnʃənl] ADJ SUFF -dimensional
diminish [dɪ'mɪnɪʃ] VI sich verringern ▶ VT verringern
diminished responsibility N verminderte Zurechnungsfähigkeit *f*
diminutive [dɪ'mɪnjutɪv] ADJ winzig ▶ N Verkleinerungsform *f*

dimly ['dɪmlɪ] ADV schwach; (*see*) undeutlich, verschwommen
dimmer ['dɪmə'] N (*Elec: also:* **dimmer switch**) Dimmer *m*; (*US Aut*) Abblendschalter *m*
dimmers ['dɪməz] (*US*) NPL (*Aut: dipped headlights*) Abblendlicht *nt*; (*parking lights*) Parklicht *nt*
dimple ['dɪmpl] N Grübchen *nt*
dim-witted ['dɪm'wɪtɪd] (*inf*) ADJ dämlich
din [dɪn] N Lärm *m*, Getöse *nt* ▶ VT (*inf*): **to ~ sth into sb** jdm etw einbläuen
dine [daɪn] VI speisen
diner ['daɪnə'] N Gast *m*; (*US: restaurant*) Esslokal *nt*
dinghy ['dɪŋgɪ] N (*also:* **rubber dinghy**) Schlauchboot *nt*; (*also:* **sailing dinghy**) Dingi *nt*
dingy ['dɪndʒɪ] ADJ schäbig; (*clothes, curtains etc*) schmuddelig
dining car ['daɪnɪŋ-] (BRIT) N Speisewagen *m*
dining room ['daɪnɪŋ-] N Esszimmer *nt*; (*in hotel*) Speiseraum *m*
dinkum ['dɪŋkəm] ADJ (AUST, NZ *inf*): **(fair) ~** echt, wirklich; **he's a ~ Aussie** er ist ein waschechter Australier (*inf*)
dinner ['dɪnə'] N (*evening meal*) Abendessen *nt*; (*lunch*) Mittagessen *nt*; (*banquet*) (Fest)essen *nt*
dinner jacket N Smokingjackett *nt*
dinner party N Abendgesellschaft *f* (mit Essen)
dinner service N Tafelservice *nt*
dinner time N Essenszeit *f*
dinosaur ['daɪnəsɔː'] N Dinosaurier *m*
dint [dɪnt] N: **by ~ of** durch *+acc*
diocese ['daɪəsɪs] N Diözese *f*
dioxide [daɪ'ɔksaɪd] N Dioxid *nt*
dip [dɪp] N Senke *f*; (*in sea*) kurzes Bad *nt*; (*Culin*) Dip *m*; (*for sheep*) Desinfektionslösung *f* ▶ VT eintauchen; (BRIT *Aut*) abblenden ▶ VI abfallen
Dip. (BRIT) ABBR = **diploma**
diphtheria [dɪf'θɪərɪə] N Diphtherie *f*
diphthong ['dɪfθɔŋ] N Diphthong *m*
diploma [dɪ'pləumə] N Diplom *nt*
diplomacy [dɪ'pləuməsɪ] N Diplomatie *f*
diplomat ['dɪpləmæt] N Diplomat(in) *m(f)*
diplomatic [dɪplə'mætɪk] ADJ diplomatisch; **to break off ~ relations (with)** die diplomatischen Beziehungen abbrechen (mit)
diplomatic corps N diplomatisches Korps *nt*
diplomatic immunity N Immunität *f*
dip rod (US) N Ölmessstab *m*
dipstick ['dɪpstɪk] (BRIT) N Ölmessstab *m*
dip switch (BRIT) N Abblendschalter *m*
dire [daɪə'] ADJ schrecklich
direct [daɪ'rɛkt] ADJ, ADV direkt ▶ VT richten; (*company, project, programme etc*) leiten; (*play, film*) Regie führen bei; **to ~ sb to do sth** jdn anweisen, etw zu tun; **can you ~ me to ...?** können Sie mir den Weg nach ... sagen?
direct access N (*Comput*) Direktzugriff *m*
direct cost N direkte Kosten *pl*
direct current N Gleichstrom *m*
direct debit (BRIT) N Einzugsauftrag *m*; (*transaction*) automatische Abbuchung *f*
direct dialling N Selbstwahl *f*
direct hit N Volltreffer *m*
direction [dɪ'rɛkʃən] N Richtung *f*; (*TV, Radio*) Leitung *f*; (*Cine*) Regie *f*; **directions** NPL (*instructions*) Anweisungen *pl*; **sense of ~** Orientierungssinn *m*; **directions for use** Gebrauchsanweisung *f*, Gebrauchsanleitung *f*; **to ask for directions** nach dem Weg fragen; **in the ~ of** in Richtung
directional [dɪ'rɛkʃənl] ADJ (*aerial*) Richt-
directive [dɪ'rɛktɪv] N Direktive *f*, Weisung *f*; **government ~** Regierungserlass *m*
direct labour N (*Comm*) Produktionsarbeit *f*; (BRIT) eigene Arbeitskräfte *pl*
directly [dɪ'rɛktlɪ] ADV direkt; (*at once*) sofort, gleich
direct mail N Werbebriefe *pl*
direct mailshot (BRIT) N Direktwerbung *f* per Post
directness [daɪ'rɛktnɪs] N Direktheit *f*
director [dɪ'rɛktə'] N Direktor(in) *m(f)*; (*of project, TV, Radio*) Leiter(in) *m(f)*; (*Cine*) Regisseur(in) *m(f)*
Director of Public Prosecutions (BRIT) N ≈ Generalstaatsanwalt *m*, ≈ Generalstaatsanwältin *f*
directory [dɪ'rɛktərɪ] N (*also:* **telephone directory**) Telefonbuch *nt*; (*also:* **street directory**) Einwohnerverzeichnis *nt*; (*Comput*) Verzeichnis *nt*; (*Comm*) Branchenverzeichnis *nt*
directory enquiries, (US) **directory assistance** N (Fernsprech)auskunft *f*
dirt [dəːt] N Schmutz *m*; (*earth*) Erde *f*; **to treat sb like ~** jdn wie (den letzten) Dreck behandeln
dirt-cheap ['dəːt'tʃiːp] ADJ spottbillig
dirt road N unbefestigte Straße *f*
dirty ['dəːtɪ] ADJ schmutzig; (*story*) unanständig ▶ VT beschmutzen
dirty bomb N schmutzige Bombe
dirty trick N gemeiner Trick *m*
disability [dɪsə'bɪlɪtɪ] N Behinderung *f*
disability allowance N Behindertenbeihilfe *f*
disable [dɪs'eɪbl] VT zum Invaliden machen; (*tank, gun*) unbrauchbar machen
disabled [dɪs'eɪbld] ADJ behindert ▶ NPL: **the ~** die Behinderten *pl*
disabuse [dɪsə'bjuːz] VT: **to ~ sb (of)** jdn befreien (von)
disadvantage [dɪsəd'vɑːntɪdʒ] N Nachteil *m*; (*detriment*) Schaden *m*; **to be at a ~** benachteiligt *or* im Nachteil sein
disadvantaged [dɪsəd'vɑːntɪdʒd] ADJ benachteiligt
disaffected [dɪsə'fɛktɪd] ADJ entfremdet
disaffection [dɪsə'fɛkʃən] N Entfremdung *f*
disagree [dɪsə'griː] VI nicht übereinstimmen; (*to be against, think differently*): **to ~ (with)** nicht einverstanden sein (mit); **I ~ with you** ich bin anderer Meinung; **garlic disagrees with me** ich vertrage keinen Knoblauch, Knoblauch bekommt mir nicht
disagreeable [dɪsə'griːəbl] ADJ unangenehm; (*person*) unsympathisch
disagreement [dɪsə'griːmənt] N Uneinigkeit *f*; (*argument*) Meinungsverschiedenheit *f*; **to have a ~ with sb** sich mit jdm nicht einig sein

d

disallow [dɪsə'laʊ] VT (*appeal*) abweisen; (*goal*) nicht anerkennen, nicht geben
disappear [dɪsə'pɪəʳ] VI verschwinden; (*custom etc*) aussterben
disappearance [dɪsə'pɪərəns] N Verschwinden *nt*; Aussterben *nt*
disappoint [dɪsə'pɔɪnt] VT enttäuschen
disappointed [dɪsə'pɔɪntɪd] ADJ enttäuscht
disappointing [dɪsə'pɔɪntɪŋ] ADJ enttäuschend
disappointment [dɪsə'pɔɪntmənt] N Enttäuschung *f*
disapproval [dɪsə'pruːvəl] N Missbilligung *f*
disapprove [dɪsə'pruːv] VI dagegen sein; **to ~ of** missbilligen *+acc*
disapproving [dɪsə'pruːvɪŋ] ADJ missbilligend
disarm [dɪs'ɑːm] VT entwaffnen; (*criticism*) zum Verstummen bringen ▶ VI abrüsten
disarmament [dɪs'ɑːməmənt] N Abrüstung *f*
disarming [dɪs'ɑːmɪŋ] ADJ entwaffnend
disarray [dɪsə'reɪ] N: **in ~** (*army, organization*) in Auflösung (begriffen); (*hair, clothes*) unordentlich; (*thoughts*) durcheinander; **to throw into ~** durcheinanderbringen
disaster [dɪ'zɑːstəʳ] N Katastrophe *f*; (*Aviat etc*) Unglück *nt*; (*fig: mess*) Fiasko *nt*
disaster area N Katastrophengebiet *nt*; (*fig: person*) Katastrophe *f*; **my office is a ~** in meinem Büro sieht es katastrophal aus
disastrous [dɪ'zɑːstrəs] ADJ katastrophal
disband [dɪs'bænd] VT auflösen ▶ VI sich auflösen
disbelief [dɪsbə'liːf] N Ungläubigkeit *f*; **in ~** ungläubig
disbelieve [dɪsbə'liːv] VT (*person*) nicht glauben *+dat*; (*story*) nicht glauben; **I don't ~ you** ich bezweifle nicht, was Sie sagen
disc [dɪsk] N (*Anat*) Bandscheibe *f*; (*record*) Platte *f*; (*Comput*) = **disk**
disc. ABBR (*Comm*) = **discount**
discard [dɪs'kɑːd] VT ausrangieren; (*fig: idea, plan*) verwerfen
disc brake N Scheibenbremse *f*
discern [dɪ'səːn] VT wahrnehmen; (*identify*) erkennen
discernible [dɪ'səːnəbl] ADJ erkennbar; (*object*) wahrnehmbar
discerning [dɪ'səːnɪŋ] ADJ (*judgement*) scharfsinnig; (*look*) kritisch; (*listeners etc*) anspruchsvoll
discharge [dɪs'tʃɑːdʒ] VT (*duties*) nachkommen *+dat*; (*debt*) begleichen; (*waste*) ablassen; (*Elec*) entladen; (*Med*) ausscheiden, absondern; (*patient, employee, soldier*) entlassen; (*defendant*) freisprechen ▶ N (*of gas*) Ausströmen *nt*; (*of liquid*) Ausfließen *nt*; (*Elec*) Entladung *f*; (*Med*) Ausfluss *m*; (*of patient, employee, soldier*) Entlassung *f*; (*of defendant*) Freispruch *m*; **to ~ a gun** ein Gewehr abfeuern
discharged bankrupt [dɪs'tʃɑːdʒd-] N (*Law*) entlasteter Konkursschuldner *m*, entlastete Konkursschuldnerin *f*
disciple [dɪ'saɪpl] N Jünger *m*; (*fig: follower*) Schüler(in) *m(f)*
disciplinary ['dɪsɪplɪnərɪ] ADJ (*powers etc*) Disziplinar-; **to take ~ action against sb** ein Disziplinarverfahren gegen jdn einleiten
discipline ['dɪsɪplɪn] N Disziplin *f* ▶ VT disziplinieren; (*punish*) bestrafen; **to ~ o.s. to do sth** sich dazu anhalten *or* zwingen, etw zu tun
disc jockey N Discjockey *m*
disclaim [dɪs'kleɪm] VT (*knowledge*) abstreiten; (*responsibility*) von sich weisen
disclaimer [dɪs'kleɪməʳ] N Dementi *nt*; **to issue a ~** eine Gegenerklärung abgeben
disclose [dɪs'kləuz] VT enthüllen, bekannt geben
disclosure [dɪs'kləuʒəʳ] N Enthüllung *f*
disco ['dɪskəu] N = **discotheque**
discolor *etc* [dɪs'kʌləʳ] (*US*) = **discolour** *etc*
discolour [dɪs'kʌləʳ] VT verfärben ▶ VI sich verfärben
discolouration [dɪskʌlə'reɪʃən] N Verfärbung *f*
discoloured [dɪs'kʌləd] ADJ verfärbt
discomfort [dɪs'kʌmfət] N (*unease*) Unbehagen *nt*; (*physical*) Beschwerden *pl*
disconcert [dɪskən'səːt] VT beunruhigen, irritieren
disconcerting [dɪskən'səːtɪŋ] ADJ beunruhigend, irritierend
disconnect [dɪskə'nɛkt] VT abtrennen; (*Elec, Radio*) abstellen; **I've been disconnected** (*Tel*) das Gespräch ist unterbrochen worden; (*supply, connection*) man hat mir das Telefon/den Strom/das Gas *etc* abgestellt
disconnected [dɪskə'nɛktɪd] ADJ unzusammenhängend
disconsolate [dɪs'kɔnsəlɪt] ADJ niedergeschlagen
discontent [dɪskən'tɛnt] N Unzufriedenheit *f*
discontented [dɪskən'tɛntɪd] ADJ unzufrieden
discontinue [dɪskən'tɪnjuː] VT einstellen; **"discontinued"** (*Comm*) „ausgelaufene Serie"
discord ['dɪskɔːd] N Zwietracht *f*; (*Mus*) Dissonanz *f*
discordant [dɪs'kɔːdənt] ADJ unharmonisch
discotheque ['dɪskəutɛk] N Diskothek *f*
discount N ['dɪskaunt] Rabatt *m* ▶ VT [dɪs'kaunt] nachlassen; (*idea, fact*) unberücksichtigt lassen; **to give sb a ~ on sth** jdm auf etw *acc* Rabatt geben; **~ for cash** Skonto *m or nt* (bei Barzahlung); **at a ~** mit Rabatt
discount house N Diskontbank *f*; (*also:* **discount store**) Diskontgeschäft *nt*
discount rate N Diskontsatz *m*
discourage [dɪs'kʌrɪdʒ] VT entmutigen; **to ~ sb from doing sth** jdm davon abraten, etw zu tun
discouragement [dɪs'kʌrɪdʒmənt] N Mutlosigkeit *f*; **to act as a ~ to sb** entmutigend für jdn sein
discouraging [dɪs'kʌrɪdʒɪŋ] ADJ entmutigend
discourteous [dɪs'kəːtɪəs] ADJ unhöflich
discover [dɪs'kʌvəʳ] VT entdecken; (*missing person*) finden; **to ~ that …** herausfinden, dass …
discovery [dɪs'kʌvərɪ] N Entdeckung *f*

discredit [dɪsˈkrɛdɪt] VT in Misskredit bringen ▶ N: **to sb's ~** zu jds Schande
discreet [dɪsˈkriːt] ADJ diskret; (*unremarkable*) dezent
discreetly [dɪsˈkriːtlɪ] ADV diskret; (*unremarkably*) dezent
discrepancy [dɪsˈkrɛpənsɪ] N Diskrepanz *f*
discretion [dɪsˈkrɛʃən] N Diskretion *f*; **at the ~ of** im Ermessen *+gen*; **use your own ~** Sie müssen nach eigenem Ermessen handeln
discretionary [dɪsˈkrɛʃənrɪ] ADJ: **~ powers** Ermessensspielraum *m*; **~ payments** Ermessenszahlungen *pl*
discriminate [dɪsˈkrɪmɪneɪt] VI: **to ~ between** unterscheiden zwischen *+dat*; **to ~ against** diskriminieren *+acc*
discriminating [dɪsˈkrɪmɪneɪtɪŋ] ADJ anspruchsvoll, kritisch; (*tax, duty*) Differenzial-
discrimination [dɪskrɪmɪˈneɪʃən] N Diskriminierung *f*; (*discernment*) Urteilsvermögen *nt*; **racial ~** Rassendiskriminierung *f*; **sexual ~** Diskriminierung aufgrund des Geschlechts
discus [ˈdɪskəs] N Diskus *m*; (*event*) Diskuswerfen *nt*
discuss [dɪsˈkʌs] VT besprechen; (*debate*) diskutieren; (*analyse*) erörtern, behandeln
discussion [dɪsˈkʌʃən] N Besprechung *f*; (*debate*) Diskussion *f*; **under ~** in der Diskussion
disdain [dɪsˈdeɪn] N Verachtung *f* ▶ VT verachten ▶ VI: **to ~ to do sth** es für unter seiner Würde halten, etw zu tun
disease [dɪˈziːz] N Krankheit *f*
diseased [dɪˈziːzd] ADJ krank; (*tree*) befallen
disembark [dɪsɪmˈbɑːk] VT ausschiffen ▶ VI (*passengers*) von Bord gehen
disembarkation [dɪsɛmbɑːˈkeɪʃən] N Ausschiffung *f*
disembodied [dɪsɪmˈbɔdɪd] ADJ (*voice*) geisterhaft; (*hand*) körperlos
disembowel [dɪsɪmˈbauəl] VT die Eingeweide herausnehmen *+dat*
disenchanted [dɪsɪnˈtʃɑːntɪd] ADJ: **~ (with)** enttäuscht (von)
disenfranchise [dɪsɪnˈfræntʃaɪz] VT (*Pol*) das Wahlrecht entziehen *+dat*; (*Comm*) die Konzession entziehen *+dat*
disengage [dɪsɪnˈgeɪdʒ] VT (*Tech*) ausrasten; **to ~ the clutch** auskuppeln
disengagement [dɪsɪnˈgeɪdʒmənt] N (*Pol*) Disengagement *nt*
disentangle [dɪsɪnˈtæŋgl] VT befreien; (*wool, wire*) entwirren
disfavour, (US) **disfavor** [dɪsˈfeɪvəʳ] N Missfallen *nt*; **to fall into ~ (with sb)** (bei jdm) in Ungnade fallen
disfigure [dɪsˈfɪgəʳ] VT entstellen; (*object, place*) verunstalten
disgorge [dɪsˈgɔːdʒ] VT (*liquid*) ergießen; (*people*) ausspeien
disgrace [dɪsˈgreɪs] N Schande *f*; (*scandal*) Skandal *m* ▶ VT Schande bringen über *+acc*
disgraceful [dɪsˈgreɪsful] ADJ skandalös
disgruntled [dɪsˈgrʌntld] ADJ verärgert
disguise [dɪsˈgaɪz] N Verkleidung *f* ▶ VT: **to ~ (as)** (*person*) verkleiden (als); (*object*) tarnen (als); **in ~** (*person*) verkleidet; **there's no disguising the fact that ...** es kann nicht geleugnet werden, dass ...; **to ~ o.s. as** sich verkleiden als
disgust [dɪsˈgʌst] N Abscheu *m* ▶ VT anwidern; **she walked off in ~** sie ging voller Empörung weg
disgusting [dɪsˈgʌstɪŋ] ADJ widerlich
dish [dɪʃ] N Schüssel *f*; (*flat*) Schale *f*; (*recipe, food*) Gericht *nt*; (*also*: **satellite dish**) Parabolantenne *f*, Schüssel (*inf*); **to do** *or* **wash the dishes** Geschirr spülen, abwaschen
▶ **dish out** VT verteilen; (*food, money*) austeilen; (*advice*) erteilen
▶ **dish up** VT (*food*) auftragen, servieren; (*facts, statistics*) auftischen (*inf*)
dishcloth [ˈdɪʃklɔθ] N Spültuch *nt*, Spüllappen *m*
dishearten [dɪsˈhɑːtn] VT entmutigen
dishevelled, (US) **disheveled** [dɪˈʃɛvəld] ADJ unordentlich; (*hair*) zerzaust
dishonest [dɪsˈɔnɪst] ADJ unehrlich; (*means*) unlauter
dishonesty [dɪsˈɔnɪstɪ] N Unehrlichkeit *f*
dishonor *etc* [dɪsˈɔnəʳ] (US) = **dishonour** *etc*
dishonour [dɪsˈɔnəʳ] N Schande *f*
dishonourable [dɪsˈɔnərəbl] ADJ unehrenhaft
dish soap (US) N Spülmittel *nt*
dishtowel [ˈdɪʃtauəl] (US) N Geschirrtuch *nt*
dishwasher [ˈdɪʃwɔʃəʳ] N (*machine*) (Geschirr)spülmaschine *f*
dishy [ˈdɪʃɪ] (*inf*: BRIT) ADJ attraktiv
disillusion [dɪsɪˈluːʒən] VT desillusionieren ▶ N = **disillusionment**; **to become disillusioned (with)** seine Illusionen (über *+acc*) verlieren
disillusionment [dɪsɪˈluːʒənmənt] N Desillusionierung *f*
disincentive [dɪsɪnˈsɛntɪv] N Entmutigung *f*; **it's a ~** es hält die Leute ab; **to be a ~ to sb** jdm keinen Anreiz bieten
disinclined [dɪsɪnˈklaɪnd] ADJ: **to be ~ to do sth** abgeneigt sein, etw zu tun
disinfect [dɪsɪnˈfɛkt] VT desinfizieren
disinfectant [dɪsɪnˈfɛktənt] N Desinfektionsmittel *nt*
disinflation [dɪsɪnˈfleɪʃən] N (*Econ*) Rückgang *m* einer inflationären Entwicklung
disinformation [dɪsɪnfəˈmeɪʃən] N Desinformation *f*
disingenuous [dɪsɪnˈdʒɛnjuəs] ADJ unaufrichtig
disinherit [dɪsɪnˈhɛrɪt] VT enterben
disintegrate [dɪsˈɪntɪgreɪt] VI zerfallen; (*marriage, partnership*) scheitern; (*organization*) sich auflösen
disinterested [dɪsˈɪntrəstɪd] ADJ (*advice*) unparteiisch, unvoreingenommen; (*help*) uneigennützig
disjointed [dɪsˈdʒɔɪntɪd] ADJ unzusammenhängend
disk [dɪsk] N Diskette *f*; **single-/double-sided ~** einseitige/zweiseitige Diskette

disk drive N Diskettenlaufwerk *nt*
diskette [dɪs'kɛt] (*US*) N = **disk**
disk operating system N Betriebssystem *nt*
dislike [dɪs'laɪk] N Abneigung *f* ▶ VT nicht mögen; **to take a ~ to sb/sth** eine Abneigung gegen jdn/etw entwickeln; **I ~ the idea** die Idee gefällt mir nicht; **he dislikes it** er kann es nicht leiden, er mag es nicht
dislocate ['dɪsləkeɪt] VT verrenken, ausrenken; **he has dislocated his shoulder** er hat sich *dat* den Arm ausgekugelt
dislodge [dɪs'lɔdʒ] VT verschieben
disloyal [dɪs'lɔɪəl] ADJ illoyal
dismal ['dɪzml] ADJ trübe, trostlos; (*song, person, mood*) trübsinnig; (*failure*) kläglich
dismantle [dɪs'mæntl] VT (*machine*) demontieren
dismast [dɪs'mɑːst] VT (*Naut*) entmasten
dismay [dɪs'meɪ] N Bestürzung *f* ▶ VT bestürzen; **much to my ~** zu meiner Bestürzung; **in ~** bestürzt
dismiss [dɪs'mɪs] VT entlassen; (*case*) abweisen; (*possibility, idea*) abtun
dismissal [dɪs'mɪsl] N Entlassung *f*
dismount [dɪs'maunt] VI absteigen
disobedience [dɪsə'biːdɪəns] N Ungehorsam *m*
disobedient [dɪsə'biːdɪənt] ADJ ungehorsam
disobey [dɪsə'beɪ] VT nicht gehorchen *+dat*; (*order*) nicht befolgen
disorder [dɪs'ɔːdə^r] N Unordnung *f*; (*rioting*) Unruhen *pl*; (*Med*) (Funktions)störung *f*; **civil ~** öffentliche Unruhen *pl*
disorderly [dɪs'ɔːdəlɪ] ADJ unordentlich; (*meeting*) undiszipliniert; (*behaviour*) ungehörig
disorderly conduct N (*Law*) ungebührliches Benehmen *nt*
disorganize [dɪs'ɔːgənaɪz] VT durcheinanderbringen
disorganized [dɪs'ɔːgənaɪzd] ADJ chaotisch
disorientated [dɪs'ɔːrɪenteɪtɪd] ADJ desorientiert, verwirrt
disown [dɪs'əun] VT (*action*) verleugnen; (*child*) verstoßen
disparaging [dɪs'pærɪdʒɪŋ] ADJ (*remarks*) abschätzig, geringschätzig; **to be ~ about sb/sth** (*person*) abschätzig *or* geringschätzig über jdn/etw urteilen
disparate ['dɪspərɪt] ADJ völlig verschieden
disparity [dɪs'pærɪtɪ] N Unterschied *m*
dispassionate [dɪs'pæʃənət] ADJ nüchtern
dispatch [dɪs'pætʃ] VT senden, schicken; (*deal with*) erledigen; (*kill*) töten ▶ N Senden *nt*, Schicken *nt*; (*Press*) Bericht *m*; (*Mil*) Depesche *f*
dispatch department N Versandabteilung *f*
dispatch rider N (*Mil*) Meldefahrer *m*
dispel [dɪs'pɛl] VT (*myths*) zerstören; (*fears*) zerstreuen
dispensable [dɪ'spensəbl] ADJ entbehrlich
dispensary [dɪs'pɛnsərɪ] N Apotheke *f*; (*in chemist's*) *Raum in einer Apotheke, wo Arzneimittel abgefüllt werden*
dispensation [dɪspən'seɪʃən] N (*of treatment*) Vergabe *f*; (*special permission*) Dispens *m*; **~ of justice** Rechtsprechung *f*
dispense [dɪs'pɛns] VT (*medicines*) abgeben; (*charity*) austeilen; (*advice*) erteilen
▶ **dispense with** VT FUS verzichten auf *+acc*
dispenser [dɪs'pɛnsə^r] N (*machine*) Automat *m*
dispensing chemist [dɪs'pɛnsɪŋ-] (BRIT) N (*shop*) Apotheke *f*
dispersal [dɪs'pəːsl] N (*of objects*) Verstreuen *nt*; (*of group, crowd*) Auflösung *f*, Zerstreuen *nt*
disperse [dɪs'pəːs] VT (*objects*) verstreuen; (*crowd etc*) auflösen, zerstreuen; (*knowledge, information*) verbreiten ▶ VI (*crowd*) sich auflösen *or* zerstreuen
dispirited [dɪs'pɪrɪtɪd] ADJ entmutigt
displace [dɪs'pleɪs] VT ablösen
displaced person [dɪs'pleɪst-] N Verschleppte(r) *f*(*m*)
displacement [dɪs'pleɪsmənt] N Ablösung *f*; (*of people*) Vertreibung *f*; (*Phys*) Verdrängung *f*
display [dɪs'pleɪ] N (*in shop*) Auslage *f*; (*exhibition*) Ausstellung *f*; (*of feeling*) Zeigen *nt*; (*pej*) Zurschaustellung *f*; (*Comput, Tech*) Anzeige *f* ▶ VT zeigen; (*ostentatiously*) zur Schau stellen; (*results, departure times*) aushängen; **on ~** ausgestellt
display advertising N Displaywerbung *f*
displease [dɪs'pliːz] VT verstimmen, verärgern
displeased [dɪs'pliːzd] ADJ: **I am very ~ with you** ich bin sehr enttäuscht von dir
displeasure [dɪs'plɛʒə^r] N Missfallen *nt*
disposable [dɪs'pəuzəbl] ADJ (*lighter*) Wegwerf-; (*bottle*) Einweg-; (*income*) verfügbar
disposable nappy (BRIT) N Wegwerfwindel *f*
disposal [dɪs'pəuzl] N (*of goods for sale*) Loswerden *nt*; (*of property, belongings: by selling*) Verkauf *m*; (*: by giving away*) Abgeben *nt*; (*of rubbish*) Beseitigung *f*; **at one's ~** zur Verfügung; **to put sth at sb's ~** jdm etw zur Verfügung stellen
dispose [dɪs'pəuz]: **~ of** *vt fus* (*body*) aus dem Weg schaffen; (*unwanted goods*) loswerden; (*problem, task*) erledigen; (*stock*) verkaufen
disposed [dɪs'pəuzd] ADJ: **to be ~ to do sth** (*inclined*) geneigt sein, etw zu tun; (*willing*) bereit sein, etw zu tun; **to be well ~ towards sb** jdm wohlwollen
disposition [dɪspə'zɪʃən] N (*nature*) Veranlagung *f*; (*inclination*) Neigung *f*
dispossess ['dɪspə'zɛs] VT enteignen; **to ~ sb of his/her land** jds Land enteignen
disproportion [dɪsprə'pɔːʃən] N Missverhältnis *nt*
disproportionate [dɪsprə'pɔːʃənət] ADJ unverhältnismäßig; (*amount*) unverhältnismäßig hoch/niedrig
disprove [dɪs'pruːv] VT widerlegen
dispute [dɪs'pjuːt] N Streit *m*; (*also:* **industrial dispute**) Auseinandersetzung *f* zwischen Arbeitgebern und Arbeitnehmern; (*Pol, Mil*) Streitigkeiten *pl* ▶ VT bestreiten; (*ownership etc*) anfechten; **to be in** *or* **under ~** umstritten sein
disqualification [dɪskwɔlɪfɪ'keɪʃən] N: **~ (from)** Ausschluss *m* (von); (*Sport*) Disqualifizierung *f* (von); **~ (from driving)** (BRIT) Führerscheinentzug *m*

disqualify [dɪs'kwɔlɪfaɪ] VT disqualifizieren; **to ~ sb for sth** jdn für etw ungeeignet machen; **to ~ sb from doing sth** jdn ungeeignet machen, etw zu tun; **to ~ sb from driving** (BRIT) jdm den Führerschein entziehen
disquiet [dɪs'kwaɪət] N Unruhe *f*
disquieting [dɪs'kwaɪətɪŋ] ADJ beunruhigend
disregard [dɪsrɪ'gɑ:d] VT nicht beachten, ignorieren ▸ N: **~ (for)** Missachtung *f* (*+gen*); (*for danger, money*) Geringschätzung *f* (*+gen*)
disrepair [dɪsrɪ'pɛəʳ] N: **to fall into ~** (*machine*) vernachlässigt werden; (*building*) verfallen
disreputable [dɪs'rɛpjutəbl] ADJ (*person*) unehrenhaft; (*behaviour*) unfein
disrepute [dɪsrɪ'pju:t] N schlechter Ruf *m*; **to bring/fall into ~** in Verruf bringen/kommen
disrespectful [dɪsrɪ'spɛktful] ADJ respektlos
disrupt [dɪs'rʌpt] VT (*plans*) durcheinanderbringen; (*conversation, proceedings*) unterbrechen
disruption [dɪs'rʌpʃən] N Unterbrechung *f*; (*disturbance*) Störung *f*
disruptive [dɪs'rʌptɪv] ADJ störend; (*action*) Stör-
dissatisfaction [dɪssætɪs'fækʃən] N Unzufriedenheit *f*
dissatisfied [dɪs'sætɪsfaɪd] ADJ: **~ (with)** unzufrieden (mit)
dissect [dɪ'sɛkt] VT sezieren
disseminate [dɪ'sɛmɪneɪt] VT verbreiten
dissent [dɪ'sɛnt] N abweichende Meinungen *pl*
dissenter [dɪ'sɛntəʳ] N Abweichler(in) *m(f)*
dissertation [dɪsə'teɪʃən] N (*speech*) Vortrag *m*; (*piece of writing*) Abhandlung *f*; (*for PhD*) Dissertation *f*
disservice [dɪs'sə:vɪs] N: **to do sb a ~** jdm einen schlechten Dienst erweisen
dissident ['dɪsɪdnt] ADJ andersdenkend; (*voice*) kritisch ▸ N Dissident(in) *m(f)*
dissimilar [dɪ'sɪmɪləʳ] ADJ: **~ (to)** anders (als)
dissipate ['dɪsɪpeɪt] VT (*heat*) neutralisieren; (*clouds*) auflösen; (*money, effort*) verschwenden
dissipated ['dɪsɪpeɪtɪd] ADJ zügellos, ausschweifend
dissociate [dɪ'səuʃɪeɪt] VT trennen; **to ~ o.s. from** sich distanzieren von
dissolute ['dɪsəlu:t] ADJ zügellos, ausschweifend
dissolution [dɪsə'lu:ʃən] N Auflösung *f*
dissolve [dɪ'zɔlv] VT auflösen ▸ VI sich auflösen; **to ~ in(to) tears** in Tränen zerfließen
dissuade [dɪ'sweɪd] VT: **to ~ sb (from sth)** jdn (von etw) abbringen
distaff ['dɪstɑ:f] N: **the ~ side** die mütterliche Seite
distance ['dɪstns] N Entfernung *f*; (*in time*) Abstand *m*; (*reserve*) Abstand, Distanz *f* ▸ VT: **to ~ o.s. (from)** sich distanzieren (von); **in the ~** in der Ferne; **what's the ~ to London?** wie weit ist es nach London?; **it's within walking ~** es ist zu Fuß erreichbar; **at a ~ of 2 metres** in 2 Meter(n) Entfernung; **keep your ~!** halten Sie Abstand!
distant ['dɪstnt] ADJ (*place*) weit entfernt, fern; (*time*) weit zurückliegend; (*relative*) entfernt; (*manner*) distanziert, kühl
distaste [dɪs'teɪst] N Widerwille *m*
distasteful [dɪs'teɪstful] ADJ widerlich; **to be ~ to sb** jdm zuwider sein
Dist. Atty. (US) ABBR = **district attorney**
distemper [dɪs'tɛmpəʳ] N (*paint*) Temperafarbe *f*; (*disease of dogs*) Staupe *f*
distend [dɪs'tɛnd] VT blähen ▸ VI sich blähen
distended [dɪs'tɛndɪd] ADJ aufgebläht
distil, (US) distill [dɪs'tɪl] VT destillieren; (*fig*) (heraus)destillieren
distillery [dɪs'tɪlərɪ] N Brennerei *f*
distinct [dɪs'tɪŋkt] ADJ deutlich, klar; (*possibility*) eindeutig; (*different*) verschieden; **as ~ from** im Unterschied zu
distinction [dɪs'tɪŋkʃən] N Unterschied *m*; (*honour*) Ehre *f*; (*in exam*) Auszeichnung *f*; **to draw a ~ between** einen Unterschied machen zwischen *+dat*; **a writer of ~** ein Schriftsteller von Rang
distinctive [dɪs'tɪŋktɪv] ADJ unverwechselbar
distinctly [dɪs'tɪŋktlɪ] ADV deutlich, klar; (*tell*) ausdrücklich; (*unhappy*) ausgesprochen; (*better*) entschieden
distinguish [dɪs'tɪŋgwɪʃ] VT unterscheiden; (*details etc*) erkennen, ausmachen; **to ~ (between)** unterscheiden (zwischen *+dat*); **to ~ o.s.** sich hervortun
distinguished [dɪs'tɪŋgwɪʃt] ADJ von hohem Rang; (*career*) hervorragend; (*in appearance*) distinguiert
distinguishing [dɪs'tɪŋgwɪʃɪŋ] ADJ charakteristisch
distort [dɪs'tɔ:t] VT verzerren; (*argument*) verdrehen
distortion [dɪs'tɔ:ʃən] N Verzerrung *f*; Verdrehung *f*
distract [dɪs'trækt] VT ablenken
distracted [dɪs'træktɪd] ADJ unaufmerksam; (*anxious*) besorgt, beunruhigt
distraction [dɪs'trækʃən] N Unaufmerksamkeit *f*; (*confusion*) Verstörtheit *f*; (*sth which distracts*) Ablenkung *f*; (*amusement*) Zerstreuung *f*; **to drive sb to ~** jdn zur Verzweiflung treiben
distraught [dɪs'trɔ:t] ADJ verzweifelt
distress [dɪs'trɛs] N Verzweiflung *f* ▸ VT Kummer machen *+dat*; **in ~** (*ship*) in Seenot; (*person*) verzweifelt; **distressed area** (BRIT) Notstandsgebiet *nt*
distressing [dɪs'trɛsɪŋ] ADJ beunruhigend
distress signal N Notsignal *nt*
distribute [dɪs'trɪbju:t] VT verteilen; (*profits*) aufteilen
distribution [dɪstrɪ'bju:ʃən] N Vertrieb *m*; (*of profits*) Aufteilung *f*
distribution costs NPL Vertriebskosten *pl*
distribution management N (*Comm*) Vertriebscontrolling *nt*
distributor [dɪs'trɪbjutəʳ] N (*Comm*) Vertreiber(in) *m(f)*; (*Aut, Tech*) Verteiler *m*

district [ˈdɪstrɪkt] N Gebiet *nt*; (*of town*) Stadtteil *m*; (*Admin*) (Verwaltungs)bezirk *m*
district attorney (US) N Bezirksstaatsanwalt *m*, Bezirksstaatsanwältin *f*

> **District Council** heißt der in jedem der britischen **districts** (Bezirke) alle vier Jahre neu gewählte Bezirksrat, der für bestimmte Bereiche der Kommunalverwaltung (Gesundheitswesen, Wohnungsbeschaffung, Baugenehmigungen, Müllabfuhr) zuständig ist. Die district councils werden durch Kommunalabgaben und durch einen Zuschuss von der Regierung finanziert. Ihre Ausgaben werden von einer unabhängigen Prüfungskommission kontrolliert, und bei zu hohen Ausgaben wird der Regierungszuschuss gekürzt.

district nurse (BRIT) N Gemeindeschwester *f*
distrust [dɪsˈtrʌst] N Misstrauen *nt* ▸ VT misstrauen *+dat*
distrustful [dɪsˈtrʌstful] ADJ: **~ (of)** misstrauisch (gegenüber *+dat*)
disturb [dɪsˈtəːb] VT stören; (*upset*) beunruhigen; (*disorganize*) durcheinanderbringen; **sorry to ~ you** entschuldigen Sie bitte die Störung
disturbance [dɪsˈtəːbəns] N Störung *f*; (*political etc*) Unruhe *f*; (*violent event*) Unruhen *pl*; (*by drunks etc*) (Ruhe)störung *f*; **to cause a ~** Unruhe/eine Ruhestörung verursachen; **~ of the peace** Ruhestörung
disturbed [dɪsˈtəːbd] ADJ beunruhigt; (*childhood*) unglücklich; **mentally/emotionally ~** geistig/seelisch gestört
disturbing [dɪsˈtəːbɪŋ] ADJ beunruhigend
disuse [dɪsˈjuːs] N: **to fall into ~** nicht mehr benutzt werden
disused [dɪsˈjuːzd] ADJ (*building*) leer stehend; (*airfield*) stillgelegt
ditch [dɪtʃ] N Graben *m* ▸ VT (*inf*: *partner*) sitzen lassen; (*: plan*) sausen lassen; (*: car etc*) loswerden
dither [ˈdɪðəʳ] (*pej*) VI zaudern
ditto [ˈdɪtəu] ADV dito, ebenfalls
divan [dɪˈvæn] N (*also*: **divan bed**) Polsterbett *nt*
dive [daɪv] N Sprung *m*; (*underwater*) Tauchen *nt*; (*of submarine*) Untertauchen *nt*; (*pej*: *place*) Spelunke *f* (*inf*) ▸ VI springen; (*under water*) tauchen; (*bird*) einen Sturzflug machen; (*submarine*) untertauchen; **to ~ into** (*bag, drawer etc*) greifen in *+acc*; (*shop, car etc*) sich stürzen in *+acc*
diver [ˈdaɪvəʳ] N Taucher(in) *m(f)*; (*also*: **deep-sea diver**) Tiefseetaucher(in) *m(f)*
diverge [daɪˈvəːdʒ] VI auseinandergehen
divergent [daɪˈvəːdʒənt] ADJ unterschiedlich; (*views*) voneinander abweichend; (*interests*) auseinandergehend
diverse [daɪˈvəːs] ADJ verschiedenartig
diversification [daɪvəːsɪfɪˈkeɪʃən] N Diversifikation *f*
diversify [daɪˈvəːsɪfaɪ] VI diversifizieren
diversion [daɪˈvəːʃən] N (BRIT *Aut*) Umleitung *f*; (*distraction*) Ablenkung *f*; (*of funds*) Umlenkung *f*
diversionary [daɪˈvəːʃənrɪ] ADJ: **~ tactics** Ablenkungsmanöver *pl*
diversity [daɪˈvəːsɪtɪ] N Vielfalt *f*
divert [daɪˈvəːt] VT (*sb's attention*) ablenken; (*funds*) umlenken; (*re-route*) umleiten
divest [daɪˈvɛst] VT: **to ~ sb of office/his authority** jdn seines Amtes entkleiden/seiner Macht entheben
divide [dɪˈvaɪd] VT trennen; (*Math*) dividieren, teilen; (*share out*) verteilen ▸ VI sich teilen; (*road*) sich gabeln; (*people, groups*) sich aufteilen ▸ N Kluft *f*; **to ~ (between** *or* **among)** aufteilen (unter *+dat*); **40 divided by 5** 40 geteilt *or* dividiert durch 5
▸ **divide out** VT: **to ~ out (between** *or* **among)** aufteilen (unter *+dat*)
divided [dɪˈvaɪdɪd] ADJ geteilt; **to be ~ about** *or* **over sth** geteilter Meinung über etw *acc* sein
divided highway (US) N ≈ Schnellstraße *f*
dividend [ˈdɪvɪdɛnd] N Dividende *f*; (*fig*): **to pay dividends** sich bezahlt machen
dividend cover N (*Comm*) Dividendendeckung *f*
dividers [dɪˈvaɪdəz] NPL (*Math, Tech*) Stechzirkel *m*; (*between pages*) Register *nt*
divine [dɪˈvaɪn] ADJ göttlich ▸ VT (*future*) weissagen, prophezeien; (*truth*) erahnen; (*water, metal*) aufspüren
diving [ˈdaɪvɪŋ] N Tauchen *nt*; (*Sport*) Kunstspringen *nt*
diving board N Sprungbrett *nt*
diving suit N Taucheranzug *m*
divinity [dɪˈvɪnɪtɪ] N Göttlichkeit *f*; (*god or goddess*) Gottheit *f*; (*Scol*) Theologie *f*
divisible [dɪˈvɪzəbl] ADJ: **~ (by)** teilbar (durch); **to be ~ into** teilbar sein in *+acc*
division [dɪˈvɪʒən] N Teilung *f*; (*Math*) Teilen *nt*, Division *f*; (*sharing out*) Verteilung *f*; (*disagreement*) Uneinigkeit *f*; (BRIT *Pol*) Abstimmung *f* durch Hammelsprung; (*Comm*) Abteilung *f*; (*Mil*) Division *f*; (*esp Football*) Liga *f*; **~ of labour** Arbeitsteilung *f*
divisive [dɪˈvaɪsɪv] ADJ: **to be ~** (*tactics*) auf Spaltung abzielen; (*system*) zu Feindseligkeit führen
divorce [dɪˈvɔːs] N Scheidung *f* ▸ VT sich scheiden lassen von; (*dissociate*) trennen
divorced [dɪˈvɔːst] ADJ geschieden
divorcee [dɪvɔːˈsiː] N Geschiedene(r) *f(m)*
divot [ˈdɪvət] N *vom Golfschläger etc ausgehacktes Rasenstück*
divulge [daɪˈvʌldʒ] VT preisgeben
DIY (BRIT) N ABBR = **do-it-yourself**
dizziness [ˈdɪzɪnɪs] N Schwindel *m*
dizzy [ˈdɪzɪ] ADJ schwind(e)lig; (*turn, spell*) Schwindel-; (*height*) schwindelerregend; **I feel ~** mir ist *or* ich bin schwind(e)lig
DJ N ABBR = **disc jockey**
dj N ABBR = **dinner jacket**
Djakarta [dʒəˈkaːtə] N Jakarta *nt*
DJIA (US) N ABBR (= *Dow-Jones Industrial Average*) Dow-Jones-Index *m*

dl ABBR (= *decilitre*) dl
DLit, DLitt N ABBR (= *Doctor of Literature, Doctor of Letters*) *akademischer Grad in Literaturwissenschaft*
dm ABBR (= *decimetre*) dm
DMus N ABBR (= *Doctor of Music*) *Doktor der Musikwissenschaft*
DMZ N ABBR = **demilitarized zone**
DNA N ABBR (= *deoxyribonucleic acid*) DNS *f*
DNA test N DNS-Test *m*

KEYWORD

do [du:] (*pt* **did**, *pp* **done**) AUX VB **1** (*in negative constructions*): **I don't understand** ich verstehe nicht
2 (*to form questions*): **didn't you know?** wusstest du das nicht?; **what do you think?** was meinst du?
3 (*for emphasis*): **she does seem rather upset** sie scheint wirklich recht aufgeregt zu sein; **do sit down/help yourself** bitte nehmen Sie Platz/bedienen Sie sich; **oh do shut up!** halte endlich den Mund!
4 (*to avoid repeating vb*): **she swims better than I do** sie schwimmt besser als ich; **she lives in Glasgow — so do I** sie wohnt in Glasgow — ich auch; **who made this mess? — I did** wer hat dieses Durcheinander gemacht? — ich
5 (*in question tags*): **you like him, don't you?** du magst ihn, nicht wahr?; **I don't know him, do I?** ich kenne ihn nicht, oder?
▸ VT **1** (*carry out, perform*) tun, machen; **what are you doing tonight?** was machen Sie heute Abend?; **what do you do (for a living)?** was machen Sie beruflich?; **to do one's teeth** sich *dat* die Zähne putzen
2 (*Aut etc*) fahren; **the car was doing 100** das Auto fuhr 100
▸ VI **1** (*act, behave*): **do as I do** mach es wie ich
2 (*get on, fare*): **he's doing well/badly at school** er ist gut/schlecht in der Schule; **the company is doing well** der Firma geht es gut; **how do you do?** guten Tag/Morgen/Abend!
3 (*suit, be sufficient*) reichen; **will that do?** reicht das?; **will this dress do for the party?** ist dieses Kleid gut genug für die Party?; **will £10 do?** reichen £10?; **that'll do** das reicht; (*in annoyance*) jetzt reichts aber!; **to make do with** auskommen mit
▸ N (*inf: party etc*) Party *f*, Fete *f*; **it was quite a do** es war ganz schön was los
▸ **do away with** VT FUS (*get rid of*) abschaffen
▸ **do for** (*inf*) VT FUS: **to be done for** erledigt sein
▸ **do in** (*inf*) VT (*kill*) umbringen
▸ **do out of** (*inf*) VT (*deprive*) bringen um
▸ **do up** VT FUS (*laces, dress, buttons*) zumachen; (*renovate: room, house*) renovieren
▸ **do with** VT FUS (*need*) brauchen; **I could do with some help/a drink** ich könnte Hilfe/einen Drink gebrauchen; **it has to do with money** es hat mit Geld zu tun
▸ **do without** VT FUS auskommen ohne

do. ABBR = **ditto**
DOA ABBR (= *dead on arrival*) bei Einlieferung ins Krankenhaus bereits tot
d.o.b. ABBR = **date of birth**
doc [dɔk] (*inf*) N Doktor *m*
docile ['dəusaɪl] ADJ sanft(mütig)
dock [dɔk] N Dock *nt*; (*Law*) Anklagebank *f*; (*Bot*) Ampfer *m* ▸ VI anlegen; (*Space*) docken ▸ VT: **they docked a third of his wages** sie kürzten seinen Lohn um ein Drittel; **docks** NPL (*Naut*) Hafen *m*
dock dues [-dju:z] NPL Hafengebühr *f*
docker ['dɔkə^r] N Hafenarbeiter *m*, Docker *m*
docket ['dɔkɪt] N Inhaltserklärung *f*; (*on parcel etc*) Warenbegleitschein *m*, Laufzettel *m*
dockyard ['dɔkjɑ:d] N Werft *f*
doctor ['dɔktə^r] N Arzt *m*, Ärztin *f*; (*PhD etc*) Doktor *m* ▸ VT: **to ~ a drink** *etc* einem Getränk *etc* etwas beimischen; **~'s office** (*US*) Sprechzimmer *nt*
doctorate ['dɔktərɪt] N Doktorwürde *f*

> **Doctorate** ist der höchste akademische Grad auf jedem Wissensgebiet und wird nach erfolgreicher Vorlage einer Doktorarbeit verliehen. Die Studienzeit (meist mindestens 3 Jahre) und Länge der Doktorarbeit ist je nach Hochschule verschieden. Am häufigsten wird der Titel **PhD** (Doctor of Philosophy) auf dem Gebiet der Geisteswissenschaften, Naturwissenschaften und des Ingenieurwesens verliehen, obwohl es auch andere Doktortitel (in Musik, Jura usw.) gibt. Siehe auch **Bachelor's degree, Master's degree.**

Doctor of Philosophy N Doktor *m* der Philosophie
doctrine ['dɔktrɪn] N Doktrin *f*
docudrama ['dɔkjudrɑ:mə] N Dokumentarspiel *nt*
document N ['dɔkjumənt] Dokument *nt* ▸ VT ['dɔkjumɛnt] dokumentieren
documentary [dɔkju'mɛntərɪ] ADJ dokumentarisch ▸ N Dokumentarfilm *m*
documentation [dɔkjumən'teɪʃən] N Dokumentation *f*
DOD (*US*) N ABBR (= *Department of Defense*) Verteidigungsministerium *nt*
doddering ['dɔdərɪŋ] ADJ (*shaky, unsteady*) zittrig
doddery ['dɔdərɪ] ADJ = **doddering**
doddle ['dɔdl] (*inf*) N: **a ~** ein Kinderspiel *nt*
Dodecanese [dəudɪkə'ni:z] NPL: **the ~ (Islands)** der Dodekanes
dodge [dɔdʒ] N Trick *m* ▸ VT ausweichen *+dat*; (*tax*) umgehen ▸ VI ausweichen; **to ~ out of the way** zur Seite springen; **to ~ through the traffic** sich durch den Verkehr schlängeln
Dodgems® ['dɔdʒəmz] (*Brit*) NPL Autoskooter *pl*
dodgy ['dɔdʒɪ] (*inf*) ADJ (*person*) zweifelhaft; (*plan etc*) gewagt
DOE N ABBR (*Brit*: = *Department of the Environment*) *Umweltministerium*; (*US*: = *Department of Energy*) *Energieministerium*

doe [dəu] N Reh *nt*, Ricke *f*; (*rabbit*) (Kaninchen)weibchen *nt*
does [dʌz] VB *see* **do**
doesn't ['dʌznt] = **does not**
dog [dɔg] N Hund *m* ▶ VT (*subj*: *person*) auf den Fersen bleiben *+dat*; (: *bad luck, memory etc*) verfolgen; **to go to the dogs** (*inf*) vor die Hunde gehen
dog biscuits NPL Hundekuchen *pl*
dog collar N Hundehalsband *nt*; (*Rel*) Kragen *m* des Geistlichen
dog-eared ['dɔgɪəd] ADJ mit Eselsohren
dog food N Hundefutter *nt*
dogged ['dɔgɪd] ADJ beharrlich
doggy ['dɔgɪ] N Hündchen *nt*
doggy bag N *Tüte für Essensreste, die man nach Hause mitnehmen möchte*
dogma ['dɔgmə] N Dogma *nt*
dogmatic [dɔg'mætɪk] ADJ dogmatisch
do-gooder [du:'gudə^r] (*pej*) N Weltverbesserer(in) *m(f)*
dogsbody ['dɔgzbɔdɪ] (BRIT *inf*) N Mädchen *nt* für alles
doily ['dɔɪlɪ] N Deckchen *nt*
doing ['duɪŋ] N: **this is your ~** das ist dein Werk
doings ['duɪŋz] NPL Treiben *nt*
do-it-yourself ['du:ɪtjɔ:'sɛlf] N Heimwerken *nt*, Do-it-yourself *nt*
doldrums ['dɔldrəmz] NPL: **to be in the ~** (*person*) niedergeschlagen sein; (*business*) in einer Flaute stecken
dole [dəul] (BRIT) N Arbeitslosenunterstützung *f*; **on the ~** arbeitslos
▶ **dole out** VT austeilen, verteilen
doleful ['dəulful] ADJ traurig
doll [dɔl] N (*toy, also US*: *inf*: *woman*) Puppe *f*
dollar ['dɔlə^r] (*US etc*) N Dollar *m*
dollar area N Dollarblock *m*
dolled up (*inf*) ADJ aufgedonnert
dollop ['dɔləp] (*inf*) N Schlag *m*
dolly ['dɔlɪ] (*inf*) N (*doll, woman*) Puppe *f*
Dolomites ['dɔləmaɪts] NPL: **the ~** die Dolomiten *pl*
dolphin ['dɔlfɪn] N Delfin *m*
domain [də'meɪn] N Bereich *m*; (*empire*) Reich *nt*
dome [dəum] N Kuppel *f*
domestic [də'mɛstɪk] ADJ (*trade*) Innen-; (*situation*) innenpolitisch; (*news*) Inland-, aus dem Inland; (*tasks, appliances*) Haushalts-; (*animal*) Haus-; (*duty, happiness*) häuslich
domesticated [də'mɛstɪkeɪtɪd] ADJ (*animal*) zahm; (*person*) häuslich
domestic flight N Inlandsflug *m*
domesticity [dəumɛs'tɪsɪtɪ] N häusliches Leben *nt*
domestic servant N Hausangestellte(r) *f(m)*
domicile ['dɔmɪsaɪl] N Wohnsitz *m*
dominant ['dɔmɪnənt] ADJ dominierend; (*share*) größte(r, s)
dominate ['dɔmɪneɪt] VT dominieren, beherrschen
domination [dɔmɪ'neɪʃən] N (Vor)herrschaft *f*
domineering [dɔmɪ'nɪərɪŋ] ADJ herrschsüchtig
Dominican Republic [də'mɪnɪkən-] N: **the ~** die Dominikanische Republik
dominion [də'mɪnɪən] N (*territory*) Herrschaftsgebiet *nt*; (*authority*): **to have ~ over** Macht haben über *+acc*
domino ['dɔmɪnəu] (*pl* **dominoes**) N (*block*) Domino(stein) *m*
domino effect N Dominoeffekt *m*
dominoes ['dɔmɪnəuz] N (*game*) Domino(spiel) *nt*
don [dɔn] N (BRIT) (Universitäts)dozent *m* (*besonders in Oxford und Cambridge*) ▶ VT anziehen
donate [də'neɪt] VT: **to ~ (to)** (*organization, cause*) spenden (für)
donation [də'neɪʃən] N (*act of donating*) Spenden *nt*; (*contribution*) Spende *f*
done [dʌn] PP *of* **do**
doner (kebab) ['dɔnəkə'bæb] N Döner (Kebab) *m*
dongle ['dɔŋgl] N Dongle *m*
donkey ['dɔŋkɪ] N Esel *m*
donkey-work ['dɔŋkɪwə:k] (BRIT *inf*) N Dreckarbeit *f*
donor ['dəunə^r] N Spender(in) *m(f)*
donor card N Organspenderausweis *m*
donor conference N (*Pol, Econ*) Geberkonferenz *f*
donor fatigue N Spendenmüdigkeit *f*
don't [dəunt] = **do not**
donut ['dəunʌt] (*US*) N = **doughnut**
doodle ['du:dl] VI Männchen malen ▶ N Kritzelei *f*
doom [du:m] N Unheil *nt* ▶ VT: **to be doomed to failure** zum Scheitern verurteilt sein
doomsday ['du:mzdeɪ] N der Jüngste Tag
door [dɔ:^r] N Tür *f*; **to go from ~ to ~** von Tür zu Tür gehen
door bell N Türklingel *f*
door handle N Türklinke *f*; (*of car*) Türgriff *m*
doorman ['dɔ:mən] N (*irreg*) Portier *m*
doormat ['dɔ:mæt] N Fußmatte *f*; (*fig*) Fußabtreter *m*
doorpost ['dɔ:pəust] N Türpfosten *m*
doorstep ['dɔ:stɛp] N Eingangsstufe *f*, Türstufe *f*; **on the ~** vor der Haustür
door-to-door ['dɔ:tə'dɔ:^r] ADJ (*selling*) von Haus zu Haus; **~ salesman** Vertreter *m*
doorway ['dɔ:weɪ] N Eingang *m*
dope [dəup] N (*inf*) Stoff *m*, Drogen *pl*; (: *person*) Esel *m*, Trottel *m*; (: *information*) Informationen *pl* ▶ VT dopen
dopey ['dəupɪ] (*inf*) ADJ (*groggy*) benebelt; (*stupid*) blöd, bekloppt
dormant ['dɔ:mənt] ADJ (*plant*) ruhend; (*volcano*) untätig; (*idea, report etc*): **to lie ~** schlummern
dormer ['dɔ:mə^r] N (*also*: **dormer window**) Mansardenfenster *nt*
dormice ['dɔ:maɪs] NPL *of* **dormouse**
dormitory ['dɔ:mɪtrɪ] N Schlafsaal *m*; (*US*: *building*) Wohnheim *nt*
dormouse ['dɔ:maus] (*pl* **dormice**) N Haselmaus *f*
DOS [dɔs] N ABBR (*Comput*: = *disk operating system*) DOS

dosage ['dəusɪdʒ] N Dosis *f*; (*on label*) Dosierung *f*
dose [dəus] N Dosis *f*; (BRIT: *bout*) Ration *f*; **a ~ of flu** eine Grippe
dosser ['dɔsə^r] (BRIT *inf*) N Penner(in) *m(f)*
dosshouse ['dɔshaus] (BRIT *inf*) N Obdachlosenheim *nt*
dossier ['dɔsɪeɪ] N Dossier *nt*
DOT (US) N ABBR (= *Department of Transportation*) ≈ Verkehrsministerium *nt*
dot [dɔt] N Punkt *m* ▶ VT: **dotted with** übersät mit; **on the ~** (auf die Minute) pünktlich
dote [dəut]: **~ on** *vt fus* abgöttisch lieben
dot-matrix printer [dɔt'meɪtrɪks-] N Nadeldrucker *m*
dotted line ['dɔtɪd-] N punktierte Linie *f*; **to sign on the ~** (*fig*) seine formelle Zustimmung geben
dotty ['dɔtɪ] (*inf*) ADJ schrullig
double ['dʌbl] ADJ doppelt; (*chin*) Doppel- ▶ ADV (*cost*) doppelt so viel ▶ N Doppelgänger(in) *m(f)* ▶ VT verdoppeln; (*paper, blanket*) (einmal) falten ▶ VI sich verdoppeln; **~ five two six (5526)** (BRIT *Tel*) fünfundfünfzig sechsundzwanzig; **it's spelt with a ~ "l"** es wird mit zwei l geschrieben; **an egg with a ~ yolk** ein Ei mit zwei Dottern; **on the ~, at the ~** (*quickly*) schnell; (*immediately*) unverzüglich; **to ~ as ...** (*person*) auch als ... fungieren; (*thing*) auch als ... dienen
▶ **double back** VI kehrtmachen, zurückgehen/-fahren
▶ **double up** VI sich krümmen; (*share room*) sich ein Zimmer teilen
double bass N Kontrabass *m*
double bed N Doppelbett *nt*
double bend (BRIT) N S-Kurve *f*
double-blind ['dʌbl'blaɪnd] ADJ: **~ experiment** Doppelblindversuch *m*
double-breasted ['dʌbl'brɛstɪd] ADJ (*jacket, coat*) zweireihig
double-check ['dʌbl'tʃɛk] VT noch einmal (über)prüfen ▶ VI es noch einmal (über)prüfen
double-click ['dʌbl'klɪk] VT (*Comput*) doppelklicken
double-clutch ['dʌbl'klʌtʃ] (US) VI mit Zwischengas schalten
double cream (BRIT) N Sahne *f* mit hohem Fettgehalt, ≈ Schlagsahne *f*
double-cross [dʌbl'krɔs] VT ein Doppelspiel treiben mit
double-decker [dʌbl'dɛkə^r] N Doppeldecker *m*
double-declutch ['dʌbldi:'klʌtʃ] (BRIT) VI mit Zwischengas schalten
double exposure N doppelt belichtetes Foto *nt*
double glazing [-'gleɪzɪŋ] (BRIT) N Doppelverglasung *f*
double-page spread ['dʌblpeɪdʒ-] N Doppelseite *f*
double-parking [dʌbl'pɑ:kɪŋ] N Parken *nt* in der zweiten Reihe
double room N Doppelzimmer *nt*
doubles ['dʌblz] N (*Tennis*) Doppel *nt*
double time N doppelter Lohn *m*
double whammy [-'wæmɪ] (*inf*) N Doppelschlag *m*
doubly ['dʌblɪ] ADV (ganz) besonders
doubt [daut] N Zweifel *m* ▶ VT bezweifeln; **without (a) ~** ohne Zweifel; **to ~ sb** jdm nicht glauben; **I ~ it (very much)** das bezweifle ich (sehr), das möchte ich (stark) bezweifeln; **to ~ if** *or* **whether ...** bezweifeln, dass ...; **I don't ~ that ...** ich bezweifle nicht, dass ...
doubtful ['dautful] ADJ zweifelhaft; **to be ~ about sth** an etw *dat* zweifeln; **to be ~ about doing sth** Bedenken haben, ob man etw tun soll; **I'm a bit ~** ich bin nicht ganz sicher
doubtless ['dautlɪs] ADV ohne Zweifel, sicherlich
dough [dəu] N Teig *m*; (*inf: money*) Kohle *f*, Knete *f*
doughnut, (US) **donut** ['dəunʌt] N ≈ Berliner (Pfannkuchen) *m*
dour [duə^r] ADJ mürrisch, verdrießlich
douse [dauz] VT Wasser schütten über +*acc*; (*extinguish*) löschen; **to ~ with** übergießen mit
dove [dʌv] N Taube *f*
Dover ['dəuvə^r] N Dover *nt*
dovetail ['dʌvteɪl] VI übereinstimmen ▶ N (*also*: **dovetail joint**) Schwalbenschwanzverbindung *f*
dowager ['dauədʒə^r] N (adlige) Witwe *f*
dowdy ['daudɪ] ADJ ohne jeden Schick; (*clothes*) unmodern
Dow-Jones average ['dau'dʒəunz-] (US) N Dow-Jones-Index *m*
down [daun] N Daunen *pl* ▶ ADV hinunter, herunter; (*on the ground*) unten ▶ PREP hinunter, herunter; (*movement along*) entlang ▶ VT (*inf: drink*) runterkippen; **~ there/here** da/hier unten; **the price of meat is ~** die Fleischpreise sind gefallen; **I've got it ~ in my diary** ich habe es in meinem Kalender notiert; **to pay £2 ~** £2 anzahlen; **England is two goals ~** England liegt mit zwei Toren zurück; **to ~ tools** (BRIT) die Arbeit niederlegen; **~ with ...!** nieder mit ...!
down-and-out ['daunəndaut] N Penner(in) *m(f)* (*inf*)
down-at-heel ['daunət'hi:l] ADJ (*appearance, person*) schäbig, heruntergekommen; (*shoes*) abgetreten
downbeat ['daunbi:t] N (*Mus*) erster betonter Taktteil *m* ▶ ADJ zurückhaltend
downcast ['daunkɑ:st] ADJ niedergeschlagen
downer ['daunə^r] (*inf*) N (*drug*) Beruhigungsmittel *nt*; **to be on a ~** deprimiert sein
downfall ['daunfɔ:l] N Ruin *m*; (*of dictator etc*) Sturz *m*, Fall *m*
downgrade ['daungreɪd] VT herunterstufen
downhearted ['daun'hɑ:tɪd] ADJ niedergeschlagen, entmutigt
downhill ['daun'hɪl] ADV bergab ▶ N (*Ski*: *also*: **downhill race**) Abfahrtslauf *m*; **to go ~** (*road*) bergab führen; (*person*) hinuntergehen,

herunterfahren; (*fig*) auf dem absteigenden Ast sein

herunterfahren; (*fig*) auf dem absteigenden Ast sein

Downing Street ist die Straße in London, die von Whitehall zum St James Park führt und in der sich der offizielle Wohnsitz des Premierministers (Nr.10) und des Finanzministers (Nr. 11) befindet. Im weiteren Sinne bezieht sich der Begriff Downing Street auf die britische Regierung.

download ['daunləud] VT (*Comput*) herunterladen, downloaden ▸ N Download *m*
downloadable [daun'ləudəbl] ADJ (*Comput*) herunterladbar
down-market ['daun'mɑːkɪt] ADJ (*product*) für den Massenmarkt
down payment N Anzahlung *f*
downplay ['daunpleɪ] (*US*) VT herunterspielen
downpour ['daunpɔːʳ] N Wolkenbruch *m*
downright ['daunraɪt] ADJ (*liar etc*) ausgesprochen; (*refusal, lie*) glatt
Downs [daunz] (BRIT) NPL: **the ~** die Downs *pl*, *Hügellandschaft in Südengland*
downscale ['daunskeɪl] ADJ (*US*) wenig anspruchsvoll; (*goods, products*) minderwertig; (*service*) mangelhaft; (*restaurant, hotel*) der unteren Preisklasse
downsize ['daunsaɪz] VI (*Econ: company*) sich verkleinern
Down's syndrome N (*Med*) Downsyndrom *nt*
downstairs ['daun'stɛəz] ADV unten; (*downwards*) nach unten
downstream ['daunstriːm] ADV flussabwärts, stromabwärts
downtime ['dauntaɪm] N Ausfallzeit *f*
down-to-earth ['dauntu'əːθ] ADJ (*person*) nüchtern; (*solution*) praktisch
downtown ['daun'taun] (*esp US*) ADV im Zentrum, in der (Innen)stadt; (*go*) ins Zentrum, in die (Innen)stadt ▸ ADJ: **~ Chicago** das Zentrum von Chicago
downtrodden ['dauntrɔdn] ADJ unterdrückt, geknechtet
down under ADV (*be*) in Australien/Neuseeland; (*go*) nach Australien/Neuseeland
downward ['daunwəd] ADJ, ADV nach unten; **a ~ trend** ein Abwärtstrend *m*
downwards ['daunwədz] ADV = **downward**
dowry ['daurɪ] N Mitgift *f*
doz. ABBR = **dozen**
doze [dəuz] VI ein Nickerchen *nt* machen
▸ **doze off** VI einschlafen, einnicken
dozen ['dʌzn] N Dutzend *nt*; **a ~ books** ein Dutzend Bücher; **80p a ~** 80 Pence das Dutzend; **dozens of** Dutzende von
DPh N ABBR (= *Doctor of Philosophy*) ≈ Dr. phil.
DPhil N ABBR (= *Doctor of Philosophy*) ≈ Dr. phil.
DPP (BRIT) N ABBR = **Director of Public Prosecutions**
DPT N ABBR (= *diphtheria, pertussis, tetanus*) Diphtherie, Keuchhusten und Tetanus
Dr ABBR = **doctor**; (*in street names:* = *Drive*) ≈ Str.
dr ABBR (*Comm*) = **debtor**
drab [dræb] ADJ trist
draft [drɑːft] N Entwurf *m*; (*also:* **bank draft**) Tratte *f*; (*US: call-up*) Einberufung *f* ▸ VT entwerfen; *see also* **draught**
draftsman *etc* ['drɑːftsmən] (*US*) N (*irreg*) = **draughtsman** *etc*
drag [dræg] VT schleifen, schleppen; (*river*) absuchen ▸ VI sich hinziehen ▸ N (*Aviat*) Luftwiderstand *m*; (*Naut*) Wasserwiderstand *m*; (*inf*): **to be a ~** (*boring*) langweilig sein; (*a nuisance*) lästig sein; (*women's clothing*): **in ~** in Frauenkleidung
▸ **drag away** VT: **to ~ away (from)** wegschleppen *or* wegziehen (von)
▸ **drag on** VI sich hinziehen
dragnet ['drægnɛt] N Schleppnetz *nt*; (*fig*) groß angelegte Polizeiaktion *f*
dragon ['drægn] N Drache *m*
dragonfly ['drægənflaɪ] N Libelle *f*
dragoon [drə'guːn] N Dragoner *m* ▸ VT: **to ~ sb into doing sth** (BRIT) jdn zwingen, etw zu tun
drain [dreɪn] N Belastung *f*; (*in street*) Gully *m* ▸ VT entwässern; (*pond*) trockenlegen; (*vegetables*) abgießen; (*glass, cup*) leeren ▸ VI ablaufen; **to feel drained (of energy/emotion)** sich ausgelaugt fühlen
drainage ['dreɪnɪdʒ] N Entwässerungssystem *nt*; (*process*) Entwässerung *f*
draining board ['dreɪnɪŋ-], (*US*) **drainboard** ['dreɪnbɔːd] N Ablaufbrett *nt*
drainpipe ['dreɪnpaɪp] N Abflussrohr *nt*
drake [dreɪk] N Erpel *m*, Enterich *m*
dram [dræm] (SCOT) N (*drink*) Schluck *m*
drama ['drɑːmə] N Drama *nt*
drama festival N Theaterfestival *nt*
dramatic [drə'mætɪk] ADJ dramatisch; (*theatrical*) theatralisch
dramatically [drə'mætɪklɪ] ADV dramatisch; (*say, announce, pause*) theatralisch
dramatist ['dræmətɪst] N Dramatiker(in) *m(f)*
dramatize ['dræmətaɪz] VT dramatisieren; (*for TV/cinema*) für das Fernsehen/den Film bearbeiten
drank [dræŋk] PT *of* **drink**
drape [dreɪp] VT drapieren
drapes [dreɪps] (*US*) NPL Vorhänge *pl*
drastic ['dræstɪk] ADJ drastisch
drastically ['dræstɪklɪ] ADV drastisch
draught, (*US*) **draft** [drɑːft] N (Luft)zug *m*; (*Naut*) Tiefgang *m*; (*of chimney*) Zug *m*; **on ~** vom Fass
draught beer N Bier *nt* vom Fass
draughtboard ['drɑːftbɔːd] (BRIT) N Damebrett *nt*
draughts [drɑːfts] (BRIT) N Damespiel *nt*
draughtsman, (*US*) **draftsman** ['drɑːftsmən] N (*irreg*) Zeichner(in) *m(f)*; (*as job*) technischer Zeichner *m*, technische Zeichnerin *f*
draughtsmanship, draftsmanship (*US*) ['drɑːftsmənʃɪp] N zeichnerisches Können *nt*; (*art*) Zeichenkunst *f*
draughty ADJ zugig

draw [drɔː] (*pt* **drew**, *pp* **drawn**) VT zeichnen; (*cart, gun, tooth, conclusion*) ziehen; (*curtain: open*) aufziehen; (*: close*) zuziehen; (*admiration, attention*) erregen; (*money*) abheben; (*wages*) bekommen ▸ VI (*Sport*) unentschieden spielen ▸ N (*Sport*) Unentschieden *nt*; (*lottery*) Lotterie *f*; (*: picking of ticket*) Ziehung *f*; **to ~ a comparison/distinction (between)** einen Vergleich ziehen/Unterschied machen (zwischen +*dat*); **to ~ near** näher kommen; (*event*) nahen; **to ~ to a close** zu Ende gehen
▸ **draw back** VI: **to ~ back (from)** zurückweichen (von)
▸ **draw in** VI (BRIT: *car*) anhalten; (*: train*) einfahren; (*nights*) länger werden
▸ **draw on** VT (*resources*) zurückgreifen auf +*acc*; (*imagination*) zu Hilfe nehmen; (*person*) einsetzen
▸ **draw out** VI länger werden ▸ VT (*money*) abheben
▸ **draw up** VI (an)halten ▸ VT (*chair etc*) heranziehen; (*document*) aufsetzen

drawback ['drɔːbæk] N Nachteil *m*

drawbridge ['drɔːbrɪdʒ] N Zugbrücke *f*

drawee [drɔː'iː] N Bezogene(r) *f*(*m*)

drawer [drɔːʳ] N Schublade *f*

drawing ['drɔːɪŋ] N Zeichnung *f*; (*skill, discipline*) Zeichnen *nt*

drawing board N Reißbrett *nt*; **back to the ~** (*fig*) das muss noch einmal neu überdacht werden

drawing pin (BRIT) N Reißzwecke *f*

drawing room N Salon *m*

drawl [drɔːl] N schleppende Sprechweise *f* ▸ VI schleppend sprechen

drawn [drɔːn] PP *of* **draw** ▸ ADJ abgespannt

drawstring ['drɔːstrɪŋ] N Kordel *f* zum Zuziehen

dread [drɛd] N Angst *f*, Furcht *f* ▸ VT große Angst haben vor +*dat*

dreadful ['drɛdful] ADJ schrecklich, furchtbar; **I feel ~!** (*ill*) ich fühle mich schrecklich; (*ashamed*) es ist mir schrecklich peinlich

dream [driːm] (*pt, pp* **dreamed** *or* **dreamt**) N Traum *m* ▸ VT, VI träumen; **to have a ~ about sb/sth** von jdm/etw träumen; **sweet dreams!** träume süß!
▸ **dream up** VT sich *dat* einfallen lassen, sich *dat* ausdenken

dreamer ['driːməʳ] N Träumer(in) *m*(*f*)

dreamt [drɛmt] PT, PP *of* **dream**

dream world N Traumwelt *f*

dreamy ['driːmɪ] ADJ verträumt; (*music*) zum Träumen

dreary ['drɪərɪ] ADJ langweilig; (*weather*) trüb

dredge [drɛdʒ] VT ausbaggern
▸ **dredge up** VT ausbaggern; (*fig: unpleasant facts*) ausgraben

dredger ['drɛdʒəʳ] N (*ship*) Schwimmbagger *m*; (*machine*) Bagger *m*; (BRIT: *also*: **sugar dredger**) Zuckerstreuer *m*

dregs [drɛgz] NPL Bodensatz *m*; (*of humanity*) Abschaum *m*

drench [drɛntʃ] VT durchnässen; **drenched to the skin** nass bis auf die Haut

dress [drɛs] N Kleid *nt*; (*no pl: clothing*) Kleidung *f* ▸ VT anziehen; (*wound*) verbinden ▸ VI sich anziehen; **she dresses very well** sie kleidet sich sehr gut; **to ~ a shop window** ein Schaufenster dekorieren; **to get dressed** sich anziehen
▸ **dress up** VI sich fein machen; (*in fancy dress*) sich verkleiden

dress circle (BRIT) N (*Theat*) erster Rang *m*

dress designer N Modezeichner(in) *m*(*f*)

dresser ['drɛsəʳ] N (BRIT) Anrichte *f*; (*US*) Kommode *f*; (*also*: **window dresser**) Dekorateur(in) *m*(*f*)

dressing ['drɛsɪŋ] N Verband *m*; (*Culin*) (Salat)soße *f*

dressing gown (BRIT) N Morgenrock *m*

dressing room N Umkleidekabine *f*; (*Theat*) (Künstler)garderobe *f*

dressing table N Frisierkommode *f*

dressmaker ['drɛsmeɪkəʳ] N (Damen)schneider(in) *m*(*f*)

dressmaking ['drɛsmeɪkɪŋ] N Schneidern *nt*

dress rehearsal N Generalprobe *f*

dressy ['drɛsɪ] (*inf*) ADJ elegant

drew [druː] PT *of* **draw**

dribble ['drɪbl] VI tropfen; (*baby*) sabbern; (*Football*) dribbeln ▸ VT (*ball*) dribbeln mit

dried [draɪd] ADJ (*fruit*) getrocknet, Dörr-; **~ egg** Trockenei *nt*, Eipulver *nt*; **~ milk** Trockenmilch *f*, Milchpulver *nt*

drier ['draɪəʳ] N = **dryer**

drift [drɪft] N Strömung *f*; (*of snow*) Schneewehe *f*; (*of questions*) Richtung *f* ▸ VI treiben; (*sand*) wehen; **to let things ~** die Dinge treiben lassen; **to ~ apart** sich auseinanderleben; **I get** *or* **catch your ~** ich verstehe, worauf Sie hinauswollen

drifter ['drɪftəʳ] N: **to be a ~** sich treiben lassen

driftwood ['drɪftwud] N Treibholz *nt*

drill [drɪl] N Bohrer *m*; (*machine*) Bohrmaschine *f*; (*Mil*) Drill *m* ▸ VT bohren; (*troops*) drillen ▸ VI: **to ~ (for)** bohren (nach); **to ~ pupils in grammar** mit den Schülern Grammatik pauken

drilling ['drɪlɪŋ] N Bohrung *f*

drilling rig N Bohrturm *m*; (*at sea*) Bohrinsel *f*

drily ['draɪlɪ] ADV = **dryly**

drink [drɪŋk] (*pt* **drank**, *pp* **drunk**) N Getränk *nt*; (*alcoholic*) Glas *nt*, Drink *m*; (*sip*) Schluck *m* ▸ VT, VI trinken; **to have a ~** etwas trinken; **a ~ of water** etwas Wasser; **we had drinks before lunch** vor dem Mittagessen gab es einen Drink; **would you like something to ~?** möchten Sie etwas trinken?
▸ **drink in** VT (*fresh air*) einatmen, einsaugen; (*story, sight*) (begierig) in sich aufnehmen

drinkable ['drɪŋkəbl] ADJ trinkbar

drink-driving ['drɪŋk'draɪvɪŋ] N Trunkenheit *f* am Steuer

drinker ['drɪŋkəʳ] N Trinker(in) *m*(*f*)

drinking ['drɪŋkɪŋ] N Trinken *nt*

drinking fountain N Trinkwasserbrunnen *m*
drinking water N Trinkwasser *nt*
drip [drɪp] N Tropfen *nt*; (*one drip*) Tropfen *m*; (*Med*) Tropf *m* ▶ VI tropfen; (*wall*) triefnass sein
drip-dry ['drɪp'draɪ] ADJ bügelfrei
drip-feed ['drɪpfi:d] VT künstlich ernähren ▶ N: **to be on a ~** künstlich ernährt werden
dripping ['drɪpɪŋ] N Bratenfett *nt* ▶ ADJ triefend; **I'm ~** ich bin klatschnass (*inf*); **~ wet** triefnass
drive [draɪv] (*pt* **drove**, *pp* **driven**) N Fahrt *f*; (*also*: **driveway**) Einfahrt *f*; (*: longer*) Auffahrt *f*; (*energy*) Schwung *m*, Elan *m*; (*campaign*) Aktion *f*; (*Sport*) Treibschlag *m*; (*Comput*: *also*: **disk drive**) Laufwerk *nt* ▶ VT fahren; (*Tech*) antreiben; (*animal*) treiben; (*ball*) weit schlagen; (*incite, encourage*: *also*: **drive on**) antreiben ▶ VI fahren; **to go for a ~** ein bisschen (raus)fahren; **it's 3 hours' ~ from London** es ist drei Stunden Fahrt von London (entfernt); **left-/right-hand ~** Links-/Rechtssteuerung *f*; **front-/rear-wheel ~** Vorderrad-/Hinterradantrieb *m*; **he drives a taxi** er ist Taxifahrer; **to ~ sth into sth** (*nail, stake etc*) etw in etw schlagen *acc*; **to ~ sb home/to the airport** jdn nach Hause/zum Flughafen fahren; **to ~ sb mad** jdn verrückt machen; **to ~ sb to (do) sth** jdn dazu treiben, etw zu tun; **to ~ at 50 km an hour** mit (einer Geschwindigkeit von) 50 Stundenkilometern fahren; **what are you driving at?** worauf wollen Sie hinaus?
▶ **drive away, drive off** VT vertreiben
▶ **drive out** VT (*evil spirit*) austreiben; (*person*) verdrängen
drive-by shooting ['draɪvbaɪ-] N *Schusswaffenangriff aus einem vorbeifahrenden Wagen*
drive-in ['draɪvɪn] (*esp US*) ADJ, N: **~ (cinema)** Autokino *nt*; **~ (restaurant)** Autorestaurant *nt*
drive-in window (*US*) N Autoschalter *m*
drivel ['drɪvl] (*inf*) N Blödsinn *m*
driven ['drɪvn] PP *of* **drive**
driver ['draɪvəʳ] N Fahrer(in) *m(f)*; (*Rail*) Führer(in) *m(f)*
driver's license ['draɪvəz-] (*US*) N Führerschein *m*
driveway ['draɪvweɪ] N Einfahrt *f*; (*longer*) Auffahrt *f*
driving ['draɪvɪŋ] N Fahren *nt* ▶ ADJ: **~ rain** strömender Regen *m*; **~ snow** Schneetreiben *nt*
driving belt N Treibriemen *m*
driving force N treibende Kraft *f*
driving instructor N Fahrlehrer(in) *m(f)*
driving lesson N Fahrstunde *f*
driving licence (BRIT) N Führerschein *m*
driving mirror N Rückspiegel *m*
driving school N Fahrschule *f*
driving test N Fahrprüfung *f*
drizzle ['drɪzl] N Nieselregen *m* ▶ VI nieseln
droll [drəul] ADJ drollig
dromedary ['drɔmədərɪ] N Dromedar *nt*
drone [drəun] N Brummen *nt*; (*male bee*) Drohne *f* ▶ VI brummen; (*bee*) summen; (*also*: **drone on**) eintönig sprechen
drool [dru:l] VI sabbern; **to ~ over sth/sb** etw/jdn sehnsüchtig anstarren
droop [dru:p] VI (*flower*) den Kopf hängen lassen; **his shoulders/head drooped** er ließ die Schultern/den Kopf herabhängen
drop [drɔp] N Tropfen *m*; (*lessening*) Rückgang *m*; (*distance*) Höhenunterschied *m*; (*in salary*) Verschlechterung *f*; (*also*: **parachute drop**) (Ab)sprung *m* ▶ VT fallen lassen; (*voice, eyes, price*) senken; (*set down from car*) absetzen; (*omit*) weglassen ▶ VI (herunter)fallen; (*wind*) sich legen; **drops** NPL Tropfen *pl*; **a 300 ft ~** ein Höhenunterschied von 300 Fuß; **a ~ of 10%** ein Rückgang um 10%; **cough drops** Hustentropfen *pl*; **to ~ anchor** ankern, vor Anker gehen; **to ~ sb a line** jdm ein paar Zeilen schreiben
▶ **drop by, drop in** (*inf*) VI vorbeikommen; **to ~ in (on sb)** (bei jdm) vorbeikommen
▶ **drop off** VI einschlafen ▶ VT (*passenger*) absetzen
▶ **drop out** VI (*withdraw*) ausscheiden; (*student*) sein Studium abbrechen
droplet ['drɔplɪt] N Tröpfchen *nt*
dropout ['drɔpaut] N Aussteiger(in) *m(f)*; (*Scol*) Studienabbrecher(in) *m(f)*
dropper ['drɔpəʳ] N Pipette *f*
droppings ['drɔpɪŋz] NPL Kot *m*
dross [drɔs] N Schlacke *f*; (*fig*) Schund *m*
drought [draut] N Dürre *f*
drove [drəuv] PT *of* **drive** ▶ N: **droves of people** Scharen *pl* von Menschen
drown [draun] VT ertränken; (*fig*: *also*: **drown out**) übertönen ▶ VI ertrinken
drowse [drauz] VI (vor sich *acc* hin) dösen *or* dämmern
drowsy ['drauzɪ] ADJ schläfrig
drudge [drʌdʒ] N Arbeitstier *nt*
drudgery ['drʌdʒərɪ] N (stumpfsinnige) Plackerei *f* (*inf*); **housework is sheer ~** Hausarbeit ist eine einzige Plackerei
drug [drʌg] N Medikament *nt*, Arzneimittel *nt*; (*narcotic*) Droge *f*, Rauschgift *nt* ▶ VT betäuben; **to be on drugs** drogensüchtig sein; **hard/soft drugs** harte/weiche Drogen *pl*
drug abuse N Drogenmissbrauch *m*; **~ prevention** Drogenprävention *f*
drug addict N Drogensüchtige(r) *f(m)*, Rauschgiftsüchtige(r) *f(m)*
drug dealer N Drogenhändler(in) *m(f)*, Dealer *m* (*inf*)
drug-driving [drʌg'draɪvɪŋ] N Fahren *nt* unter Drogeneinfluss
druggist ['drʌgɪst] (*US*) N Drogist(in) *m(f)*
drugstore ['drʌgstɔ:ʳ] (*US*) N Drogerie *f*
drum [drʌm] N Trommel *f*; (*for oil, petrol*) Fass *nt* ▶ VI trommeln; **drums** NPL (*kit*) Schlagzeug *nt*
▶ **drum up** VT (*enthusiasm*) erwecken; (*support*) auftreiben
drummer ['drʌməʳ] N Trommler(in) *m(f)*; (*in band, pop group*) Schlagzeuger(in) *m(f)*
drum roll N Trommelwirbel *m*

drumstick ['drʌmstɪk] N Trommelstock *m*; (*of chicken*) Keule *f*
drunk [drʌŋk] PP *of* **drink** ▶ ADJ betrunken ▶ N (*also*: **drunkard**) Trinker(in) *m(f)*; **to get ~** sich betrinken; **a ~ driving offence** Trunkenheit *f* am Steuer
drunken ['drʌŋkən] ADJ betrunken; (*party*) feucht-fröhlich; **~ driving** Trunkenheit *f* am Steuer
drunkenness ['drʌŋkənnɪs] N (*state*) Betrunkenheit *f*; (*habit*) Trunksucht *f*
dry [draɪ] ADJ trocken ▶ VT, VI trocknen; **on ~ land** auf festem Boden; **to ~ one's hands/hair/eyes** sich *dat* die Hände (ab)trocknen/die Haare trocknen/die Tränen abwischen; **to ~ the dishes** (das Geschirr) abtrocknen
▶ **dry up** VI austrocknen; (*in speech*) den Faden verlieren
dry-clean ['draɪ'kli:n] VT chemisch reinigen
dry-cleaner ['draɪ'kli:nər] N (*job*) Inhaber(in) *m(f)* einer chemischen Reinigung; (*shop*: *also*: **dry-cleaner's**) chemische Reinigung *f*
dry-cleaning ['draɪ'kli:nɪŋ] N (*process*) chemische Reinigung *f*
dry dock N Trockendock *nt*
dryer ['draɪər] N Wäschetrockner *m*; (*US*: *spin-dryer*) Wäscheschleuder *f*
dry goods NPL Kurzwaren *pl*
dry ice N Trockeneis *nt*
dryly ['draɪlɪ] ADV (*say, remark*) trocken
dryness ['draɪnɪs] N Trockenheit *f*
dry rot N (Haus)schwamm *m*, (Holz)schwamm *m*
dry run N (*fig*) Probe *f*
dry ski slope N Trockenskipiste *f*
DSc N ABBR (= *Doctor of Science*) ≈ Dr. rer. nat.
DSL N ABBR (*Comput*: = *digital subscriber line*) DSL
DSL connection N (*Comput*) DSL-Anschluss *m*
DSS (BRIT) N ABBR (= *Department of Social Security*) *Ministerium für Sozialfürsorge*
DST ABBR = **daylight-saving time**
DTI (BRIT) N ABBR (= *Department of Trade and Industry*) ≈ Wirtschaftsministerium *nt*
DTP N ABBR (= *desktop publishing*) DTP *nt*; (= *diphtheria, tetanus, pertussis*) Diphtherie, Tetanus und Keuchhusten
DT's (*inf*) NPL ABBR (= *delirium tremens*) Delirium tremens *nt*; **to have the ~** vom Trinken den Tatterich haben (*inf*)
dual ['djuəl] ADJ doppelt; (*personality*) gespalten
dual carriageway (BRIT) N ≈ Schnellstraße *f*
dual nationality N doppelte Staatsangehörigkeit *f*
dual-purpose ['djuəl'pə:pəs] ADJ zweifach verwendbar
dubbed [dʌbd] ADJ synchronisiert; (*nicknamed*) getauft
dubious ['dju:bɪəs] ADJ zweifelhaft; **I'm very ~ about it** ich habe da (doch) starke Zweifel
Dublin ['dʌblɪn] N Dublin *nt*
Dubliner ['dʌblɪnər] N Dubliner(in) *m(f)*
duchess ['dʌtʃɪs] N Herzogin *f*
duck [dʌk] N Ente *f* ▶ VI (*also*: **duck down**) sich ducken ▶ VT (*blow*) ausweichen *+dat*; (*duty, responsibility*) aus dem Weg gehen *+dat*
duckling ['dʌklɪŋ] N Entenküken *nt*; (*Culin*) (junge) Ente *f*
duct [dʌkt] N Rohr *nt*; (*Anat*) Röhre *f*; **tear ~** Tränenkanal *m*
dud [dʌd] N Niete *f* (*inf*); (*note*) Blüte *f* (*inf*) ▶ ADJ: **~ cheque** (BRIT) ungedeckter Scheck *m*
due [dju:] ADJ fällig; (*attention etc*) gebührend; (*consideration*) reiflich ▶ N: **to give sb his/her ~** jdn gerecht behandeln ▶ ADV: **~ north** direkt nach Norden; **dues** NPL Beitrag *m*; (*in harbour*) Gebühren *pl*; **in ~ course** zu gegebener Zeit; (*eventually*) im Laufe der Zeit; **~ to** (*owing to*) wegen *+gen*, aufgrund *+gen*; **to be ~ to do sth** etw tun sollen; **the rent is ~ on the 30th** die Miete ist am 30. fällig; **the train is ~ at 8** der Zug soll (laut Fahrplan) um 8 ankommen; **she is ~ back tomorrow** sie müsste morgen zurück sein; **I am ~ 6 days' leave** mir stehen 6 Tage Urlaub zu
due date N Fälligkeitsdatum *nt*
duel ['djuəl] N Duell *nt*
duet [dju:'ɛt] N Duett *nt*
duff [dʌf] (BRIT *inf*) ADJ kaputt
▶ **duff up** VT vermöbeln
duffel bag ['dʌfl-] N Matchbeutel *m*
duffel coat ['dʌfl-] N Dufflecoat *m*
duffer ['dʌfər] (*inf*) N Versager *m*, Flasche *f*
dug [dʌg] PT, PP *of* **dig**
dugout ['dʌgaut] N (*canoe*) Einbaum *m*; (*shelter*) Unterstand *m*
duke [dju:k] N Herzog *m*
dull [dʌl] ADJ trüb; (*intelligence, wit*) schwerfällig, langsam; (*event*) langweilig; (*sound, pain*) dumpf ▶ VT (*pain, grief*) betäuben; (*mind, senses*) abstumpfen
duly ['dju:lɪ] ADV (*properly*) gebührend; (*on time*) pünktlich
dumb [dʌm] ADJ stumm; (*pej*: *stupid*) dumm, doof (*inf*); **he was struck ~** es verschlug ihm die Sprache
▶ **dumb down** VI an Niveau *or* Qualität verlieren, verflachen ▶ VT verdummen, dumm machen
dumbbell ['dʌmbɛl] N Hantel *f*
dumbfounded [dʌm'faundɪd] ADJ verblüfft
dumbing down [dʌmɪŋ'daʊn] N Verdummung *f*, Qualitätsverlust *m*
dummy ['dʌmɪ] N (Schneider)puppe *f*; (*mock-up*) Attrappe *f*; (*Sport*) Finte *f*; (BRIT: *for baby*) Schnuller *m* ▶ ADJ (*firm*) fiktiv; **~ bullets** Übungsmunition *f*
dummy run N Probe *f*
dump [dʌmp] N (*also*: **rubbish dump**) Abfallhaufen *m*; (*inf*: *place*) Müllkippe *f*; (*Mil*) Depot *nt* ▶ VT fallen lassen; (*get rid of*) abladen; (*car*) abstellen; (*Comput*: *data*) ausgeben; **to be down in the dumps** (*inf*) deprimiert *or* down sein; **"no dumping"** „Schuttabladen verboten"
dumpling ['dʌmplɪŋ] N Kloß *m*, Knödel *m*

dumpy ['dʌmpɪ] ADJ pummelig
dunce [dʌns] N Niete *f*
dune [dju:n] N Düne *f*
dung [dʌŋ] N (*Agr*) Dünger *m*, Mist *m*; (*Zool*) Dung *m*
dungarees [dʌŋgə'ri:z] NPL Latzhose *f*
dungeon ['dʌndʒən] N Kerker *m*, Verlies *nt*
dunk [dʌŋk] VT (ein)tunken
Dunkirk [dʌn'kə:k] N Dünkirchen *nt*
duo ['dju:əu] N Duo *nt*
duodenal [dju:əu'di:nl] ADJ Duodenal-; **~ ulcer** Zwölffingerdarmgeschwür *nt*
duodenum [dju:əu'di:nəm] N Zwölffingerdarm *m*
dupe [dju:p] N Betrogene(r) *f(m)* ▸ VT betrügen
duplex ['dju:plɛks] (*US*) N Zweifamilienhaus *nt*; (*apartment*) zweistöckige Wohnung *f*
duplicate N ['dju:plɪkət] (*also*: **duplicate copy**) Duplikat *nt*, Kopie *f*; (*also*: **duplicate key**) Zweitschlüssel *m* ▸ ADJ ['dju:plɪkət] doppelt ▸ VT ['dju:plɪkeɪt] kopieren; (*repeat*) wiederholen; **in ~** in doppelter Ausfertigung
duplicating machine ['dju:plɪkeɪtɪŋ-] N Vervielfältigungsapparat *m*
duplicator ['dju:plɪkeɪtə^r] N Vervielfältigungsapparat *m*
duplicity [dju:'plɪsɪtɪ] N Doppelspiel *nt*
Dur. (BRIT) ABBR (*Post*) = **Durham**
durability [djuərə'bɪlɪtɪ] N Haltbarkeit *f*
durable ['djuərəbl] ADJ haltbar
duration [djuə'reɪʃən] N Dauer *f*
duress [djuə'rɛs] N: **under ~** unter Zwang
Durex® ['djuərɛks] (BRIT) N Gummi *m* (*inf*)
during ['djuərɪŋ] PREP während *+gen*
dusk [dʌsk] N (Abend)dämmerung *f*
dusky ['dʌskɪ] ADJ (*room*) dunkel; (*light*) Dämmer-
dust [dʌst] N Staub *m* ▸ VT abstauben; (*cake etc*): **to ~ with** bestäuben mit
▸ **dust off** VT abwischen, wegwischen; (*fig*) hervorkramen
dustbin ['dʌstbɪn] (BRIT) N Mülltonne *f*
dustbin liner (BRIT) N Müllsack *m*
duster ['dʌstə^r] N Staubtuch *nt*
dust jacket N (Schutz)umschlag *m*
dustman ['dʌstmən] (BRIT) N (*irreg*) Müllmann *m*
dustpan ['dʌstpæn] N Kehrschaufel *f*, Müllschaufel *f*
dusty ['dʌstɪ] ADJ staubig
Dutch [dʌtʃ] ADJ holländisch, niederländisch ▸ N Holländisch *nt*, Niederländisch *nt* ▸ ADV: **to go ~** (*inf*) getrennte Kasse machen; **the Dutch** NPL die Holländer *pl*, die Niederländer *pl*
Dutch auction N *Versteigerung mit stufenweise erniedrigtem Ausbietungspreis*
Dutchman ['dʌtʃmən] N (*irreg*) Holländer *m*, Niederländer *m*
Dutchwoman ['dʌtʃwumən] N (*irreg*) Holländerin *f*, Niederländerin *f*
dutiable ['dju:tɪəbl] ADJ zollpflichtig
dutiful ['dju:tɪful] ADJ pflichtbewusst; (*son, daughter*) gehorsam
duty ['dju:tɪ] N Pflicht *f*; (*tax*) Zoll *m*; **duties** NPL (*functions*) Aufgaben *pl*; **to make it one's ~ to do sth** es sich *dat* zur Pflicht machen, etw zu tun; **to pay ~ on sth** Zoll auf etw *acc* zahlen; **on/off ~** im/nicht im Dienst
duty-free ['dju:tɪ'fri:] ADJ zollfrei; **~ shop** Dutyfreeshop *m*, Duty-free-Shop *m*
duty officer N Offizier *m* vom Dienst
duvet ['du:veɪ] (BRIT) N Federbett *nt*
DV ABBR (= *Deo volente*) so Gott will
DVD N ABBR (= *digital versatile or video disc*) DVD *f*
DVD player N DVD-Player *m*
DVD recorder N DVD-Rekorder *m*
DVLA (BRIT) N ABBR (= *Driver and Vehicle Licensing Authority*) *Zulassungsbehörde für Kraftfahrzeuge*
DVM (US) N ABBR (= *Doctor of Veterinary Medicine*) ≈ Dr. med. vet.
dwarf [dwɔ:f] (*pl* **dwarves**) N Zwerg(in) *m(f)* ▸ VT: **to be dwarfed by sth** neben etw *dat* klein erscheinen
dwarves [dwɔ:vz] NPL *of* **dwarf**
dwell [dwɛl] (*pt, pp* **dwelt**) VI wohnen, leben
▸ **dwell on** VT FUS (in Gedanken) verweilen bei
dweller ['dwɛlə^r] N Bewohner(in) *m(f)*; **city ~** Stadtbewohner(in) *m(f)*
dwelling ['dwɛlɪŋ] N Wohnhaus *nt*
dwelt [dwɛlt] PT, PP *of* **dwell**
dwindle ['dwɪndl] VI abnehmen; (*interest*) schwinden; (*attendance*) zurückgehen
dwindling ['dwɪndlɪŋ] ADJ (*strength, interest*) schwindend; (*resources, supplies*) versiegend
dye [daɪ] N Farbstoff *m*; (*for hair*) Färbemittel *nt* ▸ VT färben
dyestuffs ['daɪstʌfs] NPL Farbstoffe *pl*
dying ['daɪɪŋ] ADJ sterbend; (*moments, words*) letzte(r, s)
dyke [daɪk] N (BRIT: *wall*) Deich *m*, Damm *m*; (*channel*) (Entwässerungs)graben *m*; (*causeway*) Fahrdamm *m*
dynamic [daɪ'næmɪk] ADJ dynamisch
dynamics [daɪ'næmɪks] N OR NPL Dynamik *f*
dynamite ['daɪnəmaɪt] N Dynamit *nt* ▸ VT sprengen
dynamo ['daɪnəməu] N Dynamo *m*; (*Aut*) Lichtmaschine *f*
dynasty ['dɪnəstɪ] N Dynastie *f*
dysentery ['dɪsntrɪ] N (*Med*) Ruhr *f*
dyslexia [dɪs'lɛksɪə] N Legasthenie *f*
dyslexic [dɪs'lɛksɪk] ADJ legasthenisch ▸ N Legastheniker(in) *m(f)*
dyspepsia [dɪs'pɛpsɪə] N Dyspepsie *f*, Verdauungsstörung *f*
dystrophy ['dɪstrəfɪ] N Dystrophie *f*, Ernährungsstörung *f*; **muscular ~** Muskelschwund *m*

Ee

E¹, e [iː] N (*letter*) E *nt*, e *nt*; **E for Edward**, **E for Easy** (*US*) E wie Emil
E² [iː] N (*Mus*) E *nt*, e *nt*
E³ [iː] ABBR (= *east*) O ▶ N ABBR (*drug*: = *Ecstasy*) Ecstasy *nt*
e- PREF E-, elektronisch
E111 N ABBR (*also*: **form E111**) E111-Formular *nt*
ea. ABBR = **each**
each [iːtʃ] ADJ, PRON jede(r, s); **~ other** sich, einander; **they hate ~ other** sie hassen sich *or* einander; **you are jealous of ~ other** ihr seid eifersüchtig aufeinander; **~ day** jeden Tag; **they have 2 books ~** sie haben je 2 Bücher; **they cost £5 ~** sie kosten 5 Pfund das Stück; **~ of us** jede(r, s) von uns
eager [ˈiːgəʳ] ADJ eifrig; **to be ~ to do sth** etw unbedingt tun wollen; **to be ~ for sth** auf etw *acc* erpicht *or* aus (*inf*) sein
eagerly [ˈiːgəlɪ] ADV eifrig; (*awaited*) gespannt, ungeduldig
eagle [ˈiːgl] N Adler *m*
ear [ɪəʳ] N Ohr *nt*; (*of corn*) Ähre *f*; **to be up to one's ears in debt/work** bis über beide Ohren in Schulden/Arbeit stecken; **to be up to one's ears in paint/baking** mitten im Anstreichen/Backen stecken; **to give sb a thick ~** jdm ein paar hinter die Ohren geben; **we'll play it by ~** (*fig*) wir werden es auf uns zukommen lassen
earache [ˈɪəreɪk] N Ohrenschmerzen *pl*
eardrum [ˈɪədrʌm] N Trommelfell *nt*
earful [ˈɪəful] (*inf*) N: **to give sb an ~** jdm was erzählen; **to get an ~** was zu hören bekommen
earl [əːl] (BRIT) N Graf *m*
earlier [ˈəːlɪəʳ] ADJ, ADV früher; **I can't come any ~** ich kann nicht früher *or* eher kommen
early [ˈəːlɪ] ADV früh; (*ahead of time*) zu früh ▶ ADJ früh; (*Christians*) Ur-; (*death, departure*) vorzeitig; (*reply*) baldig; **~ in the morning** früh am Morgen; **to have an ~ night** früh ins Bett gehen; **in the ~ hours** in den frühen Morgenstunden; **in the ~** *or* **~ in the spring/19th century** Anfang des Frühjahrs/des 19. Jahrhunderts; **take the ~ train** nimm den früheren Zug; **you're ~!** Sie sind früh dran!; **she's in her ~ forties** sie ist Anfang Vierzig; **at your earliest convenience** so bald wie möglich
early retirement N: **to take ~** vorzeitig in den Ruhestand gehen
early retirement benefits NPL Vorruhestandsleistungen *pl*
early warning system N Frühwarnsystem *nt*
earmark [ˈɪəmɑːk] VT: **to ~ (for)** bestimmen (für), vorsehen (für)
earn [əːn] VT verdienen; (*interest*) bringen; **to ~ one's living** seinen Lebensunterhalt verdienen; **this earned him much praise, he earned much praise for this** das trug ihm viel Lob ein; **he's earned his rest/reward** er hat sich seine Pause/Belohnung verdient
earned income [əːnd-] N Arbeitseinkommen *nt*
earnest [ˈəːnɪst] ADJ ernsthaft; (*wish, desire*) innig ▶ N (*also*: **earnest money**) Angeld *nt*; **in ~** (*begin*) richtig; **to be in ~** es ernst meinen; **work on the tunnel soon began in ~** die Tunnelarbeiten begannen bald richtig; **is the Minister in ~ about these proposals?** meint der Minister diese Vorschläge ernst?
earnings [ˈəːnɪŋz] NPL Verdienst *m*; (*of company etc*) Ertrag *m*
ear, nose and throat specialist N Hals-Nasen-Ohren-Arzt *m*, Hals-Nasen-Ohren-Ärztin *f*
earphones [ˈɪəfəunz] NPL Kopfhörer *pl*
earplugs [ˈɪəplʌgz] NPL Ohropax® *nt*
earring [ˈɪərɪŋ] N Ohrring *m*
earset [ˈɪəsɛt] N (*Tel*) Earset *nt*, Ohrhörer *m*
earshot [ˈɪəʃɔt] N: **within/out of ~** in/außer Hörweite
earth [əːθ] N Erde *f*; (*of fox*) Bau *m* ▶ VT (BRIT *Elec*) erden
earthenware [ˈəːθnwɛəʳ] N Tongeschirr *nt* ▶ ADJ Ton-
earthly [ˈəːθlɪ] ADJ irdisch; **~ paradise** Paradies *nt* auf Erden; **there is no ~ reason to think …** es besteht nicht der geringste Grund für die Annahme …
earthquake [ˈəːθkweɪk] N Erdbeben *nt*
earthshattering [ˈəːθʃætərɪŋ] ADJ (*fig*) weltbewegend
earth tremor N Erdstoß *m*
earthworks [ˈəːθwəːks] NPL Erdarbeiten *pl*
earthworm [ˈəːθwəːm] N Regenwurm *m*
earthy [ˈəːθɪ] ADJ (*humour*) derb
earwig [ˈɪəwɪg] N Ohrwurm *m*
ease [iːz] N Leichtigkeit *f*; (*comfort*) Behagen *nt* ▶ VT (*problem*) vereinfachen; (*pain*) lindern;

(*tension*) verringern; (*loosen*) lockern ▶ VI nachlassen; (*situation*) sich entspannen; **to ~ sth in/out** (*push/pull*) etw behutsam hineinschieben/herausziehen; **at ~!** (*Mil*) rührt euch!; **with ~** mit Leichtigkeit; **life of ~** Leben *nt* der Muße; **to ~ in the clutch** die Kupplung behutsam kommen lassen
▶ **ease off** VI nachlassen; (*slow down*) langsamer werden
▶ **ease up** VI = **ease off**
easel ['i:zl] N Staffelei *f*
easily ['i:zɪlɪ] ADV leicht; ungezwungen; bequem
easiness ['i:zɪnɪs] N Leichtigkeit *f*; (*of manner*) Ungezwungenheit *f*
east [i:st] N Osten *m* ▶ ADJ (*coast, Asia etc*) Ost- ▶ ADV ostwärts, nach Osten; **the E~** der Osten
Easter ['i:stə^r] N Ostern *nt* ▶ ADJ (*holidays etc*) Oster-
Easter egg N Osterei *nt*
Easter Island N Osterinsel *f*
easterly ['i:stəlɪ] ADJ östlich; (*wind*) Ost-
Easter Monday N Ostermontag *m*
eastern ['i:stən] ADJ östlich; **E~ Europe** Osteuropa *nt*; **the E~ bloc** (*formerly*) der Ostblock
Easter Sunday N Ostersonntag *m*
East Germany N (*formerly*) die DDR *f*
eastward ['i:stwəd], **eastwards** ['i:stwədz] ADV ostwärts, nach Osten
easy ['i:zɪ] ADJ leicht; (*relaxed*) ungezwungen; (*comfortable*) bequem ▶ ADV: **to take it/things ~** (*go slowly*) sich *dat* Zeit lassen; (*not worry*) es nicht so schwernehmen; (*rest*) sich schonen; **payment on ~ terms** Zahlung zu günstigen Bedingungen; **that's easier said than done** das ist leichter gesagt als getan; **I'm ~** (*inf*) mir ist alles recht
easy chair N Sessel *m*
easy-going ['i:zɪ'gəuɪŋ] ADJ gelassen
easy touch (*inf*) N: **to be an ~** (*for money etc*) leicht anzuzapfen sein
eat [i:t] (*pt* **ate**, *pp* **eaten**) VT, VI essen; (*animal*) fressen
▶ **eat away** VT (*subj: sea*) auswaschen; (*: acid*) zerfressen
▶ **eat away at** VT FUS (*metal*) anfressen; (*savings*) angreifen
▶ **eat into** VT FUS = **eat away at**
▶ **eat out** VI essen gehen
▶ **eat up** VT aufessen; **it eats up electricity** es verbraucht viel Strom
eatable ['i:təbl] ADJ genießbar
eau de Cologne ['əudəkə'ləun] N Kölnischwasser *nt*, Eau de Cologne *nt*
eaves [i:vz] NPL Dachvorsprung *m*
eavesdrop ['i:vzdrɔp] VI lauschen; **to ~ on** belauschen *+acc*
ebb [ɛb] N Ebbe *f* ▶ VI ebben; (*fig: also*: **ebb away**) dahinschwinden; (*: feeling*) abebben; **the ~ and flow** (*fig*) das Auf und Ab; **to be at a low ~** (*fig*) auf einem Tiefpunkt angelangt sein
ebb tide N Ebbe *f*
ebony ['ɛbənɪ] N Ebenholz *nt*
e-book ['i:buk] N E-Book *nt*
ebullient [ɪ'bʌlɪənt] ADJ überschäumend, übersprudelnd
EC N ABBR (= *European Community*) EG *f*
e-card ['i:kɑ:d] N ABBR (= *electronic card*) E-Card *nt*, *elektronische Grußkarte*
ECB N ABBR (= *European Central Bank*) EZB *f*
eccentric [ɪk'sɛntrɪk] ADJ exzentrisch ▶ N Exzentriker(in) *m(f)*
ecclesiastic [ɪkli:zɪ'æstɪk], **ecclesiastical** [ɪkli:zɪ'æstɪkl] ADJ kirchlich
ECG N ABBR (= *electrocardiogram*) EKG *nt*
echo ['ɛkəu] (*pl* **echoes**) N Echo *nt* ▶ VT wiederholen ▶ VI widerhallen; (*place*) hallen
éclair [eɪ'klɛə^r] N Eclair *nt*
eclipse [ɪ'klɪps] N Finsternis *f* ▶ VT in den Schatten stellen
eco- ['i:kəu] PREF Öko-, öko-
ecofriendly [i:kəu'frɛndlɪ] ADJ umweltfreundlich
ecological [i:kə'lɔdʒɪkəl] ADJ ökologisch; (*damage, disaster*) Umwelt-
ecologist [ɪ'kɔlədʒɪst] N Ökologe *m*, Ökologin *f*
ecology [ɪ'kɔlədʒɪ] N Ökologie *f*
e-commerce [i:'kɔmɜ:s] N E-Commerce *nt*, elektronischer Handel
economic [i:kə'nɔmɪk] ADJ (*system, policy etc*) Wirtschafts-; (*profitable*) wirtschaftlich
economical [i:kə'nɔmɪkl] ADJ wirtschaftlich; (*person*) sparsam
economically [i:kə'nɔmɪklɪ] ADV wirtschaftlich; (*thriftily*) sparsam
economics [i:kə'nɔmɪks] N Wirtschaftswissenschaften *pl* ▶ NPL Wirtschaftlichkeit *f*; (*of situation*) wirtschaftliche Seite *f*
economist [ɪ'kɔnəmɪst] N Wirtschaftswissenschaftler(in) *m(f)*
economize [ɪ'kɔnəmaɪz] VI sparen
economy [ɪ'kɔnəmɪ] N Wirtschaft *f*; (*financial prudence*) Sparsamkeit *f*; **economies of scale** (*Comm*) Einsparungen *pl* durch erhöhte Produktion
economy class N Touristenklasse *f*
economy size N Sparpackung *f*
ecosystem ['i:kəusɪstəm] N Ökosystem *nt*
ecotourism ['i:kəu'tuərɪzm] N Ökotourismus *m*
ECSC N ABBR (= *European Coal and Steel Community*) *Europäische Gemeinschaft für Kohle und Stahl*
ecstasy ['ɛkstəsɪ] N Ekstase *f*; (*drug*) Ecstasy *nt*; **to go into ecstasies over** in Verzückung geraten über *+acc*; **in ~** verzückt
ecstatic [ɛks'tætɪk] ADJ ekstatisch
ECT N ABBR = **electroconvulsive therapy**
Ecuador ['ɛkwədɔ:^r] N Ecuador *nt*, Ekuador *nt*
ecumenical [i:kju'mɛnɪkl] ADJ ökumenisch
eczema ['ɛksɪmə] N Ekzem *nt*
eddy ['ɛdɪ] N Strudel *m*
edge [ɛdʒ] N Rand *m*; (*of table, chair*) Kante *f*; (*of lake*) Ufer *nt*; (*of knife etc*) Schneide *f* ▶ VT einfassen ▶ VI: **to ~ forward** sich nach vorne

schieben; **on ~** (*fig*) = **edgy**; **to have the ~ on** überlegen sein +*dat*; **to ~ away from** sich allmählich entfernen von; **to ~ past** sich vorbeischieben, sich vorbeidrücken
edgeways ['ɛdʒweɪz] ADV: **he couldn't get a word in ~** er kam überhaupt nicht zu Wort
edging ['ɛdʒɪŋ] N Einfassung *f*
edgy ['ɛdʒɪ] ADJ nervös
edible ['ɛdɪbl] ADJ essbar, genießbar
edict ['i:dɪkt] N Erlass *m*
edifice ['ɛdɪfɪs] N Gebäude *nt*
edifying ['ɛdɪfaɪɪŋ] ADJ erbaulich
Edinburgh ['ɛdɪnbərə] N Edinburg(h) *nt*
edit ['ɛdɪt] VT (*text*) redigieren; (*book*) lektorieren; (*film, broadcast*) schneiden, cutten; (*newspaper, magazine*) herausgeben; (*Comput*) editieren
edition [ɪ'dɪʃən] N Ausgabe *f*
editor ['ɛdɪtə^r] N Redakteur(in) *m(f)*; (*of newspaper, magazine*) Herausgeber(in) *m(f)*; (*of book*) Lektor(in) *m(f)*; (*Cine, Radio, TV*) Cutter(in) *m(f)*
editorial [ɛdɪ'tɔ:rɪəl] ADJ redaktionell; (*staff*) Redaktions- ▶ N Leitartikel *m*
EDP N ABBR (*Comput: = electronic data processing*) EDV *f*
EDT (*US*) ABBR (*= Eastern Daylight Time*) *ostamerikanische Sommerzeit*
educate ['ɛdjukeɪt] VT erziehen; **educated at …** zur Schule/Universität gegangen in …
educated ['ɛdjʊkeɪtɪd] ADJ gebildet
educated guess N wohl begründete Vermutung *f*
education [ɛdju'keɪʃən] N Erziehung *f*; (*schooling*) Ausbildung *f*; (*knowledge, culture*) Bildung *f*; **primary ~, elementary ~** (*US*) Grundschul(aus)bildung *f*; **secondary ~** höhere Schul(aus)bildung *f*
educational [ɛdju'keɪʃənl] ADJ pädagogisch; (*experience*) lehrreich; (*toy*) pädagogisch wertvoll; **~ technology** Unterrichtstechnologie *f*
Edwardian [ɛd'wɔ:dɪən] ADJ aus der Zeit Edwards VII
EE ABBR = **electrical engineer**
EEG N ABBR (*= electroencephalogram*) EEG *nt*
eel [i:l] N Aal *m*
EEOC (*US*) N ABBR (*= Equal Employment Opportunity Commission*) *Kommission für Gleichberechtigung am Arbeitsplatz*
eerie ['ɪərɪ] ADJ unheimlich
EET ABBR (*= Eastern European Time*) OEZ *f*
efface [ɪ'feɪs] VT auslöschen; **to ~ o.s.** sich im Hintergrund halten
effect [ɪ'fɛkt] N Wirkung *f*, Effekt *m* ▶ VT bewirken; (*repairs*) durchführen; **effects** NPL Effekten *pl*; (*Theat, Cine etc*) Effekte *pl*; **to take ~** (*law*) in Kraft treten; (*drug*) wirken; **to put into ~** in Kraft setzen; **to have an ~ on sb/sth** eine Wirkung auf jdn/etw haben; **in ~** eigentlich, praktisch; **his letter is to the ~ that …** sein Brief hat zum Inhalt, dass …
effective [ɪ'fɛktɪv] ADJ effektiv, wirksam; (*actual*) eigentlich, wirklich; **to become ~** in Kraft treten; **~ date** Zeitpunkt *m* des Inkrafttretens
effectively [ɪ'fɛktɪvlɪ] ADV effektiv
effectiveness [ɪ'fɛktɪvnɪs] N Wirksamkeit *f*, Effektivität *f*
effeminate [ɪ'fɛmɪnɪt] ADJ feminin, effeminiert
effervescent [ɛfə'vɛsnt] ADJ sprudelnd
efficacy ['ɛfɪkəsɪ] N Wirksamkeit *f*
efficiency [ɪ'fɪʃənsɪ] N Fähigkeit *f*, Tüchtigkeit *f*; Rationalität *f*; Leistungsfähigkeit *f*
efficiency apartment (*US*) N Einzimmerwohnung *f*
efficient [ɪ'fɪʃənt] ADJ fähig, tüchtig; (*organization*) rationell; (*machine*) leistungsfähig
efficiently [ɪ'fɪʃəntlɪ] ADV gut, effizient
effigy ['ɛfɪdʒɪ] N Bildnis *nt*
effluent ['ɛfluənt] N Abwasser *nt*
effort ['ɛfət] N Anstrengung *f*; (*attempt*) Versuch *m*; **to make an ~ to do sth** sich bemühen, etw zu tun
effortless ['ɛfətlɪs] ADJ mühelos; (*style*) flüssig
effrontery [ɪ'frʌntərɪ] N Unverschämtheit *f*; **to have the ~ to do sth** die Frechheit besitzen, etw zu tun
effusive [ɪ'fju:sɪv] ADJ überschwänglich
EFL N ABBR (*Scol: = English as a Foreign Language*) Englisch *nt* als Fremdsprache
EFTA ['ɛftə] N ABBR (*= European Free Trade Association*) EFTA *f*
e.g. ADV ABBR (*= exempli gratia*) z. B.
egalitarian [ɪgælɪ'tɛərɪən] ADJ egalitär; (*principles*) Gleichheits- ▶ N Verfechter(in) *m(f)* des Egalitarismus
egg [ɛg] N Ei *nt*; **hard-boiled/soft-boiled ~** hart/weich gekochtes Ei *nt*
▶ **egg on** VT anstacheln
egg cup N Eierbecher *m*
eggplant ['ɛgplɑ:nt] N (*esp US*) Aubergine *f*
eggshell ['ɛgʃɛl] N Eierschale *f* ▶ ADJ eierschalenfarben
egg timer N Eieruhr *f*
egg white N Eiweiß *nt*
egg yolk N Eigelb *nt*
ego ['i:gəu] N (*self-esteem*) Selbstbewusstsein *nt*
egoism ['ɛgəuɪzəm] N Egoismus *m*
egoist ['ɛgəuɪst] N Egoist(in) *m(f)*
egotism ['ɛgəutɪzəm] N Ichbezogenheit *f*, Egotismus *m*
egotist ['ɛgəutɪst] N ichbezogener Mensch *m*, Egotist(in) *m(f)*
ego trip (*inf*) N Egotrip *m*
Egypt ['i:dʒɪpt] N Ägypten *nt*
Egyptian [ɪ'dʒɪpʃən] ADJ ägyptisch ▶ N Ägypter(in) *m(f)*
eiderdown ['aɪdədaun] N Federbett *nt*, Daunendecke *f*
eight [eɪt] NUM acht
eighteen [eɪ'ti:n] NUM achtzehn
eighteenth [eɪ'ti:nθ] NUM achtzehnte(r, s)
eighth [eɪtθ] NUM achte(r, s) ▶ N Achtel *nt*
eightieth ['eɪtɪəθ] ADJ achtzigste(r, s)
eighty ['eɪtɪ] NUM achtzig
Eire ['ɛərə] N (Republik *f*) Irland *nt*

EIS N ABBR (= *Educational Institute of Scotland*) *schottische Lehrergewerkschaft*
either ['aɪðə^r] ADJ (*one or other*) eine(r, s) (von beiden); (*both, each*) beide *pl*, jede(r, s) ▸ PRON: **~ (of them)** eine(r, s) (davon) ▸ ADV auch nicht ▸ CONJ: **~ yes or no** entweder ja oder nein; **on ~ side** (*on both sides*) auf beiden Seiten; (*on one or other side*) auf einer der beiden Seiten; **I don't like ~** ich mag beide nicht *or* keinen von beiden; **no, I don't ~** nein, ich auch nicht; **I haven't seen ~ one or the other** ich habe weder den einen noch den anderen gesehen
ejaculation [ɪdʒækju'leɪʃən] N Ejakulation *f*, Samenerguss *m*
eject [ɪ'dʒɛkt] VT ausstoßen; (*tenant, gatecrasher*) hinauswerfen ▸ VI den Schleudersitz betätigen
ejector seat [ɪ'dʒɛktə-] N Schleudersitz *m*
eke out [i:k-] VT (*make last*) strecken
EKG (*US*) N ABBR = **electrocardiogram**
el [ɛl] (*US inf*) N ABBR = **elevated railroad**
elaborate ADJ [ɪ'læbərɪt] kompliziert; (*plan*) ausgefeilt ▸ VT [ɪ'læbəreɪt] näher ausführen; (*refine*) ausarbeiten ▸ VI mehr ins Detail gehen; **to ~ on** näher ausführen
elapse [ɪ'læps] VI vergehen, verstreichen
elastic [ɪ'læstɪk] N Gummi *nt* ▸ ADJ elastisch
elastic band (BRIT) N Gummiband *nt*
elasticity [ɪlæs'tɪsɪtɪ] N Elastizität *f*
elated [ɪ'leɪtɪd] ADJ: **to be ~** hocherfreut *or* in Hochstimmung sein
elation [ɪ'leɪʃən] N große Freude *f*, Hochstimmung *f*
elbow ['ɛlbəu] N Ell(en)bogen *m* ▸ VT: **to ~ one's way through the crowd** sich durch die Menge boxen
elbow grease (*inf*) N Muskelkraft *f*
elbowroom ['ɛlbəurum] N Ellbogenfreiheit *f*
elder ['ɛldə^r] ADJ älter ▸ N (*Bot*) Holunder *m*; (*older person: gen pl*) Ältere(r) *f(m)*
elderly ['ɛldəlɪ] ADJ ältere(r, s) ▸ NPL: **the ~** ältere Leute *pl*
elder statesman N (*irreg*) erfahrener Staatsmann *m*
eldest ['ɛldɪst] ADJ älteste(r, s) ▸ N Älteste(r) *f(m)*
elect [ɪ'lɛkt] VT wählen ▸ ADJ: **the president ~** der designierte *or* künftige Präsident; **to ~ to do sth** sich dafür entscheiden, etw zu tun
election [ɪ'lɛkʃən] N Wahl *f*; **to hold an ~** eine Wahl abhalten
election campaign N Wahlkampf *m*
election debacle N Wahldebakel *nt*
electioneering [ɪlɛkʃə'nɪərɪŋ] N Wahlkampf *m*
elector [ɪ'lɛktə^r] N Wähler(in) *m(f)*
electoral [ɪ'lɛktərəl] ADJ Wähler-
electoral college N Wahlmännergremium *nt*
electorate [ɪ'lɛktərɪt] N Wähler *pl*, Wählerschaft *f*
electric [ɪ'lɛktrɪk] ADJ elektrisch
electrical [ɪ'lɛktrɪkl] ADJ elektrisch; (*appliance*) Elektro-; (*failure*) Strom-
electrical engineer N Elektrotechniker *m*
electric blanket N Heizdecke *f*
electric chair (*US*) N elektrischer Stuhl *m*
electric cooker N Elektroherd *m*
electric current N elektrischer Strom *m*
electric fire (BRIT) N elektrisches Heizgerät *nt*
electrician [ɪlɛk'trɪʃən] N Elektriker(in) *m(f)*
electricity [ɪlɛk'trɪsɪtɪ] N Elektrizität *f*; (*supply*) (elektrischer) Strom *m* ▸ CPD Strom-; **to switch on/off the ~** den Strom an-/abschalten
electricity board (BRIT) N Elektrizitätswerk *nt*
electricity price N Strompreis *m*
electricity rate N Stromtarif *m*
electric light N elektrisches Licht *nt*
electric shock N elektrischer Schlag *m*, Stromschlag *m*
electrify [ɪ'lɛktrɪfaɪ] VT (*fence*) unter Strom setzen; (*rail network*) elektrifizieren; (*audience*) elektrisieren
electro... [ɪ'lɛktrəu] PREF Elektro-
electrocardiogram [ɪ'lɛktrə'kɑ:dɪəgræm] N Elektrokardiogramm *nt*
electroconvulsive therapy [ɪ'lɛktrəkən'vʌlsɪv-] N Elektroschocktherapie *f*
electrocute [ɪ'lɛktrəkju:t] VT durch einen Stromschlag töten; (*US: criminal*) auf dem elektrischen Stuhl hinrichten
electrode [ɪ'lɛktrəud] N Elektrode *f*
electroencephalogram [ɪ'lɛktrəuɛn'sɛfələgræm] N Elektroenzephalogramm *nt*
electrolysis [ɪlɛk'trɔlɪsɪs] N Elektrolyse *f*
electromagnetic [ɪ'lɛktrəmæg'nɛtɪk] ADJ elektromagnetisch
electron [ɪ'lɛktrɔn] N Elektron *nt*
electronic [ɪlɛk'trɔnɪk] ADJ elektronisch
electronic data processing N elektronische Datenverarbeitung *f*
electronic mail N elektronische Post *f*
electronics [ɪlɛk'trɔnɪks] N Elektronik *f*
electronic tag N elektronische Fußfessel *f*
electron microscope N Elektronenmikroskop *nt*
electroplated [ɪ'lɛktrə'pleɪtɪd] ADJ galvanisiert
electrotherapy [ɪ'lɛktrə'θɛrəpɪ] N Elektrotherapie *f*
elegance ['ɛlɪgəns] N Eleganz *f*
elegant ['ɛlɪgənt] ADJ elegant
element ['ɛlɪmənt] N Element *nt*; (*of heater, kettle etc*) Heizelement *nt*
elementary [ɛlɪ'mɛntərɪ] ADJ grundlegend; **~ school** (*US*) Grundschule *f*; **~ education** Elementarunterricht *m*; **~ maths/French** Grundbegriffe *pl* der Mathematik/des Französischen

> **Elementary school** ist in den USA und Kanada eine Grundschule, an der ein Kind die ersten sechs bis acht Schuljahre verbringt. In den USA heißt diese Schule auch grade school oder grammar school. Siehe auch **high school**.

elephant ['ɛlɪfənt] N Elefant *m*
elevate ['ɛlɪveɪt] VT erheben; (*physically*) heben
elevated railroad ['ɛlɪveɪtɪd-] (*US*) N Hochbahn *f*
elevation [ɛlɪ'veɪʃən] N Erhebung *f*; (*height*) Höhe *f* über dem Meeresspiegel; (*Archit*) Aufriss *m*

elevator ['ɛlɪveɪtəʳ] N (*US*) Aufzug *m*, Fahrstuhl *m*; (*in warehouse etc*) Lastenaufzug *m*
eleven [ɪ'lɛvn] NUM elf
elevenses [ɪ'lɛvnzɪz] (BRIT) NPL zweites Frühstück *nt*
eleventh [ɪ'lɛvnθ] NUM elfte(r, s); **at the ~ hour** (*fig*) in letzter Minute
elf [ɛlf] (*pl* **elves**) N Elf *m*, Elfe *f*; (*mischievous*) Kobold *m*
elicit [ɪ'lɪsɪt] VT: **to ~ (from sb)** (*information*) (aus jdm) herausbekommen; (*reaction, response*) (von jdm) bekommen
eligible ['ɛlɪdʒəbl] ADJ (*marriage partner*) begehrt; **to be ~ for sth** für etw infrage kommen; **to be ~ for a pension** pensionsberechtigt sein
eliminate [ɪ'lɪmɪneɪt] VT beseitigen; (*candidate etc*) ausschließen; (*team, contestant*) aus dem Wettbewerb werfen
elimination [ɪlɪmɪ'neɪʃən] N Beseitigung *f*; Ausschluss *m*; Ausscheiden *nt*; **by process of ~** durch negative Auslese
élite [eɪ'li:t] N Elite *f*
elitist [eɪ'li:tɪst] (*pej*) ADJ elitär
elixir [ɪ'lɪksəʳ] N Elixier *nt*
Elizabethan [ɪlɪzə'bi:θən] ADJ elisabethanisch
ellipse [ɪ'lɪps] N Ellipse *f*
elliptical [ɪ'lɪptɪkl] ADJ elliptisch
elm [ɛlm] N Ulme *f*
elocution [ɛlə'kju:ʃən] N Sprechtechnik *f*
elongated ['i:lɔŋgeɪtɪd] ADJ lang gestreckt; (*shadow*) verlängert
elope [ɪ'ləup] VI weglaufen
elopement [ɪ'ləupmənt] N Weglaufen *nt*
eloquence ['ɛləkwəns] N Beredtheit *f*, Wortgewandtheit *f*; Ausdrucksfülle *f*
eloquent ['ɛləkwənt] ADJ beredt, wortgewandt; (*speech, description*) ausdrucksvoll
else [ɛls] ADV andere(r, s); **something ~** etwas anderes; **somewhere ~** woanders, anderswo; **everywhere ~** sonst überall; **where ~?** wo sonst?; **is there anything ~ I can do?** kann ich sonst noch etwas tun?; **there was little ~ to do** es gab nicht viel anderes zu tun; **everyone ~** alle anderen; **nobody ~ spoke** niemand anders sagte etwas, sonst sagte niemand etwas
elsewhere [ɛls'wɛəʳ] ADV woanders, anderswo; (*go*) woandershin, anderswohin
ELT N ABBR (*Scol*: = *English Language Teaching*) *Englisch als Unterrichtsfach*
elucidate [ɪ'lu:sɪdeɪt] VT erläutern
elude [ɪ'lu:d] VT (*captor*) entkommen *+dat*; (*capture*) sich entziehen *+dat*; **this fact/idea eluded him** diese Tatsache/Idee entging ihm
elusive [ɪ'lu:sɪv] ADJ schwer zu fangen; (*quality*) unerreichbar; **he's very ~** er ist sehr schwer zu erreichen
elves [ɛlvz] NPL *of* **elf**
emaciated [ɪ'meɪsɪeɪtɪd] ADJ abgezehrt, ausgezehrt
email ['i:meɪl] N ABBR (= *electronic mail*) E-Mail *f* ▸ VI, VT mailen (sth to sb jdm etw)
email address N E-Mail-Adresse *f*
emanate ['ɛməneɪt] VI: **to ~ from** stammen von; (*sound, light etc*) ausgehen von
emancipate [ɪ'mænsɪpeɪt] VT (*women*) emanzipieren; (*poor*) befreien; (*slave*) freilassen
emancipation [ɪmænsɪ'peɪʃən] N Emanzipation *f*; Befreiung *f*; Freilassung *f*
emasculate [ɪ'mæskjuleɪt] VT schwächen
embalm [ɪm'bɑ:m] VT einbalsamieren
embankment [ɪm'bæŋkmənt] N Böschung *f*; (*of railway*) Bahndamm *m*; (*of river*) Damm *m*
embargo [ɪm'bɑ:gəu] (*pl* **embargoes**) N Embargo *nt* ▸ VT mit einem Embargo belegen; **to put** *or* **impose** *or* **place an ~ on sth** ein Embargo über etw *acc* verhängen; **to lift an ~** ein Embargo aufheben
embark [ɪm'bɑ:k] VT einschiffen ▸ VI: **to ~ (on)** sich einschiffen (auf); **to ~ on** (*journey*) beginnen; (*task*) in Angriff nehmen; (*course of action*) einschlagen
embarkation [ɛmbɑ:'keɪʃən] N Einschiffung *f*
embarkation card N Bordkarte *f*
embarrass [ɪm'bærəs] VT in Verlegenheit bringen
embarrassed [ɪm'bærəst] ADJ verlegen
embarrassing [ɪm'bærəsɪŋ] ADJ peinlich
embarrassment [ɪm'bærəsmənt] N Verlegenheit *f*; (*embarrassing problem*) Peinlichkeit *f*
embassy ['ɛmbəsɪ] N Botschaft *f*; **the Swiss E~** die Schweizer Botschaft
embedded [ɪm'bɛdɪd] ADJ eingebettet; (*attitude, belief, feeling*) verwurzelt
embellish [ɪm'bɛlɪʃ] VT (*account*) ausschmücken; **to be embellished with** geschmückt sein mit
embers ['ɛmbəz] NPL Glut *f*
embezzle [ɪm'bɛzl] VT unterschlagen
embezzlement [ɪm'bɛzlmənt] N Unterschlagung *f*
embezzler [ɪm'bɛzləʳ] N *jd, der eine Unterschlagung begangen hat*
embitter [ɪm'bɪtəʳ] VT verbittern
embittered [ɪm'bɪtəd] ADJ verbittert
emblem ['ɛmbləm] N Emblem *nt*; (*symbol*) Wahrzeichen *nt*
embodiment [ɪm'bɔdɪmənt] N Verkörperung *f*; **to be the ~ of ...** (*subj: thing*) ... verkörpern; (*: person*) ... in Person sein
embody [ɪm'bɔdɪ] VT verkörpern; (*include, contain*) enthalten
embolden [ɪm'bəuldn] VT ermutigen
embolism ['ɛmbəlɪzəm] N Embolie *f*
embossed [ɪm'bɔst] ADJ geprägt; **~ with a logo** mit geprägtem Logo
embrace [ɪm'breɪs] VT umarmen; (*include*) umfassen ▸ VI sich umarmen ▸ N Umarmung *f*
embroider [ɪm'brɔɪdəʳ] VT (*cloth*) besticken; (*fig: story*) ausschmücken
embroidery [ɪm'brɔɪdərɪ] N Stickerei *f*; (*activity*) Sticken *nt*
embroil [ɪm'brɔɪl] VT: **to become embroiled (in sth)** (in etw *acc*) verwickelt *or* hineingezogen werden
embryo ['ɛmbrɪəu] N Embryo *m*; (*fig*) Keim *m*

e

emcee [ɛm'si:] N Conférencier *m*
emend [ɪ'mɛnd] VT verbessern, korrigieren
emerald ['ɛmərəld] N Smaragd *m*
emerge [ɪ'mə:dʒ] VI: **to ~ (from)** auftauchen (aus); (*from sleep*) erwachen (aus); (*from imprisonment*) entlassen werden (aus); (*from discussion etc*) sich herausstellen (bei); (*new idea, industry, society*) entstehen (aus); **it emerges that** (BRIT) es stellt sich heraus, dass
emergence [ɪ'mə:dʒəns] N Entstehung *f*
emergency [ɪ'mə:dʒənsɪ] N Notfall *m* ▸ CPD Not-; (*repair*) notdürftig; **in an ~** im Notfall; **state of ~** Notstand *m*
emergency cord (*US*) N Notbremse *f*
emergency exit N Notausgang *m*
emergency landing N Notlandung *f*
emergency lane (*US*) N Seitenstreifen *m*
emergency road service (*US*) N Pannendienst *m*
emergency services NPL: **the ~** der Notdienst
emergency stop (BRIT) N Vollbremsung *f*
emergent [ɪ'mə:dʒənt] ADJ jung, aufstrebend
emeritus [ɪ'mɛrɪtəs] ADJ emeritiert
emery board ['ɛmərɪ-] N Papiernagelfeile *f*
emery paper ['ɛmərɪ-] N Schmirgelpapier *nt*
emetic [ɪ'mɛtɪk] N Brechmittel *nt*
emigrant ['ɛmɪgrənt] N Auswanderer *m*, Auswanderin *f*, Emigrant(in) *m(f)*
emigrate ['ɛmɪgreɪt] VI auswandern, emigrieren
emigration [ɛmɪ'greɪʃən] N Auswanderung *f*, Emigration *f*
émigré ['ɛmɪgreɪ] N Emigrant(in) *m(f)*
eminence ['ɛmɪnəns] N Bedeutung *f*
eminent ['ɛmɪnənt] ADJ bedeutend
eminently ['ɛmɪnəntlɪ] ADV ausgesprochen
emirate ['ɛmɪrɪt] N Emirat *nt*
emission [ɪ'mɪʃən] N Emission *f*
emissions [ɪ'mɪʃənz] NPL Emissionen *pl*
emit [ɪ'mɪt] VT abgeben; (*smell*) ausströmen; (*light, heat*) ausstrahlen
emolument [ɪ'mɔljumənt] N (*often pl*) Vergütung *f*; (*fee*) Honorar *nt*; (*salary*) Bezüge *pl*
emoticon [ɪ'məutɪkən] N (*Comput*) Emoticon *nt*
emotion [ɪ'məuʃən] N Gefühl *nt*
emotional [ɪ'məuʃənl] ADJ emotional; (*exhaustion*) seelisch; (*scene*) ergreifend; (*speech*) gefühlsbetont
emotionally [ɪ'məuʃnəlɪ] ADV emotional; (*be involved*) gefühlsmäßig; (*speak*) gefühlvoll; **~ disturbed** seelisch gestört
emotive [ɪ'məutɪv] ADJ emotional
empathy ['ɛmpəθɪ] N Einfühlungsvermögen *nt*; **to feel ~ with sb** sich in jdn einfühlen
emperor ['ɛmpərə^r] N Kaiser *m*
emphases ['ɛmfəsi:z] NPL *of* **emphasis**
emphasis ['ɛmfəsɪs] (*pl* **emphases**) N Betonung *f*; (*importance*) (Schwer)gewicht *nt*; **to lay** *or* **place ~ on sth** etw betonen; **the ~ is on reading** das Schwergewicht liegt auf dem Lesen
emphasize ['ɛmfəsaɪz] VT betonen; (*feature*) hervorheben; **I must ~ that ...** ich möchte betonen, dass ...
emphatic [ɛm'fætɪk] ADJ nachdrücklich; (*denial*) energisch; (*person, manner*) bestimmt, entschieden
emphatically [ɛm'fætɪklɪ] ADV nachdrücklich; (*certainly*) eindeutig
emphysema [ɛmfɪ'si:mə] N Emphysem *nt*
empire ['ɛmpaɪə^r] N Reich *nt*
empirical [ɛm'pɪrɪkl] ADJ empirisch
employ [ɪm'plɔɪ] VT beschäftigen; (*tool, weapon*) verwenden; **he's employed in a bank** er ist bei einer Bank angestellt
employee [ɪmplɔɪ'i:] N Angestellte(r) *f(m)*
employer [ɪm'plɔɪə^r] N Arbeitgeber(in) *m(f)*
employment [ɪm'plɔɪmənt] N Arbeit *f*; **to find ~** Arbeit *or* eine (An)stellung finden; **without ~** stellungslos; **your place of ~** Ihre Arbeitsstätte *f*
employment agency N Stellenvermittlung *f*
employment exchange (BRIT) N Arbeitsamt *nt*
empower [ɪm'pauə^r] VT: **to ~ sb to do sth** jdn ermächtigen, etw zu tun
empress ['ɛmprɪs] N Kaiserin *f*
empties ['ɛmptɪz] NPL Leergut *nt*
emptiness ['ɛmptɪnɪs] N Leere *f*
empty ['ɛmptɪ] ADJ leer; (*house, room*) leer stehend; (*space*) frei ▸ VT leeren; (*place, house etc*) räumen ▸ VI sich leeren; (*liquid*) abfließen; (*river*) münden; **on an ~ stomach** auf nüchternen Magen; **to ~ into** (*river*) münden *or* sich ergießen in *+acc*
empty-handed ['ɛmptɪ'hændɪd] ADJ mit leeren Händen; **he returned ~** er kehrte unverrichteter Dinge zurück
empty-headed ['ɛmptɪ'hɛdɪd] ADJ strohdumm
EMS N ABBR (= *European Monetary System*) EWS *nt*
EMT (*US*) N ABBR (= *emergency medical technician*) ≈ Sanitäter(in) *m(f)*
EMU N ABBR (= *Economic and Monetary Union*) EWU *f*
emu ['i:mju:] N Emu *m*
emulate ['ɛmjuleɪt] VT nacheifern *+dat*
emulsion [ɪ'mʌlʃən] N Emulsion *f*; (*also*: **emulsion paint**) Emulsionsfarbe *f*
enable [ɪ'neɪbl] VT: **to ~ sb to do sth** (*permit*) es jdm erlauben, etw zu tun; (*make possible*) es jdm ermöglichen, etw zu tun
enact [ɪ'nækt] VT (*law*) erlassen; (*play*) aufführen; (*role*) darstellen, spielen
enamel [ɪ'næməl] N Email *nt*, Emaille *f*; (*also*: **enamel paint**) Email(le)lack *m*; (*of tooth*) Zahnschmelz *m*
enamoured [ɪ'næməd] ADJ: **to be ~ of** (*person*) verliebt sein in *+acc*; (*pastime, idea, belief*) angetan sein von
encampment [ɪn'kæmpmənt] N Lager *nt*
encased [ɪn'keɪst] ADJ: **~ in** (*shell*) umgeben von; **to be ~ in** (*limb*) in Gips liegen *or* sein
encash [ɪn'kæʃ] (BRIT) VT einlösen
enchant [ɪn'tʃɑ:nt] VT bezaubern
enchanted [ɪn'tʃɑ:ntɪd] ADJ verzaubert
enchanting [ɪn'tʃɑ:ntɪŋ] ADJ bezaubernd
encircle [ɪn'sə:kl] VT umgeben; (*person*) umringen; (*building: police etc*) umstellen
encl. ABBR (*on letters etc*: = *enclosed, enclosure*) Anl.

enclave ['ɛnkleɪv] N: **an ~ (of)** eine Enklave *(+gen)*
enclose [ɪn'kləuz] VT umgeben; *(land, space)* begrenzen; *(with fence)* einzäunen; *(letter etc)*: **to ~ (with)** beilegen *(+dat)*; **please find enclosed** als Anlage übersenden wir Ihnen
enclosure [ɪn'kləuʒəʳ] N eingefriedeter Bereich *m*; *(in letter etc)* Anlage *f*
encoder [ɪn'kəudəʳ] N Codierer *m*
encompass [ɪn'kʌmpəs] VT umfassen
encore [ɔŋ'kɔːʳ] EXCL Zugabe! ▸ N Zugabe *f*
encounter [ɪn'kauntəʳ] N Begegnung *f* ▸ VT begegnen *+dat*; *(problem)* stoßen auf *+acc*
encourage [ɪn'kʌrɪdʒ] VT *(activity, attitude)* unterstützen; *(growth, industry)* fördern; **to ~ sb (to do sth)** jdn ermutigen(, etw zu tun)
encouragement [ɪn'kʌrɪdʒmənt] N Unterstützung *f*; Förderung *f*; Ermutigung *f*
encouraging [ɪn'kʌrɪdʒɪŋ] ADJ ermutigend
encroach [ɪn'krəutʃ] VI: **to ~ (up)on** *(rights)* eingreifen in *+acc*; *(property)* eindringen in *+acc*; *(time)* in Anspruch nehmen
encrusted [ɪn'krʌstɪd] ADJ: **~ with** *(gems)* besetzt mit; *(snow, dirt)* verkrustet mit
encrypt [ɪn'krɪpt] VT verschlüsseln
encumber [ɪn'kʌmbəʳ] VT: **to be encumbered with** beladen sein mit; *(debts)* belastet sein mit
encyclopaedia, encyclopedia [ɛnsaɪkləu'piːdɪə] N Lexikon *nt*, Enzyklopädie *f*
end [ɛnd] N Ende *nt*; *(of film, book)* Schluss *m*, Ende *nt*; *(of table)* Schmalseite *f*; *(of pointed object)* Spitze *f*; *(aim)* Zweck *m*, Ziel *nt* ▸ VT *(also*: **bring to an end, put an end to**) beenden ▸ VI enden; **from ~ to ~** von einem Ende zum anderen; **to come to an ~** zu Ende gehen; **to be at an ~** zu Ende sein; **in the ~** schließlich; **on ~** hochkant; **to stand on ~** *(hair)* zu Berge stehen; **for hours on ~** stundenlang ununterbrochen; **for 5 hours on ~** 5 Stunden ununterbrochen; **at the ~ of the street** am Ende der Straße; **at the ~ of the day** (BRIT *fig*) letztlich; **to this ~, with this ~ in view** mit diesem Ziel vor Augen
▸ **end up** VI: **to ~ up in** *(place)* landen in *+dat*; **to ~ up in trouble** Ärger bekommen; **to ~ up doing sth** etw schließlich tun
endanger [ɪn'deɪndʒəʳ] VT gefährden; **an endangered species** eine vom Aussterben bedrohte Art
endear [ɪn'dɪəʳ] VT: **to ~ o.s. to sb** sich bei jdm beliebt machen
endearing [ɪn'dɪərɪŋ] ADJ gewinnend
endearment [ɪn'dɪəmənt] N: **to whisper endearments** zärtliche Worte flüstern; **term of ~** Kosewort *nt*, Kosename *m*
endeavour, *(US)* **endeavor** [ɪn'dɛvəʳ] N Anstrengung *f*, Bemühung *f*; *(effort)* Bestrebung *f* ▸ VI: **to ~ to do sth** *(attempt)* sich anstrengen *or* bemühen, etw zu tun; *(strive)* bestrebt sein, etw zu tun
endemic [ɛn'dɛmɪk] ADJ endemisch, verbreitet
ending ['ɛndɪŋ] N Ende *nt*, Schluss *m*; *(Ling)* Endung *f*
endive ['ɛndaɪv] N Endivie *f*; *(chicory)* Chicorée *m or f*
endless ['ɛndlɪs] ADJ endlos; *(patience, resources, possibilities)* unbegrenzt
endorse [ɪn'dɔːs] VT *(cheque)* indossieren, auf der Rückseite unterzeichnen; *(proposal, plan)* billigen; *(candidate)* unterstützen
endorsee [ɪndɔː'siː] N Indossat *m*
endorsement [ɪn'dɔːsmənt] N Billigung *f*; *(of candidate)* Unterstützung *f*; (BRIT: *on driving licence)* Strafvermerk *m*
endow [ɪn'dau] VT *(institution)* eine Stiftung machen an *+acc*; **to be endowed with** besitzen
endowment [ɪn'daumənt] N Stiftung *f*; *(quality)* Begabung *f*
endowment assurance N Versicherung *f* auf den Erlebensfall, Erlebensversicherung *f*
endowment mortgage N Hypothek *f* mit Lebensversicherung
end product N Endprodukt *nt*; *(fig)* Produkt *nt*
end result N Endergebnis *nt*
endurable [ɪn'djuərəbl] ADJ erträglich
endurance [ɪn'djuərəns] N Durchhaltevermögen *nt*; *(patience)* Geduld *f*
endurance test N Belastungsprobe *f*
endure [ɪn'djuəʳ] VT ertragen ▸ VI Bestand haben
enduring [ɪn'djuərɪŋ] ADJ dauerhaft
end user N *(Comput)* Endbenutzer *m*
enema ['ɛnɪmə] N Klistier *nt*, Einlauf *m*
enemy ['ɛnəmɪ] ADJ feindlich; *(strategy)* des Feindes ▸ N Feind(in) *m(f)*; **to make an ~ of sb** sich *dat* jdn zum Feind machen
energetic [ɛnə'dʒɛtɪk] ADJ aktiv
energy ['ɛnədʒɪ] N Energie *f*; **Department of E~** Energieministerium *nt*
energy crisis N Energiekrise *f*
energy drink N Energiegetränk *nt*, Energydrink *m*
energy-saving ['ɛnədʒɪ'seɪvɪŋ] ADJ energiesparend; *(policy)* energiebewusst
enervating ['ɛnəveɪtɪŋ] ADJ strapazierend
enforce [ɪn'fɔːs] VT *(law, rule, decision)* Geltung verschaffen *+dat*
enforced [ɪn'fɔːst] ADJ erzwungen
enfranchise [ɪn'fræntʃaɪz] VT das Wahlrecht geben *or* erteilen *+dat*
engage [ɪn'geɪdʒ] VT in Anspruch nehmen; *(employ)* einstellen; *(lawyer)* sich *dat* nehmen; *(Mil)* angreifen ▸ VI *(Tech)* einrasten; **to ~ the clutch** einkuppeln; **to ~ sb in conversation** jdn in ein Gespräch verwickeln; **to ~ in** sich beteiligen an *+dat*; **to ~ in commerce** kaufmännisch tätig sein; **to ~ in study** studieren
engaged [ɪn'geɪdʒd] ADJ verlobt; (BRIT: *busy, in use)* besetzt; **to get ~** sich verloben; **he is ~ in research/a survey** er ist mit Forschungsarbeit/einer Umfrage beschäftigt
engaged tone (BRIT) N Besetztzeichen *nt*
engagement [ɪn'geɪdʒmənt] N Verabredung *f*; *(booking)* Engagement *nt*; *(to marry)* Verlobung *f*; *(Mil)* Gefecht *nt*, Kampf *m*; **I have a previous ~** ich habe schon eine Verabredung

e

engagement ring N Verlobungsring *m*
engaging [ɪn'geɪdʒɪŋ] ADJ einnehmend
engender [ɪn'dʒɛndəʳ] VT erzeugen
engine ['ɛndʒɪn] N Motor *m*; (*Rail*) Lok(omotive) *f*
engine driver N (*Rail*) Lok(omotiv)führer(in) *m(f)*
engineer [ɛndʒɪ'nɪəʳ] N Ingenieur(in) *m(f)*; (BRIT: *for repairs*) Techniker(in) *m(f)*; (*US Rail*) Lok(omotiv)führer(in) *m(f)*; (*on ship*) Maschinist(in) *m(f)*; **civil/mechanical ~** Bau-/Maschinenbauingenieur(in) *m(f)*
engineering [ɛndʒɪ'nɪərɪŋ] N Technik *f*; (*design, construction*) Konstruktion *f* ▶ CPD: **~ works** *or* **factory** Maschinenfabrik *f*
engine failure N Maschinenschaden *m*; (*Aut*) Motorschaden *m*
engine trouble N Maschinenschaden *m*; (*Aut*) Motorschaden *m*
England ['ɪŋglənd] N England *nt*
English ['ɪŋglɪʃ] ADJ englisch ▶ N Englisch *nt*; **the English** NPL die Engländer *pl*; **an ~ speaker** *jd, der Englisch spricht*
English Channel N: **the ~** der Ärmelkanal
Englishman ['ɪŋglɪʃmən] N (*irreg*) Engländer *m*
English-speaking ['ɪŋglɪʃspiːkɪŋ] ADJ (*country*) englischsprachig
Englishwoman ['ɪŋglɪʃwumən] N (*irreg*) Engländerin *f*
engrave [ɪn'greɪv] VT gravieren; (*name etc*) eingravieren; (*fig*) einprägen
engraving [ɪn'greɪvɪŋ] N Stich *m*
engrossed [ɪn'grəust] ADJ: **~ in** vertieft in *+acc*
engulf [ɪn'gʌlf] VT verschlingen; (*subj: panic, fear*) überkommen
enhance [ɪn'hɑːns] VT verbessern; (*enjoyment, beauty*) erhöhen
enigma [ɪ'nɪgmə] N Rätsel *nt*
enigmatic [ɛnɪg'mætɪk] ADJ rätselhaft
enjoy [ɪn'dʒɔɪ] VT genießen; (*health, fortune*) sich erfreuen *+gen*; (*success*) haben; **to ~ o.s.** sich amüsieren; **I ~ dancing** ich tanze gerne
enjoyable [ɪn'dʒɔɪəbl] ADJ nett, angenehm
enjoyment [ɪn'dʒɔɪmənt] N Vergnügen *nt*; (*activity*) Freude *f*
enlarge [ɪn'lɑːdʒ] VT vergrößern; (*scope*) erweitern ▶ VI: **to ~ on** weiter ausführen
enlarged [ɪn'lɑːdʒd] ADJ erweitert; (*Med*) vergrößert
enlargement [ɪn'lɑːdʒmənt] N Vergrößerung *f*
enlighten [ɪn'laɪtn] VT aufklären
enlightened [ɪn'laɪtnd] ADJ aufgeklärt
enlightening [ɪn'laɪtnɪŋ] ADJ aufschlussreich
enlightenment [ɪn'laɪtnmənt] N (*also Hist: Enlightenment*) Aufklärung *f*
enlist [ɪn'lɪst] VT anwerben; (*support, help*) gewinnen ▶ VI: **to ~ in** eintreten in *+acc*; **enlisted man** (*US Mil*) gemeiner Soldat *m*; (*US: in navy*) Matrose *m*
enliven [ɪn'laɪvn] VT beleben
enmity ['ɛnmɪtɪ] N Feindschaft *f*
ennoble [ɪ'nəubl] VT adeln; (*fig: dignify*) erheben
enormity [ɪ'nɔːmɪtɪ] N ungeheure Größe *f*
enormous [ɪ'nɔːməs] ADJ gewaltig, ungeheuer; (*pleasure, success etc*) riesig
enormously [ɪ'nɔːməslɪ] ADV enorm; (*rich*) ungeheuer
enough [ɪ'nʌf] ADJ genug, genügend ▶ PRON genug ▶ ADV: **big ~** groß genug; **he has not worked ~** er hat nicht genug *or* genügend gearbeitet; **have you got ~?** haben Sie genug?; **~ to eat** genug zu essen; **will 5 be ~?** reichen 5?; **I've had ~!** jetzt reichts mir aber!; **it's hot ~ (as it is)** es ist heiß genug; **he was kind ~ to lend me the money** er war so gut und hat mir das Geld geliehen; **~! es reicht!**; **that's ~, thanks** danke, das reicht *or* ist genug; **I've had ~ of him** ich habe genug von ihm; **funnily/oddly ~ ...** komischerweise ...
enquire [ɪn'kwaɪəʳ] VT, VI = **inquire**
enquiry [ɪn'kwaɪərɪ] = **inquiry**
enrage [ɪn'reɪdʒ] VT wütend machen
enrich [ɪn'rɪtʃ] VT bereichern
enrol, (US) enroll [ɪn'rəul] VT anmelden; (*at university*) einschreiben, immatrikulieren ▶ VI sich anmelden; sich einschreiben, sich immatrikulieren
enrolment, (US) enrollment [ɪn'rəulmənt] N Anmeldung *f*; Einschreibung *f*, Immatrikulation *f*
en route [ɔn'ruːt] ADV unterwegs; **~ for** auf dem Weg nach; **~ from London to Berlin** auf dem Weg von London nach Berlin
ensconced [ɪn'skɔnst] ADJ: **she is ~ in ...** sie hat es sich *dat* in ... *dat* gemütlich gemacht
ensemble [ɔn'sɔmbl] N Ensemble *nt*
enshrine [ɪn'ʃraɪn] VT bewahren; **to be enshrined in** verankert sein in *+dat*
ensue [ɪn'sjuː] VI folgen
ensuing [ɪn'sjuːɪŋ] ADJ folgend
en suite [ɔn'swiːt] ADJ, N: **room with ~ bathroom** Zimmer *nt* mit eigenem Bad
ensure [ɪn'ʃuəʳ] VT garantieren; **to ~ that** sicherstellen, dass
ENT N ABBR (*Med: = ear, nose, and throat*) HNO
entail [ɪn'teɪl] VT mit sich bringen
entangled [ɪn'tæŋgld] ADJ: **to become ~ (in)** sich verfangen (in *+dat*)
enter ['ɛntəʳ] VT betreten; (*club*) beitreten *+dat*; (*army*) gehen zu; (*profession*) ergreifen; (*race, contest*) sich beteiligen an *+dat*; (*sb for a competition*) anmelden; (*write down*) eintragen; (*Comput: data*) eingeben ▶ VI (*come in*) hereinkommen; (*go in*) hineingehen
▶ **enter for** VT FUS anmelden für
▶ **enter into** VT FUS (*discussion, negotiations*) aufnehmen; (*correspondence*) treten in *+acc*; (*agreement*) schließen
▶ **enter up** VT eintragen
▶ **enter (up)on** VT FUS (*career, policy*) einschlagen
enteritis [ɛntə'raɪtɪs] N Dünndarmentzündung *f*
enterprise ['ɛntəpraɪz] N Unternehmen *nt*; (*initiative*) Initiative *f*; **free ~** freies Unternehmertum *nt*; **private ~** Privatunternehmertum *nt*

enterprising [ˈɛntəpraɪzɪŋ] ADJ einfallsreich
entertain [ɛntəˈteɪn] VT unterhalten; (*invite*) einladen; (*idea, plan*) erwägen
entertainer [ɛntəˈteɪnəʳ] N Unterhalter(in) *m(f)*, Entertainer(in) *m(f)*
entertaining [ɛntəˈteɪnɪŋ] ADJ amüsant ▶ N: **to do a lot of ~** sehr oft Gäste haben
entertainment [ɛntəˈteɪnmənt] N Unterhaltung *f*; (*show*) Darbietung *f*
entertainment allowance N Aufwandspauschale *f*
enthral [ɪnˈθrɔːl] VT begeistern; (*story*) fesseln
enthralled [ɪnˈθrɔːld] ADJ gefesselt; **he was ~ by** *or* **with the book** das Buch fesselte ihn
enthralling [ɪnˈθrɔːlɪŋ] ADJ fesselnd; (*details*) spannend
enthuse [ɪnˈθuːz] VI: **to ~ about** *or* **over** schwärmen von
enthusiasm [ɪnˈθuːzɪæzəm] N Begeisterung *f*
enthusiast [ɪnˈθuːzɪæst] N Enthusiast(in) *m(f)*; **he's a jazz/sports ~** er begeistert sich für Jazz/Sport
enthusiastic [ɪnθuːzɪˈæstɪk] ADJ begeistert; (*response, reception*) enthusiastisch; **to be ~ about** begeistert sein von
entice [ɪnˈtaɪs] VT locken; (*tempt*) verleiten
enticing [ɪnˈtaɪsɪŋ] ADJ verlockend
entire [ɪnˈtaɪəʳ] ADJ ganz
entirely [ɪnˈtaɪəlɪ] ADV völlig
entirety [ɪnˈtaɪərətɪ] N: **in its ~** in seiner Gesamtheit
entitle [ɪnˈtaɪtl] VT: **to ~ sb to sth** jdn zu etw berechtigen; **to ~ sb to do sth** jdn dazu berechtigen, etw zu tun
entitled [ɪnˈtaɪtld] ADJ: **a book/film** *etc* **~ ...** ein Buch/Film *etc* mit dem Titel ...; **to be ~ to do sth** das Recht haben, etw zu tun
entity [ˈɛntɪtɪ] N Wesen *nt*
entourage [ɔntuˈrɑːʒ] N Gefolge *nt*
entrails [ˈɛntreɪlz] NPL Eingeweide *pl*
entrance N [ˈɛntrns] Eingang *m*; (*arrival*) Ankunft *f*; (*on stage*) Auftritt *m* ▶ VT [ɪnˈtrɑːns] bezaubern; **to gain ~ to** (*building etc*) sich *dat* Zutritt verschaffen zu; (*university*) die Zulassung erhalten zu; (*profession etc*) Zugang erhalten zu
entrance examination N Aufnahmeprüfung *f*
entrance fee N Eintrittsgeld *nt*
entrance ramp (US) N Auffahrt *f*
entrancing [ɪnˈtrɑːnsɪŋ] ADJ bezaubernd
entrant [ˈɛntrnt] N Teilnehmer(in) *m(f)*; (BRIT: *in exam*) Prüfling *m*
entreat [ɛnˈtriːt] VT: **to ~ sb to do sth** jdn anflehen, etw zu tun
entreaty [ɛnˈtriːtɪ] N (flehentliche) Bitte *f*
entrée [ˈɔntreɪ] N Hauptgericht *nt*
entrenched [ɛnˈtrɛntʃt] ADJ verankert; (*ideas*) festgesetzt
entrepreneur [ˈɔntrəprəˈnəːʳ] N Unternehmer(in) *m(f)*
entrepreneurial [ˈɔntrəprəˈnəːrɪəl] ADJ unternehmerisch
entrust [ɪnˈtrʌst] VT: **to ~ sth to sb** jdm etw anvertrauen; **to ~ sb with sth** (*task*) jdn mit etw betrauen; (*secret, valuables*) jdm etw anvertrauen
entry [ˈɛntrɪ] N Eingang *m*; (*in competition*) Meldung *f*; (*in register, account book, reference book*) Eintrag *m*; (*arrival*) Eintritt *m*; (*to country*) Einreise *f*; **"no ~"** „Zutritt verboten"; (*Aut*) „Einfahrt verboten"; **single/double ~ book-keeping** einfache/doppelte Buchführung *f*
entry form N Anmeldeformular *nt*
entry phone (BRIT) N Türsprechanlage *f*
entwine [ɪnˈtwaɪn] VT verflechten
E-number [ˈiːnʌmbəʳ] N (*food additive*) E-Nummer *f*
enumerate [ɪˈnjuːməreɪt] VT aufzählen
enunciate [ɪˈnʌnsɪeɪt] VT artikulieren; (*principle, plan etc*) formulieren
envelop [ɪnˈvɛləp] VT einhüllen
envelope [ˈɛnvələup] N Umschlag *m*
enviable [ˈɛnvɪəbl] ADJ beneidenswert
envious [ˈɛnvɪəs] ADJ neidisch; **to be ~ of sth/sb** auf etw/jdn neidisch sein
environment [ɪnˈvaɪərnmənt] N Umwelt *f*; **Department of the E~** (BRIT) Umweltministerium *nt*
environmental [ɪnvaɪərnˈmɛntl] ADJ (*problems, pollution etc*) Umwelt-; **~ expert** Umweltexperte *m*, Umweltexpertin *f*; **~ studies** Umweltkunde *f*
environmentalist [ɪnvaɪərnˈmɛntlɪst] N Umweltschützer(in) *m(f)*
Environmental Protection Agency (US) N *staatliche Umweltbehörde der USA*
environment-friendly [ɪnˈvaɪərnməntˈfrɛndlɪ] ADJ umweltfreundlich
envisage [ɪnˈvɪzɪdʒ] VT sich *dat* vorstellen; **I ~ that ...** ich stelle mir vor, dass ...
envision [ɪnˈvɪʒən] (US) VT = **envisage**
envoy [ˈɛnvɔɪ] N Gesandte(r) *f(m)*
envy [ˈɛnvɪ] N Neid *m* ▶ VT beneiden; **to ~ sb sth** jdn um etw beneiden
enzyme [ˈɛnzaɪm] N Enzym *nt*
eon [ˈiːən] N Äon *m*, Ewigkeit *f*
EPA (US) N ABBR = **Environmental Protection Agency**
ephemeral [ɪˈfɛmərl] ADJ kurzlebig
epic [ˈɛpɪk] N Epos *nt* ▶ ADJ (*journey*) lang und abenteuerlich
epicentre, (US) epicenter [ˈɛpɪsɛntəʳ] N Epizentrum *nt*
epidemic [ɛpɪˈdɛmɪk] N Epidemie *f*
epigram [ˈɛpɪgræm] N Epigramm *nt*
epilepsy [ˈɛpɪlɛpsɪ] N Epilepsie *f*
epileptic [ɛpɪˈlɛptɪk] ADJ epileptisch ▶ N Epileptiker(in) *m(f)*
epilogue [ˈɛpɪlɔg] N Epilog *m*, Nachwort *nt*
Epiphany [ɪˈpɪfənɪ] N Dreikönigsfest *nt*
episcopal [ɪˈpɪskəpl] ADJ bischöflich; **the E~ Church** die Episkopalkirche
episode [ˈɛpɪsəud] N Episode *f*; (TV, Radio) Folge *f*
epistle [ɪˈpɪsl] N Epistel *f*; (Rel) Brief *m*
epitaph [ˈɛpɪtɑːf] N Epitaph *nt*; (*on gravestone etc*) Grab(in)schrift *f*

e

epithet [ˈɛpɪθɛt] N Beiname *m*
epitome [ɪˈpɪtəmɪ] N Inbegriff *m*
epitomize [ɪˈpɪtəmaɪz] VT verkörpern
epoch [ˈiːpɔk] N Epoche *f*
epoch-making [ˈiːpɔkmeɪkɪŋ] ADJ epochal; (*discovery*) epochemachend
eponymous [ɪˈpɔnɪməs] ADJ namengebend
equable [ˈɛkwəbl] ADJ ausgeglichen; (*reply*) sachlich
equal [ˈiːkwl] ADJ gleich ▸ N Gleichgestellte(r) *f*(*m*) ▸ VT gleichkommen *+dat*; (*number*) gleich sein *+dat*; **they are roughly ~ in size** sie sind ungefähr gleich groß; **the number of exports should be ~ to imports** Export- und Importzahlen sollten gleich sein; **~ opportunities** Chancengleichheit *f*; **to be ~ to** (*task*) gewachsen sein *+dat*; **two times two equals four** zwei mal zwei ist (gleich) vier
equality [iːˈkwɔlɪtɪ] N Gleichheit *f*; **~ of opportunity** Chancengleichheit *f*
equalize [ˈiːkwəlaɪz] VT angleichen ▸ VI (*Sport*) ausgleichen
equalizer [ˈiːkwəlaɪzə^r^] N (*Sport*) Ausgleichstreffer *m*
equally [ˈiːkwəlɪ] ADV gleichmäßig; (*good, bad etc*) gleich; **they are ~ clever** sie sind beide gleich klug
Equal Opportunities Commission, (US) **Equal Employment Opportunity Commission** N Ausschuss *m* für Chancengleichheit am Arbeitsplatz
equal sign, equals sign N Gleichheitszeichen *nt*
equanimity [ɛkwəˈnɪmɪtɪ] N Gleichmut *m*, Gelassenheit *f*
equate [ɪˈkweɪt] VT: **to ~ sth with** etw gleichsetzen mit ▸ VT (*compare*) auf die gleiche Stufe stellen; **to ~ A to B** A und B auf die gleiche Stufe stellen
equation [ɪˈkweɪʃən] N Gleichung *f*
equator [ɪˈkweɪtə^r^] N Äquator *m*
equatorial [ɛkwəˈtɔːrɪəl] ADJ äquatorial
Equatorial Guinea N Äquatorial-Guinea *nt*
equestrian [ɪˈkwɛstrɪən] ADJ (*sport, dress etc*) Reit-; (*statue*) Reiter- ▸ N Reiter(in) *m*(*f*)
equilibrium [iːkwɪˈlɪbrɪəm] N Gleichgewicht *nt*
equinox [ˈiːkwɪnɔks] N Tagundnachtgleiche *f*; **the spring/autumn ~** die Frühjahrs-/die Herbst-Tagundnachtgleiche *f*
equip [ɪˈkwɪp] VT: **to ~ (with)** (*person, army*) ausrüsten (mit); (*room, car etc*) ausstatten (mit); **to ~ sb for** jdn vorbereiten auf *+acc*; **to be well equipped** gut ausgerüstet sein
equipment [ɪˈkwɪpmənt] N Ausrüstung *f*
equitable [ˈɛkwɪtəbl] ADJ gerecht
equities [ˈɛkwɪtɪz] (BRIT) NPL Stammaktien *pl*
equity [ˈɛkwɪtɪ] N Gerechtigkeit *f*
equity capital N Eigenkapital *nt*
equivalent [ɪˈkwɪvələnt] ADJ gleich, gleichwertig ▸ N Gegenstück *nt*; **to be ~ to** *or* **the ~ of** entsprechen *+dat*
equivocal [ɪˈkwɪvəkl] ADJ vieldeutig; (*open to suspicion*) zweifelhaft
equivocate [ɪˈkwɪvəkeɪt] VI ausweichen, ausweichend antworten
equivocation [ɪkwɪvəˈkeɪʃən] N Ausflucht *f*, ausweichende Antwort *f*
ER (BRIT) ABBR (= *Elizabeth Regina*) *offizieller Namenszug der Königin*
ERA (US) N ABBR (*Pol*: = *Equal Rights Amendment*) *Artikel der amerikanischen Verfassung zur Gleichberechtigung*; (*Baseball*: = *earned run average*) *durch Eigenleistung erzielte Läufe*
era [ˈɪərə] N Ära *f*, Epoche *f*
eradicate [ɪˈrædɪkeɪt] VT ausrotten
erase [ɪˈreɪz] VT (*tape, Comput*) löschen; (*writing*) ausradieren; (*thought, feeling*) auslöschen
eraser [ɪˈreɪzə^r^] N Radiergummi *m*
e-reader, eReader [ˈiːˈriːdə^r^] N E-Reader *m*; E-Book-Reader *m*
erect [ɪˈrɛkt] ADJ aufrecht; (*tail*) hoch erhoben; (*ears*) gespitzt ▸ VT bauen; (*assemble*) aufstellen
erection [ɪˈrɛkʃən] N Bauen *nt*; (*of statue*) Errichten *nt*; (*of tent, machinery etc*) Aufstellen *nt*; (*Physiol*) Erektion *f*
ergonomics [əːgəˈnɔmɪks] N SING Ergonomie *f*, Ergonomik *f*
ERISA (US) N ABBR (= *Employee Retirement Income Security Act*) *Gesetz zur Regelung der Rentenversicherung*
Eritrea [ɛrɪˈtreɪə] N Eritrea *nt*
ERM N ABBR (= *Exchange Rate Mechanism*) Wechselkursmechanismus *m*
ermine [ˈəːmɪn] N (*fur*) Hermelin *m*
Ernie [ˈəːnɪ] (BRIT) N ABBR (= *Electronic Random Number Indicator Equipment*) *Gerät zur Ermittlung von Gewinnnummern für Prämiensparer*
erode [ɪˈrəud] VT erodieren, auswaschen; (*metal*) zerfressen; (*confidence, power*) untergraben
erogenous [ɪˈrɔdʒənəs] ADJ erogen
erosion [ɪˈrəuʒən] N Erosion *f*, Auswaschen *nt*; Zerfressen *nt*; Untergraben *nt*
erotic [ɪˈrɔtɪk] ADJ erotisch
eroticism [ɪˈrɔtɪsɪzəm] N Erotik *f*
errand [ˈɛrənd] N Besorgung *f*; (*to give a message etc*) Botengang *m*; **to run errands** Besorgungen/Botengänge machen; **~ of mercy** Rettungsaktion *f*
erratic [ɪˈrætɪk] ADJ unberechenbar; (*bus link etc*) unregelmäßig; (*performance*) unbeständig
erroneous [ɪˈrəunɪəs] ADJ irrig
error [ˈɛrə^r^] N Fehler *m*; **typing/spelling ~** Tipp-/Rechtschreibfehler *m*; **in ~** irrtümlicherweise; **errors and omissions excepted** Irrtum vorbehalten
error message N Fehlermeldung *f*
erstwhile [ˈəːstwaɪl] ADJ einstig, vormalig
erudite [ˈɛrjudaɪt] ADJ gelehrt
erupt [ɪˈrʌpt] VI ausbrechen
eruption [ɪˈrʌpʃən] N Ausbruch *m*
ESA N ABBR (= *European Space Agency*) Europäische Weltraumbehörde *f*
escalate [ˈɛskəleɪt] VI eskalieren, sich ausweiten
escalation [ɛskəˈleɪʃən] N Eskalation *f*

escalator ['ɛskəleɪtəʳ] N Rolltreppe *f*
escalator clause N Gleitklausel *f*
escapade [ɛskə'peɪd] N Eskapade *f*
escape [ɪs'keɪp] N Flucht *f*; (*Tech: of liquid*) Ausfließen *nt*; (*of gas*) Ausströmen *nt*; (*of air, heat*) Entweichen *nt* ▶ VI entkommen; (*from prison*) ausbrechen; (*liquid*) ausfließen; (*gas*) ausströmen; (*air, heat*) entweichen ▶ VT (*pursuers etc*) entkommen *+dat*; (*punishment etc*) entgehen *+dat*; **his name escapes me** sein Name ist mir entfallen; **to ~ from** flüchten aus; (*prison*) ausbrechen aus; (*person*) entkommen *+dat*; **to ~ to Peru** nach Peru fliehen; **to ~ to safety** sich in Sicherheit bringen; **to ~ notice** unbemerkt bleiben
escape artist N Entfesselungskünstler(in) *m(f)*
escape clause N (*in contract*) Befreiungsklausel *f*
escapee [ɪskeɪ'piː] N entwichener Häftling *m*
escape hatch N Notluke *f*
escape key N (*Comput*) Escape-Taste *f*
escape route N Fluchtweg *m*
escapism [ɪs'keɪpɪzəm] N Wirklichkeitsflucht *f*, Eskapismus *m*
escapist [ɪs'keɪpɪst] ADJ eskapistisch
escapologist [ɛskə'pɔlədʒɪst] (BRIT) N = **escape artist**
escarpment [ɪs'kɑːpmənt] N Steilhang *m*
eschew [ɪs'tʃuː] VT meiden
escort N ['ɛskɔːt] Eskorte *f*; (*companion*) Begleiter(in) *m(f)* ▶ VT [ɪs'kɔːt] begleiten; **his ~** seine Begleiterin; **her ~** ihr Begleiter
escort agency N Agentur *f* für Begleiter(innen)
Eskimo ['ɛskɪməu] N Eskimo(frau) *m(f)*
ESL N ABBR (*Scol: = English as a Second Language*) Englisch *nt* als Zweitsprache
esophagus [iː'sɔfəgəs] (US) N = **oesophagus**
esoteric [ɛsə'tɛrɪk] ADJ esoterisch
ESP N ABBR = **extrasensory perception**; (*Scol: = English for Specific (or Special) Purposes*) *Englischunterricht für spezielle Fachbereiche*
esp. ABBR = **especially**
especially [ɪs'pɛʃlɪ] ADV besonders
espionage ['ɛspɪənɑːʒ] N Spionage *f*
esplanade [ɛsplə'neɪd] N Promenade *f*
espouse [ɪs'pauz] VT eintreten für
Esquire [ɪs'kwaɪəʳ] N (*abbr Esq.*): **J. Brown, ~** Herrn J. Brown
essay ['ɛseɪ] N Aufsatz *m*; (*Liter*) Essay *m or nt*
essence ['ɛsns] N Wesen *nt*; (*Culin*) Essenz *f*; **in ~** im Wesentlichen; **speed is of the ~** Geschwindigkeit ist von entscheidender Bedeutung
essential [ɪ'sɛnʃl] ADJ notwendig; (*basic*) wesentlich ▶ N Notwendigste(s) *nt*; Wesentliche(s) *nt*; **it is ~ that** es ist unbedingt *or* absolut erforderlich, dass
essentially [ɪ'sɛnʃəlɪ] ADV im Grunde genommen
EST (US) ABBR (*= Eastern Standard Time*) *ostamerikanische Standardzeit*
est. ABBR = **established**; **estimate**; **estimated**
establish [ɪs'tæblɪʃ] VT gründen; (*facts*) feststellen; (*proof*) erstellen; (*relations, contact*) aufnehmen; (*reputation*) sich *dat* verschaffen
established [ɪs'tæblɪʃt] ADJ üblich; (*business*) eingeführt
establishment [ɪs'tæblɪʃmənt] N Gründung *f*; Feststellung *f*; Erstellung *f*; Aufnahme *f*; (*of reputation*) Begründung *f*; (*shop etc*) Unternehmen *nt*; **the E~** das Establishment
estate [ɪs'teɪt] N Gut *nt*; (BRIT: *also*: **housing estate**) Siedlung *f*; (*Law*) Nachlass *m*
estate agency (BRIT) N Maklerbüro *nt*
estate agent (BRIT) N Immobilienmakler(in) *m(f)*
estate car (BRIT) N Kombiwagen *m*
esteem [ɪs'tiːm] N: **to hold sb in high ~** eine hohe Meinung von jdm haben
esthetic [ɪs'θɛtɪk] (US) ADJ = **aesthetic**
estimate N ['ɛstɪmət] Schätzung *f*; (*assessment*) Einschätzung *f*; (*Comm*) (Kosten)voranschlag *m* ▶ VT ['ɛstɪmeɪt] schätzen ▶ VI (BRIT *Comm*): **to ~ for** einen Kostenvoranschlag machen für; **to give sb an ~ of sth** jdm eine Vorstellung von etw geben; **to ~ for** einen Kostenvoranschlag machen für; **at a rough ~** grob geschätzt, über den Daumen gepeilt (*inf*); **I ~ that** ich schätze, dass
estimation [ɛstɪ'meɪʃən] N Schätzung *f*; (*opinion*) Einschätzung *f*; **in my ~** meiner Einschätzung nach
estimator ['ɛstɪmeɪtəʳ] N Schätzer(in) *m(f)*
Estonia [ɛs'təunɪə] N Estland *nt*
Estonian [ɛs'təunɪən] ADJ estnisch ▶ N Este *m*, Estin *f*; (*Ling*) Estnisch *nt*
estranged [ɪs'treɪndʒd] ADJ entfremdet; (*from spouse*) getrennt; (*couple*) getrennt lebend
estrangement [ɪs'treɪndʒmənt] N Entfremdung *f*; (*from spouse*) Trennung *f*
estrogen ['iːstrəudʒən] (US) N = **oestrogen**
estuary ['ɛstjuərɪ] N Mündung *f*
ET (BRIT) N ABBR (*= Employment Training*) *Ausbildungsmaßnahmen für Arbeitslose*
ETA N ABBR (*= estimated time of arrival*) voraussichtliche Ankunftszeit *f*
et al. ABBR (*= et alii*) u. a.
etc. ABBR (*= et cetera*) etc.
etch [ɛtʃ] VT (*design, surface: with needle*) radieren; (*: with acid*) ätzen; (*: with chisel*) meißeln; **it will be etched on my memory** es wird sich tief in mein Gedächtnis eingraben
ETD N ABBR (*= estimated time of departure*) voraussichtliche Abflugzeit *f*
eternal [ɪ'təːnl] ADJ ewig
eternity [ɪ'təːnɪtɪ] N Ewigkeit *f*
ether ['iːθəʳ] N Äther *m*
ethereal [ɪ'θɪərɪəl] ADJ ätherisch
ethical ['ɛθɪkl] ADJ ethisch
ethics ['ɛθɪks] N Ethik *f* ▶ NPL (*morality*) Moral *f*
Ethiopia [iːθɪ'əupɪə] N Äthiopien *nt*
Ethiopian [iːθɪ'əupɪən] ADJ äthiopisch ▶ N Äthiopier(in) *m(f)*
ethnic ['ɛθnɪk] ADJ ethnisch; (*music*) folkloristisch; (*culture etc*) urwüchsig
ethnic cleansing [-'klɛnzɪŋ] N ethnische Säuberung *f*
ethnic minority N ethnische Minderheit *f*

e

ethnology [εθ'nɔlədʒɪ] N Ethnologie *f*, Völkerkunde *f*
ethos ['iːθɔs] N Ethos *nt*
e-ticket ['iːtɪkɪt] N ABBR (= *electronic ticket*) E-Ticket *nt*, *elektronische Eintrittskarte/Fahrkarte etc*
etiquette ['εtɪkεt] N Etikette *f*
ETV (US) N ABBR (= *educational television*) *Fernsehsender, der Bildungs- und Kulturprogramme ausstrahlt*
etymology [εtɪ'mɔlədʒɪ] N Etymologie *f*; (*of word*) Herkunft *f*
EU N ABBR (= *European Union*) EU *f*
eucalyptus [juːkə'lɪptəs] N Eukalyptus *m*
Eucharist ['juːkərɪst] N: **the ~** die Eucharistie, das (heilige) Abendmahl
eulogy ['juːlədʒɪ] N Lobrede *f*
euphemism ['juːfəmɪzəm] N Euphemismus *m*
euphemistic [juːfə'mɪstɪk] ADJ euphemistisch, verhüllend
euphoria [juː'fɔːrɪə] N Euphorie *f*
Eurasia [juə'reɪʃə] N Eurasien *nt*
Eurasian [juə'reɪʃən] ADJ eurasisch ▶ N Eurasier(in) *m(f)*
Euratom [juə'rætəm] N ABBR (= *European Atomic Energy Community*) Euratom *f*
euro ['juərəu] N (*Fin*) Euro *m*
Euro- ['juərəu] PREF Euro-
euro cent N Eurocent *m*
Eurocrat ['juərəukræt] N Eurokrat(in) *m(f)*
Eurodollar ['juərəudɔlə^r] N Eurodollar *m*
Euroland ['juərəulænd] N (*Fin*) Eurozone *f*
Europe ['juərəp] N Europa *nt*
European [juərə'piːən] ADJ europäisch ▶ N Europäer(in) *m(f)*
European Central Bank N: **the ~** die Europäische Zentralbank
European Community N: **the ~** die Europäische Gemeinschaft
European Convention N Europäische(r) Konvent *m*, EU-Konvent *m*
European Court of Justice N: **the ~** der Europäische Gerichtshof
European Economic Community N (*formerly*): **the ~** die Europäische Wirtschaftsgemeinschaft
Euro-sceptic ['juərəuskεptɪk] N Euroskeptiker(in) *m(f)*
euthanasia [juːθə'neɪzɪə] N Euthanasie *f*
evacuate [ɪ'vækjueɪt] VT evakuieren; (*place*) räumen
evacuation [ɪvækju'eɪʃən] N Evakuierung *f*; Räumung *f*
evacuee [ɪvækju'iː] N Evakuierte(r) *f(m)*
evade [ɪ'veɪd] VT (*person, question*) ausweichen *+dat*; (*tax*) hinterziehen; (*duty, responsibility*) sich entziehen *+dat*
evaluate [ɪ'væljueɪt] VT bewerten; (*situation*) einschätzen
evangelical [iːvæn'dʒεlɪkl] ADJ evangelisch
evangelist [ɪ'vændʒəlɪst] N Evangelist(in) *m(f)*
evangelize [ɪ'vændʒəlaɪz] VI evangelisieren
evaporate [ɪ'væpəreɪt] VI verdampfen; (*feeling, attitude*) dahinschwinden
evaporated milk [ɪ'væpəreɪtɪd-] N Kondensmilch *f*, Büchsenmilch *f*
evaporation [ɪvæpə'reɪʃən] N Verdampfung *f*
evasion [ɪ'veɪʒən] N Ausweichen *nt*; (*of tax*) Hinterziehung *f*
evasive [ɪ'veɪsɪv] ADJ ausweichend; **to take ~ action** ein Ausweichmanöver machen
eve [iːv] N: **on the ~ of** am Tag vor *+dat*; **Christmas E~** Heiligabend *m*; **New Year's E~** Silvester *m or nt*
even ['iːvn] ADJ (*level*) eben; (*smooth*) glatt; (*equal*) gleich; (*number*) gerade ▶ ADV sogar, selbst; (*introducing a comparison*) sogar noch; **~ if, ~ though** selbst wenn; **~ more** sogar noch mehr; **he loves her ~ more** er liebt sie umso mehr; **it's going ~ faster now** es fährt jetzt sogar noch schneller; **~ so** (aber) trotzdem; **not ~** nicht einmal; **~ he was there** sogar er war da; **to break ~** die Kosten decken; **to get ~ with sb** es jdm heimzahlen
▶ **even out** VI sich ausgleichen ▶ VT ausgleichen
even-handed ['iːvnhændɪd] ADJ gerecht
evening ['iːvnɪŋ] N Abend *m*; **in the ~** abends, am Abend; **this ~** heute Abend; **tomorrow/yesterday ~** morgen/gestern Abend
evening class N Abendkurs *m*
evening dress N (*no pl*) Abendkleidung *f*; (*woman's*) Abendkleid *nt*
evenly ['iːvnlɪ] ADV gleichmäßig
evensong ['iːvnsɔŋ] N Abendandacht *f*
event [ɪ'vεnt] N Ereignis *nt*; (*Sport*) Wettkampf *m*; **in the normal course of events** normalerweise; **in the ~ of** im Falle *+gen*; **in the ~** schließlich; **at all events** (BRIT), **in any ~** auf jeden Fall
eventful [ɪ'vεntful] ADJ ereignisreich
eventing [ɪ'vεntɪŋ] N (*Horseriding*) Military *f*
eventual [ɪ'vεntʃuəl] ADJ schließlich; (*goal*) letztlich
eventuality [ɪvεntʃu'ælɪtɪ] N Eventualität *f*
eventually [ɪ'vεntʃuəlɪ] ADV endlich; (*in time*) schließlich
ever ['εvə^r] ADV immer; (*at any time*) je(mals); **why ~ not?** warum denn bloß nicht?; **the best ~** der/die/das Allerbeste; **have you ~ seen it?** haben Sie es schon einmal gesehen?; **for ~** für immer; **hardly ~** kaum je(mals); **better than ~** besser als je zuvor; **~ since** (*as adv*) seitdem; (*as conj*) seit, seitdem; **~ so pretty** unheimlich hübsch (*inf*); **thank you ~ so much** ganz herzlichen Dank; **yours ~** (BRIT: *in letters*) alles Liebe
Everest ['εvərɪst] N (*also*: **Mount Everest**) Mount Everest *m*
evergreen ['εvəgriːn] N (*tree/bush*) immergrüner Baum/Strauch *m*
everlasting [εvə'lɑːstɪŋ] ADJ ewig

KEYWORD

every ['εvrɪ] ADJ **1** jede(r, s); **every one of them** (*persons*) jede(r) (Einzelne) von ihnen; (*objects*) jedes einzelne Stück; **every day** jeden Tag; **every week** jede Woche; **every other car** jedes

zweite Auto; **every other/third day** alle zwei/drei Tage; **every shop in the town was closed** alle Geschäfte der Stadt waren geschlossen; **every now and then** ab und zu, hin und wieder
2 (*all possible*): **I have every confidence in him** ich habe volles Vertrauen in ihn; **we wish you every success** wir wünschen Ihnen alles Gute

everybody ['ɛvrɪbɔdɪ] PRON jeder, alle *pl*; **~ knows about it** alle wissen es; **~ else** alle anderen *pl*
everyday ['ɛvrɪdeɪ] ADJ täglich; (*usual, common*) alltäglich; (*life, language*) Alltags-
everyone ['ɛvrɪwʌn] PRON = **everybody**
everything ['ɛvrɪθɪŋ] PRON alles; **he did ~ possible** er hat sein Möglichstes getan
everywhere ['ɛvrɪwɛəʳ] ADV überall; (*wherever*) wo auch *or* immer; **~ you go you meet ...** wo man auch *or* wo immer man hingeht, trifft man ...
evict [ɪ'vɪkt] VT zur Räumung zwingen
eviction [ɪ'vɪkʃən] N Ausweisung *f*
eviction notice N Räumungskündigung *f*
eviction order N Räumungsbefehl *m*
evidence ['ɛvɪdns] N Beweis *m*; (*of witness*) Aussage *f*; (*sign, indication*) Zeichen *nt*, Spur *f*; **to give ~** (als Zeuge) aussagen; **to show ~ of** zeigen; **in ~** sichtbar
evident ['ɛvɪdnt] ADJ offensichtlich
evidently ['ɛvɪdntlɪ] ADV offensichtlich
evil ['i:vl] ADJ böse; (*influence*) schlecht ▸ N Böse(s) *nt*; (*unpleasant situation or activity*) Übel *nt*
evocative [ɪ'vɔkətɪv] ADJ evokativ
evoke [ɪ'vəuk] VT hervorrufen; (*memory*) wecken
evolution [i:və'lu:ʃən] N Evolution *f*; (*development*) Entwicklung *f*
evolve [ɪ'vɔlv] VT entwickeln ▸ VI sich entwickeln
ewe [ju:] N Mutterschaf *nt*
ewer ['ju:əʳ] N (Wasser)krug *m*
ex- [ɛks] PREF Ex-, frühere(r, s); **the price ~works** der Preis ab Werk
exacerbate [ɛks'æsəbeɪt] VT verschärfen; (*pain*) verschlimmern
exact [ɪg'zækt] ADJ genau; (*word*) richtig ▸ VT: **to ~ sth (from)** etw verlangen (von); (*payment*) etw eintreiben (von)
exacting [ɪg'zæktɪŋ] ADJ anspruchsvoll
exactly [ɪg'zæktlɪ] ADV genau; **~!** (ganz) genau!; **not ~** (*hardly*) nicht gerade
exaggerate [ɪg'zædʒəreɪt] VT, VI übertreiben
exaggerated [ɪg'zædʒəreɪtɪd] ADJ übertrieben
exaggeration [ɪgzædʒə'reɪʃən] N Übertreibung *f*
exalt [ɪg'zɔ:lt] VT preisen
exalted [ɪg'zɔ:ltɪd] ADJ hoch; (*elated*) exaltiert
exam [ɪg'zæm] N ABBR = **examination**
examination [ɪgzæmɪ'neɪʃən] N Untersuchung *f*; Prüfung *f*; Verhör *nt*; **to take an ~, to sit an ~** (BRIT) eine Prüfung machen; **the matter is under ~** die Angelegenheit wird geprüft *or* untersucht
examine [ɪg'zæmɪn] VT untersuchen; (*accounts, candidate*) prüfen; (*witness*) verhören
examiner [ɪg'zæmɪnəʳ] N Prüfer(in) *m(f)*
example [ɪg'zɑ:mpl] N Beispiel *nt*; **for ~** zum Beispiel; **to set a good/bad ~** ein gutes/schlechtes Beispiel geben
exasperate [ɪg'zɑ:spəreɪt] VT (*annoy*) verärgern; (*frustrate*) zur Verzweiflung bringen; **exasperated by** *or* **with** verärgert/verzweifelt über *+acc*
exasperating [ɪg'zɑ:spəreɪtɪŋ] ADJ ärgerlich; (*job*) leidig
exasperation [ɪgzɑ:spə'reɪʃən] N Verzweiflung *f*; **in ~** verzweifelt
excavate ['ɛkskəveɪt] VT ausgraben; (*hole*) graben ▸ VI Ausgrabungen machen
excavation [ɛkskə'veɪʃən] N Ausgrabung *f*
excavator ['ɛkskəveɪtəʳ] N Bagger *m*
exceed [ɪk'si:d] VT übersteigen; (*hopes*) übertreffen; (*limit, budget, powers*) überschreiten
exceedingly [ɪk'si:dɪŋlɪ] ADV äußerst
excel [ɪk'sɛl] VT übertreffen ▸ VI: **to ~ (in** *or* **at)** sich auszeichnen (in *+dat*); **to ~ o.s.** (BRIT) sich selbst übertreffen
excellence ['ɛksələns] N hervorragende Leistung *f*
Excellency ['ɛksələnsɪ] N: **His ~** Seine Exzellenz
excellent ['ɛksələnt] ADJ ausgezeichnet, hervorragend
except [ɪk'sɛpt] PREP (*also*: **except for**) außer *+dat* ▸ VT: **to ~ sb (from)** jdn ausnehmen (bei); **~ if, ~ when** außer wenn; **~ that** nur dass
excepting [ɪk'sɛptɪŋ] PREP außer *+dat*, mit Ausnahme *+gen*
exception [ɪk'sɛpʃən] N Ausnahme *f*; **to take ~ to** Anstoß nehmen an *+dat*; **with the ~ of** mit Ausnahme von
exceptional [ɪk'sɛpʃənl] ADJ außergewöhnlich
excerpt ['ɛksə:pt] N Auszug *m*
excess [ɪk'sɛs] N Übermaß *nt*; (*Insurance*) Selbstbeteiligung *f*; **excesses** NPL Exzesse *pl*; **an ~ of £15, a £15 ~** eine Selbstbeteiligung von £15; **in ~ of** über *+dat*
excess baggage N Übergepäck *nt*
excess fare (BRIT) N Nachlösegebühr *f*
excessive [ɪk'sɛsɪv] ADJ übermäßig
excess supply N Überangebot *nt*
exchange [ɪks'tʃeɪndʒ] N Austausch *m*; (*conversation*) Wortwechsel *m*; (*also*: **telephone exchange**) Fernsprechamt *nt* ▸ VT: **to ~ (for)** tauschen (gegen); (*in shop*) umtauschen (gegen); **in ~ for** für; **foreign ~** Devisenhandel *m*; (*money*) Devisen *pl*
exchange control N Devisenkontrolle *f*
exchange market N Devisenmarkt *m*
exchange rate N Wechselkurs *m*
Exchequer [ɪks'tʃɛkəʳ] (BRIT) N: **the ~** das Finanzministerium
excisable [ɪk'saɪzəbl] ADJ steuerpflichtig
excise N ['ɛksaɪz] Verbrauchssteuer *f* ▸ VT [ɛk'saɪz] entfernen
excise duties NPL Verbrauchssteuern *pl*
excitable [ɪk'saɪtəbl] ADJ (leicht) erregbar

excite [ɪk'saɪt] VT aufregen; (*arouse*) erregen; **to get excited** sich aufregen
excitement [ɪk'saɪtmənt] N Aufregung *f*; (*exhilaration*) Hochgefühl *nt*
exciting [ɪk'saɪtɪŋ] ADJ aufregend
excl. ABBR = **excluding; exclusive (of)**
exclaim [ɪks'kleɪm] VI aufschreien
exclamation [ɛksklə'meɪʃən] N Ausruf *m*; **~ of joy** Freudenschrei *m*
exclamation mark N Ausrufezeichen *nt*
exclude [ɪks'klu:d] VT ausschließen
excluding [ɪks'klu:dɪŋ] PREP: **~ VAT** ohne Mehrwertsteuer
exclusion [ɪks'klu:ʒən] N Ausschluss *m*; **to concentrate on sth to the ~ of everything else** sich ausschließlich auf etw *dat* konzentrieren
exclusion clause N Freizeichnungsklausel *f*
exclusion zone N Sperrzone *f*
exclusive [ɪks'klu:sɪv] ADJ exklusiv; (*story, interview*) Exklusiv-; (*use*) ausschließlich ▶ N Exklusivbericht *m* ▶ ADV: **from 1st to 15th March ~** vom 1. bis zum 15. März ausschließlich; **~ of postage** ohne *or* exklusive Porto; **~ of tax** ausschließlich *or* exklusive Steuern; **to be mutually ~** sich *or* einander ausschließen
exclusively [ɪks'klu:sɪvlɪ] ADV ausschließlich
exclusive rights NPL Exklusivrechte *pl*
excommunicate [ɛkskə'mju:nɪkeɪt] VT exkommunizieren
excrement ['ɛkskrəmənt] N Kot *m*, Exkremente *pl*
excruciating [ɪks'kru:ʃieɪtɪŋ] ADJ grässlich, fürchterlich; (*noise, embarrassment*) unerträglich
excursion [ɪks'kə:ʃən] N Ausflug *m*
excursion ticket N verbilligte Fahrkarte *f*
excusable [ɪks'kju:zəbl] ADJ verzeihlich, entschuldbar
excuse N [ɪks'kju:s] Entschuldigung *f* ▶ VT [ɪks'kju:z] entschuldigen; (*forgive*) verzeihen; **to ~ sb from sth** jdm etw erlassen; **to ~ sb from doing sth** jdn davon befreien, etw zu tun; **~ me!** entschuldigen Sie!, Entschuldigung!; **if you will ~ me ...** entschuldigen Sie mich bitte ...; **to ~ o.s. for sth** sich für *or* wegen etw entschuldigen; **to ~ o.s. for doing sth** sich entschuldigen, dass man etw tut; **to make excuses for sb** jdn entschuldigen; **that's no ~!** das ist keine Ausrede!
ex-directory ['ɛksdɪ'rɛktərɪ] (BRIT) ADJ (*number*) geheim; **she's ~** sie steht nicht im Telefonbuch
execrable ['ɛksɪkrəbl] ADJ scheußlich; (*manners*) abscheulich
execute ['ɛksɪkju:t] VT ausführen; (*person*) hinrichten
execution [ɛksɪ'kju:ʃən] N Ausführung *f*; Hinrichtung *f*
executioner [ɛksɪ'kju:ʃnə[r]] N Scharfrichter *m*
executive [ɪg'zɛkjutɪv] N leitende(r) Angestellte(r) *f(m)*; (*committee*) Vorstand *m* ▶ ADJ geschäftsführend; (*role*) führend; (*secretary*) Chef-; (*car, chair*) für gehobene Ansprüche; (*toys*) Manager-; (*plane*) ≈ Privat-
executive director N leitender Direktor *m*, leitende Direktorin *f*
executor [ɪg'zɛkjutə[r]] N Testamentsvollstrecker(in) *m(f)*
exemplary [ɪg'zɛmplərɪ] ADJ vorbildlich, beispielhaft; (*punishment*) exemplarisch
exemplify [ɪg'zɛmplɪfaɪ] VT verkörpern; (*illustrate*) veranschaulichen
exempt [ɪg'zɛmpt] ADJ: **~ from** befreit von ▶ VT: **to ~ sb from** jdn befreien von
exemption [ɪg'zɛmpʃən] N Befreiung *f*
exercise ['ɛksəsaɪz] N Übung *f*; (*no pl: keep-fit*) Gymnastik *f*; (*: energetic movement*) Bewegung *f*; (*: of authority etc*) Ausübung *f* ▶ VT (*patience*) üben; (*right*) ausüben; (*dog*) ausführen; (*mind*) beschäftigen ▶ VI (*also:* **to take exercise**) Sport treiben
exercise bike N Heimtrainer *m*
exercise book N (Schul)heft *nt*
exert [ɪg'zə:t] VT (*influence*) ausüben; (*authority*) einsetzen; **to ~ o.s.** sich anstrengen
exertion [ɪg'zə:ʃən] N Anstrengung *f*
ex gratia ['ɛks'greɪʃə] ADJ: **~ payment** freiwillige Zahlung *f*
exhale [ɛks'heɪl] VT, VI ausatmen
exhaust [ɪg'zɔ:st] N (*also:* **exhaust pipe**) Auspuff *m*; (*fumes*) Auspuffgase *pl* ▶ VT erschöpfen; (*money*) aufbrauchen; (*topic*) erschöpfend behandeln; **to ~ o.s.** sich verausgaben
exhausted [ɪg'zɔ:stɪd] ADJ erschöpft
exhausting [ɪg'zɔ:stɪŋ] ADJ anstrengend
exhaustion [ɪg'zɔ:stʃən] N Erschöpfung *f*; **nervous ~** nervöse Erschöpfung
exhaustive [ɪg'zɔ:stɪv] ADJ erschöpfend
exhibit [ɪg'zɪbɪt] N Ausstellungsstück *nt*; (*Law*) Beweisstück *nt* ▶ VT zeigen, an den Tag legen; (*paintings*) ausstellen
exhibition [ɛksɪ'bɪʃən] N Ausstellung *f*; **to make an ~ of o.s.** sich unmöglich aufführen; **an ~ of bad manners** schlechte Manieren *pl*; **an ~ of draughtsmanship** zeichnerisches Können *nt*
exhibitionist [ɛksɪ'bɪʃənɪst] N Exhibitionist(in) *m(f)*
exhibitor [ɪg'zɪbɪtə[r]] N Aussteller(in) *m(f)*
exhilarating [ɪg'zɪləreɪtɪŋ] ADJ erregend, berauschend; (*news*) aufregend
exhilaration [ɪgzɪlə'reɪʃən] N Hochgefühl *nt*
exhort [ɪg'zɔ:t] VT: **to ~ sb to do sth** jdn ermahnen, etw zu tun
exile ['ɛksaɪl] N Exil *nt*; (*person*) Verbannte(r) *f(m)* ▶ VT verbannen; **in ~** im Exil
exist [ɪg'zɪst] VI existieren
existence [ɪg'zɪstəns] N Existenz *f*; **to be in ~** existieren
existentialism [ɛgzɪs'tɛnʃlɪzəm] N Existenzialismus *m*
existing [ɪg'zɪstɪŋ] ADJ bestehend
exit ['ɛksɪt] N Ausgang *m*; (*from motorway*) Ausfahrt *f*; (*departure*) Abgang *m* ▶ VI (*Theat*) abgehen; (*Comput: from program/file etc*) das

Programm/die Datei *etc* verlassen; **to ~ from** hinausgehen aus; (*motorway etc*) abfahren von
exit poll N *bei Wählern unmittelbar nach Verlassen der Wahllokale durchgeführte Umfrage*
exit ramp (*US*) N Ausfahrt *f*
exit visa N Ausreisevisum *nt*
exodus ['ɛksədəs] N Auszug *m*; **the ~ to the cities** die Abwanderung in die Städte
ex officio ['ɛksə'fɪʃɪəu] ADJ von Amts wegen ▸ ADV kraft seines Amtes
exonerate [ɪg'zɔnəreɪt] VT: **to ~ from** entlasten von
exorbitant [ɪg'zɔːbɪtnt] ADJ (*prices, rents*) astronomisch, unverschämt; (*demands*) maßlos, übertrieben
exorcize ['ɛksɔːsaɪz] VT exorzieren; (*spirit*) austreiben
exotic [ɪg'zɔtɪk] ADJ exotisch
expand [ɪks'pænd] VT erweitern; (*staff, numbers etc*) vergrößern; (*influence*) ausdehnen ▸ VI expandieren; (*population*) wachsen; (*gas, metal*) sich ausdehnen; **to ~ on** weiter ausführen
expanse [ɪks'pæns] N Weite *f*
expansion [ɪks'pænʃən] N Expansion *f*; (*of population*) Wachstum *nt*; (*of gas, metal*) Ausdehnung *f*
expansionism [ɪks'pænʃənɪzəm] N Expansionspolitik *f*
expansionist [ɪks'pænʃənɪst] ADJ Expansions-, expansionistisch
expatriate [ɛks'pætrɪət] N im Ausland Lebende(r) *f*(*m*)
expect [ɪks'pɛkt] VT erwarten; (*suppose*) denken, glauben; (*count on*) rechnen mit ▸ VI: **to be expecting** ein Kind erwarten; **to ~ sb to do sth** erwarten, dass jd etw tut; **to ~ to do sth** vorhaben, etw zu tun; **as expected** wie erwartet; **I ~ so** ich glaube schon
expectancy [ɪks'pɛktənsɪ] N Erwartung *f*; **life ~** Lebenserwartung *f*
expectant [ɪks'pɛktənt] ADJ erwartungsvoll
expectantly [ɪks'pɛktəntlɪ] ADV erwartungsvoll
expectant mother N werdende Mutter *f*
expectation [ɛkspɛk'teɪʃən] N Erwartung *f*; (*hope*) Hoffnung *f*; **in ~ of** in Erwartung *+gen*; **against** *or* **contrary to all ~(s)** wider Erwarten; **to come** *or* **live up to sb's expectations** jds Erwartungen *dat* entsprechen
expedience [ɪks'piːdɪəns] N = **expediency**
expediency [ɪks'piːdɪənsɪ] N Zweckmäßigkeit *f*; **for the sake of ~** aus Gründen der Zweckmäßigkeit
expedient [ɪks'piːdɪənt] ADJ zweckmäßig ▸ N Hilfsmittel *nt*
expedite ['ɛkspədaɪt] VT beschleunigen
expedition [ɛkspə'dɪʃən] N Expedition *f*; (*for shopping etc*) Tour *f*
expeditionary force [ɛkspə'dɪʃənrɪ-] N Expeditionskorps *nt*
expeditious [ɛkspə'dɪʃəs] ADJ schnell
expel [ɪks'pɛl] VT (*from school*) verweisen; (*from organization*) ausschließen; (*from place*) vertreiben; (*gas, liquid*) ausstoßen
expend [ɪks'pɛnd] VT ausgeben; (*time, energy*) aufwenden
expendable [ɪks'pɛndəbl] ADJ entbehrlich
expenditure [ɪks'pɛndɪtʃəʳ] N Ausgaben *pl*; (*of energy, time*) Aufwand *m*
expense [ɪks'pɛns] N Kosten *pl*; (*expenditure*) Ausgabe *f*; **expenses** NPL Spesen *pl*; **at the ~ of** auf Kosten *+gen*; **to go to the ~ of buying a new car** (viel) Geld für ein neues Auto anlegen; **at great/little ~** mit hohen/geringen Kosten
expense account N Spesenkonto *nt*
expensive [ɪks'pɛnsɪv] ADJ teuer; **to have ~ tastes** einen teuren Geschmack haben
experience [ɪks'pɪərɪəns] N Erfahrung *f*; (*event, activity*) Erlebnis *nt* ▸ VT erleben; **by** *or* **from ~** aus Erfahrung; **to learn by ~** durch eigene Erfahrung lernen
experienced [ɪks'pɪərɪənst] ADJ erfahren
experiment [ɪks'pɛrɪmənt] N Experiment *nt*, Versuch *m* ▸ VI: **to ~ (with/on)** experimentieren (mit/an *+dat*); **to perform** *or* **carry out an ~** einen Versuch *or* ein Experiment durchführen; **as an ~** versuchsweise
experimental [ɪkspɛrɪ'mɛntl] ADJ experimentell; **at the ~ stage** im Versuchsstadium
expert ['ɛkspəːt] ADJ ausgezeichnet, geschickt; (*opinion, help etc*) eines Fachmanns ▸ N Fachmann *m*, Fachfrau *f*, Experte *m*, Expertin *f*; **to be ~ in** *or* **at doing sth** etw ausgezeichnet können; **an ~ on sth/on the subject of sth** ein Experte für etw/auf dem Gebiet einer Sache *gen*; **~ witness** (*Law*) sachverständiger Zeuge *m*
expertise [ɛkspəː'tiːz] N Sachkenntnis *f*
expire [ɪks'paɪəʳ] VI ablaufen
expiry [ɪks'paɪərɪ] N Ablauf *m*
expiry date N Ablauftermin *m*; (*of voucher, special offer etc*) Verfallsdatum *nt*
explain [ɪks'pleɪn] VT erklären
▸ **explain away** VT eine Erklärung finden für
explanation [ɛksplə'neɪʃən] N Erklärung *f*; **to find an ~ for sth** eine Erklärung für etw finden
explanatory [ɪks'plænətrɪ] ADJ erklärend
expletive [ɪks'pliːtɪv] N Kraftausdruck *m*
explicable [ɪks'plɪkəbl] ADJ erklärbar; **for no ~ reason** aus unerfindlichen Gründen
explicit [ɪks'plɪsɪt] ADJ ausdrücklich; (*sex, violence*) deutlich, unverhüllt; **to be ~** (*frank*) sich deutlich ausdrücken
explode [ɪks'pləud] VI explodieren; (*population*) sprunghaft ansteigen ▸ VT zur Explosion bringen; (*myth, theory*) zu Fall bringen
exploit N ['ɛksplɔɪt] Heldentat *f* ▸ VT [ɪks'plɔɪt] ausnutzen; (*workers etc*) ausbeuten; (*resources*) nutzen
exploitation [ɛksplɔɪ'teɪʃən] N Ausnutzung *f*; Ausbeutung *f*; Nutzung *f*
exploration [ɛksplə'reɪʃən] N Erforschung *f*; Erkundung *f*; Untersuchung *f*
exploratory [ɪks'plɔrətrɪ] ADJ exploratorisch; (*expedition*) Forschungs-; **~ operation** (*Med*) Explorationsoperation *f*; **~ talks** Sondierungsgespräche *pl*

explore [ɪks'plɔːʳ] VT erforschen; (*with hands etc, idea*) untersuchen
explorer [ɪks'plɔːrəʳ] N Forschungsreisende(r) *f(m)*; (*of place*) Erforscher(in) *m(f)*
explosion [ɪks'pləuʒən] N Explosion *f*; (*outburst*) Ausbruch *m*
explosive [ɪks'pləusɪv] ADJ explosiv; (*device*) Spreng-; (*temper*) aufbrausend ▸ N Sprengstoff *m*; (*device*) Sprengkörper *m*
exponent [ɪks'pəunənt] N Vertreter(in) *m(f)*, Exponent(in) *m(f)*; (*Math*) Exponent *m*
exponential [ɛkspəu'nɛnʃl] ADJ exponentiell; (*Math: function etc*) Exponential-
export [ɛks'pɔːt] VT exportieren, ausführen; (*ideas, values*) verbreiten ▸ N Export *m*, Ausfuhr *f*; (*product*) Exportgut *nt* ▸ CPD Export-, Ausfuhr-
exportation [ɛkspɔː'teɪʃən] N Export *m*, Ausfuhr *f*
exporter [ɛks'pɔːtəʳ] N Exporteur *m*
expose [ɪks'pəuz] VT freilegen; (*to heat, radiation*) aussetzen; (*unmask*) entlarven; **to ~ o.s.** sich entblößen
exposé [ɪk'spəuzeɪ] N Enthüllung *f*
exposed [ɪks'pəuzd] ADJ ungeschützt; (*wire*) bloßliegend; **to be ~ to** (*radiation, heat etc*) ausgesetzt sein *+dat*
exposition [ɛkspə'zɪʃən] N Erläuterung *f*; (*exhibition*) Ausstellung *f*
exposure [ɪks'pəuʒəʳ] N (*to heat, radiation*) Aussetzung *f*; (*publicity*) Publicity *f*; (*of person*) Entlarvung *f*; (*Phot*) Belichtung *f*; (*: shot*) Aufnahme *f*; **to be suffering from ~** an Unterkühlung leiden; **to die from ~** erfrieren
exposure meter N Belichtungsmesser *m*
expound [ɪks'paund] VT darlegen, erläutern
express [ɪks'prɛs] ADJ ausdrücklich; (*intention*) bestimmt; (BRIT: *letter etc*) Express-, Eil- ▸ N (*train*) Schnellzug *m*; (*bus*) Schnellbus *m* ▸ ADV (*send*) per Express ▸ VT ausdrücken; (*view, emotion*) zum Ausdruck bringen; **to ~ o.s.** sich ausdrücken
expression [ɪks'prɛʃən] N Ausdruck *m*; (*on face*) (Gesichts)ausdruck *m*
expressionism [ɪks'prɛʃənɪzəm] N Expressionismus *m*
expressive [ɪks'prɛsɪv] ADJ ausdrucksvoll; **~ ability** Ausdrucksfähigkeit *f*
expressly [ɪks'prɛslɪ] ADV ausdrücklich; (*intentionally*) absichtlich
expressway [ɪks'prɛsweɪ] (*US*) N Schnellstraße *f*
expropriate [ɛks'prəuprɪeɪt] VT enteignen
expulsion [ɪks'pʌlʃən] N (*Scol*) Verweisung *f*; (*Pol*) Ausweisung *f*; (*of gas, liquid etc*) Ausstoßen *nt*
expurgate ['ɛkspəːgeɪt] VT zensieren; **the expurgated version** die zensierte *or* bereinigte Fassung
exquisite [ɛks'kwɪzɪt] ADJ exquisit, erlesen; (*keenly felt*) köstlich
exquisitely [ɛks'kwɪzɪtlɪ] ADV exquisit; (*carved*) kunstvoll; (*polite, sensitive*) äußerst
ex-serviceman ['ɛks'səːvɪsmən] N (*irreg*) ehemaliger Soldat *m*
ext. ABBR (*Tel*) = **extension**
extemporize [ɪks'tɛmpəraɪz] VI improvisieren
extend [ɪks'tɛnd] VT verlängern; (*building*) anbauen an *+acc*; (*offer, invitation*) aussprechen; (*arm, hand*) ausstrecken; (*deadline*) verschieben ▸ VI sich erstrecken; (*period*) dauern
extension [ɪks'tɛnʃən] N Verlängerung *f*; (*of building*) Anbau *m*; (*of time*) Aufschub *m*; (*of campaign, rights*) Erweiterung *f*; (*Tel*) (Neben)anschluss *m*; **~ 3718** (*Tel*) Apparat 3718
extension cable N Verlängerungskabel *nt*
extension lead N Verlängerungsschnur *f*
extensive [ɪks'tɛnsɪv] ADJ ausgedehnt; (*effect*) weitreichend; (*damage*) beträchtlich; (*coverage, discussion*) ausführlich; (*inquiries*) umfangreich; (*use*) häufig
extensively [ɪks'tɛnsɪvlɪ] ADV: **he's travelled ~** er ist viel gereist
extent [ɪks'tɛnt] N Ausdehnung *f*; (*of problem, damage, loss etc*) Ausmaß *nt*; **to some ~** bis zu einem gewissen Grade; **to a certain ~** in gewissem Maße; **to a large ~** in hohem Maße; **to the ~ of ...** (*debts*) in Höhe von ...; **to go to the ~ of doing sth** so weit gehen, etw zu tun; **to such an ~ that ...** dermaßen, dass ...; **to what ~?** inwieweit?
extenuating [ɪks'tɛnjueɪtɪŋ] ADJ: **~ circumstances** mildernde Umstände *pl*
exterior [ɛks'tɪərɪəʳ] ADJ (*surface, angle, world*) Außen- ▸ N Außenseite *f*; (*appearance*) Äußere(s) *nt*
exterminate [ɪks'təːmɪneɪt] VT ausrotten
extermination [ɪkstəːmɪ'neɪʃən] N Ausrottung *f*
external [ɛks'təːnl] ADJ (*wall etc*) Außen-; (*use*) äußerlich; (*evidence*) unabhängig; (*examiner, auditor*) extern ▸ N: **the externals** die Äußerlichkeiten *pl*; **for ~ use only** nur äußerlich (anzuwenden); **~ affairs** (*Pol*) auswärtige Angelegenheiten *pl*
externally [ɛks'təːnəlɪ] ADV äußerlich
extinct [ɪks'tɪŋkt] ADJ ausgestorben; (*volcano*) erloschen
extinction [ɪks'tɪŋkʃən] N Aussterben *nt*
extinguish [ɪks'tɪŋgwɪʃ] VT löschen; (*hope*) zerstören
extinguisher [ɪks'tɪŋgwɪʃəʳ] N (*also*: **fire extinguisher**) Feuerlöscher *m*
extol, (*US*) **extoll** [ɪks'təul] VT preisen, rühmen
extort [ɪks'tɔːt] VT erpressen; (*confession*) erzwingen
extortion [ɪks'tɔːʃən] N Erpressung *f*; Erzwingung *f*
extortionate [ɪks'tɔːʃnɪt] ADJ überhöht; (*price*) Wucher-
extra ['ɛkstrə] ADJ zusätzlich ▸ ADV extra ▸ N Extra *nt*; (*surcharge*) zusätzliche Kosten *pl*; (*Cine, Theat*) Statist(in) *m(f)*; **wine will cost ~** Wein wird extra berechnet
extra... ['ɛkstrə] PREF außer-, extra-
extract VT [ɪks'trækt] (*tooth*) ziehen; (*mineral*) gewinnen ▸ N ['ɛkstrækt] Auszug *m*; (*also*: **malt extract, vanilla extract etc**)

Extrakt *m*; **to ~ (from)** (*object*) herausziehen (aus); (*money*) herausholen (aus); (*promise*) abringen *+dat*
extraction [ɪks'trækʃən] N Ziehen *nt*; Gewinnung *f*; Herausziehen *nt*; Herausholen *nt*; Abringen *nt*; (*Dentistry*) Extraktion *f*; (*descent*) Herkunft *f*, Abstammung *f*; **to be of Scottish ~, to be Scottish by ~** schottischer Herkunft *or* Abstammung sein
extractor fan [ɪks'træktə-] N Sauglüfter *m*
extracurricular ['ɛkstrəkə'rɪkjuləʳ] ADJ außerhalb des Lehrplans
extradite ['ɛkstrədaɪt] VT ausliefern
extradition [ɛkstrə'dɪʃən] N Auslieferung *f* ▸ CPD Auslieferungs-
extramarital ['ɛkstrə'mærɪtl] ADJ außerehelich
extramural ['ɛkstrə'mjuərl] ADJ außerhalb der Universität; **~ classes** von der Universität veranstaltete Teilzeitkurse *pl*
extraneous [ɛks'treɪnɪəs] ADJ unwesentlich
extraordinary [ɪks'trɔ:dnrɪ] ADJ ungewöhnlich; (*special*) außerordentlich; **the ~ thing is that ...** das Merkwürdige ist, dass ...
extraordinary general meeting N außerordentliche Hauptversammlung *f*
extrapolation [ɛkstræpə'leɪʃən] N Extrapolation *f*
extrasensory perception ['ɛkstrə'sɛnsərɪ-] N außersinnliche Wahrnehmung *f*
extra time N (*Football*) Verlängerung *f*
extravagance [ɪks'trævəgəns] N (*no pl*) Verschwendungssucht *f*; (*example of spending*) Luxus *m*
extravagant [ɪks'trævəgənt] ADJ extravagant; (*tastes, gift*) teuer; (*wasteful*) verschwenderisch; (*praise*) übertrieben; (*ideas*) ausgefallen
extreme [ɪks'tri:m] ADJ extrem; (*point, edge, poverty*) äußerste(r, s) ▸ N Extrem *nt*; **the ~ right/left** (*Pol*) die äußerste *or* extreme Rechte/Linke; **extremes of temperature** extreme Temperaturen *pl*
extremely [ɪks'tri:mlɪ] ADV äußerst, extrem
extremist [ɪks'tri:mɪst] N Extremist(in) *m(f)* ▸ ADJ extremistisch
extremities [ɪks'trɛmɪtɪz] NPL Extremitäten *pl*
extremity [ɪks'trɛmɪtɪ] N Rand *m*; (*end*) äußerstes Ende *nt*; (*of situation*) Ausmaß *nt*
extricate ['ɛkstrɪkeɪt] VT: **to ~ sb/sth (from)** jdn/etw befreien (aus)
extrovert ['ɛkstrəvə:t] N extravertierter Mensch *m*
exuberance [ɪg'zju:bərns] N Überschwänglichkeit *f*
exuberant [ɪg'zju:bərnt] ADJ überschwänglich; (*imagination etc*) lebhaft
exude [ɪg'zju:d] VT ausstrahlen; (*liquid*) absondern; (*smell*) ausströmen
exult [ɪg'zʌlt] VI: **to ~ (in)** jubeln (über *+acc*)
exultant [ɪg'zʌltənt] ADJ jubelnd; (*shout*) Jubel-; **to be ~** jubeln
exultation [ɛgzʌl'teɪʃən] N Jubel *m*
eye [aɪ] N Auge *nt*; (*of needle*) Öhr *nt* ▸ VT betrachten; **to keep an ~ on** aufpassen auf *+acc*; **as far as the ~ can see** so weit das Auge reicht; **in the public ~** im Blickpunkt der Öffentlichkeit; **to have an ~ for sth** einen Blick für etw haben; **with an ~ to doing sth** (BRIT) mit der Absicht, etw zu tun; **there's more to this than meets the ~** da steckt mehr dahinter(, als man auf den ersten Blick meint)
eyeball ['aɪbɔ:l] N Augapfel *m*
eyebath ['aɪbɑ:θ] (BRIT) N Augenbadewanne *f*
eyebrow ['aɪbrau] N Augenbraue *f*
eyebrow pencil N Augenbrauenstift *m*
eye-catching ['aɪkætʃɪŋ] ADJ auffallend
eyecup ['aɪkʌp] (US) N = **eyebath**
eye drops NPL Augentropfen *pl*
eyeful ['aɪful] N: **to get an ~ of sth** (*lit*) etw ins Auge bekommen; (*fig: have a good look*) einiges von etw zu sehen bekommen; **she's quite an ~** sie hat allerhand zu bieten
eyeglass ['aɪglɑ:s] N Augenglas *nt*
eyelash ['aɪlæʃ] N Augenwimper *f*
eyelet ['aɪlɪt] N Öse *f*
eyelevel ['aɪlɛvl] ADJ in Augenhöhe
eye level N: **at ~** in Augenhöhe
eyelid ['aɪlɪd] N Augenlid *nt*
eyeliner ['aɪlaɪnəʳ] N Eyeliner *m*
eye-opener ['aɪəupnəʳ] N Überraschung *f*; **to be an ~ to sb** jdm die Augen öffnen
eye shadow N Lidschatten *m*
eyesight ['aɪsaɪt] N Sehvermögen *nt*
eyesore ['aɪsɔ:ʳ] N Schandfleck *m*
eyestrain ['aɪstreɪn] N: **to get ~** seine Augen überanstrengen
eyetooth ['aɪtu:θ] (*pl* **eyeteeth**) N Eckzahn *m*, Augenzahn *m*; **to give one's eyeteeth for sth** alles für etw geben; **to give one's eyeteeth to do sth** alles darum geben, etw zu tun
eyewash ['aɪwɔʃ] N Augenwasser *nt*; (*fig*) Gewäsch *nt*
eyewitness ['aɪwɪtnɪs] N Augenzeuge *m*, Augenzeugin *f*
eyrie ['ɪərɪ] N Horst *m*

F¹, f [ɛf] N (*letter*) F *nt*, f *nt*; **F for Frederick, F for Fox** (*US*) ≈ F wie Friedrich
F² [ɛf] N (*Mus*) F *nt*, f *nt*
F³ [ɛf] ABBR (= *Fahrenheit*) F
FA (BRIT) N ABBR (= *Football Association*) *englischer Fußball-Dachverband*, ≈ DFB *m*
FAA (US) N ABBR (= *Federal Aviation Administration*) *amerikanische Luftfahrtbehörde*
fable ['feɪbl] N Fabel *f*
fabric ['fæbrɪk] N Stoff *m*; (*of society*) Gefüge *nt*; (*of building*) Bausubstanz *f*
fabricate ['fæbrɪkeɪt] VT herstellen; (*story*) erfinden; (*evidence*) fälschen
fabrication [fæbrɪ'keɪʃən] N Herstellung *f*; (*lie*) Erfindung *f*
fabric ribbon N (*for typewriter*) Gewebefarbband *nt*
fabulous ['fæbjuləs] ADJ fabelhaft, toll (*inf*); (*extraordinary*) sagenhaft; (*mythical*) legendär
façade [fə'sɑːd] N Fassade *f*
face [feɪs] N Gesicht *nt*; (*expression*) Gesichtsausdruck *m*; (*grimace*) Grimasse *f*; (*of clock*) Zifferblatt *nt*; (*of mountain, cliff*) (Steil)wand *f*; (*of building*) Fassade *f*; (*side, surface*) Seite *f* ▸ VT (*subj: person*) gegenübersitzen/-stehen *+dat etc*; (*: building, street etc*) liegen zu; (*: north, south etc*) liegen nach; (*unpleasant situation*) sich gegenübersehen *+dat*; (*facts*) ins Auge sehen *+dat*; **~ down** mit dem Gesicht nach unten; (*card*) mit der Bildseite nach unten; (*object*) mit der Vorderseite nach unten; **to lose/save ~** das Gesicht verlieren/wahren; **to make** *or* **pull a ~** das Gesicht verziehen; **in the ~ of** trotz *+gen*; **on the ~ of it** so, wie es aussieht; **to come ~ to ~ with sb** jdn treffen; **to come ~ to ~ with a problem** einem Problem gegenüberstehen; **to ~ each other** einander gegenüberstehen/-liegen/-sitzen *etc*; **to ~ the fact that ...** der Tatsache ins Auge sehen, dass ...; **the man facing me** der Mann mir gegenüber
▸ **face up to** VT FUS (*obligations, difficulty*) auf sich *acc* nehmen; (*situation, possibility*) sich abfinden mit; (*danger, fact*) ins Auge sehen *+dat*
Facebook® ['feɪsbʊk] N Facebook® *nt*
facebook ['feɪsbʊk] VI eine Facebook-Nachricht schicken
face cloth (BRIT) N Waschlappen *m*
face cream N Gesichtscreme *f*
faceless ['feɪslɪs] ADJ (*fig*) anonym
face-lift ['feɪslɪft] N Facelifting *nt*; (*of building etc*) Verschönerung *f*
face powder N Gesichtspuder *m*
face-saving ['feɪs'seɪvɪŋ] ADJ: **a ~ excuse/tactic** eine Entschuldigung/Taktik, um das Gesicht zu wahren
facet ['fæsɪt] N Seite *f*, Aspekt *m*; (*of gem*) Facette *f*
face time N (*US*) *Zeit, die man mit jemandem im direkten persönlichen Gespräch verbringt*
facetious [fə'siːʃəs] ADJ witzelnd
face-to-face [feɪstə'feɪs] ADJ persönlich; (*confrontation*) direkt
face value N Nennwert *m*; **to take sth at ~** (*fig*) etw für bare Münze nehmen
facia ['feɪʃə] N = **fascia**
facial ['feɪʃl] ADJ (*expression, massage etc*) Gesichts- ▸ N kosmetische Gesichtsbehandlung *f*
facile ['fæsaɪl] ADJ oberflächlich; (*comment*) nichtssagend
facilitate [fə'sɪlɪteɪt] VT erleichtern
facilities [fə'sɪlɪtɪz] NPL Einrichtungen *pl*; **cooking ~** Kochgelegenheit *f*; **credit ~** Kreditmöglichkeiten *pl*
facility [fə'sɪlɪtɪ] N Einrichtung *f*; **to have a ~ for** (*skill, aptitude*) eine Begabung haben für
facing ['feɪsɪŋ] PREP gegenüber *+dat* ▸ N (*Sewing*) Besatz *m*
facsimile [fæk'sɪmɪlɪ] N Faksimile *nt*; (*also:* **facsimile machine**) Fernkopierer *m*, (Tele)faxgerät *nt*; (*transmitted document*) Fernkopie *f*, (Tele)fax *nt*
fact [fækt] N Tatsache *f*; (*truth*) Wirklichkeit *f*; **in ~** eigentlich; (*in reality*) tatsächlich, in Wirklichkeit; **to know for a ~ that ...** ganz genau wissen, dass ...; **the ~ (of the matter) is that ...** die Sache ist die, dass ...; **it's a ~ of life that ...** es ist eine Tatsache, dass ...; **to tell sb the facts of life** (*sex*) jdn aufklären
fact-finding ['fæktfaɪndɪŋ] ADJ: **a ~ tour** *or* **mission** eine Informationstour *f*
faction ['fækʃən] N Fraktion *f*
factional ['fækʃənl] ADJ (*dispute, system*) Fraktions-
factor ['fæktəʳ] N Faktor *m*; (*Comm*) Kommissionär *m*; (*: agent*) Makler *m*; **safety ~**

Sicherheitsfaktor *m*; **human ~** menschlicher Faktor

factory ['fæktərɪ] N Fabrik *f*

factory farming (BRIT) N industriell betriebene Viehzucht *f*

factory floor N: **the ~** (*workers*) die Fabrikarbeiter *pl*; **on the ~** bei *or* unter den Fabrikarbeitern

factory ship N Fabrikschiff *nt*

factual ['fæktjuəl] ADJ sachlich; (*information*) Sach-

faculty ['fækəltɪ] N Vermögen *nt*, Kraft *f*; (*ability*) Talent *nt*; (*of university*) Fakultät *f*; (*US: teaching staff*) Lehrkörper *m*

fad [fæd] N Fimmel *m*, Tick *m*

fade [feɪd] VI verblassen; (*light*) nachlassen; (*sound*) schwächer werden; (*flower*) verblühen; (*hope*) zerrinnen; (*smile*) verschwinden
▸ **fade in** VT SEP allmählich einblenden
▸ **fade out** VT SEP ausblenden

faeces, (US) **feces** ['fi:si:z] NPL Kot *m*

fag [fæg] N (BRIT *inf: cigarette*) Glimmstängel *m*; (*: chore*) Schinderei *f* (*inf*), Plackerei *f* (*inf*); (*US inf: homosexual*) Schwule(r) *m*

fail [feɪl] VT (*exam*) nicht bestehen; (*candidate*) durchfallen lassen; (*subj: courage*) verlassen; (*: leader, memory*) im Stich lassen ▸ VI (*candidate*) durchfallen; (*attempt*) fehlschlagen; (*brakes*) versagen; (*also:* **be failing**: *health*) sich verschlechtern; (*: eyesight, light*) nachlassen; **to ~ to do sth** etw nicht tun; (*neglect*) (es) versäumen, etw zu tun; **without ~** ganz bestimmt

failing ['feɪlɪŋ] N Schwäche *f*, Fehler *m* ▸ PREP in Ermangelung *+gen*; **~ that** (oder) sonst, und wenn das nicht möglich ist

fail-safe ['feɪlseɪf] ADJ (ab)gesichert

failure ['feɪljə^r] N Misserfolg *m*; (*person*) Versager(in) *m(f)*; (*of brakes, heart*) Versagen *nt*; (*of engine, power*) Ausfall *m*; (*of crops*) Missernte *f*; (*in exam*) Durchfall *m*; **his ~ to turn up meant that we had to …** weil er nicht kam, mussten wir …; **it was a complete ~** es war ein totaler Fehlschlag

faint [feɪnt] ADJ schwach; (*breeze, trace*) leicht ▸ N Ohnmacht *f* ▸ VI ohnmächtig werden, in Ohnmacht fallen; **she felt ~** ihr wurde schwach

faintest ['feɪntɪst] ADJ, N: **I haven't the ~ (idea)** ich habe keinen blassen Schimmer

faint-hearted ['feɪnt'hɑ:tɪd] ADJ zaghaft

faintly ['feɪntlɪ] ADV schwach

fair [fɛə^r] ADJ gerecht, fair; (*size, number*) ansehnlich; (*chance, guess*) recht gut; (*hair*) blond; (*skin, complexion*) hell; (*weather*) schön ▸ ADV: **to play ~** fair spielen ▸ N (*also:* **trade fair**) Messe *f*; (BRIT: *funfair*) Jahrmarkt *m*, Rummel *m*; **it's not ~!** das ist nicht fair!; **a ~ amount of** ziemlich viel

fair copy N Reinschrift *f*

fair game N: **to be ~ (for)** (*for attack, criticism*) Freiwild *nt* sein (für)

fairground ['fɛəgraund] N Rummelplatz *m*

fair-haired [fɛə'hɛəd] ADJ blond

fairly ['fɛəlɪ] ADV gerecht; (*quite*) ziemlich; **I'm ~ sure** ich bin (mir) ziemlich sicher

fairness ['fɛənɪs] N Gerechtigkeit *f*; **in all ~** gerechterweise, fairerweise

fair play N faires Verhalten *nt*, Fair Play *nt*

fair trade N Fairer Handel

fairway ['fɛəweɪ] N (*Golf*): **the ~** das Fairway

fairy ['fɛərɪ] N Fee *f*

fairy godmother N gute Fee *f*

fairy lights (BRIT) NPL bunte Lichter *pl*

fairy tale N Märchen *nt*

faith [feɪθ] N Glaube *m*; (*trust*) Vertrauen *nt*; **to have ~ in sb** jdm vertrauen; **to have ~ in sth** Vertrauen in etw *acc* haben

faithful ['feɪθful] ADJ (*account*) genau; **~ (to)** (*person*) treu *+dat*

faithfully ['feɪθfəlɪ] ADV genau; treu

faith healer N Gesundbeter(in) *m(f)*

fake [feɪk] N Fälschung *f*; (*person*) Schwindler(in) *m(f)* ▸ ADJ gefälscht ▸ VT fälschen; (*illness, emotion*) vortäuschen; **his illness is a ~** er simuliert seine Krankheit nur

falcon ['fɔ:lkən] N Falke *m*

Falkland Islands ['fɔ:lklənd-] NPL: **the ~** die Falklandinseln *pl*

fall [fɔ:l] (*pt* **fell**, *pp* **fallen**) N Fall *m*; (*of price, temperature*) Sinken *nt*; (*: sudden*) Sturz *m*; (*US: autumn*) Herbst *m* ▸ VI fallen; (*night, darkness*) hereinbrechen; (*silence*) eintreten; **falls** NPL (*waterfall*) Wasserfall *m*; **a ~ of snow** ein Schneefall *m*; **a ~ of earth** ein Erdrutsch *m*; **to ~ flat** auf die Nase fallen; (*plan*) ins Wasser fallen; (*joke*) nicht ankommen; **to ~ in love (with sb/sth)** sich (in jdn/etw) verlieben; **to ~ short of sb's expectations** jds Erwartungen nicht erfüllen
▸ **fall apart** VI auseinanderfallen, kaputtgehen; (*inf: emotionally*) durchdrehen
▸ **fall back** VI zurückweichen
▸ **fall back on** VI zurückgreifen auf *+acc*; **to have sth to ~ back on** auf etw *acc* zurückgreifen können
▸ **fall behind** VI zurückbleiben; (*fig: with payment*) in Rückstand geraten
▸ **fall down** VI hinfallen; (*building*) einstürzen
▸ **fall for** VT FUS (*trick, story*) hereinfallen auf *+acc*; (*person*) sich verlieben in *+acc*
▸ **fall in** VI einstürzen; (*Mil*) antreten
▸ **fall in with** VT FUS eingehen auf *+acc*
▸ **fall off** VI herunterfallen; (*takings, attendance*) zurückgehen
▸ **fall out** VI (*hair, teeth*) ausfallen; **to ~ out with sb** sich mit jdm zerstreiten
▸ **fall over** VI hinfallen; (*object*) umfallen ▸ VT: **to ~ over o.s. to do sth** sich *dat* die größte Mühe geben, etw zu tun
▸ **fall through** VI (*plan, project*) ins Wasser fallen

fallacy ['fæləsɪ] N Irrtum *m*

fall-back ['fɔ:lbæk] ADJ: **~ position** Rückzugsbasis *f*

fallen ['fɔ:lən] PP *of* **fall**

fallible ['fæləbl] ADJ fehlbar

falling ['fɔːlɪŋ] ADJ: **~ market** (*Comm*) Baissemarkt *m*
falling off N Rückgang *m*
falling-out ['fɔːlɪŋ'aut] N (*break-up*) Bruch *m*
Fallopian tube [fə'ləupɪən-] N Eileiter *m*
fallout ['fɔːlaut] N radioaktiver Niederschlag *m*
fallout shelter N Atombunker *m*
fallow ['fæləu] ADJ brach(liegend)
false [fɔːls] ADJ falsch; (*imprisonment*) widerrechtlich
false alarm N falscher *or* blinder Alarm *m*
falsehood ['fɔːlshud] N Unwahrheit *f*
falsely ['fɔːlslɪ] ADV (*accuse*) zu Unrecht
false pretences NPL: **under ~** unter Vorspiegelung falscher Tatsachen
false teeth (BRIT) NPL Gebiss *nt*
falsify ['fɔːlsɪfaɪ] VT fälschen
falter ['fɔːltə^r] VI stocken; (*hesitate*) zögern
fame [feɪm] N Ruhm *m*
familiar [fə'mɪlɪə^r] ADJ vertraut; (*intimate*) vertraulich; **to be ~ with** vertraut sein mit; **to make o.s. ~ with sth** sich mit etw vertraut machen; **to be on ~ terms with sb** mit jdm auf vertrautem Fuß stehen
familiarity [fəmɪlɪ'ærɪtɪ] N Vertrautheit *f*; Vertraulichkeit *f*
familiarize [fə'mɪlɪəraɪz] VT: **to ~ o.s. with sth** sich mit etw vertraut machen
family ['fæmɪlɪ] N Familie *f*; (*relations*) Verwandtschaft *f*
family business, family company N Familienunternehmen *nt or* -betrieb *m*
family credit N *Beihilfe für einkommensschwache Familien*
family doctor N Hausarzt *m*, Hausärztin *f*
family life N Familienleben *nt*
family man N (*irreg*) (*home-loving*) häuslich veranlagter Mann *m*; (*with a family*) Familienvater *m*
family planning N Familienplanung *f*; **~ clinic** ≈ Familienberatungsstelle *f*
family tree N Stammbaum *m*
famine ['fæmɪn] N Hungersnot *f*
famished ['fæmɪʃt] (*inf*) ADJ ausgehungert; **I'm ~** ich sterbe vor Hunger
famous ['feɪməs] ADJ berühmt
famously ['feɪməslɪ] ADV (*get on*) prächtig
fan [fæn] N (*person*) Fan *m*; (*object: folding*) Fächer *m*; (*: Elec*) Ventilator *m* ▸ VT fächeln; (*fire*) anfachen; (*quarrel*) schüren
▸ **fan out** VI ausschwärmen; (*unfurl*) sich fächerförmig ausbreiten
fanatic [fə'nætɪk] N Fanatiker(in) *m(f)*; (*enthusiast*) Fan *m*
fanatical [fə'nætɪkl] ADJ fanatisch
fan belt N (*Aut*) Keilriemen *m*
fanciful ['fænsɪful] ADJ (*idea*) abstrus, seltsam; (*design, name*) fantasievoll; (*object*) reich verziert
fan club N Fanklub *m*
fancy ['fænsɪ] N Laune *f*; (*imagination*) Fantasie *f*; (*fantasy*) Fantasievorstellung *f* ▸ ADJ (*clothes, hat*) toll, chic *inv*; (*hotel*) fein, vornehm; (*food*) ausgefallen ▸ VT mögen; (*imagine*) sich *dat* einbilden; (*think*) glauben; **to take a ~ to sth** Lust auf etw *acc* bekommen; **when the ~ takes him** wenn ihm gerade danach ist; **it took** *or* **caught my ~** es gefiel mir; **to ~ that ...** meinen, dass ...; **~ that!** (nein) so was!; **he fancies her** (*inf*) sie gefällt ihm
fancy dress N Verkleidung *f*, (Masken)kostüm *nt*
fancy-dress ball ['fænsɪdrɛs-] N Maskenball *m*
fancy goods NPL Geschenkartikel *pl*
fanfare ['fænfɛə^r] N Fanfare *f*
fanfold paper ['fænfəuld-] N Endlospapier *nt*
fang [fæŋ] N (*tooth*) Fang *m*; (*: of snake*) Giftzahn *m*
fan heater (BRIT) N Heizlüfter *m*
fanlight ['fænlaɪt] N Oberlicht *nt*
fanny ['fænɪ] N (*US inf: bottom*) Po *m*; (BRIT *inf!: genitals*) Möse *f* (*inf!*)
fantasize ['fæntəsaɪz] VI fantasieren
fantastic [fæn'tæstɪk] ADJ fantastisch
fantasy ['fæntəsɪ] N Fantasie *f*; (*dream*) Traum *m*
fanzine ['fænziːn] N Fanmagazin *nt*
FAO N ABBR (= *Food and Agriculture Organization*) FAO *f*
FAQ ABBR (*Comput:* = *frequently-asked questions*) FAQ *pl*
far [fɑː^r] ADJ: **at the ~ side** auf der anderen Seite ▸ ADV weit; **at the ~ end** am anderen Ende; **the ~ left/right** die extreme Linke/Rechte; **~ away, ~ off** weit entfernt *or* weg; **her thoughts were ~ away** sie war mit ihren Gedanken weit weg; **~ from** (*fig*) alles andere als; **by ~** bei Weitem; **is it ~ to London?** ist es weit bis nach London?; **it's not ~ from here** es ist nicht weit von hier; **go as ~ as the church** gehen/fahren Sie bis zur Kirche; **as ~ back as the 13th century** schon im 13. Jahrhundert; **as ~ as I know** soweit ich weiß; **as ~ as possible** so weit wie möglich; **how ~?** wie weit?; **how ~ have you got with your work?** wie weit sind Sie mit Ihrer Arbeit (gekommen)?
faraway ['fɑːrəweɪ] ADJ weit entfernt; (*look, voice*) abwesend
farce [fɑːs] N Farce *f*
farcical ['fɑːsɪkl] ADJ absurd, grotesk
fare [fɛə^r] N Fahrpreis *m*; (*money*) Fahrgeld *nt*; (*passenger*) Fahrgast *m*; (*food*) Kost *f* ▸ VI: **he fared well/badly** es ging ihm gut/schlecht; **half/full ~** halber/voller Fahrpreis; **how did you ~?** wie ist es Ihnen ergangen?; **they fared badly in the recent elections** sie haben bei den letzten Wahlen schlecht abgeschnitten
Far East N: **the ~** der Ferne Osten
farewell [fɛə'wɛl] EXCL lebe/lebt *etc* wohl! ▸ N Abschied *m* ▸ CPD Abschieds-
far-fetched ['fɑː'fɛtʃt] ADJ weit hergeholt
farm [fɑːm] N Bauernhof *m* ▸ VT bebauen
▸ **farm out** VT (*work etc*) vergeben
farmer ['fɑːmə^r] N Bauer *m*, Bäu(e)rin *f*, Landwirt(in) *m(f)*
farm hand N Landarbeiter(in) *m(f)*
farmhouse ['fɑːmhaus] N Bauernhaus *nt*

farming ['fɑ:mɪŋ] N Landwirtschaft *f*; (*of crops*) Ackerbau *m*; (*of animals*) Viehzucht *f*; **sheep ~** Schafzucht *f*; **intensive ~** (*of crops*) Intensivanbau *m*; (*of animals*) Intensivhaltung *f*
farm labourer N = **farm hand**
farmland ['fɑ:mlænd] N Ackerland *nt*
farm produce N landwirtschaftliche Produkte *pl*
farm worker N = **farm hand**
farmyard ['fɑ:mjɑ:d] N Hof *m*
Faroe Islands ['fɛərəu-] NPL: **the ~** die Färöer *pl*
Faroes ['fɛərəuz] NPL = **Faroe Islands**
far-reaching ['fɑ:'ri:tʃɪŋ] ADJ weitreichend
far-sighted ['fɑ:'saɪtɪd] ADJ weitsichtig; (*fig*) weitblickend
fart [fɑ:t] VI furzen (*inf!*) ▶ N Furz *m* (*inf!*)
farther ['fɑ:ðə^r] ADV weiter ▶ ADJ weiter entfernt
farthest ['fɑ:ðɪst] SUPERL *of* **far**
FAS, (BRIT) **f.a.s.** ABBR (= *free alongside ship*) frei Kai
fascia ['feɪʃə] N (*Aut*) Armaturenbrett *nt*
fascinate ['fæsɪneɪt] VT faszinieren
fascinating ['fæsɪneɪtɪŋ] ADJ faszinierend
fascination [fæsɪ'neɪʃən] N Faszination *f*
fascism ['fæʃɪzəm] N Faschismus *m*
fascist ['fæʃɪst] ADJ faschistisch ▶ N Faschist(in) *m(f)*
fashion ['fæʃən] N Mode *f*; (*manner*) Art *f* ▶ VT formen; **in ~** modern; **out of ~** unmodern; **after a ~** recht und schlecht; **in the Greek ~** im griechischen Stil
fashionable ['fæʃnəbl] ADJ modisch, modern; (*subject*) Mode-; (*club, writer*) in Mode
fashion designer N Modezeichner(in) *m(f)*
fashion show N Modenschau *f*
fashion victim N Modesklave *m*, Modesklavin *f*
fast [fɑ:st] ADJ schnell; (*dye, colour*) farbecht ▶ ADV schnell; (*stuck, held*) fest ▶ N Fasten *nt*; (*period of fasting*) Fastenzeit *f* ▶ VI fasten; **my watch is (5 minutes) ~** meine Uhr geht (5 Minuten) vor; **to be ~ asleep** tief *or* fest schlafen; **as ~ as I can** so schnell ich kann; **to make a boat ~** (BRIT) ein Boot festmachen
fasten ['fɑ:sn] VT festmachen; (*coat, belt etc*) zumachen ▶ VI festgemacht werden; zugemacht werden
▶ **fasten (up)on** VT FUS sich *dat* in den Kopf setzen
fastener ['fɑ:snə^r] N Verschluss *m*
fastening ['fɑ:snɪŋ] N = **fastener**
fast food N Fast Food *nt*, Schnellgerichte *pl*
fast-food ['fɑ:stfu:d] CPD (*industry, chain*) Fast-Food-; **~ restaurant** Schnellimbiss *m*
fastidious [fæs'tɪdɪəs] ADJ penibel
fast lane N (*Aut*): **the ~** die Überholspur
fat [fæt] ADJ dick; (*person*) dick, fett (*pej*); (*animal*) fett; (*profit*) üppig ▶ N Fett *nt*; **that's a ~ lot of use** (*inf*) das hilft herzlich wenig; **to live off the ~ of the land** wie Gott in Frankreich *or* wie die Made im Speck leben
fatal ['feɪtl] ADJ tödlich; (*mistake*) verhängnisvoll
fatalistic [feɪtə'lɪstɪk] ADJ fatalistisch
fatality [fə'tælɪtɪ] N Todesopfer *nt*
fatally ['feɪtəlɪ] ADV tödlich; verhängnisvoll
fate [feɪt] N Schicksal *nt*; **to meet one's ~** vom Schicksal ereilt werden
fated ['feɪtɪd] ADJ (*person*) unglückselig; (*project*) zum Scheitern verurteilt; (*governed by fate*) vorherbestimmt
fateful ['feɪtful] ADJ schicksalhaft
fat-free ['fæt'fri:] ADJ fettfrei
father ['fɑ:ðə^r] N Vater *m*
Father Christmas N der Weihnachtsmann
fatherhood ['fɑ:ðəhud] N Vaterschaft *f*
father-in-law ['fɑ:ðərənlɔ:] N Schwiegervater *m*
fatherland ['fɑ:ðəlænd] N Vaterland *nt*
fatherly ['fɑ:ðəlɪ] ADJ väterlich
fathom ['fæðəm] N (*Naut*) Faden *m* ▶ VT (*also*: **fathom out**) verstehen
fatigue [fə'ti:g] N Erschöpfung *f*; **fatigues** NPL (*Mil*) Arbeitsanzug *m*; **metal ~** Metallermüdung *f*
fatness ['fætnɪs] N Dicke *f*
fatten ['fætn] VT mästen ▶ VI (*person*) dick werden; (*animal*) fett werden; **chocolate is fattening** Schokolade macht dick
fatty ['fætɪ] ADJ fett ▶ N (*inf*) Dickerchen *nt*
fatuous ['fætjuəs] ADJ albern, töricht
faucet ['fɔ:sɪt] (US) N (Wasser)hahn *m*
fault [fɔ:lt] N Fehler *m*; (*blame*) Schuld *f*; (*in machine*) Defekt *m*; (*Geog*) Verwerfung *f* ▶ VT (*also*: **find fault with**) etwas auszusetzen haben an *+dat*; **it's my ~** es ist meine Schuld; **at ~** im Unrecht; **generous to a ~** übermäßig großzügig
faultless ['fɔ:ltlɪs] ADJ fehlerlos
faulty ['fɔ:ltɪ] ADJ defekt
fauna ['fɔ:nə] N Fauna *f*
faux pas ['fəu'pɑ:] N INV Fauxpas *m*
favor *etc* ['feɪvə^r] (US) = **favour** *etc*
favour, (US) **favor** ['feɪvə^r] N (*approval*) Wohlwollen *nt*; (*help*) Gefallen *m* ▶ VT bevorzugen; (*be favourable for*) begünstigen; **to ask a ~ of sb** jdn um einen Gefallen bitten; **to do sb a ~** jdm einen Gefallen tun; **to find ~ with sb** bei jdm Anklang finden; **in ~ of** (*biased*) zugunsten von; (*rejected*) zugunsten *+gen*; **to be in ~ of sth** für etw sein; **to be in ~ of doing sth** dafür sein, etw zu tun
favourable ['feɪvrəbl] ADJ günstig; (*reaction*) positiv; (*comparison*) vorteilhaft
favourably ['feɪvrəblɪ] ADV (*react*) positiv; (*compare*) vorteilhaft
favourite ['feɪvrɪt] ADJ Lieblings- ▶ N Liebling *m*; (*in race*) Favorit(in) *m(f)*
favouritism ['feɪvrɪtɪzəm] N Günstlingswirtschaft *f*
fawn [fɔ:n] N Rehkitz *nt* ▶ ADJ (*also*: **fawn-coloured**) hellbraun ▶ VI: **to ~ (up)on** sich einschmeicheln bei
fax [fæks] N Fax *nt*; (*machine*) Fax(gerät) *nt* ▶ VT faxen
fax number N Faxnummer *f*
faze [feɪz] VT (*inf*) aus der Fassung bringen

f

FBI (US) N ABBR (= *Federal Bureau of Investigation*) FBI *nt*
FCC (US) N ABBR (= *Federal Communications Commission*) *Aufsichtsbehörde im Medienbereich*
FCO (BRIT) N ABBR (= *Foreign and Commonwealth Office*) ≈ Auswärtiges Amt *nt*
FD (US) N ABBR = **fire department**
FDA (US) N ABBR (= *Food and Drug Administration*) *Nahrungs- und Arzneimittelbehörde*
fear [fɪəʳ] N Furcht *f*, Angst *f* ▸ VT fürchten, Angst haben vor *+dat*; (*be worried about*) befürchten ▸ VI sich fürchten; **~ of heights** Höhenangst *f*; **for ~ of doing sth** aus Angst, etw zu tun; **to ~ for** fürchten um; **to ~ that ...** befürchten, dass ...
fearful ['fɪəful] ADJ (*frightening*) furchtbar, schrecklich; (*apprehensive*) ängstlich; **to be ~ of** Angst haben vor *+dat*
fearfully ['fɪəfəlɪ] ADV ängstlich; (*inf: very*) furchtbar, schrecklich
fearless ['fɪəlɪs] ADJ furchtlos
fearsome ['fɪəsəm] ADJ furchterregend
feasibility [fi:zə'bɪlɪtɪ] N Durchführbarkeit *f*
feasibility study N Machbarkeits- *or* Durchführbarkeitsstudie *f*
feasible ['fi:zəbl] ADJ machbar; (*proposal, plan*) durchführbar
feast [fi:st] N Festmahl *nt*; (*Rel: also:* **feast day**) Festtag *m*, Feiertag *m* ▸ VI schlemmen; **to ~ on** sich gütlich tun an *+dat*
feat [fi:t] N Leistung *f*
feather ['fɛðəʳ] N Feder *f* ▸ CPD Feder-; (*mattress*) Federkern- ▸ VT: **to ~ one's nest** (*fig*) sein Schäfchen ins Trockene bringen
featherweight ['fɛðəweɪt] N Leichtgewicht *nt*; (*Boxing*) Federgewicht *nt*
feature ['fi:tʃəʳ] N Merkmal *nt*; (*Press, TV*) Feature *nt* ▸ VT: **the film features Marlon Brando** Marlon Brando spielt in dem Film mit ▸ VI: **to ~ in** vorkommen in *+dat*; (*film*) mitspielen in *+dat*; **features** NPL (*of face*) (Gesichts)züge *pl*; **it featured prominently in** es spielte eine große Rolle in *+dat*; **a special ~ on sth/sb** ein Sonderbeitrag *m* über etw/jdn
feature film N Spielfilm *m*
featureless ['fi:tʃəlɪs] ADJ (*landscape*) eintönig
Feb. ABBR (= *February*) Feb.
February ['fɛbruərɪ] N Februar *m*; *see also* **July**
feces ['fi:si:z] (US) NPL = **faeces**
feckless ['fɛklɪs] ADJ nutzlos
Fed [fɛd] (*US inf*) N ABBR: **the ~ = Federal Reserve Board**
fed [fɛd] PT, PP *of* **feed**
Fed. (US) ABBR = **federal; federation**
federal ['fɛdərəl] ADJ föderalistisch
Federal Republic of Germany N Bundesrepublik *f* Deutschland
Federal Reserve Board (US) N *Kontrollorgan der US-Zentralbank*
Federal Trade Commission (US) N *Handelskontrollbehörde*
federation [fɛdə'reɪʃən] N Föderation *f*, Bund *m*
fed up ADJ: **to be ~ with** die Nase vollhaben von

fee [fi:] N Gebühr *f*; (*of doctor, lawyer*) Honorar *nt*; **school fees** Schulgeld *nt*; **entrance ~** Eintrittsgebühr *f*; **membership ~** Mitgliedsbeitrag *m*; **for a small ~** gegen eine geringe Gebühr
feeble ['fi:bl] ADJ schwach; (*joke*) lahm
feeble-minded ['fi:bl'maɪndɪd] ADJ dümmlich
feed [fi:d] (*pt, pp* **fed**) N Mahlzeit *f*; (*of animal*) Fütterung *f*; (*on printer*) Papiervorschub *m* ▸ VT füttern; (*family etc*) ernähren; (*machine*) versorgen; **to ~ sth into sth** etw in etw *acc* einfüllen *or* eingeben; (*data, information*) etw in etw *acc* eingeben; **to ~ material into sth** Material in etw *acc* eingeben
▸ **feed back** VT zurückleiten
▸ **feed on** VT FUS sich nähren von
feedback ['fi:dbæk] N Feedback *nt*, Rückmeldung *f*; (*from person*) Reaktion *f*
feeder ['fi:dəʳ] N (*road*) Zubringer *m*; (*railway line, air route*) Zubringerlinie *f*; (*baby's bottle*) Flasche *f*
feeding bottle ['fi:dɪŋ-] (BRIT) N Flasche *f*
feel [fi:l] (*pt, pp* **felt**) N (*sensation, touch*) Gefühl *nt*; (*impression*) Atmosphäre *f* ▸ VT (*object*) fühlen; (*desire, anger, grief*) empfinden; (*pain*) spüren; (*cold*) leiden unter *+dat*; (*think, believe*): **I ~ that you ought to do it** ich meine *or* ich bin der Meinung, dass Sie es tun sollten; **it has a soft ~** es fühlt sich weich an; **I ~ hungry** ich habe Hunger; **I ~ cold** mir ist kalt; **to ~ lonely/better** sich einsam/besser fühlen; **I don't ~ well** mir geht es nicht gut; **I ~ sorry for him** er tut mir leid; **it feels soft** es fühlt sich weich an; **it feels colder here** es kommt mir hier kälter vor; **it feels like velvet** es fühlt sich wie Samt an; **to ~ like** (*desire*) Lust haben auf *+acc*; **to ~ like doing sth** Lust haben, etw zu tun; **to get the ~ of sth** ein Gefühl für etw bekommen; **I'm still feeling my way** ich versuche noch, mich zu orientieren
▸ **feel about** VI umhertasten; **to ~ about** *or* **around in one's pocket for** in seiner Tasche herumsuchen nach
▸ **feel around** VI = **feel about**
feelbad factor ['fi:lbæd-] N (*inf*) Frustfaktor *m*
feeler ['fi:ləʳ] N Fühler *m*; **to put out a ~** *or* **feelers** (*fig*) seine Fühler ausstrecken
feelgood ['fi:lgud] ADJ (*film, song*) Feelgood-
feeling ['fi:lɪŋ] N Gefühl *nt*; (*impression*) Eindruck *m*; **feelings ran high about it** man ereiferte sich sehr darüber; **what are your feelings about the matter?** was meinen Sie dazu?; **I have a ~ that ...** ich habe das Gefühl, dass ...; **my ~ is that ...** meine Meinung ist, dass ...; **to hurt sb's feelings** jdn verletzen
fee-paying ['fi:peɪɪŋ] ADJ (*school*) Privat-; **~ pupils** *Schüler, deren Eltern Schulgeld zahlen*
feet [fi:t] NPL *of* **foot**
feign [feɪn] VT vortäuschen
feigned [feɪnd] ADJ vorgetäuscht
feint [feɪnt] N fein liniertes Papier *nt*
felicitous [fɪ'lɪsɪtəs] ADJ glücklich
feline ['fi:laɪn] ADJ (*eyes etc*) Katzen-; (*features, grace*) katzenartig

fell [fɛl] PT *of* **fall** ▸ VT fällen; (*opponent*) niederstrecken ▸ N (BRIT: *mountain*) Berg *m*; (: *moorland*): **the fells** das Moor(land) ▸ ADJ: **in one ~ swoop** auf einen Schlag
fellow ['fɛləu] N Mann *m*, Typ *m* (*inf*); (*comrade*) Kamerad *m*; (*of learned society*) Mitglied *nt*; (*of university*) Fellow *m*; **their ~ prisoners/ students** ihre Mitgefangenen/Kommilitonen (und Kommilitoninnen); **his ~ workers** seine Kollegen (und Kolleginnen)
fellow citizen N Mitbürger(in) *m(f)*
fellow countryman N (*irreg*) Landsmann *m*, Landsmännin *f*
fellow men NPL Mitmenschen *pl*
fellowship ['fɛləuʃɪp] N Kameradschaft *f*; (*society*) Gemeinschaft *f*; (*Scol*) Forschungsstipendium *nt*
fell-walking ['fɛlwɔːkɪŋ] (BRIT) N Bergwandern *nt*
felon ['fɛlən] N (*Law*) (Schwer)verbrecher *m*
felony ['fɛlənɪ] N (*Law*) (schweres) Verbrechen *nt*
felt [fɛlt] PT, PP *of* **feel** ▸ N Filz *m*
felt-tip pen ['fɛlttɪp-] N Filzstift *m*
female ['fiːmeɪl] N Weibchen *nt*; (*pej: woman*) Frau *f*, Weib *nt* (*pej*) ▸ ADJ weiblich; (*vote etc*) Frauen-; (*Elec: connector, plug*) Mutter-, Innen-; **male and ~ students** Studenten und Studentinnen
Femidom® ['fɛmɪdɔm] N Kondom *nt* für die Frau, Femidom® *nt*
feminine ['fɛmɪnɪn] ADJ weiblich, feminin ▸ N Femininum *nt*
femininity [fɛmɪ'nɪnɪtɪ] N Weiblichkeit *f*
feminism ['fɛmɪnɪzəm] N Feminismus *m*
feminist ['fɛmɪnɪst] N Feminist(in) *m(f)*
fen [fɛn] (BRIT) N: **the Fens** *die Niederungen in East Anglia*
fence [fɛns] N Zaun *m*; (*Sport*) Hindernis *nt* ▸ VT (*also*: **fence in**) einzäunen ▸ VI (*Sport*) fechten; **to sit on the ~** (*fig*) neutral bleiben, nicht Partei ergreifen
fencing ['fɛnsɪŋ] N (*Sport*) Fechten *nt*
fend [fɛnd] VI: **to ~ for o.s.** für sich (selbst) sorgen, sich allein durchbringen
▸ **fend off** VT abwehren
fender ['fɛndə^r] N Kamingitter *nt*; (*on boat*) Fender *m*; (*US: of car*) Kotflügel *m*
fennel ['fɛnl] N Fenchel *m*
ferment VI [fə'mɛnt] gären ▸ N [fəːmɛnt] (*fig: unrest*) Unruhe *f*
fermentation [fəːmɛn'teɪʃən] N Gärung *f*
fern [fəːn] N Farn *m*
ferocious [fə'rəuʃəs] ADJ wild; (*behaviour*) heftig; (*competition*) scharf
ferocity [fə'rɔsɪtɪ] N Wildheit *f*; Heftigkeit *f*; Schärfe *f*
ferret ['fɛrɪt] N Frettchen *nt*
▸ **ferret about** VI herumstöbern
▸ **ferret around** VI = **ferret about**
▸ **ferret out** VT aufspüren
ferry ['fɛrɪ] N (*also*: **ferryboat**) Fähre *f* ▸ VT transportieren; **to ~ sth/sb across** *or* **over** jdn/ etw übersetzen
ferryman ['fɛrɪmən] N (*irreg*) Fährmann *m*
fertile ['fəːtaɪl] ADJ fruchtbar; **~ period** fruchtbare Tage *pl*
fertility [fə'tɪlɪtɪ] N Fruchtbarkeit *f*
fertility drug N Fruchtbarkeitsmedikament *nt*
fertilization [fəːtɪlaɪ'zeɪʃən] N (*Biol*) Befruchtung *f*
fertilize ['fəːtɪlaɪz] VT düngen; (*Biol*) befruchten
fertilizer ['fəːtɪlaɪzə^r] N Dünger *m*
fervent ['fəːvənt] ADJ leidenschaftlich; (*admirer*) glühend
fervour, (*US*) **fervor** ['fəːvə^r] N Leidenschaft *f*
fester ['fɛstə^r] VI (*wound*) eitern; (*insult*) nagen; (*row*) sich verschlimmern
festival ['fɛstɪvəl] N Fest *nt*; (*Art, Mus*) Festival *nt*, Festspiele *pl*
festive ['fɛstɪv] ADJ festlich; **the ~ season** (BRIT: *Christmas and New Year*) die Festzeit *f*
festivities [fɛs'tɪvɪtɪz] NPL Feierlichkeiten *pl*
festoon [fɛs'tuːn] VT: **to ~ with** schmücken mit
fetch [fɛtʃ] VT holen; (*sell for*) (ein)bringen; **would you ~ me a glass of water please?** kannst du mir bitte ein Glas Wasser bringen?; **how much did it ~?** wie viel hat es eingebracht?
▸ **fetch up** (*inf*) VI landen (*inf*)
fetching ['fɛtʃɪŋ] ADJ bezaubernd, reizend
fête [feɪt] N Fest *nt*
fetid ['fɛtɪd] ADJ übel riechend
fetish ['fɛtɪʃ] N Fetisch *m*
fetter ['fɛtə^r] VT fesseln; (*horse*) anpflocken; (*fig*) in Fesseln legen
fetters ['fɛtəz] NPL Fesseln *pl*
fettle ['fɛtl] (BRIT) N: **in fine ~** in bester Form
fetus ['fiːtəs] (*US*) N = **foetus**
feud [fjuːd] N Streit *m* ▸ VI im Streit liegen; **a family ~** ein Familienstreit *m*
feudal ['fjuːdl] ADJ (*society etc*) Feudal-
feudalism ['fjuːdlɪzəm] N Feudalismus *m*
fever ['fiːvə^r] N Fieber *nt*; **he has a ~** er hat Fieber
feverish ['fiːvərɪʃ] ADJ fiebrig; (*activity, emotion*) fieberhaft
few [fjuː] ADJ wenige; **a ~** (*adj*) ein paar, einige; (*pron*) ein paar; **a ~ more (days)** noch ein paar (Tage); **they were ~** sie waren nur wenige; **~ succeed** nur wenigen gelingt es; **very ~ survive** nur sehr wenige überleben; **I know a ~** ich kenne einige; **a good ~, quite a ~** ziemlich viele; **in the next/past ~ days** in den nächsten/letzten paar Tagen; **every ~ days/ months** alle paar Tage/Monate
fewer ['fjuːə^r] ADJ weniger; **there are ~ buses on Sundays** Sonntags fahren weniger Busse
fewest ['fjuːɪst] ADJ die wenigsten
FHA (*US*) N ABBR (= *Federal Housing Administration*): **~ loan** Baudarlehen *nt*
fiancé [fɪ'ɑ̃ːŋseɪ] N Verlobte(r) *m*
fiancée [fɪ'ɑ̃ːŋseɪ] N Verlobte *f*
fiasco [fɪ'æskəu] N Fiasko *nt*
fib [fɪb] N Flunkerei *f* (*inf*)
fibre, (*US*) **fiber** ['faɪbə^r] N Faser *f*; (*cloth*) (Faser)stoff *m*; (*roughage*) Ballaststoffe *pl*; (*Anat: tissue*) Gewebe *nt*

f

fibreboard, (*US*) **fiberboard** ['faɪbəbɔːd] N Faserplatte *f*
fibreglass, (*US*) **fiberglass** ['faɪbəglɑːs] N Fiberglas *nt*
fibrositis [faɪbrə'saɪtɪs] N Bindegewebsentzündung *f*
FICA (*US*) N ABBR (= *Federal Insurance Contributions Act*) *Abgabe zur Sozialversicherung*
fickle ['fɪkl] ADJ unbeständig; (*weather*) wechselhaft
fiction ['fɪkʃən] N Erfindung *f*; (*Liter*) Erzählliteratur *f*, Prosaliteratur *f*
fictional ['fɪkʃənl] ADJ erfunden
fictionalize ['fɪkʃnəlaɪz] VT fiktionalisieren
fictitious [fɪk'tɪʃəs] ADJ (*false*) falsch; (*invented*) fiktiv, frei erfunden
fiddle ['fɪdl] N Fiedel *f* (*inf*), Geige *f*; (*fraud, swindle*) Schwindelei *f* ▸ VT (BRIT: *accounts*) frisieren (*inf*); **tax ~** Steuermanipulation *f*; **to work a ~** ein krummes Ding drehen (*inf*)
▸ **fiddle with** VT FUS herumspielen mit
fiddler ['fɪdlə[r]] N Geiger(in) *m(f)*
fiddly ['fɪdlɪ] ADJ knifflig (*inf*); (*object*) fummelig
fidelity [fɪ'dɛlɪtɪ] N Treue *f*; (*accuracy*) Genauigkeit *f*
fidget ['fɪdʒɪt] VI zappeln
fidgety ['fɪdʒɪtɪ] ADJ zappelig
fiduciary [fɪ'djuːʃɪərɪ] N (*Law*) Treuhänder *m*
field [fiːld] N Feld *nt*; (*Sport: ground*) Platz *m*; (*subject, area of interest*) Gebiet *nt*; (*Comput*) Datenfeld *nt* ▸ CPD Feld-; **to lead the ~** das Feld anführen; **~ trip** Exkursion *f*
field day N: **to have a ~** einen herrlichen Tag haben
field glasses NPL Feldstecher *m*
field hospital N Feldlazarett *nt*
field marshal N Feldmarschall *m*
field work N Feldforschung *f*; (*Archaeology, Geog*) Arbeit *f* im Gelände
fiend [fiːnd] N Teufel *m*
fiendish ['fiːndɪʃ] ADJ teuflisch; (*problem*) verzwickt
fierce [fɪəs] ADJ wild; (*look*) böse; (*fighting, wind*) heftig; (*loyalty*) leidenschaftlich; (*enemy*) erbittert; (*heat*) glühend
fiery ['faɪərɪ] ADJ glühend; (*temperament*) feurig, hitzig
FIFA ['fiːfə] N ABBR (= *Fédération Internationale de Football Association*) FIFA *f*
fifteen [fɪf'tiːn] NUM fünfzehn
fifteenth [fɪf'tiːnθ] NUM fünfzehnte(r, s)
fifth [fɪfθ] NUM fünfte(r, s) ▸ N Fünftel *nt*
fiftieth ['fɪftɪɪθ] NUM fünfzigste(r, s)
fifty ['fɪftɪ] NUM fünfzig
fifty-fifty ['fɪftɪ'fɪftɪ] ADJ, ADV halbe-halbe, fifty-fifty; **to go/share ~ with sb** mit jdm halbe-halbe *or* fifty-fifty machen; **we have a ~ chance (of success)** unsere Chancen stehen fifty-fifty
fig [fɪg] N Feige *f*
fight [faɪt] (*pt, pp* **fought**) N Kampf *m*; (*quarrel*) Streit *m*; (*punch-up*) Schlägerei *f* ▸ VT kämpfen mit *or* gegen; (*prejudice etc*) bekämpfen; (*election*) kandidieren bei; (*emotion*) ankämpfen gegen; (*Law: case*) durchkämpfen, durchfechten ▸ VI kämpfen; (*quarrel*) sich streiten; (*punch-up*) sich schlagen; **to put up a ~** sich zur Wehr setzen; **to ~ one's way through a crowd/the undergrowth** sich *dat* einen Weg durch die Menge/das Unterholz bahnen; **to ~ against** bekämpfen; **to ~ for one's rights** für seine Rechte kämpfen
▸ **fight back** VI zurückschlagen; (*Sport*) zurückkämpfen; (*after illness*) zu Kräften kommen ▸ VT FUS unterdrücken
▸ **fight down** VT unterdrücken
▸ **fight off** VT abwehren; (*sleep, urge*) ankämpfen gegen
▸ **fight out** VT: **to ~ it out** es untereinander ausfechten
fighter ['faɪtə[r]] N Kämpfer(in) *m(f)*; (*plane*) Jagdflugzeug *nt*; (*fig*) Kämpfernatur *f*
fighter pilot N Jagdflieger *m*
fighting ['faɪtɪŋ] N Kämpfe *pl*; (*brawl*) Schlägereien *pl*
figment ['fɪgmənt] N: **a ~ of the imagination** ein Hirngespinst *nt*, pure Einbildung *f*
figurative ['fɪgjurətɪv] ADJ bildlich, übertragen; (*style*) gegenständlich
figure ['fɪgə[r]] N Figur *f*; (*illustration*) Abbildung *f*; (*number, statistic, cipher*) Zahl *f*; (*person*) Gestalt *f*; (*personality*) Persönlichkeit *f* ▸ VT (*esp US*) glauben, schätzen ▸ VI eine Rolle spielen; **to put a ~ on sth** eine Zahl für etw angeben; **public ~** Persönlichkeit *f* des öffentlichen Lebens
▸ **figure out** VT ausrechnen
figurehead ['fɪgəhɛd] N Galionsfigur *f*
figure of speech N Redensart *f*, Redewendung *f*
figure skating N Eiskunstlaufen *nt*
Fiji ['fiːdʒiː] N, **Fiji Islands** NPL Fidschi-Inseln *pl*
filament ['fɪləmənt] N Glühfaden *m*; (*Bot*) Staubfaden *m*
filch [fɪltʃ] (*inf*) VT filzen
file [faɪl] N Akte *f*; (*folder*) (Akten)ordner *m*; (*for loose leaf*) (Akten)mappe *f*; (*Comput*) Datei *f*; (*row*) Reihe *f*; (*tool*) Feile *f* ▸ VT ablegen, abheften; (*claim*) einreichen; (*wood, metal, fingernails*) feilen ▸ VI: **to ~ in/out** nacheinander hereinkommen/hinausgehen; **to ~ a suit against sb** eine Klage gegen jdn erheben; **to ~ past** in einer Reihe vorbeigehen; **to ~ for divorce** die Scheidung einreichen
filename ['faɪlneɪm] N (*Comput*) Dateiname *m*
file sharing [-ʃɛərɪŋ] N Filesharing *nt*
filibuster ['fɪlɪbʌstə[r]] (*esp US Pol*) N (*also:* **filibusterer**) Dauerredner(in) *m(f)* ▸ VI filibustern, Obstruktion betreiben
filing ['faɪlɪŋ] N Ablegen *nt*, Abheften *nt*
filing cabinet N Aktenschrank *m*
filing clerk N Angestellte(r) *f(m)* in der Registratur
Filipino [fɪlɪ'piːnəu] N Filipino *m*, Filipina *f*; (*Ling*) Philippinisch *nt*
fill [fɪl] VT füllen; (*space, area*) ausfüllen; (*tooth*) plombieren; (*need*) erfüllen ▸ VI sich füllen

▸ N: **to eat one's ~** sich satt essen; **we've already filled that vacancy** wir haben diese Stelle schon besetzt
▸ **fill in** VT füllen; (*time*) überbrücken; (*form*) ausfüllen ▸ VI: **to ~ in for sb** für jdn einspringen; **to ~ sb in on sth** (*inf*) jdn über etw *acc* ins Bild setzen
▸ **fill out** VT ausfüllen
▸ **fill up** VT füllen ▸ VI (*Aut*) tanken; **~ it up, please** (*Aut*) bitte volltanken
fillet ['fɪlɪt] N Filet *nt* ▸ VT filetieren
fillet steak N Filetsteak *nt*
filling ['fɪlɪŋ] N Füllung *f*; (*for tooth*) Plombe *f*
filling station N Tankstelle *f*
fillip ['fɪlɪp] N (*stimulus*) Ansporn *m*
filly ['fɪlɪ] N Stutfohlen *nt*
film [fɪlm] N Film *m*; (*of powder etc*) Schicht *f*; (*for wrapping*) Plastikfolie *f* ▸ VT, VI filmen
film star N Filmstar *m*
film strip N Filmstreifen *m*
film studio N Filmstudio *nt*
Filofax® ['faɪləufæks] N Filofax® *nt*, Terminplaner *m*
filter ['fɪltəʳ] N Filter *m* ▸ VT filtern
▸ **filter in** VI durchsickern
▸ **filter through** VI = **filter in**
filter coffee N Filterkaffee *m*
filter lane (BRIT) N Abbiegespur *f*
filter tip N Filter *m*
filter-tipped ['fɪltə'tɪpt] ADJ (*cigarette*) Filter-
filth [fɪlθ] N Dreck *m*, Schmutz *m*
filthy ['fɪlθɪ] ADJ dreckig, schmutzig; (*language*) unflätig
fin [fɪn] N Flosse *f*; (*Tech*) Seitenflosse *f*
final ['faɪnl] ADJ letzte(r, s); (*ultimate*) letztendlich; (*definitive*) endgültig ▸ N Finale *nt*, Endspiel *nt*; **finals** NPL (*Univ*) Abschlussprüfung *f*
final demand N letzte Zahlungsaufforderung *f*
finale [fɪ'nɑːlɪ] N Finale *nt*; (*Theat*) Schlussszene *f*
finalist ['faɪnəlɪst] N Endrundenteilnehmer(in) *m(f)*, Finalist(in) *m(f)*
finality [faɪ'nælɪtɪ] N Endgültigkeit *f*; **with an air of ~** mit Bestimmtheit
finalize ['faɪnəlaɪz] VT endgültig festlegen
finally ['faɪnəlɪ] ADV endlich, schließlich; (*lastly*) schließlich, zum Schluss; (*irrevocably*) endgültig
finance [faɪ'næns] N Geldmittel *pl*; (*money management*) Finanzwesen *nt* ▸ VT finanzieren; **finances** NPL (*personal*) Finanzen *pl*, Finanzlage *f*
financial [faɪ'nænʃəl] ADJ finanziell; **~ statement** Bilanz *f*
financially [faɪ'nænʃəlɪ] ADV finanziell
financial year N Geschäftsjahr *nt*
financier [faɪ'nænsɪəʳ] N Finanzier *m*
find [faɪnd] (*pt, pp* **found**) VT finden; (*discover*) entdecken ▸ N Fund *m*; **to ~ sb guilty** jdn für schuldig befinden; **to ~ (some) difficulty in doing sth** (einige) Schwierigkeiten haben, etw zu tun
▸ **find out** VT herausfinden; (*person*) erwischen ▸ VI: **to ~ out about** etwas herausfinden über *+acc*; (*by chance*) etwas erfahren über *+acc*
findings ['faɪndɪŋz] NPL (*Law*) Urteil *nt*; (*of report*) Ergebnis *nt*
fine [faɪn] ADJ fein; (*excellent*) gut; (*thin*) dünn ▸ ADV gut; (*small*) fein ▸ N Geldstrafe *f* ▸ VT mit einer Geldstrafe belegen; **he's ~** es geht ihm gut; **the weather is ~** das Wetter ist schön; **that's cutting it (a bit) ~** das ist aber (ein bisschen) knapp; **you're doing ~** das machen Sie gut
fine arts NPL schöne Künste *pl*
finely ['faɪnlɪ] ADV schön; (*chop*) klein; (*slice*) dünn; (*adjust*) fein
fine print N: **the ~** das Kleingedruckte
finery ['faɪnərɪ] N (*of dress*) Staat *m*
finesse [fɪ'nɛs] N Geschick *nt*
fine-tooth comb ['faɪntuːθ-] N: **to go through sth with a ~** (*fig*) etw genau unter die Lupe nehmen
finger ['fɪŋgəʳ] N Finger *m* ▸ VT befühlen; **little ~** kleiner Finger; **index ~** Zeigefinger *m*
fingernail ['fɪŋgəneɪl] N Fingernagel *m*
fingerprint ['fɪŋgəprɪnt] N Fingerabdruck *m* ▸ VT Fingerabdrücke abnehmen *+dat*
fingerstall ['fɪŋgəstɔːl] N Fingerling *m*
fingertip ['fɪŋgətɪp] N Fingerspitze *f*; **to have sth at one's fingertips** (*to hand*) etw parat haben; (*know well*) etw aus dem Effeff kennen (*inf*)
finicky ['fɪnɪkɪ] ADJ pingelig
finish ['fɪnɪʃ] N Schluss *m*, Ende *nt*; (*Sport*) Finish *nt*; (*polish etc*) Verarbeitung *f* ▸ VT fertig sein mit; (*work*) erledigen; (*book*) auslesen; (*use up*) aufbrauchen ▸ VI enden; (*person*) fertig sein; **to ~ doing sth** mit etw fertig werden; **to ~ third** als Dritter durchs Ziel gehen; **to have finished with sth** mit etw fertig sein; **she's finished with him** sie hat mit ihm Schluss gemacht
▸ **finish off** VT fertig machen; (*kill*) den Gnadenstoß geben
▸ **finish up** VT (*food*) aufessen; (*drink*) austrinken ▸ VI (*end up*) landen
finished ['fɪnɪʃt] ADJ fertig; (*performance*) ausgereift; (*inf: tired*) erledigt
finishing line ['fɪnɪʃɪŋ-] N Ziellinie *f*
finishing school ['fɪnɪʃɪŋ-] N höhere Mädchenschule *f* (*in der auch Etikette und gesellschaftliches Verhalten gelehrt wird*)
finishing touches ['fɪnɪʃɪŋ-] NPL: **the ~** der letzte Schliff
finite ['faɪnaɪt] ADJ begrenzt; (*verb*) finit
Finland ['fɪnlənd] N Finnland *nt*
Finn [fɪn] N Finne *m*, Finnin *f*
Finnish ['fɪnɪʃ] ADJ finnisch ▸ N (*Ling*) Finnisch *nt*
fiord [fjɔːd] N = **fjord**
fir [fəːʳ] N Tanne *f*
fire ['faɪəʳ] N Feuer *nt*; (*in hearth*) (Kamin)feuer *nt*; (*accidental fire*) Brand *m* ▸ VT abschießen; (*imagination*) beflügeln; (*enthusiasm*) befeuern; (*inf: dismiss*) feuern ▸ VI feuern, schießen;

f

to ~ a gun ein Gewehr abschießen; **to be on ~** brennen; **to set ~ to sth, set sth on ~** etw anzünden; **insured against ~** feuerversichert; **electric/gas ~** Elektro-/Gasofen *m*; **to come/be under ~ (from)** unter Beschuss (von) geraten/stehen

fire alarm N Feuermelder *m*

firearm ['faɪərɑ:m] N Feuerwaffe *f*, Schusswaffe *f*

fire brigade N Feuerwehr *f*

fire chief N Branddirektor *m*

fire department (US) N Feuerwehr *f*

fire door N Feuertür *f*

fire drill N Probealarm *m*

fire engine N Feuerwehrauto *nt*

fire escape N Feuertreppe *f*

fire exit N Notausgang *m*

fire-extinguisher ['faɪərɪk'stɪŋgwɪʃəʳ] N Feuerlöscher *m*

firefighter ['faɪəfaɪtəʳ] N Feuerwehrmann *m*, Feuerwehrfrau *f*

fireguard ['faɪəgɑ:d] (BRIT) N (Schutz)gitter *nt* (*vor dem Kamin*)

fire hazard N: **that's a ~** das ist feuergefährlich

fire hydrant N Hydrant *m*

fire insurance N Feuerversicherung *f*

fireman ['faɪəmən] N (*irreg*) Feuerwehrmann *m*

fireplace ['faɪəpleɪs] N Kamin *m*

fireplug ['faɪəplʌg] (US) N = **fire hydrant**

fire practice N = **fire drill**

fireproof ['faɪəpru:f] ADJ feuerfest

fire regulations NPL Brandschutzbestimmungen *pl*

fire screen N Ofenschirm *m*

fireside ['faɪəsaɪd] N: **by the ~** am Kamin

fire station N Feuerwache *f*

firewood ['faɪəwud] N Brennholz *nt*

fireworks ['faɪəwə:ks] NPL Feuerwerkskörper *pl*; (*display*) Feuerwerk *nt*

firing line ['faɪərɪŋ-] N Feuerlinie *f*, Schusslinie *f*; **to be in the ~** (*fig*) in der Schusslinie sein

firing squad ['faɪərɪŋ-] N Exekutionskommando *nt*

firm [fə:m] ADJ fest; (*mattress*) hart; (*measures*) durchgreifend ▸ N Firma *f*; **to be a ~ believer in sth** fest von etw überzeugt sein

firmly ['fə:mlɪ] ADV fest; hart; (*definitely*) entschlossen

firmness ['fə:mnɪs] N Festigkeit *f*; Härte *f*; (*definiteness*) Entschlossenheit *f*

first [fə:st] ADJ erste(r, s) ▸ ADV als Erste(r, s); (*before other things*) zuerst; (*when listing reasons etc*) erstens; (*for the first time*) zum ersten Mal ▸ N Erste(r, s); (*Aut*: *also*: **first gear**) der erste Gang; (BRIT *Scol*) ≈ Eins *f*; **the ~ of January** der erste Januar; **at ~** zuerst, zunächst; **~ of all** vor allem; **in the ~ instance** zuerst *or* zunächst einmal; **I'll do it ~ thing (tomorrow)** ich werde es (morgen) als Erstes tun; **from the very ~** gleich von Anfang an

first aid N erste Hilfe *f*

first-aid kit [fə:st'eɪd-] N Erste-Hilfe-Ausrüstung *f*

first-class ['fə:st'klɑ:s] ADJ erstklassig; (*carriage, ticket*) Erste(r)-Klasse-; (*post*) bevorzugt befördert ▸ ADV (*travel, send*) erster Klasse

first-hand ['fə:st'hænd] ADJ aus erster Hand

first lady (US) N First Lady *f*; **the ~ of jazz** die Königin des Jazz

firstly ['fə:stlɪ] ADV erstens, zunächst einmal

first name N Vorname *m*

first night N Premiere *f*

first-rate ['fə:st'reɪt] ADJ erstklassig

first-time buyer ['fə:sttaɪm-] N *jd, der zum ersten Mal ein Haus/eine Wohnung kauft*

fir tree N Tannenbaum *m*

fiscal ['fɪskl] ADJ (*year*) Steuer-; (*policies*) Finanz-

fish [fɪʃ] N INV Fisch *m* ▸ VT (*area*) fischen in *+dat*; (*river*) angeln in *+dat* ▸ VI fischen; (*as sport, hobby*) angeln; **to go fishing** fischen/angeln gehen
▸ **fish out** VT herausfischen

fish bone N (Fisch)gräte *f*

fish cake N Fischfrikadelle *f*

fisherman ['fɪʃəmən] N (*irreg*) Fischer *m*

fishery ['fɪʃərɪ] N Fischereigebiet *nt*

fish factory (BRIT) N Fischfabrik *f*

fish farm N Fischzucht(anlage) *f*

fishfingers [fɪʃ'fɪŋgəz] (BRIT) NPL Fischstäbchen *pl*

fish-hook ['fɪʃhuk] N Angelhaken *m*

fishing ['fɪʃɪŋ] N Fischen *nt*; (*with rod*) Angeln *nt*; (*as industry*) Fischerei *f*

fishing boat N Fischerboot *nt*

fishing line N Angelschnur *f*

fishing net N Fischnetz *nt*

fishing rod N Angelrute *f*

fishing tackle N Angelgeräte *pl*

fish market N Fischmarkt *m*

fishmonger ['fɪʃmʌŋgəʳ] (*esp* BRIT) N Fischhändler(in) *m(f)*

fishmonger's ['fɪʃmʌŋgəz], **fishmonger's shop** (*esp* BRIT) N Fischgeschäft *nt*

fish slice (BRIT) N Fischvorlegemesser *nt*

fish sticks (US) NPL = **fishfingers**

fish tank N Aquarium *nt*

fishy ['fɪʃɪ] (*inf*) ADJ verdächtig, faul

fission ['fɪʃən] N Spaltung *f*; **atomic** *or* **nuclear ~** Atomspaltung *f*, Kernspaltung *f*

fissure ['fɪʃəʳ] N Riss *m*, Spalte *f*

fist [fɪst] N Faust *f*

fist fight N Faustkampf *m*

fit [fɪt] ADJ geeignet; (*healthy*) gesund; (*Sport*) fit ▸ VT passen *+dat*; (*adjust*) anpassen; (*match*) entsprechen *+dat*; (*be suitable for*) passen auf *+acc*; (*put in*) einbauen; (*attach*) anbringen; (*equip*) ausstatten ▸ VI passen; (*parts*) zusammenpassen; (*in space, gap*) hineinpassen ▸ N (*Med*) Anfall *m*; **to ~ the description** der Beschreibung entsprechen; **~ to** bereit zu; **~ to eat** essbar; **~ to drink** trinkbar; **to be ~ to keep** es wert sein, aufbewahrt zu werden; **~ for** geeignet für; **~ for work** arbeitsfähig; **to keep ~** sich fit halten; **do as you think** *or* **see ~** tun Sie, was Sie für richtig halten; **a ~ of anger** ein Wutanfall *m*; **a ~ of pride** eine Anwandlung von Stolz; **to have a ~** einen Anfall haben;

(*inf, fig*) einen Anfall kriegen; **this dress is a good ~** dieses Kleid sitzt *or* passt gut; **by fits and starts** unregelmäßig
▸ **fit in** VI (*person*) sich einfügen; (*object*) hineinpassen ▸ VT (*fig: appointment*) unterbringen, einschieben; (*visitor*) Zeit finden für; **to ~ in with sb's plans** sich mit jds Plänen vereinbaren lassen
fitful ['fɪtful] ADJ unruhig
fitment ['fɪtmənt] N Einrichtungsgegenstand *m*
fitness ['fɪtnɪs] N Gesundheit *f*; (*Sport*) Fitness *f*
fitness instructor N Fitnesstrainer(in) *m(f)*
fitted carpet ['fɪtɪd-] N Teppichboden *m*
fitted cupboards ['fɪtɪd-] NPL Einbauschränke *pl*
fitted kitchen ['fɪtɪd-] (BRIT) N Einbauküche *f*
fitter ['fɪtə^r] N Monteur *m*; (*for machines*) (Maschinen)schlosser *m*
fitting ['fɪtɪŋ] ADJ passend; (*thanks*) gebührend ▸ N (*of dress*) Anprobe *f*; (*of piece of equipment*) Installation *f*; **fittings** NPL Ausstattung *f*
fitting room N Anprobe(kabine) *f*
five [faɪv] NUM fünf
five-day week ['faɪvdeɪ-] N Fünftagewoche *f*
fiver ['faɪvə^r] (*inf*) N (BRIT) Fünfpfundschein *m*; (US) Fünfdollarschein *m*
fix [fɪks] VT (*attach*) befestigen; (*arrange*) festsetzen, festlegen; (*mend*) reparieren; (*meal, drink*) machen; (*inf*) manipulieren ▸ N: **to be in a ~** in der Patsche *or* Klemme sitzen; **to ~ sth to/on sth** etw an/auf etw *dat* befestigen; **to ~ one's eyes/attention on** seinen Blick/seine Aufmerksamkeit richten auf *+acc*; **the fight was a ~** (*inf*) der Kampf war eine abgekartete Sache
▸ **fix up** VT arrangieren; **to ~ sb up with sth** jdm etw besorgen
fixation [fɪk'seɪʃən] N Fixierung *f*
fixative ['fɪksətɪv] N Fixativ *nt*
fixed [fɪkst] ADJ fest; (*ideas*) fix; (*smile*) starr; **~ charge** Pauschale *f*; **how are you ~ for money?** wie sieht es bei dir mit dem Geld aus?
fixed assets NPL Anlagevermögen *nt*
fixture ['fɪkstʃə^r] N Ausstattungsgegenstand *m*; (*Football etc*) Spiel *nt*; (*Athletics etc*) Veranstaltung *f*
fizz [fɪz] VI sprudeln; (*firework*) zischen
fizzle out ['fɪzl-] VI (*plan*) im Sande verlaufen; (*interest*) sich verlieren
fizzy ['fɪzɪ] ADJ sprudelnd
fjord [fjɔ:d] N Fjord *m*
FL, Fla. (US) ABBR (*Post*) = **Florida**
flabbergasted ['flæbəgɑ:stɪd] ADJ verblüfft
flabby ['flæbɪ] ADJ schwammig, wabbelig (*inf*)
flag [flæg] N Fahne *f*; (*of country*) Flagge *f*; (*for signalling*) Signalflagge *f*; (*also*: **flagstone**) (Stein)platte *f* ▸ VI erlahmen; **~ of convenience** Billigflagge *f*; **to ~ down** anhalten
flagon ['flægən] N Flasche *f*; (*jug*) Krug *m*
flagpole ['flægpəul] N Fahnenstange *f*
flagrant ['fleɪgrənt] ADJ flagrant; (*injustice*) himmelschreiend
flagship ['flægʃɪp] N Flaggschiff *nt*
flagstone ['flægstəun] N (Stein)platte *f*
flag stop (US) N Bedarfshaltestelle *f*
flair [flɛə^r] N Talent *nt*; (*style*) Flair *nt*
flak [flæk] N Flakfeuer *nt*; **to get a lot of ~ (for sth)** (*inf: criticism*) (wegen etw) unter Beschuss geraten
flake [fleɪk] N Splitter *m*; (*of snow, soap powder*) Flocke *f* ▸ VI (*also*: **flake off**) abblättern, absplittern
▸ **flake out** (*inf*) VI aus den Latschen kippen; (*go to sleep*) einschlafen
flaky ['fleɪkɪ] ADJ brüchig; (*skin*) schuppig
flaky pastry N Blätterteig *m*
flamboyant [flæm'bɔɪənt] ADJ extravagant
flame [fleɪm] N Flamme *f*; **to burst into flames** in Flammen aufgehen; **an old ~** (*inf*) eine alte Flamme
flaming ['fleɪmɪŋ] (*inf!*) ADJ verdammt
flamingo [flə'mɪŋgəu] N Flamingo *m*
flammable ['flæməbl] ADJ leicht entzündbar
flan [flæn] N Kuchen *m*; **~ case** Tortenboden *m*
Flanders ['flɑ:ndəz] N Flandern *nt*
flange [flændʒ] N Flansch *m*
flank [flæŋk] N Flanke *f* ▸ VT flankieren
flannel ['flænl] N Flanell *m*; (BRIT: *also*: **face flannel**) Waschlappen *m*; (*inf*) Geschwafel *nt*; **flannels** NPL (*trousers*) Flanellhose *f*
flannelette [flænə'lɛt] N Baumwollflanell *m*, Biber *m or nt*
flap [flæp] N Klappe *f*; (*of envelope*) Lasche *f* ▸ VT schlagen mit ▸ VI flattern; (*inf*: *also*: **be in a flap**) in heller Aufregung sein
flapjack ['flæpdʒæk] N (*US: pancake*) Pfannkuchen *m*; (BRIT: *biscuit*) Haferkeks *m*
flare [flɛə^r] N Leuchtsignal *nt*; (*in skirt etc*) Weite *f*
▸ **flare up** VI auflodern; (*person*) aufbrausen; (*fighting, violence, trouble*) ausbrechen; *see also* **flared**
flared ['flɛəd] ADJ (*trousers*) mit Schlag; (*skirt*) ausgestellt
flash [flæʃ] N Aufblinken *nt*; (*also*: **newsflash**) Eilmeldung *f*; (*Phot*) Blitz *m*, Blitzlicht *nt*; (*US: torch*) Taschenlampe *f* ▸ VT aufleuchten lassen; (*news, message*) durchgeben; (*look, smile*) zuwerfen ▸ VI aufblinken; (*light on ambulance*) blinken; (*eyes*) blitzen; **in a ~** im Nu; **quick as a ~** blitzschnell; **~ of inspiration** Geistesblitz *m*; **to ~ one's headlights** die Lichthupe betätigen; **the thought flashed through his mind** der Gedanke schoss ihm durch den Kopf; **to ~ by** *or* **past** vorbeiflitzen (*inf*)
flashback ['flæʃbæk] N Rückblende *f*
flashbulb ['flæʃbʌlb] N Blitzbirne *f*
flash card N Leselernkarte *f*
flashcube ['flæʃkju:b] N Blitzwürfel *m*
flash drive N USB-Stick *m*
flasher ['flæʃə^r] N (*Aut*) Lichthupe *f*; (*inf!: man*) Exhibitionist *m*
flashlight ['flæʃlaɪt] N Blitzlicht *nt*
flash point N (*fig*): **to be at ~** auf dem Siedepunkt sein
flashy ['flæʃɪ] (*pej*) ADJ auffällig, protzig

flask [flɑ:sk] N Flakon *m*; (*Chem*) Glaskolben *m*; (*also*: **vacuum flask**) Thermosflasche® *f*
flat [flæt] ADJ flach; (*surface*) eben; (*tyre*) platt; (*battery*) leer; (*beer*) schal; (*refusal, denial*) glatt; (*note, voice*) zu tief; (*rate, fee*) Pauschal- ▶ N (BRIT: *apartment*) Wohnung *f*; (*Aut*) (Reifen)panne *f*; (*Mus*) Erniedrigungszeichen *nt*; **to work ~ out** auf Hochtouren arbeiten; **~ rate of pay** Pauschallohn *m*
flat-footed ['flæt'futɪd] ADJ: **to be ~** Plattfüße *pl* haben
flatly ['flætlɪ] ADV (*refuse, deny*) glatt, kategorisch
flatmate ['flætmeɪt] (BRIT) N Mitbewohner(in) *m(f)*
flatness ['flætnɪs] N Flachheit *f*
flat screen N Flachbildschirm *m*
flat-screen monitor ['flætskri:n-] N Flachbildschirm *m*
flatten ['flætn] VT (*also*: **flatten out**) (ein)ebnen; (*paper, fabric etc*) glätten; (*building, city*) dem Erdboden gleichmachen; (*crop*) zu Boden drücken; (*inf*: *person*) umhauen; **to ~ o.s. against a wall/door** *etc* sich platt gegen *or* an eine Wand/Tür *etc* drücken
flatter ['flætəʳ] VT schmeicheln +*dat*
flatterer ['flætərəʳ] N Schmeichler(in) *m(f)*
flattering ['flætərɪŋ] ADJ schmeichelhaft; (*dress etc*) vorteilhaft
flattery ['flætərɪ] N Schmeichelei *f*
flatulence ['flætjuləns] N Blähungen *pl*
flaunt [flɔ:nt] VT zur Schau stellen, protzen mit
flavour, (US) **flavor** ['fleɪvəʳ] N Geschmack *m*; (*of ice-cream etc*) Geschmacksrichtung *f* ▶ VT Geschmack verleihen +*dat*; **to give** *or* **add ~ to** Geschmack verleihen +*dat*; **music with an African ~** (*fig*) Musik mit einer afrikanischen Note; **strawberry-flavoured** mit Erdbeergeschmack
flavouring, (US) **flavoring** ['fleɪvərɪŋ] N Aroma *nt*
flaw [flɔ:] N Fehler *m*
flawless ['flɔ:lɪs] ADJ (*performance*) fehlerlos; (*complexion*) makellos
flax [flæks] N Flachs *m*
flaxen ['flæksən] ADJ (*hair*) flachsblond
flea [fli:] N Floh *m*
flea market N Flohmarkt *m*
fleck [flɛk] N Tupfen *m*, Punkt *m*; (*of dust*) Flöckchen *nt*; (*of mud, paint, colour*) Fleck(en) *m* ▶ VT bespritzen; **brown flecked with white** braun mit weißen Punkten
fled [flɛd] PT, PP *of* **flee**
fledgeling, fledgling ['flɛdʒlɪŋ] N Jungvogel *m* ▶ ADJ (*inexperienced*: *actor etc*) Nachwuchs-; (*newly started*: *business etc*) jung
flee [fli:] (*pt, pp* **fled**) VT fliehen *or* flüchten vor +*dat*; (*country*) fliehen *or* flüchten aus ▶ VI fliehen, flüchten
fleece [fli:s] N Schafwolle *f*; (*sheep's coat*) Schaffell *nt*, Vlies *nt* ▶ VT (*inf*: *cheat*) schröpfen
fleecy ['fli:sɪ] ADJ flauschig; (*cloud*) Schäfchen-
fleet [fli:t] N Flotte *f*; (*of lorries, cars*) Fuhrpark *m*
fleeting ['fli:tɪŋ] ADJ flüchtig
Flemish ['flɛmɪʃ] ADJ flämisch ▶ N (*Ling*) Flämisch *nt*; **the Flemish** NPL die Flamen
flesh [flɛʃ] N Fleisch *nt*; (*of fruit*) Fruchtfleisch *nt*
▶ **flesh out** VT ausgestalten
flesh wound [-wu:nd] N Fleischwunde *f*
flew [flu:] PT *of* **fly**
flex [flɛks] N Kabel *nt* ▶ VT beugen; (*muscles*) spielen lassen
flexibility [flɛksɪ'bɪlɪtɪ] N Flexibilität *f*; Biegsamkeit *f*
flexible ['flɛksəbl] ADJ flexibel; (*material*) biegsam
flexitime ['flɛksɪtaɪm] N gleitende Arbeitszeit *f*, Gleitzeit *f*
flick [flɪk] N (*of finger*) Schnipsen *nt*; (*of hand*) Wischen *nt*; (*of whip*) Schnalzen *nt*; (*of towel etc*) Schlagen *nt*; (*of switch*) Knipsen *nt* ▶ VT schnipsen; (*with hand*) wischen; (*whip*) knallen mit; (*switch*) knipsen; **flicks** NPL (*inf*) Kino *nt*; **to ~ a towel at sb** mit einem Handtuch nach jdm schlagen
▶ **flick through** VT FUS durchblättern
flicker ['flɪkəʳ] VI flackern; (*eyelids*) zucken ▶ N Flackern *nt*; (*of pain, fear*) Aufflackern *nt*; (*of smile*) Anflug *m*; (*of eyelid*) Zucken *nt*
flick knife (BRIT) N Klappmesser *nt*
flier ['flaɪəʳ] N Flieger(in) *m(f)*
flight [flaɪt] N Flug *m*; (*escape*) Flucht *f*; (*also*: **flight of steps**) Treppe *f*; **to take ~** die Flucht ergreifen; **to put to ~** in die Flucht schlagen
flight attendant (US) N Flugbegleiter(in) *m(f)*
flight crew N Flugbesatzung *f*
flight deck N (*Aviat*) Cockpit *nt*; (*Naut*) Flugdeck *nt*
flight path N Flugbahn *f*
flight recorder N Flugschreiber *m*
flimsy ['flɪmzɪ] ADJ leicht, dünn; (*building*) leicht gebaut; (*excuse*) fadenscheinig; (*evidence*) nicht stichhaltig
flinch [flɪntʃ] VI zusammenzucken; **to ~ from** zurückschrecken vor +*dat*
fling [flɪŋ] (*pt, pp* **flung**) VT schleudern; (*arms*) werfen; (*oneself*) stürzen ▶ N (flüchtige) Affäre *f*
flint [flɪnt] N Feuerstein *m*
flip [flɪp] VT (*switch*) knipsen; (*coin*) werfen; (US: *pancake*) umdrehen ▶ VI: **to ~ for sth** (US) um etw mit einer Münze knobeln
▶ **flip through** VT FUS durchblättern; (*records etc*) durchgehen
flipchart ['flɪptʃɑ:t] N Flipchart *nt*
flippant ['flɪpənt] ADJ leichtfertig
flipper ['flɪpəʳ] N Flosse *f*; (*for swimming*) (Schwimm)flosse *f*
flip side N (*of record*) B-Seite *f*
flirt [flə:t] VI flirten; (*with idea*) liebäugeln ▶ N: **he/she is a ~** er/sie flirtet gern
flirtation [flə:'teɪʃən] N Flirt *m*
flit [flɪt] VI flitzen; (*expression, smile*) huschen
float [fləut] N Schwimmkork *m*; (*for fishing*) Schwimmer *m*; (*lorry*) Festwagen *m*; (*money*) Wechselgeld *nt* ▶ VI schwimmen; (*swimmer*) treiben; (*through air*) schweben; (*currency*)

floaten ▶ VT (*currency*) freigeben, floaten lassen; (*company*) gründen; (*idea, plan*) in den Raum stellen
▶ **float around** VI im Umlauf sein; (*person*) herumschweben (*inf*); (*object*) herumfliegen (*inf*)

flock [flɔk] N Herde *f*; (*of birds*) Schwarm *m* ▶ VI: **to ~ to** (*place*) strömen nach; (*event*) in Scharen kommen zu

floe [fləu] N (*also*: **ice floe**) Eisscholle *f*

flog [flɔg] VT auspeitschen; (*inf: sell*) verscherbeln

flood [flʌd] N Überschwemmung *f*; (*of letters, imports etc*) Flut *f* ▶ VT überschwemmen; (*Aut*) absaufen lassen (*inf*) ▶ VI überschwemmt werden; **to be in ~** Hochwasser führen; **to ~ the market** den Markt überschwemmen; **to ~ into Hungary/the square/the palace** nach Ungarn/auf den Platz/in den Palast strömen

flooding ['flʌdɪŋ] N Überschwemmung *f*

floodlight ['flʌdlaɪt] N Flutlicht *nt* ▶ VT (*irreg: like* **light**) (mit Flutlicht) beleuchten; (*building*) anstrahlen

floodlit ['flʌdlɪt] PT, PP *of* **floodlight** ▶ ADJ (mit Flutlicht) beleuchtet; (*building*) angestrahlt

flood tide N Flut *f*

floodwater ['flʌdwɔːtəʳ] N Hochwasser *nt*

floor [flɔːʳ] N (Fuß)boden *m*; (*storey*) Stock *nt*; (*of sea, valley*) Boden *m* ▶ VT (*subj: blow*) zu Boden werfen; (*: question, remark*) die Sprache verschlagen *+dat*; **on the ~** auf dem Boden; **ground ~** (BRIT), **first ~** (US) Erdgeschoss *nt*, Erdgeschoß *nt* (ÖSTERR); **first ~** (BRIT), **second ~** (US) erster Stock *m*; **top ~** oberstes Stockwerk *nt*; **to have the ~** (*speaker: at meeting*) das Wort haben

floorboard ['flɔːbɔːd] N Diele *f*

flooring ['flɔːrɪŋ] N (Fuß)boden *m*; (*covering*) Fußbodenbelag *m*

floor lamp (US) N Stehlampe *f*

floor show N Show *f*, Vorstellung *f*

floorwalker ['flɔːwɔːkəʳ] (*esp US*) N Ladenaufsicht *f*

floozy ['fluːzɪ] (*inf*) N Flittchen *nt*

flop [flɔp] N Reinfall *m* ▶ VI (*play, book*) durchfallen; (*fall*) sich fallen lassen; (*scheme*) ein Reinfall sein

floppy ['flɔpɪ] ADJ schlaff, schlapp ▶ N (*also*: **floppy disk**) Diskette *f*, Floppy Disk *f*; **~ hat** Schlapphut *m*

floppy disk N Diskette *f*, Floppy Disk *f*

flora ['flɔːrə] N Flora *f*

floral ['flɔːrl] ADJ geblümt

Florence ['flɔrəns] N Florenz *nt*

Florentine ['flɔrəntaɪn] ADJ florentinisch

florid ['flɔrɪd] ADJ (*style*) blumig; (*complexion*) kräftig

florist ['flɔrɪst] N Blumenhändler(in) *m(f)*

florist's ['flɔrɪsts], **florist's shop** N Blumengeschäft *nt*

flotation [fləu'teɪʃən] N (*of shares*) Auflegung *f*; (*of company*) Umwandlung *f* in eine Aktiengesellschaft

flotsam ['flɔtsəm] N (*also*: **flotsam and jetsam**) Strandgut *nt*; (*floating*) Treibgut *nt*

flounce [flauns] N Volant *m*
▶ **flounce out** VI hinausstolzieren

flounder ['flaundəʳ] VI sich abstrampeln; (*fig: speaker*) ins Schwimmen kommen; (*economy*) in Schwierigkeiten geraten ▶ N Flunder *f*

flour ['flauəʳ] N Mehl *nt*

flourish ['flʌrɪʃ] VI gedeihen; (*business*) blühen, florieren ▶ VT schwenken ▶ N (*in writing*) Schnörkel *m*; (*bold gesture*): **with a ~** mit einer schwungvollen Bewegung

flourishing ['flʌrɪʃɪŋ] ADJ gut gehend, florierend

flout [flaut] VT sich hinwegsetzen über *+acc*

flow [fləu] N Fluss *m*; (*of sea*) Flut *f* ▶ VI fließen; (*clothes, hair*) wallen

flow chart N Flussdiagramm *nt*

flow diagram N = **flow chart**

flower ['flauəʳ] N Blume *f*; (*blossom*) Blüte *f* ▶ VI blühen; **to be in ~** blühen

flowerbed ['flauəbɛd] N Blumenbeet *nt*

flowerpot ['flauəpɔt] N Blumentopf *m*

flowery ['flauərɪ] ADJ blumig; (*pattern*) Blumen-

flown [fləun] PP *of* **fly**

flu [fluː] N Grippe *f*

fluctuate ['flʌktjueɪt] VI schwanken; (*opinions, attitudes*) sich ändern

fluctuation [flʌktju'eɪʃən] N: **~ (in)** Schwankung *f* (*+gen*)

flue [fluː] N Rauchfang *m*, Rauchabzug *m*

fluency ['fluːənsɪ] N Flüssigkeit *f*; **his ~ in German** sein flüssiges Deutsch

fluent ['fluːənt] ADJ flüssig; **he speaks ~ German, he's ~ in German** er spricht fließend Deutsch

fluently ['fluːəntlɪ] ADV flüssig; (*speak a language*) fließend

fluff [flʌf] N Fussel *m*; (*fur*) Flaum *m* ▶ VT (*inf: do badly*) verpatzen; (*also*: **fluff out**) aufplustern

fluffy ['flʌfɪ] ADJ flaumig; (*jacket etc*) weich, kuschelig; **~ toy** Kuscheltier *nt*

fluid ['fluːɪd] ADJ fließend; (*situation, arrangement*) unklar ▶ N Flüssigkeit *f*

fluid ounce (BRIT) N flüssige Unze *f* (*= 28 ml*)

fluke [fluːk] (*inf*) N Glücksfall *m*; **by a ~** durch einen glücklichen Zufall

flummox ['flʌməks] VT verwirren, durcheinanderbringen

flung [flʌŋ] PT, PP *of* **fling**

flunky ['flʌŋkɪ] N Lakai *m*

fluorescent [fluə'rɛsnt] ADJ fluoreszierend; (*paint*) Leucht-; (*light*) Neon-

fluoride ['fluəraɪd] N Fluorid *nt*

fluorine ['fluəriːn] N Fluor *nt*

flurry ['flʌrɪ] N (*of snow*) Gestöber *nt*; **a ~ of activity/excitement** hektische Aktivität/Aufregung

flush [flʌʃ] N Röte *f*; (*fig: of beauty etc*) Blüte *f* ▶ VT (durch)spülen, (aus)spülen ▶ VI erröten ▶ ADJ: **~ with** auf gleicher Ebene mit; **~ against** direkt an *+dat*; **in the first ~ of youth** in der ersten Jugendblüte; **in the first ~ of freedom** im ersten Freiheitstaumel; **hot flushes** (BRIT)

f

Hitzewallungen *pl*; **to ~ the toilet** spülen, die Wasserspülung betätigen
▸**flush out** VT aufstöbern
flushed [flʌʃt] ADJ rot
fluster ['flʌstəʳ] N: **in a ~** nervös; (*confused*) durcheinander ▸VT nervös machen; (*confuse*) durcheinanderbringen
flustered ['flʌstəd] ADJ nervös; (*confused*) durcheinander
flute [flu:t] N Querflöte *f*
fluted ['flu:tɪd] ADJ gerillt; (*column*) kanneliert
flutter ['flʌtəʳ] N Flattern *nt*; (*of panic, nerves*) kurzer Anfall *m*; (*of excitement*) Beben *nt* ▸VI flattern; (*person*) tänzeln; **to have a ~** (BRIT *inf*: *gamble*) sein Glück (beim Wetten) versuchen
flux [flʌks] N: **in a state of ~** im Fluss
fly [flaɪ] (*pt* **flew**, *pp* **flown**) N Fliege *f*; (*on trousers*: *also*: **flies**) (Hosen)schlitz *m* ▸VT fliegen; (*kite*) steigen lassen ▸VI fliegen; (*escape*) fliehen; (*flag*) wehen; **to ~ open** auffliegen; **to ~ off the handle** an die Decke gehen (*inf*); **pieces of metal went flying everywhere** überall flogen Metallteile herum; **she came flying into the room** sie kam ins Zimmer gesaust; **her glasses flew off** die Brille flog ihr aus dem Gesicht
▸**fly away** VI wegfliegen
▸**fly in** VI einfliegen; **he flew in yesterday** er ist gestern mit dem Flugzeug gekommen
▸**fly off** VI = **fly away**
▸**fly out** VI ausfliegen; **he flew out yesterday** er ist gestern hingeflogen
fly-drive ['flaɪdraɪv] N Urlaub *m* mit Flug und Mietwagen
fly-fishing ['flaɪfɪʃɪŋ] N Fliegenfischen *nt*
flying ['flaɪɪŋ] N Fliegen *nt* ▸ADJ: **a ~ visit** ein Blitzbesuch *m*; **he doesn't like ~** er fliegt nicht gerne; **with ~ colours** mit fliegenden Fahnen
flying buttress N Strebebogen *m*
flying picket N mobiler Streikposten *m*
flying saucer N fliegende Untertasse *f*
flying squad N mobiles Einsatzkommando *nt*
flying start N: **to get off to a ~** (*Sport*) hervorragend wegkommen; (*fig*) einen glänzenden Start haben
flyleaf ['flaɪli:f] N Vorsatzblatt *nt*
flyover ['flaɪəuvəʳ] N (BRIT) Überführung *f*; (US) Luftparade *f*
fly-past ['flaɪpɑ:st] N Luftparade *f*
flysheet ['flaɪʃi:t] N (*for tent*) Überzelt *nt*
flyweight ['flaɪweɪt] N Fliegengewicht *nt*
flywheel ['flaɪwi:l] N Schwungrad *nt*
FM ABBR (BRIT *Mil*) = **field marshal**; (*Radio*: = *frequency modulation*) FM, ≈ UKW
FMB (US) N ABBR (= *Federal Maritime Board*) *Dachausschuss der Handelsmarine*
FMCS (US) N ABBR (= *Federal Mediation and Conciliation Service*) *Schlichtungsstelle für Arbeitskonflikte*
FO (BRIT) N ABBR = **Foreign Office**
foal [fəul] N Fohlen *nt*
foam [fəum] N Schaum *m*; (*also*: **foam rubber**) Schaumgummi *m* ▸VI schäumen
fob [fɔb] VT: **to ~ sb off** jdn abspeisen ▸N (*also*: **watch fob**) Uhrkette *f*
f.o.b. ABBR (*Comm*: = *free on board*) frei Schiff
foc (BRIT) ABBR (*Comm*: = *free of charge*) gratis
focal point ['fəukl-] N Mittelpunkt *m*; (*of camera, telescope etc*) Brennpunkt *m*
focus ['fəukəs] (*pl* **focuses**) N Brennpunkt *m*; (*of storm*) Zentrum *nt* ▸VT einstellen; (*light rays*) bündeln ▸VI: **to ~ (on)** (*with camera*) klar *or* scharf einstellen +*acc*; (*person*) sich konzentrieren (auf +*acc*); **in/out of ~** (*camera etc*) scharf/unscharf eingestellt; (*photograph*) scharf/unscharf
focus group N (*Pol*) Fokusgruppe *f*
fodder ['fɔdəʳ] N Futter *nt*
FoE N ABBR (= *Friends of the Earth*) *Umweltschutzorganisation*
foe [fəu] N Feind(in) *m(f)*
foetus, (US) **fetus** ['fi:təs] N Fötus *m*, Fetus *m*
fog [fɔg] N Nebel *m*
fogbound ['fɔgbaund] ADJ (*airport*) wegen Nebel geschlossen
foggy ['fɔgɪ] ADJ neb(e)lig
fog lamp, (US) **fog light** N (*Aut*) Nebelscheinwerfer *m*
foible ['fɔɪbl] N Eigenheit *f*
foil [fɔɪl] VT vereiteln ▸N Folie *f*; (*complement*) Kontrast *m*; (*Fencing*) Florett *nt*; **to act as a ~ to** einen Kontrast darstellen zu
foist [fɔɪst] VT: **to ~ sth on sb** (*goods*) jdm etw andrehen; (*task*) etw an jdn abschieben; (*ideas, views*) jdm etw aufzwingen
fold [fəuld] N Falte *f*; (*Agr*) Pferch *m*; (*fig*) Schoß *m* ▸VT (zusammen)falten; (*arms*) verschränken ▸VI (*business*) eingehen (*inf*)
▸**fold up** VI sich zusammenfalten lassen; (*bed, table*) sich zusammenklappen lassen; (*business*) eingehen (*inf*) ▸VT zusammenfalten
folder ['fəuldəʳ] N Aktenmappe *f*; (*binder*) Hefter *m*; (*brochure*) Informationsblatt *nt*
folding ['fəuldɪŋ] ADJ (*chair, bed*) Klapp-
foliage ['fəulɪɪdʒ] N Laubwerk *nt*
folk [fəuk] NPL Leute *pl* ▸CPD Volks-; **my folks** (*parents*) meine alten Herrschaften
folklore ['fəuklɔ:ʳ] N Folklore *f*
folk music N Volksmusik *f*; (*contemporary*) Folk *m*
folk song N Volkslied *nt*; (*contemporary*) Folksong *m*
follow ['fɔləu] VT folgen +*dat*; (*with eyes*) verfolgen; (*advice, instructions*) befolgen ▸VI folgen; **to ~ in sb's footsteps** in jds Fußstapfen *acc* treten; **I don't quite ~ you** ich kann Ihnen nicht ganz folgen; **it follows that** daraus folgt, dass; **to ~ suit** (*fig*) jds Beispiel *dat* folgen
▸**follow on** VI (*continue*): **to ~ on from** aufbauen auf +*dat*
▸**follow out** VT (*idea, plan*) zu Ende verfolgen
▸**follow through** VT = **follow out**
▸**follow up** VT nachgehen +*dat*; (*offer*) aufgreifen; (*case*) weiterverfolgen
follower ['fɔləuəʳ] N Anhänger(in) *m(f)*

ollowing ['fɔləuɪŋ] ADJ folgend ▶ N Anhängerschaft *f*
ollow-up ['fɔləuʌp] N Weiterführung *f* ▶ ADJ: **~ treatment** Nachbehandlung *f*
olly ['fɔlɪ] N Torheit *f*; (*building*) exzentrisches Bauwerk *nt*
ond [fɔnd] ADJ liebevoll; (*memory*) lieb; (*hopes, dreams*) töricht; **to be ~ of** mögen; **she's ~ of swimming** sie schwimmt gerne
ondle ['fɔndl] VT streicheln
ondly ['fɔndlɪ] ADV liebevoll; (*naïvely*) törichterweise; **he ~ believed that …** er war so naiv zu glauben, dass …
ondness ['fɔndnɪs] N (*for things*) Vorliebe *f*; (*for people*) Zuneigung *f*; **a special ~ for** eine besondere Vorliebe für/Zuneigung zu
ont [fɔnt] N Taufbecken *nt*; (*Typ*) Schrift *f*
ood [fu:d] N Essen *nt*; (*for animals*) Futter *nt*; (*nourishment*) Nahrung *f*; (*groceries*) Lebensmittel *pl*
ood chain N Nahrungskette *f*
ood combining [-kəm'baɪnɪŋ] N Trennkost *f*
ood mixer N Küchenmixer *m*
ood poisoning N Lebensmittelvergiftung *f*
ood processor N Küchenmaschine *f*
ood stamp N Lebensmittelmarke *f*
oodstuffs ['fu:dstʌfs] NPL Lebensmittel *pl*
ool [fu:l] N Dummkopf *m*; (*Culin*) *Sahnespeise aus Obstpüree* ▶ VT hereinlegen, täuschen ▶ VI herumalbern; **to make a ~ of sb** jdn lächerlich machen; (*trick*) jdn hereinlegen; **to make a ~ of o.s.** sich blamieren; **you can't ~ me** du kannst mich nicht zum Narren halten
▶ **fool about** (*pej*) VI herumtrödeln; (*behave foolishly*) herumalbern
▶ **fool around** VI = **fool about**
oolhardy ['fu:lhɑ:dɪ] ADJ tollkühn
oolish ['fu:lɪʃ] ADJ dumm
oolishly ['fu:lɪʃlɪ] ADV dumm; **~, I forgot …** dummerweise habe ich … vergessen
oolishness ['fu:lɪʃnɪs] N Dummheit *f*
oolproof ['fu:lpru:f] ADJ idiotensicher
oolscap ['fu:lskæp] N ≈ Kanzleipapier *nt*
oot [fut] (*pl* **feet**) N Fuß *m*; (*of animal*) Pfote *f* ▶ VT (*bill*) bezahlen; **on ~** zu Fuß; **to find one's feet** sich eingewöhnen; **to put one's ~ down** (*Aut*) Gas geben; (*say no*) ein Machtwort sprechen
ootage ['futɪdʒ] N Filmmaterial *nt*
oot-and-mouth [futənd'mauθ], **foot-and-mouth disease** N Maul- und Klauenseuche *f*
ootball ['futbɔ:l] N Fußball *m*; (*US*) Football *m*, amerikanischer Fußball *m*
ootballer ['futbɔ:lə[r]] (BRIT) N Fußballspieler(in) *m(f)*
ootball ground N Fußballplatz *m*
ootball match (BRIT) N Fußballspiel *nt*
ootball player N (BRIT) Fußballspieler(in) *m(f)*; (*US*) Footballspieler(in) *m(f)*

> **Football Pools**, umgangssprachlich auch **the pools** genannt, ist das in Großbritannien sehr beliebte Fußballtoto, bei dem auf die Ergebnisse der samstäglichen Fußballspiele gewettet wird. Die Gewinne können sehr hoch sein und gelegentlich Millionen von Pfund betragen.

foot brake N Fußbremse *f*
footbridge ['futbrɪdʒ] N Fußgängerbrücke *f*
foothills ['futhɪlz] NPL (Gebirgs)ausläufer *pl*
foothold ['futhəuld] N Halt *m*; **to get a ~** Fuß fassen
footing ['futɪŋ] N Stellung *f*; (*relationship*) Verhältnis *nt*; **to lose one's ~** den Halt verlieren; **on an equal ~** auf gleicher Basis
footlights ['futlaɪts] NPL Rampenlicht *nt*
footman ['futmən] N (*irreg*) Lakai *m*
footnote ['futnəut] N Fußnote *f*
footpath ['futpɑ:θ] N Fußweg *m*; (*in street*) Bürgersteig *m*
footprint ['futprɪnt] N Fußabdruck *m*; (*of animal*) Spur *f*
footrest ['futrɛst] N Fußstütze *f*
Footsie ['futsɪ] (*inf*) N = **FTSE 100 Index**
footsie ['futsɪ] (*inf*) N: **to play ~ with sb** mit jdm füßeln
footsore ['futsɔ:[r]] ADJ: **to be ~** wunde Füße haben
footstep ['futstɛp] N Schritt *m*; (*footprint*) Fußabdruck *m*; **to follow in sb's footsteps** in jds Fußstapfen *acc* treten
footwear ['futwɛə[r]] N Schuhe *pl*, Schuhwerk *nt*

KEYWORD

for [fɔ:[r]] PREP **1** für *+acc*; **is this for me?** ist das für mich?; **the train for London** der Zug nach London; **it's time for lunch** es ist Zeit zum Mittagessen; **what's it for?** wofür ist das?; **he works for the government/a local firm** er arbeitet für die Regierung/eine Firma am Ort; **he's mature for his age** er ist reif für sein Alter; **I sold it for £20** ich habe es für £20 verkauft; **I'm all for it** ich bin ganz dafür; **G for George** ≈ G wie Gustav
2 (*because of*): **for this reason** aus diesem Grund; **for fear of being criticised** aus Angst, kritisiert zu werden
3 (*referring to distance*): **there are roadworks for 5 km** die Straßenbauarbeiten erstrecken sich über 5 km; **we walked for miles** wir sind meilenweit gelaufen
4 (*referring to time*): **he was away for 2 years** er war 2 Jahre lang weg; **I have known her for years** ich kenne sie bereits seit Jahren
5 (*with infinitive clause*): **it is not for me to decide** es liegt nicht an mir, das zu entscheiden; **for this to be possible …** um dies möglich zu machen, …
6 (*in spite of*) trotz *+gen or dat*; **for all his complaints, he is very fond of her** trotz seiner vielen Klagen mag er sie sehr
▶ CONJ (*formal: since, as*) denn; **she was very angry, for he was late again** sie war sehr böse, denn er kam wieder zu spät

f.o.r. ABBR (*Comm:* = *free on rail*) frei Bahn

forage ['fɔrɪdʒ] N Futter *nt* ▶ VI herumstöbern; **to ~ (for food)** nach Futter suchen
forage cap N Schiffchen *nt*
foray ['fɔreɪ] N (Raub)überfall *m*
forbad, forbade [fə'bæd] PT *of* **forbid**
forbearing [fɔː'bɛərɪŋ] ADJ geduldig
forbid [fə'bɪd] (*pt* **forbade**, *pp* **forbidden**) VT verbieten; **to ~ sb to do sth** jdm verbieten, etw zu tun
forbidden [fə'bɪdn] PP *of* **forbid** ▶ ADJ verboten
forbidding [fə'bɪdɪŋ] ADJ (*look*) streng; (*prospect*) grauenhaft
force [fɔːs] N Kraft *f*; (*violence*) Gewalt *f*; (*of blow, impact*) Wucht *f*; (*influence*) Macht *f* ▶ VT zwingen; (*push*) drücken; (*: person*) drängen; (*lock, door*) aufbrechen; **the Forces** NPL (BRIT) die Streitkräfte*pl*; **in ~** (*law etc*) geltend; (*people: arrive etc*) zahlreich; **to come into ~** in Kraft treten; **to join forces** sich zusammentun; **a ~ 5 wind** Windstärke 5; **the sales ~** das Verkaufspersonal; **to ~ o.s./sb to do sth** sich/jdn zwingen, etw zu tun
▶ **force back** VT zurückdrängen; (*tears*) unterdrücken
▶ **force down** VT (*food*) hinunterwürgen (*inf*)
forced [fɔːst] ADJ gezwungen; **~ labour** Zwangsarbeit *f*; **~ landing** Notlandung *f*
force-feed ['fɔːsfiːd] VT zwangsernähren; (*animal*) stopfen
forceful ['fɔːsful] ADJ energisch; (*attack*) wirkungsvoll; (*point*) überzeugend
forceps ['fɔːsɛps] NPL Zange *f*
forcible ['fɔːsəbl] ADJ gewaltsam; (*reminder, lesson*) eindringlich
forcibly ['fɔːsəblɪ] ADV mit Gewalt; (*express*) eindringlich
ford [fɔːd] N Furt *f* ▶ VT durchqueren; (*on foot*) durchwaten
fore [fɔːʳ] N: **to come to the ~** ins Blickfeld geraten
forearm ['fɔːrɑːm] N Unterarm *m*
forebear ['fɔːbɛəʳ] N Vorfahr(in) *m(f)*, Ahn(e) *m(f)*
foreboding [fɔː'bəudɪŋ] N Vorahnung *f*
forecast ['fɔːkɑːst] N Prognose *f*; (*of weather*) (Wetter)vorhersage *f* ▶ VT (*irreg: like* **cast**) voraussagen
foreclose [fɔː'kləuz] VT (*Law: also:* **foreclose on**) kündigen; **to ~ sb** (*on loan/mortgage*) jds Darlehen/Hypothek kündigen
foreclosure [fɔː'kləuʒəʳ] N Zwangsvollstreckung *f*
forecourt ['fɔːkɔːt] N Vorplatz *m*
forefathers ['fɔːfɑːðəz] NPL Vorfahren *pl*
forefinger ['fɔːfɪŋgəʳ] N Zeigefinger *m*
forefront ['fɔːfrʌnt] N: **in the ~ of** an der Spitze *+gen*
forego [fɔː'gəu] VT (*irreg: like* **go**) verzichten auf *+acc*
foregoing ['fɔːgəuɪŋ] ADJ vorhergehend ▶ N: **the ~** das Vorhergehende
foregone ['fɔːgɔn] PP *of* **forego** ▶ ADJ: **it's a ~ conclusion** es steht von vornherein fest
foreground ['fɔːgraund] N Vordergrund *m*
forehand ['fɔːhænd] N (*Tennis*) Vorhand *f*
forehead ['fɔrɪd] N Stirn *f*
foreign ['fɔrɪn] ADJ ausländisch; (*holiday*) im Ausland; (*customs, appearance*) fremdartig; (*trade, policy*) Außen-; (*correspondent*) Auslands-; (*object, matter*) fremd; **goods from ~ countries/a ~ country** Waren aus dem Ausland
foreign body N Fremdkörper *m*
foreign currency N Devisen *pl*
foreigner ['fɔrɪnəʳ] N Ausländer(in) *m(f)*
foreign exchange N Devisenhandel *m*; (*money*) Devisen *pl*
foreign exchange market N Devisenmarkt *m*
foreign exchange rate N Devisenkurs *m*
foreign investment N Auslandsinvestition *f*
foreign language N Fremdsprache *f*
foreign minister N Außenminister(in) *m(f)*
Foreign Office (BRIT) N Außenministerium *nt*
foreign policy N Außenpolitik *f*
Foreign Secretary (BRIT) N Außenminister(in) *m(f)*
foreleg ['fɔːlɛg] N Vorderbein *nt*
foreman ['fɔːmən] N (*irreg*) Vorarbeiter *m*; (*of jury*) Obmann *m*
foremost ['fɔːməust] ADJ führend ▶ ADV: **first and ~** zunächst, vor allem
forename ['fɔːneɪm] N Vorname *m*
forensic [fə'rɛnsɪk] ADJ (*test*) forensisch; (*medicine*) Gerichts-; (*expert*) Spurensicherungs-
foreplay ['fɔːpleɪ] N Vorspiel *nt*
forerunner ['fɔːrʌnəʳ] N Vorläufer *m*
foresee [fɔː'siː] VT (*irreg: like* **see**) vorhersehen
foreseeable [fɔː'siːəbl] ADJ vorhersehbar; **in the ~ future** in absehbarer Zeit
foreseen [fɔː'siːn] PP *of* **foresee**
foreshadow [fɔː'ʃædəu] VT andeuten
foreshore ['fɔːʃɔːʳ] N Strand *m*
foreshorten [fɔː'ʃɔːtn] VT perspektivisch verkürzen
foresight ['fɔːsaɪt] N Voraussicht *f*, Weitblick *m*
foreskin ['fɔːskɪn] N (*Anat*) Vorhaut *f*
forest ['fɔrɪst] N Wald *m*
forestall [fɔː'stɔːl] VT zuvorkommen *+dat*; (*discussion*) im Keim ersticken
forestry ['fɔrɪstrɪ] N Forstwirtschaft *f*
foretaste ['fɔːteɪst] N: **a ~ of** ein Vorgeschmack von
foretell [fɔː'tɛl] VT (*irreg: like* **tell**) vorhersagen
forethought ['fɔːθɔːt] N Vorbedacht *m*
foretold [fɔː'təuld] PT, PP *of* **foretell**
forever [fə'rɛvəʳ] ADV für immer; (*endlessly*) ewig; (*consistently*) dauernd, ständig; **you're ~ finding difficulties** du findest ständig *or* dauernd neue Schwierigkeiten
forewarn [fɔː'wɔːn] VT vorwarnen
forewent [fɔː'wɛnt] PT *of* **forego**
forewoman ['fɔːwumən] N (*irreg*) Vorarbeiterin *f*; (*of jury*) Obmännin *f*
foreword ['fɔːwəːd] N Vorwort *nt*
forfeit ['fɔːfɪt] N Strafe *f*, Buße *f* ▶ VT (*right*) verwirken; (*friendship etc*) verlieren; (*one's happiness, health*) einbüßen

forgave [fə'geɪv] PT *of* **forgive**
forge [fɔːdʒ] N Schmiede *f* ▶ VT fälschen; (*wrought iron*) schmieden
▶ **forge ahead** VI große *or* schnelle Fortschritte machen
forger ['fɔːdʒə^r] N Fälscher(in) *m(f)*
forgery ['fɔːdʒərɪ] N Fälschung *f*
forget [fə'gɛt] (*pt* **forgot**, *pp* **forgotten**) VT vergessen ▶ VI es vergessen; **to ~ o.s.** sich vergessen
forgetful [fə'gɛtful] ADJ vergesslich; **~ of sth** (*of duties etc*) nachlässig gegenüber etw
forgetfulness [fə'gɛtfulnɪs] N Vergesslichkeit *f*; (*oblivion*) Vergessenheit *f*
forget-me-not [fə'gɛtmɪnɔt] N Vergissmeinnicht *nt*
forgive [fə'gɪv] (*pt* **forgave**, *pp* **forgiven**) VT verzeihen *+dat*, vergeben *+dat*; **to ~ sb for sth** jdm etw verzeihen *or* vergeben; **to ~ sb for doing sth** jdm verzeihen *or* vergeben, dass er etw getan hat; **~ me, but …** entschuldigen Sie, aber …; **they could be forgiven for thinking that …** es ist verständlich, wenn sie denken, dass …
forgiveness [fə'gɪvnɪs] N Verzeihung *f*
forgiving [fə'gɪvɪŋ] ADJ versöhnlich
forgo [fɔː'gəu] (*pt* **forwent**, *pp* **forgone**) VT = **forego**
forgot [fə'gɔt] PT *of* **forget**
forgotten [fə'gɔtn] PP *of* **forget**
fork [fɔːk] N Gabel *f*; (*in road, river, railway*) Gabelung *f* ▶ VI (*road*) sich gabeln
▶ **fork out** (*inf*) VT, VI (*pay*) blechen
forked [fɔːkt] ADJ (*lightning*) zickzackförmig
fork-lift truck ['fɔːklɪft-] N Gabelstapler *m*
forlorn [fə'lɔːn] ADJ verlassen; (*person*) einsam und verlassen; (*attempt*) verzweifelt; (*hope*) schwach
form [fɔːm] N Form *f*; (*Scol*) Klasse *f*; (*questionnaire*) Formular *nt* ▶ VT formen, gestalten; (*queue, organization, group*) bilden; (*idea, habit*) entwickeln; **in the ~ of** in Form von *or +gen*; **in the ~ of Peter** in Gestalt von Peter; **to be in good ~** gut in Form sein; **in top ~** in Hochform; **on ~** in Form; **to ~ part of sth** Teil von etw sein
formal ['fɔːməl] ADJ offiziell; (*person, behaviour*) förmlich, formell; (*occasion, dinner*) feierlich; (*clothes*) Gesellschafts-; (*garden*) formell angelegt; (*Art, Philosophy*) formal; **~ dress** Gesellschaftskleidung *f*
formalities [fɔː'mælɪtɪz] NPL Formalitäten *pl*
formality [fɔː'mælɪtɪ] N Förmlichkeit *f*; (*procedure*) Formalität *f*
formalize ['fɔːməlaɪz] VT formell machen
formally ['fɔːməlɪ] ADV offiziell; förmlich, formell; feierlich; **to be ~ invited** ausdrücklich eingeladen sein
format ['fɔːmæt] N Format *nt*; (*form, style*) Aufmachung *f* ▶ VT (*Comput*) formatieren
formation [fɔː'meɪʃən] N Bildung *f*; (*of theory*) Entstehung *f*; (*of business*) Gründung *f*; (*pattern: of rocks, clouds*) Formation *f*
formative ['fɔːmətɪv] ADJ (*influence*) prägend; (*years*) entscheidend
former ['fɔːmə^r] ADJ früher; **the ~ … the latter …** Erstere(r, s, r) … Letztere(s); **the ~ president** der ehemalige Präsident; **the ~ East Germany** die ehemalige DDR
formerly ['fɔːməlɪ] ADV früher
form feed N (*on printer*) Papiervorschub *m*
Formica® [fɔː'maɪkə] N Resopal® *nt*
formidable ['fɔːmɪdəbl] ADJ (*task*) gewaltig, enorm; (*opponent*) furchterregend
formula ['fɔːmjulə] (*pl* **formulae** *or* **formulas**) N Formel *f*; **F~ One** (*Aut*) Formel Eins
formulate ['fɔːmjuleɪt] VT formulieren
fornicate ['fɔːnɪkeɪt] VI Unzucht treiben
forsake [fə'seɪk] (*pt* **forsook**, *pp* **forsaken**) VT im Stich lassen; (*belief*) aufgeben
forsook [fə'suk] PT *of* **forsake**
fort [fɔːt] N Fort *nt*; **to hold the ~** die Stellung halten
forte ['fɔːtɪ] N Stärke *f*, starke Seite *f*
forth [fɔːθ] ADV aus; **back and ~** hin und her; **to go back and ~** auf und ab gehen; **to bring ~** hervorbringen; **and so ~** und so weiter
forthcoming [fɔːθ'kʌmɪŋ] ADJ (*event*) bevorstehend; (*person*) mitteilsam; **to be ~** (*help*) erfolgen; (*evidence*) geliefert werden
forthright ['fɔːθraɪt] ADJ offen
forthwith ['fɔːθ'wɪθ] ADV umgehend
fortieth ['fɔːtɪɪθ] NUM vierzigste(r, s)
fortification [fɔːtɪfɪ'keɪʃən] N Befestigung *f*, Festungsanlage *f*
fortified wine ['fɔːtɪfaɪd-] N weinhaltiges Getränk *nt* (*Sherry, Portwein etc*)
fortitude ['fɔːtɪtjuːd] N innere Kraft *or* Stärke *f*
fortnight ['fɔːtnaɪt] (BRIT) N vierzehn Tage *pl*, zwei Wochen *pl*; **it's a ~ since …** es ist vierzehn Tage *or* zwei Wochen her, dass …
fortnightly ['fɔːtnaɪtlɪ] ADJ vierzehntägig, zweiwöchentlich ▶ ADV alle vierzehn Tage, alle zwei Wochen
FORTRAN ['fɔːtræn] N FORTRAN *nt*
fortress ['fɔːtrɪs] N Festung *f*
fortuitous [fɔː'tjuːɪtəs] ADJ zufällig
fortunate ['fɔːtʃənɪt] ADJ glücklich; **to be ~** Glück haben; **he is ~ to have …** er kann sich glücklich schätzen, … zu haben; **it is ~ that …** es ist ein Glück, dass …
fortunately ['fɔːtʃənɪtlɪ] ADV glücklicherweise, zum Glück
fortune ['fɔːtʃən] N Glück *nt*; (*wealth*) Vermögen *nt*; **to make a ~** ein Vermögen machen; **to tell sb's ~** jdm wahrsagen
fortune-teller ['fɔːtʃəntɛlə^r] N Wahrsager(in) *m(f)*
forty ['fɔːtɪ] NUM vierzig
forum ['fɔːrəm] N Forum *nt*
forward ['fɔːwəd] ADJ vordere(r, s); (*movement*) Vorwärts-; (*not shy*) dreist; (*Comm: buying, price*) Termin- ▶ ADV nach vorn; (*movement*) vorwärts; (*in time*) voraus ▶ N (*Sport*) Stürmer *m* ▶ VT (*letter etc*) nachsenden; (*career, plans*) voranbringen;

~ **planning** Vorausplanung *f*; **to move ~** vorwärtskommen; **"please ~"** „bitte nachsenden"
forwards ['fɔ:wədz] ADV nach vorn; (*movement*) vorwärts; (*in time*) voraus
fossick ['fɔsɪk] VI (AUST, NZ *inf*) suchen (for nach); **to ~ around** herumstöbern (*inf*); **to ~ for gold** nach Gold graben
fossil ['fɔsl] N Fossil *nt*
fossil fuel N fossiler Brennstoff *m*
foster ['fɔstə^r] VT (*child*) in Pflege nehmen; (*idea, activity*) fördern
foster child N (*irreg*) Pflegekind *nt*
foster mother N Pflegemutter *f*
foster sister N Ziehschwester *f*
fought [fɔ:t] PT, PP *of* **fight**
foul [faul] ADJ abscheulich; (*taste, smell, temper*) übel; (*water*) faulig; (*air*) schlecht; (*language*) unflätig ▸ N (*Sport*) Foul *nt* ▸ VT beschmutzen; (*Sport*) foulen; (*entangle*) sich verheddern in *+dat*
foul play N unnatürlicher *or* gewaltsamer Tod *m*; **~ is not suspected** es besteht kein Verdacht auf ein Verbrechen
found [faund] PT, PP *of* **find** ▸ VT gründen
foundation [faun'deɪʃən] N Gründung *f*; (*base: also fig*) Grundlage *f*; (*organization*) Stiftung *f*; (*also*: **foundation cream**) Grundierungscreme *f*; **foundations** NPL (*of building*) Fundament *nt*; **the rumours are without ~** die Gerüchte entbehren jeder Grundlage; **to lay the foundations** (*fig*) die Grundlagen schaffen
foundation stone N Grundstein *m*
founder ['faundə^r] N Gründer(in) *m(f)* ▸ VI (*ship*) sinken
founder member N Gründungsmitglied *nt*
founding ['faundɪŋ] ADJ: **~ fathers** (*esp US*) Väter *pl*
foundry ['faundrɪ] N Gießerei *f*
fount [faunt] N Quelle *f*; (*Typ*) Schrift *f*
fountain ['fauntɪn] N Brunnen *m*
fountain pen N Füllfederhalter *m*, Füller *m*
four [fɔ:^r] NUM vier; **on all fours** auf allen vieren
four-by-four [fɔ:baɪ'fɔ:^r] N Geländewagen *m*, Fahrzeug *nt* mit Vierradantrieb
four-letter word ['fɔ:lɛtə-] N Vulgärausdruck *m*
four-poster ['fɔ:'pəustə^r] N (*also*: **four-poster bed**) Himmelbett *nt*
foursome ['fɔ:səm] N Quartett *nt*; **in** *or* **as a ~** zu viert
fourteen ['fɔ:'ti:n] NUM vierzehn
fourteenth ['fɔ:'ti:nθ] NUM vierzehnte(r, s)
fourth [fɔ:θ] NUM vierte(r, s) ▸ N (*Aut*: *also*: **fourth gear**) der vierte (Gang)
four-wheel drive ['fɔ:wi:l-] N (*Aut*): **with ~** mit Vierradantrieb *m*
fowl [faul] N Vogel *m* (*besonders Huhn, Gans, Ente etc*)
fox [fɔks] N Fuchs *m* ▸ VT verblüffen
foxglove ['fɔksglʌv] N (*Bot*) Fingerhut *m*
fox-hunting ['fɔkshʌntɪŋ] N Fuchsjagd *f*
foxtrot ['fɔkstrɔt] N Foxtrott *m*
foyer ['fɔɪeɪ] N Foyer *nt*
FPA (BRIT) N ABBR (= *Family Planning Association*) *Organisation für Familienplanung*
Fr. ABBR (*Rel*) = **father**; **friar**
fr. ABBR (= *franc*) Fr.
fracas ['frækɑ:] N Aufruhr *m*, Tumult *m*
fraction ['frækʃən] N Bruchteil *m*; (*Math*) Bruch *m*
fractionally ['frækʃnəlɪ] ADV geringfügig
fractious ['frækʃəs] ADJ verdrießlich
fracture ['fræktʃə^r] N Bruch *m* ▸ VT brechen
fragile ['frædʒaɪl] ADJ zerbrechlich; (*economy*) schwach; (*health*) zart; (*person*) angeschlagen
fragment N ['frægmənt] Stück *nt* ▸ VT [fræg'mɛnt] aufsplittern ▸ VI sich aufsplittern
fragmentary ['frægməntərɪ] ADJ fragmentarisch, bruchstückhaft
fragrance ['freɪgrəns] N Duft *m*
frail [freɪl] ADJ schwach, gebrechlich; (*structure*) zerbrechlich
frame [freɪm] N Rahmen *m*; (*of building*) (Grund)gerippe *nt*; (*of human, animal*) Gestalt *f*; (*of spectacles*: *also*: **frames**) Gestell *nt* ▸ VT (*picture*) rahmen; (*reply*) formulieren; (*law, theory*) entwerfen; **~ of mind** Stimmung *f*, Laune *f*; **to ~ sb** (*inf*) jdm etwas anhängen
framework ['freɪmwə:k] N Rahmen *m*
France [frɑ:ns] N Frankreich *nt*
franchise ['fræntʃaɪz] N Wahlrecht *nt*; (*Comm*) Konzession *f*, Franchise *f*
franchisee [fræntʃaɪ'zi:] N Franchisenehmer(in) *m(f)*
franchiser ['fræntʃaɪzə^r] N Franchisegeber(in) *m(f)*
frank [fræŋk] ADJ offen ▸ VT (*letter*) frankieren
Frankfurt ['fræŋkfə:t] N Frankfurt *nt*
frankfurter ['fræŋkfə:tə^r] N (Frankfurter) Würstchen *nt*
franking machine ['fræŋkɪŋ-] N Frankiermaschine *f*
frankly ['fræŋklɪ] ADV ehrlich gesagt; (*candidly*) offen
frankness ['fræŋknɪs] N Offenheit *f*
frantic ['fræntɪk] ADJ verzweifelt; (*hectic*) hektisch; (*desperate*) übersteigert
frantically ['fræntɪklɪ] ADV verzweifelt; (*hectically*) hektisch
fraternal [frə'tə:nl] ADJ brüderlich
fraternity [frə'tə:nɪtɪ] N Brüderlichkeit *f*; (*US Univ*) Verbindung *f*; **the legal/medical/golfing ~** die Juristen/Mediziner/Golfer *pl*
fraternize ['frætənaɪz] VI Umgang haben
fraud [frɔ:d] N Betrug *m*; (*person*) Betrüger(in) *m(f)*
fraudulent ['frɔ:djulənt] ADJ betrügerisch
fraught [frɔ:t] ADJ (*person*) nervös; **to be ~ with danger/problems** voller Gefahren/Probleme sein
fray [freɪ] N: **the ~** der Kampf ▸ VI (*cloth*) ausfransen; (*rope*) sich durchscheuern; **to return to the ~** sich wieder ins Getümmel stürzen; **tempers were frayed** die Gemüter erhitzten sich; **her nerves were frayed** sie war mit den Nerven am Ende

FRB (*US*) N ABBR = **Federal Reserve Board**
FRCM (BRIT) N ABBR (= *Fellow of the Royal College of Music*) *Qualifikationsnachweis in Musik*
FRCO (BRIT) N ABBR (= *Fellow of the Royal College of Organists*) *Qualifikationsnachweis für Organisten*
FRCP (BRIT) N ABBR (= *Fellow of the Royal College of Physicians*) *Qualifikationsnachweis für Ärzte*
FRCS (BRIT) N ABBR (= *Fellow of the Royal College of Surgeons*) *Qualifikationsnachweis für Chirurgen*
freak [fri:k] N Irre(r) *f*(*m*); (*in appearance*) Missgeburt *f*; (*event, accident*) außergewöhnlicher Zufall *m*; (*pej: fanatic*): **health ~** Gesundheitsapostel *m*
▸ **freak out** (*inf*) VI aussteigen; (*on drugs*) ausflippen
freakish ['fri:kɪʃ] ADJ verrückt
freckle ['frɛkl] N Sommersprosse *f*
freckled ['frɛkld] ADJ sommersprossig
free [fri:] ADJ frei; (*costing nothing*) kostenlos, gratis ▸ VT freilassen, frei lassen; (*jammed object*) lösen; **to give sb a ~ hand** jdm freie Hand lassen; **~ and easy** ungezwungen; **admission ~** Eintritt frei; **~ (of charge), for ~** umsonst, gratis
free agent N: **to be a ~** sein eigener Herr sein
freebie ['fri:bɪ] (*inf*) N (*promotional gift*) Werbegeschenk *nt*
freedom ['fri:dəm] N Freiheit *f*
freedom fighter N Freiheitskämpfer(in) *m*(*f*)
free enterprise N freies Unternehmertum *nt*
Freefone® ['fri:fəun] N: **call ~ 0800** rufen Sie gebührenfrei 0800 an
free-for-all ['fri:fərɔ:l] N Gerangel *nt*; **the fight turned into a ~** schließlich beteiligten sich alle an der Schlägerei
free gift N Werbegeschenk *nt*
freehold ['fri:həuld] N (*of property*) Besitzrecht *nt*
free kick N Freistoß *m*
freelance ['fri:lɑ:ns] ADJ (*journalist etc*) frei(schaffend), freiberuflich tätig
freelance work N freiberufliche Arbeit *f*
freeloader ['fri:ləudəʳ] (*pej*) N Schmarotzer(in) *m*(*f*)
freely ['fri:lɪ] ADV frei; (*spend*) mit vollen Händen; (*liberally*) großzügig; **drugs are ~ available in the city** Drogen sind in der Stadt frei erhältlich
free-market economy [fri:'mɑ:kɪt-] N freie Marktwirtschaft *f*
Freemason ['fri:meɪsn] N Freimaurer *m*
Freemasonry ['fri:meɪsnrɪ] N Freimaurerei *f*
Freepost® ['fri:pəust] N ≈ „Gebühr zahlt Empfänger"
free-range ['fri:'reɪndʒ] ADJ (*eggs*) von frei laufenden Hühnern
free sample N Gratisprobe *f*
freesia ['fri:zɪə] N Freesie *f*
free speech N Redefreiheit *f*
freestyle ['fri:staɪl] N Freistil *m*
free trade N Freihandel *m*
freeway ['fri:weɪ] (*US*) N Autobahn *f*
freewheel [fri:'wi:l] VI im Freilauf fahren
free will N freier Wille *m*; **of one's own ~** aus freien Stücken
freeze [fri:z] (*pt* **froze**, *pp* **frozen**) VI frieren; (*liquid*) gefrieren; (*pipe*) einfrieren; (*person: stop moving*) erstarren ▸ VT einfrieren; (*water, lake*) gefrieren ▸ N Frost *m*; (*on arms, wages*) Stopp *m*
▸ **freeze over** VI (*river*) überfrieren; (*windscreen, windows*) vereisen
▸ **freeze up** VI zufrieren
freeze-dried ['fri:zdraɪd] ADJ gefriergetrocknet
freezer ['fri:zəʳ] N Tiefkühltruhe *f*; (*upright*) Gefrierschrank *m*; (*in fridge: also:* **freezer compartment**) Gefrierfach *nt*
freezing ['fri:zɪŋ] ADJ: **~ (cold)** eiskalt ▸ N: **3 degrees below ~** 3 Grad unter null; **I'm ~** mir ist eiskalt
freezing point N Gefrierpunkt *m*
freight [freɪt] N Fracht *f*; (*money charged*) Frachtkosten *pl*; **~ forward** Fracht gegen Nachnahme; **~ inward** Eingangsfracht *f*
freight car (*US*) N Güterwagen *m*
freighter ['freɪtəʳ] N (*Naut*) Frachter *m*, Frachtschiff *nt*; (*Aviat*) Frachtflugzeug *nt*
freight forwarder [-'fɔ:wədəʳ] N Spediteur *m*
freight train (*US*) N Güterzug *m*
French [frɛntʃ] ADJ französisch ▸ N (*Ling*) Französisch *nt*; **the French** NPL die Franzosen *pl*
French bean (BRIT) N grüne Bohne *f*
French bread N Baguette *f*
French Canadian ADJ frankokanadisch ▸ N Frankokanadier(in) *m*(*f*)
French dressing N Vinaigrette *f*
French fried potatoes NPL Pommes frites *pl*
French fries [-fraɪz] (*US*) NPL = **French fried potatoes**
French Guiana [-gaɪ'ænə] N Französisch-Guyana *nt*
Frenchman ['frɛntʃmən] N (*irreg*) Franzose *m*
French Riviera N: **the ~** die französische Riviera
French stick N Stangenbrot *nt*
French window N Verandatür *f*
Frenchwoman ['frɛntʃwumən] N (*irreg*) Französin *f*
frenetic [frə'nɛtɪk] ADJ frenetisch, rasend
frenzied ['frɛnzɪd] ADJ rasend
frenzy ['frɛnzɪ] N Raserei *f*; (*of joy, excitement*) Taumel *m*; **to drive sb into a ~** jdn zum Rasen bringen; **to be in a ~** in wilder Aufregung sein
frequency ['fri:kwənsɪ] N Häufigkeit *f*; (*Radio*) Frequenz *f*
frequency modulation N Frequenzmodulation *f*
frequent ADJ ['fri:kwənt] häufig ▸ VT [frɪ'kwɛnt] (*pub, restaurant*) oft *or* häufig besuchen
frequently ['fri:kwəntlɪ] ADV oft, häufig
fresco ['frɛskəu] N Fresko *nt*
fresh [frɛʃ] ADJ frisch; (*instructions, approach, start*) neu; (*cheeky*) frech; **to make a ~ start** einen neuen Anfang machen
freshen ['frɛʃən] VI (*wind*) auffrischen; (*air*) frisch werden
▸ **freshen up** VI sich frisch machen

f

freshener ['frɛʃnəʳ] N: **skin ~** Gesichtswasser *nt*; **air ~** Raumspray *m or nt*
fresher ['frɛʃəʳ] (BRIT *inf*) N Erstsemester(in) *m(f)*
freshly ['frɛʃlɪ] ADV frisch
freshman ['frɛʃmən] (US) N (*irreg*) = **fresher**
freshness ['frɛʃnɪs] N Frische *f*
freshwater ['frɛʃwɔːtəʳ] ADJ (*fish etc*) Süßwasser-
fret [frɛt] VI sich *dat* Sorgen machen
fretful ['frɛtful] ADJ (*child*) quengelig
Freudian ['frɔɪdɪən] ADJ freudianisch, freudsch; **~ slip** freudscher Versprecher *m*
FRG N ABBR (*Hist*: = *Federal Republic of Germany*) BRD *f*
Fri. ABBR (= *Friday*) Fr.
friar ['fraɪəʳ] N Mönch *m*, (Ordens)bruder *m*
friction ['frɪkʃən] N Reibung *f*; (*between people*) Reibereien *pl*
friction feed N (*on printer*) Friktionsvorschub *m*
Friday ['fraɪdɪ] N Freitag *m*; *see also* **Tuesday**
fridge [frɪdʒ] (BRIT) N Kühlschrank *m*
fridge-freezer ['frɪdʒ'friːzəʳ] N Kühl- und Gefrierkombination *f*
fried [fraɪd] PT, PP *of* **fry** ▶ ADJ gebraten; **~ egg** Spiegelei *nt*; **~ fish** Bratfisch *m*
friend [frɛnd] N Freund(in) *m(f)*; (*less intimate*) Bekannte(r) *f(m)* ▶ VT (*Internet*): **to ~ sb** einen Freund/eine Freundin hinzufügen; **to make friends with** sich anfreunden mit
friendliness ['frɛndlɪnɪs] N Freundlichkeit *f*
friendly ['frɛndlɪ] ADJ freundlich; (*government*) befreundet; (*game, match*) Freundschafts- ▶ N (*also*: **friendly match**) Freundschaftsspiel *nt*; **to be ~ with** befreundet sein mit; **to be ~ to** freundlich *or* nett sein zu
friendly fire N Beschuss *m* durch die eigene Seite
friendly society N Versicherungsverein *m* auf Gegenseitigkeit
friendship ['frɛndʃɪp] N Freundschaft *f*
frieze [friːz] N Fries *m*
frigate ['frɪgɪt] N Fregatte *f*
fright [fraɪt] N Schreck(en) *m*; **to take ~** es mit der Angst zu tun bekommen; **she looks a ~** sie sieht verboten *or* zum Fürchten aus (*inf*)
frighten ['fraɪtn] VT erschrecken
▶ **frighten away, frighten off** VT verscheuchen
frightened ['fraɪtnd] ADJ ängstlich; **to be ~ (of)** Angst haben (vor *+dat*)
frightening ['fraɪtnɪŋ] ADJ furchterregend
frightful ['fraɪtful] ADJ schrecklich, furchtbar
frightfully ['fraɪtfəlɪ] ADV schrecklich, furchtbar; **I'm ~ sorry** es tut mir schrecklich leid
frigid ['frɪdʒɪd] ADJ frigide
frigidity [frɪ'dʒɪdɪtɪ] N Frigidität *f*
frill [frɪl] N Rüsche *f*; **without frills** (*fig*) schlicht
fringe [frɪndʒ] N (BRIT: *of hair*) Pony *m*; (*decoration*) Fransen *pl*; (*edge*: *also fig*) Rand *m*
fringe benefits NPL zusätzliche Leistungen *pl*
fringe theatre N avantgardistisches Theater *nt*
Frisbee® ['frɪzbɪ] N Frisbee® *nt*
frisk [frɪsk] VT durchsuchen, filzen (*inf*) ▶ VI umhertollen
frisky ['frɪskɪ] ADJ lebendig, ausgelassen
fritter ['frɪtəʳ] N Schmalzgebackenes *nt inv* mit Füllung
▶ **fritter away** VT vergeuden
frivolity [frɪ'vɔlɪtɪ] N Frivolität *f*
frivolous ['frɪvələs] ADJ frivol; (*activity*) leichtfertig
frizzy ['frɪzɪ] ADJ kraus
fro [frəu] ADV: **to and ~** hin und her; (*walk*) auf und ab
frock [frɔk] N Kleid *nt*
frog [frɔg] N Frosch *m*; **to have a ~ in one's throat** einen Frosch im Hals haben
frogman ['frɔgmən] N (*irreg*) Froschmann *m*
frogmarch ['frɔgmɑːtʃ] (BRIT) VT: **to ~ sb in/out** jdn herein-/herausschleppen
frolic ['frɔlɪk] VI umhertollen ▶ N Ausgelassenheit *f*; (*fun*) Spaß *m*

KEYWORD

from [frɔm] PREP **1** (*indicating starting place, origin*) von *+dat*; **where do you come from?** woher kommen Sie?; **from London to Glasgow** von London nach Glasgow; **a letter/telephone call from my sister** ein Brief/Anruf von meiner Schwester; **to drink from the bottle** aus der Flasche trinken
2 (*indicating time*) von (... an); **from one o'clock to** *or* **until** *or* **till now** von ein Uhr bis jetzt; **from January (on)** von Januar an, ab Januar
3 (*indicating distance*) von ... entfernt; **the hotel is 1 km from the beach** das Hotel ist 1 km vom Strand entfernt
4 (*indicating price, number etc*): **trousers from £20** Hosen ab £20; **prices range from £10 to £50** die Preise liegen zwischen £10 und £50
5 (*indicating difference*): **he can't tell red from green** er kann Rot und Grün nicht unterscheiden; **to be different from sb/sth** anders sein als jd/etw
6 (*because of, on the basis of*): **from what he says** nach dem, was er sagt; **to act from conviction** aus Überzeugung handeln; **weak from hunger** schwach vor Hunger

frond [frɔnd] N Wedel *m*
front [frʌnt] N Vorderseite *f*; (*of dress*) Vorderteil *nt*; (*promenade*: *also*: **sea front**) Strandpromenade *f*; (*Mil, Met*) Front *f*; (*fig*: *appearances*) Fassade *f* ▶ ADJ vorderste(r, s); (*wheel, tooth, view*) Vorder- ▶ VI: **to ~ onto sth** (*house*) auf etw *acc* hinausliegen; (*window*) auf etw *acc* hinausgehen; **in ~** vorne; **in ~ of** vor; **at the ~ of the coach/train/car** vorne im Bus/Zug/Auto; **on the political ~, little progress has been made** an der politischen Front sind kaum Fortschritte gemacht worden
frontage ['frʌntɪdʒ] N Vorderseite *f*, Front *f*; (*of shop*) Front
frontal ['frʌntl] ADJ (*attack etc*) Frontal-

front bench (BRIT) N (*Pol*) vorderste *or* erste Reihe *f*

> **Front Bench** bezeichnet im britischen Unterhaus die vorderste Bank auf der Regierungs- und Oppositionsseite zur Rechten und Linken des Sprechers. Im weiteren Sinne bezieht sich front bench auf die Spitzenpolitiker der verschiedenen Parteien, die auf dieser Bank sitzen (auch „frontbenchers" genannt), d. h. die Minister auf der einen Seite und die Mitglieder des Schattenkabinetts auf der anderen.

front desk (*US*) N Rezeption *f*
front door N Haustür *f*
frontier ['frʌntɪəʳ] N Grenze *f*
frontispiece ['frʌntɪspiːs] N zweite Titelseite *f*, Frontispiz *nt*
front page N erste Seite *f*, Titelseite *f*
front room (BRIT) N Wohnzimmer *nt*
frontrunner ['frʌntrʌnəʳ] N Spitzenreiter *m*
front-wheel drive ['frʌntwiːl-] N (*Aut*) Vorderradantrieb *m*
frost [frɔst] N Frost *m*; (*also*: **hoarfrost**) Raureif *m*
frostbite ['frɔstbaɪt] N Erfrierungen *pl*
frosted ['frɔstɪd] ADJ (*glass*) Milch-; (*esp US*) glasiert, mit Zuckerguss überzogen
frosting ['frɔstɪŋ] (*esp US*) N Zuckerguss *m*
frosty ['frɔstɪ] ADJ frostig; (*look*) eisig; (*window*) bereift
froth [frɔθ] N Schaum *m*
frothy ['frɔθɪ] ADJ schäumend
frown [fraun] N Stirnrunzeln *nt* ▸ VI die Stirn runzeln
▸ **frown on** VT FUS missbilligen
froze [frəuz] PT *of* **freeze**
frozen ['frəuzn] PP *of* **freeze** ▸ ADJ tiefgekühlt; (*food*) Tiefkühl-; (*Comm*) eingefroren
FRS N ABBR (BRIT: = *Fellow of the Royal Society*) *Auszeichnung für Naturwissenschaftler*; (US: = *Federal Reserve System*) *amerikanische Zentralbank*
frugal ['fruːgl] ADJ genügsam; (*meal*) einfach
fruit [fruːt] N INV Frucht *f*; (*collectively*) Obst *nt*; (*fig: results*) Früchte *pl*
fruiterer ['fruːtərəʳ] (*esp* BRIT) N Obsthändler(in) *m(f)*
fruit fly N Fruchtfliege *f*
fruitful ['fruːtful] ADJ fruchtbar
fruition [fruː'ɪʃən] N: **to come to ~** (*plan*) Wirklichkeit werden; (*efforts*) Früchte tragen; (*hope*) in Erfüllung gehen
fruit juice N Fruchtsaft *m*
fruitless ['fruːtlɪs] ADJ fruchtlos, ergebnislos
fruit machine (BRIT) N Spielautomat *m*
fruit salad N Obstsalat *m*
fruity ['fruːtɪ] ADJ (*taste, smell etc*) Frucht-, Obst-; (*wine*) fruchtig; (*voice, laugh*) volltönend
frump [frʌmp] N: **to feel a ~** sich *dat* wie eine Vogelscheuche vorkommen
frustrate [frʌs'treɪt] VT frustrieren; (*attempt*) vereiteln; (*plan*) durchkreuzen
frustrated [frʌs'treɪtɪd] ADJ frustriert
frustrating [frʌs'treɪtɪŋ] ADJ frustrierend
frustration [frʌs'treɪʃən] N Frustration *f*; (*of attempt*) Vereitelung *f*; (*of plan*) Zerschlagung *f*
fry [fraɪ] (*pt, pp* **fried**) VT braten; *see also* **small**
frying pan ['fraɪɪŋ-] N Bratpfanne *f*
FT (BRIT) N ABBR (= *Financial Times*) *Wirtschaftszeitung*; **the FT index** der Aktienindex der „Financial Times"
ft. ABBR = **foot; feet**
FTC (US) N ABBR = **Federal Trade Commission**
FTSE 100 Index N *Aktienindex der „Financial Times"*
fuchsia ['fjuːʃə] N Fuchsie *f*
fuck [fʌk] (*inf!*) VT, VI ficken (*inf!*); **~ off!** (*inf!*) verpiss dich! (*inf!*)
fuddled ['fʌdld] ADJ verwirrt
fuddy-duddy ['fʌdɪdʌdɪ] (*pej*) N Langweiler *m*
fudge [fʌdʒ] N Fondant *m* ▸ VT (*issue, problem*) ausweichen *+dat*, aus dem Weg gehen *+dat*
fuel ['fjuəl] N Brennstoff *m*; (*for vehicle*) Kraftstoff *m*; (*: petrol*) Benzin *nt*; (*for aircraft, rocket*) Treibstoff *m* ▸ VT (*furnace etc*) betreiben; (*aircraft, ship etc*) antreiben
fuel consumption N Kraftstoffverbrauch *m*
fuel gauge N Benzinuhr *f*
fuel oil N Gasöl *nt*
fuel poverty N *durch hohe Energiekosten verursachte Armut*
fuel pump N (*Aut*) Benzinpumpe *f*
fuel tank N Öltank *m*; (*in vehicle*) (Benzin)tank *m*
fug [fʌg] (BRIT *inf*) N Mief *m* (*inf*)
fugitive ['fjuːdʒɪtɪv] N Flüchtling *m*
fulfil, (US) **fulfill** [ful'fɪl] VT erfüllen; (*order*) ausführen
fulfilled [ful'fɪld] ADJ ausgefüllt
fulfilment, (US) **fulfillment** [ful'fɪlmənt] N Erfüllung *f*
full [ful] ADJ voll; (*complete*) vollständig; (*skirt*) weit; (*life*) ausgefüllt ▸ ADV: **to know ~ well that ...** sehr wohl wissen, dass ...; **~ up** (*hotel etc*) ausgebucht; **I'm ~ (up)** ich bin satt; **a ~ two hours** volle zwei Stunden; **~ marks** die beste Note, ≈ eine Eins; (*fig*) höchstes Lob *nt*; **at ~ speed** in voller Fahrt; **in ~** ganz, vollständig; **to pay in ~** den vollen Betrag bezahlen; **to write one's name** *etc* **in ~** seinen Namen *etc* ausschreiben
fullback ['fulbæk] N (*Rugby, Football*) Verteidiger *m*
full beam N (*Aut*) Fernlicht *nt*
full-blooded ['ful'blʌdɪd] ADJ (*vigorous*) kräftig; (*virile*) vollblütig
full board N Vollpension *f*
full-cream ['ful'kriːm] ADJ: **~ milk** (BRIT) Vollmilch *f*
full employment N Vollbeschäftigung *f*
full grown ADJ ausgewachsen
full-length ['ful'lɛŋθ] ADJ (*film*) abendfüllend; (*coat*) lang; (*portrait*) lebensgroß; (*mirror*) groß; **~ novel** Roman *m*
full moon N Vollmond *m*
fullness ['fulnɪs] N: **in the ~ of time** zu gegebener Zeit
full-page ['fulpeɪdʒ] ADJ ganzseitig

full-scale ['fulskeɪl] ADJ (*war*) richtig; (*attack*) Groß-; (*model*) in Originalgröße; (*search*) groß angelegt
full-sized ['ful'saɪzd] ADJ lebensgroß
full stop N Punkt *m*
full-time ['ful'taɪm] ADJ (*work*) Ganztags-; (*study*) Voll- ▶ ADV ganztags
fully ['fulɪ] ADV völlig; **~ as big as** mindestens so groß wie
fully fledged [-'flɛdʒd] ADJ richtiggehend; (*doctor etc*) voll qualifiziert; (*member*) Voll-; (*bird*) flügge
fulsome ['fulsəm] (*pej*) ADJ übertrieben
fumble ['fʌmbl] VI: **to ~ with** herumfummeln an *+dat* ▶ VT (*ball*) nicht sicher fangen
fume [fju:m] VI wütend sein, kochen (*inf*)
fumes [fju:mz] NPL (*of fire*) Rauch *m*; (*of fuel*) Dämpfe *pl*; (*of car*) Abgase *pl*
fumigate ['fju:mɪgeɪt] VT ausräuchern
fun [fʌn] N Spaß *m*; **he's good ~ (to be with)** es macht viel Spaß, mit ihm zusammen zu sein; **for ~** aus *or* zum Spaß; **it's not much ~** es macht keinen Spaß; **to make ~ of, to poke ~ at** sich lustig machen über *+acc*
function ['fʌŋkʃən] N Funktion *f*; (*social occasion*) Veranstaltung *f*, Feier *f* ▶ VI funktionieren; **to ~ as** (*thing*) dienen als; (*person*) fungieren als
functional ['fʌŋkʃənl] ADJ (*operational*) funktionsfähig; (*practical*) funktionell, zweckmäßig
functional food ADJ Functional Food *nt*, Funktionsnahrung *f*
function key N (*Comput*) Funktionstaste *f*
fund [fʌnd] N (*of money*) Fonds *m*; (*source, store*) Schatz *m*, Vorrat *m*; **funds** NPL (*money*) Mittel *pl*, Gelder *pl*
fundamental [fʌndə'mɛntl] ADJ fundamental, grundlegend
fundamentalism [fʌndə'mɛntəlɪzəm] N Fundamentalismus *m*
fundamentalist [fʌndə'mɛntəlɪst] N Fundamentalist(in) *m(f)*
fundamentally [fʌndə'mɛntəlɪ] ADV im Grunde; (*radically*) von Grund auf
fundamentals [fʌndə'mɛntlz] NPL Grundbegriffe *pl*
funding ['fʌndɪŋ] N Finanzierung *f*
fund-raising ['fʌndreɪzɪŋ] N Geldbeschaffung *f*
funeral ['fju:nərəl] N Beerdigung *f*
funeral director N Beerdigungsunternehmer(in) *m(f)*
funeral parlour N Leichenhalle *f*
funeral service N Trauergottesdienst *m*
funereal [fju:'nɪərɪəl] ADJ traurig, trübselig
funfair ['fʌnfɛə^r] (BRIT) N Jahrmarkt *m*
fungi ['fʌŋgaɪ] NPL *of* **fungus**
fungus ['fʌŋgəs] (*pl* **fungi**) N Pilz *m*; (*mould*) Schimmel(pilz) *m*
funicular [fju:'nɪkjulə^r] N (*also:* **funicular railway**) Seilbahn *f*
funky ['fʌŋkɪ] ADJ (*music*) Funk-
funnel ['fʌnl] N Trichter *m*; (*of ship*) Schornstein *m*
funnily ['fʌnɪlɪ] ADV komisch; **~ enough** komischerweise
funny ['fʌnɪ] ADJ komisch; (*strange*) seltsam, komisch
funny bone N Musikantenknochen *m*
fun run N ≈ Volkslauf *m*
fur [fə:^r] N Fell *nt*, Pelz *m*; (BRIT: *in kettle etc*) Kesselstein *m*
fur coat N Pelzmantel *m*
furious ['fjuərɪəs] ADJ wütend; (*exchange, argument*) heftig; (*effort*) riesig; (*speed*) rasend; **to be ~ with sb** wütend auf jdn sein
furiously ['fjuərɪəslɪ] ADV wütend; (*struggle etc*) heftig; (*run*) schnell
furl [fə:l] VT (*Naut*) einrollen
furlong ['fə:lɔŋ] N Achtelmeile *f* (*= 201,17 m*)
furlough ['fə:ləu] N (*Mil*) Urlaub *m*
furnace ['fə:nɪs] N (*in foundry*) Schmelzofen *m*; (*in power plant*) Hochofen *m*
furnish ['fə:nɪʃ] VT einrichten; (*room*) möblieren; **to ~ sb with sth** jdm etw liefern; **furnished flat, furnished apartment** (US) möblierte Wohnung *f*
furnishings ['fə:nɪʃɪŋz] NPL Einrichtung *f*
furniture ['fə:nɪtʃə^r] N Möbel *pl*; **piece of ~** Möbelstück *nt*
furniture polish N Möbelpolitur *f*
furore [fjuə'rɔ:rɪ] N (*protests*) Proteste *pl*; (*enthusiasm*) Furore *f or nt*
furrier ['fʌrɪə^r] N Kürschner(in) *m(f)*
furrow ['fʌrəu] N Furche *f*; (*in skin*) Runzel *f* ▶ VT (*brow*) runzeln
furry ['fə:rɪ] ADJ (*coat, tail*) flauschig; (*animal*) Pelz-; (*toy*) Plüsch-
further ['fə:ðə^r] ADJ weitere(r, s) ▶ ADV weiter; (*moreover*) darüber hinaus ▶ VT fördern; **until ~ notice** bis auf Weiteres; **how much ~ is it?** wie weit ist es noch?; **~ to your letter of ...** (*Comm*) Bezug nehmend auf Ihr Schreiben vom ...
further education (BRIT) N Weiterbildung *f*, Fortbildung *f*
furthermore [fə:ðə'mɔ:^r] ADV außerdem
furthermost ['fə:ðəməust] ADJ äußerste(r, s)
furthest ['fə:ðɪst] SUPERL *of* **far**
furtive ['fə:tɪv] ADJ verstohlen
furtively ['fə:tɪvlɪ] ADV verstohlen
fury ['fjuərɪ] N Wut *f*; **to be in a ~** in Rage sein
fuse, (US) fuze [fju:z] N (*Elec*) Sicherung *f*; (*for bomb etc*) Zündschnur *f* ▶ VT (*pieces of metal*) verschmelzen; (*fig*) vereinigen ▶ VI (*pieces of metal*) sich verbinden; (*fig*) sich vereinigen; **to ~ the lights** (BRIT) die Sicherung durchbrennen lassen; **a ~ has blown** eine Sicherung ist durchgebrannt
fuse box N Sicherungskasten *m*
fuselage ['fju:zəlɑ:ʒ] N Rumpf *m*
fuse wire N Schmelzdraht *m*
fusillade [fju:zɪ'leɪd] N Salve *f*
fusion ['fju:ʒən] N Verschmelzung *f*; (*also:* **nuclear fusion**) Kernfusion *f*
fuss [fʌs] N Theater *nt* (*inf*) ▶ VI sich (unnötig) aufregen ▶ VT keine Ruhe lassen *+dat*; **to make**

a ~ Krach schlagen (*inf*); **to make a ~ of sb** viel Getue um jdn machen (*inf*)
▸ **fuss over** VT FUS bemuttern

fusspot ['fʌspɔt] N Nörgler(in) *m*(*f*)

fussy ['fʌsɪ] ADJ kleinlich, pingelig (*inf*); (*clothes, room etc*) verspielt; **I'm not ~** es ist mir egal

fusty ['fʌstɪ] ADJ muffig

futile ['fju:taɪl] ADJ vergeblich; (*existence*) sinnlos; (*comment*) zwecklos

futility [fju:'tɪlɪtɪ] N Vergeblichkeit *f*; Sinnlosigkeit *f*; Zwecklosigkeit *f*

futon ['fu:tɔn] N Futon *m*

future ['fju:tʃəʳ] ADJ zukünftig ▸ N Zukunft *f*; (*Ling*) Futur *nt*; **futures** NPL (*Comm*) Termingeschäfte *pl*; **in (the) ~** in Zukunft; **in the near ~** in der nahen Zukunft; **in the immediate ~** sehr bald

futuristic [fju:tʃə'rɪstɪk] ADJ futuristisch

fuze [fju:z] (*US*) N, VT, VI = **fuse**

fuzz [fʌz] (*inf*) N (*police*): **the ~** die Bullen *pl*

fuzzy ['fʌzɪ] ADJ verschwommen; (*hair*) kraus; (*thoughts*) verworren

fwd. ABBR = **forward**

fwy (*US*) ABBR = **freeway**

FYI ABBR (= *for your information*) zu Ihrer Information

Gg

G¹, g¹ [dʒiː] N (*letter*) G *nt*, g *nt*; **G for George** ≈ G wie Gustav
G² [dʒiː] N (*Mus*) G *nt*, g *nt*
G³ [dʒiː] N ABBR (BRIT *Scol*) = **good**; (*US Cine*: = *general (audience)*) *Klassifikation für jugendfreie Filme*; (*Phys*): **G-force** g-Druck *m*
g² ABBR (= *gram(me)*) g; (*Phys*) = **gravity**
G8 N ABBR (*Pol*: = *Group of Eight*) G-8 *f*
G20 N ABBR (*Pol*: = *Group of Twenty*) G-20 *f*
GA (*US*) N ABBR (*Post*) = **Georgia**
gab [gæb] (*inf*) N: **to have the gift of the ~** reden können, nicht auf den Mund gefallen sein
gabble ['gæbl] VI brabbeln (*inf*)
gaberdine [gæbə'diːn] N Gabardine *m*
gable ['geɪbl] N Giebel *m*
Gabon [gə'bɔn] N Gabun *nt*
gad about [gæd-] (*inf*) VI herumziehen
gadget ['gædʒɪt] N Gerät *nt*
gadgetry ['gædʒɪtrɪ] N Geräte *pl*
Gaelic ['geɪlɪk] ADJ gälisch ▸ N (*Ling*) Gälisch *nt*
gaffe [gæf] N Fauxpas *m*
gaffer ['gæfəʳ] (BRIT *inf*) N (*boss*) Chef *m*; (*foreman*) Vorarbeiter *m*; (*old man*) Alte(r) *m*
gag [gæg] N Knebel *m*; (*joke*) Gag *m* ▸ VT knebeln ▸ VI würgen
gaga ['gɑːgɑː] (*inf*) ADJ: **to go ~** verkalken
gage [geɪdʒ] (US) N, VT = **gauge**
gaiety ['geɪɪtɪ] N Fröhlichkeit *f*
gaily ['geɪlɪ] ADV fröhlich; **~ coloured** farbenfroh, farbenprächtig
gain [geɪn] N Gewinn *m* ▸ VT gewinnen ▸ VI (*clock, watch*) vorgehen; **to do sth for ~** etw aus Berechnung tun; (*for money*) etw des Geldes wegen tun; **~ (in)** (*increase*) Zunahme *f* (an *+dat*); (*in rights, conditions*) Verbesserung *f +gen*; **to ~ ground** (an) Boden gewinnen; **to ~ speed** schneller werden; **to ~ weight** zunehmen; **to ~ 3lbs (in weight)** 3 Pfund zunehmen; **to ~ (in) confidence** sicherer werden; **to ~ from sth** von etw profitieren; **to ~ in strength** stärker werden; **to ~ by doing sth** davon profitieren, etw zu tun; **to ~ on sb** jdn einholen
gainful ['geɪnful] ADJ: **~ employment** Erwerbstätigkeit *f*
gainfully ['geɪnfəlɪ] ADV: **~ employed** erwerbstätig
gainsay [geɪn'seɪ] VT (*irreg: like* **say**) widersprechen *+dat*; (*fact*) leugnen
gait [geɪt] N Gang *m*; **to walk with a slow/confident ~** mit langsamen Schritten/selbstbewusst gehen
gal. ABBR = **gallon**
gala ['gɑːlə] N Galaveranstaltung *f*; **swimming ~** großes Schwimmfest *nt*
Galapagos [gə'læpəgəs], **Galapagos Islands** NPL: **(the) ~ (Islands)** die Galapagosinseln *pl*
galaxy ['gæləksɪ] N Galaxis *f*, Sternsystem *nt*
gale [geɪl] N Sturm *m*; **~ force 10** Sturmstärke 10
gall [gɔːl] N Galle *f*; (*fig*: *impudence*) Frechheit *f* ▸ VT maßlos ärgern
gall. ABBR = **gallon**
gallant ['gælənt] ADJ tapfer; (*polite*) galant
gallantry ['gæləntrɪ] N Tapferkeit *f*; Galanterie *f*
gall bladder N Gallenblase *f*
galleon ['gælɪən] N Galeone *f*
gallery ['gælərɪ] N (*also*: **art gallery**) Galerie *f*, Museum *nt*; (*private*) (Privat)galerie *f*; (*in hall, church*) Galerie *f*; (*in theatre*) oberster Rang *m*, Balkon *m*
galley ['gælɪ] N Kombüse *f*; (*ship*) Galeere *f*; (*also*: **galley proof**) Fahne *f*, Fahnenabzug *m*
Gallic ['gælɪk] ADJ gallisch; (*French*) französisch
galling ['gɔːlɪŋ] ADJ äußerst ärgerlich
gallon ['gæln] N Gallone *f* (BRIT = *4,5 l*, US = *3,8 l*)
gallop ['gæləp] N Galopp *m* ▸ VI galoppieren; **galloping inflation** galoppierende Inflation *f*
gallows ['gæləuz] N Galgen *m*
gallstone ['gɔːlstəun] N Gallenstein *m*
Gallup poll ['gæləp-] N Meinungsumfrage *f*
galore [gə'lɔːʳ] ADV in Hülle und Fülle
galvanize ['gælvənaɪz] VT (*fig*) mobilisieren; **to ~ sb into action** jdn plötzlich aktiv werden lassen
galvanized ['gælvənaɪzd] ADJ (*metal*) galvanisiert
Gambia ['gæmbɪə] N Gambia *nt*
gambit ['gæmbɪt] N: **(opening) ~** (einleitender) Schachzug *m*; (*in conversation*) (einleitende) Bemerkung *f*
gamble ['gæmbl] N Risiko *nt* ▸ VT einsetzen ▸ VI ein Risiko eingehen; (*bet*) spielen; (*on horses etc*) wetten; **to ~ on the Stock Exchange** an der Börse spekulieren; **to ~ on sth** (*horses, race*) auf etw *acc* wetten; (*success, outcome etc*) sich auf etw *acc* verlassen
gambler ['gæmbləʳ] N Spieler(in) *m(f)*

gambling ['gæmblɪŋ] N Spielen *nt*; (*on horses etc*) Wetten *nt*
gambol ['gæmbl] VI herumtollen
game [geɪm] N Spiel *nt*; (*sport*) Sport *m*; (*strategy, scheme*) Vorhaben *nt*; (*Culin, Hunting*) Wild *nt* ▸ ADJ: **to be ~ (for)** mitmachen (bei); **games** NPL (*Scol*) Sport *m*; **to play a ~ of football/tennis** Fußball/(eine Partie) Tennis spielen; **big ~** Großwild *nt*
game bird N Federwild *nt inv*
gamekeeper ['geɪmki:pəʳ] N Wildhüter(in) *m(f)*
gamely ['geɪmlɪ] ADV mutig
gamer ['geɪməʳ] N Gamer(in) *m(f)*, Computerspieler(in) *m(f)*
game reserve N Wildschutzreservat *nt*
games console ['geɪmz-] N Spielkonsole *f*
game show N (*TV*) Spielshow *f*
gamesmanship ['geɪmzmənʃɪp] N Gerissenheit *f* beim Spiel
gaming ['geɪmɪŋ] N (*gambling*) Spielen *nt*
gammon ['gæmən] N Schinken *m*
gamut ['gæmət] N Skala *f*; **to run the ~ of** die ganze Skala *+gen* durchlaufen
gander ['gændəʳ] N Gänserich *m*
gang [gæŋ] N Bande *f*; (*of friends*) Haufen *m*; (*of workmen*) Kolonne *f*
▸ **gang up** VI: **to ~ up on sb** sich gegen jdn zusammentun
Ganges ['gændʒi:z] N: **the ~** der Ganges
gangland ['gæŋlænd] ADJ (*killer, boss*) Unterwelt-
gangling ['gæŋglɪŋ] ADJ schlaksig, hoch aufgeschossen
gangly ['gæŋglɪ] ADJ schlaksig
gangplank ['gæŋplæŋk] N Laufplanke *f*
gangrene ['gæŋgri:n] N (*Med*) Brand *m*
gangster ['gæŋstəʳ] N Gangster *m*
gangway ['gæŋweɪ] N Laufplanke *f*, Gangway *f*; (*in cinema, bus, plane etc*) Gang *m*
gantry ['gæntrɪ] N (*for crane*) Portal *nt*; (*for railway signal*) Signalbrücke *f*; (*for rocket*) Abschussrampe *f*
GAO (US) N ABBR (= *General Accounting Office*) *Rechnungshof der USA*
gaol [dʒeɪl] (BRIT) N, VT = **jail**
gap [gæp] N Lücke *f*; (*in time*) Pause *f*; (*difference*): **~ (between)** Kluft *f* (zwischen *+dat*)
gape [geɪp] VI starren, gaffen; (*hole*) gähnen; (*shirt*) offen stehen
gaping ['geɪpɪŋ] ADJ (*hole*) gähnend; (*shirt*) offen
gap year N *Jahr zwischen Schulabschluss und Studium, das oft zu Auslandsaufenthalten genutzt wird*
garage ['gærɑ:ʒ] N Garage *f*; (*for car repairs*) (Reparatur)werkstatt *f*; (*petrol station*) Tankstelle *f*
garb [gɑ:b] N Gewand *nt*, Kluft *f*
garbage ['gɑ:bɪdʒ] N (*US: rubbish*) Abfall *m*, Müll *m*; (*inf: nonsense*) Blödsinn *m*, Quatsch *m*; (*fig: film, book*) Schund *m*
garbage can (US) N Mülleimer *m*, Abfalleimer *m*
garbage collector (US) N Müllmann *m*
garbage disposal, garbage disposal unit N Müllschlucker *m*
garbage truck (US) N Müllwagen *m*
garbled ['gɑ:bld] ADJ (*account*) wirr; (*message*) unverständlich
garden ['gɑ:dn] N Garten *m* ▸ VI gärtnern; **gardens** NPL (*public park*) Park *m*; (*private*) Gartenanlagen *pl*; **she was gardening** sie arbeitete im Garten
garden centre N Gartencenter *nt*
garden city N Gartenstadt *f*
gardener ['gɑ:dnəʳ] N Gärtner(in) *m(f)*
gardening ['gɑ:dnɪŋ] N Gartenarbeit *f*
gargle ['gɑ:gl] VI gurgeln ▸ N Gurgelwasser *nt*
gargoyle ['gɑ:gɔɪl] N Wasserspeier *m*
garish ['gɛərɪʃ] ADJ grell
garland ['gɑ:lənd] N Kranz *m*
garlic ['gɑ:lɪk] N Knoblauch *m*
garlic bread N Knoblauchbrot *nt*
garment ['gɑ:mənt] N Kleidungsstück *nt*
garner ['gɑ:nəʳ] VT sammeln
garnish ['gɑ:nɪʃ] VT garnieren
garret ['gærɪt] N Dachkammer *f*, Mansarde *f*
garrison ['gærɪsn] N Garnison *f*
garrulous ['gærʊləs] ADJ geschwätzig
garter ['gɑ:təʳ] N Strumpfband *nt*; (*US: suspender*) Strumpfhalter *m*
garter belt (US) N Strumpfgürtel *m*, Hüftgürtel *m*
gas [gæs] N Gas *nt*; (*US: gasoline*) Benzin *nt* ▸ VT mit Gas vergiften; (*Mil*) vergasen; **to be given ~** (*as anaesthetic*) Lachgas bekommen
gas cooker (BRIT) N Gasherd *m*
gas cylinder N Gasflasche *f*
gaseous ['gæsɪəs] ADJ gasförmig
gas fire (BRIT) N Gasofen *m*
gas-fired ['gæsfaɪəd] ADJ (*heater etc*) Gas-
gash [gæʃ] N klaffende Wunde *f*; (*tear*) tiefer Schlitz *m* ▸ VT aufschlitzen
gasket ['gæskɪt] N Dichtung *f*
gas mask N Gasmaske *f*
gas meter N Gaszähler *m*
gasoline ['gæsəli:n] (US) N Benzin *nt*
gasp [gɑ:sp] N tiefer Atemzug *m* ▸ VI keuchen; (*in surprise*) nach Luft schnappen; **to give a ~ (of shock/horror)** (vor Schreck/Entsetzen) die Luft anhalten; **to be gasping for** sich sehnen nach *+dat*
▸ **gasp out** VT hervorstoßen
gas permeable ADJ (*lenses*) luftdurchlässig
gas ring N Gasbrenner *m*
gas station (US) N Tankstelle *f*
gas stove N (*cooker*) Gasherd *m*; (*for camping*) Gaskocher *m*
gassy ['gæsɪ] ADJ (*drink*) kohlensäurehaltig
gas tank N Benzintank *m*
gastric ['gæstrɪk] ADJ (*upset, ulcer etc*) Magen-
gastric band N Magenband *nt*
gastric flu N Darmgrippe *f*
gastroenteritis ['gæstrəuɛntə'raɪtɪs] N Magen-Darm-Katarrh *m*
gastronomy [gæs'trɔnəmɪ] N Gastronomie *f*
gasworks ['gæswə:ks] N Gaswerk *nt*
gate [geɪt] N (*of garden*) Pforte *f*; (*of field*) Gatter *nt*; (*of building*) Tor *nt*; (*at airport*) Flugsteig *m*; (*of level crossing*) Schranke *f*; (*of lock*) Tor *nt*

g

gateau ['gætəu] (*pl* **gateaux**) N Torte *f*
gate-crash ['geɪtkræʃ] (BRIT) VT (*party*) ohne Einladung besuchen; (*concert*) eindringen in *+acc* ▶ VI ohne Einladung hingehen; eindringen
gate-crasher ['geɪtkræʃəʳ] N ungeladener Gast *m*
gated community ['geɪtɪd-] N bewachte Wohnanlage *f*
gatehouse ['geɪthaus] N Pförtnerhaus *nt*
gateway ['geɪtweɪ] N (*also fig*) Tor *nt*
gather ['gæðəʳ] VT sammeln; (*flowers, fruit*) pflücken; (*understand*) schließen; (*Sewing*) kräuseln ▶ VI (*assemble*) sich versammeln; (*dust*) sich ansammeln; (*clouds*) sich zusammenziehen; **to ~ (from)** schließen (aus); **to ~ (that)** annehmen(, dass); **as far as I can ~** so wie ich es sehe; **to ~ speed** schneller werden
gathering ['gæðərɪŋ] N Versammlung *f*
GATT [gæt] N ABBR (= *General Agreement on Tariffs and Trade*) GATT *nt*
gauche [gəuʃ] ADJ linkisch
gaudy ['gɔːdɪ] ADJ knallig
gauge, (US) gage [geɪdʒ] N Messgerät *nt*, Messinstrument *nt*; (*Rail*) Spurweite *f* ▶ VT messen; (*fig*) beurteilen; **petrol ~, fuel ~, gas gage** (US) Benzinuhr *f*; **to ~ the right moment** den richtigen Moment abwägen
Gaul [gɔːl] N Gallien *nt*; (*person*) Gallier(in) *m(f)*
gaunt [gɔːnt] ADJ (*haggard*) hager; (*bare, stark*) öde
gauntlet ['gɔːntlɪt] N (Stulpen)handschuh *m*; (*fig*): **to run the ~** Spießruten laufen; **to throw down the ~** den Fehdehandschuh hinwerfen
gauze [gɔːz] N Gaze *f*
gave [geɪv] PT *of* **give**
gavel ['gævl] N Hammer *m*
gawk [gɔːk] (*inf*) VI gaffen, glotzen
gawky ['gɔːkɪ] ADJ schlaksig
gawp [gɔːp] VI: **to ~ at** angaffen, anglotzen (*inf*)
gay [geɪ] ADJ (*homosexual*) schwul; (*cheerful*) fröhlich; (*dress*) bunt
gay marriage N gleichgeschlechtliche Ehe *f*, Homoehe *f* (*inf*)
gaze [geɪz] N Blick *m* ▶ VI: **to ~ at sth** etw anstarren
gazelle [gə'zɛl] N Gazelle *f*
gazette [gə'zɛt] N Zeitung *f*; (*official*) Amtsblatt *nt*
gazetteer [gæzə'tɪəʳ] N alphabetisches Ortsverzeichnis *nt*
gazump [gə'zʌmp] (BRIT) VT: **to be gazumped** *ein mündlich zugesagtes Haus an einen Höherbietenden verlieren*
GB ABBR (= *Great Britain*) GB
GBH (BRIT) N ABBR (*Law*) = **grievous bodily harm**
GC (BRIT) N ABBR (= *George Cross*) *britische Tapferkeitsmedaille*
GCE (BRIT) N ABBR (= *General Certificate of Education*) *Schulabschlusszeugnis*, ≈ Abitur *nt*
GCHQ (BRIT) N ABBR (= *Government Communications Headquarters*) *Zentralstelle des britischen Nachrichtendienstes*
GCSE (BRIT) N ABBR (= *General Certificate of Secondary Education*) *Schulabschlusszeugnis*, ≈ mittlere Reife *f*
Gdns ABBR (*in street names*: = *Gardens*) ≈ Str.
GDP N ABBR = **gross domestic product**
GDR N ABBR (*Hist*: = *German Democratic Republic*) DDR *f*
gear [gɪəʳ] N (*equipment*) Ausrüstung *f*; (*belongings*) Sachen *pl*; (*Tech*) Getriebe *nt*; (*Aut*) Gang *m*; (*on bicycle*) Gangschaltung *f* ▶ VT (*fig*: *adapt*): **to ~ sth to** etw ausrichten auf *+acc*; **top/low/bottom ~, high/low/bottom ~** (US) hoher/niedriger/erster Gang; **to put a car into ~** einen Gang einlegen; **to leave the car in ~** den Gang eingelegt lassen; **to leave out of ~** im Leerlauf lassen; **our service is geared to meet the needs of the disabled** unser Betrieb ist auf die Bedürfnisse von Behinderten eingerichtet
▶ **gear up** VT, VI: **to ~ (o.s.) up (to)** sich vorbereiten (auf *+acc*); **to ~ o.s. up to do sth** sich darauf vorbereiten, etw zu tun
gearbox ['gɪəbɔks] N Getriebe *nt*
gear lever, (US) gear shift N Schalthebel *m*
GED (US) N ABBR (*Scol*: = *general educational development*) *allgemeine Lernentwicklung*
geek-speak ['giːkspiːk] (*US inf*) N Fachchinesisch *nt*
geese [giːs] NPL *of* **goose**
geezer ['giːzəʳ] (*inf*) N Kerl *m*, Typ *m*
Geiger counter ['gaɪgə-] N Geigerzähler *m*
gel [dʒɛl] N Gel *nt*
gelatin, gelatine ['dʒɛlətiːn] N Gelatine *f*
gelignite ['dʒɛlɪgnaɪt] N Plastiksprengstoff *m*
gem [dʒɛm] N Edelstein *m*; **she/the house is a ~** (*fig*) sie/das Haus ist ein Juwel; **a ~ of an idea** eine ausgezeichnete Idee
Gemini ['dʒɛmɪnaɪ] N (*Astrol*) Zwillinge *pl*; **to be ~** (ein) Zwilling sein
gen [dʒɛn] (BRIT *inf*) N: **to give sb the ~ on sth** jdn über etw *acc* informieren
Gen. ABBR (*Mil*: = *General*) Gen.
gen. ABBR = **general**; **generally**
gender ['dʒɛndəʳ] N Geschlecht *nt*
gene [dʒiːn] N Gen *nt*
genealogy [dʒiːnɪ'ælədʒɪ] N Genealogie *f*, Stammbaumforschung *f*; (*family history*) Stammbaum *m*
general ['dʒɛnərl] N General *m* ▶ ADJ allgemein; (*widespread*) weitverbreitet; (*non-specific*) generell; **in ~** im Allgemeinen; **the ~ public** die Öffentlichkeit, die Allgemeinheit; **~ audit** (*Comm*) Jahresabschlussprüfung *f*
general anaesthetic N Vollnarkose *f*
general delivery (US) N: **to send sth ~** etw postlagernd schicken
general election N Parlamentswahlen *pl*
generalization [dʒɛnrəlaɪ'zeɪʃən] N Verallgemeinerung *f*
generalize ['dʒɛnrəlaɪz] VI verallgemeinern
generally ['dʒɛnrəlɪ] ADV im Allgemeinen
general manager N Hauptgeschäftsführer(in) *m(f)*
general practitioner N praktischer Arzt *m*, praktische Ärztin *f*
general strike N Generalstreik *m*

generate ['dʒɛnəreɪt] VT erzeugen; *(jobs)* schaffen; *(profits)* einbringen
generation [dʒɛnə'reɪʃən] N Generation *f*; *(of electricity etc)* Erzeugung *f*
generator ['dʒɛnəreɪtə^r] N Generator *m*
generic [dʒɪ'nɛrɪk] ADJ allgemein; **~ term** Oberbegriff *m*
generosity [dʒɛnə'rɔsɪtɪ] N Großzügigkeit *f*
generous ['dʒɛnərəs] ADJ großzügig; *(measure, remuneration)* reichlich
genesis ['dʒɛnɪsɪs] N Entstehung *f*
genetic [dʒɪ'nɛtɪk] ADJ genetisch
genetically ADV genetisch; **~ modified** genmanipuliert
genetic engineering N Gentechnologie *f*
genetic fingerprint N genetischer Fingerabdruck *m*
genetics [dʒɪ'nɛtɪks] N Genetik *f*
Geneva [dʒɪ'ni:və] N Genf *nt*
genial ['dʒi:nɪəl] ADJ freundlich; *(climate)* angenehm
genitals ['dʒɛnɪtlz] NPL Genitalien *pl*, Geschlechtsteile *pl*
genitive ['dʒɛnɪtɪv] N Genitiv *m*
genius ['dʒi:nɪəs] N Talent *nt*; *(person)* Genie *nt*
Genoa ['dʒɛnəuə] N Genua *nt*
genocide ['dʒɛnəusaɪd] N Völkermord *m*
Genoese [dʒɛnəu'i:z] ADJ genuesisch ▶ N INV Genuese *m*, Genuesin *f*
genome ['dʒi:nəum] N Genom *nt*
gent [dʒɛnt] (BRIT *inf*) N ABBR = **gentleman**
genteel [dʒɛn'ti:l] ADJ vornehm, fein
gentle ['dʒɛntl] ADJ sanft; *(movement, breeze)* leicht; **a ~ hint** ein zarter Hinweis
gentleman ['dʒɛntlmən] N *(irreg)* Herr *m*; *(referring to social position or good manners)* Gentleman *m*; **~'s agreement** Vereinbarung *f* auf Treu und Glauben
gentlemanly ['dʒɛntlmənlɪ] ADJ zuvorkommend
gentleness ['dʒɛntlnɪs] N Sanftheit *f*; Leichtheit *f*; Zartheit *f*
gently ['dʒɛntlɪ] ADV sanft; leicht; zart
gentry ['dʒɛntrɪ] N INV: **the ~** die Gentry, der niedere Adel
gents [dʒɛnts] N: **the ~** die Herrentoilette
genuine ['dʒɛnjuɪn] ADJ echt; *(person)* natürlich, aufrichtig
genuinely ['dʒɛnjuɪnlɪ] ADV wirklich
geographer [dʒɪ'ɔgrəfə^r] N Geograf(in) *m(f)*
geographic [dʒɪə'græfɪk], **geographical** [dʒɪə'græfɪkl] ADJ geografisch
geography [dʒɪ'ɔgrəfɪ] N Geografie *f*; *(Scol)* Erdkunde *f*
geological [dʒɪə'lɔdʒɪkl] ADJ geologisch
geologist [dʒɪ'ɔlədʒɪst] N Geologe *m*, Geologin *f*
geology [dʒɪ'ɔlədʒɪ] N Geologie *f*
geometric [dʒɪə'mɛtrɪk], **geometrical** [dʒɪə'mɛtrɪkl] ADJ geometrisch
geometry [dʒɪ'ɔmətrɪ] N Geometrie *f*
Geordie ['dʒɔ:dɪ] *(inf)* N *aus dem Gebiet von Newcastle stammende oder dort wohnhafte Person*
Georgia ['dʒɔ:dʒə] N *(in Eastern Europe)* Georgien *nt*
Georgian ['dʒɔ:dʒən] ADJ georgisch ▶ N Georgier(in) *m(f)*; *(Ling)* Georgisch *nt*
geranium [dʒɪ'reɪnɪəm] N Geranie *f*
gerbil ['dʒɜ:bəl] N *(Zool)* Wüstenrennmaus *f*
geriatric [dʒɛrɪ'ætrɪk] ADJ geriatrisch ▶ N Greis(in) *m(f)*
germ [dʒə:m] N Bazillus *m*; *(Biol, fig)* Keim *m*
German ['dʒə:mən] ADJ deutsch ▶ N Deutsche(r) *f(m)*; *(Ling)* Deutsch *nt*
German Democratic Republic N *(formerly)* Deutsche Demokratische Republik *f*
germane [dʒə:'meɪn] ADJ: **~ (to)** von Belang (für)
German measles (BRIT) N Röteln *pl*
German Shepherd, German Shepherd dog *(esp US)* N Schäferhund *m*
Germany ['dʒə:mənɪ] N Deutschland *nt*
germinate ['dʒə:mɪneɪt] VI keimen; *(fig)* aufkeimen
germination [dʒə:mɪ'neɪʃən] N Keimung *f*
germ warfare N biologische Kriegsführung *f*, Bakterienkrieg *m*
gerrymandering ['dʒɛrɪmændərɪŋ] N Wahlkreisschiebungen *pl*
gestation [dʒɛs'teɪʃən] N *(of animals)* Trächtigkeit *f*; *(of humans)* Schwangerschaft *f*
gesticulate [dʒɛs'tɪkjuleɪt] VI gestikulieren
gesture ['dʒɛstjə^r] N Geste *f*; **as a ~ of friendship** als Zeichen der Freundschaft

KEYWORD

get [gɛt] *(pt, pp* **got**, *US pp* **gotten**) VI **1** *(become, be)* werden; **to get old/tired/cold** alt/müde/kalt werden; **to get dirty** sich schmutzig machen; **to get killed** getötet werden; **to get married** heiraten
2 *(go)*: **to get (from ...) to ...** (von ...) nach ... kommen; **how did you get here?** wie sind Sie hierhin gekommen?
3 *(begin)*: **to get to know sb** jdn kennenlernen; **let's get going** *or* **started** fangen wir an!
▶ MODAL AUX VB: **you've got to do it** du musst es tun
▶ VT **1**: **to get sth done** *(do oneself)* etw gemacht bekommen; *(have done)* etw machen lassen; **to get one's hair cut** sich *dat* die Haare schneiden lassen; **to get the car going** *or* **to go** das Auto in Gang bringen; **to get sb to do sth** etw von jdm machen lassen; *(persuade)* jdn dazu bringen, etw zu tun
2 *(obtain: money, permission, results)* erhalten
3 *(fetch: person, doctor, object)* holen
4 *(find: job, flat)* finden; **to get sth for sb** jdm etw besorgen; **can I get you a drink?** kann ich Ihnen etwas zu trinken anbieten?
5 *(receive, acquire: present, prize)* bekommen; **how much did you get for the painting?** wie viel haben Sie für das Bild bekommen?
6 *(catch)* bekommen, kriegen *(inf)*
7 *(hit: target etc)* treffen; **to get sb by the arm/throat** jdn am Arm/Hals packen; **the bullet got him in the leg** die Kugel traf ihn ins Bein
8 *(take, move)* bringen; **to get sth to sb** jdm etw zukommen lassen

g

9 (*plane, bus etc: take*) nehmen; (*: catch*) bekommen
10 (*understand: joke etc*) verstehen; **I get it** ich verstehe
11 (*have, possess*): **to have got** haben; **how many have you got?** wie viele hast du?
▸ **get about** VI (*person*) herumkommen; (*news, rumour*) sich verbreiten
▸ **get across** VT (*message, meaning*) klarmachen
▸ **get along** VI (*be friends*) (miteinander) auskommen; (*depart*) sich auf den Weg machen
▸ **get around** VT FUS = **get round**
▸ **get at** VT FUS (*attack, criticize*) angreifen; (*reach*) herankommen an *+acc*; **what are you getting at?** worauf willst du hinaus?
▸ **get away** VI (*leave*) wegkommen; (*on holiday*) verreisen; (*escape*) entkommen
▸ **get away with** VT FUS (*stolen goods*) entkommen mit; **he'll never get away with it!** damit kommt er nicht durch
▸ **get back** VI (*return*) zurückkommen ▸ VT (*regain*) zurückbekommen; **get back!** zurück!
▸ **get back at** (*inf*) VT FUS: **to get back at sb for sth** jdm etw heimzahlen
▸ **get back to** VT FUS (*return to*) zurückkehren zu; (*contact again*) zurückkommen auf *+acc*; **to get back to sleep** wieder einschlafen
▸ **get by** VI (*pass*) vorbeikommen; (*manage*) zurechtkommen; **I can get by in German** ich kann mich auf Deutsch verständlich machen
▸ **get down** VI (*from tree, ladder etc*) heruntersteigen; (*from horse*) absteigen; (*leave table*) aufstehen; (*bend down*) sich bücken; (*duck*) sich ducken ▸ VT (*depress: person*) fertigmachen; (*write*) aufschreiben
▸ **get down to** VT FUS: **to get down to sth** (*work*) etw in Angriff nehmen; (*find time*) zu etw kommen; **to get down to business** (*fig*) zur Sache kommen
▸ **get in** VI (*be elected, candidate, party*) gewählt werden; (*arrive*) ankommen ▸ VT (*bring in: harvest*) einbringen; (*: shopping, supplies*) (herein)holen
▸ **get into** VT FUS (*conversation, argument, fight*) geraten in *+acc*; (*vehicle*) einsteigen in *+acc*; (*clothes*) hineinkommen in *+acc*; **to get into bed** ins Bett gehen; **to get into the habit of doing sth** sich *dat* angewöhnen, etw zu tun
▸ **get off** VI (*from train etc*) aussteigen; (*escape punishment*) davonkommen ▸ VT (*remove: clothes*) ausziehen; (*: stain*) herausbekommen ▸ VT FUS (*leave: train, bus*) aussteigen aus; **we get 3 days off at Christmas** zu Weihnachten bekommen wir 3 Tage frei; **to get off to a good start** (*fig*) einen guten Anfang machen
▸ **get on** VI (*be friends*) (miteinander) auskommen ▸ VT FUS (*bus, train*) einsteigen in *+acc*; **how are you getting on?** wie kommst du zurecht?; **time is getting on** es wird langsam spät
▸ **get on to** (BRIT) VT FUS (*subject, topic*) übergehen zu; (*contact: person*) sich in Verbindung setzen mit
▸ **get on with** VT FUS (*person*) auskommen mit; (*meeting, work etc*) weitermachen mit
▸ **get out** VI (*leave: on foot*) hinausgehen; (*of vehicle*) aussteigen; (*news etc*) herauskommen ▸ VT (*take out: book etc*) herausholen; (*remove: stain*) herausbekommen
▸ **get out of** VT FUS (*money: bank etc*) abheben von; (*avoid: duty etc*) herumkommen um ▸ VT (*extract: confession etc*) herausbekommen aus; (*derive: pleasure*) haben an *+dat*; (*: benefit*) haben von
▸ **get over** VT FUS (*overcome*) überwinden; (*: illness*) sich erholen von; (*communicate: idea etc*) verständlich machen ▸ VT: **to get it over with** (*finish*) es hinter sich *acc* bringen
▸ **get round** VT FUS (*law, rule*) umgehen; (*person*) herumkriegen
▸ **get round to** VT FUS: **to get round to doing sth** dazu kommen, etw zu tun
▸ **get through** VI (*Tel*) durchkommen ▸ VT FUS (*finish: work*) schaffen; (*: book*) lesen
▸ **get through to** VT FUS (*Tel*) durchkommen zu; (*make o.s. understood*) durchdringen zu
▸ **get together** VI (*people*) zusammenkommen ▸ VT (*people*) zusammenbringen; (*project, plan etc*) zusammenstellen
▸ **get up** VI (*rise*) aufstehen ▸ VT: **to get up enthusiasm for sth** Begeisterung für etw aufbringen
▸ **get up to** VT FUS (*prank etc*) anstellen

getaway ['gɛtəweɪ] N: **to make a/one's ~** sich davonmachen
getaway car N Fluchtauto *nt*
get-together ['gɛttəgɛðə^r] N Treffen *nt*; (*party*) Party *f*
get-up ['gɛtʌp] (*inf*) N Aufmachung *f*
get-well card [gɛt'wɛl-] N Karte *f* mit Genesungswünschen
geyser ['gi:zə^r] N Geiser *m*; (BRIT: *water heater*) Durchlauferhitzer *m*
Ghana ['gɑ:nə] N Ghana *nt*
Ghanaian [gɑ:'neɪən] ADJ ghanaisch ▸ N Ghanaer(in) *m(f)*
ghastly ['gɑ:stlɪ] ADJ grässlich; (*complexion*) totenblass; **you look ~!** (*ill*) du siehst grässlich aus!
gherkin ['gə:kɪn] N Gewürzgurke *f*
ghetto ['gɛtəu] N G(h)etto *nt*
ghetto blaster [-'blɑ:stə^r] (*inf*) N Gettoblaster *m*
ghost [gəust] N Geist *m*, Gespenst *nt* ▸ VT für jdn (als Ghostwriter) schreiben; **to give up the ~** den Geist aufgeben
ghost town N Geisterstadt *f*
ghostwriter ['gəustraɪtə^r] N Ghostwriter(in) *m(f)*
ghoul [gu:l] N böser Geist *m*
ghoulish ['gu:lɪʃ] ADJ makaber
GHQ N ABBR (*Mil: = General Headquarters*) Hauptquartier *nt*
GHz ABBR (*= gigahertz*) GHz
GI (*US inf*) N ABBR (*= government issue*) GI *m*
giant ['dʒaɪənt] N (*also fig*) Riese *m* ▸ ADJ riesig, riesenhaft; **~ (size) packet** Riesenpackung *f*

giant killer N (*fig*) Goliathbezwinger(in) *m(f)*
gibber ['dʒɪbəʳ] VI brabbeln
gibberish ['dʒɪbərɪʃ] N Quatsch *m*
gibe [dʒaɪb] N spöttische Bemerkung *f* ▶ VI: **to ~ at** spöttische Bemerkungen machen über *+acc*
Gibraltar [dʒɪ'brɔːltəʳ] N Gibraltar *nt*
giddiness ['gɪdɪnɪs] N Schwindelgefühl *nt*
giddy ['gɪdɪ] ADJ: **I am/feel ~** mir ist schwind(e)lig; (*height*) schwindelerregend; **~ with excitement** vor Aufregung ganz ausgelassen
gift [gɪft] N Geschenk *nt*; (*donation*) Spende *f*; (*Comm*: *also*: **free gift**) (Werbe)geschenk *nt*; (*ability*) Gabe *f*; **to have a ~ for sth** ein Talent für etw haben
gift card N (*US*) elektronische Guthabenkarte *f*, Gift Card *f* (*häufig in Form eines Gutscheins*)
gifted ['gɪftɪd] ADJ begabt
gift token N Geschenkgutschein *m*
gift voucher N = **gift token**
gig [gɪg] N (*performance*) Gig *m*; (*gigabyte*) Gigabyte *f*
gigabyte ['dʒɪgəbaɪt] N Gigabyte *nt*
gigantic [dʒaɪ'gæntɪk] ADJ riesig, riesengroß
giggle ['gɪgl] VI kichern ▶ N Spaß *m*; **to do sth for a ~** etw aus Spaß tun
GIGO ['gaɪgəu] (*inf*) ABBR (*Comput*: = *garbage in, garbage out*) GIGO
gild [gɪld] VT vergolden
gill [dʒɪl] N Gill *nt* (*BRIT* = *15 cl*, *US* = *12 cl*)
gills [gɪlz] NPL Kiemen *pl*
gilt [gɪlt] ADJ vergoldet ▶ N Vergoldung *f*; **gilts** NPL (*Comm*) mündelsichere Wertpapiere *pl*
gilt-edged ['gɪltɛdʒd] ADJ (*stocks, securities*) mündelsicher
gimlet ['gɪmlɪt] N Handbohrer *m*
gimmick ['gɪmɪk] N Gag *m*; **sales ~** Verkaufsmasche *f*, Verkaufstrick *m*
gin [dʒɪn] N Gin *m*
ginger ['dʒɪndʒəʳ] N Ingwer *m* ▶ ADJ (*hair*) rötlich; (*cat*) rötlich gelb
ginger ale N Gingerale *nt*
ginger beer N Ingwerbier *nt*
gingerbread ['dʒɪndʒəbrɛd] N (*cake*) Ingwerkuchen *m*; (*biscuit*) ≈ Pfefferkuchen *m*
ginger group (BRIT) N Aktionsgruppe *f*
gingerly ['dʒɪndʒəlɪ] ADV vorsichtig
gingham ['gɪŋəm] N Gingan *m*, Gingham *m*
ginseng ['dʒɪnsɛŋ] N Ginseng *m*
gipsy ['dʒɪpsɪ] N Zigeuner(in) *m(f)*
gipsy caravan N Zigeunerwagen *m*
giraffe [dʒɪ'rɑːf] N Giraffe *f*
girder ['gəːdəʳ] N Träger *m*
girdle ['gəːdl] N Hüftgürtel *m*, Hüfthalter *m* ▶ VT (*fig*) umgeben
girl [gəːl] N Mädchen *nt*; (*young unmarried woman*) (junges) Mädchen *nt*; (*daughter*) Tochter *f*; **this is my little ~** das ist mein Töchterchen; **an English ~** eine Engländerin
girlfriend ['gəːlfrɛnd] N Freundin *f*
Girl Guide N Pfadfinderin *f*
girlish ['gəːlɪʃ] ADJ mädchenhaft
Girl Scout (US) N Pfadfinderin *f*
Giro ['dʒaɪrəu] N: **the National ~** (BRIT) der Postscheckdienst
giro ['dʒaɪrəu] N Giro *nt*, Giroverkehr *m*; (*post office giro*) Postscheckverkehr *m*; (BRIT: *welfare cheque*) Sozialhilfescheck *m*
girth [gəːθ] N Umfang *m*; (*of horse*) Sattelgurt *m*
gist [dʒɪst] N Wesentliche(s) *nt*

KEYWORD

give [gɪv] (*pt* **gave**, *pp* **given**) VT **1** (*hand over*): **to give sb sth, give sth to sb** jdm etw geben; **I'll give you £5 for it** ich gebe dir £5 dafür
2 (*used with noun to replace a verb*): **to give a sigh/cry/laugh** *etc* seufzen/schreien/lachen *etc*; **to give a speech/a lecture** eine Rede/einen Vortrag halten; **to give three cheers** ein dreifaches Hoch ausbringen
3 (*tell, deliver*: *news, message etc*) mitteilen; (: *advice, answer*) geben
4 (*supply, provide*: *opportunity, job etc*) geben; (: *surprise*) bereiten; (: *bestow*: *title, honour, right*) geben, verleihen; **that's given me an idea** dabei kommt mir eine Idee
5 (*devote*: *time, one's life*) geben; (: *attention*) schenken
6 (*organize*: *party, dinner etc*) geben
▶ VI **1** (*break, collapse*: *also*: **give way**) nachgeben
2 (*stretch*: *fabric*) sich dehnen
▶ **give away** VT (*money, opportunity*) verschenken; (*secret, information*) verraten; (*bride*) zum Altar führen; **that immediately gave him away** dadurch verriet er sich sofort
▶ **give back** VT (*money, book etc*) zurückgeben
▶ **give in** VI (*yield*) nachgeben ▶ VT (*essay etc*) abgeben
▶ **give off** VT (*heat, smoke*) abgeben
▶ **give out** VT (*prizes, books, drinks etc*) austeilen
▶ VI (*be exhausted*: *supplies*) zu Ende gehen; (*fail*) versagen
▶ **give up** VT, VI aufgeben; **to give up smoking** das Rauchen aufgeben; **to give o.s. up** sich stellen; (*after siege etc*) sich ergeben
▶ **give way** VI (*yield, collapse*) nachgeben; (BRIT *Aut*) die Vorfahrt achten

give-and-take ['gɪvənd'teɪk] N (gegenseitiges) Geben und Nehmen *nt*
giveaway ['gɪvəweɪ] (*inf*) N: **her expression was a ~** ihr Gesichtsausdruck verriet alles; **the exam was a ~!** die Prüfung war geschenkt!; **~ prices** Schleuderpreise *pl*
given ['gɪvn] PP *of* **give** ▶ ADJ (*time, amount*) bestimmt ▶ CONJ: **~ the circumstances ...** unter den Umständen ...; **~ that ...** angesichts der Tatsache, dass ...
glacial ['gleɪsɪəl] ADJ (*landscape etc*) Gletscher-; (*fig*) eisig
glacier ['glæsɪəʳ] N Gletscher *m*
glad [glæd] ADJ froh; **to be ~ about sth** sich über etw *acc* freuen; **to be ~ that** sich freuen, dass; **I was ~ of his help** ich war froh über seine Hilfe
gladden ['glædn] VT erfreuen

glade [gleɪd] N Lichtung *f*
gladioli [glædɪ'əulaɪ] NPL Gladiolen *pl*
gladly ['glædlɪ] ADV gern(e)
glamorous ['glæmərəs] ADJ reizvoll; (*model etc*) glamourös
glamour ['glæmə^r] N Glanz *m*, Reiz *m*
glance [glɑ:ns] N Blick *m* ▶ VI: **to ~ at** einen Blick werfen auf *+acc*
▶ **glance off** VT FUS abprallen von
glancing ['glɑ:nsɪŋ] ADJ: **to strike sth a ~ blow** etw streifen
gland [glænd] N Drüse *f*
glandular fever ['glændjulə-] (BRIT) N Drüsenfieber *nt*
glare [glɛə^r] N wütender Blick *m*; (*of light*) greller Schein *m*; (*of publicity*) grelles Licht *nt* ▶ VI (*light*) grell scheinen; **to ~ at** (wütend) anstarren
glaring ['glɛərɪŋ] ADJ eklatant
glasnost ['glæznɔst] N Glasnost *f*
glass [glɑ:s] N Glas *nt*; **glasses** NPL (*spectacles*) Brille *f*
glass-blowing ['glɑ:sbləuɪŋ] N Glasbläserei *f*
glass ceiling N (*fig*) gläserne Decke *f*
glass fibre N Glasfaser *f*
glasshouse ['glɑ:shaus] N Gewächshaus *nt*
glassware ['glɑ:swɛə^r] N Glaswaren *pl*
glassy ['glɑ:sɪ] ADJ glasig
Glaswegian [glæs'wi:dʒən] ADJ Glasgower ▶ N Glasgower(in) *m(f)*
glaze [gleɪz] VT (*door, window*) verglasen; (*pottery*) glasieren ▶ N Glasur *f*
glazed [gleɪzd] ADJ (*eyes*) glasig; (*pottery, tiles*) glasiert
glazier ['gleɪzɪə^r] N Glaser(in) *m(f)*
gleam [gli:m] VI (*light*) schimmern; (*polished surface, eyes*) glänzen ▶ N: **a ~ of hope** ein Hoffnungsschimmer *m*
gleaming ['gli:mɪŋ] ADJ schimmernd, glänzend
glean [gli:n] VT (*information*) herausbekommen, ausfindig machen
glee [gli:] N Freude *f*
gleeful ['gli:ful] ADJ fröhlich
glen [glɛn] N Tal *nt*
glib [glɪb] ADJ (*person*) glatt; (*promise, response*) leichthin gemacht
glibly ['glɪblɪ] ADV (*talk*) gewandt; (*answer*) leichthin
glide [glaɪd] VI gleiten ▶ N Gleiten *nt*
glider ['glaɪdə^r] N Segelflugzeug *nt*
gliding ['glaɪdɪŋ] N Segelfliegen *nt*
glimmer ['glɪmə^r] N Schimmer *m*; (*of interest, hope*) Funke *m* ▶ VI schimmern
glimpse [glɪmps] N Blick *m* ▶ VT einen Blick werfen auf *+acc*; **to catch a ~ (of)** einen flüchtigen Blick erhaschen (von *+dat*)
glint [glɪnt] VI glitzern; (*eyes*) funkeln ▶ N Glitzern *nt*; Funkeln *nt*
glisten ['glɪsn] VI glänzen
glitter ['glɪtə^r] VI glitzern; (*eyes*) funkeln ▶ N Glitzern *nt*; Funkeln *nt*
glittering ['glɪtərɪŋ] ADJ glitzernd; (*eyes*) funkelnd; (*career*) glänzend
glitz [glɪts] (*inf*) N Glanz *m*
glitzy [glɪtsɪ] ADJ (*inf*) glanzvoll, Schickimicki-
gloat [gləut] VI: **to ~ (over)** (*own success*) sich brüsten (mit); (*sb's failure*) sich hämisch freuen (über *+acc*)
global ['gləubl] ADJ global
globalization [gləublaɪ'zeɪʃn] N (*Pol, Econ*) Globalisierung *f*
global player N (*Econ*) Weltfirma *f*, Global Player *m*
global warming [-'wɔ:mɪŋ] N Erwärmung *f* der Erdatmosphäre
globe [gləub] N Erdball *m*; (*model*) Globus *m*; (*shape*) Kugel *f*
globetrotter ['gləubtrɔtə^r] N Globetrotter(in) *m(f)*, Weltenbummler(in) *m(f)*
globule ['glɔbju:l] N Tröpfchen *nt*
gloom [glu:m] N Düsterkeit *f*; (*sadness*) düstere *or* gedrückte Stimmung *f*
gloomily ['glu:mɪlɪ] ADV düster
gloomy ['glu:mɪ] ADJ düster; (*person*) bedrückt; (*situation*) bedrückend
glorification [glɔ:rɪfɪ'keɪʃən] N Verherrlichung *f*
glorify ['glɔ:rɪfaɪ] VT verherrlichen
glorious ['glɔ:rɪəs] ADJ herrlich; (*victory*) ruhmreich; (*future*) glanzvoll
glory ['glɔ:rɪ] N Ruhm *m*; (*splendour*) Herrlichkeit *f* ▶ VI: **to ~ in** sich sonnen in *+dat*
glory hole (*inf*) N Rumpelkammer *f*
Glos (BRIT) ABBR (*Post*) = **Gloucestershire**
gloss [glɔs] N Glanz *m*; (*also*: **gloss paint**) Lack *m*, Lackfarbe *f*
▶ **gloss over** VT FUS vom Tisch wischen
glossary ['glɔsərɪ] N Glossar *nt*
glossy ['glɔsɪ] ADJ glänzend; (*photograph, magazine*) Hochglanz- ▶ N (*also*: **glossy magazine**) (Hochglanz)magazin *nt*
glove [glʌv] N Handschuh *m*
glove compartment N Handschuhfach *nt*
glow [gləu] VI glühen; (*stars, eyes*) leuchten ▶ N Glühen *nt*; Leuchten *nt*
glower ['glauə^r] VI: **to ~ at sb** jdn finster ansehen
glowing ['gləuɪŋ] ADJ glühend; (*complexion*) blühend; (*fig: report, description etc*) begeistert
glow-worm ['gləuwə:m] N Glühwürmchen *nt*
glucose ['glu:kəus] N Traubenzucker *m*
glue [glu:] N Klebstoff *m* ▶ VT: **to ~ sth onto sth** etw an etw *acc* kleben; **to ~ sth into place** etw festkleben
glue-sniffing ['glu:snɪfɪŋ] N (Klebstoff-)schnüffeln *nt*
glum [glʌm] ADJ bedrückt, niedergeschlagen
glut [glʌt] N: **~ (of)** Überangebot *nt* (an *+dat*) ▶ VT: **to be glutted (with)** überschwemmt sein (mit); **a ~ of pears** eine Birnenschwemme
glutinous ['glu:tɪnəs] ADJ klebrig
glutton ['glʌtn] N Vielfraß *m*; **a ~ for work** ein Arbeitstier *nt*; **a ~ for punishment** ein Masochist *m*
gluttonous ['glʌtənəs] ADJ gefräßig
gluttony ['glʌtənɪ] N Völlerei *f*
glycerin, glycerine ['glɪsəri:n] N Glyzerin *nt*
GM ABBR = **genetically modified**

gm ABBR (= *gram(me)*) g
GMAT ['dʒi:mæt] (US) N ABBR (= *Graduate Management Admissions Test*) *Zulassungsprüfung für Handelsschulen*
GM crop N ABBR GV-Pflanze *f*
GM foods N GV-Lebensmittel *pl*
GMT ABBR (= *Greenwich Mean Time*) WEZ *f*
gnarled [nɑ:ld] ADJ (*tree*) knorrig; (*hand*) knotig
gnash [næʃ] VT: **to ~ one's teeth** mit den Zähnen knirschen
gnat [næt] N (Stech)mücke *f*
gnaw [nɔ:] VT nagen an *+dat* ▸ VI (*fig*): **to ~ at** quälen
gnome [nəum] N Gnom *m*; (*in garden*) Gartenzwerg *m*
GNP N ABBR (= *gross national product*) BSP *nt*
GNVQ (BRIT) N ABBR (= *General National Vocational Qualification*) *allgemeine, auf die Arbeitswelt bezogene Qualifikation*

KEYWORD

go [gəu] (*pt* **went**, *pp* **gone**) VI **1** gehen; (*travel*) fahren; **a car went by** ein Auto fuhr vorbei
2 (*depart*) gehen; **"I must go," she said** „ich muss gehen", sagte sie; **she has gone to Sheffield/Australia** (*permanently*) sie ist nach Sheffield/Australien gegangen
3 (*attend, take part in activity*) gehen; **she went to university in Oxford** sie ist in Oxford zur Universität gegangen; **to go for a walk** spazieren gehen; **to go dancing** tanzen gehen
4 (*work*) funktionieren; **the tape recorder was still going** das Tonband lief noch
5 (*become*): **to go pale/mouldy** blass/schimmelig werden
6 (*be sold*): **to go for £100** für £100 weggehen *or* verkauft werden
7 (*be about to, intend to*): **we're going to stop in an hour** wir hören in einer Stunde auf; **are you going to come?** kommst du?, wirst du kommen?
8 (*time*) vergehen
9 (*event, activity*) ablaufen; **how did it go?** wie wars?
10 (*be given*): **the job is to go to someone else** die Stelle geht an jemand anders
11 (*break etc*) kaputtgehen; **the fuse went** die Sicherung ist durchgebrannt
12 (*be placed*) hingehören; **the milk goes in the fridge** die Milch kommt in den Kühlschrank
▸ N **1** (*try*): **to have a go at sth** etw versuchen; **I'll have a go at mending it** ich will versuchen, es zu reparieren; **to have a go** es versuchen
2 (*turn*): **whose go is it?** wer ist dran *or* an der Reihe?
3 (*move*): **to be on the go** auf Trab sein
▸ **go about** VI (*also*: **go around**: *rumour*) herumgehen ▸ VT FUS: **how do I go about this?** wie soll ich vorgehen?; **to go about one's business** seinen eigenen Geschäften nachgehen
▸ **go after** VT FUS (*pursue: person*) nachgehen *+dat*; (*: job etc*) sich bemühen um; (*: record*) erreichen wollen
▸ **go against** VT FUS (*be unfavourable to*) ungünstig verlaufen für; (*disregard: advice, wishes etc*) handeln gegen
▸ **go ahead** VI (*proceed*) weitergehen; **to go ahead with** weitermachen mit
▸ **go along** VI gehen
▸ **go along with** VT FUS (*agree with*) zustimmen *+dat*; (*accompany*) mitgehen mit
▸ **go away** VI (*leave*) weggehen
▸ **go back** VI zurückgehen
▸ **go back on** VT FUS (*promise*) zurücknehmen
▸ **go by** VI (*years, time*) vergehen ▸ VT FUS (*rule etc*) sich richten nach
▸ **go down** VI (*descend*) hinuntergehen; (*ship, sun*) untergehen; (*price, level*) sinken ▸ VT FUS (*stairs, ladder*) hinuntergehen; **his speech went down well** seine Rede kam gut an
▸ **go for** VT FUS (*fetch*) holen (gehen); (*like*) mögen; (*attack*) losgehen auf *+acc*; (*apply to*) gelten für
▸ **go in** VI (*enter*) hineingehen
▸ **go in for** VT FUS (*competition*) teilnehmen an *+dat*; (*favour*) stehen auf *+acc*
▸ **go into** VT FUS (*enter*) hineingehen in *+acc*; (*investigate*) sich befassen mit; (*career*) gehen in *+acc*
▸ **go off** VI (*leave*) weggehen; (*food*) schlecht werden; (*bomb, gun*) losgehen; (*event*) verlaufen; (*lights etc*) ausgehen ▸ VT FUS (*inf*): **I've gone off it/him** ich mache mir nichts mehr daraus/aus ihm; **the gun went off** das Gewehr ging los; **to go off to sleep** einschlafen; **the party went off well** die Party verlief gut
▸ **go on** VI (*continue*) weitergehen; (*happen*) vor sich gehen; (*lights*) angehen ▸ VT FUS (*be guided by*) sich stützen auf *+acc*; **to go on doing sth** mit etw weitermachen; **what's going on here?** was geht hier vor?, was ist hier los?
▸ **go on at** (*inf*) VT FUS (*nag*) herumnörgeln an *+dat*
▸ **go on with** VT FUS weitermachen mit
▸ **go out** VT FUS (*leave*) hinausgehen ▸ VI (*for entertainment*) ausgehen; (*fire, light*) ausgehen; (*couple*): **they went out for 3 years** sie gingen 3 Jahre lang miteinander
▸ **go over** VI hinübergehen ▸ VT (*check*) durchgehen; **to go over sth in one's mind** etw überdenken
▸ **go round** VI (*circulate: news, rumour*) umgehen; (*revolve*) sich drehen; (*suffice*) ausreichen; (*visit*): **to go round (to sb's)** (bei jdm) vorbeigehen; **there's not enough to go round** es reicht nicht (für alle)
▸ **go through** VT FUS (*place*) gehen durch; (*by car*) fahren durch; (*undergo*) durchmachen; (*search through: files, papers*) durchsuchen; (*describe: list, book, story*) durchgehen; (*perform*) durchgehen
▸ **go through with** VT FUS (*plan, crime*) durchziehen; **I couldn't go through with it** ich brachte es nicht fertig

▸ **go under** VI (*sink*: *person*) untergehen; (*fig*: *business, project*) scheitern
▸ **go up** VI (*ascend*) hinaufgehen; (*price, level*) steigen; **to go up in flames** in Flammen aufgehen
▸ **go with** VT FUS (*suit*) passen zu
▸ **go without** VT FUS (*food, treats*) verzichten auf *+acc*

goad [gəud] VT aufreizen
▸ **goad on** VT anstacheln
go-ahead ['gəuəhɛd] ADJ zielstrebig; (*firm*) fortschrittlich ▸ N grünes Licht *nt*; **to give sb the ~** jdm grünes Licht geben
goal [gəul] N Tor *nt*; (*aim*) Ziel *nt*; **to score a ~** ein Tor schießen *or* erzielen
goal difference N Tordifferenz *f*
goalie ['gəulı] (*inf*) N Tormann *m*
goalkeeper ['gəulki:pər] N Torwart *m*
goal post N Torpfosten *m*
goat [gəut] N Ziege *f*
gob [gɔb] N (BRIT *inf*) Maul *nt* ▸ VI spucken; **shut your ~** halt's Maul!
gobble ['gɔbl] VT (*also*: **gobble down, gobble up**) verschlingen
go-between ['gəubıtwi:n] N Vermittler(in) *m(f)*
Gobi Desert ['gəubı-] N: **the ~** die Wüste Gobi
goblet ['gɔblıt] N Pokal *m*
goblin ['gɔblın] N Kobold *m*
gobsmacked ['gɔbsmækt] ADJ (*inf*: *surprised*) platt
go-cart ['gəukɑ:t] N Gokart *m*
God [gɔd] N Gott *m* ▸ EXCL o Gott!
god [gɔd] N Gott *m*
god-awful [gɔd'ɔ:fəl] (*inf*) ADJ beschissen (*inf!*)
godchild ['gɔdtʃaıld] N (*irreg*) Patenkind *nt*
goddamn ['gɔddæm], (US) **goddamned** ['gɔddæmd] (*inf*) ADJ gottverdammt
goddaughter ['gɔddɔ:tər] N Patentochter *f*
goddess ['gɔdıs] N Göttin *f*
godfather ['gɔdfɑ:ðər] N Pate *m*
God-fearing ['gɔdfıərıŋ] ADJ gottesfürchtig
godforsaken ['gɔdfəseıkən] ADJ gottverlassen
godmother ['gɔdmʌðər] N Patin *f*
godparent ['gɔdpɛərənt] N Pate *m*, Patin *f*
godsend ['gɔdsɛnd] N Geschenk *nt* des Himmels
godson ['gɔdsʌn] N Patensohn *m*
goes [gəuz] VB *see* **go**
gofer ['gəufər] (*inf*) N Mädchen *nt* für alles
go-getter ['gəugɛtər] (*inf*) N Ellbogentyp *m* (*pej, inf*)
goggle ['gɔgl] (*inf*) VI: **to ~ at** anstarren, anglotzen
goggles ['gɔglz] NPL Schutzbrille *f*
going ['gəuıŋ] N: **it was slow/hard ~** (*fig*) es ging nur langsam/schwer voran ▸ ADJ: **the ~ rate** der gängige Preis; **when the ~ gets tough** wenn es schwierig wird; **a ~ concern** ein gut gehendes Unternehmen
going-over [gəuıŋ'əuvər] (*inf*) N (*check*) Untersuchung *f*; (*beating-up*) Abreibung *f*; **to give sb a good ~** jdm eine tüchtige Abreibung verpassen
goings-on ['gəuıŋz'ɔn] (*inf*) NPL Vorgänge *pl*, Dinge *pl*
go-kart ['gəukɑ:t] N = **go-cart**
gold [gəuld] N Gold *nt*; (*also*: **gold medal**) Gold *nt*, Goldmedaille *f* ▸ ADJ golden; (*reserves, jewellery, tooth*) Gold-
golden ['gəuldən] ADJ (*also fig*) golden
golden age N Blütezeit *f*
golden handshake (BRIT) N Abstandssumme *f*
golden rule N goldene Regel *f*
goldfish ['gəuldfıʃ] N Goldfisch *m*
gold leaf N Blattgold *nt*
gold medal N Goldmedaille *f*
gold mine N (*also fig*) Goldgrube *f*
gold-plated ['gəuld'pleıtıd] ADJ vergoldet
goldsmith ['gəuldsmıθ] N Goldschmied(in) *m(f)*
gold standard N Goldstandard *m*
golf [gɔlf] N Golf *nt*
golf ball N (*for game*) Golfball *m*; (*on typewriter*) Kugelkopf *m*
golf club N Golfklub *m*; (*stick*) Golfschläger *m*
golf course N Golfplatz *m*
golfer ['gɔlfər] N Golfspieler(in) *m(f)*, Golfer(in) *m(f)*
golfing ['gɔlfıŋ] N Golf(spielen) *nt* ▸ CPD Golf-; **he does a lot of ~** er spielt viel Golf
gondola ['gɔndələ] N Gondel *f*
gondolier [gɔndə'lıər] N Gondoliere *m*
gone [gɔn] PP *of* **go** ▸ ADJ weg; (*days*) vorbei
goner ['gɔnər] (*inf*) N: **to be a ~** hinüber sein
gong [gɔŋ] N Gong *m*
good [gud] ADJ gut; (*well-behaved*) brav, lieb ▸ N (*virtue, morality*) Gute(s) *nt*; (*benefit*) Wohl *nt*;
goods NPL (*Comm*) Güter *pl*; **to have a ~ time** sich (gut) amüsieren; **to be ~ at sth** (*swimming, talking etc*) etw gut können; (*science, sports etc*) gut in etw *dat* sein; **to be ~ for sb/sth** gut für jdn/zu etw *dat* sein; **it's ~ for you** das tut dir gut; **it's a ~ thing you were there** gut, dass Sie da waren; **she is ~ with children** sie kann gut mit Kindern umgehen; **she is ~ with her hands** sie ist geschickt; **to feel ~** sich wohlfühlen; **it's ~ to see you** (es ist) schön, Sie zu sehen; **would you be ~ enough to ...?** könnten Sie bitte ...?; **that's very ~ of you** das ist wirklich nett von Ihnen; **a ~ deal (of)** ziemlich viel; **a ~ many** ziemlich viele; **take a ~ look** sieh dir das genau *or* gut an; **a ~ while ago** vor einiger Zeit; **to make ~** (*damage*) wiedergutmachen; (*loss*) ersetzen; **it's no ~ complaining** es ist sinnlos *or* es nützt nichts, sich zu beklagen; **~ morning/afternoon/evening!** guten Morgen/Tag/Abend!; **~ night!** gute Nacht!; **he's up to no ~** er führt nichts Gutes im Schilde; **for the common ~** zum Wohle aller; **is this any ~?** (*will it help you?*) können Sie das gebrauchen?; (*is it good enough?*) reicht das?; **is the book/film any ~?** was halten Sie von dem Buch/Film?; **for ~** für immer; **goods and chattels** Hab und Gut *nt*
goodbye [gud'baı] EXCL auf Wiedersehen!; **to say ~** sich verabschieden
good-for-nothing ['gudfənʌθıŋ] ADJ nichtsnutzig

Good Friday N Karfreitag *m*
good-humoured ['gud'hju:məd] ADJ gut gelaunt; (*good-natured*) gutmütig; (*remark, joke*) harmlos
good-looking ['gud'lukɪŋ] ADJ gut aussehend
good-natured ['gud'neɪtʃəd] ADJ gutmütig; (*discussion*) freundlich
goodness ['gudnɪs] N Güte *f*; **for ~ sake!** um Himmels willen!; **~ gracious!** ach du liebe *or* meine Güte!
goods train (BRIT) N Güterzug *m*
goodwill [gud'wɪl] N Wohlwollen *nt*; (*Comm*) Goodwill *m*
goody ['gudɪ] (*inf*) N Gute(r) *m*, Held *m*
goody-goody ['gudɪgudɪ] (*pej*) N Tugendlamm *nt*, Musterkind (*inf*) *nt*
gooey ['gu:ɪ] (*inf*) ADJ (*sticky*) klebrig; (*cake*) üppig; (*fig: sentimental*) rührselig
Google® ['gu:gl] N Google® *nt* ▸ VT: **to google** googeln
goose [gu:s] (*pl* **geese**) N Gans *f*
gooseberry ['guzbərɪ] N Stachelbeere *f*; **to play ~** (BRIT) das fünfte Rad am Wagen sein
goose bumps N = **goose pimples**
goose flesh N = **goose pimples**
goose pimples NPL Gänsehaut *f*
goose step N Stechschritt *m*
GOP (*US inf*) N ABBR (*Pol: = Grand Old Party*) *Republikanische Partei*
gopher ['gəufə^r] N (*Zool*) Taschenratte *f*
gore [gɔ:^r] VT aufspießen ▸ N Blut *nt*
gorge [gɔ:dʒ] N Schlucht *f* ▸ VT: **to ~ o.s. (on)** sich vollstopfen (mit)
gorgeous ['gɔ:dʒəs] ADJ herrlich; (*person*) hinreißend
gorilla [gə'rɪlə] N Gorilla *m*
gormless ['gɔ:mlɪs] (BRIT *inf*) ADJ doof
gorse [gɔ:s] N Stechginster *m*
gory ['gɔ:rɪ] ADJ blutig
go-slow ['gəu'sləu] (BRIT) N Bummelstreik *m*
gospel ['gɔspl] N Evangelium *nt*; (*doctrine*) Lehre *f*
gossamer ['gɔsəmə^r] N Spinnfäden *pl*; (*light fabric*) hauchdünne Gaze *f*
gossip ['gɔsɪp] N (*rumours*) Klatsch *m*, Tratsch *m*; (*chat*) Schwatz *m*; (*person*) Klatschbase *f* ▸ VI schwatzen; **a piece of ~** eine Neuigkeit
gossip column N Klatschkolumne *f*, Klatschspalte *f*
got [gɔt] PT, PP *of* **get**
Gothic ['gɔθɪk] ADJ gotisch
gotten ['gɔtn] (US) PP *of* **get**
gouge [gaudʒ] VT (*also*: **gouge out**: *hole etc*) bohren; (*: initials*) eingravieren; **to ~ sb's eyes out** jdm die Augen ausstechen
gourd [guəd] N (*container*) Kürbisflasche *f*
gourmet ['guəmeɪ] N Feinschmecker(in) *m(f)*, Gourmet *m*
gout [gaut] N Gicht *f*
govern ['gʌvən] VT (*also Ling*) regieren; (*event, conduct*) bestimmen
governess ['gʌvənɪs] N Gouvernante *f*
governing ['gʌvənɪŋ] ADJ (*Pol*) regierend
governing body N Vorstand *m*
government ['gʌvnmənt] N Regierung *f* ▸ CPD Regierungs-; **local ~** Kommunalverwaltung *f*, Gemeindeverwaltung *f*
governmental [gʌvn'mɛntl] ADJ Regierungs-
government stocks NPL Staatspapiere *pl*, Staatsanleihen *pl*
governor ['gʌvənə^r] N Gouverneur(in) *m(f)*; (*of bank, hospital, Brit: of prison*) Direktor(in) *m(f)*; (*of school*) ≈ Mitglied *nt* des Schulbeirats
Govt ABBR = **government**
gown [gaun] N (Abend)kleid *nt*; (*of teacher, Brit: of judge*) Robe *f*
GP N ABBR = **general practitioner**
GPMU (BRIT) N ABBR (= *Graphical Paper and Media Union*) *Mediengewerkschaft*
GPO N ABBR (BRIT: *formerly: = general post office*) Postbehörde *f*; (*US: = Government Printing Office*) *regierungsamtliche Druckanstalt*
GPS ABBR (= *global positioning system*) GPS *nt*
gr. ABBR (*Comm*) = **gross**; (= *gram(me)*) g
grab [græb] VT packen; (*chance, opportunity*) (beim Schopf) ergreifen ▸ VI: **to ~ at** greifen *or* grapschen nach *+dat*; **to ~ some food** schnell etwas essen; **to ~ a few hours sleep** ein paar Stunden schlafen
grace [greɪs] N Gnade *f*; (*gracefulness*) Anmut *f* ▸ VT (*honour*) beehren; (*adorn*) zieren; **5 days' ~** 5 Tage Aufschub; **with (a) good ~** anstandslos; **with (a) bad ~** widerwillig; **his sense of humour is his saving ~** was einen mit ihm versöhnt, ist sein Sinn für Humor; **to say ~** das Tischgebet sprechen
graceful ['greɪsful] ADJ anmutig; (*style, shape*) gefällig; (*refusal, behaviour*) charmant
gracious ['greɪʃəs] ADJ (*kind, courteous*) liebenswürdig; (*compassionate*) gnädig; (*smile*) freundlich; (*house, mansion etc*) stilvoll; (*living etc*) kultiviert ▸ EXCL: **(good) ~!** (ach) du meine Güte!, (ach du) lieber Himmel!
gradation [grə'deɪʃən] N Abstufung *f*
grade [greɪd] N (*Comm*) (Güte)klasse *f*; (*in hierarchy*) Rang *m*; (*Scol: mark*) Note *f*; (*US: school class*) Klasse *f*; (*: gradient: upward*) Neigung *f*, Steigung *f*; (*: downward*) Neigung *f*, Gefälle *nt* ▸ VT klassifizieren; (*work, student*) einstufen; **to make the ~** (*fig*) es schaffen
grade crossing (US) N Bahnübergang *m*
grade school (US) N Grundschule *f*
gradient ['greɪdɪənt] N (*upward*) Neigung *f*, Steigung *f*; (*downward*) Neigung, Gefälle *nt*; (*Geom*) Gradient *m*
gradual ['grædjuəl] ADJ allmählich
gradually ['grædjuəlɪ] ADV allmählich
graduate N ['grædjuɪt] (*of university*) Hochschulabsolvent(in) *m(f)*; (*US: of high school*) Schulabgänger(in) *m(f)* ▸ VI ['grædjueɪt] (*from university*) graduieren; (US) die (Schul)abschlussprüfung bestehen
graduated pension ['grædjueɪtɪd-] N gestaffelte Rente *f*
graduation [grædju'eɪʃən] N (Ab)schlussfeier *f*
graffiti [grə'fi:tɪ] N, NPL Graffiti *pl*

g

graft [grɑ:ft] N (*Agr*) (Pfropf)reis *nt*; (*Med*) Transplantat *nt*; (BRIT *inf: hard work*) Schufterei *f*; (*bribery*) Schiebung *f* ▶ VT: **to ~ (onto)** (*Agr*) (auf)pfropfen (auf +*acc*); (*Med*) übertragen (auf +*acc*), einpflanzen (in +*acc*); (*fig*) aufpfropfen +*dat*
grain [greɪn] N Korn *nt*; (*no pl: cereals*) Getreide *nt*; (*US: corn*) Getreide *nt*, Korn; (*of wood*) Maserung *f*; **it goes against the ~** (*fig*) es geht einem gegen den Strich
gram [græm] N Gramm *nt*
grammar ['græməʳ] N Grammatik *f*, Sprachlehre *f*
grammar school (BRIT) N ≈ Gymnasium *nt*
grammatical [grə'mætɪkl] ADJ grammat(ikal)isch
gramme [græm] N = **gram**
gramophone ['græməfəun] (BRIT) N Grammofon *nt*
gran [græn] (*inf*) N Oma *f*
granary ['grænərɪ] N Kornspeicher *m*; **G~® bread/loaf** Körnerbrot *nt*
grand [grænd] ADJ großartig; (*inf: wonderful*) fantastisch ▶ N (*inf*) ≈ Riese *m* (1000 *Pfund/Dollar*)
grandchild ['græntʃaɪld] N (*irreg*) Enkelkind *nt*, Enkel(in) *m(f)*
granddad ['grændæd] (*inf*) N Opa *m*
granddaughter ['grændɔ:təʳ] N Enkelin *f*
grandeur ['grændjəʳ] N (*of scenery etc*) Erhabenheit *f*; (*of building*) Vornehmheit *f*
grandfather ['grændfɑ:ðəʳ] N Großvater *m*
grandiose ['grændɪəus] (*also pej*) ADJ grandios
grand jury (*US*) N Großes Geschworenengericht *nt*
grandma ['grænmɑ:] (*inf*) N Oma *f*
grandmother ['grænmʌðəʳ] N Großmutter *f*
grandpa ['grænpɑ:] (*inf*) N Opa *m*
grandparents ['grændpɛərənts] NPL Großeltern *pl*
grand piano N Flügel *m*
Grand Prix ['grɑ̃:'pri:] N (*Aut*) Grand Prix *m*
grandson ['grænsʌn] N Enkel *m*
grandstand ['grændstænd] N Haupttribüne *f*
grand total N Gesamtsumme *f*, Endsumme *f*
granite ['grænɪt] N Granit *m*
granny ['grænɪ] (*inf*) N Oma *f*
grant [grɑ:nt] VT (*money*) bewilligen; (*request etc*) gewähren; (*visa*) erteilen; (*admit*) zugeben ▶ N Stipendium *nt*; (*subsidy*) Subvention *f*; **to take sth for granted** etw für selbstverständlich halten; **to take sb for granted** jdn als selbstverständlich hinnehmen; **to ~ that** zugeben, dass
granulated sugar ['grænjuleɪtɪd-] N (Zucker)raffinade *f*
granule ['grænju:l] N Körnchen *nt*
grape [greɪp] N (Wein)traube *f*; **a bunch of grapes** eine (ganze) Weintraube
grapefruit ['greɪpfru:t] (*pl* **~** *or* **grapefruits**) N Pampelmuse *f*, Grapefruit *f*
grapevine ['greɪpvaɪn] N Weinstock *m*; **I heard it on the ~** (*fig*) es ist mir zu Ohren gekommen
graph [grɑ:f] N (*diagram*) grafische Darstellung *f*, Schaubild *nt*
graphic ['græfɪk] ADJ plastisch, anschaulich; (*art, design*) grafisch; *see also* **graphics**
graphic designer N Grafiker(in) *m(f)*
graphic equalizer [-i:kwəlaɪzəʳ] N (Graphic) Equalizer *m*
graphics ['græfɪks] N Grafik *f* ▶ NPL (*drawings*) Zeichnungen *pl*, grafische Darstellungen *pl*
graphite ['græfaɪt] N Grafit *m*
graph paper N Millimeterpapier *nt*
grapple ['græpl] VI: **to ~ with sb/sth** mit jdm/etw kämpfen; **to ~ with a problem** sich mit einem Problem herumschlagen
grasp [grɑ:sp] VT (*seize*) ergreifen; (*hold*) festhalten; (*understand*) begreifen ▶ N Griff *m*; (*understanding*) Verständnis *nt*; **it slipped from my ~** es entglitt mir; **to have sth within one's ~** etw in greifbarer Nähe haben; **to have a good ~ of sth** (*fig*) etw gut beherrschen
▶ **grasp at** VT FUS greifen nach; (*fig: opportunity*) ergreifen
grasping ['grɑ:spɪŋ] ADJ habgierig
grass [grɑ:s] N Gras *nt*; (*lawn*) Rasen *m*; (BRIT *inf: informer*) (Polizei)spitzel *m*
grasshopper ['grɑ:shɔpəʳ] N Grashüpfer *m*, Heuschrecke *f*
grass-roots ['grɑ:sru:ts] NPL (*of party etc*) Basis *f* ▶ ADJ (*opinion*) des kleinen Mannes; **at ~ level** an der Basis
grass snake N Ringelnatter *f*
grassy ['grɑ:sɪ] ADJ Gras-, grasig
grate [greɪt] N (Feuer)rost *m* ▶ VT reiben; (*carrots etc*) raspeln ▶ VI: **to ~ (on)** kratzen (auf +*dat*)
grateful ['greɪtful] ADJ dankbar; (*thanks*) aufrichtig
gratefully ['greɪtfəlɪ] ADV dankbar
grater ['greɪtəʳ] N Reibe *f*
gratification [grætɪfɪ'keɪʃən] N (*pleasure*) Genugtuung *f*; (*satisfaction*) Befriedigung *f*
gratify ['grætɪfaɪ] VT (*please*) erfreuen; (*satisfy*) befriedigen
gratifying ['grætɪfaɪɪŋ] ADJ erfreulich; befriedigend
grating ['greɪtɪŋ] N Gitter *nt* ▶ ADJ (*noise*) knirschend; (*voice*) schrill
gratitude ['grætɪtju:d] N Dankbarkeit *f*
gratuitous [grə'tju:ɪtəs] ADJ unnötig
gratuity [grə'tju:ɪtɪ] N Trinkgeld *nt*
grave [greɪv] N Grab *nt* ▶ ADJ (*decision, mistake*) schwer (wiegend), schwerwiegend; (*expression, person*) ernst
grave digger N Totengräber *m*
gravel ['grævl] N Kies *m*
gravely ['greɪvlɪ] ADV schwer, ernst; **~ ill** schwer krank
gravestone ['greɪvstəun] N Grabstein *m*
graveyard ['greɪvjɑ:d] N Friedhof *m*
gravitas ['grævɪtæs] N Seriosität *f*
gravitate ['grævɪteɪt] VI: **to ~ towards** angezogen werden von
gravity ['grævɪtɪ] N Schwerkraft *f*; (*seriousness*) Ernst *m*, Schwere *f*
gravy ['greɪvɪ] N (*juice*) (Braten)saft *m*; (*sauce*) (Braten)soße *f*

gravy boat N Sauciere *f*, Soßenschüssel *f*
gravy train (*inf*) N: **to ride the ~** leichtes Geld machen
gray [greɪ] (*US*) ADJ = **grey**
graze [greɪz] VI grasen, weiden ▸ VT streifen; (*scrape*) aufschürfen ▸ N (*Med*) Abschürfung *f*
grazing ['greɪzɪŋ] N Weideland *nt*
grease [gri:s] N (*lubricant*) Schmiere *f*; (*fat*) Fett *nt* ▸ VT schmieren; fetten; **to ~ the skids** (*US fig*) die Maschinerie in Gang halten
grease gun N Fettspritze *f*, Fettpresse *f*
greasepaint ['gri:speɪnt] N (Fett)schminke *f*
greaseproof paper ['gri:spru:f-] (BRIT) N Pergamentpapier *nt*
greasy ['gri:sɪ] ADJ fettig; (*food: containing grease*) fett; (*tools*) schmierig, ölig; (*clothes*) speckig; (BRIT: *road, surface*) glitschig, schlüpfrig
great [greɪt] ADJ groß; (*city*) bedeutend; (*inf: terrific*) prima, toll; **they're ~ friends** sie sind gute Freunde; **we had a ~ time** wir haben uns glänzend amüsiert; **it was ~!** es war toll!; **the ~ thing is that ...** das Wichtigste ist, dass ...
Great Barrier Reef N: **the ~** das Große Barriereriff
Great Britain N Großbritannien *nt*
greater ['greɪtə^r] ADJ größer; bedeutender; **people in G~ Calcutta** die Leute in Kalkutta und Umgebung; **G~ Manchester** Groß-Manchester *nt*
great-grandchild [greɪt'græntʃaɪld] N (*irreg*) Urenkel(in) *m(f)*
great-grandfather [greɪt'grænfɑ:ðə^r] N Urgroßvater *m*
great-grandmother [greɪt'grænmʌðə^r] N Urgroßmutter *f*
Great Lakes NPL: **the ~** die Großen Seen *pl*
greatly ['greɪtlɪ] ADV sehr; (*influenced*) stark
greatness ['greɪtnɪs] N Bedeutung *f*
Grecian ['gri:ʃən] ADJ griechisch
Greece [gri:s] N Griechenland *nt*
greed [gri:d] N (*also*: **greediness**): **~ for** Gier *f* nach; **~ for power** Machtgier *f*; **~ for money** Geldgier *f*
greedily ['gri:dɪlɪ] ADV gierig
greedy ['gri:dɪ] ADJ gierig
Greek [gri:k] ADJ griechisch ▸ N Grieche *m*, Griechin *f*; (*Ling*) Griechisch *nt*; **ancient/modern ~** Alt-/Neugriechisch *nt*
green [gri:n] ADJ (*also ecological*) grün ▸ N (*also Golf*) Grün *nt*; (*stretch of grass*) Rasen *m*, Grünfläche *f*; (*also*: **village green**) Dorfwiese *f*, Anger *m*; **greens** NPL (*vegetables*) Grüngemüse *nt*; **the Greens** (*Pol*) die Grünen *pl*; **to have ~ fingers, to have a ~ thumb** (*US*) eine Hand für Pflanzen haben; **to give sb the ~ light** jdm grünes Licht geben
green belt N Grüngürtel *m*
green card N (*Aut*) grüne (Versicherungs)karte *f*; (*US*) ≈ Aufenthaltserlaubnis *f*
greenery ['gri:nərɪ] N Grün *nt*
greenfly ['gri:nflaɪ] (BRIT) N Blattlaus *f*
greengage ['gri:ngeɪdʒ] N Reneklode *f*
greengrocer ['gri:ngrəusə^r] (BRIT) N Obst- und Gemüsehändler(in) *m(f)*
greenhouse ['gri:nhaus] N Gewächshaus *nt*, Treibhaus *nt*; **~ effect** Treibhauseffekt *m*; **~ gas** Treibhausgas *nt*
greenish ['gri:nɪʃ] ADJ grünlich
Greenland ['gri:nlənd] N Grönland *nt*
Greenlander ['gri:nləndə^r] N Grönländer(in) *m(f)*
green light N grünes Licht *nt*; **to give sb the ~** jdm grünes Licht *or* freie Fahrt geben
Green Party N (*Pol*): **the ~** die Grünen *pl*
green pepper N grüne Paprikaschote *f*
green pound N grünes Pfund *nt*
green tax N Umweltsteuer *f*
Greenwich Mean Time ['grɛnɪdʒ-] N westeuropäische Zeit
greet [gri:t] VT begrüßen; (*news*) aufnehmen
greeting ['gri:tɪŋ] N Gruß *m*; (*welcome*) Begrüßung *f*; **Christmas greetings** Weihnachtsgrüße *pl*; **birthday greetings** Geburtstagsglückwünsche *pl*; **Season's greetings** frohe Weihnachten und ein glückliches neues Jahr
greeting card, greetings card N Grußkarte *f*; (*congratulating*) Glückwunschkarte *f*
gregarious [grə'gɛərɪəs] ADJ gesellig
grenade [grə'neɪd] N (*also*: **hand grenade**) (Hand)granate *f*
grew [gru:] PT *of* **grow**
grey, (*US***) gray** [greɪ] ADJ grau; (*dismal*) trüb, grau; **to go ~** grau werden
grey-haired [greɪ'hɛəd] ADJ grauhaarig
greyhound ['greɪhaund] N Windhund *m*
grey vote N ≈ die älteren Wähler *fpl*
grid [grɪd] N Gitter *nt*; (*Elec*) (Verteiler)netz *nt*; (*US Aut: intersection*) Kreuzung *f*
griddle [grɪdl] N *gusseiserne Pfanne zum Braten und Pfannkuchenbacken*
gridiron ['grɪdaɪən] N Bratrost *m*
gridlock ['grɪdlɔk] N (*esp US: on road*) totaler Stau *m*; (*stalemate*) Patt *nt* ▸ VT: **to be gridlocked** (*roads*) total verstopft sein; (*talks etc*) festgefahren sein
grief [gri:f] N Kummer *m*, Trauer *f*; **to come to ~** (*plan*) scheitern; (*person*) zu Schaden kommen; **good ~!** ach du liebe Gute!
grievance ['gri:vəns] N Beschwerde *f*; (*feeling of resentment*) Groll *m*
grieve [gri:v] VI trauern ▸ VT Kummer bereiten *+dat*, betrüben; **to ~ for** trauern um
grievous ['gri:vəs] ADJ (*mistake*) schwer; (*situation*) betrüblich; **~ bodily harm** (*Law*) schwere Körperverletzung *f*
grill [grɪl] N Grill *m*; (*grilled food: also*: **mixed grill**) Grillgericht *nt*; (*restaurant*) = **grillroom** ▸ VT (BRIT) grillen; (*inf: question*) in die Zange nehmen, ausquetschen
grille [grɪl] N (*screen*) Gitter *nt*; (*Aut*) Kühlergrill *m*
grillroom ['grɪlrum] N Grillrestaurant *nt*
grim [grɪm] ADJ trostlos; (*serious, stern*) grimmig
grimace [grɪ'meɪs] N Grimasse *f* ▸ VI Grimassen schneiden
grime [graɪm] N Dreck *m*, Schmutz *m*

grimy ['graɪmɪ] ADJ dreckig, schmutzig
grin [grɪn] N Grinsen *nt* ▶ VI grinsen; **to ~ at sb** jdn angrinsen
grind [graɪnd] (*pt, pp* **ground**) VT zerkleinern; (*coffee, pepper etc*) mahlen; (*US: meat*) hacken, durch den Fleischwolf drehen; (*knife*) schleifen, wetzen; (*gem, lens*) schleifen ▶ VI (*car gears*) knirschen ▶ N (*work*) Schufterei *f*; **to ~ one's teeth** mit den Zähnen knirschen; **to ~ to a halt** (*vehicle*) quietschend zum Stehen kommen; (*fig: talks, scheme*) sich festfahren; (*work*) stocken; (*production*) zum Erliegen kommen; **the daily ~** (*inf*) der tägliche Trott
grinder ['graɪndə^r] N (*for coffee*) Kaffemühle *f*; (*for waste disposal etc*) Müllzerkleinerungsanlage *f*
grindstone ['graɪndstəun] N: **to keep one's nose to the ~** hart arbeiten
grip [grɪp] N Griff *m*; (*of tyre, shoe*) Halt *m*; (*holdall*) Reisetasche *f* ▶ VT packen; (*audience, attention*) fesseln; **to come to grips with sth** etw in den Griff bekommen; **to lose one's ~** den Halt verlieren; (*fig*) nachlassen; **to ~ the road** (*car*) gut auf der Straße liegen
gripe [graɪp] (*inf*) N (*complaint*) Meckerei *f* ▶ VI meckern; **the gripes** (*Med*) Kolik *f*, Bauchschmerzen *pl*
gripping ['grɪpɪŋ] ADJ fesselnd, packend
grisly ['grɪzlɪ] ADJ grässlich, grausig
grist [grɪst] N (*fig*): **it's all ~ to the mill** das kann man alles verwerten
gristle ['grɪsl] N Knorpel *m*
grit [grɪt] N (*for icy roads: sand*) Sand *m*; (*crushed stone*) Splitt *m*; (*determination, courage*) Mut *m* ▶ VT (*road*) streuen; **grits** NPL (*US*) Grütze *f*; **I've got a piece of ~ in my eye** ich habe ein Staubkorn im Auge; **to ~ one's teeth** die Zähne zusammenbeißen
grizzle ['grɪzl] (BRIT) VI quengeln
grizzly ['grɪzlɪ] N (*also*: **grizzly bear**) Grizzlybär *m*
groan [grəun] N Stöhnen *nt* ▶ VI stöhnen; (*tree, floorboard etc*) ächzen, knarren
grocer ['grəusə^r] N Lebensmittelhändler(in) *m(f)*
groceries ['grəusərɪz] NPL Lebensmittel *pl*
grocer's ['grəusəz], **grocer's shop** N Lebensmittelgeschäft *nt*
grog [grɔg] N Grog *m*
groggy ['grɔgɪ] ADJ angeschlagen
groin [grɔɪn] N Leistengegend *f*
groom [gru:m] N Stallbursche *m*; (*also*: **bridegroom**) Bräutigam *m* ▶ VT (*horse*) striegeln; (*fig*): **to ~ sb for** (*job*) jdn aufbauen für; **well-groomed** gepflegt
groove [gru:v] N Rille *f*
grope [grəup] VI: **to ~ for** tasten nach; (*fig: try to think of*) suchen nach
grosgrain ['grəugreɪn] N grob gerippter Stoff *m*
gross [grəus] ADJ (*neglect*) grob; (*injustice*) krass; (*behaviour, speech*) grob, derb; (*Comm: income, weight*) Brutto- ▶ N INV Gros *nt* ▶ VT: **to ~ £500,000** £500 000 brutto einnehmen
gross domestic product N Bruttoinlandsprodukt *nt*
grossly ['grəuslɪ] ADV äußerst; (*exaggerated*) grob
gross national product N Bruttosozialprodukt *nt*
grotesque [grə'tɛsk] ADJ grotesk
grotto ['grɔtəu] N Grotte *f*
grotty ['grɔtɪ] (*inf*) ADJ mies
grouch [grautʃ] (*inf*) VI schimpfen ▶ N (*person*) Miesepeter *m*, Muffel *m*
ground [graund] PT, PP *of* **grind** ▶ N Boden *m*, Erde *f*; (*land*) Land *nt*; (*Sport*) Platz *m*, Feld *nt*; (*US Elec: also*: **ground wire**) Erde *f*; (*reason: gen pl*) Grund *m* ▶ VT (*plane*) aus dem Verkehr ziehen; (*US Elec*) erden ▶ ADJ (*coffee etc*) gemahlen ▶ VI (*ship*) auflaufen; **grounds** NPL (*of coffee etc*) Satz *m*; (*gardens etc*) Anlagen *pl*; **below ~** unter der Erde; **to gain/lose ~** Boden gewinnen/verlieren; **common ~** Gemeinsame(s) *nt*; **on the grounds that** mit der Begründung, dass
ground cloth (US) N = **groundsheet**
ground control N (*Aviat, Space*) Bodenkontrolle *f*
ground floor N Erdgeschoss *nt*, Erdgeschoß *nt* (ÖSTERR)
grounding ['graundɪŋ] N (*in education*) Grundwissen *nt*
groundless ['graundlɪs] ADJ grundlos, unbegründet
groundnut ['graundnʌt] N Erdnuss *f*
ground rent (BRIT) N Erbbauzins *m*
ground rule N Grundregel *f*
groundsheet ['graundʃi:t] (BRIT) N Zeltboden *m*
groundskeeper ['graundzki:pə^r] (US) N = **groundsman**
groundsman ['graundzmən] N (*irreg: Sport*) Platzwart *m*
ground staff N (*Aviat*) Bodenpersonal *nt*
ground swell N: **there was a ~ of public opinion against him** die Öffentlichkeit wandte sich gegen ihn
ground-to-air missile ['graundtə'ɛə^r-] N Boden-Luft-Rakete *f*
ground-to-ground missile ['graundtə'graund-] N Boden-Boden-Rakete *f*
groundwork ['graundwə:k] N Vorarbeit *f*
group [gru:p] N Gruppe *f*; (*Comm*) Konzern *m* ▶ VT (*also*: **group together**: *in one group*) zusammentun; (: *in several groups*) in Gruppen einteilen ▶ VI (*also*: **group together**) sich zusammentun
groupie ['gru:pɪ] (*inf*) N Groupie *nt*
group therapy N Gruppentherapie *f*
grouse [graus] N INV schottisches Moorhuhn *nt* ▶ VI (*complain*) schimpfen
grove [grəuv] N Hain *m*, Wäldchen *nt*
grovel ['grɔvl] VI (*crawl*) kriechen; (*fig*): **to ~ (before)** kriechen (vor +*dat*)
grow [grəu] (*pt* **grew**, *pp* **grown**) VI wachsen; (*increase*) zunehmen; (*become*) werden ▶ VT (*roses*) züchten; (*vegetables*) anbauen, ziehen; (*beard*) sich *dat* wachsen lassen; **to ~ tired of waiting** das Warten leid sein; **to ~ (out of** *or* **from)** (*develop*) entstehen (aus)
▶ **grow apart** VI (*fig*) sich auseinanderentwickeln

▸ **grow away from** VT FUS (*fig*) sich entfremden +*dat*
▸ **grow on** VT FUS: **that painting is growing on me** allmählich finde ich Gefallen an dem Bild
▸ **grow out of** VT FUS (*clothes*) herauswachsen aus; (*habit*) ablegen; **he'll ~ out of it** diese Phase geht auch vorbei
▸ **grow up** VI aufwachsen; (*mature*) erwachsen werden; (*idea, friendship*) entstehen

grower ['grəuəʳ] N (*Bot*) Züchter(in) *m(f)*; (*Agr*) Pflanzer(in) *m(f)*
growing ['grəuɪŋ] ADJ wachsend; (*number*) zunehmend; **~ pains** Wachstumsschmerzen *pl*; (*fig*) Kinderkrankheiten *pl*, Anfangsschwierigkeiten *pl*
growl [graul] VI knurren
grown [grəun] PP *of* **grow**
grown-up [grəun'ʌp] N Erwachsene(r) *f(m)*
growth [grəuθ] N Wachstum *nt*; (*what has grown: of weeds, beard etc*) Wuchs *m*; (*of person, character*) Entwicklung *f*; (*Med*) Gewächs *nt*, Wucherung *f*
growth rate N Wachstumsrate *f*, Zuwachsrate *f*
grub [grʌb] N (*larva*) Larve *f*; (*inf: food*) Fressalien *pl*, Futter *nt* ▸ VI: **to ~ about** *or* **around (for)** (herum)wühlen (nach)
grubby ['grʌbɪ] ADJ (*dirty*) schmuddelig; (*fig*) schmutzig
grudge [grʌdʒ] N Groll *m* ▸ VT: **to ~ sb sth** jdm etw nicht gönnen; **to bear sb a ~** jdm böse sein, einen Groll gegen jdn hegen
grudging ['grʌdʒɪŋ] ADJ widerwillig
grudgingly ['grʌdʒɪŋlɪ] ADV widerwillig
gruelling, (US) **grueling** ['gruəlɪŋ] ADJ (*encounter*) aufreibend; (*trip, journey*) äußerst strapaziös
gruesome ['gru:səm] ADJ grauenhaft
gruff [grʌf] ADJ barsch, schroff
grumble ['grʌmbl] VI murren, schimpfen
grumpy ['grʌmpɪ] ADJ mürrisch, brummig
grunge [grʌndʒ] (*inf*) N Grunge *nt*
grunt [grʌnt] VI grunzen ▸ N Grunzen *nt*
G-string ['dʒi:strɪŋ] N Minislip *m*, Tangaslip *m*
GT ABBR (*Aut: = gran turismo*) GT
GU (US) ABBR (*Post*) = **Guam**
guarantee [gærən'ti:] N Garantie *f* ▸ VT garantieren; **he can't ~ (that) he'll come** er kann nicht dafür garantieren, dass er kommt
guarantor [gærən'tɔ:ʳ] N (*Comm*) Bürge *m*
guard [gɑ:d] N Wache *f*; (*Boxing, Fencing*) Deckung *f*; (BRIT *Rail*) Schaffner(in) *m(f)*; (*on machine*) Schutz *m*, Schutzvorrichtung *f*; (*also:* **fireguard**) (Schutz)gitter *nt* ▸ VT (*prisoner*) bewachen; (*protect*): **to ~ (against)** (be)schützen (vor +*dat*); (*secret*) hüten (vor +*dat*); **to be on one's ~** auf der Hut sein
▸ **guard against** VT FUS (*disease*) vorbeugen +*dat*; (*damage, accident*) verhüten
guard dog N Wachhund *m*
guarded ['gɑ:dɪd] ADJ vorsichtig, zurückhaltend
guardian ['gɑ:dɪən] N Vormund *m*; (*defender*) Hüter *m*
guardrail ['gɑ:dreɪl] N (Schutz)geländer *nt*
guard's van (BRIT) N (*Rail*) Schaffnerabteil *nt*, Dienstwagen *m*
Guatemala [gwɑ:tɪ'mɑ:lə] N Guatemala *nt*
Guatemalan [gwɑ:tɪ'mɑ:lən] ADJ guatemaltekisch, aus Guatemala
Guernsey ['gə:nzɪ] N Guernsey *nt*
guerrilla [gə'rɪlə] N Guerilla *m*, Guerillakämpfer(in) *m(f)*
guerrilla warfare N Guerillakrieg *m*
guess [gɛs] VT schätzen; (*answer*) (er)raten; (*US: think*) schätzen (*inf*) ▸ VI schätzen; raten ▸ N Vermutung *f*; **I ~ you're right** da haben Sie wohl recht; **to keep sb guessing** jdn im Ungewissen lassen; **to take** *or* **have a ~** raten; (*estimate*) schätzen; **my ~ is that ...** ich schätze *or* vermute, dass ...
guesstimate ['gɛstɪmɪt] (*inf*) N grobe Schätzung *f*
guesswork ['gɛswə:k] N Vermutungen *pl*; **I got the answer by ~** ich habe die Antwort nur geraten
guest [gɛst] N Gast *m*; **be my ~** (*inf*) nur zu!
guesthouse ['gɛsthaus] N Pension *f*
guest room N Gästezimmer *nt*
guff [gʌf] (*inf*) N Quatsch *m*, Käse *m*
guffaw [gʌ'fɔ:] VI schallend lachen ▸ N schallendes Lachen *nt*
guidance ['gaɪdəns] N Rat *m*, Beratung *f*; **under the ~ of** unter der Leitung von; **vocational ~** Berufsberatung *f*; **marriage ~** Eheberatung *f*
guide [gaɪd] N (*person*) Führer(in) *m(f)*; (*book*) Führer *m*; (BRIT: *also*: **girl guide**) Pfadfinderin *f* ▸ VT führen; (*direct*) lenken; **to be guided by sb/sth** sich von jdm/etw leiten lassen
guidebook ['gaɪdbuk] N Führer *m*
guided missile ['gaɪdɪd-] N Lenkwaffe *f*
guide dog N Blindenhund *m*
guidelines ['gaɪdlaɪnz] NPL Richtlinien *pl*
guild [gɪld] N Verein *m*
guildhall ['gɪldhɔ:l] (BRIT) N Gildehaus *nt*
guile [gaɪl] N Arglist *f*
guileless ['gaɪllɪs] ADJ arglos
guillotine ['gɪləti:n] N Guillotine *f*, Fallbeil *nt*; (*for paper*) (Papier)schneidemaschine *f*
guilt [gɪlt] N Schuld *f*; (*remorse*) Schuldgefühl *nt*
guilty ['gɪltɪ] ADJ schuldig; (*expression*) schuldbewusst; (*secret*) dunkel; **to plead ~/not ~** sich schuldig/nicht schuldig bekennen; **to feel ~ about doing sth** ein schlechtes Gewissen haben, etw zu tun
Guinea ['gɪnɪ] N: **Republic of ~** Guinea *nt*
guinea ['gɪnɪ] (BRIT) N (*old*) Guinee *f*
guinea pig N Meerschweinchen *nt*; (*fig: person*) Versuchskaninchen *nt*
guise [gaɪz] N: **in** *or* **under the ~ of** in der Form +*gen*, in Gestalt +*gen*
guitar [gɪ'tɑ:ʳ] N Gitarre *f*
guitarist [gɪ'tɑ:rɪst] N Gitarrist(in) *m(f)*
gulch [gʌltʃ] (US) N Schlucht *f*
gulf [gʌlf] N Golf *m*; (*abyss*) Abgrund *m*; (*fig: difference*) Kluft *f*; **the (Persian) G~** der (Persische) Golf
Gulf States NPL: **the ~** die Golfstaaten *pl*

Gulf Stream N: **the ~** der Golfstrom
Gulf War N: **the ~** der Golfkrieg
gull [gʌl] N Möwe *f*
gullet ['gʌlɪt] N Speiseröhre *f*
gullibility [gʌlɪ'bɪlɪtɪ] N Leichtgläubigkeit *f*
gullible ['gʌlɪbl] ADJ leichtgläubig
gully ['gʌlɪ] N Schlucht *f*
gulp [gʌlp] VI schlucken ▸ VT (*also*: **gulp down**) hinunterschlucken ▸ N: **at one ~** mit einem Schluck
gum [gʌm] N (*Anat*) Zahnfleisch *nt*; (*glue*) Klebstoff *m*; (*also*: **gumdrop**) Weingummi *nt*; (*also*: **chewing-gum**) Kaugummi *m* ▸ VT: **to ~ (together)** (zusammen)kleben
▸ **gum up** VT: **to ~ up the works** (*inf*) alles vermasseln
gumboots ['gʌmbu:ts] (BRIT) NPL Gummistiefel *pl*
gumption ['gʌmpʃən] N Grips *m* (*inf*)
gumtree ['gʌmtri:] N: **to be up a ~** (*fig, inf*) aufgeschmissen sein
gun [gʌn] N (*small*) Pistole *f*; (*medium-sized*) Gewehr *nt*; (*large*) Kanone *f* ▸ VT (*also*: **gun down**) erschießen; **to stick to one's guns** (*fig*) nicht nachgeben, festbleiben
gunboat ['gʌnbəut] N Kanonenboot *nt*
gun dog N Jagdhund *m*
gunfire ['gʌnfaɪəʳ] N Geschützfeuer *nt*
gunge [gʌndʒ] (*inf*) N Schmiere *f*
gung ho ['gʌŋ'həu] (*inf*) ADJ übereifrig
gunman ['gʌnmən] N (*irreg*) bewaffneter Verbrecher *m*
gunner ['gʌnəʳ] N Kanonier *m*, Artillerist *m*
gunpoint ['gʌnpɔɪnt] N: **at ~** mit vorgehaltener Pistole; mit vorgehaltenem Gewehr
gunpowder ['gʌnpaudəʳ] N Schießpulver *nt*
gunrunner ['gʌnrʌnəʳ] N Waffenschmuggler(in) *m(f)*, Waffenschieber(in) *m(f)*
gunrunning ['gʌnrʌnɪŋ] N Waffenschmuggel *m*, Waffenschieberei *f*
gunshot ['gʌnʃɔt] N Schuss *m*
gunsmith ['gʌnsmɪθ] N Büchsenmacher *m*
gurgle ['gə:gl] VI (*baby*) glucksen; (*water*) gluckern
guru ['guru:] N Guru *m*
gush [gʌʃ] VI hervorquellen, hervorströmen; (*person*) schwärmen ▸ N Strahl *m*
gushing ['gʌʃɪŋ] ADJ (*fig*) überschwänglich
gusset ['gʌsɪt] N Keil *m*, Zwickel *m*
gust [gʌst] N Windstoß *m*, Bö(e) *f*; (*of smoke*) Wolke *f*
gusto ['gʌstəu] N: **with ~** mit Genuss, mit Schwung
gusty ['gʌstɪ] ADJ (*wind*) böig; (*day*) stürmisch
gut [gʌt] N (*Anat*) Darm *m*; (*for violin, racket*) Darmsaiten *pl* ▸ VT (*poultry, fish*) ausnehmen; (*building*) ausräumen; (*by fire*) ausbrennen; **guts** NPL (*Anat*) Eingeweide *pl*; (*inf: courage*) Mumm *m*; **to hate sb's guts** jdn auf den Tod nicht ausstehen können
gut reaction N rein gefühlsmäßige Reaktion *f*
gutsy ['gʌtsɪ] (*inf*) ADJ (*vivid*) rasant; (*courageous*) mutig
gutter ['gʌtəʳ] N (*in street*) Gosse *f*, Rinnstein *m*; (*of roof*) Dachrinne *f*
gutter press N Boulevardpresse *f*
guttural ['gʌtərl] ADJ guttural
guy [gaɪ] N (*inf: man*) Typ *m*, Kerl *m*; (*also*: **guyrope**) Haltetau *nt*, Halteseil *nt*; (*for Guy Fawkes' night*) (Guy-Fawkes-)Puppe *f*

> **Guy Fawkes' Night**, auch „bonfire night" genannt, erinnert an den „Gunpowder Plot", einen Attentatsversuch auf James I. und sein Parlament am 5. November 1605. Einer der Verschwörer, Guy Fawkes, wurde auf frischer Tat ertappt, als er das Parlamentsgebäude in die Luft sprengen wollte. Vor der Guy Fawkes' Night basteln Kinder in Großbritannien eine Puppe des Guy Fawkes, mit der sie Geld für Feuerwerkskörper von Passanten erbetteln, und die dann am 5. November auf einem Lagerfeuer mit Feuerwerk verbrannt wird.

Guyana [gaɪ'ænə] N Guyana *nt*
guzzle ['gʌzl] VT (*food*) futtern; (*drink*) saufen (*inf*)
gym [dʒɪm] N (*also*: **gymnasium**) Turnhalle *f*; (*also*: **gymnastics**) Gymnastik *f*, Turnen *nt*
gymkhana [dʒɪm'kɑ:nə] N Reiterfest *nt*
gymnasium [dʒɪm'neɪzɪəm] N Turnhalle *f*
gymnast ['dʒɪmnæst] N Turner(in) *m(f)*
gymnastics [dʒɪm'næstɪks] N Gymnastik *f*, Turnen *nt*
gym shoes NPL Turnschuhe *pl*
gymslip ['dʒɪmslɪp] (BRIT) N (Schul)trägerrock *m*
gynaecologist, (US) **gynecologist** [gaɪnɪ'kɔlədʒɪst] N Gynäkologe *m*, Gynäkologin *f*, Frauenarzt *m*, Frauenärztin *f*
gynaecology, (US) **gynecology** [gaɪnɪ'kɔlədʒɪ] N Gynäkologie *f*, Frauenheilkunde *f*
gypsy ['dʒɪpsɪ] N = **gipsy**
gyrate [dʒaɪ'reɪt] VI kreisen, sich drehen
gyroscope ['dʒaɪərəskəup] N Gyroskop *nt*

H, h [eɪtʃ] N (*letter*) H, h *nt*; **H for Harry, H for How** (*US*) ≈ H wie Heinrich
habeas corpus ['heɪbɪəs'kɔ:pəs] N Habeaskorpusakte *f*
haberdashery [hæbə'dæʃərɪ] (BRIT) N Kurzwaren *pl*
habit ['hæbɪt] N Gewohnheit *f*; (*esp undesirable*) Angewohnheit *f*; (*addiction*) Sucht *f*; (*Rel*) Habit *m or nt*; **to get out of/into the ~ of doing sth** sich abgewöhnen/angewöhnen, etw zu tun; **to be in the ~ of doing sth** die (An)gewohnheit haben, etw zu tun
habitable ['hæbɪtəbl] ADJ bewohnbar
habitat ['hæbɪtæt] N Heimat *f*; (*of animals*) Lebensraum *m*, Heimat *f*
habitation [hæbɪ'teɪʃən] N Wohnstätte *f*; **fit for human ~** für Wohnzwecke geeignet, bewohnbar
habitual [hə'bɪtjuəl] ADJ (*action*) gewohnt; (*drinker*) Gewohnheits-; (*liar*) gewohnheitsmäßig
habitually [hə'bɪtjuəlɪ] ADV ständig
hack [hæk] VT, VI (*also Comput*) hacken ▶ N (*pej: writer*) Schreiberling *m*; (*horse*) Mietpferd *nt*
hacker ['hækə^r] N (*Comput*) Hacker *m*
hackles ['hæklz] NPL: **to make sb's ~ rise** (*fig*) jdn auf die Palme bringen (*inf*)
hackney cab ['hæknɪ-] N Taxi *nt*
hackneyed ['hæknɪd] ADJ abgedroschen
hacksaw ['hæksɔ:] N Metallsäge *f*
had [hæd] PT, PP *of* **have**
haddock ['hædək] (*pl* **~** *or* **haddocks**) N Schellfisch *m*
hadn't ['hædnt] = **had not**
haematology, (*US*) **hematology** ['hi:mə'tɔlədʒɪ] N Hämatologie *f*
haemoglobin, (*US*) **hemoglobin** ['hi:mə'gləubɪn] N Hämoglobin *nt*
haemophilia, (*US*) **hemophilia** ['hi:mə'fɪlɪə] N Bluterkrankheit *f*
haemorrhage, (*US*) **hemorrhage** ['hɛmərɪdʒ] N Blutung *f*
haemorrhoids, (*US*) **hemorrhoids** ['hɛmərɔɪdz] NPL Hämorr(ho)iden *pl*
hag [hæg] N alte Hexe *f*; (*witch*) Hexe *f*
haggard ['hægəd] ADJ ausgezehrt; (*from worry*) abgehärmt; (*from tiredness*) abgespannt
haggis ['hægɪs] (SCOT) N *Gericht aus gehackten Schafsinnereien und Haferschrot, im Schafsmagen gekocht*
haggle ['hægl] VI: **to ~ (over)** feilschen (um)
haggling ['hæglɪŋ] N Feilschen *nt*
Hague [heɪg] N: **The ~** Den Haag *m*
hail [heɪl] N Hagel *m* ▶ VT (*person*) zurufen *+dat*; (*taxi*) herbeiwinken, anhalten; (*acclaim: person*) zujubeln *+dat*; (*: event etc*) bejubeln ▶ VI hageln; **he hails from Scotland** er kommt *or* stammt aus Schottland
hailstone ['heɪlstəun] N Hagelkorn *nt*
hair [hɛə^r] N (*collectively: of person*) Haar *nt*, Haare *pl*; (*: of animal*) Fell *nt*; (*single hair*) Haar *nt*; **to do one's ~** sich frisieren; **by a ~'s breadth** um Haaresbreite
hairbrush ['hɛəbrʌʃ] N Haarbürste *f*
haircut ['hɛəkʌt] N Haarschnitt *m*; (*style*) Frisur *f*
hairdo ['hɛədu:] N Frisur *f*
hairdresser ['hɛədrɛsə^r] N Friseur *m*, Friseuse *f*
hairdresser's ['hɛədrɛsəz] N Friseursalon *m*
hair dryer N Haartrockner *m*, Föhn *f*, Fön® *m*
-haired [hɛəd] SUFF: **fair~** blond; **long~** langhaarig
hair gel N Haargel *nt*
hairgrip ['hɛəgrɪp] N Haarklemme *f*
hairline ['hɛəlaɪn] N Haaransatz *m*
hairline fracture N Haarriss *m*
hairnet ['hɛənɛt] N Haarnetz *nt*
hair oil N Haaröl *nt*
hairpiece ['hɛəpi:s] N Haarteil *nt*; (*for men*) Toupet *nt*
hairpin ['hɛəpɪn] N Haarnadel *f*
hairpin bend, (*US*) **hairpin curve** N Haarnadelkurve *f*
hair-raising ['hɛəreɪzɪŋ] ADJ haarsträubend
hair remover N Enthaarungscreme *f*
hair slide N Haarspange *f*
hair spray N Haarspray *nt*
hair straighteners NPL Haarglätter *m*
hairstyle ['hɛəstaɪl] N Frisur *f*
hairy ['hɛərɪ] ADJ behaart; (*inf: situation*) brenzlig, haarig
Haiti ['heɪtɪ] N Haiti *nt*
haka [hɑ:kə] N (*NZ*) Haka *m* (*Ritualtanz der Maori*), *dem Haka ähnlicher Tanz, der vor allem von*

neuseeländischen Rugby-Teams vor Spielbeginn aufgeführt wird
hake [heɪk] (*pl* ~ *or* **hakes**) N Seehecht *m*
halcyon ['hælsɪən] ADJ glücklich
hale [heɪl] ADJ: ~ **and hearty** gesund und munter
half [hɑːf] (*pl* **halves**) N Hälfte *f*; (*of beer etc*) kleines Bier *nt etc*; (*Rail, bus*) Fahrkarte *f* zum halben Preis ▶ ADJ, ADV halb; **first/second** ~ (*Sport*) erste/zweite Halbzeit *f*; **two and a** ~ zweieinhalb; ~**-an-hour** eine halbe Stunde; ~ **a dozen/pound** ein halbes Dutzend/Pfund; **a week and a** ~ eineinhalb *or* anderthalb Wochen; ~ **(of it)** die Hälfte; ~ **(of)** die Hälfte (von *or* +*gen*); ~ **the amount of** die halbe Menge an +*dat*; **to cut sth in** ~ etw halbieren; ~ **past three** halb vier; **to go halves (with sb)** (mit jdm) halbe-halbe machen; **she never does things by halves** sie macht keine halben Sachen; **he's too clever by** ~ er ist ein richtiger Schlaumeier; ~ **empty** halb leer; ~ **closed** halb geschlossen
half-baked ['hɑːf'beɪkt] ADJ blödsinnig (*inf*)
half board N Halbpension *f*
half-breed ['hɑːfbriːd] (*pej*) N = **half-caste**
half-brother ['hɑːfbrʌðəʳ] N Halbbruder *m*
half-caste ['hɑːfkɑːst] (*pej*) N Mischling *m*
half-day [hɑːf'deɪ] N halber freier Tag *m*
half-hearted ['hɑːf'hɑːtɪd] ADJ halbherzig, lustlos
half-hour [hɑːf'auəʳ] N halbe Stunde *f*
half-life ['hɑːflaɪf] N (*Tech*) Halbwertszeit *f*
half-mast ['hɑːf'mɑːst] ADV: **at** ~ (auf) halbmast
halfpenny ['heɪpnɪ] (BRIT) N halber Penny *m*
half-price ['hɑːf'praɪs] ADJ, ADV zum halben Preis
half-sister ['hɑːfsɪstəʳ] N Halbschwester *f*
half term (BRIT) N kleine Ferien *pl* (*in der Mitte des Trimesters*)
half-timbered [hɑːf'tɪmbəd] ADJ (*house*) Fachwerk-
half-time [hɑːf'taɪm] N (*Sport*) Halbzeit *f*
halfway ['hɑːf'weɪ] ADV: ~ **to** auf halbem Wege nach; ~ **through** mitten in +*dat*; **to meet sb** ~ (*fig*) jdm auf halbem Wege entgegenkommen
halfway house N (*hostel*) offene Anstalt *f*; (*fig*) Zwischending *nt*; (: *compromise*) Kompromiss *m*
half-yearly [hɑːf'jɪəlɪ] ADV halbjährlich, jedes halbe Jahr ▶ ADJ halbjährlich
halibut ['hælɪbət] N INV Heilbutt *m*
halitosis [hælɪ'təusɪs] N schlechter Atem *m*, Mundgeruch *m*
hall [hɔːl] N Diele *f*, (Haus)flur *m*; (*corridor*) Korridor *m*, Flur *m*; (*mansion*) Herrensitz *m*, Herrenhaus *nt*; (*for concerts etc*) Halle *f*; **to live in** ~ (BRIT) im Wohnheim wohnen
hallmark ['hɔːlmɑːk] N (*on gold, silver*) (Feingehalts)stempel *m*; (*of writer, artist etc*) Kennzeichen *nt*
hallo [hə'ləu] EXCL = **hello**
hall of residence (*pl* **halls of residence**) (BRIT) N Studentenwohnheim *nt*
hallowed ['hæləud] ADJ (*ground*) heilig; (*fig: respected, revered*) geheiligt
Hallowe'en ['hæləu'iːn] N der Tag vor Allerheiligen

> **Hallowe'en** ist der 31. Oktober, der Vorabend von Allerheiligen und nach altem Glauben der Abend, an dem man Geister und Hexen sehen kann. In Großbritannien und vor allem in den USA feiern die Kinder Hallowe'en, indem sie sich verkleiden und mit selbst gemachten Laternen aus Kürbissen von Tür zu Tür ziehen.

hallucination [həluːsɪ'neɪʃən] N Halluzination *f*
hallucinogenic [həluːsɪnəu'dʒɛnɪk] ADJ (*drug*) halluzinogen ▶ N Halluzinogen *nt*
hallway ['hɔːlweɪ] N Diele *f*, (Haus)flur *m*
halo ['heɪləu] N Heiligenschein *m*; (*circle of light*) Hof *m*
halt [hɔːlt] VT anhalten; (*progress etc*) zum Stillstand bringen ▶ VI anhalten, zum Stillstand kommen ▶ N: **to come to a** ~ zum Stillstand kommen; **to call a** ~ **to sth** (*fig*) einer Sache *dat* ein Ende machen
halter ['hɔːltəʳ] N Halfter *nt*
halter-neck ['hɔːltənɛk] ADJ (*dress*) rückenfrei mit Nackenverschluss
halve [hɑːv] VT halbieren
halves [hɑːvz] PL *of* **half**
ham [hæm] N Schinken *m*; (*inf*: *also*: **radio ham**) Funkamateur *m*; (*actor*) Schmierenkomödiant(in) *m(f)*
Hamburg ['hæmbəːg] N Hamburg *nt*
hamburger ['hæmbəːgəʳ] N Hamburger *m*
ham-fisted ['hæm'fɪstɪd], (*US*) **ham-handed** ['hæm'hændɪd] ADJ ungeschickt
hamlet ['hæmlɪt] N Weiler *m*, kleines Dorf *nt*
hammer ['hæməʳ] N Hammer *m* ▶ VT hämmern; (*fig: criticize*) vernichtend kritisieren; (: *defeat*) vernichtend schlagen ▶ VI hämmern; **to** ~ **sth into sb, to** ~ **sth across to sb** jdm etw einhämmern *or* einbläuen
▶ **hammer out** VT hämmern; (*solution, agreement*) ausarbeiten
hammock ['hæmək] N Hängematte *f*
hamper ['hæmpəʳ] VT behindern ▶ N Korb *m*
hamster ['hæmstəʳ] N Hamster *m*
hamstring ['hæmstrɪŋ] N Kniesehne *f* ▶ VT einengen
hand [hænd] N Hand *f*; (*of clock*) Zeiger *m*; (*handwriting*) Hand(schrift) *f*; (*worker*) Arbeiter(in) *m(f)*; (*of cards*) Blatt *nt*; (*measurement: of horse*) ≈ 10 cm ▶ VT geben, reichen; **to give** *or* **lend sb a** ~ jdm helfen; **at** ~ (*place*) in der Nähe; (*time*) unmittelbar bevorstehend; **by** ~ von Hand; **in** ~ (*time*) zur Verfügung; (*job*) anstehend; (*situation*) unter Kontrolle; **we have the matter in** ~ wir haben die Sache im Griff; **on** ~ zur Verfügung; **out of** ~ *adj* außer Kontrolle; *adv* (*reject etc*) rundweg; **to** ~ zur Hand; **on the one** ~ **…, on the other** ~ **…** einerseits … andererseits …; **to force sb's** ~ jdn zwingen; **to have a free** ~ freie Hand haben; **to change hands** den Besitzer wechseln;

to have in one's ~ (*also fig*) in der Hand halten; **"hands off!"** „Hände weg!"
▸ **hand down** VT (*knowledge*) weitergeben; (*possessions*) vererben; (*Law: judgement, sentence*) fällen
▸ **hand in** VT abgeben, einreichen
▸ **hand out** VT verteilen; (*information*) austeilen; (*punishment*) verhängen
▸ **hand over** VT übergeben
▸ **hand round** VT (BRIT) verteilen; (*chocolates etc*) herumreichen
handbag ['hændbæg] N Handtasche *f*
hand baggage N Handgepäck *nt*
handball ['hændbɔːl] N Handball *m*
hand basin N Handwaschbecken *nt*
handbook ['hændbuk] N Handbuch *nt*
handbrake ['hændbreɪk] N Handbremse *f*
h & c (BRIT) ABBR (= *hot and cold (water)*) h. u. k.
hand cream N Handcreme *f*
handcuff ['hændkʌf] VT Handschellen anlegen *+dat*
handcuffs ['hændkʌfs] NPL Handschellen *pl*
handful ['hændful] N Handvoll *f*
hand-held ['hænd'hɛld] ADJ (*camera*) Hand-
handicap ['hændɪkæp] N Behinderung *f*; (*disadvantage*) Nachteil *m*; (*Sport*) Handicap *nt* ▸ VT benachteiligen; **mentally/physically handicapped** geistig/körperlich behindert
handicraft ['hændɪkrɑːft] N Kunsthandwerk *nt*; (*object*) Kunsthandwerksarbeit *f*
handiwork ['hændɪwəːk] N Arbeit *f*; **this looks like his ~** (*pej*) das sieht nach seiner Arbeit aus
handkerchief ['hæŋkətʃɪf] N Taschentuch *nt*
handle ['hændl] N Griff *m*; (*of door*) Klinke *f*; (*of cup*) Henkel *m*; (*of broom, brush etc*) Stiel *m*; (*for winding*) Kurbel *f*; (*Radio: name*) Sendezeichen *nt* ▸ VT anfassen, berühren; (*problem etc*) sich befassen mit; (*: successfully*) fertig werden mit; (*people*) umgehen mit; **"~ with care"** „Vorsicht – zerbrechlich"; **to fly off the ~** an die Decke gehen; **to get a ~ on a problem** (*inf*) ein Problem in den Griff bekommen
handlebar ['hændlbɑːʳ] N, **handlebars** ['hændlbɑːz] NPL Lenkstange *f*
handling ['hændlɪŋ] N: **~ (of)** (*of plant, animal, issue etc*) Behandlung *f +gen*; (*of person, tool, machine etc*) Umgang *m* (mit); (*Admin*) Bearbeitung *f +gen*
handling charges NPL Bearbeitungsgebühr *f*; (*Banking*) Kontoführungsgebühr *f*
hand luggage N Handgepäck *nt*
handmade ['hænd'meɪd] ADJ handgearbeitet
hand-out ['hændaut] N (*money, food etc*) Unterstützung *f*; (*publicity leaflet*) Flugblatt *nt*; (*summary*) Informationsblatt *nt*
hand-picked ['hænd'pɪkt] ADJ von Hand geerntet; (*staff etc*) handverlesen
handrail ['hændreɪl] N Geländer *nt*
handset ['hændsɛt] N (*Tel*) Hörer *m*
hands-free ['hændzfriː] ADJ (*telephone, microphone*) Freisprech-
handshake ['hændʃeɪk] N Händedruck *m*
handsome ['hænsəm] ADJ gut aussehend; (*building*) schön; (*gift*) großzügig; (*profit, return*) ansehnlich
hands-on ['hændz'ɔn] ADJ (*training*) praktisch; (*approach etc*) aktiv; **~ experience** praktische Erfahrung
handstand ['hændstænd] N: **to do a ~** einen Handstand machen
hand-to-mouth ['hændtə'mauθ] ADJ: **to lead a ~ existence** von der Hand in den Mund leben
handwriting ['hændraɪtɪŋ] N Handschrift *f*
handwritten ['hændrɪtn] ADJ handgeschrieben
handy ['hændɪ] ADJ praktisch; (*skilful*) geschickt; (*close at hand*) in der Nähe; **to come in ~** sich als nützlich erweisen
handyman ['hændɪmæn] N (*irreg*) (*at home*) Heimwerker *m*; (*in hotel etc*) Faktotum *nt*
hang [hæŋ] (*pt, pp* **hung**) VT aufhängen; (*pt, pp* **hanged**: *criminal*) hängen; (*head*) hängen lassen ▸ VI hängen; (*hair, drapery*) fallen ▸ N: **to get the ~ of sth** (*inf*) den richtigen Dreh (bei etw) herauskriegen
▸ **hang about** VI herumlungern
▸ **hang around** VI = **hang about**
▸ **hang back** VI: **to ~ back (from doing sth)** zögern(, etw zu tun)
▸ **hang on** VI warten ▸ VT FUS (*depend on*) abhängen von; **to ~ on to** festhalten *+dat*; (*for protection, support*) sich festhalten an *+dat*; (*hope, position*) sich klammern an *+acc*; (*ideas*) festhalten an *+dat*; (*keep*) behalten
▸ **hang out** VT draußen aufhängen ▸ VI heraushängen; (*inf: live*) wohnen
▸ **hang together** VI (*argument*) folgerichtig *or* zusammenhängend sein; (*story, explanation*) zusammenhängend sein; (*statements*) zusammenpassen
▸ **hang up** VT aufhängen ▸ VI (*Tel*): **to ~ up (on sb)** einfach auflegen
hangar ['hæŋəʳ] N Hangar *m*, Flugzeughalle *f*
hangdog ['hæŋdɔg] ADJ zerknirscht
hanger ['hæŋəʳ] N Bügel *m*
hanger-on [hæŋər'ɔn] N (*parasite*) Trabant *m* (*inf*); **the hangers-on** der Anhang
hang-glide ['hæŋglaɪd] VI drachenfliegen
hang-glider ['hæŋglaɪdəʳ] N (Flug)drachen *m*
hang-gliding ['hæŋglaɪdɪŋ] N Drachenfliegen *nt*
hanging ['hæŋɪŋ] N (*execution*) Hinrichtung *f* durch den Strang; (*for wall*) Wandbehang *m*
hangman ['hæŋmən] N (*irreg*) Henker *m*
hangover ['hæŋəuvəʳ] N Kater *m*; (*from past*) Überbleibsel *nt*
hang-up ['hæŋʌp] N Komplex *m*
hank [hæŋk] N Strang *m*
hanker ['hæŋkəʳ] VI: **to ~ after** sich sehnen nach
hankering ['hæŋkərɪŋ] N: **~ (for)** Verlangen *nt* (nach)
hankie, hanky ['hæŋkɪ] N = **handkerchief**
haphazard [hæp'hæzəd] ADJ planlos, wahllos
hapless ['hæplɪs] ADJ glücklos

happen ['hæpən] VI geschehen; **to ~ to do sth** zufällig(erweise) etw tun; **as it happens** zufälligerweise; **what's happening?** was ist los?; **she happened to be free** sie hatte zufällig(erweise) gerade Zeit; **if anything happened to him** wenn ihm etwas zustoßen *or* passieren sollte
▶ **happen (up)on** VT FUS zufällig stoßen auf *+acc*; *(person)* zufällig treffen
happening ['hæpnɪŋ] N Ereignis *nt*, Vorfall *m*
happily ['hæpɪlɪ] ADV *(luckily)* glücklicherweise; *(cheerfully)* fröhlich
happiness ['hæpɪnɪs] N Glück *nt*
happy ['hæpɪ] ADJ glücklich; *(cheerful)* fröhlich; **to be ~ (with)** zufrieden sein (mit); **to be ~ to do sth** etw gerne tun; **~ birthday!** herzlichen Glückwunsch zum Geburtstag!
happy-go-lucky ['hæpɪgəu'lʌkɪ] ADJ unbekümmert
happy hour N *Zeit, in der Bars, Pubs usw Getränke zu ermäßigten Preisen anbieten*
harangue [hə'ræŋ] VT predigen *+dat (inf)*
harass ['hærəs] VT schikanieren
harassed ['hærəst] ADJ geplagt
harassment ['hærəsmənt] N Schikanierung *f*; **sexual ~** sexuelle Belästigung *f*
harbour, *(US)* **harbor** ['hɑːbəʳ] N Hafen *m* ▶ VT *(hope, fear, grudge etc)* hegen; *(criminal, fugitive)* Unterschlupf gewähren *+dat*
harbour dues NPL Hafengebühren *pl*
harbour master N Hafenmeister *m*
hard [hɑːd] ADJ hart; *(question, problem)* schwierig; *(evidence)* gesichert ▶ ADV *(work)* hart, schwer; *(think)* scharf; *(try)* sehr; **~ luck!** Pech!; **no ~ feelings!** ich nehme es dir nicht übel; **to be ~ of hearing** schwerhörig sein; **to be ~ done by** ungerecht behandelt werden; **I find it ~ to believe that …** ich kann es kaum glauben, dass …; **to look ~ at sth** *(object)* sich *+dat* etw genau ansehen; *(idea)* etw gründlich prüfen
hard-and-fast ['hɑːdən'fɑːst] ADJ fest
hardback ['hɑːdbæk] N gebundene Ausgabe *f*
hardboard ['hɑːdbɔːd] N Hartfaserplatte *f*
hard-boiled egg ['hɑːd'bɔɪld-] N hart gekochtes Ei *nt*
hard cash N Bargeld *nt*
hard copy N *(Comput)* Ausdruck *m*
hard core N harter Kern *m*
hard-core ['hɑːd'kɔːʳ] ADJ *(pornography)* hart; *(supporters)* zum harten Kern gehörend
hard court N *(Tennis)* Hartplatz *m*
hard disk N *(Comput)* Festplatte *f*
harden ['hɑːdn] VT härten; *(attitude, person)* verhärten ▶ VI hart werden, sich verhärten
hardened ['hɑːdnd] ADJ *(criminal)* Gewohnheits-; **to be ~ to sth** gegen etw abgehärtet sein
hardening ['hɑːdnɪŋ] N Verhärtung *f*
hard graft N: **by sheer ~** durch harte Arbeit
hard-headed ['hɑːd'hɛdɪd] ADJ nüchtern
hardhearted ['hɑːd'hɑːtɪd] ADJ hartherzig
hard-hitting ['hɑːd'hɪtɪŋ] ADJ *(fig: speech, journalist etc)* knallhart
hard labour N Zwangsarbeit *f*
hardliner [hɑːd'laɪnəʳ] N Vertreter(in) *m(f)* der harten Linie
hard-luck story ['hɑːdlʌk-] N Leidensgeschichte *f*
hardly ['hɑːdlɪ] ADV kaum; *(harshly)* hart, streng; **it's ~ the case** *(ironic)* das ist wohl kaum der Fall; **I can ~ believe it** ich kann es kaum glauben
hard-nosed [hɑːd'nəuzd] ADJ abgebrüht
hard-pressed [hɑːd'prɛst] ADJ: **to be ~** unter Druck sein; **~ for money** in Geldnot
hard sell N aggressive Verkaufstaktik *f*
hardship ['hɑːdʃɪp] N Not *f*
hard shoulder (BRIT) N *(Aut)* Seitenstreifen *m*
hard up *(inf)* ADJ knapp bei Kasse
hardware ['hɑːdwɛəʳ] N Eisenwaren *pl*; *(household goods)* Haushaltswaren *pl*; *(Comput)* Hardware *f*; *(Mil)* Waffen *pl*
hardware shop N Eisenwarenhandlung *f*
hard-wearing [hɑːd'wɛərɪŋ] ADJ strapazierfähig
hard-won [hɑːd'wʌn] ADJ schwer erkämpft
hard-working [hɑːd'wəːkɪŋ] ADJ fleißig
hardy ['hɑːdɪ] ADJ *(animals)* zäh; *(people)* abgehärtet; *(plant)* winterhart
hare [hɛəʳ] N Hase *m*
harebrained ['hɛəbreɪnd] ADJ verrückt
harelip ['hɛəlɪp] N Hasenscharte *f*
harem [hɑː'riːm] N Harem *m*
hark back [hɑːk-] VI: **to ~ to** zurückkommen auf *+acc*
harm [hɑːm] N Schaden *m*; *(injury)* Verletzung *f* ▶ VT schaden *+dat*; *(person: physically)* verletzen; **to mean no ~** es nicht böse meinen; **out of ~'s way** in Sicherheit; **there's no ~ in trying** es kann nicht schaden, es zu versuchen
harmful ['hɑːmful] ADJ schädlich
harmless ['hɑːmlɪs] ADJ harmlos
harmonic [hɑː'mɔnɪk] ADJ harmonisch
harmonica [hɑː'mɔnɪkə] N Harmonika *f*
harmonics [hɑː'mɔnɪks] NPL Harmonik *f*
harmonious [hɑː'məunɪəs] ADJ harmonisch
harmonium [hɑː'məunɪəm] N Harmonium *nt*
harmonize ['hɑːmənaɪz] VI *(Mus)* mehrstimmig singen/spielen; *(: one person)* die zweite Stimme singen/spielen; *(colours, ideas)* harmonieren
harmony ['hɑːmənɪ] N Einklang *m*; *(Mus)* Harmonie *f*
harness ['hɑːnɪs] N *(for horse)* Geschirr *nt*; *(for child)* Laufgurt *m*; *(also:* **safety harness***)* Sicherheitsgurt *m* ▶ VT *(resources, energy etc)* nutzbar machen; *(horse, dog)* anschirren
harp [hɑːp] N Harfe *f* ▶ VI: **to ~ on about** *(pej)* herumreiten auf *+dat*
harpist ['hɑːpɪst] N Harfenspieler(in) *m(f)*
harpoon [hɑː'puːn] N Harpune *f*
harpsichord ['hɑːpsɪkɔːd] N Cembalo *nt*
harried ['hærɪd] ADJ bedrängt
harrow ['hærəu] N Egge *f*
harrowing ['hærəuɪŋ] ADJ *(film)* erschütternd; *(experience)* grauenhaft
harry ['hærɪ] VT bedrängen, zusetzen *+dat*

harsh [hɑːʃ] ADJ (*sound, light*) grell; (*judge, winter*) streng; (*criticism, life*) hart
harshly ['hɑːʃlɪ] ADV (*judge*) streng; (*say*) barsch; (*criticize*) hart
harshness ['hɑːʃnɪs] N Grelle *f*; Strenge *f*; Härte *f*
harvest ['hɑːvɪst] N Ernte *f* ▸ VT ernten
harvester ['hɑːvɪstəʳ] N (*also*: **combine harvester**) Mähdrescher *m*
has [hæz] VB *see* **have**
has-been ['hæzbiːn] (*inf*) N: **he's/she's a ~** er/sie ist eine vergangene *or* vergessene Größe
hash [hæʃ] N (*Culin*) Haschee *nt*; (*fig*): **to make a ~ of sth** etw verpfuschen (*inf*) ▸ N ABBR (*inf*: = *hashish*) Hasch *nt*
hashish ['hæʃɪʃ] N Haschisch *nt*
hash tag N (*esp on Twitter*) Hashtag *nt*
hasn't ['hæznt] = **has not**
hassle ['hæsl] (*inf*) N (*bother*) Theater *nt* ▸ VT schikanieren
haste [heɪst] N Hast *f*; (*speed*) Eile *f*; **in ~** in Eile; **to make ~ (to do sth)** sich beeilen(, etw zu tun)
hasten ['heɪsn] VT beschleunigen ▸ VI: **to ~ to do sth** sich beeilen, etw zu tun; **I ~ to add ...** ich muss allerdings hinzufügen, ...; **she hastened back to the house** sie eilte zum Haus zurück
hastily ['heɪstɪlɪ] ADV hastig, eilig; vorschnell
hasty ['heɪstɪ] ADJ hastig, eilig; (*rash*) vorschnell
hat [hæt] N Hut *m*; **to keep sth under one's ~** etw für sich behalten
hatbox ['hætbɔks] N Hutschachtel *f*
hatch [hætʃ] N (*Naut*: *also*: **hatchway**) Luke *f*; (*also*: **service hatch**) Durchreiche *f* ▸ VI (*bird*) ausschlüpfen ▸ VT ausbrüten; **the eggs hatched after 10 days** nach 10 Tagen schlüpften die Jungen aus
hatchback ['hætʃbæk] N (*Aut*: *car*) Heckklappenmodell *nt*
hatchet ['hætʃɪt] N Beil *nt*; **to bury the ~** das Kriegsbeil begraben
hatchet job (*inf*) ADJ: **to do a ~ on sb** jdn fertigmachen
hatchet man (*inf*) N (*irreg*: *fig*) Vollstrecker *m*
hate [heɪt] VT hassen ▸ N Hass *m*; **I ~ him/milk** ich kann ihn/ Milch nicht ausstehen; **to ~ to do/doing sth** es hassen, etw zu tun; (*weaker*) etw ungern tun; **I ~ to trouble you, but ...** es ist mir sehr unangenehm, dass ich Sie belästigen muss, aber ...
hateful ['heɪtful] ADJ abscheulich
hater ['heitəʳ] N Hasser(in) *m(f)*; **cop-~** Bullenhasser(in) *m(f)*; **woman-~** Frauenhasser *m*
hatred ['heɪtrɪd] N Hass *m*; (*dislike*) Abneigung *f*
hat trick N Hattrick *m*
haughty ['hɔːtɪ] ADJ überheblich
haul [hɔːl] VT ziehen; (*by lorry*) transportieren; (*Naut*) den Kurs ändern *+gen* ▸ N Beute *f*; (*of fish*) Fang *m*; **he hauled himself out of the pool** er stemmte sich aus dem Schwimmbecken
haulage ['hɔːlɪdʒ] N (*cost*) Transportkosten *pl*; (*business*) Transport *m*
haulage contractor (BRIT) N Transportunternehmen *nt*, Spedition *f*; (*person*) Transportunternehmer(in) *m(f)*, Spediteur *m*
hauler ['hɔːləʳ] (*US*) N Transportunternehmer(in) *m(f)*, Spediteur *m*
haulier ['hɔːlɪəʳ] (BRIT) N Transportunternehmer(in) *m(f)*, Spediteur *m*
haunch [hɔːntʃ] N Hüftpartie *f*; (*of meat*) Keule *f*
haunt [hɔːnt] VT (*place*) spuken in *+dat*, umgehen in *+dat*; (*person, fig*) verfolgen ▸ N Lieblingsplatz *m*; (*of crooks etc*) Treffpunkt *m*
haunted ['hɔːntɪd] ADJ (*expression*) gehetzt, gequält; **this building/room is ~** in diesem Gebäude/Zimmer spukt es
haunting ['hɔːntɪŋ] ADJ (*music*) eindringlich; **a ~ sight** ein Anblick, der einen nicht loslässt
Havana [hə'vænə] N Havanna *nt*

KEYWORD

have [hæv] (*pt, pp* **had**) AUX VB **1** haben; (*with verbs of motion*) sein; **to have arrived/gone** angekommen/gegangen sein; **to have eaten/slept** gegessen/geschlafen haben; **he has been promoted** er ist befördert worden; **having eaten** *or* **when he had eaten, he left** nachdem er gegessen hatte, ging er
2 (*in tag questions*): **you've done it, haven't you?** du hast es gemacht, nicht wahr?; **he hasn't done it, has he?** er hat es nicht gemacht, oder?
3 (*in short answers and questions*): **you've made a mistake — no I haven't/so I have** du hast einen Fehler gemacht — nein(, das habe ich nicht)/ja, stimmt; **we haven't paid — yes we have!** wir haben nicht bezahlt — doch!; **I've been there before — have you?** ich war schon einmal da — wirklich *or* tatsächlich?
▸ MODAL AUX VB (*be obliged*): **to have (got) to do sth** etw tun müssen; **this has (got) to be a mistake** das muss ein Fehler sein
▸ VT **1** (*possess*) haben; **she has (got) blue eyes/dark hair** sie hat blaue Augen/dunkle Haare; **I have (got) an idea** ich habe eine Idee
2 (*referring to meals etc*): **to have breakfast** frühstücken; **to have lunch/dinner** zu Mittag/Abend essen; **to have a drink** etwas trinken; **to have a cigarette** eine Zigarette rauchen
3 (*receive, obtain etc*) haben; **may I have your address?** kann ich Ihre Adresse haben *or* bekommen?; **to have a baby** ein Kind bekommen
4 (*allow*): **I won't have this nonsense** dieser Unsinn kommt nicht infrage!; **we can't have that** das kommt nicht infrage
5: **to have sth done** etw machen lassen; **to have one's hair cut** sich *dat* die Haare schneiden lassen; **to have sb do sth** (*order*) jdn etw tun lassen; **he soon had them all laughing/working** bald hatte er alle zum Lachen/Arbeiten gebracht
6 (*experience, suffer*): **to have a cold/flu** eine Erkältung/die Grippe haben; **she had her bag stolen** ihr *dat* wurde die Tasche gestohlen

h

7 (*+ noun: take, hold etc*): **to have a swim** schwimmen gehen; **to have a walk** spazieren gehen; **to have a rest** sich ausruhen; **to have a meeting** eine Besprechung haben; **to have a party** eine Party geben
8 (*inf: dupe*): **you've been had** man hat dich hereingelegt
▸ **have in** (*inf*) VT: **to have it in for sb** jdn auf dem Kieker haben
▸ **have on** VT (*wear*) anhaben; (BRIT *inf: tease*) auf den Arm nehmen; **I don't have any money on me** ich habe kein Geld bei mir; **do you have** *or* **have you anything on tomorrow?** haben Sie morgen etwas vor?
▸ **have out** VT: **to have it out with sb** (*settle a problem etc*) ein Wort mit jdm reden

haven ['heɪvn] N Hafen *m*; (*safe place*) Zufluchtsort *m*
haven't ['hævnt] = **have not**
haversack ['hævəsæk] N Rucksack *m*
haves [hævz] (*inf*) NPL: **the ~ and the have-nots** die Betuchten und die Habenichtse
havoc ['hævək] N Verwüstung *f*; (*confusion*) Chaos *nt*; **to play ~ with sth** (*disrupt*) etw völlig durcheinanderbringen
Hawaii [hə'waiː] N Hawaii *nt*
Hawaiian [hə'waɪjən] ADJ hawaiisch ▸ N Hawaiianer(in) *m(f)*; (*Ling*) Hawaiisch *nt*
hawk [hɔːk] N Habicht *m*
hawker ['hɔːkə^r] N Hausierer(in) *m(f)*
hawkish ['hɔːkɪʃ] ADJ (*person, approach*) knallhart
hawthorn ['hɔːθɔːn] N Weißdorn *m*, Rotdorn *m*
hay [heɪ] N Heu *nt*
hay fever N Heuschnupfen *m*
haystack ['heɪstæk] N Heuhaufen *m*; **like looking for a needle in a ~** als ob man eine Stecknadel im Heuhaufen suchte
haywire ['heɪwaɪə^r] (*inf*) ADJ: **to go ~** (*machine*) verrücktspielen; (*plans etc*) über den Haufen geworfen werden
hazard ['hæzəd] N Gefahr *f* ▸ VT riskieren; **to be a health/fire ~** eine Gefahr für die Gesundheit/feuergefährlich sein; **to ~ a guess** (es) wagen, eine Vermutung anzustellen
hazard lights, hazard warning lights NPL (*Aut*) Warnblinkanlage *f*
hazardous ['hæzədəs] ADJ gefährlich
hazard pay (US) N Gefahrenzulage *f*
haze [heɪz] N Dunst *m*
hazel ['heɪzl] N Hasel(nuss)strauch *m*, Haselbusch *m* ▸ ADJ haselnussbraun
hazelnut ['heɪzlnʌt] N Haselnuss *f*
hazy ['heɪzɪ] ADJ dunstig, diesig; (*idea, memory*) unklar, verschwommen; **I'm rather ~ about the details** an die Einzelheiten kann ich mich nur vage *or* verschwommen erinnern; (*ignorant*) die genauen Einzelheiten sind mir nicht bekannt
H-bomb ['eɪtʃbɔm] N H-Bombe *f*
HD N ABBR (= *high definition*) hochauflösend
HDTV N ABBR (= *high definition television*) hochauflösendes Fernsehen
HE ABBR (*Rel, Diplomacy*: = *His/Her Excellency*) Seine/Ihre Exzellenz; (= *high explosive*) hochexplosiver Sprengstoff *m*
he [hiː] PRON er ▸ PREF männlich; **he who …** wer …
head [hɛd] N Kopf *m*; (*of table*) Kopfende *nt*; (*of queue*) Spitze *f*; (*of company, organization*) Leiter(in) *m(f)*; (*of school*) Schulleiter(in) *m(f)*; (*on coin*) Kopfseite *f*; (*on tape recorder*) Tonkopf *m* ▸ VT anführen, an der Spitze stehen von; (*group, company*) leiten; (*Football: ball*) köpfen; **heads (or tails)** Kopf (oder Zahl); **~ over heels** Hals über Kopf; (*in love*) bis über beide Ohren; **£10 a** *or* **per ~** 10 Pfund pro Kopf; **at the ~ of the list** oben auf der Liste; **to have a ~ for business** einen guten Geschäftssinn haben; **to have no ~ for heights** nicht schwindelfrei sein; **to come to a ~** sich zuspitzen; **they put their heads together** sie haben sich zusammengesetzt; **off the top of my** *etc* **~** ohne lange zu überlegen; **on your own ~ be it!** auf Ihre eigene Verantwortung *or* Kappe (*inf*)!; **to bite** *or* **snap sb's ~ off** jdn grob anfahren; **he won't bite your ~ off** er wird dir schon nicht den Kopf abreißen; **it went to my ~** es ist mir in den Kopf *or* zu Kopf gestiegen; **to lose/keep one's ~** den Kopf verlieren/nicht verlieren; **I can't make ~ nor tail of this** hieraus werde ich nicht schlau; **he's off his ~!** (*inf*) er ist nicht (ganz) bei Trost!
▸ **head for** VT FUS (*on foot*) zusteuern auf *+acc*; (*by car*) in Richtung … fahren; (*plane, ship*) Kurs nehmen auf *+acc*; **you are heading for trouble** du wirst Ärger bekommen
▸ **head off** VT abwenden
headache ['hɛdeɪk] N Kopfschmerzen *pl*, Kopfweh *nt*; (*fig*) Problem *nt*; **to have a ~** Kopfschmerzen *or* Kopfweh haben
headband ['hɛdbænd] N Stirnband *nt*
headboard ['hɛdbɔːd] N Kopfteil *nt*
head cold N Kopfgrippe *f*
headdress ['hɛddrɛs] (BRIT) N Kopfschmuck *m*
headed notepaper ['hɛdɪd-] N Schreibpapier *nt* mit Briefkopf
header ['hɛdə^r] (BRIT *inf*) N (*Football*) Kopfball *m*
headfirst ['hɛd'fəːst] ADV (*lit*) kopfüber; (*fig*) Hals über Kopf
headgear ['hɛdgɪə^r] N Kopfbedeckung *f*
head-hunt ['hɛdhʌnt] VT abwerben
head-hunter ['hɛdhʌntə^r] N (*Comm*) Kopfjäger(in) *m(f)*
heading ['hɛdɪŋ] N Überschrift *f*
headlamp ['hɛdlæmp] (BRIT) N = **headlight**
headland ['hɛdlənd] N Landspitze *f*
headlight ['hɛdlaɪt] N Scheinwerfer *m*
headline ['hɛdlaɪn] N Schlagzeile *f*; (*Radio, TV*): **(news) headlines** Nachrichtenüberblick *m*
headlong ['hɛdlɔŋ] ADV kopfüber; (*rush*) Hals über Kopf
headmaster [hɛd'mɑːstə^r] N Schulleiter *m*
headmistress [hɛd'mɪstrɪs] N Schulleiterin *f*
head office N Zentrale *f*

head of state (*pl* **heads of state**) N Staatsoberhaupt *nt*
head-on ['hɛd'ɔn] ADJ (*collision*) frontal; (*confrontation*) direkt
headphones ['hɛdfəunz] NPL Kopfhörer *pl*
headquarters ['hɛdkwɔ:təz] NPL Zentrale *f*; (*Mil*) Hauptquartier *nt*
headrest ['hɛdrɛst] N (*Aut*) Kopfstütze *f*
headroom ['hɛdrum] N (*in car*) Kopfraum *m*; (*under bridge*) lichte Höhe *f*
headscarf ['hɛdska:f] N Kopftuch *nt*
headset ['hɛdsɛt] N = **headphones**
head start N Vorsprung *m*
headstone ['hɛdstəun] N Grabstein *m*
headstrong ['hɛdstrɔŋ] ADJ eigensinnig
head teacher N Schulleiter(in) *m(f)*
head waiter N Oberkellner *m*
headway ['hɛdweɪ] N: **to make ~** vorankommen
headwind ['hɛdwɪnd] N Gegenwind *m*
heady ['hɛdɪ] ADJ (*experience etc*) aufregend; (*drink, atmosphere*) berauschend
heal [hi:l] VT, VI heilen
health [hɛlθ] N Gesundheit *f*
health care N Gesundheitsfürsorge *f*
health centre (BRIT) N Ärztezentrum *nt*
health club N Fitnesscenter *nt*
health food N Reformkost *f*, Naturkost *f*
health food shop N Reformhaus *nt*, Naturkostladen *m*
health hazard N Gefahr *f* für die Gesundheit
health insurance N Krankenversicherung *f*
health service (BRIT) N: **the Health Service** das Gesundheitswesen
healthy ['hɛlθɪ] ADJ gesund; (*profit*) ansehnlich
heap [hi:p] N Haufen *m* ▸ VT: **to ~ (up)** (auf)häufen; **heaps of** (*inf*) jede Menge; **to ~ sth with** etw beladen mit; **to ~ sth on** etw häufen auf *+acc*; **to ~ favours/gifts** *etc* **on sb** jdn mit Gefälligkeiten/Geschenken *etc* überhäufen; **to ~ praises on sb** jdn mit Lob überschütten
hear [hɪəʳ] (*pt, pp* **heard**) VT hören; (*Law: case*) verhandeln; (*: witness*) vernehmen; **to ~ about** hören von; **to ~ from sb** von jdm hören; **I've never heard of that book** von dem Buch habe ich noch nie etwas gehört; **I wouldn't ~ of it!** davon will ich nichts hören
▸ **hear out** VT ausreden lassen
heard [hə:d] PT, PP *of* **hear**
hearing ['hɪərɪŋ] N Gehör *nt*; (*of facts, by committee*) Anhörung *f*; (*of witnesses*) Vernehmung *f*; (*of a case*) Verhandlung *f*; **to give sb a ~** (BRIT) jdn anhören
hearing aid N Hörgerät *nt*
hearsay ['hɪəseɪ] N Gerüchte *pl*; **by ~** vom Hörensagen
hearse [hə:s] N Leichenwagen *m*
heart [ha:t] N Herz *nt*; (*of problem*) Kern *m*; **hearts** NPL (*Cards*) Herz *nt*; **to lose ~** den Mut verlieren; **to take ~** Mut fassen; **at ~** im Grunde; **by ~** auswendig; **to set one's ~ on sth** sein Herz an etw *acc* hängen; **to set one's ~ on doing sth** alles daransetzen, etw zu tun; **the ~ of the matter** der Kern der Sache
heartache ['ha:teɪk] N Kummer *m*
heart attack N Herzanfall *m*
heartbeat ['ha:tbi:t] N Herzschlag *m*
heartbreak ['ha:tbreɪk] N großer Kummer *m*, Leid *nt*
heartbreaking ['ha:tbreɪkɪŋ] ADJ herzzerreißend
heartbroken ['ha:tbrəukən] ADJ: **to be ~** todunglücklich sein
heartburn ['ha:tbə:n] N Sodbrennen *nt*
-hearted ['ha:tɪd] SUFF: **kind~** gutherzig
heartening ['ha:tnɪŋ] ADJ ermutigend
heart failure N Herzversagen *nt*
heartfelt ['ha:tfɛlt] ADJ tief empfunden
hearth [ha:θ] N ≈ Kamin *m*
heartily ['ha:tɪlɪ] ADV (laut und) herzlich; herzhaft; tief; ungeteilt
heartland ['ha:tlænd] N Herz *nt*; **Britain's industrial ~** Großbritanniens Industriezentrum *nt*
heartless ['ha:tlɪs] ADJ herzlos
heartstrings ['ha:tstrɪŋz] NPL: **to tug at sb's ~** bei jdm auf die Tränendrüsen drücken
heart-throb ['ha:tθrɔb] (*inf*) N Schwarm *m*
heart-to-heart ['ha:ttə'ha:t] ADJ, ADV ganz im Vertrauen
heart transplant N Herztransplantation *f*, Herzverpflanzung *f*
heart-warming ['ha:twɔ:mɪŋ] ADJ herzerfreuend
hearty ['ha:tɪ] ADJ (*person*) laut und herzlich; (*laugh, appetite*) herzhaft; (*welcome*) herzlich; (*dislike*) tief; (*support*) ungeteilt
heat [hi:t] N Hitze *f*; (*warmth*) Wärme *f*; (*temperature*) Temperatur *f*; (*Sport: also:* **qualifying heat**) Vorrunde *f* ▸ VT erhitzen, heiß machen; (*room, house*) heizen; **in ~, on ~** (BRIT) (*Zool*) brünstig, läufig
▸ **heat up** VI sich erwärmen, warm werden ▸ VT aufwärmen; (*water, room*) erwärmen
heated ['hi:tɪd] ADJ geheizt; (*pool*) beheizt; (*argument*) hitzig
heater ['hi:təʳ] N (Heiz)ofen *m*; (*in car*) Heizung *f*
heath [hi:θ] (BRIT) N Heide *f*
heathen ['hi:ðn] N Heide *m*, Heidin *f*
heather ['hɛðəʳ] N Heidekraut *nt*, Erika *f*
heating ['hi:tɪŋ] N Heizung *f*
heat-resistant ['hi:trɪzɪstənt] ADJ hitzebeständig
heat-seeking ['hi:tsi:kɪŋ] ADJ Wärme suchend
heatstroke ['hi:tstrəuk] N Hitzschlag *m*
heat wave N Hitzewelle *f*
heave [hi:v] VT (*pull*) ziehen; (*push*) schieben; (*lift*) (hoch)heben ▸ VI sich heben und senken; (*retch*) sich übergeben ▸ N Zug *m*; Stoß *m*; Heben *nt*; **to ~ a sigh** einen Seufzer ausstoßen
▸ **heave to** (*pt, pp* **hove**) VI (*Naut*) beidrehen
heaven ['hɛvn] N Himmel *m*; **thank ~!** Gott sei Dank!; **~ forbid!** bloß nicht!; **for ~'s sake!** um Himmels *or* Gottes willen!
heavenly ['hɛvnlɪ] ADJ himmlisch

h

heaven-sent [hɛvn'sɛnt] ADJ ideal
heavily ['hɛvɪlɪ] ADV schwer; (*drink, smoke, depend, rely*) stark; (*sleep, sigh*) tief; (*say*) mit schwerer Stimme
heavy ['hɛvɪ] ADJ schwer; (*clothes*) dick; (*rain, snow, drinker, smoker*) stark; (*build, frame*) kräftig; (*breathing, sleep*) tief; (*schedule, week*) anstrengend; (*weather*) drückend, schwül; **the conversation was ~ going** die Unterhaltung war mühsam; **the book was ~ going** das Buch las sich schwer
heavy cream (*US*) N *Sahne mit hohem Fettgehalt*, ≈ Schlagsahne *f*
heavy-duty ['hɛvɪ'dju:tɪ] ADJ strapazierfähig
heavy goods vehicle N Lastkraftwagen *m*
heavy-handed ['hɛvɪ'hændɪd] ADJ schwerfällig, ungeschickt
heavy industry N Schwerindustrie *f*
heavy metal N (*Mus*) Heavymetal *nt*
heavyset ['hɛvɪ'sɛt] (*esp US*) ADJ kräftig gebaut
heavyweight ['hɛvɪweɪt] N (*Sport*) Schwergewicht *nt*
Hebrew ['hi:bru:] ADJ hebräisch ▸ N (*Ling*) Hebräisch *nt*
Hebrides ['hɛbrɪdi:z] NPL: **the ~** die Hebriden *pl*
heck [hɛk] (*inf*) EXCL: **oh ~!** zum Kuckuck! ▸ N: **a ~ of a lot** irrsinnig viel
heckle ['hɛkl] VT durch Zwischenrufe stören
heckler ['hɛklə^r] N Zwischenrufer(in) *m(f)*, Störer(in) *m(f)*
hectare ['hɛktɑ:^r] (BRIT) N Hektar *m or nt*
hectic ['hɛktɪk] ADJ hektisch
hector ['hɛktə^r] VT tyrannisieren
he'd [hi:d] = **he would**; **he had**
hedge [hɛdʒ] N Hecke *f* ▸ VI ausweichen, sich nicht festlegen ▸ VT: **to ~ one's bets** (*fig*) sich absichern; **as a ~ against inflation** als Absicherung *or* Schutz gegen die Inflation
▸ **hedge in** VT (*person*) (in seiner Freiheit) einschränken; (*proposals etc*) behindern
hedgehog ['hɛdʒhɔg] N Igel *m*
hedgerow ['hɛdʒrəu] N Hecke *f*
hedonism ['hi:dənɪzəm] N Hedonismus *m*
heed [hi:d] VT (*also*: **take heed of**) beachten ▸ N: **to pay (no) ~ to, take (no) ~ of** (nicht) beachten
heedless ['hi:dlɪs] ADJ achtlos; **~ of sb/sth** ohne auf jdn/etw zu achten
heel [hi:l] N Ferse *f*; (*of shoe*) Absatz *m* ▸ VT (*shoe*) mit einem neuen Absatz versehen; **to bring to ~** (*dog*) bei Fuß gehen lassen; (*fig: person*) an die Kandare nehmen; **to take to one's heels** (*inf*) sich aus dem Staub machen
hefty ['hɛftɪ] ADJ kräftig; (*parcel etc*) schwer; (*profit*) ansehnlich
heifer ['hɛfə^r] N Färse *f*
height [haɪt] N Höhe *f*; (*of person*) Größe *f*; (*fig: of luxury, good taste etc*) Gipfel *m*; **what ~ are you?** wie groß bist du?; **of average ~** durchschnittlich groß; **to be afraid of heights** nicht schwindelfrei sein; **it's the ~ of fashion** das ist die neueste Mode; **at the ~ of the tourist season** in der Hauptsaison
heighten ['haɪtn] VT erhöhen
heinous ['heɪnəs] ADJ abscheulich, verabscheuungswürdig
heir [ɛə^r] N Erbe *m*; **the ~ to the throne** der Thronfolger
heir apparent N gesetzlicher Erbe *m*
heiress ['ɛərɛs] N Erbin *f*
heirloom ['ɛəlu:m] N Erbstück *nt*
heist [haɪst] (*US inf*) N Raubüberfall *m*
held [hɛld] PT, PP *of* **hold**
helicopter ['hɛlɪkɔptə^r] N Hubschrauber *m*
heliport ['hɛlɪpɔ:t] N Hubschrauberflugplatz *m*, Heliport *m*
helium ['hi:lɪəm] N Helium *nt*
hell [hɛl] N Hölle *f*; **~!** (*inf!*) verdammt! (*inf!*); **a ~ of a lot** (*inf*) verdammt viel (*inf*); **a ~ of a mess** (*inf*) ein wahnsinniges Chaos (*inf*); **a ~ of a noise** (*inf*) ein Höllenlärm *m*; **a ~ of a nice guy** ein wahnsinnig netter Typ
he'll [hi:l] = **he will**; **he shall**
hellbent [hɛl'bɛnt] ADJ: **~ (on)** versessen (auf +*acc*)
hellish ['hɛlɪʃ] (*inf*) ADJ höllisch
hello [hə'ləu] EXCL hallo; (*expressing surprise*) nanu, he
Hell's Angels NPL Hell's Angels *pl*
helm [hɛlm] N Ruder *nt*, Steuer *nt*; **at the ~** am Ruder
helmet ['hɛlmɪt] N Helm *m*
helmsman ['hɛlmzmən] N (*irreg*) Steuermann *m*
help [hɛlp] N Hilfe *f*; (*charwoman*) (Haushalts)hilfe *f* ▸ VT helfen +*dat*; **with the ~ of** (*person*) mit (der) Hilfe +*gen*; (*tool etc*) mithilfe +*gen*; **to be of ~ to sb** jdm behilflich sein, jdm helfen; **can I ~ you?** (*in shop*) womit kann ich Ihnen dienen?; **~ yourself** bedienen Sie sich; **he can't ~ it** er kann nichts dafür; **I can't ~ thinking that ...** ich kann mir nicht helfen, ich glaube, dass ...
help desk N (*esp Comput*) Benutzerunterstützung *f*, Helpdesk *nt m*
helper ['hɛlpə^r] N Helfer(in) *m(f)*
helpful ['hɛlpful] ADJ hilfsbereit; (*advice, suggestion*) nützlich, hilfreich
helping ['hɛlpɪŋ] N Portion *f*
helping hand N: **to give** *or* **lend sb a ~** jdm behilflich sein
helpless ['hɛlplɪs] ADJ hilflos
helplessly ['hɛlplɪslɪ] ADV hilflos
helpline ['hɛlplaɪn] N (*for emergencies*) Notruf *m*; (*for information*) Informationsdienst *m*
Helsinki ['hɛlsɪŋkɪ] N Helsinki *nt*
helter-skelter ['hɛltə'skɛltə^r] (BRIT) N Rutschbahn *f*
hem [hɛm] N Saum *m* ▸ VT säumen
▸ **hem in** VT einschließen, umgeben; **to feel hemmed in** (*fig*) sich eingeengt fühlen
hematology ['hi:mə'tɔlədʒɪ] (*US*) N = **haematology**
hemisphere ['hɛmɪsfɪə^r] N Hemisphäre *f*; (*of sphere*) Halbkugel *f*
hemlock ['hɛmlɔk] N Schierling *m*

hemoglobin ['hi:mə'gləubɪn] (*US*) N = **haemoglobin**
hemophilia ['hi:mə'fɪlɪə] (*US*) N = **haemophilia**
hemorrhage ['hɛmərɪdʒ] (*US*) N = **haemorrhage**
hemorrhoids ['hɛmərɔɪdz] (*US*) NPL = **haemorrhoids**
hemp [hɛmp] N Hanf *m*
hen [hɛn] N Henne *f*, Huhn *nt*; (*female bird*) Weibchen *nt*
hence [hɛns] ADV daher; **2 years ~** in zwei Jahren
henceforth [hɛns'fɔ:θ] ADV von nun an; (*from that time on*) von da an
henchman ['hɛntʃmən] N (*irreg: pej*) Spießgeselle *m*
henna ['hɛnə] N Henna *nt*
hen night, hen party (*inf*) N Damenkränzchen *nt*

Als **hen night** bezeichnet man eine feuchtfröhliche Frauenparty, die kurz vor einer Hochzeit von der Braut und ihren Freundinnen meist in einem Gasthaus oder Nachtklub abgehalten wird und bei der die Freundinnen dafür sorgen, dass vor allem die Braut große Mengen an Alkohol konsumiert. Siehe auch **stag night**.

henpecked ['hɛnpɛkt] ADJ: **to be ~** unter dem Pantoffel stehen; **~ husband** Pantoffelheld *m*
hepatitis [hɛpə'taɪtɪs] N Hepatitis *f*
her [hə:ʳ] PRON sie; (*indirect*) ihr ▶ ADJ ihr; **I see ~** ich sehe sie; **give ~ a book** gib ihr ein Buch; **after ~** nach ihr; *see also* **me; my**
herald ['hɛrəld] N (Vor)bote *m* ▶ VT ankündigen
heraldic [hɛ'rældɪk] ADJ heraldisch, Wappen-
heraldry ['hɛrəldrɪ] N Wappenkunde *f*, Heraldik *f*; (*coats of arms*) Wappen *pl*
herb [hə:b] N Kraut *nt*
herbaceous [hə:'beɪʃəs] ADJ: **~ border** Staudenrabatte *f*; **~ plant** Staude *f*
herbal ['hə:bl] ADJ (*tea, medicine*) Kräuter-
herbicide ['hə:bɪsaɪd] N Unkrautvertilgungsmittel *nt*, Herbizid *nt*
herd [hə:d] N Herde *f*; (*of wild animals*) Rudel *nt* ▶ VT treiben; (*gather*) zusammentreiben; **herded together** zusammengetrieben
here [hɪəʳ] ADV hier; **she left ~ yesterday** sie ist gestern von hier abgereist; **~ is/are...** hier ist/sind...; **~ you are** (*giving*) (hier,) bitte; **~ we are!** (*finding sth*) da ist es ja!; **~ she is!** da ist sie ja!; **~ she comes** da kommt sie ja; **come ~!** komm hierher *or* hierhin!; **~ and there** hier und da; **"~'s to ..."** „auf ... *acc*"
hereabouts ['hɪərə'bauts] ADV hier
hereafter [hɪər'ɑ:ftəʳ] ADV künftig
hereby [hɪə'baɪ] ADV hiermit
hereditary [hɪ'rɛdɪtrɪ] ADJ erblich, Erb-
heredity [hɪ'rɛdɪtɪ] N Vererbung *f*
heresy ['hɛrəsɪ] N Ketzerei *f*
heretic ['hɛrətɪk] N Ketzer(in) *m(f)*
heretical [hɪ'rɛtɪkl] ADJ ketzerisch
herewith [hɪə'wɪð] ADV hiermit
heritage ['hɛrɪtɪdʒ] N Erbe *nt*; **our national ~** unser nationales Erbe
hermetically [hə:'mɛtɪklɪ] ADV: **~ sealed** hermetisch verschlossen
hermit ['hə:mɪt] N Einsiedler(in) *m(f)*
hernia ['hə:nɪə] N Bruch *m*
hero ['hɪərəu] (*pl* **heroes**) N Held *m*; (*idol*) Idol *nt*
heroic [hɪ'rəuɪk] ADJ heroisch; (*figure, person*) heldenhaft
heroin ['hɛrəuɪn] N Heroin *nt*
heroin addict N Heroinsüchtige(r) *f(m)*
heroine ['hɛrəuɪn] N Heldin *f*; (*idol*) Idol *nt*
heroism ['hɛrəuɪzəm] N Heldentum *nt*
heron ['hɛrən] N Reiher *m*
hero worship N Heldenverehrung *f*
herring ['hɛrɪŋ] N Hering *m*
hers [hə:z] PRON ihre(r, s); **a friend of ~** ein Freund von ihr; **this is ~** das gehört ihr; *see also* **mine²**
herself [hə:'sɛlf] PRON sich; (*emphatic*) (sie) selbst; *see also* **oneself**
Herts [hɑ:ts] (*BRIT*) ABBR (*Post*) = **Hertfordshire**
he's [hi:z] = **he is; he has**
hesitant ['hɛzɪtənt] ADJ zögernd; **to be ~ about doing sth** zögern, etw zu tun
hesitate ['hɛzɪteɪt] VI zögern; (*be unwilling*) Bedenken haben; **to ~ about** Bedenken haben wegen; **don't ~ to see a doctor if you are worried** gehen Sie ruhig zum Arzt, wenn Sie sich Sorgen machen
hesitation [hɛzɪ'teɪʃən] N Zögern *nt*; Bedenken *pl*; **to have no ~ in saying sth** etw ohne Weiteres sagen können
hessian ['hɛsɪən] N Sackleinwand *f*, Rupfen *m*
heterogenous [hɛtə'rɔdʒɪnəs] ADJ heterogen
heterosexual ['hɛtərəu'sɛksjuəl] ADJ heterosexuell ▶ N Heterosexuelle(r) *f(m)*
het up [hɛt-] (*inf*) ADJ: **to get ~ (about)** sich aufregen (über *+acc*)
HEW (*US*) N ABBR (= *Department of Health, Education and Welfare*) *Ministerium für Gesundheit, Erziehung und Sozialfürsorge*
hew [hju:] (*pt, pp* **hewed** *or* **hewn**) VT (*stone*) behauen; (*wood*) hacken
hex [hɛks] (*US*) N Fluch *m* ▶ VT verhexen
hexagon ['hɛksəgən] N Sechseck *nt*
hexagonal [hɛk'sægənl] ADJ sechseckig
hey [heɪ] EXCL he; (*to attract attention*) he du/Sie
heyday ['heɪdeɪ] N: **the ~ of** (*person*) die Glanzzeit *+gen*; (*nation, group etc*) die Blütezeit *+gen*
HF N ABBR (= *high frequency*) HF
HGV (*BRIT*) N ABBR (= *heavy goods vehicle*) Lkw *m*
HI (*US*) ABBR (*Post*) = **Hawaii**
hi [haɪ] EXCL hallo
hiatus [haɪ'eɪtəs] N Unterbrechung *f*
hibernate ['haɪbəneɪt] VI Winterschlaf halten *or* machen
hibernation [haɪbə'neɪʃən] N Winterschlaf *m*
hiccough ['hɪkʌp] VI hicksen
hiccoughs ['hɪkʌps] NPL Schluckauf *m*; **to have (the) ~** den Schluckauf haben
hiccup ['hɪkʌp] VI = **hiccough**
hiccups ['hɪkʌps] NPL = **hiccoughs**
hick [hɪk] (*US inf*) N Hinterwäldler *m*

h

hid [hɪd] PT *of* **hide**
hidden ['hɪdn] PP *of* **hide** ▸ ADJ (*advantage, danger*) unsichtbar; (*place*) versteckt; **there are no ~ extras** es gibt keine versteckten Extrakosten
hide [haɪd] (*pt* **hid**, *pp* **hidden**) N Haut *f*, Fell *nt*; (*of birdwatcher etc*) Versteck *nt* ▸ VT verstecken; (*feeling, information*) verbergen; (*obscure*) verdecken ▸ VI: **to ~ (from sb)** sich (vor jdm) verstecken; **to ~ sth (from sb)** etw (vor jdm) verstecken
hide-and-seek ['haɪdən'si:k] N Versteckspiel *nt*; **to play ~** Verstecken spielen
hideaway ['haɪdəweɪ] N Zufluchtsort *m*
hideous ['hɪdɪəs] ADJ scheußlich; (*conditions*) furchtbar
hideously ['hɪdɪəslɪ] ADV furchtbar
hide-out ['haɪdaut] N Versteck *nt*
hiding ['haɪdɪŋ] N Tracht *f* Prügel; **to be in ~** (*concealed*) sich versteckt halten
hiding place N Versteck *nt*
hierarchy ['haɪərɑ:kɪ] N Hierarchie *f*
hieroglyphics [haɪərə'glɪfɪks] NPL Hieroglyphen *pl*
hi-fi ['haɪfaɪ] N ABBR (= *high fidelity*) Hi-Fi *nt* ▸ ADJ (*equipment etc*) Hi-Fi-
higgledy-piggledy ['hɪgldɪ'pɪgldɪ] ADJ durcheinander
high [haɪ] ADJ hoch; (*wind*) stark; (*risk*) groß; (*quality*) gut; (*inf: on drugs*) high; (*: on drink*) blau; (BRIT: *food*) schlecht; (*: game*) anbrüchig ▸ ADV hoch ▸ N: **exports have reached a new ~** der Export hat einen neuen Höchststand erreicht; **to pay a ~ price for sth** etw teuer bezahlen; **it's ~ time you did it** es ist *or* wird höchste Zeit, dass du es machst; **~ in the air** hoch oben in der Luft
highball ['haɪbɔ:l] (*US*) N Highball *m*
highboy ['haɪbɔɪ] (*US*) N hohe Kommode *f*
highbrow ['haɪbrau] ADJ intellektuell; (*book, discussion etc*) anspruchsvoll
highchair ['haɪtʃɛəʳ] N Hochstuhl *m*
high-class ['haɪ'klɑ:s] ADJ erstklassig; (*neighbourhood*) vornehm

> **High Court** ist in England und Wales die Kurzform für „High Court of Justice" und bildet zusammen mit dem Berufungsgericht den Obersten Gerichtshof. In Schottland ist es die Kurzform für „High Court of Justiciary", das höchste Strafgericht in Schottland, das in Edinburgh und anderen Großstädten (immer mit Richter und Geschworenen) zusammentritt und für Verbrechen wie Mord, Vergewaltigung und Hochverrat zuständig ist. Weniger schwere Verbrechen werden vor dem „sheriff court" verhandelt und leichtere Vergehen vor dem „district court".

higher ['haɪəʳ] ADJ (*form of study, life etc*) höher (entwickelt) ▸ ADV höher ▸ N (SCOT *Scol*): **H~** *mit „Higher" wird die vorgeschrittenenstufe des „Scottish certificate of education" und auch der Abschluss dieses Ausbildungsjahr bezeichnet*
higher education N Hochschulbildung *f*
highfalutin [haɪfə'lu:tɪn] (*inf*) ADJ hochtrabend
high finance N Hochfinanz *f*
high-flier, high-flyer [haɪ'flaɪəʳ] N Senkrechtstarter(in) *m(f)*
high-flying [haɪ'flaɪɪŋ] ADJ (*person*) erfolgreich; (*lifestyle*) exklusiv
high-handed [haɪ'hændɪd] ADJ eigenmächtig
high-heeled [haɪ'hi:ld] ADJ hochhackig
high heels NPL hochhackige Schuhe *pl*
high jump N Hochsprung *m*
Highlands ['haɪləndz] NPL: **the ~** das Hochland
high-level ['haɪlɛvl] ADJ (*talks etc*) auf höchster Ebene; **~ language** (*Comput*) höhere Programmiersprache *f*
highlight ['haɪlaɪt] N (*of event*) Höhepunkt *m*; (*in hair*) Strähnchen *nt* ▸ VT (*problem, need*) ein Schlaglicht werfen auf *+acc*
highlighter ['haɪlaɪtəʳ] N Textmarker *m*
highly ['haɪlɪ] ADV hoch-; **to speak ~ of** sich sehr positiv äußern über *+acc*; **to think ~ of** eine hohe Meinung haben von
highly strung ADJ nervös
High Mass N Hochamt *nt*
highness ['haɪnɪs] N: **Her/His/Your H~** Ihre/Seine/Eure Hoheit *f*
high-pitched [haɪ'pɪtʃt] ADJ hoch
high point N Höhepunkt *m*
high-powered ['haɪ'pauəd] ADJ (*engine*) Hochleistungs-; (*job*) Spitzen-; (*businessman*) dynamisch; (*person*) äußerst fähig; (*course*) anspruchsvoll
high-pressure ['haɪprɛʃəʳ] ADJ (*area, system*) Hochdruck-; (*inf: sales technique*) aggressiv
high-rise ['haɪraɪz] ADJ (*apartment, block*) Hochhaus-; **~ building/flats** Hochhaus *nt*
high school N ≈ Oberschule *f*

> **High school** ist eine weiterführende Schule in den USA. Man unterscheidet zwischen „junior high school" (im Anschluss an die Grundschule, umfasst das 7., 8. und 9. Schuljahr) und „senior high school" (10., 11. und 12. Schuljahr, mit akademischen und berufsbezogenen Fächern). Weiterführende Schulen in Großbritannien werden manchmal auch als high school bezeichnet. Siehe auch **elementary school**.

high season (BRIT) N Hochsaison *f*
high-speed ADJ Schnell-; **~ train** Hochgeschwindigkeitszug *m*
high spirits NPL Hochstimmung *f*
high street (BRIT) N Hauptstraße *f*
high strung (*US*) ADJ = **highly strung**
high tide N Flut *f*
highway ['haɪweɪ] (*US*) N Straße *f*; (*between towns, states*) Landstraße *f*; **information ~** Datenautobahn *f*
Highway Code (BRIT) N Straßenverkehrsordnung *f*
highwayman ['haɪweɪmən] N (*irreg*) Räuber *m*, Wegelagerer *m*
hijack ['haɪdʒæk] VT entführen ▸ N (*also:* **hijacking**) Entführung *f*

hijacker ['haɪdʒækəʳ] N Entführer(in) *m(f)*
hike [haɪk] VI wandern ▶ N Wanderung *f*; (*inf: in prices etc*) Erhöhung *f* ▶ VT (*inf*) erhöhen
hiker ['haɪkəʳ] N Wanderer *m*, Wanderin *f*
hiking ['haɪkɪŋ] N Wandern *nt*
hilarious [hɪ'lɛərɪəs] ADJ urkomisch
hilarity [hɪ'lærɪtɪ] N übermütige Ausgelassenheit *f*
hill [hɪl] N Hügel *m*; (*fairly high*) Berg *m*; (*slope*) Hang *m*; (*on road*) Steigung *f*
hillbilly ['hɪlbɪlɪ] (*US*) N Hillbilly *m*; (*pej*) Hinterwäldler(in) *m(f)*, Landpomeranze *f*
hillock ['hɪlək] N Hügel *m*, Anhöhe *f*
hillside ['hɪlsaɪd] N Hang *m*
hill start N (*Aut*) Anfahren *nt* am Berg
hilltop ['hɪltɔp] N Gipfel *m*
hill walking N Bergwandern *nt*
hilly ['hɪlɪ] ADJ hügelig
hilt [hɪlt] N (*of sword, knife*) Heft *nt*; **to the ~** voll und ganz
him [hɪm] PRON ihn; (*indirect*) ihm; *see also* **me**
Himalayas [hɪmə'leɪəz] NPL: **the ~** der Himalaja
himself [hɪm'sɛlf] PRON sich; (*emphatic*) (er) selbst; *see also* **oneself**
hind [haɪnd] ADJ (*legs*) Hinter- ▶ N (*female deer*) Hirschkuh *f*
hinder ['hɪndəʳ] VT behindern; **to ~ sb from doing sth** jdn daran hindern, etw zu tun
hindquarters ['haɪnd'kwɔːtəz] NPL Hinterteil *nt*
hindrance ['hɪndrəns] N Behinderung *f*
hindsight ['haɪndsaɪt] N: **with ~** im Nachhinein
Hindu ['hɪnduː] ADJ hinduistisch, Hindu-
hinge [hɪndʒ] N (*on door*) Angel *f* ▶ VI: **to ~ on** anhängen von
hint [hɪnt] N Andeutung *f*; (*advice*) Tipp *m*; (*sign, glimmer*) Spur *f* ▶ VT: **to ~ that** andeuten, dass ▶ VI: **to ~ at** andeuten; **to drop a ~** eine Andeutung machen; **give me a ~** geben Sie mir einen Hinweis; **white with a ~ of pink** weiß mit einem Hauch von Rosa
hip [hɪp] N Hüfte *f*
hip flask N Taschenflasche *f*, Flachmann *m* (*inf*)
hip-hop ['hɪphɔp] N Hip-Hop *nt*
hippie ['hɪpɪ] N Hippie *m*
hippo ['hɪpəu] N Nilpferd *nt*
hip pocket N Gesäßtasche *f*
hippopotamus [hɪpə'pɔtəməs] (*pl* **hippopotamuses** *or* **hippopotami**) N Nilpferd *nt*
hippy ['hɪpɪ] N = **hippie**
hire ['haɪəʳ] VT (BRIT) mieten; (*worker*) einstellen ▶ N (BRIT) Mieten *nt*; **for ~** (*taxi*) frei; (*boat*) zu vermieten; **on ~** gemietet
▶ **hire out** VT vermieten
hire car, (BRIT) **hired car** N Mietwagen *m*, Leihwagen *m*
hire-purchase [haɪə'pəːtʃɪs] (BRIT) N Ratenkauf *m*; **to buy sth on ~** etw auf Raten kaufen
his [hɪz] PRON seine(r, s) ▶ ADJ sein; *see also* **my**; **mine²**
hiss [hɪs] VI zischen; (*cat*) fauchen ▶ N Zischen *nt*; (*of cat*) Fauchen *nt*
histogram ['hɪstəgræm] N Histogramm *nt*
historian [hɪ'stɔːrɪən] N Historiker(in) *m(f)*
historic [hɪ'stɔrɪk] ADJ historisch
historical [hɪ'stɔrɪkl] ADJ historisch
history ['hɪstərɪ] N Geschichte *f*; **there's a ~ of heart disease in his family** Herzleiden liegen bei ihm in der Familie; **medical ~** Krankengeschichte *f*
hit [hɪt] (*pt, pp* **~**) VT schlagen; (*reach, affect*) treffen; (*vehicle: another vehicle*) zusammenstoßen mit; (*: wall, tree*) fahren gegen; (*: more violently*) prallen gegen; (*: person*) anfahren ▶ N Schlag *m*; (*success*) Erfolg *m*; (*song*) Hit *m*; **to ~ it off with sb** sich gut mit jdm verstehen; **to ~ the headlines** Schlagzeilen machen; **to ~ the road** (*inf*) sich auf den Weg *or* die Socken (*inf*) machen; **to ~ the roof** (*inf*) an die Decke *or* in die Luft gehen
▶ **hit back** VI: **to ~ back at sb** jdn zurückschlagen; (*fig*) jdm Kontra geben
▶ **hit out at** VT FUS auf jdn losschlagen; (*fig*) jdn scharf angreifen
▶ **hit (up)on** VT FUS stoßen auf *+acc*, finden
hit-and-miss ['hɪtən'mɪs] ADJ = **hit-or-miss**
hit-and-run driver ['hɪtən'rʌn-] N unfallflüchtiger Fahrer *m*, unfallflüchtige Fahrerin *f*
hitch [hɪtʃ] VT festmachen, anbinden; (*trousers, skirt: also:* **hitch up**) hochziehen ▶ N Schwierigkeit *f*, Problem *nt*; **to ~ a lift** trampen, per Anhalter fahren; **technical ~** technische Panne *f*
▶ **hitch up** VT anspannen; *see also* **hitch**
hitchhike ['hɪtʃhaɪk] VI trampen, per Anhalter fahren
hitchhiker ['hɪtʃhaɪkəʳ] N Tramper(in) *m(f)*, Anhalter(in) *m(f)*
hitchhiking ['hɪtʃhaɪkɪŋ] N Trampen *nt*
hi-tech ['haɪ'tɛk] ADJ Hightech-, hoch technisiert ▶ N Hightech *nt*, Hochtechnologie *f*
hitherto [hɪðə'tuː] ADV bisher, bis jetzt
hit list N Abschussliste *f*
hit man (*inf*) N Killer *m*
hit-or-miss ['hɪtə'mɪs] ADJ ungeplant; **to be a ~ affair** eine unsichere Sache sein; **it's ~ whether ...** es ist nicht zu sagen, ob ...
hit parade N Hitparade *f*
hits counter N (*on website*) Zugriffs- *or* Besucherzähler *m*, Counter *m*
HIV N ABBR (= *human immunodeficiency virus*) HIV; **~-negative** HIV-negativ; **~-positive** HIV-positiv
hive [haɪv] N Bienenkorb *m*; **to be a ~ of activity** einem Bienenhaus gleichen
▶ **hive off** (*inf*) VT ausgliedern, abspalten
hl ABBR (= *hectolitre*) hl
HM ABBR (= *His/Her Majesty*) S./I.M.
HMG (BRIT) ABBR (= *His/Her Majesty's Government*) die Regierung Seiner/Ihrer Majestät
HMI (BRIT) N ABBR (*Scol:* = *His/Her Majesty's Inspector*) *regierungsamtlicher Schulaufsichtsbeauftragter*

HMO (US) N ABBR (= *Health Maintenance Organization*) *Organisation zur Gesundheitsfürsorge*
HMS (BRIT) ABBR (= *His (or Her) Majesty's Ship*) *Namensteil von Schiffen der Kriegsmarine*
HNC (BRIT) N ABBR (= *Higher National Certificate*) *Berufsschulabschluss*
HND (BRIT) N ABBR (= *Higher National Diploma*) *Qualifikationsnachweis in technischen Fächern*
hoard [hɔːd] N (*of food*) Vorrat *m*; (*of money, treasure*) Schatz *m* ▸ VT (*food*) hamstern; (*money*) horten
hoarding ['hɔːdɪŋ] (BRIT) N Plakatwand *f*
hoarfrost ['hɔːfrɔst] N (Rau)reif *m*
hoarse [hɔːs] ADJ heiser
hoax [həuks] N (*false alarm*) blinder Alarm *m*
hob [hɔb] N Kochmulde *f*
hobble ['hɔbl] VI humpeln
hobby ['hɔbɪ] N Hobby *nt*, Steckenpferd *nt*
hobbyhorse ['hɔbɪhɔːs] N (*fig*) Lieblingsthema *nt*
hobnail boot ['hɔbneɪl-] N Nagelschuh *m*
hobnob ['hɔbnɔb] VI: **to ~ with** auf Du und Du stehen mit
hobo ['həubəu] (US) N Penner *m* (*inf*)
hock [hɔk] N (BRIT) weißer Rheinwein *m*; (*of animal*) Sprunggelenk *nt*; (*US Culin*) Gelenkstück *nt*; (*inf*): **to be in ~** (*person: in debt*) in Schulden stecken; (*object*) verpfändet *or* im Leihhaus sein
hockey ['hɔkɪ] N Hockey *nt*
hocus-pocus ['həukəs'pəukəs] N Hokuspokus *m*; (*trickery*) faule Tricks *pl*; (*jargon*) Jargon *m*
hod [hɔd] N (*for bricks etc*) Tragemulde *f*
hodgepodge ['hɔdʒpɔdʒ] (US) N = **hotchpotch**
hoe [həu] N Hacke *f* ▸ VT hacken
hog [hɔg] N (Mast)schwein *nt* ▸ VT (*road*) für sich beanspruchen; (*telephone etc*) in Beschlag nehmen; **to go the whole ~** Nägel mit Köpfen machen
Hogmanay [hɔgmə'neɪ] (SCOT) N Silvester *nt*
hogwash ['hɔgwɔʃ] (*inf*) N (*nonsense*) Quatsch *m*
ho hum ['həu'hʌm] EXCL na gut
hoist [hɔɪst] N Hebevorrichtung *f* ▸ VT hochheben; (*flag, sail*) hissen
hoity-toity [hɔɪtɪ'tɔɪtɪ] (*inf, pej*) ADJ hochnäsig
hold [həuld] (*pt, pp* **held**) VT halten; (*contain*) enthalten; (*power, qualification*) haben; (*opinion*) vertreten; (*meeting*) abhalten; (*conversation*) führen; (*prisoner, hostage*) festhalten ▸ VI halten; (*be valid*) gelten; (*weather*) sich halten ▸ N (*grasp*) Griff *m*; (*of ship, plane*) Laderaum *m*; **to ~ one's head up** den Kopf hochhalten; **to ~ sb responsible/liable** *etc* jdn verantwortlich/haftbar *etc* machen; **~ the line!** (*Tel*) bleiben Sie am Apparat!; **~ it!** Moment mal!; **to ~ one's own** sich behaupten; **he holds the view that …** er ist der Meinung *or* er vertritt die Ansicht, dass …; **to ~ firm** *or* **fast** halten; **~ still!, ~ steady!** stillhalten!; **his luck held** das Glück blieb ihm treu; **I don't ~ with …** ich bin gegen …; **to catch** *or* **get (a) ~ of** sich festhalten an *+dat*; **to get ~ of** (*fig*) finden, auftreiben; **to get ~ of o.s.** sich in den Griff bekommen; **to have a ~ over** in der Hand haben
▸ **hold back** VT zurückhalten; (*tears, laughter*) unterdrücken; (*secret*) verbergen; (*information*) geheim halten
▸ **hold down** VT niederhalten; (*job*) sich halten in *+dat*
▸ **hold forth** VI: **to ~ forth (about)** sich ergehen *or* sich auslassen (über *+acc*)
▸ **hold off** VT abwehren ▸ VI: **if the rain holds off** wenn es nicht regnet
▸ **hold on** VI sich festhalten; (*wait*) warten; **~ on!** (*Tel*) einen Moment bitte!
▸ **hold on to** VT FUS sich festhalten an *+dat*; (*keep*) behalten
▸ **hold out** VT (*hand*) ausstrecken; (*hope*) haben; (*prospect*) bieten ▸ VI nicht nachgeben
▸ **hold over** VT vertagen
▸ **hold up** VT hochheben; (*support*) stützen; (*delay*) aufhalten; (*rob*) überfallen
holdall ['həuldɔːl] (BRIT) N Tasche *f*; (*for clothes*) Reisetasche *f*
holder ['həuldəʳ] N Halter *m*; (*of ticket, record, office, title etc*) Inhaber(in) *m(f)*
holding ['həuldɪŋ] N (*share*) Anteil *m*; (*small farm*) Gut *nt* ▸ ADJ (*operation, tactic*) zur Schadensbegrenzung
holding company N Dachgesellschaft *f*, Holdinggesellschaft *f*
hold-up ['həuldʌp] N bewaffneter Raubüberfall *m*; (*delay*) Verzögerung *f*; (BRIT: *in traffic*) Stockung *f*
hole [həul] N Loch *nt*; (*unpleasant town*) Kaff *nt* (*inf*) ▸ VT (*ship*) leckschlagen; (*building etc*) durchlöchern; **~ in the heart** Loch im Herz(en); **to pick holes** (*fig*) (über)kritisch sein; **to pick holes in sth** (*fig*) an etw *dat* herumkritisieren
▸ **hole up** VI sich verkriechen
holiday ['hɔlɪdeɪ] N (BRIT) Urlaub *m*; (*Scol*) Ferien *pl*; (*day off*) freier Tag *m*; (*also*: **public holiday**) Feiertag *m*; **on ~** im Urlaub, in den Ferien
holiday camp (BRIT) N (*also*: **holiday centre**) Feriendorf *nt*
holiday home N Ferienhaus *nt*
holiday-maker ['hɔlɪdɪmeɪkəʳ] (BRIT) N Urlauber(in) *m(f)*
holiday pay N *Lohn-/Gehaltsfortzahlung während des Urlaubs*
holiday resort N Ferienort *m*
holiday season N Urlaubszeit *f*
holiness ['həulɪnɪs] N Heiligkeit *f*
holistic [həu'lɪstɪk] ADJ holistisch
Holland ['hɔlənd] N Holland *nt*
holler ['hɔləʳ] (*inf*) VI brüllen ▸ N Schrei *m*
hollow ['hɔləu] ADJ hohl; (*eyes*) tief liegend; (*laugh*) unecht; (*sound*) dumpf; (*fig*) leer; (*: victory, opinion*) wertlos ▸ N Vertiefung *f* ▸ VT: **to ~ out** aushöhlen
holly ['hɔlɪ] N Stechpalme *f*, Ilex *m*; (*leaves*) Stechpalmenzweige *pl*
hollyhock ['hɔlɪhɔk] N Malve *f*
Hollywood ['hɔlɪwud] N Hollywood *nt*
holocaust ['hɔləkɔːst] N Inferno *nt*; (*in Third Reich*) Holocaust *m*

hologram ['hɔləgræm] N Hologramm *nt*
hols [hɔlz] (*inf*) NPL Ferien *pl*
holster ['həulstəʳ] N Pistolenhalfter *m or nt*
holy ['həulɪ] ADJ heilig
Holy Communion N heilige Kommunion *f*
Holy Father N Heiliger Vater *m*
Holy Ghost N Heiliger Geist *m*
Holy Land N: **the ~** das Heilige Land
holy orders NPL Priesterweihe *f*
Holy Spirit N Heiliger Geist *m*
homage ['hɔmɪdʒ] N Huldigung *f*; **to pay ~ to** huldigen *+dat*
home [həum] N Heim *nt*; (*house, flat*) Zuhause *nt*; (*area, country*) Heimat *f*; (*institution*) Anstalt *f* ▸ CPD Heim-; (*Econ, Pol*) Innen- ▸ ADV (*go etc*) nach Hause, heim; **at ~** zu Hause; (*in country*) im Inland; **to be** *or* **feel at ~** (*fig*) sich wohlfühlen; **make yourself at ~** machen Sie es sich *dat* gemütlich *or* bequem; **to make one's ~ somewhere** sich irgendwo niederlassen; **the ~ of free enterprise/jazz** *etc* die Heimat des freien Unternehmertums/Jazz *etc*; **when will you be ~?** wann bist du wieder zu Hause?; **a ~ from ~** ein zweites Zuhause *nt*; **~ and dry** aus dem Schneider; **to drive a nail ~** einen Nagel einschlagen; **to bring sth ~ to sb** jdm etw klarmachen
▸ **home in on** VT FUS (*missiles*) sich ausrichten auf *+acc*
home address N Heimatanschrift *f*
home-brew [həum'bru:] N selbst gebrautes Bier *nt*
homecoming ['həumkʌmɪŋ] N Heimkehr *f*
home computer N Heimcomputer *m*
Home Counties (BRIT) NPL: **the ~** *die Grafschaften, die an London angrenzen*
home economics N Hauswirtschaft(slehre) *f*
home ground N (*Sport*) eigener Platz *m*; **to be on ~** (*fig*) sich auf vertrautem Terrain bewegen
home-grown ['həumgrəun] ADJ (*not foreign*) einheimisch; (*from garden*) selbst gezogen
home help N Haushaltshilfe *f*
homeland ['həumlænd] N Heimat *f*, Heimatland *nt*
homeless ['həumlɪs] ADJ obdachlos; (*refugee*) heimatlos
home loan N Hypothek *f*
homely ['həumlɪ] ADJ einfach; (*US: plain*) unscheinbar
home-made [həum'meɪd] ADJ selbst gemacht
Home Office (BRIT) N Innenministerium *nt*
homeopath ['həumɪəupæθ] (*US*) N = **homoeopath**
homeopathy [həumɪ'ɔpəθɪ] (*US*) N = **homoeopathy**
home page N (*Comput*) Homepage *f*
home rule N Selbstbestimmung *f*, Selbstverwaltung *f*
Home Secretary (BRIT) N Innenminister(in) *m(f)*
homesick ['həumsɪk] ADJ heimwehkrank; **to be ~** Heimweh haben
homestead ['həumstɛd] N Heimstätte *f*; (*farm*) Gehöft *nt*
home town N Heimatstadt *f*
home truth N bittere Wahrheit *f*; **to tell sb some home truths** jdm deutlich die Meinung sagen
homeward ['həumwəd] ADJ (*journey*) Heim- ▸ ADV = **homewards**
homewards ['həumwədz] ADV nach Hause, heim
homework ['həumwə:k] N Hausaufgaben *pl*
homicidal [hɔmɪ'saɪdl] ADJ gemeingefährlich
homicide ['hɔmɪsaɪd] (*US*) N Mord *m*
homily ['hɔmɪlɪ] N Predigt *f*
homing ['həumɪŋ] ADJ (*device, missile*) mit Zielsucheinrichtung; **~ pigeon** Brieftaube *f*
homoeopath, (*US*) **homeopath** ['həumɪəupæθ] N Homöopath(in) *m(f)*
homoeopathy, (*US*) **homeopathy** [həumɪ'ɔpəθɪ] N Homöopathie *f*
homogeneous [hɔməu'dʒi:nɪəs] ADJ homogen
homogenize [hə'mɔdʒənaɪz] VT homogenisieren
homosexual [hɔməu'sɛksjuəl] ADJ homosexuell ▸ N Homosexuelle(r) *f(m)*
Hon. ABBR = **honourable; honorary**
Honduras [hɔn'djuərəs] N Honduras *nt*
hone [həun] N Schleifstein *m* ▸ VT schleifen; (*fig: groom*) erziehen
honest ['ɔnɪst] ADJ ehrlich; (*trustworthy*) redlich; (*sincere*) aufrichtig; **to be quite ~ with you ...** um ehrlich zu sein, ...
honestly ['ɔnɪstlɪ] ADV ehrlich; redlich; aufrichtig
honesty ['ɔnɪstɪ] N Ehrlichkeit *f*; Redlichkeit *f*; Aufrichtigkeit *f*
honey ['hʌnɪ] N Honig *m*; (*US inf*) Schätzchen *nt*
honeycomb ['hʌnɪkəum] N Bienenwabe *f*; (*pattern*) Wabe *f* ▸ VT: **to ~ with** durchlöchern mit
honeymoon ['hʌnɪmu:n] N Flitterwochen *pl*; (*trip*) Hochzeitsreise *f*
honeysuckle ['hʌnɪsʌkl] N Geißblatt *nt*
Hong Kong ['hɔŋ'kɔŋ] N Hongkong *nt*
honk [hɔŋk] VI (*Aut*) hupen
Honolulu [hɔnə'lu:lu:] N Honolulu *nt*
honor *etc* ['ɔnəʳ] (*US*) = **honour** *etc*
honorary ['ɔnərərɪ] ADJ ehrenamtlich; (*title, degree*) Ehren-
honour, (*US*) **honor** ['ɔnəʳ] VT ehren; (*commitment, promise*) stehen zu ▸ N Ehre *f*; (*tribute*) Auszeichnung *f*; **in ~ of** zu Ehren von *or +gen*
honourable ['ɔnərəbl] ADJ (*person*) ehrenwert; (*action, defeat*) ehrenvoll
honour-bound ['ɔnə'baund] ADJ: **to be ~ to do sth** moralisch verpflichtet sein, etw zu tun
honours degree ['ɔnəz-] N *akademischer Grad mit Prüfung im Spezialfach*

> **Honours Degree** ist ein Universitätsabschluss mit einer guten Note, also der Note I (first class), II:1 (upper second class), II:2 (lower second class), oder III (third class). Wer ein honours degree erhalten hat, darf die

Abkürzung **Hons** nach seinem Namen und Titel führen, z. B. Mary Smith MA Hons. Heute sind fast alle Universitätsabschlusse in Großbritannien honours degrees. Siehe auch **ordinary degree**.

honours list N *Liste verliehener/zu verleihender Ehrentitel*

Honours list ist eine Liste von Adelstiteln und Orden, die der britische Monarch zweimal jährlich (zu Neujahr und am offiziellen Geburtstag des Monarchen) an Bürger in Großbritannien und im Commonwealth verleiht. Die Liste wird vom Premierminister zusammengestellt, aber drei Orden (der Hosenbandorden, der Verdienstorden und der Victoria-Orden) werden vom Monarchen persönlich vergeben. Erfolgreiche Geschäftsleute, Militärangehörige, Sportler und andere Prominente, aber auch im sozialen Bereich besonders aktive Bürger werden auf diese Weise geehrt.

Hons. ABBR (*Univ*) = **Honours degree**

hood [hud] N (*of coat etc*) Kapuze *f*; (*of cooker*) Abzugshaube *f*; (*Aut*: BRIT: *folding roof*) Verdeck *nt*; (: *US*: *bonnet*) (Motor)haube *f*

hooded ['hudɪd] ADJ maskiert; (*jacket etc*) mit Kapuze

hoodlum ['hu:dləm] N Gangster *m*

hoodwink ['hudwɪŋk] VT (he)reinlegen

hoof [hu:f] (*pl* **hooves**) N Huf *m*

hook [huk] N Haken *m* ▸ VT festhaken; (*fish*) an die Angel bekommen; **by ~ or by crook** auf Biegen und Brechen; **to be hooked on** (*inf*: *film, exhibition, etc*) fasziniert sein von; (: *drugs*) abhängig sein von; (: *person*) stehen auf *+acc*
▸ **hook up** VT (*Radio, TV etc*) anschließen

hook and eye (*pl* **hooks and eyes**) N Haken und Öse *pl*

hooligan ['hu:lɪgən] N Rowdy *m*

hooliganism ['hu:lɪgənɪzəm] N Rowdytum *nt*

hoop [hu:p] N Reifen *m*; (*for croquet*: *arch*) Tor *nt*

hooray [hu:'reɪ] EXCL = **hurrah**

hoot [hu:t] VI hupen; (*siren*) heulen; (*owl*) schreien, rufen; (*person*) johlen ▸ VT (*horn*) drücken auf *+acc* ▸ N Hupen *nt*; Heulen *nt*; Schreien *nt*, Rufen *nt*; Johlen *nt*; **to ~ with laughter** in johlendes Gelächter ausbrechen

hooter ['hu:tə^r] N (BRIT *Aut*) Hupe *f*; (*Naut, of factory*) Sirene *f*

Hoover® ['hu:və^r] (BRIT) N Staubsauger *m* ▸ VT: **to hoover** (*carpet*) saugen

hooves [hu:vz] NPL *of* **hoof**

hop [hɔp] VI hüpfen ▸ N Hüpfer *m*; *see also* **hops**

hope [həup] VI hoffen ▸ N Hoffnung *f* ▸ VT: **to ~ that** hoffen, dass; **I ~ so** ich hoffe es, hoffentlich; **I ~ not** ich hoffe nicht, hoffentlich nicht; **to ~ for the best** das Beste hoffen; **to have no ~ of sth/doing sth** keine Hoffnung auf etw *+acc* haben/darauf haben, etw zu tun; **in the ~ of/that** in der Hoffnung auf/, dass; **to ~ to do sth** hoffen, etw zu tun

hopeful ['həupful] ADJ hoffnungsvoll; (*situation*) vielversprechend; **I'm ~ that she'll manage** ich hoffe, dass sie es schafft

hopefully ['həupfulɪ] ADV hoffnungsvoll; (*one hopes*) hoffentlich; **~, he'll come back** hoffentlich kommt er wieder

hopeless ['həuplɪs] ADJ hoffnungslos; (*situation*) aussichtslos; (*useless*): **to be ~ at sth** etw überhaupt nicht können

hopper ['hɔpə^r] N Einfülltrichter *m*

hops [hɔps] NPL Hopfen *m*

horde [hɔ:d] N Horde *f*

horizon [hə'raɪzn] N Horizont *m*

horizontal [hɔrɪ'zɔntl] ADJ horizontal

hormone ['hɔ:məun] N Hormon *nt*

hormone replacement therapy N Hormonersatztherapie *f*

horn [hɔ:n] N Horn *nt*; (*Aut*) Hupe *f*

horned [hɔ:nd] ADJ (*animal*) mit Hörnern

hornet ['hɔ:nɪt] N Hornisse *f*

horn-rimmed ['hɔ:n'rɪmd] ADJ (*spectacles*) Horn-

horny ['hɔ:nɪ] (*inf*) ADJ (*aroused*) scharf, geil

horoscope ['hɔrəskəup] N Horoskop *nt*

horrendous [hə'rɛndəs] ADJ abscheulich, entsetzlich

horrible ['hɔrɪbl] ADJ fürchterlich, schrecklich; (*scream, dream*) furchtbar

horrid ['hɔrɪd] ADJ entsetzlich, schrecklich

horrific [hɔ'rɪfɪk] ADJ entsetzlich, schrecklich

horrify ['hɔrɪfaɪ] VT entsetzen

horrifying ['hɔrɪfaɪɪŋ] ADJ schrecklich, fürchterlich, entsetzlich

horror ['hɔrə^r] N Entsetzen *nt*, Grauen *nt*; **~ (of sth)** (*abhorrence*) Abscheu *m* (vor etw *dat*); **the horrors of war** die Schrecken *pl* des Krieges

horror film N Horrorfilm *m*

horror-stricken ['hɔrəstrɪkn] ADJ = **horror-struck**

horror-struck ['hɔrəstrʌk] ADJ von Entsetzen *or* Grauen gepackt

hors d'œuvre [ɔ:'də:vrə] N Hors d'œuvre *nt*, Vorspeise *f*

horse [hɔ:s] N Pferd *nt*

horseback ['hɔ:sbæk] N: **on ~** zu Pferd

horsebox ['hɔ:sbɔks] N Pferdetransporter *m*

horse chestnut N Rosskastanie *f*

horse-drawn ['hɔ:sdrɔ:n] ADJ von Pferden gezogen

horsefly ['hɔ:sflaɪ] N (Pferde)bremse *f*

horseman ['hɔ:smən] N (*irreg*) Reiter *m*

horsemanship ['hɔ:smənʃɪp] N Reitkunst *f*

horseplay ['hɔ:spleɪ] N Alberei *f*, Balgerei *f*

horsepower ['hɔ:spauə^r] N Pferdestärke *f*

horse racing N Pferderennen *nt*

horseradish ['hɔ:srædɪʃ] N Meerrettich *m*

horse riding N Reiten *nt*

horseshoe ['hɔ:sʃu:] N Hufeisen *nt*

horse show N Reitturnier *nt*

horse trading N Kuhhandel *m*

horse trials NPL = **horse show**

horsewhip ['hɔ:swɪp] N Reitpeitsche *f* ▸ VT auspeitschen

horsewoman ['hɔ:swumən] N (*irreg*) Reiterin *f*

horsey ['hɔ:sɪ] ADJ pferdenärrisch; (*appearance*) pferdeähnlich
horticulture ['hɔ:tɪkʌltʃəʳ] N Gartenbau *m*
hose [həuz] N (*also*: **hose pipe**) Schlauch *m*
▸ **hose down** VT abspritzen
hosiery ['həuzɪərɪ] N Strumpfwaren *pl*
hospice ['hɔspɪs] N Pflegeheim *nt* (*für unheilbar Kranke*)
hospitable ['hɔspɪtəbl] ADJ gastfreundlich; (*climate*) freundlich
hospital ['hɔspɪtl] N Krankenhaus *nt*; **in ~, in the ~** (*US*) im Krankenhaus
hospitality [hɔspɪ'tælɪtɪ] N Gastfreundschaft *f*
hospitalize ['hɔspɪtəlaɪz] VT ins Krankenhaus einweisen
host [həust] N Gastgeber *m*; (*Rel*) Hostie *f* ▸ ADJ Gast- ▸ VT Gastgeber sein bei; **a ~ of** eine Menge
hostage ['hɔstɪdʒ] N Geisel *f*; **to be taken/held ~** als Geisel genommen/festgehalten werden
hostel ['hɔstl] N (Wohn)heim *nt*; (*also*: **youth hostel**) Jugendherberge *f*
hostelling ['hɔstlɪŋ] N: **to go (youth) ~** in Jugendherbergen übernachten
hostess ['həustɪs] N Gastgeberin *f*; (BRIT: *also*: **air hostess**) Stewardess *f*; (*in night-club*) Hostess *f*
hostile ['hɔstaɪl] ADJ (*conditions*) ungünstig; (*environment*) unwirtlich; (*person*): **~ (to** *or* **towards)** feindselig (gegenüber *+dat*)
hostility [hɔ'stɪlɪtɪ] N Feindseligkeit *f*; **hostilities** NPL (*fighting*) Feindseligkeiten *pl*
hot [hɔt] ADJ heiß; (*moderately hot*) warm; (*spicy*) scharf; (*temper*) hitzig; **I am** *or* **feel ~** mir ist heiß; **to be ~ on sth** (*knowledgeable etc*) sich gut mit etw auskennen; (*strict*) sehr auf etw *acc* achten
▸ **hot up** (BRIT *inf*) VI (*situation*) sich verschärfen *or* zuspitzen; (*party*) in Schwung kommen ▸ VT (*pace*) steigern; (*engine*) frisieren
hot air N leeres Gerede *nt*
hot-air balloon [hɔt'ɛəʳ-] N Heißluftballon *m*
hotbed ['hɔtbɛd] N (*fig*) Brutstätte *f*
hot-blooded [hɔt'blʌdɪd] ADJ heißblütig
hotchpotch ['hɔtʃpɔtʃ] (BRIT) N Durcheinander *nt*, Mischmasch *m*
hot dog N Hotdog *m or nt*
hotel [həu'tɛl] N Hotel *nt*
hotelier [həu'tɛlɪəʳ] N Hotelier(in) *m(f)*
hotel industry N Hotelgewerbe *nt*
hotel room N Hotelzimmer *nt*
hot flash (*US*) N = **hot flush**
hot flush N (*Med*) Hitzewallung *f*
hotfoot ['hɔtfut] ADV eilends
hothead ['hɔthɛd] N Hitzkopf *m*
hot-headed [hɔt'hɛdɪd] ADJ hitzköpfig
hothouse ['hɔthaus] N Treibhaus *nt*
hot line N (*Pol*) heißer Draht *m*
hotly ['hɔtlɪ] ADV (*contest*) heiß; (*speak, deny*) heftig
hotplate ['hɔtpleɪt] N Kochplatte *f*
hotpot ['hɔtpɔt] (BRIT) N Fleischeintopf *m*
hot potato (*fig, inf*) N heißes Eisen *nt*; **to drop sb like a ~** jdn wie eine heiße Kartoffel fallen lassen
hot seat N: **to be in the ~** auf dem Schleudersitz sitzen
hotspot ['hɔtspɔt] N (*Comput*) Hotspot *m*
hot spot N (*fig*) Krisenherd *m*
hot spring N heiße Quelle *f*, Thermalquelle *f*
hot stuff N große Klasse *f*
hot-tempered ['hɔt'tɛmpəd] ADJ leicht aufbrausend, jähzornig
hot-water bottle [hɔt'wɔ:təʳ-] N Wärmflasche *f*
hot-wire (*inf*) VT (*car*) kurzschließen
hound [haund] VT hetzen, jagen ▸ N Jagdhund *m*; **the hounds** die Meute
hour ['auəʳ] N Stunde *f*; (*time*) Zeit *f*; **at 60 miles an ~** mit 60 Meilen in der Stunde; **lunch ~** Mittagspause *f*; **to pay sb by the ~** jdn stundenweise bezahlen
hourly ['auəlɪ] ADJ stündlich; (*rate*) Stunden- ▸ ADV stündlich, jede Stunde; (*soon*) jederzeit
house [haus] N Haus *nt*; (*household*) Haushalt *m*; (*dynasty*) Geschlecht *nt*, Haus *nt*; (*Theat: performance*) Vorstellung *f* ▸ VT unterbringen; **at my ~** bei mir (zu Hause); **to my ~** zu mir (nach Hause); **on the ~** (*fig*) auf Kosten des Hauses; **the H~ (of Commons)** (BRIT) das Unterhaus; **the H~ (of Lords)** (BRIT) das Oberhaus; **the H~ (of Representatives)** (*US*) das Repräsentantenhaus
house arrest N Hausarrest *m*
houseboat ['hausbəut] N Hausboot *nt*
housebound ['hausbaund] ADJ ans Haus gefesselt
housebreaking ['hausbreɪkɪŋ] N Einbruch *m*
house-broken ['hausbrəukn] (*US*) ADJ = **house-trained**
housecoat ['hauskəut] N Morgenrock *m*
household ['haushəuld] N Haushalt *m*; **to be a ~ name** ein Begriff sein
householder ['haushəuldəʳ] N Hausinhaber(in) *m(f)*; (*of flat*) Wohnungsinhaber(in) *m(f)*
house-hunting ['haushʌntɪŋ] N: **to go ~** nach einem Haus suchen
housekeeper ['hauski:pəʳ] N Haushälterin *f*
housekeeping ['hauski:pɪŋ] N Hauswirtschaft *f*; (*money*) Haushaltsgeld *nt*, Wirtschaftsgeld *nt*
houseman ['hausmən] (BRIT) N (*irreg*) (*Med*) Assistenzarzt *m*, Assistenzärztin *f*

> Das **House of Commons** ist das Unterhaus des britischen Parlaments, mit 651 Abgeordneten, die in Wahlkreisen in allgemeiner Wahl gewählt werden. Das Unterhaus hat die Regierungsgewalt inne und tagt etwa 175 Tage im Jahr unter Vorsitz des Sprechers. Als **House of Lords** wird das Oberhaus des britischen Parlaments bezeichnet. Die Mitglieder sind nicht gewählt, sondern werden auf Lebenszeit ernannt („life peers") oder sie haben ihren

Oberhaussitz geerbt („hereditary peers"). Das House of Lords setzt sich aus Kirchenmännern und Adeligen zusammen („Lords Spiritual/Temporal"). Es hat im Grunde keine Regierungsgewalt, kann aber vom Unterhaus erlassene Gesetze abändern und ist das oberste Berufungsgericht in Großbritannien (außer Schottland).

Das **House of Representatives** bildet zusammen mit dem Senat die amerikanische gesetzgebende Versammlung (den Kongress). Es besteht aus 435 Abgeordneten, die entsprechend den Bevölkerungszahlen auf die einzelnen Bundesstaaten verteilt sind und jeweils für 2 Jahre direkt vom Volk gewählt werden. Es tritt im **Capitol** in Washington zusammen. Siehe auch **Congress**.

house owner N Hausbesitzer(in) *m(f)*

house party N mehrtägige Einladung *f*; (*people*) Gesellschaft *f*

house plant N Zimmerpflanze *f*

house-proud ['hauspraud] ADJ auf Ordnung und Sauberkeit im Haushalt bedacht

house-to-house ['haustə'haus] ADJ von Haus zu Haus

house-trained ['haustreınd] (BRIT) ADJ (*animal*) stubenrein

house-warming ['hauswɔːmıŋ], **house-warming party** N Einzugsparty *f*

housewife ['hauswaıf] N (*irreg*) Hausfrau *f*

house wine N Hauswein *m*

housework ['hauswəːk] N Hausarbeit *f*

housing ['hauzıŋ] N Wohnungen *pl*; (*provision*) Wohnungsbeschaffung *f* ▶ CPD Wohnungs-

housing association N Wohnungsbaugesellschaft *f*

housing benefit N ≈ Wohngeld *nt*

housing conditions NPL Wohnbedingungen *pl*, Wohnverhältnisse *pl*

housing development N (Wohn)siedlung *f*

housing estate N (Wohn)siedlung *f*

hovel ['hɔvl] N (armselige) Hütte *f*

hover ['hɔvə^r] VI schweben; (*person*) herumstehen; **to ~ round sb** jdm nicht von der Seite weichen

hovercraft ['hɔvəkrɑːft] N Hovercraft *nt*, Luftkissenfahrzeug *nt*

hoverport ['hɔvəpɔːt] N Anlegestelle *f* für Hovercrafts

KEYWORD

how [hau] ADV **1** (*in what way*) wie; **how was the film?** wie war der Film?; **how is school?** was macht die Schule?; **how are you?** wie geht es Ihnen?
2 (*to what degree*): **how much milk?** wie viel Milch?; **how many people?** wie viele Leute?; **how long have you been here?** wie lange sind Sie schon hier?; **how old are you?** wie alt bist du?; **how lovely/awful!** wie schön/furchtbar!

however [hau'ɛvə^r] CONJ jedoch, aber ▶ ADV wie ... auch; (*in questions*) wie ... bloß *or* nur

howl [haul] VI heulen; (*animal*) jaulen; (*baby, person*) schreien ▶ N Heulen *nt*; Jaulen *nt*; Schreien *nt*

howler ['haulə^r] (*inf*) N (*mistake*) Schnitzer *m*

howling ['haulıŋ] ADJ (*wind, gale*) heulend

HP (BRIT) N ABBR = **hire-purchase**

h.p. ABBR (*Aut*: = *horsepower*) PS

HQ ABBR = **headquarters**

HR (US) N ABBR (*Pol*: = *House of Representatives*) Repräsentantenhaus *nt*; = **Human Resources**

hr ABBR (= *hour*) Std.

HRH (BRIT) ABBR (= *His/Her Royal Highness*) Seine/Ihre Königliche Hoheit

hrs ABBR (= *hours*) Std.

HST (US) ABBR (= *Hawaiian Standard Time*) *Normalzeit in Hawaii*

HTML (*Comput*) ABBR (= *hypertext markup language*) HTML *f*

hub [hʌb] N (Rad)nabe *f*; (*fig: centre*) Mittelpunkt *m*, Zentrum *nt*

hubbub ['hʌbʌb] N Lärm *m*; (*commotion*) Tumult *m*

hubcap ['hʌbkæp] N Radkappe *f*

HUD (US) N ABBR (= *Department of Housing and Urban Development*) *Ministerium für Wohnungsbau und Stadtentwicklung*

huddle ['hʌdl] VI: **to ~ together** sich zusammendrängen ▶ N: **in a ~** dicht zusammengedrängt

hue [hjuː] N Farbton *m*

hue and cry N großes Geschrei *nt*

huff [hʌf] N: **in a ~** beleidigt, eingeschnappt ▶ VI: **to ~ and puff** sich aufregen

huffy ['hʌfı] (*inf*) ADJ beleidigt

hug [hʌg] VT umarmen; (*thing*) umklammern ▶ N Umarmung *f*; **to give sb a ~** jdn umarmen

huge [hjuːdʒ] ADJ riesig

hugely ['hjuːdʒlı] ADV ungeheuer

hulk [hʌlk] N (*wrecked ship*) Wrack *nt*; (*person, building etc*) Klotz *m*

hulking ['hʌlkıŋ] ADJ: **~ great** massig

hull [hʌl] N Schiffsrumpf *m*; (*of nuts*) Schale *f*; (*of fruit*) Blättchen *nt* ▶ VT (*fruit*) entstielen

hullaballoo [hʌləbə'luː] (*inf*) N Spektakel *m*

hullo [hə'ləu] EXCL = **hello**

hum [hʌm] VT summen ▶ VI summen; (*machine*) brummen ▶ N Summen *nt*; (*of traffic*) Brausen *nt*; (*of machines*) Brummen *nt*; (*of voices*) Gemurmel *nt*

human ['hjuːmən] ADJ menschlich ▶ N (*also*: **human being**) Mensch *m*

humane [hjuː'meın] ADJ human

humanism ['hjuːmənızəm] N Humanismus *m*

humanitarian [hjuːmænı'tɛərıən] ADJ humanitär

humanity [hjuː'mænıtı] N Menschlichkeit *f*; (*mankind*) Menschheit *f*; (*humaneness*) Humanität *f*; **humanities** NPL (*Scol*): **the humanities** die Geisteswissenschaften *pl*

humanly ['hjuːmənlı] ADV menschlich; **if (at all) ~ possible** wenn es irgend möglich ist

humanoid ['hju:mənɔɪd] ADJ menschenähnlich ▶ N menschenähnliches Wesen *nt*
human rights NPL Menschenrechte *pl*
humble ['hʌmbl] ADJ bescheiden ▶ VT demütigen
humbly ['hʌmblɪ] ADV bescheiden
humbug ['hʌmbʌg] N Humbug *m*, Mumpitz *m*; (BRIT: *sweet*) Pfefferminzbonbon *m or nt*
humdrum ['hʌmdrʌm] ADJ eintönig, langweilig
humid ['hju:mɪd] ADJ feucht
humidifier [hju:'mɪdɪfaɪəʳ] N Luftbefeuchter *m*
humidity [hju:'mɪdɪtɪ] N Feuchtigkeit *f*
humiliate [hju:'mɪlɪeɪt] VT demütigen
humiliating [hju:'mɪlɪeɪtɪŋ] ADJ demütigend
humiliation [hju:mɪlɪ'eɪʃən] N Demütigung *f*
humility [hju:'mɪlɪtɪ] N Bescheidenheit *f*
humor *etc* ['hju:məʳ] (US) = **humour** *etc*; **humorous**; **humour**
humorist ['hju:mərɪst] N Humorist(in) *m(f)*
humorous ['hju:mərəs] ADJ (*remark*) witzig; (*book*) lustig; (*person*) humorvoll
humour, (US) **humor** ['hju:məʳ] N Humor *m*; (*mood*) Stimmung *f* ▶ VT seinen Willen lassen *+dat*; **sense of ~** (Sinn *m* für) Humor; **to be in good/bad ~** gute/schlechte Laune haben
humourless ['hju:məlɪs] ADJ humorlos
hump [hʌmp] N Hügel *m*; (*of camel*) Höcker *m*; (*deformity*) Buckel *m*
humpbacked ['hʌmpbækt] ADJ: **~ bridge** gewölbte Brücke *f*
humus ['hju:məs] N Humus *m*
hunch [hʌntʃ] N Gefühl *nt*, Ahnung *f*; **I have a ~ that ...** ich habe den (leisen) Verdacht, dass ...
hunchback ['hʌntʃbæk] N Bucklige(r) *f(m)*
hunched [hʌntʃt] ADJ gebeugt; (*shoulders*) hochgezogen; (*back*) krumm
hundred ['hʌndrəd] NUM hundert; **a** *or* **one ~ books/people/dollars** (ein)hundert Bücher/Personen/Dollar; **hundreds of** Hunderte von; **I'm a ~ per cent sure** ich bin absolut sicher
hundredth ['hʌndrədθ] NUM hundertste(r, s)
hundredweight ['hʌndrɪdweɪt] N *Gewichtseinheit (BRIT = 50,8 kg; US = 45,3 kg)*, ≈ Zentner *m*
hung [hʌŋ] PT, PP *of* **hang**
Hungarian [hʌŋ'gɛərɪən] ADJ ungarisch ▶ N Ungar(in) *m(f)*; (*Ling*) Ungarisch *nt*
Hungary ['hʌŋgərɪ] N Ungarn *nt*
hunger ['hʌŋgəʳ] N Hunger *m* ▶ VI: **to ~ for** hungern nach
hunger strike N Hungerstreik *m*
hung over (*inf*) ADJ verkatert
hungrily ['hʌŋgrəlɪ] ADV hungrig
hungry ['hʌŋgrɪ] ADJ hungrig; **to be ~** Hunger haben; **to be ~ for** hungern nach; (*news*) sehnsüchtig warten auf; **to go ~** hungern
hung up (*inf*) ADJ: **to be ~ on** (*person*) ein gestörtes Verhältnis haben zu; **to be ~ about** nervös sein wegen
hunk [hʌŋk] N großes Stück *nt*; (*inf*: *man*) (großer, gut aussehender) Mann *m*
hunt [hʌnt] VT jagen; (*criminal, fugitive*) fahnden nach ▶ VI (*Sport*) jagen ▶ N Jagd *f*; Fahndung *f*; (*search*) Suche *f*; **to ~ for** (*search*) suchen (nach)
▶ **hunt down** VT Jagd machen auf *+acc*
hunter ['hʌntəʳ] N Jäger(in) *m(f)*
hunting ['hʌntɪŋ] N Jagd *f*, Jagen *nt*
hurdle ['hə:dl] N Hürde *f*
hurl [hə:l] VT schleudern; **to ~ sth at sb** (*also fig*) jdm etw entgegenschleudern
hurling ['hə:lɪŋ] N (*Sport*) Hurling *nt*, *irische Hockeyart*
hurly-burly ['hə:lɪ'bə:lɪ] N Rummel *m*
hurrah [hu'rɑ:] N Hurra *nt* ▶ EXCL hurra
hurray [hu'reɪ] N = **hurrah**
hurricane ['hʌrɪkən] N Orkan *m*
hurried ['hʌrɪd] ADJ eilig; (*departure*) überstürzt
hurriedly ['hʌrɪdlɪ] ADV eilig
hurry ['hʌrɪ] N Eile *f* ▶ VI eilen; (*to do sth*) sich beeilen ▶ VT (zur Eile) antreiben; (*work*) beschleunigen; **to be in a ~** es eilig haben; **to do sth in a ~** etw schnell tun; **there's no ~** es eilt nicht; **what's the ~?** warum so eilig?; **they hurried to help him** sie eilten ihm zu Hilfe; **to ~ home** nach Hause eilen
▶ **hurry along** VI sich beeilen
▶ **hurry away** VI schnell weggehen, forteilen
▶ **hurry off** VI = **hurry away**
▶ **hurry up** VT (zur Eile) antreiben ▶ VI sich beeilen
hurt [hə:t] (*pt, pp* **~**) VT wehtun *+dat*; (*injure, fig*) verletzen ▶ VI wehtun ▶ ADJ verletzt; **I've ~ my arm** ich habe mir am Arm wehgetan; (*injured*) ich habe mir den Arm verletzt; **where does it ~?** wo tut es weh?
hurtful ['hə:tful] ADJ verletzend
hurtle ['hə:tl] VI: **to ~ past** vorbeisausen; **to ~ down** (*fall*) hinunterfallen
husband ['hʌzbənd] N (Ehe)mann *m*
hush [hʌʃ] N Stille *f* ▶ VT zum Schweigen bringen; **~!** pst!
▶ **hush up** VT vertuschen
hushed [hʌʃt] ADJ still; (*voice*) gedämpft
hush-hush [hʌʃ'hʌʃ] (*inf*) ADJ streng geheim
husk [hʌsk] N Schale *f*; (*of wheat*) Spelze *f*; (*of maize*) Hüllblatt *nt*
husky ['hʌskɪ] ADJ (*voice*) rau ▶ N Schlittenhund *m*
hustings ['hʌstɪŋz] (BRIT) NPL (*Pol*) Wahlkampf *m*
hustle ['hʌsl] VT drängen ▶ N: **~ and bustle** Geschäftigkeit *f*
hut [hʌt] N Hütte *f*
hutch [hʌtʃ] N (Kaninchen)stall *m*
hyacinth ['haɪəsɪnθ] N Hyazinthe *f*
hybrid ['haɪbrɪd] N (*plant, animal*) Kreuzung *f*; (*mixture*) Mischung *f* ▶ ADJ Misch-; **~ car** Hybridauto *nt*
hydrant ['haɪdrənt] N (*also*: **fire hydrant**) Hydrant *m*
hydraulic [haɪ'drɔ:lɪk] ADJ hydraulisch
hydraulics [haɪ'drɔ:lɪks] N Hydraulik *f*
hydrochloric acid ['haɪdrəu'klɔrɪk-] N Salzsäure *f*

h

hydroelectric ['haɪdrəuɪ'lɛktrɪk] ADJ hydroelektrisch
hydrofoil ['haɪdrəfɔɪl] N Tragflächenboot *nt*, Tragflügelboot *nt*
hydrogen ['haɪdrədʒən] N Wasserstoff *m*
hydrogen bomb N Wasserstoffbombe *f*
hydrophobia ['haɪdrə'fəubɪə] N Hydrophobie *f*, Wasserscheu *f*
hydroplane ['haɪdrəpleɪn] N Gleitboot *nt*; (*plane*) Wasserflugzeug *nt* ▸ VI (*boat*) abheben
hyena [haɪ'i:nə] N Hyäne *f*
hygiene ['haɪdʒi:n] N Hygiene *f*
hygienic [haɪ'dʒi:nɪk] ADJ hygienisch
hymn [hɪm] N Kirchenlied *nt*
hype [haɪp] (*inf*) N Rummel *m*
hyperactive ['haɪpər'æktɪv] ADJ überaktiv
hyperinflation ['haɪpərɪn'fleɪʃən] N galoppierende Inflation *f*
hyperlink ['haɪpəlɪŋk] N Hyperlink *m*
hypermarket ['haɪpəmɑ:kɪt] (BRIT) N Verbrauchermarkt *m*
hypertension ['haɪpə'tɛnʃən] N Hypertonie *f*, Bluthochdruck *m*
hypertext ['haɪpətɛkst] N (*Comput*) Hypertext *m*
hyphen ['haɪfn] N Bindestrich *m*; (*at end of line*) Trennungsstrich *m*
hyphenated ['haɪfəneɪtɪd] ADJ mit Bindestrich (geschrieben)
hypnosis [hɪp'nəusɪs] N Hypnose *f*
hypnotic [hɪp'nɔtɪk] ADJ hypnotisierend; (*trance*) hypnotisch
hypnotism ['hɪpnətɪzəm] N Hypnotismus *m*
hypnotist ['hɪpnətɪst] N Hypnotiseur *m*, Hypnotiseuse *f*
hypnotize ['hɪpnətaɪz] VT hypnotisieren
hypoallergenic ['haɪpəuælə'dʒɛnɪk] ADJ für äußerst empfindliche Haut
hypochondriac [haɪpə'kɔndrɪæk] N Hypochonder *m*
hypocrisy [hɪ'pɔkrɪsɪ] N Heuchelei *f*
hypocrite ['hɪpəkrɪt] N Heuchler(in) *m(f)*
hypocritical [hɪpə'krɪtɪkl] ADJ heuchlerisch
hypodermic [haɪpə'də:mɪk] ADJ (*injection*) subkutan ▸ N (Injektions)spritze *f*
hypotenuse [haɪ'pɔtɪnju:z] N Hypotenuse *f*
hypothermia [haɪpə'θə:mɪə] N Unterkühlung *f*
hypothesis [haɪ'pɔθɪsɪs] (*pl* **hypotheses**) N Hypothese *f*
hypothesize [haɪ'pɔθɪsaɪz] VI Hypothesen aufstellen ▸ VT annehmen
hypothetic [haɪpəu'θɛtɪk], **hypothetical** [haɪpəu'θɛtɪkl] ADJ hypothetisch
hysterectomy [hɪstə'rɛktəmɪ] N Hysterektomie *f*
hysteria [hɪ'stɪərɪə] N Hysterie *f*
hysterical [hɪ'stɛrɪkl] ADJ hysterisch; (*situation*) wahnsinnig komisch; **to become ~** hysterisch werden
hysterically [hɪ'stɛrɪklɪ] ADV hysterisch; **~ funny** wahnsinnig komisch
hysterics [hɪ'stɛrɪks] NPL: **to be in** *or* **to have ~** einen hysterischen Anfall haben; (*laughter*) einen Lachanfall haben
Hz ABBR (= *hertz*) Hz.

I¹, i [aɪ] N (*letter*) I *nt*, i *nt*; **I for Isaac, I for Item** (*US*) ≈ I wie Ida
I² [aɪ] PRON ich
I. ABBR = **island; isle**
IA (*US*) ABBR (*Post*) = **Iowa**
IAEA N ABBR = **International Atomic Energy Agency**
ib ABBR (= *ibidem*) ib(id).
Iberian [aɪ'bɪərɪən] ADJ: **the ~ Peninsula** die Iberische Halbinsel
ibid ABBR (= *ibidem*) ib(id).
i/c (BRIT) ABBR (= *in charge (of)*) *see* **charge**
ICBM N ABBR (= *intercontinental ballistic missile*) Interkontinentalrakete *f*
ICC N ABBR = **International Chamber of Commerce**; (*US*: = *Interstate Commerce Commission*) *Kommission zur Regelung des Warenverkehrs zwischen den US-Bundesstaaten*
ice [aɪs] N Eis *nt*; (*on road*) Glatteis *nt* ▸ VT (*cake*) mit Zuckerguss überziehen, glasieren ▸ VI (*also:* **ice over, ice up**) vereisen; (*puddle etc*) zufrieren; **to put sth on ~** (*fig*) etw auf Eis legen
Ice Age N Eiszeit *f*
ice axe N Eispickel *m*
iceberg ['aɪsbəːg] N Eisberg *m*; **the tip of the ~** (*fig*) die Spitze des Eisbergs
icebox ['aɪsbɔks] N (*US*: *fridge*) Kühlschrank *m*; (BRIT: *compartment*) Eisfach *nt*; (*insulated box*) Kühltasche *f*
icebreaker ['aɪsbreɪkə^r] N Eisbrecher *m*
ice bucket N Eiskühler *m*
icecap ['aɪskæp] N Eisdecke *f*; (*polar*) Eiskappe *f*
ice-cold ['aɪs'kəuld] ADJ eiskalt
ice cream N Eis *nt*
ice-cream soda ['aɪskriːm-] N *Eisbecher mit Sirup und Sodawasser*
ice cube N Eiswürfel *m*
iced [aɪst] ADJ (*cake*) mit Zuckerguss überzogen, glasiert; (*beer etc*) eisgekühlt; (*tea, coffee*) Eis-
ice hockey N Eishockey *nt*
Iceland ['aɪslənd] N Island *nt*
Icelander ['aɪsləndə^r] N Isländer(in) *m(f)*
Icelandic [aɪs'lændɪk] ADJ isländisch ▸ N (*Ling*) Isländisch *nt*
ice lolly (BRIT) N Eis *nt* am Stiel
ice pick N Eispickel *m*
ice rink N (Kunst)eisbahn *f*, Schlittschuhbahn *f*
ice skate N Schlittschuh *m*
ice-skate ['aɪsskeɪt] VI Schlittschuh laufen
ice-skating ['aɪsskeɪtɪŋ] N Eislauf *m*, Schlittschuhlaufen *nt*
icicle ['aɪsɪkl] N Eiszapfen *m*
icing ['aɪsɪŋ] N (*Culin*) Zuckerguss *m*; (*Aviat etc*) Vereisung *f*
icing sugar (BRIT) N Puderzucker *m*
ICJ N ABBR = **International Court of Justice**
icon ['aɪkɔn] N Ikone *f*; (*Comput*) Ikon *nt*
ICR (*US*) N ABBR (= *Institute for Cancer Research*) *Krebsforschungsinstitut*
ICT (BRIT) N ABBR (*Scol*) = **information and communication technology**
ICU N ABBR (*Med*) = **intensive care unit**
icy ['aɪsɪ] ADJ eisig; (*road*) vereist
ID ABBR (*US Post*) = **Idaho**; = **identification (document)**
I'd [aɪd] = **I would; I had**
Ida. (*US*) ABBR (*Post*) = **Idaho**
ID card N = **identity card**
IDD (BRIT) N ABBR (*Tel*: = *international direct dialling*) *Selbstwählferndienst ins Ausland*
idea [aɪ'dɪə] N Idee *f*; (*opinion*) Ansicht *f*; (*notion*) Vorstellung *f*; (*objective*) Ziel *nt*; **good ~!** gute Idee!; **to have a good ~ that** sich *dat* ziemlich sicher sein, dass; **I haven't the least ~** ich habe nicht die leiseste Ahnung
ideal [aɪ'dɪəl] N Ideal *nt* ▸ ADJ ideal
idealist [aɪ'dɪəlɪst] N Idealist(in) *m(f)*
ideally [aɪ'dɪəlɪ] ADV ideal; **~ the book should …** idealerweise *or* im Idealfall sollte das Buch …; **she's ~ suited for …** sie eignet sich hervorragend für …
identical [aɪ'dɛntɪkl] ADJ identisch; (*twins*) eineiig
identification [aɪdɛntɪfɪ'keɪʃən] N Identifizierung *f*; **(means of) ~** Ausweispapiere *pl*
identify [aɪ'dɛntɪfaɪ] VT (*recognize*) erkennen; (*distinguish*) identifizieren; **to ~ sb/sth with** jdn/etw identifizieren mit
Identikit® [aɪ'dɛntɪkɪt] N: **~ (picture)** Phantombild *nt*
identity [aɪ'dɛntɪtɪ] N Identität *f*
identity card N (Personal)ausweis *m*
identity papers NPL Ausweispapiere *pl*
identity parade (BRIT) N Gegenüberstellung *f*
identity theft N Identitätsdiebstahl *m*

ideological [aɪdɪə'lɔdʒɪkl] ADJ ideologisch, weltanschaulich
ideology [aɪdɪ'ɔlədʒɪ] N Ideologie *f*, Weltanschauung *f*
idiocy ['ɪdɪəsɪ] N Idiotie *f*, Dummheit *f*
idiom ['ɪdɪəm] N (*style*) Ausdrucksweise *f*; (*phrase*) Redewendung *f*
idiomatic [ɪdɪə'mætɪk] ADJ idiomatisch
idiosyncrasy [ɪdɪəu'sɪŋkrəsɪ] N Eigenheit *f*, Eigenart *f*
idiosyncratic [ɪdɪəusɪŋ'krætɪk] ADJ eigenartig; (*way, method, style*) eigen
idiot ['ɪdɪət] N Idiot(in) *m(f)*, Dummkopf *m*
idiotic [ɪdɪ'ɔtɪk] ADJ idiotisch, blöd(sinnig)
idle ['aɪdl] ADJ untätig; (*lazy*) faul; (*unemployed*) unbeschäftigt; (*machinery, factory*) stillstehend; (*question*) müßig; (*conversation, pleasure*) leer ▶ VI leerlaufen, im Leerlauf sein; **to lie ~** (*machinery*) außer Betrieb sein; (*factory*) die Arbeit eingestellt haben
▶ **idle away** VT (*time*) vertrödeln, verbummeln
idleness ['aɪdlnɪs] N Untätigkeit *f*; (*laziness*) Faulheit *f*
idler ['aɪdləʳ] N Faulenzer(in) *m(f)*
idle time N (*Comm*) Leerlaufzeit *f*
idly ['aɪdlɪ] ADV untätig; (*glance*) abwesend
idol ['aɪdl] N Idol *nt*; (*Rel*) Götzenbild *nt*
idolize ['aɪdəlaɪz] VT vergöttern
idyllic [ɪ'dɪlɪk] ADJ idyllisch
i.e. ABBR (= *id est*) d. h.
IED ABBR (= *improvised explosive device*) USBV *f* (= *unbekannte Spreng- und Brandvorrichtung*)

KEYWORD

if [ɪf] CONJ **1** (*given that, providing that etc*) wenn, falls; **if anyone comes in** wenn *or* falls jemand hereinkommt; **if necessary** wenn *or* falls nötig; **if I were you** wenn ich Sie wäre, an Ihrer Stelle
2 (*whenever*) wenn
3 (*although*): **(even) if** auch *or* selbst wenn; **I like it, (even) if you don't** mir gefällt es, auch wenn du es nicht magst
4 (*whether*) ob; **ask him if he can come** frag ihn, ob er kommen kann
5: **if so/not** falls ja/nein; **if only** wenn nur; *see also* **as**

iffy ['ɪfɪ] (*inf*) ADJ (*uncertain*) unsicher; (*plan, proposal*) fragwürdig; **he was a bit ~ about it** er hat sich sehr vage ausgedrückt
igloo ['ɪglu:] N Iglu *m or nt*
ignite [ɪg'naɪt] VT entzünden ▶ VI sich entzünden
ignition [ɪg'nɪʃən] N (*Aut*) Zündung *f*
ignition key N (*Aut*) Zündschlüssel *m*
ignoble [ɪg'nəubl] ADJ schändlich, unehrenhaft
ignominious [ɪgnə'mɪnɪəs] ADJ schmachvoll
ignoramus [ɪgnə'reɪməs] N Ignorant(in) *m(f)*
ignorance ['ɪgnərəns] N Unwissenheit *f*, Ignoranz *f*; **to keep sb in ~ of sth** jdn in Unkenntnis über etw *acc* lassen
ignorant ['ɪgnərənt] ADJ unwissend, ignorant; **to be ~ of** (*subject*) sich nicht auskennen in +*dat*; (*events*) nicht informiert sein über +*acc*
ignore [ɪg'nɔːʳ] VT ignorieren; (*fact*) außer Acht lassen
ikon ['aɪkɔn] N = **icon**
IL (*US*) ABBR (*Post*) = **Illinois**
ill [ɪl] ADJ krank; (*effects*) schädlich ▶ N Übel *nt*; (*trouble*) Schlechte(s) *nt* ▶ ADV: **to speak ~ of sb** Schlechtes über jdn sagen; **to be taken ~** krank werden; **to think ~ of sb** schlecht von jdm denken
I'll [aɪl] = **I will**; **I shall**
ill-advised [ɪləd'vaɪzd] ADJ unklug; (*person*) schlecht beraten
ill at ease ADJ unbehaglich
ill-considered [ɪlkən'sɪdəd] ADJ unüberlegt
ill-disposed [ɪldɪs'pəuzd] ADJ: **to be ~ toward sb/sth** jdm/etw nicht wohlgesinnt sein
illegal [ɪ'li:gl] ADJ illegal
illegally [ɪ'li:gəlɪ] ADV illegal
illegible [ɪ'lɛdʒɪbl] ADJ unleserlich
illegitimate [ɪlɪ'dʒɪtɪmət] ADJ (*child*) unehelich; (*activity, treaty*) unzulässig
ill-fated [ɪl'feɪtɪd] ADJ unglückselig
ill-favoured, (*US*) **ill-favored** [ɪl'feɪvəd] ADJ ungestalt (*liter*), hässlich
ill feeling N Verstimmung *f*
ill-gotten ['ɪlgɔtn] ADJ: **~ gains** unrechtmäßig erworbener Gewinn *m*
ill health N schlechter Gesundheitszustand *m*
illicit [ɪ'lɪsɪt] ADJ verboten
ill-informed [ɪlɪn'fɔ:md] ADJ (*judgement*) wenig sachkundig; (*person*) schlecht informiert *or* unterrichtet
illiterate [ɪ'lɪtərət] ADJ (*person*) des Lesens und Schreibens unkundig; (*letter*) voller Fehler
ill-mannered [ɪl'mænəd] ADJ unhöflich
illness ['ɪlnɪs] N Krankheit *f*
illogical [ɪ'lɔdʒɪkl] ADJ unlogisch
ill-suited [ɪl'su:tɪd] ADJ nicht zusammenpassend; **he is ~ to the job** er ist für die Stelle ungeeignet
ill-timed [ɪl'taɪmd] ADJ ungelegen, unpassend
ill-treat [ɪl'tri:t] VT misshandeln
ill-treatment [ɪl'tri:tmənt] N Misshandlung *f*
illuminate [ɪ'lu:mɪneɪt] VT beleuchten
illuminated sign [ɪ'lu:mɪneɪtɪd-] N Leuchtzeichen *nt*
illuminating [ɪ'lu:mɪneɪtɪŋ] ADJ aufschlussreich
illumination [ɪlu:mɪ'neɪʃən] N Beleuchtung *f*; **illuminations** NPL (*decorative lights*) festliche Beleuchtung *f*, Illumination *f*
illusion [ɪ'lu:ʒən] N Illusion *f*; (*trick*) (Zauber)trick *m*; **to be under the ~ that ...** sich *dat* einbilden, dass ...
illusive [ɪ'lu:sɪv] ADJ = **illusory**
illusory [ɪ'lu:sərɪ] ADJ illusorisch, trügerisch
illustrate ['ɪləstreɪt] VT veranschaulichen; (*book*) illustrieren
illustration [ɪlə'streɪʃən] N Illustration *f*; (*example*) Veranschaulichung *f*

illustrator ['ɪləstreɪtəʳ] N Illustrator(in) *m(f)*
illustrious [ɪ'lʌstrɪəs] ADJ (*career*) glanzvoll; (*predecessor*) berühmt
ill will N böses Blut *nt*
ILO N ABBR = **International Labour Organization**
IM N ABBR (= *instant messaging*) IM *nt*
I'm [aɪm] = **I am**
image ['ɪmɪdʒ] N Bild *nt*; (*public face*) Image *nt*; (*reflection*) Abbild *nt*
image-building campaign ['ɪmɪdʒbɪldɪŋ-] N Imagekampagne *f*
imagery ['ɪmɪdʒərɪ] N (*in writing*) Metaphorik *f*; (*in painting etc*) Symbolik *f*
imaginable [ɪ'mædʒɪnəbl] ADJ vorstellbar, denkbar; **we've tried every ~ solution** wir haben jede denkbare Lösung ausprobiert; **she had the prettiest hair ~** sie hatte das schönste Haar, das man sich vorstellen kann
imaginary [ɪ'mædʒɪnərɪ] ADJ erfunden; (*being*) Fantasie-; (*danger*) eingebildet
imagination [ɪmædʒɪ'neɪʃən] N Fantasie *f*; (*illusion*) Einbildung *f*; **it's just your ~** das bildest du dir nur ein
imaginative [ɪ'mædʒɪnətɪv] ADJ fantasievoll; (*solution*) einfallsreich
imagine [ɪ'mædʒɪn] VT sich *dat* vorstellen; (*dream*) sich *dat* träumen lassen; (*suppose*) vermuten
imbalance [ɪm'bæləns] N Unausgeglichenheit *f*
imbecile ['ɪmbəsiːl] N Schwachkopf *m*, Idiot *m*
imbue [ɪm'bjuː] VT: **to ~ sb/sth with** jdn/etw durchdringen mit
IMF N ABBR (= *International Monetary Fund*) IWF *m*
imitate ['ɪmɪteɪt] VT imitieren; (*mimic*) nachahmen
imitation [ɪmɪ'teɪʃən] N Imitation *f*, Nachahmung *f*
imitator ['ɪmɪteɪtəʳ] N Imitator(in) *m(f)*, Nachahmer(in) *m(f)*
immaculate [ɪ'mækjulət] ADJ makellos; (*appearance, piece of work*) tadellos; (*Rel*) unbefleckt
immaterial [ɪmə'tɪərɪəl] ADJ unwichtig, unwesentlich
immature [ɪmə'tjuəʳ] ADJ unreif; (*organism*) noch nicht voll entwickelt
immaturity [ɪmə'tjuərɪtɪ] N Unreife *f*
immeasurable [ɪ'meʒrəbl] ADJ unermesslich groß
immediacy [ɪ'miːdɪəsɪ] N Unmittelbarkeit *f*, Direktheit *f*; (*of needs*) Dringlichkeit *f*
immediate [ɪ'miːdɪət] ADJ sofortig; (*need*) dringend; (*neighbourhood, family*) nächste(r, s)
immediately [ɪ'miːdɪətlɪ] ADV sofort; (*directly*) unmittelbar; **~ next to** direkt neben
immense [ɪ'mens] ADJ riesig, enorm
immensely [ɪ'menslɪ] ADV unheimlich; (*grateful, complex etc*) äußerst
immensity [ɪ'mensɪtɪ] N ungeheure Größe *f*, Unermesslichkeit *f*; (*of problems etc*) gewaltiges Ausmaß *nt*
immerse [ɪ'məːs] VT eintauchen; **to ~ sth in** etw tauchen in *+acc*; **to be immersed in** (*fig*) vertieft sein in *+acc*
immersion heater [ɪ'məːʃən-] (BRIT) N elektrischer Heißwasserboiler *m*
immigrant ['ɪmɪgrənt] N Einwanderer *m*, Einwanderin *f*
immigration [ɪmɪ'greɪʃən] N Einwanderung *f*; (*at airport etc*) Einwanderungsstelle *f* ▶ CPD Einwanderungs-
imminent ['ɪmɪnənt] ADJ bevorstehend
immobile [ɪ'məubaɪl] ADJ unbeweglich
immobilize [ɪ'məubɪlaɪz] VT (*person*) handlungsunfähig machen; (*machine*) zum Stillstand bringen
immobilizer [ɪ'məubɪlaɪzəʳ] N (*Aut*) Wegfahrsperre *f*
immoderate [ɪ'mɔdərət] ADJ unmäßig; (*opinion, reaction*) extrem; (*demand*) maßlos
immodest [ɪ'mɔdɪst] ADJ unanständig; (*boasting*) unbescheiden
immoral [ɪ'mɔrl] ADJ unmoralisch; (*behaviour*) unsittlich
immorality [ɪmɔ'rælɪtɪ] N Unmoral *f*; Unsittlichkeit *f*
immortal [ɪ'mɔːtl] ADJ unsterblich
immortality [ɪmɔː'tælɪtɪ] N Unsterblichkeit *f*
immortalize [ɪ'mɔːtlaɪz] VT unsterblich machen
immovable [ɪ'muːvəbl] ADJ unbeweglich; (*person, opinion*) fest
immune [ɪ'mjuːn] ADJ: **~ (to)** (*disease*) immun (gegen); (*flattery*) unempfänglich (für); (*criticism*) unempfindlich (gegen); (*attack*) sicher (vor *+dat*)
immune system N Immunsystem *nt*
immunity [ɪ'mjuːnɪtɪ] N Immunität *f*; Unempfänglichkeit *f*; Unempfindlichkeit *f*; Sicherheit *f*; (*of diplomat, from prosecution*) Immunität *f*
immunization [ɪmjunaɪ'zeɪʃən] N Immunisierung *f*
immunize ['ɪmjunaɪz] VT: **to ~ (against)** immunisieren (gegen)
imp [ɪmp] N Kobold *m*; (*child*) Racker *m* (*inf*)
impact ['ɪmpækt] N Aufprall *m*; (*of crash*) Wucht *f*; (*of law, measure*) (Aus)wirkung *f*
impair [ɪm'peəʳ] VT beeinträchtigen
impaired [ɪm'peəd] ADJ beeinträchtigt; (*hearing*) schlecht; **~ vision** schlechte Augen *pl*
impale [ɪm'peɪl] VT: **to ~ sth (on)** etw aufspießen (auf *+dat*)
impart [ɪm'pɑːt] VT: **to ~ (to)** (*information*) mitteilen *+dat*; (*flavour*) verleihen *+dat*
impartial [ɪm'pɑːʃl] ADJ unparteiisch
impartiality [ɪmpɑːʃɪ'ælɪtɪ] N Unparteilichkeit *f*
impassable [ɪm'pɑːsəbl] ADJ unpassierbar
impasse [æm'pɑːs] N Sackgasse *f*
impassive [ɪm'pæsɪv] ADJ gelassen
impatience [ɪm'peɪʃəns] N Ungeduld *f*
impatient [ɪm'peɪʃənt] ADJ ungeduldig; **to get** *or* **grow ~** ungeduldig werden; **to be ~ to do sth** es nicht erwarten können, etw zu tun
impatiently [ɪm'peɪʃəntlɪ] ADV ungeduldig
impeach [ɪm'piːtʃ] VT anklagen; (*public official*) eines Amtsvergehens anklagen

impeachment [ɪm'piːtʃmənt] N Anklage *f* wegen eines Amtsvergehens, Impeachment *nt*
impeccable [ɪm'pɛkəbl] ADJ (*dress*) untadelig; (*manners*) tadellos
impecunious [ɪmpɪ'kjuːnɪəs] ADJ mittellos
impede [ɪm'piːd] VT behindern
impediment [ɪm'pɛdɪmənt] N Hindernis *nt*; (*also*: **speech impediment**) Sprachfehler *m*
impel [ɪm'pɛl] VT: **to ~ sb to do sth** jdn (dazu) nötigen, etw zu tun
impending [ɪm'pɛndɪŋ] ADJ bevorstehend; (*catastrophe*) drohend
impenetrable [ɪm'pɛnɪtrəbl] ADJ undurchdringlich; (*fig*) unergründlich
imperative [ɪm'pɛrətɪv] ADJ dringend; (*tone*) Befehls- ▶ N (*Ling*) Imperativ *m*, Befehlsform *f*
imperceptible [ɪmpə'sɛptɪbl] ADJ nicht wahrnehmbar, unmerklich
imperfect [ɪm'pəːfɪkt] ADJ mangelhaft; (*goods*) fehlerhaft ▶ N (*Ling*: *also*: **imperfect tense**) Imperfekt *nt*, Vergangenheit *f*
imperfection [ɪmpəː'fɛkʃən] N Fehler *m*
imperial [ɪm'pɪərɪəl] ADJ kaiserlich; (BRIT: *measure*) britisch
imperialism [ɪm'pɪərɪəlɪzəm] N Imperialismus *m*
imperil [ɪm'pɛrɪl] VT gefährden
imperious [ɪm'pɪərɪəs] ADJ herrisch, gebieterisch
impersonal [ɪm'pəːsənl] ADJ unpersönlich
impersonate [ɪm'pəːsəneɪt] VT sich ausgeben als; (*Theat*) imitieren
impersonation [ɪmpəːsə'neɪʃən] N (*Theat*) Imitation *f*; **~ of** (*Law*) Auftreten *nt* als
impertinence [ɪm'pɜːtɪnəns] N Unverschämtheit *f*, Zumutung *f*
impertinent [ɪm'pəːtɪnənt] ADJ unverschämt
imperturbable [ɪmpə'təːbəbl] ADJ unerschütterlich
impervious [ɪm'pəːvɪəs] ADJ: **~ to** (*criticism, pressure*) unberührt von; (*charm, influence*) unempfänglich für
impetuous [ɪm'pɛtjuəs] ADJ ungestüm, stürmisch; (*act*) impulsiv
impetus ['ɪmpətəs] N Schwung *m*; (*fig: driving force*) treibende Kraft *f*
impinge [ɪm'pɪndʒ]: **~ on** *vt fus* sich auswirken auf +*acc*; (*rights*) einschränken
impish ['ɪmpɪʃ] ADJ schelmisch
implacable [ɪm'plækəbl] ADJ unerbittlich, erbittert
implant [ɪm'plɑːnt] VT (*Med*) einpflanzen; (*fig: idea, principle*) einimpfen
implausible [ɪm'plɔːzɪbl] ADJ unglaubwürdig
implement N ['ɪmplɪmənt] Gerät *nt*, Werkzeug *nt* ▶ VT ['ɪmplɪmɛnt] durchführen
implicate ['ɪmplɪkeɪt] VT verwickeln
implication [ɪmplɪ'keɪʃən] N Auswirkung *f*; (*involvement*) Verwicklung *f*; **by ~** implizit
implicit [ɪm'plɪsɪt] ADJ (*inferred*) implizit, unausgesprochen; (*unquestioning*) absolut
implicitly [ɪm'plɪsɪtlɪ] ADV implizit; absolut
implore [ɪm'plɔːʳ] VT anflehen
imply [ɪm'plaɪ] VT andeuten; (*mean*) bedeuten
impolite [ɪmpə'laɪt] ADJ unhöflich
imponderable [ɪm'pɔndərəbl] ADJ unberechenbar ▶ N unberechenbare Größe *f*
import VT [ɪm'pɔːt] importieren, einführen ▶ N ['ɪmpɔːt] Import *m*, Einfuhr *f*; (*article*) Importgut *nt* ▶ CPD Import-, Einfuhr-
importance [ɪm'pɔːtns] N Wichtigkeit *f*; Bedeutung *f*; **to be of little/great ~** nicht besonders wichtig/sehr wichtig sein
important [ɪm'pɔːtənt] ADJ wichtig; (*influential*) bedeutend; **it's not ~** es ist unwichtig
importantly [ɪm'pɔːtəntlɪ] ADV wichtigtuerisch; **but more ~ ...** aber was noch wichtiger ist, ...
importation [ɪmpɔː'teɪʃən] N Import *m*, Einfuhr *f*
imported [ɪm'pɔːtɪd] ADJ importiert, eingeführt
importer [ɪm'pɔːtəʳ] N Importeur *m*
impose [ɪm'pəuz] VT auferlegen; (*sanctions*) verhängen ▶ VI: **to ~ on sb** jdm zur Last fallen
imposing [ɪm'pəuzɪŋ] ADJ eindrucksvoll
imposition [ɪmpə'zɪʃən] N (*of tax etc*) Auferlegung *f*; **to be an ~ on** eine Zumutung sein für
impossibility [ɪmpɔsə'bɪlɪtɪ] N Unmöglichkeit *f*
impossible [ɪm'pɔsɪbl] ADJ unmöglich; **it's ~ for me to leave now** ich kann jetzt unmöglich gehen
impossibly [ɪm'pɔsɪblɪ] ADV unmöglich
imposter [ɪm'pɔstəʳ] N = **impostor**
impostor [ɪm'pɔstəʳ] N Hochstapler(in) *m(f)*
impotence ['ɪmpətns] N Machtlosigkeit *f*; Impotenz *f*
impotent ['ɪmpətnt] ADJ machtlos; (*Med*) impotent
impound [ɪm'paund] VT beschlagnahmen
impoverished [ɪm'pɔvərɪʃt] ADJ verarmt
impracticable [ɪm'præktɪkəbl] ADJ (*idea*) undurchführbar; (*solution*) unbrauchbar
impractical [ɪm'præktɪkl] ADJ (*plan*) undurchführbar; (*person*) unpraktisch
imprecise [ɪmprɪ'saɪs] ADJ ungenau
impregnable [ɪm'prɛgnəbl] ADJ uneinnehmbar; (*fig*) unerschütterlich
impregnate ['ɪmprɛgneɪt] VT tränken
impresario [ɪmprɪ'sɑːrɪəu] N (*Theat*) Impresario *m*
impress [ɪm'prɛs] VT beeindrucken; (*mark*) aufdrücken; **to ~ sth on sb** jdm etw einschärfen
impression [ɪm'prɛʃən] N Eindruck *m*; (*of stamp, seal*) Abdruck *m*; (*imitation*) Nachahmung *f*, Imitation *f*; **to make a good/bad ~ on sb** einen guten/schlechten Eindruck auf jdn machen; **to be under the ~ that ...** den Eindruck haben, dass ...
impressionable [ɪm'prɛʃnəbl] ADJ leicht zu beeindrucken
impressionist [ɪm'prɛʃənɪst] N Impressionist(in) *m(f)*; (*entertainer*) Imitator(in) *m(f)*
impressive [ɪm'prɛsɪv] ADJ beeindruckend

imprint ['ımprınt] N (*of hand etc*) Abdruck *m*; (*Publishing*) Impressum *nt*
imprinted [ım'prıntıd] ADJ: **it is ~ on my memory/mind** es hat sich mir eingeprägt
imprison [ım'prızn] VT inhaftieren, einsperren
imprisonment [ım'prıznmənt] N Gefangenschaft *f*; **three years' ~** drei Jahre Gefängnis *or* Freiheitsstrafe
improbable [ım'prɔbəbl] ADJ unwahrscheinlich
impromptu [ım'prɔmptju:] ADJ improvisiert
improper [ım'prɔpə^r] ADJ ungehörig; (*procedure*) unrichtig; (*dishonest*) unlauter
impropriety [ımprə'praıətı] N Ungehörigkeit *f*; Unrichtigkeit *f*; Unlauterkeit *f*
improve [ım'pru:v] VT verbessern ▸ VI sich bessern; **the patient is improving** dem Patienten geht es besser
▸ **improve (up)on** VT FUS verbessern
improvement [ım'pru:vmənt] N: **~ (in)** Verbesserung *f* (*+gen*); **to make improvements to** Verbesserungen durchführen an *+dat*
improvisation [ımprəvaı'zeıʃən] N Improvisation *f*
improvise ['ımprəvaız] VT, VI improvisieren
imprudence [ım'pru:dns] N Unklugheit *f*
imprudent [ım'pru:dnt] ADJ unklug
impudent ['ımpjudnt] ADJ unverschämt
impugn [ım'pju:n] VT angreifen; (*sincerity, motives, reputation*) in Zweifel ziehen
impulse ['ımpʌls] N Impuls *m*; (*urge*) Drang *m*; **to act on ~** aus einem Impuls heraus handeln
impulse buy N Impulsivkauf *m*
impulsive [ım'pʌlsıv] ADJ impulsiv, spontan; (*purchase*) Impulsiv-
impunity [ım'pju:nıtı] N: **with ~** ungestraft
impure [ım'pjuə^r] ADJ unrein; (*adulterated*) verunreinigt
impurity [ım'pjuərıtı] N Verunreinigung *f*
IN (*US*) ABBR (*Post*) = **Indiana**

KEYWORD

in [ın] PREP **1** (*indicating place, position*) in *+dat*; (*: with motion*) in *+acc*; **in the house/garden** im Haus/Garten; **in town** in der Stadt; **in the country** auf dem Land; **in here** hierin; **in there** darin
2 (*with place names: of town, region, country*) in *+dat*; **in London/Bavaria** in London/Bayern
3 (*indicating time*) in *+dat*; **in spring/summer/May** im Frühling/Sommer/Mai; **in 1994** 1994; **in the afternoon** am Nachmittag; **at 4 o'clock in the afternoon** um 4 Uhr nachmittags; **I did it in 3 hours/days** ich habe es in 3 Stunden/Tagen gemacht; **in 2 weeks** *or* **2 weeks' time** in 2 Wochen
4 (*indicating manner, circumstances, state*) in *+dat*; **in a loud/soft voice** mit lauter/weicher Stimme; **in English/German** auf Englisch/Deutsch; **in the sun** in der Sonne; **in the rain** im Regen; **in good condition** in guter Verfassung
5 (*with ratios, numbers*): **1 in 10** eine(r, s) von 10; **20 pence in the pound** 20 Pence pro Pfund; **they lined up in twos** sie stellten sich in Zweierreihen auf
6 (*referring to people, works*): **the disease is common in children** die Krankheit ist bei Kindern verbreitet; **in (the works of) Dickens** bei Dickens; **they have a good leader in him** in ihm haben sie einen guten Führer
7 (*indicating profession etc*): **to be in teaching/the army** Lehrer(in)/beim Militär sein
8 (*with present participle*): **in saying this, I ...** wenn ich das sage, ...
▸ ADV: **to be in** (*person: at home, work*) da sein; (*train, ship, plane*) angekommen sein; (*in fashion*) in sein; **to ask sb in** jdn hereinbitten; **to run/limp** *etc* **in** hereinlaufen/-humpeln *etc*
▸ N: **the ins and outs** (*of proposal, situation etc*) die Einzelheiten *pl*

in. ABBR = **inch**
inability [ınə'bılıtı] N Unfähigkeit *f*
inaccessible [ınək'sɛsıbl] ADJ unzugänglich
inaccuracy [ın'ækjurəsı] N Ungenauigkeit *f*; Unrichtigkeit *f*; (*mistake*) Fehler *m*
inaccurate [ın'ækjurət] ADJ ungenau; (*not correct*) unrichtig
inaction [ın'ækʃən] N Untätigkeit *f*
inactive [ın'æktıv] ADJ untätig
inactivity [ınæk'tıvıtı] N Untätigkeit *f*
inadequacy [ın'ædıkwəsı] N Unzulänglichkeit *f*
inadequate [ın'ædıkwət] ADJ unzulänglich
inadmissible [ınəd'mısəbl] ADJ unzulässig
inadvertently [ınəd'və:tntlı] ADV ungewollt
inadvisable [ınəd'vaızəbl] ADJ unratsam; **it is ~ to ...** es ist nicht ratsam, zu ...
inane [ı'neın] ADJ dumm
inanimate [ın'ænımət] ADJ unbelebt
inapplicable [ın'æplıkəbl] ADJ unzutreffend
inappropriate [ınə'prəuprıət] ADJ unpassend; (*word, expression*) unangebracht
inapt [ın'æpt] ADJ unpassend
inarticulate [ınɑ:'tıkjulət] ADJ (*speech*) unverständlich; **he is ~** er kann sich nur schlecht ausdrücken
inasmuch as [ınəz'mʌtʃ-] ADV da, weil; (*in so far as*) insofern als
inattention [ınə'tɛnʃən] N Unaufmerksamkeit *f*
inattentive [ınə'tɛntıv] ADJ unaufmerksam
inaudible [ın'ɔ:dıbl] ADJ unhörbar
inaugural [ı'nɔ:gjurəl] ADJ (*speech, meeting*) Eröffnungs-
inaugurate [ı'nɔ:gjureıt] VT einführen; (*president, official*) (feierlich) in sein/ihr Amt einführen
inauguration [ınɔ:gju'reıʃən] N Einführung *f*; (feierliche) Amtseinführung *f*
inauspicious [ınɔ:s'pıʃəs] ADJ Unheil verheißend
in-between [ınbı'twi:n] ADJ Mittel-, Zwischen-
inborn [ın'bɔ:n] ADJ angeboren
inbox ['ınbɔks] N (*Comput*) Posteingang *m*; (*US: in-tray*) Ablage *f* für Eingänge

inbred [ɪn'brɛd] ADJ angeboren; **an ~ family** eine Familie, in der Inzucht herrscht
inbreeding [ɪn'bri:dɪŋ] N Inzucht *f*
in-built ['ɪnbɪlt] ADJ (*quality*) ihm/ihr *etc* eigen; (*feeling etc*) angeboren
Inc. ABBR = **incorporated company**
Inca ['ɪŋkə] ADJ (*also:* **Incan**) Inka-, inkaisch ▸ N Inka *mf*
incalculable [ɪn'kælkjuləbl] ADJ (*effect*) unabsehbar; (*loss*) unermesslich
incapable [ɪn'keɪpəbl] ADJ hilflos; **to be ~ of sth** unfähig zu etw sein; **to be ~ of doing sth** unfähig sein, etw zu tun
incapacitate [ɪnkə'pæsɪteɪt] VT: **to ~ sb** jdn unfähig machen
incapacitated [ɪnkə'pæsɪteɪtɪd] ADJ (*Law*) entmündigt
incapacity [ɪnkə'pæsɪtɪ] N Hilflosigkeit *f*; (*inability*) Unfähigkeit *f*
incarcerate [ɪn'kɑ:səreɪt] VT einkerkern
incarnate [ɪn'kɑ:nɪt] ADJ leibhaftig, in Person; **evil ~** das leibhaftige Böse
incarnation [ɪnkɑ:'neɪʃən] N Inbegriff *m*; (*Rel*) Menschwerdung *f*
incendiary [ɪn'sɛndɪərɪ] ADJ (*bomb*) Brand-; **~ device** Brandsatz *m*
incense N ['ɪnsɛns] Weihrauch *m*; (*perfume*) Duft *m* ▸ VT [ɪn'sɛns] wütend machen
incense burner N Weihrauchschwenker *m*
incentive [ɪn'sɛntɪv] N Anreiz *m*
inception [ɪn'sɛpʃən] N Beginn *m*, Anfang *m*
incessant [ɪn'sɛsnt] ADJ unablässig
incessantly [ɪn'sɛsntlɪ] ADV unablässig
incest ['ɪnsɛst] N Inzest *m*
inch [ɪntʃ] N Zoll *m*; **to be within an ~ of sth** kurz vor etw *dat* stehen; **he didn't give an ~** (*fig*) er gab keinen Fingerbreit nach
▸ **inch forward** VI sich millimeterweise vorwärtsschieben
incidence ['ɪnsɪdns] N Häufigkeit *f*
incident ['ɪnsɪdnt] N Vorfall *m*; (*diplomatic etc*) Zwischenfall *m*
incidental [ɪnsɪ'dɛntl] ADJ zusätzlich; (*unimportant*) nebensächlich; **~ to** verbunden mit; **~ expenses** Nebenkosten *pl*
incidentally [ɪnsɪ'dɛntəlɪ] ADV übrigens
incidental music N Begleitmusik *f*
incident room N Einsatzzentrale *f*
incinerate [ɪn'sɪnəreɪt] VT verbrennen
incinerator [ɪn'sɪnəreɪtə^r] N (*for waste, refuse*) (Müll)verbrennungsanlage *f*
incipient [ɪn'sɪpɪənt] ADJ einsetzend
incision [ɪn'sɪʒən] N Einschnitt *m*
incisive [ɪn'saɪsɪv] ADJ treffend
incisor [ɪn'saɪzə^r] N Schneidezahn *m*
incite [ɪn'saɪt] VT (*rioters*) aufhetzen; (*violence, hatred*) schüren
incl. ABBR = **including; inclusive (of)**
inclement [ɪn'klɛmənt] ADJ (*weather*) rau, unfreundlich
inclination [ɪnklɪ'neɪʃən] N Neigung *f*
incline N ['ɪnklaɪn] Abhang *m* ▸ VT [ɪn'klaɪn] neigen ▸ VI sich neigen; **to be inclined to** neigen zu; **to be well inclined towards sb** jdm geneigt *or* gewogen sein
include [ɪn'klu:d] VT einbeziehen; (*in price*) einschließen; **the tip is not included in the price** Trinkgeld ist im Preis nicht inbegriffen
including [ɪn'klu:dɪŋ] PREP einschließlich; **~ service charge** inklusive Bedienung
inclusion [ɪn'klu:ʒən] N Einbeziehung *f*; Einschluss *m*
inclusive [ɪn'klu:sɪv] ADJ (*terms*) inklusive; (*price*) Inklusiv-, Pauschal-; **~ of** einschließlich *+gen*
incognito [ɪnkɔg'ni:təu] ADV inkognito
incoherent [ɪnkəu'hɪərənt] ADJ zusammenhanglos; (*speech*) wirr; (*person*) sich unklar *or* undeutlich ausdrückend
income ['ɪnkʌm] N Einkommen *nt*; (*from property, investment, pension*) Einkünfte *pl*; **gross/net ~** Brutto-/Nettoeinkommen *nt*; **~ and expenditure account** Gewinn- und Verlustrechnung *f*; **~ bracket** Einkommensklasse *f*
income support N ≈ Sozialhilfe *f*
income tax N Einkommenssteuer *f* ▸ CPD Steuer-
incoming ['ɪnkʌmɪŋ] ADJ (*passenger*) ankommend; (*flight*) landend; (*call, mail*) eingehend; (*government, official*) neu; (*wave*) hereinbrechend; **~ tide** Flut *f*
incommunicado ['ɪnkəmjunɪ'kɑ:dəu] ADJ: **to hold sb ~** jdn ohne jede Verbindung zur Außenwelt halten
incomparable [ɪn'kɔmpərəbl] ADJ unvergleichlich
incompatible [ɪnkəm'pætɪbl] ADJ unvereinbar
incompetence [ɪn'kɔmpɪtns] N Unfähigkeit *f*
incompetent [ɪn'kɔmpɪtnt] ADJ unfähig; (*job*) unzulänglich
incomplete [ɪnkəm'pli:t] ADJ unfertig; (*partial*) unvollständig
incomprehensible [ɪnkɔmprɪ'hɛnsɪbl] ADJ unverständlich
inconceivable [ɪnkən'si:vəbl] ADJ: **it is ~ (that …)** es ist unvorstellbar *or* undenkbar(, dass …)
inconclusive [ɪnkən'klu:sɪv] ADJ (*experiment, discussion*) ergebnislos; (*evidence, argument*) nicht überzeugend; (*result*) unbestimmt
incongruous [ɪn'kɔŋgruəs] ADJ (*strange*) absurd; (*inappropriate*) unpassend
inconsequential [ɪnkɔnsɪ'kwɛnʃl] ADJ unbedeutend, unwichtig
inconsiderable [ɪnkən'sɪdərəbl] ADJ: **not ~** beachtlich; (*sum*) nicht unerheblich
inconsiderate [ɪnkən'sɪdərət] ADJ rücksichtslos
inconsistency [ɪnkən'sɪstənsɪ] N Widersprüchlichkeit *f*; Inkonsequenz *f*; Unbeständigkeit *f*
inconsistent [ɪnkən'sɪstnt] ADJ widersprüchlich; (*person*) inkonsequent; (*work*) unbeständig; **to be ~ with** im Widerspruch stehen zu
inconsolable [ɪnkən'səuləbl] ADJ untröstlich
inconspicuous [ɪnkən'spɪkjuəs] ADJ unauffällig; **to make o.s. ~** sich unauffällig benehmen

incontinence [ɪn'kɔntɪnəns] N (*Med*) Unfähigkeit *f*, Stuhl und/oder Harn zurückzuhalten, Inkontinenz *f*
incontinent [ɪn'kɔntɪnənt] ADJ (*Med*) unfähig, Stuhl und/oder Harn zurückzuhalten, inkontinent
inconvenience [ɪnkən'vi:njəns] N Unannehmlichkeit *f*; (*trouble*) Umstände *pl* ▸ VT Umstände bereiten *+dat*; **don't ~ yourself** machen Sie sich keine Umstände
inconvenient [ɪnkən'vi:njənt] ADJ (*time, place*) ungünstig; (*house*) unbequem, unpraktisch; (*visitor*) ungelegen
incorporate [ɪn'kɔ:pəreɪt] VT aufnehmen; (*contain*) enthalten; **safety features have been incorporated in the design** in der Konstruktion sind auch Sicherheitsvorkehrungen enthalten
incorporated company [ɪn'kɔ:pəreɪtɪd-] (*US*) N eingetragene Gesellschaft *f*
incorrect [ɪnkə'rɛkt] ADJ falsch
incorrigible [ɪn'kɔrɪdʒɪbl] ADJ unverbesserlich
incorruptible [ɪnkə'rʌptɪbl] ADJ unbestechlich
increase VI [ɪn'kri:s] (*level etc*) zunehmen; (*price*) steigen; (*in size*) sich vergrößern; (*in number, quantity*) sich vermehren ▸ VT vergrößern; (*price*) erhöhen ▸ N ['ɪnkri:s]: **~ (in)** Zunahme *f +gen*; (*in wages, spending etc*) Erhöhung *f +gen*; **an ~ of 5%** eine Erhöhung von 5%, eine Zunahme um 5%; **to be on the ~** zunehmen
increasing [ɪn'kri:sɪŋ] ADJ zunehmend
increasingly [ɪn'kri:sɪŋlɪ] ADV zunehmend
incredible [ɪn'krɛdɪbl] ADJ unglaublich; (*amazing, wonderful*) unwahrscheinlich (*inf*), sagenhaft (*inf*)
incredulity [ɪnkrɪ'dju:lɪtɪ] N Ungläubigkeit *f*
incredulous [ɪn'krɛdjuləs] ADJ ungläubig
increment ['ɪnkrɪmənt] N (*in salary*) Erhöhung *f*, Zulage *f*
incriminate [ɪn'krɪmɪneɪt] VT belasten
incriminating [ɪn'krɪmɪneɪtɪŋ] ADJ belastend
incrusted [ɪn'krʌstɪd] ADJ = **encrusted**
incubate ['ɪnkjubeɪt] VT ausbrüten ▸ VI ausgebrütet werden; (*disease*) zum Ausbruch kommen
incubation [ɪnkju'beɪʃən] N Ausbrüten *nt*; (*of illness*) Inkubation *f*
incubation period N Inkubationszeit *f*
incubator ['ɪnkjubeɪtə^r] N (*for babies*) Brutkasten *m*, Inkubator *m*
inculcate ['ɪnkʌlkeɪt] VT: **to ~ sth in(to) sb** jdm etw einprägen
incumbent [ɪn'kʌmbənt] N Amtsinhaber(in) *m(f)* ▸ ADJ: **it is ~ on him to ...** es obliegt ihm *or* es ist seine Pflicht, zu ...
incur [ɪn'kə:^r] VT (*expenses, debt*) machen; (*loss*) erleiden; (*disapproval, anger*) sich *dat* zuziehen
incurable [ɪn'kjuərəbl] ADJ unheilbar
incursion [ɪn'kə:ʃən] N (*Mil*) Einfall *m*
Ind. (*US*) ABBR (*Post*) = **Indiana**
indebted [ɪn'dɛtɪd] ADJ: **to be ~ to sb** jdm (zu Dank) verpflichtet sein
indecency [ɪn'di:snsɪ] N Unanständigkeit *f*, Anstößigkeit *f*
indecent [ɪn'di:snt] ADJ unanständig, anstößig; (*haste*) ungebührlich
indecent assault (BRIT) N Sexualverbrechen *nt*
indecent exposure N Erregung *f* öffentlichen Ärgernisses
indecipherable [ɪndɪ'saɪfərəbl] ADJ unleserlich; (*expression, glance etc*) unergründlich
indecision [ɪndɪ'sɪʒən] N Unentschlossenheit *f*
indecisive [ɪndɪ'saɪsɪv] ADJ unentschlossen
indeed [ɪn'di:d] ADV aber sicher; (*in fact*) tatsächlich, in der Tat; (*furthermore*) sogar; **yes ~!** oh ja!, das kann man wohl sagen!
indefatigable [ɪndɪ'fætɪgəbl] ADJ unermüdlich
indefensible [ɪndɪ'fɛnsɪbl] ADJ (*conduct*) unentschuldbar
indefinable [ɪndɪ'faɪnəbl] ADJ undefinierbar
indefinite [ɪn'dɛfɪnɪt] ADJ unklar, vage; (*period, number*) unbestimmt
indefinite article N (*Ling*) unbestimmter Artikel *m*
indefinitely [ɪn'dɛfɪnɪtlɪ] ADV (*continue*) endlos; (*wait*) unbegrenzt (lange); (*postpone*) auf unbestimmte Zeit
indelible [ɪn'dɛlɪbl] ADJ (*mark, stain*) nicht zu entfernen; **~ pen** Tintenstift *m*; **~ ink** Wäschetinte *f*
indelicate [ɪn'dɛlɪkɪt] ADJ taktlos; (*not polite*) ungehörig
indemnify [ɪn'dɛmnɪfaɪ] VT entschädigen
indemnity [ɪn'dɛmnɪtɪ] N (*insurance*) Versicherung *f*; (*compensation*) Entschädigung *f*
indent [ɪn'dɛnt] VT (*text*) einrücken, einziehen
indentation [ɪndɛn'teɪʃən] N Einkerbung *f*; (*Typ*) Einrückung *f*, Einzug *m*; (*on metal*) Delle *f*
indenture [ɪn'dɛntʃə^r] N Ausbildungsvertrag *m*, Lehrvertrag *m*
independence [ɪndɪ'pɛndns] N Unabhängigkeit *f*

> **Independence Day** (der 4. Juli) ist in den USA ein gesetzlicher Feiertag zum Gedenken an die Unabhängigkeitserklärung vom 4. Juli 1776, mit der die 13 amerikanischen Kolonien ihre Freiheit und Unabhängigkeit von Großbritannien erklärten.

independent [ɪndɪ'pɛndnt] ADJ unabhängig
independently [ɪndɪ'pɛndntlɪ] ADV unabhängig
in-depth ['ɪndɛpθ] ADJ eingehend
indescribable [ɪndɪs'kraɪbəbl] ADJ unbeschreiblich
indestructible [ɪndɪs'trʌktəbl] ADJ unzerstörbar
indeterminate [ɪndɪ'tə:mɪnɪt] ADJ unbestimmt
index ['ɪndɛks] (*pl* **indexes**) N (*in book*) Register *nt*; (*in library etc*) Katalog *m*; (*also*: **card index**) Kartei *f*; (*pl* **indices**: *ratio*) Index *m*; (: *sign*) (An)zeichen *nt*
index card N Karteikarte *f*
indexed ['ɪndɛkst] (*US*) ADJ = **index-linked**
index finger N Zeigefinger *m*

index-linked [ˈɪndɛksˈlɪŋkt] ADJ der Inflationsrate *dat* angeglichen
India [ˈɪndɪə] N Indien *nt*
Indian [ˈɪndɪən] ADJ indisch; (*American Indian*) indianisch ▶ N Inder(in) *m(f)*; **American ~** Indianer(in) *m(f)*
Indian Ocean N: **the ~** der Indische Ozean
Indian summer N Altweibersommer *m*
India paper N Dünndruckpapier *nt*
India rubber N Gummi *m*, Kautschuk *m*
indicate [ˈɪndɪkeɪt] VT (an)zeigen; (*point to*) deuten auf *+acc*; (*mention*) andeuten ▶ VI (BRIT *Aut*): **to ~ left/right** links/rechts blinken
indication [ɪndɪˈkeɪʃən] N (An)zeichen *nt*
indicative [ɪnˈdɪkətɪv] N (*Ling*) Indikativ *m*, Wirklichkeitsform *f* ▶ ADJ: **to be ~ of sth** auf etw *acc* schließen lassen
indicator [ˈɪndɪkeɪtəʳ] N (*instrument, gauge*) Anzeiger *m*; (*fig*) (An)zeichen *nt*; (*Aut*) Richtungsanzeiger *m*, Blinker *m*
indices [ˈɪndɪsiːz] NPL *of* **index**
indict [ɪnˈdaɪt] VT anklagen
indictable [ɪnˈdaɪtəbl] ADJ (*person*) strafrechtlich verfolgbar; **~ offence** strafbare Handlung *f*
indictment [ɪnˈdaɪtmənt] N Anklage *f*; **to be an ~ of sth** (*fig*) ein Armutszeugnis *nt* für etw sein
indifference [ɪnˈdɪfrəns] N Gleichgültigkeit *f*
indifferent [ɪnˈdɪfrənt] ADJ gleichgültig; (*mediocre*) mittelmäßig
indigenous [ɪnˈdɪdʒɪnəs] ADJ einheimisch
indigestible [ɪndɪˈdʒɛstɪbl] ADJ unverdaulich
indigestion [ɪndɪˈdʒɛstʃən] N Magenverstimmung *f*
indignant [ɪnˈdɪɡnənt] ADJ: **to be ~ at sth/with sb** entrüstet über etw/jdn sein
indignation [ɪndɪɡˈneɪʃən] N Entrüstung *f*
indignity [ɪnˈdɪɡnɪtɪ] N Demütigung *f*
indigo [ˈɪndɪɡəu] N Indigo *m or nt*
indirect [ɪndɪˈrɛkt] ADJ indirekt; **~ way** *or* **route** Umweg *m*
indirectly [ɪndɪˈrɛktlɪ] ADV indirekt
indiscreet [ɪndɪsˈkriːt] ADJ indiskret
indiscretion [ɪndɪsˈkrɛʃən] N Indiskretion *f*
indiscriminate [ɪndɪsˈkrɪmɪnət] ADJ wahllos; (*taste*) unkritisch
indispensable [ɪndɪsˈpɛnsəbl] ADJ unentbehrlich
indisposed [ɪndɪsˈpəuzd] ADJ unpässlich
indisputable [ɪndɪsˈpjuːtəbl] ADJ unbestreitbar
indistinct [ɪndɪsˈtɪŋkt] ADJ undeutlich; (*image*) verschwommen; (*noise*) schwach
indistinguishable [ɪndɪsˈtɪŋɡwɪʃəbl] ADJ: **~ from** nicht zu unterscheiden von
individual [ɪndɪˈvɪdjuəl] N Individuum *nt*, Einzelne(r) *f(m)* ▶ ADJ eigen; (*single*) einzeln; (*case, portion*) Einzel-; (*particular*) individuell
individualist [ɪndɪˈvɪdjuəlɪst] N Individualist(in) *m(f)*
individuality [ɪndɪvɪdjuˈælɪtɪ] N Individualität *f*
individually [ɪndɪˈvɪdjuəlɪ] ADV einzeln, individuell
indivisible [ɪndɪˈvɪzɪbl] ADJ unteilbar
Indochina [ɪndəuˈtʃaɪnə] N Indochina *nt*
indoctrinate [ɪnˈdɔktrɪneɪt] VT indoktrinieren
indoctrination [ɪndɔktrɪˈneɪʃən] N Indoktrination *f*
indolence [ˈɪndələns] N Trägheit *f*
indolent [ˈɪndələnt] ADJ träge
Indonesia [ɪndəˈniːzɪə] N Indonesien *nt*
Indonesian [ɪndəˈniːzɪən] ADJ indonesisch ▶ N Indonesier(in) *m(f)*; (*Ling*) Indonesisch *nt*
indoor [ˈɪndɔːʳ] ADJ (*plant, aerial*) Zimmer-; (*clothes, shoes*) Haus-; (*swimming pool, sport*) Hallen-; (*games*) im Haus
indoors [ɪnˈdɔːz] ADV drinnen; **to go ~** hineingehen
indubitable [ɪnˈdjuːbɪtəbl] ADJ unzweifelhaft
indubitably [ɪnˈdjuːbɪtəblɪ] ADV zweifellos
induce [ɪnˈdjuːs] VT herbeiführen; (*persuade*) dazu bringen; (*Med: birth*) einleiten; **to ~ sb to do sth** jdn dazu bewegen *or* bringen, etw zu tun
inducement [ɪnˈdjuːsmənt] N Anreiz *m*; (*pej: bribe*) Bestechung *f*
induct [ɪnˈdʌkt] VT (in sein/ihr *etc* Amt) einführen
induction [ɪnˈdʌkʃən] N (*Med: of birth*) Einleitung *f*
induction course (BRIT) N Einführungskurs *m*
indulge [ɪnˈdʌldʒ] VT nachgeben *+dat*; (*person, child*) verwöhnen ▶ VI: **to ~ in** sich hingeben *+dat*
indulgence [ɪnˈdʌldʒəns] N (*pleasure*) Luxus *m*; (*leniency*) Nachgiebigkeit *f*
indulgent [ɪnˈdʌldʒənt] ADJ nachsichtig
industrial [ɪnˈdʌstrɪəl] ADJ industriell; (*accident*) Arbeits-; (*city*) Industrie-
industrial action N Arbeitskampfmaßnahmen *pl*
industrial design N Industriedesign *nt*
industrial estate (BRIT) N Industriegebiet *nt*
industrialist [ɪnˈdʌstrɪəlɪst] N Industrielle(r) *f(m)*
industrialize [ɪnˈdʌstrɪəlaɪz] VT industrialisieren
industrial park (US) N = **industrial estate**
industrial relations NPL *Beziehungen zwischen Arbeitgebern, Arbeitnehmern und Gewerkschaften*
industrial tribunal (BRIT) N Arbeitsgericht *nt*
industrial unrest (BRIT) N Arbeitsunruhen *pl*
industrious [ɪnˈdʌstrɪəs] ADJ fleißig
industry [ˈɪndəstrɪ] N Industrie *f*; (*diligence*) Fleiß *m*
inebriated [ɪˈniːbrɪeɪtɪd] ADJ betrunken
inedible [ɪnˈɛdɪbl] ADJ ungenießbar
ineffective [ɪnɪˈfɛktɪv] ADJ wirkungslos; (*government*) unfähig
ineffectual [ɪnɪˈfɛktʃuəl] ADJ = **ineffective**
inefficiency [ɪnɪˈfɪʃənsɪ] N Ineffizienz *f*; Leistungsunfähigkeit *f*
inefficient [ɪnɪˈfɪʃənt] ADJ ineffizient; (*machine*) leistungsunfähig
inelegant [ɪnˈɛlɪɡənt] ADJ unelegant
ineligible [ɪnˈɛlɪdʒɪbl] ADJ (*candidate*) nicht wählbar; **to be ~ for sth** zu etw nicht berechtigt sein

inept [ɪ'nɛpt] ADJ (*politician*) unfähig; (*management*) stümperhaft
ineptitude [ɪ'nɛptɪtju:d] N Unfähigkeit *f*; Stümperhaftigkeit *f*
inequality [ɪnɪ'kwɔlɪtɪ] N Ungleichheit *f*
inequitable [ɪn'ɛkwɪtəbl] ADJ ungerecht
inert [ɪ'nə:t] ADJ unbeweglich; **~ gas** Edelgas *nt*
inertia [ɪ'nə:ʃə] N Trägheit *f*
inertia-reel seat belt [ɪ'nə:ʃə'ri:l-] N Automatikgurt *m*
inescapable [ɪnɪ'skeɪpəbl] ADJ unvermeidlich; (*conclusion*) zwangsläufig
inessential [ɪnɪ'sɛnʃl] ADJ unwesentlich; (*furniture etc*) entbehrlich
inessentials [ɪnɪ'sɛnʃlz] NPL Nebensächlichkeiten *pl*
inestimable [ɪn'ɛstɪməbl] ADJ unschätzbar
inevitability [ɪnɛvɪtə'bɪlɪtɪ] N Unvermeidlichkeit *f*; **it is an ~** es ist nicht zu vermeiden
inevitable [ɪn'ɛvɪtəbl] ADJ unvermeidlich; (*result*) zwangsläufig
inevitably [ɪn'ɛvɪtəblɪ] ADV zwangsläufig; **~, he was late** es konnte ja nicht ausbleiben, dass er zu spät kam; **as ~ happens ...** wie es immer so ist ...
inexact [ɪnɪg'zækt] ADJ ungenau
inexcusable [ɪnɪks'kju:zəbl] ADJ unentschuldbar, unverzeihlich
inexhaustible [ɪnɪg'zɔ:stɪbl] ADJ unerschöpflich
inexorable [ɪn'ɛksərəbl] ADJ unaufhaltsam
inexpensive [ɪnɪk'spɛnsɪv] ADJ preisgünstig
inexperience [ɪnɪk'spɪərɪəns] N Unerfahrenheit *f*
inexperienced [ɪnɪk'spɪərɪənst] ADJ unerfahren; (*swimmer etc*) ungeübt; **to be ~ in sth** wenig Erfahrung mit etw haben
inexplicable [ɪnɪk'splɪkəbl] ADJ unerklärlich
inexpressible [ɪnɪk'sprɛsɪbl] ADJ unbeschreiblich
inextricable [ɪnɪk'strɪkəbl] ADJ unentwirrbar; (*dilemma*) unlösbar
inextricably [ɪnɪk'strɪkəblɪ] ADV unentwirrbar; (*linked*) untrennbar
infallibility [ɪnfælə'bɪlɪtɪ] N Unfehlbarkeit *f*
infallible [ɪn'fælɪbl] ADJ unfehlbar
infamous ['ɪnfəməs] ADJ niederträchtig
infamy ['ɪnfəmɪ] N Verrufenheit *f*
infancy ['ɪnfənsɪ] N frühe Kindheit *f*; (*of movement, firm*) Anfangsstadium *nt*
infant ['ɪnfənt] N Säugling *m*; (*young child*) Kleinkind *nt* ▶ CPD Säuglings-
infantile ['ɪnfəntaɪl] ADJ kindisch, infantil; (*disease*) Kinder-
infantry ['ɪnfəntrɪ] N Infanterie *f*
infantryman ['ɪnfəntrɪmən] N (*irreg*) Infanterist *m*
infant school (BRIT) N Grundschule *f* (*für die ersten beiden Jahrgänge*)
infatuated [ɪn'fætjueɪtɪd] ADJ: **~ with** vernarrt in *+acc*; **to become ~ with** sich vernarren in *+acc*
infatuation [ɪnfætju'eɪʃən] N Vernarrtheit *f*
infect [ɪn'fɛkt] VT anstecken (*also fig*), infizieren; (*food*) verseuchen; **to become infected** (*wound*) sich entzünden
infection [ɪn'fɛkʃən] N Infektion *f*, Entzündung *f*; (*contagion*) Ansteckung *f*
infectious [ɪn'fɛkʃəs] ADJ ansteckend
infer [ɪn'fə:ʳ] VT schließen; (*imply*) andeuten
inference ['ɪnfərəns] N Schluss *m*; Andeutung *f*
inferior [ɪn'fɪərɪəʳ] ADJ (*in rank*) untergeordnet, niedriger; (*in quality*) minderwertig; (*in quantity, number*) geringer ▶ N Untergebene(r) *f*(*m*); **to feel ~ (to sb)** sich (jdm) unterlegen fühlen
inferiority [ɪnfɪərɪ'ɔrətɪ] N untergeordnete Stellung *f*, niedriger Rang *m*; Minderwertigkeit *f*; geringere Zahl *f*
inferiority complex N Minderwertigkeitskomplex *m*
infernal [ɪn'fə:nl] ADJ höllisch; (*temper*) schrecklich
inferno [ɪn'fə:nəu] N (*blaze*) Flammenmeer *nt*
infertile [ɪn'fə:taɪl] ADJ unfruchtbar
infertility [ɪnfə:'tɪlɪtɪ] N Unfruchtbarkeit *f*
infested [ɪn'fɛstɪd] ADJ: **~ (with)** verseucht (mit)
infidelity [ɪnfɪ'dɛlɪtɪ] N Untreue *f*
infighting ['ɪnfaɪtɪŋ] N interne Machtkämpfe *pl*
infiltrate ['ɪnfɪltreɪt] VT (*organization etc*) infiltrieren, unterwandern; (*: to spy*) einschleusen
infinite ['ɪnfɪnɪt] ADJ unendlich; (*time, money*) unendlich viel
infinitely ['ɪnfɪnɪtlɪ] ADV unendlich viel
infinitesimal [ɪnfɪnɪ'tɛsɪməl] ADJ unendlich klein, winzig
infinitive [ɪn'fɪnɪtɪv] N (*Ling*) Infinitiv *m*, Grundform *f*
infinity [ɪn'fɪnɪtɪ] N Unendlichkeit *f*; (*Math, Phot*) Unendliche *nt*; **an ~ of ...** unendlich viel(e) ...
infirm [ɪn'fə:m] ADJ schwach, gebrechlich
infirmary [ɪn'fə:mərɪ] N Krankenhaus *nt*
infirmity [ɪn'fə:mɪtɪ] N Schwäche *f*, Gebrechlichkeit *f*
inflame [ɪn'fleɪm] VT aufbringen
inflamed [ɪn'fleɪmd] ADJ entzündet
inflammable [ɪn'flæməbl] ADJ feuergefährlich
inflammation [ɪnflə'meɪʃən] N Entzündung *f*
inflammatory [ɪn'flæmətərɪ] ADJ (*speech*) aufrührerisch, Hetz-
inflatable [ɪn'fleɪtəbl] ADJ aufblasbar; (*dinghy*) Schlauch-
inflate [ɪn'fleɪt] VT aufpumpen; (*balloon*) aufblasen; (*price*) hochtreiben; (*expectation*) steigern; (*position, ideas etc*) hochspielen
inflated [ɪn'fleɪtɪd] ADJ (*value, price*) überhöht
inflation [ɪn'fleɪʃən] N Inflation *f*
inflationary [ɪn'fleɪʃənərɪ] ADJ inflationär; (*spiral*) Inflations-
inflexible [ɪn'flɛksɪbl] ADJ inflexibel; (*rule*) starr
inflict [ɪn'flɪkt] VT: **to ~ sth on sb** (*damage, suffering, wound*) jdm etw zufügen; (*punishment*) jdm etw auferlegen; (*fig: problems*) jdn mit etw belasten

infliction [ɪn'flɪkʃən] N Zufügen *nt*; Auferlegung *f*; Belastung *f*
in-flight ['ɪnflaɪt] ADJ während des Fluges
inflow ['ɪnfləu] N Zustrom *m*
influence ['ɪnfluəns] N Einfluss *m* ▸ VT beeinflussen; **under the ~ of alcohol** unter Alkoholeinfluss
influential [ɪnflu'ɛnʃl] ADJ einflussreich
influenza [ɪnflu'ɛnzə] N (*Med*) Grippe *f*
influx ['ɪnflʌks] N (*of refugees*) Zustrom *m*; (*of funds*) Zufuhr *f*
inform [ɪn'fɔ:m] VT: **to ~ sb of sth** jdn von etw unterrichten, jdn über etw *acc* informieren ▸ VI: **to ~ on sb** jdn denunzieren
informal [ɪn'fɔ:ml] ADJ ungezwungen; (*manner, clothes*) leger; (*unofficial*) inoffiziell; (*announcement, invitation*) informell
informality [ɪnfɔ:'mælɪtɪ] N Ungezwungenheit *f*; legere Art *f*; inoffizieller Charakter *m*; informeller Charakter *m*
informally [ɪn'fɔ:məlɪ] ADV ungezwungen; leger; inoffiziell; informell
informant [ɪn'fɔ:mənt] N Informant(in) *m(f)*
information [ɪnfə'meɪʃən] N Informationen *pl*, Auskunft *f*; (*knowledge*) Wissen *nt*; **to get ~ on** sich informieren über *+acc*; **a piece of ~** eine Auskunft *or* Information; **for your ~** zu Ihrer Information
information and communication technology (BRIT) N (*Scol*) ≈ Informations- und Kommunikationstechnologie
information bureau N Auskunftsbüro *nt*
information desk N Auskunftsschalter *m*
information office N Auskunftsbüro *nt*
information processing N Informationsverarbeitung *f*
information retrieval N Informationsabruf *m*, Datenabruf *m*
information science N Informatik *f*
information superhighway N (*Comput*) Datenautobahn *f*
information technology N Informationstechnik *f*
informative [ɪn'fɔ:mətɪv] ADJ aufschlussreich
informed [ɪn'fɔ:md] ADJ informiert; (*guess, opinion*) wohlbegründet; **to be well/better ~** gut/besser informiert sein
informer [ɪn'fɔ:mə^r] N Informant(in) *m(f)*; (*also:* **police informer**) Polizeispitzel *m*
infra dig ['ɪnfrə'dɪg] (*inf*) ADJ ABBR (= *infra dignitatem*) unter meiner/seiner *etc* Würde
infrared [ɪnfrə'rɛd] ADJ infrarot
infrastructure ['ɪnfrəstrʌktʃə^r] N Infrastruktur *f*
infrequent [ɪn'fri:kwənt] ADJ selten
infringe [ɪn'frɪndʒ] VT (*law*) verstoßen gegen, übertreten ▸ VI: **to ~ on** (*rights*) verletzen
infringement [ɪn'frɪndʒmənt] N Verstoß *m*, Übertretung *f*; Verletzung *f*
infuriate [ɪn'fjuərɪeɪt] VT wütend machen
infuriating [ɪn'fjuərɪeɪtɪŋ] ADJ äußerst ärgerlich
infuse [ɪn'fju:z] VT (*tea etc*) aufgießen; **to ~ sb with sth** (*fig*) jdm etw einflößen
infusion [ɪn'fju:ʒən] N (*tea etc*) Aufguss *m*
ingenious [ɪn'dʒi:njəs] ADJ genial
ingenuity [ɪndʒɪ'nju:ɪtɪ] N Einfallsreichtum *m*; (*skill*) Geschicklichkeit *f*
ingenuous [ɪn'dʒɛnjuəs] ADJ offen, aufrichtig; (*innocent*) naiv
ingot ['ɪŋgət] N Barren *m*
ingrained [ɪn'greɪnd] ADJ (*habit*) fest; (*belief*) unerschütterlich
ingratiate [ɪn'greɪʃɪeɪt] VT: **to ~ o.s. with sb** sich bei jdm einschmeicheln
ingratiating [ɪn'greɪʃɪeɪtɪŋ] ADJ schmeichlerisch
ingratitude [ɪn'grætɪtju:d] N Undank *m*
ingredient [ɪn'gri:dɪənt] N (*of cake etc*) Zutat *f*; (*of situation*) Bestandteil *m*
ingrowing ['ɪngrəuɪŋ] ADJ: **~ toenail** eingewachsener Zehennagel *m*
inhabit [ɪn'hæbɪt] VT bewohnen, wohnen in *+dat*
inhabitant [ɪn'hæbɪtnt] N Einwohner(in) *m(f)*; (*of street, house*) Bewohner(in) *m(f)*
inhale [ɪn'heɪl] VT einatmen ▸ VI einatmen; (*when smoking*) inhalieren
inhaler [ɪn'heɪlə^r] N Inhalationsapparat *m*
inherent [ɪn'hɪərənt] ADJ: **~ in** *or* **to** eigen *+dat*
inherently [ɪn'hɪərəntlɪ] ADV von Natur aus
inherit [ɪn'hɛrɪt] VT erben
inheritance [ɪn'hɛrɪtəns] N Erbe *nt*
inhibit [ɪn'hɪbɪt] VT hemmen
inhibited [ɪn'hɪbɪtɪd] ADJ gehemmt
inhibiting [ɪn'hɪbɪtɪŋ] ADJ hemmend; **~ factor** Hemmnis *nt*
inhibition [ɪnhɪ'bɪʃən] N Hemmung *f*
inhospitable [ɪnhɔs'pɪtəbl] ADJ ungastlich; (*place, climate*) unwirtlich
in-house ['ɪn'haus] ADJ, ADV hausintern
inhuman [ɪn'hju:mən] ADJ (*behaviour*) unmenschlich; (*appearance*) nicht menschlich
inhumane [ɪnhju:'meɪn] ADJ inhuman; (*treatment*) menschenunwürdig
inimitable [ɪ'nɪmɪtəbl] ADJ unnachahmlich
iniquitous [ɪ'nɪkwɪtəs] ADJ (*unfair*) ungerecht
iniquity [ɪ'nɪkwɪtɪ] N Ungerechtigkeit *f*; (*wickedness*) Ungeheuerlichkeit *f*
initial [ɪ'nɪʃl] ADJ anfänglich; (*stage*) Anfangs- ▸ N Initiale *f*, Anfangsbuchstabe *m* ▸ VT (*document*) abzeichnen; **initials** NPL Initialen *pl*; (*as signature*) Namenszeichen *nt*
initialize [ɪ'nɪʃəlaɪz] VT initialisieren
initially [ɪ'nɪʃəlɪ] ADV zu Anfang; (*first*) zuerst
initiate [ɪ'nɪʃɪeɪt] VT (*talks*) eröffnen; (*process*) einleiten; (*new member*) feierlich aufnehmen; **to ~ sb into a secret** jdn in ein Geheimnis einweihen; **to ~ proceedings against sb** (*Law*) einen Prozess gegen jdn anstrengen
initiation [ɪnɪʃɪ'eɪʃən] N (*beginning*) Einführung *f*; (*into secret etc*) Einweihung *f*
initiative [ɪ'nɪʃətɪv] N Initiative *f*; **to take the ~** die Initiative ergreifen
inject [ɪn'dʒɛkt] VT (ein)spritzen; (*fig: funds*) hineinpumpen; **to ~ sb with sth** jdm etw spritzen *or* injizieren; **to ~ money into sth** (*fig*) Geld in etw *acc* pumpen

injection [ɪn'dʒɛkʃən] N Spritze *f*, Injektion *f*; **to give/have an ~** eine Spritze *or* Injektion geben/bekommen; **an ~ of money/funds** (*fig*) eine Finanzspritze
injudicious [ɪndʒu'dɪʃəs] ADJ unklug
injunction [ɪn'dʒʌŋkʃən] N (*Law*) gerichtliche Verfügung *f*
injure ['ɪndʒə^r] VT verletzen; (*reputation*) schaden *+dat*; **to ~ o.s.** sich verletzen
injured ['ɪndʒəd] ADJ verletzt; (*tone*) gekränkt; **~ party** (*Law*) Geschädigte(r) *f(m)*
injurious [ɪn'dʒuərɪəs] ADJ: **to be ~ to** schaden *+dat*, schädlich sein *+dat*
injury ['ɪndʒərɪ] N Verletzung *f*; **to escape without ~** unverletzt davonkommen
injury time N (*Sport*) Nachspielzeit *f*; **to play ~** nachspielen
injustice [ɪn'dʒʌstɪs] N Ungerechtigkeit *f*; **you do me an ~** Sie tun mir unrecht
ink [ɪŋk] N Tinte *f*; (*in printing*) Druckfarbe *f*
ink-jet printer ['ɪŋkdʒɛt-] N Tintenstrahldrucker *m*
inkling ['ɪŋklɪŋ] N (dunkle) Ahnung *f*; **to have an ~ of** ahnen
ink pad N Stempelkissen *nt*
inky ['ɪŋkɪ] ADJ tintenschwarz; (*fingers*) tintenbeschmiert
inlaid ['ɪnleɪd] ADJ eingelegt
inland ['ɪnlənd] ADJ (*port, sea, waterway*) Binnen- ▸ ADV (*travel*) landeinwärts
Inland Revenue (BRIT) N ≈ Finanzamt *nt*
in-laws ['ɪnlɔːz] NPL (*parents-in-law*) Schwiegereltern *pl*; (*other relatives*) angeheiratete Verwandte *pl*
inlet ['ɪnlɛt] N (schmale) Bucht *f*
inlet pipe N Zuleitung *f*, Zuleitungsrohr *nt*
inmate ['ɪnmeɪt] N Insasse *m*, Insassin *f*
inmost ['ɪnməust] ADJ innerst
inn [ɪn] N Gasthaus *nt*
innards ['ɪnədz] (*inf*) NPL Innereien *pl*
innate [ɪ'neɪt] ADJ angeboren
inner ['ɪnə^r] ADJ innere(r, s); (*courtyard*) Innen-
inner city N Innenstadt *f*
innermost ['ɪnəməust] ADJ = **inmost**
inner tube N (*of tyre*) Schlauch *m*
innings ['ɪnɪŋz] N (*Cricket*) Innenrunde *f*; **he's had a good ~** (*fig*) er kann auf ein langes, ausgefülltes Leben zurückblicken
innocence ['ɪnəsns] N Unschuld *f*
innocent ['ɪnəsnt] ADJ unschuldig
innocuous [ɪ'nɔkjuəs] ADJ harmlos
innovation [ɪnəu'veɪʃən] N Neuerung *f*
innuendo [ɪnju'ɛndəu] (*pl* **innuendoes**) N versteckte Andeutung *f*
innumerable [ɪ'njuːmrəbl] ADJ unzählig
inoculate [ɪ'nɔkjuleɪt] VT: **to ~ sb against sth** jdn gegen etw impfen; **to ~ sb with sth** jdm etw einimpfen
inoculation [ɪnɔkju'leɪʃən] N Impfung *f*
inoffensive [ɪnə'fɛnsɪv] ADJ harmlos
inopportune [ɪn'ɔpətjuːn] ADJ unangebracht; (*moment*) ungelegen
inordinate [ɪ'nɔːdɪnət] ADJ (*thirst etc*) unmäßig; (*amount, pleasure*) ungeheuer
inordinately [ɪ'nɔːdɪnətlɪ] ADV (*proud*) unmäßig; (*long, large etc*) ungeheuer
inorganic [ɪnɔː'gænɪk] ADJ anorganisch
inpatient ['ɪnpeɪʃənt] N stationär behandelter Patient *m*, stationär behandelte Patientin *f*
input ['ɪnput] N (*of capital, manpower*) Investition *f*; (*of energy*) Zufuhr *f*; (*Comput*) Eingabe *f*, Input *m or nt* ▸ VT (*Comput*) eingeben
inquest ['ɪnkwɛst] N gerichtliche Untersuchung *f* der Todesursache
inquire [ɪn'kwaɪə^r] VI: **to ~ about** sich erkundigen nach, fragen nach ▸ VT sich erkundigen nach, fragen nach; **to ~ when/where/whether** fragen *or* sich erkundigen, wann/wo/ob
▸ **inquire after** VT FUS sich erkundigen nach
▸ **inquire into** VT FUS untersuchen
inquiring [ɪn'kwaɪərɪŋ] ADJ wissensdurstig
inquiry [ɪn'kwaɪərɪ] N Untersuchung *f*; (*question*) Anfrage *f*; **to hold an ~ into sth** eine Untersuchung *+gen* durchführen
inquiry desk (BRIT) N Auskunft *f*, Auskunftsschalter *m*
inquiry office (BRIT) N Auskunft *f*, Auskunftsbüro *nt*
inquisition [ɪnkwɪ'zɪʃən] N Untersuchung *f*; (*Rel*): **the I~** die Inquisition
inquisitive [ɪn'kwɪzɪtɪv] ADJ neugierig
inroads ['ɪnrəudz] NPL: **to make ~ into** (*savings, supplies*) angreifen
ins ABBR (= *inches*) *see* **inch**
insane [ɪn'seɪn] ADJ wahnsinnig; (*Med*) geisteskrank
insanitary [ɪn'sænɪtərɪ] ADJ unhygienisch
insanity [ɪn'sænɪtɪ] N Wahnsinn *m*; (*Med*) Geisteskrankheit *f*
insatiable [ɪn'seɪʃəbl] ADJ unersättlich
inscribe [ɪn'skraɪb] VT (*on ring*) eingravieren; (*on stone*) einmeißeln; (*on banner*) schreiben; **to ~ a ring/stone/banner with sth** etw in einen Ring eingravieren/in einen Stein einmeißeln/auf ein Spruchband schreiben; **to ~ a book** eine Widmung in ein Buch schreiben
inscription [ɪn'skrɪpʃən] N Inschrift *f*; (*in book*) Widmung *f*
inscrutable [ɪn'skruːtəbl] ADJ (*comment*) unergründlich; (*expression*) undurchdringlich
inseam measurement ['ɪnsiːm-] (*US*) N innere Beinlänge *f*
insect ['ɪnsɛkt] N Insekt *nt*
insect bite N Insektenstich *m*
insecticide [ɪn'sɛktɪsaɪd] N Insektizid *nt*, Insektengift *nt*
insect repellent N Insektenbekämpfungsmittel *nt*
insecure [ɪnsɪ'kjuə^r] ADJ unsicher
insecurity [ɪnsɪ'kjuərɪtɪ] N Unsicherheit *f*
insemination [ɪnsɛmɪ'neɪʃən] N: **artificial ~** künstliche Besamung *f*
insensible [ɪn'sɛnsɪbl] ADJ bewusstlos; **~ to** unempfindlich gegen; **~ of** nicht bewusst *+gen*
insensitive [ɪn'sɛnsɪtɪv] ADJ gefühllos

insensitivity [ɪnsɛnsɪ'tɪvɪtɪ] N Gefühllosigkeit *f*
inseparable [ɪn'sɛprəbl] ADJ untrennbar; (*friends*) unzertrennlich
insert VT [ɪn'sə:t] einfügen; (*into sth*) hineinstecken ▶ N ['ɪnsə:t] (*in newspaper etc*) Beilage *f*; (*in shoe*) Einlage *f*
insertion [ɪn'sə:ʃən] N Hineinstecken *nt*; (*of needle*) Einstechen *nt*; (*of comment*) Einfügen *nt*
in-service ['ɪn'sə:vɪs] ADJ: **~ training** (berufsbegleitende) Fortbildung *f*; **~ course** Fortbildungslehrgang *m*
inshore ['ɪn'ʃɔ:ʳ] ADJ (*fishing, waters*) Küsten- ▶ ADV in Küstennähe; (*move*) auf die Küste zu
inside ['ɪn'saɪd] N Innere(s) *nt*, Innenseite *f*; (*of road: in Britain*) linke Spur *f*; (*: in US, Europe etc*) rechte Spur *f* ▶ ADJ innere(r, s); (*pocket, cabin, light*) Innen- ▶ ADV (*go*) nach innen, hinein; (*be*) drinnen ▶ PREP (*location*) in *+dat*; (*motion*) in *+acc*; **insides** NPL (*inf*) Bauch *m*; (*innards*) Eingeweide *pl*; **~ 10 minutes** innerhalb von 10 Minuten
inside forward N (*Sport*) Halbstürmer *m*
inside information N Insiderinformation *f*
inside knowledge N Insiderwissen *nt*
inside lane N (BRIT) linke Spur *f*; (*in US, Europe etc*) rechte Spur *f*
inside leg measurement (BRIT) N innere Beinlänge *f*
inside out ADV (*know*) in- und auswendig; (*piece of clothing: be*) links *or* verkehrt herum; (*: turn*) nach links
insider [ɪn'saɪdəʳ] N Insider *m*, Eingeweihte(r) *f(m)*
insider dealing, insider trading N (*Stock Exchange*) Insiderhandel *m or* -geschäfte *pl*
inside story N Insidestory *f*, Inside Story *f*
insidious [ɪn'sɪdɪəs] ADJ heimtückisch
insight ['ɪnsaɪt] N Verständnis *nt*; **to gain (an) ~ into** einen Einblick gewinnen in *+acc*
insignia [ɪn'sɪgnɪə] NPL Insignien *pl*
insignificant [ɪnsɪg'nɪfɪknt] ADJ belanglos
insincere [ɪnsɪn'sɪəʳ] ADJ unaufrichtig, falsch
insincerity [ɪnsɪn'sɛrɪtɪ] N Unaufrichtigkeit *f*, Falschheit *f*
insinuate [ɪn'sɪnjueɪt] VT anspielen auf *+acc*
insinuation [ɪnsɪnju'eɪʃən] N Anspielung *f*
insipid [ɪn'sɪpɪd] ADJ fad(e); (*person*) geistlos; (*colour*) langweilig
insist [ɪn'sɪst] VI bestehen; **to ~ on** bestehen auf *+dat*; **to ~ that** darauf bestehen, dass; (*claim*) behaupten, dass
insistence [ɪn'sɪstəns] N (*determination*) Bestehen *nt*
insistent [ɪn'sɪstənt] ADJ (*determined*) hartnäckig; (*continual*) andauernd, penetrant (*pej*)
in so far as ADV insofern als
insole ['ɪnsəul] N Einlegesohle *f*
insolence ['ɪnsələns] N Frechheit *f*, Unverschämtheit *f*
insolent ['ɪnsələnt] ADJ frech, unverschämt
insoluble [ɪn'sɔljubl] ADJ unlösbar
insolvency [ɪn'sɔlvənsɪ] N Zahlungsunfähigkeit *f*
insolvent [ɪn'sɔlvənt] ADJ zahlungsunfähig
insomnia [ɪn'sɔmnɪə] N Schlaflosigkeit *f*
insomniac [ɪn'sɔmnɪæk] N: **to be an ~** an Schlaflosigkeit leiden
inspect [ɪn'spɛkt] VT kontrollieren; (*examine*) prüfen; (*troops*) inspizieren
inspection [ɪn'spɛkʃən] N Kontrolle *f*; Prüfung *f*; Inspektion *f*
inspector [ɪn'spɛktəʳ] N Inspektor(in) *m(f)*; (BRIT: *on buses, trains*) Kontrolleur(in) *m(f)*; (*: Police*) Kommissar(in) *m(f)*
inspiration [ɪnspə'reɪʃən] N Inspiration *f*; (*idea*) Eingebung *f*
inspire [ɪn'spaɪəʳ] VT inspirieren; (*confidence, hope etc*) (er)wecken
inspired [ɪn'spaɪəd] ADJ genial; **in an ~ moment** in einem Augenblick der Inspiration
inspiring [ɪn'spaɪərɪŋ] ADJ inspirierend
inst. (BRIT) ABBR (*Comm*) = **instant**; **of the 16th inst.** vom 16. d. M.
instability [ɪnstə'bɪlɪtɪ] N Instabilität *f*; (*of person*) Labilität *f*
install [ɪn'stɔ:l] VT installieren; (*telephone*) anschließen; (*official*) einsetzen; **to ~ o.s.** sich niederlassen
installation [ɪnstə'leɪʃən] N Installation *f*; (*of telephone*) Anschluss *m*; (*Industry, Mil: plant*) Anlage *f*
installment plan (*US*) N Ratenzahlung *f*
instalment, (*US*) **installment** [ɪn'stɔ:lmənt] N Rate *f*; (*of story*) Fortsetzung *f*; (*of TV serial etc*) (Sende)folge *f*; **in instalments** in Raten
instance ['ɪnstəns] N Beispiel *nt*; **for ~** zum Beispiel; **in that ~** in diesem Fall; **in many instances** in vielen Fällen; **in the first ~** zuerst *or* zunächst (einmal)
instant ['ɪnstənt] N Augenblick *m* ▶ ADJ (*reaction*) unmittelbar; (*success*) sofortig; **~ food** Schnellgerichte *pl*; **~ coffee** Instantkaffee *m*; **the 10th ~** (*Comm, Admin*) der 10. dieses Monats
instantaneous [ɪnstən'teɪnɪəs] ADJ unmittelbar
instantly ['ɪnstəntlɪ] ADV sofort
instant message N Sofortnachricht *f*
instant messaging [-'mɛsɪdʒɪŋ] N Instant Messaging *nt*
instant replay N (TV) Wiederholung *f*
instead [ɪn'stɛd] ADV stattdessen; **~ of** statt *+gen*; **~ of sb** an jds Stelle *dat*; **~ of doing sth** anstatt *or* anstelle etw zu tun
instep ['ɪnstɛp] N (*of foot*) Spann *m*; (*of shoe*) Blatt *nt*
instigate ['ɪnstɪgeɪt] VT anstiften, anzetteln; (*talks etc*) initiieren
instigation [ɪnstɪ'geɪʃən] N Anstiftung *f*, Anzettelung *f*; Initiierung *f*; **at sb's ~** auf jds Betreiben *acc*
instil [ɪn'stɪl] VT: **to ~ sth into sb** (*confidence, fear etc*) jdm etw einflößen
instinct ['ɪnstɪŋkt] N Instinkt *m*; (*reaction, inclination*) instinktive Reaktion *f*
instinctive [ɪn'stɪŋktɪv] ADJ instinktiv
instinctively [ɪn'stɪŋktɪvlɪ] ADV instinktiv

institute [ˈɪnstɪtjuːt] N Institut *nt*; (*for teaching*) Hochschule *f*; (*professional body*) Bund *m*, Verband *m* ▶ VT einführen; (*inquiry, course of action*) einleiten; (*proceedings*) anstrengen
institution [ɪnstɪˈtjuːʃən] N Einführung *f*; (*organization*) Institution *f*, Einrichtung *f*; (*hospital, mental home*) Anstalt *f*, Heim *nt*
institutional [ɪnstɪˈtjuːʃənl] ADJ (*education*) institutionell; (*value, quality etc*) institutionalisiert; **~ care** Unterbringung *f* in einem Heim *or* einer Anstalt; **to be in ~ care** in einem Heim *or* einer Anstalt sein
instruct [ɪnˈstrʌkt] VT: **to ~ sb in sth** jdn in etw *dat* unterrichten; **to ~ sb to do sth** jdn anweisen, etw zu tun
instruction [ɪnˈstrʌkʃən] N Unterricht *m*; **instructions** NPL (*orders*) Anweisungen *pl*; **instructions (for use)** Gebrauchsanweisung *f*, Gebrauchsanleitung *f*; **~ book/manual/leaflet** *etc* Bedienungsanleitung *f*
instructive [ɪnˈstrʌktɪv] ADJ lehrreich; (*response*) aufschlussreich
instructor [ɪnˈstrʌktəʳ] N Lehrer(in) *m(f)*
instrument [ˈɪnstrumənt] N Instrument *nt*; (*Mus*) (Musik)instrument *nt*
instrumental [ɪnstruˈmɛntl] ADJ (*Mus: music, accompaniment*) Instrumental-; **to be ~ in** eine bedeutende Rolle spielen bei
instrumentalist [ɪnstruˈmɛntəlɪst] N Instrumentalist(in) *m(f)*
instrument panel N Armaturenbrett *nt*
insubordination [ɪnsəbɔːdɪˈneɪʃən] N Gehorsamsverweigerung *f*
insufferable [ɪnˈsʌfrəbl] ADJ unerträglich
insufficient [ɪnsəˈfɪʃənt] ADJ unzureichend
insufficiently [ɪnsəˈfɪʃəntlɪ] ADV unzureichend
insular [ˈɪnsjuləʳ] ADJ engstirnig
insulate [ˈɪnsjuleɪt] VT isolieren; (*person, group*) abschirmen
insulating tape [ˈɪnsjuleɪtɪŋ-] N Isolierband *nt*
insulation [ɪnsjuˈleɪʃən] N Isolierung *f*; Abschirmung *f*
insulator [ˈɪnsjuleɪtəʳ] N Isolierstoff *m*
insulin [ˈɪnsjulɪn] N Insulin *nt*
insult N [ˈɪnsʌlt] Beleidigung *f* ▶ VT [ɪnˈsʌlt] beleidigen
insulting [ɪnˈsʌltɪŋ] ADJ beleidigend
insuperable [ɪnˈsjuːprəbl] ADJ unüberwindlich
insurance [ɪnˈʃuərəns] N Versicherung *f*; **fire/life ~** Brand-/Lebensversicherung *f*; **to take out ~ (against)** eine Versicherung abschließen (gegen)
insurance agent N Versicherungsvertreter(in) *m(f)*
insurance broker N Versicherungsmakler(in) *m(f)*
insurance policy N Versicherungspolice *f*
insurance premium N Versicherungsprämie *f*
insure [ɪnˈʃuəʳ] VT versichern; **to ~ o.s./sth against sth** sich/etw gegen etw versichern; **to ~ o.s.** *or* **one's life** eine Lebensversicherung abschließen; **to ~ (o.s.) against sth** (*fig*) sich gegen etw absichern; **to be insured for £5,000** für £5000 versichert sein
insured [ɪnˈʃuəd] N: **the ~** der/die Versicherte
insurer [ɪnˈʃuərəʳ] N Versicherer *m*
insurgent [ɪnˈsəːdʒənt] ADJ aufständisch ▶ N Aufständische(r) *f(m)*
insurmountable [ɪnsəˈmauntəbl] ADJ unüberwindlich
insurrection [ɪnsəˈrɛkʃən] N Aufstand *m*
intact [ɪnˈtækt] ADJ intakt; (*whole*) ganz; (*unharmed*) unversehrt
intake [ˈɪnteɪk] N (*of food*) Aufnahme *f*; (*of air*) Zufuhr *f*; (BRIT *Scol*): **an ~ of 200 a year** 200 neue Schüler pro Jahr
intangible [ɪnˈtændʒɪbl] ADJ unbestimmbar; (*idea*) vage; (*benefit*) immateriell
integer [ˈɪntɪdʒəʳ] N (*Math*) ganze Zahl *f*
integral [ˈɪntɪgrəl] ADJ wesentlich
integrate [ˈɪntɪgreɪt] VT integrieren ▶ VI sich integrieren
integrated circuit [ˈɪntɪgreɪtɪd-] N (*Comput*) integrierter Schaltkreis *m*
integration [ɪntɪˈgreɪʃən] N Integration *f*; **racial ~** Rassenintegration *f*
integrity [ɪnˈtɛgrɪtɪ] N Integrität *f*; (*of group*) Einheit *f*; (*of culture, text*) Unversehrtheit *f*
intellect [ˈɪntəlɛkt] N Intellekt *m*
intellectual [ɪntəˈlɛktjuəl] ADJ intellektuell, geistig ▶ N Intellektuelle(r) *f(m)*
intelligence [ɪnˈtɛlɪdʒəns] N Intelligenz *f*; (*information*) Informationen *pl*
intelligence quotient N Intelligenzquotient *m*
intelligence service N Nachrichtendienst *m*, Geheimdienst *m*
intelligence test N Intelligenztest *m*
intelligent [ɪnˈtɛlɪdʒənt] ADJ intelligent; (*decision*) klug
intelligently [ɪnˈtɛlɪdʒəntlɪ] ADV intelligent
intelligentsia [ɪntɛlɪˈdʒɛntsɪə] N: **the ~** die Intelligenz
intelligible [ɪnˈtɛlɪdʒɪbl] ADJ verständlich
intemperate [ɪnˈtɛmpərət] ADJ unmäßig; (*remark*) überzogen
intend [ɪnˈtɛnd] VT: **to be intended for sb** für jdn gedacht sein; **to ~ to do sth** beabsichtigen, etw zu tun
intended [ɪnˈtɛndɪd] ADJ (*effect, victim*) beabsichtigt; (*journey*) geplant; (*insult*) absichtlich
intense [ɪnˈtɛns] ADJ intensiv; (*anger, joy*) äußerst groß; (*person*) ernsthaft
intensely [ɪnˈtɛnslɪ] ADV äußerst; **I dislike him ~** ich verabscheue ihn
intensify [ɪnˈtɛnsɪfaɪ] VT intensivieren, verstärken
intensity [ɪnˈtɛnsɪtɪ] N Intensität *f*; (*of anger*) Heftigkeit *f*
intensive [ɪnˈtɛnsɪv] ADJ intensiv
intensive care N: **to be in ~** auf der Intensivstation sein
intensive care unit N Intensivstation *f*
intent [ɪnˈtɛnt] N Absicht *f* ▶ ADJ (*attentive*) aufmerksam; (*absorbed*): **~ (on)** versunken (in

i

+acc); **to all intents and purposes** im Grunde; **to be ~ on doing sth** entschlossen sein, etw zu tun
intention [ɪnˈtɛnʃən] N Absicht *f*
intentional [ɪnˈtɛnʃənl] ADJ absichtlich
intentionally [ɪnˈtɛnʃnəlɪ] ADV absichtlich
intently [ɪnˈtɛntlɪ] ADV konzentriert
inter [ɪnˈtəːʳ] VT bestatten
interact [ɪntərˈækt] VI (*people*) interagieren; (*things*) aufeinander einwirken; (*ideas*) sich gegenseitig beeinflussen; **to ~ with** interagieren mit; einwirken auf *+acc*; beeinflussen
interaction [ɪntərˈækʃən] N Interaktion *f*; gegenseitige Einwirkung *f*; gegenseitige Beeinflussung *f*
interactive [ɪntərˈæktɪv] ADJ (*also Comput*) interaktiv
intercede [ɪntəˈsiːd] VI: **to ~ (with sb/on behalf of sb)** sich (bei jdm/für jdn) einsetzen
intercept [ɪntəˈsɛpt] VT abfangen
interception [ɪntəˈsɛpʃən] N Abfangen *nt*
interchange [ˈɪntətʃeɪndʒ] N Austausch *m*; (*on motorway*) (Autobahn)kreuz *nt*
interchangeable [ɪntəˈtʃeɪndʒəbl] ADJ austauschbar
intercity [ɪntəˈsɪtɪ] ADJ: **~ train** Intercityzug *m*
intercom [ˈɪntəkɔm] N (Gegen)sprechanlage *f*
interconnect [ɪntəkəˈnɛkt] VI (*rooms*) miteinander verbunden sein
intercontinental [ˈɪntəkɔntɪˈnɛntl] ADJ (*flight, missile*) Interkontinental-
intercourse [ˈɪntəkɔːs] N (*sexual*) (Geschlechts)verkehr *m*; (*social, verbal*) Verkehr *m*
intercultural [ɪntəˈkʌltʃərəl] ADJ interkulturell
interdependence [ɪntədɪˈpɛndəns] N gegenseitige Abhängigkeit *f*
interdependent [ɪntədɪˈpɛndənt] ADJ voneinander abhängig
interest [ˈɪntrɪst] N Interesse *nt*; (*Comm: in company*) Anteil *m*; (*: sum of money*) Zinsen *pl* ▶ VT interessieren; **compound ~** Zinseszins *m*; **simple ~** einfache Zinsen; **British interests in the Middle East** britische Interessen im Nahen Osten; **his main ~ is …** er interessiert sich hauptsächlich für …
interested [ˈɪntrɪstɪd] ADJ interessiert; (*party, body etc*) beteiligt; **to be ~ in sth** sich für etw interessieren; **to be ~ in doing sth** daran interessiert sein, etw zu tun
interest-free [ˈɪntrɪstˈfriː] ADJ, ADV zinslos
interesting [ˈɪntrɪstɪŋ] ADJ interessant
interest rate N Zinssatz *m*
interface [ˈɪntəfeɪs] N Verbindung *f*; (*Comput*) Schnittstelle *f*
interfere [ɪntəˈfɪəʳ] VI: **to ~ in** sich einmischen in *+acc*; **to ~ with** (*object*) sich zu schaffen machen an *+dat*; (*plans*) durchkreuzen; (*career, duty, decision*) beeinträchtigen; **don't ~** misch dich nicht ein
interference [ɪntəˈfɪərəns] N Einmischung *f*; (*Radio, TV*) Störung *f*
interfering [ɪntəˈfɪərɪŋ] ADJ (*person*) sich ständig einmischend
interim [ˈɪntərɪm] ADJ (*agreement, government etc*) Übergangs- ▶ N: **in the ~** in der Zwischenzeit
interim dividend N (*Comm*) Abschlagsdividende *f*
interior [ɪnˈtɪərɪəʳ] N Innere(s) *nt*; (*decor etc*) Innenausstattung *f* ▶ ADJ Innen-
interior decorator N Innenausstatter(in) *m(f)*
interior designer N Innenarchitekt(in) *m(f)*
interjection [ɪntəˈdʒɛkʃən] N Einwurf *m*; (*Ling*) Interjektion *f*
interlock [ɪntəˈlɔk] VI ineinandergreifen
interloper [ˈɪntələupəʳ] N Eindringling *m*
interlude [ˈɪntəluːd] N Unterbrechung *f*, Pause *f*; (*Theat*) Zwischenspiel *nt*
intermarry [ɪntəˈmærɪ] VI untereinander heiraten
intermediary [ɪntəˈmiːdɪərɪ] N Vermittler(in) *m(f)*
intermediate [ɪntəˈmiːdɪət] ADJ (*stage*) Zwischen-; **an ~ student** ein fortgeschrittener Anfänger
interment [ɪnˈtəːmənt] N Bestattung *f*
interminable [ɪnˈtəːmɪnəbl] ADJ endlos
intermission [ɪntəˈmɪʃən] N Pause *f*
intermittent [ɪntəˈmɪtnt] ADJ (*noise*) periodisch auftretend; (*publication*) in unregelmäßigen Abständen veröffentlicht
intermittently [ɪntəˈmɪtntlɪ] ADV periodisch; in unregelmäßigen Abständen
intern VT [ɪnˈtəːn] internieren ▶ N [ˈɪntəːn] (*US*) Assistenzarzt *m*, Assistenzärztin *f*
internal [ɪnˈtəːnl] ADJ innere(r, s); (*pipes*) im Haus; (*politics*) Innen-; (*dispute, reform, memo, structure etc*) intern
internally [ɪnˈtəːnəlɪ] ADV: **"not to be taken ~"** „nicht zum Einnehmen"
Internal Revenue Service (*US*) N ≈ Finanzamt *nt*
international [ɪntəˈnæʃənl] ADJ international ▶ N (*BRIT Sport*) Länderspiel *nt*
International Atomic Energy Agency N *Internationale Atomenergiebehörde*
International Chamber of Commerce N Internationale Handelskammer *f*
International Court of Justice N Internationaler Gerichtshof *m*
international date line N Datumsgrenze *f*
International Labour Organization N Internationale Arbeitsorganisation *f*
internationally [ɪntəˈnæʃnəlɪ] ADV international
International Monetary Fund N Internationaler Währungsfonds *m*
international relations NPL zwischenstaatliche Beziehungen *pl*
internecine [ɪntəˈniːsaɪn] ADJ mörderisch; (*war*) Vernichtungs-
internee [ɪntəːˈniː] N Internierte(r) *f(m)*
Internet [ˈɪntənɛt] N Internet *nt*
Internet access N Internetzugang *m*
Internet auction N Internetauktion *f*

Internet banking N Onlinebanking *nt*
Internet café N Internetcafé *nt*
Internet connection N Internetanschluss *m*
Internet provider N Internetprovider *m*
internment [ɪn'tə:nmənt] N Internierung *f*
interplay ['ɪntəpleɪ] N: **~ (of** *or* **between)** Zusammenspiel *nt* (von)
Interpol ['ɪntəpɔl] N Interpol *f*
interpret [ɪn'tə:prɪt] VT auslegen, interpretieren; (*translate*) dolmetschen ▸ VI dolmetschen
interpretation [ɪntə:prɪ'teɪʃən] N Auslegung *f*, Interpretation *f*; Dolmetschen *nt*
interpreter [ɪn'tə:prɪtə^r] N Dolmetscher(in) *m(f)*
interpreting [ɪn'tə:prɪtɪŋ] N Dolmetschen *nt*
interrelated [ɪntərɪ'leɪtɪd] ADJ zusammenhängend
interrogate [ɪn'tɛrəugeɪt] VT verhören; (*witness*) vernehmen
interrogation [ɪntɛrəu'geɪʃən] N Verhör *nt*; Vernehmung *f*
interrogative [ɪntə'rɔgətɪv] ADJ (*Ling: pronoun*) Interrogativ-, Frage-
interrogator [ɪn'tɛrəgeɪtə^r] N (*Police*) Vernehmungsbeamte(r) *m*; **the hostage's ~** derjenige, der die Geisel verhörte
interrupt [ɪntə'rʌpt] VT, VI unterbrechen
interruption [ɪntə'rʌpʃən] N Unterbrechung *f*
intersect [ɪntə'sɛkt] VI sich kreuzen ▸ VT durchziehen; (*Math*) schneiden
intersection [ɪntə'sɛkʃən] N Kreuzung *f*; (*Math*) Schnittpunkt *m*
intersperse [ɪntə'spə:s] VT: **to be interspersed with** durchsetzt sein mit; **he interspersed his lecture with …** er spickte seine Rede mit …
intertwine [ɪntə'twaɪn] VI sich ineinander verschlingen
interval ['ɪntəvl] N Pause *f*; (*Mus*) Intervall *nt*; **bright intervals** (*in weather*) Aufheiterungen *pl*; **at intervals** in Abständen
intervene [ɪntə'vi:n] VI eingreifen; (*event*) dazwischenkommen; (*time*) dazwischenliegen
intervening [ɪntə'vi:nɪŋ] ADJ (*period, years*) dazwischenliegend
intervention [ɪntə'vɛnʃən] N Eingreifen *nt*
interview ['ɪntəvju:] N (*for job*) Vorstellungsgespräch *nt*; (*for place at college etc*) Auswahlgespräch *nt*; (*Radio, TV etc*) Interview *nt* ▸ VT ein Vorstellungsgespräch/ Auswahlgespräch führen mit; interviewen
interviewee [ɪntəvju'i:] N (*for job*) Stellenbewerber(in) *m(f)*; (*TV etc*) Interviewgast *m*
interviewer ['ɪntəvjuə^r] N Leiter(in) *m(f)* des Vorstellungsgesprächs/Auswahlgesprächs; (*Radio, TV etc*) Interviewer(in) *m(f)*
intestate [ɪn'tɛsteɪt] ADV: **to die ~** ohne Testament sterben
intestinal [ɪn'tɛstɪnl] ADJ (*infection etc*) Darm-
intestine [ɪn'tɛstɪn] N Darm *m*
intimacy ['ɪntɪməsɪ] N Vertrautheit *f*
intimate ADJ ['ɪntɪmət] eng; (*sexual, also restaurant, dinner, atmosphere*) intim; (*conversation, matter, detail*) vertraulich; (*knowledge*) gründlich ▸ VT ['ɪntɪmeɪt] andeuten; (*make known*) zu verstehen geben
intimately ['ɪntɪmətlɪ] ADV eng; intim; vertraulich; gründlich
intimation [ɪntɪ'meɪʃən] N Andeutung *f*
intimidate [ɪn'tɪmɪdeɪt] VT einschüchtern
intimidation [ɪntɪmɪ'deɪʃən] N Einschüchterung *f*

KEYWORD

into ['ɪntu] PREP **1** (*indicating motion or direction*) in *+acc*; **to go into town** in die Stadt gehen; **he worked late into the night** er arbeitete bis spät in die Nacht; **the car bumped into the wall** der Wagen fuhr gegen die Mauer
2 (*indicating change of condition, result*): **it broke into pieces** es zerbrach in Stücke; **she translated into English** sie übersetzte ins Englische; **to change pounds into dollars** Pfund in Dollar wechseln; **5 into 25** 25 durch 5

intolerable [ɪn'tɔlərəbl] ADJ unerträglich
intolerance [ɪn'tɔlərns] N Intoleranz *f*
intolerant [ɪn'tɔlərnt] ADJ: **~ (of)** intolerant (gegenüber)
intonation [ɪntəu'neɪʃən] N Intonation *f*
intoxicated [ɪn'tɔksɪkeɪtɪd] ADJ betrunken; (*fig*) berauscht
intoxication [ɪntɔksɪ'keɪʃən] N (Be)trunkenheit *f*; (*fig*) Rausch *m*
intractable [ɪn'træktəbl] ADJ hartnäckig; (*child*) widerspenstig; (*temper*) unbeugsam
intranet ['ɪntrənɛt] N (*Comput*) Intranet *nt*
intransigence [ɪn'trænsɪdʒəns] N Unnachgiebigkeit *f*
intransigent [ɪn'trænsɪdʒənt] ADJ unnachgiebig
intransitive [ɪn'trænsɪtɪv] ADJ (*Ling*) intransitiv
intrauterine device ['ɪntrə'ju:təraɪn-] N (*Med*) Intrauterinpessar *nt*, Spirale *f* (*inf*)
intravenous [ɪntrə'vi:nəs] ADJ intravenös
in-tray ['ɪntreɪ] N Ablage *f* für Eingänge
intrepid [ɪn'trɛpɪd] ADJ unerschrocken
intricacy ['ɪntrɪkəsɪ] N Kompliziertheit *f*
intricate ['ɪntrɪkət] ADJ kompliziert
intrigue [ɪn'tri:g] N Intrigen *pl* ▸ VT faszinieren
intriguing [ɪn'tri:gɪŋ] ADJ faszinierend
intrinsic [ɪn'trɪnsɪk] ADJ wesentlich
introduce [ɪntrə'dju:s] VT (*sth new*) einführen; (*speaker, TV show etc*) ankündigen; **to ~ sb (to sb)** jdn (jdm) vorstellen; **to ~ sb to** (*pastime, technique*) jdn einführen in *+acc*; **may I ~ …?** darf ich … vorstellen?
introduction [ɪntrə'dʌkʃən] N Einführung *f*; (*of person*) Vorstellung *f*; (*to book*) Einleitung *f*; **a letter of ~** ein Einführungsschreiben *nt*
introductory [ɪntrə'dʌktərɪ] ADJ Einführungs-; **~ remarks** einführende Bemerkungen *pl*; **~ offer** Einführungsangebot *nt*
introspection [ɪntrəu'spɛkʃən] N Selbstbeobachtung *f*, Introspektion *f*
introspective [ɪntrəu'spɛktɪv] ADJ in sich gekehrt

i

introvert [ˈɪntrəuvəːt] N Introvertierte(r) *f(m)* ▸ ADJ (*also*: **introverted**) introvertiert
intrude [ɪnˈtruːd] VI eindringen; **to ~ on** stören; (*conversation*) sich einmischen in *+acc*; **am I intruding?** störe ich?
intruder [ɪnˈtruːdəʳ] N Eindringling *m*
intrusion [ɪnˈtruːʒən] N Eindringen *nt*
intrusive [ɪnˈtruːsɪv] ADJ aufdringlich
intuition [ɪntjuːˈɪʃən] N Intuition *f*
intuitive [ɪnˈtjuːɪtɪv] ADJ intuitiv; (*feeling*) instinktiv
inundate [ˈɪnʌndeɪt] VT: **to ~ with** überschwemmen mit
inure [ɪnˈjuəʳ] VT: **to ~ o.s. to** sich gewöhnen an *+acc*
invade [ɪnˈveɪd] VT einfallen in *+acc*; (*fig*) heimsuchen
invader [ɪnˈveɪdəʳ] N Invasor *m*
invalid N [ˈɪnvəlɪd] Kranke(r) *f(m)*; (*disabled*) Invalide *m* ▸ ADJ [ɪnˈvælɪd] ungültig
invalidate [ɪnˈvælɪdeɪt] VT entkräften; (*law, marriage, election*) ungültig machen
invaluable [ɪnˈvæljuəbl] ADJ unschätzbar
invariable [ɪnˈvɛərɪəbl] ADJ unveränderlich
invariably [ɪnˈvɛərɪəblɪ] ADV ständig, unweigerlich; **she is ~ late** sie kommt immer zu spät
invasion [ɪnˈveɪʒən] N Invasion *f*; **an ~ of privacy** ein Eingriff *m* in die Privatsphäre
invective [ɪnˈvɛktɪv] N Beschimpfungen *pl*
inveigle [ɪnˈviːgl] VT: **to ~ sb into sth/doing sth** jdn zu etw verleiten/dazu verleiten, etw zu tun
invent [ɪnˈvɛnt] VT erfinden
invention [ɪnˈvɛnʃən] N Erfindung *f*
inventive [ɪnˈvɛntɪv] ADJ erfinderisch
inventiveness [ɪnˈvɛntɪvnɪs] N Einfallsreichtum *m*
inventor [ɪnˈvɛntəʳ] N Erfinder(in) *m(f)*
inventory [ˈɪnvəntrɪ] N Inventar *nt*
inventory control N (*Comm*) Bestandskontrolle *f*
inverse [ɪnˈvəːs] ADJ umgekehrt; **in ~ proportion (to)** im umgekehrten Verhältnis (zu)
invert [ɪnˈvəːt] VT umdrehen
invertebrate [ɪnˈvəːtɪbrət] N wirbelloses Tier *nt*
inverted commas [ɪnˈvəːtɪd-] (BRIT) NPL Anführungszeichen *pl*
invest [ɪnˈvɛst] VT investieren ▸ VI: **~ in** investieren in *+acc*; (*fig*) sich *dat* anschaffen; **to ~ sb with sth** jdm etw verleihen
investigate [ɪnˈvɛstɪgeɪt] VT untersuchen
investigation [ɪnvɛstɪˈgeɪʃən] N Untersuchung *f*
investigative [ɪnˈvɛstɪgətɪv] ADJ: **~ journalism** Enthüllungsjournalismus *m*
investigator [ɪnˈvɛstɪgeɪtəʳ] N Ermittler(in) *m(f)*; **private ~** Privatdetektiv(in) *m(f)*
investiture [ɪnˈvɛstɪtʃəʳ] N (*of chancellor*) Amtseinführung *f*; (*of prince*) Investitur *f*
investment [ɪnˈvɛstmənt] N Investition *f*
investment income N Kapitalerträge *pl*
investment trust N Investmenttrust *m*
investor [ɪnˈvɛstəʳ] N (Kapital)anleger(in) *m(f)*
inveterate [ɪnˈvɛtərət] ADJ unverbesserlich
invidious [ɪnˈvɪdɪəs] ADJ (*task, job*) unangenehm; (*comparison, decision*) ungerecht
invigilator [ɪnˈvɪdʒɪleɪtəʳ] N Aufsicht *f*
invigorating [ɪnˈvɪgəreɪtɪŋ] ADJ belebend; (*experience etc*) anregend
invincible [ɪnˈvɪnsɪbl] ADJ unbesiegbar; (*belief, conviction*) unerschütterlich
inviolate [ɪnˈvaɪələt] ADJ sicher; (*truth*) unantastbar
invisible [ɪnˈvɪzɪbl] ADJ unsichtbar
invisible mending N Kunststopfen *nt*
invitation [ɪnvɪˈteɪʃən] N Einladung *f*; **by ~ only** nur auf Einladung; **at sb's ~** auf jds Aufforderung *acc* (hin)
invite [ɪnˈvaɪt] VT einladen; (*discussion*) auffordern zu; (*criticism*) herausfordern; **to ~ sb to do sth** jdn auffordern, etw zu tun; **to ~ sb to dinner** jdn zum Abendessen einladen
▸ **invite out** VT einladen
inviting [ɪnˈvaɪtɪŋ] ADJ einladend; (*desirable*) verlockend
invoice [ˈɪnvɔɪs] N Rechnung *f* ▸ VT in Rechnung stellen; **to ~ sb for goods** jdm für Waren eine Rechnung ausstellen
invoke [ɪnˈvəuk] VT anrufen; (*feelings, memories etc*) heraufbeschwören
involuntary [ɪnˈvɔləntrɪ] ADJ unbeabsichtigt; (*reflex*) unwillkürlich
involve [ɪnˈvɔlv] VT (*person*) beteiligen; (*thing*) verbunden sein mit; (*concern, affect*) betreffen; **to ~ sb in sth** jdn in etw *acc* verwickeln
involved [ɪnˈvɔlvd] ADJ kompliziert; **the work/problems ~** die damit verbundene Arbeit/verbundenen Schwierigkeiten; **to be ~ in** beteiligt sein an *+dat*; (*be engrossed*) engagiert sein in *+dat*; **to become ~ with sb** Umgang mit jdm haben; (*emotionally*) mit jdm eine Beziehung anfangen
involvement [ɪnˈvɔlvmənt] N Engagement *nt*; (*participation*) Beteiligung *f*
invulnerable [ɪnˈvʌlnərəbl] ADJ unverwundbar; (*ship, building etc*) uneinnehmbar
inward [ˈɪnwəd] ADJ innerste(r, s); (*movement*) nach innen ▸ ADV nach innen
inwardly [ˈɪnwədlɪ] ADV innerlich
inwards [ˈɪnwədz] ADV nach innen
I/O ABBR (*Comput*: = *input/output*) E/A
IOC N ABBR (= *International Olympic Committee*) IOC *nt*, IOK *nt*
iodine [ˈaɪəudiːn] N Jod *nt*
IOM (BRIT) ABBR (*Post*) = **Isle of Man**
ion [ˈaɪən] N Ion *nt*
Ionian Sea [aɪˈəunɪən-] N: **the ~** das Ionische Meer
ionizer [ˈaɪənaɪzəʳ] N Ionisator *m*
iota [aɪˈəutə] N Jota *nt*
IOU N ABBR (= *I owe you*) Schuldschein *m*
IOW (BRIT) ABBR (*Post*) = **Isle of Wight**
IP ABBR (*Comput*: = *Internet Protocol*) IP
IPA N ABBR (= *International Phonetic Alphabet*) internationale Lautschrift *f*

iPad® ['aɪpæd] N iPad® *nt*; I-Pad *nt*
iPhone® ['aɪfəʊn] N iPhone® *nt*; I-Phone *nt*
iPod® ['aɪpɔd] N iPod® *m*
IQ N ABBR (= *intelligence quotient*) IQ *m*
IRA N ABBR (= *Irish Republican Army*) IRA *f*; (US: = *individual retirement account*) *privates Rentensparkonto*
Iran [ɪ'rɑ:n] N (der) Iran
Iranian [ɪ'reɪnɪən] ADJ iranisch ▸ N Iraner(in) *m(f)*; (*Ling*) Iranisch *nt*
Iraq [ɪ'rɑ:k] N (der) Irak
Iraqi [ɪ'rɑ:kɪ] ADJ irakisch ▸ N Iraker(in) *m(f)*
irascible [ɪ'ræsɪbl] ADJ jähzornig
irate [aɪ'reɪt] ADJ zornig
Ireland ['aɪələnd] N Irland *nt*; **the Republic of ~** die Republik Irland
iris ['aɪrɪs] (*pl* **irises**) N (*Anat*) Iris *f*, Regenbogenhaut *f*; (*Bot*) Iris, Schwertlilie *f*
Irish ['aɪrɪʃ] ADJ irisch ▸ NPL: **the ~** die Iren *pl*, die Irländer *pl*
Irishman ['aɪrɪʃmən] N (*irreg*) Ire *m*, Irländer *m*
Irish Sea N: **the ~** die Irische See
Irishwoman ['aɪrɪʃwumən] N (*irreg*) Irin *f*, Irländerin *f*
irk [ə:k] VT ärgern
irksome ['ə:ksəm] ADJ lästig
IRN N ABBR (= *Independent Radio News*) *Nachrichtendienst des kommerziellen Rundfunks*
iron ['aɪən] N Eisen *nt*; (*for clothes*) Bügeleisen *nt* ▸ CPD Eisen-; (*will, discipline etc*) eisern ▸ VT bügeln
▸ **iron out** VT (*fig*) aus dem Weg räumen
Iron Curtain N: **the ~** der Eiserne Vorhang
ironic [aɪ'rɔnɪk], **ironical** [aɪ'rɔnɪkl] ADJ ironisch; (*situation*) paradox, witzig
ironically [aɪ'rɔnɪklɪ] ADV ironisch; **~, the intelligence chief was the last to find out** witzigerweise war der Geheimdienstchef der Letzte, der es erfuhr
ironing ['aɪənɪŋ] N Bügeln *nt*; (*clothes*) Bügelwäsche *f*
ironing board N Bügelbrett *nt*
iron lung N (*Med*) eiserne Lunge *f*
ironmonger ['aɪənmʌŋgə^r] (BRIT) N Eisen- und Haushaltswarenhändler(in) *m(f)*
ironmonger's ['aɪənmʌŋgəz], **ironmonger's shop** (BRIT) N Eisen- und Haushaltswarenhandlung *f*
iron ore N Eisenerz *nt*
irons ['aɪəns] NPL Hand- und Fußschellen *pl*; **to clap sb in ~** jdn in Eisen legen
irony ['aɪrənɪ] N Ironie *f*; **the ~ of it is that …** das Ironische daran ist, dass …
irrational [ɪ'ræʃənl] ADJ irrational
irreconcilable [ɪrɛkən'saɪləbl] ADJ unvereinbar
irredeemable [ɪrɪ'di:məbl] ADJ (*Comm*) nicht einlösbar; (*loan*) unkündbar; (*fault, character*) unverbesserlich
irrefutable [ɪrɪ'fju:təbl] ADJ unwiderlegbar
irregular [ɪ'rɛgjulə^r] ADJ unregelmäßig; (*surface*) uneben; (*behaviour*) ungehörig
irregularity [ɪrɛgju'lærɪtɪ] N Unregelmäßigkeit *f*; Unebenheit *f*; Ungehörigkeit *f*
irrelevance [ɪ'rɛləvəns] N Irrelevanz *f*
irrelevant [ɪ'rɛləvənt] ADJ unwesentlich, irrelevant
irreligious [ɪrɪ'lɪdʒəs] ADJ unreligiös
irreparable [ɪ'rɛprəbl] ADJ nicht wiedergutzumachen
irreplaceable [ɪrɪ'pleɪsəbl] ADJ unersetzlich
irrepressible [ɪrɪ'prɛsəbl] ADJ (*good humour*) unerschütterlich; (*enthusiasm etc*) unbändig; (*person*) nicht unterzukriegen
irreproachable [ɪrɪ'prəutʃəbl] ADJ untadelig
irresistible [ɪrɪ'zɪstɪbl] ADJ unwiderstehlich
irresolute [ɪ'rɛzəlu:t] ADJ unentschlossen
irrespective [ɪrɪ'spɛktɪv]: **~ of** *prep* ungeachtet *+gen*
irresponsible [ɪrɪ'spɔnsɪbl] ADJ verantwortungslos; (*action*) unverantwortlich
irretrievable [ɪrɪ'tri:vəbl] ADJ (*object*) nicht mehr wiederzubekommen; (*loss*) unersetzlich; (*damage*) nicht wiedergutzumachen
irreverent [ɪ'rɛvərnt] ADJ respektlos
irrevocable [ɪ'rɛvəkəbl] ADJ unwiderruflich
irrigate ['ɪrɪgeɪt] VT bewässern
irrigation [ɪrɪ'geɪʃən] N Bewässerung *f*
irritable ['ɪrɪtəbl] ADJ reizbar
irritant ['ɪrɪtənt] N Reizerreger *m*; (*situation etc*) Ärgernis *nt*
irritate ['ɪrɪteɪt] VT ärgern, irritieren; (*Med*) reizen
irritating ['ɪrɪteɪtɪŋ] ADJ ärgerlich, irritierend; **he is ~** er kann einem auf die Nerven gehen
irritation [ɪrɪ'teɪʃən] N Ärger *m*; (*Med*) Reizung *f*; (*annoying thing*) Ärgernis *nt*
IRS (US) N ABBR (= *Internal Revenue Service*) *Steuereinzugsbehörde*
is [ɪz] VB *see* **be**
ISA ['aɪsə] (BRIT) N ABBR (= *individual savings account*) *steuerfreies Sparsystem mit begrenzter Einlagenhöhe*
ISBN N ABBR (= *International Standard Book Number*) ISBN *f*
ISDN N ABBR (= *Integrated Services Digital Network*) ISDN *nt*
Islam ['ɪzlɑ:m] N der Islam; (*Islamic countries*) die islamischen Länder *pl*
Islamic [ɪz'læmɪk] ADJ islamisch
island ['aɪlənd] N Insel *f*; (*also*: **traffic island**) Verkehrsinsel *f*
islander ['aɪləndə^r] N Inselbewohner(in) *m(f)*
isle [aɪl] N Insel *f*; (*in names*): **the I~ of Man** die Insel Man; **the I~ of Wight** die Insel Wight; **the British Isles** die Britischen Inseln
isn't ['ɪznt] = **is not**
isobar ['aɪsəubɑ:^r] N Isobare *f*
isolate ['aɪsəleɪt] VT isolieren
isolated ['aɪsəleɪtɪd] ADJ isoliert; (*place*) abgelegen; **~ incident** Einzelfall *m*
isolation [aɪsə'leɪʃən] N Isolierung *f*
isolationism [aɪsə'leɪʃənɪzəm] N Isolationismus *m*
isotope ['aɪsəutəup] N Isotop *nt*
ISP (*Comput*) N ABBR (= *Internet Service Provider*) Provider *m*
Israel ['ɪzreɪl] N Israel *nt*

Israeli [ɪz'reɪlɪ] ADJ israelisch ▸ N Israeli *mf*

issue ['ɪʃuː] N Frage *f*; (*subject*) Thema *nt*; (*problem*) Problem *nt*; (*of book, stamps etc*) Ausgabe *f*; (*offspring*) Nachkommenschaft *f* ▸ VT ausgeben; (*statement*) herausgeben; (*documents*) ausstellen ▸ VI: **to ~ (from)** dringen (aus); (*liquid*) austreten (aus); **the point at ~** der Punkt, um den es geht; **to avoid the ~** ausweichen; **to confuse** *or* **obscure the ~** es unnötig kompliziert machen; **to ~ sth to sb** *or* **~ sb with sth** jdm etw geben; (*documents*) jdm etw ausstellen; (*gun etc*) jdn mit etw ausstatten; **to take ~ with sb (over)** jdm widersprechen (in *+dat*); **to make an ~ of sth** etw aufbauschen

isthmus ['ɪsməs] N Landenge *f*, Isthmus *m*

IT N ABBR = **information technology**

KEYWORD

it [ɪt] PRON **1** (*specific: subject*) er/sie/es; (*: direct object*) ihn/sie/es; (*: indirect object*) ihm/ihr/ihm; **it's on the table** es ist auf dem Tisch; **I can't find it** ich kann es nicht finden; **give it to me** gib es mir; **about it** darüber; **from it** davon; **in it** darin; **of it** davon; **what did you learn from it?** was hast du daraus gelernt?; **I'm proud of it** ich bin stolz darauf
2 (*impersonal*) es; **it's raining** es regnet; **it's Friday tomorrow** morgen ist Freitag; **who is it? — it's me** wer ist da? — ich bins

ITA, (BRIT) **i.t.a.** N ABBR (= *initial teaching alphabet*) *Alphabet zum Lesenlernen*

Italian [ɪ'tæljən] ADJ italienisch ▸ N Italiener(in) *m(f)*; (*Ling*) Italienisch *nt*; **the Italians** die Italiener *pl*

italics [ɪ'tælɪks] NPL Kursivschrift *f*

Italy ['ɪtəlɪ] N Italien *nt*

ITC (BRIT) N ABBR (= *Independent Television Commission*) *Fernseh-Aufsichtsgremium*

itch [ɪtʃ] N Juckreiz *m* ▸ VI jucken; **I am itching all over** mich juckt es überall; **to ~ to do sth** darauf brennen, etw zu tun

itchy ['ɪtʃɪ] ADJ juckend; **my back is ~** mein Rücken juckt

it'd ['ɪtd] = **it would; it had**

item ['aɪtəm] N Punkt *m*; (*of collection*) Stück *nt*; (*also*: **news item**) Meldung *f*; (*: in newspaper*) Zeitungsnotiz *f*; **items of clothing** Kleidungsstücke *pl*

itemize ['aɪtəmaɪz] VT einzeln aufführen

itemized bill ['aɪtəmaɪzd-] N *Rechnung, auf der die Posten einzeln aufgeführt sind*

itinerant [ɪ'tɪnərənt] ADJ (*labourer, priest etc*) Wander-; (*salesman*) reisend

itinerary [aɪ'tɪnərərɪ] N Reiseroute *f*

it'll ['ɪtl] = **it will; it shall**

ITN (BRIT) N ABBR (*TV*: = *Independent Television News*) *Nachrichtendienst des kommerziellen Fernsehens*

its [ɪts] ADJ sein(e), ihr(e) ▸ PRON seine(r, s), ihre(r, s)

it's [ɪts] = **it is; it has**

itself [ɪt'sɛlf] PRON sich; (*emphatic*) selbst

ITV (BRIT) N ABBR (*TV*: = *Independent Television*) *kommerzieller Fernsehsender*

> **ITV** steht für „Independent Television" und ist ein landesweiter privater Fernsehsender in Großbritannien. Unter der Oberaufsicht einer unabhängigen Rundfunkbehörde produzieren Privatfirmen die Programme für die verschiedenen Sendegebiete. ITV, das seit 1955 Programme ausstrahlt, wird ganz durch Werbung finanziert und bietet etwa ein Drittel Informationssendungen (Nachrichten, Dokumentarfilme, Aktuelles) und ansonsten Unterhaltung (Sport, Komödien, Drama, Spielshows, Filme).

IUD N ABBR = **intrauterine device**

I've [aɪv] = **I have**

ivory ['aɪvərɪ] N Elfenbein *nt*

Ivory Coast N Elfenbeinküste *f*

ivory tower N (*fig*) Elfenbeinturm *m*

ivy ['aɪvɪ] N Efeu *m*

Ivy League (*US*) N *Eliteuniversitäten der USA*

> Als **Ivy League** bezeichnet man die acht renommiertesten Universitäten im Nordosten der Vereinigten Staaten (Brown, Columbia, Cornell, Dartmouth College, Harvard, Princeton, University of Pennsylvania, Yale), die untereinander Sportwettkämpfe austragen. Der Name bezieht sich auf die efeubewachsenen Mauern der Universitätsgebäude.

J, j [dʒeɪ] N (*letter*) J *nt*, j *nt*; **J for Jack, J for Jig** (*US*) ≈ J wie Julius
JA N ABBR = **judge advocate; joint account**
J/A ABBR = **joint account**
jab [dʒæb] VT stoßen; (*with finger, needle*) stechen ▸ N (*inf*) Spritze *f* ▸ VI: **to ~ at** einstechen auf *+acc*; **to ~ sth into sth** etw in etw *acc* stoßen/stechen
jack [dʒæk] N (*Aut*) Wagenheber *m*; (*Bowls*) Zielkugel *f*; (*Cards*) Bube *m*
▸ **jack in** (*inf*) VT aufgeben
▸ **jack up** VT (*Aut*) aufbocken
jackal ['dʒækl] N Schakal *m*
jackass ['dʒækæs] (*inf*) N (*person*) Esel *m*
jackdaw ['dʒækdɔː] N Dohle *f*
jacket ['dʒækɪt] N Jackett *nt*; (*of book*) Schutzumschlag *m*; **potatoes in their jackets, ~ potatoes** in der Schale gebackene Kartoffeln *pl*
jack-in-the-box ['dʒækɪnðəbɔks] N Schachtelteufel *m*, Kastenteufel *m*
jack-knife ['dʒæknaɪf] N Klappmesser *nt* ▸ VI: **the lorry jack-knifed** der Anhänger (des Lastwagens) hat sich quer gestellt
jack-of-all-trades ['dʒækəv'ɔːltreɪdz] N Alleskönner *m*
jack plug N Bananenstecker *m*
jackpot ['dʒækpɔt] N Hauptgewinn *m*; **to hit the ~** (*fig*) das große Los ziehen
Jacuzzi® [dʒə'kuːzɪ] N Whirlpool *m*
jade [dʒeɪd] N Jade *m or f*
jaded ['dʒeɪdɪd] ADJ abgespannt; **to get ~** die Nase vollhaben
JAG N ABBR = **Judge Advocate General**
jagged ['dʒægɪd] ADJ gezackt
jaguar ['dʒægjuəʳ] N Jaguar *m*
jail [dʒeɪl] N Gefängnis *nt* ▸ VT einsperren
jailbird ['dʒeɪlbəːd] N Knastbruder *m* (*inf*)
jailbreak ['dʒeɪlbreɪk] N (Gefängnis)ausbruch *m*
jalopy [dʒə'lɔpɪ] (*inf*) N alte (Klapper)kiste *f or* Mühle *f*
jam [dʒæm] N Marmelade *f*, Konfitüre *f*; (*also*: **traffic jam**) Stau *m*; (*inf: difficulty*) Klemme *f* ▸ VT blockieren; (*mechanism, drawer etc*) verklemmen; (*Radio*) stören ▸ VI klemmen; (*gun*) Ladehemmung haben; **I'm in a real ~** (*inf*) ich stecke wirklich in der Klemme; **to get sb out of a ~** (*inf*) jdm aus der Klemme helfen; **to ~ sth into sth** etw in etw *acc* stopfen; **the telephone lines are jammed** die Leitungen sind belegt
Jamaica [dʒə'meɪkə] N Jamaika *nt*
Jamaican [dʒə'meɪkən] ADJ jamaikanisch ▸ N Jamaikaner(in) *m(f)*
jamb [dʒæm] N (*of door*) (Tür)pfosten *m*; (*of window*) (Fenster)pfosten *m*
jamboree [dʒæmbə'riː] N Fest *nt*
jam-packed [dʒæm'pækt] ADJ: **~ (with)** vollgestopft (mit)
jam session N (*Mus*) Jamsession *f*
Jan. ABBR (= *January*) Jan.
jangle ['dʒæŋgl] VI klimpern
janitor ['dʒænɪtəʳ] N Hausmeister(in) *m(f)*
January ['dʒænjuərɪ] N Januar *m*; *see also* **July**
Japan [dʒə'pæn] N Japan *nt*
Japanese [dʒæpə'niːz] ADJ japanisch ▸ N INV Japaner(in) *m(f)*; (*Ling*) Japanisch *nt*
jar [dʒɑːʳ] N Topf *m*, Gefäß *nt*; (*glass*) Glas *nt* ▸ VI (*sound*) gellen; (*colours*) nicht harmonieren, sich beißen ▸ VT erschüttern; **to ~ on sb** jdm auf die Nerven gehen
jargon ['dʒɑːgən] N Jargon *m*
jarring ['dʒɑːrɪŋ] ADJ (*sound*) gellend, schrill; (*colour*) schreiend
jasmine ['dʒæzmɪn] N Jasmin *m*
jaundice ['dʒɔːndɪs] N Gelbsucht *f*
jaundiced ['dʒɔːndɪst] ADJ (*view, attitude*) zynisch
jaunt [dʒɔːnt] N Spritztour *f*
jaunty ['dʒɔːntɪ] ADJ munter; (*step*) schwungvoll
Java ['dʒɑːvə] N Java *nt*
javelin ['dʒævlɪn] N Speer *m*
jaw [dʒɔː] N Kiefer *m*
jawbone ['dʒɔːbəun] N Kieferknochen *m*
jay [dʒeɪ] N Eichelhäher *m*
jaywalker ['dʒeɪwɔːkəʳ] N unachtsamer Fußgänger *m*, unachtsame Fußgängerin *f*
jazz [dʒæz] N Jazz *m*
▸ **jazz up** VT aufpeppen (*inf*)
jazz band N Jazzband *f*
JCB® N Erdräummaschine *f*
JCS (*US*) N ABBR (= *Joint Chiefs of Staff*) Stabschefs *pl*
JD (*US*) N ABBR (= *Doctor of Laws*) ≈ Dr. jur.; (= *Justice Department*) ≈ Justizministerium *nt*
jealous ['dʒɛləs] ADJ eifersüchtig; (*envious*) neidisch

jealously [ˈdʒɛləslɪ] ADV eifersüchtig; (*enviously*) neidisch; (*watchfully*) sorgsam
jealousy [ˈdʒɛləsɪ] N Eifersucht *f*; (*envy*) Neid *m*
jeans [dʒiːnz] NPL Jeans *pl*
Jeep® [dʒiːp] N Jeep® *m*
jeer [dʒɪəʳ] VI höhnische Bemerkungen machen; **to ~ at** verhöhnen
jeering [ˈdʒɪərɪŋ] ADJ höhnisch; (*crowd*) johlend ▶ N Johlen *nt*
jeers [ˈdʒɪəz] NPL Buhrufe *pl*
jelly [ˈdʒɛlɪ] N Götterspeise *f*; (*jam*) Gelee *m or nt*
jelly baby (BRIT) N Gummibärchen *nt*
jellyfish [ˈdʒɛlɪfɪʃ] N Qualle *f*
jeopardize [ˈdʒɛpədaɪz] VT gefährden
jeopardy [ˈdʒɛpədɪ] N: **to be in ~** gefährdet sein
jerk [dʒəːk] N Ruck *m*; (*inf: idiot*) Trottel *m* ▶ VT reißen ▶ VI (*vehicle*) ruckeln
jerkin [ˈdʒəːkɪn] N Wams *nt*
jerky [ˈdʒəːkɪ] ADJ ruckartig
jerry-built [ˈdʒɛrɪbɪlt] ADJ schlampig gebaut
jerry can [ˈdʒɛrɪ-] N großer Blechkanister *m*
Jersey [ˈdʒəːzɪ] N Jersey *nt*
jersey [ˈdʒəːzɪ] N Pullover *m*; (*fabric*) Jersey *m*
Jerusalem [dʒəˈruːsləm] N Jerusalem *nt*
jest [dʒɛst] N Scherz *m*
jester [ˈdʒɛstəʳ] N Narr *m*
Jesus [ˈdʒiːzəs] N Jesus *m*; **~ Christ** Jesus Christus *m*
jet [dʒɛt] N Strahl *m*; (*Aviat*) Düsenflugzeug *nt*; (*Mineralogy, Jewellery*) Jett *m or nt*, Gagat *m*
jet-black [ˈdʒɛtˈblæk] ADJ pechschwarz
jet engine N Düsentriebwerk *nt*
jet lag N Jetlag *nt*
jet-propelled [ˈdʒɛtprəˈpɛld] ADJ Düsen-, mit Düsenantrieb
jetsam [ˈdʒɛtsəm] N Strandgut *nt*; (*floating*) Treibgut *nt*
jet-setter [ˈdʒɛtsɛtəʳ] N: **to be a ~** zum Jetset gehören
jettison [ˈdʒɛtɪsn] VT abwerfen; (*from ship*) über Bord werfen
jetty [ˈdʒɛtɪ] N Landesteg *m*, Pier *m*
Jew [dʒuː] N Jude *m*, Jüdin *f*
jewel [ˈdʒuːəl] N Edelstein *m*, Juwel *nt* (*also fig*); (*in watch*) Stein *m*
jeweller, (US) **jeweler** [ˈdʒuːələʳ] N Juwelier *m*
jeweller's, jeweller's shop N Juwelier *m*, Juweliergeschäft *nt*
jewellery, (US) **jewelry** [ˈdʒuːəlrɪ] N Schmuck *m*
Jewess [ˈdʒuːɪs] N Jüdin *f*
Jewish [ˈdʒuːɪʃ] ADJ jüdisch
JFK (US) N ABBR (= *John Fitzgerald Kennedy International Airport*) John-F.-Kennedy-Flughafen *m*
jib [dʒɪb] N (*Naut*) Klüver *m*; (*of crane*) Ausleger *m* ▶ VI (*horse*) scheuen, bocken; **to ~ at doing sth** sich dagegen sträuben, etw zu tun
jibe [dʒaɪb] N = **gibe**
jiffy [ˈdʒɪfɪ] (*inf*) N: **in a ~** sofort
jig [dʒɪg] N *lebhafter Volkstanz*
jigsaw [ˈdʒɪgsɔː] N (*also:* **jigsaw puzzle**) Puzzle(spiel) *nt*; (*tool*) Stichsäge *f*
jilt [dʒɪlt] VT sitzen lassen
jingle [ˈdʒɪŋgl] N (*tune*) Jingle *m* ▶ VI (*bracelets*) klimpern; (*bells*) bimmeln
jingoism [ˈdʒɪŋgəuɪzəm] N Hurrapatriotismus *m*
jinx [dʒɪŋks] (*inf*) N Fluch *m*; **there's a ~ on it** es ist verhext
jitters [ˈdʒɪtəz] (*inf*) NPL: **to get the ~** das große Zittern bekommen
jittery [ˈdʒɪtərɪ] (*inf*) ADJ nervös, rappelig
jiujitsu [dʒuːˈdʒɪtsuː] N Jiu-Jitsu *nt*
job [dʒɔb] N Arbeit *f*; (*post, employment*) Stelle *f*, Job *m*; **it's not my ~** es ist nicht meine Aufgabe; **a part-time ~** eine Teilzeitbeschäftigung; **a full-time ~** eine Ganztagsstelle; **he's only doing his ~** er tut nur seine Pflicht; **it's a good ~ that ...** nur gut, dass ...; **just the ~!** genau das Richtige!
jobber [ˈdʒɔbəʳ] (BRIT) N Börsenhändler *m*
jobbing [ˈdʒɔbɪŋ] (BRIT) ADJ Gelegenheits-
job centre (BRIT) N Arbeitsamt *nt*
job creation scheme N Arbeitsbeschaffungsmaßnahmen *pl*
job description N Tätigkeitsbeschreibung *f*
job-hunting N: **to go ~** auf Arbeitssuche gehen
job interview N Vorstellungs- *or* Bewerbungsgespräch *nt*
jobless [ˈdʒɔblɪs] ADJ arbeitslos ▶ NPL: **the ~** die Arbeitslosen *pl*
job lot N (Waren)posten *m*
job satisfaction N Zufriedenheit *f* am Arbeitsplatz
job security N Sicherheit *f* des Arbeitsplatzes
jobseeker's allowance N Arbeitslosengeld *nt*
job sharing N Jobsharing *nt*, Arbeitsplatzteilung *f*
job specification N Tätigkeitsbeschreibung *f*
Jock [dʒɔk] (*inf*) N Schotte *m*
jockey [ˈdʒɔkɪ] N Jockey *m* ▶ VI: **to ~ for position** um eine gute Position rangeln
jockey box (US) N (*Aut*) Handschuhfach *nt*
jocular [ˈdʒɔkjuləʳ] ADJ spaßig, witzig
jog [dʒɔg] VT (an)stoßen ▶ VI joggen, Dauerlauf machen; **to ~ sb's memory** jds Gedächtnis *dat* nachhelfen
▶ **jog along** VI entlangzuckeln (*inf*)
jogger [ˈdʒɔgəʳ] N Jogger(in) *m(f)*
jogging [ˈdʒɔgɪŋ] N Jogging *nt*, Joggen *nt*
john [dʒɔn] (*US inf*) N (*toilet*) Klo *nt*
join [dʒɔɪn] VT (*club, party*) beitreten *+dat*; (*queue*) sich stellen in *+acc*; (*things, places*) verbinden; (*group of people*) sich anschließen *+dat* ▶ VI (*roads*) sich treffen; (*rivers*) zusammenfließen ▶ N Verbindungsstelle *f*; **to ~ forces (with)** (*fig*) sich zusammentun (mit); **will you ~ us for dinner?** wollen Sie mit uns zu Abend essen?; **I'll ~ you later** ich komme später
▶ **join in** VI mitmachen ▶ VT FUS sich beteiligen an *+dat*
▶ **join up** VI sich treffen; (*Mil*) zum Militär gehen
joiner [ˈdʒɔɪnəʳ] (BRIT) N Schreiner(in) *m(f)*

joinery ['dʒɔɪnərɪ] (BRIT) N Schreinerei *f*
joint [dʒɔɪnt] N (*in woodwork*) Fuge *f*; (*in pipe etc*) Verbindungsstelle *f*; (*Anat*) Gelenk *nt*; (BRIT *Culin*) Braten *m*; (*inf: place*) Laden *m*; (: *of cannabis*) Joint *m* ▶ ADJ gemeinsam; (*combined*) vereint
joint account N gemeinsames Konto *nt*
jointly ['dʒɔɪntlɪ] ADV gemeinsam
joint ownership N Miteigentum *nt*
joint-stock company ['dʒɔɪnt'stɔk-] N Aktiengesellschaft *f*
joint venture N Gemeinschaftsunternehmen *nt*, Joint Venture *nt*
joist [dʒɔɪst] N Balken *m*, Träger *m*
joke [dʒəuk] N Witz *m*; (*also:* **practical joke**) Streich *m* ▶ VI Witze machen; **to play a ~ on sb** jdm einen Streich spielen
joker ['dʒəukər] N (*Cards*) Joker *m*
joking ['dʒəukɪŋ] ADJ scherzhaft
jokingly ['dʒəukɪŋlɪ] ADV scherzhaft, im Spaß
jollity ['dʒɔlɪtɪ] N Fröhlichkeit *f*
jolly ['dʒɔlɪ] ADJ fröhlich; (*enjoyable*) lustig ▶ ADV (BRIT *inf: very*) ganz (schön) ▶ VT (BRIT): **to ~ sb along** jdm aufmunternd zureden; **~ good!** prima!
jolt [dʒəult] N Ruck *m*; (*shock*) Schock *m* ▶ VT schütteln; (*subj: bus etc*) durchschütteln; (*emotionally*) aufrütteln
Jordan ['dʒɔ:dən] N Jordanien *nt*; (*river*) Jordan *m*
Jordanian [dʒɔ:'deɪnɪən] ADJ jordanisch ▶ N Jordanier(in) *m(f)*
joss stick [dʒɔs-] N Räucherstäbchen *nt*
jostle ['dʒɔsl] VT anrempeln ▶ VI drängeln
jot [dʒɔt] N: **not one ~** kein bisschen
▶ **jot down** VT notieren
jotter ['dʒɔtər] (BRIT) N Notizbuch *nt*; (*pad*) Notizblock *m*
journal ['dʒə:nl] N Zeitschrift *f*; (*diary*) Tagebuch *nt*
journalese [dʒə:nə'li:z] (*pej*) N Pressejargon *m*
journalism ['dʒə:nəlɪzəm] N Journalismus *m*
journalist ['dʒə:nəlɪst] N Journalist(in) *m(f)*
journey ['dʒə:nɪ] N Reise *f* ▶ VI reisen; **a 5-hour ~** eine Fahrt von 5 Stunden; **return ~** Rückreise *f*; (*both ways*) Hin- und Rückreise *f*
jovial ['dʒəuvɪəl] ADJ fröhlich; (*atmosphere*) freundlich, herzlich
jowl [dʒaul] N Backe *f*
joy [dʒɔɪ] N Freude *f*
joyful ['dʒɔɪful] ADJ freudig
joyride ['dʒɔɪraɪd] N *Spritztour in einem gestohlenen Auto*
joyrider ['dʒɔɪraɪdər] N *Autodieb, der den Wagen nur für eine Spritztour benutzt*
joystick ['dʒɔɪstɪk] N (*Aviat*) Steuerknüppel *m*; (*Comput*) Joystick *m*
JP N ABBR = **Justice of the Peace**
Jr ABBR (*in names:* = *junior*) jun.
JTPA (US) N ABBR (= *Job Training Partnership Act*) *Arbeitsbeschaffungsprogramm für benachteiligte Bevölkerungsteile und Minderheiten*
jubilant ['dʒu:bɪlnt] ADJ überglücklich
jubilation [dʒu:bɪ'leɪʃən] N Jubel *m*
jubilee ['dʒu:bɪli:] N Jubiläum *nt*; **silver ~** 25-jähriges Jubiläum; **golden ~** 50-jähriges Jubiläum
judge [dʒʌdʒ] N Richter(in) *m(f)*; (*in competition*) Preisrichter(in) *m(f)*; (*fig: expert*) Kenner(in) *m(f)* ▶ VT (*Law: person*) die Verhandlung führen über *+acc*; (: *case*) verhandeln; (*competition*) Preisrichter(in) sein bei; (*person etc*) beurteilen; (*consider*) halten für; (*estimate*) einschätzen ▶ VI: **judging by** *or* **to ~ by his expression** seinem Gesichtsausdruck nach zu urteilen; **she's a good ~ of character** sie ist ein guter Menschenkenner; **I'll be the ~ of that** das müssen Sie mich schon selbst beurteilen lassen; **as far as I can ~** soweit ich es beurteilen kann; **I judged it necessary to inform him** ich hielt es für nötig, ihn zu informieren
judge advocate N (*Mil*) Beisitzer(in) *m(f)* bei einem Kriegsgericht
Judge Advocate General N (*Mil*) *Vorsitzender des obersten Militärgerichts*
judgment, judgement ['dʒʌdʒmənt] N Urteil *nt*; (*Rel*) Gericht *nt*; (*view, opinion*) Meinung *f*; (*discernment*) Urteilsvermögen *nt*; **in my judg(e)ment** meiner Meinung nach; **to pass judg(e)ment (on)** (*Law*) das Urteil sprechen (über *+acc*); (*fig*) ein Urteil fällen (über *+acc*)
judicial [dʒu:'dɪʃl] ADJ gerichtlich, Justiz-; (*fig*) kritisch; **~ review** gerichtliche Überprüfung *f*
judiciary [dʒu:'dɪʃɪərɪ] N: **the ~** die Gerichtsbehörden *pl*
judicious [dʒu:'dɪʃəs] ADJ klug
judo ['dʒu:dəu] N Judo *nt*
jug [dʒʌg] N Krug *m*
jugged hare ['dʒʌgd-] (BRIT) N ≈ Hasenpfeffer *m*
juggernaut ['dʒʌgənɔ:t] (BRIT) N Fernlastwagen *m*
juggle ['dʒʌgl] VI jonglieren
juggler ['dʒʌglər] N Jongleur *m*
Jugoslav *etc* ['ju:gəu'slɑ:v] = **Yugoslav** *etc*
jugular ['dʒʌgjulər] ADJ: **~ (vein)** Drosselvene *f*
juice [dʒu:s] N Saft *m*; (*inf: petrol*): **we've run out of ~** wir haben keinen Sprit mehr
juicy ['dʒu:sɪ] ADJ saftig
jukebox ['dʒu:kbɔks] N Musikbox *f*
Jul. ABBR = **July**
July [dʒu:'laɪ] N Juli *m*; **the first of ~** der erste Juli; **on the eleventh of ~** am elften Juli; **in the month of ~** im (Monat) Juli; **at the beginning/end of ~** Anfang/Ende Juli; **in the middle of ~** Mitte Juli; **during ~** im Juli; **in ~ of next year** im Juli nächsten Jahres; **each** *or* **every ~** jedes Jahr im Juli; **~ was wet this year** der Juli war dieses Jahr ein nasser Monat
jumble ['dʒʌmbl] N Durcheinander *nt*; (*items for sale*) gebrauchte Sachen *pl* ▶ VT (*also:* **jumble up**) durcheinanderbringen

> **Jumble sale** ist ein Wohltätigkeitsbasar, meist in einer Aula oder einem Gemeindehaus abgehalten, bei dem alle möglichen Gebrauchtwaren (vor allem Kleidung, Spielzeug, Bücher, Geschirr und

Möbel) verkauft werden. Der Erlös fließt entweder einer Wohltätigkeitsorganisation zu oder wird für örtliche Zwecke verwendet, z. B. die Pfadfinder, die Grundschule, Reparatur der Kirche usw.

jumbo ['dʒʌmbəu], **jumbo jet** N Jumbo(jet) *m*

jumbo-size ['dʒʌmbəusaɪz] ADJ (*packet etc*) Riesen-

jump [dʒʌmp] VI springen; (*with fear, surprise*) zusammenzucken; (*increase*) sprunghaft ansteigen ▸ VT springen über *+acc* ▸ N Sprung *m*; Zusammenzucken *nt*; sprunghafter Anstieg *m*; **to ~ the queue** (BRIT) sich vordrängeln

▸ **jump about** VI herumspringen

▸ **jump at** VT FUS (*idea*) sofort aufgreifen; (*chance*) sofort ergreifen; **he jumped at the offer** er griff bei dem Angebot sofort zu

▸ **jump down** VI herunterspringen

▸ **jump up** VI hochspringen; (*from seat*) aufspringen

jumped-up ['dʒʌmptʌp] (BRIT *pej*) ADJ eingebildet

jumper ['dʒʌmpəʳ] N (BRIT) Pullover *m*; (US: *dress*) Trägerkleid *nt*; (*Sport*) Springer(in) *m*(*f*)

jumper cables (US) NPL = **jump leads**

jumping jack N Knallfrosch *m*

jump jet N Senkrechtstarter *m*

jump leads (BRIT) NPL Starthilfekabel *nt*

jump-start ['dʒʌmpstɑːt] VT (*Aut: engine*) durch Anschieben des Wagens in Gang bringen

jump suit N Overall *m*

jumpy ['dʒʌmpɪ] ADJ nervös

Jun. ABBR = **June**

junction ['dʒʌŋkʃən] (BRIT) N Kreuzung *f*; (*Rail*) Gleisanschluss *m*

juncture ['dʒʌŋktʃəʳ] N: **at this ~** zu diesem Zeitpunkt

June [dʒuːn] N Juni *m*; *see also* **July**

jungle ['dʒʌŋgl] N Urwald *m*, Dschungel *m* (*also fig*)

junior ['dʒuːnɪəʳ] ADJ jünger; (*subordinate*) untergeordnet ▸ N Jüngere(r) *f*(*m*); (*young person*) Junior *m*; **he's ~ to me (by 2 years), he's my ~ (by 2 years)** (*younger*) er ist (2 Jahre) jünger als ich; **he's ~ to me** (*subordinate*) er steht unter mir

junior executive N Zweiter Geschäftsführer *m*, Zweite Geschäftsführerin *f*

junior high school (US) N ≈ Mittelschule *f*

junior minister (BRIT) N Staatssekretär(in) *m*(*f*)

junior partner N Juniorpartner(in) *m*(*f*)

junior school (BRIT) N ≈ Grundschule *f*

junior sizes NPL (*Comm*) Kindergrößen *pl*

juniper ['dʒuːnɪpəʳ] N: **~ berry** Wacholderbeere *f*

junk [dʒʌŋk] N (*rubbish*) Gerümpel *nt*; (*cheap goods*) Ramsch *m*; (*ship*) Dschunke *f* ▸ VT (*inf*) ausrangieren

junk bond N (*Fin*) *niedrig eingestuftes Wertpapier mit hohen Ertragschancen bei erhöhtem Risiko*

junket ['dʒʌŋkɪt] N Dickmilch *f*; (*inf, pej: free trip*): **to go on a ~** eine Reise auf Kosten des Steuerzahlers machen

junk food N ungesundes Essen *nt*

junkie ['dʒʌŋkɪ] (*inf*) N Fixer(in) *m*(*f*)

junk mail N (Post)wurfsendungen *pl*

junk room N Rumpelkammer *f*

junk shop N Trödelladen *m*

Junr ABBR (*in names:* = *junior*) jun.

junta ['dʒʌntə] N Junta *f*

Jupiter ['dʒuːpɪtəʳ] N Jupiter *m*

jurisdiction [dʒuərɪs'dɪkʃən] N Gerichtsbarkeit *f*; (*Admin*) Zuständigkeit *f*, Zuständigkeitsbereich *m*; **it falls** *or* **comes within/outside my ~** dafür bin ich zuständig/nicht zuständig

jurisprudence [dʒuərɪs'pruːdəns] N Jura *no art*, Rechtswissenschaft *f*

juror ['dʒuərəʳ] N Schöffe *m*, Schöffin *f*; (*for capital crimes*) Geschworene(r) *f*(*m*); (*in competition*) Preisrichter(in) *m*(*f*)

jury ['dʒuərɪ] N: **the ~** die Schöffen *pl*; (*for capital crimes*) die Geschworenen *pl*; (*for competition*) die Jury, das Preisgericht

jury box N Schöffenbank *f*; Geschworenenbank *f*

juryman ['dʒuərɪmən] N (*irreg*) = **juror**

just [dʒʌst] ADJ gerecht ▸ ADV (*exactly*) genau; (*only*) nur; **he's ~ done it/left** er hat es gerade getan/ist gerade gegangen; **~ as I expected** genau wie ich erwartet habe; **~ right** genau richtig; **~ two o'clock** erst zwei Uhr; **we were ~ going** wir wollten gerade gehen; **I was ~ about to phone** ich wollte gerade anrufen; **she's ~ as clever as you** sie ist genauso klug wie du; **it's ~ as well (that …)** nur gut, dass …; **~ as he was leaving** gerade als er gehen wollte; **~ before** gerade noch; **~ enough** gerade genug; **~ here** genau hier, genau an dieser Stelle; **he ~ missed** er hat genau danebengetroffen; **it's ~ me** ich bins nur; **it's ~ a mistake** es ist nur ein Fehler; **~ listen** hör mal; **~ ask someone the way** frage doch einfach jemanden nach dem Weg; **not ~ now** nicht gerade jetzt; **~ a minute!, ~ one moment!** einen Moment, bitte!

justice ['dʒʌstɪs] N Justiz *f*; (*of cause, complaint*) Berechtigung *f*; (*fairness*) Gerechtigkeit *f*; (US: *judge*) Richter(in) *m*(*f*); **Lord Chief J~** (BRIT) *oberster Richter in Großbritannien*; **to do ~ to** (*fig*) gerecht werden *+dat*

Justice of the Peace N Friedensrichter(in) *m*(*f*)

justifiable [dʒʌstɪ'faɪəbl] ADJ gerechtfertigt, berechtigt

justifiably [dʒʌstɪ'faɪəblɪ] ADV zu Recht, berechtigterweise

justification [dʒʌstɪfɪ'keɪʃən] N Rechtfertigung *f*; (*Typ*) Justierung *f*

justify ['dʒʌstɪfaɪ] VT rechtfertigen; (*text*) justieren; **to be justified in doing sth** etw zu *or* mit Recht tun

justly ['dʒʌstlɪ] ADV zu *or* mit Recht; (*deservedly*) gerecht

jut [dʒʌt] VI (*also:* **jut out**) vorstehen

jute [dʒuːt] N Jute *f*

uvenile ['dʒu:vənaɪl] ADJ (*crime, offenders*) Jugend-; (*humour, mentality*) kindisch, unreif ▶ N Jugendliche(r) *f(m)*
uvenile delinquency N Jugendkriminalität *f*
uvenile delinquent N jugendlicher Straftäter *m*, jugendliche Straftäterin *f*
juxtapose ['dʒʌkstəpəuz] VT nebeneinanderstellen
juxtaposition ['dʒʌkstəpə'zɪʃən] N Nebeneinanderstellung *f*

K¹, k [keɪ] N (*letter*) K *nt*, k *nt*; **K for King** ≈ K wie Kaufmann
K² [keɪ] ABBR (= *one thousand*) K; (*Comput*: = *kilobyte*) KB; (BRIT: *in titles*) = **knight**
kaftan ['kæftæn] N Kaftan *m*
Kalahari Desert [kælə'hɑːrɪ-] N: **the ~** die Kalahari
kale [keɪl] N Grünkohl *m*
kaleidoscope [kə'laɪdəskəup] N Kaleidoskop *nt*
kamikaze ['kæmɪ'kɑːzɪ] ADJ (*mission etc*) Kamikaze-, Selbstmord-
Kampala [kæm'pɑːlə] N Kampala *nt*
Kampuchea [kæmpu'tʃɪə] N Kampuchea *nt*
Kampuchean [kæmpu'tʃɪən] ADJ kampucheanisch
kangaroo [kæŋgə'ruː] N Känguru *nt*
Kans. (US) ABBR (*Post*) = **Kansas**
kaput [kə'put] (*inf*) ADJ: **to be ~** kaputt sein
karaoke [kɑːrə'əukɪ] N Karaoke *nt*
karate [kə'rɑːtɪ] N Karate *nt*
kart [kɑːt] N Gokart *m*
Kashmir [kæʃmɪəʳ] N Kaschmir *nt*
kayak ['kaɪæk] N Kajak *m or nt*
Kazakhstan [kæzæk'stɑːn] N Kasachstan *nt*
KC (BRIT) N ABBR (*Law*: = *King's Counsel*) Kronanwalt *m*
kebab [kə'bæb] N Kebab *m*
keel [kiːl] N Kiel *m*; **on an even ~** (*fig*) stabil
▸ **keel over** VI kentern; (*person*) umkippen
keen [kiːn] ADJ begeistert, eifrig; (*interest*) groß; (*desire*) heftig; (*eye, intelligence, competition, edge*) scharf; **to be ~ to do** *or* **on doing sth** scharf darauf sein, etw zu tun (*inf*); **to be ~ on sth** an etw *dat* sehr interessiert sein; **to be ~ on sb** von jdm sehr angetan sein; **I'm not ~ on going** ich brenne nicht gerade darauf, zu gehen
keenly ['kiːnlɪ] ADV (*enthusiastically*) begeistert; (*feel*) leidenschaftlich; (*look*) aufmerksam
keenness ['kiːnnɪs] N Begeisterung *f*, Eifer *m*; **his ~ to go is suspicious** dass er so unbedingt gehen will, ist verdächtig
keep [kiːp] (*pt, pp* **kept**) VT behalten; (*preserve, store*) aufbewahren; (*house, shop, accounts, diary*) führen; (*garden etc*) pflegen; (*chickens, bees, promise*) halten; (*family etc*) versorgen, unterhalten; (*detain*) aufhalten; (*prevent*) abhalten ▸ VI (*remain*) bleiben; (*food*) sich halten ▸ N (*food etc*) Unterhalt *m*; (*of castle*) Bergfried *m*; **to ~ doing sth** etw immer wieder tun; **to ~ sb happy** jdn zufriedenstellen; **to ~ a room tidy** ein Zimmer in Ordnung halten; **to ~ sb waiting** jdn warten lassen; **to ~ an appointment** eine Verabredung einhalten; **to ~ a record of sth** über etw *acc* Buch führen; **to ~ sth to o.s.** etw für sich behalten; **to ~ sth (back) from sb** etw vor jdm geheim halten; **to ~ sb from doing sth** jdn davon abhalten, etw zu tun; **to ~ sth from happening** etw verhindern; **to ~ time** (*clock*) genau gehen; **enough for his ~** genug für seinen Unterhalt
▸ **keep away** VT fernhalten ▸ VI: **to ~ away (from)** wegbleiben (von)
▸ **keep back** VT zurückhalten; (*tears*) unterdrücken; (*money*) einbehalten ▸ VI zurückbleiben
▸ **keep down** VT (*prices*) niedrig halten; (*spending*) einschränken; (*food*) bei sich behalten ▸ VI unten bleiben
▸ **keep in** VT im Haus behalten; (*at school*) nachsitzen lassen ▸ VI (*inf*): **to ~ in with sb** sich mit jdm gut stellen
▸ **keep off** VT fernhalten ▸ VI wegbleiben; **"~ off the grass"** „Betreten des Rasens verboten"; **~ your hands off** Hände weg
▸ **keep on** VI: **to ~ on doing sth** (*continue*) etw weiter tun; **to ~ on (about sth)** unaufhörlich (von etw) reden
▸ **keep out** VT fernhalten; **"~ out"** „Zutritt verboten"
▸ **keep up** VT (*payments*) weiterbezahlen; (*standards etc*) aufrechterhalten ▸ VI: **to ~ up (with)** mithalten können (mit)
keeper ['kiːpəʳ] N Wärter(in) *m(f)*
keep fit N Fitnesstraining *nt*
keeping ['kiːpɪŋ] N (*care*) Obhut *f*; **in ~ with** in Übereinstimmung mit; **out of ~ with** nicht in Einklang mit; **I'll leave this in your ~** ich vertraue dies deiner Obhut an
keeps [kiːps] N: **for ~** (*inf*) für immer
keepsake ['kiːpseɪk] N Andenken *nt*
keg [kɛg] N Fässchen *nt*; **~ beer** Bier *nt* vom Fass
Ken. (US) ABBR (*Post*) = **Kentucky**
kennel ['kɛnl] N Hundehütte *f*
kennels ['kɛnlz] N Hundeheim *nt*; **we had to leave our dog in ~ over Christmas** wir mussten unseren Hund über Weihnachten in ein Heim geben

Kenya ['kɛnjə] N Kenia *nt*
Kenyan ['kɛnjən] ADJ kenianisch ▸ N Kenianer(in) *m(f)*
kept [kɛpt] PT, PP *of* **keep**
kerb [kəːb] (BRIT) N Bordstein *m*
kerb crawler [-'krɔːlə^r] (*inf*) N Freier *m* im Autostrich
kernel ['kəːnl] N Kern *m*
kerosene ['kɛrəsiːn] N Kerosin *nt*
kestrel ['kɛstrəl] N Turmfalke *m*
ketchup ['kɛtʃəp] N Ket(s)chup *m or nt*
kettle ['kɛtl] N Kessel *m*
kettledrum ['kɛtldrʌm] N (Kessel)pauke *f*
kettling ['kɛtəlɪŋ] N (*by police*) Einkesselung *f*
key [kiː] N Schlüssel *m*; (*Mus*) Tonart *f*; (*of piano, computer, typewriter*) Taste *f* ▸ CPD (*issue etc*) Schlüssel- ▸ VT (*also*: **key in**) eingeben
keyboard ['kiːbɔːd] N Tastatur *f*
keyboarder ['kiːbɔːdə^r] N Datentypist(in) *m(f)*
keyed up [kiːd-] ADJ: **to be (all) ~** (ganz) aufgedreht sein (*inf*)
keyhole ['kiːhəul] N Schlüsselloch *nt*
keyhole surgery N Schlüssellochchirurgie *f*, minimal invasive Chirurgie *f*
keynote ['kiːnəut] N Grundton *m*; (*of speech*) Leitgedanke *m*
keypad ['kiːpæd] N Tastenfeld *nt*
key ring N Schlüsselring *m*
keystroke ['kiːstrəuk] N Anschlag *m*
kg ABBR (= *kilogram*) kg
KGB N ABBR (*Pol: formerly*) KGB *m*
khaki ['kɑːkɪ] N K(h)aki *nt*
kHz ABBR (= *kilohertz*) kHz
kibbutz [kɪ'buts] N Kibbuz *m*
kick [kɪk] VT treten; (*table, ball*) treten gegen *+acc*; (*inf: habit*) ablegen; (*: addiction*) wegkommen von ▸ VI (*horse*) ausschlagen ▸ N Tritt *m*; (*to ball*) Schuss *m*; (*of rifle*) Rückstoß *m*; (*thrill*): **he does it for kicks** er macht es zum Spaß
▸ **kick around** (*inf*) VI (*person*) rumhängen; (*thing*) rumliegen
▸ **kick off** VI (*Sport*) anstoßen
▸ **kick out** VT (*inf*) rausschmeißen (of aus)
kickoff ['kɪkɔf] N (*Sport*) Anstoß *m*
kick start N (*Aut: also*: **kick starter**) Kickstarter *m*
kid [kɪd] N (*inf: child*) Kind *nt*; (*animal*) Kitz *nt*; (*leather*) Ziegenleder *nt*, Glacéleder *nt* ▸ VI (*inf*) Witze machen; **~ brother** kleiner Bruder *m*; **~ sister** kleine Schwester *f*
kid gloves NPL: **to treat sb with ~** (*fig*) jdn mit Samthandschuhen anfassen
kidnap ['kɪdnæp] VT entführen, kidnappen
kidnapper ['kɪdnæpə^r] N Entführer(in) *m(f)*, Kidnapper(in) *m(f)*
kidnapping ['kɪdnæpɪŋ] N Entführung *f*, Kidnapping *nt*
kidney ['kɪdnɪ] N Niere *f*
kidney bean N Gartenbohne *f*
kidney machine N (*Med*) künstliche Niere *f*
Kilimanjaro [kɪlɪmən'dʒɑːrəu] N: **Mount ~** der Kilimandscharo
kill [kɪl] VT töten; (*murder*) ermorden, umbringen; (*plant*) eingehen lassen; (*proposal*) zu Fall bringen; (*rumour*) ein Ende machen *+dat* ▸ N Abschuss *m*; **to ~ time** die Zeit totschlagen; **to ~ o.s. to do sth** (*fig*) sich fast umbringen, um etw zu tun; **to ~ o.s. (laughing)** (*fig*) sich totlachen
▸ **kill off** VT abtöten; (*fig: romance*) beenden
killer ['kɪlə^r] N Mörder(in) *m(f)*
killer instinct N (*fig*) Tötungsinstinkt *m*
killing ['kɪlɪŋ] N Töten *nt*; (*instance*) Mord *m*; **to make a ~** (*inf*) einen Riesengewinn machen
killjoy ['kɪldʒɔɪ] N Spielverderber(in) *m(f)*
kiln [kɪln] N Brennofen *m*
kilo ['kiːləu] N Kilo *nt*
kilobyte ['kɪləubaɪt] N Kilobyte *nt*
kilogram, kilogramme ['kɪləugræm] N Kilogramm *nt*
kilohertz ['kɪləuhəːts] N INV Kilohertz *nt*
kilometre, (*US*) **kilometer** ['kɪləmiːtə^r] N Kilometer *m*
kilowatt ['kɪləuwɔt] N Kilowatt *nt*
kilt [kɪlt] N Kilt *m*, Schottenrock *m*
kilter ['kɪltə^r] N: **out of ~** nicht in Ordnung
kimono [kɪ'məunəu] N Kimono *m*
kin [kɪn] N *see* **kith**; **next**
kind [kaɪnd] ADJ freundlich ▸ N Art *f*; (*sort*) Sorte *f*; **would you be ~ enough to ...?, would you be so ~ as to ...?** wären Sie (vielleicht) so nett und ...?; **it's very ~ of you (to do ...)** es ist wirklich nett von Ihnen(, ... zu tun); **in ~** (*Comm*) in Naturalien; **a ~ of ...** eine Art ...; **they are two of a ~** sie sind beide von der gleichen Art; (*people*) sie sind vom gleichen Schlag
kindergarten ['kɪndəgɑːtn] N Kindergarten *m*
kind-hearted [kaɪnd'hɑːtɪd] ADJ gutherzig
Kindle® ['kɪndl] N Kindle® *m*
kindle ['kɪndl] VT anzünden; (*emotion*) wecken
kindling ['kɪndlɪŋ] N Anzündholz *nt*
kindly ['kaɪndlɪ] ADJ, ADV freundlich, nett; **will you ~ ...** würden Sie bitte ...; **he didn't take it ~** er konnte sich damit nicht anfreunden
kindness ['kaɪndnɪs] N Freundlichkeit *f*
kindred ['kɪndrɪd] ADJ: **~ spirit** Gleichgesinnte(r) *f(m)*
kinetic [kɪ'nɛtɪk] ADJ kinetisch
king [kɪŋ] N (*also fig*) König *m*
kingdom ['kɪŋdəm] N Königreich *nt*
kingfisher ['kɪŋfɪʃə^r] N Eisvogel *m*
kingpin ['kɪŋpɪn] N (*Tech*) Bolzen *m*; (*Aut*) Achsschenkelbolzen *m*; (*fig*) wichtigste Stütze *f*
king-size ['kɪŋsaɪz], **king-sized** ['kɪŋsaɪzd] ADJ extragroß; (*cigarette*) Kingsize-
kink [kɪŋk] N Knick *m*; (*in hair*) Welle *f*; (*fig*) Schrulle *f*
kinky ['kɪŋkɪ] (*pej*) ADJ schrullig; (*sexually*) abartig
kinship ['kɪnʃɪp] N Verwandtschaft *f*
kinsman ['kɪnzmən] N (*irreg*) Verwandte(r) *m*
kinswoman ['kɪnzwumən] N (*irreg*) Verwandte *f*
kiosk ['kiːɔsk] N Kiosk *m*; (BRIT) (Telefon)zelle *f*; (*also*: **newspaper kiosk**) (Zeitungs)kiosk *m*
kipper ['kɪpə^r] N Räucherhering *m*
Kirghizia [kəː'gɪzɪə] N Kirgistan *nt*

k

kiss [kɪs] N Kuß *m* ▸ VT küssen ▸ VI sich küssen; **to ~ (each other)** sich küssen; **to ~ sb goodbye** jdm einen Abschiedskuss geben
kissagram ['kɪsəgræm] N *durch eine(n) Angestellte(n) einer Agentur persönlich übermittelter Kuss*
kiss of life (BRIT) N: **the ~** Mund-zu-Mund-Beatmung *f*
kit [kɪt] N Zeug *nt*, Sachen *pl*; (*equipment, also Mil*) Ausrüstung *f*; (*set of tools*) Werkzeug *nt*; (*for assembly*) Bausatz *m*
▸ **kit out** (BRIT) VT ausrüsten, ausstatten
kitbag ['kɪtbæg] N Seesack *m*
kitchen ['kɪtʃɪn] N Küche *f*
kitchen garden N Küchengarten *m*
kitchen sink N Spüle *f*
kitchen unit (BRIT) N Küchenschrank *m*
kitchenware ['kɪtʃɪnwɛəʳ] N Küchengeräte *pl*
kite [kaɪt] N Drachen *m*; (*Zool*) Milan *m*
kith [kɪθ] N: **~ and kin** Freunde und Verwandte *pl*
kitten ['kɪtn] N Kätzchen *nt*
kitty ['kɪtɪ] N (gemeinsame) Kasse *f*
kiwi ['ki:wi:], **kiwi fruit** N Kiwi(frucht) *f*
KKK (*US*) N ABBR (= *Ku Klux Klan*) Ku-Klux-Klan *m*
Kleenex® ['kli:nɛks] N Tempo(taschentuch)® *nt*
kleptomaniac [klɛptəu'meɪnɪæk] N Kleptomane *m*, Kleptomanin *f*
km ABBR (= *kilometre*) km
km/h ABBR (= *kilometres per hour*) km/h
knack [næk] N: **to have the ~ of doing sth** es heraushaben, wie man etw macht; **there's a ~ to doing this** da ist ein Trick *or* Kniff dabei
knackered ['nækəd] (*BRIT inf*) ADJ kaputt
knapsack ['næpsæk] N Rucksack *m*
knead [ni:d] VT kneten
knee [ni:] N Knie *nt*
kneecap ['ni:kæp] N Kniescheibe *f*
kneecapping ['ni:kæpɪŋ] N Durchschießen *nt* der Kniescheibe
knee-deep ['ni:'di:p] ADJ, ADV: **the water was ~** das Wasser ging mir *etc* bis zum Knie; **~ in mud** knietief *or* bis zu den Knien im Schlamm
kneejerk reaction ['ni:dʒə:k-] N (*fig*) instinktive Reaktion *f*
kneel [ni:l] (*pt, pp* **knelt**) VI knien; (*also*: **kneel down**) niederknien
kneepad ['ni:pæd] N Knieschützer *m*
knell [nɛl] N Totengeläut(e) *nt*; (*fig*) Ende *nt*
knelt [nɛlt] PT, PP *of* **kneel**
knew [nju:] PT *of* **know**
knickers ['nɪkəz] (BRIT) NPL Schlüpfer *m*
knick-knacks ['nɪknæks] NPL Nippsachen *pl*
knife [naɪf] (*pl* **knives**) N Messer *nt* ▸ VT (*injure, attack*) einstechen auf *+acc*; **~, fork and spoon** Messer, Gabel und Löffel
knife edge N: **to be balanced on a ~** (*fig*) auf Messers Schneide stehen
knight [naɪt] N (BRIT) Ritter *m*; (*Chess*) Springer *m*, Pferd *nt*
knighthood ['naɪthud] (BRIT) N: **to get a ~** in den Adelsstand erhoben werden
knit [nɪt] VT stricken ▸ VI stricken; (*bones*) zusammenwachsen; **to ~ one's brows** die Stirn runzeln
knitted ['nɪtɪd] ADJ gestrickt, Strick-
knitting ['nɪtɪŋ] N Stricken *nt*; (*garment being made*) Strickzeug *nt*
knitting machine N Strickmaschine *f*
knitting needle N Stricknadel *f*
knitting pattern N Strickmuster *nt*
knitwear ['nɪtwɛəʳ] N Strickwaren *pl*
knives [naɪvz] NPL *of* **knife**
knob [nɔb] N Griff *m*; (*of stick*) Knauf *m*; (*on radio, TV etc*) Knopf *m*; **a ~ of butter** (BRIT) ein Stückchen *nt* Butter
knobbly ['nɔblɪ], (*US*) **knobby** ['nɔbɪ] ADJ (*wood*) knorrig; (*surface*) uneben; **~ knees** Knubbelknie *pl* (*inf*)
knock [nɔk] VT schlagen; (*bump into*) stoßen gegen *+acc*; (*inf: criticize*) runtermachen ▸ VI klopfen ▸ N Schlag *m*; (*bump*) Stoß *m*; (*on door*) Klopfen *nt*; **to ~ a nail into sth** einen Nagel in etw *acc* schlagen; **to ~ some sense into sb** jdn zur Vernunft bringen; **to ~ at/on** klopfen an/auf *+acc*; **he knocked at the door** er klopfte an, er klopfte an die Tür
▸ **knock about** (*inf*) VT schlagen, verprügeln ▸ VI rumziehen; **~ about with** sich rumtreiben mit
▸ **knock around** VT, VI = **knock about**
▸ **knock back** (*inf*) VT (*drink*) sich *dat* hinter die Binde kippen
▸ **knock down** VT anfahren; (*fatally*) überfahren; (*building etc*) abreißen; (*price: buyer*) herunterhandeln; (*: seller*) heruntergehen mit
▸ **knock off** VI (*inf*) Feierabend machen ▸ VT (*from price*) nachlassen; (*inf: steal*) klauen; **to ~ off £10** £10 nachlassen
▸ **knock out** VT bewusstlos schlagen; (*subj: drug*) bewusstlos werden lassen; (*Boxing*) k. o. schlagen; (*in game, competition*) besiegen
▸ **knock over** VT umstoßen; (*with car*) anfahren
knockdown ['nɔkdaun] ADJ: **~ price** Schleuderpreis *m*
knocker ['nɔkəʳ] N Türklopfer *m*
knock-for-knock ['nɔkfə'nɔk] (BRIT) ADJ: **~ agreement** *Vereinbarung, bei der jede Versicherungsgesellschaft den Schaden am von ihr versicherten Fahrzeug übernimmt*
knocking ['nɔkɪŋ] N Klopfen *nt*
knock-kneed [nɔk'ni:d] ADJ X-beinig; **to be ~** X-Beine haben
knockout ['nɔkaut] N (*Boxing*) K.-o.-Schlag *m* ▸ CPD (*competition etc*) Ausscheidungs-
knock-up ['nɔkʌp] N (*Tennis*): **to have a ~** ein paar Bälle schlagen
knot [nɔt] N Knoten *m*; (*in wood*) Ast *m* ▸ VT einen Knoten machen in *+acc*; (*knot together*) verknoten; **to tie a ~** einen Knoten machen
knotty ['nɔtɪ] ADJ (*fig: problem*) verwickelt
know [nəu] (*pt* **knew**, *pp* **known**) VT kennen; (*facts*) wissen; (*language*) können ▸ VI: **to ~ about** *or* **of sth/sb** von etw/jdm gehört haben; **to ~ how to swim** schwimmen können; **to get to ~ sth** etw erfahren; (*place*) etw kennenlernen; **I don't ~ him** ich kenne ihn nicht; **to ~ right from wrong** Gut und Böse unterscheiden können; **as far as I ~** soviel

ich weiß; **yes, I ~** ja, ich weiß; **I don't ~** ich weiß (es) nicht

▸ **know about** VT Bescheid wissen über *+acc*; (*subject*) sich auskennen in *+dat*; (*cars, horses etc*) sich auskennen mit

know-all ['nəuɔ:l] (BRIT *pej*) N Alleswisser *m*

know-how ['nəuhau] N Know-how *nt*, Sachkenntnis *f*

knowing ['nəuɪŋ] ADJ wissend

knowingly ['nəuɪŋlɪ] ADV (*purposely*) bewusst; (*smile, look*) wissend

know-it-all ['nəuɪtɔ:l] (*US*) N = **know-all**

knowledge ['nɔlɪdʒ] N Wissen *nt*, Kenntnis *f*; (*learning, things learnt*) Kenntnisse *pl*; **to have no ~ of** nichts wissen von; **not to my ~** nicht, dass ich wüsste; **without my ~** ohne mein Wissen; **it is common ~ that ...** es ist allgemein bekannt, dass ...; **it has come to my ~ that ...** ich habe erfahren, dass ...; **to have a working ~ of French** Grundkenntnisse in Französisch haben

knowledgeable ['nɔlɪdʒəbl] ADJ informiert

known [nəun] PP *of* **know** ▸ ADJ bekannt; (*expert*) anerkannt

knuckle ['nʌkl] N (Finger)knöchel *m*

▸ **knuckle down** (*inf*) VI sich dahinter klemmen; **to ~ down to work** sich an die Arbeit machen

▸ **knuckle under** (*inf*) VI sich fügen, spuren

knuckle-duster ['nʌkl'dʌstə^r] N Schlagring *m*

KO N ABBR (= *knockout*) K. o. *m* ▸ VT k. o. schlagen

koala [kəu'ɑ:lə] N (*also*: **koala bear**) Koala(bär) *m*

kook [ku:k] (*US inf*) N Spinner *m*

Koran [kɔ'rɑ:n] N: **the ~** der Koran

Korea [kə'rɪə] N Korea *nt*; **North ~** Nordkorea *nt*; **South ~** Südkorea *nt*

Korean [kə'rɪən] ADJ koreanisch ▸ N Koreaner(in) *m(f)*

kosher ['kəuʃə^r] ADJ koscher

Kosovo ['kɒsɒvəʊ] N der Kosovo

kowtow ['kau'tau] VI: **to ~ to sb** vor jdm dienern *or* einen Kotau machen

Kremlin ['krɛmlɪn] N: **the ~** der Kreml

KS (*US*) ABBR (*Post*) = **Kansas**

Kt (BRIT) ABBR (*in titles*) = **knight**

Kuala Lumpur ['kwɑ:lə'lumpuə^r] N Kuala Lumpur *nt*

kudos ['kju:dɔs] N Ansehen *nt*, Ehre *f*

Kurd [kə:d] N Kurde *m*, Kurdin *f*

Kuwait [ku'weɪt] N Kuwait *nt*

Kuwaiti [ku'weɪtɪ] ADJ kuwaitisch ▸ N Kuwaiter(in) *m(f)*

kW ABBR (= *kilowatt*) kW

KY (*US*) ABBR (*Post*) = **Kentucky**

Ll

L[1], l[1] [ɛl] N (*letter*) L *nt*, l *nt*; **L for Lucy, L for Love** (*US*) ≈ L wie Ludwig

L[2] [ɛl] ABBR (BRIT *Aut*: = *learner*) *am Auto angebrachtes Kennzeichen für Fahrschüler*; = **lake**; (= *large*) gr.; (= *left*) l.

l[2] ABBR (= *litre*) l

LA (*US*) N ABBR = **Los Angeles** ▸ ABBR (*Post*) = **Louisiana**

La. (*US*) ABBR (*Post*) = **Louisiana**

lab [læb] N ABBR = **laboratory**

label ['leɪbl] N Etikett *nt*; (*brand: of record*) Label *nt* ▸ VT etikettieren; (*fig: person*) abstempeln

labor *etc* ['leɪbə^r] (*US*) N = **labour** *etc*

laboratory [lə'bɔrətərɪ] N Labor *nt*

> **Labor Day** ist in den USA und Kanada der Name für den Tag der Arbeit. Er wird dort als gesetzlicher Feiertag am ersten Montag im September begangen.

laborious [lə'bɔːrɪəs] ADJ mühsam

labor union (*US*) N Gewerkschaft *f*

labour, (*US*) **labor** ['leɪbə^r] N Arbeit *f*; (*work force*) Arbeitskräfte *pl*; (*Med*): **to be in ~** in den Wehen liegen ▸ VI: **to ~ (at sth)** sich (mit etw) abmühen ▸ VT: **to ~ a point** auf einem Thema herumreiten; **L~, the L~ Party** (BRIT) die Labour Party; **hard ~** Zwangsarbeit *f*

labour camp N Arbeitslager *nt*

labour cost N Lohnkosten *pl*

labour dispute N Arbeitskampf *m*

laboured ['leɪbəd] ADJ (*breathing*) schwer; (*movement, style*) schwerfällig

labourer ['leɪbərə^r] N Arbeiter(in) *m(f)*; **farm ~** Landarbeiter(in) *m(f)*

labour force N Arbeiterschaft *f*

labour intensive ADJ arbeitsintensiv

labour market N Arbeitsmarkt *m*

labour pains NPL Wehen *pl*

labour relations NPL Beziehungen *pl* zwischen Arbeitnehmern, Arbeitgebern und Gewerkschaften

labour-saving ['leɪbəseɪvɪŋ] ADJ arbeitsparend

laburnum [lə'bəːnəm] N (*Bot*) Goldregen *m*

labyrinth ['læbɪrɪnθ] N Labyrinth *nt*

lace [leɪs] N (*fabric*) Spitze *f*; (*of shoe etc*) (Schuh)band *nt*, Schnürsenkel *m* ▸ VT (*also*: **lace up**) (zu)schnüren; **to ~ a drink** einen Schuss Alkohol in ein Getränk geben

lacemaking ['leɪsmeɪkɪŋ] N Klöppelei *f*

lacerate ['læsəreɪt] VT zerschneiden

laceration [læsə'reɪʃən] N Schnittwunde *f*

lace-up ['leɪsʌp] ADJ (*shoes etc*) Schnür-

lack [læk] N Mangel *m* ▸ VT, VI: **sb lacks sth, sb is lacking in sth** jdm fehlt es an etw *dat*; **through** *or* **for ~ of** aus Mangel an *+dat*; **to be lacking** fehlen

lackadaisical [lækə'deɪzɪkl] ADJ lustlos

lackey ['lækɪ] (*pej*) N Lakai *m*

lacklustre, (*US*) **lackluster** ['læklʌstə^r] ADJ farblos, langweilig

laconic [lə'kɔnɪk] ADJ lakonisch

lacquer ['lækə^r] N Lack *m*; (*also*: **hair lacquer**) Haarspray *nt*

lacrosse [lə'krɔs] N Lacrosse *nt*

lacy ['leɪsɪ] ADJ Spitzen-; (*like lace*) spitzenartig

lad [læd] N Junge *m*

ladder ['lædə^r] N (*also fig*) Leiter *f*; (BRIT: *in tights*) Laufmasche *f* ▸ VT (BRIT) Laufmaschen bekommen in *+dat* ▸ VI (BRIT) Laufmaschen bekommen

laden ['leɪdn] ADJ: **~ (with)** beladen (mit); **fully ~** vollbeladen

ladle ['leɪdl] N Schöpflöffel *m*, (Schöpf)kelle *f* ▸ VT schöpfen
▸ **ladle out** VT (*fig*) austeilen

lad mag N Männerzeitschrift *f*

lady ['leɪdɪ] N (*woman*) Frau *f*; (*: dignified, graceful etc*) Dame *f*; (BRIT: *title*) Lady *f*; **ladies and gentlemen ...** meine Damen und Herren ...; **young ~** junge Dame; **the ladies' (room)** die Damentoilette

ladybird ['leɪdɪbəːd], (*US*) **ladybug** ['leɪdɪbʌg] N Marienkäfer *m*

lady-in-waiting ['leɪdɪɪn'weɪtɪŋ] N Hofdame *f*

lady-killer ['leɪdɪkɪlə^r] N Herzensbrecher *m*

ladylike ['leɪdɪlaɪk] ADJ damenhaft

ladyship ['leɪdɪʃɪp] N: **your L~** Ihre Ladyschaft

lag [læg] N (*period of time*) Zeitabstand *m* ▸ VI (*also*: **lag behind**) zurückbleiben; (*trade, investment etc*) zurückgehen ▸ VT (*pipes etc*) isolieren; **old ~** (*inf: prisoner*) (ehemaliger) Knacki *m*

lager ['lɑːgə^r] N helles Bier *nt*

lager lout (BRIT *inf*) N betrunkener Rowdy *m*

lagging ['lægɪŋ] N Isoliermaterial *nt*

lagoon [lə'guːn] N Lagune *f*

Lagos ['leɪgɔs] N Lagos *nt*

laid [leɪd] PT, PP *of* **lay**

laid-back [leɪd'bæk] (*inf*) ADJ locker
laid up ADJ: **to be ~ (with)** im Bett liegen (mit)
lain [leɪn] PP *of* **lie²**
lair [lɛəʳ] N Lager *nt*; (*cave*) Höhle *f*; (*den*) Bau *m*
laissez faire [lɛseɪ'fɛəʳ] N Laisser-faire *nt*
laity ['leɪətɪ] N OR NPL Laien *pl*
lake [leɪk] N See *m*
Lake District (BRIT) N: **the ~** der Lake Distrikt, *Seengebiet im NW Englands*
lamb [læm] N Lamm *nt*; (*meat*) Lammfleisch *nt*
lamb chop N Lammkotelett *nt*
lambskin ['læmskɪn] N Lammfell *nt*
lambswool ['læmzwul] N Lammwolle *f*
lame [leɪm] ADJ lahm; (*argument, answer*) schwach
lame duck N (*person*) Niete *f*; (*business*) unwirtschaftliche Firma *f*
lamely ['leɪmlɪ] ADV lahm
lament [lə'mɛnt] N Klage *f* ▸ VT beklagen
lamentable ['læməntəbl] ADJ beklagenswert
laminated ['læmɪneɪtɪd] ADJ laminiert; (*metal*) geschichtet; **~ glass** Verbundglas *nt*; **~ wood** Sperrholz *nt*
lamp [læmp] N Lampe *f*
lamplight ['læmplaɪt] N: **by ~** bei Lampenlicht
lampoon [læm'pu:n] N Schmähschrift *f* ▸ VT verspotten
lamppost ['læmppəust] (BRIT) N Laternenpfahl *m*
lampshade ['læmpʃeɪd] N Lampenschirm *m*
lance [lɑ:ns] N Lanze *f* ▸ VT (*Med*) aufschneiden
lance corporal (BRIT) N Obergefreite(r) *m*
lancet ['lɑ:nsɪt] N (*Med*) Lanzette *f*
Lancs [læŋks] (BRIT) ABBR (*Post*) = **Lancashire**
land [lænd] N Land *nt*; (*as property*) Grund und Boden *m* ▸ VI (*Aviat, fig*) landen; (*from ship*) an Land gehen ▸ VT (*passengers*) absetzen; (*goods*) an Land bringen; **to own ~** Land besitzen; **to go** *or* **travel by ~** auf dem Landweg reisen; **to ~ on one's feet** (*fig*) auf die Füße fallen; **to ~ sb with sth** (*inf*) jdm etw aufhalsen
▸ **land up** VI; **to ~ up in/at** landen in *+dat*
landed gentry ['lændɪd-] N Landadel *m*
landfill site ['lændfɪl-] N ≈ Mülldeponie *f*
landing ['lændɪŋ] N (*of house*) Flur *m*; (*outside flat door*) Treppenabsatz *m*; (*Aviat*) Landung *f*
landing card N Einreisekarte *f*
landing craft N INV Landungsboot *nt*
landing gear N (*Aviat*) Fahrgestell *nt*
landing stage N Landesteg *m*
landing strip N Landebahn *f*
landlady ['lændleɪdɪ] N Vermieterin *f*; (*of pub*) Wirtin *f*
landline ['lændlaɪn] N Festnetz *nt*
landlocked ['lændlɔkt] ADJ von Land eingeschlossen; **~ country** Binnenstaat *m*
landlord ['lændlɔ:d] N Vermieter *m*; (*of pub*) Wirt *m*
landlubber ['lændlʌbəʳ] (*old*) N Landratte *f*
landmark ['lændmɑ:k] N Orientierungspunkt *m*; (*famous building*) Wahrzeichen *nt*; (*fig*) Meilenstein *m*
landowner ['lændəunəʳ] N Grundbesitzer(in) *m(f)*
landscape ['lændskeɪp] N Landschaft *f* ▸ VT landschaftlich *or* gärtnerisch gestalten
landscape architect N Landschaftsarchitekt(in) *m(f)*
landscape gardener N Landschaftsgärtner(in) *m(f)*
landscape painting N Landschaftsmalerei *f*
landslide ['lændslaɪd] N Erdrutsch *m*; (*fig: electoral*) Erdrutschsieg *m*
lane [leɪn] N (*in country*) Weg *m*; (*in town*) Gasse *f*; (*of carriageway*) Spur *f*; (*of race course, swimming pool*) Bahn *f*; **shipping ~** Schifffahrtsweg *m*
language ['læŋgwɪdʒ] N Sprache *f*; **bad ~** Kraftausdrücke *pl*
language laboratory N Sprachlabor *nt*
languid ['læŋgwɪd] ADJ träge, matt
languish ['læŋgwɪʃ] VI schmachten; (*project, case*) erfolglos bleiben
lank [læŋk] ADJ (*hair*) strähnig
lanky ['læŋkɪ] ADJ schlaksig
lanolin, lanoline ['lænəlɪn] N Lanolin *nt*
lantern ['læntən] N Laterne *f*
Laos [laus] N Laos *nt*
lap [læp] N Schoß *m*; (*in race*) Runde *f* ▸ VT (*also*: **lap up**) aufschlecken ▸ VI (*water*) plätschern
▸ **lap up** VT (*fig*) genießen
lapdog ['læpdɔg] (*pej*) N (*fig*) Schoßhund *m*
lapel [lə'pɛl] N Aufschlag *m*, Revers *m or nt*
Lapland ['læplænd] N Lappland *nt*
Lapp [læp] ADJ lappländisch ▸ N Lappe *m*, Lappin *f*; (*Ling*) Lappländisch *nt*
lapse [læps] N (*bad behaviour*) Fehltritt *m*; (*of memory etc*) Schwäche *f*; (*of time*) Zeitspanne *f* ▸ VI ablaufen; (*law*) ungültig werden; **to ~ into bad habits** in schlechte Gewohnheiten verfallen
laptop ['læptɔp] (*Comput*) N Laptop *m* ▸ CPD Laptop-
larceny ['lɑ:sənɪ] N Diebstahl *m*
larch [lɑ:tʃ] N Lärche *f*
lard [lɑ:d] N Schweineschmalz *nt*
larder ['lɑ:dəʳ] N Speisekammer *f*; (*cupboard*) Speiseschrank *m*
large [lɑ:dʒ] ADJ groß; (*person*) korpulent; **to make larger** vergrößern; **a ~ number of people** eine große Anzahl von Menschen; **on a ~ scale** im großen Rahmen; (*extensive*) weitreichend; **at ~** (*as a whole*) im Allgemeinen; (*at liberty*) auf freiem Fuß; **by and ~** im Großen und Ganzen
large goods vehicle N Lastkraftwagen *m*
largely ['lɑ:dʒlɪ] ADV (*mostly*) zum größten Teil; (*mainly*) hauptsächlich
large-scale ['lɑ:dʒ'skeɪl] ADJ im großen Rahmen; (*extensive*) weitreichend; (*map, diagram*) in einem großen Maßstab
largesse [lɑ:'ʒɛs] N Großzügigkeit *f*
lark [lɑ:k] N (*bird*) Lerche *f*; (*joke*) Spaß *m*, Jux *m*
▸ **lark about** VI herumalbern
larva ['lɑ:və] (*pl* **larvae**) N Larve *f*
larvae ['lɑ:vi:] NPL *of* **larva**

laryngitis [lærɪn'dʒaɪtɪs] N Kehlkopfentzündung *f*
larynx ['lærɪŋks] N Kehlkopf *m*
lasagne [lə'zænjə] N Lasagne *pl*
lascivious [lə'sɪvɪəs] ADJ lüstern
laser ['leɪzə^r] N Laser *m*
laser beam N Laserstrahl *m*
laser printer N Laserdrucker *m*
lash [læʃ] N (*also:* **eyelash**) Wimper *f*; (*blow with whip*) Peitschenhieb *m* ▸ VT peitschen; (*rain, wind*) peitschen gegen; (*tie*): **to ~ to** festbinden an *+dat*; **to ~ together** zusammenbinden
▸ **lash down** VT festbinden ▸ VI (*rain*) niederprasseln
▸ **lash out** VI um sich schlagen; **to ~ out at sb** auf jdn losschlagen; **to ~ out at** *or* **against sb** (*criticize*) gegen jdn wettern
lashing ['læʃɪŋ] N: **lashings of** (BRIT *inf*) massenhaft
lass [læs] (BRIT) N Mädchen *nt*
lasso [læ'su:] N Lasso *nt* ▸ VT mit dem Lasso einfangen
last [lɑ:st] ADJ letzte(r, s) ▸ ADV (*most recently*) zuletzt, das letzte Mal; (*finally*) als Letztes ▸ VI (*continue*) dauern; (*: in good condition*) sich halten; (*money, commodity*) reichen; **~ week** letzte Woche; **~ night** gestern Abend; **~ but one** vorletzte(r, s); **the ~ time** das letzte Mal; **at ~** endlich; **it lasts (for) 2 hours** es dauert 2 Stunden
last-ditch ['lɑ:st'dɪtʃ] ADJ (*attempt*) allerletzte(r, s)
lasting ['lɑ:stɪŋ] ADJ dauerhaft
lastly ['lɑ:stlɪ] ADV (*finally*) schließlich; (*last of all*) zum Schluss
last-minute ['lɑ:stmɪnɪt] ADJ in letzter Minute
latch [lætʃ] N Riegel *m*; **to be on the ~** nur eingeklinkt sein
▸ **latch on to** VT FUS (*person*) sich anschließen *+dat*; (*idea*) abfahren auf *+acc* (*inf*)
latchkey ['lætʃki:] N Hausschlüssel *m*
latchkey child N Schlüsselkind *nt*
late [leɪt] ADJ spät; (*not on time*) verspätet ▸ ADV spät; (*behind time*) zu spät; (*recently*): **~ of Glasgow** bis vor Kurzem in Glasgow wohnhaft; **the ~ Mr X** (*deceased*) der verstorbene Herr X; **in ~ May** Ende Mai; **to be (10 minutes) ~** (10 Minuten) zu spät kommen; (*train etc*) (10 Minuten) Verspätung haben; **to work ~** länger arbeiten; **~ in life** relativ spät (im Leben); **of ~** in letzter Zeit
latecomer ['leɪtkʌmə^r] N Nachzügler(in) *m(f)*
lately ['leɪtlɪ] ADV in letzter Zeit
lateness ['leɪtnɪs] N (*of person*) Zuspätkommen *nt*; (*of train, event*) Verspätung *f*
latent ['leɪtnt] ADJ (*energy*) ungenutzt; (*skill, ability*) verborgen
late opening N verlängerte Öffnungszeiten *pl*
later ['leɪtə^r] ADJ, ADV später; **~ on** nachher
lateral ['lætərəl] ADJ seitlich; **~ thinking** kreatives Denken *nt*
latest ['leɪtɪst] ADJ neueste(r, s) ▸ N: **at the ~** spätestens
latex ['leɪtɛks] N Latex *m*
lathe [leɪð] N Drehbank *f*
lather ['lɑ:ðə^r] N (Seifen)schaum *m* ▸ VT einschäumen
Latin ['lætɪn] N Latein *nt*; (*person*) Südländer(in) *m(f)* ▸ ADJ lateinisch; (*temperament etc*) südländisch
Latin America N Lateinamerika *nt*
Latin American ADJ lateinamerikanisch ▸ N Lateinamerikaner(in) *m(f)*
Latino [læ'ti:nəu] (*US*) ADJ aus Lateinamerika stammend ▸ N Latino *mf*, *in den USA lebende(r) Lateinamerikaner(in)*
latitude ['lætɪtju:d] N (*Geog*) Breite *f*; (*fig: freedom*) Freiheit *f*
latrine [lə'tri:n] N Latrine *f*
latter ['lætə^r] ADJ (*of two*) letztere(r, s); (*later*) spätere(r, s); (*second part of period*) zweite(r, s); (*recent*) letzte(r, s) ▸ N: **the ~** der/die/das Letztere, die Letzteren
latter-day ['lætədeɪ] ADJ modern
latterly ['lætəlɪ] ADV in letzter Zeit
lattice ['lætɪs] N Gitter *nt*
lattice window N Gitterfenster *nt*
Latvia ['lætvɪə] N Lettland *nt*
Latvian ['lætvɪən] ADJ lettisch ▸ N Lette *m*, Lettin *f*; (*Ling*) Lettisch *nt*
laudable ['lɔ:dəbl] ADJ lobenswert
laudatory ['lɔ:dətrɪ] ADJ (*comments*) lobend; (*speech*) Lob-
laugh [lɑ:f] N Lachen *nt* ▸ VI lachen; **(to do sth) for a ~** (etw) aus Spaß (tun)
▸ **laugh at** VT FUS lachen über *+acc*
▸ **laugh off** VT mit einem Lachen abtun
laughable ['lɑ:fəbl] ADJ lächerlich, lachhaft
laughing gas ['lɑ:fɪŋ-] N Lachgas *nt*
laughing matter N: **this is no ~** das ist nicht zum Lachen
laughing stock N: **to be the ~ of** zum Gespött *+gen* werden
laughter ['lɑ:ftə^r] N Lachen *nt*, Gelächter *nt*
launch [lɔ:ntʃ] N (*of rocket, missile*) Abschuss *m*; (*of satellite*) Start *m*; (*Comm: of product*) Einführung *f*; (*: with publicity*) Lancierung *f*; (*motorboat*) Barkasse *f* ▸ VT (*ship*) vom Stapel lassen; (*rocket, missile*) abschießen; (*satellite*) starten; (*fig: start*) beginnen mit; (*Comm*) auf den Markt bringen; (*: with publicity*) lancieren
▸ **launch into** VT FUS (*speech*) vom Stapel lassen; (*activity*) in Angriff nehmen
▸ **launch out** VI; **to ~ out (into)** beginnen (mit)
launching ['lɔ:ntʃɪŋ] N (*of ship*) Stapellauf *m*; (*of rocket, missile*) Abschuss *m*; (*of satellite*) Start *m*; (*fig: start*) Beginn *m*; (*Comm: of product*) Einführung *f*; (*: with publicity*) Lancierung *f*
launching pad, launch pad N Startrampe *f*, Abschussrampe *f*
launder ['lɔ:ndə^r] VT waschen und bügeln; (*pej: money*) waschen
Launderette® [lɔ:n'drɛt] (BRIT) N Waschsalon *m*
Laundromat® ['lɔ:ndrəmæt] (*US*) N Waschsalon *m*

laundry ['lɔːndrɪ] N Wäsche *f*; (*dirty*) (schmutzige) Wäsche; (*business*) Wäscherei *f*; (*room*) Waschküche *f*; **to do the ~** (Wäsche) waschen
laureate ['lɔːrɪət] ADJ *see* **poet laureate**
laurel ['lɔrl] N (*tree*) Lorbeer(baum) *m*; **to rest on one's laurels** sich auf seinen Lorbeeren ausruhen
Lausanne [ləu'zæn] N Lausanne *nt*
lava ['lɑːvə] N Lava *f*
lavatory ['lævətərɪ] N Toilette *f*
lavatory paper N Toilettenpapier *nt*
lavender ['lævəndəʳ] N Lavendel *m*
lavish ['lævɪʃ] ADJ großzügig; (*meal*) üppig; (*surroundings*) feudal; (*wasteful*) verschwenderisch ▸ VT: **to ~ sth on sb** jdn mit etw überhäufen
lavishly ['lævɪʃlɪ] ADV (*generously*) großzügig; (*sumptuously*) aufwendig
law [lɔː] N Recht *nt*; (*a rule: also of nature, science*) Gesetz *nt*; (*professions connected with law*) Rechtswesen *nt*; (*Scol*) Jura *no art*; **against the ~** rechtswidrig; **to study ~** Jura *or* Recht(swissenschaft) studieren; **to go to ~** vor Gericht gehen; **to break the ~** gegen das Gesetz verstoßen
law-abiding ['lɔːəbaɪdɪŋ] ADJ gesetzestreu
law and order N Ruhe und Ordnung *f*
lawbreaker ['lɔːbreɪkəʳ] N Rechtsbrecher(in) *m(f)*
law court N Gerichtshof *m*, Gericht *nt*
lawful ['lɔːful] ADJ rechtmäßig
lawfully ['lɔːfəlɪ] ADV rechtmäßig
lawless ['lɔːlɪs] ADJ gesetzwidrig
Law Lord (BRIT) N *Mitglied des Oberhauses mit besonderem Verantwortungsbereich in Rechtsfragen*
lawn [lɔːn] N Rasen *m*
lawn mower N Rasenmäher *m*
lawn tennis N Rasentennis *nt*
law school (US) N juristische Hochschule *f*
law student N Jurastudent(in) *m(f)*
lawsuit ['lɔːsuːt] N Prozess *m*
lawyer ['lɔːjəʳ] N (Rechts)anwalt *m*, (Rechts)anwältin *f*
lax [læks] ADJ lax
laxative ['læksətɪv] N Abführmittel *nt*
laxity ['læksɪtɪ] N Laxheit *f*; **moral ~** lockere *or* laxe Moral *f*
lay [leɪ] (*pt, pp* **laid**) PT *of* **lie²** ▸ ADJ (*Rel: preacher etc*) Laien- ▸ VT legen; (*table*) decken; (*carpet, cable etc*) verlegen; (*plans*) schmieden; (*trap*) stellen; **the ~ person** (*not expert*) der Laie; **to ~ facts/ proposals before sb** jdm Tatsachen vorlegen/ Vorschläge unterbreiten; **to ~ one's hands on sth** (*fig*) etw in die Finger bekommen; **to get laid** (*inf!*) bumsen (*inf!*)
▸ **lay aside** VT weglegen, zur Seite legen
▸ **lay by** VT beiseitelegen, auf die Seite legen
▸ **lay down** VT hinlegen; (*rules, laws etc*) festlegen; **to ~ down the law** Vorschriften machen; **to ~ down one's life** sein Leben geben
▸ **lay in** VT (*supply*) anlegen
▸ **lay into** VT FUS losgehen auf +*acc*; (*criticize*) herunterputzen
▸ **lay off** VT (*workers*) entlassen
▸ **lay on** VT (*meal*) auftischen; (*entertainment etc*) sorgen für; (*water, gas*) anschließen; (*paint*) auftragen
▸ **lay out** VT ausbreiten; (*inf: spend*) ausgeben
▸ **lay up** VT (*illness*) außer Gefecht setzen; *see also* **lay by**
layabout ['leɪəbaut] (*inf, pej*) N Faulenzer *m*
lay-by ['leɪbaɪ] (BRIT) N Parkbucht *f*
lay days NPL Liegezeit *f*
layer ['leɪəʳ] N Schicht *f*
layette [leɪ'ɛt] N Babyausstattung *f*
layman ['leɪmən] N (*irreg*) Laie *m*
lay-off ['leɪɔf] N Entlassung *f*
layout ['leɪaut] N (*of garden*) Anlage *f*; (*of building*) Aufteilung *f*; (*Typ*) Layout *nt*
laze [leɪz] VI (*also:* **laze about**) (herum)faulenzen
laziness ['leɪzɪnɪs] N Faulheit *f*
lazy ['leɪzɪ] ADJ faul; (*movement, action*) langsam, träge
LB (CANADA) ABBR = **Labrador**
lb ABBR (= *pound (weight)*) *britisches Pfund (0,45 kg)*, ≈ Pfd.
lbw ABBR (*Cricket: = leg before wicket*) *Regelverletzung beim Kricket*
LC (US) N ABBR (= *Library of Congress*) *Bibliothek des US-Parlaments*
lc ABBR (*Typ: = lower case*) *see* **case**
L/C ABBR = **letter of credit**
lcd, LCD N ABBR (= *liquid-crystal display*) LCD *nt*
Ld (BRIT) ABBR (*in titles*) = **lord**
LDS N ABBR (BRIT: = *Licentiate in Dental Surgery*) ≈ Dr. med. dent. ▸ N ABBR (= *Latter-day Saints*) Heilige *pl* der Letzten Tage
LEA (BRIT) N ABBR (= *Local Education Authority*) *örtliche Schulbehörde*
lead¹ [liːd] (*pt, pp* **led**) N (*Sport, fig*) Führung *f*; (*clue*) Spur *f*; (*in play, film*) Hauptrolle *f*; (*for dog*) Leine *f*; (*Elec*) Kabel *nt* ▸ VT anführen; (*guide*) führen; (*organization, orchestra*) leiten ▸ VI führen; **to be in the ~** (*Sport, fig*) in Führung liegen; **to take the ~** (*Sport*) in Führung gehen; **to ~ the way** vorangehen; **to ~ sb astray** jdn vom rechten Weg abführen; (*mislead*) jdn irreführen; **to ~ sb to believe that ...** jdm den Eindruck vermitteln, dass ...; **to ~ sb to do sth** jdn dazu bringen, etw zu tun
▸ **lead away** VT wegführen; (*prisoner etc*) abführen
▸ **lead back** VT zurückführen
▸ **lead off** VI (*in conversation etc*) den Anfang machen; (*room, road*) abgehen ▸ VT FUS abgehen von
▸ **lead on** VT (*tease*) aufziehen
▸ **lead to** VT FUS führen zu
▸ **lead up to** VT FUS (*events*) vorangehen +*dat*; (*in conversation*) hinauswollen auf +*acc*
lead² [lɛd] N Blei *nt*; (*in pencil*) Mine *f*
leaded ['lɛdɪd] ADJ (*window*) bleiverglast; (*petrol*) verbleit

leaden ['lɛdn] ADJ (*sky, sea*) bleiern; (*movements*) bleischwer
leader ['li:dəʳ] N Führer(in) *m(f)*; (*Sport*) Erste(r) *f(m)*; (*in newspaper*) Leitartikel *m*; **the L~ of the House (of Commons/of Lords)** (BRIT) der Führer des Unterhauses/des Oberhauses
leadership ['li:dəʃɪp] N Führung *f*; (*position*) Vorsitz *m*; (*quality*) Führungsqualitäten *pl*
lead-free ['lɛdfri:] ADJ (*old*) bleifrei
leading ['li:dɪŋ] ADJ führend; (*role*) Haupt-; (*first, front*) vorderste(r, s)
leading lady N (*Theat*) Hauptdarstellerin *f*
leading light N führende Persönlichkeit *f*
leading man N (*irreg: Theat*) Hauptdarsteller *m*
leading question N Suggestivfrage *f*
lead pencil [lɛd-] N Bleistift *m*
lead poisoning [lɛd-] N Bleivergiftung *f*
lead singer [li:d-] N Leadsänger(in) *m(f)*
lead time [li:d-] N (*Comm: for production*) Produktionszeit *f*; (*: for delivery*) Lieferzeit *f*
lead-up ['li:dʌp] N: **the ~ to sth** die Zeit vor etw *dat*
leaf [li:f] (*pl* **leaves**) N Blatt *nt*; (*of table*) Ausziehplatte *f*; **to turn over a new ~** einen neuen Anfang machen; **to take a ~ out of sb's book** sich *dat* von jdm eine Scheibe abschneiden
▸ **leaf through** VT FUS durchblättern
leaflet ['li:flɪt] N Informationsblatt *nt*
leafy ['li:fɪ] ADJ (*tree, branch*) belaubt; (*lane, suburb*) grün
league [li:g] N (*of people, clubs*) Verband *m*; (*of countries*) Bund *m*; (*Football*) Liga *f*; **to be in ~ with sb** mit jdm gemeinsame Sache machen
league table N Tabelle *f*
leak [li:k] N Leck *nt*; (*in roof, pipe etc*) undichte Stelle *f*; (*piece of information*) zugespielte Information *f* ▸ VI (*shoes, roof, pipe*) undicht sein; (*ship*) lecken; (*liquid*) auslaufen; (*gas*) ausströmen ▸ VT (*information*) durchsickern lassen; **to ~ sth to sb** jdm etw zuspielen
▸ **leak out** VI (*liquid*) auslaufen; (*news, information*) durchsickern
leakage ['li:kɪdʒ] N (*of liquid*) Auslaufen *nt*; (*of gas*) Ausströmen *nt*
leaky ['li:kɪ] ADJ (*roof, container*) undicht
lean [li:n] (*pt, pp* **leaned** *or* **leant**) ADJ (*person*) schlank; (*meat, time*) mager ▸ VT: **to ~ sth on sth** etw an etw *acc* lehnen; (*rest*) etw auf etw *acc* stützen ▸ VI (*slope*) sich neigen; **to ~ against** sich lehnen gegen; **to ~ on** sich stützen auf *+acc*; **to ~ forward/back** sich vorbeugen/zurücklehnen; **to ~ towards** tendieren zu
▸ **lean out** VI sich hinauslehnen
▸ **lean over** VI sich vorbeugen
leaning ['li:nɪŋ] N Hang *m*, Neigung *f*
leant [lɛnt] PT, PP *of* **lean**
lean-to ['li:ntu:] N Anbau *m*
leap [li:p] (*pt, pp* **leaped** *or* **leapt**) N Sprung *m*; (*in price, number etc*) sprunghafter Anstieg *m* ▸ VI springen; (*price, number etc*) sprunghaft (an)steigen
▸ **leap at** VT FUS (*offer*) sich stürzen auf *+acc*; (*opportunity*) beim Schopf ergreifen
▸ **leap up** VI aufspringen
leapfrog ['li:pfrɔg] N Bockspringen *nt*
leapt [lɛpt] PT, PP *of* **leap**
leap year N Schaltjahr *nt*
learn [lə:n] (*pt, pp* **learned** *or* **learnt**) VT lernen; (*facts*) erfahren ▸ VI lernen; **to ~ about** *or* **of sth** von etw erfahren; **to ~ about sth** (*study*) etw lernen; **to ~ that ...** (*hear, read*) erfahren, dass ...; **to ~ to do sth** etw lernen
learned ['lə:nɪd] ADJ gelehrt; (*book, paper*) wissenschaftlich
learner ['lə:nəʳ] (BRIT) N (*also*: **learner driver**) Fahrschüler(in) *m(f)*
learning ['lə:nɪŋ] N Gelehrsamkeit *f*
learnt [lə:nt] PT, PP *of* **learn**
lease [li:s] N Pachtvertrag *m* ▸ VT: **to ~ sth (to sb)** etw (an jdn) verpachten; **on ~ (to)** verpachtet (an *+acc*); **to ~ sth (from sb)** etw (von jdm) pachten
▸ **lease back** VT rückmieten
▸ **lease out** VT vermieten
leaseback ['li:sbæk] N Verkauf und Rückmiete *pl*
leasehold ['li:shəuld] N Pachtbesitz *m* ▸ ADJ gepachtet
leash [li:ʃ] N Leine *f*
least [li:st] ADV am wenigsten ▸ ADJ: **the ~** (*+ noun*) der/die/das wenigste; (*slightest*) der/die/das geringste; **the ~ expensive car** das billigste Auto; **at ~** mindestens; (*still, rather*) wenigstens; **you could at ~ have written** du hättest wenigstens schreiben können; **not in the ~** nicht im Geringsten; **it was the ~ I could do** das war das wenigste, was ich tun konnte
leather ['lɛðəʳ] N Leder *nt*
leave [li:v] (*pt, pp* **left**) VT verlassen; (*leave behind*) zurücklassen; (*mark, stain*) hinterlassen; (*object: accidentally*) liegen lassen, stehen lassen; (*food*) übrig lassen; (*space, time etc*) lassen ▸ VI (*go away*) (weg)gehen; (*bus, train*) abfahren ▸ N Urlaub *m*; **to ~ sth to sb** (*money etc*) jdm etw hinterlassen; **to ~ sb with sth** (*impose*) jdm etw aufhalsen; (*possession*) jdm etw lassen; **they were left with nothing** ihnen blieb nichts; **to be left** übrig sein; **to be left over** (*remain*) übrig (geblieben) sein; **to ~ for** gehen/fahren nach; **to take one's ~ of sb** sich von jdm verabschieden; **on ~** auf Urlaub
▸ **leave behind** VT zurücklassen; (*object: accidentally*) liegen lassen, stehen lassen
▸ **leave off** VT (*cover, lid*) ablassen; (*heating, light*) auslassen ▸ VI (*inf: stop*) aufhören
▸ **leave on** VT (*light, heating*) anlassen
▸ **leave out** VT auslassen
leave of absence N Beurlaubung *f*
leaves [li:vz] NPL *of* **leaf**
leaving do [li:vɪŋdu:] N Abschiedsfeier *f*
Lebanese [lɛbə'ni:z] ADJ libanesisch ▸ N INV Libanese *m*, Libanesin *f*
Lebanon ['lɛbənən] N Libanon *m*
lecherous ['lɛtʃərəs] (*pej*) ADJ lüstern

lectern ['lɛktə:n] N Rednerpult *nt*
lecture ['lɛktʃə^r] N Vortrag *m*; (*Univ*) Vorlesung *f* ▶ VI Vorträge/Vorlesungen halten ▶ VT (*scold*): **to ~ sb on** *or* **about sth** jdm wegen etw eine Strafpredigt halten; **to give a ~ on** einen Vortrag/eine Vorlesung halten über *+acc*
lecture hall N Hörsaal *m*
lecturer ['lɛktʃərə^r] (BRIT) N Dozent(in) *m(f)*; (*speaker*) Redner(in) *m(f)*
lecture theatre N Hörsaal *m*
LED N ABBR (*Elec*: = *light-emitting diode*) LED *f*
led [lɛd] PT, PP *of* **lead²**
ledge [lɛdʒ] N (*of mountain*) (Fels)vorsprung *m*; (*of window*) Fensterbrett *nt*; (*on wall*) Leiste *f*
ledger ['lɛdʒə^r] N (*Comm*) Hauptbuch *nt*
lee [li:] N Windschatten *m*; (*Naut*) Lee *f*
leech [li:tʃ] N Blutegel *m*; (*fig*) Blutsauger *m*
leek [li:k] N Porree *m*, Lauch *m*
leer [lɪə^r] VI: **to ~ at sb** jdm lüsterne Blicke zuwerfen
leeward ['li:wəd] (*Naut*) ADJ (*side etc*) Lee- ▶ ADV leewärts ▶ N: **to ~** an der Leeseite; (*direction*) nach der Leeseite
leeway ['li:weɪ] N (*fig*): **to have some ~** etwas Spielraum haben; **there's a lot of ~ to make up** ein großer Rückstand muss aufgeholt werden
left [lɛft] PT, PP *of* **leave** ▶ ADJ (*remaining*) übrig; (*of position*) links; (*of direction*) nach links ▶ N linke Seite *f* ▶ ADV links; nach links; **on the ~, to the ~** links; **the L~** (*Pol*) die Linke
left-click ['lɛftklɪk] (*Comput*) VT links klicken ▶ VI links klicken auf *+acc*
left-hand drive ['lɛfthænd-] ADJ mit Linkssteuerung
left-handed [lɛft'hændɪd] ADJ linkshändig
left-hand side ['lɛfthænd-] N linke Seite *f*
leftie ['lɛftɪ] (*inf*) N Linke(r) *f(m)*
leftist ['lɛftɪst] (*Pol*) N Linke(r) *f(m)* ▶ ADJ linke(r, s)
left-luggage [lɛft'lʌgɪdʒ], **left-luggage office** (BRIT) N Gepäckaufbewahrung *f*
left-luggage locker N Gepäckschließfach *nt*
leftovers ['lɛftəuvəz] NPL Reste *pl*
left wing N linker Flügel
left-wing ['lɛft'wɪŋ] ADJ (*Pol*) linke(r, s)
left-winger ['lɛft'wɪŋgə^r] N (*Pol*) Linke(r) *f(m)*
lefty ['lɛftɪ] N = **leftie**
leg [lɛg] N Bein *nt*; (*Culin*) Keule *f*; (*Sport*) Runde *f*; (: *of relay race*) Teilstrecke *f*; (*of journey etc*) Etappe *f*; **to stretch one's legs** sich *dat* die Beine vertreten; **to get one's ~ over** (*inf*) bumsen
legacy ['lɛgəsɪ] N Erbschaft *f*; (*fig*) Erbe *nt*
legal ['li:gl] ADJ (*requirement*) rechtlich, gesetzlich; (*system*) Rechts-; (*allowed by law*) legal, rechtlich zulässig; **to take ~ action** *or* **proceedings against sb** jdn verklagen
legal adviser N juristischer Berater *m*
legal holiday (US) N gesetzlicher Feiertag *m*
legality [lɪ'gælɪtɪ] N Legalität *f*
legalize ['li:gəlaɪz] VT legalisieren
legally ['li:gəlɪ] ADV rechtlich, gesetzlich; (*in accordance with the law*) rechtmäßig; **~ binding** rechtsverbindlich
legal tender N gesetzliches Zahlungsmittel *nt*
legation [lɪ'geɪʃən] N Gesandtschaft *f*
legend ['lɛdʒənd] N Legende *f*, Sage *f*; (*fig*: *person*) Legende *f*
legendary ['lɛdʒəndərɪ] ADJ legendär; (*very famous*) berühmt
-legged ['lɛgɪd] SUFF -beinig
leggings ['lɛgɪŋz] NPL Leggings *pl*, Leggins *pl*
leggy ['lɛgɪ] ADJ langbeinig
legibility [lɛdʒɪ'bɪlɪtɪ] N Lesbarkeit *f*
legible ['lɛdʒəbl] ADJ leserlich
legibly ['lɛdʒəblɪ] ADV leserlich
legion ['li:dʒən] N Legion *f* ▶ ADJ zahlreich
legionnaire [li:dʒə'nɛə^r] N Legionär *m*
legionnaire's disease N Legionärskrankheit *f*
legislate ['lɛdʒɪsleɪt] VI Gesetze/ein Gesetz erlassen
legislation [lɛdʒɪs'leɪʃən] N Gesetzgebung *f*; (*laws*) Gesetze *pl*
legislative ['lɛdʒɪslətɪv] ADJ gesetzgebend; **~ reforms** Gesetzesreformen *pl*
legislator ['lɛdʒɪsleɪtə^r] N Gesetzgeber *m*
legislature ['lɛdʒɪslətʃə^r] N Legislative *f*
legitimacy [lɪ'dʒɪtɪməsɪ] N (*validity*) Berechtigung *f*; (*legality*) Rechtmäßigkeit *f*
legitimate [lɪ'dʒɪtɪmət] ADJ (*reasonable*) berechtigt; (*excuse*) begründet; (*legal*) rechtmäßig
legitimize [lɪ'dʒɪtɪmaɪz] VT legitimieren
legless ['lɛglɪs] (*inf*) ADJ (*drunk*) sternhagelvoll
legroom ['lɛgru:m] N Beinfreiheit *f*
Leics (BRIT) ABBR (*Post*) = **Leicestershire**
leisure ['lɛʒə^r] N Freizeit *f*; **at ~** in Ruhe
leisure centre N Freizeitzentrum *nt*
leisurely ['lɛʒəlɪ] ADJ geruhsam
leisure suit N Freizeitanzug *m*
lemon ['lɛmən] N Zitrone *f*; (*colour*) Zitronengelb *nt*
lemonade [lɛmə'neɪd] N Limonade *f*
lemon cheese N = **lemon curd**
lemon curd N *zähflüssiger Brotaufstrich mit Zitronengeschmack*
lemon juice N Zitronensaft *m*
lemon sole N Seezunge *f*
lemon squeezer N Zitronenpresse *f*
lemon tea N Zitronentee *m*
lend [lɛnd] (*pt, pp* **lent**) VT: **to ~ sth to sb** jdm etw leihen; **to ~ sb a hand (with sth)** jdm (bei etw) helfen; **it lends itself to ...** es eignet sich für ...
lender ['lɛndə^r] N Verleiher(in) *m(f)*
lending library ['lɛndɪŋ-] N Leihbücherei *f*
length [lɛŋθ] N Länge *f*; (*piece*) Stück *nt*; (*amount of time*) Dauer *f*; **the ~ of the island** (*all along*) die ganze Insel entlang; **2 metres in ~** 2 Meter lang; **at ~** (*at last*) schließlich; (*for a long time*) lange; **to go to great lengths to do sth** sich *dat* sehr viel Mühe geben, etw zu tun; **to fall full-~** lang hinfallen; **to lie full-~** in voller Länge daliegen

lengthen ['lɛŋθn] VT verlängern ▸ VI länger werden
lengthways ['lɛŋθweɪz] ADV der Länge nach
lengthy ['lɛŋθɪ] ADJ lang
leniency ['li:nɪənsɪ] N Nachsicht *f*
lenient ['li:nɪənt] ADJ nachsichtig
leniently ['li:nɪəntlɪ] ADV nachsichtig
lens [lɛnz] N (*of spectacles*) Glas *nt*; (*of camera*) Objektiv *nt*; (*of telescope*) Linse *f*
Lent [lɛnt] N Fastenzeit *f*
lent [lɛnt] PT, PP *of* **lend**
lentil ['lɛntɪl] N Linse *f*
Leo ['li:əu] N Löwe *m*; **to be ~** Löwe sein
leopard ['lɛpəd] N Leopard *m*
leotard ['li:ətɑ:d] N Gymnastikanzug *m*
leper ['lɛpə^r] N Leprakranke(r) *f*(*m*)
leper colony N Leprasiedlung *f*
leprosy ['lɛprəsɪ] N Lepra *f*
lesbian ['lɛzbɪən] ADJ lesbisch ▸ N Lesbierin *f*
lesion ['li:ʒən] N Verletzung *f*
Lesotho [lɪ'su:tu:] N Lesotho *nt*
less [lɛs] ADJ, PRON, ADV weniger ▸ PREP: **~ tax/10% discount** abzüglich Steuer/10% Rabatt; **~ than half** weniger als die Hälfte; **~ than ever** weniger denn je; **~ and ~** immer weniger; **the ~ he works …** je weniger er arbeitet …; **the Prime Minister, no ~** kein Geringerer als der Premierminister
lessee [lɛ'si:] N Pächter(in) *m*(*f*)
lessen ['lɛsn] VI nachlassen, abnehmen ▸ VT verringern
lesser ['lɛsə^r] ADJ geringer; **to a ~ extent** in geringerem Maße
lesson ['lɛsn] N (*class*) Stunde *f*; (*example, warning*) Lehre *f*; **to teach sb a ~** (*fig*) jdm eine Lektion erteilen
lessor ['lɛsɔ:^r] N Verpächter(in) *m*(*f*)
lest [lɛst] CONJ damit … nicht
let [lɛt] (*pt, pp* **~**) VT (*allow*) lassen; (BRIT: *lease*) vermieten; **to ~ sb do sth** jdn etw tun lassen, jdm erlauben, etw zu tun; **to ~ sb know sth** jdn etw wissen lassen; **~'s go** gehen wir!; **~ him come** lassen Sie ihn kommen; **"to ~"** „zu vermieten"
▸ **let down** VT (*tyre etc*) die Luft herauslassen aus; (*person*) im Stich lassen; (*dress etc*) länger machen; (*hem*) auslassen; **to ~ one's hair down** (*fig*) aus sich herausgehen
▸ **let go** VI loslassen ▸ VT (*release*) freilassen; **to ~ go of** loslassen; **to ~ o.s. go** aus sich herausgehen; (*neglect o.s.*) sich gehen lassen
▸ **let in** VT hereinlassen; (*water*) durchlassen
▸ **let off** VT (*culprit*) laufen lassen; (*firework, bomb*) hochgehen lassen; (*gun*) abfeuern; **to ~ sb off sth** (*excuse*) jdm etw erlassen; **to ~ off steam** (*inf: fig*) sich abreagieren
▸ **let on** VI verraten
▸ **let out** VT herauslassen; (*sound*) ausstoßen; (*house, room*) vermieten
▸ **let up** VI (*cease*) aufhören; (*diminish*) nachlassen
letdown ['lɛtdaun] N Enttäuschung *f*
lethal ['li:θl] ADJ tödlich
lethargic [lɛ'θɑ:dʒɪk] ADJ träge, lethargisch
lethargy ['lɛθədʒɪ] N Trägheit *f*, Lethargie *f*
letter ['lɛtə^r] N Brief *m*; (*of alphabet*) Buchstabe *m*; **small/capital ~** Klein-/Großbuchstabe *m*
letter bomb N Briefbombe *f*
letter box (BRIT) N Briefkasten *m*
letterhead ['lɛtəhɛd] N Briefkopf *m*
lettering ['lɛtərɪŋ] N Beschriftung *f*
letter of credit N Akkreditiv *nt*
letter opener N Brieföffner *m*
letterpress ['lɛtəprɛs] N Hochdruck *m*
letter-quality printer ['lɛtəkwɔlɪtɪ-] N Schönschreibdrucker *m*
letters patent NPL Patent *nt*, Patenturkunde *f*
lettuce ['lɛtɪs] N Kopfsalat *m*
let-up ['lɛtʌp] N Nachlassen *nt*; **there was no ~** es ließ nicht nach
leukaemia, (US) **leukemia** [lu:'ki:mɪə] N Leukämie *f*
level ['lɛvl] ADJ eben ▸ N (*on scale, of liquid*) Stand *m*; (*of lake, river*) Wasserstand *m*; (*height*) Höhe *f*; (*fig: standard*) Niveau *nt*; (*also:* **spirit level**) Wasserwaage *f* ▸ VT (*building*) abreißen; (*forest etc*) einebnen ▸ VI: **to ~ with sb** (*inf*) ehrlich mit jdm sein ▸ ADV: **to draw ~ with** einholen; **to be ~ with** auf gleicher Höhe sein mit; **to do one's ~ best** sein Möglichstes tun; **"A" levels** (BRIT) ≈ Abitur *nt*; **"O" levels** (BRIT) ≈ mittlere Reife *f*; **on the ~** (*fig: honest*) ehrlich, reell; **to ~ a gun at sb** ein Gewehr auf jdn richten; **to ~ an accusation at** *or* **against sb** eine Anschuldigung gegen jdn erheben; **to ~ a criticism at** *or* **against sb** Kritik an jdm üben
▸ **level off** VI (*prices etc*) sich beruhigen
▸ **level out** VI = **level off**
level crossing (BRIT) N (beschrankter) Bahnübergang *m*
level-headed [lɛvl'hɛdɪd] ADJ (*calm*) ausgeglichen
levelling ['lɛvlɪŋ] N Nivellierung *f*
level playing field N Chancengleichheit *f*; **to compete on a ~** unter gleichen Bedingungen antreten
lever ['li:və^r] N Hebel *m*; (*bar*) Brechstange *f*; (*fig*) Druckmittel *nt* ▸ VT: **to ~ up** hochhieven; **to ~ out** heraushieven
leverage ['li:vərɪdʒ] N Hebelkraft *f*; (*fig: influence*) Einfluss *m*
levity ['lɛvɪtɪ] N Leichtfertigkeit *f*
levy ['lɛvɪ] N (*tax*) Steuer *f*; (*charge*) Gebühr *f* ▸ VT erheben
lewd [lu:d] ADJ (*look etc*) lüstern; (*remark*) anzüglich
lexicographer [lɛksɪ'kɔgrəfə^r] N Lexikograf(in) *m*(*f*)
lexicography [lɛksɪ'kɔgrəfɪ] N Lexikografie *f*
LGBT ABBR (= *lesbian, gay, bisexual and transgender*) LGBT, LSBT (*Sammelbegriff für Lesben, Schwule, Bisexuelle und Transsexuelle*)
LGV (BRIT) N ABBR (= *large goods vehicle*) Lkw *m*
LI (US) ABBR = **Long Island**

liability [laɪəˈbɪlətɪ] N Belastung *f*; (*Law*) Haftung *f*; **liabilities** NPL (*Comm*) Verbindlichkeiten *pl*
liable [ˈlaɪəbl] ADJ: **to be ~ to** (*subject to*) unterliegen *+dat*; (*prone to*) anfällig sein für; **~ for** (*responsible*) haftbar für; **to be ~ to do sth** dazu neigen, etw zu tun
liaise [liːˈeɪz] VI: **to ~ (with)** sich in Verbindung setzen (mit)
liaison [liːˈeɪzɔn] N Zusammenarbeit *f*; (*sexual relationship*) Liaison *f*
liar [ˈlaɪə[r]] N Lügner(in) *m(f)*
Lib Dem [lɪbˈdem] ABBR = **Liberal Democrat**
libel [ˈlaɪbl] N Verleumdung *f* ▸ VT verleumden
libellous, (*US*) **libelous** [ˈlaɪbləs] ADJ verleumderisch
liberal [ˈlɪbərl] ADJ (*Pol*) liberal; (*tolerant*) aufgeschlossen; (*generous: offer*) großzügig; (*: amount etc*) reichlich ▸ N (*tolerant person*) liberal eingestellter Mensch *m*; (*Pol*): **L~** Liberale(r) *f(m)*; **~ with** großzügig mit
Liberal Democrat N Liberaldemokrat(in) *m(f)*
liberalize [ˈlɪbərəlaɪz] VT liberalisieren
liberally [ˈlɪbrəlɪ] ADV großzügig
liberal-minded [ˈlɪbərlˈmaɪndɪd] ADJ liberal (eingestellt)
liberate [ˈlɪbəreɪt] VT befreien
liberation [lɪbəˈreɪʃən] N Befreiung *f*
liberation theology N Befreiungstheologie *f*
Liberia [laɪˈbɪərɪə] N Liberia *nt*
Liberian [laɪˈbɪərɪən] ADJ liberianisch ▸ N Liberianer(in) *m(f)*
liberty [ˈlɪbətɪ] N Freiheit *f*; **to be at ~** (*criminal*) auf freiem Fuß sein; **to be at ~ to do sth** etw tun dürfen; **to take the ~ of doing sth** sich *dat* erlauben, etw zu tun
libido [lɪˈbiːdəu] N Libido *f*
Libra [ˈliːbrə] N Waage *f*; **to be ~** Waage sein
librarian [laɪˈbrɛərɪən] N Bibliothekar(in) *m(f)*
library [ˈlaɪbrərɪ] N Bibliothek *f*; (*institution*) Bücherei *f*
library book N Buch *nt* aus der Bücherei
libretto [lɪˈbrɛtəu] N Libretto *nt*
Libya [ˈlɪbɪə] N Libyen *nt*
Libyan [ˈlɪbɪən] ADJ libysch ▸ N Libyer(in) *m(f)*
lice [laɪs] NPL *of* **louse**
licence, (*US*) **license** [ˈlaɪsns] N (*document*) Genehmigung *f*; (*also*: **driving licence**) Führerschein *m*; (*Comm*) Lizenz *f*; (*excessive freedom*) Zügellosigkeit *f*; **to get a TV ~** ≈ Fernsehgebühren bezahlen; **under ~** (*Comm*) in Lizenz
license [ˈlaɪsns] N (*US*) = **licence** ▸ VT (*person, organization*) eine Lizenz vergeben an *+acc*; (*activity*) eine Genehmigung erteilen für
licensed [ˈlaɪsnst] ADJ: **the car is ~** die Kfz-Steuer für das Auto ist bezahlt; **~ hotel/restaurant** Hotel/Restaurant mit Schankerlaubnis
licensee [laɪsənˈsiː] N (*of bar*) Inhaber(in) *m(f)* einer Schankerlaubnis
license plate (*US*) N Nummernschild *nt*
licensing hours [ˈlaɪsnsɪŋ-] (*Brit*) NPL Ausschankzeiten *pl*
licentious [laɪˈsɛnʃəs] ADJ ausschweifend, zügellos
lichen [ˈlaɪkən] N Flechte *f*
lick [lɪk] VT lecken; (*stamp etc*) lecken an *+dat*; (*inf: defeat*) in die Pfanne hauen ▸ N Lecken *nt*; **to ~ one's lips** sich *dat* die Lippen lecken; (*fig*) sich *dat* die Finger lecken; **a ~ of paint** ein Anstrich *m*
licorice [ˈlɪkərɪs] (*US*) N = **liquorice**
lid [lɪd] N Deckel *m*; (*eyelid*) Lid *nt*; **to take the ~ off sth** (*fig*) etw enthüllen *or* aufdecken
lido [ˈlaɪdəu] (*Brit*) N Freibad *nt*
lie[1] [laɪ] (*pt, pp* **lied**) VI lügen ▸ N Lüge *f*; **to tell lies** lügen
lie[2] [laɪ] (*pt* **lay**, *pp* **lain**) VI (*lit, fig*) liegen; **to ~ low** (*fig*) untertauchen
▸ **lie about** VI herumliegen
▸ **lie around** VI = **lie about**
▸ **lie back** VI sich zurücklehnen; (*fig: accept the inevitable*) sich fügen
▸ **lie down** VI sich hinlegen
▸ **lie up** VI (*hide*) untertauchen; (*rest*) im Bett bleiben
Liechtenstein [ˈlɪktənstaɪn] N Liechtenstein *nt*
lie detector N Lügendetektor *m*
lie-down [ˈlaɪdaun] (*Brit*) N: **to have a ~** ein Schläfchen machen
lie-in [ˈlaɪɪn] (*Brit*) N: **to have a ~** (sich) ausschlafen
lieu [luː]: **in ~ of** *prep* anstelle von, anstatt *+gen*
Lieut. ABBR (*Mil: = lieutenant*) Lt.
lieutenant [lɛfˈtɛnənt, (*US*) luːˈtɛnənt] N Leutnant *m*
lieutenant colonel N Oberstleutnant *m*
life [laɪf] (*pl* **lives**) N Leben *nt*; (*of machine etc*) Lebensdauer *f*; **true to ~** lebensecht; **painted from ~** aus dem Leben gegriffen; **to be sent to prison for ~** zu einer lebenslänglichen Freiheitsstrafe verurteilt werden; **such is ~** so ist das Leben; **to come to ~** (*fig: person*) munter werden; (*: party etc*) in Schwung kommen
life annuity N Leibrente *f*
life assurance (*Brit*) N = **life insurance**
life belt (*Brit*) N Rettungsgürtel *m*
lifeblood [ˈlaɪfblʌd] N (*fig*) Lebensnerv *m*
lifeboat [ˈlaɪfbəut] N Rettungsboot *nt*
life buoy N Rettungsring *m*
life expectancy N Lebenserwartung *f*
lifeguard [ˈlaɪfgɑːd] N (*at beach*) Rettungsschwimmer(in) *m(f)*; (*at swimming pool*) Bademeister(in) *m(f)*
life imprisonment N lebenslängliche Freiheitsstrafe *f*
life insurance N Lebensversicherung *f*
life jacket N Schwimmweste *f*
lifeless [ˈlaɪflɪs] ADJ leblos; (*fig: person, party etc*) langweilig
lifelike [ˈlaɪflaɪk] ADJ lebensecht; (*painting*) naturgetreu
lifeline [ˈlaɪflaɪn] N (*fig*) Rettungsanker *m*; (*rope*) Rettungsleine *f*
lifelong [ˈlaɪflɔŋ] ADJ lebenslang
life preserver (*US*) N = **life belt**; **life jacket**

lifer [ˈlaɪfəʳ] (*inf*) N Lebenslängliche(r) *f(m)*
life raft N Rettungsfloß *nt*
life-saver [ˈlaɪfseɪvəʳ] N Lebensretter(in) *m(f)*
life-saving ADJ lebensrettend
life sciences NPL Biowissenschaften *pl*
life sentence N lebenslängliche Freiheitsstrafe *f*
life-size [ˈlaɪfsaɪz], **life-sized** [ˈlaɪfsaɪzd] ADJ in Lebensgröße
life span N Lebensdauer *f*; (*of person*) Lebenszeit *f*
life style [ˈlaɪfstaɪl] N Lebensstil *m*
life-support system [ˈlaɪfsəpɔːt-] N (*Med*) Lebenserhaltungssystem *nt*
lifetime [ˈlaɪftaɪm] N Lebenszeit *f*; (*of thing*) Lebensdauer *f*; (*of parliament*) Legislaturperiode *f*; **in my ~** während meines Lebens; **the chance of a ~** eine einmalige Chance
lift [lɪft] VT (*raise*) heben; (*end: ban etc*) aufheben; (*plagiarize*) abschreiben; (*inf: steal*) mitgehen lassen, klauen ▶ VI (*fog*) sich auflösen ▶ N (BRIT) Aufzug *m*, Fahrstuhl *m*; **to take the ~** mit dem Aufzug *or* Fahrstuhl fahren; **to give sb a ~** (BRIT) jdn (im Auto) mitnehmen
▶ **lift off** VI abheben
▶ **lift up** VT hochheben
liftoff [ˈlɪftɔf] N Abheben *nt*
ligament [ˈlɪgəmənt] N (*Anat*) Band *nt*
light [laɪt] (*pt, pp* **lit**) N Licht *nt* ▶ VT (*candle, cigarette, fire*) anzünden; (*room*) beleuchten ▶ ADJ leicht; (*pale, bright*) hell; (*traffic etc*) gering; (*music*) Unterhaltungs- ▶ ADV: **to travel ~** mit leichtem Gepäck reisen; **lights** NPL (*Aut: also:* **traffic lights**) Ampel *f*; **the lights** (*of car*) die Beleuchtung; **have you got a ~?** haben Sie Feuer?; **to turn the ~ on/off** das Licht an-/ausmachen; **to come to ~** ans Tageslicht kommen; **to cast** *or* **shed** *or* **throw ~ on** (*fig*) Licht bringen in *+acc*; **in the ~ of** angesichts *+gen*; **to make ~ of sth** (*fig*) etw auf die leichte Schulter nehmen; **~ blue/green** *etc* hellblau/-grün *etc*
▶ **light up** VI (*face*) sich erhellen ▶ VT (*illuminate*) beleuchten, erhellen
light bulb N Glühbirne *f*
lighten [ˈlaɪtn] VT (*make less heavy*) leichter machen ▶ VI (*become less dark*) sich aufhellen
lighter [ˈlaɪtəʳ] N (*also:* **cigarette lighter**) Feuerzeug *nt*
light-fingered [laɪtˈfɪŋgəd] (*inf*) ADJ langfingerig
light-headed [laɪtˈhɛdɪd] ADJ (*dizzy*) benommen; (*excited*) ausgelassen
light-hearted [laɪtˈhɑːtɪd] ADJ unbeschwert; (*question, remark etc*) scherzhaft
lighthouse [ˈlaɪthaus] N Leuchtturm *m*
lighting [ˈlaɪtɪŋ] N Beleuchtung *f*
lighting-up time [laɪtɪŋˈʌp-] N *Zeitpunkt, zu dem die Fahrzeugbeleuchtung eingeschaltet werden muss*
lightly [ˈlaɪtlɪ] ADV leicht; (*not seriously*) leichthin; **to get off ~** glimpflich davonkommen
light meter N Belichtungsmesser *m*
lightness [ˈlaɪtnɪs] N (*in weight*) Leichtigkeit *f*
lightning [ˈlaɪtnɪŋ] N Blitz *m* ▶ ADJ (*attack etc*) Blitz-; **with ~ speed** blitzschnell
lightning conductor N Blitzableiter *m*
lightning rod (US) N = **lightning conductor**
light pen N Lichtstift *m*, Lichtgriffel *m*
lightship [ˈlaɪtʃɪp] N Feuerschiff *nt*
lightweight [ˈlaɪtweɪt] ADJ leicht ▶ N (*Boxing*) Leichtgewichtler *m*
light year N Lichtjahr *nt*
like [laɪk] VT mögen ▶ PREP wie; (*such as*) wie (zum Beispiel) ▶ N: **and the ~** und dergleichen; **I would ~, I'd ~** ich hätte *or* möchte gern; **would you ~ a coffee?** möchten Sie einen Kaffee?; **if you ~** wenn Sie wollen; **to be/look ~ sb/sth** jdm/etw ähnlich sein/sehen; **something ~ that** so etwas Ähnliches; **what does it look/taste/sound ~?** wie sieht es aus/schmeckt es/hört es sich an?; **what's he/the weather ~?** wie ist er/das Wetter?; **I feel ~ a drink** ich möchte gerne etwas trinken; **there's nothing ~ ...** es geht nichts über *+acc*; **that's just ~ him** das sieht ihm ähnlich; **do it ~ this** mach es so; **it is nothing ~** (*+noun*) es ist ganz anders als; (*+adj*) es ist alles andere als; **it is nothing ~ as ...** es ist bei Weitem nicht so ...; **his likes and dislikes** seine Vorlieben und Abneigungen
likeable [ˈlaɪkəbl] ADJ sympathisch
likelihood [ˈlaɪklɪhud] N Wahrscheinlichkeit *f*; **there is every ~ that ...** es ist sehr wahrscheinlich, dass ...; **in all ~** aller Wahrscheinlichkeit nach
likely [ˈlaɪklɪ] ADJ wahrscheinlich; **to be ~ to do sth** wahrscheinlich etw tun; **not ~!** (*inf*) wohl kaum!
like-minded [ˈlaɪkˈmaɪndɪd] ADJ gleich gesinnt
liken [ˈlaɪkən] VT: **to ~ sth to sth** etw mit etw vergleichen
likeness [ˈlaɪknɪs] N Ähnlichkeit *f*; **that's a good ~** (*photo, portrait*) das ist ein gutes Bild von ihm/ihr *etc*
likewise [ˈlaɪkwaɪz] ADV ebenso; **to do ~** das Gleiche tun
liking [ˈlaɪkɪŋ] N: **~ (for)** (*person*) Zuneigung *f* (zu); (*thing*) Vorliebe *f* (für); **to be to sb's ~** nach jds Geschmack sein; **to take a ~ to sb** an jdm Gefallen finden
lilac [ˈlaɪlək] N (*Bot*) Flieder *m* ▶ ADJ fliederfarben, (zart)lila
Lilo® [ˈlaɪləu] N Luftmatratze *f*
lilt [lɪlt] N singender Tonfall *m*
lilting [ˈlɪltɪŋ] ADJ singend
lily [ˈlɪlɪ] N Lilie *f*
lily of the valley N Maiglöckchen *nt*
Lima [ˈliːmə] N Lima *nt*
limb [lɪm] N Glied *nt*; (*of tree*) Ast *m*; **to be out on a ~** (*fig*) (ganz) allein (da)stehen
limber up [ˈlɪmbəʳ-] VI Lockerungsübungen machen
limbo [ˈlɪmbəu] N: **to be in ~** (*fig: plans etc*) in der Schwebe sein; (*: person*) in der Luft hängen (*inf*)

lime [laɪm] N (*fruit*) Limone *f*; (*tree*) Linde *f*; (*also*: **lime juice**) Limonensaft *m*; (*for soil*) Kalk *m*; (*rock*) Kalkstein *m*
limelight ['laɪmlaɪt] N: **to be in the ~** im Rampenlicht stehen
limerick ['lɪmərɪk] N Limerick *m*
limestone ['laɪmstəun] N Kalkstein *m*
limit ['lɪmɪt] N Grenze *f*; (*restriction*) Beschränkung *f* ▸ VT begrenzen, einschränken; **within limits** innerhalb gewisser Grenzen
limitation [lɪmɪ'teɪʃən] N Einschränkung *f*; **limitations** NPL (*shortcomings*) Grenzen *pl*
limited ['lɪmɪtɪd] ADJ begrenzt, beschränkt; **to be ~ to** beschränkt sein auf *+acc*
limited company, (BRIT) limited liability company N ≈ Gesellschaft *f* mit beschränkter Haftung
limited edition N beschränkte Ausgabe *f*
limitless ['lɪmɪtlɪs] ADJ grenzenlos
limousine ['lɪməzi:n] N Limousine *f*
limp [lɪmp] ADJ schlaff; (*material etc*) weich ▸ VI hinken ▸ N: **to have a ~** hinken
limpet ['lɪmpɪt] N Napfschnecke *f*
limpid ['lɪmpɪd] ADJ klar
limply ['lɪmplɪ] ADV schlaff
linchpin ['lɪntʃpɪn] N (*fig*) wichtigste Stütze *f*
Lincs [lɪŋks] (BRIT) ABBR (*Post*) = **Lincolnshire**
line [laɪn] N Linie *f*; (*written, printed*) Zeile *f*; (*wrinkle*) Falte *f*; (*row: of people*) Schlange *f*; (*: of things*) Reihe *f*; (*for fishing, washing*) Leine *f*; (*wire, Tel*) Leitung *f*; (*railway track*) Gleise *pl*; (*fig: attitude*) Standpunkt *m*; (*: business*) Branche *f*; (*Comm: of product(s)*) Art *f* ▸ VT (*road*) säumen; (*container*) auskleiden; (*clothing*) füttern; **hold the ~ please!** (*Tel*) bleiben Sie am Apparat!; **to cut in ~** (*US*) sich vordrängeln; **in ~** in einer Reihe; **in ~ with** im Einklang mit, in Übereinstimmung mit; **to be in ~ for sth** mit etw an der Reihe sein; **to bring sth into ~ with sth** etw auf die gleiche Linie wie etw *acc* bringen; **on the right lines** auf dem richtigen Weg; **I draw the ~ at that** da mache ich nicht mehr mit; **to ~ sth with sth** etw mit etw auskleiden; (*drawers etc*) etw mit etw auslegen; **to ~ the streets** die Straßen säumen
▸ **line up** VI sich aufstellen ▸ VT (*in a row*) aufstellen; (*engage*) verpflichten; (*prepare*) arrangieren; **to have sb lined up** jdn verpflichtet haben; **to have sth lined up** etw geplant haben
linear ['lɪnɪə^r] ADJ linear; (*shape, form*) gerade
lined [laɪnd] ADJ (*face*) faltig; (*paper*) liniert; (*skirt, jacket*) gefüttert
line editing N (*Comput*) zeilenweise Aufbereitung *f*
line feed N (*Comput*) Zeilenvorschub *m*
lineman ['laɪnmən] (*US*) N (*irreg: Football*) Stürmer *m*
linen ['lɪnɪn] N (*cloth*) Leinen *nt*; (*tablecloths, sheets etc*) Wäsche *f*
line printer N (*Comput*) Zeilendrucker *m*
liner ['laɪnə^r] N (*ship*) Passagierschiff *nt*; (*also*: **bin liner**) Müllbeutel *m*
linesman ['laɪnzmən] N (*irreg: Sport*) Linienrichter *m*
line-up ['laɪnʌp] N (*US: queue*) Schlange *f*; (*Sport*) Aufstellung *f*; (*at concert etc*) Künstleraufgebot *nt*; (*identity parade*) Gegenüberstellung *f*
linger ['lɪŋgə^r] VI (*smell*) sich halten; (*tradition etc*) fortbestehen; (*person*) sich aufhalten
lingerie ['lænʒəri:] N (Damen)unterwäsche *f*
lingering ['lɪŋgərɪŋ] ADJ bleibend
lingo ['lɪŋgəu] (*pl* **lingoes**) N (*inf*) Sprache *f*
linguist ['lɪŋgwɪst] N (*person who speaks several languages*) Sprachkundige(r) *f(m)*
linguistic [lɪŋ'gwɪstɪk] ADJ sprachlich
linguistics [lɪŋ'gwɪstɪks] N Sprachwissenschaft *f*
liniment ['lɪnɪmənt] N Einreibemittel *nt*
lining ['laɪnɪŋ] N (*cloth*) Futter *nt*; (*Anat: of stomach*) Magenschleimhaut *f*; (*Tech*) Auskleidung *f*; (*of brakes*) (Brems)belag *m*
link [lɪŋk] N Verbindung *f*, Beziehung *f*; (*communications link*) Verbindung; (*of a chain*) Glied *nt*; (*Comput*) Link *m* ▸ VI (*Comput*): **to ~ to a site** einen Link zu einer Website haben ▸ VT (*join*) verbinden; (*Comput*) per Link verbinden; **links** NPL (*Golf*) Golfplatz *m*; **rail ~** Bahnverbindung *f*
▸ **link up** VT verbinden ▸ VI verbunden werden
linkup ['lɪŋkʌp] N Verbindung *f*; (*of spaceships*) Koppelung *f*
lino ['laɪnəu] N = **linoleum**
linoleum [lɪ'nəulɪəm] N Linoleum *nt*
linseed oil ['lɪnsi:d-] N Leinöl *nt*
lint [lɪnt] N Mull *m*
lintel ['lɪntl] N (*Archit*) Sturz *m*
lion ['laɪən] N Löwe *m*
lion cub N Löwenjunge(s) *nt*
lioness ['laɪənɪs] N Löwin *f*
lip [lɪp] N (*Anat*) Lippe *f*; (*of cup etc*) Rand *m*; (*inf: insolence*) Frechheiten *pl*
liposuction ['lɪpəusʌkʃən] N Liposuktion *f*
lip-read ['lɪpri:d] VI (*irreg: like* **read**) von den Lippen ablesen
lip salve N Fettstift *m*
lip service (*pej*) N: **to pay ~ to sth** ein Lippenbekenntnis *nt* zu etw ablegen
lipstick ['lɪpstɪk] N Lippenstift *m*
liquefy ['lɪkwɪfaɪ] VT verflüssigen ▸ VI sich verflüssigen
liqueur [lɪ'kjuə^r] N Likör *m*
liquid ['lɪkwɪd] ADJ flüssig ▸ N Flüssigkeit *f*
liquid assets NPL flüssige Vermögenswerte *pl*
liquidate ['lɪkwɪdeɪt] VT liquidieren
liquidation [lɪkwɪ'deɪʃən] N Liquidation *f*
liquidation sale (*US*) N Verkauf *m* wegen Geschäftsaufgabe
liquidator ['lɪkwɪdeɪtə^r] N Liquidator *m*
liquid-crystal display ['lɪkwɪd'krɪstl-] N Flüssigkristallanzeige *f*
liquidity [lɪ'kwɪdɪtɪ] N Liquidität *f*
liquidize ['lɪkwɪdaɪz] VT (im Mixer) pürieren
liquidizer ['lɪkwɪdaɪzə^r] N Mixer *m*
liquor ['lɪkə^r] N Spirituosen *pl*, Alkohol *m*; **hard ~** harte Drinks *pl*

l

liquorice ['lɪkərɪs] (BRIT) N Lakritze *f*
liquor store (US) N Spirituosengeschäft *nt*
Lisbon ['lɪzbən] N Lissabon *nt*
lisp [lɪsp] N Lispeln *nt* ▶ VI lispeln
list [lɪst] N Liste *f* ▶ VT aufführen; (*Comput*) auflisten; (*write down*) aufschreiben ▶ VI (*ship*) Schlagseite haben
listed building ['lɪstɪd-] (BRIT) N unter Denkmalschutz stehendes Gebäude *nt*
listed company N börsennotierte Firma *f*
listen ['lɪsn] VI hören; **to ~ (out) for** horchen auf *+acc*; **to ~ to sb** jdm zuhören; **to ~ to sth** etw hören; **~!** hör zu!
listener ['lɪsnə^r] N Zuhörer(in) *m(f)*; (*Radio*) Hörer(in) *m(f)*
listeria [lɪs'tɪərɪə] N Listeriose *f*
listing ['lɪstɪŋ] N Auflistung *f*; (*entry*) Eintrag *m*
listless ['lɪstlɪs] ADJ lustlos
listlessly ['lɪstlɪslɪ] ADV lustlos
list price N Listenpreis *m*
lit [lɪt] PT, PP *of* **light**
litany ['lɪtənɪ] N Litanei *f*
liter ['li:tə^r] (US) N = **litre**
literacy ['lɪtərəsɪ] N die Fähigkeit, lesen und schreiben zu können
literacy campaign N Kampagne *f* gegen das Analphabetentum
literal ['lɪtərəl] ADJ wörtlich, eigentlich; (*translation*) (wort)wörtlich
literally ['lɪtrəlɪ] ADV buchstäblich
literary ['lɪtərərɪ] ADJ literarisch
literate ['lɪtərət] ADJ (*educated*) gebildet; **to be ~** lesen und schreiben können
literature ['lɪtrɪtʃə^r] N Literatur *f*; (*printed information*) Informationsmaterial *nt*
lithe [laɪð] ADJ gelenkig; (*animal*) geschmeidig
lithography [lɪ'θɔgrəfɪ] N Lithografie *f*
Lithuania [lɪθju'eɪnɪə] N Litauen *nt*
Lithuanian [lɪθju'eɪnɪən] ADJ litauisch ▶ N Litauer(in) *m(f)*; (*Ling*) Litauisch *nt*
litigation [lɪtɪ'geɪʃən] N Prozess *m*
litmus paper ['lɪtməs-] N Lackmuspapier *nt*
litre, (US) **liter** ['li:tə^r] N Liter *m or nt*
litter ['lɪtə^r] N (*rubbish*) Abfall *m*; (*young animals*) Wurf *m*
litter bin (BRIT) N Abfalleimer *m*
litterbug ['lɪtəbʌg] N Dreckspatz *m*
littered ['lɪtəd] ADJ: **~ with** (*scattered*) übersät mit
litter lout N Dreckspatz *m*
little ['lɪtl] ADJ klein; (*short*) kurz ▶ ADV wenig; **a ~** ein wenig, ein bisschen; **a ~ bit** ein kleines bisschen; **to have ~ time/money** wenig Zeit/Geld haben; **~ by ~** nach und nach
little finger N kleiner Finger *m*
little-known ['lɪtl'nəun] ADJ wenig bekannt
liturgy ['lɪtədʒɪ] N Liturgie *f*
live VI [lɪv] leben; (*in house, town*) wohnen ▶ ADJ [laɪv] lebend; (*TV, Radio*) live; (*performance, pictures etc*) Live-; (*Elec*) Strom führend; (*bullet, bomb etc*) scharf
▶ **live down** VT hinwegkommen über *+acc*
▶ **live for** VT leben für
▶ **live in** VI (*student/servant*) im Wohnheim/Haus wohnen
▶ **live off** VT FUS leben von; (*parents etc*) auf Kosten *+gen* leben
▶ **live on** VT FUS leben von
▶ **live out** VI (BRIT: *student/servant*) außerhalb (des Wohnheims/Hauses) wohnen ▶ VT; **to ~ out one's days** *or* **life** sein Leben verbringen
▶ **live together** VI zusammenleben
▶ **live up** VT: **to ~ it up** einen draufmachen (*inf*)
▶ **live up to** VT FUS erfüllen, entsprechen *+dat*
▶ **live with** VT (*parents etc*) wohnen bei; (*partner*) zusammenleben mit; **you'll just have to ~ with it** du musst dich/Sie müssen sich eben damit abfinden
live-in ['lɪvɪn] ADJ (*cook, maid*) im Haus wohnend; **her ~ lover** ihr Freund, der bei ihr wohnt
livelihood ['laɪvlɪhud] N Lebensunterhalt *m*
liveliness ['laɪvlɪnɪs] N Lebhaftigkeit *f*; Lebendigkeit *f*
lively ['laɪvlɪ] ADJ lebhaft; (*place, event, book etc*) lebendig
liven up ['laɪvn-] VT beleben, Leben bringen in *+acc*; (*person*) aufmuntern ▶ VI (*person*) aufleben; (*discussion, evening etc*) in Schwung kommen
liver ['lɪvə^r] N (*Anat, Culin*) Leber *f*
liverish ['lɪvərɪʃ] ADJ: **to be ~** sich unwohl fühlen
Liverpudlian [lɪvə'pʌdlɪən] ADJ Liverpooler ▶ N Liverpooler(in) *m(f)*
livery ['lɪvərɪ] N Livree *f*
lives [laɪvz] NPL *of* **life**
livestock ['laɪvstɔk] N Vieh *nt*
live wire (*inf*) N (*person*) Energiebündel *nt*
livid ['lɪvɪd] ADJ (*colour*) bleifarben; (*inf: furious*) fuchsteufelswild
living ['lɪvɪŋ] ADJ lebend ▶ N: **to earn** *or* **make a ~** sich *dat* seinen Lebensunterhalt verdienen; **within ~ memory** seit Menschengedenken; **the cost of ~** die Lebenshaltungskosten *pl*
living conditions NPL Wohnverhältnisse *pl*
living expenses NPL Lebenshaltungskosten *pl*
living room N Wohnzimmer *nt*
living standards NPL Lebensstandard *m*
living wage N ausreichender Lohn *m*
living will N Patientenverfügung *f*
lizard ['lɪzəd] N Eidechse *f*
llama ['lɑ:mə] N Lama *nt*
LLB N ABBR (= *Bachelor of Laws*) *akademischer Grad für Juristen*
LLD N ABBR (= *Doctor of Laws*) ≈ Dr. jur.
LMT (US) ABBR (= *Local Mean Time*) *Ortszeit*
load [ləud] N Last *f*; (*of vehicle*) Ladung *f*; (*weight, Elec*) Belastung *f* ▶ VT (*also*: **load up**) beladen; (*gun, program, data*) laden; **that's a ~ of rubbish** (*inf*) das ist alles Blödsinn; **loads of, a ~ of** (*fig*) jede Menge; **to ~ a camera** einen Film einlegen
loaded ['ləudɪd] ADJ (*inf: rich*) steinreich; (*dice*) präpariert; (*vehicle*): **to be ~ with** beladen sein mit; **a ~ question** eine Fangfrage
loading bay ['ləudɪŋ-] N Ladeplatz *m*

loaf [ləuf] (*pl* **loaves**) N Brot *nt*, Laib *m* ▸ VI (*also*: **loaf about, loaf around**) faulenzen; **use your ~!** (*inf*) streng deinen Grips an!
loam [ləum] N Lehmerde *f*
loan [ləun] N Darlehen *nt* ▸ VT: **to ~ sth to sb** jdm etw leihen; **on ~** geliehen
loan account N Darlehenskonto *nt*
loan capital N Anleihekapital *nt*
loan shark (*inf*) N Kredithai *m*
loath [ləuθ] ADJ: **to be ~ to do sth** etw ungern tun
loathe [ləuð] VT verabscheuen
loathing ['ləuðɪŋ] N Abscheu *m*
loathsome ['ləuðsəm] ADJ abscheulich
loaves [ləuvz] NPL *of* **loaf**
lob [lɔb] VT (*ball*) lobben
lobby ['lɔbɪ] N (*of building*) Eingangshalle *f*; (*Pol*: *pressure group*) Interessenverband *m* ▸ VT Einfluss nehmen auf *+acc*
lobbyist ['lɔbɪɪst] N Lobbyist(in) *m*(*f*)
lobe [ləub] N Ohrläppchen *nt*
lobster ['lɔbstə^r] N Hummer *m*
lobster pot N Hummer(fang)korb *m*
local ['ləukl] ADJ örtlich; (*council*) Stadt-, Gemeinde-; (*paper*) Lokal- ▸ N (*pub*) Stammkneipe *f*; **the locals** NPL (*local inhabitants*) die Einheimischen *pl*
local anaesthetic N örtliche Betäubung *f*
local authority N Gemeindeverwaltung *f*, Stadtverwaltung *f*
local call N Ortsgespräch *nt*
locale [ləu'kɑːl] N Umgebung *f*
local government N Kommunalverwaltung *f*
locality [ləu'kælɪtɪ] N Gegend *f*
localize ['ləukəlaɪz] VT lokalisieren
locally ['ləukəlɪ] ADV am Ort
lo-carb [ləu'kɑːb] ADJ = **low-carb**
locate [ləu'keɪt] VT (*find*) ausfindig machen; **to be located in** sich befinden in *+dat*
location [ləu'keɪʃən] N Ort *m*; (*position*) Lage *f*; (*Cine*) Drehort *m*; **he's on ~ in Mexico** er ist bei Außenaufnahmen in Mexiko; **to be filmed on ~** als Außenaufnahme gedreht werden
loch [lɔx] (SCOT) N See *m*
lock [lɔk] N (*of door etc*) Schloss *nt*; (*on canal*) Schleuse *f*; (*also*: **lock of hair**) Locke *f* ▸ VT (*door etc*) abschließen; (*steering wheel*) sperren; (*Comput*: *keyboard*) verriegeln ▸ VI (*door etc*) sich abschließen lassen; (*wheels, mechanism etc*) blockieren; **on full ~** (*Aut*) voll eingeschlagen; **~, stock and barrel** mit allem Drum und Dran; **his jaw locked** er hatte Mundsperre
▸ **lock away** VT wegschließen; (*criminal*) einsperren
▸ **lock in** VT einschließen
▸ **lock out** VT aussperren
▸ **lock up** VT (*criminal etc*) einsperren; (*house*) abschließen ▸ VI abschließen
locker ['lɔkə^r] N Schließfach *nt*
locker room N Umkleideraum *m*
locket ['lɔkɪt] N Medaillon *nt*
lockjaw ['lɔkdʒɔː] N Wundstarrkrampf *m*
lockout ['lɔkaut] N Aussperrung *f*
locksmith ['lɔksmɪθ] N Schlosser *m*
lockup ['lɔkʌp] N (*US inf*: *jail*) Gefängnis *nt*; (*also*: **lock-up garage**) Garage *f*
locomotive [ləukə'məutɪv] N Lokomotive *f*
locum ['ləukəm] N (*Med*) Vertreter(in) *m*(*f*)
locust ['ləukəst] N Heuschrecke *f*
lodge [lɔdʒ] N Pförtnerhaus *nt*; (*also*: **hunting lodge**) Hütte *f*; (*Freemasonry*) Loge *f* ▸ VT (*complaint, protest etc*) einlegen ▸ VI (*bullet*) stecken bleiben; (*person*): **to ~ (with)** zur Untermiete wohnen (bei)
lodger ['lɔdʒə^r] N Untermieter(in) *m*(*f*)
lodging ['lɔdʒɪŋ] N Unterkunft *f*
lodging house N Pension *f*
lodgings ['lɔdʒɪŋz] NPL möbliertes Zimmer *nt*; (*several rooms*) Wohnung *f*
loft [lɔft] N Boden *m*, Speicher *m*
lofty ['lɔftɪ] ADJ (*noble*) hoch(fliegend); (*self-important*) hochmütig; (*high*) hoch
log [lɔg] N (*of wood*) Holzblock *m*, Holzklotz *m*; (*written account*) Log *nt* ▸ N ABBR (*Math*: = *logarithm*) log ▸ VT (ins Logbuch) eintragen
▸ **log in** VI (*Comput*) sich anmelden
▸ **log into** VT FUS (*Comput*) sich anmelden bei
▸ **log off** VI (*Comput*) sich abmelden
▸ **log on** VI (*Comput*) = **log in**
▸ **log out** VI (*Comput*) = **log off**
logarithm ['lɔgərɪðm] N Logarithmus *m*
logbook ['lɔgbuk] N (*Naut*) Logbuch *nt*; (*Aviat*) Bordbuch *nt*; (*of car*) Kraftfahrzeugbrief *m*; (*of lorry driver*) Fahrtenbuch *nt*; (*of events*) Tagebuch *nt*; (*of movement of goods etc*) Dienstbuch *nt*
log fire N Holzfeuer *nt*
logger ['lɔgə^r] N (*lumberjack*) Holzfäller *m*
loggerheads ['lɔgəhɛdz] NPL: **to be at ~** Streit haben
logic ['lɔdʒɪk] N Logik *f*
logical ['lɔdʒɪkl] ADJ logisch
logically ['lɔdʒɪkəlɪ] ADV logisch; (*reasonably*) logischerweise
login ['lɔgɪn] N (*Comput*) Log-in *nt*, Anmeldung *f*
logistics [lɔ'dʒɪstɪks] N Logistik *f*
log jam N (*fig*) Blockierung *f*; **to break the ~** freie Bahn schaffen
logo ['ləugəu] N Logo *nt*
loin [lɔɪn] N Lende *f*
loincloth ['lɔɪnklɔθ] N Lendenschurz *m*
loiter ['lɔɪtə^r] VI sich aufhalten
lol ABBR (*Internet, Tel*: = *laugh out loud*) lol (*lautes Lachen*)
loll [lɔl] VI (*person*: *also*: **loll about**) herumhängen; (*head*) herunterhängen; (*tongue*) heraushängen
lollipop ['lɔlɪpɔp] N Lutscher *m*
lollipop lady (BRIT) N ≈ Schülerlotsin *f*
lollipop man (BRIT) N ≈ Schülerlotse *m*

> **Lollipop man/lady** heißen in Großbritannien die Männer bzw. Frauen, die mithilfe eines runden Stoppschildes den Verkehr anhalten, damit Schulkinder die Straße gefahrlos überqueren können. Der Name bezieht sich auf die Form des Schildes, die an einen Lutscher erinnert.

lollop ['lɔləp] VI zockeln
lolly ['lɔlɪ] (*inf*) N (*lollipop*) Lutscher *m*; (*money*) Mäuse *pl*
London ['lʌndən] N London *nt*
Londoner ['lʌndənəʳ] N Londoner(in) *m(f)*
lone [ləun] ADJ einzeln, einsam; (*only*) einzig
loneliness ['ləunlɪnɪs] N Einsamkeit *f*
lonely ['ləunlɪ] ADJ einsam
lonely hearts ADJ: **~ ad** Kontaktanzeige *f*; **the ~ column** die Kontaktanzeigen *pl*
lone parent N Alleinerziehende(r) *f(m)*
loner ['ləunəʳ] N Einzelgänger(in) *m(f)*
long [lɔŋ] ADJ lang ▶ ADV lang(e) ▶ VI: **to ~ for sth** sich nach etw sehnen; **in the ~ run** auf die Dauer; **how ~ is the lesson?** wie lange dauert die Stunde?; **6 metres/months ~** 6 Meter/ Monate lang; **so** *or* **as ~ as** (*on condition that*) solange; (*while*) während; **don't be ~!** bleib nicht so lange!; **all night ~** die ganze Nacht; **he no longer comes** er kommt nicht mehr; **~ ago** vor langer Zeit; **~ before/after** lange vorher/danach; **before ~** bald; **at ~ last** schließlich und endlich; **the ~ and the short of it is that …** kurz gesagt, …
long-distance [lɔŋ'dɪstəns] ADJ (*travel, phone call*) Fern-; (*race*) Langstrecken-
longevity [lɔn'dʒɛvɪtɪ] N Langlebigkeit *f*
long-haired ['lɔŋ'hɛəd] ADJ langhaarig; (*animal*) Langhaar-
longhand ['lɔŋhænd] N Langschrift *f*
longing ['lɔŋɪŋ] N Sehnsucht *f*
longingly ['lɔŋɪŋlɪ] ADV sehnsüchtig
longitude ['lɔŋgɪtju:d] N Länge *f*
long johns [-dʒɔnz] NPL lange Unterhose *f*
long jump N Weitsprung *m*
long-life ['lɔŋlaɪf] ADJ (*batteries etc*) mit langer Lebensdauer; **~ milk** H-Milch *f*
long-lost ['lɔŋlɔst] ADJ verloren geglaubt
long-playing record ['lɔŋpleɪɪŋ-] N Langspielplatte *f*
long-range ['lɔŋ'reɪndʒ] ADJ (*plan, forecast*) langfristig; (*missile, plane etc*) Langstrecken-
longshoreman ['lɔŋʃɔ:mən] (US) N (*irreg*) Hafenarbeiter *m*
long-sighted ['lɔŋ'saɪtɪd] ADJ weitsichtig
long-standing ['lɔŋ'stændɪŋ] ADJ langjährig
long-suffering [lɔŋ'sʌfərɪŋ] ADJ schwer geprüft
long-term ['lɔŋtə:m] ADJ langfristig
long wave N Langwelle *f*
long-winded [lɔŋ'wɪndɪd] ADJ umständlich, langatmig
loo [lu:] (BRIT *inf*) N Klo *nt*
loofah ['lu:fə] N Luffa(schwamm) *m*
look [luk] VI sehen, schauen, gucken (*inf*); (*seem, appear*) aussehen ▶ N (*glance*) Blick *m*; (*appearance*) Aussehen *nt*; (*expression*) Miene *f*; (*Fashion*) Look *m*; **looks** NPL (*good looks*) (gutes) Aussehen; **to ~ (out) onto the sea/south** (*building etc*) Blick aufs Meer/nach Süden haben; **~ (here)!** (*expressing annoyance*) hör (mal) zu!; **~!** (*expressing surprise*) sieh mal!; **to ~ like sb/sth** wie jd/etw aussehen; **it looks like him** es sieht ihm ähnlich; **it looks about 4 metres long** es scheint etwa 4 Meter lang zu sein; **it looks all right to me** es scheint mir in Ordnung zu sein; **to ~ ahead** vorausschauen; **to have a ~ at sth** sich *dat* etw ansehen; **let me have a ~** lass mich mal sehen; **to have a ~ for sth** nach etw suchen
▶ **look after** VT FUS sich kümmern um
▶ **look at** VT FUS ansehen; (*read quickly*) durchsehen; (*study, consider*) betrachten
▶ **look back** VI: **to ~ back (on)** zurückblicken (auf +*acc*); **to ~ back at sth/sb** sich nach jdm/ etw umsehen
▶ **look down on** VT FUS (*fig*) herabsehen auf +*acc*
▶ **look for** VT FUS suchen
▶ **look forward to** VT FUS sich freuen auf +*acc*; **we ~ forward to hearing from you** (*in letters*) wir hoffen, bald von Ihnen zu hören
▶ **look in** VI: **to ~ in on sb** bei jdm vorbeikommen
▶ **look into** VT FUS (*investigate*) untersuchen
▶ **look on** VI (*watch*) zusehen
▶ **look out** VI (*beware*) aufpassen
▶ **look out for** VT FUS Ausschau halten nach
▶ **look over** VT (*essay etc*) durchsehen; (*house, town etc*) sich *dat* ansehen; (*person*) mustern
▶ **look round** VI sich umsehen
▶ **look through** VT FUS durchsehen
▶ **look to** VT FUS (*rely on*) sich verlassen auf +*acc*
▶ **look up** VI aufsehen; (*situation*) sich bessern ▶ VT (*word etc*) nachschlagen; **things are looking up** es geht bergauf
▶ **look up to** VT FUS aufsehen zu
lookalike ['lukəlaɪk] N Doppelgänger(in) *m(f)*
look-in ['lukɪn] N: **to get a ~** (*inf*) eine Chance haben
lookout ['lukaut] N (*tower etc*) Ausguck *m*; (*person*) Wachtposten *m*; **to be on the ~ for sth** nach etw Ausschau halten
loom [lu:m] VI (*object, shape: also:* **loom up**) sich abzeichnen; (*event*) näher rücken ▶ N Webstuhl *m*
loony ['lu:nɪ] (*inf*) ADJ verrückt ▶ N Verrückte(r) *f(m)*
loop [lu:p] N Schlaufe *f*; (*Comput*) Schleife *f* ▶ VT: **to ~ sth around sth** etw um etw schlingen
loophole ['lu:phəul] N Hintertürchen *nt*; **a ~ in the law** eine Lücke im Gesetz
loose [lu:s] ADJ lose, locker; (*clothes etc*) weit; (*long hair*) offen; (*not strictly controlled, promiscuous*) locker; (*definition*) ungenau; (*translation*) frei ▶ VT (*animal*) loslassen; (*prisoner*) freilassen; (*set off, unleash*) entfesseln ▶ N: **to be on the ~** frei herumlaufen
loose change N Kleingeld *nt*
loose chippings NPL Schotter *m*
loose end N: **to be at a ~, to be at loose ends** (US) nichts mit sich *dat* anzufangen wissen; **to tie up loose ends** die offenstehenden Probleme lösen
loose-fitting ['lu:sfɪtɪŋ] ADJ weit
loose-leaf ['lu:sli:f] ADJ Loseblatt-; **~ binder** Ringbuch *nt*

loose-limbed [lu:s'lɪmd] ADJ gelenkig, beweglich
loosely ['lu:slɪ] ADV lose, locker
loosely-knit ['lu:slɪ'nɪt] ADJ (*fig*) locker
loosen ['lu:sn] VT lösen, losmachen; (*clothing, belt etc*) lockern
loosen up VI (*before game*) sich auflockern; (*relax*) auftauen
loot [lu:t] N (*inf*) Beute *f* ▸ VT plündern
looter ['lu:tə^r] N Plünderer *m*
looting ['lu:tɪŋ] N Plünderung *f*
lop off [lɔp-] VT abhacken
lopsided ['lɔp'saɪdɪd] ADJ schief
lord [lɔ:d] N (BRIT) Lord *m*; **L~ Smith** Lord Smith; **the L~** (*Rel*) der Herr; **my ~** (*to bishop*) Exzellenz; (*to noble*) Mylord; (*to judge*) Euer Ehren; **good L~!** ach, du lieber Himmel!; **the (House of) Lords** (BRIT) das Oberhaus
lordly ['lɔ:dlɪ] ADJ hochmütig
lordship ['lɔ:dʃɪp] N: **your L~** Eure Lordschaft
lore [lɔ:^r] N Überlieferungen *pl*
lorry ['lɔrɪ] (BRIT) N Lastwagen *m*, Lkw *m*
lorry driver (BRIT) N Lastwagenfahrer *m*
lose [lu:z] (*pt, pp* **lost**) VT verlieren; (*opportunity*) verpassen; (*pursuers*) abschütteln ▸ VI verlieren; **to ~ (time)** (*clock*) nachgehen; **to ~ weight** abnehmen; **to ~ 5 pounds** 5 Pfund abnehmen; **to ~ sight of sth** (*also fig*) etw aus den Augen verlieren
loser ['lu:zə^r] N Verlierer(in) *m(f)*; (*inf: failure*) Versager *m*; **to be a good/bad ~** ein guter/schlechter Verlierer sein
loss [lɔs] N Verlust *m*; **to make a ~ (of £1,000)** (1000 Pfund) Verlust machen; **to sell sth at a ~** etw mit Verlust verkaufen; **heavy losses** schwere Verluste *pl*; **to cut one's losses** aufgeben, bevor es noch schlimmer wird; **to be at a ~** nicht mehr weiterwissen
loss adjuster N Schadenssachverständige(r) *f(m)*
loss leader N (*Comm*) Lockvogelangebot *nt*
lost [lɔst] PT, PP *of* **lose** ▸ ADJ (*person, animal*) vermisst; (*object*) verloren; **to be ~** sich verlaufen/verfahren haben; **to get ~** sich verlaufen/verfahren; **get ~!** (*inf*) verschwinde!; **~ in thought** in Gedanken verloren
lost and found (US) N = **lost property**
lost cause N aussichtslose Sache *f*
lost property (BRIT) N Fundsachen *pl*; (*also*: **lost property office**) Fundbüro *nt*
lot [lɔt] N (*kind*) Art *f*; (*group*) Gruppe *f*; (*at auctions, destiny*) Los *nt*; **to draw lots** losen, Lose ziehen; **the ~** alles; **a ~ (of)** (*a large number (of)*) viele; (*a great deal (of)*) viel; **lots of** viele; **I read a ~** ich lese viel; **this happens a ~** das kommt oft vor
loth [ləuθ] ADJ = **loath**
lotion ['ləuʃən] N Lotion *f*
lottery ['lɔtərɪ] N Lotterie *f*
loud [laud] ADJ laut; (*clothes*) schreiend ▸ ADV laut; **to be ~ in one's support of sb/sth** jdn/etw lautstark unterstützen; **out ~** (*read, laugh etc*) laut
loud-hailer [laud'heɪlə^r] (BRIT) N Megafon *nt*
loudly ['laudlɪ] ADV laut
loudmouthed ['laudmauθt] ADJ großmäulig
loudspeaker [laud'spi:kə^r] N Lautsprecher *m*
lounge [laundʒ] N (*in house*) Wohnzimmer *nt*; (*in hotel*) Lounge *f*; (*at airport, station*) Wartehalle *f*; (BRIT: *also*: **lounge bar**) Salon *m* ▸ VI faulenzen
▸ **lounge about** VI herumliegen, herumsitzen, herumstehen
▸ **lounge around** VI = **lounge about**
lounge suit (BRIT) N Straßenanzug *m*
louse [laus] (*pl* **lice**) N Laus *f*
▸ **louse up** (*inf*) VT vermasseln
lousy ['lauzɪ] (*inf*) ADJ (*bad-quality*) lausig, mies; (*despicable*) fies, gemein; (*ill*): **to feel ~** sich miserabel *or* elend fühlen
lout [laut] N Lümmel *m*, Flegel *m*
louvre, (US) **louver** ['lu:və^r] ADJ (*door, window*) Lamellen-
lovable ['lʌvəbl] ADJ liebenswert
love [lʌv] N Liebe *f* ▸ VT lieben; (*thing, activity etc*) gern mögen; **"~ (from) Anne"** (*on letter*) „mit herzlichen Grüßen, Anne"; **to be in ~ with** verliebt sein in *+acc*; **to fall in ~ with** sich verlieben in *+acc*; **to make ~** sich lieben; **~ at first sight** Liebe auf den ersten Blick; **to send one's ~ to sb** jdn grüßen lassen; **"fifteen ~"** (*Tennis*) „fünfzehn null"; **to ~ doing sth** etw gern tun; **I'd ~ to come** ich würde sehr gerne kommen; **I ~ chocolate** ich esse Schokolade liebend gern
love affair N Verhältnis *nt*, Liebschaft *f*
love child N (*irreg*) uneheliches Kind *nt*, Kind *nt* der Liebe
loved ones ['lʌvdwʌnz] NPL enge Freunde und Verwandte *pl*
love-hate relationship ['lʌvheɪt-] N Hassliebe *f*
love letter N Liebesbrief *m*
love life N Liebesleben *nt*
lovely ['lʌvlɪ] ADJ (*beautiful*) schön; (*delightful*) herrlich; (*person*) sehr nett
lover ['lʌvə^r] N Geliebte(r) *f(m)*; (*person in love*) Liebende(r) *f(m)*; **~ of art/music** Kunst-/Musikliebhaber(in) *m(f)*; **to be lovers** ein Liebespaar sein
lovesick ['lʌvsɪk] ADJ liebeskrank
love song N Liebeslied *nt*
loving ['lʌvɪŋ] ADJ liebend; (*actions*) liebevoll
low [ləu] ADJ niedrig; (*bow, curtsey*) tief; (*quality*) schlecht; (*sound: deep*) tief; (: *quiet*) leise; (*depressed*) niedergeschlagen, bedrückt ▸ ADV (*sing*) leise; (*fly*) tief ▸ N (*Met*) Tief *nt*; **to be/run ~** knapp sein/werden; **sb is running ~ on sth** jdm wird etw knapp; **to reach a new** *or* **an all-time ~** einen neuen Tiefstand erreichen
low-alcohol ['ləu'ælkəhɔl] ADJ alkoholarm
lowbrow ['ləubrau] ADJ (geistig) anspruchslos
low-calorie ['ləu'kælərɪ] ADJ kalorienarm
low-carb [ləu'kɑ:b] ADJ low-carb, kohlenhydratarm; **~ bread** kohlenhydratarmes Brot
low-cut ['ləukʌt] ADJ (*dress*) tief ausgeschnitten
lowdown ['ləudaun] (*inf*) N: **he gave me the ~ on it** er hat mich darüber informiert

low-emission ADJ schadstoffarm
lower ['ləuə^r] ADJ untere(r, s); *(lip, jaw, arm)* Unter- ▸ VT senken
low-fat ['ləu'fæt] ADJ fettarm
low-key ['ləu'ki:] ADJ zurückhaltend; *(not obvious)* unaufdringlich
lowlands ['ləuləndz] NPL Flachland *nt*
low-level language ['ləulɛvl-] N *(Comput)* niedere Programmiersprache *f*
low-loader ['ləu'ləudə^r] N Tieflader *m*
lowly ['ləulɪ] ADJ *(position)* niedrig; *(origin)* bescheiden
low-lying [ləu'laɪɪŋ] ADJ tief gelegen
low-paid [ləu'peɪd] ADJ schlecht bezahlt
low-rise ['ləuraɪz] ADJ niedrig (gebaut)
low-tech ['ləutɛk] ADJ nicht mit Hightech ausgestattet
low tide [ləʊ'taɪd] N Ebbe *f*
loyal ['lɔɪəl] ADJ treu; *(support)* loyal
loyalist ['lɔɪəlɪst] N Loyalist(in) *m(f)*
loyalty ['lɔɪəltɪ] N Treue *f*; Loyalität *f*
loyalty card (BRIT) N *(Comm)* Paybackkarte *f*
lozenge ['lɔzɪndʒ] N Pastille *f*; *(shape)* Raute *f*
LP N ABBR *(= long player)* LP *f*; *see also* **long-playing record**
LPG N ABBR *(= liquefied petroleum gas)* Flüssiggas *nt*

> Als **L-plates** werden in Großbritannien die weißen Schilder mit einem roten „L" bezeichnet, die vorne und hinten an jedem von einem Fahrschüler geführten Fahrzeug befestigt werden müssen. Fahrschüler müssen einen vorläufigen Führerschein beantragen und dürfen damit unter der Aufsicht eines erfahrenen Autofahrers auf allen Straßen außer Autobahnen fahren.

LPN (US) N ABBR *(= Licensed Practical Nurse)* staatlich anerkannte Krankenschwester *f*, staatlich anerkannter Krankenpfleger *m*
LRAM (BRIT) N ABBR *(= Licentiate of the Royal Academy of Music) Qualifikationsnachweis in Musik*
LSAT (US) N ABBR *(= Law School Admissions Test) Zulassungsprüfung für juristische Hochschulen*
LSD N ABBR *(= lysergic acid diethylamide)* LSD *nt*; (BRIT: *= pounds, shillings and pence) früheres britisches Währungssystem*
LSE (BRIT) N ABBR *(= London School of Economics) LondonerWirtschaftshochschule*
Lt ABBR *(Mil: = lieutenant)* Lt.
Ltd ABBR *(Comm: = limited (liability))* ≈ GmbH *f*
lubricant ['lu:brɪkənt] N Schmiermittel *nt*
lubricate ['lu:brɪkeɪt] VT schmieren, ölen
lucid ['lu:sɪd] ADJ klar; *(person)* bei klarem Verstand
lucidity [lu:'sɪdɪtɪ] N Klarheit *f*
luck [lʌk] N *(esp good luck)* Glück *nt*; **bad ~** Unglück *nt*; **good ~!** viel Glück!; **bad** *or* **hard** *or* **tough ~!** so ein Pech!; **hard** *or* **tough ~!** *(showing no sympathy)* Pech gehabt!; **to be in ~** Glück haben; **to be out of ~** kein Glück haben
luckily ['lʌkɪlɪ] ADV glücklicherweise
luckless ['lʌklɪs] ADJ glücklos
lucky ['lʌkɪ] ADJ *(situation, event)* glücklich; *(object)* Glück bringend; *(person)*: **to be ~** Glück haben; **to have a ~ escape** noch einmal davonkommen; **~ charm** Glücksbringer *m*
lucrative ['lu:krətɪv] ADJ einträglich
ludicrous ['lu:dɪkrəs] ADJ grotesk
ludo ['lu:dəu] N Mensch, ärgere dich nicht *nt*
lug [lʌg] *(inf)* VT schleppen
luggage ['lʌgɪdʒ] N Gepäck *nt*
luggage car (US) N = **luggage van**
luggage compartment N Gepäckraum *m*
luggage rack N Gepäckträger *m*; *(in train)* Gepäckablage *f*
luggage van (BRIT) N *(Rail)* Gepäckwagen *m*
lugubrious [lu'gu:brɪəs] ADJ schwermütig
lukewarm ['lu:kwɔ:m] ADJ lauwarm; *(fig: person, reaction etc)* lau
lull [lʌl] N Pause *f* ▸ VT: **to ~ sb to sleep** jdn einlullen *or* einschläfern; **to be lulled into a false sense of security** in trügerische Sicherheit gewiegt werden
lullaby ['lʌləbaɪ] N Schlaflied *nt*
lumbago [lʌm'beɪgəu] N Hexenschuss *m*
lumber ['lʌmbə^r] N *(wood)* Holz *nt*; *(junk)* Gerümpel *nt* ▸ VI: **to ~ about/along** herum-/entlangtapsen
▸ **lumber with** VT; **to be/get lumbered with sth** etw am Hals haben/aufgehalst bekommen
lumberjack ['lʌmbədʒæk] N Holzfäller *m*
lumber room (BRIT) N Rumpelkammer *f*
lumberyard ['lʌmbəjɑ:d] (US) N Holzlager *nt*
luminous ['lu:mɪnəs] ADJ leuchtend, Leucht-
lump [lʌmp] N Klumpen *m*; *(on body)* Beule *f*; *(in breast)* Knoten *m*; *(also*: **sugar lump**) Stück *nt* (Zucker) ▸ VT: **to ~ together** in einen Topf werfen; **a ~ sum** eine Pauschalsumme
lumpy ['lʌmpɪ] ADJ klumpig
lunacy ['lu:nəsɪ] N Wahnsinn *m*
lunar ['lu:nə^r] ADJ Mond-
lunatic ['lu:nətɪk] ADJ wahnsinnig ▸ N Wahnsinnige(r) *f(m)*, Irre(r) *f(m)*
lunatic asylum N Irrenanstalt *f*
lunatic fringe N: **the ~** die Extremisten *pl*
lunch [lʌntʃ] N Mittagessen *nt*; *(time)* Mittagszeit *f* ▸ VI zu Mittag essen
lunch break N Mittagspause *f*
luncheon ['lʌntʃən] N Mittagessen *nt*
luncheon meat N Frühstücksfleisch *nt*
luncheon voucher (BRIT) N Essensmarke *f*
lunch hour N Mittagspause *f*
lunch time N Mittagszeit *f*
lung [lʌŋ] N Lunge *f*
lunge [lʌndʒ] VI *(also*: **lunge forward**) sich nach vorne stürzen; **to ~ at** sich stürzen auf *+acc*
lupin ['lu:pɪn] N Lupine *f*
lurch [lə:tʃ] VI ruckeln; *(person)* taumeln ▸ N Ruck *m*; *(of person)* Taumeln *nt*; **to leave sb in the ~** jdn im Stich lassen
lure [luə^r] N Verlockung *f* ▸ VT locken
lurid ['luərɪd] ADJ *(story etc)* reißerisch; *(pej: brightly coloured)* grell, in grellen Farben
lurk [lə:k] VI *(also fig)* lauern
luscious ['lʌʃəs] ADJ *(attractive)* fantastisch; *(food)* köstlich, lecker

lush [lʌʃ] ADJ (*fields*) saftig; (*gardens*) üppig; (*luxurious*) luxuriös
lust [lʌst] (*pej*) N (*sexual*) (sinnliche) Begierde *f*; (*for money, power etc*) Gier *f*
▸ **lust after** VT FUS (*sexually*) begehren; (*crave*) gieren nach
▸ **lust for** VT FUS = **lust after**
lustful ['lʌstful] ADJ lüstern
lustre, (US) **luster** ['lʌstəʳ] N Schimmer *m*, Glanz *m*
lusty ['lʌstɪ] ADJ gesund und munter
lute [lu:t] N Laute *f*
luvvie, luvvy ['lʌvɪ] N (*inf*) Schätzchen *nt*
Luxembourg ['lʌksəmbə:g] N Luxemburg *nt*
luxuriant [lʌg'zjuərɪənt] ADJ üppig
luxuriate [lʌg'zjuərɪeɪt] VI: **to ~ in sth** sich in etw *dat* aalen
luxurious [lʌg'zjuərɪəs] ADJ luxuriös
luxury ['lʌkʃərɪ] N Luxus *m* (*no pl*) ▸ CPD (*hotel, car etc*) Luxus-; **little luxuries** kleine Genüsse
LV (BRIT) N ABBR = **luncheon voucher**
LW ABBR (*Radio*: = *long wave*) LW
Lycra® ['laɪkrə] N Lycra *nt*
lying ['laɪɪŋ] N Lügen *nt* ▸ ADJ verlogen
lynch [lɪntʃ] VT lynchen
lynx [lɪŋks] N Luchs *m*
lyric ['lɪrɪk] ADJ lyrisch
lyrical ['lɪrɪkl] ADJ lyrisch; (*fig: praise etc*) schwärmerisch
lyricism ['lɪrɪsɪzəm] N Lyrik *f*
lyrics ['lɪrɪks] NPL (*of song*) Text *m*

l

Mm

M¹, m¹ [ɛm] N (*letter*) M *nt*, m *nt*; **M for Mary, M for Mike** (*US*) ≈ M wie Martha
M² [ɛm] N ABBR (BRIT: = *motorway*): **the M8** ≈ die A8 ▸ ABBR = **medium**
m² ABBR (= *metre*) m; = **mile**; (= *million*) Mio.
MA N ABBR (= *Master of Arts*) *akademischer Grad für Geisteswissenschaftler*; (= *military academy*) Militärakademie *f* ▸ ABBR (*US Post*) = **Massachusetts**
mac [mæk] (BRIT) N Regenmantel *m*
macabre [mə'kɑːbrə] ADJ makaber
macaroni [mækə'rəunɪ] N Makkaroni *pl*
macaroon [mækə'ruːn] N Makrone *f*
mace [meɪs] N (*weapon*) Keule *f*; (*ceremonial*) Amtsstab *m*; (*spice*) Muskatblüte *f*
Macedonia [mæsɪ'dəunɪə] N Makedonien *nt*
Macedonian [mæsɪ'dəunɪən] ADJ makedonisch ▸ N Makedonier(in) *m(f)*; (*Ling*) Makedonisch *nt*
machinations [mækɪ'neɪʃənz] NPL Machenschaften *pl*
machine [mə'ʃiːn] N Maschine *f*; (*fig: party machine etc*) Apparat *m* ▸ VT (*Tech*) maschinell herstellen *or* bearbeiten; (*dress etc*) mit der Maschine nähen
machine code N Maschinencode *m*
machine gun N Maschinengewehr *nt*
machine language N Maschinensprache *f*
machine-readable [mə'ʃiːnriːdəbl] ADJ maschinenlesbar
machinery [mə'ʃiːnərɪ] N Maschinen *pl*; (*fig: of government*) Apparat *m*
machine shop N Maschinensaal *m*
machine tool N Werkzeugmaschine *f*
machine washable ADJ waschmaschinenfest
machinist [mə'ʃiːnɪst] N Maschinist(in) *m(f)*
macho ['mætʃəu] ADJ Macho-; **a ~ man** ein Macho *m*
mackerel ['mækrl] N INV Makrele *f*
mackintosh ['mækɪntɔʃ] (BRIT) N Regenmantel *m*
macro... ['mækrəu] PREF Makro-, makro-
macroeconomics ['mækrəuiːkə'nɔmɪks] NPL Makroökonomie *f*
mad [mæd] ADJ wahnsinnig, verrückt; (*angry*) böse, sauer (*inf*); **to be ~ about** verrückt sein auf +*acc*; **to be ~ at sb** böse *or* sauer auf jdn sein; **to go ~** (*insane*) verrückt *or* wahnsinnig werden; (*angry*) böse *or* sauer werden
madam ['mædəm] N gnädige Frau *f*; **yes, ~** ja(wohl); **M~ Chairman** Frau Vorsitzende
madcap ['mædkæp] ADJ (*idea*) versponnen; (*tricks*) toll
mad cow disease N Rinderwahn *m*
madden ['mædn] VT ärgern, fuchsen (*inf*)
maddening ['mædnɪŋ] ADJ unerträglich
made [meɪd] PT, PP *of* **make**
Madeira [mə'dɪərə] N Madeira *nt*; (*wine*) Madeira *m*
made-to-measure ['meɪdtə'mɛʒəʳ] (BRIT) ADJ maßgeschneidert
madhouse ['mædhaus] N (*also fig*) Irrenhaus *nt*
madly ['mædlɪ] ADV wie verrückt; **~ in love** bis über beide Ohren verliebt
madman ['mædmən] N (*irreg*) Verrückte(r) *m*, Irre(r) *m*
madness ['mædnɪs] N Wahnsinn *m*
Madrid [mə'drɪd] N Madrid *nt*
Mafia ['mæfɪə] N Mafia *f*
mag [mæg] (BRIT *inf*) N = **magazine**
magazine [mægə'ziːn] N Zeitschrift *f*; (*Radio, TV, of firearm*) Magazin *nt*; (*Mil: store*) Depot *nt*
maggot ['mægət] N Made *f*
magic ['mædʒɪk] N Magie *f*; (*conjuring*) Zauberei *f* ▸ ADJ magisch; (*formula*) Zauber-; (*fig: place, moment etc*) zauberhaft
magical ['mædʒɪkl] ADJ magisch; (*experience, evening*) zauberhaft
magician [mə'dʒɪʃən] N (*wizard*) Magier *m*; (*conjurer*) Zauberer *m*
magistrate ['mædʒɪstreɪt] N Friedensrichter(in) *m(f)*
magnanimous [mæg'nænɪməs] ADJ großmütig
magnate ['mægneɪt] N Magnat *m*
magnesium [mæg'niːzɪəm] N Magnesium *nt*
magnet ['mægnɪt] N Magnet *m*
magnetic [mæg'nɛtɪk] ADJ magnetisch; (*field, compass, pole etc*) Magnet-; (*personality*) anziehend
magnetic disk N (*Comput*) Magnetplatte *f*
magnetic tape N Magnetband *nt*
magnetism ['mægnɪtɪzəm] N Magnetismus *m*; (*of person*) Anziehungskraft *f*
magnetize ['mægnɪtaɪz] VT magnetisieren
magnification [mægnɪfɪ'keɪʃən] N Vergrößerung *f*

magnificence [mæg'nɪfɪsns] N Großartigkeit *f*; (*of robes*) Pracht *f*
magnificent [mæg'nɪfɪsnt] ADJ großartig; (*robes*) prachtvoll
magnify ['mægnɪfaɪ] VT vergrößern; (*sound*) verstärken; (*fig: exaggerate*) aufbauschen
magnifying glass ['mægnɪfaɪɪŋ-] N Vergrößerungsglas *nt*, Lupe *f*
magnitude ['mægnɪtju:d] N (*size*) Ausmaß *nt*, Größe *f*; (*importance*) Bedeutung *f*
magnolia [mæg'nəulɪə] N Magnolie *f*
magpie ['mægpaɪ] N Elster *f*
mahogany [mə'hɔgənɪ] N Mahagoni *nt* ▸ CPD Mahagoni-
maid [meɪd] N Dienstmädchen *nt*; **old ~** (*pej*) alte Jungfer
maiden ['meɪdn] N (*liter*) Mädchen *nt* ▸ ADJ unverheiratet; (*speech, voyage*) Jungfern-
maiden name N Mädchenname *m*
mail [meɪl] N Post *f* ▸ VT aufgeben; **by ~** mit der Post
mailbox ['meɪlbɔks] N (*US*) Briefkasten *m*; (*Comput*) Mailbox *f*, elektronischer Briefkasten *m*
mailing list ['meɪlɪŋ-] N Anschriftenliste *f*
mailman ['meɪlmæn] (*US*) N (*irreg*) Briefträger *m*, Postbote *m*
mail order N (*system*) Versand *m* ▸ CPD: **mail-order firm** *or* **business** Versandhaus *nt*; **mail-order catalogue** Versandhauskatalog *m*; **by ~** durch Bestellung per Post
mailshot ['meɪlʃɔt] (BRIT) N Werbebrief *m*
mail train N Postzug *m*
mail truck (*US*) N Postauto *nt*
mail van (BRIT) N (*Aut*) Postauto *nt*; (*Rail*) Postwagen *m*
maim [meɪm] VT verstümmeln
main [meɪn] ADJ Haupt-, wichtigste(r, s); (*door, entrance, meal*) Haupt- ▸ N Hauptleitung *f*; **the mains** NPL (*Elec*) das Stromnetz; (*gas, water*) die Hauptleitung; **in the ~** im Großen und Ganzen
main course N (*Culin*) Hauptgericht *nt*
mainframe ['meɪnfreɪm] N (*Comput*) Großrechner *m*
mainland ['meɪnlənd] N Festland *nt*
mainline ['meɪnlaɪn] ADJ: **~ station** Fernbahnhof *m* ▸ VT (*drugs slang*) spritzen ▸ VI (*drugs slang*) fixen
main line N Hauptstrecke *f*
mainly ['meɪnlɪ] ADV hauptsächlich
main road N Hauptstraße *f*
mainstay ['meɪnsteɪ] N (*foundation*) (wichtigste) Stütze *f*; (*chief constituent*) Hauptbestandteil *m*
mainstream ['meɪnstri:m] N Hauptrichtung *f* ▸ ADJ (*cinema etc*) populär; (*politics*) der Mitte
main street N (*US*) Hauptstraße *f*
maintain [meɪn'teɪn] VT (*preserve*) aufrechterhalten; (*keep up*) beibehalten; (*provide for*) unterhalten; (*look after: building*) instand halten; (*: equipment*) warten; (*affirm: opinion*) vertreten; (*: innocence*) beteuern; **to ~ that ...** behaupten, dass ...
maintenance ['meɪntənəns] N (*of building*) Instandhaltung *f*; (*of equipment*) Wartung *f*; (*preservation*) Aufrechterhaltung *f*; (*Law: alimony*) Unterhalt *m*
maintenance contract N Wartungsvertrag *m*
maintenance order N (*Law*) Unterhaltsurteil *nt*
maisonette [meɪzə'nɛt] (BRIT) N Maisonettewohnung *f*
maize [meɪz] N Mais *m*
Maj. ABBR (*Mil*) = **major**
majestic [mə'dʒɛstɪk] ADJ erhaben
majesty ['mædʒɪstɪ] N (*title*): **Your M~** Eure Majestät; (*splendour*) Erhabenheit *f*
major ['meɪdʒər] N Major *m* ▸ ADJ bedeutend; (*Mus*) Dur ▸ VI (*US*): **to ~ in French** Französisch als Hauptfach belegen; **a ~ operation** eine größere Operation
Majorca [mə'jɔ:kə] N Mallorca *nt*
major general N Generalmajor *m*
majority [mə'dʒɔrɪtɪ] N Mehrheit *f* ▸ CPD (*verdict, holding*) Mehrheits-
make [meɪk] (*pt, pp* **made**) VT machen; (*clothes*) nähen; (*cake*) backen; (*speech*) halten; (*manufacture*) herstellen; (*earn*) verdienen; (*cause to be*): **to ~ sb sad** jdn traurig machen; (*force*): **to ~ sb do sth** jdn zwingen, etw zu tun; (*cause*) jdn dazu bringen, etw zu tun; (*equal*): **2 and 2 ~ 4** 2 und 2 ist *or* macht 4 ▸ N Marke *f*, Fabrikat *nt*; **to ~ a fool of sb** jdn lächerlich machen; **to ~ a profit/loss** Gewinn/Verlust machen; **to ~ it** (*arrive*) es schaffen; (*succeed*) Erfolg haben; **what time do you ~ it?** wie spät hast du?; **to ~ good** erfolgreich sein; (*threat*) wahr machen; (*promise*) einlösen; (*damage*) wiedergutmachen; (*loss*) ersetzen; **to ~ do with** auskommen mit
▸ **make for** VT FUS (*place*) zuhalten auf *+acc*
▸ **make off** VI sich davonmachen
▸ **make out** VT (*decipher*) entziffern; (*understand*) verstehen; (*see*) ausmachen; (*write: cheque*) ausstellen; (*claim, imply*) behaupten; (*pretend*) so tun, als ob; **to ~ out a case for sth** für etw argumentieren
▸ **make over** VT: **to ~ over (to)** überschreiben *+dat*
▸ **make up** VT (*constitute*) bilden; (*invent*) erfinden; (*prepare: bed*) zurechtmachen; (*: parcel*) zusammenpacken ▸ VI (*after quarrel*) sich versöhnen; (*with cosmetics*) sich schminken; **to ~ up one's mind** sich entscheiden; **to be made up of** bestehen aus
▸ **make up for** VT FUS (*loss*) ersetzen; (*disappointment etc*) ausgleichen
make-believe ['meɪkbɪli:v] N Fantasie *f*; **a world of ~** eine Fantasiewelt; **it's just ~** es ist nicht wirklich
makeover ['meɪkəuvər] N *grundlegende Veränderung des Aussehens*; **to give sb a ~** jdm ein neues Aussehen verpassen
maker ['meɪkər] N Hersteller *m*; **film ~** Filmemacher(in) *m(f)*
makeshift ['meɪkʃɪft] ADJ behelfsmäßig
make-up ['meɪkʌp] N Make-up *nt*, Schminke *f*
make-up bag N Kosmetiktasche *f*

m

make-up remover N Make-up-Entferner *m*
making ['meɪkɪŋ] N (*fig*): **in the ~** im Entstehen; **to have the makings of** das Zeug haben zu
maladjusted [mælə'dʒʌstɪd] ADJ verhaltensgestört
maladroit [mælə'drɔɪt] ADJ ungeschickt
malaise [mæ'leɪz] N Unbehagen *nt*
malaria [mə'lɛərɪə] N Malaria *f*
Malawi [mə'lɑ:wɪ] N Malawi *nt*
Malay [mə'leɪ] ADJ malaiisch ▶ N Malaie *m*, Malaiin *f*; (*Ling*) Malaiisch *nt*
Malaya [mə'leɪə] N Malaya *nt*
Malayan [mə'leɪən] ADJ, N = **Malay**
Malaysia [mə'leɪzɪə] N Malaysia *nt*
Malaysian [mə'leɪzɪən] ADJ malaysisch ▶ N Malaysier(in) *m(f)*
Maldives ['mɔ:ldaɪvz] NPL Malediven *pl*
male [meɪl] N (*animal*) Männchen *nt*; (*man*) Mann *m* ▶ ADJ männlich; (*Elec*): **~ plug** Stecker *m*; **because he is ~** weil er ein Mann/Junge ist; **~ and female students** Studenten und Studentinnen; **a ~ child** ein Junge
male chauvinist N Chauvinist *m*
male nurse N Krankenpfleger *m*
malevolence [mə'lɛvələns] N Boshaftigkeit *f*; (*of action*) Böswilligkeit *f*
malevolent [mə'lɛvələnt] ADJ boshaft; (*intention*) böswillig
malfunction [mæl'fʌŋkʃən] N (*of computer*) Funktionsstörung *f*; (*of machine*) Defekt *m* ▶ VI (*computer*) eine Funktionsstörung haben; (*machine*) defekt sein
malice ['mælɪs] N Bosheit *f*
malicious [mə'lɪʃəs] ADJ boshaft; (*Law*) böswillig
malign [mə'laɪn] VT verleumden ▶ ADJ (*influence*) schlecht; (*interpretation*) böswillig
malignant [mə'lɪgnənt] ADJ bösartig; (*intention*) böswillig
malingerer [mə'lɪŋgərə^r] N Simulant(in) *m(f)*
mall [mɔ:l] N (*also*: **shopping mall**) Einkaufszentrum *nt*
malleable ['mælɪəbl] ADJ (*lit, fig*) formbar
mallet ['mælɪt] N Holzhammer *m*
malnutrition [mælnju:'trɪʃən] N Unterernährung *f*
malpractice [mæl'præktɪs] N Berufsvergehen *nt*
malt [mɔ:lt] N Malz *nt*; (*also*: **malt whisky**) Malt Whisky *m*
Malta ['mɔ:ltə] N Malta *nt*
Maltese [mɔ:l'ti:z] ADJ maltesisch ▶ N INV Malteser(in) *m(f)*; (*Ling*) Maltesisch *nt*
maltreat [mæl'tri:t] VT schlecht behandeln; (*violently*) misshandeln
malware ['mælwɛə^r] N (*Comput*) Schadprogramm *nt*, Malware *f*
mammal ['mæml] N Säugetier *nt*
mammoth ['mæməθ] N Mammut *nt* ▶ ADJ (*task*) Mammut-
man [mæn] (*pl* **men**) N Mann *m*; (*mankind*) der Mensch, die Menschen *pl*; (*Chess*) Figur *f* ▶ VT (*ship*) bemannen; (*gun, machine*) bedienen; (*post*) besetzen; **~ and wife** Mann und Frau
manage ['mænɪdʒ] VI: **to ~ to do sth** es schaffen, etw zu tun; (*get by financially*) zurechtkommen ▶ VT (*business, organization*) leiten; (*control*) zurechtkommen mit; **to ~ without sb/sth** ohne jdn/etw auskommen; **well managed** (*business, shop etc*) gut geführt
manageable ['mænɪdʒəbl] ADJ (*task*) zu bewältigen; (*number*) überschaubar
management ['mænɪdʒmənt] N Leitung *f*, Führung *f*; (*persons*) Unternehmensleitung *f*; **"under new ~"** „unter neuer Leitung"
management accounting N Kosten- und Leistungsrechnung *f*
management consultant N Unternehmensberater(in) *m(f)*
manager ['mænɪdʒə^r] N (*of business*) Geschäftsführer(in) *m(f)*; (*of institution etc*) Direktor(in) *m(f)*; (*of department*) Leiter(in) *m(f)*; (*of pop star*) Manager(in) *m(f)*; (*Sport*) Trainer(in) *m(f)*; **sales ~** Verkaufsleiter(in) *m(f)*
manageress [mænɪdʒə'rɛs] N (*of shop, business*) Geschäftsführerin *f*; (*of office, department etc*) Leiterin *f*
managerial [mænɪ'dʒɪərɪəl] ADJ (*role, post*) leitend; (*decisions*) geschäftlich; **~ staff/skills** Führungskräfte *pl*/-qualitäten *pl*
managing director ['mænɪdʒɪŋ-] N Geschäftsführer(in) *m(f)*
Mancunian [mæŋ'kju:nɪən] N Bewohner(in) *m(f)* Manchesters
mandarin ['mændərɪn] N (*also*: **mandarin orange**) Mandarine *f*; (*official: Chinese*) Mandarin *m*; (*: gen*) Funktionär *m*
mandate ['mændeɪt] N Mandat *nt*; (*task*) Auftrag *m*
mandatory ['mændətərɪ] ADJ obligatorisch
mandolin, mandoline ['mændəlɪn] N Mandoline *f*
mane [meɪn] N Mähne *f*
maneuver *etc* [mə'nu:və^r] (*US*) = **manoeuvre** *etc*
manfully ['mænfəlɪ] ADV mannhaft, beherzt
manganese [mæŋgə'ni:z] N Mangan *nt*
mangetout ['mɔnʒ'tu:] (BRIT) N Zuckererbse *f*
mangle ['mæŋgl] VT (übel) zurichten ▶ N Mangel *f*
mango ['mæŋgəu] (*pl* **mangoes**) N Mango *f*
mangrove ['mæŋgrəuv] N Mangrove(n)baum *m*
mangy ['meɪndʒɪ] ADJ (*animal*) räudig
manhandle ['mænhændl] VT (*mistreat*) grob behandeln; (*move by hand*) (von Hand) befördern
manhole ['mænhəul] N Kanalschacht *m*
manhood ['mænhud] N Mannesalter *nt*
man-hour ['mænauə^r] N Arbeitsstunde *f*
manhunt ['mænhʌnt] N Fahndung *f*
mania ['meɪnɪə] N Manie *f*; (*craze*) Sucht *f*; **persecution ~** Verfolgungswahn *m*
maniac ['meɪnɪæk] N Wahnsinnige(r) *f(m)*, Verrückte(r) *f(m)*; (*fig*) Fanatiker(in) *m(f)*
manic ['mænɪk] ADJ (*behaviour*) manisch; (*activity*) rasend
manic-depressive ['mænɪkdɪ'prɛsɪv] N Manisch-Depressive(r) *f(m)* ▶ ADJ manisch-depressiv

manicure ['mænɪkjuə^r] N Maniküre *f* ▸ VT maniküren
manicure set N Nageletui *nt*, Maniküreetui *nt*
manifest ['mænɪfɛst] VT zeigen, bekunden ▸ ADJ offenkundig ▸ N Manifest *nt*
manifestation [mænɪfɛs'teɪʃən] N Anzeichen *nt*
manifesto [mænɪ'fɛstəu] N Manifest *nt*
manifold ['mænɪfəuld] ADJ vielfältig ▸ N: **exhaust** ~ Auspuffkrümmer *m*
Manila [mə'nɪlə] N Manila *nt*
manila [mə'nɪlə] ADJ: ~ **envelope** brauner Briefumschlag *m*
manipulate [mə'nɪpjuleɪt] VT manipulieren
manipulation [mənɪpju'leɪʃən] N Manipulation *f*
mankind [mæn'kaɪnd] N Menschheit *f*
manliness ['mænlɪnɪs] N Männlichkeit *f*
manly ['mænlɪ] ADJ männlich
man-made ['mæn'meɪd] ADJ künstlich; (*fibre*) synthetisch
manna ['mænə] N Manna *nt*
mannequin ['mænɪkɪn] N (*dummy*) Schaufensterpuppe *f*; (*fashion model*) Mannequin *nt*
manner ['mænə^r] N (*way*) Art *f*, Weise *f*; (*behaviour*) Art *f*; (*type, sort*): **all ~ of things** die verschiedensten Dinge; **manners** NPL (*conduct*) Manieren *pl*, Umgangsformen *pl*; **bad manners** schlechte Manieren; **that's bad manners** das gehört sich nicht
mannerism ['mænərɪzəm] N Eigenheit *f*
mannerly ['mænəlɪ] ADJ wohlerzogen
manning ['mænɪŋ] N Besatzung *f*
manoeuvrable, (*US*) **maneuverable** [mə'nu:vrəbl] ADJ manövrierfähig
manoeuvre, (*US*) **maneuver** [mə'nu:və^r] VT manövrieren; (*situation*) manipulieren ▸ VI manövrieren ▸ N (*skilful move*) Manöver *nt*; **manoeuvres** NPL (*Mil*) Manöver *nt*, Truppenübungen *pl*; **to ~ sb into doing sth** jdn dazu bringen, etw zu tun
manor ['mænə^r] N (*also*: **manor house**) Herrenhaus *nt*
manpower ['mænpauə^r] N Personal *nt*, Arbeitskräfte *pl*
Manpower Services Commission (BRIT) N *Behörde für Arbeitsbeschaffung, Arbeitsvermittlung und Berufsausbildung*
manservant ['mænsə:vənt] (*pl* **menservants**) N Diener *m*
mansion ['mænʃən] N Villa *f*
manslaughter ['mænslɔ:tə^r] N Totschlag *m*
mantelpiece ['mæntlpi:s] N Kaminsims *m or nt*
mantle ['mæntl] N Decke *f*; (*fig*) Deckmantel *m*
man-to-man ['mæntə'mæn] ADJ, ADV von Mann zu Mann
manual ['mænjuəl] ADJ manuell, Hand-; (*controls*) von Hand ▸ N Handbuch *nt*
manufacture [mænju'fæktʃə^r] VT herstellen ▸ N Herstellung *f*
manufactured goods NPL Fertigerzeugnisse *pl*
manufacturer [mænju'fæktʃərə^r] N Hersteller *m*
manufacturing [mænju'fæktʃərɪŋ] N Herstellung *f*
manure [mə'njuə^r] N Dung *m*
manuscript ['mænjuskrɪpt] N Manuskript *nt*; (*old document*) Handschrift *f*
many ['mɛnɪ] ADJ, PRON viele; **a great ~** eine ganze Reihe; **how ~?** wie viele?; **too ~ difficulties** zu viele Schwierigkeiten; **twice as ~** doppelt so viele; **~ a time** so manches Mal
Maori ['maurɪ] ADJ maorisch ▸ N Maori *mf*
map [mæp] N (Land)karte *f*; (*of town*) Stadtplan *m* ▸ VT eine Karte anfertigen von
▸ **map out** VT planen; (*plan*) entwerfen; (*essay*) anlegen
maple ['meɪpl] N (*tree, wood*) Ahorn *m*
mar [mɑ:^r] VT (*appearance*) verunstalten; (*day*) verderben; (*event*) stören
Mar. ABBR = **March**
marathon ['mærəθən] N Marathon *m* ▸ ADJ: **a ~ session** eine Marathonsitzung
marathon runner N Marathonläufer(in) *m(f)*
marauder [mə'rɔ:də^r] N (*robber*) Plünderer *m*; (*killer*) Mörder *m*
marble ['mɑ:bl] N Marmor *m*; (*toy*) Murmel *f*
marbles ['mɑ:blz] N (*game*) Murmeln *pl*
March [mɑ:tʃ] N März *m*; *see also* **July**
march [mɑ:tʃ] VI marschieren; (*protesters*) ziehen ▸ N Marsch *m*; (*demonstration*) Demonstration *f*; **to ~ out of/into** (heraus)marschieren aus *+dat*/ (herein)marschieren in *+acc*
marcher ['mɑ:tʃə^r] N Demonstrant(in) *m(f)*
marching orders ['mɑ:tʃɪŋ-] NPL: **to give sb his/her ~** (*employee*) jdn entlassen; (*lover*) jdm den Laufpass geben
march past N Vorbeimarsch *m*
mare [mɛə^r] N Stute *f*
margarine [mɑ:dʒə'ri:n] N Margarine *f*
marge [mɑ:dʒ] (BRIT *inf*) N = **margarine**
margin ['mɑ:dʒɪn] N Rand *m*; (*of votes*) Mehrheit *f*; (*for safety, error etc*) Spielraum *m*; (*Comm*) Gewinnspanne *f*
marginal ['mɑ:dʒɪnl] ADJ geringfügig; (*note*) Rand-
marginally ['mɑ:dʒɪnəlɪ] ADV nur wenig, geringfügig
marginal (seat) N (*Pol*) *mit knapper Mehrheit gewonnener Wahlkreis*
marigold ['mærɪgəuld] N Ringelblume *f*
marijuana [mærɪ'wɑ:nə] N Marihuana *nt*
marina [mə'ri:nə] N Jachthafen *m*
marinade [mærɪ'neɪd] N Marinade *f* ▸ VT = **marinate**
marinate ['mærɪneɪt] VT marinieren
marine [mə'ri:n] ADJ (*plant, biology*) Meeres- ▸ N (BRIT: *soldier*) Marineinfanterist *m*; (*US: sailor*) Marinesoldat *m*; **~ engineer** Schiff(s)bauingenieur *m*; **~ engineering** Schiff(s)bau *m*
marine insurance N Seeversicherung *f*
marital ['mærɪtl] ADJ ehelich; (*problem*) Ehe-; **~ status** Familienstand *m*

m

maritime ['mærɪtaɪm] ADJ (*nation*) Seefahrer-; (*museum*) Seefahrts-; (*law*) See-
marjoram ['mɑ:dʒərəm] N Majoran *m*
mark [mɑ:k] N Zeichen *nt*; (*stain*) Fleck *m*; (*in snow, mud etc*) Spur *f*; (BRIT *Scol*) Note *f*; (*level, point*): **the halfway ~** die Hälfte *f*; (*currency*) Mark *f*; (BRIT *Tech*): **M~ 2/3** Version *f* 2/3 ▶ VT (*with pen*) beschriften; (*with shoes etc*) schmutzig machen; (*with tyres etc*) Spuren hinterlassen auf *+dat*; (*damage*) beschädigen; (*stain*) Flecken machen auf *+dat*; (*indicate*) markieren; (*: price*) auszeichnen; (*commemorate*) begehen; (*characterize*) kennzeichnen; (BRIT *Scol*) korrigieren (und benoten); (*Sport: player*) decken; **punctuation marks** Satzzeichen *pl*; **to be quick off the ~ (in doing sth)** (*fig*) blitzschnell reagieren (und etw tun); **to be up to the ~** den Anforderungen entsprechen; **to ~ time** auf der Stelle treten
▶ **mark down** VT (*prices, goods*) herabsetzen, heruntersetzen
▶ **mark off** VT (*tick off*) abhaken
▶ **mark out** VT markieren; (*person*) auszeichnen
▶ **mark up** VT (*price*) heraufsetzen
marked [mɑ:kt] ADJ deutlich
markedly ['mɑ:kɪdlɪ] ADV deutlich
marker ['mɑ:kə[r]] N Markierung *f*; (*bookmark*) Lesezeichen *nt*
market ['mɑ:kɪt] N Markt *m* ▶ VT (*sell*) vertreiben; (*new product*) auf den Markt bringen; **to be on the ~** auf dem Markt sein; **on the open ~** auf dem freien Markt; **to play the ~** (*Stock Exchange*) an der Börse spekulieren
marketable ['mɑ:kɪtəbl] ADJ marktfähig
market analysis N Marktanalyse *f*
market day N Markttag *m*
market demand N Marktbedarf *m*
market economy N Marktwirtschaft *f*
market expert N Marktexperte *m*, Marktexpertin *f*
market forces NPL Marktkräfte *pl*
market garden (BRIT) N Gemüseanbaubetrieb *m*
marketing ['mɑ:kɪtɪŋ] N Marketing *nt*
marketing manager N Marketingmanager(in) *m(f)*
market leader N Marktführer *m*
marketplace ['mɑ:kɪtpleɪs] N Marktplatz *m*; (*Comm*) Markt *m*
market price N Marktpreis *m*
market research N Marktforschung *f*
market sector N Marktsegment *nt or* -sektor *m*
market value N Marktwert *m*
marking ['mɑ:kɪŋ] N (*on animal*) Zeichnung *f*; (*on road*) Markierung *f*
marksman ['mɑ:ksmən] N (*irreg*) Scharfschütze *m*
marksmanship ['mɑ:ksmənʃɪp] N Treffsicherheit *f*
mark-up ['mɑ:kʌp] N (*Comm: margin*) Handelsspanne *f*; (*: increase*) (Preis)aufschlag *m*
marmalade ['mɑ:məleɪd] N Orangenmarmelade *f*
maroon [mə'ru:n] VT: **to be marooned** festsitzen ▶ ADJ kastanienbraun
marquee [mɑ:'ki:] N Festzelt *nt*
marquess, marquis ['mɑ:kwɪs] N Marquis *m*
Marrakech, Marrakesh [mærə'kɛʃ] N Marrakesch *nt*
marriage ['mærɪdʒ] N Ehe *f*; (*institution*) die Ehe; (*wedding*) Hochzeit *f*; **~ of convenience** Vernunftehe *f*
marriage bureau N Ehevermittlung *f*
marriage certificate N Heiratsurkunde *f*
marriage guidance, (*US*) **marriage counseling** N Eheberatung *f*
married ['mærɪd] ADJ verheiratet; (*life*) Ehe-; (*love*) ehelich; **to get ~** heiraten
marrow ['mærəu] N (*vegetable*) Kürbis *m*; (*also*: **bone marrow**) (Knochen)mark *nt*
marry ['mærɪ] VT heiraten; (*father*) verheiraten; (*priest*) trauen ▶ VI heiraten
Mars [mɑ:z] N Mars *m*
Marseilles [mɑ:'seɪlz] N Marseilles *nt*
marsh [mɑ:ʃ] N Sumpf *m*; (*also*: **salt marsh**) Salzsumpf *m*
marshal ['mɑ:ʃl] N (*Mil: also*: **field marshal**) (Feld)marschall *m*; (*official*) Ordner *m*; (*US: of police*) Bezirkspolizeichef *m* ▶ VT (*thoughts*) ordnen; (*support*) auftreiben; (*soldiers*) aufstellen
marshalling yard ['mɑ:ʃlɪŋ-] N (*Rail*) Rangierbahnhof *m*
marshmallow [mɑ:ʃ'mæləu] N (*Bot*) Eibisch *m*; (*sweet*) Marshmallow *nt*
marshy ['mɑ:ʃɪ] ADJ sumpfig
marsupial [mɑ:'su:pɪəl] N Beuteltier *nt*
martial ['mɑ:ʃl] ADJ kriegerisch
martial arts NPL Kampfsport *m*; **the ~** die Kampfkunst *sing*
martial law N Kriegsrecht *nt*
Martian ['mɑ:ʃən] N Marsmensch *m*
martin ['mɑ:tɪn] N (*also*: **house martin**) Schwalbe *f*
martyr ['mɑ:tə[r]] N Märtyrer(in) *m(f)* ▶ VT martern
martyrdom ['mɑ:tədəm] N Martyrium *nt*
marvel ['mɑ:vl] N Wunder *nt* ▶ VI: **to ~ (at)** staunen (über *+acc*)
marvellous, (*US*) **marvelous** ['mɑ:vləs] ADJ wunderbar
Marxism ['mɑ:ksɪzəm] N Marxismus *m*
Marxist ['mɑ:ksɪst] ADJ marxistisch ▶ N Marxist(in) *m(f)*
marzipan ['mɑ:zɪpæn] N Marzipan *nt*
mascara [mæs'kɑ:rə] N Wimperntusche *f*
mascot ['mæskət] N Maskottchen *nt*
masculine ['mæskjulɪn] ADJ männlich; (*atmosphere, woman*) maskulin; (*Ling*) männlich, maskulin
masculinity [mæskju'lɪnɪtɪ] N Männlichkeit *f*
MASH [mæʃ] (*US*) N ABBR (= *mobile army surgical hospital*) mobiles Lazarett *nt*
mash [mæʃ] VT zerstampfen
mashed potatoes [mæʃt-] NPL Kartoffelpüree *nt*, Kartoffelbrei *m*

mask [mɑ:sk] N Maske *f* ▸ VT (*cover*) verdecken; (*hide*) verbergen; **surgical ~** Mundschutz *m*
masking tape ['mɑ:skɪŋ-] N Abdeckband *nt*
masochism ['mæsəukɪzəm] N Masochismus *m*
masochist ['mæsəukɪst] N Masochist(in) *m(f)*
mason ['meɪsn] N (*also*: **stone mason**) Steinmetz *m*; (*also*: **freemason**) Freimaurer *m*
masonic [mə'sɔnɪk] ADJ (*lodge etc*) Freimaurer-
masonry ['meɪsnrɪ] N Mauerwerk *nt*
masquerade [mæskə'reɪd] VI: **to ~ as** sich ausgeben als ▸ N Maskerade *f*
mass [mæs] N Masse *f*; (*of people*) Menge *f*; (*large amount*) Fülle *f*; (*Rel*): **M~** Messe *f* ▸ CPD Massen- ▸ VI (*troops*) sich massieren; (*protesters*) sich versammeln; **the masses** NPL (*ordinary people*) die Masse, die Massen *pl*; **to go to M~** zur Messe gehen; **masses of** (*inf*) massenhaft, jede Menge
Mass. (*US*) ABBR (*Post*) = **Massachusetts**
massacre ['mæsəkə^r] N Massaker *nt* ▸ VT massakrieren
massage ['mæsɑ:ʒ] N Massage *f* ▸ VT massieren
masseur [mæ'sə:^r] N Masseur *m*
masseuse [mæ'sə:z] N Masseurin *f*
massive ['mæsɪv] ADJ (*furniture, person*) wuchtig; (*support*) massiv; (*changes, increase*) enorm
mass market N Massenmarkt *m*
mass media NPL Massenmedien *pl*
mass meeting N Massenveranstaltung *f*; (*of everyone concerned*) Vollversammlung *f*; (*Pol*) Massenkundgebung *f*
mass-produce ['mæsprə'dju:s] VT in Massenproduktion herstellen
mass-production ['mæsprə'dʌkʃən] N Massenproduktion *f*
mast [mɑ:st] N (*Naut*) Mast *m*; (*Radio etc*) Sendeturm *m*
mastectomy [mæs'tɛktəmɪ] N Brustamputation *f*
master ['mɑ:stə^r] N Herr *m*; (*teacher*) Lehrer *m*; (*title*): **M~ X** (der junge) Herr X; (*Art, Mus, of craft etc*) Meister *m* ▸ CPD: **~ baker/plumber** *etc* Bäcker-/Klempnermeister *etc m* ▸ VT meistern; (*feeling*) unter Kontrolle bringen; (*skill, language*) beherrschen
master disk N (*Comput*) Stammdiskette *f*
masterful ['mɑ:stəful] ADJ gebieterisch; (*skilful*) meisterhaft
master key N Hauptschlüssel *m*
masterly ['mɑ:stəlɪ] ADJ meisterhaft
mastermind ['mɑ:stəmaɪnd] N (führender) Kopf *m* ▸ VT planen und ausführen
Master of Arts N Magister *m* der philosophischen Fakultät
Master of Ceremonies N Zeremonienmeister *m*; (*for variety show etc*) Conférencier *m*
Master of Science N Magister *m* der naturwissenschaftlichen Fakultät
masterpiece ['mɑ:stəpi:s] N Meisterwerk *nt*
master plan N kluger Plan *m*

> **Master's Degree** ist ein höherer akademischer Grad, den man in der Regel nach dem **bachelor's degree** erwerben kann. Je nach Universität erhält man ein master's degree nach einem entsprechenden Studium und/oder einer Dissertation. Die am häufigsten verliehenen Grade sind **MA** (= Master of Arts) und **MSc** (= Master of Science), die beide Studium und Dissertation erfordern, während für **MLitt** (= Master of Letters) und **MPhil** (= Master of Philosophy) meist nur eine Dissertation nötig ist. Siehe auch **bachelor's degree, doctorate**.

masterstroke ['mɑ:stəstrəuk] N Meisterstück *nt*
mastery ['mɑ:stərɪ] N (*of language etc*) Beherrschung *f*; (*skill*) (meisterhaftes) Können *nt*
mastiff ['mæstɪf] N Dogge *f*
masturbate ['mæstəbeɪt] VI masturbieren, onanieren
masturbation [mæstə'beɪʃən] N Masturbation *f*, Onanie *f*
mat [mæt] N Matte *f*; (*also*: **doormat**) Fußmatte *f*; (*also*: **table mat**) Untersetzer *m*; (: *of cloth*) Deckchen *nt* ▸ ADJ = **matt**
match [mætʃ] N Wettkampf *m*; (*team game*) Spiel *nt*; (*Tennis*) Match *nt*; (*for lighting fire etc*) Streichholz *nt*; (*equivalent*): **to be a good/perfect ~** gut/perfekt zusammenpassen ▸ VT (*go well with*) passen zu; (*equal*) gleichkommen *+dat*; (*correspond to*) entsprechen *+dat*; (*suit*) sich anpassen *+dat*; (*pair*: *also*: **match up**) passend zusammenbringen ▸ VI zusammenpassen; **to be a good ~** gut zusammenpassen; **to be no ~ for** sich nicht messen können mit; **with shoes to ~** mit (dazu) passenden Schuhen
▸ **match up** VI zusammenpassen
matchbox ['mætʃbɔks] N Streichholzschachtel *f*
matching ['mætʃɪŋ] ADJ (dazu) passend
matchless ['mætʃlɪs] ADJ unvergleichlich
mate [meɪt] N (*inf*: *friend*) Freund(in) *m(f)*, Kumpel *m*; (*animal*) Männchen *nt*, Weibchen *nt*; (*assistant*) Gehilfe *m*, Gehilfin *f*; (*in merchant navy*) Maat *m* ▸ VI (*animals*) sich paaren
material [mə'tɪərɪəl] N Material *nt*; (*cloth*) Stoff *m* ▸ ADJ (*possessions, existence*) materiell; (*relevant*) wesentlich; **materials** NPL (*equipment*) Material *nt*
materialistic [mətɪərɪə'lɪstɪk] ADJ materialistisch
materialize [mə'tɪərɪəlaɪz] VI (*event*) zustande kommen; (*plan*) verwirklicht werden; (*hope*) sich verwirklichen; (*problem*) auftreten; (*crisis, difficulty*) eintreten
maternal [mə'tə:nl] ADJ mütterlich, Mutter-
maternity [mə'tə:nɪtɪ] N Mutterschaft *f* ▸ CPD (*ward etc*) Entbindungs-; (*care*) für werdende und junge Mütter
maternity benefit N Mutterschaftsgeld *nt*
maternity dress N Umstandskleid *nt*

m

maternity hospital N Entbindungsheim *nt*
maternity leave N Mutterschaftsurlaub *m*
matey ['meɪtɪ] (BRIT *inf*) ADJ kumpelhaft
math [mæθ] (*US*) N = **maths**
mathematical [mæθə'mætɪkl] ADJ mathematisch
mathematician [mæθəmə'tɪʃən] N Mathematiker(in) *m(f)*
mathematics [mæθə'mætɪks] N Mathematik *f*
maths [mæθs], (*US*) **math** [mæθ] N Mathe *f*
matinée ['mætɪneɪ] N Nachmittagsvorstellung *f*
mating ['meɪtɪŋ] N Paarung *f*
mating call N Lockruf *m*
mating season N Paarungszeit *f*
matriarchal [meɪtrɪ'ɑ:kl] ADJ matriarchalisch
matrices ['meɪtrɪsi:z] NPL *of* **matrix**
matriculation [mətrɪkju'leɪʃən] N Immatrikulation *f*
matrimonial [mætrɪ'məunɪəl] ADJ Ehe-
matrimony ['mætrɪmənɪ] N Ehe *f*
matrix ['meɪtrɪks] (*pl* **matrices**) N (*Math*) Matrix *f*; (*framework*) Gefüge *nt*
matron ['meɪtrən] N (*in hospital*) Oberschwester *f*; (*in school*) Schwester *f*
matronly ['meɪtrənlɪ] ADJ matronenhaft
matt [mæt] ADJ matt; (*paint*) Matt-
matted ['mætɪd] ADJ verfilzt
matter ['mætə^r] N (*event, situation*) Sache *f*, Angelegenheit *f*; (*Phys*) Materie *f*; (*substance, material*) Stoff *m*; (*Med: pus*) Eiter *m* ▸ VI (*be important*) wichtig sein; **matters** NPL (*affairs*) Angelegenheiten *pl*, Dinge *pl*; (*situation*) Lage *f*; **what's the ~?** was ist los?; **no ~ what** egal was (passiert); **that's another ~** das ist etwas anderes; **as a ~ of course** selbstverständlich; **as a ~ of fact** eigentlich; **it's a ~ of habit** es ist eine Gewohnheitssache; **vegetable ~** pflanzliche Stoffe *pl*; **printed ~** Drucksachen *pl*; **reading ~** (BRIT) Lesestoff *m*; **it doesn't ~** es macht nichts
matter-of-fact ['mætərəv'fækt] ADJ sachlich
matting ['mætɪŋ] N Matten *pl*; **rush ~** Binsenmatten *pl*
mattress ['mætrɪs] N Matratze *f*
mature [mə'tjuə^r] ADJ reif; (*wine*) ausgereift ▸ VI reifen; (*Comm*) fällig werden
mature student N älterer Student *m*, ältere Studentin *f*
maturity [mə'tjuərɪtɪ] N Reife *f*; **to have reached ~** (*person*) erwachsen sein; (*animal*) ausgewachsen sein
maudlin ['mɔ:dlɪn] ADJ gefühlsselig
maul [mɔ:l] VT (anfallen und) übel zurichten
Mauritania [mɔ:rɪ'teɪnɪə] N Mauritanien *nt*
Mauritius [mə'rɪʃəs] N Mauritius *nt*
mausoleum [mɔ:sə'lɪəm] N Mausoleum *nt*
mauve [məuv] ADJ mauve
maverick ['mævrɪk] N (*dissenter*) Abtrünnige(r) *m*; (*independent thinker*) Querdenker *m*
mawkish ['mɔ:kɪʃ] ADJ rührselig
max. ABBR = **maximum**
maxim ['mæksɪm] N Maxime *f*
maxima ['mæksɪmə] NPL *of* **maximum**
maximize ['mæksɪmaɪz] VT maximieren
maximum ['mæksɪməm] (*pl* **maxima** *or* **maximums**) ADJ (*amount, speed etc*) Höchst-; (*efficiency*) maximal ▸ N Maximum *nt*
May [meɪ] N Mai *m*; *see also* **July**
may [meɪ] (*conditional* **might**) VI (*be possible*) können; (*have permission*) dürfen; **he ~ come** vielleicht kommt er; **~ I smoke?** darf ich rauchen?; **~ God bless you!** (*wish*) Gott segne dich!; **~ I sit here?** kann ich mich hier hinsetzen?; **he might be there** er könnte da sein; **you might like to try** vielleicht möchten Sie es mal versuchen; **you ~ as well go** Sie können ruhig gehen
maybe ['meɪbi:] ADV vielleicht; **~ he'll …** es kann sein, dass er …; **~ not** vielleicht nicht
Mayday ['meɪdeɪ] N Maydaysignal *nt*, ≈ SOS-Ruf *m*
May Day N der 1. Mai
mayhem ['meɪhɛm] N Chaos *nt*
mayonnaise [meɪə'neɪz] N Mayonnaise *f*
mayor [mɛə^r] N Bürgermeister *m*
mayoress ['mɛərɛs] N Bürgermeisterin *f*; (*partner*) Frau *f* des Bürgermeisters
maypole ['meɪpəul] N Maibaum *m*
maze [meɪz] N Irrgarten *m*; (*fig*) Wirrwarr *m*
MB ABBR (*Comput: = megabyte*) MB; (CANADA) = **Manitoba**
MBA N ABBR (= *Master of Business Administration*) *akademischer Grad in Betriebswirtschaft*
MBE (BRIT) N ABBR (= *Member of (the Order of) the British Empire*) *britischer Ordenstitel*
MC N ABBR = **Master of Ceremonies**
MCAT (*US*) N ABBR (= *Medical College Admissions Test*) *Zulassungsprüfung für medizinische Fachschulen*
m-commerce ['ɛm'kɔmə:s] N (*Comm*) M-Commerce *m*, mobiler Handel *m*
MD N ABBR (= *Doctor of Medicine*) ≈ Dr. med.; (*Comm*) = **managing director** ▸ ABBR (*US Post*) = **Maryland**
MDT (*US*) ABBR (= *Mountain Daylight Time*) *amerikanische Sommerzeitzone*
ME N ABBR (*US*) = **medical examiner**; (*Med:* = *myalgic encephalomyelitis*) *krankhafter Energiemangel (oft nach Viruserkrankungen)* ▸ ABBR (*US Post*) = **Maine**

KEYWORD

me [mi:] PRON **1** (*direct*) mich; **can you hear me?** können Sie mich hören?; **it's me** ich bins
2 (*indirect*) mir; **he gave me the money, he gave the money to me** er gab mir das Geld
3 (*after prep*): **it's for me** es ist für mich; **with me** mit mir; **give them to me** gib sie mir; **without me** ohne mich

meadow ['mɛdəu] N Wiese *f*
meagre, (*US*) **meager** ['mi:gə^r] ADJ (*amount*) kläglich; (*meal*) dürftig
meal [mi:l] N Mahlzeit *f*; (*food*) Essen *nt*; (*flour*) Schrotmehl *nt*; **to go out for a ~** essen gehen; **to make a ~ of sth** (*fig*) etw auf sehr umständliche Art machen

meals on wheels N SING Essen *nt* auf Rädern
mealtime ['mi:ltaɪm] N Essenszeit *f*
mealy-mouthed ['mi:lɪmauðd] ADJ unaufrichtig; (*politician*) schönfärberisch
mean [mi:n] (*pt, pp* **meant**) ADJ (*with money*) geizig; (*unkind*) gemein; (*US inf: animal*) bösartig; (*shabby*) schäbig; (*average*) Durchschnitts-, mittlere(r, s) ▸ VT (*signify*) bedeuten; (*refer to*) meinen; (*intend*) beabsichtigen ▸ N (*average*) Durchschnitt *m*; **means** NPL (*way*) Möglichkeit *f*; (*money*) Mittel *pl*; **by means of** durch; **by all means!** aber natürlich *or* selbstverständlich!; **do you ~ it?** meinst du das ernst?; **what do you ~?** was willst du damit sagen?; **to be meant for sb/sth** für jdn/etw bestimmt sein; **to ~ to do sth** etw tun wollen
meander [mɪ'ændəʳ] VI (*river*) sich schlängeln; (*person: walking*) schlendern; (*: talking*) abschweifen
meaning ['mi:nɪŋ] N Sinn *m*; (*of word, gesture*) Bedeutung *f*
meaningful ['mi:nɪŋful] ADJ sinnvoll; (*glance, remark*) vielsagend, bedeutsam; (*relationship*) tiefer gehend
meaningless ['mi:nɪŋlɪs] ADJ sinnlos; (*word, song*) bedeutungslos
meanness ['mi:nnɪs] N (*with money*) Geiz *m*; (*unkindness*) Gemeinheit *f*; (*shabbiness*) Schäbigkeit *f*
means test [mi:nz-] N Überprüfung *f* der Einkommens- und Vermögensverhältnisse
means-tested ['mi:nztɛstɪd] ADJ von den Einkommens- und Vermögensverhältnissen abhängig
meant [mɛnt] PT, PP *of* **mean**
meantime ['mi:ntaɪm] ADV (*also*: **in the meantime**) inzwischen
meanwhile ['mi:nwaɪl] ADV = **meantime**
measles ['mi:zlz] N Masern *pl*
measly ['mi:zlɪ] (*inf*) ADJ mick(e)rig
measurable ['mɛʒərəbl] ADJ messbar
measure ['mɛʒəʳ] VT, VI messen ▸ N (*amount*) Menge *f*; (*ruler*) Messstab *m*; (*of achievement*) Maßstab *m*; (*action*) Maßnahme *f*; **a litre ~** ein Messbecher *m*, der einen Liter fasst; **a/some ~ of** ein gewisses Maß an *+dat*; **to take measures to do sth** Maßnahmen ergreifen, um etw zu tun
▸ **measure up** VI: **to ~ up to** herankommen an *+acc*
measured ['mɛʒəd] ADJ (*tone*) bedächtig; (*step*) gemessen
measurement ['mɛʒəmənt] N (*measure*) Maß *nt*; (*act*) Messung *f*; **chest/hip ~** Brust-/Hüftumfang *m*
measurements ['mɛʒəmənts] NPL Maße *pl*; **to take sb's ~** bei jdm Maß nehmen
meat [mi:t] N Fleisch *nt*; **cold meats** (BRIT) Aufschnitt *m*; **crab ~** Krabbenfleisch *nt*
meatball ['mi:tbɔ:l] N Fleischkloß *m*
meat pie N Fleischpastete *f*
meaty ['mi:tɪ] ADJ (*meal, dish*) mit viel Fleisch; (*fig: satisfying: book etc*) gehaltvoll; (*: brawny: person*) kräftig (gebaut)
Mecca ['mɛkə] N (*Geog, fig*) Mekka *nt*
mechanic [mɪ'kænɪk] N Mechaniker(in) *m(f)*
mechanical [mɪ'kænɪkl] ADJ mechanisch
mechanical engineering N Maschinenbau *m*
mechanics [mɪ'kænɪks] N (*Phys*) Mechanik *f* ▸ NPL (*of reading etc*) Technik *f*; (*of government etc*) Mechanismus *m*
mechanism ['mɛkənɪzəm] N Mechanismus *m*
mechanization [mɛkənaɪ'zeɪʃən] N Mechanisierung *f*
mechanize ['mɛkənaɪz] VT, VI mechanisieren
MEd N ABBR (= *Master of Education*) *akademischer Grad für Lehrer*
medal ['mɛdl] N Medaille *f*; (*decoration*) Orden *m*
medallion [mɪ'dælɪən] N Medaillon *nt*
medallist, (US) **medalist** ['mɛdlɪst] N Medaillengewinner(in) *m(f)*
meddle ['mɛdl] VI: **to ~ (in)** sich einmischen (in *+acc*); **to ~ with sb** sich mit jdm einlassen; **to ~ with sth** (*tamper*) sich *dat* an etw *dat* zu schaffen machen
meddlesome ['mɛdlsəm], **meddling** ['mɛdlɪŋ] ADJ sich ständig einmischend
media ['mi:dɪə] NPL Medien *pl*
media bashing N (*inf*) Medienschelte *f*
media circus N Medienrummel *m*
mediaeval [mɛdɪ'i:vl] ADJ = **medieval**
median ['mi:dɪən] (US) N (*also*: **median strip**) Mittelstreifen *m*
mediate ['mi:dɪeɪt] VI vermitteln
mediation [mi:dɪ'eɪʃən] N Vermittlung *f*
mediator ['mi:dɪeɪtəʳ] N Vermittler(in) *m(f)*
Medicaid ['mɛdɪkeɪd] (US) N *staatliche Krankenversicherung und Gesundheitsfürsorge für Einkommensschwache*
medical ['mɛdɪkl] ADJ (*care*) medizinisch; (*treatment*) ärztlich ▸ N (ärztliche) Untersuchung *f*
medical certificate N (*confirming health*) ärztliches Gesundheitszeugnis *nt*; (*confirming illness*) ärztliches Attest *nt*
medical examiner (US) N ≈ Gerichtsmediziner(in) *m(f)*; (*performing autopsy*) Leichenbeschauer *m*
medical student N Medizinstudent(in) *m(f)*
Medicare ['mɛdɪkɛəʳ] (US) N *staatliche Krankenversicherung und Gesundheitsfürsorge für ältere Bürger*
medicated ['mɛdɪkeɪtɪd] ADJ medizinisch
medication [mɛdɪ'keɪʃən] N Medikamente *pl*
medicinal [mɛ'dɪsɪnl] ADJ (*substance*) Heil-; (*qualities*) heilend; (*purposes*) medizinisch
medicine ['mɛdsɪn] N Medizin *f*; (*drug*) Arznei *f*
medicine ball N Medizinball *m*
medicine chest N Hausapotheke *f*
medicine man N (*irreg*) Medizinmann *m*
medieval [mɛdɪ'i:vl] ADJ mittelalterlich
mediocre [mi:dɪ'əukəʳ] ADJ mittelmäßig
mediocrity [mi:dɪ'ɔkrɪtɪ] N Mittelmäßigkeit *f*
meditate ['mɛdɪteɪt] VI nachdenken; (*Rel*) meditieren
meditation [mɛdɪ'teɪʃən] N Nachdenken *nt*; (*Rel*) Meditation *f*

m

Mediterranean [mɛdɪtəˈreɪnɪən] ADJ *(country, climate etc)* Mittelmeer-; **the ~ (Sea)** das Mittelmeer
medium [ˈmiːdɪəm] *(pl* **media** *or* **mediums***)* ADJ mittlere(r, s) ▸ N *(means)* Mittel *nt*; *(substance, material)* Medium *nt*; *(pl* **mediums***: person)* Medium *nt*; **of ~ height** mittelgroß; **to strike a happy ~** den goldenen Mittelweg finden
medium-dry [ˈmiːdɪəmˈdraɪ] ADJ *(wine, sherry)* halbtrocken
medium-sized [ˈmiːdɪəmˈsaɪzd] ADJ mittelgroß
medium wave N *(Radio)* Mittelwelle *f*
medley [ˈmɛdlɪ] N Gemisch *nt*; *(Mus)* Medley *nt*
meek [miːk] ADJ sanft(mütig), duldsam
meet [miːt] *(pt, pp* **met***)* VT *(encounter)* treffen; *(by arrangement)* sich treffen mit; *(for the first time)* kennenlernen; *(go and fetch)* abholen; *(opponent)* treffen auf *+acc*; *(condition, standard)* erfüllen; *(need, expenses)* decken; *(problem)* stoßen auf *+acc*; *(challenge)* begegnen *+dat*; *(bill)* begleichen; *(join: line)* sich schneiden mit; *(: road etc)* treffen auf *+acc* ▸ VI *(encounter)* sich begegnen; *(by arrangement)* sich treffen; *(for the first time)* sich kennenlernen; *(for talks etc)* zusammenkommen; *(committee)* tagen; *(join: lines)* sich schneiden; *(: roads etc)* aufeinandertreffen ▸ N *(Brit Hunting)* Jagd *f*; *(US Sport)* Sportfest *nt*; **pleased to ~ you!** (sehr) angenehm!
▸ **meet up** VI: **to ~ up with sb** sich mit jdm treffen
▸ **meet with** VT FUS *(difficulty, success)* haben
meeting [ˈmiːtɪŋ] N *(assembly, people assembling)* Versammlung *f*; *(Comm, of committee etc)* Sitzung *f*; *(also:* **business meeting***)* Besprechung *f*; *(encounter)* Begegnung *f*; *(: arranged)* Treffen *nt*; *(Pol)* Gespräch *nt*; *(Sport)* Veranstaltung *f*; **she's at** *or* **in a ~** *(Comm)* sie ist bei einer Besprechung; **to call a ~** eine Sitzung/Versammlung einberufen
meeting-place [ˈmiːtɪŋpleɪs] N Treffpunkt *m*
megabyte [ˈmɛgəbaɪt] N Megabyte *nt*
megalomaniac [mɛgələˈmeɪnɪæk] N Größenwahnsinnige(r) *f(m)*
megaphone [ˈmɛgəfəun] N Megafon *nt*
megawatt [ˈmɛgəwɔt] N Megawatt *nt*
melancholy [ˈmɛlənkəlɪ] N Melancholie *f*, Schwermut *f* ▸ ADJ melancholisch, schwermütig
mellow [ˈmɛləu] ADJ *(sound)* voll, weich; *(light, colour, stone)* warm; *(weathered)* verwittert; *(person)* gesetzt; *(wine)* ausgereift ▸ VI *(person)* gesetzter werden
melodious [mɪˈləudɪəs] ADJ melodisch
melodrama [ˈmɛləudrɑːmə] N Melodrama *nt*
melodramatic [mɛlədrəˈmætɪk] ADJ melodramatisch
melody [ˈmɛlədɪ] N Melodie *f*
melon [ˈmɛlən] N Melone *f*
melt [mɛlt] VI *(lit, fig)* schmelzen ▸ VT schmelzen; *(butter)* zerlassen
▸ **melt down** VT einschmelzen
meltdown [ˈmɛltdaun] N *(in nuclear reactor)* Kernschmelze *f*
melting point [ˈmɛltɪŋ-] N Schmelzpunkt *m*
melting pot N *(lit, fig)* Schmelztiegel *m*; **to be in the ~** in der Schwebe sein
member [ˈmɛmbəʳ] N Mitglied *nt*; *(Anat)* Glied *nt* ▸ CPD: **~ country** Mitgliedsland *nt*; **~ state** Mitgliedsstaat *m*; **M~ of Parliament** (Brit) Abgeordnete(r) *f(m)* (des Unterhauses); **M~ of the European Parliament** (Brit) Abgeordnete(r) *f(m)* des Europaparlaments
membership [ˈmɛmbəʃɪp] N Mitgliedschaft *f*; *(members)* Mitglieder *pl*; *(number of members)* Mitgliederzahl *f*
membership card N Mitgliedsausweis *m*
membrane [ˈmɛmbreɪn] N Membran(e) *f*
memento [məˈmɛntəu] N Andenken *nt*
memo [ˈmɛməu] N Memo *nt*, Mitteilung *f*
memoir [ˈmɛmwɑːʳ] N Kurzbiografie *f*
memoirs [ˈmɛmwɑːz] NPL Memoiren *pl*
memo pad N Notizblock *m*
memorable [ˈmɛmərəbl] ADJ denkwürdig; *(unforgettable)* unvergesslich
memorandum [mɛməˈrændəm] *(pl* **memoranda***)* N Mitteilung *f*
memorial [mɪˈmɔːrɪəl] N Denkmal *nt* ▸ ADJ *(service, prize)* Gedenk-
Memorial Day (US) N ≈ Volkstrauertag *m*

> **Memorial Day** ist in den USA ein gesetzlicher Feiertag am letzten Montag im Mai zum Gedenken an die in allen Kriegen gefallenen amerikanischen Soldaten. Siehe auch **Remembrance Sunday.**

memorize [ˈmɛməraɪz] VT sich *dat* einprägen
memory [ˈmɛmərɪ] N Gedächtnis *nt*; *(sth remembered)* Erinnerung *f*; *(Comput)* Speicher *m*; **in ~ of** zur Erinnerung an *+acc*; **to have a good/bad ~** ein gutes/schlechtes Gedächtnis haben; **loss of ~** Gedächtnisschwund *m*
memory card N Speicherkarte *f*
memory stick N *(Comput)* Memorystick® *nt*
men [mɛn] NPL *of* **man**
menace [ˈmɛnɪs] N Bedrohung *f*; *(nuisance)* (Land)plage *f* ▸ VT bedrohen; **a public ~** eine Gefahr für die Öffentlichkeit
menacing [ˈmɛnɪsɪŋ] ADJ drohend
menagerie [mɪˈnædʒərɪ] N Menagerie *f*
mend [mɛnd] VT reparieren; *(darn)* flicken ▸ N: **to be on the ~** auf dem Wege der Besserung sein; **to ~ one's ways** sich bessern
mending [ˈmɛndɪŋ] N Reparaturen *pl*; *(clothes)* Flickarbeiten *pl*
menial [ˈmiːnɪəl] *(often pej)* ADJ niedrig, untergeordnet
meningitis [mɛnɪnˈdʒaɪtɪs] N Hirnhautentzündung *f*
menopause [ˈmɛnəupɔːz] N: **the ~** die Wechseljahre *pl*
menservants [ˈmɛnsəːvənts] NPL *of* **manservant**
men's room (US) N Herrentoilette *f*
menstrual [ˈmɛnstruəl] ADJ *(Biol: cycle etc)* Menstruations-; **~ period** Monatsblutung *f*

menstruate ['mɛnstrueɪt] VI die Menstruation haben
menstruation [mɛnstru'eɪʃən] N Menstruation *f*
menswear ['mɛnzwɛəʳ] N Herren(be)kleidung *f*
mental ['mɛntl] ADJ geistig; (*illness*) Geistes-; **~ arithmetic** Kopfrechnen *nt*
mental hospital N psychiatrische Klinik *f*
mentality [mɛn'tælɪtɪ] N Mentalität *f*
mentally ['mɛntlɪ] ADV: **to be ~ handicapped** geistig behindert sein
menthol ['mɛnθɔl] N Menthol *nt*
mention ['mɛnʃən] N Erwähnung *f* ▶ VT erwähnen; **don't ~ it!** (bitte,) gern geschehen!; **not to ~ …** von … ganz zu schweigen
mentor ['mɛntɔːʳ] N Mentor *m*
menu ['mɛnjuː] N Menü *nt*; (*printed*) Speisekarte *f*
menu-driven ['mɛnjuːdrɪvn] ADJ (*Comput*) menügesteuert
MEP (BRIT) N ABBR (= *Member of the European Parliament*) Abgeordnete(r) *f*(*m*) des Europaparlaments
mercantile ['məːkəntaɪl] ADJ (*class, society*) Handel treibend; (*law*) Handels-
mercenary ['məːsɪnərɪ] ADJ (*person*) geldgierig ▶ N Söldner *m*
merchandise ['məːtʃəndaɪz] N Ware *f*
merchandiser ['məːtʃəndaɪzəʳ] N Verkaufsförderungsexperte *m*
merchant ['məːtʃənt] N Kaufmann *m*; **timber/wine ~** Holz-/Weinhändler *m*
merchant bank (BRIT) N Handelsbank *f*
merchantman ['məːtʃəntmən] N (*irreg*) Handelsschiff *nt*
merchant navy, (US) **merchant marine** N Handelsmarine *f*
merciful ['məːsɪful] ADJ gnädig; **a ~ release** eine Erlösung
mercifully ['məːsɪflɪ] ADV glücklicherweise
merciless ['məːsɪlɪs] ADJ erbarmungslos
mercurial [məː'kjuərɪəl] ADJ (*unpredictable*) sprunghaft, wechselhaft; (*lively*) quecksilbrig
mercury ['məːkjurɪ] N Quecksilber *nt*
mercy ['məːsɪ] N Gnade *f*; **to have ~ on sb** Erbarmen mit jdm haben; **at the ~ of** ausgeliefert *+dat*
mercy killing N Euthanasie *f*
mere [mɪəʳ] ADJ bloß; **his ~ presence irritates her** schon *or* allein seine Anwesenheit ärgert sie; **she is a ~ child** sie ist noch ein Kind; **it's a ~ trifle** es ist eine Lappalie; **by ~ chance** rein durch Zufall
merely ['mɪəlɪ] ADV lediglich, bloß
merge [məːdʒ] VT (*combine*) vereinen; (*Comput: files*) mischen ▶ VI (*Comm*) fusionieren; (*colours, sounds, shapes*) ineinander übergehen; (*roads*) zusammenlaufen
merger ['məːdʒəʳ] N (*Comm*) Fusion *f*
meridian [mə'rɪdɪən] N Meridian *m*
meringue [mə'ræŋ] N Baiser *nt*
merit ['mɛrɪt] N (*worth, value*) Wert *m*; (*advantage*) Vorzug *m*; (*achievement*) Verdienst *nt* ▶ VT verdienen
meritocracy [mɛrɪ'tɔkrəsɪ] N Leistungsgesellschaft *f*
mermaid ['məːmeɪd] N Seejungfrau *f*, Meerjungfrau *f*
merrily ['mɛrɪlɪ] ADV vergnügt
merriment ['mɛrɪmənt] N Heiterkeit *f*
merry ['mɛrɪ] ADJ vergnügt; (*music*) fröhlich; **M~ Christmas!** fröhliche *or* frohe Weihnachten!
merry-go-round ['mɛrɪgəuraund] N Karussell *nt*
mesh [mɛʃ] N Geflecht *nt*; **wire ~** Maschendraht *m*
mesmerize ['mɛzməraɪz] VT (*fig*) faszinieren
mess [mɛs] N Durcheinander *nt*; (*dirt*) Dreck *m*; (*Mil*) Kasino *nt*; **to be in a ~** (*untidy*) unordentlich sein; (*in difficulty*) in Schwierigkeiten stecken; **to be a ~** (*fig: life*) verkorkst sein; **to get o.s. in a ~** in Schwierigkeiten geraten
▶ **mess about** (*inf*) VI (*fool around*) herumalbern
▶ **mess about with** (*inf*) VT FUS (*play around with*) herumfummeln an *+dat*
▶ **mess around** (*inf*) VI = **mess about**
▶ **mess around with** (*inf*) VT FUS = **mess about with**
▶ **mess up** VT durcheinanderbringen; (*dirty*) verdrecken
message ['mɛsɪdʒ] N Mitteilung *f*, Nachricht *f*; (*meaning*) Aussage *f* ▶ VT eine Nachricht senden *+dat*; **she messaged me on Facebook** sie schickte mir eine Facebook-Nachricht; **to get the ~** (*inf: fig*) kapieren
message board N (*on Internet*) Internetforum *nt*
message switching [-'swɪtʃɪŋ] N (*Comput*) Speichervermittlung *f*
messenger ['mɛsɪndʒəʳ] N Bote *m*
Messiah [mɪ'saɪə] N Messias *m*
Messrs ['mɛsəz] ABBR (*on letters:* = *messieurs*) An (die Herren)
messy ['mɛsɪ] ADJ (*dirty*) dreckig; (*untidy*) unordentlich
Met [mɛt] (US) N ABBR (= *Metropolitan Opera*) Met *f*
met [mɛt] PT, PP *of* **meet**
met. ADJ ABBR (= *meteorological*): **the Met. Office** das Wetteramt
metabolism [mɛ'tæbəlɪzəm] N Stoffwechsel *m*
metal ['mɛtl] N Metall *nt*
metal fatigue N Metallermüdung *f*
metalled ['mɛtld] ADJ (*road*) asphaltiert
metallic [mɪ'tælɪk] ADJ metallisch; (*made of metal*) aus Metall
metallurgy [mɛ'tælədʒɪ] N Metallurgie *f*
metalwork ['mɛtlwəːk] N Metallarbeit *f*
metamorphosis [mɛtə'mɔːfəsɪs] (*pl* **metamorphoses**) N Verwandlung *f*
metaphor ['mɛtəfəʳ] N Metapher *f*
metaphorical [mɛtə'fɔrɪkl] ADJ metaphorisch
metaphysics [mɛtə'fɪzɪks] N Metaphysik *f*
meteor ['miːtɪəʳ] N Meteor *m*
meteoric [miːtɪ'ɔrɪk] ADJ (*fig*) kometenhaft
meteorite ['miːtɪəraɪt] N Meteorit *m*

m

meteorological [mi:tɪərə'lɔdʒɪkl] ADJ (*conditions, office etc*) Wetter-
meteorology [mi:tɪə'rɔlədʒɪ] N Wetterkunde *f*, Meteorologie *f*
mete out [mi:t-] VT austeilen; **to ~ justice** Recht sprechen
meter ['mi:tə^r] N Zähler *m*; (*also*: **water meter**) Wasseruhr *f*; (*also*: **parking meter**) Parkuhr *f*; (*US*: *unit*) = **metre**
methane ['mi:θeɪn] N Methan *nt*
method ['mɛθəd] N Methode *f*; **~ of payment** Zahlungsweise *f*
methodical [mɪ'θɔdɪkl] ADJ methodisch
Methodist ['mɛθədɪst] N Methodist(in) *m(f)*
methodology [mɛθə'dɔlədʒɪ] N Methodik *f*
meths [mɛθs] (BRIT) N = **methylated spirit**
methylated spirit ['mɛθɪleɪtɪd-] (BRIT) N (Brenn)spiritus *m*
meticulous [mɪ'tɪkjuləs] ADJ sorgfältig; (*detail*) genau
metre, (*US*) **meter** ['mi:tə^r] N Meter *m or nt*
metric ['mɛtrɪk] ADJ metrisch; **to go ~** auf das metrische Maßsystem umstellen
metrical ['mɛtrɪkl] ADJ metrisch
metrication [mɛtrɪ'keɪʃən] N Umstellung *f* auf das metrische Maßsystem
metric system N metrisches Maßsystem *nt*
metric ton N Metertonne *f*
metronome ['mɛtrənəum] N Metronom *nt*
metropolis [mɪ'trɔpəlɪs] N Metropole *f*
metropolitan [mɛtrə'pɔlɪtn] ADJ großstädtisch
Metropolitan Police (BRIT) N: **the ~** die Londoner Polizei
mettle ['mɛtl] N: **to be on one's ~** auf dem Posten sein
mew [mju:] VI miauen
mews [mju:z] (BRIT) N Gasse *f* mit ehemaligen Kutscherhäuschen
Mexican ['mɛksɪkən] ADJ mexikanisch ▶ N Mexikaner(in) *m(f)*
Mexico ['mɛksɪkəu] N Mexiko *nt*
Mexico City N Mexico City *f*
mezzanine ['mɛtsəni:n] N Mezzanin *nt*
MFA (US) N ABBR (= *Master of Fine Arts*) *akademischer Grad in Kunst*
mfr ABBR = **manufacture; manufacturer**
mg ABBR (= *milligram(me)*) mg
Mgr ABBR (= *Monseigneur, Monsignor*) Mgr.; (*Comm*) = **manager**
MHR (US, AUST) N ABBR (= *Member of the House of Representatives*) Abgeordnete(r) *f(m)* des Repräsentantenhauses
MHz ABBR (= *megahertz*) MHz
MI (US) ABBR (*Post*) = **Michigan**
MI5 (BRIT) N ABBR (= *Military Intelligence, section five*) *britischer Spionageabwehrdienst*
MI6 (BRIT) N ABBR (= *Military Intelligence, section six*) *britischer Geheimdienst*
MIA ABBR (*Mil*: = *missing in action*) vermisst
miaow [mi:'au] VI miauen
mice [maɪs] NPL *of* **mouse**
Mich. (US) ABBR (*Post*) = **Michigan**
micro ['maɪkrəu] N = **microcomputer**
micro... ['maɪkrəu] PREF mikro-, Mikro-
microbe ['maɪkrəub] N Mikrobe *f*
microbiology [maɪkrəubaɪ'ɔlədʒɪ] N Mikrobiologie *f*
microblog ['maɪkrəublɔg] N Mikroblog *nt*
microchip ['maɪkrəutʃɪp] N Mikrochip *m*
microcomputer ['maɪkrəukəm'pju:tə^r] N Mikrocomputer *m*
microcosm ['maɪkrəukɔzəm] N Mikrokosmos *m*
microeconomics ['maɪkrəui:kə'nɔmɪks] N Mikroökonomie *f*
microelectronics ['maɪkrəuɪlɛk'trɔnɪks] N Mikroelektronik *f*
microfiche ['maɪkrəufi:ʃ] N Mikrofiche *m or nt*
microfilm ['maɪkrəufɪlm] N Mikrofilm *m*
microlight ['maɪkrəulaɪt] N Ultraleichtflugzeug *nt*
micrometer [maɪ'krɔmɪtə^r] N Messschraube *f*
microphone ['maɪkrəfəun] N Mikrofon *nt*
microprocessor ['maɪkrəu'prəusɛsə^r] N Mikroprozessor *m*
microscope ['maɪkrəskəup] N Mikroskop *nt*; **under the ~** unter dem Mikroskop
microscopic [maɪkrə'skɔpɪk] ADJ mikroskopisch; (*creature*) mikroskopisch klein
microwave ['maɪkrəuweɪv] N Mikrowelle *f*; (*also*: **microwave oven**) Mikrowellenherd *m*
mid- [mɪd] ADJ: **in ~May** Mitte Mai; **in ~afternoon** (mitten) am Nachmittag; **in ~air** (mitten) in der Luft; **he's in his ~thirties** er ist Mitte dreißig
midday [mɪd'deɪ] N Mittag *m*
middle ['mɪdl] N Mitte *f* ▶ ADJ mittlere(r, s); **in the ~ of the night** mitten in der Nacht; **I'm in the ~ of reading it** ich bin mittendrin; **a ~ course** ein Mittelweg *m*
middle age N mittleres Lebensalter *nt*
middle-aged [mɪdl'eɪdʒd] ADJ mittleren Alters
Middle Ages NPL Mittelalter *nt*
middle class N, **middle classes** NPL Mittelstand *m*
middle-class [mɪdl'klɑ:s] ADJ mittelständisch
Middle East N Naher Osten *m*
middleman ['mɪdlmæn] N (*irreg*) Zwischenhändler *m*
middle management N mittleres Management *nt*
middle name N zweiter Vorname *m*
middle-of-the-road ['mɪdləvðə'rəud] ADJ gemäßigt; (*politician*) der Mitte; (*Mus*) leicht
middleweight ['mɪdlweɪt] N (*Boxing*) Mittelgewicht *nt*
middling ['mɪdlɪŋ] ADJ mittelmäßig
Middx (BRIT) ABBR (*Post*) = **Middlesex**
midge [mɪdʒ] N Mücke *f*
midget ['mɪdʒɪt] N Liliputaner(in) *m(f)*
midi system ['mɪdɪ-] N Midi-System *nt*
Midlands ['mɪdləndz] (BRIT) NPL: **the ~** Mittelengland *nt*
midnight ['mɪdnaɪt] N Mitternacht *f* ▶ CPD Mitternachts-; **at ~** um Mitternacht
midriff ['mɪdrɪf] N Taille *f*

midst [mɪdst] N: **in the ~ of** mitten in *+dat*; **to be in the ~ of doing sth** mitten dabei sein, etw zu tun
midsummer [mɪd'sʌməʳ] N Hochsommer *m*; **M~('s) Day** Sommersonnenwende *f*
midway [mɪd'weɪ] ADJ: **we have reached the ~ point** wir haben die Hälfte hinter uns *dat* ▸ ADV auf halbem Weg; **~ between** (*in space*) auf halbem Weg zwischen; **~ through** (*in time*) mitten in *+dat*
midweek [mɪd'wi:k] ADV mitten in der Woche ▸ ADJ Mitte der Woche
midwife ['mɪdwaɪf] (*pl* **midwives**) N Hebamme *f*
midwifery ['mɪdwɪfərɪ] N Geburtshilfe *f*
midwinter [mɪd'wɪntəʳ] N: **in ~** im tiefsten Winter
miffed [mɪft] (*inf*) ADJ: **to be ~** eingeschnappt sein
might [maɪt] VB *see* **may** ▸ N Macht *f*; **with all one's ~** mit aller Kraft
mighty ['maɪtɪ] ADJ mächtig
migraine ['mi:greɪn] N Migräne *f*
migrant ['maɪgrənt] ADJ (*bird*) Zug-; (*worker*) Wander- ▸ N (*bird*) Zugvogel *m*; (*worker*) Wanderarbeiter(in) *m(f)*
migrate [maɪ'greɪt] VI (*bird*) ziehen; (*person*) abwandern
migration [maɪ'greɪʃən] N Wanderung *f*; (*to cities*) Abwanderung *f*; (*of birds*) (Vogel)zug *m*
mike [maɪk] N = **microphone**
Milan [mɪ'læn] N Mailand *nt*
mild [maɪld] ADJ mild; (*gentle*) sanft; (*slight: infection etc*) leicht; (*: interest*) gering
mildew ['mɪldju:] N Schimmel *m*
mildly ['maɪldlɪ] ADV (*say*) sanft; (*slight*) leicht; **to put it ~** gelinde gesagt
mildness ['maɪldnɪs] N Milde *f*; (*gentleness*) Sanftheit *f*; (*of infection etc*) Leichtigkeit *f*
mile [maɪl] N Meile *f*; **to do 30 miles per gallon** ≈ 9 Liter auf 100 km verbrauchen
mileage ['maɪlɪdʒ] N Meilenzahl *f*; (*fig*) Nutzen *m*; **to get a lot of ~ out of sth** etw gründlich ausnutzen; **there is a lot of ~ in the idea** aus der Idee lässt sich viel machen
mileage allowance N ≈ Kilometergeld *nt*
mileometer [maɪ'lɔmɪtəʳ] N ≈ Kilometerzähler *m*
milestone ['maɪlstəun] N (*lit, fig*) Meilenstein *m*
milieu ['mi:ljə:] N Milieu *nt*
militant ['mɪlɪtnt] ADJ militant ▸ N Militante(r) *f(m)*
militarism ['mɪlɪtərɪzəm] N Militarismus *m*
militaristic [mɪlɪtə'rɪstɪk] ADJ militaristisch
military ['mɪlɪtərɪ] ADJ (*history, leader etc*) Militär- ▸ N: **the ~** das Militär
military police N Militärpolizei *f*
military service N Militärdienst *m*
militate ['mɪlɪteɪt] VI: **to ~ against** negative Auswirkungen haben auf *+acc*
militia [mɪ'lɪʃə] N Miliz *f*
milk [mɪlk] N Milch *f* ▸ VT (*lit, fig*) melken
milk chocolate N Vollmilchschokolade *f*
milk float (BRIT) N Milchwagen *m*
milking ['mɪlkɪŋ] N Melken *nt*
milkman ['mɪlkmən] N (*irreg*) Milchmann *m*
milk shake N Milchmixgetränk *nt*
milk tooth N Milchzahn *m*
milk truck (US) N = **milk float**
milky ['mɪlkɪ] ADJ milchig; (*drink*) mit viel Milch; **~ coffee** Milchkaffee *m*
Milky Way N Milchstraße *f*
mill [mɪl] N Mühle *f*; (*factory*) Fabrik *f*; (*woollen mill*) Spinnerei *f* ▸ VT mahlen ▸ VI (*also*: **mill about**) umherlaufen
millennium [mɪ'lɛnɪəm] (*pl* **millenniums** *or* **millennia**) N Jahrtausend *nt*
millennium bug N (*Comput*) Jahrtausendfehler *m*
miller ['mɪləʳ] N Müller *m*
millet ['mɪlɪt] N Hirse *f*
milli... ['mɪlɪ] PREF Milli-
milligram, milligramme ['mɪlɪgræm] N Milligramm *nt*
millilitre, (US) **milliliter** ['mɪlɪli:təʳ] N Milliliter *m or nt*
millimetre, (US) **millimeter** ['mɪlɪmi:təʳ] N Millimeter *m or nt*
millinery ['mɪlɪnərɪ] N Hüte *pl*
million ['mɪljən] N Million *f*; **a ~ times** (*fig*) tausend Mal, x-mal
millionaire [mɪljə'nɛəʳ] N Millionär *m*
millipede ['mɪlɪpi:d] N Tausendfüßler *m*
millstone ['mɪlstəun] N (*fig*): **it's a ~ round his neck** es ist für ihn ein Klotz am Bein
millwheel ['mɪlwi:l] N Mühlrad *nt*
milometer [maɪ'lɔmɪtəʳ] N = **mileometer**
mime [maɪm] N Pantomime *f*; (*actor*) Pantomime *m* ▸ VT pantomimisch darstellen
mimic ['mɪmɪk] N Imitator *m* ▸ VT (*for amusement*) parodieren; (*animal, person*) imitieren, nachahmen
mimicry ['mɪmɪkrɪ] N Nachahmung *f*
Min. (BRIT) ABBR (*Pol*) = **ministry**
min. ABBR (= *minute*) Min.; = **minimum**
minaret [mɪnə'rɛt] N Minarett *nt*
mince [mɪns] VT (*meat*) durch den Fleischwolf drehen ▸ VI (*in walking*) trippeln ▸ N (BRIT: *meat*) Hackfleisch *nt*; **he does not ~ (his) words** er nimmt kein Blatt vor den Mund
mincemeat ['mɪnsmi:t] N *süße Gebäckfüllung aus Dörrobst und Sirup*; (US: *meat*) Hackfleisch *nt*; **to make ~ of sb** (*inf*) Hackfleisch aus jdm machen
mince pie N *mit Mincemeat gefülltes Gebäck*
mincer ['mɪnsəʳ] N Fleischwolf *m*
mincing ['mɪnsɪŋ] ADJ (*walk*) trippelnd; (*voice*) geziert
mind [maɪnd] N Geist *m*, Verstand *m*; (*thoughts*) Gedanken *pl*; (*memory*) Gedächtnis *nt* ▸ VT aufpassen auf *+acc*; (*office etc*) nach dem Rechten sehen in *+dat*; (*object to*) etwas haben gegen; **to my ~** meiner Meinung nach; **to be out of one's ~** verrückt sein; **it is on my ~** es beschäftigt mich; **to keep** *or* **bear sth in ~** etw nicht vergessen, an etw denken; **to make up one's ~** sich entscheiden; **to change one's ~** es sich *dat* anders überlegen; **to be in two minds**

m

about sth sich *dat* über etw *acc* nicht im Klaren sein; **to have it in ~ to do sth** die Absicht haben, etw zu tun; **to have sb/sth in ~** an jdn/etw denken; **it slipped my ~** ich habe es vergessen; **to bring** *or* **call sth to ~** etw in Erinnerung rufen; **I can't get it out of my ~** es geht mir nicht aus dem Kopf; **his ~ was on other things** er war mit den Gedanken woanders; **"~ the step"** „Vorsicht Stufe"; **do you ~ if ...?** macht es Ihnen etwas aus, wenn ...?; **I don't ~** es ist mir egal; **~ you, ...** allerdings ...; **never ~!** (*it makes no odds*) ist doch egal!; (*don't worry*) macht nichts!

mind-boggling ['maɪndbɔglɪŋ] (*inf*) ADJ atemberaubend

-minded ['maɪndɪd] ADJ: **fair~** gerecht; **an industrially~ nation** ein auf Industrie ausgerichtetes Land

minder ['maɪndə^r] N Betreuer(in) *m(f)*; (*inf: bodyguard*) Aufpasser(in) *m(f)*

mindful ['maɪndful] ADJ: **~ of** unter Berücksichtigung *+gen*

mindless ['maɪndlɪs] ADJ (*violence*) sinnlos; (*work*) geistlos

mine[1] [maɪn] N (*also*: **coal mine, gold mine**) Bergwerk *nt*; (*bomb*) Mine *f* ▸ VT (*coal*) abbauen; (*beach etc*) verminen; (*ship*) eine Mine befestigen an *+dat*

mine[2] [maɪn] PRON meine(r, s); **that book is ~** das Buch ist mein(e)s, das Buch gehört mir; **this is ~** das ist meins; **a friend of ~** ein Freund/eine Freundin von mir

mine detector N Minensuchgerät *nt*

minefield ['maɪnfi:ld] N Minenfeld *nt*; (*fig*) brisante Situation *f*

miner ['maɪnə^r] N Bergmann *m*, Bergarbeiter *m*

mineral ['mɪnərəl] ADJ (*deposit, resources*) Mineral- ▸ N Mineral *nt*; **minerals** NPL (BRIT: *soft drinks*) Erfrischungsgetränke *pl*

mineralogy [mɪnə'rælədʒɪ] N Mineralogie *f*

mineral water N Mineralwasser *nt*;

minesweeper ['maɪnswi:pə^r] N Minensuchboot *nt*

mingle ['mɪŋgl] VI: **to ~ (with)** sich vermischen (mit); **to ~ with** (*people*) Umgang haben mit; (*at party etc*) sich unterhalten mit; **you should ~ a bit** du solltest dich unter die Leute mischen

mingy ['mɪndʒɪ] (*inf*) ADJ knick(e)rig; (*amount*) mick(e)rig

mini... ['mɪnɪ] PREF Mini-

miniature ['mɪnətʃə^r] ADJ winzig; (*version etc*) Miniatur- ▸ N Miniatur *f*; **in ~** im Kleinen, im Kleinformat

minibus ['mɪnɪbʌs] N Kleinbus *m*

minicab ['mɪnɪkæb] N Kleintaxi *nt*

minicomputer ['mɪnɪkəm'pju:tə^r] N Minicomputer *m*

minim ['mɪnɪm] N (*Mus*) halbe Note *f*

minima ['mɪnɪmə] NPL *of* **minimum**

minimal ['mɪnɪml] ADJ minimal

minimalist ['mɪnɪməlɪst] ADJ minimalistisch

minimize ['mɪnɪmaɪz] VT auf ein Minimum reduzieren; (*play down*) herunterspielen

minimum ['mɪnɪməm] (*pl* **minima**) N Minimum *nt* ▸ ADJ (*income, speed*) Mindest-; **to reduce to a ~** auf ein Mindestmaß reduzieren; **~ wage** Mindestlohn *m*

minimum lending rate N Diskontsatz *m*

mining ['maɪnɪŋ] N Bergbau *m* ▸ CPD Bergbau-

minion ['mɪnjən] (*pej*) N Untergebene(r) *f(m)*

miniseries ['mɪnɪsɪəri:z] N Miniserie *f*

miniskirt ['mɪnɪskə:t] N Minirock *m*

minister ['mɪnɪstə^r] N (BRIT *Pol*) Minister(in) *m(f)*; (*Rel*) Pfarrer *m* ▸ VI: **to ~ to** sich kümmern um; (*needs*) befriedigen

ministerial [mɪnɪs'tɪərɪəl] (BRIT) ADJ (*Pol*) ministeriell

ministry ['mɪnɪstrɪ] N (BRIT *Pol*) Ministerium *nt*; **to join the ~** (*Rel*) Geistliche(r) werden

Ministry of Defence (BRIT) N Verteidigungsministerium *nt*

mink [mɪŋk] (*pl* **minks** *or* **~**) N Nerz *m*

mink coat N Nerzmantel *m*

Minn. (US) ABBR (*Post*) = **Minnesota**

minnow ['mɪnəu] N Elritze *f*

minor ['maɪnə^r] ADJ kleinere(r, s); (*poet*) unbedeutend; (*planet*) klein; (*Mus*) Moll ▸ N Minderjährige(r) *f(m)*

Minorca [mɪ'nɔ:kə] N Menorca *nt*

minority [maɪ'nɔrɪtɪ] N Minderheit *f*; **to be in a ~** in der Minderheit sein

minster ['mɪnstə^r] N Münster *nt*

minstrel ['mɪnstrəl] N Spielmann *m*

mint [mɪnt] N Minze *f*; (*sweet*) Pfefferminz(bonbon) *nt*; (*place*): **the M~** die Münzanstalt ▸ VT (*coins*) prägen; **in ~ condition** neuwertig

mint sauce N Minzsoße *f*

minuet [mɪnju'ɛt] N Menuett *nt*

minus ['maɪnəs] N (*also*: **minus sign**) Minuszeichen *nt* ▸ PREP minus, weniger; **~ 24°C** 24 Grad unter null

minuscule ['mɪnəskju:l] ADJ winzig

minute[1] [maɪ'nju:t] ADJ winzig; (*search*) peinlich genau; (*detail*) kleinste(r, s); **in ~ detail** in allen Einzelheiten

minute[2] ['mɪnɪt] N Minute *f*; (*fig*) Augenblick *m*, Moment *m*; **minutes** NPL (*of meeting*) Protokoll *nt*; **it is 5 minutes past 3** es ist 5 Minuten nach 3; **wait a ~!** einen Augenblick *or* Moment!; **up-to-the-~** (*news*) hochaktuell; (*technology*) allerneueste(r, s); **at the last ~** in letzter Minute; **minute book** N Protokollbuch *nt*; **minute hand** N Minutenzeiger *m*; **minutely** [maɪ'nju:tlɪ] ADV (*in detail*) genauestens; (*by a small amount*) ganz geringfügig

minutiae [mɪ'nju:ʃɪi:] NPL Einzelheiten *pl*

miracle ['mɪrəkl] N (*Rel, fig*) Wunder *nt*

miraculous [mɪ'rækjuləs] ADJ wunderbar; (*powers, effect, cure*) Wunder-; (*success, change*) unglaublich; **to have a ~ escape** wie durch ein Wunder entkommen

mirage ['mɪrɑ:ʒ] N Fata Morgana *f*; (*fig*) Trugbild *nt*

mire ['maɪə^r] N Morast *m*

mirror ['mɪrəʳ] N Spiegel *m* ▶ VT (*lit, fig*) widerspiegeln
mirror image N Spiegelbild *nt*
mirth [mə:θ] N Heiterkeit *f*
misadventure [mɪsəd'vɛntʃəʳ] N Missgeschick *nt*; **death by ~** (BRIT) Tod *m* durch Unfall
misanthropist [mɪ'zænθrəpɪst] N Misanthrop *m*, Menschenfeind *m*
misapply [mɪsə'plaɪ] VT (*term*) falsch verwenden; (*rule*) falsch anwenden
misapprehension ['mɪsæprɪ'hɛnʃən] N Missverständnis *nt*; **you are under a ~** Sie befinden sich im Irrtum
misappropriate [mɪsə'prəuprɪeɪt] VT veruntreuen
misappropriation ['mɪsəprəuprɪ'eɪʃən] N Veruntreuung *f*
misbehave [mɪsbɪ'heɪv] VI sich schlecht benehmen
misbehaviour, (*US*) **misbehavior** [mɪsbɪ'heɪvjəʳ] N schlechtes Benehmen *nt*
misc. ABBR = **miscellaneous**
miscalculate [mɪs'kælkjuleɪt] VT falsch berechnen; (*misjudge*) falsch einschätzen
miscalculation ['mɪskælkju'leɪʃən] N Rechenfehler *m*; (*misjudgement*) Fehleinschätzung *f*
miscarriage ['mɪskærɪdʒ] N (*Med*) Fehlgeburt *f*; **~ of justice** (*Law*) Justizirrtum *m*
miscarry [mɪs'kærɪ] VI (*Med*) eine Fehlgeburt haben; (*fail: plans*) fehlschlagen
miscellaneous [mɪsɪ'leɪnɪəs] ADJ verschieden; (*subjects, items*) divers; **~ expenses** sonstige Unkosten *pl*
mischance [mɪs'tʃɑ:ns] N unglücklicher Zufall *m*
mischief ['mɪstʃɪf] N (*bad behaviour*) Unfug *m*; (*playfulness*) Verschmitztheit *f*; (*harm*) Schaden *m*; (*pranks*) Streiche *pl*; **to get into ~** etwas anstellen; **to do sb a ~** jdm etwas antun
mischievous ['mɪstʃɪvəs] ADJ (*naughty*) ungezogen; (*playful*) verschmitzt
misconception ['mɪskən'sɛpʃən] N fälschliche Annahme *f*
misconduct [mɪs'kɔndʌkt] N Fehlverhalten *nt*; **professional ~** Berufsvergehen *nt*
misconstrue [mɪskən'stru:] VT missverstehen
miscount [mɪs'kaunt] VT falsch zählen ▶ VI sich verzählen
misdemeanour, (*US*) **misdemeanor** [mɪsdɪ'mi:nəʳ] N Vergehen *nt*
misdirect [mɪsdɪ'rɛkt] VT (*person*) in die falsche Richtung schicken; (*talent*) vergeuden
miser ['maɪzəʳ] N Geizhals *m*
miserable ['mɪzərəbl] ADJ (*unhappy*) unglücklich; (*wretched*) erbärmlich, elend; (*unpleasant: weather*) trostlos; (*: person*) gemein; (*contemptible: offer, donation*) armselig; (*: failure*) kläglich; **to feel ~** sich elend fühlen
miserably ['mɪzərəblɪ] ADV (*fail*) kläglich; (*live*) elend; (*smile, speak*) unglücklich; (*small*) jämmerlich
miserly ['maɪzəlɪ] ADJ geizig; (*amount*) armselig
misery ['mɪzərɪ] N (*unhappiness*) Kummer *m*; (*wretchedness*) Elend *nt*; (*inf: person*) Miesepeter *m*
misfire [mɪs'faɪəʳ] VI (*plan*) fehlschlagen; (*car engine*) fehlzünden
misfit ['mɪsfɪt] N Außenseiter(in) *m(f)*
misfortune [mɪs'fɔ:tʃən] N Pech *nt*, Unglück *nt*
misgiving [mɪs'gɪvɪŋ] N Bedenken *pl*; **to have misgivings about sth** sich bei etw nicht wohlfühlen
misguided [mɪs'gaɪdɪd] ADJ töricht; (*opinion, view*) irrig; (*misplaced*) unangebracht
mishandle [mɪs'hændl] VT falsch handhaben
mishap ['mɪshæp] N Missgeschick *nt*
mishear [mɪs'hɪəʳ] VT (*irreg: like* **hear**) falsch hören ▶ VI sich verhören
misheard [mɪs'hə:d] PT, PP *of* **mishear**
mishmash ['mɪʃmæʃ] (*inf*) N Mischmasch *m*
misinform [mɪsɪn'fɔ:m] VT falsch informieren
misinterpret [mɪsɪn'tə:prɪt] VT (*gesture, situation*) falsch auslegen; (*comment*) falsch auffassen
misinterpretation ['mɪsɪntə:prɪ'teɪʃən] N falsche Auslegung *f*
misjudge [mɪs'dʒʌdʒ] VT falsch einschätzen
mislay [mɪs'leɪ] VT (*irreg: like* **lay**) verlegen
mislead [mɪs'li:d] VT (*irreg: like* **lead[1]**) irreführen
misleading [mɪs'li:dɪŋ] ADJ irreführend
misled [mɪs'lɛd] PT, PP *of* **mislead**
mismanage [mɪs'mænɪdʒ] VT (*business*) herunterwirtschaften; (*institution*) schlecht führen
mismanagement [mɪs'mænɪdʒmənt] N Misswirtschaft *f*
misnomer [mɪs'nəuməʳ] N unzutreffende Bezeichnung *f*
misogynist [mɪ'sɔdʒɪnɪst] N Frauenfeind *m*
misplaced [mɪs'pleɪst] ADJ (*misguided*) unangebracht; (*wrongly positioned*) an der falschen Stelle
misprint ['mɪsprɪnt] N Druckfehler *m*
mispronounce [mɪsprə'nauns] VT falsch aussprechen
misquote ['mɪs'kwəut] VT falsch zitieren
misread [mɪs'ri:d] VT (*irreg: like* **read**) falsch lesen; (*misinterpret*) falsch verstehen
misrepresent [mɪsrɛprɪ'zɛnt] VT falsch darstellen; **he was misrepresented** seine Worte wurden verfälscht wiedergegeben
Miss [mɪs] N Fräulein *nt*; **Dear ~ Smith** Liebe Frau Smith
miss [mɪs] VT (*train etc, chance, opportunity*) verpassen; (*target*) verfehlen; (*notice loss of, regret absence of*) vermissen; (*class, meeting*) fehlen bei ▶ VI danebentreffen; (*missile, object*) danebengehen ▶ N Fehltreffer *m*; **you can't ~ it** du kannst es nicht verfehlen; **the bus just missed the wall** der Bus wäre um ein Haar gegen die Mauer gefahren; **you're missing the point** das geht an der Sache vorbei
▶ **miss out** (BRIT) VT auslassen
▶ **miss out on** VT FUS (*party*) verpassen; (*fun*) zu kurz kommen bei
missal ['mɪsl] N Messbuch *nt*
misshapen [mɪs'ʃeɪpən] ADJ missgebildet

m

missile ['mɪsaɪl] N (*Mil*) Rakete *f*; (*object thrown*) (Wurf)geschoss *nt*, (Wurf)geschoß *nt* (Österr)
missile base N Raketenbasis *f*
missile launcher [-'lɔːntʃə^r] N Startrampe *f*
missing ['mɪsɪŋ] ADJ (*lost: person*) vermisst; (*: object*) verschwunden; (*absent, removed*) fehlend; **to be ~** fehlen; **to go ~** verschwinden; **~ person** Vermisste(r) *f(m)*
mission ['mɪʃən] N (*task*) Mission *f*, Auftrag *m*; (*representatives*) Gesandtschaft *f*; (*Mil*) Einsatz *m*; (*Rel*) Mission *f*; **on a ~ to ...** (*to place/people*) im Einsatz in *+dat*/bei ...
missionary ['mɪʃənrɪ] N Missionar(in) *m(f)*
missive ['mɪsɪv] (*form*) N Schreiben *nt*
misspell ['mɪs'spɛl] VT (*irreg: like* **spell**) falsch schreiben
misspent ['mɪs'spɛnt] ADJ (*youth*) vergeudet
mist [mɪst] N Nebel *m*; (*light*) Dunst *m* ▸ VI (*eyes: also*: **mist over**) sich verschleiern; (Brit: *windows: also*: **mist over, mist up**) beschlagen
mistake [mɪs'teɪk] N Fehler *m* ▸ VT (*irreg: like* **take**) sich irren in *+dat*; (*intentions*) falsch verstehen; **by ~** aus Versehen; **to make a ~** (*in writing, calculation*) sich vertun; **to make a ~ (about sb/sth)** sich (in jdm/etw) irren; **to ~ A for B** A mit B verwechseln
mistaken [mɪs'teɪkən] PP *of* **mistake** ▸ ADJ falsch; **to be ~** sich irren
mistaken identity N Verwechslung *f*
mistakenly [mɪs'teɪkənlɪ] ADV irrtümlicherweise
mister ['mɪstə^r] (*inf*) N (*sir*) *not translated*; *see* **Mr**
mistletoe ['mɪsltəu] N Mistel *f*
mistook [mɪs'tuk] PT *of* **mistake**
mistranslation [mɪstræns'leɪʃən] N falsche Übersetzung *f*
mistreat [mɪs'triːt] VT schlecht behandeln
mistress ['mɪstrɪs] N (*lover*) Geliebte *f*; (*of house, servant, situation*) Herrin *f*; (Brit: *teacher*) Lehrerin *f*
mistrust [mɪs'trʌst] VT misstrauen *+dat* ▸ N: **~ (of)** Misstrauen *nt* (gegenüber)
mistrustful [mɪs'trʌstful] ADJ: **~ (of)** misstrauisch (gegenüber)
misty ['mɪstɪ] ADJ (*day etc*) neblig; (*glasses, windows*) beschlagen
misty-eyed ['mɪstɪ'aɪd] ADJ mit verschleiertem Blick
misunderstand [mɪsʌndə'stænd] VT (*irreg: like* **understand**) missverstehen, falsch verstehen ▸ VI es falsch verstehen
misunderstanding ['mɪsʌndə'stændɪŋ] N Missverständnis *nt*; (*disagreement*) Meinungsverschiedenheit *f*
misunderstood [mɪsʌndə'stud] PT, PP *of* **misunderstand**
misuse N [mɪs'juːs] Missbrauch *m* ▸ VT [mɪs'juːz] missbrauchen; (*word*) falsch gebrauchen
MIT (US) N ABBR (= *Massachusetts Institute of Technology*) *private technische Fachhochschule*
mite [maɪt] N (*small quantity*) bisschen *nt*; (Brit: *small child*) Würmchen *nt*
miter ['maɪtə^r] (*US*) N = **mitre**
mitigate ['mɪtɪgeɪt] VT mildern; **mitigating circumstances** mildernde Umstände *pl*
mitigation [mɪtɪ'geɪʃən] N Milderung *f*
mitre, (US) miter ['maɪtə^r] N (*of bishop*) Mitra *f*; (*Carpentry*) Gehrung *f*
mitt ['mɪt], **mitten** ['mɪtn] N Fausthandschuh *m*
mix [mɪks] VT mischen; (*drink*) mixen; (*sauce, cake*) zubereiten; (*ingredients*) verrühren ▸ VI: **to ~ (with)** verkehren (mit) ▸ N Mischung *f*; **to ~ sth with sth** etw mit etw vermischen; **to ~ business with pleasure** das Angenehme mit dem Nützlichen verbinden; **cake ~** Backmischung *f*
▸ **mix in** VT (*eggs etc*) unterrühren
▸ **mix up** VT (*people*) verwechseln; (*things*) durcheinanderbringen; **to be mixed up in sth** in etw *acc* verwickelt sein
mixed [mɪkst] ADJ gemischt; **~ marriage** Mischehe *f*
mixed-ability ['mɪkstə'bɪlɪtɪ] ADJ (*group etc*) mit unterschiedlichen Fähigkeiten
mixed bag N (*of things, problems*) Sammelsurium *nt*; (*of people*) gemischter Haufen *m*
mixed blessing N: **it's a ~** das ist ein zweischneidiges Schwert
mixed doubles NPL gemischtes Doppel *nt*
mixed economy N gemischte Wirtschaftsform *f*
mixed grill (Brit) N Grillteller *m*
mixed-up [mɪkst'ʌp] ADJ durcheinander
mixer ['mɪksə^r] N (*for food*) Mixer *m*; (*drink*) *Tonic etc zum Auffüllen von alkoholischen Mixgetränken*; **to be a good ~** (*sociable person*) kontaktfreudig sein
mixer tap N Mischbatterie *f*
mixture ['mɪkstʃə^r] N Mischung *f*; (*Culin*) Gemisch *nt*; (*: for cake*) Teig *m*; (*Med*) Mixtur *f*
mix-up ['mɪksʌp] N Durcheinander *nt*
MK (Brit) ABBR (*Tech*) = **mark**
mkt ABBR = **market**
ml ABBR (= *millilitre*) ml
MLA (Brit) N ABBR (*Pol*: = *Member of the Legislative Assembly (of Northern Ireland)*) Abgeordnete(r) *f(m)* der gesetzgebenden Versammlung
MLitt N ABBR (= *Master of Literature, Master of Letters*) *akademischer Grad in Literaturwissenschaft*
MLR (Brit) N ABBR = **minimum lending rate**
mm ABBR (= *millimetre*) mm
MMS N ABBR (= *Multimedia Messaging Service*) MMS® *m*
MN ABBR (Brit) = **merchant navy**; (*US Post*) = **Minnesota**
MO N ABBR (= *medical officer*) Sanitätsoffizier *m*; (*US inf*) = **modus operandi**
moan [məun] N Stöhnen *nt* ▸ VI stöhnen; (*inf: complain*): **to ~ (about)** meckern (über *+acc*)
moaner ['məunə^r] (*inf*) N Miesmacher(in) *m(f)*
moat [məut] N Wassergraben *m*
mob [mɔb] N Mob *m*; (*organized*) Bande *f* ▸ VT herfallen über *+acc*
mobile ['məubaɪl] ADJ beweglich; (*workforce, society*) mobil ▸ N (*decoration*) Mobile *nt*; (*phone*)

Handy *nt*; **applicants must be ~** Bewerber müssen motorisiert sein
mobile home N Wohnwagen *m*
mobile (phone) N Funktelefon *nt*, Handy *nt*
mobile-phone mast N Handymast *m*
mobility [məu'bılıtı] N Beweglichkeit *f*; (*of workforce etc*) Mobilität *f*
mobility allowance N *Beihilfe für Gehbehinderte*
mobilize ['məubılaız] VT mobilisieren; (*Mil*) mobil machen ▸ VI (*Mil*) mobil machen
moccasin ['mɔkəsın] N Mokassin *m*
mock [mɔk] VT sich lustig machen über *+acc* ▸ ADJ (*fake: Elizabethan etc*) Pseudo-; (*exam*) Probe-; (*battle*) Schein-
mockery ['mɔkərı] N Spott *m*; **to make a ~ of sb** jdn zum Gespött machen; **to make a ~ of sth** etw zur Farce machen
mocking ['mɔkıŋ] ADJ spöttisch
mockingbird ['mɔkıŋbə:d] N Spottdrossel *f*
mock-up ['mɔkʌp] N Modell *nt*
MOD (BRIT) N ABBR = **Ministry of Defence**
mod cons ['mɔd'kɔnz] (BRIT) NPL (= *modern conveniences*) Komfort *m*
mode [məud] N Form *f*; (*Comput, Tech*) Betriebsart *f*; **~ of life** Lebensweise *f*; **~ of transport** Transportmittel *nt*
model ['mɔdl] N Modell *nt*; (*also*: **fashion model**) Mannequin *nt*; (*example*) Muster *nt* ▸ ADJ (*excellent*) vorbildlich; (*small scale: railway etc*) Modell- ▸ VT (*clothes*) vorführen; (*with clay etc*) modellieren, formen ▸ VI (*for designer, photographer etc*) als Modell arbeiten; **to ~ o.s. on sb** sich *dat* jdn zum Vorbild nehmen
modeller, (*US*) **modeler** ['mɔdlə^r] N Modellbauer *m*
model railway N Modelleisenbahn *f*
modem ['məudɛm] N Modem *nt*
moderate ADJ ['mɔdərət] gemäßigt; (*amount*) nicht allzu groß; (*change*) leicht ▸ N Gemäßigte(r) *f(m)* ▸ VI ['mɔdəreıt] (*storm, wind etc*) nachlassen ▸ VT (*tone, demands*) mäßigen
moderately ['mɔdərətlı] ADV mäßig; (*expensive, difficult*) nicht allzu; (*pleased, happy*) einigermaßen; **~ priced** nicht allzu teuer
moderation [mɔdə'reıʃən] N Mäßigung *f*; **in ~** in *or* mit Maßen
moderator ['mɔdəreıtə^r] N (*Eccl*) Synodalpräsident *m*
modern ['mɔdən] ADJ modern; **~ languages** moderne Fremdsprachen *pl*
modernization [mɔdənaı'zeıʃən] N Modernisierung *f*
modernize ['mɔdənaız] VT modernisieren
modest ['mɔdıst] ADJ bescheiden; (*chaste*) schamhaft
modestly ['mɔdıstlı] ADV bescheiden; (*behave*) schamhaft; (*to a moderate extent*) mäßig
modesty ['mɔdıstı] N Bescheidenheit *f*; (*chastity*) Schamgefühl *nt*
modicum ['mɔdıkəm] N: **a ~ of** ein wenig *or* bisschen
modification [mɔdıfı'keıʃən] N Änderung *f*; (*to policy etc*) Modifizierung *f*; **to make modifications to** (Ver)änderungen vornehmen an *+dat*, modifizieren
modify ['mɔdıfaı] VT (ver)ändern; (*policy etc*) modifizieren
modish ['məudıʃ] ADJ (*fashionable*) modisch
Mods [mɔdz] (BRIT) N ABBR (*Scol*: = (*Honour*) *Moderations*) *akademische Prüfung an der Universität Oxford*
modular ['mɔdjulə^r] ADJ (*unit, furniture*) aus Bauelementen (zusammengesetzt); (*Comput*) modular
modulate ['mɔdjuleıt] VT modulieren; (*process, activity*) umwandeln
modulation [mɔdju'leıʃən] N Modulation *f*; (*modification*) Veränderung *f*
module ['mɔdju:l] N (Bau)element *nt*; (*Space*) Raumkapsel *f*; (*Scol*) Kurs *m*
modus operandi ['məudəsɔpə'rændi:] N Modus Operandi *m*
Mogadishu [mɔgə'dıʃu:] N Mogadischu *nt*
mogul ['məugl] N (*fig*) Mogul *m*
MOH (BRIT) N ABBR (= *Medical Officer of Health*) Amtsarzt *m*, Amtsärztin *f*
mohair ['məuhɛə^r] N Mohair *m*
Mohammed [mə'hæmɛd] N Mohammed *m*
moist [mɔıst] ADJ feucht
moisten ['mɔısn] VT anfeuchten
moisture ['mɔıstʃə^r] N Feuchtigkeit *f*
moisturize ['mɔıstʃəraız] VT (*skin*) mit einer Feuchtigkeitscreme behandeln
moisturizer ['mɔıstʃəraızə^r] N Feuchtigkeitscreme *f*
molar ['məulə^r] N Backenzahn *m*
molasses [mə'læsız] N Melasse *f*
mold *etc* [məuld] (*US*) N, VT = **mould** *etc*
Moldavia [mɔl'deıvıə] N Moldawien *nt*
Moldavian [mɔl'deıvıən] ADJ moldawisch
Moldova [mɔl'dəuvə] N Moldawien *nt*
Moldovan ADJ moldawisch
mole [məul] N (*on skin*) Leberfleck *m*; (*Zool*) Maulwurf *m*; (*fig: spy*) Spion(in) *m(f)*
molecular [məu'lɛkjulə^r] ADJ molekular; (*biology*) Molekular-
molecule ['mɔlıkju:l] N Molekül *nt*
molehill ['məulhıl] N Maulwurfshaufen *m*
molest [mə'lɛst] VT (*assault sexually*) sich vergehen an *+dat*; (*harass*) belästigen
mollusc ['mɔləsk] N Weichtier *nt*
mollycoddle ['mɔlıkɔdl] VT verhätscheln
Molotov cocktail ['mɔlətɔf-] N Molotowcocktail *m*
molt [məult] (*US*) VI = **moult**
molten ['məultən] ADJ geschmolzen, flüssig
mom [mɔm] (*US*) N = **mum**
moment ['məumənt] N Moment *m*, Augenblick *m*; (*importance*) Bedeutung *f*; **for a ~** (für) einen Moment *or* Augenblick; **at that ~** in diesem Moment *or* Augenblick; **at the ~** momentan; **for the ~** vorläufig; **in a ~** gleich; **"one ~ please"** (*Tel*) „bleiben Sie am Apparat"
momentarily ['məuməntrılı] ADV für einen Augenblick *or* Moment; (*US: very soon*) jeden Augenblick *or* Moment

m

momentary ['məuməntərɪ] ADJ (*brief*) kurz
momentous [məu'mɛntəs] ADJ (*occasion*) bedeutsam; (*decision*) von großer Tragweite
momentum [məu'mɛntəm] N (*Phys*) Impuls *m*; (*fig: of movement*) Schwung *m*; (*: of events, change*) Dynamik *f*; **to gather ~** schneller werden; (*fig*) richtig in Gang kommen
mommy ['mɔmɪ] (*US*) N = **mummy**
Mon. ABBR (= *Monday*) Mo.
Monaco ['mɔnəkəu] N Monaco *nt*
monarch ['mɔnək] N Monarch(in) *m(f)*
monarchist ['mɔnəkɪst] N Monarchist(in) *m(f)*
monarchy ['mɔnəkɪ] N Monarchie *f*; **the M~** (*royal family*) die königliche Familie
monastery ['mɔnəstərɪ] N Kloster *nt*
monastic [mə'næstɪk] ADJ Kloster-, klösterlich; (*fig*) mönchisch, klösterlich einfach
Monday ['mʌndɪ] N Montag *m*; *see also* **Tuesday**
Monegasque [mɔnə'gæsk] ADJ monegassisch ▶ N Monegasse *m*, Monegassin *f*
monetarist ['mʌnɪtərɪst] N Monetarist(in) *m(f)* ▶ ADJ monetaristisch
monetary ['mʌnɪtərɪ] ADJ (*system, union*) Währungs-
money ['mʌnɪ] N Geld *nt*; **to make ~** (*person*) Geld verdienen; (*business*) etwas einbringen; **danger ~** (*BRIT*) Gefahrenzulage *f*; **I've got no ~ left** ich habe kein Geld mehr
moneyed ['mʌnɪd] (*form*) ADJ begütert
moneylender ['mʌnɪlɛndə^r] N Geldverleiher(in) *m(f)*
moneymaker ['mʌnɪmeɪkə^r] N (*person*) Finanzgenie *nt*; (*idea*) einträgliche Sache *f*; (*product*) Verkaufserfolg *m*
moneymaking ['mʌnɪmeɪkɪŋ] ADJ einträglich
money market N Geldmarkt *m*
money order N Zahlungsanweisung *f*
money-spinner ['mʌnɪspɪnə^r] (*inf*) N Verkaufsschlager *m*; (*person, business*) Goldgrube *f*
money supply N Geldvolumen *nt*
Mongol ['mɔŋgəl] N Mongole *m*, Mongolin *f*; (*Ling*) Mongolisch *nt*
mongol ['mɔŋgəl] (*offensive*) N Mongoloide(r) *f(m)*
Mongolia [mɔŋ'gəulɪə] N die Mongolei
Mongolian [mɔŋ'gəulɪən] ADJ mongolisch ▶ N Mongole *m*, Mongolin *f*; (*Ling*) Mongolisch *nt*
mongoose ['mɔŋgu:s] N Mungo *m*
mongrel ['mʌŋgrəl] N Promenadenmischung *f*
monitor ['mɔnɪtə^r] N Monitor *m* ▶ VT überwachen; (*broadcasts*) mithören
monk [mʌŋk] N Mönch *m*
monkey ['mʌŋkɪ] N Affe *m*
monkey business (*inf*) N faule Sachen *pl*
monkey nut (*BRIT*) N Erdnuss *f*
monkey tricks NPL = **monkey business**
monkey wrench N verstellbarer Schraubenschlüssel *m*
mono ['mɔnəu] ADJ (*recording etc*) Mono-
monochrome ['mɔnəkrəum] ADJ (*photograph, television*) Schwarzweiß-; (*Comput: screen*) Monochrom-
monogamous [mə'nɔgəməs] ADJ monogam
monogamy [mə'nɔgəmɪ] N Monogamie *f*
monogram ['mɔnəgræm] N Monogramm *nt*
monolith ['mɔnəlɪθ] N Monolith *m*
monolithic [mɔnə'lɪθɪk] ADJ monolithisch
monologue ['mɔnəlɔg] N Monolog *m*
monoplane ['mɔnəpleɪn] N Eindecker *m*
monopolize [mə'nɔpəlaɪz] VT beherrschen; (*person*) mit Beschlag belegen; (*conversation*) an sich *acc* reißen
monopoly [mə'nɔpəlɪ] N Monopol *nt*; **to have a ~ on** *or* **of sth** (*fig: domination*) etw für sich gepachtet haben; **Monopolies and Mergers Commission** (*BRIT*) ≈ Kartellamt *nt*
monorail ['mɔnəureɪl] N Einschienenbahn *f*
monosodium glutamate [mɔnə'səudɪəm'glu:təmeɪt] N Glutamat *nt*
monosyllabic [mɔnəsɪ'læbɪk] ADJ einsilbig
monosyllable ['mɔnəsɪləbl] N einsilbiges Wort *nt*
monotone ['mɔnətəun] N: **in a ~** monoton
monotonous [mə'nɔtənəs] ADJ monoton, eintönig
monotony [mə'nɔtənɪ] N Monotonie *f*, Eintönigkeit *f*
monsoon [mɔn'su:n] N Monsun *m*
monster ['mɔnstə^r] N Ungetüm *nt*, Monstrum *nt*; (*imaginary creature*) Ungeheuer *nt*, Monster *nt*; (*person*) Unmensch *m*
monstrosity [mɔn'strɔsɪtɪ] N Ungetüm *nt*, Monstrum *nt*
monstrous ['mɔnstrəs] ADJ (*huge*) riesig; (*ugly*) abscheulich; (*atrocious*) ungeheuerlich
Mont. (*US*) ABBR (*Post*) = **Montana**
montage [mɔn'tɑ:ʒ] N Montage *f*
Mont Blanc [mɔ̃ blɑ̃] N Montblanc *m*
month [mʌnθ] N Monat *m*; **every ~** jeden Monat; **300 dollars a ~** 300 Dollar im Monat
monthly ['mʌnθlɪ] ADJ monatlich; (*ticket, magazine*) Monats- ▶ ADV monatlich; **twice ~** zweimal im Monat
Montreal [mɔntrɪ'ɔ:l] N Montreal *nt*
monument ['mɔnjumənt] N Denkmal *nt*
monumental [mɔnju'mɛntl] ADJ (*building, statue*) gewaltig, monumental; (*book, piece of work*) unsterblich; (*storm, row*) ungeheuer
moo [mu:] VI muhen
mood [mu:d] N Stimmung *f*; (*of person*) Laune *f*, Stimmung *f*; **to be in a good/bad ~** gut/schlecht gelaunt sein; **to be in the ~ for** aufgelegt sein zu
moodily ['mu:dɪlɪ] ADV launisch; (*sullenly*) schlecht gelaunt
moody ['mu:dɪ] ADJ launisch; (*sullen*) schlecht gelaunt
moon [mu:n] N Mond *m*
moonlight ['mu:nlaɪt] N Mondschein *m* ▶ VI (*inf*) schwarzarbeiten
moonlighting ['mu:nlaɪtɪŋ] (*inf*) N Schwarzarbeit *f*
moonlit ['mu:nlɪt] ADJ (*night*) mondhell
moonshot ['mu:nʃɔt] N Mondflug *m*
moor [muə^r] N (Hoch)moor *nt*, Heide *f* ▶ VT vertäuen ▶ VI anlegen

mooring ['muərɪŋ] N Anlegeplatz *m*; **moorings** NPL (*chains*) Verankerung *f*
Moorish ['muərɪʃ] ADJ maurisch
moorland ['muələnd] N Moorlandschaft *f*, Heidelandschaft *f*
moose [mu:s] N INV Elch *m*
moot [mu:t] VT: **to be mooted** vorgeschlagen werden ▸ ADJ: **it's a ~ point** das ist fraglich
mop [mɔp] N (*for floor*) Mop *m*; (*for dishes*) Spülbürste *f*; (*of hair*) Mähne *f* ▸ VT (*floor*) wischen; (*face*) abwischen; (*eyes*) sich *dat* wischen; **to ~ the sweat from one's brow** sich *dat* den Schweiß von der Stirn wischen
▸ **mop up** VT aufwischen
mope [məup] VI Trübsal blasen
▸ **mope about** VI mit einer Jammermiene herumlaufen
▸ **mope around** VI = **mope about**
moped ['məupɛd] N Moped *nt*
moquette [mɔ'kɛt] N Mokett *m*
MOR ADJ ABBR (*Mus*) = **middle-of-the-road**
moral ['mɔrl] ADJ moralisch; (*welfare, values*) sittlich; (*behaviour*) moralisch einwandfrei ▸ N Moral *f*; **morals** NPL (*principles, values*) Moralvorstellungen *pl*; **~ support** moralische Unterstützung *f*
morale [mɔ'rɑ:l] N Moral *f*
morality [mə'rælɪtɪ] N Sittlichkeit *f*; (*system of morals*) Moral *f*, Ethik *f*; (*correctness*) moralische Richtigkeit *f*
moralize ['mɔrəlaɪz] VI moralisieren; **to ~ about** sich moralisch entrüsten über *+acc*
morally ['mɔrəlɪ] ADV moralisch; (*live, behave*) moralisch einwandfrei
moral victory N moralischer Sieg *m*
morass [mə'ræs] N Morast *m*, Sumpf *m* (*also fig*)
moratorium [mɔrə'tɔ:rɪəm] N Stopp *m*; Moratorium *nt*
morbid ['mɔ:bɪd] ADJ (*imagination*) krankhaft; (*interest*) unnatürlich; (*comments, behaviour*) makaber

KEYWORD

more [mɔ:ʳ] ADJ **1** (*greater in number etc*) mehr; **more people/work/letters than we expected** mehr Leute/Arbeit/Briefe, als wir erwarteten; **I have more wine/money than you** ich habe mehr Wein/Geld als du
2 (*additional*): **do you want (some) more tea?** möchten Sie noch mehr Tee?; **is there any more wine?** ist noch Wein da?; **I have no more money, I don't have any more money** ich habe kein Geld mehr
▸ PRON **1** (*greater amount*) mehr; **more than 10** mehr als 10; **it cost more than we expected** es kostete mehr, als wir erwarteten
2 (*further or additional amount*): **is there any more?** gibt es noch mehr?; **there's no more** es ist nichts mehr da; **many/much more** viel mehr
▸ ADV mehr; **more dangerous/difficult/easily** *etc* **(than)** gefährlicher/schwerer/leichter *etc* (als); **more and more** mehr und mehr, immer mehr; **more and more excited/expensive** immer aufgeregter/teurer; **more or less** mehr oder weniger; **more than ever** mehr denn je, mehr als jemals zuvor; **more beautiful than ever** schöner denn je; **no more, not any more** nicht mehr

moreover [mɔ:'rəuvəʳ] ADV außerdem, zudem
morgue [mɔ:g] N Leichenschauhaus *nt*
MORI ['mɔ:rɪ] (BRIT) N ABBR (= *Market and Opinion Research Institute*) *Markt- und Meinungsforschungsinstitut*
moribund ['mɔrɪbʌnd] ADJ dem Untergang geweiht
Mormon ['mɔ:mən] N Mormone *m*, Mormonin *f*
morning ['mɔ:nɪŋ] N Morgen *m*; (*as opposed to afternoon*) Vormittag *m* ▸ CPD Morgen-; **in the ~** morgens; vormittags; (*tomorrow*) morgen früh; **7 o'clock in the ~** 7 Uhr morgens; **this ~** heute Morgen
morning-after pill ['mɔ:nɪŋ'ɑ:ftə-] N Pille *f* danach
morning market N (*Econ*) Vormittagsmarkt *m*
morning sickness N (Schwangerschafts)übelkeit *f*
Moroccan [mə'rɔkən] ADJ marokkanisch ▸ N Marokkaner(in) *m(f)*
Morocco [mə'rɔkəu] N Marokko *nt*
moron ['mɔ:rɔn] (*inf*) N Schwachkopf *m*
moronic [mə'rɔnɪk] (*inf*) ADJ schwachsinnig
morose [mə'rəus] ADJ missmutig
morphine ['mɔ:fi:n] N Morphium *nt*
morris dancing ['mɔrɪs-] N Moriskentanz *m*, *alter englischer Volkstanz*
Morse [mɔ:s] N (*also*: **Morse code**) Morsealphabet *nt*
morsel ['mɔ:sl] N Stückchen *nt*
mortal ['mɔ:tl] ADJ sterblich; (*wound, combat*) tödlich; (*danger*) Todes-; (*sin, enemy*) Tod- ▸ N (*human being*) Sterbliche(r) *f(m)*
mortality [mɔ:'tælɪtɪ] N Sterblichkeit *f*; (*number of deaths*) Todesfälle *pl*
mortality rate N Sterblichkeitsziffer *f*
mortally ADV tödlich
mortar ['mɔ:təʳ] N (*Mil*) Minenwerfer *m*; (*Constr*) Mörtel *m*; (*Culin*) Mörser *m*
mortgage ['mɔ:gɪdʒ] N Hypothek *f* ▸ VT mit einer Hypothek belasten; **to take out a ~** eine Hypothek aufnehmen
mortgage company (*US*) N Hypothekenbank *f*
mortgagee [mɔ:gə'dʒi:] N Hypothekengläubiger *m*
mortgagor ['mɔ:gədʒəʳ] N Hypothekenschuldner *m*
mortician [mɔ:'tɪʃən] (*US*) N Bestattungsunternehmer *m*
mortified ['mɔ:tɪfaɪd] ADJ: **he was ~** er empfand das als beschämend; (*embarrassed*) es war ihm schrecklich peinlich
mortify ['mɔ:tɪfaɪ] VT beschämen
mortise lock ['mɔ:tɪs-] N Einsteckschloss *nt*
mortuary ['mɔ:tjuərɪ] N Leichenhalle *f*

mosaic [məu'zeɪɪk] N Mosaik *nt*
Moscow ['mɔskəu] N Moskau *nt*
Moslem ['mɔzləm] ADJ, N = **Muslim**
mosque [mɔsk] N Moschee *f*
mosquito [mɔs'ki:təu] (*pl* **mosquitoes**) N Stechmücke *f*; (*in tropics*) Moskito *m*
mosquito net N Moskitonetz *nt*
moss [mɔs] N Moos *nt*
mossy ['mɔsɪ] ADJ bemoost

KEYWORD

most [məust] ADJ **1** (*almost all: people, things etc*) meiste(r, s); **most people** die meisten Leute
2 (*largest, greatest: interest, money etc*) meiste(r, s); **who has (the) most money?** wer hat das meiste Geld?
▶ PRON (*greatest quantity, number*) der/die/das meiste; **most of it** das meiste (davon); **most of them** die meisten von ihnen; **most of the time/work** die meiste Zeit/Arbeit; **most of the time he's very helpful** er ist meistens sehr hilfsbereit; **to make the most of sth** das Beste aus etw machen; **for the most part** zum größten Teil; **at the (very) most** (aller)höchstens
▶ ADV (*+ vb: spend, eat, work etc*) am meisten; (*+ adv: carefully, easily etc*) äußerst; (*very: polite, interesting etc*) höchst; (*+ adj*): **the most intelligent/expensive** *etc* der/die/das intelligenteste/teuerste … *etc*; **a most interesting book** ein höchst interessantes Buch

mostly ['məustlɪ] ADV (*chiefly*) hauptsächlich; (*usually*) meistens
MOT (BRIT) N ABBR (= *Ministry of Transport*): **~ (test)** ≈ TÜV *m*; **the car failed its ~** das Auto ist nicht durch den TÜV gekommen
motel [məu'tɛl] N Motel *nt*
moth [mɔθ] N Nachtfalter *m*; (*also*: **clothes moth**) Motte *f*
mothball ['mɔθbɔ:l] N Mottenkugel *f*
moth-eaten ['mɔθi:tn] (*pej*) ADJ mottenzerfressen
mother ['mʌðə^r] N Mutter *f* ▶ ADJ (*country*) Heimat-; (*company*) Mutter- ▶ VT großziehen; (*pamper, protect*) bemuttern
motherboard ['mʌðəbɔ:d] N (*Comput*) Hauptplatine *f*
motherhood ['mʌðəhud] N Mutterschaft *f*
mother-in-law ['mʌðərɪnlɔ:] N Schwiegermutter *f*
motherly ['mʌðəlɪ] ADJ mütterlich
mother-of-pearl ['mʌðərəv'pə:l] N Perlmutt *nt*
mother's help N Haushaltshilfe *f*
mother-to-be ['mʌðətə'bi:] N werdende Mutter *f*
mother tongue N Muttersprache *f*
mothproof ['mɔθpru:f] ADJ mottenfest
motif [məu'ti:f] N Motiv *nt*
motion ['məuʃən] N Bewegung *f*; (*proposal*) Antrag *m*; (BRIT: *also*: **bowel motion**) Stuhlgang *m* ▶ VT, VI: **to ~ (to) sb to do sth** jdm ein Zeichen geben, dass er/sie etw tun solle; **to be in ~** (*vehicle*) fahren; **to set in ~** in Gang bringen; **to go through the motions (of doing sth)** (*fig*) etw der Form halber tun; (*pretend*) so tun, als ob (man etw täte)
motionless ['məuʃənlɪs] ADJ reg(ungs)los
motion picture N Film *m*
motivate ['məutɪveɪt] VT motivieren
motivated ['məutɪveɪtɪd] ADJ motiviert; **~ by** getrieben von
motivation [məutɪ'veɪʃən] N Motivation *f*
motive ['məutɪv] N Motiv *nt*, Beweggrund *m* ▶ ADJ (*power, force*) Antriebs-; **from the best (of) motives** mit den besten Absichten
motley ['mɔtlɪ] ADJ bunt (gemischt)
motor ['məutə^r] N Motor *m*; (BRIT *inf*: *car*) Auto *nt* ▶ CPD (*industry, trade*) Auto(mobil)-
motorbike ['məutəbaɪk] N Motorrad *nt*
motorboat ['məutəbəut] N Motorboot *nt*
motorcade ['məutəkeɪd] N Fahrzeugkolonne *f*
motorcar ['məutəkɑ:] (BRIT) N (Personenkraft)wagen *m*
motorcoach ['məutəkəutʃ] (BRIT) N Reisebus *m*
motorcycle ['məutəsaɪkl] N Motorrad *nt*
motorcycle racing N Motorradrennen *nt*
motorcyclist ['məutəsaɪklɪst] N Motorradfahrer(in) *m(f)*
motoring ['məutərɪŋ] (BRIT) N Autofahren *nt* ▶ CPD Auto-; (*offence, accident*) Verkehrs-
motorist ['məutərɪst] N Autofahrer(in) *m(f)*
motorized ['məutəraɪzd] ADJ motorisiert
motor oil N Motorenöl *nt*
motor racing (BRIT) N Autorennen *nt*
motor scooter N Motorroller *m*
motor show N Automobilausstellung *f*
motor vehicle N Kraftfahrzeug *nt*
motorway ['məutəweɪ] (BRIT) N Autobahn *f*
mottled ['mɔtld] ADJ gesprenkelt
motto ['mɔtəu] (*pl* **mottoes**) N Motto *nt*
mould, (US) mold [məuld] N (*cast*) Form *f*; (*: for metal*) Gussform *f*; (*mildew*) Schimmel *m* ▶ VT (*lit, fig*) formen
moulder ['məuldə^r] VI (*decay*) vermodern
moulding ['məuldɪŋ] N (*Archit*) Zierleiste *f*
mouldy ['məuldɪ] ADJ schimmelig; (*smell*) moderig
moult, (US) molt [məult] VI (*animal*) sich haaren; (*bird*) sich mausern
mound [maund] N (*of earth*) Hügel *m*; (*heap*) Haufen *m*
mount [maunt] N (*in proper names*): **M~ Carmel** der Berg Karmel; (*horse*) Pferd *nt*; (*for picture*) Passepartout *nt* ▶ VT (*horse*) besteigen; (*exhibition etc*) vorbereiten; (*jewel*) (ein)fassen; (*picture*) mit einem Passepartout versehen; (*staircase*) hochgehen; (*stamp*) aufkleben; (*attack, campaign*) organisieren ▶ VI (*increase*) steigen; (*: problems*) sich häufen; (*on horse*) aufsitzen
▶ **mount up** VI (*costs, savings*) sich summieren, sich zusammenläppern (*inf*)
mountain ['mauntɪn] N Berg *m* ▶ CPD (*road, stream*) Gebirgs-; **to make a ~ out of a molehill** aus einer Mücke einen Elefanten machen
mountain bike N Mountainbike *nt*

mountaineer [mauntɪˈnɪəʳ] N Bergsteiger(in) *m(f)*
mountaineering [mauntɪˈnɪərɪŋ] N Bergsteigen *nt*; **to go ~** bergsteigen gehen
mountainous [ˈmauntɪnəs] ADJ gebirgig
mountain range N Gebirgskette *f*
mountain rescue team N Bergwacht *f*
mountainside [ˈmauntɪnsaɪd] N (Berg)hang *m*
mounted [ˈmauntɪd] ADJ (*police*) beritten
Mount Everest N Mount Everest *m*
mourn [mɔːn] VT betrauern ▸ VI: **to ~ (for)** trauern (um)
mourner [ˈmɔːnəʳ] N Trauernde(r) *f(m)*
mournful [ˈmɔːnful] ADJ traurig
mourning [ˈmɔːnɪŋ] N Trauer *f*; **to be in ~** trauern; (*wear special clothes*) Trauer tragen
mouse [maus] (*pl* **mice**) N (*Zool, Comput*) Maus *f*; (*fig: person*) schüchternes Mäuschen *nt*
mouse mat, (*US*) **mouse pad** N Mauspad *nt*
mouse potato N (*inf*) Computerjunkie *m*, Mouse Potato *f*
mousetrap [ˈmaustræp] N Mausefalle *f*
moussaka [muˈsɑːkə] N Moussaka *f*
mousse [muːs] N (*Culin*) Mousse *f*; (*cosmetic*) Schaumfestiger *m*
moustache, (*US*) **mustache** [məsˈtɑːʃ] N Schnurrbart *m*
mousy [ˈmausɪ] ADJ (*hair*) mausgrau
mouth [mauθ] (*pl* **mouths**) N Mund *m*; (*of cave, hole, bottle*) Öffnung *f*; (*of river*) Mündung *f*
mouthful [ˈmauθful] N (*of food*) Bissen *m*; (*of drink*) Schluck *m*
mouth organ N Mundharmonika *f*
mouthpiece [ˈmauθpiːs] N Mundstück *nt*; (*spokesman*) Sprachrohr *nt*
mouth-to-mouth [ˈmauθtəˈmauθ] ADJ: **~ resuscitation** Mund-zu-Mund-Beatmung *f*
mouthwash [ˈmauθwɔʃ] N Mundwasser *nt*
mouth-watering [ˈmauθwɔːtərɪŋ] ADJ appetitlich
movable [ˈmuːvəbl] ADJ beweglich; **~ feast** beweglicher Feiertag *m*
move [muːv] N (*movement*) Bewegung *f*; (*in game*) Zug *m*; (*change: of house*) Umzug *m*; (*: of job*) Stellenwechsel *m* ▸ VT bewegen; (*furniture*) (ver)rücken; (*car*) umstellen; (*in game*) ziehen mit; (*emotionally*) bewegen, ergreifen; (*Pol: resolution etc*) beantragen ▸ VI sich bewegen; (*traffic*) vorankommen; (*in game*) ziehen; (*also*: **move house**) umziehen; (*develop*) sich entwickeln; **it's my ~** ich bin am Zug; **to get a ~ on** sich beeilen; **to ~ sb to do sth** jdn (dazu) veranlassen, etw zu tun; **to ~ towards** sich nähern *+dat*
▸ **move about** VI sich (hin- und her)bewegen; (*travel*) unterwegs sein; (*from place to place*) umherziehen; (*change residence*) umziehen; (*change job*) die Stelle wechseln; **I can hear him moving about** ich höre ihn herumlaufen
▸ **move along** VI weitergehen
▸ **move around** VI = **move about**
▸ **move away** VI (*from town, area*) wegziehen
▸ **move back** VI (*return*) zurückkommen
▸ **move forward** VI (*advance*) vorrücken
▸ **move in** VI (*to house*) einziehen; (*police, soldiers*) anrücken
▸ **move off** VI (*car*) abfahren
▸ **move on** VI (*leave*) weitergehen; (*travel*) weiterfahren ▸ VT (*onlookers*) zum Weitergehen auffordern
▸ **move out** VI (*of house*) ausziehen
▸ **move over** VI (*to make room*) (zur Seite) rücken
▸ **move up** VI (*employee*) befördert werden; (*pupil*) versetzt werden; (*deputy*) aufrücken
moveable [ˈmuːvəbl] ADJ = **movable**
movement [ˈmuːvmənt] N (*action, group*) Bewegung *f*; (*freedom to move*) Bewegungsfreiheit *f*; (*transportation*) Beförderung *f*; (*shift*) Trend *m*; (*Mus*) Satz *m*; (*Med: also*: **bowel movement**) Stuhlgang *m*
mover [ˈmuːvəʳ] N (*of proposal*) Antragsteller(in) *m(f)*
movie [ˈmuːvɪ] N Film *m*; **to go to the movies** ins Kino gehen
movie camera N Filmkamera *f*
moviegoer [ˈmuːvɪgəuəʳ] (US) N Kinogänger(in) *m(f)*
moving [ˈmuːvɪŋ] ADJ beweglich; (*emotional*) ergreifend; (*instigating*): **the ~ spirit/force** die treibende Kraft
mow [məu] (*pt* **mowed**, *pp* **mowed** *or* **mown**) VT mähen
▸ **mow down** VT (*kill*) niedermähen
mower [ˈməuəʳ] N (*also*: **lawnmower**) Rasenmäher *m*
Mozambique [məuzəmˈbiːk] N Mosambik *nt*
MP N ABBR (= *Member of Parliament*) ≈ MdB; = **military police**; (CANADA: = *Mounted Police*) berittene Polizei *f*
MP3 ABBR (*Comput*) MP3
MP3 player N (*Comput*) MP3-Spieler *m*
mpg N ABBR (= *miles per gallon*) *see* **mile**
mph ABBR (= *miles per hour*) Meilen pro Stunde
MPhil N ABBR (= *Master of Philosophy*) ≈ M.A.
MPS (BRIT) N ABBR (= *Member of the Pharmaceutical Society*) *Qualifikationsnachweis für Pharmazeuten*
Mr, (US) **Mr.** [ˈmɪstəʳ] N: **Mr Smith** Herr Smith
MRC (BRIT) N ABBR (= *Medical Research Council*) *medizinischer Forschungsausschuss*
MRCP (BRIT) N ABBR (= *Member of the Royal College of Physicians*) *höchster akademischer Grad in Medizin*
MRCS (BRIT) N ABBR (= *Member of the Royal College of Surgeons*) *höchster akademischer Grad für Chirurgen*
MRCVS (BRIT) N ABBR (= *Member of the Royal College of Veterinary Surgeons*) *höchster akademischer Grad für Tiermediziner*
Mrs, (US) **Mrs.** [ˈmɪsɪz] N: **~ Smith** Frau Smith
MS N ABBR (= *multiple sclerosis*) MS *f*; (US: = *Master of Science*) *akademischer Grad in Naturwissenschaften* ▸ ABBR (*US Post*) = **Mississippi**
Ms, (US) **Ms.** [mɪz] N (= *Miss or Mrs*): **Ms Smith** Frau Smith
MS. (*pl* **MSS.**) N ABBR (= *manuscript*) Ms.
MSA (US) N ABBR (= *Master of Science in Agriculture*) *akademischer Grad in Agronomie*
MSc N ABBR (= *Master of Science*) *akademischer Grad in Naturwissenschaften*

m

MSG N ABBR = **monosodium glutamate**
MSP (BRIT) N ABBR (*Pol: = Member of the Scottish Parliament*) Abgeordnete(r) *f*(*m*) des schottischen Parlaments
MST (US) ABBR (= *Mountain Standard Time*) *amerikanische Standardzeitzone*
MSW (US) N ABBR (= *Master of Social Work*) *akademischer Grad in Sozialwissenschaft*
MT N ABBR (*Comput, Ling: = machine translation*) maschinelle Übersetzung *f*
Mt ABBR (*Geog*) = **mount**
MTV (*esp US*) N ABBR (= *music television*) MTV *nt*

KEYWORD

much [mʌtʃ] ADJ (*time, money, effort*) viel; **how much money/time do you need?** wie viel Geld/Zeit brauchen Sie?; **he's done so much work for us** er hat so viel für uns gearbeitet; **as much as** so viel wie; **I have as much money/intelligence as you** ich besitze genauso viel Geld/Intelligenz wie du
▸ PRON viel; **how much is it?** was kostet es?
▸ ADV **1** (*greatly, a great deal*) sehr; **thank you very much** vielen Dank, danke sehr; **I read as much as I can** ich lese so viel wie ich kann
2 (*by far*) viel; **I'm much better now** mir geht es jetzt viel besser
3 (*almost*) fast; **how are you feeling? — much the same** wie fühlst du dich? — fast genauso; **the two books are much the same** die zwei Bücher sind sich sehr ähnlich

muck [mʌk] N (*dirt*) Dreck *m*
▸ **muck about** (*inf*) VI (*fool about*) herumalbern
▸ VT: **to ~ sb about** mit jdm beliebig umspringen
▸ **muck around** VI = **muck about**
▸ **muck in** (BRIT *inf*) VI mit anpacken
▸ **muck out** VT (*stable*) ausmisten
▸ **muck up** (*inf*) VT (*exam etc*) verpfuschen
muckraking ['mʌkreɪkɪŋ] (*fig: inf*) N Sensationsmache *f* ▸ ADJ sensationslüstern
mucky ['mʌkɪ] ADJ (*dirty*) dreckig; (*field*) matschig
mucus ['mju:kəs] N Schleim *m*
mud [mʌd] N Schlamm *m*
muddle ['mʌdl] N (*mess*) Durcheinander *nt*; (*confusion*) Verwirrung *f* ▸ VT (*person*) verwirren; (*also*: **muddle up**) durcheinanderbringen; **to be in a ~** völlig durcheinander sein; **to get in a ~** (*person*) konfus werden; (*things*) durcheinandergeraten
▸ **muddle along** VI vor sich *acc* hin wursteln
▸ **muddle through** VI (*get by*) sich durchschlagen
muddled ADJ konfus
muddle-headed [mʌdl'hɛdɪd] ADJ zerstreut
muddy ['mʌdɪ] ADJ (*floor*) schmutzig; (*field*) schlammig
mud flats NPL Watt(enmeer) *nt*
mudguard ['mʌdgɑ:d] (BRIT) N Schutzblech *nt*
mudpack ['mʌdpæk] N Schlammpackung *f*
mud-slinging ['mʌdslɪŋɪŋ] N (*fig*) Schlechtmacherei *f*

muesli ['mju:zlɪ] N Müsli *nt*
muffin ['mʌfɪn] N (BRIT) *weiches, flaches Milchbrötchen, meist warm gegessen*; (US) *kleiner runder Rührkuchen*
muffle ['mʌfl] VT (*sound*) dämpfen; (*against cold*) einmummeln
muffled ['mʌfld] ADJ gedämpft; eingemummelt
muffler ['mʌflə^r] N (*US Aut*) Auspufftopf *m*; (*scarf*) dicker Schal *m*
mufti ['mʌftɪ] N: **in ~** in Zivil
mug [mʌg] N (*cup*) Becher *m*; (*for beer*) Krug *m*; (*inf: face*) Visage *f*; (*: fool*) Trottel *m* ▸ VT (auf der Straße) überfallen; **it's a ~'s game** (BRIT) das ist doch Schwachsinn
▸ **mug up** (BRIT *inf*) VT (*also*: **mug up on**) pauken
mugger ['mʌgə^r] N Straßenräuber *m*
mugging ['mʌgɪŋ] N Straßenraub *m*
muggins ['mʌgɪnz] (BRIT *inf*) N Dummkopf *m*; **... and ~ does all the work** ... und ich bin mal wieder der/die Dumme und mache die ganze Arbeit
muggy ['mʌgɪ] ADJ (*weather, day*) schwül
mug shot (*inf*) N (*of criminal*) Verbrecherfoto *nt*; (*for passport*) Passbild *nt*
mulatto [mju:'lætəu] (*pl* **mulattoes**) N Mulatte *m*, Mulattin *f*
mulberry ['mʌlbrɪ] N (*fruit*) Maulbeere *f*; (*tree*) Maulbeerbaum *m*
mule [mju:l] N Maultier *nt*
mulled [mʌld] ADJ: **~ wine** Glühwein *m*
mullioned ['mʌlɪənd] ADJ (*windows*) längs unterteilt
mull over [mʌl-] VT sich *dat* durch den Kopf gehen lassen
multi... ['mʌltɪ] PREF multi-, Multi-
multi-access ['mʌltɪ'æksɛs] ADJ (*Comput: system etc*) Mehrplatz-
multicoloured, (US) **multicolored** ['mʌltɪkʌləd] ADJ mehrfarbig
multicultural ADJ multikulturell
multifarious [mʌltɪ'fɛərɪəs] ADJ vielfältig
multifocals ['mʌltɪfəuklz] NPL Gleitsichtgläser *pl*
multilateral [mʌltɪ'lætərl] ADJ multilateral
multi-level ['mʌltɪlɛvl] (US) ADJ = **multistorey**
multilingual ADJ mehrsprachig
multimillionaire [mʌltɪmɪljə'nɛə^r] N Multimillionär *m*
multinational [mʌltɪ'næʃənl] ADJ multinational ▸ N multinationaler Konzern *m*, Multi *m* (*inf*)
multiple ['mʌltɪpl] ADJ (*injuries*) mehrfach; (*interests, causes*) vielfältig ▸ N Vielfache(s) *nt*; **~ collision** Massenkarambolage *f*
multiple-choice ['mʌltɪpltʃɔɪs] ADJ (*question etc*) Multiple-Choice-
multiple sclerosis N multiple Sklerose *f*
multiplex ['mʌltɪplɛks] N: **~ transmitter** Multiplexsender *m*; **~ (cinema)** Multiplexkino *nt* ▸ ADJ (*Tech*) Mehrfach- ▸ VT (*Tel*) gleichzeitig senden
multiplication [mʌltɪplɪ'keɪʃən] N Multiplikation *f*; (*increase*) Vervielfachung *f*

multiplication table N Multiplikationstabelle *f*
multiplicity [mʌltɪ'plɪsɪtɪ] N: **a ~ of** eine Vielzahl von
multiply ['mʌltɪplaɪ] VT multiplizieren ▸ VI (*increase: problems*) stark zunehmen; (*: number*) sich vervielfachen; (*breed*) sich vermehren
multi-purpose ['mʌltɪ'pɜːpəs] ADJ Mehrzweck-
multiracial [mʌltɪ'reɪʃl] ADJ gemischtrassig; (*school*) ohne Rassentrennung; **~ policy** Politik *f* der Rassenintegration
multistorey [mʌltɪ'stɔːrɪ] (BRIT) ADJ (*building, car park*) mehrstöckig
multitude ['mʌltɪtjuːd] N Menge *f*; **a ~ of** eine Vielzahl von, eine Menge
mum [mʌm] (BRIT *inf*) N Mutti *f*, Mama *f* ▸ ADJ: **to keep ~** den Mund halten; **~'s the word** nichts verraten!
mumble ['mʌmbl] VT, VI (*indistinctly*) nuscheln; (*quietly*) murmeln
mumbo jumbo ['mʌmbəu-] N (*nonsense*) Geschwafel *nt*
mummify ['mʌmɪfaɪ] VT mumifizieren
mummy ['mʌmɪ] N (BRIT: *mother*) Mami *f*; (*embalmed body*) Mumie *f*
mumps [mʌmps] N Mumps *m or f*
munch [mʌntʃ] VT, VI mampfen
mundane [mʌn'deɪn] ADJ (*life*) banal; (*task*) stumpfsinnig
Munich ['mjuːnɪk] N München *nt*
municipal [mjuː'nɪsɪpl] ADJ städtisch, Stadt-; (*elections, administration*) Kommunal-
municipality [mjuːnɪsɪ'pælɪtɪ] N Gemeinde *f*, Stadt *f*
munitions [mjuː'nɪʃənz] NPL Munition *f*
mural ['mjuərl] N Wandgemälde *nt*
murder ['məːdə^r] N Mord *m* ▸ VT ermorden; (*spoil: piece of music, language*) verhunzen; **to commit ~** einen Mord begehen
murderer ['məːdərə^r] N Mörder *m*
murderess ['məːdərɪs] N Mörderin *f*
murderous ['məːdərəs] ADJ blutrünstig; (*attack*) Mord-; (*fig: look, attack*) vernichtend; (*: pace, heat*) mörderisch
murk [məːk] N Düsternis *f*
murky ['məːkɪ] ADJ düster; (*water*) trübe
murmur ['məːmə^r] N (*of voices*) Murmeln *nt*; (*of wind, waves*) Rauschen *nt* ▸ VT, VI murmeln; **heart ~** Herzgeräusche *pl*
MusB, MusBac N ABBR (= *Bachelor of Music*) *akademischer Grad in Musikwissenschaft*
muscle ['mʌsl] N Muskel *m*; (*fig: strength*) Macht *f*
▸ **muscle in** VI: **to ~ in (on sth)** (bei etw) mitmischen
muscular ['mʌskjulə^r] ADJ (*pain, dystrophy*) Muskel-; (*person, build*) muskulös
muscular dystrophy N Muskeldystrophie *f*
MusD, MusDoc N ABBR (= *Doctor of Music*) *Doktorat in Musikwissenschaft*
muse [mjuːz] VI nachgrübeln ▸ N Muse *f*
museum [mjuː'zɪəm] N Museum *nt*
mush [mʌʃ] N Brei *m*; (*pej*) Schmalz *m*
mushroom ['mʌʃrum] N (*edible*) (essbarer) Pilz *m*; (*poisonous*) Giftpilz *m*; (*button mushroom*) Champignon *m* ▸ VI (*fig: buildings etc*) aus dem Boden schießen; (*: town, organization*) explosionsartig wachsen
mushroom cloud N Atompilz *m*
mushy ['mʌʃɪ] ADJ matschig; (*consistency*) breiig; (*inf: sentimental*) rührselig; **~ peas** Erbsenbrei *m*
music ['mjuːzɪk] N Musik *f*; (*written music, score*) Noten *pl*
musical ['mjuːzɪkl] ADJ musikalisch; (*sound, tune*) melodisch ▸ N Musical *nt*
musical box N = **music box**
musical chairs N die Reise *f* nach Jerusalem
musical instrument N Musikinstrument *nt*
musically ADV musikalisch
music box N Spieldose *f*
music centre N Musikcenter *nt*
music hall N Varieté *nt*
musician [mjuː'zɪʃən] N Musiker(in) *m(f)*
music stand N Notenständer *m*
musk [mʌsk] N Moschus *m*
musket ['mʌskɪt] N Muskete *f*
muskrat ['mʌskræt] N Bisamratte *f*
musk rose N Moschusrose *f*
Muslim ['mʌzlɪm] ADJ moslemisch ▸ N Moslem *m*, Moslime *f*
muslin ['mʌzlɪn] N Musselin *m*
musquash ['mʌskwɔʃ] N Bisamratte *f*; (*fur*) Bisam *m*
mussel ['mʌsl] N (Mies)muschel *f*
must [mʌst] AUX VB müssen; (*in negative*) dürfen ▸ N Muss *nt*; **I ~ do it** ich muss es tun; **you ~ not do that** das darfst du nicht tun; **he ~ be there by now** jetzt müsste er schon dort sein; **you ~ come and see me soon** Sie müssen mich bald besuchen; **why ~ he behave so badly?** warum muss er sich so schlecht benehmen?; **I ~ have made a mistake** ich muss mich geirrt haben; **the film is a ~** den Film muss man unbedingt gesehen haben
mustache ['mʌstæʃ] (US) N = **moustache**
mustard ['mʌstəd] N Senf *m*
mustard gas N (*Mil*) Senfgas *nt*
muster ['mʌstə^r] VT (*support*) zusammenbekommen; (*energy, strength, courage: also:* **muster up**) aufbringen; (*troops, members*) antreten lassen ▸ N: **to pass ~** den Anforderungen genügen
mustiness ['mʌstɪnɪs] N Muffigkeit *f*
mustn't ['mʌsnt] = **must not**
musty ['mʌstɪ] ADJ muffig; (*building*) moderig
mutant ['mjuːtənt] N Mutante *f*
mutate [mjuː'teɪt] VI (*Biol*) mutieren
mutation [mjuː'teɪʃən] N (*Biol*) Mutation *f*; (*alteration*) Veränderung *f*
mute [mjuːt] ADJ stumm
muted ['mjuːtɪd] ADJ (*colour*) gedeckt; (*reaction, criticism*) verhalten; (*sound, trumpet, Mus*) gedämpft
mutilate ['mjuːtɪleɪt] VT verstümmeln

m

mutilation [mju:tɪ'leɪʃən] N Verstümmelung *f*
mutinous ['mju:tɪnəs] ADJ meuterisch; (*attitude*) rebellisch
mutiny ['mju:tɪnɪ] N Meuterei *f* ▶ VI meutern
mutter ['mʌtəʳ] VT, VI murmeln
mutton ['mʌtn] N Hammelfleisch *nt*
mutual ['mju:tʃuəl] ADJ (*feeling, attraction*) gegenseitig; (*benefit*) beiderseitig; (*interest, friend*) gemeinsam; **the feeling was ~** das beruhte auf Gegenseitigkeit
mutually ['mju:tʃuəlɪ] ADV (*beneficial, satisfactory*) für beide Seiten; (*accepted*) von beiden Seiten; **to be ~ exclusive** einander ausschließen; **~ incompatible** nicht miteinander vereinbar
Muzak® ['mju:zæk] N Berieselungsmusik *f* (*inf*)
muzzle ['mʌzl] N (*of dog*) Maul *nt*; (*of gun*) Mündung *f*; (*guard: for dog*) Maulkorb *m* ▶ VT (*dog*) einen Maulkorb anlegen *+dat*; (*fig: press, person*) mundtot machen
MV ABBR (= *motor vessel*) MS
MVP (US) N ABBR (*Sport: = most valuable player*) wertvollster Spieler *m*, wertvollste Spielerin *f*
MW ABBR (*Radio: = medium wave*) MW

KEYWORD

my [maɪ] ADJ mein(e); **this is my brother/sister/house** das ist mein Bruder/meine Schwester/mein Haus; **I've washed my hair/cut my finger** ich habe mir die Haare gewaschen/mir *or* mich in den Finger geschnitten; **is this my pen or yours?** ist das mein Stift oder deiner?

Myanmar ['maɪænma:ʳ] N Myanmar *nt*
myopic [maɪ'ɔpɪk] ADJ (*Med, fig*) kurzsichtig
myriad ['mɪrɪəd] N Unzahl *f*
myrrh [mə:ʳ] N Myrr(h)e *f*
myself [maɪ'sɛlf] PRON (*acc*) mich; (*dat*) mir; (*emphatic*) selbst; *see also* **oneself**
mysterious [mɪs'tɪərɪəs] ADJ geheimnisvoll, mysteriös
mysteriously [mɪs'tɪərɪəslɪ] ADV auf mysteriöse Weise; (*smile*) geheimnisvoll
mystery ['mɪstərɪ] N (*puzzle*) Rätsel *nt*; (*strangeness*) Rätselhaftigkeit *f* ▶ CPD (*guest, voice*) mysteriös; **~ tour** Fahrt *f* ins Blaue
mystery caller N Testanrufer(in) *m(f)*
mystery calling N Testanruf *m*
mystery shopper N Testkäufer(in) *m(f)*
mystery story N Kriminalgeschichte *f*
mystery visitor N Testbesucher(in) *m(f)*
mystic ['mɪstɪk] N Mystiker(in) *m(f)* ▶ ADJ mystisch
mystical ['mɪstɪkl] ADJ mystisch
mystify ['mɪstɪfaɪ] VT vor ein Rätsel stellen
mystique [mɪs'ti:k] N geheimnisvoller Nimbus *m*
myth [mɪθ] N Mythos *m*; (*fallacy*) Märchen *nt*
mythical ['mɪθɪkl] ADJ mythisch; (*jobs, opportunities etc*) fiktiv
mythological [mɪθə'lɔdʒɪkl] ADJ mythologisch
mythology [mɪ'θɔlədʒɪ] N Mythologie *f*

Nn

N¹, n [ɛn] N (*letter*) N *nt*, n *nt*; **N for Nellie, N for Nan** (*US*) ≈ N wie Nordpol
N² [ɛn] ABBR (= *north*) N
NA (*US*) N ABBR (= *Narcotics Anonymous*) *Hilfsorganisation für Drogensüchtige*; (= *National Academy*) *Dachverband verschiedener Forschungsunternehmen*
n/a ABBR (= *not applicable*) entf.
NAACP (*US*) N ABBR (= *National Association for the Advancement of Colored People*) *Vereinigung zur Förderung Farbiger*
NAAFI ['næfɪ] (BRIT) N ABBR (= *Navy, Army & Air Force Institutes*) *Laden für britische Armeeangehörige*
NACU (*US*) N ABBR (= *National Association of Colleges and Universities*) *Fachhochschul- und Universitätsverband*
nadir ['neɪdɪəʳ] N (*fig*) Tiefstpunkt *m*; (*Astron*) Nadir *m*
NAFTA N ABBR (= *North Atlantic Free Trade Agreement*) *amerikanische Freihandelszone*
nag [næg] VT herumnörgeln an *+dat* ▶ VI nörgeln ▶ N (*pej: horse*) Gaul *m*; (*: person*) Nörgler(in) *m(f)*; **to ~ at sb** jdn plagen, jdm keine Ruhe lassen
nagging ['nægɪŋ] ADJ (*doubt, suspicion*) quälend; (*pain*) dumpf
nail [neɪl] N Nagel *m* ▶ VT (*inf: thief etc*) drankriegen; (*: fraud*) aufdecken; **to ~ sth to sth** etw an etw *acc* nageln; **to ~ sb down (to sth)** jdn (auf etw *acc*) festnageln
nailbrush ['neɪlbrʌʃ] N Nagelbürste *f*
nail clippers NPL Nagelknipser *m*
nailfile ['neɪlfaɪl] N Nagelfeile *f*
nail polish N Nagellack *m*
nail polish remover N Nagellackentferner *m*
nail scissors NPL Nagelschere *f*
nail varnish (BRIT) N = **nail polish**
Nairobi [naɪ'rəubɪ] N Nairobi *nt*
naive [nɑː'iːv] ADJ naiv
naïveté [nɑːiːv'teɪ] N = **naivety**
naivety [naɪ'iːvtɪ] N Naivität *f*
naked ['neɪkɪd] ADJ nackt; (*flame, light*) offen; **with the ~ eye** mit bloßem Auge; **to the ~ eye** für das bloße Auge
nakedness ['neɪkɪdnɪs] N Nacktheit *f*
NAM (*US*) N ABBR (= *National Association of Manufacturers*) *nationaler Verband der verarbeitenden Industrie*
name [neɪm] N Name *m* ▶ VT nennen; (*ship*) taufen; (*identify*) (beim Namen) nennen; (*date etc*) bestimmen, festlegen; **what's your ~?** wie heißen Sie?; **my ~ is Peter** ich heiße Peter; **by ~** mit Namen; **in the ~ of** im Namen *+gen*; **to give one's ~ and address** Namen und Adresse angeben; **to make a ~ for o.s.** sich *dat* einen Namen machen; **to give sb a bad ~** jdn in Verruf bringen; **to call sb names** jdn beschimpfen; **to be named after sb/sth** nach jdm/etw benannt werden
name-dropping ['neɪmdrɔpɪŋ] N Angeberei *f* mit berühmten Namen
nameless ['neɪmlɪs] ADJ namenlos; **who/which shall remain ~** der/die/das ungenannt bleiben soll
namely ['neɪmlɪ] ADV nämlich
nameplate ['neɪmpleɪt] N Namensschild *nt*
namesake ['neɪmseɪk] N Namensvetter(in) *m(f)*
nan bread [nɑːn-] N Nan-Brot *nt*, *fladenförmiges Weißbrot als Beilage zu indischen Gerichten*
nanny ['nænɪ] N Kindermädchen *nt*
nanny-goat ['nænɪgəut] N Geiß *f*
nap [næp] N Schläfchen *nt*; (*of fabric*) Strich *m* ▶ VI: **to be caught napping** (*fig*) überrumpelt werden; **to have a ~** ein Schläfchen *or* ein Nickerchen (*inf*) machen
NAPA (*US*) N ABBR (= *National Association of Performing Artists*) *Künstlergewerkschaft*
napalm ['neɪpɑːm] N Napalm *nt*
nape [neɪp] N: **the ~ of the neck** der Nacken
napkin ['næpkɪn] N (*also:* **table napkin**) Serviette *f*
Naples ['neɪplz] N Neapel *nt*
Napoleonic [nəpəulɪ'ɔnɪk] ADJ napoleonisch
nappy ['næpɪ] (BRIT) N Windel *f*
nappy liner (BRIT) N Windeleinlage *f*
nappy rash N Wundsein *nt*
narcissistic [nɑːsɪ'sɪstɪk] ADJ narzisstisch
narcissus [nɑː'sɪsəs] (*pl* **narcissi** [-saɪ]) N Narzisse *f*
narcotic [nɑː'kɔtɪk] ADJ narkotisch ▶ N Narkotikum *nt*; **narcotics** NPL (*drugs*) Drogen *pl*; **~ drug** Rauschgift *nt*
nark [nɑːk] (BRIT *inf*) VT: **to be narked at sth** sauer über etw *acc* sein
narrate [nə'reɪt] VT erzählen; (*film, programme*) kommentieren

narration [nəˈreɪʃən] N Kommentar *m*
narrative [ˈnærətɪv] N Erzählung *f*; (*of journey etc*) Schilderung *f*
narrator [nəˈreɪtəʳ] N Erzähler(in) *m(f)*; (*in film etc*) Kommentator(in) *m(f)*
narrow [ˈnærəu] ADJ eng; (*ledge etc*) schmal; (*majority, advantage, victory, defeat*) knapp; (*ideas, view*) engstirnig ▸ VI sich verengen; (*gap, difference*) sich verringern ▸ VT (*gap, difference*) verringern; (*eyes*) zusammenkneifen; **to have a ~ escape** mit knapper Not davonkommen; **to ~ sth down (to sth)** etw (auf etw *acc*) beschränken
narrow gauge [ˈnærəugeɪdʒ] ADJ (*Rail*) Schmalspur-
narrowly [ˈnærəulɪ] ADV knapp; (*escape*) mit knapper Not
narrow-minded [nærəuˈmaɪndɪd] ADJ engstirnig
NAS (*US*) N ABBR (= *National Academy of Sciences*) *Akademie der Wissenschaften*
NASA [ˈnæsə] (*US*) N ABBR (= *National Aeronautics and Space Administration*) NASA *f*
nasal [ˈneɪzl] ADJ Nasen-; (*voice*) näselnd
Nassau [ˈnæsɔː] N Nassau *nt*
nastily [ˈnɑːstɪlɪ] ADV gemein; (*say*) gehässig
nastiness [ˈnɑːstɪnɪs] N Gemeinheit *f*; (*of remark*) Gehässigkeit *f*; (*of smell, taste etc*) Ekelhaftigkeit *f*
nasturtium [nəsˈtəːʃəm] N Kapuzinerkresse *f*
nasty [ˈnɑːstɪ] ADJ (*remark*) gehässig; (*person*) gemein; (*taste, smell*) ekelhaft; (*wound, disease, accident, shock*) schlimm; (*problem, question*) schwierig; (*weather, temper*) abscheulich; **to turn ~** unangenehm werden; **it's a ~ business** es ist schrecklich; **he's got a ~ temper** mit ihm ist nicht gut Kirschen essen
NAS/UWT (*Brit*) N ABBR (= *National Association of Schoolmasters/Union of Women Teachers*) *Lehrergewerkschaft*
nation [ˈneɪʃən] N Nation *f*; (*people*) Volk *nt*
national [ˈnæʃənl] ADJ (*character, flag*) National-; (*interests*) Staats-; (*newspaper*) überregional ▸ N Staatsbürger(in) *m(f)*; **foreign ~** Ausländer(in) *m(f)*
national anthem N Nationalhymne *f*
National Curriculum N *zentraler Lehrplan für Schulen in England und Wales*
national debt N Staatsverschuldung *f*
national dress N Nationaltracht *f*
National Guard (*US*) N Nationalgarde *f*
National Health Service N (*Brit*) Staatlicher Gesundheitsdienst *m*
National Insurance N (*Brit*) Sozialversicherung *f*
nationalism [ˈnæʃnəlɪzəm] N Nationalismus *m*
nationalist [ˈnæʃnəlɪst] ADJ nationalistisch ▸ N Nationalist(in) *m(f)*
nationality [næʃəˈnælɪtɪ] N Staatsangehörigkeit *f*, Nationalität *f*
nationalization [næʃnəlaɪˈzeɪʃən] N Verstaatlichung *f*
nationalize [ˈnæʃnəlaɪz] VT verstaatlichen
National Lottery N ≈ Lotto *nt*
nationally [ˈnæʃnəlɪ] ADV landesweit
national park N Nationalpark *m*
national press N überregionale Presse *f*
National Security Council (*US*) N Nationaler Sicherheitsrat *m*
national service N Wehrdienst *m*
National Trust (*Brit*) N *Organisation zum Schutz historischer Bauten und Denkmäler sowie zum Landschaftsschutz*

> Der **National Trust** ist ein 1895 gegründeter Natur- und Denkmalschutzverband in Großbritannien, der Gebäude und Gelände von besonderem historischem oder ästhetischem Interesse erhält und der Öffentlichkeit zugänglich macht. Viele Gebäude im Besitz des National Trust sind (z. T. gegen ein Eintrittsgeld) zu besichtigen.

nationwide [ˈneɪʃənwaɪd] ADJ, ADV landesweit
native [ˈneɪtɪv] N Einheimische(r) *f(m)* ▸ ADJ einheimisch; (*country*) Heimat-; (*language*) Mutter-; (*innate*) angeboren; **a ~ of Germany, a ~ German** ein gebürtiger Deutscher, eine gebürtige Deutsche; **~ to** beheimatet in *+dat*
Native American ADJ indianisch, der Ureinwohner Amerikas ▸ N Ureinwohner(in) *m(f)* Amerikas
native speaker N Muttersprachler(in) *m(f)*
Nativity [nəˈtɪvɪtɪ] N: **the ~** Christi Geburt *f*
nativity play N Krippenspiel *nt*
NATO [ˈneɪtəu] N ABBR (= *North Atlantic Treaty Organization*) NATO *f*
natter [ˈnætəʳ] (*Brit*) VI quatschen (*inf*) ▸ N: **to have a ~** einen Schwatz halten
natural [ˈnætʃrəl] ADJ natürlich; (*disaster*) Natur-; (*innate*) angeboren; (*born*) geboren; (*Mus*) ohne Vorzeichen; **to die of ~ causes** eines natürlichen Todes sterben; **~ foods** Naturkost *f*; **she played F ~ not F sharp** sie spielte f statt fis
natural childbirth N natürliche Geburt *f*
natural gas N Erdgas *nt*
natural history N Naturkunde *f*; **the ~ of England** die Naturgeschichte Englands
naturalist [ˈnætʃrəlɪst] N Naturforscher(in) *m(f)*
naturalize [ˈnætʃrəlaɪz] VT: **to become naturalized** eingebürgert werden
naturally [ˈnætʃrəlɪ] ADV natürlich; (*happen*) auf natürlichem Wege; (*die*) eines natürlichen Todes; (*occur, cheerful, talented, blonde*) von Natur aus
naturalness [ˈnætʃrəlnɪs] N Natürlichkeit *f*
natural resources NPL Naturschätze *pl*
natural selection N natürliche Auslese *f*
natural wastage N natürliche Personalreduzierung *f*
nature [ˈneɪtʃəʳ] N (*also*: **Nature**) Natur *f*; (*kind, sort*) Art *f*; (*character*) Wesen *nt*; **by ~** von Natur aus; **by its (very) ~** naturgemäß; **documents of a confidential ~** Unterlagen vertraulicher Art

-natured ['neɪtʃəd] SUFF: **good~** gutmütig; **ill~** bösartig
nature reserve (BRIT) N Naturschutzgebiet *nt*
nature trail N Naturlehrpfad *m*
naturist ['neɪtʃərɪst] N Anhänger(in) *m(f)* der Freikörperkultur
naught [nɔːt] N = **nought**
naughtiness ['nɔːtɪnɪs] N Unartigkeit *f*, Ungezogenheit *f*; Unanständigkeit *f*
naughty ['nɔːtɪ] ADJ (*child*) unartig, ungezogen; (*story, film, words*) unanständig
nausea ['nɔːsɪə] N Übelkeit *f*
nauseate ['nɔːsɪeɪt] VT Übelkeit verursachen *+dat*; (*fig*) anwidern
nauseating ['nɔːsɪeɪtɪŋ] ADJ ekelerregend; (*fig*) widerlich
nauseous ['nɔːsɪəs] ADJ ekelhaft; **I feel ~** mir ist übel
nautical ['nɔːtɪkl] ADJ (*chart*) See-; (*uniform*) Seemanns-
nautical mile N Seemeile *f*
naval ['neɪvl] ADJ Marine-; (*battle, forces*) See-
naval officer N Marineoffizier *m*
nave [neɪv] N Hauptschiff *nt*, Mittelschiff *nt*
navel ['neɪvl] N Nabel *m*
navel piercing ['neɪvl] N Nabelpiercing *nt*
navigable ['nævɪgəbl] ADJ schiffbar
navigate ['nævɪgeɪt] VT (*river*) befahren; (*path*) begehen ▸ VI navigieren; (*Aut*) den Fahrer dirigieren
navigation [nævɪ'geɪʃən] N Navigation *f*
navigator ['nævɪgeɪtəʳ] N (*Naut*) Steuermann *m*; (*Aviat*) Navigator(in) *m(f)*; (*Aut*) Beifahrer(in) *m(f)*
navvy ['nævɪ] (BRIT) N Straßenarbeiter *m*
navy ['neɪvɪ] N (Kriegs)marine *f*; (*ships*) (Kriegs)flotte *f* ▸ ADJ marineblau; **Department of the N~** (*US*) Marineministerium *nt*
navy-blue ['neɪvɪ'bluː] ADJ marineblau
Nazareth ['næzərɪθ] N Nazareth *nt*
Nazi ['nɑːtsɪ] N Nazi *m*
NB ABBR (= *nota bene*) NB; (CANADA) = **New Brunswick**
NBA (*US*) N ABBR (= *National Basketball Association*) *Basketball-Dachverband*; (= *National Boxing Association*) *Boxsport-Dachverband*
NBC (*US*) N ABBR (= *National Broadcasting Company*) *Fernsehsender*
NBS (*US*) N ABBR (= *National Bureau of Standards*) *amerikanischer Normenausschuss*
NC ABBR (*Comm etc*: = *no charge*) frei; (*US Post*) = **North Carolina**
NCC (*US*) N ABBR (= *National Council of Churches*) *Zusammenschluss protestantischer und orthodoxer Kirchen*
NCCL (BRIT) N ABBR (= *National Council for Civil Liberties*) *Organisation zum Schutz von Freiheitsrechten*
NCO N ABBR (*Mil*: = *noncommissioned officer*) Uffz.
ND (*US*) ABBR (*Post*) = **North Dakota**
N.Dak. (*US*) ABBR (*Post*) = **North Dakota**
NE ABBR = **north-east**; (*US Post*) = **New England**; **Nebraska**
NEA (*US*) N ABBR (= *National Education Association*) *Verband für das Erziehungswesen*
neap [niːp] N (*also*: **neap tide**) Nippflut *f*
Neapolitan [nɪə'pɔlɪtən] ADJ neapolitanisch ▸ N Neapolitaner(in) *m(f)*
near [nɪəʳ] ADJ nahe ▸ ADV nahe; (*almost*) fast, beinahe ▸ PREP (*also*: **near to**: *in space*) nahe an *+dat*; (: *in time*) um *acc* ... herum; (: *in situation, in intimacy*) nahe *+dat* ▸ VT sich nähern *+dat*; (*state, situation*) kurz vor *+dat* stehen; **Christmas is ~** bald ist Weihnachten; **£25,000 or nearest offer** (BRIT) £25.000 oder das nächstbeste Angebot; **in the ~ future** in naher Zukunft, bald; **in ~ darkness** fast im Dunkeln; **a ~ tragedy** beinahe eine Tragödie; **~ here/there** hier/dort in der Nähe; **to be ~ (to) doing sth** nahe daran sein, etw zu tun; **the building is nearing completion** der Bau steht kurz vor dem Abschluss
nearby [nɪə'baɪ] ADJ nahe gelegen ▸ ADV in der Nähe
Near East N: **the ~** der Nahe Osten
nearer ['nɪərəʳ] ADJ COMP, ADV COMP *of* **near**
nearest ['nɪərəst] SUPERL, ADV SUPERL *of* **near**
nearly ['nɪəlɪ] ADV fast; **I ~ fell** ich wäre beinahe gefallen; **it's not ~ big enough** es ist bei Weitem nicht groß genug; **she was ~ crying** sie war den Tränen nahe
near miss N Beinahezusammenstoß *m*; **that was a ~** (*shot*) das war knapp daneben
nearness ['nɪənɪs] N Nähe *f*
nearside ['nɪəsaɪd] (*Aut*) ADJ (*when driving on left*) linksseitig; (*when driving on right*) rechtsseitig ▸ N: **the ~** (*when driving on left*) die linke Seite; (*when driving on right*) die rechte Seite
near-sighted [nɪə'saɪtɪd] ADJ kurzsichtig
neat [niːt] ADJ ordentlich; (*handwriting*) sauber; (*plan, solution*) elegant; (*description*) prägnant; (*spirits*) pur; **I drink it ~** ich trinke es pur
neatly ['niːtlɪ] ADV ordentlich; (*conveniently*) sauber
neatness ['niːtnɪs] N Ordentlichkeit *f*; (*of solution, plan*) Sauberkeit *f*
Nebr. (*US*) ABBR (*Post*) = **Nebraska**
nebulous ['nɛbjuləs] ADJ vage, unklar
necessarily ['nɛsɪsrɪlɪ] ADV notwendigerweise; **not ~** nicht unbedingt
necessary ['nɛsɪsrɪ] ADJ notwendig, nötig; (*inevitable*) unausweichlich; **if ~** wenn nötig, nötigenfalls; **it is ~ to ...** man muss ...
necessitate [nɪ'sɛsɪteɪt] VT erforderlich machen
necessity [nɪ'sɛsɪtɪ] N Notwendigkeit *f*; **of ~** notgedrungen; **out of ~** aus Not; **the necessities (of life)** das Notwendigste (zum Leben)
neck [nɛk] N Hals *m*; (*of shirt, dress, jumper*) Ausschnitt *m* ▸ VI (*inf*) knutschen; **~ and ~** Kopf an Kopf; **to stick one's ~ out** (*inf*) seinen Kopf riskieren
necklace ['nɛklɪs] N (Hals)kette *f*
neckline ['nɛklaɪn] N Ausschnitt *m*
necktie ['nɛktaɪ] (*esp US*) N Krawatte *f*

n

nectar ['nɛktəʳ] N Nektar *m*
nectarine ['nɛktərɪn] N Nektarine *f*
née [neɪ] PREP: **~ Scott** geborene Scott
need [ni:d] N Bedarf *m*; (*necessity*) Notwendigkeit *f*; (*requirement*) Bedürfnis *nt*; (*poverty*) Not *f* ▶ VT brauchen; (*could do with*) nötig haben; **in ~** bedürftig; **to be in ~ of sth** etw nötig haben; **£10 will meet my immediate needs** mit £10 komme ich erst einmal aus; **(there's) no ~** (das ist) nicht nötig; **there's no ~ to get so worked up about it** du brauchst dich darüber nicht so aufzuregen; **he had no ~ to work** er hatte es nicht nötig zu arbeiten; **I ~ to do it** ich muss es tun; **you don't ~ to go, you needn't go** du brauchst nicht zu gehen; **a signature is needed** das bedarf einer Unterschrift *gen*
needle ['ni:dl] N Nadel *f* ▶ VT (*fig: inf: goad*) ärgern, piesacken
needless ['ni:dlɪs] ADJ unnötig; **~ to say** natürlich
needlessly ['ni:dlɪslɪ] ADV unnötig
needlework ['ni:dlwə:k] N Handarbeit *f*
needn't ['ni:dnt] = **need not**
needy ['ni:dɪ] ADJ bedürftig ▶ NPL: **the ~** die Bedürftigen *pl*
negation [nɪ'geɪʃən] N Verweigerung *f*
negative ['nɛgətɪv] ADJ negativ; (*answer*) abschlägig ▶ N (*Phot*) Negativ *nt*; (*Ling*) Verneinungswort *nt*, Negation *f*; **to answer in the ~** eine verneinende Antwort geben
negative equity N *Differenz zwischen gefallenem Wert und hypothekarischer Belastung eines Wohnungseigentums*
neglect [nɪ'glɛkt] VT vernachlässigen; (*writer, artist*) unterschätzen ▶ N Vernachlässigung *f*
neglected [nɪ'glɛktɪd] ADJ vernachlässigt; (*writer, artist*) unterschätzt
neglectful [nɪ'glɛktful] ADJ nachlässig; (*father*) pflichtvergessen; **to be ~ of sth** etw vernachlässigen
negligee ['nɛglɪʒeɪ] N Negligee *nt*, Negligé *nt*
negligence ['nɛglɪdʒəns] N Nachlässigkeit *f*; (*Law*) Fahrlässigkeit *f*
negligent ['nɛglɪdʒənt] ADJ nachlässig; (*Law*) fahrlässig; (*casual*) lässig
negligently ['nɛglɪdʒəntlɪ] ADV nachlässig; fahrlässig; lässig
negligible ['nɛglɪdʒɪbl] ADJ geringfügig
negotiable [nɪ'gəuʃɪəbl] ADJ verhandlungsfähig; (*path, river*) passierbar; **not ~** (*on cheque etc*) nicht übertragbar
negotiate [nɪ'gəuʃɪeɪt] VI verhandeln ▶ VT aushandeln; (*obstacle, hill*) überwinden; (*bend*) nehmen; **to ~ with sb (for sth)** mit jdm (über etw *acc*) verhandeln
negotiating table [nɪ'gəuʃɪeɪtɪŋ-] N Verhandlungstisch *m*
negotiation [nɪgəuʃɪ'eɪʃən] N Verhandlung *f*; **the matter is still under ~** über die Sache wird noch verhandelt
negotiator [nɪ'gəuʃɪeɪtəʳ] N Unterhändler(in) *m(f)*
Negress ['ni:grɪs] N Negerin *f*
Negro ['ni:grəu] (*pl* **Negroes**) ADJ (*boy, slave*) Neger- ▶ N Neger *m*
neigh [neɪ] VI wiehern
neighbour, (US) neighbor ['neɪbəʳ] N Nachbar(in) *m(f)*
neighbourhood ['neɪbəhud] N (*place*) Gegend *f*; (*people*) Nachbarschaft *f*; **in the ~ of …** in der Nähe von …; (*sum of money*) so um die …
neighbourhood watch N *Vereinigung von Bürgern, die Straßenwachen etc zur Unterstützung der Polizei bei der Verbrechensbekämpfung organisiert*
neighbouring ['neɪbərɪŋ] ADJ benachbart, Nachbar-
neighbourly ['neɪbəlɪ] ADJ nachbarlich
neither ['naɪðəʳ] CONJ: **I didn't move and ~ did John** ich bewegte mich nicht und John auch nicht ▶ PRON keine(r, s) (von beiden) ▶ ADV: **~ … nor …** weder … noch …; **~ story is true** keine der beiden Geschichten stimmt; **~ is true** beides stimmt nicht; **~ do I/have I** ich auch nicht
neo… ['ni:əu] PREF neo-, Neo-
neolithic [nɪə'lɪθɪk] ADV jungsteinzeitlich, neolithisch
neologism [nɪ'ɔlədʒɪzəm] N (Wort)neubildung *f*, Neologismus *m*
neon ['ni:ɔn] N Neon *nt*
neon light N Neonlampe *f*
neon sign N Neonreklame *f*
Nepal [nɪ'pɔ:l] N Nepal *nt*
nephew ['nɛvju:] N Neffe *m*
nepotism ['nɛpətɪzəm] N Vetternwirtschaft *f*
nerd [nə:d] (*inf*) N Schwachkopf *m*
nerve [nə:v] N (*Anat*) Nerv *m*; (*courage*) Mut *m*; (*impudence*) Frechheit *f*; **nerves** NPL (*anxiety*) Nervosität *f*; (*emotional strength*) Nerven *pl*; **he gets on my nerves** er geht mir auf die Nerven; **to lose one's ~** die Nerven verlieren
nerve-centre, (US) nerve-center ['nə:vsɛntəʳ] N (*fig*) Schaltzentrale *f*
nerve gas N Nervengas *nt*
nerve-racking ['nə:vrækɪŋ] ADJ nervenaufreibend
nervous ['nə:vəs] ADJ Nerven-, nervlich; (*anxious*) nervös; **to be ~ of/about** Angst haben vor +*dat*
nervous breakdown N Nervenzusammenbruch *m*
nervously ['nə:vəslɪ] ADV nervös
nervousness ['nə:vəsnɪs] N Nervosität *f*
nervous system N Nervensystem *nt*
nervous wreck (*inf*) N Nervenbündel *nt*; **to be a ~** mit den Nerven völlig am Ende sein
nervy ['nə:vɪ] (*inf*) ADJ (BRIT: *tense*) nervös; (*US: cheeky*) dreist
nest [nɛst] N Nest *nt* ▶ VI nisten; **a ~ of tables** ein Satz Tische *or* von Tischen
nest egg N Notgroschen *m*
nestle ['nɛsl] VI sich kuscheln; (*house*) eingebettet sein
nestling ['nɛstlɪŋ] N Nestling *m*
Net [nɛt] N: **the ~** (*Comput*) das Internet

net [nɛt] N Netz *nt*; (*fabric*) Tüll *m* ▶ ADJ (*Comm*) Netto-; (*final: result, effect*) End- ▶ VT (mit einem Netz) fangen; (*profit*) einbringen; (*deal, sale, fortune*) an Land ziehen; **~ of tax** steuerfrei; **he earns £10,000 ~ per year** er verdient £ 10.000 netto im Jahr; **it weighs 250g ~** es wiegt 250 g netto
netball ['nɛtbɔːl] N Netzball *m*
net curtains NPL Gardinen *pl*, Stores *pl*
Netherlands ['nɛðələndz] NPL: **the ~** die Niederlande *pl*
netiquette ['nɛtıkɛt] N Netiquette *f*
nett [nɛt] ADJ = **net**
netting ['nɛtıŋ] N (*for fence etc*) Maschendraht *m*; (*fabric*) Netzgewebe *nt*, Tüll *m*
nettle ['nɛtl] N Nessel *f*; **to grasp the ~** (*fig*) in den sauren Apfel beißen
network ['nɛtwəːk] N Netz *nt*; (*TV, Radio*) Sendenetz *nt* ▶ VT (*Radio, TV*) im ganzen Netzbereich ausstrahlen; (*computers*) in einem Netzwerk zusammenschließen
neuralgia [njuə'rældʒə] N Neuralgie *f*, Nervenschmerzen *pl*
neurological [njuərə'lɔdʒıkl] ADJ neurologisch
neurotic [njuə'rɔtık] ADJ neurotisch ▶ N Neurotiker(in) *m(f)*
neuter ['njuːtə^r] ADJ (*Ling*) sächlich ▶ VT kastrieren; (*female*) sterilisieren
neutral ['njuːtrəl] ADJ neutral ▶ N (*Aut*) Leerlauf *m*
neutrality [njuː'trælıtı] N Neutralität *f*
neutralize ['njuːtrəlaız] VT neutralisieren, aufheben
neutron ['njuːtrɔn] N Neutron *nt*
neutron bomb N Neutronenbombe *f*
Nev. (*US*) ABBR (*Post*) = **Nevada**
never ['nɛvə^r] ADV nie; (*not*) nicht; **~ in my life** noch nie; **~ again** nie wieder; **well I ~!** nein, so was!; *see also* **mind**
never-ending [nɛvər'ɛndıŋ] ADJ endlos
nevertheless [nɛvəðə'lɛs] ADV trotzdem, dennoch
new [njuː] ADJ neu; (*mother*) jung; **as good as ~** so gut wie neu; **to be ~ to sb** jdm neu sein
New Age N New Age *nt*
newbie ['njuːbı] (*inf*) N Neuling *m*
newborn ['njuːbɔːn] ADJ neugeboren
newcomer ['njuːkʌmə^r] N Neuankömmling *m*; (*in job*) Neuling *m*
new-fangled ['njuː'fæŋgld] (*pej*) ADJ neumodisch
new-found ['njuːfaund] ADJ neu entdeckt; (*confidence*) neu geschöpft
Newfoundland ['njuːfənlənd] N Neufundland *nt*
New Guinea N Neuguinea *nt*
newly ['njuːlı] ADV neu
newly-weds ['njuːlıwɛdz] NPL Neuvermählte *pl*, Frischvermählte *pl*
new moon N Neumond *m*
newness ['njuːnıs] N Neuheit *f*; (*of cheese, bread etc*) Frische *f*
New Orleans [-'ɔːliːənz] N New Orleans *nt*
news [njuːz] N Nachricht *f*; **a piece of ~** eine Neuigkeit; **the ~** (*Radio, TV*) die Nachrichten *pl*; **good/bad ~** gute/schlechte Nachrichten
news agency N Nachrichtenagentur *f*
newsagent ['njuːzeıdʒənt] (BRIT) N Zeitungshändler(in) *m(f)*
news bulletin N Bulletin *nt*
newscaster ['njuːzkɑːstə^r] N Nachrichtensprecher(in) *m(f)*
newsdealer ['njuːzdiːlə^r] (*US*) N = **newsagent**
newsflash ['njuːzflæʃ] N Kurzmeldung *f*
newsgroup N (*Comput*) Diskussionsforum *nt*, Newsgroup *f*
newsletter ['njuːzlɛtə^r] N Rundschreiben *nt*, Mitteilungsblatt *nt*
newspaper ['njuːzpeıpə^r] N Zeitung *f*; **daily/weekly ~** Tages-/Wochenzeitung *f*
newsprint ['njuːzprınt] N Zeitungspapier *nt*
newsreader ['njuːzriːdə^r] N = **newscaster**
newsreel ['njuːzriːl] N Wochenschau *f*
newsroom ['njuːzruːm] N Nachrichtenredaktion *f*; (*Radio, TV*) Nachrichtenstudio *nt*
newsstand ['njuːzstænd] N Zeitungsstand *m*
newsworthy ['njuːzwəːðı] ADJ: **to be ~** Neuigkeitswert haben
newt [njuːt] N Wassermolch *m*
new town (BRIT) N *neue, teilweise mit Regierungsgeldern errichtete städtische Siedlung*
New Year N neues Jahr *nt*; (*New Year's Day*) Neujahr *nt*; **Happy ~!** (ein) glückliches *or* frohes neues Jahr!
New Year's Day N Neujahr *nt*, Neujahrstag *m*
New Year's Eve N Silvester *nt*
New York [-'jɔːk] N New York *nt*; (*also*: **New York State**) der Staat New York
New Zealand [-'ziːlənd] N Neuseeland *nt* ▶ ADJ neuseeländisch
New Zealander [-'ziːləndə^r] N Neuseeländer(in) *m(f)*
next [nɛkst] ADJ nächste(r, s); (*room*) Neben- ▶ ADV dann; (*do, happen*) als Nächstes; (*afterwards*) danach; **the ~ day** am nächsten *or* folgenden Tag; **~ time** das nächste Mal; **~ year** nächstes Jahr; **~ please!** der Nächste bitte!; **who's ~?** wer ist der Nächste?; **"turn to the ~ page"** „bitte umblättern"; **the week after ~** übernächste Woche; **the ~ on the right/left** der/die/das Nächste rechts/links; **the ~ thing I knew** das Nächste, woran ich mich erinnern konnte; **~ to** neben *+dat*; **~ to nothing** so gut wie nichts; **when do we meet ~?** wann treffen wir uns wieder *or* das nächste Mal?; **the ~ best** der/die/das Nächstbeste
next door ADV nebenan ▶ ADJ: **next-door** nebenan; **the house ~** das Nebenhaus; **to go ~** nach nebenan gehen; **my next-door neighbour** mein direkter Nachbar
next-of-kin ['nɛkstəv'kın] N nächster Verwandter *m*, nächste Verwandte *f*
NF N ABBR (BRIT *Pol*: = *National Front*) *rechtsradikale Partei* ▶ ABBR (CANADA) = **Newfoundland**

n

NFL (*US*) N ABBR (= *National Football League*) *Fußball-Nationalliga*
NG (*US*) ABBR = **National Guard**
NGO N ABBR (= *nongovernmental organization*) *nichtstaatliche Organisation*
NH (*US*) ABBR (*Post*) = **New Hampshire**
NHL (*US*) N ABBR (= *National Hockey League*) *Hockey-Nationalliga*
NHS (*BRIT*) N ABBR = **National Health Service**
NI ABBR = **Northern Ireland**; (*BRIT*) = **National Insurance**
Niagara Falls [naɪ'ægərə-] NPL Niagarafälle *pl*
nib [nɪb] N Feder *f*
nibble ['nɪbl] VT knabbern; (*bite*) knabbern an *+dat* ▶ VI: **to ~ at** knabbern an *+dat*
Nicaragua [nɪkə'rægjuə] N Nicaragua *nt*
Nicaraguan [nɪkə'rægjuən] ADJ nicaraguanisch ▶ N Nicaraguaner(in) *m(f)*
Nice [ni:s] N Nizza *nt*
nice [naɪs] ADJ nett; (*holiday, weather, picture etc*) schön; (*taste*) gut; (*person, clothes etc*) hübsch
nicely ['naɪslɪ] ADV (*attractively*) hübsch; (*politely*) nett; (*satisfactorily*) gut; **that will do ~** das reicht (vollauf)
niceties ['naɪsɪtɪz] NPL: **the ~** die Feinheiten *pl*
niche [ni:ʃ] N Nische *f*; (*job, position*) Plätzchen *nt*
nick [nɪk] N Kratzer *m*; (*in metal, wood etc*) Kerbe *f* ▶ VT (*BRIT inf: steal*) klauen; (: *arrest*) einsperren, einlochen; (*cut*): **to ~ o.s.** sich schneiden; **in good ~** (*BRIT inf*) gut in Schuss; **in the ~** (*BRIT inf: in prison*) im Knast; **in the ~ of time** gerade noch rechtzeitig
nickel ['nɪkl] N Nickel *nt*; (*US*) Fünfcentstück *nt*
nickname ['nɪkneɪm] N Spitzname *m* ▶ VT betiteln, taufen (*inf*)
Nicosia [nɪkə'si:ə] N Nikosia *nt*
nicotine ['nɪkəti:n] N Nikotin *nt*
nicotine patch N Nikotinpflaster *nt*
niece [ni:s] N Nichte *f*
nifty ['nɪftɪ] (*inf*) ADJ flott; (*gadget, tool*) schlau
Niger ['naɪdʒə'] N Niger *m*
Nigeria [naɪ'dʒɪərɪə] N Nigeria *nt*
Nigerian [naɪ'dʒɪərɪən] ADJ nigerianisch ▶ N Nigerianer(in) *m(f)*
niggardly ['nɪgədlɪ] ADJ knauserig; (*allowance, amount*) armselig
nigger [nɪgə'] (*offensive*) N Nigger *m* (*inf!*)
niggle ['nɪgl] VT plagen, zu schaffen machen *+dat* ▶ VI herumkritisieren
niggling ['nɪglɪŋ] ADJ quälend; (*pain, ache*) bohrend
night [naɪt] N Nacht *f*; (*evening*) Abend *m*; **the ~ before last** vorletzte Nacht, vorgestern Abend; **at ~, by ~** nachts, abends; **nine o'clock at ~** neun Uhr abends; **in the ~, during the ~** in der Nacht; **~ and day** Tag und Nacht
nightcap ['naɪtkæp] N Schlaftrunk *m*
nightclub ['naɪtklʌb] N Nachtlokal *nt*
nightdress ['naɪtdrɛs] N Nachthemd *nt*
nightfall ['naɪtfɔ:l] N Einbruch *m* der Dunkelheit
nightgown ['naɪtgaun] N = **nightdress**
nightie ['naɪtɪ] N = **nightdress**
nightingale ['naɪtɪŋgeɪl] N Nachtigall *f*
nightlife ['naɪtlaɪf] N Nachtleben *nt*
nightly ['naɪtlɪ] ADJ (all)nächtlich, Nacht-; (*every evening*) (all)abendlich, Abend- ▶ ADV jede Nacht; (*every evening*) jeden Abend
nightmare ['naɪtmɛə'] N Albtraum *m*
night porter N Nachtportier *m*
night safe N Nachtsafe *m*
night school N Abendschule *f*
nightshade ['naɪtʃeɪd] N: **deadly ~** Tollkirsche *f*
night shift N Nachtschicht *f*
night-time ['naɪttaɪm] N Nacht *f*
night watchman N (*irreg*) Nachtwächter *m*
nihilism ['naɪɪlɪzəm] N Nihilismus *m*
nil [nɪl] N Nichts *nt*; (*BRIT Sport*) Null *f*
Nile [naɪl] N: **the ~** der Nil
nimble ['nɪmbl] ADJ flink; (*mind*) beweglich
nine [naɪn] NUM neun
nineteen ['naɪn'ti:n] NUM neunzehn
nineteenth [naɪn'ti:nθ] NUM neunzehnte(r, s)
ninetieth ['naɪntɪɪθ] ADJ neunzigste(r, s)
ninety ['naɪntɪ] NUM neunzig
ninth [naɪnθ] NUM neunte(r, s) ▶ N Neuntel *nt*
nip [nɪp] VT zwicken ▶ N Biss *m*; (*drink*) Schlückchen *nt* ▶ VI (*BRIT inf*): **to ~ out/down/up** kurz raus-/runter-/raufgehen; **to ~ into a shop** (*BRIT inf*) kurz in einen Laden gehen
nipple ['nɪpl] N (*Anat*) Brustwarze *f*
nippy ['nɪpɪ] (*BRIT*) ADJ (*quick: person*) flott; (: *car*) spritzig; (*cold*) frisch
nit [nɪt] N Nisse *f*; (*inf: idiot*) Dummkopf *m*
nitpicking ['nɪtpɪkɪŋ] (*inf*) N Kleinigkeitskrämerei *f*
nitrogen ['naɪtrədʒən] N Stickstoff *m*
nitroglycerin, nitroglycerine ['naɪtrəu'glɪsəri:n] N Nitroglyzerin *nt*
nitty-gritty ['nɪtɪ'grɪtɪ] (*inf*) N: **to get down to the ~** zur Sache kommen
nitwit ['nɪtwɪt] (*inf*) N Dummkopf *m*
NJ (*US*) ABBR (*Post*) = **New Jersey**
NLF N ABBR (= *National Liberation Front*) *vietnamesische Befreiungsbewegung während des Vietnamkrieges*
NLRB (*US*) N ABBR (= *National Labor Relations Board*) *Ausschuss zur Regelung der Beziehungen zwischen Arbeitgebern und Arbeitnehmern*
NM, (US) N.Mex. ABBR (*Post*) = **New Mexico**

KEYWORD

no [nəu] (*pl* **noes**) ADV (*opposite of "yes"*) nein; **no thank you** nein danke

▶ ADJ (*not any*) kein(e); **I have no money/time/books** ich habe kein Geld/keine Zeit/keine Bücher; **"no entry"** „kein Zutritt"; **"no smoking"** „Rauchen verboten"

▶ N Nein *nt*; **there were 20 noes and one abstention** es gab 20 Neinstimmen und eine Enthaltung; **I won't take no for an answer** ich bestehe darauf

no. ABBR (= *number*) Nr.
nobble [nɔbl] (*BRIT inf*) VT (*bribe*) (sich *dat*) kaufen; (*grab*) sich *dat* schnappen; (*Racing: horse, dog*) lahmlegen

Nobel Prize [nəu'bɛl-] N Nobelpreis *m*
nobility [nəu'bɪlɪtɪ] N Adel *m*; (*quality*) Edelmut *m*
noble ['nəubl] ADJ edel, nobel; (*aristocratic*) ad(e)lig; (*impressive*) prächtig
nobleman ['nəublmən] N (*irreg*) Ad(e)lige(r) *f*(*m*)
nobly ['nəublɪ] ADV edel
nobody ['nəubədɪ] PRON niemand, keiner ▶ N: **he's a ~** er ist ein Niemand *m*
no-claims bonus [nəu'kleɪmz-] N Schadenfreiheitsrabatt *m*
nocturnal [nɔk'tə:nl] ADJ nächtlich; (*animal*) Nacht-
nod [nɔd] VI nicken; (*fig: flowers etc*) wippen ▶ VT: **to ~ one's head** mit dem Kopf nicken ▶ N Nicken *nt*; **they nodded their agreement** sie nickten zustimmend
▶ **nod off** VI einnicken
no-fly zone [nəu'flaɪ-] N Sperrzone *f* für den Flugverkehr
noise [nɔɪz] N Geräusch *nt*; (*din*) Lärm *m*
noiseless ['nɔɪzlɪs] ADJ geräuschlos
noisily ['nɔɪzɪlɪ] ADV laut
noisy ['nɔɪzɪ] ADJ laut
nomad ['nəumæd] N Nomade *m*, Nomadin *f*
nomadic [nəu'mædɪk] ADJ Nomaden-, nomadisch
no-man's-land ['nəumænzlænd] N Niemandsland *nt*
nominal ['nɔmɪnl] ADJ nominell
nominate ['nɔmɪneɪt] VT nominieren; (*appoint*) ernennen
nomination [nɔmɪ'neɪʃən] N Nominierung *f*; (*appointment*) Ernennung *f*
nominee [nɔmɪ'ni:] N Kandidat(in) *m*(*f*)
non- [nɔn] PREF nicht-, Nicht-
non-alcoholic [nɔnælkə'hɔlɪk] ADJ alkoholfrei
non-aligned [nɔnə'laɪnd] ADJ blockfrei
non-breakable [nɔn'breɪkəbl] ADJ unzerbrechlich
nonce word ['nɔns-] N Ad-hoc-Bildung *f*
nonchalant ['nɔnʃələnt] ADJ lässig, nonchalant
noncommissioned officer [nɔnkə'mɪʃənd-] N Unteroffizier *m*
non-committal [nɔnkə'mɪtl] ADJ zurückhaltend; (*answer*) unverbindlich
nonconformist [nɔnkən'fɔ:mɪst] N Nonkonformist(in) *m*(*f*) ▶ ADJ nonkonformistisch
non-cooperation ['nɔnkəuɔpə'reɪʃən] N unkooperative Haltung *f*
nondescript ['nɔndɪskrɪpt] ADJ unauffällig; (*colour*) unbestimmbar
none [nʌn] PRON (*not one*) kein(e, er, es); (*not any*) nichts; **~ of us** keiner von uns; **I've ~ left** (*not any*) ich habe nichts übrig; (*not one*) ich habe kein(e, en, es) übrig; **~ at all** (*not any*) überhaupt nicht; (*not one*) überhaupt kein(e, er, es); **I was ~ the wiser** ich war auch nicht klüger; **she would have ~ of it** sie wollte nichts davon hören; **it was ~ other than X** es war kein anderer als X
nonentity [nɔ'nɛntɪtɪ] N (*person*) Nichts *nt*, unbedeutende Figur *f*
non-essential [nɔnɪ'sɛnʃl] ADJ unnötig ▶ N: **non-essentials** nicht (lebens)notwendige Dinge *pl*
nonetheless ['nʌnðə'lɛs] ADV nichtsdestoweniger, trotzdem
non-event [nɔnɪ'vɛnt] N Reinfall *m*
non-existent [nɔnɪg'zɪstənt] ADJ nicht vorhanden
non-fiction [nɔn'fɪkʃən] N Sachbücher *pl* ▶ ADJ (*book*) Sach-; (*prize*) Sachbuch-
non-flammable [nɔn'flæməbl] ADJ nicht entzündbar
non-intervention ['nɔnɪntə'vɛnʃən] N Nichteinmischung *f*, Nichteingreifen *nt*
no-no ['nəunəu] N: **it's a ~** (*inf*) das kommt nicht infrage
non obst. ABBR (= *non obstante*) dennoch
no-nonsense [nəu'nɔnsəns] ADJ (*approach, look*) nüchtern
non-payment [nɔn'peɪmənt] N Nichtzahlung *f*, Zahlungsverweigerung *f*
nonplussed [nɔn'plʌst] ADJ verdutzt, verblüfft
non-profit making ['nɔn'prɔfɪt-] ADJ (*organization*) gemeinnützig
non-returnable [nɔnrə'tə:nəbl] ADJ: **~ bottle** Einwegflasche *f*
nonsense ['nɔnsəns] N Unsinn *m*; **~!** Unsinn!, Quatsch!; **it is ~ to say that ...** es ist dummes Gerede zu sagen, dass ...; **to make (a) ~ of sth** etw ad absurdum führen
nonsensical [nɔn'sɛnsɪkl] ADJ (*idea, action etc*) unsinnig
non-shrink [nɔn'ʃrɪŋk] (BRIT) ADJ nicht einlaufend
non-smoker ['nɔn'sməukə^r] N Nichtraucher(in) *m*(*f*)
nonstarter [nɔn'stɑ:tə^r] N (*fig*): **it's a ~** (*idea etc*) es hat keine Erfolgschance
non-stick ['nɔn'stɪk] ADJ kunststoffbeschichtet, Teflon-®
non-stop ['nɔn'stɔp] ADJ ununterbrochen; (*flight*) Nonstop-, Non-Stop- ▶ ADV ununterbrochen; (*fly*) nonstop
non-taxable [nɔn'tæksəbl] ADJ nicht steuerpflichtig
non-U [nɔn'ju:] (BRIT *inf*) ADJ ABBR (= *non-upper class*) nicht vornehm
non-white ['nɔn'waɪt] ADJ farbig ▶ N Farbige(r) *f*(*m*)
noodles ['nu:dlz] NPL Nudeln *pl*
nook [nuk] N: **every ~ and cranny** jeder Winkel
noon [nu:n] N Mittag *m*
no-one ['nəuwʌn] PRON = **nobody**
noose [nu:s] N Schlinge *f*
nor [nɔ:^r] CONJ, ADV = **neither**
Norf (BRIT) ABBR (*Post*) = **Norfolk**
norm [nɔ:m] N Norm *f*
normal ['nɔ:məl] ADJ normal ▶ N: **to return to ~** sich wieder normalisieren
normality [nɔ:'mælɪtɪ] N Normalität *f*
normally ['nɔ:məlɪ] ADV normalerweise; (*act, behave*) normal

n

Normandy ['nɔːməndɪ] N Normandie *f*
north [nɔːθ] N Norden *m* ▶ ADJ nördlich, Nord- ▶ ADV nach Norden; **~ of** nördlich von
North Africa N Nordafrika *nt*
North African ADJ nordafrikanisch ▶ N Nordafrikaner(in) *m(f)*
North America N Nordamerika *nt*
North American ADJ nordamerikanisch ▶ N Nordamerikaner(in) *m(f)*
Northants [nɔː'θænts] (BRIT) ABBR (*Post*) = **Northamptonshire**
northbound ['nɔːθbaund] ADJ in Richtung Norden; (*carriageway*) nach Norden (führend)
Northd (BRIT) ABBR (*Post*) = **Northumberland**
north-east [nɔːθ'iːst] N Nordosten *m* ▶ ADJ nordöstlich, Nordost- ▶ ADV nach Nordosten; **~ of** nordöstlich von
northerly ['nɔːðəlɪ] ADJ nördlich
northern ['nɔːðən] ADJ nördlich, Nord-
Northern Ireland N Nordirland *nt*
North Korea N Nordkorea *nt*
North Pole N: **the ~** der Nordpol
North Sea N: **the ~** die Nordsee *f*
North Sea oil N Nordseeöl *nt*
northward ['nɔːθwəd], **northwards** ['nɔːθwədz] ADV nach Norden, nordwärts
north-west [nɔːθ'wɛst] N Nordwesten *m* ▶ ADJ nordwestlich, Nordwest- ▶ ADV nach Nordwesten; **~ of** nordwestlich von
Norway ['nɔːweɪ] N Norwegen *nt*
Norwegian [nɔː'wiːdʒən] ADJ norwegisch ▶ N Norweger(in) *m(f)*; (*Ling*) Norwegisch *nt*
nos. ABBR (= *numbers*) Nrn.
nose [nəuz] N Nase *f*; (*of car*) Schnauze *f* ▶ VI (*also*: **nose one's way**) sich schieben; **to follow one's ~** immer der Nase nach gehen; **to get up one's ~** (*inf*) auf die Nerven gehen +*dat*; **to have a (good) ~ for sth** eine (gute) Nase für etw haben; **to keep one's ~ clean** (*inf*) eine saubere Weste behalten; **to look down one's ~ at sb/sth** (*inf*) auf jdn/etw herabsehen; **to pay through the ~ (for sth)** (*inf*) (für etw) viel blechen; **to rub sb's ~ in sth** (*inf*) jdm etw unter die Nase reiben; **to turn one's ~ up at sth** (*inf*) die Nase über etw *acc* rümpfen; **under sb's ~** vor jds Augen
▶ **nose about** VI herumschnüffeln
▶ **nose around** VI = **nose about**
nosebleed ['nəuzbliːd] N Nasenbluten *nt*
nose-dive ['nəuzdaɪv] N (*of plane*) Sturzflug *m* ▶ VI (*plane*) im Sturzflug herabgehen
nose drops NPL Nasentropfen *pl*
nosey ['nəuzɪ] (*inf*) ADJ = **nosy**
nostalgia [nɔs'tældʒɪə] N Nostalgie *f*
nostalgic [nɔs'tældʒɪk] ADJ nostalgisch
nostril ['nɔstrɪl] N Nasenloch *nt*; (*of animal*) Nüster *f*
nosy ['nəuzɪ] (*inf*) ADJ neugierig

KEYWORD

not [nɔt] ADV nicht; **he is not** *or* **isn't here** er ist nicht hier; **you must not** *or* **you mustn't do that** das darfst du nicht tun; **it's too late, isn't it?** es ist zu spät, nicht wahr?; **not that I don't like him** nicht, dass ich ihn nicht mag; **not yet** noch nicht; **not now** nicht jetzt; *see also* **all**; **only**

notable ['nəutəbl] ADJ bemerkenswert
notably ['nəutəblɪ] ADV hauptsächlich; (*markedly*) bemerkenswert
notary ['nəutərɪ] N (*also*: **notary public**) Notar(in) *m(f)*
notation [nəu'teɪʃən] N Notation *f*; (*Mus*) Notenschrift *f*
notch [nɔtʃ] N Kerbe *f*; (*in blade, saw*) Scharte *f*; (*fig*) Klasse *f*
▶ **notch up** VT erzielen; (*victory*) erringen
note [nəut] N Notiz *f*; (*of lecturer*) Manuskript *nt*; (*of student etc*) Aufzeichnung *f*; (*in book etc*) Anmerkung *f*; (*letter*) paar Zeilen *pl*; (*banknote*) Note *f*, Schein *m*; (*Mus*: *sound*) Ton *m*; (: *symbol*) Note *f*; (*tone*) Ton *m*, Klang *m* ▶ VT beachten; (*point out*) anmerken; (*also*: **note down**) notieren; **of ~** bedeutend; **to make a ~ of sth** sich *dat* etw notieren; **to take notes** Notizen machen, mitschreiben; **to take ~ of sth** etw zur Kenntnis nehmen
notebook ['nəutbuk] N Notizbuch *nt*; (*for shorthand*) Stenoblock *m*
notecase ['nəutkeɪs] (BRIT) N Brieftasche *f*
noted ['nəutɪd] ADJ bekannt
notepad ['nəutpæd] N Notizblock *m*
notepaper ['nəutpeɪpə[r]] N Briefpapier *nt*
noteworthy ['nəutwəːðɪ] ADJ beachtenswert
nothing ['nʌθɪŋ] N nichts; **~ new/worse** *etc* nichts Neues/Schlimmeres *etc*; **~ much** nicht viel; **~ else** sonst nichts; **for ~** umsonst; **~ at all** überhaupt nichts
notice ['nəutɪs] N Bekanntmachung *f*; (*sign*) Schild *nt*; (*warning*) Ankündigung *f*; (*dismissal*) Kündigung *f*; (BRIT: *review*) Kritik *f*, Rezension *f* ▶ VT bemerken; **to bring sth to sb's ~** jdn auf etw *acc* aufmerksam machen; **to take no ~ of** ignorieren, nicht beachten; **to escape sb's ~** jdm entgehen; **it has come to my ~ that ...** es ist mir zu Ohren gekommen, dass ...; **to give sb ~ of sth** jdm von etw Bescheid geben; **without ~** ohne Ankündigung; **advance ~** Vorankündigung *f*; **at short/a moment's ~** kurzfristig/innerhalb kürzester Zeit; **until further ~** bis auf Weiteres; **to hand in one's ~** kündigen; **to be given one's ~** gekündigt werden +*dat*
noticeable ['nəutɪsəbl] ADJ deutlich
noticeboard ['nəutɪsbɔːd] (BRIT) N Anschlagbrett *nt*
notification [nəutɪfɪ'keɪʃən] N Benachrichtigung *f*
notify ['nəutɪfaɪ] VT: **to ~ sb (of sth)** jdn (von etw) benachrichtigen
notion ['nəuʃən] N Vorstellung *f*; **notions** NPL (*US*: *haberdashery*) Kurzwaren *pl*
notoriety [nəutə'raɪətɪ] N traurige Berühmtheit *f*
notorious [nəu'tɔːrɪəs] ADJ berüchtigt

notoriously [nəu'tɔ:rɪəslɪ] ADV notorisch
Notts [nɔts] (BRIT) ABBR (*Post*) = **Nottinghamshire**
notwithstanding [nɔtwɪθ'stændɪŋ] ADV trotzdem ▸ PREP trotz +*dat*
nougat ['nu:gɑ:] N Nugat *m*
nought [nɔ:t] N Null *f*
noughties ['nɔ:tɪz] NPL (*inf*) *das erste Jahrzehnt des dritten Jahrtausends*, Nullerjahre *pl*
noun [naun] N Hauptwort *nt*, Substantiv *nt*
nourish ['nʌrɪʃ] VT nähren
nourishing ['nʌrɪʃɪŋ] ADJ nahrhaft
nourishment ['nʌrɪʃmənt] N Nahrung *f*
Nov. ABBR (= *November*) Nov.
Nova Scotia ['nəuvə'skəuʃə] N Neuschottland *nt*
novel ['nɔvl] N Roman *m* ▸ ADJ neu(artig)
novelist ['nɔvəlɪst] N Romanschriftsteller(in) *m(f)*
novelty ['nɔvəltɪ] N Neuheit *f*; (*object*) Kleinigkeit *f*
November [nəu'vɛmbə^r] N November *m*; *see also* **July**
novice ['nɔvɪs] N Neuling *m*, Anfänger(in) *m(f)*; (*Rel*) Novize *m*, Novizin *f*
NOW [nau] (US) N ABBR (= *National Organization for Women*) *Frauenvereinigung*
now [nau] ADV jetzt; (*these days*) heute ▸ CONJ: **~ (that)** jetzt, wo; **right ~** gleich, sofort; **by ~** inzwischen, mittlerweile; **that's the fashion just ~** das ist gerade modern; **I saw her just ~** ich habe sie gerade gesehen; **(every) ~ and then, (every) ~ and again** ab und zu, gelegentlich; **from ~ on** von nun an; **in 3 days from ~** (heute) in 3 Tagen; **between ~ and Monday** bis Montag; **that's all for ~** das ist erst einmal alles; **any day ~** jederzeit; **~ then** also
nowadays ['nauədeɪz] ADV heute
nowhere ['nəuwɛə^r] ADV (*be*) nirgends, nirgendwo; (*go*) nirgendwohin; **~ else** nirgendwo anders
no-win situation [nəu'wɪn-] N aussichtslose Lage *f*
noxious ['nɔkʃəs] ADJ (*gas, fumes*) schädlich; (*smell*) übel
nozzle ['nɔzl] N Düse *f*
NP N ABBR (*Law*) = **notary public**
NS (CANADA) ABBR = **Nova Scotia**
NSC (US) N ABBR = **National Security Council**
NSF (US) N ABBR (= *National Science Foundation*) *Organisation zur Förderung der Wissenschaft*
NSPCC (BRIT) N ABBR (= *National Society for the Prevention of Cruelty to Children*) Kinderschutzbund *m*
NSW (AUST) ABBR (*Post*) = **New South Wales**
NT N ABBR (*Bible*: = *New Testament*) NT
nth [ɛnθ] (*inf*) ADJ: **to the ~ degree** in der n-ten Potenz
nuance ['nju:ɑ̃:ns] N Nuance *f*
nubile ['nju:baɪl] ADJ gut entwickelt
nuclear ['nju:klɪə^r] ADJ (*bomb, industry etc*) Atom-; **~ physics** Kernphysik *f*; **~ war** Atomkrieg *m*
nuclear disarmament N nukleare *or* atomare Abrüstung *f*
nuclear family N Kleinfamilie *f*, Kernfamilie *f*
nuclear-free zone ['nju:klɪə'fri:-] N atomwaffenfreie Zone *f*
nuclear waste N Atommüll *m*
nuclei ['nju:klɪaɪ] NPL *of* **nucleus**
nucleus ['nju:klɪəs] (*pl* **nuclei**) N Kern *m*
NUCPS (BRIT) N ABBR (= *National Union of Civil and Public Servants*) *Gewerkschaft für Beschäftigte im öffentlichen Dienst*
nude [nju:d] ADJ nackt ▸ N (*Art*) Akt *m*; **in the ~** nackt
nudge [nʌdʒ] VT anstoßen
nudist ['nju:dɪst] N Nudist(in) *m(f)*
nudist colony N FKK-Kolonie *f*
nudity ['nju:dɪtɪ] N Nacktheit *f*
nugget ['nʌgɪt] N (*of gold*) Klumpen *m*; (*fig: of information*) Brocken *m*
nuisance ['nju:sns] N: **to be a ~** lästig sein; (*situation*) ärgerlich sein; **he's a ~** er geht einem auf die Nerven; **what a ~!** wie ärgerlich/lästig!
NUJ (BRIT) N ABBR (= *National Union of Journalists*) *Journalistengewerkschaft*
null [nʌl] ADJ: **~ and void** null und nichtig
nullify ['nʌlɪfaɪ] VT zunichtemachen; (*claim, law*) für null und nichtig erklären
NUM (BRIT) N ABBR (= *National Union of Mineworkers*) *Bergarbeitergewerkschaft*
numb [nʌm] ADJ taub, gefühllos; (*fig: with fear etc*) wie betäubt ▸ VT taub *or* gefühllos machen; (*pain, mind*) betäuben
number ['nʌmbə^r] N Zahl *f*; (*quantity*) (An)zahl *f*; (*of house, bank account, bus etc*) Nummer *f* ▸ VT (*pages etc*) nummerieren; (*amount to*) zählen; **a ~ of** einige; **any ~ of** beliebig viele; (*reasons*) alle möglichen; **wrong ~** (*Tel*) falsch verbunden; **to be numbered among** zählen zu
number plate (BRIT) N (*Aut*) Nummernschild *nt*
Number Ten (BRIT) N (*Pol*: = *10 Downing Street*) Nummer zehn *f* (Downing Street)
numbness ['nʌmnɪs] N Taubheit *f*, Starre *f*; (*fig*) Benommenheit *f*, Betäubung *f*
numbskull ['nʌmskʌl] N = **numskull**
numeral ['nju:mərəl] N Ziffer *f*
numerate ['nju:mərɪt] (BRIT) ADJ: **to be ~** rechnen können
numerical [nju:'mɛrɪkl] ADJ numerisch
numerous ['nju:mərəs] ADJ zahlreich
numskull ['nʌmskʌl] (*inf*) N Holzkopf *m*
nun [nʌn] N Nonne *f*
nunnery ['nʌnərɪ] N (Nonnen)kloster *nt*
nuptial ['nʌpʃəl] ADJ (*feast, celebration*) Hochzeits-; **~ bliss** Eheglück *nt*
nurse [nə:s] N Krankenschwester *f*; (*also*: **nursemaid**) Kindermädchen *nt* ▸ VT pflegen; (*cold, toothache etc*) auskurieren; (*baby*) stillen; (*fig: desire, grudge*) hegen
nursery ['nə:sərɪ] N Kindergarten *m*; (*room*) Kinderzimmer *nt*; (*for plants*) Gärtnerei *f*
nursery rhyme N Kinderreim *m*
nursery school N Kindergarten *m*
nursery slope (BRIT) N (*Ski*) Anfängerhügel *m*

nursing ['nəːsɪŋ] N Krankenpflege *f*; (*care*) Pflege *f*
nursing home N Pflegeheim *nt*
nursing mother N stillende Mutter *f*
nurture ['nəːtʃə^r] VT hegen und pflegen; (*fig: ideas, creativity*) fördern
NUS (BRIT) N ABBR (= *National Union of Students*) *Studentengewerkschaft*
NUT (BRIT) N ABBR (= *National Union of Teachers*) *Lehrergewerkschaft*
nut [nʌt] N (*Tech*) (Schrauben)mutter *f*; (*Bot*) Nuss *f*; (*inf: lunatic*) Spinner(in) *m(f)*
nutcase ['nʌtkeɪs] (*inf*) N Spinner(in) *m(f)*
nutcrackers ['nʌtkrækəz] NPL Nussknacker *m*
nutmeg ['nʌtmɛg] N Muskat *m*, Muskatnuss *f*
nutrient ['njuːtrɪənt] N Nährstoff *m*
nutrition [njuː'trɪʃən] N Ernährung *f*; (*nourishment*) Nahrung *f*
nutritionist [njuː'trɪʃənɪst] N Ernährungswissenschaftler(in) *m(f)*
nutritious [njuː'trɪʃəs] ADJ nahrhaft
nuts [nʌts] (*inf*) ADJ verrückt; **he's ~** er spinnt
nutshell ['nʌtʃɛl] N Nussschale *f*; **in a ~** (*fig*) kurz gesagt
nutty ['nʌtɪ] ADJ (*flavour*) Nuss-; (*inf: idea etc*) bekloppt
nuzzle ['nʌzl] VI: **to ~ up to** sich drücken *or* schmiegen an *+acc*
NV (*US*) ABBR (*Post*) = **Nevada**
NVQ N ABBR (= *National Vocational Qualification*) *Qualifikation für berufsbegleitende Ausbildungsinhalte*
NW ABBR = **north-west**
NY (*US*) ABBR (*Post*) = **New York**
nylon ['naɪlɔn] N Nylon *nt* ▶ ADJ Nylon-;
nylons NPL (*stockings*) Nylonstrümpfe *pl*
nymph [nɪmf] N Nymphe *f*
nymphomaniac ['nɪmfəu'meɪnɪæk] N Nymphomanin *f*
NYSE (*US*) N ABBR (= *New York Stock Exchange*) *New Yorker Börse*
NZ ABBR = **New Zealand**

Oo

O, o [əu] N *(letter)* O *nt*, o *nt*; *(US Scol: outstanding)* ≈ Eins *f*; *(Tel etc)* Null *f*; **O for Olive, O for Oboe** *(US)* ≈ O wie Otto
oaf [əuf] N Trottel *m*
oak [əuk] N *(tree, wood)* Eiche *f* ▶ ADJ *(furniture, door)* Eichen-
O & M N ABBR *(= organization and method)* Organisation und Arbeitsweise *pl*
OAP (BRIT) N ABBR = **old age pensioner**
oar [ɔːʳ] N Ruder *nt*; **to put** *or* **shove one's ~ in** *(inf: fig)* mitmischen, sich einmischen
oarsman [ˈɔːzmən] N *(irreg)* Ruderer *m*
oarswoman [ˈɔːzwumən] N *(irreg)* Ruderin *f*
OAS N ABBR *(= Organization of American States)* OAS *f*
oasis [əuˈeɪsɪs] *(pl* **oases***)* N *(lit, fig)* Oase *f*
oath [əuθ] N *(promise)* Eid *m*, Schwur *m*; *(swear word)* Fluch *m*; **on ~** (BRIT), **under ~** unter Eid; **to take the ~** *(Law)* vereidigt werden
oatmeal [ˈəutmiːl] N Haferschrot *m*; *(colour)* Hellbeige *nt*
oats [əuts] NPL Hafer *m*; **he's getting his ~** (BRIT *inf: fig)* er kommt im Bett auf seine Kosten
obdurate [ˈɔbdjurɪt] ADJ unnachgiebig
OBE (BRIT) N ABBR *(= Officer of (the order of) the British Empire) britischer Ordenstitel*
obedience [əˈbiːdɪəns] N Gehorsam *m*; **in ~ to** gemäß *+dat*
obedient [əˈbiːdɪənt] ADJ gehorsam; **to be ~ to sb** jdm gehorchen
obelisk [ˈɔbɪlɪsk] N Obelisk *m*
obese [əuˈbiːs] ADJ fettleibig
obesity [əuˈbiːsɪtɪ] N Fettleibigkeit *f*
obey [əˈbeɪ] VT *(person)* gehorchen *+dat*, folgen *+dat*; *(orders, law)* befolgen ▶ VI gehorchen
obituary [əˈbɪtjuərɪ] N Nachruf *m*
object N [ˈɔbdʒɪkt] *(also Ling)* Objekt *nt*; *(aim, purpose)* Ziel *nt*, Zweck *m* ▶ VI [əbˈdʒɛkt] dagegen sein; **to be an ~ of ridicule** *(person)* sich lächerlich machen; *(thing)* lächerlich wirken; **money is no ~** Geld spielt keine Rolle; **he objected that …** er wandte ein, dass …; **I ~!** ich protestiere!; **do you ~ to my smoking?** haben Sie etwas dagegen, wenn ich rauche?
objection [əbˈdʒɛkʃən] N *(argument)* Einwand *m*; **I have no ~ to …** ich habe nichts dagegen, dass …; **if you have no ~** wenn Sie nichts dagegen haben; **to raise** *or* **voice an ~** einen Einwand erheben *or* vorbringen
objectionable [əbˈdʒɛkʃənəbl] ADJ *(language, conduct)* anstößig; *(person)* unausstehlich
objective [əbˈdʒɛktɪv] ADJ objektiv ▶ N Ziel *nt*
objectively [əbˈdʒɛktɪvlɪ] ADV objektiv
objectivity [ɔbdʒɪkˈtɪvɪtɪ] N Objektivität *f*
object lesson N: **an ~ in** ein Paradebeispiel *nt* für
objector [əbˈdʒɛktəʳ] N Gegner(in) *m(f)*
obligation [ɔblɪˈgeɪʃən] N Pflicht *f*; **to be under an ~ to do sth** verpflichtet sein, etw zu tun; **to be under an ~ to sb** jdm verpflichtet sein; **"no ~ to buy"** *(Comm)* „kein Kaufzwang"
obligatory [əˈblɪgətərɪ] ADJ obligatorisch
oblige [əˈblaɪdʒ] VT *(compel)* zwingen; *(do a favour for)* einen Gefallen tun *+dat*; **I felt obliged to invite him in** ich fühlte mich verpflichtet, ihn hereinzubitten; **to be obliged to sb for sth** *(grateful)* jdm für etw dankbar sein; **anything to ~!** *(inf)* stets zu Diensten!
obliging [əˈblaɪdʒɪŋ] ADJ entgegenkommend
oblique [əˈbliːk] ADJ *(line, angle)* schief; *(reference, compliment)* indirekt, versteckt ▶ N (BRIT: *also:* **oblique stroke**) Schrägstrich *m*
obliterate [əˈblɪtəreɪt] VT *(village etc)* vernichten; *(fig: memory, error)* auslöschen
oblivion [əˈblɪvɪən] N *(unconsciousness)* Bewusstlosigkeit *f*; *(being forgotten)* Vergessenheit *f*; **to sink into ~** *(event etc)* in Vergessenheit geraten
oblivious [əˈblɪvɪəs] ADJ: **he was ~ of** *or* **to it** er war sich dessen nicht bewusst
oblong [ˈɔblɔŋ] ADJ rechteckig ▶ N Rechteck *nt*
obnoxious [əbˈnɔkʃəs] ADJ widerwärtig, widerlich
o.b.o. (US) ABBR *(in classified ads: = or best offer)* bzw. Höchstgebot
oboe [ˈəubəu] N Oboe *f*
obscene [əbˈsiːn] ADJ obszön; *(fig: wealth)* unanständig; *(income etc)* unverschämt
obscenity [əbˈsɛnɪtɪ] N Obszönität *f*
obscure [əbˈskjuəʳ] ADJ *(little known)* unbekannt, obskur; *(difficult to understand)* unklar ▶ VT *(obstruct, conceal)* verdecken
obscurity [əbˈskjuərɪtɪ] N *(of person, book)* Unbekanntheit *f*; *(of remark etc)* Unklarheit *f*
obsequious [əbˈsiːkwɪəs] ADJ unterwürfig
observable [əbˈzəːvəbl] ADJ wahrnehmbar; *(noticeable)* erkennbar

observance [əb'zə:vəns] N (*of law etc*) Befolgung *f*; **religious observances** religiöse Feste *pl*
observant [əb'zə:vənt] ADJ aufmerksam
observation [ɔbzə'veɪʃən] N (*remark*) Bemerkung *f*; (*act of observing, Med*) Beobachtung *f*; **she's in hospital under ~** sie ist zur Beobachtung im Krankenhaus
observation post N Beobachtungsposten *m*
observatory [əb'zə:vətrɪ] N Observatorium *nt*
observe [əb'zə:v] VT (*watch*) beobachten; (*notice, comment*) bemerken; (*abide by: rule etc*) einhalten
observer [əb'zə:vəʳ] N Beobachter(in) *m(f)*
obsess [əb'sɛs] VT verfolgen; **to be obsessed by** *or* **with sb/sth** von jdm/etw besessen sein
obsession [əb'sɛʃən] N Besessenheit *f*
obsessive [əb'sɛsɪv] ADJ (*person*) zwanghaft; (*interest, hatred, tidiness*) krankhaft; **to be ~ about cleaning/tidying up** einen Putz-/ Ordnungsfimmel haben (*inf*)
obsolescence [ɔbsə'lɛsns] N Veralten *nt*; **built-in** *or* **planned ~** (*Comm*) geplanter Verschleiß *m*
obsolete ['ɔbsəli:t] ADJ veraltet
obstacle ['ɔbstəkl] N (*lit, fig*) Hindernis *nt*
obstacle race N Hindernisrennen *nt*
obstetrician [ɔbstə'trɪʃən] N Geburtshelfer(in) *m(f)*
obstetrics [ɔb'stɛtrɪks] N Geburtshilfe *f*
obstinacy ['ɔbstɪnəsɪ] N (*of person*) Starrsinn *m*
obstinate ['ɔbstɪnɪt] ADJ (*person*) starrsinnig, stur; (*refusal, cough etc*) hartnäckig
obstruct [əb'strʌkt] VT (*road, path*) blockieren; (*traffic, fig*) behindern
obstruction [əb'strʌkʃən] N (*object*) Hindernis *nt*; (*of plan, law*) Behinderung *f*
obstructive [əb'strʌktɪv] ADJ hinderlich, obstruktiv (*esp Pol*); **she's being ~** sie macht Schwierigkeiten
obtain [əb'teɪn] VT erhalten, bekommen ▶ VI (*form: exist, be the case*) gelten
obtainable [əb'teɪnəbl] ADJ erhältlich
obtrusive [əb'tru:sɪv] ADJ aufdringlich; (*conspicuous*) auffällig
obtuse [əb'tju:s] ADJ (*person, remark*) einfältig; (*Math*) stumpf
obverse ['ɔbvə:s] N (*of situation, argument*) Kehrseite *f*
obviate ['ɔbvɪeɪt] VT (*need, problem etc*) vorbeugen *+dat*
obvious ['ɔbvɪəs] ADJ offensichtlich; (*lie*) klar; (*predictable*) naheliegend
obviously ['ɔbvɪəslɪ] ADV (*clearly*) offensichtlich; (*of course*) natürlich; **~!** selbstverständlich!; **~ not** offensichtlich nicht; **he was ~ not drunk** er war natürlich nicht betrunken; **he was not ~ drunk** offenbar war er nicht betrunken
OCAS N ABBR (= *Organization of Central American States*) *mittelamerikanischer Staatenbund*
occasion [ə'keɪʒən] N Gelegenheit *f*; (*celebration etc*) Ereignis *nt* ▶ VT (*form: cause*) verursachen; **on ~** (*sometimes*) gelegentlich; **on that ~** bei der Gelegenheit; **to rise to the ~** sich der Lage gewachsen zeigen
occasional [ə'keɪʒənl] ADJ gelegentlich; **he likes the ~ cigar** er raucht gelegentlich gern eine Zigarre
occasionally [ə'keɪʒənəlɪ] ADV gelegentlich; **very ~** sehr selten
occasional table N Beistelltisch *m*
occult [ɔ'kʌlt] N: **the ~** der Okkultismus ▶ ADJ okkult
occupancy ['ɔkjupənsɪ] N (*of room etc*) Bewohnen *nt*
occupant ['ɔkjupənt] N (*of house etc*) Bewohner(in) *m(f)*; (*temporary: of car*) Insasse *m*, Insassin *f*; **the ~ of this table/office** derjenige, der an diesem Tisch sitzt/in diesem Büro arbeitet
occupation [ɔkju'peɪʃən] N (*job*) Beruf *m*; (*pastime*) Beschäftigung *f*; (*of building, country etc*) Besetzung *f*
occupational guidance [ɔkju'peɪʃənl-] (BRIT) N Berufsberatung *f*
occupational hazard N Berufsrisiko *nt*
occupational pension scheme N betriebliche Altersversorgung *f*
occupational therapy N Beschäftigungstherapie *f*
occupied ADJ (*country, seat, toilet*) besetzt; (*person*) beschäftigt; **to keep sb/oneself ~** jdn/sich beschäftigen; **to be ~ in** *or* **with sth** mit etw beschäftigt sein; **to be ~ in** *or* **with doing sth** damit beschäftigt sein, etw zu tun
occupier ['ɔkjupaɪəʳ] N Bewohner(in) *m(f)*
occupy ['ɔkjupaɪ] VT (*house, office*) bewohnen; (*place etc*) belegen; (*building, country etc*) besetzen; (*time, attention*) beanspruchen; (*position, space*) einnehmen; **to ~ o.s. (in** *or* **with sth)** sich (mit etw) beschäftigen; **to ~ o.s. in** *or* **with doing sth** sich damit beschäftigen, etw zu tun
occur [ə'kə:ʳ] VI (*take place*) geschehen, sich ereignen; (*exist*) vorkommen; **to ~ to sb** jdm einfallen
occurrence [ə'kʌrəns] N (*event*) Ereignis *nt*; (*incidence*) Auftreten *nt*
ocean ['əuʃən] N Ozean *m*, Meer *nt*; **oceans of** (*inf*) jede Menge
ocean bed N Meeresgrund *m*
ocean-going ['əuʃəngəuɪŋ] ADJ (*ship, vessel*) Hochsee-
Oceania [əuʃɪ'eɪnɪə] N Ozeanien *nt*
ocean liner N Ozeandampfer *m*
ochre, (*US*) **ocher** ['əukəʳ] ADJ ockerfarben
o'clock [ə'klɔk] ADV: **it is 5 ~** es ist 5 Uhr
OCR N ABBR (*Comput*) = **optical character reader**; **optical character recognition**
Oct. ABBR (= *October*) Okt.
octagonal [ɔk'tægənl] ADJ achteckig
octane ['ɔkteɪn] N Oktan *nt*; **high-~ petrol, high-~ gas** (*US*) Benzin *nt* mit hoher Oktanzahl
octave ['ɔktɪv] N Oktave *f*
October [ɔk'təubəʳ] N Oktober *m*; *see also* **July**
octogenarian ['ɔktəudʒɪ'nɛərɪən] N Achtzigjährige(r) *f(m)*

octopus [ˈɔktəpəs] N Tintenfisch *m*
odd [ɔd] ADJ (*person*) sonderbar, komisch; (*behaviour, shape*) seltsam; (*number*) ungerade; (*sock, shoe etc*) einzeln; (*occasional*) gelegentlich; **60-~** etwa 60; **at ~ times** ab und zu; **to be the ~ one out** der Außenseiter/die Außenseiterin sein; **add meat or the ~ vegetable to the soup** fügen Sie der Suppe Fleisch oder auch etwas Gemüse bei
oddball [ˈɔdbɔːl] (*inf*) N komischer Kauz *m*
oddity [ˈɔdɪtɪ] N (*person*) Sonderling *m*; (*thing*) Merkwürdigkeit *f*
odd-job man [ɔdˈdʒɔb-] N (*irreg*) Mädchen *nt* für alles
odd jobs NPL Gelegenheitsarbeiten *pl*
oddly [ˈɔdlɪ] ADV (*behave, dress*) seltsam; *see also* **enough**
oddments [ˈɔdmənts] NPL (*Comm*) Restposten *m*
odds [ɔdz] NPL (*in betting*) Gewinnquote *f*; (*fig*) Chancen *pl*; **the ~ are in favour of/against his coming** es sieht so aus, als ob er kommt/nicht kommt; **to succeed against all the ~** allen Erwartungen zum Trotz erfolgreich sein; **it makes no ~** es spielt keine Rolle; **to be at ~ (with)** (*in disagreement*) uneinig sein (mit); (*at variance*) sich nicht vertragen (mit)
odds and ends NPL Kleinigkeiten *pl*
odds-on [ɔdzˈɔn] ADJ: **the ~ favourite** der klare Favorit ▸ ADV: **it's ~ that she'll win** es ist so gut wie sicher, dass sie gewinnt
ode [əud] N Ode *f*
odious [ˈəudɪəs] ADJ widerwärtig
odometer [ɔˈdɔmɪtə^r] (US) N Tacho(meter) *m*
odor *etc* (US) = **odour** *etc*
odour, (US) **odor** [ˈəudə^r] N Geruch *m*
odourless [ˈəudəlɪs] ADJ geruchlos
OECD N ABBR (= *Organization for Economic Cooperation and Development*) OECD *f*
oesophagus, (US) **esophagus** [iːˈsɔfəgəs] N Speiseröhre *f*
oestrogen, (US) **estrogen** [ˈiːstrəudʒən] N Östrogen *nt*

KEYWORD

of [ɔv] PREP **1** von; **the history of Germany** die Geschichte Deutschlands; **a friend of ours** ein Freund von uns; **a boy of ten** ein Junge von zehn Jahren, ein zehnjähriger Junge; **that was kind of you** das war nett von Ihnen; **the city of New York** die Stadt New York
2 (*expressing quantity, amount, dates etc*): **a kilo of flour** ein Kilo Mehl; **how much of this do you need?** wie viel brauchen Sie davon?; **3 of them** (*people*) 3 von ihnen; (*objects*) 3 davon; **a cup of tea** eine Tasse Tee; **a vase of flowers** eine Vase mit Blumen; **the 5th of July** der 5. Juli
3 (*from, out of*) aus; **a bracelet of solid gold** ein Armband aus massivem Gold; **made of wood** aus Holz (gemacht)

Ofcom [ˈɔfkɔm] (BRIT) N ABBR (= *Office of Communications Regulation*) *Regulierungsbehörde für die Kommunikationsindustrie*

KEYWORD

off [ɔf] ADV **1** (*referring to distance, time*): **it's a long way off** es ist sehr weit weg; **the game is 3 days off** es sind noch 3 Tage bis zum Spiel
2 (*departure*): **to go off to Paris/Italy** nach Paris/Italien fahren; **I must be off** ich muss gehen
3 (*removal*): **to take off one's coat/clothes** seinen Mantel/sich ausziehen; **the button came off** der Knopf ging ab; **10 % off** (*Comm*) 10% Nachlass
4: **to be off** (*on holiday*) im Urlaub sein; (*due to sickness*) krank sein; **I'm off on Fridays** freitags habe ich frei; **he was off on Friday** Freitag war er nicht da; **to have a day off** (*from work*) einen Tag freihaben; **to be off sick** wegen Krankheit fehlen
▸ ADJ **1** (*not turned on: machine, light, engine etc*) aus; (*: water, gas*) abgedreht; (*: tap*) zu
2: **to be off** (*meeting, match*) ausfallen; (*agreement*) nicht mehr gelten
3 (BRIT: *not fresh*) verdorben, schlecht
4: **on the off chance that …** für den Fall, dass …; **to have an off day** (*not as good as usual*) nicht in Form sein; **to be badly off** sich schlecht stehen
▸ PREP **1** (*indicating motion, removal etc*) von *+dat*; **to fall off a cliff** von einer Klippe fallen; **to take a picture off the wall** ein Bild von der Wand nehmen
2 (*distant from*): **5 km off the main road** 5 km von der Hauptstraße entfernt; **an island off the coast** eine Insel vor der Küste
3: **I'm off meat/beer** (*no longer eat/drink it*) ich esse kein Fleisch/trinke kein Bier mehr; (*no longer like it*) ich kann kein Fleisch/Bier *etc* mehr sehen

offal [ˈɔfl] N (*Culin*) Innereien *pl*
off-beat [ˈɔfbiːt] ADJ (*clothes, ideas*) ausgefallen
off-centre, (US) **off-center** [ɔfˈsɛntə^r] ADJ nicht genau in der Mitte, links/rechts von der Mitte ▸ ADV asymmetrisch
off-colour [ˈɔfˈkʌlə^r] (BRIT) ADJ (*ill*) unpässlich; **to feel ~** sich unwohl fühlen
offence, (US) **offense** [əˈfɛns] N (*crime*) Vergehen *nt*; (*insult*) Beleidigung *f*, Kränkung *f*; **to commit an ~** eine Straftat begehen; **to take ~ (at)** Anstoß nehmen (an *+dat*); **to give ~ (to)** Anstoß erregen (bei); **"no ~"** „nichts für ungut"
offend [əˈfɛnd] VT (*upset*) kränken; **to ~ against** (*law, rule*) verstoßen gegen
offender [əˈfɛndə^r] N Straftäter(in) *m(f)*
offending [əˈfɛndɪŋ] ADJ (*item etc*) anstoßerregend
offense [əˈfɛns] (US) N = **offence**
offensive [əˈfɛnsɪv] ADJ (*remark, behaviour*) verletzend; (*smell etc*) übel; (*weapon*) Angriffs- ▸ N (*Mil*) Offensive *f*
offer [ˈɔfə^r] N Angebot *nt* ▸ VT anbieten; (*money, opportunity, service*) bieten; (*reward*) aussetzen; **to make an ~ for sth** ein Angebot für etw machen; **on ~** (*Comm: available*) erhältlich;

O

(: *cheaper*) im Angebot; **to ~ sth to sb** jdm etw anbieten; **to ~ to do sth** anbieten, etw zu tun
offering ['ɔfərɪŋ] N Darbietung *f*; (*Rel*) Opfergabe *f*
off-grid [ɔf'grɪd] ADJ netzunabhängig
off-hand [ɔf'hænd] ADJ (*casual*) lässig; (*impolite*) kurz angebunden ▶ ADV auf Anhieb; **I can't tell you ~** das kann ich Ihnen auf Anhieb nicht sagen
office ['ɔfɪs] N Büro *nt*; (*position*) Amt *nt*; **doctor's ~** (*US*) Praxis *f*; **to take ~** das Amt antreten; **in ~** (*minister etc*) im Amt; **through his good offices** durch seine guten Dienste; **O~ of Fair Trading** (BRIT) Behörde *f* gegen unlauteren Wettbewerb
office block, (*US*) **office building** N Bürogebäude *nt*
office boy N Bürogehilfe *m*
office holder N Amtsinhaber(in) *m(f)*
office hours NPL (*Comm*) Bürostunden *pl*; (*US Med*) Sprechstunde *f*
office manager N Büroleiter(in) *m(f)*
officer ['ɔfɪsə^r] N (*Mil etc*) Offizier *m*; (*also*: **police officer**) Polizeibeamte(r) *m*, Polizeibeamtin *f*; (*of organization*) Funktionär *m*
office work N Büroarbeit *f*
office worker N Büroangestellte(r) *f(m)*
official [ə'fɪʃl] ADJ offiziell ▶ N (*in government*) Beamte(r) *m*, Beamtin *f*; (*in trade union etc*) Funktionär *m*
officialdom [ə'fɪʃldəm] (*pej*) N Bürokratie *f*
officially [ə'fɪʃəlɪ] ADV offiziell
official receiver N (*Comm*) Konkursverwalter *m*
officiate [ə'fɪʃɪeɪt] VI amtieren; **to ~ at a marriage** eine Trauung vornehmen
officious [ə'fɪʃəs] ADJ übereifrig
offing ['ɔfɪŋ] N: **in the ~** in Sicht
off-key [ɔf'ki:] ADJ (*Mus: sing, play*) falsch; (*instrument*) verstimmt
off-licence ['ɔflaɪsns] (BRIT) N ≈ Wein- und Spirituosenhandlung *f*

> **Off-licence** ist ein Geschäft (oder eine Theke in einer Gaststätte), wo man alkoholische Getränke kaufen kann, die aber anderswo konsumiert werden müssen. In solchen Geschäften, die oft von landesweiten Ketten betrieben werden, kann man auch andere Getränke, Süßigkeiten, Zigaretten und Knabbereien kaufen.

off-limits [ɔf'lɪmɪts] ADJ verboten
off-line [ɔf'laɪn] (*Comput*) ADJ Offline- ▶ ADV offline; (*switched off*) abgetrennt
off-load ['ɔfləud] VT abladen
off-peak ['ɔf'pi:k] ADJ (*heating*) Nachtspeicher-; (*electricity*) Nacht-; (*train*) außerhalb der Stoßzeit; **~ ticket** Fahrkarte *f* zur Fahrt außerhalb der Stoßzeit
off-putting ['ɔfputɪŋ] (BRIT) ADJ (*remark, behaviour*) abstoßend
off-season ['ɔf'si:zn] ADJ, ADV außerhalb der Saison
offset ['ɔfsɛt] VT (*irreg: like* **set**) (*counteract*) ausgleichen
offshoot ['ɔfʃu:t] N (*Bot, fig*) Ableger *m*
offshore [ɔf'ʃɔ:^r] ADJ (*breeze*) ablandig; (*oil rig, fishing*) küstennah
offside ['ɔf'saɪd] ADJ (*Sport*) im Abseits; (*Aut: when driving on left*) rechtsseitig; (: *when driving on right*) linksseitig ▶ N: **the ~** (*Aut: when driving on left*) die rechte Seite; (: *when driving on right*) die linke Seite
offspring ['ɔfsprɪŋ] N INV Nachwuchs *m*
offstage [ɔf'steɪdʒ] ADV hinter den Kulissen
off-the-cuff [ɔfðə'kʌf] ADJ (*remark*) aus dem Stegreif
off-the-job ['ɔfðə'dʒɔb] ADJ: **~ training** außerbetriebliche Weiterbildung *f*
off-the-peg ['ɔfðə'pɛg], (*US*) **off-the-rack** ['ɔfðə'ræk] ADV von der Stange
off-the-record ['ɔfðə'rɛkɔ:d] ADJ (*conversation, briefing*) inoffiziell; **that's strictly ~** das ist ganz im Vertrauen
off-white ['ɔfwaɪt] ADJ gebrochen weiß
Ofgem ['ɔfgɛm] N *Überwachungsgremium zum Verbraucherschutz nach Privatisierung der Stromindustrie*
often ['ɔfn] ADV oft; **how ~?** wie oft?; **more ~ than not** meistens; **as ~ as not** ziemlich oft; **every so ~** ab und zu
Ofwat ['ɔfwɔt] N *Überwachungsgremium zum Verbraucherschutz nach Privatisierung der Wasserindustrie*
ogle ['əugl] VT schielen nach, begaffen (*pej*)
ogre ['əugə^r] N (*monster*) Menschenfresser *m*
OH (*US*) ABBR (*Post*) = **Ohio**
oh [əu] EXCL oh
ohm [əum] N Ohm *nt*
OHMS (BRIT) ABBR (= *On His/Her Majesty's Service*) *Aufdruck auf amtlichen Postsendungen*
oil [ɔɪl] N Öl *nt*; (*petroleum*) (Erd)öl *nt* ▶ VT ölen
oilcan ['ɔɪlkæn] N Ölkanne *f*
oil change N Ölwechsel *m*
oilcloth ['ɔɪlklɔθ] N Wachstuch *nt*
oilfield ['ɔɪlfi:ld] N Ölfeld *nt*
oil filter N Ölfilter *m*
oil-fired ['ɔɪlfaɪəd] ADJ (*boiler, central heating*) Öl-
oil gauge N Ölstandsmesser *m*
oil painting N Ölgemälde *nt*
oil refinery N Ölraffinerie *f*
oil rig N Ölförderturm *m*; (*at sea*) Bohrinsel *f*
oilskins ['ɔɪlskɪnz] NPL Ölzeug *nt*
oil slick N Ölteppich *m*
oil tanker N (*ship*) (Öl)tanker *m*; (*truck*) Tankwagen *m*
oil well N Ölquelle *f*
oily ['ɔɪlɪ] ADJ (*substance*) ölig; (*rag*) öldurchtränkt; (*food*) fettig
ointment ['ɔɪntmənt] N Salbe *f*
OK (*US*) ABBR (*Post*) = **Oklahoma**
O.K. ['əu'keɪ] (*inf*) EXCL okay; (*granted*) gut ▶ ADJ (*average*) einigermaßen; (*acceptable*) in Ordnung ▶ VT genehmigen ▶ N: **to give sb/sth the O.K.** jdm/etw seine Zustimmung geben; **is it O.K.?** ist es in Ordnung?; **are you O.K.?** bist du in Ordnung?; **are you O.K. for money?** hast du (noch) genug Geld?; **it's O.K. with** *or* **by me** mir ist es recht

okay ['əu'keɪ] EXCL = **O.K.**
Okla. (*US*) ABBR (*Post*) = **Oklahoma**
old [əuld] ADJ alt; **how ~ are you?** wie alt bist du?; **he's 10 years ~** er ist 10 Jahre alt; **older brother** ältere(r) Bruder; **any ~ thing will do for him** ihm ist alles recht
old age N Alter *nt*
old age pension N Rente *f*
old age pensioner N (*BRIT*) Rentner(in) *m(f)*
old-fashioned ['əuld'fæʃnd] ADJ altmodisch
old hand N alter Hase *m*
old hat ADJ: **to be ~** ein alter Hut sein
old maid N alte Jungfer *f*
old people's home N Altersheim *nt*
old-style ['əuldstaɪl] ADJ im alten Stil
old-time dancing ['əuldtaɪm-] N Tänze *pl* im alten Stil
old-timer [əuld'taɪmə^r] (*esp US*) N Veteran *m*
old wives' tale N Ammenmärchen *nt*
oleander [əulɪ'ændə^r] N Oleander *m*
O level (*BRIT*) N (*formerly*) ≈ Abschluss *m* der Sekundarstufe 1, ≈ mittlere Reife *f*
olive ['ɔlɪv] N Olive *f*; (*tree*) Olivenbaum *m* ▶ ADJ (*also*: **olive-green**) olivgrün; **to offer an ~ branch to sb** (*fig*) jdm ein Friedensangebot machen
olive oil N Olivenöl *nt*
Olympic [əu'lɪmpɪk] ADJ olympisch
Olympic Games NPL: **the ~** (*also*: **the Olympics**) die Olympischen Spiele *pl*
OM (*BRIT*) N ABBR (= *Order of Merit*) *britischer Verdienstorden*
Oman [əu'mɑːn] N Oman *nt*
OMB (*US*) N ABBR (= *Office of Management and Budget*) *Regierungsbehörde für Verwaltung und Etat*
ombudsman ['ɔmbudzmən] N Ombudsmann *m*
omelette, (*US*) **omelet** ['ɔmlɪt] N Omelett *nt*; **ham/cheese omelet(te)** Schinken-/Käseomelett *nt*
omen ['əumən] N Omen *nt*
OMG (*inf*) ABBR (= *Oh my God*); Oh Gott, Mein Gott
ominous ['ɔmɪnəs] ADJ (*silence, warning*) ominös; (*clouds, smoke*) bedrohlich
omission [əu'mɪʃən] N (*thing omitted*) Auslassung *f*; (*act of omitting*) Auslassen *nt*
omit [əu'mɪt] VT (*deliberately*) unterlassen; (*by mistake*) auslassen ▶ VI: **to ~ to do sth** es unterlassen, etw zu tun
omnivorous [ɔm'nɪvrəs] ADJ: **to be ~** Allesfresser sein
ON (*CANADA*) ABBR = **Ontario**

KEYWORD

on [ɔn] PREP **1** (*indicating position*) auf +*dat*; (*with vb of motion*) auf +*acc*; **it's on the table** es ist auf dem Tisch; **she put the book on the table** sie legte das Buch auf den Tisch; **on the left** links; **on the right** rechts; **the house is on the main road** das Haus liegt an der Hauptstraße
2 (*indicating means, method, condition etc*): **on foot** (*go, be*) zu Fuß; **to be on the train/plane** im Zug/Flugzeug sein; **to go on the train/plane** mit dem Zug/Flugzeug reisen; **(to be wanted) on the telephone** am Telefon (verlangt werden); **on the radio/television** im Radio/Fernsehen; **to be on drugs** Drogen nehmen; **to be on holiday** im Urlaub sein; **I'm here on business** ich bin geschäftlich hier
3 (*referring to time*): **on Friday** am Freitag; **on Fridays** freitags; **on June 20th** am 20. Juni; **on Friday, June 20th** am Freitag, dem 20. Juni; **a week on Friday** Freitag in einer Woche; **on (his) arrival he went straight to his hotel** bei seiner Ankunft ging er direkt in sein Hotel; **on seeing this he ...** als er das sah, ... er ...
4 (*about, concerning*) über +*acc*; **a book on physics** ein Buch über Physik
▶ ADV **1** (*referring to dress*): **to have one's coat on** seinen Mantel anhaben; **what's she got on?** was hat sie an?
2 (*referring to covering*): **screw the lid on tightly** dreh den Deckel fest zu
3 (*further, continuously*): **to walk/drive/read on** weitergehen/-fahren/-lesen
▶ ADJ **1** (*functioning, in operation: machine, radio, TV, light*) an; (*: tap*) auf; (*: handbrake*) angezogen; **there's a good film on at the cinema** im Kino läuft ein guter Film
2: **that's not on!** (*inf: of behaviour*) das ist nicht drin!

once [wʌns] ADV (*on one occasion*) einmal; (*formerly*) früher; (*a long time ago*) früher einmal ▶ CONJ (*as soon as*) sobald; **at ~** (*immediately*) sofort; (*simultaneously*) gleichzeitig; **~ a week** einmal pro Woche; **~ more** *or* **again** noch einmal; **~ and for all** ein für alle Mal; **~ upon a time** es war einmal; **~ in a while** ab und zu; **all at ~** (*suddenly*) plötzlich; **for ~** ausnahmsweise (einmal); **~ or twice** ein paarmal; **~ he had left** sobald er gegangen war; **~ it was done** nachdem es getan war
oncoming ['ɔnkʌmɪŋ] ADJ (*traffic etc*) entgegenkommend

KEYWORD

one [wʌn] NUM ein(e); (*counting*) eins; **one hundred and fifty** (ein)hundert(und)fünfzig; **one day there was a sudden knock at the door** eines Tages klopfte es plötzlich an der Tür; **one by one** einzeln
▶ ADJ **1** (*sole*) einzige(r, s); **the one book which ...** das einzige Buch, das ...
2 (*same*): **they came in the one car** sie kamen in demselben Wagen; **they all belong to the one family** sie alle gehören zu ein und derselben Familie
▶ PRON **1**: **this one** diese(r, s); **that one** der/die/das (da); **which one?** welcher/welche/welches?; **he is one of us** er ist einer von uns; **I've already got one/a red one**

ich habe schon eins/ein rotes
2: **one another** einander; **do you two ever see one another?** seht ihr zwei euch jemals?
3 (*impersonal*) man; **one never knows** man weiß nie; **to cut one's finger** sich *dat* in den Finger schneiden

one-day excursion ['wʌndeɪ-] (*US*) N (*day return*) Tagesrückfahrkarte *f*
one-man ['wʌn'mæn] ADJ (*business, show*) Einmann-
one-man band N Einmannkapelle *f*
one-off [wʌn'ɔf] (*BRIT inf*) N einmaliges Ereignis *nt*
one-parent family ['wʌnpɛərənt-] N Familie *f* mit nur einem Elternteil
one-piece ['wʌnpi:s] ADJ: **~ swimsuit** einteiliger Badeanzug *m*
onerous ['ɔnərəs] ADJ (*duty etc*) schwer

KEYWORD

oneself [wʌn'sɛlf] PRON (*reflexive: after prep*) sich; (*: emphatic*) selbst; **to hurt oneself** sich *dat* wehtun; **to keep sth for oneself** etw für sich behalten; **to talk to oneself** Selbstgespräche führen

one-shot ['wʌnʃɔt] (*US*) N = **one-off**
one-sided [wʌn'saɪdɪd] ADJ einseitig
one-time ['wʌntaɪm] ADJ ehemalig
one-to-one ['wʌntəwʌn] ADJ (*relationship, tuition*) Einzel-
one-upmanship [wʌn'ʌpmənʃɪp] N: **the art of ~** die Kunst, anderen um einen Schritt voraus zu sein
one-way ['wʌnweɪ] ADJ (*street, traffic*) Einbahn-; (*ticket*) Einzel-
ongoing ['ɔngəuɪŋ] ADJ (*project*) laufend; (*situation etc*) andauernd
onion ['ʌnjən] N Zwiebel *f*
on-line ['ɔnlaɪn] (*Comput*) ADJ (*printer, database*) Online-; (*switched on*) gekoppelt ▶ ADV online
onlooker ['ɔnlukə^r] N Zuschauer(in) *m(f)*
only ['əunlɪ] ADV nur ▶ ADJ einzige(r, s) ▶ CONJ nur, bloß; **I ~ took one** ich nahm nur eins; **I saw her ~ yesterday** ich habe sie erst gestern gesehen; **I'd be ~ too pleased to help** ich würde allzu gern helfen; **not ~ … but (also) …** nicht nur …, sondern auch …; **an ~ child** ein Einzelkind *nt*; **I would come, ~ I'm too busy** ich würde kommen, wenn ich nicht so viel zu tun hätte
ono (*BRIT*) ABBR (*in classified ads: = or near(est) offer*) *see* **near**
onset ['ɔnsɛt] N Beginn *m*
onshore ['ɔnʃɔ:^r] ADJ (*wind*) auflandig, See-
onslaught ['ɔnslɔ:t] N Attacke *f*
on-the-job ['ɔnðə'dʒɔb] ADJ: **~ training** Ausbildung *f* am Arbeitsplatz
onto ['ɔntu] PREP = **on to**
onus ['əunəs] N Last *f*, Pflicht *f*; **the ~ is on him to prove it** er trägt die Beweislast

onward ['ɔnwəd], **onwards** ['ɔnwədz] ADV weiter ▶ ADJ fortschreitend; **from that time ~(s)** von der Zeit an
onyx ['ɔnɪks] N Onyx *m*
ooze [u:z] VI (*mud, water etc*) triefen
opacity [əu'pæsɪtɪ] N (*of substance*) Undurchsichtigkeit *f*
opal ['əupl] N Opal *m*
opaque [əu'peɪk] ADJ (*substance*) undurchsichtig, trüb
OPEC ['əupɛk] N ABBR (= *Organization of Petroleum-Exporting Countries*) OPEC *f*
open ['əupn] ADJ offen; (*packet, shop, museum*) geöffnet; (*view*) frei; (*meeting, debate*) öffentlich; (*ticket, return*) unbeschränkt; (*vacancy*) verfügbar ▶ VT öffnen, aufmachen; (*book, paper etc*) aufschlagen; (*account*) eröffnen; (*blocked road*) frei machen ▶ VI (*door, eyes, mouth*) sich öffnen; (*shop, bank etc*) aufmachen; (*commence*) beginnen; (*film, play*) Premiere haben; (*flower*) aufgehen; **in the ~ (air)** im Freien; **the ~ sea** das offene Meer; **to have an ~ mind on sth** etw *dat* aufgeschlossen gegenüberstehen; **to be ~ to** (*ideas etc*) offen sein für; **to be ~ to criticism** der Kritik *dat* ausgesetzt sein; **to be ~ to the public** für die Öffentlichkeit zugänglich sein; **to ~ one's mouth** (*speak*) den Mund aufmachen
▶ **open on to** VT FUS (*room, door*) führen auf +*acc*
▶ **open up** VI (*unlock*) aufmachen; (*confide*) sich äußern
open-air [əupn'ɛə^r] ADJ im Freien; **~ concert** Open-Air-Konzert *nt*; **~ swimming pool** Freibad *nt*
open-and-shut ['əupnən'ʃʌt] ADJ: **~ case** klarer Fall *m*
open day N Tag *m* der offenen Tür
open-ended [əupn'ɛndɪd] ADJ (*question etc*) mit offenem Ausgang; (*contract*) unbefristet
opener ['əupnə^r] N (*also*: **tin opener, can opener**) Dosenöffner *m*
open-heart [əupn'hɑ:t] ADJ: **~ surgery** Eingriff *m* am offenen Herzen
opening ['əupnɪŋ] ADJ (*commencing: stages, scene*) erste(r, s); (*remarks, ceremony etc*) Eröffnungs- ▶ N (*gap, hole*) Öffnung *f*; (*of play etc*) Anfang *m*; (*of new building etc*) Eröffnung *f*; (*opportunity*) Gelegenheit *f*
opening hours NPL Öffnungszeiten *pl*
opening night N (*Theat*) Eröffnungsabend *m*
open learning N *Weiterbildungssystem auf Teilzeitbasis*
openly ['əupnlɪ] ADV offen
open-minded [əupn'maɪndɪd] ADJ aufgeschlossen
open-necked ['əupnnɛkt] ADJ (*shirt*) mit offenem Kragen
openness ['əupnnɪs] N (*frankness*) Offenheit *f*
open-plan ['əupn'plæn] ADJ (*office*) Großraum-
open prison N offenes Gefängnis *nt*
open sandwich N belegtes Brot *nt*
open shop N *Unternehmen ohne Gewerkschaftszwang*

Open University (BRIT) N ≈ Fernuniversität *f*

Open University ist eine 1969 in Großbritannien gegründete Fernuniversität für Spätstudierende. Der Unterricht findet durch Fernseh- und Radiosendungen statt, schriftliche Arbeiten werden mit der Post verschickt, und der Besuch von Sommerkursen ist Pflicht. Die Studenten müssen eine bestimmte Anzahl von Unterrichtseinheiten in einem bestimmten Zeitraum absolvieren und für die Verleihung eines akademischen Grades eine Mindestzahl von Scheinen machen.

open verdict N (*Law*) *Todesfeststellung ohne Angabe der Todesursache*
opera ['ɔpərə] N Oper *f*
opera glasses NPL Opernglas *nt*
opera house N Opernhaus *nt*
opera singer N Opernsänger(in) *m(f)*
operate ['ɔpəreɪt] VT (*machine etc*) bedienen ▸ VI (*machine etc*) funktionieren; (*company*) arbeiten; (*laws, forces*) wirken; (*Med*) operieren; **to ~ on sb** jdn operieren
operatic [ɔpə'rætɪk] ADJ (*singer etc*) Opern-
operating room ['ɔpəreɪtɪŋ-] (*US*) N Operationssaal *m*
operating system N (*Comput*) Betriebssystem *nt*
operating table N (*Med*) Operationstisch *m*
operating theatre N (*Med*) Operationssaal *m*
operation [ɔpə'reɪʃən] N (*activity*) Unternehmung *f*; (*of machine etc*) Betrieb *m*; (*Mil, Med*) Operation *f*; (*Comm*) Geschäft *nt*; **to be in ~** (*law, scheme*) in Kraft sein; **to have an ~** (*Med*) operiert werden; **to perform an ~** (*Med*) eine Operation vornehmen
operational [ɔpə'reɪʃənl] ADJ (*machine etc*) einsatzfähig
operative ['ɔpərətɪv] ADJ (*measure, system*) wirksam; (*law*) gültig ▸ N (*in factory*) Maschinenarbeiter(in) *m(f)*; **the ~ word** das entscheidende Wort
operator ['ɔpəreɪtə^r] N (*Tel*) Vermittlung *f*; (*of machine*) Bediener(in) *m(f)*
operetta [ɔpə'rɛtə] N Operette *f*
ophthalmic [ɔf'θælmɪk] ADJ (*department*) Augen-
ophthalmic optician N Augenoptiker(in) *m(f)*
ophthalmologist [ɔfθæl'mɔlədʒɪst] N Augenarzt *m*, Augenärztin *f*
opinion [ə'pɪnjən] N Meinung *f*; **in my ~** meiner Meinung nach; **to have a good/high ~ of sb/o.s.** eine gute/hohe Meinung von jdm/sich haben; **to be of the ~ that ...** der Ansicht *or* Meinung sein, dass ...; **to get a second ~** (*Med etc*) ein zweites Gutachten einholen
opinionated [ə'pɪnjəneɪtɪd] (*pej*) ADJ rechthaberisch
opinion poll N Meinungsumfrage *f*
opium ['əupɪəm] N Opium *nt*
opponent [ə'pəunənt] N Gegner(in) *m(f)*
opportune ['ɔpətju:n] ADJ (*moment*) günstig
opportunism [ɔpə'tju:nɪsəm] (*pej*) N Opportunismus *m*
opportunist [ɔpə'tju:nɪst] (*pej*) N Opportunist(in) *m(f)*
opportunity [ɔpə'tju:nɪtɪ] N Gelegenheit *f*, Möglichkeit *f*; (*prospects*) Chance *f*; **to take the ~ of doing sth** die Gelegenheit ergreifen, etw zu tun
oppose [ə'pəuz] VT (*opinion, plan*) ablehnen; **to be opposed to sth** gegen etw sein; **as opposed to** im Gegensatz zu
opposing [ə'pəuzɪŋ] ADJ (*side, team*) gegnerisch; (*ideas, tendencies*) entgegengesetzt
opposite ['ɔpəzɪt] ADJ (*house, door*) gegenüberliegend; (*end, direction*) entgegengesetzt; (*point of view, effect*) gegenteilig ▸ ADV gegenüber ▸ PREP (*in front of*) gegenüber; (*next to: on list, form etc*) neben ▸ N: **the ~** das Gegenteil; **the ~ sex** das andere Geschlecht; **"see ~ page"** „siehe gegenüber"
opposite number N (*person*) Gegenspieler(in) *m(f)*
opposition [ɔpə'zɪʃən] N (*resistance*) Widerstand *m*; (*Sport*) Gegner *pl*; **the O~** (*Pol*) die Opposition
oppress [ə'prɛs] VT unterdrücken
oppressed [ə'prɛst] ADJ unterdrückt
oppression [ə'prɛʃən] N Unterdrückung *f*
oppressive [ə'prɛsɪv] ADJ (*weather, heat*) bedrückend; (*political regime*) repressiv
opprobrium [ə'prəubrɪəm] N (*form*) Schande *f*, Schmach *f*
opt [ɔpt] VI: **to ~ for** sich entscheiden für; **to ~ to do sth** sich entscheiden, etw zu tun
▸ **opt out (of)** VI (*not participate*) sich nicht beteiligen (an +*dat*); (*of insurance scheme etc*) kündigen; **to ~ out (of local authority control)** (*Pol: hospital, school*) aus der Kontrolle der Gemeindeverwaltung austreten
optical ['ɔptɪkl] ADJ optisch
optical character reader N optischer Klarschriftleser *m*
optical character recognition N optische Zeichenerkennung *f*
optical illusion N optische Täuschung *f*
optician [ɔp'tɪʃən] N Optiker(in) *m(f)*
optics ['ɔptɪks] N Optik *f*
optimism ['ɔptɪmɪzəm] N Optimismus *m*
optimist ['ɔptɪmɪst] N Optimist(in) *m(f)*
optimistic [ɔptɪ'mɪstɪk] ADJ optimistisch
optimum ['ɔptɪməm] ADJ optimal
option ['ɔpʃən] N (*choice*) Möglichkeit *f*; (*Scol*) Wahlfach *nt*; (*Comm*) Option *f*; **to keep one's options open** sich *dat* alle Möglichkeiten offenhalten; **to have no ~** keine (andere) Wahl haben
optional ['ɔpʃənl] ADJ freiwillig; **~ extras** (*Comm*) Extras *pl*
opulence ['ɔpjuləns] N Reichtum *m*
opulent ['ɔpjulənt] ADJ (*very wealthy*) reich, wohlhabend
OR (*US*) ABBR (*Post*) = **Oregon**
or [ɔ:^r] CONJ oder; **he hasn't seen or heard anything** er hat weder etwas gesehen noch gehört; **or else** (*otherwise*) sonst; **fifty or sixty people** fünfzig bis sechzig Leute

O

oracle ['ɔrəkl] N Orakel *nt*
oral ['ɔ:rəl] ADJ (*test, report*) mündlich; (*Med: vaccine, contraceptive*) zum Einnehmen ▸ N (*exam*) mündliche Prüfung *f*
orange ['ɔrɪndʒ] N Orange *f*, Apfelsine *f* ▸ ADJ (*colour*) orange
orangeade [ɔrɪndʒ'eɪd] N Orangenlimonade *f*
orange juice N Orangensaft *m*
oration [ɔ:'reɪʃən] N Ansprache *f*
orator ['ɔrətəʳ] N Redner(in) *m(f)*
oratorio [ɔrə'tɔ:rɪəu] N (*Mus*) Oratorium *nt*
orb [ɔ:b] N Kugel *f*
orbit ['ɔ:bɪt] N (*of planet etc*) Umlaufbahn *f* ▸ VT umkreisen
orbital motorway ['ɔ:bɪtəl-] N Ringautobahn *f*
orchard ['ɔ:tʃəd] N Obstgarten *m*; **apple ~** Obstgarten mit Apfelbäumen
orchestra ['ɔ:kɪstrə] N Orchester *nt*; (*US: stalls*) Parkett *nt*
orchestral [ɔ:'kɛstrəl] ADJ (*piece, musicians*) Orchester-
orchestrate ['ɔ:kɪstreɪt] VT orchestrieren
orchid ['ɔ:kɪd] N Orchidee *f*
ordain [ɔ:'deɪn] VT (*Rel*) ordinieren; (*decree*) verfügen
ordeal [ɔ:'di:l] N Qual *f*
order ['ɔ:dəʳ] N (*command*) Befehl *m*; (*Comm, in restaurant*) Bestellung *f*; (*sequence*) Reihenfolge *f*; (*discipline, organization*) Ordnung *f*; (*Rel*) Orden *m* ▸ VT (*command*) befehlen; (*Comm, in restaurant*) bestellen; (*also:* **put in order**) ordnen; **in ~** (*permitted*) in Ordnung; **in (working) ~** betriebsfähig; **in ~ to do sth** um etw zu tun; **in ~ of size** nach Größe (geordnet); **on ~** (*Comm*) bestellt; **out of ~** (*not working*) außer Betrieb; (*in the wrong sequence*) durcheinander; (*motion, proposal*) nicht zulässig; **to place an ~ for sth with sb** eine Bestellung für etw bei jdm aufgeben; **made to ~** (*Comm*) auf Bestellung (gemacht); **to be under orders to do sth** die Anweisung haben, etw zu tun; **to take orders** Befehle entgegennehmen; **a point of ~** (*in debate etc*) eine Verfahrensfrage; **"pay to the ~ of ..."** „zahlbar an *+dat* ..."; **of** *or* **in the ~ of** in der Größenordnung von; **to ~ sb to do sth** jdn anweisen, etw zu tun
▸ **order around, order about** VT herumkommandieren
order book N (*Comm*) Auftragsbuch *nt*
order form N Bestellschein *m*
orderly ['ɔ:dəlɪ] N (*Mil*) Offiziersbursche *m*; (*Med*) Pfleger(in) *m(f)* ▸ ADJ (*manner*) ordentlich; (*sequence, system*) geordnet
order number N (*Comm*) Bestellnummer *f*
ordinal ['ɔ:dɪnl] ADJ: **~ number** Ordinalzahl *f*
ordinarily ['ɔ:dnrɪlɪ] ADV normalerweise
ordinary ['ɔ:dnrɪ] ADJ (*everyday*) gewöhnlich, normal; (*pej: mediocre*) mittelmäßig; **out of the ~** außergewöhnlich

> **Ordinary degree** ist ein Universitätsabschluss, der an Studenten vergeben wird, die entweder die für ein **honours degree** nötige Note nicht erreicht haben, aber trotzdem nicht durchgefallen sind, oder die sich nur für ein ordinary degree eingeschrieben haben, wobei das Studium meist kürzer ist.

ordinary seaman (BRIT) N (*irreg*) Leichtmatrose *m*
ordinary shares NPL Stammaktien *pl*
ordination [ɔ:dɪ'neɪʃən] N (*Rel*) Ordination *f*
ordnance ['ɔ:dnəns] N (*unit*) Technische Truppe *f* ▸ ADJ (*factory, supplies*) Munitions-
Ordnance Survey (BRIT) N Landesvermessung *f*
ore [ɔ:ʳ] N Erz *nt*
Ore. (*US*) ABBR (*Post*) = **Oregon**
organ ['ɔ:gən] N (*Anat*) Organ *nt*; (*Mus*) Orgel *f*
organic [ɔ:'gænɪk] ADJ organisch; (*farming, vegetables*) Bio-, Öko-; **~ food** Biokost *f*
organism ['ɔ:gənɪzəm] N Organismus *m*
organist ['ɔ:gənɪst] N Organist(in) *m(f)*
organization [ɔ:gənaɪ'zeɪʃən] N Organisation *f*
organization chart N Organisationsplan *m*
organize ['ɔ:gənaɪz] VT organisieren; **to get organized** sich fertig machen
organized crime N organisiertes Verbrechen *nt*
organized labour N organisierte Arbeiterschaft *f*
organizer ['ɔ:gənaɪzəʳ] N (*of conference etc*) Organisator *m*, Veranstalter *m*
orgasm ['ɔ:gæzəm] N Orgasmus *m*
orgy ['ɔ:dʒɪ] N Orgie *f*; **an ~ of destruction** eine Zerstörungsorgie
Orient ['ɔ:rɪənt] N: **the ~** der Orient
orient ['ɔ:rɪənt] VT: **to ~ o.s. (to)** sich orientieren (in *+dat*); **to be oriented towards** ausgerichtet sein auf *+acc*
oriental [ɔ:rɪ'ɛntl] ADJ orientalisch
orientate ['ɔ:rɪənteɪt] VT: **to ~ o.s.** sich orientieren; (*fig*) sich zurechtfinden; **to be orientated towards** ausgerichtet sein auf *+acc*
orifice ['ɔrɪfɪs] N (*Anat*) Öffnung *f*
origin ['ɔrɪdʒɪn] N Ursprung *m*; (*of person*) Herkunft *f*; **country of ~** Herkunftsland *nt*
original [ə'rɪdʒɪnl] ADJ (*first*) ursprünglich; (*genuine*) original; (*imaginative*) originell ▸ N Original *nt*
originality [ərɪdʒɪ'nælɪtɪ] N Originalität *f*
originally [ə'rɪdʒɪnəlɪ] ADV (*at first*) ursprünglich
originate [ə'rɪdʒɪneɪt] VI: **to ~ in** (*idea, custom etc*) entstanden sein in *+dat*; **to ~ with** *or* **from** stammen von
originator [ə'rɪdʒɪneɪtəʳ] N (*of idea, custom*) Urheber(in) *m(f)*
Orkneys ['ɔ:knɪz] NPL: **the ~** (*also:* **the Orkney Islands**) die Orkneyinseln *pl*
ornament ['ɔ:nəmənt] N (*object*) Ziergegenstand *m*; (*decoration*) Verzierungen *pl*
ornamental [ɔ:nə'mɛntl] ADJ (*garden, pond*) Zier-
ornamentation [ɔ:nəmɛn'teɪʃən] N Verzierungen *pl*
ornate [ɔ:'neɪt] ADJ (*necklace, design*) kunstvoll
ornithologist [ɔ:nɪ'θɔlədʒɪst] N Ornithologe *m*, Ornithologin *f*
ornithology [ɔ:nɪ'θɔlədʒɪ] N Ornithologie *f*, Vogelkunde *f*

orphan ['ɔ:fn] N Waise *f*, Waisenkind *nt* ▸ VT: **to be orphaned** zur Waise werden
orphanage ['ɔ:fənɪdʒ] N Waisenhaus *nt*
orthodox ['ɔ:θədɔks] ADJ orthodox; **~ medicine** die konventionelle Medizin
orthodoxy ['ɔ:θədɔksɪ] N Orthodoxie *f*
orthopaedic, (*US*) **orthopedic** [ɔ:θə'pi:dɪk] ADJ orthopädisch
OS ABBR (BRIT) = **Ordnance Survey**; (*Naut*) = **ordinary seaman**; (*Dress*) = **outsize**
o.s. ABBR (*Comm*: = *out of stock*) nicht auf Lager
Oscar ['ɔskə[r]] N Oscar *m*
oscillate ['ɔsɪleɪt] VI (*Elec, Phys*) schwingen, oszillieren; (*fig*) schwanken
OSHA (*US*) N ABBR (= *Occupational Safety and Health Administration*) *Regierungsstelle für Arbeitsschutzvorschriften*
Oslo ['ɔzləu] N Oslo *nt*
OST N ABBR (= *Office of Science and Technology*) *Ministerium für Wissenschaft und Technologie*
ostensible [ɔs'tɛnsɪbl] ADJ vorgeblich, angeblich
ostensibly [ɔs'tɛnsɪblɪ] ADV angeblich
ostentation [ɔstɛn'teɪʃən] N Pomp *m*, Protz *m*
ostentatious [ɔstɛn'teɪʃəs] ADJ (*building, car etc*) pompös; (*person*) protzig
osteopath ['ɔstɪəpæθ] N Osteopath(in) *m(f)*
ostracize ['ɔstrəsaɪz] VT ächten
ostrich ['ɔstrɪtʃ] N Strauß *m*
OT ABBR (*Bible*: = *Old Testament*) AT
OTB (*US*) N ABBR (= *offtrack betting*) *Wetten außerhalb des Rennbahngeländes*
OTE ABBR (*Comm*: = *on-target earnings*) Einkommensziel *nt*
other ['ʌðə[r]] ADJ andere(r, s) ▸ PRON: **the ~ (one)** der/die/das andere; **others** andere *pl*; **the others** die anderen *pl*; **~ than** (*apart from*) außer; **the ~ day** (*recently*) neulich; **some actor or ~** irgendein Schauspieler; **somebody or ~** irgendjemand; **the car was none ~ than Robert's** das Auto gehörte keinem anderen als Robert
otherwise ['ʌðəwaɪz] ADV (*differently*) anders; (*apart from that, if not*) sonst, ansonsten; **an ~ good piece of work** eine im Übrigen gute Arbeit
OTT (*inf*) ABBR (= *over the top*) *see* **top**
otter ['ɔtə[r]] N Otter *m*
OU (BRIT) N ABBR = **Open University**
ouch [autʃ] EXCL autsch
ought [ɔ:t] (*pt* **~**) AUX VB: **I ~ to do it** ich sollte es tun; **this ~ to have been corrected** das hätte korrigiert werden müssen; **he ~ to win** (*he probably will win*) er dürfte wohl gewinnen; **you ~ to go and see it** das solltest du dir ansehen
ounce [auns] N Unze *f*; (*fig*: *small amount*) bisschen *nt*
our ['auə[r]] ADJ unsere(r, s); *see also* **my**
ours [auəz] PRON unsere(r, s); *see also* **mine²**
ourselves [auə'sɛlvz] PL PRON uns (selbst); (*emphatic*) selbst; **we did it (all) by ~** wir haben alles selbst gemacht; *see also* **oneself**
oust [aust] VT (*forcibly remove*) verdrängen

KEYWORD

out¹ [aut] ADV **1** (*not in*) draußen; **out in the rain/snow** draußen im Regen/Schnee; **out here** hier; **out there** dort; **to go/come** *etc* **out** hinausgehen/-kommen *etc*; **to speak out loud** laut sprechen
2 (*not at home, absent*) nicht da
3 (*indicating distance*): **the boat was 10 km out** das Schiff war 10 km weit draußen; **3 days out from Plymouth** 3 Tage nach dem Auslaufen von Plymouth
4 (*Sport*) aus; **the ball is out/has gone out** der Ball ist aus
▸ ADJ **1**: **to be out** (*person*) (*unconscious*) bewusstlos sein; (*out of game*) ausgeschieden sein; (*out of fashion*: *style, singer*) out sein
2 (*have appeared*: *flowers*) da; (: *news, secret*) heraus
3 (*extinguished, finished*: *fire, light, gas*) aus; **before the week was out** ehe die Woche zu Ende war
4: **to be out to do sth** (*intend*) etw tun wollen
5 (*wrong*): **to be out in one's calculations** sich in seinen Berechnungen irren

out² [aut] VT (*inf*: *expose as homosexual*) outen
outage ['autɪdʒ] (*esp US*) N (*power failure*) Stromausfall *m*
out-and-out ['autəndaut] ADJ (*liar, thief etc*) ausgemacht
outback ['autbæk] N (*in Australia*): **the ~** das Hinterland
outbid [aut'bɪd] VT (*irreg*: *like* **bid**) überbieten
outboard ['autbɔ:d] N (*also*: **outboard motor**) Außenbordmotor *m*
outbound ['autbaund] ADJ (*ship*) auslaufend
outbox ['autbɔks] N (*Comput*) Postausgang *m*; (*US*: *out-tray*) Ablage *f* für Ausgänge
outbreak ['autbreɪk] N (*of war, disease etc*) Ausbruch *m*
outbuilding ['autbɪldɪŋ] N Nebengebäude *nt*
outburst ['autbə:st] N (*of anger etc*) Gefühlsausbruch *m*
outcast ['autkɑ:st] N Ausgestoßene(r) *f(m)*
outclass [aut'klɑ:s] VT deklassieren
outcome ['autkʌm] N Ergebnis *nt*, Resultat *nt*
outcrop ['autkrɔp] N (*of rock*) Block *m*
outcry ['autkraɪ] N Aufschrei *m*
outdated [aut'deɪtɪd] ADJ (*custom, idea*) veraltet
outdo [aut'du:] VT (*irreg*: *like* **do**) übertreffen
outdoor [aut'dɔ:[r]] ADJ (*activities*) im Freien; (*clothes*) für draußen; **~ swimming pool** Freibad *nt*; **she's an ~ person** sie liebt die freie Natur
outdoors [aut'dɔ:z] ADV (*play, sleep*) draußen, im Freien
outer ['autə[r]] ADJ äußere(r, s); **~ suburbs** (äußere) Vorstädte *pl*; **the ~ office** das Vorzimmer
outer space N der Weltraum
outfit ['autfɪt] N (*clothes*) Kleidung *f*; (*inf*: *team*) Verein *m*
outfitter's ['autfɪtəz] (BRIT) N (*shop*) Herrenausstatter *m*

outgoing ['autgəuɪŋ] ADJ (*extrovert*) kontaktfreudig; (*retiring: president etc*) scheidend; (*mail etc*) ausgehend
outgoings ['autgəuɪŋz] (BRIT) NPL Ausgaben *pl*
outgrow [aut'grəu] VT (*irreg: like* **grow**) (*clothes*) herauswachsen aus; (*habits etc*) ablegen
outhouse ['authaus] N Nebengebäude *nt*
outing ['autɪŋ] N Ausflug *m*
outlandish [aut'lændɪʃ] ADJ eigenartig, seltsam
outlast [aut'lɑːst] VT überleben
outlaw ['autlɔː] N Geächtete(r) *f(m)* ▶ VT verbieten
outlay ['autleɪ] N Auslagen *pl*
outlet ['autlɛt] N (*hole, pipe*) Abfluss *m*; (*US Elec*) Steckdose *f*; (*Comm: also:* **retail outlet**) Verkaufsstelle *f*; (*fig: for grief, anger etc*) Ventil *nt*
outline ['autlaɪn] N (*shape*) Umriss *m*; (*brief explanation*) Abriss *m*; (*rough sketch*) Skizze *f* ▶ VT (*fig: theory, plan etc*) umreißen, skizzieren
outlive [aut'lɪv] VT (*survive*) überleben
outlook ['autluk] N (*attitude*) Einstellung *f*; (*prospects*) Aussichten *pl*; (*for weather*) Vorhersage *f*
outlying ['autlaɪɪŋ] ADJ (*area, town etc*) entlegen
outmanoeuvre, (US) **outmaneuver** [autmə'nuːvə^r] VT ausmanövrieren
outmoded [aut'məudɪd] ADJ veraltet
outnumber [aut'nʌmbə^r] VT zahlenmäßig überlegen sein *+dat*; **to be outnumbered (by) 5 to 1** im Verhältnis 5 zu 1 in der Minderheit sein

KEYWORD

out of PREP **1** (*outside, beyond: position*) nicht in *+dat*; (*: motion*) aus *+dat*; **to look out of the window** aus dem Fenster blicken; **to be out of danger** außer Gefahr sein
2 (*cause, origin*) aus *+dat*; **out of curiosity/fear/greed** aus Neugier/Angst/Habgier; **to drink sth out of a cup** etw aus einer Tasse trinken
3 (*from among*) von *+dat*; **one out of every three smokers** einer von drei Rauchern
4 (*without*): **to be out of sugar/milk/petrol** *etc* keinen Zucker/keine Milch/kein Benzin *etc* mehr haben

out of bounds ADJ: **to be ~** verboten sein
out-of-court [autəv'kɔːt] ADJ (*settlement*) außergerichtlich; *see also* **court**
out-of-date [autəv'deɪt] ADJ (*passport, ticket etc*) abgelaufen; (*clothes, idea*) veraltet
out-of-doors [autəv'dɔːz] ADV (*play, stay etc*) im Freien
out-of-the-way ['autəvðə'weɪ] ADJ (*place*) entlegen; (*pub, restaurant etc*) kaum bekannt
out-of-work ['autəvwəːk] ADJ arbeitslos
outpatient ['autpeɪʃənt] N ambulanter Patient *m*, ambulante Patientin *f*
outpost ['autpəust] N (*Mil, Comm*) Vorposten *m*
outpouring ['autpɔːrɪŋ] N (*of emotion etc*) Erguss *m*
output ['autput] N (*production: of factory, writer etc*) Produktion *f*; (*Comput*) Output *m*, Ausgabe *f* ▶ VT (*Comput*) ausgeben

outrage ['autreɪdʒ] N (*scandal*) Skandal *m*; (*atrocity*) Verbrechen *nt*, Ausschreitung *f*; (*anger*) Empörung *f* ▶ VT (*shock, anger*) empören
outrageous [aut'reɪdʒəs] ADJ (*remark etc*) empörend; (*clothes*) unmöglich; (*scandalous*) skandalös
outrider ['autraɪdə^r] N (*on motorcycle*) Kradbegleiter *m*
outright [aut'raɪt] ADV (*kill*) auf der Stelle; (*win*) überlegen; (*buy*) auf einen Schlag; (*ask, refuse*) ohne Umschweife ▶ ADJ (*winner, victory*) unbestritten; (*refusal, hostility*) total
outrun [aut'rʌn] VT (*irreg: like* **run**) schneller laufen als
outset ['autsɛt] N Anfang *m*, Beginn *m*; **from the ~** von Anfang an; **at the ~** am Anfang
outshine [aut'ʃaɪn] VT (*irreg: like* **shine**) (*fig*) in den Schatten stellen
outside [aut'saɪd] N (*of building etc*) Außenseite *f* ▶ ADJ (*wall, lavatory*) Außen- ▶ ADV (*be, wait*) draußen; (*go*) nach draußen ▶ PREP außerhalb *+gen*; (*door etc*) vor *+dat*; **at the ~** (*at the most*) höchstens; (*at the latest*) spätestens; **an ~ chance** eine geringe Chance
outside broadcast N außerhalb des Studios produzierte Sendung *f*
outside lane N Überholspur *f*
outside line N (*Tel*) Amtsanschluss *m*
outsider [aut'saɪdə^r] N (*stranger*) Außenstehende(r) *f(m)*; (*odd one out, in race etc*) Außenseiter(in) *m(f)*
outsize ['autsaɪz] ADJ (*clothes*) übergroß
outskirts ['autskəːts] NPL (*of town*) Stadtrand *m*
outsmart [aut'smɑːt] VT austricksen (*inf*)
outspoken [aut'spəukən] ADJ offen
outspread [aut'sprɛd] ADJ (*wings, arms etc*) ausgebreitet
outstanding [aut'stændɪŋ] ADJ (*exceptional*) hervorragend; (*remaining*) ausstehend; **your account is still ~** Ihr Konto weist noch Außenstände auf
outstay [aut'steɪ] VT: **to ~ one's welcome** länger bleiben als erwünscht
outstretched [aut'strɛtʃt] ADJ ausgestreckt
outstrip [aut'strɪp] VT (*competitors, supply*): **to ~ (in)** übertreffen (an *+dat*)
out tray N Ablage *f* für Ausgänge
outvote [aut'vəut] VT überstimmen
outward ['autwəd] ADJ (*sign, appearances*) äußere(r, s) ▶ ADV (*move, face*) nach außen; **~ journey** Hinreise *f*
outwardly ['autwədlɪ] ADV (*on the surface*) äußerlich
outwards ['autwədz] ADV (*move, face*) nach außen
outweigh [aut'weɪ] VT schwerer wiegen als
outwit [aut'wɪt] VT überlisten
ova ['əuvə] NPL *of* **ovum**
oval ['əuvl] ADJ oval ▶ N Oval *nt*

> **Oval Office**, ein großer ovaler Raum im Weißen Haus, ist das private Büro des amerikanischen Präsidenten. Im weiteren Sinne bezieht sich dieser Begriff oft auf die Präsidentschaft selbst.

ovarian [əu'vɛərɪən] ADJ (*Anat*) des Eierstocks/der Eierstöcke; **~ cyst** Zyste *f* im Eierstock
ovary ['əuvərɪ] N (*Anat, Med*) Eierstock *m*
ovation [əu'veɪʃən] N Ovation *f*
oven ['ʌvn] N (*Culin*) Backofen *m*
ovenproof ['ʌvnpru:f] ADJ (*dish etc*) feuerfest
oven-ready ['ʌvnrɛdɪ] ADJ backfertig
ovenware ['ʌvnwɛə^r] N feuerfestes Geschirr *nt*

KEYWORD

over ['əuvə^r] ADV **1** (*across: walk, jump, fly etc*) hinüber; **over here** hier; **over there** dort (drüben); **to ask sb over** (*to one's house*) jdn zu sich einladen
2 (*indicating movement*): **to fall over** (*person*) hinfallen; (*object*) umfallen; **to knock sth over** etw umstoßen; **to turn over** (*in bed*) sich umdrehen; **to bend over** sich bücken
3 (*finished*): **to be over** (*game, life, relationship etc*) vorbei sein, zu Ende sein
4 (*excessively: clever, rich, fat etc*) übermäßig
5 (*remaining: money, food etc*) übrig; **is there any cake (left) over?** ist noch Kuchen übrig?
6: **all over** (*everywhere*) überall
7 (*repeatedly*): **over and over (again)** immer (und immer) wieder; **five times over** fünfmal
▶ PREP **1** (*on top of, above*) über *+dat*; (*with vb of motion*) über *+acc*; **to spread a sheet over sth** ein Laken über etw *acc* breiten
2 (*on the other side of*): **the pub over the road** die Kneipe gegenüber; **he jumped over the wall** er sprang über die Mauer
3 (*more than*) über *+acc*; **over 200 people** über 200 Leute; **over and above my normal duties** über meine normalen Pflichten hinaus; **over and above that** darüber hinaus
4 (*during*) während; **let's discuss it over dinner** wir sollten es beim Abendessen besprechen

over... ['əuvə^r] PREF über-
overact [əuvər'ækt] VI übertreiben
overall ['əuvərɔ:l] ADJ (*length, cost etc*) Gesamt-; (*impression, view*) allgemein ▶ ADV (*measure, cost*) insgesamt; (*generally*) im Allgemeinen ▶ N (BRIT) Kittel *m*; **overalls** NPL Overall *m*
overall majority N absolute Mehrheit *f*
overanxious [əuvər'æŋkʃəs] ADJ überängstlich
overawe [əuvər'ɔ:] VT: **to be overawed (by)** überwältigt sein (von)
overbalance [əuvə'bæləns] VI das Gleichgewicht verlieren
overbearing [əuvə'bɛərɪŋ] ADJ (*person, manner*) aufdringlich
overboard ['əuvəbɔ:d] ADV (*Naut*) über Bord; **to go ~** (*fig*) es übertreiben, zu weit gehen
overbook [əuvə'buk] VT überbuchen
overcame [əuvə'keɪm] PT *of* **overcome**
overcapitalize [əuvə'kæpɪtəlaɪz] VT überkapitalisieren
overcast ['əuvəkɑ:st] ADJ (*day, sky*) bedeckt
overcharge [əuvə'tʃɑ:dʒ] VT zu viel berechnen *+dat*
overcoat ['əuvəkəut] N Mantel *m*
overcome [əuvə'kʌm] VT (*irreg: like* **come**) (*problem, fear*) überwinden ▶ ADJ überwältigt; **she was ~ with grief** der Schmerz übermannte sie
overconfident [əuvə'kɔnfɪdənt] ADJ zu selbstsicher
overcooked [əuvə'kukt] ADJ verkocht; (*meat*) zu lange gebraten
overcrowded [əuvə'kraudɪd] ADJ überfüllt
overcrowding [əuvə'kraudɪŋ] N Überfüllung *f*
overdo [əuvə'du:] VT (*irreg: like* **do**) übertreiben; **to ~ it** es übertreiben
overdone ADJ übertrieben; (*food*) zu lange gekocht; (*meat*) zu lange gebraten
overdose ['əuvədəus] N Überdosis *f*
overdraft ['əuvədrɑ:ft] N Kontoüberziehung *f*; **to have an ~** sein Konto überziehen
overdrawn [əuvə'drɔ:n] ADJ (*account*) überzogen; **I am ~** ich habe mein Konto überzogen
overdrive ['əuvədraɪv] N (*Aut*) Schongang *m*
overdue [əuvə'dju:] ADJ überfällig; **that change was long ~** diese Änderung war schon lange fällig
overemphasis [əuvər'ɛmfəsɪs] N: **~ on** Überbetonung *+gen*
overestimate [əuvər'ɛstɪmeɪt] VT überschätzen
overexcited [əuvərɪk'saɪtɪd] ADJ ganz aufgeregt
overexertion [əuvərɪg'zə:ʃən] N Überanstrengung *f*
overexpose [əuvərɪk'spəuz] VT (*Phot*) überbelichten
overflow [əuvə'fləu] VI (*river*) über die Ufer treten; (*bath, jar etc*) überlaufen ▶ N (*also*: **overflow pipe**) Überlaufrohr *nt*
overgenerous [əuvə'dʒɛnərəs] ADJ allzu großzügig
overgrown [əuvə'grəun] ADJ (*garden*) verwildert; **he's just an ~ schoolboy** er ist nur ein großes Kind
overhang ['əuvə'hæŋ] VT (*irreg: like* **hang**) herausragen über *+acc* ▶ VI überhängen ▶ N Überhang *m*
overhaul [əuvə'hɔ:l] VT (*equipment, car etc*) überholen ▶ N Überholung *f*
overhead [əuvə'hɛd] ADV (*above*) oben; (*in the sky*) in der Luft ▶ ADJ (*lighting*) Decken-; (*cables, wires*) Überland- ▶ N (US) = **overheads**; **overheads** NPL allgemeine Unkosten *pl*
overhear [əuvə'hɪə^r] VT (*irreg: like* **hear**) (zufällig) mit anhören
overheat [əuvə'hi:t] VI (*engine*) heißlaufen
overjoyed [əuvə'dʒɔɪd] ADJ überglücklich; **to be ~ (at)** überglücklich sein (über *+acc*)
overkill ['əuvəkɪl] N (*fig*): **it would be ~** das wäre zu viel des Guten
overland ['əuvəlænd] ADJ (*journey*) Überland- ▶ ADV (*travel*) über Land
overlap [əuvə'læp] VI (*figures, ideas etc*) sich überschneiden
overleaf [əuvə'li:f] ADV umseitig, auf der Rückseite
overload [əuvə'ləud] VT (*vehicle*) überladen; (*Elec*) überbelasten; (*fig: with work etc*) überlasten

O

overlook [əuvəˈluk] VT (*have view over*) überblicken; (*fail to notice*) übersehen; (*excuse, forgive*) hinwegsehen über *+acc*
overlord [ˈəuvəlɔːd] N oberster Herr *m*
overmanning [əuvəˈmænɪŋ] N Überbesetzung *f*
overnight [əuvəˈnaɪt] ADV über Nacht ▸ ADJ (*bag, clothes*) Reise-; (*accommodation, stop*) für die Nacht; **to travel ~** nachts reisen; **he'll be away ~** (*tonight*) er kommt erst morgen zurück; **to stay ~** über Nacht bleiben; **~ stay** Übernachtung *f*
overpass [ˈəuvəpɑːs] (*esp US*) N Überführung *f*
overpay [əuvəˈpeɪ] VT (*irreg: like* **pay**): **to ~ sb by £50** jdm £ 50 zu viel bezahlen
overplay [əuvəˈpleɪ] VT (*overact*) übertrieben darstellen; **to ~ one's hand** den Bogen überspannen
overpower [əuvəˈpauəʳ] VT überwältigen
overpowering [əuvəˈpauərɪŋ] ADJ (*heat*) unerträglich; (*stench*) durchdringend; (*feeling, desire*) überwältigend
overproduction [ˈəuvəprəˈdʌkʃən] N Überproduktion *f*
overrate [əuvəˈreɪt] VT überschätzen
overreach [əuvəˈriːtʃ] VT: **to ~ o.s.** sich übernehmen
overreact [əuvəriːˈækt] VI übertrieben reagieren
override [əuvəˈraɪd] VT (*irreg: like* **ride**) (*order etc*) sich hinwegsetzen über *+acc*
overriding [əuvəˈraɪdɪŋ] ADJ vorrangig
overrule [əuvəˈruːl] VT (*claim, person*) zurückweisen; (*decision*) aufheben
overrun [əuvəˈrʌn] VT (*irreg: like* **run**) (*country, continent*) einfallen in *+acc* ▸ VI (*meeting etc*) zu lange dauern; **the town is ~ with tourists** die Stadt ist von Touristen überlaufen
overseas [əuvəˈsiːz] ADV (*live, work*) im Ausland; (*travel*) ins Ausland ▸ ADJ (*market, trade*) Übersee-; (*student, visitor*) aus dem Ausland
oversee [əuvəˈsiː] VT (*irreg: like* **see**) (*supervise*) beaufsichtigen, überwachen
overseer [ˈəuvəsɪəʳ] N Aufseher(in) *m(f)*
overshadow [əuvəˈʃædəu] VT (*place, building etc*) überschatten; (*fig*) in den Schatten stellen
overshoot [əuvəˈʃuːt] VT (*irreg: like* **shoot**) (*target, runway*) hinausschießen über *+acc*
oversight [ˈəuvəsaɪt] N Versehen *nt*; **due to an ~** aus Versehen
oversimplify [əuvəˈsɪmplɪfaɪ] VT zu stark vereinfachen
oversleep [əuvəˈsliːp] VI (*irreg: like* **sleep**) verschlafen
overspend [əuvəˈspɛnd] VI (*irreg: like* **spend**) zu viel ausgeben; **we have overspent by 5,000 dollars** wir haben 5000 Dollar zu viel ausgegeben
overspill [ˈəuvəspɪl] N (*excess population*) Bevölkerungsüberschuss *m*
overstaffed [əuvəˈstɑːft] ADJ: **to be ~** überbesetzt sein
overstate [əuvəˈsteɪt] VT (*exaggerate*) zu sehr betonen
overstatement [əuvəˈsteɪtmənt] N Übertreibung *f*
overstay [əuvəˈsteɪ] VT *see* **outstay**
overstep [əuvəˈstɛp] VT: **to ~ the mark** zu weit gehen
overstock [əuvəˈstɔk] VT zu große Bestände anlegen in *+dat*
overstretched [əuvəˈstrɛtʃt] ADJ (*person, resources*) überfordert
overstrike [ˈəuvəstraɪk] N (*on printer*) Mehrfachdruck *m* ▸ VT (*irreg: like* **strike**) mehrfachdrucken
oversubscribed [əuvəsəbˈskraɪbd] ADJ (*Comm etc*) überzeichnet
overt [əuˈvəːt] ADJ offen
overtake [əuvəˈteɪk] VT (*irreg: like* **take**) (*Aut*) überholen; (*event, change*) hereinbrechen über *+acc*; (*emotion*) befallen ▸ VI (*Aut*) überholen
overtaking [əuvəˈteɪkɪŋ] N (*Aut*) Überholen *nt*
overtax [əuvəˈtæks] VT (*Econ*) zu hoch besteuern; (*strength, patience*) überfordern; **to ~ o.s.** sich übernehmen
overthrow [əuvəˈθrəu] VT (*irreg: like* **throw**) (*government etc*) stürzen
overtime [ˈəuvətaɪm] N Überstunden *pl*; **to do** *or* **work ~** Überstunden machen
overtime ban N Überstundenverbot *nt*
overtone [ˈəuvətəun] N (*fig: also:* **overtones**): **overtones of** Untertöne *pl* von
overture [ˈəuvətʃuəʳ] N (*Mus*) Ouvertüre *f*; (*fig*) Annäherungsversuch *m*
overturn [əuvəˈtəːn] VT (*car, chair*) umkippen; (*fig: decision*) aufheben; (*: government*) stürzen ▸ VI (*train etc*) umkippen; (*car*) sich überschlagen; (*boat*) kentern
overview [ˈəuvəvjuː] N Überblick *m*
overweight [əuvəˈweɪt] ADJ (*person*) übergewichtig
overwhelm [əuvəˈwɛlm] VT überwältigen
overwhelming [əuvəˈwɛlmɪŋ] ADJ überwältigend; **one's ~ impression is of heat/noise** man bemerkt vor allem die Hitze/den Lärm
overwhelmingly [əuvəˈwɛlmɪŋlɪ] ADV (*vote, reject*) mit überwältigender Mehrheit; (*appreciative, generous etc*) über alle Maßen; (*opposed etc*) überwiegend
overwork [əuvəˈwəːk] N Überarbeitung *f* ▸ VT (*person*) (mit Arbeit) überlasten; (*cliché etc*) überstrapazieren ▸ VI sich überarbeiten
overworked ADJ überarbeitet
overwrite [əuvəˈraɪt] VT (*irreg: like* **write**) (*Comput*) überschreiben
overwrought [əuvəˈrɔːt] ADJ (*person*) überreizt
ovulate [ˈɔvjuleɪt] VI ovulieren
ovulation [ɔvjuˈleɪʃən] N Eisprung *m*, Ovulation *f*
ovum [ˈəuvəm] (*pl* **ova**) N Eizelle *f*
owe [əu] VT: **to ~ sb sth, to ~ sth to sb** (*lit, fig*) jdm etw schulden; (*life, talent, good looks etc*) jdm etw verdanken
owing to [ˈəuɪŋ-] PREP (*because of*) wegen *+gen*, aufgrund *+gen*
owl [aul] N Eule *f*
own [əun] VT (*possess*) besitzen ▸ VI (*Brit form*): **to**

~ up to sth etw zugeben ▸ ADJ eigen; **a room of my ~** mein eigenes Zimmer; **to get one's ~ back** (*take revenge*) sich rächen; **on one's ~** allein; **to come into one's ~** sich entfalten
▸ **own up** VI gestehen, es zugeben
own brand N (*Comm*) Hausmarke *f*
owner ['əunəʳ] N Besitzer(in) *m(f)*, Eigentümer(in) *m(f)*
owner-occupier ['əunər'ɔkjupaɪəʳ] N (*Admin, Law*) Bewohner(in) *m(f)* im eigenen Haus
ownership ['əunəʃɪp] N Besitz *m*; **under new ~** (*shop etc*) unter neuer Leitung
own goal N (*also fig*) Eigentor *nt*
ox [ɔks] (*pl* **oxen**) N Ochse *m*

> **Oxbridge**, eine Mischung aus Ox(ford) und (Cam)bridge, bezieht sich auf die traditionsreichen Universitäten von Oxford und Cambridge. Dieser Begriff ist oft wertend und bringt das Prestige und die Privilegien zum Ausdruck, die traditionellerweise mit diesen Universitäten in Verbindung gebracht werden.

OXFAM (BRIT) N ABBR (= *Oxford Committee for Famine Relief*) *karitative Vereinigung zur Hungerhilfe*
oxide ['ɔksaɪd] N Oxid *nt*
oxidize ['ɔksɪdaɪz] VI oxidieren
Oxon. ['ɔksn] (BRIT) ABBR (*Post*) = **Oxfordshire**; (*in degree titles: = Oxoniensis*) *der Universität Oxford*
oxtail ['ɔksteɪl] N: **~ soup** Ochsenschwanzsuppe *f*
oxyacetylene ['ɔksɪə'sɛtɪliːn] ADJ (*flame*) Azetylensauerstoff-; **~ burner** Schweißbrenner *m*; **~ welding** Autogenschweißen *nt*
oxygen ['ɔksɪdʒən] N Sauerstoff *m*
oxygen mask N Sauerstoffmaske *f*
oxygen tent N Sauerstoffzelt *nt*
oyster ['ɔɪstəʳ] N Auster *f*
Oz ['ɒz] N (*inf*) Australien *nt*
oz ABBR = **ounce**
ozone ['əuzəun] N Ozon *nt*
ozone hole N Ozonloch *nt*
ozone layer N: **the ~** die Ozonschicht

Pp

P[1], p [piː] N (*letter*) P *nt*, p *nt*; **P for Peter** ≈ P wie Paula
P. ABBR = **president; prince**
p[2] (BRIT) ABBR = **penny; pence**
p. ABBR (= *page*) S.
PA N ABBR = **personal assistant; public-address system** ▶ ABBR (*US Post*) = **Pennsylvania**
pa [pɑː] (*inf*) N Papa *m*
p.a. ABBR (= *per annum*) p.a.
PAC (US) N ABBR (= *political action committee*) *politisches Aktionskomitee*
pace [peɪs] N (*step*) Schritt *m*; (*speed*) Tempo *nt* ▶ VI: **to ~ up and down** auf und ab gehen; **to keep ~ with** Schritt halten mit; **to set the ~** das Tempo angeben; **to put sb through his/her paces** (*fig*) jdn auf Herz und Nieren prüfen
pacemaker ['peɪsmeɪkər] N (*Med*) (Herz)schrittmacher *m*; (*Sport*: *pacesetter*) Schrittmacher *m*
pacesetter ['peɪssetər] N (*Sport*) = **pacemaker**
Pacific [pə'sɪfɪk] N (*Geog*): **the ~ (Ocean)** der Pazifik, der Pazifische Ozean
pacific [pə'sɪfɪk] ADJ (*intentions etc*) friedlich
pacifier ['pæsɪfaɪər] (US) N (*dummy*) Schnuller *m*
pacifist ['pæsɪfɪst] N Pazifist(in) *m(f)*
pacify ['pæsɪfaɪ] VT (*person, fears*) beruhigen
pack [pæk] N (*packet*) Packung *f*; (*US*: *of cigarettes*) Schachtel *f*; (*of people, hounds*) Meute *f*; (*also*: **back pack**) Rucksack *m*; (*of cards*) (Karten)spiel *nt* ▶ VT (*clothes etc*) einpacken; (*suitcase etc, Comput*) packen; (*press down*) pressen ▶ VI packen; **to ~ one's bags** (*fig*) die Koffer packen; **to ~ into** (*cram*: *people, objects*) hineinstopfen in *+acc*; **to send sb packing** (*inf*) jdn kurz abfertigen
▶ **pack in** (BRIT *inf*) VT (*job*) hinschmeißen; **~ it in!** hör auf!
▶ **pack off** VT schicken
▶ **pack up** VI (BRIT *inf*: *machine*) den Geist aufgeben; (: *person*) Feierabend machen ▶ VT (*belongings*) zusammenpacken
package ['pækɪdʒ] N (*parcel, Comput*) Paket *nt*; (*also*: **package deal**) Pauschalangebot *nt* ▶ VT verpacken
package holiday, (US) **package tour** N Pauschalreise *f*
packaging ['pækɪdʒɪŋ] N Verpackung *f*
packaging industry N Verpackungsindustrie *f*
packed [pækt] ADJ (*crowded*) randvoll
packed lunch (BRIT) N Lunchpaket *nt*
packer ['pækər] N Packer(in) *m(f)*
packet ['pækɪt] N Packung *f*; (*of cigarettes*) Schachtel *m*; **to make a ~** (BRIT *inf*) einen Haufen Geld verdienen
packet switching N (*Comput*) Paketvermittlung *f*
pack ice ['pækaɪs] N Packeis *nt*
packing ['pækɪŋ] N (*act*) Packen *nt*; (*material*) Verpackung *f*
packing case N Kiste *f*
pact [pækt] N Pakt *m*
pad [pæd] N (*paper*) Block *m*; (*to prevent damage*) Polster *nt*; (*inf*: *home*) Bude *f* ▶ VT (*upholstery etc*) polstern ▶ VI: **to ~ about/in** herum-/hereintrotten
padded cell ['pædɪd-] N Gummizelle *f*
padded envelope N wattierter Umschlag
padding ['pædɪŋ] N (*material*) Polsterung *f*; (*fig*) Füllwerk *nt*
paddle ['pædl] N (*oar*) Paddel *nt*; (*US*: *for table tennis*) Schläger *m* ▶ VT paddeln ▶ VI (*at seaside*) plan(t)schen
paddle steamer N Raddampfer *m*
paddling pool ['pædlɪŋ-] (BRIT) N Plan(t)schbecken *nt*
paddock ['pædək] N (*small field*) Koppel *f*; (*at race course*) Sattelplatz *m*
paddy field ['pædɪ-] N Reisfeld *nt*
padlock ['pædlɔk] N Vorhängeschloss *nt* ▶ VT (mit einem Vorhängeschloss) verschließen
padre ['pɑːdrɪ] N (*Rel*) Feldgeistliche(r) *m*
paediatrician [piːdɪə'trɪʃən] N Kinderarzt *m*, Kinderärztin *f*
paediatrics, (US) **pediatrics** [piːdɪ'ætrɪks] N Kinderheilkunde *f*, Pädiatrie *f*
paedophile ['piːdəufaɪl] N Pädophile(r) *f(m)* ▶ ADJ pädophil
paedophilia [piːdəu'fɪlɪə] N Pädophilie *f*
pagan ['peɪgən] ADJ heidnisch ▶ N Heide *m*, Heidin *f*
page [peɪdʒ] N (*of book etc*) Seite *f*; (*in hotel*: *also*: **pageboy**) Page *m* ▶ VT (*in hotel etc*) ausrufen lassen
pageant ['pædʒənt] N (*historical procession*) Festzug *m*; (*show*) Historienspiel *nt*
pageantry ['pædʒəntrɪ] N Prunk *m*

pageboy ['peɪdʒbɔɪ] N *see* **page**
pager ['peɪdʒəʳ] N Funkrufempfänger *m*, Piepser *m* (*inf*)
paginate ['pædʒɪneɪt] VT paginieren
pagination [pædʒɪ'neɪʃən] N Paginierung *f*
pagoda [pə'gəudə] N Pagode *f*
paid [peɪd] PT, PP *of* **pay** ▸ ADJ bezahlt; **to put ~ to** (BRIT) zunichtemachen
paid-in ['peɪdɪn] (US) ADJ = **paid-up**
paid-up ['peɪdʌp], (US) **paid-in** ['peɪdɪn] ADJ (*member*) zahlend; (*Comm: shares*) eingezahlt; **~ capital** eingezahltes Kapital *nt*
pail [peɪl] N Eimer *m*
pain [peɪn] N Schmerz *m*; (*inf: also:* **pain in the neck**: *nuisance*) Plage *f*; **to have a ~ in the chest/arm** Schmerzen in der Brust/im Arm haben; **to be in ~** Schmerzen haben; **to take pains to do sth** (*make an effort*) sich *dat* Mühe geben, etw zu tun; **on ~ of death** bei Todesstrafe; **he is/it is a right ~ (in the neck)** (*inf*) er/das geht einem auf den Wecker
pained [peɪnd] ADJ (*expression*) gequält
painful ['peɪnful] ADJ (*back, injury etc*) schmerzhaft; (*sight, decision etc*) schmerzlich; (*laborious*) mühsam; (*embarrassing*) peinlich
painfully ['peɪnfəlɪ] ADV (*fig: extremely*) furchtbar
painkiller ['peɪnkɪləʳ] N schmerzstillendes Mittel *nt*
painless ['peɪnlɪs] ADJ schmerzlos
painstaking ['peɪnzteɪkɪŋ] ADJ (*work, person*) gewissenhaft
paint [peɪnt] N Farbe *f* ▸ VT (*door, house etc*) anstreichen; (*person, picture*) malen; (*fig*) zeichnen; **a tin of ~** eine Dose Farbe; **to ~ the door blue** die Tür blau streichen; **to ~ in oils** in Öl malen
paintbox ['peɪntbɔks] N Farbkasten *m*, Malkasten *m*
paintbrush ['peɪntbrʌʃ] N Pinsel *m*
painter ['peɪntəʳ] N (*artist*) Maler(in) *m(f)*; (*decorator*) Anstreicher(in) *m(f)*
painting ['peɪntɪŋ] N (*activity: of artist*) Malerei *f*; (*: of decorator*) Anstreichen *nt*; (*picture*) Bild *nt*, Gemälde *nt*
paint stripper N Abbeizmittel *nt*
paintwork ['peɪntwəːk] N (*of wall etc*) Anstrich *m*; (*of car*) Lack *m*
pair [pɛəʳ] N Paar *nt*; **a ~ of scissors** eine Schere; **a ~ of trousers** eine Hose
▸ **pair off** VI: **to ~ off with sb** sich jdm anschließen
pajamas [pə'dʒɑːməz] (US) NPL Schlafanzug *m*, Pyjama *m*
Pakistan [pɑːkɪ'stɑːn] N Pakistan *nt*
Pakistani [pɑːkɪ'stɑːnɪ] ADJ pakistanisch ▸ N Pakistani *m*, Pakistaner(in) *m(f)*
PAL N ABBR (TV: = *phase alternation line*) PAL *nt*
pal [pæl] (*inf*) N (*friend*) Kumpel *m*, Freund(in) *m(f)*
palace ['pæləs] N Palast *m*
palaeontology [pælɪɔn'tɔlədʒɪ] N Paläontologie *f*
palatable ['pælɪtəbl] ADJ (*food, drink*) genießbar; (*fig: idea, fact etc*) angenehm
palate ['pælɪt] N (*Anat*) Gaumen *m*; (*sense of taste*) Geschmackssinn *m*
palatial [pə'leɪʃəl] ADJ (*residence etc*) prunkvoll
palaver [pə'lɑːvəʳ] (*inf*) N (*fuss*) Theater *nt*
pale [peɪl] ADJ blass; (*light*) fahl ▸ VI erblassen ▸ N: **beyond the ~** (*unacceptable: behaviour*) indiskutabel; **to grow** *or* **turn ~** erblassen, blass werden; **~ blue** zartblau; **to ~ into insignificance (beside)** zur Bedeutungslosigkeit herabsinken (gegenüber *+dat*)
paleness ['peɪlnɪs] N Blässe *f*
Palestine ['pælɪstaɪn] N Palästina *nt*
Palestinian [pælɪs'tɪnɪən] ADJ palästinensisch ▸ N Palästinenser(in) *m(f)*
palette ['pælɪt] N Palette *f*
palings ['peɪlɪŋz] NPL (*fence*) Lattenzaun *m*
palisade [pælɪ'seɪd] N Palisade *f*
pall [pɔːl] N (*cloud of smoke*) (Rauch)wolke *f* ▸ VI an Reiz verlieren
pallet ['pælɪt] N (*for goods*) Palette *f*
palliative ['pælɪətɪv] N (*Med*) Linderungsmittel *nt*; (*fig*) Beschönigung *f*
pallid ['pælɪd] ADJ bleich
pallor ['pæləʳ] N Bleichheit *f*
pally ['pælɪ] (*inf*) ADJ: **they're very ~** sie sind dicke Freunde
palm [pɑːm] N (*also:* **palm tree**) Palme *f*; (*of hand*) Handteller *m* ▸ VT: **to ~ sth off on sb** (*inf*) jdm etw andrehen
palmistry ['pɑːmɪstrɪ] N Handlesekunst *f*
Palm Sunday N Palmsonntag *m*
palpable ['pælpəbl] ADJ (*obvious*) offensichtlich
palpitations [pælpɪ'teɪʃənz] NPL (*Med*) Herzklopfen *nt*
paltry ['pɔːltrɪ] ADJ (*amount, wage*) armselig
pamper ['pæmpəʳ] VT verwöhnen
pamphlet ['pæmflət] N Broschüre *f*; (*political*) Flugschrift *f*
pan [pæn] N (*also:* **saucepan**) Topf *m*; (*also:* **frying pan**) Pfanne *f* ▸ VI (*Cine, TV*) schwenken ▸ VT (*inf: book, film*) verreißen; **to ~ for gold** Gold waschen
panacea [pænə'sɪə] N Allheilmittel *nt*
panache [pə'næʃ] N Elan *m*, Schwung *m*
Panama ['pænəmɑː] N Panama *nt*
panama [pænə'mɑː] N (*also:* **panama hat**) Panamahut *m*
Panama Canal N: **the ~** der Panamakanal
Panamanian [pænə'meɪnɪən] ADJ panamaisch ▸ N Panamaer(in) *m(f)*
pancake ['pænkeɪk] N Pfannkuchen *m*
Pancake Day (BRIT) N Fastnachtsdienstag *m*
pancake roll N *gefüllte Pfannkuchenrolle*
pancreas ['pæŋkrɪəs] N Bauchspeicheldrüse *f*
panda ['pændə] N Panda *m*
panda car (BRIT) N Streifenwagen *m*
pandemic [pændɛmɪk] N Pandemie *f*
pandemonium [pændɪ'məunɪəm] N Chaos *nt*
pander ['pændəʳ] VI: **to ~ to** (*person, desire etc*) sich richten nach, entgegenkommen *+dat*
p & h (US) ABBR (= *postage and handling*) Porto und Bearbeitungsgebühr

P

P & L ABBR (= *profit and loss*) Gewinn und Verlust; *see also* **profit**

p & p (BRIT) ABBR (= *postage and packing*) Porto und Verpackung

pane [peɪn] N (*of glass*) Scheibe *f*

panel ['pænl] N (*wood, metal, glass etc*) Platte *f*, Tafel *f*; (*group of experts etc*) Diskussionsrunde *f*; **~ of judges** Jury *f*

panel game (BRIT) N Ratespiel *nt*

panelling, (US) **paneling** ['pænəlɪŋ] N Täfelung *f*

panellist, (US) **panelist** ['pænəlɪst] N Diskussionsteilnehmer(in) *m(f)*

pang [pæŋ] N: **to have** *or* **feel a ~ of regret** Reue empfinden; **hunger pangs** quälender Hunger *m*; **pangs of conscience** Gewissensbisse *pl*

panhandler ['pænhændləʳ] (*US inf*) N Bettler(in) *m(f)*

panic ['pænɪk] N Panik *f* ▸ VI in Panik geraten

panic buying [-baɪɪŋ] N Panikkäufe *pl*

panicky ['pænɪkɪ] ADJ (*person*) überängstlich; (*feeling*) Angst-; (*reaction*) Kurzschluss-

panic-stricken ['pænɪkstrɪkən] ADJ (*person, face*) von Panik erfasst

pannier ['pænɪəʳ] N (*on bicycle*) Satteltasche *f*; (*on animal*) (Trage)korb *m*

panorama [pænə'rɑːmə] N (*view*) Panorama *nt*

panoramic [pænə'ræmɪk] ADJ (*view*) Panorama-

pansy ['pænzɪ] N (*Bot*) Stiefmütterchen *nt*; (*inf, pej: sissy*) Tunte *f*

pant [pænt] VI (*person*) keuchen; (*animal*) hecheln

pantechnicon [pæn'tɛknɪkən] (BRIT) N Möbelwagen *m*

panther ['pænθəʳ] N Pant(h)er *m*

panties ['pæntɪz] NPL Höschen *nt*

panto ['pæntəu], **pantomime** ['pæntəumaɪm] N *siehe Info-Artikel*

> **Pantomime** oder umgangssprächlich **panto** ist in Großbritannien ein zur Weihnachtszeit aufgeführtes Märchenspiel mit possenhaften Elementen, Musik, Standardrollen (ein als Frau verkleideter Mann, ein Junge, ein Bösewicht) und aktuellen Witzen. Publikumsbeteiligung wird gern gesehen (z. B. warnen die Kinder den Helden mit dem Ruf „He's behind you" vor einer drohenden Gefahr), und viele der Witze sprechen vor allem Erwachsene an, sodass pantomimes Unterhaltung für die ganze Familie bieten.

pantry ['pæntrɪ] N (*cupboard*) Vorratsschrank *m*; (*room*) Speisekammer *f*

pants [pænts] NPL (BRIT: *woman's*) Höschen *nt*; (: *man's*) Unterhose *f*; (*US: trousers*) Hose *f*

panty hose (US) NPL Strumpfhose *f*

papacy ['peɪpəsɪ] N Papsttum *nt*; **during the ~ of Paul VI** während der Amtszeit von Papst Paul VI

papal ['peɪpəl] ADJ päpstlich

paparazzi [pæpə'rætsiː] NPL Pressefotografen *pl*, Paparazzi *pl*

paper ['peɪpəʳ] N Papier *nt*; (*also*: **newspaper**) Zeitung *f*; (*exam*) Arbeit *f*; (*academic essay*) Referat *nt*; (*document*) Dokument *nt*, Papier; (*wallpaper*) Tapete *f* ▸ ADJ (*made from paper: hat, plane etc*) Papier-, aus Papier ▸ VT (*room*) tapezieren; **papers** NPL (*also*: **identity papers**) Papiere *pl*; **a piece of ~** (*odd bit*) ein Stück *nt* Papier, ein Zettel *m*; (*sheet*) ein Blatt *nt* Papier; **to put sth down on ~** etw schriftlich festhalten

paper advance N (*on printer*) Papiervorschub *m*

paperback ['peɪpəbæk] N Taschenbuch *nt*, Paperback *nt* ▸ ADJ: **~ edition** Taschenbuchausgabe *f*

paper bag N Tüte *f*

paperboy ['peɪpəbɔɪ] N Zeitungsjunge *m*

paperclip ['peɪpəklɪp] N Büroklammer *f*

paper hankie N Tempotaschentuch® *nt*

paper mill N Papierfabrik *f*

paper money N Papiergeld *nt*

paper round N: **to do a ~** Zeitungen austragen

paper shop N Zeitungsladen *m*

paperweight ['peɪpəweɪt] N Briefbeschwerer *m*

paperwork ['peɪpəwəːk] N Schreibarbeit *f*

papier-mâché [pæpjeɪ'mæʃeɪ] N Papiermaschee *nt*

paprika ['pæprɪkə] N Paprika *m*

Pap Smear, Pap Test N (*Med*) Abstrich *m*

par [pɑːʳ] N (*Golf*) Par *nt*; **to be on a ~ with** sich messen können mit; **at ~** (*Comm*) zum Nennwert; **above/below ~** (*Comm*) über/unter dem Nennwert; **above** *or* **over ~** (*Golf*) über dem Par; **below** *or* **under ~** (*Golf*) unter dem Par; **to feel below** *or* **under ~** sich nicht auf der Höhe fühlen; **to be ~ for the course** (*fig*) zu erwarten sein

parable ['pærəbl] N Gleichnis *nt*

parabola [pə'ræbələ] N (*Math*) Parabel *f*

paracetamol [pærə'siːtəmɒl] N (*tablet*) Paracetamoltablette *f*

parachute ['pærəʃuːt] N Fallschirm *m*

parachute jump N Fallschirmabsprung *m*

parachutist ['pærəʃuːtɪst] N Fallschirmspringer(in) *m(f)*

parade [pə'reɪd] N (*procession*) Parade *f*; (*ceremony*) Zeremonie *f* ▸ VT (*people*) aufmarschieren lassen; (*wealth, knowledge etc*) zur Schau stellen ▸ VI (*Mil*) aufmarschieren; **fashion ~** Modenschau *f*

parade ground N Truppenübungsplatz *m*, Exerzierplatz *m*

paradise ['pærədaɪs] N (*also fig*) Paradies *nt*

paradox ['pærədɔks] N Paradox *nt*

paradoxical [pærə'dɔksɪkl] ADJ (*situation*) paradox

paradoxically [pærə'dɔksɪklɪ] ADV paradoxerweise

paraffin ['pærəfɪn] (BRIT) N (*also*: **paraffin oil**) Petroleum *nt*; **liquid ~** Paraffinöl *nt*

paraffin heater (BRIT) N Petroleumofen *m*

paraffin lamp (BRIT) N Petroleumlampe *f*

paragon ['pærəgən] N: **a ~ of** (*honesty, virtue etc*) ein Muster *nt* an +*dat*

paragraph [ˈpærəgrɑːf] N Absatz *m*, Paragraf *m*; **to begin a new ~** einen neuen Absatz beginnen
parallel [ˈpærəlɛl] ADJ (*also Comput*) parallel; (*fig: similar*) vergleichbar ▶ N Parallele *f*; (*Geog*) Breitenkreis *m*; **to run ~ (with** *or* **to)** (*lit, fig*) parallel verlaufen (zu); **to draw parallels between/with** Parallelen ziehen zwischen/mit; **in ~** (*Elec*) parallel
paralyse [ˈpærəlaɪz] (BRIT) VT (*also fig*) lähmen
paralysis [pəˈrælɪsɪs] (*pl* **paralyses**) N Lähmung *f*
paralytic [pærəˈlɪtɪk] ADJ paralytisch, Lähmungs-; (BRIT *inf: drunk*) sternhagelvoll
paralyze [ˈpærəlaɪz] (*US*) VT = **paralyse**
paramedic [pærəˈmɛdɪk] N Sanitäter(in) *m(f)*; (*in hospital*) medizinisch-technischer Assistent *m*, medizinisch-technische Assistentin *f*
parameter [pəˈræmɪtə^r] N (*Math*) Parameter *m*; (*fig: factor*) Faktor *m*; (*: limit*) Rahmen *m*
paramilitary [pærəˈmɪlɪtərɪ] ADJ paramilitärisch
paramount [ˈpærəmaunt] ADJ vorherrschend; **of ~ importance** von höchster *or* größter Wichtigkeit
paranoia [pærəˈnɔɪə] N Paranoia *f*
paranoid [ˈpærənɔɪd] ADJ paranoid
paranormal [pærəˈnɔːml] ADJ übersinnlich, paranormal ▶ N: **the ~** das Übersinnliche
parapet [ˈpærəpɪt] N Brüstung *f*
paraphernalia [pærəfəˈneɪlɪə] N Utensilien *pl*
paraphrase [ˈpærəfreɪz] VT umschreiben
paraplegic [pærəˈpliːdʒɪk] N Paraplegiker(in) *m(f)*, doppelseitig Gelähmte(r) *f(m)*
parapsychology [pærəsaɪˈkɔlədʒɪ] N Parapsychologie *f*
parasite [ˈpærəsaɪt] N (*also fig*) Parasit *m*
parasol [ˈpærəsɔl] N Sonnenschirm *m*
paratrooper [ˈpærətruːpə^r] N Fallschirmjäger *m*
parcel [ˈpɑːsl] N Paket *nt* ▶ VT (*also*: **parcel up**) verpacken
▶ **parcel out** VT aufteilen
parcel bomb (BRIT) N Paketbombe *f*
parcel post N Paketpost *f*
parch [pɑːtʃ] VT ausdörren, austrocknen
parched [pɑːtʃt] ADJ ausgetrocknet; **I'm ~** (*inf: thirsty*) ich bin am Verdursten
parchment [ˈpɑːtʃmənt] N Pergament *nt*
pardon [ˈpɑːdn] N (*Law*) Begnadigung *f* ▶ VT (*forgive*) verzeihen +*dat*, vergeben +*dat*; (*Law*) begnadigen; **~ me!, I beg your ~!** (*I'm sorry!*) verzeihen Sie bitte!; **(I beg your) ~?, ~ me?** (*US*) (*what did you say?*) bitte?
pare [pɛə^r] VT (BRIT: *nails*) schneiden; (*fruit etc*) schälen; (*fig: costs etc*) reduzieren
parent [ˈpɛərənt] N (*mother*) Mutter *f*; (*father*) Vater *m*; **parents** NPL (*mother and father*) Eltern *pl*
parentage [ˈpɛərəntɪdʒ] N Herkunft *f*; **of unknown ~** unbekannter Herkunft
parental [pəˈrɛntl] ADJ (*love, control etc*) elterlich
parent company N Mutterunternehmen *nt*
parentheses [pəˈrɛnθɪsiːz] NPL *of* **parenthesis**
parenthesis [pəˈrɛnθɪsɪs] (*pl* **parentheses**) N Klammer *f*; **in ~** in Klammern
parenthood [ˈpɛərənthud] N Elternschaft *f*
parenting [ˈpɛərəntɪŋ] N elterliche Pflege *f*
Paris [ˈpærɪs] N Paris *nt*
parish [ˈpærɪʃ] N Gemeinde *f*
parish council (BRIT) N Gemeinderat *m*
parishioner [pəˈrɪʃənə^r] N Gemeindemitglied *nt*
Parisian [pəˈrɪzɪən] ADJ Pariser *inv*, paris(er)isch ▶ N Pariser(in) *m(f)*
parity [ˈpærɪtɪ] N (*equality*) Gleichstellung *f*
park [pɑːk] N Park *m* ▶ VT, VI (*Aut*) parken
parka [ˈpɑːkə] N Parka *m*
park and ride N Park-and-Ride(-System) *nt*, Parken und Reisen *nt*
parking [ˈpɑːkɪŋ] N Parken *nt*; **"no ~"** „Parken verboten"
parking lights NPL Parklicht *nt*
parking lot (*US*) N Parkplatz *m*
parking meter N Parkuhr *f*
parking offence (BRIT) N Parkvergehen *nt*
parking place N Parkplatz *m*
parking ticket N Strafzettel *m*
parking violation (*US*) N = **parking offence**
Parkinson's [ˈpɑːkɪnsənz], **Parkinson's disease** N parkinsonsche Krankheit *f*
parkway [ˈpɑːkweɪ] (*US*) N Allee *f*
parlance [ˈpɑːləns] N: **in common/modern ~** im allgemeinen/modernen Sprachgebrauch
parliament [ˈpɑːləmənt] N Parlament *nt*

> **Parliament** ist die höchste gesetzgebende Versammlung in Großbritannien und tritt im Parlamentsgebäude in London zusammen. Die Legislaturperiode beträgt normalerweise 5 Jahre von einer Wahl zur nächsten. Das Parlament besteht aus zwei Kammern, dem Oberhaus (siehe **House of Lords** und dem Unterhaus (siehe **House of Commons**).

parliamentary [pɑːləˈmɛntərɪ] ADJ parlamentarisch
parlour, (*US***) parlor** [ˈpɑːlə^r] N Salon *m*
parlous [ˈpɑːləs] ADJ (*state*) prekär
Parmesan [pɑːmɪˈzæn] N (*also*: **Parmesan cheese**) Parmesan(käse) *m*
parochial [pəˈrəukɪəl] (*pej*) ADJ (*person, attitude*) engstirnig
parody [ˈpærədɪ] N Parodie *f* ▶ VT parodieren
parole [pəˈrəul] N (*Law*) Bewährung *f*; **on ~** auf Bewährung
paroxysm [ˈpærəksɪzəm] N (*also Med*) Anfall *m*
parquet [ˈpɑːkeɪ] N (*also*: **parquet floor(ing)**) Parkettboden *m*
parrot [ˈpærət] N Papagei *m*
parrot-fashion [ˈpærətfæʃən] ADV (*say, learn*) mechanisch; (*repeat*) wie ein Papagei
parry [ˈpærɪ] VT (*blow, argument*) parieren, abwehren
parsimonious [pɑːsɪˈməunɪəs] ADJ geizig
parsley [ˈpɑːslɪ] N Petersilie *f*
parsnip [ˈpɑːsnɪp] N Pastinake *f*
parson [ˈpɑːsn] N Pfarrer *m*
part [pɑːt] N Teil *m*; (*Tech*) Teil *nt*; (*Theat, Cine etc: role*) Rolle *f*; (*US: in hair*) Scheitel *m*; (*Mus*)

Stimme *f* ▶ ADV = **partly** ▶ VT (*separate*) trennen; (*hair*) scheiteln ▶ VI (*roads, people*) sich trennen; (*crowd*) sich teilen; **to take ~ in** teilnehmen an +*dat*; **to take sth in good ~** etw nicht übel nehmen; **to take sb's ~** (*support*) sich auf jds Seite *acc* stellen; **on his ~** seinerseits; **for my ~** für meinen Teil; **for the most ~** (*generally*) zumeist; **for the better** *or* **best ~ of the day** die meiste Zeit des Tages; **to be ~ and parcel of** dazugehören zu; **~ of speech** (*Ling*) Wortart *f*
▶ **part with** VT FUS sich trennen von

partake [pɑːˈteɪk] VI (*irreg: like* **take**) (*form*): **to ~ of sth** etw zu sich nehmen

part exchange (BRIT) N: **to give/take sth in ~** etw in Zahlung geben/nehmen

partial [ˈpɑːʃl] ADJ (*victory, solution*) Teil-; (*support*) teilweise; (*biassed*) parteiisch; **to be ~ to** (*person, drink etc*) eine Vorliebe haben für

partially [ˈpɑːʃəlɪ] ADV (*to some extent*) teilweise, zum Teil

participant [pɑːˈtɪsɪpənt] N Teilnehmer(in) *m(f)*

participate [pɑːˈtɪsɪpeɪt] VI sich beteiligen; **to ~ in** teilnehmen an +*dat*

participation [pɑːtɪsɪˈpeɪʃən] N Teilnahme *f*

participle [ˈpɑːtɪsɪpl] N Partizip *nt*

particle [ˈpɑːtɪkl] N Teilchen *nt*, Partikel *f*

particular [pəˈtɪkjuləʳ] ADJ (*distinct: person, time, place etc*) bestimmt, speziell; (*special*) speziell, besondere(r, s) ▶ N: **in ~** im Besonderen, besonders; **particulars** NPL Einzelheiten *pl*; (*name, address etc*) Personalien *pl*; **to be very ~ about sth** (*fussy*) in Bezug auf etw *acc* sehr eigen sein

particularly [pəˈtɪkjuləlɪ] ADV besonders

parting [ˈpɑːtɪŋ] N (*action*) Teilung *f*; (*farewell*) Abschied *m*; (BRIT: *in hair*) Scheitel *m* ▶ ADJ (*words, gift etc*) Abschieds-; **his ~ shot was ...** (*fig*) seine Bemerkung zum Abschied war ...

partisan [pɑːtɪˈzæn] ADJ (*politics, views*) voreingenommen ▶ N (*supporter*) Anhänger(in) *m(f)*; (*fighter*) Partisan *m*

partition [pɑːˈtɪʃən] N (*wall, screen*) Trennwand *f*; (*of country*) Teilung *f* ▶ VT (*room, office*) aufteilen; (*country*) teilen

partly [ˈpɑːtlɪ] ADV teilweise, zum Teil

partner [ˈpɑːtnəʳ] N Partner(in) *m(f)*; (*Comm*) Partner(in), Teilhaber(in) *m(f)* ▶ VT (*at dance, cards etc*) als Partner(in) haben

partnership [ˈpɑːtnəʃɪp] N (*Pol etc*) Partnerschaft *f*; (*Comm*) Teilhaberschaft *f*; **to go into ~ (with sb), form a ~ (with sb)** (mit jdm) eine Partnerschaft eingehen

part payment N Anzahlung *f*

partridge [ˈpɑːtrɪdʒ] N Rebhuhn *nt*

part-time [ˈpɑːtˈtaɪm] ADJ (*work, staff*) Teilzeit-, Halbtags- ▶ ADV: **to work ~** Teilzeit arbeiten; **to study ~** Teilzeitstudent(in) *m(f)* sein

part-timer [pɑːtˈtaɪməʳ] N (*also:* **part-time worker**) Teilzeitbeschäftigte(r) *f(m)*

party [ˈpɑːtɪ] N (*Pol, Law*) Partei *f*; (*celebration, social event*) Party *f*, Fete *f*; (*group of people*) Gruppe *f*, Gesellschaft *f* ▶ CPD (*Pol*) Partei-; **dinner ~** Abendgesellschaft *f*; **to give** *or* **throw a ~** eine Party geben, eine Fete machen; **we're having a ~ next Saturday** bei uns ist nächsten Samstag eine Party; **our son's birthday ~** die Geburtstagsfeier unseres Sohnes; **to be a ~ to a crime** an einem Verbrechen beteiligt sein

party dress N Partykleid *nt*

party line N (*Tel*) Gemeinschaftsanschluss *m*; (*Pol*) Parteilinie *f*

party piece (*inf*) N: **to do one's ~** auf einer Party etwas zum Besten geben

party political ADJ parteipolitisch

party political broadcast N parteipolitische Sendung *f*

par value N (*Comm: of share, bond*) Nennwert *m*

pass [pɑːs] VT (*spend: time*) verbringen; (*hand over*) reichen, geben; (*go past*) vorbeikommen an +*dat*; (*: in car*) vorbeifahren an +*dat*; (*overtake*) überholen; (*fig: exceed*) übersteigen; (*exam*) bestehen; (*law, proposal*) genehmigen ▶ VI (*go past*) vorbeigehen; (*: in car*) vorbeifahren; (*in exam*) bestehen ▶ N (*permit*) Ausweis *m*; (*in mountains, Sport*) Pass *m*; **to ~ sth through sth** etw durch etw führen; **to ~ the ball to** den Ball zuspielen +*dat*; **could you ~ the vegetables round?** könnten Sie das Gemüse herumreichen?; **to get a ~ in ...** (*Scol*) die Prüfung in ... bestehen; **things have come to a pretty ~ when ...** (BRIT *inf*) so weit ist es schon gekommen, dass ...; **to make a ~ at sb** (*inf*) jdn anmachen
▶ **pass away** VI (*die*) dahinscheiden
▶ **pass by** VI (*go past*) vorbeigehen; (*: in car*) vorbeifahren ▶ VT (*ignore*) vorbeigehen an +*dat*
▶ **pass down** VT (*customs, inheritance*) weitergeben
▶ **pass for** VT: **she could ~ for 25** sie könnte für 25 durchgehen
▶ **pass on** VI (*die*) verscheiden ▶ VT: **to ~ on (to)** weitergeben (an +*acc*)
▶ **pass out** VI (*faint*) ohnmächtig werden; (BRIT *Mil*) die Ausbildung beenden
▶ **pass over** VT (*ignore*) übergehen ▶ VI (*die*) entschlafen
▶ **pass up** VT (*opportunity*) sich *dat* entgehen lassen

passable [ˈpɑːsəbl] ADJ (*road*) passierbar; (*acceptable*) passabel

passage [ˈpæsɪdʒ] N Gang *m*; (*in book*) Passage *f*; (*way through crowd etc, Anat*) Weg *m*; (*act of passing: of train etc*) Durchfahrt *f*; (*journey: on boat*) Überfahrt *f*

passageway [ˈpæsɪdʒweɪ] N Gang *m*

passenger [ˈpæsɪndʒəʳ] N (*in boat, plane*) Passagier *m*; (*in car*) Fahrgast *m*

passer-by [pɑːsəˈbaɪ] (*pl* **passers-by**) N Passant(in) *m(f)*

passing [ˈpɑːsɪŋ] ADJ (*moment, thought etc*) flüchtig; **in ~** (*incidentally*) beiläufig, nebenbei; **to mention sth in ~** etw beiläufig *or* nebenbei erwähnen

passing place N (*Aut*) Ausweichstelle *f*

passion [ˈpæʃən] N Leidenschaft *f*; **to have a ~ for sth** eine Leidenschaft für etw haben

passionate ['pæʃənɪt] ADJ leidenschaftlich
passion fruit N Passionsfrucht *f*, Maracuja *f*
Passion play N Passionsspiel *nt*
passive ['pæsɪv] ADJ passiv; (*Ling*) Passiv- ▶ N (*Ling*) Passiv *nt*
passive smoking N passives Rauchen, Passivrauchen *nt*
passkey ['pɑːskiː] N Hauptschlüssel *m*
Passover ['pɑːsəuvəʳ] N Passah(fest) *nt*
passport ['pɑːspɔːt] N Pass *m*; (*fig: to success etc*) Schlüssel *m*
passport control N Passkontrolle *f*
passport office N Passamt *nt*
password ['pɑːswəːd] N Kennwort *nt*; (*Comput*) Passwort *nt*
past [pɑːst] PREP (*in front of*) vorbei an *+dat*; (*beyond*) hinter *+dat*; (*later than*) nach ▶ ADJ (*government etc*) früher, ehemalig; (*week, month etc*) vergangen ▶ N Vergangenheit *f* ▶ ADV: **to run ~** vorbeilaufen; **he's ~ 40** er ist über 40; **it's ~ midnight** es ist nach Mitternacht; **ten/quarter ~ eight** zehn/Viertel nach acht; **he ran ~ me** er lief an mir vorbei; **I'm ~ caring** es kümmert mich nicht mehr; **to be ~ it** (BRIT *inf: person*) es nicht mehr bringen; **for the ~ few/3 days** während der letzten Tage/3 Tage; **in the ~** (*also Ling*) in der Vergangenheit
pasta ['pæstə] N Nudeln *pl*
paste [peɪst] N (*wet mixture*) Teig *m*; (*glue*) Kleister *m*; (*jewellery*) Strass *m*; (*fish, tomato paste*) Paste *f* ▶ VT (*stick*) kleben
pastel ['pæstl] ADJ (*colour*) Pastell-
pasteurized ['pæstʃəraɪzd] ADJ pasteurisiert
pastille ['pæstɪl] N Pastille *f*
pastime ['pɑːstaɪm] N Zeitvertreib *m*, Hobby *nt*
past master (BRIT) N: **to be a ~ at sth** ein Experte *m* in etw *dat* sein
pastor ['pɑːstəʳ] N Pastor(in) *m(f)*
pastoral ['pɑːstərl] ADJ (*Rel: duties etc*) als Pastor
pastry ['peɪstrɪ] N (*dough*) Teig *m*; (*cake*) Gebäckstück *nt*
pasture ['pɑːstʃəʳ] N Weide *f*
pasty N ['pæstɪ] (*pie*) Pastete *f* ▶ ADJ ['peɪstɪ] (*complexion*) blässlich
pat [pæt] VT (*with hand*) tätscheln ▶ ADJ (*answer, remark*) glatt ▶ N: **to give sb/o.s. a ~ on the back** (*fig*) jdm/sich auf die Schulter klopfen; **he knows it off ~, he has it down ~** (*US*) er kennt das in- und auswendig
patch [pætʃ] N (*piece of material*) Flicken *m*; (*also: eye patch*) Augenklappe *f*; (*damp, bald etc*) Fleck *m*; (*of land*) Stück *nt*; (*: for growing vegetables etc*) Beet *nt* ▶ VT (*clothes*) flicken; **(to go through) a bad ~** eine schwierige Zeit (durchmachen)
▶ **patch up** VT (*clothes etc*) flicken; (*quarrel*) beilegen
patchwork ['pætʃwəːk] N (*Sewing*) Patchwork *nt*
patchy ['pætʃɪ] ADJ (*colour*) ungleichmäßig; (*information, knowledge etc*) lückenhaft
pate [peɪt] N: **a bald ~** eine Glatze
pâté ['pæteɪ] N Pastete *f*
patent ['peɪtnt] N Patent *nt* ▶ VT patentieren lassen ▶ ADJ (*obvious*) offensichtlich
patent leather N Lackleder *nt*
patently ['peɪtntlɪ] ADV (*obvious, wrong*) vollkommen
patent medicine N patentrechtlich geschütztes Arzneimittel *nt*
Patent Office N Patentamt *nt*
paternal [pə'təːnl] ADJ väterlich; **my ~ grandmother** meine Großmutter väterlicherseits
paternalistic [pətəːnə'lɪstɪk] ADJ patriarchalisch
paternity [pə'təːnɪtɪ] N Vaterschaft *f*
paternity leave N Vaterschaftsurlaub *m*
paternity suit N Vaterschaftsprozess *m*
path [pɑːθ] N (*also fig*) Weg *m*; (*trail, track*) Pfad *m*; (*trajectory: of bullet, aircraft, planet*) Bahn *f*
pathetic [pə'θɛtɪk] ADJ (*pitiful*) mitleiderregend; (*very bad*) erbärmlich
pathological [pæθə'lɔdʒɪkl] ADJ (*liar, hatred*) krankhaft; (*Med*) pathologisch
pathologist [pə'θɔlədʒɪst] N Pathologe *m*, Pathologin *f*
pathology [pə'θɔlədʒɪ] N Pathologie *f*
pathos ['peɪθɔs] N Pathos *nt*
pathway ['pɑːθweɪ] N Pfad *m*, Weg *m*; (*fig*) Weg
patience ['peɪʃns] N Geduld *f*; (BRIT *Cards*) Patience *f*; **to lose (one's) ~** die Geduld verlieren
patient ['peɪʃnt] N Patient(in) *m(f)* ▶ ADJ geduldig; **to be ~ with sb** Geduld mit jdm haben
patiently ['peɪʃntlɪ] ADV geduldig
patio ['pætɪəu] N Terrasse *f*
patriot ['peɪtrɪət] N Patriot(in) *m(f)*
patriotic [pætrɪ'ɔtɪk] ADJ patriotisch
patriotism ['pætrɪətɪzəm] N Patriotismus *m*
patrol [pə'trəul] N (*Mil*) Patrouille *f*; (*Police*) Streife *f* ▶ VT (*Mil, Police: city, streets etc*) patrouillieren; **to be on ~** (*Mil*) auf Patrouille sein; (*Police*) auf Streife sein
patrol boat N Patrouillenboot *nt*
patrol car N Streifenwagen *m*
patrolman [pə'trəulmən] (*US*) N (*irreg*) (*Police*) (Streifen)polizist *m*
patron ['peɪtrən] N (*customer*) Kunde *m*, Kundin *f*; (*benefactor*) Förderer *m*; **~ of the arts** Kunstmäzen *m*
patronage ['pætrənɪdʒ] N (*of artist, charity etc*) Förderung *f*
patronize ['pætrənaɪz] VT (*pej: look down on*) von oben herab behandeln; (*artist etc*) fördern; (*shop, club*) besuchen
patronizing ['pætrənaɪzɪŋ] ADJ herablassend
patron saint N Schutzheilige(r) *f(m)*
patter ['pætəʳ] N (*of feet*) Trappeln *nt*; (*of rain*) Prasseln *nt*; (*sales talk etc*) Sprüche *pl* ▶ VI (*footsteps*) trappeln; (*rain*) prasseln
pattern ['pætən] N Muster *nt*; (*Sewing*) Schnittmuster *nt*; **behaviour patterns** Verhaltensmuster *pl*
patterned ['pætənd] ADJ gemustert; **~ with flowers** mit Blumenmuster
paucity ['pɔːsɪtɪ] N: **a ~ of** ein Mangel *m* an *+dat*
paunch [pɔːntʃ] N Bauch *m*, Wanst *m*

P

pauper ['pɔːpə^r] N Arme(r) *f(m)*; **~'s grave** Armengrab *nt*
pause [pɔːz] N Pause *f* ▶ VI eine Pause machen; (*hesitate*) innehalten; **to ~ for breath** eine Verschnaufpause einlegen
pave [peɪv] VT (*street, yard etc*) pflastern; **to ~ the way for** (*fig*) den Weg bereiten *or* bahnen für
pavement ['peɪvmənt] N (BRIT) Bürgersteig *m*; (*US: roadway*) Straße *f*
pavilion [pə'vɪlɪən] N (*Sport*) Klubhaus *nt*
paving ['peɪvɪŋ] N (*material*) Straßenbelag *m*
paving stone N Pflasterstein *m*
paw [pɔː] N (*of cat, dog etc*) Pfote *f*; (*of lion, bear etc*) Tatze *f*, Pranke *f* ▶ VT (*pej: touch*) betatschen; **to ~ the ground** (*animal*) scharren
pawn [pɔːn] N (*Chess*) Bauer *m*; (*fig*) Schachfigur *f* ▶ VT versetzen
pawnbroker ['pɔːnbrəukə^r] N Pfandleiher *m*
pawnshop ['pɔːnʃɔp] N Pfandhaus *nt*
pay [peɪ] (*pt, pp* **paid**) N (*wage*) Lohn *m*; (*salary*) Gehalt *nt* ▶ VT (*sum of money, wage*) zahlen; (*bill, person*) bezahlen ▶ VI (*be profitable*) sich bezahlt machen; (*fig*) sich lohnen; **how much did you ~ for it?** wie viel hast du dafür bezahlt?; **I paid 10 pounds for that book** ich habe 10 Pfund für das Buch bezahlt, das Buch hat mich 10 Pfund gekostet; **to ~ one's way** seinen Beitrag leisten; **to ~ dividends** (*fig*) sich bezahlt machen; **to ~ the price/penalty for sth** (*fig*) den Preis/die Strafe für etw zahlen; **to ~ sb a compliment** jdm ein Kompliment machen; **to ~ attention (to)** achtgeben (auf *+acc*); **to ~ sb a visit** jdn besuchen; **to ~ one's respects to sb** jdm seine Aufwartung machen
▶ **pay back** VT zurückzahlen; **I'll ~ you back next week** ich gebe dir das Geld nächste Woche zurück
▶ **pay for** VT FUS (*also fig*) (be)zahlen für
▶ **pay in** VT einzahlen
▶ **pay off** VT (*debt*) abbezahlen; (*person*) auszahlen; (*creditor*) befriedigen; (*mortgage*) tilgen ▶ VI sich auszahlen; **to ~ sth off in instalments** etw in Raten (ab)zahlen
▶ **pay out** VT (*money*) ausgeben; (*rope*) ablaufen lassen
▶ **pay up** VI zahlen
payable ['peɪəbl] ADJ zahlbar; **to make a cheque ~ to sb** einen Scheck auf jdn ausstellen
pay award N Lohn-/Gehaltserhöhung *f*
payday ['peɪdeɪ] N Zahltag *m*
PAYE (BRIT) N ABBR (= *pay as you earn*) *Lohnsteuerabzugsverfahren*
payee [peɪ'iː] N Zahlungsempfänger *m*
pay envelope (US) N = **pay packet**
paying guest ['peɪɪŋ-] N zahlender Gast *m*
payload ['peɪləud] N Nutzlast *f*
payment ['peɪmənt] N (*act*) Zahlung *f*, Bezahlung *f*; (*of bill*) Begleichung *f*; (*sum of money*) Zahlung *f*; **advance ~** (*part sum*) Anzahlung *f*; (*total sum*) Vorauszahlung *f*; **deferred ~, ~ by instalments** Ratenzahlung *f*; **monthly ~** (*sum of money*) Monatsrate *f*; **on ~ of** gegen Zahlung von
pay packet (BRIT) N Lohntüte *f*
pay-per-click ['peɪpə'klɪk] N (*Comput*) Pay-per-Click *nt*
payphone ['peɪfəun] N Münztelefon *nt*; (*card phone*) Kartentelefon *nt*
payroll ['peɪrəul] N Lohnliste *f*; **to be on a firm's ~** bei einer Firma beschäftigt sein
pay slip (BRIT) N Lohnstreifen *m*; Gehaltsstreifen *m*
pay station (US) N = **payphone**
pay TV N Pay-TV *nt*
paywall ['peɪwɔːl] N (*Comput*) Bezahlschranke *f*
PBS (US) N ABBR (= *Public Broadcasting Service*) *öffentliche Rundfunkanstalt*
PC N ABBR (= *personal computer*) PC *m*; (BRIT) = **police constable** ▶ ADJ ABBR = **politically correct** ▶ ABBR (BRIT) = **Privy Councillor**
pc ABBR = **per cent; postcard**
p/c ABBR = **petty cash**
PCB N ABBR (*Elec, Comput*) = **printed circuit board**; (= *polychlorinated biphenyl*) PCB *nt*
pcm ABBR (= *per calendar month*) pro Monat
PD (US) N ABBR = **police department**
pd ABBR (= *paid*) bez.
PDA ABBR (*Comput:* = *personal digital assistant*) PDA *m*
pdq (*inf*) ADV ABBR (= *pretty damn quick*) verdammt schnell
PDSA (BRIT) N ABBR (= *People's Dispensary for Sick Animals*) *kostenloses Behandlungszentrum für Haustiere*
PDT (US) ABBR (= *Pacific Daylight Time*) *pazifische Sommerzeit*
PE N ABBR (*Scol*) = **physical education**
pea [piː] N Erbse *f*
peace [piːs] N Frieden *m*; **to be at ~ with sb/sth** mit jdm/etw in Frieden leben; **to keep the ~** (*policeman*) die öffentliche Ordnung aufrechterhalten; (*citizen*) den Frieden wahren
peaceable ['piːsəbl] ADJ friedlich
peaceful ['piːsful] ADJ friedlich
peacekeeper ['piːskiːpə^r] N Friedenswächter(in) *m(f)*
peacekeeping force ['piːskiːpɪŋ-] N Friedenstruppen *pl*
peace offering N Friedensangebot *nt*
peach [piːtʃ] N Pfirsich *m*
peacock ['piːkɔk] N Pfau *m*
peak [piːk] N (*of mountain*) Spitze *f*, Gipfel *m*; (*of cap*) Schirm *m*; (*fig*) Höhepunkt *m*
peak hours NPL Stoßzeit *f*
peak period N Spitzenzeit *f*, Stoßzeit *f*
peak rate N Höchstrate *f*
peaky ['piːkɪ] (BRIT *inf*) ADJ blass
peal [piːl] N (*of bells*) Läuten *nt*; **peals of laughter** schallendes Gelächter *nt*
peanut ['piːnʌt] N Erdnuss *f*
peanut butter N Erdnussbutter *f*
pear [pɛə^r] N Birne *f*
pearl [pəːl] N Perle *f*
peasant ['pɛznt] N Bauer *m*
peat [piːt] N Torf *m*
pebble ['pɛbl] N Kieselstein *m*

pecan [pɪ'kæn] N Pekannuss
peck [pɛk] VT (*bird*) picken; (*also*: **peck at**) picken an +*dat* ▸ N (*of bird*) Schnabelhieb *m*; (*kiss*) Küsschen *nt*
pecking order ['pɛkɪŋ-] N (*fig*) Hackordnung *f*
peckish ['pɛkɪʃ] (BRIT *inf*) ADJ (*hungry*) leicht hungrig; **I'm feeling ~** ich könnte was zu essen gebrauchen
peculiar [pɪ'kju:lɪəʳ] ADJ (*strange*) seltsam; **~ to** (*exclusive to*) charakteristisch für
peculiarity [pɪkju:lɪ'ærɪtɪ] N (*strange habit*) Eigenart *f*; (*distinctive feature*) Besonderheit *f*, Eigentümlichkeit *f*
peculiarly [pɪ'kju:lɪəlɪ] ADV (*oddly*) seltsam; (*distinctively*) unverkennbar
pecuniary [pɪ'kju:nɪərɪ] ADJ finanziell
pedal ['pɛdl] N Pedal *nt* ▸ VI in die Pedale treten
pedal bin (BRIT) N Treteimer *m*
pedant ['pɛdənt] N Pedant(in) *m(f)*
pedantic [pɪ'dæntɪk] ADJ pedantisch
peddle ['pɛdl] VT (*goods*) feilbieten, verkaufen; (*drugs*) handeln mit; (*gossip*) verbreiten
peddler ['pɛdləʳ] N (*also*: **drug peddler**) Pusher *m*
pedestal ['pɛdəstl] N Sockel *m*
pedestrian [pɪ'dɛstrɪən] N Fußgänger(in) *m(f)* ▸ ADJ Fußgänger-; (*fig*) langweilig
pedestrian crossing (BRIT) N Fußgängerüberweg *m*
pedestrian mall (US) N Fußgängerzone *f*
pedestrian precinct (BRIT) N Fußgängerzone *f*
pediatrics [pi:dɪ'ætrɪks] (US) N = **paediatrics**
pedigree ['pɛdɪgri:] N (*of animal*) Stammbaum *m*; (*fig*: *background*) Vorgeschichte *f* ▸ CPD (*dog*) Rasse-, reinrassig
pee [pi:] (*inf*) VI pinkeln
peek [pi:k] VI: **to ~ at/over/into** *etc* gucken nach/über +*acc*/in +*acc etc* ▸ N: **to have** *or* **take a ~ (at)** einen (kurzen) Blick werfen (auf +*acc*)
peel [pi:l] N Schale *f* ▸ VT schälen ▸ VI (*paint*) abblättern; (*wallpaper*) sich lösen; (*skin, back etc*) sich schälen
▸ **peel back** VT abziehen
peeler ['pi:ləʳ] N (*potato peeler etc*) Schälmesser *nt*
peelings ['pi:lɪŋz] NPL Schalen *pl*
peep [pi:p] N (*look*) kurzer Blick *m*; (*sound*) Pieps *m* ▸ VI (*look*) gucken; **to have** *or* **take a ~ (at)** einen kurzen Blick werfen (auf +*acc*)
▸ **peep out** VI (*be visible*) hervorgucken
peephole ['pi:phəul] N Guckloch *nt*
peer [pɪəʳ] N (*noble*) Peer *m*; (*equal*) Gleichrangige(r) *f(m)*; (*contemporary*) Gleichaltrige(r) *f(m)* ▸ VI: **to ~ at** starren auf +*acc*
peerage ['pɪərɪdʒ] N (*title*) Adelswürde *f*; (*position*) Adelsstand *m*; **the ~** (*all the peers*) der Adel
peerless ['pɪəlɪs] ADJ unvergleichlich
peeved [pi:vd] ADJ verärgert, sauer (*inf*)
peevish ['pi:vɪʃ] ADJ (*bad-tempered*) mürrisch
peg [pɛg] N (*hook, knob*) Haken *m*; (BRIT: *also*: **clothes peg**) Wäscheklammer *f*; (*also*: **tent peg**) Zeltpflock *m*, Hering *m* ▸ VT (*washing*) festklammern; (*prices*) festsetzen; **off the ~** von der Stange
pejorative [pɪ'dʒɔrətɪv] ADJ abwertend
Pekin [pi:'kɪn] N = **Peking**
Pekinese [pi:kɪ'ni:z] N = **Pekingese**
Peking [pi:'kɪŋ] N Peking *nt*
Pekingese [pi:kɪ'ni:z] N (*dog*) Pekinese *m*
pelican ['pɛlɪkən] N Pelikan *m*
pelican crossing (BRIT) N (*Aut*) Fußgängerüberweg *m* mit Ampel
pellet ['pɛlɪt] N (*of paper etc*) Kügelchen *nt*; (*of mud etc*) Klümpchen *nt*; (*for shotgun*) Schrotkugel *f*
pell-mell ['pɛl'mɛl] ADV in heillosem Durcheinander
pelmet ['pɛlmɪt] N (*wooden*) Blende *f*; (*fabric*) Querbehang *m*
pelt [pɛlt] VI (*rain*: *also*: **pelt down**) niederprasseln; (*inf*: *run*) rasen ▸ N (*animal skin*) Pelz *m*, Fell *nt* ▸ VT: **to ~ sb with sth** jdn mit etw bewerfen
pelvis ['pɛlvɪs] N Becken *nt*
pen [pɛn] N (*also*: **fountain pen**) Füller *m*; (*also*: **ballpoint pen**) Kugelschreiber *m*; (*also*: **felt-tip pen**) Filzstift *m*; (*enclosure*: *for sheep, pigs etc*) Pferch *m*; (US *inf*: *prison*) Knast *m*; **to put ~ to paper** zur Feder greifen
penal ['pi:nl] ADJ (*Law*: *colony, institution*) Straf-; (: *system, reform*) Strafrechts-; **~ code** Strafgesetzbuch *nt*
penalize ['pi:nəlaɪz] VT (*punish*) bestrafen; (*fig*) benachteiligen
penal servitude [-'sə:vɪtju:d] N Zwangsarbeit *f*
penalty ['pɛnltɪ] N Strafe *f*; (*Sport*) Strafstoß *m*; (: *Football*) Elfmeter *m*
penalty area (BRIT) N (*Sport*) Strafraum *m*
penalty clause N Strafklausel *f*
penalty kick N (*Rugby*) Strafstoß *m*; (*Football*) Elfmeter *m*
penalty shoot-out [-'ʃu:taut] N (*Football*) Elfmeterschießen *nt*
penance ['pɛnəns] N (*Rel*): **to do ~ for one's sins** für seine Sünden Buße tun
pence [pɛns] NPL *of* **penny**
penchant ['pɑ̃:ʃɑ̃:ŋ] N Vorliebe *f*, Schwäche *f*; **to have a ~ for** eine Schwäche haben für
pencil ['pɛnsl] N Bleistift *m* ▸ VT: **to ~ sb/sth in** jdn/etw vormerken
pencil case N Federmäppchen *nt*
pencil sharpener N Bleistiftspitzer *m*
pendant ['pɛndnt] N Anhänger *m*
pending ['pɛndɪŋ] ADJ anstehend ▸ PREP: **~ his return** bis zu seiner Rückkehr; **~ a decision** bis eine Entscheidung getroffen ist
pendulum ['pɛndjuləm] N Pendel *nt*
penetrate ['pɛnɪtreɪt] VT (*person*: *territory etc*) durchdringen; (*light, water, sound*) eindringen in +*acc*
penetrating ['pɛnɪtreɪtɪŋ] ADJ (*sound, gaze*) durchdringend; (*mind, observation*) scharf
penetration [pɛnɪ'treɪʃən] N Durchdringen *nt*
pen friend (BRIT) N Brieffreund(in) *m(f)*
penguin ['pɛŋgwɪn] N Pinguin *m*
penicillin [pɛnɪ'sɪlɪn] N Penizillin *nt*
peninsula [pə'nɪnsjulə] N Halbinsel *f*
penis ['pi:nɪs] N Penis *m*
penitence ['pɛnɪtns] N Reue *f*

P

penitent ['pɛnɪtnt] ADJ reuig
penitentiary [pɛnɪ'tɛnʃərɪ] (*US*) N Gefängnis *nt*
penknife ['pɛnnaɪf] N Taschenmesser *nt*
Penn. (*US*) ABBR (*Post*) = **Pennsylvania**
pen name N Pseudonym *nt*
pennant ['pɛnənt] N (*Naut*) Wimpel *m*
penniless ['pɛnɪlɪs] ADJ mittellos
Pennines ['pɛnaɪnz] NPL: **the ~** die Pennines *pl*
penny ['pɛnɪ] (*pl* **pennies** *or* BRIT **pence**) N Penny *m*; (*US*) Cent *m*; **it was worth every ~** es war jeden Pfennig wert; **it won't cost you a ~** es kostet dich keinen Pfennig
pen pal N Brieffreund(in) *m(f)*
penpusher ['pɛnpuʃəʳ] N Schreiberling *m*
pension ['pɛnʃən] N Rente *f*
▸ **pension off** VT (vorzeitig) pensionieren
pensionable ['pɛnʃənəbl] ADJ (*age*) Pensions-; (*job*) mit Pensionsberechtigung
pensioner ['pɛnʃənəʳ] (BRIT) N Rentner(in) *m(f)*
pension scheme, pension plan N Rentenversicherung *f*
pensive ['pɛnsɪv] ADJ nachdenklich
pentagon ['pɛntəgən] (*US*) N: **the P~** das Pentagon

> **Pentagon** heißt das fünfeckige Gebäude in Arlington, Virginia, in dem das amerikanische Verteidigungsministerium untergebracht ist. Im weiteren Sinne bezieht sich dieses Wort auf die amerikanische Militärführung.

Pentecost ['pɛntɪkɔst] N (*in Judaism*) Erntefest *nt*; (*in Christianity*) Pfingsten *nt*
penthouse ['pɛnthaus] N Penthouse *nt*
pent-up ['pɛntʌp] ADJ (*feelings*) aufgestaut
penultimate [pɛ'nʌltɪmət] ADJ vorletzte(r, s)
penury ['pɛnjurɪ] N Armut *f*, Not *f*
people ['pi:pl] NPL (*persons*) Leute *pl*; (*inhabitants*) Bevölkerung *f* ▸ N (*nation, race*) Volk *nt*; **old ~** alte Menschen *or* Leute; **young ~** junge Leute; **the room was full of ~** das Zimmer war voller Leute *or* Menschen; **several ~ came** mehrere (Leute) kamen; **~ say that …** man sagt, dass …; **the ~** (*Pol*) das Volk; **a man of the ~** ein Mann des Volkes
PEP N ABBR (= *personal equity plan*) *steuerbegünstigte Kapitalinvestition*
pep [pɛp] (*inf*) N Schwung *m*, Pep *m*
▸ **pep up** VT (*person*) aufmöbeln; (*food*) pikanter machen
pepper ['pɛpəʳ] N (*spice*) Pfeffer *m*; (*vegetable*) Paprika *m* ▸ VT: **to ~ with** (*fig*) übersäen mit; **two peppers** zwei Paprikaschoten
peppercorn ['pɛpəkɔ:n] N Pfefferkorn *nt*
pepper mill N Pfeffermühle *f*
peppermint ['pɛpəmɪnt] N (*sweet*) Pfefferminz *nt*; (*plant*) Pfefferminze *f*
pepperoni [pɛpə'rəunɪ] N ≈ Pfeffersalami *f*
pepper pot N Pfefferstreuer *m*
pep talk (*inf*) N aufmunternde Worte *pl*
per [pə:ʳ] PREP (*for each*) pro; **~ day/person/kilo** pro Tag/Person/Kilo; **~ annum** pro Jahr; **as ~ your instructions** gemäß Ihren Anweisungen
per capita [-'kæpɪtə] ADJ (*income*) Pro-Kopf- ▸ ADV pro Kopf
perceive [pə'si:v] VT (*see*) wahrnehmen; (*view, understand*) verstehen
per cent N Prozent *nt*; **a 20 ~ discount** 20 Prozent Rabatt
percentage [pə'sɛntɪdʒ] N Prozentsatz *m*; **on a ~ basis** auf Prozentbasis
percentage point N Prozent *nt*
perceptible [pə'sɛptɪbl] ADJ (*difference, change*) wahrnehmbar, merklich
perception [pə'sɛpʃən] N (*insight*) Einsicht *f*; (*opinion, understanding*) Erkenntnis *f*; (*faculty*) Wahrnehmung *f*
perceptive [pə'sɛptɪv] ADJ (*person*) aufmerksam; (*analysis etc*) erkenntnisreich
perch [pə:tʃ] N (*for bird*) Stange *f*; (*fish*) Flussbarsch *m* ▸ VI: **to ~ (on)** (*bird*) sitzen (auf +*dat*); (*person*) hocken (auf +*dat*)
percolate ['pə:kəleɪt] VT (*coffee*) (mit einer Kaffeemaschine) zubereiten ▸ VI (*coffee*) durchlaufen; **to ~ through/into** (*idea, light etc*) durchsickern durch/in +*acc*
percolator ['pə:kəleɪtəʳ] N (*also*: **coffee percolator**) Kaffeemaschine *f*
percussion [pə'kʌʃən] N (*Mus*) Schlagzeug *nt*
peremptory [pə'rɛmptərɪ] (*pej*) ADJ (*person*) herrisch; (*order*) kategorisch
perennial [pə'rɛnɪəl] ADJ (*plant*) mehrjährig; (*fig: problem, feature etc*) immer wiederkehrend ▸ N (*Bot*) mehrjährige Pflanze *f*
perfect ADJ ['pə:fɪkt] perfekt; (*nonsense, idiot etc*) ausgemacht ▸ VT [pə'fɛkt] (*technique*) perfektionieren ▸ N ['pə:fɪkt]: **the ~** (*also*: **the perfect tense**) das Perfekt; **he's a ~ stranger to me** er ist mir vollkommen fremd
perfection [pə'fɛkʃən] N Perfektion *f*, Vollkommenheit *f*
perfectionist [pə'fɛkʃənɪst] N Perfektionist(in) *m(f)*
perfectly ['pə:fɪktlɪ] ADV vollkommen; (*faultlessly*) perfekt; **I'm ~ happy with the situation** ich bin mit der Lage vollkommen zufrieden; **you know ~ well that …** Sie wissen ganz genau, dass …
perforate ['pə:fəreɪt] VT perforieren
perforated ulcer ['pə:fəreɪtəd-] N durchgebrochenes Geschwür *nt*
perforation [pə:fə'reɪʃən] N (*small hole*) Loch *nt*; (*line of holes*) Perforation *f*
perform [pə'fɔ:m] VT (*operation, ceremony etc*) durchführen; (*task*) erfüllen; (*piece of music, play etc*) aufführen ▸ VI auftreten; **to ~ well/badly** eine gute/schlechte Leistung zeigen
performance [pə'fɔ:məns] N Leistung *f*; (*of play, show*) Vorstellung *f*; **the team put up a good ~** die Mannschaft zeigte eine gute Leistung
performer [pə'fɔ:məʳ] N Künstler(in) *m(f)*
performing [pə'fɔ:mɪŋ] ADJ (*animal*) dressiert
performing arts NPL: **the ~** die darstellenden Künste *pl*
perfume ['pə:fju:m] N Parfüm *nt*; (*fragrance*) Duft *m* ▸ VT parfümieren

perfunctory [pəˈfʌŋktərɪ] ADJ flüchtig
perhaps [pəˈhæps] ADV vielleicht; **~ he'll come** er kommt vielleicht; **~ not** vielleicht nicht
peril [ˈpɛrɪl] N Gefahr *f*
perilous [ˈpɛrɪləs] ADJ gefährlich
perilously [ˈpɛrɪləslɪ] ADV: **they came ~ close to being caught** sie wären um ein Haar gefangen worden
perimeter [pəˈrɪmɪtə^r] N Umfang *m*
perimeter fence N Umzäunung *f*
period [ˈpɪərɪəd] N (*length of time*) Zeitraum *m*, Periode *f*; (*era*) Zeitalter *nt*; (*Scol*) Stunde *f*; (*esp US: full stop*) Punkt *m*; (*Med: also*: **menstrual period**) Periode ▶ ADJ (*costume etc*) zeitgenössisch; **for a ~ of 3 weeks** für eine Dauer *or* einen Zeitraum von 3 Wochen; **the holiday ~** (BRIT) die Urlaubszeit; **I won't do it. P~.** ich mache das nicht, und damit basta!
periodic [pɪərɪˈɔdɪk] ADJ periodisch
periodical [pɪərɪˈɔdɪkl] N Zeitschrift *f* ▶ ADJ periodisch
periodically [pɪərɪˈɔdɪklɪ] ADV periodisch
period pains (BRIT) NPL Menstruationsschmerzen *pl*
peripatetic [pɛrɪpəˈtɛtɪk] ADJ (*BRIT: teacher*) an mehreren Schulen tätig; **~ life** Wanderleben *nt*
peripheral [pəˈrɪfərəl] ADJ (*feature, issue*) Rand-, nebensächlich; (*vision*) peripher ▶ N (*Comput*) Peripheriegerät *nt*
periphery [pəˈrɪfərɪ] N Peripherie *f*
periscope [ˈpɛrɪskəup] N Periskop *nt*
perish [ˈpɛrɪʃ] VI (*die*) umkommen; (*rubber, leather etc*) verschleißen
perishable [ˈpɛrɪʃəbl] ADJ (*food*) leicht verderblich
perishables [ˈpɛrɪʃəblz] NPL leicht verderbliche Waren *pl*
perishing [ˈpɛrɪʃɪŋ] (BRIT *inf*) ADJ: **it's ~ (cold)** es ist eisig kalt
peritonitis [pɛrɪtəˈnaɪtɪs] N Bauchfellentzündung *f*
perjure [ˈpəːdʒə^r] VT: **to ~ o.s.** einen Meineid leisten
perjury [ˈpəːdʒərɪ] N (*in court*) Meineid *m*; (*breach of oath*) Eidesverletzung *f*
perks [pəːks] (*inf*) NPL (*extras*) Vergünstigungen *pl*
perk up VI (*cheer up*) munter werden
perky [ˈpəːkɪ] ADJ (*cheerful*) munter
perm [pəːm] N Dauerwelle *f* ▶ VT: **to have one's hair permed** sich *dat* eine Dauerwelle machen lassen
permanence [ˈpəːmənəns] N Dauerhaftigkeit *f*
permanent [ˈpəːmənənt] ADJ dauerhaft; (*job, position*) fest; **~ address** ständiger Wohnsitz *m*; **I'm not ~ here** ich bin hier nicht fest angestellt
permanently [ˈpəːmənəntlɪ] ADV (*damage*) dauerhaft; (*stay, live*) ständig; (*locked, open, frozen etc*) dauernd
permeable [ˈpəːmɪəbl] ADJ durchlässig
permeate [ˈpəːmɪeɪt] VT durchdringen ▶ VI: **to ~ through** dringen durch
permissible [pəˈmɪsɪbl] ADJ zulässig
permission [pəˈmɪʃən] N Erlaubnis *f*, Genehmigung *f*; **to give sb ~ to do sth** jdm die Erlaubnis geben, etw zu tun
permissive [pəˈmɪsɪv] ADJ permissiv
permit N [ˈpəːmɪt] Genehmigung *f* ▶ VT [pəˈmɪt] (*allow*) erlauben; (*make possible*) gestatten; **fishing ~** Angelschein *m*; **to ~ sb to do sth** jdm erlauben, etw zu tun; **weather permitting** wenn das Wetter es zulässt
permutation [pəːmjuˈteɪʃən] N Permutation *f*; (*fig*) Variation *f*
pernicious [pəːˈnɪʃəs] ADJ (*lie, nonsense*) bösartig; (*effect*) schädlich
pernickety [pəˈnɪkɪtɪ] (*inf*) ADJ pingelig
perpendicular [pəːpənˈdɪkjulə^r] ADJ senkrecht ▶ N: **the ~** die Senkrechte; **~ to** senkrecht zu
perpetrate [ˈpəːpɪtreɪt] VT (*crime*) begehen
perpetual [pəˈpɛtjuəl] ADJ ständig, dauernd
perpetuate [pəˈpɛtjueɪt] VT (*custom, belief etc*) bewahren; (*situation*) aufrechterhalten
perpetuity [pəːpɪˈtjuːɪtɪ] N: **in ~** auf ewig
perplex [pəˈplɛks] VT verblüffen
perplexing [pəːˈplɛksɪŋ] ADJ verblüffend
perquisites [ˈpəːkwɪzɪts] (*form*) NPL Vergünstigungen *pl*
per se [-seɪ] ADV an sich
persecute [ˈpəːsɪkjuːt] VT verfolgen
persecution [pəːsɪˈkjuːʃən] N Verfolgung *f*
perseverance [pəːsɪˈvɪərns] N Beharrlichkeit *f*, Ausdauer *f*
persevere [pəːsɪˈvɪə^r] VI durchhalten, beharren
Persia [ˈpəːʃə] N Persien *nt*
Persian [ˈpəːʃən] ADJ persisch ▶ N (*Ling*) Persisch *nt*; **the ~ Gulf** der Persische Golf
Persian cat N Perserkatze *f*
persist [pəˈsɪst] VI: **to ~ (with** *or* **in)** beharren (auf *+dat*), festhalten (an *+dat*); **to ~ in doing sth** darauf beharren, etw zu tun
persistence [pəˈsɪstəns] N Beharrlichkeit *f*
persistent [pəˈsɪstənt] ADJ (*person, noise*) beharrlich; (*smell, cough etc*) hartnäckig; (*lateness, rain*) andauernd; **~ offender** Wiederholungstäter(in) *m*(*f*)
persnickety [pəˈsnɪkɪtɪ] (*US inf*) ADJ = **pernickety**
person [ˈpəːsn] N Person *f*, Mensch *m*; **in ~** persönlich; **on** *or* **about one's ~** bei sich; **~ to ~ call** (*Tel*) Gespräch *nt* mit Voranmeldung
personable [ˈpəːsnəbl] ADJ von angenehmer Erscheinung
personal [ˈpəːsnl] ADJ persönlich; (*life*) Privat-; **nothing ~!** nehmen Sie es nicht persönlich!
personal allowance N (*Tax*) persönlicher Steuerfreibetrag *m*
personal assistant N persönlicher Referent *m*, persönliche Referentin *f*
personal column N private Kleinanzeigen *pl*
personal computer N Personal Computer *m*
personal details NPL Personalien *pl*
personal hygiene N Körperhygiene *f*
personal identification number N Geheimnummer *f*, PIN-Nummer *f*
personality [pəːsəˈnælɪtɪ] N (*character, person*) Persönlichkeit *f*

personal loan N Personaldarlehen *nt*
personally ['pə:snəlɪ] ADV persönlich; **to take sth ~** etw persönlich nehmen
personal organizer N Terminplaner *m*
personal, social and health education (BRIT) N (*Scol*) ≈ Persönlichkeits-, gesellschafts- und gesundheitsbezogene Erziehung
personal stereo N Walkman® *m*
personal trainer N (persönlicher) Fitnesstrainer *m*, (persönliche) Fitnesstrainerin *f*
personify [pə:'sɔnɪfaɪ] VT personifizieren; (*embody*) verkörpern
personnel [pə:sə'nɛl] N Personal *nt*
personnel department N Personalabteilung *f*
personnel manager N Personalleiter(in) *m(f)*
perspective [pə'spɛktɪv] N (*also fig*) Perspektive *f*; **to get sth into ~** (*fig*) etw in Relation zu anderen Dingen sehen
Perspex® ['pə:spɛks] N Acrylglas *nt*
perspicacity [pə:spɪ'kæsɪtɪ] N Scharfsinn *m*
perspiration [pə:spɪ'reɪʃən] N Transpiration *f*
perspire [pə'spaɪə^r] VI transpirieren
persuade [pə'sweɪd] VT: **to ~ sb to do sth** jdn dazu überreden, etw zu tun; **to ~ sb that** jdn davon überzeugen, dass; **to be persuaded of sth** von etw überzeugt sein
persuasion [pə'sweɪʒən] N (*act*) Überredung *f*; (*creed*) Überzeugung *f*
persuasive [pə'sweɪsɪv] ADJ (*person, argument*) überzeugend
pert [pə:t] ADJ (*person*) frech; (*nose, buttocks*) keck; (*hat*) kess
pertaining [pə:'teɪnɪŋ]: **~ to** *prep* betreffend *+acc*
pertinent ['pə:tɪnənt] ADJ relevant
perturb [pə'tə:b] VT beunruhigen
Peru [pə'ru:] N Peru *nt*
perusal [pə'ru:zl] N Durchsicht *f*
peruse [pə'ru:z] VT durchsehen
Peruvian [pə'ru:vjən] ADJ peruanisch ▶ N Peruaner(in) *m(f)*
pervade [pə'veɪd] VT (*smell, feeling*) erfüllen
pervasive [pə'veɪzɪv] ADJ (*smell*) durchdringend; (*influence*) weitreichend; (*mood, atmosphere*) allumfassend
perverse [pə'və:s] ADJ (*person*) borniert; (*behaviour*) widernatürlich, pervers
perversion [pə'və:ʃən] N (*sexual*) Perversion *f*; (*of truth, justice*) Verzerrung *f*, Pervertierung *f*
perversity [pə'və:sɪtɪ] N Widernatürlichkeit *f*
pervert N ['pə:və:t] (*sexual deviant*) perverser Mensch *m* ▶ VT [pə'və:t] (*person, mind*) verderben; (*distort: truth, custom*) verfälschen
perverted [pə'vɜ:tɪd] ADJ pervers
pessimism ['pɛsɪmɪzəm] N Pessimismus *m*
pessimist ['pɛsɪmɪst] N Pessimist(in) *m(f)*
pessimistic [pɛsɪ'mɪstɪk] ADJ pessimistisch
pest [pɛst] N (*insect*) Schädling *m*; (*fig: nuisance*) Plage *f*
pest control N Schädlingsbekämpfung *f*
pester ['pɛstə^r] VT belästigen
pesticide ['pɛstɪsaɪd] N Schädlingsbekämpfungsmittel *nt*, Pestizid *nt*
pestilence ['pɛstɪləns] N Pest *f*
pestle ['pɛsl] N Stößel *m*
pet [pɛt] N (*animal*) Haustier *nt* ▶ ADJ (*theory etc*) Lieblings- ▶ VT (*stroke*) streicheln ▶ VI (*inf: sexually*) herumknutschen; **teacher's ~** (*favourite*) Lehrers Liebling *m*; **a ~ rabbit/snake** *etc* ein Kaninchen/eine Schlange *etc* (als Haustier); **that's my ~ hate** das hasse ich besonders
petal ['pɛtl] N Blütenblatt *nt*
peter out ['pi:tə-] VI (*road etc*) allmählich aufhören, zu Ende gehen; (*conversation, meeting*) sich totlaufen
petite [pə'ti:t] ADJ (*woman*) zierlich
petition [pə'tɪʃən] N (*signed document*) Petition *f*; (*Law*) Klage *f* ▶ VT ersuchen ▶ VI: **to ~ for divorce** die Scheidung einreichen
pet name (BRIT) N Kosename *m*
petrified ['pɛtrɪfaɪd] ADJ (*fig: terrified*) starr vor Angst
petrify ['pɛtrɪfaɪ] VT (*fig: terrify*) vor Angst erstarren lassen
petrochemical [pɛtrə'kɛmɪkl] ADJ petrochemisch
petrodollars ['pɛtrəudɔləz] NPL Petrodollar *pl*
petrol ['pɛtrəl] (BRIT) N Benzin *nt*; **two-star ~** Normalbenzin *nt*; **four-star ~** Super(benzin) *nt*; **unleaded ~** bleifreies *or* unverbleites Benzin
petrol bomb N Benzinbombe *f*
petrol can (BRIT) N Benzinkanister *m*
petrol engine (BRIT) N Benzinmotor *m*
petroleum [pə'trəulɪəm] N Petroleum *nt*
petroleum jelly N Vaseline *f*
petrol pump (BRIT) N (*in garage*) Zapfsäule *f*; (*in engine*) Benzinpumpe *f*
petrol station (BRIT) N Tankstelle *f*
petrol tank (BRIT) N Benzintank *m*
petticoat ['pɛtɪkəut] N (*underskirt: full-length*) Unterkleid *nt*; (*: waist*) Unterrock *m*
pettifogging ['pɛtɪfɔgɪŋ] ADJ kleinlich
pettiness ['pɛtɪnɪs] N Kleinlichkeit *f*
petty ['pɛtɪ] ADJ (*trivial*) unbedeutend; (*small-minded*) kleinlich; (*crime*) geringfügig; (*official*) untergeordnet; (*excuse*) billig; (*remark*) spitz
petty cash N (*in office*) Portokasse *f*
petty officer N Maat *m*
petulant ['pɛtjulənt] ADJ (*person, expression*) gereizt
pew [pju:] N (*in church*) Kirchenbank *f*
pewter ['pju:tə^r] N Zinn *nt*
PG N ABBR (*Cine: = parental guidance*) *Klassifikation für Filme, die Kinder nur in Begleitung Erwachsener sehen dürfen*
PGA N ABBR (*= Professional Golfers' Association*) *Golf-Profiverband*
PGA 13 (*US*) ABBR (*Cine: = Parental Guidance 13*) *Klassifikation für Kinofilme, welche Kinder unter 13 Jahren nur in Begleitung Erwachsener sehen dürfen*
pH N ABBR (*= potential of hydrogen*) pH
PHA (*US*) N ABBR (*= Public Housing Administration*) *Regierungsbehörde für sozialen Wohnungsbau*
phallic ['fælɪk] ADJ phallisch; (*symbol*) Phallus-
phantom ['fæntəm] N Phantom *nt* ▶ ADJ (*fig*) Phantom-

Pharaoh ['fɛərəu] N Pharao *m*
pharmaceutical [fɑːmə'sjuːtɪkl] ADJ pharmazeutisch
pharmaceuticals [fɑːmə'sjuːtɪklz] NPL Arzneimittel *pl*, Pharmaka *pl*
pharmacist ['fɑːməsɪst] N Apotheker(in) *m(f)*
pharmacy ['fɑːməsɪ] N (*shop*) Apotheke *f*; (*science*) Pharmazie *f*
phase [feɪz] N Phase *f* ▸ VT: **to ~ sth in/out** etw stufenweise einführen/abschaffen
phat [fæt] ADJ (*inf*) abgefahren, geil
PhD N ABBR (= *Doctor of Philosophy*) ≈ Dr. phil.
pheasant ['fɛznt] N Fasan *m*
phenomena [fə'nɔmɪnə] NPL *of* **phenomenon**
phenomenal [fə'nɔmɪnl] ADJ phänomenal
phenomenon [fə'nɔmɪnən] (*pl* **phenomena**) N Phänomen *nt*
phew [fjuː] EXCL puh!
phial ['faɪəl] N Fläschchen *nt*
philanderer [fɪ'lændərə^r^] N Schwerenöter *m*
philanthropic [fɪlən'θrɔpɪk] ADJ philanthropisch
philanthropist [fɪ'lænθrəpɪst] N Philanthrop(in) *m(f)*
philatelist [fɪ'lætəlɪst] N Philatelist(in) *m(f)*
philately [fɪ'lætəlɪ] N Philatelie *f*
Philippines ['fɪlɪpiːnz] NPL: **the ~** die Philippinen *pl*
Philistine ['fɪlɪstaɪn] N (*boor*) Banause *m*
philosopher [fɪ'lɔsəfə^r^] N Philosoph(in) *m(f)*
philosophical [fɪlə'sɔfɪkl] ADJ philosophisch; (*fig: calm, resigned*) gelassen
philosophize [fɪ'lɔsəfaɪz] VI philosophieren
philosophy [fɪ'lɔsəfɪ] N Philosophie *f*
phlegm [flɛm] N (*Med*) Schleim *m*
phlegmatic [flɛg'mætɪk] ADJ phlegmatisch
phobia ['fəubjə] N Phobie *f*
phone [fəun] N Telefon *nt* ▸ VT anrufen ▸ VI anrufen, telefonieren; **to be on the ~** (*possess a phone*) Telefon haben; (*be calling*) telefonieren
▸ **phone back** VT, VI zurückrufen
▸ **phone up** VT, VI anrufen
phone book N Telefonbuch *nt*
phone booth N Telefonzelle *f*
phone box (BRIT) N Telefonzelle *f*
phone call N Anruf *m*
phonecard ['fəunkɑːd] N Telefonkarte *f*
phone-in ['fəunɪn] (BRIT) N (*Radio, TV*) *Radio-/Fernsehsendung mit Hörer-/Zuschauerbeteiligung per Telefon*, Phone-in *nt* ▸ ADJ mit Hörer-/Zuschaueranrufen
phone tapping [-tæpɪŋ] N Abhören *nt* von Telefonleitungen
phonetics [fə'nɛtɪks] N Phonetik *f*
phoney ['fəunɪ] ADJ (*address*) falsch; (*accent*) unecht; (*person*) unaufrichtig
phonograph ['fəunəgrɑːf] (US) N Grammofon *nt*
phony ['fəunɪ] ADJ = **phoney**
phosphate ['fɔsfeɪt] N Phosphat *nt*
phosphorus ['fɔsfərəs] N Phosphor *m*
photo ['fəutəu] N Foto *nt*
photo... ['fəutəu] PREF Foto-
photocopier ['fəutəukɔpɪə^r^] N Fotokopierer *m*
photocopy ['fəutəukɔpɪ] N Fotokopie *f* ▸ VT fotokopieren
photoelectric [fəutəuɪ'lɛktrɪk] ADJ (*effect*) fotoelektrisch; (*cell*) Photo-
photo finish N Fotofinish *nt*
Photofit® ['fəutəufɪt] N, **Photofit picture**® N Phantombild *nt*
photogenic [fəutəu'dʒɛnɪk] ADJ fotogen
photograph ['fəutəgræf] N Fotografie *f* ▸ VT fotografieren; **to take a ~ of sb** jdn fotografieren
photographer [fə'tɔgrəfə^r^] N Fotograf(in) *m(f)*
photographic [fəutə'græfɪk] ADJ (*equipment etc*) fotografisch, Foto-
photography [fə'tɔgrəfɪ] N Fotografie *f*
photo opportunity N Fototermin *m*; (*accidental*) Fotogelegenheit *f*
Photoshop® ['fəutəuʃɔp] N Photoshop® *nt*
photostat ['fəutəustæt] N Fotokopie *f*
photosynthesis [fəutəu'sɪnθəsɪs] N Fotosynthese *f*
phrase [freɪz] N Satz *m*; (*Ling*) Redewendung *f*; (*Mus*) Phrase *f* ▸ VT ausdrücken; (*letter*) formulieren
phrase book N Sprachführer *m*
physical ['fɪzɪkl] ADJ (*bodily*) körperlich; (*geography, properties*) physikalisch; (*law, explanation*) natürlich; **~ examination** ärztliche Untersuchung *f*; **the ~ sciences** die Naturwissenschaften
physical education N Sportunterricht *m*
physically ['fɪzɪklɪ] ADV (*fit, attractive*) körperlich
physician [fɪ'zɪʃən] N Arzt *m*, Ärztin *f*
physicist ['fɪzɪsɪst] N Physiker(in) *m(f)*
physics ['fɪzɪks] N Physik *f*
physiological ['fɪzɪə'lɔdʒɪkl] ADJ physiologisch
physiology [fɪzɪ'ɔlədʒɪ] N Physiologie *f*
physiotherapist [fɪzɪəu'θɛrəpɪst] N Physiotherapeut(in) *m(f)*
physiotherapy [fɪzɪəu'θɛrəpɪ] N Physiotherapie *f*
physique [fɪ'ziːk] N Körperbau *m*
pianist ['piːənɪst] N Pianist(in) *m(f)*
piano [pɪ'ænəu] N Klavier *nt*, Piano *nt*
piano accordion (BRIT) N Akkordeon *nt*
piccolo ['pɪkələu] N Piccoloflöte *f*
pick [pɪk] N (*also*: **pickaxe**) Spitzhacke *f* ▸ VT (*select*) aussuchen; (*gather: fruit, mushrooms*) sammeln; (*: flowers*) pflücken; (*remove, take out*) herausnehmen; (*lock*) knacken; (*scab, spot*) kratzen an *+dat*; **take your ~** (*choose*) Sie haben die Wahl; **the ~ of** (*best*) das Beste *+gen*; **to ~ one's nose** in der Nase bohren; **to ~ one's teeth** in den Zähnen stochern; **to ~ sb's brains** jdn als Informationsquelle nutzen; **to ~ sb's pocket** jdn bestehlen; **to ~ a quarrel (with sb)** einen Streit (mit jdm) anfangen
▸ **pick at** VT FUS (*food*) herumstochern in *+dat*
▸ **pick off** VT (*shoot*) abschießen
▸ **pick on** VT FUS (*criticize*) herumhacken auf *+dat*
▸ **pick out** VT (*distinguish*) ausmachen; (*select*) aussuchen
▸ **pick up** VI (*health*) sich verbessern; (*economy*) sich erholen ▸ VT (*from floor etc*) aufheben;

P

(*arrest*) festnehmen; (*collect: person, parcel etc*) abholen; (*hitchhiker*) mitnehmen; (*for sexual encounter*) aufreißen; (*learn: skill etc*) mitbekommen; (*Radio*) empfangen; **to ~ up where one left off** da weitermachen, wo man aufgehört hat; **to ~ up speed** schneller werden; **to ~ o.s. up** (*after falling etc*) sich aufrappeln

pickaxe, (*US*) **pickax** ['pɪkæks] N Spitzhacke *f*

picket ['pɪkɪt] N (*in strike*) Streikposten *m* ▶ VT (*factory etc*) Streikposten aufstellen vor *+dat*

picketing ['pɪkɪtɪŋ] N Aufstellen *nt* von Streikposten

picket line N Streikpostenkette *f*

pickings ['pɪkɪŋz] NPL: **there are rich ~ to be had here** hier ist die Ausbeute gut

pickle ['pɪkl] N (*also*: **pickles**) Pickles *pl* ▶ VT einlegen; **to be in a ~** in der Klemme sitzen; **to get in a ~** in eine Klemme geraten

pick-me-up ['pɪkmiːʌp] N Muntermacher *m*

pickpocket ['pɪkpɔkɪt] N Taschendieb(in) *m(f)*

pick-up ['pɪkʌp] N (*also*: **pick-up truck**) offener Kleintransporter *m*; (*BRIT*: *on record player*) Tonabnehmer *m*

picnic ['pɪknɪk] N Picknick *nt* ▶ VI picknicken

picnicker ['pɪknɪkə^r] N Picknicker(in) *m(f)*

pictorial [pɪk'tɔːrɪəl] ADJ (*record, coverage etc*) bildlich

picture ['pɪktʃə^r] N Bild *nt*; (*film*) Film *m* ▶ VT (*imagine*) sich *dat* vorstellen; **the pictures** (*BRIT inf*: *the cinema*) das Kino; **to take a ~ of sb** ein Bild von jdm machen; **to put sb in the ~** jdn ins Bild setzen

picture book N Bilderbuch *nt*

picture messaging N Picture Messaging *nt*

picturesque [pɪktʃə'rɛsk] ADJ malerisch

picture window N Aussichtsfenster *nt*

piddling ['pɪdlɪŋ] (*inf*) ADJ lächerlich

pidgin ['pɪdʒɪn] ADJ: **~ English** Pidginenglisch *nt*

pie [paɪ] N (*vegetable, meat*) Pastete *f*; (*fruit*) Torte *f*

piebald ['paɪbɔːld] ADJ (*horse*) scheckig

piece [piːs] N Stück *nt*; (*Draughts etc*) Stein *m*; (*Chess*) Figur *f*; **in pieces** (*broken*) kaputt; (*taken apart*) auseinandergenommen, in Einzelteilen; **a ~ of clothing/furniture/music** ein Kleidungs-/Möbel-/Musikstück *nt*; **a ~ of machinery** eine Maschine; **a ~ of research** eine Forschungsarbeit; **a ~ of advice** ein Rat *m*; **to take sth to pieces** etw auseinandernehmen; **in one ~** (*object*) unbeschädigt; (*person*) wohlbehalten; **a 10p ~** (*BRIT*) ein 10-Pence-Stück *nt*; **~ by ~** Stück für Stück; **a six-~ band** eine sechsköpfige Band; **let her say her ~** lass sie ausreden
▶ **piece together** VT zusammenfügen

piecemeal ['piːsmiːl] ADV stückweise, Stück für Stück

piecework ['piːswəːk] N Akkordarbeit *f*

pie chart N Tortendiagramm *nt*

pier [pɪə^r] N Pier *m*

pierce [pɪəs] VT durchstechen; **to have one's ears pierced** sich *dat* die Ohrläppchen durchstechen lassen

pierced [pɪəst] ADJ (*part of body*) gepierct

piercing ['pɪəsɪŋ] ADJ (*fig*: *cry, eyes, stare*) durchdringend; (*wind*) schneidend

piety ['paɪətɪ] N Frömmigkeit *f*

piffling ['pɪflɪŋ] (*inf*) ADJ lächerlich

pig [pɪg] N (*also pej*) Schwein *nt*; (*greedy person*) Vielfraß *m*

pigeon ['pɪdʒən] N Taube *f*

pigeonhole ['pɪdʒənhəul] N (*for letters etc*) Fach *nt*; (*fig*) Schublade *f* ▶ VT (*fig*: *person*) in eine Schublade stecken

pigeon-toed ['pɪdʒəntəud] ADJ mit einwärtsgerichteten Zehen

piggy bank ['pɪgɪ-] N Sparschwein *nt*

pig-headed ['pɪg'hɛdɪd] (*pej*) ADJ dickköpfig

piglet ['pɪglɪt] N Schweinchen *nt*, Ferkel *nt*

pigment ['pɪgmənt] N Pigment *nt*

pigmentation [pɪgmən'teɪʃən] N Pigmentierung *f*, Färbung *f*

pigmy ['pɪgmɪ] N = **pygmy**

pigskin ['pɪgskɪn] N Schweinsleder *nt*

pigsty ['pɪgstaɪ] N (*also fig*) Schweinestall *m*

pigtail ['pɪgteɪl] N Zopf *m*

pike [paɪk] N (*fish*) Hecht *m*; (*spear*) Spieß *m*

pilchard ['pɪltʃəd] N Sardine *f*

pile [paɪl] N (*heap*) Haufen *m*; (*stack*) Stapel *m*; (*of carpet, velvet*) Flor *m*; (*pillar*) Pfahl *m* ▶ VT (*also*: **pile up**) (auf)stapeln; **in a ~** in einem Haufen; **to ~ into/out of** (*vehicle*) sich drängen in *+acc*/aus
▶ **pile on** VT: **to ~ it on** (*inf*) zu dick auftragen
▶ **pile up** VI sich stapeln

piles [paɪlz] NPL (*Med*) Hämorr(ho)iden *pl*

pile-up ['paɪlʌp] N (*Aut*) Massenkarambolage *f*

pilfer ['pɪlfə^r] VT, VI stehlen

pilfering ['pɪlfərɪŋ] N Diebstahl *m*

pilgrim ['pɪlgrɪm] N Pilger(in) *m(f)*

pilgrimage ['pɪlgrɪmɪdʒ] N Pilgerfahrt *f*, Wallfahrt *f*

pill [pɪl] N Tablette *f*, Pille *f*; **the ~** (*contraceptive*) die Pille; **to be on the ~** die Pille nehmen

pillage ['pɪlɪdʒ] N Plünderung *f* ▶ VT plündern

pillar ['pɪlə^r] N Säule *f*; **a ~ of society** (*fig*) eine Säule *or* Stütze der Gesellschaft

pillar box (*BRIT*) N Briefkasten *m*

pillion ['pɪljən] N: **to ride ~** (*on motorcycle*) auf dem Soziussitz mitfahren; (*on horse*) hinten auf dem Pferd mitreiten

pillory ['pɪlərɪ] VT (*criticize*) anprangern ▶ N Pranger *m*

pillow ['pɪləu] N (Kopf)kissen *nt*

pillowcase ['pɪləukeɪs] N (Kopf)kissenbezug *m*

pillowslip ['pɪləuslɪp] N = **pillowcase**

pilot ['paɪlət] N (*Aviat*) Pilot(in) *m(f)*; (*Naut*) Lotse *m* ▶ ADJ (*scheme, study etc*) Pilot- ▶ VT (*aircraft*) steuern; (*fig*: *new law, scheme*) sich zum Fürsprecher machen *+gen*

pilot boat N Lotsenboot *nt*

pilot light N (*on cooker, boiler*) Zündflamme *f*

pilot test N Pilot- *od* Modellversuch *m*

pimento [pɪ'mɛntəu] N (*spice*) Piment *nt*

pimp [pɪmp] N Zuhälter *m*

pimple ['pɪmpl] N Pickel *m*

pimply ['pɪmplɪ] ADJ pick(e)lig

PIN N ABBR (= *personal identification number*) PIN; **~ number** PIN-Nummer *f*
pin [pɪn] N (*metal: for clothes, papers*) Stecknadel *f*; (*Tech*) Stift *m*; (BRIT: *also*: **drawing pin**) Heftzwecke *f*; (*in grenade*) Sicherungsstift *m*; (BRIT *Elec*) Pol *m* ▶ VT (*fasten with pin*) feststecken; **pins and needles** (*in arms, legs etc*) Kribbeln *nt*; **to ~ sb against/to sth** jdn gegen/an etw *acc* pressen; **to ~ sth on sb** (*fig*) jdm etw anhängen ▶ **pin down** VT (*fig: person*) festnageln; **there's something strange here but I can't quite ~ it down** hier stimmt etwas nicht, aber ich weiß nicht genau was
pinafore [ˈpɪnəfɔːʳ] (BRIT) N (*also*: **pinafore dress**) Trägerkleid *nt*
pinball [ˈpɪnbɔːl] N (*game*) Flippern *nt*; (*machine*) Flipper *m*
pincers [ˈpɪnsəz] NPL (*tool*) Kneifzange *f*; (*of crab, lobster etc*) Schere *f*
pinch [pɪntʃ] N (*of salt etc*) Prise *f* ▶ VT (*with finger and thumb*) zwicken, kneifen; (*inf: steal*) klauen ▶ VI (*shoe*) drücken; **at a ~** zur Not; **to feel the ~** (*fig*) die schlechte Lage zu spüren bekommen
pinched [pɪntʃt] ADJ (*face*) erschöpft; **~ with cold** verfroren
pincushion [ˈpɪnkuʃən] N Nadelkissen *nt*
pine [paɪn] N (*also*: **pine tree**) Kiefer *f*; (*wood*) Kiefernholz *nt* ▶ VI: **to ~ for** sich sehnen nach ▶ **pine away** VI sich (vor Kummer) verzehren
pineapple [ˈpaɪnæpl] N Ananas *f*
pine cone N Kiefernzapfen *m*
pine needles NPL Kiefernnadeln *pl*
ping [pɪŋ] N (*noise*) Klingeln *nt*
Ping-Pong® [ˈpɪŋpɔŋ] N Pingpong *nt*
pink [pɪŋk] ADJ rosa *inv* ▶ N (*colour*) Rosa *nt*; (*Bot*) Gartennelke *f*
pinking shears NPL Zickzackschere *f*
pin money (BRIT *inf*) N Nadelgeld *nt*
pinnacle [ˈpɪnəkl] N (*of building, mountain*) Spitze *f*; (*fig*) Gipfel *m*
pinpoint [ˈpɪnpɔɪnt] VT (*identify*) genau festlegen, identifizieren; (*position of sth*) genau aufzeigen
pinstripe [ˈpɪnstraɪp], **pinstriped** [ˈpɪnstraɪpt] ADJ: **~ suit** Nadelstreifenanzug *m*
pint [paɪnt] N (BRIT: = *568 cc*) (britisches) Pint *nt*; (US: = *473 cc*) (amerikanisches) Pint; **a ~** (BRIT *inf: of beer*) ≈ eine Halbe
pin-up [ˈpɪnʌp] N (*picture*) Pin-up-Foto *nt*
pioneer [paɪəˈnɪəʳ] N (*lit, fig*) Pionier *m* ▶ VT (*invention etc*) Pionierarbeit leisten für
pious [ˈpaɪəs] ADJ fromm
pip [pɪp] N (*of apple, orange*) Kern *m* ▶ VT: **to be pipped at the post** (BRIT *fig*) um Haaresbreite geschlagen werden; **the pips** NPL (BRIT *Radio*) das Zeitzeichen
pipe [paɪp] N (*for water, gas*) Rohr *nt*; (*for smoking*) Pfeife *f*; (*Mus*) Flöte *f* ▶ VT (*water, gas, oil*) (durch Rohre) leiten; **pipes** NPL (*also*: **bagpipes**) Dudelsack *m*
▶ **pipe down** (*inf*) VI (*be quiet*) ruhig sein
pipe cleaner N Pfeifenreiniger *m*
piped music [paɪpt-] N Berieselungsmusik *f*
pipe dream N Hirngespinst *nt*
pipeline [ˈpaɪplaɪn] N Pipeline *f*; **it's in the ~** (*fig*) es ist in Vorbereitung
piper [ˈpaɪpəʳ] N (*bagpipe player*) Dudelsackspieler(in) *m(f)*
pipe tobacco N Pfeifentabak *m*
piping [ˈpaɪpɪŋ] ADV: **~ hot** kochend heiß
piquant [ˈpiːkənt] ADJ (*also fig*) pikant
pique [ˈpiːk] N: **in a fit of ~** eingeschnappt, pikiert
piracy [ˈpaɪərəsɪ] N Piraterie *f*, Seeräuberei *f*; (*Comm*): **to commit ~** ein Plagiat *nt* begehen
pirate [ˈpaɪərət] N Pirat *m*, Seeräuber *m* ▶ VT (*Comm: video tape, cassette etc*) illegal herstellen
pirate radio station (BRIT) N Piratensender *m*
pirouette [pɪruˈɛt] N Pirouette *f* ▶ VI Pirouetten drehen
Pisces [ˈpaɪsiːz] N Fische *pl*; **to be ~** Fische *or* (ein) Fisch sein
piss [pɪs] (*inf!*) VI pissen (*inf!*) ▶ N Pisse *f* (*inf!*); **~ off!** verpiss dich!; **to be pissed off (with sb/sth)** (von jdm/etw) die Schnauze vollhaben; **it's pissing down** (BRIT: *raining*) es schifft; **to take the ~ out of sb** (BRIT) jdn verarschen
pissed [pɪst] (*inf!*) ADJ (*drunk*) besoffen
pistachio [pɪˈstɑːʃɪəʊ] (*pl* **pistachios**) N Pistazie *f*
pistol [ˈpɪstl] N Pistole *f*
piston [ˈpɪstən] N Kolben *m*
pit [pɪt] N Grube *f*; (*in surface of road*) Schlagloch *nt*; (*coal mine*) Zeche *f*; (*also*: **orchestra pit**) Orchestergraben *m* ▶ VT: **to ~ one's wits against sb** seinen Verstand mit jdm messen; **the pits** NPL (*Aut*) die Box; **to ~ o.s. against sth** den Kampf gegen etw aufnehmen; **to ~ sb against sb** jdn gegen jdn antreten lassen; **the ~ of one's stomach** die Magengrube
pitapat [ˈpɪtəˈpæt] (BRIT) ADV: **to go ~** (*heart*) pochen, klopfen; (*rain*) prasseln
pitch [pɪtʃ] N (BRIT *Sport: field*) Spielfeld *nt*; (*Mus*) Tonhöhe *f*; (*fig: level, degree*) Grad *m*; (*tar*) Pech *nt*; (*also*: **sales pitch**) Verkaufsmasche *f*; (*Naut*) Stampfen *nt* ▶ VT (*throw*) werfen, schleudern; (*set: price, message*) ansetzen ▶ VI (*fall forwards*) hinschlagen; (*Naut*) stampfen; **to ~ a tent** ein Zelt aufschlagen; **to be pitched forward** vornüber geworfen werden
pitch-black [ˈpɪtʃˈblæk] ADJ pechschwarz
pitched battle [pɪtʃt-] N offene Schlacht *f*
pitcher [ˈpɪtʃəʳ] N (*jug*) Krug *m*; (*US Baseball*) Werfer *m*
pitchfork [ˈpɪtʃfɔːk] N Heugabel *f*
piteous [ˈpɪtɪəs] ADJ kläglich, erbärmlich
pitfall [ˈpɪtfɔːl] N Falle *f*
pith [pɪθ] N (*of orange etc*) weiße Haut *f*; (*of plant*) Mark *nt*; (*fig*) Kern *m*
pithead [ˈpɪthɛd] N Schachtanlagen *pl* über Tage
pithy [ˈpɪθɪ] ADJ (*comment etc*) prägnant
pitiable [ˈpɪtɪəbl] ADJ mitleiderregend
pitiful [ˈpɪtɪful] ADJ (*sight etc*) mitleiderregend; (*excuse, attempt*) jämmerlich, kläglich
pitifully [ˈpɪtɪfəlɪ] ADV (*thin, frail*) jämmerlich; (*inadequate, ill-equipped*) fürchterlich
pitiless [ˈpɪtɪlɪs] ADJ mitleidlos

P

pittance ['pɪtns] N Hungerlohn *m*
pitted ['pɪtɪd] ADJ: **~ with** übersät mit; **~ with rust** voller Rost
pity ['pɪtɪ] N Mitleid *nt* ▸ VT bemitleiden, bedauern; **what a ~!** wie schade!; **it is a ~ that you can't come** schade, dass du nicht kommen kannst; **to take ~ on sb** Mitleid mit jdm haben
pitying ['pɪtɪɪŋ] ADJ mitleidig
pivot ['pɪvət] N (*Tech*) Drehpunkt *m*; (*fig*) Dreh- und Angelpunkt *m* ▸ VI sich drehen
▸ **pivot on** VT FUS (*depend on*) abhängen von
pixel ['pɪksl] N (*Comput*) Pixel *nt*
pixie ['pɪksɪ] N Elf *m*, Elfe *f*
pizza ['pi:tsə] N Pizza *f*
placard ['plækɑ:d] N Plakat *nt*, Aushang *m*; (*in march etc*) Transparent *nt*
placate [plə'keɪt] VT beschwichtigen, besänftigen
placatory [plə'keɪtərɪ] ADJ beschwichtigend, besänftigend
place [pleɪs] N Platz *m*; (*position*) Stelle *f*, Ort *m*; (*seat: on committee etc*) Sitz *m*; (*home*) Wohnung *f*; (*in street names*) ≈ Straße *f* ▸ VT (*put: object*) stellen, legen; (*identify: person*) unterbringen; **~ of birth** Geburtsort *m*; **to take ~** (*happen*) geschehen, passieren; **at/to his ~** (*home*) bei/zu ihm; **from ~ to ~** von Ort zu Ort; **all over the ~** überall; **in places** stellenweise; **in sb's/sth's ~** anstelle von jdm/etw; **to take sb's/sth's ~** an die Stelle von jdm/etw treten, jdn/etw ersetzen; **out of ~** (*inappropriate*) unangebracht; **I feel out of ~ here** ich fühle mich hier fehl am Platze; **in the first ~** (*first of all*) erstens; **to change places with sb** mit jdm den Platz tauschen; **to put sb in his ~** (*fig*) jdn in seine Schranken weisen; **he's going places** er bringt es noch mal weit; **it's not my ~ to do it** es ist nicht an mir, das zu tun; **to be placed** (*in race, exam*) platziert sein; **to be placed third** den dritten Platz belegen; **to ~ an order with sb (for sth)** eine Bestellung bei jdm (für etw) aufgeben; **how are you placed next week?** wie sieht es bei Ihnen nächste Woche aus?
placebo [plə'si:bəu] N Placebo *nt*; (*fig*) Beruhigungsmittel *nt*
place mat N Set *m or nt*
placement ['pleɪsmənt] N Platzierung *f*
place name N Ortsname *m*
placenta [plə'sɛntə] N Plazenta *f*
place setting N Gedeck *nt*
placid ['plæsɪd] ADJ (*person*) ruhig, gelassen; (*place, river etc*) friedvoll
plagiarism ['pleɪdʒjərɪzəm] N Plagiat *nt*
plagiarist ['pleɪdʒjərɪst] N Plagiator(in) *m(f)*
plagiarize ['pleɪdʒjəraɪz] VT (*idea, work*) kopieren, plagiieren
plague [pleɪg] N (*Med*) Seuche *f*; (*fig: of locusts etc*) Plage *f* ▸ VT (*fig: problems etc*) plagen; **to ~ sb with questions** jdn mit Fragen quälen
plaice [pleɪs] N INV Scholle *f*
plaid [plæd] N Plaid *nt*
plain [pleɪn] ADJ (*unpatterned*) einfarbig; (*simple*) einfach, schlicht; (*clear, easily understood*) klar; (*not beautiful*) unattraktiv; (*frank*) offen ▸ ADV (*wrong, stupid etc*) einfach ▸ N (*area of land*) Ebene *f*; (*Knitting*) rechte Masche *f*; **to make sth ~ to sb** jdm etw klarmachen
plain chocolate N Bitterschokolade *f*
plain-clothes ['pleɪnkləuðz] ADJ (*police officer*) in Zivil
plainly ['pleɪnlɪ] ADV (*obviously*) eindeutig; (*clearly*) deutlich, klar
plainness ['pleɪnnɪs] N (*of person*) Reizlosigkeit *f*
plain speaking N Offenheit *f*; **a bit of ~** ein paar offene Worte
plain-spoken ['pleɪn'spəukn] ADJ offen
plaintiff ['pleɪntɪf] N Kläger(in) *m(f)*
plaintive ['pleɪntɪv] ADJ (*cry, voice*) klagend; (*song*) schwermütig; (*look*) traurig
plait [plæt] N (*of hair*) Zopf *m*; (*of rope, leather*) Geflecht *nt* ▸ VT flechten
plan [plæn] N Plan *m* ▸ VT planen; (*building, schedule*) entwerfen ▸ VI planen; **to ~ to do sth** planen *or* vorhaben, etw zu tun; **how long do you ~ to stay?** wie lange haben Sie vor, zu bleiben?; **to ~ for** *or* **on** (*expect*) sich einstellen auf *+acc*; **to ~ on doing sth** vorhaben, etw zu tun
plane [pleɪn] N (*Aviat*) Flugzeug *nt*; (*Math*) Ebene *f*; (*fig: level*) Niveau *nt*; (*tool*) Hobel *m*; (*also:* **plane tree**) Platane *f* ▸ VT (*wood*) hobeln ▸ VI (*Naut, Aut*) gleiten
planet ['plænɪt] N Planet *m*
planetarium [plænɪ'tɛərɪəm] N Planetarium *nt*
plank [plæŋk] N (*of wood*) Brett *nt*; (*fig: of policy etc*) Schwerpunkt *m*
plankton ['plæŋktən] N Plankton *nt*
planned economy ['plænd-] N Planwirtschaft *f*
planner ['plænə^r] N Planer(in) *m(f)*
planning ['plænɪŋ] N Planung *f*
planning permission (BRIT) N Baugenehmigung *f*
plant [plɑ:nt] N (*Bot*) Pflanze *f*; (*machinery*) Maschinen *pl*; (*factory*) Anlage *f* ▸ VT (*seed, plant, crops*) pflanzen; (*field, garden*) bepflanzen; (*microphone, bomb etc*) anbringen; (*incriminating evidence*) schleusen; (*fig: object*) stellen; (*: kiss*) drücken
plantation [plæn'teɪʃən] N Plantage *f*; (*wood*) Anpflanzung *f*
plant pot (BRIT) N Blumentopf *m*
plaque [plæk] N (*on building etc*) Tafel *f*, Plakette *f*; (*on teeth*) Zahnbelag *m*
plasma ['plæzmə] N Plasma *nt*
plaster ['plɑ:stə^r] N (*for walls*) Putz *m*; (*also:* **plaster of Paris**) Gips *m*; (BRIT: *also:* **sticking plaster**) Pflaster *nt* ▸ VT (*wall, ceiling*) verputzen; **in ~** (BRIT) in Gips; **to ~ with** (*cover*) bepflastern mit
plasterboard ['plɑ:stəbɔ:d] N Gipskarton *m*
plaster cast N (*Med*) Gipsverband *m*; (*model, statue*) Gipsform *f*
plastered ['plɑ:stəd] (*inf*) ADJ (*drunk*) sturzbesoffen
plasterer ['plɑ:stərə^r] N Gipser *m*
plastic ['plæstɪk] N Plastik *nt* ▸ ADJ (*bucket, cup etc*) Plastik-; (*flexible*) formbar; **the ~ arts** die bildende Kunst

plastic bag N Plastiktüte *f*
plastic bullet N Plastikgeschoss *nt*
plastic explosive N Plastiksprengstoff *m*
Plasticine® ['plæstɪsi:n] N Plastilin *nt*
plastic surgery N plastische Chirurgie *f*
plate [pleɪt] N Teller *m*; *(metal cover)* Platte *f*; *(Typ)* Druckplatte *f*; *(Aut)* Nummernschild *nt*; *(in book: picture)* Tafel *f*; *(also:* **dental plate***)* Gaumenplatte *f*; *(on door)* Schild *nt*; **gold/silver ~** vergoldeter/versilberter Artikel *m*; **that necklace is just ~** die Halskette ist nur vergoldet/versilbert
plateau ['plætəu] *(pl* **plateaus** *or* **plateaux***)* N *(Geog)* Plateau *nt*, Hochebene *f*; *(fig)* stabiler Zustand *m*
plateful ['pleɪtful] N Teller *m*
plate glass N Tafelglas *nt*
platen ['plætən] N *(on typewriter, printer)* (Schreib)walze *f*
plate rack N Geschirrständer *m*
platform ['plætfɔ:m] N *(stage)* Podium *nt*; *(for landing, loading on etc, Brit: of bus)* Plattform *f*; *(Rail)* Bahnsteig *m*; *(Pol)* Programm *nt*; **the train leaves from ~ 7** der Zug fährt von Gleis 7 ab
platform ticket (BRIT) N *(Rail)* Bahnsteigkarte *f*
platinum ['plætɪnəm] N Platin *nt*
platitude ['plætɪtju:d] N Plattitüde *f*, Gemeinplatz *m*
platonic [plə'tɔnɪk] ADJ *(relationship)* platonisch
platoon [plə'tu:n] N Zug *m*
platter ['plætəʳ] N Platte *f*
plaudits ['plɔ:dɪts] NPL Ovationen *pl*
plausible ['plɔ:zɪbl] ADJ *(theory, excuse)* plausibel; *(liar etc)* glaubwürdig
play [pleɪ] N *(Theat)* (Theater)stück *nt*; *(TV)* Fernsehspiel *nt*; *(Radio)* Hörspiel *nt*; *(activity)* Spiel *nt* ▸ VT spielen; *(team, opponent)* spielen gegen ▸ VI spielen; **to bring into ~** ins Spiel bringen; **a ~ on words** ein Wortspiel *nt*; **to ~ a trick on sb** jdn hereinlegen; **to ~ a part** *or* **role in sth** *(fig)* eine Rolle bei etw spielen; **to ~ for time** *(fig)* auf Zeit spielen, Zeit gewinnen wollen; **to ~ safe** auf Nummer sicher gehen; **to ~ into sb's hands** jdm in die Hände spielen
▸ **play about with** VT FUS = **play around with**
▸ **play along with** VT FUS *(person)* sich richten nach; *(plan, idea)* eingehen auf *+acc*
▸ **play around with** VT FUS *(fiddle with)* herumspielen mit
▸ **play at** VT FUS *(do casually)* spielen mit; **to ~ at being sb/sth** jdn/etw spielen; **what are you playing at?** was soll das?
▸ **play back** VT *(recording)* abspielen
▸ **play down** VT herunterspielen
▸ **play on** VT FUS *(sb's feelings etc)* ausnutzen; **to ~ on sb's mind** jdm im Kopf herumgehen
▸ **play up** VI *(machine, knee etc)* Schwierigkeiten machen; *(children)* frech werden
play-act ['pleɪækt] VI Theater spielen
playacting N Schauspielerei *f*
playboy ['pleɪbɔɪ] N Playboy *m*
player ['pleɪəʳ] N *(Sport, Mus)* Spieler(in) *m(f)*; *(Theat)* Schauspieler(in) *m(f)*
playful ['pleɪful] ADJ *(person, gesture)* spielerisch; *(animal)* verspielt
playgoer ['pleɪgəuəʳ] N Theaterbesucher(in) *m(f)*
playground ['pleɪgraund] N *(in park)* Spielplatz *m*; *(in school)* Schulhof *m*
playgroup ['pleɪgru:p] N Spielgruppe *f*
playing card ['pleɪɪŋ-] N Spielkarte *f*
playing field N Sportplatz *m*
playmaker ['pleɪmeɪkəʳ] N *(Sport)* Spielmacher(in) *m(f)*
playmate ['pleɪmeɪt] N Spielkamerad(in) *m(f)*
play-off ['pleɪɔf] N Ausscheidungsspiel *nt*, Play-off *nt*
playpen ['pleɪpɛn] N Laufstall *m*
playroom ['pleɪru:m] N Spielzimmer *nt*
playschool ['pleɪsku:l] N = **playgroup**
plaything ['pleɪθɪŋ] N *(also fig)* Spielzeug *nt*
playtime ['pleɪtaɪm] N (kleine) Pause *f*
playwright ['pleɪraɪt] N Dramatiker(in) *m(f)*
plc (BRIT) N ABBR *(= public limited company)* ≈ AG *f*
plea [pli:] N *(request)* Bitte *f*; *(Law)*: **to enter a ~ of guilty/not guilty** sich schuldig/unschuldig erklären; *(excuse)* Vorwand *m*
plea bargaining N *Verhandlungen zwischen Anklage und Verteidigung mit dem Ziel, bestimmte Anklagepunkte fallen zu lassen, wenn der Angeklagte sich in anderen Punkten schuldig bekennt*
plead [pli:d] VI *(Law) vor Gericht eine Schuld-/Unschuldserklärung abgeben* ▸ VT *(Law)*: **to ~ sb's case** jdn vertreten; *(give as excuse: ignorance, ill health etc)* vorgeben, sich berufen auf *+acc*; **to ~ with sb** *(beg)* jdn inständig bitten; **to ~ for sth** um etw nachsuchen; **to ~ guilty/not guilty** sich schuldig/nicht schuldig bekennen
pleasant ['plɛznt] ADJ angenehm; *(smile)* freundlich
pleasantly ['plɛzntlɪ] ADV *(surprised)* angenehm; *(say, behave)* freundlich
pleasantries ['plɛzntrɪz] NPL Höflichkeiten *pl*, Nettigkeiten *pl*
please [pli:z] EXCL bitte ▸ VT *(satisfy)* zufriedenstellen ▸ VI *(give pleasure)* gefällig sein; **~ Miss/Sir!** *(to attract teacher's attention)* ≈ Frau/Herr X!; **yes, ~** ja, bitte; **my bill, ~** die Rechnung, bitte; **~ don't cry!** bitte wein doch nicht!; **~ yourself!** *(inf)* wie du willst!; **do as you ~** machen Sie, was Sie für richtig halten
pleased [pli:zd] ADJ *(happy)* erfreut; *(satisfied)* zufrieden; **~ to meet you** freut mich(, Sie kennenzulernen); **~ with** zufrieden mit; **we are ~ to inform you that ...** wir freuen uns, Ihnen mitzuteilen, dass ...
pleasing ['pli:zɪŋ] ADJ *(remark, picture etc)* erfreulich; *(person)* sympathisch
pleasurable ['plɛʒərəbl] ADJ angenehm
pleasure ['plɛʒəʳ] N *(happiness, satisfaction)* Freude *f*; *(fun, enjoyable experience)* Vergnügen *nt*; **it's a ~, my ~** gern geschehen; **with ~** gern, mit Vergnügen; **is this trip for business or ~?** ist diese Reise geschäftlich oder zum Vergnügen?
pleasure boat N Vergnügungsschiff *nt*
pleasure cruise N Vergnügungsfahrt *f*

P

pleat [pli:t] N Falte *f*
pleb [plɛb] (*inf, pej*) N Prolet *m*
plebiscite ['plɛbɪsɪt] N Volksentscheid *m*, Plebiszit *nt*
plectrum ['plɛktrəm] N Plektron *nt*, Plektrum *nt*
pledge [plɛdʒ] N (*promise*) Versprechen *nt* ▶ VT (*promise*) versprechen; **to ~ sb to secrecy** jdn zum Schweigen verpflichten
plenary ['pli:nərɪ] ADJ (*powers*) unbeschränkt; **~ session** Plenarsitzung *f*; **~ meeting** Vollversammlung *f*
plentiful ['plɛntɪful] ADJ reichlich
plenty ['plɛntɪ] N (*lots*) eine Menge; (*sufficient*) reichlich; **~ of** eine Menge; **we've got ~ of time to get there** wir haben jede Menge Zeit, dorthin zu kommen
plethora ['plɛθərə] N: **a ~ of** eine Fülle von, eine Unmenge an *+dat*
pleurisy ['pluərɪsɪ] N Rippenfellentzündung *f*
Plexiglas® ['plɛksɪglɑ:s] (US) N Plexiglas® *nt*
pliable ['plaɪəbl] ADJ (*material*) biegsam; (*fig: person*) leicht beeinflussbar
pliant ['plaɪənt] ADJ = **pliable**
pliers ['plaɪəz] NPL Zange *f*
plight [plaɪt] N (*of person, country*) Not *f*
plimsolls ['plɪmsəlz] (BRIT) NPL Turnschuhe *pl*
plinth [plɪnθ] N Sockel *m*
PLO N ABBR (= *Palestine Liberation Organization*) PLO *f*
plod [plɔd] VI (*walk*) trotten; (*fig*) sich abplagen
plodder ['plɔdə^r] (*pej*) N (*slow worker*) zäher Arbeiter *m*, zähe Arbeiterin *f*
plonk [plɔŋk] (*inf*) N (BRIT: *wine*) (billiger) Wein *m* ▶ VT: **to ~ sth down** etw hinknallen
plot [plɔt] N (*secret plan*) Komplott *nt*, Verschwörung *f*; (*of story, play, film*) Handlung *f* ▶ VT (*sb's downfall etc*) planen; (*on chart, graph*) markieren ▶ VI (*conspire*) sich verschwören; **a ~ of land** ein Grundstück *nt*; **a vegetable ~** (BRIT) ein Gemüsebeet *nt*
plotter ['plɔtə^r] N (*instrument, Comput*) Plotter *m*
plough, (US) **plow** [plau] N Pflug *m* ▶ VT pflügen; **to ~ money into sth** (*project etc*) Geld in etw *acc* stecken
▶ **plough back** VT (*Comm*) reinvestieren
▶ **plough into** VT FUS (*crowd*) rasen in *+acc*
ploughman, (US) **plowman** ['plaumən] N (*irreg*) Pflüger *m*
ploughman's lunch ['plaumənz-] (BRIT) N *Imbiss aus Brot, Käse und Pickles*
plow *etc* (US) = **plough** *etc*
ploy [plɔɪ] N Trick *m*
pls ABBR (= *please*) b
pluck [plʌk] VT (*fruit, flower, leaf*) pflücken; (*musical instrument, eyebrows*) zupfen; (*bird*) rupfen ▶ N (*courage*) Mut *m*; **to ~ up courage** allen Mut zusammennehmen
plucky ['plʌkɪ] (*inf*) ADJ (*person*) tapfer
plug [plʌg] N (*Elec*) Stecker *m*; (*stopper*) Stöpsel *m*; (*Aut: also:* **spark(ing) plug**) Zündkerze *f* ▶ VT (*hole*) zustopfen; (*inf: advertise*) Reklame machen für; **to give sb/sth a ~** für jdn/etw Reklame machen
▶ **plug in** VT (*Elec*) einstöpseln, anschließen ▶ VI angeschlossen werden
plughole ['plʌghəul] (BRIT) N Abfluss *m*
plug-in ['plʌgɪn] N (*Comput*) Zusatzprogramm *nt*, Plug-in *nt*
plum [plʌm] N (*fruit*) Pflaume *f* ▶ ADJ (*inf*): **a ~ job** ein Traumjob *m*
plumage ['plu:mɪdʒ] N Gefieder *nt*
plumb [plʌm] VT: **to ~ the depths of despair/humiliation** die tiefste Verzweiflung/Erniedrigung erleben
▶ **plumb in** VT anschließen, installieren
plumber ['plʌmə^r] N Installateur *m*, Klempner *m*
plumbing ['plʌmɪŋ] N (*piping*) Installationen *pl*, Rohrleitungen *pl*; (*trade*) Klempnerei *f*; (*work*) Installationsarbeiten *pl*
plumb line N Lot *nt*, Senkblei *nt*
plume [plu:m] N (*of bird*) Feder *f*; (*on helmet, horse's head*) Federbusch *m*; **~ of smoke** Rauchfahne *f*
plummet ['plʌmɪt] VI (*bird, aircraft*) (hinunter)stürzen; (*price, rate*) rapide absacken
plump [plʌmp] ADJ (*person*) füllig, mollig
▶ **plump for** (*inf*) VT FUS sich entscheiden für
▶ **plump up** VT (*cushion*) aufschütteln
plunder ['plʌndə^r] N (*activity*) Plünderung *f*; (*stolen things*) Beute *f* ▶ VT (*city, tomb*) plündern
plunge [plʌndʒ] N (*of bird, person*) Sprung *m*; (*fig: of prices, rates etc*) Sturz *m* ▶ VT (*hand, knife*) stoßen ▶ VI (*thing*) stürzen; (*bird, person*) sich stürzen; (*fig: prices, rates etc*) abfallen, stürzen; **to take the ~** (*fig*) den Sprung wagen; **the room was plunged into darkness** das Zimmer war in Dunkelheit getaucht
plunger ['plʌndʒə^r] N (*for sink*) Sauger *m*
plunging ['plʌndʒɪŋ] ADJ: **~ neckline** tiefer Ausschnitt *m*
pluperfect [plu:'pə:fɪkt] N: **the ~** das Plusquamperfekt
plural ['pluərl] ADJ Plural- ▶ N Plural *m*, Mehrzahl *f*
plus [plʌs] N (*also:* **plus sign**) Pluszeichen *nt* ▶ PREP, ADJ plus; **it's a ~** (*fig*) es ist ein Vorteil *or* ein Pluspunkt; **ten/twenty ~** (*more than*) über zehn/zwanzig; **B ~** (*Scol*) ≈ Zwei plus
plus fours NPL Überfallhose *f*
plush [plʌʃ] ADJ (*car, hotel etc*) feudal ▶ N (*fabric*) Plüsch *m*
plus-one ['plʌs'wʌn] N Begleitperson *f*; **he was my ~ for the party** er war meine Begleitperson auf der Party
plutonium [plu:'təunɪəm] N Plutonium *nt*
ply [plaɪ] VT (*a trade*) ausüben, nachgehen *+dat*; (*tool*) gebrauchen, anwenden ▶ VI (*ship*) verkehren ▶ N (*of wool, rope*) Stärke *f*; (*also:* **plywood**) Sperrholz *nt*; **to ~ sb with drink** jdn ausgiebig bewirten; **to ~ sb with questions** jdm viele Fragen stellen; **two-/three-~ wool** zwei-/dreifädige Wolle
plywood ['plaɪwud] N Sperrholz *nt*
PM (BRIT) ABBR = **Prime Minister**
p.m. ADV ABBR (= *post meridiem*) nachmittags; (*later*) abends
PMT ABBR = **premenstrual tension**

pneumatic [nju:ˈmætɪk] ADJ pneumatisch
pneumatic drill N Pressluftbohrer *m*
pneumonia [nju:ˈməunɪə] N Lungenentzündung *f*
PO N ABBR = **Post Office**; (*Mil*) = **petty officer**
p.o. ABBR = **postal order**
POA (BRIT) N ABBR (= *Prison Officers' Association*) *Gewerkschaft der Gefängnisbeamten*
poach [pəutʃ] VT (*steal: fish, animals, birds*) illegal erbeuten, wildern; (*Culin: egg*) pochieren; (*: fish*) dünsten ▸ VI (*steal*) wildern
poached [pəutʃt] ADJ: **~ eggs** verlorene Eier
poacher [ˈpəutʃəʳ] N Wilderer *m*
PO Box N ABBR (= *Post Office Box*) Postf.
pocket [ˈpɔkɪt] N Tasche *f*; (*fig: small area*) vereinzelter Bereich *m* ▸ VT (*put in one's pocket, steal*) einstecken; **to be out of ~** (BRIT) Verlust machen; **~ of resistance** Widerstandsnest *nt*
pocketbook [ˈpɔkɪtbuk] N (*notebook*) Notizbuch *nt*; (*US: wallet*) Brieftasche *f*; (*: handbag*) Handtasche *f*
pocket calculator N Taschenrechner *m*
pocketknife [ˈpɔkɪtnaɪf] N Taschenmesser *nt*
pocket money N Taschengeld *nt*
pocket-sized [ˈpɔkɪtsaɪzd] ADJ im Taschenformat
pockmarked [ˈpɔkmɑ:kt] ADJ (*face*) pockennarbig
pod [pɔd] N Hülse *f*
podcast [ˈpɔdkɑ:st] N Podcast *m*
podgy [ˈpɔdʒɪ] (*inf*) ADJ rundlich, pummelig
podiatrist [pɔˈdi:ətrɪst] (*US*) N Fußspezialist(in) *m(f)*
podiatry [pɔˈdi:ətrɪ] (*US*) N Fußpflege *f*
podium [ˈpəudɪəm] N Podium *nt*
POE N ABBR (= *port of embarkation*) Ausgangshafen *m*; (= *port of entry*) Eingangshafen *m*
poem [ˈpəuɪm] N Gedicht *nt*
poet [ˈpəuɪt] N Dichter(in) *m(f)*
poetic [pəuˈɛtɪk] ADJ poetisch, dichterisch; (*fig*) malerisch
poetic justice N ausgleichende Gerechtigkeit *f*
poetic licence N dichterische Freiheit *f*
poet laureate [-lɔriət] N Hofdichter *m*

> **Poet laureate** ist in Großbritannien ein Dichter, der ein Gehalt als Hofdichter bezieht und kraft seines Amtes ein lebenslanges Mitglied des britischen Königshofes ist. Der Poet Laureate schrieb traditionellerweise ausführliche Gedichte zu Staatsanlässen; ein Brauch, der heute kaum noch befolgt wird. Der erste Poet Laureate 1616 war Ben Jonson.

poetry [ˈpəuɪtrɪ] N (*poems*) Gedichte *pl*; (*writing*) Poesie *f*
poignant [ˈpɔɪnjənt] ADJ ergreifend; (*situation*) herzzerreißend
point [pɔɪnt] N Punkt *m*; (*of needle, knife etc*) Spitze *f*; (*purpose*) Sinn *m*, Zweck *m*; (*significant part*) Entscheidende(s) *nt*; (*moment*) Zeitpunkt *m*; (*Elec: also*: **power point**) Steckdose *f*; (*also*: **decimal point**) ≈ Komma *nt* ▸ VT (*show, mark*) deuten auf *+acc* ▸ VI (*with finger, stick etc*) zeigen, deuten; **points** NPL (*Aut*) (Unterbrecher)kontakte *pl*; (*Rail*) Weichen *pl*; **two ~ five** (= *2.5*) zwei Komma fünf; **good/bad points** (*of person*) gute/schlechte Seiten *or* Eigenschaften; **the train stops at Carlisle and all points south** der Zug hält in Carlisle und allen Orten weiter südlich; **to be on the ~ of doing sth** im Begriff sein, etw zu tun; **to make a ~ of doing sth** besonders darauf achten, etw zu tun; (*make a habit of*) Wert darauf legen, etw zu tun; **to get/miss the ~** verstehen/nicht verstehen, worum es geht; **to come** *or* **get to the ~** zur Sache kommen; **to make one's ~** seinen Standpunkt klarmachen; **that's the whole ~!** darum geht es ja gerade!; **what's the ~?** was solls?; **to be beside the ~** unwichtig *or* irrelevant sein; **there's no ~ talking to you** es ist sinnlos, mit dir zu reden; **you've got a ~ there!** da könnten Sie recht haben!; **in ~ of fact** in Wirklichkeit; **~ of sale** (*Comm*) Verkaufsstelle *f*; **to ~ sth at sb** (*gun etc*) etw auf jdn richten; (*finger*) mit etw auf jdn *acc* zeigen; **to ~ at** zeigen auf *+acc*; **to ~ to** zeigen auf *+acc*; (*fig*) hinweisen auf *+acc*
▸ **point out** VT hinweisen auf *+acc*
▸ **point to** VT FUS hindeuten auf *+acc*
point-blank [ˈpɔɪntˈblæŋk] ADV (*say, ask*) direkt; (*refuse*) glatt; (*also*: **at point-blank range**) aus unmittelbarer Entfernung
point duty (BRIT) N: **to be on ~** Verkehrsdienst haben
pointed [ˈpɔɪntɪd] ADJ spitz; (*fig: remark*) spitz, scharf
pointedly [ˈpɔɪntɪdlɪ] ADV (*ask, reply etc*) spitz, scharf
pointer [ˈpɔɪntəʳ] N (*on chart, machine*) Zeiger *m*; (*fig: piece of information or advice*) Hinweis *m*; (*stick*) Zeigestock *m*; (*dog*) Pointer *m*
pointing [ˈpɔɪntɪŋ] N (*Constr*) Ausfugung *f*
pointless [ˈpɔɪntlɪs] ADJ sinnlos, zwecklos
point of view N Ansicht *f*, Standpunkt *m*; **from a practical ~** von einem praktischen Standpunkt aus
poise [pɔɪz] N (*composure*) Selbstsicherheit *f*; (*balance*) Haltung *f* ▸ VT: **to be poised for sth** (*fig*) bereit zu etw sein
poison [ˈpɔɪzn] N Gift *nt* ▸ VT vergiften
poisoning [ˈpɔɪznɪŋ] N Vergiftung *f*
poisonous [ˈpɔɪznəs] ADJ (*animal, plant*) Gift-; (*fumes, chemicals etc*) giftig; (*fig: rumours etc*) zersetzend
poison-pen letter [pɔɪznˈpɛn] N anonymer Brief *m* (*mit Indiskretionen*)
poke [pəuk] VT (*with finger, stick etc*) stoßen; (*fire*) schüren ▸ N (*jab*) Stoß *m*, Schubs *m* (*inf*); **to ~ sth in(to)** (*put*) etw stecken in *+acc*; **to ~ one's head out of the window** seinen Kopf aus dem Fenster strecken; **to ~ fun at sb** sich über jdn lustig machen
▸ **poke about** VI (*search*) herumstochern
▸ **poke out** VI (*stick out*) vorstehen
poker [ˈpəukəʳ] N (*metal bar*) Schürhaken *m*; (*Cards*) Poker *nt*

poker-faced ['pəukə'feɪst] ADJ mit unbewegter Miene, mit Pokergesicht
poky ['pəukɪ] *(pej)* ADJ *(room, house)* winzig
Poland ['pəulənd] N Polen *nt*
polar ['pəulər] ADJ *(icecap)* polar; *(region)* Polar-
polar bear N Eisbär *m*
polarize ['pəuləraɪz] VT polarisieren
Pole [pəul] N Pole *m*, Polin *f*
pole [pəul] N *(post, stick)* Stange *f*; *(flag pole, telegraph pole etc)* Mast *m*; *(Geog, Elec)* Pol *m*; **to be poles apart** *(fig)* durch Welten (voneinander) getrennt sein
poleaxe, *(US)* **poleax** ['pəulæks] VT *(fig)* umhauen
pole bean *(US)* N *(runner bean)* Stangenbohne *f*
polecat ['pəulkæt] N Iltis *m*
Pol. Econ. ['pɔlɪkɔn] N ABBR (= *political economy*) Volkswirtschaft *f*
polemic [pɔ'lɛmɪk] N Polemik *f*
Pole Star N Polarstern *m*
pole vault ['pəulvɔːlt] N Stabhochsprung *m*
police [pə'liːs] NPL *(organization)* Polizei *f*; *(members)* Polizisten *pl*, Polizeikräfte *pl* ▶ VT *(street, area, town)* kontrollieren; **a large number of ~ were hurt** viele Polizeikräfte wurden verletzt
police car N Polizeiauto *nt*
police constable (BRIT) N Polizist(in) *m(f)*, Polizeibeamte(r) *m*, Polizeibeamtin *f*
police department *(US)* N Polizei *f*
police force N Polizei *f*
policeman [pə'liːsmən] N *(irreg)* Polizist *m*
police officer N = **police constable**
police record N: **to have a ~** vorbestraft sein
police state N *(Pol)* Polizeistaat *m*
police station N Polizeiwache *f*
policewoman [pə'liːswumən] N *(irreg)* Polizistin *f*
policy ['pɔlɪsɪ] N *(Pol, Econ)* Politik *f*; *(also:* **insurance policy***)* (Versicherungs)police *f*; *(of newspaper)* Grundsatz *m*; **to take out a ~** *(Insurance)* eine Versicherung abschließen
policyholder ['pɔlɪsɪ'həuldər] N *(Insurance)* Versicherungsnehmer(in) *m(f)*
policy making N Strategieplanung *f*
polio ['pəulɪəu] N Kinderlähmung *f*, Polio *f*
Polish ['pəulɪʃ] ADJ polnisch ▶ N *(Ling)* Polnisch *nt*
polish ['pɔlɪʃ] N *(for shoes)* Creme *f*; *(for furniture)* Politur *f*; *(for floors)* Bohnerwachs *nt*; *(shine: on shoes, floor etc)* Glanz *m*; *(fig: refinement)* Schliff *m* ▶ VT *(shoes)* putzen; *(floor, furniture etc)* polieren ▶ **polish off** VT *(work)* erledigen; *(food)* verputzen
polished ['pɔlɪʃt] ADJ *(fig: person)* mit Schliff; *(: style)* geschliffen
polite [pə'laɪt] ADJ höflich; *(company, society)* fein; **it's not ~ to do that** es gehört sich nicht, das zu tun
politely [pə'laɪtlɪ] ADV höflich
politeness [pə'laɪtnɪs] N Höflichkeit *f*
politic ['pɔlɪtɪk] ADJ klug, vernünftig
political [pə'lɪtɪkl] ADJ politisch
political asylum N politisches Asyl *nt*
politically [pə'lɪtɪklɪ] ADV politisch; **~ correct** politisch korrekt
politician [pɔlɪ'tɪʃən] N Politiker(in) *m(f)*
politics ['pɔlɪtɪks] N Politik *f* ▶ NPL *(beliefs, opinions)* politische Ansichten *pl*
polka ['pɔlkə] N Polka *f*
poll [pəul] N *(also:* **opinion poll***)* (Meinungs)umfrage *f*; *(election)* Wahl *f* ▶ VT *(in opinion poll)* befragen; *(number of votes)* erhalten; **to go to the polls** *(voters)* zur Wahl gehen; *(government)* sich den Wählern stellen
pollen ['pɔlən] N Pollen *m*, Blütenstaub *m*
pollen count N Pollenkonzentration *f*
pollinate ['pɔlɪneɪt] VT bestäuben
polling booth ['pəulɪŋ-] (BRIT) N Wahlkabine *f*
polling day (BRIT) N Wahltag *m*
polling station (BRIT) N Wahllokal *nt*
pollster ['pəulstər] N Meinungsforscher(in) *m(f)*
poll tax N Kopfsteuer *f*
pollutant [pə'luːtənt] N Schadstoff *m*
pollute [pə'luːt] VT verschmutzen
pollution [pə'luːʃən] N *(process)* Verschmutzung *f*; *(substances)* Schmutz *m*
polo ['pəuləu] N Polo *nt*
polo neck N *(jumper)* Rollkragenpullover *m*
polo-necked ['pəuləunɛkt] ADJ *(jumper, sweater)* Rollkragen-
poltergeist ['pɔːltəgaɪst] N Poltergeist *m*
poly ['pɔlɪ] (BRIT) N = **polytechnic**
poly bag *(inf)* N Plastiktüte *f*
polyester [pɔlɪ'ɛstər] N Polyester *m*
polygamy [pə'lɪgəmɪ] N Polygamie *f*
polygraph ['pɔlɪgrɑːf] *(US)* N *(lie detector)* Lügendetektor *m*
Polynesia [pɔlɪ'niːzɪə] N Polynesien *nt*
Polynesian [pɔlɪ'niːzɪən] ADJ polynesisch ▶ N Polynesier(in) *m(f)*
polyp ['pɔlɪp] N Polyp *m*
polystyrene [pɔlɪ'staɪriːn] N ≈ Styropor® *nt*
polytechnic [pɔlɪ'tɛknɪk] N technische Hochschule *f*
polythene ['pɔlɪθiːn] N Polyäthylen *nt*
polythene bag N Plastiktüte *f*
polyurethane [pɔlɪ'juərɪθeɪn] N Polyurethan *nt*
pomegranate ['pɔmɪgrænɪt] N Granatapfel *m*
pommel ['pɔml] N *(on saddle)* Sattelknopf *m* ▶ VT *(US)* = **pummel**
po-mo ['pəuməu] ABBR (= *postmodern*) postmodern; (= *postmodernism*) Postmoderne *f*
pomp [pɔmp] N Pomp *m*, Prunk *m*
pompom ['pɔmpɔm] N Troddel *f*
pompous ['pɔmpəs] *(pej)* ADJ *(person)* aufgeblasen; *(piece of writing)* geschwollen
pond [pɔnd] N Teich *m*
ponder ['pɔndər] VT nachdenken über *+acc* ▶ VI nachdenken
ponderous ['pɔndərəs] ADJ *(style, language)* schwerfällig
pong [pɔŋ] (BRIT *inf*) N Gestank *m* ▶ VI stinken
pontiff ['pɔntɪf] N Papst *m*
pontificate [pɔn'tɪfɪkeɪt] VI dozieren
pontoon [pɔn'tuːn] N *(floating platform)* Ponton *m*; *(Cards)* Siebzehnundvier *nt*

pony ['pəunɪ] N Pony *nt*
ponytail ['pəunɪteɪl] N Pferdeschwanz *m*; **to have one's hair in a ~** einen Pferdeschwanz tragen
pony trekking (BRIT) N Ponytrecken *nt*
poodle ['pu:dl] N Pudel *m*
pooh-pooh ['pu:'pu:] VT verächtlich abtun
pool [pu:l] N (*pond*) Teich *m*; (*also*: **swimming pool**) Schwimmbad *nt*; (*of blood*) Lache *f*; (*Sport*) Poolbillard *nt*; (*of cash, workers*) Bestand *m*; (*Cards: kitty*) Kasse *f*; (*Comm: consortium*) Interessengemeinschaft *f* ▶ VT (*money*) zusammenlegen; (*knowledge, resources*) vereinigen; **pools** NPL (*also*: **football pools**) ≈ Fußballtoto *nt*; **a ~ of sunlight/shade** eine sonnige/schattige Stelle; **car ~** Fahrgemeinschaft *f*; **typing ~, secretary ~** (*US*) Schreibzentrale *f*; **to do the (football) pools** ≈ im Fußballtoto spielen
poor [puəʳ] ADJ arm; (*bad*) schlecht ▶ NPL: **the ~** die Armen *pl*; **~ in** (*resources etc*) arm an +*dat*; **~ Bob** der arme Bob
poorly ['puəlɪ] ADJ (*ill*) elend, krank ▶ ADV (*badly: designed, paid, furnished*) schlecht
pop [pɔp] N (*Mus*) Pop *m*; (*fizzy drink*) Limonade *f*; (*US inf: father*) Papa *m*; (*sound*) Knall *m* ▶ VI (*balloon*) platzen; (*cork*) knallen ▶ VT: **to ~ sth into/onto sth** etw schnell in etw *acc* stecken/auf etw *acc* legen; **his eyes popped out of his head** (*inf*) ihm fielen fast die Augen aus dem Kopf; **she popped her head out of the window** sie streckte den Kopf aus dem Fenster
▶ **pop in** VI vorbeikommen
▶ **pop out** VI kurz weggehen
▶ **pop up** VI auftauchen; (*Comput: window*) aufpoppen
popcorn ['pɔpkɔ:n] N Popcorn *nt*
pope [pəup] N Papst *m*
poplar ['pɔpləʳ] N Pappel *f*
poplin ['pɔplɪn] N Popeline *f*
popper ['pɔpəʳ] (BRIT *inf*) N (*for fastening*) Druckknopf *m*
poppy ['pɔpɪ] N Mohn *m*
poppycock ['pɔpɪkɔk] (*inf*) N Humbug *m*, dummes Zeug *nt*
Popsicle® ['pɔpsɪkl] (*US*) N Eis *nt* am Stiel
pop star N Popstar *m*
populace ['pɔpjuləs] N: **the ~** die Bevölkerung, das Volk
popular ['pɔpjuləʳ] ADJ (*well-liked, fashionable*) beliebt, populär; (*general, non-specialist*) allgemein; (*idea*) weitverbreitet; (*Pol: movement*) Volks-; (*: cause*) des Volkes; **to be ~ with** beliebt sein bei; **the ~ press** die Boulevardpresse
popularity [pɔpju'lærɪtɪ] N Beliebtheit *f*, Popularität *f*
popularize ['pɔpjuləraɪz] VT (*sport, music, fashion*) populär machen; (*science, ideas*) popularisieren
popularly ['pɔpjuləlɪ] ADV (*commonly*) allgemein
population [pɔpju'leɪʃən] N Bevölkerung *f*; (*of a species*) Zahl *f*, Population *f*; **a prison ~ of 44,000** (eine Zahl von) 44.000 Gefängnisinsassen; **the civilian ~** die Zivilbevölkerung
population explosion N Bevölkerungsexplosion *f*
populous ['pɔpjuləs] ADJ dicht besiedelt
pop-up ['pɔpʌp] ADJ (*esp Comput*) Pop-up-, Popup- ▶ N (*also shop, restaurant*) Pop-up *nt*
pop-up window N (*Comput*) Popup-Fenster *nt*
porcelain ['pɔ:slɪn] N Porzellan *nt*
porch [pɔ:tʃ] N (*entrance*) Vorbau *m*; (*US*) Veranda *f*
porcupine ['pɔ:kjupaɪn] N Stachelschwein *nt*
pore [pɔ:ʳ] N Pore *f* ▶ VI: **to ~ over** (*book etc*) gründlich studieren
pork [pɔ:k] N Schweinefleisch *nt*
pork chop N Schweinekotelett *nt*
porn [pɔ:n] (*inf*) N Porno *m*; **~ channel/magazine/shop** Pornokanal *m*/-magazin *nt*/-laden *m*
pornographic [pɔ:nə'græfɪk] ADJ pornografisch
pornography [pɔ:'nɔgrəfɪ] N Pornografie *f*
porous ['pɔ:rəs] ADJ porös
porpoise ['pɔ:pəs] N Tümmler *m*
porridge ['pɔrɪdʒ] N Haferbrei *m*, Porridge *nt*
port [pɔ:t] N (*harbour*) Hafen *m*; (*Naut: left side*) Backbord *nt*; (*wine*) Portwein *m*; (*Comput*) Port *m* ▶ ADJ (*Naut*) Backbord-; **to ~** (*Naut*) an Backbord; **~ of call** (*Naut*) Anlaufhafen *nt*
portable ['pɔ:təbl] ADJ (*television, typewriter etc*) tragbar, portabel
portal ['pɔ:tl] N Portal *nt*
portaloo ['pɔ:təlu:] N Mobiltoilette *f*
portcullis [pɔ:t'kʌlɪs] N Fallgitter *nt*
portend [pɔ:'tɛnd] VT hindeuten auf +*acc*
portent ['pɔ:tɛnt] N Vorzeichen *nt*
porter ['pɔ:təʳ] N (*for luggage*) Gepäckträger *m*; (*doorkeeper*) Pförtner *m*; (*US Rail*) Schlafwagenschaffner(in) *m(f)*
portfolio [pɔ:t'fəulɪəu] N (*case*) Aktenmappe *f*; (*Pol*) Geschäftsbereich *m*; (*Fin*) Portefeuille *nt*; (*of artist*) Kollektion *f*
porthole ['pɔ:thəul] N Bullauge *nt*
portico ['pɔ:tɪkəu] N Säulenhalle *f*
portion ['pɔ:ʃən] N (*part*) Teil *m*; (*helping of food*) Portion *f*
portly ['pɔ:tlɪ] ADJ beleibt, korpulent
portrait ['pɔ:treɪt] N Porträt *nt*
portray [pɔ:'treɪ] VT darstellen
portrayal [pɔ:'treɪəl] N Darstellung *f*
Portugal ['pɔ:tjugl] N Portugal *nt*
Portuguese [pɔ:tju'gi:z] ADJ portugiesisch ▶ N INV (*person*) Portugiese *m*, Portugiesin *f*; (*Ling*) Portugiesisch *nt*
Portuguese man-of-war [-mænəv'wɔ:ʳ] N (*Zool*) Röhrenqualle *f*, Portugiesische Galeere *f*
pose [pəuz] N Pose *f* ▶ VT (*question, problem*) aufwerfen; (*danger*) mit sich bringen ▶ VI: **to ~ as** (*pretend*) sich ausgeben als; **to strike a ~** sich in Positur werfen; **to ~ for** (*painting etc*) Modell sitzen für, posieren für
poser ['pəuzəʳ] N (*problem, puzzle*) harte Nuss *f* (*inf*); (*person*) = **poseur**
poseur [pəu'zə:ʳ] (*pej*) N Angeber(in) *m(f)*
posh [pɔʃ] (*inf*) ADJ vornehm; **to talk ~** vornehm daherreden

position [pəˈzɪʃən] N (*place: of thing, person*) Position *f*, Lage *f*; (*of person's body*) Stellung *f*; (*job*) Stelle *f*; (*in race etc*) Platz *m*; (*attitude*) Haltung *f*, Standpunkt *m*; (*situation*) Lage ▸ VT (*person, thing*) stellen; **to be in a ~ to do sth** in der Lage sein, etw zu tun

positive [ˈpɒzɪtɪv] ADJ positiv; (*certain*) sicher; (*decisive: action, policy*) konstruktiv

positively [ˈpɒzɪtɪvlɪ] ADV (*emphatic: rude, stupid etc*) eindeutig; (*encouragingly, Elec*) positiv; **the body has been ~ identified** die Leiche ist eindeutig identifiziert worden

posse [ˈpɒsɪ] (*US*) N (Polizei)truppe *f*

possess [pəˈzɛs] VT besitzen; (*subj: feeling, belief*) Besitz ergreifen von; **like a man possessed** wie besessen; **whatever possessed you to do it?** was ist in dich gefahren, das zu tun?

possession [pəˈzɛʃən] N Besitz *m*; **possessions** NPL (*belongings*) Besitz *m*; **to take ~ of** Besitz ergreifen von

possessive [pəˈzɛsɪv] ADJ (*nature etc*) besitzergreifend; (*Ling: pronoun*) Possessiv-; (*: adjective*) besitzanzeigend; **to be ~ about sb/sth** Besitzansprüche an jdn/etw *acc* stellen

possessiveness [pəˈzɛsɪvnɪs] N besitzergreifende Art *f*

possessor [pəˈzɛsəʳ] N Besitzer(in) *m(f)*

possibility [pɒsɪˈbɪlɪtɪ] N Möglichkeit *f*

possible [ˈpɒsɪbl] ADJ möglich; **it's ~** (*may be true*) es ist möglich, es kann sein; **it's ~ to do it** es ist machbar *or* zu machen; **as far as ~** so weit wie möglich; **if ~** falls *or* wenn möglich; **as soon as ~** so bald wie möglich

possibly [ˈpɒsɪblɪ] ADV (*perhaps*) möglicherweise, vielleicht; (*conceivably*) überhaupt; **if you ~ can** falls überhaupt möglich; **what could they ~ want?** was um alles in der Welt wollen sie?; **I cannot ~ come** ich kann auf keinen Fall kommen

post [pəust] N (*Brit*) Post *f*; (*pole, goal post*) Pfosten *m*; (*job*) Stelle *f*; (*Mil*) Posten *m*; (*on internet forum*) Posting *nt*; (*also:* **trading post**) Handelsniederlassung *f* ▸ VT (*Brit: letter*) aufgeben; (*on website*) posten; (*Mil*) aufstellen; **by ~** (*Brit*) per Post; **by return of ~** (*Brit*) postwendend, umgehend; (*to internet*) posten; **to keep sb posted** (*informed*) jdn auf dem Laufenden halten; **to ~ sb to** (*town, country*) jdn versetzen nach; (*embassy, office*) jdn versetzen zu; (*Mil*) jdn abkommandieren nach
▸ **post up** VT anschlagen

post... [pəust] PREF Post-, post-; **post...-1990** nach 1990

postage [ˈpəustɪdʒ] N Porto *nt*

postage stamp N Briefmarke *f*

postal [ˈpəustl] ADJ (*charges, service*) Post-

postal order (*Brit*) N Postanweisung *f*

postbag [ˈpəustbæg] (*Brit*) N Postsack *m*; (*letters*) Posteingang *m*

postbox [ˈpəustbɒks] N Briefkasten *m*

postcard [ˈpəustkɑːd] N Postkarte *f*

postcode [ˈpəustkəud] (*Brit*) N Postleitzahl *f*

postdate [ˈpəustˈdeɪt] VT (*cheque*) vordatieren

poster [ˈpəustəʳ] N Poster *nt*, Plakat *nt*

poste restante [pəustˈrɛstɑ̃ːnt] (*Brit*) N Stelle *f* für postlagernde Sendungen ▸ ADV postlagernd

posterior [pɒsˈtɪərɪəʳ] (*hum*) N Allerwerteste(r) *m*

posterity [pɒsˈtɛrɪtɪ] N die Nachwelt

poster paint N Plakatfarbe *f*

post exchange (*US*) N (*Mil*) *Laden für US-Militärpersonal*

post-free [pəustˈfriː] (*Brit*) ADJ, ADV portofrei

postgraduate [ˈpəustˈgrædjuət] N Graduierte(r) *f(m)* (*im Weiterstudium*)

posthumous [ˈpɒstjuməs] ADJ posthum

posthumously [ˈpɒstjuməslɪ] ADV posthum

posting [ˈpəustɪŋ] N (*job*) Stelle *f*

postman [ˈpəustmən] N (*irreg*) Briefträger *m*, Postbote *m*

postmark [ˈpəustmɑːk] N Poststempel *m*

postmaster [ˈpəustmɑːstəʳ] N Postmeister *m*

Postmaster General N ≈ Postminister(in) *m(f)*

postmistress [ˈpəustmɪstrɪs] N Postmeisterin *f*

postmortem [pəustˈmɔːtəm] N (*Med*) Obduktion *f*; (*fig*) nachträgliche Erörterung *f*

postnatal [ˈpəustˈneɪtl] ADJ nach der Geburt, postnatal

post office N (*building*) Post *f*, Postamt *nt*; **the Post Office** (*organization*) die Post

Post Office Box N Postfach *nt*

post-paid [ˈpəustˈpeɪd] ADJ, ADV = **post-free**

postpone [pəusˈpəun] VT verschieben

postponement [pəusˈpəunmənt] N Aufschub *m*

postscript [ˈpəustskrɪpt] N (*to letter*) Nachschrift *f*, PS *nt*

postulate [ˈpɒstjuleɪt] VT ausgehen von, postulieren

posture [ˈpɒstʃəʳ] N (*also fig*) Haltung *f* ▸ VI (*pej*) posieren

postwar [pəustˈwɔːʳ] ADJ Nachkriegs-

posy [ˈpəuzɪ] N Blumensträußchen *nt*

pot [pɒt] N Topf *m*; (*teapot, coffee pot, potful*) Kanne *f*; (*inf: marijuana*) Pot *nt* ▸ VT (*plant*) eintopfen; **to go to ~** (*inf*) auf den Hund kommen; **pots of** (*Brit inf*) jede Menge

potash [ˈpɒtæʃ] N Pottasche *f*

potassium [pəˈtæsɪəm] N Kalium *nt*

potato [pəˈteɪtəu] (*pl* **potatoes**) N Kartoffel *f*

potato chips (*US*) NPL = **potato crisps**

potato crisps NPL Kartoffelchips *pl*

potato flour N Kartoffelmehl *nt*

potato peeler N Kartoffelschäler *m*

potbellied [ˈpɒtbɛlɪd] ADJ (*from overeating*) dickbäuchig; (*from malnutrition*) blähbäuchig

potency [ˈpəutnsɪ] N (*sexual*) Potenz *f*; (*of drink, drug*) Stärke *f*

potent [ˈpəutnt] ADJ (*powerful*) stark; (*sexually*) potent

potentate [ˈpəutnteɪt] N Machthaber *m*, Potentat *m*

potential [pəˈtɛnʃl] ADJ potenziell ▸ N Potenzial *nt*; **to have ~** (*person, machine*) Fähigkeiten *or* Potenzial haben; (*idea, plan*) ausbaufähig sein

potentially [pəˈtɛnʃəlɪ] ADV potenziell; **it's ~ dangerous** es könnte gefährlich sein

pothole ['pɔthəul] N (*in road*) Schlagloch *nt*; (*cave*) Höhle *f*
potholing ['pɔthəulɪŋ] (BRIT) N: **to go ~** Höhlenforschung betreiben
potion ['pəuʃən] N Elixier *nt*
potluck [pɔt'lʌk] N: **to take ~** sich überraschen lassen
potpourri [pəu'puri:] N (*dried petals*) Duftsträußchen *nt*; (*fig*) Sammelsurium *nt*
pot roast N Schmorbraten *m*
pot shot N: **to take a ~ at** aufs Geratewohl schießen auf *+acc*
potted ['pɔtɪd] ADJ (*food*) eingemacht; (*plant*) Topf-; (*abbreviated: history etc*) Kurz-, kurz gefasst
potter ['pɔtə^r] N Töpfer(in) *m(f)* ▶ VI: **to ~ around, ~ about** (BRIT) herumhantieren; **to ~ around the house** im Haus herumwerkeln
potter's wheel N Töpferscheibe *f*
pottery ['pɔtərɪ] N (*pots, dishes etc*) Keramik *f*, Töpferwaren *pl*; (*work, hobby*) Töpfern *nt*; (*factory, workshop*) Töpferei *f*; **a piece of ~** ein Töpferstück *nt*
potty ['pɔtɪ] ADJ (*inf: mad*) verrückt ▶ N (*for child*) Töpfchen *nt*
potty-training ['pɔtɪtreɪnɪŋ] N Entwöhnung *f* vom Windeltragen
pouch [pautʃ] N Beutel *m* (*also Zool*)
pouf, pouffe [pu:f] N (*stool*) gepolsterter Hocker *m*
poultice ['pəultɪs] N Umschlag *m*
poultry ['pəultrɪ] N Geflügel *nt*
poultry farm N Geflügelfarm *f*
poultry farmer N Geflügelzüchter(in) *m(f)*
pounce [pauns] VI: **to ~ on** (*also fig*) sich stürzen auf *+acc*
pound [paund] N (*unit of money*) Pfund *nt*; (*unit of weight*) (britisches) Pfund (*= 453,6g*); (*for dogs*) Zwinger *m*; (*for cars*) Abholstelle *f* (*für abgeschleppte Fahrzeuge*) ▶ VT (*beat: table, wall etc*) herumhämmern auf *+dat*; (*crush: grain, spice etc*) zerstoßen; (*bombard*) beschießen ▶ VI (*heart*) klopfen, pochen; (*head*) dröhnen; **half a ~ of butter** ein halbes Pfund Butter; **a five-~ note** ein Fünfpfundschein *m*
pounding ['paundɪŋ] N: **to take a ~** (*fig*) schwer angegriffen werden; (*team*) eine Schlappe einstecken müssen
pound sterling N Pfund *nt* Sterling
pour [pɔ:^r] VT (*tea, wine etc*) gießen; (*cereal etc*) schütten ▶ VI strömen; **to ~ sb a glass of wine/a cup of tea** jdm ein Glas Wein/eine Tasse Tee einschenken; **to ~ with rain** in Strömen gießen
▶ **pour away** VT wegschütten
▶ **pour in** VI (*people*) hereinströmen; (*letters etc*) massenweise eintreffen
▶ **pour out** VI (*people*) herausströmen ▶ VT (*tea, wine etc*) eingießen; (*fig: thoughts, feelings, etc*) freien Lauf lassen *+dat*
pouring ['pɔ:rɪŋ] ADJ: **~ rain** strömender Regen *m*
pout [paut] VI einen Schmollmund ziehen
poverty ['pɔvətɪ] N Armut *f*
poverty line N Armutsgrenze *f*
poverty risk N Armutsrisiko *f*
poverty-stricken ['pɔvətɪstrɪkn] ADJ verarmt, Not leidend
poverty trap (BRIT) N *gleichbleibend schlechte wirtschaftliche Situation aufgrund des Wegfalls von Sozialleistungen bei verbessertem Einkommen*, Armutsfalle *f*
POW N ABBR = **prisoner of war**
powder ['paudə^r] N Pulver *nt* ▶ VT: **to ~ one's face** sich *dat* das Gesicht pudern; **to ~ one's nose** (*euph*) kurz mal verschwinden
powder compact N Puderdose *f*
powdered milk ['paudəd-] N Milchpulver *nt*
powder keg N (*also fig*) Pulverfass *nt*
powder puff N Puderquaste *f*
powder room (*euph*) N Damentoilette *f*
power ['pauə^r] N (*control, legal right*) Macht *f*; (*ability*) Fähigkeit *f*; (*of muscles, ideas, words*) Kraft *f*; (*of explosion, engine*) Gewalt *f*; (*electricity*) Strom *m*; **2 to the ~ (of) 3** (*Math*) 2 hoch 3; **to do everything in one's ~ to help** alles in seiner Macht Stehende tun, um zu helfen; **a world ~** eine Weltmacht; **the powers that be** (*authority*) diejenigen, die das Sagen haben; **~ of attorney** Vollmacht *f*; **to be in ~** (*Pol etc*) an der Macht sein
powerboat ['pauəbəut] N schnelles Motorboot *nt*, Rennboot *nt*
power cut N Stromausfall *m*
powered ['pauəd] ADJ: **~ by** angetrieben von; **nuclear-~ submarine** atomgetriebenes U-Boot
power failure N Stromausfall *m*
powerful ['pauəful] ADJ (*person, organization*) mächtig; (*body, voice, blow etc*) kräftig; (*engine*) stark; (*unpleasant: smell*) streng; (*emotion*) überwältigend; (*argument, evidence*) massiv
powerhouse ['pauəhaus] N: **he is a ~ of ideas** er hat ständig neue Ideen
powerless ['pauəlɪs] ADJ machtlos; **to be ~ to do sth** nicht die Macht haben, etw zu tun
power line N Stromkabel *nt*
power point (BRIT) N Steckdose *f*
power station N Kraftwerk *nt*
power steering N (*Aut*) Servolenkung *f*
powwow ['pauwau] N Besprechung *f*
pp ABBR (*= per procurationem*) ppa.
pp. ABBR (*= pages*) S.
PPE (BRIT) N ABBR (*Univ: = philosophy, politics, and economics*) *Studiengang bestehend aus Philosophie, Politologie und Volkswirtschaft*
PPS N ABBR (*= post postscriptum*) PPS; (BRIT: *= parliamentary private secretary*) *Privatsekretär eines Ministers*
PQ (CANADA) ABBR = **Province of Quebec**
PR N ABBR = **public relations**; (*Pol*) = **proportional representation** ▶ ABBR (*US Post*) = **Puerto Rico**
Pr. ABBR = **prince**
practicability [præktɪkə'bɪlɪtɪ] N Durchführbarkeit *f*
practicable ['præktɪkəbl] ADJ (*scheme, idea*) durchführbar
practical ['præktɪkl] ADJ praktisch; (*person: good with hands*) praktisch veranlagt; (*ideas, methods*) praktikabel

P

practicality [præktɪ'kælɪtɪ] N *(of person)* praktische Veranlagung *f*; **practicalities** NPL *(of situation etc)* praktische Einzelheiten *pl*
practical joke N Streich *m*
practically ['præktɪklɪ] ADV praktisch
practice ['præktɪs] N *(also Med, Law)* Praxis *f*; *(custom)* Brauch *m*; *(exercise)* Übung *f* ▸ VT, VI *(US)* = **practise**; **in ~** in der Praxis; **out of ~** aus der Übung; **2 hours' piano ~** 2 Stunden Klavierübungen; **it's common** *or* **standard ~** es ist allgemein üblich; **to put sth into ~** etw in die Praxis umsetzen; **target ~** Zielschießen *nt*
practice match N Übungsspiel *nt*
practise, *(US)* **practice** ['præktɪs] VT *(train at)* üben; *(carry out: custom)* pflegen; *(: activity etc)* ausüben; *(profession)* praktizieren ▸ VI *(train)* üben; *(lawyer, doctor etc)* praktizieren
practised ['præktɪst] (BRIT) ADJ *(person, liar)* geübt; *(performance)* gekonnt; **with a ~ eye** mit geschultem Auge
practising ['præktɪsɪŋ] ADJ praktizierend
practitioner [præk'tɪʃənə^r] N: **medical ~** praktischer Arzt *m*, praktische Ärztin *f*; **legal ~** Rechtsanwalt *m*, Rechtsanwältin *f*
pragmatic [præg'mætɪk] ADJ pragmatisch
pragmatism ['prægmətɪzəm] N Pragmatismus *m*
Prague [prɑːg] N Prag *nt*
prairie ['prɛərɪ] N (Gras)steppe *f*; **the prairies** *(US)* die Prärien
praise [preɪz] N Lob *nt* ▸ VT loben; *(Rel)* loben, preisen
praiseworthy ['preɪzwəːðɪ] ADJ lobenswert
pram [præm] (BRIT) N Kinderwagen *m*
prance [prɑːns] VI *(horse)* tänzeln; **to ~ about/in/out** *(person)* herum-/hinein-/hinausstolzieren
prank [præŋk] N Streich *m*
prat [præt] (BRIT *inf*) N *(idiot)* Trottel *m*
prattle ['prætl] VI: **to ~ on (about)** pausenlos plappern (über *+acc*)
prawn [prɔːn] N *(Culin, Zool)* Garnele *f*, Krabbe *f*; **~ cocktail** Krabbencocktail *m*
pray [preɪ] VI beten; **to ~ for sb/sth** *(Rel, fig)* für jdn/um etw beten
prayer [prɛə^r] N Gebet *nt*; **to say one's prayers** beten
prayer book N Gebetbuch *nt*
pre... [priː] PREF Prä-, prä-; **pre...-1970** vor 1970
preach [priːtʃ] VI *(Rel)* predigen; *(pej: moralize)* Predigten halten ▸ VT *(sermon)* direkt halten; *(fig: advocate)* predigen, verkünden; **to ~ at sb** *(fig)* jdm Moralpredigten halten; **to ~ to the converted** *(fig)* offene Türen einrennen
preacher ['priːtʃə^r] N Prediger(in) *m(f)*
preamble [prɪ'æmbl] N Vorbemerkung *f*
prearranged [priːə'reɪndʒd] ADJ (vorher) vereinbart
precarious [prɪ'kɛərɪəs] ADJ prekär
precaution [prɪ'kɔːʃən] N Vorsichtsmaßnahme *f*; **to take precautions** Vorsichtsmaßnahmen treffen
precautionary [prɪ'kɔːʃənrɪ] ADJ *(measure)* vorbeugend, Vorsichts-
precede [prɪ'siːd] VT *(event)* vorausgehen *+dat*; *(person)* vorangehen *+dat*; *(words, sentences)* vorangestellt sein *+dat*
precedence ['prɛsɪdəns] N *(priority)* Vorrang *m*; **to take ~ over** Vorrang haben vor *+dat*
precedent ['prɛsɪdənt] N *(Law)* Präzedenzfall *m*; **without ~** noch nie da gewesen; **to establish** *or* **set a ~** einen Präzedenzfall schaffen
preceding [prɪ'siːdɪŋ] ADJ vorhergehend
precept ['priːsɛpt] N Grundsatz *m*, Regel *f*
precinct ['priːsɪŋkt] N *(US: part of city)* Bezirk *m*; **precincts** NPL *(of cathedral, palace)* Gelände *nt*; **shopping ~** (BRIT) Einkaufsviertel *nt*; *(under cover)* Einkaufscenter *nt*
precious ['prɛʃəs] ADJ wertvoll, kostbar; *(pej: person, writing)* geziert; *(ironic: damned)* heiß geliebt, wundervoll ▸ ADV *(inf)*: **~ little/few** herzlich wenig/wenige
precious stone N Edelstein *m*
precipice ['prɛsɪpɪs] N *(also fig)* Abgrund *m*
precipitate VT [prɪ'sɪpɪteɪt] *(event)* heraufbeschwören ▸ ADJ [prɪ'sɪpɪtɪt] *(hasty)* überstürzt, übereilt
precipitation [prɪsɪpɪ'teɪʃən] N *(rain)* Niederschlag *m*
precipitous [prɪ'sɪpɪtəs] ADJ *(steep)* steil; *(hasty)* übereilt
précis ['preɪsiː] N INV Zusammenfassung *f*
precise [prɪ'saɪs] ADJ genau, präzise; **at 4 o'clock to be ~** um 4 Uhr, um genau zu sein
precisely [prɪ'saɪslɪ] ADV genau, exakt; *(emphatic)* ganz genau; **~!** genau!
precision [prɪ'sɪʒən] N Genauigkeit *f*, Präzision *f*
preclude [prɪ'kluːd] VT ausschließen; **to ~ sb from doing sth** jdn daran hindern, etw zu tun
precocious [prɪ'kəuʃəs] ADJ *(child, behaviour)* frühreif
preconceived [priːkən'siːvd] ADJ *(idea)* vorgefasst
preconception ['priːkən'sɛpʃən] N vorgefasste Meinung *f*
precondition ['priːkən'dɪʃən] N Vorbedingung *f*
precursor [priː'kəːsə^r] N Vorläufer *m*
predate ['priː'deɪt] VT *(precede)* vorausgehen *+dat*
predator ['prɛdətə^r] N *(Zool)* Raubtier *nt*; *(fig)* Eindringling *m*
predatory ['prɛdətərɪ] ADJ *(animal)* Raub-; *(person, organization)* auf Beute lauernd
predecessor ['priːdɪsɛsə^r] N Vorgänger(in) *m(f)*
predestination [priːdɛstɪ'neɪʃən] N Vorherbestimmung *f*
predetermine [priːdɪ'təːmɪn] VT vorherbestimmen
predicament [prɪ'dɪkəmənt] N Notlage *f*, Dilemma *nt*; **to be in a ~** in einer Notlage *or* einem Dilemma stecken
predicate ['prɛdɪkɪt] N *(Ling)* Prädikat *nt*
predict [prɪ'dɪkt] VT vorhersagen
predictable [prɪ'dɪktəbl] ADJ vorhersagbar

predictably [prɪ'dɪktəblɪ] ADV (*behave, react*) wie vorherzusehen; **~ she didn't come** wie vorherzusehen war, kam sie nicht
prediction [prɪ'dɪkʃən] N Voraussage *f*
predispose ['pri:dɪs'pəuz] VT: **to ~ sb to sth** jdn zu etw veranlassen; **to be predisposed to do sth** geneigt sein, etw zu tun
predominance [prɪ'dɔmɪnəns] N Vorherrschaft *f*
predominant [prɪ'dɔmɪnənt] ADJ vorherrschend; **to become ~** vorherrschend werden
predominantly [prɪ'dɔmɪnəntlɪ] ADV überwiegend
predominate [prɪ'dɔmɪneɪt] VI (*in number, size*) vorherrschen; (*in strength, influence*) überwiegen
pre-eminent [pri:'ɛmɪnənt] ADJ herausragend
pre-empt [pri:'ɛmt] VT zuvorkommen *+dat*
pre-emptive [pri:'ɛmtɪv] ADJ: **~ strike** Präventivschlag *m*
preen [pri:n] VT: **to ~ itself** (*bird*) sich putzen; **to ~ o.s.** sich herausputzen
prefab ['pri:fæb] N Fertighaus *nt*
prefabricated [pri:'fæbrɪkeɪtɪd] ADJ vorgefertigt
preface ['prɛfəs] N Vorwort *nt* ▸ VT: **to ~ with/by** (*speech, action*) einleiten mit/durch
prefect ['pri:fɛkt] (BRIT) N (*in school*) Aufsichtsschüler(in) *m(f)*
prefer [prɪ'fə:ʳ] VT (*like better*) vorziehen; **to ~ charges** (*Law*) Anklage erheben; **to ~ doing** *or* **to do sth** (es) vorziehen, etw zu tun; **I ~ tea to coffee** ich mag lieber Tee als Kaffee
preferable ['prɛfrəbl] ADJ: **to be ~ (to)** vorzuziehen sein (*+dat*)
preferably ['prɛfrəblɪ] ADV vorzugsweise, am besten
preference ['prɛfrəns] N: **to have a ~ for** (*liking*) eine Vorliebe haben für; **I drink beer in ~ to wine** ich trinke lieber Bier als Wein; **to give ~ to** (*priority*) vorziehen, Vorrang einräumen *+dat*
preference shares (BRIT) NPL (*Comm*) Vorzugsaktien *pl*
preferential [prɛfə'rɛnʃəl] ADJ: **~ treatment** bevorzugte Behandlung *f*; **to give sb ~ treatment** jdn bevorzugt behandeln
preferred stock [prɪ'fəd-] (*US*) NPL = **preference shares**
prefix ['pri:fɪks] N (*Ling*) Präfix *nt*
pregnancy ['prɛgnənsɪ] N (*of woman*) Schwangerschaft *f*; (*of female animal*) Trächtigkeit *f*
pregnancy test N Schwangerschaftstest *m*
pregnant ['prɛgnənt] ADJ (*woman*) schwanger; (*female animal*) trächtig; (*fig: pause, remark*) bedeutungsschwer; **3 months ~** im vierten Monat (schwanger)
prehistoric ['pri:hɪs'tɔrɪk] ADJ prähistorisch, vorgeschichtlich
prehistory [pri:'hɪstərɪ] N Vorgeschichte *f*
prejudge [pri:'dʒʌdʒ] VT vorschnell beurteilen
prejudice ['prɛdʒudɪs] N (*bias against*) Vorurteil *nt*; (*bias in favour*) Voreingenommenheit *f* ▸ VT beeinträchtigen; **without ~ to** (*form*) unbeschadet *+gen*, ohne Beeinträchtigung *+gen*; **to ~ sb in favour of/against sth** jdn für/gegen etw einnehmen
prejudiced ['prɛdʒudɪst] ADJ (*person, view*) voreingenommen
prelate ['prɛlət] N Prälat *m*
preliminaries [prɪ'lɪmɪnərɪz] NPL Vorbereitungen *pl*; (*of competition*) Vorrunde *f*
preliminary [prɪ'lɪmɪnərɪ] ADJ (*step, arrangements*) vorbereitend; (*remarks*) einleitend
pre-loaded [pri'ləudɪd] ADJ (*Comput: program etc*) vorinstalliert
prelude ['prɛlju:d] N (*Mus*) Präludium *nt*; (*: as introduction*) Vorspiel *nt*; **a ~ to** (*fig*) ein Vorspiel *or* ein Auftakt zu
premarital ['pri:'mærɪtl] ADJ vorehelich
premature ['prɛmətʃuəʳ] ADJ (*earlier than expected*) vorzeitig; (*too early*) verfrüht; **you are being a little ~** Sie sind etwas voreilig; **~ baby** Frühgeburt *f*
premeditated [pri:'mɛdɪteɪtɪd] ADJ vorsätzlich
premeditation [pri:mɛdɪ'teɪʃən] N Vorsatz *m*
premenstrual tension [pri:'mɛnstruəl-] N prämenstruelles Syndrom *nt*
premier ['prɛmɪəʳ] ADJ (*best*) beste(r, s), bedeutendste(r, s) ▸ N (*Pol*) Premierminister(in) *m(f)*
premiere ['prɛmɪɛəʳ] N Premiere *f*
premise ['prɛmɪs] N (*of argument*) Voraussetzung *f*; **premises** NPL (*of business etc*) Räumlichkeiten *pl*; **on the premises** im Hause
premium ['pri:mɪəm] N (*Comm, Insurance*) Prämie *f*; **to be at a ~** (*expensive*) zum Höchstpreis gehandelt werden; (*hard to get*) Mangelware sein
premium bond (BRIT) N Prämienanleihe *f*

> **Premium bonds**, eigentlich **premium savings bonds**, sind Lotterieaktien, die seit 1956 vom britischen Finanzministerium ausgegeben werden und keine Zinsen bringen, sondern stattdessen an einer monatlichen Auslosung teilnehmen. Die Gewinnnummern für die verschiedenen Geldpreise werden in Blackpool von einem Computer namens „ERNIE" (Electronic Random Number Indicator Equipment) ermittelt.

premium gasoline (*US*) N Super(benzin) *nt*
premonition [prɛmə'nɪʃən] N Vorahnung *f*
preoccupation [pri:ɔkju'peɪʃən] N: **~ with** (vorrangige) Beschäftigung mit
preoccupied [pri:'ɔkjupaɪd] ADJ (*thoughtful*) gedankenverloren; (*with work, family*) beschäftigt
pre-owned [pri:'əund] ADJ gebraucht
prep [prɛp] (*Scol*) ADJ (= *preparatory*) *see* **preparatory school** ▸ N (= *preparation*) Hausaufgaben *pl*
prepaid [pri:'peɪd] ADJ (*paid in advance*) im Voraus bezahlt; (*envelope*) frankiert
preparation [prɛpə'reɪʃən] N Vorbereitung *f*; (*food, medicine, cosmetic*) Zubereitung *f*;

P

preparations NPL Vorbereitungen *pl*; **in ~ for sth** als Vorbereitung für etw
preparatory [prɪ'pærətərɪ] ADJ vorbereitend; **~ to sth/to doing sth** als Vorbereitung für etw/, um etw zu tun

Preparatory school ist in Großbritannien eine meist private Schule für Kinder im Alter von 7 bis 13 Jahren, die auf eine weiterführende Privatschule vorbereiten soll.

prepare [prɪ'pɛəʳ] VT vorbereiten; (*food, meal*) zubereiten ▸ VI: **to ~ for** sich vorbereiten auf *+acc*
prepared [prɪ'pɛəd] ADJ: **to be ~ to do sth** (*willing*) bereit sein, etw zu tun; **to be ~ for sth** (*ready*) auf etw *acc* vorbereitet sein
preponderance [prɪ'pɔndərns] N Übergewicht *nt*
preposition [prɛpə'zɪʃən] N Präposition *f*
prepossessing [pri:pə'zɛsɪŋ] ADJ von angenehmer Erscheinung
preposterous [prɪ'pɔstərəs] ADJ grotesk, widersinnig
prep school N = **preparatory school**
prerecorded ['pri:rɪ'kɔ:dɪd] ADJ (*broadcast*) aufgezeichnet; (*cassette, video*) bespielt
prerequisite [pri:'rɛkwɪzɪt] N Vorbedingung *f*, Grundvoraussetzung *f*
prerogative [prɪ'rɔgətɪv] N Vorrecht *nt*, Privileg *nt*
Presbyterian [prɛzbɪ'tɪərɪən] ADJ presbyterianisch ▸ N Presbyterianer(in) *m(f)*
presbytery ['prɛzbɪtərɪ] N Pfarrhaus *nt*
preschool ['pri:'sku:l] ADJ (*age, child, education*) Vorschul-
prescribe [prɪ'skraɪb] VT (*Med*) verschreiben; (*demand*) anordnen, vorschreiben
prescribed ADJ (*duties, period*) vorgeschrieben
prescription [prɪ'skrɪpʃən] N (*Med: slip of paper*) Rezept *nt*; (*: medicine*) Medikament *nt*; **to make up a ~, to fill a ~** (US) ein Medikament zubereiten; **"only available on ~"** „rezeptpflichtig"
prescription charges (BRIT) NPL Rezeptgebühr *f*
prescriptive [prɪ'skrɪptɪv] ADJ normativ
presence ['prɛzns] N Gegenwart *f*, Anwesenheit *f*; (*fig: personality*) Ausstrahlung *f*; (*spirit, invisible influence*) Erscheinung *f*; **in sb's ~** in jds *dat* Gegenwart *or* Beisein; **~ of mind** Geistesgegenwart *f*
present ADJ ['prɛznt] (*current*) gegenwärtig, derzeitig; (*in attendance*) anwesend ▸ N ['prɛznt] (*gift*) Geschenk *nt*; (*Ling: also:* **present tense**) Präsens *nt*, Gegenwart *f* ▸ VT [prɪ'zɛnt] (*give: prize etc*) überreichen; (*plan, report*) vorlegen; (*cause, provide, portray*) darstellen; (*information, view*) darlegen; (*Radio, TV*) leiten; **to be ~ at** anwesend *or* zugegen sein bei; **those ~** die Anwesenden; **to give sb a ~** jdm ein Geschenk geben; **the ~** (*actuality*) die Gegenwart; **at ~** gegenwärtig, im Augenblick; **to ~ sth to sb, ~ sb with sth** jdm etw übergeben *or* überreichen; **to ~ sb (to)** (*formally: introduce*) jdn vorstellen *+dat*; **to ~ itself** (*opportunity*) sich bieten
presentable [prɪ'zɛntəbl] ADJ (*person*) präsentabel, ansehnlich
presentation [prɛzn'teɪʃən] N (*of prize*) Überreichung *f*; (*of plan, report etc*) Vorlage *f*; (*appearance*) Erscheinungsbild *nt*; (*talk*) Vortrag *m*; **on ~ of** (*voucher etc*) gegen Vorlage *+gen*
present-day ['prɛzntdeɪ] ADJ heutig, gegenwärtig
presenter [prɪ'zɛntəʳ] N (*on radio, TV*) Moderator(in) *m(f)*
presently ['prɛzntlɪ] ADV (*soon after*) gleich darauf; (*soon*) bald, in Kürze; (*currently*) derzeit, gegenwärtig
present participle N Partizip *nt* Präsens
preservation [prɛzə'veɪʃən] N (*of peace, standards etc*) Erhaltung *f*; (*of furniture, building*) Konservierung *f*
preservative [prɪ'zə:vətɪv] N Konservierungsmittel *nt*
preserve [prɪ'zə:v] VT erhalten; (*peace*) wahren; (*wood*) schützen; (*food*) konservieren ▸ N (*often pl: jam, chutney etc*) Eingemachte(s) *nt*; (*for game, fish*) Revier *nt*; **a male ~** (*fig*) eine männliche Domäne; **a working class ~** (*fig*) eine Domäne der Arbeiterklasse
preshrunk ['pri:'ʃrʌŋk] ADJ (*jeans etc*) vorgewaschen
preside [prɪ'zaɪd] VI: **to ~ over** (*meeting etc*) vorsitzen *+dat*, den Vorsitz haben bei
presidency ['prɛzɪdənsɪ] N (*Pol*) Präsidentschaft *f*; (*US: of company*) Vorsitz *m*
president ['prɛzɪdənt] N (*Pol*) Präsident(in) *m(f)*; (*of organization*) Vorsitzende(r) *f(m)*
presidential [prɛzɪ'dɛnʃl] ADJ (*election, campaign etc*) Präsidentschafts-; (*adviser, representative etc*) des Präsidenten
press [prɛs] N (*also:* **printing press**) Presse *f*; (*of switch, bell*) Druck *m*; (*for wine*) Kelter *f* ▸ VT drücken, pressen; (*button, sb's hand etc*) drücken; (*iron: clothes*) bügeln; (*put pressure on: person*) drängen; (*pursue: idea, claim*) vertreten ▸ VI (*squeeze*) drücken, pressen; **the P~** (*newspapers, journalists*) die Presse; **to go to ~** (*newspaper*) in Druck gehen; **to be in ~** (*at the printer's*) im Druck sein; **to be in the ~** (*in the newspapers*) in der Zeitung stehen; **at the ~ of a button** auf Knopfdruck; **to ~ sth (up)on sb** (*force*) jdm etw aufdrängen; **we are pressed for time/money** wir sind in Geldnot/Zeitnot; **to ~ sb for an answer** auf jds *acc* Antwort drängen; **to ~ sb to do** *or* **into doing sth** jdn drängen, etw zu tun; **to ~ charges (against sb)** (*Law*) Klage (gegen jdn) erheben; **to ~ for** (*changes etc*) drängen auf *+acc*
▸ **press ahead** VI weitermachen; **to ~ ahead with sth** etw durchziehen
▸ **press on** VI weitermachen
press agency N Presseagentur *f*
press clipping N Zeitungsausschnitt *m*
press conference N Pressekonferenz *f*

press cutting N = **press clipping**
press-gang ['prɛsgæŋ] VT: **to ~ sb into doing sth** jdn bedrängen, etw zu tun
pressing ['prɛsɪŋ] ADJ (*urgent*) dringend
press officer N Pressesprecher(in) *m(f)*
press release N Pressemitteilung *f*
press stud N (BRIT) Druckknopf *m*
press-up ['prɛsʌp] (BRIT) N Liegestütz *m*
pressure ['prɛʃəʳ] N (*also fig*) Druck *m* ▶ VT: **to ~ sb to do sth** jdn dazu drängen, etw zu tun; **to put ~ on sb (to do sth)** Druck auf jdn ausüben(, etw zu tun); **high/low ~** (*Tech, Met*) Hoch-/Tiefdruck *m*
pressure cooker N Schnellkochtopf *m*
pressure gauge N Druckmesser *m*, Manometer *nt*
pressure group N Interessenverband *m*, Pressuregroup *f*
pressurize ['prɛʃəraɪz] VT: **to ~ sb (to do sth** *or* **into doing sth)** jdn unter Druck setzen(, etw zu tun)
pressurized ['prɛʃəraɪzd] ADJ (*cabin, container etc*) Druck-
Prestel® ['prɛstɛl] N ≈ Bildschirmtext *m*, Btx *nt*
prestige [prɛs'tiːʒ] N Prestige *nt*
prestigious [prɛs'tɪdʒəs] ADJ (*institution, appointment*) mit hohem Prestigewert
presumably [prɪ'zjuːməblɪ] ADV vermutlich; **~ he did it** vermutlich *or* wahrscheinlich hat er es getan
presume [prɪ'zjuːm] VT: **to ~ (that)** (*assume*) annehmen(, dass); **to ~ to do sth** (*dare*) sich anmaßen, etw zu tun; **I ~ so** das nehme ich an
presumption [prɪ'zʌmpʃən] N (*supposition*) Annahme *f*; (*audacity*) Anmaßung *f*
presumptuous [prɪ'zʌmpʃəs] ADJ anmaßend
presuppose [priːsə'pəuz] VT voraussetzen
presupposition [priːsʌpə'zɪʃən] N Voraussetzung *f*
pretax [priː'tæks] ADJ (*profit*) vor (Abzug der) Steuern
pretence, (*US*) **pretense** [prɪ'tɛns] N (*false appearance*) Vortäuschung *f*; **under false pretences** unter Vorspiegelung falscher Tatsachen; **she is devoid of all ~** sie ist völlig natürlich; **to make a ~ of doing sth** vortäuschen, etw zu tun
pretend [prɪ'tɛnd] VT (*feign*) vorgeben ▶ VI (*feign*) sich verstellen, so tun, als ob; **I don't ~ to understand it** (*claim*) ich erhebe nicht den Anspruch, es zu verstehen
pretense [prɪ'tɛns] (US) N = **pretence**
pretentious [prɪ'tɛnʃəs] ADJ anmaßend
preterite ['prɛtərɪt] N Imperfekt *nt*, Präteritum *nt*
pretext ['priːtɛkst] N Vorwand *m*; **on** *or* **under the ~ of doing sth** unter dem Vorwand, etw zu tun
pretty ['prɪtɪ] ADJ hübsch, nett ▶ ADV: **~ clever** ganz schön schlau; **~ good** ganz gut
prevail [prɪ'veɪl] VI (*be current*) vorherrschen; (*triumph*) siegen; **to ~ (up)on sb to do sth** (*persuade*) jdn dazu bewegen *or* überreden, etw zu tun
prevailing [prɪ'veɪlɪŋ] ADJ (*wind, fashion etc*) vorherrschend
prevalent ['prɛvələnt] ADJ (*belief, custom*) vorherrschend
prevaricate [prɪ'værɪkeɪt] VI (*by saying sth*) Ausflüchte machen; (*by doing sth*) Ausweichmanöver machen
prevarication [prɪværɪ'keɪʃən] N Ausflucht *f*; Ausweichmanöver *nt*
prevent [prɪ'vɛnt] VT verhindern; **to ~ sb from doing sth** jdn daran hindern, etw zu tun; **to ~ sth from happening** verhindern, dass etw geschieht
preventable [prɪ'vɛntəbl] ADJ verhütbar, vermeidbar
preventative [prɪ'vɛntətɪv] ADJ = **preventive**
prevention [prɪ'vɛnʃən] N Verhütung *f*
preventive [prɪ'vɛntɪv] ADJ (*measures, medicine*) vorbeugend
preview ['priːvjuː] N (*of film*) Vorpremiere *f*; (*of exhibition*) Vernissage *f*
previous ['priːvɪəs] ADJ (*earlier*) früher; (*preceding*) vorhergehend; **~ to** vor *+dat*
previously ['priːvɪəslɪ] ADV (*before*) zuvor; (*formerly*) früher
prewar [priː'wɔːʳ] ADJ (*period*) Vorkriegs-
prey [preɪ] N Beute *f*; **to fall ~ to** (*fig*) zum Opfer fallen *+dat*
▶ **prey on** VT FUS (*animal*) Jagd machen auf *+acc*; **it was preying on his mind** es ließ ihn nicht los
price [praɪs] N (*also fig*) Preis *m* ▶ VT (*goods*) auszeichnen; **what is the ~ of ...?** was kostet ...?; **to go up** *or* **rise in ~** im Preis steigen, teurer werden; **to put a ~ on sth** (*also fig*) einen Preis für etw festsetzen; **what ~ his promises now?** wie steht es jetzt mit seinen Versprechungen?; **he regained his freedom, but at a ~** er hat seine Freiheit wieder, aber zu welchem Preis!; **to be priced at £30** £30 kosten; **to ~ o.s. out of the market** durch zu hohe Preise konkurrenzunfähig werden
price control N Preiskontrolle *f*
price-cutting ['praɪskʌtɪŋ] N Preissenkungen *pl*
priceless ['praɪslɪs] ADJ (*diamond, painting*) von unschätzbarem Wert; (*inf: amusing*) unbezahlbar, köstlich
price list N Preisliste *f*
price range N Preisklasse *f*; **it's within my ~** ich kann es mir leisten
price tag N Preisschild *nt*; (*fig*) Preis *m*
price war N Preiskrieg *m*
pricey ['praɪsɪ] (*inf*) ADJ kostspielig
prick [prɪk] N (*sting*) Stich *m*; (*inf!: penis*) Schwanz *m*; (*: idiot*) Arsch *m* (*inf!*) ▶ VT stechen; (*sausage, balloon*) einstechen; **to ~ up one's ears** die Ohren spitzen
prickle ['prɪkl] N (*of plant*) Dorn *m*, Stachel *m*; (*sensation*) Prickeln *nt*
prickly ['prɪklɪ] ADJ (*plant*) stachelig; (*fabric*) kratzig
prickly heat N Hitzebläschen *pl*

prickly pear N Feigenkaktus *m*
pride [praɪd] N Stolz *m*; (*pej: arrogance*) Hochmut *m* ▸ VT: **to ~ o.s. on** sich rühmen *+gen*; **to take (a) ~ in** stolz sein auf *+acc*; **to take a ~ in doing sth** etw mit Stolz tun; **to have** *or* **take ~ of place** (BRIT) die Krönung sein
priest [pri:st] N Priester *m*
priestess ['pri:stɪs] N Priesterin *f*
priesthood ['pri:sthud] N Priestertum *nt*
prig [prɪg] N: **he's a ~** er hält sich für ein Tugendlamm
prim [prɪm] (*pej*) ADJ (*person*) etepetete
primacy ['praɪməsɪ] N (*supremacy*) Vorrang *m*; (*position*) Vorrangstellung *f*
prima-facie ['praɪmə'feɪʃɪ] ADJ: **to have a ~ case** (*Law*) eine gute Beweisgrundlage haben
primal ['praɪməl] ADJ ursprünglich; **~ scream** Urschrei *m*
primarily ['praɪmərɪlɪ] ADV in erster Linie, hauptsächlich
primary ['praɪmərɪ] ADJ (*principal*) Haupt-, hauptsächlich; (*education, teacher*) Grundschul- ▸ N (*US: election*) Vorwahl *f*

> Als **primary** wird im amerikanischen Präsidentschaftswahlkampf eine Vorwahl bezeichnet, die mitentscheidet, welche Präsidentschaftskandidaten die beiden großen Parteien aufstellen. Vorwahlen werden nach komplizierten Regeln von Februar (New Hampshire) bis Juni in etwa 35 Staaten abgehalten. Der von den Kandidaten in den primaries erzielte Stimmenanteil bestimmt, wie viele Abgeordnete bei der endgültigen Auswahl der demokratischen bzw. republikanischen Kandidaten auf den nationalen Parteitagen im Juli/August für sie stimmen.

primary colour N Primärfarbe *f*
primary school (BRIT) N Grundschule *f*

> **Primary school** ist in Großbritannien eine Grundschule für Kinder im Alter von 5 bis 11 Jahren. Oft wird sie aufgeteilt in „infant school" (5 bis 7 Jahre) und „junior school" (7 bis 11 Jahre). Siehe auch **secondary school**.

primate ['praɪmɪt] N (*Zool*) Primat *m*; (*Rel*) Primas *m*
prime [praɪm] ADJ (*most important*) oberste(r, s); (*best quality*) erstklassig ▸ N (*of person's life*) die besten Jahre *pl* ▸ VT (*wood*) grundieren; (*fig: person*) informieren; (*gun*) schussbereit machen; (*pump*) auffüllen; **~ example** erstklassiges Beispiel; **in the ~ of life** im besten Alter
Prime Minister N Premierminister(in) *m(f)*
primer ['praɪməʳ] N (*paint*) Grundierung *f*; (*book*) Einführung *f*
prime time N (*Radio, TV*) Hauptsendezeit *f*
primeval [praɪ'mi:vl] ADJ (*beast*) urzeitlich; (*fig: feelings*) instinktiv; **~ forest** Urwald *m*
primitive ['prɪmɪtɪv] ADJ (*tribe, tool, conditions etc*) primitiv; (*life form, machine etc*) frühzeitlich; (*man*) der Urzeit
primrose ['prɪmrəuz] N Primel *f*, gelbe Schlüsselblume *f*
primula ['prɪmjulə] N Primel *f*
Primus® ['praɪməs], (BRIT) **Primus stove** N Primuskocher *m*
prince [prɪns] N Prinz *m*
Prince Charming (*hum*) N Märchenprinz *m*
princess [prɪn'sɛs] N Prinzessin *f*
principal ['prɪnsɪpl] ADJ (*most important*) Haupt-, wichtigste(r, s) ▸ N (*of school, college*) Rektor(in) *m(f)*; (*Theat*) Hauptdarsteller(in) *m(f)*; (*Fin*) Kapitalsumme *f*
principality [prɪnsɪ'pælɪtɪ] N Fürstentum *nt*
principally ['prɪnsɪplɪ] ADV vornehmlich
principle ['prɪnsɪpl] N Prinzip *nt*; **in ~** im Prinzip, prinzipiell; **on ~** aus Prinzip
print [prɪnt] N (*Art*) Druck *m*; (*Phot*) Abzug *m*; (*fabric*) bedruckter Stoff *m* ▸ VT (*produce*) drucken; (*publish*) veröffentlichen; (*cloth, pattern*) bedrucken; (*write in capitals*) in Druckschrift schreiben; **prints** NPL (*fingerprints etc*) Abdrücke *pl*; **out of ~** vergriffen; **in ~** erhältlich; **the fine** *or* **small ~** das Kleingedruckte
▸ **print out** VT (*Comput*) ausdrucken
printed circuit ['prɪntɪd-] N gedruckte Schaltung *f*
printed circuit board N Leiterplatte *f*
printed matter N Drucksache *f*
printer ['prɪntəʳ] N (*person*) Drucker(in) *m(f)*; (*firm*) Druckerei *f*; (*machine*) Drucker *m*
printhead ['prɪnthɛd] N Druckkopf *m*
printing ['prɪntɪŋ] N (*activity*) Drucken *nt*
printing press N Druckerpresse *f*
print-out ['prɪntaut] (*Comput*) N Ausdruck *m*
print run N Auflage *f*
printwheel ['prɪntwi:l] N (*Comput*) Typenrad *nt*
prior ['praɪəʳ] ADJ (*previous: knowledge, warning*) vorherig; (*: engagement*) früher; (*more important: claim, duty*) vorrangig ▸ N (*Rel*) Prior *m*; **without ~ notice** ohne vorherige Ankündigung; **to have a ~ claim on sth** ein Vorrecht auf etw *acc* haben; **~ to** vor *+dat*
priority [praɪ'ɔrɪtɪ] N vorrangige Angelegenheit *f*; **priorities** NPL Prioritäten *pl*; **to take** *or* **have ~ (over sth)** Vorrang (vor etw *dat*) haben; **to give ~ to sb/sth** jdm/etw Vorrang einräumen
priory ['praɪərɪ] N Kloster *nt*
prise [praɪz] (BRIT) VT: **to ~ open** aufbrechen
prism ['prɪzəm] N Prisma *nt*
prison ['prɪzn] N Gefängnis *nt* ▸ CPD (*officer, food, cell etc*) Gefängnis-
prison camp N Gefangenenlager *nt*
prisoner ['prɪznəʳ] N Gefangene(r) *f(m)*; **the ~ at the bar** (*Law*) der/die Angeklagte; **to take sb ~** jdn gefangen nehmen
prisoner of war N Kriegsgefangene(r) *f(m)*
prissy ['prɪsɪ] (*pej*) ADJ zimperlich
pristine ['prɪsti:n] ADJ makellos; **in ~ condition** in makellosem Zustand
privacy ['prɪvəsɪ] N Privatsphäre *f*
private ['praɪvɪt] ADJ privat; (*life*) Privat-; (*thoughts, plans etc*) persönlich; (*place*) abgelegen;

(*secretive: person*) verschlossen ▸ N (*Mil*) Gefreite(r) *m*; **"~"** (*on envelope*) „vertraulich"; (*on door*) „privat"; **in ~** privat; **in (his) ~ life** in seinem Privatleben; **to be in ~ practice** (*Med*) Privatpatienten haben; **~ hearing** (*Law*) nicht öffentliche Verhandlung *f*
private enterprise N Privatunternehmen *nt*
private eye N Privatdetektiv *m*
private limited company (BRIT) N (*Comm*) ≈ Aktiengesellschaft *f*
privately [ˈpraɪvɪtlɪ] ADV privat; (*secretly*) insgeheim; **a ~ owned company** eine Firma im Privatbesitz
private parts NPL (*Anat*) Geschlechtsteile *pl*
private property N Privatbesitz *m*
private school N (*fee-paying*) Privatschule *f*
privation [praɪˈveɪʃən] N Not *f*
privatize [ˈpraɪvɪtaɪz] VT privatisieren
privet [ˈprɪvɪt] N Liguster *m*
privilege [ˈprɪvɪlɪdʒ] N (*advantage*) Privileg *nt*; (*honour*) Ehre *f*
privileged [ˈprɪvɪlɪdʒd] ADJ privilegiert; **to be ~ to do sth** das Privileg *or* die Ehre haben, etw zu tun
privy [ˈprɪvɪ] ADJ: **to be ~ to** eingeweiht sein in *+acc*

> **Privy Council** ist eine Gruppe von königlichen Beratern, die ihren Ursprung im normannischen England hat. Heute hat dieser Rat eine rein formale Funktion. Kabinettsmitglieder und andere bedeutende politische, kirchliche oder juristische Persönlichkeiten sind automatisch Mitglieder.

Privy Councillor (BRIT) N Geheimer Rat *m*
prize [praɪz] N Preis *m* ▸ ADJ (*prize-winning*) preisgekrönt; (*classic: example*) erstklassig ▸ VT schätzen; **~ idiot** (*inf*) Vollidiot *m*
prizefighter [ˈpraɪzfaɪtə^r] N Preisboxer *m*
prizegiving [ˈpraɪzgɪvɪŋ] N Preisverleihung *f*
prize money N Geldpreis *m*
prizewinner [ˈpraɪzwɪnə^r] N Preisträger(in) *m(f)*
prizewinning [ˈpraɪzwɪnɪŋ] ADJ preisgekrönt
PRO N ABBR = **public relations officer**
pro [prəu] N (*Sport*) Profi *m* ▸ PREP (*in favour of*) pro *+acc*, für *+acc*; **the pros and cons** das Für und Wider
pro- [prəu] PREF (*in favour of*) Pro-, pro-; **~disarmament campaign** Kampagne *f* für Abrüstung
proactive [prəuˈæktɪv] ADJ proaktiv
probability [prɔbəˈbɪlɪtɪ] N Wahrscheinlichkeit *f*; **in all ~** aller Wahrscheinlichkeit nach
probable [ˈprɔbəbl] ADJ wahrscheinlich; **it seems ~ that …** es ist wahrscheinlich, dass …
probably [ˈprɔbəblɪ] ADV wahrscheinlich
probate [ˈprəubɪt] N gerichtliche Testamentsbestätigung *f*
probation [prəˈbeɪʃən] N: **on ~** (*lawbreaker*) auf Bewährung; (*employee*) auf Probe
probationary [prəˈbeɪʃənrɪ] ADJ (*period*) Probe-
probationer [prəˈbeɪʃənə^r] N (*nurse: female*) Lernschwester *f*; (*: male*) Lernpfleger *m*
probation officer N Bewährungshelfer(in) *m(f)*
probe [prəub] N (*Med, Space*) Sonde *f*; (*enquiry*) Untersuchung *f* ▸ VT (*investigate*) untersuchen; (*poke*) bohren in *+dat*
probity [ˈprəubɪtɪ] N Rechtschaffenheit *f*
problem [ˈprɔbləm] N Problem *nt*; **to have problems with the car** Probleme *or* Schwierigkeiten mit dem Auto haben; **what's the ~?** wo fehlts?; **I had no ~ finding her** ich habe sie ohne Schwierigkeiten gefunden; **no ~!** kein Problem!
problematic [prɔbləˈmætɪk], **problematical** [prɔbləˈmætɪkl] ADJ problematisch
problem-solving [ˈprɔbləmsɔlvɪŋ] ADJ (*skills, ability*) zur Problemlösung ▸ N Problemlösung *f*
procedural [prəˈsiːdjurəl] ADJ (*agreement, problem*) verfahrensmäßig
procedure [prəˈsiːdʒə^r] N Verfahren *nt*
proceed [prəˈsiːd] VI (*carry on*) fortfahren; (*person: go*) sich bewegen; **to ~ to do sth** etw tun; **to ~ with** fortfahren mit; **I am not sure how to ~** ich bin nicht sicher über die weitere Vorgehensweise; **to ~ against sb** (*Law*) gegen jdn gerichtlich vorgehen
proceedings [prəˈsiːdɪŋz] NPL (*organized events*) Vorgänge *pl*; (*Law*) Verfahren *nt*; (*records*) Protokoll *nt*
proceeds [ˈprəusiːdz] NPL Erlös *m*
process [ˈprəusɛs] N (*series of actions*) Verfahren *nt*; (*Biol, Chem*) Prozess *m* ▸ VT (*raw materials, food, Comput: data*) verarbeiten; (*application*) bearbeiten; (*Phot*) entwickeln; **in the ~** dabei; **to be in the ~ of doing sth** (gerade) dabei sein, etw zu tun
processed cheese [ˈprəusɛst-], (*US*) **process cheese** N Schmelzkäse *m*
processing [ˈprəusɛsɪŋ] N (*Phot*) Entwickeln *nt*
procession [prəˈsɛʃən] N Umzug *m*, Prozession *f*; **wedding/funeral ~** Hochzeits-/Trauerzug *m*
processor [ˈprəusɛsə^r] N (*Comput*) Prozessor *m*; (*Culin*) Küchenmaschine *f*
proclaim [prəˈkleɪm] VT verkünden, proklamieren
proclamation [prɔkləˈmeɪʃən] N Proklamation *f*
proclivity [prəˈklɪvɪtɪ] (*form*) N Vorliebe *f*
procrastinate [prəuˈkræstɪneɪt] VI zögern, zaudern
procrastination [prəukræstɪˈneɪʃən] N Zögern *nt*, Zaudern *nt*
procreation [prəukrɪˈeɪʃən] N Fortpflanzung *f*
procurator fiscal [ˈprɔkjureɪtə-] (SCOT) N (*pl* **procurators fiscal**) ≈ Staatsanwalt *m*, ≈ Staatsanwältin *f*
procure [prəˈkjuə^r] VT (*obtain*) beschaffen
procurement [prəˈkjuəmənt] N (*Comm*) Beschaffung *f*
prod [prɔd] VT (*push: with finger, stick etc*) stoßen, stupsen (*inf*); (*fig: urge*) anspornen ▸ N (*with finger, stick etc*) Stoß *m*, Stups *m* (*inf*); (*fig: reminder*) mahnender Hinweis *m*
prodigal [ˈprɔdɪgl] ADJ: **~ son** verlorener Sohn *m*
prodigious [prəˈdɪdʒəs] ADJ (*cost, memory*) ungeheuer

prodigy ['prɔdɪdʒɪ] N (*person*) Naturtalent *nt*; **child ~** Wunderkind *nt*
produce N ['prɔdju:s] (*Agr*) (Boden)produkte *pl* ▸ VT [prə'dju:s] (*result etc*) hervorbringen; (*goods, commodity*) produzieren, herstellen; (*Biol, Chem*) erzeugen; (*fig: evidence etc*) liefern; (*: passport etc*) vorlegen; (*play, film, programme*) produzieren
producer [prə'dju:sə^r] N (*person*) Produzent(in) *m(f)*; (*country, company*) Produzent *m*, Hersteller *m*
product ['prɔdʌkt] N Produkt *nt*
production [prə'dʌkʃən] N Produktion *f*; (*Theat*) Inszenierung *f*; **to go into ~** (*goods*) in Produktion gehen; **on ~ of** gegen Vorlage *+gen*
production agreement (*US*) N Produktivitätsabkommen *nt*
production line N Fließband *nt*, Fertigungsstraße *f*
production manager N Produktionsleiter(in) *m(f)*
productive [prə'dʌktɪv] ADJ produktiv
productivity [prɔdʌk'tɪvɪtɪ] N Produktivität *f*
productivity agreement (BRIT) N Produktivitätsabkommen *nt*
productivity bonus N Leistungszulage *f*
Prof. N ABBR (= *professor*) Prof.
profane [prə'feɪn] ADJ (*language etc*) profan; (*secular*) weltlich
profess [prə'fɛs] VT (*claim*) vorgeben; (*express: feeling, opinion*) zeigen, bekunden; **I do not ~ to be an expert** ich behaupte nicht, ein Experte zu sein
professed [prə'fɛst] ADJ (*self-declared*) erklärt
profession [prə'fɛʃən] N Beruf *m*; (*people*) Berufsstand *m*; **the professions** die gehobenen Berufe
professional [prə'fɛʃənl] ADJ (*organization, musician etc*) Berufs-; (*misconduct, advice*) beruflich; (*skilful*) professionell ▸ N (*doctor, lawyer, teacher etc*) Fachmann *m*, Fachfrau *f*; (*Sport*) Profi *m*; (*skilled person*) Experte *m*, Expertin *f*; **to seek ~ advice** fachmännischen Rat einholen
professionalism [prə'fɛʃnəlɪzəm] N fachliches Können *nt*
professionally [prə'fɛʃnəlɪ] ADV beruflich; (*for a living*) berufsmäßig; **I only know him ~** ich kenne ihn nur beruflich
professor [prə'fɛsə^r] N (BRIT) Professor(in) *m(f)*; (*US, CANADA*) Dozent(in) *m(f)*
professorship [prə'fɛsəʃɪp] N Professur *f*
proffer ['prɔfə^r] VT (*advice, drink, one's hand*) anbieten; (*apologies*) aussprechen; (*plate etc*) hinhalten
proficiency [prə'fɪʃənsɪ] N Können *nt*, Fertigkeiten *pl*
proficient [prə'fɪʃənt] ADJ fähig; **to be ~ at** *or* **in** gut sein in *+dat*
profile ['prəufaɪl] N (*of person's face*) Profil *nt*; (*fig: biography*) Porträt *nt*; **to keep a low ~** (*fig*) sich zurückhalten; **to have a high ~** (*fig*) eine große Rolle spielen

profit ['prɔfɪt] N (*Comm*) Gewinn *m*, Profit *m* ▸ VI: **to ~ by** *or* **from** (*fig*) profitieren von; **~ and loss account** Gewinn-und-Verlust-Rechnung; **to make a ~** einen Gewinn machen; **to sell (sth) at a ~** (etw) mit Gewinn verkaufen
profitability [prɔfɪtə'bɪlɪtɪ] N Rentabilität *f*
profitable ['prɔfɪtəbl] ADJ (*business, deal*) rentabel, einträglich; (*fig: useful*) nützlich
profit centre N Bilanzabteilung *f*
profiteering [prɔfɪ'tɪərɪŋ] (*pej*) N Profitmacherei *f*
profit-making ['prɔfɪtmeɪkɪŋ] ADJ (*organization*) gewinnorientiert
profit margin N Gewinnspanne *f*
profit-sharing ['prɔfɪtʃɛərɪŋ] N Gewinnbeteiligung *f*
profits tax (BRIT) N Ertragssteuer *f*
profligate ['prɔflɪgɪt] ADJ (*person, spending*) verschwenderisch; (*waste*) sinnlos; **~ with** (*extravagant*) verschwenderisch mit
pro forma ['prəu'fɔ:mə] ADJ: **~ invoice** Pro-forma-Rechnung *f*
profound [prə'faund] ADJ (*shock*) schwer, tief; (*effect, differences*) weitreichend; (*idea, book*) tief schürfend
profuse [prə'fju:s] ADJ (*apologies*) überschwänglich
profusely [prə'fju:slɪ] ADV (*apologise, thank*) vielmals; (*sweat, bleed*) stark
profusion [prə'fju:ʒən] N Überfülle *f*
progeny ['prɔdʒɪnɪ] N Nachkommenschaft *f*
prognoses [prɔg'nəusi:z] NPL *of* **prognosis**
prognosis [prɔg'nəusɪs] (*pl* **prognoses**) N (*Med, fig*) Prognose *f*
program ['prəugræm] (*Comput*) N Programm *nt* ▸ VT programmieren
programme, (*US*) **program** ['prəugræm] N Programm *nt* ▸ VT (*machine, system*) programmieren
programmer ['prəugræmə^r] N Programmierer(in) *m(f)*
programming, (*US*) **programing** ['prəugræmɪŋ] N Programmierung *f*
programming language N Programmiersprache *f*
progress N ['prəugrɛs] Fortschritt *m*; (*improvement*) Fortschritte *pl* ▸ VI [prə'grɛs] (*advance*) vorankommen; (*become higher in rank*) aufsteigen; (*continue*) sich fortsetzen; **in ~** (*meeting, battle, match*) im Gange; **to make ~** Fortschritte machen
progression [prə'grɛʃən] N (*development*) Fortschritt *m*, Entwicklung *f*; (*series*) Folge *f*
progressive [prə'grɛsɪv] ADJ (*enlightened*) progressiv, fortschrittlich; (*gradual*) fortschreitend
progressively [prə'grɛsɪvlɪ] ADV (*gradually*) zunehmend
progress report N (*Med*) Fortschrittsbericht *m*; (*Admin*) Tätigkeitsbericht *m*
prohibit [prə'hɪbɪt] VT (*ban*) verbieten; **to ~ sb from doing sth** jdm verbieten *or* untersagen, etw zu tun; **"smoking prohibited"** „Rauchen verboten"

rohibition [prəuɪ'bɪʃən] N Verbot *nt*; **P~** (*US*) Prohibition *f*

rohibitive [prə'hɪbɪtɪv] ADJ (*cost etc*) untragbar

roject N ['prɔdʒɛkt] (*plan, scheme*) Projekt *nt*; (*Scol*) Referat *nt* ▶ VT [prə'dʒɛkt] (*plan*) planen; (*estimate*) schätzen, voraussagen; (*light, film, picture*) projizieren ▶ VI (*stick out*) hervorragen

rojectile [prə'dʒɛktaɪl] N Projektil *nt*, Geschoss *nt*, Geschoß *nt* (ÖSTERR)

rojection [prə'dʒɛkʃən] N (*estimate*) Schätzung *f*, Voraussage *f*; (*overhang*) Vorsprung *m*; (*Cine*) Projektion *f*

rojectionist [prə'dʒɛkʃənɪst] N Filmvorführer(in) *m(f)*

rojection room N Vorführraum *m*

rojector [prə'dʒɛktə^r] N Projektor *m*

roletarian [prəulɪ'tɛərɪən] ADJ proletarisch

roletariat [prəulɪ'tɛərɪət] N: **the ~** das Proletariat

roliferate [prə'lɪfəreɪt] VI sich vermehren

roliferation [prəlɪfə'reɪʃən] N Vermehrung *f*, Verbreitung *f*

rolific [prə'lɪfɪk] ADJ (*artist, writer*) produktiv

rologue, (*US*) **prolog** ['prəulɔg] N (*of play, book*) Prolog *m*

rolong [prə'lɔŋ] VT verlängern

rom [prɔm] N ABBR = **promenade**; (*Mus*) = **promenade concert**; (*US, CANADA*: *college ball*) Studentenball *m*

Prom (promenade concert) ist in Großbritannien ein Konzert, bei dem ein Teil der Zuhörer steht (ursprünglich spazieren ging). Die seit 1895 alljährlich stattfindenden Proms (seit 1941 immer in der Londoner Royal Albert Hall) zählen zu den bedeutendsten Musikereignissen in England. Der letzte Abend der Proms steht ganz um Zeichen des Patriotismus und gipfelt im Singen des Lieds „Land of Hope and Glory". In den USA und Kanada steht das Wort für **promenade**, ein Ball an einer **high school** oder einem **college**.

romenade [prɔmə'nɑ:d] N Promenade *f*

romenade concert (BRIT) N Promenadenkonzert *nt*

romenade deck N Promenadendeck *nt*

rominence ['prɔmɪnəns] N (*importance*) Bedeutung *f*; **to rise to ~** bekannt werden

rominent ['prɔmɪnənt] ADJ (*person*) prominent; (*thing*) bedeutend; (*very noticeable*) herausragend; **he is ~ in the field of science** er ist eine führende Persönlichkeit im naturwissenschaftlichen Bereich

rominently ['prɔmɪnəntlɪ] ADV (*display, set*) deutlich sichtbar; **he figured ~ in the case** er spielte in dem Fall eine bedeutende Rolle

romiscuity [prɔmɪs'kju:ɪtɪ] N Promiskuität *f*

romiscuous [prə'mɪskjuəs] ADJ promisk

romise ['prɔmɪs] N (*vow*) Versprechen *nt*; (*potential, hope*) Hoffnung *f* ▶ VI versprechen ▶ VT: **to ~ sb sth, ~ sth to sb** jdm etw versprechen; **to make/break/keep a ~** ein Versprechen geben/brechen/halten; **a young man of ~** ein vielversprechender junger Mann; **she shows ~** sie gibt zu Hoffnungen Anlass; **it promises to be lively** es verspricht lebhaft zu werden; **to ~ (sb) to do sth** (jdm) versprechen, etw zu tun

promising ['prɔmɪsɪŋ] ADJ vielversprechend

promissory note ['prɔmɪsərɪ-] N Schuldschein *m*

promontory ['prɔməntrɪ] N Felsvorsprung *m*

promote [prə'məut] VT (*employee*) befördern; (*advertise*) werben für; (*encourage*: *peace etc*) fördern; **the team was promoted to the first division** (BRIT *Football*) die Mannschaft stieg in die erste Division auf

promoter [prə'məutə^r] N (*of concert, event*) Veranstalter(in) *m(f)*; (*of cause, idea*) Förderer *m*, Förderin *f*

promotion [prə'məuʃən] N (*at work*) Beförderung *f*; (*of product, event*) Werbung *f*; (*of idea*) Förderung *f*; (*publicity campaign*) Werbekampagne *f*

prompt [prɔmpt] ADJ prompt, sofortig ▶ ADV (*exactly*) pünktlich ▶ N (*Comput*) Prompt *m* ▶ VT (*cause*) veranlassen; (*when talking*) auf die Sprünge helfen *+dat*; (*Theat*) soufflieren *+dat*; **they're very ~** (*punctual*) sie sind sehr pünktlich; **he was ~ to accept** er nahm unverzüglich an; **at 8 o'clock ~** (um) Punkt 8 Uhr; **to ~ sb to do sth** jdn dazu veranlassen, etw zu tun

prompter ['prɔmptə^r] N (*Theat*) Souffleur *m*, Souffleuse *f*

promptly ['prɔmptlɪ] ADV (*immediately*) sofort; (*exactly*) pünktlich

promptness ['prɔmptnɪs] N Promptheit *f*

promulgate ['prɔməlgeɪt] VT (*policy*) bekannt machen, verkünden; (*idea*) verbreiten

prone [prəun] ADJ (*face down*) in Bauchlage; **to be ~ to sth** zu etw neigen; **she is ~ to burst into tears if ...** sie neigt dazu, in Tränen auszubrechen, wenn ...

prong [prɔŋ] N (*of fork*) Zinke *f*

pronoun ['prəunaun] N Pronomen *nt*, Fürwort *nt*

pronounce [prə'nauns] VT (*word*) aussprechen; (*give verdict, opinion*) erklären ▶ VI: **to ~ (up)on** sich äußern zu; **they pronounced him dead/unfit to drive** sie erklärten ihn für tot/fahruntüchtig

pronounced [prə'naunst] ADJ (*noticeable*) ausgeprägt, deutlich

pronouncement [prə'naunsmənt] N Erklärung *f*

pronto ['prɔntəu] (*inf*) ADV fix

pronunciation [prənʌnsɪ'eɪʃən] N Aussprache *f*

proof [pru:f] N (*evidence*) Beweis *m*; (*Typ*) (Korrektur)fahne *f* ▶ ADJ: **~ against** sicher vor *+dat*; **to be 70 % ~** (*alcohol*) ≈ einen Alkoholgehalt von 40% haben

proofreader ['pru:fri:də^r] N Korrektor(in) *m(f)*

prop [prɔp] N (*support*) Stütze *f* ▶ VT (*lean*): **to ~ sth against sth** etw an etw *acc* lehnen

▸ **prop up** VT SEP (*thing*) (ab)stützen; (*fig: government, industry*) unterstützen

Prop. ABBR (*Comm*: = *proprietor*) Inh.

propaganda [prɔpə'gændə] N Propaganda *f*

propagate ['prɔpəgeɪt] VT (*plants*) züchten; (*ideas etc*) propagieren ▸ VI (*plants, animals*) sich fortpflanzen

propagation [prɔpə'geɪʃən] N (*of ideas etc*) Propagierung *f*; (*of plants, animals*) Fortpflanzung *f*

propel [prə'pɛl] VT (*vehicle, machine*) antreiben; (*person*) schubsen; (*fig: person*) treiben

propeller [prə'pɛlə^{r}] N Propeller *m*

propelling pencil [prə'pɛlɪŋ-] (BRIT) N Drehbleistift *m*

propensity [prə'pɛnsɪtɪ] N: **a ~ for** *or* **to sth** ein Hang *m or* eine Neigung zu etw; **to have a ~ to do sth** dazu neigen, etw zu tun

proper ['prɔpə^{r}] ADJ (*genuine, correct*) richtig; (*socially acceptable*) schicklich; (*inf: real*) echt; **the town/city ~** die Stadt selbst; **to go through the ~ channels** den Dienstweg einhalten

properly ['prɔpəlɪ] ADV (*eat, work*) richtig; (*behave*) anständig

proper noun N Eigenname *m*

property ['prɔpətɪ] N (*possessions*) Eigentum *nt*; (*building and its land*) Grundstück *nt*; (*quality*) Eigenschaft *f*; **it's their ~** es gehört ihnen

property developer N ≈ Grundstücksmakler(in) *m(f)*

property market N Immobilienmarkt *m*

property owner N Grundbesitzer(in) *m(f)*

property tax N Vermögenssteuer *f*

prophecy ['prɔfɪsɪ] N Prophezeiung *f*

prophesy ['prɔfɪsaɪ] VT prophezeien ▸ VI Prophezeiungen machen

prophet ['prɔfɪt] N Prophet *m*; **~ of doom** Unheilsprophet(in) *m(f)*

prophetic [prə'fɛtɪk] ADJ prophetisch

proportion [prə'pɔ:ʃən] N (*part*) Teil *m*; (*number, of people, things*) Anteil *m*; (*ratio*) Verhältnis *nt*; **in ~ to** im Verhältnis zu; **to be out of all ~ to sth** in keinem Verhältnis zu etw stehen; **to get sth in/out of ~** etw im richtigen/falschen Verhältnis sehen; **a sense of ~** (*fig*) ein Sinn für das Wesentliche

proportional [prə'pɔ:ʃənl] ADJ: **~ to** proportional zu

proportional representation N Verhältniswahlrecht *nt*

proportionate [prə'pɔ:ʃənɪt] ADJ = **proportional**

proposal [prə'pəuzl] N (*plan*) Vorschlag *m*; **~ (of marriage)** Heiratsantrag *m*

propose [prə'pəuz] VT (*plan, idea*) vorschlagen; (*motion*) einbringen; (*toast*) ausbringen ▸ VI (*offer marriage*) einen Heiratsantrag machen; **to ~ to do sth** *or* **doing sth** (*intend*) die Absicht haben, etw zu tun

proposer [prə'pəuzə^{r}] N (*of motion etc*) Antragsteller(in) *m(f)*

proposition [prɔpə'zɪʃən] N (*statement*) These *f*; (*offer*) Angebot *nt*; **to make sb a ~** jdm ein Angebot machen

propound [prə'paund] VT (*idea etc*) darlegen

proprietary [prə'praɪətərɪ] ADJ (*brand, medicine*) Marken-; (*tone, manner*) besitzergreifend

proprietor [prə'praɪətə^{r}] N (*of hotel, shop etc*) Inhaber(in) *m(f)*; (*of newspaper*) Besitzer(in) *m(f)*

propriety [prə'praɪətɪ] N (*seemliness*) Schicklichkeit *f*

props [prɔps] NPL (*Theat*) Requisiten *pl*

propulsion [prə'pʌlʃən] N Antrieb *m*

pro rata [prəu'rɑ:tə] ADJ, ADV anteilmäßig; **on a ~ basis** anteilmäßig

prosaic [prəu'zeɪɪk] ADJ prosaisch, nüchtern

Pros. Atty. (*US*) ABBR = **prosecuting attorney**

proscribe [prə'skraɪb] (*form*) VT verbieten, untersagen

prose [prəuz] N (*not poetry*) Prosa *f*; (BRIT *Scol: translation*) Übersetzung *f* in die Fremdsprache

prosecute ['prɔsɪkju:t] VT (*Law: person*) strafrechtlich verfolgen; (*: case*) die Anklage vertreten in *+dat*

prosecuting attorney ['prɔsɪkju:tɪŋ-] (*US*) N Staatsanwalt *m*, Staatsanwältin *f*

prosecution [prɔsɪ'kju:ʃən] N (*Law: action*) strafrechtliche Verfolgung *f*; (*: accusing side*) Anklage(vertretung) *f*

prosecutor ['prɔsɪkju:tə^{r}] N Anklagevertreter(in) *m(f)*; (*also*: **public prosecutor**) Staatsanwalt *m*, Staatsanwältin *f*

prospect N ['prɔspɛkt] Aussicht *f* ▸ VI [prə'spɛkt]: **to ~ (for)** suchen (nach); **prospects** NPL (*for work etc*) Aussichten *pl*, Chancen *pl*; **we are faced with the ~ of higher unemployment** wir müssen mit der Möglichkeit rechnen, dass die Arbeitslosigkei[t] steigt

prospecting ['prɔspɛktɪŋ] N (*for gold, oil etc*) Suche *f*

prospective [prə'spɛktɪv] ADJ (*son-in-law*) zukünftig; (*customer, candidate*) voraussichtlich

prospectus [prə'spɛktəs] N (*of college, company*) Prospekt *m*

prosper ['prɔspə^{r}] VI (*person*) Erfolg haben; (*business, city etc*) gedeihen, florieren

prosperity [prɔ'spɛrɪtɪ] N Wohlstand *m*

prosperous ['prɔspərəs] ADJ (*person*) wohlhabend; (*business, city etc*) blühend

prostate ['prɔsteɪt] N (*also*: **prostate gland**) Prostata *f*

prostitute ['prɔstɪtju:t] N (*female*) Prostituierte *f*; (*male*) männliche(r) Prostituierte(r) *m*, Strichjunge *m* (*inf*) ▸ VT: **to ~ o.s.** (*fig*) sich prostituieren, sich unter Wert verkaufen

prostitution [prɔstɪ'tju:ʃən] N Prostitution *f*

prostrate ['prɔstreɪt] ADJ (*face down*) ausgestreckt (liegend); (*fig*) niedergeschmettert ▸ VT: **to ~ o.s. before** sich zu Boden werfen vor *+dat*

protagonist [prə'tægənɪst] N (*of idea, movement*) Verfechter(in) *m(f)*; (*Theat, Liter*) Protagonist(in) *m(f)*

protect [prə'tɛkt] VT schützen

protection [prə'tɛkʃən] N Schutz *m*; **police ~** Polizeischutz *m*

protectionism [prəˈtɛkʃənɪzəm] N Protektionismus *m*
protection racket N Organisation *f* zur Erpressung von Schutzgeld
protective [prəˈtɛktɪv] ADJ (*clothing, layer etc*) Schutz-; (*person*) fürsorglich; **~ custody** Schutzhaft *f*
protector [prəˈtɛktəʳ] N (*person*) Beschützer(in) *m(f)*; (*device*) Schutz *m*
protégé, protégée [ˈprəutɪʒeɪ] N Schützling *m*
protein [ˈprəutiːn] N Protein *nt*, Eiweiß *nt*
pro tem [prəuˈtɛm] ADV ABBR (= *pro tempore*) vorläufig
protest N [ˈprəutɛst] Protest *m* ▸ VI [prəˈtɛst]: **to ~ about** *or* **against** *or* **at sth** gegen etw protestieren ▸ VT: **to ~ (that)** (*insist*) beteuern(, dass)
Protestant [ˈprɔtɪstənt] ADJ protestantisch ▸ N Protestant(in) *m(f)*
protester [prəˈtɛstəʳ] N (*in demonstration*) Demonstrant(in) *m(f)*
protest march N Protestmarsch *m*
protestor [prəˈtɛstəʳ] N = **protester**
protocol [ˈprəutəkɔl] N Protokoll *nt*
prototype [ˈprəutətaɪp] N Prototyp *m*
protracted [prəˈtræktɪd] ADJ (*meeting etc*) langwierig, sich hinziehend; (*absence*) länger
protractor [prəˈtræktəʳ] N (*Geom*) Winkelmesser *m*
protrude [prəˈtruːd] VI (*rock, ledge, teeth*) vorstehen
protuberance [prəˈtjuːbərəns] N Auswuchs *m*
proud [praud] ADJ stolz; (*arrogant*) hochmütig; **~ of sb/sth** stolz auf jdn/etw; **to be ~ to do sth** stolz (darauf) sein, etw zu tun; **to do sb/o.s. ~** (*inf*) jdn/sich verwöhnen
proudly [ˈpraudlɪ] ADV stolz
prove [pruːv] VT beweisen ▸ VI: **to ~ (to be) correct** sich als richtig herausstellen *or* erweisen; **to ~ (o.s./itself) (to be) useful** sich als nützlich erweisen; **he was proved right in the end** er hat schließlich recht behalten
proverb [ˈprɔvəːb] N Sprichwort *nt*
proverbial [prəˈvəːbɪəl] ADJ sprichwörtlich
provide [prəˈvaɪd] VT (*food, money, shelter etc*) zur Verfügung stellen; (*answer, example etc*) liefern; **to ~ sb with sth** jdm etw zur Verfügung stellen
▸ **provide for** VT FUS (*person*) sorgen für; (*future event*) vorsorgen für
provided [prəˈvaɪdɪd] CONJ: **~ (that)** vorausgesetzt(, dass)
Providence [ˈprɔvɪdəns] N die Vorsehung
providing [prəˈvaɪdɪŋ] CONJ: **~ (that)** vorausgesetzt(, dass)
province [ˈprɔvɪns] N (*of country*) Provinz *f*; (*responsibility etc*) Bereich *m*, Gebiet *nt*; **provinces** NPL: **the provinces** *außerhalb der Hauptstadt liegende Landesteile*, Provinz *f*
provincial [prəˈvɪnʃəl] ADJ (*town, newspaper etc*) Provinz-; (*pej: parochial*) provinziell
provision [prəˈvɪʒən] N (*supplying*) Bereitstellung *f*; (*preparation*) Vorsorge *f*, Vorkehrungen *pl*; (*stipulation, clause*) Bestimmung *f*; **provisions** NPL (*food*) Proviant *m*; **to make ~ for** vorsorgen für; (*for people*) sorgen für; **there's no ~ for this in the contract** dies ist im Vertrag nicht vorgesehen
provisional [prəˈvɪʒənl] ADJ vorläufig, provisorisch ▸ N: **P~** (IRISH *Pol*) *Mitglied der provisorischen Irisch-Republikanischen Armee*
provisional licence (BRIT) N (*Aut*) vorläufige Fahrerlaubnis *f*
provisionally [prəˈvɪʒnəlɪ] ADV vorläufig
proviso [prəˈvaɪzəu] N Vorbehalt *m*; **with the ~ that …** unter dem Vorbehalt, dass …
Provo [ˈprɔvəu] (IRISH *inf*) N ABBR (*Pol*) = **Provisional**
provocation [prɔvəˈkeɪʃən] N Provokation *f*, Herausforderung *f*; **to be under ~** provoziert werden
provocative [prəˈvɔkətɪv] ADJ provozierend, herausfordernd; (*sexually stimulating*) aufreizend
provoke [prəˈvəuk] VT (*person*) provozieren, herausfordern; (*fight*) herbeiführen; (*reaction etc*) hervorrufen; **to ~ sb to do** *or* **into doing sth** jdn dazu provozieren, etw zu tun
provost [ˈprɔvəst] N (BRIT: *of university*) Dekan *m*; (SCOT) Bürgermeister(in) *m(f)*
prow [prau] N (*of boat*) Bug *m*
prowess [ˈprauɪs] N Können *nt*, Fähigkeiten *pl*; **his ~ as a footballer** sein fußballerisches Können
prowl [praul] VI (*also*: **prowl about, prowl around**) schleichen ▸ N: **on the ~** auf Streifzug
prowler [ˈprauləʳ] N Herumtreiber *m*
proximity [prɔkˈsɪmɪtɪ] N Nähe *f*
proxy [ˈprɔksɪ] N: **by ~** durch einen Stellvertreter
prude [pruːd] N: **to be a ~** prüde sein
prudence [ˈpruːdns] N Klugheit *f*, Umsicht *f*
prudent [ˈpruːdnt] ADJ (*sensible*) klug
prudish [ˈpruːdɪʃ] ADJ prüde
prune [pruːn] N Backpflaume *f* ▸ VT (*plant*) stutzen, beschneiden
pry [praɪ] VI: **to ~ (into)** seine Nase hineinstecken (in +*acc*), herumschnüffeln (in +*dat*)
PS ABBR (= *postscript*) PS
psalm [sɑːm] N Psalm *m*
PSAT® (US) N ABBR (= *Preliminary Scholastic Aptitude Test*) *Schuleignungstest*
PSBR (BRIT) N ABBR (*Econ*: = *public sector borrowing requirement*) staatlicher Kreditbedarf *m*
pseud [sjuːd] (BRIT *inf, pej*) N Angeber(in) *m(f)*
pseudo- [ˈsjuːdəu] PREF Pseudo-
pseudonym [ˈsjuːdənɪm] N Pseudonym *nt*
PSHE (BRIT) N ABBR (*Scol*) = **personal, social and health education**
PST (US) ABBR (= *Pacific Standard Time*) *pazifische Standardzeit*
psyche [ˈsaɪkɪ] N Psyche *f*
psychedelic [saɪkəˈdɛlɪk] ADJ (*drug*) psychedelisch; (*clothes, colours*) in psychedelischen Farben
psychiatric [saɪkɪˈætrɪk] ADJ psychiatrisch
psychiatrist [saɪˈkaɪətrɪst] N Psychiater(in) *m(f)*

P

psychiatry [saɪ'kaɪətrɪ] N Psychiatrie *f*

psychic ['saɪkɪk] ADJ (*person*) übersinnlich begabt; (*damage, disorder*) psychisch ▶ N Mensch *m* mit übersinnlichen Fähigkeiten

psycho ['saɪkəu] (*US inf*) N Verrückte(r) *f(m)*

psychoanalyse [saɪkəu'ænəlaɪz] VT psychoanalytisch behandeln, psychoanalysieren

psychoanalysis [saɪkəuə'nælɪsɪs] N Psychoanalyse *f*

psychoanalyst [saɪkəu'ænəlɪst] N Psychoanalytiker(in) *m(f)*

psychological [saɪkə'lɔdʒɪkl] ADJ psychologisch

psychologist [saɪ'kɔlədʒɪst] N Psychologe *m*, Psychologin *f*

psychology [saɪ'kɔlədʒɪ] N (*science*) Psychologie *f*; (*character*) Psyche *f*

psychopath ['saɪkəupæθ] N Psychopath(in) *m(f)*

psychoses [saɪ'kəusi:z] NPL *of* **psychosis**

psychosis [saɪ'kəusɪs] (*pl* **psychoses**) N Psychose *f*

psychosomatic ['saɪkəusə'mætɪk] ADJ psychosomatisch

psychotherapy [saɪkəu'θɛrəpɪ] N Psychotherapie *f*

psychotic [saɪ'kɔtɪk] ADJ psychotisch

PT (BRIT) N ABBR (*Scol: = physical training*) Turnen *nt*

Pt ABBR (*in place names: = Point*) Pt.

pt ABBR = **pint**; **point**

PTA N ABBR (= *Parent-Teacher Association*) *Lehrer- und Elternverband*

Pte (BRIT) ABBR (*Mil*) = **private**

PTO ABBR (= *please turn over*) b. w.

PTV (US) N ABBR (= *pay television*) Pay-TV *nt*; (= *public television*) öffentliches Fernsehen *nt*

pub [pʌb] N = **public house**

> **Pub** ist ein Gasthaus mit einer Lizenz zum Ausschank von alkoholischen Getränken. Ein Pub besteht meist aus verschiedenen gemütlichen (lounge, snug) oder einfacheren Räumen (public bar), in der oft auch Spiele wie Darts, Domino und Poolbilliard zur Verfügung stehen. In Pubs werden vor allem mittags oft auch Mahlzeiten angeboten. Pubs sind normalerweise von 11 bis 23 Uhr geöffnet, aber manchmal nachmittags geschlossen.

pub-crawl ['pʌbkrɔ:l] (*inf*) N: **to go on a ~** eine Kneipentour machen

puberty ['pju:bətɪ] N Pubertät *f*

pubic ['pju:bɪk] ADJ (*hair*) Scham-; **~ bone** Schambein *nt*

public ['pʌblɪk] ADJ öffentlich ▶ N: **the ~** (*in general*) die Öffentlichkeit; (*particular set of people*) das Publikum; **to be ~ knowledge** allgemein bekannt sein; **to make sth ~** etw bekannt machen; **to go ~** (*Comm*) in eine Aktiengesellschaft umgewandelt werden; **in ~** in aller Öffentlichkeit; **the general ~** die Allgemeinheit

public-address system [pʌblɪkə'drɛs-] N Lautsprecheranlage *f*

publican ['pʌblɪkən] N Gastwirt(in) *m(f)*

publication [pʌblɪ'keɪʃən] N Veröffentlichung *f*

public company N Aktiengesellschaft *f*

public convenience (BRIT) N öffentliche Toilette *f*

public holiday N gesetzlicher Feiertag *m*

public house (BRIT) N Gaststätte *f*

publicity [pʌb'lɪsɪtɪ] N (*information*) Werbung *f*; (*attention*) Publicity *f*

publicity tour N Werbetour *f*; **to be on a ~** auf Werbetour sein

publicize ['pʌblɪsaɪz] VT (*fact*) bekannt machen; (*event*) Publicity machen für

public limited company N ≈ Aktiengesellschaft *f*

publicly ['pʌblɪklɪ] ADV öffentlich; **to be ~ owned** (*Comm*) in Staatsbesitz sein

public opinion N die öffentliche Meinung

public ownership N: **to be taken into ~** verstaatlicht werden

Public Prosecutor N Staatsanwalt *m*, Staatsanwältin *f*

public relations N Public Relations *pl*, Öffentlichkeitsarbeit *f*

public relations officer N Beauftragte(r) *f(m)* für Öffentlichkeitsarbeit

public school N (BRIT) Privatschule *f*; (US) staatliche Schule *f*

> **Public school** bezeichnet vor allem in England eine weiterführende Privatschule, meist eine Internatsschule mit hohem Prestige, an die oft auch eine **preparatory school** angeschlossen ist. Public schools werden von einem Schulbeirat verwaltet und durch Stiftungen und Schulgelder, die an den bekanntesten Schulen wie Eton, Harrow und Westminster sehr hoch sein konnen, finanziert. Die meisten Schüler einer public school gehen zur Universität, oft nach Oxford oder Cambridge. Viele Industrielle, Abgeordnete und hohe Beamte haben eine public school besucht. In Schottland und den USA bedeutet public school eine öffentliche, vom Steuerzahler finanzierte Schule.

public sector N: **the ~** der öffentliche Sektor

public-service vehicle [pʌblɪk'sə:vɪs-] (BRIT) N öffentliches Verkehrsmittel *nt*

public-spirited [pʌblɪk'spɪrɪtɪd] ADJ gemeinsinnig

public transport N öffentliche Verkehrsmittel *pl*

public utility N öffentlicher Versorgungsbetrieb *m*

public works NPL öffentliche Bauprojekte *pl*

publish ['pʌblɪʃ] VT veröffentlichen

publisher ['pʌblɪʃə[r]] N (*person*) Verleger(in) *m(f)*; (*company*) Verlag *m*

publishing ['pʌblɪʃɪŋ] N (*profession*) das Verlagswesen

publishing company N Verlag *m*, Verlagshaus *nt*

pub lunch N *in Pubs servierter Imbiss*

puce [pju:s] ADJ (*face*) hochrot
puck [pʌk] N (*Ice Hockey*) Puck *m*
pucker ['pʌkəʳ] VI (*lips, face*) sich verziehen; (*fabric etc*) Falten werfen ▸ VT (*lips, face*) verziehen; (*fabric etc*) Falten machen in *+acc*
pudding ['pudɪŋ] N (*cooked sweet food*) Süßspeise *f*; (BRIT: *dessert*) Nachtisch *m*; **rice ~** Milchreis *m*; **black ~, blood ~** (*US*) ≈ Blutwurst *f*
puddle ['pʌdl] N (*of rain*) Pfütze *f*; (*of blood*) Lache *f*
puerile ['pjuəraɪl] ADJ kindisch
Puerto Rico ['pwə:təu'ri:kəu] N Puerto Rico *nt*
puff [pʌf] N (*of cigarette, pipe*) Zug *m*; (*gasp*) Schnaufer *m*; (*of air*) Stoß *m*; (*of smoke*) Wolke *f* ▸ VT (*cigarette, pipe*: *also*: **puff on, puff at**) ziehen an *+dat* ▸ VI (*gasp*) keuchen, schnaufen
▸ **puff out** VT (*one's chest*) herausdrücken; (*one's cheeks*) aufblasen
puffed [pʌft] (*inf*) ADJ außer Puste
puffin ['pʌfɪn] N Papageientaucher *m*
puff pastry, (*US*) **puff paste** N Blätterteig *m*
puffy ['pʌfɪ] ADJ (*eye*) geschwollen; (*face*) aufgedunsen
pugnacious [pʌg'neɪʃəs] ADJ (*person*) streitsüchtig
pull [pul] VT (*rope, handle etc*) ziehen an *+dat*; (*cart etc*) ziehen; (*close*: *curtain*) zuziehen; (: *blind*) herunterlassen; (*inf*: *attract*: *people*) anlocken; (: *sexual partner*) aufreißen; (*pint of beer*) zapfen ▸ VI ziehen ▸ N (*also fig*: *attraction*) Anziehungskraft *f*; **to ~ the trigger** abdrücken; **to ~ a face** ein Gesicht schneiden; **to ~ a muscle** sich *dat* einen Muskel zerren; **not to ~ one's** *or* **any punches** (*fig*) sich *dat* keine Zurückhaltung auferlegen; **to ~ to pieces** (*fig*) zerreißen; **to ~ one's weight** (*fig*) sich ins Zeug legen; **to ~ o.s. together** sich zusammenreißen; **to ~ sb's leg** (*fig*) jdn auf den Arm nehmen; **to ~ strings (for sb)** seine Beziehungen (für jdn) spielen lassen; **to give sth a ~** an etw *dat* ziehen
▸ **pull apart** VT (*separate*) trennen
▸ **pull away** VI (*Aut*) losfahren
▸ **pull back** VI (*retreat*) sich zurückziehen; (*fig*) einen Rückzieher machen (*inf*)
▸ **pull down** VT (*building*) abreißen
▸ **pull in** VI (*Aut*: *at kerb*) anhalten; (*Rail*) einfahren ▸ VT (*inf*: *money*) einsacken; (*crowds, people*) anlocken; (*police*: *suspect*) sich *dat* schnappen (*inf*)
▸ **pull off** VT (*clothes etc*) ausziehen; (*fig*: *difficult thing*) schaffen, bringen (*inf*)
pullback ['pulbæk] N (*retreat*) Rückzug *m*
pulley ['pulɪ] N Flaschenzug *m*
pull on VT (*clothes*) anziehen
▸ **pull out** VI (*Aut*: *from kerb*) losfahren; (: *when overtaking*) ausscheren; (*Rail*) ausfahren; (*withdraw*) sich zurückziehen ▸ VT (*extract*) herausziehen
▸ **pull over** VI (*Aut*) an den Straßenrand fahren
▸ **pull through** VI (*Med*) durchkommen
▸ **pull up** VI (*Aut, Rail*: *stop*) anhalten ▸ VT (*raise*) hochziehen; (*uproot*) herausreißen; (*chair*) heranrücken
pull-out ['pulaut] N (*in magazine*) Beilage *f* (*zum Heraustrennen*)
pullover ['puləuvəʳ] N Pullover *m*
pulp [pʌlp] N (*of fruit*) Fruchtfleisch *nt*; (*for paper*) (Papier)brei *m*; (*Liter*: *pej*) Schund *m* ▸ ADJ (*pej*: *magazine, novel*) Schund-; **to reduce sth to a ~** etw zu Brei machen
pulpit ['pulpɪt] N Kanzel *f*
pulsate [pʌl'seɪt] VI (*heart*) klopfen; (*music*) pulsieren
pulse [pʌls] N (*Anat*) Puls *m*; (*rhythm*) Rhythmus *m*; **pulses** NPL (*Bot*) Hülsenfrüchte *pl*; (*Tech*) Impuls *m* ▸ VI pulsieren; **to take** *or* **feel sb's ~** jdm den Puls fühlen; **to have one's finger on the ~ (of sth)** (*fig*) den Finger am Puls (einer Sache *gen*) haben
pulverize ['pʌlvəraɪz] VT pulverisieren; (*fig*: *destroy*) vernichten
puma ['pju:mə] N Puma *m*
pumice ['pʌmɪs] N (*also*: **pumice stone**) Bimsstein *m*
pummel ['pʌml] VT mit Faustschlägen bearbeiten
pump [pʌmp] N Pumpe *f*; (*also*: **petrol pump**) Zapfsäule *f*; (*shoe*) Turnschuh *m* ▸ VT pumpen; **to ~ sb for information** jdn aushorchen; **she had her stomach pumped** ihr wurde der Magen ausgepumpt
▸ **pump up** VT (*inflate*) aufpumpen
pumpkin ['pʌmpkɪn] N Kürbis *m*
pun [pʌn] N Wortspiel *nt*
punch [pʌntʃ] N (*blow*) Schlag *m*; (*fig*: *force*) Schlagkraft *f*; (*tool*) Locher *m*; (*drink*) Bowle *f*, Punsch *m* ▸ VT (*hit*) schlagen; (*make a hole in*) lochen; **to ~ a hole in sth** ein Loch in etw *acc* stanzen
▸ **punch in** (*US*) VI (bei Arbeitsbeginn) stempeln
▸ **punch out** (*US*) VI (bei Arbeitsende) stempeln
Punch and Judy show N ≈ Kasper(le)theater *nt*
punch card, (*US*) **punched card** [pʌntʃt-] N Lochkarte *f*
punch-drunk ['pʌntʃdrʌŋk] (BRIT) ADJ (*boxer*) angeschlagen
punch line N Pointe *f*
punch-up ['pʌntʃʌp] (BRIT *inf*) N Schlägerei *f*
punctual ['pʌŋktjuəl] ADJ pünktlich
punctuality [pʌŋktju'ælɪtɪ] N Pünktlichkeit *f*
punctually ['pʌŋktjuəlɪ] ADV pünktlich; **it will start ~ at 6** es beginnt um Punkt 6 *or* pünktlich um 6
punctuation [pʌŋktju'eɪʃən] N Zeichensetzung *f*
punctuation mark N Satzzeichen *nt*
puncture ['pʌŋktʃəʳ] N (*Aut*) Reifenpanne *f* ▸ VT durchbohren; **I have a ~** ich habe eine Reifenpanne
pundit ['pʌndɪt] N Experte *m*, Expertin *f*
pungent ['pʌndʒənt] ADJ (*smell, taste*) scharf; (*fig*: *speech, article etc*) spitz, scharf
punish ['pʌnɪʃ] VT bestrafen; **to ~ sb for sth** jdn für etw bestrafen; **to ~ sb for doing sth** jdn dafür bestrafen, dass er etw getan hat
punishable ['pʌnɪʃəbl] ADJ strafbar

P

punishing [ˈpʌnɪʃɪŋ] ADJ (*fig: exercise, ordeal*) hart
punishment [ˈpʌnɪʃmənt] N (*act*) Bestrafung *f*; (*way of punishing*) Strafe *f*; **to take a lot of ~** (*fig: car, person etc*) viel abbekommen
punitive [ˈpjuːnɪtɪv] ADJ (*action*) Straf-, zur Strafe; (*measure*) (extrem) hart
punk [pʌŋk] N (*also:* **punk rocker**) Punker(in) *m(f)*; (*also:* **punk rock**) Punk *m*; (*US inf: hoodlum*) Gangster *m*
punnet [ˈpʌnɪt] N (*of raspberries etc*) Körbchen *nt*
punt¹ [pʌnt] N (*boat*) Stechkahn *m* ▶ VI mit dem Stechkahn fahren
punt² [pʌnt] (IRISH) N (*currency*) irisches Pfund *nt*
punter [ˈpʌntəʳ] (BRIT) N (*gambler*) Wetter(in) *m(f)*; **the punters** (*inf: customers*) die Leute; **the average ~** (*inf*) Otto Normalverbraucher
puny [ˈpjuːnɪ] ADJ (*person, arms etc*) schwächlich; (*efforts*) kläglich, kümmerlich
pup [pʌp] N (*young dog*) Welpe *m*, junger Hund *m*; **seal ~** Welpenjunge(s) *nt*
pupil [ˈpjuːpl] N (*Scol*) Schüler(in) *m(f)*; (*of eye*) Pupille *f*
puppet [ˈpʌpɪt] N Handpuppe *f*; (*with strings, fig: person*) Marionette *f*
puppet government N Marionettenregierung *f*
puppy [ˈpʌpɪ] N (*young dog*) Welpe *m*, junger Hund *m*
purchase [ˈpəːtʃɪs] N Kauf *m*; (*grip*) Halt *m* ▶ VT kaufen; **to get** *or* **gain (a) ~ on** (*grip*) Halt finden an *+dat*
purchase order N Bestellung *f*
purchase price N Kaufpreis *m*
purchaser [ˈpəːtʃɪsəʳ] N Käufer(in) *m(f)*
purchase tax N Kaufsteuer *f*
purchasing power [ˈpəːtʃɪsɪŋ-] N Kaufkraft *f*
pure [pjuəʳ] ADJ rein; **a ~ wool jumper** ein Pullover aus reiner Wolle; **it's laziness ~ and simple** es ist nichts als reine Faulheit
purebred [ˈpjuəbrɛd] ADJ reinrassig
puree [ˈpjʊəreɪ] N Püree *nt*
purely [ˈpjuəlɪ] ADV rein
purgatory [ˈpəːgətərɪ] N (*Rel*) das Fegefeuer; (*fig*) die Hölle
purge [pəːdʒ] N (*Pol*) Säuberung *f* ▶ VT (*Pol: organization*) säubern; (*: extremists etc*) entfernen; (*fig: thoughts, mind etc*) befreien
purification [pjuərɪfɪˈkeɪʃən] N Reinigung *f*
purify [ˈpjuərɪfaɪ] VT reinigen
purist [ˈpjuərɪst] N Purist(in) *m(f)*
puritan [ˈpjuərɪtən] N Puritaner(in) *m(f)*
puritanical [pjuərɪˈtænɪkl] ADJ puritanisch
purity [ˈpjuərɪtɪ] N Reinheit *f*
purl [pəːl] (*Knitting*) N linke Masche *f* ▶ VT links stricken
purloin [pəːˈlɔɪn] (*form*) VT entwenden
purple [ˈpəːpl] ADJ violett
purport [pəːˈpɔːt] VI: **to ~ to be/do sth** vorgeben, etw zu sein/tun
purpose [ˈpəːpəs] N (*reason*) Zweck *m*; (*aim*) Ziel *nt*, Absicht *f*; **on ~** absichtlich; **for illustrative purposes** zu Illustrationszwecken; **for all practical purposes** praktisch (gesehen); **for the purposes of this meeting** zum Zweck dieses Treffens; **to little ~** mit wenig Erfolg; **to no ~** ohne Erfolg; **a sense of ~** ein Zielbewusstsein *nt*
purpose-built [ˈpəːpəsˈbɪlt] (BRIT) ADJ speziell angefertigt, Spezial-
purposeful [ˈpəːpəsful] ADJ entschlossen
purposely [ˈpəːpəslɪ] ADV absichtlich, bewusst
purr [pəːʳ] VI (*cat*) schnurren
purse [pəːs] N (BRIT: *for money*) Geldbörse *f*, Portemonnaie *nt*; (*US: handbag*) Handtasche *f* ▶ VT (*lips*) kräuseln
purser [ˈpəːsəʳ] N (*Naut*) Zahlmeister *m*
purse-snatcher [ˈpəːssnætʃəʳ] (*US*) N Handtaschendieb *m*
pursue [pəˈsjuː] VT (*person, vehicle, plan, aim*) verfolgen; (*fig: interest etc*) nachgehen *+dat*
pursuer [pəˈsjuːəʳ] N Verfolger(in) *m(f)*
pursuit [pəˈsjuːt] N (*chase*) Verfolgung *f*; (*pastime*) Beschäftigung *f*; (*fig*): **~ of** (*of happiness etc*) Streben *nt* nach; **in ~ of** (*person, car etc*) auf der Jagd nach; (*fig: happiness etc*) im Streben nach
purveyor [pəˈveɪəʳ] (*form*) N (*of goods etc*) Lieferant *m*
pus [pʌs] N Eiter *m*
push [puʃ] N Stoß *m*, Schub *m* ▶ VT (*press*) drücken; (*shove*) schieben; (*fig: put pressure on: person*) bedrängen; (*: promote: product*) werben für; (*inf: sell: drugs*) pushen ▶ VI (*press*) drücken; (*shove*) schieben; **at the ~ of a button** auf Knopfdruck; **at a ~** (BRIT *inf*) notfalls; **to ~ a door open/shut** eine Tür auf-/zudrücken; **"~"** (*on door*) „drücken"; (*on bell*) „klingeln"; **to be pushed for time/money** (*inf*) in Zeitnot/Geldnot sein; **she is pushing fifty** (*inf*) sie geht auf die fünfzig zu; **to ~ for** (*demand*) drängen auf *+acc*
▶ **push around** VT (*bully*) herumschubsen
▶ **push aside** VT beiseiteschieben
▶ **push in** VI sich dazwischendrängeln
▶ **push off** (*inf*) VI abhauen
▶ **push on** VI (*continue*) weitermachen
▶ **push over** VT umstoßen
▶ **push through** VT (*measure etc*) durchdrücken
▶ **push up** VT (*total, prices*) hochtreiben
push-bike [ˈpuʃbaɪk] (BRIT) N Fahrrad *nt*
push-button [ˈpuʃbʌtn] ADJ (*machine, calculator*) Drucktasten-
pushchair [ˈpuʃtʃɛəʳ] (BRIT) N Sportwagen *m*
pusher [ˈpuʃəʳ] N (*drug dealer*) Pusher *m*
pushover [ˈpuʃəuvəʳ] (*inf*) N: **it's a ~** das ist ein Kinderspiel
push-up [ˈpuʃʌp] (*US*) N Liegestütz *m*
pushy [ˈpuʃɪ] (*pej*) ADJ aufdringlich
puss [pus] (*inf*) N Mieze *f*
pussy [ˈpusɪ], **pussycat** [ˈpusɪkæt] (*inf*) N Mieze(katze) *f*
put [put] (*pt, pp* **~**) VT (*thing*) tun; (*: upright*) stellen; (*: flat*) legen; (*person: in room, institution etc*) stecken; (*: in state, situation*) versetzen; (*express: idea etc*) ausdrücken; (*present: case, view*) vorbringen; (*ask: question*) stellen; (*classify*) einschätzen; (*write, type*) schreiben; **to ~ sb in a**

good/bad mood jdn gut/schlecht stimmen; **to ~ sb to bed** jdn ins Bett bringen; **to ~ sb to a lot of trouble** jdm viele Umstände machen; **how shall I ~ it?** wie soll ich es sagen *or* ausdrücken?; **to ~ a lot of time into sth** viel Zeit auf etw *acc* verwenden; **to ~ money on a horse** Geld auf ein Pferd setzen; **the cost is now ~ at 2 million pounds** die Kosten werden jetzt auf 2 Millionen Pfund geschätzt; **I ~ it to you that ...** (BRIT) ich behaupte, dass ...; **to stay ~** (an Ort und Stelle) bleiben

▸ **put about** VI (*Naut*) den Kurs ändern ▸ VT (*rumour*) verbreiten

▸ **put across** VT (*ideas etc*) verständlich machen

▸ **put around** VT = **put about**

▸ **put aside** VT (*work*) zur Seite legen; (*idea, problem*) unbeachtet lassen; (*sum of money*) zurücklegen

▸ **put away** VT (*store*) wegräumen; (*inf: consume*) verdrücken; (*save: money*) zurücklegen; (*imprison*) einsperren

▸ **put back** VT (*replace*) zurücktun; (*: upright*) zurückstellen; (*: flat*) zurücklegen; (*postpone*) verschieben; (*delay*) zurückwerfen

▸ **put by** VT (*money, supplies etc*) zurücklegen

▸ **put down** VT (*upright*) hinstellen; (*flat*) hinlegen; (*cup, glass*) absetzen; (*in writing*) aufschreiben; (*riot, rebellion*) niederschlagen; (*humiliate*) demütigen; (*kill*) töten

▸ **put down to** VT (*attribute*) zurückführen auf *+acc*

▸ **put forward** VT (*ideas etc*) vorbringen; (*watch, clock*) vorstellen; (*date, meeting*) vorverlegen

▸ **put in** VT (*application, complaint*) einreichen; (*time, effort*) investieren; (*gas, electricity etc*) installieren ▸ VI (*Naut*) einlaufen

▸ **put in for** VT FUS (*promotion*) sich bewerben um; (*leave*) beantragen

▸ **put off** VT (*delay*) verschieben; (*distract*) ablenken; **to ~ sb off sth** (*discourage*) jdn von etw abbringen

▸ **put on** VT (*clothes, brake*) anziehen; (*glasses, kettle*) aufsetzen; (*make-up, ointment etc*) auftragen; (*light, TV*) anmachen; (*play etc*) aufführen; (*record, tape, video*) auflegen; (*dinner etc*) aufsetzen; (*assume: look, behaviour etc*) annehmen; (*inf: tease*) auf den Arm nehmen; (*extra bus, train etc*) einsetzen; **to ~ on airs** sich zieren; **to ~ on weight** zunehmen

▸ **put on to** VT (*tell about*) vermitteln

▸ **put out** VT (*fire, light*) ausmachen; (*take out: rubbish*) herausbringen; (*: cat etc*) vor die Tür setzen; (*one's hand*) ausstrecken; (*story, announcement*) verbreiten; (BRIT: *dislocate: shoulder etc*) verrenken; (*inf: inconvenience*) Umstände machen *+dat* ▸ VI (*Naut*): **to ~ out to sea** in See stechen; **to ~ out from Plymouth** von Plymouth auslaufen

▸ **put through** VT (*Tel: person*) verbinden; (*: call*) durchstellen; (*plan, agreement*) durchbringen; **~ me through to Ms Blair** verbinden Sie mich mit Frau Blair

▸ **put together** VT (*furniture etc*) zusammenbauen; (*plan, campaign*) ausarbeiten; **more than the rest of them ~ together** mehr als alle anderen zusammen

▸ **put up** VT (*fence, building*) errichten; (*tent*) aufstellen; (*umbrella*) aufspannen; (*hood*) hochschlagen; (*poster, sign etc*) anbringen; (*price, cost*) erhöhen; (*accommodate*) unterbringen; **to ~ up resistance** Widerstand leisten; **to ~ up a fight** sich zur Wehr setzen; **to ~ sb up to sth** jdn zu etw anstiften; **to ~ sb up to doing sth** jdn dazu anstiften, etw zu tun; **to ~ sth up for sale** etw zum Verkauf anbieten

▸ **put upon** VT FUS: **to be ~ upon** (*imposed on*) ausgenutzt werden

▸ **put up with** VT FUS sich abfinden mit

putative ['pju:tətɪv] ADJ mutmaßlich

putrid ['pju:trɪd] ADJ (*mess, meat*) faul

putt [pʌt] N Putt *m*

putter ['pʌtə^r] N (*Golf*) Putter *m* ▸ VI (*US*) = **potter**

putting green ['pʌtɪŋ-] N kleiner Golfplatz *m* zum Putten

putty ['pʌtɪ] N Kitt *m*

put-up ['putʌp] ADJ: **a ~ job** ein abgekartetes Spiel *nt*

puzzle ['pʌzl] N (*game, toy*) Geschicklichkeitsspiel *nt*; (*mystery*) Rätsel *nt* ▸ VT verwirren ▸ VI: **to ~ over sth** sich *dat* über etw *acc* den Kopf zerbrechen; **to be puzzled as to why ...** vor einem Rätsel stehen, warum ...

puzzling ['pʌzlɪŋ] ADJ verwirrend; (*mysterious*) rätselhaft

PVC N ABBR (= *polyvinyl chloride*) PVC *nt*

Pvt. (*US*) ABBR (*Mil*) = **private**

p.w. ABBR (= *per week*) pro Woche

pygmy ['pɪgmɪ] N Pygmäe *m*

pyjamas, (*US*) **pajamas** [pə'dʒɑ:məz] NPL Pyjama *m*, Schlafanzug *m*; **a pair of ~** ein Schlafanzug

pylon ['paɪlən] N Mast *m*

pyramid ['pɪrəmɪd] N Pyramide *f*

Pyrenean [pɪrə'ni:ən] ADJ pyrenäisch

Pyrenees [pɪrə'ni:z] NPL: **the ~** die Pyrenäen *pl*

Pyrex® ['paɪrɛks] N ≈ Jenaer Glas® *nt* ▸ ADJ (*dish, bowl*) aus Jenaer Glas®

python ['paɪθən] N Pythonschlange *f*

Qq

Q, q [kju:] N (*letter*) Q *nt*, q *nt*; **Q for Queen** ≈ Q wie Quelle
Qatar [kæ'tɑ:ʳ] N Katar *nt*
QC (BRIT) N ABBR (*Law*: = *Queen's Counsel*) Kronanwalt *m*

> **QC** (kurz für Queen's Counsel, bzw. **KC** für King's Counsel) ist in Großbritannien ein hochgestellter **barrister**, der auf Empfehlung des Lordkanzlers ernannt wird und zum Zeichen seines Amtes einen seidenen Umhang trägt und daher auch als **silk** bezeichnet wird. Ein QC muss vor Gericht in Begleitung eines rangniedrigeren Anwaltes erscheinen.

QCA (BRIT) N ABBR (= *Qualifications and Curriculum Authority*) *Behörde, die in England für die Entwicklung von Lehrplänen und deren Beachtung zuständig ist*
QED ABBR (= *quod erat demonstrandum*) q. e. d.
QM N ABBR (*Mil*) = **quartermaster**
q.t. (*inf*) N ABBR (= *quiet*): **on the q.t.** heimlich
quack [kwæk] N (*of duck*) Schnattern *nt*, Quaken *nt*; (*inf, pej*: *doctor*) Quacksalber *m* ▶ VI schnattern, quaken
quad [kwɔd] ABBR = **quadrangle**; (= *quadruplet*) Vierling *m*
quadrangle ['kwɔdræŋgl] N (*courtyard*) Innenhof *m*
quadrilateral [kwɔdrɪ'lætərəl] N Viereck *nt*
quadruped ['kwɔdrupɛd] N Vierfüßer *m*
quadruple [kwɔ'dru:pl] VT vervierfachen ▶ VI sich vervierfachen
quadruplets [kwɔ'dru:plɪts] NPL Vierlinge *pl*
quagmire ['kwægmaɪəʳ] N (*also fig*) Sumpf *m*
quail [kweɪl] N Wachtel *f* ▶ VI: **he quailed at the thought/before her anger** ihm schauderte bei dem Gedanken/vor ihrem Zorn
quaint [kweɪnt] ADJ (*house, village*) malerisch; (*ideas, customs*) urig, kurios
quake [kweɪk] VI beben, zittern ▶ N = **earthquake**
Quaker ['kweɪkəʳ] N Quäker(in) *m(f)*
qualification [kwɔlɪfɪ'keɪʃən] N (*often pl*: *degree etc*) Qualifikation *f*; (*attribute*) Voraussetzung *f*; (*reservation*) Vorbehalt *m*; **what are your qualifications?** welche Qualifikationen haben Sie?
qualified ['kwɔlɪfaɪd] ADJ (*trained*: *doctor etc*) qualifiziert, ausgebildet; (*limited*: *agreement, praise*) bedingt; **to be/feel ~ to do sth** (*fit, competent*) qualifiziert sein/sich qualifiziert fühlen, etw zu tun; **it was a ~ success** es war kein voller Erfolg; **he's not ~ for the job** ihm fehlen die Qualifikationen für die Stelle
qualify ['kwɔlɪfaɪ] VT (*entitle*) qualifizieren; (*modify*: *statement*) einschränken ▶ VI (*pass examination*) sich qualifizieren; **to ~ for** (*be eligible*) die Berechtigung erlangen für; (*in competition*) sich qualifizieren für; **to ~ as an engineer** die Ausbildung zum Ingenieur abschließen
qualifying ['kwɔlɪfaɪɪŋ] ADJ: **~ exam** Auswahlprüfung *f*; **~ game** Vorrunden- *or* Qualifikationsspiel *f*; **~ group** Vorrunden- *or* Qualifikationsgruppe *f*; **~ round** Qualifikationsrunde *f*
qualitative ['kwɔlɪtətɪv] ADJ qualitativ
quality ['kwɔlɪtɪ] N Qualität *f*; (*characteristic*) Eigenschaft *f* ▶ CPD Qualitäts-; **of good/poor ~** von guter/schlechter Qualität; **~ of life** Lebensqualität *f*
quality control N Qualitätskontrolle *f*
quality papers (BRIT) NPL: **the ~** die seriösen Zeitungen *pl*

> **Quality press** bezeichnet die seriösen Tages- und Wochenzeitungen im Gegensatz zu den Massenblättern. Diese Zeitungen sind fast alle großformatig und wenden sich an den anspruchsvolleren Leser, der voll informiert sein möchte und bereit ist, für die Zeitungslektüre viel Zeit aufzuwenden. Siehe auch **tabloid press**.

qualm [kwɑ:m] N Bedenken *pl*; **to have qualms about sth** Bedenken wegen etw haben
quandary ['kwɔndrɪ] N: **to be in a ~** in einem Dilemma sein
quango ['kwæŋgəu] (BRIT) N ABBR (= *quasi-autonomous nongovernmental organization*) ≈ (regierungsunabhängige) Kommission *f*
quantifiable ['kwɔntɪfaɪəbl] ADJ quantifizierbar
quantitative ['kwɔntɪtətɪv] ADJ quantitativ
quantity ['kwɔntɪtɪ] N (*amount*) Menge *f*; **in large/small quantities** in großen/kleinen Mengen; **in ~** (*in bulk*) in großen Mengen; **an unknown ~** (*fig*) eine unbekannte Größe
quantity surveyor N Baukostenkalkulator(in) *m(f)*

quantum leap ['kwɔntəm-] N (*Phys*) Quantensprung *m*; (*fig*) Riesenschritt *m*
quarantine ['kwɔrnti:n] N Quarantäne *f*; **in ~** in Quarantäne
quark [kwɑ:k] N (*cheese*) Quark *m*; (*Phys*) Quark *nt*
quarrel ['kwɔrl] N (*argument*) Streit *m* ▸ VI sich streiten; **to have a ~ with sb** sich mit jdm streiten; **I've no ~ with him** ich habe nichts gegen ihn; **I can't ~ with that** dagegen kann ich nichts einwenden
quarrelsome ['kwɔrəlsəm] ADJ streitsüchtig
quarry ['kwɔrɪ] N (*for stone*) Steinbruch *m*; (*prey*) Beute *f* ▸ VT (*marble etc*) brechen
quart [kwɔ:t] N Quart *nt*
quarter ['kwɔ:tə^r] N Viertel *nt*; (*US: coin*) 25-Cent-Stück *nt*; (*of year*) Quartal *nt*; (*district*) Viertel *nt* ▸ VT (*divide*) vierteln; (*Mil: lodge*) einquartieren; **quarters** NPL (*Mil*) Quartier *nt*; (*also*: **living quarters**) Unterkünfte *pl*; **a ~ of an hour** eine viertel Stunde; **it's a ~ to three, it's a ~ of three** (*US*) es ist Viertel vor drei; **it's a ~ past three, it's a ~ after three** (*US*) es ist Viertel nach drei; **from all quarters** aus allen Richtungen; **at close quarters** aus unmittelbarer Nähe
quarterback ['kwɔ:təbæk] N (*American Football*) Quarterback *m*
quarterdeck ['kwɔ:tədɛk] N (*Naut*) Quarterdeck *nt*
quarterfinal ['kwɔ:tə'faɪnl] N Viertelfinale *nt*
quarterly ['kwɔ:təlɪ] ADJ, ADV vierteljährlich ▸ N Vierteljahresschrift *f*
quartermaster ['kwɔ:təmɑ:stə^r] N (*Mil*) Quartiermeister *m*
quartet [kwɔ:'tɛt] N (*Mus*) Quartett *nt*
quarto ['kwɔ:təu] N (*size of paper*) Quartformat *nt*; (*book*) im Quartformat
quartz [kwɔ:ts] N Quarz *m* ▸ CPD (*watch, clock*) Quarz-
quash [kwɔʃ] VT (*verdict*) aufheben
quasi- ['kweɪzaɪ] PREF quasi-
quaver ['kweɪvə^r] N (*BRIT Mus*) Achtelnote *f* ▸ VI (*voice*) beben, zittern
quay [ki:] N Kai *m*
quayside ['ki:saɪd] N Kai *m*
queasiness ['kwi:zɪnɪs] N Übelkeit *f*
queasy ['kwi:zɪ] ADJ (*nauseous*) übel; **I feel ~** mir ist übel *or* schlecht
Quebec [kwɪ'bɛk] N Quebec *nt*
queen [kwi:n] N (*also Zool*) Königin *f*; (*Cards, Chess*) Dame *f*
queen mother N Königinmutter *f*
Queen's speech (BRIT) N ≈ Regierungserklärung *f*

> **Queen's Speech** (bzw. **King's Speech**) ist eine vom britischen Monarchen bei der alljährlichen feierlichen Parlamentseröffnung im Oberhaus vor dem versammelten Ober- und Unterhaus verlesene Rede. Sie wird vom Premierminister in Zusammenarbeit mit dem Kabinett verfasst und enthält die Regierungserklärung.

queer [kwɪə^r] ADJ (*odd*) sonderbar, seltsam ▸ N (*inf!, pej: male homosexual*) Schwule(r) *m*; **I feel ~** (BRIT: *unwell*) mir ist ganz komisch
quell [kwɛl] VT (*riot*) niederschlagen; (*fears*) überwinden
quench [kwɛntʃ] VT: **to ~ one's thirst** seinen Durst stillen
querulous ['kwɛruləs] ADJ nörglerisch
query ['kwɪərɪ] N Anfrage *f* ▸ VT (*check*) nachfragen bezüglich *+gen*; (*express doubt about*) bezweifeln
quest [kwɛst] N Suche *f*
question ['kwɛstʃən] N Frage *f* ▸ VT (*interrogate*) befragen; (*doubt*) bezweifeln; **to ask sb a ~, put a ~ to sb** jdm eine Frage stellen; **to bring** *or* **call sth into ~** etw infrage stellen; **the ~ is ...** die Frage ist ...; **there's no ~ of him playing for England** es ist ausgeschlossen, dass er für England spielt; **the person/night in ~** die fragliche Person/Nacht; **to be beyond ~** außer Frage stehen; **to be out of the ~** nicht infrage kommen
questionable ['kwɛstʃənəbl] ADJ fraglich
questioner ['kwɛstʃənə^r] N Fragesteller(in) *m(f)*
questioning ['kwɛstʃənɪŋ] ADJ (*look*) fragend; (*mind*) forschend ▸ N (*Police*) Vernehmung *f*
question mark N Fragezeichen *nt*
questionnaire [kwɛstʃə'nɛə^r] N Fragebogen *m*
queue [kju:] (BRIT) N Schlange *f* ▸ VI (*also*: **queue up**) Schlange stehen
quibble ['kwɪbl] VI: **to ~ about** *or* **over** sich streiten über *+acc*; **to ~ with** herumnörgeln an *+dat* ▸ N Krittelei *f*
quiche [ki:ʃ] N Quiche *f*
quick [kwɪk] ADJ schnell; (*mind, wit*) wach; (*look, visit*) flüchtig ▸ ADV schnell ▸ N: **to cut sb to the ~** (*fig*) jdn tief verletzen; **be ~!** mach schnell!; **to be ~ to act** schnell handeln; **she was ~ to see that ...** sie begriff schnell, dass ...; **she has a ~ temper** sie wird leicht hitzig
quicken ['kwɪkən] VT beschleunigen ▸ VI schneller werden, sich beschleunigen
quick-fire ['kwɪkfaɪə^r] ADJ (*questions*) wie aus der Pistole
quick fix N Sofortlösung *f*
quicklime ['kwɪklaɪm] N ungelöschter Kalk *m*
quickly ['kwɪklɪ] ADV schnell
quickness ['kwɪknɪs] N Schnelligkeit *f*; **~ of mind** Scharfsinn *m*
quicksand ['kwɪksænd] N Treibsand *m*
quickstep ['kwɪkstɛp] N Quickstepp *m*
quick-tempered [kwɪk'tɛmpəd] ADJ hitzig, leicht erregbar
quick-witted [kwɪk'wɪtɪd] ADJ schlagfertig
quid [kwɪd] (BRIT *inf*) N INV Pfund *nt*
quid pro quo ['kwɪdprəu'kwəu] N Gegenleistung *f*
quiet ['kwaɪət] ADJ leise; (*place*) ruhig, still; (*silent, reserved*) still; (*business, day*) ruhig; (*without fuss etc: wedding*) in kleinem Rahmen ▸ N (*peacefulness*) Stille *f*, Ruhe *f*; (*silence*) Ruhe *f* ▸ VT, VI (*US*) = **quieten**; **keep** *or* **be ~!** sei still!; **I'll have a ~ word with him** ich werde mal unter

vier Augen mit ihm reden; **on the ~** (*in secret*) heimlich
quieten ['kwaɪətn] (Brit) vi (*also*: **quieten down**) ruhiger werden ▸ vt (*person, animal*: *also*: **quieten down**) beruhigen
quietly ['kwaɪətlɪ] adv leise; (*silently*) still; (*calmly*) ruhig; **~ confident** insgeheim sicher
quietness ['kwaɪətnɪs] n (*peacefulness*) Ruhe *f*; (*silence*) Stille *f*
quill [kwɪl] n (*pen*) Feder *f*; (*of porcupine*) Stachel *m*
quilt [kwɪlt] n Decke *f*; (*also*: **continental quilt**) Federbett *nt*
quin [kwɪn] (Brit) n abbr (= *quintuplet*) Fünfling *m*
quince [kwɪns] n Quitte *f*
quinine [kwɪ'ni:n] n Chinin *nt*
quintet [kwɪn'tɛt] n (*Mus*) Quintett *nt*
quintuplets [kwɪn'tju:plɪts] npl Fünflinge *pl*
quip [kwɪp] n witzige *or* geistreiche Bemerkung *f* ▸ vt witzeln
quire ['kwaɪəʳ] n (*of paper*) 24 Bogen Papier
quirk [kwə:k] n Marotte *f*; **a ~ of fate** eine Laune des Schicksals
quit [kwɪt] (*pt, pp* **~** *or* **quitted**) vt (*smoking*) aufgeben; (*job*) kündigen; (*premises*) verlassen ▸ vi (*give up*) aufgeben; (*resign*) kündigen; **to ~ doing sth** aufhören, etw zu tun; **~ stalling!** (*US inf*) weichen Sie nicht ständig aus!; **notice to ~** (Brit) Kündigung *f*
quite [kwaɪt] adv (*rather*) ziemlich; (*entirely*) ganz; **not ~** nicht ganz; **I ~ like it** ich mag es ganz gern; **I ~ understand** ich verstehe; **I don't ~ remember** ich erinnere mich nicht genau; **not ~ as many as the last time** nicht ganz so viele wie das letzte Mal; **that meal was ~ something!** das Essen konnte sich sehen lassen!; **it was ~ a sight** das war vielleicht ein Anblick; **~ a few of them** eine ganze Reihe von Ihnen; **~ (so)!** ganz recht!
quits [kwɪts] adj: **we're ~** wir sind quitt; **let's call it ~** lassen wirs dabei
quiver ['kwɪvəʳ] vi zittern
quiz [kwɪz] n (*game*) Quiz *nt* ▸ vt (*question*) befragen
quizzical ['kwɪzɪkl] adj (*look, smile*) wissend
quoits [kwɔɪts] npl (*game*) *Wurfspiel mit Ringen*
quorum ['kwɔ:rəm] n Quorum *nt*
quota ['kwəutə] n (*allowance*) Quote *f*
quotation [kwəu'teɪʃən] n (*from book etc*) Zitat *nt*; (*estimate*) Preisangabe *f*; (Comm) Kostenvoranschlag *m*
quotation marks npl Anführungszeichen *pl*
quote [kwəut] n (*from book etc*) Zitat *nt*; (*estimate*) Kostenvoranschlag *m* ▸ vt zitieren; (*fact, example*) anführen; (*price*) nennen; **quotes** npl (*quotation marks*) Anführungszeichen *pl*; **in quotes** in Anführungszeichen; **the figure quoted for the repairs** die für die Reparatur genannte Summe; **~ … unquote** Zitat Anfang … Zitat Ende
quotient ['kwəuʃənt] n Quotient *m*
qv abbr (= *quod vide*) s.d.
qwerty keyboard ['kwə:tɪ-] n Qwerty-Tastatur *f*

Rr

R¹, r [ɑːʳ] N *(letter)* R *nt*, r *nt*; **R for Robert, R for Roger** *(US)* ≈ R wie Richard
R² [ɑːʳ] ABBR *(= Réaumur (scale))* R; *(US Cine: = restricted) Klassifikation für nicht jugendfreie Filme*
R. ABBR *(= right)* r.; = **river**; *(US Pol)* = **republican**; *(BRIT: = Rex) König; (= Regina) Königin*
RA ABBR *(Mil)* = **rear admiral** ▸ N ABBR *(BRIT: = Royal Academy) Gesellschaft zur Förderung der Künste; (= Royal Academician) Mitglied der Royal Academy*
RAAF N ABBR *(Mil: = Royal Australian Air Force)* australische Luftwaffe *f*
Rabat [rəˈbɑːt] N Rabat *nt*
rabbi [ˈræbaɪ] N Rabbi *m*
rabbit [ˈræbɪt] N Kaninchen *nt* ▸ VI *(BRIT inf: also:* **rabbit on***)* quatschen, schwafeln
rabbit hole N Kaninchenbau *m*
rabbit hutch N Kaninchenstall *m*
rabble [ˈræbl] *(pej)* N Pöbel *m*
rabid [ˈræbɪd] ADJ *(animal)* tollwütig; *(fig: fanatical)* fanatisch
rabies [ˈreɪbiːz] N Tollwut *f*
RAC *(BRIT)* N ABBR *(= Royal Automobile Club) Autofahrerorganisation*, ≈ ADAC *m*
raccoon, racoon [rəˈkuːn] N Waschbär *m*
race [reɪs] N *(species)* Rasse *f*; *(competition)* Rennen *nt*; *(for power, control)* Wettlauf *m* ▸ VT *(horse, pigeon)* an Wettbewerben teilnehmen lassen; *(car etc)* ins Rennen schicken; *(person)* um die Wette laufen mit ▸ VI *(compete)* antreten; *(hurry)* rennen; *(pulse, heart)* rasen; *(engine)* durchdrehen; **the human ~** die Menschheit; **a ~ against time** ein Wettlauf mit der Zeit; **he raced across the road** er raste über die Straße; **to ~ in/out** hinein-/hinausstürzen
race car *(US)* N = **racing car**
race car driver *(US)* N = **racing driver**
racecourse [ˈreɪskɔːs] N Rennbahn *f*
racehorse [ˈreɪshɔːs] N Rennpferd *nt*
race meeting N Rennveranstaltung *f*
race relations NPL Beziehungen *pl* zwischen den Rassen
racetrack [ˈreɪstræk] N Rennbahn *f*; *(US)* = **racecourse**
racial [ˈreɪʃl] ADJ Rassen-
racialism [ˈreɪʃlɪzəm] N Rassismus *m*
racialist [ˈreɪʃlɪst] ADJ rassistisch ▸ N *(pej)* Rassist(in) *m(f)*
racing [ˈreɪsɪŋ] N *(also:* **horse racing***)* Pferderennen *nt*; *(also:* **motor racing***)* Rennsport *m*
racing car *(BRIT)* N Rennwagen *m*
racing driver *(BRIT)* N Rennfahrer(in) *m(f)*
racism [ˈreɪsɪzəm] N Rassismus *m*
racist [ˈreɪsɪst] ADJ rassistisch ▸ N *(pej)* Rassist(in) *m(f)*
rack [ræk] N *(also:* **luggage rack***)* Gepäckablage *f*; *(also:* **roof rack***)* Dachgepäckträger *m*; *(for dresses etc)* Ständer *m*; *(for dishes)* Gestell *nt* ▸ VT: **racked by** *(pain etc)* gemartert von; **magazine/toast ~** Zeitungs-/Toastständer *m*; **to ~ one's brains** sich *dat* den Kopf zerbrechen; **to go to ~ and ruin** *(building)* zerfallen; *(business, country)* herunterkommen
racket [ˈrækɪt] N *(for tennis etc)* Schläger *m*; *(noise)* Krach *m*, Radau *m*; *(swindle)* Schwindel *m*
racketeer [rækɪˈtɪəʳ] *(esp US)* N Gangster *m*
racquet [ˈrækɪt] N *(for tennis etc)* Schläger *m*
racy [ˈreɪsɪ] ADJ *(book, story)* rasant
RADA [rɑːdə] *(BRIT)* N ABBR *(= Royal Academy of Dramatic Art) Schauspielschule*
radar [ˈreɪdɑːʳ] N Radar *m or nt* ▸ CPD Radar-
radar trap N Radarfalle *f*
radial [ˈreɪdɪəl] ADJ *(roads)* strahlenförmig verlaufend; *(pattern)* strahlenförmig ▸ N *(also:* **radial tyre***)* Gürtelreifen *m*
radiance [ˈreɪdɪəns] N Glanz *m*
radiant [ˈreɪdɪənt] ADJ strahlend; *(Phys: heat)* Strahlungs-
radiate [ˈreɪdɪeɪt] VT *(lit, fig)* ausstrahlen ▸ VI *(lines, roads)* strahlenförmig verlaufen
radiation [reɪdɪˈeɪʃən] N *(radioactivity)* radioaktive Strahlung *f*; *(from sun etc)* Strahlung *f*
radiation sickness N Strahlenkrankheit *f*
radiator [ˈreɪdɪeɪtəʳ] N *(heater)* Heizkörper *m*; *(Aut)* Kühler *m*
radiator cap N *(Aut)* Kühlerdeckel *m*
radiator grill N *(Aut)* Kühlergrill *m*
radical [ˈrædɪkl] ADJ radikal ▸ N *(person)* Radikale(r) *f(m)*
radii [ˈreɪdɪaɪ] NPL *of* **radius**
radio [ˈreɪdɪəu] N *(broadcasting)* Radio *nt*, Rundfunk *m*; *(device: for receiving broadcasts)*

radio – raise

Radio *nt*; (*: for transmitting and receiving*) Funkgerät *nt* ▸ VI: **to ~ to sb** mit jdm per Funk sprechen ▸ VT (*person*) per Funk verständigen; (*message, position*) per Funk durchgeben; **on the ~** im Radio

radio... ['reɪdɪəu] PREF Radio..., radio...

radioactive ['reɪdɪəu'æktɪv] ADJ radioaktiv

radioactivity ['reɪdɪəuæk'tɪvɪtɪ] N Radioaktivität *f*

radio announcer N Rundfunksprecher(in) *m(f)*

radio-controlled ['reɪdɪəukən'trəuld] ADJ ferngesteuert

radiographer [reɪdɪ'ɔgrəfəʳ] N Röntgenologe *m*, Röntgenologin *f*

radiography [reɪdɪ'ɔgrəfɪ] N Röntgenografie *f*

radiologist [reɪdɪ'ɔlədʒɪst] N Radiologe *m*, Radiologin *f*

radiology [reɪdɪ'ɔlədʒɪ] N Radiologie *f*

radio station N Radiosender *m*

radio taxi N Funktaxi *nt*

radiotelephone ['reɪdɪəu'tɛlɪfəun] N Funksprechgerät *nt*

radio telescope N Radioteleskop *nt*

radiotherapist ['reɪdɪəu'θɛrəpɪst] N Strahlentherapeut(in) *m(f)*

radiotherapy ['reɪdɪəu'θɛrəpɪ] N Strahlentherapie *f*

radish ['rædɪʃ] N Radieschen *nt*; (*long white variety*) Rettich *m*

radium ['reɪdɪəm] N Radium *nt*

radius ['reɪdɪəs] (*pl* **radii**) N Radius *m*; (*area*) Umkreis *m*; **within a ~ of 50 miles** in einem Umkreis von 50 Meilen

RAF (BRIT) N ABBR = **Royal Air Force**

raffia ['ræfɪə] N Bast *m*

raffish ['ræfɪʃ] ADJ (*person*) verwegen; (*place*) verkommen

raffle ['ræfl] N Verlosung *f*, Tombola *f* ▸ VT (*prize*) verlosen; **~ ticket** Los *nt*

raft [rɑ:ft] N Floß *nt*; (*also*: **life raft**) Rettungsfloß *nt*

rafter ['rɑ:ftəʳ] N Dachsparren *m*

rag [ræg] N (*piece of cloth*) Lappen *m*; (*torn cloth*) Fetzen *m*; (*pej: newspaper*) Käseblatt *nt*; (BRIT *Univ*) *studentische Wohltätigkeitsveranstaltung* ▸ VT (BRIT: *tease*) aufziehen; **rags** NPL (*torn clothes*) Lumpen *pl*; **in rags** (*person*) zerlumpt; **his was a rags-to-riches story** er brachte es vom Tellerwäscher zum Millionär

rag-and-bone man [rægən'bəun-] (BRIT) N (*irreg*) Lumpensammler *m*

ragbag ['rægbæg] N (*assortment*) Sammelsurium *nt*

> **Rag Day/Week** heißt der Tag bzw. die Woche, wenn Studenten Geld für wohltätige Zwecke sammeln. Diverse gesponserte Aktionen wie Volksläufe, Straßentheater und Kneipentouren werden zur Unterhaltung der Studenten und der Bevölkerung organisiert. Studentenzeitschriften mit schlüpfrigen Witzen werden auf der Straße verkauft, und fast alle Universitäten und Colleges halten einen Ball ab. Der Erlös aller Veranstaltungen fließt Wohltätigkeitsorganisationen zu.

rag doll N Stoffpuppe *f*

rage [reɪdʒ] N (*fury*) Wut *f*, Zorn *m* ▸ VI toben, wüten; **it's all the ~** (*fashionable*) es ist der letzte Schrei; **to fly into a ~** einen Wutanfall bekommen

ragged ['rægɪd] ADJ (*jagged*) zackig; (*clothes, person*) zerlumpt; (*beard*) ausgefranst

raging ['reɪdʒɪŋ] ADJ (*sea, storm, torrent*) tobend, tosend; (*fever*) heftig; (*thirst*) brennend; (*toothache*) rasend

rag trade (*inf*) N: **the ~** die Modebranche *f*

raid [reɪd] N (*Mil*) Angriff *m*, Überfall *m*; (*by police*) Razzia *f*; (*by criminal: forcefully*) Überfall *m*; (*: secretly*) Einbruch *m* ▸ VT (*Mil*) angreifen, überfallen; (*police*) stürmen; (*criminal: forcefully*) überfallen; (*: secretly*) einbrechen in *+acc*

rail [reɪl] N Geländer *nt*; (*on deck of ship*) Reling *f*; **rails** NPL (*for train*) Schienen *pl*; **by ~** mit der Bahn

railcard ['reɪlkɑ:d] (BRIT) N (*for young people*) ≈ Juniorenpass *m*; (*for pensioners*) ≈ Seniorenpass *m*

railing ['reɪlɪŋ] N, **railings** ['reɪlɪŋz] NPL (*fence*) Zaun *m*

railroad ['reɪlrəud] (US) N = **railway**

railway ['reɪlweɪ] (BRIT) N Eisenbahn *f*; (*track*) Gleis *nt*; (*company*) Bahn *f*

railway engine (BRIT) N Lokomotive *f*

railway line (BRIT) N Bahnlinie *f*; (*track*) Gleis *nt*

railwayman ['reɪlweɪmən] (BRIT) N (*irreg*) Eisenbahner *m*

railway station (BRIT) N Bahnhof *m*

rain [reɪn] N Regen *m* ▸ VI regnen; **in the ~** im Regen; **as right as ~** voll auf der Höhe; **it's raining** es regnet; **it's raining cats and dogs** es regnet in Strömen

rainbow ['reɪnbəu] N Regenbogen *m*

rainbow family N *gleichgeschlechtliches Paar mit Kind/Kindern*, Regenbogenfamilie *f*

rainbow flag N Regenbogenfahne *f or* -flagge *f*

rain check (US) N: **to take a ~ on sth** sich *dat* etw noch einmal überlegen

raincoat ['reɪnkəut] N Regenmantel *m*

raindrop ['reɪndrɔp] N Regentropfen *m*

rainfall ['reɪnfɔ:l] N Niederschlag *m*

rainforest ['reɪnfɔrɪst] N Regenwald *m*

rainproof ['reɪnpru:f] ADJ wasserfest

rainstorm ['reɪnstɔ:m] N schwere Regenfälle *pl*

rainwater ['reɪnwɔ:təʳ] N Regenwasser *nt*

rainy ['reɪnɪ] ADJ (*day*) regnerisch, verregnet; (*area*) regenreich; **~ season** Regenzeit *f*; **to save sth for a ~ day** etw für schlechte Zeiten aufheben

raise [reɪz] N (*pay rise*) Gehaltserhöhung *f* ▸ VT (*lift: hand*) hochheben; (*: window*) hochziehen; (*siege*) beenden; (*embargo*) aufheben; (*increase*) erhöhen; (*improve*) verbessern; (*question etc*) zur Sprache bringen; (*doubts etc*) vorbringen; (*child, cattle*) aufziehen; (*crop*) anbauen; (*army*) aufstellen; (*funds*) aufbringen; (*loan*) aufnehmen; **to ~ a glass to sb/sth** das Glas auf jdn/etw erheben; **to ~ one's voice** die Stimme erheben; **to ~ sb's hopes** jdm Hoffnungen machen; **to ~ a laugh/smile** Gelächter/ein Lächeln hervorrufen; **this raises the question ...** das wirft die Frage auf ...

raisin ['reɪzn] N Rosine *f*

Raj [rɑːdʒ] N: **the ~** *britische Regierung in Indien vor 1947*

rajah ['rɑːdʒə] N Radscha *m*

rake [reɪk] N Harke *f*; (*old: person*) Schwerenöter *m* ▸ VT harken; (*light, gun: area*) bestreichen; **he's raking it in** (*inf*) er scheffelt das Geld nur so

rake-off ['reɪkɔf] (*inf*) N Anteil *m*

rally ['rælɪ] N (*Pol etc*) Kundgebung *f*; (*Aut*) Rallye *f*; (*Tennis etc*) Ballwechsel *m* ▸ VT (*support*) sammeln ▸ VI (*sick person, Stock Exchange*) sich erholen
▸ **rally round** VI sich zusammentun ▸ VT FUS zu Hilfe kommen *+dat*

rallying point ['rælɪɪŋ-] N Sammelstelle *f*

RAM [ræm] N ABBR (*Comput: = random access memory*) RAM

ram [ræm] N Widder *m* ▸ VT rammen

ramble ['ræmbl] N Wanderung *f* ▸ VI wandern; (*talk: also:* **ramble on**) schwafeln

rambler ['ræmblə^r] N Wanderer *m*, Wanderin *f*; (*Bot*) Kletterrose *f*

rambling ['ræmblɪŋ] ADJ (*speech, letter*) weitschweifig; (*house*) weitläufig; (*Bot*) rankend, Kletter-

rambunctious [ræm'bʌŋkʃəs] (*US*) ADJ = **rumbustious**

RAMC (BRIT) N ABBR (= *Royal Army Medical Corps*) *Verband zur Versorgung der Armee mit Stabsärzten und Sanitätern*

ramifications [ræmɪfɪ'keɪʃənz] NPL Auswirkungen *pl*

ramp [ræmp] N Rampe *f*; (*in garage*) Hebebühne *f*; **on ~** (*US Aut*) Auffahrt *f*; **off ~** (*US Aut*) Ausfahrt *f*

rampage [ræm'peɪdʒ] N: **to be/go on the ~** randalieren ▸ VI: **they went rampaging through the town** sie zogen randalierend durch die Stadt

rampant ['ræmpənt] ADJ: **to be ~** (*crime, disease etc*) wild wuchern

rampart ['ræmpɑːt] N Schutzwall *m*

ram raiding [-reɪdɪŋ] N *Einbruchdiebstahl, wobei die Diebe mit einem Wagen in die Schaufensterfront eines Ladens eindringen*

ramshackle ['ræmʃækl] ADJ (*house*) baufällig; (*cart*) klapprig; (*table*) altersschwach

RAN N ABBR (= *Royal Australian Navy*) australische Marine *f*

ran [ræn] PT *of* **run**

ranch [rɑːntʃ] N Ranch *f*

rancher ['rɑːntʃə^r] N Rancher(in) *m(f)*; (*worker*) Farmhelfer(in) *m(f)*

rancid ['rænsɪd] ADJ ranzig

rancour, (*US*) **rancor** ['ræŋkə^r] N Verbitterung *f*

R & B N ABBR (= *rhythm and blues*) R & B

R & D N ABBR = **research and development**

random ['rændəm] ADJ (*arrangement*) willkürlich; (*selection*) zufällig; (*Comput*) wahlfrei; (*Math*) Zufalls- ▸ N: **at ~** aufs Geratewohl

random access N (*Comput*) wahlfreier Zugriff *m*

random access memory N (*Comput*) Schreib-Lese-Speicher *m*

R & R (*US*) N ABBR (*Mil: = rest and recreation*) Urlaub *m*

randy ['rændɪ] (BRIT *inf*) ADJ geil, scharf

rang [ræŋ] PT *of* **ring**

range [reɪndʒ] N (*of mountains*) Kette *f*; (*of missile*) Reichweite *f*; (*of voice*) Umfang *m*; (*series*) Reihe *f*; (*of products*) Auswahl *f*; (*Mil: also:* **rifle range**) Schießstand *m*; (*also:* **kitchen range**) Herd *m* ▸ VT (*place in a line*) anordnen ▸ VI: **to ~ over** (*extend*) sich erstrecken über *+acc*; **price ~** Preisspanne *f*; **do you have anything else in this price ~?** haben Sie noch etwas anderes in dieser Preisklasse?; **within (firing) ~** in Schussweite; **at close ~** aus unmittelbarer Entfernung; **ranged left/right** (*text*) links-/rechtsbündig; **to ~ from ... to ...** sich zwischen ... und ... bewegen

ranger ['reɪndʒə^r] N Förster(in) *m(f)*

Rangoon [ræŋ'guːn] N Rangun *nt*

rank [ræŋk] N (*row*) Reihe *f*; (*Mil*) Rang *m*; (*social class*) Schicht *f*; (BRIT: *also:* **taxi rank**) Taxistand *m* ▸ VI: **to ~ as/among** zählen zu ▸ VT: **he is ranked third in the world** er steht weltweit an dritter Stelle ▸ ADJ (*stinking*) stinkend; (*sheer: hypocrisy etc*) rein; **the ranks** NPL (*Mil*) die Mannschaften *pl*; **the ~ and file** (*ordinary members*) die Basis *f*; **to close ranks** (*Mil, fig*) die Reihen schließen

rankle ['ræŋkl] VI (*insult*) nachwirken; **to ~ with sb** jdn wurmen

rank outsider N totaler Außenseiter *m*, totale Außenseiterin *f*

ransack ['rænsæk] VT (*search*) durchwühlen; (*plunder*) plündern

ransom ['rænsəm] N (*money*) Lösegeld *nt*; **to hold sb to ~** (*hostage*) jdn als Geisel halten; (*fig*) jdn erpressen

rant [rænt] VI schimpfen, wettern; **to ~ and rave** herumwettern

ranting ['ræntɪŋ] N Geschimpfe *nt*

rap [ræp] VI klopfen ▸ VT: **to ~ sb's knuckles** jdm auf die Finger klopfen ▸ N (*at door*) Klopfen *nt*; (*also:* **rap music**) Rap *m*

rape [reɪp] N Vergewaltigung *f*; (*Bot*) Raps *m* ▸ VT vergewaltigen

rape oil, rapeseed oil ['reɪpsiːd-] N Rapsöl *nt*

rapid ['ræpɪd] ADJ schnell; (*growth, change*) schnell, rapide

rapidity [rə'pɪdɪtɪ] N Schnelligkeit *f*

rapidly ['ræpɪdlɪ] ADV schnell; (*grow, change*) schnell, rapide

rapids ['ræpɪdz] NPL Stromschnellen *pl*

rapist ['reɪpɪst] N Vergewaltiger *m*

rapport [ræ'pɔː^r] N enges Verhältnis *nt*

r

rapprochement [ræ'prɔʃmɑ̃:ŋ] N Annäherung *f*
rapt [ræpt] ADJ (*attention*) gespannt; **to be ~ in thought** in Gedanken versunken sein
rapture ['ræptʃəʳ] N Entzücken *nt*; **to go into raptures over** ins Schwärmen geraten über *+acc*
rapturous ['ræptʃərəs] ADJ (*applause, welcome*) stürmisch
rare [rɛəʳ] ADJ selten; (*steak*) nur angebraten, englisch (gebraten); **it is ~ to find that ...** es kommt nur selten vor, dass ...
rarebit ['rɛəbɪt] N *see* **Welsh rarebit**
rarefied ['rɛərɪfaɪd] ADJ (*air, atmosphere*) dünn; (*fig*) exklusiv
rarely ['rɛəlɪ] ADV selten
raring ['rɛərɪŋ] ADJ: **~ to go** (*inf*) in den Startlöchern
rarity ['rɛərɪtɪ] N Seltenheit *f*
rascal ['rɑ:skl] N (*child*) Frechdachs *m*; (*rogue*) Schurke *m*
rash [ræʃ] ADJ (*person*) unbesonnen; (*promise, act*) übereilt ▸ N (*Med*) Ausschlag *m*; (*of events etc*) Flut *f*; **to come out in a ~** einen Ausschlag bekommen
rasher ['ræʃəʳ] N (*of bacon*) Scheibe *f*
rashly ['ræʃlɪ] ADV (*promise etc*) voreilig
rasp [rɑ:sp] N (*tool*) Raspel *f*; (*sound*) Kratzen *nt* ▸ VT, VI krächzen
raspberry ['rɑ:zbərɪ] N Himbeere *f*; **~ bush** Himbeerstrauch *m*; **to blow a ~** (*inf*) verächtlich schnauben
rasping ['rɑ:spɪŋ] ADJ: **a ~ noise** ein kratzendes Geräusch
Rastafarian N Rastafarier *m*
rat [ræt] N Ratte *f*
ratable ['reɪtəbl] ADJ = **rateable**
ratchet ['rætʃɪt] N Sperrklinke *f*; **~ wheel** Sperrrad *nt*
rate [reɪt] N (*speed: of change etc*) Tempo *nt*; (*of inflation, unemployment etc*) Rate *f*; (*of interest, taxation*) Satz *m*; (*price*) Preis *m* ▸ VT einschätzen; **rates** NPL (BRIT: *property tax*) Kommunalabgaben *pl*; **at a ~ of 60 kph** mit einem Tempo von 60 km/h; **~ of growth** (*Econ*) Wachstumsrate *f*; **~ of return** (*Fin*) Rendite *f*; **pulse ~** Pulszahl *f*; **at this/that ~** wenn es so weitergeht; **at any ~** auf jeden Fall; **to ~ sb/sth as** jdn/etw einschätzen als; **to ~ sb/sth among** jdn/etw zählen zu; **to ~ sb/sth highly** jdn/etw hoch einschätzen
rateable ['reɪtəbl] ADJ: **~ value** (BRIT) steuerbarer Wert *m*
ratepayer ['reɪtpeɪəʳ] (BRIT) N Steuerzahler(in) *m(f)*
rather ['rɑ:ðəʳ] ADV (*somewhat*) etwas; (*very*) ziemlich; **~ a lot** ziemlich *or* recht viel; **I would ~ go** ich würde lieber gehen; **~ than** (*instead of*) anstelle von; **or ~** (*more accurately*) oder vielmehr; **I'd ~ not say** das möchte ich lieber nicht sagen; **I ~ think he won't come** ich glaube eher, dass er nicht kommt
ratification [rætɪfɪ'keɪʃən] N Ratifikation *f*
ratify ['rætɪfaɪ] VT (*treaty etc*) ratifizieren
rating ['reɪtɪŋ] N (*score*) Rate *f*; (*assessment*) Beurteilung *f*; (BRIT *Naut: sailor*) Matrose *m*; **ratings** NPL (*Radio, TV*) Einschaltquote *f*; **ratings hit** Quotenhit *m*
ratio ['reɪʃɪəu] N Verhältnis *nt*; **a ~ of 5 to 1** ein Verhältnis von 5 zu 1
ration ['ræʃən] N Ration *f* ▸ VT rationieren; **rations** NPL (*Mil*) Rationen *pl*
rational ['ræʃənl] ADJ rational, vernünftig
rationale [ræʃə'nɑ:l] N Grundlage *f*
rationalization [ræʃnəlaɪ'zeɪʃən] N (*justification*) Rechtfertigung *f*; (*of company, system*) Rationalisierung *f*
rationalize ['ræʃnəlaɪz] VT rechtfertigen, rationalisieren
rationally ['ræʃnəlɪ] ADV vernünftig, rational
rationing ['ræʃnɪŋ] N Rationierung *f*
ratpack (BRIT *inf*) N (*reporters*) Pressemeute *f*
rat poison N Rattengift *nt*
rat race N: **the ~** der ständige *or* tägliche Konkurrenzkampf *m*
rattan [ræ'tæn] N Rattan *nt*, Peddigrohr *nt*
rattle ['rætl] N (*of door, window, snake*) Klappern *nt*; (*of train, car etc*) Rattern *nt*; (*of chain*) Rasseln *nt*; (*toy*) Rassel *f* ▸ VI (*chains*) rasseln; (*windows*) klappern; (*bottles*) klirren ▸ VT (*shake noisily*) rütteln an *+dat*; (*fig: unsettle*) nervös machen; **to ~ along** (*car, bus*) dahinrattern
rattlesnake ['rætlsneɪk] N Klapperschlange *f*
ratty ['rætɪ] (*inf*) ADJ gereizt
raucous ['rɔ:kəs] ADJ (*voice etc*) rau
raucously ['rɔ:kəslɪ] ADV rau
raunchy ['rɔ:ntʃɪ] ADJ (*voice, song*) lüstern, geil
ravage ['rævɪdʒ] VT verwüsten
ravages ['rævɪdʒɪz] NPL (*of war*) Verwüstungen *pl*; (*of weather*) zerstörende Auswirkungen *pl*; (*of time*) Spuren *pl*
rave [reɪv] VI (*in anger*) toben ▸ ADJ (*inf: review*) glänzend; (*scene, culture*) Rave- ▸ N (BRIT *inf: party*) Rave *m*, Fete *f*
▸ **rave about** VT schwärmen von
raven ['reɪvən] N Rabe *m*
ravenous ['rævənəs] ADJ (*person*) ausgehungert; (*appetite*) unersättlich
ravine [rə'vi:n] N Schlucht *f*
raving ['reɪvɪŋ] ADJ: **a ~ lunatic** ein total verrückter Typ
ravings ['reɪvɪŋz] NPL Fantastereien *pl*
ravioli [rævɪ'əulɪ] N Ravioli *pl*
ravishing ['rævɪʃɪŋ] ADJ hinreißend
raw [rɔ:] ADJ roh; (*sore*) wund; (*inexperienced*) unerfahren; (*weather, day*) rau; **to get a ~ deal** ungerecht behandelt werden
Rawalpindi [rɔ:l'pɪndɪ] N Rawalpindi *nt*
raw material N Rohmaterial *nt*
ray [reɪ] N Strahl *m*; **~ of hope** Hoffnungsschimmer *m*
rayon ['reɪɔn] N Reyon *nt*
raze [reɪz] VT (*also*: **to raze to the ground**) dem Erdboden gleichmachen
razor ['reɪzəʳ] N Rasierapparat *m*; (*open razor*) Rasiermesser *nt*
razor blade N Rasierklinge *f*

razzle ['ræzl] (BRIT *inf*) N: **to be/go on the ~** einen draufmachen

razzmatazz ['ræzmə'tæz] (*inf*) N Trubel *m*

RC ABBR (= *Roman Catholic*) r.-k.

RCAF N ABBR (= *Royal Canadian Air Force*) kanadische Luftwaffe *f*

RCMP N ABBR (= *Royal Canadian Mounted Police*) *kanadische berittene Polizei*

RCN N ABBR (= *Royal Canadian Navy*) kanadische Marine

RD (US) ABBR (*Post*: = *rural delivery*) Landpostzustellung *f*

Rd ABBR (= *road*) Str.

RDC (BRIT) N ABBR = **rural district council**

RE (BRIT) N ABBR (*Scol*) = **religious education**; (*Mil*: = *Royal Engineers*) *Königliches Pionierkorps*

re [ri:] PREP (*with regard to*) bezüglich *+gen*

reach [ri:tʃ] N (*range*) Reichweite *f* ▶ VT erreichen; (*conclusion, decision*) kommen zu; (*be able to touch*) kommen an *+acc* ▶ VI (*stretch out one's arm*) langen; **reaches** NPL (*of river*) Gebiete *pl*; **within/out of ~** in/außer Reichweite; **within easy ~ of the supermarket/station** ganz in der Nähe des Supermarkts/Bahnhofs; **beyond the ~ of sb/sth** außerhalb der Reichweite von jdm/etw; **"keep out of the ~ of children"** „von Kindern fernhalten"; **can I ~ you at your hotel?** kann ich Sie in Ihrem Hotel erreichen?

▶ **reach for** VT greifen nach

▶ **reach out** VT (*hand*) ausstrecken ▶ VI die Hand ausstrecken; **to ~ out for sth** nach etw greifen

react [ri:'ækt] VI: **to ~ (to)** (*also Med*) reagieren (auf *+acc*); (*Chem*): **to ~ (with)** reagieren (mit); **to ~ (against)** (*rebel*) sich wehren (gegen)

reaction [ri:'ækʃən] N Reaktion *f*; **reactions** NPL (*reflexes*) Reaktionen *pl*; **a ~ against sth** Widerstand gegen etw

reactionary [ri:'ækʃənrɪ] ADJ reaktionär ▶ N Reaktionär(in) *m(f)*

reactor [ri:'æktə^r] N (*also*: **nuclear reactor**) Kernreaktor *m*

read [ri:d] (*pt, pp* ~ [rɛd]) VI lesen; (*piece of writing etc*) sich lesen ▶ VT lesen; (*meter, thermometer etc*) ablesen; (*understand: mood, thoughts*) sich versetzen in *+acc*; (*meter, thermometer etc: measurement*) anzeigen; (*study*) studieren; **to ~ sb's lips** jdm von den Lippen ablesen; **to ~ sb's mind** jds Gedanken lesen; **to ~ between the lines** zwischen den Zeilen lesen; **to take sth as ~** (*self-evident*) etw für selbstverständlich halten; **you can take it as ~ that ...** Sie können davon ausgehen, dass ...; **do you ~ me?** (*Tel*) verstehen Sie mich?; **to ~ sth into sb's remarks** etw in jds Bemerkungen hineininterpretieren

▶ **read out** VT vorlesen

▶ **read over** VT durchlesen

▶ **read through** VT durchlesen

▶ **read up on** VT FUS sich informieren über *+acc*

readable ['ri:dəbl] ADJ (*legible*) lesbar; (*book, author etc*) lesenswert

reader ['ri:də^r] N (*person*) Leser(in) *m(f)*; (*book*) Lesebuch *nt*; (BRIT: *at university*) ≈ Dozent(in) *m(f)*; **to be an avid/slow ~** eifrig/langsam lesen

readership ['ri:dəʃɪp] N (*of newspaper etc*) Leserschaft *f*

readily ['rɛdɪlɪ] ADV (*without hesitation*) bereitwillig; (*easily*) ohne Weiteres

readiness ['rɛdɪnɪs] N Bereitschaft *f*; **in ~ for** bereit für

reading ['ri:dɪŋ] N Lesen *nt*; (*understanding*) Verständnis *nt*; (*from bible, of poetry etc*) Lesung *f*; (*on meter, thermometer etc*) Anzeige *f*

reading glasses NPL Lesebrille *f*

reading lamp N Leselampe *f*

reading matter N Lesestoff *m*

reading room N Lesesaal *m*

readjust [ri:ə'dʒʌst] VT (*position, knob, instrument etc*) neu einstellen ▶ VI: **to ~ (to)** sich anpassen (an *+acc*)

readjustment [ri:ə'dʒʌstmənt] N (*fig*) Neuorientierung *f*

ready ['rɛdɪ] ADJ (*prepared*) bereit, fertig; (*willing*) bereit; (*easy*) leicht; (*available*) fertig ▶ N: **at the ~** (*Mil*) einsatzbereit; (*fig*) griffbereit; **~ for use** gebrauchsfertig; **to be ~ to do sth** bereit sein, etw zu tun; **to get ~** sich fertig machen; **to get sth ~** etw bereitmachen

ready cash N Bargeld *nt*

ready-cooked ['rɛdɪkukt] ADJ vorgekocht

ready-made ['rɛdɪ'meɪd] ADJ (*clothes*) von der Stange, Konfektions-; **~ meal** Fertiggericht *nt*

ready-mix ['rɛdɪmɪks] N (*for cakes etc*) Backmischung *f*; (*concrete*) Fertigbeton *m*

ready money N = **ready cash**

ready reckoner [-'rɛkənə^r] (BRIT) N Rechentabelle *f*

ready-to-wear ['rɛdɪtə'wɛə^r] ADJ (*clothes*) von der Stange, Konfektions-

reaffirm [ri:ə'fə:m] VT bestätigen

reagent [ri:'eɪdʒənt] N: **chemical ~** Reagens *nt*, Reagenz *nt*

real [rɪəl] ADJ (*reason, result etc*) wirklich; (*leather, gold etc*) echt; (*life, feeling*) wahr; (*for emphasis*) echt ▶ ADV (*US inf: very*) echt; **in ~ life** im wahren *or* wirklichen Leben; **in ~ terms** effektiv

real ale N Real Ale *nt*

real estate N Immobilien *pl* ▶ CPD (*US: agent, business etc*) Immobilien-

realign VT neu ausrichten

realism ['rɪəlɪzəm] N (*also Art*) Realismus *m*

realist ['rɪəlɪst] N Realist(in) *m(f)*

realistic [rɪə'lɪstɪk] ADJ realistisch

reality [ri:'ælɪtɪ] N Wirklichkeit *f*, Realität *f*; **in ~** in Wirklichkeit

reality TV N Reality-TV *nt*

realization [rɪəlaɪ'zeɪʃən] N (*understanding*) Erkenntnis *f*; (*fulfilment*) Verwirklichung *f*, Realisierung *f*; (*Fin: of asset*) Realisation *f*

realize ['rɪəlaɪz] VT (*understand*) verstehen; (*fulfil*) verwirklichen, realisieren; (*Fin: amount, profit*) realisieren; **I ~ that ...** es ist mir klar, dass ...

r

really ['rɪəlɪ] ADV wirklich; **what ~ happened** was wirklich geschah; **~?** wirklich?; **~!** (*indicating annoyance*) also wirklich!
realm [rɛlm] N (*fig: field*) Bereich *m*; (*kingdom*) Reich *nt*
real-time ['ri:ltaɪm] ADJ (*Comput: processing etc*) Echtzeit-
Realtor® ['rɪəltɔ:ʳ] (*US*) N Immobilienmakler(in) *m(f)*
ream [ri:m] N (*of paper*) Ries *nt*; **reams** NPL (*inf: fig*) Bände *pl*
reap [ri:p] VT (*crop*) einbringen, ernten; (*fig: benefits*) ernten; (*: rewards*) bekommen
reaper ['ri:pəʳ] N (*machine*) Mähdrescher *m*
reappear [ri:ə'pɪəʳ] VI wieder auftauchen
reappearance [ri:ə'pɪərəns] N Wiederauftauchen *nt*
reapply [ri:ə'plaɪ] VI: **to ~ for** sich erneut bewerben um
reappoint [ri:ə'pɔɪnt] VT (*to job*) wiedereinstellen
reappraisal [ri:ə'preɪzl] N (*of idea etc*) Neubeurteilung *f*
rear [rɪəʳ] ADJ hintere(r, s); (*wheel etc*) Hinter- ▸ N Rückseite *f*; (*buttocks*) Hinterteil *nt* ▸ VT (*family, animals*) aufziehen ▸ VI (*horse: also:* **rear up**) sich aufbäumen
rear admiral N Konteradmiral *m*
rear-engined ['rɪər'ɛndʒɪnd] ADJ mit Heckmotor
rearguard ['rɪəgɑ:d] N (*Mil*) Nachhut *f*; **to fight a ~ action** (*fig*) sich erbittert wehren
rearm [ri:'ɑ:m] VI (*country*) wiederaufrüsten ▸ VT wiederbewaffnen
rearmament [ri:'ɑ:məmənt] N Wiederaufrüstung *f*
rearrange [ri:ə'reɪndʒ] VT (*furniture*) umstellen; (*meeting*) den Termin ändern *+gen*
rear-view mirror ['rɪəvju:-] N Rückspiegel *m*
reason ['ri:zn] N (*cause*) Grund *m*; (*rationality*) Verstand *m*; (*common sense*) Vernunft *f* ▸ VI: **to ~ with sb** vernünftig mit jdm reden; **the ~ for/why** der Grund für/, warum; **we have ~ to believe that …** wir haben Grund zu der Annahme, dass …; **it stands to ~ that …** es ist zu erwarten, dass …; **she claims with good ~ that …** sie behauptet mit gutem Grund *or* mit Recht, dass …; **all the more ~ why …** ein Grund mehr, warum …; **yes, but within ~** ja, solange es sich im Rahmen hält
reasonable ['ri:znəbl] ADJ vernünftig; (*number, amount*) angemessen; (*not bad*) ganz ordentlich; **be ~!** sei doch vernünftig!
reasonably ['ri:znəblɪ] ADV (*fairly*) ziemlich; (*sensibly*) vernünftig; **one could ~ assume that …** man könnte durchaus annehmen, dass …
reasoned ['ri:znd] ADJ (*argument*) durchdacht
reasoning ['ri:znɪŋ] N Argumentation *f*
reassemble [ri:ə'sɛmbl] VT (*machine*) wieder zusammensetzen ▸ VI sich wieder versammeln
reassert [ri:ə'sə:t] VT: **to ~ oneself/one's authority** seine Autorität wieder geltend machen
reassurance [ri:ə'ʃuərəns] N (*comfort*) Beruhigung *f*; (*guarantee*) Bestätigung *f*
reassure [ri:ə'ʃuəʳ] VT beruhigen
reassuring [ri:ə'ʃuərɪŋ] ADJ beruhigend
reawakening [ri:ə'weɪknɪŋ] N Wiedererwachen *nt*
rebate ['ri:beɪt] N (*on tax etc*) Rückerstattung *f*; (*discount*) Ermäßigung *f*
rebel ['rɛbl] N Rebell(in) *m(f)* ▸ VI rebellieren
rebellion [rɪ'bɛljən] N Rebellion *f*
rebellious [rɪ'bɛljəs] ADJ rebellisch
rebirth [ri:'bə:θ] N Wiedergeburt *f*
reboot [ri:'bu:t] VT, VI (*Comput*) rebooten
rebound [rɪ'baund] VI (*ball*) zurückprallen ▸ N: **on the ~** (*fig*) als Tröstung
rebuff [rɪ'bʌf] N Abfuhr *f* ▸ VT zurückweisen
rebuild [ri:'bɪld] VT (*irreg: like* **build**) wiederaufbauen; (*confidence*) wiederherstellen
rebuke [rɪ'bju:k] VT zurechtweisen, tadeln ▸ N Zurechtweisung *f*, Tadel *m*
rebut [rɪ'bʌt] (*form*) VT widerlegen
rebuttal [rɪ'bʌtl] (*form*) N Widerlegung *f*
recalcitrant [rɪ'kælsɪtrənt] ADJ aufsässig
recall [rɪ'kɔ:l] VT (*remember*) sich erinnern an *+acc*; (*ambassador*) abberufen; (*product*) zurückrufen ▸ N (*of memories*) Erinnerung *f*; (*of ambassador*) Abberufung *f*; (*of product*) Rückruf *m*; **beyond ~** unwiederbringlich
recant [rɪ'kænt] VI widerrufen
recap ['ri:kæp] VT, VI zusammenfassen ▸ N Zusammenfassung *f*
recapitulate [ri:kə'pɪtjuleɪt] VT, VI = **recap**
recapture [ri:'kæptʃəʳ] VT (*town*) wiedereinnehmen; (*prisoner*) wiederergreifen; (*atmosphere etc*) heraufbeschwören
rec'd ABBR (*Comm: = received*) erh.
recede [rɪ'si:d] VI (*tide*) zurückgehen; (*lights etc*) verschwinden; (*memory, hope*) schwinden; **his hair is beginning to ~** er bekommt eine Stirnglatze
receding [rɪ'si:dɪŋ] ADJ (*hairline*) zurückweichend; (*chin*) fliehend
receipt [rɪ'si:t] N (*document*) Quittung *f*; (*act of receiving*) Erhalt *m*; **receipts** NPL (*Comm*) Einnahmen *pl*; **on ~ of** bei Erhalt *+gen*; **to be in ~ of sth** etw erhalten
receivable [rɪ'si:vəbl] ADJ (*Comm*) zulässig; (*owing*) ausstehend
receive [rɪ'si:v] VT erhalten, bekommen; (*injury*) erleiden; (*treatment*) erhalten; (*visitor, guest*) empfangen; **to be on the receiving end of sth** der/die Leidtragende von etw sein; **"received with thanks"** (*Comm*) „dankend erhalten"

> **Received Pronunciation** oder **RP** ist die hochsprachliche Standardaussprache des britischen Englisch, die bis vor Kurzem in der Ober- und Mittelschicht vorherrschte und auch noch großes Ansehen unter höheren Beamten genießt.

receiver [rɪ'si:vəʳ] N (*Tel*) Hörer *m*; (*Radio, TV*) Empfänger *m*; (*of stolen goods*) Hehler(in) *m(f)*; (*Comm*) Empfänger(in) *m(f)*

receivership [rɪ'si:vəʃɪp] N: **to go into ~** in Konkurs gehen
recent ['ri:snt] ADJ (*event*) kürzlich; (*times*) letzte(r, s); **in ~ years** in den letzten Jahren
recently ['ri:sntlɪ] ADV (*not long ago*) kürzlich; (*lately*) in letzter Zeit; **as ~ as** erst; **until ~** bis vor Kurzem
receptacle [rɪ'sɛptɪkl] N Behälter *m*
reception [rɪ'sɛpʃən] N (*in hotel, office etc*) Rezeption *f*; (*party, Radio, TV*) Empfang *m*; (*welcome*) Aufnahme *f*
reception centre (BRIT) N Aufnahmelager *nt*
reception desk N Rezeption *f*
receptionist [rɪ'sɛpʃənɪst] N (*in hotel*) Empfangschef *m*, Empfangsdame *f*; (*in doctor's surgery*) Sprechstundenhilfe *f*
receptive [rɪ'sɛptɪv] ADJ aufnahmebereit
recess [rɪ'sɛs] N (*in room*) Nische *f*; (*secret place*) Winkel *m*; (*Pol etc: holiday*) Ferien *pl*; (*US Law: short break*) Pause *f*; (*esp US Scol*) Pause *f*
recession [rɪ'sɛʃən] N (*Econ*) Rezession *f*
recessionista [rɪsɛʃə'nɪstə] N *modebewusste Person, die in Zeiten der Rezession auf die Kosten ihres Lebensstils achtet*
recharge [ri:'tʃɑ:dʒ] VT (*battery*) aufladen
rechargeable [ri:'tʃɑ:dʒəbl] ADJ (*battery*) aufladbar
recipe ['rɛsɪpɪ] N Rezept *nt*; **a ~ for success** ein Erfolgsrezept *nt*; **to be a ~ for disaster** in die Katastrophe führen
recipient [rɪ'sɪpɪənt] N Empfänger(in) *m(f)*
reciprocal [rɪ'sɪprəkl] ADJ gegenseitig
reciprocate [rɪ'sɪprəkeɪt] VT (*invitation, feeling*) erwidern ▸ VI sich revanchieren
recital [rɪ'saɪtl] N (*concert*) Konzert *nt*
recitation [rɛsɪ'teɪʃən] N (*of poem etc*) Vortrag *m*
recite [rɪ'saɪt] VT (*poem*) vortragen; (*complaints etc*) aufzählen
reckless ['rɛkləs] ADJ (*driving, driver*) rücksichtslos; (*spending*) leichtsinnig
recklessly ['rɛkləslɪ] ADV (*drive*) rücksichtslos; (*spend, gamble*) leichtsinnig
reckon ['rɛkən] VT (*consider*) halten für; (*calculate*) berechnen ▸ VI: **he is somebody to be reckoned with** mit ihm muss man rechnen; **I ~ that ...** (*think*) ich schätze, dass ...; **to ~ without sb/sth** nicht mit jdm/etw rechnen
▸ **reckon on** VT FUS rechnen mit
reckoning ['rɛknɪŋ] N (*calculation*) Berechnung *f*; **the day of ~** der Tag der Abrechnung
reclaim [rɪ'kleɪm] VT (*luggage*) abholen; (*tax etc*) zurückfordern; (*land*) gewinnen; (*waste materials*) zur Wiederverwertung sammeln
reclamation [rɛklə'meɪʃən] N (*of land*) Gewinnung *f*
recline [rɪ'klaɪn] VI (*sit or lie back*) zurückgelehnt sitzen
reclining [rɪ'klaɪnɪŋ] ADJ (*seat*) Liege-
recluse [rɪ'klu:s] N Einsiedler(in) *m(f)*
recognition [rɛkəg'nɪʃən] N (*of person, place*) Erkennen *nt*; (*of problem, fact*) Erkenntnis *f*; (*of achievement*) Anerkennung *f*; **in ~ of** in Anerkennung *+gen*; **to gain ~** Anerkennung finden; **she had changed beyond ~** sie war nicht wieder zu erkennen
recognizable ['rɛkəgnaɪzəbl] ADJ erkennbar
recognize ['rɛkəgnaɪz] VT (*person, place, voice*) wiedererkennen; (*sign, problem*) erkennen; (*qualifications, government, achievement*) anerkennen; **to ~ sb by/as** jdn erkennen an *+dat*/als
recoil [rɪ'kɔɪl] VI (*person*): **to ~ from** zurückweichen vor *+dat*; (*fig*) zurückschrecken vor *+dat* ▸ N (*of gun*) Rückstoß *m*
recollect [rɛkə'lɛkt] VT (*remember*) sich erinnern an *+acc*
recollection [rɛkə'lɛkʃən] N Erinnerung *f*; **to the best of my ~** soweit ich mich erinnern *or* entsinnen kann
recommend [rɛkə'mɛnd] VT empfehlen; **she has a lot to ~ her** es spricht sehr viel für sie
recommendation [rɛkəmɛn'deɪʃən] N Empfehlung *f*; **on the ~ of** auf Empfehlung *+gen*
recommended retail price (BRIT) N (*Comm*) unverbindlicher Richtpreis *m*
recompense ['rɛkəmpɛns] N (*reward*) Belohnung *f*; (*compensation*) Entschädigung *f*
reconcilable ['rɛkənsaɪləbl] ADJ (*ideas*) (miteinander) vereinbar
reconcile ['rɛkənsaɪl] VT (*people*) versöhnen; (*facts, beliefs*) (miteinander) vereinbaren, in Einklang bringen; **to ~ o.s. to sth** sich mit etw abfinden
reconciliation [rɛkənsɪlɪ'eɪʃən] N (*of people*) Versöhnung *f*; (*of facts, beliefs*) Vereinbarung *f*
recondite [rɪ'kɔndaɪt] ADJ obskur
recondition [ri:kən'dɪʃən] VT (*machine*) überholen
reconditioned [ri:kən'dɪʃənd] ADJ (*engine, TV*) generalüberholt
reconnaissance [rɪ'kɔnɪsns] N (*Mil*) Aufklärung *f*
reconnoitre, (US) **reconnoiter** [rɛkə'nɔɪtə[r]] VT (*Mil*) erkunden
reconsider [ri:kən'sɪdə[r]] VT (noch einmal) überdenken ▸ VI es sich *dat* noch einmal überlegen
reconstitute [ri:'kɔnstɪtju:t] VT (*organization*) neu bilden; (*food*) wiederherstellen
reconstruct [ri:kən'strʌkt] VT (*building*) wiederaufbauen; (*policy, system*) neu organisieren; (*event, crime*) rekonstruieren
reconstruction [ri:kən'strʌkʃən] N Wiederaufbau *m*; (*of crime*) Rekonstruktion *f*
reconvene [ri:kən'vi:n] VI (*meet again*) wieder zusammenkommen ▸ VT (*meeting etc*) wiedereinberufen
record N ['rɛkɔ:d] (*written account*) Aufzeichnung *f*; (*of meeting*) Protokoll *nt*; (*of decision*) Beleg *m*; (*Comput*) Datensatz *m*; (*file*) Akte *f*; (*Mus: disc*) Schallplatte *f*; (*history*) Vorgeschichte *f*; (*also:* **criminal record**) Vorstrafen *pl*; (*Sport*) Rekord *m* ▸ VT [rɪ'kɔ:d] aufzeichnen; (*song etc*) aufnehmen; (*temperature, speed etc*) registrieren

r

▶ ADJ ['rɛkɔ:d] (*sales, profits*) Rekord- ▶ ADV ['rɛkɔ:d] (*speak*) im Vertrauen; **~ of attendance** Anwesenheitsliste *f*; **public records** Urkunden *pl* des Nationalarchivs; **to keep a ~ of sth** etw schriftlich festhalten; **to have a good/poor ~** gute/schlechte Leistungen vorzuweisen haben; **to have a (criminal) ~** vorbestraft sein; **to set** *or* **put the ~ straight** (*fig*) Klarheit schaffen; **he is on ~ as saying that ...** er hat nachweislich gesagt, dass ...; **off the ~** (*remark*) inoffiziell; **in ~ time** in Rekordzeit

recorded delivery [rɪ'kɔ:dɪd-] (BRIT) N (*Post*) Einschreiben *nt*; **to send sth (by) ~** etw per Einschreiben senden

recorder [rɪ'kɔ:dəʳ] N (*Mus*) Blockflöte *f*; (*Law*) *nebenamtlich als Richter tätiger Rechtsanwalt*

record holder N (*Sport*) Rekordinhaber(in) *m(f)*

recording [rɪ'kɔ:dɪŋ] N Aufnahme *f*

recording studio N Aufnahmestudio *nt*

record library N Schallplattenverleih *m*

record player N Plattenspieler *m*

recount [rɪ'kaunt] VT (*story etc*) erzählen

re-count ['ri:kaunt] N (*of votes*) Nachzählung *f* ▶ VT (*votes*) nachzählen

recoup [rɪ'ku:p] VT: **to ~ one's losses** seine Verluste ausgleichen

recourse [rɪ'kɔ:s] N: **to have ~ to sth** Zuflucht zu etw nehmen

recover [rɪ'kʌvəʳ] VT (*get back*) zurückbekommen; (*stolen goods*) sicherstellen; (*wreck, body*) bergen; (*financial loss*) ausgleichen ▶ VI sich erholen

re-cover [ri:'kʌvəʳ] VT (*chair etc*) neu beziehen

recovery [rɪ'kʌvərɪ] N (*from illness etc*) Erholung *f*; (*in economy*) Aufschwung *m*; (*of lost items*) Wiederfinden *nt*; (*of stolen goods*) Sicherstellung *f*; (*of wreck, body*) Bergung *f*; (*of financial loss*) Ausgleich *m*

re-create [ri:krɪ'eɪt] VT (*atmosphere, situation*) wiederherstellen

recreation [rɛkrɪ'eɪʃən] N (*leisure*) Erholung *f*, Entspannung *f*

recreational [rɛkrɪ'eɪʃənl] ADJ (*facilities etc*) Freizeit-

recreational drug N Freizeitdroge *f*

recreational vehicle (US) N Caravan *m*

recrimination [rɪkrɪmɪ'neɪʃən] N gegenseitige Anschuldigungen *pl*

recruit [rɪ'kru:t] N (*Mil*) Rekrut *m*; (*in company*) neuer Mitarbeiter *m*, neue Mitarbeiterin *f* ▶ VT (*Mil*) rekrutieren; (*staff, new members*) anwerben

recruiting office [rɪ'kru:tɪŋ-] N (*Mil*) Rekrutierungsbüro *nt*

recruitment [rɪ'kru:tmənt] N (*of staff*) Anwerbung *f*

recruitment agency N Personalagentur *f*

rectangle ['rɛktæŋgl] N Rechteck *nt*

rectangular [rɛk'tæŋgjuləʳ] ADJ (*shape*) rechteckig

rectify ['rɛktɪfaɪ] VT (*mistake etc*) korrigieren

rector ['rɛktəʳ] N (*Rel*) Pfarrer(in) *m(f)*

rectory ['rɛktərɪ] N Pfarrhaus *nt*

rectum ['rɛktəm] N Rektum *nt*, Mastdarm *m*

recuperate [rɪ'kju:pəreɪt] VI (*recover*) sich erholen

recur [rɪ'kə:ʳ] VI (*error, event*) sich wiederholen; (*pain etc*) wiederholt auftreten

recurrence [rɪ'kʌrns] N Wiederholung *f*; wiederholtes Auftreten *nt*

recurrent [rɪ'kʌrnt] ADJ sich wiederholend; wiederholt auftretend

recurring [rɪ'kə:rɪŋ] ADJ (*problem, dream*) sich wiederholend; (*Math*): **six point five four ~** sechs Komma fünf Periode vier

recyclable [ri:'saɪkləbl] ADJ recycelbar, wiederverwertbar

recycle [ri:'saɪkl] VT (*waste, paper etc*) recyceln, wiederverwerten

recycling [ri:'saɪklɪŋ] N Recycling *nt*; **~ site** Recycling- *or* Wertstoffhof *m*

red [rɛd] N Rot *nt*; (*pej, Pol*) Rote(r) *f(m)* ▶ ADJ rot; **to be in the ~** (*business etc*) in den roten Zahlen sein

red alert N: **to be on ~** in höchster Alarmbereitschaft sein

red-blooded ['rɛd'blʌdɪd] ADJ heißblütig

> Als **redbrick university** werden die jüngeren britischen Universitäten bezeichnet, die im späten 19. und Anfang des 20. Jh. in Städten wie Manchester, Liverpool und Bristol gegründet wurden. Der Name steht im Gegensatz zu Oxford und Cambridge und bezieht sich auf die roten Backsteinmauern der Universitätsgebäude.

red cabbage N Rotkohl *m*

red carpet treatment N: **to give sb the ~** den roten Teppich für jdn ausrollen

Red Cross N Rotes Kreuz *nt*

redcurrant ['rɛdkʌrənt] N Rote Johannisbeere *f*

redden ['rɛdn] VT röten ▶ VI (*blush*) erröten

reddish ['rɛdɪʃ] ADJ rötlich

redecorate [ri:'dɛkəreɪt] VT, VI renovieren

redecoration [ri:dɛkə'reɪʃən] N Renovierung *f*

redeem [rɪ'di:m] VT (*situation etc*) retten; (*voucher, sth in pawn*) einlösen; (*loan*) abzahlen; (*Rel*) erlösen; **to ~ oneself for sth** etw wiedergutmachen

redeemable [rɪ'di:məbl] ADJ (*voucher etc*) einlösbar

redeeming [rɪ'di:mɪŋ] ADJ (*feature, quality*) versöhnend

redefine [ri:dɪ'faɪn] VT neu definieren

redemption [rɪ'dɛmʃən] N (*Rel*) Erlösung *f*; **past** *or* **beyond ~** nicht mehr zu retten

redeploy [ri:dɪ'plɔɪ] VT (*resources, staff*) umverteilen; (*Mil*) verlegen

redeployment [ri:dɪ'plɔɪmənt] N Umverteilung *f*; Verlegung *f*

redevelop [ri:dɪ'vɛləp] VT (*area*) sanieren

redevelopment [ri:dɪ'vɛləpmənt] N Sanierung *f*

red-handed [rɛd'hændɪd] ADJ: **to be caught ~** auf frischer Tat ertappt werden

redhead ['rɛdhɛd] N Rotschopf *m*

red herring N (*fig*) falsche Spur *f*

red-hot [rɛd'hɔt] ADJ (*metal*) rot glühend
redirect [ri:daɪ'rɛkt] VT (*mail*) nachsenden; (*traffic*) umleiten
rediscover [ri:dɪs'kʌvəʳ] VT wiederentdecken
redistribute [ri:dɪs'trɪbju:t] VT umverteilen
red-letter day ['rɛdlɛtə-] N besonderer Tag *m*
red light N (*Aut*): **to go through a ~** eine Ampel bei Rot überfahren
red-light district ['rɛdlaɪt-] N Rotlichtviertel *nt*
red meat N *Rind- und Lammfleisch*
redness ['rɛdnɪs] N Röte *f*
redo [ri:'du:] VT (*irreg: like* **do**) noch einmal machen
redolent ['rɛdələnt] ADJ: **to be ~ of sth** nach etw riechen; (*fig*) an etw erinnern
redouble [ri:'dʌbl] VT: **to ~ one's efforts** seine Anstrengungen verdoppeln
redraft [ri:'drɑ:ft] VT (*agreement*) neu abfassen
redraw [ri:'drɔ:] VT neu zeichnen
redress [rɪ'drɛs] N (*compensation*) Wiedergutmachung *f* ▸ VT (*error etc*) wiedergutmachen; **to ~ the balance** das Gleichgewicht wiederherstellen
Red Sea N: **the ~** das Rote Meer
redskin ['rɛdskɪn] (*old: offensive*) N Rothaut *f*
red tape N (*fig*) Bürokratie *f*
reduce [rɪ'dju:s] VT (*spending, numbers, risk etc*) vermindern, reduzieren; **to ~ sth by/to 5%** etw um/auf 5% *acc* reduzieren; **to ~ sb to tears/silence** jdn zum Weinen/Schweigen bringen; **to ~ sb to begging/stealing** jdn zur Bettelei/zum Diebstahl zwingen; **"~ speed now"** (*Aut*) „langsam fahren"
reduced [rɪ'dju:st] ADJ (*goods, ticket etc*) ermäßigt; **"greatly ~ prices"** „Preise stark reduziert"
reduction [rɪ'dʌkʃən] N (*in price etc*) Ermäßigung, Reduzierung *f*; (*in numbers*) Verminderung *f*
redundancy [rɪ'dʌndənsɪ] (BRIT) N (*dismissal*) Entlassung *f*; (*unemployment*) Arbeitslosigkeit *f*; **compulsory ~** Entlassung *f*; **voluntary ~** freiwilliger Verzicht *m* auf den Arbeitsplatz
redundancy payment (BRIT) N Abfindung *f*
redundant [rɪ'dʌndnt] ADJ (BRIT: *worker*) arbeitslos; (*word, object*) überflüssig; **to be made ~** (*worker*) den Arbeitsplatz verlieren
red wine [red'waɪn] N Rotwein *m*
reed [ri:d] N (*Bot*) Schilf *nt*; (*Mus: of clarinet etc*) Rohrblatt *nt*
re-educate [ri:'ɛdjukeɪt] VT umerziehen
reedy ['ri:dɪ] ADJ (*voice*) Fistel-
reef [ri:f] N (*at sea*) Riff *nt*
reek [ri:k] VI: **to ~ (of)** (*lit, fig*) stinken (nach)
reel [ri:l] N (*of thread etc, on fishing-rod*) Rolle *f*; (*Cine: scene*) Szene *f*; (*of film, tape*) Spule *f*; (*dance*) Reel *m* ▸ VI (*sway*) taumeln; **my head is reeling** mir dreht sich der Kopf
▸ **reel in** VT (*fish, line*) einholen
▸ **reel off** VT (*say*) herunterrasseln
re-election [ri:ɪ'lɛkʃən] N Wiederwahl *f*
re-enter [ri:'ɛntəʳ] VT (*country*) wieder einreisen in +*acc*; (*Space*) wieder eintreten in +*acc*
re-entry [ri:'ɛntrɪ] N Wiedereinreise *f*; (*Space*) Wiedereintritt *m*
re-examine [ri:ɪg'zæmɪn] VT (*proposal etc*) nochmals prüfen; (*witness*) nochmals vernehmen
re-export ['ri:ɪks'pɔ:t] VT wiederausführen ▸ N Wiederausfuhr *f*; (*commodity*) wiederausgeführte Ware *f*
ref [rɛf] (*inf*) N ABBR (*Sport*) = **referee**
ref. ABBR (*Comm: = with reference to*) betr.; **your ref.** Ihr Zeichen:
refectory [rɪ'fɛktərɪ] N (*in university*) Mensa *f*
refer [rɪ'fə:ʳ] VT: **to ~ sb to** (*book etc*) jdn verweisen auf +*acc*; (*doctor, hospital*) jdn überweisen zu; **to ~ sth to** (*task, problem*) etw übergeben an +*acc*; **he referred me to the manager** er verwies mich an den Geschäftsführer
▸ **refer to** VT FUS (*mention*) erwähnen; (*relate to*) sich beziehen auf +*acc*; (*consult*) hinzuziehen
referee [rɛfə'ri:] N (*Sport*) Schiedsrichter(in) *m(f)*; (BRIT: *for job application*) Referenz *f* ▸ VT als Schiedsrichter(in) leiten
reference ['rɛfrəns] N (*mention*) Hinweis *m*; (*in book, article*) Quellenangabe *f*; (*for job application, person*) Referenz *f*; **with ~ to** mit Bezug auf +*acc*; **"please quote this ~"** (*Comm*) „bitte dieses Zeichen angeben"
reference book N Nachschlagewerk *nt*
reference library N Präsenzbibliothek *f*
reference number N Aktenzeichen *nt*
referenda [rɛfə'rɛndə] NPL *of* **referendum**
referendum [rɛfə'rɛndəm] (*pl* **referenda**) N Referendum *nt*, Volksentscheid *m*
referral [rɪ'fə:rəl] N (*of matter, problem*) Weiterleitung *f*; (*to doctor, specialist*) Überweisung *f*
refill [ri:'fɪl] VT nachfüllen ▸ N (*for pen etc*) Nachfüllmine *f*; (*drink*) Nachfüllung *f*
refine [rɪ'faɪn] VT (*sugar, oil*) raffinieren; (*theory, idea*) verfeinern
refined [rɪ'faɪnd] ADJ (*person*) kultiviert; (*taste*) fein, vornehm; (*sugar, oil*) raffiniert
refinement [rɪ'faɪnmənt] N (*of person*) Kultiviertheit *f*; (*of system, ideas*) Verfeinerung *f*
refinery [rɪ'faɪnərɪ] N (*for oil etc*) Raffinerie *f*
refit [ri:'fɪt] (*Naut*) N Überholung *f* ▸ VT (*ship*) überholen
reflate [ri:'fleɪt] VT (*economy*) ankurbeln
reflation [ri:'fleɪʃən] N (*Econ*) Reflation *f*
reflationary [ri:'fleɪʃənrɪ] ADJ (*Econ*) reflationär
reflect [rɪ'flɛkt] VT reflektieren; (*fig*) widerspiegeln ▸ VI (*think*) nachdenken
▸ **reflect on** VT FUS (*discredit*) ein schlechtes Licht werfen auf +*acc*
reflection [rɪ'flɛkʃən] N (*image*) Spiegelbild *nt*; (*of light, heat*) Reflexion *f*; (*fig*) Widerspiegelung *f*; (*: thought*) Gedanke *m*; **on ~** nach genauerer Überlegung; **this is a ~ on ...** (*criticism*) das sagt einiges über ...
reflector [rɪ'flɛktəʳ] N (*Aut etc*) Rückstrahler *m*; (*for light, heat*) Reflektor *m*
reflex ['ri:flɛks] ADJ Reflex-; **reflexes** NPL (*Physiol, Psych*) Reflexe *pl*

r

reflexive [rɪ'flɛksɪv] ADJ (*Ling*) reflexiv
reform [rɪ'fɔ:m] N Reform *f* ▶ VT reformieren ▶ VI (*criminal etc*) sich bessern
reformat [ri:'fɔ:mæt] VT (*Comput*) neu formatieren
Reformation [rɛfə'meɪʃən] N: **the ~** die Reformation
reformatory [rɪ'fɔ:mətərɪ] (*US*) N Besserungsanstalt *f*
reformed [rɪ'fɔ:md] ADJ (*character, alcoholic*) gewandelt
refrain [rɪ'freɪn] VI: **to ~ from doing sth** etw unterlassen ▶ N (*of song*) Refrain *m*
refresh [rɪ'frɛʃ] VT erfrischen; **to ~ one's memory** sein Gedächtnis auffrischen
refresher course [rɪ'frɛʃə-] N Auffrischungskurs *m*
refreshing [rɪ'frɛʃɪŋ] ADJ erfrischend; (*sleep*) wohltuend; (*idea etc*) angenehm
refreshment [rɪ'frɛʃmənt] N Erfrischung *f*
refreshments [rɪ'frɛʃmənts] NPL (*food and drink*) Erfrischungen *pl*
refrigeration [rɪfrɪdʒə'reɪʃən] N Kühlung *f*
refrigerator [rɪ'frɪdʒəreɪtə[r]] N Kühlschrank *m*
refuel [ri:'fjuəl] VT, VI auftanken
refuelling [ri:'fjuəlɪŋ] N Auftanken *nt*
refuge ['rɛfju:dʒ] N Zuflucht *f*; **to seek/take ~ in** Zuflucht suchen/nehmen in *+dat*
refugee [rɛfju'dʒi:] N Flüchtling *m*; **a political ~** ein politischer Flüchtling
refugee camp N Flüchtlingslager *nt*
refund ['ri:fʌnd] N Rückerstattung *f* ▶ VT (*money*) zurückerstatten
refurbish [ri:'fə:bɪʃ] VT (*shop etc*) renovieren
refurbishment [ri:fə:bɪʃmənt] N (*of shop etc*) Renovierung *f*
refurnish [ri:'fə:nɪʃ] VT neu möblieren
refusal [rɪ'fju:zəl] N Ablehnung *f*; **a ~ to do sth** eine Weigerung, etw zu tun; **to give sb first ~ on sth** jdm etw zuerst anbieten
refuse[1] [rɪ'fju:z] VT (*request, offer etc*) ablehnen; (*gift*) zurückweisen; (*permission*) verweigern ▶ VI ablehnen; (*horse*) verweigern; **to ~ to do sth** sich weigern, etw zu tun
refuse[2] ['rɛfju:s] N (*rubbish*) Abfall *m*, Müll *m*
refuse collection ['rɛfju:s-] N Müllabfuhr *f*
refuse disposal ['rɛfju:s-] N Müllbeseitigung *f*
refusenik [rɪ'fju:znɪk] N (*inf*) Verweigerer(in) *m(f)*; (*in former USSR*) *sowjetischer Jude, dem die Emigration nach Israel verweigert wurde*
refute [rɪ'fju:t] VT (*argument*) widerlegen
regain [rɪ'geɪn] VT wiedererlangen
regal ['ri:gl] ADJ königlich
regale [rɪ'geɪl] VT: **to ~ sb with sth** jdn mit etw verwöhnen
regalia [rɪ'geɪlɪə] N (*costume*) Amtstracht *f*
regard [rɪ'gɑ:d] N (*esteem*) Achtung *f* ▶ VT (*consider*) ansehen, betrachten; (*view*) betrachten; **to give one's regards to sb** jdm Grüße bestellen; **"with kindest regards"** „mit freundlichen Grüßen"; **as regards, with ~ to** bezüglich *+gen*
regarding [rɪ'gɑ:dɪŋ] PREP bezüglich *+gen*
regardless [rɪ'gɑ:dlɪs] ADV trotzdem ▶ ADJ: **~ of** ohne Rücksicht auf *+acc*
regatta [rɪ'gætə] N Regatta *f*
regency ['ri:dʒənsɪ] N Regentschaft *f* ▶ ADJ: **R~** (*furniture etc*) Regency-
regenerate [rɪ'dʒɛnəreɪt] VT (*inner cities, arts*) erneuern; (*person, feelings*) beleben ▶ VI (*Biol*) sich regenerieren
regent ['ri:dʒənt] N Regent(in) *m(f)*
reggae ['rɛgeɪ] N Reggae *m*
regime [reɪ'ʒi:m] N (*government*) Regime *nt*; (*diet etc*) Kur *f*
regiment ['rɛdʒɪmənt] N (*Mil*) Regiment *nt* ▶ VT reglementieren
regimental [rɛdʒɪ'mɛntl] ADJ Regiments-
regimentation [rɛdʒɪmɛn'teɪʃən] N Reglementierung *f*
region ['ri:dʒən] N (*of land*) Gebiet *nt*; (*of body*) Bereich *m*; (*administrative division of country*) Region *f*; **in the ~ of** (*approximately*) im Bereich von
regional ['ri:dʒənl] ADJ regional
regional development N regionale Entwicklung *f*
regionalize ['ri:dʒənəlaɪz] VT regionalisieren
register ['rɛdʒɪstə[r]] N (*list, Mus*) Register *nt*; (*also*: **electoral register**) Wählerverzeichnis *nt*; (*Scol*) Klassenbuch *nt* ▶ VT registrieren; (*car*) anmelden; (*letter*) als Einschreiben senden; (*amount, measurement*) verzeichnen ▶ VI (*person*) sich anmelden; (*: at doctor's*) sich (als Patient) eintragen; (*amount etc*) registriert werden; (*make impression*) (einen) Eindruck machen; **to ~ a protest** Protest anmelden
registered ['rɛdʒɪstəd] ADJ (*letter, parcel*) eingeschrieben; (*drug addict, childminder etc*) (offiziell) eingetragen
registered company N eingetragene Gesellschaft *f*
registered nurse (*US*) N staatlich geprüfte Krankenschwester *f*, staatlich geprüfter Krankenpfleger *m*
registered trademark N eingetragenes Warenzeichen *nt*
register office N = **registry office**
registrar ['rɛdʒɪstrɑ:[r]] N (*in registry office*) Standesbeamte(r) *m*, Standesbeamtin *f*; (*in college etc*) Kanzler *m*; (BRIT: *in hospital*) Krankenhausarzt *m*, Krankenhausärztin *f*
registration [rɛdʒɪs'treɪʃən] N Registrierung *f*; (*of students, unemployed etc*) Anmeldung *f*
registration number (BRIT) N (*Aut*) polizeiliches Kennzeichen *nt*
registry ['rɛdʒɪstrɪ] N Registratur *f*
registry office (BRIT) N Standesamt *nt*; **to get married in a ~** standesamtlich heiraten
regret [rɪ'grɛt] N Bedauern *nt* ▶ VT bedauern; **with ~** mit Bedauern; **to have no regrets** nichts bereuen; **we ~ to inform you that ...** wir müssen Ihnen leider mitteilen, dass ...
regretfully [rɪ'grɛtfəlɪ] ADV mit Bedauern
regrettable [rɪ'grɛtəbl] ADJ bedauerlich

regrettably [rɪ'grɛtəblɪ] ADV bedauerlicherweise; **~, he said ...** bedauerlicherweise sagte er ...
Regt ABBR *(Mil: = regiment)* Rgt.
regular ['rɛgjuləʳ] ADJ *(also Ling)* regelmäßig; *(usual: time, doctor)* üblich; *(: customer)* Stamm-; *(soldier)* Berufs-; *(Comm: size)* normal ▶ N *(client)* Stammkunde *m*, Stammkundin *f*
regularity [rɛgju'lærɪtɪ] N Regelmäßigkeit *f*
regularly ['rɛgjuləlɪ] ADV regelmäßig; *(breathe, beat: evenly)* gleichmäßig
regulate ['rɛgjuleɪt] VT regulieren
regulation [rɛgju'leɪʃən] N Regulierung *f*; *(rule)* Vorschrift *f*
regulatory [rɛgju'leɪtrɪ] ADJ *(system)* Regulierungs-; *(body, agency)* Überwachungs-
rehabilitate [ri:ə'bɪlɪteɪt] VT *(criminal, drug addict)* (in die Gesellschaft) wiedereingliedern; *(invalid)* rehabilitieren
rehabilitation ['ri:əbɪlɪ'teɪʃən] N Wiedereingliederung *f* (in die Gesellschaft); Rehabilitation *f*
rehash [ri:'hæʃ] *(inf)* VT *(idea etc)* aufwärmen
rehearsal [rɪ'hə:səl] N *(Theat)* Probe *f*; **dress ~** Generalprobe *f*
rehearse [rɪ'hə:s] VT *(play, speech etc)* proben
rehouse [ri:'hauz] VT neu unterbringen
reign [reɪn] N *(lit, fig)* Herrschaft *f* ▶ VI *(lit, fig)* herrschen
reigning ['reɪnɪŋ] ADJ regierend; *(champion)* amtierend
reimburse [ri:ɪm'bə:s] VT die Kosten erstatten *+dat*
rein [reɪn] N Zügel *m*; **to give sb free ~** *(fig)* jdm freie Hand lassen; **to keep a tight ~ on sth** *(fig)* bei etw die Zügel kurz halten
reincarnation [ri:ɪnkɑ:'neɪʃən] N *(belief)* die Wiedergeburt *f*; *(person)* Reinkarnation *f*
reindeer ['reɪndɪəʳ] N INV Ren(tier) *nt*
reinforce [ri:ɪn'fɔ:s] VT *(strengthen)* verstärken; *(support: idea etc)* stützen; *(: prejudice)* stärken
reinforced concrete N Stahlbeton *m*
reinforcement [ri:ɪn'fɔ:smənt] N *(strengthening)* Verstärkung *f*; *(of attitude etc)* Stärkung *f*; **reinforcements** NPL *(Mil)* Verstärkung *f*
reinstate [ri:ɪn'steɪt] VT *(employee)* wiedereinstellen; *(tax, law)* wiedereinführen; *(text)* wiedereinfügen
reinstatement [ri:ɪn'steɪtmənt] N *(of employee)* Wiedereinstellung *f*
reissue [ri:'ɪʃju:] VT neu herausgeben
reiterate [ri:'ɪtəreɪt] VT wiederholen
reject ['ri:dʒɛkt] N *(Comm)* Ausschuss *m inv* ▶ VT ablehnen; *(admirer)* abweisen; *(goods)* zurückweisen; *(machine: coin)* nicht annehmen; *(Med: heart, kidney)* abstoßen
rejection [rɪ'dʒɛkʃən] N Ablehnung *f*; *(of admirer)* Abweisung *f*; *(Med)* Abstoßung *f*
rejoice [rɪ'dʒɔɪs] VI: **to ~ at** *or* **over** jubeln über *+acc*
rejoinder [rɪ'dʒɔɪndəʳ] N Erwiderung *f*
rejuvenate [rɪ'dʒu:vəneɪt] VT *(person)* verjüngen; *(organization etc)* beleben
rekindle [ri:'kɪndl] VT *(interest, emotion etc)* wiedererwecken
relapse [rɪ'læps] N *(Med)* Rückfall *m* ▶ VI: **to ~ into** zurückfallen in *+acc*
relate [rɪ'leɪt] VT *(tell)* berichten; *(connect)* in Verbindung bringen ▶ VI: **to ~ to** *(empathize with: person, subject)* eine Beziehung finden zu; *(connect with)* zusammenhängen mit
related [rɪ'leɪtɪd] ADJ: **to be ~** (miteinander) verwandt sein; *(issues etc)* zusammenhängen
relating to [rɪ'leɪtɪŋ-] PREP bezüglich *+gen*, mit Bezug auf *+acc*
relation [rɪ'leɪʃən] N *(member of family)* Verwandte(r) *f(m)*; *(connection)* Beziehung *f*; **relations** NPL *(contact)* Beziehungen *pl*; **diplomatic/international relations** diplomatische/internationale Beziehungen; **in ~ to** im Verhältnis zu; **to bear no ~ to** in keinem Verhältnis stehen zu
relationship [rɪ'leɪʃənʃɪp] N Beziehung *f*; *(between countries)* Beziehungen *pl*; *(affair)* Verhältnis *nt*; **they have a good ~** sie haben ein gutes Verhältnis zueinander
relative ['rɛlətɪv] N Verwandte(r) *f(m)* ▶ ADJ relativ; **all her relatives** ihre ganze Verwandtschaft; **~ to** im Vergleich zu; **it's all ~** es ist alles relativ
relatively ['rɛlətɪvlɪ] ADV relativ
relative pronoun N Relativpronomen *nt*
relax [rɪ'læks] VI *(person, muscle)* sich entspannen; *(calm down)* sich beruhigen ▶ VT *(one's grip)* lockern; *(mind, person)* entspannen; *(control etc)* lockern
relaxation [ri:læk'seɪʃən] N Entspannung *f*; *(of control etc)* Lockern *nt*
relaxed [rɪ'lækst] ADJ *(person, atmosphere)* entspannt; *(discussion)* locker
relaxing [rɪ'læksɪŋ] ADJ entspannend
relay ['ri:leɪ] N *(race)* Staffel *f*, Staffellauf *m* ▶ VT *(message etc)* übermitteln; *(broadcast)* übertragen
release [rɪ'li:s] N *(from prison)* Entlassung *f*; *(from obligation, situation)* Befreiung *f*; *(of documents, funds etc)* Freigabe *f*; *(of gas etc)* Freisetzung *f*; *(of film, book, record)* Herausgabe *f*; *(record, film)* Veröffentlichung *f*; *(Tech: device)* Auslöser *m* ▶ VT *(from prison)* entlassen; *(person: from obligation, from wreckage)* befreien; *(gas etc)* freisetzen; *(Tech, Aut: catch, brake etc)* lösen; *(record, film)* herausbringen; *(news, figures)* bekannt geben; **on general ~** *(film)* überall in den Kinos; *see also* **press release**
relegate ['rɛləgeɪt] VT *(downgrade)* herunterstufen; (BRIT *Sport*): **to be relegated** absteigen
relent [rɪ'lɛnt] VI *(give in)* nachgeben
relentless [rɪ'lɛntlɪs] ADJ *(heat, noise)* erbarmungslos; *(enemy etc)* unerbittlich
relevance ['rɛləvəns] N Relevanz *f*, Bedeutung *f*; **the ~ of religion to society** die Relevanz *or* Bedeutung der Religion für die Gesellschaft
relevant ['rɛləvənt] ADJ relevant; *(chapter, area)* entsprechend; **~ to** relevant für
reliability [rɪlaɪə'bɪlɪtɪ] N Zuverlässigkeit *f*

r

reliable [rɪ'laɪəbl] ADJ zuverlässig
reliably [rɪ'laɪəblɪ] ADV: **to be ~ informed that ...** zuverlässige Informationen darüber haben, dass ...
reliance [rɪ'laɪəns] N: **~ (on)** (*person*) Angewiesenheit *f* (auf *+acc*); (*drugs, financial support*) Abhängigkeit *f* (von)
reliant [rɪ'laɪənt] ADJ: **to be ~ on sth/sb** auf etw/jdn angewiesen sein
relic ['rɛlɪk] N (*Rel*) Reliquie *f*; (*of the past*) Relikt *nt*
relief [rɪ'li:f] N (*from pain etc*) Erleichterung *f*; (*aid*) Hilfe *f*; (*Art, Geog*) Relief *nt* ▸ CPD (*bus*) Entlastungs-; (*driver*) zur Ablösung; **light ~** leichte Abwechslung *f*
relief map N Reliefkarte *f*
relief road (BRIT) N Entlastungsstraße *f*
relieve [rɪ'li:v] VT (*pain*) lindern; (*fear, worry*) mildern; (*take over from*) ablösen; **to ~ sb of sth** (*load*) jdm etw abnehmen; (*duties, post*) jdn einer Sache *gen* entheben; **to ~ o.s.** (*euphemism*) sich erleichtern
relieved [rɪ'li:vd] ADJ erleichtert; **I'm ~ to hear it** es erleichtert mich, das zu hören
religion [rɪ'lɪdʒən] N Religion *f*
religious [rɪ'lɪdʒəs] ADJ religiös
religious education N Religionsunterricht *m*
religiously [rɪ'lɪdʒəslɪ] ADV (*regularly, thoroughly*) gewissenhaft
relinquish [rɪ'lɪŋkwɪʃ] VT (*control etc*) aufgeben; (*claim*) verzichten auf *+acc*
relish ['rɛlɪʃ] N (*Culin*) würzige Soße *f*, Relish *nt*; (*enjoyment*) Genuss *m* ▸ VT (*enjoy*) genießen; **to ~ doing sth** etw mit Genuss tun
relive [ri:'lɪv] VT noch einmal durchleben
reload [ri:'ləud] VT (*gun*) neu laden
relocate [ri:ləu'keɪt] VT verlegen ▸ VI den Standort wechseln; **to ~ in** seinen Standort verlegen nach
reluctance [rɪ'lʌktəns] N Widerwille *m*
reluctant [rɪ'lʌktənt] ADJ unwillig, widerwillig; **I'm ~ to do that** es widerstrebt mir, das zu tun
reluctantly [rɪ'lʌktəntlɪ] ADV widerwillig, nur ungern
rely on [rɪ'laɪ-] VT FUS (*be dependent on*) abhängen von; (*trust*) sich verlassen auf *+acc*
remain [rɪ'meɪn] VI bleiben; (*survive*) übrig bleiben; **to ~ silent** weiterhin schweigen; **to ~ in control** die Kontrolle behalten; **much remains to be done** es ist noch viel zu tun; **the fact remains that ...** Tatsache ist und bleibt, dass ...; **it remains to be seen whether ...** es bleibt abzuwarten, ob ...
remainder [rɪ'meɪndə^r] N Rest *m* ▸ VT (*Comm*) zu ermäßigtem Preis anbieten
remaining [rɪ'meɪnɪŋ] ADJ übrig
remains [rɪ'meɪnz] NPL (*of meal*) Überreste *pl*; (*of building etc*) Ruinen *pl*; (*of body*) sterbliche Überreste *pl*
remand [rɪ'mɑ:nd] N: **to be on ~** in Untersuchungshaft sein ▸ VT: **to be remanded in custody** in Untersuchungshaft bleiben müssen
remand home (*formerly*: BRIT) N Untersuchungsgefängnis *nt* für Jugendliche
remark [rɪ'mɑ:k] N Bemerkung *f* ▸ VT bemerken ▸ VI: **to ~ on sth** Bemerkungen über etw *acc* machen; **to ~ that** die Bemerkung machen, dass
remarkable [rɪ'mɑ:kəbl] ADJ bemerkenswert
remarry [ri:'mærɪ] VI wieder heiraten
remedial [rɪ'mi:dɪəl] ADJ (*tuition, classes*) Förder-; **~ exercise** Heilgymnastik *f*
remedy ['rɛmədɪ] N (*lit, fig*) (Heil)mittel *nt* ▸ VT (*mistake, situation*) abhelfen *+dat*
remember [rɪ'mɛmbə^r] VT (*call back to mind*) sich erinnern an *+acc*; (*bear in mind*) denken an *+acc*; **~ me to him** (*send greetings*) grüße ihn von mir; **I ~ seeing it, I ~ having seen it** ich erinnere mich (daran), es gesehen zu haben; **she remembered to do it** sie hat daran gedacht, es zu tun
remembrance [rɪ'mɛmbrəns] N Erinnerung *f*; **in ~ of sb/sth** im Gedenken an *+acc*
Remembrance Sunday (BRIT) N ≈ Volkstrauertag *m*

> **Remembrance Sunday** oder **Remembrance Day** ist der britische Gedenktag für die Gefallenen der beiden Weltkriege und anderer Konflikte. Er fällt auf einen Sonntag vor oder nach dem 11. November (am 11. November 1918 endete der Erste Weltkrieg) und wird mit einer Schweigeminute, Kranzniederlegungen an Kriegerdenkmälern und dem Tragen von Anstecknadeln in Form einer Mohnblume begangen.

remind [rɪ'maɪnd] VT: **to ~ sb to do sth** jdn daran erinnern, etw zu tun; **to ~ sb of sth** jdn an etw *acc* erinnern; **to ~ sb that ...** jdn daran erinnern, dass ...; **she reminds me of her mother** sie erinnert mich an ihre Mutter; **that reminds me!** dabei fällt mir etwas ein!
reminder [rɪ'maɪndə^r] N (*of person, place etc*) Erinnerung *f*; (*letter*) Mahnung *f*
reminisce [rɛmɪ'nɪs] VI: **to ~ (about)** sich in Erinnerungen ergehen (über *+acc*)
reminiscences [rɛmɪ'nɪsnsɪz] NPL Erinnerungen *pl*
reminiscent [rɛmɪ'nɪsnt] ADJ: **to be ~ of sth** an etw *acc* erinnern
remiss [rɪ'mɪs] ADJ nachlässig; **it was ~ of him** es war nachlässig von ihm
remission [rɪ'mɪʃən] N (*of sentence*) Straferlass *m*; (*Med*) Remission *f*; (*Rel*) Erlass *m*
remit [rɪ'mɪt] VT (*money*) überweisen ▸ N (*of official etc*) Aufgabenbereich *m*
remittance [rɪ'mɪtns] N Überweisung *f*
remnant ['rɛmnənt] N Überrest *m*; (*Comm: of cloth*) Rest *m*
remonstrate ['rɛmənstreɪt] VI: **to ~ (with sb about sth)** sich beschweren (bei jdm wegen etw)
remorse [rɪ'mɔ:s] N Reue *f*
remorseful [rɪ'mɔ:sful] ADJ reumütig

remorseless [rɪ'mɔːslɪs] ADJ (*noise, pain*) unbarmherzig
remote [rɪ'məut] ADJ (*distant: place, time*) weit entfernt; (*aloof*) distanziert; (*slight: chance etc*) entfernt; **there is a ~ possibility that ...** es besteht eventuell die Möglichkeit, dass ...
remote control N Fernsteuerung *f*; (*TV etc*) Fernbedienung *f*
remote-controlled [rɪ'məutkən'trəuld] ADJ ferngesteuert
remotely [rɪ'məutlɪ] ADV (*slightly*) entfernt
remoteness [rɪ'məutnɪs] N (*of place*) Entlegenheit *f*; (*of person*) Distanziertheit *f*
remould ['riːməuld] (BRIT) N (*Aut*) runderneuerter Reifen *m*
removable [rɪ'muːvəbl] ADJ (*detachable*) abnehmbar
removal [rɪ'muːvəl] N (*of object etc*) Entfernung *f*; (*of threat etc*) Beseitigung *f*; (BRIT: *from house*) Umzug *m*; (*dismissal*) Entlassung *f*; (*Med: of kidney etc*) Entfernung *f*
removal man (BRIT) N (*irreg*) Möbelpacker *m*
removal van (BRIT) N Möbelwagen *m*
remove [rɪ'muːv] VT entfernen; (*clothing*) ausziehen; (*bandage etc*) abnehmen; (*employee*) entlassen; (*name: from list*) streichen; (*doubt, threat, obstacle*) beseitigen; **my first cousin once removed** mein Vetter ersten Grades
remover [rɪ'muːvə^r] N (*for paint, varnish*) Entferner *m*; **stain ~** Fleckentferner *m*; **make-up ~** Make-up-Entferner *m*
remunerate [rɪ'mjuːnəreɪt] VT vergüten
remuneration [rɪmjuːnə'reɪʃən] N Vergütung *f*
Renaissance [rɪ'neɪsɑ̃ːs] N: **the ~** die Renaissance
renal ['riːnl] ADJ (*Med*) Nieren-
renal failure N Nierenversagen *nt*
rename [riː'neɪm] VT umbenennen
rend [rɛnd] (*pt, pp* **rent**) VT (*air, silence*) zerreißen
render ['rɛndə^r] VT (*give: assistance, aid*) leisten; (*cause to become: unconscious, harmless, useless*) machen; (*submit*) vorlegen
rendering ['rɛndərɪŋ] (BRIT) N = **rendition**
rendezvous ['rɔndɪvuː] N (*meeting*) Rendezvous *nt*; (*place*) Treffpunkt *m* ▸ VI (*people*) sich treffen; (*spacecraft*) ein Rendezvousmanöver durchführen; **to ~ with sb** sich mit jdm treffen
rendition [rɛn'dɪʃən] N (*of song etc*) Vortrag *m*
renegade ['rɛnɪgeɪd] N Renegat(in) *m(f)*, Überläufer(in) *m(f)*
renew [rɪ'njuː] VT erneuern; (*attack, negotiations*) wiederaufnehmen; (*loan, contract etc*) verlängern; (*relationship etc*) wiederaufleben lassen
renewable ADJ (*energy*) erneuerbar
renewables NPL erneuerbare Energien *pl*
renewal [rɪ'njuːəl] N Erneuerung *f*; (*of conflict*) Wiederaufnahme *f*; (*of contract etc*) Verlängerung *f*
renounce [rɪ'nauns] VT verzichten auf +*acc*; (*belief*) aufgeben
renovate ['rɛnəveɪt] VT (*building*) restaurieren; (*machine*) überholen
renovation [rɛnə'veɪʃən] N Restaurierung *f*; Überholung *f*
renown [rɪ'naun] N Ruf *m*
renowned [rɪ'naund] ADJ berühmt
rent [rɛnt] PT, PP *of* **rend** ▸ N (*for house*) Miete *f* ▸ VT mieten; (*also*: **rent out**) vermieten
rental ['rɛntl] N (*for television, car*) Mietgebühr *f*
rent boy (*inf*) N Strichjunge *m*
rent strike N Mietstreik *m*
renunciation [rɪnʌnsɪ'eɪʃən] N Verzicht *m*; (*of belief*) Aufgabe *f*; (*self-denial*) Selbstverleugnung *f*
reopen [riː'əupən] VT (*shop etc*) wiedereröffnen; (*negotiations, legal case etc*) wiederaufnehmen
reopening [riː'əupnɪŋ] N Wiedereröffnung *f*; Wiederaufnahme *f*
reorder [riː'ɔːdə^r] VT (*rearrange*) umordnen
reorganization ['riːɔːgənaɪ'zeɪʃən] N Umorganisation *f*
reorganize [riː'ɔːgənaɪz] VT umorganisieren
rep [rɛp] N ABBR (*Comm*) = **representative**; (*Theat*) = **repertory**
Rep. (US) ABBR (*Pol*) = **representative**; **Republican**
repair [rɪ'pɛə^r] N Reparatur *f* ▸ VT reparieren; (*clothes, road*) ausbessern; **in good/bad ~** in gutem/schlechtem Zustand; **beyond ~** nicht mehr zu reparieren; **to be under ~** (*road*) ausgebessert werden
repair kit N (*for bicycle*) Flickzeug *nt*
repair man N (*irreg*) Handwerker *m*
repair shop N Reparaturwerkstatt *f*
repartee [rɛpɑː'tiː] N (*exchange*) Schlagabtausch *m*; (*reply*) schlagfertige Bemerkung *f*
repast [rɪ'pɑːst] (*form*) N Mahl *nt*
repatriate [riː'pætrɪeɪt] VT repatriieren
repay [riː'peɪ] VT (*irreg: like* **pay**) zurückzahlen; (*sb's efforts, attention*) belohnen; (*favour*) erwidern; **I'll ~ you next week** ich zahle es dir nächste Woche zurück
repayment [riː'peɪmənt] N Rückzahlung *f*
repeal [rɪ'piːl] N (*of law*) Aufhebung *f* ▸ VT (*law*) aufheben
repeat [rɪ'piːt] N (*Radio, TV*) Wiederholung *f* ▸ VT, VI wiederholen ▸ CPD (*performance*) Wiederholungs-; (*order*) Nach-; **to ~ o.s./itself** sich wiederholen; **to ~ an order for sth** etw nachbestellen
repeatedly [rɪ'piːtɪdlɪ] ADV wiederholt
repel [rɪ'pɛl] VT (*drive away*) zurückschlagen; (*disgust*) abstoßen
repellent [rɪ'pɛlənt] ADJ abstoßend ▸ N: **insect ~** Insekten(schutz)mittel *nt*
repent [rɪ'pɛnt] VI: **to ~ of sth** etw bereuen
repentance [rɪ'pɛntəns] N Reue *f*
repercussions [riːpə'kʌʃənz] NPL Auswirkungen *pl*
repertoire ['rɛpətwɑː^r] N (*Mus, Theat*) Repertoire *nt*; (*fig*) Spektrum *nt*
repertory ['rɛpətərɪ] N (*also*: **repertory theatre**) Repertoiretheater *nt*
repertory company N Repertoire-Ensemble *nt*

r

repetition [rɛpɪˈtɪʃən] N (*repeat*) Wiederholung *f*
repetitious [rɛpɪˈtɪʃəs] ADJ (*speech etc*) voller Wiederholungen
repetitive [rɪˈpɛtɪtɪv] ADJ eintönig, monoton
replace [rɪˈpleɪs] VT (*put back: upright*) zurückstellen; (*: flat*) zurücklegen; (*take the place of*) ersetzen; **to ~ X with Y** X durch Y ersetzen; **"~ the receiver"** (*Tel*) „Hörer auflegen"
replacement [rɪˈpleɪsmənt] N Ersatz *m*
replacement part N Ersatzteil *nt*
replay [ˈriːpleɪ] N (*of match*) Wiederholungsspiel *nt* ▸ VT (*match*) wiederholen; (*track, song: on tape*) nochmals abspielen
replenish [rɪˈplɛnɪʃ] VT (*glass, stock etc*) auffüllen
replete [rɪˈpliːt] ADJ (*after meal*) gesättigt; **~ with** reichlich ausgestattet mit
replica [ˈrɛplɪkə] N (*of object*) Nachbildung *f*
reply [rɪˈplaɪ] N Antwort *f* ▸ VI: **to ~ (to sb/sth)** (jdm/auf etw *acc*) antworten; **in ~ to** als Antwort auf *+acc*; **there's no ~** (*Tel*) es meldet sich niemand
reply coupon N Antwortschein *m*
report [rɪˈpɔːt] N Bericht *m*; (Brit: *also*: **school report**) Zeugnis *nt*; (*of gun*) Knall *m* ▸ VT berichten; (*casualties, damage, theft etc*) melden; (*person: to police*) anzeigen ▸ VI (*make a report*) Bericht erstatten; **to ~ to sb** (*present o.s. to*) sich bei jdm melden; (*be responsible to*) jdm unterstellt sein; **to ~ on sth** über etw *acc* Bericht erstatten; **to ~ sick** sich krankmelden; **it is reported that** es wird berichtet *or* gemeldet, dass ...
report card (*US, Scot*) N Zeugnis *nt*
reportedly [rɪˈpɔːtɪdlɪ] ADV: **she is ~ living in Spain** sie lebt angeblich in Spanien
reported speech N (*Ling*) indirekte Rede *f*
reporter [rɪˈpɔːtə^r] N Reporter(in) *m(f)*
repose [rɪˈpəuz] N: **in ~** in Ruhestellung
repository [rɪˈpɔzɪtərɪ] N (*person: of knowledge*) Quelle *f*; (*place: of collection etc*) Lager *nt*
repossess [ˈriːpəˈzɛs] VT (wieder) in Besitz nehmen
repossession order [riːpəˈzɛʃən-] N Beschlagnahmungsverfügung *f*
reprehensible [rɛprɪˈhɛnsɪbl] ADJ verwerflich
represent [rɛprɪˈzɛnt] VT (*person, nation*) vertreten; (*show: view, opinion*) darstellen; (*symbolize: idea*) symbolisieren, verkörpern; **to ~ sth as** (*describe*) etw darstellen als
representation [rɛprɪzɛnˈteɪʃən] N (*state of being represented*) Vertretung *f*; (*picture etc*) Darstellung *f*; **representations** NPL (*protest*) Proteste *pl*
representative [rɛprɪˈzɛntətɪv] N (*also Comm*) Vertreter(in) *m(f)*; (*US Pol*) Abgeordnete(r) *f(m)* des Repräsentantenhauses ▸ ADJ repräsentativ; **~ of** repräsentativ für
repress [rɪˈprɛs] VT unterdrücken
repression [rɪˈprɛʃən] N Unterdrückung *f*
repressive [rɪˈprɛsɪv] ADJ repressiv
reprieve [rɪˈpriːv] N (*cancellation*) Begnadigung *f*; (*postponement*) Strafaufschub *m*; (*fig*) Gnadenfrist *f* ▸ VT: **he was reprieved** er wurde begnadigt; ihm wurde Strafaufschub gewährt
reprimand [ˈrɛprɪmɑːnd] N Tadel *m* ▸ VT tadeln
reprint [ˈriːprɪnt] N Nachdruck *m* ▸ VT nachdrucken
reprisal [rɪˈpraɪzl] N Vergeltung *f*; **reprisals** NPL Repressalien *pl*; (*in war*) Vergeltungsaktionen *pl*; **to take reprisals** zu Repressalien greifen; (*in war*) Vergeltungsaktionen durchführen
reproach [rɪˈprəutʃ] N (*rebuke*) Vorwurf *m* ▸ VT: **to ~ sb for sth** jdm etw zum Vorwurf machen; **beyond ~** über jeden Vorwurf erhaben; **to ~ sb with sth** jdm etw vorwerfen
reproachful [rɪˈprəutʃful] ADJ vorwurfsvoll
reproduce [riːprəˈdjuːs] VT reproduzieren ▸ VI (*Biol*) sich vermehren
reproduction [riːprəˈdʌkʃən] N Reproduktion *f*; (*Biol*) Fortpflanzung *f*
reproductive [riːprəˈdʌktɪv] ADJ (*system, organs*) Fortpflanzungs-
reproof [rɪˈpruːf] N (*rebuke*) Tadel *m*; **with ~** tadelnd
reprove [rɪˈpruːv] VT tadeln; **to ~ sb for sth** jdn wegen etw tadeln
reproving [rɪˈpruːvɪŋ] ADJ tadelnd
reptile [ˈrɛptaɪl] N Reptil *nt*
Repub. (*US*) ABBR (*Pol*) = **Republican**
republic [rɪˈpʌblɪk] N Republik *f*
republican [rɪˈpʌblɪkən] ADJ republikanisch ▸ N Republikaner(in) *m(f)*; **the Republicans** (*US Pol*) die Republikaner
repudiate [rɪˈpjuːdɪeɪt] VT (*accusation*) zurückweisen; (*violence*) ablehnen; (*old: friend, wife etc*) verstoßen
repugnance [rɪˈpʌgnəns] N Abscheu *m*
repugnant [rɪˈpʌgnənt] ADJ abstoßend
repulse [rɪˈpʌls] VT (*attack etc*) zurückschlagen; (*sight, picture etc*) abstoßen
repulsion [rɪˈpʌlʃən] N Abscheu *m*
repulsive [rɪˈpʌlsɪv] ADJ widerwärtig, abstoßend
reputable [ˈrɛpjutəbl] ADJ (*make, company etc*) angesehen
reputation [rɛpjuˈteɪʃən] N Ruf *m*; **to have a ~ for** einen Ruf haben für; **he has a ~ for being awkward** er gilt als schwierig
repute [rɪˈpjuːt] N: **of ~** angesehen; **to be held in high ~** in hohem Ansehen stehen
reputed [rɪˈpjuːtɪd] ADJ angeblich; **he is ~ to be rich** er ist angeblich reich
reputedly [rɪˈpjuːtɪdlɪ] ADV angeblich
request [rɪˈkwɛst] N (*polite*) Bitte *f*; (*formal*) Ersuchen *nt*; (*Radio*) Musikwunsch *m* ▸ VT (*politely*) bitten um; (*formally*) ersuchen; **at the ~ of** auf Wunsch von; **"you are requested not to smoke"** „bitte nicht rauchen"
request stop (Brit) N Bedarfshaltestelle *f*
requiem [ˈrɛkwɪəm] N (*Rel: also*: **requiem mass**) Totenmesse *f*; (*Mus*) Requiem *nt*
require [rɪˈkwaɪə^r] VT (*need*) benötigen; (*: situation*) erfordern; (*demand*) verlangen; **to ~ sb to do sth** von jdm verlangen, etw zu tun; **if required** falls nötig; **what qualifications are required?** welche Qualifikationen werden verlangt?; **required by law** gesetzlich vorgeschrieben

required [rɪˈkwaɪəd] ADJ erforderlich
requirement [rɪˈkwaɪəmənt] N *(need)* Bedarf *m*; *(condition)* Anforderung *f*; **to meet sb's requirements** jds Anforderungen erfüllen
requisite [ˈrɛkwɪzɪt] ADJ erforderlich; **requisites** NPL: **toilet/travel requisites** Toiletten-/Reiseartikel *pl*
requisition [rɛkwɪˈzɪʃən] N: **~ (for)** *(demand)* Anforderung *f* (von) ▸ VT *(Mil)* beschlagnahmen
reroute [riːˈruːt] VT *(train etc)* umleiten
resale [riːˈseɪl] N Weiterverkauf *m*; **"not for ~"** „nicht zum Weiterverkauf bestimmt"
resale price maintenance N Preisbindung *f*
rescind [rɪˈsɪnd] VT *(law, order)* aufheben; *(decision)* rückgängig machen; *(agreement)* widerrufen
rescue [ˈrɛskjuː] N Rettung *f* ▸ VT retten; **to come to sb's ~** jdm zu Hilfe kommen
rescue party N Rettungsmannschaft *f*
rescuer [ˈrɛskjuəʳ] N Retter(in) *m(f)*
research [rɪˈsəːtʃ] N Forschung *f* ▸ VT erforschen ▸ VI: **to ~ into sth** etw erforschen; **to do ~** Forschung betreiben; **a piece of ~** eine Forschungsarbeit; **~ and development** Forschung und Entwicklung
researcher [rɪˈsəːtʃəʳ] N Forscher(in) *m(f)*
research work N Forschungsarbeit *f*
research worker N = **researcher**
resell [riːˈsɛl] VT *(irreg: like* **sell***)* weiterverkaufen
resemblance [rɪˈzɛmbləns] N Ähnlichkeit *f*; **to bear a strong ~ to** starke Ähnlichkeit haben mit; **it bears no ~ to ...** es hat keine Ähnlichkeit mit ...
resemble [rɪˈzɛmbl] VT ähneln *+dat*, gleichen *+dat*
resent [rɪˈzɛnt] VT *(attitude, treatment)* missbilligen; *(person)* ablehnen
resentful [rɪˈzɛntful] ADJ *(person)* gekränkt; *(attitude)* missbilligend
resentment [rɪˈzɛntmənt] N Verbitterung *f*
reservation [rɛzəˈveɪʃən] N *(booking)* Reservierung *f*; *(doubt)* Vorbehalt *m*; *(land)* Reservat *nt*; **to make a ~** *(in hotel etc)* eine Reservierung vornehmen; **with ~(s)** *(doubts)* unter Vorbehalt
reservation desk N Reservierungsschalter *m*
reserve [rɪˈzəːv] N Reserve *f*, Vorrat *m*; *(fig: of talent etc)* Reserve *f*; *(Sport)* Reservespieler(in) *m(f)*; *(also:* **nature reserve***)* Naturschutzgebiet *nt*; *(restraint)* Zurückhaltung *f* ▸ VT reservieren; *(table, ticket)* reservieren lassen; **reserves** NPL *(Mil)* Reserve *f*; **in ~** in Reserve
reserve currency N Reservewährung *f*
reserved [rɪˈzəːvd] ADJ *(restrained)* zurückhaltend; *(seat)* reserviert
reserve price (BRIT) N Mindestpreis *m*
reserve team (BRIT) N Reservemannschaft *f*
reservist [rɪˈzəːvɪst] N *(Mil)* Reservist *m*
reservoir [ˈrɛzəvwɑːʳ] N *(lit, fig)* Reservoir *nt*
reset [riːˈsɛt] VT *(irreg: like* **set***)* *(watch)* neu stellen; *(broken bone)* wieder einrichten; *(Comput)* zurückstellen
reshape [riːˈʃeɪp] VT *(policy, view)* umgestalten
reshuffle [riːˈʃʌfl] N: **cabinet ~** Kabinettsumbildung *f*
reside [rɪˈzaɪd] VI *(live: person)* seinen/ihren Wohnsitz haben
▸ **reside in** VT FUS *(exist)* liegen in *+dat*
residence [ˈrɛzɪdəns] N *(form: home)* Wohnsitz *m*; *(length of stay)* Aufenthalt *m*; **to take up ~** sich niederlassen; **in ~** *(queen etc)* anwesend; **writer/artist in ~** *Schriftsteller/Künstler, der in einer Ausbildungsstätte bei freier Unterkunft lehrt und arbeitet*
residence permit (BRIT) N Aufenthaltserlaubnis *f*
resident [ˈrɛzɪdənt] N *(of country, town)* Einwohner(in) *m(f)*; *(in hotel)* Gast *m* ▸ ADJ *(in country, town)* wohnhaft; *(population)* ansässig; *(doctor)* hauseigen; *(landlord)* im Hause wohnend
residential [rɛzɪˈdɛnʃəl] ADJ *(area)* Wohn-; *(course)* mit Wohnung am Ort; *(staff)* im Hause wohnend
residue [ˈrɛzɪdjuː] N *(Chem)* Rückstand *m*; *(fig)* Überrest *m*
resign [rɪˈzaɪn] VT *(one's post)* zurücktreten von ▸ VI *(from post)* zurücktreten; **to ~ o.s. to** *(situation etc)* sich abfinden mit
resignation [rɛzɪgˈneɪʃən] N *(from post)* Rücktritt *m*; *(state of mind)* Resignation *f*; **to tender one's ~** seine Kündigung einreichen
resigned [rɪˈzaɪnd] ADJ: **to be ~ to sth** sich mit etw abgefunden haben
resilience [rɪˈzɪlɪəns] N *(of material)* Widerstandsfähigkeit *f*; *(of person)* Unverwüstlichkeit *f*
resilient [rɪˈzɪlɪənt] ADJ widerstandsfähig; unverwüstlich
resin [ˈrɛzɪn] N Harz *nt*
resist [rɪˈzɪst] VT *(change, demand)* sich widersetzen *+dat*; *(attack etc)* Widerstand leisten *+dat*; *(urge etc)* widerstehen *+dat*; **I couldn't ~ (doing) it** ich konnte nicht widerstehen(, es zu tun)
resistance [rɪˈzɪstəns] N *(also Elec)* Widerstand *m*; *(to illness)* Widerstandsfähigkeit *f*
resistant [rɪˈzɪstənt] ADJ: **~ (to)** *(to change etc)* widerstandsfähig (gegenüber); *(to antibiotics etc)* resistent (gegen)
resit [riːˈsɪt] (BRIT) VT *(irreg: like* **sit***)* wiederholen ▸ N [ˈriːsɪt] Wiederholungsprüfung *f*
resolute [ˈrɛzəluːt] ADJ *(person)* entschlossen, resolut; *(refusal)* entschieden
resolution [rɛzəˈluːʃən] N *(decision)* Beschluss *m*; *(determination)* Entschlossenheit *f*; *(of problem)* Lösung *f*; **to make a ~** einen Entschluss fassen
resolve [rɪˈzɔlv] N *(determination)* Entschlossenheit *f* ▸ VT *(problem)* lösen; *(difficulty)* beseitigen ▸ VI: **to ~ to do sth** beschließen, etw zu tun
resolved [rɪˈzɔlvd] ADJ *(determined)* entschlossen
resonance [ˈrɛzənəns] N Resonanz *f*
resonant [ˈrɛzənənt] ADJ *(sound, voice)* volltönend; *(place)* widerhallend

r

resort [rɪ'zɔːt] N (*town*) Urlaubsort *m*; (*recourse*) Zuflucht *f* ▶ VI: **to ~ to** Zuflucht nehmen zu; **seaside ~** Seebad *nt*; **winter sports ~** Wintersportort *m*; **as a last ~** als letzter Ausweg; **in the last ~** schlimmstenfalls
resound [rɪ'zaund] VI: **to ~ (with)** widerhallen (von)
resounding [rɪ'zaundɪŋ] ADJ (*noise*) widerhallend; (*voice*) schallend; (*fig: success*) durchschlagend; (*: victory*) überlegen
resource [rɪ'sɔːs] N (*raw material*) Bodenschatz *m*; **resources** NPL (*coal, oil etc*) Energiequellen *pl*; (*money*) Mittel *pl*, Ressourcen *pl*; **natural resources** Naturschätze *pl*
resourceful [rɪ'sɔːsful] ADJ einfallsreich
resourcefulness [rɪ'sɔːsfulnɪs] N Einfallsreichtum *m*
respect [rɪs'pɛkt] N (*consideration, esteem*) Respekt *m* ▶ VT respektieren; **respects** NPL (*greetings*) Grüße *pl*; **to have ~ for sb/sth** Respekt vor jdm/etw haben; **to show sb/sth ~** Respekt vor jdm/etw zeigen; **out of ~ for** aus Rücksicht auf *+acc*; **with ~ to, in ~ of** in Bezug auf *+acc*; **in this ~** in dieser Hinsicht; **in some/many respects** in gewisser/vielfacher Hinsicht; **with (all due) ~** bei allem Respekt
respectability [rɪspɛktə'bɪlɪtɪ] N Anständigkeit *f*
respectable [rɪs'pɛktəbl] ADJ anständig; (*amount, income*) ansehnlich; (*standard, mark etc*) ordentlich
respected [rɪs'pɛktɪd] ADJ angesehen
respectful [rɪs'pɛktful] ADJ respektvoll
respectfully [rɪs'pɛktfəlɪ] ADV (*behave*) respektvoll
respective [rɪs'pɛktɪv] ADJ jeweilig
respectively [rɪs'pɛktɪvlɪ] ADV beziehungsweise; **Germany and Britain were 3rd and 4th ~** Deutschland und Großbritannien belegten den 3. beziehungsweise 4. Platz
respiration [rɛspɪ'reɪʃən] N *see* **artificial**
respirator ['rɛspɪreɪtə[r]] N Respirator *m*, Beatmungsgerät *nt*
respiratory ['rɛspərətərɪ] ADJ (*system, failure*) Atmungs-
respite ['rɛspaɪt] N (*rest*) Ruhepause *f*
resplendent [rɪs'plɛndənt] ADJ (*clothes*) prächtig
respond [rɪs'pɔnd] VI (*answer*) antworten; (*react*) reagieren
respondent [rɪs'pɔndənt] N (*Law*) Beklagte(r) *f(m)*
response [rɪs'pɔns] N (*to question*) Antwort *f*; (*to event etc*) Reaktion *f*; **in ~ to** als Antwort/Reaktion auf *+acc*
responsibility [rɪspɔnsɪ'bɪlɪtɪ] N Verantwortung *f*; **to take ~ for sth/sb** die Verantwortung für etw/jdn übernehmen
responsible [rɪs'pɔnsɪbl] ADJ verantwortlich; (*reliable, important*) verantwortungsvoll; **to be ~ for sth** für etw verantwortlich sein; **to be ~ for doing sth** dafür verantwortlich sein, etw zu tun; **to be ~ to sb** jdm gegenüber verantwortlich sein
responsibly [rɪs'pɔnsɪblɪ] ADV verantwortungsvoll
responsive [rɪs'pɔnsɪv] ADJ (*person*) ansprechbar
rest [rɛst] N (*relaxation*) Ruhe *f*; (*pause*) Ruhepause *f*; (*remainder*) Rest *m*; (*support*) Stütze *f*; (*Mus*) Pause *f* ▶ VI (*relax*) sich ausruhen ▶ VT (*eyes, legs etc*) ausruhen; **the ~ of them** die Übrigen; **to put** *or* **set sb's mind at ~** jdn beruhigen; **to come to ~** (*object*) zum Stillstand kommen; **to lay sb to ~** jdn zur letzten Ruhe betten; **to ~ on sth** (*lit, fig*) sich auf etw *acc* stützen; **to let the matter ~** die Sache auf sich beruhen lassen; **~ assured that …** seien Sie versichert, dass …; **I won't ~ until …** ich werde nicht ruhen, bis …; **may he/she ~ in peace** möge er/sie in Frieden ruhen; **to ~ sth on/against sth** (*lean*) etw an *acc*/gegen etw lehnen; **to ~ one's eyes** *or* **gaze on sth** den Blick auf etw heften; **I ~ my case** mehr brauche ich dazu wohl nicht zu sagen
restart [riː'stɑːt] VT (*engine*) wieder anlassen; (*work*) wiederaufnehmen
restaurant ['rɛstərɔŋ] N Restaurant *nt*
restaurant car (BRIT) N (*Rail*) Speisewagen *m*
rest cure N Erholung *f*
restful ['rɛstful] ADJ (*music*) ruhig; (*lighting*) beruhigend; (*atmosphere*) friedlich
rest home N Pflegeheim *nt*
restitution [rɛstɪ'tjuːʃən] N: **to make ~ to sb of sth** jdm etw zurückerstatten; (*as compensation*) jdn für etw entschädigen
restive ['rɛstɪv] ADJ (*person, crew*) unruhig; (*horse*) störrisch
restless ['rɛstlɪs] ADJ rastlos; (*audience*) unruhig; **to get ~** unruhig werden
restlessly ['rɛstlɪslɪ] ADV (*walk around*) rastlos; (*turn over*) unruhig
restock [riː'stɔk] VT (*shop, freezer*) wieder auffüllen; (*lake, river: with fish*) wieder besetzen
restoration [rɛstə'reɪʃən] N (*of painting etc*) Restauration *f*; (*of law and order, health, sight etc*) Wiederherstellung *f*; (*of land, rights*) Rückgabe *f*; (*Hist*): **the R~** die Restauration
restorative [rɪ'stɔrətɪv] ADJ (*power, treatment*) stärkend ▶ N (*old: drink*) Stärkungsmittel *nt*
restore [rɪ'stɔː[r]] VT (*painting etc*) restaurieren; (*law and order, faith, health etc*) wiederherstellen; (*property*) zurückgeben; **to ~ sth to** (*to former state*) etw zurückverwandeln in *+acc*; **to ~ sb to power** jdn wieder an die Macht bringen
restorer [rɪ'stɔːrə[r]] N (*Art etc*) Restaurator(in) *m(f)*
restrain [rɪs'treɪn] VT (*person*) zurückhalten; (*feeling*) unterdrücken; (*growth, inflation*) dämpfen; **to ~ sb from doing sth** jdn davon abhalten, etw zu tun; **to ~ o.s. from doing sth** sich beherrschen, etw nicht zu tun
restrained [rɪs'treɪnd] ADJ (*person*) beherrscht; (*style etc*) zurückhaltend
restraint [rɪs'treɪnt] N (*restriction*) Einschränkung *f*; (*moderation*) Zurückhaltung *f*; **wage ~** Zurückhaltung *f* bei Lohnforderungen

restrict [rɪs'trɪkt] VT beschränken
restricted ADJ beschränkt
restricted area (BRIT) N (*Aut*) Bereich *m* mit Geschwindigkeitsbeschränkung
restriction [rɪs'trɪkʃən] N Beschränkung *f*
restrictive [rɪs'trɪktɪv] ADJ (*law, measure*) restriktiv; (*clothing*) beengend
restrictive practices (BRIT) NPL (*Industry*) wettbewerbshemmende Geschäftspraktiken *pl*
rest room (US) N Toilette *f*
restructure [ri:'strʌktʃəʳ] VT umstrukturieren
result [rɪ'zʌlt] N Resultat *nt*; (*of match, election, exam etc*) Ergebnis *nt* ▸ VI: **to ~ in** führen zu; **as a ~ of the accident** als Folge des Unfalls; **he missed the train as a ~ of sleeping in** er verpasste den Zug, weil er verschlafen hatte; **to ~ from** resultieren *or* sich ergeben aus; **as a ~ it is too expensive** folglich ist es zu teuer
resultant [rɪ'zʌltənt] ADJ resultierend, sich ergebend
resume [rɪ'zju:m] VT (*work, journey*) wiederaufnehmen; (*seat*) wieder einnehmen ▸ VI (*start again*) von Neuem beginnen
résumé ['reɪzju:meɪ] N Zusammenfassung *f*; (*US: curriculum vitae*) Lebenslauf *m*
resumption [rɪ'zʌmpʃən] N (*of work etc*) Wiederaufnahme *f*
resurgence [rɪ'sə:dʒəns] N Wiederaufleben *nt*
resurrection [rɛzə'rɛkʃən] N (*of hopes, fears*) Wiederaufleben *nt*; (*of custom etc*) Wiederbelebung *f*; (*Rel*): **the R~** die Auferstehung *f*
resuscitate [rɪ'sʌsɪteɪt] VT (*Med, fig*) wiederbeleben
resuscitation [rɪsʌsɪ'teɪʃən] N Wiederbelebung *f*
retail ['ri:teɪl] ADJ (*trade, department*) Verkaufs-; (*shop, goods*) Einzelhandels- ▸ ADV im Einzelhandel ▸ VT (*sell*) (im Einzelhandel) verkaufen ▸ VI: **to ~ at** (im Einzelhandel) kosten; **this product retails at £25** dieses Produkt kostet im Laden £25
retailer ['ri:teɪləʳ] N Einzelhändler(in) *m(f)*
retail outlet N Einzelhandelsverkaufsstelle *f*
retail price N Einzelhandelspreis *m*
retail price index N Einzelhandelspreisindex *m*
retain [rɪ'teɪn] VT (*keep*) behalten; (*: heat, moisture*) zurückhalten
retainer [rɪ'teɪnəʳ] N (*fee*) Vorauszahlung *f*
retaliate [rɪ'tælɪeɪt] VI Vergeltung üben
retaliation [rɪtælɪ'eɪʃən] N Vergeltung *f*; **in ~ for** als Vergeltung für
retaliatory [rɪ'tælɪətərɪ] ADJ (*move, attack*) Vergeltungs-
retarded [rɪ'tɑ:dɪd] ADJ zurückgeblieben; **mentally ~** geistig zurückgeblieben
retch [rɛtʃ] VI würgen
retention [rɪ'tɛnʃən] N (*of tradition etc*) Beibehaltung *f*; (*of land, memories*) Behalten *nt*; (*of heat, fluid etc*) Zurückhalten *nt*
retentive [rɪ'tɛntɪv] ADJ (*memory*) merkfähig
rethink ['ri:'θɪŋk] VT noch einmal überdenken
reticence ['rɛtɪsns] N Zurückhaltung *f*
reticent ['rɛtɪsnt] ADJ zurückhaltend
retina ['rɛtɪnə] N Netzhaut *f*
retinue ['rɛtɪnju:] N Gefolge *nt*
retire [rɪ'taɪəʳ] VI (*give up work*) in den Ruhestand treten; (*withdraw, go to bed*) sich zurückziehen
retired [rɪ'taɪəd] ADJ (*person*) im Ruhestand
retirement [rɪ'taɪəmənt] N (*state*) Ruhestand *m*; (*act*) Pensionierung *f*
retirement age N Rentenalter *nt*
retiring [rɪ'taɪərɪŋ] ADJ (*leaving*) ausscheidend; (*shy*) zurückhaltend
retort [rɪ'tɔ:t] VI erwidern ▸ N (*reply*) Erwiderung *f*
retrace [ri:'treɪs] VT: **to ~ one's steps** (*lit, fig*) seine Schritte zurückverfolgen
retract [rɪ'trækt] VT (*promise*) zurücknehmen; (*confession*) zurückziehen; (*claws, undercarriage*) einziehen
retractable [rɪ'træktəbl] ADJ (*undercarriage, aerial*) einziehbar
retrain [ri:'treɪn] VT umschulen ▸ VI umgeschult werden
retraining [ri:'treɪnɪŋ] N Umschulung *f*
retread ['ri:trɛd] N (*tyre*) runderneuerter Reifen *m*
retreat [rɪ'tri:t] N (*place*) Zufluchtsort *m*; (*withdrawal: also Mil*) Rückzug *m* ▸ VI sich zurückziehen; **to beat a hasty ~** schleunigst den Rückzug antreten
retrial [ri:'traɪəl] N erneute Verhandlung *f*
retribution [rɛtrɪ'bju:ʃən] N Strafe *f*
retrieval [rɪ'tri:vəl] N (*of object*) Zurückholen *nt*; (*Comput*) Abruf *m*
retrieve [rɪ'tri:v] VT (*object*) zurückholen; (*situation*) retten; (*error*) wiedergutmachen; (*dog*) apportieren; (*Comput*) abrufen
retriever [rɪ'tri:vəʳ] N (*dog*) Apportierhund *m*
retroactive [rɛtrəu'æktɪv] ADJ rückwirkend
retrograde ['rɛtrəgreɪd] ADJ (*step*) Rück-
retrospect ['rɛtrəspɛkt] N: **in ~** rückblickend, im Rückblick
retrospective [rɛtrə'spɛktɪv] ADJ (*opinion etc*) im Nachhinein; (*law, tax*) rückwirkend ▸ N (*Art*) Retrospektive *f*
return [rɪ'tə:n] N (*going or coming back*) Rückkehr *f*; (*of sth stolen etc*) Rückgabe *f*; (*BRIT: also:* **return ticket**) Rückfahrkarte *f*; (*Fin: from investment etc*) Ertrag *m*; (*of merchandise*) Rücksendung *f*; (*official report*) Erklärung *f* ▸ CPD (*journey*) Rück- ▸ VI (*person etc: come or go back*) zurückkehren; (*feelings, symptoms etc*) wiederkehren ▸ VT (*favour, greetings etc*) erwidern; (*sth stolen etc*) zurückgeben; (*Law: verdict*) fällen; (*Pol: candidate*) wählen; (*ball*) zurückspielen; **returns** NPL (*Comm*) Gewinne *pl*; **in ~ (for)** als Gegenleistung (für); **by ~ of post** postwendend; **many happy returns (of the day)!** herzlichen Glückwunsch zum Geburtstag!; **~ match** Rückspiel *nt*
▸ **return to** VT FUS (*regain: consciousness, power*) wiedererlangen
returnable [rɪ'tə:nəbl] ADJ (*bottle etc*) Mehrweg-
returner N *jd, der nach längerer Abwesenheit wieder in die Arbeitswelt zurückkehrt*

r

returning officer [rɪˈtəːnɪŋ-] (BRIT) N Wahlleiter(in) *m(f)*
return key N (*Comput*) Return-Taste *f*
retweet [riːˈtwiːt] VT (*on Twitter*) weitertwittern
reunification [riːjuːnɪfɪˈkeɪʃən] N Wiedervereinigung *f*
reunion [riːˈjuːnɪən] N Treffen *nt*; (*after long separation*) Wiedervereinigung *f*
reunite [riːjuːˈnaɪt] VT wiedervereinigen
reusable [riːˈjuːzəbl] ADJ wiederverwendbar
rev [rɛv] N ABBR (*Aut*: = *revolution*) Umdrehung *f* ▸ VT (*engine*: *also*: **rev up**) aufheulen lassen
Rev. ABBR (*Rel*) = **Reverend**
revaluation [riːvæljuˈeɪʃən] N (*of property*) Neuschätzung *f*; (*of currency*) Aufwertung *f*; (*of attitudes*) Neubewertung *f*
revamp [riːˈvæmp] VT (*company, system*) auf Vordermann bringen
rev counter (BRIT) N (*Aut*) Drehzahlmesser *m*
Revd. ABBR (*Rel*) = **Reverend**
reveal [rɪˈviːl] VT (*make known*) enthüllen; (*make visible*) zum Vorschein bringen
revealing [rɪˈviːlɪŋ] ADJ (*comment, action*) aufschlussreich; (*dress*) tief ausgeschnitten
reveille [rɪˈvælɪ] N (*Mil*) Wecksignal *nt*
revel [ˈrɛvl] VI: **to ~ in sth** in etw schwelgen; **to ~ in doing sth** es genießen, etw zu tun
revelation [rɛvəˈleɪʃən] N (*disclosure*) Enthüllung *f*
reveller [ˈrɛvlə^r] N Zecher(in) *m(f)*
revelry [ˈrɛvlrɪ] N Gelage *nt*
revenge [rɪˈvɛndʒ] N (*for insult etc*) Rache *f* ▸ VT rächen; **to get one's ~ (for sth)** seine Rache (für etw) bekommen; **to ~ o.s.** *or* **take one's ~ (on sb)** sich (an jdm) rächen
revengeful [rɪˈvɛndʒful] ADJ rachsüchtig
revenue [ˈrɛvənjuː] N (*of person, company*) Einnahmen *pl*; (*of government*) Staatseinkünfte *pl*
reverberate [rɪˈvəːbəreɪt] VI (*sound etc*) widerhallen; (*fig*: *shock etc*) Nachwirkungen haben
reverberation [rɪvəːbəˈreɪʃən] N (*of sound*) Widerhall *m*; (*fig*: *of event etc*) Nachwirkungen *pl*
revere [rɪˈvɪə^r] VT verehren
reverence [ˈrɛvərəns] N Ehrfurcht *f*
Reverend [ˈrɛvərənd] ADJ (*in titles*) Pfarrer; **the ~ John Smith** Pfarrer John Smith
reverent [ˈrɛvərənt] ADJ ehrfürchtig
reverie [ˈrɛvərɪ] N Träumerei *f*
reversal [rɪˈvəːsl] N (*of policy, trend*) Umkehr *f*; **a ~ of roles** ein Rollentausch *m*
reverse [rɪˈvəːs] N (*opposite*) Gegenteil *nt*; (*back*: *of cloth*) linke Seite *f*; (: *of coin, paper*) Rückseite *f*; (*Aut*: *also*: **reverse gear**) Rückwärtsgang *m*; (*setback*) Rückschlag *m* ▸ ADJ (*side*) Rück-; (*process*) umgekehrt ▸ VT (*position, trend etc*) umkehren; (*Law*: *verdict*) revidieren; (*roles*) vertauschen; (*car*) zurücksetzen ▸ VI (BRIT *Aut*) zurücksetzen; **in ~** umgekehrt; **to go into ~** den Rückwärtsgang einlegen; **in ~ order** in umgekehrter Reihenfolge; **to ~ direction** sich um 180 Grad drehen
reverse-charge call [rɪˈvəːstʃɑːdʒ-] (BRIT) N R-Gespräch *nt*
reverse video N (*Comput*) invertierte Darstellung *f*
reversible [rɪˈvəːsəbl] ADJ (*garment*) auf beiden Seiten tragbar; (*decision, operation*) umkehrbar
reversing lights [rɪˈvəːsɪŋ-] (BRIT) NPL Rückfahrscheinwerfer *m*
reversion [rɪˈvəːʃən] N: **~ to** Rückfall in +*acc*; (*Zool*) Rückentwicklung *f*
revert [rɪˈvəːt] VI: **to ~ to** (*former state*) zurückkehren zu, zurückfallen in +*acc*; (*Law*: *money, property*) zurückfallen an +*acc*
review [rɪˈvjuː] N (*magazine*) Zeitschrift *f*; (*Mil*) Inspektion *f*; (*of book, film etc*) Kritik *f*, Besprechung *f*, Rezension *f*; (*of policy etc*) Überprüfung *f* ▸ VT (*Mil*: *troops*) inspizieren; (*book, film etc*) besprechen, rezensieren; (*policy etc*) überprüfen; **to be/come under ~** überprüft werden
reviewer [rɪˈvjuːə^r] N Kritiker(in) *m(f)*, Rezensent(in) *m(f)*
revile [rɪˈvaɪl] VT schmähen
revise [rɪˈvaɪz] VT (*manuscript*) überarbeiten, revidieren; (*opinion etc*) ändern; (*price, procedure*) revidieren ▸ VI (*study*) wiederholen; **revised edition** überarbeitete Ausgabe
revision [rɪˈvɪʒən] N (*of manuscript, law etc*) Überarbeitung *f*, Revision *f*; (*for exam*) Wiederholung *f*
revitalize [riːˈvaɪtəlaɪz] VT neu beleben
revival [rɪˈvaɪvəl] N (*recovery*) Aufschwung *m*; (*of interest, faith*) Wiederaufleben *nt*; (*Theat*) Wiederaufnahme *f*
revive [rɪˈvaɪv] VT (*person*) wiederbeleben; (*economy etc*) Auftrieb geben +*dat*; (*custom*) wiederaufleben lassen; (*hope, interest etc*) neu beleben; (*play*) wiederaufnehmen ▸ VI (*person*) wieder zu sich kommen; (*activity, economy etc*) wieder aufblühen; (*hope, interest etc*) wiedererweckt werden
revoke [rɪˈvəuk] VT (*law etc*) aufheben; (*title, licence*) entziehen +*dat*; (*promise, decision*) widerrufen
revolt [rɪˈvəult] N Revolte *f*, Aufstand *m* ▸ VI rebellieren ▸ VT abstoßen; **to ~ against sb/sth** gegen jdn/etw rebellieren
revolting [rɪˈvəultɪŋ] ADJ (*disgusting*) abscheulich, ekelhaft
revolution [rɛvəˈluːʃən] N (*Pol etc*) Revolution *f*; (*rotation*) Umdrehung *f*
revolutionary [rɛvəˈluːʃənrɪ] ADJ revolutionär; (*leader, army*) Revolutions- ▸ N Revolutionär(in) *m(f)*
revolutionize [rɛvəˈluːʃənaɪz] VT revolutionieren
revolve [rɪˈvɔlv] VI sich drehen; **to ~ (a)round** sich drehen um
revolver [rɪˈvɔlvə^r] N Revolver *m*
revolving [rɪˈvɔlvɪŋ] ADJ (*chair*) Dreh-; (*sprinkler etc*) drehbar
revolving door N Drehtür *f*
revue [rɪˈvjuː] N (*Theat*) Revue *f*

revulsion [rɪ'vʌlʃən] N (*disgust*) Abscheu *m*, Ekel *m*
reward [rɪ'wɔːd] N Belohnung *f*; (*satisfaction*) Befriedigung *f* ▸ VT belohnen
reward card N Kundenkarte *f*, Pay-back-Karte® *f*
rewarding [rɪ'wɔːdɪŋ] ADJ lohnend; **financially** ~ einträglich
rewind [riː'waɪnd] VT (*irreg: like* **wind²**) (*tape etc*) zurückspulen
rewire [riː'waɪəʳ] VT neu verkabeln
reword [riː'wəːd] VT (*message, note*) umformulieren
rework [riː'wəːk] VT (*use again: theme etc*) wiederverarbeiten; (*revise*) neu fassen
rewritable [riː'raɪtəbl] ADJ (*CD, DVD*) wiederbeschreibbar
rewrite [riː'raɪt] VT (*irreg: like* **write**) neu schreiben
Reykjavik ['reɪkjəviːk] N Reykjavik *nt*
RFD (*US*) ABBR (*Post: = rural free delivery*) *freie Landpostzustellung*
RGN (BRIT) N ABBR (*= Registered General Nurse*) staatlich geprüfte Krankenschwester *f*, staatlich geprüfter Krankenpfleger *m*
Rh ABBR (*Med: = rhesus*) Rh.
rhapsody ['ræpsədɪ] N (*Mus*) Rhapsodie *f*
rhesus negative ADJ Rhesus negativ
rhesus positive ADJ Rhesus positiv
rhetoric ['rɛtərɪk] N Rhetorik *f*
rhetorical [rɪ'tɔrɪkl] ADJ rhetorisch
rheumatic [ruː'mætɪk] ADJ rheumatisch
rheumatism ['ruːmətɪzəm] N Rheuma *nt*, Rheumatismus *m*
rheumatoid arthritis ['ruːmətɔɪd-] N Gelenkrheumatismus *m*
Rhine [raɪn] N: **the** ~ der Rhein
rhinestone ['raɪnstəun] N Rheinkiesel *m*
rhinoceros [raɪ'nɔsərəs] N Rhinozeros *nt*
Rhodes [rəudz] N Rhodos *nt*
rhododendron [rəudə'dɛndrən] N Rhododendron *m or nt*
Rhone [rəun] N: **the** ~ die Rhone
rhubarb ['ruːbɑːb] N Rhabarber *m*
rhyme [raɪm] N Reim *m*; (*verse*) Verse *pl* ▸ VI: **to ~ (with)** sich reimen (mit); **without ~ or reason** ohne Sinn und Verstand
rhythm ['rɪðm] N Rhythmus *m*
rhythmic ['rɪðmɪk], **rhythmical** ['rɪðmɪkl] ADJ rhythmisch
rhythmically ['rɪðmɪklɪ] ADV (*move, beat*) rhythmisch, im Rhythmus
rhythm method N Knaus-Ogino-Methode *f*
RI N ABBR (BRIT *Scol: = religious instruction*) Religionsunterricht *m* ▸ ABBR (*US Post*) = **Rhode Island**
rib [rɪb] N Rippe *f* ▸ VT (*mock*) aufziehen
ribald ['rɪbəld] ADJ (*laughter, joke*) rüde; (*person*) anzüglich
ribbed [rɪbd] ADJ (*socks, sweater*) gerippt
ribbon ['rɪbən] N (*for hair, decoration*) Band *nt*; (*of typewriter*) Farbband *nt*; **in ribbons** (*torn*) in Fetzen
rice [raɪs] N Reis *m*
ricefield ['raɪsfiːld] N Reisfeld *nt*
rice pudding N Milchreis *m*
rich [rɪtʃ] ADJ reich; (*soil*) fruchtbar; (*food*) schwer; (*diet*) reichhaltig; (*colour*) satt; (*voice*) volltönend; (*tapestries, silks*) prächtig ▸ NPL: **the** ~ die Reichen; ~ **in** reich an +*dat*
riches ['rɪtʃɪz] NPL Reichtum *m*
richly ['rɪtʃlɪ] ADV (*decorated, carved*) reich; (*reward, benefit*) reichlich; **~ deserved/earned** wohlverdient
richness ['rɪtʃnɪs] N (*wealth*) Reichtum *m*; (*of life, culture, food*) Reichhaltigkeit *f*; (*of soil*) Fruchtbarkeit *f*; (*of costumes, furnishings*) Pracht *f*
rickets ['rɪkɪts] N Rachitis *f*
rickety ['rɪkɪtɪ] ADJ (*chair etc*) wackelig
rickshaw ['rɪkʃɔː] N Rikscha *f*
ricochet ['rɪkəʃeɪ] VI abprallen ▸ N Abpraller *m*
rid [rɪd] (*pt, pp* **~**) VT: **to ~ sb/sth of** jdn/etw befreien von; **to get ~ of** loswerden; (*inhibitions, illusions etc*) sich befreien von
riddance ['rɪdns] N: **good ~!** gut, dass wir den/die/das los sind!
ridden ['rɪdn] PP *of* **ride**
riddle ['rɪdl] N Rätsel *nt* ▸ VT: **to be riddled with** (*guilt, doubts*) geplagt sein von; (*holes, corruption*) durchsetzt sein von
ride [raɪd] (*pt* **rode**, *pp* **ridden**) N (*in car, on bicycle*) Fahrt *f*; (*on horse*) Ritt *m*; (*path*) Reitweg *m* ▸ VI (*on horse*) reiten; (*on bicycle, bus etc*) fahren ▸ VT reiten; fahren; **car** ~ Autofahrt *f*; **to go for a ~** eine Fahrt/einen Ausritt machen; **to take sb for a ~** (*fig*) jdn hereinlegen; **we rode all day/ all the way** wir sind den ganzen Tag/den ganzen Weg geritten/gefahren; **to ~ at anchor** (*Naut*) vor Anker liegen; **can you ~ a bike?** kannst du Fahrrad fahren?
▸ **ride out** VT: **to ~ out the storm** (*fig*) den Sturm überstehen
rider ['raɪdəʳ] N (*on horse*) Reiter(in) *m(f)*; (*on bicycle etc*) Fahrer(in) *m(f)*; (*in document etc*) Zusatz *m*
ridge [rɪdʒ] N (*of hill*) Grat *m*; (*of roof*) First *m*; (*in sand etc*) Rippelmarke *f*
ridicule ['rɪdɪkjuːl] N Spott *m* ▸ VT (*person*) verspotten; (*proposal, system etc*) lächerlich machen; **she was the object of ~** alle machten sich über sie lustig
ridiculous [rɪ'dɪkjuləs] ADJ lächerlich
riding ['raɪdɪŋ] N Reiten *nt*
riding school N Reitschule *f*
rife [raɪf] ADJ: **to be ~** (*corruption, disease etc*) grassieren; **to be ~ with** (*rumours etc*) durchsetzt sein von
riffraff ['rɪfræf] N Gesindel *nt*
rifle ['raɪfl] N (*gun*) Gewehr *nt* ▸ VT (*wallet etc*) plündern
▸ **rifle through** VT FUS (*papers etc*) durchwühlen
rifle range N Schießstand *m*
rift [rɪft] N Spalt *m*; (*fig*) Kluft *f*
rig [rɪg] N (*also*: **oil rig**: *at sea*) Bohrinsel *f*; (: *on land*) Bohrturm *m* ▸ VT (*election, game etc*) manipulieren

r

▸ **rig out** (BRIT) VT; **to ~ sb out as/in** jdn ausstaffieren als/in *+dat*

▸ **rig up** VT (*device*) montieren

rigging ['rɪgɪŋ] N (*Naut*) Takelage *f*

right [raɪt] ADJ (*correct*) richtig; (*not left*) rechte(r, s) ▸ N Recht *nt* ▸ ADV (*correctly, properly*) richtig; (*directly, exactly*) genau; (*not on the left*) rechts ▸ VT (*ship, car etc*) aufrichten; (*fault, situation*) korrigieren, berichtigen ▸ EXCL okay; **the ~ time** (*exact*) die genaue Zeit; (*most suitable*) die richtige Zeit; **to be ~** (*person*) recht haben; (*answer, fact*) richtig sein; (*clock*) genau gehen; (*reading etc*) korrekt sein; **to get sth ~** etw richtig machen; **let's get it ~ this time!** diesmal machen wir es richtig!; **you did the ~ thing** du hast das Richtige getan; **to put sth ~** (*mistake etc*) etw berichtigen; **on/to the ~** rechts; **the R~** (*Pol*) die Rechte; **by rights** richtig genommen; **to be in the ~** im Recht sein; **you're within your rights (to do that)** es ist dein gutes Recht(, das zu tun); **he is a well-known author in his own ~** er ist selbst auch ein bekannter Autor; **film rights** Filmrechte *pl*; **~ now** im Moment; **~ before/after the party** gleich vor/nach der Party; **~ against the wall** unmittelbar an der Wand; **~ ahead** geradeaus; **~ away** (*immediately*) sofort; **~ in the middle** genau in der Mitte; **he went ~ to the end of the road** er ging bis ganz ans Ende der Straße

right angle N rechter Winkel *m*

right-click ['raɪtklɪk] (*Comput*) VI rechts klicken ▸ VT rechts klicken auf *+acc*

righteous ['raɪtʃəs] ADJ (*person*) rechtschaffen; (*indignation*) gerecht

righteousness ['raɪtʃəsnɪs] N Rechtschaffenheit *f*

rightful ['raɪtful] ADJ rechtmäßig

rightfully ['raɪtfəlɪ] ADV von Rechts wegen

right-hand drive ADJ (*vehicle*) mit Rechtssteuerung

right-handed [raɪt'hændɪd] ADJ rechtshändig

right-hand man N (*irreg*) rechte Hand *f*

right-hand side N rechte Seite *f*

rightly ['raɪtlɪ] ADV (*with reason*) zu Recht; **if I remember ~** (BRIT) wenn ich mich recht entsinne

right-minded [raɪt'maɪndɪd] ADJ vernünftig

right of way N (*on path etc*) Durchgangsrecht *f*; (*Aut*) Vorfahrt *f*

rights issue N (*Stock Exchange*) Bezugsrechtsemission *f*

right wing N (*Pol, Sport*) rechter Flügel *m*

right-wing [raɪt'wɪŋ] ADJ (*Pol*) rechtsgerichtet

right-winger [raɪt'wɪŋə^r] N (*Pol*) Rechte(r) *f(m)*; (*Sport*) Rechtsaußen *m*

rigid ['rɪdʒɪd] ADJ (*structure, views*) starr; (*principle, control etc*) streng

rigidity [rɪ'dʒɪdɪtɪ] N (*of structure etc*) Starrheit *f*; (*of attitude, views etc*) Strenge *f*

rigidly ['rɪdʒɪdlɪ] ADV (*hold, fix etc*) starr; (*control, interpret*) streng

rigmarole ['rɪgmərəul] N Gedöns *nt* (*inf*)

rigor ['rɪgə^r] (*US*) N = **rigour**

rigor mortis ['rɪgə'mɔːtɪs] N Totenstarre *f*

rigorous ['rɪgərəs] ADJ (*control etc*) streng; (*training*) gründlich

rigorously ['rɪgərəslɪ] ADV (*test, assess etc*) streng

rigour, (US) rigor ['rɪgə^r] N (*of argument, law*) Strenge *f*; (*of research*) Gründlichkeit; **the rigours of life/winter** die Härten des Lebens/des Winters

rig-out ['rɪgaut] (BRIT *inf*) N Aufzug *m*

rile [raɪl] VT ärgern

rim [rɪm] N (*of glass, spectacles*) Rand *m*; (*of wheel*) Felge *f*, Radkranz *m*

rimless ['rɪmlɪs] ADJ (*spectacles*) randlos

rimmed [rɪmd] ADJ: **~ with** umrandet von; **gold-~ spectacles** Brille *f* mit Goldfassung *or* Goldrand

rind [raɪnd] N (*of bacon*) Schwarte *f*; (*of lemon, melon*) Schale *f*; (*of cheese*) Rinde *f*

ring [rɪŋ] (*pt* **rang**, *pp* **rung**) N Ring *m*; (*of people, objects*) Kreis *m*; (*of circus*) Manege *f*; (*bullring*) Arena *f*; (*sound of telephone*) Klingeln *nt*; (*sound of bell*) Läuten *nt*; (*on cooker*) Kochstelle *m* ▸ VI (*Tel: person*) anrufen; (*telephone, doorbell*) klingeln; (*bell*) läuten; (*also*: **ring out**) ertönen ▸ VT (BRIT *Tel*) anrufen; (*bell etc*) läuten; (*encircle*) einen Kreis machen um; **to give sb a ~** (BRIT *Tel*) jdn anrufen; **that has a ~ of truth about it** das könnte stimmen; **to run rings round sb** (*inf: fig*) jdn in die Tasche stecken; **to ~ true/false** wahr/falsch klingen; **my ears are ringing** mir klingen die Ohren; **to ~ the doorbell** klingeln; **the name doesn't ~ a bell (with me)** der Name sagt mir nichts

▸ **ring back** (BRIT) VT, VI (*Tel*) zurückrufen

▸ **ring off** (BRIT) VI (*Tel*) (den Hörer) auflegen

▸ **ring up** (BRIT) VT (*Tel*) anrufen

ring binder N Ringbuch *nt*

ring-fence [rɪŋ'fɛns] VT (*money, tax*) zweckbinden

ring finger N Ringfinger *m*

ringing ['rɪŋɪŋ] N (*of telephone*) Klingeln *nt*; (*of bell*) Läuten *nt*; (*in ears*) Klingen *nt*

ringing tone (BRIT) N (*Tel*) Rufzeichen *nt*

ringleader ['rɪŋliːdə^r] N Rädelsführer(in) *m(f)*

ringlets ['rɪŋlɪts] NPL Ringellocken *pl*; **in ~** in Ringellocken

ring road (BRIT) N Ringstraße *f*

ringtone ['rɪŋtəun] N (*of mobile phone*) Klingelton *m*

rink [rɪŋk] N (*also*: **ice rink**) Eisbahn *f*; (*also*: **roller skating rink**) Rollschuhbahn *f*

rinse [rɪns] N Spülen *nt*; (*of hands*) Abspülen *nt*; (*hair dye*) Tönung *f* ▸ VT spülen; (*hands*) abspülen; (*also*: **rinse out**: *clothes*) auswaschen; (: *mouth*) ausspülen; **to give sth a ~** etw spülen; (*dishes*) etw abspülen

Rio ['riːəu], **Rio de Janeiro** ['riːəudədʒə'nɪərəu] N Rio (de Janeiro) *nt*

riot ['raɪət] N (*disturbance*) Aufruhr *m* ▸ VI randalieren; **a ~ of colours** ein Farbenmeer *nt*; **to run ~** randalieren

rioter ['raɪətə^r] N Randalierer *m*

riot gear N Schutzausrüstung *f*
riotous ['raɪətəs] ADJ (*crowd*) randalierend; (*nights, party*) ausschweifend; (*welcome etc*) tumultartig
riotously ['raɪətəslɪ] ADV: **~ funny** *or* **comic** urkomisch
riot police N Bereitschaftspolizei *f*; **hundreds of ~** Hunderte von Bereitschaftspolizisten
RIP ABBR (= *requiescat or requiescant in pace*) R.I.P.
rip [rɪp] N (*tear*) Riss *m* ▸ VT zerreißen ▸ VI reißen
▸ **rip off** VT (*clothes*) herunterreißen; (*inf: swindle*) übers Ohr hauen
▸ **rip up** VT zerreißen
ripcord ['rɪpkɔːd] N Reißleine *f*
ripe [raɪp] ADJ reif; **to be ~ for sth** (*fig*) reif für etw sein; **he lived to a ~ old age** er erreichte ein stolzes Alter
ripen ['raɪpn] VT reifen lassen ▸ VI reifen
ripeness ['raɪpnɪs] N Reife *f*
rip-off ['rɪpɔf] (*inf*) N: **it's a ~!** das ist Wucher!
riposte [rɪ'pɔst] N scharfe Entgegnung *f*
ripple ['rɪpl] N (*wave*) kleine Welle *f*; (*of laughter, applause*) Welle *f* ▸ VI (*water*) sich kräuseln; (*muscles*) spielen ▸ VT (*surface*) kräuseln
rise [raɪz] (*pt* **rose**, *pp* **risen**) N (*incline*) Steigung *f*; (BRIT: *salary increase*) Gehaltserhöhung *f*; (*in prices, temperature etc*) Anstieg *m*; (*fig: to fame etc*) Aufstieg *m* ▸ VI (*prices, water*) steigen; (*sun, moon*) aufgehen; (*wind*) aufkommen; (*from bed, chair*) aufstehen; (*sound, voice*) ansteigen; (*tower, rebel: also:* **rise up**) sich erheben; (*in rank*) aufsteigen; **to give ~ to** Anlass geben zu; **to ~ to power** an die Macht kommen
risen [rɪzn] PP *of* **rise**
rising ['raɪzɪŋ] ADJ (*increasing*) steigend; (*up-and-coming*) aufstrebend
rising damp N aufsteigende Feuchtigkeit *f*
rising star N (*fig: person*) Aufsteiger(in) *m(f)*
risk [rɪsk] N (*danger, chance*) Gefahr *f*; (*deliberate*) Risiko *nt* ▸ VT riskieren; **to take a ~** ein Risiko eingehen; **to run the ~ of sth** etw zu fürchten haben; **to run the ~ of doing sth** Gefahr laufen, etw zu tun; **at ~** in Gefahr; **at one's own ~** auf eigene Gefahr; **at the ~ of sounding rude ...** auf die Gefahr hin, unhöflich zu klingen, ...; **it's a fire/health ~** es ist ein Feuer-/Gesundheitsrisiko; **I'll ~ it** ich riskiere es
risk capital N Risikokapital *nt*
risky ['rɪskɪ] ADJ riskant
risqué ['riːskeɪ] ADJ (*joke*) gewagt
rissole ['rɪsəul] N (*of meat, fish etc*) Frikadelle *f*
rite [raɪt] N Ritus *m*; **last rites** (*Rel*) Letzte Ölung *f*
ritual ['rɪtjuəl] ADJ (*law, murder*) Ritual-; (*dance*) rituell ▸ N Ritual *nt*
rival ['raɪvl] N Rivale *m*, Rivalin *f* ▸ ADJ (*firm, newspaper etc*) Konkurrenz-; (*teams, groups etc*) rivalisierend ▸ VT (*match*) sich messen können mit; **to ~ sth/sb in sth** sich mit etw/jdm in Bezug auf etw messen können
rivalry ['raɪvlrɪ] N Rivalität *f*
river ['rɪvəʳ] N Fluss *m*; (*fig: of blood etc*) Strom *m* ▸ CPD (*port, traffic*) Fluss-; **up/down ~** flussaufwärts/-abwärts
river bank N Flussufer *nt*
river bed N Flussbett *nt*
riverside ['rɪvəsaɪd] N = **river bank**
rivet ['rɪvɪt] N Niete *f* ▸ VT (*fig: attention*) fesseln; (*: eyes*) heften
riveting ['rɪvɪtɪŋ] ADJ (*fig*) fesselnd
Riviera [rɪvɪ'ɛərə] N: **the (French) ~** die (französische) Riviera; **the Italian ~** die italienische Riviera
Riyadh [rɪ'jɑːd] N Riad *nt*
RMT N ABBR (= *National Union of Rail, Maritime and Transport Workers*) *Gewerkschaft der Eisenbahner, Seeleute und Transportarbeiter*
RN N ABBR (BRIT) = **Royal Navy**; (US) = **registered nurse**
RNA N ABBR (= *ribonucleic acid*) RNS *f*
RNLI (BRIT) N ABBR (= *Royal National Lifeboat Institution*) *durch Spenden finanzierter Seenot-Rettungsdienst*, ≈ DLRG *f*
RNZAF N ABBR (= *Royal New Zealand Air Force*) neuseeländische Luftwaffe *f*
RNZN N ABBR (= *Royal New Zealand Navy*) neuseeländische Marine *f*
road [rəud] N Straße *f*; (*fig*) Weg *m* ▸ CPD (*accident, sense*) Verkehrs-; **main ~** Hauptstraße *f*; **it takes four hours by ~** man braucht vier Stunden mit dem Auto; **let's hit the ~** machen wir uns auf den Weg!; **to be on the ~** (*salesman etc*) unterwegs sein; (*pop group etc*) auf Tournee sein; **on the ~ to success** auf dem Weg zum Erfolg; **major/minor ~** Haupt-/Nebenstraße *f*
road accident N Verkehrsunfall *m*
roadblock ['rəudblɔk] N Straßensperre *f*
road haulage N Spedition *f*
roadhog ['rəudhɔg] N Verkehrsrowdy *m*
road map N Straßenkarte *f*
road rage N Aggressivität *f* im Straßenverkehr
road safety N Verkehrssicherheit *f*
roadside ['rəudsaɪd] N Straßenrand *m* ▸ CPD (*building, sign etc*) am Straßenrand; **by the ~** am Straßenrand
road sign N Verkehrszeichen *nt*
roadsweeper ['rəudswiːpəʳ] (BRIT) N (*person*) Straßenkehrer(in) *m(f)*; (*vehicle*) Straßenkehrmaschine *f*
road tax N Kraftfahrzeugssteuer *f*
road user N Verkehrsteilnehmer(in) *m(f)*
roadway ['rəudweɪ] N Fahrbahn *f*
road works NPL Straßenbauarbeiten *pl*, Straßenbau *sing*
roadworthy ['rəudwəːðɪ] ADJ verkehrstüchtig
roam [rəum] VI wandern, streifen ▸ VT (*streets, countryside*) durchstreifen
roar [rɔːʳ] N (*of animal, crowd*) Brüllen *nt*; (*of vehicle*) Getöse *nt*; (*of storm*) Heulen *nt* ▸ VI (*animal, person*) brüllen; (*engine, wind etc*) heulen; **roars of laughter** brüllendes Gelächter; **to ~ with laughter** vor Lachen brüllen
roaring ['rɔːrɪŋ] ADJ: **a ~ fire** ein prasselndes Feuer; **a ~ success** ein Bombenerfolg *m*; **to do**

r

a ~ trade (in sth) ein Riesengeschäft (mit etw) machen
roast [rəust] N Braten *m* ▸ VT (*meat, potatoes*) braten; (*coffee*) rösten
roast beef N Roastbeef *nt*
roasting ['rəustɪŋ] (*inf*) ADJ (*hot*) knallheiß ▸ N (*criticism*) Verriss *m*; (*telling-off*) Standpauke *f*; **to give sb a ~** (*criticize*) jdn verreißen; (*scold*) jdm eine Standpauke halten
rob [rɔb] VT (*person*) bestehlen; (*house, bank*) ausrauben; **to ~ sb of sth** jdm etw rauben; (*fig: deprive*) jdm etw vorenthalten
robber ['rɔbə^r] N Räuber(in) *m(f)*
robbery ['rɔbərɪ] N Raub *m*
robe [rəub] N (*for ceremony etc*) Gewand *nt*; (*also*: **bath robe**) Bademantel *m*; (*US*) Morgenrock *m* ▸ VT: **to be robed in** (*form*) (festlich) in etw *acc* gekleidet sein
robin ['rɔbɪn] N Rotkehlchen *nt*
robot ['rəubɔt] N Roboter *m*
robotics [rə'bɔtɪks] N Robotik *f*
robust [rəu'bʌst] ADJ robust; (*appetite*) gesund
rock [rɔk] N (*substance*) Stein *m*; (*boulder*) Felsen *m*; (*US: small stone*) Stein *m*; (BRIT: *sweet*) ≈ Zuckerstange *f*; (*Mus: also*: **rock music**) Rock *m*, Rockmusik *f* ▸ VT (*swing gently: cradle*) schaukeln; (*: child*) wiegen; (*shake: also fig*) erschüttern ▸ VI (*object*) schwanken; (*person*) schaukeln; **on the rocks** (*drink*) mit Eis; (*ship*) (auf Felsen) aufgelaufen; (*marriage etc*) gescheitert; **to ~ the boat** (*fig*) Unruhe stiften
rock and roll N Rock and Roll *m*
rock bottom ['rɔk'bɔtəm] ADJ (*prices*) Tiefst- ▸ N: **to reach** *or* **touch** *or* **hit ~** (*person, prices*) den Tiefpunkt erreichen
rock cake N ≈ Rosinenbrötchen *nt*
rock climber N Felsenkletterer(in) *m(f)*
rock climbing N Felsenklettern *nt*
rockery ['rɔkərɪ] N Steingarten *m*
rocket ['rɔkɪt] N Rakete *f* ▸ VI (*prices*) in die Höhe schießen
rocket launcher N Raketenwerfer *m*
rock face N Felswand *f*
rock fall N Steinschlag *m*
rocking chair ['rɔkɪŋ-] N Schaukelstuhl *m*
rocking horse N Schaukelpferd *nt*
rocky ['rɔkɪ] ADJ (*path, ground*) felsig; (*fig: business, marriage*) wackelig
Rocky Mountains NPL: **the ~** die Rocky Mountains *pl*
rod [rɔd] N (*also Tech*) Stange *f*; (*also*: **fishing rod**) Angelrute *f*
rode [rəud] PT *of* **ride**
rodent ['rəudnt] N Nagetier *nt*
rodeo ['rəudɪəu] (*US*) N Rodeo *nt*
roe [rəu] N (*Culin*): **hard ~** Rogen *m*; **soft ~** Milch *f*
roe deer N INV Reh *nt*
rogue [rəug] N Gauner *m*
roguish ['rəugɪʃ] ADJ schelmisch
role [rəul] N Rolle *f*
role model N Rollenmodell *nt*
role play N Rollenspiel *nt*
roll [rəul] N (*of paper*) Rolle *f*; (*of cloth*) Ballen *m*; (*of banknotes*) Bündel *nt*; (*also*: **bread roll**) Brötchen *nt*; (*register, list*) Verzeichnis *nt*; (*of drums etc*) Wirbel *m* ▸ VT rollen; (*also*: **roll up**: *string*) aufrollen; (*: sleeves*) aufkrempeln; (*cigarette*) drehen; (*pastry: also*: **roll out**) ausrollen; (*flatten: lawn, road*) walzen ▸ VI rollen; (*drum*) wirbeln; (*thunder*) grollen; (*ship*) schlingern; (*tears, sweat*) fließen; (*camera, printing press*) laufen; **cheese/ham ~** Käse-/Schinkenbrötchen *nt*; **he's rolling in it** (*inf: rich*) er schwimmt im Geld
▸ **roll about** VI sich wälzen
▸ **roll around** VI = **roll about**
▸ **roll in** VI (*money, invitations*) hereinströmen
▸ **roll over** VI sich umdrehen
▸ **roll up** VI (*inf: arrive*) aufkreuzen ▸ VT (*carpet, umbrella etc*) aufrollen; **to ~ o.s. up into a ball** sich zusammenrollen
roll call N namentlicher Aufruf *m*
rolled gold [rəuld-] N Doublégold *nt*
roller ['rəulə^r] N Rolle *f*; (*for lawn, road*) Walze *f*; (*for hair*) Lockenwickler *m*
Rollerblades® NPL Rollerblades *pl*
rollerblading N Inlineskaten *nt*
roller blind N Rollo *nt*
roller coaster N Achterbahn *f*
roller skates NPL Rollschuhe *pl*
roller-skating N Rollschuhlaufen *nt*
rollicking ['rɔlɪkɪŋ] ADJ toll, Mords-; **to have a ~ time** sich ganz toll amüsieren
rolling ['rəulɪŋ] ADJ (*hills*) wellig
rolling mill N Walzwerk *nt*
rolling pin N Nudelholz *nt*
rolling stock N (*Rail*) Fahrzeuge *pl*
roll-on-roll-off ['rəulɔn'rəulɔf] (BRIT) ADJ (*ferry*) Roll-on-roll-off-
roly-poly ['rəulɪ'pəulɪ] (BRIT) N ≈ Strudel *m*
ROM [rɔm] N ABBR (*Comput*: = *read only memory*) ROM
Roman ['rəumən] ADJ römisch ▸ N (*person*) Römer(in) *m(f)*
Roman Catholic ADJ römisch-katholisch ▸ N Katholik(in) *m(f)*
romance [rə'mæns] N (*love affair*) Romanze *f*; (*romanticism*) Romantik *f*; (*novel*) fantastische Erzählung *f*
Romanesque [rəumə'nɛsk] ADJ romanisch
Romania [rəu'meɪnɪə] N Rumänien *nt*
Romanian [rəu'meɪnɪən] ADJ rumänisch ▸ N (*person*) Rumäne *m*, Rumänin *f*; (*Ling*) Rumänisch *nt*
Roman numeral N römische Ziffer *f*
romantic [rə'mæntɪk] ADJ romantisch
romanticism [rə'mæntɪsɪzəm] N (*also Art, Liter*) Romantik *f*
Romany ['rɔmənɪ] ADJ Roma- ▸ N (*person*) Roma *mf*; (*Ling*) Romani *nt*
Rome [rəum] N Rom *nt*
romp [rɔmp] N Klamauk *m* ▸ VI (*also*: **romp about**) herumtollen; **to ~ home** (*horse*) spielend gewinnen
rompers ['rɔmpəz] NPL (*clothing*) *einteiliger Spielanzug für Babys*

rondo ['rɔndəu] N (*Mus*) Rondo *nt*
roof [ru:f] (*pl* **roofs**) N Dach *nt* ▶ VT (*house etc*) überdachen; **the ~ of the mouth** der Gaumen
roof garden N Dachgarten *m*
roofing ['ru:fɪŋ] N Deckung *f*; **~ felt** Dachpappe *f*
roof rack N Dachgepäckträger *m*
rook [ruk] N (*bird*) Saatkrähe *f*; (*Chess*) Turm *m*
rookie ['ruki:] (*inf*) N (*esp Mil*) Grünschnabel *m*
room [ru:m] N (*in house, hotel*) Zimmer *nt*; (*space*) Raum *m*, Platz *m*; (*scope: for change etc*) Raum *m* ▶ VI: **to ~ with sb** (*esp US*) ein Zimmer mit jdm teilen; **rooms** NPL (*lodging*) Zimmer *pl*; **"rooms to let"**, **"rooms for rent"** (*US*) „Zimmer zu vermieten"; **single/double ~** Einzel-/ Doppelzimmer *nt*; **is there ~ for this?** ist dafür Platz vorhanden?; **to make ~ for sb** für jdn Platz machen; **there is ~ for improvement** es gibt Möglichkeiten zur Verbesserung
rooming house ['ru:mɪŋ-] (*US*) N Mietshaus *nt*
roommate ['ru:mmeɪt] N Zimmergenosse *m*, Zimmergenossin *f*
room service N Zimmerservice *m*
room temperature N Zimmertemperatur *f*
roomy ['ru:mɪ] ADJ (*building, car*) geräumig
roost [ru:st] VI (*birds*) sich niederlassen
rooster ['ru:stər] (*esp US*) N Hahn *m*
root [ru:t] N (*also Math*) Wurzel *f* ▶ VI (*plant*) Wurzeln schlagen ▶ VT: **to be rooted in** verwurzelt sein in *+dat*; **roots** NPL (*family origins*) Wurzeln *pl*; **to take ~** (*plant, idea*) Wurzeln schlagen; **the ~ cause of the problem** die Wurzel des Problems
▶ **root about** VI (*search*) herumwühlen
▶ **root for** VT FUS (*support*) anfeuern
▶ **root out** VT ausrotten
root beer (*US*) N *kohlensäurehaltiges Getränk aus Wurzel- und Kräuterextrakten*
rope [rəup] N Seil *nt*; (*Naut*) Tau *nt* ▶ VT (*tie*) festbinden; (*also:* **rope together**) zusammenbinden; **to know the ropes** (*fig*) sich auskennen
▶ **rope in** VT (*fig: person*) einspannen
▶ **rope off** VT (*area*) mit einem Seil absperren
rope ladder N Strickleiter *f*
ropey, ropy ['rəupɪ] (*inf*) ADJ (*ill, poor quality*) miserabel
rort [rɔ:t] N (*AUST, NZ inf*) Betrugsschema *nt*, Abzocke *f* (*inf*) ▶ VT austricksen (*inf*); (*money*) abschöpfen
rosary ['rəuzərɪ] N Rosenkranz *m*
rose [rəuz] PT *of* **rise** ▶ N (*flower*) Rose *f*; (*also:* **rosebush**) Rosenstrauch *m*; (*on watering can*) Brause *f* ▶ ADJ rosarot
rosé ['rəuzeɪ] N (*wine*) Rosé *m*
rosebed ['rəuzbɛd] N Rosenbeet *nt*
rosebud ['rəuzbʌd] N Rosenknospe *f*
rosebush ['rəuzbuʃ] N Rosenstrauch *m*
rosemary ['rəuzmərɪ] N Rosmarin *m*
rosette [rəu'zɛt] N Rosette *f*
ROSPA ['rɔspə] (BRIT) N ABBR (= *Royal Society for the Prevention of Accidents*) *Verband, der Maßnahmen zur Unfallverhütung propagiert*
roster ['rɔstər] N: **duty ~** Dienstplan *m*
rostrum ['rɔstrəm] N Rednerpult *nt*
rosy ['rəuzɪ] ADJ (*colour*) rosarot; (*face, situation*) rosig; **a ~ future** eine rosige Zukunft
rot [rɔt] N (*decay*) Fäulnis *f*; (*fig: rubbish*) Quatsch *m* ▶ VT verfaulen lassen ▶ VI (*teeth, wood, fruit etc*) verfaulen; **to stop the ~** (BRIT *fig*) den Verfall stoppen; **dry ~** Holzschwamm *m*; **wet ~** Nassfäule *f*
rota ['rəutə] N Dienstplan *m*; **on a ~ basis** reihum nach Plan
rotary ['rəutərɪ] ADJ (*cutter*) rotierend; (*motion*) Dreh-
rotate [rəu'teɪt] VT (*spin*) drehen, rotieren lassen; (*crops*) im Wechsel anbauen; (*jobs*) turnusmäßig wechseln ▶ VI (*revolve*) rotieren, sich drehen
rotating [rəu'teɪtɪŋ] ADJ (*revolving*) rotierend; (*drum, mirror*) Dreh-
rotation [rəu'teɪʃən] N (*of planet, drum etc*) Rotation *f*, Drehung *f*; (*of crops*) Wechsel *m*; (*of jobs*) turnusmäßiger Wechsel *m*; **in ~** der Reihe nach
rote [rəut] N: **by ~** auswendig
rotor ['rəutər] N (*also:* **rotor blade**) Rotor *m*
rotten ['rɔtn] ADJ (*decayed*) faul, verfault; (*inf: person, situation*) gemein; (*: film, weather, driver etc*) mies; **to feel ~** sich elend fühlen
rotund [rəu'tʌnd] ADJ (*person*) rundlich
rouble, (US) **ruble** ['ru:bl] N Rubel *m*
rouge [ru:ʒ] N Rouge *nt*
rough [rʌf] ADJ rau; (*terrain, road*) uneben; (*person, plan, drawing, guess*) grob; (*life, conditions, journey*) hart; (*sea, crossing*) stürmisch ▶ N (*Golf*): **in the ~** im Rough ▶ VT: **to ~ it** primitiv *or* ohne Komfort leben; **the sea is ~ today** die See ist heute stürmisch; **to have a ~ time** eine harte Zeit durchmachen; **can you give me a ~ idea of the cost?** können Sie mir eine ungefähre Vorstellung von den Kosten geben?; **to feel ~** (BRIT) sich elend fühlen; **to sleep ~** (BRIT) im Freien übernachten; **to play ~** (*fig*) auf die grobe Tour kommen
▶ **rough out** VT (*drawing, idea etc*) skizzieren
roughage ['rʌfɪdʒ] N Ballaststoffe *pl*
rough-and-ready ['rʌfən'rɛdɪ] ADJ provisorisch
rough-and-tumble ['rʌfən'tʌmbl] N (*fighting*) Balgerei *f*; (*fig*) Schlachtfeld *nt*
roughcast ['rʌfkɑ:st] N Rauputz *m*
rough copy N Entwurf *m*
rough draft N = **rough copy**
rough justice N Justizwillkür *f*
roughly ['rʌflɪ] ADV grob; (*approximately*) ungefähr; **~ speaking** grob gesagt
roughness ['rʌfnɪs] N Rauheit *f*; (*of manner*) Grobheit *f*
roughshod ['rʌfʃɔd] ADV: **to ride ~ over** sich rücksichtslos hinwegsetzen über *+acc*
roulette [ru:'lɛt] N Roulette *nt*
Roumania *etc* [ru:'meɪnɪə] N = **Romania** *etc*
round [raund] ADJ rund ▶ N Runde *f*; (*of ammunition*) Ladung *f* ▶ VT (*corner*) biegen um; (*cape*) umrunden ▶ PREP um ▶ ADV: **all ~**

r

rundherum; **in ~ figures** rund gerechnet; **the daily ~** (*fig*) der tägliche Trott; **a ~ of applause** Beifall *m*; **a ~ (of drinks)** eine Runde; **a ~ of sandwiches** ein Butterbrot; **a ~ of toast** (BRIT) eine Scheibe Toast; **it's just ~ the corner** (*fig*) es steht vor der Tür; **to go ~ the back** hinten herum gehen; **to go ~ (an obstacle)** (um ein Hindernis) herumgehen; **~ the clock** rund um die Uhr; **~ his neck/the table** um seinen Hals/den Tisch; **to sail ~ the world** die Welt umsegeln; **to walk ~ the room/park** im Zimmer/Park herumgehen; **~ about 300** (*approximately*) ungefähr 300; **the long way ~** auf Umwegen; **all (the) year ~** das ganze Jahr über; **the wrong way ~** falsch herum; **to ask sb ~** jdn zu sich einladen; **I'll be ~ at 6 o'clock** ich komme um 6 Uhr; **to go ~** (*rotate*) sich drehen; **to go ~ to sb's (house)** jdn (zu Hause) besuchen; **enough to go ~** genug für alle
▸ **round off** VT abrunden
▸ **round up** VT (*cattle etc*) zusammentreiben; (*people*) versammeln; (*figure*) aufrunden

roundabout ['raundəbaut] (BRIT) N (*Aut*) Kreisverkehr *m*; (*at fair*) Karussell *nt* ▸ ADJ: **by a ~ route** auf Umwegen; **in a ~ way** auf Umwegen

rounded ['raundɪd] ADJ (*hill, figure etc*) rundlich

rounders ['raundəz] N ≈ Schlagball *m*

roundly ['raundlɪ] ADV (*fig: criticize etc*) nachdrücklich

round robin (*esp US*) N (*Sport*) *Wettkampf, bei dem jeder gegen jeden spielt*

round-shouldered ['raund'ʃəuldəd] ADJ mit runden Schultern

round trip N Rundreise *f*

round-trip ticket N (US) Rückfahrkarte *f*; (*for plane*) Rückflugticket *nt*

roundup ['raundʌp] N (*of news etc*) Zusammenfassung *f*; (*of animals*) Zusammentreiben *nt*; (*of criminals*) Aufgreifen *nt*; **a ~ of the latest news** ein Nachrichtenüberblick *m*

rouse [rauz] VT (*wake up*) aufwecken; (*stir up*) reizen

rousing ['rauzɪŋ] ADJ (*speech*) mitreißend; (*welcome*) stürmisch

rout [raut] (*Mil*) N totale Niederlage *f* ▸ VT (*defeat*) vernichtend schlagen

route [ru:t] N Strecke *f*; (*of bus, train, shipping*) Linie *f*; (*of procession, fig*) Weg *m*; **"all routes"** (*Aut*) „alle Richtungen"; **the best ~ to London** der beste Weg nach London

route map (BRIT) N Streckenkarte *f*

routine [ru:'ti:n] ADJ (*work, check etc*) Routine- ▸ N (*habits*) Routine *f*; (*drudgery*) Stumpfsinn *m*; (*Theat*) Nummer *f*; **~ procedure** Routinesache *f*

rove [rəuv] VT (*area, streets*) ziehen durch

roving reporter ['rəuvɪŋ-] N Reporter(in) *m(f)* im Außendienst

row¹ [rəu] N (*line*) Reihe *f* ▸ VI (*in boat*) rudern ▸ VT (*boat*) rudern; **three times in a ~** dreimal hintereinander

row² [rau] N (*din*) Krach *m*, Lärm *m*; (*dispute*) Streit *m* ▸ VI (*argue*) sich streiten; **to have a ~** sich streiten

rowboat ['rəubəut] (US) N = **rowing boat**

rowdiness ['raudɪnɪs] N Rowdytum *nt*

rowdy ['raudɪ] ADJ (*person*) rüpelhaft; (*party etc*) lärmend

rowdyism ['raudɪɪzəm] N = **rowdiness**

rowing ['rəuɪŋ] N (*sport*) Rudern *nt*

rowing boat (BRIT) N Ruderboot *nt*

rowlock ['rɔlək] (BRIT) N Dolle *f*

royal ['rɔɪəl] ADJ königlich; **the ~ family** die königliche Familie

> Die **Royal Academy** oder **Royal Academy of Arts**, eine Akademie zur Förderung der Malerei, Bildhauerei und Architektur, wurde 1768 unter der Schirmherrschaft von George II. gegründet und befindet sich seit 1869 in Burlington House, Piccadilly, London. Jeden Sommer findet dort eine Ausstellung mit Werken zeitgenössischer Künstler statt. Die Royal Academy unterhält auch Schulen, an denen Malerei, Bildhauerei und Architektur unterrichtet wird.

Royal Air Force (BRIT) N: **the ~** die Königliche Luftwaffe

royal blue ADJ königsblau

royalist ['rɔɪəlɪst] N Royalist(in) *m(f)* ▸ ADJ royalistisch

Royal Navy (BRIT) N: **the ~** die Königliche Marine

royalty ['rɔɪəltɪ] N (*royal persons*) die königliche Familie; **royalties** NPL (*to author*) Tantiemen *pl*; (*to inventor*) Honorar *nt*

RP (BRIT) N ABBR (= *received pronunciation*) *Standardaussprache des Englischen*; *see also* **Received Pronunciation**

rpm ABBR (= *revolutions per minute*) U/min.

RR (US) ABBR = **railroad**

RRP (BRIT) N ABBR = **recommended retail price**

RSA (BRIT) N ABBR (= *Royal Society of Arts*) *akademischer Verband zur Vergabe von Diplomen*; (= *Royal Scottish Academy*) *Kunstakademie*

RSI N ABBR (*Med*: = *repetitive strain injury*) RSI *nt*, *Schmerzempfindung durch ständige Wiederholung bestimmter Bewegungen*

RSPB (BRIT) N ABBR (= *Royal Society for the Protection of Birds*) *Vogelschutzorganisation*

RSPCA (BRIT) N ABBR (= *Royal Society for the Prevention of Cruelty to Animals*) Tierschutzverein *m*

RSVP ABBR (= *répondez s'il vous plaît*) u. A. w. g.

RTA N ABBR (= *road traffic accident*) Verkehrsunfall *m*

Rt Hon. (BRIT) ABBR (= *Right Honourable*) *Titel für Abgeordnete des Unterhauses*

Rt Rev. ABBR (*Rel*: = *Right Reverend*) *Titel für Bischöfe*

rub [rʌb] VT reiben ▸ N: **to give sth a ~** (*polish*) etw polieren; **he rubbed his hands together** er rieb sich *dat* die Hände; **to ~ sb up the wrong way, to ~ sb the wrong way** (US) bei jdm anecken
▸ **rub down** VT (*body, horse*) abreiben

▸ rub in VT (*ointment*) einreiben; **don't ~ it in!** (*fig*) reite nicht so darauf herum!
▸ rub off VI (*paint*) abfärben
▸ rub off on VT FUS abfärben auf +*acc*
▸ rub out VT (*with eraser*) ausradieren
rubber ['rʌbə^r] N (*also inf: condom*) Gummi *m or nt*; (BRIT: *eraser*) Radiergummi *m*
rubber band N Gummiband *nt*
rubber bullet N Gummigeschoss *nt*
rubber plant N Gummibaum *m*
rubber ring N (*for swimming*) Schwimmreifen *m*
rubber stamp N Stempel *m*
rubber-stamp [rʌbə'stæmp] VT (*fig: decision*) genehmigen
rubbery ['rʌbərɪ] ADJ (*material*) gummiartig; (*meat, food*) wie Gummi
rubbish ['rʌbɪʃ] (BRIT) N (*waste*) Abfall *m*; (*fig: junk*) Schrott *m*; (: *pej: nonsense*) Quatsch *m* ▸ VT (*inf*) heruntermachen; **~!** Quatsch!
rubbish bin (BRIT) N Abfalleimer *m*
rubbish dump (BRIT) N Müllabladeplatz *m*
rubbishy ['rʌbɪʃɪ] (BRIT *inf*) ADJ miserabel, mies
rubble ['rʌbl] N (*debris*) Trümmer *pl*; (*Constr*) Schutt *m*
ruble ['ru:bl] (US) N = **rouble**
ruby ['ru:bɪ] N (*gem*) Rubin *m* ▸ ADJ (*red*) rubinrot
RUC (BRIT) N ABBR (= *Royal Ulster Constabulary*) *nordirische Polizeibehörde*
rucksack ['rʌksæk] N Rucksack *m*
ructions ['rʌkʃənz] (*inf*) NPL Krach *m*, Ärger *m*
rudder ['rʌdə^r] N (*of ship, plane*) Ruder *nt*
ruddy ['rʌdɪ] ADJ (*complexion etc*) rötlich; (*inf: damned*) verdammt
rude [ru:d] ADJ (*impolite*) unhöflich; (*naughty*) unanständig; (*unexpected: shock etc*) böse; (*crude: table, shelter etc*) primitiv; **to be ~ to sb** unhöflich zu jdm sein; **a ~ awakening** ein böses Erwachen
rudely ['ru:dlɪ] ADV (*interrupt*) unhöflich; (*say, push*) grob
rudeness ['ru:dnɪs] N (*impoliteness*) Unhöflichkeit *f*
rudimentary [ru:dɪ'mɛntərɪ] ADJ (*equipment*) primitiv; (*knowledge*) Grund-
rudiments ['ru:dɪmənts] NPL Grundlagen *pl*
rue [ru:] VT bereuen
rueful ['ru:ful] ADJ (*expression, person*) reuevoll
ruff [rʌf] N (*collar*) Halskrause *f*
ruffian ['rʌfiən] N Rüpel *m*
ruffle ['rʌfl] VT (*hair, feathers*) zerzausen; (*water*) kräuseln; (*fig: person*) aus der Fassung bringen
rug [rʌg] N (*on floor*) Läufer *m*; (BRIT: *blanket*) Decke *f*
rugby ['rʌgbɪ] N (*also:* **rugby football**) Rugby *nt*
rugged ['rʌgɪd] ADJ (*landscape*) rau; (*man*) robust; (*features, face*) markig; (*determination, independence*) wild
rugger ['rʌgə^r] (BRIT *inf*) N Rugby *nt*
ruin ['ru:ɪn] N (*destruction, downfall*) Ruin *m*; (*remains*) Ruine *f* ▸ VT ruinieren; (*building*) zerstören; (*clothes, carpet etc*) verderben; **ruins** NPL (*of castle*) Ruinen *pl*; (*of building*) Trümmer *pl*; **in ruins** (*lit, fig*) in Trümmern
ruination [ru:ɪ'neɪʃən] N (*of building etc*) Zerstörung *f*; (*of person, life*) Ruinierung *f*
ruinous ['ru:ɪnəs] ADJ (*expense, interest*) ruinös
rule [ru:l] N (*norm*) Regel *f*; (*regulation*) Vorschrift *f*; (*government*) Herrschaft *f*; (*ruler*) Lineal *nt* ▸ VT (*country, people*) herrschen über +*acc* ▸ VI (*monarch etc*) herrschen; **it's against the rules** das ist nicht gestattet; **as a ~ of thumb** als Faustregel; **under British ~** unter britischer Herrschaft; **as a ~** in der Regel; **to ~ in favour of/against/on sth** (*Law*) für/gegen/über etw *acc* entscheiden; **to ~ that ...** (*umpire, judge etc*) entscheiden, dass ...
▸ rule out VT (*possibility etc*) ausschließen; **murder cannot be ruled out** Mord ist nicht auszuschließen
ruled [ru:ld] ADJ (*paper*) liniert
ruler ['ru:lə^r] N (*sovereign*) Herrscher(in) *m(f)*; (*for measuring*) Lineal *nt*
ruling ['ru:lɪŋ] ADJ (*party*) Regierungs-; (*body*) maßgebend ▸ N (*Law*) Entscheidung *f*; **the ~ class** die herrschende Klasse
rum [rʌm] N Rum *m* ▸ ADJ (BRIT *inf: peculiar*) komisch
Rumania *etc* N = **Romania** *etc*
rumble ['rʌmbl] N (*of thunder*) Grollen *nt*; (*of traffic*) Rumpeln *nt*; (*of guns*) Donnern *nt*; (*of voices*) Gemurmel *nt* ▸ VI (*stomach*) knurren; (*thunder*) grollen; (*traffic*) rumpeln; (*guns*) donnern
rumbustious [rʌm'bʌstʃəs] ADJ (*person*) ungebärdig
ruminate ['ru:mɪneɪt] VI (*person*) grübeln; (*cow, sheep etc*) wiederkäuen
rummage ['rʌmɪdʒ] VI herumstöbern
rummage sale (US) N Trödelmarkt *m*
rumour, (US) **rumor** ['ru:mə^r] N Gerücht *nt* ▸ VT: **it is rumoured that ...** man sagt, dass ...
rump [rʌmp] N (*of animal*) Hinterteil *nt*; (*of group etc*) Rumpf *m*
rumple ['rʌmpl] VT (*clothes etc*) zerknittern; (*hair*) zerzausen
rump steak N Rumpsteak *nt*
rumpus ['rʌmpəs] N Krach *m*; **to kick up a ~** Krach schlagen
run [rʌn] (*pt* **ran**, *pp* **~**) N (*as exercise, sport*) Lauf *m*; (*in car, train etc*) Fahrt *f*; (*series*) Serie *f*; (*Ski*) Abfahrt *f*; (*Cricket, Baseball*) Run *m*; (*Theat*) Spielzeit *f*; (*in tights etc*) Laufmasche *f* ▸ VT (*race, distance*) laufen, rennen; (*operate: business*) leiten; (: *hotel, shop*) führen; (: *competition, course*) durchführen; (*Comput: program*) laufen lassen; (*hand, fingers*) streichen mit; (*water, bath*) einlaufen lassen; (*Press: feature, article*) bringen ▸ VI laufen, rennen; (*flee*) weglaufen; (*bus, train*) fahren; (*river, tears*) fließen; (*colours*) auslaufen; (*jumper*) färben; (*in election*) antreten; (*road, railway etc*) verlaufen; **to go for a ~** (*as exercise*) einen Dauerlauf machen; **to break into a ~** zu laufen *or* rennen beginnen; **a ~ of good/bad luck** eine Glücks-/Pechsträhne; **to have the ~ of sb's house** jds Haus zur freien Verfügung haben; **there was a ~ on ...** (*meat, tickets*) es gab

r

einen Ansturm auf *+acc*; **in the long ~** langfristig; **in the short ~** kurzfristig; **to make a ~ for it** die Beine in die Hand nehmen; **on the ~** *(fugitive)* auf der Flucht; **I'll ~ you to the station** ich fahre dich zum Bahnhof; **to ~ the risk of doing sth** Gefahr laufen, etw zu tun; **she ran her finger down the list** sie ging die Liste mit dem Finger durch; **it's very cheap to ~** *(car, machine)* es ist sehr billig im Verbrauch; **to ~ a bath** das Badewasser einlaufen lassen; **to be ~ off one's feet** (BRIT) ständig auf Trab sein; **the baby's nose was running** dem Baby lief die Nase; **the train runs between Gatwick and Victoria** der Zug verkehrt zwischen Gatwick und Victoria; **the bus runs every 20 minutes** der Bus fährt alle 20 Minuten; **to ~ on petrol/off batteries** mit Benzin/auf Batterie laufen; **to ~ for president** für das Amt des Präsidenten kandidieren; **to ~ dry** *(well etc)* austrocknen; **tempers were running high** alle waren sehr erregt; **unemployment is running at 20 per cent** die Arbeitslosigkeit beträgt 20 Prozent; **blonde hair runs in the family** blonde Haare liegen in der Familie

▸ **run about** VI herumlaufen

▸ **run across** VT FUS *(find)* stoßen auf *+acc*

▸ **run after** VT FUS nachlaufen *+dat*

▸ **run away** VI weglaufen

▸ **run down** VT *(production)* verringern; *(factory)* allmählich stilllegen; *(Aut: person)* überfahren; *(criticize)* schlechtmachen ▸ VI *(battery)* leer werden

▸ **run in** (BRIT) VT *(car)* einfahren

▸ **run into** VT FUS *(meet: person)* begegnen *+dat*; *(: trouble etc)* bekommen; *(collide with)* laufen/fahren gegen; **to ~ into debt** in Schulden geraten; **their losses ran into millions** ihre Schulden gingen in die Millionen

▸ **run off** VT *(liquid)* ablassen; *(copies)* machen ▸ VI weglaufen

▸ **run out** VI *(time, passport)* ablaufen; *(money)* ausgehen; *(luck)* zu Ende gehen

▸ **run out of** VT FUS: **we're running out of money/petrol** uns geht das Geld/das Benzin aus; **we're running out of time** wir haben keine Zeit mehr

▸ **run over** VT *(Aut)* überfahren ▸ VT FUS *(repeat)* durchgehen ▸ VI *(bath, water)* überlaufen

▸ **run through** VT FUS *(instructions, lines)* durchgehen

▸ **run up** VT *(debt)* anhäufen

▸ **run up against** VT FUS *(difficulties)* stoßen auf *+acc*

runabout ['rʌnəbaut] N *(Aut)* Flitzer *m*

run-around ['rʌnəraund] *(inf)* N: **to give sb the ~** jdn an der Nase herumführen

runaway ['rʌnəweɪ] ADJ *(horse)* ausgerissen; *(truck, train)* außer Kontrolle geraten; *(child, slave)* entlaufen; *(fig: inflation)* unkontrollierbar; *(: success)* überwältigend

rundown ['rʌndaun] N *(of industry etc)* allmähliche Stillegung *f* ▸ ADJ: **to be run-down** *(person)* total erschöpft sein; *(building, area)* heruntergekommen

rung [rʌŋ] PP *of* **ring** ▸ N *(also fig)* Sprosse *f*

run-in ['rʌnɪn] *(inf)* N Auseinandersetzung *f*

runner ['rʌnə^r^] N Läufer(in) *m(f)*; *(horse)* Rennpferd *nt*; *(on sledge, drawer etc)* Kufe *f*

runner bean (BRIT) N Stangenbohne *f*

runner-up [rʌnər'ʌp] N Zweitplatzierte(r) *f(m)*

running ['rʌnɪŋ] N *(sport)* Laufen *nt*; *(of business etc)* Leitung *f*; *(of machine etc)* Betrieb *m* ▸ ADJ *(water, stream)* laufend; **to be in/out of the ~ for sth** bei etw im Rennen liegen/aus dem Rennen sein; **to make the ~** *(in race, fig)* das Rennen machen; **6 days ~** 6 Tage hintereinander; **to have a ~ battle with sb** ständig im Streit mit jdm liegen; **to give a ~ commentary on sth** etw fortlaufend kommentieren; **a ~ sore** eine nässende Wunde

running costs NPL *(of car, machine)* Unterhaltskosten *pl*

running head N *(Typ, Comput)* Kolumnentitel *m*

running mate (US) N *(Pol)* Vizepräsidentschaftskandidat *m*

runny ['rʌnɪ] ADJ *(egg, butter)* dünnflüssig; *(nose, eyes)* triefend

run-off ['rʌnɔf] N *(in contest, election)* Entscheidungsrunde *f*; *(extra race)* Entscheidungsrennen *nt*

run-of-the-mill ['rʌnəvðə'mɪl] ADJ gewöhnlich

runt [rʌnt] N *(animal) kleinstes und schwächstes Tier eines Wurfs*; *(pej: person)* Zwerg *m*

run-through ['rʌnθru:] N *(rehearsal)* Probe *f*

run-up ['rʌnʌp] N: **the ~ to** *(election etc)* die Zeit vor *+dat*

runway ['rʌnweɪ] N *(Aviat)* Start- und Landebahn *f*

rupee [ru:'pi:] N Rupie *f*

rupture ['rʌptʃə^r^] N *(Med)* Bruch *m*; *(conflict)* Spaltung *f* ▸ VT: **to ~ o.s.** *(Med)* sich *dat* einen Bruch zuziehen

rural ['ruərl] ADJ ländlich; *(crime)* auf dem Lande

rural district council (BRIT) N Landbezirksverwaltung *f*

ruse [ru:z] N List *f*

rush [rʌʃ] N *(hurry)* Eile *f*, Hetze *f*; *(Comm: sudden demand)* starke Nachfrage *f*; *(of water, air)* Stoß *m*; *(of feeling)* Woge *f* ▸ VT *(lunch, job etc)* sich beeilen bei; *(person, supplies etc)* schnellstens bringen ▸ VI *(person)* sich beeilen; *(air, water)* strömen; **rushes** NPL *(Bot)* Schilf *nt*; *(for chair, basket etc)* Binsen *pl*; **is there any ~ for this?** eilt das?; **we've had a ~ of orders** wir hatten einen Zustrom von Bestellungen; **I'm in a ~ (to do sth)** ich habe es eilig (, etw zu tun); **gold ~** Goldrausch *m*; **don't ~ me!** drängen Sie mich nicht!; **to ~ sth off** *(send)* etw schnellstens abschicken; **to ~ sb into doing sth** jdn dazu drängen, etw zu tun

▸ **rush through** VT *(order, application)* schnellstens erledigen

rush hour N Hauptverkehrszeit *f*, Rushhour *f*

rush job N Eilauftrag *m*

rush matting N Binsenmatte *f*
rusk [rʌsk] N Zwieback *m*
Russia ['rʌʃə] N Russland *nt*
Russian ['rʌʃən] ADJ russisch ▸ N (*person*) Russe *m*, Russin *f*; (*Ling*) Russisch *nt*
rust [rʌst] N Rost *m* ▸ VI rosten
rustic ['rʌstɪk] ADJ (*style, furniture*) rustikal ▸ N (*pej: person*) Bauer *m*
rustle ['rʌsl] VI (*paper, leaves*) rascheln ▸ VT (*paper*) rascheln mit; (*US: cattle*) stehlen
rustproof ['rʌstpru:f] ADJ nicht rostend
rustproofing ['rʌstpru:fɪŋ] N Rostschutz *m*
rusty ['rʌstɪ] ADJ (*car*) rostig; (*fig: skill etc*) eingerostet
rut [rʌt] N (*in path etc*) Furche *f*; (*Zool: season*) Brunft *f*, Brunst *f*; **to be in a ~** (*fig*) im Trott stecken
rutabaga [ru:tə'beɪgə] (*US*) N Steckrübe *f*
ruthless ['ru:θlɪs] ADJ rücksichtslos
ruthlessness ['ru:θlɪsnɪs] N Rücksichtslosigkeit *f*
RV ABBR (*Bible: = revised version*) *englische Bibelübersetzung von 1885* ▸ N ABBR (*US*) = **recreational vehicle**
Rwanda [ru'ændə] N Ruanda *nt*
Rwandan [ru'ændən] ADJ ruandisch
rye [raɪ] N (*cereal*) Roggen *m*
rye bread N Roggenbrot *nt*

r

Ss

S[1], s [ɛs] N (*letter*) S *nt*, s *nt*; (*US Scol: satisfactory*) ≈ 3; **S for sugar** ≈ S wie Samuel

S[2] [ɛs] ABBR (= *south*) S; (= *saint*) St.; (= *small*) kl.

SA ABBR = **South Africa**; **South America**; (= *South Australia*) Südaustralien *nt*

Sabbath ['sæbəθ] N (*Jewish*) Sabbat *m*; (*Christian*) Sonntag *m*

sabbatical [sə'bætɪkl] N (*also*: **sabbatical year**) Forschungsjahr *nt*

sabotage ['sæbətɑːʒ] VT (*plan, meeting*) sabotieren, einen Sabotageakt verüben auf *+acc* ▸ N Sabotage *f*

sabre ['seɪbə[r]] N Säbel *m*

sabre-rattling ['seɪbərætlɪŋ] N Säbelrasseln *nt*

saccharin, saccharine ['sækərɪn] N Sa(c)charin *nt* ▸ ADJ (*fig*) zuckersüß

sachet ['sæʃeɪ] N (*of shampoo*) Beutel *m*; (*of sugar etc*) Tütchen *nt*

sack [sæk] N Sack *m* ▸ VT (*dismiss*) entlassen; (*plunder*) plündern; **to get the ~** rausfliegen (*inf*); **to give sb the ~** jdn rausschmeißen (*inf*)

sackful ['sækful] N: **a ~ of** ein Sack

sacking ['sækɪŋ] N (*dismissal*) Entlassung *f*; (*material*) Sackleinen *nt*

sacrament ['sækrəmənt] N Sakrament *nt*

sacred ['seɪkrɪd] ADJ heilig; (*music, history*) geistlich; (*memory*) geheiligt; (*building*) sakral

sacred cow N (*lit, fig*) heilige Kuh *f*

sacrifice ['sækrɪfaɪs] N Opfer *nt* ▸ VT opfern; **to make sacrifices (for sb)** (für jdn) Opfer bringen

sacrilege ['sækrɪlɪdʒ] N Sakrileg *nt*; **that would be ~** das wäre ein Sakrileg

sacrosanct ['sækrəusæŋkt] ADJ (*lit, fig*) sakrosankt

sad [sæd] ADJ traurig; **he was ~ to see her go** er war traurig (darüber), dass sie wegging

sadden ['sædn] VT betrüben

saddle ['sædl] N Sattel *m* ▸ VT (*horse*) satteln; **to be saddled with sb/sth** (*inf*) jdn/etw am Hals haben

saddlebag ['sædlbæg] N Satteltasche *f*

sadism ['seɪdɪzəm] N Sadismus *m*

sadist ['seɪdɪst] N Sadist(in) *m(f)*

sadistic [sə'dɪstɪk] ADJ sadistisch

sadly ['sædlɪ] ADV (*unfortunately*) leider, bedauerlicherweise, traurig, betrübt; (*seriously*) schwer; **he is ~ lacking in humour** ihm fehlt leider jeglicher Humor

sadness ['sædnɪs] N Traurigkeit *f*

sadomasochism [seɪdəu'mæsəkɪzəm] N Sadomasochismus *m*

s.a.e. (BRIT) ABBR (= *stamped addressed envelope*) *see* **stamp**

safari [sə'fɑːrɪ] N Safari *f*; **to go on ~** auf Safari gehen

safari park N Safaripark *m*

safe [seɪf] ADJ sicher; (*out of danger*) in Sicherheit ▸ N Safe *m or nt*, Tresor *m*; **~ from** sicher vor *+dat*; **~ and sound** gesund und wohlbehalten; **(just) to be on the ~ side** (nur) um sicherzugehen; **to play ~** auf Nummer sicher gehen (*inf*); **it is ~ to say that ...** man kann wohl sagen, dass ...; **~ journey!** gute Fahrt *or* Reise!

safe bet N: **it's a ~ that ...** es ist sicher, dass ...

safe-breaker ['seɪfbreɪkə[r]] (BRIT) N Safeknacker *m* (*inf*)

safe-conduct [seɪf'kɔndʌkt] N freies *or* sicheres Geleit *nt*

safe-cracker ['seɪfkrækə[r]] N = **safe-breaker**

safe-deposit ['seɪfdɪpɔzɪt] N (*vault*) Tresorraum *m*; (*also*: **safe-deposit box**) Banksafe *m*

safeguard ['seɪfgɑːd] N Schutz *m* ▸ VT schützen; (*interests*) wahren; (*future*) sichern; **as a ~ against** zum Schutz gegen

safe haven N Zufluchtsort *m*

safe house N geheimer Unterschlupf *m*

safekeeping ['seɪf'kiːpɪŋ] N sichere Aufbewahrung *f*

safely ['seɪflɪ] ADV sicher; (*assume, say*) wohl, ruhig; (*arrive*) wohlbehalten; **I can ~ say ...** ich kann wohl sagen ...

safe passage N sichere Durchreise *f*

safe sex N Safer Sex *m*

safety ['seɪftɪ] N Sicherheit *f*; **~ first!** Sicherheit geht vor!

safety belt N Sicherheitsgurt *m*

safety catch N (*on gun*) Sicherung *f*; (*on window, door*) Sperre *f*

safety net N Sprungnetz *nt*, Sicherheitsnetz *nt*; (*fig*) Sicherheitsvorkehrung *f*

safety pin N Sicherheitsnadel *f*

safety valve N Sicherheitsventil *nt*

saffron ['sæfrən] N Safran *m*

sag [sæg] VI durchhängen; (*breasts*) hängen; (*fig: spirits, demand*) sinken

saga ['sɑːgə] N Saga *f*; (*fig*) Geschichte *f*

sage [seɪdʒ] N (*herb*) Salbei *m*; (*wise man*) Weise(r) *m*
Sagittarius [sædʒɪ'tɛərɪəs] N Schütze *m*; **to be ~** Schütze sein
sago ['seɪgəu] N Sago *m*
Sahara [sə'hɑːrə] N: **the ~ (Desert)** die (Wüste) Sahara
Sahel [sæ'hɛl] N Sahel *m*, Sahelzone *f*
said [sɛd] PT, PP *of* **say**
Saigon [saɪ'gɔn] N Saigon *nt*
sail [seɪl] N Segel *nt* ▸ VT segeln ▸ VI fahren; (*Sport*) segeln; (*begin voyage: ship*) auslaufen; (*: passenger*) abfahren; (*fig: ball etc*) fliegen, segeln; **to go for a ~** segeln gehen; **to set ~** losfahren, abfahren
▸ **sail through** VT FUS (*fig: exam etc*) spielend schaffen
sailboat ['seɪlbəut] (*US*) N = **sailing boat**
sailing ['seɪlɪŋ] N (*Sport*) Segeln *nt*; (*voyage*) Überfahrt *f*; **to go ~** segeln gehen
sailing boat N Segelboot *nt*
sailing ship N Segelschiff *nt*
sailor ['seɪlə^r] N Seemann *m*, Matrose *m*
saint [seɪnt] N (*lit, fig*) Heilige(r) *f(m)*
saintly ['seɪntlɪ] ADJ heiligmäßig; (*expression*) fromm
sake [seɪk] N: **for the ~ of sb/sth, for sb's/sth's ~** um jds/einer Sache *gen* willen; (*out of consideration for*) jdm/etw zuliebe; **he enjoys talking for talking's ~** er redet gerne, nur damit etwas gesagt wird; **for the ~ of argument** rein theoretisch; **art for art's ~** Kunst um der Kunst willen; **for heaven's ~!** um Gottes willen!
salad ['sæləd] N Salat *m*; **tomato ~** Tomatensalat *m*; **green ~** grüner Salat *m*
salad bowl N Salatschüssel *f*
salad cream (*BRIT*) N ≈ Mayonnaise *f*
salad dressing N Salatsoße *f*
salami [sə'lɑːmɪ] N Salami *f*
salaried ['sælərɪd] ADJ: **~ staff** Gehaltsempfänger *pl*
salary ['sælərɪ] N Gehalt *nt*
salary scale N Gehaltsskala *f*
sale [seɪl] N Verkauf *m*; (*at reduced prices*) Ausverkauf *m*; (*auction*) Auktion *f*; **sales** NPL (*total amount sold*) Absatz *m* ▸ CPD (*campaign*) Verkaufs-; (*conference*) Vertreter-; (*figures*) Absatz-; **"for ~"** „zu verkaufen"; **on ~** im Handel; **on ~ or return** auf Kommissionsbasis; **closing-down ~, liquidation ~** (*US*) Räumungsverkauf *m*
sale and lease back N (*Comm*) Verkauf *m* mit Rückmiete
saleroom ['seɪlruːm] N Auktionsraum *m*
sales assistant, (*US*) **sales clerk** [seɪlz-] N Verkäufer(in) *m(f)*
sales force N Vertreterstab *m*
salesman ['seɪlzmən] N (*irreg*) Verkäufer *m*; (*representative*) Vertreter *m*
sales manager N Verkaufsleiter *m*
salesmanship ['seɪlzmənʃɪp] N Verkaufstechnik *f*
sales tax (*US*) N Verkaufssteuer *f*
saleswoman ['seɪlzwumən] N (*irreg*) Verkäuferin *f*; (*representative*) Vertreterin *f*
salient ['seɪlɪənt] ADJ (*features*) hervorstechend; (*points*) Haupt-
saline ['seɪlaɪn] ADJ (*solution etc*) Salz-
saliva [sə'laɪvə] N Speichel *m*
sallow ['sæləu] ADJ (*complexion*) fahl
sally forth ['sælɪ-] (*old*) VI sich aufmachen
sally out VI = **sally forth**
salmon ['sæmən] N INV Lachs *m*
salmon trout N Lachsforelle *f*
salon ['sælɔn] N Salon *m*
saloon [sə'luːn] N (*US: bar*) Saloon *m*; (*BRIT Aut*) Limousine *f*; (*ship's lounge*) Salon *m*
SALT [sɔːlt] N ABBR (= *Strategic Arms Limitation Talks/Treaty*) SALT
salt [sɔːlt] N Salz *nt* ▸ VT (*put salt on*) salzen; (*road*) mit Salz streuen; (*preserve*) einsalzen ▸ CPD Salz-; (*pork, beef*) gepökelt; **the ~ of the earth** (*fig*) das Salz der Erde; **to take sth with a pinch** *or* **grain of ~** (*fig*) etw nicht ganz so ernst nehmen
salt cellar N Salzstreuer *m*
salt-free ['sɔːlt'friː] ADJ salzlos
salt mine N Salzbergwerk *nt*
saltwater ['sɔːlt'wɔːtə^r] ADJ (*fish, plant*) Meeres-
salty ['sɔːltɪ] ADJ salzig
salubrious [sə'luːbrɪəs] ADJ (*district etc*) fein; (*air, living conditions*) gesund
salutary ['sæljutərɪ] ADJ heilsam
salute [sə'luːt] N (*Mil, greeting*) Gruß *m*; (*Mil: with guns*) Salut *m* ▸ VT (*Mil*) grüßen, salutieren vor *+dat*; (*fig*) begrüßen
salvage ['sælvɪdʒ] VT bergen; (*fig*) retten ▸ N Bergung *f*; (*things saved*) Bergungsgut *nt*
salvage vessel N Bergungsschiff *nt*
salvation [sæl'veɪʃən] N (*Rel*) Heil *nt*; (*economic etc*) Rettung *f*
Salvation Army N Heilsarmee *f*
salver ['sælvə^r] N Tablett *nt*
salvo ['sælvəu] (*pl* **salvoes**) N Salve *f*
Samaritan [sə'mærɪtən] N: **the Samaritans** ≈ die Telefonseelsorge
same [seɪm] ADJ (*similar*) gleiche(r, s); (*identical*) selbe(r, s) ▸ PRON: **the ~** (*similar*) der/die/das Gleiche; (*identical*) derselbe/dieselbe/dasselbe; **the ~ book as** das gleiche Buch wie; **they are the ~ age** sie sind gleichaltrig; **they are exactly the ~** sie sind genau gleich; **on the ~ day** am gleichen *or* selben Tag; **at the ~ time** (*simultaneously*) gleichzeitig, zur gleichen Zeit; (*yet*) doch; **they're one and the ~** (*person*) das ist doch ein und derselbe/dieselbe; (*thing*) das ist doch dasselbe; **~ again** (*in bar etc*) das Gleiche noch mal; **all** *or* **just the ~** trotzdem; **to do the ~ (as sb)** das Gleiche (wie jd) tun; **the ~ to you!** (danke) gleichfalls!; **~ here!** ich/wir *etc* auch!; **thanks all the ~** trotzdem vielen Dank; **it's all the ~ to me** es ist mir egal
same-sex marriage ['seɪmsɛks-] N gleichgeschlechtliche Ehe *f*, Homoehe *f* (*inf*)
same-sex relationship ['seɪmsɛks-] N gleichgeschlechtliche Beziehung *f*

S

sample ['sɑːmpl] N Probe *f*; (*of merchandise*) Muster *nt*, Probe *f* ▶ VT probieren; **to take a ~** eine Stichprobe machen; **free ~** kostenlose Probe
sanatorium [sænəˈtɔːrɪəm] (*pl* **sanatoria**) N Sanatorium *nt*
sanctify ['sæŋktɪfaɪ] VT heiligen
sanctimonious [sæŋktɪ'məunɪəs] ADJ scheinheilig
sanction ['sæŋkʃən] N Zustimmung *f* ▶ VT sanktionieren; **sanctions** NPL (*Pol*) Sanktionen *pl*; **to impose economic sanctions on** *or* **against** Wirtschaftssanktionen verhängen gegen
sanctity ['sæŋktɪtɪ] N (*holiness*) Heiligkeit *f*; (*inviolability*) Unantastbarkeit *f*
sanctuary ['sæŋktjuərɪ] N (*for birds/animals*) Schutzgebiet *nt*; (*place of refuge*) Zuflucht *f*; (*Rel: in church*) Altarraum *m*
sand [sænd] N Sand *m* ▶ VT (*also:* **sand down**) abschmirgeln; *see also* **sands**
sandal ['sændl] N Sandale *f*
sandbag ['sændbæg] N Sandsack *m*
sandblast ['sændblɑːst] VT sandstrahlen
sandbox ['sændbɔks] (*US*) N Sandkasten *m*; (*Comput: antivirus software*) Sandbox *f*
sandcastle ['sændkɑːsl] N Sandburg *f*
sand dune N Sanddüne *f*
sander ['sændəʳ] N (*tool*) Schleifmaschine *f*
S & M (*US*) N ABBR (= *sadomasochism*) S/M
sandpaper ['sændpeɪpəʳ] N Schmirgelpapier *nt*
sandpit ['sændpɪt] N Sandkasten *m*; (*Comput: antivirus software*) Sandbox *f*
sands [sændz] NPL (*beach*) Sandstrand *m*
sandstone ['sændstəun] N Sandstein *m*
sandstorm ['sændstɔːm] N Sandsturm *m*
sandwich ['sændwɪtʃ] N Sandwich *nt* ▶ VT: **sandwiched between** eingequetscht zwischen; **cheese/ham ~** Käse-/Schinkenbrot *nt*
sandwich board N Reklametafel *f*
sandwich course (Brit) N *Ausbildungsgang, bei dem sich Theorie und Praxis abwechseln*
sandwich man N (*irreg*) Sandwichmann *m*, Plakatträger *m*
sandy ['sændɪ] ADJ sandig; (*beach*) Sand-; (*hair*) rotblond
sane [seɪn] ADJ geistig gesund; (*sensible*) vernünftig
sang [sæŋ] PT *of* **sing**
sanguine ['sæŋgwɪn] ADJ zuversichtlich
sanitarium [sænɪ'tɛərɪəm] (*US*) (*pl* **sanitaria**) N = **sanatorium**
sanitary ['sænɪtərɪ] ADJ hygienisch; (*facilities*) sanitär; (*inspector*) Gesundheits-
sanitary towel, (*US*) **sanitary napkin** N Damenbinde *f*
sanitation [sænɪ'teɪʃən] N Hygiene *f*; (*toilets etc*) sanitäre Anlagen *pl*; (*drainage*) Kanalisation *f*
sanitation department (*US*) N Stadtreinigung *f*
sanity ['sænɪtɪ] N geistige Gesundheit *f*; (*common sense*) Vernunft *f*
sank [sæŋk] PT *of* **sink**
Santa Claus [sæntə'klɔːz] N ≈ der Weihnachtsmann
Santiago [sæntɪ'ɑːgəu] N (*also:* **Santiago de Chile**) Santiago (de Chile) *nt*
sap [sæp] N Saft *m* ▶ VT (*strength*) zehren an +*dat*; (*confidence*) untergraben
sapling ['sæplɪŋ] N junger Baum *m*
sapphire ['sæfaɪəʳ] N Saphir *m*
sarcasm ['sɑːkæzm] N Sarkasmus *m*
sarcastic [sɑː'kæstɪk] ADJ sarkastisch
sarcophagus [sɑː'kɔfəgəs] (*pl* **sarcophagi**) N Sarkophag *m*
sardine [sɑː'diːn] N Sardine *f*
Sardinia [sɑː'dɪnɪə] N Sardinien *nt*
Sardinian [sɑː'dɪnɪən] ADJ sardinisch, sardisch ▶ N (*person*) Sardinier(in) *m(f)*; (*Ling*) Sardinisch *nt*
sardonic [sɑː'dɔnɪk] ADJ (*smile*) süffisant
sari ['sɑːrɪ] N Sari *m*
SARS [sɑːz] N ABBR (= *severe acute respiratory syndrome*) SARS *nt*
sartorial [sɑː'tɔːrɪəl] ADJ: **his ~ elegance** seine elegante Art, sich zu kleiden
SAS (Brit) N ABBR (*Mil:* = *Special Air Service*) *Spezialeinheit der britischen Armee*
SASE (*US*) N ABBR (= *self-addressed stamped envelope*) frankierter Rückumschlag *m*
sash [sæʃ] N Schärpe *f*; (*of window*) Fensterrahmen *m*
sash window N Schiebefenster *nt*
SAT (*US*) N ABBR (= *Scholastic Aptitude Test*) *Hochschulaufnahmeprüfung*
sat [sæt] PT, PP *of* **sit**
Sat. ABBR (= *Saturday*) Sa.
Satan ['seɪtn] N Satan *m*
satanic [sə'tænɪk] ADJ satanisch
satanism ['seɪtnɪzəm] N Satanismus *m*
satchel ['sætʃl] N (*child's*) Schultasche *f*
sated ['seɪtɪd] ADJ gesättigt; **to be ~ with sth** (*fig*) von etw übersättigt sein
satellite ['sætəlaɪt] N Satellit *m*; (*also:* **satellite state**) Satellitenstaat *m*
satellite dish N Satellitenantenne *f*, Parabolantenne *f*
satellite receiver N Satellitenempfänger *m*
satellite television N Satellitenfernsehen *nt*
satiate ['seɪʃɪeɪt] VT (*food*) sättigen; (*fig: pleasure etc*) übersättigen
satin ['sætɪn] N Satin *m* ▶ ADJ (*dress etc*) Satin-; **with a ~ finish** mit Seidenglanz
satire ['sætaɪəʳ] N Satire *f*
satirical [sə'tɪrɪkl] ADJ satirisch
satirist ['sætɪrɪst] N Satiriker(in) *m(f)*
satirize ['sætɪraɪz] VT satirisch darstellen
satisfaction [sætɪs'fækʃən] N Befriedigung *f*; **to get ~ from sb** (*refund, apology etc*) Genugtuung von jdm erhalten; **has it been done to your ~?** sind Sie damit zufrieden?
satisfactorily [sætɪs'fæktərɪlɪ] ADV zufriedenstellend
satisfactory [sætɪs'fæktərɪ] ADJ zufriedenstellend

satisfied ['sætɪsfaɪd] ADJ zufrieden
satisfy ['sætɪsfaɪ] VT zufriedenstellen; (*needs, demand*) befriedigen; (*requirements, conditions*) erfüllen; **to ~ sb/o.s. that …** jdn/sich davon überzeugen, dass …
satisfying ['sætɪsfaɪɪŋ] ADJ befriedigend; (*meal*) sättigend
satsuma [sæt'suːmə] N Satsuma *f*
saturate ['sætʃəreɪt] VT: **to ~ (with)** durchnässen (mit); (*Chem: market*) sättigen; (*fig: area etc*) überschwemmen
saturated fat ['sætʃəreɪtɪd-] N gesättigtes Fett *nt*
saturation [sætʃə'reɪʃən] N (*Chem*) Sättigung *f*; **~ advertising** flächendeckende Werbung *f*; **~ bombing** Flächenbombardierung *f*
Saturday ['sætədɪ] N Samstag *m*; *see also* **Tuesday**
sauce [sɔːs] N Soße *f*
saucepan ['sɔːspən] N Kochtopf *m*
saucer ['sɔːsə[r]] N Untertasse *f*
saucy ['sɔːsɪ] ADJ frech
Saudi, Saudi Arabian ['saudi-] ADJ saudisch, saudi-arabisch
Saudi Arabia ['saudɪ-] N Saudi-Arabien *nt*
sauna ['sɔːnə] N Sauna *f*
saunter ['sɔːntə[r]] VI schlendern
sausage ['sɔsɪdʒ] N Wurst *f*
sausage roll N Wurst *f* im Schlafrock
sauté ['səuteɪ] VT kurz anbraten ▸ ADJ: **sautéed potatoes** Bratkartoffeln *pl*
savage ['sævɪdʒ] ADJ (*attack etc*) brutal; (*dog*) gefährlich; (*criticism*) schonungslos ▸ N (*old: pej*) Wilde(r) *f(m)* ▸ VT (*maul*) zerfleischen; (*fig: criticize*) verreißen
savagely ['sævɪdʒlɪ] ADV (*attack etc*) brutal; (*criticize*) schonungslos
savagery ['sævɪdʒrɪ] N (*of attack*) Brutalität *f*
save [seɪv] VT (*rescue*) retten; (*money, time*) sparen; (*food etc*) aufheben; (*work, trouble*) (er)sparen; (*keep: receipts etc*) aufbewahren; (*: seat etc*) frei halten; (*Comput: file*) abspeichern; (*Sport: shot, ball*) halten ▸ VI (*also*: **save up**) sparen ▸ N (*Sport*) (Ball)abwehr *f* ▸ PREP (*form*) außer +*dat*; **it will ~ me an hour** dadurch spare ich eine Stunde; **to ~ face** das Gesicht wahren; **God ~ the Queen!** Gott schütze die Königin!
saving ['seɪvɪŋ] N (*on price etc*) Ersparnis *f* ▸ ADJ: **the ~ grace of sth** das einzig Gute an etw *dat*; **savings** NPL (*money*) Ersparnisse *pl*; **to make savings** sparen
savings account N Sparkonto *nt*
savings bank N Sparkasse *f*
saviour, (*US*) **savior** ['seɪvjə[r]] N Retter(in) *m(f)*; (*Rel*) Erlöser *m*
savoir-faire ['sævwɑːfɛə[r]] N Gewandtheit *f*
savour, (*US*) **savor** ['seɪvə[r]] VT genießen ▸ N (*of food*) Geschmack *m*
savoury, (*US*) **savory** ['seɪvərɪ] ADJ pikant
savvy ['sævɪ] (*inf*) N Grips *m*; **he hasn't got much ~** er hat keine Ahnung
saw [sɔː] (*pt* **sawed**, *pp* **sawed** *or* **sawn**) VT sägen ▸ N Säge *f* ▸ PT *of* **see**; **to ~ sth up** etw zersägen
sawdust ['sɔːdʌst] N Sägemehl *nt*
sawmill ['sɔːmɪl] N Sägewerk *nt*
sawn [sɔːn] PP *of* **saw**
sawn-off ['sɔːnɔf], (*US*) **sawed-off** ['sɔːdɔf] ADJ: **~ shotgun** Gewehr *nt* mit abgesägtem Lauf
saxophone ['sæksəfəun] N Saxofon *nt*
say [seɪ] (*pt, pp* **said**) VT sagen ▸ N: **to have one's ~** seine Meinung äußern; **could you ~ that again?** können Sie das wiederholen?; **my watch says 3 o'clock** auf meiner Uhr ist es 3 Uhr; **it says on the sign "No Smoking"** auf dem Schild steht „Rauchen verboten"; **shall we ~ Tuesday?** sagen wir Dienstag?; **come for dinner at, ~, 8 o'clock** kommt um, sagen wir mal 8 Uhr, zum Essen; **that doesn't ~ much for him** das spricht nicht gerade für ihn; **when all is said and done** letzten Endes; **there is something/a lot to be said for it** es spricht einiges/vieles dafür; **you can ~ that again!** das kann man wohl sagen!; **that is to ~** das heißt; **that goes without saying** das versteht sich von selbst; **to ~ nothing of …** von … ganz zu schweigen; **~ (that) …** angenommen, (dass) …; **to have a** *or* **some ~ in sth** ein Mitspracherecht bei etw haben
saying ['seɪɪŋ] N Redensart *f*
say-so ['seɪsəu] N Zustimmung *f*; **to do sth on sb's ~** etw auf jds Anweisung *acc* hin tun
SBA (*US*) N ABBR (= *Small Business Administration*) *Regierungsstelle zur Unterstützung kleiner und mittelständischer Betriebe*
SC (*US*) N ABBR = **Supreme Court** ▸ ABBR (*Post*) = **South Carolina**
s/c ABBR = **self-contained**
scab [skæb] N (*on wound*) Schorf *m*; (*pej*) Streikbrecher(in) *m(f)*
scabby ['skæbɪ] (*pej*) ADJ (*hands, skin*) schorfig
scaffold ['skæfəld] N (*for execution*) Schafott *nt*
scaffolding ['skæfəldɪŋ] N Gerüst *nt*
scald [skɔːld] N Verbrühung *f* ▸ VT (*burn*) verbrühen
scalding ['skɔːldɪŋ] ADJ (*also*: **scalding hot**) siedend heiß
scale [skeɪl] N Skala *f*; (*of fish*) Schuppe *f*; (*Mus*) Tonleiter *f*; (*size, extent*) Ausmaß *nt*, Umfang *m*; (*of map, model*) Maßstab *m* ▸ VT (*cliff, tree*) erklettern; **(pair of) scales** NPL (*for weighing*) Waage *f*; **pay ~** Lohnskala *f*; **to draw sth to ~** etw maßstabgetreu zeichnen; **a small-~ model** ein Modell in verkleinertem Maßstab; **on a large ~** im großen Rahmen; **~ of charges** Gebührenordnung *f*
▸ **scale down** VT verkleinern; (*fig*) verringern
scaled-down [skeɪld'daun] ADJ verkleinert; (*project, forecast*) eingeschränkt
scale drawing N maßstabgetreue Zeichnung *f*
scallion ['skæljən] N Frühlingszwiebel *f*; (*US: shallot*) Schalotte *f*; (*: leek*) Lauch *m*
scallop ['skɔləp] N (*Zool*) Kammmuschel *f*; (*Sewing*) Bogenkante *f*
scalp [skælp] N Kopfhaut *f* ▸ VT skalpieren
scalpel ['skælpl] N Skalpell *nt*
scalper ['skælpə[r]] (*US inf*) N (*ticket tout*) (Karten)schwarzhändler(in) *m(f)*

S

scam [skæm] (*inf*) N Betrug *m*
scamp [skæmp] (*inf*) N Frechdachs *m*
scamper ['skæmpəʳ] VI: **to ~ away** *or* **off** verschwinden
scampi ['skæmpɪ] (*BRIT*) NPL Scampi *pl*
scan [skæn] VT (*horizon*) absuchen; (*newspaper etc*) überfliegen; (*TV, Radar*) abtasten ▸ VI (*poetry*) das richtige Versmaß haben ▸ N (*Med*) Scan *m*
▸ **scan in** VT (*Comput*) einscannen
scandal ['skændl] N Skandal *m*; (*gossip*) Skandalgeschichten *pl*
scandalize ['skændəlaɪz] VT schockieren
scandalous ['skændələs] ADJ skandalös
Scandinavia [skændɪ'neɪvɪə] N Skandinavien *nt*
Scandinavian [skændɪ'neɪvɪən] ADJ skandinavisch ▸ N Skandinavier(in) *m(f)*
scanner ['skænəʳ] N (*Med*) Scanner *m*; (*Radar*) Richtantenne *f*
scant [skænt] ADJ wenig
scantily ['skæntɪlɪ] ADV: **~ clad** *or* **dressed** spärlich bekleidet
scanty ['skæntɪ] ADJ (*information*) dürftig; (*meal*) kärglich; (*bikini*) knapp
scapegoat ['skeɪpgəut] N Sündenbock *m*
scar [skɑ:] N Narbe *f*; (*fig*) Wunde *f* ▸ VT eine Narbe hinterlassen auf +*dat*; (*fig*) zeichnen
scarce [skɛəs] ADJ knapp; **to make o.s. ~** (*inf*) verschwinden
scarcely ['skɛəslɪ] ADV kaum; (*certainly not*) wohl kaum; **~ anybody** kaum jemand; **I can ~ believe it** ich kann es kaum glauben
scarcity ['skɛəsɪtɪ] N Knappheit *f*; **~ value** Seltenheitswert *m*
scare [skɛəʳ] N (*public fear*) Panik *f*; (*fright*) Schreck(en) *m* ▸ VT (*frighten*) erschrecken; (*worry*) Angst machen +*dat*; **to give sb a ~** jdm einen Schrecken einjagen; **bomb ~** Bombendrohung *f*
▸ **scare away** VT (*animal*) verscheuchen; (*investor, buyer*) abschrecken
▸ **scare off** VT = **scare away**
scarecrow ['skɛəkrəu] N Vogelscheuche *f*
scared ['skɛəd] ADJ: **to be ~** Angst haben; **to be ~ stiff** fürchterliche Angst haben
scaremonger ['skɛəmʌŋgəʳ] N Panikmacher *m*
scarf [skɑ:f] (*pl* **scarfs** *or* **scarves**) N Schal *m*; (*headscarf*) Kopftuch *nt*
scarlet ['skɑ:lɪt] ADJ (scharlach)rot
scarlet fever N Scharlach *m*
scarper ['skɑ:pəʳ] (*BRIT inf*) VI abhauen
scarred [skɑ:d] ADJ narbig; (*fig*) gezeichnet
SCART socket ['skɑ:tsɔkɪt] N (*Comput*) SCART-Büchse *f*
scarves [skɑ:vz] NPL *of* **scarf**
scary ['skɛərɪ] (*inf*) ADJ unheimlich; (*film*) gruselig
scathing ['skeɪðɪŋ] ADJ (*comments*) bissig; (*attack*) scharf; **to be ~ about sth** bissige Bemerkungen über etw *acc* machen
scatter ['skætəʳ] VT verstreuen; (*flock of birds*) aufscheuchen; (*crowd*) zerstreuen ▸ VI (*crowd*) sich zerstreuen
scatterbrained ['skætəbreɪnd] (*inf*) ADJ schusselig
scattered ['skætəd] ADJ verstreut; **~ showers** vereinzelte Regenschauer *pl*
scatty ['skætɪ] (*BRIT inf*) ADJ schusselig
scavenge ['skævəndʒ] VI: **to ~ for sth** nach etw suchen
scavenger ['skævəndʒəʳ] N (*person*) Aasgeier *m* (*inf*); (*animal, bird*) Aasfresser *m*
SCE N ABBR (= *Scottish Certificate of Education*) *Schulabschlusszeugnis in Schottland*
scenario [sɪ'nɑ:rɪəu] N (*Theat, Cine*) Szenarium *nt*; (*fig*) Szenario *nt*
scene [si:n] N (*lit, fig*) Szene *f*; (*of crime*) Schauplatz *m*; (*of accident*) Ort *m*; (*sight*) Anblick *m*; **behind the scenes** (*fig*) hinter den Kulissen; **to make a ~** (*inf: fuss*) eine Szene machen; **to appear on the ~** (*fig*) auftauchen, auf der Bildfläche erscheinen; **the political ~** die politische Landschaft
scenery ['si:nərɪ] N (*Theat*) Bühnenbild *nt*; (*landscape*) Landschaft *f*
scenic ['si:nɪk] ADJ malerisch, landschaftlich schön
scent [sɛnt] N (*fragrance*) Duft *m*; (*track*) Fährte *f*; (*fig*) Spur *f*; (*liquid perfume*) Parfüm *nt*; **to put** *or* **throw sb off the ~** (*fig*) jdn von der Spur abbringen
sceptic, (*US*) **skeptic** ['skɛptɪk] N Skeptiker(in) *m(f)*
sceptical, (*US*) **skeptical** ['skɛptɪkl] ADJ skeptisch
scepticism, (*US*) **skepticism** ['skɛptɪsɪzəm] N Skepsis *f*
sceptre, (*US*) **scepter** ['sɛptəʳ] N Zepter *nt*
schedule ['ʃɛdju:l, (*US*) 'skɛdju:l] N (*of trains, buses*) Fahrplan *m*; (*of events*) Programm *nt*; (*of prices, details etc*) Liste *f* ▸ VT planen; (*visit, meeting etc*) ansetzen; **on ~** wie geplant, pünktlich; **we are working to a very tight ~** wir arbeiten nach einem sehr knappen Zeitplan; **everything went according to ~** alles ist planmäßig verlaufen; **to be ahead of/behind ~** dem Zeitplan voraus sein/im Rückstand sein; **he was scheduled to leave yesterday** laut Zeitplan hätte er gestern abfahren sollen
scheduled ['ʃɛdju:ld, (*US*) 'skɛdju:ld] ADJ (*train, bus, stop*) planmäßig; (*date, time*) vorgesehen; (*visit, event*) geplant
scheduled flight N Linienflug *m*
schematic [skɪ'mætɪk] ADJ schematisch
scheme [ski:m] N (*personal plan*) Plan *m*; (*plot*) raffinierter Plan *m*, Komplott *nt*; (*formal plan*) Programm *nt* ▸ VI Pläne schmieden, intrigieren; **colour ~** Farbzusammenstellung *f*; **pension ~** Rentenversicherung *f*
scheming ['ski:mɪŋ] ADJ intrigierend ▸ N Machenschaften *pl*
schism ['skɪzəm] N Spaltung *f*
schizophrenia [skɪtsə'fri:nɪə] N Schizophrenie *f*
schizophrenic [skɪtsə'frɛnɪk] ADJ schizophren ▸ N Schizophrene(r) *f(m)*

scholar ['skɔləʳ] N Gelehrte(r) *f(m)*; *(pupil)* Student(in) *m(f)*, Schüler(in) *m(f)*; *(scholarship holder)* Stipendiat(in) *m(f)*
scholarly ['skɔləlɪ] ADJ gelehrt; *(text, approach)* wissenschaftlich
scholarship ['skɔləʃɪp] N Gelehrsamkeit *f*; *(grant)* Stipendium *nt*
school [sku:l] N Schule *f*; *(US inf: university)* Universität *f*; *(of whales, porpoises etc)* Schule *f*, Schwarm *m* ▸ CPD Schul-
school age N Schulalter *nt*
school bag N Schultasche *f*
schoolbook ['sku:lbuk] N Schulbuch *nt*
schoolboy ['sku:lbɔɪ] N Schüler *m*, Schuljunge *m*
school bus N Schulbus *m*
schoolchildren ['sku:ltʃɪldrən] NPL Schulkinder *pl*, Schüler *pl*
schooldays ['sku:ldeɪz] NPL Schulzeit *f*
schooled [sku:ld] ADJ geschult; **to be ~ in sth** über etw *acc* gut Bescheid wissen
schoolgirl ['sku:lgə:l] N Schülerin *f*, Schulmädchen *nt*
schooling ['sku:lɪŋ] N Schulbildung *f*
school-leaver [sku:l'li:vəʳ] (BRIT) N Schulabgänger(in) *m(f)*
schoolmaster ['sku:lmɑ:stəʳ] N Lehrer *m*
schoolmistress ['sku:lmɪstrɪs] N Lehrerin *f*
school report (BRIT) N Zeugnis *nt*
schoolroom ['sku:lru:m] N Klassenzimmer *nt*
schoolteacher ['sku:lti:tʃəʳ] N Lehrer(in) *m(f)*
schoolyard ['sku:ljɑ:d] N Schulhof *m*
schooner ['sku:nəʳ] N *(ship)* Schoner *m*; (BRIT: *for sherry)* großes Sherryglas *nt*; *(US etc: for beer)* großes Bierglas *nt*
sciatica [saɪ'ætɪkə] N Ischias *m or nt*
science ['saɪəns] N Naturwissenschaft *f*; *(branch of knowledge)* Wissenschaft *f*; **the sciences** Naturwissenschaften *pl*
science fiction N Science-Fiction *f*
scientific [saɪən'tɪfɪk] ADJ wissenschaftlich
scientist ['saɪəntɪst] N Wissenschaftler(in) *m(f)*
sci-fi ['saɪfaɪ] *(inf)* N ABBR (= *science fiction*) SF
Scillies ['sɪlɪz] NPL = **Scilly Isles**
Scilly Isles ['sɪlɪ'aɪlz] NPL: **the ~** die Scillyinseln *pl*
scintillating ['sɪntɪleɪtɪŋ] ADJ *(fig: conversation)* faszinierend; *(wit)* sprühend
scissors ['sɪzəz] NPL Schere *f*; **a pair of ~** eine Schere
sclerosis [sklɪ'rəusɪs] N Sklerose *f*
scoff [skɔf] VT (BRIT *inf: eat)* futtern, verputzen ▸ VI: **to ~ (at)** *(mock)* spotten (über *+acc*), sich lustig machen (über *+acc*)
scold [skəuld] VT ausschimpfen
scolding ['skəuldɪŋ] N Schelte *f*; **to get a ~** ausgeschimpft werden
scone [skɔn] N *brötchenartiges Teegebäck*
scoop [sku:p] N *(amount)* Kugel *f*; *(Press)* Knüller *m*; *(for flour etc)* Schaufel *f*; *(for ice cream etc)* Portionierer *m*
▸ **scoop out** VT aushöhlen
▸ **scoop up** VT aufschaufeln; *(liquid)* aufschöpfen
scooter ['sku:təʳ] N *(also:* **motor scooter**) Motorroller *m*; *(toy)* (Tret)roller *m*
scope [skəup] N *(opportunity)* Möglichkeiten *pl*; *(range)* Umfang *m*, Ausmaß *nt*; *(freedom)* Freiheit *f*; **within the ~ of** im Rahmen *+gen*; **there is plenty of ~ for improvement** (BRIT) es könnte noch viel verbessert werden
scorch [skɔ:tʃ] VT versengen; *(earth, grass)* verbrennen
scorched earth policy N *(Mil)* Politik *f* der verbrannten Erde
scorcher ['skɔ:tʃəʳ] *(inf)* N heißer Tag *m*
scorching ['skɔ:tʃɪŋ] ADJ *(day, weather)* brütend heiß
score [skɔ:ʳ] N *(number of points)* (Punkte)stand *m*; *(of game)* Spielstand *m*; *(Mus)* Partitur *f*; *(twenty)* zwanzig ▸ VT *(goal)* schießen; *(point, success)* erzielen; *(mark)* einkerben; *(cut)* einritzen ▸ VI *(keep score)* (Punkte) zählen; *(in game)* einen Punkt/Punkte erzielen; *(Football etc)* ein Tor schießen; **to settle an old ~ with sb** *(fig)* eine alte Rechnung mit jdm begleichen; **what's the ~?** *(Sport)* wie stehts?; **scores of** Hunderte von; **on that ~** in dieser Hinsicht; **to ~ well** gut abschneiden; **to ~ 6 out of 10** 6 von 10 Punkten erzielen; **to ~ (a point) over sb** *(fig)* jdn ausstechen
▸ **score out** VT ausstreichen
scoreboard ['skɔ:bɔ:d] N Anzeigetafel *f*
scorecard ['skɔ:kɑ:d] N *(Sport)* Spielprotokoll *nt*
score line N *(Sport)* Spielstand *m*; (: *final score)* Endergebnis *nt*
scorer ['skɔ:rəʳ] N *(Football etc)* Torschütze *m*, Torschützin *f*; *(person keeping score)* Anschreiber(in) *m(f)*
scorn [skɔ:n] N Verachtung *f* ▸ VT verachten; *(reject)* verschmähen
scornful ['skɔ:nful] ADJ verächtlich, höhnisch
Scorpio ['skɔ:pɪəu] N Skorpion *m*; **to be ~** Skorpion sein
scorpion ['skɔ:pɪən] N Skorpion *m*
Scot [skɔt] N Schotte *m*, Schottin *f*
Scotch [skɔtʃ] N Scotch *m*
scotch [skɔtʃ] VT *(rumour)* aus der Welt schaffen; *(plan, idea)* unterbinden
Scotch tape® N ≈ Tesafilm® *m*
scot-free ['skɔt'fri:] ADV: **to get off ~** ungeschoren davonkommen
Scotland ['skɔtlənd] N Schottland *nt*
Scots [skɔts] ADJ schottisch
Scotsman ['skɔtsmən] N *(irreg)* Schotte *m*
Scotswoman ['skɔtswumən] N *(irreg)* Schottin *f*
Scottish ['skɔtɪʃ] ADJ schottisch
Scottish National Party N *Partei, die für die Unabhängigkeit Schottlands eintritt*
scoundrel ['skaundrl] N Schurke *m*
scour ['skauəʳ] VT *(search)* absuchen; *(clean)* scheuern
scourer ['skauərəʳ] N Topfkratzer *m*
scourge [skə:dʒ] N *(lit, fig)* Geißel *f*
scout [skaut] N *(also:* **boy scout**) Pfadfinder *m*; *(Mil)* Kundschafter *m*, Späher *m*; **girl ~** (US) Pfadfinderin *f*
▸ **scout around** VI sich umsehen

S

scowl [skaul] VI ein böses Gesicht machen ▸ N böses Gesicht *nt*; **to ~ at sb** jdn böse ansehen

scrabble ['skræbl] VI (*also*: **scrabble around**) herumtasten ▸ N: **S~**® Scrabble® *nt*; **to ~ at sth** nach etw krallen; **to ~ about** *or* **around for sth** nach etw herumsuchen

scraggy ['skrægɪ] ADJ (*animal*) mager; (*body, neck etc*) dürr

scram [skræm] (*inf*) VI abhauen, verschwinden

scramble ['skræmbl] N (*climb*) Kletterpartie *f*; (*rush*) Hetze *f*; (*struggle*) Gerangel *nt* ▸ VI: **to ~ up/over** klettern auf/über +*acc*; **to ~ for** sich drängeln um; **to go scrambling** (*Sport*) Querfeldeinrennen fahren

scrambled eggs ['skræmbld-] N Rührei *nt*

scrap [skræp] N (*bit*) Stückchen *nt*; (*fig: of truth, evidence*) Spur *f*; (*fight*) Balgerei *f*; (*also*: **scrap metal**) Schrott *m*, Altmetall *nt* ▸ VT (*machines etc*) verschrotten; (*fig: plans etc*) fallen lassen ▸ VI (*fight*) sich balgen; **scraps** NPL (*leftovers*) Reste *pl*; **to sell sth for ~** etw als Schrott *or* zum Verschrotten verkaufen

scrapbook ['skræpbuk] N Sammelalbum *nt*

scrap dealer N Schrotthändler(in) *m(f)*

scrape [skreɪp] VT abkratzen; (*hand etc*) abschürfen; (*car*) verschrammen ▸ N: **to get into a ~** (*difficult situation*) in Schwulitäten *pl* kommen (*inf*)
▸ **scrape through** VT (*exam etc*) durchrutschen durch (*inf*)
▸ **scrape together** VT (*money*) zusammenkratzen

scraper ['skreɪpəʳ] N Kratzer *m*

scrap heap N: **to be on the ~** (*fig*) zum alten Eisen gehören

scrap merchant (Brit) N Schrotthändler(in) *m(f)*

scrap metal N Schrott *m*, Altmetall *nt*

scrap paper N Schmierpapier *nt*

scrappy ['skræpɪ] ADJ zusammengestoppelt (*inf*)

scrap yard N Schrottplatz *m*

scratch [skrætʃ] N Kratzer *m* ▸ VT kratzen; (*one's nose etc*) sich kratzen an +*dat*; (*paint, car, record*) verkratzen; (*Comput*) löschen ▸ VI sich kratzen ▸ CPD (*team, side*) zusammengewürfelt; **to start from ~** ganz von vorne anfangen; **to be up to ~** den Anforderungen entsprechen; **to ~ the surface** (*fig*) an der Oberfläche bleiben

scratch pad (US) N Notizblock *m*

scrawl [skrɔ:l] N Gekritzel *nt*; (*handwriting*) Klaue *f* (*inf*) ▸ VT hinkritzeln

scrawny ['skrɔ:nɪ] ADJ dürr

scream [skri:m] N Schrei *m* ▸ VI schreien; **to be a ~** (*inf*) zum Schreien sein; **to ~ at sb (to do sth)** jdn anschreien(, etw zu tun)

scree [skri:] N Geröll *nt*

screech [skri:tʃ] VI kreischen; (*tyres, brakes*) quietschen ▸ N Kreischen *nt*; (*of tyres, brakes*) Quietschen *nt*

screen [skri:n] N (*Cine*) Leinwand *f*; (*TV, Comput*) Bildschirm *m*; (*movable barrier*) Wandschirm *m*; (*fig: cover*) Tarnung *f*; (*also*: **windscreen**) Windschutzscheibe *f* ▸ VT (*protect*) abschirmen; (*from the wind etc*) schützen; (*conceal*) verdecken; (*film*) zeigen, vorführen; (*programme*) senden; (*candidates etc*) überprüfen; (*for illness*): **to ~ sb for sth** jdn auf etw *acc* (hin) untersuchen

screen editing N (*Comput*) Bildschirmaufbereitung *f*

screening ['skri:nɪŋ] N (*Med*) Untersuchung *f*; (*of film*) Vorführung *f*; (*TV*) Sendung *f*; (*for security*) Überprüfung *f*

screen memory N (*Comput*) Bildschirmspeicher *m*

screenplay ['skri:npleɪ] N Drehbuch *nt*

screen saver N (*Comput*) Bildschirmschoner *m*

screenshot ['skri:nʃɔt] N (*Comput*) Screenshot *m*, Bildschirmfoto *nt*

screen test N Probeaufnahmen *pl*

screw [skru:] N Schraube *f* ▸ VT schrauben; (*inf!*) bumsen (*inf!*); **to ~ sth in** etw einschrauben; **to ~ sth to the wall** etw an der Wand festschrauben; **to have one's head screwed on** (*fig*) ein vernünftiger Mensch sein
▸ **screw up** VT (*paper etc*) zusammenknüllen; (*inf: ruin*) vermasseln; **to ~ up one's eyes** die Augen zusammenkneifen

screwdriver ['skru:draɪvəʳ] N Schraubenzieher *m*

screwed-up ['skru:d'ʌp] (*inf*) ADJ: **to be/get ~ about sth** sich wegen etw ganz verrückt machen

screw top N Schraubverschluss *m*

screwy ['skru:ɪ] (*inf*) ADJ verrückt

scribble ['skrɪbl] N Gekritzel *nt* ▸ VT, VI kritzeln; **to ~ sth down** etw hinkritzeln

scribe [skraɪb] N Schreiber *m*

script [skrɪpt] N (*Cine*) Drehbuch *nt*; (*of speech, play etc*) Text *m*; (*alphabet*) Schrift *f*; (*in exam*) schriftliche Arbeit *f*

scripted ['skrɪptɪd] ADJ vorbereitet

scripture ['skrɪptʃəʳ] N, **scriptures** ['skrɪptʃəz] NPL (heilige) Schrift *f*; **the S~(s)** (*the Bible*) die Heilige Schrift *f*

scriptwriter ['skrɪptraɪtəʳ] N (*Radio, TV*) Autor(in) *m(f)*; (*Cine*) Drehbuchautor(in) *m(f)*

scroll [skrəul] N Schriftrolle *f* ▸ VI (*Comput*) scrollen

scroll bar N (*Comput*) Bildaufleiste *f*

scroll down ['skrəul'daun] VI (*Comput*) runterscrollen

scroll up VI (*Comput*) raufscrollen

scrotum ['skrəutəm] N Hodensack *m*

scrounge [skraundʒ] (*inf*) VT: **to ~ sth off sb** etw bei jdm schnorren ▸ VI schnorren ▸ N: **on the ~** am Schnorren

scrounger ['skraundʒəʳ] (*inf*) N Schnorrer(in) *m(f)*

scrub [skrʌb] N Gestrüpp *nt* ▸ VT (*floor etc*) schrubben; (*inf: idea, plan*) fallen lassen

scrubbing brush ['skrʌbɪŋ-] N Scheuerbürste *f*

scruff [skrʌf] N: **by the ~ of the neck** am Genick

scruffy ['skrʌfɪ] ADJ gammelig, verwahrlost

scrum ['skrʌm], **scrummage** ['skrʌmɪdʒ] N (*Rugby*) Gedränge *nt*

scruple ['skru:pl] N (*gen pl*) Skrupel *m*, Bedenken *nt*; **to have no scruples about doing sth** keine Skrupel *or* Bedenken haben, etw zu tun
scrupulous ['skru:pjuləs] ADJ gewissenhaft; (*honesty*) unbedingt
scrupulously ['skru:pjuləslı] ADV gewissenhaft; (*honest, fair*) äußerst; (*clean*) peinlich
scrutinize ['skru:tınaız] VT prüfend ansehen; (*data, records etc*) genau prüfen *or* untersuchen
scrutiny ['skru:tını] N genaue Untersuchung *f*; **under the ~ of sb** unter jds prüfendem Blick
scuba ['sku:bə] N (Schwimm)tauchgerät *nt*
scuba diving N Sporttauchen *nt*
scuff [skʌf] VT (*shoes, floor*) abwetzen
scuffle ['skʌfl] N Handgemenge *nt*
scull [skʌl] N Skull *nt*
scullery ['skʌlərı] N (*old*) Spülküche *f*
sculptor ['skʌlptə^r] N Bildhauer(in) *m(f)*
sculpture ['skʌlptʃə^r] N (*art*) Bildhauerei *f*; (*object*) Skulptur *f*
scum [skʌm] N (*on liquid*) Schmutzschicht *f*; (*pej*) Abschaum *m*
scupper ['skʌpə^r] (BRIT *inf*) VT (*plan, idea*) zerschlagen
scurrilous ['skʌrıləs] ADJ verleumderisch
scurry ['skʌrı] VI huschen
▶ **scurry off** VI forthasten
scurvy ['skə:vı] N Skorbut *m*
scuttle ['skʌtl] N (*also:* **coal scuttle**) Kohleneimer *m* ▶ VT (*ship*) versenken ▶ VI: **to ~ away** *or* **off** verschwinden
scythe [saıð] N Sense *f*
SD, (US) **S.Dak.** ABBR (*Post*) = **South Dakota**
SDI (US) N ABBR (*Mil:* = *Strategic Defense Initiative*) SDI *f*
SDLP (BRIT) N ABBR (*Pol:* = *Social Democratic and Labour Party*) *sozialdemokratische Partei in Nordirland*
SE ABBR (= *south-east*) SO
sea [si:] N Meer *nt*, See *f*; (*fig*) Meer *nt* ▶ CPD See-; **by ~** (*travel*) mit dem Schiff; **beside** *or* **by the ~** (*holiday*) am Meer, an der See; (*village*) am Meer; **on the ~** (*boat*) auf See; **at ~** auf See; **to be all at ~** (*fig*) nicht durchblicken (*inf*); **out to ~** aufs Meer (hinaus); **to look out to ~** aufs Meer hinausblicken; **heavy/rough ~(s)** schwere/raue See *f*
sea anemone N Seeanemone *f*
sea bed N Meeresboden *m*
seaboard ['si:bɔ:d] N Küste *f*
seafarer ['si:fɛərə^r] N Seefahrer *m*
seafaring ['si:fɛərıŋ] ADJ (*life, nation*) Seefahrer-
seafood ['si:fu:d] N Meeresfrüchte *pl*
seafront ['si:frʌnt] N Strandpromenade *f*
seagoing ['si:gəuıŋ] ADJ hochseetüchtig
seagull ['si:gʌl] N Möwe *f*
seal [si:l] N (*animal*) Seehund *m*; (*official stamp*) Siegel *nt*; (*in machine etc*) Dichtung *f*; (*on bottle etc*) Verschluss *m* ▶ VT (*envelope*) zukleben; (*crack, opening*) abdichten; (*with seal*) versiegeln; (*agreement, sb's fate*) besiegeln; **to give sth one's ~ of approval** einer Sache *dat* seine offizielle Zustimmung geben
▶ **seal off** VT (*place*) abriegeln
sea level N Meeresspiegel *m*; **2,000 ft above/below ~** 2000 Fuß über/unter dem Meeresspiegel
sealing wax ['si:lıŋ-] N Siegelwachs *nt*
sea lion N Seelöwe *m*
sealskin ['si:lskın] N Seehundfell *nt*
seam [si:m] N Naht *f*; (*lit, fig: where edges join*) Übergang *m*; (*of coal etc*) Flöz *nt*; **the hall was bursting at the seams** der Saal platzte aus allen Nähten
seaman ['si:mən] N (*irreg*) Seemann *m*
seamanship ['si:mənʃıp] N Seemannschaft *f*
seamless ['si:mlıs] ADJ (*lit, fig*) nahtlos
seamy ['si:mı] ADJ zwielichtig; **the ~ side of life** die Schattenseite des Lebens
séance ['seıɔns] N spiritistische Sitzung *f*
seaplane ['si:pleın] N Wasserflugzeug *nt*
seaport ['si:pɔ:t] N Seehafen *m*
search [sə:tʃ] N Suche *f*; (*inspection*) Durchsuchung *f*; (*Comput*) Suchlauf *m* ▶ VT durchsuchen; (*mind, memory*) durchforschen ▶ VI: **to ~ for** suchen nach; **"~ and replace"** (*Comput*) „suchen und ersetzen"; **in ~ of** auf der Suche nach
▶ **search through** VT FUS durchsuchen
search engine N (*Comput*) Suchmaschine *f*
searcher ['sə:tʃə^r] N Suchende(r) *f(m)*
searching ['sə:tʃıŋ] ADJ (*question*) bohrend; (*look*) prüfend; (*examination*) eingehend
searchlight ['sə:tʃlaıt] N Suchscheinwerfer *m*
search party N Suchtrupp *m*; **to send out a ~** einen Suchtrupp ausschicken
search warrant N Durchsuchungsbefehl *m*
searing ['sıərıŋ] ADJ (*heat*) glühend; (*pain*) scharf
seashell ['si:ʃel] N Muschel *f*
seashore ['si:ʃɔ:^r] N Strand *m*; **on the ~** am Strand
seasick ['si:sık] ADJ seekrank
seasickness ['si:sıknıs] N Seekrankheit *f*
seaside ['si:saıd] N Meer *nt*, See *f*; **to go to the ~** ans Meer *or* an die See fahren; **at the ~** am Meer, an der See
seaside resort N Badeort *m*
season ['si:zn] N Jahreszeit *f*; (*Agr*) Zeit *f*; (*Sport, of films etc*) Saison *f*; (*Theat*) Spielzeit *f* ▶ VT (*food*) würzen; **strawberries are in ~/out of ~** für Erdbeeren ist jetzt die richtige Zeit/nicht die richtige Zeit; **the busy ~** die Hochsaison *f*; **the open ~** (*Hunting*) die Jagdzeit *f*
seasonal ['si:znl] ADJ (*work*) Saison-
seasoned ['si:znd] ADJ (*fig: traveller*) erfahren; (*wood*) abgelagert; **she's a ~ campaigner** sie ist eine alte Kämpferin
seasoning ['si:znıŋ] N Gewürz *nt*
season ticket N (*Rail*) Zeitkarte *f*; (*Sport*) Dauerkarte *f*; (*Theat*) Abonnement *nt*
seat [si:t] N (*chair, of government, Pol*) Sitz *m*; (*place*) Platz *m*; (*buttocks*) Gesäß *nt*; (*of trousers*) Hosenboden *m*; (*of learning*) Stätte *f* ▶ VT setzen; (*have room for*) Sitzplätze bieten für; **are there any seats left?** sind noch Plätze frei?; **to take one's ~** sich setzen; **please be seated** bitte nehmen Sie Platz; **to be seated** sitzen
seat belt N Sicherheitsgurt *m*

S

seating arrangements ['si:tɪŋ-] NPL Sitzordnung *f*
seating capacity N Sitzplätze *pl*
SEATO ['si:təu] N ABBR (= *Southeast Asia Treaty Organization*) SEATO *f*
sea urchin N Seeigel *m*
sea view ['si:vju:] N Seeblick *m*
sea water N Meerwasser *nt*
seaweed ['si:wi:d] N Seetang *m*
seaworthy ['si:wə:ðɪ] ADJ seetüchtig
SEC (*US*) N ABBR (= *Securities and Exchange Commission*) *amerikanische Börsenaufsichtsbehörde*
sec. ABBR (= *second*) Sek.
secateurs [sɛkə'tə:z] NPL Gartenschere *f*
secede [sɪ'si:d] VI (*Pol*): **to ~ (from)** sich abspalten (von)
secluded [sɪ'klu:dɪd] ADJ (*place*) abgelegen; (*life*) zurückgezogen
seclusion [sɪ'klu:ʒən] N Abgeschiedenheit *f*; **in ~** zurückgezogen
second¹ [sɪ'kɔnd] (BRIT) VT (*employee*) abordnen
second² ['sɛkənd] ADJ zweite(r, s) ▶ ADV (*come, be placed*) Zweite(r, s); (*when listing*) zweitens ▶ N (*time*) Sekunde *f*; (*Aut*: *also*: **second gear**) der zweite Gang; (*person*) Zweite(r) *f*(*m*); (*Comm*: *imperfect*) zweite Wahl *f* ▶ VT (*motion*) unterstützen; **upper/lower ~** (BRIT *Univ*) ≈ Zwei plus/minus; **Charles the S~** Karl der Zweite; **just a ~!** einen Augenblick!; **~ floor** (BRIT) zweiter Stock *m*; (*US*) erster Stock *m*; **to ask for a ~ opinion** ein zweites Gutachten einholen
secondary ['sɛkəndərɪ] ADJ weniger wichtig
secondary education N höhere Schulbildung *f*
secondary picketing N *Aufstellung von Streikposten bei nur indirekt beteiligten Firmen*
secondary school N höhere Schule *f*

> **Secondary school** ist in Großbritannien eine weiterführende Schule für Kinder von 11 bis 18 Jahren. Manche Schüler gehen schon mit 16 Jahren, wenn die allgemeine Schulpflicht endet, von der Schule ab. Die meisten secondary schools sind heute Gesamtschulen, obwohl es auch noch selektive Schulen gibt. Siehe auch **comprehensive school, primary school.**

second-best [sɛkənd'bɛst] ADJ zweitbeste(r, s) ▶ N: **as a ~** als Ausweichlösung; **don't settle for ~** gib dich nur mit dem Besten zufrieden
second-class ['sɛkənd'klɑ:s] ADJ zweitklassig; (*citizen*) zweiter Klasse; (*Rail, Post*) Zweite-Klasse- ▶ ADV (*Rail, Post*) zweiter Klasse; **to send sth ~** etw zweiter Klasse schicken; **to travel ~** zweiter Klasse reisen
second cousin N Cousin *m*/Cousine *f* zweiten Grades
seconder ['sɛkəndəʳ] N Befürworter(in) *m*(*f*)
second-guess ['sɛkənd'gɛs] VT vorhersagen; **to ~ sb** vorhersagen, was jd machen wird
second hand N (*on clock*) Sekundenzeiger *m*
second-hand ['sɛkənd'hænd] ADJ gebraucht; (*clothing*) getragen ▶ ADV (*buy*) gebraucht; **to hear sth ~** etw aus zweiter Hand haben; **~ car** Gebrauchtwagen *m*; **~ smoking** (*US*) Passivrauchen *nt*
second-in-command ['sɛkəndɪnkə'mɑ:nd] N (*Mil*) stellvertretender Kommandeur *m*; (*Admin*) stellvertretender Leiter *m*
secondly ['sɛkəndlɪ] ADV zweitens
secondment [sɪ'kɔndmənt] (BRIT) N Abordnung *f*; **to be on ~** abgeordnet sein
second-rate ['sɛkənd'reɪt] ADJ zweitklassig
second thoughts NPL: **on ~, on second thought** (*US*) wenn ich es mir (recht) überlege; **to have ~ (about doing sth)** es sich *dat* anders überlegen (und etw doch nicht tun)
Second World War N: **the ~** der Zweite Weltkrieg
secrecy ['si:krəsɪ] N Geheimhaltung *f*; (*of person*) Verschwiegenheit *f*; **in ~** heimlich
secret ['si:krɪt] ADJ geheim; (*admirer*) heimlich ▶ N Geheimnis *nt*; **in ~** heimlich; **~ passage** Geheimgang *m*; **to keep sth ~ from sb** etw vor jdm geheim halten; **can you keep a ~?** kannst du schweigen?; **to make no ~ of sth** kein Geheimnis *or* keinen Hehl aus etw machen
secret agent N Geheimagent(in) *m*(*f*)
secretarial [sɛkrɪ'tɛərɪəl] ADJ (*work*) Büro-; (*course*) Sekretärinnen-; (*staff*) Sekretariats-
secretariat [sɛkrɪ'tɛərɪət] N (*Pol, Admin*) Sekretariat *nt*
secretary ['sɛkrətərɪ] N (*Comm*) Sekretär(in) *m*(*f*); (*of club*) Schriftführer(in) *m*(*f*); **S~ of State (for)** (BRIT *Pol*) Minister(in) *m*(*f*) (für); **S~ of State** (*US Pol*) Außenminister(in) *m*(*f*)
secretary-general ['sɛkrətərɪ'dʒɛnərl] (*pl* **secretaries-general**) N Generalsekretär(in) *m*(*f*)
secrete [sɪ'kri:t] VT (*Anat, Biol, Med*) absondern; (*hide*) verbergen
secretion [sɪ'kri:ʃən] N (*substance*) Sekret *nt*
secretive ['si:krətɪv] ADJ verschlossen; (*pej*) geheimnistuerisch
secretly ['si:krɪtlɪ] ADV heimlich; (*hope*) insgeheim
secret police N Geheimpolizei *f*
secret service N Geheimdienst *m*
sect [sɛkt] N Sekte *f*
sectarian [sɛk'tɛərɪən] ADJ (*killing etc*) konfessionell motiviert; **~ violence** gewalttätige Konfessionsstreitigkeiten *pl*
section ['sɛkʃən] N (*part*) Teil *m*; (*department*) Abteilung *f*; (*of document*) Absatz *m*; (*cross-section*) Schnitt *m* ▶ VT (*divide*) teilen; **the business/sport ~** (*Press*) der Wirtschafts-/Sportteil
sectional ['sɛkʃənl] ADJ: **~ drawing** Darstellung *f* im Schnitt
sector ['sɛktəʳ] N Sektor *m*
secular ['sɛkjuləʳ] ADJ weltlich
secure [sɪ'kjuəʳ] ADJ sicher; (*firmly fixed*) fest ▶ VT (*fix*) festmachen; (*votes etc*) erhalten; (*contract etc*) (sich *dat*) sichern; (*Comm*: *loan*) (ab)sichern; **to make sth ~** etw sichern; **to ~ sth for sb** jdm etw sichern
secured creditor [sɪ'kjuəd-] N (*Comm*) abgesicherter Gläubiger *m*
securely [sɪ'kjuəlɪ] ADV (*firmly*) fest; (*safely*) sicher

security [sɪ'kjuərɪtɪ] N Sicherheit *f*; (*freedom from anxiety*) Geborgenheit *f*; **securities** NPL (*Stock Exchange*) Effekten *pl*, Wertpapiere *pl*; **securities market** Wertpapiermarkt *m*; **to increase/tighten ~** die Sicherheitsvorkehrungen verschärfen; **~ of tenure** Kündigungsschutz *m*

Security Council N Sicherheitsrat *m*

security forces NPL Sicherheitskräfte *pl*

security guard N Sicherheitsbeamte(r) *m*; (*transporting money*) Wachmann *m*

security risk N Sicherheitsrisiko *nt*

secy. ABBR = **secretary**

sedan [sə'dæn] (US) N (*Aut*) Limousine *f*

sedate [sɪ'deɪt] ADJ (*person*) ruhig, gesetzt; (*life*) geruhsam; (*pace*) gemächlich ▸ VT (*Med*) Beruhigungsmittel geben *+dat*

sedation [sɪ'deɪʃən] N (*Med*) Beruhigungsmittel *pl*; **to be under ~** unter dem Einfluss von Beruhigungsmitteln stehen

sedative ['sɛdɪtɪv] N (*Med*) Beruhigungsmittel *nt*

sedentary ['sɛdntrɪ] ADJ (*occupation, work*) sitzend

sediment ['sɛdɪmənt] N (*in bottle*) (Boden)satz *m*; (*in lake etc*) Ablagerung *f*

sedimentary [sɛdɪ'mɛntərɪ] ADJ (*Geog*) sedimentär; **~ rock** Sedimentgestein *nt*

sedition [sɪ'dɪʃən] N Aufwiegelung *f*

seduce [sɪ'dju:s] VT verführen; **to ~ sb into doing sth** jdn dazu verleiten, etw zu tun

seduction [sɪ'dʌkʃən] N (*attraction*) Verlockung *f*; (*act of seducing*) Verführung *f*

seductive [sɪ'dʌktɪv] ADJ verführerisch; (*fig: offer*) verlockend

see [si:] (*pt* **saw**, *pp* **seen**) VT sehen; (*look at*) sich *dat* ansehen; (*understand*) verstehen, (ein)sehen; (*doctor etc*) aufsuchen ▸ VI sehen ▸ N (*Rel*) Bistum *nt*; **to ~ that** (*ensure*) dafür sorgen, dass; **to ~ sb to the door** jdn zur Tür bringen; **there was nobody to be seen** es war niemand zu sehen; **to go and ~ sb** jdn besuchen (gehen); **to ~ a doctor** zum Arzt gehen; **~ you!** tschüss! (*inf*); **~ you soon!** bis bald!; **let me ~** (*show me*) lass mich mal sehen; (*let me think*) lass mich mal überlegen; **I ~** ich verstehe, aha; (*annoyed*) ach so; **you ~** weißt du, siehst du; **~ for yourself** überzeug dich doch selbst; **I don't know what she sees in him** ich weiß nicht, was sie an ihm findet; **as far as I can ~** so wie ich das sehe

▸ **see about** VT FUS sich kümmern um *+acc*

▸ **see off** VT verabschieden

▸ **see out** VT (*show out*) zur Tür bringen

▸ **see through** VT FUS durchschauen ▸ VT; **to ~ sb through sth** jdm in etw *dat* beistehen; **to ~ sth through to the end** etw zu Ende bringen; **this should ~ you through** das müsste dir reichen

▸ **see to** VT FUS sich kümmern um *+acc*

seed [si:d] N Samen *m*; (*of fruit*) Kern *m*; (*fig: usu pl*) Keim *m*; (*Tennis*) gesetzter Spieler *m*, gesetzte Spielerin *f*; **to go to ~** (*plant*) Samen bilden; (*lettuce etc*) schießen; (*fig: person*) herunterkommen

seedless ['si:dlɪs] ADJ kernlos

seedling ['si:dlɪŋ] N (*Bot*) Sämling *m*

seedy ['si:dɪ] ADJ (*person, place*) zwielichtig, zweifelhaft

seeing ['si:ɪŋ] CONJ: **~ as** *or* **that** da

seek [si:k] (*pt, pp* **sought**) VT suchen; **to ~ advice from sb** jdn um Rat fragen; **to ~ help from sb** jdn um Hilfe bitten

▸ **seek out** VT ausfindig machen

seem [si:m] VI scheinen; **there seems to be a mistake** da scheint ein Fehler zu sein; **it seems (that)** es scheint(, dass); **it seems to me that ...** mir scheint, dass ...; **what seems to be the trouble?** worum geht es denn?; (*doctor*) was fehlt Ihnen denn?

seemingly ['si:mɪŋlɪ] ADV anscheinend

seemly ['si:mlɪ] ADJ schicklich

seen [si:n] PP *of* **see**

seep [si:p] VI sickern

seersucker ['sɪəsʌkə^r] N Krepp *m*, Seersucker *m*

seesaw ['si:sɔ:] N Wippe *f*

seethe [si:ð] VI: **to ~ with** (*place*) wimmeln von; **to ~ with anger** vor Wut kochen

see-through ['si:θru:] ADJ durchsichtig

segment ['sɛgmənt] N Teil *m*; (*of orange*) Stück *nt*

segregate ['sɛgrɪgeɪt] VT trennen, absondern

segregation [sɛgrɪ'geɪʃən] N Trennung *f*

Seine [seɪn] N: **the ~** die Seine *f*

seismic shock N Erdstoß *m*

seize [si:z] VT packen, ergreifen; (*fig: opportunity*) ergreifen; (*power, control*) an sich *acc* reißen; (*territory, airfield*) besetzen; (*hostage*) nehmen; (*Law*) beschlagnahmen

▸ **seize up** VI (*engine*) sich festfressen

▸ **seize (up)on** VT FUS sich stürzen auf *+acc*

seizure ['si:ʒə^r] N (*Med*) Anfall *m*; (*of power*) Ergreifung *f*; (*Law*) Beschlagnahmung *f*

seldom ['sɛldəm] ADV selten

select [sɪ'lɛkt] ADJ exklusiv ▸ VT (aus)wählen; (*Sport*) aufstellen; **a ~ few** wenige Auserwählte *pl*

selection [sɪ'lɛkʃən] N (*range*) Auswahl *f*; (*being chosen*) Wahl *f*

selection committee N Auswahlkomitee *nt*

selective [sɪ'lɛktɪv] ADJ wählerisch; (*not general*) selektiv

selector [sɪ'lɛktə^r] N (*Sport*) Mannschaftsaufsteller(in) *m(f)*; (*Tech*) Wählschalter *m*; (*: button*) Taste *f*

self [sɛlf] (*pl* **selves**) N Selbst *nt*, Ich *nt*; **she was her normal ~ again** sie war wieder ganz die Alte

self... [sɛlf] PREF selbst-, Selbst-

self-addressed ['sɛlfə'drɛst] ADJ: **~ envelope** adressierter Rückumschlag *m*

self-adhesive [sɛlfəd'hi:zɪv] ADJ selbstklebend

self-appointed [sɛlfə'pɔɪntɪd] ADJ selbst ernannt

self-assertive [sɛlfə'sə:tɪv] ADJ selbstbewusst

self-assurance [sɛlfə'ʃuərəns] N Selbstsicherheit *f*

self-assured [sɛlfə'ʃuəd] ADJ selbstsicher

self-catering [sɛlf'keɪtərɪŋ] (BRIT) ADJ (*holiday, flat*) für Selbstversorger

S

self-centred, (*US*) **self-centered** [sɛlfˈsɛntəd] ADJ egozentrisch, ichbezogen
self-cleaning [sɛlfˈkliːnɪŋ] ADJ selbstreinigend
self-confessed [sɛlfkənˈfɛst] ADJ erklärt
self-confidence [sɛlfˈkɔnfɪdns] N Selbstbewusstsein *nt*, Selbstvertrauen *nt*
self-confident [sɛlfˈkɔnfɪdənt] ADJ selbstbewusst, selbstsicher
self-conscious [sɛlfˈkɔnʃəs] ADJ befangen, gehemmt
self-contained [sɛlfkənˈteɪnd] (BRIT) ADJ (*flat*) abgeschlossen; (*person*) selb(st)ständig
self-control [sɛlfkənˈtrəul] N Selbstbeherrschung *f*
self-defeating [sɛlfdɪˈfiːtɪŋ] ADJ unsinnig
self-defence, (*US*) **self-defense** [sɛlfdɪˈfɛns] N Selbstverteidigung *f*; (*Law*) Notwehr *f*; **in ~** zu seiner/ihrer *etc* Verteidigung; (*Law*) in Notwehr
self-discipline [sɛlfˈdɪsɪplɪn] N Selbstdisziplin *f*
self-employed [sɛlfɪmˈplɔɪd] ADJ selbstständig
self-esteem [sɛlfɪsˈtiːm] N Selbstachtung *f*
self-evident [sɛlfˈɛvɪdnt] ADJ offensichtlich
self-explanatory [sɛlfɪksˈplænətrɪ] ADJ unmittelbar verständlich
self-financing [sɛlffaɪˈnænsɪŋ] ADJ selbstfinanzierend
self-governing [sɛlfˈgʌvənɪŋ] ADJ selbst verwaltet
self-harm [sɛlfˈhɑːm] N selbstverletzendes Verhalten *nt*
self-help [ˈsɛlfˈhɛlp] N Selbsthilfe *f*
self-importance [sɛlfɪmˈpɔːtns] N Aufgeblasenheit *f*
self-indulgent [sɛlfɪnˈdʌldʒənt] ADJ genießerisch; **to be ~** sich verwöhnen
self-inflicted [sɛlfɪnˈflɪktɪd] ADJ selbst zugefügt
self-interest [sɛlfˈɪntrɪst] N Eigennutz *m*
selfish [ˈsɛlfɪʃ] ADJ egoistisch, selbstsüchtig
selfishly [ˈsɛlfɪʃlɪ] ADV egoistisch, selbstsüchtig
selfishness [ˈsɛlfɪʃnɪs] N Egoismus *m*, Selbstsucht *f*
selfless [ˈsɛlflɪs] ADJ selbstlos
selflessly [ˈsɛlflɪslɪ] ADV selbstlos
selflessness [ˈsɛlflɪsnɪs] N Selbstlosigkeit *f*
self-made [ˈsɛlfmeɪd] ADJ: **~ man** Selfmademan *m*
self-pity [sɛlfˈpɪtɪ] N Selbstmitleid *nt*
self-portrait [sɛlfˈpɔːtreɪt] N Selbstporträt *nt*, Selbstbildnis *nt*
self-possessed [sɛlfpəˈzɛst] ADJ selbstbeherrscht
self-preservation [ˈsɛlfprɛzəˈveɪʃən] N Selbsterhaltung *f*
self-raising [sɛlfˈreɪzɪŋ], (*US*) **self-rising** [ˈsɛlfˈraɪzɪŋ] ADJ: **~ flour** *Mehl mit bereits beigemischtem Backpulver*
self-reliant [sɛlfrɪˈlaɪənt] ADJ selb(st)ständig
self-respect [sɛlfrɪsˈpɛkt] N Selbstachtung *f*
self-respecting [sɛlfrɪsˈpɛktɪŋ] ADJ mit Selbstachtung; (*genuine*) der/die/das etwas auf sich hält
self-righteous [sɛlfˈraɪtʃəs] ADJ selbstgerecht
self-rising [sɛlfˈraɪzɪŋ] (*US*) ADJ = **self-raising**
self-sacrifice [sɛlfˈsækrɪfaɪs] N Selbstaufopferung *f*
self-same [ˈsɛlfseɪm] ADJ: **the ~** genau derselbe/dieselbe/dasselbe
self-satisfied [sɛlfˈsætɪsfaɪd] ADJ selbstzufrieden
self-sealing [sɛlfˈsiːlɪŋ] ADJ selbstklebend
self-service [sɛlfˈsəːvɪs] ADJ (*shop, restaurant etc*) Selbstbedienungs-
self-styled [ˈsɛlfstaɪld] ADJ selbst ernannt
self-sufficient [sɛlfsəˈfɪʃənt] ADJ (*country*) autark; (*person*) selb(st)ständig, unabhängig; **to be ~ in coal** seinen Kohlebedarf selbst decken können
self-supporting [sɛlfsəˈpɔːtɪŋ] ADJ (*business*) sich selbst tragend
self-taught [sɛlfˈtɔːt] ADJ: **to be ~** Autodidakt sein; **he is a ~ pianist** er hat sich das Klavierspielen selbst beigebracht
self-test [ˈsɛlftɛst] N (*Comput*) Selbsttest *m*
sell [sɛl] (*pt, pp* **sold**) VT verkaufen; (*shop: goods*) haben (*inf*), führen; (*fig: idea*) schmackhaft machen *+dat*, verkaufen (*inf*) ▸ VI sich verkaufen (lassen); **to ~ at** *or* **for 10 pounds** für 10 Pfund verkauft werden; **to ~ sb sth** jdm etw verkaufen; **to ~ o.s.** sich verkaufen
▸ **sell off** VT verkaufen
▸ **sell out** VI: **we/the tickets are sold out** wir/die Karten sind ausverkauft; **we have sold out of …** wir haben kein … mehr, … ist ausverkauft
▸ **sell up** VI sein Haus/seine Firma *etc* verkaufen
sell-by date [ˈsɛlbaɪ-] N ≈ Haltbarkeitsdatum *nt*
seller [ˈsɛlə^r] N Verkäufer(in) *m(f)*; **~'s market** Verkäufermarkt *m*
selling point [ˈsɛlɪŋ-] N Verkaufsanreiz *m or* -argument *nt*
selling price [ˈsɛlɪŋ-] N Verkaufspreis *m*
Sellotape® [ˈsɛləuteɪp] (BRIT) N ≈ Tesafilm® *m*, Klebeband *nt*
sellout [ˈsɛlaut] N (*inf: betrayal*) Verrat *m*; **the match was a ~** das Spiel war ausverkauft
selves [sɛlvz] PL *of* **self**
semantic [sɪˈmæntɪk] ADJ semantisch
semantics [sɪˈmæntɪks] N (*Ling*) Semantik *f*
semaphore [ˈsɛməfɔː^r] N Flaggenalphabet *nt*
semblance [ˈsɛmblns] N Anschein *m*
semen [ˈsiːmən] N Samenflüssigkeit *f*, Sperma *nt*
semester [sɪˈmɛstə^r] (*esp US*) N Semester *nt*
semi [ˈsɛmɪ] N = **semidetached**
semi… [ˈsɛmɪ] PREF halb-, Halb-
semibreve [ˈsɛmɪbriːv] (BRIT) N (*Mus*) ganze Note *f*
semicircle [ˈsɛmɪsəːkl] N Halbkreis *m*
semicircular [ˈsɛmɪˈsəːkjulə^r] ADJ halbkreisförmig
semicolon [sɛmɪˈkəulən] N Semikolon *nt*, Strichpunkt *m*
semiconductor [sɛmɪkənˈdʌktə^r] N Halbleiter *m*
semiconscious [sɛmɪˈkɔnʃəs] ADJ halb bewusstlos
semidetached [sɛmɪdɪˈtætʃt], **semidetached house** (BRIT) N Doppelhaushälfte *f*

semifinal [sɛmɪˈfaɪnl] N Halbfinale *nt*
seminar [ˈsɛmɪnɑːʳ] N Seminar *nt*
seminary [ˈsɛmɪnərɪ] N (*Rel*) Priesterseminar *nt*
semi-precious stone N Halbedelstein *m*
semiquaver [ˈsɛmɪkweɪvəʳ] (BRIT) N (*Mus*) Sechzehntelnote *f*
semiskilled [sɛmɪˈskɪld] ADJ (*work*) Anlern-; (*worker*) angelernt
semi-skimmed [sɛmɪˈskɪmd] ADJ (*milk*) teilentrahmt, Halbfett-
semitone [ˈsɛmɪtəun] N (*Mus*) Halbton *m*
semolina [sɛməˈliːnə] N Grieß *m*
Sen., sen. ABBR (*US*) = **senator**; (*in names*: = *senior*) sen.
senate [ˈsɛnɪt] N Senat *m*

> **Senate** ist das Oberhaus des amerikanischen Kongresses (das Unterhaus ist das **House of Representatives**. Der Senat besteht aus 100 Senatoren, zwei für jeden Bundesstaat, die für sechs Jahre gewählt werden, wobei ein Drittel alle zwei Jahre neu gewählt wird. Die Senatoren werden in direkter Wahl vom Volk gewählt. Siehe auch **congress**.

senator [ˈsɛnɪtəʳ] N Senator(in) *m(f)*
send [sɛnd] (*pt, pp* **sent**) VT schicken; (*transmit*) senden; **to ~ sth by post, to ~ sth by mail** (*US*) etw mit der Post schicken; **to ~ sb for sth** (*for check-up etc*) jdn zu etw schicken; **to ~ word that ...** Nachricht geben, dass ...; **she sends (you) her love** sie lässt dich grüßen; **to ~ sb to Coventry** (BRIT) jdn schneiden (*inf*); **to ~ sb to sleep** jdn einschläfern; **to ~ sth flying** etw umwerfen
▶ **send away** VT wegschicken
▶ **send away for** VT FUS (per Post) anfordern
▶ **send back** VT zurückschicken
▶ **send for** VT FUS (per Post) anfordern; (*doctor, police*) rufen
▶ **send in** VT einsenden, einschicken
▶ **send off** VT abschicken; (BRIT: *player*) vom Platz weisen
▶ **send on** VT (BRIT: *letter*) nachsenden; (*luggage etc*) vorausschicken
▶ **send out** VT verschicken; (*light, heat*) abgeben; (*signal*) aussenden
▶ **send round** VT schicken; (*circulate*) zirkulieren lassen
▶ **send up** VT (*astronaut*) hochschießen; (*price, blood pressure*) hochtreiben; (BRIT: *parody*) verulken (*inf*)
sender [ˈsɛndəʳ] N Absender(in) *m(f)*
sending-off [ˈsɛndɪŋɔf] N (*Sport*) Platzverweis *m*
send-off [ˈsɛndɔf] N: **a good ~** eine große Verabschiedung
send-up [ˈsɛndʌp] N Verulkung *f* (*inf*)
Senegal [sɛnɪˈgɔːl] N Senegal *nt*
Senegalese [sɛnɪgəˈliːz] ADJ senegalesisch ▶ N INV Senegalese *m*, Senegalesin *f*
senile [ˈsiːnaɪl] ADJ senil
senility [sɪˈnɪlɪtɪ] N Senilität *f*
senior [ˈsiːnɪəʳ] ADJ (*staff, manager*) leitend; (*officer*) höher; (*post, position*) leitend ▶ N (*Scol*): **the seniors** die Oberstufenschüler *pl*; **to be ~ to sb** jdm übergeordnet sein; **she is 15 years his ~** sie ist 15 Jahre älter als er; **P. Jones ~** P. Jones senior
senior citizen N Senior(in) *m(f)*
senior high school (*US*) N Oberstufe *f*
seniority [siːnɪˈɔrɪtɪ] N (*in service*) (längere) Betriebszugehörigkeit *f*; (*in rank*) (höhere) Position *f*
sensation [sɛnˈseɪʃən] N (*feeling*) Gefühl *nt*; (*great success*) Sensation *f*; **to cause a ~** großes Aufsehen erregen
sensational [sɛnˈseɪʃənl] ADJ (*wonderful*) wunderbar; (*result*) sensationell; (*headlines etc*) reißerisch
sense [sɛns] N Sinn *m*; (*feeling*) Gefühl *nt*; (*good sense*) Verstand *m*, gesunder Menschenverstand *m*; (*meaning*) Bedeutung *f*, Sinn *m* ▶ VT spüren; **~ of smell** Geruchssinn *m*; **it makes ~** (*can be understood*) es ergibt einen Sinn; (*is sensible*) es ist vernünftig *or* sinnvoll; **there's no ~ in that** das hat keinen Sinn; **there is no ~ in doing that** es hat keinen Sinn, das zu tun; **to come to one's senses** Vernunft annehmen; **to take leave of one's senses** den Verstand verlieren
senseless [ˈsɛnslɪs] ADJ (*pointless*) sinnlos; (*unconscious*) besinnungslos, bewusstlos
sense of humour N Sinn *m* für Humor
sensibility [sɛnsɪˈbɪlɪtɪ] N Empfindsamkeit *f*; (*sensitivity*) Empfindlichkeit *f*; **to offend sb's sensibilities** jds Zartgefühl verletzen
sensible [ˈsɛnsɪbl] ADJ vernünftig; (*shoes, clothes*) praktisch
sensitive [ˈsɛnsɪtɪv] ADJ empfindlich; (*understanding*) einfühlsam; (*touchy*: *person*) sensibel; (: *issue*) heikel; **to be ~ to sth** in Bezug auf etw *acc* empfindlich sein; **he is very ~ about it/to criticism** er reagiert sehr empfindlich darauf/auf Kritik
sensitivity [sɛnsɪˈtɪvɪtɪ] N Empfindlichkeit *f*; (*understanding*) Einfühlungsvermögen *nt*; (*of issue etc*) heikle Natur *f*; **an issue of great ~** ein sehr heikles Thema
sensual [ˈsɛnsjuəl] ADJ sinnlich; (*person, life*) sinnenfroh
sensuous [ˈsɛnsjuəs] ADJ sinnlich
sent [sɛnt] PT, PP *of* **send**
sentence [ˈsɛntns] N (*Ling*) Satz *m*; (*Law*: *judgement*) Urteil *nt*; (: *punishment*) Strafe *f* ▶ VT: **to ~ sb to death/to 5 years in prison** jdn zum Tode/zu 5 Jahren Haft verurteilen; **to pass ~ on sb** das Urteil über jdn verkünden; (*fig*) jdn verurteilen; **to serve a life ~** eine lebenslängliche Freiheitsstrafe verbüßen
sentiment [ˈsɛntɪmənt] N Sentimentalität *f*; (*also pl*: *opinion*) Ansicht *f*
sentimental [sɛntɪˈmɛntl] ADJ sentimental
sentimentality [sɛntɪmɛnˈtælɪtɪ] N Sentimentalität *f*
sentry [ˈsɛntrɪ] N Wachtposten *m*
sentry duty N: **to be on ~** auf Wache sein
Seoul [səul] N Seoul *nt*
separable [ˈsɛprəbl] ADJ: **to be ~ from** trennbar sein von

S

separate ['sɛprɪt] ADJ getrennt; (*occasions*) verschieden; (*rooms*) separat ▸ VT trennen ▸ VI sich trennen; **~ from** getrennt von; **to go ~ ways** getrennte Wege gehen; **under ~ cover** (*Comm*) mit getrennter Post; **to ~ into** aufteilen in *+acc*; *see also* **separates**
separately ['sɛprɪtlɪ] ADV getrennt
separates ['sɛprɪts] NPL (*clothes*) kombinierbare Einzelteile *pl*
separation [sɛpə'reɪʃən] N Trennung *f*
sepia ['si:pjə] ADJ sepiafarben
Sept. ABBR (= *September*) Sept.
September [sɛp'tɛmbə[r]] N September *m*; *see also* **July**
septic ['sɛptɪk] ADJ vereitert, septisch; **to go ~** eitern
septicaemia, (*US*) **septicemia** [sɛptɪ'si:mɪə] N Blutvergiftung *f*
septic tank N Faulbehälter *m*
sequel ['si:kwl] N (*of film, story*) Fortsetzung *f*; (*follow-up*) Nachspiel *nt*
sequence ['si:kwəns] N Folge *f*; (*dance/film sequence*) Sequenz *f*; **in ~** der Reihe nach
sequential [sɪ'kwɛnʃəl] ADJ aufeinanderfolgend; **~ access** (*Comput*) sequenzieller Zugriff *m*
sequestrate [sɪ'kwɛstreɪt] VT (*Law, Comm*) sequestrieren, beschlagnahmen
sequin ['si:kwɪn] N Paillette *f*
Serbia ['sə:bɪə] N Serbien *nt*
Serbian ['sə:bɪən] ADJ serbisch ▸ N Serbier(in) *m(f)*; (*Ling*) Serbisch *nt*
Serbo-Croat ['sə:bəu'krəuæt] N (*Ling*) Serbokroatisch *nt*
serenade [sɛrə'neɪd] N Serenade *f* ▸ VT ein Ständchen *nt* bringen *+dat*
serene [sɪ'ri:n] ADJ (*landscape etc*) friedlich; (*expression*) heiter; (*person*) gelassen
serenity [sə'rɛnɪtɪ] N (*of landscape*) Friedlichkeit *f*; (*of expression*) Gelassenheit *f*
sergeant ['sɑ:dʒənt] N (*Mil etc*) Feldwebel *m*; (*Police*) Polizeimeister *m*
sergeant-major ['sɑ:dʒənt'meɪdʒə[r]] N Oberfeldwebel *m*
serial ['sɪərɪəl] N (*TV*) Serie *f*; (*Radio*) Sendereihe *f*; (*in magazine*) Fortsetzungsroman *m* ▸ ADJ (*Comput*) seriell
serialize ['sɪərɪəlaɪz] VT in Fortsetzungen veröffentlichen; (*TV, Radio*) in Fortsetzungen senden
serial killer N Serienmörder(in) *m(f)*
serial number N Seriennummer *f*
series ['sɪərɪz] N INV (*of books*) Reihe *f*; (*TV*) Serie *f*; (*group*) Serie *f*, Reihe *f*
serious ['sɪərɪəs] ADJ ernst; (*important*) wichtig; (*: illness*) schwer; (*: condition*) bedenklich; **are you ~ (about it)?** meinst du das ernst?
seriously ['sɪərɪəslɪ] ADV ernst; (*talk, interested*) ernsthaft; (*ill, hurt, damaged*) schwer; (*not jokingly*) im Ernst; **to take sb/sth ~** jdn/etw ernst nehmen; **do you ~ believe that ...** glauben Sie ernsthaft *or* im Ernst, dass ...
seriousness ['sɪərɪəsnɪs] N Ernst *m*, Ernsthaftigkeit *f*; (*of problem*) Bedenklichkeit *f*
sermon ['sə:mən] N Predigt *f*; (*fig*) Moralpredigt *f*
serrated [sɪ'reɪtɪd] ADJ gezackt; **~ knife** Sägemesser *nt*
serum ['sɪərəm] N Serum *nt*
servant ['sə:vənt] N (*lit, fig*) Diener(in) *m(f)*; (*domestic*) Hausangestellte(r) *f(m)*
serve [sə:v] VT dienen *+dat*; (*in shop, with food/drink*) bedienen; (*food, meal*) servieren; (*purpose*) haben; (*apprenticeship*) durchmachen; (*prison term*) verbüßen ▸ VI (*at table*) auftragen, servieren; (*Tennis*) aufschlagen; (*soldier*) dienen; (*be useful*): **to ~ as/for** dienen als ▸ N (*Tennis*) Aufschlag *m*; **are you being served?** werden Sie schon bedient?; **to ~ its purpose** seinen Zweck erfüllen; **to ~ sb's purpose** jds Zwecken dienen; **it serves him right** das geschieht ihm recht; **to ~ on a committee** einem Ausschuss angehören; **to ~ on a jury** Geschworene(r) *f(m)* sein; **it's my turn to ~** (*Tennis*) ich habe Aufschlag; **it serves to show/explain ...** das zeigt/erklärt ...
▸ **serve out** VT (*food*) auftragen, servieren
▸ **serve up** VT = **serve out**
server N (*Comput*) Server *m*
service ['sə:vɪs] N Dienst *m*; (*commercial*) Dienstleistung *f*; (*in hotel, restaurant*) Bedienung *f*, Service *m*; (*also:* **train service**) Bahnverbindung *f*; (*: generally*) Zugverkehr *m*; (*Rel*) Gottesdienst *m*; (*Aut*) Inspektion *f*; (*Tennis*) Aufschlag *m*; (*plates etc*) Service *nt* ▸ VT (*car, machine*) warten; **the Services** NPL (*army, navy etc*) die Streitkräfte *pl*; **military/national ~** Militärdienst *m*; **to be of ~ to sb** jdm nützen; **to do sb a ~** jdm einen Dienst erweisen; **to put one's car in for a ~** sein Auto zur Inspektion geben; **dinner ~** Essservice *nt*
serviceable ['sə:vɪsəbl] ADJ zweckmäßig
service area N (*on motorway*) Raststätte *f*
service charge (BRIT) N Bedienungsgeld *nt*
service contract N Wartungsvertrag *m*
service industry N Dienstleistungsbranche *f*
serviceman ['sə:vɪsmən] N (*irreg*) Militärangehörige(r) *m*
service provider N (*Comput*) Provider *m*
service station N Tankstelle *f*
serviette [sə:vɪ'ɛt] (BRIT) N Serviette *f*
servile ['sə:vaɪl] ADJ unterwürfig
session ['sɛʃən] N Sitzung *f*; (*US, Scot: Scol*) Studienjahr *nt*; (*: term*) Semester *nt*; **recording ~** Aufnahme *f*; **to be in ~** tagen
session musician N Session-Musiker(in) *m(f)*
set [sɛt] (*pt, pp* **~**) N (*of saucepans, books, keys etc*) Satz *m*; (*group*) Reihe *f*; (*of cutlery*) Garnitur *f*; (*also:* **radio set**) Radio(gerät) *nt*; (*also:* **TV set**) Fernsehgerät *nt*; (*Tennis*) Satz *m*; (*group of people*) Kreis *m*; (*Math*) Menge *f*; (*Theat: stage*) Bühne *f*; (*: scenery*) Bühnenbild *nt*; (*Cine*) Drehort *m*; (*Hairdressing*) (Ein)legen *nt* ▸ ADJ (*fixed*) fest; (*ready*) bereit, fertig ▸ VT (*table*) decken; (*place*) auflegen; (*time, price, rules etc*) festsetzen; (*record*)

aufstellen; (*alarm, watch, task*) stellen; (*exam*) zusammenstellen; (*Typ*) setzen ▸ VI (*sun*) untergehen; (*jam, jelly, concrete*) fest werden; (*bone*) zusammenwachsen; **a ~ of false teeth** ein Gebiss *nt*; **a ~ of dining-room furniture** eine Esszimmergarnitur; **a chess ~** ein Schachspiel *nt*; **to be ~ on doing sth** etw unbedingt tun wollen; **to be all ~ to do sth** bereit sein, etw zu tun; **he's ~ in his ways** er ist in seinen Gewohnheiten festgefahren; **a ~ phrase** eine feste Redewendung; **a novel ~ in Rome** ein Roman, der in Rom spielt; **to ~ to music** vertonen; **to ~ on fire** anstecken; **to ~ free** freilassen; **to ~ sail** losfahren

▸ **set about** VT FUS (*task*) anpacken; **to ~ about doing sth** sich daranmachen, etw zu tun

▸ **set aside** VT (*money etc*) beiseitelegen; (*time*) einplanen

▸ **set back** VT: **to ~ sb back 5 pounds** jdn 5 Pfund kosten; **to ~ sb back (by)** (*in time*) jdn zurückwerfen (um); **a house ~ back from the road** ein Haus, das etwas von der Straße abliegt

▸ **set in** VI (*bad weather*) einsetzen; (*infection*) sich einstellen; **the rain has ~ in for the day** es hat sich für heute eingeregnet

▸ **set off** VI (*depart*) aufbrechen ▸ VT (*alarm, chain of events*) auslösen; (*show up well*) hervorheben; (*bomb*) losgehen lassen

▸ **set out** VI (*depart*) aufbrechen ▸ VT (*chairs etc*) aufstellen; (*arguments*) darlegen; (*goods etc*) ausbreiten; **to ~ out to do sth** sich *dat* vornehmen, etw zu tun; **to ~ out from home** zu Hause aufbrechen

▸ **set up** VT (*organization*) gründen; (*monument*) errichten; **to ~ up shop** ein Geschäft eröffnen; (*fig*) sich selb(st)ständig machen

setback ['sɛtbæk] N Rückschlag *m*

set menu N Menü *nt*

set square N Zeichendreieck *nt*

settee [sɛ'tiː] N Sofa *nt*

setting ['sɛtɪŋ] N (*background*) Rahmen *m*; (*position*) Einstellung *f*; (*of jewel*) Fassung *f*

setting lotion N (Haar)festiger *m*

settle ['sɛtl] VT (*matter*) regeln; (*argument*) beilegen; (*accounts*) begleichen; (*affairs, business*) in Ordnung bringen; (*colonize: land*) besiedeln ▸ VI (*also:* **settle down**) sich niederlassen; (*sand, dust etc*) sich legen; (*sediment*) sich setzen; (*calm down*) sich beruhigen; **to ~ one's stomach** den Magen beruhigen; **that's settled then!** das ist also abgemacht!; **to ~ down to work** sich an die Arbeit setzen; **to ~ down to watch TV** es sich *dat* vor dem Fernseher gemütlich machen

▸ **settle for** VT FUS sich zufriedengeben mit

▸ **settle in** VI sich einleben; (*in job etc*) sich eingewöhnen

▸ **settle on** VT FUS sich entscheiden für

▸ **settle up** VI: **to ~ up with sb** mit jdm abrechnen

settlement ['sɛtlmənt] N (*payment*) Begleichung *f*; (*Law*) Vergleich *m*; (*agreement*) Übereinkunft *f*; (*of conflict*) Beilegung *f*; (*village etc*) Siedlung *f*, Niederlassung *f*; (*colonization*) Besiedelung *f*; **in ~ of our account** (*Comm*) zum Ausgleich unseres Kontos

settler ['sɛtləʳ] N Siedler(in) *m(f)*

setup, set-up ['sɛtʌp] N (*organization*) Organisation *f*; (*system*) System *nt*; (*Comput*) Setup *nt*

seven ['sɛvn] NUM sieben

seventeen [sɛvn'tiːn] NUM siebzehn

seventeenth ADJ siebzehnte(r, s); *see also* **eighth**

seventh ['sɛvnθ] NUM siebte(r, s)

seventieth ['sɛvntɪɪθ] ADJ siebzigste(r, s); *see also* **eighth**

seventy ['sɛvntɪ] NUM siebzig

sever ['sɛvəʳ] VT durchtrennen; (*fig: relations*) abbrechen; (*: ties*) lösen

several ['sɛvərl] ADJ mehrere, einige ▸ PRON einige; **~ of us** einige von uns; **~ times** einige Male, mehrmals

severance ['sɛvərəns] N (*of relations*) Abbruch *m*

severance pay N Abfindung *f*

severe [sɪ'vɪəʳ] ADJ (*damage, shortage*) schwer; (*pain*) stark; (*person, expression, dress, winter*) streng; (*punishment*) hart; (*climate*) rau

severely [sɪ'vɪəlɪ] ADV (*punish*) hart; (*wounded, ill*) schwer; (*damage*) stark

severity [sɪ'vɛrɪtɪ] N (*gravity: of punishment*) Härte *f*; (*: of manner, voice, winter*) Strenge *f*; (*: of weather*) Rauheit *f*; (*austerity*) Strenge *f*

sew [səu] (*pt* **sewed**, *pp* **sewn**) VT, VI nähen

▸ **sew up** VT (zusammen)nähen; **it is all sewn up** (*fig*) es ist unter Dach und Fach

sewage ['suːɪdʒ] N Abwasser *nt*

sewage works N Kläranlage *f*

sewer ['suːəʳ] N Abwasserkanal *m*

sewing ['səuɪŋ] N Nähen *nt*; (*items*) Näharbeit *f*

sewing machine N Nähmaschine *f*

sewn [səun] PP *of* **sew**

sex [sɛks] N (*gender*) Geschlecht *nt*; (*lovemaking*) Sex *m*; **to have ~ with sb** (Geschlechts)verkehr mit jdm haben

sex act N Geschlechtsakt *m*

sex appeal N Sex-Appeal *m*

sex education N Sexualerziehung *f*

sexism ['sɛksɪzəm] N Sexismus *m*

sexist ['sɛksɪst] ADJ sexistisch

sex life N Sexualleben *nt*

sex object N Sexualobjekt *nt*

sextet [sɛks'tɛt] N Sextett *nt*

sexual ['sɛksjuəl] ADJ sexuell; (*reproduction*) geschlechtlich; (*equality*) der Geschlechter

sexual assault N Vergewaltigung *f*

sexual harassment N sexuelle Belästigung *f*

sexual intercourse N Geschlechtsverkehr *m*

sexuality [sɛksjʊ'ælɪtɪ] N Sexualität *f*

sexually ['sɛksjuəlɪ] ADV sexuell; (*segregate*) nach Geschlechtern; (*discriminate*) aufgrund des Geschlechts; (*reproduce*) geschlechtlich

sexual orientation N sexuelle Orientierung *f*

sexy ['sɛksɪ] ADJ sexy; (*pictures, underwear*) sexy, aufreizend

Seychelles [seɪ'ʃɛl(z)] NPL: **the ~** die Seychellen *pl*

SF N ABBR (= *science fiction*) SF

S

SG (*US*) N ABBR (*Mil, Med*) = **Surgeon General**
Sgt ABBR (*Police, Mil*) = **sergeant**
shabbiness ['ʃæbɪnɪs] N Schäbigkeit *f*
shabby ['ʃæbɪ] ADJ schäbig
shack [ʃæk] N Hütte *f*
▸ **shack up** (*inf*) VI: **to ~ up (with sb)** (mit jdm) zusammenziehen
shackles ['ʃæklz] NPL Ketten *pl*; (*fig*) Fesseln *pl*
shade [ʃeɪd] N Schatten *m*; (*for lamp*) (Lampen)schirm *m*; (*of colour*) (Farb)ton *m*; (*US: also*: **window shade**) Jalousie *f*, Rollo *nt* ▸ VT beschatten; (*eyes*) abschirmen; **shades** NPL (*inf: sunglasses*) Sonnenbrille *f*; **in the ~** im Schatten; **a ~ of blue** ein Blauton; **a ~ (more/too large)** (*small quantity*) etwas *or* eine Spur (mehr/zu groß)
shadow ['ʃædəu] N Schatten *m* ▸ VT (*follow*) beschatten; **without** *or* **beyond a ~ of a doubt** ohne den geringsten Zweifel
shadow cabinet (BRIT) N Schattenkabinett *nt*
shadow economy N (*Econ*) Schattenwirtschaft *f*
shadowy ['ʃædəuɪ] ADJ schattig; (*figure, shape*) schattenhaft
shady ['ʃeɪdɪ] ADJ schattig; (*fig: dishonest*) zwielichtig; **~ deals** dunkle Geschäfte
shaft [ʃɑ:ft] N (*of arrow, spear*) Schaft *m*; (*Aut, Tech*) Welle *f*; (*of mine, lift*) Schacht *m*; (*of light*) Strahl *m*; **ventilation ~** Luftschacht *m*
shaggy ['ʃægɪ] ADJ zottelig; (*dog, sheep*) struppig
shake [ʃeɪk] (*pt* **shook**, *pp* **shaken**) VT schütteln; (*weaken, upset, surprise*) erschüttern; (*weaken: resolve*) ins Wanken bringen ▸ VI zittern, beben; (*building, table*) wackeln; (*earth*) beben ▸ N Schütteln *nt*; **to ~ one's head** den Kopf schütteln; **to ~ hands with sb** jdm die Hand schütteln; **to ~ one's fist (at sb)** (jdm) mit der Faust drohen; **give it a good ~** schütteln Sie es gut durch; **a ~ of the head** ein Kopfschütteln
▸ **shake off** VT (*lit, fig*) abschütteln
▸ **shake up** VT schütteln; (*fig: upset*) erschüttern
shake-out ['ʃeɪkaut] N Freisetzung *f* von Arbeitskräften
shake-up ['ʃeɪkʌp] N (radikale) Veränderung *f*
shakily ['ʃeɪkɪlɪ] ADV (*reply*) mit zittriger Stimme; (*walk, stand*) unsicher, wackelig
shaky ['ʃeɪkɪ] ADJ (*hand, voice*) zittrig; (*knowledge, prospects, future, start*) unsicher; (*memory*) schwach
shale [ʃeɪl] N Schiefer *m*
shall [ʃæl] AUX VB: **I ~ go** ich werde gehen; **~ I open the door?** soll ich die Tür öffnen?; **I'll go, ~ I?** soll ich gehen?
shallot [ʃə'lɔt] (BRIT) N Schalotte *f*
shallow ['ʃæləu] ADJ flach; (*fig*) oberflächlich; **the shallows** NPL die Untiefen *pl*
sham [ʃæm] N Heuchelei *f*; (*person*) Heuchler(in) *m(f)*; (*object*) Attrappe *f* ▸ ADJ unecht; (*fight*) Schein- ▸ VT vortäuschen
shambles ['ʃæmblz] N heilloses Durcheinander *nt*; **the economy is (in) a complete ~** die Wirtschaft befindet sich in einem totalen Chaos
shambolic [ʃæm'bɔlɪk] (*inf*) ADJ chaotisch
shame [ʃeɪm] N Scham *f*; (*disgrace*) Schande *f* ▸ VT beschämen; **it is a ~ that …** es ist eine Schande, dass …; **what a ~!** wie schade!; **to bring ~ on** Schande bringen über +*acc*; **to put sb/sth to ~** jdn/etw in den Schatten stellen
shamefaced ['ʃeɪmfeɪst] ADJ betreten
shameful ['ʃeɪmful] ADJ schändlich
shameless ['ʃeɪmlɪs] ADJ schamlos
shampoo [ʃæm'pu:] N Shampoo(n) *nt* ▸ VT waschen
shampoo and set N Waschen und Legen *nt*
shamrock ['ʃæmrɔk] N (*plant*) Klee *m*; (*leaf*) Kleeblatt *nt*
shandy ['ʃændɪ] N Bier *nt* mit Limonade, Radler *m*
shan't [ʃɑ:nt] = **shall not**
shantytown ['ʃæntɪtaun] N Elendsviertel *nt*
SHAPE [ʃeɪp] N ABBR (*Mil: = Supreme Headquarters Allied Powers, Europe*) *Hauptquartier der alliierten Streitkräfte in Europa während des 2. Weltkriegs*
shape [ʃeɪp] N Form *f* ▸ VT gestalten; (*form*) formen; (*sb's ideas*) prägen; (*sb's life*) bestimmen; **to take ~** Gestalt annehmen; **in the ~ of a heart** in Herzform; **I can't bear gardening in any ~ or form** ich kann Gartenarbeit absolut nicht ausstehen; **to get (o.s.) into ~** in Form kommen
▸ **shape up** VI sich entwickeln
-shaped [ʃeɪpt] SUFF: **heart~** herzförmig
shapeless ['ʃeɪplɪs] ADJ formlos
shapely ['ʃeɪplɪ] ADJ (*woman*) wohlproportioniert; (*legs*) wohlgeformt
share [ʃɛə^r] N (*part*) Anteil *m*; (*contribution*) Teil *m*; (*Comm*) Aktie *f* ▸ VT teilen; (*room, bed, taxi*) sich *dat* teilen; (*have in common*) gemeinsam haben; **to ~ in** (*joy, sorrow*) teilen; (*profits*) beteiligt sein an +*dat*; (*work*) sich beteiligen an +*dat*
▸ **share out** VT aufteilen
share capital N Aktienkapital *nt*
share certificate N Aktienurkunde *f*
shareholder ['ʃɛəhəuldə^r] N Aktionär(in) *m(f)*
share index N Aktienindex *m*; **the 100 Share Index** *Aktienindex der Financial Times*
share issue N Aktienemission *f*
shark [ʃɑ:k] N Hai(fisch) *m*
sharp [ʃɑ:p] ADJ scharf; (*point, nose, chin*) spitz; (*pain*) heftig; (*cold*) schneidend; (*Mus*) zu hoch; (*increase*) stark; (*person: quick-witted*) clever; (*: dishonest*) gerissen ▸ N (*Mus*) Kreuz *nt* ▸ ADV: **at 2 o'clock ~** um Punkt 2 Uhr; **turn ~ left** biegen Sie scharf nach links ab; **to be ~ with sb** schroff mit jdm sein; **~ practices** (*Comm*) unsaubere Geschäfte *pl*; **C ~** (*Mus*) Cis *nt*; **look ~!** (ein bisschen) dalli! (*inf*)
sharpen ['ʃɑ:pn] VT schärfen, schleifen; (*pencil, stick etc*) (an)spitzen; (*fig: appetite*) anregen
sharpener ['ʃɑ:pnə^r] N (*also*: **pencil sharpener**) (Bleistift)spitzer *m*; (*also*: **knife sharpener**) Schleifgerät *nt*
sharp-eyed [ʃɑ:p'aɪd] ADJ scharfsichtig
sharpish ['ʃɑ:pɪʃ] (*inf*) ADJ (*instantly*) auf der Stelle

sharply ['ʃɑ:plɪ] ADV scharf; (*stop*) plötzlich; (*retort*) schroff
sharp-tempered [ʃɑ:p'tɛmpəd] ADJ jähzornig
sharp-witted [ʃɑ:p'wɪtɪd] ADJ scharfsinnig
shatter ['ʃætə^r] VT zertrümmern; (*fig: hopes, dreams*) zunichtemachen; (*: confidence*) zerstören ▸VI zerspringen, zerbrechen
shattered ['ʃætəd] ADJ erschüttert; (*inf: exhausted*) fertig, kaputt
shattering ['ʃætərɪŋ] ADJ erschütternd, niederschmetternd; (*exhausting*) äußerst anstrengend
shatterproof ['ʃætəpru:f] ADJ splitterfest, splitterfrei
shave [ʃeɪv] VT rasieren ▸VI sich rasieren ▸N: **to have a ~** sich rasieren
▸**shave off** VT: **to ~ one's beard off** sich den Bart abrasieren
shaven ['ʃeɪvn] ADJ (*head*) kahl geschoren
shaver ['ʃeɪvə^r] N (*also*: **electric shaver**) Rasierapparat *m*
shaving ['ʃeɪvɪŋ] N Rasieren *nt*; **shavings** NPL (*of wood etc*) Späne *pl*
shaving brush N Rasierpinsel *m*
shaving cream N Rasiercreme *f*
shaving foam N Rasierschaum *m*
shaving point N Steckdose *f* für Rasierapparate
shaving soap N Rasierseife *f*
shawl [ʃɔ:l] N (Woll)tuch *nt*
she [ʃi:] PRON sie ▸PREF weiblich; **~-bear** Bärin *f*; **there ~ is** da ist sie
sheaf [ʃi:f] (*pl* **sheaves**) N (*of corn*) Garbe *f*; (*of papers*) Bündel *nt*
shear [ʃɪə^r] (*pt* **sheared**, *pp* **shorn**) VT scheren
▸**shear off** VI abbrechen
shears ['ʃɪəz] NPL (*for hedge*) Heckenschere *f*
sheath [ʃi:θ] N (*of knife*) Scheide *f*; (*contraceptive*) Kondom *nt*
sheathe [ʃi:ð] VT ummanteln; (*sword*) in die Scheide stecken
sheath knife N Fahrtenmesser *nt*
sheaves [ʃi:vz] NPL *of* **sheaf**
shed [ʃɛd] (*pt, pp* **~**) N Schuppen *m*; (*Industry, Rail*) Halle *f* ▸VT (*tears, blood*) vergießen; (*load*) verlieren; (*workers*) entlassen; **to ~ its skin** sich häuten; **to ~ light on** (*problem*) erhellen
she'd [ʃi:d] = **she had; she would**
sheen [ʃi:n] N Glanz *m*
sheep [ʃi:p] N INV Schaf *nt*
sheepdog ['ʃi:pdɔg] N Hütehund *m*
sheep farmer N Schaffarmer *m*
sheepish ['ʃi:pɪʃ] ADJ verlegen
sheepskin ['ʃi:pskɪn] N Schaffell *nt* ▸CPD Schaffell-
sheer [ʃɪə^r] ADJ (*utter*) rein; (*steep*) steil; (*almost transparent*) (hauch)dünn ▸ADV (*straight up*) senkrecht; **by ~ chance** rein zufällig
sheet [ʃi:t] N (*on bed*) (Bett)laken *nt*; (*of paper*) Blatt *nt*; (*of glass, metal*) Platte *f*; (*of ice*) Fläche *f*
sheet feed N (*on printer*) Papiereinzug *m*
sheet lightning N Wetterleuchten *nt*
sheet metal N Walzblech *nt*
sheet music N Notenblätter *pl*
sheik, sheikh [ʃeɪk] N Scheich *m*
shelf [ʃɛlf] (*pl* **shelves**) N Brett *nt*, Bord *nt*; **set of shelves** Regal *nt*
shelf life N Lagerfähigkeit *f*
shell [ʃɛl] N (*on beach*) Muschel *f*; (*of egg, nut etc*) Schale *f*; (*explosive*) Granate *f*; (*of building*) Mauern *pl* ▸VT (*peas*) enthülsen; (*Mil: fire on*) (mit Granaten) beschießen
▸**shell out** (*inf*) VT: **to ~ out (for)** blechen (für)
she'll [ʃi:l] = **she will; she shall**
shellfish ['ʃɛlfɪʃ] N INV Schalentier *nt*; (*scallop etc*) Muschel *f*; (*as food*) Meeresfrüchte *pl*
shelter ['ʃɛltə^r] N (*building*) Unterstand *m*; (*refuge*) Schutz *m*; (*also*: **bus shelter**) Wartehäuschen *nt*; (*also*: **night shelter**) Obdachlosenasyl *nt* ▸VT (*protect*) schützen; (*homeless, refugees*) aufnehmen; (*wanted man*) Unterschlupf gewähren +*dat* ▸VI sich unterstellen; (*from storm*) Schutz suchen; **to take ~ (from)** (*from danger*) sich in Sicherheit bringen (vor +*dat*); (*from storm etc*) Schutz suchen (vor +*dat*)
sheltered ['ʃɛltəd] ADJ (*life*) behütet; (*spot*) geschützt; **~ housing** (*for old people*) Altenwohnungen *pl*; (*for handicapped people*) Behindertenwohnungen *pl*
shelve [ʃɛlv] VT (*fig: plan*) ad acta legen
shelves [ʃɛlvz] NPL *of* **shelf**
shelving ['ʃɛlvɪŋ] N Regale *pl*
shepherd ['ʃɛpəd] N Schäfer *m* ▸VT (*guide*) führen
shepherdess ['ʃɛpədɪs] N Schäferin *f*
shepherd's pie (BRIT) N *Auflauf aus Hackfleisch und Kartoffelbrei*
sherbet ['ʃə:bət] N (BRIT: *powder*) Brausepulver *nt*; (*US: water ice*) Fruchteis *nt*
sheriff ['ʃɛrɪf] (US) N Sheriff *m*
sherry ['ʃɛrɪ] N Sherry *m*
she's [ʃi:z] = **she is; she has**
Shetland ['ʃɛtlənd] N (*also*: **the Shetland Islands**) die Shetlandinseln *pl*
Shetland pony N Shetlandpony *nt*
shield [ʃi:ld] N (*Mil*) Schild *m*; (*trophy*) Trophäe *f*; (*fig: protection*) Schutz *m* ▸VT: **to ~ (from)** schützen (vor +*dat*)
shift [ʃɪft] N (*change*) Änderung *f*; (*work-period, workers*) Schicht *f* ▸VT (*furniture*) (ver)rücken; (*stain*) herausbekommen; (*move*) bewegen ▸VI (*move*) sich bewegen; (*wind*) drehen; **a ~ in demand** (*Comm*) eine Nachfrageverschiebung
shift key N Umschalttaste *f*
shiftless ['ʃɪftlɪs] ADJ träge
shift work N Schichtarbeit *f*; **to do ~** Schicht arbeiten
shifty ['ʃɪftɪ] ADJ verschlagen
Shiite ['ʃi:aɪt] ADJ schiitisch ▸N Schiit(in) *m(f)*
shilling ['ʃɪlɪŋ] (BRIT: *old*) N Shilling *m*
shilly-shally ['ʃɪlɪʃælɪ] VI unschlüssig sein
shimmer ['ʃɪmə^r] VI schimmern
shimmering ['ʃɪmərɪŋ] ADJ schimmernd
shin [ʃɪn] N Schienbein *nt* ▸VI: **to ~ up a tree** einen Baum hinaufklettern
shindig ['ʃɪndɪg] (*inf*) N Remmidemmi *nt*

S

shine [ʃaɪn] (*pt, pp* **shone**) N Glanz *m* ▸ VI (*sun, light*) scheinen; (*eyes*) leuchten; (*hair: fig: person*) glänzen ▸ VT (*pt, pp* **shined**) (*polish*) polieren; **to ~ a torch on sth** etw mit einer Taschenlampe anleuchten

shingle [ˈʃɪŋgl] N (*on beach*) Kiesel(steine) *pl*; (*on roof*) Schindel *f*

shingles [ˈʃɪŋglz] NPL (*Med*) Gürtelrose *f*

shining [ˈʃaɪnɪŋ] ADJ glänzend; (*example*) leuchtend

shiny [ˈʃaɪnɪ] ADJ glänzend

ship [ʃɪp] N Schiff *nt* ▸ VT verschiffen; (*send*) versenden; (*water*) übernehmen; **on board ~** an Bord

shipbuilder [ˈʃɪpbɪldəʳ] N Schiffbauer *m*

shipbuilding [ˈʃɪpbɪldɪŋ] N Schiffbau *m*

ship canal N Seekanal *m*

ship chandler [-ˈtʃɑːndləʳ] N Schiffsausrüster *m*

shipment [ˈʃɪpmənt] N (*of goods*) Versand *m*; (*amount*) Sendung *f*

shipowner [ˈʃɪpəunəʳ] N Schiffseigner *m*; (*of many ships*) Reeder *m*

shipper [ˈʃɪpəʳ] N (*person*) Spediteur *m*; (*company*) Spedition *f*

shipping [ˈʃɪpɪŋ] N (*transport*) Versand *m*; (*ships*) Schiffe *pl*

shipping agent N Reeder *m*

shipping company N Schifffahrtslinie *f*, Reederei *f*

shipping lane N Schifffahrtsstraße *f*

shipping line N = **shipping company**

shipshape [ˈʃɪpʃeɪp] ADJ tipptopp (*inf*)

shipwreck [ˈʃɪprɛk] N Schiffbruch *m*; (*ship*) Wrack *nt* ▸ VT: **to be shipwrecked** schiffbrüchig sein

shipyard [ˈʃɪpjɑːd] N Werft *f*

shire [ˈʃaɪəʳ] (BRIT) N Grafschaft *f*

shirk [ʃəːk] VT sich drücken vor +*dat*

shirt [ʃəːt] N (Ober)hemd *nt*; (*woman's*) (Hemd)bluse *f*; **in (one's) ~ sleeves** in Hemdsärmeln

shirty [ˈʃəːtɪ] (BRIT *inf*) ADJ sauer (*inf*)

shit [ʃɪt] (*inf!*) EXCL Scheiße (*inf!*)

shitty [ˈʃɪtɪ] ADJ (*inf*) beschissen

shiver [ˈʃɪvəʳ] N Schauer *m* ▸ VI zittern; **to ~ with cold** vor Kälte zittern

shoal [ʃəul] N (*of fish*) Schwarm *m*; (*fig: also:* **shoals**) Scharen *pl*

shock [ʃɔk] N Schock *m*; (*impact*) Erschütterung *f*; (*also:* **electric shock**) Schlag *m* ▸ VT (*offend*) schockieren; (*upset*) erschüttern; **to be suffering from ~** (*Med*) einen Schock haben; **to be in ~** unter Schock stehen; **it gave us a ~** es hat uns erschreckt; **it came as a ~ to hear that ...** wir hörten mit Bestürzung, dass ...

shock absorber N (*Aut*) Stoßdämpfer *m*

shocked ADJ schockiert (by über +*acc*)

shocker [ˈʃɔkəʳ] (*inf*) N (*film etc*) Schocker *m*, Reißer *m*; **that's a real ~** (*event etc*) das haut einen echt um

shocking [ˈʃɔkɪŋ] ADJ fürchterlich, schrecklich; (*outrageous*) schockierend

shockproof [ˈʃɔkpruːf] ADJ stoßfest

shock therapy N Schocktherapie *f*

shock treatment N = **shock therapy**

shock wave N (*lit*) Druckwelle *f*; (*fig*) Schockwelle *f*

shod [ʃɔd] PT, PP *of* **shoe**

shoddy [ˈʃɔdɪ] ADJ minderwertig

shoe [ʃuː] (*pt, pp* **shod**) N Schuh *m*; (*for horse*) Hufeisen *nt*; (*also:* **brake shoe**) Bremsbacke *f* ▸ VT (*horse*) beschlagen

shoebrush [ˈʃuːbrʌʃ] N Schuhbürste *f*

shoelace [ˈʃuːleɪs] N Schnürsenkel *m*

shoemaker [ˈʃuːmeɪkəʳ] N Schuhmacher *m*, Schuster *m*

shoe polish N Schuhcreme *f*

shoe shop N Schuhgeschäft *nt*

shoestring [ˈʃuːstrɪŋ] N (*fig*): **on a ~** mit ganz wenig Geld

shoetree [ˈʃuːtriː] N Schuhspanner *m*

shone [ʃɔn] PT, PP *of* **shine**

shonky [ˈʃɔŋkɪ] ADJ (AUST, NZ *inf*) schäbig; (*work*) stümperhaft

shoo [ʃuː] EXCL (*to dog etc*) pfui ▸ VT (*also:* **shoo away, shoo off** *etc*) verscheuchen; (*somewhere*) scheuchen

shook [ʃuk] PT *of* **shake**

shoot [ʃuːt] (*pt, pp* **shot**) N (*on branch*) Trieb *m*; (*seedling*) Sämling *m*; (*Sport*) Jagd *f* ▸ VT (*arrow, goal*) schießen; (*kill, execute*) erschießen; (*wound*) anschießen; (*gun*) abfeuern; (BRIT: *game birds*) schießen; (*film*) drehen ▸ VI: **to ~ (at)** schießen (auf +*acc*); **to ~ past (sb/sth)** (an jdm/etw) vorbeischießen

▸ **shoot down** VT abschießen

▸ **shoot in** VI hereingeschossen kommen

▸ **shoot out (of)** VI herausgeschossen kommen (aus +*dat*)

▸ **shoot up** VI (*fig: increase*) in die Höhe schnellen

shooting [ˈʃuːtɪŋ] N Schießen *nt*, Schüsse *pl*; (*attack*) Schießerei *f*; (*murder*) Erschießung *f*; (*Cine*) Drehen *nt*; (*Hunting*) Jagen *nt*

shooting range N Schießplatz *m*

shooting star N Sternschnuppe *f*

shop [ʃɔp] N Geschäft *nt*, Laden *m*; (*workshop*) Werkstatt *f* ▸ VI (*also:* **go shopping**) einkaufen (gehen); **repair ~** Reparaturwerkstatt *f*; **to talk ~** (*fig*) über die Arbeit reden

▸ **shop around** VI Preise vergleichen; (*fig*) sich umsehen

shopaholic [ˈʃɔpəˈhɔlɪk] (*inf*) N: **to be a ~** einen Einkaufsfimmel haben

shop assistant (BRIT) N Verkäufer(in) *m(f)*

shop floor (BRIT) N (*workers*) Arbeiter *pl*; **on the ~** bei *or* unter den Arbeitern

shopkeeper [ˈʃɔpkiːpəʳ] N Geschäftsinhaber(in) *m(f)*, Ladenbesitzer(in) *m(f)*

shoplifter [ˈʃɔplɪftəʳ] N Ladendieb(in) *m(f)*

shoplifting [ˈʃɔplɪftɪŋ] N Ladendiebstahl *m*

shopper [ˈʃɔpəʳ] N Käufer(in) *m(f)*

shopping [ˈʃɔpɪŋ] N (*goods*) Einkäufe *pl*

shopping bag N Einkaufstasche *f*

shopping cart N (*US*) Einkaufswagen *m*

shopping centre, (*US*) **shopping center** N Einkaufszentrum *nt*

shopping list N Einkaufszettel *m*
shopping mall N Shoppingcenter *nt*
shopping trolley N (BRIT) Einkaufswagen *m*
shop-soiled ['ʃɔpsɔɪld] ADJ angeschmutzt
shop steward (BRIT) N gewerkschaftlicher Vertrauensmann *m*
shop window N Schaufenster *nt*
shore [ʃɔːʳ] N Ufer *nt*; (*beach*) Strand *m* ▸ VT: **to ~ (up)** abstützen; **on ~** an Land
shore leave N (*Naut*) Landurlaub *m*
shorn [ʃɔːn] PP *of* **shear**; **to be ~ of** (*power etc*) entkleidet sein *+gen*
short [ʃɔːt] ADJ kurz; (*person*) klein; (*curt*) schroff, kurz angebunden (*inf*); (*scarce*) knapp ▸ N (*also*: **short film**) Kurzfilm *m*; **to be ~ of ...** zu wenig ... haben; **I'm 3 ~** ich habe 3 zu wenig, mir fehlen 3; **in ~** kurz gesagt; **to be in ~ supply** knapp sein; **it is ~ for ...** es ist die Kurzform von ...; **a ~ time ago** vor Kurzem; **in the ~ term** auf kurze Sicht; **~ of doing sth** außer etw zu tun; **to cut ~** abbrechen; **everything ~ of ...** alles außer ... *+dat*; **to fall ~ of sth** etw nicht erreichen; (*expectations*) etw nicht erfüllen; **to run ~ of ...** nicht mehr viel ... haben; **to stop ~** plötzlich innehalten; **to stop ~ of** haltmachen vor *+dat*; *see also* **shorts**
shortage ['ʃɔːtɪdʒ] N: **a ~ of** ein Mangel *m* an *+dat*
shortbread ['ʃɔːtbrɛd] N Mürbegebäck *nt*
short-change [ʃɔːt'tʃeɪndʒ] VT: **to ~ sb** jdm zu wenig Wechselgeld geben
short circuit N Kurzschluss *m*
shortcrust pastry, (*US*) **short pastry** N Mürbeteig *m*
short cut N Abkürzung *f*; (*fig*) Schnellverfahren *nt*
shorten ['ʃɔːtn] VT verkürzen
shortening ['ʃɔːtnɪŋ] N (Back)fett *nt*
shortfall ['ʃɔːtfɔːl] N Defizit *nt*
shorthand ['ʃɔːthænd] N Stenografie *f*, Kurzschrift *f*; (*fig*) Kurzform *f*; **to take sth down in ~** etw stenografieren
shorthand notebook (BRIT) N Stenoblock *m*
shorthand typist (BRIT) N Stenotypist(in) *m(f)*
short list (BRIT) N Auswahlliste *f*; **to be on the ~** in der engeren Wahl sein
short-list ['ʃɔːtlɪst] (BRIT) VT in die engere Wahl ziehen; **to be short-listed** in die engere Wahl kommen
short-lived ['ʃɔːt'lɪvd] ADJ kurzlebig; **to be ~** nicht von Dauer sein
shortly ['ʃɔːtlɪ] ADV bald
shorts [ʃɔːts] NPL: **(a pair of) ~** Shorts *pl*
short-sighted [ʃɔːt'saɪtɪd] (BRIT) ADJ (*lit, fig*) kurzsichtig
short-sightedness [ʃɔːt'saɪtɪdnɪs] N Kurzsichtigkeit *f*
short-sleeved ADJ kurzärmelig
short-staffed [ʃɔːt'stɑːft] ADJ: **to be ~** zu wenig Personal haben
short story N Kurzgeschichte *f*
short-tempered [ʃɔːt'tɛmpəd] ADJ gereizt
short-term ['ʃɔːttəːm] ADJ kurzfristig
short time N: **to work ~, to be on ~** kurzarbeiten, Kurzarbeit haben
short-wave ['ʃɔːtweɪv] (*Radio*) N Kurzwelle *f* ▸ ADJ auf Kurzwelle
shot [ʃɔt] PT, PP *of* **shoot** ▸ N Schuss *m*; (*shotgun pellets*) Schrot *m*; (*injection*) Spritze *f*; (*Phot*) Aufnahme *f*; **to fire a ~ at sb/sth** einen Schuss auf jdn/etw abgeben; **to have a ~ at (doing) sth** etw mal versuchen; **to get ~ of sb/sth** (*inf*) jdn/etw loswerden; **a big ~** (*inf*) ein hohes Tier; **a good/poor ~** (*person*) ein guter/schlechter Schütze; **like a ~** sofort
shotgun ['ʃɔtgʌn] N Schrotflinte *f*
should [ʃud] AUX VB: **I ~ go now** ich sollte jetzt gehen; **he ~ be there now** er müsste eigentlich schon da sein; **I ~ go if I were you** an deiner Stelle würde ich gehen; **I ~ like to** ich möchte gerne, ich würde gerne; **~ he phone ...** falls er anruft ...
shoulder ['ʃəuldəʳ] N Schulter *f* ▸ VT (*fig*) auf sich *acc* nehmen; **to rub shoulders with sb** (*fig*) mit jdm in Berührung kommen; **to give sb the cold ~** (*fig*) jdm die kalte Schulter zeigen
shoulder bag N Umhängetasche *f*
shoulder blade N Schulterblatt *nt*
shoulder strap N (*on clothing*) Träger *m*; (*on bag*) Schulterriemen *m*
shouldn't ['ʃudnt] = **should not**
should've ['ʃudəv] = **should have**
shout [ʃaut] N Schrei *m*, Ruf *m* ▸ VT rufen, schreien ▸ VI (*also*: **shout out**) aufschreien; **to give sb a ~** jdn rufen
▸ **shout down** VT niederbrüllen
shouting ['ʃautɪŋ] N Geschrei *nt*
shouting match (*inf*) N: **to have a ~** sich gegenseitig anschreien
shove [ʃʌv] VT schieben; (*with one push*) stoßen, schubsen (*inf*) ▸ N: **to give sb a ~** jdn stoßen *or* schubsen (*inf*); **to give sth a ~** etw verrücken; (*door*) gegen etw stoßen; **to ~ sth in sth** (*inf: put*) etw in etw *acc* stecken; **he shoved me out of the way** er stieß mich zur Seite
▸ **shove off** (*inf*) VI abschieben
shovel ['ʃʌvl] N Schaufel *f*; (*mechanical*) Bagger *m* ▸ VT schaufeln
show [ʃəu] (*pt* **showed**, *pp* **shown**) N (*exhibition*) Ausstellung *f*, Schau *f*; (*Theat*) Aufführung *f*; (*TV*) Show *f*; (*Cine*) Vorstellung *f* ▸ VT zeigen; (*exhibit*) ausstellen ▸ VI: **it shows** man sieht es; (*is evident*) man merkt es; **to ask for a ~ of hands** um Handzeichen bitten; **without any ~ of emotion** ohne jede Gefühlsregung; **it's just for ~** es ist nur zur Schau; **on ~** ausgestellt, zu sehen; **who's running the ~ here?** (*inf*) wer ist hier verantwortlich?; **to ~ sb to his seat/to the door** jdn an seinen Platz/zur Tür bringen; **to ~ a profit/loss** Gewinn/Verlust aufweisen; **it just goes to ~ that ...** da sieht mans mal wieder, dass
▸ **show in** VT hereinführen
▸ **show off** (*pej*) VI angeben ▸ VT vorführen
▸ **show out** VT hinausbegleiten
▸ **show up** VI (*inf: turn up*) auftauchen; (*stand out*) sich abheben ▸ VT (*uncover*) deutlich erkennen lassen; (*shame*) blamieren

showbiz N = **show business**
show business N Showgeschäft *nt*
showcase ['ʃəukeɪs] N Schaukasten *m*; (*fig*) Werbung *f*
showdown ['ʃəudaun] N Kraftprobe *f*
shower ['ʃauə^r] N (*of rain*) Schauer *m*; (*for bathing in*) Dusche *f*; (*of stones etc*) Hagel *m*; (*US: party*) *Party, bei der jeder ein Geschenk für den Ehrengast mitbringt* ▸ VI duschen ▸ VT: **to ~ sb with** (*gifts etc*) jdn überschütten mit; (*missiles, abuse etc*) auf jdn niederhageln lassen; **to have** *or* **take a ~** duschen; **a ~ of sparks** ein Funkenregen *m*
showercap ['ʃauəkæp] N Duschhaube *f*
shower gel N Duschgel *nt*
showerproof ['ʃauəpru:f] ADJ regenfest
showery ['ʃauərɪ] ADJ regnerisch
showground ['ʃəugraund] N Ausstellungsgelände *nt*
showing ['ʃəuɪŋ] N (*of film*) Vorführung *f*
show jumping N Springreiten *nt*
showman ['ʃəumən] N (*irreg*) (*at fair*) Schausteller *m*; (*at circus*) Artist *m*; (*fig*) Schauspieler *m*
showmanship ['ʃəumənʃɪp] N Talent *nt* für effektvolle Darbietung
shown [ʃəun] PP *of* **show**
show-off ['ʃəuɔf] (*inf*) N Angeber(in) *m(f)*
showpiece ['ʃəupi:s] N (*of exhibition etc*) Schaustück *nt*; (*best example*) Paradestück *nt*; (*prime example*) Musterbeispiel *nt*
showroom ['ʃəurum] N Ausstellungsraum *m*
show trial N Schauprozess *m*
showy ['ʃəuɪ] ADJ auffallend
shrank [ʃræŋk] PT *of* **shrink**
shrapnel ['ʃræpnl] N Schrapnell *nt*
shred [ʃrɛd] N (*gen pl*) Fetzen *m*; (*fig*): **not a ~ of truth** kein Fünkchen Wahrheit; **not a ~ of evidence** keine Spur eines Beweises ▸ VT zerfetzen; (*Culin*) raspeln
shredder ['ʃrɛdə^r] N (*also*: **document shredder**) Reißwolf *m*; (*also*: **vegetable shredder**) Raspel *f*; (*also*: **garden shredder**) Häcksler *m*
shrew [ʃru:] N (*Zool*) Spitzmaus *f*; (*pej: woman*) Xanthippe *f*
shrewd [ʃru:d] ADJ klug
shrewdness ['ʃru:dnɪs] N Klugheit *f*
shriek [ʃri:k] N schriller Schrei *m* ▸ VI schreien; **to ~ with laughter** vor Lachen quietschen
shrift [ʃrɪft] N: **to give sb short ~** jdn kurz abfertigen
shrill [ʃrɪl] ADJ schrill
shrimp [ʃrɪmp] N Garnele *f*
shrine [ʃraɪn] N Schrein *m*; (*fig*) Gedenkstätte *f*
shrink [ʃrɪŋk] (*pt* **shrank**, *pp* **shrunk**) VI (*cloth*) einlaufen; (*profits, audiences*) schrumpfen; (*forests*) schwinden; (*also*: **shrink away**) zurückweichen ▸ VT (*cloth*) einlaufen lassen ▸ N (*inf, pej*) Klapsdoktor *m*; **to ~ from sth** vor etw *dat* zurückschrecken; **to ~ from doing sth** davor zurückschrecken, etw zu tun
shrinkage ['ʃrɪŋkɪdʒ] N (*of clothes*) Einlaufen *nt*
shrink-wrap ['ʃrɪŋkræp] VT einschweißen
shrivel ['ʃrɪvl], **shrivel up** VI austrocknen, verschrumpeln ▸ VT austrocknen
shroud [ʃraud] N Leichentuch *nt* ▸ VT: **shrouded in mystery** von einem Geheimnis umgeben
Shrove Tuesday ['ʃrəuv-] N Fastnachtsdienstag *m*
shrub [ʃrʌb] N Strauch *m*, Busch *m*
shrubbery ['ʃrʌbərɪ] N Gebüsch *nt*
shrug [ʃrʌg] N: **~ (of the shoulders)** Achselzucken *nt* ▸ VI, VT: **to ~ (one's shoulders)** mit den Achseln zucken
▸ **shrug off** VT (*criticism*) auf die leichte Schulter nehmen; (*illness*) abschütteln
shrunk [ʃrʌŋk] PP *of* **shrink**
shrunken ['ʃrʌŋkn] ADJ (ein)geschrumpft
shudder ['ʃʌdə^r] VI schaudern ▸ N Schauder *m*; **I ~ to think of it** (*fig*) mir graut, wenn ich nur daran denke
shuffle ['ʃʌfl] VT (*cards*) mischen ▸ VI schlurfen; **to ~ (one's feet)** mit den Füßen scharren
shun [ʃʌn] VT meiden; (*publicity*) scheuen
shunt [ʃʌnt] VT rangieren
shunting yard ['ʃʌntɪŋ-] N Rangierbahnhof *m*
shush [ʃuʃ] EXCL pst!, sch!
shut [ʃʌt] (*pt, pp* **~**) VT schließen, zumachen (*inf*) ▸ VI sich schließen, zugehen; (*shop*) schließen, zumachen (*inf*)
▸ **shut down** VT (*factory etc*) schließen; (*machine*) abschalten ▸ VI schließen, zumachen (*inf*)
▸ **shut in** VT einschließen
▸ **shut off** VT (*gas, electricity*) abstellen; (*oil supplies etc*) abschneiden
▸ **shut out** VT (*person*) aussperren; (*cold, noise*) nicht hereinlassen; (*view*) versperren; (*memory, thought*) verdrängen
▸ **shut up** VI (*inf: keep quiet*) den Mund halten ▸ VT (*silence*) zum Schweigen bringen
shutdown ['ʃʌtdaun] N Schließung *f*
shutter ['ʃʌtə^r] N Fensterladen *m*; (*Phot*) Verschluss *m*
shutter speed N Belichtungszeit *f*
shuttle ['ʃʌtl] N (*plane*) Pendelflugzeug *nt*; (*train*) Pendelzug *m*; (*also*: **space shuttle**) Raumtransporter *m*; (*also*: **shuttle service**) Pendelverkehr *m*; (*for weaving*) Schiffchen *nt* ▸ VI: **to ~ to and fro** pendeln; **to ~ between** pendeln zwischen ▸ VT (*passengers*) transportieren
shuttlecock ['ʃʌtlkɔk] N Federball *m*
shuttle diplomacy N Reisediplomatie *f*
shy [ʃaɪ] ADJ schüchtern; (*animal*) scheu ▸ VI: **to ~ away from doing sth** (*fig*) davor zurückschrecken, etw zu tun; **to fight ~ of** aus dem Weg gehen +*dat*; **to be ~ of doing sth** Hemmungen haben, etw zu tun
shyly ['ʃaɪlɪ] ADV schüchtern, scheu
shyness ['ʃaɪnɪs] N Schüchternheit *f*, Scheu *f*
Siam [saɪ'æm] N Siam *nt*
Siamese [saɪə'mi:z] ADJ: **~ cat** Siamkatze *f*; **~ twins** siamesische Zwillinge *pl*
Siberia [saɪ'bɪərɪə] N Sibirien *nt*
sibling ['sɪblɪŋ] N Geschwister *nt*
Sicilian [sɪ'sɪlɪən] ADJ sizilianisch ▸ N Sizilianer(in) *m(f)*

Sicily ['sɪsɪlɪ] N Sizilien *nt*
sick [sɪk] ADJ krank; (*humour, joke*) makaber; **to be ~** (*vomit*) sich übergeben, brechen; **I feel ~** mir ist schlecht; **to fall ~** krank werden; **to be (off) ~** wegen Krankheit fehlen; **a ~ person** ein Kranker, eine Kranke; **to be ~ of** (*fig*) satthaben *+acc*
sickbag ['sɪkbæg] N Spucktüte *f*
sickbay ['sɪkbeɪ] N Krankenrevier *nt*
sickbed ['sɪkbɛd] N Krankenbett *nt*
sick building syndrome N *Kopfschmerzen, Allergien etc, die in modernen, vollklimatisierten Bürogebäuden entstehen*
sicken ['sɪkn] VT (*disgust*) anwidern ▸ VI: **to be sickening for a cold/flu** eine Erkältung/Grippe bekommen
sickening ['sɪknɪŋ] ADJ (*fig*) widerlich, ekelhaft
sickle ['sɪkl] N Sichel *f*
sick leave N: **to be on ~** krankgeschrieben sein
sickle-cell anaemia N Sichelzellenanämie *f*
sick list N: **to be on the ~** auf der Krankenliste stehen
sickly ['sɪklɪ] ADJ kränklich; (*causing nausea*) widerlich, ekelhaft
sickness ['sɪknɪs] N Krankheit *f*; (*vomiting*) Erbrechen *nt*
sickness benefit N Krankengeld *nt*
sick note N Krankmeldung *f*
sick pay N Lohnfortzahlung *f* im Krankheitsfall; (*paid by insurance*) Krankengeld *nt*
sickroom ['sɪkru:m] N Krankenzimmer *nt*
side [saɪd] N Seite *f*; (*team*) Mannschaft *f*; (*in conflict etc*) Partei *f*, Seite *f*; (*of hill*) Hang *m* ▸ ADJ (*door, entrance*) Seiten-, Neben- ▸ VI: **to ~ with sb** jds Partei ergreifen; **by the ~ of** neben *+dat*; **~ by ~** Seite an Seite; **the right/wrong ~** (*of cloth*) die rechte/linke Seite; **they are on our ~** sie stehen auf unserer Seite; **she never left my ~** sie wich mir nicht von der Seite; **to put sth to one ~** etw beiseitelegen; **from ~ to ~** von einer Seite zur anderen; **to take sides (with)** Partei ergreifen (für); **a ~ of beef** ein halbes Rind; **a ~ of bacon** eine Speckseite
sideboard ['saɪdbɔ:d] N Sideboard *nt*; **sideboards** NPL (BRIT) = **sideburns**
sideburns ['saɪdbə:nz] NPL Koteletten *pl*
sidecar ['saɪdkɑ:ʳ] N Beiwagen *m*
side dish N Beilage *f*
side drum N kleine Trommel *f*
side effect N (*Med, fig*) Nebenwirkung *f*
sidekick ['saɪdkɪk] (*inf*) N Handlanger *m*
sidelight ['saɪdlaɪt] N (*Aut*) Begrenzungsleuchte *f*
sideline ['saɪdlaɪn] N (*Sport*) Seitenlinie *f*; (*fig: job*) Nebenerwerb *m*; **to stand on the sidelines** (*fig*) unbeteiligter Zuschauer sein; **to wait on the sidelines** (*fig*) in den Kulissen warten
sidelong ['saɪdlɔŋ] ADJ (*glance*) Seiten-; (*: surreptitious*) verstohlen; **to give sb a ~ glance** jdn kurz aus den Augenwinkeln ansehen
side plate N kleiner Teller *m*
side road N Nebenstraße *f*
side-saddle ['saɪdsædl] ADV (*ride*) im Damensitz
sideshow ['saɪdʃəu] N Nebenattraktion *f*
sidestep ['saɪdstɛp] VT (*problem*) umgehen; (*question*) ausweichen *+dat* ▸ VI (*Boxing etc*) seitwärts ausweichen
side street N Seitenstraße *f*
sidetrack ['saɪdtræk] VT (*fig*) ablenken
sidewalk ['saɪdwɔ:k] (*US*) N Bürgersteig *m*
sideways ['saɪdweɪz] ADV seitwärts; (*lean, look*) zur Seite
siding ['saɪdɪŋ] N Abstellgleis *nt*
sidle ['saɪdl] VI: **to ~ up (to)** sich heranschleichen (an *+acc*)
SIDS N ABBR (*Med: = sudden infant death syndrome*) plötzlicher Kindstod *m*
siege [si:dʒ] N Belagerung *f*; **to be under ~** belagert sein; **to lay ~ to** belagern
siege economy N Belagerungswirtschaft *f*
siege mentality N Belagerungsmentalität *f*
Sierra Leone [sɪ'ɛrəlɪ'əun] N Sierra Leone *f*
siesta [sɪ'ɛstə] N Siesta *f*
sieve [sɪv] N Sieb *nt* ▸ VT sieben
sift [sɪft] VT sieben; (*also*: **sift through**) durchgehen
sigh [saɪ] VI seufzen ▸ N Seufzer *m*; **to breathe a ~ of relief** erleichtert aufseufzen
sight [saɪt] N (*faculty*) Sehvermögen *nt*, Augenlicht *nt*; (*spectacle*) Anblick *m*; (*on gun*) Visier *nt* ▸ VT sichten; **in ~** in Sicht; **on ~** (*shoot*) sofort; **out of ~** außer Sicht; **at ~** (*Comm*) bei Sicht; **at first ~** auf den ersten Blick; **I know her by ~** ich kenne sie vom Sehen; **to catch ~ of sb/sth** jdn/etw sehen; **to lose ~ of sth** (*fig*) etw aus den Augen verlieren; **to set one's sights on sth** ein Auge auf etw werfen
sighted ['saɪtɪd] ADJ sehend; **partially ~** sehbehindert
sightseeing ['saɪtsi:ɪŋ] N Besichtigungen *pl*; **to go ~** auf Besichtigungstour gehen
sightseer ['saɪtsi:əʳ] N Tourist(in) *m(f)*
sign [saɪn] N Zeichen *nt*; (*notice*) Schild *nt*; (*evidence*) Anzeichen *nt*; (*also*: **road sign**) Verkehrsschild *nt* ▸ VT unterschreiben; (*player*) verpflichten; **a ~ of the times** ein Zeichen unserer Zeit; **it's a good/bad ~** es ist ein gutes/schlechtes Zeichen; **plus/minus ~** Plus-/Minuszeichen *nt*; **there's no ~ of her changing her mind** nichts deutet darauf hin, dass sie es sich anders überlegen wird; **he was showing signs of improvement** er ließ Anzeichen einer Verbesserung erkennen; **to ~ one's name** unterschreiben; **to ~ sth over to sb** jdm etw überschreiben
▸ **sign away** VT (*rights etc*) verzichten auf *+acc*
▸ **sign in** VI sich eintragen
▸ **sign off** VI (*Radio, TV*) sich verabschieden; (*in letter*) Schluss machen
▸ **sign on** VI (BRIT: *as unemployed*) sich arbeitslos melden; (*Mil*) sich verpflichten; (*for course*) sich einschreiben ▸ VT (*Mil*) verpflichten; (*employee*) anstellen
▸ **sign out** VI (*from hotel etc*) sich (aus dem Hotelgästebuch *etc*) austragen

S

▸ **sign up** VI (*Mil*) sich verpflichten; (*for course*) sich einschreiben ▸ VT (*player, recruit*) verpflichten
signal ['sɪgnl] N Zeichen *nt*; (*Rail*) Signal *nt* ▸ VI (*Aut*) Zeichen/ein Zeichen geben ▸ VT ein Zeichen geben *+dat*; **to ~ a right/left turn** (*Aut*) rechts/links blinken
signal box N Stellwerk *nt*
signalman ['sɪgnlmən] N (*irreg*) Stellwerkswärter *m*
signatory ['sɪgnətərɪ] N Unterzeichner *m*; (*state*) Signatarstaat *m*
signature ['sɪgnətʃəʳ] N Unterschrift *f*; (*Zool, Biol*) Kennzeichen *nt*
signature tune N Erkennungsmelodie *f*
signet ring ['sɪgnət-] N Siegelring *m*
significance [sɪg'nɪfɪkəns] N Bedeutung *f*; **that is of no ~** das ist belanglos *or* bedeutungslos
significant [sɪg'nɪfɪkənt] ADJ bedeutend, wichtig; (*look, smile*) bedeutsam, vielsagend; **it is ~ that ...** es ist bezeichnend, dass ...
significantly [sɪg'nɪfɪkəntlɪ] ADV bedeutend; (*smile*) vielsagend, bedeutsam
signify ['sɪgnɪfaɪ] VT bedeuten; (*person*) zu erkennen geben
sign language N Zeichensprache *f*
signpost ['saɪnpəust] N (*lit, fig*) Wegweiser *m*
Sikh [si:k] N Sikh *mf* ▸ ADJ (*province etc*) Sikh-
silage ['saɪlɪdʒ] N Silage *f*, Silofutter *nt*
silence ['saɪləns] N Stille *f*; (*of person*) Schweigen *nt* ▸ VT zum Schweigen bringen; **in ~** still; (*not talking*) schweigend
silencer ['saɪlənsəʳ] N (*on gun*) Schalldämpfer *m*; (Brit *Aut*) Auspufftopf *m*
silent ['saɪlənt] ADJ still; (*machine*) ruhig; **~ film** Stummfilm *m*; **to remain ~** still bleiben; (*about sth*) sich nicht äußern
silently ['saɪləntlɪ] ADV lautlos; (*not talking*) schweigend
silent partner N stiller Teilhaber *m*
silhouette [sɪlu:'ɛt] N Silhouette *f*, Umriss *m* ▸ VT: **to be silhouetted against sth** sich als Silhouette gegen etw abheben
silicon ['sɪlɪkən] N Silizium *nt*
silicon chip N Silikonchip *m*
silicone ['sɪlɪkəun] N Silikon *nt*
silk [sɪlk] N Seide *f* ▸ ADJ (*dress etc*) Seiden-
silky ['sɪlkɪ] ADJ seidig
sill [sɪl] N (*also:* **window sill**) (Fenster)sims *m or nt*; (*of door*) Schwelle *f*; (*Aut*) Türleiste *f*
silly ['sɪlɪ] ADJ (*person*) dumm; **to do something ~** etwas Dummes tun
silo ['saɪləu] N Silo *nt*; (*for missile*) Raketensilo *nt*
silt [sɪlt] N Schlamm *m*, Schlick *m*
▸ **silt up** VI verschlammen ▸ VT verschlämmen
silver ['sɪlvəʳ] N Silber *nt*; (*coins*) Silbergeld *nt* ▸ ADJ silbern
silver foil (Brit) N Alufolie *f*
silver paper (Brit) N Silberpapier *nt*
silver-plated [sɪlvə'pleɪtɪd] ADJ versilbert
silversmith ['sɪlvəsmɪθ] N Silberschmied(in) *m(f)*
silverware ['sɪlvəwɛəʳ] N Silber *nt*
silver wedding, silver wedding anniversary N Silberhochzeit *f*
silvery ['sɪlvrɪ] ADJ silbern; (*sound*) silberhell
SIM card ['sɪmkɑ:d] N (*Tel: = Subscriber Identity Module card*) SIM-Karte *f*
similar ['sɪmɪləʳ] ADJ: **~ (to)** ähnlich (wie *or +dat*)
similarity [sɪmɪ'lærɪtɪ] N Ähnlichkeit *f*
similarly ['sɪmɪləlɪ] ADV ähnlich; (*likewise*) genauso
simile ['sɪmɪlɪ] N (*Ling*) Vergleich *m*
simmer ['sɪməʳ] VI auf kleiner Flamme kochen
▸ **simmer down** (*inf*) VI (*fig*) sich abregen
simper ['sɪmpəʳ] VI geziert lächeln
simpering ['sɪmprɪŋ] ADJ geziert
simple ['sɪmpl] ADJ einfach; (*dress*) schlicht, einfach; (*foolish*) einfältig; **the ~ truth is that ...** es ist einfach so, dass ...
simple interest N Kapitalzinsen *pl*
simple-minded [sɪmpl'maɪndɪd] (*pej*) ADJ einfältig
simpleton ['sɪmpltən] (*pej*) N Einfaltspinsel *m*
simplicity [sɪm'plɪsɪtɪ] N Einfachheit *f*; (*of dress*) Schlichtheit *f*
simplification [sɪmplɪfɪ'keɪʃən] N Vereinfachung *f*
simplify ['sɪmplɪfaɪ] VT vereinfachen
simply ['sɪmplɪ] ADV (*just, merely*) bloß, nur; (*in a simple way*) einfach
simulate ['sɪmjuleɪt] VT vortäuschen, spielen; (*illness*) simulieren
simulated ['sɪmjuleɪtɪd] ADJ (*hair, fur*) imitiert; (*Tech*) simuliert
simulation [sɪmju'leɪʃən] N Vortäuschung *f*; (*simulated object*) Imitation *f*; (*Tech*) Simulation *f*
simultaneous [sɪməl'teɪnɪəs] ADJ gleichzeitig; (*translation, interpreting*) Simultan-
simultaneously [sɪməl'teɪnɪəslɪ] ADV gleichzeitig
sin [sɪn] N Sünde *f* ▸ VI sündigen
since [sɪns] ADV inzwischen, seitdem ▸ PREP seit ▸ CONJ (*time*) seit(dem); (*because*) da; **~ then, ever ~** seitdem
sincere [sɪn'sɪəʳ] ADJ aufrichtig, offen; (*apology, belief*) aufrichtig
sincerely [sɪn'sɪəlɪ] ADV aufrichtig, offen; **yours ~** (*in letter*) mit freundlichen Grüßen
sincerity [sɪn'sɛrɪtɪ] N Aufrichtigkeit *f*
sine [saɪn] N Sinus *m*
sine qua non [sɪnɪkwɑ:'nɔn] N unerlässliche Voraussetzung *f*
sinew ['sɪnju:] N Sehne *f*
sinful ['sɪnful] ADJ sündig, sündhaft
sing [sɪŋ] (*pt* **sang**, *pp* **sung**) VT, VI singen
Singapore [sɪŋgə'pɔ:ʳ] N Singapur *nt*
singe [sɪndʒ] VT versengen; (*lightly*) ansengen
singer ['sɪŋəʳ] N Sänger(in) *m(f)*
Singhalese [sɪŋə'li:z] ADJ = **Sinhalese**
singing ['sɪŋɪŋ] N Singen *nt*, Gesang *m*; **a ~ in the ears** ein Dröhnen in den Ohren
single ['sɪŋgl] ADJ (*solitary*) einzige(r, s); (*individual*) einzeln; (*unmarried*) ledig, unverheiratet; (*not double*) einfach ▸ N (Brit:

also: **single ticket**) Einzelfahrschein *m*; (*record*) Single *f*; **not a ~ one was left** es war kein Einziges mehr übrig; **every ~ day** jeden Tag; **~ spacing** einfacher Zeilenabstand *m*
▸ **single out** VT auswählen; **to ~ out for praise** lobend erwähnen
single bed N Einzelbett *nt*
single-breasted ['sɪŋglbrɛstɪd] ADJ einreihig
Single European Market N: **the ~** der Europäische Binnenmarkt
single file N: **in ~** im Gänsemarsch
single-handed [sɪŋgl'hændɪd] ADV ganz allein
single-minded [sɪŋgl'maɪndɪd] ADJ zielstrebig
single parent N Alleinerziehende(r) *f*(*m*)
single parent family N Einelternfamilie *f*
single room N Einzelzimmer *nt*
singles ['sɪŋglz] NPL (*Tennis*) Einzel *nt*
singles bar N Singles-Bar *f*
single-sex school N reine Jungen-/Mädchenschule *f*; **education in single-sex schools** nach Geschlechtern getrennte Schulerziehung
singly ['sɪŋglɪ] ADV einzeln
singsong ['sɪŋsɔŋ] ADJ (*tone*) singend ▸ N: **to have a ~** zusammen singen
singular ['sɪŋgjulə^r] ADJ (*odd*) eigenartig; (*outstanding*) einzigartig; (*Ling*: *form etc*) Singular- ▸ N (*Ling*) Singular *m*, Einzahl *f*; **in the ~** im Singular
singularly ['sɪŋgjuləlɪ] ADV außerordentlich
Sinhalese [sɪnhə'li:z] ADJ singhalesisch
sinister ['sɪnɪstə^r] ADJ unheimlich
sink [sɪŋk] (*pt* **sank**, *pp* **sunk**) N Spülbecken *nt* ▸ VT (*ship*) versenken; (*well*) bohren; (*foundations*) absenken ▸ VI (*ship*) sinken, untergehen; (*ground*) sich senken; (*person*) sinken; **to ~ one's teeth/claws into sth** die Zähne/seine Klauen in etw *acc* schlagen; **his heart/spirits sank at the thought** bei dem Gedanken verließ ihn der Mut; **he sank into the mud/a chair** er sank in den Schlamm ein/in einen Sessel
▸ **sink back** VI (zurück)sinken
▸ **sink down** VI (nieder)sinken
▸ **sink in** VI (*fig*) verstanden werden; **it's only just sunk in** ich begreife es erst jetzt
sinking ['sɪŋkɪŋ] N (*of ship*) Untergang *m*; (: *deliberate*) Versenkung *f* ▸ ADJ: **~ feeling** flaues Gefühl *nt* (im Magen)
sinking fund N Tilgungsfonds *m*
sink unit N Spüle *f*
sinner ['sɪnə^r] N Sünder(in) *m*(*f*)
Sinn Féin [ʃɪn'feɪn] N *republikanisch-nationalistische irische Partei*
Sino- ['saɪnəu] PREF chinesisch-
sinuous ['sɪnjuəs] ADJ (*snake*) gewunden; (*dance*) geschmeidig
sinus ['saɪnəs] N (Nasen)nebenhöhle *f*
sip [sɪp] N Schlückchen *nt* ▸ VT nippen an *+dat*
siphon ['saɪfən] N Heber *m*; (*also*: **soda siphon**) Siphon *m*
▸ **siphon off** VT absaugen; (*petrol*) abzapfen
SIPS N ABBR (= *side impact protection system*) Seitenaufprallschutz *m*
sir [sə^r] N mein Herr, Herr X; **S~ John Smith** Sir John Smith; **yes, ~** ja(, Herr X); **Dear S~ (or Madam)** (*in letter*) Sehr geehrte (Damen und) Herren!
siren ['saɪərn] N Sirene *f*
sirloin ['sə:lɔɪn] N (*also*: **sirloin steak**) Filetsteak *nt*
sirocco [sɪ'rɔkəu] N Schirokko *m*
sisal ['saɪsəl] N Sisal *m*
sissy ['sɪsɪ] (*inf*, *pej*) N Waschlappen *m* ▸ ADJ weichlich
sister ['sɪstə^r] N Schwester *f*; (*nun*) (Ordens)schwester *f*; (BRIT: *nurse*) Oberschwester *f* ▸ CPD: **~ organization** Schwesterorganisation *f*; **~ ship** Schwesterschiff *nt*
sister-in-law ['sɪstərɪnlɔ:] N Schwägerin *f*
sit [sɪt] (*pt*, *pp* **sat**) VI (*sit down*) sich setzen; (*be sitting*) sitzen; (*assembly*) tagen; (*for painter*) Modell sitzen ▸ VT (*exam*) machen; **to ~ on a committee** in einem Ausschuss sitzen; **to ~ tight** abwarten
▸ **sit about** VI herumsitzen
▸ **sit around** VI = **sit about**
▸ **sit back** VI sich zurücklehnen
▸ **sit down** VI sich (hin)setzen; **to be sitting down** sitzen
▸ **sit in on** VT FUS dabei sein bei
▸ **sit up** VI sich aufsetzen; (*straight*) sich gerade hinsetzen; (*not go to bed*) aufbleiben
sitcom ['sɪtkɔm] N ABBR (*TV*) = **situation comedy**
sit-down ['sɪtdaun] ADJ: **a ~ strike** ein Sitzstreik *m*; **a ~ meal** eine richtige Mahlzeit
site [saɪt] N (*place*) Platz *m*; (*of crime*) Ort *m*; (*also*: **building site**) Baustelle *f*; (*Comput*) Site *f* ▸ VT (*factory*) legen; (*missiles*) stationieren
sit-in ['sɪtɪn] N Sit-in *nt*
siting ['saɪtɪŋ] N (*location*) Lage *f*
sits vac ABBR (= *situations vacant*) Stellenangebote *pl*
sitter ['sɪtə^r] N (*for painter*) Modell *nt*; (*also*: **baby-sitter**) Babysitter *m*
sitting ['sɪtɪŋ] N Sitzung *f*; **we have two sittings for lunch** bei uns wird das Mittagessen in zwei Schüben serviert; **at a single ~** auf einmal
sitting member N (*Pol*) (derzeitiger) Abgeordnete(r) *m*, (derzeitige) Abgeordnete *f*
sitting room N Wohnzimmer *nt*
sitting tenant (BRIT) N (derzeitiger) Mieter *m*
situate ['sɪtjueɪt] VT legen
situated ['sɪtjueɪtɪd] ADJ gelegen; **to be ~** liegen
situation [sɪtju'eɪʃən] N Situation *f*, Lage *f*; (*job*) Stelle *f*; (*location*) Lage *f*; **"situations vacant** *or* **wanted"** „Stellenangebote"
situation comedy N (*TV*) Situationskomödie *f*
six [sɪks] NUM sechs
six-pack ['sɪkspæk] N Sechserpack *m*
sixteen [sɪks'ti:n] NUM sechzehn
sixteenth ADJ sechzehnte(r, s); *see also* **eighth**
sixth [sɪksθ] NUM sechste(r, s); **the upper/lower ~** (BRIT *Scol*) ≈ die Ober-/Unterprima

S

sixtieth ['sɪkstɪɪθ] ADJ sechzigste(r, s); *see also* **eighth**
sixty ['sɪkstɪ] NUM sechzig
size [saɪz] N Größe *f*; (*extent*) Ausmaß *nt*; **I take ~ 14** ich habe Größe 14; **the small/large ~** (*of soap powder etc*) die kleine/große Packung; **it's the ~ of …** es ist so groß wie …; **cut to ~** auf die richtige Größe zurechtgeschnitten
▸ **size up** VT einschätzen
sizeable ['saɪzəbl] ADJ ziemlich groß; (*income etc*) ansehnlich
sizzle ['sɪzl] VI brutzeln
SK (CANADA) ABBR = **Saskatchewan**
skate [skeɪt] N (*also*: **ice skate**) Schlittschuh *m*; (*also*: **roller skate**) Rollschuh *m*; (*fish*: *pl inv*) Rochen *m* ▸ VI Schlittschuh laufen
▸ **skate around** VT FUS (*problem, issue*) einfach übergehen
▸ **skate over** VT FUS = **skate around**
skateboard ['skeɪtbɔ:d] N Skateboard *nt*
skater ['skeɪtə^r] N Schlittschuhläufer(in) *m(f)*
skating ['skeɪtɪŋ] N Eislauf *m*
skating rink N Eisbahn *f*
skeleton ['skɛlɪtn] N Skelett *nt* ▸ CPD (*plan, outline*) skizzenhaft
skeleton key N Dietrich *m*; Nachschlüssel *m*
skeleton staff N Minimalbesetzung *f*
skeptic *etc* ['skɛptɪk] (*US*) = **sceptic** *etc*
sketch [skɛtʃ] N Skizze *f*; (*Theat, TV*) Sketch *m* ▸ VT skizzieren; (*ideas*: *also*: **sketch out**) umreißen
sketchbook ['skɛtʃbuk] N Skizzenbuch *nt*
sketchpad ['skɛtʃpæd] N Skizzenblock *m*
sketchy ['skɛtʃɪ] ADJ (*coverage*) oberflächlich; (*notes etc*) bruchstückhaft
skew [skju:] ADJ schief
skewed [skju:d] ADJ (*distorted*) verzerrt
skewer ['skju:ə^r] N Spieß *m*
ski [ski:] N Ski *m* ▸ VI Ski laufen *or* fahren
ski boot N Skistiefel *m*
skid [skɪd] N (*Aut*) Schleudern *nt* ▸ VI rutschen; (*Aut*) schleudern; **to go into a ~** ins Schleudern geraten *or* kommen
skid marks NPL Reifenspuren *pl*; (*from braking*) Bremsspuren *pl*
skier ['ski:ə^r] N Skiläufer(in) *m(f)*, Skifahrer(in) *m(f)*
skiing ['ski:ɪŋ] N Skilaufen *nt*, Skifahren *nt*; **to go ~** Ski laufen *or* Ski fahren gehen
ski instructor N Skilehrer(in) *m(f)*
ski jump N (*event*) Skispringen *nt*; (*ramp*) Sprungschanze *f*
skilful, (*US*) **skillful** ['skɪlful] ADJ geschickt
skilfully ADV geschickt
ski lift N Skilift *m*
skill [skɪl] N (*ability*) Können *nt*; (*dexterity*) Geschicklichkeit *f*; **skills** NPL (*acquired abilities*) Fähigkeiten *pl*; **computer/language skills** Computer-/Sprachkenntnisse *pl*; **to learn a new ~** etwas Neues lernen
skilled [skɪld] ADJ (*skilful*) geschickt; (*trained*) ausgebildet; (*work*) qualifiziert
skillet ['skɪlɪt] N Bratpfanne *f*
skillful *etc* ['skɪlful] (*US*) = **skilful** *etc*
skim [skɪm] VT (*cream, fat*: *also*: **skim off**) abschöpfen; (*glide over*) gleiten über *+acc* ▸ VI: **to ~ through** (*book etc*) überfliegen
skimmed milk [skɪmd-] N Magermilch *f*
skimp [skɪmp]: **~ on** *vt* (*work etc*) nachlässig machen; (*cloth etc*) sparen an *+dat*
skimpy ['skɪmpɪ] ADJ (*meagre*) dürftig; (*too small*) knapp
skin [skɪn] N Haut *f*; (*fur*) Fell *nt*; (*of fruit*) Schale *f* ▸ VT (*animal*) häuten; **wet** *or* **soaked to the ~** nass bis auf die Haut
skin cancer N Hautkrebs *m*
skin-deep ['skɪn'di:p] ADJ oberflächlich
skin diver N Sporttaucher(in) *m(f)*
skin diving N Sporttauchen *nt*
skinflint ['skɪnflɪnt] N Geizkragen *m*
skin graft N Hautverpflanzung *f*
skinhead ['skɪnhɛd] N Skinhead *m*
skinny ['skɪnɪ] ADJ dünn
skin test N Hauttest *m*
skintight ['skɪntaɪt] ADJ hauteng
skip [skɪp] N Sprung *m*, Hüpfer *m*; (BRIT: *container*) (Müll)container *m* ▸ VI springen, hüpfen; (*with rope*) seilspringen ▸ VT überspringen; (*miss*: *lunch, lecture*) ausfallen lassen; **to ~ school** (*esp US*) die Schule schwänzen
ski pants NPL Skihose *f*
ski pass N Skipass *nt*
ski pole N Skistock *m*
skipper ['skɪpə^r] N (*Naut*) Kapitän *m*; (*inf*: *Sport*) Mannschaftskapitän *m* ▸ VT: **to ~ a boat/team** Kapitän eines Schiffes/einer Mannschaft sein
skipping rope ['skɪpɪŋ-] (BRIT) N Sprungseil *nt*
ski resort N Wintersportort *m*
skirmish ['skə:mɪʃ] N (*Mil*) Geplänkel *nt*; (*political etc*) Zusammenstoß *m*
skirt [skə:t] N Rock *m* ▸ VT (*fig*) umgehen
skirting board ['skə:tɪŋ-] (BRIT) N Fußleiste *f*
ski run N Skipiste *f*
ski slope N Skipiste *f*
ski suit N Skianzug *m*
skit [skɪt] N Parodie *f*
ski tow N Schlepplift *m*
skittle ['skɪtl] N Kegel *m*
skittles ['skɪtlz] N (*game*) Kegeln *nt*
skive [skaɪv] (BRIT *inf*) VI blaumachen; (*from school*) schwänzen
skulk [skʌlk] VI sich herumdrücken
skull [skʌl] N Schädel *m*
skullcap ['skʌlkæp] N Scheitelkäppchen *nt*
skunk [skʌŋk] N Skunk *m*, Stinktier *nt*; (*fur*) Skunk *m*
sky [skaɪ] N Himmel *m*; **to praise sb to the skies** jdn in den Himmel heben
sky-blue [skaɪ'blu:] ADJ himmelblau
skydiving ['skaɪdaɪvɪŋ] N Fallschirmspringen *nt*
sky-high ['skaɪ'haɪ] ADJ (*prices, confidence*) himmelhoch ▸ ADV: **to blow a bridge ~** eine Brücke in die Luft sprengen
skylark ['skaɪlɑ:k] N Feldlerche *f*

skylight ['skaɪlaɪt] N Dachfenster *nt*
skyline ['skaɪlaɪn] N (*horizon*) Horizont *m*; (*of city*) Skyline *f*, Silhouette *f*
Skype® [skaɪp] (*Internet, Tel*) N Skype® *nt* ▶ VT skypen
skyscraper ['skaɪskreɪpəʳ] N Wolkenkratzer *m*
slab [slæb] N (*stone*) Platte *f*; (*of wood*) Tafel *f*; (*of cake, cheese*) großes Stück *nt*
slack [slæk] ADJ (*loose*) locker; (*rope*) durchhängend; (*skin*) schlaff; (*careless*) nachlässig; (*Comm: market*) flau; (*: demand*) schwach; (*period*) ruhig ▶ N (*in rope etc*) durchhängendes Teil *nt*; **slacks** NPL (*trousers*) Hose *f*; **business is ~** das Geschäft geht schlecht
slacken ['slækn] VI (*also*: **slacken off**: *speed, rain*) nachlassen; (*: pace*) langsamer werden; (*: demand*) zurückgehen ▶ VT (*grip*) lockern; (*speed*) verringern; (*pace*) verlangsamen
slag heap [slæg-] N Schlackenhalde *f*
slag off (BRIT *inf*) VT (*criticize*) (he)runtermachen
slain [sleɪn] PP *of* **slay**
slake [sleɪk] VT (*thirst*) stillen
slalom ['slɑːləm] N Slalom *m*
slam [slæm] VT (*door*) zuschlagen, zuknallen (*inf*); (*throw*) knallen (*inf*); (*criticize*) verreißen ▶ VI (*door*) zuschlagen, zuknallen (*inf*); **to ~ on the brakes** (*Aut*) auf die Bremse steigen (*inf*)
slammer ['slæməʳ] (*inf*) N (*prison*) Knast *m*
slander ['slɑːndəʳ] N (*Law*) Verleumdung *f*; (*insult*) Beleidigung *f* ▶ VT verleumden
slanderous ['slɑːndrəs] ADJ verleumderisch
slang [slæŋ] N Slang *m*; (*jargon*) Jargon *m*
slanging match ['slæŋɪŋ-] N gegenseitige Beschimpfungen *pl*
slant [slɑːnt] N Neigung *f*, Schräge *f*; (*fig: approach*) Perspektive *f* ▶ VI (*floor*) sich neigen; (*ceiling*) schräg sein
slanted ['slɑːntɪd] ADJ (*roof*) schräg; (*eyes*) schräg gestellt
slanting ['slɑːntɪŋ] ADJ = **slanted**
slap [slæp] N Klaps *m*, Schlag *m* ▶ VT schlagen ▶ ADV (*inf: directly*) direkt; **to ~ sth on sth** etw auf etw *acc* klatschen; **it fell ~(-bang) in the middle** es fiel genau in die Mitte
slapdash ['slæpdæʃ] ADJ nachlässig, schludrig (*inf*)
slapstick ['slæpstɪk] N Klamauk *m*
slap-up ['slæpʌp] ADJ: **a ~ meal** (BRIT) ein Essen mit allem Drum und Dran
slash [slæʃ] VT aufschlitzen; (*fig: prices*) radikal senken; **to ~ one's wrists** sich *dat* die Pulsadern aufschneiden
slat [slæt] N Leiste *f*, Latte *f*
slate [sleɪt] N Schiefer *m*; (*piece*) Schieferplatte *f* ▶ VT (*criticize*) verreißen
slaughter ['slɔːtəʳ] N (*of animals*) Schlachten *nt*; (*of people*) Gemetzel *nt* ▶ VT (*animals*) schlachten; (*people*) abschlachten
slaughterhouse ['slɔːtəhaus] N Schlachthof *m*
Slav [slɑːv] ADJ slawisch ▶ N Slawe *m*, Slawin *f*
slave [sleɪv] N Sklave *m*, Sklavin *f* ▶ VI (*also*: **slave away**) schuften (*inf*), sich abplagen; **to ~ (away) at sth** sich mit etw herumschlagen
slave-driver ['sleɪvdraɪvəʳ] N Sklaventreiber(in) *m(f)*
slave labour N Sklavenarbeit *f*; **it's just ~** (*fig*) es ist die reinste Sklavenarbeit
slaver ['slævəʳ] VI (*dribble*) geifern
slavery ['sleɪvərɪ] N Sklaverei *f*
Slavic ['slævɪk] ADJ slawisch
slavish ['sleɪvɪʃ] ADJ sklavisch
slavishly ['sleɪvɪʃlɪ] ADV sklavisch
Slavonic [slə'vɔnɪk] ADJ slawisch
slay [sleɪ] (*pt* **slew**, *pp* **slain**) VT (*liter*) erschlagen
sleaze [sliːz] N (*corruption*) Korruption *f*
sleazy ['sliːzɪ] ADJ schäbig
sledge [slɛdʒ] N Schlitten *m*
sledgehammer ['slɛdʒhæməʳ] N Vorschlaghammer *m*
sleek [sliːk] ADJ glatt, glänzend; (*car, boat etc*) schnittig
sleep [sliːp] (*pt, pp* **slept**) N Schlaf *m* ▶ VI schlafen ▶ VT: **we can ~ 4** bei uns können 4 Leute schlafen; **to go to ~** einschlafen; **to have a good night's ~** sich richtig ausschlafen; **to put to ~** (*euph: kill*) einschläfern; **to ~ lightly** einen leichten Schlaf haben; **to ~ with sb** (*euph: have sex*) mit jdm schlafen
▶ **sleep around** VI mit jedem/jeder schlafen
▶ **sleep in** VI (*oversleep*) verschlafen; (*rise late*) lange schlafen
sleeper ['sliːpəʳ] N (*train*) Schlafwagenzug *m*; (*berth*) Platz *m* im Schlafwagen; (BRIT: *on track*) Schwelle *f*; (*person*) Schläfer(in) *m(f)*
sleepily ['sliːpɪlɪ] ADV müde, schläfrig
sleeping accommodation N (*beds etc*) Schlafgelegenheiten *pl*
sleeping arrangements NPL Bettenverteilung *f*
sleeping bag N Schlafsack *m*
sleeping car N Schlafwagen *m*
sleeping partner (BRIT) = **silent partner**
sleeping pill N Schlaftablette *f*
sleeping sickness N Schlafkrankheit *f*
sleepless ['sliːplɪs] ADJ (*night*) schlaflos
sleeplessness ['sliːplɪsnɪs] N Schlaflosigkeit *f*
sleepover ['sliːpəuvəʳ] N Übernachtung *f* (*bei Freunden etc*)
sleepwalk ['sliːpwɔːk] VI schlafwandeln
sleepwalker ['sliːpwɔːkəʳ] N Schlafwandler(in) *m(f)*
sleepy ['sliːpɪ] ADJ müde, schläfrig; (*fig: village etc*) verschlafen; **to be** *or* **feel ~** müde sein
sleet [sliːt] N Schneeregen *m*
sleeve [sliːv] N Ärmel *m*; (*of record*) Hülle *f*; **to have sth up one's ~** (*fig*) etw in petto haben
sleeveless ['sliːvlɪs] ADJ (*garment*) ärmellos
sleigh [sleɪ] N (Pferde)schlitten *m*
sleight [slaɪt] N: **~ of hand** Fingerfertigkeit *f*
slender ['slɛndəʳ] ADJ schlank, schmal; (*small*) knapp
slept [slɛpt] PT, PP *of* **sleep**
sleuth [sluːθ] N Detektiv *m*
slew [sluː] VI (BRIT: *also*: **slew round**) herumschwenken ▶ PT *of* **slay**; **the bus slewed across the road** der Bus rutschte über die Straße

S

slice [slaɪs] N Scheibe *f*; (*utensil*) Wender *m* ▶ VT (in Scheiben) schneiden; **sliced bread** aufgeschnittenes Brot *nt*; **the best thing since sliced bread** der/die/das Allerbeste
slick [slɪk] ADJ professionell; (*pej*) glatt ▶ N (*also:* **oil slick**) Ölteppich *m*
slid [slɪd] PT, PP *of* **slide**
slide [slaɪd] (*pt, pp* **slid**) N (*in playground*) Rutschbahn *f*; (*Phot*) Dia *nt*; (BRIT: *also:* **hair slide**) Spange *f*; (*on ice etc*) Rutschen *nt*; (*fig: to ruin etc*) Abgleiten *nt*; (*microscope slide*) Objektträger *m*; (*in prices*) Preisrutsch *m* ▶ VT schieben ▶ VI (*slip*) rutschen; (*glide*) gleiten; **to let things ~** (*fig*) die Dinge schleifen lassen
slide projector N Diaprojektor *m*
slide rule N Rechenschieber *m*
slide show N Diavortrag *m*; (*Comput*) Bildschirmpräsentation *f*
sliding ['slaɪdɪŋ] ADJ (*door, window etc*) Schiebe-
sliding roof N (*Aut*) Schiebedach *nt*
sliding scale N gleitende Skala *f*
slight [slaɪt] ADJ zierlich; (*small*) gering; (*error, accent, pain etc*) leicht; (*trivial*) leicht ▶ N: **a ~ (on sb/sth)** ein Affront *m* (gegen jdn/etw); **the slightest noise** der geringste Lärm; **the slightest problem** das kleinste Problem; **I haven't the slightest idea** ich habe nicht die geringste Ahnung; **not in the slightest** nicht im Geringsten
slightly ['slaɪtlɪ] ADV etwas, ein bisschen; **~ built** zierlich
slim [slɪm] ADJ schlank; (*chance*) gering ▶ VI eine Schlankheitskur machen, abnehmen
slime [slaɪm] N Schleim *m*
slimming ['slɪmɪŋ] N Abnehmen *nt*
slimy ['slaɪmɪ] ADJ (*lit, fig*) schleimig
sling [slɪŋ] (*pt, pp* **slung**) N Schlinge *f*; (*for baby*) Tragetuch *nt*; (*weapon*) Schleuder *f* ▶ VT schleudern; **to have one's arm in a ~** den Arm in der Schlinge tragen
slingshot ['slɪŋʃɔt] N Steinschleuder *f*
slink [slɪŋk] (*pt, pp* **slunk**) VI: **to ~ away** *or* **off** sich davonschleichen
slinky ['slɪŋkɪ] ADJ (*dress*) eng anliegend
slip [slɪp] N (*fall*) Ausrutschen *nt*; (*mistake*) Fehler *m*, Schnitzer *m*; (*underskirt*) Unterrock *m*; (*also:* **slip of paper**) Zettel *m* ▶ VT (*slide*) stecken ▶ VI ausrutschen; (*decline*) fallen; **he had a nasty ~** er ist ausgerutscht und böse gefallen; **to give sb the ~** jdm entwischen; **a ~ of the tongue** ein Versprecher *m*; **to ~ into/out of sth, to ~ sth on/off** in etw *acc*/aus etw schlüpfen; **to let a chance ~ by** eine Gelegenheit ungenutzt lassen; **it slipped from her hand** es rutschte ihr aus der Hand
▶ **slip away** VI sich davonschleichen
▶ **slip in** VT stecken in *+acc*
▶ **slip out** VI kurz weggehen
▶ **slip up** VI sich vertun (*inf*)
slip-on ['slɪpɔn] ADJ zum Überziehen; **~ shoes** Slipper *pl*
slipped disc [slɪpt-] N Bandscheibenschaden *m*
slipper ['slɪpə^r] N Hausschuh *m*, Pantoffel *m*
slippery ['slɪpərɪ] ADJ (*lit, fig*) glatt; (*fish etc*) schlüpfrig
slippy ['slɪpɪ] ADJ (*slippery*) glatt
slip road (BRIT) N (*to motorway etc*) Auffahrt *f*; (*from motorway etc*) Ausfahrt *f*
slipshod ['slɪpʃɔd] ADJ schludrig (*inf*)
slipstream ['slɪpstri:m] N (*Tech*) Sog *m*; (*Aut*) Windschatten *m*
slip-up ['slɪpʌp] N Fehler *m*, Schnitzer *m*
slipway ['slɪpweɪ] N (*Naut*) Ablaufbahn *f*
slit [slɪt] (*pt, pp* **~**) N Schlitz *m*; (*tear*) Riss *m* ▶ VT aufschlitzen; **to ~ sb's throat** jdm die Kehle aufschlitzen
slither ['slɪðə^r] VI rutschen; (*snake etc*) gleiten
sliver ['slɪvə^r] N (*of glass, wood*) Splitter *m*; (*of cheese etc*) Scheibchen *nt*
slob [slɔb] (*inf*) N Drecksau *f* (*inf!*)
slog [slɔg] (BRIT) VI (*work hard*) schuften ▶ N: **it was a hard ~** es war eine ganz schöne Schufterei; **to ~ away at sth** sich mit etw abrackern
slogan ['sləugən] N Slogan *m*
slop [slɔp] VI schwappen ▶ VT verschütten
▶ **slop out** VI (*in prison etc*) den Toiletteneimer ausleeren
slope [sləup] N Hügel *m*; (*side of mountain*) Hang *m*; (*ski slope*) Piste *f*; (*slant*) Neigung *f* ▶ VI: **to ~ down** abfallen; **to ~ up** ansteigen
sloping ['sləupɪŋ] ADJ (*roof, handwriting*) schräg; (*upwards*) ansteigend; (*downwards*) abfallend
sloppy ['slɔpɪ] ADJ (*appearance*) schlampig; (*sentimental*) rührselig; (*work*) nachlässig
slops [slɔps] NPL Abfallbrühe *f*
slosh [slɔʃ] (*inf*) VI: **to ~ around** *or* **about** (*person*) herumplan(t)schen; (*liquid*) herumschwappen
sloshed [slɔʃt] (*inf*) ADJ (*drunk*) blau
slot [slɔt] N Schlitz *m*; (*fig: in timetable*) Termin *m*; (*: Radio, TV*) Sendezeit *f* ▶ VT: **to ~ sth in** etw hineinstecken ▶ VI: **to ~ into** sich einfügen lassen in *+acc*
sloth [sləuθ] N (*laziness*) Trägheit *f*, Faulheit *f*; (*Zool*) Faultier *nt*
slot machine N (BRIT) Münzautomat *m*; (*for gambling*) Spielautomat *m*
slot meter (BRIT) N Münzzähler *m*
slouch [slautʃ] VI eine krumme Haltung haben; (*when walking*) krumm gehen ▶ N: **he's no ~** er hat etwas los (*inf*); **she was slouched in a chair** sie hing auf einem Stuhl
Slovak ['sləuvæk] ADJ slowakisch ▶ N Slowake *m*, Slowakin *f*; (*Ling*) Slowakisch *nt*; **the ~ Republic** die Slowakische Republik
Slovakia [sləu'vækɪə] N die Slowakei
Slovakian [sləu'vækɪən] ADJ, N = **Slovak**
Slovene ['sləuvi:n] N Slowene *m*, Slowenin *f*; (*Ling*) Slowenisch *nt* ▶ ADJ slowenisch
Slovenia [sləu'vi:nɪə] N Slowenien *nt*
Slovenian [sləu'vi:nɪən] ADJ, N = **Slovene**
slovenly ['slʌvənlɪ] ADJ schlampig; (*careless*) nachlässig, schludrig (*inf*)
slow [sləu] ADJ langsam; (*not clever*) langsam, begriffsstutzig ▶ ADV langsam ▶ VT (*also:* **slow down, slow up**) verlangsamen; (*business*)

verschlechtern ▶ VI (*also*: **slow down, slow up**) sich verlangsamen; (*business*) schlechter gehen; **to be ~** (*watch, clock*) nachgehen; **"~"** „langsam fahren"; **at a ~ speed** langsam; **to be ~ to act** sich *dat* Zeit lassen; **to be ~ to decide** lange brauchen, um sich zu entscheiden; **my watch is 20 minutes ~** meine Uhr geht 20 Minuten nach; **business is ~** das Geschäft geht schlecht; **to go ~** (*driver*) langsam fahren; (BRIT: *in industrial dispute*) einen Bummelstreik machen

slow-acting [sləu'æktɪŋ] ADJ mit Langzeitwirkung

slow food N Slow Food *nt*

slowly ['sləulɪ] ADV langsam

slow motion N: **in ~** in Zeitlupe

slow-moving [sləu'mu:vɪŋ] ADJ langsam; (*traffic*) kriechend

slowness ['sləunɪs] N Langsamkeit *f*

sludge [slʌdʒ] N Schlamm *m*

slue [slu:] (US) VI = **slew**

slug [slʌg] N Nacktschnecke *f*; (*US inf*: *bullet*) Kugel *f*

sluggish ['slʌgɪʃ] ADJ träge; (*engine*) lahm; (*Comm*) flau

sluice [slu:s] N Schleuse *f*; (*channel*) (Wasch)rinne *f* ▶ VT: **to ~ down** *or* **out** abspritzen

slum [slʌm] N Slum *m*, Elendsviertel *nt*

slumber ['slʌmbə^r] N Schlaf *m*

slump [slʌmp] N Rezession *f* ▶ VI fallen; **~ in sales** Absatzflaute *f*; **~ in prices** Preissturz *m*; **he was slumped over the wheel** er war über dem Steuer zusammengesackt

slung [slʌŋ] PT, PP *of* **sling**

slunk [slʌŋk] PT, PP *of* **slink**

slur [slə:^r] N (*fig*): **~ (on)** Beleidigung *f* (für) ▶ VT (*words*) undeutlich aussprechen; **to cast a ~ on** verunglimpfen

slurp [slə:p] (*inf*) VT, VI schlürfen

slurred [slə:d] ADJ (*speech, voice*) undeutlich

slush [slʌʃ] N (*melted snow*) Schneematsch *m*

slush fund N Schmiergelder *pl*, Schmiergeldfonds *m*

slushy ['slʌʃɪ] ADJ matschig; (BRIT *fig*) schmalzig

slut [slʌt] (*pej*) N Schlampe *f*

sly [slaɪ] ADJ (*smile, expression*) wissend; (*remark*) vielsagend; (*person*) schlau, gerissen; **on the ~** heimlich

S/M N ABBR (= *sadomasochism*) S/M

smack [smæk] N Klaps *m*; (*on face*) Ohrfeige *f* ▶ VT (*hit*) schlagen; (: *child*) einen Klaps geben +*dat*; (: *on face*) ohrfeigen ▶ VI: **to ~ of** riechen nach ▶ ADV: **it fell ~ in the middle** (*inf*) es fiel genau in die Mitte; **to ~ one's lips** schmatzen

smacker ['smækə^r] (*inf*) N (*kiss*) Schmatzer *m*

small [smɔ:l] ADJ klein ▶ N: **the ~ of the back** das Kreuz; **to get** *or* **grow smaller** (*thing*) kleiner werden; (*numbers*) zurückgehen; **to make smaller** (*amount, income*) kürzen; (*object, garment*) kleiner machen; **a ~ shopkeeper** der Inhaber eines kleinen Geschäfts; **a ~ business** ein Kleinunternehmen *nt*

small ads (BRIT) NPL Kleinanzeigen *pl*

small arms N Handfeuerwaffen *pl*

small business N Kleinunternehmen *nt*

small change N Kleingeld *nt*

small fry NPL (*unimportant people*) kleine Fische *pl*

smallholder ['smɔ:lhəuldə^r] (BRIT) N Kleinbauer *m*

smallholding ['smɔ:lhəuldɪŋ] (BRIT) N kleiner Landbesitz *m*

small hours NPL: **in the ~** in den frühen Morgenstunden

smallish ['smɔ:lɪʃ] ADJ ziemlich klein

small-minded [smɔ:l'maɪndɪd] ADJ engstirnig

smallpox ['smɔ:lpɔks] N Pocken *pl*

small print N: **the ~** das Kleingedruckte

small-scale ['smɔ:lskeɪl] ADJ (*map, model*) in verkleinertem Maßstab; (*business, farming*) klein angelegt

small talk N (oberflächliche) Konversation *f*

small-time ['smɔ:ltaɪm] ADJ (*farmer etc*) klein; **a ~ thief** ein kleiner Ganove

small-town ['smɔ:ltaun] ADJ kleinstädtisch

smarmy ['smɑ:mɪ] (BRIT *pej*) ADJ schmierig

smart [smɑ:t] ADJ (*neat*) ordentlich, gepflegt; (*fashionable*) chic *inv*, elegant; (*clever*) intelligent, clever (*inf*); (*quick*) schnell ▶ VI (*sting*) brennen; (*suffer*) leiden; **the ~ set** die Schickeria (*inf*); **and look ~ (about it)!** und zwar ein bisschen plötzlich! (*inf*)

smart card N Chipkarte *f*

smarten up ['smɑ:tn-] VI sich fein machen ▶ VT verschönern

smartphone N (*Tel*) Smartphone *nt*

smash [smæʃ] N (*also*: **smash-up**) Unfall *m*; (*sound*) Krachen *nt*; (*song, play, film*) Superhit *m*; (*Tennis*) Schmetterball *m* ▶ VT (*break*) zerbrechen; (*car etc*) kaputt fahren; (*hopes*) zerschlagen; (*Sport*: *record*) haushoch schlagen ▶ VI (*break*) zerbrechen; (*against wall, into sth etc*) krachen ▶ **smash up** VT (*car*) kaputt fahren; (*room*) kurz und klein schlagen (*inf*)

smash hit N Superhit *m*

smashing ['smæʃɪŋ] (*inf*) ADJ super, toll

smattering ['smætərɪŋ] N: **a ~ of Greek** *etc* ein paar Brocken Griechisch *etc*

smear [smɪə^r] N (*trace*) verschmierter Fleck *m*; (*insult*) Verleumdung *f*; (*Med*) Abstrich *m* ▶ VT (*spread*) verschmieren; (*make dirty*) beschmieren; **his hands were smeared with oil/ink** seine Hände waren mit Öl/Tinte beschmiert

smear campaign N Verleumdungskampagne *f*

smear test N Abstrich *m*

smell [smɛl] (*pt, pp* **smelt** *or* **smelled**) N Geruch *m*; (*sense*) Geruchssinn *m* ▶ VT riechen ▶ VI riechen; (*pej*) stinken; (*pleasantly*) duften; **to ~ of** riechen nach

smelly ['smɛlɪ] (*pej*) ADJ stinkend

smelt [smɛlt] PT, PP *of* **smell** ▶ VT schmelzen

smile [smaɪl] N Lächeln *nt* ▶ VI lächeln

smiling ['smaɪlɪŋ] ADJ lächelnd

smirk [smə:k] (*pej*) N Grinsen *nt*

smithy ['smɪðɪ] N Schmiede *f*

smitten ['smɪtn] ADJ: **~ with** vernarrt in +*acc*

smock [smɔk] N Kittel *m*; (*US*: *overall*) Overall *m*

S

smog [smɔg] N Smog *m*
smoke [sməuk] N Rauch *m* ▸ VI, VT rauchen; **to have a ~** eine rauchen; **to go up in ~** in Rauch (und Flammen) aufgehen; (*fig*) sich in Rauch auflösen; **do you ~?** rauchen Sie?
smoke alarm N Rauchmelder *m*
smoked [sməukt] ADJ geräuchert, Räucher-; **~ glass** Rauchglas *nt*
smokeless fuel ['sməuklɪs-] N rauchlose Kohle *f*
smokeless zone (BRIT) N rauchfreie Zone *f*
smoker ['sməukə^r] N Raucher(in) *m(f)*; (*Rail*) Raucherabteil *nt*
smoke screen N Rauchvorhang *m*; (*fig*) Deckmantel *m*
smoke shop (*US*) N Tabakladen *m*
smoking ['sməukɪŋ] N Rauchen *nt*; **"no ~"** „Rauchen verboten"
smoking compartment, (*US*) **smoking car** N Raucherabteil *nt*
smoking room N Raucherzimmer *nt*
smoky ['sməukɪ] ADJ verraucht; (*taste*) rauchig
smolder ['sməuldə^r] (*US*) VI = **smoulder**
smoochy ['smu:tʃɪ] ADJ (*music, tape*) zum Schmusen
smooth [smu:ð] ADJ (*lit, fig: pej*) glatt; (*flavour, whisky*) weich; (*movement*) geschmeidig; (*flight*) ruhig
▸ **smooth out** VT glätten; (*fig: difficulties*) aus dem Weg räumen
▸ **smooth over** VT: **to ~ things over** (*fig*) die Sache bereinigen
smoothly ['smu:ðlɪ] ADV reibungslos, glatt; **everything went ~** alles ging glatt über die Bühne
smoothness ['smu:ðnɪs] N Glätte *f*; (*of flight*) Ruhe *f*
smother ['smʌðə^r] VT (*fire, person*) ersticken; (*repress*) unterdrücken
smoulder, (*US*) **smolder** ['sməuldə^r] VI (*lit, fig*) glimmen, schwelen
SMS N ABBR (= *Short Message Service*) SMS *m*
smudge [smʌdʒ] N Schmutzfleck *m* ▸ VT verwischen
smug [smʌg] (*pej*) ADJ selbstgefällig
smuggle ['smʌgl] VT schmuggeln; **to ~ in/out** einschmuggeln/herausschmuggeln
smuggler ['smʌglə^r] N Schmuggler(in) *m(f)*
smuggling ['smʌglɪŋ] N Schmuggel *m*
smut [smʌt] N (*grain of soot*) Rußflocke *f*; (*in conversation etc*) Schmutz *m*
smutty ['smʌtɪ] ADJ (*fig: joke, book*) schmutzig
snack [snæk] N Kleinigkeit *f* (zu essen); **to have a ~** eine Kleinigkeit essen
snack bar N Imbissstube *f*
snag [snæg] N Haken *m*, Schwierigkeit *f*
snail [sneɪl] N Schnecke *f*
snake [sneɪk] N Schlange *f*
snap [snæp] N Knacken *nt*; (*photograph*) Schnappschuss *m*; (*card game*) ≈ Schnippschnapp *nt* ▸ ADJ (*decision*) spontan, plötzlich ▸ VT (*break*) (zer)brechen ▸ VI (*break*) (zer)brechen; (*rope, thread etc*) reißen; **a cold ~** ein Kälteeinbruch *m*; **his patience snapped** ihm riss der Geduldsfaden; **his temper snapped** er verlor die Beherrschung; **to ~ one's fingers** mit den Fingern schnipsen *or* schnalzen; **to ~ open/shut** auf-/zuschnappen
▸ **snap at** VT FUS (*dog*) schnappen nach; (*fig: person*) anschnauzen (*inf*)
▸ **snap off** VT (*break*) abbrechen
▸ **snap up** VT (*bargains*) wegschnappen
snap fastener N Druckknopf *m*
snappy ['snæpɪ] (*inf*) ADJ (*answer*) kurz und treffend; (*slogan*) zündend; **make it ~** ein bisschen dalli!; **he is a ~ dresser** er zieht sich flott an
snapshot ['snæpʃɔt] N Schnappschuss *m*
snare [snɛə^r] N Falle *f* ▸ VT (*lit, fig*) fangen
snarl [snɑ:l] VI knurren ▸ VT: **to get snarled up** (*plans*) durcheinanderkommen; (*traffic*) stocken
snarl-up ['snɑ:lʌp] N Verkehrschaos *nt*
snatch [snætʃ] N (*of conversation*) Fetzen *m*; (*of song*) paar Takte *pl* ▸ VT (*grab*) greifen; (*steal*) stehlen, klauen (*inf*); (*child*) entführen; (*fig: opportunity*) ergreifen; (*: look*) werfen ▸ VI: **don't ~!** nicht grapschen!; **to ~ a sandwich** schnell ein Butterbrot essen; **to ~ some sleep** etwas Schlaf ergattern
▸ **snatch up** VT schnappen
snazzy ['snæzɪ] (*inf*) ADJ flott
sneak [sni:k] (*US pt* **snuck**) VI: **to ~ in/out** sich einschleichen/sich hinausschleichen ▸ VT: **to ~ a look at sth** heimlich auf etw *acc* schielen ▸ N (*inf, pej*) Petze *f*
▸ **sneak up** VI: **to ~ up on sb** sich an jdn heranschleichen
sneakers ['sni:kəz] NPL Freizeitschuhe *pl*
sneaking ['sni:kɪŋ] ADJ: **to have a ~ feeling/suspicion that ...** das ungute Gefühl/den leisen Verdacht haben, dass ...
sneaky ['sni:kɪ] (*pej*) ADJ raffiniert
sneer [snɪə^r] VI (*smile nastily*) spöttisch lächeln; (*mock*): **to ~ at** verspotten ▸ N (*smile*) spöttisches Lächeln *nt*; (*remark*) spöttische Bemerkung *f*
sneeze [sni:z] N Niesen *nt* ▸ VI niesen
▸ **sneeze at** VT FUS: **it's not to be sneezed at** es ist nicht zu verachten
snicker ['snɪkə^r] VI *see* **snigger**
snide [snaɪd] (*pej*) ADJ abfällig
sniff [snɪf] VI schniefen ▸ VT schnuppern an +*dat*, riechen; (*glue*) schnüffeln ▸ N Schniefen *nt*; (*smell*) Schnüffeln *nt*
sniffer dog ['snɪfə-] N Spürhund *m*
snigger ['snɪgə^r] VI kichern
snip [snɪp] N Schnitt *m*; (BRIT *inf: bargain*) Schnäppchen *nt* ▸ VT schnippeln; **to ~ sth off/through sth** etw abschnippeln/durchschnippeln
sniper ['snaɪpə^r] N Heckenschütze *m*
snippet ['snɪpɪt] N (*of information*) Bruchstück *nt*; (*of conversation*) Fetzen *m*
snivelling, (*US*) **sniveling** ['snɪvlɪŋ] ADJ heulend
snob [snɔb] N Snob *m*
snobbery ['snɔbərɪ] N Snobismus *m*

snobbish ['snɔbɪʃ] ADJ versnobt (*inf*), snobistisch
snog [snɔg] (BRIT *inf*) VI (rum)knutschen ▸ N Knutscherei *f*; **to have a ~ with sb** mit jdm (rum)knutschen
snooker ['snu:kə^r] N Snooker *nt* ▸ VT (BRIT *inf*): **to be snookered** festsitzen
snoop [snu:p] VI: **to ~ about** herumschnüffeln; **to ~ on sb** jdm nachschnüffeln
snooper ['snu:pə^r] N Schnüffler(in) *m(f)*
snooty ['snu:tɪ] ADJ hochnäsig
snooze [snu:z] N Schläfchen *nt* ▸ VI ein Schläfchen machen
snore [snɔ:^{r}] VI schnarchen ▸ N Schnarchen *nt*
snoring ['snɔ:rɪŋ] N Schnarchen *nt*
snorkel ['snɔ:kl] N Schnorchel *m*
snort [snɔ:t] N Schnauben *nt* ▸ VI (*animal*) schnauben; (*person*) prusten ▸ VT (*inf*: *cocaine*) schnüffeln
snotty ['snɔtɪ] (*inf*) ADJ (*handkerchief, nose*) Rotz-; (*pej*: *snobbish*) hochnäsig
snout [snaut] N Schnauze *f*
snow [snəu] N Schnee *m* ▸ VI schneien ▸ VT: **to be snowed under with work** mit Arbeit reichlich eingedeckt sein; **it's snowing** es schneit
snowball ['snəubɔ:l] N Schneeball *m* ▸ VI (*fig*: *problem*) eskalieren; (: *campaign*) ins Rollen kommen
snowboard N Snowboard *nt*
snowboarding N Snowboarding *nt*
snowbound ['snəubaund] ADJ eingeschneit
snow-capped ['snəukæpt] ADJ schneebedeckt
snowdrift ['snəudrɪft] N Schneewehe *f*
snowdrop ['snəudrɔp] N Schneeglöckchen *nt*
snowfall ['snəufɔ:l] N Schneefall *m*
snowflake ['snəufleɪk] N Schneeflocke *f*
snowline ['snəulaɪn] N Schneegrenze *f*
snowman ['snəumæn] N (*irreg*) Schneemann *m*
snowplough, (*US*) **snowplow** ['snəuplau] N Schneepflug *m*
snowshoe ['snəuʃu:] N Schneeschuh *m*
snowstorm ['snəustɔ:m] N Schneesturm *m*
snowy ['snəuɪ] ADJ schneeweiß; (*covered with snow*) verschneit
SNP (BRIT) N ABBR (*Pol*) = **Scottish National Party**
snub [snʌb] VT (*person*) vor den Kopf stoßen ▸ N Abfuhr *f*
snub-nosed [snʌb'nəuzd] ADJ stupsnasig
snuff [snʌf] N Schnupftabak *m* ▸ VT (*candle*: *also*: **snuff out**) auslöschen
snuff movie N *Pornofilm, in dem jemand tatsächlich stirbt*
snug [snʌg] ADJ gemütlich, behaglich; (*well-fitting*) gut sitzend; **it's a ~ fit** es passt genau
snuggle ['snʌgl] VI: **to ~ up to sb** sich an jdn kuscheln; **to ~ down in bed** sich ins Bett kuscheln
snugly ['snʌglɪ] ADV behaglich; **it fits ~** (*object in pocket etc*) es passt genau hinein; (*garment*) es passt wie angegossen
SO N ABBR (*Banking*) = **standing order**

KEYWORD

so [səu] ADV **1** (*thus, likewise*) so; **so saying he walked away** mit diesen Worten ging er weg; **if so** falls ja; **I didn't do it — you did so!** ich hab es nicht getan — hast du wohl!; **so do I, so am I** *etc* ich auch; **it's 5 o'clock — so it is!** es ist 5 Uhr — tatsächlich!; **I hope/think so** ich hoffe/glaube ja; **so far** bis jetzt
2 (*in comparisons etc*: *to such a degree*) so; **so big/quickly (that)** so groß/schnell(, dass); **I'm so glad to see you** ich bin ja so froh, dich zu sehen
3: **so much** so viel; **I've got so much work** ich habe so viel Arbeit; **I love you so much** ich liebe dich so sehr; **so many** so viele
4 (*phrases*): **10 or so** 10 oder so; **so long!** (*inf*: *goodbye*) tschüss!
▸ CONJ **1** (*expressing purpose*): **so as to do sth** um etw zu tun; **so (that)** damit
2 (*expressing result*) also; **so I was right after all** ich hatte also doch Recht; **so you see, I could have gone** wie Sie sehen, hätte ich gehen können; **so (what)?** na und?

soak [səuk] VT (*drench*) durchnässen; (*steep*) einweichen ▸ VI einweichen; **to be soaked through** völlig durchnässt sein
▸ **soak in** VI einziehen
▸ **soak up** VT aufsaugen
soaking ['səukɪŋ] ADJ (*also*: **soaking wet**) patschnass
so-and-so ['səuənsəu] N (*somebody*) Soundso *no art*; **Mr/Mrs ~** Herr/Frau Soundso; **the little ~!** (*pej*) das Biest!
soap [səup] N Seife *f*; (*TV*: *also*: **soap opera**) Fernsehserie *f*, Seifenoper *f* (*inf*)
soapbox ['səupbɔks] N (*lit*) Seifenkiste *f*; (*fig*: *platform*) Apfelsinenkiste *f*
soapflakes ['səupfleɪks] NPL Seifenflocken *pl*
soap opera N (*TV*) Fernsehserie *f*, Seifenoper *f* (*inf*)
soap powder N Seifenpulver *nt*
soapsuds ['səupsʌds] NPL Seifenschaum *m*
soapy ['səupɪ] ADJ seifig; **~ water** Seifenwasser *nt*
soar [sɔ:^{r}] VI aufsteigen; (*price, temperature*) hochschnellen; (*building etc*) aufragen
soaring ['sɔ:rɪŋ] ADJ (*prices*) in die Höhe schnellend; (*inflation*) unaufhaltsam
sob [sɔb] N Schluchzer *m* ▸ VI schluchzen
s.o.b. (*US inf!*) N ABBR (= *son of a bitch*) Scheißkerl *m*
sober ['səubə^r] ADJ nüchtern; (*serious*) ernst; (*colour*) gedeckt; (*style*) schlicht
▸ **sober up** VI nüchtern werden ▸ VT nüchtern machen
sobriety [sə'braɪətɪ] N Nüchternheit *f*; (*seriousness*) Ernst *m*
sobriquet ['səubrɪkeɪ] N Spitzname *m*
sob story N rührselige Geschichte *f*
Soc. ABBR (= *society*) Ges.
so-called ['səu'kɔ:ld] ADJ sogenannt
soccer ['sɔkə^r] N Fußball *m*

S

soccer pitch N Fußballplatz *m*
soccer player N Fußballspieler(in) *m(f)*
sociable ['səuʃəbl] ADJ gesellig
social ['səuʃl] ADJ sozial; (*history*) Sozial-; (*structure*) Gesellschafts-; (*event, contact*) gesellschaftlich; (*person*) gesellig; (*animal*) gesellig lebend ▸ N (*party*) geselliger Abend *m*; **~ life** gesellschaftliches Leben *nt*; **to have no ~ life** nicht mit anderen Leuten zusammenkommen
social class N Gesellschaftsklasse *f*
social climber (*pej*) N Emporkömmling *m*, sozialer Aufsteiger *m*
social club N Klub *m* für geselliges Beisammensein
Social Democrat N Sozialdemokrat(in) *m(f)*
social insurance (*US*) N Sozialversicherung *f*
socialism ['səuʃəlɪzəm] N Sozialismus *m*
socialist ['səuʃəlɪst] ADJ sozialistisch ▸ N Sozialist(in) *m(f)*
socialite ['səuʃəlaɪt] N Angehörige(r) *f(m)* der Schickeria
socialize ['səuʃəlaɪz] VI unter die Leute kommen; **to ~ with** (*meet socially*) gesellschaftlich verkehren mit; (*chat to*) sich unterhalten mit
socially ['səuʃəlɪ] ADV (*visit*) privat; (*acceptable*) in Gesellschaft
social media N soziale Medien *fpl*
social networking [-'nɛtwə:kɪŋ] N Netzwerken *nt*
social networking site [-'nɛtwə:kɪŋ-] N soziales Netzwerk *nt*
social science N Sozialwissenschaft *f*
social security (BRIT) N Sozialhilfe *f*; **Department of Social Security** Ministerium *nt* für Soziales
social services NPL soziale Einrichtungen *pl*
social welfare N soziales Wohl *nt*
social work N Sozialarbeit *f*
social worker N Sozialarbeiter(in) *m(f)*
society [sə'saɪətɪ] N Gesellschaft *f*; (*people, their lifestyle*) die Gesellschaft; (*club*) Verein *m*; (*also*: **high society**) High Society *f* ▸ CPD (*party, lady*) Gesellschafts-
socioeconomic ['səusɪəui:kə'nɔmɪk] ADJ sozioökonomisch
sociological [səusɪə'lɔdʒɪkl] ADJ soziologisch
sociologist [səusɪ'ɔlədʒɪst] N Soziologe *m*, Soziologin *f*
sociology [səusɪ'ɔlədʒɪ] N Soziologie *f*
sock [sɔk] N Socke *f* ▸ VT (*inf*: *hit*) hauen; **to pull one's socks up** (*fig*) sich am Riemen reißen
socket ['sɔkɪt] N (*BRIT Elec*: *also*: **wall socket**) Steckdose *f*; (*of eye*) Augenhöhle *f*; (*of joint*) Gelenkpfanne *f*; (*: for light bulb*) Fassung *f*
sod [sɔd] N (*earth*) Sode *f*; (BRIT *inf!*) Sau *f* (*inf!*); **the poor ~** das arme Schwein
▸ **sod off** (BRIT *inf!*) VI: **~ off!** verpiss dich!
soda ['səudə] N Soda *nt*; (*also*: **soda water**) Soda(wasser) *nt*; (*US*: *also*: **soda pop**) Brause *f*
sodden ['sɔdn] ADJ durchnässt
sodium ['səudɪəm] N Natrium *nt*
sodium chloride N Natriumchlorid *nt*, Kochsalz *nt*
sofa ['səufə] N Sofa *nt*
sofa bed N Schlafcouch *f*
Sofia ['səufɪə] N Sofia *nt*
soft [sɔft] ADJ weich; (*not rough*) zart; (*voice, music light, colour*) gedämpft; (*lenient*) nachsichtig; **~ in the head** (*inf*) nicht ganz richtig im Kopf
soft benefits NPL (*Econ*) nicht monetäre (betriebliche) Leistungen *pl*
soft-boiled ['sɔftbɔɪld] ADJ (*egg*) weich (gekocht
soft drink N alkoholfreies Getränk *nt*
soft drugs NPL weiche Drogen *pl*
soften ['sɔfn] VT weich machen; (*effect, blow*) mildern ▸ VI weich werden; (*voice, expression*) sanfter werden
softener ['sɔfnə[r]] N (*also*: **water softener**) Enthärtungsmittel *nt*; (*also*: **fabric softener**) Weichspüler *m*
soft fruit (BRIT) N Beerenobst *nt*
soft furnishings NPL Raumtextilien *pl*
soft-hearted [sɔft'hɑ:tɪd] ADJ weichherzig
softly ['sɔftlɪ] ADV (*gently*) sanft; (*quietly*) leise
softness ['sɔftnɪs] N Weichheit *f*; (*gentleness*) Sanftheit *f*
soft option N Weg *m* des geringsten Widerstandes
soft sell N weiche Verkaufstaktik *f*
soft spot N: **to have a ~ for sb** eine Schwäche für jdn haben
soft target N leicht verwundbares Ziel *nt*
soft toy N Stofftier *nt*
software ['sɔftwɛə[r]] N (*Comput*) Software *f*
software package N (*Comput*) Softwarepaket *n*
soft water N weiches Wasser *nt*
soggy ['sɔgɪ] ADJ (*ground*) durchweicht; (*sandwiches etc*) matschig
soil [sɔɪl] N Erde *f*, Boden *m* ▸ VT beschmutzen
soiled [sɔɪld] ADJ schmutzig
sojourn ['sɔdʒə:n] (*form*) N Aufenthalt *m*
solace ['sɔlɪs] N Trost *m*
solar ['səulə[r]] ADJ (*eclipse, power station etc*) Sonnen-
solarium [sə'lɛərɪəm] (*pl* **solaria**) N Solarium *nt*
solar panel N Sonnenkollektor *m*
solar plexus [-'plɛksəs] N (*Anat*) Solarplexus *m*, Magengrube *f*
solar power N Sonnenenergie *f*
solar system N Sonnensystem *nt*
solar wind N Sonnenwind *m*
sold [səuld] PT, PP *of* **sell**
solder ['səuldə[r]] VT löten ▸ N Lötmittel *nt*
soldier ['səuldʒə[r]] N Soldat *m* ▸ VI: **to ~ on** unermüdlich weitermachen; **toy ~** Spielzeugsoldat *m*
sold out ADJ ausverkauft
sole [səul] N Sohle *f*; (*fish*: *pl inv*) Seezunge *f* ▸ AD einzig, Allein-; (*exclusive*) alleinig; **the ~ reaso** der einzige Grund
solely ['səullɪ] ADV nur, ausschließlich; **I will hold you ~ responsible** ich mache Sie allein dafür verantwortlich
solemn ['sɔləm] ADJ feierlich; (*person*) ernst

sole trader N (*Comm*) Einzelunternehmer *m*
solicit [sə'lɪsɪt] VT (*request*) erbitten, bitten um ▸ VI (*prostitute*) Kunden anwerben
solicitor [sə'lɪsɪtə^r] (BRIT) N Rechtsanwalt *m*, Rechtsanwältin *f*
solid ['sɔlɪd] ADJ (*not hollow, pure*) massiv; (*not liquid*) fest; (*reliable*) zuverlässig; (*strong: structure*) stabil; (*: foundations*) solide; (*substantial: advice*) gut; (*: experience*) solide; (*unbroken*) ununterbrochen ▸ N (*solid object*) Festkörper *m*; **solids** NPL (*food*) feste Nahrung *f*; **to be on ~ ground** (*fig*) sich auf festem Boden befinden; **I read for 2 hours ~** ich habe 2 Stunden ununterbrochen gelesen
solidarity [sɔlɪ'dærɪtɪ] N Solidarität *f*
solid fuel N fester Brennstoff *m*
solidify [sə'lɪdɪfaɪ] VI fest werden ▸ VT fest werden lassen
solidity [sə'lɪdɪtɪ] N (*of structure*) Stabilität *f*; (*of foundations*) Solidität *f*
solidly ['sɔlɪdlɪ] ADV (*built*) solide; (*in favour*) geschlossen, einmütig; **a ~ respectable family** eine durch und durch respektable Familie
solid-state ['sɔlɪdsteɪt] ADJ (*Elec: equipment*) Halbleiter-
soliloquy [sə'lɪləkwɪ] N Monolog *m*
solitaire [sɔlɪ'tɛə^r] N (*gem*) Solitär *m*; (*game*) Patience *f*
solitary ['sɔlɪtərɪ] ADJ einsam; (*single*) einzeln
solitary confinement N Einzelhaft *f*
solitude ['sɔlɪtju:d] N Einsamkeit *f*; **to live in ~** einsam leben
solo ['səuləu] N Solo *nt* ▸ ADV (*fly*) allein; (*play, perform*) solo; **~ flight** Alleinflug *m*
soloist ['səuləuɪst] N Solist(in) *m(f)*
Solomon Islands ['sɔləmən-] NPL: **the ~** die Salomoninseln *pl*
solstice ['sɔlstɪs] N Sonnenwende *f*
soluble ['sɔljubl] ADJ löslich
solution [sə'lu:ʃən] N (*answer, liquid*) Lösung *f*; (*to crossword*) Auflösung *f*
solve [sɔlv] VT lösen; (*mystery*) enträtseln
solvency ['sɔlvənsɪ] N (*Comm*) Zahlungsfähigkeit *f*
solvent ['sɔlvənt] ADJ (*Comm*) zahlungsfähig ▸ N (*Chem*) Lösungsmittel *nt*
solvent abuse N Lösungsmittelmissbrauch *m*
Som. (BRIT) ABBR (*Post*) = **Somerset**
Somali [sə'mɑ:lɪ] ADJ somalisch ▸ N Somalier(in) *m(f)*
Somalia [sə'mɑ:lɪə] N Somalia *nt*
Somaliland N (*formerly*) Somaliland *nt*
sombre, (*US*) **somber** ['sɔmbə^r] ADJ (*dark*) düster, dunkel; (*serious*) finster

KEYWORD

some [sʌm] ADJ **1** (*a certain amount or number of*) einige; **some tea/water/money** etwas Tee/Wasser/Geld; **some biscuits** ein paar Plätzchen; **some children came** einige Kinder kamen; **he asked me some questions** er stellte mir ein paar Fragen
2 (*certain: in contrasts*) manche(r, s); **some people say that ...** manche Leute sagen, dass ...; **some films were excellent** einige *or* manche Filme waren ausgezeichnet
3 (*unspecified*) irgendein(e); **some woman was asking for you** eine Frau hat nach Ihnen gefragt; **some day** eines Tages; **some day next week** irgendwann nächste Woche; **that's some house!** das ist vielleicht ein Haus!
▸ PRON **1** (*a certain number*) einige; **I've got some** (*books etc*) ich habe welche
2 (*a certain amount*) etwas; **I've got some** (*money, milk*) ich habe welche(s); **I've read some of the book** ich habe das Buch teilweise gelesen
▸ ADV: **some 10 people** etwa 10 Leute

somebody ['sʌmbədɪ] PRON = **someone**
someday ['sʌmdeɪ] ADV irgendwann
somehow ['sʌmhau] ADV irgendwie
someone ['sʌmwʌn] PRON (irgend)jemand; **there's ~ coming** es kommt jemand; **I saw ~ in the garden** ich habe jemanden im Garten gesehen
someplace ['sʌmpleɪs] (*US*) ADV = **somewhere**
somersault ['sʌməsɔ:lt] N Salto *m* ▸ VI einen Salto machen; (*vehicle*) sich überschlagen
something ['sʌmθɪŋ] PRON etwas; **~ nice** etwas Schönes; **there's ~ wrong** da stimmt etwas nicht; **would you like ~ to eat/drink?** möchten Sie etwas zu essen/trinken?
sometime ['sʌmtaɪm] ADV irgendwann; **~ last month** irgendwann letzten Monat; **I'll finish it ~** ich werde es irgendwann fertig machen
sometimes ['sʌmtaɪmz] ADV manchmal
somewhat ['sʌmwɔt] ADV ein wenig, etwas; **~ to my surprise** ziemlich zu meiner Überraschung
somewhere ['sʌmwɛə^r] ADV (*be*) irgendwo; (*go*) irgendwohin; **~ (or other) in Scotland** irgendwo in Schottland; **~ else** (*be*) woanders; (*go*) woandershin
son [sʌn] N Sohn *m*
sonar ['səunɑ:^r] N Sonar(gerät) *nt*, Echolot *nt*
sonata [sə'nɑ:tə] N Sonate *f*
song [sɔŋ] N Lied *nt*; (*of bird*) Gesang *m*
songbook ['sɔŋbuk] N Liederbuch *nt*
songwriter ['sɔŋraɪtə^r] N Liedermacher *m*
sonic ['sɔnɪk] ADJ (*speed*) Schall-; **~ boom** Überschallknall *m*
son-in-law ['sʌnɪnlɔ:] N Schwiegersohn *m*
sonnet ['sɔnɪt] N Sonett *nt*
sonny ['sʌnɪ] (*inf*) N Junge *m*
soon [su:n] ADV bald; (*a short time after*) bald, schnell; (*early*) früh; **~ afterwards** kurz *or* bald danach; **quite ~** ziemlich bald; **how ~ can you finish it?** bis wann haben Sie es fertig?; **how ~ can you come back?** wann können Sie frühestens wiederkommen?; **see you ~!** bis bald!; *see also* **as**
sooner ['su:nə^r] ADV (*time*) früher, eher; (*preference*) lieber; **I would ~ do that** das würde ich lieber tun; **~ or later** früher oder später; **the ~ the better** je eher, desto besser; **no ~**

S

said than done gesagt, getan; **no ~ had we left than …** wir waren gerade gegangen, da …
soot [sut] N Ruß *m*
soothe [suːð] VT beruhigen; (*pain*) lindern
soothing ['suːðɪŋ] ADJ beruhigend; (*ointment etc*) schmerzlindernd; (*drink*) wohltuend; (*bath*) entspannend
SOP N ABBR (= *standard operating procedure*) normale Vorgehensweise *f*
sop [sɔp] N: **that's only a ~** das soll nur zur Beschwichtigung dienen
sophisticated [sə'fɪstɪkeɪtɪd] ADJ (*woman, lifestyle*) kultiviert; (*audience*) anspruchsvoll; (*machinery*) hoch entwickelt; (*arguments*) differenziert
sophistication [səfɪstɪ'keɪʃən] N (*of person*) Kultiviertheit *f*; (*of machine*) hoher Entwicklungsstand *m*; (*of argument etc*) Differenziertheit *f*
sophomore ['sɔfəmɔːʳ] (*US*) N *Student(in) im 2. Studienjahr*
soporific [sɔpə'rɪfɪk] ADJ einschläfernd ▶ N Schlafmittel *nt*
sopping ['sɔpɪŋ] ADJ: **~ (wet)** völlig durchnässt
soppy ['sɔpɪ] (*pej*) ADJ (*person*) sentimental; (*film*) schmalzig
soprano [sə'prɑːnəu] N Sopranist(in) *m(f)*
sorbet ['sɔːbeɪ] N Sorbet *m or nt*, Fruchteis *nt*
sorcerer ['sɔːsərəʳ] N Hexenmeister *m*
sordid ['sɔːdɪd] ADJ (*dirty*) verkommen; (*wretched*) elend
sore [sɔːʳ] ADJ wund; (*esp US: offended*) verärgert, sauer (*inf*) ▶ N wunde Stelle *f*; **to have a ~ throat** Halsschmerzen haben; **it's a ~ point** (*fig*) es ist ein wunder Punkt
sorely ['sɔːlɪ] ADV: **I am ~ tempted (to)** ich bin sehr in Versuchung(, zu)
soreness ['sɔːnɪs] N (*pain*) Schmerz *m*
sorrel ['sɔrəl] N (*Bot*) (großer) Sauerampfer *m*
sorrow ['sɔrəu] N Trauer *f*; **sorrows** NPL (*troubles*) Sorgen und Nöte *pl*
sorrowful ['sɔrəuful] ADJ traurig
sorry ['sɔrɪ] ADJ traurig; (*excuse*) faul; (*sight*) jämmerlich; **~!** Entschuldigung!, Verzeihung!; **~?** wie bitte?; **I feel ~ for him** er tut mir leid; **I'm ~ to hear that …** es tut mir leid, dass …; **I'm ~ about …** es tut mir leid wegen …
sort [sɔːt] N Sorte *f*; (*make: of car etc*) Marke *f* ▶ VT (*also*: **sort out**) sortieren; (*: problems*) ins Reine bringen; (*Comput*) sortieren; **all sorts of reasons** alle möglichen Gründe; **what ~ do you want?** welche Sorte möchten Sie?; **what ~ of car?** was für ein Auto?; **I'll do nothing of the ~!** das kommt überhaupt nicht infrage!; **it's ~ of awkward** (*inf*) es ist irgendwie schwierig; **to ~ sth out** etw in Ordnung bringen
sort code N Bankleitzahl *f*
sortie ['sɔːtɪ] N (*Mil*) Ausfall *m*; (*fig*) Ausflug *m*
sorting office ['sɔːtɪŋ-] N Postverteilstelle *f*
SOS N ABBR (= *save our souls*) SOS *nt*
so-so ['səusəu] ADV, ADJ so lala
soufflé ['suːfleɪ] N Soufflé *nt*
sought [sɔːt] PT, PP *of* **seek**
sought-after ['sɔːtɑːftəʳ] ADJ begehrt, gesucht; **a much ~ item** ein viel begehrtes Stück
soul [səul] N Seele *f*; (*Mus*) Soul *m*; **the poor ~ had nowhere to sleep** der Ärmste hatte keine Unterkunft; **I didn't see a ~** ich habe keine Menschenseele gesehen
soul-destroying ['səuldɪstrɔɪɪŋ] ADJ geisttötend
soulful ['səulful] ADJ (*eyes*) seelenvoll; (*music*) gefühlvoll
soulless ['səullɪs] ADJ (*place*) seelenlos; (*job*) eintönig
soul mate N Seelenfreund(in) *m(f)*
soul-searching ['səulsəːtʃɪŋ] N: **after much ~** nach reiflicher Überlegung
sound [saund] ADJ (*healthy*) gesund; (*safe, secure*) sicher; (*not damaged*) einwandfrei; (*reliable*) solide; (*thorough*) gründlich; (*sensible, valid*) vernünftig ▶ ADV: **to be ~ asleep** tief und fest schlafen ▶ N Geräusch *nt*; (*Mus*) Klang *m*; (*on TV etc*) Ton *m*; (*Geog*) Meerenge *f*, Sund *m* ▶ VT: **to ~ the alarm** Alarm schlagen ▶ VI (*fig: seem*) klingen, sich anhören; (*alarm, horn*) ertönen; **to be of ~ mind** bei klarem Verstand sein; **I don't like the ~ of it** das klingt gar nicht gut; **to ~ one's horn** (*Aut*) hupen; **to ~ like** sich anhören wie; **that sounds like them arriving** das hört sich so an, als ob sie ankommen; **it sounds as if …** es klingt *or* es hört sich so an, als ob …
▶ **sound off** (*inf*) VI: **to ~ off (about)** sich auslassen (über +*acc*)
▶ **sound out** VT (*person*) aushorchen; (*opinion*) herausbekommen
sound barrier N Schallmauer *f*
sound bite N prägnantes Zitat *nt*
soundcard N (*Comput*) Soundkarte *f*
sound effects NPL Toneffekte *pl*
sound engineer N Toningenieur(in) *m(f)*
sounding ['saundɪŋ] N (*Naut*) Loten *nt*, Peilung *f*
sounding board N (*Mus*) Resonanzboden *m*; (*fig*): **to use sb as a ~ for one's ideas** seine Ideen an jdm testen
soundly ['saundlɪ] ADV (*sleep*) tief und fest; (*beat*) tüchtig
soundproof ['saundpruːf] ADJ schalldicht ▶ VT schalldicht machen
sound system N Verstärkersystem *nt*
soundtrack ['saundtræk] N Filmmusik *f*
sound wave N Schallwelle *f*
soup [suːp] N Suppe *f*; **to be in the ~** (*fig*) in der Tinte sitzen
soup kitchen N Suppenküche *f*
soup plate N Suppenteller *m*
soupspoon ['suːpspuːn] N Suppenlöffel *m*
sour ['sauəʳ] ADJ sauer; (*fig: bad-tempered*) säuerlich; **to go** *or* **turn ~** (*milk, wine*) sauer werden; (*fig: relationship*) sich trüben; **it's ~ grapes** (*fig*) die Trauben hängen zu hoch
source [sɔːs] N Quelle *f*; (*fig: of problem, anxiety*) Ursache *f*; **I have it from a reliable ~ that …** ich habe es aus sicherer Quelle, dass …

south [sauθ] N Süden *m* ▶ ADJ Süd-, südlich ▶ ADV nach Süden; **(to the) ~ of** im Süden *or* südlich von; **to travel ~** nach Süden fahren; **the S~ of France** Südfrankreich *nt*
South Africa N Südafrika *nt*
South African ADJ südafrikanisch ▶ N Südafrikaner(in) *m(f)*
South America N Südamerika *nt*
South American ADJ südamerikanisch ▶ N Südamerikaner(in) *m(f)*
southbound ['sauθbaund] ADJ in Richtung Süden; *(carriageway)* Richtung Süden
south-east [sauθ'i:st] N Südosten *m*
South-East Asia N Südostasien *nt*
southerly ['sʌðəlɪ] ADJ südlich; *(wind)* aus südlicher Richtung
southern ['sʌðən] ADJ südlich, Süd-; **the ~ hemisphere** die südliche Halbkugel *or* Hemisphäre
South Korea N Südkorea *nt*
South Pole N Südpol *m*
South Sea Islands NPL Südseeinseln *pl*
South Seas NPL Südsee *f*
southward ['sauθwəd], **southwards** ['sauθwədz] ADV nach Süden, in Richtung Süden
south-west [sauθ'wɛst] N Südwesten *m*
souvenir [su:və'nɪə^r] N Andenken *nt*, Souvenir *nt*
sovereign ['sɔvrɪn] N Herrscher(in) *m(f)*
sovereignty ['sɔvrɪntɪ] N Oberhoheit *f*, Souveränität *f*
soviet ['səuvɪət] *(formerly)* ADJ sowjetisch ▶ N Sowjetbürger(in) *m(f)*; **the S~ Union** die Sowjetunion *f*
sow¹ [sau] N Sau *f*
sow² [səu] *(pt* **sowed**, *pp* **sown**) VT *(lit, fig)* säen
soya ['sɔɪə], **soy** [sɔɪ] *(US)* N: **~ bean** Sojabohne *f*; **~ sauce** Sojasoße *f*
sozzled ['sɔzld] *(BRIT inf)* ADJ besoffen
spa [spɑ:] N *(town)* Heilbad *nt*; *(US: also:* **health spa**) Fitnesszentrum *nt*
space [speɪs] N Platz *m*, Raum *m*; *(gap)* Lücke *f*; *(beyond Earth)* der Weltraum; *(interval, period)* Zeitraum *m* ▶ CPD Raum- ▶ VT *(also:* **space out**) verteilen; **to clear a ~ for sth** für etw Platz schaffen; **in a confined ~** auf engem Raum; **in a short ~ of time** in kurzer Zeit; **(with)in the ~ of an hour** innerhalb einer Stunde
space bar N *(on keyboard)* Leertaste *f*
spacecraft ['speɪskrɑ:ft] N Raumfahrzeug *nt*
spaceman ['speɪsmæn] N *(irreg)* Raumfahrer *m*
spaceship ['speɪsʃɪp] N Raumschiff *nt*
space shuttle N Raumtransporter *m*
spacesuit ['speɪssu:t] N Raumanzug *m*
spacewoman ['speɪswumən] N *(irreg)* Raumfahrerin *f*
spacing ['speɪsɪŋ] N Abstand *m*; **single/double ~** einfacher/doppelter Zeilenabstand
spacious ['speɪʃəs] ADJ geräumig
spade [speɪd] N Spaten *m*; *(child's)* Schaufel *f*; **spades** NPL *(Cards)* Pik *nt*
spadework ['speɪdwə:k] N *(fig)* Vorarbeit *f*
spaghetti [spə'gɛtɪ] N Spag(h)etti *pl*
Spain [speɪn] N Spanien *nt*
spam [spæm] *(Comput)* N Spam *m* ▶ VT mit Werbung bombardieren
span [spæn] N *(of bird, plane, arch)* Spannweite *f*; *(in time)* Zeitspanne *f* ▶ VT überspannen; *(fig: time)* sich erstrecken über *+acc*
Spaniard ['spænjəd] N Spanier(in) *m(f)*
spaniel ['spænjəl] N Spaniel *m*
Spanish ['spænɪʃ] ADJ spanisch ▶ N *(Ling)* Spanisch *nt*; **the Spanish** NPL die Spanier *pl*; **~ omelette** *Omelett mit Paprikaschoten, Zwiebeln, Tomaten etc*
spank [spæŋk] VT: **to ~ sb's bottom** jdm den Hintern versohlen *(inf)*
spanner ['spænə^r] *(BRIT)* N Schraubenschlüssel *m*
spar [spɑ:^r] N *(Naut)* Sparren *m* ▶ VI *(Boxing)* ein Sparring *nt* machen
spare [spɛə^r] ADJ *(free)* frei; *(extra: part, fuse etc)* Ersatz- ▶ N = **spare part** ▶ VT *(save: trouble etc)* (er)sparen; *(make available)* erübrigen; *(afford to give)* (übrig) haben; *(refrain from hurting)* verschonen; **these 2 are going ~** diese beiden sind noch übrig; **to ~** *(surplus)* übrig; **to ~ no expense** keine Kosten scheuen, an nichts sparen; **can you ~ the time?** haben Sie Zeit?; **I've a few minutes to ~** ich habe ein paar Minuten Zeit; **there is no time to ~** es ist keine Zeit; **~ me the details** verschone mich mit den Einzelheiten
spare part N Ersatzteil *nt*
spare room N Gästezimmer *nt*
spare time N Freizeit *f*
spare tyre N Reservereifen *m*
spare wheel N Reserverad *nt*
sparing ['spɛərɪŋ] ADJ: **to be ~ with** sparsam umgehen mit
sparingly ['spɛərɪŋlɪ] ADV sparsam
spark [spɑ:k] N *(lit, fig)* Funke *m*
sparking plug ['spɑ:kɪŋ-] N = **spark plug**
sparkle ['spɑ:kl] VI funkeln, glitzern ▶ N Funkeln *nt*, Glitzern *nt*
sparkler ['spɑ:klə^r] N *(firework)* Wunderkerze *f*
sparkling ['spɑ:klɪŋ] ADJ *(water)* mit Kohlensäure; *(conversation)* vor Geist sprühend; *(performance)* glänzend; **~ wine** Schaumwein *m*
spark plug N Zündkerze *f*
sparring partner ['spɑ:rɪŋ-] N *(also fig)* Sparringspartner *m*
sparrow ['spærəu] N Spatz *m*
sparse [spɑ:s] ADJ spärlich; *(population)* dünn
spartan ['spɑ:tən] ADJ *(fig)* spartanisch
spasm ['spæzəm] N *(Med)* Krampf *m*; *(fig: of anger etc)* Anfall *m*
spasmodic [spæz'mɔdɪk] ADJ *(fig)* sporadisch
spastic ['spæstɪk] *(old)* N Spastiker(in) *m(f)* ▶ ADJ spastisch
spat [spæt] PT, PP *of* **spit** ▶ N *(US: quarrel)* Krach *m*
spate [speɪt] N *(fig)*: **a ~ of** eine Flut von; **to be in full ~** *(river)* Hochwasser führen
spatial ['speɪʃl] ADJ räumlich
spatter ['spætə^r] VT *(liquid)* verspritzen; *(surface)* bespritzen ▶ VI spritzen

S

spatula ['spætjulə] N (*Culin*) Spachtel *m*; (*Med*) Spatel *m*
spawn [spɔ:n] VI laichen ▸ VT hervorbringen, erzeugen ▸ N Laich *m*
SPCA (*US*) N ABBR (= *Society for the Prevention of Cruelty to Animals*) Tierschutzverein *m*
SPCC (*US*) N ABBR (= *Society for the Prevention of Cruelty to Children*) Kinderschutzbund *m*
speak [spi:k] (*pt* **spoke**, *pp* **spoken**) VT (*language*) sprechen; (*say*) sagen ▸ VI sprechen, reden; (*make a speech*) sprechen; **to ~ one's mind** seine Meinung sagen; **to ~ to sb/of** *or* **about sth** mit jdm/über etw *acc* sprechen *or* reden; **~ up!** sprich lauter!; **to ~ at a conference** bei einer Tagung einen Vortrag halten; **to ~ in a debate** in einer Debatte sprechen; **he has no money to ~ of** er hat so gut wie kein Geld; **so to ~** sozusagen
▸ **speak for** VT FUS: **to ~ for sb** (*on behalf of*) in jds Namen *dat or* für jdn sprechen; **that picture is already spoken for** (*in shop*) das Bild ist schon verkauft *or* vergeben; **~ for yourself!** das meinst auch nur du!
speaker ['spi:kə^r] N (*in public*) Redner(in) *m(f)*; (*also*: **loudspeaker**) Lautsprecher *m*; (*Pol*): **the S~** (BRIT, *US*) der Sprecher, die Sprecherin; **are you a Welsh ~?** sprechen Sie Walisisch?
speaking ['spi:kɪŋ] ADJ sprechend; **Italian-~ people** Italienischsprechende *pl*; **to be on ~ terms** miteinander reden *or* sprechen; **~ clock** telefonische Zeitansage
spear [spɪə^r] N Speer *m* ▸ VT aufspießen
spearhead ['spɪəhɛd] VT (*Mil, fig*) anführen
spearmint ['spɪəmɪnt] N Grüne Minze *f*
spec [spɛk] (*inf*) N: **on ~** auf Verdacht, auf gut Glück; **to buy/go on ~** auf gut Glück kaufen/hingehen
spec. N ABBR (*Tech*) = **specification**
special ['spɛʃl] ADJ besondere(r, s); (*service, performance, adviser, permission, school*) Sonder- ▸ N (*train*) Sonderzug *m*; **take ~ care** pass besonders gut auf; **nothing ~** nichts Besonderes; **today's ~** (*at restaurant*) Tagesgericht *nt*
special agent N Agent(in) *m(f)*
special correspondent N Sonderberichterstatter(in) *m(f)*
special delivery N (*Post*): **by ~** durch Eilzustellung
special effects NPL Spezialeffekte *pl*
specialist ['spɛʃəlɪst] N Spezialist(in) *m(f)*; (*Med*) Facharzt *m*, Fachärztin *f*; **heart ~** Facharzt *m*/Fachärztin *f* für Herzkrankheiten
speciality [spɛʃɪ'ælɪtɪ] N Spezialität *f*; (*study*) Spezialgebiet *nt*
specialize ['spɛʃəlaɪz] VI: **to ~ (in)** sich spezialisieren (auf +*acc*)
specially ['spɛʃlɪ] ADV besonders, extra
special offer N Sonderangebot *nt*
specialty ['spɛʃəltɪ] (*esp US*) = **speciality**
species ['spi:ʃi:z] N INV Art *f*
specific [spə'sɪfɪk] ADJ (*fixed*) bestimmt; (*exact*) genau; **to be ~ to** eigentümlich sein für
specifically [spə'sɪfɪklɪ] ADV (*specially*) speziell; (*exactly*) genau; **more ~** und zwar
specification [spɛsɪfɪ'keɪʃən] N genaue Angabe *f*; (*requirement*) Bedingung *f*; **specifications** NPL (*Tech*) technische Daten *pl*
specify ['spɛsɪfaɪ] VT angeben; **unless otherwise specified** wenn nicht anders angegeben
specimen ['spɛsɪmən] N Exemplar *nt*; (*Med*) Probe *f*
specimen copy N Belegexemplar *nt*, Probeexemplar *nt*
specimen signature N Unterschriftsprobe *f*
speck [spɛk] N Fleckchen *nt*; (*of dust*) Körnchen *nt*
speckled ['spɛkld] ADJ gesprenkelt
specs [spɛks] (*inf*) NPL Brille *f*
spectacle ['spɛktəkl] N (*scene*) Schauspiel *nt*; (*sight*) Anblick *m*; (*grand event*) Spektakel *nt*; **spectacles** NPL (*glasses*) Brille *f*
spectacle case (BRIT) N Brillenetui *nt*
spectacular [spɛk'tækjulə^r] ADJ sensationell; (*success*) spektakulär ▸ N (*Theat etc*) Show *f*
spectator [spɛk'teɪtə^r] N Zuschauer(in) *m(f)*; **~ sport** Publikumssport *m*
spectra ['spɛktrə] NPL *of* **spectrum**
spectre, (*US*) **specter** ['spɛktə^r] N Gespenst *nt*; (*fig*) (Schreck)gespenst *nt*
spectrum ['spɛktrəm] (*pl* **spectra**) N (*lit, fig*) Spektrum *nt*
speculate ['spɛkjuleɪt] VI (*Fin*) spekulieren; **to ~ about** spekulieren *or* Vermutungen anstellen über +*acc*
speculation [spɛkju'leɪʃən] N Spekulation *f*
speculative ['spɛkjulətɪv] ADJ spekulativ
speculator ['spɛkjuleɪtə^r] N Spekulant(in) *m(f)*
sped [spɛd] PT, PP *of* **speed**
speech [spi:tʃ] N Sprache *f*; (*manner of speaking*) Sprechweise *f*; (*enunciation*) (Aus)sprache *f*; (*formal talk: Theat*) Rede *f*
speech day (BRIT) N (*Scol*) ≈ Schulfeier *f*
speech impediment N Sprachfehler *m*
speechless ['spi:tʃlɪs] ADJ sprachlos
speech recognition software N (*Comput*) Spracherkennungssoftware *f*
speech therapist N Logopäde *m*, Logopädin *f*, Sprachtherapeut(in) *m(f)*
speech therapy N Logopädie *f*, Sprachtherapie *f*
speed [spi:d] (*pt, pp* **sped**) N Geschwindigkeit *f*, Schnelligkeit *f* ▸ VI (*exceed speed limit*) zu schnell fahren; **to ~ along** dahinsausen; **to ~ by** (*car etc*) vorbeischießen; (*years*) verfliegen; **at ~** (BRIT) mit hoher Geschwindigkeit; **at full** *or* **top ~** mit Höchstgeschwindigkeit; **at a ~ of 70km/h** mit (einer Geschwindigkeit *or* einem Tempo von) 70 km/h; **shorthand/typing speeds** Silben/Anschläge pro Minute; **a five-~ gearbox** ein Fünfganggetriebe *nt*
▸ **speed up** (*pt, pp* **speeded up**) VI beschleunigen; (*fig*) sich beschleunigen ▸ VT beschleunigen
speedboat ['spi:dbəut] N Rennboot *nt*
speed bump N Bodenschwelle *f*
speed camera N Blitzgerät *nt*

speed dial (*Tel*) N Kurzwahl *f* ▶ ADJ Kurzwahl-; **~ button** Kurzwahltaste *f*
speedily ['spi:dɪlɪ] ADV schnell
speeding ['spi:dɪŋ] N Geschwindigkeitsüberschreitung *f*
speed limit N Geschwindigkeitsbegrenzung *f*, Tempolimit *nt*
speedometer [spɪ'dɔmɪtəʳ] N Tachometer *m*
speed trap N Radarfalle *f*
speedway ['spi:dweɪ] N (*also*: **speedway racing**) Speedway-Rennen *nt*
speedy ['spi:dɪ] ADJ schnell; (*reply, settlement*) prompt
speleologist [spɛlɪ'ɔlədʒɪst] N Höhlenkundler(in) *m(f)*
spell [spɛl] (*pt, pp* **spelt** *or* **spelled**) N (*also*: **magic spell**) Zauber *m*; (*incantation*) Zauberspruch *m*; (*period of time*) Weile *f*, Zeit *f* ▶ VT schreiben; (*aloud*: *also*: **spell out**) buchstabieren; (*signify*) bedeuten; **to cast a ~ on sb** jdn verzaubern; **cold ~** Kältewelle *f*; **how do you ~ your name?** wie schreibt sich Ihr Name?; **can you ~ it for me?** können Sie das bitte buchstabieren?; **he can't ~** er kann keine Rechtschreibung
spellbound ['spɛlbaund] ADJ gebannt
spellchecker N (*Comput*) Rechtschreibprüfung *f*
spelling ['spɛlɪŋ] N Schreibweise *f*; (*ability*) Rechtschreibung *f*; **~ mistake** Rechtschreibfehler *m*
spelt [spɛlt] PT, PP *of* **spell**
spend [spɛnd] (*pt, pp* **spent**) VT (*money*) ausgeben; (*time, life*) verbringen; **to ~ time/money/effort on sth** Zeit/Geld/Mühe für etw aufbringen
spending ['spɛndɪŋ] N Ausgaben *pl*; **government ~** öffentliche Ausgaben *pl*
spending money N Taschengeld *nt*
spending power N Kaufkraft *f*
spendthrift ['spɛndθrɪft] N Verschwender(in) *m(f)*
spent [spɛnt] PT, PP *of* **spend** ▶ ADJ (*patience*) erschöpft; (*cartridge, bullets*) verbraucht; (*match*) abgebrannt
sperm [spə:m] N Samenzelle *f*, Spermium *nt*
sperm bank N Samenbank *f*
sperm whale N Pottwal *m*
spew [spju:] VT (*also*: **spew up**) erbrechen; (*fig*) ausspucken
sphere [sfɪəʳ] N Kugel *f*; (*area*) Gebiet *nt*, Bereich *m*
spherical ['sfɛrɪkl] ADJ kugelförmig
sphinx [sfɪŋks] N Sphinx *f*
spice [spaɪs] N Gewürz *nt* ▶ VT würzen
spick-and-span ['spɪkən'spæn] ADJ blitzsauber
spicy ['spaɪsɪ] ADJ stark gewürzt
spider ['spaɪdəʳ] N Spinne *f*; **~'s web** Spinnengewebe *nt*, Spinnennetz *nt*
spidery ['spaɪdərɪ] ADJ (*handwriting*) krakelig
spiel [spi:l] (*inf*) N Sermon *m*
spike [spaɪk] N (*point*) Spitze *f*; (*Bot*) Ähre *f*; (*Elec*) Spannungsspitze *f*; **spikes** NPL (*Sport*) Spikes *pl*
spike heel (*US*) N Pfennigabsatz *m*
spiky ['spaɪkɪ] ADJ stachelig; (*branch*) dornig
spill [spɪl] (*pt, pp* **spilt** *or* **spilled**) VT verschütten ▶ VI verschüttet werden; **to ~ the beans** (*inf*: *fig*) alles ausplaudern
▶ **spill out** VI (*people*) herausströmen
▶ **spill over** VI überlaufen; (*fig*: *spread*) sich ausbreiten; **to ~ over into** sich auswirken auf +*acc*
spillage ['spɪlɪdʒ] N (*act*) Verschütten *nt*; (*quantity*) verschüttete Menge *f*
spin [spɪn] (*pt* **spun** *or* **span**, *pp* **spun**) N (*revolution*) Drehung *f*; (*trip*) Spritztour *f*; (*Aviat*) Trudeln *nt*; (*on ball*) Drall *m* ▶ VT (*wheel*) drehen; (*ball, coin*) (hoch)werfen; (*wool etc*) spinnen; (BRIT: *also*: **spin-dry**) schleudern ▶ VI (*person*) sich drehen; (*make thread*) spinnen; (*car etc*) schleudern; **to ~ a yarn** Seemannsgarn spinnen; **to ~ a coin** (BRIT) eine Münze werfen; **my head is spinning** mir dreht sich alles
▶ **spin out** VT (*talk*) ausspinnen; (*job, holiday*) in die Länge ziehen; (*money*) strecken
spina bifida ['spaɪnə'bɪfɪdə] N offene Wirbelsäule *f*, Spina bifida *f*
spinach ['spɪnɪtʃ] N Spinat *m*
spinal ['spaɪnl] ADJ (*injury etc*) Rückgrat-
spinal column N Wirbelsäule *f*
spinal cord N Rückenmark *nt*
spindly ['spɪndlɪ] ADJ spindeldürr
spin doctor N PR-Fachmann *m*, PR-Fachfrau *f*
spin-dry ['spɪn'draɪ] VT schleudern
spin-dryer [spɪn'draɪəʳ] (BRIT) N (Wäsche)schleuder *f*
spine [spaɪn] N (*Anat*) Rückgrat *nt*; (*thorn*) Stachel *m*
spine-chilling ['spaɪntʃɪlɪŋ] ADJ schaurig, gruselig
spineless ['spaɪnlɪs] ADJ (*fig*) rückgratlos
spinner ['spɪnəʳ] N (*of thread*) Spinner(in) *m(f)*
spinning ['spɪnɪŋ] N (*art*) Spinnen *nt*
spinning top N Kreisel *m*
spinning wheel N Spinnrad *nt*
spin-off ['spɪnɔf] N (*fig*) Nebenprodukt *nt*
spinster ['spɪnstəʳ] N unverheiratete Frau; (*pej*) alte Jungfer
spiral ['spaɪərl] N Spirale *f* ▶ VI (*fig*: *prices etc*) in die Höhe klettern; **the inflationary ~** die Inflationsspirale
spiral staircase N Wendeltreppe *f*
spire ['spaɪəʳ] N Turmspitze *f*
spirit ['spɪrɪt] N Geist *m*; (*soul*) Seele *f*; (*energy*) Elan *m*, Schwung *m*; (*courage*) Mut *m*; (*sense*) Geist *m*, Sinn *m*; (*frame of mind*) Stimmung *f*; **spirits** NPL (*drink*) Spirituosen *pl*; **in good spirits** guter Laune; **community ~** Gemeinschaftssinn *m*
spirited ['spɪrɪtɪd] ADJ (*resistance, defence*) mutig; (*performance*) lebendig
spirit level N Wasserwaage *f*
spiritual ['spɪrɪtjuəl] ADJ geistig, seelisch; (*religious*) geistlich ▶ N (*also*: **Negro spiritual**) Spiritual *nt*
spiritualism ['spɪrɪtjuəlɪzəm] N Spiritismus *m*
spit [spɪt] (*pt, pp* **spat**) N (*for roasting*) Spieß *m*; (*saliva*) Spucke *f* ▶ VI spucken; (*fire*) Funken

S

sprühen; (*cooking*) spritzen; (*inf: rain*) tröpfeln
▸ **spit out** VT ausspucken
spite [spaɪt] N Boshaftigkeit *f* ▸ VT ärgern; **in ~ of** trotz *+gen*
spiteful ['spaɪtful] ADJ boshaft, gemein
spitroast ['spɪtrəust] N Spießbraten *m*
spitting ['spɪtɪŋ] ADJ: **to be the ~ image of sb** jdm wie aus dem Gesicht geschnitten sein ▸ N: **"~ prohibited"** „Spucken verboten"
spittle ['spɪtl] N Speichel *m*, Spucke *f*
spiv [spɪv] (BRIT *inf, pej*) N schmieriger Typ *m*
splash [splæʃ] N (*sound*) Platschen *nt*; (*of colour*) Tupfer *m* ▸ EXCL platsch! ▸ VT bespritzen ▸ VI (*also*: **splash about**) herumplan(t)schen; (*water, rain*) spritzen; **to ~ paint on the floor** den Fußboden mit Farbe bespritzen
splashdown ['splæʃdaun] N (*Space*) Wasserung *f*
splayfooted ['spleɪfutɪd] ADJ mit nach außen gestellten Füßen
spleen [spli:n] N Milz *f*
splendid ['splɛndɪd] ADJ hervorragend, ausgezeichnet; (*impressive*) prächtig
splendour, (US) **splendor** ['splɛndə^r] N Pracht *f*; **splendours** NPL Pracht *f*
splice [splaɪs] VT spleißen, kleben
splint [splɪnt] N Schiene *f*
splinter ['splɪntə^r] N Splitter *m* ▸ VI (zer)splittern
splinter group N Splittergruppe *f*
split [splɪt] (*pt, pp* **~**) N (*tear*) Riss *m*; (*fig: division*) Aufteilung *f*; (*: difference*) Kluft *f*; (*Pol*) Spaltung *f* ▸ VT (*party*) spalten; (*share equally*) teilen; (*divide*) aufteilen ▸ VI (*divide*) sich aufteilen; (*tear*) reißen; **to do the splits** (einen) Spagat machen; **let's ~ the difference** teilen wir uns die Differenz
▸ **split up** VI sich trennen; (*meeting*) sich auflösen
split-level ['splɪtlɛvl] ADJ mit versetzten Geschossen
split peas NPL getrocknete (halbe) Erbsen *pl*
split personality N gespaltene Persönlichkeit *f*
split second N Bruchteil *m* einer Sekunde
splitting ['splɪtɪŋ] ADJ: **a ~ headache** rasende Kopfschmerzen *pl*
splutter ['splʌtə^r] VI (*engine etc*) stottern; (*person*) prusten
spoil [spɔɪl] (*pt, pp* **spoilt** *or* **spoiled**) VT verderben; (*child*) verwöhnen; (*ballot paper, vote*) ungültig machen ▸ VI: **to be spoiling for a fight** Streit suchen
spoils [spɔɪlz] NPL Beute *f*; (*fig*) Gewinn *m*
spoilsport ['spɔɪlspɔ:t] (*pej*) N Spielverderber *m*
spoilt [spɔɪlt] PT, PP *of* **spoil** ▸ ADJ (*child*) verwöhnt; (*ballot paper*) ungültig
spoke [spəuk] PT *of* **speak** ▸ N Speiche *f*
spoken ['spəukn] PP *of* **speak**
spokesman ['spəuksmən] N (*irreg*) Sprecher *m*
spokesperson ['spəukspə:sn] N Sprecher(in) *m(f)*
spokeswoman ['spəukswumən] N (*irreg*) Sprecherin *f*
sponge [spʌndʒ] N Schwamm *m*; (*also*: **sponge cake**) Biskuit(kuchen) *m* ▸ VT mit einem Schwamm waschen ▸ VI: **to ~ off** *or* **on sb** jdm auf der Tasche liegen
sponge bag (BRIT) N Kulturbeutel *m*, Waschbeutel *m*
sponge cake N Biskuitkuchen *m*
sponger ['spʌndʒə^r] (*pej*) N Schmarotzer *m*
spongy ['spʌndʒɪ] ADJ schwammig
sponsor ['spɔnsə^r] N Sponsor(in) *m(f)*, Geldgeber(in) *m(f)*; (BRIT: *for charitable event*) Sponsor(in) *m(f)*; (*for application, bill etc*) Befürworter(in) *m(f)* ▸ VT sponsern, finanziell unterstützen; (*fund-raiser*) sponsern; (*applicant*) unterstützen; (*proposal, bill etc*) befürworten; **I sponsored him at 3p a mile** (*in fund-raising race*) ich habe mich verpflichtet, ihm 3 Pence pro Meile zu geben
sponsorship ['spɔnsəʃɪp] N finanzielle Unterstützung *f*
spontaneity [spɔntə'neɪɪtɪ] N Spontaneität *f*
spontaneous [spɔn'teɪnɪəs] ADJ spontan; **~ combustion** Selbstentzündung *f*
spoof [spu:f] N (*parody*) Parodie *f*; (*hoax*) Ulk *m*
spooky ['spu:kɪ] (*inf*) ADJ gruselig
spool [spu:l] N Spule *f*
spoon [spu:n] N Löffel *m*
spoon-feed ['spu:nfi:d] VT (mit dem Löffel) füttern; (*fig*) gängeln
spoonful ['spu:nful] N Löffel *m*
sporadic [spə'rædɪk] ADJ sporadisch, vereinzelt
sport [spɔ:t] N Sport *m*; (*type*) Sportart *f*; (*person: also*: **good sport**) feiner Kerl *m* ▸ VT (*wear*) tragen; **indoor sports** Hallensport *m*; **outdoor sports** Sport *m* im Freien
sporting ['spɔ:tɪŋ] ADJ (*event etc*) Sport-; (*generous*) großzügig; **to give sb a ~ chance** jdm eine faire Chance geben
sport jacket (US) N = **sports jacket**
sports car N Sportwagen *m*
sports centre N Sportzentrum *nt*
sports drink N Sportgetränk *nt*
sports ground N Sportplatz *m*
sports jacket (BRIT) N Sakko *m*
sportsman ['spɔ:tsmən] N (*irreg*) Sportler *m*
sportsmanship ['spɔ:tsmənʃɪp] N Sportlichkeit *f*
sports page N Sportseite *f*
sportswear ['spɔ:tswɛə^r] N Sportkleidung *f*
sportswoman ['spɔ:tswumən] N (*irreg*) Sportlerin *f*
sporty ['spɔ:tɪ] ADJ sportlich
spot [spɔt] N (*mark*) Fleck *m*; (*dot*) Punkt *m*; (*on skin*) Pickel *m*; (*place*) Stelle *f*, Platz *m*; (*Radio, TV*) Nummer *f*, Auftritt *m*; (*also*: **spot advertisement**) Werbespot *m*; (*small amount*): **a ~ of** ein bisschen ▸ VT entdecken; **on the ~** (*in that place*) an Ort und Stelle; (*immediately*) auf der Stelle; **to be in a ~** in der Klemme sitzen; **to put sb on the ~** jdn in Verlegenheit bringen; **to come out in spots** Pickel bekommen
spot check N Stichprobe *f*
spotless ['spɔtlɪs] ADJ makellos sauber

spotlight ['spɔtlaɪt] N Scheinwerfer *m*; (*in room*) Strahler *m*
spot-on [spɔt'ɔn] (BRIT *inf*) ADJ genau richtig
spot price N Kassapreis *m*
spotted ['spɔtɪd] ADJ gepunktet
spotty ['spɔtɪ] ADJ pickelig
spouse [spaus] N (*male*) Gatte *m*; (*female*) Gattin *f*
spout [spaut] N (*of jug, teapot*) Tülle *f*; (*of pipe*) Ausfluss *m*; (*of liquid*) Strahl *m* ▸ VI spritzen; (*flames*) sprühen
sprain [spreɪn] N Verstauchung *f* ▸ VT: **to ~ one's ankle/wrist** sich *dat* den Knöchel/das Handgelenk verstauchen
sprang [spræŋ] PT *of* **spring**
sprawl [sprɔ:l] VI (*person*) sich ausstrecken; (*place*) wild wuchern ▸ N: **urban ~** wild wuchernde Ausbreitung des Stadtgebietes; **to send sb sprawling** jdn zu Boden werfen
spray [spreɪ] N (*small drops*) Sprühnebel *m*; (*sea spray*) Gischt *m or f*; (*container*) Sprühdose *f*; (*garden spray*) Sprühgerät *nt*; (*of flowers*) Strauß *m* ▸ VT sprühen, spritzen; (*crops*) spritzen ▸ CPD (*deodorant*) Sprüh-; **~ can** Sprühdose *f*
spread [sprɛd] (*pt, pp* **~**) N (*distribution*) Verteilung *f*; (*for bread*) (Brot)aufstrich *m*; (*range*) Spektrum *nt*; (*selection*) Auswahl *f*; (*inf: food*) Festessen *nt*; (*Press, Typ: two pages*) Doppelseite *f* ▸ VT ausbreiten; (*butter*) streichen; (*workload, wealth, repayments etc*) verteilen; (*scatter*) verstreuen; (*rumour, disease*) verbreiten ▸ VI (*disease, news*) sich verbreiten; (*stain: also:* **spread out**) sich ausbreiten; **to get a middle-age ~** in den mittleren Jahren Speck ansetzen
▸ **spread out** VI (*move apart*) sich verteilen
spread-eagled ['sprɛdi:gld] ADJ mit ausgestreckten Armen und Beinen; **to be** *or* **lie ~** mit ausgestreckten Armen und Beinen daliegen
spreadsheet ['sprɛdʃi:t] N (*Comput*) Tabellenkalkulation *f*
spree [spri:] N: **to go on a ~** (*drinking*) eine Zechtour machen; (*spending*) groß einkaufen gehen
sprig [sprɪg] N Zweig *m*
sprightly ['spraɪtlɪ] ADJ rüstig
spring [sprɪŋ] (*pt* **sprang**, *pp* **sprung**) N (*coiled metal*) Sprungfeder *f*; (*season*) Frühling *m*, Frühjahr *nt*; (*of water*) Quelle *f* ▸ VI (*leap*) springen ▸ VT: **to ~ a leak** (*pipe etc*) undicht werden; **in ~** im Frühling *or* Frühjahr; **to walk with a ~ in one's step** mit federnden Schritten gehen; **to ~ from** (*result*) herrühren von; **to ~ into action** aktiv werden; **he sprang the news on me** er hat mich mit der Nachricht überrascht
▸ **spring up** VI (*building, plant*) aus dem Boden schießen
springboard ['sprɪŋbɔ:d] N (*Sport, fig*) Sprungbrett *nt*
spring-clean [sprɪŋ'kli:n], **spring-cleaning** [sprɪŋ'kli:nɪŋ] N Frühjahrsputz *m*
spring onion (BRIT) N Frühlingszwiebel *f*
spring roll N Frühlingsrolle *f*
springtime ['sprɪŋtaɪm] N Frühling *m*
springy ['sprɪŋɪ] ADJ federnd; (*mattress*) weich gefedert
sprinkle ['sprɪŋkl] VT (*liquid*) sprenkeln; (*salt, sugar*) streuen; **to ~ water on, ~ with water** mit Wasser besprengen; **to ~ sugar** *etc* **on, ~ with sugar** *etc* mit Zucker *etc* bestreuen
sprinkler ['sprɪŋkləʳ] N (*for lawn*) Rasensprenger *m*; (*to put out fire*) Sprinkler *m*
sprinkling ['sprɪŋklɪŋ] N: **a ~ of** (*water*) ein paar Tropfen; (*salt, sugar*) eine Prise; (*fig*) ein paar ...
sprint [sprɪnt] VI rennen; (*Sport*) sprinten ▸ N Sprint *m*; **the 200 metres ~** der 200-Meter-Lauf
sprinter ['sprɪntəʳ] N Sprinter(in) *m(f)*
sprite [spraɪt] N Kobold *m*
spritzer ['sprɪtsəʳ] N Schorle *f*
sprocket ['sprɔkɪt] N Kettenzahnrad *nt*
sprout [spraut] VI sprießen; (*vegetable*) keimen
sprouts [sprauts] NPL (*also:* **Brussels sprouts**) Rosenkohl *m*
spruce [spru:s] N INV Fichte *f* ▸ ADJ gepflegt, adrett
▸ **spruce up** VT auf Vordermann bringen (*inf*); **to ~ o.s. up** sein Äußeres pflegen
sprung [sprʌŋ] PP *of* **spring**
spry [spraɪ] ADJ rüstig
SPUC N ABBR (= *Society for the Protection of the Unborn Child*) *Gesellschaft zum Schutz des ungeborenen Lebens*
spud [spʌd] (*inf*) N Kartoffel *f*
spun [spʌn] PT, PP *of* **spin**
spur [spə:ʳ] N Sporn *m*; (*fig*) Ansporn *m* ▸ VT (*fig: also:* **spur on**) anspornen; **on the ~ of the moment** ganz spontan
spurious ['spjuərɪəs] ADJ falsch
spurn [spə:n] VT verschmähen
spurt [spə:t] N (*of blood etc*) Strahl *m*; (*of energy*) Anwandlung *f* ▸ VI (*blood*) (heraus)spritzen; **to put on a ~** (*lit, fig*) einen Spurt einlegen
sputter ['spʌtəʳ] VI = **splutter**
spy [spaɪ] N Spion(in) *m(f)* ▸ VI: **to ~ on** nachspionieren *+dat* ▸ VT sehen ▸ CPD (*film, story*) Spionage-
spying ['spaɪɪŋ] N Spionage *f*
spyware ['spaɪwɛəʳ] N (*Comput*) Spyware *f*, Spionagesoftware *f*
Sq. ABBR (*in address:* = *square*) ≈ Pl.
sq. ABBR = **square**
squabble ['skwɔbl] VI (sich) zanken ▸ N Streit *m*
squad [skwɔd] N (*Police*) Kommando *nt*; (*: drug/fraud squad*) Dezernat *nt*; (*Sport*) Mannschaft *f*; (*Mil*) Trupp *m*; **flying ~** (*Police*) Überfallkommando *nt*
squad car (BRIT) N (*Police*) Streifenwagen *m*
squaddie ['skwɔdɪ] (BRIT) N (*private soldier*) Gefreite(r) *m*
squadron ['skwɔdrn] N (*Mil*) Schwadron *f*; (*Aviat*) Staffel *f*; (*Naut*) Geschwader *nt*
squalid ['skwɔlɪd] ADJ verkommen; (*conditions*) elend; (*sordid*) erbärmlich
squall [skwɔ:l] N Bö(e) *f*
squalor ['skwɔləʳ] N Elend *nt*

S

squander ['skwɔndəʳ] VT verschwenden; (*chances*) vertun
square [skwɛəʳ] N Quadrat *nt*; (*in town*) Platz *m*; (*US: block of houses*) Block *m*; (*also*: **set square**) Zeichendreieck *nt*; (*inf: person*) Spießer *m* ▶ ADJ quadratisch; (*inf: ideas, person*) spießig ▶ VT (*arrange*) ausrichten; (*Math*) quadrieren; (*reconcile*) in Einklang bringen ▶ VI (*accord*) übereinstimmen; **we're back to ~ one** jetzt sind wir wieder da, wo wir angefangen haben; **all ~** (*Sport*) unentschieden; (*fig*) quitt; **a ~ meal** eine ordentliche Mahlzeit; **2 metres ~** 2 Meter im Quadrat; **2 ~ metres** 2 Quadratmeter; **I'll ~ it with him** (*inf*) ich mache das mit ihm ab; **can you ~ it with your conscience?** können Sie das mit Ihrem Gewissen vereinbaren?
▶ **square up** (BRIT) VI abrechnen
square bracket N eckige Klammer *f*
squarely ['skwɛəlɪ] ADV (*directly*) direkt, genau; (*firmly*) fest; (*honestly*) ehrlich; (*fairly*) gerecht, fair
square root N Quadratwurzel *f*
squash [skwɔʃ] N (BRIT): **lemon/orange ~** Zitronen-/Orangensaftgetränk *nt*; (*US: marrow etc*) Kürbis *m*; (*Sport*) Squash *nt* ▶ VT zerquetschen
squat [skwɔt] VI (*also*: **squat down**) sich (hin)hocken ▶ ADJ gedrungen; (*on property*): **to ~ (in a house)** ein Haus besetzen
squatter ['skwɔtəʳ] N Hausbesetzer(in) *m(f)*
squawk [skwɔ:k] VI kreischen
squeak [skwi:k] VI quietschen; (*mouse etc*) piepsen ▶ N Quietschen *nt*; (*of mouse etc*) Piepsen *nt*
squeaky-clean [skwi:kɪ'kli:n] (*inf*) ADJ blitzsauber
squeal [skwi:l] VI quietschen
squeamish ['skwi:mɪʃ] ADJ empfindlich
squeeze [skwi:z] N Drücken *nt*; (*Econ*) Beschränkung *f*; (*also*: **credit squeeze**) Kreditbeschränkung *f* ▶ VT drücken; (*lemon etc*) auspressen ▶ VI: **to ~ under sth** sich unter etw *dat* durchzwängen; **to ~ past sth** sich an etw *dat* vorbeidrücken; **to give sth a ~** etw drücken; **a ~ of lemon** ein Spritzer *m* Zitronensaft
▶ **squeeze out** VT (*juice etc*) (her)auspressen; (*fig: exclude*) hinausdrängen
squelch [skwɛltʃ] VI (*mud etc*) quatschen
squib [skwɪb] N Knallfrosch *m*
squid [skwɪd] N Tintenfisch *m*
squiggle ['skwɪgl] N Schnörkel *m*
squint [skwɪnt] VI (*in the sunlight*) blinzeln ▶ N (*Med*) Schielen *nt*; **he has a ~** er schielt
squire ['skwaɪəʳ] (BRIT) N Gutsherr *m*; (*inf*) Chef *m*
squirm [skwə:m] VI (*lit, fig*) sich winden
squirrel ['skwɪrəl] N Eichhörnchen *nt*
squirt [skwə:t] VI, VT spritzen
Sr ABBR (*in names*: = *senior*) sen.; (*Rel*) = **sister**
SRC (BRIT) N ABBR (= *Students' Representative Council*) *studentische Vertretung*
Sri Lanka [srɪ'læŋkə] N Sri Lanka *nt*
SRO (US) ABBR (= *standing room only*) nur Stehplätze
SS ABBR = **steamship**
SSA (US) N ABBR (= *Social Security Administration*) *Sozialversicherungsbehörde*
SST (US) N ABBR (= *supersonic transport*) Überschallverkehr *m*
ST (US) ABBR = **standard time**
St ABBR (= *saint*) St.; (= *street*) Str.
stab [stæb] VT (*body*) einstechen auf +*acc*; (*person*) niederstechen ▶ N Stich *m*, Stoß *m*; (*inf: try*): **to have a ~ at sth** etw probieren; **a ~ of pain** ein stechender Schmerz; **to ~ sb to death** jdn erstechen
stabbing ['stæbɪŋ] ADJ (*pain*) stechend ▶ N Messerstecherei *f*
stability [stə'bɪlɪtɪ] N Stabilität *f*
stabilization [steɪbəlaɪ'zeɪʃən] N Stabilisierung *f*
stabilize ['steɪbəlaɪz] VT stabilisieren ▶ VI sich stabilisieren
stabilizer ['steɪbəlaɪzəʳ] N (*Aviat*) Stabilisierungsfläche *f*; (*Naut, food additive*) Stabilisator *m*
stable ['steɪbl] ADJ stabil; (*marriage*) dauerhaft ▶ N Stall *m*; **riding stables** Reitstall *m*
staccato [stə'kɑ:təu] ADV (*Mus*) stakkato ▶ ADJ abgehackt
stack [stæk] N Stapel *m*; (*of books etc*) Stoß *m* ▶ VT (*also*: **stack up**) aufstapeln; **stacks of time** (BRIT *inf*) jede Menge Zeit; **to ~ with** vollstapeln mit
stadia ['steɪdɪə] NPL *of* **stadium**
stadium ['steɪdɪəm] (*pl* **stadia** *or* **stadiums**) N Stadion *nt*
staff [stɑ:f] N (*workforce, servants*) Personal *nt*; (BRIT: *also*: **teaching staff**) (Lehrer)kollegium *nt*; (*stick: Mil*) Stab *m* ▶ VT (mit Personal) besetzen; **one of his ~** einer seiner Mitarbeiter; **a member of ~** ein(e) Mitarbeiter(in) *m(f)*; (*Scol*) ein(e) Lehrer(in) *m(f)*
staffroom ['stɑ:fru:m] N (*Scol*) Lehrerzimmer *nt*
Staffs (BRIT) ABBR (*Post*) = **Staffordshire**
stag [stæg] N Hirsch *m*; (BRIT *Stock Exchange*) Spekulant *m* (*der junge Aktien aufkauft*); **~ market** (BRIT *Stock Exchange*) Spekulantenmarkt *m*
stage [steɪdʒ] N Bühne *f*; (*platform*) Podium *nt*; (*point, period*) Stadium *nt* ▶ VT (*play*) aufführen; (*demonstration*) organisieren; (*perform: recovery etc*) schaffen; **the ~** das Theater, die Bühne; **in stages** etappenweise; **to go through a difficult ~** eine schwierige Phase durchmachen; **in the early/final stages** im Anfangs-/Endstadium
stagecoach ['steɪdʒkəutʃ] N Postkutsche *f*
stage door N Bühneneingang *m*
stage fright N Lampenfieber *nt*
stagehand ['steɪdʒhænd] N Bühnenarbeiter(in) *m(f)*
stage-manage ['steɪdʒmænɪdʒ] VT (*fig*) inszenieren
stage manager N Inspizient(in) *m(f)*
stagger ['stægəʳ] VI schwanken, taumeln ▶ VT (*amaze*) die Sprache verschlagen +*dat*; (*hours, holidays*) staffeln

staggering ['stægərɪŋ] ADJ (*amazing*) atemberaubend
staging post ['steɪdʒɪŋ-] N Zwischenstation *f*
stagnant ['stægnənt] ADJ (*water*) stehend; (*economy etc*) stagnierend
stagnate [stæg'neɪt] VI (*economy etc*) stagnieren; (*person*) verdummen
stagnation [stæg'neɪʃən] N Stagnation *f*
stag night, stag party N Herrenabend *m*

> Als **stag night** bezeichnet man eine feuchtfröhliche Männerparty, die kurz vor einer Hochzeit vom Bräutigam und seinen Freunden meist in einem Gasthaus oder Nachtklub abgehalten wird. Diese Feiern sind oft sehr ausgelassen und können manchmal auch zu weit gehen (wenn dem betrunkenen Bräutigam ein Streich gespielt wird). Siehe auch **hen night**.

staid [steɪd] ADJ gesetzt
stain [steɪn] N Fleck *m*; (*colouring*) Beize *f* ▸ VT beflecken; (*wood*) beizen
stained glass window [steɪnd-] N buntes Glasfenster *nt*
stainless steel ['steɪnlɪs-] N (rostfreier) Edelstahl *m*
stain remover N Fleckentferner *m*
stair [stɛəʳ] N (*step*) Stufe *f*; **stairs** NPL (*flight of steps*) Treppe *f*; **on the stairs** auf der Treppe
staircase ['stɛəkeɪs] N Treppe *f*
stairway ['stɛəweɪ] N = **staircase**
stairwell ['stɛəwɛl] N Treppenhaus *nt*
stake [steɪk] N (*post*) Pfahl *m*, Pfosten *m*; (*Comm*) Anteil *m*; (*Betting: gen pl*) Einsatz *m* ▸ VT (*money*) setzen; (*area: also:* **stake out**) abstecken; **to be at ~** auf dem Spiel stehen; **to have a ~ in sth** einen Anteil an etw *dat* haben; **to ~ a claim (to sth)** sich *dat* ein Anrecht (auf etw *acc*) sichern; **to ~ one's life on sth** seinen Kopf auf etw *acc* wetten; **to ~ one's reputation on sth** sich für etw verbürgen
stakeout ['steɪkaut] N (*surveillance*) Überwachung *f*
stalactite ['stæləktaɪt] N Stalaktit *m*
stalagmite ['stæləgmaɪt] N Stalagmit *m*
stale [steɪl] ADJ (*bread*) altbacken; (*food*) alt; (*smell*) muffig; (*air*) verbraucht; (*beer*) schal
stalemate ['steɪlmeɪt] N (*Chess*) Patt *nt*; (*fig*) Sackgasse *f*
stalk [stɔːk] N Stiel *m* ▸ VT sich heranpirschen an *+acc* ▸ VI: **to ~ out/off** hinaus-/davonstolzieren
stall [stɔːl] N (BRIT: *in market etc*) Stand *m*; (*in stable*) Box *f* ▸ VT (*engine, car*) abwürgen; (*fig: person*) hinhalten; (*: decision etc*) hinauszögern ▸ VI (*engine*) absterben; (*car*) stehen bleiben; (*fig: person*) ausweichen; **stalls** NPL (BRIT: *in cinema, theatre*) Parkett *nt*; **a seat in the stalls** ein Platz im Parkett; **a clothes/flower ~** ein Kleidungs-/Blumenstand; **to ~ for time** versuchen, Zeit zu gewinnen
stallholder ['stɔːlhəuldəʳ] (BRIT) N Standbesitzer(in) *m(f)*
stallion ['stæljən] N Hengst *m*
stalwart ['stɔːlwət] ADJ treu
stamen ['steɪmɛn] N Staubgefäß *nt*
stamina ['stæmɪnə] N Ausdauer *f*
stammer ['stæməʳ] N Stottern *nt* ▸ VI stottern; **to have a ~** stottern
stamp [stæmp] N (*lit, fig*) Stempel *m*; (*also:* **postage stamp**) Briefmarke *f* ▸ VI stampfen; (*also:* **stamp one's foot**) (mit dem Fuß) aufstampfen ▸ VT stempeln; (*with postage stamp*) frankieren; **stamped addressed envelope** frankierter Rückumschlag
▸ **stamp out** VT (*fire*) austreten; (*fig: crime*) ausrotten; (*: opposition*) unterdrücken
stamp album N Briefmarkenalbum *nt*
stamp collecting N Briefmarkensammeln *nt*
stamp duty (BRIT) N (Stempel)gebühr *f*
stampede [stæm'piːd] N (*of animals*) wilde Flucht *f*; (*fig*) Massenandrang *m*
stamp machine N Briefmarkenautomat *m*
stance [stæns] N Haltung *f*; (*fig*) Einstellung *f*
stand [stænd] (*pt, pp* **stood**) N (*Comm*) Stand *m*; (*Sport*) Tribüne *f*; (*piece of furniture*) Ständer *m* ▸ VI stehen; (*rise*) aufstehen; (*remain*) bestehen bleiben; (*in election etc*) kandidieren ▸ VT stellen; (*tolerate, withstand*) ertragen; **to make a ~ against sth** Widerstand gegen etw leisten; **to take a ~ on sth** einen Standpunkt zu etw vertreten; **to take the ~** (*US Law*) in den Zeugenstand treten; **to ~ at** (*value, score etc*) betragen; (*level*) liegen bei; **to ~ for parliament** (BRIT) in den Parlamentswahlen kandidieren; **to ~ to gain/lose sth** etw gewinnen/verlieren können; **it stands to reason** es ist einleuchtend; **as things ~** nach Lage der Dinge; **to ~ sb a drink/meal** jdm einen Drink/ein Essen spendieren; **I can't ~ him** ich kann ihn nicht leiden *or* ausstehen; **we don't ~ a chance** wir haben keine Chance; **to ~ trial** vor Gericht stehen
▸ **stand around** VI herumstehen
▸ **stand by** VI (*be ready*) sich bereithalten; (*fail to help*) (unbeteiligt) danebenstehen ▸ VT FUS (*opinion, decision*) stehen zu; (*person*) halten zu
▸ **stand down** VI zurücktreten
▸ **stand for** VT FUS (*represent*) stehen für; (*tolerate*) sich *dat* gefallen lassen; (*signify*) bedeuten
▸ **stand in for** VT FUS vertreten
▸ **stand out** VI hervorstechen
▸ **stand up** VI aufstehen
▸ **stand up for** VT FUS eintreten für
▸ **stand up to** VT FUS standhalten *+dat*; (*person*) sich behaupten gegenüber *+dat*
stand-alone ['stændələun] ADJ (*Comput*) selb(st)ständig
standard ['stændəd] N (*norm*) Norm *f*; (*criterion*) Maßstab *m*; (*level*) Niveau *nt*; (*flag*) Standarte *f* ▸ ADJ (*size, model, value etc*) Standard-; (*normal*) normal; **standards** NPL (*morals*) (sittliche) Maßstäbe *pl*; **to be** *or* **to come up to ~** den Anforderungen genügen; **to apply a double ~** mit zweierlei Maß messen
Standard Grade (SCOT) N (*Scol*) *Schulabschlusszeugnis*, ≈ mittlere Reife *f*

S

standardization [stændədaɪ'zeɪʃən] N Vereinheitlichung *f*
standardize ['stændədaɪz] VT vereinheitlichen
standard lamp (BRIT) N Stehlampe *f*
standard of living N Lebensstandard *m*
standard time N Normalzeit *f*
standby, stand-by ['stændbaɪ] N Reserve *f*; (*also*: **standby ticket**) Stand-by-Ticket *nt* ▸ ADJ (*generator*) Reserve-, Ersatz-; **to be on stand-by** (*crew, firemen etc*) in Bereitschaft sein, einsatzbereit sein; (*doctor*) Bereitschaftsdienst haben
standby ticket N Stand-by-Ticket *nt*
stand-in ['stændɪn] N Ersatz *m*
standing ['stændɪŋ] ADJ (*permanent*) ständig; (*army*) stehend ▸ N (*status*) Rang *m*, Stellung *f*; **a ~ ovation** stürmischer Beifall; **of many years' ~** von langjähriger Dauer; **a relationship of 6 months' ~** eine seit 6 Monaten bestehende Beziehung; **a man of some ~** ein angesehener Mann
standing joke N Standardwitz *m*
standing order (BRIT) N (*at bank*) Dauerauftrag *m*
standing room N Stehplätze *pl*
standoff N (*situation*) ausweglose *or* verfahrene Situation *f*
stand-offish [stænd'ɔfɪʃ] ADJ distanziert
standpat ['stændpæt] (US) ADJ konservativ
standpipe ['stændpaɪp] N Steigrohr *nt*
standpoint ['stændpɔɪnt] N Standpunkt *m*
standstill ['stændstɪl] N: **to be at a ~** stillstehen; (*fig: negotiations*) in eine Sackgasse geraten sein; **to come to a ~** (*traffic*) zum Stillstand kommen
stank [stæŋk] PT *of* **stink**
stanza ['stænzə] N Strophe *f*
staple ['steɪpl] N (*for papers*) Heftklammer *f*; (*chief product*) Hauptartikel *m* ▸ ADJ (*food, diet*) Grund-, Haupt- ▸ VT heften
stapler ['steɪpləʳ] N Hefter *m*
star [stɑːʳ] N Stern *m*; (*celebrity*) Star *m* ▸ VT (*Theat, Cine*) in der Hauptrolle zeigen ▸ VI: **to ~ in** die Hauptrolle haben in; **the stars** NPL (*horoscope*) das Horoskop; **4-~ hotel** 4-Sterne-Hotel *nt*; **2-~ petrol** (BRIT) Normal(benzin) *nt*; **4-~ petrol** (BRIT) Super(benzin) *nt*
star attraction N Hauptattraktion *f*
starboard ['stɑːbɔːd] ADJ (*side*) Steuerbord-; **to ~** (nach) Steuerbord
starch [stɑːtʃ] N Stärke *f*
starched [stɑːtʃt] ADJ gestärkt
starchy ['stɑːtʃɪ] ADJ (*food*) stärkehaltig; (*pej: person*) steif
stardom ['stɑːdəm] N Berühmtheit *f*
stare [stɛəʳ] VI: **to ~ at** anstarren ▸ N starrer Blick *m*
starfish ['stɑːfɪʃ] N Seestern *m*
stark [stɑːk] ADJ (*bleak*) kahl; (*simplicity*) schlicht; (*colour*) eintönig; (*reality, poverty*) nackt ▸ ADV: **~ naked** splitternackt
starkers ['stɑːkəz] (*inf*) ADJ splitter(faser)nackt
starlet ['stɑːlɪt] N (Film)sternchen *nt*, Starlet *nt*
starlight ['stɑːlaɪt] N Sternenlicht *nt*
starling ['stɑːlɪŋ] N Star *m*
starlit ['stɑːlɪt] ADJ sternklar
starry ['stɑːrɪ] ADJ sternklar; **~ sky** Sternenhimmel *m*
starry-eyed [stɑːrɪ'aɪd] ADJ (*innocent*) arglos, blauäugig; (*from wonder*) verzückt
Stars and Stripes N SING Sternenbanner *nt*
star sign N Sternzeichen *nt*
star-studded ['stɑːstʌdɪd] ADJ: **a ~ cast** eine Starbesetzung *f*
START N ABBR (*Mil: = Strategic Arms Reduction Talks*) START
start [stɑːt] N Beginn *m*, Anfang *m*; (*departure*) Aufbruch *m*; (*advantage*) Vorsprung *m* ▸ VT anfangen mit; (*panic*) auslösen; (*fire*) anzünden; (*found*) gründen; (*: restaurant etc*) eröffnen; (*engine*) anlassen; (*car*) starten ▸ VI anfangen; (*with fright*) zusammenfahren; (*engine etc*) anspringen; **at the ~** am Anfang, zu Beginn; **for a ~** erstens; **to make an early ~** frühzeitig aufbrechen; **to give a ~** zusammenfahren; **to wake up with a ~** aus dem Schlaf hochschrecken; **to ~ doing** *or* **to do sth** anfangen, etw zu tun; **to ~ (off) with ...** (*firstly*) erstens; (*at the beginning*) zunächst
▸ **start off** VI (*begin*) anfangen; (*begin moving*) losgehen/-fahren
▸ **start out** VI (*leave*) sich aufmachen
▸ **start over** (US) VI noch einmal von vorn anfangen
▸ **start up** VT (*business*) gründen; (*restaurant etc*) eröffnen; (*car*) starten; (*engine*) anlassen
starter ['stɑːtəʳ] N (*Aut*) Anlasser *m*; (*Sport: official, runner, horse*) Starter *m*; (BRIT *Culin*) Vorspeise *f*; **for starters** (*inf*) für den Anfang
starting point ['stɑːtɪŋ-] N (*lit, fig*) Ausgangspunkt *m*
starting price N (*at auction*) Ausgangsangebot *nt*
startle ['stɑːtl] VT erschrecken
startling ['stɑːtlɪŋ] ADJ (*news etc*) überraschend
star turn (BRIT) N Sensation *f*, Hauptattraktion *f*
starvation [stɑː'veɪʃən] N Hunger *m*; **to die of/from ~** verhungern
starve [stɑːv] VI hungern; (*to death*) verhungern ▸ VT hungern lassen; (*fig: deprive*): **to ~ sb of sth** jdm etw vorenthalten; **I'm starving** ich sterbe vor Hunger
Star Wars N Krieg *m* der Sterne
stash [stæʃ] VI (*also*: **stash away**) beiseiteschaffen ▸ N (*secret store*) geheimes Lager *nt*
state [steɪt] N (*condition*) Zustand *m*; (*Pol*) Staat *m* ▸ VT (*say*) feststellen; (*declare*) erklären; **the States** NPL (*Geog*) die (Vereinigten) Staaten *pl*; **to be in a ~** aufgeregt sein; (*on edge*) nervös sein; (*in a mess*) in einem schrecklichen Zustand sein; **to get into a ~** durchdrehen (*inf*); **in ~** feierlich; **to lie in ~** (feierlich) aufgebahrt sein; **~ of emergency** Notstand *m*; **~ of mind** Verfassung *f*
state control N staatliche Kontrolle *f*
stated ['steɪtɪd] ADJ erklärt

State Department (*US*) N Außenministerium *nt*
state education (*BRIT*) N staatliche Erziehung *f*; (*system*) staatliches Bildungswesen *nt*
stateless ['steɪtlɪs] ADJ staatenlos
stately ['steɪtlɪ] ADJ würdevoll; (*walk*) gemessen; **~ home** Schloss *nt*
statement ['steɪtmənt] N (*declaration*) Erklärung *f*; (*Fin*) (Konto)auszug *m*; **official ~** (amtliche) Erklärung *f*; **bank ~** Kontoauszug *m*; (*thing said*) Feststellung *f*
state of the art N: **the ~** der neueste Stand der Technik ▶ ADJ: **state-of-the-art** auf dem neuesten Stand der Technik; (*technology*) Spitzen-
state-owned ['steɪtəund] ADJ staatseigen
state school N öffentliche Schule *f*
state secret N Staatsgeheimnis *nt*
statesman ['steɪtsmən] N (*irreg*) Staatsmann *m*
statesmanship ['steɪtsmənʃɪp] N Staatskunst *f*
static ['stætɪk] ADJ (*not moving*) konstant ▶ N (*Radio, TV*) atmosphärische Störungen *pl*
static electricity N Reibungselektrizität *f*
station ['steɪʃən] N (*Rail*) Bahnhof *m*; (*also*: **bus station**) Busbahnhof *m*; (*also*: **police station**) (Polizei)wache *f*; (*Radio*) Sender *m* ▶ VT (*soldiers etc*) stationieren; (*guards etc*) postieren; **action stations** (*Mil*) Stellung *f*; **above one's ~** über seinem Stand
stationary ['steɪʃnərɪ] ADJ (*vehicle*) haltend; **to be ~** stehen
stationer ['steɪʃənə^r] N Schreibwarenhändler(in) *m(f)*
stationer's, stationer's shop N Schreibwarenhandlung *f*
stationery ['steɪʃnərɪ] N Schreibwaren *pl*; (*writing paper*) Briefpapier *nt*
stationmaster ['steɪʃənmɑːstə^r] N Bahnhofsvorsteher *m*
station wagon (*US*) N Kombi(wagen) *m*
statistic [stə'tɪstɪk] N Statistik *f*
statistical [stə'tɪstɪkl] ADJ statistisch
statistics [stə'tɪstɪks] N (*science*) Statistik *f*
statue ['stætjuː] N Statue *f*
statuesque [stætju'ɛsk] ADJ stattlich
statuette [stætju'ɛt] N Statuette *f*
stature ['stætʃə^r] N Wuchs *m*, Statur *f*; (*fig: reputation*) Format *nt*
status ['steɪtəs] N Status *m*; (*position*) Stellung *f*; **the ~ quo** der Status quo
status bar, status line N (*Comput*) Statuszeile *f*
status symbol N Statussymbol *nt*
statute ['stætjuːt] N Gesetz *nt*; **statutes** NPL (*of club etc*) Satzung *f*
statute book N: **to be on the ~** geltendes Recht sein
statutory ['stætjutrɪ] ADJ gesetzlich; **~ declaration** eidesstattliche Erklärung *f*
staunch [stɔːntʃ] ADJ treu ▶ VT (*flow*) stauen; (*blood*) stillen
stave [steɪv] N (*Mus*) Notensystem *nt*
▶ **stave off** VT (*attack*) abwehren; (*threat*) abwenden

stay [steɪ] N Aufenthalt *m* ▶ VI bleiben; (*with sb, as guest*) wohnen; (*in hotel*) übernachten; **~ of execution** (*Law*) Aussetzung *f*; **to ~ put** bleiben; **to ~ with friends** bei Freunden untergebracht sein; **to ~ the night** übernachten
▶ **stay away** VI wegbleiben; **to ~ away from sb** sich von jdm fernhalten
▶ **stay behind** VI zurückbleiben
▶ **stay in** VI (*at home*) zu Hause bleiben
▶ **stay on** VI bleiben
▶ **stay out** VI (*of house*) wegbleiben; (*remain on strike*) weiterstreiken
▶ **stay up** VI (*at night*) aufbleiben
staying power ['steɪɪŋ-] N Stehvermögen *nt*, Durchhaltevermögen *nt*
STD N ABBR (*BRIT Tel*: = *subscriber trunk dialling*) Selbstwählferndienst *m*; (*Med*: = *sexually transmitted disease*) durch Geschlechtsverkehr übertragene Krankheit *f*
stead [stɛd] N: **in sb's ~** an jds Stelle; **to stand sb in good ~** jdm zugute- *or* zustattenkommen
steadfast ['stɛdfɑːst] ADJ standhaft
steadily ['stɛdɪlɪ] ADV (*regularly*) regelmäßig; (*constantly*) stetig; (*fixedly*) fest, unverwandt
steady ['stɛdɪ] ADJ (*job, boyfriend, girlfriend, look*) fest; (*income*) regelmäßig; (*speed*) gleichmäßig; (*rise*) stetig; (*person, character*) zuverlässig, solide; (*voice, hand etc*) ruhig ▶ VT (*nerves*) beruhigen; (*stabilize*) ruhig halten; **to ~ o.s. on sth** sich auf etw *acc* stützen; **to ~ o.s. against sth** sich an etw *dat* abstützen
steak [steɪk] N Steak *nt*; (*fish*) Filet *nt*
steakhouse ['steɪkhaus] N Steakrestaurant *nt*
steal [stiːl] (*pt* **stole**, *pp* **stolen**) VT stehlen ▶ VI stehlen; (*move secretly*) sich stehlen, schleichen
▶ **steal away** VI sich davonschleichen
stealth [stɛlθ] N: **by ~** heimlich
stealthy ['stɛlθɪ] ADJ heimlich, verstohlen
steam [stiːm] N Dampf *m* ▶ VT (*Culin*) dämpfen, dünsten ▶ VI dampfen; **covered with ~** (*window etc*) beschlagen; **under one's own ~** (*fig*) allein, ohne Hilfe; **to run out of ~** (*fig*) den Schwung verlieren; **to let off ~** (*inf: fig*) Dampf ablassen
▶ **steam up** VI (*window*) beschlagen; **to get steamed up about sth** (*inf: fig*) sich über etw *acc* aufregen
steam engine N (*Rail*) Dampflok(omotive) *f*
steamer ['stiːmə^r] N Dampfer *m*; (*Culin*) Dämpfer *m*
steam iron N Dampfbügeleisen *nt*
steamroller ['stiːmrəulə^r] N Dampfwalze *f*
steamship ['stiːmʃɪp] N = **steamer**
steamy ['stiːmɪ] ADJ (*room*) dampfig; (*window*) beschlagen; (*book, film*) heiß
steed [stiːd] (*liter*) N Ross *nt*
steel [stiːl] N Stahl *m* ▶ ADJ (*girder, wool etc*) Stahl-
steel band N (*Mus*) Steelband *f*
steel industry N Stahlindustrie *f*
steel mill N Stahlwalzwerk *nt*
steelworks ['stiːlwəːks] N Stahlwerk *nt*
steely ['stiːlɪ] ADJ (*determination*) eisern; (*eyes, gaze*) hart, stählern

S

steep [sti:p] ADJ steil; (*increase, rise*) stark; (*price, fees*) gepfeffert ▸ VT einweichen; **to be steeped in history** geschichtsträchtig sein
steeple ['sti:pl] N Kirchturm *m*
steeplechase ['sti:pltʃeɪs] N (*for horses*) Hindernisrennen *nt*; (*for runners*) Hindernislauf *m*
steeplejack ['sti:pldʒæk] N Turmarbeiter *m*
steeply ['sti:plɪ] ADV steil
steer [stɪəʳ] VT steuern; (*car etc*) lenken; (*person*) lotsen ▸ VI steuern; (*in car etc*) lenken; **to ~ for** zusteuern auf +*acc*; **to ~ clear of sb** (*fig*) jdm aus dem Weg gehen; **to ~ clear of sth** (*fig*) etw meiden
steering ['stɪərɪŋ] N (*Aut*) Lenkung *f*
steering column N (*Aut*) Lenksäule *f*
steering committee N Lenkungsausschuss *m*
steering wheel N (*Aut*) Lenkrad *nt*, Steuer *nt*
stellar ['stɛləʳ] ADJ stellar
stem [stɛm] N Stiel *m*; (*of pipe*) Hals *m* ▸ VT aufhalten; (*flow*) eindämmen; (*bleeding*) zum Stillstand bringen
▸ **stem from** VT FUS zurückgehen auf +*acc*
stench [stɛntʃ] (*pej*) N Gestank *m*
stencil ['stɛnsl] N Schablone *f* ▸ VT mit Schablone zeichnen
stenographer [stɛ'nɔgrəfəʳ] (*US*) N Stenograf(in) *m(f)*
stenography [stɛ'nɔgrəfɪ] (*US*) N Stenografie *f*
step [stɛp] N (*lit, fig*) Schritt *m*; (*of stairs*) Stufe *f* ▸ VI: **to ~ forward/back** vor-/zurücktreten; **steps** NPL (BRIT) = **stepladder**; **~ by ~** (*fig*) Schritt für Schritt; **in/out of ~ (with)** im/nicht im Tritt (mit); (*fig*) im/nicht im Gleichklang (mit)
▸ **step down** VI (*fig: resign*) zurücktreten
▸ **step in** VI (*fig*) eingreifen
▸ **step off** VT FUS aussteigen aus +*dat*
▸ **step on** VT FUS treten auf +*acc*
▸ **step over** VT FUS steigen über +*acc*
▸ **step up** VT (*efforts*) steigern; (*pace etc*) beschleunigen
stepbrother ['stɛpbrʌðəʳ] N Stiefbruder *m*
stepchild ['stɛptʃaɪld] N (*irreg*) Stiefkind *nt*
stepdaughter ['stɛpdɔ:təʳ] N Stieftochter *f*
stepfather ['stɛpfɑ:ðəʳ] N Stiefvater *m*
stepladder ['stɛplædəʳ] (BRIT) N Trittleiter *f*
stepmother ['stɛpmʌðəʳ] N Stiefmutter *f*
stepping stone ['stɛpɪŋ-] N Trittstein *m*; (*fig*) Sprungbrett *nt*
stepsister ['stɛpsɪstəʳ] N Stiefschwester *f*
stepson ['stɛpsʌn] N Stiefsohn *m*
stereo ['stɛrɪəu] N (*system*) Stereoanlage *f* ▸ ADJ (*sound etc*) Stereo-; **in ~** in Stereo
stereotype ['stɪərɪətaɪp] N Klischee *nt*, Klischeevorstellung *f* ▸ VT in ein Klischee zwängen; **stereotyped** stereotyp
sterile ['stɛraɪl] ADJ steril, keimfrei; (*barren*) unfruchtbar; (*fig: debate*) fruchtlos
sterility [stɛ'rɪlɪtɪ] N Unfruchtbarkeit *f*
sterilization [stɛrɪlaɪ'zeɪʃən] N Sterilisation *f*, Sterilisierung *f*
sterilize ['stɛrɪlaɪz] VT sterilisieren
sterling ['stə:lɪŋ] N (*Econ*) das Pfund Sterling, das englische Pfund ▸ ADJ (*silver*) Sterling-; (*fig*) gediegen; **one pound ~** ein Pfund Sterling
sterling area N (*Econ*) Sterlingländer *pl*
stern [stə:n] ADJ streng ▸ N Heck *nt*
sternum ['stə:nəm] N Brustbein *nt*
steroid ['stɪərɔɪd] N Steroid *nt*
stethoscope ['stɛθəskəup] N Stethoskop *nt*
stevedore ['sti:vədɔ:ʳ] N Stauer *m*, Schauermann *m*
stew [stju:] N Eintopf *m* ▸ VT schmoren; (*fruit, vegetables*) dünsten ▸ VI schmoren; **stewed tea** bitterer Tee *m*; **stewed fruit** (Obst)kompott *nt*
steward ['stju:əd] N Steward *m*; (*at public event*) Ordner(in) *m(f)*; (*also*: **shop steward**) gewerkschaftliche Vertrauensperson *f*
stewardess ['stjuədɛs] N Stewardess *f*
stewardship ['stjuədʃɪp] N Verwaltung *f*
stewing steak, (*US*) **stew meat** ['stju:ɪŋ-] N (Rinder)schmorfleisch *nt*
St. Ex. ABBR = **stock exchange**
stg ABBR = **sterling**
stick [stɪk] (*pt, pp* **stuck**) N Zweig *m*; (*of dynamite, celery*) Stange *f*; (*of chalk etc*) Stück *nt*; (*as weapon*) Stock *m*; (*also*: **walking stick**) (Spazier)stock *m* ▸ VT (*with glue etc*) kleben; (*inf: put*) tun, stecken; (*: tolerate*) aushalten; (*thrust*) stoßen ▸ VI: **to ~ (to)** kleben (an +*dat*); (*remain*) (hängen) bleiben; (*door etc*) klemmen; (*lift*) stecken bleiben; **to get hold of the wrong end of the ~** (BRIT *fig*) es falsch verstehen; **to ~ in sb's mind** jdm im Gedächtnis (haften) bleiben
▸ **stick around** (*inf*) VI hier-/dableiben
▸ **stick out** VI (*ears etc*) abstehen ▸ VT: **to ~ it out** (*inf*) durchhalten
▸ **stick to** VT FUS (*agreement, rules*) sich halten an +*acc*; (*one's word, promise*) halten; (*the truth, facts*) bleiben bei
▸ **stick up** VI hochstehen
▸ **stick up for** VT FUS eintreten für
sticker ['stɪkəʳ] N Aufkleber *m*
sticking plaster ['stɪkɪŋ-] N Heftpflaster *nt*
sticking point N Hindernis *nt*; (*in discussion etc*) strittiger Punkt *m*
stickleback ['stɪklbæk] N Stichling *m*
stickler ['stɪkləʳ] N: **to be a ~ for sth** es mit etw peinlich genau nehmen
stick shift (*US*) N Schaltknüppel *m*; (*car*) Wagen *m* mit Handschaltung
stick-up ['stɪkʌp] (*inf*) N Überfall *m*
sticky ['stɪkɪ] ADJ klebrig; (*label, tape*) Klebe-; (*weather, day*) schwül
stiff [stɪf] ADJ steif; (*hard, firm*) hart; (*paste, egg-white*) fest; (*door, zip etc*) schwer gehend; (*competition*) hart; (*sentence*) schwer; (*drink*) stark ▸ ADV (*bored, worried, scared*) zu Tode; **to be** *or* **feel ~** steif sein; **to have a ~ neck** einen steifen Hals haben; **to keep a ~ upper lip** (BRIT *fig*) die Haltung bewahren
stiffen ['stɪfn] VI steif werden; (*body*) erstarren
stiffness ['stɪfnɪs] N Steifheit *f*
stifle ['staɪfl] VT unterdrücken; (*heat*) erdrücken
stifling ['staɪflɪŋ] ADJ (*heat*) drückend

stigma ['stɪgmə] N Stigma *nt*; (*Bot*) Narbe *f*, Stigma *nt*; **stigmata** NPL (*Med*) Wundmal *nt*
stile [staɪl] N Zaunübertritt *m*
stiletto [stɪ'lɛtəu] (BRIT) N (*also*: **stiletto heel**) Bleistiftabsatz *m*
still [stɪl] ADJ (*air, water*) still; (BRIT: *drink*) ohne Kohlensäure; (*motionless*) bewegungslos; (*tranquil*) ruhig ▸ ADV (immer) noch; (*yet, even*) noch; (*nonetheless*) trotzdem ▸ N (*Cine*) Standfoto *nt*; **to stand ~** (*machine, motor*) stillstehen; (*motionless*) still stehen; **keep ~!** halte still!; **he ~ hasn't arrived** er ist immer noch nicht angekommen
stillborn ['stɪlbɔːn] ADJ tot geboren
still life N Stillleben *nt*
stilt [stɪlt] N (*pile*) Pfahl *m*; (*for walking on*) Stelze *f*
stilted ['stɪltɪd] ADJ gestelzt
stimulant ['stɪmjulənt] N Anregungsmittel *nt*
stimulate ['stɪmjuleɪt] VT anregen, stimulieren; (*demand*) ankurbeln
stimulating ['stɪmjuleɪtɪŋ] ADJ anregend, stimulierend
stimulation [stɪmju'leɪʃən] N Anregung *f*, Stimulation *f*
stimuli ['stɪmjulaɪ] NPL *of* **stimulus**
stimulus ['stɪmjuləs] (*pl* **stimuli**) N (*incentive*) Anreiz *m*; (*Biol*) Reiz *m*; (*Psych*) Stimulus *m*
sting [stɪŋ] (*pt, pp* **stung**) N Stich *m*; (*pain*) Stechen *nt*; (*organ: of insect*) Stachel *m*; (*inf: confidence trick*) Ding *nt* ▸ VT stechen; (*fig*) treffen, verletzen ▸ VI stechen; (*eyes, ointment, plant etc*) brennen; **my eyes are stinging** mir brennen die Augen
stingy ['stɪndʒɪ] (*pej*) ADJ geizig, knauserig
stink [stɪŋk] (*pt* **stank**, *pp* **stunk**) N Gestank *m* ▸ VI stinken
stinker ['stɪŋkə^r] (*inf*) N (*problem*) harter Brocken *m*; (*person*) Ekel *nt*
stinking ['stɪŋkɪŋ] (*inf*) ADJ (*fig*) beschissen (*inf!*); **a ~ cold** eine scheußliche Erkältung; **~ rich** stinkreich
stint [stɪnt] N (*period*) Zeit *f*; (*batch of work*) Pensum *nt*; (*share*) Teil *m* ▸ VI: **to ~ on** sparen mit
stipend ['staɪpɛnd] N Gehalt *nt*
stipendiary [staɪ'pɛndɪərɪ] ADJ: **~ magistrate** bezahlter Friedensrichter *m*
stipulate ['stɪpjuleɪt] VT festsetzen; (*condition*) stellen
stipulation [stɪpju'leɪʃən] N Bedingung *f*, Auflage *f*
stir [stəː^r] VT umrühren; (*fig: emotions*) aufwühlen; (*: person*) bewegen ▸ VI sich bewegen ▸ N (*fig*) Aufsehen *nt*; **to give sth a ~** etw umrühren; **to cause a ~** Aufsehen erregen ▸ **stir up** VT: **to ~ up trouble** Unruhe stiften; **to ~ things up** stänkern
stir-fry ['stəː'fraɪ] VT unter Rühren kurz anbraten ▸ N Pfannengericht *nt* (*das unter Rühren kurz angebraten wurde*)
stirring ['stəːrɪŋ] ADJ bewegend
stirrup ['stɪrəp] N Steigbügel *m*
stitch [stɪtʃ] N (*Sewing*) Stich *m*; (*Knitting*) Masche *f*; (*Med*) Faden *m*; (*pain*) Seitenstiche *pl* ▸ VT nähen; **he had to have stitches** er musste genäht werden
stoat [stəut] N Wiesel *nt*
stock [stɔk] N Vorrat *m*; (*Comm*) Bestand *m*; (*Agr*) Vieh *nt*; (*Culin*) Brühe *f*; (*descent, origin*) Abstammung *f*, Herkunft *f*; (*Fin*) Wertpapiere *pl*; (*Rail: also*: **rolling stock**) rollendes Material *nt* ▸ ADJ (*reply, excuse etc*) Standard- ▸ VT (*in shop*) führen; **in/out of ~** vorrätig/nicht vorrätig; **stocks and shares** (Aktien und) Wertpapiere *pl*; **government ~** Staatsanleihe *f*; **to take ~ of** (*fig*) Bilanz ziehen über *+acc*; **well-stocked** (*shop*) mit gutem Sortiment
▸ **stock up** VI: **to ~ up (with)** sich eindecken (mit)
stockade [stɔ'keɪd] N Palisade *f*
stockbroker ['stɔkbrəukə^r] N Börsenmakler *m*
stock control N Bestandsüberwachung *f*
stock cube (BRIT) N Brühwürfel *m*
stock exchange N Börse *f*
stockholder ['stɔkhəuldə^r] (*esp US*) N Aktionär(in) *m(f)*
Stockholm ['stɔkhəum] N Stockholm *nt*
stocking ['stɔkɪŋ] N Strumpf *m*
stock-in-trade ['stɔkɪn'treɪd] N (*fig*): **it's his ~** es gehört zu seinem festen Repertoire
stockist ['stɔkɪst] (BRIT) N Händler *m*
stock market (BRIT) N Börse *f*
stock phrase N Standardsatz *m*
stockpile ['stɔkpaɪl] N Vorrat *m*; (*of weapons*) Lager *nt* ▸ VT horten
stockroom ['stɔkruːm] N Lager *nt*, Lagerraum *m*
stocktaking ['stɔkteɪkɪŋ] (BRIT) N Inventur *f*
stocky ['stɔkɪ] ADJ stämmig
stodgy ['stɔdʒɪ] ADJ (*food*) pampig (*inf*), schwer
stoic ['stəuɪk] N Stoiker(in) *m(f)* ▸ ADJ stoisch
stoical ['stəuɪkl] ADJ stoisch
stoke [stəuk] VT (*fire*) schüren; (*furnace, boiler*) heizen
stoker ['stəukə^r] N Heizer *m*
stole [stəul] PT *of* **steal** ▸ N Stola *f*
stolen ['stəuln] PP *of* **steal**
stolid ['stɔlɪd] ADJ phlegmatisch, stur (*inf*)
stomach ['stʌmək] N Magen *m*; (*belly*) Bauch *m* ▸ VT (*fig*) vertragen
stomach ache N Magenschmerzen *pl*
stomach pump N Magenpumpe *f*
stomach ulcer N Magengeschwür *nt*
stomp [stɔmp] VI stapfen
stone [stəun] N Stein *m*; (BRIT: *weight*) Gewichtseinheit (= 6,35 kg) ▸ ADJ (*wall, jar etc*) Stein-, steinern ▸ VT (*person*) mit Steinen bewerfen; (*fruit*) entkernen, entsteinen; **within a ~'s throw of the station** nur einen Katzensprung vom Bahnhof entfernt
Stone Age N Steinzeit *f*
stone-cold ['stəun'kəuld] ADJ eiskalt
stoned [stəund] (*inf*) ADJ (*on drugs*) stoned; (*drunk*) total zu
stone-deaf ['stəun'dɛf] ADJ stocktaub
stonemason ['stəunmeɪsn] N Steinmetz *m*
stonewall [stəun'wɔːl] VI mauern; (*in answering questions*) ausweichen
stonework ['stəunwəːk] N Mauerwerk *nt*

S

stony ['stəunɪ] ADJ steinig; (*fig: silence etc*) steinern
stood [stud] PT, PP *of* **stand**
stooge [stu:dʒ] N (*inf*) Handlanger(in) *m(f)*; (*Theat*) Stichwortgeber(in) *m(f)*
stool [stu:l] N Hocker *m*
stoop [stu:p] VI (*also*: **stoop down**) sich bücken; (*walk*) gebeugt gehen; **to ~ to sth** (*fig*) sich zu etw herablassen; **to ~ to doing sth** sich dazu herablassen, etw zu tun
stop [stɔp] N Halt *m*; (*short stay*) Aufenthalt *m*; (*in punctuation: also*: **full stop**) Punkt *m*; (*bus stop etc*) Haltestelle *f* ▶ VT stoppen; (*car etc*) anhalten; (*block*) sperren; (*prevent*) verhindern ▶ VI (*car etc*) anhalten; (*train*) halten; (*pedestrian, watch, clock*) stehen bleiben; (*end*) aufhören; **to come to a ~** anhalten; **to put a ~ to** einen Riegel vorschieben *+dat*; **to ~ doing sth** aufhören, etw zu tun; **to ~ sb (from) doing sth** jdn davon abhalten, etw zu tun; **~ it!** lass das!, hör auf!
▶ **stop by** VI kurz vorbeikommen
▶ **stop off** VI kurz haltmachen, Zwischenstation machen
▶ **stop over** VI Halt machen; (*overnight*) übernachten
▶ **stop up** VT (*hole*) zustopfen
stopcock ['stɔpkɔk] N Absperrhahn *m*
stopgap ['stɔpgæp] N (*person*) Lückenbüßer *m*; (*thing*) Notbehelf *m*; **~ measure** Überbrückungsmaßnahme *f*
stop-go [stɔp'gəu] ADJ (*economic cycle etc*) mit ständigem Auf und Ab
stoplights ['stɔplaɪts] NPL (*Aut*) Bremslichter *pl*
stopover ['stɔpəuvə[r]] N Zwischenaufenthalt *m*; (*Aviat*) Zwischenlandung *f*
stoppage ['stɔpɪdʒ] N (*strike*) Streik *m*; (*blockage*) Unterbrechung *f*; (*of pay, cheque*) Sperrung *f*; (*deduction*) Abzug *m*
stopper ['stɔpə[r]] N Stöpsel *m*
stop press N letzte Meldungen *pl*
stop sign N Stoppschild *nt*
stopwatch ['stɔpwɔtʃ] N Stoppuhr *f*
storage ['stɔ:rɪdʒ] N Lagerung *f*; (*also*: **storage space**) Stauraum *m*; (*Comput*) Speicherung *f*
storage capacity N (*Comput*) Speicherkapazität *f*
storage heater (BRIT) N (Nacht)speicherofen *m*
store [stɔ:[r]] N Vorrat *m*; (*depot*) Lager *nt*; (BRIT: *large shop*) Geschäft *nt*, Kaufhaus *nt*; (US: *shop*) Laden *m*; (*fig*): **a ~ of** eine Fülle an *+dat* ▶ VT lagern; (*information etc, Comput*) speichern; (*food, medicines etc*) aufbewahren; (*in filing system*) ablegen; **stores** NPL (*provisions*) Vorräte *pl*; **in ~** eingelagert; **who knows what's in ~ for us?** wer weiß, was uns bevorsteht?; **to set great/little ~ by sth** viel/wenig von etw halten
▶ **store up** VT einen Vorrat anlegen von; (*memories*) im Gedächtnis bewahren
storehouse ['stɔ:haus] N (*US Comm*) Lager(haus) *nt*; (*fig*) Fundgrube *f*
storekeeper ['stɔ:ki:pə[r]] (US) N Ladenbesitzer(in) *m(f)*
storeroom ['stɔ:ru:m] N Lagerraum *m*
storey, (*US*) **story** ['stɔ:rɪ] N Stock *m*, Stockwerk *nt*
stork [stɔ:k] N Storch *m*
storm [stɔ:m] N (*lit, fig*) Sturm *m*; (*bad weather*) Unwetter *nt*; (*also*: **electrical storm**) Gewitter *nt* ▶ VI (*fig*) toben ▶ VT (*attack*) stürmen
storm cloud N Gewitterwolke *f*
storm door N äußere Windfangtür *f*
stormy ['stɔ:mɪ] ADJ (*lit, fig*) stürmisch
story ['stɔ:rɪ] N Geschichte *f*; (*Press*) Artikel *m*; (*lie*) Märchen *nt*; (*US*) = **storey**
storybook ['stɔ:rɪbuk] N Geschichtenbuch *nt*
storyteller ['stɔ:rɪtɛlə[r]] N Geschichtenerzähler(in) *m(f)*
stout [staut] ADJ (*fat*) untersetzt; (*strong*) stark; (*resolute*) energisch ▶ N Starkbier *nt*
stove [stəuv] N Herd *m*; (*small*) Kocher *m*; (*for heating*) (Heiz)ofen *m*; **gas ~** Gasherd *m*
stow [stəu] VT (*also*: **stow away**) verstauen
stowaway ['stəuəweɪ] N blinder Passagier *m*
straddle ['strædl] VT (*sitting*) rittlings sitzen auf *+dat*; (*standing*) breitbeinig stehen über *+dat*; (*jumping*) grätschen über *+acc*; (*fig*) überspannen
strafe [strɑ:f] VT beschießen
straggle ['strægl] VI (*houses etc*) verstreut liegen; (*people etc*) zurückbleiben
straggler ['stræglə[r]] N Nachzügler *m*
straggly ['stræglɪ] ADJ (*hair*) unordentlich
straight [streɪt] ADJ gerade; (*hair*) glatt; (*honest*) offen, direkt; (*simple*) einfach; (*: fight*) direkt; (*Theat*) ernst; (*inf: heterosexual*) hetero; (*whisky etc*) pur ▶ ADV (*in time*) sofort; (*in direction*) direkt; (*drink*) pur ▶ N (*Sport*) Gerade *f*; **to put** *or* **get sth ~** (*make clear*) etw klären; (*make tidy*) etw in Ordnung bringen; **let's get this ~** das wollen wir mal klarstellen; **10 ~ wins** 10 Siege hintereinander; **to win in ~ sets** (*Tennis*) ohne Satzverlust gewinnen; **to go ~ home** direkt nach Hause gehen; **~ out** rundheraus; **~ away, ~ off** sofort, gleich
straighten ['streɪtn] VT (*skirt, sheet etc*) gerade ziehen
▶ **straighten out** VT (*fig*) klären
straighteners ['streɪtnəz] NPL (*for hair*) Haarglätter *m*
straight-faced [streɪt'feɪst] ADJ: **to be/remain ~** ernst bleiben ▶ ADV ohne zu lachen
straightforward [streɪt'fɔ:wəd] ADJ (*simple*) einfach; (*honest*) offen
straight sets NPL (*Tennis*): **to win in ~** ohne Satzverlust gewinnen
strain [streɪn] N Belastung *f*; (*Med*: *also*: **back strain**) überanstrengter Rücken *m*; (*tension*) Überlastung *f*; (*of virus*) Art *f*; (*breed*) Sorte *f* ▶ VT (*back etc*) überanstrengen; (*resources*) belasten; (*Culin*) abgießen ▶ VI: **to ~ to do sth** sich anstrengen, etw zu tun; **strains** NPL (*Mus*) Klänge *pl*; **he's been under a lot of ~** er hat unter großem Stress gestanden
strained [streɪnd] ADJ (*muscle*) gezerrt; (*forced*) gezwungen; (*relations*) gespannt; (*back*) überanstrengt

strainer ['streɪnəʳ] N Sieb *nt*

strait [streɪt] N Meerenge *f*, Straße *f*; **straits** NPL (*fig*): **to be in dire straits** in großen Nöten sein

straitjacket ['streɪtdʒækɪt] N Zwangsjacke *f*

strait-laced [streɪt'leɪst] ADJ prüde, puritanisch

strand [strænd] N (*lit, fig*) Faden *m*; (*of wire*) Litze *f*; (*of hair*) Strähne *f*

stranded ['strændɪd] ADJ: **to be ~** (*traveller*) festsitzen; (*ship, sea creature*) gestrandet

strange [streɪndʒ] ADJ fremd; (*odd*) seltsam, merkwürdig

strangely ['streɪndʒlɪ] ADV seltsam, merkwürdig; *see also* **enough**

stranger ['streɪndʒəʳ] N Fremde(r) *f*(*m*); **I'm a ~ here** ich bin hier fremd

strangle ['stræŋgl] VT erdrosseln, erwürgen; (*fig: economy etc*) ersticken

stranglehold ['stræŋglhəuld] N (*fig*) absolute Machtposition *f*

strangulation [stræŋgju'leɪʃən] N Erwürgen *nt*, Erdrosseln *nt*

strap [stræp] N Riemen *m*; (*of dress etc*) Träger *m* ▸ VT (*also*: **strap in**) anschnallen; (*also*: **strap on**) umschnallen

straphanging ['stræphæŋɪŋ] N Pendeln *nt* (als stehender Fahrgast)

strapless ['stræplɪs] ADJ trägerlos, schulterfrei

strapped [stræpt] (*inf*) ADJ: **~ (for cash)** pleite

strapping ['stræpɪŋ] ADJ stramm

Strasbourg ['stræzbəːg] N Straßburg *nt*

strata ['strɑːtə] NPL *of* **stratum**

stratagem ['strætɪdʒəm] N List *f*

strategic [strə'tiːdʒɪk] ADJ strategisch; (*error*) taktisch

strategist ['strætɪdʒɪst] N Stratege *m*, Strategin *f*

strategy ['strætɪdʒɪ] N Strategie *f*

stratosphere ['strætəsfɪəʳ] N Stratosphäre *f*

stratum ['strɑːtəm] (*pl* **strata**) N Schicht *f*

straw [strɔː] N Stroh *nt*; (*also*: **drinking straw**) Strohhalm *m*; **that's the last ~!** das ist der Gipfel!

strawberry ['strɔːbərɪ] N Erdbeere *f*

stray [streɪ] ADJ (*animal*) streunend; (*bullet*) verirrt; (*scattered*) einzeln, vereinzelt ▸ VI (*animals*) streunen; (*children*) sich verirren; (*thoughts*) abschweifen

streak [striːk] N Streifen *m*; (*in hair*) Strähne *f*; (*fig: of madness etc*) Zug *m* ▸ VT streifen ▸ VI: **to ~ past** vorbeiflitzen; **a winning/losing ~** eine Glücks-/Pechsträhne

streaker ['striːkəʳ] (*inf*) N Blitzer(in) *m*(*f*)

streaky ['striːkɪ] ADJ (*bacon*) durchwachsen

stream [striːm] N (*small river*) Bach *m*; (*current*) Strömung *f*; (*of people, vehicles*) Strom *m*; (*of questions, insults etc*) Flut *f*, Schwall *m*; (*of smoke*) Schwaden *m*; (*Scol*) Leistungsgruppe *f* ▸ VT (*Scol*) in Leistungsgruppen einteilen ▸ VI strömen; **against the ~** gegen den Strom; **to come on ~** (*new power plant etc*) in Betrieb genommen werden

streamer ['striːməʳ] N Luftschlange *f*

stream feed N automatischer Papiereinzug *m*

streamline ['striːmlaɪn] VT Stromlinienform geben *+dat*; (*fig*) rationalisieren

streamlined ['striːmlaɪnd] ADJ stromlinienförmig; (*Aviat, Aut*) windschlüpfrig; (*fig*) rationalisiert

street [striːt] N Straße *f*; **the back streets** die Seitensträßchen *pl*; **to be on the streets** (*homeless*) obdachlos sein; (*as prostitute*) auf den Strich gehen

streetcar ['striːtkɑːʳ] (*US*) N Straßenbahn *f*

street cred [-krɛd] (*inf*) N Glaubwürdigkeit *f*

street lamp N Straßenlaterne *f*

street lighting N Straßenbeleuchtung *f*

street map N Stadtplan *m*

street market N Straßenmarkt *m*

street plan N Stadtplan *m*

streetwise ['striːtwaɪz] (*inf*) ADJ: **to be ~** wissen, wos langgeht

strength [strɛŋθ] N (*lit, fig*) Stärke *f*; (*physical*) Kraft *f*, Stärke *f*; (*of girder etc*) Stabilität *f*; (*of knot etc*) Festigkeit *f*; (*of chemical solution*) Konzentration *f*; (*of wine*) Schwere *f*; **on the ~ of** aufgrund *+gen*; **at full ~** vollzählig; **to be below ~** nicht die volle Stärke haben

strengthen ['strɛŋθn] VT (*lit, fig*) verstärken; (*muscle*) kräftigen; (*economy, currency, relationship*) festigen

strenuous ['strɛnjuəs] ADJ anstrengend; (*determined*) unermüdlich

strenuously ['strɛnjuəslɪ] ADV energisch; **she ~ denied the rumour** sie leugnete das Gerücht hartnäckig

stress [strɛs] N Druck *m*; (*mental*) Stress *m*, Belastung *f*; (*Ling*) Betonung *f*; (*emphasis*) Akzent *m*, Gewicht *nt* ▸ VT betonen; **to lay great ~ on sth** großen Wert auf etw *acc* legen; **to be under ~** unter Stress stehen, großen Belastungen ausgesetzt sein

stressed ADJ: **~ out** gestresst

stressful ['strɛsful] ADJ anstrengend, stressig; (*situation*) angespannt

stretch [strɛtʃ] N (*of sand, water etc*) Stück *nt*; (*of time*) Zeit *f* ▸ VI (*person, animal*) sich strecken; (*land, area*) sich erstrecken ▸ VT (*pull*) spannen; (*fig: job, task*) fordern; **at a ~** an einem Stück, ohne Unterbrechung; **by no ~ of the imagination** beim besten Willen nicht; **to ~ to** *or* **as far as the frontier** (*extend*) sich bis zur Grenze erstrecken; **to ~ one's legs** sich *dat* die Beine vertreten

▸ **stretch out** VI sich ausstrecken ▸ VT ausstrecken

▸ **stretch to** VT FUS (*be enough*) reichen für

stretcher ['strɛtʃəʳ] N (Trag)bahre *f*

stretcher-bearer ['strɛtʃəbɛərəʳ] N Krankenträger *m*

stretch marks NPL Dehnungsstreifen *pl*; (*through pregnancy*) Schwangerschaftsstreifen *pl*

strewn [struːn] ADJ: **~ with** übersät mit

stricken ['strɪkən] ADJ (*person*) leidend; (*city, industry etc*) Not leidend; **~ with** (*disease*) geschlagen mit; (*fear etc*) erfüllt von

S

strict [strɪkt] ADJ streng; (*precise*) genau; **in the strictest confidence** streng vertraulich; **in the ~ sense of the word** streng genommen
strictly ['strɪktlɪ] ADV streng; (*exactly*) genau; (*solely*) ausschließlich; **~ confidential** streng vertraulich; **~ speaking** genau genommen; **not ~ true** nicht ganz richtig; **~ between ourselves** ganz unter uns
strictness ['strɪktnɪs] N Strenge *f*
stridden ['strɪdn] PP *of* **stride**
stride [straɪd] (*pt* **strode**, *pp* **stridden**) N Schritt *m* ▸ VI schreiten; **to take sth in one's ~** (*fig*) mit etw spielend fertig werden
strident ['straɪdnt] ADJ schrill, durchdringend; (*demands*) lautstark
strife [straɪf] N Streit *m*, Zwietracht *f*
strike [straɪk] (*pt, pp* **struck**) N Streik *m*, Ausstand *m*; (*Mil*) Angriff *m* ▸ VT (*hit*) schlagen; (*fig: idea, thought*) in den Sinn kommen *+dat*; (*oil etc*) finden, stoßen auf *+acc*; (*bargain, deal*) aushandeln; (*coin, medal*) prägen ▸ VI streiken; (*illness, killer*) zuschlagen; (*disaster*) hereinbrechen; (*clock*) schlagen; **on ~** streikend; **to be on ~** streiken; **to ~ a balance** einen Mittelweg finden; **to be struck by lightning** vom Blitz getroffen werden; **to ~ a match** ein Streichholz anzünden
▸ **strike back** VI (*Mil*) zurückschlagen; (*fig*) sich wehren
▸ **strike down** VT niederschlagen
▸ **strike off** VT (*from list*) (aus)streichen; (*doctor etc*) die Zulassung entziehen *+dat*
▸ **strike out** VI losziehen, sich aufmachen ▸ VT (*word, sentence*) (aus)streichen
▸ **strike up** VT (*conversation*) anknüpfen; (*friendship*) schließen; (*Mus*) anstimmen
strikebreaker ['straɪkbreɪkəʳ] N Streikbrecher *m*
strike pay N Streikgeld *nt*
striker ['straɪkəʳ] N Streikende(r) *f(m)*; (*Sport*) Stürmer *m*
striking ['straɪkɪŋ] ADJ auffallend; (*attractive*) attraktiv
strimmer ['strɪməʳ] N Rasentrimmer *m*
string [strɪŋ] (*pt, pp* **strung**) N Schnur *f*; (*of islands*) Kette *f*; (*of people, cars*) Schlange *f*; (*series*) Serie *f*; (*Comput*) Zeichenfolge *f*; (*Mus*) Saite *f* ▸ VT: **to ~ together** aneinanderreihen; **the strings** NPL (*Mus*) die Streichinstrumente *pl*; **to pull strings** (*fig*) Beziehungen spielen lassen; **with no strings attached** (*fig*) ohne Bedingungen; **to ~ sth out** etw verteilen
string bean N grüne Bohne *f*
stringed instrument N Saiteninstrument *nt*
stringent ['strɪndʒənt] ADJ streng; (*measures*) drastisch
string quartet N Streichquartett *nt*
strip [strɪp] N Streifen *m*; (*of metal*) Band *nt*; (*Sport*) Trikot *nt*, Dress *m* ▸ VT (*undress*) ausziehen; (*paint*) abbeizen; (*machine etc: also:* **strip down**) auseinandernehmen ▸ VI (*undress*) sich ausziehen
strip cartoon N Comic(strip) *m*
stripe [straɪp] N Streifen *m*; **stripes** NPL (*Mil, Police*) (Ärmel)streifen *pl*
striped [straɪpt] ADJ gestreift
strip lighting (BRIT) N Neonlicht *nt*
strip mall N Einkaufsmeile *nt*
stripper ['strɪpəʳ] N Stripper(in) *m(f)*, Stripteasetänzer(in) *m(f)*
strip-search ['strɪpsətʃ] N Leibesvisitation *f* (*bei der man sich ausziehen muss*) ▸ VT: **to be strip-searched** sich ausziehen müssen und durchsucht werden
striptease ['strɪpti:z] N Striptease *m or nt*
strive [straɪv] (*pt* **strove**, *pp* **striven**) VI: **to ~ for sth** nach etw streben; **to ~ to do sth** danach streben, etw zu tun
striven ['strɪvn] PP *of* **strive**
strobe [strəub] N (*also:* **strobe lights**) Stroboskoplicht *nt*
strode [strəud] PT *of* **stride**
stroke [strəuk] N Schlag *m*, Hieb *m*; (*Swimming: style*) Stil *m*; (*Med*) Schlaganfall *m*; (*of clock*) Schlag *m*; (*of paintbrush*) Strich *m* ▸ VT (*caress*) streicheln; **at a ~** mit einem Schlag; **on the ~ of 5** Punkt 5 (Uhr); **a ~ of luck** ein Glücksfall *m*; **a 2-~ engine** ein Zweitaktmotor *m*
stroll [strəul] N Spaziergang *m* ▸ VI spazieren; **to go for a ~, have** *or* **take a ~** einen Spaziergang machen
stroller ['strəuləʳ] (*US*) N (*pushchair*) Sportwagen *m*
strong [strɔŋ] ADJ stark; (*person, arms, grip*) stark, kräftig; (*healthy*) kräftig; (*object, material*) stabil, solide; (*letter*) geharnischt; (*measure*) drastisch; (*language*) derb; (*nerves*) gut; (*taste, smell*) streng ▸ ADV: **to be going ~** (*company*) sehr erfolgreich sein; (*person*) gut in Schuss sein; **I have no ~ feelings about it** es ist mir ziemlich egal; **they are 50 ~** sie sind insgesamt 50
strong-arm ['strɔŋɑ:m] ADJ brutal
strongbox ['strɔŋbɔks] N (Geld)kassette *f*
stronghold ['strɔŋhəuld] N Festung *f*; (*fig*) Hochburg *f*
strongly ['strɔŋlɪ] ADV (*solidly*) stabil; (*forcefully*) entschieden; (*deeply*) fest; **to feel ~ that …** fest davon überzeugt sein, dass …; **I feel ~ about it** mir liegt sehr viel daran; (*negatively*) ich bin sehr dagegen
strongman ['strɔŋmæn] N (*irreg: lit, fig*) starker Mann *m*
strongroom ['strɔŋru:m] N Tresorraum *m*
stroppy ['strɔpɪ] (BRIT *inf*) ADJ pampig; (*obstinate*) stur
strove [strəuv] PT *of* **strive**
struck [strʌk] PT, PP *of* **strike**
structural ['strʌktʃrəl] ADJ strukturell; (*damage*) baulich; (*defect*) Konstruktions-
structurally ['strʌktʃrəlɪ] ADV: **~ sound** mit guter Bausubstanz
structure ['strʌktʃəʳ] N Struktur *f*, Aufbau *m*; (*building*) Gebäude *nt*
struggle ['strʌgl] N Kampf *m*; (*difficulty*) Anstrengung *f* ▸ VI (*try hard*) sich abmühen; (*fight*) kämpfen; (*in self-defence*) sich wehren; **to**

have a ~ to do sth Mühe haben, etw zu tun; **to be a ~ for sb** jdm große Schwierigkeiten bereiten

strum [strʌm] VT *(guitar)* klimpern auf *+dat*

strung [strʌŋ] PT, PP *of* **string**

strut [strʌt] N Strebe *f*, Stütze *f* ▸ VI stolzieren

strychnine ['strɪkni:n] N Strychnin *nt*

stub [stʌb] N *(of cheque, ticket etc)* Abschnitt *m*; *(of cigarette)* Kippe *f* ▸ VT: **to ~ one's toe** sich *dat* den Zeh stoßen

▸ **stub out** VT *(cigarette)* ausdrücken

stubble ['stʌbl] N Stoppeln *pl*

stubborn ['stʌbən] ADJ hartnäckig; *(child)* störrisch

stubby ['stʌbɪ] ADJ kurz und dick

stucco ['stʌkəu] N Stuck *m*

stuck [stʌk] PT, PP *of* **stick** ▸ ADJ: **to be ~** *(jammed)* klemmen; *(unable to answer)* nicht klarkommen; **to get ~** stecken bleiben; *(fig)* nicht weiterkommen

stuck-up [stʌk'ʌp] *(inf)* ADJ hochnäsig

stud [stʌd] N *(on clothing etc)* Niete *f*; *(on collar)* Kragenknopf *m*; *(earring)* Ohrstecker *m*; *(on boot)* Stollen *m*; *(also:* **stud farm***)* Gestüt *nt*; *(also:* **stud horse***)* Zuchthengst *m* ▸ VT *(fig)*: **studded with** übersät mit; *(with jewels)* dicht besetzt mit

student ['stju:dənt] N Student(in) *m(f)*; *(at school)* Schüler(in) *m(f)* ▸ CPD Studenten-; **law/ medical ~** Jura-/Medizinstudent(in) *m(f)*; **~ nurse** Krankenpflegeschüler(in) *m(f)*; **~ teacher** Referendar(in) *m(f)*

student driver *(US)* N Fahrschüler(in) *m(f)*

students' union ['stju:dənts-] *(Brit)* N Studentenvereinigung *f*, ≈ AStA *m*; *(building)* Gebäude *nt* der Studentenvereinigung

studied ['stʌdɪd] ADJ *(expression)* einstudiert; *(attitude)* berechnet

studio ['stju:dɪəu] N Studio *nt*; *(sculptor's etc)* Atelier *nt*

studio flat, *(US)* **studio apartment** N Einzimmerwohnung *f*

studious ['stju:dɪəs] ADJ lernbegierig

studiously ['stju:dɪəslɪ] ADV *(carefully)* sorgsam

study ['stʌdɪ] N Studium *nt*, Lernen *nt*; *(room)* Arbeitszimmer *nt* ▸ VT studieren; *(face)* prüfend ansehen; *(evidence)* prüfen ▸ VI studieren, lernen; **studies** NPL *(studying)* Studien *pl*; **to make a ~ of sth** etw untersuchen; *(academic)* etw studieren; **to ~ for an exam** sich auf eine Prüfung vorbereiten

stuff [stʌf] N Zeug *nt* ▸ VT ausstopfen; *(Culin)* füllen; *(inf: push)* stopfen; **my nose is stuffed up** ich habe eine verstopfte Nase; **get stuffed!** *(inf!)* du kannst mich mal!

stuffed toy [stʌft-] N Stofftier *nt*

stuffing ['stʌfɪŋ] N Füllung *f*; *(in sofa etc)* Polstermaterial *nt*

stuffy ['stʌfɪ] ADJ *(room)* stickig; *(person, ideas)* spießig

stumble ['stʌmbl] VI stolpern; **to ~ across** *or* **on** *(fig)* (zufällig) stoßen auf *+acc*

stumbling block ['stʌmblɪŋ-] N Hürde *f*, Hindernis *nt*

stump [stʌmp] N Stumpf *m* ▸ VT: **to be stumped** überfragt sein

stun [stʌn] VT betäuben; *(news)* fassungslos machen

stung [stʌŋ] PT, PP *of* **sting**

stunk [stʌŋk] PP *of* **stink**

stunning ['stʌnɪŋ] ADJ *(news, event)* sensationell; *(girl, dress)* hinreißend

stunt [stʌnt] N *(in film)* Stunt *m*; *(publicity stunt)* (Werbe)gag *m*

stunted ['stʌntɪd] ADJ verkümmert

stuntman ['stʌntmæn] N *(irreg)* Stuntman *m*

stupefaction [stju:pɪ'fækʃən] N Verblüffung *f*

stupefy ['stju:pɪfaɪ] VT benommen machen; *(fig)* verblüffen

stupendous [stju:'pɛndəs] ADJ enorm

stupid ['stju:pɪd] ADJ dumm

stupidity [stju:'pɪdɪtɪ] N Dummheit *f*

stupidly ['stju:pɪdlɪ] ADV dumm

stupor ['stju:pər] N Benommenheit *f*; **in a ~** benommen

sturdily ['stə:dɪlɪ] ADV: **~ built** *(person)* kräftig gebaut; *(thing)* stabil gebaut

sturdy ['stə:dɪ] ADJ *(person)* kräftig; *(thing)* stabil

sturgeon ['stə:dʒən] N Stör *m*

stutter ['stʌtər] N Stottern *nt* ▸ VI stottern; **to have a ~** stottern

Stuttgart ['stutgɑ:t] N Stuttgart *nt*

sty [staɪ] N Schweinestall *m*

stye [staɪ] N Gerstenkorn *nt*

style [staɪl] N Stil *m*; *(design)* Modell *nt*; **in the latest ~** nach der neuesten Mode; **hair ~** Frisur *f*

styli ['staɪlaɪ] NPL *of* **stylus**

stylish ['staɪlɪʃ] ADJ elegant

stylist ['staɪlɪst] N *(hair stylist)* Friseur *m*, Friseuse *f*; *(literary stylist)* Stilist(in) *m(f)*

stylized ['staɪlaɪzd] ADJ stilisiert

stylus ['staɪləs] *(pl* **styli** *or* **styluses***)* N Nadel *f*

Styrofoam® ['staɪrəfəum] N ≈ Styropor® *nt*

suave [swɑ:v] ADJ zuvorkommend

sub [sʌb] N ABBR *(Naut)* = **submarine**; *(Admin)* = **subscription**; *(Brit Press)* = **subeditor**

sub... [sʌb] PREF Unter-, unter-

subcommittee ['sʌbkəmɪtɪ] N Unterausschuss *m*

subconscious [sʌb'kɔnʃəs] ADJ unterbewusst

subcontinent [sʌb'kɔntɪnənt] N: **the (Indian) ~** der (indische) Subkontinent

subcontract VT ['sʌbkən'trækt] (verträglich) weitervergeben ▸ N ['sʌb'kɔntrækt] Nebenvertrag *m*

subcontractor ['sʌbkən'træktər] N Subunternehmer *m*

subdivide [sʌbdɪ'vaɪd] VT unterteilen

subdivision ['sʌbdɪvɪʒən] N Unterteilung *f*

subdue [səb'dju:] VT unterwerfen; *(emotions)* dämpfen

subdued [səb'dju:d] ADJ *(light)* gedämpft; *(person)* bedrückt

subeditor [sʌb'ɛdɪtər] *(Brit)* N Redakteur(in) *m(f)*

S

subject [*n* 'sʌbdʒɪkt, *vt* səb'dʒɛkt] N (*matter*) Thema *nt*; (*Scol*) Fach *nt*; (*of country*) Staatsbürger(in) *m(f)*; (*Gram*) Subjekt *nt* ▶ VT: **to ~ sb to sth** jdn einer Sache *dat* unterziehen; (*expose*) jdn einer Sache *dat* aussetzen; **to change the ~** das Thema wechseln; **to be ~ to** (*law, tax*) unterworfen sein *+dat*; (*heart attacks etc*) anfällig sein für; **~ to confirmation in writing** vorausgesetzt, es wird schriftlich bestätigt
subjection [səb'dʒɛkʃən] N Unterwerfung *f*
subjective [səb'dʒɛktɪv] ADJ subjektiv
subject matter N Stoff *m*; (*content*) Inhalt *m*
sub judice [sʌb'dju:dɪsɪ] ADJ (*Law*): **to be ~** verhandelt werden
subjugate ['sʌbdʒugeɪt] VT unterwerfen
subjunctive [səb'dʒʌŋktɪv] N Konjunktiv *m*; **in the ~** im Konjunktiv
sublet [sʌb'lɛt] VT (*irreg: like* **let**) untervermieten
sublime [sə'blaɪm] ADJ erhaben, vollendet; **that's going from the ~ to the ridiculous** das ist ein Abstieg ins Profane
subliminal [sʌb'lɪmɪnl] ADJ unterschwellig
submachine gun ['sʌbmə'ʃi:n-] N Maschinenpistole *f*
submarine [sʌbmə'ri:n] N U-Boot *nt*, Unterseeboot *nt*
submerge [səb'mə:dʒ] VT untertauchen; (*flood*) überschwemmen ▶ VI tauchen; **submerged** unter Wasser
submersion [səb'mə:ʃən] N Untertauchen *nt*; (*of submarine*) Tauchen *nt*; (*by flood*) Überschwemmung *f*
submission [səb'mɪʃən] N (*subjection*) Unterwerfung *f*; (*of plan, application etc*) Einreichung *f*; (*proposal*) Vorlage *f*
submissive [səb'mɪsɪv] ADJ gehorsam; (*gesture*) demütig
submit [səb'mɪt] VT (*application etc*) einreichen; (*proposal*) vorlegen ▶ VI: **to ~ to sth** sich einer Sache *dat* unterwerfen
subnormal [sʌb'nɔ:ml] ADJ (*below average*) unterdurchschnittlich; (*old: child etc*) minderbegabt; **educationally ~** lernbehindert
subordinate [sə'bɔ:dɪnət] N Untergebene(r) *f(m)*; (*Ling*): **~ clause** Nebensatz *m* ▶ ADJ untergeordnet; **to be ~ to sb** jdm untergeordnet sein
subpoena [səb'pi:nə] N (*Law*) Vorladung *f* ▶ VT vorladen
subprime ['sʌbpraɪm] ADJ (*borrower, loan*) risikoreich; **~ mortgage** Subprime-Hypothek *f*
subroutine [sʌbru:'ti:n] N (*Comput*) Unterprogramm *nt*
subscribe [səb'skraɪb] VI spenden; **to ~ to** (*magazine etc*) abonnieren; (*opinion, theory*) sich anschließen *+dat*; (*fund, charity*) regelmäßig spenden an *+acc*
subscriber [səb'skraɪbə^r] N (*to magazine*) Abonnent(in) *m(f)*; (*Tel*) Teilnehmer(in) *m(f)*
subscript ['sʌbskrɪpt] N tiefgestelltes Zeichen *nt*
subscription [səb'skrɪpʃən] N (*to magazine etc*) Abonnement *nt*; (*membership dues*) (Mitglieds)beitrag *m*; **to take out a ~ to** (*magazine etc*) abonnieren
subsequent ['sʌbsɪkwənt] ADJ nachfolgend, später; (*further*) weiter; **~ to** im Anschluss an *+acc*
subsequently ['sʌbsɪkwəntlɪ] ADV später
subservient [səb'sə:vɪənt] ADJ unterwürfig; (*less important*) untergeordnet; **to be ~ to** untergeordnet sein *+dat*
subside [səb'saɪd] VI (*flood*) sinken; (*earth*) sich senken; (*feeling, pain*) nachlassen
subsidence [səb'saɪdns] N Senkung *f*
subsidiarity [səbsɪdɪ'ærɪtɪ] N Subsidiarität *f*
subsidiary [səb'sɪdɪərɪ] ADJ (*question, role, Brit: Scol: subject*) Neben- ▶ N (*also:* **subsidiary company**) Tochtergesellschaft *f*
subsidize ['sʌbsɪdaɪz] VT subventionieren
subsidy ['sʌbsɪdɪ] N Subvention *f*
subsist [səb'sɪst] VI: **to ~ on sth** sich von etw ernähren
subsistence [səb'sɪstəns] N Existenz *f*; **enough for ~** genug zum (Über)leben
subsistence allowance N Unterhaltszuschuss *m*
subsistence level N Existenzminimum *nt*
substance ['sʌbstəns] N Substanz *f*, Stoff *m*; (*fig: essence*) Kern *m*; **a man of ~** ein vermögender Mann; **to lack ~** (*book*) keine Substanz haben; (*argument*) keine Durchschlagskraft haben
substance abuse N *Missbrauch von Alkohol, Drogen, Arzneimitteln etc*
substandard [sʌb'stændəd] ADJ minderwertig; (*housing*) unzulänglich
substantial [səb'stænʃl] ADJ (*solid*) solide; (*considerable*) beträchtlich, größere(r, s); (*meal*) kräftig
substantially [səb'stænʃəlɪ] ADV erheblich; (*in essence*) im Wesentlichen
substantiate [səb'stænʃɪeɪt] VT erhärten, untermauern
substitute ['sʌbstɪtju:t] N Ersatz *m* ▶ VT: **to ~ A for B** B durch A ersetzen
substitute teacher (*US*) N Vertretung *f*
substitution [sʌbstɪ'tju:ʃən] N Ersetzen *nt*; (*Football*) Auswechseln *nt*
subterfuge ['sʌbtəfju:dʒ] N Tricks *pl*; (*trickery*) Täuschung *f*
subterranean [sʌbtə'reɪnɪən] ADJ unterirdisch
subtitle ['sʌbtaɪtl] N Untertitel *m*
subtle ['sʌtl] ADJ fein; (*indirect*) raffiniert
subtlety ['sʌtltɪ] N Feinheit *f*; (*art of being subtle*) Finesse *f*
subtly ['sʌtlɪ] ADV (*change, vary*) leicht; (*different*) auf subtile Weise; (*persuade*) raffiniert
subtotal [sʌb'təutl] N Zwischensumme *f*
subtract [səb'trækt] VT abziehen, subtrahieren
subtraction [səb'trækʃən] N Abziehen *nt*, Subtraktion *f*
subtropical [sʌb'trɔpɪkl] ADJ subtropisch
suburb ['sʌbə:b] N Vorort *m*
suburban [sə'bə:bən] ADJ (*train etc*) Vorort-; (*lifestyle etc*) spießig, kleinbürgerlich
suburbia [sə'bə:bɪə] N die Vororte *pl*

subvention [səb'vɛnʃən] N Subvention *f*
subversion [səb'və:ʃən] N Subversion *f*
subversive [səb'və:sɪv] ADJ subversiv
subway ['sʌbweɪ] N (*US*) U-Bahn *f*, Untergrundbahn *f*; (BRIT: *underpass*) Unterführung *f*
sub-zero [sʌb'zɪərəu] ADJ: **~ temperatures** Temperaturen unter null
succeed [sək'si:d] VI (*person*) erfolgreich sein, Erfolg haben; (*plan etc*) gelingen, erfolgreich sein ▸ VT (*in job*) Nachfolger werden *+gen*; (*in order*) folgen *+dat*; **he succeeded in doing it** es gelang ihm(, es zu tun)
succeeding [sək'si:dɪŋ] ADJ folgend; **~ generations** spätere *or* nachfolgende Generationen *pl*
success [sək'sɛs] N Erfolg *m*; **without ~** ohne Erfolg, erfolglos
successful [sək'sɛsful] ADJ erfolgreich; **to be ~** erfolgreich sein, Erfolg haben; **sb is ~ in doing sth** es gelingt jdm, etw zu tun
successfully [sək'sɛsfəlɪ] ADV erfolgreich, mit Erfolg
succession [sək'sɛʃən] N Folge *f*, Serie *f*; (*to throne etc*) Nachfolge *f*; **3 years in ~** 3 Jahre nacheinander *or* hintereinander
successive [sək'sɛsɪv] ADJ aufeinanderfolgend; **on 3 ~ days** 3 Tage nacheinander *or* hintereinander
successor [sək'sɛsə^r] N Nachfolger(in) *m(f)*
succinct [sək'sɪŋkt] ADJ knapp, prägnant
succulent ['sʌkjulənt] ADJ saftig ▸ N Fettpflanze *f*, Sukkulente *f*
succumb [sə'kʌm] VI: **to ~ to** (*temptation*) erliegen *+dat*; (*illness: become affected by*) bekommen; (*: die of*) erliegen *+dat*
such [sʌtʃ] ADJ (*of that kind*): **~ a book** so ein Buch; (*so much*): **~ courage** so viel Mut; (*emphasizing similarity*): **or some ~ place/name** *etc* oder so ähnlich ▸ ADV so; **~ books** solche Bücher; **~ a lot of** so viel; **she made ~ a noise that …** sie machte so einen Lärm, dass …; **~ books as I have** was ich an Büchern habe; **I said no ~ thing** das habe ich nie gesagt; **~ a long trip** so eine lange Reise; **~ as** wie (zum Beispiel); **as ~** an sich
such-and-such ['sʌtʃənsʌtʃ] ADJ die und die, der und der, das und das
suchlike ['sʌtʃlaɪk] (*inf*) PRON: **and ~** und dergleichen
suck [sʌk] VT (*sweet etc*) lutschen; (*pump, machine*) saugen; (*ice-lolly*) lutschen an *+dat*; (*baby*) saugen an *+dat*
sucker ['sʌkə^r] N (*Zool*) Saugnapf *m*; (*Tech*) Saugfuß *m*; (*Bot*) unterirdischer Ausläufer *m*; (*inf*) Dummkopf *m*
suckle ['sʌkl] VT (*baby*) stillen; (*animal*) säugen
sucrose ['su:krəuz] N (pflanzlicher) Zucker *m*
suction ['sʌkʃən] N Saugwirkung *f*
suction pump N Saugpumpe *f*
Sudan [su'dɑ:n] N der Sudan
Sudanese [su:də'ni:z] ADJ sudanesisch ▸ N Sudanese *m*, Sudanesin *f*
sudden ['sʌdn] ADJ plötzlich; **all of a ~** ganz plötzlich
sudden death N (*also*: **sudden-death play-off**) Stichkampf *m*
suddenly ['sʌdnlɪ] ADV plötzlich
sudoku [sʊ'dəʊku:] N Sudoku *nt*
suds [sʌdz] NPL Seifenschaum *m*
sue [su:] VT verklagen ▸ VI klagen, vor Gericht gehen; **to ~ sb for damages** jdn auf Schadenersatz verklagen; **to ~ for divorce** die Scheidung einreichen
suede [sweɪd] N Wildleder *nt* ▸ CPD Wildleder-
suet ['suɪt] N Nierenfett *nt*
Suez ['su:ɪz] N: **the ~ Canal** der Suezkanal
Suff. (BRIT) ABBR (*Post*) = **Suffolk**
suffer ['sʌfə^r] VT erleiden; (*rudeness etc*) ertragen ▸ VI leiden; **to ~ from** leiden an *+dat*; **to ~ the effects of sth** an den Folgen von etw leiden
sufferance ['sʌfərns] N: **he was only there on ~** er wurde dort nur geduldet
sufferer ['sʌfərə^r] N Leidende(r) *f(m)*
suffering ['sʌfərɪŋ] N Leid *nt*
suffice [sə'faɪs] VI genügen
sufficient [sə'fɪʃənt] ADJ ausreichend; **~ money** genug Geld
sufficiently [sə'fɪʃəntlɪ] ADV ausreichend, genug; **~ powerful/enthusiastic** mächtig/begeistert genug
suffix ['sʌfɪks] N Suffix *nt*, Nachsilbe *f*
suffocate ['sʌfəkeɪt] VI (*lit, fig*) ersticken
suffocation [sʌfə'keɪʃən] N Ersticken *nt*
suffrage ['sʌfrɪdʒ] N Wahlrecht *nt*
suffragette [sʌfrə'dʒɛt] N Suffragette *f*
suffused [sə'fju:zd] ADJ: **~ with** erfüllt von; **~ with light** lichtdurchflutet
sugar ['ʃugə^r] N Zucker *m* ▸ VT zuckern
sugar beet N Zuckerrübe *f*
sugar bowl N Zuckerdose *f*
sugar cane N Zuckerrohr *nt*
sugar-coated ['ʃugə'kəutɪd] ADJ mit Zucker überzogen
sugar lump N Zuckerstück *nt*
sugar refinery N Zuckerraffinerie *f*
sugary ['ʃugərɪ] ADJ süß; (*fig: smile, phrase*) süßlich
suggest [sə'dʒɛst] VT vorschlagen; (*indicate*) andeuten, hindeuten auf *+acc*; **what do you ~ I do?** was schlagen Sie vor?
suggestion [sə'dʒɛstʃən] N Vorschlag *m*; (*indication*) Anflug *m*; (*trace*) Spur *f*
suggestive [sə'dʒɛstɪv] (*pej*) ADJ anzüglich
suicidal [suɪ'saɪdl] ADJ selbstmörderisch; (*person*) selbstmordgefährdet; **to be** *or* **feel ~** Selbstmordgedanken haben
suicide ['suɪsaɪd] N (*lit, fig*) Selbstmord *m*; (*person*) Selbstmörder(in) *m(f)*; *see also* **commit**
suicide attack N Selbstmordanschlag *m*
suicide attacker N Selbstmordattentäter(in) *m(f)*
suicide attempt, suicide bid N Selbstmordversuch *m*
suicide bomber N Selbstmordattentäter(in) *m(f)*

S

suit [su:t] N (*man's*) Anzug *m*; (*woman's*) Kostüm *nt*; (*Cards*) Farbe *f*; (*Law*) Prozess *m*, Verfahren *nt* ▶ VT passen *+dat*; (*colour, clothes*) stehen *+dat*; **to bring a ~ against sb** (*Law*) gegen jdn Klage erheben *or* einen Prozess anstrengen; **to follow ~** (*fig*) das Gleiche tun; **to ~ sth to** etw anpassen an *+acc*; **to be suited to do sth** sich dafür eignen, etw zu tun; **~ yourself!** wie du willst!; **well suited** (*couple*) gut zusammenpassend
suitability [su:tə'bɪlɪtɪ] N Eignung *f*
suitable ['su:təbl] ADJ (*appropriate*) geeignet; (*convenient*) passend; **would tomorrow be ~?** würde Ihnen morgen passen?; **Monday isn't ~** Montag passt nicht; **we found somebody ~** wir haben jemand Passenden gefunden
suitably ['su:təblɪ] ADV passend; (*impressed*) gebührend
suitcase ['su:tkeɪs] N Koffer *m*
suite [swi:t] N (*of rooms*) Suite *f*, Zimmerflucht *f*; (*Mus*) Suite *f*; **bedroom/dining room ~** Schlafzimmer-/Esszimmereinrichtung *f*; **a three-piece ~** eine dreiteilige Polstergarnitur
suitor ['su:tə^r] N Kläger(in) *m(f)*
sulfate ['sʌlfeɪt] (*US*) N = **sulphate**
sulfur ['sʌlfə^r] (*US*) N = **sulphur**
sulfuric [sʌl'fjuərɪk] (*US*) ADJ = **sulphuric**
sulk [sʌlk] VI schmollen
sulky ['sʌlkɪ] ADJ schmollend
sullen ['sʌlən] ADJ mürrisch, verdrossen
sulphate, (*US*) **sulfate** ['sʌlfeɪt] N Sulfat *nt*, schwefelsaures Salz *nt*
sulphur, (*US*) **sulfur** ['sʌlfə^r] N Schwefel *m*
sulphur dioxide N Schwefeldioxid *nt*
sulphuric, (*US*) **sulfuric** [sʌl'fjuərɪk] ADJ: **~ acid** Schwefelsäure *f*
sultan ['sʌltən] N Sultan *m*
sultana [sʌl'tɑ:nə] N Sultanine *f*
sultry ['sʌltrɪ] ADJ schwül
sum [sʌm] N (*calculation*) Rechenaufgabe *f*; (*amount*) Summe *f*, Betrag *m*
▶ **sum up** VT zusammenfassen; (*evaluate rapidly*) einschätzen ▶ VI zusammenfassen
Sumatra [su'mɑ:trə] N Sumatra *nt*
summarize ['sʌməraɪz] VT zusammenfassen
summary ['sʌmərɪ] N Zusammenfassung *f* ▶ ADJ (*justice, executions*) im Schnellverfahren
summer ['sʌmə^r] N Sommer *m* ▶ CPD Sommer-; **in ~** im Sommer
summer camp (*US*) N Ferienlager *nt*
summer holidays NPL Sommerferien *pl*
summerhouse ['sʌməhaus] N (*in garden*) Gartenhaus *nt*, Gartenlaube *f*
summertime ['sʌmətaɪm] N Sommer *m*, Sommerszeit *f*
summery ['sʌmərɪ] ADJ sommerlich
summing-up [sʌmɪŋ'ʌp] N (*Law*) Resümee *nt*
summit ['sʌmɪt] N Gipfel *m*; (*also*: **summit conference/meeting**) Gipfelkonferenz *f*/-treffen *nt*
summon ['sʌmən] VT rufen, kommen lassen; (*help*) holen; (*meeting*) einberufen; (*Law*: *witness*) vorladen
▶ **summon up** VT aufbringen
summons ['sʌmənz] N (*Law*) Vorladung *f*; (*fig*) Aufruf *m* ▶ VT (*Law*) vorladen; **to serve a ~ on sb** jdn vor Gericht laden
sumo ['su:məu], **sumo wrestling** N Sumo(-Ringen) *nt*
sump [sʌmp] (BRIT) N Ölwanne *f*
sumptuous ['sʌmptjuəs] ADJ (*meal*) üppig; (*costume*) aufwendig
sun [sʌn] N Sonne *f*; **to catch the ~** einen Sonnenbrand bekommen; **everything under the ~** alles Mögliche
Sun. ABBR (= *Sunday*) So.
sunbathe ['sʌnbeɪð] VI sich sonnen
sunbeam ['sʌnbi:m] N Sonnenstrahl *m*
sunbed ['sʌnbɛd] N (*with sun lamp*) Sonnenbank *f*
sunblock N Sonnenschutzcreme *f*
sunburn ['sʌnbə:n] N Sonnenbrand *m*
sunburned ['sʌnbə:nd] ADJ = **sunburnt**
sunburnt ['sʌnbə:nt] ADJ sonnenverbrannt, sonnengebräunt; **to be ~** (*painfully*) einen Sonnenbrand haben
sun-cream ['sʌnkri:m] N Sonnencreme *f*
sundae ['sʌndeɪ] N Eisbecher *m*
Sunday ['sʌndɪ] N Sonntag *m*; *see also* **Tuesday**
Sunday paper N Sonntagszeitung *f*

> Die **Sunday papers** umfassen sowohl Massenblätter als auch seriöse Zeitungen. „The Observer" ist die älteste überregionale Sonntagszeitung der Welt. Die Sonntagszeitungen sind alle sehr umfangreich mit vielen Farb- und Sonderbeilagen. Zu den meisten Tageszeitungen gibt es parallele Sonntagsblätter, die aber separate Redaktionen haben.

Sunday school N Sonntagsschule *f*
sundial ['sʌndaɪəl] N Sonnenuhr *f*
sundown ['sʌndaun] (*esp US*) N Sonnenuntergang *m*
sundries ['sʌndrɪz] NPL Verschiedenes *nt*
sundry ['sʌndrɪ] ADJ verschiedene; **all and ~** jedermann
sunflower ['sʌnflauə^r] N Sonnenblume *f*
sunflower oil N Sonnenblumenöl *nt*
sung [sʌŋ] PP *of* **sing**
sunglasses ['sʌnglɑ:sɪz] NPL Sonnenbrille *f*
sunk [sʌŋk] PP *of* **sink**
sunken ['sʌŋkn] ADJ versunken; (*eyes*) tief liegend; (*cheeks*) eingefallen; (*bath*) eingelassen
sunlamp ['sʌnlæmp] N Höhensonne *f*
sunlight ['sʌnlaɪt] N Sonnenlicht *nt*
sunlit ['sʌnlɪt] ADJ sonnig, sonnenbeschienen
sunny ['sʌnɪ] ADJ sonnig; (*fig*) heiter
sunrise ['sʌnraɪz] N Sonnenaufgang *m*
sun roof N (*Aut*) Schiebedach *nt*; (*on building*) Sonnenterrasse *f*
sun screen N Sonnenschutzmittel *nt*
sunset ['sʌnsɛt] N Sonnenuntergang *m*
sunshade ['sʌnʃeɪd] N Sonnenschirm *m*
sunshine ['sʌnʃaɪn] N Sonnenschein *m*
sunspot ['sʌnspɔt] N Sonnenfleck *m*
sunstroke ['sʌnstrəuk] N Sonnenstich *m*

suntan ['sʌntæn] N (Sonnen)bräune *f*; **to get a ~** braun werden
suntan lotion N Sonnenmilch *f*
suntanned ['sʌntænd] ADJ braun (gebrannt)
suntan oil N Sonnenöl *nt*
suntrap ['sʌntræp] N sonniges Eckchen *nt*
super ['su:pəʳ] (*inf*) ADJ toll, fantastisch
superannuation [su:pərænju'eɪʃən] N Beitrag *m* zur Rentenversicherung
superb [su:'pə:b] ADJ ausgezeichnet, großartig; (*meal*) vorzüglich
Super Bowl N Superbowl *m*, Super Bowl *m*, *American-Football-Turnier zwischen den Spitzenreitern der Nationalligen*
supercilious [su:pə'sɪlɪəs] ADJ herablassend
superconductor [su:pəkən'dʌktəʳ] N (*Phys*) Superleiter *m*
superficial [su:pə'fɪʃəl] ADJ oberflächlich
superficially [su:pə'fɪʃəlɪ] ADV oberflächlich; (*from a superficial point of view*) oberflächlich gesehen
superfluous [su'pə:fluəs] ADJ überflüssig
superglue ['su:pəglu:] N Sekundenkleber *m*
superhighway (*US*) N ≈ Autobahn *f*; **information ~** Datenautobahn *f*
superhuman [su:pə'hju:mən] ADJ übermenschlich
superimpose ['su:pərɪm'pəuz] VT (*two things*) übereinanderlegen; **to ~ on** legen auf *+acc*; **to ~ with** überlagern mit
superintend [su:pərɪn'tɛnd] VT beaufsichtigen, überwachen
superintendent [su:pərɪn'tɛndənt] N Aufseher(in) *m(f)*; (*Police*) Kommissar(in) *m(f)*
superior [su'pɪərɪəʳ] ADJ besser, überlegen *+dat*; (*more senior*) höhergestellt; (*smug*) überheblich; (*: smile*) überlegen ▶ N Vorgesetzte(r) *f(m)*; **Mother S~** (*Rel*) Mutter Oberin
superiority [supɪərɪ'ɔrɪtɪ] N Überlegenheit *f*
superlative [su'pə:lətɪv] N Superlativ *m* ▶ ADJ überragend
superman ['su:pəmæn] N (*irreg*) Übermensch *m*
supermarket ['su:pəmɑ:kɪt] N Supermarkt *m*
supermodel ['su:pəmɔdl] N Supermodell *nt*
supernatural [su:pə'nætʃərəl] ADJ übernatürlich ▶ N: **the ~** das Übernatürliche
supernova [su:pə'nəuvə] N Supernova *f*
superpower ['su:pəpauəʳ] N Supermacht *f*
superscript ['su:pəskrɪpt] N hochgestelltes Zeichen *nt*
supersede [su:pə'si:d] VT ablösen, ersetzen
supersonic ['su:pə'sɔnɪk] ADJ (*aircraft etc*) Überschall-
superstar ['su:pəstɑ:ʳ] N Superstar *m*
superstition [su:pə'stɪʃən] N Aberglaube *m*
superstitious [su:pə'stɪʃəs] ADJ abergläubisch
superstore ['su:pəstɔ:ʳ] (BRIT) N Großmarkt *m*
supertanker ['su:pətæŋkəʳ] N Supertanker *m*
supertax ['su:pətæks] N Höchststeuer *f*
supervise ['su:pəvaɪz] VT beaufsichtigen
supervision [su:pə'vɪʒən] N Beaufsichtigung *f*; **under medical ~** unter ärztlicher Aufsicht
supervisor ['su:pəvaɪzəʳ] N Aufseher(in) *m(f)*; (*of students*) Tutor(in) *m(f)*
supervisory ['su:pəvaɪzərɪ] ADJ beaufsichtigend, Aufsichts-
supine ['su:paɪn] ADJ: **to be ~** auf dem Rücken liegen ▶ ADV auf dem Rücken
supper ['sʌpəʳ] N Abendessen *nt*; **to have ~** zu Abend essen
supplant [sə'plɑ:nt] VT ablösen, ersetzen
supple ['sʌpl] ADJ geschmeidig; (*person*) gelenkig
supplement ['sʌplɪmənt] N Zusatz *m*; (*of newspaper etc*) Beilage *f*; (*of book*) Ergänzungsband *m* ▶ VT ergänzen
supplementary [sʌplɪ'mɛntərɪ] ADJ zusätzlich, ergänzend
supplementary benefit (BRIT: *old*) N ≈ Sozialhilfe *f*
supplementary budget N (*Pol*) ≈ Nachtragshaushalt *m or* -etat *m*
supplier [sə'plaɪəʳ] N Lieferant(in) *m(f)*
supply [sə'plaɪ] VT liefern; (*provide*) sorgen für; (*a need*) befriedigen ▶ N Vorrat *m*; (*supplying*) Lieferung *f*; **supplies** NPL (*food*) Vorräte *pl*; (*Mil*) Nachschub *m*; **to ~ sth to sb** jdm etw liefern; **to ~ sth with sth** etw mit etw versorgen; **it comes supplied with an adaptor** es wird mit einem Adapter geliefert; **office supplies** Bürobedarf *m*; **to be in short ~** knapp sein; **the electricity/water/gas ~** die Strom-/Wasser-/Gasversorgung *f*; **~ and demand** Angebot *nt* und Nachfrage
supply teacher (BRIT) N Vertretung *f*
support [sə'pɔ:t] N Unterstützung *f*; (*Tech*) Stütze *f* ▶ VT unterstützen, eintreten für; (*financially: family etc*) unterhalten; (*: party etc*) finanziell unterstützen; (*Tech*) (ab)stützen; (*theory etc*) untermauern; **they stopped work in ~ of ...** sie sind in den Streik getreten, um für ... einzutreten; **to ~ o.s.** (*financially*) finanziell unabhängig sein; **to ~ Arsenal** Arsenal-Fan sein
supporter [sə'pɔ:təʳ] N (*Pol etc*) Anhänger(in) *m(f)*; (*Sport*) Fan *m*
supporting [sə'pɔ:tɪŋ] ADJ: **~ role** Nebenrolle *f*; **~ actor** Schauspieler *m* in einer Nebenrolle; **~ film** Vorfilm *m*
supportive [sə'pɔ:tɪv] ADJ hilfreich; **to be ~ of sb/sth** jdn/etw unterstützen
suppose [sə'pəuz] VT annehmen, glauben; (*imagine*) sich *dat* vorstellen; **to be supposed to do sth** etw tun sollen; **it was worse than she'd supposed** es war schlimmer, als sie es sich vorgestellt hatte; **I don't ~ she'll come** ich glaube kaum, dass sie kommt; **he's about sixty, I ~** er muss wohl so um die Sechzig sein; **he's supposed to be an expert** er ist angeblich ein Experte; **I ~ so/not** ich glaube schon/nicht
supposedly [sə'pəuzɪdlɪ] ADV angeblich
supposing [sə'pəuzɪŋ] CONJ angenommen
supposition [sʌpə'zɪʃən] N Annahme *f*
suppository [sə'pɔzɪtrɪ] N Zäpfchen *nt*
suppress [sə'prɛs] VT unterdrücken; (*publication*) verbieten
suppression [sə'prɛʃən] N Unterdrückung *f*

S

suppressor [sə'presəʳ] N (*Elec etc*) Entstörungselement *nt*
supremacy [su'preməsi] N Vormachtstellung *f*
supreme [su'pri:m] ADJ Ober-, oberste(r, s); (*effort*) äußerste(r, s); (*achievement*) höchste(r, s)
Supreme Court (US) N Oberster Gerichtshof *m*
supremo [su'pri:məu] (BRIT *inf*) N Boss *m*
Supt ABBR (*Police*) = **superintendent**
surcharge ['sə:tʃɑ:dʒ] N Zuschlag *m*
sure [ʃuəʳ] ADJ sicher; (*reliable*) zuverlässig, sicher ▶ ADV (*inf: esp US*): **that ~ is pretty, that's ~ pretty** das ist aber schön; **to make ~ of sth** sich einer Sache *gen* vergewissern; **to make ~ that** sich vergewissern, dass; **I'm ~ of it** ich bin mir da sicher; **I'm not ~ how/why/when** ich bin mir nicht sicher *or* ich weiß nicht genau, wie/warum/wann; **to be ~ of o.s.** selbstsicher sein; **~!** klar!; **~ enough** tatsächlich
sure-fire ['ʃuəfaɪəʳ] (*inf*) ADJ todsicher
sure-footed [ʃuə'futɪd] ADJ trittsicher
surely ['ʃuəlɪ] ADV sicherlich, bestimmt; **~ you don't mean that!** das meinen Sie doch bestimmt *or* sicher nicht (so)!
surety ['ʃuərətɪ] N Bürgschaft *f*, Sicherheit *f*; **to go** *or* **stand ~ for sb** für jdn bürgen
surf [sə:f] N Brandung *f*
surface ['sə:fɪs] N Oberfläche *f* ▶ VT (*road*) mit einem Belag versehen ▶ VI (*lit, fig*) auftauchen; (*feeling*) hochkommen; (*rise from bed*) hochkommen; **on the ~** (*fig*) oberflächlich betrachtet
surface area N Fläche *f*
surface mail N Post *f* auf dem Land-/Seeweg
surface-to-surface ['sə:fɪstə'sə:fɪs] ADJ (*missile*) Boden-Boden-
surfboard ['sə:fbɔ:d] N Surfbrett *nt*
surfeit ['sə:fɪt] N: **a ~ of** ein Übermaß an *+dat*
surfer ['sə:fəʳ] N Surfer(in) *m(f)*
surfing ['sə:fɪŋ] N Surfen *nt*; **to go ~** surfen gehen
surge [sə:dʒ] N Anstieg *m*; (*fig: of emotion*) Woge *f*; (*Elec*) Spannungsstoß *m* ▶ VI (*water*) branden; (*people*) sich drängen; (*vehicles*) sich wälzen; (*emotion*) aufwallen; (*Elec: power*) ansteigen; **to ~ forward** nach vorne drängen
surgeon ['sə:dʒən] N Chirurg(in) *m(f)*
Surgeon General (US) N (*Med*) ≈ Gesundheitsminister(in) *m(f)*; (*Mil*) Sanitätsinspekteur(in) *m(f)*
surgery ['sə:dʒərɪ] N Chirurgie *f*; (BRIT: *room*) Sprechzimmer *nt*; (: *building*) Praxis *f*; (*of doctor, MP etc: also*: **surgery hours**) Sprechstunde *f*; **to have ~** operiert werden; **to need ~** operiert werden müssen
surgical ['sə:dʒɪkl] ADJ chirurgisch; (*treatment*) operativ
surgical spirit (BRIT) N Wundbenzin *nt*
surly ['sə:lɪ] ADJ verdrießlich, mürrisch
surmise [sə:'maɪz] VT vermuten, mutmaßen
surmount [sə:'maunt] VT (*fig*) überwinden
surname ['sə:neɪm] N Nachname *m*
surpass [sə:'pɑ:s] VT übertreffen
surplus ['sə:pləs] N Überschuss *m* ▶ ADJ überschüssig; **it is ~ to our requirements** das benötigen wir nicht
surprise [sə'praɪz] N Überraschung *f* ▶ VT überraschen; (*astonish*) erstaunen; (*army*) überrumpeln; (*thief*) ertappen; **to take sb by ~** jdn überraschen
surprising [sə'praɪzɪŋ] ADJ überraschend; (*situation*) erstaunlich; **it is ~ how/that** es ist erstaunlich, wie/dass
surprisingly [sə'praɪzɪŋlɪ] ADV überraschend, erstaunlich; **(somewhat) ~, he agreed** erstaunlicherweise war er damit einverstanden
surrealism [sə'rɪəlɪzəm] N Surrealismus *m*
surrealist [sə'rɪəlɪst] ADJ surrealistisch
surrender [sə'rendəʳ] VI sich ergeben ▶ VT aufgeben ▶ N Kapitulation *f*
surrender value N Rückkaufswert *m*
surreptitious [sʌrəp'tɪʃəs] ADJ heimlich, verstohlen
surrogate ['sʌrəgɪt] N Ersatz *m* ▶ ADJ (*parents*) Ersatz-
surrogate mother N Leihmutter *f*
surround [sə'raund] VT umgeben; (*Mil, Police etc*) umstellen
surrounding [sə'raundɪŋ] ADJ umliegend; **the ~ area** die Umgebung
surroundings [sə'raundɪŋz] NPL Umgebung *f*
surtax ['sə:tæks] N Steuerzuschlag *m*
surveillance [sə:'veɪləns] N Überwachung *f*; **to be under ~** überwacht werden
survey ['sə:veɪ] N (*of land*) Vermessung *f*; (*of house*) Begutachtung *f*; (*investigation*) Untersuchung *f*; (*report*) Gutachten *nt*; (*comprehensive view*) Überblick *m* ▶ VT (*land*) vermessen; (*house*) inspizieren; (*look at*) betrachten
surveying [sə'veɪɪŋ] N (*of land*) Vermessung *f*
surveyor [sə'veɪəʳ] N (*of land*) Landvermesser(in) *m(f)*; (*of house*) Baugutachter(in) *m(f)*
survival [sə'vaɪvl] N Überleben *nt*; (*relic*) Überbleibsel *nt*; **~ course/kit** Überlebenstraining *nt*/-ausrüstung *f*; **~ bag** Expeditionsschlafsack *m*
survive [sə'vaɪv] VI überleben; (*custom etc*) weiter bestehen ▶ VT überleben
survivor [sə'vaɪvəʳ] N Überlebende(r) *f(m)*
susceptible [sə'septəbl] ADJ: **~ (to)** anfällig (für); (*influenced by*) empfänglich (für)
sushi ['su:ʃɪ] N Sushi *nt*
suspect ['sʌspekt] ADJ verdächtig ▶ N Verdächtige(r) *f(m)* ▶ VT: **to ~ sb of** jdn verdächtigen *+gen*; (*think*) vermuten; (*doubt*) bezweifeln
suspected [səs'pektɪd] ADJ (*terrorist etc*) mutmaßlich; **he is a ~ member of this organization** er steht im Verdacht, Mitglied dieser Organisation zu sein
suspend [səs'pend] VT (*hang*) (auf)hängen; (*delay, stop*) einstellen; (*from employment*) suspendieren; **to be suspended (from)** (*hang*) hängen (an *+dat*)

suspended animation [səs'pɛndɪd-] N *vorübergehender Stillstand aller Körperfunktionen*
suspended sentence [səs'pɛndɪd-] N (*Law*) zur Bewährung ausgesetzte Strafe *f*
suspender belt [səs'pɛndəʳ-] N Strumpfhaltergürtel *m*
suspenders [səs'pɛndəz] NPL (BRIT) Strumpfhalter *pl*; (US) Hosenträger *pl*
suspense [səs'pɛns] N Spannung *f*; (*uncertainty*) Ungewissheit *f*; **to keep sb in ~** jdn auf die Folter spannen
suspension [səs'pɛnʃən] N (*from job*) Suspendierung *f*; (*from team*) Sperrung *f*; (*Aut*) Federung *f*; (*of driving licence*) zeitweiliger Entzug *m*; (*of payment*) zeitweilige Einstellung *f*
suspension bridge N Hängebrücke *f*
suspicion [səs'pɪʃən] N Verdacht *m*; (*distrust*) Misstrauen *nt*; (*trace*) Spur *f*; **to be under ~** unter Verdacht stehen; **arrested on ~ of murder** wegen Mordverdacht(s) festgenommen
suspicious [səs'pɪʃəs] ADJ (*suspecting*) misstrauisch; (*causing suspicion*) verdächtig; **to be ~ of** *or* **about sb/sth** jdn/etw mit Misstrauen betrachten
suss out [sʌs-] (BRIT *inf*) VT (*discover*) rauskriegen; (*understand*) durchschauen
sustain [səs'teɪn] VT (*continue*) aufrechterhalten; (*food, drink*) bei Kräften halten; (*suffer: injury*) erleiden
sustainable [səs'teɪnəbl] ADJ: **to be ~** aufrechtzuerhalten sein; **~ growth** stetiges Wachstum *nt*
sustained [səs'teɪnd] ADJ (*effort*) ausdauernd; (*attack*) anhaltend
sustenance ['sʌstɪnəns] N Nahrung *f*
suture ['su:tʃəʳ] N Naht *f*
SUV ABBR (= *sport utility vehicle*) SUV *m*, Geländewagen *m*
SVQ N ABBR (= *Scottish Vocational Qualification*) *Qualifikation für berufsbegleitende Ausbildungsinhalte in Schottland*
SW ABBR (= *south-west*) SW; (*Radio*: = *short-wave*) KW
swab [swɔb] N (*Med*) Tupfer *m* ▸ VT (*Naut*: *also*: **swab down**) wischen
swagger ['swægəʳ] VI stolzieren
swallow ['swɔləu] N (*bird*) Schwalbe *f*; (*of food, drink etc*) Schluck *m* ▸ VT (herunter)schlucken; (*fig: story, insult, one's pride*) schlucken; **to ~ one's words** (*speak indistinctly*) seine Worte verschlucken; (*retract*) alles zurücknehmen
▸ **swallow up** VT verschlingen
swam [swæm] PT *of* **swim**
swamp [swɔmp] N Sumpf *m* ▸ VT (*lit, fig*) überschwemmen
swampy ['swɔmpɪ] ADJ sumpfig
swan [swɔn] N Schwan *m*
swank [swæŋk] (*inf*) VI angeben
swan song N (*fig*) Schwanengesang *m*
swap [swɔp] VT: **to ~ (for)** (ein)tauschen (gegen) ▸ N Tausch *m*
SWAPO ['swɑ:pəu] N ABBR (= *South-West Africa People's Organization*) SWAPO *f*
swarm [swɔ:m] N Schwarm *m*; (*of people*) Schar *f* ▸ VI (*bees, people*) schwärmen; **to be swarming with** wimmeln von
swarthy ['swɔ:ðɪ] ADJ (*person, face*) dunkelhäutig; (*complexion*) dunkel
swastika ['swɔstɪkə] N Hakenkreuz *nt*
SWAT (US) N ABBR (= *Special Weapons and Tactics*): **~ team** ≈ schnelle Eingreiftruppe *f*
swat [swɔt] VT totschlagen ▸ N (BRIT: *also*: **fly swat**) Fliegenklatsche *f*
swathe [sweɪð] VT: **to ~ in** wickeln in *+acc*
swatter ['swɔtəʳ] N (*also*: **fly swatter**) Fliegenklatsche *f*
sway [sweɪ] VI schwanken ▸ VT (*influence*) beeinflussen ▸ N: **to hold ~** herrschen; **to hold ~ over sb** jdn beherrschen *or* in seiner Macht haben
swear [swɛəʳ] (*pt* **swore**, *pp* **sworn**) VI (*curse*) fluchen ▸ VT (*promise*) schwören; **to ~ an oath** einen Eid ablegen
▸ **swear in** VT vereidigen
swear by VT (*have faith in*) schwören auf *+acc*
swearword ['swɛəwə:d] N Fluch *m*, Kraftausdruck *m*
sweat [swɛt] N Schweiß *m* ▸ VI schwitzen; **to be in a ~** schwitzen
sweatband ['swɛtbænd] N Schweißband *nt*
sweater ['swɛtəʳ] N Pullover *m*
sweatshirt ['swɛtʃə:t] N Sweatshirt *nt*
sweatshop ['swɛtʃɔp] (*pej*) N Ausbeuterbetrieb *m*
sweaty ['swɛtɪ] ADJ verschwitzt; (*hands*) schweißig
Swede [swi:d] N Schwede *m*, Schwedin *f*
swede [swi:d] (BRIT) N Steckrübe *f*
Sweden ['swi:dn] N Schweden *nt*
Swedish ['swi:dɪʃ] ADJ schwedisch ▸ N Schwedisch *nt*
sweep [swi:p] (*pt, pp* **swept**) VT fegen, kehren; (*current*) reißen ▸ VI (*wind*) fegen; (*through air*) gleiten ▸ N (*curve*) Bogen *m*; (*range*) Bereich *m*; (*also*: **chimney sweep**) Kaminkehrer *m*, Schornsteinfeger *m*; **to give sth a ~** etw fegen *or* kehren
▸ **sweep away** VT hinwegfegen
▸ **sweep past** VI vorbeirauschen
▸ **sweep up** VI zusammenfegen, zusammenkehren
sweeper ['swi:pəʳ] N (*Football*) Ausputzer *m*
sweeping ['swi:pɪŋ] ADJ (*gesture*) weit ausholend; (*changes, reforms*) weitreichend; (*statement*) verallgemeinernd
sweepstake ['swi:psteɪk] N *Pferdewette, bei der der Preis aus der Summe der Einsätze besteht*
sweet [swi:t] N (*candy*) Bonbon *m or nt*; (BRIT *Culin*) Nachtisch *m* ▸ ADJ süß; (*kind*) lieb; (*air, water*) frisch ▸ ADV: **to smell/taste ~** süß duften/schmecken; **~ and sour** süß-sauer
sweetbread ['swi:tbrɛd] N Bries *nt*
sweetcorn ['swi:tkɔ:n] N Mais *m*
sweeten ['swi:tn] VT süßen; (*temper*) bessern; (*person*) gnädig stimmen
sweetener ['swi:tnəʳ] N Süßstoff *m*; (*fig*) Anreiz *m*

S

sweetheart ['swi:thɑ:t] N Freund(in) *m(f)*; (*in speech, writing*) Schatz *m*, Liebling *m*
sweetness ['swi:tnɪs] N Süße *f*; (*kindness*) Liebenswürdigkeit *f*
sweet pea N (Garten)wicke *f*
sweet potato N Süßkartoffel *f*, Batate *f*
sweet shop (BRIT) N Süßwarengeschäft *nt*
sweet tooth N: **to have a ~** gern Süßes essen
swell [swɛl] (*pt* **swelled**, *pp* **swollen** *or* **swelled**) ADJ (*US inf*) toll, prima ▸ VI (*also*: **swell up**) anschwellen; (*increase*) anwachsen; (*sound*) anschwellen; (*feeling*) stärker werden ▸ N Seegang *m*
swelling ['swɛlɪŋ] N Schwellung *f*
sweltering ['swɛltərɪŋ] ADJ (*heat*) glühend; (*weather, day*) glühend heiß
swept [swɛpt] PT, PP *of* **sweep**
swerve [swə:v] VI (*animal*) ausbrechen; (*driver, vehicle*) ausschwenken; **to ~ off the road** ausschwenken und von der Straße abkommen
swift [swɪft] ADJ schnell ▸ N Mauersegler *m*
swiftly ['swɪftlɪ] ADV schnell
swiftness ['swɪftnɪs] N Schnelligkeit *f*
swig [swɪg] (*inf*) N Schluck *m* ▸ VT herunterkippen
swill [swɪl] VT (*also*: **swill out**) ausspülen; (*also*: **swill down**) abspülen ▸ N (*for pigs*) Schweinefutter *nt*
swim [swɪm] (*pt* **swam**, *pp* **swum**) VI schwimmen; (*before one's eyes*) verschwimmen ▸ VT (*the Channel etc*) durchschwimmen; (*a length*) schwimmen ▸ N: **to go for a ~** schwimmen gehen; **to go swimming** schwimmen gehen; **my head is swimming** mir dreht sich der Kopf
swimmer ['swɪmə[r]] N Schwimmer(in) *m(f)*
swimming ['swɪmɪŋ] N Schwimmen *nt*
swimming baths (BRIT) NPL Schwimmbad *nt*
swimming cap N Badekappe *f*, Bademütze *f*
swimming costume (BRIT) N Badeanzug *m*
swimmingly ['swɪmɪŋlɪ] (*inf*) ADV glänzend
swimming pool N Schwimmbad *nt*
swimming trunks NPL Badehose *f*
swimsuit ['swɪmsu:t] N Badeanzug *m*
swindle ['swɪndl] VT: **to ~ sb (out of sth)** jdn (um etw) betrügen *or* beschwindeln ▸ N Schwindel *m*, Betrug *m*
swindler ['swɪndlə[r]] N Schwindler(in) *m(f)*
swine [swaɪn] (*inf!*) N Schwein *nt*
swine flu N Schweinegrippe *f*
swing [swɪŋ] (*pt, pp* **swung**) N (*in playground*) Schaukel *f*; (*movement*) Schwung *m*; (*change*) Umschwung *m*; (*Mus*) Swing *m* ▸ VT (*arms, legs*) schwingen (mit); (*also*: **swing round**) herumschwenken ▸ VI schwingen; (*also*: **swing round**) sich umdrehen; (*vehicle*) herumschwenken; **a ~ to the left** (*Pol*) ein Linksruck *m*; **to get into the ~ of things** richtig reinkommen; **to be in full ~** (*party etc*) in vollem Gang sein
swing bridge N Drehbrücke *f*
swing door, (US) **swinging door** N Pendeltür *f*
swingeing ['swɪndʒɪŋ] (BRIT) ADJ (*blow*) hart; (*attack*) scharf; (*cuts, increases*) extrem
swinging ['swɪŋɪŋ] ADJ (*music*) schwungvoll; (*movement*) schaukelnd
swipe [swaɪp] VT (*inf: steal*) klauen; (*also*: **swipe at**) schlagen nach ▸ N Schlag *m*
swirl [swə:l] VI wirbeln ▸ N Wirbeln *nt*
swish [swɪʃ] VI rauschen; (*tail*) schlagen ▸ N Rauschen *nt*; (*of tail*) Schlagen *nt* ▸ ADJ (*inf*) chic *inv*, schick
Swiss [swɪs] ADJ schweizerisch, Schweizer ▸ N INV Schweizer(in) *m(f)*
Swiss French ADJ französischschweizerisch
Swiss German ADJ deutsch-schweizerisch
Swiss roll N Biskuitrolle *f*
switch [swɪtʃ] N Schalter *m*; (*change*) Änderung *f* ▸ VT (*change*) ändern; (*exchange*) tauschen, wechseln; **to ~ (round** *or* **over)** vertauschen
▸ **switch off** VT abschalten; (*light*) ausschalten ▸ VI (*fig*) abschalten
▸ **switch on** VT einschalten; (*radio*) anstellen; (*engine*) anlassen
switchback ['swɪtʃbæk] (BRIT) N (*road*) auf und ab führende Straße *f*; (*roller-coaster*) Achterbahn *f*
switchblade ['swɪtʃbleɪd] N Schnappmesser *nt*
switchboard ['swɪtʃbɔ:d] N Vermittlung *f*, Zentrale *f*
switchboard operator N Telefonist(in) *m(f)*
Switzerland ['swɪtsələnd] N die Schweiz *f*
swivel ['swɪvl] VI (*also*: **swivel round**) sich (herum)drehen
swollen ['swəulən] PP *of* **swell** ▸ ADJ geschwollen; (*lake etc*) angeschwollen
swoon [swu:n] VI beinahe ohnmächtig werden ▸ N Ohnmacht *f*
swoop [swu:p] N (*by police etc*) Razzia *f*; (*of bird etc*) Sturzflug *m* ▸ VI (*bird: also*: **swoop down**) herabstoßen; (*plane*) einen Sturzflug machen
swop [swɔp] = **swap**
sword [sɔ:d] N Schwert *nt*
swordfish ['sɔ:dfɪʃ] N Schwertfisch *m*
swore [swɔ:[r]] PT *of* **swear**
sworn [swɔ:n] PP *of* **swear** ▸ ADJ (*statement*) eidlich; (*evidence*) unter Eid; (*enemy*) geschworen
swot [swɔt] VI pauken ▸ N (*pej*) Streber(in) *m(f)*
▸ **swot up** VT: **to ~ up (on)** pauken (*+acc*)
swum [swʌm] PP *of* **swim**
swung [swʌŋ] PT, PP *of* **swing**
sycamore ['sɪkəmɔ:[r]] N Bergahorn *m*
sycophant ['sɪkəfænt] N Kriecher *m*, Speichellecker *m*
sycophantic [sɪkə'fæntɪk] ADJ kriecherisch
Sydney ['sɪdnɪ] N Sydney *nt*
syllable ['sɪləbl] N Silbe *f*
syllabus ['sɪləbəs] N Lehrplan *m*; **on the ~** im Lehrplan
symbol ['sɪmbl] N Symbol *nt*
symbolic [sɪm'bɔlɪk], **symbolical** [sɪm'bɔlɪkl] ADJ symbolisch; **to be ~(al) of sth** etw symbolisieren, ein Symbol für etw sein
symbolism ['sɪmbəlɪzəm] N Symbolismus *m*
symbolize ['sɪmbəlaɪz] VT symbolisieren
symmetrical [sɪ'mɛtrɪkl] ADJ symmetrisch

symmetry ['sɪmɪtrɪ] N Symmetrie *f*
sympathetic [sɪmpə'θɛtɪk] ADJ (*understanding*) verständnisvoll; (*showing pity*) mitfühlend; (*likeable*) sympathisch; (*supportive*) wohlwollend; **to be ~ to a cause** (*well-disposed*) einer Sache wohlwollend gegenüberstehen
sympathetically [sɪmpə'θɛtɪklɪ] ADV (*showing understanding*) verständnisvoll; (*showing support*) wohlwollend
sympathize ['sɪmpəθaɪz] VI: **to ~ with** (*person*) Mitleid haben mit; (*feelings*) Verständnis haben für; (*cause*) sympathisieren mit
sympathizer ['sɪmpəθaɪzə[r]] N (*Pol*) Sympathisant(in) *m(f)*
sympathy ['sɪmpəθɪ] N Mitgefühl *nt*; **sympathies** NPL (*support, tendencies*) Sympathien *pl*; **with our deepest ~** mit aufrichtigem *or* herzlichem Beileid; **to come out in ~** (*workers*) in einen Sympathiestreik treten
symphonic [sɪm'fɔnɪk] ADJ sinfonisch
symphony ['sɪmfənɪ] N Sinfonie *f*
symphony orchestra N Sinfonieorchester *nt*
symposia [sɪm'pəuzɪə] NPL *of* **symposium**
symposium [sɪm'pəuzɪəm] (*pl* **symposiums** *or* **symposia**) N Symposium *nt*
symptom ['sɪmptəm] N (*Med, fig*) Symptom *nt*, Anzeichen *nt*
symptomatic [sɪmptə'mætɪk] ADJ: **~ of** symptomatisch für
synagogue ['sɪnəgɔg] N Synagoge *f*
sync [sɪŋk] N ABBR (= *synchronization*): **in ~** synchron; **out of ~** nicht synchron
synchromesh [sɪŋkrəu'mɛʃ] N Synchrongetriebe *nt*
synchronize ['sɪŋkrənaɪz] VT (*watches*) gleichstellen; (*movements*) aufeinander abstimmen; (*sound*) synchronisieren ▸ VI: **to ~ with** (*sound*) synchron sein mit
synchronized swimming ['sɪŋkrənaɪzd-] N Synchronschwimmen *nt*
syncopated ['sɪŋkəpeɪtɪd] ADJ synkopiert
syndicate ['sɪndɪkɪt] N Interessengemeinschaft *f*; (*of businesses*) Verband *m*; (*of newspapers*) Pressezentrale *f*
syndrome ['sɪndrəum] N Syndrom *nt*; (*fig*) Phänomen *nt*
synonym ['sɪnənɪm] N Synonym *nt*
synonymous [sɪ'nɔnɪməs] ADJ (*fig*): **~ (with)** gleichbedeutend (mit)
synopses [sɪ'nɔpsi:z] NPL *of* **synopsis**
synopsis [sɪ'nɔpsɪs] (*pl* **synopses**) N Abriss *m*, Zusammenfassung *f*
syntactic [sɪn'tæktɪk] ADJ syntaktisch
syntax ['sɪntæks] N Syntax *f*
syntax error N (*Comput*) Syntaxfehler *m*
syntheses ['sɪnθəsi:z] NPL *of* **synthesis**
synthesis ['sɪnθəsɪs] (*pl* **syntheses**) N Synthese *f*
synthesizer ['sɪnθəsaɪzə[r]] N Synthesizer *m*
synthetic [sɪn'θɛtɪk] ADJ synthetisch; (*speech*) künstlich; **synthetics** NPL (*man-made fabrics*) Synthetik *f*
syphilis ['sɪfɪlɪs] N Syphilis *f*
syphon ['saɪfən] = **siphon**
Syria ['sɪrɪə] N Syrien *nt*
Syrian ['sɪrɪən] ADJ syrisch ▸ N Syrer(in) *m(f)*
syringe [sɪ'rɪndʒ] N Spritze *f*
syrup ['sɪrəp] N Sirup *m*; (*also*: **golden syrup**) (gelber) Sirup *m*
syrupy ['sɪrəpɪ] ADJ sirupartig; (*pej*: *fig*: *sentimental*) schmalzig
system ['sɪstəm] N System *nt*; (*body*) Körper *m*; (*Anat*) Apparat *m*, System *nt*; **it was a shock to his ~** er hatte schwer damit zu schaffen
systematic [sɪstə'mætɪk] ADJ systematisch
system disk N (*Comput*) Systemdiskette *f*
systems administrator ['sɪstəmz-] N (*Comput*) Systembetreuer(in) *m(f)*
systems analyst ['sɪstəmz-] N (*Comput*) Systemanalytiker(in) *m(f)*
systems engineer ['sɪstəmz-] N (*Comput*) Systemtechniker(in) *m(f)*

S

Tt

T, t [ti:] N (*letter*) T *nt*, t *nt*; **T for Tommy** ≈ T wie Theodor
TA (BRIT) N ABBR = **Territorial Army**
ta [tɑ:] (BRIT *inf*) EXCL danke
tab [tæb] N ABBR = **tabulator** ▸ N (*on garment*) Etikett *nt*; (*on drinks can*) Ring *m*; **to keep tabs on sb/sth** (*fig*) jdn/etw im Auge behalten
tabby ['tæbɪ] N (*also*: **tabby cat**) getigerte Katze *f*
tabernacle ['tæbənækl] N Tabernakel *nt*
table ['teɪbl] N Tisch *m*; (*Math, Chem etc*) Tabelle *f* ▸ VT (BRIT *Parl*: *motion etc*) einbringen; **to lay** *or* **set the ~** den Tisch decken; **to clear the ~** den Tisch abräumen; **league ~** (BRIT *Sport*) Tabelle *f*
tablecloth ['teɪblklɔθ] N Tischdecke *f*
table d'hôte [tɑ:bl'dəut] ADJ (*menu, meal*) Tagesmenü *nt*
table lamp N Tischlampe *f*
tablemat ['teɪblmæt] N (*of cloth*) Set *m or nt*; (*for hot dish*) Untersatz *m*
table of contents N Inhaltsverzeichnis *nt*
table salt N Tafelsalz *nt*
tablespoon ['teɪblspu:n] N Esslöffel *m*; (*also*: **tablespoonful**) Esslöffel(voll) *m*
tablet ['tæblɪt] N (*Med*) Tablette *f*; (*Hist*: *for writing*) Tafel *f*; (*plaque*) Plakette *f*; **~ of soap** (BRIT) Stück *nt* Seife
table tennis N Tischtennis *nt*
table wine N Tafelwein *m*
tabloid ['tæblɔɪd] N (*newspaper*) Boulevardzeitung *f*; **the tabloids** die Boulevardpresse

> Des Ausdruck **tabloid press** bezieht sich auf kleinformatige Zeitungen (ca 30 x 40 cm); diese sind in Großbritannien fast ausschließlich Massenblätter. Im Gegensatz zur **quality press** verwenden sie viele Fotos und einen knappern, oft reißerischen Stil. Sie kommen denjenigen Lesern entgegen, die mehr Wert auf Unterhaltung legen.

taboo [tə'bu:] N Tabu *nt* ▸ ADJ tabu; **a ~ subject/word** ein Tabuthema/Tabuwort
tabulate ['tæbjuleɪt] VT tabellarisieren
tabulator ['tæbjuleɪtə^r] N (*on typewriter*) Tabulator *m*
tachograph ['tækəgrɑ:f] N Fahrtenschreiber *m*
tachometer [tæ'kɔmɪtə^r] N Tachometer *m*
tacit ['tæsɪt] ADJ stillschweigend
taciturn ['tæsɪtə:n] ADJ schweigsam
tack [tæk] N (*nail*) Stift *m* ▸ VT (*nail*) anheften; (*stitch*) heften ▸ VI (*Naut*) kreuzen; **to change ~** (*fig*) den Kurs ändern; **to ~ sth on to (the end of) sth** etw (hinten) an etw *acc* anheften
tackle ['tækl] N (*for fishing*) Ausrüstung *f*; (*Football, Rugby*) Angriff *m*; (*for lifting*) Flaschenzug *m* ▸ VT (*deal with*: *difficulty*) in Angriff nehmen; (*challenge*: *person*) zur Rede stellen; (*physically, also Sport*) angreifen
tacky ['tækɪ] ADJ (*sticky*) klebrig; (*pej*: *cheap-looking*) schäbig
tact [tækt] N Takt *m*
tactful ['tæktful] ADJ taktvoll; **to be ~** taktvoll sein
tactfully ['tæktfəlɪ] ADV taktvoll
tactical ['tæktɪkl] ADJ taktisch; **~ error** taktischer Fehler; **~ voting** taktische Stimmabgabe
tactician [tæk'tɪʃən] N Taktiker(in) *m(f)*
tactics ['tæktɪks] NPL Taktik *f*
tactless ['tæktlɪs] ADJ taktlos
tactlessly ['tæktlɪslɪ] ADV taktlos
tadpole ['tædpəul] N Kaulquappe *f*
taffy ['tæfɪ] (US) N (*toffee*) Toffee *nt*, Sahnebonbon *nt*
tag [tæg] N (*label*) Anhänger *m*; **price/name ~** Preis-/Namensschild *nt*; **(electronic) ~** (elektronische) Fußfessel *f*
▸ **tag along** VI sich anschließen
Tahiti [tɑ:'hi:tɪ] N Tahiti *nt*
tail [teɪl] N (*of animal*) Schwanz *m*; (*of plane*) Heck *nt*; (*of shirt, coat*) Schoß *m* ▸ VT (*follow*) folgen +*dat*; **tails** NPL (*formal suit*) Frack *m*; **to turn ~** die Flucht ergreifen; *see also* **head**
▸ **tail off** VI (*in size etc*) abnehmen; (*voice*) schwächer werden
tailback ['teɪlbæk] (BRIT) N (*Aut*) Stau *m*
tail coat N = **tails**
tail end N Ende *nt*
tailgate ['teɪlgeɪt] N (*Aut*) Heckklappe *f*
taillight ['teɪllaɪt] N (*Aut*) Rücklicht *nt*
tailor ['teɪlə^r] N Schneider(in) *m(f)* ▸ VT: **to ~ sth (to)** etw abstimmen (auf +*acc*); **~'s shop** Schneiderei *f*
tailoring ['teɪlərɪŋ] N (*craft*) Schneiderei *f*; (*cut*) Verarbeitung *f*

tailor-made ['teɪlə'meɪd] ADJ (*also fig*) maßgeschneidert
tailwind ['teɪlwɪnd] N Rückenwind *m*
taint [teɪnt] VT (*meat, food*) verderben; (*fig: reputation etc*) beschmutzen
tainted ['teɪntɪd] ADJ (*food, water, air*) verdorben; (*fig: profits, reputation etc*): **~ with** behaftet mit
Taiwan ['taɪ'wɑ:n] N Taiwan *nt*
Tajikistan [tɑ:dʒɪkɪ'stɑ:n] N Tadschikistan *nt*
take [teɪk] (*pt* **took**, *pp* **taken**) VT nehmen; (*photo, notes*) machen; (*decision*) fällen; (*require: courage, time*) erfordern; (*tolerate: pain etc*) ertragen; (*hold: passengers etc*) fassen; (*accompany: person*) begleiten; (*carry, bring*) mitnehmen; (*exam, test*) machen; (*conduct: meeting*) leiten; (*: class*) unterrichten ▸ VI (*have effect: drug*) wirken; (*: dye*) angenommen werden ▸ N (*Cine*) Aufnahme *f*; **to ~ sth from** (*drawer etc*) etw nehmen aus *+dat*; **I ~ it (that)** ich nehme an(, dass); **I took him for a doctor** (*mistake*) ich hielt ihn für einen Arzt; **to ~ sb's hand** jds Hand nehmen; **to ~ sb for a walk** mit jdm spazieren gehen; **to be taken ill** krank werden; **to ~ it upon o.s. to do sth** es auf sich nehmen, etw zu tun; **~ the first (street) on the left** nehmen Sie die erste Straße links; **to ~ Russian at university** Russisch studieren; **it won't ~ long** es dauert nicht lange; **I was quite taken with her/it** (*attracted to*) ich war von ihr/davon recht angetan
▸ **take after** VT FUS (*resemble*) ähneln *+dat*, ähnlich sein *+dat*
▸ **take along** VT mitnehmen
▸ **take apart** VT auseinandernehmen
▸ **take away** VT wegnehmen; (*carry off*) wegbringen; (*Math*) abziehen ▸ VI: **to ~ away from** (*detract from*) schmälern, beeinträchtigen
▸ **take back** VT (*return*) zurückbringen; (*one's words*) zurücknehmen
▸ **take down** VT (*write down*) aufschreiben; (*dismantle*) abreißen
▸ **take in** VT (*deceive: person*) hereinlegen, täuschen; (*understand*) begreifen; (*include*) einschließen; (*lodger*) aufnehmen; (*orphan, stray dog*) zu sich nehmen; (*dress, waistband*) enger machen
▸ **take off** VI (*Aviat*) starten; (*go away*) sich absetzen ▸ VT (*clothes*) ausziehen; (*glasses*) abnehmen; (*make-up*) entfernen; (*time*) freinehmen; (*imitate: person*) nachmachen
▸ **take on** VT (*work, responsibility*) übernehmen; (*employee*) einstellen; (*compete against*) antreten gegen
▸ **take out** VT (*invite*) ausgehen mit; (*remove: tooth*) herausnehmen; (*licence*) erwerben; **to ~ sth out of sth** (*drawer, pocket etc*) etw aus etw nehmen; **don't ~ it out on me!** lass es nicht an mir aus!
▸ **take over** VT (*business*) übernehmen; (*country*) Besitz ergreifen von ▸ VI (*replace*): **to ~ over from sb** jdn ablösen
▸ **take to** VT FUS (*person, thing*) mögen; (*activity*) Gefallen finden an *+dat*; (*form habit of*): **to ~ to doing sth** sich *dat* angewöhnen, etw zu tun
▸ **take up** VT (*hobby, sport*) anfangen mit; (*job*) antreten; (*idea etc*) annehmen; (*time, space*) beanspruchen; (*continue: task, story*) fortfahren mit; (*shorten: hem, garment*) kürzer machen ▸ VI (*befriend*): **to ~ up with sb** sich mit jdm anfreunden; **to ~ sb up on an offer/a suggestion** auf jds Angebot/Vorschlag eingehen
takeaway ['teɪkəweɪ] (BRIT) N (*shop, restaurant*) ≈ Schnellimbiss *m*; (*food*) Imbiss *m* (*zum Mitnehmen*)
take-home pay ['teɪkhəum-] N Nettolohn *m*
taken ['teɪkən] PP *of* **take**
takeoff ['teɪkɔf] N (*Aviat*) Start *m*
takeout ['teɪkaut] (US) N = **takeaway**
takeover ['teɪkəuvə^r] N (*Comm*) Übernahme *f*; (*of country*) Inbesitznahme *f*
takeover bid N Übernahmeangebot *nt*
takings ['teɪkɪŋz] NPL Einnahmen *pl*
talc [tælk] N (*also*: **talcum powder**) Talkumpuder *nt*
tale [teɪl] N Geschichte *f*; **to tell tales (to sb)** (*child*) (jdm) Geschichten erzählen
talent ['tælnt] N Talent *nt*
talented ['tæləntɪd] ADJ talentiert, begabt
talent scout N Talentsucher(in) *m(f)*
talisman ['tælɪzmən] N Talisman *m*
talk [tɔ:k] N (*speech*) Vortrag *m*; (*conversation, discussion*) Gespräch *nt*; (*gossip*) Gerede *nt* ▸ VI (*speak*) sprechen; (*chat*) reden; (*gossip*) klatschen; **talks** NPL (*Pol etc*) Gespräche *pl*; **to give a ~** einen Vortrag halten; **to ~ about** (*discuss*) sprechen *or* reden über; **talking of films, have you seen ...?** da wir gerade von Filmen sprechen: hast du ... gesehen?; **to ~ sb into doing sth** jdn zu etw überreden; **to ~ sb out of doing sth** jdm etw ausreden
▸ **talk over** VT (*problem etc*) besprechen, bereden
talkative ['tɔ:kətɪv] ADJ gesprächig
talker ['tɔ:kə^r] N: **to be a good/entertaining/fast** *etc* **~** gut/amüsant/schnell *etc* reden können
talking point ['tɔ:kɪŋ-] N Gesprächsthema *nt*
talking-to ['tɔ:kɪŋtu] N: **to give sb a (good) ~** jdm eine (ordentliche) Standpauke halten (*inf*)
talk show N Talkshow *f*
tall [tɔ:l] ADJ (*person*) groß; (*glass, bookcase, tree, building*) hoch; (*ladder*) lang; **to be 6 feet ~** (*person*) ≈ 1,80m groß sein; **how ~ are you?** wie groß bist du?
tallboy ['tɔ:lbɔɪ] (BRIT) N Kommode *f*
tallness ['tɔ:lnɪs] N (*of person*) Größe *f*; (*of tree, building etc*) Höhe *f*
tall story N unglaubliche Geschichte *f*
tally ['tælɪ] N (*of marks, amounts etc*) aktueller Stand *m* ▸ VI: **to ~ (with)** (*figures, stories etc*) übereinstimmen mit; **to keep a ~ of sth** über etw *acc* Buch führen
talon ['tælən] N Kralle *f*
tambourine [tæmbə'ri:n] N Tamburin *nt*
tame [teɪm] ADJ (*animal, bird*) zahm; (*fig: story, party, performance*) lustlos, lahm (*inf*)

t

Tamil ['tæmɪl] ADJ tamilisch ▶ N Tamile *m*, Tamilin *f*; (*Ling*) Tamil *nt*
tamper ['tæmpəʳ] VI: **to ~ with sth** an etw *dat* herumpfuschen (*inf*)
tampon ['tæmpɔn] N Tampon *m*
tan [tæn] N (*also*: **suntan**) (Sonnen)bräune *f* ▶ VI (*person, skin*) braun werden ▶ VT (*hide*) gerben; (*skin*) bräunen ▶ ADJ (*colour*) hellbraun; **to get a ~** braun werden
tandem ['tændəm] N Tandem *nt*; (*together*): **in ~** (*fig*) zusammen
tandoori [tæn'duərɪ] N: **~ oven** Tandoori-Ofen *m*; **~ chicken** *im Tandoori-Ofen gebratenes Huhn*
tang [tæŋ] N (*smell*) Geruch *m*; (*taste*) Geschmack *m*
tangent ['tændʒənt] N (*Math*) Tangente *f*; **to go off at a ~** (*fig*) vom Thema abschweifen
tangerine [tændʒə'ri:n] N (*fruit*) Mandarine *f*; (*colour*) Orangerot *nt*
tangible ['tændʒəbl] ADJ greifbar; **~ assets** (*Comm*) Sachanlagevermögen *nt*
Tangier [tæn'dʒɪəʳ] N Tanger *nt*
tangle ['tæŋgl] N (*of branches, wire etc*) Gewirr *nt*; **to be in a ~** verheddert sein; (*fig*) durcheinander sein; **to get in a ~** sich verheddern; (*fig*) durcheinandergeraten
tango ['tæŋgəu] N Tango *m*
tank [tæŋk] N Tank *m*; (*for photographic processing*) Wanne *f*; (*also*: **fish tank**) Aquarium *nt*; (*Mil*) Panzer *m*
tankard ['tæŋkəd] N Bierkrug *m*
tanker ['tæŋkəʳ] N (*ship*) Tanker *m*; (*truck*) Tankwagen *m*
tankini [tæn'ki:nɪ] N Tankini *m*
tanned [tænd] ADJ (*person*) braun gebrannt; (*hide*) gegerbt
tannin ['tænɪn] N Tannin *nt*
tanning ['tænɪŋ] N (*of leather*) Gerben *nt*
Tannoy® ['tænɔɪ] (BRIT) N Lautsprechersystem *nt*; **over the ~** über Lautsprecher
tantalizing ['tæntəlaɪzɪŋ] ADJ (*smell*) verführerisch; (*possibility*) verlockend
tantamount ['tæntəmaunt] ADJ: **~ to** gleichbedeutend mit
tantrum ['tæntrəm] N Wutanfall *m*; **to throw a ~** einen Wutanfall bekommen
Tanzania [tænzə'nɪə] N Tansania *nt*
Tanzanian [tænzə'nɪən] ADJ tansanisch ▶ N (*person*) Tansanier(in) *m(f)*
tap [tæp] N (*on sink, gas tap*) Hahn *m*; (*gentle blow*) leichter Schlag *m*, Klaps *m* ▶ VT (*hit gently*) klopfen; (*exploit: resources, energy*) nutzen; (*telephone*) abhören, anzapfen; **on ~** (*fig: resources, information*) zur Verfügung; (*beer*) vom Fass
tap-dancing ['tæpdɑ:nsɪŋ] N Stepptanz *m*
tape [teɪp] N (*also*: **magnetic tape**) Tonband *nt*; (*cassette*) Kassette *f*; (*also*: **sticky tape**) Klebeband *nt*; (*for tying*) Band *nt* ▶ VT (*record, conversation*) aufnehmen, aufzeichnen; (*stick with tape*) mit Klebeband befestigen; **on ~** (*song etc*) auf Band
tape deck N Tapedeck *nt*
tape measure N Bandmaß *nt*
taper ['teɪpəʳ] N (*candle*) lange, dünne Kerze ▶ VI sich verjüngen
tape recorder N Tonband(gerät) *nt*
tape recording N Tonbandaufnahme *f*
tapered ['teɪpəd] ADJ (*skirt, jacket*) nach unten enger werdend
tapering ['teɪpərɪŋ] ADJ spitz zulaufend
tapestry ['tæpɪstrɪ] N (*on wall*) Wandteppich *m*; (*fig*) Kaleidoskop *nt*
tapeworm ['teɪpwə:m] N Bandwurm *m*
tapioca [tæpɪ'əukə] N Tapioka *f*
tappet ['tæpɪt] N (*Aut*) Stößel *m*
tap water ['tæpwɔ:təʳ] N Leitungswasser *nt*
tar [tɑ:] N Teer *m*; **low/middle ~ cigarettes** Zigaretten mit niedrigem/mittlerem Teergehalt
tarantula [tə'ræntjulə] N Tarantel *f*
tardy ['tɑ:dɪ] ADJ (*reply, letter*) verspätet; (*progress*) langsam
target ['tɑ:gɪt] N Ziel *nt*; (*fig: of joke, criticism etc*) Zielscheibe *f*; **to be on ~** (*project, work*) nach Plan verlaufen
target practice N Zielschießen *nt*
tariff ['tærɪf] N (*tax on goods*) Zoll *m*; (BRIT: *in hotels etc*) Preisliste *f*
tariff barrier N Zollschranke *f*
tarmac® ['tɑ:mæk] N (*Aviat*): **on the ~** auf dem Rollfeld; (BRIT: *on road*) Asphalt *m* ▶ VT (BRIT: *road etc*) asphaltieren
tarn [tɑ:n] N Bergsee *m*
tarnish ['tɑ:nɪʃ] VT (*silver, brass etc*) stumpf werden lassen; (*fig: reputation etc*) beflecken, in Mitleidenschaft ziehen
tarot ['tærəu] N Tarot *m or nt*
tarpaulin [tɑ:'pɔ:lɪn] N Plane *f*
tarragon ['tærəgən] N Estragon *m*
tart [tɑ:t] N (*Culin*) Torte *f*; (*: small*) Törtchen *nt*; (BRIT *inf: prostitute*) Nutte *f* ▶ ADJ (*apple, grapefruit etc*) säuerlich
▶ **tart up** (BRIT *inf*) VT (*room, building*) aufmotzen; **to ~ o.s. up** sich fein machen; (*pej*) sich auftakeln
tartan ['tɑ:tn] N Schottenstoff *m*, Tartan *m* ▶ ADJ (*scarf etc*) mit Schottenmuster
tartar ['tɑ:təʳ] N (*on teeth*) Zahnstein *m*; (*pej: person*) Tyrann(in) *m(f)*
tartar sauce, tartare sauce ['tɑ:tə-] N Remouladensoße *f*
task [tɑ:sk] N Aufgabe *f*; **to take sb to ~** jdn ins Gebet nehmen
taskbar N (*Comput*) Taskbar *f*
task force N (*Mil*) Sonderkommando *nt*; (*Police*) Spezialeinheit *f*
taskmaster ['tɑ:skmɑ:stəʳ] N: **a hard ~** ein strenger Lehrmeister
Tasmania [tæz'meɪnɪə] N Tasmanien *nt*
tassel ['tæsl] N Quaste *f*
taste [teɪst] N Geschmack *m*; (*sample*) Kostprobe *f*; (*fig: of suffering, freedom etc*) Vorgeschmack *m* ▶ VT (*get flavour of*) schmecken; (*test*) probieren, versuchen ▶ VI: **to ~ of/like sth** nach/wie etw schmecken; **sense of ~** Geschmackssinn *m*; **to have a ~ of sth** (*sample*) etw probieren; **to**

acquire a ~ for sth (*liking*) Geschmack an etw *dat* finden; **to be in good/bad ~** (*joke etc*) geschmackvoll/geschmacklos sein; **you can ~ the garlic (in it)** (*detect*) man schmeckt den Knoblauch durch; **what does it ~ like?** wie schmeckt es?
taste buds NPL Geschmacksknospen *pl*
tasteful ['teɪstful] ADJ geschmackvoll
tastefully ['teɪstfəlɪ] ADV geschmackvoll
tasteless ['teɪstlɪs] ADJ geschmacklos
tasty ['teɪstɪ] ADJ schmackhaft
tattered ['tætəd] ADJ (*clothes, paper etc*) zerrissen; (*fig: hopes etc*) angeschlagen
tatters ['tætəz] NPL: **to be in ~** (*clothes*) in Fetzen sein
tattoo [tə'tu:] N (*on skin*) Tätowierung *f*; (*spectacle*) Zapfenstreich *m* ▸ VT: **to ~ sth on sth** etw auf etw *acc* tätowieren
tatty ['tætɪ] (BRIT *inf*) ADJ schäbig
taught [tɔ:t] PT, PP *of* **teach**
taunt [tɔ:nt] N höhnische Bemerkung *f* ▸ VT (*person*) verhöhnen
Taurus ['tɔ:rəs] N Stier *m*; **to be ~** (ein) Stier sein
taut [tɔ:t] ADJ (*skin, thread etc*) straff
tavern ['tævən] N Taverne *f*
tawdry ['tɔ:drɪ] ADJ billig
tawny ['tɔ:nɪ] ADJ gelbbraun
tawny owl N Waldkauz *m*
tax [tæks] N Steuer *f* ▸ VT (*earnings, goods etc*) besteuern; (*fig: memory, knowledge*) strapazieren; (*: patience etc*) auf die Probe stellen; **before/ after ~** vor/nach Abzug der Steuern; **free of ~** steuerfrei
taxable ['tæksəbl] ADJ steuerpflichtig; (*income*) steuerbar
tax allowance N Steuerfreibetrag *m*
taxation [tæk'seɪʃən] N (*system*) Besteuerung *f*; (*money paid*) Steuern *pl*
tax avoidance N Steuerumgehung *f*
tax collector N Steuerbeamte(r) *m*, Steuerbeamtin *f*
tax disc (BRIT) N (*Aut*) Steuerplakette *f*
tax evasion N Steuerhinterziehung *f*
tax exemption N Steuerbefreiung *f*
tax exile (*person*) N Steuerflüchtling *m*
tax-free ['tæksfri:] ADJ steuerfrei
tax haven N Steuerparadies *nt*
taxi ['tæksɪ] N Taxi *nt* ▸ VI (*Aviat: plane*) rollen
taxidermist ['tæksɪdə:mɪst] N Taxidermist(in) *m(f)*, Tierpräparator(in) *m(f)*
taxi driver N Taxifahrer(in) *m(f)*
tax inspector (BRIT) N Steuerinspektor(in) *m(f)*
taxi rank (BRIT) N Taxistand *m*
taxi stand N = **taxi rank**
taxpayer ['tækspeɪə^r] N Steuerzahler(in) *m(f)*
tax rebate N Steuerrückvergütung *f*
tax relief N Steuernachlass *m*
tax return N Steuererklärung *f*
tax shelter N (*Comm*) *System zur Verhinderung von Steuerbelastung*
tax year N Steuerjahr *nt*
TB N ABBR (= *tuberculosis*) Tb *f*, Tbc *f*
tbc ABBR (= *to be confirmed*) noch zu bestätigen
TD (*US*) N ABBR = **Treasury Department**; (*Football*) = **touchdown**
tea [ti:] N (*drink*) Tee *m*; (BRIT: *evening meal*) Abendessen *nt*; **afternoon ~** (BRIT) Nachmittagstee *m*
tea bag N Teebeutel *m*
tea break (BRIT) N Teepause *f*
teacake ['ti:keɪk] (BRIT) N Rosinenbrötchen *nt*
teach [ti:tʃ] (*pt, pp* **taught**) VT: **to ~ sb sth, ~ sth to sb** (*instruct*) jdm etw beibringen; (*in school*) jdn in etw *dat* unterrichten ▸ VI unterrichten; **it taught him a lesson** (*fig*) er hat seine Lektion gelernt
teacher ['ti:tʃə^r] N Lehrer(in) *m(f)*; **German ~** Deutschlehrer(in) *m(f)*
teacher training college N (*for primary schools*) ≈ pädagogische Hochschule *f*; (*for secondary schools*) ≈ Studienseminar *nt*
teaching ['ti:tʃɪŋ] N (*work of teacher*) Unterricht *m*
teaching aids NPL Lehrmittel *pl*
teaching hospital (BRIT) N Ausbildungskrankenhaus *nt*
teaching staff (BRIT) N Lehrerkollegium *nt*
tea cosy N Teewärmer *m*
teacup ['ti:kʌp] N Teetasse *f*
teak [ti:k] N Teak *nt*
tea leaves NPL Teeblätter *pl*
team [ti:m] N (*Sport*) Mannschaft *f*, Team *nt*; (*of experts etc*) Team *nt*; (*of horses, oxen*) Gespann *nt*
▸ **team up** VI: **to ~ up (with)** sich zusammentun (mit)
team game N Mannschaftsspiel *nt*
team spirit N Teamgeist *m*
teamwork ['ti:mwə:k] N Teamarbeit *f*, Teamwork *nt*
tea party N Teegesellschaft *f*
teapot ['ti:pɔt] N Teekanne *f*
tear[1] [tɛə^r] (*pt* **tore**, *pp* **torn**) N (*hole*) Riss *m* ▸ VT (*rip*) zerreißen ▸ VI (*become torn*) reißen; **to ~ sth to pieces** *or* **bits** *or* **shreds** (*lit, fig*) etw in Stücke reißen; **to ~ sb to pieces** jdn fertigmachen
▸ **tear along** VI (*rush: driver, car*) entlangrasen
▸ **tear apart** VT (*book, clothes, people*) auseinanderreißen; (*upset: person*) hin- und herreißen
▸ **tear away** VT: **to ~ o.s. away (from sth)** (*fig*) sich (von etw) losreißen
▸ **tear out** VT (*sheet of paper etc*) herausreißen
▸ **tear up** VT (*sheet of paper etc*) zerreißen
tear[2] [tɪə^r] N (*in eye*) Träne *f*; **in tears** in Tränen; **to burst into tears** in Tränen ausbrechen
tearaway ['tɛərəweɪ] (BRIT *inf*) N Rabauke *m*
teardrop ['tɪədrɔp] N Träne *f*
tearful ['tɪəful] ADJ (*person*) weinend; (*face*) tränenüberströmt
tear gas [tɪə-] N Tränengas *nt*
tearing ['tɛərɪŋ] ADJ: **to be in a ~ hurry** es unheimlich eilig haben
tearoom ['ti:ru:m] N = **teashop**
tease [ti:z] VT necken; (*unkindly*) aufziehen ▸ N: **she's a real ~** sie zieht einen ständig auf
tea set N Teeservice *nt*
teashop ['ti:ʃɔp] (BRIT) N Teestube *f*

t

Teasmade® ['ti:zmeɪd] N Teemaschine *f* (*mit Zeiteinstellung*)
teaspoon ['ti:spu:n] N Teelöffel *m*; (*measure: also:* **teaspoonful**) Teelöffel(voll) *m*
tea strainer N Teesieb *nt*
teat [ti:t] N (*on bottle*) Sauger *m*
teatime ['ti:taɪm] N Teestunde *f*
tea towel (BRIT) N Geschirrtuch *nt*
tea urn N Teespender *m*
tech [tɛk] (*inf*) N ABBR = **technical college**; **technology**
technical ['tɛknɪkl] ADJ technisch; (*terms, language*) Fach-
technical college (BRIT) N technische Fachschule *f*
technicality [tɛknɪ'kælɪtɪ] N (*point of law*) Formalität *f*; (*detail*) technische Einzelheit *f*; **on a (legal) ~** aufgrund einer (juristischen) Formalität
technically ['tɛknɪklɪ] ADV (*regarding technique*) technisch (gesehen); (*strictly speaking*) genau genommen
technician [tɛk'nɪʃən] N Techniker(in) *m(f)*
technique [tɛk'ni:k] N Technik *f*
techno ['tɛknəu] N (*Mus*) Techno *nt*
technocrat ['tɛknəkræt] N Technokrat(in) *m(f)*
technological [tɛknə'lɔdʒɪkl] ADJ technologisch
technologist [tɛk'nɔlədʒɪst] N Technologe *m*, Technologin *f*
technology [tɛk'nɔlədʒɪ] N Technologie *f*
technology college N *Oberstufenkolleg mit technischem Schwerpunkt*
teddy ['tɛdɪ], **teddy bear** N Teddy(bär) *m*
tedious ['ti:dɪəs] ADJ langweilig
tedium ['ti:dɪəm] N Langeweile *f*
tee [ti:] N (*Golf*) Tee *nt*
▸ **tee off** VI (vom Tee) abschlagen
teem [ti:m] VI: **to ~ with** (*tourists etc*) wimmeln von; **it is teeming down** es gießt in Strömen
teenage ['ti:neɪdʒ] ADJ (*fashions etc*) Jugend-; (*children*) im Teenageralter
teenager ['ti:neɪdʒə^r] N Teenager *m*, Jugendliche(r) *f(m)*
teens [ti:nz] NPL: **to be in one's ~** im Teenageralter sein
tee shirt N = **T-shirt**
teeter ['ti:tə^r] VI (*also fig*) schwanken, taumeln
teeth [ti:θ] NPL *of* **tooth**
teethe [ti:ð] VI Zähne bekommen, zahnen
teething ring ['ti:ðɪŋ-] N Beißring *m*
teething troubles NPL (*fig*) Kinderkrankheiten *pl*
teetotal ['ti:'təutl] ADJ (*person*) abstinent
teetotaller, (*US*) **teetotaler** ['ti:'təutlə^r] N Abstinenzler(in) *m(f)*, Antialkoholiker(in) *m(f)*
TEFL ['tɛfl] N ABBR (= *Teaching of English as a Foreign Language*) *Unterricht in Englisch als Fremdsprache*
Teflon® ['tɛflɔn] N Teflon® *nt*
Teheran [tɛə'rɑ:n] N Teheran *nt*
tel. ABBR (= *telephone*) Tel.
Tel Aviv ['tɛlə'vi:v] N Tel Aviv *nt*
telecast ['tɛlɪkɑ:st] N Fernsehsendung *f*
telecommunications ['tɛlɪkəmju:nɪ'keɪʃənz] N Nachrichtentechnik *f*
teleconferencing [tɛlɪ'kɔnfərənsɪŋ] N Telekonferenzen *pl*
telegram ['tɛlɪgræm] N Telegramm *nt*
telegraph ['tɛlɪgrɑ:f] N (*system*) Telegraf *m*
telegraphic [tɛlɪ'græfɪk] ADJ (*equipment*) telegrafisch
telegraph pole N Telegrafenmast *m*
telegraph wire N Telegrafenleitung *f*
telepathic [tɛlɪ'pæθɪk] ADJ telepathisch
telepathy [tə'lɛpəθɪ] N Telepathie *f*
telephone ['tɛlɪfəun] N Telefon *nt* ▸ VT (*person*) anrufen ▸ VI telefonieren, anrufen; **to be on the ~** (*talking*) telefonieren; (*possessing phone*) ein Telefon haben
telephone box, (*US*) **telephone booth** N Telefonzelle *f*
telephone call N Anruf *m*
telephone directory N Telefonbuch *nt*
telephone exchange N Telefonzentrale *f*
telephone number N Telefonnummer *f*
telephone operator N Telefonist(in) *m(f)*
telephone tapping N Abhören *nt* von Telefonleitungen
telephonist [tə'lɛfənɪst] (BRIT) N Telefonist(in) *m(f)*
telephoto ['tɛlɪ'fəutəu] ADJ: **~ lens** Teleobjektiv *nt*
teleprinter ['tɛlɪprɪntə^r] N Fernschreiber *m*
Teleprompter® ['tɛlɪprɔmptə^r] (*US*) N Teleprompter *m*
telesales ['tɛlɪseɪlz] N Verkauf *m* per Telefon
telescope ['tɛlɪskəup] N Teleskop *nt* ▸ VI (*fig: bus, lorry*) sich ineinanderschieben ▸ VT (*make shorter*) zusammenschieben
telescopic [tɛlɪ'skɔpɪk] ADJ (*legs, aerial*) ausziehbar; **~ lens** Fernrohrlinse *f*
Teletext® ['tɛlɪtɛkst] N Videotext *m*
telethon ['tɛlɪθɔn] N *Spendenaktion für wohltätige Zwecke in Form einer vielstündigen Fernsehsendung*
televise ['tɛlɪvaɪz] VT (im Fernsehen) übertragen
television ['tɛlɪvɪʒən] N Fernsehen *nt*; (*set*) Fernseher *m*, Fernsehapparat *m*; **to be on ~** im Fernsehen sein
television licence (BRIT) N Fernsehgenehmigung *f*
television programme N Fernsehprogramm *nt*
television set N Fernseher *m*, Fernsehapparat *m*
teleworking ['tɛlɪwə:kɪŋ] N Telearbeit *f*
telex ['tɛlɛks] N (*system, machine, message*) Telex *nt* ▸ VT (*message*) telexen; (*person*) ein Telex schicken *+dat* ▸ VI telexen
tell [tɛl] (*pt, pp* **told**) VT (*say*) sagen; (*relate: story*) erzählen; (*distinguish*): **to ~ sth from** etw unterscheiden von; (*be sure*) wissen ▸ VI (*have an effect*) sich auswirken; **to ~ sb to do sth** jdm sagen, etw zu tun; **to ~ sb of** *or* **about sth** jdm von etw erzählen; **to be able to ~ the time** (*know how to*) die Uhr kennen; **can you ~ me the time?** können Sie mir sagen, wie spät es ist?; **(I) ~ you what, let's go to the cinema** weißt du was? Lass uns ins Kino gehen!; **I can't ~**

them apart ich kann sie nicht unterscheiden
▸ **tell off** VT: **to ~ sb off** jdn ausschimpfen
▸ **tell on** VT FUS (*inform against*) verpetzen

teller ['tɛləʳ] N (*in bank*) Kassierer(in) *m(f)*

telling ['tɛlɪŋ] ADJ (*remark etc*) verräterisch

telltale ['tɛlteɪl] ADJ verräterisch ▸ N (*pej*) Petzer *m*, Petze *f*

telly ['tɛlɪ] (BRIT *inf*) N ABBR = **television**

temerity [tə'mɛrɪtɪ] N Unverschämtheit *f*

temp [tɛmp] (BRIT *inf*) N ABBR (= *temporary office worker*) Zeitarbeitskraft *f* ▸ VI als Zeitarbeitskraft arbeiten

temper ['tɛmpəʳ] N (*mood*) Laune *f*; (*nature*) Naturell *nt* ▸ VT (*moderate*) mildern; **a (fit of) ~** ein Wutanfall *m*; **to be in a ~** gereizt sein; **to lose one's ~** die Beherrschung verlieren

temperament ['tɛmprəmənt] N Temperament *nt*

temperamental [tɛmprə'mɛntl] ADJ (*person, car*) launisch

temperate ['tɛmprət] ADJ gemäßigt

temperature ['tɛmprətʃəʳ] N Temperatur *f*; **to have** *or* **run a ~** Fieber haben; **to take sb's ~** bei jdm Fieber messen

temperature chart N (*Med*) Fiebertabelle *f*

tempered ['tɛmpəd] ADJ (*steel*) gehärtet

tempest ['tɛmpɪst] N Sturm *m*

tempestuous [tɛm'pɛstjuəs] ADJ (*also fig*) stürmisch; (*person*) leidenschaftlich

tempi ['tɛmpi:] NPL *of* **tempo**

template ['tɛmplɪt] N Schablone *f*

temple ['tɛmpl] N (*building*) Tempel *m*; (*Anat*) Schläfe *f*

tempo ['tɛmpəu] (*pl* **tempos** *or* **tempi**) N (*Mus, fig*) Tempo *nt*

temporal ['tɛmpərl] ADJ (*non-religious*) weltlich; (*relating to time*) zeitlich

temporarily ['tɛmpərərɪlɪ] ADV vorübergehend; (*unavailable, alone etc*) zeitweilig

temporary ['tɛmpərərɪ] ADJ (*arrangement*) provisorisch; (*worker, job*) Aushilfs-; **~ refugee** Flüchtling *m* mit zeitlich begrenzter Aufenthaltserlaubnis; **~ secretary** Sekretärin zur Aushilfe; **~ teacher** Aushilfslehrer(in) *m(f)*

temporize ['tɛmpəraɪz] VI ausweichen

tempt [tɛmpt] VT in Versuchung führen; **to ~ sb into doing sth** jdn dazu verleiten, etw zu tun; **to be tempted to do sth** versucht sein, etw zu tun

temptation [tɛmp'teɪʃən] N Versuchung *f*

tempting ['tɛmptɪŋ] ADJ (*offer*) verlockend; (*food*) verführerisch

ten [tɛn] NUM zehn ▸ N: **tens of thousands** Zehntausende *pl*

tenable ['tɛnəbl] ADJ (*argument, position*) haltbar

tenacious [tə'neɪʃəs] ADJ zäh, hartnäckig

tenacity [tə'næsɪtɪ] N Zähigkeit *f*, Hartnäckigkeit *f*

tenancy ['tɛnənsɪ] N (*of room*) Mietverhältnis *nt*; (*of land*) Pachtverhältnis *nt*

tenant ['tɛnənt] N (*of room*) Mieter(in) *m(f)*; (*of land*) Pächter(in) *m(f)*

tend [tɛnd] VT (*crops, sick person*) sich kümmern um ▸ VI: **to ~ to do sth** dazu neigen *or* tendieren, etw zu tun

tendency ['tɛndənsɪ] N (*of person*) Neigung *f*; (*of thing*) Tendenz *f*

tender ['tɛndəʳ] ADJ (*person, care*) zärtlich; (*heart*) gut; (*sore*) empfindlich; (*meat, age*) zart ▸ N (*Comm*) Angebot *nt*; (*money*): **legal ~** gesetzliches Zahlungsmittel *nt* ▸ VT (*offer*) vorlegen; (*resignation*) einreichen; (*apology*) anbieten; **to put in a ~ (for)** ein Angebot vorlegen (für); **to put work out to ~** (BRIT) Arbeiten ausschreiben

tenderize ['tɛndəraɪz] VT (*meat*) zart machen

tenderly ['tɛndəlɪ] ADV zärtlich, liebevoll

tenderness ['tɛndənɪs] N (*affection*) Zärtlichkeit *f*; (*of meat*) Zartheit *f*

tendon ['tɛndən] N Sehne *f*

tendril ['tɛndrɪl] N (*Bot*) Ranke *f*; (*of hair etc*) Strähne *f*

tenement ['tɛnəmənt] N Mietshaus *nt*

Tenerife [tɛnə'ri:f] N Teneriffa *nt*

tenet ['tɛnət] N Prinzip *nt*

Tenn. (US) ABBR (*Post*) = **Tennessee**

tenner ['tɛnəʳ] (BRIT *inf*) N Zehner *m*

tennis ['tɛnɪs] N Tennis *nt*

tennis ball N Tennisball *m*

tennis club N Tennisklub *m*

tennis court N Tennisplatz *m*

tennis elbow N (*Med*) Tennisell(en)bogen *m*

tennis match N Tennismatch *nt*

tennis player N Tennisspieler(in) *m(f)*

tennis racket N Tennisschläger *m*

tennis shoes NPL Tennisschuhe *pl*

tenor ['tɛnəʳ] N (*Mus*) Tenor *m*; (*of speech etc*) wesentlicher Gehalt *m*

tenpin bowling ['tɛnpɪn-] (BRIT) N Bowling *nt*

tense [tɛns] ADJ (*person, muscle*) angespannt; (*smile*) verkrampft; (*period, situation*) gespannt ▸ N (*Ling*) Zeit *f*, Tempus *nt* ▸ VT (*muscles*) anspannen

tenseness ['tɛnsnɪs] N Gespanntheit *f*

tension ['tɛnʃən] N (*nervousness*) Angespanntheit *f*; (*between ropes etc*) Spannung *f*

tent [tɛnt] N Zelt *nt*

tentacle ['tɛntəkl] N (*Zool*) Fangarm *m*; (*fig*) Klaue *f*

tentative ['tɛntətɪv] ADJ (*person, smile*) zögernd; (*step*) unsicher; (*conclusion, plans*) vorläufig

tentatively ['tɛntətɪvlɪ] ADV (*suggest*) versuchsweise; (*wave etc*) zögernd

tenterhooks ['tɛntəhuks] NPL: **to be on ~** wie auf glühenden Kohlen sitzen

tenth [tɛnθ] NUM zehnte(r, s) ▸ N Zehntel *nt*

tent peg N Hering *m*

tent pole N Zeltstange *f*

tenuous ['tɛnjuəs] ADJ (*hold, links etc*) schwach

tenure ['tɛnjuəʳ] N (*of land etc*) Nutzungsrecht *nt*; (*of office*) Amtszeit *f*; (*Univ*): **to have ~** eine Dauerstellung haben

tepid ['tɛpɪd] ADJ (*also fig*) lauwarm

Ter. ABBR (*in street names*: = *terrace*) ≈ Str.

term [tə:m] N (*word*) Ausdruck *m*; (*period in power etc*) Amtszeit *f*; (*Scol*: *three per year*) Trimester *nt* ▸ VT (*call*) nennen; **terms** NPL (*also Comm*) Bedingungen *pl*; **in economic/political terms** wirtschaftlich/politisch gesehen; **in terms of**

t

business was das Geschäft angeht *or* betrifft; **~ of imprisonment** Gefängnisstrafe *f*; **"easy terms"** (*Comm*) „günstige Bedingungen"; **in the short/long ~** auf kurze/lange Sicht; **to be on good terms with sb** sich mit jdm gut verstehen; **to come to terms with** (*problem*) sich abfinden mit

terminal ['tə:mɪnl] ADJ (*disease, patient*) unheilbar ▸ N (*Aviat, Comm, Comput*) Terminal *nt*; (*Elec*) Anschluss *m*; (BRIT: *also*: **bus terminal**) Endstation *f*

terminally ADV (*ill*) unheilbar

terminate ['tə:mɪneɪt] VT beenden ▸ VI: **to ~ in** enden in *+dat*

termination [tə:mɪ'neɪʃən] N Beendigung *f*; (*expiry: of contract*) Ablauf *m*; (*Med: of pregnancy*) Abbruch *m*

termini ['tə:mɪnaɪ] NPL *of* **terminus**

terminology [tə:mɪ'nɔlədʒɪ] N Terminologie *f*

terminus ['tə:mɪnəs] (*pl* **termini**) N (*for buses, trains*) Endstation *f*

termite ['tə:maɪt] N Termite *f*

term paper (US) N (*Univ*) ≈ Semesterarbeit *f*

Terr. ABBR (*in street names: = terrace*) ≈ Str.

terrace ['tɛrəs] N (BRIT: *row of houses*) Häuserreihe *f*; (*Agr, patio*) Terrasse *f*; **the terraces** NPL (BRIT *Sport*) die Ränge *pl*

terraced ['tɛrəst] ADJ (*garden*) terrassenförmig angelegt; (*house*) Reihen-

terracotta ['tɛrə'kɔtə] N (*clay*) Terrakotta *f*; (*colour*) Braunrot *nt* ▸ ADJ (*pot, roof etc*) Terrakotta-

terrain [tɛ'reɪn] N Gelände *nt*, Terrain *nt*

terrible ['tɛrɪbl] ADJ schrecklich, furchtbar

terribly ['tɛrɪblɪ] ADV (*very*) furchtbar; (*very badly*) entsetzlich

terrier ['tɛrɪə^r^] N Terrier *m*

terrific [tə'rɪfɪk] ADJ (*time, party*) sagenhaft; (*very great: thunderstorm, speed*) unheimlich

terrify ['tɛrɪfaɪ] VT erschrecken; **to be terrified** schreckliche Angst haben

terrifying ['tɛrɪfaɪɪŋ] ADJ entsetzlich, grauenvoll

territorial [tɛrɪ'tɔ:rɪəl] ADJ (*boundaries, dispute*) territorial, Gebiets-; (*waters*) Hoheits- ▸ N (*Mil*) Soldat *m* der Territorialarmee

Territorial Army (BRIT) N (*Mil*): **the ~** die Territorialarmee

territorial waters NPL Hoheitsgewässer *pl*

territory ['tɛrɪtərɪ] N (*also fig*) Gebiet *nt*

terror ['tɛrə^r^] N (*great fear*) panische Angst *f*

terrorism ['tɛrərɪzəm] N Terrorismus *m*

terrorist ['tɛrərɪst] N Terrorist(in) *m(f)*

terrorize ['tɛrəraɪz] VT terrorisieren

terse [tə:s] ADJ knapp

tertiary ['tə:ʃərɪ] ADJ tertiär; **~ education** (BRIT) Universitätsausbildung *f*

Terylene® ['tɛrɪli:n] N Terylen® *nt* ▸ ADJ Terylen-

TESL ['tɛsl] N ABBR (= *Teaching of English as a Second Language*) *Unterricht in Englisch als Zweitsprache*

TESSA ['tɛsə] (BRIT) N ABBR (= *Tax Exempt Special Savings Account*) *steuerfreies Sparsystem mit begrenzter Einlagehöhe*

test [tɛst] N Test *m*; (*of courage etc*) Probe *f*; (*Scol*) Prüfung *f*; (*also*: **driving test**) Fahrprüfung *f* ▸ VT testen; (*check, Scol*) prüfen; **to put sth to the ~** etw auf die Probe stellen; **to ~ sth for sth** etw auf etw *acc* prüfen

testament ['tɛstəmənt] N Zeugnis *nt*; **the Old/New T~** das Alte/Neue Testament; **last will and ~** Testament *nt*

test ban N (*also*: **nuclear test ban**) Teststopp *m*

test card N (*TV*) Testbild *nt*

test case N (*Law*) Musterfall *m*; (*fig*) Musterbeispiel *nt*

testes ['tɛsti:z] NPL Testikel *pl*, Hoden *pl*

test flight N Testflug *m*

testicle ['tɛstɪkl] N Hoden *m*

testify ['tɛstɪfaɪ] VI (*Law*) aussagen; **to ~ to sth** (*Law, fig*) etw bezeugen

testimonial [tɛstɪ'məunɪəl] N (BRIT: *reference*) Referenz *f*; (*Sport: also*: **testimonial match**) *Benefizspiel, dessen Erlös einem verdienten Spieler zugutekommt*

testimony ['tɛstɪmənɪ] N (*statement*) Aussage *f*; (*clear proof*): **to be (a) ~ to** ein Zeugnis *nt* sein für

testing ['tɛstɪŋ] ADJ schwierig

test match N (*Cricket, Rugby*) Testmatch *nt*, Test Match *nt*, Länderspiel *nt*

testosterone [tɛs'tɔstərəun] N Testosteron *nt*

test paper N (*Scol*) Klassenarbeit *f*

test pilot N Testpilot(in) *m(f)*

test tube N Reagenzglas *nt*

test-tube baby ['tɛsttju:b-] N Retortenbaby *nt*

testy ['tɛstɪ] ADJ gereizt

tetanus ['tɛtənəs] N Tetanus *m*

tetchy ['tɛtʃɪ] ADJ gereizt

tether ['tɛðə^r^] VT (*animal*) festbinden ▸ N: **to be at the end of one's ~** völlig am Ende sein

text [tɛkst] N Text *m*; (*sent by mobile phone*) SMS *f* ▸ VT (*on mobile phone*): **to ~ sb** jdm eine SMS schicken

textbook ['tɛkstbuk] N Lehrbuch *nt*

textiles ['tɛkstaɪlz] NPL Textilien *pl*

texting ['tekstɪŋ] N SMS-Messaging *nt*

text message N (*Tel*) SMS *f*

text messaging N (*Tel*) Textnachrichten *pl*

textual ['tɛkstjuəl] ADJ (*analysis etc*) Text-

texture ['tɛkstʃə^r^] N Beschaffenheit *f*, Struktur *f*

TGWU (BRIT) N ABBR (= *Transport and General Workers' Union*) *Transportarbeitergewerkschaft*

Thai [taɪ] ADJ thailändisch ▸ N Thailänder(in) *m(f)*

Thailand ['taɪlænd] N Thailand *nt*

thalidomide® [θə'lɪdəmaɪd] N Contergan® *nt*

Thames [tɛmz] N: **the ~** die Themse

than [ðæn] CONJ (*in comparisons*) als; **more ~ 10** mehr als 10; **she is older ~ you think** sie ist älter, als Sie denken; **more ~ once** mehr als einmal

thank [θæŋk] VT danken *+dat*; **~ you** danke; **~ you very much** vielen Dank; **~ God!** Gott sei Dank!

thankful ['θæŋkful] ADJ: **~ (for/that)** dankbar (für/, dass)

thankfully [ˈθæŋkfəlɪ] ADV dankbar; **~ there were few victims** zum Glück gab es nur wenige Opfer
thankless [ˈθæŋklɪs] ADJ undankbar
thanks [θæŋks] NPL Dank *m* ▸ EXCL (*also*: **many thanks, thanks a lot**) danke, vielen Dank; **~ to** dank *+gen*
Thanksgiving [ˈθæŋksgɪvɪŋ], (*US*) **Thanksgiving Day** N Thanksgiving Day *m*

> **Thanksgiving (Day)** ist ein Feiertag in den USA, der auf den vierten Donnerstag im November fällt. Er soll daran erinnern, wie die Pilgerväter die gute Ernte im Jahre 1621 feierten. In Kanada gibt es einen ähnlichen Erntedanktag (der aber nichts mit den Pilgervätern zu tun hat) am zweiten Montag im Oktober.

KEYWORD

that [ðæt, ðət] (*pl* **those**) ADJ (*demonstrative*) der/die/das; **that man** der Mann; **that woman** die Frau; **that book** das Buch; **that one** der/die/das da; **I want this one, not that one** ich will dieses (hier), nicht das (da)
▸ PRON **1** (*demonstrative*) das; **who's/what's that?** wer/was ist das?; **is that you?** bist du das?; **will you eat all that?** isst du das alles?; **that's what he said** das hat er gesagt; **what happened after that?** was geschah danach?; **that is (to say)** das heißt; **and that's that!** und damit Schluss!
2 (*relative: subject*) der/die/das; (*: pl*) die; (*: direct object*) den/die/das; (*: pl*) die; (*: indirect object*) dem/der/dem; (*: pl*) denen; **the man that I saw** der Mann, den ich gesehen habe; **all that I have** alles was ich habe; **the people that I spoke to** die Leute, mit denen ich geredet habe
3 (*relative: of time*): **the day that he came** der Tag, an dem er kam; **the winter that he came to see us** der Winter, in dem er uns besuchte
▸ CONJ dass; **he thought that I was ill** er dachte, dass ich krank sei, er dachte, ich sei krank
▸ ADV (*demonstrative*) so; **I can't work that much** ich kann nicht so viel arbeiten; **that high** so hoch

thatched [θætʃt] ADJ strohgedeckt
Thatcherism [ˈθætʃərɪzəm] N Thatcherismus *m*
Thatcherite [ˈθætʃəraɪt] ADJ thatcheristisch ▸ N Thatcher-Anhänger(in) *m(f)*
thaw [θɔː] N Tauwetter *nt* ▸ VI (*ice*) tauen; (*food*) auftauen ▸ VT (*also*: **thaw out**) auftauen; **it's thawing** es taut

KEYWORD

the [ðiː, ðə] DEF ART **1** (*before masculine noun*) der; (*: before feminine noun*) die; (*: before neuter noun*) das; (*: before plural noun*) die; **to play the piano/violin** Klavier/Geige spielen; **I'm going to the butcher's/the cinema** ich gehe zum Metzger/ins Kino
2 (*+ adj to form noun*): **the rich and the poor** die Reichen und die Armen; **to attempt the impossible** das Unmögliche versuchen
3 (*in titles*): **Elizabeth the First** Elisabeth die Erste; **Peter the Great** Peter der Große
4 (*in comparisons*): **the more he works the more he earns** je mehr er arbeitet, desto mehr verdient er; **the sooner the better** je eher, desto besser

theatre, (*US*) **theater** [ˈθɪətə^r] N Theater *nt*; (*also*: **lecture theatre**) Hörsaal *m*; (*also*: **operating theatre**) Operationssaal *m*
theatre-goer [ˈθɪətəgəuə^r] N Theaterbesucher(in) *m(f)*
theatrical [θɪˈætrɪkl] ADJ (*event, production*) Theater-; (*gestures etc*) theatralisch
theft [θɛft] N Diebstahl *m*
their [ðɛə^r] ADJ ihr
theirs [ðɛəz] PRON ihre(r, s); **it is ~** es gehört ihnen; **a friend of ~** ein Freund/eine Freundin von ihnen; *see also* **my**; **mine²**
them [ðɛm] PRON (*direct*) sie; (*indirect*) ihnen; **I see ~** ich sehe sie; **give ~ the book** gib ihnen das Buch; **give me a few of ~** geben Sie mir ein paar davon; **with ~** mit ihnen; **without ~** ohne sie; *see also* **me**
theme [θiːm] N (*also Mus*) Thema *nt*
theme park N Themenpark *m*
theme song N Titelmusik *f*
theme tune N Titelmelodie *f*
themselves [ðəmˈsɛlvz] PL PRON (*reflexive, after prep*) sich; (*emphatic, alone*) selbst; **between ~** unter sich
then [ðɛn] ADV (*at that time*) damals; (*next, later*) dann ▸ CONJ (*therefore*) also ▸ ADJ: **the ~ president** der damalige Präsident; **by ~** (*past*) bis dahin; (*future*) bis dann; **from ~ on** von da an; **before ~** davor; **until ~** bis dann; **and ~ what?** und was dann?; **what do you want me to do ~?** was soll ich dann machen?; **... but ~ (again) he's the boss** ... aber er ist ja der Chef
theologian [θɪəˈləudʒən] N Theologe *m*, Theologin *f*
theological [θɪəˈlɔdʒɪkl] ADJ theologisch
theology [θɪˈɔlədʒɪ] N Theologie *f*
theorem [ˈθɪərəm] N Lehrsatz *m*
theoretical [θɪəˈrɛtɪkl] ADJ theoretisch
theorize [ˈθɪəraɪz] VI theoretisieren
theory [ˈθɪərɪ] N Theorie *f*; **in ~** theoretisch
therapeutic [θɛrəˈpjuːtɪk] ADJ therapeutisch
therapist [ˈθɛrəpɪst] N Therapeut(in) *m(f)*
therapy [ˈθɛrəpɪ] N Therapie *f*

KEYWORD

there [ðɛə^r] ADV **1**: **there is/are** da ist/sind; (*there exist(s)*) es gibt; **there are 3 of them** es gibt 3 davon; **there has been an accident** da war ein Unfall; **there will be a meeting tomorrow** morgen findet ein Treffen statt
2 (*referring to place*) da, dort; **down/over there** da unten/drüben; **put it in/on there** leg es dorthinein/-hinauf; **I want that book there** ich möchte das Buch da; **there he is!** da ist er ja!
3: **there, there** (*esp to child*) ist ja gut

t

thereabouts [ðɛərə'bauts] ADV: **or ~** (*amount, time*) oder so; (*place*) oder dortherum
thereafter [ðɛər'ɑ:ftəʳ] ADV danach
thereby ['ðɛəbaɪ] ADV dadurch
therefore ['ðɛəfɔ:ʳ] ADV daher, deshalb
there's ['ðɛəz] = **there is; there has**
thereupon [ðɛərə'pɔn] ADV (*at that point*) darauf(hin)
thermal ['θə:ml] ADJ (*springs*) Thermal-; (*underwear, paper, printer*) Thermo-
thermodynamics ['θə:mədaɪ'næmɪks] N Thermodynamik *f*
thermometer [θə'mɔmɪtəʳ] N Thermometer *nt*
thermonuclear ['θə:məu'nju:klɪəʳ] ADJ thermonuklear
Thermos® ['θə:məs] N (*also*: **Thermos flask**) Thermosflasche® *f*
thermostat ['θə:məustæt] N Thermostat *m*
thesaurus [θɪ'sɔ:rəs] N Synonymwörterbuch *nt*
these [ði:z] PL ADJ, PL PRON diese
theses ['θi:si:z] NPL *of* **thesis**
thesis ['θi:sɪs] (*pl* **theses**) N These *f*; (*for doctorate etc*) Doktorarbeit *f*, Dissertation *f*
they [ðeɪ] PL PRON sie; **~ say that ...** (*it is said that*) man sagt, dass ...
they'd [ðeɪd] = **they had; they would**
they'll [ðeɪl] = **they shall; they will**
they're [ðɛəʳ] = **they are**
they've [ðeɪv] = **they have**
thick [θɪk] ADJ dick; (*sauce etc*) dickflüssig; (*fog, forest, hair etc*) dicht; (*inf: stupid*) blöd ▶ N: **in the ~ of the battle** mitten im Gefecht; **it's 20 cm ~** es ist 20 cm dick
thicken ['θɪkn] VI (*fog etc*) sich verdichten ▶ VT (*sauce etc*) eindicken; **the plot thickens** die Sache wird immer verwickelter
thicket ['θɪkɪt] N Dickicht *nt*
thickly ['θɪklɪ] ADV (*spread, cut*) dick; **~ populated** dicht bevölkert
thickness ['θɪknɪs] N (*of rope, wire*) Dicke *f*; (*layer*) Lage *f*
thickset [θɪk'sɛt] ADJ (*person, body*) gedrungen
thick-skinned [θɪk'skɪnd] ADJ (*also fig*) dickhäutig
thief [θi:f] (*pl* **thieves**) N Dieb(in) *m(f)*
thieves [θi:vz] NPL *of* **thief**
thieving ['θi:vɪŋ] N Stehlen *nt*
thigh [θaɪ] N Oberschenkel *m*
thighbone ['θaɪbəun] N Oberschenkelknochen *m*
thimble ['θɪmbl] N Fingerhut *m*
thin [θɪn] ADJ dünn; (*fog*) leicht; (*hair, crowd*) spärlich ▶ VT: **to ~ (down)** (*sauce, paint*) verdünnen ▶ VI (*fog, crowd*) sich lichten; **his hair is thinning** sein Haar lichtet sich
thing [θɪŋ] N Ding *nt*; (*matter*) Sache *f*; (*inf*): **to have a ~ about sth** (*be fascinated by*) wie besessen sein von etw; (*hate*) etw nicht ausstehen können; **things** NPL (*belongings*) Sachen *pl*; **to do sth first ~ (every morning/tomorrow morning)** etw (morgens/morgen früh) als Erstes tun; **I look awful first ~ in the morning** ich sehe frühmorgens immer furchtbar aus; **to do sth last ~ (at night)** etw als Letztes (am Abend) tun; **the ~ is ...** die Sache ist die: ...; **for one ~** zunächst mal; **don't worry about a ~** du brauchst dir überhaupt keine Sorgen zu machen; **you'll do no such ~!** das lässt du schön bleiben!; **poor ~** armes Ding; **the best ~ would be to ...** das Beste wäre, zu ...; **how are things?** wie gehts?
think [θɪŋk] (*pt, pp* **thought**) VI (*reason*) denken; (*reflect*) nachdenken ▶ VT (*be of the opinion*) denken; (*believe*) glauben; **to ~ of** denken an *+acc*; (*recall*) sich erinnern an *+acc*; **what did you ~ of them?** was hielten Sie von ihnen?; **to ~ about sth/sb** (*ponder*) über etw/jdn nachdenken; **I'll ~ about it** ich werde es mir überlegen; **to ~ of doing sth** daran denken, etw zu tun; **to ~ highly of sb** viel von jdm halten; **to ~ aloud** laut nachdenken; **~ again!** denk noch mal nach!; **I ~ so/not** ich glaube ja/nein
▶ **think over** VT (*offer, suggestion*) überdenken; **I'd like to ~ things over** ich möchte mir die Sache noch einmal überlegen
▶ **think through** VT durchdenken
▶ **think up** VT sich *dat* ausdenken
thinking ['θɪŋkɪŋ] N Denken *nt*; **to my (way of) ~** meiner Meinung *or* Ansicht nach
think-tank ['θɪŋktæŋk] N Expertengremium *nt*
thinly ['θɪnlɪ] ADV dünn; (*disguised, veiled*) kaum
thinness ['θɪnnɪs] N Dünne *f*
third [θə:d] NUM dritte(r, s) ▶ N (*fraction*) Drittel *nt*; (*Aut: also*: **third gear**) dritter Gang *m*; (BRIT *Scol: degree*) ≈ Ausreichend *nt*; **a ~ of** ein Drittel *+gen*
third-degree burns ['θə:ddɪgri:-] NPL Verbrennungen *pl* dritten Grades
thirdly ['θə:dlɪ] ADV drittens
third party insurance (BRIT) N ≈ Haftpflichtversicherung *f*
third-rate ['θə:d'reɪt] (*pej*) ADJ drittklassig
Third World N: **the ~** die Dritte Welt ▶ ADJ der Dritten Welt
thirst [θə:st] N Durst *m*
thirsty ['θə:stɪ] ADJ durstig; **to be ~** Durst haben; **gardening is ~ work** Gartenarbeit macht durstig
thirteen [θə:'ti:n] NUM dreizehn
thirteenth ['θə:'ti:nθ] NUM dreizehnte(r, s)
thirtieth ['θə:tɪɪθ] NUM dreißigste(r, s)
thirty ['θə:tɪ] NUM dreißig

KEYWORD

this [ðɪs] (*pl* **these**) ADJ (*demonstrative*) diese(r, s); **this man** dieser Mann; **this woman** diese Frau; **this book** dieses Buch; **this one** diese(r, s) (hier)
▶ PRON (*demonstrative*) dies, das; **who/what is this?** wer/was ist das?; **this is where I live** hier wohne ich; **this is what he said** das hat er gesagt; **this is Mr Brown** (*in introductions, photo*) das ist Herr Brown; (*on telephone*) hier ist Herr Brown
▶ ADV (*demonstrative*): **this high/long** *etc* so hoch/lang *etc*

thistle ['θɪsl] N Distel *f*
thong [θɔŋ] N Riemen *m*
thorn [θɔ:n] N Dorn *m*
thorny ['θɔ:nɪ] ADJ dornig; (*fig: problem*) heikel
thorough ['θʌrə] ADJ gründlich
thoroughbred ['θʌrəbrɛd] N (*horse*) Vollblüter *m*
thoroughfare ['θʌrəfɛəʳ] N (*road*) Durchgangsstraße *f*; **"no ~"** (BRIT) „Durchfahrt verboten"
thoroughgoing ['θʌrəgəuɪŋ] ADJ (*changes, reform*) grundlegend; (*investigation*) gründlich
thoroughly ['θʌrəlɪ] ADV gründlich; (*very*) äußerst; **I ~ agree** ich stimme vollkommen zu
thoroughness ['θʌrənɪs] N Gründlichkeit *f*
those [ðəuz] PL ADJ, PL PRON die (da); **~ (of you) who ...** diejenigen (von Ihnen), die ...
though [ðəu] CONJ obwohl ▸ ADV aber; **even ~** obwohl; **it's not easy, ~** es ist aber nicht einfach
thought [θɔ:t] PT, PP *of* **think** ▸ N Gedanke *m*; **thoughts** NPL (*opinion*) Gedanken *pl*; **after much ~** nach langer Überlegung; **I've just had a ~** mir ist gerade etwas eingefallen; **to give sth some ~** sich *dat* Gedanken über etw *acc* machen
thoughtful ['θɔ:tful] ADJ (*deep in thought*) nachdenklich; (*considerate*) aufmerksam
thoughtfully ['θɔ:tfəlɪ] ADV (*look etc*) nachdenklich; (*behave etc*) rücksichtsvoll; (*provide*) rücksichtsvollerweise
thoughtless ['θɔ:tlɪs] ADJ gedankenlos
thoughtlessly ['θɔ:tlɪslɪ] ADV gedankenlos
thoughtlessness ['θɔ:tlɪsnɪs] N Gedankenlosigkeit *f*
thought-out [θɔ:t'aut] ADJ durchdacht
thought-provoking ['θɔ:tprəvəukɪŋ] ADJ: **to be ~** Denkanstöße geben
thousand ['θauzənd] NUM (ein)tausend; **two ~** zweitausend; **thousands of** Tausende von
thousandth ['θauzəntθ] NUM tausendste(r, s)
thrash [θræʃ] VT (*beat*) verprügeln; (*defeat*) (vernichtend) schlagen
▸ **thrash about** VI um sich schlagen
▸ **thrash around** VI = **thrash about**
▸ **thrash out** VT (*problem*) ausdiskutieren
thrashing ['θræʃɪŋ] N: **to give sb a ~** jdn verprügeln
thread [θrɛd] N (*yarn*) Faden *m*; (*of screw*) Gewinde *nt* ▸ VT (*needle*) einfädeln; **to ~ one's way between** sich hindurchschlängeln zwischen
threadbare ['θrɛdbɛəʳ] ADJ (*clothes*) abgetragen; (*carpet*) abgelaufen
threat [θrɛt] N Drohung *f*; (*fig*): **~ (to)** Gefahr *f* (für); **to be under ~ of** (*closure etc*) bedroht sein von
threaten ['θrɛtn] VI bedrohen ▸ VT: **to ~ sb with sth** jdm mit etw drohen; **to ~ to do sth** (damit) drohen, etw zu tun
threatening ['θrɛtnɪŋ] ADJ bedrohlich, drohend
three [θri:] NUM drei
three-dimensional [θri:dɪ'mɛnʃənl] ADJ dreidimensional
threefold ['θri:fəuld] ADV: **to increase ~** dreifach *or* um das Dreifache ansteigen
three-piece suit ['θri:pi:s-] N dreiteiliger Anzug *m*
three-piece suite N dreiteilige Polstergarnitur *f*
three-ply [θri:'plaɪ] ADJ (*wool*) dreifädig; (*wood*) dreilagig
three-quarters [θri:'kwɔ:təz] NPL drei Viertel *pl*; **~ full** drei viertel voll
three-wheeler ['θri:'wi:ləʳ] N (*car*) Dreiradwagen *m*
thresh [θrɛʃ] VT dreschen
threshing machine ['θrɛʃɪŋ-] N Dreschmaschine *f*
threshold ['θrɛʃhəuld] N Schwelle *f*; **to be on the ~ of sth** (*fig*) an der Schwelle zu etw sein *or* stehen
threshold agreement N (*Econ*) *Tarifvereinbarung über der Inflationsrate angeglichene Lohnerhöhungen*
threw [θru:] PT *of* **throw**
thrift [θrɪft] N Sparsamkeit *f*
thrifty ['θrɪftɪ] ADJ sparsam
thrill [θrɪl] N (*excitement*) Aufregung *f*; (*shudder*) Erregung *f* ▸ VI zittern ▸ VT (*person, audience*) erregen; **to be thrilled** (*with gift etc*) sich riesig freuen
thriller ['θrɪləʳ] N Thriller *m*
thrilling ['θrɪlɪŋ] ADJ (*news*) aufregend; (*ride, performance etc*) erregend
thrive [θraɪv] (*pt* **thrived** *or* **throve**, *pp* **thrived**) VI gedeihen; **to ~ on sth** von etw leben
thriving ['θraɪvɪŋ] ADJ (*business, community*) blühend, florierend
throat [θrəut] N Kehle *f*; **to have a sore ~** Halsschmerzen haben
throb [θrɔb] N (*of heart*) Klopfen *nt*; (*pain*) Pochen *nt*; (*of engine*) Dröhnen *nt* ▸ VI (*heart*) klopfen; (*pain*) pochen; (*machine*) dröhnen; **my head is throbbing** ich habe rasende Kopfschmerzen
throes [θrəuz] NPL: **in the ~ of** (*war, moving house etc*) mitten in *+dat*; **death ~** Todeskampf *m*
thrombosis [θrɔm'bəusɪs] N Thrombose *f*
throne [θrəun] N Thron *m*; **on the ~** auf dem Thron
throng ['θrɔŋ] N Masse *f* ▸ VT (*streets etc*) sich drängen in *+dat* ▸ VI: **to ~ to** strömen zu; **a ~ of people** eine Menschenmenge; **to be thronged with** wimmeln von
throttle ['θrɔtl] N (*in car*) Gaspedal *nt*; (*on motorcycle*) Gashebel *m* ▸ VT (*strangle*) erdrosseln
through [θru:] PREP durch; (*time*) während; (*owing to*) infolge *+gen* ▸ ADJ (*ticket, train*) durchgehend ▸ ADV durch; **(from) Monday ~ Friday** (US) von Montag bis Freitag; **to be ~** (*Tel*) verbunden sein; **to be ~ with sb/sth** mit jdm/etw fertig sein; **we're ~!** es ist aus zwischen uns!; **"no ~ road"**, **"no ~ traffic"** (US) „keine Durchfahrt"; **to let sb ~** jdn durchlassen; **to put sb ~ to sb** (*Tel*) jdn mit jdm verbinden
throughout [θru:'aut] ADV (*everywhere*) überall; (*the whole time*) die ganze Zeit über ▸ PREP (*place*) überall in *+dat*; (*time*): **~ the morning/**

t

afternoon während des ganzen Morgens/ Nachmittags; **~ her life** ihr ganzes Leben lang
throughput ['θru:put] N (*also Comput*) Durchsatz *m*
throve [θrəuv] PT *of* **thrive**
throw [θrəu] (*pt* **threw**, *pp* **thrown**) N Wurf *m* ▸ VT werfen; (*rider*) abwerfen; (*fig: confuse*) aus der Fassung bringen; (*pottery*) töpfern; **to ~ a party** eine Party geben; **to ~ open** (*doors, windows*) aufreißen; (*debate*) öffnen
▸ **throw about** VT (*money*) herumwerfen mit
▸ **throw around** VT = **throw about**
▸ **throw away** VT wegwerfen; (*waste*) verschwenden
▸ **throw off** VT (*get rid of: burden*) abwerfen
▸ **throw out** VT (*rubbish*) wegwerfen; (*idea*) verwerfen; (*person*) hinauswerfen
▸ **throw together** VT (*meal*) hinhauen; (*clothes*) zusammenpacken
▸ **throw up** VI (*vomit*) sich übergeben
throwaway ['θrəuəweɪ] ADJ (*cutlery etc*) Einweg-; (*line, remark*) beiläufig
throwback ['θrəubæk] N: **it's a ~ to** (*reminder*) es erinnert an *+acc*
throw-in ['θrəuɪn] N (*Football*) Einwurf *m*
thrown [θrəun] PP *of* **throw**
thru [θru:] (US) PREP, ADJ, ADV = **through**
thrush [θrʌʃ] N (*bird*) Drossel *f*; (*Med: esp in children*) Soor *m*; (: BRIT: *in women*) vaginale Pilzerkrankung *f*
thrust [θrʌst] (*pt, pp* **~**) VT stoßen ▸ N (*Tech*) Schubkraft *f*; (*push*) Stoß *m*; (*fig: impetus*) Stoßkraft *f*
thud [θʌd] N dumpfes Geräusch *nt*
thug [θʌg] N Schlägertyp *m*
thumb [θʌm] N Daumen *m* ▸ VT: **to ~ a lift** per Anhalter fahren; **to give sb/sth the thumbs up** (*approve*) jdm/etw *dat* grünes Licht geben; **to give sb/sth the thumbs down** (*disapprove*) jdn/ etw ablehnen
▸ **thumb through** VT FUS (*book*) durchblättern
thumb index N Daumenregister *nt*
thumbnail ['θʌmneɪl] N Daumennagel *m*
thumbnail sketch N kurze Darstellung *f*
thumbtack ['θʌmtæk] (US) N Heftzwecke *f*
thump [θʌmp] N (*blow*) Schlag *m*; (*sound*) dumpfer Schlag *m* ▸ VT schlagen auf *+acc* ▸ VI (*heart etc*) heftig pochen
thumping ['θʌmpɪŋ] ADJ (*majority, victory etc*) Riesen-; (*headache, cold*) fürchterlich
thunder ['θʌndə^r] N Donner *m* ▸ VI donnern; (*shout angrily*) brüllen; **to ~ past** (*train etc*) vorbeidonnern
thunderbolt ['θʌndəbəult] N Blitzschlag *m*
thunderclap ['θʌndəklæp] N Donnerschlag *m*
thunderous ['θʌndrəs] ADJ donnernd
thunderstorm ['θʌndəstɔ:m] N Gewitter *nt*
thunderstruck ['θʌndəstrʌk] ADJ: **to be ~** (*shocked*) wie von Donner gerührt sein
thundery ['θʌndərɪ] ADJ (*weather*) gewitterig
Thur., Thurs. ABBR (= *Thursday*) Do.
Thursday ['θə:zdɪ] N Donnerstag *m*; *see also* **Tuesday**
thus [ðʌs] ADV (*in this way*) so; (*consequently*) somit
thwart [θwɔ:t] VT (*person*) einen Strich durch die Rechnung machen *+dat*; (*plans*) vereiteln
thyme [taɪm] N Thymian *m*
thyroid ['θaɪrɔɪd] N (*also:* **thyroid gland**) Schilddrüse *f*
tiara [tɪ'ɑ:rə] N Diadem *nt*
Tiber ['taɪbə^r] N: **the ~** der Tiber
Tibet [tɪ'bɛt] N Tibet *nt*
Tibetan [tɪ'bɛtən] ADJ tibetanisch ▸ N (*person*) Tibetaner(in) *m(f)*; (*Ling*) Tibetisch *nt*
tibia ['tɪbɪə] N Schienbein *nt*
tic [tɪk] N nervöse Zuckung *f*, Tic *m*, Tick *m*
tick [tɪk] N (*mark*) Häkchen *nt*; (*sound*) Ticken *nt*; (*Zool*) Zecke *f*; (BRIT *inf: moment*) Augenblick *m*; (: *credit*): **to buy sth on ~** etw auf Pump kaufen ▸ VI (*clock, watch*) ticken ▸ VT (*item on list*) abhaken; **to put a ~ against sth** etw abhaken; **what makes him ~?** was ist er für ein Mensch?
▸ **tick off** VT (*item on list*) abhaken; (*person*) rüffeln
▸ **tick over** VI (*engine*) im Leerlauf sein; (*fig: business etc*) sich über Wasser halten
ticker tape ['tɪkəteɪp] N Lochstreifen *m*; (US: *in celebrations*) ≈ Luftschlangen *pl*
ticket ['tɪkɪt] N (*for public transport*) Fahrkarte *f*; (*for theatre etc*) Eintrittskarte *f*; (*in shop: on goods*) Preisschild *nt*; (: *from cash register*) Kassenbon *m*; (*for raffle*) Los *nt*; (*for library*) Ausweis *m*; (*fine: also:* **parking ticket**) Strafzettel *m*; (*US Pol*) Wahlliste *f*; **to get a (parking) ~** (*Aut*) einen Strafzettel bekommen
ticket agency N (*Theat*) Vorverkaufsstelle *f*
ticket collector N (*Rail: at station*) Fahrkartenkontrolleur(in) *m(f)*; (*on train*) Schaffner(in) *m(f)*
ticket holder N Karteninhaber(in) *m(f)*
ticket inspector N Fahrkartenkontrolleur(in) *m(f)*
ticket machine N (*for public transport*) Fahrscheinautomat *m*; (*in car park*) Parkscheinautomat *m*
ticket office N (*Rail*) Fahrkartenschalter *m*; (*Theat*) Theaterkasse *f*
tickle ['tɪkl] VT kitzeln; (*fig: amuse*) amüsieren ▸ VI kitzeln; **it tickles!** das kitzelt!
ticklish ['tɪklɪʃ] ADJ (*person, situation*) kitzlig
tidal ['taɪdl] ADJ (*force*) Gezeiten-, der Gezeiten; (*river*) Tide-
tidal wave N Flutwelle *f*
tidbit ['tɪdbɪt] (US) N = **titbit**
tiddlywinks ['tɪdlɪwɪŋks] N Flohhüpfen *nt*
tide [taɪd] N (*in sea*) Gezeiten *pl*; (*fig: of events, opinion etc*) Trend *m*; **high ~** Flut *f*; **low ~** Ebbe *f*; **the ~ is in/out** es ist Flut/Ebbe; **the ~ is coming in** die Flut kommt
▸ **tide over** VT über die Runden helfen *+dat*
tidily ['taɪdɪlɪ] ADV ordentlich
tidiness ['taɪdɪnɪs] N Ordentlichkeit *f*
tidy ['taɪdɪ] ADJ (*room, desk*) ordentlich, aufgeräumt; (*person*) ordnungsliebend; (*sum, income*) ordentlich ▸ VT (*also:* **tidy up**) aufräumen

tie [taɪ] N (BRIT: *also*: **necktie**) Krawatte *f*; (*string etc*) Band *nt*; (*fig: link*) Verbindung *f*; (*Sport: match*) Spiel *nt*; (*in competition: draw*) Unentschieden *nt* ▸ VT (*ribbon*) binden; (*parcel*) verschnüren; (*shoelaces*) zubinden ▸ VI (*Sport etc*): **to ~ with sb for first place** sich mit jdm den ersten Platz teilen; **"black ~"** „Abendanzug"; **"white ~"** „Frackzwang"; **family ties** familiäre Bindungen; **to ~ sth in a bow** etw zu einer Schleife binden; **to ~ a knot in sth** einen Knoten in etw *acc* machen
▸ **tie down** VT (*fig: restrict*) binden; (*: to date, price etc*) festlegen
▸ **tie in** VI: **to ~ in with** zusammenpassen mit
▸ **tie on** VT (BRIT) anbinden
▸ **tie up** VT (*parcel*) verschnüren; (*dog*) anbinden; (*boat*) festmachen; (*person*) fesseln; (*arrangements*) unter Dach und Fach bringen; **to be tied up** (*busy*) zu tun haben, beschäftigt sein

tie-break ['taɪbreɪk], **tie-breaker** ['taɪbreɪkə^r] N (*Tennis*) Tiebreak *m*; (*in quiz*) Entscheidungsfrage *f*

tie-on ['taɪɔn] (BRIT) ADJ (*label*) Anhänge-

tiepin ['taɪpɪn] (BRIT) N Krawattennadel *f*

tier [tɪə^r] N (*of stadium etc*) Rang *m*; (*of cake*) Lage *f*

tie-tack ['taɪtæk] (US) N = **tiepin**

tiff [tɪf] N Krach *m*

tiger ['taɪgə^r] N Tiger *m*

tiger economy N (*Econ*) Tigerstaat *m*

tight [taɪt] ADJ (*screw, knot, grip*) fest; (*shoes, clothes, bend*) eng; (*security*) streng; (*budget, money*) knapp; (*schedule*) gedrängt; (*inf: drunk*) voll; (*: stingy*) knickerig ▸ ADV fest; **to be packed ~** (*suitcase*) prallvoll sein; (*room*) gerammelt voll sein; **everybody hold ~!** alle festhalten!

tighten ['taɪtn] VT (*rope, strap*) straffen; (*screw, bolt*) anziehen; (*grip*) festigen; (*security*) verschärfen ▸ VI (*grip*) sich festigen; (*rope etc*) sich spannen

tightfisted [taɪt'fɪstɪd] ADJ knickerig (*inf*)

tight-lipped ['taɪt'lɪpt] ADJ (*fig: silence*) eisern; **to be ~ about sth** über etw *acc* schweigen

tightly ['taɪtlɪ] ADV fest

tightrope ['taɪtrəup] N Seil *nt*; **to be on** *or* **walking a ~** (*fig*) einen Balanceakt vollführen

tightrope walker N Seiltänzer(in) *m(f)*

tights [taɪts] (BRIT) NPL Strumpfhose *f*

tigress ['taɪgrɪs] N Tigerin *f*

tilde ['tɪldə] N Tilde *f*

tile [taɪl] N (*on roof*) Ziegel *m*; (*on floor*) Fliese *f*; (*on wall*) Kachel *f* ▸ VT (*floor*) mit Fliesen auslegen; (*bathroom*) kacheln

tiled [taɪld] ADJ (*floor*) mit Fliesen ausgelegt; (*wall*) gekachelt

till [tɪl] N (*in shop etc*) Kasse *f* ▸ VT (*land*) bestellen ▸ PREP, CONJ = **until**

tiller ['tɪlə^r] N (*Naut*) Ruderpinne *f*

tilt [tɪlt] VT neigen ▸ VI sich neigen ▸ N (*slope*) Neigung *f*; **to wear one's hat at a ~** den Hut schief aufhaben; **(at) full ~** mit Volldampf

timber ['tɪmbə^r] N (*material*) Holz *nt*; (*trees*) Nutzholz *nt*

time [taɪm] N Zeit *f*; (*occasion*) Mal *nt*, Gelegenheit *f*; (*Mus*) Takt *m* ▸ VT (*measure time of*) die Zeit messen bei; (*runner*) stoppen; (*fix moment for: visit etc*) den Zeitpunkt festlegen für; **a long ~** eine lange Zeit; **for the ~ being** vorläufig; **4 at a ~** 4 auf einmal; **from ~ to ~** von Zeit zu Zeit; **~ after ~, ~ and again** immer (und immer) wieder; **at times** manchmal, zuweilen; **in ~** (*soon enough*) rechtzeitig; (*eventually*) mit der Zeit; (*Mus*) im Takt; **in a week's ~** in einer Woche; **in no ~** im Handumdrehen; **any ~** jederzeit; **on ~** rechtzeitig; **to be 30 minutes behind/ahead of ~** 30 Minuten zurück/voraus sein; **by the ~ he arrived** als er ankam; **5 times 5** 5 mal 5; **what ~ is it?** wie spät ist es?; **to have a good ~** sich amüsieren; **we/they** *etc* **had a hard ~** wir/sie *etc* hatten es schwer; **~'s up!** die Zeit ist um!; **I've no ~ for it** (*fig*) dafür habe ich nichts übrig; **he'll do it in his own (good) ~** (*without being hurried*) er macht es, ohne sich hetzen zu lassen; **he'll do it in his own ~**, (US) **he'll do it on his own ~** (*out of working hours*) er macht es in seiner Freizeit; **to be behind the times** rückständig sein; **to ~ sth well/badly** den richtigen/falschen Zeitpunkt für etw wählen; **the bomb was timed to go off 5 minutes later** die Bombe war so eingestellt, dass sie 5 Minuten später explodieren sollte

time-and-motion study ['taɪmənd'məuʃən-] N Arbeitsstudie *f*

time bomb N (*also fig*) Zeitbombe *f*

time card N Stechkarte *f*

time clock N (*in factory etc*) Stechuhr *f*

time-consuming ['taɪmkənsju:mɪŋ] ADJ zeitraubend

time difference N Zeitunterschied *m*

time frame N zeitlicher Rahmen *m*

time-honoured, (US) **time-honored** ['taɪmɔnəd] ADJ althergebracht

timekeeper ['taɪmki:pə^r] N: **she's a good ~** sie erfüllt ihr Zeitsoll

time-lag ['taɪmlæg] N Verzögerung *f*

timeless ['taɪmlɪs] ADJ zeitlos

time limit N zeitliche Grenze *f*

timely ['taɪmlɪ] ADJ (*arrival*) rechtzeitig; (*reminder*) zur rechten Zeit

time management N Zeitmanagement *nt*

time off N: **to take ~** sich *dat* freinehmen

timer ['taɪmə^r] N (*time switch*) Schaltuhr *f*; (*on cooker*) Zeitmesser *m*; (*on video*) Timer *m*

time-saving ['taɪmseɪvɪŋ] ADJ zeitsparend

timescale ['taɪmskeɪl] (BRIT) N Zeitspanne *f*

time-share ['taɪmʃɛə^r] N Ferienwohnung *f* auf Timesharingbasis

time-sharing ['taɪmʃɛərɪŋ] N (*of property, Comput*) Timesharing *nt*

time sheet N = **time card**

time signal N (*Radio*) Zeitzeichen *nt*

time switch N Zeitschalter *m*

timetable ['taɪmteɪbl] N (*Rail etc*) Fahrplan *m*; (*Scol*) Stundenplan *m*; (*programme of events*) Programm *nt*

time zone N Zeitzone *f*

timid ['tɪmɪd] ADJ (*person*) schüchtern; (*animal*) scheu
timidity [tɪ'mɪdɪtɪ] N (*shyness*) Schüchternheit *f*
timing ['taɪmɪŋ] N (*Sport*) Timing *nt*; **the ~ of his resignation** der Zeitpunkt seines Rücktritts
timing device N (*on bomb*) Zeitzünder *m*
timpani ['tɪmpənɪ] NPL Kesselpauken *pl*
tin [tɪn] N (*metal*) Blech *nt*; (*container*) Dose *f*; (*: for baking*) Form *f*; (*: BRIT: can*) Dose *f*, Büchse *f*; **two tins of paint** zwei Dosen Farbe
tinfoil ['tɪnfɔɪl] N Alufolie *f*
tinge [tɪndʒ] N (*of colour*) Färbung *f*; (*fig: of emotion etc*) Anflug *m*, Anstrich *m* ▸ VT: **tinged with blue/red** leicht blau/rot gefärbt; **to be tinged with sth** (*fig: emotion etc*) einen Anstrich von etw haben
tingle ['tɪŋgl] VI prickeln; (*from cold*) kribbeln; **I was tingling with excitement** ich zitterte vor Aufregung
tinker ['tɪŋkə^r] N (*gipsy*) Kesselflicker *m*
▸ **tinker with** VT FUS herumbasteln an *+dat*
tinkle ['tɪŋkl] VI klingeln ▸ N (*inf*): **to give sb a ~** (*Tel*) bei jdm anklingeln
tin mine N Zinnbergwerk *nt*
tinned [tɪnd] (BRIT) ADJ (*food, peas*) Dosen-, in Dosen
tinnitus ['tɪnɪtəs] N Tinnitus *m*, Ohrensummen *nt*
tinny ['tɪnɪ] (*pej*) ADJ (*sound*) blechern; (*car etc*) Schrott-
tin-opener ['tɪnəupnə^r] (BRIT) N Dosenöffner *m*
tinsel ['tɪnsl] N Rauschgoldgirlanden *pl*
tint [tɪnt] N (*colour*) Ton *m*; (*for hair*) Tönung *f* ▸ VT (*hair*) tönen
tinted ['tɪntɪd] ADJ getönt
tiny ['taɪnɪ] ADJ winzig
tip [tɪp] N (*end*) Spitze *f*; (*gratuity*) Trinkgeld *nt*; (BRIT: *for rubbish*) Müllkippe *f*; (*: for coal*) Halde *f*; (*advice*) Tipp *m*, Hinweis *m* ▸ VT (*waiter*) ein Trinkgeld geben *+dat*; (*tilt*) kippen; (*overturn: also*: **tip over**) umkippen; (*empty: also*: **tip out**) leeren; (*predict: winner etc*) tippen *or* setzen auf *+acc*; **he tipped out the contents of the box** er kippte den Inhalt der Kiste aus
▸ **tip off** VT einen Tipp *or* Hinweis geben *+dat*
tip-off ['tɪpɔf] N Hinweis *m*
tipped ['tɪpt] ADJ (BRIT: *cigarette*) Filter-; **steel-~** mit Stahlspitze
Tipp-Ex® ['tɪpɛks] N Tipp-Ex® *nt*
tipple ['tɪpl] (BRIT) VI picheln ▸ N: **to have a ~** einen trinken
tipster ['tɪpstə^r] N *jd, der bei Pferderennen, Börsengeschäften etc Tipps gegen Bezahlung weitergibt*
tipsy ['tɪpsɪ] (*inf*) ADJ beschwipst
tiptoe ['tɪptəu] N: **on ~** auf Zehenspitzen
tip-top ['tɪp'tɔp] ADJ: **in ~ condition** tipptopp
tirade [taɪ'reɪd] N Tirade *f*
tire ['taɪə^r] N (US) = **tyre** ▸ VT müde machen, ermüden ▸ VI (*become tired*) müde werden; **to ~ of sth** genug von etw haben
▸ **tire out** VT erschöpfen
tired ['taɪəd] ADJ müde; **to be/look ~** müde sein/aussehen; **to feel ~** sich müde fühlen; **to be ~ of sth** etw satthaben; **to be ~ of doing sth** es satthaben, etw zu tun
tiredness ['taɪədnɪs] N Müdigkeit *f*
tireless ['taɪəlɪs] ADJ unermüdlich
tiresome ['taɪəsəm] ADJ lästig
tiring ['taɪərɪŋ] ADJ ermüdend, anstrengend
tissue ['tɪʃu:] N (*Anat, Biol*) Gewebe *nt*; (*paper handkerchief*) Papiertaschentuch *nt*
tissue paper N Seidenpapier *nt*
tit [tɪt] N (*bird*) Meise *f*; (*inf: breast*) Titte *f*; **~ for tat** wie du mir, so ich dir
titanium [tɪ'teɪnɪəm] N Titan *nt*
titbit, (US) **tidbit** ['tɪtbɪt] N (*food, news*) Leckerbissen *m*
titillate ['tɪtɪleɪt] VT erregen, reizen
titivate ['tɪtɪveɪt] VT fein machen
title ['taɪtl] N Titel *m*; (*Law*): **~ to** Anspruch auf *+acc*
title deed N Eigentumsurkunde *f*
title page N Titelseite *f*
title role N Titelrolle *f*
title track N Titelstück *nt*
titter ['tɪtə^r] VI kichern
tittle-tattle ['tɪtltætl] (*inf*) N Klatsch *m*, Gerede *nt*
tizzy ['tɪzɪ] N: **to be in a ~** aufgeregt sein; **to get in a ~** sich aufregen
T-junction ['ti:'dʒʌŋkʃən] N T-Kreuzung *f*
TM ABBR (= *trademark*) Wz; = **transcendental meditation**
TN (US) ABBR (*Post*) = **Tennessee**
TNT N ABBR (= *trinitrotoluene*) TNT *nt*

KEYWORD

to [tu:] PREP **1** (*direction*) nach *+dat*, zu *+dat*; **to go to France/London/school/the station** nach Frankreich/nach London/zur Schule/zum Bahnhof gehen; **to the left/right** nach links/rechts; **I have never been to Germany** ich war noch nie in Deutschland
2 (*as far as*) bis; **to count to 10** bis 10 zählen
3 (*with expressions of time*) vor *+dat*; **a quarter to 5** (BRIT) Viertel vor 5
4 (*for, of*): **the key to the front door** der Schlüssel für die Haustür; **a letter to his wife** ein Brief an seine Frau
5 (*expressing indirect object*): **to give sth to sb** jdm etw geben; **to talk to sb** mit jdm sprechen; **I sold it to a friend** ich habe es an einen Freund verkauft; **you've done something to your hair** du hast etwas mit deinem Haar gemacht
6 (*in relation to*) zu; **A is to B as C is to D** A verhält sich zu B wie C zu D; **3 goals to 2** 3 zu 2 Tore; **40 miles to the gallon** 40 Meilen pro Gallone
7 (*purpose, result*) zu; **to sentence sb to death** jdn zum Tode verurteilen; **to my surprise** zu meiner Überraschung
▸ PREP (*with vb*) **1** (*simple infinitive*): **to go** gehen; **to eat** essen
2 (*following another vb*): **to want to do sth** etw tun wollen; **to try/start to do sth** versuchen/anfangen, etw zu tun

3 (*with vb omitted*): **I don't want to** ich will nicht; **you ought to** du solltest es tun
4 (*purpose, result*) (um ...) zu; **I did it to help you** ich habe es getan, um dir zu helfen
5 (*equivalent to relative clause*) zu; **he has a lot to lose** er hat viel zu verlieren; **the main thing is to try** die Hauptsache ist, es zu versuchen
6 (*after adjective etc*): **ready to use** gebrauchsfertig; **too old/young to ...** zu alt/jung, um zu ...; **it's too heavy to lift** es ist zu schwer zu heben
▶ ADV: **to push/pull the door to** die Tür zudrücken/zuziehen; **to and fro** hin und her

toad [təud] N Kröte *f*
toadstool ['təudstu:l] N Giftpilz *m*
toady ['təudɪ] (*pej*) VI: **to ~ to sb** vor jdm kriechen
toast [təust] N (*bread, drink*) Toast *m* ▶ VT (*bread etc*) toasten; (*drink to*) einen Toast *or* Trinkspruch ausbringen auf *+acc*; **a piece** *or* **slice of ~** eine Scheibe Toast
toaster ['təustə^r] N Toaster *m*
toastmaster ['təustmɑ:stə^r] N Zeremonienmeister *m*
toast rack N Toastständer *m*
tobacco [tə'bækəu] N Tabak *m*; **pipe ~** Pfeifentabak *m*
tobacconist [tə'bækənɪst] N Tabakhändler(in) *m(f)*
tobacconist's [tə'bækənɪsts], **tobacconist's shop** N Tabakwarenladen *m*
Tobago [tə'beɪgəu] N *see* **Trinidad and Tobago**
toboggan [tə'bɔgən] N Schlitten *m*
today [tə'deɪ] ADV, N heute; **what day is it ~?** welcher Tag ist heute?; **what date is it ~?** der Wievielte ist heute?; **~ is the 4th of March** heute ist der 4. März; **a week ago ~** heute vor einer Woche; **~'s paper** die Zeitung von heute
toddle ['tɔdl] (*inf*) VI: **to ~ in/off/along** herein-/davon-/entlangwatscheln
toddler ['tɔdlə^r] N Kleinkind *nt*
to-do [tə'du:] N Aufregung *f*, Theater *nt*
toe [təu] N Zehe *f*, Zeh *m*; (*of shoe, sock*) Spitze *f*; **to ~ the line** (*fig*) auf Linie bleiben; **big/little ~** großer/kleiner Zeh
toehold ['təuhəuld] N (*in climbing*) Halt *m* für die Fußspitzen; (*fig*): **to get/gain a ~ (in)** einen Einstieg bekommen/sich *dat* einen Einstieg verschaffen (in *+dat*)
toenail ['təuneɪl] N Zehennagel *m*
toffee ['tɔfɪ] N Toffee *m*
toffee apple (BRIT) N ≈ kandierter Apfel *m*
tofu ['təufu:] N Tofu *m*
toga ['təugə] N Toga *f*
together [tə'gɛðə^r] ADV zusammen; (*at the same time*) gleichzeitig; **~ with** gemeinsam mit
togetherness [tə'gɛðənɪs] N Beisammensein *nt*
toggle switch ['tɔgl-] N (*Comput*) Toggle-Schalter *m*
Togo ['təugəu] N Togo *nt*
togs [tɔgz] (*inf*) NPL Klamotten *pl*
toil [tɔɪl] N Mühe *f* ▶ VI sich abmühen
toilet ['tɔɪlət] N Toilette *f* ▶ CPD (*kit, accessories etc*) Toiletten-; **to go to the ~** auf die Toilette gehen
toilet bag (BRIT) N Kulturbeutel *m*
toilet bowl N Toilettenbecken *nt*
toilet paper N Toilettenpapier *nt*
toiletries ['tɔɪlətrɪz] NPL Toilettenartikel *pl*
toilet roll N Rolle *f* Toilettenpapier
toilet soap N Toilettenseife *f*
toilet water N Toilettenwasser *nt*
to-ing and fro-ing ['tu:ɪŋən'frəuɪŋ] (BRIT) N Hin und Her *nt*
token ['təukən] N (*sign, souvenir*) Zeichen *nt*; (*substitute coin*) Wertmarke *f* ▶ ADJ (*strike, payment etc*) symbolisch; **by the same ~** (*fig*) in gleicher Weise; **book/record/gift ~** (BRIT) Bücher-/Platten-/Geschenkgutschein *m*
tokenism ['təukənɪzəm] N: **to be (pure) ~** (nur) eine Alibifunktion haben
Tokyo ['təukjəu] N Tokio *nt*
told [təuld] PT, PP *of* **tell**
tolerable ['tɔlərəbl] ADJ (*bearable*) erträglich; (*fairly good*) passabel
tolerably ['tɔlərəblɪ] ADV: **~ good** ganz annehmbar *or* passabel
tolerance ['tɔlərns] N Toleranz *f*
tolerant ['tɔlərnt] ADJ tolerant; **to be ~ of sth** tolerant gegenüber etw sein
tolerate ['tɔləreɪt] VT (*pain, noise*) erdulden, ertragen; (*injustice*) tolerieren
toleration [tɔlə'reɪʃən] N (*of person, pain etc*) Duldung *f*; (*Rel, Pol*) Toleranz *f*
toll [təul] N (*of casualties, deaths*) (Gesamt)zahl *f*; (*tax, charge*) Gebühr *f* ▶ VI (*bell*) läuten; **the work took its ~ on us** die Arbeit blieb nicht ohne Auswirkungen auf uns
tollbridge ['təulbrɪdʒ] N gebührenpflichtige Brücke *f*, Mautbrücke *f*
toll call (US) N Ferngespräch *nt*
toll-free ['təulfri:] (US) ADJ gebührenfrei
toll road N gebührenpflichtige Straße *f*, Mautstraße *f*
tomato [tə'mɑ:təu] (*pl* **tomatoes**) N Tomate *f*
tomato ketchup N Tomatenketchup *m or nt*
tomato purée N Tomatenmark *nt*
tomato sauce N Tomatensoße *f*; (BRIT: *ketchup*) Tomatenketchup *m or nt*
tomb [tu:m] N Grab *nt*
tombola [tɔm'bəulə] N Tombola *f*
tomboy ['tɔmbɔɪ] N Wildfang *m*
tombstone ['tu:mstəun] N Grabstein *m*
tomcat ['tɔmkæt] N Kater *m*
tome [təum] (*form*) N Band *m*
tomorrow [tə'mɔrəu] ADV morgen ▶ N morgen; (*future*) Zukunft *f*; **the day after ~** übermorgen; **a week ~** morgen in einer Woche; **~ morning** morgen früh
ton [tʌn] N (BRIT) (britische) Tonne *f*; (US: *also*: **short ton**) (US-)Tonne *f* (*ca. 907 kg*); (*also*: **metric ton**) (metrische) Tonne *f*; **tons of** (*inf*) Unmengen von
tonal ['təunl] ADJ (*Mus*) klanglich, tonal
tone [təun] N Ton *m* ▶ VI (*colours*: *also*: **tone in**) (farblich) passen

t

▶ **tone down** VT (*also fig*) abschwächen
▶ **tone up** VT (*muscles*) kräftigen
tone-deaf [təun'dɛf] ADJ ohne Gefühl für Tonhöhen
toner ['təunə^r] N (*for photocopier*) Toner *m*
toner cartridge N Tonerpatrone *f*
Tonga [tɔŋə] N Tonga *nt*
tongs [tɔŋz] NPL Zange *f*; (*also*: **curling tongs**) Lockenstab *m*
tongue [tʌŋ] N Zunge *f*; (*form: language*) Sprache *f*; **~-in-cheek** (*speak, say*) ironisch
tongue-tied ['tʌŋtaɪd] ADJ (*fig*) sprachlos
tongue-twister ['tʌŋtwɪstə^r] N Zungenbrecher *m*
tonic ['tɔnɪk] N (*Med*) Tonikum *nt*; (*fig*) Wohltat *f*; (*also*: **tonic water**) Tonic *nt*; (*Mus*) Tonika *f*, Grundton *m*
tonight [tə'naɪt] ADV (*this evening*) heute Abend; (*this night*) heute Nacht ▶ N (*this evening*) der heutige Abend; (*this night*) die kommende Nacht; **(I'll) see you ~!** bis heute Abend!
tonnage ['tʌnɪdʒ] N Tonnage *f*
tonne [tʌn] (BRIT) N (*metric ton*) Tonne *f*
tonsil ['tɔnsl] N Mandel *f*; **to have one's tonsils out** sich *dat* die Mandeln herausnehmen lassen
tonsillitis [tɔnsɪ'laɪtɪs] N Mandelentzündung *f*
too [tu:] ADV (*excessively*) zu; (*also*) auch; **it's ~ sweet** es ist zu süß; **I went ~** ich bin auch mitgegangen; **~ much** (*adj*) zu viel; (*adv*) zu sehr; **~ many** zu viele; **~ bad!** das ist eben Pech!
took [tuk] PT *of* **take**
tool [tu:l] N (*also fig*) Werkzeug *nt*
toolbar N (*Comput*) Symbolleiste *f*
tool box N Werkzeugkasten *m*
tool kit N Werkzeugsatz *m*
toot [tu:t] N (*of horn*) Hupton *m*; (*of whistle*) Pfeifton *m* ▶ VI (*with car-horn*) hupen
tooth [tu:θ] (*pl* **teeth**) N (*also Tech*) Zahn *m*; **to have a ~ out, to have a ~ pulled** (*US*) sich *dat* einen Zahn ziehen lassen; **to brush one's teeth** sich *dat* die Zähne putzen; **by the skin of one's teeth** (*fig*) mit knapper Not
toothache ['tu:θeɪk] N Zahnschmerzen *pl*; **to have ~** Zahnschmerzen haben
toothbrush ['tu:θbrʌʃ] N Zahnbürste *f*
toothpaste ['tu:θpeɪst] N Zahnpasta *f*
toothpick ['tu:θpɪk] N Zahnstocher *m*
tooth powder N Zahnpulver *nt*
top [tɔp] N (*of mountain, tree, ladder*) Spitze *f*; (*of cupboard, table, box*) Oberseite *f*; (*of street*) Ende *nt*; (*lid*) Verschluss *m*; (*Aut: also*: **top gear**) höchster Gang *m*; (*toy: also*: **spinning top**) Kreisel *m*; (*blouse etc*) Oberteil *nt*; (*of pyjamas*) Jacke *f* ▶ ADJ höchste(r, s); (*highest in rank*) oberste(r, s); (*: golfer etc*) Top- ▶ VT (*poll, vote, list*) anführen; (*estimate etc*) übersteigen; **at the ~ of the stairs/page** oben auf der Treppe/Seite; **at the ~ of the street** am Ende der Straße; **on ~ of** (*above*) auf *+dat*; (*in addition to*) zusätzlich zu; **from ~ to bottom** von oben bis unten; **from ~ to toe** (BRIT) von Kopf bis Fuß; **at the ~ of the list** oben auf der Liste; **at the ~ of his voice** so laut er konnte; **over the ~** (*inf: behaviour etc*) übertrieben; **to go over the ~** (*inf*) übertreiben; **at ~ speed** bei Höchstgeschwindigkeit
▶ **top up, (US) top off** VT (*drink*) nachfüllen; (*salary*) aufbessern
topaz ['təupæz] N Topas *m*
top-class ['tɔp'klɑ:s] ADJ erstklassig; (*hotel, player etc*) Spitzen-
topcoat ['tɔpkəut] N (*overcoat*) Mantel *m*; (*of paint*) Deckanstrich *m*
top floor N oberster Stock *m*
top hat N Zylinder *m*
top-heavy [tɔp'hɛvɪ] ADJ (*also fig*) kopflastig
topic ['tɔpɪk] N Thema *nt*
topical ['tɔpɪkl] ADJ (*issue etc*) aktuell
topless ['tɔplɪs] ADJ (*waitress*) Oben-ohne-; (*bather*) barbusig ▶ ADV oben ohne
top-level ['tɔplɛvl] ADJ auf höchster Ebene
topmost ['tɔpməust] ADJ oberste(r, s)
top-notch ['tɔp'nɔtʃ] ADJ erstklassig
topography [tə'pɔgrəfɪ] N Topografie *f*
topping ['tɔpɪŋ] N (*Culin*) Überzug *m*
topple ['tɔpl] VT (*government etc*) stürzen ▶ VI (*person*) stürzen; (*object*) fallen
top-ranking ['tɔpræŋkɪŋ] ADJ (*official*) hochgestellt
top-secret ['tɔp'si:krɪt] ADJ streng geheim
top-security ['tɔpsə'kjuərɪtɪ] (BRIT) ADJ (*prison, wing*) Hochsicherheits-
topsy-turvy ['tɔpsɪ'tə:vɪ] ADJ auf den Kopf gestellt ▶ ADV durcheinander; (*fall, land*) verkehrt herum
top-up ['tɔpʌp] N: **would you like a ~?** darf ich Ihnen nachschenken?
top-up loan N Ergänzungsdarlehen *nt*
torch [tɔ:tʃ] N Fackel *f*; (BRIT: *electric*) Taschenlampe *f*
tore [tɔ:^r] PT *of* **tear²**
torment N ['tɔ:mɛnt] Qual *f* ▶ VT [tɔ:'mɛnt] quälen; (*annoy*) ärgern
torn [tɔ:n] PP *of* **tear²** ▶ ADJ: **~ between** (*fig*) hin- und hergerissen zwischen
tornado [tɔ:'neɪdəu] (*pl* **tornadoes**) N (*storm*) Tornado *m*
torpedo [tɔ:'pi:dəu] (*pl* **torpedoes**) N Torpedo *m*
torpedo boat N Torpedoboot *nt*
torpor ['tɔ:pə^r] N Trägheit *f*
torrent ['tɔrnt] N (*flood*) Strom *m*; (*fig*) Flut *f*
torrential [tɔ'rɛnʃl] ADJ (*rain*) wolkenbruchartig
torrid ['tɔrɪd] ADJ (*weather, love affair*) heiß
torso ['tɔ:səu] N Torso *m*
tortoise ['tɔ:təs] N Schildkröte *f*
tortoiseshell ['tɔ:təʃɛl] ADJ (*jewellery, ornaments*) aus Schildpatt; (*cat*) braungelbschwarz, braun-gelb-schwarz
tortuous ['tɔ:tjuəs] ADJ (*path*) gewunden; (*argument, mind*) umständlich
torture ['tɔ:tʃə^r] N Folter *f*; (*fig*) Qual *f* ▶ VT foltern; (*fig: torment*) quälen; **it was ~** (*fig*) es war eine Qual
torturer ['tɔ:tʃərə^r] N Folterer *m*
Tory ['tɔ:rɪ] (BRIT *Pol*) ADJ konservativ ▶ N Tory *m*, Konservative(r) *f*(*m*)

toss [tɔs] VT (*throw*) werfen; (*one's head*) zurückwerfen; (*salad*) anmachen; (*pancake*) wenden ▸ N: **with a ~ of her head** mit einer Kopfbewegung; **to ~ a coin** eine Münze werfen; **to win/lose the ~** die Entscheidung per Münzwurf gewinnen/verlieren; **to ~ up for sth** etw per Münzwurf entscheiden; **to ~ and turn** (*in bed*) sich hin und her wälzen
tot [tɔt] N (BRIT: *drink*) Schluck *m*; (*child*) Knirps *m*
▸ **tot up** (BRIT) VT (*figures*) zusammenzählen
total ['təutl] ADJ (*number etc*) gesamt; (*failure, wreck etc*) völlig, total ▸ N Gesamtzahl *f* ▸ VT (*add up to*) sich belaufen auf; (*add up*) zusammenzählen; **in ~** insgesamt
totalitarian [təutælɪ'tɛərɪən] ADJ totalitär
totality [təu'tælɪtɪ] N Gesamtheit *f*
totally ['təutəlɪ] ADV völlig
totem pole ['təutəm-] N Totempfahl *m*
totter ['tɔtəʳ] VI (*person*) wanken, taumeln; (*fig: government*) im Wanken sein
touch [tʌtʃ] N (*sense of touch*) Gefühl *nt*; (*contact*) Berührung *f*; (*skill: of pianist etc*) Hand *f* ▸ VT berühren; (*tamper with*) anrühren; (*emotionally*) rühren ▸ VI (*make contact*) sich berühren; **the personal ~** die persönliche Note; **to put the finishing touches to sth** letzte Hand an etw *acc* legen; **a ~ of** (*fig: frost etc*) etwas, ein Hauch von; **in ~ with** (*person, group*) in Verbindung mit; **to get in ~ with sb** mit jdm in Verbindung treten; **I'll be in ~** ich melde mich; **to lose ~** (*friends*) den Kontakt verlieren; **to be out of ~ with sb** keine Verbindung mehr zu jdm haben; **to be out of ~ with events** nicht auf dem Laufenden sein; **~ wood!** hoffen wir das Beste!
▸ **touch on** VT FUS (*topic*) berühren
▸ **touch up** VT (*car etc*) ausbessern
touch-and-go ['tʌtʃən'gəu] ADJ (*situation*) auf der Kippe; **it was ~ whether we'd succeed** es war völlig offen, ob wir Erfolg haben würden
touchdown ['tʌtʃdaun] N (*of rocket, plane*) Landung *f*; (*US Football*) Touchdown *m*
touched [tʌtʃt] ADJ (*moved*) gerührt; (*inf: mad*) plemplem
touching ['tʌtʃɪŋ] ADJ rührend
touchline ['tʌtʃlaɪn] N (*Sport*) Seitenlinie *f*
touch screen N (*Tech*) Berührungsbildschirm *m*, Touchscreen *m*
touch screen mobile N Touchscreen-Handy *nt*
touch screen technology N Touchscreen-Technologie *f*
touch-sensitive ['tʌtʃsensɪtɪv] ADJ berührungsempfindlich; (*switch*) Kontakt-
touch-type ['tʌtʃtaɪp] VI blindschreiben
touchy ['tʌtʃɪ] ADJ (*person, subject*) empfindlich
tough [tʌf] ADJ (*strong, firm, difficult*) hart; (*resistant*) widerstandsfähig; (*meat, animal, person*) zäh; (*rough*) rau; **~ luck!** Pech!
toughen ['tʌfn] VT (*sb's character*) hart machen; (*glass etc*) härten
toughness ['tʌfnɪs] N Härte *f*
toupee ['tu:peɪ] N Toupet *nt*
tour ['tuəʳ] N (*journey*) Tour *f*, Reise *f*; (*of factory, museum etc*) Rundgang *m*; (*also*: **guided tour**) Führung *f*; (*by pop group etc*) Tournee *f* ▸ VT (*country, factory etc: on foot*) ziehen durch; (*: in car*) fahren durch; **to go on a ~ of a museum/castle** an einer Museums-/Schlossführung teilnehmen; **to go on a ~ of the Highlands** die Highlands bereisen; **to go/be on ~** (*pop group, theatre company etc*) auf Tournee gehen/sein
tour guide N Reiseleiter(in) *m(f)*
touring ['tuərɪŋ] N Umherreisen *nt*
tourism ['tuərɪzm] N Tourismus *m*
tourist ['tuərɪst] N Tourist(in) *m(f)* ▸ CPD (*attractions, season*) Touristen-; **the ~ trade** die Tourismusbranche
tourist class N Touristenklasse *f*
tourist guide N (*book*) Reiseführer *m*; (*person*) Fremdenführer(in) *m(f)*
tourist information centre (BRIT) N Touristen-Informationszentrum *nt*
tourist office N Verkehrsamt *nt*
tournament ['tuənəmənt] N Turnier *nt*
tourniquet ['tuənɪkeɪ] N Aderpresse *f*
tour operator (BRIT) N Reiseveranstalter *m*
tousled ['tauzld] ADJ (*hair*) zerzaust
tout [taut] VI: **to ~ for business** die Reklametrommel schlagen; **to ~ for custom** auf Kundenfang gehen ▸ N (*also*: **ticket tout**) *Schwarzhändler, der Eintrittskarten zu überhöhten Preisen verkauft*
tow [təu] VT (*vehicle*) abschleppen; (*caravan, trailer*) ziehen ▸ N: **to give sb a ~** (*Aut*) jdn abschleppen; **"on ~"**, **"in ~"** (*US*) „Fahrzeug wird abgeschleppt"
▸ **tow away** VT (*vehicle*) abschleppen
toward [tə'wɔ:d], **towards** [tə'wɔ:dz] PREP (*direction*) zu; (*attitude*) gegenüber +*dat*; (*purpose*) für; (*in time*) gegen; **~(s) noon/the end of the year** gegen Mittag/Ende des Jahres; **to feel friendly ~(s) sb** jdm freundlich gesinnt sein
towel ['tauəl] N Handtuch *nt*; **to throw in the ~** (*fig*) das Handtuch werfen
towelling ['tauəlɪŋ] N Frottee *m or nt*
towel rail, (*US*) **towel rack** N Handtuchstange *f*
tower ['tauəʳ] N Turm *m* ▸ VI aufragen; **to ~ above** *or* **over sb/sth** über jdm/etw aufragen
tower block (BRIT) N Hochhaus *nt*
towering ['tauərɪŋ] ADJ hoch aufragend
towline ['təulaɪn] N Abschleppseil *nt*
town [taun] N Stadt *f*; **to go (in)to ~** in die Stadt gehen; **to go to ~ on sth** (*fig*) sich bei etw ins Zeug legen; **in ~** in der Stadt; **to be out of ~** (*person*) nicht in der Stadt sein
town centre N Stadtzentrum *nt*
town clerk N Stadtdirektor(in) *m(f)*
town council N Stadtrat *m*
town crier [-'kraɪəʳ] N Ausrufer *m*
town hall N Rathaus *nt*
town house N (städtisches) Wohnhaus *nt*; (*US: in a complex*) Reihenhaus *nt*
townie ['taunɪ] (*inf*) N (*town-dweller*) Städter(in) *m(f)*
town plan N Stadtplan *m*
town planner N Stadtplaner(in) *m(f)*
town planning N Stadtplanung *f*

t

township ['taunʃɪp] N Stadt(gemeinde) *f*; (*formerly: in South Africa*) Township *f*
townspeople ['taunzpi:pl] NPL Stadtbewohner *pl*
towpath ['təupɑ:θ] N Leinpfad *m*
towrope ['təurəup] N Abschleppseil *nt*
tow truck (US) N Abschleppwagen *m*
toxic ['tɔksɪk] ADJ giftig, toxisch
toxic asset N (*Econ*) faule Wertpapiere *pl*
toxic bank N (*Econ*) Bad Bank *f*
toxin ['tɔksɪn] N Gift *nt*, Giftstoff *m*
toy [tɔɪ] N Spielzeug *nt*
▸ **toy with** VT FUS (*object, idea*) spielen mit
toyshop ['tɔɪʃɔp] N Spielzeugladen *m*
trace [treɪs] N (*sign, small amount*) Spur *f* ▸ VT (*draw*) nachzeichnen; (*follow*) verfolgen; (*locate*) aufspüren; **without ~** (*disappear*) spurlos; **there was no ~ of it** es war spurlos verschwunden
trace element N Spurenelement *nt*
tracer ['treɪsə^r] N (*Mil: also*: **tracer bullet**) Leuchtspurgeschoss *nt*; (*Med*) Indikator *m*
trachea [trə'kɪə] N Luftröhre *f*
tracing paper ['treɪsɪŋ-] N Pauspapier *nt*
track [træk] N Weg *m*; (*of comet, Sport*) Bahn *f*; (*of suspect, animal*) Spur *f*; (*Rail*) Gleis *nt*; (*on tape, record*) Stück *nt*, Track *m* ▸ VT (*follow*) verfolgen; **to keep ~ of sb/sth** (*fig*) jdn/etw im Auge behalten; **to be on the right ~** (*fig*) auf der richtigen Spur sein
▸ **track down** VT aufspüren
tracker dog ['trækə-] (BRIT) N Spürhund *m*
track events NPL Laufwettbewerbe *f*
tracking station ['trækɪŋ-] N Bodenstation *f*
track meet (US) N (*Sport*) Leichtathletikwettkampf *m*
track record N: **to have a good ~** (*fig*) gute Leistungen vorzuweisen haben
tracksuit ['træksu:t] N Trainingsanzug *m*
tract [trækt] N (*Geog*) Gebiet *nt*; (*pamphlet*) Traktat *m or nt*; **respiratory ~** Atemwege *pl*
traction ['trækʃən] N (*power*) Zugkraft *f*; (*Aut: grip*) Bodenhaftung *f*; (*Med*): **in ~** im Streckverband
traction engine N Zugmaschine *f*
tractor ['træktə^r] N Traktor *m*
trade [treɪd] N (*activity*) Handel *m*; (*skill, job*) Handwerk *nt* ▸ VI (*do business*) handeln ▸ VT: **to ~ sth (for sth)** etw (gegen etw) eintauschen; **foreign ~** Außenhandel *m*; **Department of T~ and Industry** (BRIT) ≈ Wirtschaftsministerium *nt*; **to ~ with** Handel treiben mit; **to ~ in** (*merchandise*) handeln in *+dat*
▸ **trade in** VT in Zahlung geben
trade barrier N Handelsschranke *f*
trade deficit N Handelsdefizit *nt*
Trade Descriptions Act (BRIT) N *Gesetz über korrekte Warenbeschreibungen*
trade discount N Händlerrabatt *m*
trade fair N Handelsmesse *f*
trade figures NPL Handelsziffern *pl*
trade-in ['treɪdɪn] N: **to take sth as a ~** etw in Zahlung nehmen
trade-in value N Gebrauchtwert *m*
trademark ['treɪdmɑ:k] N Warenzeichen *nt*
trade mission N Handelsmission *f*
trade name N Handelsname *m*
trade-off ['treɪdɔf] N Handel *m*; **there's bound to be a ~ between speed and quality** es gibt entweder Einbußen bei der Schnelligkeit oder bei der Qualität
trader ['treɪdə^r] N Händler(in) *m(f)*
trade secret N (*also fig*) Betriebsgeheimnis *nt*
tradesman ['treɪdzmən] N (*irreg: shopkeeper*) Händler *m*
trade union N Gewerkschaft *f*
trade unionist [-'ju:njənɪst] N Gewerkschaftler(in) *m(f)*
trade wind N Passat *m*
trading ['treɪdɪŋ] N Handel *m*
trading estate (BRIT) N Industriegelände *nt*
trading stamp N Rabattmarke *f*
tradition [trə'dɪʃən] N Tradition *f*
traditional [trə'dɪʃənl] ADJ traditionell
traditionally [trə'dɪʃnəlɪ] ADV traditionell
traffic ['træfɪk] N Verkehr *m*; (*in drugs etc*) Handel *m* ▸ VI: **to ~ in** handeln mit
traffic calming N Verkehrsberuhigung *f*
traffic circle (US) N Kreisverkehr *m*
traffic island N Verkehrsinsel *f*
traffic jam N Stau *m*, Verkehrsstauung *f*
trafficker ['træfɪkə^r] N Händler(in) *m(f)*
traffic lights NPL Ampel *f*
traffic offence (BRIT) N Verkehrsdelikt *nt*
traffic sign N Verkehrszeichen *nt*
traffic violation (US) N = **traffic offence**
traffic warden N *Verkehrspolizist für Parkvergehen*; (*woman*) ≈ Politesse *f*
tragedy ['trædʒədɪ] N Tragödie *f*
tragic ['trædʒɪk] ADJ tragisch
tragically ['trædʒɪkəlɪ] ADV tragisch
trail [treɪl] N (*path*) Weg *m*; (*track*) Spur *f*; (*of smoke, dust*) Wolke *f* ▸ VT (*drag*) schleifen; (*follow*) folgen *+dat* ▸ VI (*hang loosely*) schleifen; (*in game, contest*) zurückliegen; **to be on sb's ~** jdm auf der Spur sein
▸ **trail away** VI (*sound, voice*) sich verlieren
▸ **trail behind** VI hinterhertrotten
▸ **trail off** VI = **trail away**
trailer ['treɪlə^r] N (*Aut*) Anhänger *m*; (*US: caravan*) Wohnwagen *m*, Caravan *m*; (*Cine, TV*) Trailer *m*
trailer truck (US) N Sattelschlepper *m*
train [treɪn] N (*Rail*) Zug *m*; (*of dress*) Schleppe *f* ▸ VT (*apprentice etc*) ausbilden; (*dog*) abrichten; (*athlete*) trainieren; (*mind*) schulen; (*plant*) ziehen; (*point: camera, gun etc*): **to ~ on** richten auf *+acc* ▸ VI (*Sport*) trainieren; (*learn a skill*) ausgebildet werden; **~ of thought** Gedankengang *m*; **to go by ~** mit dem Zug fahren; **~ of events** Ereignisfolge *f*; **to ~ sb to do sth** jdn dazu ausbilden, etw zu tun
train attendant (US) N Schlafwagenschaffner *m*
trained [treɪnd] ADJ (*teacher*) ausgebildet; (*worker*) gelernt; (*animal*) dressiert; (*eye*) geschult
trainee [treɪ'ni:] N Auszubildende(r) *f(m)*
traineeship N Praktikum *nt*

trainer ['treɪnəʳ] N (*Sport: coach*) Trainer(in) *m(f)*; (*: shoe*) Trainingsschuh *m*; (*of animals*) Dresseur(in) *m(f)*
training ['treɪnɪŋ] N (*for occupation*) Ausbildung *f*; (*Sport*) Training *nt*; **in ~** (*Sport*) im Training
training college N (*for teachers*) ≈ pädagogische Hochschule *f*
training course N Ausbildungskurs *m*
train station N Bahnhof *m*
train wreck N (*fig*) unabwendbare Katastrophe; **He's a complete ~** Er ist ein Wrack
traipse [treɪps] VI: **to ~ in/out** hinein-/herauslatschen
trait [treɪt] N Zug *m*, Eigenschaft *f*
traitor ['treɪtəʳ] N Verräter(in) *m(f)*
trajectory [trə'dʒɛktərɪ] N Flugbahn *f*
tram [træm] (BRIT) N (*also*: **tramcar**) Straßenbahn *f*
tramline ['træmlaɪn] N Straßenbahnschiene *f*
tramp [træmp] N Landstreicher *m*; (*pej: woman*) Flittchen *nt* ▸ VI stapfen ▸ VT (*walk through: town, streets*) latschen durch
trample ['træmpl] VT: **to ~ (underfoot)** niedertrampeln ▸ VI (*also fig*): **to ~ on** herumtrampeln auf *+dat*
trampoline ['træmpəli:n] N Trampolin *nt*
trance [trɑ:ns] N Trance *f*; **to go into a ~** in Trance verfallen
tranquil ['træŋkwɪl] ADJ ruhig, friedlich
tranquillity, (*US*) **tranquility** [træŋ'kwɪlɪtɪ] N Ruhe *f*
tranquillizer, (*US*) **tranquilizer** ['træŋkwɪlaɪzəʳ] N Beruhigungsmittel *nt*
transact [træn'zækt] VT (*business*) abwickeln
transaction [træn'zækʃən] N Geschäft *nt*; **cash ~** Bargeldtransaktion *f*
transatlantic ['trænzət'læntɪk] ADJ transatlantisch; (*phone-call*) über den Atlantik
transcend [træn'sɛnd] VT überschreiten
transcendental [trænsɛn'dɛntl] ADJ: **~ meditation** transzendentale Meditation *f*
transcribe [træn'skraɪb] VT transkribieren
transcript ['trænskrɪpt] N Niederschrift *f*, Transkription *f*
transcription [træn'skrɪpʃən] N Transkription *f*
transept ['trænsɛpt] N Querschiff *nt*
transfer ['trænsfəʳ] N (*of money*) Überweisung *f*; (*of employees*) Versetzung *f*; (*of power*) Übertragung *f*; (*Sport*) Transfer *m*; (*picture, design*) Abziehbild *nt* ▸ VT (*employees*) versetzen; (*money*) überweisen; (*power, ownership*) übertragen; **by bank ~** per Banküberweisung; **to ~ the charges** (BRIT *Tel*) ein R-Gespräch führen
transferable [træns'fə:rəbl] ADJ übertragbar; **"not ~"** „nicht übertragbar"
transfix [træns'fɪks] VT aufspießen; **transfixed with fear** (*fig*) starr vor Angst
transform [træns'fɔ:m] VT umwandeln
transformation [trænsfə'meɪʃən] N Umwandlung *f*
transformer [træns'fɔ:məʳ] N (*Elec*) Transformator *m*
transfusion [træns'fju:ʒən] N (*also*: **blood transfusion**) Bluttransfusion *f*
transgress [træns'grɛs] VT (*go beyond*) überschreiten; (*violate: rules, law*) verletzen
transient ['trænzɪənt] ADJ vorübergehend
transistor [træn'zɪstəʳ] N (*Elec*) Transistor *m*; (*also*: **transistor radio**) Transistorradio *nt*
transit ['trænzɪt] N: **in ~** unterwegs
transit camp N Durchgangslager *nt*
transition [træn'zɪʃən] N Übergang *m*
transitional [træn'zɪʃənl] ADJ (*period, stage*) Übergangs-
transitive ['trænzɪtɪv] ADJ (*verb*) transitiv
transit lounge N Transithalle *f*
transitory ['trænzɪtərɪ] ADJ (*emotion, arrangement etc*) vorübergehend
transit visa N Transitvisum *nt*
translate [trænz'leɪt] VT übersetzen; **to ~ (from/into)** übersetzen (aus/in *+acc*)
translation [trænz'leɪʃən] N Übersetzung *f*; **in ~** als Übersetzung
translator [trænz'leɪtəʳ] N Übersetzer(in) *m(f)*
translucent [trænz'lu:snt] ADJ (*object*) lichtdurchlässig
transmission [trænz'mɪʃən] N (*Aut*) Getriebe *nt*; (*also TV*) Übertragung *f*; (*of information*) Übermittlung *f*
transmission rate N (*Tel, Comput*) Übertragungsrate *f*
transmit [trænz'mɪt] VT (*also TV*) übertragen; (*message, signal*) übermitteln
transmitter [trænz'mɪtəʳ] N (*TV, Radio*) Sender *m*
transparency [træns'pɛərnsɪ] N (*of glass etc*) Durchsichtigkeit *f*; (BRIT *Phot*) Dia *nt*
transparent [træns'pærnt] ADJ durchsichtig; (*fig: obvious*) offensichtlich
transpire [træns'paɪəʳ] VI (*turn out*) bekannt werden; (*happen*) passieren; **it finally transpired that ...** schließlich sickerte durch, dass ...
transplant VT [træns'plɑ:nt] (*organ, seedlings*) verpflanzen ▸ N ['trɑ:nsplɑ:nt] (*Med*) Transplantation *f*; **to have a heart ~** sich einer Herztransplantation unterziehen
transport ['trænspɔ:t] N Beförderung *f*, Transport *m* ▸ VT transportieren; **do you have your own ~?** haben Sie ein Auto?; **public ~** öffentliche Verkehrsmittel *pl*; **Department of T~** (BRIT) Verkehrsministerium *nt*
transportation ['trænspɔ:'teɪʃən] N Transport *m*, Beförderung *f*; (*means of transport*) Beförderungsmittel *nt*; **Department of T~** (*US*) Verkehrsministerium *nt*
transport café (BRIT) N Fernfahrerlokal *nt*
transpose [træns'pəuz] VT versetzen
transsexual [trænz'sɛksuəl] ADJ transsexuell ▸ N Transsexuelle(r) *f(m)*
transverse ['trænzvə:s] ADJ (*beam etc*) Quer-
transvestite [trænz'vɛstaɪt] N Transvestit *m*
trap [træp] N (*also fig*) Falle *f*; (*carriage*) zweirädriger Pferdewagen *m* ▸ VT (*animal*) (mit einer Falle) fangen; (*person: trick*) in die Falle locken; (*: confine*) gefangen halten; (*immobilize*) festsetzen; (*capture: energy*) stauen; **to set** *or* **lay**

t

a ~ **(for sb)** (jdm) eine Falle stellen; **to shut one's ~** (*inf*) die Klappe halten; **to ~ one's finger in the door** sich *dat* den Finger in der Tür einklemmen
trap door N Falltür *f*
trapeze [trə'pi:z] N Trapez *nt*
trapper ['træpə^r] N Fallensteller *m*, Trapper *m*
trappings ['træpɪŋz] NPL äußere Zeichen *pl*; (*of power*) Insignien *pl*
trash [træʃ] N (*rubbish*) Abfall *m*, Müll *m*; (*pej: nonsense*) Schund *m*, Mist *m*
trash can (*US*) N Mülleimer *m*
trashy ['træʃɪ] ADJ (*goods*) minderwertig, wertlos; (*novel etc*) Schund-
trauma ['trɔ:mə] N Trauma *nt*
traumatic [trɔ:'mætɪk] ADJ traumatisch
traumatize ['trɔ:mətaɪz] VT traumatisieren
travel ['trævl] N (*travelling*) Reisen *nt* ▶ VI reisen; (*short distance*) fahren; (*move: car, aeroplane*) sich bewegen; (*sound etc*) sich fortpflanzen; (*news*) sich verbreiten ▶ VT (*distance*) zurücklegen; **travels** NPL (*journeys*) Reisen *pl*; **this wine doesn't ~ well** dieser Wein verträgt den Transport nicht
travel agency N Reisebüro *nt*
travel agent N Reisebürokaufmann *m*, Reisebürokauffrau *f*
travel brochure N Reiseprospekt *m*
traveling *etc* (*US*) = **travelling** *etc*
travel insurance N Reiseversicherung *f*
traveller, (*US*) **traveler** ['trævlə^r] N Reisende(r) *f*(*m*); (*Comm*) Vertreter(in) *m*(*f*)
traveller's cheque, (*US*) **traveler's check** N Reisescheck *m*
travelling, (*US*) **traveling** ['trævlɪŋ] N Reisen *nt* ▶ CPD (*circus, exhibition*) Wander-; (*bag, clock*) Reise-; ~ **expenses** Reisespesen *pl*
travelling salesman N (*irreg*) Vertreter *m*
travelogue ['trævəlɔg] N Reisebericht *m*
travel sickness N Reisekrankheit *f*
traverse ['trævəs] VT durchqueren
travesty ['trævəstɪ] N Travestie *f*
trawler ['trɔ:lə^r] N Fischdampfer *m*
tray [treɪ] N (*for carrying*) Tablett *nt*; (*on desk: also:* **in-tray/out-tray**) Ablage *f* für Eingänge/Ausgänge
treacherous ['trɛtʃərəs] ADJ (*person, look*) verräterisch; (*ground, tide*) tückisch; **road conditions are ~** die Straßen sind in gefährlichem Zustand
treachery ['trɛtʃərɪ] N Verrat *m*
treacle ['tri:kl] N Sirup *m*
tread [trɛd] (*pt* **trod**, *pp* **trodden**) N (*of tyre*) Profil *nt*; (*footstep*) Schritt *m*; (*of stair*) Stufe *f* ▶ VI gehen ▶ **tread on** VT FUS treten auf *+acc*
treadle ['trɛdl] N Pedal *nt*
treas. ABBR = **treasurer**
treason ['tri:zn] N Verrat *m*
treasure ['trɛʒə^r] N (*also fig*) Schatz *m* ▶ VT schätzen; **treasures** NPL (*art treasures etc*) Schätze *pl*, Kostbarkeiten *pl*
treasure hunt N Schatzsuche *f*
treasurer ['trɛʒərə^r] N Schatzmeister(in) *m*(*f*)
treasury ['trɛʒərɪ] N: **the T~, the T~ Department** (*US*) das Finanzministerium
treasury bill N kurzfristiger Schatzwechsel *m*
treat [tri:t] N (*present*) (besonderes) Vergnügen *nt* ▶ VT (*also Med, Tech*) behandeln; **it came as a ~** es war eine besondere Freude; **to ~ sth as a joke** etw als Witz ansehen; **to ~ sb to sth** jdm etw spendieren
treatment ['tri:tmənt] N Behandlung *f*; **to have ~ for sth** wegen etw in Behandlung sein
treaty ['tri:tɪ] N Vertrag *m*
treble ['trɛbl] ADJ (*triple*) dreifach; (*Mus: voice, part*) (Knaben)sopran-; (*instrument*) Diskant- ▶ N (*singer*) (Knaben)sopran *m*; (*on hi-fi, radio etc*) Höhen *pl* ▶ VT verdreifachen ▶ VI sich verdreifachen; **to be ~ the amount/size of sth** dreimal so viel/so groß wie etw sein
treble clef N Violinschlüssel *m*
tree [tri:] N Baum *m*
tree-lined ['tri:laɪnd] ADJ baumbestanden
treetop ['tri:tɔp] N Baumkrone *f*
tree trunk N Baumstamm *m*
trek [trɛk] N Treck *m*; (*tiring walk*) Marsch *m* ▶ VI trecken
trellis ['trɛlɪs] N Gitter *nt*
tremble ['trɛmbl] VI (*voice, body, trees*) zittern; (*ground*) beben
trembling ['trɛmblɪŋ] N (*of ground*) Beben *nt*, Erschütterung *f*; (*of trees*) Zittern *nt* ▶ ADJ (*hand, voice etc*) zitternd
tremendous [trɪ'mɛndəs] ADJ (*amount, success etc*) gewaltig, enorm; (*holiday, view etc*) fantastisch
tremendously [trɪ'mɛndəslɪ] ADV (*difficult, exciting*) ungeheuer; **he enjoyed it ~** es hat ihm ausgezeichnet gefallen
tremor ['trɛmə^r] N Zittern *nt*; (*also:* **earth tremor**) Beben *nt*, Erschütterung *f*
trench [trɛntʃ] N Graben *m*
trench coat N Trenchcoat *m*
trench warfare N Stellungskrieg *m*
trend [trɛnd] N Tendenz *f*; (*fashion*) Trend *m*; **a ~ towards/away from sth** eine Tendenz zu/weg von etw; **to set a/the ~** richtungsweisend sein
trendy ['trɛndɪ] ADJ modisch
trepidation [trɛpɪ'deɪʃən] N (*apprehension*) Beklommenheit *f*; **in ~** beklommen
trespass ['trɛspəs] VI: **to ~ on** (*private property*) unbefugt betreten; **"no trespassing"** „Betreten verboten"
trespasser ['trɛspəsə^r] N Unbefugte(r) *f*(*m*); **"trespassers will be prosecuted"** „widerrechtliches Betreten wird strafrechtlich verfolgt"
tress [trɛs] N (*of hair*) Locke *f*
trestle ['trɛsl] N Bock *m*
trestle table N Klapptisch *m*
trial ['traɪəl] N (*Law*) Prozess *m*; (*test, of machine, drug etc*) Versuch *m*; (*worry*) Plage *f*; **trials** NPL (*unpleasant experiences*) Schwierigkeiten *pl*; **~ by jury** Schwurgerichtsverfahren *nt*; **to be sent for ~** vor Gericht gestellt werden; **to be/go on ~** (*Law*) angeklagt sein/werden; **by ~ and error** durch Ausprobieren

trial balance N Probebilanz *f*
trial basis N: **on a ~** probeweise
trial period N Probezeit *f*
trial run N Versuch *m*
triangle ['traɪæŋgl] N Dreieck *nt*; (*US: set square*) (Zeichen)dreieck *nt*; (*Mus*) Triangel *f*
triangular [traɪ'æŋgjuləʳ] ADJ dreieckig
triathlon [traɪ'æθlən] N Triathlon *nt*
tribal ['traɪbl] ADJ (*warrior, warfare, dance*) Stammes-
tribe [traɪb] N Stamm *m*
tribesman ['traɪbzmən] N (*irreg*) Stammesangehörige(r) *m*
tribulations [trɪbju'leɪʃənz] NPL Kümmernisse *pl*
tribunal [traɪ'bju:nl] N Gericht *nt*
tributary ['trɪbjutərɪ] N (*of river*) Nebenfluss *m*
tribute ['trɪbju:t] N Tribut *m*; **to pay ~ to** Tribut zollen *+dat*
trice [traɪs] N: **in a ~** im Handumdrehen
trick [trɪk] N Trick *m*; (*Cards*) Stich *m* ▶ VT hereinlegen; **to play a ~ on sb** jdm einen Streich spielen; **it's a ~ of the light** das Licht täuscht; **that should do the ~** das müsste hinhauen; **to ~ sb into doing sth** jdn (mit einem Trick) dazu bringen, etw zu tun; **to ~ sb out of sth** jdn um etw prellen
trickery ['trɪkərɪ] N Tricks *pl*, Betrügerei *f*
trickle ['trɪkl] N (*of water etc*) Rinnsal *nt* ▶ VI (*water, rain etc*) rinnen; (*people*) sich langsam bewegen
trick photography N Trickfotografie *f*
trick question N Fangfrage *f*
trickster ['trɪkstəʳ] N Betrüger(in) *m(f)*
tricky ['trɪkɪ] ADJ (*job, problem*) schwierig
tricycle ['traɪsɪkl] N Dreirad *nt*
trifle ['traɪfl] N (*detail*) Kleinigkeit *f*; (*Culin*) Trifle *nt* ▶ ADV: **a ~ long** ein bisschen lang ▶ VI: **to ~ with sb/sth** jdn/etw nicht ernst nehmen; **he is not (someone) to be trifled with** mit ihm ist nicht zu spaßen
trifling ['traɪflɪŋ] ADJ (*detail*) unbedeutend
trigger ['trɪgəʳ] N Abzug *m*
▶ **trigger off** VT FUS auslösen
trigonometry [trɪgə'nɔmətrɪ] N Trigonometrie *f*
trilby ['trɪlbɪ] (BRIT) N (*also*: **trilby hat**) Filzhut *m*
trill [trɪl] N (*Mus*) Triller *m*; (*of birds*) Trillern *nt*
trilogy ['trɪlədʒɪ] N Trilogie *f*
trim [trɪm] ADJ (*house, garden*) gepflegt; (*figure, person*) schlank ▶ N (*haircut etc*): **to have a ~** sich *dat* die Haare nachschneiden lassen; (*on clothes, car*) Besatz *m* ▶ VT (*hair, beard*) nachschneiden; (*decorate*): **to ~ (with)** besetzen (mit); (*Naut: a sail*) trimmen mit; **to keep o.s. in (good) ~** (gut) in Form bleiben
trimmings ['trɪmɪŋz] NPL (*Culin*): **with all the ~** mit allem Drum und Dran; (*cuttings, of pastry etc*) Reste *pl*
Trinidad and Tobago ['trɪnɪdæd-] N Trinidad und Tobago *nt*
trinity ['trɪnɪtɪ] N (*Rel*) Dreieinigkeit *f*
trinket ['trɪŋkɪt] N (*ornament*) Schmuckgegenstand *m*; (*piece of jewellery*) Schmuckstück *nt*
trio ['tri:əu] N Trio *nt*
trip [trɪp] N (*journey*) Reise *f*; (*outing*) Ausflug *m* ▶ VI (*stumble*) stolpern; (*go lightly*) trippeln; **on a ~** auf Reisen
▶ **trip over** VT FUS stolpern über *+acc*
▶ **trip up** VI stolpern ▶ VT (*person*) zu Fall bringen
tripartite [traɪ'pɑ:taɪt] ADJ (*agreement, talks*) dreiseitig
tripe [traɪp] N (*Culin*) Kaldaunen *pl*; (*pej: rubbish*) Stuss *m*
triple ['trɪpl] ADJ dreifach ▶ ADV: **~ the distance/the speed** dreimal so weit/schnell; **~ the amount** dreimal so viel
triple jump N Dreisprung *m*
triplets ['trɪplɪts] NPL Drillinge *pl*
triplicate ['trɪplɪkət] N: **in ~** in dreifacher Ausfertigung
tripod ['traɪpɔd] N (*Phot*) Stativ *nt*
Tripoli ['trɪpəlɪ] N Tripolis *nt*
tripper ['trɪpəʳ] (BRIT) N Ausflügler(in) *m(f)*
tripwire ['trɪpwaɪəʳ] N Stolperdraht *m*
trite [traɪt] (*pej*) ADJ (*comment, idea etc*) banal
triumph ['traɪʌmf] N Triumph *m* ▶ VI: **to ~ (over)** triumphieren (über *+acc*)
triumphal [traɪ'ʌmfl] ADJ (*return*) triumphal
triumphant [traɪ'ʌmfənt] ADJ triumphal; (*victorious*) siegreich
triumphantly [traɪ'ʌmfəntlɪ] ADV triumphierend
trivia ['trɪvɪə] (*pej*) NPL Trivialitäten *pl*
trivial ['trɪvɪəl] ADJ trivial
triviality [trɪvɪ'ælɪtɪ] N Trivialität *f*
trivialize ['trɪvɪəlaɪz] VT trivialisieren
trod [trɔd] PT *of* **tread**
trodden [trɔdn] PP *of* **tread**
troll [trɔl] N (*also Comput*) Troll *m*
trolley ['trɔlɪ] N (*for luggage*) Kofferkuli *m*; (*for shopping*) Einkaufswagen *m*; (*table on wheels*) Teewagen *m*; (*also*: **trolley bus**) Oberleitungsomnibus *m*, Obus *m*
trollop ['trɔləp] (*pej*) N (*woman*) Schlampe *f*
trombone [trɔm'bəun] N Posaune *f*
troop [tru:p] N (*of people, monkeys etc*) Gruppe *f* ▶ VI: **to ~ in/out** hinein-/hinausströmen;
troops NPL (*Mil*) Truppen *pl*
troop carrier N Truppentransporter *m*; (*Naut: also*: **troopship**) Truppentransportschiff *nt*
trooper ['tru:pəʳ] N (*Mil*) Kavallerist *m*; (*US: policeman*) Polizist *m*
trooping the colour ['tru:pɪŋ-] (BRIT) N (*ceremony*) Fahnenparade *f*
troopship ['tru:pʃɪp] N Truppentransportschiff *nt*
trophy ['trəufɪ] N Trophäe *f*
tropic ['trɔpɪk] N Wendekreis *m*; **the tropics** NPL die Tropen *pl*; **T~ of Cancer/Capricorn** Wendekreis des Krebses/Steinbocks
tropical ['trɔpɪkl] ADJ tropisch
trot [trɔt] N (*fast pace*) Trott *m*; (*of horse*) Trab *m* ▶ VI (*horse*) traben; (*person*) trotten; **on the ~** (BRIT *fig*) hintereinander
▶ **trot out** VT (*facts, excuse etc*) vorbringen

t

trouble ['trʌbl] N Schwierigkeiten *pl*; (*bother, effort*) Umstände *pl*; (*unrest*) Unruhen *pl* ▸ VT (*worry*) beunruhigen; (*disturb: person*) belästigen ▸ VI: **to ~ to do sth** sich *dat* die Mühe machen, etw zu tun; **troubles** NPL (*personal*) Probleme *pl*; (*Pol etc*) Unruhen *pl*; **to be in ~** in Schwierigkeiten sein; **to have ~ doing sth** Schwierigkeiten *or* Probleme haben, etw zu tun; **to go to the ~ of doing sth** sich *dat* die Mühe machen, etw zu tun; **it's no ~!** das macht mir nichts aus!; **the ~ is ...** das Problem ist ...; **what's the ~?** wo fehlts?; **stomach** *etc* **~** Probleme mit dem Magen *etc*; **please don't ~ yourself** bitte bemühen Sie sich nicht
troubled [trʌbld] ADJ (*person*) besorgt; (*country, life, era*) von Problemen geschüttelt
trouble-free ['trʌblfri:] ADJ problemlos
troublemaker ['trʌblmeɪkə^r] N Unruhestifter(in) *m(f)*
troubleshooter ['trʌblʃu:tə^r] N Vermittler(in) *m(f)*
troublesome ['trʌblsəm] ADJ (*cough etc*) lästig; (*child*) schwierig
trouble spot N (*Mil*) Unruheherd *m*
troubling ['trʌblɪŋ] ADJ (*question etc*) beunruhigend
trough [trɔf] N (*also*: **drinking trough**) Wassertrog *m*; (*also*: **feeding trough**) Futtertrog *m*; (*channel*) Rinne *f*; (*low point*) Tief *nt*; **a ~ of low pressure** ein Tiefdruckkeil *m*
trounce [trauns] VT (*defeat*) vernichtend schlagen
troupe [tru:p] N Truppe *f*
trouser press ['trauzə-] N Hosenpresse *f*
trousers ['trauzəz] NPL Hose *f*; **short ~** kurze Hose; **a pair of ~** eine Hose
trousseau ['tru:səu] (*pl* **trousseaux** *or* **trousseaus**) N Aussteuer *f*
trout [traut] N INV Forelle *f*
trowel ['trauəl] N (*garden tool*) Pflanzkelle *f*; (*builder's tool*) (Maurer)kelle *f*
truant ['truənt] (BRIT) N: **to play ~** die Schule schwänzen
truce [tru:s] N Waffenstillstand *m*
truck [trʌk] N (*lorry*) Lastwagen *m*; (*Rail*) Güterwagen *m*; (*for luggage*) Gepäckwagen *m*; **to have no ~ with sb** nichts mit jdm zu tun haben
truck driver N Lkw-Fahrer(in) *m(f)*
trucker ['trʌkə^r] (US) N Lkw-Fahrer(in) *m(f)*
truck farm (US) N Gemüsefarm *f*
trucking ['trʌkɪŋ] (US) N Transport *m*
trucking company (US) N Spedition *f*
truculent ['trʌkjulənt] ADJ aufsässig
trudge [trʌdʒ] VI (*also*: **trudge along**) sich dahinschleppen
true [tru:] ADJ wahr; (*accurate*) genau; (*genuine*) echt; (*faithful: friend*) treu; (*wall, beam*) gerade; (*circle*) rund; **to come ~** wahr werden; **~ to life** lebensecht
truffle ['trʌfl] N (*fungus, sweet*) Trüffel *f*
truly ['tru:lɪ] ADV wirklich, wahrhaft; (*truthfully*) wirklich; **yours ~** (*in letter*) mit freundlichen Grüßen
trump [trʌmp] N (*also*: **trump card**: *fig*) Trumpf *m*; **to turn up trumps** (*fig*) sich als Retter in der Not erweisen
trumped-up ADJ: **a ~ charge** eine erfundene Anschuldigung
trumpet ['trʌmpɪt] N Trompete *f*
truncated [trʌŋ'keɪtɪd] ADJ (*message, object*) verstümmelt
truncheon ['trʌntʃən] (BRIT) N Gummiknüppel *m*
trundle ['trʌndl] VT (*trolley etc*) rollen ▸ VI: **to ~ along** (*person*) dahinschlendern; (*vehicle*) dahinrollen
trunk [trʌŋk] N (*of tree*) Stamm *m*; (*of person*) Rumpf *m*; (*of elephant*) Rüssel *m*; (*case*) Schrankkoffer *m*; (*US Aut*) Kofferraum *m*; **trunks** NPL (*also*: **swimming trunks**) Badehose *f*
trunk call (BRIT) N Ferngespräch *nt*
trunk road (BRIT) N Fernstraße *f*
truss [trʌs] N (*Med*) Bruchband *nt* ▸ **truss (up)** VT (*Culin*) dressieren; (*person*) fesseln
trust [trʌst] N Vertrauen *nt*; (*Comm: for charity etc*) Stiftung *f* ▸ VT vertrauen *+dat*; **to take sth on ~** (*advice etc*) etw einfach glauben; **to be in ~** (*Law*) treuhänderisch verwaltet werden; **to ~ (that)** (*hope*) hoffen(, dass)
trust company N Trust *m*
trusted ['trʌstɪd] ADJ (*friend, servant*) treu
trustee [trʌs'ti:] N (*Law*) Treuhänder(in) *m(f)*; (*of school etc*) Aufsichtsratsmitglied *nt*
trustful ['trʌstful] ADJ vertrauensvoll
trust fund N Treuhandvermögen *nt*
trusting ['trʌstɪŋ] ADJ vertrauensvoll
trustworthy ['trʌstwə:ðɪ] ADJ (*person*) vertrauenswürdig
trusty ['trʌstɪ] ADJ getreu
truth [tru:θ] (*pl* **truths**) N: **the ~** die Wahrheit *f*
truthful ['tru:θful] ADJ (*person*) ehrlich; (*answer etc*) wahrheitsgemäß
truthfully ['tru:θfəlɪ] ADV (*answer*) wahrheitsgemäß
truthfulness ['tru:θfəlnɪs] N Ehrlichkeit *f*
try [traɪ] N (*also Rugby*) Versuch *m* ▸ VT (*attempt*) versuchen; (*test*) probieren; (*Law*) vor Gericht stellen; (*strain: patience*) auf die Probe stellen ▸ VI es versuchen; **to have a ~** es versuchen, einen Versuch machen; **to ~ to do sth** versuchen, etw zu tun; **to ~ one's (very) best** *or* **hardest** sein Bestes versuchen *or* tun ▸ **try on** VT (*clothes*) anprobieren; **she's trying it on** (*fig*) sie probiert, wie weit sie gehen kann ▸ **try out** VT ausprobieren
trying ['traɪɪŋ] ADJ (*person*) schwierig; (*experience*) schwer
tsar [zɑ:^r] N Zar *m*
T-shirt ['ti:ʃə:t] N T-Shirt *nt*
T-square ['ti:skwɛə^r] N (*Tech*) Reißschiene *f*
TT ADJ ABBR (BRIT *inf*) = **teetotal** ▸ ABBR (*US Post: = Trust Territories*) *der US-Verwaltungshoheit unterstellte Gebiete*
tub [tʌb] N (*container*) Kübel *m*; (*bath*) Wanne *f*
tuba ['tju:bə] N Tuba *f*

tubby ['tʌbɪ] ADJ rundlich
tube [tjuːb] N *(pipe)* Rohr *nt*; *(container)* Tube *f*; (BRIT: *underground*) U-Bahn *f*; (*US inf*): **the ~** *(television)* die Röhre
tubeless ['tjuːblɪs] ADJ *(tyre)* schlauchlos
tuber ['tjuːbəʳ] N *(Bot)* Knolle *f*
tuberculosis [tjubəːkju'ləusɪs] N Tuberkulose *f*
tube station (BRIT) N U-Bahn-Station *f*
tubing ['tjuːbɪŋ] N Schlauch *m*; **a piece of ~** ein Schlauch
tubular ['tjuːbjuləʳ] ADJ röhrenförmig
TUC (BRIT) N ABBR (= *Trades Union Congress*) *britischer Gewerkschafts-Dachverband*
tuck [tʌk] VT *(put)* stecken ▶ N *(Sewing)* Biese *f*
▶ **tuck away** VT *(money)* wegstecken; **to be tucked away** *(building)* versteckt liegen
▶ **tuck in** VT *(clothing)* feststecken; *(child)* zudecken ▶ VI *(eat)* zulangen
▶ **tuck up** VT *(invalid, child)* zudecken
tucker ['tʌkəʳ] N (AUST, *NZ inf*) Essen *nt*, Fressalien *pl (inf)*
tuck shop N Süßwarenladen *m*
Tue., Tues. ABBR (= *Tuesday*) Di.
Tuesday ['tjuːzdɪ] N Dienstag *m*; **it is ~ 23rd March** heute ist Dienstag, der 23. März; **on ~** am Dienstag; **on Tuesdays** dienstags; **every ~** jeden Dienstag; **every other ~** jeden zweiten Dienstag; **last/next ~** letzten/nächsten Dienstag; **the following ~** am Dienstag darauf; **~'s newspaper** die Zeitung von Dienstag; **a week/fortnight on ~** Dienstag in einer Woche/in vierzehn Tagen; **the ~ before last** der vorletzte Dienstag; **the ~ after next** der übernächste Dienstag; **~ morning/lunchtime/afternoon/evening** Dienstag Morgen/Mittag/Nachmittag/Abend; **~ night** *(overnight)* Dienstag Nacht
tuft [tʌft] N Büschel *nt*
tug [tʌg] N *(ship)* Schlepper *m* ▶ VT zerren
tug of love N Tauziehen *nt (um das Sorgerecht für Kinder)*
tug-of-war [tʌgəv'wɔːʳ] N *(also fig)* Tauziehen *nt*
tuition [tjuː'ɪʃən] N (BRIT) Unterricht *m*; (*US: school fees*) Schulgeld *nt*
tulip ['tjuːlɪp] N Tulpe *f*
tumble ['tʌmbl] VI *(fall)* stürzen ▶ N *(fall)* Sturz *m*
▶ **tumble to** *(inf)* VT FUS kapieren
tumbledown ['tʌmbldaun] ADJ *(building)* baufällig
tumble dryer (BRIT) N Wäschetrockner *m*
tumbler ['tʌmbləʳ] N *(glass)* Trinkglas *nt*
tummy ['tʌmɪ] *(inf)* N Bauch *m*
tumour, (*US*) **tumor** ['tjuːməʳ] N *(Med)* Tumor *m*, Geschwulst *f*
tumult ['tjuːmʌlt] N Tumult *m*
tumultuous [tjuː'mʌltjuəs] ADJ *(welcome, applause etc)* stürmisch
tuna ['tjuːnə] N INV (*also:* **tuna fish**) T(h)unfisch *m*
tune [tjuːn] N *(melody)* Melodie *f* ▶ VT *(Mus)* stimmen; *(Radio, TV, Aut)* einstellen; **to be in/out of ~** *(instrument)* richtig gestimmt/verstimmt sein; *(singer)* richtig/falsch singen; **to be in/out of ~ with** *(fig)* in Einklang/nicht in Einklang stehen mit; **she was robbed to the ~ of 10,000 pounds** sie wurde um einen Betrag in Höhe von 10.000 Pfund beraubt
▶ **tune in** VI *(Radio, TV)* einschalten; **to ~ in to BBC1** BBC1 einschalten
▶ **tune up** VI *(Mus)* (das Instrument/die Instrumente) stimmen
tuneful ['tjuːnful] ADJ melodisch
tuner ['tjuːnəʳ] N *(radio set)* Tuner *m*; **piano ~** Klavierstimmer(in) *m(f)*
tuner amplifier N Steuergerät *nt*
tungsten ['tʌŋstən] N Wolfram *nt*
tunic ['tjuːnɪk] N Hemdbluse *f*
tuning fork ['tjuːnɪŋ-] N Stimmgabel *f*
Tunis ['tjuːnɪs] N Tunis *nt*
Tunisia [tjuː'nɪzɪə] N Tunesien *nt*
Tunisian [tjuː'nɪzɪən] ADJ tunesisch ▶ N *(person)* Tunesier(in) *m(f)*
tunnel ['tʌnl] N Tunnel *m*; *(in mine)* Stollen *m* ▶ VI einen Tunnel bauen
tunnel vision N *(Med)* Gesichtsfeldeinengung *f*; *(fig)* Engstirnigkeit *f*
tunny ['tʌnɪ] N T(h)unfisch *m*
turban ['təːbən] N Turban *m*
turbid ['təːbɪd] ADJ *(water)* trüb; *(air)* schmutzig
turbine ['təːbaɪn] N Turbine *f*
turbo ['təːbəu] N Turbo *m*; **~ engine** Turbomotor *m*
turbojet [təːbəu'dʒɛt] N Düsenflugzeug *nt*
turboprop [təːbəu'prɔp] N *(engine)* Turbo-Prop-Turbine *f*
turbot ['təːbət] N INV Steinbutt *m*
turbulence ['təːbjuləns] N *(Aviat)* Turbulenz *f*
turbulent ['təːbjulənt] ADJ *(water, seas)* stürmisch; *(fig: career, period)* turbulent
tureen [tə'riːn] N Terrine *f*
turf [təːf] N *(grass)* Rasen *m*; *(clod)* Sode *f* ▶ VT *(area)* mit Grassoden bedecken; **the T~** *(horse-racing)* der Pferderennsport
▶ **turf out** *(inf)* VT *(person)* rausschmeißen
turf accountant (BRIT) N Buchmacher *m*
turgid ['təːdʒɪd] ADJ geschwollen
Turin ['tjuə'rɪn] N Turin *nt*
Turk [təːk] N Türke *m*, Türkin *f*
Turkey ['təːkɪ] N die Türkei *f*
turkey ['təːkɪ] N *(bird)* Truthahn *m*, Truthenne *f*; *(meat)* Puter *m*
Turkish ['təːkɪʃ] ADJ türkisch ▶ N *(Ling)* Türkisch *nt*
Turkish bath N türkisches Bad *nt*
Turkish delight N *geleeartige Süßigkeit, mit Puderzucker oder Schokolade überzogen*
turmeric ['təːmərɪk] N Kurkuma *f*
turmoil ['təːmɔɪl] N Aufruhr *m*; **in ~** in Aufruhr
turn [təːn] N *(rotation)* Drehung *f*; *(performance)* Nummer *f*; *(change)* Wende *f*; *(in road)* Kurve *f*; *(inf: Med)* Anfall *m* ▶ VT *(handle, key)* drehen; *(page)* umblättern; *(collar, steak)* wenden; *(shape: wood)* drechseln; *(: metal)* drehen ▶ VI *(object)* sich drehen; *(person)* sich umdrehen; *(change direction)* abbiegen; *(milk)* sauer werden; **to do sb a good ~** jdm einen guten Dienst erweisen; **a ~ of events** eine Wendung der Dinge; **it gave**

t

me quite a ~ (*inf*) das hat mir einen schönen Schrecken eingejagt; **"no left ~"** (*Aut*) „Linksabbiegen verboten"; **it's your ~** du bist dran; **in ~** der Reihe nach; **to take turns (at)** sich abwechseln (bei); **at the ~ of the century/year** zur Jahrhundertwende/Jahreswende; **to take a ~ for the worse** (*events*) sich zum Schlechten wenden; **his health** *or* **he has taken a ~ for the worse** sein Befinden hat sich verschlechtert; **to ~ nasty/forty/grey** unangenehm/vierzig/grau werden
▸ **turn against** VT FUS sich wenden gegen
▸ **turn around** VI sich umdrehen; (*in car*) wenden
▸ **turn away** VT (*applicants*) abweisen; (*business*) zurückweisen ▸ VI sich abwenden
▸ **turn back** VI umkehren ▸ VT (*person, vehicle*) zurückweisen
▸ **turn down** VT (*request*) ablehnen; (*heating*) kleiner stellen; (*radio etc*) leiser stellen; (*bedclothes*) aufschlagen
▸ **turn in** VI (*inf: go to bed*) sich hinhauen ▸ VT (*to police*) anzeigen; **to ~ o.s. in** sich stellen
▸ **turn into** VT FUS (*change*) sich verwandeln in +*acc* ▸ VT machen zu
▸ **turn off** VI (*from road*) abbiegen ▸ VT (*light, radio etc*) ausmachen; (*tap*) zudrehen; (*engine*) abstellen
▸ **turn on** VT (*light, radio etc*) anmachen; (*tap*) aufdrehen; (*engine*) anstellen
▸ **turn out** VT (*light*) ausmachen; (*gas*) abstellen ▸ VI (*appear, attend*) erscheinen; **to ~ out to be** (*prove to be*) sich erweisen als; **to ~ out well/badly** (*situation*) gut/schlecht enden
▸ **turn over** VI (*person*) sich umdrehen ▸ VT (*object*) umdrehen, wenden; (*page*) umblättern; **to ~ sth over to** (*to sb*) etw übertragen +*dat*; (*to sth*) etw verlagern zu
▸ **turn round** VI sich umdrehen; (*vehicle*) wenden
▸ **turn up** VI (*person*) erscheinen; (*lost object*) wieder auftauchen ▸ VT (*heater*) höher stellen; (*radio etc*) lauter stellen; (*collar*) hochklappen

turnabout ['tə:nəbaut] N (*fig*) Kehrtwendung *f*

turnaround ['tə:nəraund] N = **turnabout**

turncoat ['tə:nkəut] N Überläufer(in) *m(f)*

turned-up ['tə:ndʌp] ADJ: **~ nose** Stupsnase *f*

turning ['tə:nɪŋ] N (*in road*) Abzweigung *f*; **the first ~ on the right** die erste Straße rechts

turning circle (BRIT) N (*Aut*) Wendekreis *m*

turning point N (*fig*) Wendepunkt *m*

turning radius (*US*) N = **turning circle**

turnip ['tə:nɪp] N Rübe *f*

turnout ['tə:naut] N (*of voters etc*) Beteiligung *f*

turnover ['tə:nəuvəʳ] N (*Comm: amount of money*) Umsatz *m*; (*: of staff*) Fluktuation *f*; (*Culin*): **apple ~** Apfeltasche *f*; **there is a rapid ~ in staff** der Personalbestand wechselt ständig

turnpike ['tə:npaɪk] (*US*) N gebührenpflichtige Autobahn *f*

turnstile ['tə:nstaɪl] N Drehkreuz *nt*

turntable ['tə:nteɪbl] N (*on record player*) Plattenteller *m*

turn-up ['tə:nʌp] (BRIT) N (*on trousers*) Aufschlag *m*; **that's a ~ for the books!** (*inf*) das ist eine echte Überraschung!

turpentine ['tə:pəntaɪn] N (*also*: **turps**) Terpentin *nt*

turquoise ['tə:kwɔɪz] ADJ (*colour*) türkis ▸ N (*stone*) Türkis *m*

turret ['tʌrɪt] N Turm *m*

turtle ['tə:tl] N Schildkröte *f*

turtleneck ['tə:tlnɛk], **turtleneck sweater** N Pullover *m* mit rundem Kragen

Tuscan ['tʌskən] ADJ toskanisch ▸ N (*person*) Toskaner(in) *m(f)*

Tuscany ['tʌskənɪ] N die Toskana

tusk [tʌsk] N (*of elephant*) Stoßzahn *m*

tussle ['tʌsl] N Gerangel *nt*

tutor ['tju:təʳ] N Tutor(in) *m(f)*; (*private tutor*) Privatlehrer(in) *m(f)*

tutorial [tju:'tɔ:rɪəl] N Kolloquium *nt*

tuxedo [tʌk'si:dəu], (*US*) **tux** N Smoking *m*

TV [ti:'vi:] N ABBR (= *television*) TV *nt*

TV dinner N Fertiggericht *nt*

twaddle ['twɔdl] (*inf*) N dummes Zeug *nt*

twang [twæŋ] N (*of instrument*) singender Ton *m*; (*of voice*) näselnder Ton *m* ▸ VI einen singenden Ton von sich geben ▸ VT (*guitar*) zupfen

tweak [twi:k] VT kneifen

tweed [twi:d] N Tweed *m* ▸ ADJ (*jacket, skirt*) Tweed-

tweet [twi:t] VI (*on Twitter*) twittern

tweezers ['twi:zəz] NPL Pinzette *f*

twelfth [twɛlfθ] NUM zwölfte(r, s) ▸ N Zwölftel *nt*

Twelfth Night N ≈ Dreikönige *nt*

twelve [twɛlv] NUM zwölf; **at ~ (o'clock)** (*midday*) um zwölf Uhr (mittags); (*midnight*) um zwölf Uhr nachts

twentieth ['twɛntɪɪθ] NUM zwanzigste(r, s)

twenty ['twɛntɪ] NUM zwanzig

twenty-four seven ['twɛntɪfɔ:'sɛvn] N (*store*) Geschäft, das an sieben Tagen die Woche und 24 Stunden am Tag geöffnet hat ▸ ADJ rund um die Uhr; **~ service** Service, der rund um die Uhr zur Verfügung steht

twerp [twə:p] (*inf*) N Schwachkopf *m*

twice [twaɪs] ADV zweimal; **~ as much** zweimal so viel; **~ a week** zweimal die Woche; **she is ~ your age** sie ist doppelt so alt wie du

twiddle ['twɪdl] VT drehen an +*dat* ▸ VI: **to ~ (with)** herumdrehen (an +*dat*); **to ~ one's thumbs** (*fig*) Däumchen drehen

twig [twɪg] N Zweig *m* ▸ VI, VT (BRIT *inf: realize*) kapieren

twilight ['twaɪlaɪt] N Dämmerung *f*; **in the ~** in der Dämmerung

twill [twɪl] N (*cloth*) Köper *m*

twin [twɪn] ADJ (*sister, brother*) Zwillings-; (*towers*) Doppel- ▸ N Zwilling *m*; (*room in hotel etc*) Zweibettzimmer *nt* ▸ VT (*towns etc*): **to be twinned with ...** ... als Partnerstadt haben

twin-bedded room ['twɪn'bɛdɪd-] N Zweibettzimmer *nt*

twin beds NPL zwei (gleiche) Einzelbetten *pl*

twin-carburettor ['twɪnkɑ:bju'rɛtə^r] ADJ Doppelvergaser-
twine [twaɪn] N Bindfaden *m* ▸ VI sich winden
twin-engined [twɪn'ɛndʒɪnd] ADJ zweimotorig
twinge [twɪndʒ] N (*of pain*) Stechen *nt*; **a ~ of conscience** Gewissensbisse *pl*; **a ~ of fear/guilt** ein Angst-/Schuldgefühl *nt*
twinkle ['twɪŋkl] VI funkeln ▸ N Funkeln *nt*
twin room ['twɪn'ru:m] N Zweibettzimmer *nt*
twin town N Partnerstadt *f*
twirl [twə:l] VT herumwirbeln ▸ VI wirbeln ▸ N Wirbel *m*
twist [twɪst] N (*action*) Drehung *f*; (*in road*) Kurve; (*in coil, flex*) Biegung *f*; (*in story*) Wendung *f* ▸ VT (*turn*) drehen; (*injure, ankle etc*) verrenken; (*twine*) wickeln; (*fig: meaning etc*) verdrehen ▸ VI (*road, river*) sich winden; **~ my arm!** (*inf*) überreden Sie mich einfach!
twisted ['twɪstɪd] ADJ (*wire, rope*) gedreht; (*ankle*) verrenkt; (*fig: logic, mind*) verdreht
twit [twɪt] (*inf*) N Trottel *m*
twitch [twɪtʃ] N (*jerky movement*) Zucken *nt* ▸ VI zucken
Twitter® [twɪtə^r] N Twitter® *nt* ▸ VI twittern
two [tu:] NUM zwei; **~ by ~, in twos** zu zweit; **to put ~ and ~ together** (*fig*) zwei und zwei zusammenzählen
two-bit [tu:'bɪt] (*inf*) ADJ (*worthless*) mies
two-dimensional ADJ zweidimensional; (*fig*) oberflächlich
two-door [tu:'dɔ:^r] ADJ zweitürig
two-faced [tu:'feɪst] (*pej*) ADJ scheinheilig
twofold ['tu:fəuld] ADV: **to increase ~** um das Doppelte ansteigen ▸ ADJ (*increase*) um das Doppelte; (*aim, value etc*) zweifach
two-piece ['tu:pi:s] N (*also:* **two-piece suit**) Zweiteiler *m*; (*also:* **two-piece swimsuit**) zweiteiliger Badeanzug *m*
two-ply ['tu:plaɪ] ADJ (*wool*) zweifädig; (*tissues*) zweilagig
two-seater ['tu:'si:tə^r] N (*car*) Zweisitzer *m*
twosome ['tu:səm] N (*people*) Paar *nt*
two-stroke ['tu:strəuk] N (*also:* **two-stroke engine**) Zweitakter *m* ▸ ADJ (*engine*) Zweitakt-
two-tone ['tu:'təun] ADJ (*in colour*) zweifarbig
two-way ['tu:weɪ] ADJ: **~ traffic** Verkehr *m* in beiden Richtungen; **~ radio** Funksprechgerät *nt*
TX (*US*) ABBR (*Post*) = **Texas**
tycoon [taɪ'ku:n] N Magnat *m*
type [taɪp] N (*category, model, example*) Typ *m*; (*Typ*) Schrift *f* ▸ VT (*letter etc*) tippen, (mit der) Maschine schreiben; **a ~ of** eine Art von; **what ~ do you want?** welche Sorte möchten Sie?; **in bold/italic ~** in Fett-/Kursivdruck
typecast ['taɪpkɑ:st] VT (*irreg: like* **cast**) (*actor*) (auf eine Rolle) festlegen
typeface ['taɪpfeɪs] N Schrift *f*, Schriftbild *nt*
typescript ['taɪpskrɪpt] N (maschinengeschriebenes) Manuskript *nt*
typeset ['taɪpsɛt] VT (*irreg: like* **set**) setzen
typesetter ['taɪpsɛtə^r] N Setzer(in) *m(f)*
typewriter ['taɪpraɪtə^r] N Schreibmaschine *f*
typewritten ['taɪprɪtn] ADJ maschine(n)geschrieben
typhoid ['taɪfɔɪd] N Typhus *m*
typhoon [taɪ'fu:n] N Taifun *m*
typhus ['taɪfəs] N Fleckfieber *nt*
typical ['tɪpɪkl] ADJ typisch; **~ (of)** typisch (für); **that's ~!** das ist typisch!
typify ['tɪpɪfaɪ] VT typisch sein für
typing ['taɪpɪŋ] N Maschine(n)schreiben *nt*
typing error N Tippfehler *m*
typing pool N Schreibzentrale *f*
typist ['taɪpɪst] N Schreibkraft *f*
typo ['taɪpəu] (*inf*) N ABBR (= *typographical error*) Druckfehler *m*
typography [tɪ'pɔgrəfɪ] N Typografie *f*
tyranny ['tɪrənɪ] N Tyrannei *f*
tyrant ['taɪərnt] N Tyrann(in) *m(f)*
tyre, (*US*) **tire** ['taɪə^r] N Reifen *m*
tyre pressure N Reifendruck *m*
Tyrol [tɪ'rəul] N Tirol *nt*
Tyrolean [tɪrə'li:ən] ADJ Tiroler ▸ N (*person*) Tiroler(in) *m(f)*
Tyrolese [tɪrə'li:z] = **Tyrolean**
Tyrrhenian Sea [tɪ'ri:nɪən-] N: **the ~** das Tyrrhenische Meer
tzar [zɑ:^r] N = **tsar**

t

Uu

U¹, u [juː] N (*letter*) U *nt*, u *nt*; **U for Uncle** ≈ U wie Ulrich
U² [juː] (BRIT) N ABBR (*Cine*: = *universal*) *Klassifikation für jugendfreie Filme*
UAW (US) N ABBR (= *United Automobile Workers*) *Automobilarbeitergewerkschaft*
UB40 (BRIT) N ABBR (= *unemployment benefit form 40*) Arbeitslosenausweis *m*
U-bend ['juːbɛnd] N (*in pipe*) U-Krümmung *f*
ubiquitous [juː'bɪkwɪtəs] ADJ allgegenwärtig
UCCA ['ʌkə] (BRIT) N ABBR (= *Universities Central Council on Admissions*) *akademische Zulassungsstelle*, ≈ ZVS *f*
UDA (BRIT) N ABBR (= *Ulster Defence Association*) *paramilitärische protestantische Organisation in Nordirland*
UDC (BRIT) N ABBR (= *Urban District Council*) Stadtverwaltung *f*
udder ['ʌdəʳ] N Euter *nt*
UDI (BRIT) N ABBR (*Pol*: = *unilateral declaration of independence*) einseitige Unabhängigkeitserklärung *f*
UDR (BRIT) N ABBR (= *Ulster Defence Regiment*) *Regiment aus Teilzeitsoldaten zur Unterstützung der britischen Armee und Polizei in Nordirland*
UEFA [juː'eɪfə] N ABBR (= *Union of European Football Associations*) UEFA *f*
UFO ['juːfəu] N ABBR (= *unidentified flying object*) UFO *nt*
Uganda [juː'gændə] N Uganda *nt*
Ugandan [juː'gændən] ADJ ugandisch ▶ N Ugander(in) *m(f)*
UGC (BRIT) N ABBR (= *University Grants Committee*) *Ausschuss zur Verteilung von Geldern an Universitäten*
ugh [əːh] EXCL igitt
ugliness ['ʌglɪnɪs] N Hässlichkeit *f*
ugly ['ʌglɪ] ADJ hässlich; (*nasty*) schlimm
UHF ABBR (= *ultrahigh frequency*) UHF
UHT ABBR (= *ultra heat treated*): **~ milk** H-Milch *f*
UK N ABBR = **United Kingdom**
Ukraine [juː'kreɪn] N Ukraine *f*
Ukrainian [juː'kreɪnɪən] ADJ ukrainisch ▶ N Ukrainer(in) *m(f)*; (*Ling*) Ukrainisch *nt*
ulcer ['ʌlsəʳ] N (*stomach ulcer etc*) Geschwür *nt*; (*also*: **mouth ulcer**) Abszess *m* im Mund
Ulster ['ʌlstəʳ] N Ulster *nt*
ulterior [ʌl'tɪərɪəʳ] ADJ: **~ motive** Hintergedanke *m*
ultimata [ʌltɪ'meɪtə] NPL *of* **ultimatum**
ultimate ['ʌltɪmət] ADJ (*final*) letztendlich; (*greatest*) größte(r, s); (: *deterrent*) äußerste(r, s); (: *authority*) höchste(r, s) ▶ N: **the ~ in luxury** das Äußerste *or* Höchste an Luxus
ultimately ['ʌltɪmətlɪ] ADV (*in the end*) schließlich, letzten Endes; (*basically*) im Grunde (genommen)
ultimatum [ʌltɪ'meɪtəm] (*pl* **ultimatums** *or* **ultimata**) N Ultimatum *nt*
ultrasonic [ʌltrə'sɔnɪk] ADJ (*sound*) Ultraschall-
ultrasound ['ʌltrəsaund] N Ultraschall *m*
ultraviolet ['ʌltrə'vaɪəlɪt] ADJ ultraviolett
umbilical cord [ʌm'bɪlɪkl-] N Nabelschnur *f*
umbrage ['ʌmbrɪdʒ] N: **to take ~ at** Anstoß nehmen an *+dat*
umbrella [ʌm'brɛlə] N (*for rain*) (Regen)schirm *m*; (*for sun*) Sonnenschirm *m*; (*fig*): **under the ~ of** unter der Leitung von
umlaut ['umlaut] N Umlaut *m*; (*mark*) Umlautzeichen *nt*
umpire ['ʌmpaɪəʳ] N Schiedsrichter(in) *m(f)* ▶ VT (*game*) als Schiedsrichter leiten
umpteen [ʌmp'tiːn] ADJ zig
umpteenth [ʌmp'tiːnθ] ADJ: **for the ~ time** zum x-ten Mal
UMWA N ABBR (= *United Mineworkers of America*) *amerikanische Bergarbeitergewerkschaft*
UN N ABBR (= *United Nations*) UNO *f*
unabashed [ʌnə'bæʃt] ADJ: **to be/seem ~** unbeeindruckt sein/scheinen
unabated [ʌnə'beɪtɪd] ADJ unvermindert ▶ ADV: **to continue ~** nicht nachlassen
unable [ʌn'eɪbl] ADJ: **to be ~ to do sth** etw nicht tun können
unabridged [ʌnə'brɪdʒd] ADJ ungekürzt
unacceptable [ʌnək'sɛptəbl] ADJ unannehmbar, nicht akzeptabel
unaccompanied [ʌnə'kʌmpənɪd] ADJ (*child, song*) ohne Begleitung; (*luggage*) unbegleitet
unaccountably [ʌnə'kauntəblɪ] ADV unerklärlich
unaccounted [ʌnə'kauntɪd] ADJ: **to be ~ for** (*passengers, money etc*) (noch) fehlen
unaccustomed [ʌnə'kʌstəmd] ADJ: **to be ~ to** nicht gewöhnt sein an *+acc*
unacquainted [ʌnə'kweɪntɪd] ADJ: **to be ~ with** nicht vertraut sein mit

unadulterated [ʌnəˈdʌltəreɪtɪd] ADJ rein
unaffected [ʌnəˈfɛktɪd] ADJ (*person, behaviour*) natürlich, ungekünstelt; **to be ~ by sth** von etw nicht berührt werden
unafraid [ʌnəˈfreɪd] ADJ: **to be ~** keine Angst haben
unaided [ʌnˈeɪdɪd] ADV ohne fremde Hilfe
unanimity [juːnəˈnɪmɪtɪ] N Einstimmigkeit *f*
unanimous [juːˈnænɪməs] ADJ einstimmig
unanimously [juːˈnænɪməslɪ] ADV einstimmig
unanswered [ʌnˈɑːnsəd] ADJ unbeantwortet
unappetizing [ʌnˈæpɪtaɪzɪŋ] ADJ (*food*) unappetitlich
unappreciative [ʌnəˈpriːʃɪətɪv] ADJ (*person*) undankbar; (*audience*) verständnislos
unarmed [ʌnˈɑːmd] ADJ unbewaffnet; **~ combat** Nahkampf *m* ohne Waffen
unashamed [ʌnəˈʃeɪmd] ADJ (*pleasure, greed etc*) unverhohlen
unassisted [ʌnəˈsɪstɪd] ADV ohne fremde Hilfe
unassuming [ʌnəˈsjuːmɪŋ] ADJ bescheiden
unattached [ʌnəˈtætʃt] ADJ (*single: person*) ungebunden; (*unconnected*) ohne Verbindung
unattended [ʌnəˈtɛndɪd] ADJ (*car, luggage, child*) unbeaufsichtigt
unattractive [ʌnəˈtræktɪv] ADJ unattraktiv
unauthorized [ʌnˈɔːθəraɪzd] ADJ (*visit, use*) unbefugt; (*version*) nicht unautorisiert
unavailable [ʌnəˈveɪləbl] ADJ (*article, room*) nicht verfügbar; (*person*) nicht zu erreichen; **~ for comment** nicht zu sprechen
unavoidable [ʌnəˈvɔɪdəbl] ADJ unvermeidlich
unavoidably [ʌnəˈvɔɪdəblɪ] ADV (*delayed etc*) auf unvermeidliche Weise
unaware [ʌnəˈwɛəʳ] ADJ: **he was ~ of it** er war sich *dat* dessen nicht bewusst
unawares [ʌnəˈwɛəz] ADV (*catch, take*) unerwartet
unbalanced [ʌnˈbælənst] ADJ (*report*) unausgewogen; **(mentally) ~** geistig gestört
unbearable [ʌnˈbɛərəbl] ADJ unerträglich
unbeatable [ʌnˈbiːtəbl] ADJ unschlagbar
unbeaten [ʌnˈbiːtn] ADJ ungeschlagen
unbecoming [ʌnbɪˈkʌmɪŋ] ADJ (*language, behaviour*) unpassend; (*garment*) unvorteilhaft
unbeknown [ʌnbɪˈnəun], **unbeknownst** [ʌnbɪˈnəunst] ADV: **~(st) to me/Peter** ohne mein/Peters Wissen
unbelief [ʌnbɪˈliːf] N Ungläubigkeit *f*
unbelievable [ʌnbɪˈliːvəbl] ADJ unglaublich
unbelievably [ʌnbɪˈliːvəblɪ] ADV unglaublich
unbend [ʌnˈbɛnd] VI (*irreg: like* **bend**) (*relax*) aus sich herausgehen ▶ VT (*wire etc*) gerade biegen
unbending [ʌnˈbɛndɪŋ] ADJ (*person, attitude*) unnachgiebig
unbiased, unbiassed [ʌnˈbaɪəst] ADJ unvoreingenommen
unblemished [ʌnˈblɛmɪʃt] ADJ (*also fig*) makellos
unblock [ʌnˈblɔk] VT (*pipe*) frei machen
unborn [ʌnˈbɔːn] ADJ ungeboren
unbounded [ʌnˈbaundɪd] ADJ grenzenlos
unbreakable [ʌnˈbreɪkəbl] ADJ (*object*) unzerbrechlich
unbridled [ʌnˈbraɪdld] ADJ ungezügelt
unbroken [ʌnˈbrəukən] ADJ (*seal*) unversehrt; (*silence*) ununterbrochen; (*record, series*) ungebrochen
unbuckle [ʌnˈbʌkl] VT aufschnallen
unburden [ʌnˈbəːdn] VT: **to ~ o.s. (to sb)** (jdm) sein Herz ausschütten
unbusinesslike [ʌnˈbɪznɪslaɪk] ADJ ungeschäftsmäßig
unbutton [ʌnˈbʌtn] VT aufknöpfen
uncalled-for [ʌnˈkɔːldfɔːʳ] ADJ (*remark etc*) unnötig
uncanny [ʌnˈkænɪ] ADJ unheimlich
unceasing [ʌnˈsiːsɪŋ] ADJ (*search, flow etc*) unaufhörlich; (*loyalty*) unermüdlich
unceremonious [ʌnsɛrɪˈməunɪəs] ADJ (*abrupt, rude*) brüsk, barsch
uncertain [ʌnˈsəːtn] ADJ (*person*) unsicher; (*future, outcome*) ungewiss; **to be ~ about sth** unsicher über etw *acc* sein; **in no ~ terms** unzweideutig
uncertainty [ʌnˈsəːtntɪ] N Ungewissheit *f*; **uncertainties** NPL (*doubts*) Unsicherheiten *pl*
unchallenged [ʌnˈtʃælɪndʒd] ADJ unbestritten ▶ ADV (*walk, enter*) ungehindert; **to go ~** unangefochten bleiben
unchanged [ʌnˈtʃeɪndʒd] ADJ unverändert
uncharitable [ʌnˈtʃærɪtəbl] ADJ (*remark, behaviour etc*) unfreundlich
uncharted [ʌnˈtʃɑːtɪd] ADJ (*land, sea*) unverzeichnet
unchecked [ʌnˈtʃɛkt] ADV (*grow, continue*) ungehindert
uncivil [ʌnˈsɪvɪl] ADJ (*person*) grob
uncivilized [ʌnˈsɪvɪlaɪzd] ADJ unzivilisiert
uncle [ˈʌŋkl] N Onkel *m*
unclear [ʌnˈklɪəʳ] ADJ unklar; **I'm still ~ about what I'm supposed to do** mir ist immer noch nicht klar, was ich tun soll
uncoil [ʌnˈkɔɪl] VT (*rope, wire*) abwickeln ▶ VI (*snake*) sich strecken
uncomfortable [ʌnˈkʌmfətəbl] ADJ (*person, chair*) unbequem; (*room*) ungemütlich; (*nervous*) unbehaglich; (*unpleasant: situation, fact*) unerfreulich
uncomfortably [ʌnˈkʌmfətəblɪ] ADV (*sit*) unbequem; (*smile*) unbehaglich
uncommitted [ʌnkəˈmɪtɪd] ADJ nicht engagiert; **~ to** nicht festgelegt auf +*acc*
uncommon [ʌnˈkɔmən] ADJ ungewöhnlich
uncommunicative [ʌnkəˈmjuːnɪkətɪv] ADJ (*person*) schweigsam
uncomplicated [ʌnˈkɔmplɪkeɪtɪd] ADJ unkompliziert
uncompromising [ʌnˈkɔmprəmaɪzɪŋ] ADJ (*person, belief*) kompromisslos
unconcerned [ʌnkənˈsəːnd] ADJ (*person*) unbekümmert; **to be ~ about sth** sich nicht um etw kümmern
unconditional [ʌnkənˈdɪʃənl] ADJ bedingungslos; (*acceptance*) vorbehaltlos
uncongenial [ʌnkənˈdʒiːnɪəl] ADJ (*surroundings*) unangenehm

unconnected [ʌnkə'nɛktɪd] ADJ (*unrelated*) ohne Verbindung; **to be ~ with sth** nicht mit etw in Beziehung stehen
unconscious [ʌn'kɔnʃəs] ADJ (*in faint*) bewusstlos; (*unaware*): **~ of** nicht bewusst *+gen* ▶ N: **the ~** das Unbewusste; **to knock sb ~** jdn bewusstlos schlagen
unconsciously [ʌn'kɔnʃəslɪ] ADV unbewusst
unconsciousness [ʌn'kɔnʃəsnɪs] N Bewusstlosigkeit *f*
unconstitutional ['ʌnkɔnstɪ'tju:ʃənl] ADJ verfassungswidrig
uncontested [ʌnkən'tɛstɪd] ADJ (*Pol: seat, election*) ohne Gegenkandidat; (*divorce*) ohne Einwände der Gegenseite
uncontrollable [ʌnkən'trəuləbl] ADJ unkontrollierbar; (*laughter*) unbändig
uncontrolled [ʌnkən'trəuld] ADJ (*behaviour*) ungezähmt; (*price rises etc*) ungehindert
unconventional [ʌnkən'vɛnʃənl] ADJ unkonventionell
unconvinced [ʌnkən'vɪnst] ADJ: **to be/remain ~** nicht überzeugt sein/bleiben
unconvincing [ʌnkən'vɪnsɪŋ] ADJ nicht überzeugend
uncork [ʌn'kɔ:k] VT (*bottle*) entkorken
uncorroborated [ʌnkə'rɔbəreɪtɪd] ADJ (*evidence*) unbestätigt
uncouth [ʌn'ku:θ] ADJ (*person, behaviour*) ungehobelt
uncover [ʌn'kʌvəʳ] VT aufdecken
unctuous ['ʌŋktjuəs] (*form*) ADJ (*person, behaviour*) salbungsvoll
undamaged [ʌn'dæmɪdʒd] ADJ unbeschädigt
undaunted [ʌn'dɔ:ntɪd] ADJ (*person*) unverzagt; **~, she struggled on** sie kämpfte unverzagt weiter
undecided [ʌndɪ'saɪdɪd] ADJ (*person*) unentschlossen; (*question*) unentschieden
undelivered [ʌndɪ'lɪvəd] ADJ (*goods*) nicht geliefert; (*letters*) nicht zugestellt; **if ~ return to sender** (*on envelope*) falls unzustellbar, zurück an Absender
undeniable [ʌndɪ'naɪəbl] ADJ unbestreitbar
undeniably [ʌndɪ'naɪəblɪ] ADV (*true*) zweifellos; (*handsome*) unbestreitbar
under ['ʌndəʳ] PREP (*position*) unter *+dat*; (*motion*) unter *+acc*; (*according to: law etc*) nach, gemäß *+dat* ▶ ADV (*go, fly etc*) darunter; **to come from ~ sth** unter etw *dat* hervorkommen; **~ there** darunter; **in ~ 2 hours** in weniger als 2 Stunden; **~ anaesthetic** unter Narkose; **to be ~ discussion** diskutiert werden; **~ repair** in Reparatur; **~ the circumstances** unter den Umständen
under... ['ʌndəʳ] PREF Unter-, unter-
underage [ʌndər'eɪdʒ] ADJ (*person*) minderjährig; **~ drinking** Alkoholgenuss *m* von Minderjährigen
underarm ['ʌndərɑ:m] ADV (*bowl, throw*) von unten ▶ ADJ (*throw, shot*) von unten; (*deodorant*) Achselhöhlen-
undercapitalized ['ʌndə'kæpɪtəlaɪzd] ADJ unterkapitalisiert
undercarriage ['ʌndəkærɪdʒ] N (*Aviat*) Fahrgestell *nt*
undercharge [ʌndə'tʃɑ:dʒ] VT zu wenig berechnen *+dat*
underclass ['ʌndəklɑ:s] N Unterklasse *f*
underclothes ['ʌndəkləuðz] NPL Unterwäsche *f*
undercoat ['ʌndəkəut] N (*paint*) Grundierung *f*
undercover [ʌndə'kʌvəʳ] ADJ (*duty, agent*) Geheim- ▶ ADV (*work*) insgeheim
undercurrent ['ʌndəkʌrnt] N (*also fig*) Unterströmung *f*
undercut [ʌndə'kʌt] VT (*irreg: like* **cut**) (*person, prices*) unterbieten
underdeveloped ['ʌndədɪ'vɛləpt] ADJ unterentwickelt
underdog ['ʌndədɔg] N: **the ~** der/die Benachteiligte
underdone [ʌndə'dʌn] ADJ (*food*) nicht gar; (*: meat*) nicht durchgebraten
underemployment ['ʌndərɪm'plɔɪmənt] N Unterbeschäftigung *f*
underestimate ['ʌndər'ɛstɪmeɪt] VT unterschätzen
underexposed ['ʌndərɪks'pəuzd] ADJ (*Phot*) unterbelichtet
underfed [ʌndə'fɛd] ADJ unterernährt
underfoot [ʌndə'fut] ADV: **to crush sth ~** etw am Boden zerdrücken; **to trample sth ~** auf etw *dat* herumtrampeln
underfunded ['ʌndə'fʌndɪd] ADJ unterfinanziert
undergo [ʌndə'gəu] VT (*irreg: like* **go**) (*change*) durchmachen; (*test, operation*) sich unterziehen; **the car is undergoing repairs** das Auto wird gerade repariert
undergraduate [ʌndə'grædjuɪt] N Student(in) *m(f)* ▶ CPD: **~ courses** Kurse *pl* für nicht graduierte Studenten
underground ['ʌndəgraund] ADJ unterirdisch; (*Pol: newspaper, activities*) Untergrund- ▶ ADV (*work*) unterirdisch; (*: miners*) unter Tage; (*Pol*): **to go ~** untertauchen ▶ N: **the ~** (BRIT) die U-Bahn; (*Pol*) die Untergrundbewegung; **~ car park** Tiefgarage *f*
underground station N U-Bahn-Station *f*
undergrowth ['ʌndəgrəuθ] N Unterholz *nt*
underhand [ʌndə'hænd], **underhanded** [ʌndə'hændɪd] ADJ (*fig: behaviour, person*) hinterhältig
underinsured [ʌndərɪn'ʃuəd] ADJ unterversichert
underlay [ʌndə'leɪ] N Unterlage *f*
underlie [ʌndə'laɪ] VT (*irreg: like* **lie²**) (*fig: be basis of*) zugrunde liegen *+dat*; **the underlying cause** der eigentliche Grund
underline [ʌndə'laɪn] VT unterstreichen; (*fig: emphasize*) betonen
underling ['ʌndəlɪŋ] (*pej*) N Befehlsempfänger(in) *m(f)*
underlying [ʌndə'laɪɪŋ] ADJ zugrunde liegend
undermanning [ʌndə'mænɪŋ] N Personalmangel *m*

undermentioned [ʌndəˈmɛnʃənd] ADJ unten genannt
undermine [ʌndəˈmaɪn] VT unterminieren, unterhöhlen
underneath [ʌndəˈni:θ] ADV darunter ▸ PREP (*position*) unter *+dat*; (*motion*) unter *+acc*
undernourished [ʌndəˈnʌrɪʃt] ADJ unterernährt
underpaid [ʌndəˈpeɪd] ADJ unterbezahlt
underpants [ˈʌndəpænts] NPL Unterhose *f*
underpass [ˈʌndəpɑ:s] (BRIT) N Unterführung *f*
underpin [ʌndəˈpɪn] VT (*argument*) untermauern
underplay [ʌndəˈpleɪ] (BRIT) VT herunterspielen
underpopulated [ʌndəˈpɔpjuleɪtɪd] ADJ unterbevölkert
underprice [ʌndəˈpraɪs] VT (*goods*) zu billig anbieten
underprivileged [ʌndəˈprɪvɪlɪdʒd] ADJ unterprivilegiert
underrate [ʌndəˈreɪt] VT unterschätzen
underscore [ʌndəˈskɔ:ʳ] VT unterstreichen
underseal [ʌndəˈsi:l] (BRIT) VT (*car*) mit Unterbodenschutz versehen ▸ N (*of car*) Unterbodenschutz *m*
undersecretary [ˈʌndəˈsɛkrətərɪ] N (*Pol*) Staatssekretär(in) *m(f)*
undersell [ʌndəˈsɛl] VT (*irreg: like* **sell**) (*competitors*) unterbieten
undershirt [ˈʌndəʃə:t] (*US*) N Unterhemd *nt*
undershorts [ˈʌndəʃɔ:ts] (*US*) NPL Unterhose *f*
underside [ˈʌndəsaɪd] N Unterseite *f*
undersigned [ˈʌndəsaɪnd] ADJ unterzeichnet ▸ N: **the ~** der/die Unterzeichnete; **we the ~ agree that ...** wir, die Unterzeichneten, kommen überein, dass ...
underskirt [ˈʌndəskə:t] (BRIT) N Unterrock *m*
understaffed [ʌndəˈstɑ:ft] ADJ unterbesetzt
understand [ʌndəˈstænd] VT, VI (*irreg: like* **stand**) verstehen; **I ~ (that) you have ...** (*believe*) soweit ich weiß, haben Sie ...; **to make o.s. understood** sich verständlich machen
understandable [ʌndəˈstændəbl] ADJ verständlich
understanding [ʌndəˈstændɪŋ] ADJ verständnisvoll ▸ N Verständnis *nt*; **to come to an ~ with sb** mit jdm übereinkommen; **on the ~ that ...** unter der Voraussetzung, dass ...
understate [ʌndəˈsteɪt] VT herunterspielen
understatement [ˈʌndəsteɪtmənt] N Understatement *nt*, Untertreibung *f*; **that's an ~!** das ist untertrieben!
understood [ʌndəˈstud] PT, PP *of* **understand** ▸ ADJ (*agreed*) abgemacht; (*implied*) impliziert
understudy [ˈʌndəstʌdɪ] N zweite Besetzung *f*
undertake [ʌndəˈteɪk] VT (*irreg: like* **take**) (*task*) übernehmen ▸ VI: **to ~ to do sth** es übernehmen, etw zu tun
undertaker [ˈʌndəteɪkəʳ] N (Leichen)bestatter *m*
undertaking [ˈʌndəteɪkɪŋ] N (*job*) Unternehmen *nt*; (*promise*) Zusicherung *f*
undertone [ˈʌndətəun] N (*of criticism etc*) Unterton *m*; **in an ~** mit gedämpfter Stimme
undervalue [ʌndəˈvælju:] VT (*person, work etc*) unterbewerten
underwater [ˈʌndəˈwɔ:təʳ] ADV (*swim etc*) unter Wasser ▸ ADJ (*exploration, camera etc*) Unterwasser-
underwear [ˈʌndəwɛəʳ] N Unterwäsche *f*
underweight [ʌndəˈweɪt] ADJ: **to be ~** Untergewicht haben
underworld [ˈʌndəwə:ld] N Unterwelt *f*
underwrite [ʌndəˈraɪt] VT (*irreg: like* **write**) (*Fin*) garantieren; (*Insurance*) versichern
underwriter [ˈʌndəraɪtəʳ] N (*Insurance*) Versicherer(in) *m(f)*
undeserved [ʌndɪˈzə:vd] ADJ unverdient
undesirable [ʌndɪˈzaɪərəbl] ADJ unerwünscht
undeveloped [ʌndɪˈvɛləpt] ADJ (*land*) unentwickelt; (*resources*) ungenutzt
undies [ˈʌndɪz] (*inf*) NPL Unterwäsche *f*
undiluted [ˈʌndaɪˈlu:tɪd] ADJ (*substance*) unverdünnt; (*emotion*) unverfälscht
undiplomatic [ˈʌndɪpləˈmætɪk] ADJ undiplomatisch
undischarged [ˈʌndɪsˈtʃɑ:dʒd] ADJ: **~ bankrupt** nicht entlasteter Konkursschuldner *m*, nicht entlastete Konkursschuldnerin *f*
undisciplined [ʌnˈdɪsɪplɪnd] ADJ undiszipliniert
undiscovered [ˈʌndɪsˈkʌvəd] ADJ unentdeckt
undisguised [ˈʌndɪsˈgaɪzd] ADJ (*dislike, amusement etc*) unverhohlen
undisputed [ˈʌndɪsˈpju:tɪd] ADJ unbestritten
undistinguished [ˈʌndɪsˈtɪŋgwɪʃt] ADJ (*career, person*) mittelmäßig; (*appearance*) durchschnittlich
undisturbed [ʌndɪsˈtə:bd] ADJ ungestört; **to leave sth ~** etw unberührt lassen
undivided [ʌndɪˈvaɪdɪd] ADJ: **you have my ~ attention** Sie haben meine ungeteilte Aufmerksamkeit
undo [ʌnˈdu:] VT (*irreg: like* **do**) (*unfasten*) aufmachen; (*spoil*) zunichtemachen
undoing [ʌnˈdu:ɪŋ] N Verderben *nt*
undone [ʌnˈdʌn] PP *of* **undo** ▸ ADJ: **to come ~** (*shoelaces etc*) aufgehen
undoubted [ʌnˈdautɪd] ADJ unzweifelhaft
undoubtedly [ʌnˈdautɪdlɪ] ADV zweifellos
undress [ʌnˈdrɛs] VI sich ausziehen ▸ VT ausziehen
undrinkable [ʌnˈdrɪŋkəbl] ADJ (*unpalatable*) ungenießbar; (*poisonous*) nicht trinkbar
undue [ʌnˈdju:] ADJ (*excessive*) übertrieben
undulating [ˈʌndjuleɪtɪŋ] ADJ (*movement*) Wellen-; (*hills*) sanft
unduly [ʌnˈdju:lɪ] ADV (*excessively*) übermäßig
undying [ʌnˈdaɪɪŋ] ADJ (*love, loyalty etc*) ewig
unearned [ʌnˈə:nd] ADJ (*praise*) unverdient; **~ income** Kapitaleinkommen *nt*
unearth [ʌnˈə:θ] VT (*skeleton etc*) ausgraben; (*fig: secrets etc*) ausfindig machen
unearthly [ʌnˈə:θlɪ] ADJ (*eerie*) unheimlich; **at some ~ hour** zu nachtschlafender Zeit

unease [ʌn'i:z] N Unbehagen *nt*
uneasy [ʌn'i:zɪ] ADJ (*person*) unruhig; (*feeling*) unbehaglich; (*peace, truce*) unsicher; **to feel ~ about doing sth** ein ungutes Gefühl dabei haben, etw zu tun
uneconomic ['ʌni:kə'nɔmɪk] ADJ unwirtschaftlich
uneconomical ['ʌni:kə'nɔmɪkl] ADJ unwirtschaftlich
uneducated [ʌn'ɛdjukeɪtɪd] ADJ ungebildet
unemployed [ʌnɪm'plɔɪd] ADJ arbeitslos ▶ NPL: **the ~** die Arbeitslosen *pl*
unemployment [ʌnɪm'plɔɪmənt] N Arbeitslosigkeit *f*
unemployment benefit (BRIT) N Arbeitslosenunterstützung *f*
unemployment compensation (US) N = **unemployment benefit**
unending [ʌn'ɛndɪŋ] ADJ endlos
unenviable [ʌn'ɛnvɪəbl] ADJ (*task, conditions etc*) wenig beneidenswert
unequal [ʌn'i:kwəl] ADJ ungleich; **to feel ~ to** sich nicht gewachsen fühlen +*dat*
unequalled, (US) **unequaled** [ʌn'i:kwəld] ADJ unübertroffen
unequivocal [ʌnɪ'kwɪvəkl] ADJ (*answer*) unzweideutig; **to be ~ about sth** eine klare Haltung zu etw haben
unerring [ʌn'ə:rɪŋ] ADJ unfehlbar
UNESCO [ju:'nɛskəu] N ABBR (= *United Nations Educational, Scientific and Cultural Organization*) UNESCO *f*
unethical [ʌn'ɛθɪkl] ADJ (*methods*) unlauter; (*doctor's behaviour*) unethisch
uneven [ʌn'i:vn] ADJ (*teeth, road etc*) uneben; (*performance*) ungleichmäßig
uneventful [ʌnɪ'vɛntful] ADJ ereignislos
unexceptional [ʌnɪk'sɛpʃənl] ADJ durchschnittlich
unexciting [ʌnɪk'saɪtɪŋ] ADJ (*film, news*) wenig aufregend
unexpected [ʌnɪks'pɛktɪd] ADJ unerwartet
unexpectedly [ʌnɪks'pɛktɪdlɪ] ADV unerwartet
unexplained [ʌnɪks'pleɪnd] ADJ (*mystery, failure*) ungeklärt
unexploded [ʌnɪks'pləudɪd] ADJ nicht explodiert
unfailing [ʌn'feɪlɪŋ] ADJ (*support, energy*) unerschöpflich
unfair [ʌn'fɛə^r] ADJ unfair, ungerecht; (*advantage*) ungerechtfertigt; **~ to** unfair *or* ungerecht zu
unfair dismissal N ungerechtfertigte Entlassung *f*
unfairly [ʌn'fɛəlɪ] ADV (*treat*) unfair, ungerecht; (*dismiss*) ungerechtfertigt
unfaithful [ʌn'feɪθful] ADJ (*lover, spouse*) untreu
unfamiliar [ʌnfə'mɪlɪə^r] ADJ ungewohnt; (*person*) fremd; **to be ~ with sth** mit etw nicht vertraut sein
unfashionable [ʌn'fæʃnəbl] ADJ (*clothes, ideas*) unmodern; (*place*) unbeliebt
unfasten [ʌn'fɑ:sn] VT (*seat belt, strap*) lösen
unfathomable [ʌn'fæðəməbl] ADJ unergründlich
unfavourable, (US) **unfavorable** [ʌn'feɪvrəbl] ADJ (*circumstances, weather*) ungünstig; (*opinion, report*) negativ
unfavourably, (US) **unfavorably** [ʌn'feɪvrəblɪ] ADV: **to compare ~ (with sth)** im Vergleich (mit etw) ungünstig sein; **to compare ~ (with sb)** im Vergleich (mit jdm) schlechter abschneiden; **to look ~ on** (*suggestion etc*) ablehnend gegenüberstehen +*dat*
unfeeling [ʌn'fi:lɪŋ] ADJ gefühllos
unfinished [ʌn'fɪnɪʃt] ADJ unvollendet
unfit [ʌn'fɪt] ADJ (*physically*) nicht fit; (*incompetent*) unfähig; **~ for work** arbeitsunfähig; **~ for human consumption** zum Verzehr ungeeignet
unflagging [ʌn'flægɪŋ] ADJ (*attention, energy*) unermüdlich
unflappable [ʌn'flæpəbl] ADJ unerschütterlich
unflattering [ʌn'flætərɪŋ] ADJ (*dress, hairstyle*) unvorteilhaft; (*remark*) wenig schmeichelhaft
unflinching [ʌn'flɪntʃɪŋ] ADJ unerschrocken
unfold [ʌn'fəuld] VT (*sheets, map*) auseinanderfalten ▶ VI (*situation, story*) sich entfalten
unforeseeable [ʌnfɔ:'si:əbl] ADJ unvorhersehbar
unforeseen ['ʌnfɔ:'si:n] ADJ unvorhergesehen
unforgettable [ʌnfə'gɛtəbl] ADJ unvergesslich
unforgivable [ʌnfə'gɪvəbl] ADJ unverzeihlich
unformatted [ʌn'fɔ:mætɪd] ADJ (*disk, text*) unformatiert
unfortunate [ʌn'fɔ:tʃənət] ADJ (*unlucky*) unglücklich; (*regrettable*) bedauerlich; **it is ~ that ...** es ist bedauerlich, dass ...
unfortunately [ʌn'fɔ:tʃənətlɪ] ADV leider
unfounded [ʌn'faundɪd] ADJ (*allegations, fears*) unbegründet
unfriend [ʌn'frɛnd] VT (*on social network*) entfreunden
unfriendly [ʌn'frɛndlɪ] ADJ unfreundlich
unfulfilled [ʌnful'fɪld] ADJ (*ambition, prophecy*) unerfüllt; (*person*) unausgefüllt
unfurl [ʌn'fə:l] VT (*flag etc*) entrollen
unfurnished [ʌn'fə:nɪʃt] ADJ unmöbliert
ungainly [ʌn'geɪnlɪ] ADJ (*person*) unbeholfen
ungodly [ʌn'gɔdlɪ] ADJ (*annoying*) heillos; **at some ~ hour** zu nachtschlafender Zeit
ungrateful [ʌn'greɪtful] ADJ undankbar
unguarded [ʌn'gɑ:dɪd] ADJ: **in an ~ moment** in einem unbedachten Augenblick
unhappily [ʌn'hæpɪlɪ] ADV (*miserably*) unglücklich; (*unfortunately*) leider
unhappiness [ʌn'hæpɪnɪs] N Traurigkeit *f*
unhappy [ʌn'hæpɪ] ADJ unglücklich; **~ about/with** (*dissatisfied*) unzufrieden über +*acc*/mit
unharmed [ʌn'hɑ:md] ADJ (*person, animal*) unversehrt
UNHCR N ABBR (= *United Nations High Commission for Refugees*) *Flüchtlingskommission der Vereinten Nationen*

unhealthy [ʌn'hɛlθɪ] ADJ (*person*) nicht gesund; (*place*) ungesund; (*fig: interest*) krankhaft
unheard-of [ʌn'hə:dɔv] ADJ (*unknown*) unbekannt; (*outrageous*) unerhört
unhelpful [ʌn'hɛlpful] ADJ (*person*) nicht hilfreich; (*advice*) nutzlos
unhesitating [ʌn'hɛzɪteɪtɪŋ] ADJ (*loyalty*) bereitwillig; (*reply, offer*) prompt
unholy [ʌn'həulɪ] (*inf*) ADJ (*fig: alliance*) übel; (*: mess*) heillos; (*: row*) furchtbar
unhook [ʌn'huk] VT (*unfasten*) losmachen
unhurt [ʌn'hə:t] ADJ unverletzt
unhygienic ['ʌnhaɪ'dʒi:nɪk] ADJ unhygienisch
UNICEF ['ju:nɪsɛf] N ABBR (= *United Nations International Children's Emergency Fund*) UNICEF *f*
unicorn ['ju:nɪkɔ:n] N Einhorn *nt*
unidentified [ʌnaɪ'dɛntɪfaɪd] ADJ (*unknown*) unbekannt; (*unnamed*) ungenannt; *see also* **UFO**
unification [ju:nɪfɪ'keɪʃən] N Vereinigung *f*
unification process N Einigungsprozess *m*
uniform ['ju:nɪfɔ:m] N Uniform *f* ▶ ADJ (*length, width etc*) einheitlich
uniformity [ju:nɪ'fɔ:mɪtɪ] N Einheitlichkeit *f*
unify ['ju:nɪfaɪ] VT vereinigen
unilateral [ju:nɪ'lætərəl] ADJ einseitig
unimaginable [ʌnɪ'mædʒɪnəbl] ADJ unvorstellbar
unimaginative [ʌnɪ'mædʒɪnətɪv] ADJ fantasielos
unimpaired [ʌnɪm'pɛəd] ADJ unbeeinträchtigt
unimportant [ʌnɪm'pɔ:tənt] ADJ unwichtig
unimpressed [ʌnɪm'prɛst] ADJ unbeeindruckt
uninhabited [ʌnɪn'hæbɪtɪd] ADJ unbewohnt
uninhibited [ʌnɪn'hɪbɪtɪd] ADJ (*person*) ohne Hemmungen; (*behaviour*) hemmungslos
uninjured [ʌn'ɪndʒəd] ADJ unverletzt
uninspiring [ʌnɪn'spaɪərɪŋ] ADJ wenig aufregend; (*person*) trocken, nüchtern
uninstall [ʌnɪn'stɔ:l] VT (*Comput*) deinstallieren
unintelligent [ʌnɪn'tɛlɪdʒənt] ADJ unintelligent
unintentional [ʌnɪn'tɛnʃənəl] ADJ unbeabsichtigt
unintentionally [ʌnɪn'tɛnʃnəlɪ] ADV unabsichtlich
uninvited [ʌnɪn'vaɪtɪd] ADJ (*guest*) ungeladen
uninviting [ʌnɪn'vaɪtɪŋ] ADJ (*food*) unappetitlich; (*place*) wenig einladend
union ['ju:njən] N (*unification*) Vereinigung *f*; (*also:* **trade union**) Gewerkschaft *f* ▶ CPD (*activities, leader etc*) Gewerkschafts-; **the U~** (*US*) die Vereinigten Staaten
unionize ['ju:njənaɪz] VT (*employees*) gewerkschaftlich organisieren
Union Jack N Union Jack *m*
union shop N gewerkschaftspflichtiger Betrieb *m*
unique [ju:'ni:k] ADJ (*object etc*) einmalig; (*ability, skill*) einzigartig; **to be ~ to** charakteristisch sein für
unisex ['ju:nɪsɛks] ADJ (*clothes*) Unisex-; (*hairdresser*) für Damen und Herren
UNISON ['ju:nɪsn] N *Gewerkschaft der Angestellten im öffentlichen Dienst*
unison ['ju:nɪsn] N: **in ~** (*say, sing*) einstimmig; (*act*) in Übereinstimmung
unit ['ju:nɪt] N Einheit *f*; **production ~** Produktionsabteilung *f*; **kitchen ~** Küchen-Einbauelement *nt*
unitary ['ju:nɪtrɪ] ADJ (*state, system etc*) einheitlich
unit cost N (*Comm*) Stückkosten *pl*
unite [ju:'naɪt] VT vereinigen ▶ VI sich zusammenschließen
united [ju:'naɪtɪd] ADJ (*agreed*) einig; (*country, party*) vereinigt
United Arab Emirates NPL: **the ~** die Vereinigten Arabischen Emirate *pl*
United Kingdom N: **the ~** das Vereinigte Königreich
United Nations NPL: **the ~** die Vereinten Nationen *pl*
United States, United States of America N: **the ~ (of America)** die Vereinigten Staaten *pl* (von Amerika)
unit price N (*Comm*) Einzelpreis *m*
unit trust (BRIT) N (*Comm*) Investmenttrust *m*
unity ['ju:nɪtɪ] N Einheit *f*
Univ. ABBR = **university**
universal [ju:nɪ'və:sl] ADJ allgemein
universe ['ju:nɪvə:s] N Universum *nt*
university [ju:nɪ'və:sɪtɪ] N Universität *f* ▶ CPD (*student, professor*) Universitäts-; (*education, year*) akademisch
university degree N Universitätsabschluss *m*
unjust [ʌn'dʒʌst] ADJ ungerecht; (*society*) unfair
unjustifiable ['ʌndʒʌstɪ'faɪəbl] ADJ nicht zu rechtfertigen
unjustified [ʌn'dʒʌstɪfaɪd] ADJ (*belief, action*) ungerechtfertigt; (*text*) nicht bündig
unkempt [ʌn'kɛmpt] ADJ ungepflegt
unkind [ʌn'kaɪnd] ADJ (*person, comment etc*) unfreundlich
unkindly [ʌn'kaɪndlɪ] ADV unfreundlich
unknown [ʌn'nəun] ADJ unbekannt; **~ to me, …** ohne dass ich es wusste, …; **~ quantity** (*fig*) unbekannte Größe
unladen [ʌn'leɪdn] ADJ (*ship*) ohne Ladung; (*weight*) Leer-
unlawful [ʌn'lɔ:ful] ADJ gesetzwidrig
unleaded ['ʌn'lɛdɪd] ADJ (*petrol*) bleifrei, unverbleit; **I use ~** ich fahre bleifrei
unleash [ʌn'li:ʃ] VT (*fig: feeling, forces etc*) entfesseln
unleavened [ʌn'lɛvnd] ADJ (*bread*) ungesäuert
unless [ʌn'lɛs] CONJ es sei denn; **~ he comes** wenn er nicht kommt; **~ otherwise stated** wenn nicht anders angegeben; **~ I am mistaken** wenn ich mich nicht irre; **there will be a strike ~ …** es wird zum Streik kommen, es sei denn, …
unlicensed [ʌn'laɪsnst] (BRIT) ADJ (*restaurant*) ohne Schankkonzession
unlike [ʌn'laɪk] ADJ (*not alike*) unähnlich ▶ PREP (*different from*) verschieden von; **~ me, she is**

u

very tidy im Gegensatz zu mir ist sie sehr ordentlich
unlikelihood [ʌn'laɪklɪhud] N Unwahrscheinlichkeit *f*
unlikely [ʌn'laɪklɪ] ADJ unwahrscheinlich; (*combination etc*) merkwürdig; **in the ~ event of/that ...** im unwahrscheinlichen Fall *+gen*/ dass ...
unlimited [ʌn'lɪmɪtɪd] ADJ unbeschränkt
unlisted ['ʌn'lɪstɪd] ADJ (*Stock Exchange*) nicht notiert; (*US Tel*): **to be ~** nicht im Telefonbuch stehen
unlit [ʌn'lɪt] ADJ (*room etc*) unbeleuchtet
unload [ʌn'ləud] VT (*box etc*) ausladen; (*car etc*) entladen
unlock [ʌn'lɔk] VT aufschließen
unlucky [ʌn'lʌkɪ] ADJ (*object*) Unglück bringend; (*number*) Unglücks-; **to be ~** (*person*) Pech haben
unmanageable [ʌn'mænɪdʒəbl] ADJ (*tool, vehicle*) kaum zu handhaben; (*person, hair*) widerspenstig; (*situation*) unkontrollierbar
unmanned [ʌn'mænd] ADJ (*station, spacecraft etc*) unbemannt
unmarked [ʌn'mɑːkt] ADJ (*unstained*) fleckenlos; (*unscarred*) nicht gezeichnet; (*unblemished*) makellos; **~ police car** nicht gekennzeichneter Streifenwagen *m*
unmarried [ʌn'mærɪd] ADJ unverheiratet
unmarried mother N ledige Mutter *f*
unmask [ʌn'mɑːsk] VT (*reveal*) enthüllen
unmatched [ʌn'mætʃt] ADJ unübertroffen
unmentionable [ʌn'mɛnʃnəbl] ADJ (*topic, word*) Tabu-; **to be ~** tabu sein
unmerciful [ʌn'məːsɪful] ADJ erbarmungslos
unmistakable, unmistakeable [ʌnmɪs'teɪkəbl] ADJ unverkennbar
unmistakably, unmistakeably [ʌnmɪs'teɪkəblɪ] ADV unverkennbar
unmitigated [ʌn'mɪtɪgeɪtɪd] ADJ (*disaster etc*) total
unnamed [ʌn'neɪmd] ADJ (*nameless*) namenlos; (*anonymous*) ungenannt
unnatural [ʌn'nætʃrəl] ADJ unnatürlich; (*against nature: habit*) widernatürlich
unnecessarily [ʌn'nɛsəsərɪlɪ] ADV (*worry etc*) unnötigerweise; (*severe etc*) übertrieben
unnecessary [ʌn'nɛsəsərɪ] ADJ unnötig
unnerve [ʌn'nəːv] VT entnerven
unnoticed [ʌn'nəutɪst] ADJ: **to go** *or* **pass ~** unbemerkt bleiben
UNO ['juːnəu] N ABBR (= *United Nations Organization*) UNO *f*
unobservant [ʌnəb'zəːvənt] ADJ unaufmerksam
unobtainable [ʌnəb'teɪnəbl] ADJ (*item*) nicht erhältlich; **this number is ~** (*Tel*) kein Anschluss unter dieser Nummer
unobtrusive [ʌnəb'truːsɪv] ADJ unauffällig
unoccupied [ʌn'ɔkjupaɪd] ADJ (*seat*) frei; (*house*) leer (stehend)
unofficial [ʌnə'fɪʃl] ADJ inoffiziell
unopened [ʌn'əupənd] ADJ ungeöffnet
unopposed [ʌnə'pəuzd] ADJ: **to be ~** (*suggestion*) nicht auf Widerstand treffen; (*motion, bill*) ohne Gegenstimmen angenommen werden
unorthodox [ʌn'ɔːθədɔks] ADJ (*also Rel*) unorthodox
unpack [ʌn'pæk] VT, VI auspacken
unpaid [ʌn'peɪd] ADJ unbezahlt
unpalatable [ʌn'pælətəbl] ADJ (*meal*) ungenießbar; (*truth*) bitter
unparalleled [ʌn'pærəlɛld] ADJ beispiellos
unpatriotic ['ʌnpætrɪ'ɔtɪk] ADJ unpatriotisch
unplanned [ʌn'plænd] ADJ ungeplant
unpleasant [ʌn'plɛznt] ADJ unangenehm; (*person, manner*) unfreundlich
unplug [ʌn'plʌg] VT (*iron, record player etc*) den Stecker herausziehen *+gen*
unpolluted [ʌnpə'luːtɪd] ADJ unverschmutzt
unpopular [ʌn'pɔpjuləʳ] ADJ unpopulär; **to make o.s. ~ (with)** sich unbeliebt machen (bei)
unprecedented [ʌn'prɛsɪdɛntɪd] ADJ noch nie da gewesen; (*decision*) einmalig
unpredictable [ʌnprɪ'dɪktəbl] ADJ (*person, weather*) unberechenbar; (*reaction*) unvorhersehbar
unprejudiced [ʌn'prɛdʒudɪst] ADJ unvoreingenommen
unprepared [ʌnprɪ'pɛəd] ADJ unvorbereitet
unprepossessing ['ʌnpriːpə'zɛsɪŋ] ADJ (*person, place*) unattraktiv
unpretentious [ʌnprɪ'tɛnʃəs] ADJ (*building, person*) schlicht
unprincipled [ʌn'prɪnsɪpld] ADJ (*person*) charakterlos
unproductive [ʌnprə'dʌktɪv] ADJ (*land*) unfruchtbar, ertragsarm; (*discussion*) unproduktiv
unprofessional [ʌnprə'fɛʃənl] ADJ unprofessionell
unprofitable [ʌn'prɔfɪtəbl] ADJ nicht profitabel, unrentabel
UNPROFOR N ABBR (= *United Nations Protection Force*) UNPROFOR *f*; **~ troops** UNPROFOR-Truppen, UNO-Schutztruppen
unprotected ['ʌnprə'tɛktɪd] ADJ ungeschützt
unprovoked [ʌnprə'vəukt] ADJ (*attack*) grundlos
unpunished [ʌn'pʌnɪʃt] ADJ: **to go ~** straflos bleiben
unqualified [ʌn'kwɔlɪfaɪd] ADJ unqualifiziert; (*disaster, success*) vollkommen
unquestionably [ʌn'kwɛstʃənəblɪ] ADV fraglos
unquestioning [ʌn'kwɛstʃənɪŋ] ADJ bedingungslos
unravel [ʌn'rævl] VT (*also fig*) entwirren
unreal [ʌn'rɪəl] ADJ (*artificial*) unecht; (*peculiar*) unwirklich
unrealistic ['ʌnrɪə'lɪstɪk] ADJ unrealistisch
unreasonable [ʌn'riːznəbl] ADJ (*person, attitude*) unvernünftig; (*demand, length of time*) unzumutbar
unrecognizable [ʌn'rɛkəgnaɪzəbl] ADJ nicht zu erkennen
unrecognized [ʌn'rɛkəgnaɪzd] ADJ (*talent etc*) unerkannt; (*Pol: regime*) nicht anerkannt

unreconstructed ['ʌnri:kən'strʌktɪd] (*esp US*) ADJ (*unwilling to accept change*) unverbesserlich
unrecorded [ʌnrə'kɔ:dɪd] ADJ (*piece of music etc*) nicht aufgenommen; (*incident, statement*) nicht schriftlich festgehalten
unrefined [ʌnrə'faɪnd] ADJ (*sugar, petroleum*) nicht raffiniert
unrehearsed [ʌnrɪ'hə:st] ADJ (*Theat etc*) nicht geprobt; (*spontaneous*) spontan
unrelated [ʌnrɪ'leɪtɪd] ADJ (*incidents*) ohne Beziehung; (*people*) nicht verwandt
unrelenting [ʌnrɪ'lɛntɪŋ] ADJ (*person, behaviour etc*) unnachgiebig
unreliable [ʌnrɪ'laɪəbl] ADJ unzuverlässig
unrelieved [ʌnrɪ'li:vd] ADJ ungemindert
unremitting [ʌnrɪ'mɪtɪŋ] ADJ (*efforts, attempts*) unermüdlich
unrepeatable [ʌnrɪ'pi:təbl] ADJ (*offer*) einmalig; (*comment*) nicht wiederholbar
unrepentant [ʌnrɪ'pɛntənt] ADJ: **to be ~ about sth** etw nicht bereuen; **he's an ~ Marxist** er bereut es nicht, nach wie vor Marxist zu sein
unrepresentative ['ʌnrɛprɪ'zɛntətɪv] ADJ: **~ (of)** nicht repräsentativ (für)
unrepresented ['ʌnrɛprɪ'zɛntɪd] ADJ nicht vertreten
unreserved [ʌnrɪ'zə:vd] ADJ (*seat*) unreserviert; (*approval etc*) uneingeschränkt, vorbehaltlos
unreservedly [ʌnrɪ'zə:vɪdlɪ] ADV ohne Vorbehalt
unresponsive [ʌnrɪs'pɔnsɪv] ADJ unempfänglich
unrest [ʌn'rɛst] N Unruhen *pl*
unrestricted [ʌnrɪ'strɪktɪd] ADJ unbeschränkt; **to have ~ access to** ungehinderten Zugang haben zu
unrewarded [ʌnrɪ'wɔ:dɪd] ADJ unbelohnt
unripe [ʌn'raɪp] ADJ unreif
unrivalled, (*US*) **unrivaled** [ʌn'raɪvəld] ADJ unübertroffen
unroll [ʌn'rəul] VT entrollen ▶ VI sich entrollen
unruffled [ʌn'rʌfld] ADJ unbewegt; (*hair*) unzerzaust
unruly [ʌn'ru:lɪ] ADJ (*child, behaviour*) ungebärdig; (*hair*) widerspenstig
unsafe [ʌn'seɪf] ADJ unsicher; (*machine, bridge, car etc*) gefährlich; **~ to eat/drink** ungenießbar
unsaid [ʌn'sɛd] ADJ: **to leave sth ~** etw ungesagt lassen
unsaleable, (*US*) **unsalable** [ʌn'seɪləbl] ADJ unverkäuflich
unsatisfactory ['ʌnsætɪs'fæktərɪ] ADJ unbefriedigend
unsatisfied [ʌn'sætɪsfaɪd] ADJ unzufrieden
unsavoury, (*US*) **unsavory** [ʌn'seɪvərɪ] ADJ (*fig: person, place*) widerwärtig
unscathed [ʌn'skeɪðd] ADJ unversehrt
unscientific ['ʌnsaɪən'tɪfɪk] ADJ unwissenschaftlich
unscrew [ʌn'skru:] VT losschrauben
unscrupulous [ʌn'skru:pjuləs] ADJ skrupellos
unseat [ʌn'si:t] VT (*rider*) abwerfen; (*from office*) aus dem Amt drängen
unsecured ['ʌnsɪ'kjuəd] ADJ: **~ creditor** nicht gesicherter Gläubiger *m*; **~ loan** Blankokredit *m*
unseeded [ʌn'si:dɪd] ADJ (*player*) nicht gesetzt
unseemly [ʌn'si:mlɪ] ADJ unschicklich
unseen [ʌn'si:n] ADJ (*person, danger*) unsichtbar
unselfish [ʌn'sɛlfɪʃ] ADJ selbstlos
unsettled [ʌn'sɛtld] ADJ (*person*) unruhig; (*future*) unsicher; (*question*) ungeklärt; (*weather*) unbeständig
unsettling [ʌn'sɛtlɪŋ] ADJ beunruhigend
unshakable, unshakeable [ʌn'ʃeɪkəbl] ADJ unerschütterlich
unshaven [ʌn'ʃeɪvn] ADJ unrasiert
unsightly [ʌn'saɪtlɪ] ADJ unansehnlich
unskilled [ʌn'skɪld] ADJ (*work, worker*) ungelernt
unsociable [ʌn'səuʃəbl] ADJ ungesellig
unsocial [ʌn'səuʃl] ADJ: **to work ~ hours** außerhalb der normalen Arbeitszeit arbeiten
unsold [ʌn'səuld] ADJ unverkauft
unsolicited [ʌnsə'lɪsɪtɪd] ADJ unerbeten
unsophisticated [ʌnsə'fɪstɪkeɪtɪd] ADJ (*person*) anspruchslos; (*method, device*) simpel
unsound [ʌn'saund] ADJ (*floor, foundations*) unsicher; (*policy, advice*) unklug; **of ~ mind** unzurechnungsfähig
unspeakable [ʌn'spi:kəbl] ADJ (*indescribable*) unsagbar; (*awful*) abscheulich
unspoken [ʌn'spəukn] ADJ (*word*) unausgesprochen; (*agreement etc*) stillschweigend
unstable [ʌn'steɪbl] ADJ (*piece of furniture*) nicht stabil; (*government*) instabil; (*person: mentally*) labil
unsteady [ʌn'stɛdɪ] ADJ (*step, voice, legs*) unsicher; (*ladder*) wack(e)lig
unstinting [ʌn'stɪntɪŋ] ADJ (*support*) vorbehaltlos; (*generosity*) unbegrenzt
unstuck [ʌn'stʌk] ADJ: **to come ~** (*label etc*) sich lösen; (*fig: plan, idea etc*) versagen
unsubstantiated ['ʌnsəb'stænʃɪeɪtɪd] ADJ (*rumour*) unbestätigt; (*accusation*) unbegründet
unsuccessful [ʌnsək'sɛsful] ADJ erfolglos; (*marriage*) gescheitert; **to be ~** keinen Erfolg haben
unsuccessfully [ʌnsək'sɛsfəlɪ] ADV ohne Erfolg, vergeblich
unsuitable [ʌn'su:təbl] ADJ (*time*) unpassend; (*clothes, person*) ungeeignet
unsuited [ʌn'su:tɪd] ADJ: **to be ~ for** *or* **to sth** für etw ungeeignet sein
unsung ['ʌnsʌŋ] ADJ: **an ~ hero** ein unbesungener Held
unsure [ʌn'ʃuə^r] ADJ unsicher; **to be ~ of o.s.** unsicher sein
unsuspecting [ʌnsəs'pɛktɪŋ] ADJ ahnungslos
unsweetened [ʌn'swi:tnd] ADJ ungesüßt
unswerving [ʌn'swə:vɪŋ] ADJ unerschütterlich
unsympathetic ['ʌnsɪmpə'θɛtɪk] ADJ (*showing little understanding*) abweisend; (*unlikeable*) unsympathisch; **to be ~ to(wards) sth** einer Sache *dat* ablehnend gegenüberstehen
untangle [ʌn'tæŋgl] VT entwirren
untapped [ʌn'tæpt] ADJ (*resources*) ungenutzt

U

untaxed [ʌn'tækst] ADJ (*goods, income*) steuerfrei
unthinkable [ʌn'θɪŋkəbl] ADJ undenkbar
unthinking [ʌn'θɪŋkɪŋ] ADJ (*uncritical*) bedenkenlos; (*thoughtless*) gedankenlos
untidy [ʌn'taɪdɪ] ADJ unordentlich
untie [ʌn'taɪ] VT (*knot, parcel*) aufschnüren; (*prisoner, dog*) losbinden
until [ən'tɪl] PREP bis *+acc*; (*after negative*) vor *+dat* ▸ CONJ bis; (*after negative*) bevor; **not ~** erst; **~ now** bis jetzt; **~ then** bis dann; **from morning ~ night** von morgens bis abends; **~ he comes** bis er kommt
untimely [ʌn'taɪmlɪ] ADJ (*moment*) unpassend; (*arrival*) ungelegen; (*death*) vorzeitig
untold [ʌn'təuld] ADJ (*joy, suffering, wealth*) unermesslich; **the ~ story** die Hintergründe
untouched [ʌn'tʌtʃt] ADJ unberührt; (*undamaged*) unversehrt; **~ by** (*unaffected*) unberührt von
untoward [ʌntə'wɔ:d] ADJ (*events, effects etc*) ungünstig
untrained ['ʌn'treɪnd] ADJ unausgebildet; (*eye, hands*) ungeschult
untrammelled [ʌn'træmld] ADJ (*person*) ungebunden; (*behaviour*) unbeschränkt
untranslatable [ʌntrænz'leɪtəbl] ADJ unübersetzbar
untried [ʌn'traɪd] ADJ (*policy, remedy*) unerprobt; (*prisoner*) noch nicht vor Gericht gestellt
untrue [ʌn'tru:] ADJ unwahr
untrustworthy [ʌn'trʌstwə:ðɪ] ADJ unzuverlässig
unusable [ʌn'ju:zəbl] ADJ (*object*) unbrauchbar; (*room*) nicht benutzbar
unused¹ [ʌn'ju:zd] ADJ (*new*) unbenutzt
unused² [ʌn'ju:st] ADJ: **to be ~ to sth** an etw *acc* nicht gewöhnt sein; **to be ~ to doing sth** nicht daran gewöhnt sein, etw zu tun
unusual [ʌn'ju:ʒuəl] ADJ ungewöhnlich; (*exceptional*) außergewöhnlich
unusually [ʌn'ju:ʒuəlɪ] ADV (*large, high etc*) ungewöhnlich
unveil [ʌn'veɪl] VT (*also fig*) enthüllen
unwanted [ʌn'wɔntɪd] ADJ unerwünscht
unwarranted [ʌn'wɔrəntɪd] ADJ ungerechtfertigt
unwary [ʌn'wεərɪ] ADJ unachtsam
unwavering [ʌn'weɪvərɪŋ] ADJ (*faith, support*) unerschütterlich; (*gaze*) fest
unwelcome [ʌn'wεlkəm] ADJ (*guest*) unwillkommen; (*news*) unerfreulich; **to feel ~** sich nicht willkommen fühlen
unwell [ʌn'wεl] ADJ: **to be ~, to feel ~** sich nicht wohlfühlen
unwieldy [ʌn'wi:ldɪ] ADJ (*object*) unhandlich; (*system*) schwerfällig
unwilling [ʌn'wɪlɪŋ] ADJ: **to be ~ to do sth** etw nicht tun wollen
unwillingly [ʌn'wɪlɪŋlɪ] ADV widerwillig
unwind [ʌn'waɪnd] VT (*irreg: like* **wind²**) abwickeln ▸ VI sich abwickeln; (*relax*) sich entspannen
unwise [ʌn'waɪz] ADJ unklug
unwitting [ʌn'wɪtɪŋ] ADJ (*accomplice*) unwissentlich; (*victim*) ahnungslos
unworkable [ʌn'wə:kəbl] ADJ (*plan*) undurchführbar
unworthy [ʌn'wə:ðɪ] ADJ unwürdig; **to be ~ of sth** einer Sache *gen* nicht wert *or* würdig sein; **to be ~ to do sth** es nicht wert sein, etw zu tun; **that remark is ~ of you** diese Bemerkung ist unter deiner Würde
unwrap [ʌn'ræp] VT auspacken
unwritten [ʌn'rɪtn] ADJ (*law*) ungeschrieben; (*agreement*) stillschweigend
unzip [ʌn'zɪp] VT aufmachen

KEYWORD

up [ʌp] PREP: **to be up sth** (oben) auf etw *dat* sein; **to go up sth** (auf) etw *acc* hinaufgehen; **go up that road and turn left** gehen Sie die Straße hinauf und biegen Sie links ab
▸ ADV **1** (*upwards, higher*) oben; **put it a bit higher up** stelle es etwas höher; **up there** dort oben; **up above** hoch oben
2: **to be up** (*out of bed*) auf sein; (*prices, level*) gestiegen sein; (*building, tent*) stehen; **time's up** die Zeit ist um *or* vorbei
3: **up to** (*as far as*) bis; **up to now** bis jetzt
4: **to be up to** (*depending on*) abhängen von; **it's up to you** das hängt von dir ab; **it's not up to me to decide** es liegt nicht bei mir, das zu entscheiden
5: **to be up to** (*equal to*) gewachsen sein *+dat*; **he's not up to it** (*job, task etc*) er ist dem nicht gewachsen; **his work is not up to the required standard** seine Arbeit entspricht nicht dem gewünschten Niveau
6: **to be up to** (*inf: be doing*) vorhaben; **what is he up to?** (*showing disapproval, suspicion*) was führt er im Schilde?
▸ N: **ups and downs** (*in life, career*) Höhen und Tiefen*pl*
▸ VI (*inf*): **she upped and left** sie sprang auf und rannte davon
▸ VT (*inf: price*) heraufsetzen

up-and-coming [ʌpənd'kʌmɪŋ] ADJ (*actor, company etc*) kommend
upbeat ['ʌpbi:t] N (*Mus*) Auftakt *m*; (*in economy etc*) Aufschwung *m* ▸ ADJ (*optimistic*) optimistisch
upbraid [ʌp'breɪd] VT tadeln
upbringing ['ʌpbrɪŋɪŋ] N Erziehung *f*
upcoming ['ʌpkʌmɪŋ] (*esp US*) ADJ kommend
update [ʌp'deɪt] VT aktualisieren
upend [ʌp'εnd] VT auf den Kopf stellen
upfront [ʌp'frʌnt] ADJ (*person*) offen ▸ ADV: **20% ~** 20% (als) Vorschuss, 20% im Voraus
upgrade [ʌp'greɪd] VT (*house*) Verbesserungen durchführen in *+dat*; (*job*) verbessern; (*employee*) befördern; (*Comput*) nachrüsten
upheaval [ʌp'hi:vl] N Unruhe *f*
uphill ['ʌp'hɪl] ADJ bergaufwärts (führend); (*fig: task*) mühsam ▸ ADV (*push, move*) bergaufwärts; (*go*) bergauf

uphold [ʌp'həuld] VT (*irreg: like* **hold**) (*law, principle*) wahren; (*decision*) unterstützen
upholstery [ʌp'həulstərɪ] N Polsterung *f*
upkeep ['ʌpki:p] N (*maintenance*) Instandhaltung *f*
upload [ʌp'ləud] VT hochladen
up-market [ʌp'mɑ:kɪt] ADJ anspruchsvoll
upon [ə'pɔn] PREP (*position*) auf *+dat*; (*motion*) auf *+acc*
upper ['ʌpə^r] ADJ obere(r, s) ▸ N (*of shoe*) Oberleder *nt*
upper class N: **the ~** die Oberschicht
upper-class ['ʌpə'klɑ:s] ADJ vornehm
uppercut ['ʌpəkʌt] N Uppercut *m*
upper hand N: **to have the ~** die Oberhand haben
Upper House N (*Pol*) Oberhaus *nt*
uppermost ['ʌpəməust] ADJ oberste(r, s); **what was ~ in my mind** woran ich in erster Linie dachte
Upper Volta [-'vɔltə] N (*formerly*) Obervolta *nt*
upright ['ʌpraɪt] ADJ (*vertical*) vertikal; (*fig: honest*) rechtschaffen ▸ ADV (*sit, stand*) aufrecht ▸ N (*Constr*) Pfosten *m*
uprising ['ʌpraɪzɪŋ] N Aufstand *m*
uproar ['ʌprɔ:^r] N Aufruhr *m*
uproarious [ʌp'rɔ:rɪəs] ADJ (*laughter*) brüllend; (*joke*) brüllend komisch; (*mirth*) überwältigend
uproot [ʌp'ru:t] VT (*tree*) entwurzeln; (*fig: people*) aus der gewohnten Umgebung reißen; (*: in war etc*) entwurzeln
upset VT [ʌp'sɛt] (*irreg: like* **set**) (*knock over*) umstoßen; (*person: offend, make unhappy*) verletzen; (*routine, plan*) durcheinanderbringen ▸ ADJ [ʌp'sɛt] (*unhappy*) aufgebracht; (*stomach*) verstimmt ▸ N ['ʌpsɛt]: **to have/get a stomach ~** (BRIT) eine Magenverstimmung haben/bekommen; **to get ~** sich aufregen
upset price ['ʌpsɛt-] (US, SCOT) N Mindestpreis *m*
upsetting [ʌp'sɛtɪŋ] ADJ (*distressing*) erschütternd
upshot ['ʌpʃɔt] N Ergebnis *nt*; **the ~ of it all was that …** es lief schließlich darauf hinaus, dass …
upside down ['ʌpsaɪd-] ADV verkehrt herum; **to turn a room ~** (*fig*) ein Zimmer auf den Kopf stellen
upstage ['ʌp'steɪdʒ] ADV (*Theat*) im Bühnenhintergrund ▸ VT: **to ~ sb** (*fig*) jdn ausstechen, jdm die Schau stehlen (*inf*)
upstairs [ʌp'stɛəz] ADV (*be*) oben; (*go*) nach oben ▸ ADJ (*room*) obere(r, s); (*window*) im oberen Stock ▸ N oberes Stockwerk *nt*; **there's no ~** das Haus hat kein Obergeschoss
upstart ['ʌpstɑ:t] (*pej*) N Emporkömmling *m*
upstream [ʌp'stri:m] ADV, ADJ flussaufwärts
upsurge ['ʌpsə:dʒ] N (*of enthusiasm etc*) Schwall *m*
uptake ['ʌpteɪk] N: **to be quick on the ~** schnell kapieren; **to be slow on the ~** schwer von Begriff sein
uptight [ʌp'taɪt] (*inf*) ADJ nervös
up-to-date ['ʌptə'deɪt] ADJ (*modern*) modern; (*person*) up to date
upturn ['ʌptə:n] N (*in economy*) Aufschwung *m*
upturned ['ʌptə:nd] ADJ: **~ nose** Stupsnase *f*
upward ['ʌpwəd] ADJ (*movement*) Aufwärts-; (*glance*) nach oben gerichtet
upwardly mobile ['ʌpwədlɪ-] ADJ: **to be ~** ein Aufsteigertyp *m* sein
upwards ['ʌpwədz] ADV (*move*) aufwärts; (*glance*) nach oben; **upward(s) of** (*more than*) über *+acc*
URA (US) N ABBR (= *Urban Renewal Administration*) *Stadtsanierungsbehörde*
Ural Mountains ['juərəl-] NPL: **the ~** (*also:* **the Urals**) der Ural
uranium [juə'reɪnɪəm] N Uran *nt*
Uranus [juə'reɪnəs] N Uranus *m*
urban ['ə:bən] ADJ städtisch; (*unemployment*) in den Städten
urbane [ə:'beɪn] ADJ weltgewandt
urbanization ['ə:bənaɪ'zeɪʃən] N Urbanisierung *f*, Verstädterung *f*
urchin ['ə:tʃɪn] (*pej*) N Gassenkind *nt*
Urdu ['uədu:] N Urdu *nt*
urge [ə:dʒ] N (*need, desire*) Verlangen *nt* ▸ VT: **to ~ sb to do sth** jdn eindringlich bitten, etw zu tun; **to ~ caution** zur Vorsicht mahnen
▸ **urge on** VT antreiben
urgency ['ə:dʒənsɪ] N Dringlichkeit *f*
urgent ['ə:dʒənt] ADJ dringend; (*voice*) eindringend
urgently ['ə:dʒəntlɪ] ADV dringend
urinal ['juərɪnl] N (*building*) Pissoir *nt*; (*vessel*) Urinal *nt*
urinate ['juərɪneɪt] VI urinieren
urine ['juərɪn] N Urin *m*
URL ABBR = **uniform resource locator**; (*Comput*) URL-Adresse *f*, Internetadresse *f*
urn [ə:n] N Urne *f*; (*also:* **tea urn**) Teekessel *m*
Uruguay ['juərəgwaɪ] N Uruguay *nt*
Uruguayan [juərə'gwaɪən] ADJ uruguayisch ▸ N (*person*) Uruguayer(in) *m(f)*
US N ABBR (= *United States*) USA *pl*
us [ʌs] PL PRON uns; (*emphatic*) wir; *see also* **me**
USA N ABBR (= *United States of America*) USA *f*; (*Mil:* = *United States Army*) US-Armee *f*
usable ['ju:zəbl] ADJ brauchbar
USAF N ABBR (= *United States Air Force*) US-Luftwaffe *f*
usage ['ju:zɪdʒ] N (*Ling*) (Sprach)gebrauch *m*
USB ABBR (= *universal serial bus*) US
USB stick [ju:es'bi:stɪk] N USB-Stick *m*
USCG N ABBR (= *United States Coast Guard*) *Küstenwache der USA*
USDA N ABBR (= *United States Department of Agriculture*) *US-Landwirtschaftsministerium*
USDAW ['ʌzdɔ:] (BRIT) N ABBR (= *Union of Shop, Distributive, and Allied Workers*) *Einzelhandelsgewerkschaft*
USDI N ABBR (= *United States Department of the Interior*) *US-Innenministerium*
use N [ju:s] (*using*) Gebrauch *m*, Verwendung *f*; (*usefulness, purpose*) Nutzen *m* ▸ VT [ju:z] benutzen, gebrauchen; (*phrase*) verwenden;

in ~ in Gebrauch; **out of ~** außer Gebrauch; **to be of ~** nützlich *or* von Nutzen sein; **to make ~ of sth** Gebrauch von etw machen; **it's no ~** es hat keinen Zweck; **to have the ~ of sth** über etw *acc* verfügen können; **what's this used for?** wofür wird das gebraucht?; **to be used to sth** etw gewohnt sein; **to get used to sth** sich an etw *acc* gewöhnen; **she used to do it** sie hat es früher gemacht
▸ **use up** VT (*food, leftovers*) aufbrauchen; (*money*) verbrauchen
used [ju:zd] ADJ gebraucht; (*car*) Gebraucht-
useful ['ju:sful] ADJ nützlich; **to come in ~** sich als nützlich erweisen
usefulness ['ju:sfəlnɪs] N Nützlichkeit *f*
useless ['ju:slɪs] ADJ nutzlos; (*person: hopeless*) hoffnungslos
user ['ju:zəʳ] N Benutzer(in) *m(f)*; (*of petrol, gas etc*) Verbraucher(in) *m(f)*
user-friendly ['ju:zə'frɛndlɪ] ADJ benutzerfreundlich
username ['ju:zəneɪm] N Benutzername *m*
usher ['ʌʃəʳ] N (*at wedding*) Platzanweiser *m* ▸ VT: **to ~ sb in** jdn hineinführen
usherette [ʌʃə'rɛt] N Platzanweiserin *f*
USIA N ABBR (= *United States Information Agency*) *US-Informations- und Kulturinstitut*
USM N ABBR (= *United States Mint*) *US-Münzanstalt*; (= *United States Mail*) *US-Postbehörde*
USN N ABBR (= *United States Navy*) US-Marine *f*
USPHS N ABBR (= *United States Public Health Service*) *US-Gesundheitsbehörde*
USPO N ABBR (= *United States Post Office*) *US-Postbehörde*
USS ABBR (= *United States Ship*) *Namensteil von Schiffen der Kriegsmarine*
USSR N ABBR (*formerly*: = *Union of Soviet Socialist Republics*) UdSSR *f*
usu. ABBR = **usually**
usual ['ju:ʒuəl] ADJ üblich, gewöhnlich; **as ~** wie gewöhnlich
usually ['ju:ʒuəlɪ] ADV gewöhnlich
usurer ['ju:ʒərəʳ] N Wucherer *m*
usurp [ju:'zə:p] VT (*title, position*) an sich *acc* reißen
usury ['ju:ʒurɪ] N Wucher *m*
UT (*US*) ABBR (*Post*) = **Utah**
ute [ju:t] N (*inf*: AUST, NZ) Kleintransporter *m*
utensil [ju:'tɛnsl] N Gerät *nt*; **kitchen utensils** Küchengeräte *pl*
uterus ['ju:tərəs] N Gebärmutter *f*, Uterus *m*
utilitarian [ju:tɪlɪ'tɛərɪən] ADJ (*building, object*) praktisch; (*Philosophy*) utilitaristisch
utility [ju:'tɪlɪtɪ] N (*usefulness*) Nützlichkeit *f*; (*public utility*) Versorgungsbetrieb *m*
utility room N ≈ Hauswirtschaftsraum *m*
utilization [ju:tɪlaɪ'zeɪʃən] N Verwendung *f*
utilize ['ju:tɪlaɪz] VT verwenden
utmost ['ʌtməust] ADJ äußerste(r, s) ▸ N: **to do one's ~** sein Möglichstes tun; **of the ~ importance** von äußerster Wichtigkeit
utter ['ʌtəʳ] ADJ (*amazement*) äußerste(r, s); (*rubbish, fool*) total ▸ VT (*sounds, words*) äußern
utterance ['ʌtərəns] N Äußerung *f*
utterly ['ʌtəlɪ] ADV (*totally*) vollkommen
U-turn ['ju:'tə:n] N (*also fig*) Kehrtwendung *f*
Uzbekistan [ʌzbɛkɪ'stɑ:n] N Usbekistan *nt*

V[1], v [viː] N (*letter*) V *nt*, v *nt*; **V for Victor** ≈ V wie Viktor
V[2] ABBR (= *volt*) V
v. ABBR = **verse**; (= *versus*) vs.; (= *vide*) s.
VA (US) ABBR (*Post*) = **Virginia**
vac [væk] (BRIT *inf*) N = **vacation**
vacancy [ˈveɪkənsɪ] N (BRIT: *job*) freie Stelle *f*; (*room in hotel etc*) freies Zimmer *nt*; **"no vacancies"** „belegt"; **have you any vacancies?** (*hotel*) haben Sie Zimmer frei?; (*office*) haben Sie freie Stellen?
vacant [ˈveɪkənt] ADJ (*room, seat, job*) frei; (*look*) leer
vacant lot (US) N unbebautes Grundstück *nt*
vacate [vəˈkeɪt] VT (*house*) räumen; (*one's seat*) frei machen; (*job*) aufgeben
vacation [vəˈkeɪʃən] (*esp US*) N (*holiday*) Urlaub *m*; (*Scol*) Ferien *pl*; **to take a ~** Urlaub machen; **on ~** im Urlaub
vacation course N Ferienkurs *m*
vaccinate [ˈvæksɪneɪt] VT: **to ~ sb (against sth)** jdn (gegen etw) impfen
vaccination [væksɪˈneɪʃən] N Impfung *f*
vaccine [ˈvæksiːn] N Impfstoff *m*
vacuum [ˈvækjum] N (*empty space*) Vakuum *nt*
vacuum cleaner N Staubsauger *m*
vacuum flask (BRIT) N Thermosflasche® *f*
vacuum-packed [ˈvækjumˈpækt] ADJ vakuumverpackt
vagabond [ˈvægəbɔnd] N Vagabund *m*
vagary [ˈveɪgərɪ] N: **the vagaries of** die Launen *+gen*
vagina [vəˈdʒaɪnə] N Scheide *f*, Vagina *f*
vagrancy [ˈveɪgrənsɪ] N Landstreicherei *f*; (*in towns, cities*) Stadtstreicherei *f*
vagrant [ˈveɪgrənt] N Landstreicher(in) *m(f)*; (*in town, city*) Stadtstreicher(in) *m(f)*
vague [veɪg] ADJ (*memory*) vage; (*outline*) undeutlich; (*look, idea, instructions*) unbestimmt; (*person: not precise*) unsicher; (: *evasive*) unbestimmt; **to look ~** (*absent-minded*) zerstreut aussehen; **I haven't the vaguest idea** ich habe nicht die leiseste Ahnung
vaguely [ˈveɪglɪ] ADV (*unclearly*) vage, unbestimmt; (*slightly*) in etwa
vagueness [ˈveɪgnɪs] N Unbestimmtheit *f*
vain [veɪn] ADJ (*person*) eitel; (*attempt, action*) vergeblich; **in ~** vergebens; **to die in ~** umsonst sterben
vainly [ˈveɪnlɪ] ADV vergebens
valance [ˈvæləns] N (*of bed*) Volant *m*
valedictorian [vælɪdɪkˈtɔːrɪən] (US) N (*Scol*) *Abschiedsredner(in) bei der Schulentlassungsfeier*
valedictory [vælɪˈdɪktərɪ] ADJ (*speech*) Abschieds-; (*remarks*) zum Abschied
valentine [ˈvæləntaɪn] N (*also*: **valentine card**) Valentinsgruß *m*; (*person*) *Freund/Freundin, dem/der man am Valentinstag einen Gruß schickt*
Valentine's Day N Valentinstag *m*
valet [ˈvælɪt] N Kammerdiener *m*
valet parking N Einparken *nt* (*durch Hotelangestellte etc*)
valet service N Reinigungsdienst *m*
valiant [ˈvælɪənt] ADJ (*effort*) tapfer
valid [ˈvælɪd] ADJ (*ticket, document*) gültig; (*argument, reason*) stichhaltig
validate [ˈvælɪdeɪt] VT (*contract, document*) für gültig erklären; (*argument, claim*) bestätigen
validity [vəˈlɪdɪtɪ] N (*soundness*) Gültigkeit *f*
valise [vəˈliːz] N kleiner Koffer *m*
valley [ˈvælɪ] N Tal *nt*
valour, (US) **valor** [ˈvæləʳ] N Tapferkeit *f*
valuable [ˈvæljuəbl] ADJ wertvoll; (*time*) kostbar
valuables [ˈvæljuəblz] NPL Wertsachen *pl*
valuation [væljuˈeɪʃən] N (*of house etc*) Schätzung *f*; (*judgement of quality*) Einschätzung *f*
value [ˈvæljuː] N Wert *m*; (*usefulness*) Nutzen *m* ▶ VT schätzen; **values** NPL (*principles, beliefs*) Werte *pl*; **you get good ~ (for money) in that shop** in dem Laden bekommt man etwas für sein Geld; **to lose (in) ~** an Wert verlieren; **to gain (in) ~** im Wert steigen; **to be of great ~ (to sb)** (*fig*) von großem Wert (für jdn) sein
value-added tax [væljuːˈædɪd-] (BRIT) N Mehrwertsteuer *f*
valued [ˈvæljuːd] ADJ (*customer, advice*) geschätzt
valuer [ˈvæljuəʳ] N Schätzer(in) *m(f)*
valve [vælv] N Ventil *nt*; (*Med*) Klappe *f*
vampire [ˈvæmpaɪəʳ] N Vampir *m*
van [væn] N (*Aut*) Lieferwagen *m*; (BRIT *Rail*) Wa(g)gon *m*
V and A (BRIT) N ABBR (= *Victoria and Albert Museum*) *Londoner Museum*
vandal [ˈvændl] N Rowdy *m*
vandalism [ˈvændəlɪzəm] N Vandalismus *m*
vandalize [ˈvændəlaɪz] VT mutwillig zerstören

vanguard ['væŋgɑːd] N (*fig*): **in the ~ of** an der Spitze *+gen*
vanilla [və'nɪlə] N Vanille *f*
vanilla ice cream N Vanilleeis *nt*
vanish ['vænɪʃ] VI verschwinden
vanity ['vænɪtɪ] N (*of person*) Eitelkeit *f*
vanity case N Kosmetikkoffer *m*
vantage point ['vɑːntɪdʒ-] N Aussichtspunkt *m*; (*fig*): **from our ~** aus unserer Sicht
vaporize ['veɪpəraɪz] VT verdampfen ▶ VI verdunsten
vapour, (*US*) **vapor** ['veɪpə^r] N (*gas, steam*) Dampf *m*; (*mist*) Dunst *m*
vapour trail N (*Aviat*) Kondensstreifen *m*
variable ['vɛərɪəbl] ADJ (*likely to change: mood, quality, weather*) veränderlich, wechselhaft; (*able to be changed: temperature, height, speed*) variabel ▶ N veränderlicher Faktor *m*; (*Math*) Variable *f*
variance ['vɛərɪəns] N: **to be at ~ (with)** nicht übereinstimmen (mit)
variant ['vɛərɪənt] N Variante *f*
variation [vɛərɪ'eɪʃən] N (*change*) Veränderung *f*; (*different form: of plot, theme etc*) Variation *f*
varicose ['værɪkəus] ADJ: **~ veins** Krampfadern *pl*
varied ['vɛərɪd] ADJ (*diverse*) unterschiedlich; (*full of changes*) abwechslungsreich
variety [və'raɪətɪ] N (*diversity*) Vielfalt *f*; (*varied collection*) Auswahl *f*; (*type*) Sorte *f*; **a wide ~ of ...** eine Vielfalt an *+acc* ...; **for a ~ of reasons** aus verschiedenen Gründen
variety show N Varietévorführung *f*
various ['vɛərɪəs] ADJ (*reasons, people*) verschiedene; **at ~ times** (*different*) zu verschiedenen Zeiten; (*several*) mehrmals, mehrfach
varnish ['vɑːnɪʃ] N Lack *m* ▶ VT (*wood, one's nails*) lackieren
vary ['vɛərɪ] VT verändern ▶ VI (*be different*) variieren; **to ~ with** (*weather, season etc*) sich ändern mit
varying ['vɛərɪɪŋ] ADJ unterschiedlich
vase [vɑːz] N Vase *f*
vasectomy [væ'sɛktəmɪ] N Vasektomie *f*
Vaseline® ['væsɪliːn] N Vaseline *f*
vast [vɑːst] ADJ (*knowledge*) enorm; (*expense, area*) riesig
vastly ['vɑːstlɪ] ADV (*superior, improved*) erheblich
vastness ['vɑːstnɪs] N ungeheure Größe *f*
VAT [væt] (BRIT) N ABBR (= *value-added tax*) MwSt *f*
vat [væt] N Fass *nt*
Vatican ['vætɪkən] N: **the ~** der Vatikan
vatman ['vætmæn] (*inf*) N (*irreg*) ≈ Fiskus *m* (*bezüglich Einbehaltung der Mehrwertsteuer*)
vaudeville ['vəudəvɪl] N Varieté *nt*
vault [vɔːlt] N (*of roof*) Gewölbe *nt*; (*tomb*) Gruft *f*; (*in bank*) Tresorraum *m*; (*jump*) Sprung *m* ▶ VT (*also*: **vault over**) überspringen
vaunted ['vɔːntɪd] ADJ: **much-~** viel gepriesen
VC N ABBR = **vice-chairman**; (BRIT: = *Victoria Cross*) Viktoriakreuz *nt*, *höchste britische Tapferkeitsauszeichnung*
VCR N ABBR = **video cassette recorder**
VD N ABBR = **venereal disease**
VDU N ABBR (*Comput*) = **visual display unit**
veal [viːl] N Kalbfleisch *nt*
veer [vɪə^r] VI (*wind*) sich drehen; (*vehicle*) ausscheren
veg (BRIT *inf*) N ABBR = **vegetable**; **vegetables**
vegan ['viːgən] N Veganer(in) *m(f)* ▶ ADJ radikal vegetarisch
vegeburger ['vɛdʒɪbəːgə^r] N vegetarischer Hamburger *m*
vegetable ['vɛdʒtəbl] N (*plant*) Gemüse *nt*; (*plant life*) Pflanzen *pl* ▶ CPD (*oil etc*) Pflanzen-; (*garden, plot*) Gemüse-
vegetarian [vɛdʒɪ'tɛərɪən] N Vegetarier(in) *m(f)* ▶ ADJ vegetarisch
vegetate ['vɛdʒɪteɪt] VI (*fig: person*) dahinvegetieren
vegetation [vɛdʒɪ'teɪʃən] N (*plants*) Vegetation *f*
vegetative ['vɛdʒɪtətɪv] ADJ vegetativ
veggieburger ['vɛdʒɪbəːgə^r] N = **vegeburger**
vehemence ['viːɪməns] N Vehemenz *f*, Heftigkeit *f*
vehement ['viːɪmənt] ADJ heftig
vehicle ['viːɪkl] N (*machine*) Fahrzeug *nt*; (*fig: means*) Mittel *nt*
vehicular [vɪ'hɪkjulə^r] ADJ: **"no ~ traffic"** „kein Fahrzeugverkehr"
veil [veɪl] N Schleier *m* ▶ VT (*also fig*) verschleiern; **under a ~ of secrecy** unter einem Schleier von Geheimnissen
veiled [veɪld] ADJ (*also fig: threat*) verschleiert
vein [veɪn] N Ader *f*; (*fig: mood, style*) Stimmung *f*
Velcro® ['vɛlkrəu] N (*also*: **Velcro fastener** *or* **fastening**) Klettverschluss *m*
vellum ['vɛləm] N (*writing paper*) Pergament *nt*
velocity [vɪ'lɔsɪtɪ] N Geschwindigkeit *f*
velours [və'luə^r] N Velours *m*
velvet ['vɛlvɪt] N Samt *m* ▶ ADJ (*skirt, jacket*) Samt-
vendetta [vɛn'dɛtə] N Vendetta *f*; (*between families*) Blutrache *f*
vending machine ['vɛndɪŋ-] N Automat *m*
vendor ['vɛndə^r] N Verkäufer(in) *m(f)*; **street ~** Straßenhändler(in) *m(f)*
veneer [və'nɪə^r] N (*on furniture*) Furnier *nt*; (*fig*) Anstrich *m*
venerable ['vɛnərəbl] ADJ ehrwürdig; (*Rel*) hochwürdig
venereal [vɪ'nɪərɪəl] ADJ: **~ disease** Geschlechtskrankheit *f*
Venetian [vɪ'niːʃən] ADJ (*Geog*) venezianisch ▶ N (*person*) Venezianer(in) *m(f)*
Venetian blind N Jalousie *f*
Venezuela [vɛnɛ'zweɪlə] N Venezuela *nt*
Venezuelan [vɛnɛ'zweɪlən] ADJ venezolanisch ▶ N (*person*) Venezolaner(in) *m(f)*
vengeance ['vɛndʒəns] N Rache *f*; **with a ~** (*fig: fiercely*) gewaltig; **he broke the rules with a ~** er verstieß die Regeln – und nicht zu knapp
vengeful ['vɛndʒful] ADJ rachsüchtig
Venice ['vɛnɪs] N Venedig *nt*
venison ['vɛnɪsn] N Rehfleisch *nt*
venom ['vɛnəm] N (*poison*) Gift *nt*; (*bitterness, anger*) Gehässigkeit *f*

venomous ['vɛnəməs] ADJ (*snake, insect*) giftig; (*look*) gehässig
vent [vɛnt] N (*also*: **air vent**) Abzug *m*; (*in jacket*) Schlitz *m* ▶ VT (*fig*: *feelings*) abreagieren
ventilate ['vɛntɪleɪt] VT (*building*) belüften; (*room*) lüften
ventilation [vɛntɪ'leɪʃən] N Belüftung *f*
ventilation shaft N Luftschacht *m*
ventilator ['vɛntɪleɪtəʳ] N (*Tech*) Ventilator *m*; (*Med*) Beatmungsgerät *nt*
ventriloquist [vɛn'trɪləkwɪst] N Bauchredner(in) *m(f)*
venture ['vɛntʃəʳ] N Unternehmung *f* ▶ VT (*opinion*) zu äußern wagen ▶ VI (*dare to go*) sich wagen; **a business ~** ein geschäftliches Unternehmen; **to ~ to do sth** es wagen, etw zu tun
venture capital N Risikokapital *nt*
venue ['vɛnju:] N (*for meeting*) Treffpunkt *m*; (*for big events*) Austragungsort *m*
Venus ['vi:nəs] N Venus *f*
veracity [və'ræsɪtɪ] N (*of person*) Aufrichtigkeit *f*; (*of evidence etc*) Richtigkeit *f*
veranda, verandah [və'rændə] N Veranda *f*
verb [və:b] N Verb *nt*
verbal ['və:bl] ADJ verbal; (*skills*) sprachlich; (*translation*) wörtlich
verbally ['və:bəlɪ] ADV (*communicate etc*) mündlich, verbal
verbatim [və:'beɪtɪm] ADJ wörtlich ▶ ADV Wort für Wort
verbose [və:'bəus] ADJ (*person*) wortreich; (*writing*) weitschweifig
verdict ['və:dɪkt] N (*Law, fig*) Urteil *nt*; **~ of guilty/not guilty** Schuld-/Freispruch *m*
verge [və:dʒ] (BRIT) N (*of road*) Rand *m*, Bankett *nt*; **"soft verges"** (BRIT *Aut*) „Seitenstreifen nicht befahrbar"; **to be on the ~ of doing sth** im Begriff sein, etw zu tun
▶ **verge on** VT FUS grenzen an *+acc*
verger ['və:dʒəʳ] N (*Rel*) Küster *m*
verification [vɛrɪfɪ'keɪʃən] N Bestätigung *f*; Überprüfung *f*
verify ['vɛrɪfaɪ] VT (*confirm*) bestätigen; (*check*) überprüfen
veritable ['vɛrɪtəbl] ADJ (*real*) wahr
vermin ['və:mɪn] NPL Ungeziefer *nt*
vermouth ['və:məθ] N Wermut *m*
vernacular [və'nækjuləʳ] N (*of country*) Landessprache *f*; (*of region*) Dialekt *m*
verruca [ve'ru:kə] N Warze *f*
versatile ['və:sətaɪl] ADJ vielseitig
versatility [və:sə'tɪlɪtɪ] N Vielseitigkeit *f*
verse [və:s] N (*poetry*) Poesie *f*; (*stanza*) Strophe *f*; (*in bible*) Vers *m*; **in ~** in Versform
versed [və:st] ADJ: **(well-)~ in** (gut) bewandert in *+dat*
version ['və:ʃən] N Version *f*
versus ['və:səs] PREP gegen
vertebra ['və:tɪbrə] (*pl* **vertebrae**) N Rückenwirbel *m*
vertebrae ['və:tɪbri:] NPL *of* **vertebra**
vertebrate ['və:tɪbrɪt] N Wirbeltier *nt*
vertical ['və:tɪkl] ADJ vertikal, senkrecht ▶ N Vertikale *f*
vertically ['və:tɪklɪ] ADV vertikal
vertigo ['və:tɪgəu] N Schwindelgefühle *pl*; **to suffer from ~** leicht schwindlig werden
verve [və:v] N Schwung *m*
very ['vɛrɪ] ADV sehr ▶ ADJ: **the ~ book which …** genau das Buch, das …; **the ~ last** der/die/das Allerletzte; **at the ~ least** allerwenigstens; **~ well/little** sehr gut/wenig; **~ much** sehr viel; (*like, hope*) sehr; **the ~ thought (of it) alarms me** der bloße Gedanke (daran) beunruhigt mich; **at the ~ end** ganz am Ende
vespers ['vɛspəz] NPL (*Rel*) Vesper *f*
vessel ['vɛsl] N Gefäß *nt*; (*Naut*) Schiff *nt*; *see* **blood**
vest [vɛst] N (BRIT: *underwear*) Unterhemd *nt*; (US: *waistcoat*) Weste *f* ▶ VT: **to ~ sb with sth, ~ sth in sb** jdm etw verleihen
vested interest ['vɛstɪd-] N (*Comm*) finanzielles Interesse *nt*; **to have a ~ in doing sth** ein besonderes Interesse daran haben, etw zu tun
vestibule ['vɛstɪbju:l] N Vorhalle *f*
vestige ['vɛstɪdʒ] N Spur *f*
vestment ['vɛstmənt] N (*Rel*) Ornat *nt*
vestry ['vɛstrɪ] N Sakristei *f*
Vesuvius [vɪ'su:vɪəs] N Vesuv *m*
vet [vɛt] (BRIT) N = **veterinary surgeon**; (US) = **veteran** ▶ VT (*examine*) überprüfen
veteran ['vɛtərn] N Veteran(in) *m(f)* ▶ ADJ: **she's a ~ campaigner for …** sie ist eine altgediente Kämpferin für …
veteran car N Oldtimer *m* (*vor 1919 gebaut*)
veterinarian [vɛtrɪ'nɛərɪən] (US) N = **veterinary surgeon**
veterinary ['vɛtrɪnərɪ] ADJ (*practice, medicine*) Veterinär-; (*care, training*) tierärztlich
veterinary surgeon (BRIT) N Tierarzt *m*, Tierärztin *f*
veto ['vi:təu] (*pl* **vetoes**) N Veto *nt* ▶ VT ein Veto einlegen gegen; **to put a ~ on sth** gegen etw ein Veto einlegen
vetting ['vɛtɪŋ] N Überprüfung *f*
vex [vɛks] VT (*irritate, upset*) ärgern
vexed [vɛkst] ADJ (*upset*) verärgert; (*question*) umstritten
VFD (US) N ABBR (= *volunteer fire department*) ≈ freiwillige Feuerwehr *f*
VG (BRIT) N ABBR (*Scol etc*: = *very good*) ≈ „sehr gut"
VHF ABBR (*Radio*: = *very high frequency*) VHF
VI (US) ABBR (*Post*) = **Virgin Islands**
via ['vaɪə] PREP über *+acc*
viability [vaɪə'bɪlɪtɪ] N Durchführbarkeit *f*; Rentabilität *f*
viable ['vaɪəbl] ADJ (*project*) durchführbar; (*company*) rentabel
viaduct ['vaɪədʌkt] N Viadukt *m*
vial ['vaɪəl] N Fläschchen *nt*
vibes [vaɪbz] NPL (*Mus*) *see* **vibraphone**; (*inf*: *vibrations*): **I get good/bad ~ from it/him** das/er macht mich an/nicht an
vibrant ['vaɪbrnt] ADJ (*lively*) dynamisch; (*bright*) lebendig; (*full of emotion*: *voice*) volltönend
vibraphone ['vaɪbrəfəun] N Vibrafon *nt*

V

vibrate [vaɪ'breɪt] VI (*house*) zittern, beben; (*machine, sound etc*) vibrieren
vibration [vaɪ'breɪʃən] N (*act of vibrating*) Vibrieren *nt*; (*instance*) Vibration *f*
vibrator [vaɪ'breɪtə^r] N Vibrator *m*
vicar ['vɪkə^r] N Pfarrer *m*
vicarage ['vɪkərɪdʒ] N Pfarrhaus *nt*
vicarious [vɪ'kɛərɪəs] ADJ (*pleasure, experience*) indirekt
vice [vaɪs] N (*moral fault*) Laster *nt*; (*Tech*) Schraubstock *m*
vice- [vaɪs] PREF Vize-
vice-chairman [vaɪs'tʃɛəmən] N (*irreg*) stellvertretender Vorsitzender *m*
vice chancellor (BRIT) N (*of university*) ≈ Rektor *m*
vice president N Vizepräsident(in) *m(f)*
viceroy ['vaɪsrɔɪ] N Vizekönig *m*
vice squad N (*Police*) Sittendezernat *nt*
vice versa ['vaɪsɪ'və:sə] ADV umgekehrt
vicinity [vɪ'sɪnɪtɪ] N: **in the ~ (of)** in der Nähe *or* Umgebung (*+gen*)
vicious ['vɪʃəs] ADJ (*attack, blow*) brutal; (*words, look*) gemein; (*horse, dog*) bösartig
vicious circle N Teufelskreis *m*
viciousness ['vɪʃəsnɪs] N Bösartigkeit *f*, Gemeinheit *f*
vicissitudes [vɪ'sɪsɪtju:dz] NPL Wechselfälle *pl*
victim ['vɪktɪm] N Opfer *nt*; **to be the ~ of an attack** einem Angriff zum Opfer fallen
victimization ['vɪktɪmaɪ'zeɪʃən] N Schikanierung *f*
victimize ['vɪktɪmaɪz] VT schikanieren
victor ['vɪktə^r] N Sieger(in) *m(f)*
Victorian [vɪk'tɔ:rɪən] ADJ viktorianisch
victorious [vɪk'tɔ:rɪəs] ADJ (*team*) siegreich; (*shout*) triumphierend
victory ['vɪktərɪ] N Sieg *m*; **to win a ~ over sb** einen Sieg über jdn erringen
video ['vɪdɪəu] N (*film, cassette, recorder*) Video *nt* ▸ VT auf Video aufnehmen ▸ CPD Video-
video camera N Videokamera *f*
video cassette N Videokassette *f*
video cassette recorder N Videorekorder *m*
videodisc, videodisk ['vɪdɪəudɪsk] N Bildplatte *f*
video game N Videospiel *nt*, Telespiel *nt*
video nasty N *Video mit übertriebenen Gewaltszenen und/oder pornografischem Inhalt*
videophone ['vɪdɪəufəun] N Bildtelefon *nt*
video recorder N Videorekorder *m*
video recording N Videoaufnahme *f*
video tape N Videoband *nt*
vie [vaɪ] VI: **to ~ with sb/for sth** mit jdm/um etw wetteifern
Vienna [vɪ'ɛnə] N Wien *nt*
Viennese [vɪə'ni:z] ADJ Wiener
Vietnam ['vjɛt'næm] N Vietnam *nt*
Viet Nam ['vjɛt'næm] N = **Vietnam**
Vietnamese [vjɛtnə'mi:z] ADJ vietnamesisch ▸ N INV (*person*) Vietnamese *m*, Vietnamesin *f*; (*Ling*) Vietnamesisch *nt*
view [vju:] N (*from window etc*) Aussicht *f*; (*sight*) Blick *m*; (*outlook*) Sicht *f*; (*opinion*) Ansicht *f* ▸ VT betrachten; (*house*) besichtigen; **to be on ~** (*in museum etc*) ausgestellt sein; **in full ~ of** vor den Augen *+gen*; **to take the ~ that …** der Ansicht sein, dass …; **in ~ of the weather/the fact that** in Anbetracht des Wetters/der Tatsache, dass …; **in my ~** meiner Ansicht nach; **an overall ~ of the situation** ein allgemeiner Überblick über die Lage; **with a ~ to doing sth** mit der Absicht, etw zu tun
viewdata® ['vju:deɪtə] (BRIT) N Bildschirmtext *m*
viewer ['vju:ə^r] N (*person*) Zuschauer(in) *m(f)*; (*viewfinder*) Sucher *m*
viewfinder ['vju:faɪndə^r] N Sucher *m*
viewpoint ['vju:pɔɪnt] N (*attitude*) Standpunkt *m*; (*place*) Aussichtspunkt *m*
vigil ['vɪdʒɪl] N Wache *f*; **to keep ~** Wache halten
vigilance ['vɪdʒɪləns] N Wachsamkeit *f*
vigilance committee (US) N Bürgerwehr *f*
vigilant ['vɪdʒɪlənt] ADJ wachsam
vigilante [vɪdʒɪ'læntɪ] N *Mitglied einer Selbstschutzorganisation oder Bürgerwehr* ▸ ADJ (*group, patrol*) Bürgerwehr-, Selbstschutz-
vigorous ['vɪgərəs] ADJ (*action, campaign*) energisch, dynamisch; (*plant*) kräftig
vigour, (US) vigor ['vɪgə^r] N (*of person, campaign*) Energie *f*, Dynamik *f*
vile [vaɪl] ADJ abscheulich
vilify ['vɪlɪfaɪ] VT diffamieren
villa ['vɪlə] N Villa *f*
village ['vɪlɪdʒ] N Dorf *nt*
villager ['vɪlɪdʒə^r] N Dorfbewohner(in) *m(f)*
villain ['vɪlən] N (*scoundrel*) Schurke *m*; (*in novel etc*) Bösewicht *m*; (BRIT: *criminal*) Verbrecher(in) *m(f)*
VIN (US) N ABBR (= *vehicle identification number*) amtliches Kennzeichen *nt*
vinaigrette [vɪneɪ'grɛt] N Vinaigrette *f*
vindicate ['vɪndɪkeɪt] VT (*person*) rehabilitieren; (*action*) rechtfertigen
vindication [vɪndɪ'keɪʃən] N Rechtfertigung *f*
vindictive [vɪn'dɪktɪv] ADJ (*person*) nachtragend; (*action*) aus Rache
vine [vaɪn] N (*Bot: producing grapes*) Weinrebe *f*; (*: in jungle*) Rebengewächs *nt*
vinegar ['vɪnɪgə^r] N Essig *m*
vine grower N Weinbauer *m*
vine-growing ['vaɪngrəuɪŋ] ADJ (*region*) Weinbau- ▸ N Weinbau *m*
vineyard ['vɪnjɑ:d] N Weinberg *m*
vintage ['vɪntɪdʒ] N (*of wine*) Jahrgang *m* ▸ CPD (*classic*) klassisch; **the 1980 ~** (*of wine*) der Jahrgang 1980
vintage car N Oldtimer *m* (*zwischen 1919 und 1930 gebaut*)
vintage wine N erlesener Wein *m*
vinyl ['vaɪnl] N Vinyl *nt*; (*records*) Schallplatten *pl*
viola [vɪ'əulə] N Bratsche *f*
violate ['vaɪəleɪt] VT (*agreement*) verletzen; (*peace*) stören; (*graveyard*) schänden
violation [vaɪə'leɪʃən] N (*of agreement etc*) Verletzung *f*; **in ~ of** (*rule, law*) unter Verletzung *+gen*

violence ['vaɪələns] N Gewalt *f*; (*strength*) Heftigkeit *f*
violent ['vaɪələnt] ADJ (*behaviour*) gewalttätig; (*death*) gewaltsam; (*explosion, criticism, emotion*) heftig; **a ~ dislike of sb/sth** eine heftige Abneigung gegen jdn/etw
violently ['vaɪələntlɪ] ADV heftig; (*ill*) schwer; (*angry*) äußerst
violet ['vaɪələt] ADJ violett ▸ N (*colour*) Violett *nt*; (*plant*) Veilchen *nt*
violin [vaɪə'lɪn] N Geige *f*, Violine *f*
violinist [vaɪə'lɪnɪst] N Violinist(in) *m(f)*, Geiger(in) *m(f)*
VIP N ABBR (= *very important person*) VIP *m*
viper ['vaɪpəʳ] N Viper *f*
viral ['vaɪərəl] ADJ (*disease, infection*) Virus-
virgin ['və:dʒɪn] N Jungfrau *f* ▸ ADJ (*snow, forest etc*) unberührt; **she is a ~** sie ist Jungfrau; **the Blessed V~** die Heilige Jungfrau
virgin birth N unbefleckte Empfängnis *f*; (*Biol*) Jungfernzeugung *f*
virginity [və:'dʒɪnɪtɪ] N (*of person*) Jungfräulichkeit *f*
Virgo ['və:gəu] N (*sign*) Jungfrau *f*; **to be ~** Jungfrau sein
virile ['vɪraɪl] ADJ (*person*) männlich
virility [vɪ'rɪlɪtɪ] N (*masculine qualities*) Männlichkeit *f*
virtual ['və:tjuəl] ADJ (*Comput, Phys*) virtuell; **it's a ~ impossibility** es ist so gut wie unmöglich; **to be the ~ leader** eigentlich *or* praktisch der Führer sein
virtually ['və:tjuəlɪ] ADV praktisch, nahezu; **it is ~ impossible** es ist so gut wie unmöglich
virtual reality N virtuelle Realität *f*
virtue ['və:tju:] N Tugend *f*; (*advantage*) Vorzug *m*; **by ~ of** aufgrund *+gen*
virtuosi [və:tju'əuzɪ] NPL *of* **virtuoso**
virtuosity [və:tju'ɔsɪtɪ] N Virtuosität *f*
virtuoso [və:tju'əuzəu] (*pl* **virtuosos** *or* **virtuosi**) N Virtuose *m*
virtuous ['və:tjuəs] ADJ tugendhaft
virulence ['vɪruləns] N (*of disease*) Bösartigkeit *f*; (*hatred*) Feindseligkeit *f*
virulent ['vɪrulənt] ADJ (*disease*) bösartig; (*actions, feelings*) feindselig
virus ['vaɪərəs] N (*Med, Comput*) Virus *m or nt*
visa ['vi:zə] N Visum *nt*
vis-à-vis [vi:zə'vi:] PREP gegenüber
viscose ['vɪskəus] N (*also Chem*) Viskose *f*
viscount ['vaɪkaunt] N Viscount *m*
viscous ['vɪskəs] ADJ zähflüssig
vise [vaɪs] (*US*) N (*Tech*) = **vice**
visibility [vɪzɪ'bɪlɪtɪ] N (*range of vision*) Sicht(weite) *f*
visible ['vɪzəbl] ADJ sichtbar; **~ exports/imports** sichtbare Ausfuhren/Einfuhren
visibly ['vɪzəblɪ] ADV sichtlich
vision ['vɪʒən] N (*sight*) Sicht *f*; (*foresight*) Weitblick *m*; (*in dream*) Vision *f*
visionary ['vɪʒənrɪ] ADJ (*with foresight*) vorausblickend
visit ['vɪzɪt] N Besuch *m* ▸ VT besuchen; **a private/official ~** ein privater/offizieller Besuch
visiting ['vɪzɪtɪŋ] ADJ (*speaker, team*) Gast-
visiting card N Visitenkarte *f*
visiting hours NPL Besuchszeiten *pl*
visiting professor N Gastprofessor(in) *m(f)*
visitor ['vɪzɪtəʳ] N Besucher(in) *m(f)*
visitor centre N Informationszentrum *nt*
visitors' book ['vɪzɪtəz-] N Gästebuch *nt*
visor ['vaɪzəʳ] N (*of helmet etc*) Visier *nt*
VISTA ['vɪstə] (*US*) N ABBR (= *Volunteers In Service To America*) *staatliches Förderprogramm für strukturschwache Gebiete*
vista ['vɪstə] N Aussicht *f*
visual ['vɪzjuəl] ADJ (*image etc*) visuell; **the ~ arts** die darstellenden Künste
visual aid N Anschauungsmaterial *nt*
visual display unit N (Daten)sichtgerät *nt*
visualize ['vɪzjuəlaɪz] VT sich *dat* vorstellen
visually ['vɪzjuəlɪ] ADV visuell; **~ appealing** optisch ansprechend; **~ handicapped** sehbehindert
vital ['vaɪtl] ADJ (*essential*) unerlässlich; (*organ*) lebenswichtig; (*full of life*) vital; **of ~ importance (to sb/sth)** von größter Wichtigkeit (für jdn/etw)
vitality [vaɪ'tælɪtɪ] N (*liveliness*) Vitalität *f*
vitally ['vaɪtəlɪ] ADV: **~ important** äußerst wichtig
vital statistics NPL (*fig: of woman*) Körpermaße *pl*; (*of population*) Bevölkerungsstatistik *f*
vitamin ['vɪtəmɪn] N Vitamin *nt* ▸ CPD (*pill, deficiencies*) Vitamin-
vitiate ['vɪʃieɪt] VT (*spoil*) verunreinigen
vitreous ['vɪtrɪəs] ADJ: **~ china** Porzellanemail *nt*; **~ enamel** Glasemail *nt*
vitriolic [vɪtrɪ'ɔlɪk] ADJ (*fig: language, behaviour*) hasserfüllt
viva ['vaɪvə] N (*Scol: also:* **viva voce**) mündliche Prüfung *f*
vivacious [vɪ'veɪʃəs] ADJ lebhaft
vivacity [vɪ'væsɪtɪ] N Lebendigkeit *f*
vivid ['vɪvɪd] ADJ (*description*) lebendig; (*memory, imagination*) lebhaft; (*colour*) leuchtend; (*light*) hell
vividly ['vɪvɪdlɪ] ADV (*describe*) lebendig; (*remember*) lebhaft
vivisection [vɪvɪ'sɛkʃən] N Vivisektion *f*
vixen ['vɪksn] N (*Zool*) Füchsin *f*; (*pej: woman*) Drachen *m*
viz [vɪz] ABBR (= *videlicet*) nämlich
VLF ABBR (*Radio:* = *very low frequency*) VLF
V-neck ['vi:nɛk] N (*also:* **V-neck jumper** *or* **pullover**) Pullover *m* mit V-Ausschnitt
VOA N ABBR (= *Voice of America*) Stimme *f* Amerikas
vocabulary [vəu'kæbjulərɪ] N (*words known*) Vokabular *nt*, Wortschatz *m*
vocal ['vəukl] ADJ (*of the voice*) stimmlich; (*articulate*) lautstark
vocal cords NPL Stimmbänder *pl*
vocalist ['vəukəlɪst] N Sänger(in) *m(f)*
vocals ['vəuklz] NPL (*Mus*) Gesang *m*

vocation [vəu'keɪʃən] N *(calling)* Berufung *f*; *(profession)* Beruf *m*
vocational [vəu'keɪʃənl] ADJ *(training, guidance etc)* Berufs-
vociferous [və'sɪfərəs] ADJ *(protesters, demands)* lautstark
vodka ['vɔdkə] N Wodka *m*
vogue [vəug] N *(fashion)* Mode *f*; *(popularity)* Popularität *f*; **in ~** in Mode
voice [vɔɪs] N *(also fig)* Stimme *f* ▸ VT *(opinion)* zum Ausdruck bringen; **in a loud/soft ~** mit lauter/leiser Stimme; **to give ~ to** Ausdruck verleihen *+dat*
voice mail N *(Comput)* Voicemail *f*
voice-over ['vɔɪsəuvəʳ] N (Film)kommentar *m*
void [vɔɪd] N *(hole)* Loch *nt*; *(fig: emptiness)* Leere *f* ▸ ADJ *(invalid)* ungültig; **~ of** *(empty)* ohne
voile [vɔɪl] N Voile *m*
vol. ABBR (= *volume*) Bd.
volatile ['vɔlətaɪl] ADJ *(person)* impulsiv; *(situation)* unsicher; *(liquid etc)* flüchtig
volcanic [vɔl'kænɪk] ADJ *(rock, eruption)* vulkanisch, Vulkan-
volcano [vɔl'keɪnəu] (*pl* **volcanoes**) N Vulkan *m*
volition [və'lɪʃən] N: **of one's own ~** aus freiem Willen
volley ['vɔlɪ] N *(of gunfire)* Salve *f*; *(of stones, questions)* Hagel *m*; *(Tennis etc)* Volley *m*
volleyball ['vɔlɪbɔːl] N Volleyball *m*
volt [vəult] N Volt *nt*
voltage ['vəultɪdʒ] N Spannung *f*; **high/low ~** Hoch-/Niederspannung *f*
volte-face ['vɔlt'fɑːs] N Kehrtwendung *f*
voluble ['vɔljubl] ADJ *(person)* redselig; *(speech)* wortreich
volume ['vɔljuːm] N *(space)* Volumen *nt*; *(amount)* Umfang *m*, Ausmaß *nt*; *(book)* Band *m*; *(sound level)* Lautstärke *f*; **~ one/two** *(of book)* Band eins/zwei; **his expression spoke volumes** sein Gesichtsausdruck sprach Bände
volume control N *(Radio, TV)* Lautstärkeregler *m*
volume discount N *(Comm)* Mengenrabatt *m*
voluminous [və'luːmɪnəs] ADJ *(clothes)* sehr weit; *(correspondence, notes)* umfangreich
voluntarily ['vɔləntrɪlɪ] ADV freiwillig
voluntary ['vɔləntərɪ] ADJ freiwillig
voluntary liquidation N freiwillige Liquidation *f*
volunteer [vɔlən'tɪəʳ] N Freiwillige(r) *f(m)* ▸ VT *(information)* vorbringen ▸ VI *(for army etc)* sich freiwillig melden; **to ~ to do sth** sich anbieten, etw zu tun
voluptuous [və'lʌptjuəs] ADJ sinnlich, wollüstig
vomit ['vɔmɪt] N Erbrochene(s) *nt* ▸ VT erbrechen ▸ VI sich übergeben
voracious [və'reɪʃəs] ADJ *(person)* gefräßig; **~ appetite** Riesenappetit *m*
vortal ['vɔːtl] N *(Comput)* Vortal *nt*
vote [vəut] N Stimme *f*; *(votes cast)* Stimmen *pl*; *(right to vote)* Wahlrecht *nt*; *(ballot)* Abstimmung *f* ▸ VT *(elect)*: **to be voted chairman** *etc* zum Vorsitzenden *etc* gewählt werden; *(propose)*: **to ~ that** vorschlagen, dass ▸ VI *(in election etc)* wählen; **to put sth to the ~, (take a) ~ on sth** über etw *acc* abstimmen; **~ of censure** Tadelsantrag *m*; **to pass a ~ of confidence/no confidence** ein Vertrauens-/Misstrauensvotum annehmen; **to ~ to do sth** dafür stimmen, etw zu tun; **to ~ yes/no** mit Ja/Nein stimmen; **to ~ Labour/Green** *etc* Labour/die Grünen *etc* wählen; **to ~ for** *or* **in favour of sth/against sth** für/gegen etw stimmen
vote of thanks N Danksagung *f*
voter ['vəutəʳ] N Wähler(in) *m(f)*
voting ['vəutɪŋ] N Wahl *f*
voting paper (BRIT) N Stimmzettel *m*
voting right N Stimmrecht *nt*
vouch [vautʃ]: **~ for** *vt fus* bürgen für
voucher ['vautʃəʳ] N Gutschein *m*; *(receipt)* Beleg *m*; **gift ~** Geschenkgutschein *m*; **luncheon ~** Essensmarke *f*; **travel ~** Reisegutschein *m*
vow [vau] N Versprechen *nt* ▸ VT: **to ~ to do sth/that** geloben, etw zu tun/dass; **to take** *or* **make a ~ to do sth** geloben, etw zu tun
vowel ['vauəl] N Vokal *m*
voyage ['vɔɪɪdʒ] N Reise *f*
voyeur [vwɑː'jəːʳ] N Voyeur(in) *m(f)*
voyeurism [vwɑː'jəːrɪzəm] N Voyeurismus *m*
VP N ABBR = **vice president**
vs ABBR (= *versus*) vs.
V-sign ['viːsaɪn] (BRIT) N: **to give sb the ~** ≈ jdm den Vogel zeigen
VSO (BRIT) N ABBR (= *Voluntary Service Overseas*) *britischer Entwicklungsdienst*
VT (US) ABBR *(Post)* = **Vermont**
vulgar ['vʌlgəʳ] ADJ *(remarks, gestures)* vulgär; *(decor, ostentation)* geschmacklos
vulgarity [vʌl'gærɪtɪ] N Vulgarität *f*; Geschmacklosigkeit *f*
vulnerability [vʌlnərə'bɪlɪtɪ] N Verletzlichkeit *f*
vulnerable ['vʌlnərəbl] ADJ *(person, position)* verletzlich
vulture ['vʌltʃəʳ] N *(also fig)* Geier *m*
vulva ['vʌlvə] N Vulva *f*

W¹, w ['dʌblju:] N (*letter*) W *nt*, w *nt*; **W for William** ≈ W wie Wilhelm
W² ['dʌblju:] ABBR (*Elec*: = *watt*) W; (= *west*) W
WA ABBR (*US Post*) = **Washington**; (AUST) = **Western Australia**
wad [wɔd] N (*of cotton wool*) Bausch *m*; (*of paper, banknotes*) Bündel *nt*
wadding ['wɔdɪŋ] N Füllmaterial *nt*
waddle ['wɔdl] VI watscheln
wade [weɪd] VI: **to ~ across** (*a river, stream*) waten durch; **to ~ through** (*fig: a book*) sich durchkämpfen durch
wafer ['weɪfəʳ] N (*biscuit*) Waffel *f*
wafer-thin ['weɪfə'θɪn] ADJ hauchdünn
waffle ['wɔfl] N (*Culin*) Waffel *f*; (*inf: empty talk*) Geschwafel *nt* ▸ VI (*in speech etc*) schwafeln
waffle iron N Waffeleisen *nt*
waft [wɔft] VT, VI wehen
wag [wæg] VT (*tail*) wedeln mit; (*finger*) drohen mit ▸ VI (*tail*) wedeln; **the dog wagged its tail** der Hund wedelte mit dem Schwanz
wage [weɪdʒ] N (*also*: **wages**) Lohn *m* ▸ VT: **to ~ war** Krieg führen; **a day's wages** ein Tageslohn
wage claim N Lohnforderung *f*
wage differential N Lohnunterschied *m*
wage earner [-ə:nəʳ] N Lohnempfänger(in) *m(f)*
wage freeze N Lohnstopp *m*
wage packet N Lohntüte *f*
wager ['weɪdʒəʳ] N Wette *f* ▸ VT wetten
waggle ['wægl] VT (*ears etc*) wackeln mit ▸ VI wackeln
wagon, waggon ['wægən] N (*horse-drawn*) Fuhrwerk *nt*; (BRIT *Rail*) Wa(g)gon *m*
wail [weɪl] N (*of person*) Jammern *nt*; (*of siren*) Heulen *nt* ▸ VI (*person*) jammern; (*siren*) heulen
waist [weɪst] N (*Anat, of clothing*) Taille *f*
waistcoat ['weɪskəut] (BRIT) N Weste *f*
waistline ['weɪstlaɪn] N Taille *f*
wait [weɪt] N Wartezeit *f* ▸ VI warten; **to lie in ~ for sb** jdm auflauern; **to keep sb waiting** jdn warten lassen; **I can't ~ to …** (*fig*) ich kann es kaum erwarten, zu …; **to ~ for sb/sth** auf jdn/etw warten; **~ a minute!** Moment mal!; **"repairs while you ~"** „Reparaturen sofort"
▸ **wait behind** VI zurückbleiben
▸ **wait on** VT FUS (*serve*) bedienen
▸ **wait up** VI aufbleiben; **don't ~ up for me** warte nicht auf mich

waiter ['weɪtəʳ] N Kellner *m*
waiting ['weɪtɪŋ] N: **"no ~"** (BRIT *Aut*) „Halten verboten"
waiting list N Warteliste *f*
waiting room N (*in surgery*) Wartezimmer *nt*; (*in railway station*) Wartesaal *m*
waitress ['weɪtrɪs] N Kellnerin *f*
waive [weɪv] VT (*rule*) verzichten auf *+acc*
waiver ['weɪvəʳ] N Verzicht *m*
wake [weɪk] (*pt* **woke** *or* **waked**, *pp* **woken** *or* **waked**) VT (*also*: **wake up**) wecken ▸ VI (*also*: **wake up**) aufwachen ▸ N (*for dead person*) Totenwache *f*; (*Naut*) Kielwasser *nt*; **to ~ up to** (*fig*) sich *dat* bewusst werden *+gen*; **in the ~ of** (*fig*) unmittelbar nach, im Gefolge *+gen*; **to follow in sb's ~** (*fig*) hinter jdm herziehen
waken ['weɪkn] VT = **wake**
wake-up call N (*Tel*) Weckruf *m*
Wales [weɪlz] N Wales *nt*; **the Prince of ~** der Prinz von Wales
walk [wɔ:k] N (*hike*) Wanderung *f*; (*shorter*) Spaziergang *m*; (*gait*) Gang *m*; (*path*) Weg *m*; (*in park, along coast etc*) (Spazier)weg *m* ▸ VI gehen; (*instead of driving*) zu Fuß gehen; (*for pleasure, exercise*) spazieren gehen ▸ VT (*distance*) gehen, laufen; (*dog*) ausführen; **it's 10 minutes' ~ from here** es ist 10 Minuten zu Fuß von hier; **to go for a ~** spazieren gehen; **to slow to a ~** im Schritttempo weitergehen; **people from all walks of life** Leute aus allen Gesellschaftsschichten; **to ~ in one's sleep** schlafwandeln; **I'd rather ~ than take the bus** ich gehe lieber zu Fuß als mit dem Bus zu fahren; **I'll ~ you home** ich bringe dich nach Hause
▸ **walk out** VI (*audience*) den Saal verlassen; (*workers*) in Streik treten
▸ **walk out on** (*inf*) VT FUS (*family etc*) verlassen
walkabout ['wɔ:kəbaut] N: **the Queen/president went on a ~** die Königin/der Präsident mischte sich unters Volk *or* nahm ein Bad in der Menge
walker ['wɔ:kəʳ] N (*person*) Spaziergänger(in) *m(f)*
walkie-talkie ['wɔ:kɪ'tɔ:kɪ] N Walkie-Talkie *nt*
walking ['wɔ:kɪŋ] N Wandern *nt*; **it's within ~ distance** es ist zu Fuß erreichbar
walking holiday N Wanderurlaub *m*

walking shoes NPL Wanderschuhe *pl*
walking stick N Spazierstock *m*
Walkman® ['wɔːkmən] N Walkman® *m*
walk-on ['wɔːkɔn] ADJ (*Theat*): **~ part** Statistenrolle *f*
walkout ['wɔːkaut] N (*of workers*) Streik *m*
walkover ['wɔːkəuvəʳ] (*inf*) N (*competition, exam etc*) Kinderspiel *nt*
walkway ['wɔːkweɪ] N Fußweg *m*
wall [wɔːl] N Wand *f*; (*exterior, city wall etc*) Mauer *f*; **to go to the ~** (*fig: firm etc*) kaputtgehen ▶ **wall in** VT (*enclose*) ummauern
wall cupboard N Wandschrank *m*
walled [wɔːld] ADJ von Mauern umgeben
wallet ['wɔlɪt] N Brieftasche *f*
wallflower ['wɔːlflauəʳ] N (*Bot*) Goldlack *m*; **to be a ~** (*fig*) ein Mauerblümchen sein
wall hanging N Wandbehang *m*
wallop ['wɔləp] (BRIT *inf*) VT verprügeln
wallow ['wɔləu] VI (*in mud, water*) sich wälzen; (*in guilt, grief*) schwelgen
wallpaper ['wɔːlpeɪpəʳ] N Tapete *f* ▶ VT tapezieren
wall-to-wall ['wɔːltə'wɔːl] ADJ: **~ carpeting** Teppichboden *m*
wally [wɔlɪ] (*inf*) N Trottel *m*
walnut ['wɔːlnʌt] N (*nut*) Walnuss *f*; (*tree*) Walnussbaum *m*; (*wood*) Nussbaumholz *nt*
walrus ['wɔːlrəs] (*pl* ~ *or* **walruses**) N Walross *nt*
waltz [wɔːlts] N Walzer *m* ▶ VI Walzer tanzen
wan [wɔn] ADJ bleich; (*smile*) matt
wand [wɔnd] N (*also*: **magic wand**) Zauberstab *m*
wander ['wɔndəʳ] VI (*person*) herumlaufen; (*mind, thoughts*) wandern ▶ VT (*the streets, the hills etc*) durchstreifen
wanderer ['wɔndərəʳ] N Wandervogel *m*
wandering ['wɔndrɪŋ] ADJ (*tribe*) umherziehend; (*minstrel, actor*) fahrend
wane [weɪn] VI (*moon*) abnehmen; (*influence etc*) schwinden
wangle ['wæŋgl] (BRIT *inf*) VT sich *dat* verschaffen
wanker ['wæŋkəʳ] (*inf!*) N Wichser *m*
wannabe, wannabee ['wɔnəbiː] (*inf*) N Möchtegern *m*; **James Bond ~(e)** Möchtegern-James-Bond *m*
want [wɔnt] VT (*wish for*) wollen; (*need*) brauchen ▶ N (*lack*): **for ~ of** aus Mangel an +*dat*; **wants** NPL (*needs*) Bedürfnisse *pl*; **to ~ to do sth** etw tun wollen; **to ~ sb to do sth** wollen, dass jd etw tut; **to ~ in/out** herein-/hinauswollen; **you're wanted on the phone** Sie werden am Telefon verlangt; **he is wanted by the police** er wird von der Polizei gesucht; **a ~ of foresight** ein Mangel *m* an Voraussicht
want ads (US) NPL Kaufgesuche *pl*
wanted ['wɔntɪd] ADJ (*criminal etc*) gesucht; **"cook ~"** „Koch/Köchin gesucht"
wanting ['wɔntɪŋ] ADJ: **to be found ~** sich als unzulänglich erweisen
wanton ['wɔntn] ADJ (*violence*) mutwillig; (*promiscuous: woman*) schamlos
WAP [wæp] N ABBR (*Comput*: = *wireless application protocol*) WAP *nt*
war [wɔːʳ] N Krieg *m*; **to go to ~** (*start*) einen Krieg anfangen; **to be at ~ (with)** sich im Kriegszustand befinden (mit); **to make ~ (on)** Krieg führen (gegen); **a ~ on drugs/crime** ein Feldzug gegen Drogen/das Verbrechen
warble ['wɔːbl] N Trällern *nt* ▶ VI trällern
war cry N Kriegsruf *m*; (*fig: slogan*) Schlachtruf *m*
ward [wɔːd] N (*in hospital*) Station *f*; (*Pol*) Wahlbezirk *m*; (*Law*: *also*: **ward of court**) Mündel *nt* unter Amtsvormundschaft ▶ **ward off** VT (*attack, enemy, illness*) abwehren
warden ['wɔːdn] N (*of park etc*) Aufseher(in) *m(f)*; (*of jail*) Wärter(in) *m(f)*; (BRIT: *of youth hostel*) Herbergsvater *m*, Herbergsmutter *f*; (: *in university*) Wohnheimleiter(in) *m(f)*; (*also*: **traffic warden**) Verkehrspolizist(in) *m(f)*
warder ['wɔːdəʳ] (BRIT) N Gefängniswärter(in) *m(f)*
wardrobe ['wɔːdrəub] N (*for clothes*) Kleiderschrank *m*; (*collection of clothes*) Garderobe *f*; (*Cine, Theat*) Kostüme *pl*
warehouse ['wɛəhaus] N Lager *nt*
wares [wɛəz] NPL Waren *pl*
warfare ['wɔːfɛəʳ] N Krieg *m*
war game N Kriegsspiel *nt*
warhead ['wɔːhɛd] N Sprengkopf *m*
warily ['wɛərɪlɪ] ADV vorsichtig
Warks (BRIT) ABBR (*Post*) = **Warwickshire**
warlike ['wɔːlaɪk] ADJ kriegerisch
warm [wɔːm] ADJ warm; (*thanks, applause, welcome, person*) herzlich; **it's ~** es ist warm; **I'm ~** mir ist warm; **to keep sth ~** etw warm halten; **with my warmest thanks/ congratulations** mit meinem herzlichsten Dank/meinen herzlichsten Glückwünschen ▶ **warm up** VI warm werden; (*athlete*) sich aufwärmen ▶ VT aufwärmen
warm-blooded ['wɔːm'blʌdɪd] ADJ warmblütig
war memorial N Kriegerdenkmal *nt*
warm-hearted [wɔːm'hɑːtɪd] ADJ warmherzig
warmly ['wɔːmlɪ] ADV (*applaud, welcome*) herzlich; (*dress*) warm
warmonger ['wɔːmʌŋgəʳ] (*pej*) N Kriegshetzer *m*
warmongering ['wɔːmʌŋgrɪŋ] (*pej*) N Kriegshetze *f*
warmth [wɔːmθ] N Wärme *f*; (*friendliness*) Herzlichkeit *f*
warm-up ['wɔːmʌp] N Aufwärmen *nt*; **~ exercise** Aufwärmübung *f*
warn [wɔːn] VT: **to ~ sb that …** jdn warnen, dass …; **to ~ sb of sth** jdn vor etw *dat* warnen; **to ~ sb not to do sth** *or* **against doing sth** jdn davor warnen, etw zu tun
warning ['wɔːnɪŋ] N Warnung *f*; **without (any) ~** (*suddenly*) unerwartet; (*without notifying*) ohne Vorwarnung; **gale ~** Sturmwarnung *f*
warning light N Warnlicht *nt*
warning triangle N (*Aut*) Warndreieck *nt*
warp [wɔːp] VI (*wood etc*) sich verziehen ▶ VT (*fig: character*) entstellen ▶ N (*Textiles*) Kette *f*
warpath ['wɔːpɑːθ] N: **to be on the ~** auf dem Kriegspfad sein
warped [wɔːpt] ADJ (*wood*) verzogen; (*fig: character, sense of humour etc*) abartig

warrant ['wɔrnt] N (*Law: for arrest*) Haftbefehl *m*; (*also*: **search warrant**) Durchsuchungsbefehl *m* ▸ VT (*justify, merit*) rechtfertigen
warrant officer N (*Mil*) *Dienstgrad zwischen Offizier und Unteroffizier*
warranty ['wɔrəntɪ] N Garantie *f*; **under ~** (*Comm*) unter Garantie
warren ['wɔrən] N (*of rabbits*) Bau *m*; (*fig: of passages, streets*) Labyrinth *nt*
warring ['wɔ:rɪŋ] ADJ (*nations*) Krieg führend; (*interests*) gegensätzlich; (*factions*) verfeindet
warrior ['wɔrɪə^r] N Krieger *m*
Warsaw ['wɔ:sɔ:] N Warschau *nt*
warship ['wɔ:ʃɪp] N Kriegsschiff *nt*
wart [wɔ:t] N Warze *f*
wartime ['wɔ:taɪm] N: **in ~** im Krieg
wary ['wɛərɪ] ADJ (*person*) vorsichtig; **to be ~ about** *or* **of doing sth** Bedenken haben, etw zu tun
was [wɔz] PT *of* **be**
wash [wɔʃ] VT waschen; (*dishes*) spülen, abwaschen; (*remove grease, paint etc*) ausspülen ▸ VI (*person*) sich waschen ▸ N (*clothes etc*) Wäsche *f*; (*washing programme*) Waschgang *m*; (*of ship*) Kielwasser *nt*; **he was washed overboard** er wurde über Bord gespült; **to ~ over/against sth** (*sea etc*) über/gegen etw *acc* spülen; **to have a ~** sich waschen; **to give sth a ~** etw waschen
▸ **wash away** VT wegspülen
▸ **wash down** VT (*wall, car*) abwaschen; (*food: with wine etc*) hinunterspülen
▸ **wash off** VI sich herauswaschen ▸ VT abwaschen
▸ **wash out** VT (*stain*) herauswaschen
▸ **wash up** VI (*Brit: wash dishes*) spülen, abwaschen; (*US: have a wash*) sich waschen
Wash. (*US*) ABBR (*Post*) = **Washington**
washable ['wɔʃəbl] ADJ (*fabric*) waschbar; (*wallpaper*) abwaschbar
washbasin ['wɔʃbeɪsn], (*US*) **washbowl** ['wɔʃbəul] N Waschbecken *nt*
washcloth ['wɔʃklɔθ] (*US*) N Waschlappen *m*
washer ['wɔʃə^r] N (*on tap etc*) Dichtungsring *m*
washing ['wɔʃɪŋ] N Wäsche *f*
washing line (*Brit*) N Wäscheleine *f*
washing machine N Waschmaschine *f*
washing powder (*Brit*) N Waschpulver *nt*
Washington ['wɔʃɪŋtən] N Washington *nt*
washing-up [wɔʃɪŋ'ʌp] N Abwasch *m*; **to do the ~** spülen, abwaschen
washing-up liquid (*Brit*) N (Geschirr)spülmittel *nt*
wash-out ['wɔʃaut] (*inf*) N (*failed event*) Reinfall *m*
washroom ['wɔʃrum] (*US*) N Waschraum *m*
wasn't ['wɔznt] = **was not**
WASP, Wasp [wɔsp] (*US inf*) N ABBR (= *White Anglo-Saxon Protestant*) weißer angelsächsischer Protestant *m*
wasp [wɔsp] N Wespe *f*
waspish ['wɔspɪʃ] ADJ giftig
wastage ['weɪstɪdʒ] N Verlust *m*; **natural ~** natürliche Personalreduzierung
waste [weɪst] N Verschwendung *f*; (*rubbish*) Abfall *m* ▸ ADJ (*material*) Abfall-; (*left over: paper etc*) ungenutzt ▸ VT verschwenden; (*opportunity*) vertun; **wastes** NPL (*area of land*) Wildnis *f*; **it's a ~ of money** das ist Geldverschwendung; **to go to ~** umkommen; **to lay ~** (*area, town*) verwüsten
▸ **waste away** VI verkümmern
wastebasket ['weɪstbɑ:skɪt] (*US*) N = **wastepaper basket**
waste disposal unit (*Brit*) N Müllschlucker *m*
wasteful ['weɪstful] ADJ (*person*) verschwenderisch; (*process*) aufwendig
waste ground (*Brit*) N unbebautes Grundstück *nt*
wasteland ['weɪstlənd] N Ödland *nt*; (*in town*) ödes Gebiet *nt*; (*fig*) Einöde *f*
wastepaper basket ['weɪstpeɪpə-] (*Brit*) N Papierkorb *m*
waste pipe N Abflussrohr *nt*
waste products NPL Abfallprodukte *pl*
waster ['weɪstə^r] N Verschwender(in) *m(f)*; (*good-for-nothing*) Taugenichts *m*
watch [wɔtʃ] N (*also*: **wristwatch**) (Armband)uhr *f*; (*surveillance*) Bewachung *f*; (*Mil, Naut: group of guards*) Wachmannschaft *f*; (*Naut: spell of duty*) Wache *f* ▸ VT (*look at*) betrachten; (*: match, programme*) sich *dat* ansehen; (*spy on, guard*) beobachten; (*be careful of*) aufpassen auf *+acc* ▸ VI (*look*) zusehen; **to be on ~** Wache halten; **to keep a close ~ on sb/sth** jdn/etw genau im Auge behalten; **to ~ TV** fernsehen; **~ what you're doing!** pass auf!; **~ how you drive!** fahr vorsichtig!
▸ **watch out** VI aufpassen; **~ out!** Vorsicht!
watchband ['wɔtʃbænd] (*US*) N = **watchstrap**
watchdog ['wɔtʃdɔg] N (*dog*) Wachhund *m*; (*fig*) Aufpasser(in) *m(f)*
watchful ['wɔtʃful] ADJ wachsam
watchmaker ['wɔtʃmeɪkə^r] N Uhrmacher(in) *m(f)*
watchman ['wɔtʃmən] N (*irreg*) *see* **night watchman**
watch stem (*US*) N (*winder*) Krone *f*, Aufziehrädchen *nt*
watchstrap ['wɔtʃstræp] N Uhrarmband *nt*
watchword ['wɔtʃwə:d] N Parole *f*
water ['wɔ:tə^r] N Wasser *nt* ▸ VT (*plant*) gießen; (*garden*) bewässern ▸ VI (*eyes*) tränen; **a drink of ~** ein Schluck Wasser; **in British waters** in britischen (Hoheits)gewässern; **to pass ~** (*urinate*) Wasser lassen; **my mouth is watering** mir läuft das Wasser im Mund zusammen; **to make sb's mouth ~** jdm den Mund wässrig machen
▸ **water down** VT (*also fig*) verwässern
water biscuit N Cracker *m*
water cannon N Wasserwerfer *m*
water closet (*Brit: old*) N Wasserklosett *nt*
watercolour, (*US*) **watercolor** ['wɔ:təkʌlə^r] N (*picture*) Aquarell *nt*; **watercolours** NPL (*paints*) Wasserfarben *pl*
water-cooled ['wɔ:təku:ld] ADJ wassergekühlt
water-cooler ['wɔ:təku:lə^r] N Wasserkühler *m*; **~ talks** (*inf*) Flurfunk *m*
watercress ['wɔ:təkrɛs] N Brunnenkresse *f*

W

waterfall ['wɔːtəfɔːl] N Wasserfall *m*
waterfront ['wɔːtəfrʌnt] N (*at seaside*) Ufer *nt*; (*at docks*) Hafengegend *f*
water heater N Heißwassergerät *nt*
water hole N Wasserloch *nt*
water ice N Fruchteis *nt* (*auf Wasserbasis*)
watering can ['wɔːtərɪŋ-] N Gießkanne *f*
water level N Wasserstand *m*; (*of flood*) Pegelstand *m*
water lily N Seerose *f*
water line N Wasserlinie *f*
waterlogged ['wɔːtəlɔgd] ADJ (*ground*) unter Wasser
water main N Hauptwasserleitung *f*
watermark ['wɔːtəmɑːk] N (*on paper*) Wasserzeichen *nt*
watermelon ['wɔːtəmɛlən] N Wassermelone *f*
waterproof ['wɔːtəpruːf] ADJ (*trousers, jacket etc*) wasserdicht
water-repellent ['wɔːtərɪ'pɛlnt] ADJ Wasser abstoßend
watershed ['wɔːtəʃɛd] N (*Geog*) Wasserscheide *f*; (*fig*) Wendepunkt *m*
water-skiing ['wɔːtəskiːɪŋ] N Wasserski *nt*
water softener N Wasserenthärter *m*
water sports NPL Wassersport *m*
water tank N Wassertank *m*
watertight ['wɔːtətaɪt] ADJ wasserdicht; (*fig: excuse, case, agreement etc*) hieb- und stichfest
water vapour N Wasserdampf *m*
waterway ['wɔːtəweɪ] N Wasserstraße *f*
waterworks ['wɔːtəwəːks] N Wasserwerk *nt*; (*inf: fig: bladder*) Blase *f*
watery ['wɔːtərɪ] ADJ (*coffee, soup etc*) wässrig; (*eyes*) tränend
watt [wɔt] N Watt *nt*
wattage ['wɔtɪdʒ] N Wattleistung *f*
wattle ['wɔtl] N Flechtwerk *nt*
wattle and daub N Lehmgeflecht *nt*
wave [weɪv] N (*also fig*) Welle *f*; (*of hand*) Winken *nt* ▸ VI (*signal*) winken; (*branches*) sich hin und her bewegen; (*grass*) wogen; (*flag*) wehen ▸ VT (*hand, flag etc*) winken mit; (*gun, stick*) schwenken; (*hair*) wellen; **short/medium/long ~** (*Radio*) Kurz-/Mittel-/Langwelle *f*; **the new ~** (*Cine, Mus*) die neue Welle *f*; **he waved us over to his table** er winkte uns zu seinem Tisch hinüber; **to ~ goodbye to sb** jdm zum Abschied winken
▸ **wave aside** VT (*fig: suggestion etc*) zurückweisen
waveband ['weɪvbænd] N (*Radio*) Wellenbereich *m*
wavelength ['weɪvlɛŋθ] N (*Radio*) Wellenlänge *f*; **on the same ~** (*fig*) auf derselben Wellenlänge
waver ['weɪvə^r] VI (*voice*) schwanken; (*eyes*) zucken; (*love, person*) wanken
wavy ['weɪvɪ] ADJ (*line*) wellenförmig; (*hair*) wellig
wax [wæks] N Wachs *nt*; (*for sealing*) Siegellack *m*; (*in ear*) Ohrenschmalz *nt* ▸ VT (*floor*) bohnern; (*car, skis*) wachsen ▸ VI (*moon*) zunehmen
waxed [wækst] ADJ (*jacket*) gewachst
waxen [wæksn] ADJ (*face*) wachsbleich
waxworks ['wækswəːks] NPL (*models*) Wachsfiguren *pl* ▸ N (*place*) Wachsfigurenkabinett *nt*
way [weɪ] N Weg *m*; (*distance*) Strecke *f*; (*direction*) Richtung *f*; (*manner*) Art *f*; (*method*) Art und Weise *f*; (*habit*) Gewohnheit *f*; **which ~ to ...?** wo geht es zu ...?; **this ~, please** hier entlang, bitte; **on the ~** (*en route*) auf dem Weg, unterwegs; **to be on one's ~** auf dem Weg sein; **to fight one's ~ through a crowd** sich *acc* durch die Menge kämpfen; **to lie one's ~ out of sth** sich aus etw herauslügen; **to keep out of sb's ~** jdm aus dem Weg gehen; **it's a long ~ away** es ist weit entfernt; (*event*) das ist noch lange hin; **the village is rather out of the ~** das Dorf ist recht abgelegen; **to go out of one's ~ to do sth** sich sehr bemühen, etw zu tun; **to be in the ~** im Weg sein; **to lose one's ~** sich verirren; **under ~** (*project etc*) im Gang; **the ~ back** der Rückweg; **to make ~ (for sb/sth)** (für jdn/etw) Platz machen; **to get one's own ~** seinen Willen bekommen; **put it the right ~ up** (BRIT) stell es richtig herum hin; **to be the wrong ~ round** verkehrt herum sein; **he's in a bad ~** ihm geht es schlecht; **in a ~** in gewisser Weise; **in some ways** in mancher Hinsicht; **no ~!** (*inf*) kommt nicht infrage!; **by the ~ ...** übrigens ...; **"~ in"** (BRIT) „Eingang"; **"~ out"** (BRIT) „Ausgang"; **"give ~"** (BRIT *Aut*) „Vorfahrt beachten"; **~ of life** Lebensstil *m*
waybill ['weɪbɪl] N Frachtbrief *m*
waylay [weɪ'leɪ] VT (*irreg: like* **lay**) auflauern *+dat*; **to get waylaid** (*fig*) abgefangen werden
wayside ['weɪsaɪd] ADJ am Straßenrand ▸ N Straßenrand *m*; **to fall by the ~** (*fig*) auf der Strecke bleiben
way station (*US*) N (*Rail*) kleiner Bahnhof *m*; (*fig*) Zwischenstation *f*
wayward ['weɪwəd] ADJ (*behaviour*) eigenwillig; (*child*) eigensinnig
WC (BRIT) N ABBR (= *water closet*) WC *nt*
WCC N ABBR (= *World Council of Churches*) Weltkirchenrat *m*
we [wiː] PL PRON wir; **here we are** (*arriving*) da sind wir; (*finding sth*) na bitte
weak [wiːk] ADJ schwach; (*tea, coffee*) dünn; **to grow ~(er)** schwächer werden
weaken ['wiːkn] VI (*resolve, person*) schwächer werden; (*influence, power*) nachlassen ▸ VT schwächen
weak-kneed ['wiːk'niːd] ADJ (*fig*) schwächlich
weakling ['wiːklɪŋ] N Schwächling *m*
weakly ['wiːklɪ] ADV schwach
weakness ['wiːknɪs] N Schwäche *f*; **to have a ~ for** eine Schwäche haben für
wealth [wɛlθ] N Reichtum *m*; (*of details, knowledge etc*) Fülle *f*
wealth tax N Vermögenssteuer *f*
wealthy ['wɛlθɪ] ADJ wohlhabend, reich
wean [wiːn] VT (*also fig*) entwöhnen
weapon ['wɛpən] N Waffe *f*; **weapons of mass destruction** Massenvernichtungswaffen *pl*

wear [wɛəʳ] (*pt* **wore**, *pp* **worn**) VT (*clothes, shoes, beard*) tragen; (*put on*) anziehen ▶ VI (*last*) halten; (*become old: carpet, jeans*) sich abnutzen ▶ N (*damage*) Verschleiß *m*; (*use*): **I got a lot of/ very little ~ out of the coat** der Mantel hat lange/nicht sehr lange gehalten; **babywear** Babykleidung *f*; **sportswear** Sportkleidung *f*; **evening ~** Kleidung für den Abend; **to ~ a hole in sth** (*coat etc*) etw durchwetzen
▶ **wear away** VT verschleißen ▶ VI (*inscription etc*) verwittern
▶ **wear down** VT (*heels*) abnutzen; (*person, strength*) zermürben
▶ **wear off** VI (*pain etc*) nachlassen
▶ **wear on** VI sich hinziehen
▶ **wear out** VT (*shoes, clothing*) verschleißen; (*person, strength*) erschöpfen
wearable ['wɛərəbl] ADJ tragbar
wear and tear [-tɛəʳ] N Verschleiß *m*
wearer ['wɛərəʳ] N Träger(in) *m(f)*
wearily ['wɪərɪlɪ] ADV (*say, sit*) lustlos, müde
weariness ['wɪərɪnɪs] N (*tiredness*) Müdigkeit *f*
wearisome ['wɪərɪsəm] ADJ (*boring*) langweilig; (*tiring*) ermüdend
weary ['wɪərɪ] ADJ (*tired*) müde; (*dispirited*) lustlos ▶ VI: **to ~ of sb/sth** jds/etw *gen* überdrüssig werden
weasel ['wi:zl] N Wiesel *nt*
weather ['wɛðəʳ] N Wetter *nt* ▶ VT (*storm, crisis*) überstehen; (*rock, wood*) verwittern; **what's the ~ like?** wie ist das Wetter?; **under the ~** (*fig: ill*) angeschlagen
weather-beaten ['wɛðəbi:tn] ADJ (*face*) vom Wetter gegerbt; (*building, stone*) verwittert
weathercock ['wɛðəkɔk] N Wetterhahn *m*
weather forecast N Wettervorhersage *f*
weatherman ['wɛðəmæn] N (*irreg*) Mann *m* vom Wetteramt, Wetterfrosch *m* (*inf, hum*)
weatherproof ['wɛðəpru:f] ADJ wetterfest
weather report N Wetterbericht *m*
weather vane [-veɪn] N = **weathercock**
weave [wi:v] (*pt* **wove**, *pp* **woven**) VT (*cloth*) weben; (*basket*) flechten ▶ VI (*fig: pt, pp weaved: move in and out*) sich schlängeln
weaver ['wi:vəʳ] N Weber(in) *m(f)*
weaving ['wi:vɪŋ] N Weberei *f*
web [wɛb] N (*also fig*) Netz *nt*; (*Comput*): **the W~** das Web, das Internet; (*on duck's foot*) Schwimmhaut *f*
webbed ['wɛbd] ADJ (*foot*) Schwimm-
webbing ['wɛbɪŋ] N (*on chair*) Gewebe *nt*
webcam ['wɛbkæm] N Webcam *f*
webinar ['wɛbɪnɑ:ʳ] N (*Comput*) Webinar *nt*, Web-Seminar *nt*
webmail ['wɛbmeɪl] N (*Comput*) Webmail *nt*
web page N Webseite *f*
website ['wɛbsaɪt] N (*Comput*) Website *f*, Webseite *f*
wed [wɛd] (*pt, pp* **wedded**) VT, VI heiraten ▶ N: **the newly-weds** die Jungvermählten *pl*
Wed. ABBR (= *Wednesday*) Mi.
we'd [wi:d] = **we had; we would**
wedded ['wɛdɪd] PT, PP *of* **wed** ▶ ADJ: **to be ~ to sth** (*idea etc*) mit etw eng verbunden sein
wedding [wɛdɪŋ] N Hochzeit *f*; **silver/golden ~** silberne/goldene Hochzeit
wedding day N Hochzeitstag *m*
wedding dress N Hochzeitskleid *nt*
wedding present N Hochzeitsgeschenk *nt*
wedding ring N Trauring *m*
wedge [wɛdʒ] N Keil *m*; (*of cake*) Stück *nt* ▶ VT (*fasten*) festklemmen; (*pack tightly*) einkeilen
wedge-heeled shoes ['wɛdʒhi:ld-] NPL Schuhe *pl* mit Keilabsätzen
wedlock ['wɛdlɔk] N Ehe *f*
Wednesday ['wɛdnzdɪ] N Mittwoch *m*; *see also* **Tuesday**
wee [wi:] (SCOT) ADJ klein
weed [wi:d] N (*Bot*) Unkraut *nt*; (*pej: person*) Schwächling *m* ▶ VT (*garden*) jäten
▶ **weed out** VT (*fig*) aussondern
weedkiller ['wi:dkɪləʳ] N Unkrautvertilger *m*
weedy ['wi:dɪ] ADJ (*person*) schwächlich
week [wi:k] N Woche *f*; **once/twice a ~** einmal/ zweimal die Woche; **in two weeks' time** in zwei Wochen; **a ~ today/on Friday** heute/ Freitag in einer Woche
weekday ['wi:kdeɪ] N Wochentag *m*; (*Comm: Monday to Saturday*) Werktag *m*; **on weekdays** an Wochentagen/Werktagen
weekend [wi:k'ɛnd] N Wochenende *nt*; **this/ next/last ~** an diesem/am nächsten/am letzten Wochenende; **what are you doing at the ~?** was machen Sie am Wochenende?; **open at weekends** an Wochenenden geöffnet
weekly ['wi:klɪ] ADV wöchentlich ▶ ADJ (*newspaper*) Wochen- ▶ N (*newspaper*) Wochenzeitung *f*; (*magazine*) Wochenzeitschrift *f*
weep [wi:p] (*pt, pp* **wept**) VI (*person*) weinen; (*wound*) nässen
weeping willow ['wi:pɪŋ-] N (*tree*) Trauerweide *f*
weepy ['wi:pɪ] ADJ (*person*) weinerlich; (*film*) rührselig ▶ N (*film etc*) Schmachtfetzen *m*
weigh [weɪ] VT wiegen; (*fig: evidence, risks*) abwägen ▶ VI wiegen; **to ~ anchor** den Anker lichten
▶ **weigh down** VT niederdrücken
▶ **weigh out** VT (*goods*) auswiegen
▶ **weigh up** VT (*person, offer, risk*) abschätzen
weighbridge ['weɪbrɪdʒ] N Brückenwaage *f*
weighing machine ['weɪɪŋ-] N Waage *f*
weight [weɪt] N Gewicht *nt* ▶ VT (*fig*): **to be weighted in favour of sb/sth** jdn/etw begünstigen; **to be sold by ~** nach Gewicht verkauft werden; **to lose ~** abnehmen; **to put on ~** zunehmen; **weights and measures** Maße und Gewichte
weighting ['weɪtɪŋ] N (*allowance*) Zulage *f*
weightlessness ['weɪtlɪsnɪs] N Schwerelosigkeit *f*
weightlifter ['weɪtlɪftəʳ] N Gewichtheber *m*
weightlifting N Gewichtheben *nt*
weight limit N Gewichtsbeschränkung *f*
weight training N Krafttraining *nt*
weighty ['weɪtɪ] ADJ schwer; (*fig: important*) gewichtig

W

weir [wɪəʳ] N *(in river)* Wehr *nt*
weird [wɪəd] ADJ *(object, situation, effect)* komisch; *(person)* seltsam
weirdo ['wɪədəu] *(inf)* N verrückter Typ *m*
welcome ['wɛlkəm] ADJ willkommen ▶ N Willkommen *nt* ▶ VT begrüßen, willkommen heißen; **~ to London!** willkommen in London!; **to make sb ~** jdn freundlich aufnehmen; **you're ~ to try** du kannst es gern versuchen; **thank you — you're ~!** danke — nichts zu danken!
welcoming ['wɛlkəmɪŋ] ADJ *(smile, room)* einladend; *(person)* freundlich
weld [wɛld] N Schweißnaht *f* ▶ VT schweißen
welder ['wɛldəʳ] N *(person)* Schweißer(in) *m(f)*
welding ['wɛldɪŋ] N Schweißen *nt*
welfare ['wɛlfɛəʳ] N *(well-being)* Wohl *nt*; *(social aid)* Sozialhilfe *f*
welfare state N Wohlfahrtsstaat *m*
welfare work N Fürsorgearbeit *f*
well [wɛl] N *(for water)* Brunnen *m*; *(oil well)* Quelle *f* ▶ ADV gut; *(for emphasis with adj)* durchaus ▶ ADJ: **to be ~** *(person)* gesund sein ▶ EXCL nun!, na!; **as ~** *(in addition)* ebenfalls; **you might as ~ tell me** sag es mir ruhig; **he did as ~ as he could** er machte es so gut er konnte; **pretty as ~ as rich** sowohl hübsch als auch reich; **~ done!** gut gemacht!; **to do ~** *(person)* gut vorankommen; *(business)* gut gehen; **~ before dawn** lange vor Tagesanbruch; **~ over 40** weit über 40; **I don't feel ~** ich fühle mich nicht gut *or* wohl; **get ~ soon!** gute Besserung!; **~, as I was saying ...** also, wie ich bereits sagte, ... ▶ **well up** VI *(tears, emotions)* aufsteigen
we'll [wi:l] = **we will; we shall**
well-behaved ['wɛlbɪ'heɪvd] ADJ wohlerzogen
well-being ['wɛl'bi:ɪŋ] N Wohl(ergehen) *nt*
well-bred ['wɛl'brɛd] ADJ *(person)* gut erzogen
well-built ['wɛl'bɪlt] ADJ gut gebaut
well-chosen ['wɛl'tʃəuzn] ADJ gut gewählt
well-deserved ['wɛldɪ'zə:vd] ADJ wohlverdient
well-developed ['wɛldɪ'vɛləpt] ADJ gut entwickelt
well-disposed ['wɛl'dɪspəuzd] ADJ: **~ to(wards)** freundlich gesonnen *+dat*
well-done ADJ *(steak)* durchgebraten
well-dressed ['wɛl'drɛst] ADJ gut gekleidet
well-earned ['wɛl'ə:nd] ADJ *(rest)* wohlverdient
well-groomed ['wɛl'gru:md] ADJ gepflegt
well-heeled ['wɛl'hi:ld] *(inf)* ADJ betucht
well-informed ['wɛlɪn'fɔ:md] ADJ gut informiert
Wellington ['wɛlɪŋtən] N *(Geog)* Wellington *nt*
wellingtons ['wɛlɪŋtənz] NPL *(also:* **wellington boots**) Gummistiefel *pl*
well-kept ['wɛl'kɛpt] ADJ *(house, grounds)* gepflegt; *(secret)* gut gehütet
well-known ['wɛl'nəun] ADJ wohlbekannt
well-mannered ['wɛl'mænəd] ADJ wohlerzogen
well-meaning ['wɛl'mi:nɪŋ] ADJ *(person)* wohlmeinend; *(offer etc)* gut gemeint
well-nigh ['wɛl'naɪ] ADV: **~ impossible** geradezu unmöglich
well-off ['wɛl'ɔf] ADJ *(rich)* begütert
well-paid ADJ gut bezahlt
well-read ['wɛl'rɛd] ADJ belesen
well-spoken ['wɛl'spəukn] ADJ: **to be ~** sich gut *or* gewandt ausdrücken
well-stocked ['wɛl'stɔkt] ADJ gut bestückt
well-timed ['wɛl'taɪmd] ADJ gut abgepasst
well-to-do ['wɛltə'du:] ADJ wohlhabend
well-wisher ['wɛlwɪʃəʳ] N *(friend, admirer)* wohlmeinender Mensch *m*; **scores of well-wishers had gathered** eine große Gefolgschaft hatte sich versammelt; **letters from well-wishers** Briefe von Leuten, die es gut meinen
well-woman clinic ['wɛlwumən-] N ≈ Frauensprechstunde *f*
Welsh [wɛlʃ] ADJ walisisch ▶ N *(Ling)* Walisisch *nt*; **the Welsh** NPL die Waliser *pl*
Welshman ['wɛlʃmən] N *(irreg)* Waliser *m*
Welsh rarebit N überbackenes Käsebrot *nt*
Welshwoman ['wɛlʃwumən] N *(irreg)* Waliserin *f*
welter ['wɛltəʳ] N: **a ~ of** eine Flut von
went [wɛnt] PT *of* **go**
wept [wɛpt] PT, PP *of* **weep**
were [wə:ʳ] PT *of* **be**
we're [wɪəʳ] = **we are**
weren't [wə:nt] = **were not**
werewolf ['wɪəwulf] *(pl* **werewolves**) N Werwolf *m*
werewolves ['wɪəwulvz] NPL *of* **werewolf**
west [wɛst] N Westen *m* ▶ ADJ *(wind, side, coast)* West-, westlich ▶ ADV *(to or towards the west)* westwärts; **the W~** *(Pol)* der Westen
westbound ['wɛstbaund] ADJ *(traffic, carriageway)* in Richtung Westen
West Country (BRIT) N: **the ~** Südwestengland *nt*
westerly ['wɛstəlɪ] ADJ westlich
western ['wɛstən] ADJ westlich ▶ N *(Cine)* Western *m*
westerner ['wɛstənəʳ] N Abendländer(in) *m(f)*
westernized ['wɛstənaɪzd] ADJ *(society etc)* verwestlicht
West German ADJ westdeutsch ▶ N *(person)* Westdeutsche(r) *f(m)*
West Germany N *(formerly)* Bundesrepublik *f* Deutschland
West Indian ADJ westindisch ▶ N *(person)* Westinder(in) *m(f)*
West Indies [-'ɪndɪz] NPL: **the ~** Westindien *nt*
Westminster ['wɛstmɪnstəʳ] N Westminster *nt*; *(parliament)* das britische Parlament
westward ['wɛstwəd], **westwards** ['wɛstwədz] ADV westwärts
wet [wɛt] ADJ nass ▶ N (BRIT *Pol*) Gemäßigte(r) *f(m)*, Waschlappen *m (pej)*; **to get ~** nass werden; **"~ paint"** „frisch gestrichen"; **to be a ~ blanket** *(fig: pej: person)* ein(e) Spielverderber(in) *m(f)* sein; **to ~ one's pants/o.s.** sich *dat* in die Hosen machen
wetness ['wɛtnɪs] N Nässe *f*; *(of climate)* Feuchtigkeit *f*

wet suit N Taucheranzug *m*
we've [wi:v] = **we have**
whack [wæk] VT schlagen
whacked [wækt] (BRIT *inf*) ADJ (*exhausted*) erschlagen
whale [weɪl] N Wal *m*
whaler ['weɪlə^r] N Walfänger *m*
whaling ['weɪlɪŋ] N Walfang *m*
wharf [wɔ:f] (*pl* **wharves**) N Kai *m*
wharves [wɔ:vz] NPL *of* **wharf**

KEYWORD

what [wɔt] ADJ **1** (*in direct/indirect questions*) welche(r, s); **what colour/shape is it?** welche Farbe/Form hat es?; **for what reason?** aus welchem Grund?
2 (*in exclamations*) was für ein(e); **what a mess!** was für ein Durcheinander!; **what a fool I am!** was bin ich doch (für) ein Idiot!
▸ PRON (*interrogative, relative*) was; **what are you doing?** was machst du?; **what are you talking about?** wovon redest du?; **what is it called?** wie heißt das?; **what about me?** und ich?; **what about a cup of tea?** wie wärs mit einer Tasse Tee?; **what about going to the cinema?** sollen wir ins Kino gehen?; **I saw what you did/what was on the table** ich habe gesehen, was du getan hast/was auf dem Tisch war; **tell me what you're thinking about** sag mir, woran du denkst
▸ EXCL (*disbelieving*) was, wie; **what, no coffee!** was *or* wie, kein Kaffee?

whatever [wɔt'ɛvə^r] ADJ: **~ book** welches Buch auch immer ▸ PRON: **do ~ is necessary/you want** tun Sie, was nötig ist/was immer Sie wollen; **~ happens** was auch passiert; **no reason ~** *or* **whatsoever** überhaupt kein Grund; **nothing ~** *or* **whatsoever** überhaupt nichts
whatsoever [wɔtsəu'ɛvə^r] ADJ = **whatever**
wheat [wi:t] N Weizen *m*
wheatgerm ['wi:tdʒə:m] N Weizenkeim *m*
wheatmeal ['wi:tmi:l] N Weizenmehl *nt*
wheedle ['wi:dl] VT: **to ~ sb into doing sth** jdn beschwatzen, etw zu tun; **to ~ sth out of sb** jdm etw abluchsen
wheel [wi:l] N Rad *nt*; (*also*: **steering wheel**) Lenkrad *nt*; (*Naut*) Steuer *nt* ▸ VT (*pram etc*) schieben ▸ VI (*birds*) kreisen; (*person*: *also*: **wheel round**) sich herumdrehen
wheelbarrow ['wi:lbærəu] N Schubkarre *f*
wheelbase ['wi:lbeɪs] N Radstand *m*
wheelchair ['wi:ltʃɛə^r] N Rollstuhl *m*
wheel clamp N Parkkralle *f*
wheeler-dealer ['wi:lə'di:lə^r] (*pej*) N Geschäftemacher(in) *m(f)*
wheelie-bin ['wi:lɪbɪn] N Mülltonne *f* auf Rädern
wheeling ['wi:lɪŋ] N: **~ and dealing** (*pej*) Geschäftemacherei *f*
wheeze [wi:z] VI (*person*) keuchen ▸ N (*idea, joke etc*) Scherz *m*
wheezy ['wi:zɪ] ADJ (*person*) mit pfeifendem Atem; (*cough*) keuchend; (*breath*) pfeifend; (*laugh*) asthmatisch

KEYWORD

when [wɛn] ADV wann
▸ CONJ **1** (*at, during, after the time that*) wenn; **she was reading when I came in** als ich hereinkam, las sie gerade; **be careful when you cross the road** sei vorsichtig, wenn du die Straße überquerst
2 (*on, at which*) als; **on the day when I met him** am Tag, als ich ihn traf
3 (*whereas*) wo ... doch, obwohl; **why did you buy that when you can't afford it?** warum hast du das gekauft, obwohl du es dir nicht leisten kannst?

whenever [wɛn'ɛvə^r] ADV, CONJ (*any time that*) wann immer; (*every time that*) (jedes Mal,) wenn; **I go ~ I can** ich gehe, wann immer ich kann
where [wɛə^r] ADV, CONJ wo; **this is ~ ...** hier ...; **~ possible** so weit möglich; **~ are you from?** woher kommen Sie?
whereabouts [wɛərə'bauts] ADV wo ▸ N: **nobody knows his ~** keiner weiß, wo er ist
whereas [wɛər'æz] CONJ während
whereby [wɛə'baɪ] (*form*) ADV wonach
whereupon [wɛərə'pɔn] CONJ worauf
wherever [wɛər'ɛvə^r] CONJ (*position*) wo (auch) immer; (*motion*) wohin (auch) immer ▸ ADV (*surprise*) wo (um alles in der Welt); **sit ~ you like** nehmen Sie Platz, wo immer Sie wollen
wherewithal ['wɛəwɪðɔ:l] N: **the ~ (to do sth)** (*money*) das nötige Kleingeld(, um etw zu tun)
whet [wɛt] VT (*appetite*) anregen; (*tool*) schleifen
whether ['wɛðə^r] CONJ ob; **I don't know ~ to accept or not** ich weiß nicht, ob ich annehmen soll oder nicht; **~ you go or not** ob du gehst oder nicht; **it's doubtful ~ ...** es ist zweifelhaft, ob ...
whey ['weɪ] N Molke *f*

KEYWORD

which [wɪtʃ] ADJ **1** (*interrogative: direct, indirect*) welche(r, s); **which picture?** welches Bild?; **which books?** welche Bücher?; **which one?** welche(r, s)?
2: **in which case** in diesem Fall; **by which time** zu dieser Zeit
▸ PRON **1** (*interrogative*) welche(r, s); **which of you are coming?** wer von Ihnen kommt?; **I don't mind which** mir ist gleich, welche(r, s)
2 (*relative*) der/die/das; **the apple which you ate/which is on the table** der Apfel, den du gegessen hast/der auf dem Tisch liegt; **the chair on which you are sitting** der Stuhl, auf dem Sie sitzen; **the book of which you spoke** das Buch, wovon *or* von dem Sie sprachen; **he said he saw her, which is true** er sagte, er habe sie gesehen, was auch stimmt; **after which** wonach

W

whichever [wɪtʃˈɛvəʳ] ADJ: **take ~ book you want** nehmen Sie irgendein *or* ein beliebiges Buch; **~ book you take** welches Buch Sie auch nehmen

whiff [wɪf] N (*of perfume*) Hauch *m*; (*of petrol, smoke*) Geruch *m*; **to catch a ~ of sth** den Geruch von etw wahrnehmen

while [waɪl] N Weile *f* ▸ CONJ während; **for a ~** eine Weile (lang); **in a ~** gleich; **all the ~** die ganze Zeit (über); **I'll/we'll** *etc* **make it worth your ~** es wird sich für Sie lohnen
▸ **while away** VT (*time*) sich *dat* vertreiben

whilst [waɪlst] CONJ = **while**

whim [wɪm] N Laune *f*

whimper [ˈwɪmpəʳ] N (*cry, moan*) Wimmern *nt* ▸ VI wimmern

whimsical [ˈwɪmzɪkəl] ADJ wunderlich, seltsam; (*story*) kurios

whine [waɪn] N (*of pain*) Jammern *nt*; (*of engine, siren*) Heulen *nt* ▸ VI (*person*) jammern; (*dog*) jaulen; (*engine, siren*) heulen

whip [wɪp] N Peitsche *f*; (*Pol*) ≈ Fraktionsführer *m*; *siehe Info-Artikel* ▸ VT (*person, animal*) peitschen; (*cream, eggs*) schlagen; (*move quickly*): **to ~ sth out/off** etw blitzschnell hervorholen/wegbringen
▸ **whip up** VT (*cream*) schlagen; (*inf: meal*) hinzaubern; (*arouse: support*) anheizen; (*: people*) mitreißen

> Der Ausdruck **whip** bezieht sich in der Politik auf einen Abgeordneten, der für die Einhaltung der Parteidisziplin zuständig ist, besonders für die Anwesenheit und das Wahlverhalten der Abgeordneten im Unterhaus. Die whips fordern die Abgeordneten ihrer Partei schriftlich zur Anwesenheit auf und deuten die Wichtigkeit der Abstimmungen durch ein-, zwei-, oder dreimaliges Unterstreichen an, wobei dreimaliges Unterstreichen (3-line whip) strengsten Fraktionszwang bedeutet.

whiplash [ˈwɪplæʃ] N Peitschenhieb *m*; (*Med: also*: **whiplash injury**) Schleudertrauma *nt*

whipped cream [wɪpt-] N Schlagsahne *f*

whipping boy [ˈwɪpɪŋ-] N (*fig*) Prügelknabe *m*

whip-round [ˈwɪpraund] (BRIT *inf*) N (Geld)sammlung *f*

whirl [wəːl] VT (*arms, sword etc*) herumwirbeln ▸ VI wirbeln ▸ N (*of activity, pleasure*) Wirbel *m*; **to be in a ~** (*mind, person*) völlig verwirrt sein

whirlpool [ˈwəːlpuːl] N (*lit*) Strudel *m*

whirlwind [ˈwəːlwɪnd] N (*lit*) Wirbelwind *m*

whirr [wəːʳ] VI (*motor etc*) surren

whisk [wɪsk] N (*Culin*) Schneebesen *m* ▸ VT (*cream, eggs*) schlagen; **to ~ sb away** *or* **off** jdn in Windeseile wegbringen

whiskers [ˈwɪskəz] NPL (*of animal*) Barthaare *pl*; (*of man*) Backenbart *m*

whisky, (US, IRISH) **whiskey** [ˈwɪskɪ] N Whisky *m*

whisper [ˈwɪspəʳ] N Flüstern *nt*; (*fig: of wind*) Wispern *nt* ▸ VT, VI flüstern; **to ~ sth to sb** jdm etw zuflüstern

whispering [ˈwɪspərɪŋ] N Geflüster *nt*

whist [wɪst] (BRIT) N Whist *nt*

whistle [ˈwɪsl] N (*sound*) Pfiff *m*; (*object*) Pfeife *f* ▸ VI pfeifen ▸ VT: **to ~ a tune** eine Melodie pfeifen

whistle-stop [ˈwɪslstɔp] ADJ: **to make a ~ tour of** (*fig*) eine Rundreise machen durch; (*Pol*) eine Wahlkampfreise machen durch

Whit [wɪt] N = **Whitsun**

white [waɪt] ADJ weiß ▸ N (*colour*) Weiß *nt*; (*person*) Weiße(r) *f(m)*; (*of egg, eye*) Weiße(s) *nt*; **to turn** *or* **go ~** (*person: with fear*) weiß *or* bleich werden; (*: with age*) weiße Haare bekommen; (*hair*) weiß werden; **the whites** (*washing*) die Weißwäsche *f*; **tennis/cricket whites** weiße Tennis-/Krickettrikots

whitebait [ˈwaɪtbeɪt] N *essbare Jungfische (Heringe, Sprotten etc)*

whiteboard [ˈwaɪtbɔːd] N Weißwandtafel *f*; **interactive ~** interaktive Weißwandtafel

white coffee (BRIT) N Kaffee *m* mit Milch

white-collar worker [ˈwaɪtkɔlə-] N Schreibtischarbeiter(in) *m(f)*

white elephant N (*fig: venture*) Fehlinvestition *f*

white food N weiße Lebensmittel *pl*, weißes Essen *nt*

white goods NPL (*appliances*) große Haushaltsgeräte *pl*; (*linen etc*) Weißwaren *pl*

white-hot [waɪtˈhɔt] ADJ (*metal*) weiß glühend

> **White House**, eine weiß gestrichene Villa in Washington, ist der offizielle Wohnsitz des amerikanischen Präsidenten. Im weiteren Sinne bezieht sich dieser Begriff auf die Exekutive der amerikanischen Regierung.

white lie N Notlüge *f*

whiteness [ˈwaɪtnɪs] N Weiß *nt*

white noise N weißes Rauschen *nt*

whiteout [ˈwaɪtaut] N starkes Schneegestöber *nt*

white paper N (*Pol*) Weißbuch *nt*

whitewash [ˈwaɪtwɔʃ] N (*paint*) Tünche *f*; (*inf: Sport*) totale Niederlage *f* ▸ VT (*building*) tünchen; (*fig: incident, reputation*) reinwaschen

white water N: **white-water rafting** Wildwasserflößen *nt*

white wine N Weißwein *m*

whiting [ˈwaɪtɪŋ] N INV (*fish*) Weißling *m*

Whit Monday N Pfingstmontag *m*

Whitsun [ˈwɪtsn] N Pfingsten *nt*

whittle [ˈwɪtl] VT: **to ~ away** *or* **down** (*costs etc*) verringern

whizz [wɪz] VI: **to ~ past** *or* **by** vorbeisausen

whizz kid (*inf*) N Senkrechtstarter(in) *m(f)*

WHO N ABBR (= *World Health Organization*) Weltgesundheitsorganisation *f*, WHO *f*

KEYWORD

who [huː] PRON **1** (*interrogative*) wer; (*: acc*) wen; (*: dat*) wem; **who is it?, who's there?** wer ist da?; **who did you give it to?** wem hast du es gegeben?
2 (*relative*) der/die/das; **the man/woman who spoke to me** der Mann, der/die Frau, die mit mir gesprochen hat

whodunit, whodunnit [hu:'dʌnɪt] (*inf*) N Krimi *m*
whoever [hu:'ɛvəʳ] PRON: **~ finds it** wer (auch immer) es findet; **ask ~ you like** fragen Sie, wen Sie wollen; **~ he marries** ganz gleich *or* egal, wen er heiratet; **~ told you that?** wer um alles in der Welt hat dir das erzählt?
whole [həul] ADJ (*entire*) ganz; (*not broken*) heil ▸ N Ganze(s) *nt*; **the ~ lot (of it)** alles; **the ~ lot (of them)** alle; **the ~ (of the) time** die ganze Zeit; **~ villages were destroyed** ganze Dörfer wurden zerstört; **the ~ of** der/die/das ganze; **the ~ of Glasgow/Europe** ganz Glasgow/ Europa; **the ~ of the town** die ganze Stadt; **on the ~** im Ganzen (gesehen)
wholefood ['həulfu:d] N, **wholefoods** ['həulfu:dz] NPL Vollwertkost *f*
wholefood shop N ≈ Reformhaus *nt*
wholehearted [həul'hɑ:tɪd] ADJ (*agreement etc*) rückhaltlos
wholeheartedly [həul'hɑ:tɪdlɪ] ADV (*agree etc*) rückhaltlos
wholemeal ['həulmi:l] (BRIT) ADJ (*bread, flour*) Vollkorn-
whole note (US) N ganze Note *f*
wholesale ['həulseɪl] N (*business*) Großhandel *m* ▸ ADJ (*price*) Großhandels-; (*destruction etc*) umfassend ▸ ADV (*buy, sell*) im Großhandel
wholesaler ['həulseɪləʳ] N Großhändler *m*
wholesome ['həulsəm] ADJ (*food*) gesund; (*effect*) zuträglich; (*attitude*) positiv
wholewheat ['həulwi:t] ADJ = **wholemeal**
wholly ['həulɪ] ADV ganz und gar

KEYWORD

whom [hu:m] PRON **1** (*interrogative*: *acc*) wen; (: *dat*) wem; **whom did you see?** wen hast du gesehen?; **to whom did you give it?** wem hast du es gegeben?
2 (*relative*: *acc*) den/die/das; (: *dat*) dem/der/dem; **the man whom I saw/to whom I spoke** der Mann, den ich gesehen habe/mit dem ich gesprochen habe

whooping cough ['hu:pɪŋ-] N Keuchhusten *m*
whoosh [wuʃ] VI: **to ~ along/past/down** entlang-/vorbei-/hinuntersausen ▸ N Sausen *nt*; **the skiers whooshed past, skiers came by with a ~** die Skifahrer sausten vorbei
whopper ['wɔpəʳ] (*inf*) N (*lie*) faustdicke Lüge *f*; (*large thing*) Mordsding *nt*
whopping ['wɔpɪŋ] (*inf*) ADJ Riesen-, riesig
whore [hɔ:ʳ] (*inf, pej*) N Hure *f*

KEYWORD

whose [hu:z] ADJ **1** (*possessive*: *interrogative*) wessen; **whose book is this?, whose is this book?** wessen Buch ist das?, wem gehört das Buch?; **I don't know whose it is** ich weiß nicht, wem es gehört
2 (*possessive*: *relative*) dessen/deren/dessen; **the man whose son you rescued** der Mann, dessen Sohn du gerettet hast; **the woman whose car was stolen** die Frau, deren Auto gestohlen worden war
▸ PRON: **whose is this?** wem gehört das?; **I know whose it is** ich weiß, wem es gehört

Who's Who ['hu:z'hu:] N (*book*) Who's who *nt*

KEYWORD

why [waɪ] ADV warum; **why not?** warum nicht?
▸ CONJ warum; **I wonder why he said that** ich frage mich, warum er das gesagt hat; **that's not why I'm here** ich bin nicht deswegen hier; **the reason why** der Grund, warum *or* weshalb
▸ EXCL (*expressing surprise, shock*) na so was; (: *expressing annoyance*) ach; **why, yes (of course)** aber ja doch; **why, it's you!** na so was, du bists!

WI N ABBR (BRIT: = *Women's Institute*) *britischer Frauenverband* ▸ ABBR = **West Indies**; (*US Post*) = **Wisconsin**
wick [wɪk] N Docht *m*; **he gets on my ~** (BRIT *inf*) er geht mir auf den Geist
wicked ['wɪkɪd] ADJ (*crime, person*) böse; (*smile, wit*) frech; (*inf*: *prices*) unverschämt; (: *weather*) schrecklich
wicker ['wɪkəʳ] ADJ (*chair etc*) Korb-; (*basket*) Weiden-
wickerwork ['wɪkəʳwə:k] ADJ (*chair etc*) Korb-; (*basket*) Weiden- ▸ N (*objects*) Korbwaren *pl*
wicket ['wɪkɪt] N (*Cricket*: *stumps*) Tor *nt*, Wicket *nt*; (: *grass area*) Spielbahn *f*
wicket-keeper ['wɪkɪtki:pəʳ] N Torwächter *m*
wide [waɪd] ADJ breit; (*area*) weit; (*publicity*) umfassend ▸ ADV: **to open sth ~** etw weit öffnen; **it is 3 metres ~** es ist 3 Meter breit; **to go ~** vorbeigehen
wide-angle lens ['waɪdæŋgl-] N Weitwinkelobjektiv *nt*
wide-awake [waɪdə'weɪk] ADJ hellwach
wide-eyed [waɪd'aɪd] ADJ mit großen Augen; (*fig*) unschuldig, naiv
widely ['waɪdlɪ] ADV (*differ, vary*) erheblich; (*travel*) ausgiebig, viel; (*spaced*) weit; (*believed, known*) allgemein; **to be ~ read** (*reader*) sehr belesen sein
widen ['waɪdn] VT (*road, river*) verbreitern; (*one's experience*) erweitern ▸ VI sich verbreitern
wideness ['waɪdnɪs] N (*of road, river, gap*) Breite *f*
wide open ADJ (*window, eyes, mouth*) weit geöffnet
wide-ranging [waɪd'reɪndʒɪŋ] ADJ (*effects*) weitreichend; (*interview, survey*) umfassend
widescreen TV N Breitbildfernseher *m*
widespread ['waɪdspred] ADJ weitverbreitet
widget ['wɪdʒɪt] N (*Comput*) Minianwendung *f*, Widget *nt*
widow ['wɪdəu] N Witwe *f*
widowed ['wɪdəud] ADJ verwitwet
widower ['wɪdəuəʳ] N Witwer *m*
width [wɪdθ] N Breite *f*; (*in swimming pool*) (Quer)bahn *f*; **it's 7 metres in ~** es ist 7 Meter breit
widthways ['wɪdθweɪz] ADV der Breite nach
wield [wi:ld] VT (*sword*) schwingen; (*power*) ausüben

W

wife [waɪf] (*pl* **wives**) N Frau *f*
Wi-Fi ['waɪfaɪ] N Wi-Fi *nt*
wig [wɪg] N Perücke *f*
wigging ['wɪgɪŋ] (BRIT *inf*) N Standpauke *f*
wiggle ['wɪgl] VT wackeln mit
wiggly ['wɪglɪ] ADJ: **~ line** Schlangenlinie *f*
wigwam ['wɪgwæm] N Wigwam *m*
wiki ['wɪkɪ] N (*Internet*) Wiki *nt*
wild [waɪld] ADJ wild; (*weather*) rau, stürmisch; (*person, behaviour*) ungestüm; (*idea*) weit hergeholt; (*applause*) stürmisch ▶ N: **the ~** (*natural surroundings*) die freie Natur *f*; **the wilds** NPL die Wildnis; **I'm not ~ about it** ich bin nicht versessen *or* scharf darauf
wild card N (*Comput*) Wildcard *f*, Ersatzzeichen *nt*
wildcat ['waɪldkæt] N Wildkatze *f*
wildcat strike N wilder Streik *m*
wilderness ['wɪldənɪs] N Wildnis *f*
wildfire ['waɪldfaɪə^r] N: **to spread like ~** sich wie ein Lauffeuer ausbreiten
wild-goose chase [waɪld'gu:s-] N aussichtslose Suche *f*
wildlife ['waɪldlaɪf] N (*animals*) die Tierwelt *f*
wildly ['waɪldlɪ] ADV wild; (*very: romantic*) wild-; (*: inefficient*) furchtbar
wiles [waɪlz] NPL List *f*
wilful, (*US*) **willful** ['wɪlful] ADJ (*obstinate*) eigensinnig; (*deliberate*) vorsätzlich

KEYWORD

will [wɪl] AUX VB **1** (*forming future tense*): **I will finish it tomorrow** ich werde es morgen fertig machen, ich mache es morgen fertig; **will you do it? — yes I will/no I won't** machst du es? — ja/nein
2 (*in conjectures, predictions*): **that will be the postman** das ist bestimmt der Briefträger
3 (*in commands, requests, offers*): **will you sit down** (*politely*) bitte nehmen Sie Platz; (*angrily*) nun setz dich doch; **will you be quiet!** seid jetzt still!; **will you help me?** hilfst du mir?; **will you have a cup of tea?** möchten Sie eine Tasse Tee?; **I won't put up with it!** das lasse ich mir nicht gefallen!
▶ VT (*pt, pp* **willed**): **to will sb to do sth** jdn durch Willenskraft dazu bewegen, etw zu tun; **he willed himself to go on** er zwang sich dazu, weiterzumachen
▶ N (*volition*) Wille *m*; (*: testament*) Testament *nt*; **he did it against his will** er tat es gegen seinen Willen

willful ['wɪlful] (*US*) ADJ = **wilful**
willing ['wɪlɪŋ] ADJ (*having no objection*) gewillt; (*enthusiastic*) bereitwillig; **he's ~ to do it** er ist bereit, es zu tun; **to show ~** guten Willen zeigen
willingly ['wɪlɪŋlɪ] ADV bereitwillig
willingness ['wɪlɪŋnɪs] N (*readiness*) Bereitschaft *f*; (*enthusiasm*) Bereitwilligkeit *f*
will-o'-the-wisp ['wɪləðə'wɪsp] N Irrlicht *nt*; (*fig*) Trugbild *nt*
willow ['wɪləu] N (*tree*) Weide *f*; (*wood*) Weidenholz *nt*
willpower ['wɪl'pauə^r] N Willenskraft *f*
willy-nilly ['wɪlɪ'nɪlɪ] ADV (*willingly or not*) wohl oder übel
wilt [wɪlt] VI (*plant*) welken
Wilts [wɪlts] (BRIT) ABBR (*Post*) = **Wiltshire**
wily ['waɪlɪ] ADJ listig, raffiniert
wimp [wɪmp] (*inf, pej*) N Waschlappen *m*
wimpish ['wɪmpɪʃ] (*inf*) ADJ weichlich
win [wɪn] (*pt, pp* **won**) N Sieg *m* ▶ VT gewinnen ▶ VI siegen, gewinnen
▶ **win over** VT (*persuade*) gewinnen
▶ **win round** (BRIT) VT = **win over**
wince [wɪns] VI zusammenzucken
winch [wɪntʃ] N Winde *f*
Winchester disk ['wɪntʃɪstə-] N Winchesterplatte *f*
wind¹ [wɪnd] N (*air*) Wind *m*; (*Med*) Blähungen *pl*; (*breath*) Atem *m* ▶ VT (*take breath away from*) den Atem nehmen *+dat*; **the winds** NPL (*Mus*) die Bläser *pl*; **into** *or* **against the ~** gegen den Wind; **to get ~ of sth** (*fig*) von etw Wind bekommen; **to break ~** Darmwind entweichen lassen
wind² [waɪnd] (*pt, pp* **wound**) VT (*thread, rope, bandage*) wickeln; (*clock, toy*) aufziehen ▶ VI (*road, river*) sich winden
▶ **wind down** VT (*car window*) herunterdrehen; (*fig: production*) zurückschrauben
▶ **wind up** VT (*clock, toy*) aufziehen; (*debate*) abschließen
windbreak ['wɪndbreɪk] N Windschutz *m*
windbreaker ['wɪndbreɪkə^r] (*US*) N = **windcheater**
windcheater ['wɪndtʃi:tə^r] N Windjacke *f*
winder ['waɪndə^r] (BRIT) N (*on watch*) Krone *f*, Aufziehrädchen *nt*
windfall ['wɪndfɔ:l] N (*money*) unverhoffter Glücksfall *m*; (*apple*) Fallobst *nt*
wind farm ['wɪnd-] N Windpark *m*
winding ['waɪndɪŋ] ADJ gewunden
wind instrument ['wɪnd-] N Blasinstrument *nt*
windmill ['wɪndmɪl] N Windmühle *f*
window ['wɪndəu] N (*also Comput*) Fenster *nt*; (*in shop*) Schaufenster *nt*
window box N Blumenkasten *m*
window cleaner N Fensterputzer(in) *m(f)*
window dresser N Schaufensterdekorateur(in) *m(f)*
window envelope N Fensterumschlag *m*
window frame N Fensterrahmen *m*
window ledge N Fenstersims *m*
window pane N Fensterscheibe *f*
window-shopping ['wɪndəuʃɔpɪŋ] N Schaufensterbummel *m*; **to go ~** einen Schaufensterbummel machen
windowsill ['wɪndəusɪl] N Fensterbank *f*
windpipe ['wɪndpaɪp] N Luftröhre *f*
wind power ['wɪnd-] N Windkraft *f*, Windenergie *f*
windscreen ['wɪndskri:n] N Windschutzscheibe *f*
windscreen washer N Scheibenwaschanlage *f*

windscreen wiper [-waɪpəʳ] N Scheibenwischer *m*
windshield ['wɪndʃi:ld] (US) N = **windscreen**
windsurfing ['wɪndsə:fɪŋ] N Windsurfen *nt*
windswept ['wɪndswɛpt] ADJ (*place*) vom Wind gepeitscht; (*person*) vom Wind zerzaust
wind tunnel ['wɪnd-] N Windkanal *m*
wind turbine ['wɪnd-] N Windturbine *f*
windy ['wɪndɪ] ADJ windig; **it's ~** es ist windig
wine [waɪn] N Wein *m* ▸ VT: **to ~ and dine sb** jdm zu einem guten Essen ausführen
wine bar N Weinlokal *nt*
wine cellar N Weinkeller *m*
wine glass N Weinglas *nt*
wine list N Weinkarte *f*
wine merchant N Weinhändler(in) *m(f)*
wine tasting [-teɪstɪŋ] N Weinprobe *f*
wine waiter N Weinkellner *m*
wing [wɪŋ] N (*of bird, insect, plane*) Flügel *m*; (*of building*) Trakt *m*; (*of car*) Kotflügel *m*; **the wings** NPL (*Theat*) die Kulissen *pl*
winger ['wɪŋəʳ] N (*Sport*) Flügelspieler(in) *m(f)*
wing mirror (BRIT) N Seitenspiegel *m*
wing nut N Flügelmutter *f*
wingspan ['wɪŋspæn] N Flügelspannweite *f*
wingspread ['wɪŋsprɛd] N = **wingspan**
wink [wɪŋk] N (*of eye*) Zwinkern *m* ▸ VI (*with eye*) zwinkern; (*light etc*) blinken
winkle [wɪŋkl] N Strandschnecke *f*
winner ['wɪnəʳ] N (*of race, competition*) Sieger(in) *m(f)*; (*of prize*) Gewinner(in) *m(f)*
winning ['wɪnɪŋ] ADJ (*team, entry*) siegreich; (*shot, goal*) entscheidend; (*smile*) einnehmend; *see also* **winnings**
winning post N (*lit*) Zielpfosten *m*; (*fig*) Ziel *nt*
winnings ['wɪnɪŋz] NPL Gewinn *m*
winsome ['wɪnsəm] ADJ (*expression*) gewinnend; (*person*) reizend
winter ['wɪntəʳ] N Winter *m* ▸ VI (*birds*) überwintern; **in ~** im Winter
winter sports NPL Wintersport *m*
wintry ['wɪntrɪ] ADJ (*weather, day*) winterlich, Winter-
wipe [waɪp] VT wischen; (*dry*) abtrocknen; (*clean*) abwischen; (*erase: tape*) löschen ▸ N: **to give sth a ~** etw abwischen; **to ~ one's nose** sich *dat* die Nase putzen
▸ **wipe off** VT abwischen
▸ **wipe out** VT (*destroy: city etc*) auslöschen
▸ **wipe up** VT (*mess*) aufwischen
wire ['waɪəʳ] N Draht *m*; (*US: telegram*) Telegramm *nt* ▸ VT (*US*): **to ~ sb** jdm telegrafieren; (*electrical fitting: also:* **wire up**) anschließen
wire brush N Drahtbürste *f*
wire cutters NPL Drahtschere *f*
wireless ['waɪəlɪs] (BRIT: *old*) N Funk *m*; (*set*) Rundfunkgerät *nt*
wireless phone N schnurloses Telefon *nt*
wire netting N Maschendraht *m*
wire service (US) N Nachrichtenagentur *f*
wire-tapping ['waɪə'tæpɪŋ] N Anzapfen *nt* von Leitungen
wiring ['waɪərɪŋ] N elektrische Leitungen *pl*
wiry ['waɪərɪ] ADJ (*person*) drahtig; (*hair*) borstig
Wis. (US) ABBR (*Post*) = **Wisconsin**
wisdom ['wɪzdəm] N (*of person*) Weisheit *f*; (*of action, remark*) Klugheit *f*
wisdom tooth N Weisheitszahn *m*
wise ADJ (*person*) weise; (*action, remark*) klug; **I'm none the wiser** ich bin genauso klug wie vorher
▸ **wise up** (*inf*) VI: **to ~ up to sth** hinter etw *acc* kommen
...wise [waɪz] SUFF: **timewise/moneywise** *etc* zeitmäßig/geldmäßig *etc*
wisecrack ['waɪzkræk] N Witzelei *f*
wisely ['waɪzlɪ] ADV klug, weise
wish [wɪʃ] N Wunsch *m* ▸ VT wünschen; **best wishes** (*for birthday etc*) herzliche Grüße, alle guten Wünsche; **with best wishes** (*in letter*) mit den besten Wünschen *or* Grüßen; **give her my best wishes** grüßen Sie sie herzlich von mir; **to make a ~** sich *dat* etw wünschen; **to ~ sb goodbye** jdm Auf Wiedersehen sagen; **he wished me well** er wünschte mir alles Gute; **to ~ to do sth** etw tun wollen; **to ~ sth on sb** jdm etw wünschen; **to ~ for sth** sich *dat* etw wünschen
wishbone ['wɪʃbəun] N Gabelbein *nt*
wishful ['wɪʃful] ADJ: **it's ~ thinking** das ist reines Wunschdenken
wishy-washy ['wɪʃɪ'wɔʃɪ] (*inf*) ADJ (*colour*) verwaschen; (*person*) farblos; (*ideas*) nichtssagend
wisp [wɪsp] N (*of grass*) Büschel *nt*; (*of hair*) Strähne *f*; (*of smoke*) Fahne *f*
wistful ['wɪstful] ADJ wehmütig
wit [wɪt] N (*wittiness*) geistreiche Art *f*; (*person*) geistreicher Mensch *m*; (*presence of mind*) Verstand *m*; **wits** NPL (*intelligence*) Verstand *m*; **to be at one's wits' end** mit seinem Latein am Ende sein; **to have one's wits about one** einen klaren Kopf haben; **to ~** (*namely*) und zwar
witch [wɪtʃ] N Hexe *f*
witchcraft ['wɪtʃkrɑ:ft] N Hexerei *f*
witch doctor N Medizinmann *m*
witch-hunt ['wɪtʃhʌnt] N (*fig*) Hexenjagd *f*

KEYWORD

with [wɪð] PREP **1** (*accompanying, in the company of*) mit; **we stayed with friends** wir wohnten bei Freunden; **I'll be with you in a minute** einen Augenblick, ich bin sofort da; **I'm with you** (*I understand*) ich verstehe; **to be with it** (*inf: up-to-date*) auf dem Laufenden sein; (*: alert*) da sein
2 (*descriptive, indicating manner*) mit; **the man with the grey hat/blue eyes** der Mann mit dem grauen Hut/den blauen Augen; **with tears in her eyes** mit Tränen in den Augen; **red with anger** rot vor Wut

withdraw [wɪθ'drɔ:] VT (*irreg: like* **draw**) (*object, offer*) zurückziehen; (*remark*) zurücknehmen

▸ VI (*troops*) abziehen; (*person*) sich zurückziehen; **to ~ money** (*from bank*) Geld abheben; **to ~ into o.s.** sich in sich *acc* selbst zurückziehen

withdrawal [wɪθ'drɔːəl] N (*of offer, remark*) Zurücknahme *f*; (*of troops*) Abzug *m*; (*of participation*) Ausstieg *m*; (*of services*) Streichung *f*; (*of money*) Abhebung *f*

withdrawal symptoms NPL Entzugserscheinungen *pl*

withdrawn [wɪθ'drɔːn] PP *of* **withdraw** ▸ ADJ (*person*) verschlossen

wither ['wɪðə^r] VI (*plant*) verwelken

withered ['wɪðəd] ADJ (*plant*) verwelkt; (*limb*) verkümmert

withhold [wɪθ'həuld] VT (*irreg: like* **hold**) vorenthalten

within [wɪð'ɪn] PREP (*place*) innerhalb *+gen*; (*time, distance*) innerhalb von ▸ ADV innen; **~ reach** in Reichweite; **~ sight (of)** in Sichtweite (*+gen*); **~ the week** vor Ende der Woche; **~ a mile of** weniger als eine Meile entfernt von; **~ an hour** innerhalb einer Stunde; **~ the law** im Rahmen des Gesetzes

without [wɪð'aut] PREP ohne; **~ a coat** ohne Mantel; **~ speaking** ohne zu sprechen; **it goes ~ saying** das versteht sich von selbst; **~ anyone knowing** ohne dass jemand davon wusste

withstand [wɪθ'stænd] VT (*irreg: like* **stand**) widerstehen *+dat*

witness ['wɪtnɪs] N Zeuge *m*, Zeugin *f* ▸ VT (*event*) sehen, Zeuge/Zeugin sein *+gen*; (*fig*) miterleben; **to bear ~ to sth** Zeugnis für etw ablegen; **~ for the prosecution/defence** Zeuge/Zeugin der Anklage/Verteidigung; **to ~ to sth** etw bezeugen; **to ~ having seen sth** bezeugen, etw gesehen zu haben

witness box N Zeugenstand *m*

witness stand (US) N = **witness box**

witticism ['wɪtɪsɪzəm] N geistreiche Bemerkung *f*

witty ['wɪtɪ] ADJ geistreich

wives [waɪvz] NPL *of* **wife**

wizard ['wɪzəd] N Zauberer *m*

wizened ['wɪznd] ADJ (*person*) verhutzelt; (*fruit, vegetable*) verschrumpelt

wk ABBR = **week**

Wm. ABBR = **William**

WO N ABBR (*Mil*) = **warrant officer**

wobble ['wɔbl] VI wackeln; (*legs*) zittern

wobbly ['wɔblɪ] ADJ (*hand, voice*) zitt(e)rig; (*table, chair*) wack(e)lig; **to feel ~** sich wack(e)lig fühlen

woe [wəu] N (*sorrow*) Jammer *m*; (*misfortune*) Kummer *m*

woeful ['wəuful] ADJ traurig

wok [wɔk] N Wok *m*

woke [wəuk] PT *of* **wake**

woken ['wəukn] PP *of* **wake**

wolf [wulf] (*pl* **wolves**) N Wolf *m*

wolves [wulvz] NPL *of* **wolf**

woman ['wumən] (*pl* **women**) N Frau *f*; **~ friend** Freundin *f*; **~ teacher** Lehrerin *f*; **young ~** junge Frau; **women's page** Frauenseite *f*

woman doctor N Ärztin *f*

womanize ['wumənaɪz] (*pej*) VI hinter Frauen her sein

womanly ['wumənlɪ] ADJ (*virtues etc*) weiblich

womb [wuːm] N Mutterleib *m*; (*Med*) Gebärmutter *f*

women ['wɪmɪn] NPL *of* **woman**

women's lib ['wɪmɪnz-] (*inf*) N Frauenbefreiung *f*

Women's Liberation Movement, Women's Movement N Frauenbewegung *f*

won [wʌn] PT, PP *of* **win**

wonder ['wʌndə^r] N (*miracle*) Wunder *nt*; (*awe*) Verwunderung *f* ▸ VI: **to ~ whether/why** *etc* sich fragen, ob/warum *etc*; **it's no ~ (that)** es ist kein Wunder(, dass); **to ~ at** (*marvel at*) staunen über *+acc*; **to ~ about** sich *dat* Gedanken machen über *+acc*; **I ~ if you could help me** könnten Sie mir vielleicht helfen

wonderful ['wʌndəful] ADJ wunderbar

wonderfully ['wʌndəfəlɪ] ADV wunderbar

wonky ['wɔŋkɪ] (BRIT *inf*) ADJ wack(e)lig

wont [wəunt] N: **as is his ~** wie er zu tun pflegt

won't [wəunt] = **will not**

woo [wuː] VT (*woman, audience*) umwerben

wood [wud] N (*timber*) Holz *nt*; (*forest*) Wald *m* ▸ CPD Holz-

woodcarving ['wudkɑːvɪŋ] N (*act, object*) Holzschnitzerei *f*

wooded ['wudɪd] ADJ bewaldet

wooden ['wudn] ADJ (*also fig*) hölzern

woodland ['wudlənd] N Waldland *nt*

woodpecker ['wudpɛkə^r] N Specht *m*

wood pigeon N Ringeltaube *f*

woodwind ['wudwɪnd] ADJ (*instrument*) Holzblasinstrument *nt*; **the ~** die Holzbläser *pl*

woodwork ['wudwəːk] N (*skill*) Holzarbeiten *pl*

woodworm ['wudwəːm] N Holzwurm *m*

woof [wuf] N (*of dog*) Wau *nt* ▸ VI kläffen; **~, ~!** wau, wau!

wool [wul] N Wolle *f*; **to pull the ~ over sb's eyes** (*fig*) jdn hinters Licht führen

woollen, (US) **woolen** ['wulən] ADJ (*hat*) Woll-, wollen

woollens ['wulənz] NPL Wollsachen *pl*

woolly, (US) **wooly** ['wulɪ] ADJ (*socks, hat etc*) Woll-; (*fig: ideas*) schwammig; (*person*) verworren ▸ N (*pullover*) Wollpullover *m*

woozy ['wuːzɪ] (*inf*) ADJ duselig

Worcs (BRIT) ABBR (*Post*) = **Worcestershire**

word [wəːd] N Wort *nt*; (*news*) Nachricht *f* ▸ VT (*letter, message*) formulieren; **~ for ~** Wort für Wort, (wort)wörtlich; **what's the ~ for "pen" in German?** was heißt „pen" auf Deutsch?; **to put sth into words** etw in Worte fassen; **in other words** mit anderen Worten; **to break/keep one's ~** sein Wort brechen/halten; **to have words with sb** eine Auseinandersetzung mit jdm haben; **to have a ~ with sb** mit jdm sprechen; **I'll take your ~ for it** ich verlasse mich auf Sie; **to send ~ of sth** etw verlauten lassen; **to leave ~ (with sb/for sb) that ...** (bei jdm/für jdn) die Nachricht hinterlassen, dass ...; **by ~ of mouth** durch mündliche Überlieferung

wording ['wə:dɪŋ] N (*of message, contract etc*) Wortlaut *m*, Formulierung *f*
word-perfect ['wə:d'pə:fɪkt] ADJ: **to be ~** den Text perfekt beherrschen
word processing N Textverarbeitung *f*
word processor [-prəusɛsə^r] N Textverarbeitungssystem *nt*
wordwrap ['wə:dræp] N (*Comput*) (automatischer) Zeilenumbruch *m*
wordy ['wə:dɪ] ADJ (*book*) langatmig; (*person*) wortreich
wore [wɔ:^r] PT *of* **wear**
work [wə:k] N Arbeit *f*; (*Art, Liter*) Werk *nt* ▸ VI arbeiten; (*mechanism*) funktionieren; (*be successful*: *medicine etc*) wirken ▸ VT (*clay, wood, land*) bearbeiten; (*mine*) arbeiten in; (*machine*) bedienen; (*create*: *effect, miracle*) bewirken; **to go to ~** zur Arbeit gehen; **to set to ~, to start ~** sich an die Arbeit machen; **to be at ~ (on sth)** (an etw *dat*) arbeiten; **to be out of ~** arbeitslos sein; **to be in ~** eine Stelle haben; **to ~ hard** hart arbeiten; **to ~ loose** (*part, knot*) sich lösen; **to ~ on the assumption that ...** von der Annahme ausgehen, dass ...
▸ **work on** VT FUS (*task*) arbeiten an *+dat*; (*person*: *influence*) bearbeiten; **he's working on his car** er arbeitet an seinem Auto
▸ **work out** VI (*plans etc*) klappen; (*Sport*) trainieren ▸ VT (*problem*) lösen; (*plan*) ausarbeiten; **it works out at 100 pounds** es ergibt 100 Pfund
▸ **work up** VT: **to get worked up** sich aufregen
workable ['wə:kəbl] ADJ (*system*) durchführbar; (*solution*) brauchbar
workaholic [wə:kə'hɔlɪk] N Arbeitstier *nt*
workbench ['wə:kbɛntʃ] N Werkbank *f*
worker ['wə:kə^r] N Arbeiter(in) *m(f)*; **office ~** Büroarbeiter(in) *m(f)*
workforce ['wə:kfɔ:s] N Arbeiterschaft *f*
work-in ['wə:kɪn] (BRIT) N Fabrikbesetzung *f*
working ['wə:kɪŋ] ADJ (*day, conditions*) Arbeits-; (*population*) arbeitend; (*mother*) berufstätig; **a ~ knowledge of English** (*adequate*) Grundkenntnisse in Englisch
working capital N Betriebskapital *nt*
working class N Arbeiterklasse *f*
working-class ['wə:kɪŋ'klɑ:s] ADJ (*family, town*) Arbeiter-
working man N (*irreg*) Arbeiter *m*
working order N: **in ~** in betriebsfähigem Zustand
working party (BRIT) N Ausschuss *m*
working relationship N Arbeitsbeziehung *f*
working week N Arbeitswoche *f*
work-in-progress ['wə:kɪn'prəugrɛs] N laufende Arbeiten *pl*
workload ['wə:kləud] N Arbeitsbelastung *f*
workman ['wə:kmən] N (*irreg*) Arbeiter *m*
workmanship ['wə:kmənʃɪp] N Arbeitsqualität *f*
workmate ['wə:kmeɪt] N Arbeitskollege *m*, Arbeitskollegin *f*
workout ['wə:kaut] N Fitnesstraining *nt*
work permit N Arbeitserlaubnis *f*
works [wə:ks] (BRIT) N (*factory*) Fabrik *f*, Werk *nt* ▸ NPL (*of clock*) Uhrwerk *nt*; (*of machine*) Getriebe *nt*
work sheet N Arbeitsblatt *nt*
workshop ['wə:kʃɔp] N (*building*) Werkstatt *f*; (*practical session*) Workshop *nt*
work station N Arbeitsplatz *m*; (*Comput*) Workstation *f*
work-study ['wə:kstʌdɪ] N Arbeitsstudie *f*
worktop ['wə:ktɔp] N Arbeitsfläche *f*
work-to-rule ['wə:ktə'ru:l] (BRIT) N Dienst *m* nach Vorschrift
world [wə:ld] N Welt *f* ▸ CPD (*champion, power, war*) Welt-; **all over the ~** auf der ganzen Welt; **to think the ~ of sb** große Stücke auf jdn halten; **what in the ~ is he doing?** was um alles in der Welt macht er?; **to do sb a** *or* **the ~ of good** jdm unwahrscheinlich guttun; **W~ War One/Two** der Erste/Zweite Weltkrieg; **out of this ~** fantastisch
World Cup N: **the ~** (*Football*) die Fußballweltmeisterschaft *f*
world-famous [wə:ld'feɪməs] ADJ weltberühmt
worldly ['wə:ldlɪ] ADJ weltlich; (*knowledgeable*) weltgewandt
world music N World Music *f*, *Richtung der Popmusik, die musikalische Stilelemente der Dritten Welt verwendet*
World Series (*US*) N *Endrunde der Baseball-Weltmeisterschaft zwischen den Tabellenführern der Spitzenligen*
World War N: **~ I/II, the First/Second ~** der Erste/Zweite Weltkrieg
worldwide ['wə:ld'waɪd] ADJ, ADV weltweit
World Wide Web N World Wide Web *nt*
worm [wə:m] N Wurm *m*
▸ **worm out** VT: **to ~ sth out of sb** jdm etw entlocken
worn [wɔ:n] PP *of* **wear** ▸ ADJ (*carpet*) abgenutzt; (*shoe*) abgetragen
worn-out ['wɔ:naut] ADJ (*object*) abgenutzt; (*person*) erschöpft
worried ['wʌrɪd] ADJ besorgt; **to be ~ about sth** sich wegen etw Sorgen machen
worrier ['wʌrɪə^r] N: **to be a ~** sich ständig Sorgen machen
worrisome ['wʌrɪsəm] ADJ besorgniserregend
worry ['wʌrɪ] N Sorge *f* ▸ VT beunruhigen ▸ VI sich *dat* Sorgen machen; **to ~ about** *or* **over sth/sb** sich um etw/jdn Sorgen machen
worrying ['wʌrɪɪŋ] ADJ beunruhigend
worse [wə:s] ADJ schlechter, schlimmer ▸ ADV schlechter ▸ N Schlechtere(s) *nt*, Schlimmere(s) *nt*; **to get ~** (*situation etc*) sich verschlechtern *or* verschlimmern; **he is none the ~ for it** er hat keinen Schaden dabei erlitten; **so much the ~ for you!** um so schlimmer für dich!; **a change for the ~** eine Wendung zum Schlechten
worsen ['wə:sn] VT verschlimmern ▸ VI sich verschlechtern
worse off ADJ (*also fig*) schlechter dran; **he is now ~ than before** er ist jetzt schlechter dran als zuvor

W

worship ['wəːʃɪp] N (*act*) Verehrung *f* ▶ VT (*god*) anbeten; (*person, thing*) verehren; **Your W~** (BRIT: *to mayor*) verehrter Herr Bürgermeister; (: *to judge*) Euer Ehren
worshipper ['wəːʃɪpə^r] N (*in church etc*) Kirchgänger(in) *m(f)*; (*fig*) Anbeter(in) *m(f)*, Verehrer(in) *m(f)*
worst [wəːst] ADJ schlechteste(r, s), schlimmste(r, s) ▶ ADV am schlimmsten ▶ N Schlimmste(s) *nt*; **at ~** schlimmstenfalls; **if the ~ comes to the ~** wenn alle Stricke reißen
worst-case scenario ['wəːstkeɪs-] N Schlimmstfallszenario *nt*
worsted ['wustɪd] N Kammgarn *nt*
worth [wəːθ] N Wert *m* ▶ ADJ: **to be ~** wert sein; **£2 ~ of apples** Äpfel für £ 2; **how much is it ~?** was *or* wie viel ist es wert?; **it's ~ it** (*effort, time*) es lohnt sich; **it's ~ every penny** es ist sein Geld wert
worthless ['wəːθlɪs] ADJ wertlos
worthwhile ['wəːθ'waɪl] ADJ lohnend
worthy [wəːðɪ] ADJ (*person*) würdig; (*motive*) ehrenwert; **~ of** wert *+gen*

KEYWORD

would [wud] AUX VB **1** (*conditional tense*): **if you asked him he would do it** wenn du ihn fragtest, würde er es tun; **if you had asked him he would have done it** wenn du ihn gefragt hättest, hätte er es getan
2 (*in offers, invitations, requests*): **would you like a biscuit?** möchten Sie ein Plätzchen?; **would you ask him to come in?** würden Sie ihn bitten hereinzukommen?
3 (*in indirect speech*): **I said I would do it** ich sagte, ich würde es tun
4 (*emphatic*): **it WOULD have to snow today!** ausgerechnet heute musste es schneien!
5 (*insistence*): **she wouldn't behave** sie wollte sich partout nicht benehmen
6 (*conjecture*): **it would have been midnight** es mochte etwa Mitternacht gewesen sein; **it would seem so** so scheint es wohl
7 (*indicating habit*): **he would go there on Mondays** er ging montags immer dorthin; **he would spend every day on the beach** er verbrachte jeden Tag am Strand

would-be ['wudbiː] ADJ (*singer, writer*) Möchtegern-
wouldn't ['wudnt] = **would not**
wound[1] [waund] PT, PP *of* **wind**[2]
wound[2] [wuːnd] N Wunde *f* ▶ VT verwunden; **wounded in the leg** am Bein verletzt
wove [wəuv] PT *of* **weave**
woven ['wəuvn] PP *of* **weave**
WP N ABBR = **word processing; word processor** ▶ ABBR (BRIT *inf*: = *weather permitting*) bei günstiger Witterung
WPC (BRIT) N ABBR (= *woman police constable*) Polizistin *f*
wpm ABBR (= *words per minute*) Worte pro Minute (*beim Maschineschreiben*)
WRAC (BRIT) N ABBR (= *Women's Royal Army Corps*) *Frauenkorps der Armee*
WRAF (BRIT) N ABBR (= *Women's Royal Air Force*) *Frauenkorps der Luftwaffe*
wrangle ['ræŋgl] N Gerangel *nt* ▶ VI: **to ~ with sb over sth** sich mit jdm um etw zanken
wrap [ræp] N (*shawl*) Umhang *m*; (*cape*) Cape *nt* ▶ VT einwickeln; (*pack*: *also*: **wrap up**) einpacken; (*wind*: *tape etc*) wickeln; **under wraps** (*fig*: *plan*) geheim
wrapper ['ræpə^r] N (*on chocolate*) Papier *nt*; (BRIT: *of book*) Umschlag *m*
wrapping paper ['ræpɪŋ-] N (*brown*) Packpapier *nt*; (*fancy*) Geschenkpapier *nt*
wrath [rɔθ] N Zorn *m*
wreak [riːk] VT: **to ~ havoc (on)** verheerenden Schaden anrichten (bei); **to ~ vengeance** *or* **revenge on sb** Rache an jdm üben
wreath [riːθ] (*pl* **wreaths**) N Kranz *m*
wreck [rɛk] N Wrack *nt*; (*vehicle*) Schrotthaufen *m* ▶ VT kaputt machen; (*car*) zu Schrott fahren; (*chances*) zerstören
wreckage ['rɛkɪdʒ] N (*of car, plane, building*) Trümmer *pl*; (*of ship*) Wrackteile *pl*
wrecker ['rɛkə^r] (US) N (*breakdown van*) Abschleppwagen *m*
Wren (BRIT) N ABBR *weibliches Mitglied der britischen Marine*
wren [rɛn] N (*Zool*) Zaunkönig *m*
wrench [rɛntʃ] N (*Tech*) Schraubenschlüssel *m*; (*tug*) Ruck *m*; (*fig*) schmerzhaftes Erlebnis *nt* ▶ VT (*pull*) reißen; (*injure, arm, back*) verrenken; **to ~ sth from sb** jdm etw entreißen
wrest [rɛst] VT: **to ~ sth from sb** jdm etw abringen
wrestle ['rɛsl] VI: **to ~ (with sb)** (mit jdm) ringen; **to ~ with a problem** mit einem Problem kämpfen
wrestler ['rɛslə^r] N Ringer(in) *m(f)*
wrestling ['rɛslɪŋ] N Ringen *nt*; (*also*: **all-in wrestling**) Freistilringen *nt*
wrestling match N Ringkampf *m*
wretch [rɛtʃ] N: **poor ~** (*man*) armer Schlucker *m*; (*woman*) armes Ding *nt*; **little ~!** (*often humorous*) kleiner Schlingel!
wretched ['rɛtʃɪd] ADJ (*poor*) erbärmlich; (*unhappy*) unglücklich; (*inf*: *damned*) elend
wriggle ['rɪgl] VI (*person*: *also*: **wriggle about**) zappeln; (*fish*) sich winden; (*snake etc*) sich schlängeln ▶ N Zappeln *nt*
wring [rɪŋ] (*pt, pp* **wrung**) VT (*wet clothes*) auswringen; (*hands*) wringen; (*neck*) umdrehen; **to ~ sth out of sth/sb** (*fig*) etw/jdm etw abringen
wringer ['rɪŋə^r] N Mangel *f*
wringing ['rɪŋɪŋ] ADJ (*also*: **wringing wet**) tropfnass
wrinkle ['rɪŋkl] N Falte *f* ▶ VT (*nose, forehead etc*) runzeln ▶ VI (*skin, paint etc*) sich runzeln
wrinkled ['rɪŋkld] ADJ (*fabric, paper*) zerknittert; (*surface*) gekräuselt; (*skin*) runzlig
wrinkly ['rɪŋklɪ] ADJ = **wrinkled**
wrist [rɪst] N Handgelenk *nt*

wristband ['rɪstbænd] (BRIT) N (*of shirt*) Manschette *f*; (*of watch*) Armband *nt*
wristwatch ['rɪstwɔtʃ] N Armbanduhr *f*
writ [rɪt] N (*Law*) (gerichtliche) Verfügung *f*; **to issue a ~ against sb, serve a ~ on sb** eine Verfügung gegen jdn erlassen
write [raɪt] (*pt* **wrote**, *pp* **written**) VT schreiben; (*cheque*) ausstellen ▶ VI schreiben; **to ~ to sb** jdm schreiben
▶ **write away** VI: **to ~ away for sth** etw anfordern
▶ **write down** VT aufschreiben
▶ **write off** VT (*debt, project*) abschreiben; (*wreck: car etc*) zu Schrott fahren ▶ VI = **write away**
▶ **write out** VT (*put in writing*) schreiben; (*cheque, receipt etc*) ausstellen
▶ **write up** VT (*report etc*) schreiben
write-off ['raɪtɔf] N (*Aut*) Totalschaden *m*
write-protected ['raɪtprə'tɛktɪd] ADJ (*Comput*) schreibgeschützt
writer ['raɪtə^r] N (*author*) Schriftsteller(in) *m(f)*; (*of report, document etc*) Verfasser(in) *m(f)*
write-up ['raɪtʌp] N (*review*) Kritik *f*
writhe [raɪð] VI sich krümmen
writing ['raɪtɪŋ] N Schrift *f*; (*of author*) Arbeiten *pl*; (*activity*) Schreiben *nt*; **in ~** schriftlich; **in my own ~** in meiner eigenen Handschrift
writing case N Schreibmappe *f*
writing desk N Schreibtisch *m*
writing paper N Schreibpapier *nt*
written ['rɪtn] PP *of* **write**
WRNS (BRIT) N ABBR (= *Women's Royal Naval Service*) *Frauenkorps der Marine*
wrong [rɔŋ] ADJ falsch; (*morally bad*) unrecht; (*unfair*) ungerecht ▶ ADV falsch ▶ N (*injustice*) Unrecht *nt*; (*evil*): **right and ~** Gut und Böse ▶ VT (*treat unfairly*) unrecht *or* ein Unrecht tun *+dat*; **to be ~** (*answer*) falsch sein; (*in doing, saying sth*) unrecht haben; **you are ~ to do it** es ist ein Fehler von dir, das zu tun; **it's ~ to steal, stealing is ~** Stehlen ist unrecht; **you are ~ about that, you've got it ~** da hast du unrecht; **what's ~?** wo fehlts?; **there's nothing ~** es ist alles in Ordnung; **to go ~** (*person*) einen Fehler machen; (*plan*) schiefgehen; (*machine*) versagen; **to be in the ~** im Unrecht sein
wrongdoer ['rɔŋdu:ə^r] N Übeltäter(in) *m(f)*
wrong-foot [rɔŋ'fut] VT: **to ~ sb** (*Sport*) jdn auf dem falschen Fuß erwischen; (*fig*) jdn im falschen Moment erwischen
wrongful ['rɔŋful] ADJ unrechtmäßig
wrongly ['rɔŋlɪ] ADV falsch; (*unjustly*) zu Unrecht
wrong number N (*Tel*): **you've got the ~** Sie sind falsch verbunden
wrong side N: **the ~** (*of material*) die linke Seite
wrote [rəut] PT *of* **write**
wrought [rɔ:t] ADJ: **~ iron** Schmiedeeisen *nt*
wrung [rʌŋ] PT, PP *of* **wring**
WRVS (BRIT) N ABBR (= *Women's Royal Voluntary Service*) *karitativer Frauenverband*
wry [raɪ] ADJ (*smile, humour*) trocken
wt. ABBR = **weight**
WV (US) ABBR (*Post*) = **West Virginia**
W.Va. (US) ABBR (*Post*) = **West Virginia**
WWW N ABBR (= *World Wide Web*) WWW *nt*
WY, (US) **Wyo.** ABBR (*Post*) = **Wyoming**
WYSIWYG ['wɪzɪwɪg] ABBR (*Comput*: = *what you see is what you get*) WYSIWYG *nt*

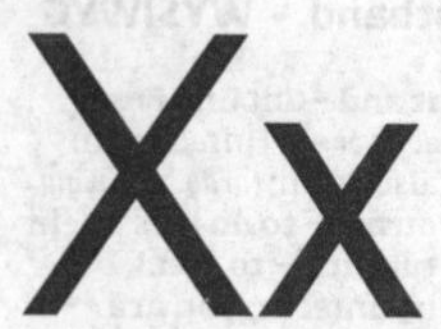

X, x [ɛks] N (*letter*) X *nt*, x *nt*; (BRIT *Cine: formerly*) *Klassifikation für nicht jugendfreie Filme*; **X for Xmas** ≈ X wie Xanthippe

xenophobia [zenəˈfəʊbɪə] N Ausländerfeindlichkeit *f*

Xerox® [ˈzɪərɔks] N (*also*: **Xerox machine**) Xerokopierer *m*; (*photocopy*) Xerokopie *f* ▶ VT xerokopieren

XL ABBR (= *extra large*) XL

Xmas [ˈɛksməs] N ABBR = **Christmas**

XML ABBR (*Comput*: = *extensible markup language*) XML

X-rated [ˈɛksˈreɪtɪd] (*US*) ADJ (*film*) nicht jugendfrei

X-ray [ˈɛksreɪ] N Röntgenstrahl *m*; (*photo*) Röntgenbild *nt* ▶ VT röntgen; **to have an ~** sich röntgen lassen

xylophone [ˈzaɪləfəun] N Xylofon *nt*

Y, y [waɪ] N (*letter*) Y *nt*, y *nt*; **Y for Yellow, Y for Yoke** (*US*) ≈ Y wie Ypsilon
yacht [jɔt] N Jacht *f*
yachting ['jɔtɪŋ] N Segeln *nt*
yachtsman ['jɔtsmən] N (*irreg*) Segler *m*
yam [jæm] N Jamswurzel *f*, Yamswurzel *f*
Yank [jæŋk] (*pej*) N Ami *m*
yank [jæŋk] VT reißen ▸ N Ruck *m*; **to give sth a ~** mit einem Ruck an etw *dat* ziehen
Yankee ['jæŋkɪ] (*pej*) N = **Yank**
yap [jæp] VI (*dog*) kläffen
yard [jɑːd] N (*of house etc*) Hof *m*; (*US: garden*) Garten *m*; (*measure*) Yard *nt* (*= 0,91 m*); **builder's ~** Bauhof *m*
yardstick ['jɑːdstɪk] N (*fig*) Maßstab *m*
yarn [jɑːn] N (*thread*) Garn *nt*; (*tale*) Geschichte *f*
yawn [jɔːn] VI gähnen ▸ N Gähnen *nt*
yawning ['jɔːnɪŋ] ADJ (*gap*) gähnend
yd ABBR = **yard**
yeah [jɛə] (*inf*) ADV ja
year [jɪəʳ] N Jahr *nt*; (*referring to wine*) Jahrgang *m*; **every ~** jedes Jahr; **this ~** dieses Jahr; **a** *or* **per ~** pro Jahr; **~ in, ~ out** jahrein, jahraus; **to be 8 years old** 8 Jahre alt sein; **an eight-~-old child** ein achtjähriges Kind
yearbook ['jɪəbuk] N Jahrbuch *nt*
yearling ['jɪəlɪŋ] N (*horse*) Jährling *m*
yearly ['jɪəlɪ] ADJ, ADV (*once a year*) jährlich; **twice ~** zweimal jährlich *or* im Jahr
yearn [jəːn] VI: **to ~ for sth** sich nach etwas sehnen; **to ~ to do sth** sich danach sehnen, etw zu tun
yearning ['jəːnɪŋ] N: **to have a ~ for sth** ein Verlangen nach etw haben; **to have a ~ to do sth** ein Verlangen danach haben, etw zu tun
yeast [jiːst] N Hefe *f*
yell [jɛl] N Schrei *m* ▸ VI schreien
yellow ['jɛləu] ADJ gelb ▸ N Gelb *nt*
yellow fever N Gelbfieber *nt*
yellowish ['jɛləuɪʃ] ADJ gelblich
Yellow Pages® NPL: **the ~** die gelben Seiten *pl*, das Branchenverzeichnis
Yellow Sea N: **the ~** das Gelbe Meer
yelp [jɛlp] N Jaulen *nt* ▸ VI jaulen
Yemen ['jɛmən] N: **(the) ~** (der) Jemen
Yemeni ['jɛmənɪ] ADJ jemenitisch ▸ N Jemenit(in) *m(f)*
yen [jɛn] N (*currency*) Yen *m*; (*craving*): **to have a ~ for** Lust auf etw haben; **to have a ~ to do sth** Lust darauf haben, etw zu tun
yeoman ['jəumən] N (*irreg*): **Y~ of the Guard** (königlicher) Leibgardist *m*
yes [jɛs] ADV ja; (*in reply to negative*) doch ▸ N Ja *nt*; **to say ~** Ja sagen; **to answer ~** mit Ja antworten
yes-man ['jɛsmæn] (*pej*) N (*irreg*) Jasager *m*
yesterday ['jɛstədɪ] ADV gestern ▸ N Gestern *nt*; **~ morning/evening** gestern Morgen/Abend; **~'s paper** die Zeitung von gestern; **the day before ~** vorgestern; **all day ~** gestern den ganzen Tag (lang)
yet [jɛt] ADV noch ▸ CONJ jedoch; **it is not finished ~** es ist noch nicht fertig; **must you go just ~?** musst du schon gehen?; **the best ~** der/die/das bisher Beste; **as ~** bisher; **it'll be a few days ~** es wird noch ein paar Tage dauern; **not for a few days ~** nicht in den nächsten paar Tagen; **~ again** wiederum
yew [juː] N (*tree*) Eibe *f*; (*wood*) Eibenholz *nt*
Y-fronts® ['waɪfrʌnts] NPL (Herren-)Slip *m* (*mit y-förmiger Vorderseite*)
YHA (BRIT) N ABBR (*= Youth Hostels Association*) *britischer Jugendherbergsverband*
Yiddish ['jɪdɪʃ] N Jiddisch *nt*
yield [jiːld] N (*Agr*) Ertrag *m*; (*Comm*) Gewinn *m* ▸ VT (*produce: results, profit*) hervorbringen; (*surrender: control etc*) abtreten ▸ VI (*surrender, give way*) nachgeben; (*US Aut*) die Vorfahrt achten; **a ~ of 5%** ein Ertrag *or* Gewinn von 5%
YMCA N ABBR (*organization: = Young Men's Christian Association*) CVJM *m*
yob ['jɔb], (BRIT) **yobbo** ['jɔbəu] (*inf, pej*) N Rowdy *m*
yodel ['jəudl] VI jodeln
yoga ['jəugə] N Yoga *m or nt*
yoghourt, yogourt ['jəugət] N = **yoghurt**
yoghurt, yogurt ['jəugət] N Joghurt *m or nt*
yoke [jəuk] N (*also fig*) Joch *nt* ▸ VT (*oxen: also:* **yoke together**) einspannen
yolk [jəuk] N (*of egg*) Eigelb *nt*, Dotter *m*
yonder ['jɔndəʳ] ADV: **(over) ~** dort drüben ▸ ADJ: **from ~ house** von dem Haus dort drüben
yonks [jɔŋks] (*inf*) N: **for ~** seit einer Ewigkeit
Yorks [jɔːks] (BRIT) ABBR (*Post*) = **Yorkshire**

KEYWORD

you [ju:] PRON **1** (*subject: familiar: singular*) du; (*: plural*) ihr; (*: polite*) Sie; **you Germans enjoy your food** ihr Deutschen esst gern gut
2 (*object: direct: familiar: singular*) dich; (*: plural*) euch; (*: polite*) Sie; (*: indirect: familiar: singular*) dir; (*: plural*) euch; (*: polite*) Ihnen; **I know you** ich kenne dich/euch/Sie; **I gave it to you** ich habe es dir/euch/Ihnen gegeben; **if I were you I would ...** an deiner/eurer/Ihrer Stelle würde ich ...
3 (*after prep, in comparisons*): **it's for you** es ist für dich/euch/Sie; **she's younger than you** sie ist jünger als du/ihr/Sie
4 (*impersonal: one*) man; **you never know** man weiß nie

you'd [ju:d] = **you had; you would**
you'll [ju:l] = **you will; you shall**
young [jʌŋ] ADJ jung; **the young** NPL (*of animal*) die Jungen *pl*; (*people*) die jungen Leute *pl*; **a ~ man** ein junger Mann; **a ~ lady** eine junge Dame
younger [jʌŋgəʳ] ADJ jünger; **the ~ generation** die jüngere Generation
youngish ['jʌŋɪʃ] ADJ recht jung
youngster ['jʌŋstəʳ] N Kind *nt*
your [jɔ:ʳ] ADJ (*familiar: sing*) dein/deine/dein; (*: pl*) euer/eure/euer; (*polite*) Ihr/Ihre/Ihr; (*one's*) sein; **you mustn't eat with ~ fingers** man darf nicht mit den Fingern essen; *see also* **my**
you're [juəʳ] = **you are**
yours [jɔ:z] PRON (*familiar: sing*) deiner/deine/dein(e)s; (*: pl*) eurer/eure/eures; (*polite*) Ihrer/Ihre/Ihres; **a friend of ~** ein Freund von dir/Ihnen; **is it ~?** gehört es dir/Ihnen?; **~ sincerely/faithfully** mit freundlichen Grüßen; *see also* **mine²**
yourself [jɔ:'sɛlf] PRON (*reflexive: familiar: sing: acc*) dich; (*: dat*) dir; (*: pl*) euch; (*: polite*) sich; (*emphatic*) selbst; **you ~ told me** das haben Sie mir selbst gesagt
yourselves [jɔ:'sɛlvz] PL PRON (*reflexive: familiar*) euch; (*: polite*) sich; (*emphatic*) selbst; *see also* **oneself**
youth [ju:θ] N Jugend *f*; (*young man: pl youths*) Jugendliche(r) *m*; **in my ~** in meiner Jugend
youth club N Jugendklub *m*
youthful ['ju:θful] ADJ jugendlich
youthfulness ['ju:θfəlnɪs] N Jugendlichkeit *f*
youth hostel N Jugendherberge *f*
youth movement N Jugendbewegung *f*
you've [ju:v] = **you have**
yowl [jaul] N (*of animal*) Jaulen *nt*; (*of person*) Heulen *nt*
yr ABBR (= *year*) J.
YT (CANADA) ABBR = **Yukon Territory**
yuck factor ['jʌkfæktəʳ] N (*inf*) Igitt-Faktor *m*
yucky ['jʌkɪ] ADJ (*inf*) eklig
Yugoslav ['ju:gəuslɑ:v] (*formerly*) ADJ jugoslawisch ▶ N Jugoslawe *m*, Jugoslawin *f*
Yugoslavia ['ju:gəu'slɑ:vɪə] (*formerly*) N Jugoslawien *nt*
Yugoslavian ['ju:gəu'slɑ:vɪən] (*formerly*) ADJ jugoslawisch
Yule log [ju:l-] N *Biskuitrolle mit Überzug, die zu Weihnachten gegessen wird*
yummy ['jʌmɪ] ADJ (*inf*) lecker
yuppie ['jʌpɪ] (*inf*) N Yuppie *m* ▶ ADJ yuppiehaft; (*job, car*) Yuppie-
YWCA N ABBR (*organization:* = *Young Women's Christian Association*) CVJF *m*

Zz

Z, z [zɛd, (*US*) zi:] N (*letter*) Z *nt*, z *nt*; **Z for Zebra** ≈ Z wie Zacharias
Zaire [zɑ:'i:əʳ] N Zaire *nt*
Zambia ['zæmbɪə] N Sambia *nt*
Zambian ['zæmbɪən] ADJ sambisch ▶ N Sambier(in) *m(f)*
zany ['zeɪnɪ] ADJ verrückt
zap [zæp] VT (*Comput: delete*) löschen
zapping N (*TV*) ständiges Umschalten, Zapping *nt*
zeal [zi:l] N Eifer *m*
zealot ['zɛlət] N Fanatiker(in) *m(f)*
zealous ['zɛləs] ADJ eifrig
zebra ['zi:brə] N Zebra *nt*
zebra crossing (BRIT) N Zebrastreifen *m*
zenith ['zɛnɪθ] N (*also fig*) Zenit *m*
zero ['zɪərəu] N (*number*) Null *f* ▶ VI: **to ~ in on sth** (*target*) etw einkreisen; **5 degrees below ~** 5 Grad unter null
zero hour N die Stunde X
zero option N (*esp Pol*) Nulllösung *f*
zero-rated ['zi:rəureɪtɪd] (BRIT) ADJ (*Tax*) mehrwertsteuerfrei
zest [zɛst] N (*for life*) Begeisterung *f*; (*of orange*) Orangenschale *f*
zigzag ['zɪgzæg] N Zickzack *m* ▶ VI sich im Zickzack bewegen
Zimbabwe [zɪm'bɑ:bwɪ] N Zimbabwe *nt*
Zimbabwean [zɪm'bɑ:bwɪən] ADJ zimbabwisch
zimmer® ['zɪməʳ] N (*also*: **zimmer frame**) Laufgestell *nt*
zinc [zɪŋk] N Zink *nt*
Zionism ['zaɪənɪzəm] N Zionismus *m*
Zionist ['zaɪənɪst] ADJ zionistisch ▶ N Zionist(in) *m(f)*
zip [zɪp] N (*also*: **zip fastener**) Reißverschluss *m* ▶ VT (*dress etc: also*: **zip up**) den Reißverschluss zumachen an *+dat*
zip code (*US*) N Postleitzahl *f*
Zip file® N (*Comput*) ZIP-Datei® *f*
zipper ['zɪpəʳ] (*US*) N = **zip**
zit [zɪt] N (*inf*) Pickel *m*
zither ['zɪðəʳ] N Zither *f*
zodiac ['zəudɪæk] N Tierkreis *m*
zombie ['zɔmbɪ] N (*fig*) Schwachkopf *m*
zone [zəun] N (*also Mil*) Zone *f*, Gebiet *nt*; (*in town*) Bezirk *m*
zonked [zɔŋkt] (*inf*) ADJ (*tired*) total geschafft; (*high on drugs*) high; (*drunk*) voll
zoo [zu:] N Zoo *m*
zoological [zuə'lɔdʒɪkl] ADJ zoologisch
zoologist [zu'ɔlədʒɪst] N Zoologe *m*, Zoologin *f*
zoology [zu:'ɔlədʒɪ] N Zoologie *f*
zoom [zu:m] VI: **to ~ past** vorbeisausen; **to ~ in (on sth/sb)** (*Phot, Cine*) (etw/jdn) näher heranholen
zoom lens N Zoomobjektiv *nt*
zucchini [zu:'ki:nɪ] (*US*) N Zucchini *pl*
Zulu ['zu:lu:] ADJ (*tribe, culture*) Zulu- ▶ N (*person*) Zulu *mf*; (*Ling*) Zulu *nt*
Zürich ['zjuərɪk] N Zürich *nt*

Grammar
Grammatik

Using the grammar

The Grammar section deals systematically and comprehensively with all the information you will need in order to communicate accurately in German. The user-friendly layout explains the grammar point on a left-hand page, leaving the facing page free for illustrative examples. The numbers, → 1 etc, direct you to the relevant example in every case.

The Grammar section also provides invaluable guidance on the danger of translating English structures by identical structures in German. Use of Numbers and Punctuation are important areas covered towards the end of the section. Finally, the index lists the main words and grammatical terms in both English and German.

Abbreviations

acc	*feminine*
ctd	*continued*
dat	*dative*
fem	*feminine*
intr	*intransitive*
masc	*masculine*
neut	*neuter*
nom	*nominative*
tr	*transitive*

Contents

Tense Formation

Tenses are either simple or compound. Once you know how to form the past participle, compound tenses are similar for all verbs (see pages 22–29). To form simple tenses you need to know whether a verb is weak, strong or mixed.

In German these are:

Present indicative → 1
Imperfect indicative → 2
Present subjunctive → 3
Imperfect subjunctive → 4

Subjunctive forms are widely used in German, especially for indirect or reported speech (see pages 66–67).

The simple tenses are formed by adding endings to a verb stem. The endings show the number, person and tense of the subject of the verb → 5

The types of verb you need to know to form simple tenses are:

Strong verbs (pages 12–15), those whose vowel usually changes in forming the imperfect indicative → 6

Weak verbs (pages 8–11), which are usually completely regular and have no vowel changes. Their endings differ from those of strong verbs → 7

Mixed verbs (pages 16–17), which have a vowel change like strong verbs, but the endings of weak verbs → 8

Examples

1	ich hole	I fetch I am fetching I do fetch
2	ich holte	I fetched I was fetching I used to fetch
3	(dass) ich hole	(that) I fetch/I fetched
4	(dass) ich holte	(that) I fetched
5	ich hole wir holen du holtest	I fetch we fetch you fetched
6	singen er singt er sang	to sing he sings he sang
7	holen er holt er holte	to fetch he fetches he fetched
8	bringen er bringt er bringte	to bring he brings he brought

Weak Verbs

Weak verbs are usually regular in conjugation. Their simple tenses are formed as follows:

Present and imperfect tenses are formed by adding the endings shown below to the verb stem. This stem is formed by removing the -en ending of the infinitive (the form found in the dictionary) → 1

Where the infinitive of a weak verb ends in -eln or -ern, only the -n is removed to form the verb stem → 2

The endings are as follows:

	PRESENT INDICATIVE	PRESENT SUBJUNCTIVE	
1st singular	-e	-e	
2nd	-st	-est	
3rd	-t	-e	→ 3
1st plural	-en	-en	
2nd	-t	-et	
3rd	-en	-en	

	IMPERFECT INDICATIVE	IMPERFECT SUBJUNCTIVE	
1st singular	-te	-te	
2nd	-test	-test	
3rd	-te	-te	→ 3
1st plural	-ten	-ten	
2nd	-tet	-tet	
3rd	-ten	-ten	

❶ **INFINITIVE** | | **STEM**

holen	to fetch	**hol-**
machen	to make	**mach-**
kauen	to chew	**kau-**

❷ **INFINITIVE** | | **STEM**

wandern	to roam	**wander-**
handeln	to trade, to act	**handel-**

❸ holen **to fetch**

PRESENT INDICATIVE	PRESENT SUBJUNCTIVE	
ich hol**e**	ich hol**e**	I fetch
du hol**st**	du hol**est**	you fetch
er/sie/es hol**t**	er/sie/es hol**e**	he/she/it fetches
wir hol**en**	wir hol**en**	we fetch
ihr hol**t**	ihr hol**et**	you (*plural*) fetch
sie/Sie hol**en**	sie/Sie hol**en**	they/you (*polite*) fetch

IMPERFECT INDICATIVE AND IMPERFECT SUBJUNCTIVE
(*These tenses are identical for weak verbs*)

ich hol**te**	I fetched
du hol**test**	you fetched
er/sie/es hol**te**	he/she/it fetched
wir hol**ten**	we fetched
ihr hol**tet**	you (*plural*) fetched
sie/Sie hol**ten**	they/you (*polite*) fetched

Weak Verbs *continued*

Where the stem of a weak verb ends in -d or -t, an extra -e- is inserted before those endings where this will ease pronunciation → ❶

Weak verbs whose stems end in -m or -n may take this extra -e-, or not, depending on whether its addition is necessary for pronunciation. If the -m or -n is preceded by a consonant other than l, r or h, the -e- is inserted → ❷

Weak (and strong) verbs whose stem ends in a sibilant sound (-s, -z, -ss, -ß) normally lose the -s- of the second person singular ending (the du form) in the present indicative → ❸

NOTE: When this sibilant is -sch, the -s- of the ending remains → ❹

Examples

1 reden **to speak** — arbeiten **to work**

PRESENT	IMPERFECT	PRESENT	IMPERFECT
ich rede	ich redete	ich arbeite	ich arbeitete
du redest	du redetest	du arbeitest	du arbeitetest
er redet	er redete	er arbeitet	er arbeitete
wir reden	wir redeten	wir arbeiten	wir arbeiteten
ihr redet	ihr redetet	ihr arbeitet	ihr arbeitetet
sie reden	sie redeten	sie arbeiten	sie arbeiteten

2 atmen **to breathe** — segnen **to bless**

PRESENT	IMPERFECT	PRESENT	IMPERFECT
ich atme	ich atmete	ich segne	ich segnete
du atmest	du atmetest	du segnest	du segnetest
er atmet	er atmete	er segnet	er segnete
wir atmen	wir atmeten	wir segnen	wir segneten
ihr atmet	ihr atmetet	ihr segnet	ihr segnetet
sie atmen	sie atmeten	sie segnen	sie segneten

BUT:

umarmen **to embrace** — lernen **to learn**

PRESENT	IMPERFECT	PRESENT	IMPERFECT
ich umarme	ich umarmte	ich lerne	ich lernte
du umarmst	du umarmtest	du lernst	du lerntest
er umarmt	er umarmte	er lernt	er lernte
wir umarmen	wir umarmten	wir lernen	wir lernten
ihr umarmt	ihr umarmtet	ihr lernt	ihr lerntet
sie umarmen	sie umarmten	sie lernen	sie lernten

3 grüßen **to greet** — 4 löschen **to extinguish**

PRESENT	PRESENT
ich grüße	ich lösche
du **grüßt**	du löschst
er grüßt	er löscht
wir grüßen	wir löschen
ihr grüßt	ihr löscht
sie grüßen	sie löschen

Strong Verbs

A table of the most useful strong verbs is given on pages 86–97.

What differentiates strong verbs from weak ones is that when forming their imperfect indicative tense, strong verbs undergo a vowel change and have a different set of endings → ①

Their past participles are also formed differently (see page 24).

To form the imperfect subjunctive of strong verbs, the endings from the appropriate table below are added to the stem of the imperfect indicative, but the vowel is modified by an umlaut where this is possible, i.e. a ä, o ö, u ü. Exceptions to this are clearly shown in the table of strong verbs → ②

The endings for the simple tenses of strong verbs are as follows:

	PRESENT INDICATIVE	PRESENT SUBJUNCTIVE	
1st singular	-e	-e	
2nd	-st	-est	
3rd	-t	-e	→ ③
1st plural	-en	-en	
2nd	-t	-et	
3rd	-en	-en	

	IMPERFECT INDICATIVE	IMPERFECT SUBJUNCTIVE	
1st singular	—	-e	
2nd	-st	-(e)st	
3rd	—	-e	→ ③
1st plural	-en	-en	
2nd	-t	-(e)t	
3rd	-en	-en	

Examples

1 Compare:

	INFINITIVE	PRESENT	IMPERFECT
WEAK	sagen **to say**	er sagt	er sagte
STRONG	rufen **to shout**	er ruft	er rief

2

	IMPERFECT INDICATIVE	IMPERFECT SUBJUNCTIVE
	er gab **he gave**	er gäbe (*umlaut added*)
BUT:	er rief **he shouted**	er riefe (*no umlaut possible*)

3 singen **to sing**

PRESENT INDICATIVE	PRESENT SUBJUNCTIVE
ich sing**e**	ich sing**e**
du sing**st**	du sing**est**
er sing**t**	er sing**e**
wir sing**en**	wir sing**en**
ihr sing**t**	ihr sing**et**
sie sing**en**	sie sing**en**
Sie sing**en**	Sie sing**en**

IMPERFECT INDICATIVE	IMPERFECT SUBJUNCTIVE
ich sang	ich säng**e**
du sang**st**	du säng**(e)st**
er sang	er säng**e**
wir sang**en**	wir säng**en**
ihr sang**t**	ihr säng**(e)t**
sie sang**en**	sie säng**en**
Sie sang**en**	Sie säng**en**

Strong Verbs *continued*

In the present tense of strong verbs, the vowel also often changes for the second and third persons singular (the du and er/sie/es forms). The pattern of possible changes is as follows:

long e	→	ie
short e	→	i
a	→	ä
au	→	äu
o	→	ö

Verbs which undergo these changes are clearly shown in the table on page 86 → ❶

Strong (and weak) verbs whose stem ends with a sibilant sound (-s, -z, -ss, -ß) normally lose the -s- of the second person singular ending (the du form) in the *present indicative*, unless the sibilant is -sch, when it remains → ❷

In the second person singular of the *imperfect* tense of strong verbs whose stem ends in a sibilant sound (including -sch) the sibilant remains, and an -e- is inserted between it and the appropriate ending → ❸

Examples

1

sehen **to see**	helfen **to help**	fahren **to drive**
ich sehe	ich helfe	ich fahre
du s**ie**hst	du h**i**lfst	du f**ä**hrst
er/sie/es s**ie**ht	er/sie/es h**i**lft	er f**ä**hrt
wir sehen	wir helfen	wir fahren
ihr seht	ihr helft	ihr fahrt
sie sehen	sie helfen	sie fahren

saufen **to booze**	stoßen **to push**
ich saufe	ich stoße
du s**äu**fst	du st**ö**ßt
er s**äu**ft	er st**ö**ßt
wir saufen	wir stoßen
ihr sauft	ihr stoßt
sie saufen	sie stoßen

2

wachsen **to grow**	waschen **to wash**
ich wachse	ich wasche
du wächst	du wäsch**s**t
er wächst	er wäscht
wir wachsen	wir waschen
ihr wachst	ihr wascht
sie wachsen	sie waschen

3

lesen **to read**	schließen **to close**	waschen **to wash**
ich las	ich schloss	ich wusch
du las**e**st	du schloss**e**st	du wusch**e**st
er las	er schloss	er wusch
wir lasen	wir schlossen	wir wuschen
ihr last	ihr schlosst	ihr wuscht
sie lasen	sie schlossen	sie wuschen

Mixed Verbs

There are nine mixed verbs in German, and, as their name implies, they are formed according to a mixture of the rules already outlined for weak and strong verbs.

The mixed verbs are:

brennen to burn	kennen to know	senden to send
bringen to bring	nennen to name	wenden to turn
denken to think	rennen to run	wissen to know

Full details of their principal parts are given in the verb table beginning on page 86.

Mixed verbs form their imperfect tense by adding the weak verb endings to a stem whose vowel has been changed as for a strong verb → 1

NOTE: Bringen and denken have a consonant change too in their imperfect forms → 2

The imperfect subjunctive forms of mixed verbs are unusual and should be noted → 3

Other tenses of mixed verbs are formed as for strong verbs.

The past participle of mixed verbs has characteristics of both weak and strong verbs, as shown on page 24.

Examples

1 IMPERFECT INDICATIVE

kennen **to know**	senden **to send**	wissen **to know**
ich k**a**nn**te**	ich s**a**nd**te**	ich w**u**ss**te**
du k**a**nn**test**	du s**a**nd**test**	du w**u**ss**test**
er k**a**nn**te**	er s**a**nd**te**	er w**u**ss**te**
wir k**a**nn**ten**	wir s**a**nd**ten**	wir w**u**ss**ten**
ihr k**a**nn**tet**	ihr s**a**nd**tet**	ihr w**u**ss**tet**
sie k**a**nn**ten**	sie s**a**nd**ten**	sie w**u**ss**ten**

2 IMPERFECT INDICATIVE

bringen **to bring**	denken **to think**
ich **brachte**	ich **dachte**
du **brachtest**	du **dachtest**
er **brachte**	er **dachte**
wir **brachten**	wir **dachten**
ihr **brachtet**	ihr **dachtet**
sie **brachten**	sie **dachten**

3 IMPERFECT SUBJUNCTIVE

brennen	kennen	senden
ich brennte	ich kennte	ich sendete
du brenntest	du kenntest	du sendetest
er brennte *etc*	er kennte *etc*	er sendete *etc*
bringen	nennen	wenden
ich brächte	ich nennte	ich wendete
du brächtest	du nenntest	du wendetest
er brächte *etc*	er nennte *etc*	er wendete *etc*
denken	rennen	wissen
ich dächte	ich rennte	ich wüsste
du dächtest	du renntest	du wüsstest
er dächte *etc*	er rennte *etc*	er wüsste *etc*

The Imperative

Ths is the form of a verb used to give an order or a command, or to make a request:

Come here/Stand up/Please bring me a beer → 1

German has three main imperative forms. These correspond to the three ways of addressing people - **Sie**, **du** and **ihr** (see page 160)

	FORMATION	EXAMPLES	
SINGULAR	stem (+ **e**)	**hol(e)!**	fetch!
PLURAL	stem + **t**	**holt**	fetch!
POLITE (*sing* and *pl*)	stem + **en Sie**	**holen Sie!**	fetch!

The **-e** of the singular form is often dropped, BUT not where the verb stem ends in **-chn**, **-ckn**, **-dn**, **-fn**, **-gn** or **-tm** → 2

Weak verbs ending in **-eln** or **-ern** take the **-e** ending in the singular form, but the additional **-e-** within the stem may be dropped → 3

Any vowel change in the present tense of a strong verb (see page 14) occurs also in its singular imperative form and no **-e** is added → 4

BUT: If the vowel modification in the present tense of a strong verb is the addition of an umlaut, this is not added in the singular form of the imperative → 5

In the imperative form of a reflexive verb (see page 30) the pronoun is placed immediately after the verb → 6

Separable prefixes (see page 72) are placed at the end of an imperative statement → 7

Examples

1

SINGULAR	Komm mal her!	**Come here!**
PLURAL	Steht auf!	**Stand up!**
POLITE	Kommen Sie herein!	**Do come in!**

2

Hör zu! **Listen!**
Hol es! **Fetch it!**

BUT:
Öffne die Tür! **Open the door!**

3

wandern **to walk**
wand(e)re! **walk!**

handeln **to act**
hand(e)le! **act!**

4

nehmen **to take**
du nimmst **you take**
nimm! **take!**

helfen **to help**
du hilfst **you help**
hilf! **help!**

BUT:
sehen **to see**
sieh(e)! **see!**

5

laufen **to run**
du läufst **you run**
lauf(e)! **run!**

stoßen **to push**
du stößt **you push**
stoß(e)! **push!**

6

sich setzen **to sit down**
Setz dich! **Sit down!**
Setzt euch! **Sit down!**
Setzen Sie sich! **Do sit down!**

7

zumachen **to close**
Mach die Tür zu!
Close the door!

aufhören **to stop**
Hör aber endlich auf!
Do stop it!

The Imperative *continued*

Imperatives are followed in German by an exclamation mark, unless the imperative is not intended as a command → 1

Du and **ihr**, though not normally present in imperative forms, may be included for emphasis → 2

An imperative form also exists for the **wir** form of the verb. It consists of the normal present tense form, but with the pronoun **wir** following the verb. It is used for making suggestions → 3

The imperative forms of **sein** (to be) are irregular → 4

The particles **auch**, **nur**, **mal**, **doch** are frequently used with imperatives. They heighten or soften the imperative effect, or add a note of encouragement to a request or command. Often they have no direct equivalent in English and are therefore not always translated → 5

Some alternatives to the imperative in German

Infinitives are often used instead of the imperative in written instructions or public announcements → 6

The impersonal passive (see page 34) may be used → 7

Nouns, adjectives or adverbs can also be used with imperative effect → 8

Some of these have become set expressions → 9

Examples

1 Lass ihn in Ruhe!
Leave him alone!
Sagen Sie mir bitte, wie spät es ist.
What's the time please?

2 Geht ihr voran! **You go on ahead.**
Sag du ihm, was los ist. **You tell him what's wrong.**

3 Nehmen wir an, dass ...
Let's assume that ...
Sagen wir mal, es habe 2.000 Euro gekostet.
Let's just say it cost 2,000 euros.

4 sein **to be**
sei!
seid!
seien wir!
seien Sie!

5 Geh doch! **Go on!/Get going!**
Sag mal, ... **Tell me ...**
Versuchen Sie es mal! **Do give it a try!**
Komm schon! **Do come/Please come!**
Mach es auch richtig! **Be sure to do it properly.**

6 Einsteigen!
All aboard!
Zwiebeln abziehen und in Ringe schneiden.
Peel the onions and slice them.

7 Jetzt wird aufgeräumt!
You're going to clear up now!

8 Ruhe! **Be quiet!/Silence!**
Vorsicht! **Careful!/Look out!**

9 Achtung! **Listen!/Attention!**
Rauchen verboten! **No smoking.**

Compound Tenses

The present and imperfect tenses in German are simple tenses, as described on pages 6–17.

All other tenses, called compound tenses, are formed for all types of verb by using the appropriate tense of an auxiliary verb plus a part of the main verb.

There are three auxiliary verbs:

haben	for past tenses
sein	also for past tenses
werden	for future and conditional tenses

The compound past tenses in German are:

Perfect indicative → 1
Perfect subjunctive → 2
Pluperfect indicative → 3
Pluperfect subjunctive → 4

These are dealt with on pages 24–27.

The future and conditional tenses in German are all compound tenses.

They are:

Future indicative → 5
Future subjunctive → 6
Future perfect → 7
Conditional → 8
Conditional perfect → 9

These are dealt with on pages 28–29.

Examples

	WITH haben	WITH sein
1	er hat geholt **he (has) fetched**	er ist gereist **he (has) travelled**
2	er habe geholt **he (has) fetched**	er sei gereist **he (has) travelled**
3	er hatte geholt **he had fetched**	er war gereist **he had travelled**
4	er hätte geholt **he had fetched**	er wäre gereist **he had travelled**
5	er wird holen **he will fetch**	er wird reisen **he will travel**
6	er werde holen **he will fetch**	er werde reisen **he will travel**
7	er wird geholt haben **he will have fetched**	er wird gereist sein **he will have travelled**
8	er würde holen **he would fetch**	er würde reisen **he would travel**
9	er würde geholt haben **he would have fetched**	er würde gereist sein **he would have travelled**

Compound Past Tenses: Formation

Compound past tenses are normally formed by using the auxiliary verb haben, plus the past participle of the main verb (see below) → 1

Certain types of verb take sein instead of haben, and this is clearly indicated in the verb table starting on page 86. They fall into three main types:

- intransitive verbs (those that take no direct object, often showing a change of state or place) → 2
- certain verbs meaning "to happen" → 3
- miscellaneous others, including:
  begegnen to meet, bleiben to remain,
  gelingen to succeed, sein to be, werden to become → 4

In some cases the verb can be conjugated with either haben or sein, depending on whether it is used transitively (with a direct object) or intransitively (where no direct object is possible) → 5

The past participle: formation (see also page 50)

Weak verbs add the prefix ge- and suffix -t to the verb stem → 6

Verbs ending in -ieren or -eien omit the ge- → 7

Strong verbs add the prefix ge- and the suffix -en to the verb stem → 8
The vowel of the stem may be modified (see verb table, page 86) → 9

Mixed verbs add the prefix ge- and the "weak" suffix -t to the stem. The stem vowel is modified as for many strong verbs → 10

Examples

1 Haben Sie gut geschlafen?
Did you sleep well?
Die Kinder hatten fleißig gearbeitet.
The children had worked hard.

2 Wir sind nach Bonn gefahren.
We went to Bonn.
Er ist schnell eingeschlafen.
He quickly fell asleep.

3 Was ist geschehen?
What happened?

4 Er ist zu Hause geblieben.
He stayed at home.
Es ist uns nicht gelungen.
We did not succeed.
Er ist einem Freund begegnet.
He met a friend.

Er ist krank gewesen.
He has been ill.
Sie ist krank geworden.
She became ill.

5 Er hat den Wagen nach Köln gefahren.
He drove the car to Cologne.
Er ist nach Köln gefahren.
He went to Cologne.

6 holen **to fetch**
geholt **fetched**

7 studieren **to study**
studiert **studied**
prophezeien **to prophesy**
prophezeit **prophesied**

8 laufen **to run**
gelaufen **run**

9 singen **to sing**
gesungen **sung**

10 enden **to send**
gesandt **sent**
bringen **to bring**
gebracht **brought**

For a full list of strong and mixed verbs see page 86.

Compound Past Tenses: Formation *continued*

The formation of past participles for weak, strong and mixed verbs is described on page 24, and a comprehensive list of the principal parts of the most commonly used strong and mixed verbs is provided for reference on pages 86–97.

How to form the compound past tenses:

Perfect indicative	the present tense of haben or sein plus the past participle of the verb → ❶
Perfect subjunctive	(used in indirect or reported speech) the present subjunctive of haben or sein plus the past participle → ❷
Pluperfect indicative	imperfect indicative of haben or sein plus the past participle → ❸
Pluperfect subjunctive	(for indirect or reported speech) imperfect subjunctive of haben or sein plus the past participle → ❹
	NOTE: The pluperfect subjunctive is a frequently used tense in German, since it can replace the much clumsier conditional perfect tense shown on page 28.

Examples

WITH haben	WITH sein
1 PERFECT INDICATIVE	
ich habe geholt	ich bin gereist
du hast geholt	du bist gereist
er/sie/es hat geholt	er/sie/es ist gereist
wir haben geholt	wir sind gereist
ihr habt geholt	ihr seid gereist
sie/Sie haben geholt	sie/Sie sind gereist
2 PERFECT SUBJUNCTIVE	
ich habe geholt	ich sei gereist
du habest geholt	du sei(e)st gereist
er/sie/es habe geholt	er/sie/es sei gereist
wir haben geholt	wir seien gereist
ihr habet geholt	ihr seiet gereist
sie/Sie haben geholt	sie/Sie seien gereist
3 PLUPERFECT INDICATIVE	
ich hatte geholt	ich war gereist
du hattest geholt	du warst gereist
er/sie/es hatte geholt	er/sie/es war gereist
wir hatten geholt	wir waren gereist
ihr hattet geholt	ihr wart gereist
sie/Sie hatten geholt	sie/Sie waren gereist
4 PLUPERFECT SUBJUNCTIVE	
ich hätte geholt	ich wäre gereist
du hättest geholt	du wär(e)st gereist
er/sie/es hätte geholt	er/sie/es wäre gereist
wir hätten geholt	wir wären gereist
ihr hättet geholt	ihr wär(e)t gereist
sie/Sie hätten geholt	sie/Sie wären gereist

Future and Conditional Tenses: Formation

The future and conditional tenses are formed in the same way for all verbs, whether weak, strong or mixed.

The auxiliary werden is used for all verbs together with the infinitive of the main verb.

The infinitive is usually placed at the end of the clause (see page 224).

How to form the future and conditional tenses:

Future indicative	present tense of werden plus the infinitive of the verb → 1
Future subjunctive	present subjunctive of werden plus the infinitive → 2
Future perfect	present indicative of werden plus the perfect infinitive (see below) → 3
Conditional imperfect	subjunctive of werden plus the infinitive → 4
Conditional perfect	imperfect subjunctive of werden plus the perfect infinitive (see below) → 5

NOTE: The conditional perfect is often replaced by the pluperfect subjunctive.

The perfect infinitive consists of the infinitive of haben/sein plus the past participle of the verb.

Examples

1 **FUTURE INDICATIVE**

ich werde holen	wir werden holen
du wirst holen	ihr werdet holen
er/sie/es wird holen	sie/Sie werden holen

2 **FUTURE SUBJUNCTIVE**

ich werde holen	wir werden holen
du werdest holen	ihr werdet holen
er/sie/es werde holen	sie/Sie werden holen

3 **FUTURE PERFECT**

ich werde geholt haben	wir werden geholt haben
du wirst geholt haben	ihr werdet geholt haben
er wird geholt haben	sie/Sie werden geholt haben

4 **CONDITIONAL IMPERFECT**

ich würde holen	wir würden holen
du würdest holen	ihr würdet holen
er/sie/es würde holen	sie/Sie würden holen

5 **CONDITIONAL PERFECT**

ich würde geholt haben	wir würden geholt haben
du würdest geholt haben	ihr würdet geholt haben
er würde geholt haben	sie/Sie würden geholt haben

NOTE: The conditional perfect is often replaced by the pluperfect subjunctive (see page 26).

Reflexive Verbs

A verb whose action is reflected back to its subject may be termed reflexive:

she washes *herself*

Reflexive verbs in German are recognized in the infinitive by the preceding reflexive pronoun sich → 1

German has many reflexive verbs, a great number of which are not reflexive in English → 1

Reflexive verbs are composed of the verb and a reflexive pronoun (see page 170). This pronoun may be either the direct object (and therefore in the accusative case) or the indirect object (and therefore in the dative case) → 2

Many verbs in German which are not essentially reflexive may become reflexive by the addition of a reflexive pronoun → 3
When a verb with an indirect object is made reflexive (see page 170) the pronoun is usually dative → 4

A direct object reflexive pronoun changes to the dative if another direct object is present → 5

In a main clause the reflexive pronoun follows the verb → 6
After inversion (see page 226), or in a subordinate clause, the reflexive pronoun must come after the subject if the subject is a personal pronoun → 7
It may precede or follow a noun subject → 8

Reflexive verbs are always conjugated with haben *except* where the pronoun is used to mean *each other*. Then the verb is normally conjugated with sein.

The imperative forms are shown on page 19.

Examples

1 sich beeilen — wir beeilen uns
to hurry — we are hurrying

2 sich (*accusative*) erinnern to remember

ich erinnere mich	wir erinnern uns
du erinnerst dich	ihr erinnert euch
er/sie/es erinnert sich	sie/Sie erinnern sich

sich (*dative*) erlauben to allow oneself

ich erlaube mir	wir erlauben uns
du erlaubst dir	ihr erlaubt euch
er/sie/es erlaubt sich	sie/Sie erlauben sich

3 etwas melden to report something

sich melden	Ich habe mich gemeldet.
to report/to volunteer	I volunteered.

4 wehtun to hurt

sich wehtun	Hast du dir wehgetan?
to get hurt	Have you hurt yourself?

kaufen to buy

Er kaufte ihr einen Mantel.	Er kaufte sich (*dative*) einen neuen Mantel.
He bought her a coat.	He bought himself a new coat.

5

Ich wasche mich.	Ich wasche mir die Hände
I am having a wash.	I am washing my hands.

6 Er wird sich darüber freuen.
He'll be pleased about that.

7 Darüber wird er sich freuen.
He'll be pleased about that.
Ich frage mich, ob er sich darüber freuen wird.
I wonder if he'll be pleased about that.

8 Langsam drehten sich die Kinder um. OR:
Langsam drehten die Kinder sich um.
The children slowly turned round.

Reflexive Verbs *continued*

Some examples of verbs which can be used with a reflexive pronoun in the accusative case:

sich anziehen **to get dressed** → 1
sich aufregen **to get excited** → 2
sich beeilen **to hurry** → 3
sich beschäftigen mit[1] **to be occupied with** → 4
sich bewerben um[1] **to apply for** → 5
sich erinnern an[1] **to remember** → 6
sich freuen auf[1] **to look forward to** → 7
sich interessieren für[1] **to be interested in** → 8
sich irren **to be wrong** → 9
sich melden **to report (for duty *etc*)/to volunteer**
sich rasieren **to shave**
sich (hin)setzen **to sit down** → 10
sich trauen[2] **to trust oneself**
sich umsehen **to look around** → 11

Some examples of verbs which can be used with a reflexive pronoun in the dative case:

sich abgewöhnen **to give up (something)** → 12
sich aneignen **to appropriate**
sich ansehen **to have a look at**
sich einbilden **to imagine (wrongly)** → 13
sich erlauben **to allow oneself** → 14
sich leisten **to treat oneself** → 15
sich nähern **to get close to**
sich vornehmen **to plan to do** → 16
sich vorstellen **to imagine** → 17
sich wünschen **to want** → 18

[1] For verbs normally followed by a preposition, see pages 76–79.

[2] trauen when non-reflexive takes the dative case.

Examples

1. Du sollst dich sofort anziehen.
   You are to get dressed immediately.
2. Reg dich doch nicht so auf!
   Calm down!
3. Wir müssen uns beeilen.
   We must hurry.
4. Sie beschäftigen sich sehr mit den Kindern.
   They spend a lot of time with the children.
5. Hast du dich um diese Stelle beworben?
   Have you applied for this post?
6. Ich erinnere mich nicht daran.
   I can't remember it.
7. Ich freue mich auf die Fahrt.
   I am looking forward to the journey.
8. Interessierst du dich für Musik?
   Are you interested in music?
9. Er hat sich geirrt.
   He was wrong.
10. Bitte, setzt euch hin!
    Please sit down!
11. Die Kinder sahen sich erstaunt um.
    The children looked around in amazement.
12. Eigentlich müsste man sich das Rauchen abgewöhnen.
    One really ought to give up smoking.
13. Bilde dir doch nichts ein!
    Don't kid yourself!
14. Eins könntest du dir doch erlauben.
    You could surely allow yourself one.
15. Wenn ich mir nur einen Mercedes leisten könnte!
    If only I could afford a Mercedes!
16. Du hast dir wieder zu viel vorgenommen!
    You've taken on too much again!
17. So hatte ich es mir oft vorgestellt.
    I had often imagined it like this.
18. Was wünscht ihr euch zu Weihnachten?
    What do you want for Christmas?

The Passive

In active tenses, the subject of a verb carries out the action of the verb, but in passive tenses the subject of the verb has something done to it.

Compare the following:

Peter kicked the cat (subject: Peter)
The cat was kicked by Peter (subject: the cat)

English uses the verb "to be" to form its passive tenses. German uses werden → ❶

A sample verb is conjugated in the passive on pages 39–41.

In English, the word "by" usually introduces the agent through which the action of a passive tense is performed. In German this agent is introduced by:

von for the performer of the action
durch for an inanimate cause → ❷

The passive can be used to add impersonality or distance to an event → ❸

It may also be used where the identity of the cause of the deed is unknown or not important → ❹

In general, however, the passive is used less in German than in English. The following are common replacements for the passive:

- an active tense with the impersonal pronoun man as subject (meaning they/one). This resembles the use of *on* in French, and man is not always translated as one or they → ❺
- sich lassen plus a verb in the infinitive → ❻

Examples

1 Das Auto wurde gekauft.
The car was bought.

2 Das ist von seinem Onkel geschickt worden.
It was sent by his uncle.

Das Kind wurde von einem Hund gebissen.
The child was bitten by a dog.

Seine Bewerbung ist von der Firma abgelehnt worden.
(*the firm is viewed as a human agent*)
His application was turned down by the firm.

Die Tür wurde durch den Wind geöffnet.
The door was opened by the wind.

Das Getreide wurde durch den Sturm niedergeschlagen.
The crop was flattened by the storm.

3 Die Praxis ist von Dr. Disselkamp übernommen worden.
The practice has been taken over by Dr Disselkamp.

Anfang 1993 wurde ein weiterer Anschlag auf sein Leben verübt.
Another attempt was made on his life early in 1993.

4 In letzter Zeit sind neue Gesetze eingeführt worden.
New laws have recently been introduced.

5 Man hatte es schon verkauft.
It had already been sold.

Man wird es verkauft haben.
It will have been sold.

6 Das lässt sich schnell herausfinden.
We'll/You'll/One will be able to find that out quickly.

The Passive *continued*

In English the indirect object of an active tense can become the subject of a passive statement e.g.

Peter gave *him* a car (*him* = to him)
He was given a car by Peter

This is not possible in German, where the indirect object (*him*) must remain in the dative case (see page 110). There are two ways of handling this in German:

1 with the direct object (*car*) as the subject of a passive verb → ❶
2 by means of an impersonal passive construction, with or without the impersonal subject es → ❶

These constructions would however normally be avoided in favour of an active tense, when the agent of the action is known → ❷

Verbs which are normally followed by the dative case in German and so have only an indirect object (see page 80) should therefore be especially noted, as they can only adopt the impersonal or man-forms of the passive → ❸

Some passive tenses are avoided in German, as they are inelegant (and difficult to use!). For instance, the future perfect passives should be replaced by an active tense or a construction using man → ❹

The conditional perfect passives are also rarely used, past conditional being shown by the pluperfect subjunctives, either passive or active → ❺

English passive constructions such as

he was heard whistling/they were thought to be dying

are not possible in German → ❻

Examples

1. Ein Auto wurde ihm von Peter geschenkt.
   OR:
   Es wurde ihm von Peter ein Auto geschenkt.
   OR:
   Ihm wurde von Peter ein Auto geschenkt.
   He was given a car by Peter.

2. Peter schenkte ihm ein Auto.
   Peter gave him a car.

3. helfen (+ *dative*) to help

Sie half mir.	Mir wurde von ihr geholfen.
She helped me.	OR:
	Es wurde mir von ihr geholfen.
	I was helped by her.

4. Er meint, es werde schon gesehen worden sein.
   He thinks that it will already have been seen.

   BETTER: Er meint, man werde es schon gesehen haben.

2. Es würde geholt worden sein / Man würde es geholt haben.
   It would have been fetched.

   BETTER: Es wäre geholt worden / Man hätte es geholt.

6. Man hörte ihn singen.
   He was heard singing.
   Man sah sie ankommen.
   She was seen arriving.
   Man glaubte, er sei betrunken.
   He was thought to be drunk.

Passive Tenses: Conjugation

Simple tenses

Present passive indicative e.g. *it is seen*	present indicative of werden + past participle of the verb → ❶
Present passive subjunctive	present subjunctive of werden + past participle of the verb → ❷
Imperfect passive indicative e.g. *it was seen*	imperfect indicative of werden + past participle of the verb → ❸
Imperfect passive subjunctive	imperfect subjunctive of werden + past participle of the verb → ❹

Compound tenses

Perfect passive indicative e.g. *it has been seen*	present indicative of sein + e.g. past participle of the verb + worden → ❺
Perfect passive subjunctive	present subjunctive of sein + past participle of the verb + worden → ❻
Pluperfect passive indicative e.g. *it had been seen*	imperfect indicative of sein + past participle of the verb + worden → ❼

Examples

1 PRESENT PASSIVE INDICATIVE

ich werde gesehen	wir werden gesehen
du wirst gesehen	ihr werdet gesehen
er/sie/es wird gesehen	sie/Sie werden gesehen

OR: man sieht mich/man sieht dich *etc*

2 PRESENT PASSIVE SUBJUNCTIVE

ich werde gesehen	wir werden gesehen
du werdest gesehen	ihr werdet gesehen
er/sie/es werde gesehen	sie/Sie werden gesehen

OR: man sehe mich/man sehe dich *etc*

3 IMPERFECT PASSIVE INDICATIVE

ich wurde gesehen/wir wurden gesehen *etc*
OR: man sah mich/man sah uns *etc*

4 IMPERFECT PASSIVE SUBJUNCTIVE

ich würde gesehen/wir würden gesehen *etc*
OR: man sähe mich/man sähe uns *etc*

5 PERFECT PASSIVE INDICATIVE

ich bin gesehen worden/wir sind gesehen worden *etc*
OR: man hat mich/uns gesehen *etc*

6 PERFECT PASSIVE SUBJUNCTIVE

ich sei gesehen worden/wir seien gesehen worden *etc*
OR: man habe mich/uns gesehen *etc*

7 PLUPERFECT PASSIVE INDICATIVE

ich war gesehen worden/wir waren gesehen worden *etc*
OR: man hatte mich/uns gesehen *etc*

Passive Tenses: Conjugation *continued*

Pluperfect passive subjunctive	imperfect subjunctive of sein + past participle of the verb + worden → 1
Present passive infinitive e.g. *to be seen*	infinitive of werden + past participle of the verb → 2
Future passive indicative e.g. *it will be seen*	present indicative of werden + present passive infinitive of the verb → 3
Future passive subjunctive	present subjunctive of werden + present passive infinitive of the verb → 4
Perfect passive infinitive e.g. *to have been seen*	past participle of the verb + worden sein → 5
Future perfect passive e.g. *it will have been seen*	present indicative of werden + perfect passive infinitive of the verb → 6
Conditional passive e.g. *it would be seen*	imperfect subjunctive of werden + present passive infinitive of the verb → 7
Conditional perfect passive e.g. *it would have been seen*	imperfect subjunctive of werden + perfect passive infinitive of the verb → 8

Examples

1 PLUPERFECT PASSIVE SUBJUNCTIVE

ich wäre gesehen worden/wir wären gesehen worden *etc*
OR: man hätte mich/uns gesehen *etc*

2 PRESENT PASSIVE INFINITIVE

gesehen werden

3 FUTURE PASSIVE INDICATIVE

ich werde gesehen werden/wir werden gesehen werden *etc*
OR: man wird mich/uns sehen *etc*

4 FUTURE PASSIVE SUBJUNCTIVE

ich werde gesehen werden/wir werden gesehen werden *etc*
OR: man werde mich/uns sehen *etc*

5 PERFECT PASSIVE INFINITIVE

gesehen worden sein

6 FUTURE PERFECT PASSIVE

ich werde/wir werden gesehen worden sein *etc*
OR: man wird mich/uns gesehen haben *etc*

7 CONDITIONAL PASSIVE

ich würde gesehen werden/wir würden gesehen werden
OR: man würde mich/uns sehen *etc*

8 CONDITIONAL PERFECT PASSIVE

ich würde/wir würden gesehen worden sein *etc*
OR: man würde mich/uns gesehen haben *etc*
OR: **pluperfect subjunctive:** man hätte mich/uns gesehen *etc*

Impersonal Verbs

These verbs are used only in the third person singular, usually with the subject es meaning *it* → 1

Intransitive verbs (verbs with no direct object) are often made impersonal in the passive to describe activity of a general nature → 2

When the verb and subject are inverted (see page 226), the es is omitted → 3

Impersonal verbs in the passive can also be used as an imperative form (see page 20) → 4

In certain expressions in the active, the impersonal pronoun es can be omitted. In this case, a personal pronoun object begins the clause → 5

In the following lists * indicates that es may be omitted in this way:

Some common impersonal verbs and expressions

es donnert	it's thundering
es fällt mir ein, dass/zu*	it occurs to me that/to → 5
es fragt sich, ob	one wonders whether → 7
es freut mich, dass/zu	I am glad that/to → 8
es friert	it is freezing → 9
es gefällt mir	I like it → 10
es geht mir gut/schlecht	I'm fine/not too good
es geht nicht	it's not possible
es geht um	it's about
es gelingt mir (zu)	I succeed (in) → 11
es geschieht	it happens → 12
es gießt	it's pouring
es handelt sich um	it's a question of

Examples

1. Es regnet.
   It's raining.

2. Es wurde viel gegessen und getrunken.
   There was a lot of eating and drinking.

3. Auf der Hochzeit wurde viel gegessen und getrunken.
   There was a lot of eating and drinking at the wedding.

4. Jetzt wird gearbeitet!
   Now you're/we're going to work!

5. Mir ist warm.
   I'm warm.

6. Nachher fiel (es) mir ein, dass der Mann ziemlich komisch angezogen war.
   Afterwards it occurred to me that the man was rather oddly dressed.

7. Es fragt sich, ob es sich lohnt, das zu machen.
   One wonders if that's worth doing.

8. Es freut mich sehr, dass du gekommen bist.
   I'm so pleased that you have come.

9. Heute Nacht hat es gefroren.
   It was below freezing last night.

10. Ihm hat es gar nicht gefallen.
    He didn't like it at all.

11. Es war ihnen gelungen, die letzten Karten zu kriegen.
    They had succeeded in getting the last tickets.

12. Und so geschah es, dass ...
    And so it came about that ...

Impersonal Verbs and Expressions *continued*

es hängt davon ab	it depends
es hat keinen Zweck (zu)	there's no point (in) → 1
es interessiert mich, dass/zu*	I am interested that/to
es ist mir egal (ob)*	it's all the same to me (if) → 2
es ist möglich(, dass)	it's possible (that) → 3
es ist nötig	it's necessary → 4
es ist mir, als ob*	I feel as if
es ist mir gut/schlecht *etc* zumute	I feel good/bad *etc* → 5
es ist schade(, dass)	it's a pity (that)
es ist (mir) wichtig*	it's important (to me)
es ist mir warm/kalt*	I'm warm/cold
es ist warm/kalt	it's *or* the weather is warm/cold
es ist zu hoffen/bedauern *etc**	it is to be hoped/regretted *etc*
es klingelt	someone's ringing the bell → 6
es klopft	someone's knocking
es kommt darauf an(, ob)	it all depends (whether)
es kommt mir vor(, als ob)	it seems to me (as if)
es läutet	the bell is ringing → 7
es liegt an	it is because of → 8
es lohnt sich (nicht)	it's (not) worth it → 9
es macht nichts	it doesn't matter
es macht nichts aus	it makes no difference → 10
es macht mir (keinen) Spaß(, zu)	it's (no) fun (to) → 11
es passiert	it happens → 12
es regnet	it's raining → 13
es scheint mir, dass/als ob*	it seems to me that/as if
es schneit	it's snowing
es stellt sich heraus, dass	it turns out that
es stimmt (nicht), dass	it's (not) true that
es tut mir leid(, dass)	I'm sorry (that)
wie geht es (dir)?	how are you? → 14
mir wird schlecht	I feel sick

Examples

1 Es hat keinen Zweck, weiter darüber zu diskutieren.
There's no point in discussing this any further.

2 Es ist mir egal, ob du kommst oder nicht.
I don't care if you come or not.

3 Es ist doch möglich, dass der Zug Verspätung hat.
It's always possible the train has been delayed.

4 Es wird nicht nötig sein, uns darüber zu informieren.
It won't be necessary to inform us of it.

5 Mir ist heute seltsam zumute.
I feel strange today.

6 Es hat gerade geklingelt.
The bell just went/The phone just rang.

7 Es hat schon geläutet.
The bell has gone.

8 Woran liegt es?
Why is that?

9 Ich weiß nicht, ob es sich lohnt oder nicht.
I don't know if it's worth it or not.

10 Mir macht es nichts aus.
It makes no difference to me.
Macht es Ihnen etwas aus, wenn ... ?
Would you mind if ... ?

11 Hauptsache, es macht Spaß.
The main thing is to enjoy yourself.

12 Ihm ist bestimmt etwas passiert.
Something must have happened to him.

13 Es hat den ganzen Tag geregnet.
It rained the whole day.

14 Wie gehts denn? — Danke, es geht.
How are things? — All right, thank you.

The Infinitive

Forms

There are four forms of the infinitive → ❶.
These forms are used in certain compound tenses (see page 28). The present active infinitive is the most widely used and is the form found in dictionaries.

Uses

Preceded by zu (*to*)

- as in English, after other verbs ("I tried *to come*") → ❷
- as in English, after adjectives ("it was easy *to see*") → ❸
- where the English equivalent is not always an infinitive:
- after nouns, where English may use an "-ing" form → ❹
- after sein, where the English equivalent may be a passive tense → ❺

Without zu, the infinitive is used after the following:

modal verbs → ❻
lassen → ❼
heißen → ❽
bleiben → ❾
gehen → ❿
verbs of perception → ⓫

NOTE: Verbs of perception can also be followed by a subordinate clause beginning with wie or dass, especially if the sentence is long or involved → ⓬

Examples

1 INFINITIVES:

PRESENT ACTIVE	PERFECT ACTIVE
holen	geholt haben
to fetch	to have fetched

PRESENT PASSIVE	PERFECT PASSIVE
geholt werden	geholt worden sein
to be fetched	to have been fetched

2 Ich versuchte zu kommen. I tried to come.

3 Es war leicht zu sehen. It was easy to see.

4 Ich liebe es, Musik zu hören.
I love listening to music.

5 Er ist zu bedauern. He is to be pitied.

6 Er kann schwimmen. He can swim.

7 Sie ließen uns warten. They kept us waiting.

8 Er hieß ihn kommen. He bade him come.

9 Er blieb sitzen. He remained seated.

10 Sie ging einkaufen. She went shopping.

11 Ich sah ihn kommen. I saw him coming.
Er hörte sie singen. He heard her singing.

12 Er sah, wie sie langsam auf und ab schlenderte.
He watched her strolling slowly up and down.

The Infinitive *continued*

Used as an imperative

The infinitive can be used as an imperative (see page 20) → ❶

Used as a noun

The infinitive can be made into a noun by giving it a capital letter. Its gender is always neuter → ❷

Used with modal verbs (see page 52)

An infinitive used with a modal verb is always placed at the end of a clause (see page 56) → ❸

If the modal verb is in a compound tense, its auxiliary will follow the subject in a main clause in the normal way, and the modal participle comes after the infinitive.

BUT: In a subordinate clause, the auxiliary immediately precedes the infinitive and the modal participle, instead of coming at the end → ❹

An infinitive expressing change of place may be omitted entirely after a modal verb (see page 56) → ❺

Used in infinitive phrases

Infinitive phrases can be formed with:

zu	ohne ... zu
um ... zu	anstatt ... zu → ❻

The infinitive comes at the end of its phrase → ❼

In separable verbs, zu is inserted *between* the verb and its prefix in the present infinitive → ❽

A reflexive pronoun comes first, immediately following an introductory word if there is one → ❾

Examples

1 Einsteigen und Türen schließen!
All aboard! Close the doors!

2 rauchen **to smoke**
Er hat das Rauchen aufgegeben.
He's given up smoking.

3 Wir müssen morgen einkaufen gehen.
We have to go shopping tomorrow.

4 Sie haben gestern aufräumen müssen.
They had to tidy up yesterday.

BUT:

Da sie gestern haben aufräumen müssen, durften sie nicht kommen.
They couldn't come as they had to tidy up yesterday.

5 Er will jetzt nach Hause.
He wants to go home now.

6

es zu tun	**to do it**
es getan zu haben	**to have done it**
um es zu tun	**in order to do it**
um es getan zu haben	**in order to have done it**
ohne es zu tun	**without doing it**
ohne es getan zu haben	**without having done it**
anstatt es zu tun	**instead of doing it**
anstatt es getan zu haben	**instead of having done it**

7 Ohne ein Wort zu sagen, verließ er das Haus.
He left the house without saying a word.
Er ging nach Hause, ohne mit ihr gesprochen zu haben.
He went home without having spoken to her.

8

aufgeben	**to give up**
um es aufzugeben	**in order to give it up**

9 Sie gingen weg, ohne sich zu verabschieden.
They left without saying goodbye.

The Present Participle

The present participle for all verbs is formed by adding **-d** to the infinitive form → ❶

The present participle may be used as an adjective. As with all adjectives, it is declined if used attributively (see page 140) → ❷

The present participle may also be used as an adjectival noun (see page 148) → ❸

The past participle

For weak verbs, the past participle is formed by prefixing **ge-** and adding **-t** to the verb stem → ❹

For strong verbs, the past participle is formed by adding the prefix **ge-** and the ending **-en** to the verb stem → ❺
The vowel is often modified too → ❻
(See table of strong and mixed verbs beginning on page 86)

Mixed verbs form their past participle by adding the **ge-** and **-t** of weak verbs, but they change their vowel as for strong verbs. (See table on page 86) → ❼

The past participles of *separable* verbs are formed according to the above rules and are joined on to the separable prefix → ❽

For *inseparable* verbs, past participles are formed without the **ge-** prefix → ❾

Many past participles can also be used as adjectives and adjectival nouns → ❿

Examples

1	lachen	to laugh	singen	to sing
	lachend	laughing	singend	singing

2	ein lachendes Kind	a laughing child
	mit klopfendem Herzen	with beating heart
3	der Vorsitzende/ein Vorsitzender	the/a chairman

4	machen	to do/make
	gemacht	done/made
5	sehen	to see
	gesehen	seen
6	singen	to sing
	gesungen	sung
7	wissen	to know
	gewusst	known

8	aufstehen	to get up	nachmachen	to copy/ imitate
	aufgestanden	got up	nachgemacht	copied/ imitated
9	bestellen	to order	entscheiden	to decide
	bestellt	ordered	entschieden	decided

10	seine verlorene Brille	his lost spectacles
	Wir aßen Gebratenes.	We ate fried food.

Modal Auxiliary Verbs

Modal verbs, sometimes called modal auxiliaries, are used to modify other verbs (to show e.g. possibility, ability, willingness, permission, necessity) much as in English:

he *can* swim
may I come?
we *shouldn't* go

In German the modal auxiliary verbs are: dürfen, können, mögen, müssen, sollen and wollen.

Modal verbs have some important differences in their uses and in their conjugation from other verbs, and these are clearly shown in the verb tables on pages 86–97.

Modal verbs have the following meanings:

dürfen
to be allowed to/may → 1
used negatively: *must not/may not* → 2
to show probability → 3
also used in some polite expressions → 4

können
to be able to/can → 5
in its subjunctive forms:
would be able to/could → 6
as an informal alternative to dürfen with the meaning:
to be allowed to/can → 7
to show possibility → 8

mögen
to like/to like to → 9
most common in its imperfect subjunctive form which expresses polite inquiry or request: *should like to/would like to* → 10
to show possibility or probability → 11

Examples

1 Darfst du mit ins Kino kommen?
Are you allowed to/can you come with us to the cinema?
Darf ich bitte mitkommen?
May I come with you please?
Ich dürfte schon, aber ich will nicht.
I could/would be allowed to, but I don't want to.

2 Hier darf man nicht rauchen.
Smoking is prohibited here.

3 Das dürfte wohl das Beste sein.
That's probably the best thing.

4 Was darf es sein?
Can I help you?/What would you like?

5 Wir konnten es nicht schaffen.
We couldn't/weren't able to do it.

6 Er könnte noch früher kommen.
He could/would be able to come even earlier.
Er meinte, er könne noch früher kommen.
He thought he could come earlier.
Wir könnten vielleicht morgen hinfahren?
Perhaps we could go there tomorrow?

7 Kann ich/darf ich ein Eis haben?
Can I/may I have an ice cream?

8 Wer könnte es gewesen sein?
Who could it have been?

Das kann sein.
That may be so.

BUT: Das kann nicht sein.
That cannot be so.

9 Magst du Butter?
Do you like butter?

10 Wir möchten bitte etwas trinken.
We should like something to drink.
Möchtest du sie besuchen?
Would you like to visit her?

11 Wie alt mag sie sein?
How old might she be?

Modal Auxiliary Verbs *continued*

müssen

to have to/must/need to → 1

certain idiomatic uses → 2

NOTE: For *must have* ..., use the relevant tense of müssen + past participle of main verb + the auxiliary haben or sein → 3

For *don't have to/need not*, a negative form of brauchen (*to need*) may be used instead of müssen → 4

sollen

ought to/should → 5

to be (supposed) to where the demand is not self-imposed → 6

to be said to be → 7

as a command, either direct or indirect → 8

wollen

to want/want to → 9

used as a less formal version of mögen to mean: *to want/wish* → 10

to be willing to → 11

to show previous intention → 12

to claim or pretend → 13

Examples

1 Er hatte jeden Tag um sechs aufstehen müssen.
He had to get up at six o'clock every day.
Man musste lachen.
One had to laugh/One couldn't help laughing.

2 Muss das sein? **Is that really necessary?**
Ein Millionär müsste man sein! **Oh to be a millionaire!**
Den Film muss man gesehen haben.
That film is worth seeing.

3 Es muss geregnet haben. **It must have been raining.**
Er meinte, es müsse am vorigen Abend passiert sein.
He thought it must have happened the previous evening.

4 Das brauchtest du nicht zu sagen.
You didn't have to say that.

5 Man sollte immer die Wahrheit sagen.
One should always tell the truth.
Er wusste nicht, was er tun sollte.
He didn't know what to do. (*what he should do*)

6 Ich soll dir helfen.
I am to help you. (*I have been told to help you*)
Du sollst sofort deine Frau anrufen.
You are to phone your wife at once. (*She has left a message asking you to ring*)

7 Er soll sehr reich sein.
I've heard he's very rich/He is said to be very rich.

8 Es soll niemand sagen, dass die Schotten geizig sind!
Let no-one say the Scots are mean!
Sie sagte mir, ich solle damit aufhören.
She told me to stop it.

9 Das Kind will Lkw-Fahrer werden.
The child wants to become a lorry driver.

10 Willst du eins? **Do you want one?**
Willst du/möchtest du etwas trinken?
Do you want/would you like something to drink?

11 Er wollte nichts sagen. **He refused to say anything.**

12 Ich wollte gerade anrufen. **I was just about to phone.**

13 Keiner will es gewesen sein. **No-one admits to doing it.**

Modal Auxiliary Verbs *continued*

Conjugation and use

Modal verbs have unusual present tenses → 1

Their principal parts are given in the verb tables on pages 86–97.

Each modal verb has two past participles.

The first, which is the more common, is the same as the infinitive form and is used where the modal is modifying a verb → 2

The second resembles a normal weak past participle and is used only where no verb is being modified (see the verb tables on page 86) → 3

The verb modified by the modal is placed in its infinitive form at the end of a clause → 4

Where the modal is used in a compound tense, its past participle in the form of the infinitive is also placed at the end of a clause, immediately after the modified verb → 5

If the modal verb is modifying a verb, and if the modal is used in a compound tense in a subordinate clause, then the normal word order for subordinate clauses (see p 228) does not apply. The auxiliary used to form the compound tense of the modal is not placed right at the end of the subordinate clause, but instead comes before both infinitives → 6

Such constructions are usually avoided in German, by using a simple tense in place of a compound. (For notes on the use of tenses in German, see pages 58–61) → 7

A modified verb which expresses motion may be omitted entirely if an adverb or adverbial phrase is present to indicate the movement or destination → 8

Examples

1

dürfen	können
ich/er/sie/es darf	ich/er/sie/es kann
du darfst	du kannst
wir/sie/Sie dürfen	wir/sie/Sie können
ihr dürft	ihr könnt

mögen	müssen
ich/er/sie/es mag	ich/er/sie/es muss
du magst	du musst
wir/sie/Sie mögen	wir/sie/Sie müssen
ihr mögt	ihr müsst

sollen	wollen
ich/er/sie/es soll	ich/er/sie/es will
du sollst	du willst
wir/sie/Sie sollen	wir/sie/Sie wollen
ihr sollt	ihr wollt

2 wollen: **past participle** wollen
Er hat kommen wollen.
He wanted to come.

3 wollen: **past participle** gewollt
Hast du es gewollt?
Did you want it?

4 Er kann gut schwimmen.
He can swim well.

5 Wir haben das Haus nicht kaufen wollen.
We didn't want to buy the house.
Sie wird dich bald sehen wollen.
She will want to see you soon.

6 COMPARE:
Obwohl wir das Haus gekauft haben, ...
Although we bought the house ...
Obwohl wir das Haus haben kaufen wollen, ...
Although we wanted to buy the house ...

7 Obwohl wir das Haus kaufen wollten ...
Although we wanted to buy the house ...

8 Ich muss nach Hause.
I must go home.
Die Kinder sollen jetzt ins Bett.
The children have to go to bed now.

Use of Tenses

Continuous forms

Unlike English, the German verb does not distinguish between its simple and continuous forms → ❶
To emphasize continuity, the following may be used:

- simple tense plus an adverb or adverbial phrase → ❷
- am or beim plus an infinitive used as a noun → ❸
- eben/gerade dabei sein zu plus an infinitive → ❹

The present

The present tense is used in German with seit or seitdem where English uses a past tense to show an action which began in the past and still continues → ❺
If the action is finished, or does not continue, a past tense is used → ❻
The present is commonly used with future meaning → ❼

The future

The present is often used as a future tense → ❼
The future tense is used however to:

- emphasize the future → ❽
- express doubt or supposition about the future → ❾
- express future intention → ❿

The future perfect

The future perfect is used as in English to mean *shall/will have done* → ⓫
It is used in German to express a supposition → ⓬
In conversation it is replaced by the perfect → ⓭

The conditional

The conditional may be used in place of the imperfect subjunctive to express improbable condition (see page 62) → ⓮
It is used in indirect statements or questions to replace the future subjunctive in conversation or where the subjunctive form is not distinctive → ⓯

Examples

1 ich tue **I do** (*simple form*) OR: **I am doing** (*continuous*)
er rauchte **he smoked** OR: **he was smoking**
sie hat gelesen **she has read** OR: **she has been reading**
es wird geschickt **it is sent** OR: **it is being sent**

2 Er kochte gerade das Abendessen.
He was cooking the supper.
Nun spricht sie mit ihm.
Now she's talking to him.

3 Ich bin am Bügeln.
I am ironing.

4 Wir waren eben dabei, einige Briefe zu schreiben.
We were just writing a few letters.

5 Ich wohne seit drei Jahren hier.
I have been living here for three years.

6 Seit er krank ist, hat er uns nicht besucht.
He hasn't visited us since he's been ill.
Seit seiner Verlobung habe ich ihn nicht geehen.
I haven't seen him since his engagement.

7 Wir fahren nächstes Jahr nach Griechenland.
We're going to Greece next year.

8 Das werde ich erst nächstes Jahr machen können.
I won't be able to do that until next year.

9 Wenn er zurückkommt, wird er mir bestimmt helfen.
He's sure to help me when he returns.

10 Ich werde ihm helfen.
I'm going to help him.

11 Bis Sonntag wird er es gelesen haben.
He will have read it by Sunday.

12 Das wird Herr Keute gewesen sein.
That must have been Herr Keute.

13 Bis du zurückkommst, haben wir alles aufgeräumt.
We'll have tidied up by the time you get back.

14 Wenn ich eins hätte, würde ich es dir geben.
If I had one I would give it to you.
Wenn er jetzt bloß kommen würde!
If only he would get here!

15 Er fragte, ob wir fahren würden.
He asked if we were going to go.

Use of Tenses *continued*

The conditional perfect

May be used in place of the pluperfect subjunctive in a sentence containing a wenn-clause → 1
But the pluperfect subjunctive is preferred → 2

The imperfect

Is used in German with seit or seitdem where the pluperfect is used in English to show an action which began in the remote past and continued to a point in the more recent past → 3
For discontinued actions the pluperfect is used → 4
Is used to describe past actions which have no link with the present as far as the speaker is concerned → 5
Is used for narrative purposes → 6
Is used for repeated, habitual or prolonged past action → 7
See also the NOTE on The perfect (below).

The perfect

Is used to translate the English perfect tense, eg:
I have spoken, he has been reading → 8
Describes past actions or events which still have a link with the present or the speaker → 9
Is used in conversation and similar communication → 10

NOTE: In practice however the perfect and imperfect are often interchangeable in German usage, and in spoken German a mixture of both is common.

The pluperfect

Is used to translate *had done/had been doing*, except in conjunction with seit/seitdem (see The imperfect above) → 11

The subjunctive

For uses of the subjunctive tenses, see pages 62–67.

Examples

1 Wenn du es gesehen hättest, würdest dus geglaubt haben.
You would have believed it if you'd seen it.

2 Hättest du es gesehen, so hättest du es geglaubt.
If you had seen it, you'd have believed it.
Wenn ich das nur nicht gemacht hätte!
If only I hadn't done it!
Wäre ich nur da gewesen!
If I'd only been there!

3 Sie war seit ihrer Heirat als Lehrerin beschäftigt.
She had been working as a teacher since her marriage.

4 Ihren Sohn hatten sie seit zwölf Jahren nicht gesehen.
They hadn't seen their son for twelve years.

5 Er kam zu spät, um teilnehmen zu können.
He arrived too late to take part.

6 Das Mädchen stand auf, wusch sich das Gesicht und verließ das Haus.
The girl got up, washed her face and went out.

7 Wir machten jeden Tag einen kleinen Spaziergang.
We went/We used to go for a little walk every day.

8 Ich habe ihn heute nicht gesehen.
I haven't seen him today.

9 Ich habe ihr nichts davon erzählt.
I didn't tell her anything about it.
Gestern sind wir in die Stadt gefahren und haben uns ein paar Sachen gekauft.
Yesterday we went into town and bought ourselves a few things.

10 Hast du den Krimi gestern Abend im Fernsehen gesehen?
Did you see the thriller on television last night?

11 Sie waren schon weggefahren.
They had already left.
Diese Bücher hatten sie schon gelesen.
They had already read these books.

The Subjunctive: when to use it

The subjunctive form in English has almost died out, leaving only a few examples such as:

> if I *were* rich
> if only he *were* to come
> so *be* it

German however makes much wider use of subjunctive forms, especially in formal, educated or literary contexts. Although there is a growing tendency to use indicatives in spoken German, subjunctives are still very common.

The indicative tenses in German display fact or certainty. The subjunctives show unreality, uncertainty, speculation about a situation or any doubt in the speaker's mind → ❶

Subjunctives are also used in indirect speech, as shown on pages 66–67.

For how to form all tenses of the subjunctive, the reader is referred to the relevant sections on Simple Tenses (pages 6–17) and Compound Tenses (pages 22–29). See also the Subjunctive in Reported Speech (page 66).

The imperfect subjunctive is very common. It is important to note that the imperfect subjunctive form does not always represent actions performed in the past → ❷

Uses of the subjunctive in German

To show improbable condition (e.g. if he *came*, he would ...).

The wenn-clause has a verb in the imperfect subjunctive and the main clause can have either an imperfect subjunctive or a conditional → ❸

Examples

1 INDICATIVE

Das stimmt.	Es ist eine Unverschämtheit.
That's true.	It's a scandal.

SUBJUNCTIVE

Es könnte doch war sein.
It could well be true.
Sie meint, es sei eine Unverschämtheit.
She thinks it's a scandal.
(*speaker not necessarily in agreement with her*)

2 *imperfect subjunctive expressing the future:*
Wenn ich morgen nur da sein könnte!
If only I could be there tomorrow!

expressing the present/immediate future:
Wenn er jetzt nur käme!
If only he would come now!

speaker's opinion, referring to present or future:
Sie wäre die Beste.
She's the best.

3 Wenn du kämest, wäre ich froh.
OR:
Wenn du kämest, würde ich froh sein.
I should be happy if you came.

Wenn es mir nicht gefiele, würde ich es nicht bezahlen.
OR:
Wenn es mir nicht gefiele, bezahlte ich es nicht.
If I wasn't happy with it, I wouldn't pay for it.

(*The second form is less likely, as the imperfect subjunctive and imperfect indicative forms of* bezahlen *are identical*)

The Subjunctive: when to use it *continued*

The imperfect of sollen or wollen, or a conditional tense might be used in the wenn-clause to replace an uncommon imperfect subjunctive, or a subjunctive which is not distinct from the same tense of the indicative → 1

To show unfulfilled condition (if he *had come*, he would have ...)

The wenn-clause requires a pluperfect subjunctive, the main clause a pluperfect subjunctive or conditional perfect → 2

NOTE: The indicative is used to express a *probable* condition, as in English → 3

Wenn can be omitted from conditional clauses. The verb must then follow the subject and dann or so usually begins the main clause → 4

With selbst wenn (*even if/even though*) → 5

With wenn ... nur (*if only ...*) → 6

To speculate or make assumptions → 7

After als (*as if/as though*) → 8

Where there is uncertainty or doubt → 9

To make a polite enquiry → 10

To indicate theoretical possibility or unreality → 11

As an alternative to the conditional perfect → 12

Examples

1. Wenn er mich so sehen würde, würde er mich für verrückt halten!
   OR:
   Wenn er mich so sehen würde, hielte er mich für verrückt!
   OR:
   Wenn er mich so sehen sollte, würde er mich für verrückt halten!
   If he saw me like this, he would think I was mad!
   (Wenn er mich so sähe *would sound rather stilted*)
2. Wenn du pünktlich gekommen wärest, hättest du ihn gesehen.
   OR:
3. Wenn du pünktlich gekommen wärest, würdest du ihn gesehen haben.
   If you had been on time, you would have seen him.
   Wenn ich ihn sehe, gebe ich es ihm.
   If I see him I'll give him it.
4. Hättest du mich nicht gesehen, so wäre ich schon weg.
   If you hadn't seen me, I would have been gone by now.
5. Selbst wenn er etwas wüsste, würde er nichts sagen.
   Even if he knew about it, he wouldn't say anything.
6. Wenn wir nur erfolgreich wären!
   If only we were successful!
7. Und wenn er recht hätte?
   What if he were right?
   Eine Frau, die das sagen würde (OR: die das sagte), müsste Feministin sein!
   Any woman who would say that must be a feminist!
8. Er sah aus, als sei er krank.
   He looked as if he were ill.
9. Er wusste nicht, wie es ihr jetzt ginge.
   He didn't know how she was.
10. Wäre da sonst noch etwas?
    Will there be anything else?
11. Er stellte sich vor, wie gut er in dem Anzug aussähe.
    He imagined how good he would look in the suit.
12. Ich hätte ihn gesehen.
    OR:
    Ich würde ihn gesehen haben.
    I would have seen him.

The Subjunctive in Indirect Speech

What a person asks or thinks can be reported in one of two ways, either directly:

Tom said, "I have been on holiday"

OR indirectly:

Tom said (that) he had been on holiday

In English, indirect (or reported) speech can be indicated by a change in tense of what has been reported:

He said, "*I know* your sister"
He said (that) *he knew* my sister

In German the change is not in tense, but from indicative to subjunctive → ➊

There are two ways of introducing indirect speech in German, similar to the parallel English constructions:

- The clause which reports what is said may be introduced by dass (*that*). The finite verb or auxiliary comes at the end of the clause → ➋

- dass may be omitted. The verb in this case must stand in second position in the clause, instead of being placed at the end → ➌

Forms of the subjunctive in indirect speech

For conjugation of verbs in the subjunctive, see pages 8–15 and 26–31. In indirect (or reported) speech, wherever the present subjunctive is identical to the present indicative form, the imperfect subjunctive is used instead → ➍

Examples

1 Er sagte: „Sie kennt deine Schwester".
He said, "She knows your sister".

Er sagte, sie kenne meine Schwester.
He said she knew my sister.

„Habe ich zu viel gesagt?", fragte er.
"Have I said too much?", he asked.

Er fragte, ob er zu viel gesagt habe.
He asked if he had said too much.

2 Er hat uns gesagt, dass er Italienisch spreche.
He told us that he spoke Italian.

3 Er hat uns gesagt, er spreche Italienisch.
He told us he spoke Italian.

4 PRESENT SUBJUNCTIVE IN INDIRECT SPEECH

WEAK VERBS

holen **to fetch**

ich holte	wir holten
du holest	**ihr holet**
er hole	sie holten

STRONG VERBS

singen **to sing**

ich sänge	wir sängen
du singest	**ihr singet**
er singe	sie sängen

Verbs with Prefixes

Many verbs in German begin with a prefix. A prefix is a word or part of a word which precedes the verb stem → 1

Often the addition of a prefix changes the meaning of the basic verb → 2

Prefixes may be found in strong, weak or mixed verbs. Adding a prefix may occasionally change the verb conjugation → 3

There are four kinds of prefix and each behaves in a slightly different way, as shown on the following pages. Prefixes may be inseparable, separable, double or variable (i.e. either separable or inseparable depending on the verb).

Inseparable prefixes

The eight inseparable prefixes are:

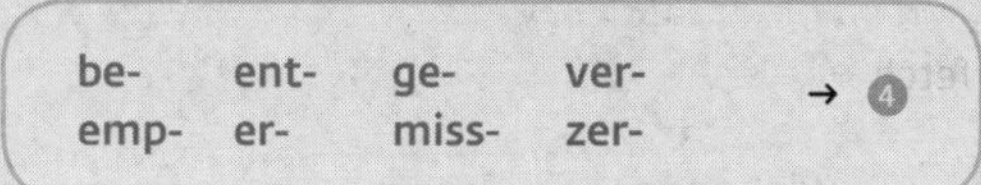

be-	ent-	ge-	ver-	→ 4
emp-	er-	miss-	zer-	

These exist only as prefixes, and cannot be words in their own right.

They are never separated from the verb stem, whatever tense of the verb is used → 5

Inseparable prefixes are always unstressed → 6

Examples

1. zu + geben = zugeben
   an + ziehen = anziehen

2.

nehmen	to take
zunehmen	to put on weight/to increase
sich benehmen	to behave

3.

WEAK		STRONG	
suchen	to look for	stehen	to stand
versuchen	to try	verstehen	to understand
besuchen	to visit	aufstehen	to get up

WEAK		STRONG	
löschen	to extinguish	erlöschen	to go out

WEAK		STRONG	
fehlen	to be missing	empfehlen	to recommend

4.

beschreiben	to describe
empfangen	to receive
enttäuschen	to disappoint
erhalten	to contain
gehören	to belong
misstrauen	to mistrust
verlieren	to lose
zerlegen	to dismantle

5. besuchen **to visit**

Er besucht uns regelmäßig.	He visits us regularly.
Er besuchte uns jeden Tag.	He used to visit us every day.
Er hat uns jeden Tag besucht.	He visited us every day.
Er wird uns morgen besuchen.	He will visit us tomorrow.
Besuche sofort deine Tante!	Visit your aunt at once!

6. **er**lau**ben**, **ver**steh**en**, **emp**fang**en**, **ver**gess**en**

Verbs with Prefixes *continued*

Separable prefixes

Some common examples are:

ab	fest	herunter	mit
an	frei	hervor	nach
auf	her	hin	nieder
aus	herab	hinab	vor
bei	heran	hinauf	vorbei
da(r)	herauf	hinaus	vorüber
davon	heraus	hindurch	weg
dazu	herbei	hinein	zu
ein	herein	hinüber	zurecht
empor	herüber	hinunter	zurück
entgegen	herum	los	zusammen

Unlike inseparable prefixes, separable prefixes may be words in their own right. Indeed, nouns, adjectives and adverbs are often used as separable prefixes → ❶

The past participle of a verb with a separable prefix is formed with ge-. It comes between the verb and the prefix → ❷

In main clauses, the prefix is placed at the end of the clause if the verb is in a simple tense (i.e. present, imperfect or imperative form) → ❸

In subordinate clauses, whatever the tense of the verb, the prefix is attached to the verb and the resulting whole placed at the end of the clause → ❹

Where an infinitive construction requiring zu is used (see page 48), the zu is placed between the infinitive and prefix to form one word → ❺

Examples

1 *noun + verb*: teilnehmen to take part
adjective + verb: loswerden to get free of
adverb + verb: niederlegen to lay down

2 Er hat nicht teilgenommen.
He did not participate.
Wir sind an der Grenze zurückgewiesen worden.
We were turned back at the border.

3 wegbringen **to take for repair/to take away**

PRESENT
Wir bringen das Auto weg

IMPERFECT
Wir brachten das Auto weg

IMPERATIVE
Bringt das Auto weg!

FUTURE
Wir werden das Auto wegbringen

CONDITIONAL
Wir würden das Auto wegbringen

PERFECT
Wir haben das Auto weggebracht

PERFECT PASSIVE
Das Auto ist weggebracht worden

PLUPERFECT SUBJUNCTIVE
Wir hätten das Auto weggebracht

4 PRESENT
Weil wir das Auto wegbringen, ...

IMPERFECT
Dass wir das Auto wegbrachten, ...

PERFECT
Nachdem wir das Auto weggebracht haben, ...

PLUPERFECT SUBJUNCTIVE
Wenn wir das Auto weggebracht hätten, ...

FUTURE
Obwohl wir das Auto wegbringen werden, ...

5 Um das Auto rechtzeitig wegzubringen, müssen wir morgen früh aufstehen.
In order to take the car in on time we shall have to get up early tomorrow.

Verbs with Prefixes *continued*

Variable prefixes

These are:

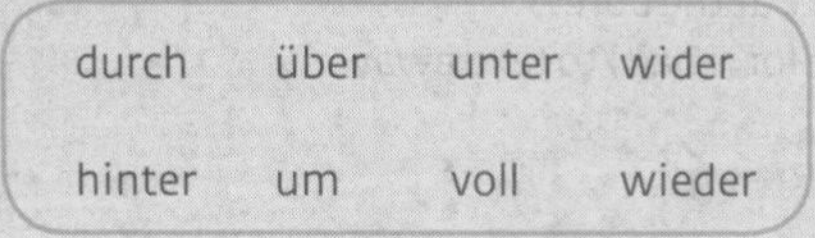

durch
über
unter
wider
hinter
um
voll
wieder

These can be separable or inseparable → 1

Often they are used separably and inseparably with the same verb. In such cases the verb and prefix will tend to retain their basic meanings if the prefix is used separably, but adopt figurative meanings when the prefix is used inseparably → 2

Variable prefixes behave as separable prefixes when used separably, and as inseparable prefixes when used inseparably → 3

Double prefixes

These occur where a verb with an inseparable prefix is preceded by a separable prefix → 4

The separable prefix behaves as described on page 70, the verb plus inseparable prefix representing the basic verb to which the separable prefix is attached → 5

Unlike other separable verbs, however, verbs with double prefixes have no ge- in their past participles → 6

Examples

1 unternehmen (*inseparable*) to undertake, take on
Wir haben in den Ferien vieles unternommen.
We did a great deal in the holidays.
Du unternimmst zu viel.
You take on too much.

untergehen (*separable*) to sink, go down
Die Sonne geht unter.
The sun is going down/is setting.
Die Sonne ist untergangen.
The sun has gone down/has set.

2 etwas wiederholen (*separable*) **to retrieve something**
etwas wiederholen (*inseparable*) **to repeat something**

3 Er holte ihr die Tasche wieder.
He brought her back her bag.
Er wiederholte den Satz.
He repeated the sentence.

4 ausverkaufen **to sell off**

5 Er verkauft alles aus.
He's selling everything off.
Um alles auszuverkaufen ...
In order to sell everything off ...
Er wird alles ausverkaufen.
He'll be selling everything off.

6 Aber er hat doch alles ausverkauft.
But he's sold everything off.

Verb Combinations

Noun + verb combinations are normally written separately → ❶

BUT: Compound verbs if they are written as one word are almost exclusively used in the infinitive or as participles → ❷

OR: if the noun element has lost its distinctive meaning → ❸

Infinitive + verb combinations are normally written separately but many may also be written as one word → ❹

Participle + verb combinations are normally written separately → ❺

Adjective/adverb + verb combinations are written as one word if the first component of the compound is not a word in its own right → ❻

Adjective + verb combinations are normally written separately but writing them as one word is also acceptable → ❼

BUT: In figurative usage, such combinations are always written as one word → ❽

Verb combinations with **-ander** are written as one word → ❾

Verb combinations with **-seits** and **-wärts** are written as one word → ❿

Verb combinations with sein are written separately → ⓫

Examples

1 Ski fahren, Schlange stehen, Klavier spielen

2 bergsteigen, brustschwimmen, kopfrechnen, sonnenbaden

3 eislaufen, kopfstehen, teilhaben

4 baden gehen, sitzen bleiben *or* sitzenbleiben, spazieren gehen *or* spazierengehen

5 gefangen nehmen, getrennt schreiben

6 abhandenkommen, fehlschlagen, kundgeben

7 bekannt machen *or* bekanntmachen, blau färben *or* blaufärben, klein schneiden *or* kleinschneiden

8 freihalten, leichtfallen, nahebringen, satthaben

9 aneinanderlegen, auseinanderlaufen, durcheinanderreden

10 abseitsstehen, abwärtsgehen

11 auf sein, zu sein

Verbs followed by Prepositions

Some verbs in English usage require a preposition (*for/with/by* etc) for their completion.

This also happens in German, though the prepositions used with German verbs may not be those expected from their English counterparts → 1

The preposition used may significantly alter the meaning of a verb in German → 2

Occasionally German verbs use a preposition where their English equivalents do not → 3

Prepositions used with verbs behave as normal prepositions and affect the *case* of the following noun (see page 198).

A verb plus preposition may be followed by a clause containing another verb rather than by a noun or pronoun. This often corresponds to an *-ing* construction in English:

Thank you for *coming*

In German, this is dealt with in two ways:

- Where the "verb-plus-preposition" construction has the same subject as the following verb, the preposition is preceded by da- or dar- and the following verb becomes an infinitive used with zu → 4
- Where the subject of the "verb-plus-preposition" is not the same as for the following verb, a dass clause is used → 5

Following clauses may also be introduced by interrogatives (ob, wie etc) if the meaning demands them → 6

Examples

1 COMPARE:

sich sehnen **nach**	to long *for*
warten **auf**	to wait *for*
bitten **um**	to ask *for*

2

bestehen	to pass (an examination/a test *etc*)
bestehen aus	to consist of
bestehen auf	to insist on
sich freuen auf	to look forward to
sich freuen über	to be pleased about

3

diskutieren über	to discuss

4 Ich freue mich sehr darauf, mal wieder mit ihm zu arbeiten.
I am looking forward to working with him again.

5 Ich freue mich sehr darauf, dass du morgen kommst.
I am looking forward to your coming tomorrow.

Er sorgte dafür, dass die Kinder immer gut gepflegt waren.
He saw to it that the children were always well cared for.

6 Er dachte lange darüber nach, ob er es wirklich kaufen wollte.
He thought for ages about whether he really wanted to buy it.

Sie freut sich darüber, wie schnell ihre Schüler gelernt haben.
She is pleased at how quickly her students have learned.

Verbs followed by Prepositions *continued*

COMMON VERBS FOLLOWED BY PREPOSITION PLUS **ACCUSATIVE CASE**:

achten auf	to pay attention to, keep an eye on → 1
sich amüsieren über	to laugh at, smile about
sich ärgern über	to get annoyed about/with
sich bewerben um	to apply for → 2
bitten um	to ask for → 3
denken an	to be thinking of → 4
denken über	to hold an opinion of, think about → 5
sich erinnern an	to remember
sich freuen auf	to look forward to
sich freuen über	to be pleased about → 6
sich gewöhnen an	to get used to → 7
sich interessieren für	to be interested in → 8
kämpfen um	to fight for
sich kümmern um	to take care of, see to
nachdenken über	to ponder, reflect on → 9
sich unterhalten über	to talk about
sich verlassen auf	to rely on, depend on → 10
warten auf	to wait for

COMMON VERBS FOLLOWED BY PREPOSITION PLUS **DATIVE CASE**:

abhängen von	to be dependent on → 11
sich beschäftigen mit	to occupy oneself with → 12
bestehen aus	to consist of → 13
leiden an/unter	to suffer from → 14
neigen zu	to be inclined to
riechen nach	to smell of → 15
schmecken nach	to taste of
sich sehnen nach	to long for
sterben an	to die of
teilnehmen an	to take part in → 16
träumen von	to dream of → 17
sich verabschieden von	to say goodbye to
sich verstehen mit	to get along with, get on with
zittern vor	to tremble with → 18

Examples

1 Er musste auf die Kinder achten.
He had to keep an eye on the children.

2 Sie hat sich um die Stelle als Sekretärin beworben.
She applied for the post of secretary.

3 Die Kinder baten ihre Mutter um Plätzchen.
The children asked their mother for some biscuits.

4 Woran denkst du?
What are you thinking about?
Daran habe ich gar nicht mehr gedacht.
I'd forgotten about that.

5 Wie denkt ihr darüber?
What do you think about it?

6 Ich freute mich sehr darüber, Johannes besucht zu haben.
I was very glad I had visited Johannes.

7 Man gewöhnt sich an alles. One gets used to anything.

8 Sie interessiert sich sehr für Politik.
She is very interested in politics.

9 Er hatte schon lange darüber nachgedacht.
He had been thinking about it for a long time.

10 Er verlässt sich darauf, dass seine Frau alles tut.
He relies on his wife to do everything.

11 Das hängt davon ab.
It all depends.

12 Sie sind im Moment sehr damit beschäftigt, ihr neues Haus in Ordnung zu bringen.
They are very busy sorting out their new house at the moment.

13 Dieser Kuchen besteht aus Eiern, Mehl und Zucker.
This cake is made from eggs, flour and sugar.

14 Sie hat lange an dieser Krankheit gelitten.
She suffered from this illness for a long time.
Alte Leute können sehr unter der Einsamkeit leiden.
Old people can suffer from dreadful loneliness.

15 Der Kuchen roch nach Zimt.
The cake smelled of cinnamon.

16 Sie hat an der Bonner Tagung teilnehmen müssen.
She had to attend the Bonn conference.

17 Er hat von seinem Urlaub geträumt.
He dreamt of his holiday.

18 Er zitterte vor Freude.
He was trembling with joy.

Verbs followed by the Dative

Some verbs have a direct object and an indirect object. In the English sentence "*He gave me a book*", *a book* is the direct object of *gave* and would be in the accusative and *me* (= *to me*) is the indirect object and would appear in the dative case in German → 1

In German, as in English, this type of verb is usually concerned with giving or telling something to someone, or with performing an action for someone → 2

The normal word order after such verbs is for the direct object to follow the indirect, *except* where the direct object is a personal pronoun (see page 224) → 2

This order may be reversed for emphasis → 3

Some examples of verbs followed by the dative in this way:

anbieten	gönnen	schicken	
bringen	kaufen	schreiben	
beweisen	leihen	schulden	→ 4
erzählen	mitteilen	verkaufen	
geben	schenken	zeigen	

Certain verbs in German however can be followed *only* by an indirect object in the dative case. These should be noted especially, since most of them are quite different from their English equivalents:

begegnen	gratulieren	schmeicheln	
danken	helfen	trauen	
fehlen	imponieren	trotzen	
gefallen	misstrauen	vorangehen	→ 5
gehören	nachgehen	wehtun	
gelingen	schaden	widersprechen	
gleichen	schmecken	widerstehen	

For how to form the passive of such verbs, see page 36.

Examples

1 Er gab mir ein Buch. He gave me a book.

2 Er wusch dem Kind (*indirect*) das Gesicht (*direct*).
He washed the child's face.
Er erzählte ihm (*indirect*) eine Geschichte (*direct*).
He told him a story.
BUT:
Er hat sie (*direct*) meiner Mutter (*indirect*) gezeigt.
He showed it to my mother.
Kaufst du es (*direct*) mir (*indirect*)?
Will you buy it for me?

3 Er wollte das Buch (*direct*) seiner Mutter (*indirect*) geben.
(*This emphasises* seiner Mutter)
He wanted to give the book to his mother.

4 Er bot ihr die Arbeitsstelle an. He offered her the job.
Bringst du mir eins? Will you bring me one?
Ich gönne dir das neue Kleid.
I want you to have the new dress.
Er hat ihr mitgeteilt, dass ... He told her that ...
Ich schenke meiner Mutter Parfüm zum Geburtstag.
I am giving my mother perfume for her birthday.
Das schulde ich ihm. I owe him that.
Zeig es mir! Show me it!

5 Er ist seinem Freund in der Stadt begegnet.
He bumped into his friend in town.
Mir fehlt der Mut dazu. I don't have the courage.
Es ist ihnen gelungen. They succeeded.
Wem gehört dieses Buch? Whose book is this?
Er wollte ihr nicht helfen. He refused to help her.
Ich gratuliere dir! Congratulations!
Rauchen schadet der Gesundheit.
Smoking is bad for your health.
Das Essen hat ihnen gut geschmeckt.
They enjoyed the meal.

There is/There are

There are three ways of expressing this in German:

Es gibt

This is always used in the singular form, and is followed by an accusative object which may be either singular or plural → 1

Es gibt is used to refer to things of a general nature or location → 2

It also has some idiomatic usages → 3

Es ist/es sind

The es here merely introduces the real subject. The verb therefore becomes plural where the real subject is plural. The real subject is in the nominative case → 4

The es is not required and is therefore omitted when the verb and real subject come together. This happens when inversion of subject and verb occurs (see page 226) and in subordinate clauses → 5

Es ist or es sind are used to refer to:

- subjects with a specific and confined location.
  This location must always be mentioned either by name or by da, darauf, darin *etc* → 6
- temporary existence → 7
- as a beginning to a story → 8

The passive voice

Often *there is/there are* in English will be rendered by a verb in the passive voice in German → 9

Examples

1. Es gibt zu viele Probleme dabei.
   There are too many problems with it.
   Es gibt kein besseres Bier.
   There's no better beer.

2. Es gibt bestimmt Regen.
   It's definitely going to rain.
   Ruhe hat es bei uns nie gegeben.
   There has never been any peace here.

3. Was gibts (=gibt es) zum Essen? — What is there to eat?
   Was gibts? — What's wrong?, What's up?
   So was gibts doch nicht! — That's impossible!

4. Es waren zwei ältere Leute unten im Hof.
   There were two elderly people down in the yard.
   Es sind so viele Touristen da.
   There are so many tourists there.

5. Unten im Hof waren zwei ältere Leute.
   Down in the yard were two elderly people.
   Wenn so viele Touristen da sind, ...
   If there are so many tourists there, ...

6. Es waren viele Flaschen Sekt im Keller.
   There were a lot of bottles of champagne in the cellar.
   Ein Brief lag auf dem Tisch. Es waren auch zwei Bücher darauf.
   A letter lay on the table. There were also two books on it.

7. Es war niemand da.
   There was no-one there.

8. Es war einmal ein König ...
   Once upon a time there was a king ...

9. Es wurde auf der Party viel getrunken.
   There was a lot of drinking at the party.

Use of "es" as an Anticipatory Object

Many verbs can have as their object a dass clause or an infinitive with zu → 1

With some verbs es is used as an object to anticipate this clause or infinitive phrase → 2

When the clause or infinitive phrase begins the sentence, es is not used in the main clause but its place may be taken by an optional das → 3

COMMON VERBS WHICH *USUALLY* HAVE THE "ES" OBJECT:

es ablehnen, zu	to refuse to
es aushalten, zu tun/dass	to stand doing → 4
es ertragen, zu tun/dass	to endure doing
es leicht haben, zu	to find it easy to → 5
es nötig haben, zu	to need to → 6
es satt haben, zu	to have had enough of (doing)
es verstehen, zu	to know how to → 7

COMMON VERBS WHICH *OFTEN* HAVE THE "ES" OBJECT:

es jemandem anhören/ansehen, dass	to tell by listening to/ looking at someone that → 8
es begreifen, dass/warum/wie	to understand that/why/ how
es bereuen, zu tun/dass	to regret having done/that
es leugnen, dass	to deny that → 9
es unternehmen, zu	to undertake to
es jemandem verbieten, zu	to forbid someone to
es jemandem vergeben, dass	to forgive someone for (doing)
es jemandem verschweigen, dass	not to tell someone that
es jemandem verzeihen, dass	to forgive someone for (doing)
es wagen zu	to dare to

Examples

1 Er wusste, dass wir pünktlich kommen würden.
He knew that we would come on time.
Sie fing an zu lachen.
She began to laugh.

2 Er hatte es abgelehnt mitzufahren.
He had refused to come.

3 Dass es Wolfgang war, das haben wir ihr verschwiegen.
OR:
Dass es Wolfgang war, haben wir ihr verschwiegen.
We didn't tell her that it was Wolfgang.

4 Ich halte es nicht mehr aus, bei ihnen zu arbeiten.
I can't stand working for them any longer.

5 Er hatte es nicht leicht, sie zu überreden.
He didn't have an easy job persuading them.

6 Ich habe es nicht nötig, mit dir darüber zu reden.
I don't have to talk to you about it.

7 Er versteht es, Autos zu reparieren.
He knows about repairing cars.

8 Man hörte es ihm sofort an, dass er kein Deutscher war.
OR:
Dass er kein Deutscher war, (das) hörte man ihm sofort an.
One could tell immediately (from the way he spoke) that he wasn't German.

Man sieht es ihm sofort an, dass er dein Bruder ist.
OR:
Dass er dein Bruder ist, (das) sieht man ihm sofort an.
One can tell at a glance that he's your brother.

9 Er hat es nie geleugnet, das Geld genommen zu haben.
He has never denied taking the money.

Strong and Mixed Verbs – Principal Parts

INFINITIVE	TRANSLATION	3RD PERSON PRESENT
backen	to bake	er bäckt
befehlen	to command	er befiehlt
beginnen	to begin	er beginnt
beißen	to bite	er beißt
bergen	to rescue	er birgt
bersten	to burst *intr*	er birst
betrügen	to deceive	er betrügt
biegen	to bend *tr*/to turn *intr*	er biegt
bieten	to offer	er bietet
binden	to tie	er bindet
bitten	to ask for	er bittet
blasen	to blow	er bläst
bleiben	to remain	er bleibt
braten	to fry	er brät
brechen	to break	er bricht
brennen	to burn	er brennt
bringen	to bring	er bringt
denken	to think	er denkt
dreschen	to thresh	er drischt
dringen	to penetrate	er dringt
dürfen	to be allowed to	er darf
empfehlen	to recommend	er empfiehlt
erlöschen	to go out (*fire, light*)	er erlischt
erschallen	to resound	er erschallt
erschrecken[1]	to be startled	er erschrickt
erwägen	to weigh up	er erwägt
essen	to eat	er isst
fahren	to travel	er fährt

[1]erschrecken **meaning "to frighten" is weak:**
erschrecken, erschreckt, erschreckte, hat erschreckt

3RD PERSON IMPERFECT	PERFECT	IMPERFECT SUBJUNCTIVE
er backte	er hat gebacken	er backte
er befahl	er hat befohlen	er befähle
er begann	er hat begonnen	er begänne
er biss	er hat gebissen	er bisse
er barg	er hat geborgen	er bärge
er barst	er ist geborsten	er bärste
er betrog	er hat betrogen	er betröge
er bog	er hat/ist gebogen	er böge
er bot	er hat geboten	er böte
er band	er hat gebunden	er bände
er bat	er hat gebeten	er bäte
er blies	er hat geblasen	er bliese
er blieb	er ist geblieben	er bliebe
er briet	er hat gebraten	er briete
er brach	er hat/ist gebrochen	er bräche
er brannte	er hat gebrannt	er brennte
er brachte	er hat gebracht	er brächte
er dachte	er hat gedacht	er dächte
er drosch	er hat gedroschen	er drösche
er drang	er ist gedrungen	er dränge
er durfte	er hat gedurft/dürfen[1]	er dürfte
er empfahl	er hat empfohlen	er empfähle
er erlosch	er ist erloschen	er erlösche
er erschallte	er ist erschollen	er erschölle
er erschrak	er ist erschrocken	er erschräke
er erwog	er hat erwogen	er erwöge
er aß	er hat gegessen	er äße
er fuhr	er ist gefahren	er führe

1 The second (infinitive) form is used when combined with an infinitive construction (see page 56).

Strong and Mixed Verbs *continued*

INFINITVE	TRANSLATION	3RD PERSON PRESENT
fallen	to fall	er fällt
fangen	to catch	er fängt
fechten	to fight	er ficht
finden	to find	er findet
fliegen	to fly	er fliegt
fliehen	to flee *tr/intr*	er flieht
fließen	to flow	er fließt
fressen	to eat (*of animals*)	er frisst
frieren	to be cold/to freeze over	er friert
gebären	to give birth to	sie gebärt
geben	to give	er gibt
gedeihen	to thrive	er gedeiht
gehen	to go	er geht
gelingen	to succeed	es gelingt
gelten	to be valid	er gilt
genesen	to get well	er genest
genießen	to enjoy	er genießt
geraten	to get into (*a state etc*)	er gerät
geschehen	to happen	es geschieht
gewinnen	to win	er gewinnt
gießen	to pour	er gießt
gleichen	to resemble/to equal	er gleicht
gleiten	to glide	er gleitet
glimmen	to glimmer	er glimmt
graben	to dig	er gräbt
greifen	to grip	er greift
haben	to have	er hat
halten	to hold/to stop	er hält
hängen[1]	to hang *intr*	er hängt
heben	to lift	er hebt
heißen	to be called	er heißt

[1] hängen is weak when used transitively:
hängen, hängt, hängte, hat gehängt

3RD PERSON IMPERFECT	PERFECT	IMPERFECT SUBJUNCTIVE
er fiel	er ist gefallen	er fiele
er fing	er hat gefangen	er finge
er focht	er hat gefochten	er föchte
er fand	er hat gefunden	er fände
er flog	er hat/ist geflogen	er flöge
er floh	er hat/ist geflohen	er flöhe
er floss	er ist geflossen	er flösse
er fraß	er hat gefressen	er fräße
er fror	er hat/ist gefroren	er fröre
sie gebar	sie hat geboren	sie gebäre
er gab	er hat gegeben	er gäbe
er gedieh	er ist gediehen	er gediehe
er ging	er ist gegangen	er ginge
es gelang	es ist gelungen	es gelänge
er galt	er hat gegolten	er gälte
er genas	er ist genesen	er genäse
er genoss	er hat genossen	er genösse
er geriet	er ist geraten	er geriete
es geschah	es ist geschehen	es geschähe
er gewann	er hat gewonnen	er gewönne
er goss	er hat gegossen	er gösse
er glich	er hat geglichen	er gliche
er glitt	er ist geglitten	er glitte
er glomm	er hat geglommen	er glömme
er grub	er hat gegraben	er grübe
er griff	er hat gegriffen	er griffe
er hatte	er hat gehabt	er hätte
er hielt	er hat gehalten	er hielte
er hing	er hat gehangen	er hinge
er hob	er hat gehoben	er höbe
er hieß	er hat geheißen	er hieße

Strong and Mixed Verbs *continued*

INFINITVE	TRANSLATION	3RD PERSON PRESENT
helfen	to help	er hilft
kennen	to know (*someone etc*)	er kennt
klingen	to sound	er klingt
kommen	to come	er kommt
kneifen	to pinch	er kneift
können	to be able to	er kann
kriechen	to crawl	er kriecht
laden	to load	er lädt
lassen	to allow	er lässt
laufen	to walk/to run	er läuft
leiden	to suffer	er leidet
leihen	to lend	er leiht
lesen	to read	er liest
liegen	to lie	er liegt
lügen	to tell a lie	er lügt
mahlen	to grind	er mahlt
messen	to measure	er misst
misslingen	to fail	es misslingt
mögen	to like to	er mag
müssen	to have to	er muss
nehmen	to take	er nimmt
nennen	to call	er nennt
pfeifen	to whistle	er pfeift
preisen	to praise	er preist
quellen	to gush	er quillt
raten	to advise/to guess	er rät
reiben	to rub	er reibt
reißen	to tear *tr/intr*	er reißt
reiten	to ride *tr/intr*	er reitet

3RD PERSON IMPERFECT	PERFECT	IMPERFECT SUBJUNCTIVE
er half	er hat geholfen	er hülfe
er kannte	er hat gekannt	er kennte
er klang	er hat geklungen	er klänge
er kam	er ist gekommen	er käme
er kniff	er hat gekniffen	er kniffe
er konnte	er hat gekonnt/können[1]	er könnte
er kroch	er ist gekrochen	er kröche
er lud	er hat geladen	er lüde
er ließ	er hat gelassen	er ließe
er lief	er ist gelaufen	er liefe
er litt	er hat gelitten	er litte
er lieh	er hat geliehen	er liehe
er las	er hat gelesen	er läse
er lag	er hat gelegen	er läge
er log	er hat gelogen	er löge
er mahlte	er hat gemahlen	er mahlte
er maß	er hat gemessen	er mäße
es misslang	es ist misslungen	es misslänge
er mochte	er hat gemocht/mögen[1]	er möchte
er musste	er hat gemusst/müssen[1]	er müsste
er nahm	er hat genommen	er nähme
er nannte	er hat genannt	er nennte
er pfiff	er hat gepfiffen	er pfiffe
er pries	er hat gepriesen	er priese
er quoll	er ist gequollen	er quölle
er riet	er hat geraten	er riete
er rieb	er hat gerieben	er riebe
er riss	er hat/ist gerissen	er risse
er ritt	er hat/ist geritten	er ritte

[1] The second (infinitive) form is used when combined with an infinitive construction (see page 56).

Strong and Mixed Verbs *continued*

INFINITVE	TRANSLATION	3RD PERSON PRESENT
rennen	to run	er rennt
riechen	to smell	er riecht
ringen	to wrestle	er ringt
rinnen	to flow	er rinnt
rufen	to shout	er ruft
salzen	to salt	er salzt
saufen	to booze/to drink	er säuft
saugen	to suck	er saugt
schaffen[1]	to create	er schafft
scheiden	to separate *tr/intr*	er scheidet
scheinen	to seem/to shine	er scheint
schelten	to scold	er schilt
scheren	to shear	er schert
schieben	to shove	er schiebt
schießen	to shoot	er schießt
schlafen	to sleep	er schläft
schlagen	to hit	er schlägt
schleichen	to creep	er schleicht
schleifen	to grind	er schleift
schließen	to close	er schließt
schlingen	to wind	er schlingt
schmeißen	to fling	er schmeißt
schmelzen	to melt *tr/intr*	er schmilzt
schneiden	to cut	er schneidet
schreiben	to write	er schreibt
schreien	to shout	er schreit
schreiten	to stride	er schreitet
schweigen	to be silent	er schweigt

[1]schaffen meaning "to work hard/to manage" is weak:
schaffen, schafft, schaffte, hat geschafft

3RD PERSON IMPERFECT	PERFECT	IMPERFECT SUBJUNCTIVE
er rannte	er ist gerannt	er rennte
er roch	er hat gerochen	er röche
er rang	er hat gerungen	er ränge
er rann	er ist geronnen	er ränne
er rief	er hat gerufen	er riefe
er salzte	er hat gesalzen	er salzte
er soff	er hat gesoffen	er söffe
er sog	er hat gesogen	er söge
er schuf	er hat geschaffen	er schüfe
er schied	er hat/ist geschieden	er schiede
er schien	er hat geschienen	er schiene
er schalt	er hat gescholten	er schölte
er schor	er hat geschoren	er schöre
er schob	er hat geschoben	er schöbe
er schoss	er hat geschossen	er schösse
er schlief	er hat geschlafen	er schliefe
er schlug	er hat geschlagen	er schlüge
er schlich	er ist geschlichen	er schliche
er schliff	er hat geschliffen	er schliffe
er schloss	er hat geschlossen	er schlösse
er schlang	er hat geschlungen	er schlänge
er schmiss	er hat geschmissen	er schmisse
er schmolz	er hat/ist geschmolzen	er schmölze
er schnitt	er hat geschnitten	er schnitte
er schrieb	er hat geschrieben	er schriebe
er schrie	er hat geschrien	er schrie
er schritt	er ist geschritten	er schritte
er schwieg	er hat geschwiegen	er schwiege

Strong and Mixed Verbs *continued*

INFINITVE	TRANSLATION	3RD PERSON PRESENT
schwellen[1]	to swell *intr*	er schwillt
schwimmen	to swim	er schwimmt
schwingen	to swing	er schwingt
schwören	to vow	er schwört
sehen	to see	er sieht
sein	to be	er ist
senden[2]	to send	er sendet
singen	to sing	er singt
sinken	to sink	er sinkt
sinnen	to ponder	er sinnt
sitzen	to sit	er sitzt
sollen	to be supposed to be	er soll
spalten	to split *tr/intr*	er spaltet
speien	to spew	er speit
spinnen	to spin	er spinnt
sprechen	to speak	er spricht
sprießen	to sprout	er sprießt
springen	to jump	er springt
stechen	to sting/to prick	er sticht
stehen	to stand	er steht
stehlen	to steal	er stiehlt
steigen	to climb	er steigt
sterben	to die	er stirbt
stinken	to stink	er stinkt
stoßen	to push	er stößt
streichen	to stroke/to wander	er streicht
streiten	to quarrel	er streitet

[1] schwellen is weak when used transitively:
schwellen, schwellt, schwellte, hat geschwellt

[2] senden meaning "to broadcast" is weak:
senden, sendet, sendete, hat gesendet

3RD PERSON IMPERFECT	PERFECT	IMPERFECT SUBJUNCTIVE
er schwoll	er ist geschwollen	er schwölle
er schwamm	er ist geschwommen	er schwömme
er schwang	er hat geschwungen	er schwänge
er schwor	er hat geschworen	er schwüre
er sah	er hat gesehen	er sähe
er war	er ist gewesen	er wäre
er sandte	er hat gesandt	er sendete
er sang	er hat gesungen	er sänge
er sank	er ist gesunken	er sänke
er sann	er hat gesonnen	er sänne
er saß	er hat gesessen	er säße
er sollte	er hat gesollt/sollen[1]	er sollte
er spaltete	er hat/ist gespalten	er spaltete
er spie	er hat gespien	er spie
er spann	er hat gesponnen	er spönne
er sprach	er hat gesprochen	er spräche
er spross	er ist gesprossen	er sprösse
er sprang	er ist gesprungen	er spränge
er stach	er hat gestochen	er stäche
er stand	er hat gestanden	er stünde
er stahl	er hat gestohlen	er stähle
er stieg	er ist gestiegen	er stiege
er starb	er ist gestorben	er stürbe
er stank	er hat gestunken	er stänke
er stieß	er hat/ist gestoßen	er stieße
er strich	er hat/ist gestrichen	er striche
er stritt	er hat gestritten	er stritte

[1] The second (infinitive) form is used when combined with an infinitive construction (see page 56).

Strong and Mixed Verbs *continued*

INFINITVE	TRANSLATION	3RD PERSON PRESENT
tragen	to carry/to wear	er trägt
treffen	to meet	er trifft
treiben	to drive/to engage in	er treibt
treten	to kick/step	er tritt
trinken	to drink	er trinkt
tun	to do	er tut
verderben	to spoil/to go bad	er verdirbt
verdrießen	to irritate	er verdrießt
vergessen	to forget	er vergisst
verlieren	to lose	er verliert
vermeiden	to avoid	er vermeidet
verschwinden	to disappear	er verschwindet
verzeihen	to pardon	er verzeiht
wachsen	to grow	er wächst
waschen	to wash	er wäscht
weichen	to yield	er weicht
weisen	to point	er weist
wenden	to turn	er wendet
werben	to recruit	er wirbt
werden	to become	er wird
werfen	to throw	er wirft
wiegen[1]	to weigh	er wiegt
winden	to wind	er windet
wissen	to know	er weiß
wollen	to want to	er will
ziehen	to pull	er zieht
zwingen	to force	er zwingt

[1]wiegen **meaning "to rock" is weak:**
wiegen, wiegt, wiegte, hat gewiegt

3RD PERSON IMPERFECT	PERFECT	IMPERFECT SUBJUNCTIVE
er trug	er hat getragen	er trüge
er traf	er hat getroffen	er träfe
er trieb	er hat getrieben	er triebe
er trat	er hat/ist getreten	er träte
er trank	er hat getrunken	er tränke
er tat	er hat getan	er täte
er verdarb	er hat/ist verdorben	er verdürbe
er verdross	er hat verdrossen	er verdrösse
er vergaß	er hat vergessen	er vergäße
er verlor	er hat verloren	er verlöre
er vermied	er hat vermieden	er vermiede
er verschwand	er ist verschwunden	er verschwände
er verzieh	er hat verziehen	er verziehe
er wuchs	er ist gewachsen	er wüchse
er wusch	er hat gewaschen	er wüsche
er wich	er ist gewichen	er wiche
er wies	er hat gewiesen	er wiese
er wandte	er hat gewandt	er wendete
er warb	er hat geworben	er würbe
er wurde	er ist geworden	er würde
er warf	er hat geworfen	er würfe
er wog	er hat gewogen	er wöge
er wand	er hat gewunden	er wände
er wusste	er hat gewusst	er wüsste
er wollte	er hat gewollt/wollen[1]	er wollte
er zog	er hat gezogen	er zöge
er zwang	er hat gezwungen	er zwänge

[1] The second (infinitive) form is used when combined with an infinitive construction (see page 56).

The Declension of Nouns

In German, all nouns may be declined. This means that they may change their form according to their:

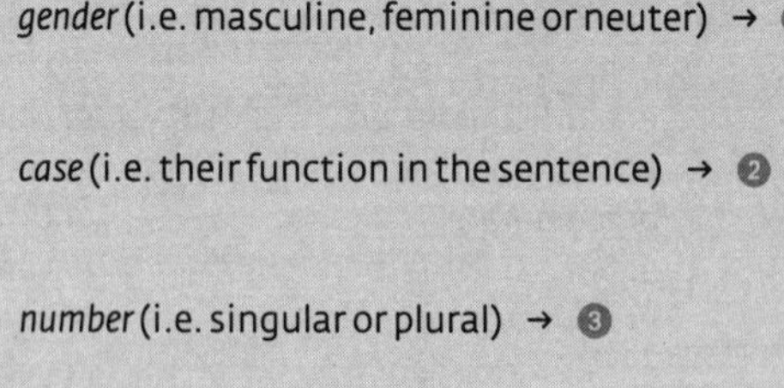

gender (i.e. masculine, feminine or neuter) → ❶

case (i.e. their function in the sentence) → ❷

number (i.e. singular or plural) → ❸

Nearly all *feminine* nouns change in the *plural* form by adding **-n** or **-en**. Many *masculine* and *neuter* nouns also change → ❹

Masculine and *neuter* nouns, with a few exceptions, add **-s** (**-s** or **-es** for nouns of one syllable) in the *genitive singular* (but see page 110) → ❺

All nouns end in **-n** or **-en** in the *dative plural*. This is added to the nominative plural form, where this does not already end in **-n** → ❻

A good dictionary will provide guidance on how to decline a noun:

The nominative singular form is given in full, followed by the gender of the noun, then the genitive singular and nominative plural endings are shown where appropriate → ❼

Adjectives used as nouns are declined as adjectives rather than nouns. Their declension endings are therefore dictated by the preceding article, as well as by number, case and gender (see page 140) → ❽

Examples

1	der Tisch (*masculine*)	the table
	die Gabel (*feminine*)	the fork
	das Mädchen (*neuter*)	the girl
2	des Tisches	of the table
	auf den Tischen	on the tables
3	die Tische	the tables
	die Gabeln	the forks
	die Mädchen	the girls

		NOM SING	NOM PLURAL
4	MASC	der Apfel	die Äpfel
	FEM	die Schule	die Schulen
	NEUT	das Kind	die Kinder

		NOM SING	GEN SING
5	MASC	der Apfel	des Apfels
	FEM	die Schule	der Schule
	NEUT	das Kind	des Kind(e)s

		DAT PLURAL
6	MASC	den Äpfeln
	FEM	den Schulen
	NEUT	den Kindern

7 Tiger *m* -s, -

NOM SING	der Tiger	the tiger
GEN SING	des Tigers	of the tiger, the tiger's
NOM PLURAL	die Tiger	the tigers

8	der Angestellte	the employee
	ein Angestellter	an employee
	(die) Angestellten	(the) employees

The Gender of Nouns

In German a noun may be masculine, feminine or neuter. Gender is relatively unpredictable and has to be learned for each noun. This is best done by learning each noun with its definite article, i.e.

der Teppich
die Zeit
das Bild

The following are intended therefore only as guidelines in helping decide the gender of a word:

Nouns denoting male people and animals are masculine → 1

Nouns denoting the female of the species, as shown on page 104, are feminine → 2

But nouns denoting an entire species can be of any gender → 3

Makes of cars identify with der Wagen and so are usually masculine → 4

Makes of aeroplane identify with die Maschine and so are usually feminine → 5

Seasons, months, days of the week, weather features and points of the compass are masculine → 6

Names of objects that perform an action are usually masculine → 7

Foreign nouns ending in -ant, -ast, -ismus, -or are masculine → 8

Nouns ending in -ich, -ig, -ing, -ling are masculine → 9

Examples

1	der Hörer	(male) listener
	der Löwe	(male) lion
	der Onkel	uncle
	der Vetter	(male) cousin
2	die Hörerin	(female) listener
	die Löwin	lioness
	die Tante	aunt
	die Kusine	(female) cousin
3	der Hund	dog
	die Schlange	snake
	das Vieh	cattle
4	der Mercedes	Mercedes
	der VW	VW, Volkswagen
5	die Boeing	Boeing
	die Concorde	Concorde
6	der Sommer	summer
	der Winter	winter
	der August	August
	der Freitag	Friday
	der Wind	wind
	der Schnee	snow
	der Norden	north
	der Osten	east
7	der Wecker	alarm clock
	der Computer	computer
8	der Ballast	ballast
	der Chauvinismus	chauvinism
9	der Essig	vinegar
	der Schmetterling	butterfly

The Gender of Nouns *continued*

Cardinal numbers are mostly feminine, but fractions are neuter → ❶

Most nouns ending in **-e** are feminine → ❷

BUT: Male people or animals are masculine → ❸
Nouns beginning with **Ge–** are normally neuter (*see below*)

Nouns ending in **-heit**, **-keit**, **-schaft**, **-ung**, **-ei** are feminine → ❹

Foreign nouns ending in **-anz**, **-enz**, **-ie**, **-ik**, **-ion**, **-tät**, **-ur** are generally feminine → ❺

Nouns denoting the young of a species are neuter → ❻

Infinitives used as nouns are neuter → ❼

Most nouns beginning with **Ge–** are neuter → ❽

-chen or **-lein** may be added to many words to give a diminutive form. These words are then neuter → ❾

NOTE: The vowel adds an umlaut where possible (i.e. on **a**, **o**, **u** or **au**) and a final **-e** is dropped before these endings → ❿

Nouns ending in **-nis** or **-tum** are neuter → ⓫

Foreign nouns ending in **-at**, **-ett**, **-fon**, **-ma**, **-ment**, **-um**, **-ium** are mainly neuter → ⓬

Adjectives and participles may be used as masculine, feminine or neuter nouns (see page 148) → ⓭

Examples

1	Er hat eine Drei gekriegt.	He got a three (*mark*).
	ein Drittel davon	a third of it
2	die Falte	crease, wrinkle
	die Brücke	bridge
3	der Löwe	lion
	der Matrose	sailor
4	die Eitelkeit	vanity
	die Gewerkschaft	trade union
	die Scheidung	divorce
	die Druckerei	printing works
5	die Distanz	distance
	die Konkurrenz	rivalry
	die Theorie	theory
	die Panik	panic
	die Union	union
	die Elektrizität	electricity
	die Partitur	score (*musical*)
6	das Baby	baby
	das Kind	child
7	das Schwimmen	swimming
8	das Geschirr	crockery, dishes
	das Geschöpf	creature
9	das Getreide	crop
	das Kindlein	child
10	das Bächlein (*from* der Bach)	(small) stream
	das Kätzchen (*from* die Katze)	kitten
11	das Ereignis	event
	das Altertum	antiquity
12	das Tablett	tray
	das Telefon	telephone
	das Testament	will
	das Podium	platform, podium
13	der Verwandte	(male) relative
	die Verwandte	(female) relative
	das Gehackte	minced meat

The Gender of Nouns *continued*

The following are some common exceptions to the gender guidelines shown on pages 100–103:

das Weib	woman, wife
die Person	person
die Waise	orphan
das Mitglied	member
das Genie	genius
die Wache	sentry, guard
das Restaurant	restaurant

The formation of feminine nouns

As in English, male and female forms are sometimes shown by two completely different words e.g.

mother/father
→ ❶
uncle/aunt etc

Where such separate forms do not exist, however, German often differentiates between male and female forms in one of two ways:

- The masculine form may sometimes be made feminine by the addition of -in in the singular and -innen in the plural → ❷

- An adjective may be used as a feminine noun (see page 148). It has feminine adjective endings which change according to the article which precedes it (see page 140) → ❸

Examples

1	der Vater father	die Mutter mother
	der Bulle bull	die Kuh cow
	der Mann man	die Frau woman
2	der Lehrer (male) teacher	die Lehrerin (female) teacher
	der König king	die Königin queen
	der Hörer (male) listener	die Hörerin (female) listener

Liebe Hörer und Hörerinnen!
Dear listeners!

unsere Leser und Leserinnen
our readers

3 eine Deutsche
a German woman
Er ist mit einer Deutschen verheiratet.
He is married to a German.

die Abgeordnete
the female MP
Nur Abgeordnete durften dabei sein.
Only MPs were allowed in.

The Gender of Nouns: Miscellaneous Points

Compound nouns

Compound nouns, i.e. nouns composed of two or more nouns put together, are a regular feature of German.

They normally take their gender and declension from the last noun of the compound word → ❶

Exceptions to this are compounds ending in -mut, -scheu and -wort, which do not always have the same gender as the last word when it stands alone → ❷

Nouns with more than one gender

A few nouns have two genders, one of which may only be used in certain regions → ❸

Other nouns have two genders, each of which gives the noun a different meaning → ❹

Abbreviations

These take the gender of their principal noun → ❺

Examples

1	die Armbanduhr (*from* die Uhr)	wristwatch
	der Tomatensalat (*from* der Salat)	tomato salad
	der Fußballspieler (*from* der Spieler)	footballer
2	der Mut	courage
	die Armut	poverty
	die Demut	humility
	die Scheu	fear, shyness, timidity
	der Abscheu	repugnance, abhorrence
	das Wort	word
	die Antwort	reply
3	das/der Marzipan	marzipan
	das/der Keks	biscuit
4	der Band	volume, book
	das Band	ribbon, band, tape, bond
	der See	lake
	die See	sea
	der Leiter	leader, manager
	die Leiter	ladder
	der Tau	dew
	das Tau	rope, hawser
5	der DGB (*from* der Deutsche Gewerkschaftsbund)	the Federation of German Trade Unions
	die EU (*from* die Europäische Gemeinschaft)	the EU
	das AKW (*from* das Atomkraftwerk)	nuclear power station

The Cases

There are four grammatical *cases* – nominative, accusative, genitive and dative – which are generally shown by the form of the article used before the noun (see page 118).

The nominative case

The nominative singular is the form shown in full in dictionary entries.

The nominative plural is formed as described on page 98.

The nominative case is used for:

- the subject of a verb → 1
- the complement of sein or werden → 2

The accusative case

The noun in the accusative case usually has the same form as in the nominative → 3

Exceptions to this are "weak" masculine nouns (see page 115) and adjectives used as nouns (see page 148).

It is used:

- for the direct object of the verb → 4
- after those prepositions which always take the accusative case (see pages 206–209) → 5
- to show change of location after prepositions of place (see page 210) → 6
- in many expressions of time and place which do not contain a preposition → 7
- in certain fixed expressions → 8

Examples

1 Das Mädchen singt. — The girl is singing.

2 Er ist ein guter Lehrer. — He's a good teacher.
Das wird ein Pullover. — It's going to be a jumper.

3

das Lied	the song	(*nominative*)
das Lied	the song	(*accusative*)
der Wagen	the car	(*nominative*)
den Wagen	the car	(*accusative*)
die Dose	the tin	(*nominative*)
die Dose	the tin	(*accusative*)

4 Er hat ein Lied gesungen. — He sang a song.

5 für seine Freundin — for his girlfriend
ohne diesen Wagen — without this car
durch das Rauchen — through smoking

6 in die Stadt (*accusative*) — into town
BUT:
in der Stadt (*dative*) — in town

7 Das macht sie jeden Donnerstag.
She does that every Thursday.
Die Schule ist einen Kilometer entfernt.
The school is a kilometre away.

8 Guten Abend! — Good evening!
Vielen Dank! — Thank you very much!

The Cases *continued*

The genitive case

In the genitive singular, *masculine* and *neuter* nouns take endings as follows:

- -s is added to nouns ending in -en, -el, -er → ❶
- -es is added to nouns ending in -tz, -sch, -st, -ss or -ß → ❷
- for nouns of one syllable, either -s or -es may be added → ❸

Feminine singular and all *plural* nouns have the same form as their nominative.

The genitive is used:

- to show possession → ❸
- after prepositions taking the genitive (see page 212) → ❹
- in expressions of time when the exact occasion is not specified → ❺

The dative case

Singular nouns in the dative have the same form as in the nominative → ❻
-e may be added to the dative singular of *masculine* and *neuter* nouns if the sentence rhythm needs it → ❼
This -e is always used in certain set phrases → ❽
Dative plural forms for all genders end in -n → ❾
The only exceptions to this are some nouns of foreign origin that end in -s in all plural forms, including the dative plural (see page 114) → ❿

The dative is used:

- as the indirect object → ⓫
- after verbs taking the dative (see page 80) → ⓬
- after prepositions taking the dative (see page 202) → ⓭
- in certain idiomatic expressions → ⓮
- instead of the possessive adjective to refer to parts of the body and items of clothing (see page 122) → ⓯

Examples

1 der Wagen **car** ► des Wagens **of the car**
das Rauchen **smoking** ► des Rauchens **of smoking**
der Computer **computer** ► des Computers **of the computer**
der Reiter **rider** ► des Reiters **of the rider**

2 der Sitz **seat; residence** ► des Sitzes **of the seat/residence**
der Arzt **doctor** ► des Arztes **of the doctor**
das Schloss **castle** ► des Schlosses **of the castle**

3 Die Zähne des Kindes waren faul geworden.
The child's teeth had decayed.
Der Name des Kinds war ihm unbekannt.
The child's name was not known to him.

4 wegen seiner Krankheit — **because of his illness**
trotz ihrer Bemühungen — **despite her efforts**

5 eines Tages — **one day**

6 dem Wagen — **to the car**
der Frau — **to the woman**
dem Mädchen — **to the girl**

7 zu welchem Zwecke? — **to what purpose?**

8 nach Hause — **home**
sich zu Tode trinken/arbeiten
to drink/work oneself to death

9 mit den Anwälten — **with the lawyers**
nach den Kindern — **after the children**

10

SINGULAR	PLURAL
das Auto	die Autos
das Auto	die Autos
des Autos	der Autos
dem Auto	den Autos

11 Er gab dem Mann das Buch. — **He gave the man the book.**

12 Sie half ihrer Mutter. — **She helped her mother.**

13 Nach dem Essen ... — **After eating ...**

14 Mir ist kalt — **I'm cold**

15 Ich habe mir die Hände gewaschen. — **I've washed my hands.**

The Formation of Plurals

The following pages show full noun declensions in all their singular and plural forms.
Those nouns shown represent the most common types of plural.

Most feminine nouns add **-n**, **-en** or **-nen** to form their plurals:

	SINGULAR	PLURAL
NOM	die Frau	die Frauen
ACC	die Frau	die Frauen
GEN	der Frau	der Frauen
DAT	der Frau	den Frauen

Many nouns have no plural ending.
These are mainly masculine or neuter nouns ending in **-en**, **-er**, **-el**:

	SINGULAR	PLURAL
NOM	der Onkel	die Onkel
ACC	den Onkel	die Onkel
GEN	des Onkels	der Onkel
DAT	dem Onkel	den Onkeln

An umlaut is sometimes added to the vowel in the plural forms:

	SINGULAR	PLURAL
NOM	der Apfel	die Äpfel
ACC	den Apfel	die Äpfel
GEN	des Apfels	der Äpfel
DAT	dem Apfel	den Äpfeln

The Formation of Plurals *continued*

Many nouns form their plurals by adding **¨e**:

	SINGULAR	PLURAL
NOM	der Stuhl	die Stühle
ACC	den Stuhl	die Stühle
GEN	des Stuhl(e)s	der Stühle
DAT	dem Stuhl	den Stühlen

	SINGULAR	PLURAL
NOM	die Angst	die Ängste
ACC	die Angst	die Ängste
GEN	der Angst	der Ängste
DAT	der Angst	den Ängsten

Masculine and neuter nouns often add **-e** in the plural:

	SINGULAR	PLURAL
NOM	das Schicksal	die Schicksale
ACC	das Schicksal	die Schicksale
GEN	des Schicksals	der Schicksale
DAT	dem Schicksal	den Schicksalen

Masculine and neuter nouns sometimes add **¨er** or **-er**:

	SINGULAR	PLURAL
NOM	das Dach	die Dächer
ACC	das Dach	die Dächer
GEN	des Dach(e)s	der Dächer
DAT	dem Dach	den Dächern

The Formation of Plurals *continued*

Some unusual plurals

SINGULAR	TRANSLATION	PLURAL
das Ministerium	department	die Ministerien
das Prinzip	principle	die Prinzipien
das Thema	theme, topic, subject	die Themen
das Drama	drama	die Dramen
der Firma	firm	die Firmen
das Konto	bank account	die Konten
das Risiko	risk	die Risiken
das Komma	comma/decimal point	die Kommas *or* Kommata
das Baby	baby	die Babys
der Klub	club	die Klubs
der Streik	strike	die Streiks
der Park	park	die Parks
der Chef	boss, chief, head	die Chefs
der Israeli	Israeli	die Israelis
das Restaurant	restaurant	die Restaurants
das Bonbon	sweet	die Bonbons
das Hotel	hotel	die Hotels
das Niveau	standard, level	die Niveaus

German singular/English plural nouns

Some nouns are always plural in English, but singular in German.

Some of the most common examples are:

eine Brille	glasses, spectacles
eine Schere	scissors
eine Hose	trousers

They are only used in the plural in German to mean more than one pair, e.g. zwei Hosen *two pairs of trousers*

The Declension of Nouns

"Weak" masculine nouns

Some masculine nouns have a weak declension, which means that in all cases apart from the nominative singular, they end in **-en** or, if the word ends in a vowel, in **-n**.

The dictionary will often show such nouns as:

Junge *m* **-n, -n** boy
Held *m* **-en, -en** hero

Weak masculine nouns are declined as follows:

	SINGULAR	PLURAL
NOM	der Junge	die Jungen
ACC	den Jungen	die Jungen
GEN	des Jungen	der Jungen
DAT	dem Jungen	den Jungen

Masculine nouns falling into this category include:

- those ending in **-og**(**e**) referring to males:
  der Psychologe, der Geologe, der Astrologe
- those ending in **-aph** (*in many cases now spelt* **-af**) or **-oph**:
  der Graph, der Paragraf, der Philosoph
- those ending in **-nom** referring to males:
  der Astronom, der Gastronom
- those ending in **-ant**:
  der Elefant, der Diamant
- those ending in **-t** referring to males:
  der Astronaut, der Komponist, der Architekt
- miscellaneous others:
  der Bauer, der Chirurg, der Franzose, der Katholik, der Kollege, der Mensch, der Ochse, der Spatz

der Name (*name*) has a different ending in the genitive singular, **-ns**: des Namens. Otherwise it is the same as der Junge shown above. Others in this category are: der Buchstabe, der Funke, der Gedanke, der Glaube.

The Declension of Proper Nouns

Names of people and places add -s in the genitive singular unless they are preceded by the definite article or a demonstrative → 1

Where proper names end in a sibilant (-s, -sch, -ss, -ß, -x, -z, -tz) and this makes the genitive form with -s almost impossible to pronounce, they are best avoided altogether by using von followed by the dative case → 2

Personal names can be given diminutive forms if desired. These may be used as a sign of affection as well as with diminutive meaning → 3

Herr (*Mr*) is always declined where it occurs as part of a proper name → 4

When articles or adjectives form part of a proper name (e.g. in the names of books, plays, hotels, restaurants etc), these are declined in the normal way (see pages 118 and 140) → 5

Surnames usually form their plurals by adding -s, unless they end in a sibilant, in which case they sometimes add -ens. They are often preceded by the definite article → 6

Nouns of measurement and quantity

These usually remain singular, even if preceded by a plural number → 7

The substance which they measure follows in the same case as the noun of quantity, and not in the genitive case as in English → 8

Examples

1 Annas Buch — Anna's book
Klaras Mantel — Klara's coat
die Werke Goethes — Goethe's works
BUT: die Versenkung der Bismarck
the sinking of the Bismarck

2 das Buch von Hans — Hans' book
die Werke von Marx — the works of Marx
die Freundin von Klaus — Klaus's girlfriend

3 von deinem Sabinchen — from your Sabine
Das kleine Kläuschen hat uns dann ein Lied gesungen.
Then little Klaus sang us a song.

4 an Herrn Schmidt — to Mr Schmidt
Sehr geehrte Herren — Dear Sirs

5 im Weißen Schwan — in the White Swan
Er hat den „Zauberberg" schon gelesen.
He has already read "The Magic Mountain".

nach Karl dem Großen — after Charlemagne

6 Die Schmidts haben uns eingeladen.
The Schmidts have invited us.
Die Zeißens haben uns eingeladen.
Mr and Mrs Zeiß have invited us.

7 Möchten Sie zwei Stück?
Would you like two?

8 Er wollte zwei Kilo Kartoffeln.
He wanted two kilos of potatoes.
Sie hat drei Tassen Kaffee getrunken.
She drank three cups of coffee.
Drei Glas Weißwein, bitte!
Three glasses of white wine please.

The Definite Article

In English the definite article *the* always keeps the same form:

the book
the books
with *the* books

In German, however, the definite article has many forms:

In its singular form it changes for masculine, feminine and neuter nouns → ❶

In its plural forms it is the same for all genders → ❷

The definite article is also used to show the function of the noun in the sentence by showing which case it is.

There are four cases, as explained more fully on page 108:

1. *nominative* for the subject or complement of the verb → ❸
2. *accusative* for the object of the verb and after some prepositions → ❹
3. *genitive* to show possession and after some prepositions → ❺
4. *dative* for an indirect object (*to* or *for*) and after some prepositions and certain verbs → ❻

The forms of the definite article are as follows:

	SINGULAR			PLURAL
	MASC	FEM	NEUT	ALL GENDERS
NOM	der	die	das	die
ACC	den	die	das	die
GEN	des	der	des	der
DAT	dem	der	dem	den

→ ❼

Examples

1 MASCULINE: der Mann — the man
der Wagen — the car
FEMININE: die Frau — the wife/woman
die Blume — the flower
NEUTER: das Ding — the thing
das Mädchen — the girl

2 die Männer — the men
die Frauen — the women
die Dinge — the things

3 Der Mann ist jung. — The man is young.
Die Frau/das Kind ist jung. — The woman/the child is young.

4 Ich kenne den Mann/die Frau/das Kind.
I know the man/the woman/the child.

5 der Kopf des Mannes/der Frau/des Kindes
the man's/woman's/child's head
wegen des Mannes/der Frau/des Kindes
because of the man/the woman/the child

6 Ich gab es dem Mann/der Frau/dem Kind.
I gave it to the man/to the woman/to the child.

7 SINGULAR

	MASC	FEM	NEUT
NOM	der Mann	die Frau	das Kind
ACC	den Mann	die Frau	das Kind
GEN	des Mann(e)s	der Frau	des Kind(e)s
DAT	dem Mann	der Frau	dem Kind

PLURAL

	MASC	FEM	NEUT
NOM	die Männer	die Frauen	die Kinder
ACC	die Männer	die Frauen	die Kinder
GEN	der Männer	der Frauen	der Kinder
DAT	den Männern	den Frauen	den Kindern

Uses of the Definite Article

When to use and when not to use the definite article in German is one of the most difficult areas for the learner. The following guidelines show where German practice varies from English.

The definite article is used with:

abstract and other nouns where something is being referred to as a whole or as a general idea → 1

Where these nouns are quantified or modified, the article is not used → 2

the genitive, unless the noun is a proper name or is acting as a proper name → 3

occasionally with proper names to make the sex or case clearer → 4

always with proper names preceded by an adjective → 5

sometimes with proper names in familiar contexts or for slight emphasis → 6

with masculine and feminine countries and districts → 7

with geographical names preceded by an adjective → 8

with names of seasons → 9

often with meals → 10

with the names of roads → 11

Examples

1 Das Leben ist schön. Life is wonderful.

2 Es braucht Mut. It needs (some) courage.
Gibt es dort Leben? Is there (any) life there?

3 das Auto des Lehrers the teacher's car
Günters Auto Günter's car
Muttis Auto Mummy's car

4 Er hat es Frau Lehmann gegeben.
Er hat es der Frau Lehmann gegeben.
He gave it to Frau Lehmann.

5 Der alte Herr Brockhaus ist gestorben.
Old Mr Brockhaus has died.

6 Ich habe heute den Christoph gesehen.
I saw Christoph today.
Du hast es aber nicht der Petra geschenkt!
You haven't given it to *Petra*!

7 Deutschland is sehr schön. Germany is very beautiful.
Die Schweiz ist auch schön. Switzerland is also lovely.

8 im (= in dem) heutigen Deutschland
in today's Germany

9 Im (= in dem) Sommer gehen wir schwimmen.
We go swimming in summer.
Der Winter kommt bald.
Soon it will be winter.

10 Das Abendessen wird ab acht Uhr serviert.
Dinner is served from eight o'clock.
Was gibts zum (= zu dem) Mittagessen?
What's for lunch?
BUT:
Um acht Uhr ist Frühstück.
Breakfast is at eight o'clock.

11 Sie wohnt jetzt in der Geisener Straße.
She lives in Geisener Road now.

Uses of the Definite Article *continued*

with months of the year except after seit/nach/vor → ❶

instead of the possessive adjective to refer to parts of the body and items of clothing → ❷

A reflexive pronoun or noun in the dative case is used if it is necessary to clarify to whom the parts of the body belong → ❸

in expressions of price, to mean *each/per/a* → ❹

with certain common expressions → ❺

Other uses

The definite article can be used with demonstrative meaning → ❻

After certain prepositions, forms of the definite article can be shortened (see pages 198–201).
Some of these forms are best used in informal situations → ❼
Others are commonly and correctly used in formal contexts → ❶ → ❺ → ❽

Omitting the definite article

The definite article may be omitted in German:

in certain set expressions → ❾

in *preposition + adjective + noun* combinations → ❿

For the declension of adjectives without the article see page 142.

Examples

1 Wir fahren im (= in dem) September weg.
We are going away in September.
Wir sind seit September hier.
We have been here since September.

2 Er legte den Hut auf den Tisch.
He laid his hat on the table.
Ich drücke Ihnen die Daumen.
I'm keeping my fingers crossed for you.

3 Er hat sich die Hände schon gewaschen.
He has already washed his hands.
Er hat dem Kind schon die Hände gewaschen.
He has already washed the child's hands.

4

Die kosten ...	**They cost ...**
... fünf Euro das Pfund	**... five euros a pound**
... sechs Euro das Stück	**... six euros each**

5

in die Stadt fahren	**to go into town**
zur (= zu der) Schule gehen	**to go to school**
mit der Post	**by post**
mit dem Zug/Bus/Auto	**by train/bus/car**
im (= in dem) Gefängnis	**in prison**

6 Du willst **das** Buch lesen!
You want to read *that* book!

7 für das ► fürs vor dem ► vorm um das ► ums *etc*

8 an dem ► am zu dem ► zum zu der ► zur *etc*

9

von Beruf	**by profession**
nach Wunsch	**as desired**
Nachrichten hören	**to listen to the news**

10

Mit gebeugtem Rücken ...	**Bending his back, ...**

The Indefinite Article

Like the definite article, the form of the indefinite article varies depending on the gender and case of the noun → ❶

It has no plural forms → ❷

The indefinite article is declined as follows:

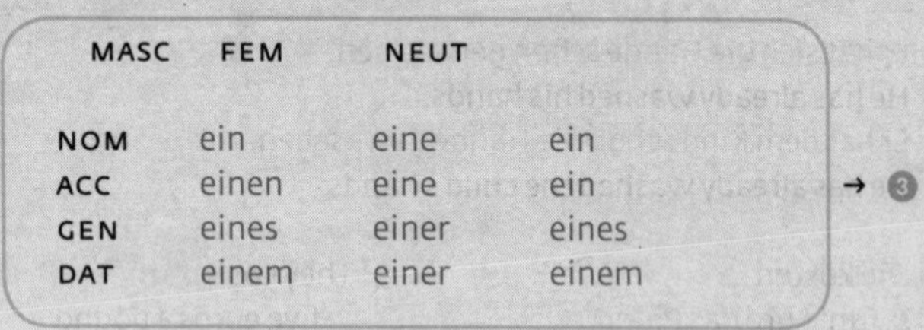

	MASC	FEM	NEUT
NOM	ein	eine	ein
ACC	einen	eine	ein
GEN	eines	einer	eines
DAT	einem	einer	einem

→ ❸

The indefinite article is omitted in the following:

- descriptions of people by profession, religion, nationality etc → ❹

BUT: Note that the article is included when an adjective precedes the noun → ❺

- in certain fixed expressions → ❻
- after als (*as a*) → ❼

Examples

1 Da ist ein Auto. — **There's a car.**
Er hat eine Wohnung. — **He has a flat.**
Sie gab es einem Kind. — **She gave it to a child.**

2 Autos sind in letzter Zeit teurer geworden.
Cars have become more expensive recently.

3

	SINGULAR		
	MASC	FEM	NEUT
NOM	ein Mann	eine Frau	ein Kind
ACC	einen Mann	eine Frau	ein Kind
GEN	eines Mann(e)s	einer Frau	eines Kind(e)s
DAT	einem Mann	einer Frau	einem Kind

4 Sie ist Kinderärztin. — **She's a paediatrician.**
Sie ist Deutsche. — **She's (a) German.**

5 Sie ist eine sehr geschickte Kinderärztin.
She's a very clever paediatrician.

6 Es ist Geschmacksache . — **It's a question of taste.**
Tatsache ist ... — **It's a fact ...**

7 Als Ausländer ist er hier nicht wahlberechtigt.
As a foreigner he doesn't have the vote here.

... und ich rede nun als Vater von vier Kindern
... and I'm talking now as a father of four

The Indefinite Article *continued*

In German, a separate negative form of the indefinite article exists. It is declined exactly like ein in the singular, and also has plural forms:

	SINGULAR			PLURAL
	MASC	FEM	NEUT	ALL GENDERS
NOM	kein	keine	kein	keine
ACC	keinen	keine	kein	keine
GEN	keines	keiner	keines	keiner
DAT	keinem	keiner	keinem	keinen

→ ❶

It has the meaning *no/not a/not one/not any* → ❷

It is used even where the equivalent *positive* phrase has no article → ❸

It is also used in many idiomatic expressions → ❹

Nicht ein may be used instead of kein where the ein is to be emphasized → ❺

Examples

1

	SINGULAR		
	MASC	FEM	NEUT
NOM	kein Mann	keine Frau	kein Kind
ACC	keinen Mann	keine Frau	kein Kind
GEN	keines Mann(e)s	keiner Frau	keines Kind(e)s
DAT	keinem Mann	keiner Frau	keinem Kind

	PLURAL		
	MASC	FEM	NEUT
NOM	keine Männer	keine Frauen	keine Kinder
ACC	keine Männer	keine Frauen	keine Kinder
GEN	keiner Männer	keiner Frauen	keiner Kinder
DAT	keinen Männern	keinen Frauen	keinen Kindern

2 Er hatte keine Geschwister. — He had no brothers or sisters.
Ich sehe keinen Unterschied. — I don't see any difference.
Das ist keine richtige Antwort. — That's no answer.
Kein Mensch hat es gesehen. — Not one person has seen it.

3 Er hatte Angst davor. — He was frightened.
Er hatte keine Angst davor. — He wasn't frightened.

4 Er hatte kein Geld mehr. — All his money was gone.
Es waren keine drei Monate vergangen, als ...
It was less than three months later that ...
Es hat mich keine zehn Euro gekostet.
It cost me less than ten euros.

5 Nicht ein Kind hat es singen können.
Not *one* child could sing it.

Words declined like the definite article

The following have endings similar to those of the definite article shown on page 118:

aller, alle, alles	all, all of them
beide	both (*plural only*)
dieser, diese, dieses	this, this one, these
einiger, einige, einiges	some, a few, a little
irgendwelcher, -e, -es	some or other
jeder, jede, jedes	each, each one, every
jener, jene, jenes	that, that one, those
mancher, manche, manches	many a/some
sämtliche	all, entire (*usually plural*)
solcher, solche, solches	such/such a
welcher, welche, welches	which, which one

These words can be used as:

- articles → 1
- pronouns → 2

They have the following endings:

	SINGULAR			PLURAL
	MASC	FEM	NEUT	ALL GENDERS
NOM	-er	-e	-es	-e
ACC	-en	-e	-es	-e
GEN	-es/-en	-er	-es/-en	-er
DAT	-em	-er	-em	-en

Example declensions are shown on pages 134–135.

einiger and irgendwelcher use the -en genitive ending before masculine or neuter nouns ending in -s → 3

jeder, welcher, mancher and solcher may also do so → 4

Examples

1 Dieser Mann kommt aus Südamerika.
This man comes from South America.

Er geht jeden Tag ins Büro.
He goes to the office every day.

Manche Leute können das nicht.
A good many people can't do it.

2 Willst du diesen?
Do you want this one?

In manchem hat er recht.
He's right about some things.

Man kann ja nicht alles wissen.
You can't know everything.

Es gibt manche, die keinen Alkohol mögen.
There are some people who don't like alcohol.

3 wegen irgendwelchen Geredes
on account of some gossip

4 der Besitz solchen Reichtums
the possession of such wealth

trotz jeden Versuchs
despite all attempts

Words declined like the definite article *continued*

Adjectives following these words have the weak declension (see page 140) → ❶

Exceptions are the plural forms of einige, which are followed by the strong declension (see page 142) → ❷

Further points

Solcher, beide, sämtliche may be used after another article or possessive adjective. They then take weak (see page 140) or mixed (see page 142) adjectival endings, as appropriate → ❸

Although beide generally has plural forms only, one singular form does exist. This is in the neuter nominative and accusative: beides → ❹

Dies often replaces the nominative and accusative dieses and diese when used as a pronoun → ❺

A fixed form all exists which is used together with other articles or possessive pronouns → ❻

Ganz can also be used to replace both the inflected form aller/alle/alles and the uninflected all das/dieses/sein *etc*. It is declined as a normal adjective (see page 140) → ❼

It must be used with collective nouns, in time phrases and geographical references → ❽

Examples

1 dieses alte Auto
this old car
aus irgendwelchem dummen Grund
for some stupid reason or other
Welche neuen Waren?
Which new goods?

2 Dies sind einige gute Freunde von mir.
These are some good friends of mine.

3 Ein solches Kleid habe ich früher auch getragen.
I used to wear a dress like that too.
Diese beiden Männer haben es gesehen.
Both of these men have seen it.

4 Beides ist richtig.
Both are right.
Sie hat beides genommen.
She took both.

5 Hast du dies schon gelesen?
Have you already read this?
Dies sind meine neuen Sachen.
These are my new things.

6 All sein Mut war verschwunden.
All his courage had vanished.
mit all diesem Geld
with all this money

7 mit dem ganzen Geld
with all the money

8 die ganze Gesellschaft
the entire company
Es hat den ganzen Tag geschneit.
It snowed the whole day long.
Im ganzen Land gab es keinen besseren Wein.
There wasn't a better wine in the whole country.

Words declined like the definite article *continued*

derjenige/diejenige/dasjenige (*the one, those*) is declined exactly as the definite article plus an adjective in the weak declension (see page 140) → ❶

derselbe/dieselbe/dasselbe (*the same, the same one*) is declined in the same way as derjenige → ❷

After prepositions, however, the normal contracted forms of the definite article are used for the appropriate parts of derselbe → ❸

Examples

1

SINGULAR

MASC FEM	NEUT	
derjenig**e** Mann	**die**jenig**e** Frau	**das**jenig**e** Kind
denjenig**en** Mann	**die**jenig**e** Frau	**das**jenig**e** Kind
desjenig**en** Mann(e)s	**der**jenig**en** Frau	**des**jenig**en** Kind(e)s
demjenig**en** Mann	**der**jenig**en** Frau	**dem**jenig**en** **Kind**

PLURAL

MASC	FEM	NEUT
diejenig**en** Männer	**die**jenig**en** Frauen	**die**jenig**en** Kinder
diejenig**en** Männer	**die**jenig**en** Frauen	**die**jenig**en** Kinder
derjenig**en** Männer	**der**jenig**en** Frauen	**der**jenig**en** Kinder
denjenig**en** Männern	**den**jenig**en** Frauen	**den**jenig**en** Kindern

2

SINGULAR

MASC	FEM	NEUT
derselb**e** Mann	**die**selb**e** Frau	**das**selb**e** Kind
denselb**en** Mann	**die**selb**e** Frau	**das**selb**e** Kind
desselb**en** Mann(e)s	**der**selb**en** Frau	**des**selb**en** Kind(e)s
demselb**en** Mann	**der**selb**en** Frau	**dem**selb**en** Kind

PLURAL

MASC	FEM	NEUT
dieselb**en** Männer	**die**selb**en** Frauen	**die**selb**en** Kinder
dieselb**en** Männer	**die**selb**en** Frauen	**die**selb**en** Kinder
derselb**en** Männer	**der**selb**en** Frauen	**der**selb**en** Kinder
denselb**en** Männern	**den**selb**en** Frauen	**den**selb**en** Kindern

3

zur selben (= zu derselben) Zeit	**at the same time**
im selben (= in demselben) Zimmer	**in the same room**

Words declined like the definite article *continued*

Sample declensions in full

dieser, diese, dieses **this, this one:**

	SINGULAR		
	MASC	FEM	NEUT
NOM	dies**er** Mann	dies**e** Frau	dies**es** Kind
ACC	dies**en** Mann	dies**e** Frau	dies**es** Kind
GEN	dies**es** Mann(e)s	dies**er** Frau	dies**es** Kind(e)s
DAT	dies**em** Mann	dies**er** Frau	dies**em** Kind

	PLURAL		
	MASC	FEM	NEUT
NOM	dies**e** Männer	dies**e** Frauen	dies**e** Kinder
ACC	dies**e** Männer	dies**e** Frauen	dies**e** Kinder
GEN	dies**er** Männer	dies**er** Frauen	dies**er** Kinder
DAT	dies**en** Männern	dies**en** Frauen	dies**en** Kindern

jener, jene, jenes **that, that one:**

	SINGULAR		
	MASC	FEM	NEUT
NOM	jen**er** Mann	jen**e** Frau	jen**es** Kind
ACC	jen**en** Mann	jen**e** Frau	jen**es** Kind
GEN	jen**es** Mann(e)s	jen**er** Frau	jen**es** Kind(e)s
DAT	jen**em** Mann	jen**er** Frau	jen**em** Kind

	PLURAL		
	MASC	FEM	NEUT
NOM	jen**e** Männer	jen**e** Frauen	jen**e** Kinder
ACC	jen**e** Männer	jen**e** Frauen	jen**e** Kinder
GEN	jen**er** Männer	jen**er** Frauen	jen**er** Kinder
DAT	jen**en** Männern	jen**en** Frauen	jen**en** Kindern

Examples

jeder, jede, jedes **each, every, everybody:**

	SINGULAR		
	MASC	FEM	NEUT
NOM	jed**er** Wagen	jed**e** Minute	jed**es** Bild
ACC	jed**en** Wagen	jed**e** Minute	jed**es** Bild
GEN	jed**es** Wagens (jed**en** Wagens)	jed**er** Minute	jed**es** Bild(e)s (jed**en** Bild(e)s)
DAT	jed**em** Wagen	jed**er** Minute	jed**em** Bild

welcher, welche, welches **which?, which:**

	SINGULAR		
	MASC	FEM	NEUT
NOM	welch**er** Preis	welch**e** Sorte	welch**es** Mädchen
ACC	welch**en** Preis	welch**e** Sorte	welch**es** Mädchen
GEN	welch**es** Preises (welch**en** Preises)	welch**er** Sorte	welch**es** Mädchens (welch**en** Mädchens)
DAT	welch**em** Preis	welch**er** Sorte	welch**em** Mädchen

	PLURAL		
	MASC	FEM	NEUT
NOM	welch**e** Preise	welch**e** Sorten	welch**e** Mädchen
ACC	welch**e** Preise	welch**e** Sorten	welch**e** Mädchen
GEN	welch**er** Preise	welch**er** Sorten	welch**er** Mädchen
DAT	welch**en** Preisen	welch**en** Sorten	welch**en** Mädchen

Words declined like the indefinite article

The following have the same declension pattern as the indefinite articles ein and kein (see pages 124 and 126):

The possessive adjectives

mein	my → 1
dein	your (*singular familiar*)
sein	his/its
ihr	her/its → 2
unser	our
euer	your (*plural familiar*)
ihr	their → 3
Ihr	your (*polite singular and plural*)

These words are declined as follows:

	SINGULAR			PLURAL
	MASC	FEM	NEUT	ALL GENDERS
NOM	—	-e	—	-e
ACC	-en	-e	—	-e
GEN	-es	-er	-es	-er
DAT	-em	-er	-em	-en

Adjectives following these determiners have the mixed declension forms (see page 142), e.g.

sein altes Auto his old car

irgendein (*some ... or other*) also follows this declension pattern in the singular. Its plural form is irgendwelche (see page 128).

Examples

1 mein, meine, mein **my**

	SINGULAR		
	MASC	FEM	NEUT
NOM	mein Bruder	mein**e** Schwester	mein Kind
ACC	mein**en** Bruder	mein**e** Schwester	mein Kind
GEN	mein**es** Bruders	mein**er** Schwester	mein**es** Kind(e)s
DAT	mein**em** Bruder	mein**er** Schwester	mein**em** Kind

	PLURAL		
	MASC	FEM	NEUT
NOM	mein**e** Brüder	mein**e** Schwestern	mein**e** Kinder
ACC	mein**e** Brüder	mein**e** Schwestern	mein**e** Kinder
GEN	mein**er** Brüder	mein**er** Schwestern	mein**er** Kinder
DAT	mein**en** Brüdern	mein**en** Schwestern	mein**en** Kindern

2 ihr, ihre, ihr **her/its/their**

	SINGULAR		
	MASC	FEM	NEUT
NOM	ihr Bruder	ihr**e** Schwester	ihr Kind
ACC	ihr**en** Bruder	ihr**e** Schwester	ihr Kind
GEN	ihr**es** Bruders	ihr**er** Schwester	ihr**es** Kind(e)s
DAT	ihr**em** Bruder	ihr**er** Schwester	ihr**em** Kind

	PLURAL		
	MASC	FEM	NEUT
NOM	ihr**e** Brüder	ihr**e** Schwestern	ihr**e** Kinder
ACC	ihr**e** Brüder	ihr**e** Schwestern	ihr**e** Kinder
GEN	ihr**er** Brüder	ihr**er** Schwestern	ihr**er** Kinder
DAT	ihr**en** Brüdern	ihr**en** Schwestern	ihr**en** Kindern

Indefinite Adjectives

These are adjectives used in place of, or together with, an article:

ander	other, different
mehrere (*plural only*)	several
viel	much, a lot, many
wenig	little, a little, few

After the definite article and words declined like it (see page 128) these adjectives have weak declension endings → ❶

Adjectives following the indefinite adjectives are also weak → ❷

After ein, kein, irgendein or the possessive adjectives they have mixed declension endings → ❸

Adjectives following the indefinite adjectives are also mixed in declension → ❹

When used without a preceding article, ander and mehrere have strong declension endings → ❺

When used without a preceding article, viel and wenig may be declined as follows, though in the singular they are usually undeclined → ❻

	SINGULAR			PLURAL
	MASC	FEM	NEUT	ALL GENDERS
NOM	viel	viel	viel	viele
ACC	viel	viel	viel	viele
GEN	vielen	vieler	vielen	vieler
DAT	viel(em)	vieler	viel(em)	vielen

Any adjective following viel or wenig has strong endings → ❼

Examples

1. Die wenigen Kuchen, die übrig geblieben waren ...
   The few cakes which were left over ...

2. die vielen interessanten Ideen, die ans Licht kamen
   the many interesting ideas which came to light

3. Ihr anderes Auto ist in der Werkstatt.
   Their other car is in for repair.

4. Mehrere gute Freunde waren gekommen.
   Several good friends had come.

5. Mehrere prominente Gäste sind eingeladen.
   Various prominent guests are invited.

   Er war anderer Meinung.
   He was of a different opinion.

6. Es wurde viel Bier getrunken.
   They drank a lot of beer.

   Sie essen nur wenig Obst.
   They don't eat a lot of fruit.

7. Er kaufte viele billige Sachen.
   He bought a lot of cheap things.

   Es wurde viel gutes Bier getrunken.
   They drank a lot of good beer.

   Sie essen wenig frisches Obst.
   They don't eat a lot of fresh fruit.

The Declension of Adjectives

There are two ways of using adjectives:

- They can be used attributively, where the adjective comes before the noun: *the new book*

- They can be used non-attributively, where the adjective comes after the verb: *the book is new*

In English the adjective does not change its form no matter how it is used.

In German, however, adjectives remain unchanged only when used non-attributively → 1

Used attributively, adjectives change to show the number, gender and case of the noun they precede → 2

The endings also depend on the nature of the article which precedes them → 3

There are three sets of endings:

1) The weak declension

These are the endings used after der and those words declined like it as shown on page 128 → 4

	SINGULAR			PLURAL
	MASC	FEM	NEUT	ALL GENDERS
NOM	-e	-e	-e	-en
ACC	-en	-e	-e	-en
GEN	-en	-en	-en	-en
DAT	-en	-en	-en	-en

Examples

1 Das Buch ist neu.
The book is new.
Der Vortrag war sehr langweilig.
The lecture was very boring.

2 Das neue Buch ist da.
The new book has arrived.
Während des langweiligen Vortrags sind wir alle eingeschlafen.
We all fell asleep during the boring lecture.

3 der junge Rechtsanwalt
the young lawyer
ein junger Rechtsanwalt
a young lawyer
manch junger Rechtsanwalt
many a young lawyer

4

SINGULAR

	MASC	FEM	NEUT
NOM	der alt**e** Mann	die alt**e** Frau	das alt**e** Haus
ACC	den alt**en** Mann	die alt**e** Frau	das alt**e** Haus
GEN	des alt**en** Mann(e)s	der alt**en** Frau	des alt**en** Hauses
DAT	dem alt**en** Mann	der alt**en** Frau	dem alt**en** Haus

PLURAL

	MASC	FEM	NEUT
NOM	die alt**en** Männer	die alt**en** Frauen	die alt**en** Häuser
ACC	die alt**en** Männer	die alt**en** Frauen	die alt**en** Häuser
GEN	der alt**en** Männer	der alt**en** Frauen	der alt**en** Häuser
DAT	den alt**en** Männern	den alt**en** Frauen	den alt**en** Häusern

The Declension of Adjectives *continued*

2) The mixed declension

These are the endings used after ein, kein, irgendein and the possessive adjectives (see page 136) → 1

	SINGULAR			PLURAL
	MASC	FEM	NEUT	ALL GENDERS
NOM	-er	-e	-es	-en
ACC	-en	-e	-es	-en
GEN	-en	-en	-en	-en
DAT	-en	-en	-en	-en

→ 2

3) The strong declension

Strong declension endings:

	SINGULAR			PLURAL
	MASC	FEM	NEUT	ALL GENDERS
NOM	-er	-e	-es	-e
ACC	-en	-e	-es	-e
GEN	-en	-er	-en	-er
DAT	-em	-er	-em	-en

→ 3

These endings are used where there is no preceding article. The article is omitted more frequently in German than in English, especially in *preposition + adjective + noun* combinations (see page 122).

These endings enable the adjective to do the work of the missing article by showing case, number and gender → 4

Examples

1 Meine neue Stelle ist bei einer großen Druckerei.
My new job is with a large printing works.
Ihre frühere Theorie ist jetzt bestätigt worden.
Her earlier theory has now been proved true.

2 SINGULAR

	MASC	FEM	NEUT
NOM	ein lang**er** Weg	eine lang**e** Reise	ein lang**es** Spiel
ACC	einen lang**en** Weg	eine lang**e** Reise	ein lang**es** Spiel
GEN	eines lang**en** Weg(e)s	einer lang**en** Reise	eines lang**en** Spiel(e)s
DAT	einem lang**en** Weg	einer lang**en** Reise	einem lang**en** Spiel

PLURAL
ALL GENDERS

NOM	ihre lang**en** Wege/Reisen/Spiele
ACC	ihre lang**en** Wege/Reisen/Spiele
GEN	ihrer lang**en** Wege/Reisen/Spiele
DAT	ihren lang**en** Wegen/Reisen/Spielen

3 SINGULAR

	MASC	FEM	NEUT
NOM	gut**er** Käse	gut**e** Marmelade	gut**es** Bier
ACC	gut**en** Käse	gut**e** Marmelade	gut**es** Bier
GEN	gut**en** Käses	gut**er** Marmelade	gut**en** Biers
DAT	gut**em** Käse	gut**er** Marmelade	gut**em** Bier

PLURAL
ALL GENDERS

NOM	gut**e** Käse/Marmeladen/Biere
ACC	gut**e** Käse/Marmeladen/Biere
GEN	gut**er** Käse/Marmeladen/Biere
DAT	gut**en** Käsen/Marmeladen/Bieren

4 nach kurzer Fahrt — after a short journey
mit gleichem Gehalt — with the same salary

The Declension of Adjectives *continued*

Strong declension endings are also used after any of the following where they are not preceded by an article or other determiner:

ein bisschen	a little, a bit of
ein wenig	a little
ein paar	a few, a couple → 1
weniger	fewer, less
einige (*plural forms only*)	some
allerlei/allerhand	all kinds of, all sorts of
keinerlei	no ... whatsoever, no ... at all
mancherlei	various, a number of
etwas	some, any (*singular*) → 2
mehr	more
lauter	nothing but, sheer, pure
solch	such
vielerlei	various, all sorts of, many different
mehrerlei	several kinds of
was für	what, what kind of
(NOTE: Was für ein takes the mixed declension)	
welcherlei	what kind of, what sort of
viel	much, many, a lot of
wievielerlei	how many kinds of
welch ...!	what ...! what a ...! → 3
manch	many a
wenig	little, few, not much → 4
zweierlei/dreierlei *etc*	two/three *etc* kinds of
zwei, drei *etc*	two, three *etc* → 5
(NOTE: The mixed declension is used after ein)	

The strong declension is also required after possessives where no other word indicates the case, gender and number → 6

Examples

1 ein paar gute Tipps (*strong declension*)
a couple of good tips

2 Etwas starken Pfeffer zugeben. (*strong*)
Add a little strong pepper.

3 Welch herrliches Wetter! (*strong*)
What splendid weather!

4 Es gab damals nur wenig frisches Obst. (*strong*)
At that time there was little fresh fruit.

BUT:

Das wenige frische Obst, das es damals gab ... (*weak*)
The little fresh fruit that was then available ...

5 Zwei große Jungen waren gekommen. (*strong*)
Two big boys had come along.

BUT:

die zwei großen Jungen, die gekommen waren (*weak*)
the two big boys who had come along

meine zwei großen Jungen (*mixed*)
my two big sons

6 Herberts altes Buch. (*strong*)
Herbert's old book.

Muttis neues Auto. (*strong*)
Mum's new car.

The Declension of Adjectives *continued*

Some spelling changes when adjectives are declined

When the adjective hoch (*high*) is declined, its stem changes to **hoh-** → ❶

Adjectives ending in **-el** lose the **-e-** when inflected, i.e. when endings are added → ❷

Adjectives with an **-er** ending often lose the **-e-** when inflected → ❸

The participles as adjectives

The present participle can be used as an adjective with normal adjectival endings (pages 140–143) → ❹

The present participles of sein and haben cannot be used in this way.

The past participle can also be used as an adjective → ❺

Adjectives followed by the dative case

The *dative case* is required after many adjectives e.g.

ähnlich	similar to
bekannt	familiar to
dankbar	grateful to
fremd	alien to
gleich	all the same to/like → ❻
leicht	easy for
nah	close to
peinlich	painful for
unbekannt	unknown to

Examples

1 Das Gebäude ist hoch. BUT: ein hohes Gebäude
The building is high. a high building

2 Das Zimmer ist dunkel. BUT: in dem dunklen Zimmer
The room is dark. in the dark room

3 Das Auto war teuer. BUT: Er kaufte ein teures Auto.
The car was expensive. He bought an expensive car.

4 die werdende Mutter
the mother-to-be

ein lachendes Kind
a laughing child

5 meine verlorene Sachen
my lost things

die ausgebeuteten Arbeiter
the exploited workers

6 Ist dir das bekannt?
Do you know about it?

Ich wäre Ihnen dankbar, wenn ...
I should be grateful to you if ...

Diese Sache ist mir etwas peinlich.
This matter is somewhat embarrassing for me.

Solche Gedanken waren ihm fremd.
Such thoughts were alien to him.

Adjectives used as Nouns

All adjectives in German, and those participles used as adjectives, can also be used as nouns. These are often called adjectival nouns.

Adjectives and participles used as nouns have:

- a capital letter like other nouns → 1
- declension endings like other adjectives, depending on the preceding article, if any (see below) → 2

Declension endings for adjectives used as nouns

After der, dieser and words like it shown on page 128, the normal *weak* adjective endings apply (see page 140) → 3
Der Junge (*the boy*) is an exception, and is declined like a weak masculine noun, as shown on page 115.

After ein, kein, irgendein and the possessive adjectives shown on page 136, the *mixed* adjective endings apply (see page 142) → 4

Where no article is present, or after those words shown on page 144, the *strong* adjective endings are used (see page 142) → 5

When another adjective precedes the adjectival noun, the *strong* endings become *weak* in two instances:

- in the *dative singular* → 6
- in the *nominative* and *accusative plural* after a possessive, where the strong endings might cause confusion with the singular feminine form → 7

Examples

1 der Angestellte
the employee

2 die Angestellte
the (female) employee
das Neue daran ist ...
the new thing about it is ...
Es bleibt beim Alten.
Things remain as they were.
Er hat den ersten Besten genommen.
He took the first that came to hand.

3 für den Angeklagten
for the accused
mit dieser Bekannten
with this (*female*) friend

4 Kein Angestellter darf hier rauchen.
No employee may smoke here.
Sie machten einen Ausflug mit ihren Bekannten zusammen.
They went on a trip with their friends.

5 Etwas Besonderes ist geschehen.
Something special has happened.

6 Ich hatte es Rudis jüngerem Verwandten versprochen.
I had promised it to Rudi's young relative.

7 Rudis jüngere Verwandten wollten es haben.
Rudi's young relatives wanted to have it.

Miscellaneous Points

Adjectives of nationality

These are not spelt with a capital letter in German except in public or official names → 1

However, when used as a noun to refer to the language, a capital letter is used → 2

In German, for expressions like *he is English/he is German etc* a noun or adjectival noun is used instead of an adjective → 3

Adjectives derived from place names

These are formed by adding -er to names of towns → 4

They are never inflected → 5

Adjectives from die Schweiz and from certain regions can also be formed in this way → 6

Such adjectives may be used as nouns denoting the inhabitants of a town.
They are then declined as normal nouns (see pages 98–99) → 7
The feminine form is made by adding -in in the singular and -innen in the plural → 8

Certain names ending in **-en** drop the **-e-** or the **-en** of their ending before adding -er → 9

A second type of adjective formed from place names exists, ending in **-isch** and spelt with a small letter. It is inflected as a normal adjective (see page 140).
It is used mainly where the speaker is referring to the mood of, or something typical of, that place → 10

Examples

1 die deutsche Sprache — das französische Volk
the German language — the French people
BUT:
die Deutsche Bahn
the German railways

2 Sie sprechen kein Englisch.
They don't speak English.

3 Er ist Deutscher. — Sie ist Deutsche.
He is German. — She is German.

4 Kölner, Frankfurter, Leipziger *etc*

5 der Kölner Dom — ein Frankfurter Würstchen
Cologne cathedral — a frankfurter sausage

6 Schweizer Käse
Swiss cheese

7 Die Sprache des Kölners heißt Kölsch.
People from Cologne speak Kölsch.
von den Frankfurtern
of the people of Frankfurt

8 die Kölnerin, die Kölnerinnen
die Londonerin, die Londonerinnen

9 München ► der Münchner
Bremen ► der Bremer
Göttingen ► der Göttinger

10 ein echt frankfurterischer Ausdruck
a real Frankfurt expression
Er spricht etwas münchnerisch.
He has something of a Munich accent.

The Comparison of Adjectives

Adjectives have three basic forms of comparison:

1) The simple form is used to describe something or someone.

e.g. a *little* house
the house is *little*

This form is fully dealt with on pages 140–147.

Simple forms are used in *as ... as / not as ... as* comparisons → 1

2) The comparative form is used to compare two things or persons.

e.g. he is *bigger* than his brother

In German, comparatives are formed by adding -er to the simple form → 2

Than in comparative statements is translated by als → 3

Unlike English, the vast majority of German adjectives, including those of several syllables, form their comparatives in this way → 4

Many adjectives modify the stem vowel when forming their comparatives → 5

Examples

1 so ... wie **as ... as**
Er ist so gut wie sein Bruder.
He is as good as his brother.

ebenso ... wie **just as ... as**
Er war ebenso glücklich wie ich.
He was just as happy as I was.

zwei-/dreimal *etc* **twice/three times** ***etc***
so ... wie **as ... as**

Er war zweimal so groß wie sein Bruder.
He was twice as big as his brother.

nicht so ... wie **not as ... as**
Er ist nicht so alt wie du
He is not as old as you

2 klein/kleiner — **small/smaller**
schön/schöner — **lovely/lovelier**

3 Er ist kleiner als seine Schwester.
He is smaller than his sister.

4 bequem/bequemer — **comfortable/more comfortable**
gebildet/gebildeter — **educated/more educated**
effektiv/effektiver — **effective/more effective**

5 alt/älter — **old/older**
stark/stärker — **strong/stronger**
schwach/schwächer — **weak/weaker**
scharf/schärfer — **sharp/sharper**
lang/länger — **long/longer**
kurz/kürzer — **short/shorter**
warm/wärmer — **warm/warmer**
kalt/kälter — **cold/colder**
hart/härter — **hard/harder**
groß/größer — **big/bigger**

The Comparison of Adjectives *continued*

Adjectives whose simple form ends in **-el** lose the **-e-** before adding the comparative ending **-er** → ①

Adjectives with a diphthong followed by **-er** in their simple forms also drop the **-e-** before adding **-er** → ②

Adjectives whose simple form ends in **-en** or **-er** may drop the **-e-** of the simple form when adjectival endings are added to their comparative forms → ③

With a few adjectives, comparative forms may be used not only for comparison, but also to render the idea of "-ish" or "rather ..." Some common examples are:

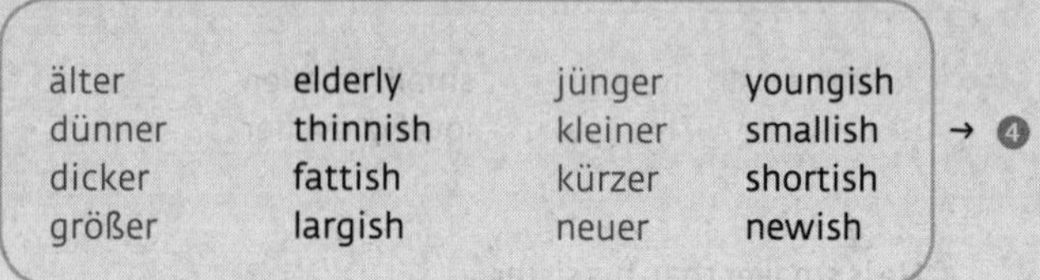

älter	elderly	jünger	youngish
dünner	thinnish	kleiner	smallish
dicker	fattish	kürzer	shortish
größer	largish	neuer	newish

→ ④

When used attributively (*before* the noun), comparative forms are declined in exactly the same way as simple adjectives (see pages 140–147) → ④ → ⑤

3) The superlative form is used to compare three or more persons or things.

e.g. he is *the biggest/the best*

Superlatives are formed by adding **-st** to the simple adjective. The vowel is modified, as for comparative forms, where applicable.

Superlative forms are generally used with an article and take endings accordingly (see page 140) → ⑥

Examples

1 eitel/eitler — vain/vainer
dunkel/dunkler — dark/darker

2 sauer/saurer — sour/more sour
die saurere Zitrone
the sourer lemon
Der Wein ist saurer geworden.
The wine has grown more sour.

teuer/teurer — expensive/more expensive
Das ist eine teurere Sorte.
That is a more expensive kind.
Die Neuen sind teurer.
The new ones are more expensive.

3 finster/finsterer — dark/darker
ein finstreres Gesicht
OR:
ein finstereres Gesicht
a grimmer face

4 ein älterer Herr
an elderly gentleman
eine größere Summe
a rather large sum
von jüngerem Aussehen
of youngish appearance

5 Die jüngere Schwester ist größer als die ältere.
The younger sister is bigger than the older one.
Mein kleinerer Bruder geht jetzt zur Schule.
My younger brother goes to school now.

6 Er ist der Jüngste.
He is the youngest.
Ihr erfolgreichster Versuch war im Herbst 2012.
Her most successful attempt was in the autumn of 2012.

The Comparison of Adjectives *continued*

Many adjectives form their superlative forms by adding -**est** instead of -**st** where pronunciation would otherwise be difficult or unaesthetic → 1

The English superlative "*most*" meaning "*very*" can be shown in German by any of the following → 2

äußerst

sehr

besonders

außerordentlich

höchst (***not with monosyllabic words***)

furchtbar (***conversational only***)

richtig (***conversational only***)

Some irregular comparative and superlative forms

SIMPLE FORM	COMPARATIVE	SUPERLATIVE
gut	besser	der beste
hoch	höher	der höchste
viel	mehr	der meiste
nah	näher	der nächste

Examples

1 der/die/das schlechteste
the worst

der/die/das schmerzhafteste
the most painful

der/die/das süßeste
the sweetest

der/die/das neueste
the newest

der/die/das stolzeste
the proudest

der/die/das frischeste
the freshest

2 Er ist ein äußerst begabter Mensch.
He is a most gifted person.

Das Essen war besonders schlecht.
The food was really/most dreadful.

Der Wein war furchtbar teuer!
The wine was dreadfully/most expensive!

Das sieht richtig komisch aus.
That looks really/most funny.

Personal Pronouns

As in English, personal pronouns change their form depending on their function in the sentence:

I saw *him*
He saw *me* → 1
We saw *her*

The personal pronouns are declined as follows:

NOMINATIVE		ACCUSATIVE		DATIVE	
ich	I	mich	me	mir	to/for me
du	you (*familiar*)	dich	you	dir	to/for you
er	he/it	ihn	him/it	ihm	to/for him/it
sie	she/it	sie	her/it	ihr	to/for her/it
es	it/he/she	es	it/him/her	ihm	to/for it/him/her → 2
wir	we	uns	us	uns	to/for us
ihr	you (*plural*)	euch	you	euch	to/for you
sie	they	sie	them	ihnen	to/for them
Sie	you (*polite*)	Sie	you	Ihnen	to/for you
man	one	einen	one	einem	to/for one

As can be seen from the above table, there are three ways of addressing people in German – du, ihr or Sie.

All three forms are illustrated on page 160.

Personal pronouns in the dative require no preposition when acting as indirect object, i.e. *to* me, *to* him *etc* → 3

Examples

1 Ich sah ihn.
I saw him.

Er sah mich.
He saw me.

Wir sahen sie.
We saw her.

2 Wir sind mit ihnen spazieren gegangen.
We went for a walk with them.

Sie haben uns eine tolle Geschichte erzählt.
They told us a great story.

Soll ich Ihnen etwas mitbringen?
Shall I bring something back for you?

3 Er hat es ihr gegeben.
He gave it to her.

Ich habe ihm ein neues Buch gekauft.
I bought a new book for him.
OR:
I bought him a new book.

Personal Pronouns *continued*

Du is a singular form, used only when speaking to one person. It is used to talk to children, close friends and relatives, animals and objects of affection such as a toy, one's car etc.

When in doubt it is always best to use the more formal Sie form.

Ihr is simply the plural form of du and is used in exactly the same situations wherever more than one person is to be addressed → 1

The familiar forms and their possessives are written with a small letter → 2

Sie is the polite, or formal, way of addressing people. It is written in all its declined forms with a capital letter, including the possessive → 3

Sie is used:

- by children talking to adults outside their immediate family.
- by adults talking to older children from mid-teens onwards. Teachers use it to their senior classes and bosses to their trainees etc.
- among adult strangers meeting for the first time.
- among colleagues, friends and acquaintances unless a suggestion has been formally made by one party and accepted by the other that the familiar forms should be used. Familiar forms must then continue to be used at all times, as a reversion to the formal might be considered insulting.

Examples

1 Kinder, was wollt ihr essen?
Children, what do you want to eat?

2 Er hat mir gesagt, du sollst deine Frau mitbringen.
He told me you were to bring your wife.

Gestern bin ich deinem Bruder begegnet.
I met your brother yesterday.

3 Was haben Sie gesagt?
What did you say?

Ich habe es Ihnen schon gegeben.
I have already given it to you.

Ja, Ihre Sachen sind jetzt fertig.
Yes, your things are ready now.

Personal Pronouns *continued*

Er/sie/es

All German nouns are masculine, feminine or neuter → 1

The personal pronoun must agree in number and in gender with the noun which it represents.

Es is used only for neuter nouns, and not for all inanimate objects → 2

Inanimate objects which are masculine use the pronoun er → 3

Feminine inanimate objects use the pronoun sie → 4

Neuter nouns referring to people have the neuter pronoun es → 5

NOTE: A common error for English speakers is to call all objects es.

Man

This is used in much the same way as the pronoun one in English, but it is much more commonly used in German → 6

It is also used to make an alternative passive form (see page 34) → 7

The genitive personal pronoun

Genitive forms of the personal pronouns do exist → 8

In practice, however, these are rarely used. Wherever possible, alternative expressions are found which do not require the genitive personal pronoun.

Special genitive forms exist for use with the prepositions wegen and willen → 9

Examples

1

der Tisch	the table (*masculine*)
die Gardine	the curtain (*feminine*)
das Baby	the baby (*neuter*)

2 Das Bild ist schön. ► Es ist schön.
The picture is beautiful. ► It is beautiful.

3 Der Tisch ist groß. ► Er ist groß.
The table is large. ► It is large.

4 Die Gardine ist weiß. ► Sie ist weiß.
The curtain is white. ► It is white.

5 Das Kind stand auf. ► Es stand auf.
The child stood up. ► He/she stood up.

6 Es tut einem gut.
It does one good.

7 Man holt mich um sieben ab.
I am being picked up at seven.

8

meiner	of me	unser	of us
deiner	of you	euer	of you (*plural*)
seiner	of him/it	ihrer	of them
ihrer	of her/it	Ihrer	of you (*polite*)

9

meinetwegen	because of me, on my account
deinetwegen	because of you, on your account *etc*
seinetwegen	
ihretwegen	
unsertwegen	
euretwegen	
Ihretwegen	

meinetwillen	for my sake, for me *etc*
deinetwillen	
ihretwillen *etc*	

Personal Pronouns *continued*

The use of pronouns after prepositions

Personal pronouns used after prepositions and referring to a person are in the *case* required by the preposition in question (see pages 198–199) → 1

When, however, a *thing* rather than a person is referred to, the construction

preposition + pronoun

becomes

da- + *preposition* → 2

Before a preposition beginning with a vowel, the form dar- + *preposition* is used → 3

This affects the following prepositions:

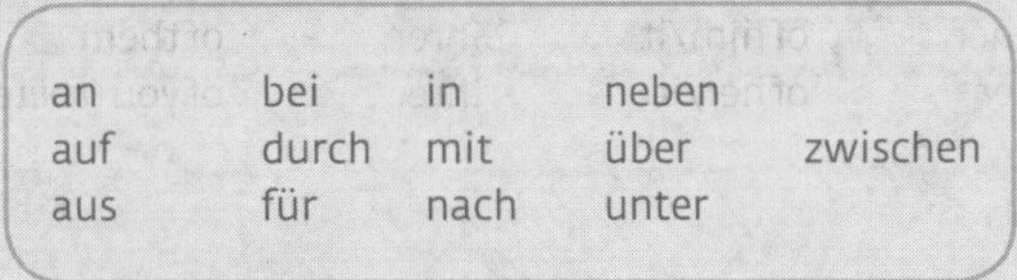

an	bei	in	neben	
auf	durch	mit	über	zwischen
aus	für	nach	unter	

These contracted forms are used after verbs followed by a preposition (see pages 76–79) → 4

After prepositions used to express motion the form with da(r)- is not felt to be sufficiently strong. Forms with hin and her are used as follows:

aus: heraus/hinaus
auf: herauf/hinauf → 5
in: herein/hinein

Examples

1 Ich bin mit ihm spazieren gegangen.
I went for a walk with him.

2 Klaus hatte ein Messer geholt und wollte damit den Kuchen schneiden.
Klaus had brought a knife and was about to cut the cake with it.

3 Lege es bitte darauf.
Put it there please.

4 Der Unterschied liegt darin, dass ...
The difference is that ...

Ich erinnere mich nicht daran.
I don't remember (it).

5 Er sah eine Treppe und ging leise hinauf.
He saw some stairs and went up them quietly.

Endlich fand er unser Zelt und kam herein.
He finally found our tent and came in.

Er öffnete den Koffer und legte das Hemd hinein.
He opened his suitcase and put in his shirt.

Possessive Pronouns

meiner	mine
deiner	yours (*familiar*)
seiner	his/its
ihrer	hers/its
uns(e)rer	ours
eu(e)rer	yours (*plural*)
ihrer	theirs
Ihrer	yours (*polite*)

These have the same endings as dieser. Their declension is therefore the same as for possessive adjectives (see page 136) except in the masculine nominative singular and the neuter nominative and accusative singular:

	SINGULAR			PLURAL
	MASC	FEM	NEUT	ALL GENDERS
NOM	-er	-e	-(e)s	-e
ACC	-en	-e	-(e)s	-e
GEN	-es	-er	-es	-er
DAT	-em	-er	-em	-en

The bracketed **(e)** is often omitted, especially in spoken German.

Possessive pronouns must agree in number, gender and case with the noun they replace → 1

Note the translation of *of mine*, *of yours* etc → 2

meiner is declined in full opposite → 3
Deiner, seiner and ihrer are declined like meiner.

Unserer and euerer are shown in full, since they have slightly different forms with an optional -e- → 4

Examples

1 Der Wagen da drüben ist meiner. Er ist kleiner als deiner.
The car over there is mine. It is smaller than yours.

2 Er ist ein Bekannter von mir.
He is an acquaintance of mine.

3 meiner **mine**

	SINGULAR			PLURAL
	MASC	FEM	NEUT	ALL GENDERS
NOM	meiner	meine	mein(e)s	meine
ACC	meinen	meine	mein(e)s	meine
GEN	meines	meiner	meines	meiner
DAT	meinem	meiner	meinem	meinen

4 uns(e)rer **ours**

	SINGULAR			PLURAL
	MASC	FEM	NEUT	ALL GENDERS
NOM	uns(e)rer	uns(e)re	uns(e)res	uns(e)re
ACC	uns(e)ren	uns(e)re	uns(e)res	uns(e)re
GEN	uns(e)res	uns(e)rer	uns(e)res	uns(e)rer
DAT	uns(e)rem	uns(e)rer	uns(e)rem	uns(e)ren

eu(e)rer **yours** (*plural*)

	SINGULAR			PLURAL
	MASC	FEM	NEUT	ALL GENDERS
NOM	eu(e)rer	eu(e)re	eu(e)res	eu(e)re
ACC	eu(e)ren	eu(e)re	eu(e)res	eu(e)re
GEN	eu(e)res	eu(e)rer	eu(e)res	eu(e)rer
DAT	eu(e)rem	eu(e)rer	eu(e)rem	eu(e)ren

Possessive Pronouns *continued*

Alternative forms

There are two alternatives to the meiner/deiner *etc* forms shown on page 167:

der, die, das meinige *or* Meinige	mine
der, die, das deinige *or* Deinige	yours (*familiar*)
der, die, das seinige *or* Seinige	his/its
der, die, das ihrige *or* Ihrige	hers/its
der, die, das uns(e)rige *or* Uns(e)rige	ours
der, die, das eu(e)rige *or* Eu(e)rige	yours (*plural*)
der, die, das ihrige *or* Ihrige	theirs
der, die, das Ihrige	yours (*polite*)

These are not as common as the meiner/deiner *etc* forms → 1

These forms are declined as the definite article followed by a weak adjective (see page 140) → 2

The bracketed (e) of the first and second person plural is often omitted in spoken German.

der, die, das meine *or* Meine	mine
der, die, das deine *or* Deine	yours (*familiar*)
der, die, das seine *or* Seine	his/its
der, die, das ihre *or* Ihre	hers/its
der, die, das uns(e)re *or* Uns(e)re	ours
der, die, das eu(e)re *or* Eu(e)re	yours (*plural*)
der, die, das ihre *or* Ihre	theirs
der, die, das Ihre	yours (*polite*)

These forms are also less common than the meiner/deiner *etc* forms. They are declined as the definite article followed by a weak adjective (see page 140) → 3

Examples

1. Ihr Auto ist aber neuer als das meinige *or* Meinige.
Your car is newer than mine.
Paul hat seiner Freundin Blumen gekauft. Ich habe der meinigen *or* Meinigen Parfüm geschenkt.
Paul bought his girlfriend some flowers. I bought mine perfume.

2. SINGULAR

	MASC	FEM	NEUT
NOM	der meinige	die meinige	das meinige
ACC	den meinigen	die meinige	das meinige
GEN	des meinigen	der meinigen	des meinigen
DAT	dem meinigen	der meinigen	dem meinigen

PLURAL
ALL GENDERS

NOM	die meinigen
ACC	die meinigen
GEN	der meinigen
DAT	den meinigen

3. SINGULAR

	MASC	FEM	NEUT
NOM	der meine	die meine	das meine
ACC	den meinen	die meine	das meine
GEN	des meinen	der meinen	des meinen
DAT	dem meinen	der meinen	dem meinen

PLURAL
ALL GENDERS

NOM	die meinen
ACC	die meinen
GEN	der meinen
DAT	den meinen

NOTE: Der/die/das meinige *etc* **can also be spelt** der/die/das Meinige *etc* **and** der/die/das meine *etc* **can also be spelt** der/die/das Meine *etc*.

Reflexive Pronouns

Reflexive pronouns, used to form reflexive verbs, have two forms, accusative and dative, as follows → 1

ACCUSATIVE	DATIVE	
mich	mir	myself
dich	dir	yourself (*familiar*)
sich	sich	himself/herself/itself/themselves
uns	uns	ourselves
euch	euch	yourselves (*plural*)
sich	sich	yourself/yourselves (*polite*)

Unlike personal pronouns and possessives, the polite forms have no capital letter → 2

For the position of reflexive pronouns within a sentence see page 30 (reflexive verbs) and pages 224–235 (sentence structure).

Reflexive pronouns are also used after prepositions when the pronoun has the function of "reflecting back" to the subject of the sentence → 3

A further use of reflexive pronouns in German is with transitive verbs where the action is performed for the benefit of the subject, as in the English phrase:

> I bought *myself* a new hat

The pronoun is not always translated in English → 4

Examples

1 Er hat sich rasiert.
He had a shave.

Du hast dich gebadet.
You had a bath.

Ich will es mir zuerst überlegen.
I'll have to think about it first.

2 Setzen Sie sich bitte.
Please take a seat.

3 Er hatte nicht genug Geld bei sich. (NOT: bei ihm)
He didn't have enough money on him.

4 Ich hole mir ein Bier.
I'm going to get a beer (for myself).

Er hat sich einen neuen Anzug gekauft.
He bought (himself) a new suit.

Reflexive Pronouns *continued*

Reflexive pronouns may be used for *reciprocal* actions, usually rendered by "each other" in English → 1

Reciprocal actions may also be expressed by einander. This does not change in form → 2

Einander is always used in place of the reflexive pronoun after prepositions. Note that the preposition and einander come together to form one word → 3

Emphatic reflexive pronouns

In English, these have the same forms as the normal reflexive pronouns:

The queen *herself* had given the order

I haven't read it *myself*, but ...

In German, this idea is expressed not by the reflexive pronouns, but by selbst or (in colloquial speech) selber placed at some point in the sentence after the noun or pronoun to which they refer → 4

selbst/selber do not change their form, regardless of number and gender of the noun to which they refer → 4

They are always stressed, regardless of their position in the sentence.

Examples

1 Wir sind uns letzte Woche begegnet.
We met (each other) last week.

Sie hatten sich auf einer Tagung kennengelernt.
They had got to know each other at a conference.

2 Wir kennen uns schon.
OR:
Wir kennen einander schon.
We already know each other.

Sie kennen sich schon.
OR:
Sie kennen einander schon.
They already know each other.

3 Sie redeten miteinander.
They were talking to each other.

4 Die Königin selbst hat es befohlen.
The queen herself has given the order.

Ich selbst habe es nicht gelesen, aber ...
I haven't read it myself, but ...

Relative Pronouns

These have the same forms as the definite article, except in the dative plural and genitive cases.

They are declined as follows:

	SINGULAR			PLURAL
	MASC	FEM	NEUT	ALL GENDERS
NOM	der	die	das	die
ACC	den	die	das	die
GEN	dessen	deren	dessen	deren
DAT	dem	der	dem	denen

Relative pronouns must agree in gender and number with the noun to which they refer. They take their case however from the function they have in their own relative clause → ❶

The relative pronoun cannot be omitted in German as it sometimes is in English → ❷

The genitive forms are used in relative clauses in much the same way as in English → ❸

NOTE, however, the translation of certain phrases → ❹

When a preposition introduces the relative clause, the relative pronoun may be replaced by **wo-** or **wor-** if the noun or pronoun it stands for refers to an inanimate object or abstract concept → ❺

The full form of relative pronoun plus preposition is however stylistically better.

Relative clauses are always divided off by commas from the rest of the sentence → ❶-❺

Examples

1. Der Mann, den ich gestern gesehen habe, kommt aus Hamburg.
   The man whom I saw yesterday comes from Hamburg.

2. Die Frau, mit der ich gestern gesprochen habe, kennt deine Mutter.
   The woman I spoke to yesterday knows your mother.

3. Das Kind, dessen Fahrrad gestohlen worden war, ...
   The child whose bicycle had been stolen ...

4. Die Kinder, von denen einige schon lesen konnten, ...
   The children, some of whom could read, ...

   Meine Freunde, von denen einer ...
   My friends, one of whom ...

5. Das Buch, woraus ich vorgelesen habe, ...
   OR:
   Das Buch, aus dem ich vorgelesen habe, ...
   The book I read aloud from ...

Relative Pronouns *continued*

Welcher

A second relative pronoun exists. This has the same forms as the interrogative adjective welcher without the genitive forms:

	SINGULAR			PLURAL
	MASC	FEM	NEUT	ALL GENDERS
NOM	welcher	welche	welches	welche
ACC	welchen	welche	welches	welche
GEN	—	—	—	—
DAT	welchem	welcher	welchem	welchen

These forms are used only infrequently as relative pronouns, where sentence rhythm might benefit.

They are also useful used as articles or adjectives to connect a noun in the relative clause with the contents of the main clause → 1

Wer, was

These are normally used as interrogative pronouns meaning *who?*, *what?* and are declined as such on page 178.

They may, however, also be used without interrogative meaning to replace both subject and relative pronoun in English:

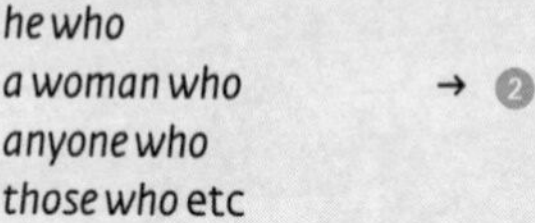

he who
a woman who → 2
anyone who
those who etc

Was is the relative pronoun used in set expressions with certain neuter forms → 3

Examples

1 Er glaubte, mit der Hausarbeit nicht helfen zu brauchen, mit welcher Idee seine Mutter nicht einverstanden war!
He thought he didn't have to help in the house, an idea with which his mother was not in agreement!

2 Wer das glaubt, ist verrückt.
Anyone who believes that is mad.

Was mich angeht, ...
For my part, ...

Was du gestern gekauft hast, steht dir ganz gut.
The things you bought yesterday suit you very well.

3

alles, was ...	**everything which**
allerlei, was ...	**all kinds of things that**
das, was ...	**that which**
dasjenige, was ...	**that which**
dasselbe, was ...	**the same one that**
einiges, was ...	**some that**
Folgendes, was ...	**the following which**
manches, was ...	**some which**
nichts, was ...	**nothing that**
vieles, was ...	**a lot that**
wenig, was ...	**little that**

Nichts, was er sagte, hat gestimmt.
Nothing that he said was right.

Das, was du jetzt machst, ist reiner Unsinn!
What you are doing now is sheer nonsense!

Mit allem, was du gesagt hast, sind wir einverstanden.
We agree with everything you said.

Interrogative Pronouns

These are the pronouns used to ask questions.

As in English, they have few forms, singular and plural being the same.

They are declined as follows:

	PERSONS	THINGS
NOM	wer?	was?
ACC	wen?	was?
GEN	wessen?	wessen?
DAT	wem?	—

They are used in direct questions → ❶

or in indirect questions → ❷

When used as the subject of a sentence, they are always followed by a singular verb → ❸

BUT: When followed by a verb and taking a noun complement, the verb may be plural if the sense demands it → ❹

The interrogative pronouns can be used in rhetorical questions or in exclamations → ❺

Examples

1 Wer hat es gemacht?
Who did it?

Mit wem bist du gekommen?
Who did you come with?

2 Ich weiß nicht, wer es gemacht hat.
I don't know who did it.

Er wollte wissen, mit wem er fahren sollte.
He wanted to know who he was to travel with.

3 Wer kommt heute?
Who's coming today?

4 Wer sind diese Leute?
Who are these people?

5 Was haben wir gelacht!
How we laughed!

Interrogative Pronouns *continued*

When used with prepositions, was usually becomes wo- and is placed in front of the preposition to form one word → 1

Where the preposition begins with a vowel, wor- is used instead → 2

This construction is similar to da(r)- + *preposition* shown on page 164.

As with da(r)- + *preposition*, this construction is not used when the preposition is intended to convey movement.

Wohin (*where to*) and woher (*where from*) are used instead → 3

Was für ein?, welcher?

These are used to mean *what kind of one?* and *which one?*

They are declined as shown on pages 124–128.

They are used to form either direct or indirect questions → 4

They may refer either to persons or to things with the appropriate declension endings → 5

Examples

1 Wonach sehnst du dich?
What do you long for?

Wodurch ist es zerstört worden?
How was it destroyed?

2 Worauf kann man sich heutzutage noch verlassen?
What is there left to rely on these days?

3 Wohin fährst du?
Where are you going?

Woher kommt das?
Where has this come from?/How has this come about?

4 Was für eins hat er?
What kind (of one) does he have?

Welches hast du gewollt?
Which one did you want?

5 Für welchen hat sie sich entschieden?
Which one (*man/hat etc*) did she choose?

Indefinite Pronouns

(irgend)jemand someone, somebody

NOM	(irgend)jemand
ACC	(irgend)jemanden, (irgend)jemand
GEN	(irgend)jemand(e)s
DAT	(irgend)jemandem, (irgend)jemand

→ 1

niemand no-one, nobody

NOM	niemand
ACC	niemanden, niemand
GEN	niemand(e)s
DAT	niemandem, niemand

→ 2

The forms without endings are used in conversational German, but the inflected forms are preferred in literary and written styles.

When niemand and (irgend)jemand are used with a following adjective, they are usually not declined, but the adjective takes a capital letter and is declined as follows:

NOM	(irgend)jemand/niemand Neues
ACC	(irgend)jemand/niemand Neues
GEN	—
DAT	(irgend)jemand/niemand Neuem

→ 3

When (irgend)jemand and niemand are followed by ander(e)s, this is written with a small letter, e.g. (irgend)jemand/niemand ander(e)s.

Examples

1 Ich habe es (irgend)jemandem (*dat*) gegeben.
I gave it to someone.

(Irgend)jemand (*nom*) hat es genommen.
Someone has stolen it.

2 Er hat niemanden (*acc*) gesehen.
He didn't see anyone.

Er ist unterwegs niemandem (*dat*) begegnet.
He encountered no-one on the way.

3 Diese Aufgabe erfordert (irgend)jemand Intelligentes.
Someone intelligent is needed for this task.

Indefinite Pronouns *continued*

keiner none

	SINGULAR			PLURAL
	MASC	FEM	NEUT	ALL GENDERS
NOM	keiner	keine	keins	keine
ACC	keinen	keine	keins	keine
GEN	keines	keiner	keines	keiner
DAT	keinem	keiner	keinem	keinen

It is declined like the article kein, keine, kein (see page 126) except in the nominative masculine and nominative and accusative neuter forms → 1

It may be used to refer to people or things → 1

einer one

	SINGULAR		
	MASC	FEM	NEUT
NOM	einer	eine	ein(e)s
ACC	einen	eine	ein(e)s
GEN	eines	einer	eines
DAT	einem	einer	einem

This pronoun may be used to refer to either people or things → 2

It exists only in the singular forms.

Examples

1 Keiner von ihnen hat es tun können.
Not one of them was able to do it.

Gibst du mir eine Zigarette? — Tut mir leid, ich habe keine.
Will you give me a cigarette? — Sorry, I haven't got any.

2 Sie ist mit einem meiner Verwandten verlobt.
She is engaged to one of my relatives.

Wo sind die anderen Kinder? Ich sehe hier nur eins.
Where are the rest of the children? I can only see one here.

Gibst du mir einen? **(e.g. *einen Whisky, einen Zehner* etc) OR:**
Gibst du mir eine? **(e.g. *eine Zigarette, eine Blume* etc) OR:**
Gibst du mir eins? **(e.g. *ein Buch, ein Butterbrot* etc)**
Will you give me one?

Indefinite Pronouns *continued*

Certain adjectives and articles can be used as pronouns.

The following are all declined to agree in gender and number with the noun or pronoun they represent → 1

aller	all
ander	other
beide	both
derjenige	that one
derselbe	the same one
dieser	this one
einiger	some
irgendwelcher	someone or other/something or other
jeder	each (one), every one
jener	that one
mancher	some, quite a few
mehrere	several
sämtliche	all, the lot
solcher	such as that, such a one
welcher	which one

The following do not change whatever the gender or number of the noun or pronoun they represent → 2

ein bisschen	a bit, a little
ein paar	a few
ein wenig	a little, a few
(irgend)etwas	some, something
mehr	more
nichts	nothing, none

When an adjective follows etwas or nichts, it takes a capital letter and declension endings, e.g. etwas/nichts Gutes

Examples

1 Andere machen es besser. (e.g. *Leute, Waschmaschinen* etc)
Others do it better.

Mit einem solchen kommst du nicht bis nach Hause.
(e.g. *Wagen* etc)
You won't make it home in one like that.

Alles, was er ihr schenkte, schickte sie sofort zurück.
Everything that he gave her she sent back at once.

Er war mit beiden zufrieden. (e.g. *Computern, Autos* etc)
He was satisfied with both.

2 Ich muss dir etwas sagen.
I must tell you something.

(Irgend)etwas ist herausgefallen.
Something fell out.

Nichts ist geschehen.
Nothing happened.

Er ist mit nichts zufrieden.
Nothing ever satisfies him.

Gibst du mir bitte ein paar?
Will you give me a few?

Er hatte ein wenig bei sich.
He had a little with him.

Er braucht immer mehr um zu überleben.
He needs more and more to survive.

Use of Adverbs

Adverbs, or phrases which are used as adverbs, may:

- modify a verb → 1
- modify an adjective → 2
- modify another adverb → 3
- modify a conjunction → 4
- ask a question → 5
- form verb prefixes (see page 72) → 6

Adverbs are also used, in much the same way as in English, to make the meaning of certain tenses more precise e.g.

- with continuous tenses → 7
- to show a future meaning where the tense used is not future → 8

Examples

1 Er ging langsam über die Brücke.
He walked slowly over the bridge.

2 Er ist ein ziemlich großer Kerl.
He's quite a big chap.

3 Sie arbeitet heute besonders tüchtig.
She's working exceptionally well today.

4 Wenn er es nur aufgeben wollte!
If only he would give it up!

5 Wann kommt er an?
When does he arrive?

6 falsch spielen
to cheat (*at cards*)

hintragen
to carry (*to a place*)

7 Er liest gerade die Zeitung.
He's just reading the paper.

8 Er wollte gerade aufstehen, als ...
He was just about to get up when ...

Wir fahren morgen nach Köln.
We're driving to Cologne tomorrow.

The Formation of Adverbs

Many German adverbs are simply adjectives used as adverbs. Used in this way, unlike adjectives, they are not declined → 1

Some adverbs are formed by adding **-weise** or **-sweise** to a noun → 2

Some adverbs are also formed by adding **-erweise** to an uninflected adjective.

Such adverbs are used mainly to show the speaker's opinion → 3

There is also a class of adverbs which are not formed from other parts of speech e.g. unten, oben, leider → 4

For the position of adverbs within a clause or sentence, see the section on sentence structure, pages 224–235.

The following are some common adverbs of time:

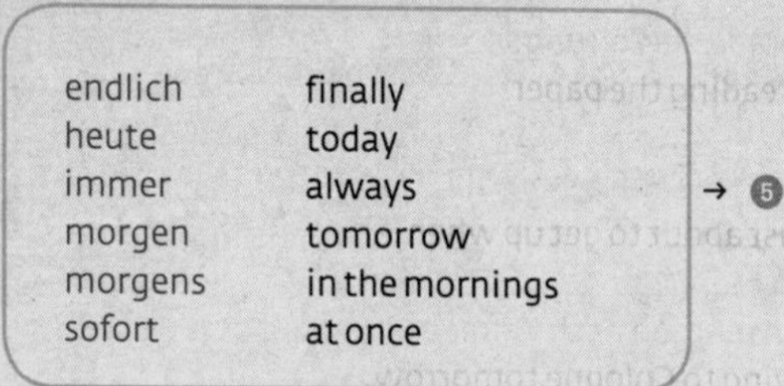

endlich	finally
heute	today
immer	always
morgen	tomorrow
morgens	in the mornings
sofort	at once

→ 5

The following are some common adverbs of degree:

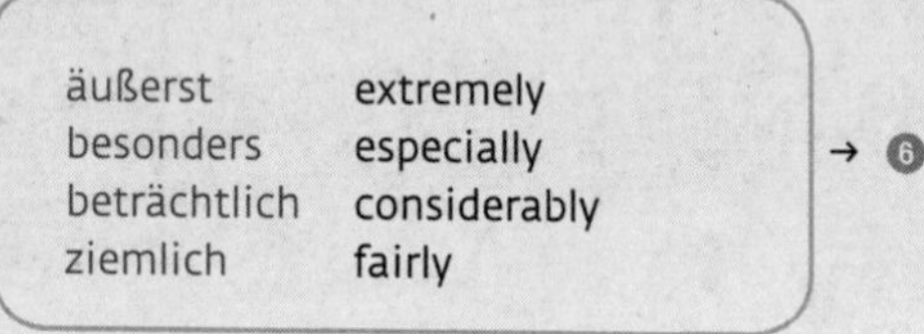

äußerst	extremely
besonders	especially
beträchtlich	considerably
ziemlich	fairly

→ 6

Examples

1 Habe ich das richtig gehört?
Is it true what I've heard?

Sie war modern angezogen.
She was fashionably dressed.

2
beispielsweise	for example
beziehungsweise	or/or rather/that is to say
schrittweise	step by step
zeitweise	at times
zwangsweise	compulsorily

3
erstaunlicherweise	astonishingly enough
glücklicherweise	fortunately
komischerweise	strangely enough

4 Unten wohnte Frau Schmidt.
Mrs Schmidt lived downstairs.

Leider können wir nicht kommen.
Unfortunately we cannot come.

5 Ich kann erst morgen kommen.
I can't come till tomorrow.

Das Kind hat immer Hunger.
The child is always hungry.

6 Das Paket war besonders schwer.
The parcel was unusually heavy.

Diese Übung ist ziemlich leicht.
This exercise is quite easy.

Adverbs of place

In certain respects German adverbs of place behave very differently from their English counterparts:

Where no movement, or merely a movement within the same place, is involved, the adverb is used in its simple dictionary form → 1

Movement *away from the speaker* is shown by the presence of hin → 2

The following compound adverbs are therefore often used when movement away from the original position is concerned, even though a simple adverb would be used in English:

dahin	(to) there
dorthin	there
hierhin	here
irgendwohin	(to) somewhere or other
überallhin	everywhere
wohin?	where (to)?

→ 3

Movement *towards the speaker* or central person is shown by the presence of her.

The following compound adverbs are therefore often used to show movement towards a person:

daher	from there
hierher	here
irgendwoher	from somewhere or other
überallher	from all over
woher?	where from?

→ 4

Examples

1 Wo ist er?
Where is he?

Er ist nicht da.
He isn't there.

Hier darf man nicht parken.
You can't park here.

2 Klaus und Ulli geben heute eine Party. Gehen wir hin?
Klaus and Ulli are having a party today. Shall we go?

3 Wohin fährst du?
Where are you going?

Sie liefen überallhin.
They ran everywhere.

4 Woher kommst du?
Where do you come from?

Woher hast du das?
Where did you get that from?

Das habe ich irgendwoher gekriegt.
I got that from somewhere or other.

Comparison of Adverbs

The comparative form of the adverb is obtained in exactly the same way as that of adjectives, i.e. by adding **-er** → 1

The superlative form is produced as follows:

am + *adverb* + **-sten/-esten**

It is not declined → 2

Note the use of the comparative adverb with immer to show progression → 3

the more ... the more ... is expressed in German by:

je ... desto ... or je ... umso ... → 4

Some adverbial superlatives are used to show the extent of a quality rather than a comparison with others. These are as follows:

bestens	very well/very warmly
höchstens	at the most/at best
meistens	mostly/most often
spätestens	at the latest
strengstens	strictly, absolutely
wenigstens	at least

→ 5

Two irregular comparatives and superlatives:

gern ► lieber ► am liebsten (used with haben) → 6
well ► better ► best

bald ► eher ► am ehesten
soon ► sooner ► soonest

Examples

1 Er läuft schneller als seine Schwester.
He runs faster than his sister.

Ich sehe ihn seltener als früher.
I see him less often than before.

2 Wer von ihnen arbeitet am schnellsten?
Which of them works fastest?

Er isst am meisten.
He eats most.

3 Die Mädchen sprachen immer lauter.
The girls were talking more and more loudly.

Er fuhr immer langsamer.
He drove more and more slowly.

4 Je eher, desto besser.
The sooner the better.

5 Er kommt meistens zu spät an.
He usually arrives late.

Rauchen strengstens verboten!
Smoking strictly prohibited.

6 Welches hast du am liebsten?
Which do you like best?

Emphasizers

These are words commonly used in German, as indeed in English, especially in the spoken language, to emphasize or modify in some way the meaning of the sentence. The following are some of the most common:

aber

Used to lend emphasis to a statement → ①

denn

As well as its uses as a conjunction (see page 214), denn is widely used to emphasize the meaning. It often cannot be directly translated → ②

doch

Used as a positive reply in order to correct negative assumptions or impressions → ③
It can strengthen an imperative → ④
It can make a question out of a statement → ⑤

mal

May be used with imperatives → ⑥
It also has several idiomatic uses → ⑦

ja

Strengthens a statement → ⑧
It also has several idiomatic uses → ⑨

schon

Is used familiarly with an imperative → ⑩
It is also used in various idiomatic ways → ⑪

Examples

1 Das ist aber schön!
Oh that's pretty!

Aber ja!
Yes indeed!

2 Was ist denn hier los?
What's going on here then?

Wo denn?
Where?

3 Hat es dir nicht gefallen? — Doch!
Didn't you like it? — Oh yes, I did!

4 Lass ihn doch!
Just leave him!

5 Das schaffst du doch?
You'll manage it, won't you?

6 Komm mal her!
Come here!

Moment mal!
Just a minute!

7 Mal sehen.
We'll see.
Er soll es nur mal versuchen!
Just let him try it!

Hören Sie mal ...
Look here now ...

8 Er sieht ja wie seine Mutter aus.
He looks like his mother.
Das kann ja sein.
That may well be.

9 Ja und?
So what?/What then?
Das ist es ja.
That's just it.

Das ist ja lächerlich.
That's ridiculous.

10 Mach schon!
Get on with it!

11 schon wieder
again

Schon gut!
Okay/Very well!

Prepositions

In English, a preposition does not affect the word or phrase which it introduces, e.g.

the women	a large meal	these events
with the women	*after* a large meal	*before* these events

In German, however, the noun following a preposition must be put in a certain *case*:

accusative → ①

dative → ②

genitive → ③

It is therefore important to learn each preposition with the case, or cases, it governs.

The following guidelines will help you:

Prepositions which take the accusative or dative cases are much more common than those taking the genitive case.

Certain prepositions may take a dative or accusative case, depending on whether *movement* is involved or not. This is explained further on pages 202–211 → ④

Prepositions are often used to complete the sense of certain verbs, as shown on pages 76–79 → ⑤

After many prepositions, a shortened or *contracted* form of the definite article may be merged with the preposition to form one word, e.g.

auf + das ► aufs

bei + dem ► beim

zu + der ► zur

Examples

1 Es ist für dich.
It's for you.

Wir sind durch die ganze Welt gereist.
We travelled all over the world.

2 Er ist mit seiner Frau gekommen.
He came with his wife.

3 Es ist ihm trotz seiner Bemühungen nicht gelungen.
Despite his efforts, he still didn't succeed.

4 Es liegt auf dem Tisch.
It's on the table.
(*dative*: no movement implied)

Lege es bitte auf den Tisch.
Please put it on the table.
(*accusative*: movement *onto* the table)

5 Ich warte auf meinen Mann.
I'm waiting for my husband.

Contracted forms

Contractions are possible with the following prepositions:

PREPOSITION	+das	+den	+dem	+der
an	ans		am	
auf	aufs*			
bei			beim	
durch	durchs*			
für	fürs*			
hinter	hinters*	hintern*	hinterm*	
in	ins		im	
über	übers*	übern*	überm*	
um	ums*			
unter	unters*	untern*	unterm*	
vor	vors*		vorm*	
von			vom	
zu			zum	zur

* NOTE: Those forms marked with an asterisk are suitable only for use in colloquial, spoken German.
All other forms (not marked with an asterisk) may be safely used in any context, formal or informal → 1

Contracted forms are not used where the article is to be stressed → 

Other contracted forms involving prepositions, as shown on pages 164 and 174, occur:

- in the introduction to relative clauses → 3
- with personal pronouns representing inanimate objects → 4

Examples

1 Wir gehen heute Abend ins Theater.
We are going to the theatre this evening.

Er geht zur Schule.
He goes to school.

Das kommt vom Trinken.
That comes from drinking.

2 In dem Anzug kann ich mich nicht sehen lassen!
I can't go out in that suit!

3 Die Bank, worauf wir saßen, war etwas wackelig.
The bench we were sitting on was rather wobbly.

4 Er war damit zufrieden.
He was satisfied with that.

Er hat es darauf gesetzt.
He put it on it.

Prepositions followed by the Dative Case

Some of the most common prepositions taking the dative case are:

aus	gegenüber	seit
außer	mit	von
bei	nach	zu

aus

as a preposition meaning: *out of/from* → 1

as a separable verbal prefix (see page 72) → 2

außer

as a preposition meaning: *out of* → 3
except → 4

bei

as a preposition meaning: *at the home/shop/work* etc *of* → 5
near → 6
in the course of/during → 7

as a separable verbal prefix (see page 72) → 8

gegenüber

as a preposition meaning: *opposite* → 9
to(wards) → 10

NOTE: When used as a preposition, gegenüber is placed *after a pronoun*, but may be placed *before or after a noun*.

as a separable verbal prefix → 11

Examples

1 Er trinkt aus der Flasche.
He is drinking out of the bottle.
Er kommt aus Essen.
He comes from Essen.

2 aushalten to endure
Ich halte es nicht mehr aus.
I can't stand it any longer.

3 außer Gefahr/Betrieb
out of danger/order

4 alle außer mir
all except me

5 bei uns in Schottland
at home in Scotland
Er wohnt immer noch bei seinen Eltern.
He still lives with his parents.

6 Er saß bei mir.
He was sitting next to me.

7 Ich singe immer beim Arbeiten.
I always sing when I'm working.
Bei unserer Ankunft ...
On our arrival ...

8 beistehen to stand by
Er stand seinem Freund bei.
He stood by his friend.

9 Er wohnt uns gegenüber.
He lives opposite us.

10 Er ist mir gegenüber immer sehr freundlich gewesen.
He has always been very friendly towards me.

11 gegenüberstehen to face/to have an attitude towards
Er steht ihnen kritisch gegenüber.
He takes a critical view of them.

Prepositions followed by the Dative Case *continued*

mit

as a preposition meaning: *with* → ①

as a separable verbal prefix (see page 72) → ②

nach

as a preposition meaning: *after* → ③
to → ④
according to (it can be placed after the noun with this meaning) → ⑤

as a separable verbal prefix (see page 72) → ⑥

seit

as a preposition meaning: *since* → ⑦
for (of time) → ⑧
NOTE: Beware of the tense!

von

as a preposition meaning: *from* → ⑨
about → ⑩

as an alternative, often preferred, to the genitive case → ⑪

as a preposition meaning: *by* (to introduce the agent of a passive action, see page 34) → ⑫

zu

as a preposition meaning: *to* → ⑬
for → ⑭

as a separable verbal prefix (see page 72) → ⑮

Examples

1 Er ging mit seinen Freunden spazieren.
He went walking with his friends.

2 jemanden mitnehmen **to give someone a lift**
Nimmst du mich bitte mit?
Will you give me a lift please?

3 Nach zwei Stunden kam er wieder.
He returned two hours later.

4 Er ist nach London gereist.
He went to London.

5 Ihrer Sprache nach ist sie Süddeutsche.
From the way she spoke I would say she is from southern Germany.

6 nachmachen **to copy**
Sie macht mir alles nach.
She copies everything I do.

7 Seit der Zeit ...
Since then ...

8 Ich wohne seit zwei Jahren in Frankfurt.
I've been living in Frankfurt for two years.

9 Von Frankfurt sind wir weiter nach München gefahren.
From Frankfurt we went on to Munich.

10 Ich weiß nichts von ihm.
I know nothing about him.

11 Die Mutter von diesen Mädchen ...
The mother of these girls ...
Sie ist eine Freundin von Horst.
She is a friend of Horst's.

12 Er ist von unseren Argumenten überzeugt worden.
He was convinced by our arguments.

13 Er ging zum Arzt.
He went to the doctor's.

14 Wir sind zum Essen eingeladen.
We're invited for dinner.

15 zumachen **to shut**
Mach die Tür zu!
Shut the door!

Prepositions followed by the Accusative Case

The most common of these are:

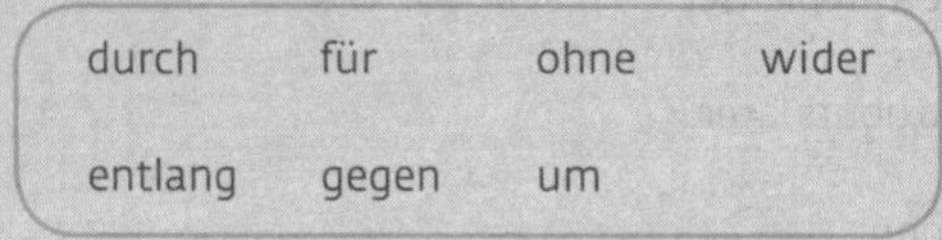

durch	für	ohne	wider
entlang	gegen	um	

durch

as a preposition meaning: *through* → 1

preceding the inanimate agent of a passive action (see page 34) → 2

as a separable verbal prefix

entlang

as a preposition meaning: *along* (it follows the noun with this meaning) → 3

as a separable verbal prefix → 4

für

as a preposition meaning: *for* → 5
to → 6

in was für/was für ein *what kind of/what* (see pages 144 and 180) → 7

gegen

as a preposition meaning: *against* → 8
towards/getting on for → 9

as a separable verbal prefix

Examples

1 durch das Fenster blicken
to look through the window

2 Durch seine Bemühungen wurden alle gerettet.
Everyone was saved through his efforts.

3 die Straße entlang
along the street

4 entlanggehen to go along
Wir gingen die Straße entlang.
We went along the street.

5 Ich habe es für dich getan.
I did it for you.

6 Das ist für ihn sehr wichtig.
That is very important to him.

7 Was für Äpfel sind das?
What kind of apples are they?

8 Stelle es gegen die Mauer.
Put it against the wall.

Haben Sie ein Mittel gegen Schnupfen?
Have you something for colds?

Ich habe nichts dagegen.
I've got nothing against it.

9 Wir sind gegen vier angekommen.
We arrived at getting on for/around four o'clock.

Prepositions followed by the Accusative Case *continued*

ohne

as a preposition meaning: *without* → 1

um

as a preposition meaning: *(a)round/round about* → 2

at (in time expressions) → 3

for (after certain verbs) → 4

about (after certain verbs) → 5

by (in expressions of quantity) → 6

as a variable verbal prefix (see page 74) → 7

wider

as a preposition meaning: *contrary to/against* → 8

as a variable verbal prefix (see page 74) → 9

Examples

1 Ohne ihn gehts nicht.
It won't work without him.

2 um die Ecke
(a)round the corner

3 Es fängt um neun Uhr an.
It begins at nine.

4 Sie baten ihre Mutter um Kekse.
They asked their mother for some biscuits.

5 Es handelt sich um dein Benehmen.
It's a question of your behaviour.

6 Es ist um zehn Euro billiger.
It is cheaper by ten euros.

7 umarmen **to embrace (*inseparable*)**
Er hat sie umarmt.
He gave her a hug.

umfallen **to fall over (*separable*)**
Er ist umgefallen.
He fell over.

8 Das geht mir wider die Natur.
That's against my nature.

9 widersprechen **to go against (*inseparable*)**
Das hat meinen Wünschen widersprochen.
That went against my wishes.

(sich) widerspiegeln **to reflect (*separable*)**
Der Baum spiegelt sich im Wasser wider.
The tree is reflected in the water.

Prepositions followed by the Accusative or the Dative Case

These prepositions are followed by:

- the accusative when *movement towards* a different place is involved.
- the dative when *position* is described as opposed to movement, or when the movement is *within* the same place.

The most common prepositions in this category are:

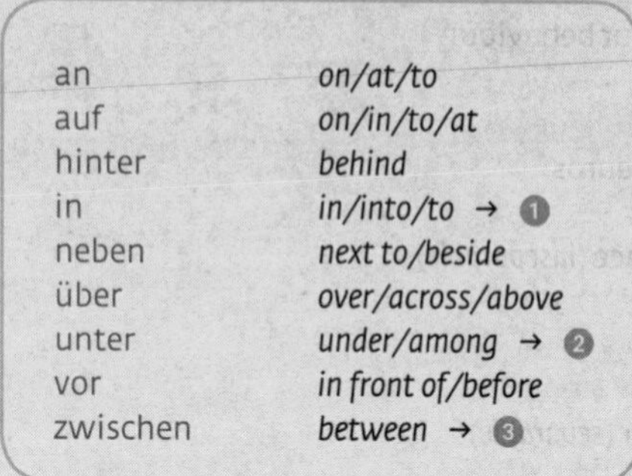

an	*on/at/to*
auf	*on/in/to/at*
hinter	*behind*
in	*in/into/to* → ❶
neben	*next to/beside*
über	*over/across/above*
unter	*under/among* → ❷
vor	*in front of/before*
zwischen	*between* → ❸

These prepositions may also be used with figurative meanings as part of a *verb + preposition* construction (see page 76).

The case following auf or an is then not the same after all verbs → 

It is therefore best to learn such constructions together with the case which follows them.

Many of these prepositions are also used as verbal prefixes in the same way as the prepositions described on pages 202–209 → ❺

Examples

1 Er ging ins Zimmer (*acc*).
He entered the room.

Im Zimmer (*dat*) warteten viele Leute auf ihn.
A lot of people were waiting for him in the room.

2 Er stellte sich unter den Baum (*acc*).
He (came and) stood under the tree.

Er lebte dort unter Freunden (*dat*).
There he lived among friends.

3 Er legte es zwischen die beiden Teller (*acc*).
He put it between the two plates.

Das Dorf liegt zwischen den Bergen (*dat*).
The village lies between the mountains.

4

sich verlassen auf (+*acc*)	**to depend on**
bestehen auf (+*dat*)	**to insist on**
glauben an (+*acc*)	**to believe in**
leiden an (+*dat*)	**to suffer from**

5 anrechnen **to charge for (*separable*)**
Das wird Ihnen später angerechnet.
You'll be charged for that later.

aufsetzen **to put on (*separable*)**
Sie setzte sich den Hut auf.
She put her hat on.

überqueren **to cross (*inseparable*)**
Sie hat die Straße überquert.
She crossed the street.

Prepositions followed by the Genitive Case

The following are some of the more common prepositions which take the genitive case:

außerhalb	*outside*
beiderseits	*on both sides of*
diesseits	*on this side of*
... halber	*for ... sake/because of ...*
hinsichtlich	*with regard to*
infolge	*as a result of*
innerhalb	*within/inside* → 1
jenseits	*on the other side of* → 2
statt*	*instead of*
trotz*	*in spite of* → 3
um ... willen	*for ... sake/because of ...*
während*	*during* → 4
wegen*	*on account of* → 5

* NOTE: Those prepositions marked with an asterisk may also be followed by the dative case → 6

NOTE: Special forms of the possessive and relative pronouns are used with wegen, halber and willen → 7

Examples

1 innerhalb dieses Zeitraums
within this period of time

2 jenseits der Grenze
on the other side of the frontier

3 trotz seiner Befürchtungen
despite his fears

4 während der Vorstellung
during the performance

5 wegen der neuen Stelle
because of the new job

6 trotz allem
in spite of everything

wegen mir
because of me

7

meinetwegen	on my account, because of me
deinetwegen	on your account, because of you (*familiar*)
seinetwegen	on his account, because of him
ihretwegen	on her/their account, because of her/them
unsertwegen	on our account, because of us
euertwegen	on your account, because of you (*plural*)
Ihretwegen	on your account, because of you (*polite*)
derentwegen	for whose sake, for her/their/its sake
dessentwegen	for whose sake, for his/its sake
meinethalben *etc*	on my *etc* account
derenthalben	on whose account, on her/their/its account
dessenthalben	on whose account, on his/its account
meinetwillen *etc*	for my *etc* sake
derentwillen	for whose sake, for her/its/their sake
dessentwillen	for whose sake, for his/its sake

Co-ordinating Conjunctions

These are used to link words, phrases or clauses.

These are the main co-ordinating conjunctions:

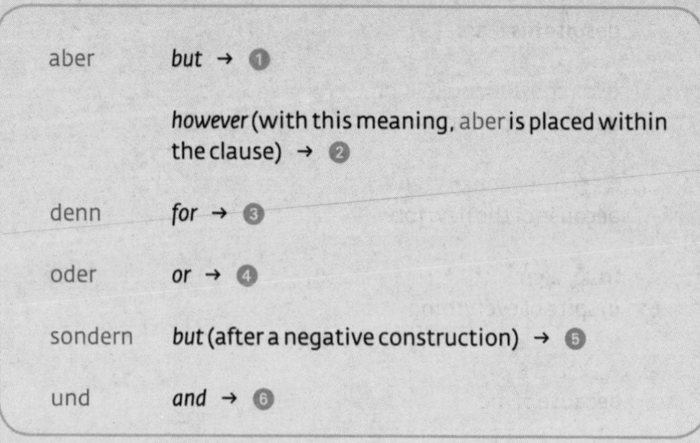

aber	*but* → ❶
	however (with this meaning, aber is placed within the clause) → ❷
denn	*for* → ❸
oder	*or* → ❹
sondern	*but* (after a negative construction) → ❺
und	*and* → ❻

These do not cause the inversion of subject and verb, i.e. the verb follows the subject in the normal way (see page 224) → ❶–❻

Inversion may however be caused by something other than the co-ordinating conjunction, e.g. dann, trotzdem, montags in the examples opposite → ❼

1 Wir wollten ins Kino, aber wir hatten kein Geld.
We wanted to go to the cinema but we had no money.

2 Ich wollte ins Theater; er aber wollte nicht mit.
I wanted to go to the theatre; however he wouldn't come.

3 Wir wollten heute fahren, denn montags ist weniger Verkehr.
We wanted to travel today because the traffic is lighter on Mondays.

4 Er hatte noch nie Whisky oder Schnaps getrunken.
He had never drunk whisky or schnapps.

Willst du eins oder hast du vielleicht keinen Hunger?
Do you want one or aren't you hungry?

5 Er ist nicht alt, sondern jung.
He isn't old, but young.

6 Horst und Veronika
Horst and Veronika

Er ging in die Stadt und kaufte sich ein neues Hemd.
He went into town and bought himself a new shirt.

7 Er hat sie besucht und dann ist er wieder nach Hause gegangen.
He paid her a visit and then went home again.

Wir wollten doch ins Kino, aber trotzdem sind wir zu Hause geblieben.
We wanted to go to the cinema, but even so we stayed at home.

Wir wollten heute fahren, denn montags ist der Verkehr geringer.
We wanted to travel today because there is less traffic on Mondays.

Double Co-ordinating Conjunctions

These conjunctions consist of two separate elements, like their English counterparts, e.g.

not only ... but also ...

The following are widely used:

sowohl.. als auch
both ... and

This may link words or phrases → 1

The verb is usually plural, whether the subjects are singular or plural → 1

weder ... noch
neither ... nor

This may link words or phrases → 2

It may also link clauses, and inversion of subject and verb then takes place in both clauses → 3

The verb is plural unless both subjects are singular → 4

1 Sowohl sein Vater als auch seine Mutter haben sich darüber gefreut.
Both his father and his mother were pleased about it.

Sowohl unser Lehrkörper als auch unsere Schüler haben teilgenommen.
Both our staff and our pupils took part.

2 Weder Georg noch sein Bruder kannte das Mädchen.
Neither Georg nor his brother knew the girl.

3 Weder mag ich ihn noch respektiere ich ihn.
I neither like nor respect him.

4 Weder die Befürworter noch die Gegner haben recht.
Neither the supporters nor the opponents are right.

Weder du noch ich würde es schaffen.
Neither you nor I would be able to do it.

Double Co-ordinating Conjunctions *continued*

nicht nur ... sondern auch
not only ... but also

This is used to link clauses as well as words and phrases → 1

The word order is: inversion of subject and verb in the first clause, and normal order in the second → 2

However, if nicht nur does not begin the clause, normal order prevails → 3

The verb agrees in number with the subject nearest to it → 4

entweder ... oder
either ... or

The verb agrees with the subject nearest it → 5

The normal word order is: inversion in the first clause, and normal order in the second → 6

However, it is possible to use normal order in the first clause, and this may lend a more threatening tone to the statement → 7

teils ... teils
partly ... partly

The verb is normally plural unless both subjects are singular → 8

Inversion of subject and verb takes place in both clauses → 9

1 Er ist nicht nur geschickt, sondern auch intelligent. OR:
Nicht nur ist er geschickt, sondern er ist auch intelligent.
He is not only skilful but also intelligent.

2 Nicht nur hat es die ganze Zeit geregnet, sondern ich habe mir auch noch das Bein gebrochen.
Not only did it rain the whole time, but I also broke my leg.

3 Es hat nicht nur die ganze Zeit geregnet, sondern ich habe mir auch noch das Bein gebrochen.
Not only did it rain the whole time, but I also broke my leg.

4 Nicht nur ich, sondern auch die Mädchen sind dafür verantwortlich.
It's not just me, but it's also the girls who are also responsible.

Nicht nur sie, sondern auch ich habe es gehört.
They weren't the only ones to hear it — I heard it too.

5 Entweder du oder Georg muss es getan haben.
It must have been either you or Georg who did it.

6 Entweder komme ich morgen vorbei, oder ich rufe dich an.
I'll either drop in tomorrow or I'll give you a ring.

7 Entweder du gibst das sofort auf, oder du kriegst kein Taschengeld mehr.
Either you stop that immediately, or you get no more pocket money.

8 Die Studenten waren teils Deutsche, teils Ausländer.
The students were partly German and partly from abroad.

9 Teils bin ich überzeugt, teils bleibe ich skeptisch.
Part of me is convinced, and part remains sceptical.

Subordinating Conjunctions

These are used to link clauses in such a way as to make one clause dependent on another for its meaning. The dependent clause is called a subordinate clause and the other a main clause.

The subordinate clause is always separated from the rest of the sentence by commas → ❶

The subordinate clause may precede the main clause. When this happens, the verb and subject of the main clause are inverted, i.e. they swap places, as shown on page 226 → ❷

The finite part of the verb (i.e. the conjugated part) is always at the end of a subordinate clause (see page 228) → ❸

For compound tenses in subordinate clauses, it is the auxiliary (the main part of the verb) which comes last, after the participle or infinitive used to form the compound tense (see pages 22–29) → ❹

Any modal verb (mögen, können etc, see pages 52–57) used in a subordinate clause is placed last in the clause → ❺

BUT: When the modal verb is in a compound tense, the order is as shown → ❻

1 **MAIN CLAUSE** **SUBORDINATE CLAUSE**

Er ist zu Fuß gekommen, weil der Bus zu teuer ist.
He came on foot because the bus is too dear.

Ich trinke viel Bier, obwohl es nicht gesund ist.
I drink a lot of beer although it isn't good for me.

Wir haben weitergefeiert, nachdem sie gegangen waren.
We carried on with the party after they went.

2 **SUBORDINATE CLAUSE** **MAIN CLAUSE**

Weil der Bus zu teuer ist, ist er zu Fuß gekommen.

Obwohl es nicht gesund ist, trinke ich viel Bier.

Nachdem sie gegangen waren, haben wir weitergefeiert.

3 Als er uns sah, ist er davongelaufen. **OR:**
Er ist davongelaufen, als er uns sah.
He ran away when he saw us.

4 Nachdem er gegessen hatte, ging er hinaus.
He went out after he had eaten.

5 Da er nicht mit uns sprechen wollte, ist er davongelaufen.
Since he didn't want to speak to us he ran away.

6 Da er nicht mit uns hat sprechen wollen, ist er davongelaufen.
Since he didn't want to speak to us he ran away.

Subordinating conjunctions *continued*

Here are some common examples of subordinating conjunctions and their uses:

als	when → 1
als ob	as if, as though
bevor	before
bis	until → 2
da	as, since → 3
damit	so (that)
indem	while
inwiefern	to what extent
nachdem	after → 4
ob	whether, if
obwohl	although
wann	when (*interrogative*) → 5
während	while → 6
weil	because → 7
wenn	when, whenever/if → 8
wie	as, like
wo	where
wohin	to where
worauf	whereupon/on which
worin	in which
seitdem	since
so dass, sodass	such that, so that
sobald	as soon as
soweit	as far as

1 Es regnete, als ich in Köln ankam. OR:
Als ich in Köln ankam, regnete es.
It was raining when I arrived in Cologne.

2 Ich warte, bis du zurückkommst.
I'll wait till you get back.

3 Da er nicht kommen wollte, ...
Since he didn't want to come ...

4 Er wird uns Bescheid sagen können, nachdem er angerufen hat. OR:
Nachdem er angerufen hat, wird er uns Bescheid sagen können.
He will be able to let us know for certain once he has phoned.

5 Er möchte wissen, wann der Zug ankommt.
He would like to know when the train is due to arrive.

6 Während seine Frau die Koffer auspackte, machte er das Abendessen. OR:
Er machte das Abendessen, während seine Frau die Koffer auspackte.
He made the supper while his wife unpacked the cases.

7 Wir haben den Hund nicht mitgenommen, weil im Auto nicht genug Platz war. OR:
Weil im Auto nicht genug Platz war, haben wir den Hund nicht mitgenommen.
We didn't take the dog because there wasn't enough room in the car.

8 Wenn ich ins Kino gehe ...
When(ever) I go to the cinema ...

Ich komme, wenn du willst.
I'll come if you like.

Word Order: Main Clauses

In a main clause the subject comes first and is followed by the verb, as in English:

His mother (*subject*) drinks (*verb*) whisky → 1

If the verb is in a compound or passive tense, the auxiliary follows the subject and the past participle or infinitive goes to the end of the clause → 2

The verb is the second concept in a main clause. The first concept may be a word, phrase or clause (see page 226) → 3

Any reflexive pronoun follows the main verb in simple tenses and the auxiliary in compound tenses → 4

The order for articles, adjectives and nouns is as in English: *article* + *adjective(s)* + *noun* → 5

A direct object usually follows an indirect, except where the direct object is a personal pronoun.

BUT: The indirect object can be placed last for emphasis, providing it is not a pronoun → 6

The position of adverbial expressions (see page 188) is not fixed. As a general rule they are placed close to the words to which they refer.

Adverbial items of *time* often come first in the clause, but this is flexible → 7

Adverbial items of *place* can be placed at the beginning of a clause when emphasis is required → 8

Adverbial items of *manner* are more likely to be within the clause, close to the word to which they refer → 9

Where there is more than one adverb, a useful rule of thumb is: "time, manner, place" → 10

Examples

1. Seine Mutter trinkt Whisky.
His mother drinks whisky.

2. Sie wird dir etwas sagen. Sie hat mir nichts gesagt.
She will tell you something. She told me nothing.
Es ist für ihn gekauft worden.
It was bought for him.

3.

1ST CONCEPT	**2ND CONCEPT**	
Die neuen Waren	kommen	morgen
(The new goods are coming tomorrow)		
Was du gesagt hast,	stimmt	nicht
(What you said isn't true)		

4. Er rasierte sich. Er hat sich rasiert.
He shaved. He (has) shaved.

5. ein alter Mann diese alten Sachen
an old man these old things

6. Ich gab dem Mann das Geld.
I gave the man the money.
Ich gab ihm das Geld. Ich gab es ihm.
I gave him the money. I gave him it/I gave it to him.
Er gab das Geld seiner Schwester.
He gave the money to his sister. (*not his brother*)

7. Gestern gingen wir ins Theater. **OR:**
Wir gingen gestern ins Theater.
We went to the theatre yesterday.

8. Dort haben sie Fußball gespielt. **OR:**
Sie haben dort Fußball gespielt.
They played football there.

9. Sie spielen gut Fußball.
They play football well.
Das war furchtbar teuer.
It was terribly expensive.

10. Wir haben gestern gut hierhin gefunden.
We found our way here all right yesterday.

Word Order: Main Clauses *continued*

A pronoun object precedes all adverbs → ❶

While the main verb must normally remain the second concept, the first concept need not always be the subject. Main clauses can begin with many things, including:

an adverb → ❷
a direct or indirect object → ❸
an infinitive phrase → ❹
a complement → ❺
a past participle → ❻
a prepositional phrase → ❼
a clause acting as the object of the verb → ❽
a subordinate clause → ❾

If the subject does not begin a main clause, the verb and subject must be turned around or "inverted" → ❷–❾

Beginning a sentence with something other than the subject is frequent in German.
It may however also be used for special effect to:

- *highlight* whatever is placed first in the clause → ❿
- *emphasize* the subject of the clause by forcing it from its initial position to the end of the clause → ⓫

After inversion, any reflexive pronoun precedes the subject, unless the subject is a pronoun → ⓬

The following do not cause inversion when placed at the beginning of a main clause, although inversion may be caused by something else placed after them:

allein, denn, oder, sondern, und → ⓭
ja and nein → ⓮
certain exclamations: ach, also, nun *etc* → ⓯
words or phrases qualifying the subject: auch, nur, sogar, *etc* → ⓰

Examples

1 Sie haben es gestern sehr billig gekauft.
They bought it very cheaply yesterday.

2 Gestern sind wir ins Theater gegangen.
We went to the theatre yesterday.

3 So ein Kind habe ich noch nie gesehen!
I've never seen such a child!
Seinen Freunden wollte er es nicht zeigen.
He wouldn't show it to his friends.

4 Seinen Freunden zu helfen, hat er nicht versucht.
He didn't try to help his friends.

5 Deine Schwester war es. It was your sister.

6 Geraucht hatte er nie. He had never smoked.

7 In diesem Haus ist Mozart auf die Welt gekommen.
Mozart was born in this house.

8 Was mit ihm los war, haben wir nicht herausgefunden.
We never discovered what was wrong with him.

9 Nachdem ich ihn gesehen hatte, ging ich nach Hause.
I went home after seeing him.

10 Dem würde ich nichts sagen!
I wouldn't tell *him* anything!

11 An der Ecke stand eine riesengroße Fabrik.
A huge factory stood on the corner.

12 Daran erinnerten sich die Zeugen nicht.
The witnesses didn't remember that.
Daran erinnerten sie sich nicht.
They didn't remember that.

13 Peter ging nach Hause und Elsa blieb auf der Party.
Peter went home and Elsa stayed at the party.
BUT: Peter ging nach Hause und unterwegs sah er Kurt.
Peter went home and on the way he saw Kurt.

14 Nein, ich will nicht. No, I don't want to.
BUT: Nein, das tue ich nicht. No, I won't do that.

15 Also, wir fahren nach Hamburg.
So we'll go to Hamburg.
BUT: Also, nach Hamburg wollt ihr fahren.
So you want to go to Hamburg.

16 Sogar seine Mutter wollte es ihm nicht glauben.
Even his mother wouldn't believe him.
BUT: Sogar mit dem Zug ginge es nicht schneller.
It would be no faster even by train.

Word Order: Subordinate Clauses

A subordinate clause may be introduced by:

- a relative pronoun (see page 174) → ①
- a subordinating conjunction (see page 222) → ②–③

The subject follows the opening conjunction or relative pronoun – see wir and er → ①–③

The main verb almost always goes to the end of a subordinate clause → ①–③

The exceptions to this are:

- in a wenn clause where wenn is omitted (see page 64) → ④
- in an indirect statement without dass (see page 64) → ⑤

The order for articles, nouns, adjectives, adverbs, direct and indirect objects is the same as for main clauses (see page 224), but they are all placed between the subject of the clause and the verb → ⑥

If the subject of a reflexive verb in a subordinate clause is a pronoun, the order is *subject pronoun + reflexive pronoun* → ⑦

If the subject is a noun, the reflexive pronoun may follow or precede it → ⑧

Where one subordinate clause lies inside another, both still obey the order rule for subordinate clauses → ⑨

Examples

1 Die Kinder, die wir gesehen haben ...

The children whom we saw ...

2 Da er nicht schwimmen wollte, ist er nicht mitgekommen.

As he didn't want to swim he didn't come.

3 Ich weiß, dass er zur Zeit in London wohnt.

I know he's living in London at the moment.

Ich weiß nicht, ob er kommt.

I don't know if he's coming.

4 Findest du meine Uhr, so ruf mich bitte an.
(= Wenn du meine Uhr findest, ruf mich bitte an.)

If you find my watch, please give me a ring.

5 Er meint, er werde es innerhalb einer Stunde schaffen.
(= Er meint, dass er es innerhalb einer Stunde schaffen werde.)

He thinks (that) he will manage it within an hour.

6 MAIN CLAUSE

Er ist gestern mit seiner Mutter in die Stadt gefahren.

He went to town with his mother yesterday.

SUBORDINATE CLAUSES

Da er gestern mit seiner Mutter in die Stadt gefahren ist, ...

Since he went to town with his mother yesterday ...

Der Junge, der gestern mit seiner Mutter in die Stadt gefahren ist, ...

The boy who went to town with his mother yesterday ...

Ich weiß, dass er gestern mit seiner Mutter in die Stadt gefahren ist.

I know that he went to town with his mother yesterday.

7 Weil er sich nicht setzen wollte, ...

Because he wouldn't sit down ...

8 Weil das Kind sich nicht setzen wollte, ... OR:
Weil sich das Kind nicht setzen wollte, ...

Because the child wouldn't sit down ...

9 Er wusste, dass der Mann, mit dem er gesprochen hatte, bei einer Baufirma arbeitete.

He knew that the man he had been speaking to worked for a construction company.

Word Order

In the imperative

- normal order → ❶
- with reflexive verbs → ❷
- with separable verbs → ❸
- with separable reflexive verbs → ❹

In direct and indirect speech

The verb of saying ("he replied/he said") must be inverted if it is placed within a quotation → ❺

The position of the verb in indirect speech depends on whether or not dass (see page 66) is used → ❻

Verbs with separable prefixes (see pages 72–75)

In main clauses the verb and prefix are separated in simple tenses and imperative forms → ❼

For compound tenses of main clauses and all tenses of subordinate clauses, the verb and its prefix are united at the end of the clause → ❽

In a present infinitive phrase (see page 46), the verb and prefix are joined together by zu and placed at the end of the phrase → ❾

Examples

1 Hol mir das Buch! (*singular*)
Holt mir das Buch! (*plural*) Fetch me that book!
Holen Sie mir das Buch! (*polite*)

2 Wasch dich sofort! (*singular*)
Wascht euch sofort! (*plural*) Wash yourself/yourselves
Waschen Sie sich sofort! (*polite*) at once!

3 Hör jetzt auf! (*singular*)
Hört jetzt auf! (*plural*) Stop it!
Hören Sie jetzt auf! (*polite*)

4 Dreh dich um! (*singular*)
Dreht euch um! (*plural*) Turn round!
Drehen Sie sich um! (*polite*)

5 „Meine Mutter" sagte er, „kommt erst morgen an".
"My mother", he said, "won't arrive till tomorrow".

6 Er sagte, dass sie erst am nächsten Tag ankomme.
He said that she would not arrive until the next day.
Er sagte, sie komme erst am nächsten Tag an.
He said she would not arrive until the next day.

7 Er machte die Tür zu.
He closed the door.
Ich räume zuerst auf.
I'll clean up first.
Hol mich um 7 ab!
Pick me up at 7!

8 Er hat die Tür zugemacht.
He closed the door.
Ich werde zuerst aufräumen.
I'll clean up first.
Er wurde um 7 abgeholt.
He was picked up at 7.
Wenn du mich um 7 abholst, ...
If you pick me up at 7 ...
Nachdem du mich abgeholt hast, ...
After you've picked me up ...

9 Um frühzeitig anzukommen, fuhren wir sofort ab.
In order to arrive early we left immediately.

Question Forms

Direct questions

In German, a direct question is formed by simply inverting the verb and subject → ❶

In compound tenses (see pages 22–27) the past participle or infinitive goes to the end of the clause → ❷

A statement can be made into a question by the addition of nicht, nicht wahr or doch, as with "isn't it" in English → ❸

Questions formed in this way normally expect the answer to be "yes".

When a question is put in the negative, doch can be used to answer it more positively than ja → ❹

Questions formed using interrogative words

When questions are formed with interrogative adverbs, the subject and verb are inverted → ❺

When questions are formed with interrogative pronouns and adjectives (see pages 144 and 176–178), the word order is that of direct statements:

- as the subject of the verb at the beginning of the clause they do not cause inversion → ❻
- if *not* the subject of the verb *and* at the beginning of the clause they do cause inversion → ❼

Indirect questions

These are questions following verbs of asking and wondering etc. The verb comes at the end of an indirect question → ❽

Examples

1 Magst du ihn?
Do you like him?

2 Gehst du ins Kino? **Do you go to the cinema?**
OR: **Are you going to the cinema?**

Hast du ihn gesehen? **Did you see him?**
OR: **Have you seen him?**

Wird sie mit ihm kommen?
Will she come with him?

3 Das stimmt, nicht (wahr)?
That's true, isn't it?

Das schaffst du doch?
You'll manage, won't you?

4 Glaubst du mir nicht? — Doch!
Don't you believe me? — Yes I do!

5 Wann ist er gekommen?
When did he come?

Wo willst du hin?
Where are you off to?

6 Wer hat das gemacht?
Who did this?

7 Wem hast du es geschenkt?
Who did you give it to?

8 Er fragte, ob du mitkommen wolltest.
He asked if you wanted to come.

Er möchte wissen, warum du nicht gekommen bist.
He would like to know why you didn't come.

Negatives

A statement or question is made negative by adding:

nicht (*not*) or nie (*never*)

The negative may be placed next to the phrase or word to which it refers. The negative meaning can be shifted from one element of the sentence to another in this way → 1

nie can be placed at the beginning of a sentence for added emphasis, in which case the subject and verb are inverted → 2

nicht comes at the end of a negative imperative, except when the verb is separable, in which case nicht *precedes* the separable prefix → 3

The combination nicht ein is usually replaced by forms of kein (see page 126) → 4

doch (see page 196) is used in place of ja to contradict a negative statement → 5

Negative comparison is made with nicht ... sondern (*not ... but*).

This construction is used to correct a previous false impression or idea → 6

Examples

1 Mit ihr wollte er nicht sprechen.
He didn't want to speak to *her*.
Er wollte nicht mit ihr sprechen.
He didn't *want* to speak to her.

Er will nicht morgen nach Hause.
OR: Morgen will er nicht nach Hause.
He doesn't want to go home *tomorrow*.
Er will morgen nicht nach Hause.
He doesn't want to go *home* tomorrow.

Wohnen Sie nicht in Dortmund?
Don't you live in Dortmund?
Warum ist er nicht mitgekommen?
Why didn't he come with you?
Waren Sie nie in Dortmund?
Have you never been to Dortmund?

2 Nie war sie glücklicher gewesen.
She had never been happier.

3 Iss das nicht!
Don't eat that!
Beeilen Sie sich nicht!
Don't hurry!
BUT: Geh nicht weg!
Don't go away!

4 Gibt es keine Plätzchen?
Aren't there any biscuits?
Kein einziges Kind hatte die Arbeit geschrieben.
Not a single child had done the work.

5 Du kommst nicht mit. — Doch, ich komme mit.
You're not coming. — Yes I am.

6 Nicht Joachim, sondern sein Bruder war es.
It wasn't Joachim, but his brother.

Numbers

Cardinal (*one, two etc*)		**Ordinal** (*first, second etc*)	
null	0		
eins	1	der erste [2]	1.
zwei [1]	2	der zweite [1]	2.
drei	3	der dritte	3.
vier	4	der vierte	4.
fünf	5	der fünfte	5.
sechs	6	der sechste	6.
sieben	7	der siebte	7.
acht	8	der achte	8.
neun	9	der neunte	9.
zehn	10	der zehnte	10.
elf	11	der elfte	11.
zwölf	12	der zwölfte	12.
dreizehn	13	der dreizehnte	13.
vierzehn	14	der vierzehnte	14.
fünfzehn	15	der fünfzehnte	15.
sechzehn	16	der sechzehnte	16.
siebzehn	17	der siebzehnte	17.
achtzehn	18	der achtzehnte	18.
neunzehn	19	der neunzehnte	19.
zwanzig	20	der zwanzigste	20.
einundzwanzig	21	der einundzwanzigste	21.
zweiundzwanzig [1]	22	der zweiundzwanzigste [1]	22.
dreißig	30	der dreißigste	30.
vierzig	40	der vierzigste	40.
fünfzig	50	der fünfzigste	50.
sechzig	60	der sechzigste	60.

[1] zwo **often replaces** zwei **in speech, to distinguish it clearly from** drei: zwo, zwoundzwanzig ***etc.***

[2] **The ordinal number and the preceding definite article (and adjective if there is one) are declined, e.g.:**

bei seinem dritten Versuch **at his third attempt**

siebzig	70	der siebzigste	70.
achtzig	80	der achtzigste	80.
neunzig	90	der neunzigste	90.
hundert	a hundred	der hundertste	100.
einhundert	one hundred		
hunderteins	101	der hunderterste	101.
hundertzwei	102	der hundertzweite	102.
hunderteinundzwanzig	121	der hunderteinundzwanzigste	121.
zweihundert	200	der zweihundertste	200.
tausend	a thousand	der tausendste	1000.
eintausend	one thousand		
tausendeins	1001	der tausenderste	1001.
zweitausend	2000	der zweitausendste	2000.
hunderttausend	100 000	der hunderttausendste	100 000.
eine Million	1 000 000	der millionste	1 000 000.

With large numbers, spaces or full stops are used where English uses a comma, e.g.:

1.000.000 or 1 000 000 for 1,000,000 (*a million*)

Decimals are written with a comma instead of a full stop, e.g.:

7,5 (sieben Komma fünf) for 7.5 (*seven point five*)

When ordinal numbers are used as nouns, they are written with a capital letter, e.g.:

sie ist die Zehnte — she's the tenth

Fractions

halb	die Hälfte	eine halbe Stunde
half (a)	half (the)	half an hour
das Drittel	zwei Drittel	das Viertel
third	two thirds	quarter
drei viertel	anderthalb, eineinhalb	zweieinhalb
three quarters	one and a half	two and a half

Time

Wie spät ist es? / Wie viel Uhr ist es?
What time is it?

Es ist ...
It's ...

00.00	Mitternacht / null Uhr / vierundzwanzig Uhr / zwölf Uhr
00.10	zehn (Minuten) nach zwölf / null Uhr zehn
00.15	Viertel nach zwölf / null Uhr fünfzehn
00.30	halb eins / null Uhr dreißig
00.40	zwanzig (Minuten) vor eins / null Uhr vierzig
00.45	Viertel vor eins / drei viertel eins / null Uhr fünfundvierzig
01.00	ein Uhr
01.10	zehn (Minuten) nach eins / ein Uhr zehn
01.15	Viertel nach eins / ein Uhr fünfzehn
01.30	halb zwei /ein Uhr dreißig
01.40	zwanzig (Minuten) vor zwei / ein Uhr vierzig
01.45	Viertel vor zwei / drei viertel zwei / ein Uhr fünfundvierzig
01.50	zehn (Minuten) vor zwei / ein Uhr fünfzig
12.00	zwölf Uhr
12.30	halb eins / zwölf Uhr dreißig
13.00	ein Uhr / dreizehn Uhr
16.30	halb fünf / sechzehn Uhr dreißig
22.00	zehn Uhr / zweiundzwanzig Uhr / zwoundzwanzig Uhr

morgen um halb drei
at half past two tomorrow

um drei Uhr (nachmittags)
at three (pm)

kurz vor zehn Uhr
just before ten o'clock

gegen vier Uhr (nachmittags)
towards four o'clock (in the afternoon)

erst um halb neun
not until half past eight

ab neun Uhr
from nine o'clock onwards

morgen früh/Abend
tomorrow morning/evening

Dates

Der Wievielte ist heute? / Welches Datum haben wir heute?
What's the date today?

Heute ist ... — It's ...
der zwanzigste März — the twentieth of March
der Zwanzigste — the twentieth

Heute haben wir ... — It's ...
den zwanzigsten März — the twentieth of March
den Zwanzigsten — the twentieth

Am Wievielten findet es statt? — When does it take place?

Es findet am ersten April statt ... — ... on the first of April

Es findet am Ersten statt — ... on the first

Es findet (am) Montag, den ersten April statt.
OR:
Es findet Montag, den 1. April statt.
It takes place on Monday, the first of April / April 1st.

Years

Er wurde 1980 geboren.
He was born in 1980.

(im Jahre) 2013
in 2013

Other expressions

im Dezember/Januar *etc*
in December/January *etc*

im Winter/Sommer/Herbst/Frühling
in winter/summer/autumn/spring

nächstes Jahr
next year

Anfang September
at the beginning of September

Punctuation

German punctuation differs from English in the following cases:

Commas

Decimal places are always shown by a comma → 1

Large numbers are separated off by means of a space or a full stop → 2

Subordinate clauses are always marked off from the rest of the sentence by a comma → 3

This applies to all types of subordinate clause, e.g.:

- clauses with an adverbial function → 3
- relative clauses → 4
- clauses containing indirect speech → 5

A comma is not required between two main clauses linked by und or oder → 6

Exclamation marks

Exclamation marks are used after imperative forms unless these are not intended as commands → 7

An exclamation mark is occasionally used after the name at the beginning of a letter, but this tends to be rather old-fashioned → 8

Examples

1 3,4 (drei Komma vier)
3.4 (three point four)

2 20 000
OR: 20.000 (zwanzigtausend)
20,000 (twenty thousand)

3 Als er nach Hause kam, war sie schon weg.
She had already gone when he came home.

Er bleibt gesund, obwohl er zu viel trinkt.
He stays healthy, even though he drinks too much.

4 Der Mann, mit dem sie verheiratet ist, soll sehr reich sein.
The man she is married to is said to be very rich.

5 Er sagt, es gefällt ihm nicht.
He says he doesn't like it.

6 Wir gehen ins Kino oder wir bleiben zu Hause.
We'll go to the cinema or stay at home.

7 Steh auf!
Get up!

Bitte nehmen Sie doch Platz.
Do please sit down.

8 Liebe Elke! ...
Dear Elke, ...

Sehr geehrter Herr Braun!...
Dear Mr Braun, ...

Index

The following index lists comprehensively both grammatical terms and *key words* in **German** and English contained in this book.